THE PORTABLE HANDBOOK OF

Texas

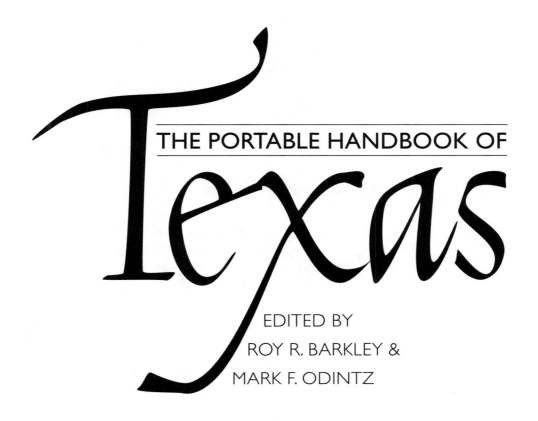

THE PORTABLE HANDBOOK OF

Texas

EDITED BY

ROY R. BARKLEY &

MARK F. ODINTZ

Austin

The Texas State Historical Association

Published by the Texas State Historical Association
in cooperation with the Center for Studies in Texas History
at the University of Texas at Austin

ISBN 0-87611-180-0

Library of Congress Cataloging-in-Publication Data

The portable handbook of Texas / edited by Roy R. Barkley and Mark F. Odintz.
    p.   cm.
   ISBN 0-87611-180-0 (alk. paper)
     1. Texas—Encyclopedias. 2. Texas—History. I. Barkley, Roy R. 1941– . II. Odintz,
Mark F., 1953– . III. Texas State Historical Association.
F384.P67 2000
976.4—dc21   00-036368

Designed by David Timmons

FOREWORD

Newcomers to Texas often puzzle over what is different about Texas. What is at the root of the prodigious attitude or spirit that Texans have exhibited for well over 150 years? a spirit so palpable that newcomers to the state often claim to "feel" it once they arrive? It has been characterized as a "can-do" attitude, an indomitable will, a simple streak of positivism combined with "no quittin' sense."

Many have suggested answers to this question ranging from land and the people who settled it to freedom and fate. Governor Peter H. Bell identified the forge on which the Texan character was wrought in an 1851 message to the legislature: "The days of the Republic were 'the days of our glory,'" he said, "deeds of devoted patriotism and daring chivalry were then performed which would have graced the heroic pages of Greece and Rome." And from a position of historical perspective almost four decades later, Mrs. Anna J. H. Pennybacker, who in 1888 published what became one of the most widely used Texas history textbooks in the state, identified that unique characteristic as the state's history: "there is not other State in the Union whose history presents such varied and romantic scenes as does that of Texas."

To provide access to that story, Walter Prescott Webb, professor of history at the University of Texas and director of the Texas State Historical Association, initiated the *Handbook of Texas* project in 1940. It resulted in a two-volume work, co-edited by H. Bailey Carroll, in 1952. One would need a whole roomful of books to obtain accurate information on all the different phases of the state's history, Webb explained in the "Introduction" to those volumes, but the *Handbook* "assembled into one usable, practical, ready-reference work the most significant information about the widest possible range of Texas topics." Eldon Stephen Branda edited a supplementary third volume in 1976, and the *Handbook* was further updated and expanded in a fourteen-year project beginning in 1982 that resulted in the *New Handbook of Texas* (6 volumes) in 1996. The *New Handbook* has received both favorable reviews and good sales, despite its expense, and is now reaching unparalleled audiences via the Internet (www.tsha.utexas.edu).

But these six volumes are formidable, thorough, and complex. With publication of the *Portable Handbook of Texas,* we hope to serve those newcomers to the state and others who may not know its storied past, those whom the writer James A. Michener had in mind in his fictional *Texas* when he recognized that the classrooms of the future would "be filled with young people who have never before studied the glories of Texas history and who will not be familiar with its unique and heroic nature." Here our intent is to extract the elemental story and facts from the larger *New Handbook*. All the regular features of the familiar *Handbook* are here—biographies of notable individuals, histories of important events and communities, descriptions of significant physical features, thematic articles—but considerably condensed. In addition, the chronological essays of the *New Handbook* have been woven into an overview of the history of Texas.

The story that the *Portable Handbook of Texas* tells is considerably more varied than the one originally presented in 1952. Beginning with the 1976 Suuplement, we have enlarged it specifically to include more information on women, African Americans, Mexican Americans, and other ethnic groups. Also included is much new material on the people and events of the last quarter of the twentieth century. But our goal remains the same as Webb's: to provide in "one usable, practical, ready-reference work the most significant information about the widest possible range of Texas topics."

Again, as with all the other editions of the *Handbook of Texas,* our efforts are dependent not only upon a dedicated staff of editors and writers, but also upon the more than 3,000 individuals who contributed articles and materials to the *New Handbook.* And now that the *Handbook* project is a permanent part of the Texas State Historical Association's programs, we will continue to add to it in the manner in which we can best serve our members and users, whether that be the internet, CD-ROM, or printed book.

Ron Tyler
March 2000

INTRODUCTION

The *Portable Handbook of Texas* is intimately related to its immediate predecessor. The present volume embodies a concentrated version of the most important information in the *New Handbook of Texas*, a six-volume, 7,000-page encyclopedia published by the Texas State Historical Association in 1996.

Before the *New Handbook* was finished, ideas for many subsequent projects took shape. Two of these, the paramount ones, have come to fruition:

- First, to put the *New Handbook* on the World Wide Web, where it would be accessible to a large and growing audience, while itself growing and improving.
- Second, to make available a crystallized version of the larger work in a convenient, one-volume format. The sheer size of the printed *New Handbook*, which weighs forty-two pounds, suggested that many readers might appreciate a less detailed and expansive, though more easily toted, general reference work on the Lone Star State—a *Portable Handbook of Texas*.

In this work we have spared no effort to maintain the quality of the six-volume encyclopedia. That book itself was designed to be a worthy successor to the original *Handbook of Texas* (1952) and its distinguished *Supplement* (1976). Renowned critics and scholars lauded the two-volume 1952 work, edited by Walter Prescott Webb and H. Bailey Carroll, as a triumph of scholarship and presentation. The 1976 supplementary volume, edited by Eldon S. Branda, drew similar accolades. By the mid-1970s, however, 1952 already seemed remote, not to say simple and halcyon. Branda was well aware that the state's rushing complexification cried out for a complete new edition of the *Handbook*, not only for a supplement. During the fourteen years after L. Tuffly Ellis inaugurated the revision project in 1982, that edition became a reality.

Structures. This volume comprises two sections of unequal length: (1) an opening survey of Texas history and (2) an alphabetically arranged encyclopedic treatment of Texas history and culture. The introductory survey provides a broad context for all that follows.

One of the basic structural and formal principles of the *New Handbook* was its breaking out of smaller topics from larger ones, so that the smaller ones could receive separate and more complete treatment. The idea was to survey a large subject in general, then to focus upon its components in separate articles. The components themselves might then be broken down into more specific subjects. The result was a collage of overlapping pyramids that moved into and out of each other like images in a painting by Lyonel Feininger. Thus, for instance, the overview article on the Republic of Texas led to a separate article on the Mier expedition, which in turn led to an account of the notorious Black-Bean Episode. Crossing all layers of this structure were not only pyramid-base articles such as biographies and minor topical entries but other overviews. The result is a kaleidoscopic treatment appropriate to a large and complicated history.

Though smaller and of friendlier heft, the *Portable Handbook* is no less kaleidoscopic. But it was necessarily produced by a different dynamic—that of combining rather than breaking out. In the interest of reducing the size while retaining the essential content, the editors sought ways to shrink articles and combine them. Thus the Aguayo expedition, for instance, became part of the article on the Marqués de Aguayo. The working principle was to omit separate articles when their content was sketched elsewhere. Most of the topics that receive summary mention in a large article—for instance, in the panoramic first article—are therefore no longer treated under separate headings. Nevertheless, the subjects of most importance to Texas history are richly represented in this volume. They are accessible through the index, which has obviated the need for cross-references in the text.

We have tried to include articles on topics that most historians would consider indispensable—the Alamo, for instance, or Sam Houston, Stephen F. Austin, and the Kennedy assassination. The next rank of importance includes a large collection of articles that, though secondary to such general topics as Education or Agriculture, the editors deemed necessary to explain the state's history and culture. Again, the process of selection was to start at the top with the most compelling subjects, then to move to those necessary supporting topics that were not treated adequately in summary statements in larger articles. In a third rank we have also included topics that belong essentially to the Texas story not so much because of their historical influence as because of their notoriety or intrinsic interest. Some stories that embody the color and smack of Texas—the account of the Crash at Crush, for instance, or the Santa Claus Bank Robbery—are just too good to omit.

One influence on the contents of this book is the Texas State Historical Association's plans for future publications. A detailed treatment of any of the general subjects covered here would require another volume, in addition not only to this one but to the six volumes of the *New Handbook*. The editors plan to produce such detailed works—on music, Mexican Americans in Texas, African Americans in Texas, Texas women, railroads, business, and other subjects. That fact helped in the selection of articles for this book. Some subjects about which we plan future volumes receive only broad coverage here. Railroads, for instance, are covered in one long article. Other topics lent themselves to a structure of general coverage with essential supporting articles. The article on Mexican Americans, for instance, is supplemented by numerous biographies and other topics such as civil rights. But the large studies of some other relevant subjects—Mexican Americans and Education, for example, or Mexican Americans and the Visual Arts—must wait for the separate volume.

This book includes many articles of the "overview" category. Such entries as those on Urbanization and Literature are intended to give the reader in-depth, stand-alone coverage of these complex subjects. Subordinate articles—e.g., on individual writers or cities—are included on their own merits, although they support the larger treatises. We would have had to include Katherine Anne Porter and the city of Houston, for instance, even without the overview pieces. The index will show just how many filiations exist between the large and small subjects in the *Portable Handbook*.

In addition to the overviews, however, we have included a few large, composite articles. The first, a general historical introduction to Texas, is essentially an overview of overviews. It is designed to present a broad chronological sketch from prehistoric times to the present—a context for all that follows. The others, on Water and Women, bring together under these headings numerous articles that might otherwise be scattered throughout the book. This convenient treatment reflects the central importance of the subjects. Naturally, additional articles abound on individual women and water features such as rivers.

Biographies. In no subject area was selection more difficult than in biographies. Initially, the editors studied a list of the more than 6,000 biographical articles in the *Handbook* files and tried to judge which subjects were genuinely important enough to include. That process, however, yielded thousands of subjects—far more than we had room for. The next approach was to ask which Texas people were the "movers and shakers" without which the state would not be what it is. Those are only a handful. A balance of these approaches produced the present contents. We couldn't have much of an encyclopedia of Texas without, say, Lyndon Johnson, a salient mover and shaker, or his mentor, Sam Rayburn. On the other hand, we couldn't omit a cultural icon such as Elizabet Ney, or a contrarian one such as Janis Joplin, although their pervasive effects on the terrain have been more subtle.

But a third principle was also operative in our selection of biographical subjects. That is, if a person not of the first rank was mentioned significantly in some other article, we often chose to let that mention suffice. The index will lead the reader to numerous such subjects, and, in many cases, to the materials for a suitable biographical sketch. At the margins, our final selection will not please everyone, though we hope all will agree on the core characters. It is our belief that all the most important Texas figures are represented in the *Portable Handbook*, although quite a few are included in articles on other topics. As in the *New Handbook of Texas*, only deceased people get their own articles.

Communities. The communities that are the subjects of articles in the present book are (1) major population centers, i.e., cities of 50,000 or more; (2) population centers of 10,000 to 50,000 with substantial histories; and (3) small or defunct communities whose historical importance belies their present insignificance. The 100 or so communities thus selected are the most important of more than 8,000 that have existed in Texas. They represent the history of all regions of the state. In addition to settlement facts, historical and current demographics, and developmental milestones, they also carry information on such cultural features as parks, museums, and educational institutions.

Natural features. The most striking large physiographic features of Texas—often synonymous with regions—receive full treatment in this book: the Panhandle, the Trans-Pecos, the Gulf of Mexico. Such articles as those on Grasslands, Wildlife Areas, Forests, Trees, and Geology also convey a sense of the geographic regions of the state. A subtext of the omnibus article on Water is the immense historical importance of this vital resource to the arid Southwest. The most important rivers, all of which have given rise to colorful history, are treated in their own articles. Such articles as those on Mineral Resources and the Oil and Gas Industry suggest the richness of the state's natural resources and their regional significance.

General articles on Mammals, Reptiles, Birds, and other representatives of the Texas fauna give the prominent features of the state's wildlife, while such articles as those on Ranching and Goat Ranching survey the history of domesticated animals. Some important animals and birds—the armadillo, the mockingbird, the prairie dog—receive separate treatment.

Education and health care. The story of Texas education merits a separate volume. We have included here an overview article on the subject and articles on the important degree-granting institutions of higher learning in the state. Junior colleges, which make up an increasingly important component of modern education, are generally named in community articles, although constricted space prohibited separate articles on them.

The subject of health care, which significantly overlaps that of education in the form of medical schools and teaching hospitals, is covered in a general article on Health and Medicine. Medical schools, being degree-granting institutions, are given separate articles. Some of the most important teaching hospitals are included in separate articles, though, again, space constraints prohibited the inclusion of hospitals as such. An encyclopedic volume on health care in Texas would be a valuable work.

Take it with you. The editors of this *Portable Handbook of Texas* believe that it includes in condensed form all of the most important information about Texas history and culture. It is our hope that it will be used as a *vade mecum* by travelers, newcomers, historians, teachers, students, entrepreneurs, and anyone else seeking a thorough and reliable reference work on the Lone Star State.

ABBREVIATIONS

In general, the abbreviations in the *Portable Handbook of Texas* are explained by their contexts. The following list includes those that often are not.

A.A.: Associate of Arts
AAUW: American Association of University Women
AFL: American Federation of Labor; American Football League
AMA: American Medical Association
ATM: Automated Teller Machine
b.: born (in)
B.B.A.: bachelor of business administration
ca.: circa
CCC: Civilian Conservation Corps
CEO: Chief Executive Officer
CIO: Congress of Industrial Organizations
CISD: Consolidated Independent School District
d.: died (in)
DAR: Daughters of the American Revolution
DEA: Drug Enforcement Agency
DRT: Daughters of the Republic of Texas
ed.: educated (at)
e.g.: for example
EPA: Environmental Protection Agency
FDIC: Federal Deposit Insurance Corporation
FERA: Federal Emergency Relief Administration
GED: General Equivalency Diploma (equivalent to a high school diploma)
HEW: United States Department of Housing, Education, and Welfare
ICBM: Intercontinental Ballistic Missile
i.e.: that is
INS: United States Immigration and Naturalization Service
IRS: Internal Revenue Service
ISD: Independent School District
IWW: International Workers of the World

LL.B.: Bachelor of Laws
LL.D.: Doctor of Laws
LULAC: League of United Latin American Citizens
m.: married
MSA: Metropolitan Statistical Area
NASA: National Aeronautics and Space Administration
NAACP: National Association for the Advancement of Colored People
NCAA: National Collegiate Athletic Association
NFL: National Football League
NYA: National Youth Administration
PWA: Public Works Administration
RAF: Royal Air Force
RFC: Reconstruction Finance Corporation
ROTC: Reserve Officers' Training Corps
spp.: species (plural)
SWC: Southwest Conference

UIL: University Interscholastic League
USDA: United States Department of Agriculture
USO: United Service Organization
VA: Veterans Administration
VJ Day: Victory in Japan Day (World War II)
WCTU: Woman's Christian Temperance Union
WPA: Work Projects Administration, subsequently Works Progress Administration

ABBREVIATIONS OF INSTITUTION NAMES IN ILLUSTRATION CREDITS

CAH: Center for American History, University of Texas at Austin
HRHRC: Harry Ransom Humanities Center, University of Texas at Austin
ITC: University of Texas Institute of Texan Cultures, San Antonio
TSL: Texas State Library, Austin

THE PORTABLE HANDBOOK OF

Texas

TEXAS FROM THE BEGINNING

Prehistory. Texas prehistory extends back at least 11,200 years and is witnessed by a variety of cultural remains of Indians. The "historic" era began with the shipwreck of Pánfilo de Narváez's expedition and the subsequent account written by Cabeza de Vaca. Indian culture was not modified, as best we can tell, by Cabeza de Vaca or by the later seventeenth-century French and Spanish exploration. Indeed, the peoples the explorers found were not severely affected until the advent of the Spanish missions and the incursion of Apaches at the beginning of the eighteenth century. It is possible, however, that Spanish diseases, introduced in central Mexico, had already begun affecting the hunter–gatherer bands of northern Mexico, causing displacement of these and similar groups in southern Texas.

The prehistory of Texas has been studied by both professional and avocational archeologists for more than 80 years. Some areas, such as Central Texas, have been intensively studied, and detailed archeological sequences of them have been established. In other regions, such as South Texas, research intensified only in the 1970s, and much remains to be learned about them. Cultural change proceeded at somewhat different rates over the vast area of Texas; in some regions, hunting and gathering cultures persisted throughout prehistory; in others, cultures with farming and settled village life appeared. Research has divided the Texas archeological record into four general periods: Paleo-Indian (9200–6000 B.C.), Archaic (6000 B.C. to around the beginning of the Christian era), Late Prehistoric (roughly A.D. 700–1600), and Historic.

Paleo-Indian. Although some claims have been made for greater antiquity, the earliest known inhabitants of the state, during the late Pleistocene (Ice Age), can be linked to the Clovis Complex around 9200 B.C. The distinctive Clovis fluted point is widespread and was used at least in some cases in mammoth hunting. A mammoth kill-site, Miami, is found in Roberts County in the Panhandle. The Gault Site in Central Texas has a Clovis occupation that includes incised pebbles, a blade core, and several Clovis points, including one made of Alibates material from the Canadian River quarries. At a deeply buried Clovis campsite at the Aubrey Site in Denton County, a Clovis point, Clovis blades, and thousands of flakes were found. The Lewisville Site near Denton is another Clovis campsite. The Folsom Complex, around 8800–8200 B.C., is distinguished by Folsom fluted points and is known from sites where now-extinct forms of bison were killed and butchered (Bonfire Shelter) or from campsites (Adair–Steadman) where the points are found along with other stone tools. The Clovis and Folsom materials might be considered to fall within the early part of this period. Although fluting ceases to be an important trait of Paleo-Indian points after Clovis and Folsom, later Paleo-Indian points maintain an overall lanceolate, parallel-sided form, often with careful parallel flaking and with the basal edges dulled to facilitate hafting. One unfluted type that may well be "early Paleo-Indian" is Midland, known from excavations at the Scharbauer Site, near Midland, in the early 1950s. A portion of a human cranium found at that site may be linked to this early cultural pattern.

Dalton and San Patrice points may date around 8000 B.C. in East

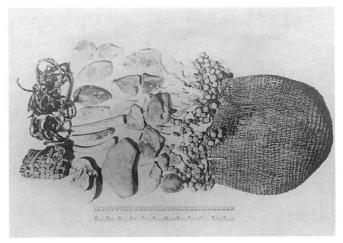

Medicine bundle from Horseshoe Ranch Caves, Val Verde County. Courtesy Texas Archeological Research Laboratory, University of Texas at Austin; neg. no. 41VV171-15. This net bag and its contents served as a tool kit, with blanks that could be fashioned into projectile points, a hammerstone, sinew and cordage, and scrapers of jackrabbit jaws. The mountain laurel and mescal seeds might have been used as hallucinogens, and the buckeye seeds could have been used to poison fish.

Texas; Plainview points found from the Panhandle into South Texas date from around 8200–8000 B.C. and are associated with kills of Pleistocene bison at Plainview and Bonfire. By around 8000 B.C., the end of the Pleistocene, remnants of the animals of that era—mammoth, bison, camel, horse, sloth—disappeared. Climates became more like those of modern times, yet in some regions, group mobility and stone toolmaking continued to follow the patterns of earlier times. There is a great diversification of point types, several of which we still cannot precisely date, in post-Pleistocene, late Paleo-Indian times. Excavations done in the 1980s and 1990s at the Wilson–Leonard Site in Williamson County may help to resolve some of these issues, as well as provide archeologists with a broader view of the cultural patterns associated with distinctive Paleo-Indian points. The Scottsbluff points in East Texas are from around 6500 B.C.; in the lower Pecos and South Texas, hunters and gatherers used Golondrina points, radiocarbon dated at 7000 B.C.. Excavations at Baker Cave, a dry rockshelter on the Devils River drainage, have yielded a wide array of information on the climate, which was essentially modern though probably drier, and the diet of peoples there 9000 years ago (the Golondrina Complex). A well-preserved cooking pit yielded the remains of small game, especially rabbits, rodents, and several species of snake; the cave also yielded charred walnut and pecan hulls as well as other organic remains. The Angostura projectile point marks the end of the Paleo-Indian period; radiocarbon dates from the Wilson–Leonard Site and the Richard Beene Site near San Antonio date it at around 6800 B.C. The peoples who made these points, like the peoples of the Golondrina Complex, were hunters and gatherers who used resources quite similar to those of the modern era.

TYPE SITES	POINT TYPES	TIME PERIODS	STAGES
Blum Smith Kyle	Perdiz Cliffton	(TOYAH FOCUS)	Neo - American
Blum Smith Kyle	Granbury Scallorn	(AUSTIN FOCUS)	
Wunderlich Smith Williams Collins	Prov. Type III Darl	TRANSITIONAL	Archaic
Oblate Wunderlich Collins	Ensor Frio Montell Marcos	LATE	
Wunderlich Crumley	Pedernales Bulverde	MIDDLE	
Wunderlich Crumley	Nolan Travis	EARLY	
			Paleo - Indian

Sequence of projectile-point types in central and south central Texas, based on excavations at Canyon Reservoir, Comal County. Drawings by Hal Story. From LeRoy Johnson, Dee Ann Suhm, and Curtis D. Tunnell, *Salvage Archeology of Canyon Reservoir* (Austin: Texas Memorial Museum, 1962).

Archaic. Much of Texas prehistory is subsumed within a long time span of hunting and gathering cultural patterns known collectively as the Archaic. The period begins around 6000 B.C. and is notable for changes in the style of projectile points and tools, the distribution of site types, and the introduction of grinding implements and ground-stone ornaments, all reflecting a gradually increasing population that utilized abundant plant and animal resources of environments similar to those of modern times. The primary weapon during the Archaic was the spearthrower or atlatl. The bow and arrow had not yet been introduced. Climatic patterns surely vacillated during the Archaic, though we have little detailed knowledge of them; a dry, warm episode known as the Altithermal (about 5000–3000 B.C.) was clearly present, but we are uncertain about its effects on local populations. The details of the Archaic sequence vary from region to region within the state. In general, the span can be divided into Early, Middle, Late, and Transitional eras. Each period is represented by changes in cultural patterns, often including specific artifact forms, hunting patterns, types of site utilized, and other elements. In some regions we have enough information to subdivide these periods into "phases" or "intervals."

The Early Archaic (6000–2500 B.C.) is poorly known in its earliest phases, though a number of point and tool types can be linked to that era. In general, settlement appears more scattered than in later times, and populations were still rather small and quite mobile. There are broader relationships among several regions, as indicated by the widespread occurrence of distinctive points, such as the Martindale, Uvalde, Early Triangular, Andice, and Bell (the latter two part of a cultural pattern known as Calf Creek, which encompasses Oklahoma and parts of Arkansas). The Middle Archaic (2500–1000 B.C.) marks a time of significant population increase, large numbers of sites, and abundant artifacts, especially projectile points of various forms. Apparently, Indian cultures became more specialized on a regional basin. Most regions appeared to be typified in the Middle Archaic by one or two distinctive points: Gary and Kent points in East Texas, for example, Pedernales in Central Texas, Langtry in the lower Pecos, and Tortugas in South Texas. In some regions, specific types of site are present, especially the burned-rock middens of Central Texas (apparently used for cooking wild plants, especially sotol bulbs) and shell middens on the coast. Additionally, cemeteries with large numbers of interments begin to appear late in the period, perhaps reflecting territoriality on the part of some hunting and gathering societies. Similarly, trade connections are established and artifacts of stone and shell are brought from distant areas, especially Arkansas. The Late Archaic (1000–300 B.C.) sees the continuation of hunting and gathering in most of Texas, again distinguished by certain types of projectile points and stone tools. In East Texas, pre-Caddo sites mark the beginning of settled village life shortly after 500 B.C. Cemeteries are more notable in some regions, such as Southeast Texas. Bison appear to be an important game resource in Central Texas and in the lower Pecos, where another bison kill occurs at Bonfire Shelter. Other bison kills are known in the Panhandle and South Plains at this time. The Transitional Archaic (300 B.C.–A.D. 700) marks an interval which in some ways is little more than a continuation of the Late Archaic. Still, it features distinctive point styles, such as Ensor, Darl, Frio, and Fairland. Although this period is important in the Archaic sequences of Central and lower Pecos Texas, it is not part of the East Texas archeological record, where village sites such as the George C. Davis Site of the Gibson Aspect (most of which is in Caddoan Mounds State Historic Site) make their initial appearance and fully develop only during the subsequent Late Prehistoric period. These sites often have large mounds, flat-topped ones sometimes used to support structures and conical ones for burials. Such sites mark the introduction of agriculture, which leads to population growth and the emergence of social and political systems.

Many Indian rock art sites in Texas, especially in the lower Pecos, date from the Archaic. Archaic pictographs at such sites as Seminole Canyon in the lower Pecos can be recognized by the presence of spearthrower motifs in the panels of polychrome Pecos River Style art. Studies using a specialized type of radiocarbon dating known as AMS (accelerator mass spectrometry) suggest that this style may date as early as 4000 B.C.

Late Prehistoric. This period (A.D. 700 to historic times) is particularly noticeable in the archeological record throughout the state. Toward the end of Late Prehistoric times the bow and arrow was introduced, along with distinctive types of stone tools. Pottery was also present, even among hunters and gatherers in Central, South, and coastal Texas. Buffalo hunting appears to have been very important in most regions. The occurrence of tiny arrow points marks the spread of the bow and arrow throughout the state. Many local types develop: Livermore in the Trans-Pecos, Friley and Catahoula on the Texas–Louisiana border, Lott and Garza on the Llano Estacado, and McGloin and Bulbar Stemmed on the coast. In some areas arrow-point styles differ clearly through time, especially with Scallorn (Austin Phase) and, later, Perdiz (Toyah Phase) in Central Texas. The Toyah Phase is of particular interest because it represents a widespread bison-hunting tradition in Central and South Texas from around A.D. 1300 to 1600; in addition to Perdiz points, its material culture includes end scrapers for hideworking, beveled knives for bison butchering, and a distinctive bone-tempered ceramic. On the central Gulf Coast, the Rockport Complex represents a population that may be ancestral to the historic Karankawas. These peoples hunted and fished along the bayshores and often moved inland to hunt bison. An asphalt-lined, thin-walled pottery called Rockport Ware is diagnostic of this complex. In the Rio Grande delta, the Brownsville Complex is unique for its trade with frontier Mesoamerican cultures (e.g., the Huastecs of Veracruz), which began around A.D. 1300–1400. Representatives of the Brownsville Complex made shell beads and other ornaments in large numbers and traded these to the Huastecs in return for pottery vessels, jadeite ornaments, and obsidian, all found in Brownsville Complex sites in the lower Rio Grande valley.

Although a hunting and gathering life continues in the Late Prehistoric as in the Archaic, the material culture, hunting patterns, settlement types and other facets of the era mark a fairly distinctive break with the past. In East Texas, agriculture provides the base for the Gibson Aspect, which marks the earliest Caddoan culture; mound building, specific types of pottery and arrow points, sedentary villages, ceremonial centers, and an established social hierarchy are salient features. Around A.D. 1200, Gibson gives way to the Fulton Aspect, which continues into the Historic era and is clearly linked with the Caddos. In the Panhandle and Llano Estacado, settled villages (also engaged in bison hunting) are found in the Antelope Creek Phase on the Canadian River around A.D. 1400 and in Andrews County. Village sites with links to southeast New Mexico appear around the same time. In the Trans-Pecos, a sequence of settled horticulturists with strong ties to the Southwest Mogollón culture begins in the early centuries A.D. and develops more fully around A.D. 600. It is marked especially by pit-house dwellings. Down the Rio Grande, near Presidio, another center of agriculturally based villages, the Bravo Valley Aspect, dates to around A.D. 1200–1400.

One distinctive aspect of the Late Prehistoric was widespread, long-distance trade, best reflected in the distribution of obsidian artifacts in parts of Texas. Artifact-quality obsidian (volcanic glass,

Overview of Archeological Chronology in Texas

Period	Dates	Characteristics	Artifacts
Historic	1600–1800	Cabeza de Vaca; Spanish missions; entry of Tonkawas	Spanish Colonial artifacts gunflints; metal arrowpoints
Late Prehistoric	700–1600	Toyah phase bison hunters; villages in the Panhandle; Caddo cultures in East Texas	pottery; introduction of bow and arrow (tiny arrowpoints); agriculture in parts of state
Transitional Archaic	300 B.C–A.D. 700	first mounds in East Texas; hunters and gatherers continue elsewhere	dart points are smaller: Ensor Frio, Fairland, Paisano
Late Archaic	1000–300	bison hunting in Panhandle, lower Pecos, Central Texas; increased trade; cemeteries in Southeast and South Texas	large points for hunting: castroville, Montell; "corner tang" knives
Middle Archaic	2500–1000	hunters and gatherers across Texas; rock art begins in lower Pecos; burned-rock middens in Central Texas	Langtry points in West Texas; Pedernales points in Central Texas
Early Archaic	6000–2500	development of modern vegetation and fauna; hunting and gathering; possible period of aridity 5500–3000 B.C.	widespread point types cut across regions; Bell, Uvalde Martindale, Gower
Paleo-Indian	9200–6000	earliest occupation by Native Americans, with Pleistocene or ice age ending around 8000 B.C.; first peoples are known as Clovis and hunted mammoths and other ice-age animals	distinctive point types; Angostura, Golondrina, Plainview Folsom, Clovis

Baker Cave, Val Verde County. Center for Archaeological Research, University of Texas at San Antonio. Indians lived in this rockshelter, one of the best preserved in the United States, about 9,000 years ago. In it archeologists found tools and weapons made of chipped stone, sandals and nets made of plant fibers, basket fragments, bone beads, a leather pouch, and a toy bow.

usually black to gray in color) does not occur in Texas. Yet at sites in deep South Texas, across Central Texas, and into the Panhandle, obsidian artifacts are often reported. The geologic origin of the obsidian can be traced using methods of nuclear chemistry, such as X-ray fluorescence or neutron activation analysis of a chemical "fingerprint" of trace minerals in a specimen. The specimen can then be linked to a specific obsidian quarry. In the Panhandle, most of the obsidian comes from sources in the Jémez Mountains of northern Mexico, and was part of Plains–Pueblo trade in Late Prehistoric times. However, some of the obsidians found in South and Central Texas can be definitively traced to sources in southern Idaho (Malad), Wyoming (Obsidian Cliff), and central Mexico. These facts reflect long-distance trade networks, especially in the case of the Idaho and Wyoming obsidian, which were part of a north–south trade system through the Great Plains that continued into Historic times.

The transition from Late Prehistoric to Historic is difficult to discern in many parts of the state. The initial European expeditions had little, if any, effect on the native cultures, which were largely unchanged for another 100 to 150 years. Texas archeologists refer to this brief span as the "Protohistoric." Perhaps it is best exemplified by sites of the sixteenth and seventeenth centuries on Galveston Island and in South Texas, where no tangible evidence of contact (e.g., glass beads) is found. However, by the early eighteenth century most peoples of these areas were affected by the Spanish missions, and their cultures began to unravel.

Historic. The Historic era (after ca. A.D. 1600) marks the beginning of the end for the Indian cultures of Texas. The Spanish and French brought change to both agriculturalists and hunter–gatherers. The latter were decimated by the mission system and the intrusion of Apaches, and later, Comanches. Archeologically, we can recognize certain sites as Historic Caddo on the basis of their pottery and arrow points. Similarly, some arrow-point types such as Harrell and Washita are found with historic hunter–gatherers and village farmers in north central Texas and the Panhandle. Rock-art sites incorporate such historic motifs as churches and horse-borne Indian warriors or Spaniards. With the advent of the missions, the Indians who adopted mission life continued for a while to make stone tools, and a distinctive point type, Guerrero, is often found in missions, ranchos, and Indian campsites of that era. However, by the late eighteenth century, stone tools gave way to glass, and brass and iron points replaced those chipped from stone, thus signaling the end of an 11,000-year tradition.

Thomas R. Hester and Ellen Sue Turner

Spanish Texas. Spanish Texas, situated on the border of Spain's North American empire, encompassed only a small portion of what is now the Lone Star State. The Spanish province lay above the Nueces River to the east of the Medina River headwaters and extended into Louisiana. Over time, Texas was a part of four provinces in the Viceroyalty of New Spain (Colonial Mexico): the El Paso area was under the jurisdiction of New Mexico, the missions founded near La Junta de los Ríos were under Nueva Vizcaya, the coastal region from the Nueces River to the Rio Grande and thence upstream to Laredo was under Nuevo Santander after 1749, and Texas was initially (and later in Mexican Texas) under joint jurisdiction with the province of Coahuila.

The uninterrupted Spanish occupation of Texas lasted for just 105 years (1716–1821). However, its legacies are lasting and significant. On reflection they seem all out of proportion to the relatively small number of Spaniards and Hispanicized Indians who became the Mexican nation in 1821. Perhaps most obvious, yet superficial in importance, is the use of Spanish names for hundreds of towns, cities, counties, and geographic features in Texas. San Antonio, the first formal municipality in Texas, is one of the 10 largest cities in the United States. Forty-two of the 254 counties in Texas bear either Hispanic names, or Anglicized derivations from Spanish such as Galveston, or misspellings such as Uvalde. The names of physiographical features such as Llano Estacado, Guadalupe Mountains, and Padre Island serve as reminders of Spanish explorers and conquistadors who crossed Texas well before the English settled the Atlantic Coast of North America. Spaniards introduced numerous European crops, irrigation at San Antonio and other mission sites, livestock, and ranching techniques. Agriculture, initially practiced by some Indian groups in Texas, was likewise expanded and improved by Spanish missionaries and settlers. The restored missions at San Antonio and Goliad stand as enduring monuments to the Franciscans who brought the mantle of Christianity to Texas Indians. With the exception of those in California, the finest examples of Spanish mission architecture in the United States are in Texas. The missions in Texas, however, are much older than their California counterparts. San José y San Miguel de Aguayo Mission in San Antonio is appropriately called the "Queen of the Missions." The reconstructed La Bahía (Nuestra Señora de Loreto) Presidio at Goliad is a fitting monument to the military pioneers of Texas. Spanish is a second language for millions of Texans; for some it is the first language. Although much of the linguistic influence on Texas English has come from Mexico since 1821, Spanish—not English, German, French, or Dutch—was the first European language spoken in Texas. The lasting impact of Spanish law on the legal system is likewise vitally important. Rules of judicial procedure, land law, water law, and the law of family relations derive from the Spanish.

Slightly more than three centuries elapsed between the time the Texas shoreline was first viewed by a Spaniard in 1519 and 21 July 1821, when the flag of Castile and León was lowered for the last time at San Antonio. Those 300 years may be divided into three stages: the era of early exploration, in which there was a preliminary evaluation of the land and its resources; the period of cultural absorption, in which the Texas Indians began to acquire Hispanic cultural elements, at first indirectly from Indian intermediaries and then directly from the Spanish themselves; and the time of defensive occupation, in which the Spanish presence in Texas was more dictated by international considerations than caused by the momentum of an expanding empire.

Early exploration. Spaniards first approached Texas from the east by sea along the coast of the Gulf of Mexico, then overland almost simultaneously from New Mexico and Louisiana. The initial contacts were the result of historical processes generated within the West Indies and the vast kingdom of New Spain. Contemporaneously with the conquest of Mexico, begun by Hernán Cortés of Cuba in 1519, the Spanish governor of Jamaica outfitted Alonso Álvarez de Pineda with four ships and 270 men and ordered him to search for wealth. Pineda sailed the northern Gulf waters from the Florida Keys to Veracruz, constructed the first map of the region, and named the Mississippi River the Río del Espíritu Santo. He and his crew were the first Europeans to view the entire Texas coast. In the ensuing conquest of Mexico, a minor participant, Pánfilo de Narváez, lost an eye and command of his army in a skirmish with Cortés. Narváez returned to Spain in the early 1520s seeking redress from the king, and was finally awarded a royal patent to establish a colony in "Florida"—a term applied to the Gulf Coast between the Florida peninsula and the province of Pánuco, situated to the north of Veracruz. Narváez left Spain in June 1527, wintered in Cuba, and landed near Tampa Bay with some 300 men in the spring of 1528. He and his men were soon separated from their support vessels and stranded on the Florida coast. On September 22 they set out from northwestern Florida for Pánuco in five improvised barges. In the first month at sea, the small flotilla passed the mouth of the Mississippi River and arrived off the Texas coast, where it was caught in a violent storm. Two of the five craft landed near the western extremity of Galveston Island in early November; their occupants were the first non-Indians to set foot on Texas soil. Of the nearly 250 men who left Florida, only four—Cabeza de Vaca, Andrés Dorantes de Carranza, his African-born slave Estevanico, and Alonso Castillo Maldonado—survived. They lived for nearly seven years amid hostile Indians and the harsh environment of the Texas coast and after an astonishing odyssey reached Mexico City in the summer of 1536. Their accounts and the later writings of Cabeza de Vaca provided the first descriptions of Texas

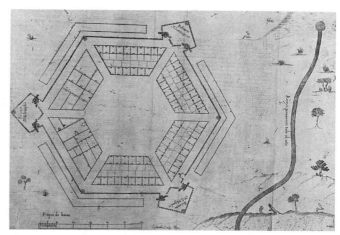

Plan of Nuestra Señora del Pilar de los Adaes Presidio, drawn by the Marqués de San Miguel de Aguayo, ca. 1722. Courtesy Archivo General de Indias, Seville. Photograph courtesy TSL.

landforms, Indians, and biota. Cabeza de Vaca in particular was the only Spaniard to record the names of the Indians of South Texas and to locate them relative to each other. His description of the Mariames, Avavares, Yguaces, and associated Texas Indians, according to one writer, supplied cultural information that "quantitatively exceeds that of all his successors combined." The collective experiences of the four men also prompted the viceroy of New Spain to sponsor the overland expedition of Francisco Vázquez de Coronado to New Mexico and Texas.

Vásquez de Coronado, from a base on the Rio Grande north of the site of present-day Albuquerque, reached the Panhandle in the spring of 1541. His army crossed the Llano Estacado, discovered Palo Duro Canyon, and encountered for the first time the Plains Indians of Texas, Oklahoma, and Kansas. On the return trip to Pueblo country, Coronado again crossed the Panhandle at its extreme northwest corner. One of his friars, Juan de Padilla, chose to return to Quivira, as the country along the Arkansas River in Kansas was called. Accompanying him were a Portuguese soldier and two Indian lay brothers. After succeeding with mission work among the Wichitas, Padilla died at the hands of unidentified Indians from farther east. His three companions, however, escaped on foot and crossed Texas from north to south en route to Mexico. Padilla's trek was another remarkable example of early pedestrian travel across the Texas landscape. The Coronado expedition is linked to that of Hernando De Soto by a chance occurrence. Both men were in the field during the early 1540s. De Soto's successor, Luis de Moscoso Alvarado, approached Texas from Louisiana as Coronado marched back to Mexico. It would appear that the Moscoso expedition entered the future Texas in late August 1542 and penetrated to the Trinity River in what is now Houston County. Moscoso made the first documented contact by Spaniards with Indians of the Hasinai Confederacy. His expedition had a greater acquaintance with an area of early importance in Spanish Texas than did Coronado's. By way of the Mississippi River and the Texas Gulf Coast, Moscoso led some 300 Spaniards in improvised boats to safety in Mexico. He finally reached Pánuco in September 1543.

The next recorded contact by Europeans with the Texas coast came in 1554 as a result of three Spanish ships wrecked off Padre

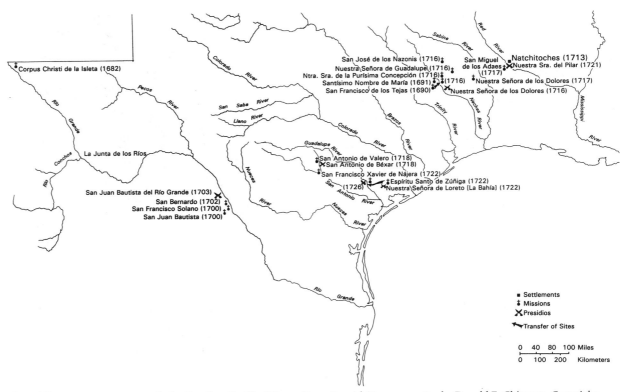

Missions and presidios, 1682–1726, cartography by Caroline Castillo Crimm. From *Spanish Texas, 1519–1821*, by Donald E. Chipman, Copyright ©1992. Courtesy the author and University of Texas Press.

Island. Perhaps 250 of the survivors were killed by hostile Indians, but a few escaped by boat and one on foot. Knowledge of the wrecks, laden with gold and silver, prompted salvage operations from Veracruz and Tampico in the late summer of that same year.

By a twist of fate, the next remarkable experience in Texas involved Englishmen. In 1568 John Hawkins placed several dozen of his countrymen ashore near Tampico after he suffered a nearly disastrous defeat by the Spanish fleet in Veracruz harbor. One of the men, David Ingram, along with two others, walked from Pánuco along the Gulf and Atlantic coasts to near Cape Breton, Nova Scotia, and lived to tell about the trek. Ingram's experiences, like those of Álvarez de Pineda, Cabeza de Vaca, Coronado, and Moscoso did little to encourage immediate settlement in Texas. Legends, however, died hard for Spaniards. Despite the reports of Coronado and Moscoso about the dearth of readily exploitable wealth in the north country, Tierra Nueva (as it was then called) continued to attract the attention of gold-hungry men in New Spain. Within five years after Coronado's return, the presumed wealth of Gran Quivira was again a topic of interest. Future explorers looked for the pearls of the Jumanos and the Great Kingdom of the Tejas. In the second half of the sixteenth century, the discovery of rich silver deposits in northern Mexico drew Spaniards into the area like a magnet attracting nails. The first of the mining boomtowns was Zacatecas, where a mountain of silver ore was discovered in 1546. By the 1570s additional strikes brought about the founding of settlements in southern Chihuahua near the headwaters of the Río Conchos. The town of Santa Bárbara in that locale became the principal staging area for entradas into New Mexico and Texas.

Development of the mining frontier, however, had spawned the Chichimeca Wars (1550–1590s) and Spain's institutional response to them. The latter comprised the Spanish missions and presidios, frontier agencies designed to convert Indians and pacify rebellious ones. From their inception, missions and presidios served as interrelated agencies of church and state and validated Spain's claim to frontier regions. The primary function of missions was the propagation of the Catholic faith. But missions also served the state by Hispanicizing the Indian population, thereby making Indians in theory into tractable and tax-paying citizens. Presidios, as the nuclei of military presence on the frontier, were clearly agencies of the state, but they also served as necessary adjuncts to the security of the missions and the discipline of the neophytes within—a lesson painfully learned by the friars in the early days of Spanish Texas. As the frontier of New Spain advanced northward, the northeastern field of missionary work, which encompassed Coahuila, Nuevo León, New Mexico, and Texas, became the primary responsibility of the Franciscan order. In the American Southwest the Friars Minor, the Little Brothers of St. Francis, established their first missions in New Mexico. Forty years after the return of the Coronado expedition, three Franciscans journeyed to Pueblo country with Francisco Sánchez Chamuscado (1581), and within a year all of the friars had suffered martyrdom. A subsequent expedition to New Mexico, led by Antonio de Espejo and Diego Pérez de Luxán (1582), brought the first Europeans into extreme Southwest Texas as they returned to Chihuahua. In the following year, the Spanish crown authorized the pacification of New Mexico by a private individual, but no formal agreement was reached for a dozen years. Finally, Juan de Oñate received a contract (1595) that led to the occupation of New Mexico in 1598 and to the establishment of more than twenty missions by 1680.

Cultural absorption. In the 82 years of continuous Spanish presence in New Mexico, Texas along the Rio Grande from modern Presidio to El Paso bordered the path from the mines, missions, and ranches of northern Mexico to the land of the Pueblos. The interior of Texas, however, remained for the most part *tierra incognita*. It was penetrated by some, however. Between 1629 and 1654 expeditions from New Mexico entered Texas to search for Indians allegedly instructed in Christian doctrine by María de Agreda, the miraculously bilocating "Woman in Blue," and to establish trade with the Jumano Indians. The Jumanos carried aspects of Spanish material culture as far as the eastern Gulf Coast and East Texas.

When the Pueblo Revolt of 1680 forced prolonged abandonment of New Mexico, El Paso del Norte, where settlement west of the river had occurred as early as 1655, became the focal point of Spanish presence on the extreme northern frontier. Its sparse population was severely tested by the arrival of nearly 2,000 Spanish and Indian refugees from New Mexico. To accommodate the Indian exiles, Spaniards founded the first mission and pueblo within the present boundaries of Texas, Corpus Christi de la Isleta, at the site of modern Ysleta. In the following years, efforts were made to found missions among the Jumano Indians at the junction of the Conchos and Rio Grande near the site of present-day Presidio. However, in the middle 1680s intelligence of French designs in the Gulf of Mexico downgraded the importance of that undertaking.

Concern centered on the extraordinary threat to Spanish realms posed by Frenchmen descending the Mississippi River from Canada. In 1682 La Salle explored the great river to its mouth and formally named the region Louisiana in honor of Louis XIV. He established that the Mississippi emptied into the Gulf of Mexico between Spanish Florida and Pánuco. If Spain closed that gap and occupied the lower Mississippi valley, Canada would lose its access to the sea and be threatened from the south. On the other hand, a French colony placed on the lower part of the river would be close to the rich mines of New Spain. La Salle returned to France in 1683 to lay his colonization plans before the court at Versailles. After some delays, occasioned by a rival and international considerations, he received generous support for his plan to challenge the Spanish empire. His expedition sailed from France in 1684, but because of misperceptions and faulty maps it overshot the Mississippi by some 400 miles and landed at Matagorda Bay in early 1685. By the time La Salle discovered that he had not landed at "his river," he was stranded on the Texas coast and had become the object of a resolute Spanish manhunt. The Spanish dispatched five sea and six land expeditions in search of La Salle's elusive colony at Fort St. Louis. In 1689 Alonso De León discovered its ruins on Garcitas Creek. By then La Salle, a victim of assassination, had been dead for two years. His colony had failed, as historian Robert S. Weddle has noted, not because of Spanish vigilance, but rather due to bad luck, hostile environment, fatal diseases, deadly Karankawa arrows, and the enmity of Frenchman toward Frenchman. But because La Salle overshot the Mississippi River and landed on the Texas coast, Spain reacted defensively. In reality, La Salle's expedition focused Spanish attention on East Texas, where success was hard to come by. The Spanish also underestimated the impending French threat to Louisiana.

Officials in Mexico City viewed the disastrous failure of La Salle's colony as evidence of God's "divine aid and favor." They were also impressed by Alonso De León's favorable account of the land and people of eastern Texas. Father Damián Massanet, who had accompanied the expedition of 1689, volunteered his services and those of his brethren of the College of Santa Cruz de Querétaro to man missions among the Tejas. De León, however, wisely suggested the placement of presidios to bridge the gap between settlements in Coahuila and the proposed new mission field. If his suggestions had been accepted, the subsequent disasters in East Texas might well have been lessened, if not avoided. Nevertheless, officials in the capital concluded, with Massanet's endorsement, that military presence would impede spreading the Gospel.

In May 1690 Father Massanet founded San Francisco de los Tejas, the first mission in East Texas, perhaps near the site of modern Augusta in northeastern Houston County. Instead of leaving 50 soldiers at the mission as De León recommended, the expedition left only three and an equal number of friars when it returned to Coahuila. Before De León departed, Massanet secured a promise from the Indian governor that he would not mistreat the three padres. However, according to the late Franciscan historian Lino Gómez Canedo, San Francisco de los Tejas was abandoned in October 1693 because of floods, epidemics, the relaxation of the French challenge, and the contempt of the Indians. The priests, expecting a rebellion, buried the cannons and bells, ignited the mission, and went back to Coahuila. But the mission effort in East Texas had familiarized Spaniards with the geography and Indians of Texas and convinced both church and government officials that future missions must be sustained by presidios and civilian settlements.

For one of the missionaries, Father Francisco Hidalgo, unfinished work among the Tejas Indians became a consuming passion. At the close of the seventeenth century, because of mining, ranching, and Hidalgo's unswerving commitment to missionary goals in East Texas, Spanish settlement in northern Mexico had advanced to the Rio Grande. San Juan Bautista, which Weddle has appropriately called the "Gateway to Spanish Texas," was founded on 1 January 1700 at the site of present-day Guerrero, Coahuila. By then the French had resurrected La Salle's plan to settle the lower Mississippi valley. Under the leadership of Pierre Le Moyne d'Iberville, a fort had been constructed at Biloxi Bay in 1699. In early 1700 the arrival of fresh supplies and reinforcements brought from France by Iberville strengthened the French presence in Louisiana. Accompanying him was a relative by marriage, Louis Juchereau de St. Denis, a Canadian-born adventurer who changed the course of Texas history. Despite Iberville's best efforts, the crown colony of Louisiana suffered neglect due in part to resumption of the costly wars of Louis XIV (1702–13). In an effort to reduce royal expenses, Louisiana was assigned as a proprietary colony to a wealthy Frenchman, Antoine Crozat. Crozat's choice as governor of the colony fell on Antoine de La Mothe, Sieur de Cadillac, who arrived in Louisiana in May 1713. Cadillac's duties were obvious. He had to run the colony in a businesslike manner and find a way to turn a profit. He concluded that the desired avenue of riches lay in establishing trade with New Spain, a commerce he knew to be forbidden by Spanish mercantile restrictions. At that juncture, however, Cadillac received a letter, drafted two years earlier, from Father Hidalgo. Hidalgo had despaired of winning support from the Spanish crown for his plans to reestablish missions among the Hasinais. His letter asked the French governor to assist him in accomplishing that goal. For Cadillac it was an invitation to do God's work and his own. He called on St. Denis, who had become skilled in diplomacy and Indian languages and had already made explorations beyond the Red River, to make overtures to the

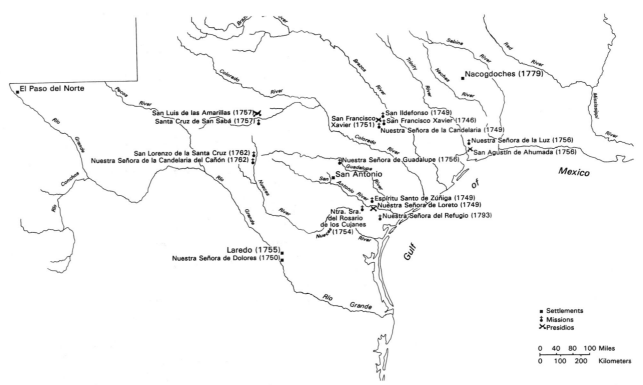

Expansion of Spanish missions, settlements, and presidios, 1682–1726, cartography by Caroline Castillo Crimm. From *Spanish Texas, 1519–1821*, by Donald E. Chipman, Copyright ©1992. Courtesy the author and University of Texas Press.

Spanish. St. Denis set out in late September and traveled to the site of Natchitoches, Louisiana, where he stored some of his merchandise. Twenty-two days after crossing the Sabine River, he reached the first Tejas villages and began trading for livestock, loosely managed by Indians, and buffalo hides. But the French adventurer had more ambitious goals. Justifying his actions on the grounds that he had not found Father Hidalgo living among the Indians, he planned to push on toward Spanish settlements.

In July 1714, St. Denis arrived at San Juan Bautista, bearing a French passport and news that the Tejas Indians earnestly desired the return of Spanish missionaries. His appearance alerted officials that the French were contacting Indians in East Texas and brought about the permanent Spanish occupation of Texas. The presidio commander, Diego Ramón, placed St. Denis under house arrest while he awaited instructions from Mexico City. The Frenchman's genial incarceration provided an opportunity to court and win a promise of marriage from Ramón's beautiful granddaughter, Manuela Sánchez. St. Denis was subsequently sent under guard to the capital, where he managed to charm the viceroy and obtain his freedom. Indeed, the chief executive of New Spain appointed St. Denis as commissary and guide for the expedition to reestablish Spanish missions in East Texas. St. Denis returned to San Juan Bautista, married his intended, and departed for Texas on 27 April 1716. Capt. Domingo Ramón, a son of the presidio commander, led more than 70 priests, lay brothers, soldiers, and civilians along a path that became the Old San Antonio Road, a *camino real*.

Responsibility for founding new missions in Texas was divided equally between the missionary colleges of Querétaro and Zacatecas. The former supplied two of the most famous Franciscans in Texas history, fathers Isidro Félix de Espinosa and

Francisco Hidalgo, and from the College of Nuestra Señora de Guadalupe de Zacatecas came the renowned Father Antonio Margil de Jesús, whose cause for canonization is ongoing. The priests reestablished Mission San Francisco at a different site and renamed it San Francisco de los Neches. They also founded five new missions—Nuestra Señora de la Purísima Concepción de Acuña, Nuestra Señora de Guadalupe de los Nacogdoches, San José de los Nazonis, Nuestra Señora de los Dolores de los Ais, and San Miguel de Linares de los Adaes (near the site of present Robeline, Louisiana). At the western edge of the mission field, Ramón built Nuestra Señora de los Dolores de los Tejas Presidio for his soldiers. The reestablishment of missions and a presidio in East Texas was very important historically, because it gave Spain a valid claim to land north of the Rio Grande, did much to determine that Texas would be Spanish, not French, and helped advance the eventual boundary between Texas and the United States to the Sabine River. For the enterprising St. Denis, the presence of Spaniards near Louisiana opened the door for the contraband trade that became a way of life on the Texas frontier.

Although the Spanish had received a friendly welcome from the Indians of East Texas, the latter were not willing to congregate in missions. To do so would require them to give up their idols and established way of life. To try to force compliance with the wishes of the missionaries was viewed as foolish, for the strength of the military guard was inadequate. Unless Spanish presence could be augmented and a halfway station established between the Rio Grande and the eastward missions, the occupation of Texas seemed destined to go as it had gone in 1693. Fortunately, the arrival in Mexico City of a new viceroy, the Marqués de Valero, signaled a positive trend for the struggling missions and presidio. The viceroy, at the instigation of Father Antonio de San Buenaventura y Olivares, made the suppression of illicit trade from Louisiana a primary objective. He also pledged support for the Franciscan missions in Texas. Father San Buenaventura had earlier visited a site on the San Antonio River in 1709, and from that time forward he was determined to found a mission and civilian settlement there. The viceroy gave formal approval for a halfway mission and presidio in late 1716, and assigned responsibility for their establishment to Martin de Alarcón, the governor of Coahuila and Texas. A series of delays, however, occasioned in part by differences between Alarcón and san Buenaventura, postponed definitive action until 1718. On 1 May on the San Antonio River the governor founded San Antonio de Valero Mission (later famous as the Alamo), and on 5 May established San Antonio de Béxar Presidio. As it turned out, these institutions came none too soon.

In 1719 a brief war in Europe between Spain and France affected Texas. From Natchitoches, Philippe Blondel and six soldiers easily captured the poorly defended Adaes mission, but in the confusion a lay brother escaped. He spread fear of an impending French attack throughout the mission outposts all the way to Presidio Dolores. There Captain Ramón viewed the situation as untenable. He ordered immediate abandonment of the six missions and the military garrison, thus bringing an inglorious close to the second effort at establishing the Spanish in East Texas. Fortunately, the retreating Spaniards found refuge at the new settlements on the San Antonio River. Soon after his arrival there, Father Margil began building a second mission, San José y San Miguel de Aguayo, named for the governor of Coahuila and Texas who replaced Alarcón in 1719.

The Marqués de Aguayo was a veteran soldier and a wealthy man, thanks to his wife, Ignacia Xaviera de Echeverez, who owned vast estates in Coahuila. At his own expense, he accepted the viceroy's request to deal with the troublesome situation in Texas and to undertake the establishment of missions in East Texas for a third time. In the early spring of 1721 Aguayo set out for Texas. He had recruited 500 men and collected 2,800 horses, 4,800 cattle, and 6,400 sheep and goats. Although livestock had accompanied previous entradas, Spanish ranching in Texas began with the arrival of these large herds in 1721. Aguayo reestablished all of the abandoned missions in East Texas; founded a new presidio, Nuestra Señora del Pilar, at Los Adaes; and made a lasting peace with St. Denis, who had become commandant of the French settlement at Natchitoches. By the spring of 1722, Domingo Ramón, under orders of Aguayo, had begun construction of Nuestra Señora del Espíritu Santo de Zúñiga Mission and Nuestra Señora de Loreto Presidio, both commonly called La Bahía, at the site of La Salle's Fort St. Louis. When Aguayo departed from Texas in May 1722 he left a province that was soon separated from Coahuila. It was secured by 268 soldiers at four presidios, two of which—at Los Adaes and La Bahía—were located where foreign aggression was most feared. Across the province were 10 missions and hundreds of potential neophytes. Although there was a continuing problem of smuggling between French Louisiana and Spanish Texas, the threat of French dominance in Texas was ended.

Peace in Europe and its implications for America prompted the king of Spain to order reforms within New Spain in the interest of economy. To that end the viceroy sent Gen. Pedro de Rivera y Villalón to make a thorough inspection of frontier posts in Texas. Rivera's recommendations in 1727 led to the reduction of troop strength at Los Adaes and to the abandonment of Presidio

Father Antonio Margil de Jesús, by Noriega, date unknown. Oil on canvas. 82" × 52". Courtesy San Jacinto Museum of History, Houston. Franciscan missionary Antonio Margil de Jesús founded four of the approximately 40 missions in Texas between 1632 and 1793, including missions in Nacogdoches (1716) and San Antonio (1719). This work of hagiography was produced to honor Margil's missionary works and, perhaps, as an early part of the effort to have him canonized.

Dolores. Without military support, the missions of San Francisco, Concepción, and San José were removed to the Colorado River and subsequently to San Antonio (1731). Unfortunately for the settlement at San Antonio, the reduction of military strength in Texas left the settlement vulnerable to raids by the Apaches at the very time it was attempting to integrate an influx of important settlers. Historians have generally marked the beginning of civilian settlement in San Antonio with the arrival of Canary Islanders on 9 March 1731, but it is well to remember that Alarcón's expedition of 1718 was not a purely military undertaking. The presidio was to protect the missions in the area and serve as a way station between the Rio Grande and the East Texas missions. San Antonio was also to be the site of a Spanish villa (San Fernando de Béxar), and to this end Alarcón had recruited frontiersmen from Coahuila and

Nuevo León. As Jesús F. de la Teja has demonstrated, "From its founding in 1718 to 1731, 47 couples married and 107 children were baptized at Mission Valero." Thus, a first generation of native Bexareños was already living in San Antonio by 1731. The arrival of the Canary Island settlers temporarily disrupted the racially harmonious community, but the threat of Indian attacks and frontier isolation soon eroded the Islanders' aloofness. Indian attacks began in the 1720s with the Apaches and worsened in the 1760s with the appearance of the Comanches at San Antonio. In the summer of 1768, Bexareños had to fight off a 22-day siege without outside assistance.

As San Antonio grew to become the most important and viable community in Spanish Texas, relations with the French remained generally peaceful. Arroyo Hondo, a small stream between Los Adaes and Natchitoches, became the accepted boundary between the two empires until the cession of Louisiana to Spain in 1762. The French, however, were much more adept than the Spanish in establishing trade with Texas Indians. At the Red River the French won favor with the Kadodachos (a Caddo group) and other Indians of the region. They were likewise successful in establishing trade with the Wichitas and Tawakonis in northern Texas. To the south, French traders crossed the Sabine in the early 1730s and initiated contact with the Orcoquizas and Bidais along the lower San Jacinto and Trinity rivers. In response to that continuing threat, in 1756 the Spanish established San Agustín de Ahumada Presidio and Nuestra Señora de la Luz Mission in the general vicinity of Anahuac. Neither establishment had much success, and both were abandoned within 15 years.

More serious external threats stemmed from continued French incursions and the English colony of Georgia in 1733. Spaniards considered Georgia to be a part of Florida and viewed the presence of foreigners there as a threat to unsettled Gulf Coast regions. Concern deepened with the outbreak of war between England and Spain in 1739, a conflict that presaged the larger War of the Austrian Succession (1740–48). Spain regarded the Costa del Seno Mexicano, between Tampico and Matagorda Bay, as especially vulnerable to English and French designs. To counter those threats the viceroy of New Spain approved the appointment of José de Escandón as military commander and governor of the recently established province of Nuevo Santander. In a burst of energy, Escandón and his lieutenants founded 24 towns and 15 missions between 1747 and 1755. Escandón also moved the mission and presidio at La Bahía from their second location on the Guadalupe River to the site of present Goliad. The founding of Laredo completed Escandón's colonization. Less successful was a simultaneous effort to expand the mission system along the San Gabriel River, called San Xavier by the Spanish, to the northeast of San Antonio. In the area of modern Rockdale three Franciscan missions and a presidio (collectively known as the San Xavier Missions) were founded in the late 1740s and early 1750s. Trouble between the presidio commander and the friars, disease, drought, and hostile Apaches doomed this undertaking to eventual failure.

In 1757 the entire properties of the San Xavier missions were redirected toward a new effort on the San Saba River, the most disastrous mission-extension project in the history of Spanish Texas. In 1757 near the site of present Menard, Col. Diego Ortiz Parrilla and Franciscan missionaries headed by Father Alonso Giraldo de Terreros set up San Luis de las Amarillas Presidio and Santa Cruz de San Sabá Mission. The settlements were established at the request of Lipan Apaches, a group generally hostile to the Spanish.

The Lipans, because of increasing pressure from the Comanches and their allies, especially the Wichitas, had been forced to set aside their dislike for the Spanish. But in forging an alliance of convenience, they further infuriated their Indian adversaries. In March 1758 the Comanches and their allies, including Tejas, Tonkawa, and Bidai Indians, attacked the mission in great numbers. They pillaged and burned it and killed eight persons, including Father Terreros. Santa Cruz de San Sabá was the only mission in Texas to be destroyed by outright Indian attack. In the following year, a major assault on the San Sabá livestock herd cost the lives of 20 soldiers and resulted in the loss of more than 700 horses, mules, and cattle. Several months later Ortiz Parrilla led a sizable force of presidial soldiers and Apache allies on a punitive expedition to the Red River, only to suffer a humiliating defeat. The San Sabá mission was never rebuilt. Missionary efforts on behalf of the Apaches continued for a time from outposts on the upper Nueces River, but they, too, had to be abandoned within a few years. Presidio San Luis de las Amarillas was strengthened and maintained for another 10 years, but it was abandoned in 1770. Thus, Spanish efforts toward expansion in Texas during the years 1731–62 were a failure, except at La Bahía and along the lower Rio Grande. Missions and presidios, although proven frontier institutions, had clearly failed north of San Antonio.

Elsewhere, events in Europe and the course of the French and Indian War in America (1754–63) had a profound effect on Texas. Before the Treaty of Paris, France had ceded to Spain all French territory west of the Mississippi River. Louisiana had been a financial disaster for France, and it became no less burdensome for Spain. Lacking resources and manpower, Spain could not defend or develop this vast territory, and it brought assertive English rather than the tolerant French to its borders. Twenty years later the English were supplanted by even more aggressive citizens of the United States. For Spain, adjustments were necessary to meet changing circumstances that confronted its North American empire. In the 1760s Charles III, an exceptionally able king of Spain, ordered a sweeping inspection of New Spain and its frontier provinces to determine what reforms were needed. The *visitador general* of importance for Texas was the Marqués de Rubí, who arrived in 1767. Rubí visited all major settlements in Texas and concluded that they could not be maintained without consolidation and new resources. His recommendations called for the strengthening of San Antonio by moving the settlers and remaining missions in East Texas to that site. Second, he suggested a new approach aimed at developing friendly relations with the powerful Comanches and Wichitas, coupled with a war of extermination against their enemies, the Apaches. The forced abandonment of East Texas was a bitter blow to its inhabitants. Because they were no longer needed as a barrier against the French, their settlements were removed to shore up the defenses of San Antonio. In the summer of 1773, Baron Juan María de Ripperdá, the governor of Texas, reluctantly ordered the closure of missions in East Texas, removal of the entire Spanish population, and designation of San Antonio as capital in place of Los Adaes. The displaced settlers often complained that native Bexareños denied them arable and irrigable lands. They petitioned to return to their homes, but were denied that right by Hugo Oconór, then inspector general on the frontier. Not dissuaded, the East Texans selected Antonio Gil Ibarvo as their spokesman and dispatched him to Mexico City for an audience with Viceroy Antonio María de Bucareli y Ursúa. Ibarvo was only partially successful. The viceroy did permit the resettlement of East Texas, but would not consent to dwellings within 100 leagues of Natchitoches, Louisiana. Still, the refugees in San Antonio viewed any concession as encouraging. In August 1774 they founded the settlement of Bucareli on the Trinity River at a site in what is now Madison County. The town had attracted 347 inhabitants by 1777, but it was plagued by floods and Comanche raids. Without authorization, the population moved again in 1779 to Nacogdoches, which became, with La Bahía, San Antonio, and Laredo, one of the first four permanent Spanish settlements within the boundaries of the future state of Texas.

Also during the mid-1770s, as part of Charles III's sweeping administrative reforms, the Provincias Internas administration was instituted for the northern provinces of New Spain, including Texas. That political arrangement, however, was in a state of flux to the end of the colonial era. The Internal Provinces began as an independent jurisdiction responsible only to the king, then passed under the viceroy of New Spain, and were finally divided into shifting military districts.

One of the major military concerns of the period was the enactment of Rubí's recommendations for an Indian policy that would destroy the Apaches and make peace with the northern tribes. Spaniards wisely called on French agents, who had remained in Louisiana after its transfer to Spain, to help implement that policy. Athanase de Mézières, the former son-in-law of St. Denis, masterminded this arrangement. He was fluent in several Indian languages. He enjoyed some success with the Wichitas—less with the Comanches—but was never able to piece together a general alliance of the northern tribes against the Apaches. Nevertheless, the talented frontiersman became highly respected by Spanish officials, and in 1779 they appointed him governor of Texas. He died, however, at San Antonio before assuming the post. Troubles with the Comanches continued until 1785, when a treaty with them brought peace that lasted, with a few interruptions, for nearly 30 years. Less successful was a final wave of missionary effort among the Karankawas and other coastal tribes. This undertaking was not new. The original Espíritu Santo Mission had been established for Karankawas. In 1754 Nuestra Señora del Rosario de los Cujanes Mission had been founded a short distance west of the site of present Goliad by the Zacatecan Franciscans. Indians in the area, however, were difficult neophytes. After they fled the mission in 1781, it was closed. For a time, the nearby La Bahía Mission served Indians of the region. The Franciscans again directed their attention to Rosario when former mission Indians asked that it be reopened. Their request was granted in December 1789. Four years later, the last of the Texas missions, Nuestra Señora del Refugio, was founded for Indians who had deserted the missions of La Bahía and Rosario. Because of unhealthful conditions, friars moved the mission in 1794 and finally reestablished it in January 1795 at the site of present Refugio. Success among the coastal tribes had proved difficult, and in the end the missions at La Bahía, Rosario, and Refugio, as elsewhere in Texas outside of San Antonio, disappointed their Franciscan founders.

Defensive occupation. The final crisis for Spanish Texas came from problems associated with the retrocession of Louisiana to France (1800), its subsequent sale to the United States (1803), and the struggle for Mexican independence, begun in 1810 by Father Miguel Hidalgo y Costilla. Spain's response to the first two situations was a determination to defend its boundaries unimpaired, to keep out American intruders, and to colonize Texas with loyal Spanish subjects. Negotiations over the western boundary of

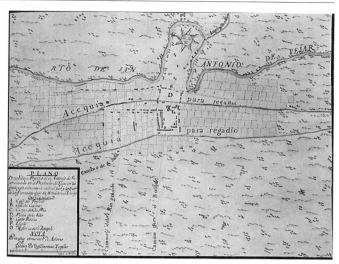

Plan for the villa and presidio of San Antonio de Béxar, by Joseph Ramón de Urrutia, ca. 1766–67. Manuscript map. By permission of the British Library; add MS 17662 T: San Antonio.

Louisiana were complex and extended, but Spain and the United States, by the Neutral Ground agreement of 1806, avoided a clash of arms when they temporarily accepted the Sabine River and Arroyo Hondo as borders of their respective lands. The boundary issue was not resolved until the Adams–Onís Treaty (1819–21). Of particular concern to the Spanish was the fear of Anglo-American intruders as agents of political discord and illicit trade. One of the famous filibusters, Philip Nolan, was killed by Spanish forces in 1801 near the site of present Waco. His fate, however, did not frighten away subsequent adventurers, who responded to the lure of wealth and recognized Spain's tenuous hold on the vast, relatively unpopulated land that was Texas.

The most complete census data for Spanish Texas in the early nineteenth century are for 1804, the first year after the sale of Louisiana to the United States. It is quite possible that this systematic count resulted from the need to assess the strength and numbers of the Spanish and Hispanicized population in the face of aggressive Americans to the east. The following population figures were compiled between January and December 1804: Nacogdoches, 789; Presidial Company of San Antonio de Béxar, 413; Mission San Juan Capistrano, 74; Mission San Antonio de Valero, 121; Presidio (Settlement) of La Bahía, 399; Presidial Company of La Bahía, 301; Missions La Bahía, Rosario, and Refugio, 224; Mission San Francisco de la Espada, 107; Villa San Fernando de Béxar and Presidio (Settlement) of Béxar, 1,177. Total: 3,605. Although the Spanish-speaking population included merchants and a few artisans such as tailors and blacksmiths, the vast majority of Texans were stock raisers and small farmers. The figures do not include unsettled Indians or black slaves; as Randolph B. Campbell has demonstrated, there were virtually no black bondsmen in Spanish Texas on the eve of Mexican independence.

The aggregate Hispanic population of Texas in 1810, when Hidalgo began his revolt against Spain, was probably fewer than 5,000. Events occurring far to the south in Mexico had a brief but important impact on Texas. Threats to Royalist authority in the form of the Casas Revolt and the Gutiérrez–Magee expedition foreshadowed the end of Spanish rule. The Gutiérrez–Magee insurgents suffered a disastrous defeat at the hands of Joaquín de

Arredondo at the battle of Medina on 18 August 1813. Subsequently, Arredondo's bloody purges, which substantially depopulated the province, left an indelible mark on Texas and assured that it would remain a Spanish province for another seven years. Those years, however, were frightfully destructive. Although Royalists successfully repelled all military invasions, the defenders of Texas had also become its predators. In the words of Antonio María Martínez, the last governor of Spanish Texas, the king's soldiers had "drained the resources of the country, and laid their hands on everything that could sustain human life."

In 1821, under the leadership of Agustín de Iturbide and Vicente Guerrero, a successful independence movement in Mexico brought Texas under that new nation. The Mexican War of Independence marked the close of an era in Texas history in which the Franciscan padres had founded and refounded missions at approximately 40 different sites. Presidios, numbering 10, had extended from Central Texas eastward to the site of present Robeline, Louisiana, and southward to Chambers County. Municipalities ranged from Laredo to San Antonio and Nacogdoches. Ranches and farms dotted the landscape. The majority of the population was probably mestizo. After Mexican independence, Hispanics were soon outstripped in numbers by Americans. Modern Texas, however, reflects its Spanish origins in many ways.

Donald E. Chipman

The Age of Mexican Independence. The nineteenth century began with the western world at war and Texas once again about to become a bone of contention between Spain and rivals who would dismember the Spanish empire. Called upon to resume its early role as an international border region, Texas underwent a series of upheavals during the first two decades of the 1800s that left it ill-prepared to face the challenges of being one of the least developed parts of the Provincias Internas at Mexican independence in 1821. Foreign encroachments, Indian warfare, and insurrectionary activity all contributed to demographic and economic collapse. In the end, desperate Spanish authorities authorized Anglo-American colonization in an effort to bolster the province and so produced a new set of problems for the Mexican authorities who soon replaced them.

In the last years of the eighteenth century Spain once again faced concerted efforts by rivals, now including the United States, to wrest from it important parts of its North American empire. Relations with the United States had come dangerously close to war over navigation rights on the Mississippi River and the expansion of Anglo-American frontier settlements into the Spanish Floridas. Napoleon's coerced acquisition of Louisiana in 1800 and his subsequent sale of the vast territory to the United States in 1803 left Spanish North America divided and vulnerable. Under these circumstances Texas assumed a geopolitical importance vastly disproportionate to its economic or demographic place in the empire. To Spanish royal officials United States claims that the Louisiana Purchase included all the territory to the Rio Grande put in jeopardy not only New Mexico, but the silver-mining regions of Zacatecas and San Luis Potosí as well. Governor Manuel Antonio Cordero y Bustamante had orders to hold on to all of Texas, which at that time stretched northward from the Medina and Nueces rivers to the Red River and eastward to the Arroyo Hondo. (Laredo at this time was part of Nuevo Santander, today Tamaulipas, and Ysleta was then part of New Mexico.) Simón de Herrera, Spanish military commander at the eastern border,

decided to make his stand on the west bank of the Sabine River. Late in 1806 he and Gen. James Wilkinson, who had orders to occupy the territory to the Sabine, signed the Neutral Ground agreement, by which both sides agreed to stay out of the area between the Sabine and the Arroyo Hondo until its sovereignty was determined by treaty.

For the next decade Spain tried to keep the United States at bay in Texas while slowly ceding ground in Florida. The Mexican-oriented activities of Philip Nolan, Aaron Burr, Zebulon Pike, and General Wilkinson concerned Spanish officials more than Anglo-American encroachments in Florida because Mexico was a richer colonial possession. The overthrow of the Spanish Bourbons by Napoleon, the resistance government in southern Spain, and the outbreak of various rebellions throughout Spanish America also contributed to loss of ground to the United States. Between 1810 and 1813 Baton Rouge and the Florida parishes and Mobile areas were incorporated into the United States. In 1814 and again in 1818 Andrew Jackson captured Pensacola. In 1817 a group of filibusters established the Republic of the Floridas on Amelia Island and resisted efforts by Spanish troops to oust them. Mexican viceregal authorities, successful in containing the Hidalgo revolt and in keeping Texas under Spanish rule, handed Ferdinand VII, the restored Bourbon monarch, at least one strong bargaining position in negotiations with the United States. Between 1816 and 1819 John Quincy Adams and Luis de Onís negotiated the conflicting territorial claims of the two continental powers. The resulting Adams–Onís Treaty, signed in Washington on 22 February 1819, recognized the obvious: the United States got the Floridas, much of which were already in Anglo-American hands; Spain retained title to Texas and got a clear demarcation of its boundary with the Louisiana territory. By terms of the treaty the Sabine and Red rivers marked the Texas–Louisiana border and the Neutral Ground became a permanent part of Louisiana.

At the beginning of the nineteenth century Texas remained a sparsely settled territory, heavily dependent on the military and continually exposed to the depredations of Indians that resisted Spanish sovereignty in the region. Crown efforts to bolster the small population and thus improve the province's viability proved unsuccessful, and the temporary advances made between 1805 and 1810 were quickly undone during the insurrectionary turmoil of 1811–13. By 1821 Texas had an even smaller Hispanic population than two decades earlier. The oldest and largest of colonial Texas communities was San Antonio de Béxar. In its 80-year history the settlement had evolved from a presidio–mission complex to the first chartered municipality and finally to the provincial capital. Its population of approximately 2,000 was composed chiefly of Mexican settlers from Coahuila, Nuevo León, and other frontier provinces mixed with a small number of Canary Islanders. After the United States acquired Louisiana, reinforcement of the Spanish military presence in Texas resulted in the transfer of the Second Flying Company of San Carlos de Parras to San Antonio, where it was headquartered in 1803 at San Antonio de Valero Mission, which had been closed. Other units from Nuevo Santander and Nuevo León swelled the population to over 3,000 by 1810. La Bahía's population of approximately 618 soldiers and civilians continued to live under military jurisdiction. Far to the northeast, near the Louisiana border, Nacogdoches was attracting increasing numbers of immigrants, legal and otherwise, from the Anglo-American frontier. Its population of 660 in 1803 continued to grow until hostilities during the Mexican War of Independence caused its virtual abandonment. Sustained contacts with Louisiana, although illegal, also brought about the reoccupation of the area between the Sabine River and the Arroyo Hondo. Bayou Pierre, an informal settlement of unknown dimensions located near the abandoned former capital of Los Adaes, was occupied by Spanish troops in 1805. Although the troops withdrew after the signing of the Neutral Ground agreement, Spanish authorities continued to claim jurisdiction there. In 1810 Governor Manuel María de Salcedo estimated the Neutral Ground population, including Bayou Pierre, at approximately 190.

The growing number of Spanish subjects in Louisiana who sought to avoid United States jurisdiction by applying for admission to Texas presented Spanish authorities with an important opportunity to address the lack of population on the frontier. Those officials who lobbied to admit the émigrés as settlers to Texas convinced policymakers that the benefits of the population increase outweighed the risks of contraband trade and disloyalty. During the latter part of 1805 Commandant-General Nemecio Salcedo authorized Governor Cordero to establish settlements on the Trinity, Brazos, Colorado, San Marcos, and Guadalupe rivers. Only two settlements came from these ambitious plans— Santísima Trinidad de Salcedo, started with five families from Bexar and seven from Louisiana, and San Marcos de Neve, with an original population of 81 from Nuevo Santander, Bexar, and La Bahía. While Salcedo grew slowly but steadily until the outbreak of insurrection, San Marcos floundered in the aftermath of a flood and Indian depredations.

Beyond the borders of what was then Texas, other settlements brought increasing numbers of Mexican colonists north of the Rio Grande. Laredo doubled in size between the end of the eighteenth century and the outbreak of Hidalgo's revolt. At this time numerous ranches were established east of Laredo and south of the Nueces River. On the eve of the independence struggle Cordero, now governor of Coahuila, ordered the establishment of Palafox Villa, half-way between San Juan Bautista and Laredo, with families from Coahuila. Although Laredo successfully held off the Indian raids that increased as Mexico sank into rebellion, the ranches to the east and Palafox to the west succumbed to the raiders and were largely abandoned by 1821.

The first decades of the nineteenth century were also notable for the arrival of new Indian settlers in Texas. United States occupation of Louisiana and the pursuit of Indian removal policies all along the Anglo-American frontier contributed to Indian flight to Spanish territory, where southern tribes had learned they would be well received. The demographic collapse of the Caddoan population, combined with Spanish perceptions of these displaced agriculturalist Indians as willing allies against the expansionist United States, also favored their settlement in Texas. Cherokees, Chickasaws, Choctaws, and Alabama–Coushattas established themselves in Texas at this time.

Prospects for the economic development of Texas improved markedly during the first decade of the nineteenth century. The enlarged military presence in the province; new settlement projects; increased, albeit illicit, trade opportunities with Louisiana; and relative peace with the Apaches and Comanches contributed to rising expectations among Texans. But the beginning of hostilities in 1811 started an economic and social disintegration that saw Texas in ruins on the eve of Mexican independence.

Military payrolls continued to be the driving force of the Texas economy in the early 1800s. The various presidio garrisons and other military units stationed in the province not only gave employment for those men who served in them, but also provided work for civilian artisans and income to local merchants, farmers, and ranchers. Steady growth in this sector of the economy came to an abrupt halt after the outbreak of the Mexican insurrection in late 1810. As the viceregal government diverted available resources to the royal armies fighting Hidalgo, José María Morelos, and the regional revolts they began, the frontier garrisons went unpaid and became burdens on the local communities. The dry-up of royal funds also had a devastating effect on Indian–Spanish relations. During the last decades of the eighteenth century Spanish policy had centered on appeasement of the Comanches and Norteños through regular gift-giving. In East Texas the Spanish government authorized Indian agents for the tribes in the region, the most prominent of which was the House of Barr and Davenport. As a result, Texas settlements enjoyed a prolonged period of peaceful trade with the various Indian peoples of the region that succeeded in maintaining their independence. Once the gifts became unavailable, the depredations renewed. Between 1810 and 1820 Indian raiders made agricultural work, ranching, and travel dangerous in the western part of the province and throughout the Rio Grande country.

Agriculture remained largely a subsistence pursuit during this period. A few farmers produced enough surplus corn to market it among the various military units, and an even smaller number produced commercial amounts of beans, chilis, and even crudely refined cane sugar (*piloncillo*). Cotton, which had once flourished at Bexar's mission farms, was no longer grown, nor was wheat. Most commercial farming took place around Bexar, the only Texas community with extensive irrigation works, although most of these fell into disrepair during the decade. Ranching also suffered. Over-harvesting and droughts during the last third of the eighteenth century contributed to a marked decline in cattle at the beginning of the nineteenth century. The expanding Anglo-American frontier brought new opportunities in horse trading, however. But the production of equine stock was an even more dangerous activity than cattle raising, as horses made a particularly attractive target for Indian raiders. Nevertheless, the high prices paid in Louisiana for mustangs afforded Texans one of the few opportunities for export earnings. The population of Nacogdoches, which had long-established, close economic ties with Louisiana, was particularly involved in this contraband trade. Contraband was, in fact, a way of life on the Texas frontier. Isolation made manufacturing impracticable in the province, yet made it attractive as a conduit for illicit trade goods flowing into and out of Mexico. The numerous reports of local officials, the recorded activities of those Texans who were caught participating in illegal trade, and the description of Anglo-American influences on the Hispanic population during this time all attest to the increasingly eastern orientation of the Texas economy. Unfortunately, because of its illegality, direct evidence of the contents and volume of this commerce is largely lacking.

Whether legal or illegal, the volume of trade that the Texas economy generated was insufficient to raise the population out of general poverty. No families in the province were rich, even by colonial standards. Governmental and ecclesiastical hierarchies were represented by the governor, some missionaries, and the parish priest at Bexar. The evidence suggests that only a handful of Tejanos had by the early nineteenth century managed to leave the province to seek a higher education. At Bexar, where the Canary

Islanders had mixed with the original presidial population, social status tended to be somewhat independent of economic position. Throughout Texas, personal accomplishment went far in establishing an individual's place in society.

Texas was the scene of two important episodes of rebellion against Spanish rule between 1811 and 1813. In succeeding years a number of invasions, some tied to the continuing struggle against Spanish colonial rule and some not, kept the Spanish military on the defensive. Surprisingly, the underpaid, ill-equipped frontier troops successfully held off the various threats to the crown's interests. The collapse of Royalist control throughout the northeastern provinces bordering Texas in late 1810 and early 1811 contributed to a similar occurrence in Texas. Frontier supporters of Hidalgo's movement found their manpower in the presidial military and provincial militias. The men in these locally recruited units were wary of exposing families and property to Indian attack and other dangers in order to go fight Hidalgo's rebels in the interior. In Texas, Juan Bautista de las Casas, a retired militia officer and Hidalgo supporter, took advantage of these very fears to lead a mutiny of the Bexar garrison on 22 January 1811. His aides met little opposition when they arrived at La Bahía and Nacogdoches to assume control. Nevertheless, disaffection, internal divisions among the rebel leadership, and loyalist leanings among local elites contributed to the quick restoration of royal rule. Gen. Joaquín de Arredondo led the counterattack in Nuevo Santander, while a counterrevolutionary junta in Coahuila liberated Governor Salcedo, who had been sent there by Casas, and organized resistance against the rebels. A similar organization of the local leadership took place at Bexar under the leadership of Juan Manuel Zambrano, son of one of the wealthier families in the community and a member of the clergy. The counter-revolutionaries proclaimed their allegiance to Ferdinand VII on 2 March 1811. Nine days later Coahuilan loyalists captured Hidalgo and the rest of the rebel leaders as they attempted to make their way to Texas in order to escape to the United States.

Eighteen months later rebellion once again engulfed Texas. José Bernardo Gutiérrez de Lara, a native of Nuevo Santander who had been sent as Hidalgo's emissary to the United States, entered Texas at the head of a force of Mexicans and Anglo-Americans styled the Republican Army of the North. He shared the command with West Point graduate Augustus W. Magee, who resigned a commission in the United States Army to help organize the Gutiérrez–Magee expedition. The expedition captured Nacogdoches in August 1812 and La Bahía in early November. Governor Salcedo failed to defeat the invaders either at La Bahía or later on the outskirts of Bexar. Following the battle of Rosillo (29 March 1813), Salcedo surrendered the Texas capital. Gutiérrez and a group of supporters declared Texas independence from Spain, but tensions among the various factions involved in the revolt left the insurrectionists unprepared to meet Arredondo's forces. Salcedo and more than a dozen other Spaniards in the province were executed, although they had been promised safe conduct out of Texas. A conservative constitution organized the province as a state within an illusory Mexican republic. Samuel Kemper, who had assumed command of the Anglo-American contingent, withdrew to the United States along with a number of other officers dissatisfied with the turn of events. At the beginning of August 1813 José Álvarez de Toledo y Dubois replaced Gutiérrez as political leader of the insurrection, just in time to be defeated by Arredondo at the battle of Medina on August 18. In the days that followed, the rebels abandoned La Bahía and Nacogdoches, thus restoring the province to Royalist rule.

After a respite of about two years, challenges to Spanish governance of Texas by armed invaders resumed. In November 1815 Henry Perry, who had served as an officer in the Gutiérrez–Magee expedition, crossed the Sabine River with a small force and occupied Point Bolivar as part of a new plan to conquer Texas. The following September privateer Louis Michel Aury seized Galveston on behalf of a group of New Orleans conspirators and declared the makeshift establishment a port of the Republic of Mexico. Francisco Xavier Mina, another insurrectionary interested in the liberation of Mexico, launched his invasion of Tamaulipas from Galveston in early 1817. Perry, who had joined Mina's expedition, abandoned the Tamaulipas venture and marched on La Bahía, where a force under Governor Antonio María Martínez defeated him on June 18. The Laffite brothers, Pierre and Jean, took over Galveston also in early 1817 and made it headquarters for their privateering and smuggling operations until May 1820. Although provincial authorities did not respond to the presence of pirates at Galveston, they did send an expedition to expel a large body of Napoleonic émigrés who attempted to establish themselves on the Trinity River at a site called Champ d'Asile in 1818. The following year Governor Martínez mounted an expedition of more than 500 troops under the command of Juan Ignacio Pérez to drive out James Long's expedition, which had been organized by Americans displeased by the boundary of the Louisiana Purchase agreed to in the Adams–Onís Treaty. Long returned to Texas in 1820 and remained at Point Bolivar for more than a year before attempting an attack on La Bahía. Pérez again took to the field and defeated Long on 8 October 1821, months after Mexican independence had been declared.

While colonial officials tried to preserve Mexico and Texas for the Spanish Bourbons, political instability on the Iberian peninsula conspired to prevent peace. Although he took an oath to the liberal constitution of 1812, Ferdinand VII grasped the first opportunity after his return from exile to reestablish autocratic rule. His unrealistic expectations of recovering lost South American colonies contributed to widespread dissatisfaction in Spain, and in 1820 a revolt of the expeditionary force about to sail for America led to the reestablishment of the Constitution of 1812. By the summer of 1821 one of the leading Royalist commanders, Agustín de Iturbide, had reached an agreement with rebel leaders still in the field and declared Mexican independence.

Texas, exhausted by its previous participation in the war of independence, by continuous Indian raids, and by periodic filibustering expeditions, embraced independence cautiously. Only in mid-July 1821, after Commandant-General Arredondo sent word of his acceptance of Iturbide's Plan de Iguala, did Governor Martínez order ceremonies to commemorate the event. At Bexar, La Bahía, and what little was left of Nacogdoches, Tejanos swore allegiance to the new Mexican nation and prepared to take their destiny into their own hands. *Jesús F. de la Teja*

Mexican Texas. The Mexican War of Independence left Mexico devastated. The new country stood in marked contrast to the rich colony that had promised great potential towards the end of the colonial era. Money barely circulated. Once-rich mines struggled to regain their former efficiency. Ranches and farms were no longer productive. With the economy in shambles, thousands faced unemployment. Entire areas were depopulated as people

Vista del presidio de Goliad antes Bahia del Espirita Santo, by Jean Louis Berlandier, 1829. Graphic. Courtesy Yale Collection of Western Americana, Beinecke Rare Book and Manuscript Library. The Congress of Coahuila and Texas declared the presidio of La Bahía a town and renamed it Goliad in 1829. Goliad was one of three municipalities in Spanish Texas. The area was settled in 1749 when a mission and presidio were moved there.

moved away looking for a livelihood. Moreover, differences over class distinctions split the nation as the landed gentry, the military, and church officials sought the preservation of the antebellum order, wherein they ruled alongside government. Additionally, many of the country's new leaders had had little prior experience in governing.

An equally urgent concern for the young country was guarding its far northern possessions from United States expansion; Texas was especially vulnerable to encroachment from that country, and colonization offered the best deterrent. But Mexico lacked the population to settle the north. Consequently, it tried enticing European and American immigrants to the region to act as defense forces against Indians and foreign powers. The political issues raised by the new settlers became the dominant topic in Texas during this period. In January 1821 the Spanish government gave Moses Austin of Missouri a contract to establish a colony on the Brazos River with 300 Catholic families. When he died on 10 June 1821, his son, Stephen F. Austin, inherited the contract, and by the end of 1821 colonists began reaching Texas, some of them establishing themselves on the main settlement, San Felipe de Austin. The Mexican government confirmed Austin's contract via the Imperial Colonization Law of January 1823.

The National Colonization Law of August 18, 1824, which superseded the Imperial Colonization Law, determined how Texas would be peopled. It stipulated that those wishing colonization contracts should make arrangements with the legislatures of individual states and not the federal government. In the case of Texas, an empresario would have to negotiate with Saltillo, the capital of Coahuila, since Texas was merged with that state. Government

officials in Coahuila would thus define the course of immigration by determining whether those receiving contracts would be Anglos, Europeans, or Mexicans. The National Colonization Law of 1824 resulted from a Federalist political philosophy advanced by some of Mexico's post-independence statesmen who envisioned establishing a republic patterned after the United States. After asserting themselves over their Centralist rivals in the latter part of 1823, they wrote the Federal Constitution of the United States of Mexico on 4 October 1824. This republican document called for a constitutional arrangement by which the national government would grant powers to the states. It resembled the United States Constitution in several ways, but also borrowed tenets from the Spanish Constitution of 1812.

In accordance with the National Colonization Law, the Federalist constituent legislature, meeting in Saltillo, passed the State Colonization Law of March 24, 1825. The legislature attempted to bring about the peopling of the state of Coahuila and Texas, encourage agriculture and ranching, and facilitate commerce. It stated that Americans could settle in the state, though Mexicans were to have first choice of lands; that for a nominal payment a settler could receive as much as a league or sitio of pastureland and a labor of land for cultivation; that immigrants were temporarily free of every kind of tax; and that newcomers had to take an oath promising to abide by the federal and state constitutions, to worship according to the Christian religion, and to display sound moral principles and good conduct. After accepting these terms and settling in Texas, immigrants earned the standing of naturalized Mexicans. The legislative provision addressing slavery was too ambiguous, and so the secretary of state at Saltillo declared

McNeil's estate near Brazoria, by J. T. Hammond. Engraving. From *A Visit to Texas* (New York: Goodrich and Wiley, 1834). Courtesy CAH; CN 02343. By 1834 approximately 20,000 Americans had settled in Texas. Many built dogtrot homes like the one depicted here. McNeil's was described as a fine estate and his hospitality as generous.

that "What is not prohibited is to be understood as permitted." Foreigners seeking land in Texas could negotiate individually, but the more common method was to act through immigration agents (empresarios), who selected families, designated land where the newcomers could settle, and saw to the obedience of the laws. In compensation, the government would award these contracting parties five sitios and five labores for each 100 families brought and settled. Among the most prominent of these colonizers were Stephen F. Austin and Green DeWitt.

By the mid-1820s Mexico began reconsidering its lenient immigration policy. Officials expressed consternation that some Americans squatted on lands without any formality and that most did not make a serious commitment to conform to the laws and traditions of their adopted land. The Americans, who were settled in the eastern part of the province, violated colonization statutes when convenient and imposed their own practices on local affairs. In 1826 the empresario Haden Edwards went so far as to proclaim the Nacogdoches area an independent republic, the Republic of Fredonia. Though the Fredonian Rebellion was short-lived, the Mexican government came to fear that continued immigration might well produce secessionist sentiments among Anglo-Texans.

In response to the troubles in Texas, the Centralists in Mexico City, who ousted the Federalists in late 1829 and espoused a strong central government patterned after the monarchist Spain of old, implemented the Law of April 6, 1830. The law voided those empresario contracts still not in compliance. It further curtailed immigration from the United States, although officials did permit continued settlement in the colonies of Austin and DeWitt because these two empresarios were ruled to have settled the required 100 families; in actuality, however, both had yet to fulfill their contracts. Military bases were to be established as a means of policing illegal immigration. Slaves, the law stipulated, were not to be imported from the United States, though blacks already in Texas would remain bondsmen. Among those inveighing against the Law of April 6 were Anglos, political leaders in Coahuila, and Tejano oligarchs who thought that inexpensive settlement from the United States portended the wealth of Texas. Federalists in Coahuila and Texas had welcomed Anglos as a way of providing security from Indians, developing the cotton lands of Texas, and establishing prosperity through commerce. With more and more foreigners seeking to convert their land into farmsteads, entrepreneurs foresaw the realization of their ambitious plan to develop the region. As commercial activity grew, they envisaged for themselves an economic network extending into Louisiana, Coahuila, and the far north of Mexico. But Anglo immigrants could be attracted only if they were permitted to use the Gulf ports, exempted from taxes, and offered other inducements. Coahuila's colonizing program of 1825 had offered such incentives.

Allowing slavery would also attract immigrants. Since the mid-1820s, the three groups opposed to the Law of April 6 had lobbied for the acceptance of human bondage. They had succeeded in 1828 when the legislature, noting the scarcity of field laborers in Coahuila and Texas, decreed that slaves could be brought to Texas under indenture contracts; in Texas, bondsmen would work to pay their owners for freedom. Thus was Mexico's own form of economic bondage—debt peonage—utilized to rationalize the existence of slavery. On September 15 of the next year President Vicente Ramón Guerrero issued the Guerrero Decree, which expressly prohibited enslavement in every form. This move revealed the president's humanitarianism, but might also have been designed to control the flow of immigration from the United States. Political leaders in Texas and Coahuila remonstrated, however, and Guerrero excluded Texas from slave manumission by a decree on December 2, 1829. Subsequently, in 1830, the Law of April 6 presented a more formidable obstacle.

Among those upset with the anti-immigration policy outlined in the Law of April 6 were Anglo-Americans who attacked the military post at Anahuac in the summer of 1832. Their pretext was the arrest for sedition of the lawyer William B. Travis by the Anahuac commander, Col. John Davis Bradburn, an Anglo-American adventurer who belonged to the Centralist faction in Mexico. Fortunately, ranking military figures defused the crisis by reassigning Bradburn and releasing Travis and other inmates. On June 13, 1832, the attackers issued the Turtle Bayou Resolutions, wherein they explained the attack as an expression of dissatisfaction with Bradburn, not the government in the interior. But Anglo volunteers and Mexican troops skirmished again at the battle of Velasco on June 26. As of 1832, however, the "War party"—as the radicals came to be labeled—lacked popular support; in fact many Anglo-Texan colonists branded them as adventurers.

In early 1833 Antonio López de Santa Anna entered Mexico City and removed the Centralists. The Federalist government then revoked the article in the Law of April 6, 1830, that curtailed immigration from the United States, and the Anglo-American influx resumed. But in May 1834 Santa Anna pronounced against his vice president, Valentín Gómez Farías, who, in Santa Anna's absence, had passed legislation that infringed on the prerogatives of the clergy, army officers, and privileged classes. Now turned Centralist, Santa Anna abrogated the Constitution of 1824 and called for a new congress composed of officials faithful to Centralist doctrine. In October 1835 the new congress disbanded legislatures and converted the states into departments governed by appointees of the president. In effect, it established a Centralist state. The rise of the Centralists incited uprisings in such states as Zacatecas, though these were not independence movements. In Coahuila, meanwhile, the Federalists rejected Centralist orders,

Ranchero de Texas, by Lino Sánchez y Tapía, ca. 1830. Watercolor. Courtesy Gilcrease Museum, Tulsa; acc. no. 4016.336, plate XXXV. Most Hispanic Texans resided in Central and South Texas and made their living off the land.

and in the spring of 1835 the legislature promulgated a law authorizing the governor to dispose of up to 400 leagues of land in order to raise the needed funds to meet the danger confronting federalism. Another decree permitted the distribution of 400 leagues to finance militia units to deal with threats from unfriendly Indian tribes. The Mexican commander in Bexar now feared that the Anglo-Texans would assemble an army against the government, and he called upon Santa Anna for reinforcements.

With reports spreading to Texas that Mexico had ordered troops into the north, a force of militant Texans under Travis's leadership headed for Anahuac on June 30, 1835, and captured the site to protect Texas from a Mexican military incursion. To Mexico, the attack on the military post was an indication of a rebellion, and the refusal of Texans to surrender the Anahuac ringleaders confirmed suspicions of widespread defiance. The initial conflict between Anglo-Americans and Mexican authorities occurred in October 1835 in the battle of Gonzales, generally considered the first battle of the Texas Revolution.

At the end of the Mexican War of Independence the population of Texas numbered approximately 2,500. Throughout the 1820s the size of the immigrant population increased, then stagnated following the adoption of the Law of April 6, 1830. Settlers arrived nonetheless; in any case the law was nullified in 1834. That year Juan N. Almonte, sent by Mexico on an inspection tour of Texas, estimated the Anglo population at about 20,000. One historian estimates that the figure probably reflected a doubling of the Anglo population from four years previous. From the three towns that existed in 1821, the number of urban sites increased to 21 by 1835; almost all owed their founding to Anglo immigrants. Principal towns established by Americans included San Felipe de Austin,

Cheraquis

Cherokees: Indigènes des E.U. du N.Amérique émigrés aux environs de Nacogdoches.

Cheraquis, by Lino Sánchez y Tapía, after José María Sánchez y Tapía, ca. 1830. Watercolor. Courtesy Gilcrease Museum, Tulsa; acc. no. 4016.336, plate XV. In Mexican Texas, the Cherokees, who came to Texas from Georgia and Alabama in 1819–20, farmed, ranched, and traded with whites in Nacogdoches. They were later expelled by the Republic of Texas.

Gonzales, Velasco, Matagorda, Brazoria, San Augustine, and Liberty.

Generally, settlers lived in isolation, for neighboring farms might be miles away. Immigrants thus struggled for survival by their own wits, living off the land by hunting and by planting small gardens. For their shelter, plain folks turned to the environment and used whatever materials they could—logs, for instance—to build their cabins. The primitive domiciles characteristically consisted of one or two rooms and lacked floors and windows.

Frontiersmen improvised in other ways. For the education of their children, Anglo settlers set up schools that they themselves subsidized, most of them similar to the academies then typical of the South. Or settlers would simply convert homes into teaching institutions, so that school buildings generally consisted of pine-log huts. Teachers, furthermore, were difficult to find. Residents of means, however, dispatched youngsters to the United States for school.

Printing in Texas originated during the years of the Mexican War of Independence, when Americans established newspaper presses on Texas soil to encourage Mexico's struggle for self-rule. Not until 1829, however, did G. B. M. Cotten establish the *Texas Gazette* at Austin's colony; this enterprise, the first newspaper to be published in the province on a regular basis, enabled Austin to explain laws and policies to the colonists. After the *Gazette* discontinued production in 1832, Anglo-Texans got their news from other publications. Among these was the *Telegraph and Texas Register*, started in October 1835. It published such official documents as letters and reports written by leading Anglo-American figures.

Though Mexico required settlers to practice only the Catholic religion, the country could hardly enforce its own laws due to a shortage of priests and other problems. Anglo-Texan settlers therefore generally went their own way in practicing their faiths.

Austin's settlers enacted their own ceremonies solemnizing births and deaths, for only briefly in 1831–32 did they have a priest among them, an Irishman named Michael Muldoon. Other colonists conducted worship services and camp meetings. The Mexican government seemed not to have been terribly concerned with the persistence of Protestantism, for in 1834 it even granted the Texans religious freedom on the condition that settlers abide by the laws they promised to observe.

For blacks, slavery came to be a way of life in the eastern settlements, even as the Mexican government had strongly expressed disapproval of the system. The immediate future of the "peculiar institution" seemed uncertain during the early years of settlement, as the Mexican government persisted in its opposition to slavery but did not enforce edicts abolishing it. Once the Federalists in Coahuila and Texas succeeded in making slavery legal, the institution took root, even as the national government reversed its position on the matter several other times. It gained a foothold because Anglo-Texans generally thought blacks destined for servitude; most of the immigrants came from the lower South, where attitudes prescribed specific roles for both races. Furthermore, the immigrants considered slavery essential for the economic growth of Texas, a conviction with which Tejano oligarchs and their colleagues in Coahuila concurred. By 1836, 5,000 slaves resided in Texas, concentrated in the Anglo settlements.

Most Hispanic Texans remained situated in central and southern Texas, where they made their livelihood as bucolic workers, but others resided in the three urban settlements founded in the early eighteenth century—San Antonio, Goliad, and Nacogdoches. According to Almonte's report in 1834, Bexar and outlying ranches had a Hispanic population of 2,400, Goliad 700, and Nacogdoches 500. The new town of Victoria, colonized by Martín De León in 1824, had 300 residents in 1834. Laredo, on the Rio Grande, had a population of about 2,000 in 1835.

The new immigration exacerbated old social divisions. A group of *ricos* occupied the upper crust of society; their standing rested on government position, family, racial background, business, and land possession. At the bottom lived *peones* and day laborers, usually mestizos and Hispanicized Indians. The aristocrats sent their children to schools in Coahuila or had private tutors for them. Throughout the Mexican era, it was the *ricos* who voiced political opinions. The society stressed frontier ruggedness and masculinity. Even as Mexican law permitted women numerous freedoms—such as the right to have their own property while married and the right to judicial redress—they nonetheless lived under numerous political and legal restraints. Women could not be officeholders or exercise the franchise. Adulteresses could faced harsh penalties and risked the loss of their property. Divorces were difficult to obtain. In the tradition of some other Western societies of that era, Texas Mexican women ate only after serving their husbands, then ate apart from the men.

While the government committed itself to a program of public education, support to communities was often inadequate, so that citizens looked to municipal taxes and individual contributions to educate their children. Hispanic Texans established schools in each of the urban areas during the 1820s, though they functioned irregularly amid weak government support, political uncertainty, the threat of Indian raids, epidemics, and the difficulty of finding qualified teachers. In 1829, the legislature decreed the establishment of instruction based on the Lancastrian system of education, which used advanced students to teach those in lower grades.

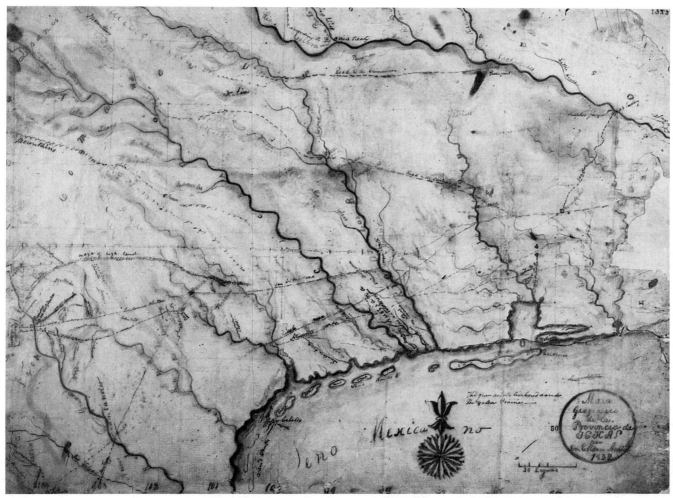

Mapa Geográfico de la Provincia de Texas, by Stephen F. Austin, 1822. Manuscript. Stephen F. Austin Map Collection, CAH; CN 00057. Stephen F. Austin carried this map when he went to Mexico City to confirm his empresario contract. It was the most complete and accurate map of Texas to that date.

Through dictation, memorization, and recitation, pupils learned the basics of arithmetic, grammar, religion, and civics.

The Indians of Texas, whom the Spaniards had sought to convert, had either been reduced by diseases, conflict, or the adverse effects of mission life and white men's institutions, pushed west into the frontier, or integrated into Hispanic society. Only remnants of groups that the Spaniards had sought to Christianize—such as the Coahuiltecans and Karankawas—survived by the 1830s, and those Indians in the San Antonio and Goliad missions were ostensibly absorbed into the towns' populations after the missions were secularized in the 1820s. The more hostile Indians situated west of the settlements survived in their traditional ways. The Comanches and their allies hunted buffalo, then turned the animals over to the women, who cut and cured the meat and treated the hides before turning them into clothes, weapons, and an assortment of items for household use. Some Plains Indians also relied on such crops as corn, beans, and pumpkins, whose cultivation and preservation was also entrusted to the women. Raids on settlements remained a way of life as the Comanches and smaller groups continued in their custom of stealing livestock. Some traded horses, mules, furs, and other stolen goods to unscrupulous

Americans for weapons. The more sedentary tribes of East Texas, meantime, struggled to earn subsistence as horticulturists. The Caddos, who numbered about 300 families in the late 1820s, planted corn, beans, and pumpkins, but they supplemented their livelihood by trading beaver, deer, and otter skins for weapons and tobacco in Louisiana. Cherokees, who had arrived in Texas from Georgia and Alabama in 1819–20 and settled on land now in Van Zandt, Cherokee, Rusk, and Smith counties, numbered about 80 families in the late 1820s. They farmed, raised cattle, and traded skins, corn, pumpkins, beans, and fruits with the whites in Nacogdoches. During the 1820s and 1830s they sought to persuade the Mexican government to grant them title to their lands, but received only a vague commitment in return. The Republic of Texas government expelled the Cherokees and numerous other Indian groups.

Frontier life determined the state of economic matters in Mexican Texas. Manufacturing of basic items was hardly known, so that Anglo settlers brought with them blankets, hats, clothing, and shoes; after they wore out their apparel, they replaced it with clothes made from animal skins. Where fiber or a spinning wheel was available, settlers produced new clothes from hand-made

19

cloth. Weapons and implements for working the land were brought by settlers, as were such luxury items as coffee, cigars, and wines. The soil provided a minimum living of corn and various vegetables. But with slaves and imported technology, Anglos initiated commercial agriculture by raising and processing cotton for export. One historian estimates that commerce with New Orleans may have totaled 7,000 bales worth about $315,000 by 1834. Other items produced in quantities large enough to sell outside the province included corn, salted meats, and bear and deer skins. Lumbering and milling appeared in the timberlands of East Texas; though the lumber industry principally met only local needs, some lumber made its way to the Matamoros market. As in colonial days, smuggling was attractive to East Texans. The Mexican government excused immigrants from paying tariff duties, but since not all imports were exempted, the immigrants smuggled what they could of these. They found markets for such contraband in Mexico and even as far west as New Mexico. Bexareños also participated in the contraband market and apparently made hefty profits from the business. Trapping was pursued to some degree. The rivers along the coast abounded in otters and beavers, and Anglos sold the pelts at Nacogdoches yearly. Hispanic ranchers tapped the market in Coahuila and Louisiana by rounding up wild cattle and mustangs in the brush country, though stock raising may not have been as brisk as in Spanish Texas. Moreover, the ranchers were still harried by government restrictions and dangers from hostile Indians. Possibly, however, Tejanos found new markets for cattle and horses among the Anglo-Texan arrivals. Farming among the Hispanic population took a subordinate position to ranching. San Antonio residents irrigated small family-owned fields and orchards to raise a variety of vegetables, grains, and fruits, but did not produce them in exportable amounts. Wealthier landholders did cultivate produce to sell for a profit to the local military. Some landowners near San Antonio or Goliad experimented with cotton production, but their crops constituted only a small portion of the total amount of cotton harvested in the province. With hard cash practically unknown, barter was the popular way of conducting business. Transactions often involved payment with cows, swine, poultry, or even land. "Money is very scarce in Texas," reported Juan Almonte in 1834, "and one may say with certainty that out of every hundred transactions made not ten involve specie." Counterfeit paper money from both Mexico and the United States appeared regularly and was a constant problem.

Immigration from the United States to Texas produced new political directions for the province from 1821 to 1836. For one thing, it caused political disagreement over immigration itself: Federalists generally encouraged the arrival of Anglo-Americans in hopes of advancing and modernizing Coahuila and Texas; but Centralists feared the Americanization of Texas and consistently clashed with the Federalists' policy and the fractious Anglo-Texans. Most significantly, of course, the new arrivals asserted themselves politically and finally usurped their hosts' authority. By the end of the Mexican period, therefore, great changes were apparent in Texas. Anglos had implemented a republican form of government, established a different language, introduced new Christian communions, brought about a social order wherein minorities, among them some Mexican Texans who assisted in the struggles of the 1830s, were subordinated. Overall, the immigrants had given the region clear Anglo-American characteristics. However, the resulting life was not radically changed. The province remained an underdeveloped frontier region that taxed the perseverance of its settlers, still depended on an agrarian economy, and continued to face serious problems in such concerns as finances and education. *Arnoldo De León*

Texas Revolution. The Texas Revolution began with the battle of Gonzales in October 1835 and ended with the battle of San Jacinto on 21 April 1836. Earlier clashes between official forces and groups of colonists, however, as well as social and political changes, were a part of the revolution. Mexican policies often did not sit well with the Anglo-American occupants of Texas. Moreover, Mexican government officials thought that the United States government was not above using colonists to cause trouble in the hope of acquiring Texas. The Fredonian Rebellion (1826) and the two episodes of the Anahuac Disturbances (1832, 1835), as well as other military actions (e.g., the battle of Velasco and the battle of Nacogdoches) preceded the decisive independence movement of the fall of 1835. Col. José Francisco Ruiz abandoned Fort Tenoxtitlán without being attacked. Santa Anna was busy leading a revolution against President Anastasio Bustamante at the time of these disturbances in Texas, and the few colonists who participated in them declared that they were cooperating with him by expelling Bustamante's garrisons from Texas.

Actually, the great mass of the colonists had no quarrel with Mexico or Mexicans and adopted resolutions assuring the authorities of their loyalty—at least, they wanted no war with Mexico. Tranquillity seemed about restored on this basis when Col. José Antonio Mexía sailed into the mouth of the Brazos with a regiment of Santanisto soldiers and inquired what was going on. With him was Stephen F. Austin, who had been in Mexico during the summer, and by Austin's advice it was decided to stand by the declaration of the insurgents for Santa Anna. After enjoying appropriate hospitalities, Mexía sailed away. His visit had, however, compelled Austin to abandon his policy of aloofness from national party contests. The summer ended with Santa Anna successful in Mexico and all garrisons expelled from Texas except those at San Antonio and Goliad.

As a result of the conventions of 1832 and 1833 the colonists had asked for a number of privileges and reforms, of which three were the most important. (1) In September 1823, Congress had given the colonists certain tariff exemptions for seven years. This liberal law expired in 1830, and friction over the tariff was an element in the disturbances in 1832. Both conventions adopted petitions asking for extension of the tariff exemptions. (2) When the federal system was instituted in 1824, Congress united Coahuila and Texas as a single state, with the somewhat indefinite assurance that the union might be dissolved when Texas was qualified for statehood. Both conventions declared that Texas was able to maintain a state government and asked for separation. The Convention of 1833 went so far as to frame a constitution for the approval of Congress, the Constitution Proposed in 1833. (3) Apprehension over the large number of colonists led Congress to pass the Law of April 6, 1830, forbidding immigrants to settle in territory adjacent to their native country. Though this law was subsequently interpreted to permit continued settlement in the Austin and DeWitt colonies, it remained a menace to the development of Texas, and the conventions petitioned for its repeal. Resolutions of the Convention of 1832 were never delivered; but Austin, elected to present the petitions of 1833, arrived in Mexico City in July. Congress repealed the immigration restriction of the Law of April 6, 1830, held the tariff plea in abeyance, and took no action on the petition for statehood.

On his way home, however, Austin was arrested at the instigation of Vice President Valentín Gómez Farías and held a prisoner in Mexico until July 1835.

Dissatisfaction over continued union with Coahuila was alleviated by state laws extending local self-government and granting Texas trial by jury and appellate courts. At the same time, however, Santa Anna's movements toward overthrowing the Constitution of 1824 and establishing a virtual dictatorship aroused bitter opposition. Details of his program included remanning the military posts evacuated in 1832 and reorganizing the state government. The first contingent of soldiers arrived at Anahuac in January 1835, and resultant friction soon led to the second of the Anahuac Disturbances. After Travis compelled Capt. Antonio Tenorio to surrender the post and conditions appeared to return to the status of 1832, numerous mass meetings condemned Travis and adopted resolutions declaring loyalty to Mexico. Reports continued, however, that Santa Anna was bent upon military occupation of Texas, and a group of colonists published a call for election of delegates to a convention, or consultation, in October. Austin, returned from his long detention in Mexico, gave his approval to the Consultation and was made chairman of a committee of safety and correspondence at San Felipe. The committee was regarded as a central advisory board to collect and distribute information.

From this time forward, only a spark was necessary to set off an explosion. At Copano Bay, Gen. Martín Perfecto de Cos landed at the head of 500 men, formed his troops, and moved on San Antonio. Austin's committee called for the immediate formation of military units to offer armed resistance. Cos announced his intention to punish those who led the uprising at Anahuac, and in his proclamation was the hint that he would drive the American settlers out of Texas. The day after Cos arrived in San Antonio on 9 October, Texans seized Goliad. There, at the battle of Gonzales, what is regarded as the first shot in the Texas Revolution was fired. This event was minor in itself. But after it, Austin, at this time in command of the embryonic revolutionary army and in the Gonzales vicinity, realized that Texas had reached the point of no return. In early October he therefore led his command, all volunteers, toward San Antonio. Two others shared the command, James Bowie and James W. Fannin, Jr. On the night of 27 October Bowie, in general command, staked out a solid defensive position on the San Antonio River not far from Nuestra Señora de la Purísima Concepcíon de Acuña Mission. On the following morning in the battle of Concepción the Texans defeated a combined force of Mexican foot and horse supported by artillery, with the Mexicans losing 60 men to the Texans' one. On November 26 the Texans again faced the Mexicans at the Grass Fight, an episode of the successful siege of Bexar. Once again Bowie was in command, but this time with Edward Burleson, who assumed Austin's command, the latter having been made commissioner to the United States by the provisional government. The Texans forced the Mexicans to retreat, killing 50 of them in the process, while losing two men with another unaccounted for. The climax of the siege came on 5 December, when, learning that Burleson was considering withdrawal to Goliad, Benjamin R. Milam raised the defiant cry, "Who will go to San Antonio with old Ben Milam?" and he and Francis W. Johnson led 300 volunteers into the heart of the city. After three days of house-to-house fighting, Milam was dead and San Antonio was the prize of the Texans. Ironically, Cos's final stand was at the Alamo. Forced to surrender, the Mexican commander was compelled to take his troops beyond the Rio Grande.

Freemen of Texas To Arms!!! To Arms!!!, October 2, 1835. Broadsides Collection, CAH; CN 01536. After Texans defeated Mexican troops at the battle of Gonzales on 2 October 1835, they issued a call for others to arm themselves and join them at their camp for a march on the Mexican soldiers stationed in San Antonio.

Taking advantage of the fact that the Texan army was divided and disintegrating despite its victories in 1835, Santa Anna, in his role as generalissimo, crossed the Rio Grande on a punitive expedition shortly after the new year. His plan was simple and direct: he would crush insurgency in Texas with the force of a hammer, treating all in arms against his government as mere pirates. The quelling of piracy, after all, required no mercy. At the beginning of his campaign, it seemed apparent that he would do just that, for Texan fortunes took a decided turn for the worse in early 1836. By 2 March the Convention of 1836, meeting at Washington-on-the-Brazos, formally voted for independence, though in view of Santa Anna's powerful force, such action might have been considered premature. The convention also appointed Sam Houston major general of the Texas army and commander of the forces at Gonzales. After crossing the Rio Grande with 6,000 troops, Santa Anna's command eventually grew to more than 8,000. It soon became apparent that his target was San Antonio and the Texans stationed there. In fact, he probably should have avoided that city, for it was not important to his success. The Texan defense stood on a triangle. On the west was San Antonio, on the south was San Patricio, and on the northeast was Goliad. Militarily speaking, Goliad was the prize. It held approximately 500 insurgents under the command of Fannin, while a divided command under Bowie and Travis at the Alamo comprised only 150 men, to which only some 30 more were soon added. Goliad was the door to East Texas, with its heavy American population. San Antonio, however, even reinforced, could not offer a real threat to Santa Anna or even to his line of communication. But military considerations aside, the general was determined to march on San Antonio, in part because of the humiliation visited upon his family there through defeat of his son-in-law, Cos.

Unfortunately for Santa Anna's army, his logistical support was spare. He apparently had hoped to supplement his supplies by living off the land, but the area south of San Antonio could not sustain him. Furthermore, the weather that spring was unusually cold and wet. Some of Santa Anna's troops, recruited from the Yucatán, died of hypothermia. Meanwhile, in San Antonio, the few Texans were drawn into the confines of San Antonio de Valero Mission. On 23 February, Santa Anna's advance force arrived in San Antonio. For 13 days the Texans held their position behind the inadequate defenses of the mission, while waiting for reinforcements that never came. It soon became apparent that Santa Anna not only wanted San Antonio as a base for operations but also desired the utter destruction of the Texan defenders, whom he wanted to make an example. He chose to force the issue with a bloody assault, whereas in fact his trenches and siege train could have handled the matter effectively. In the battle of the Alamo (6 March 1836), the Texans were overwhelmed by sheer force of numbers. In bitter fighting all of the soldiers were killed, while some 30 noncombatants—women, children, and blacks—were spared. Santa Anna lost some 600 of his men, or roughly a third of his assault force. To be sure, the generalissimo was delighted, but little of importance had been gained. Furthermore, the Alamo catastrophe subsequently led Texans to a relentless thirst for vengeance.

Simultaneously with Santa Anna's progress, cutting across the Rio Grande at Matamoros was a smaller force under Gen. José de Urrea, a canny fighter and inspiring leader, who, though a Federalist, put his politics aside and delivered a devastating blow to the Texan heartland. Urrea captured San Patricio by a swift thrust that caught the Texans by surprise. This success was followed by another at the battle of Agua Dulce Creek, in which Dr. James Grant's force was defeated. In short order, Urrea also descended upon Lt. Col. William Ward's party. But these actions, though significant in themselves, were incidental matters to Urrea, who was bound for Goliad. Fannin, the Texan commander at Goliad, had gathered men to attack Matamoros, despite Houston's opposition. When he heard that Urrea already had consolidated that position, he changed his mind and fell back to Goliad. Houston ordered him to relieve the men at the Alamo but by March 14 rescinded that order and issued a new one. Fannin was to proceed with his entire command to Victoria, where a linking of forces would occur. However, learning that Ward and Aaron King and all their men had been defeated by Urrea, Fannin vacillated between defending Goliad and retreating to Victoria. Finally, on March 19, he decided too late to leave Presidio La Bahía and move toward Houston. Urrea immediately set out in pursuit. Fannin, fearing the exhaustion of his men and animals, halted after a march of only six miles. The Texans were not far from Coleto Creek with its water

and protective treeline when Urrea's cavalry appeared, blocked Fannin's path, and seized the creek. When Urrea's main body arrived, Fannin could only form a square and wait. The next morning Urrea received reinforcements, including artillery. As Mexican cannons leveled their guns on the Texans, and as Mexican infantry formed attack columns, Fannin accepted the inevitable and asked for terms. He received what he, at least, regarded as an assurance that his army would be treated honorably as prisoners of war. The Texans were marched back to Goliad, imprisoned, and assured of their release. Upon hearing the terms of surrender, Santa Anna countermanded them and ordered the execution of the Texans, an order that was carried out on 27 March—an act of treachery that became known as the Goliad Massacre, which like the fall of the Alamo became a rallying cry for Texans.

About the same time, Houston arrived in Gonzales and assumed command of an army of fewer than 400 men. Upon hearing of the fall of the Alamo from Susanna Dickinson, Houston also learned that the Mexican army was pressing on to Gonzales. Aware of his precarious position, he decided to withdraw. Because of a lack of transport, he was forced to sink his cannons in the Guadalupe River. He burned the town to render it useless to Santa Anna and fell back to the northeast toward the Colorado River. The town's inhabitants contributed to the number of refugees already pouring northward and eastward from San Patricio, Refugio, and points in between. In time, they were joined by throngs from all over East Texas in what became known as the Runaway Scrape.

After the Alamo fell, Santa Anna assumed that the war was over, and news of Goliad only confirmed his view. It was necessary for his officers to convince him that the job was not yet finished—he still had to run down Houston and the remaining Texan forces. Finally accepting their remonstrations, he planned a three-pronged offensive through East Texas. Gen. Antonio Gaona was initially to take a northerly route via Bastrop toward Nacogdoches, but shortly thereafter Santa Anna ordered him instead to proceed from Bastrop toward San Felipe. Gen. Joaquín Ramírez y Sesma was also ordered to San Felipe, whence he would strike in an easterly direction with the probable destination of Anahuac. Ramírez's troops were to act as the spearhead of the thrust. Finally, Urrea was to secure the right flank of these movements while maintaining a northerly route in the hope of joining the main forces if a mass formation should be necessary. Houston was thus to be snared, his army crushed or captured, and the rebellion finished. On March 20 Ramírez, in torrid pursuit of Houston but at the head of only 800 men, reached the Colorado. Houston's army at this time probably outnumbered the Mexicans, but the Texas general refused to fight for several reasons. He realized that although his army was patriotically motivated, it was poorly trained. Furthermore, his enemy had artillery and he did not. Finally, Santa Anna's plan allowed for rapid communication and consequent quick reinforcement. Houston thought that he could not risk it, for if he lost, there would be nothing to stop Santa Anna from marching unimpeded across Texas. This last consideration became all the more important after 2 March, the date on which the convention approved the Texas Declaration of Independence. In Houston's mind, nothing less was at stake than independent nationhood. Nevertheless, disappointed that he did not attack, a number of his troops began to question his leadership, and a discipline problem developed that lasted all the way to San Jacinto.

When Houston learned of Fannin's destruction, his withdrawal

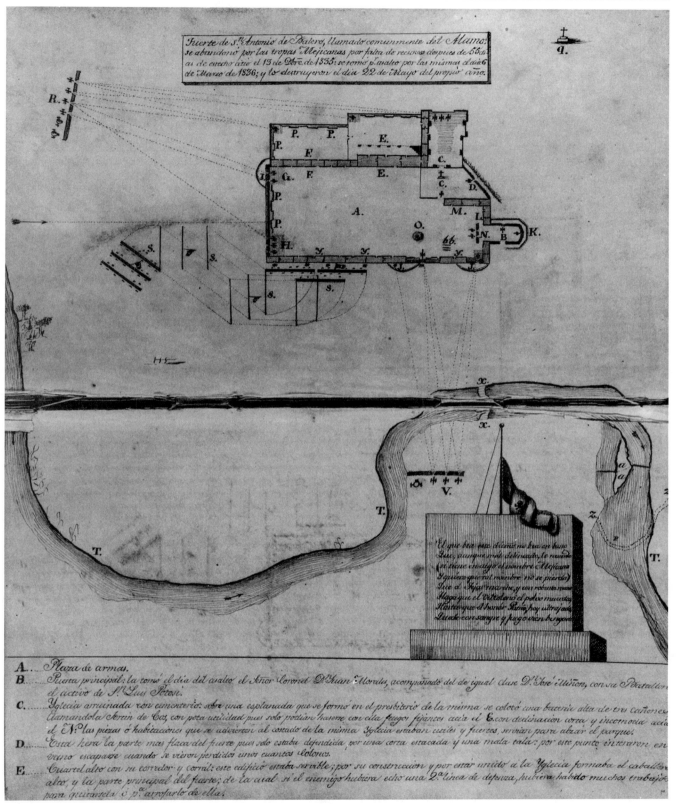

Plan of the Alamo, by José Juan Sánchez Navarro, 1836. José Sánchez Navarro Papers, CAH; CN 01579a. This manuscript map, part of an official military report on the fall of the Alamo, shows where the Mexicans positioned cannons (at R and V) and the line of attack of troops under General Cos (S).

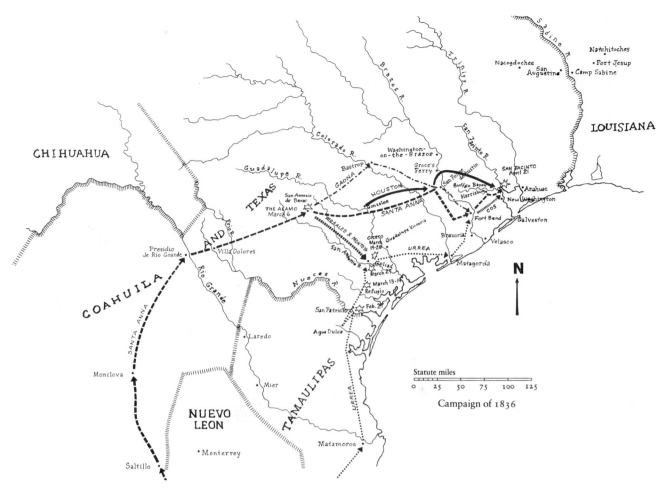

From Stephen L. Hardin, *Texian Iliad: A Military History of the Texas Revolution* (Austin: University of Texas Press, 1994), p. 100. Courtesy the author.

became a retreat, and he turned northward toward the Brazos River and Jared Groce's plantation. He went by way of San Felipe de Austin, which he torched. By now, Houston's disgruntled force had shrunk to no more than 800 men. Some allege that he wanted to retreat as far as the Trinity River, others that he merely intended to teach his little army the fundamentals of the drill while waiting for reinforcement. In either event, captains Wyly Martin and Moseley Baker balked, claiming that they would fight the enemy on their own. Houston solved the problem by ordering these men and their followers to establish a rear guard to hold up a Mexican advance. Discontent came not only from the ranks, however, but from the government. Houston was strongly criticized by President David G. Burnet as well. In the meantime, Burnet and the cabinet fled New Washington, the most recent capital of the new government, for Harrisburg. Time passed slowly at Groce's plantation, but the troops did receive the rudiments of battlefield drill and formation. The weather stayed bad, and disease became a problem. In these troubles, Houston's command was buttressed by two loyal supporters, Col. Thomas J. Rusk and Col. Edward Burleson.

Upon hearing of Burnet's flight, Santa Anna also decided to move on Harrisburg. This error diverted him from his objective, Houston's army, and required him to divide his force further.

Nevertheless, he decided on the chase and personally led the advancing force. When he arrived in Harrisburg, he discovered that the Texas government had fled again, so he ordered Col. Juan N. Almonte ahead. The colonel nearly succeeded in capturing the escaping officials. By now, however, Houston was on the move again, this time to the east. At the fork between the road to Nacogdoches and that to Harrisburg, the army swung toward the latter, and the character of the campaign changed. Houston, who had been slow and deliberate in his manner, now became swift and animated, and his strike toward Harrisburg resembled a forced march. On the way, he intercepted Mexican couriers, from whom he learned the location and size of Santa Anna's force. Gathering his men around him, Houston eloquently addressed them and called upon them to remember the Alamo and Goliad.

By now, both Houston and Santa Anna, on separate roads, were headed for Lynch's Ferry on the San Jacinto River. Still concerned about reinforcement, for he knew that Cos would soon join his adversary, Houston crossed and then destroyed Vince's Bridge. During the remainder of the campaign, the possibility of Mexican reinforcement was never far from his mind. The Texans reached Lynch's Ferry, at the confluence of the San Jacinto River and Buffalo Bayou, first. On the banks of both streams was marshland flanked by heavy foliage, mostly live oak, spread laterally. In the tree line beside Buffalo Bayou Houston aligned his force on 20 April. Later on the same day, Santa Anna's force, surprised by the Texan presence, also arrived. In the late afternoon, there was a brief but sharp clash between elements of the two armies, but nothing serious developed. Apparently, Santa Anna decided to await reinforcements, which arrived the following morning in the form of Cos's command. Meanwhile, Houston held a council of war, wherein the merits of an offensive or a defensive battle were debated. On the afternoon of 21 April he ordered his small force of perhaps 900 men forward. Santa Anna's army, numbering somewhere around 1,300 men, was resting. Santa Anna had concluded that the Texans were on the defensive, and he had decided to attack them the next day. Because of this costly miscalculation, Houston surprised and completely overran the enemy in a battle that took only 18 minutes. Shouts of "Remember the Alamo!" and "Remember Goliad!" filled the air, and in this charged atmosphere the killing continued for an hour after the issue was resolved. Virtually the entire Mexican army was killed, scattered, or captured, including Santa Anna, who managed to escape but was captured the next day. In effect, the Mexicans lost everything. The Texans lost nine men. On Houston's command, Santa Anna ordered his second-in-command, Gen. Vicente Filisola, to withdraw all his troops from Texas, and the order was obeyed. If the Mexican army had remained in Texas, it is probable that the war would have continued. Many Texans wanted Santa Anna's life, but Houston, aware of the Mexican general's value alive, spared him.

The war was concluded by the two treaties of Velasco, one public, the other secret. The first was published as soon as possible, and its contents held conditions very favorable to Texas. By its terms Texas independence was recognized, hostilities were ended, the Mexican army was retired beyond the Rio Grande, confiscated property was to be restored, and prisoners were to be exchanged. The secret treaty agreed to Santa Anna's release in exchange for his promise that he would do all he could to secure within the Mexican government all the provisions of the public treaty without exception, as well as the enforcement of them. Santa Anna agreed, as was his perceived prerogative, since by destroying the Constitution of 1824 he had assumed authority over Mexican foreign policy. Although the rest of the Mexican government refused to accept these terms, Texas became not only a *de facto* state but also a *de jure* state in the eyes of many nations.

Eugene C. Barker and James W. Pohl

Republic of Texas. As hostility toward Mexican Centralism grew, leading Texans moved toward establishing a government for an independent Texas. The colonists, both at the seat of the provisional government of the Consultation at San Felipe and on the battlefronts of the revolution, agreed that another popular assembly was needed to chart a course of action. On 10 December 1835 the General Council of the provisional government issued a call for an election on 1 February 1836 to choose 44 delegates to assemble on 1 March at Washington-on-the-Brazos. These delegates represented the 17 Texas municipalities and the small settlement at Pecan Point on the Red River. The Consultation sent Branch T. Archer, William H. Wharton, and Stephen F. Austin to the United States to solicit men, money, supplies, and sympathy for the Texas cause. At New Orleans, in early January 1836, the agents found enthusiastic support, but warned that aid would not be forthcoming so long as Texans squabbled over whether to sustain the Mexican constitution. They then proceeded to Washington and

separated: Wharton remained in the capital, Archer went to Richmond, and Austin headed for New York City.

The new convention was quite different from the Consultation. Forty-one delegates were present at the opening session (1 March 1836), and 59 individuals attended the convention at some time. Two delegates (José Francisco Ruiz and José Antonio Navarro of Bexar) were native Texans, and one (Lorenzo de Zavala) had been born in Mexico. Only 10 of the delegates had been in Texas by 1836. A majority were from other places—primarily from the United States, but also from Europe. Two-thirds of the delegates were not yet 40 years old. Several had broad political experience. Samuel P. Carson of Pecan Point and Robert Potter of Nacogdoches had served, respectively, in the North Carolina legislature and in the United States House of Representatives. Richard Ellis, representing the Red River district and president of the convention, and Martin Parmer of San Augustine, had participated in constitutional conventions in Alabama (1819) and Missouri (1821), respectively. Sam Houston, a former United States congressman and governor of Tennessee, was a close friend of United States president Andrew Jackson. Houston was chosen commander in chief of the revolutionary army and left the convention early to take charge of the forces gathering at Gonzales. He had control of all troops in the field—militia, volunteers, and regular army enlistees. The convention delegates knew they must declare independence or submit to Mexican authority. If they chose independence they had to draft a constitution for a new nation, establish a strong provisional government, and prepare to combat the Mexican armies invading Texas.

On opening day George C. Childress, who had recently visited President Jackson in Tennessee, presented a resolution calling for independence. At its adoption, the chairman of the convention appointed Childress to head a committee of five to draft a declaration of independence. When the committee met that evening, Childress drew from his pocket a statement he had brought from Tennessee that followed the outline and main features of the United States Declaration of Independence. The next day, March 2, the delegates unanimously adopted Childress's suggestion for independence. Ultimately 58 members signed the document. Thus was born the Republic of Texas.

The convention declared all able-bodied men ages 17 to 50 liable for military duty and offered land bounties of 320 to 1,280 acres for service from three months to one year. Those men who left Texas to avoid military service, refused to participate, or gave aid to the enemy would forfeit their rights of citizenship and the lands they held in the republic. The convention also halted public land sales and closed the land offices. It authorized its agents in the United States to seek a $1 million loan and to pledge land for its redemption. When independence was declared, the chairman appointed one man from each municipality to a committee to draft a constitution. If one individual can be designated the "father of the Texas Constitution," it should be David Thomas, who chaired the committee, spoke for the group, and put the draft together. The convention adopted the document about midnight on 16 March.

The Constitution of the Republic of Texas was patterned after that of the United States and several Southern states. It provided for a unitary, tripartite government consisting of a legislature, an executive, and a judiciary. The arrangement was more like that of a state than a federal system of states bound together by a central government. The document specified that the president would serve three years and could not succeed himself in office. He would be the commander in chief of the army, navy, and militia, but could not "command in person" without the permission of Congress. There would be a two-house Congress. The House of Representatives would comprise from 24 to 40 members until the population reached 100,000; thereafter the number of seats would increase from 40 to 100. Members would serve one-year terms.

The number of seats in the Senate would be "not less than one-third nor more than one-half that of the House." Senators were to serve three-year overlapping terms, with one-third elected each year. The constitution legalized slavery but prohibited the foreign slave trade. Immigrants from the United States could bring slaves with them. Free blacks could not live in Texas without the consent of Congress. No minister of the Gospel could hold public office.

Executive Officers, 1835–45

Provisional Government
November 15, 1835, to March 1, 1836

Provisional Governor	Henry Smith
Lieutenant Governor	James W. Robinson
Secretary of State	Charles Bellinger Stewart
Postmaster General	John Rice Jones, Jr.

Ad Interim Government
March 16, 1836, to October 22, 1836

President	David Gouverneur Burnet
Vice President	Lorenzo de Zavala
Secretary of State	Samuel Price Carson
	James Collinsworth
	William Houston Jack
Secretary of War	Thomas Jefferson Rusk
	Mirabeau Buonaparte Lamar
	Alexander Somervell
	Frederick A. Sawyer
	John Austin Wharton
	Henry P. Brewster
Secretary of Treasury	Bailey Hardeman
	Bernard E. Bee, Sr.
Secretary of Navy	Robert Potter
Attorney General	David Thomas
	Peter W. Grayson
Postmaster General	John Rice Jones, Jr.

Houston Administration (First)
October 22, 1836, to December 10, 1838

President	Samuel Houston
Vice President	Mirabeau Buonaparte Lamar
Secretary State	Stephen Fuller Austin
	James Pinckney Henderson
	Robert Anderson Irion
Secretary of War	Thomas Jefferson Rusk
	William S. Fisher
	Bernard E. Bee, Sr.
Secretary of Treasury	Henry Smith
Secretary of Navy	Samuel Rhoads Fisher
	William M. Shepherd
Attorney General	James Collinsworth
	James Pinckney Henderson
	Peter W. Grayson
	John Birdsall
	Algernon S. Thruston
Postmaster General	Gustavus A. Parker
	Robert Barr
Commissioner of General Land Office	John P. Borden

Lamar Administration
December 10, 1838, to December 12, 1841

President	Mirabeau Buonaparte Lamar
Vice President	David Gouverneur Burnet
Secretary of State	Bernard E. Bee, Sr.
	James Webb
	David Gouverneur Burnet
	Nathaniel C. Amory
	Abner Smith Lipscomb
	Joseph Waples (acting)
	James S. Mayfield
	Samuel A. Roberts
Secretary of War	Albert Sidney Johnston
	Branch Tanner Archer
Secretary of Treasury	Richard G. Dunlap
	James Harper Starr
	James W. Simmons
	John G. Chalmers
Secretary of Navy	Memucan Hunt
	Louis P. Cooke
Attorney General	John C. Watrous
	James Webb
	Francis A. Morris
Postmaster General	Robert Barr
	Elijah S. C. Robertson
	John Rice Jones, Jr.
Commissioner of General Land Office	John P. Borden
	Henry W. Raglin
	Thomas William Ward

Houston Administration (Second)
December 12, 1841, to December 9, 1844

President	Samuel Houston
Vice President	Edward Burleson
Secretary of State	Anson Jones
Secretary of War and Marine	George W. Hockley
	Morgan C. Hamilton (acting)
	George Washington Hill
Secretary of Treasury	E. Lawrence Stickney
	William Henry Daingerfield
	James B. Miller
Attorney General	George W. Terrell
Commissioner of General Land Office	Thomas William Ward

Jones Administration
December 9, 1844, to February 19, 1846

President	Anson Jones
Vice President	Kenneth Lewis Anderson
Secretary of State	Ebenezer Allen
	Ashbel Smith
Secretary of War and Marine	George Washington Hill
	Morgan C. Hamilton
	William Gordon Cooke
Secretary of Treasury	William Beck Ochiltree
	John Alexander Greer
Attorney General	Ebenezer Allen
	William Beck Ochiltree
Commissioner of General Land Office	Thomas William Ward

The constitution also included a bill of rights. An ad interim government would direct affairs until general elections were possible.

With news that the Alamo had fallen and Mexican armies were marching eastward, the convention hastily adopted the constitution, signed it, and elected an ad interim government: David G. Burnet, president; Lorenzo de Zavala, vice president; Samuel P. Carson, secretary of state; Thomas J. Rusk, secretary of war; Bailey Hardeman, secretary of the treasury; Robert Potter, secretary of the navy; and David Thomas, attorney general. The delegates then quickly abandoned Washington-on-the-Brazos. The government officers, learning that Houston's army had crossed the Colorado River near the site of present La Grange on 17 March and was retreating eastward, fled to Harrisburg and then to Galveston Island. With news of the Texan victory at San Jacinto, the Burnet government hastened to the battlefield and began negotiations to end the war. On 14 May at Velasco, Texas officials had Santa Anna sign two treaties, one public and one secret. The public treaty ended hostilities and restored private property. Texan and Mexican prisoners were to be released, and Mexican troops would retire beyond the Rio Grande. By the terms of the secret treaty, Texas was to take Santa Anna to Veracruz and release him. In return, he agreed to seek Mexican government approval of the two treaties and to negotiate a permanent treaty that acknowledged Texas independence and recognized the Rio Grande as its boundary. Military activity continued briefly along the Gulf Coast. On 2 June Maj. Isaac W. Burton, leading 20 mounted rangers, contacted a suspicious vessel in Copano Bay and signaled the vessel to send its boat ashore. His men captured the vessel, *Watchman*, and found it loaded with supplies for the Mexican army. On the seventeenth Burton seized the *Comanche* and the *Fannie Butler*, which were carrying provisions for the enemy valued at $25,000. Word soon reached Texas that the Mexican Congress had repudiated Santa Anna, rejected his treaties, and ordered the war with Texas to continue.

There was a widespread clamor that Santa Anna should be put to death, and on 4 June—after the dictator, his secretary, and Col. Juan N. Almonte had been put aboard the *Invincible* to be returned to Veracruz—Gen. Thomas Jefferson Green, who had just arrived from the United States with volunteers, compelled President Burnet to remove the Mexicans from the vessel and confine them. On 25 June Burnet appointed as secretary of war Mirabeau B. Lamar, a major general, to succeed Rusk, who had asked to be relieved. But with word that Gen. José de Urrea was advancing on Goliad, Rusk changed his mind about retiring. T. J. Green and Felix Huston, who had brought volunteers from Mississippi, stirred up the soldiers against Lamar, and Rusk resumed command. When Urrea failed to appear, Rusk vacated his command and the army chose Huston to replace him. Army unrest continued as the officers openly defied the government and threatened to impose a military dictatorship.

There were also other problems. On the morning of 19 May, Comanche and Caddo Indians attacked Fort Parker, on the Navasota River some 60 miles above the settlements, and carried into captivity two women and three children. The government lacked the men and resources to retaliate. Communications were poor, roads were few, and there was no regular mail system. The treasury was empty, the new nation's credit was in low repute, money was scarce. There was much confusion over land titles. Many families were nearly destitute. They had lost heavily in the Runaway Scrape after the fall of the Alamo, and upon returning home found their property ravaged and their stock consumed or scattered. By July Burnet and his cabinet began shifting responsibilities. The ad interim president called an election for the first Monday in September to set up a government under the constitution. The voters were asked to (1) approve the constitution, (2) authorize Congress to amend the constitution, (3) elect a president, other officers, and members of Congress, and (4) express their views on annexation to the United States.

The choice of a president caused concern. Henry Smith, governor of the provisional government, quickly announced his candidacy. Stephen F. Austin also entered the race, but he had accumulated enemies because of the land speculations of his business associate Samuel May Williams. Many newcomers to Texas knew little of Austin, and some thought he had been too slow in supporting the idea of independence. Rusk refused to run. Finally, just 11 days before the election, Sam Houston became an active candidate. On election day, 5 September, Houston received 5,119 votes, Smith 743, and Austin 587. Lamar, the "keenest blade" at San Jacinto, was elected vice president. Houston received strong support from the army and from those who believed that his election would ensure internal stability and hasten recognition by world powers and early annexation to the United States. He was also expected to stand firm against Mexico and seek recognition of Texas independence. The people voted overwhelmingly to accept the constitution and to seek annexation, but they denied Congress the power of amendment.

The First Texas Congress assembled at Columbia (now West Columbia) on 3 October 1836. It consisted of 14 senators and 29 representatives. The next day ad interim president Burnet delivered a valedictory address. He urged Congress to authorize land grants to the veterans of the revolution and reminded his listeners that the national debt stood at $1,250,000. On 22 October Houston took the oath of office as president before a joint session of Congress. In his inaugural he stressed the need for peace treaties with the Indians and for constant vigilance regarding "our national enemies—the Mexicans." He hoped to see Texas annexed to the United States. Houston requested the Senate to confirm his cabinet appointments. He named Austin to be secretary of state; Henry Smith, secretary of the treasury; Thomas J. Rusk and Samuel Rhoads Fisher secretary of war and secretary of the navy, respectively; and James Pinckney Henderson, attorney general. Congress adopted a flag and a seal for the new republic.

When Congress later established the office of postmaster general, Houston named Robert Barr of Nacogdoches to that post, and at Barr's death chose John Rice Jones, who had held the office under the provisional government, as his successor. Jones patterned the Texas postal system, which was placed in 1841 under the State Department, after that of the United States. All persons transporting mail for the Post Office Department during 1837 could take payment in land at 50 cents an acre and pay expenses. Postal rates were 6½ cents for the first 20 miles, and rose to 12½ cents for up to 50 miles. The rates applied to one-page letters folded over and addressed on the front. Envelopes came into use around 1845.

The court system inaugurated by Congress included a Supreme Court consisting of a chief justice appointed by the president and four associate justices, elected by a joint ballot of both houses of Congress for four-year terms and eligible for reelection. The associates also presided over four judicial districts. Houston nominated James Collinsworth to be the first chief justice. The county-court system consisted of a chief justice and two associates, chosen by a majority of the justices of the peace in the county. Each county was also to have a sheriff, a coroner, justices of the peace, and constables to serve two-year terms. Congress formed 23 counties, whose boundaries generally coincided with the existing municipalities.

The choice of a national capital proved difficult, and each house appointed a committee to make recommendations. The Senate selected Nacogdoches, while the lower house favored a site at San Jacinto. On 14 November, the two houses agreed on a temporary location. Augustus Chapman Allen and John Kirby Allen, two brothers who were promoting a new town named Houston on Buffalo Bayou, offered to provide buildings for the government and lodgings for congressmen. Congress chose Houston to be the temporary capital, and the government moved there in April 1837.

On 19 December 1836 the Texas Congress unilaterally set the boundaries of the republic. It declared the Rio Grande to be the southern boundary, even though Mexico had refused to recognize Texas independence. The eastern border with Louisiana presented problems. Houston took up the matter with the United States through diplomatic channels, and a treaty was signed in Washington on 25 April 1838, which provided that each government would appoint a commissioner and a surveyor to run the boundary. Texas chose Memucan Hunt and John Overton to join their United States counterparts at the mouth of the Sabine River. The work stalled when the commissioners could not agree on whether Sabine Lake was part of the river named in the treaty. On 24 November 1849, after annexation, the United States Congress recognized the Texas claim that the boundary ran through the middle of the lake.

National defense and frontier protection also claimed Houston's attention. Threats of a Mexican invasion and the fear of Indian raids kept the western counties in turmoil. Congress passed several acts dealing with frontier defense. In December 1836 it authorized a military force of 3,587 men and a battalion of 280 mounted riflemen, and appropriated funds to build forts and trading posts to encourage and supervise Indian trade. In case of a Mexican invasion, Congress empowered Houston to accept 40,000 volunteers from the United States. President Houston took a practical view of the situation. He downplayed Mexican threats, labeling them braggadocio and bombast. If the enemy invaded, he reasoned, Texans would rush to defend their homes. Ranger units on the frontier could handle the Indian situation. Houston's primary concern was to negotiate treaties with the Indians ensuring fair treatment. As for the army, Houston feared that Felix Huston, the commander and a military adventurer, might commit a rash act. He sent Albert Sidney Johnston to replace him. When Johnston reached Camp Independence, near Texana, on 4 February 1837, Huston challenged him to a duel and severely wounded him. Huston retained command, but later relinquished his position to Johnston. In May Johnston left for New Orleans to seek medical attention and turned over his command to a Colonel Rodgers. The temporary commander urged the soldiers to march on the capital at Houston, "chastise the President" for his weak defense policies, "kick Congress out of doors, and give laws to Texas." At the same time Huston came to Houston and raised a clamor for a campaign against Mexico. When the general visited the president, Houston treated him cordially, but promptly ordered acting secretary of war William S. Fisher to furlough three of the four army regiments. The remaining troops were gradually disbanded.

Houston planned to depend on the militia, ranger companies, and troops called for special duty. He hoped, by keeping military

units out of the Indian country and seeking treaties with various tribes, to avoid difficulties with the Indians. He sent friendly "talks" to the Shawnees, Cherokees, Alabama–Coushattas, Lipans, Tehuacanas, Tonkawas, Comanches, Kichais, and other groups. The most pressing problem involved the Cherokees, who had settled on rich lands along the Sabine and elsewhere in East Texas. Neither Spain nor Mexico had given them title to their lands. At the time of the Texas Revolution, the Consultation, hoping to keep the Cherokees and their associated bands quiet, sent Houston to make a treaty guaranteeing them title to their land, and they had remained quiet during the difficult days. When Houston became president he submitted the Cherokee treaty to the Senate for ratification, but that body killed it in December 1837. In October 1838 Houston authorized agents to run a line between the settlements and the properties of the Cherokees and associate bands, as stipulated by the treaty of 1836, but he had to halt the project when difficulties developed.

Land disposal presented another problem that Houston grappled with. In 1836 the Republic of Texas had a public domain of 251,579,800 acres (minus 26,280,000 acres granted before the revolution). This land eventually freed Texas from debt, paid for her military services and public buildings, and provided endowments for many of her institutions. The Texas Congress had voted liberal land laws in 1836. Under the constitution, the heads of families (blacks and Indians excepted) living in Texas on 2 March 1836 could apply for a square league (4,428 acres) and a labor (177.1 acres) of land. Single men over age 17 could receive one-third of a league. No one was required to live on the land. To encourage settlement, Congress also offered immigrants arriving between 2 March 1836 and 1 October 1837 a grant of 1,280 acres for heads of families and 640 acres for single men. Congress later allowed 640 acres and 320 acres, respectively, to heads of family and single men arriving after 1 October 1837 and before 1 January 1842. However, all immigrants arriving after 2 March 1836 had to live in Texas three years to receive clear title. Texas Revolution veterans arriving before 11 August 1836 received the same grants as original colonists and if permanently disabled could claim an additional 640 acres (known as a donation grant). Veterans of the battle of San Jacinto (including those wounded on 20 April before the battle and members of the baggage and camp guard), participants in the siege of Bexar, and the heirs and survivors of those who died at the Alamo or had served in the Matamoros and Goliad campaigns could receive additional land. Grants were given for postrevolution military service varying from 320 acres for three months' duty to 1,240 acres for 12 months'.

Land sales, however, ran into problems. Texas offered land scrip or land at 50 cents an acre when public land in the United States was $1.25 an acre, but the republic actually made few sales. Scrip sales ran into the problems of depreciated currency and forged certificates. Despite the cheap selling price, land acquisition could be costly, since applicants had to pay for locating, surveying, and obtaining title, services that amounted to about one-third the value of the land. Because old settlers and veterans were not required to live on the land to obtain title, they frequently sold their certificates to others who located land outside the settlements. This land often sat 10 or more years before it became part of a county. To encourage home ownership Congress enacted a homestead law on 26 January 1839. The act, patterned somewhat after legislation of Coahuila and Texas, guaranteed every citizen or head of family in the republic "fifty acres of land or one town lot, including his or her homestead, and improvements not exceeding five hundred dollars in value." Earlier, in December 1836, Congress had voted to reopen the land offices closed by the Permanent Council and the Consultation. Houston vetoed the bill, saying that existing land claims should be validated before new surveys were made. Congress passed the law over his veto, but in December 1837, before it went into effect, the succeeding Congress enacted a more comprehensive land act. It called for opening a land office for the use of old settlers and soldiers in February 1838, and for all others six months later. Houston vetoed the bill, but saw it passed over his veto. Since Congress refused to modify the land laws, Houston kept the General Land Office closed throughout his administration.

Meeting in special session in May 1837 in Houston, the First Congress instituted a commission-at-large to locate a permanent capital. The commission recommended Bastrop (first choice), Washington-on-the-Brazos, San Felipe, and Gonzales. When no action was taken, in December Congress selected a site commission from its members, and in April 1838 the group picked a vacant tract on the Colorado near La Grange. In January 1839 under the Lamar administration, Congress authorized still a third commission, drawn from its membership. It stipulated that the site be between the Trinity and Colorado rivers and north of the Old San Antonio Road and recommended that the capital be named Austin. The commissioners selected the frontier settlement of Waterloo, on the east bank of the Colorado some 35 miles above Bastrop, and purchased 7,135 acres of land there for $21,000. The site was surveyed into city lots, and construction began on government buildings, hotels, business houses, and homes. The Texas government moved to Austin in October 1839.

Two days after the constitutional convention adjourned in March 1836, President Burnet had sent George Childress and Robert Hamilton, probably the wealthiest man to sign the Texas Declaration of Independence, to Washington to seek recognition of the new republic. These two men joined the three agents (Austin, Archer, and Wharton) already there. Childress and Hamilton met with Secretary of State John Forsyth, but they carried no official documents to prove that Texas had a de facto government, and he refused to negotiate. In May, Burnet recalled all the agents and appointed James Collinsworth, who had been Burnet's secretary of state from 29 April to 23 May, and Peter W. Grayson, the attorney general, to replace them. They were instructed to ask the United States to mediate to end the hostilities between Texas and Mexico and obtain recognition of Texas independence. They also were to stress the republic's interest in annexation. During the summer of 1836 President Jackson sent Henry M. Morfit, a State Department clerk, as a special agent to Texas to collect information on the republic's population, strength, and ability to maintain independence. In August, Morfit filed his report. He estimated the population at 30,000 Anglo-Americans, 3,478 Tejanos, 14,200 Indians, of which 8,000 belonged to civilized tribes that had migrated from the United States, and a slave population of 5,000, plus a few free blacks. The population was small, Texas independence was far from secure, the government had a heavy debt, and there was a vast tract of contested vacant land between the settlements and the Rio Grande. Morfit advised the United States to delay recognition. In his annual message to Congress on 21 December 1836, Jackson cited Morfit's report and stated that the United States traditionally had accorded recognition only when a new political entity could maintain its independence. Texas was threatened by "an immense disparity of physical force on the side of Mexico," which might recover its lost dominion. Jackson left the disposition of the matter to Congress.

In the meantime Houston, recently elected president of Texas, recalled Grayson and Collinsworth and dispatched Wharton to Washington with instructions to seek recognition on both *de jure* and *de facto* grounds. If Wharton succeeded he would present his credentials as minister. Memucan Hunt soon joined him. They reported that Powhatan Ellis, United States minister to Mexico, had arrived in Washington and stated that Mexico was filled with anarchy, revolution, and bankruptcy. It would be impossible for her to invade Texas. France, Great Britain, and the United States were clamoring for the payment of claims of their citizens against Mexico. On 1 March 1837 the United States Congress, receiving memorials and petitions demanding the recognition of Texas independence, passed a resolution to provide money for "a diplomatic agent" to Texas. Jackson signed the resolution and appointed Alcée Louis La Branche of Louisiana to be *chargé d'affaires* to the Republic of Texas. The United States Congress adjourned on 9 July 1838, without acting upon the question of annexation. Houston replaced Hunt with Anson Jones, a member of the Texas Congress. Jones had introduced a resolution urging Houston to withdraw the offer of annexation, saying that Texas had grown in strength and resources and no longer needed ties with the United States. In Washington on 12 October 1838, Jones informed Secretary Forsyth that Texas had withdrawn its request for annexation. The issue lay dormant for several years.

In the fall of 1838 Houston sent James Pinckney Henderson abroad to seek recognition of Texas by England and France. The withdrawal of the annexation proposal in Washington helped facilitate his mission. France, being at war with Mexico, signed a treaty on 25 September 1839 recognizing Texas independence. England, in spite of slavery in the young republic and her desire to see the abolition of slavery worldwide, could not stand idly by and see France gain influence and trade privileges in Texas. Also, England had just settled the Maine boundary issue with the United States but faced hostilities over her claims in Oregon and the controversial Pacific Northwest boundary. She needed a supply of cotton if war came. In the fall of 1840, Lord Aberdeen announced that Her Majesty's government would recognize Texas independence, and on 13–16 November three treaties were signed that dealt with independence, commerce and navigation, and suppression of the African slave trade. A month earlier, on 18 September, Texas had concluded a treaty of amity, commerce, and navigation with the Netherlands. The three treaties with England were not ratified until December 1841, soon after Houston's election for a second term to the Texas presidency. Houston named Ashbel Smith minister to Great Britain and France and sent James Reily to represent Texas in Washington. He instructed both men to get the three nations to exert pressure on Mexico for peace and recognition.

During Houston's first administration (1836–38), the public debt of the republic soared from approximately $1,250,000 to $3,250,000. Houston's successor, Lamar, pursued aggressive policies toward Mexico and the Indians that added $4,855,000. In his second administration (1841–44) Houston and Congress pursued a policy of retrenchment and economy. The president abolished a number of offices in the government and in the army, combined or downgraded others, and cut salaries. Congress repealed the $5 million loan authorization voted earlier, since Texas had been unable to obtain money in the United States or Europe, and even

HISTORY

OF THE

CAPTIVITY AND PROVIDENTIAL RELEASE
THEREFROM OF

MRS. CAROLINE HARRIS,

Wife of the late Mr. *Richard Harris*, of Franklin County, State of New-York ; who, with Mrs. *Clarissa Plummer*, wife of Mr. *James Plummer*, were, in the Spring of 1835, (with their unfortunate husbands,) taken prisoners by the Camanche tribe of Indians, while emigrating from said Franklin County (N. Y.) to Texas ; and after having been made to witness the tragical deaths of their husbands, and held nearly two years in bondage, were providentially redeemed therefrom by two of their countrymen attached to a company of Santa Fe Fur Traders.

It was the misfortune of Mrs. *Harris*, and her unfortunate female companion (soon after the deaths of their husbands,) to be separated by, and compelled to become the companions of, and to cohabit with, two disgusting Indian Chiefs, and from whom they received the most cruel and beastly treatment.

NEW-YORK:
PERRY AND COOKE, PUBLISHERS.
1838.

Title page from *History of the Captivity and Providential Release therefrom of Mrs. Caroline Harris* . . . (New York: Perry and Cooke, 1838). Courtesy CAH. The government of the Republic of Texas, concerned about Indian captivities and possible raids, devoted a great deal of time to considering how best to deal with the "Indian problem."

reduced the pay of its own members. However, the Congress had overlooked an 1839 act that authorized the president to seek a loan of $1 million, and in June 1842, when he was considering a campaign against Mexico, Houston arranged to borrow that amount from Alexandre Bourgeois d'Orvanne of New Orleans. Congress also suspended payments on the public debt until the republic could meet its operating expenses. In his second term Houston spent $511,000, only $100,000 of which went to Indian affairs. Though income slowly began to equal expenditures, at the time of annexation the public debt had risen to about $12 million.

Although Texas had no incorporated or private bank during the days of the republic, an effort was made to form a big banking institution. The first Congress granted a 98-year charter to the Texas Railroad, Navigation, and Banking Company, whose sponsors included a number of prominent Texans. The company could capitalize at $5 million, enjoy extensive banking privileges, and offer loans to build canals and railroads to connect the Rio Grande and the Sabine River. Opposition to the company developed when Branch Archer, a sponsor, tried to pay into the Texas treasury in

discounted paper money the $25,000 required in gold and silver to launch the bank. The bank became the first political issue in the first Houston administration. The constitution empowered Congress to coin money and decreed that gold and silver coins would be lawful tender with the same value as in the United States. The republic, however, never minted any coins.

Texas met her expenses in various ways. Officials sold confiscated and captured Mexican property and sought funds among well-wishers in the United States and elsewhere. The Bank of the United States in Philadelphia lent the republic $457,380. Texas also sold land scrip in the United States for 50 cents an acre. As scrip sales were disappointing, Congress approved the issuance of paper money and, on 9 June 1837, authorized $500,000 in promissory notes bearing 10 percent interest and redeemable in 12 months. The notes began circulating on 1 November. For note redemption, Congress pledged one-fourth of the proceeds from the sale of Matagorda and Galveston islands, a half million acres of public domain, all forfeited lands, and the faith of the republic. The notes were not to be reissued at maturity; they depreciated very little. A replacement issue, called "engraved interest notes," declined in value from 65 cents on the dollar in May 1838 to forty cents by January 1839. The total face value of notes placed in circulation in 1837–38 was $1,165,139. The treasury also accepted audited government drafts. The Texas Congress approved "change notes" (treasury notes) up to $10,000 and specified that customs duties be paid in specie or treasury notes. As imports exceeded exports, gold and silver quickly drained from the republic. During the Lamar administration (1838–41), to curtail smuggling and increase tariff collection, Congress lowered rates nearly to a free-trade basis, but saw no positive effect. Direct taxes and license fees could be paid in depreciated currency until February 1842. On 19 January 1839 Congress approved non-interest-bearing promissory notes, called "red-backs." The treasury issued $2,780,361 in these notes, valued at 37½ cents on the dollar in specie; these were worthless within three years. United States notes also circulated in Texas. Lamar appointed James Hamilton, a banker and former governor of South Carolina, to negotiate the authorized $5 million loan in either Europe or the United States, but Hamilton's attempts proved fruitless.

After the defeat at San Jacinto, Mexico sought to stir up discontent in Texas. Military commanders knew that there were restless groups around Nacogdoches and among various Indian tribes, and sent agents to East Texas to promote dissension. In the late summer of 1838, a rebellion flared near Nacogdoches. Vicente Córdova, a prominent citizen, organized a Mexican–Indian combination and disclaimed allegiance to Texas. General Rusk, the local militia commander, called for volunteers. Córdova boldly attacked Rusk's camp on 16 September but was repulsed. In March 1839, with 53 Mexicans, a few Indians, and six blacks, Córdova sought to travel from the upper Trinity along the frontier to Matamoros. Near Austin, scouts discovered his trail, and Col. Edward Burleson at Bastrop gathered 80 men and broke up the Córdova party on Mill Creek near the Guadalupe River. In May, Manuel Flores, a Mexican agent, left Matamoros to contact Córdova, unaware of his flight. Texas Rangers intercepted Flores's party near Onion Creek, killed the emissary, and dispersed his men.

Upon taking office in December 1838, Lamar was convinced that the Cherokees were in treasonable correspondence with the Mexicans, and launched a campaign that drove them from Texas. Soldiers also forced the Shawnees, Alabamas, and Coushattas to abandon their hunting grounds; the last two tribes were given lands in East Texas, the Alabama–Coushatta Indian Reservation. Speculators and settlers swarmed into vacated Indian land. Lamar also wanted to end Comanche depredations on the frontier. In 1839 ranger parties based in San Antonio invaded Comanche country and fought several engagements. Aware of the Cherokee expulsion, the Comanches sent a small delegation to San Antonio to talk peace. Texas authorities agreed to negotiate if the Indians brought in their white captives. On 19 March 1840, 65 Comanches showed up with one white prisoner, a 12-year-old girl named Matilda Lockhart. Matilda said the Comanches had other prisoners. The Texans demanded the remaining prisoners and tried to hold the Indians as hostages. In what became known as the Council House Fight, 35 Indians and seven Texans were killed. Furious over the massacre, the Comanches killed their captives and descended several hundred strong on San Antonio but were unable to coax a fight and therefore rode away. Beginning in July the Comanches hit the frontier counties in force, with some 1,000 warriors descending the Guadalupe valley toward the coast. At the battle of Plum Creek, near the site of present Lockhart, Capt. Mathew Caldwell, Col. Edward Burleson, and Gen. Felix Huston combined their forces and scattered the marauders. In October Col. John H. Moore attacked Comanche camps west of the settlement line. Near the site of present-day Colorado City his force surprised and killed more than 130 Indians.

In his second term as president, Sam Houston continued to negotiate with the Indian tribes and sought to rescue white captives. His policy of conciliation proved successful and was far less expensive than Lamar's policy. In August 1842 Houston tried to contact the Apaches and other tribes in Northwest Texas, and in October he met the Lipan Apaches and Tonkawas at the Waco village on the Brazos River. The president wanted to establish trading houses on the Brazos, believing that these establishments, lying west of the settlements, would provide protection. Coffee's Station, opened in 1837 on the Red River on a north–south Indian trail, had been successful. John F. Torrey started posts at Austin, San Antonio, and New Braunfels and near Waco. Houston became a stockholder in the Torrey Trading Houses. On 29 September 1843 Edward H. Tarrant and George W. Terrell concluded a treaty with nine Indian tribes at Bird's Fort, near the site of present Arlington. The Senate ratified the treaty, but the government made no demarcation line between white and Indian territory. The largest Indian council held in the republic met in October 1844 near Waco, where a treaty was concluded with the Waco, Tawakoni, Kichai, and Wichita Indians.

Presidents of the republic could not succeed themselves. Toward the end of Houston's first term as president, which ended on 10 December 1838, Lamar announced his candidacy. Houston supporters tried to get Rusk to run, but he refused. Also Rusk lacked two months meeting the constitutional age requirement. Houston supporters next endorsed Peter W. Grayson, the attorney general, who had worked in Washington, but on his way back to Texas Grayson committed suicide. The Houstonites then approached Chief Justice James Collinsworth, but in late July he fell overboard in Galveston Bay and drowned. Lamar campaigned vigorously, promised to remedy the mistakes of the Houston administration, and won by a vote of 6,995 to 252 over Senator Robert Wilson, who represented Liberty and Harrisburg (later Harris) counties. David Burnet was elected vice president. At the Lamar inaugural in Houston on 10 December, Houston appeared in colonial costume and powdered wig and gave a three-hour "Farewell Address." Algernon P. Thompson, Lamar's secretary, reported that the new president was indisposed and read Lamar's inaugural remarks. Lamar picked Bernard E. Bee for secretary of state, retained Robert Barr as postmaster general, asked Albert Sidney Johnston to be secretary of war, and made Memucan Hunt secretary of the navy. Richard G. Dunlap and John C. Watrous were appointed secretary of the treasury and attorney general, respectively.

In his message to the Texas Congress on 21 December, President Lamar spoke against annexation. He saw no value in a tie with the United States, and predicted that Texas could someday become a great nation extending to the Pacific. Lamar called for far-reaching public programs. He recommended the establishment of a national bank owned and operated by the government, and urged the establishment of public free schools and the founding of a university. He wanted the municipal code reformed to coordinate Mexican and United States law in the republic. He also wanted increased protection for the western frontier. He declared that neither the native nor the immigrant tribes had a cause of complaint and denied that the Cherokees or others had legal claims to land. Lamar recommended the building of military posts along the frontier and the formation of a permanent military force capable of protecting the nation's borders. He promised to prosecute the war against Mexico until Mexico recognized Texas independence. He stated that Texas needed a navy to protect its commerce on the high seas and urged legislation to reserve all minerals for government use as well as a program to turn them to the advantage of the nation. Lamar favored continuing the tariff, but hoped some day to see Texas ports free and open. Congress responded to his message by authorizing a force of 15 companies to be stationed in military colonies at eight places on the frontier. These were to be located on the Red River, at the Three Forks of the Trinity, on the Brazos, on the Colorado River, on the Saint Marks (San Marcos) River, near the headwaters of Cibolo Creek, on the Frio River, and on the Nueces. At each site, three leagues of land was to be surveyed into 160-acre tracts, and each soldier who fulfilled his enlistment would receive a tract. Bona fide settlers who lived on the land for three years also would be given tracts. In addition, the government planned to build 16 trading posts near the settlement line. On 1 January 1839 the Texas Congress authorized Lamar to enroll eight companies of mounted volunteers for six months' service and appropriated $75,000 to sustain the force. Congress also set aside $5,000 to recruit and maintain a company of 56 rangers to patrol western Gonzales County for three months and three mounted companies for immediate service against the hostile Indians in Bastrop, Milam, and Robertson counties. An additional two companies were to protect San Patricio, Goliad, and Refugio counties. Congress appropriated a million dollars in promissory notes to cover the expenses for these units.

At the beginning of the Lamar administration Mexico was temporarily distracted. Because of unresolved French claims the French Navy had blockaded the Mexican coast and shelled and captured Veracruz. The Centralist Mexican government also faced a revolt by Federalists in its northern states. Tension increased when Lamar threatened to launch an offensive against Mexico if that nation refused to recognize Texas independence. Texan military units under colonels Reuben Ross, Juan N. Seguín, and William S. Fisher crossed the Rio Grande and joined the Mexican Federalists, ignoring Lamar's call to return. In February 1839

Lamar increased the pressure on Mexico. He appointed Secretary of State Bee minister extraordinary and plenipotentiary to Mexico to request recognition of Texas independence and to conclude a treaty of peace, amity, and commerce. Bee also was to seek an agreement fixing the national boundary at the Rio Grande from its mouth to its source. If Mexico refused these requests, Bee could offer $5 million for the territory that Texas claimed by the act of 19 December 1836—territory that lay outside the bounds recognized by Mexican law. When Bee reached Veracruz, the French had withdrawn and the Centralists were strengthening their position. However, Juan Vitalba, a secret agent of Santa Anna who was serving temporarily as president, made overtures and hinted at possible negotiations. Lamar asked James Treat, a former resident of Mexico who knew Santa Anna and other Mexican leaders, to act as a confidential agent and attempt negotiations. Treat reached Veracruz on 28 November 1839, when the Federalists and their Texan allies were at the gates of Matamoros. The alliance blocked his plans. A year later, in September 1840, Treat proposed to the Mexican minister of foreign affairs an extended armistice but was ignored.

A Mexican invasion of Texas was now rumored. Gen. Felix Huston proposed sending an expedition of 1,000 men into Chihuahua, believing the move would eventually force any Mexican army that crossed the Rio Grande downstream to withdraw. Congress did not act, however, and in March 1841 Lamar appointed James Webb, former attorney general, to replace Bee as secretary of state and sent him to Mexico. Webb was denied permission to land at Veracruz. On 29 June, the president recommended that Texas recognize the independence of Yucatán and Tabasco and join in a declaration of war against Mexico. Lamar also urged attention to the upper part of the Rio Grande. The Fifth Congress debated bills but refused to finance an expedition to establish Texas authority over its far-western claims. Congress also failed to appropriate money to maintain the army, and Lamar disbanded the military.

In November, with a large amount of military equipment on hand, the president urged Congress to authorize an expedition to Santa Fe. Lamar believed that the New Mexicans were restless under Governor Manuel Armijo. In April 1840 he had addressed a letter to the citizens of Santa Fe, saying that the United States and France had recognized Texas independence, and that he hoped to send commissioners to explain his concern for their wellbeing. When Santa Fe did not respond, Lamar was determined to send an expedition. He believed that Texas must extend its authority over its western claims, divert a part of the Santa Fe–St. Louis trade through its ports, and encourage the 80,000 inhabitants of New Mexico to sever their ties with Mexico and turn to Texas. If the United States took over New Mexico, however, it would extend its influence to the Pacific and complicate the Texas claims. In June 1841 the Texan Santa Fe expedition left the Austin vicinity. Military and civilians crossed the vast plains of West Texas under great hardship and on 17 September reached the village of Anton Chico, east of Santa Fe. There they met Armijo's forces and surrendered. The Mexicans marched the prisoners to Mexico City and held them until the following April.

As the Lamar administration drew to an end and the Sixth Congress assembled in Austin in 1841, the Rio Grande frontier was the scene of constant attacks by Texas renegades and Mexican outlaws. The nation was heavily in debt. Texans were in low spirits, the economy was depressed, and some people even considered moving back to the United States. During these years Texas regarded its vast public domain as critical to attracting settlers and encouraging economic development. The year before, Congress had passed a law permitting the president to issue colonization contracts to individuals or groups who would introduce a specified number of families within three years. Now Congress discussed a bill to allow the Franco-Texian Commercial and Colonization Company (also called the Franco-Texienne Company; not to be confused with the later Franco-Texan Land Company) to bring in 8,000 families and build 20 forts from the Red River to the Rio Grande. The settlers would be exempted from all taxes and tariffs for twenty years. The company would receive three million acres of land divided into 16 tracts and have trading privileges with the New Mexican settlements. The bill passed the House but died in the Senate. Lamar approved a number of colonization contracts, however. On 30 August 1841 he authorized William S. Peters and his associates to settle 600 families from the Ohio valley and northeastern states on the northern frontier south of the Red River. Heads of families in the Peters colony would each receive 640 acres of land and single men 320 acres. The settler would received title to half his land, while the contractor would hold the rest to pay for surveying, securing titles, furnishing seed, powder and shot, and providing a cabin. Other grants were made. In 1842 William Kennedy, an Englishman, with William Pringle, the Frenchman Henri Castro, and others each received permission to settle 600 or more immigrants between the Nueces and the Rio Grande. Castro sent out 300 colonists, principally from Alsace, to settle on the Medina River at Castroville. By 1845 he had introduced a total of 2,134 settlers. Kennedy and his associates planned to place families south of the Nueces River, but the colony never materialized.

During his second administration, Houston continued the settlement program. To strengthen frontier defense, he signed a contract on 7 June 1842 with Alexandre Bourgeois d'Orvanne and Armand Ducos to settle 600 French families on the headwaters of the Medina and Frio rivers and 500 families along the lower Rio Grande. Two Germans, Burchard Miller and Henry Fisher, contracted to locate 1,000 families of Germans, Swiss, Danes, Swedes, Norwegians, and Dutchmen between the Llano and Colorado rivers. The Fisher–Miller Land Grant covered nearly four million acres, but the contractors introduced very few settlers. The Adelsverein, or Association of Noblemen, was one of the most successful colonizing enterprises. In 1844 the association acquired a large tract west of San Antonio from Bourgeois d'Orvanne and sent Prince Carl of Solms–Braunfels as commissioner general to Texas. Informed that the Bourgeois grant had been forfeited, Solms purchased the Fisher–Miller grant, which ran along the Colorado River and west to the Llano River. Solms also obtained a tract at the junction of Cibolo Creek and the San Antonio River. To establish a station halfway to the Fisher–Miller grant, he bought the so-called Comal Tract and founded the town of New Braunfels. In 1846 John O. Meusebach, who succeeded Solms–Braunfels as agent, founded Fredericksburg on the Pedernales River. Although after five years the Adelsverein went bankrupt, it had brought 7,380 immigrants to Texas. Charles Fenton Mercer, an agent of the Peters colony, contracted in January 1844 to settle 100 families within five years on any unappropriated lands in the republic. A number of families came, but controversy and lawsuits plagued both the contractor and the settlers from the beginning until the 1930s.

During the period of the republic, the population of Texas increased about 7,000 per year, primarily from immigration. By

Austin, by Edward Hall, 1840. Pencil sketch. Courtesy Austin History Center, Austin Public Library; PICA 01083. Hall's crude sketch of log cabins along a single avenue reveals the newness of the capital. The legend (lower center) identifies such structures as the President's House (right center) and Bullock's Tavern (lower left). The picture was published in A. B. Lawrence, *Texas in 1840* (New York, 1840).

1847 the white population, including Mexican immigrants, had risen to 102,961, and the number of slaves to 38,753. The growth was due largely to liberal land policies and expanding opportunities. Like other frontier areas, Texas acquired a reputation as a land of sharp dealers, lawlessness, rowdiness, and fraudulence. Land frauds were numerous and law-enforcement agencies were weak or nonexistent, but Texans developed an ability to handle challenges. They elected few demagogues to office and were remarkably fortunate in their choice of leaders.

Early in his administration, Lamar promoted public education. In 1839 Congress set aside three square leagues of land in each county to support primary schools or academies. It also assigned 50 leagues of land for two universities. The next year the county allotment was increased to four leagues and teachers were required to provide certificates indicating they could teach the basic courses. The republic, however, failed to establish a public school system or to found a university. Private and denominational schools filled the void. The first Protestant church-related school was Rutersville College, near La Grange, opened in January 1840 by Methodists. Congress provided a charter and four leagues of land.

The school had preparatory and female departments, and added college work for men. During the republic, Rutersville was the foremost college in Texas. In 1842 the University of San Augustine, at San Augustine in East Texas, opened with a grammar school and female and collegiate departments. It prided itself on its laboratory work in science. McKenzie College, started near Clarksville in 1841, at one time had more than 300 boarding students. Marshall University, a coeducational institution, received its charter in 1842. Its female department eventually became a separate institution. Nacogdoches University, probably the first nonsectarian institution of higher learning in Texas, chartered on 3 February 1845, had an endowment of 29,712 acres of land and $2,699 in personal property. That same month Baylor University was opened near Independence.

In the fall of 1841 Houston and Burnet were candidates for president. Campaign issues included the Franco-Texian Bill, promoted by Houston; Houston and Burnet's questionable role in making land grants; frontier protection; making Houston the capital; instituting reforms to ensure land titles; retrenchment; and the redemption of the nation's honor, desecrated by Mexico. Houston

The *San Antonio*, Galveston, 1841. Pencil sketch. Prints and Photographs Collection, Texas Navy file, CAH; CN 00859. The *San Antonio* belonged to the second navy established under the Republic of Texas. In the fall of 1841 she was sent to help protect Yucatán, which was in rebellion and receiving support from Texas.

was pictured as representing eastern Texas (except Nacogdoches County, where the Cherokee land question made Burnet the favorite), while Burnet was the champion of the western counties. On 6 September Houston easily won a second term, and Burleson beat Hunt for vice president.

In his second administration, Houston reversed many of Lamar's policies. He sought peace treaties with the Indians, took a defensive stand against Mexico, and encouraged trade along the southern and western borders. Houston was vitally concerned with the location of the capital. Austin was on the frontier, far from the center of population. If Indian or Mexican intruders captured and burned the capital, the prestige of the government would suffer. Houston wanted the government returned to Houston, but the western counties protested and Congress balked. In early March 1842, when Gen. Rafael Vásquez crossed the Rio Grande with 700 soldiers and occupied San Antonio, Houston seized the opportunity to order removal of the national archives from Austin, but local citizens blocked the move in an act of rebellion called the Archive War. During the session of Congress called to discuss the Vásquez invasion, Houston brought up the moving of the capital, but had no success. In October he moved the government offices to Washington-on-the-Brazos. In late December, at the president's orders, Col. Thomas W. Ward, commissioner of the General Land Office, loaded the archives into wagons and sought to remove them to the new seat of government. Irate citizens overtook Ward at Kenney's Fort on Brushy Creek and retrieved the documents. Washington-on-the-Brazos remained the seat of government until July 1845.

Texas had two navies during its short history as a nation. The first was commanded by Charles E. Hawkins, who carried the title of commodore. To protect the supply line to New Orleans, in 1835 the General Council of the provisional government authorized the purchase of four schooners and granted letters of marque and reprisal to privateers until the ships were armed. The first navy included the 60-ton *Liberty*, the 125-ton *Independence*, the 125-ton *Brutus*, and the 125-ton *Invincible*. All four ships were lost by mid-1837. Early in 1838 Texas bought the merchant brig *Potomac*, but

was unable to convert it to a man-of-war, and instead used it at the Galveston Navy Yard as a receiving vessel. In March 1839 the government converted the S.S. *Charleston*, a steam side-wheeler, into a man-of-war, rechristened it the *Zavala*, and sent it on a cruise to Yucatán. It ran aground in Galveston Bay in May 1842 and subsequently was sold for scrap.

Lamar established the second Texas navy. Its fleet of six vessels included the schooners *San Jacinto*, *San Antonio*, and *San Bernard*, each 170 tons; the brigs *Wharton* and *Archer*, 400 tons each; and the sloop-of-war *Austin*, 600 tons. Commodore Edwin W. Moore made the *Austin* his flagship. In October 1840 the Texas Congress, lulled by an unofficial armistice, cut navy appropriations and tied up the fleet. The *San Jacinto*, mapping the Texas coast, was wrecked the same month. A year later Lamar agreed to participate in Yucatán's rebellion against Mexico and sent the navy to protect the Yucatán coast. Yucatán paid $8,000 a month to keep the fleet active. On becoming president again, Houston canceled Lamar's arrangements and ordered the fleet to sail home. The *San Antonio* reached Galveston in January 1842, reported on Yucatecan matters, and went on to New Orleans for repairs. There the only mutiny in the Texas Navy occurred. United States authorities captured the mutineers, and Commodore Moore later court-martialed two of the men. In April Moore arrived in New Orleans and began haggling with Houston over repair bills. In February 1843, Moore learned that Yucatán would pay these bills and sailed for Campeche. Houston, who had been planning to sell the navy, declared Moore a pirate. The commodore settled his accounts with Yucatán and returned home. After trial by a court-martial, he was restored to command. Houston ordered the vessels decommissioned. At annexation, the Texas Navy was transferred to the United States Navy, which promptly sold all the vessels except the *Austin*. Other vessels of the Texas Navy had been abandoned in Galveston harbor, lost at sea, or wrecked by storm. The United States Navy refused to accept the Texas naval officers and canceled their commissions.

On 9 October 1841, Santa Anna reestablished himself as provisional president of Mexico and determined to renew hostilities against Texas. In January 1842, Gen. Mariano Arista, commanding the Army of the North, announced his intention of invading the "Department of Texas." Subsequently, after Vásquez seized San Antonio in March, the western counties demanded a retaliatory strike at Mexico. Houston knew that such a campaign could not be sustained, but decided to let the agitators see for themselves. On 17 March he approved the undertaking and sent agents to the United States to recruit volunteers and obtain arms, munitions, and provisions. The soldiers, assembling under Gen. James Davis at Lipantitlán, on the Nueces near San Patricio, quickly became restless. Provisions were short, and gambling and drunkenness prevailed. Learning of the disorder, colonels Antonio Canales Rosillo and Cayetano Montero camped on the Rio Grande near Mier and Camargo and launched a surprise attack on the Texan camp on 7 July, but were beaten off. The Sixth Congress, meeting in special session, passed a "war bill," but Houston vetoed it since it appropriated no funds for the campaign. The army was disbanded.

The Mexican government, however, was determined to keep the Texas frontier in turmoil. Santa Anna ordered Gen. Adrián Woll to attack San Antonio and informed the Mexican Congress that he planned to resubjugate Texas. Woll crossed the Rio Grande at Presidio del Río Grande (Eagle Pass), and made a surprise attack on San Antonio on the morning of 11 September. The defenders, learning that the soldiers were Mexican regulars, surrendered. On the eighteenth Woll moved to Salado Creek, assaulted the Texans assembled on the creek east of San Antonio under Col. Mathew Caldwell, then withdrew to San Antonio. Mexican troops intercepted Capt. Nicholas M. Dawson and 53 volunteers, and the Dawson Massacre ensued. Woll sent 52 prisoners from San Antonio ahead to Mexico, evacuated San Antonio on the twentieth, and marched for the Rio Grande. Caldwell's forces and a small ranger party under Capt. John Coffee Hays harassed the Mexicans as far as the Nueces River. After the battle of Salado Creek, Texans demanded retaliation and rushed to San Antonio as individuals, in companies, and in small groups. Houston sent Brig. Gen. Alexander Somervell to take charge of the force there. On 25 November Somervell headed for the border with more than 750 men and seized Laredo. Disgusted by the Texans' plundering, 187 men soon left for home. In December Somervell led the rest downriver, crossed the Rio Grande, and seized Guerrero. Unable to find provisions, he recrossed into Texas and ordered his men to prepare to return home. A large group, 309 men, broke off from the expedition and refused to return home. They organized under Col. William S. Fisher and marched down the east side of the Rio Grande, crossed the river opposite Mier, and demanded food and clothing from the inhabitants of Mier. A large body of Mexican troops was rushed to the town, and the Texans, facing odds of ten to one, surrendered on 26 December. On their march to Mexico City, the Mier expedition prisoners overthrew their guards at Hacienda Salado, and sought to escape to Texas, but most of them were recaptured. Nicolás Bravo, the vice president, ordered that they be decimated. Seventeen drew black beans in the Black Bean Episode and were shot on 25 March 1843.

Like Lamar, Houston expressed concern over the western boundaries of Texas. In February 1843 his administration authorized Jacob Snively to raise a volunteer group to make a show of force in the northwest territory claimed by Texas. They hoped to prey on the Mexican caravans traveling the Texas section of the Santa Fe Trail. The men were to mount, arm, and equip themselves and share half the spoils; the other half would go to the republic. In August 1842, Charles A. Warfield had received a similar commission, recruited a small party largely in Missouri, and briefly occupied the New Mexican town of Mora on the overland trail. Snively organized 175 men near Coffee's Station, on the Red River, and in April 1843 they rode north. From his camp about 40 miles below where the Santa Fe Trail crossed the Arkansas River, Snively captured a New Mexican patrol guarding the trail. The ensuing foray was short-lived. Capt. Philip St. George Cooke, in command of United States dragoons escorting merchant caravans through Indian country, arrested and disarmed the Texans, allegedly for being on United States soil, and sent them home. The United States later paid for the arms they had taken from the Texans.

Internal disturbances also flared during Houston's second term. In Shelby County, Charles W. Jackson, a fugitive from Louisiana, ran for Congress and blamed his defeat on land sharks and counterfeiters of headright certificates. Joseph G. Goodbread, who headed the anti-Jackson faction, threatened to run him out of the country. In 1842 Jackson shot and killed Goodbread. At Jackson's trial, in Harrison County, the judge failed to appear on the second day and Jackson went free. He soon headed a force called the "Regulators," who sought to suppress crime in the area and harass Goodbread supporters. In response, Edward Merchant

formed the "Moderators." In the spring of 1843 a civil war broke out between the factions in Shelby, Panola, and Harrison counties. Over the three following years more than 50 men were killed and numerous homes and other property were burnt or destroyed. Judge John M. Hansford was killed by the Regulators. In August 1844, President Houston called on both parties to lay down their arms and sent Travis G. Brooks and 600 militiamen to maintain order. They arrested leaders on both sides and took them to San Augustine, where Houston persuaded them to sign a peace agreement that ended the Regulator–Moderator War.

While in Perote Prison, James W. Robinson, a former acting governor of Texas during the Consultation, sought an interview with Santa Anna. He stated that if granted an audience, he could show how to arrange a lasting peace between Mexico and Texas. Santa Anna, being at war with Yucatán, agreed to hear Robinson. Under his proposals Texas would become an independent department (state) in the Mexican federation, be represented in the Mexican Congress, and be allowed to make its own laws. Texas would be granted amnesty for past acts against Mexico, and Mexico would station no troops in Texas. The Mexican president approved the proposals on 18 February 1843 and released Robinson to convey them to Texas. Houston studied the proposals and reasoned that Santa Anna's Yucatán problem might lead the Mexican president to agree to peace terms. Houston asked Charles Elliot, the British chargé d'affaires to Texas, to ask Richard Pakenham, the British minister in Mexico, to seek an armistice. Robinson wrote Santa Anna that Houston wanted an armistice of several months to give the people of Texas an opportunity to consider the proposals. When Santa Anna received Robinson's letter, he agreed to a truce. Houston proclaimed an armistice on 15 June 1843 and sent Samuel M. Williams and George W. Hockley as commissioners to meet their counterparts at Sabinas, near the Rio Grande. They were to arrange a general armistice and request that a commission meet in Mexico City to discuss a permanent peace. Houston was cautious and proclaimed martial law between the Nueces and the Rio Grande. Pakenham informed Houston that Santa Anna would release the Mier prisoners if the Texas president would release all Mexican prisoners. Houston ordered the prisoners released, but when no Mexicans arrived on the Rio Grande, Santa Anna canceled the exchange. The Texas and Mexican commissioners agreed on a permanent armistice on 18 February 1844, but Houston filed the document away without taking action because it referred to Texas as a Mexican department.

In the Texas presidential race of 1844, Vice President Edward Burleson faced Secretary of State Anson Jones, who had the support of Houston. Jones won by a large vote. After he was inaugurated on 9 December, he launched a policy of economy, peaceful relations with the Indians, and a nonaggressive policy toward Mexico. As his administration also tackled the issue of annexation, Jones earned the sobriquet "Architect of Annexation." He, Houston, and their supporters knew that proper timing was essential in securing annexation. Upon taking office, Jones instructed Isaac Van Zandt, Texan chargé d'affaires to the United States, to decline all offers to negotiate an annexation treaty until it was known that the United States Senate definitely would ratify it. When President John Tyler reopened negotiations on annexation, Mexico became friendly to Texas. At the same time she threatened war with the United States if annexation were approved. In the United States, there was great sympathy for the Texas cause. The collapse of the Santa Fe expedition in 1841 and the Mexican inva-

Matty Meeting the Texas Question, by unknown artist, 1844. Lithograph. 13¼" × 19 7⁄16". Courtesy Amon Carter Museum, Fort Worth; acc. no. 226.67. Martin Van Buren faces the question of whether to annex Texas. Andrew Jackson encourages him to "stand up to your lick-log" and take Texas. Van Buren cannot face the question, but James K. Polk convinces George Dallas, his running mate in the 1844 presidential campaign, that they should espouse "Dame Texas."

sions of 1842 had attracted widespread attention. In March 1842 Houston instructed James Reily, the Texas representative to Washington, to sound out the government on annexation. The United States, knowing the British wanted to mediate Texas-Mexican difficulties, saw a strong British influence looming in Texas affairs. President Tyler, a Whig with Southern views on slavery, had indicated in October that he wanted to open discussions leading to the annexation of Texas by treaty. An annexation treaty was completed on 12 April 1844 and signed by Secretary of State John C. Calhoun, Isaac Van Zandt, and Van Zandt's assistant, J. Pinckney Henderson.

Great Britain and France became concerned. The British Foreign Office, with French support, advised Ashbel Smith, the Texan agent to Great Britain and France, that a "diplomatic act" was needed to force Mexico to make peace with Texas and recognize its independence. They wanted the United States to join their efforts to end Texas-Mexican hostilities. Pakenham, however, opposed the plan, and the matter was dropped. Houston favored a "diplomatic act," but president-elect Jones balked. Jones wanted annexation and thought that the threat of an alignment with England, connected with the cotton trade, was the key to achieving it. In June 1844 the United States Senate voted 35 to 16 to reject the treaty.

The annexation of Texas also became a major issue in the United States election of 1844. The Democrats ran James K. Polk, of Tennessee, for president with the campaign slogan "the Re-Annexation of Texas and the Re-Occupation of Oregon," hoping to capture the expansionists' vote both North and South. The Democrats won by a large vote. Tyler viewed Polk's election as a mandate for immediate annexation. In his annual message on 2 December he urged Congress to approve annexation by a joint resolution, which Congress passed on 28 February 1845 and Tyler signed on 1 March. He then dispatched Andrew Jackson Donelson, a nephew of Andrew Jackson, to Texas with instructions to press for its acceptance. The terms were generous. Texas would be

annexed as a slave state rather than as a territory. She would keep her public lands and pay her own public debts. She could divide herself into as many as four additional states. The terms of annexation had to be accepted by 1 January 1846. In May 1845 the United States dispatched a fleet of warships to protect the Texas coast.

The British *chargé d'affaires* and the French minister asked President Jones to postpone action on the annexation agreement for 90 days because they wanted to arrange a settlement of matters between Mexico and Texas. Jones agreed on 29 March. The British and French emissaries reached Mexico City in mid-April. Luis G. Cuevas, minister of foreign relations, placed their proposals before the Mexican Congress, and in late April Mexico recognized Texas independence. The British minister handed a copy of the document to Jones on 4 June, and he immediately announced a preliminary peace with Mexico. On the same day Jones signed a peace treaty with the last Comanche chief whose tribe had been at war with Texas, thus ending Indian hostilities for the republic.

President Jones issued a call for a convention to be elected by the people to meet in Austin on 4 July. At his call, the Texas Congress assembled on 16 June in special session at Washington-on-the-Brazos and rejected the Mexican offer for peace. They accepted the annexation agreement and approved elections for a convention. The convention met in Austin as planned and passed an ordinance to accept annexation. It then drafted the Constitution of 1845 and submitted both the annexation agreement and proposed constitution to a popular vote. On 13 October annexation was approved by a vote of 4,245 to 257, and the constitution by a vote of 4,174 to 312. The United States Congress approved the Texas state constitution, and Polk signed the act admitting Texas as a state on 29 December 1845. The fledgling republic, whose existence had spanned nearly 12 years, was no more. In a special election on 15 December, Texans had elected officers for the new state government. The First Legislature convened in Austin on 19 February 1846. In a ceremony in front of the Capitol, President Jones gave a valedictory address, the flag of the republic was lowered, and the flag of the United States was raised above it. The ceremonies concluded with the inaugural address of the newly elected governor, J. Pinckney Henderson.

Joseph Milton Nance

Antebellum Texas. In the drama of Texas history the period of early statehood, from 1846 to 1861, appears largely as an interlude between two great adventures—the Republic of Texas and the Civil War. These 15 years did indeed lack the excitement and romance of the experiment in nationhood and the "Lost Cause" of the Confederacy. Events and developments during the period, however, were critical in shaping the Lone Star State as part of the antebellum South. By 1861 Texas was so like the other Southern states economically, socially, and politically that it joined them in secession and war. Antebellum Texans cast their lot with the Old South and in the process gave their state an indelibly Southern heritage.

When President Anson Jones lowered the flag of the republic for the last time in February 1846, the framework for the development of Texas over the next 15 years was already constructed. The great majority of the new state's approximately 100,000 white inhabitants were natives of the South, who, as they settled in the eastern timberlands and south central plains, had built a life as similar as possible to that in their home states. Their economy, dependent on agriculture, was concentrated first on subsistence farming and herding and then on production of cotton as a cash crop, an enterprise that seemed to necessitate slavery. In 1846 Texas had more than 30,000 black slaves and produced an even larger number of bales of cotton. Political institutions were also characteristically Southern. The Constitution of 1845, written by a convention in which natives of three states—Tennessee, Virginia, and Georgia—constituted a majority, depended heavily on Louisiana's fundamental law as well as on the existing Constitution of the Republic of Texas. As befitted an agricultural state led by Jacksonians, the constitution prohibited banking and required a two-thirds vote of the legislature to charter any private corporation. Article VIII guaranteed the institution of slavery.

With the foundations of their society in place and the turbulence of the republic behind them, Texans in 1846 anticipated years of expansion and prosperity. Instead, however, they found themselves and their state's interests heavily involved in the Mexican War, which broke out within a few months of annexation. Differences between the United States and Mexico arose from a variety of issues, but disagreement over the southwestern boundary of Texas provided the spark for war. Mexico contended that Texas reached only to the Nueces River, whereas after 1836 the republic had claimed the Rio Grande as the border. President James K. Polk, a Jacksonian Democrat from Tennessee, backed the Texans' claims, and in January 1846, after unsuccessful attempts to make the Rio Grande the boundary and settle other differences by diplomacy, he ordered Gen. Zachary Taylor to occupy the disputed area. In March Taylor moved to the Rio Grande across from Matamoros. Battles between his troops and Mexican soldiers occurred north of the river in May, and Congress, at Polk's request, declared war. Approximately 5,000 Texans served with United States forces in the conflict that followed, fighting for both General Taylor in northern Mexico and Gen. Winfield Scott on his campaign to capture Mexico City. In the Treaty of Guadalupe Hidalgo, which ended the war in February 1848, Mexico recognized Texas as a part of the United States and confirmed the Rio Grande as its border.

Victory in the Mexican War soon led to a dispute concerning the boundary between Texas and the newly acquired Mexican Cession. This conflict arose from the Lone Star State's determination to make the most of the Rio Grande as its western boundary by claiming an area reaching to Santa Fe and encompassing the eastern half of what is now New Mexico. In March 1848 the Texas legislature decreed a Santa Fe County. Governor George T. Wood sent Spruce M. Baird to organize the local government and serve as its first judge. The people of Santa Fe, however, proved unwilling to accept Texas authority, and United States troops in the area supported them. In July 1849, after failing to organize the county, Baird left. At the same time a bitter controversy was developing in Congress between representatives of the North and the South concerning the expansion of slavery into the territory taken from Mexico. The Texans' western boundary claims became involved in this larger dispute, and the Lone Star State was drawn into the crisis of 1850 on the side of the South.

President Zachary Taylor, who took office in March 1849, proposed to handle the Mexican Cession by omitting the territorial stage and admitting California and New Mexico directly into the Union. His policy angered southerners in general and Texans in particular. First, both California and New Mexico were expected to prohibit slavery, a development that would give the free states numerical superiority in the Union. Second, Taylor's approach in effect pitted the federal government against Texas claims to the

Santa Fe area and promised to stop the expansion of slavery at the state's western boundary. Southern extremists resolved to break up the Union before accepting the president's proposals. They urged Texas to stand firm on the boundary issue, and the Mississippi state legislature called for a convention in Nashville during June 1850 "to devise and adopt some means of resistance" to Northern aggression. Southern spokesmen in Texas took up the cry, demanding that their state send delegates to Nashville and take all steps necessary to prove that it was not "submissionist."

In December 1849 the Texas legislature responded to the crisis with an act designating new boundaries for Santa Fe County, and Robert S. Neighbors was sent to organize the government there. The legislature also provided for the election in March 1850 of eight delegates to attend the Nashville Convention for "consultation and mutual action on the subject of slavery and Southern Rights." By June, when Neighbors reported that the people of Santa Fe did not want to be part of Texas, the state appeared ready to take aggressive action. Moderation prevailed, however, in Washington, Nashville, and Texas. By September 1850 Congress had worked out a compromise to settle the crisis. After much wrangling, Senator James A. Pearce of Maryland proposed that the boundary between Texas and New Mexico be a line drawn east from the Rio Grande along the 32d parallel to the 103d meridian, then north to 36°30', and finally east again to the 100th meridian. In return for its New Mexican claims, Texas would receive $10 million in United States bonds, half of which would be held to satisfy the state's public debt. Some Texans bitterly opposed the "Infamous Texas Bribery Bill," but extremism was on the wane across the state and the South as a whole. In Texas the crisis had aroused the Unionism of Sam Houston, the state's most popular politician. He made fun of the election to choose delegates to the Nashville convention. The vote had been called too late to allow effective campaigning anyhow, and of those elected only former governor J. Pinckney Henderson actually attended the meeting in Tennessee. (Incidentally, in this same election Texans approved the permanent choice of Austin as state capital.) The Nashville convention, although it urged Texas to stand by its claim to New Mexico, generally adopted a moderate tone. In November 1850 Texans voted by a two-to-one margin to accept the Pearce Bill. The crisis of 1850 demonstrated the existence of strong Unionist sentiment in Texas, but it also revealed that the state, in spite of its location on the southwestern frontier, was identified with the Old South. Charles C. Mills of Harrison County summarized this circumstance perfectly in a letter to Governor Peter H. Bell during the crisis: "Texas having so recently come into the Union, should not be foremost to dissolve it, but I trust she will not waver, when the crisis shall come."

As the boundaries of antebellum Texas were being settled and its identity shaped during the first years of statehood, new settlers poured in. A state census in 1847 reported the population at 142,009. Three years later a far more complete United States census (the first taken in Texas) enumerated 212,592 people, excluding Indians, in the state. Immigrants arriving in North Texas came primarily from the upper South and states of the old Northwest such as Illinois. Settlers entering through the Marshall–Jefferson area and Nacogdoches were largely from the lower South. On the Gulf Coast, Galveston and Indianola served as entry points for many lower southerners. Numerous foreign-born immigrants, especially Germans, also entered through these ports during the late 1840s.

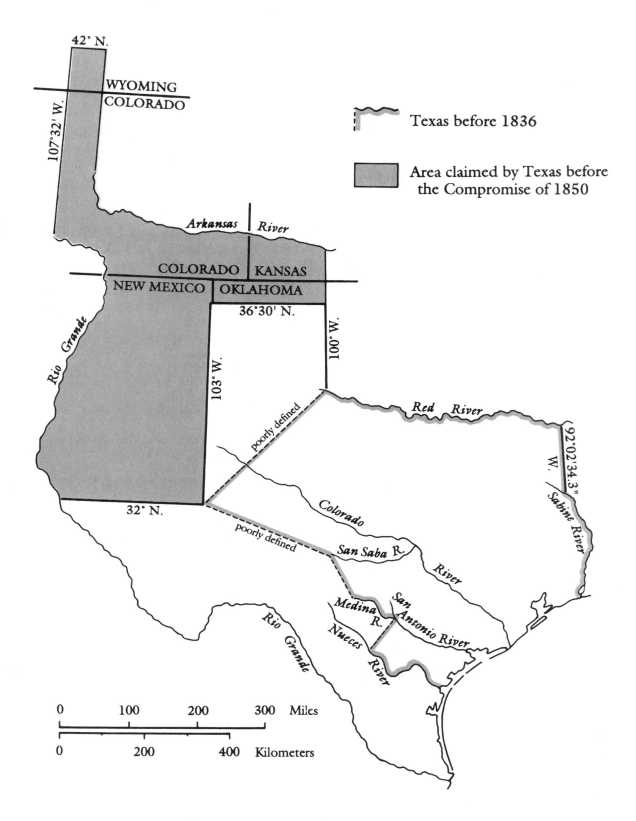

42° N.

WYOMING
COLORADO

107°32' W.

Texas before 1836

Area claimed by Texas before
the Compromise of 1850

Arkansas | River

COLORADO | KANSAS
NEW MEXICO | OKLAHOMA

36°30' N.

Rio Grande

103° W.

100° W.

Red River

92°02'34.3" W.

Sabine River

poorly defined

32° N.

Colorado

poorly defined

San Saba R.

River

Medina R.

San Antonio River

Rio Grande

Nueces River

| 0 | 100 | 200 | 300 | Miles |

| 0 | 200 | 400 | Kilometers |

Boundary settlements of 1848 and 1850. Drawn by John Cotter. As both republic and young state, Texas declared its south and west boundary to be the Rio Grande from its source to its mouth. The Treaty of Guadalupe Hidalgo of 1848 declared the Rio Grande to El Paso to be the boundary between Texas and Mexico. As part of the Compromise of 1850, Texas relinquished its claim to territory in the present-day states of New Mexico, Colorado, Wyoming, Kansas, and Oklahoma in exchange for $10 million.

The Texas to which these migrants came was a frontier state in the classic sense. That is, it had a line of settlement advancing westward as pioneers populated and cultivated new land. Also, as on most American frontiers, settlers faced problems with Indians. By the late 1840s Texas frontiersmen had reached the country of the fierce Comanches and were no doubt relieved that, since annexation, the task of defending the frontier rested with the United States Army. In 1848–49 the army built a line of eight military posts from Fort Worth to Fort Duncan, at Eagle Pass on the Rio Grande. Within two years, under the pressure to open additional lands and do a better job of protecting existing settlements, federal forces built seven new forts approximately 100 miles to the west of the existing posts. This new line of defense, when completed in 1852, ran from Fort Belknap, on the Brazos River, to Fort Clark, at the site of present-day Brackettville. Conflict with the Comanches continued for the remainder of the decade as federal troops, joined at times by companies of Texas Rangers, sought to protect the frontier. They were never entirely successful, however, and Indian warfare continued after the Civil War. With the Comanches and the lack of water and wood on the western plains both hampering its advance, the Texas frontier did not move during the 1850s beyond the seven forts completed at the beginning of the decade. Areas immediately east of the military posts continued to fill, but the rush westward slowed. In 1860 the line of settlement ran irregularly from north to south through Clay, Young, Erath, Brown, Llano, Kerr, and Uvalde counties.

Important as it was to antebellum Texas, this western frontier was home to only a small fraction of the state's population. The great majority lived well to the east in areas where moving onto unclaimed land and fighting Indians were largely things of the past by 1846. These Texans, not frontiersmen in the traditional sense, were yet part of an extremely significant frontier—the southwesterly march of slaveholding, cotton-producing farmers and planters. "King Cotton" ruled the Old South's agricultural economy, and he came to rule eastern antebellum Texas as well. Anglo-American settlers had sought from the beginning to build a plantation society in the region stretching from the Red River through the East Texas timberlands to the fertile soils along the Trinity, Brazos, Colorado, and lesser rivers that emptied into the Gulf of Mexico. During the 1850s this cotton frontier developed rapidly.

At the census of 1850, 95 percent of the 212,592 Texans lived in the eastern two-fifths of the state, an area the size of Alabama and Mississippi combined. Ten years later, although the state's population had grown to 604,215, the overwhelming majority still lived in the same region. The population had far greater ethnic variety than was common elsewhere in the South. There were large numbers of Germans in the south central counties, many Mexican Americans from San Antonio southward, and smaller groups of Poles, Czechs, and other foreign-born immigrants scattered through the interior. Nevertheless, natives of the lower South constituted the largest group of immigrants to Texas during the 1850s, and southerners headed three of every four households there in 1860. Like immigrants from the Deep South, slaves also constituted an increasingly large part of the population (27 percent in 1850 and 30 percent in 1860). Their numbers rose from 58,161 to 182,566, a growth of 214 percent, during the decade.

The expansion of slavery correlated closely with soaring cotton production, which rose from fewer than 60,000 bales in 1850 to more than 400,000 in 1860. In 1850, of the 19 counties having 1,000 or more slaves—10 in northeastern Texas and 9 stretching inland

along the Brazos and Colorado rivers—15 produced 1,000 or more bales of cotton. The census of 1860 reported 64 counties having 1,000 or more slaves, and all except 8 produced 1,000 or more bales. These included, with the exception of an area in extreme Southeast Texas, virtually every county east of a line running from Fannin County, on the Red River, southwestward through McLennan County to Comal County and then along the San Antonio River to the Gulf. Only six counties in this area managed to grow at least 1,000 bales of cotton without a matching number of slaves. Slavery and cotton thus marched hand-in-hand across antebellum Texas, increasingly dominating the state's agricultural economy. Plantations in Brazoria and Matagorda counties produced significant sugar crops, but elsewhere farmers and planters concentrated on cotton as a source of cash income. By 1860 King Cotton had the eastern two-fifths of Texas, excepting only the north central prairie area around Dallas and the plains south of the San Antonio River, firmly within his grasp.

Perhaps, as Charles W. Ramsdell suggested, the cotton frontier was approaching its natural limits in Texas during the 1850s. The soil and climate of western Texas precluded successful plantation agriculture, and proximity to Mexico, with its offer of freedom for runaways, reinforced these geographical limitations. In reality, however, regardless of these apparent natural boundaries, slavery and cotton had great potential for continued expansion in Texas after 1860. Growth had not ended anywhere in the state at that time, and the north central prairie had not even been opened for development. The fertile soils of the Blackland Prairie and Grand Prairie counties would produce hundreds of thousands of bales of cotton once adequate transportation reached that far inland, and railroads would soon have met that need. The two prairie regions combined were more than three-fourths as large as the state of South Carolina but had only 6 percent as many slaves in 1860. The cotton frontier of antebellum Texas constituted a virtual empire for slavery, and such editors as John F. Marshall of the Austin *State Gazette* wrote confidently of the day when the state would have two million bondsmen or even more.

Only a minority of antebellum Texans, however, actually owned slaves and participated directly in the cash-crop economy. Only one family in four held so much as a single slave, and more than half of those had fewer than five bondsmen. Small and large planters, defined respectively as those owning 10 to 19 and 20 or more slaves, held well over half of the state's slaves in both 1850 and 1860. This planter class profited from investments in land, labor, and cotton and, although a decided minority even among slaveholders, provided the driving force behind the state's economy.

Agriculture developed rapidly in antebellum Texas, as evidenced by a steady expansion in the number of farms, the amount of improved acreage, the value of livestock, and the size of crops produced. Slave labor contributed heavily to that growth. On the other hand, during the 1850s Texas developed very slowly in terms of industry, commerce, and urban growth. In both 1850 and 1860 only about 1 percent of Texas family heads worked at manufacturing. Texas industries in 1860 produced goods valued at $6.5 million, while, by contrast, Wisconsin, another frontier state that had entered the Union in 1846, reported nearly $28 million worth of manufactures. Commercial activity, retarded no doubt by inadequate transportation and the constitutional prohibition on banking, also occupied only a small minority of Texans. With industry and commerce so limited, no urban area in the state reached a population of 10,000 during the antebellum years. In 1860 San

Antonio (8,200), Galveston (7,307), Houston (4,800), and Austin (3,500) were the state's only "cities." By contrast, Milwaukee, Wisconsin, reported a population of 20,000 as early as 1850.

Antebellum Texans failed to diversify their economy for several reasons. Part of the explanation was geographical: climate and soil gave Texas an advantage over most regions of the United States, certainly those outside the South, in plantation agriculture and thus helped produce an overwhelmingly agricultural economy. Slavery appears also to have retarded the rise of industry and commerce. Slave labor made the plantation productive and profitable and reduced the need for the invention and manufacture of farm machinery. Planters concentrated on self-sufficiency and on the cultivation of cotton, a crop that quickly passed out of Texas for processing elsewhere with a minimum involvement of local merchants along the way. Opportunities for industry and commerce were thus reduced by the success of the plantation. Moreover, the planters, who were, after all, the richest and most enterprising men in Texas and who would have had to lead any move to diversify the economy, benefited enough financially and socially from combining land and slave labor that they generally saw no need to risk investments in industry or commerce.

Planters did have an interest in improving transportation. From the 1820s onward Texans had utilized the major rivers from the Red River to the Rio Grande to move themselves and their goods and crops, but periodic low water, sand bars, and rafts of logs and brush made transportation by water highly unreliable. Moving supplies and cotton on Texas roads, which became quagmires in wet weather, was simply too slow and expensive. Thus, as the cotton frontier advanced inland, the movement of crops and supplies, never an easy matter, became increasingly difficult. Railroads offered a solution, albeit not without more financial difficulties than promoters could imagine. The state legislature chartered the state's first railroad, the Buffalo Bayou, Brazos and Colorado, in February 1850. Intended to run from Harrisburg, near Houston, westward to Alleyton, on the Colorado River, and tap the commerce on both the Brazos and Colorado, this road became operational to Stafford's Point in 1853 and reached its destination by 1860. Dozens of other railroads received charters after 1850, but for every one that actually operated six came to nothing.

Railroad promoters, faced with a difficult task and armed with arguments about the obvious importance of improved transportation in Texas, insisted that the state should subsidize construction. Their efforts to gain public aid for railroad corporations focused on obtaining land grants and using the United States bonds acquired in the settlement of the New Mexico boundary as a basis for loans. Some Texans, however, led by Lorenzo Sherwood, a New

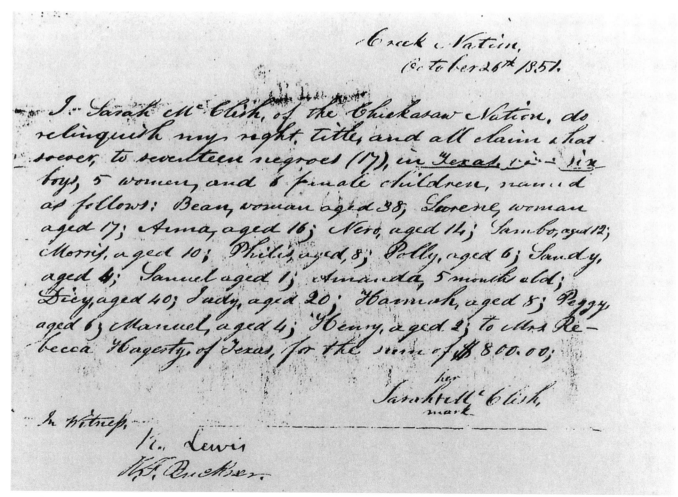

Record of slave sale, Creek Nation, October 26, 1851. Rebecca McIntosh Hawkins Hagerty Papers, CAH; CN 08001. Sarabeth McClish made her mark on this document recording her sale of 17 slaves to Rebecca Hagerty "of Texas" for a total of $800.

Mr. Polley's Plantation, Harrie's birthplace, by Sarah Ann Daniels, ca. 1856. Watercolor, gouache, and graphite on paper. Courtesy Amon Carter Museum, Fort Worth; gift of Mrs. Lucinda Shastid. This primitive watercolor shows Joseph H. Polley's two-story house and slave cabins surrounded by snake fences.

York–born lawyer who lived in Galveston, opposed the whole concept of state subsidies for private corporations. Sherwood developed a State Plan calling for the government in Austin to construct and own a thousand-mile network of railroads. Those who favored private promoters managed early in 1854 to obtain a law authorizing the granting of 16 sections of land for each mile of road built to all railroads chartered after that date. However, the struggle between those who favored loans and supporters of the State Plan continued into 1856, as Sherwood won election to the legislature and continued to fight effectively for his ideas. His opponents finally seized upon statements Sherwood made against reopening the African slave trade, accused him of opposing slavery, and forced him under the threat of violence to resign from the legislature. Within less than a month, in July 1856, the legislature passed a bill authorizing loans of $6,000 to railroad companies for every mile of road built.

Antebellum Texans thus decided that private corporations encouraged by state aid would built their railroads. Progress was limited, however. By 1860 the state had approximately 400 miles of operating railroad, but almost all of it radiated from Houston. Major lines included the Buffalo Bayou, Brazos and Colorado, from Harrisburg to Alleyton through Houston; the Galveston, Houston and Henderson, from Galveston to Houston; and the Texas and New Orleans, from Houston to Orange through Beaumont. Only the San Antonio and Mexican Gulf Railway, which ran from Port Lavaca to Victoria, and the Southern Pacific

Railroad (not to be confused with the future system of that name) in Harrison County did not connect in some fashion with Houston. Railroad building progressed slowly because antebellum Texas did not have the native capital to finance it, the industrial base to produce building materials, or the population and diversified economy to provide traffic the year around. At least the stage had been set, however, for building an adequate network of rail transportation after 1865.

Thus, as the cotton frontier of Texas developed during the 1850s, the state's economy increasingly mirrored that of the Deep South. A majority of Texans lived as small, nonslaveholding farmers, but plantation agriculture and slave labor produced the state's wealth and provided its economic leaders. At the same time, there was little development in terms of industry, commerce, urban growth, and transportation. With an economy of this nature and a Southern-born population predominant in most areas, antebellum Texas naturally developed social practices and institutions that also were Southern to the core.

Women in antebellum Texas found their role in society shaped by traditions that, while by no means unique to the South, were strongly entrenched in that region. The ideal female was a homemaker and mother, pious and pure, strong and hardworking, and yet docile and submissive. She was placed on a pedestal and admired, but she had no political rights and suffered serious disabilities before the law. Women could not, for example, serve on juries, act as lawyers, or witness a will. Texas women, however, did

Main building of Rutersville College, Rutersville, Texas. Completed 1842. Courtesy Special Collections/John G. Tower Library, Southwestern University, Georgetown, Texas. Higher education flourished before the Civil War as churches established educational institutions. Rutersville College, a Methodist school, opened in 1840. The main building had a bell tower atop its second floor.

have significant property rights inherited from Spanish law. Married women retained title to property such as land and slaves owned before they wed, had community rights to all property acquired during a marriage, and had full title to property that came into their hands after divorce or the death of a husband. These rights allowed Texas women to head families, own plantations, and manage estates in ways that were anything but passive and submissive.

Antebellum Texans favored churches in the evangelical tradition of the Old South. Methodists far outnumbered other denominations. By 1860 the Methodist Episcopal Church, South, as it was called after the North–South split of 1844, had 30,661 members. After the Methodist Church, the Baptist Church constituted the second largest denomination, followed by the Presbyterian, Disciples of Christ, Cumberland Presbyterian, Catholic, Lutheran, and Protestant Episcopal churches. These institutions provided spiritual and moral guidance and offered educational instruction as well. Moreover, religious activities brought people together in settings that encouraged friendly social interchange and relieved the isolation of rural life.

Education in antebellum Texas was largely a matter of private enterprise, both secular and church affiliated. At the most basic level, would-be teachers simply established common schools and offered primary and elementary instruction to children whose parents could pay tuition. More formal education took place in state-chartered institutions, which often bore names promising far more than they could deliver. Between 1846 and 1861 the Texas legislature chartered 117 schools, including 40 academies, 30 colleges, and 7 universities. Most of these institutions lasted only a few years, had relatively few students, and, regardless of their titles, offered little beyond secondary education. The University of San Augustine and Marshall University, for example, both chartered in 1842, had primary departments teaching reading, writing, and arithmetic. The quality of education at all levels in Texas schools suffered from a variety of problems, including the fact that teachers who were dependent for their pay on the good will of parents could not afford to be very demanding. Schools often covered

their shortcomings and bolstered their academic reputations by holding public oral examinations that the whole community could attend. Parents and most observers greatly appreciated these events and overlooked the fact that generally they were watching rehearsed performances rather than true examinations.

Regardless of its doubtful quality, private education lay beyond the means of most antebellum Texas families. In general only the well-to-do could afford to buy schooling for their children, a situation that conflicted with democratic ideals and growing American faith in education. Texans expressed considerable interest during the 1850s in establishing a public school system. Action came, however, only after the legislature devised a scheme to establish a fund that could be used for loans to promote railroad building, with the interest going to support public schools. In January 1854 the legislature set aside $2 million of the bonds received from the boundary settlement in 1850 as a "Special School Fund." Two years later another act provided for loans from this fund to railroad corporations. Interest from the school fund was to go to the counties on a per-student basis to pay the salaries of public school teachers, but counties had to provide all the necessary buildings and equipment. Knowing that this would be expensive and doubtless feeling pressure from private school interests, the legislature permitted local authorities to hire teachers in existing educational institutions. It quickly became apparent that the interest from the school fund would be totally inadequate to do more than subsidize the schooling of children from indigent families. The private schools benefited, and public education remained only a dream.

Educational opportunities notwithstanding, literacy, at least as measured by census enumerators, was high in antebellum Texas. The state's many newspapers (3 dailies, 3 triweeklies, and 65 weeklies by 1860) constituted the most widely available reading matter. Among the most influential publications were the *Telegraph and Texas Register*, the Clarksville *Northern Standard*, the Marshall *Texas Republican*, the Nacogdoches *Texas Chronicle*, the Austin *State Gazette*, the Dallas *Weekly Herald*, and the Galveston *Daily News*. What the papers lacked in news-gathering facilities they made up for with colorful editors and political partisanship. Virtually anyone who cared to could find both information on current events and entertainment in an antebellum newspaper.

Texans had a notable variety of amusements. Amateur theater groups, debating societies, and music recitals, for example, provided cultural opportunities. Many other amusements were notably less genteel. Horse racing, gambling, and drinking were popular, the last to such a degree that the temperance crusade against liquor was by far the most important reform movement of the era. Cruder amusements often sparked violence, although antebellum Texans needed very little provocation. The constitution had outlawed dueling, the Old South's traditional method of settling affairs of honor, but violence in Texas was generally more spontaneous and less stylized anyhow. In June 1860, for example, a man named Johnson spotted on the street in Hempstead one McNair, with whom he had a long-standing quarrel. Firing three times from his second-floor hotel room window, he hit McNair in the neck, side, and thigh. As Johnson prepared to ride away, a crowd gathered around the dying McNair. "By God, a good shot that," one said.

Politics in antebellum Texas reflected the state's preeminently Southern economic and social structure. Institutionally, political arrangements were highly democratic by the standards of that era. The Constitution of 1845 permitted all adult white males, without

Theatre at the Old Casino Club in San Antonio, by Carl G. von Iwonski, ca. 1860. Oil on canvas. 9½" × 14". Courtesy Witte Museum, San Antonio. The Casino Club, founded in 1854, served as the social and cultural center of the German community in San Antonio.

regard to taxpaying or property-holding status, to vote and hold any state or local office. In practice, however, wealthy slaveholders dominated officeholding at all levels and provided the state's political leadership. Their control was democratic in that they were freely elected, and they governed without having to coerce non-slaveholders into supporting their policies. Nevertheless, leadership by a minority class whose status depended on the ownership of slaves introduced an element of aristocracy and gave a pro-Southern cast to antebellum Texas politics.

Virtually all of the men who governed Texas from 1846 to 1861 were identified with the Democratic party. "We are all Democrats," Guy M. Bryan wrote in 1845, "since the glorious victory of that party, who fearlessly espoused our cause and nailed the 'Lone Star' to the topmast of their noble ship." When the Whig party displayed a lack of enthusiasm for the Mexican War and supported President Taylor in denying Texas claims to New Mexico territory in 1849–50, Bryan's statement became even more accurate. The Democrats won every presidential and gubernatorial election between 1845 and 1861. Indeed, so complete was their domination that the closest contests during these years came as a result of intraparty divisions, usually with the towering figure of Sam Houston occupying center stage.

J. Pinckney Henderson easily won the first race for state governor in December 1845 and took office in February 1846. He presided over the transition from republic to state and spent the latter part of 1846 commanding Texas troops in Mexico. Worn out from the war and in failing health, Henderson declined in 1847 to run for reelection. He was succeeded by George T. Wood, a Trinity River planter who had the support of Sam Houston. Wood served from 1847 to 1849, while the dispute over the New Mexico boundary built to crisis proportions. During his term Texans participated in their first presidential election and gave Democrat Lewis Cass 69 percent of the vote in his contest with the Whig Zachary Taylor. Wood lost the governorship to Peter Hansborough Bell in 1849, probably because of lukewarm support from Houston and Bell's promise of a more aggressive policy on the boundary question. The Compromise of 1850, although considered a shameful surrender by some extremists, did not seriously injure Bell's pro-Southern reputation. He defeated four opponents in 1851, including the Whig Benjamin H. Epperson, and served a second term before resigning in 1853 to take a seat in Congress. In the meantime the Democratic presidential candidate, Franklin Pierce, carried Texas overwhelmingly in the election of 1852. The Whigs made their most serious bid for the governorship in 1853 with the candidacy of William B. Ochiltree. Democrats met this challenge by agreeing to support one man, Elisha M. Pease, rather than their usual multiplicity of candidates. Pease's first term was significant for efforts to start a public school system and encourage railroad

Sam Recruiting, after the injunction of secrecy had been removed, 1855. Lithograph by Wilhelm C. A. Thielepape. Broadsides Collection, CAH; CN 00694. In 1854 the American (Know-Nothing) party became active in Texas, and Houston adopted some of its tenets. The "secrecy" in the cartoon title alludes to Houston's connection with this xenophobic party, which was in many ways a secret society.

building. It also marked the appearance of a new political party that offered the most serious threat to Democratic domination of state politics during the 1850s. The American party, or Know-Nothings, an antiforeign, anti-Catholic organization that had originated in the Northeast, appeared in Texas during 1855 and attracted many Whigs, whose party had disintegrated as a result of the Kansas–Nebraska Act in 1854. The Know-Nothings supported Lieutenant Governor David C. Dickson for governor in 1855 and forced the Democrats to call a hurried state convention and unify in support of Governor Pease. The new party had considerable success in legislative and local elections, but Pease defeated Dickson with relative ease. The Know-Nothings lost badly in their support of Millard Fillmore during the presidential race of 1856 and rapidly withered into insignificance thereafter.

During Pease's second term (1855–57), Texas politics came to focus on pro- and anti-Houston issues as they had not since the end of the republic. Senator Houston's consistent Unionism in the crisis of 1850 and in voting against the Kansas–Nebraska Act greatly irritated Southern Democrats in Texas. A flirtation with the Know-Nothings had the same effect. Believing that he would not be reelected to the Senate when his term ended in 1859, Houston decided to run for governor in 1857 as an independent. The regular Democrats nominated Hardin R. Runnels, a native Mississippian with strong states'-rights beliefs, and a bitter campaign followed.

Houston presented himself as a champion of the Union and his opponents as disunionists, while regular Democrats said that Old Sam was a Free-Soil traitor to Texas. Runnels won by a vote of 32,552 to 23,628, handing Houston the only defeat he ever suffered in a major political campaign. As governor, Runnels pursued an aggressive policy toward Indians in Northwest Texas, and there was more bloodshed on the frontier in 1858–59 than at any other time since 1836. The Comanches, although pushed back, mounted destructive raids on exposed settlements in 1859, creating considerable dissatisfaction with the Runnels administration. Also, during Runnels's term sectional tensions increased as the governor endorsed an extreme version of states' rights, and leading Democrats, including John Marshall, state party chairman and editor of the Austin *State Gazette*, advocated extreme policies such as reopening the African slave trade.

These developments under Runnels set the stage for another bitter and exciting gubernatorial contest in 1859. The regular Democrats renominated Runnels and Lieutenant Governor Francis R. Lubbock on a Southern platform, while Houston and Edward Clark opposed them by running as Independent or Union Democrats. This time, in his last electoral contest, Houston defeated Runnels, 36,227 to 27,500. The victory may have resulted in part from a lack of pro-Southern extremism among Texas voters, but Houston's personal popularity and the failure of Runnels's frontier policy played key roles, too. In any case, the state legislature's choice of Louis T. Wigfall as United States senator only two months after the gubernatorial election demonstrated that Unionism by no means had control in Texas. Wigfall, a native of South Carolina, was a fire-eating secessionist and one of Houston's bitterest enemies in Texas.

Houston's inaugural address, which he delivered publicly rather than to the hostile legislature, concluded with a plea for moderation. "When Texas united her destiny with that of the United States," he said, "she entered not into the North, nor South. Her connection was not sectional, but national." The governor was at least partly correct about the attitude at the time of annexation, but by 1860 Texas had become so much a part of the Old South that not even Sam Houston could restrain the state's rush toward secession. Ultrasoutherners controlled the Democratic state convention in 1860 and sent a delegation headed by Runnels and Lubbock to the national convention in Charleston, South Carolina. Rather than accept a platform favoring Stephen A. Douglas, the northern Democrat who called for popular sovereignty to decide the matter of slavery in the territories, the Texans joined other Deep South delegations in walking out of the convention. This step opened a split in the Democratic party that soon resulted in the nominations of Douglas by the Northern wing and John C. Breckinridge by the Southern. In the meantime the Republican party nominated Abraham Lincoln on a platform opposing the spread of slavery, and conservatives from the upper South formed a Constitutional Union party aimed at uniting those who wished to avoid disunion. Sam Houston received serious consideration for the presidential nomination of the new party but lost to John Bell of Tennessee.

Regular Democrats in Texas supported Breckinridge and threatened immediate secession if the "Black Republican" Abraham Lincoln won. The Opposition, as those who opposed the Democrats were now called, turned to Bell and the Constitutional Unionists in the hope of preventing disunion. This group, which generally sought to carry on the traditional unionism of the Whigs, Know-Nothings, and Houston Independent Democrats, did not oppose slavery or Southern interests. They simply argued that secession amounted to revolution and would probably hasten the destruction of slavery rather than protect it. A minority from the outset, the Opposition saw their cause weakened further during the late summer of 1860 by an outbreak of public hysteria known as the Texas Troubles. The panic began with a series of ruinous fires in North Texas. Spontaneous ignition of phosphorous matches due to extremely hot weather may have caused the fires. Several masters, however, forced their slaves to confess to arson, and Texans decided that a massive abolitionist-inspired plot threatened to destroy slavery and devastate the countryside. Slave and white suspects alike fell victim to vigilante action before the panic subsided in September. "It is better," said one citizen of Fort Worth, "for us to hang ninety-nine innocent (suspicious) men than to let one guilty one pass."

In November 1860 Breckinridge defeated Bell in Texas by a vote of 47,458 to 15,463, carrying every county in the state except three—Bandera, Gillespie, and Starr. Abraham Lincoln received no votes in Texas, but free-state votes made him the president-elect, scheduled to take office in March 1861. His victory signaled the beginning of a spontaneous popular movement that soon swept the Lone Star State out of the Union. True to its antebellum heritage as a growing part of the cotton frontier, Texas stood ready in 1860 to join the other Southern states in secession and war.

Randolph B. Campbell

Civil War. The sectional controversies that divided the North and South in the 1850s deeply troubled Texans. Although most Texans had a strong attachment to the Union that they had worked so hard to join in 1845, they expressed increasing concern over the attacks upon Southern institutions by Northern political leaders. Although only one Texas family in four owned slaves, most Texans opposed any interference with the institution of slavery, which they believed necessary for the continued growth of the state.

Many Texans, alarmed by the election of Abraham Lincoln to the presidency, urged Governor Houston to call a convention of the people to determine what course of action the state should take. Houston, devoted both to Texas and the Union, paid little heed to these requests, refusing to take any step that might aid secession. The demands for a convention increased, however, with the secession of South Carolina in December 1860 and the calling of state secession conventions in Mississippi, Florida, Alabama, Georgia, and Louisiana in early January. A group of secessionist leaders, including O. M. Roberts, John S. (Rip) Ford, George M. Flournoy, and William P. Rogers, issued an address to the people calling for the election of delegates to a state Secession Convention in early January. Houston called a special session of the legislature and recommended that it refuse to recognize the convention. Instead, the legislature gave approval to the convention, on the condition that the people ratify its outcome by a final vote.

The convention, which assembled in Austin on 28 January 1861, was dominated by secessionists. The delegates adopted an ordinance of secession by a vote of 166 to 8. This ordinance was approved by the voters of the state, 46,153 to 14,747, on 23 February. The convention reassembled in early March, declared Texas out of the Union, and adopted a measure uniting the state with other Southern states in the newly formed Confederate States of America. Houston, who would not recognize the authority of the convention to take this action, refused to take an oath of allegiance to the new government, whereupon the convention declared the

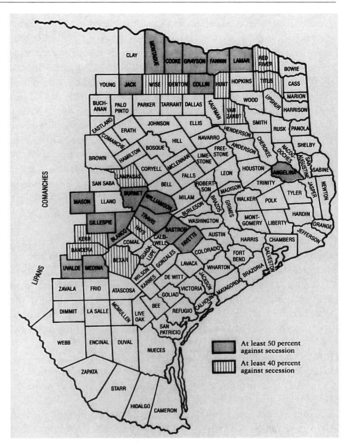

Popular referendum on secession, February 23, 1861. Map by Liz Conrad, from *Secession and the Union in Texas* by Walter Buenger, Copyright ©1984. Courtesy University of Texas Press. Photograph courtesy CAH; CN 08486.

office of governor vacant and elevated Lieutenant Governor Edward Clark to the position. President Lincoln offered to send troops to assist Houston if he would resist the convention, but Houston rejected the offer rather than bring on civil conflict within the state. He retired to his home in Huntsville, where he died two years later.

While the campaign for ratification of the secession ordinance was being waged in mid-February, the Committee of Public Safety assembled by the Secession Convention took steps to take over federal property in the state. The committee opened negotiations with Maj. Gen. David E. Twiggs, the commander of United States troops stationed in Texas. Twiggs, an aging Georgian in poor health, was awaiting orders from the War Department. On the morning of 16 February, Ben McCulloch, a veteran Texas Ranger and Mexican War hero and now colonel of Texas cavalry, led at least 500 volunteers into San Antonio, where they surrounded Twiggs and his headquarters garrison. Twiggs agreed to surrender all federal property in Texas and evacuate the 2,700 Union troops scattered in frontier forts throughout the state.

The Committee of Public Safety authorized the recruiting of volunteer troops during late February and March 1861. In addition to troops recruited by Ben McCulloch, regiments of cavalry were enrolled by Henry E. McCulloch, Ben's younger brother, and Rip Ford, veteran ranger captain and explorer. The firing on Fort Sumter in April 1861 and the subsequent call for volunteers by

Confederate president Jefferson Davis stimulated efforts by Texas authorities to raise additional troops. Governor Clark divided the state first into six and later into 11 military districts for recruiting and organizing the troops requested by Confederate authorities.

By the end of 1861, 25,000 Texans were in the Confederate Army. Two-thirds of these were in the cavalry, the branch of service preferred by Texans. Lt. Col. Arthur Fremantle of the British Coldstream Guards, who visited Texas during the war, observed this fondness for cavalry service: "it was found very difficult to raise infantry in Texas," he said, "as no Texan walks a yard if he can help it." Governor Clark observed that "the predilection of Texans for cavalry service, founded as it is upon their peerless horsemanship, is so powerful that they are unwilling in many instances to engage in service of any other description unless required by actual necessity."

Francis R. Lubbock, who defeated Clark by a narrow margin in the 1861 gubernatorial election, worked closely with Confederate authorities to meet manpower needs as the war expanded. Recruitment became more difficult as some of the early enthusiasm waned. The passage of a general conscription law by the Confederate Congress in April 1862 momentarily gave impetus to volunteering. Under this law all white males between the ages of 18 and 35 were liable for military service. In September the upper age limit was raised to 45, and in February 1864 the age limits were extended to 17 and 50. The Confederate conscription laws did contain many exemptions, however, and for a time conscripted men could hire substitutes.

Approximately 90,000 Texans saw military service in the war. Governor Lubbock reported to the legislature in November 1863 that the army numbered 90,000 Texas residents, but this figure seems high for Texans in service at any one time. The 1860 federal census lists 92,145 white males between the ages of 18 and 45 living in the state. Allowing for a slight increase in population during the four years of the war and considering that some Texans younger than 18 and older than 50 served, one may say that between 100,000 and 110,000 Texans were potential soldiers.

Two-thirds of the Texans enrolled in the military spent the war in the Southwest, either defending the state from Indian attacks and Union invasion or participating in expansionist moves into New Mexico Territory. One regiment, recruited mainly in the Houston area, served under the colorful Rip Ford in South Texas. Ford commanded the military district of the Rio Grande, which extended from the mouth of the river for more than 1,000 miles to above El Paso. During the course of the war, Ford's men battled Union invaders, hostile Comanches, and Mexican raiders led by Juan N. Cortina. Other Texas regiments patrolled North and West Texas. In May 1861 Col. William C. Young and the Eleventh Texas Cavalry, recruited in North Texas, crossed the Red River and captured federal forts Arbuckle, Cobb, and Washita. Another regiment, enrolled originally as state troops and known as the Frontier Regiment, patrolled West Texas between the Red River and the Rio Grande. The regiment, commanded first by Col. James M. Norris and later Col. James E. McCord, was transferred to Confederate service as the Forty-sixth Texas Cavalry. Part of the regiment was later moved to the Houston area, and its place on the frontier was taken by state troops commanded by Brig. Gen. James W. Throckmorton, who was appointed commander of the northern military district by state authorities.

Texans played a major role in Confederate efforts to expand into New Mexico Territory. In June 1861 four companies of Ford's cavalry, under the command of Lt. Col. John R. Baylor, were ordered to occupy extreme West Texas. Baylor reached Fort Bliss at El Paso in early July and later in the month moved into New Mexico. He occupied the small town of Mesilla, located on the left bank of the Rio Grande about forty miles north of El Paso. After a small skirmish, federal troops commanded by Maj. Isaac Lynde surrendered Fort Fillmore, on the opposite bank of the Rio Grande. On 1 August 1861, Baylor decreed the existence of the Confederate Territory of Arizona, with its capital at Mesilla and himself as the military governor.

Meanwhile, Henry H. Sibley, a West Point graduate and veteran soldier, convinced President Davis that the Confederates could capture New Mexico and Arizona. Sibley was commissioned brigadier general with orders to raise and equip a brigade of cavalry to drive federal forces from New Mexico. In August he established his headquarters in San Antonio, where he began recruiting men for the "Army of New Mexico." In early November the brigade, consisting of three regiments, began the long march to El Paso, nearly 700 miles distant. Sibley's Brigade reached El Paso on December 14. On 11 January 1862 it marched to Mesilla, where Sibley assumed command of Baylor's forces. Sibley moved northward along the west bank of the Rio Grande to Fort Craig, where he encountered Union forces commanded by Col. Edward R. S. Canby, perhaps Sibley's brother-in-law. The Confederates won a battle at nearby Valverde ford but were not strong enough to capture the fort. After the battle of Valverde, Sibley decided to bypass the fort and move northward to capture Albuquerque and Santa Fe. Morale in his army was low. Commissary supplies were virtually exhausted, the weather was bitterly cold, and many of the men were highly critical of Sibley himself. On 26 March his men fought a spirited battle with Colorado militia at Apache Canyon to the east of Santa Fe. Two days later a larger battle was fought in Glorieta Pass (the battle of Glorieta) between federals led by Col. Maj. John M. Chivington and Texans commanded by Col. William R. Scurry. In the fierce engagement the Texans drove the federals from the field. Late that afternoon, however, Scurry's supply train was captured by Union forces. The loss of the supply train was a major blow to Sibley's plans. With Union forces receiving reinforcements from Colorado and California, Sibley determined to retreat down the Rio Grande. By early May the Confederates were back at Fort Bliss, where Sibley made an address praising his men for their sacrifices. Many of the Texans who served under Sibley blamed the commander for their failure and expressed the view that better leadership would have brought success to the campaign.

The defense of the Texas coastline was more successful than the New Mexico invasion. Brig. Gen. Earl Van Dorn, commander of the Texas district from April to September 1861, organized defense companies, authorized the use of slave labor for building fortifications, and worked to secure heavy cannons for coastal defense. His successor as district commander, Brig. Gen. Paul Octave Hébert, also made efforts to secure heavy ordnance, but with only limited success. Hébert concluded that he would be unable to prevent a landing on the coast and determined to fight the enemy in the interior.

In November 1861 Union naval forces began a series of harassing activities along the Texas coast. The Confederate patrol schooner *Royal Yacht* was partially burned, and Confederate positions near Aransas Pass, Port Lavaca, and Indianola were shelled. The naval blockade of the Texas coastline was intensified in 1862; the United States bark *Arthur*, commanded by Lt. John W.

Surrender of General David E. Twiggs's federal forces and stores to Texas Confederate militia, San Antonio, February 16, 1861. Ambrotype. Courtesy TSL. This photograph was taken on Soledad Street in San Antonio, facing north, and is believed to be a scene associated with Twiggs's surrender. Terms of the surrender were negotiated in the Veramendi Palace, shown here in the center of the picture.

Kittredge, was especially active along the middle coast. In August Kittredge, commanding a small flotilla, attempted to capture Corpus Christi but was repulsed by Confederates commanded by Maj. Alfred M. Hobby. Another, more successful, Union force commanded by Lt. Frederick Crocker destroyed a small fort at Sabine Pass and burned the railroad bridge at Taylor's Bayou.

The main Union attack against the Texas coast in 1862 was aimed at the state's largest seaport, Galveston. On 4 October 1862 a small Union fleet commanded by W. B. Renshaw sailed into Galveston harbor. Confederate artillery at Fort Point opened fire but was quickly silenced by superior Union gunpower. Renshaw demanded and received the surrender of the city. The loss of Galveston was followed by a change in Confederate command in Texas. General Hébert, who had never been popular with Texans, was replaced by Gen. John Bankhead Magruder, a Virginian with a reputation as an aggressive soldier. Magruder quickly made plans for the recapture of Galveston. He called for land forces to move across the railroad bridge from the mainland at night to surprise Union garrison troops, while two river steamers converted to gunboats, the *Bayou City* and the *Neptune*, sailed into the harbor to attack federal warships. The Confederate assault began shortly after midnight on New Year's Day, 1863. At 1:00 A.M., while federal

troops slept, Magruder led his forces across the railroad bridge connecting the island and the mainland. Between 4:00 and 5:00 A.M., Confederate artillery opened fire on federal ships and positions along the waterfront. The two Confederate gunboats attacked the Union fleet soon thereafter. The *Neptune* was hit by a shell from the USS *Harriet Lane*, veered into shallow water, and sank. The *Bayou City* meanwhile moved alongside the *Harriet Lane*. The "Horse Marines" stormed aboard, captured the vessel, and hauled down her colors. Other Union ships in the harbor had troubles of their own. The Union flagship, the *Westfield*, ran aground on Pelican Spit, and efforts by a sister ship, the *Clifton*, to move her were unsuccessful. Three other small Union vessels, *Sachem*, *Owasco*, and *Corypheus*, fired on Confederate troops near the waterfront without much success. In the midst of the excitement, the *Westfield* was rocked by an internal explosion caused by premature detonation as her commander, Renshaw, prepared to destroy the ship rather than risk capture. The explosion killed Renshaw and 14 crewmen. Union naval forces now pulled out of the harbor, and the Union infantry soon surrendered to Magruder. Galveston was once again in Confederate possession.

Union naval forces continued to maintain a blockade of the Texas coastline throughout the war, but its effectiveness is difficult to measure. Ships loaded with cotton sailed out of Galveston and other Texas ports several times a week, while other vessels sailing from Havana and Caribbean ports returned with trade goods, munitions, and Enfield rifles. Unfortunately for the Confederacy, the Texas blockade runners, like those elsewhere in the South, were never adequately directed and organized for the highest degree of efficiency. Furthermore, the number of Union warships in the blockade increased with each passing month of the war. In an effort to tighten control of the Texas coastline, Maj. Gen. Nathaniel P. Banks, the Union commander of the Department of the Gulf, with headquarters in New Orleans, planned a major operation in the fall of 1863. He intended to land a large military force near Sabine Pass, march overland to Houston, and capture Galveston. To this effort he assigned 4,000 troops of the Nineteenth Army Corps, commanded by Maj. Gen. William B. Franklin. Transport vessels carrying the troops were to be protected by four light-draft gunboats, the *Clifton*, *Sachem*, *Arizona*, and *Granite City*.

The Union fleet appeared off the upper Texas coast in early September. Franklin planned to move his gunboats up the narrow channel at Sabine Pass, knock out the guns of the small Confederate fort guarding the waterway, and take his transport vessels into Sabine Lake, where they could land. The only obstacle was the rough earthwork fortification known locally as Fort Griffin and defended by a battery of Confederate artillery of 47 men commanded by Lt. Richard W. Dowling, an Irish barkeeper from Houston. On 8 September 1863, the four Union gunboats entered the channel and opened fire on Fort Griffin. The six cannons in the Confederate installation responded with high accuracy, firing 107 rounds in 36 minutes. The *Sachem* was hit on the third or fourth round and driven up against the Louisiana side of the channel, a helpless wreck. The Confederates then turned their fire on the *Clifton*. A cannonball cut her tiller rope, throwing her out of control, and she soon ran aground. Many of the crew jumped overboard and made it to shore, where they were captured by the Confederates. The two other Union gunboats, the *Arizona* and the *Granite City*, turned and withdrew from the pass. General Franklin, overestimating the size and nature of the Confederate defense, ordered a withdrawal to New Orleans. Dowling and his men were awarded medals by the Confederate government for their victory.

Union troops were temporarily more successful in southern Texas. In November 1863, 7,000 soldiers commanded by General Banks landed at the mouth of the Rio Grande and captured Brownsville, cutting the important trade between Texas and Mexico. Banks then sent one wing of his army upriver to capture Rio Grande City and another column along the coast to capture Corpus Christi, Aransas Pass, and the Matagorda Peninsula. General Magruder called upon state and Confederate authorities for additional forces to halt the advance. Fortunately for the Confederacy, many of Banks's troops were transferred to Louisiana, where a major Union offensive was planned for the spring of 1864. This allowed Confederate and state troops commanded by John S. Ford to retake most of the area occupied by Union forces. In the summer of 1864 Ford recaptured Brownsville and reopened the vital trade link with Mexico. By the end of the war the only Union holding on the lower Texas coast was Brazos Island.

Union campaigns in Arkansas and Louisiana in 1864 involved thousands of Texans. In March, General Banks moved an army of 27,000 men and a naval flotilla up the Red River toward Shreveport. He hoped to link up with federal troops under Gen. Frederick Steele, who was moving southward from Little Rock, and then extend federal control over Northeast Texas. In an effort to prevent this, Texas troops in Indian Territory commanded by Brig. Gen. Samuel Maxey—Gano's Brigade, Walker's Choctaw brigade, and Krumbhaar's battery, which was attached to Gano's brigade—were moved to Arkansas, where they joined Sterling Price in halting the Union advance at Camden. Banks, meanwhile, continued his advance in northwest Louisiana. On 8 April 1864, part of his army was defeated at Sabine Crossroads, near Mansfield, by Confederates under the command of Richard Taylor. Texans played a major role in the battle, which halted Banks's advance. Confederates resumed the attack the next day at Pleasant Hill, fourteen miles to the south, but superior Union numbers prevented a Southern victory. Once again Texas units—including Walker's Texas Division; Thomas Green's cavalry, which consisted of five brigades in three divisions led by Hamilton P. Bee, James Patrick Major, and William Steele; and Polignac's Brigade—figured prominently in the fighting. Green, one of the most popular of all the Texans, was killed three days later while leading an attack on the retreating federals at Blair's Landing. Banks continued to retreat and in mid-May crossed the Atchafalaya River, thus ending attempts to invade Northeast Texas.

Although the large battles of the Civil War were fought beyond the Mississippi River, far from Texas, the state contributed thousands of men who participated in them. Texan Albert Sidney Johnston was killed in the battle of Shiloh in April 1862 while commanding a major Confederate army. Another Texas officer, Gen. John Bell Hood, lost the use of an arm at Gettysburg and a leg at Chickamauga. The Texas Brigade, originally commanded by Hood, had one of the finest reputations of any military unit. The brigade, including the First, Fourth, and Fifth Texas Infantry regiments, fought with honor at Gaines' Mill, Second Manassas, Sharpsburg, Gettysburg, and Chickamauga. A Texas regiment, the Eighth Texas Cavalry, better known as Terry's Texas Rangers, distinguished itself on battlefields in Kentucky, Tennessee, Mississippi, Georgia, and South and North Carolina. Another brigade, commanded late in the war by Lawrence Sullivan Ross, won praise for combat in Mississippi, Tennessee, and Georgia. Granbury's Texas Brigade, commanded by Waco lawyer Col. Hiram B. Granbury, also saw extensive action in Georgia and Tennessee. Granbury himself was killed in the futile Confederate assault at Franklin, Tennessee, in November 1864. Ector's Brigade, consisting of the Tenth, Eleventh, Fourteenth, and Fifteenth Texas Dismounted Cavalry and commanded by Brig. Gen. Mathew Duncan Ector, saw action in Tennessee, Mississippi, and Georgia and participated in Hood's invasion of Tennessee.

The task of recruiting and equipping the thousands of Texans in military service required diligent efforts by state authorities. Francis R. Lubbock, who served as governor during the first half of the war, was a most capable and energetic chief executive. At his request the legislature provided for reorganization of the state militia system, passed a revenue act raising taxes, and established the Military Board of Texas, which had power to purchase military supplies and establish ordnance foundries and arms factories. Lubbock met frequently with Confederate political and military leaders in efforts to provide better cooperation in the war. Although Texas and the Southwest were cut off from the rest of the South with the fall of Vicksburg in the summer of 1863, Lubbock continued to emphasize the need for unity in support of the Confederacy.

The governor entered the military in December 1863 and did not seek reelection. In the contest to choose his successor, Pendleton Murrah, a Harrison County lawyer and former state legislator, defeated Thomas Jefferson Chambers, four-time gubernatorial candidate and pioneer Gulf Coast rancher. The election centered upon support for the war effort. Although Murrah was less well known than Chambers, the Marshall lawyer benefited from Chambers's reputation as a political maverick and a critic of Jefferson Davis's administration. Most Texans regarded Murrah as the safer candidate. In office Murrah soon found himself involved in controversy with Gen. Edmund Kirby Smith, commander of the Trans-Mississippi Department. The disagreements related to a variety of relationships between the state and the central Confederate authority, including conscription laws, impressment of slave labor, transfer of Texas troops outside the war area, and supply matters. Particularly bitter was the controversy over government purchase of cotton, a disagreement that divided Smith, who had set up the national Cotton Bureau for purchasing and selling cotton, and Murrah, who developed a state plan for the same purpose. The matter was resolved in a meeting between Smith and Murrah at Hempstead in June 1864. Shortly thereafter, the governor requested that the people of Texas deliver their cotton to the army's agents for compensation and declared that the state would no longer compete with the military for the cotton.

The majority of Texans approved the efforts of governors Clark, Lubbock, and Murrah to support the Confederacy. Even so, Unionism remained strong in some sections of the state. This was especially true in some of the German counties in the Hill Country and in a group of counties north of Dallas. Some of the early Texas Unionists such as James W. Throckmorton, who cast one of the eight votes against secession in the Secession Convention, and Ben H. Epperson, a leader of East Texans opposed to secession, accepted the Confederacy after Fort Sumter and vigorously supported the Southern cause. Others, such as David G. Burnet, Elisha M. Pease, and Sam Houston, withdrew from public life and attempted to avoid controversy. Another group left the state or attempted to do so. Some of these, such as S. M. Swenson, the father of Swedish migration to Texas, and William Marsh Rice, a native of Massachusetts who made a fortune in the mercantile business in Texas, quietly left. Others joined the Union army in their efforts to defeat the Confederacy. Though most of the Mexican Americans from Texas who fought in the war joined the Confederate Army, some joined the Union Army, partly in memory of the events of the Texas Revolution and its aftermath. The Second Texas Cavalry (U.S.), for example, was made up of mostly Texas Mexicans and Mexican nationals; the unit suffered a high desertion rate. Some 2,132 whites and 47 blacks from Texas served in the Union Army. The best known of the Texans who supported the Union were Edmund J. Davis, who organized and commanded the First Texas Cavalry Regiment (Union), and Andrew J. Hamilton, Texas legislator and congressman, whom Lincoln appointed military governor of Texas after the war.

Texas Confederates dealt harshly with those attempting to assist the enemy. In August 1862 Fritz Tegener led 65 Unionists, mostly Germans from the Hill Country, in an unsuccessful attempt to cross the Rio Grande and flee from Texas. They were overtaken near the Nueces River by state troops commanded by Lt. C. D. McRae. Thirty-five of the Unionists were killed, and several others were wounded in the battle of the Nueces. Another 50 Union sympathizers were hanged in Gillespie County several weeks later. The

Hood's Texas Brigade, in camp. Courtesy Austin History Center, Austin Public Library; Photo no. PICA 03674. Hood's Texas Brigade fought in many engagements in Virginia. Its commander, John Bell Hood, went on to become commander of the Army of Tennessee.

greatest roundup of suspected Unionists occurred in Cooke and Grayson counties, north of Dallas. A citizens' court at Gainesville tried 150 individuals for Unionist activities. Some confessed, some were convicted, and 39 were executed in what contemporaries called the Great Hanging at Gainesville.

The life of ordinary Texans was much affected by the war. Although the state suffered less economically than other Confederate states, many adjustments were necessary. The blockade resulted in shortages of many commodities, especially coffee, medicine, clothing, shoes, and farm implements. Homespun clothing was worn as in early days; Governor Lubbock was inaugurated in a homespun suit. The British visitor Colonel Fremantle reported that "the loss of coffee afflicts the Confederates even more than the loss of spirits; and they exercise their ingenuity in devising substitutes, which are not generally very successful." These substitutes included barley, corn, okra, peanuts, and sweet potatoes. Salt was so scarce that some Texans dug up the floors of their smokehouses and leached the dirt to recover the salt drippings. Thorns were used for pins, willow-bark extract and red pepper were mixed to substitute for quinine, and pieces of wallpaper served as writing paper. Several Texas newspapers suspended or discontinued operations for periods of time due to the lack of paper.

On the other hand, trade with Mexico made more materials available to Texas than to other Confederate states. In return for cotton, Texans received military supplies, medicines, dry goods, food, iron goods, liquor, coffee, and tobacco. Matamoros, on the Rio Grande across from Brownsville, and Bagdad, Tamaulipas, a seaport village at the mouth of the Rio Grande, were the centers of this activity, in which hundreds of vessels from Europe and the United States engaged in a flourishing business. The trade was interrupted from time to time by Union military activities along the lower Texas coast, but even so it provided many items needed by Texans during the war.

The war brought other changes to Texas. Some adjustments were made in agriculture as farmers planted more corn to meet food needs and requests of the government to reduce cotton production. The absence of men away at the war front placed greater responsibilities and burdens upon women and children, who assumed increased duties. The shortage of free labor was partially

Funeral of German patriots at Comfort, Texas, August 20, 1865. Engraving published in *Harper's Weekly: A Journal of Civilization,* January 20, 1866. Photograph courtesy Special Collections Libraries, University of Texas at Austin. In August 1865, in the German community of Comfort, a funeral was held and a monument erected honoring Unionists who were killed in the battle of the Nueces.

offset by the increase in the number of slaves sent from other Southern states to Texas in an attempt to avoid the invading enemy armies. On occasion, military units were assigned harvesting duties.

Transportation was seriously affected by the war. The outbreak of fighting halted all railroad building for seven years, and difficulties in maintaining rolling stock caused existing service to be interrupted. General Magruder ordered segments of the Eastern Texas road and the Texas and New Orleans torn up for coastal fortifications. Several miles of track between Swanson's Landing and Jonesville in East Texas was taken up and relaid eastward from Marshall to Waskom for military purposes. Stagecoach lines continued to operate, but coaches were overcrowded and behind schedule. Roads and bridges suffered from lack of repair as labor and materials were diverted elsewhere.

The requirements of the military and the impact of the blockade caused rapid expansion of manufacturing in the state. The Texas State Military Board had the promotion of manufacturing as one of its responsibilities. Under its direction a percussion-cap factory and a cannon foundry were established in Austin. The board established a textile mill in the Texas State Penitentiary at Huntsville. During the war three million yards of cotton and wool cloth was produced at the Huntsville facility. The Confederate quartermaster department operated, or contracted for, facilities at Houston, Dallas, Austin, Tyler, Rusk, Paris, Jefferson, Marshall,

Waco, and Hempstead for the manufacture of clothing, shoes, iron products, wagons, tents, harness, and saddles. A major ordnance works was established at Tyler, and smaller plants were located in or near Rusk, Jefferson, Houston, and Galveston. A beef-packing plant at Jefferson provided meat for the Confederate Army.

Although political and military leaders attempted to keep up the morale of Texans, military defeats in Georgia, Tennessee, and Virginia in late 1864 caused increased anxiety in the state. Newspaper editorials urged civilians to remain calm, and Governor Murrah and General Smith asked Texans to continue the struggle. News of Robert E. Lee's surrender in April 1865, followed by that of Joseph E. Johnston in North Carolina, made further resistance appear futile. Rip Ford defeated Union troops in the battle of Palmito Ranch, near Brownsville, on 13 May 1865, the last battle of the war. From captured prisoners Ford learned that Confederate forces were surrendering all over the South. Kirby Smith attempted to keep his command intact, but found his soldiers heading for their homes. Some Texans, including Murrah and former governor Clark, joined other Confederates fleeing to Mexico. On 2 June 1865 generals Smith and Magruder signed the formal terms of surrender for their commands, and on 19 June (Juneteenth) Gen. Gordon Granger arrived in Galveston with Union forces of occupation. Reconstruction was in the offing. The Civil War had ended.

Ralph A. Wooster

Reconstruction. For nine years following the Civil War, Texas was in turmoil, as its people attempted to solve political, social, and economic problems produced by the war. Emancipation changed the labor system, and the end of slavery forced a redefinition of the relationship between blacks and whites. The change in labor and the costs of the war threatened to undermine the economic power of those who had dominated antebellum economic life, which was focused on the plantation. The weakening of the antebellum elite threatened not only their economic and social position but also their political power. In 1865 Texans confronted a situation in which new directions had to be taken in economic development, political alignments, and social order.

One of the major forces of change in the state was the United States Army. Federal troops began entering the state in late May 1865. Their commanders believed that their duty, at least in part, was to ensure loyal government and to protect the rights of the blacks who were free as a result of the war. Gen. George A. Custer, stationed at Austin, expressed the military view when he recommended that the army retain control of the state until the government was "satisfied that a loyal sentiment prevails in at least a majority of the inhabitants." The military insistence upon loyalty threatened an indefinite loss of power among antebellum and wartime political leaders. Military views regarding freedmen posed, at least in the minds of white Texans, a permanent disruption of their labor system and, subsequently, their entire economy. Their fears proved groundless, at least for the most part, for a variety of factors prevented the army from effecting all the change of which it seemed capable. Rapid demobilization reduced within a year the number of troops in the state from 51,000 to 3,000, and many of those who remained were on the frontier. The small size of the occupying army thus guaranteed its ineffectiveness. Still, various military commanders attempted to intervene in local politics. Turnover among them, however, prevented the development of a sustained policy. From May 1865 to March 1870 the command of forces in the state changed eight times. Of the commanders, Charles Griffin was the most active politically, but his career ended with his death in September 1867. His successor, Joseph J. Reynolds, was also politically active, though changes in command over him and his own indecisiveness and incompetence frustrated his forays into local politics. Wavering but domineering army policies ultimately provoked the local white population into an obstinate defense of prewar political power and control over the black population.

The formation of the Freedmen's Bureau presented a further threat to prewar society. This agency began its operations in the state in September 1865 under the command of Maj. Gen. Edgar M. Gregory. The bureau was charged with overseeing all matters concerning refugees, freedmen, and abandoned lands, but its principal role was helping the new freedmen make the transition from slavery to freedom. Gregory, an abolitionist, interpreted his chief goal in the state as establishing a free labor system for the former slaves. Despite white fears, the course of Gregory and his principal successors, Joseph B. Kiddoo, Charles Griffin, and Joseph J. Reynolds, was not radical. Within a year Gregory's labor policies stabilized the black labor force. He pressured blacks to stay where they were and to sign contracts to work for wages or on shares. Without land of their own the freedmen had no alternative to going back to work for others. While planters complained publicly that free black labor was not as good as slave, in private most found the new situation of tenantry acceptable. The indebtedness of tenants to landlords

embodied its own mechanisms for controlling the freedom of the labor force. Though they possessed freedom to search for the best conditions among local landowners, blacks had few choices other than to labor on some other person's land. Other aspects of the bureau's work were not as acceptable to whites. They saw attempts to educate the freedmen as potentially destructive to good order. They also criticized the intervention of agents and bureau courts in situations where bureau agents charged that blacks were being treated unjustly. The bureau adjudicated matters ranging from violence to labor contracts. However, the challenge represented by bureau schools and courts was always more in appearance than reality. The schools did not receive the financial support necessary to serve the large black population. The courts were inadequate for the protection of the freedmen and irritated the whites brought before them. Ultimately the bureau had little effect and, like the army, served to provoke whites to even greater opposition.

Presidential Reconstruction presented a third, more substantial threat to antebellum order. Under this plan for restoring the South to the Union, the president was to appoint a provisional governor for each state. This officer was required to call a convention in order to nullify the act of secession, to abolish slavery, and to repudiate the state's Confederate debt. The delegates to the convention had to take an oath of amnesty as prescribed by the president and were to be elected by voters who had also taken the oath. Once the voters had ratified the work of the convention, they would elect a governor, a legislature, and other state officials. When the legislature had ratified the Thirteenth Amendment of the United States Constitution, the state would be fully restored to the Union. In accordance with this plan, President Andrew Johnson appointed Andrew J. Hamilton provisional governor of Texas. Hamilton represented elements of the antebellum opposition to the dominant Democratic party and received a great deal of support from Texas Unionists. The oath of amnesty was designed to exclude many antebellum political leaders from the convention and allow the Unionists to rise to power in their place. Their success would mean a different distribution of the resources of state government and the acceptance of a broader definition of freedmen's rights than many of the old order were willing to permit. In fact, Hamilton failed to prevent the resurgence of the Democrats. In the election held on 8 January 1866 the prewar power structure reasserted itself. This was made possible by the fact that although this group had suffered economically, their losses were only relative. The war had not driven them from their control of the state's economic life. They now demanded political power again, and, even though excluded by the provisions of Presidential Reconstruction, many voted and ran for the convention. When the delegates assembled at Austin in February 1866 they included a large number of prominent prewar and Confederate leaders, including H. R. Runnels, O. M. Roberts, R. S. Walker, and T. N. Waul. They made some concessions to the Reconstruction situation, however, and in the Constitutional Convention of 1866 they shared power with moderate Unionists, those who were willing to make concessions to the Democrats. Members of the coalition called themselves conservatives, and they elected James W. Throckmorton, a Unionist from northeastern Texas, as president of the convention.

The proceedings of the convention showed the reluctance of the majority to meet anything more than the president's minimum requirements for readmission to regular status in the Union. The delegates renounced the right of secession and proclaimed the state's act of secession null and void. Unionist delegates attempted

Confederate veterans, former members of Hood's Texas Brigade, two of them with war wounds, Austin, 1866. Courtesy TSL. In postwar Texas, veterans often found it hard to accept changes they experienced in their social, political, and economic positions.

unsuccessfully to have secession declared null and void *ab initio*—from the beginning. The delegates also declared their acceptance of the abolition of slavery and granted blacks basic rights, but did not concede black suffrage. They repudiated the state's war debt. Finally, in an action that fueled controversy through the rest of Reconstruction, they validated all laws of the state government during the war that were not in conflict with the United States Constitution, the state constitution prior to secession, or proclamations of the provisional governor. They set an election of ratification, at which officials were also elected, for 25 June 1866, and the proposed constitution passed. Voters also had to select state officers and choose between a conservative ticket, headed by Throckmorton, and a Unionist one, led by former governor Elisha M. Pease. The campaign centered on charges that Pease represented the interests of Radical Republicans in the North and supported extension of suffrage to the freedmen. The power of antebellum politicians again asserted itself when Throckmorton handily carried the election by a vote of 49,277 to 12,168.

The Eleventh Legislature met in August 1866, and Throckmorton took office a few days later. The governor's efforts at securing recognition were hindered by the many former secessionists who dominated the legislature. These men selected two prominent secessionists, O. M. Roberts and David G. Burnet, for seats in the United States Senate. The legislature's actions attempted to return the state as much as possible to the status quo ante bellum. They refused to ratify the Thirteenth and Fourteenth amendments. The members also enacted "black codes," a series of measures designed to regulate black labor through apprenticeship, contract labor, and vagrancy laws. These labor laws appeared to Unionists in Texas and Republicans in the north as an attempt to establish a new form of slavery. Such activity convinced even those Unionists who had not remained outside the conservative coalition that the former Confederates were back in control and unrepentant. It raised similar doubts in the minds of the local military commanders, the assistant commissioner of the Freedmen's Bureau, and the members of Congress. Neither the senators chosen by the legislature nor the congressmen elected by Texas voters were allowed to take their seats in Washington. Throckmorton

himself increased tension by his complaints against the army for interfering in civil affairs and in his efforts to protect the frontier from Indian raids by fielding ranging companies. He believed that the army and the Freedmen's Bureau meddled unreasonably in civil affairs and that the army was not doing its duty on the frontier. In turn, military officials and Unionists believed that Throckmorton, relying on local justice, had brought about a situation in which die-hard Confederates persecuted and even murdered blacks and Unionists without punishment. They also feared that the governor's rangers were intended as a political organization to block Reconstruction as much as to fight Indians.

Congress brought the course of Throckmorton, the legislature, and Presidential Reconstruction to an end in March 1867 with its First Reconstruction Act. The law broke the South into military districts under the command of the army and declared the existing governments to be provisional. Texas was placed in the Fifth Military District. From the beginning General Griffin, commander in Texas, differed from Throckmorton on policy, and on 30 July 1867, at the request of Griffin, Gen. Philip H. Sheridan, commander of the district, removed Throckmorton from office as an "impediment to Reconstruction." In his complaints to Sheridan, Griffin cited Throckmorton's failure to qualify for office under the "military bill" (the First Reconstruction Act) and his refusal to cooperate in the punishment of those who had committed outrages against loyal men, white and black. Following Throckmorton's removal, complaints from Unionists, blacks, and Freedmen's Bureau officials about local officials who refused to protect their lives and property continued to pour into military headquarters. Griffin began to move toward defenestrating these local officials, but little was done toward this end before his death in the yellow fever epidemic that swept through the eastern part of the state that summer and fall. His successor, Reynolds, continued to receive complaints, and with a series of special orders began wholesale removals in the fall of 1867. The most sweeping of these special orders, No. 195, issued in November 1867, removed more than 400 county officials in 57 counties across the state. Four days later Reynolds removed the elected city officials of San Antonio, and the day after that, their terms having expired, he replaced the officials of Austin. The men Reynolds appointed to replace these removed officials had to be capable of taking the "Test Oath," passed by Congress in 1862, stating that they had never voluntarily borne arms against the United States or given "aid, countenance, counsel, or encouragement to persons engaged in armed hostility thereto." The removals continued until most counties in the state had had at least one county official removed. Many local elected officials who remained in office after Reynolds's removals of late 1867 and early 1868 were forced to leave office in April 1869, when Gen. Edward R. S. Canby ruled that every office filled by an elected official incapable of taking the Test Oath would be considered vacant on 25 April 1869.

Under the provisions of Congressional Reconstruction, Texans had to take new steps for restoration. The state had to have another constitutional convention, with delegates elected by all male citizens over the age of 21, regardless of race, color, or "previous condition of servitude." Only felons and those who had been disfranchised for their part in the war could not participate. Congress required that the convention write a new state constitution that would provide for universal adult male suffrage. When the constitution had been written and the state had ratified the Fourteenth Amendment of the United States Constitution,

Congress would consider the case for readmission to the Union. In the spring and summer of 1867 political parties organized in preparation for the new constitutional convention. Unionists' participation in forming the state's Republican party linked them with black voters, who were for the first time to be allowed to take part in the political process. The biracial nature of the party led its opponents to refer to it usually as the Radical party. In fact, like the Unionists, the new party reflected diverse interests. Regional concerns, economic interests, race, and ideological considerations provided the motivating force behind those who joined this party. Blacks organized under white sponsorship in the Union League. A major weakness of this new organization was that its members had little in common, other than their opposition to the power and policies of the conservatives. Still, that opposition meant that their electoral triumph threatened to bring about a potential political revolution. Those opposed to the coming convention were not sure exactly how to respond. Their leaders at first encouraged voters to stay away from the polls and ensure that the convention did not receive a majority of votes. In January 1868 conservatives met at Houston and concluded that their supporters should vote against a convention and for conservative delegates, stating that they preferred military rule to the "Africanization" that would result from a convention. The result was that most conservatives did not bother to register or to vote. The Radicals carried the election by a vote of 44,689 to 11,440. The turnout indicated that most white Texans either did not believe they had a real say in the election, or they did not care, for little more than half of the eligible voters cast ballots.

The convention met at Austin in June 1868 and did not adjourn until February 1869. Though the delegates devoted as much time to special-interest legislation as to drafting the basic document, the constitution they wrote differed significantly from previous constitutions. It authorized a more centralized and bureaucratized system of government, with greater power in the hands of the governor, who received extensive powers of appointment, including the right to name district judges. The centralizing tendencies of the constitution later proved to be controversial, but in the convention this strengthening of executive power was one of the few issues that did not produce conflict between Democratic and Republican delegates. No matter what the strengths or weaknesses of the proposed constitution were, its drafting produced political turmoil. The assembly uncovered major weaknesses within the new Republican party. After disagreeing over many measures in the constitutional convention, the party split over the same issues at their convention in August 1868. A. J. Hamilton and Pease led what came to be known as the moderate wing of the party. Edmund J. Davis, James P. Newcomb, and Morgan C. Hamilton dominated the Radical wing. The terms *moderate* and *radical* referred primarily to the parties' willingness to grant rights to blacks or to make concessions to former Confederates, but the split also reflected differences over economic and other policies as well. The Radical Republicans supported greater rights for blacks, more restrictions on Confederates, and, paradoxically, a more cautious program of economic development. The moderates, however, controlled the convention and included in the new constitution liberal provisions restoring the franchise to former Confederates. This particular concession caused the Radicals to oppose, at Washington, the holding of an election to ratify the proposed constitution. The moderates, however, urged the Grant administration to accept the document. When it became clear that

Young Texas. Carte de visite by J. R. Davis, Dallas. Courtesy Lawrence T. Jones III Collection, Austin. This political cartoon depicts the state of Texas as a disheveled ne'er-do-well. He is armed with an enormous Bowie knife with which he intends to kill the Reconstruction programs imposed on him by the federal government.

the administration would hold an election for ratification and for state offices, the two factions each put candidates in the field.

Texans began preparing for an election in the spring of 1869, though the election was not held until the following December. The two Republican factions ran opposing tickets. The Radicals selected the man who had led them in the convention, E. J. Davis, and the moderates chose A. J. Hamilton. Hamilton sought support among the former Democratic leadership in the subsequent campaign. The two factions jockeyed for support from the administration of President Grant, support that ultimately went to the Davis faction, which received federal patronage after September 1869. Grant's support helped Davis to get the black vote. On 11 January 1870, General Reynolds declared that the new constitution had been ratified and that Davis had received an 800-vote majority. Hamilton Stuart, a newspaper editor, received 380 votes.

In February 1870 the elected members of the Twelfth Legislature assembled at Austin at the order of the military commander. They were to adopt the Fourteenth and Fifteenth amendments and select United States senators in preparation for readmission to the Union. They quickly approved the amendments and selected Morgan C. Hamilton for a six-year term and James W. Flanagan for a four-year term. This completed the requirements set by Congress for readmission. On 30 March 1870, Grant signed the act that readmitted Texas to the Union and ended Congressional Reconstruction.

The next month the legislature reconvened in a special session to address the numerous problems that had emerged since the war. As a whole, their program produced a significant increase in the role of state government. It also demonstrated Republican commitment to change. Of the issues addressed, none provided more controversy than that of violence. Everyone agreed that lawlessness was rampant in much of the state, but parties could not agree about the cause. Certainly much of it could be attributed to the postwar breakup. Bands of brigands roamed along the Red River and in the Big Thicket. Gangs led by such outlaws as Cullen Baker, Benjamin F. Bickerstaff, and Bob Lee preyed upon the people of Texas. Though their targets often were freedmen or federal soldiers, these murderers and horse thieves could hardly be called political activists. On the other hand, much violence clearly had racial or political overtones. The Convention of 1868 reported that of 939 murders in the state between 1865 and 1868, 379 were murders of blacks committed by whites. In 1868 General Reynolds also reported that armed organizations, generally known as the Ku Klux Klan but locally referred to as Pale Face, Knights of the White Camellia, or the White Brotherhood, were operating east of the Trinity River. Their targets were blacks and Union men. Although no evidence exists to prove a statewide organization, such groups clearly were political in motivation. As its chief measure to end this lawlessness, the legislature passed a State Police bill and established a militia, which had among its responsibilities the support of the State Police. Both forces were placed under the adjutant general. To aid the police the legislature also expanded the district court system. Although controversy surrounded these measures from the beginning, the program appeared to achieve its goals. In 1871 the police made 3,602 arrests, and in 1872 the adjutant general reported 1,204 arrests. In its first three years of existence the police force recovered $200,000 in stolen property. Many of the state's citizens began to look to the force for protection. In addition, despite some early fears, the militia was used sparingly. Still, the police measures produced many enemies. Local citizens complained that police behavior was inappropriate. The use of the police to protect pools of voters during elections incensed the Republicans' opponents, who charged that the force was only a political organization. The fact that many of the policemen were blacks and had authority over whites did not help. When Governor Davis used the militia, again composed frequently of blacks, to enforce order at the polls, that organization was also linked inextricably to the Republican regime. Declarations of martial law and the use of the militia in Madison, Hill, Walker, Limestone, and Freestone counties produced widespread condemnation. When adjutant general James Davidson fled the state in 1872 with $34,434 of state money, he added to the darkened reputation of the police.

Almost as controversial were the Davis government's school measures. The legislature did not produce a successful school law until 1871, and this act inaugurated a highly centralized system of public schools. The state supported the schools in each county; selected and tested the teachers; determined a common curriculum; and provided for a graded system of three classes, primary, elementary, and advanced. The public education system, headed by Jacob C. DeGress, grew rapidly. Enrollment peaked at 129,542, or 56 percent of the scholastic population, in 1872–73. But opponents raised objections to the education of blacks, compulsory attendance, centralization of authority, and costs. The schools generated enough enemies that they provided a major focus of Democratic aversion. Other laws also provided a basis for criticism. Opponents condemned the law that set the first state election to be held after readmission in November 1872, rather than in November 1871. This law gave the legislature a two-year term, as provided in the Constitution, but changed the election date set by the Constitution. An enabling act allowing the governor to appoint district attorneys, county surveyors, cattle and hide inspectors, public cotton weighers, and mayors and aldermen, and to fill other vacancies until regularly scheduled elections, was considered another dangerous appropriation of power.

Republican aid to railroads produced less party strife and indicated the Republicans' belief in the need to encourage economic development. The first major act was the legislature's incorporation of the International Railroad Company, which received $10,000 in 8 percent bonds for each mile of new road. In a later session the legislature gave subsidies to the Southern Trans-Continental and the Southern Pacific. Governor Davis vetoed these bills, contending that the state could support only one railroad, but a coalition of Democrats and Republicans overrode his veto. The legislature also authorized counties and towns to provide their own support for railroads through the issuance of bonds. In addition to the railroad measures, other laws designed to promote growth passed with little debate. The legislature passed two homestead laws to encourage immigration and farm expansion. The first allowed 160 acres of state land to each head of a family who did not already possess a homestead. In turn the homesteader had to occupy the land for three years and pay processing fees. Single men were allowed 80 acres. The settler wishing less than 160 acres could buy land for a dollar an acre. The second law exempted from forced sale a family homestead of not more than 200 acres of rural land or more than $5,000 worth of city property. Efforts were also made to encourage cotton and woolen textile factories by granting such concerns tax exemptions for up to five years on their stock and property used in production. The legislature also founded a bureau, headed by Gustav Loeffler, to encourage immigration. Another component of the Republican program that produced little debate was its Indian policy. The state government wanted to get rid of the Indians. A frontier protection bill provided for ranging companies of troops, although they were never funded sufficiently to have an effect. The Davis government's chief problem in Indian relations was that the Republican federal government was trying to get Indians onto reservations, while most Texans wanted them exterminated. The height of this conflict came in October 1873, when Davis was pressured by the federal government into releasing the Kiowa chiefs Satanta and Big Tree, who had been imprisoned for murder after the Warren Wagontrain Raid. Davis won few friends by giving in. In fact, however, neither the state nor federal government settled the situation on the frontier until more aggressive tactics were introduced by Ranald S. Mackenzie in 1874. His defeat of the Comanches at Palo Duro Canyon was the first step towards removing the plains Indians from the Texas frontier.

The government's overall program produced many enemies. It offended too many different interest groups. The centralizing tendencies of many of the Republican measures, their susceptibility to abuse, and their costs provided a common ground for opposition among a disparate majority, the basis of a coalition of moderate Republicans and Democrats that emerged in the early 1870s. The opposition peaked in September 1871 in the Tax-payers' Convention. This state convention, political in its nature and goals, aimed at rallying opposition to regular Republican candidates in the autumn congressional elections. Conservative businessmen who wanted to avoid taxes and planters who wanted to avoid turmoil in their black workforce joined the small farmers, who, destroyed by the war, turned all of their anger into hatred of freed blacks, the cause, it seemed, of all their woes. Thus were allied men who would otherwise have been political enemies.

The charges of high taxes proved the undoing of the Republican regime. Beginning with the 1871 elections the party encountered one defeat after another. It was never able to recover. In 1871 the Democrats carried all four congressional seats. In 1872 they elected two new congressmen at large and, more importantly, gained control of the House in the Thirteenth Legislature. Only the staggered senatorial terms prevented the Senate from also falling to Democratic control. Even so, Republicans in the Senate now appeared eager to cooperate with their opponents in undoing much of the party's Reconstruction program. The Thirteenth Legislature abolished the State Police and altered the militia law so that the governor could no longer declare martial law. The enabling act was also modified to provide for special elections to fill vacancies. The voting act was changed to make possible precinct voting and to end the practice of voting only at county seats. The legislature also effectively destroyed the state school system and placed school operations in the hands of local boards of school directors. Although the office of state superintendent of public instruction was retained, it now involved mainly record keeping. The resurgent conservatives did not interfere, however, with the economic programs of the Twelfth Legislature.

In December 1873 the state had its first general election since 1869. Davis ran again for the Republican nomination and received it, then campaigned in defense of his administration. The coalition that had opposed Davis up to this point came apart, and for the first time since the war the Democratic party ran a regular candidate, leaving its moderate Republican allies to move back to the Davis party or stay out of politics. After considerable internal upheaval, the Democratic convention nominated Richard Coke on the fifth ballot. Coke supported the continued dismantling of the Republican program, although he favored a new constitutional convention. Davis secured strong support only in the black belt and some western counties. Coke won easily, 85,549 to 42,663. For all practical purposes the Republican effort was over, but one last step had to be taken to end legislative Reconstruction. Houston Republicans attempted to overturn the election in the case of *Ex parte Rodriguez* or, as it was popularly called, the Semicolon Case. In ruling that the election was unconstitutional, the state Supreme Court set up a confrontation between Davis and the newly elected Coke known as the Coke–Davis controversy. Davis refused to step down, arguing that he must enforce the decision of the court. Coke stated his intention to take office no matter what. In fact, Davis's only hope in the matter was for intervention by federal authorities, since he faced overwhelming power in the hands of his opponents. When the president refused to intervene, Davis had to resign. In January 1874 the Democrats staged a military celebration at the state Capitol, firing a 102-gun salute for the newly inaugurated Governor Coke and his lieutenant governor, Richard Hubbard.

Joshua Houston, 1898. Courtesy Sam Houston Memorial Museum, Huntsville. Black Texans found that they now had power to make decisions that affected their own families, communities, and institutions. Houston was one of the first blacks elected alderman in Huntsville.

Coke's triumph marked a strong and lasting reaction to the Republican regime. Democrats controlled the state government for the next century.

Four years of Republican rule brought almost no change in the basic patterns of life in the state. The most important economic trend was the steady expansion of the state's railroad network. In 1861 the state had 392 miles of track in service, although it had fallen into disrepair during the war. Encouraged by prospects of government subsidies, railroad companies rapidly rebuilt their facilities and began expansion. By 1870 the miles in service had increased to 711; by 1872 the number was 1,066; and by 1873 it was 1,578. The trunk lines that served the state throughout the rest of the century were taking shape. The Houston and Texas Central had tied Houston and Galveston to Austin, Waco, and the Red River at Denison, where the line was to connect with the Missouri, Kansas and Texas. The International had completed part of its planned route from Texarkana through Austin and San Antonio to Laredo. The Texas and Pacific, formed by a merger of the Southern Pacific and Southern Trans-Continental, had started two lines, one from Longview to Dallas and a second from Sherman to Brookston. The effect of railroad development, however, was not to open wider opportunities but to fix commercial agriculture and cotton farming on the state more firmly than ever. The railroads made possible the integration of rural Texas into the national market. Steadily, the self-sufficient rural economy was supplanted by a market one, as production of wheat and corn gave way to the one marketable crop—cotton. Wheat production expanded from 1,225,000 bushels to 1,474,000 between 1870 and 1874. Corn increased from 23,690,000 bushels to 31,000,000 in the same period. Along the rail lines, however, the amount of cotton grown relative to wheat and corn steadily increased. Observers noted that even along the Red River, the one region of the state that had emphasized wheat production before the war, rust, grasshoppers, and the railroads pushed farmers to the cultivation of cotton. As a result, despite the setbacks caused by the war and problems caused by weather and insects, by the end of Reconstruction, Texas farmers had surpassed their prewar cotton production. In 1860 they had produced 431,463 bales. In 1873 they brought in a harvest of 487,771 bales. The state's economy thus remained tied to a crop that suffered from steadily declining prices through the rest of the nineteenth century.

There was some economic diversification, but it was limited. During this period, in the western counties, the range cattle industry developed. The first large-scale cattle drives to the north began in 1866, at the end of the war, usually headed for Sedalia, Missouri, for transportation by rail to the East. In 1866, 260,000 cattle went over the trails. The greatest drive in this period took place in the spring of 1871, when 700,000 Texas cattle arrived in Kansas. After 1871 lower prices caused a decline in cattle trailing. The industry received another setback in the summer of 1873, when low demand forced Texas cattlemen to hold on to their stock and borrow money to fatten it for the fall market. Entangled in debt, many ranchers were bankrupted in the general banking disaster caused by the collapse of the New York banking firm Jay Cooke and Company that year. Despite these problems, ranching had become a major component of the state's economy. The postwar years also saw an expansion in sheep ranching, with a steady growth in herds and the sale of wool. In 1870 the census indicated 1,272,000 sheep in the state. By 1874 the estimate was 1,632,971. With cotton, wool became a major export. By 1871 the wool clip was over three million pounds, and most of it was shipped out of the state. The postwar years brought about a small expansion in manufactures, but not enough to challenge agricultural domination of the economy. The firms that did appear generally processed farm products. Typical of the manufacturing that developed were the 533 flour and grist mills and 324 sawmills listed by the 1870 census. Few concerns, however, possessed the scale, organization, or technology of contemporary northern industries. By the end of Reconstruction the state had about a dozen woolen and cotton textile mills. In East Texas several small iron smelters and foundries operated. None of these, however, signaled the state's participation in the industrial expansion that revolutionized the economy of the North.

Waves of newcomers overwhelmed the antebellum population during this period. People from the older Southern states faced many economic problems as a result of the war. They saw Texas, with its extensive public lands, as a place of opportunity. Newcomers, both white and black, flooded into the state. Although the exact number of arrivals during Reconstruction is not known, the state Bureau of Immigration estimated that in 1873 as many as 125,000 people arrived, over 100,000 of these being from older Southern states. As southerners, these immigrants posed no threats to the dominant culture of the state. They did bring with them, however, economic and social problems generated by their war experiences. Some European immigrants came, as many as 24,000 in 1873. The vast majority were Germans, but Irish, French, English, Austrians, Czechs, Scots, Swedes, and Swiss continued to

arrive. Their appearance added to the mix of Texas culture. From a population of 604,215 in 1860, the count increased to 818,579 by 1870, and estimates indicated that it had reached over a million by the end of Reconstruction.

The greatest social change involved the state's black population. In 1870 the census reported 253,475 African Americans in the state. They were free but not accepted as integral members of society. They were excluded from traditional avenues for social and economic advancement. Nonetheless, Reconstruction marked a revolution for them. During this period blacks gained control over such basic community institutions as their schools and churches and made them into vehicles for improvement within their own communities. For the first time Southern blacks were able to control their own families, without the intervention made possible by the slave system. Despite the problems of separation and prejudice, they gained basic control over their economic lives. The beginnings of a free black society were rooted firmly by the end of Reconstruction.

The period also saw steady urban growth in the state. Cities were the center of an active economic and cultural life. Two cities had surpassed a population of 10,000 by 1870. Galveston, the principal city, had 13,818 people, and San Antonio had 12,256. Other towns were becoming cities, including Houston, Austin, and Jefferson. These were the centers of finance, education, commerce, and entertainment in the state. Galveston was the financial and cultural capital, with two national banks, a savings bank, a medical college, a Catholic college, an opera house, two theaters, and three concert halls. By the end of Reconstruction, Galveston had its first paved streets, gas lights, and streetcars.

Change was taking place, but still much remained the same in the end. Texans were still primarily a rural people. Of the nearly 750,000 employees in the state in 1870, more than two-thirds worked directly in agriculture. In 1870 fewer than 6½ percent of the population lived in towns with populations of over 2,000. The rhythms of farm life and the isolation of rural existence dominated the lives of these people. For the 23,520 Mexican Americans in Texas, Reconstruction changed nothing. They remained along the Rio Grande frontier for the most part. Some Texans hated them and expressed contempt for their culture. Already they were "being voted" by the *patrón* landowners of Southwest Texas. Their own views of the dominant culture around them are little known. Despite their difficulties and lack of change, most Texans expressed a remarkable optimism and the continued belief that their state had a destiny to fill. In the midst of Reconstruction, John Milton McCoy, a young Indianan who had settled in Dallas and who later became a prominent civic leader, wrote home:

> My idea is that the time will come when Texas Society will be the most refined of any in America. It will be simply the polished steel. It is now steel in the rust and rough. Send on your teachers, your preachers, your churches and schools along with your rail roads and the great Lone Star State will be the particular bright evening star of the first magnitude in the western horizon of that galaxy of stars known and read of by all men in the United States. But there is work to be done.

Carl H. Moneyhon

Late Nineteenth Century. Between the end of Reconstruction (1876) and the beginning of the Progressive era (1900) Texas hardly shared the ostentatious wealth that gave the period the title Gilded

Compress. Photograph by Henry Stark. Terrell, ca. 1895–96. Courtesy Dallas Historical Society. Texas became the leading producer of cotton in the United States in the late nineteenth century. Sadly for the farmer who could grow nothing else, cotton prices fell as production increased.

Age in the rest of the country. Yet the state did reflect a mixture of changes common to the developing western frontier and the New South. Population, economic production, and cities expanded, while society and culture began to mature. Partially separate black and Hispanic communities continued to emerge in the face of discrimination. Third parties challenged the political dominance of Democrats who struggled with issues of land policy, prohibition, and railroad regulation. New economic, social, and political organizations appeared as Texas joined other Americans in seeking more orderly approaches to major concerns.

The population of Texas grew rapidly from 1,591,749 in 1880 to 2,235,527 by 1890 and 3,048,710 in 1900. In addition to the natural growth of already resident population, a steady migration came from other states, primarily in the South. Immigration, especially from Mexico and Germany, contributed 179,357 foreign born to the population by the turn of the century. Most Texans lived and labored in rural areas—90.8 percent in 1880 and 82.9 percent in 1900. The expanding population spread westward to complete settlement of the state by establishing communities on the South Plains, in the Panhandle, and beyond the Pecos River.

The Texas economy of the late nineteenth century burgeoned, as did serious problems and major changes. Agriculture continued to dominate the economy, with a majority of Texans engaged in

farming or ranching. The number of farms and ranches grew from 174,184 with 12,650,314 improved acres and $256,084,364 in equipment and animals in 1880 to 352,190 farms and ranches with 19,576,076 improved acres and $962,476,273 in equipment and animals in 1900. Production of cotton, the primary crop grown for profit, leaped from 805,284 bales in 1880 to 2,506,212 in 1900—more than in any other state. Corn, the most significant food crop, increased from 29,065,172 bushels in 1880 to 109,970,350 in 1900. In this context of growth, national depressions struck in the 1870s and 1890s to deepen the effect of other farm problems. Farm prices fluctuated through the period but declined overall. The value of Texas farms increased because they grew in size, but the value of land per acre fell in the 1890s. These problems produced greater debts, more mortgaged farms, and a rise in percentage of tenants from 37.6 to 49.7 percent of all farmers during the last two decades of the nineteenth century.

These concerns led farmers to join the Patrons of Husbandry, or Grange, which spread from the North across the South in the 1870s. Texas membership peaked at about 40,000 in 1875. The organization promoted social gatherings, political lobbying, agricultural education, and cooperative buying and selling in a search for better prices. In the 1880s the Grange began to fade away as the Farmers' Alliance arose. The alliance developed in Lampasas

Alliance Milling Company. Photograph by Henry Stark. Denton, ca. 1895–96. Courtesy Dallas Historical Society. This mill, established by the Farmers' Alliance in 1886, remained in operation over a century later under the management of the Morrison Milling Company.

County during the late 1870s and expanded to 50,000 supporters by 1885. Although it pursued goals similar to those of the Grange, the alliance grew to over 100,000 members and spread into other states. It emphasized cooperative business efforts based on credits instead of cash. After the state business exchange failed at the end of the 1880s, many alliance members turned to politics through the Populist or People's party.

Ranching, like farming, grew impressively, as Texans drove more than three million cattle north to the railroads in Kansas between 1875 and 1885, after the Indians had been forced from the plains and the buffalo almost destroyed. Major ranchers in West Texas joined those in South Texas in raising the largest herds in the nation, which grew from 4,894,698 cattle and 3,651,633 sheep in 1880 to 8,543,635 cattle and 4,264,187 sheep in 1890. Prices began to fall because supply outran demand, disease led to quarantines, harsh winters and drought killed animals, and new settlers began to fence the plains with barbed wire. Huge ranches, some supported by foreign investment, introduced improved breeds, but the total number of animals declined to 7,279,935 cattle and 1,439,940 sheep by 1900. In 1877, to cooperate in meeting their problems, ranchers formed the Northwest Texas Cattle Raisers' Association, which became a state organization by the 1890s.

The development of commercial farming and ranching received important stimulation from the growth of railroads. Spurred on by state land grants of over 30 million acres, railroads grew from 1,650 miles of track in 1875 to 9,867 in 1900. The new track, more than half of which was laid between 1875 and 1885, crossed the state both east–west and north–south to provide faster and cheaper transportation for people and products. Yet in the

1880s control by Jay Gould and Collis P. Huntington of most railroads in Texas led to reduced competition and uniform rates. Farmers and small businessmen began to complain of monopolies and trusts, and political debates and government regulations followed. Business and manufacturing also received an important boost from improved transportation. The number of manufacturers advanced from 2,996 with about 12,000 employees producing over $20 million worth of products in 1880 to 12,289 with approximately 48,000 workers producing $119 million worth of goods by 1900. Major industries of the period included the lumber industry and milling. Meat packing, which ranked third in the 1870s, gave way to the manufacture of cottonseed oil and cake, which stood second in 1900. The Corsicana oilfield produced 65,955 barrels in 1897 and foreshadowed the twentieth-century economic development of Texas.

To improve wages, hours, and working conditions the laborers in these industries began to join labor organizations. The Knights of Labor attracted perhaps 30,000 members in the late 1880s but declined after the Great Southwest Strike of railroad workers failed in 1886. Local craft-union representatives met in state conventions during the 1890s, and some groups joined the American Federation of Labor. Between 1880 and 1900 the number of women in the workforce increased from 58,943 to 140,392, an advance from 11 percent to 13 percent of all employed persons. Women in agriculture, domestic service, and teaching formed 95 percent of those working in 1880 but declined to 90 percent by 1900 as the number of dressmakers and saleswomen increased.

Some economic growth proved short-sighted. Cattle replaced the buffalo on the plains, and hunting and fishing reduced several other species of wildlife. Lumbering steadily cut into the size of East Texas forests. In response the legislature inaugurated the office of state fish commissioner in 1879 and authorized the short-lived Texas Arbor Day and Forestry Association in 1890.

The development of industries, primarily in urban areas, stimulated the growth of Texas towns in the late nineteenth century. The number of Texans living in urban centers (towns with a population of more than 4,000) grew from 115,396 in 1880 to 454,926 in 1900, an increase from 7.2 percent to 14.9 percent of the population. The patterns of urbanization shifted, however, as newer interior towns expanded more rapidly with advancing settlement. San Antonio grew from 20,550 in 1880 to 53,321 in 1900, advancing from second largest to largest among the cities of the state as a result of South Texas railroads and cattle. Houston, a major rail center for East Texas agriculture, grew from third to second in size, as it more than doubled from 16,513 to 44,633. Dallas, the commercial center of North Texas, progressed from fifth to third with its growth from 10,358 to 42,638. The Gulf port of Galveston increased from 22,248 to 37,789 but fell from first to fourth in size. Fort Worth, with its 26,688 people in 1900, replaced Austin among the five largest Texas towns, as it became a railroad shipping point for West Texas cattle.

The emerging towns and cities also provided focal points for social and cultural developments. Religion influenced many aspects of life, with evangelical Protestants dominant in much of the state. In 1890 Baptists, with 248,523 members, and Methodists, with 218,890, led numerically. The 99,691 Catholics ranked third in the state and were most influential in South Texas. Disciples of Christ, Presbyterians, and Lutherans were the next most numer-ous Christian groups. Differences between religions emerged most clearly over the prohibition issue. One major area of church activity continued to be support for education through church-sponsored institutions. The state also entered the field of higher education by opening Texas A&M in 1876 and the University of Texas in 1883. These institutions received students from a public-education system that expanded from 176,245 students in 1880 to 515,544 in 1900. As a result literacy increased from 70.3 percent in 1880 to 85.5 percent in 1900. That advance resulted in part from the establishment in 1884 of the office of state superintendent of public instruction and school districts that could tax to fund public education.

Churches and schools also sponsored such social events as picnics and concerts. Fraternal organizations as well as local cultural and social clubs provided opportunities for relaxation. Women's groups began to appear, first missionary societies within the churches, then chapters of the Woman's Christian Temperance Union, and finally the Texas Federation of Women's Clubs, which stressed education and social reform. Recreation became more organized in urban areas, as baseball, circuses, and theaters joined hunting and horse racing. Texas League professional baseball began in 1888 and was followed by college football; the first football game in the state, between the University of Texas and Texas A&M, occurred in 1894.

Artists and writers also contributed to the leisure enjoyments of Texans. Several volumes of reminiscences appeared, such as *Early Times in Texas* (1892) by John C. Duval, as well as popular histories, including *Indian Depredations in Texas* (1889) by J. W. Wilbarger. The Texas State Historical Association was formed in 1897 and initiated a journal now entitled *Southwestern Historical*

Dipping cattle in the Texas Panhandle, ca. 1890s. Photograph by Andrew Alexander Forbes. Courtesy Western History Collections, University of Oklahoma Library. Disease, animal quarantines, harsh winters, and drought devastated herds in the late nineteenth century.

Quarterly. Charles Siringo became the forerunner of a literary field with *A Texas Cowboy; Or Fifteen Years on the Hurricane Deck of a Spanish Pony* (1886). In 1895 novelist Mollie E. Moore Davis published *Under the Man-Fig.* Some of the most famous paintings by Texans reflected the historical style of this period—*Dawn at the Alamo* (1876–83) by Henry A. McArdle and *The Surrender of Santa Anna* (1886) by William H. Huddle. Frank Reaugh began to sketch West Texas landscapes and longhorn cattle in the 1880s for oils and pastels that were displayed during 1893 as part of the Columbian Exposition in Chicago. Elisabet Ney sculpted statues of such historical subjects as Sam Houston and Stephen F. Austin, as well as pieces drawn from other sources. Texas music included analogues of Southern Anglo-American folk songs and religious spirituals and also reflected black, German, and Mexican influences. Cowboy trail songs grew in popularity. Town bands appeared, as did opera houses, and in 1886 the Texas Music Teachers' Association was founded.

The two largest racial minorities in Texas, African Americans and Mexican Americans, developed partially separate social communities during the late nineteenth century, partly because of discrimination, which produced segregation in some activities and lack of opportunity in others. The number of black Texans increased from 393,384 in 1880 to 620,722 in 1900 but declined from 24.7 to 20.4 percent of the state's population because other ethnic groups grew even more rapidly through immigration. Most blacks labored as sharecroppers, some herded cattle, and others worked on railroads, in lumber camps, on seaport docks, or as skilled craftsmen. A small but growing number acquired their own land or opened small businesses. To meet economic problems black farmers organized the Colored Farmers' Alliance in the 1880s. Some urban workers joined local unions or the Knights of Labor, yet racial discrimination limited their opportunities. Black Texans formed their own churches, primarily Baptist and Methodist, to acquire control over their religious activities. They attended segregated public schools that generally received less funding than those for whites. Nevertheless, the black literacy level rose from 24.6 percent in 1880 to 61.8 percent in 1900. The churches established several black colleges, and the state established Prairie View A&M. Black Texans formed their own fraternal and social groups and continued to celebrate emancipation each Juneteenth with parades, picnics, and games. Sutton Griggs, a native of Texas, became one of the best known black novelists in the 1890s, the same decade in which Scott Joplin of Texarkana moved north to gain fame as a ragtime musician. Segregation existed in most railroads, ships, and theaters, and blacks faced exclusion from most hotels and restaurants. They also received uneven justice as exclusion from juries became common, and they were disproportionately the victims of lynching.

Hispanic Texans increased in number, partially through immigration, to 165,000 in 1900. The population of Mexican birth in Texas grew from 43,161 in 1880 to 71,062 in 1900—about two-thirds of the Mexican-born population in the United States. Mexican Texans formed a majority in the region below San Antonio and along the Rio Grande, where they had some political power. They maintained their culture through Spanish-language newspapers, observance of Mexican holidays, and the formation of *sociedades mutualistas* (mutual-aid societies). Some owned ranches or operated small businesses, though most herded cattle or sheep and did manual labor in towns or on railroads. Conflicts with Anglos arose over land, cattle, and the salt lakes near El Paso. Gregorio Cortez

Lira and Catarino Erasmo Garza became folk heroes by avoiding prosecution under Texas law.

The economic, social, and racial issues of late nineteenth-century Texas shaped state politics in conjunction with political parties. The Democratic party dominated Texas politics after Reconstruction, under leaders who generally had been Confederate soldiers or their sons. Party members were primarily white Protestant farmers, but also ranchers and businessmen. Most Hispanic Catholics also supported the party, some under the guidance of South Texas *patrones* who provided paternalistic aid under the system of boss rule. Perhaps half of the German Lutherans and Catholics also favored the Democrats. The Democratic constituency was therefore more varied than in most Southern states. In the 1870s Democrats stood for retrenchment, white supremacy, and states' rights on racial issues—but not in the case of federal aid to river development, railroads, and frontier defense. They generally supported low tariffs in national politics.

The Republican party provided the Democrats' most lasting opposition with a membership that included blacks, former Unionists, sheep raisers, and some businessmen. The party favored expanding the civil rights of minorities, improving education, and developing economically, and survived with the aid of patronage from national Republican administrations and the hope of coalitions with third parties that arose at times. In the late 1870s and early 1880s former governor Edmund J. Davis led the larger wing of the party, which included most black Texans. A smaller group of white businessmen, such as former governor and banker E. M. Pease, struggled with limited success for control of the party.

Democrat Richard Coke won reelection as governor in 1876 with three-fourths of the votes, while his party held 80 percent of the legislative seats and elected all six congressmen. The legislature then sent Coke on to the United States Senate. Yet the depression of the 1870s, linked to limited credit and falling farm prices, stirred up a lively factional fight for the gubernatorial nomination in 1878 and gave rise to third-party opposition. Democrats broke their deadlock between Lieutenant Governor Richard B. Hubbard, who replaced Coke as governor, and former governor James W. Throckmorton, who were both criticized for their railroad connections, by nominating Oran M. Roberts, a state Supreme Court justice and former secession leader. Roberts won by a small margin over William H. Hamman, nominee of the Greenback party, which favored increasing the money in circulation to ease debt. Greenbackers formed a coalition with Republicans and elected a dozen legislators as well as a congressman, G. W. (Wash) Jones, from south central Texas. In 1880 Texas provided the Greenback party vice-presidential nominee, Barzillai J. Chambers, an able organizer, but the party faded away after another election defeat.

To replace Roberts, who cut taxes and sold state lands cheaply to reduce state debts, in 1882 Democrats nominated John Ireland, who promised to raise land prices to help pay for improved public schools. Ireland defeated Wash Jones, who was running as an independent candidate for governor. Democrats held all but one of the congressional seats, now increased to 11 as a result of population growth. The governor and legislature struggled with conflicts between ranchers fencing public land and opponents cutting fences by making both acts illegal. Texas Democrats retained control of state government in 1884 and helped elect President Grover Cleveland, who then appointed them to a wide range of federal offices from local postmaster to minister to Japan (Richard B. Hubbard).

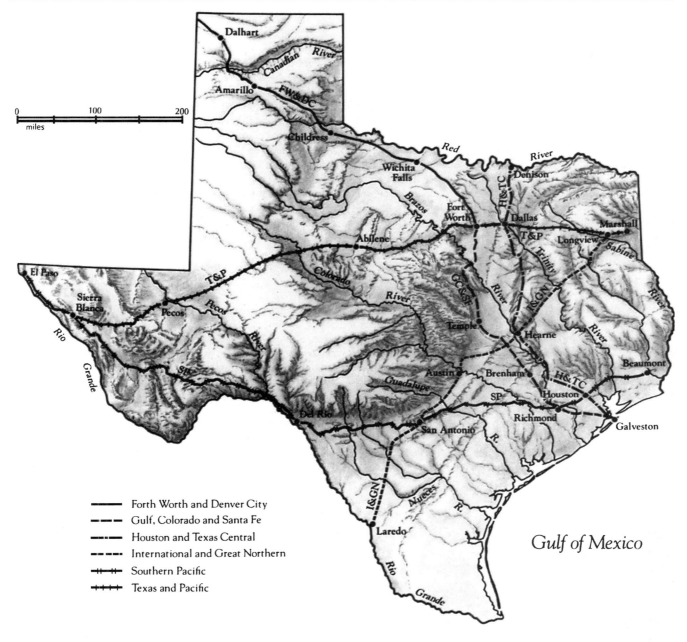

Major railroads in Texas to 1900. From *The History of Texas* by Robert A. Calvert and Arnoldo De León, ©1990 by Harlan Davidson, Inc. Reproduced by permission.

The temperance issue had arisen nationally before the Civil War. Support in Texas led to a local option clause in the Constitution of 1876 and to lobbying for complete prohibition, led by Baptist and Methodist ministers, who helped form a Prohibition party briefly in the 1880s. In 1887 the legislature placed before the voters a constitutional amendment to ban liquor sales, which led to a heated campaign including fistfights and the ringing of church bells. The Democrats were divided, and Republicans generally opposed the amendment, which former Greenbackers usually favored. Many white Protestants supported it, but most other ethnic groups joined the opposition, which was victorious. The stage was set, however, for the prohibition conflicts ahead.

The Farmers' Alliance and the Knights of Labor, formed in the 1880s in the context of farm and labor problems, also supported candidates and legislation. Sul Ross, a former Confederate general and Democrat, won the governor's race in 1886, despite some Union Labor party opposition. During his administration he supervised the completion and dedication of the new Capitol, helped to strengthen the state's educational and eleemosynary institutions, and worked to promote industrial, agricultural, and commercial growth for the state.

In Congress Texans led two efforts aimed at economic reform. John H. Reagan, former Confederate postmaster general, became a major advocate of the federal railroad regulation that resulted in establishment of the Interstate Commerce Commission in 1887. Roger Q. Mills, a former Confederate colonel, became chairman of the House Ways and Means Committee and a leading spokesman for tariff reduction. The Mills tariff bill became an issue in the presidential election of 1888 but went down to defeat with the Democratic party.

James Stephen Hogg, state attorney general and son of a Confederate general, began a new era of more active state government with his election as governor in 1890. An impressive figure because of his size and speaking ability, Hogg overcame lobbying and pushed through the legislature a Railroad Commission bill backed by farmers and small businessmen. Reagan headed the new state agency, but its impact proved less sweeping than hoped or feared. Opponents of the commission supported railroad attorney George Clark for governor in 1892, while Hogg's failure to appoint a Farmers' Alliance leader to the commission helped push many farmers into the new Populist or People's party behind Thomas Nugent. Yet Hogg won reelection in the lively three-way race.

The Populists also broke away from the Democratic party, which opposed the subtreasury plan. This proposal, supported by the Populists, was for federal loans to farmers based on crops stored in government warehouses until sold. In the heated campaigns of 1894 and 1896 Populists offered the strongest challenges to Democratic dominance since Reconstruction. Yet their efforts foundered on issues of race and culture. As they attracted more black votes through a coalition with Republicans they lost some white support, while the prohibitionists among the Populists caused Germans and Hispanics to shun the party. Although the People's party declined in the late 1890s and some of its members turned to socialism, it had pushed Democrats toward reform measures; some of its leaders reappeared as progressive Democrats in the early twentieth century.

Hogg Democrats from Texas helped nominate William Jennings Bryan for president in 1896, on a platform of free coinage of silver to expand money and ease debt pressures, but in the aftermath of his defeat the state party shifted in a more conservative direction. Charles Culberson, attorney general under Hogg, won the gubernatorial elections of 1894 and 1896 with businessman Edward M. House as his campaign manager. Through his success in organizing campaigns, House grew in political influence and formed a coalition with Joseph W. Bailey, a North Texas congressman with exceptional oratorical ability and increasing business connections, including ties with the new oil industry. Together they successfully supported the election of Culberson to the United States Senate in 1898, Joseph Sayers as governor the same year, and Bailey as the other United States senator in 1900. By supporting limited reforms they avoided more sweeping efforts to regulate economic activities.

The Republican party remained active throughout the period, especially through coalitions with third parties. After E. J. Davis died in 1883, leadership shifted to Norris Wright Cuney, a black labor and political organizer. He served as national committeeman from 1886 to 1896 and as customs collector at Galveston from 1889 to 1893. White Republicans who opposed black leadership formed a "lily-white" movement that generally proved unsuccessful in the 1890s. Supporters of winning presidential candidate William McKinley ousted Cuney in 1896 because he backed another contender. Republican congressman Robert B. Hawley of Galveston influenced patronage and became national committeeman in the late 1890s.

Black Republicans faced growing opposition to their participation in the voting process, despite the declining black percentage of state population. As early as 1878 a white men's club was formed in Harrison County to help seize control of local offices from the black majority. The Jaybirds of Fort Bend County followed a similar path in 1889, as did several organizations that opposed

Katy Station. Photograph by Henry Stark. New Braunfels, ca. 1895–96. Courtesy Dallas Historical Society. The expansion of railroads across the state stimulated agriculture and industry. Railroads also brought new settlers, products, and news from around the world.

Clerks in the ladies' ready-to-wear department of Sanger Brothers, Dallas, 1888. From Leon Joseph Rosenberg, *Sangers': Pioneer Texas Merchants* (Austin: Texas State Historical Association, 1978). The number of women in the workforce rose between 1880 and 1900. By the turn of the century, many women worked as dressmakers and saleswomen.

Populism during the 1890s. These activities foreshadowed the white primary adopted early in the twentieth century to exclude blacks from the Democratic party.

South Texas political *patrones* such as James B. Wells had Mexicans declared immigrants and thus legal voters as a means of adding support for the Democrats they favored. This practice led to controversy and a new law in 1895 requiring six months' residency before a person could vote. Unsuccessful efforts to institute a poll tax in this period foreshadowed the imposition of the tax in 1902, despite opposition from blacks, Hispanics, labor groups, and former Populists. These limitations on political participation led to a major decline in voter turnout, from over 80 percent in the 1890s to less than 50 percent by whites and no more than 15 percent by blacks after the turn of the century. The Republican party thus declined from a substantial force with 100,000 voters representing 25 percent of the electorate to a handful of leaders with a tiny following and no influence.

An increasing number of women sought the right to vote in the 1890s. Rebecca Hayes of Dallas organized the Texas Equal Rights Association in 1893. Local clubs were formed, and members pressured political parties or lobbied the legislature for woman suffrage. Disagreement over a tour by Susan B. Anthony caused the group to split and die out.

During the late nineteenth century, Texas politics evolved from preoccupation with the sectional and racial issues of Recon-

struction and agricultural problems toward concern with more varied rural and urban economic and ethnic matters, and this development limited the state's ability to focus on specific solutions, except for establishment of the Railroad Commission. Through Reagan, Mills, and the national Democratic convention of 1896, Texas also had influenced national politics. Progressive and conservative factions of 1900 foreshadowed twentieth-century divisions among Texas Democrats.

In the last quarter of the nineteenth century Texas had emerged as the leading producer of cotton and cattle, yet its agricultural economy continued to struggle with a variety of problems, while industry made limited advances, including the opening of the first Texas oilfield. The beginnings of a more complex urban society and culture had appeared, but they hardly dominated the state. Blacks and Hispanics achieved some progress in education and economic status, offset by more rigid discrimination in public accommodations and treatment under the law. While most women remained in family roles, an increasing number entered the workforce or joined church and reform societies. The Democratic party retained control of politics and government in the face of Republican and third-party challenges, by facing major issues of land policy, prohibition, and railroad regulation. In every area of activity Texans joined the national trend toward organization as a means of meeting problems and shaping their society.

Alwyn Barr

Progressive Era. In the first two decades of the twentieth century, Texans shared the optimism and confidence that permeated American society in the Progressive Era. The state was, wrote one observer, "like some boy giant of sixteen, all bulging and bursting out of his outgrown clothes, awkward and ungainly." Its agricultural economy was suspicious of business but stood on the verge of an oil boom that made Texas an international symbol of corporate power. It was solidly Democratic in politics, a fact which meant that it also rigidly segregated whites from African Americans and barely tolerated Mexican Americans. Texans embodied the tensions and contradictions of the New South while possessing what one writer termed "a coolly arrogant self-sufficiency." During these twenty years the state pursued political reform in campaigns for prohibition, woman suffrage, and the regulation of corporations, and gained important national influence in Congress and the White House during the presidency of Woodrow Wilson. The prediction of a Chicago journalist in 1911 seemed as if it might be accurate: "When Texas becomes as fully developed as Ohio and Illinois, her people will control the government of the United States."

There were 3,048,710 Texans recorded in the 1900 census; the population stood at 3,896,542 in 1910, and rose to 4,663,228 by 1920. The majority of the white population had been born within the state, and most of the rest had come from neighboring states. "Texas is predominantly Southern in thought and feeling," concluded two analysts in 1916. The state was also still essentially rural. Two-thirds of the populace lived in the country, and fewer than one of five Texans resided in towns of more than 10,000 as the century began. Agriculture dominated the economy. More than 800,000 men were farmers; the number of women and children who helped them is unknown. Products of farms and ranches totaled more than $660 million in 1912, five times the output of Texas factories. By 1919 the state led the nation in total value of crops, in cotton production, in cattle raising, and in several other categories.

Cotton was the principal cash crop. In 1909 farmers raised 2½ million bales, and the *Texas Almanac* concluded the following year that "cotton sits on the throne as the money crop of Texas." These years were prosperous for cotton farmers, with prices fluctuating at around 14 cents a pound in 1909 and 1910, well above the disastrous lows of the 1890s. During World War I prices for cotton soared to 35 cents a pound before falling back sharply in 1920–21. Despite this improvement in their condition between 1900 and 1920, farmers still complained of low profits, inequities in the marketing process, and difficulty in securing needed credit through the banking system. An animus against eastern bankers and Wall Street permeated agrarian Texas in the Progressive years.

Equally serious to many students of Texas agriculture was the problem of farm tenancy. By 1900, 49 percent of the farmers were tenants; the figure stood at 52 percent 10 years later. Landless farmers lacking capital rented their labor and gave the owner one-fourth or one-third of the cotton crop. Sharecroppers were the most impoverished of the 200,000 tenants in Texas, but poverty was widespread in the farm areas. Wives and children lived in squalor, and existing economic conditions made escape from tenant status highly improbable. "There is something rotten in Texas when over 50 per cent of our farm families are homeless renters," said the Houston *Chronicle* in 1912.

Industry remained an underdeveloped sector in Texas economic life before 1920. The principal businesses were lumber, oil, and railroads. The state's lumber industry, concentrated in East Texas, supplied about 5 percent of the national market in 1907. Increasing consolidation among lumber firms gave them dominant power over their workers, and labor relations were often embittered. The Brotherhood of Timber Workers challenged unsuccessfully the Southern Lumber Operators' Association and its leader, John Henry Kirby, in 1910–11. Some state supervision occurred in the actual conservation of Texas timber, but much less took place in the area of child labor or workmen's compensation.

The oil and gas industry had only begun to establish itself in Texas before 1920. Discovery of the Spindletop oilfield near Beaumont in January 1901 marked the opening of the prosperous phase of the business in Texas, but after 1905 the focus of exploration moved to Oklahoma. Yearly production of oil in the state had declined markedly by 1909, when Texas ranked sixth among states in petroleum production. The opening of the Electra oilfield in 1911 revived industry fortunes. During World War I large wells came in at Ranger and Burkburnett, and within a year sizable drilling operations were begun throughout the Wichita Falls area. In 1919 the legislature gave the Railroad Commission the power to supervise petroleum production for the state. By the end of the period, Texas wells were producing 85,000,000 barrels a year, and even more dramatic increases lay ahead in the 1920s.

Railroads were the other major industrial force in Texas. The Railroad Commission, established in the 1890s, closely regulated the 71 companies that used the state's 11,000 miles of track in 1904. Freight rates within the state had dramatically declined before World War I, and the rail companies found it difficult to issue new securities under Texas laws. Expansion of mileage slowed accordingly. Whatever their power had been a generation earlier, Texas railroads were politically weaker in the Progressive years. A growing interest in good highways also signaled an emerging rival for the rail lines. There were 3,591 miles of paved roads in the state in 1910, and highway proponents accelerated their campaign after the passage of the Federal Highway Act in 1916.

Attitudes toward non-Texan corporate enterprises underwent important shifts in these two decades. Although few Texans disliked the idea of successful businesses that originated within the state's borders, there was a historic suspicion of "foreign" concerns and investors that lay behind regulation of non-Texas railroads, insurance companies, and oil firms. Before 1910 one Progressive boasted that reformers were "simply keeping in advance of some of their sister States in taking a good half hitch on corporations." This mood waned before World War I, and the impulse to oversee business and to pursue social reform was eroding by 1920. "Let us throw down the bars and let business come into Texas," said one enthusiastic state legislator in 1919. From its place as a perceived national leader in the effort to achieve reform, Texas had begun its twentieth-century development into a setting for corporate power.

Although the state retained its predominantly agricultural character throughout the 20-year period, urbanization also accelerated. There were 132 "cities" in Texas in 1910, but only San Antonio, Dallas, Houston, and Fort Worth numbered more than 50,000 inhabitants. Austin, El Paso, Galveston, and Waco had between 25,000 and 50,000 residents. More than 90 of the urban areas had fewer than 5,000 people within their city limits. They were "small islands almost submerged in a great agricultural sea." Despite their modest size, however, Texas cities were governmental innovators in the era of progressivism. After the Galveston hurricane of 1900, Galveston adopted the commission form of city

Cotton bales on wharves in Galveston. Courtesy Rosenberg Library, Galveston. Cotton was the state's main cash crop during the Progressive Era.

government. The idea, which emphasized efficiency and economy through the election of commissioners on a citywide basis, spread to Houston, Dallas, Fort Worth, and numerous smaller municipalities before 1910. By lowering taxes on the middle class, simplifying administration, and weakening the influence of aldermen, commission government appealed to business and professional men who deemed the older ward style of governance as corrupt. After 1910 cities increased in population ten times faster than the countryside. Nearly one-third of the population lived in urban centers by 1919, and 15 percent resided in Houston, Dallas, and San Antonio. Rapid urban expansion fueled cultural tensions particularly over the issue of prohibition and laid the basis for the popularity of the Ku Klux Klan in the 1920s. "What is the matter?" an angry farmer asked in 1920. "Our people are all going to the cities."

White Texans gave little thought to the situation of the black and Hispanic minorities in the state in the years before 1920. Segregation kept the 690,000 blacks from offering any challenge to white supremacy. The black population comprised nearly 18 percent of all Texans in 1910 and was sprinkled throughout the eastern third of the state. But blacks were a majority in no more than counties. Law, custom, and the threat of violence kept them politically and socially subservient. They had separate schools and social services, and were generally excluded from the political affairs of the Democratic party, though they could vote in general elections and in contests over constitutional amendments. The size of the black vote was small. Of the 160,000 black men over 21, somewhere between 15,000 and 40,000 surmounted the restrictions on suffrage. So pervasive was racism in Texas that the subject rarely came up in partisan campaigns. Joseph Weldon Bailey sounded virulent antiblack sentiments in his gubernatorial race in 1920, and the more vicious of the segregationist newspapers captured small audiences. If segregation was questioned, however, retribution came swiftly. In the Longview race riot of 1919 a white mob in Longview burned buildings in the town's black district before the state militia restored order. In the following month an organizer for the NAACP was beaten badly by Travis County officials during a visit to Austin. Tolerance for black aspirations in Texas did not manifest itself for more than four decades.

The Mexican-American population, numbering about 250,000, did not confront the highly visible repression that blacks endured, but their lot in the border counties of South Texas was one of poverty and political subordination. Their votes became the virtual property of local political machines, usually led by Anglo-Americans such as James B. Wells of Cameron County and Archie Parr of Duval County. These machines provided services to the local population. Wells, said a friend, was a "Father Confessor" for a people "whose troubles he has made his own for more than thirty years." But the social cost of such patronage was high. The economic position of most Mexican Americans was desperate; some earned only 50 cents a day in 1901. South Texas politics was squalid,

Itinerant farmers, 1913. Photograph by Lewis Hine. Courtesy Photography Collections, University of Maryland, Baltimore County. Almost half of all farmers during the Progressive Era worked land they rented, often paying their rent with part of their crop.

corrupt, and often violent. Huge majorities for successful candidates became commonplace, and state politicians cultivated leaders who delivered docile legions on election day. Even the influx of white settlers into the border region after 1910 did not disrupt the established pattern of affairs in most of South Texas. To many white residents of the state, the Mexican-American community remained an unknown and despised entity before World War I. Assertion of cultural identity and ethnic pride from the state's Hispanic community did not touch the majority of Texans for several more decades.

In the assertively masculine world of early twentieth-century Texas, women also occupied a restricted place. They were expected to marry and be homemakers. State law gave males legal authority over community property, and custom allocated dominant power to the man in the marriage. For poor and lower-middle-class women, this state of affairs did not improve before 1920. In the middle class and higher, activist women pursued the goals of mild reform through the Texas Federation of Women's Clubs, under Mrs. Anna Pennybacker. The most intense political campaign sought woman suffrage. Its leaders, Minnie Cunningham, Jane McCallum, and Jessie Ames, argued that "no state can be a true democracy in which one half of the people are denied the right to vote." But the Texas Woman Suffrage Association also stressed that votes for women would offset "disloyal and disintegrating forces" such as black, Hispanic, or German-American voters. After some inconclusive efforts at the turn of the century, proponents of woman suffrage reorganized between 1912 and 1915 as the Texas

Woman Suffrage Association and gained additional strength from the progress of the national movement and the onset of World War I. Participation in the struggle to impeach Governor James Ferguson in 1917 helped the suffragists secure legislative approval of female voting in the 1918 Democratic primary. In 1919 voters rejected an amendment to the Texas constitution that would have given women the vote in general elections. However, a special session of the legislature ratified the national woman-suffrage amendment in June 1919. Out of the suffrage agitation came the League of Women Voters and a "petticoat lobby" in the early 1920s. Yet the overall role of women, outside the voting booth, remained largely domestic. "We have the vote," said Jane McCallum, "and I must give my time to my household." She did not do as she said, but many other women did.

An issue that engaged the energies of many Texans in the Progressive decades was control of alcohol. Prohibition became the dominant political topic of the period. It was, said the Dallas *Morning News* in 1916, "as perennial as it is paramount as an issue in our politics. The methods devised to keep it outside party councils have failed utterly." Statewide concern with the liquor issue was a relatively new phenomenon in Texas politics. Except for an unsuccessful fight for a prohibition amendment to the Texas constitution in 1887, voters had accepted local-option provisions that gave individual counties, municipalities, and precincts the power to ban alcohol. By 1903 most of North Texas, outside Dallas and Fort Worth, was dry, and East and Central Texas seemed likely to follow. South Texas, with its sizable Mexican and German populations, remained a wet bastion. The progress of local option after 1893 alarmed the liquor interests. They organized the Texas Brewers Association in February 1901, opposed the adoption of the poll-tax amendment in 1902, and supported a bill in 1903 that provided for a mandatory two-year period between local-option elections. The legislature narrowly defeated the latter proposal, but appearance of an active liquor lobby convinced the prohibitionists of the need for more concerted action. The Texas Local Option Association appeared in 1903 and over the next five years supplied speakers and direction for local-option contests in wet areas. However, the most the association could accomplish was a stalemate with the liquor side. Entrance of the Anti-Saloon League into Texas in 1907 accelerated the movement for statewide action against alcohol. Working through the evangelical Protestant churches and relying on ministers for leadership, the league stressed cohesive organization and intense lobbying of the Democratic party to stand against liquor. It served as a clearinghouse for political strategy and popular agitation. Its fervor and commitment soon gained the league a preeminent place among the state's prohibitionist groups.

Dry strength centered in North Texas among the rural, old-stock residents, whom prohibition leaders called the "Anglo-Saxon Democracy." In South Texas the black, Catholic Hispanic, and German population opposed liquor regulation. Most prominent in the ranks of the prohibitionists were the Protestant churches that had "locked shields for the purpose of destroying the liquor business." Baptists and Methodists were in the forefront of the campaign. Their newspapers, such as the *Baptist Standard* and the *Texas Christian Advocate*, assailed alcohol as a social evil. The only proper attitude for "any Christian man and thoughtful citizen," said Texas Baptists in 1911, was "one of ceaseless and truceless hostility against the entire liquor oligarchy, local, county, state, and national, root and branch."

The drys attacked minorities, the city, and the liquor lobby itself as reasons why alcohol had to be controlled. The brewers were "the only dangerous special interest left with any potency in the state." For many Progressives in Texas, prohibition led the agenda of reform. It was the key to "civic righteousness, clean politics, pure elections and the sanctity of the ballot box." Not all reformers shared dry convictions, but most did. As Martin M. Crane noted, "the great majority of the progressive forces in Texas are prohibitionist." Their wet opponents labeled the liquor reformers religious cranks and zealots. Antiprohibitionists played on fears that a government strong enough to ban alcohol could abridge personal freedom or attack segregation. "Civil liberty will give way to military despotism to appease fanaticism on this subject," said Governor Oscar B. Colquitt, a wet, in 1911. The wets were more united and effective than the drys before the First World War, and they won most of the political struggles in those years. Gradually the excesses of the brewers, the support of the Germans, and the connection with Pa Ferguson doomed the wet cause.

The liquor question and other political conflicts were fought out within the ranks of the Texas Democratic party between 1900 and 1920. The Republican and the Socialist parties offered only ineffectual electoral resistance to the dominant political organization in these two decades. Texas Republicans before 1920 were

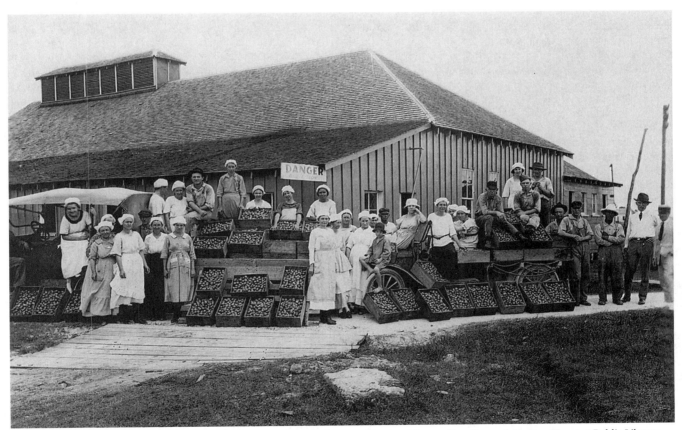

Workers standing by boxes of figs. Photograph by Frank J. Schlueter. Courtesy Houston Metropolitan Research Center, Houston Public Library. Agriculture provided some of the few employment opportunities available to women in the early years of the twentieth century.

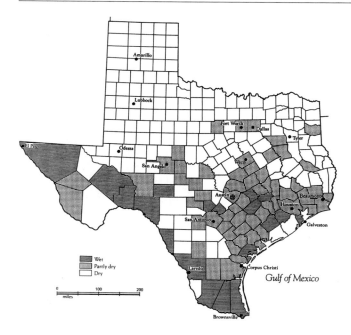

"Wet and Dry" counties of Texas, 1911. From *The History of Texas* by Robert A. Calvert and Arnoldo De León, ©1990 by Harlan Davidson, Inc. Reproduced by permission. Prohibition was the dominant political issue during the Progressive Era. Liquor selling was a local option until 1918, when the Texas legislature adopted the national prohibition amendment.

Map legend:
- Wet
- Partly dry
- Dry

essentially parts of a shadow political structure for the disposition of patronage from the federal government when their party held national power. Accordingly they mirrored the larger battles of the GOP. During Theodore Roosevelt's presidency (1901–09), Cecil A. Lyon had control of the party machinery and used it on behalf of Roosevelt and against the interests of black Republicans. From 1909 to 1913 William Howard Taft shifted patronage away from Lyon to promote his renomination in 1912. The state's delegation was bitterly contested at the Republican national convention in 1912, with the Taft forces emerging victorious. Lyon followed Roosevelt into the Progressive party, and the Republicans remained split until 1916. After the collapse of Roosevelt's third party, "amalgamation" occurred. Yet in 1920 the Republican presidential vote in Texas totaled only 115,000, less than half the Democratic vote. Texas remained a bastion of the solidly Democratic South as the 1920s opened. The Socialists gained sufficient strength in Texas before World War I to challenge the Republicans briefly for second place behind the Democrats. Keyed to the upsurge in farm tenancy, Socialist electoral power centered in the cotton belt of East Texas and in newer areas of cotton culture to the north of Abilene. In a weekly newspaper, *The Rebel*, the Socialists spread their message. Labor unrest among the timber workers added to the party's appeal. Socialism reached the peak of its voting power in the 1912 election, when Eugene V. Debs, the presidential hopeful, received nearly 26,000 votes in Texas. Democrat Jim Ferguson's gubernatorial campaign in 1914 against high rents for tenants drained off Socialist voters into the majority party. When war came in 1917, government suppression of *The Rebel* and the Socialist leadership broke the party. Nevertheless, Socialism represented an alternative to the Democrats between

1900 and 1920 that added complexity and organized dissent to the state's political scene.

The Democrats easily maintained their electoral ascendancy without serious challenge throughout the two decades. Most white, male Texans gave their allegiance to "the party of the fathers," the party that stood for states' rights, white supremacy, and limited government. Election laws supported Democratic power. The Terrell election statutes of 1903 and 1905 mandated a statewide primary for all parties whose general election totals exceeded 100,000. Participation in the primary required payment of a poll tax and the signing of a party loyalty pledge. The "white primary" was also gaining more adherents in Texas counties, though it did not become state law and party policy until the 1920s. Most blacks, some Hispanics, and many poorer Texans were effectively ruled out of the governing process. "A nomination in the Democratic primaries is tantamount to election," wrote an unhappy Republican in 1912. Personalities defined the highly factionalized Democrats before 1910. James S. Hogg died early in 1906, but the former governor spoke for a large array of party members who identified with his opposition to out-of-state railroads and corporations. His advocacy of a state government that could regulate railroads and encourage economic progress laid the basis for later progressivism. Before 1906, however, the more conservative Senator Joseph Weldon Bailey and the backstage manipulator Edward M. House overshadowed Hogg in power and policy influence.

House's precise impact on state politics between 1892 and 1906 remains clouded. An adroit promoter of his historical reputation, he left evidence that he made and unmade governors, managed senators, and was, at the same time, something of a reformer. That his wealth and campaign contributions gave him access to politicians is undeniable. That he managed campaigns for Charles A. Culberson, S. W. T. Lanham, and Joseph D. Sayers is also clear. How much he actually influenced legislation or the making of policy is less certain. House and the truth often went in different directions, and a definitive account of his role in Texas has not been written. In many ways he was conservative and considerate of the business interests whose views he shared. By 1906 House's impact on Texas was waning, and he did not regain his importance until he became a confidant of Woodrow Wilson in 1911. With that power he assisted his political associates Albert S. Burleson, Thomas Watt Gregory, and David F. Houston into the president's cabinet in 1913–14.

Bailey was as flamboyant as House was discreet. After a decade in the House of Representatives, he was elected to the United States Senate in 1900. He was the best orator in the state, with his blend of states' rights, racism, and attacks on eastern Republicans. But he also liked the good life, and scandal stuck to his financial dealings with an oil company in 1900. The issue came up again in 1906. He secured a second term in 1907 only after an embittered wrangle in the legislature. The "Bailey question" was the main issue in the battles that preceded the presidential election of 1908 in Texas; Bailey's slate of convention delegates triumphed over his opponent's, but the controversy bubbled on until 1920. Bailey came to represent older values to Democrats unhappy with change and to stand for political immorality to others who wished to make the state a Progressive bastion. Tumult followed him, but his career produced little substantive achievement. "When something practical was on the hooks," said a reporter, "Bailey was like a tree in perpetual and perennial efflorescence, all flower and no fruit."

John Frisbie in his Curtiss aeroplane stampeding U.S. Cavalry at aviation meet, El Paso, 1911. Courtesy Photography Collection, HRHRC. Among the auspicious developments in Texas during the Progressive Era was the arrival of the army's only airplane in 1910.

After 1905 support for reform gathered strength in several areas. Farmers again clamored for railroad regulation and higher cotton prices. Elements of the business community sought laws to give them an advantage over out-of-state competitors. Urban residents wanted city governments that were more honest, more efficient, and less costly. The central part of the Progressive coalition was the evangelical churches, the religious press, and the women's groups who advocated prohibition.

Governor Thomas M. Campbell gained from the new reform spirit. He had long opposed the House wing of the party, and he won the Democratic nomination in 1906 as the candidate of East Texas against three North Texas rivals. In his two terms he encouraged legislation to supervise non-Texas insurance companies through the Robertson Insurance Law of 1907, as well as measures to tax inheritances and corporations, to give the state stricter control over corporations, and to establish a guaranty deposit system for Texas banks. Campbell did not fulfill the promise of his reform rhetoric. He was more indecisive and cautious than his admirers then and later contended, but he was as much a Progressive governor as Texas had before 1920.

Toward the end of Campbell's first term, the liquor issue became paramount among Texas Democrats. An attempt to secure a prohibition amendment in 1908–09 failed in the legislature, and the drys turned their attention to the 1910 gubernatorial race. The voters urged that an antiliquor amendment be submitted to the electorate, but they also chose Oscar Colquitt, a wet, as the next governor. The prohibitionists divided their votes between two other dry candidates, and Colquitt received solid wet support. Prohibition encountered another setback when a constitutional amendment was narrowly beaten in a statewide election in July 1911. Following this defeat, the drys challenged Colquitt in 1912. Flouting the informal tradition of a nearly automatic second term for a governor, they selected a state judge to oppose the incumbent. The jurist was an inept campaigner, and Colquitt won the primary easily. Prohibition Democrats prepared to make another effort in 1914, when Colquitt would step down.

The prohibitionists lost the governor's race in part because the major focus of Progressive work in 1912 was the presidential candidacy of Woodrow Wilson. As a reformer and southerner, Wilson won the early endorsement of men such as Thomas B. Love and Thomas Watt Gregory. Only after the Wilson movement was well launched did Colonel House enter the picture. Love and his allies organized the state, defeated the conservatives in the primaries, and sent 40 dedicated delegates (the so-called "Immortal Forty") to the Democratic convention in Baltimore. Though Wilson equivocated on prohibition, his Texas reformist friends felt confident that he would assist them in making the state party both dry and progressive.

The "golden lane" of oil wells, Big Lake Oilfield, near Texon, 1925. Prints and Photographs Collection, Oil Scenes file, CAH; CN 02173a. This double row of oil wells sat on land owned by the University of Texas, one of the institutions that profited from the oil boom.

The Wilson administration disappointed these hopes during its first year in office. Under the guidance of Postmaster General Albert S. Burleson, the president rebuffed attempts to make progressivism a criterion for federal office. Wilson gave the congressional delegation a larger patronage voice than his reform supporters in an attempt to ensure votes for his legislative program. Burleson and House, who were wet, conservative, longtime residents of Austin, also allocated some of the best positions to friends and associates in the Texas capital. Only in the bitter dispute over the collectorship of customs at Brownsville did the Progressives win a patronage triumph.

The Progressives and their dry allies looked to the 1914 gubernatorial primary with more optimism. Between July 1913 and February 1914 they rallied behind a single candidate, a Houston attorney named Thomas H. Ball, and prepared to defeat the apparently disorganized wets. Ball, a lawyer for railroads and corporations, had much surface strength, but he was more of a prohibitionist than a Progressive. He had an erratic personal background, and lacked the ardor of some of his more intense supporters. Although he was the best candidate his faction could offer, he was also a vulnerable target for an opponent with stamina and a taste for demagogy. The wets found such a man in James Ferguson, a Central Texas banker who had moved on the fringes of state politics for five years. Ferguson announced his candidacy in November 1913, on a platform that emphasized the evils of farm tenancy, and promised to veto all prohibition legislation: "I will strike it where the chicken got the axe." The tenancy issue and his antiprohibition sentiments provided Ferguson with the elements of victory. He drove the other wet candidates from the field by April 1914, and brought his unique campaign style to bear on the hapless Ball. Worried drys reported that the farmers were "taking to Ferguson's land proposal like a hungry cat to a piece of fresh beef liver." Ferguson gave Ball no rest. On the stump, "Farmer Jim" used agrarian props like a gourd and wooden dipper to underscore his rural allegiance. He assailed Ball for belonging to a Houston club that sold liquor, and promised that his opponent would "go down in history as the biggest political straddler that ever lived." By mid-June a prohibitionist worker concluded: "unless some very aggressive and active efforts are made, we stand to lose." Ball's advisors turned to the Wilson administration to stave off defeat. They sought an endorsement of the dry cause and told the president that Ferguson was an agent of reaction. Wilson, Secretary of State William Jennings Bryan, and Burleson issued public statements for Ball in mid-July, a tactic that moved Ferguson to denounce federal interference in state affairs. Despite the presidential action, Ferguson combined the wet vote with the ballots of North Texas farmers concerned about tenancy and achieved a 45,000-vote majority.

Ferguson's nomination inflicted a serious setback on the progressive Democrats. The new governor was a master campaigner, a deft manipulator of wet and rural sentiment, and a clever opportunist with an eye on the state treasury and other sources of personal profit. His ability to muddy differences over prohibition and the land question perpetuated the confused condition of state politics. Drys and Progressives faced the gloomy prospect of four years of antiprohibitionist leadership in Austin.

A rapport between Ferguson and Wilson emerged during the aftermath of the primary and lasted until the spring of 1917. In contrast to Governor Colquitt, who openly bickered with Washington over Mexican policy, Ferguson deferred to the Wilson administration in his public statements and confined dissent to private correspondence. A similarly cooperative attitude marked the governor's actions on neutrality after World War I began. In 1916, after Ferguson had supported the Wilson campaign for preparedness, the administration acquiesced in the governor's domination of the state convention at San Antonio and tacitly endorsed his leadership of the Democratic delegation to the national convention. The Progressives, said Love, wanted to keep "men who wear the political collar of the liquor traffic" off the slate, but they were no match for a coalition of Ferguson backers, friends of former senator Bailey, and moderates who thought the governor was doing Wilson's bidding.

Progressives took some comfort in the defeat of Colquitt, long a wet stalwart, in the 1916 senatorial contest. Colquitt had moved away from the mild progressivism of his first term and broken with Wilson in 1914 over patronage, cotton legislation, and Mexico. In a New York *Times* interview Colquitt described the administration as "the greatest failure in the history of the Presidency." After leaving office, he supported Germany in the quarrels over neutrality, in part to preserve his base of support among the Germans in south central Texas, and continued to scold the president. He ran first in the six-man senatorial primary in June and went into a runoff with the incumbent, Culberson. This development caused dismay in the White House—a fear that Colquitt would "disgrace the State and the Senate of the United States," Thomas Watt Gregory, now Wilson's attorney general, told Love.

To defeat Colquitt, the Democrats had to opt for a politician whose loyalty to dry progressivism was doubtful. As state attorney general, governor, and senator, Culberson turned silence into a settled habit and rarely revealed his convictions. The illnesses that flowed from the excessive use of alcohol made Culberson a semi-invalid who lacked the endurance to campaign personally. Though he never set foot in the state during the campaign, Culberson rode to a runoff victory behind the votes of conservative and progressive Democrats, joined together temporarily to defeat the open enemy of a Democratic president. This kind of negative victory did not mean, however, that the prohibitionist–progressive wing had rebounded from the effects of 1914. With Ferguson a potential candidate in 1918 against the archdry Senator Morris Sheppard and no strong gubernatorial hopefuls on the horizon, prohibition Democrats still displayed their "inherent inability . . . to 'hang together'" as 1917 began.

American entry in World War I removed some of the obstacles to prohibition. Prohibition became a patriotic cause to conserve food, protect the soldiers in training camps, and injure the German-dominated brewing industry. The Wilson administration abandoned its previous coolness on the subject and endorsed wartime curbs on alcohol. In Texas, reformers marched on such wet bastions as Dallas, Waco, and Austin in the fall of 1917. A dry leader, Cullen F. Thomas, noting the progress, remarked: "Reform seems awfully slow, but wrong will not always be on the throne." Even more effective in promoting the antiliquor movement was the impeachment of Ferguson over his personal finances and protracted controversy with the University of Texas. The political repercussions of this dispute, which went on from mid-1915 until the state Senate ousted Gentleman Jim in September 1917, devastated the wet cause. By attacking the university, the governor united its alumni, the drys, the woman suffragists, and the press against him. As a result, the forces of prohibition acquired a cohesion that contrasted sharply with their earlier disunity. The revelation in Ferguson's trial of his misuse of state funds and shady financial relations with the brewers left the antiprohibitionists "practically wrecked." Over the next year the drys remained on the offensive. The acting governor, William P. Hobby, renounced his wet past and called the legislature into special session to deal with the sale of liquor near military training camps. The lawmakers went far beyond this topic, and passed a statewide prohibition law, ratified the national prohibition amendment, and gave women the vote in the Democratic primary. Ball told the state Senate that the "destruction of the liquor business" and the other achievements of the winter of 1918 "record a new high water mark in patriotism and progressive democracy."

"Progressive democracy" also prevailed in the gubernatorial primary as Hobby turned back Ferguson's bid for vindication. The same coalition of Progressives, drys, and organized women gave the Hobby campaign its thrust. Labeling Ferguson an agent of the Kaiser because of his brewery connections, the Hobby campaign made patriotism the keynote. "From a political campaign," stated the Houston *Post*, "this has become an impetuous, patriotic impulse to 'slay the beast' at home." Hobby won a smashing 244,000-vote majority, and the drys took over the party.

A final challenge to dry supremacy appeared in 1919. Bailey decided to reshape the Democratic party in accord with his states'-rights views. He was suspect among Progressives because of his financial dealings between 1900 and 1906. He also opposed Wilson's candidacy in 1912, criticized the president after 1913, and was an open foe of prohibition and woman suffrage. In August 1919 he urged party members to repudiate Wilsonian "Socialism" and sponsored a statewide convention of conservative Democrats. To assist in the selection of an anti-Wilson delegation to the national convention, he became a candidate for governor early in 1920 and began a campaign that accused the Wilson administration of extravagance, softness on the race question, and usurpation of states' rights. The Progressives, under the leadership of Hobby, Love, and Gregory, responded vigorously to the assault. Pro-administration Democrats built a campaign organization, called Bailey a traitor to the party, and soundly trounced him over the selection of delegates in May 1920. Bailey stayed in the gubernatorial contest and led the field in the first primary. In a singularly dirty runoff campaign, he lost decisively to a prohibitionist, Pat M. Neff. When Bailey's defeat was final, his enemies termed the outcome an accolade for "the achievements of the Wilson administration, prohibition and equal suffrage, the rule of right in this land of ours and for honest and progressive government conducted by honest and progressive men." The irrepressible Ferguson made a race for president in the fall election as a way of keeping his name before followers. Otherwise, the dry Democrats seemed everywhere dominant.

In many ways the 20 years after 1900 left Texas relatively unchanged. The state was still rural, agricultural, Democratic, segregated, and poor. Industrialization, the rapid growth of cities, and the great wealth that became legend were years away. Nonetheless the Progressive Era in Texas had initiated trends that later led to the emergence of the modern state. The government of Texas dealt with a wider range of responsibilities in economic policy, conservation, and social services than in 1900. The Democratic party, under the influence of Woodrow Wilson, had left much of the inaction of its negative past for a more positive philosophy of government participation, especially as it related to the regulation of alcohol. White women had the vote, liquor was prohibited, and the national government was a larger presence in state affairs. Texans in the age of reform had accomplished much and left unsolved issues for those who followed them. In the 1920s and 1930s the successive interaction of the Klan, the Fergusons, and the New Deal extended a tradition of flamboyance and controversy in the state's politics that had marked the era of Progressives and prohibitionists.

Lewis L. Gould

World War I. During the World War I years, imbedded in the Progressive Era, the war greatly influenced the lives of Texans both at home and abroad. The United States was officially neutral when the war erupted in Europe in August 1914. Nevertheless, President Woodrow Wilson's policies increasingly leaned toward the Allies as the trench warfare settled into a costly stalemate for the major European powers. Wilson's attitudes reflected the opinions of most Americans and Texans as the nation drifted closer to war. Following the sinking of the *Lusitania* by a German submarine in May 1915, the Texas Senate passed a resolution urging the United States to declare war against Germany. The Dallas *Morning News* called the attack a crime against civilization. Governor James Ferguson urged caution and said people should not be "swayed or excited by the passions of the hour." However, this first episode marked the beginning of a buildup in popular opinion in Texas and the nation to support United States entry into the European war.

Many Texans were disturbed by submarine warfare, but they were more upset by rumors of German attempts to encourage Mexico to renew hostilities against the United States. German officials knew that territorial losses to the United States in the Treaty of Guadalupe Hidalgo in 1848 were a stain on Mexico's national honor. Germany was especially interested in keeping America out of the European war and became involved in the internal affairs of Mexico during its revolution. Events along the Rio Grande and the political unrest during the prolonged revolution became major contributing factors to the United States entry into World War 1.

In Mexico, Germany supported General Victoriano Huerta, who ordered the assassination of the popular president, Francisco Madero. The unpopular Huerta resigned the presidency in July 1914 and left Mexico in a German ship. Venustiano Carranza eventually succeeded him, but clashes between the forces of Pancho Villa and Carranza in northern Mexico during 1915 and 1916 were common. Texas became a sanctuary and a source of arms for factions in the Mexican Revolution. After learning of the shootings of a number of Americans in Mexico, in June 1915 Governor Ferguson asked President Wilson to station troops in the Big Bend region to protect residents and commerce. Following Villa's raid on Columbus, New Mexico, in March 1916, President Wilson quickly ordered General John Pershing and 10,000 United States Army troops into Mexico to pursue the Villistas. The American force spent the rest of the year in the deserts and mountains of northern Mexico, where they sparred with the elusive Villa and also fought units of Carranza's army.

The lower Rio Grande valley was aflame during this same period. Many Texas newspapers carried accounts of "Mexican bandits" and their raids on ranches and small communities north of the Rio Grande. Train derailments, burned bridges, and other property damage were attributed to these mounted raiders. Many believed the attacks were instigated by the German government. However, most United States military observers blamed the violence on discrimination by whites against Mexicans and Tejanos. Many Tejano families lost their farms and dwellings during this unsettled period.

As the violence increased in South Texas, many white residents and the press blamed the Plan of San Diego for inciting the resident Tejano population. The plan called for independence for Mexican Americans from "Yankee tyranny" and the creation of a new, independent republic that would include all of Texas and the other states in the Southwest. Law enforcement authorities made wholesale arrests of suspected Mexican insurrectionists while others were executed upon apprehension. Thousands fled the state. The San Antonio *Express* reported in September 1915 that "finding of dead bodies of Mexicans suspected for various reasons of being connected with the troubles has reached a point where it creates little or no interest." According to Texas historian Walter Prescott Webb, at least 500 and perhaps as many as 5,000 Mexicans were killed, while deaths among white residents and soldiers were under 200. The *Express* stated, however, that "not an innocent Mexican citizen has suffered," as reprisals were directed only "in pursuit of bandits or in defense of life and property."

While Pershing's force was south of the Rio Grande, another attack occurred on the remote villages of Glenn Spring and Boquillas in the Big Bend region on 5 May 1916. Nine soldiers of Troop A of the Fourteenth Cavalry were stationed at the spring. The troopers took shelter in an adobe building following the nighttime assault by 50 raiders, although some accounts said as many as several hundred Mexicans participated in the foray. The attackers killed three soldiers and wounded four others. Two civilians, including a 10-year-old boy, were also shot and killed in nearby Boquillas. The Wilson Administration and the military again blamed the conflict on Villa. Governor Ferguson expressed the feelings of many when he advocated United States intervention in Mexico to "assume control of that unfortunate country." The San Antonio *Express* urged the Mexican government to cooperate with Pershing's force to pursue those who participated in "organized murder, plundering and property destruction."

The attack led to the reorganization of troops along the Rio Grande. Wilson ordered the National Guard to reinforce the army on the border, and by the end of July 1916 over 100,000 guardsmen were on patrol along the international boundary. Troops assembled at San Antonio and manned a dozen new camps along the Rio Grande in the Big Bend region. They remained stationed along the border until 1920 but saw little active fighting. W. D. Smithers, a former muleteer for the troops, said that after the 1916 raid at Glenn Spring, the soldiers had nothing to do except "watch for bandits and play baseball." Pershing's force withdrew from northern Mexico in February 1917.

Within weeks after Pershing's return to United States soil, German involvement with Mexico made headlines in an international incident surrounding the "Zimmermann Telegram." The occasion was a secret telegram from German secretary of state Arthur Zimmermann transmitted in code to his ambassadors in Washington and Mexico City. The proposal promised Mexico that if that nation would side with Germany and encourage Japan to join the Central Powers, Germany would assist Mexico to regain its lost territories of Texas, Arizona, and New Mexico. British intelligence intercepted the message and sent its contents to President Wilson only a few days before he took his second oath of office. Neither the Mexican nor the Japanese government knew of its contents until they were publicized by the Wilson Administration.

Widespread public indignation erupted when Germany's proposal became front-page news in March 1917. Many Texas newspapers reacted with alarm and inflamed passions north of the Rio Grande. The San Antonio *Light* stated that if a German–Mexican–Japanese army invaded Texas, Texans would fight to the death—just as they had at the Alamo. Other papers throughout Texas reacted more cautiously. The Houston *Post* averred that Zimmerman was "utterly ignorant of conditions in Mexico" if they believed the Carranza government could undertake a reconquest of Texas and the rest of the Southwest. The Zimmermann Telegram and its threats against United States security were one of the reasons that President Wilson, who campaigned on his ability to keep the nation out of the European conflict, reversed his position and asked Congress to declare war on Germany in April 1917. In many ways the message confirmed the suspicions of many Texans who believed on the basis of its record in Mexico that Germany posed a real threat as both an external and internal enemy.

The buildup of United States forces on the border with Mexico, along with action by the Mexican government and military, finally ended the "orgy of bloodshed" along the border. The prolonged military activity also helped prepare the United States Army for war. Texans gained valuable experience in working with large troop units with modern weapons. A large number of Texans volunteered for military service and entered the draft. Over 989,000 men registered; nearly 200,000 enlisted and saw service during the war. Several hundred Texas women served as nurses during the war. One nurse and 5,170 men died in the service. Of these deaths, one-third occurred in the United States as a result of the influenza epidemic of 1918. Four Texans received the Medal of Honor for service in the war.

Federal legislation had reorganized all state militias in 1903 into national guard units. However, they were still subject to organization within each state. The Terrell Election Laws, which disfranchised most African Americans and Mexican Americans in Texas, allowed the adjutant general to eliminate segregated black militia units and to bar most Hispanics from service by 1906. The Texas National Guard was effectively an all-white unit at the outbreak of hostilities with Mexico and the United States entry into World War I. Several thousand Texas troops entered the service and joined the United States Army's punitive expedition into Mexico in the unsuccessful pursuit of Pancho Villa.

The National Defense Act of 1916 reorganized all state militias into the National Guard. When Congress declared war on Germany in April 1917, all members of the National Guard were called into active service. Texas units assembled with those from Oklahoma and formed the Thirty-sixth Division, better known as the "Texas Division," at Camp Bowie in Tarrant County. After a period of training in Texas the division was ordered overseas under the command of Maj. Gen. William R. Smith. The troops arrived in France during the summer of 1918. In September they joined the Meuse–Argonne offensive fighting in the Aisne valley, where they suffered over 2,600 total casualties with 591 men killed in action.

The Ninetieth Division was the other major unit composed mainly of Texans and Oklahomans. The division was organized at Camp Travis, San Antonio, in August 1917 under the command of Maj. Gen. Henry T. Allen, a career army officer and veteran of Pershing's Mexico campaign. The entire unit was in France by July and participated in the St. Mihiel offensive against the Hindenberg Line. Later, the division was part of the Meuse–Argonne attack that drove the Germans across the Meuse River. After the Armistice, the division assisted in taking care of Allied prisoners of war and repatriating French civilians. In recognition of its accomplishments, the unit remained in Germany its part of the Allied occupation force until April 1919. The unit sustained 9,400, casualties of which 1,079 officers and men were killed. Following the Armistice, the German military declared the Ninetieth Division one of the most feared Allied units.

At home, military camps established to train servicemen included Camp MacArthur at Waco, Camp Travis at San Antonio, and Camp Bowie at Fort Worth. Military training schools for aviators included Hicks Field and Kelly Field in San Antonio. Nearly all of the combat fliers of World War I earned their wings at Kelly Field. Many of the future leaders for the Air Force trained at the site. Charles Lindberg also earned his wings at Kelly. The Department of War authorized two new installations in Houston for military training—Camp Logan and Ellington Field. In July 1917 the army ordered the Twenty-Fourth Infantry, which included a company of black troops, to transfer from Illinois to Houston for training. Black–white racial tensions led to the Houston Riot in August 1917. Scars from this violent interracial confrontation were notable in Houston long after the war was over.

Once war was declared in April 1917, people were encouraged to support the troops and government efforts to mobilize the peacetime economy. Each public school was required to be equipped with a flag and to spend at least 10 minutes a day teaching patriotism. Texans bought Liberty and Victory Bonds and War Savings Stamps. Food-conservation programs included wheatless Mondays, meatless Tuesdays, and porkless Thursdays. War gardens sprouted up around the state, as did new industries to supply the war effort and provide services to the military bases opened in Texas. One of the first casualties of the war was freedom of the press. The Wilson administration quickly took action against suspected critics. The first newspaper closed by the federal government was the *Rebel*, a Socialist weekly published by Thomas Hickey in Hallettsville, Texas.

Governor Ferguson appointed 40 men to serve as the Texas State Council of Defense, a branch of the National Council of Defense, on 9 April 1917. The board represented the most influential business and political leaders in the state. Judge O. E. Dunlap

of Waxahachie was the first chairman. Dunlap was an attorney, former president of the Texas Bankers' Association, and president of the Good Roads Association. Thomas H. Ball, a former opponent of Governor Ferguson and United States Congressman from Houston, became vice chairman. Robert J. Kleberg of the King Ranch also served as vice chairman. The council worked to establish county organizations and mobilize the state's resources for the war in Europe. Ten committees became active in all areas of the state to build popular support for the war, increase crop production, promote the sale of war bonds, assist the armed forces in Texas, and provide protection for the state's citizens. The state council organized 240 county councils and about 15,000 community councils. Council work continued throughout the war, and for six months after the Armistice to aid returning soldiers. The last council meeting was on 7 June 1919.

The board also formed a separate Woman's Committee, a reflection of the changing status of women during the Progressive Era. Mrs. Fred Fleming of Dallas chaired the Woman's Committee, and Mrs. Lee Joseph was vice chairman. Volunteers promoted health efforts and worked in hospitals during the influenza epidemic. They also aided in drives for War Savings and Liberty Loans. Directing their own initiatives, the committee expanded child-welfare, education, and health programs in the state while securing new job opportunities in government and service areas for women.

The state and local councils set up many programs to generate patriotism and maintain enthusiasm for the war effort. As part of this patriotic fervor, the council directed the arrest of IWW labor activists as "agitators." The German language and publications were also suppressed by the council in the many Texas communities with a strong Germanic heritage. The council sent letters to individuals "whose loyalty was questioned" and assisted the army in obtaining information on deserters and draft evaders. The department commander at Fort Sam Houston in San Antonio requested that the council prevent Mexicans from leaving the country, an exodus that "would have depleted the labor supply." Local councils also used the presence of Home Guards, whose efforts "went a long way towards suppressing people of disloyal tendencies."

The state's public schools and universities enthusiastically joined the war effort. State School Superintendent W. F. Doughty said that "education is now on trial, just as much as are democracy and liberty." Public schoolteachers and students conducted War Savings Stamp Campaigns, organized local chapters of the Junior Red Cross, the Farm Cadets, and the Victory Boys and Victory Girls. The government needed carbon from seeds to make gas masks, so students were asked to save peach and plum pits and the shells from nuts. The University of Texas announced that winning the war was "paramount to everything else" in which the institution was involved. Professors edited pamphlets, contributed articles for newspapers, and justified the nation's involvement in the war. University of Texas history professor Frederic Duncalf described Germany as "barbarous, brutal and destructive beyond all belief."

When Governor Ferguson questioned the patriotism of the university, President Robert E. Vinson responded that every student was involved in "some form of military training." A notable exception at the university was political science professor Lindley M. Keasbey, described by Walter Prescott Webb as the "greatest teacher he ever had." Keasbey joined other pacifists in the Emergency Peace Federation. Once America joined the conflict, Keasbey opposed conscription and demanded safeguards from the Wilson administration to protect civil liberties. When the university's board of regents met in July 1917, they voted to dismiss Keasbey "for the best interest of the university." Few members of the faculty or the administration came to his defense.

World War I also brought a new wartime economy. The outbreak of the war in Europe initially wrought economic havoc in Texas and the rest of the South. Cotton, the primary cash crop, dropped in price as the conflict disrupted international trade. However, by 1915, demand for cotton, oil, and other agricultural and manufactured products by the Allied forces reversed the trend. When the United States entered the war in 1917, Texas farmers and businesses benefited from the national mobilization effort. Cotton prices rose by 1919 from a low of seven cents a pound to 35 cents a pound. The Houston Ship Channel was enlarged, and the Bayou City emerged as the largest inland seaport in the nation as a result of wartime traffic. Bank deposits rose and employment increased across the state from the stimulus provided by wartime activities.

The Texas oil industry, with its history of instability in the early 1900s, declined along with cotton when the war began in Europe. But the price soon increased as exports flowed to England and France to fuel the Allied war machine. From a low of 48 cents a barrel in 1915, prices of Texas crude rose to $1.70 a barrel by 1919. Many new oil discoveries throughout the state increased production, and large refineries, pipelines, and other petroleum-related businesses began and expanded during the war years. The Texas Company (later known as Texaco), Gulf, Sun, Magnolia, and Humble Oil (later known as Exxon) all diversified as they saw their profits rise faster than a new gusher.

This diversification occurred because wartime demands for petroleum overcame legal strictures of the Texas antitrust laws. The state legislature allowed companies to combine production, refining, and marketing within one firm—a change that set the groundwork for the growth of oil companies into major corporations. Federal troops responded to pleas from Texas oil executives to break a strike of more than 10,000 unionized petroleum workers in November 1917. The strike dissolved, as the need for an uninterrupted flow of oil was judged to be more essential than oilfield workers' wages. As a result of wartime demands, the oil industry became the major industry in the state. Along with its expansion, the industry increased its political influence in both Austin and Washington. The close ties to government policy makers appeared to fulfill an early prediction of petroleum attorney James Autrey. He told Joseph Cullinan, founding president of the Texas Company, that the oil business was "the kind of shining mark which attracts the attention of average politicians."

Overall, the economic impact of the war accelerated the trend of industrialization and urbanization in a state that nevertheless remained tied to its agricultural and rural past. San Antonio, Dallas, and Houston nearly doubled in population between 1910 and 1920, when more than 100,000 people resided in each city. The state as a whole increased in population and became more oriented towards these urban commercial centers. Of the 4.6 million people living in the Texas by 1920, nearly one out of three lived in an urban area. Nearly all of the population growth from 1910 to 1920 occurred in the state's urban centers. The shift from farm to city and the business expansion during this era laid the foundations for the future economic growth of the state.

The patriotic fervor that erupted in the nation during the war was a godsend to advocates of the prohibition of alcohol and woman suffrage. Prohibition supporters argued that alcohol was a waste of vital resources, a threat to American soldiers, and a tool of the German Kaiser. On 14 April 1917, the day the United States declared war on Germany, United States Senator Morris Sheppard of Texas introduced the prohibition amendment to Congress. He said the war effort would be greatly improved "if the liquor traffic could be wiped out." At their fall convention, Texas Baptists renewed their hostility to liquor and called for a ban of alcohol around military camps "to protect our soldier boys against evils more deadly than all the horrors and carnage of the battlefields." Senator Sheppard won his battle, as Congress passed the amendment in December 1917 and sent it to the states for ratification. Sheppard became nationally known as the "Father of National Prohibition."

Local campaigns by prohibition forces increased the pressure on local politicians. Advocates linked their cause to the war as well as to longstanding arguments about the social problems associated with alcohol abuse. Ironic prohibition ads advocated "More booze and fewer shoes." The dries claimed that liquor bestows "Orphan Children, Corrupt Politics, More Divorces, Poverty," and other associated ills on society. Governor William P. Hobby announced in February 1917 that he supported a law to ban the sale of liquor within 10 miles of any military base in the state. He astutely noted that the sanction "will make Texas practically dry." At the same time, Gen. J. W. Ruckman, army commander at San Antonio, called for a ban on liquor, and the legislature overwhelmingly complied. Lawmakers also ratified the prohibition amendment and passed legislation to curb prostitution near military bases.

Suffrage advocates turned their rhetorical guns on the newspapers and the business leaders of the community to press their cause. Hortense Ward of Houston lamented that "alien enemies" of the nation could vote in elections but "loyal American women" could not. As part of their campaign, suffrage leaders enthusiastically volunteered for projects linked to the war effort. They worked on food-conservation drives, sales of war bonds, and efforts to raise medical supplies and clothing. Women's-rights activists noted that the "alien enemy has paid his poll tax" while "our sons and brothers and husbands" were in the service and effectively disfranchised.

The suffrage movement cleared a major hurdle when the special legislative session that voted for prohibition also approved a measure that allowed women the right to vote in primary elections. Women voters turned out in large numbers in the 1918 Democratic Primary to reelect Governor Hobby, now the male hero of the suffrage movement. Hobby withstood a strong challenge from former Governor James Ferguson. The following year the legislature approved the constitutional amendment granting women the right to vote. According to historian Lewis Gould, World War I moved a majority of the state to favor prohibition and played a deciding factor in the ultimate suffrage victory. Dry progressive Democrats became the dominant political force in Texas politics for many years to come. Alcohol remained a potent political issue for decades. After he became president in 1963, Lyndon Johnson noted that most Texas elections for his generation were usually decided by two simple issues: "All I heard was whether you were wet or dry, whether you were for the courthouse group or against them."

Patrick L. Cox

The 1920s. At one time historians commonly described the 1920s as a decade of sterility, in which little happened except economic excesses, symbolized by the great bull market on Wall Street, that brought on the 1929 crash. Most historians concentrated on politics and, compared with either the Progressive era that preceded or the New Deal reforms that followed, the twenties did indeed look like retrograde years. However, the period was really one of amazing vitality, of social invention and change. The twenties were the formative years of modern America. In that decade the country became urban, and a new type of industrial economy arose, typified by mass production and mass consumption. Both factors speeded the breakdown of traditional habits and thought patterns in such areas as religion, dress, moral standards, and the uses of leisure time. The popular image of the twenties is that of a "roaring" era, replete with flappers, Fords, raccoon coats, jazz, movies and radio, speakeasies, Florida real estate promotions, mail-order stock schemes, bootleggers, gangsters like Al Capone, flamboyant preachers, and the "Lone Eagle," Charles A. Lindbergh. Societies do not give up old ideals and attitudes easily; the conflicts between the spokesmen for the old order and the champions of the new day were at times both bitter and extensive.

For most southerners the dominant theme of the 1920s was economic expansion. If electrical power was the basic regional builder in the Southeast, petroleum assumed that role in the Southwest—Texas, Oklahoma, Arkansas, and Louisiana. Oil diversified the region's economy, which was previously based on agriculture and timber, and fueled the burgeoning automobile industry in the United States. By 1929 there was an automobile for every 4.3 Texans. A storied oil boom was set off in 1901, when exploratory drilling at the Spindletop oilfield, near Beaumont, resulted in a gusher of unprecedented volume. In 1902 the field produced more than 17 million barrels of oil. This discovery opened the first of the series of new oilfields discovered in Texas and Oklahoma that made these two states the nation's top producers; in 1919 Louisiana assumed third place when the Homer field was opened. Major Texas oilfields included the Ranger, Desdemona, and Breckenridge oilfields and the Sour Lake, Batson–Old, Humble, Goose Creek, and Burkburnett fields before 1920, as well as the Big Lake, Yates, East Texas, Mexia, Panhandle, Van, and McCamey fields after that date. The discovery of oil beneath school and university lands subsequently channeled billions of dollars into public education in Texas. The 1920s witnessed an oil find in Arkansas, and in 1929 the four southwestern states represented about 60 percent of the major crude-oil production in the United States. Texas pulled in front of Oklahoma by 1928. On 3 October 1930, near Henderson, a seasoned wildcatter named Columbus Marion "Dad" Joiner struck the southwestern edge of the largest oil pool discovered in the world to that time and set off a new oil boom reminiscent of Spindletop.

By 1930 Texas ranked fifth among the states in population, with 5,824,715 residents—a 24.9 percent increase over 1920. Forty-one percent were living in concentrations of more than 2,500. This was up from 32.4 percent 10 years earlier. Among major cities, Houston led with 292,352 people, Dallas had 260,475, San Antonio 231,542, and Fort Worth 163,447. Wartime inflation and demands for Southern products brought a brief period of unprecedented prosperity, and the Southern farmer held high hopes of climbing out of his economic slough of despond. The cotton crop of 1919 sold for a satisfying figure. Postwar prices continued to rise in the early months of 1920. Farm boys felt so prosperous that some of them bought silk shirts and silk underwear. But farmers who had expanded their operations and gone further into debt in order to capitalize on inflation and the increased demand for products found themselves the victims of the "cotton cycle." Cotton prices rose to a high of 42 cents a pound in New Orleans in April 1920, and that spring Southern farmers planted their largest crop since 1914. Prices held steady until the middle of the summer, when they began to decline. By December 1920 the price had fallen to 13½ cents, and the great 1920 crop, 13,429,000 bales, proved to be a disastrous financial failure. Cotton was selling for 9.8 cents a pound in March 1921. The crisis of 1920–21 inflicted near-fatal wounds.

The price break resulted in demands to cut production in 1921, and a Cotton Acreage Reduction Convention met in Memphis to encourage reduced planting in the spring of that year. The Memphis convention, the boll weevil, and a short cotton crop raised prices from 1922 to 1925 but did not solve the farmers' basic problems, which stemmed from unscientific farming, the crop-lien system, an unsatisfactory marketing system, and overproduction. From 1919 to 1926 Texas increased her cotton acreage from something over 10 million to more than 18 million acres and her production from three million to almost six million bales. Prices dropped again in 1926, to an average of 12.47 cents a pound, but not until the Great Depression did cotton fall to the disastrous average price of 5.66 cents a pound (1931). Farm tenancy continued to constitute one of the most serious social problems in the state. In 1920, 53.3 percent of farms were run by tenants, and in 1930 the figure stood at 60.9 percent. In 1920, 66.1 percent of all farms in 19 "blackland" Texas counties were so operated. Agricultural expert William B. Bizzell wrote of the farm tenancy problem in *Rural Texas* (1924): "It is impossible to build a prosperous and progressive rural civilization with more than half the farmers cultivating the land on some basis of cash or share tenancy." The farmers' persistent problems in the 1920s were accompanied by the rise and decline of numerous farm organizations. The farmer alternately joined or abandoned organizations designed to help with his problems, depending upon his state of mind or financial condition. The revived Grange, the American Farm Bureau Federation, and the Farm Labor Union used various methods to gain support for their organizations and to agitate for better farm conditions. The Texas Farm Bureau Federation claimed a membership of 70,000 in 130 counties in late 1921. The Farm Labor Union, organized in Bonham in October 1920, under the leadership of M. W. Fitzwater, represented the attitudes of the poorer tenants and laborers and was more radical than the other farm organizations. With the "cost of production plus a profit" as its slogan, the Farm Labor Union spread into parts of Oklahoma, Arkansas, Louisiana, Mississippi, Alabama, and Florida. Membership claims fluctuated from 45,000 in 1921 to 160,000 in 1925, but by 1926 the organization was in decline.

Although there was a steady stream of Mexican immigration into Texas during the 1890s, the flood began about 1920. According to the census figures, the number of people of Mexican descent in the state increased from 71,062 in 1900 to 683,681 in 1930, when 38.4 percent of them were foreign-born. Large numbers came across the border during World War I, and in the postwar period another heavy influx occurred. The rapid expansion of Texas agriculture was primarily responsible for the migration of Mexicans from 1900 to 1930. "Cotton picking suits the Mexican," was the unanimous opinion of Texas growers. Imported Mexicans did most of the work in the newly developed cottonfields of West Texas, where the plantation system was not deeply entrenched. The development of large fruit and truck farming areas in Texas between 1910 and 1930 came about by the opening of new irrigation projects and the availability of cheap Mexican labor. The *Literary Digest* judged, "The Mexican has put Texas on the map agriculturally." In a completely unorganized labor market, white, black, and Hispanic agricultural workers roamed throughout the vast reaches of Texas trying to pick up temporary employment. Because Mexicans moved readily from area to area and were available in any numbers desired, they rapidly displaced both black and white tenants and farm laborers. "There is a bird in Texas," a Mexican said, "called the road-runner, which cannot be like other birds, although it has wings. It stays on the ground and dodges in and out of the brush. The bird reminds us of our humble selves so much that we call it the *paisano*, which means countryman." Immigration authority Carey McWilliams remarked, "To the road-runner, as to the Mexican, 'the next field, the next season, always looks as if it might be better.'"

Labor organizations made little enough headway in the nation as a whole before the New Deal, but they were even less successful in the South. In addition to the surplus of unskilled labor, which lessened the probability that those workers with jobs would make demands that might alienate employers, labor unions in the South had to fight hostility, apathy, tradition, ingrained individualism, poverty, and suspicion of "Yankees." In the lumber industry, despite the determined efforts of the Brotherhood of Timber Workers in 1910 to organize workers, the operators, headed by the "Prince of the Pines," John Henry Kirby, were generally successful in preventing any union from getting a foothold. Many mills used an anti-union (yellow-dog) contract, and known organizers were harassed by sheriffs and company police until they fled from the region. Some businesses operated espionage systems that swiftly carried word of any unionization effort. The latent hostility of white and black workers was played upon to prevent an alliance, and all union organizers were denounced as a new group of "Carpetbaggers" who were coming south in an attempt to place the Negro above the Caucasian. As most companies owned an entire company town, including the streets, it was a simple matter to arrest and prosecute the would-be organizer for trespassing. This remained a favorite device for three generations. The lumber industry, however, declined in the postwar decade, as more and more companies, having exhausted their old-growth pine, moved elsewhere, often to the Pacific Coast states. The lumber and oil operators of Beaumont introduced the open shop, the so-called "Beaumont Plan," as a means of dealing with unions. Ben S. Woodhead of the Beaumont Lumber Company stated in March 1920, "So far as is known Beaumont is the first city previously working under closed shop conditions which has had the red blooded Americanism to stand upon its hindlegs and shake itself free from the tentacles and shackles of the closed shop." Under the leadership of the Beaumont group the Southwestern Open Shop Association was organized to cover Texas, Oklahoma, Arkansas, Louisiana, and New Mexico. It was succeeded by the Texas Employers' Association.

Galveston longshoremen went on strike in March 1920, demanding that their employers hire only union men and that wages be increased. After an investigation Governor William P. Hobby concluded that the only way to keep commerce moving regularly through the port was to place the city under martial law. After several months the troops were withdrawn, and several Texas Rangers remained to help local authorities maintain order. When the strike was settled in December 1920, each side made some con-

cessions. Meanwhile the legislature, in special session, passed an "open-port law," the purpose of which was to facilitate the movement of commerce by common carriers. Under its terms, it was unlawful "by or through the use of any physical violence, or by threatening the use of any physical violence, or by intimidation" to interfere with any person working at "loading or unloading or transporting any commerce within this state." Critics denounced it as an "antistrike law." Governor Hobby maintained that anyone could strike but could not compel others to do so. In July 1922 Governor Pat M. Neff invoked the law against striking railroad shopmen in North Texas. Although this strike failed, in 1926 the Texas Court of Criminal Appeals held the open-port law unconstitutional.

Progressivism did not disappear from the South in the 1920s. Instead, as historian George B. Tindall has shown, it was "transformed through greater emphasis upon certain of its tendencies and the distortion of others. The impulse for 'good government' and public services remained strong; the impulse for reform somehow turned into a drive for moral righteousness and conformity. The Ku Klux Klan and the fundamentalist movement inherited the reform spirit but channeled it into new crusades." Fundamentalists saw in Charles Darwin's theory of evolution an even more direct challenge to the old-time religion than that presented by modernism. The Bible was said to affirm that man was the product of fiat creation, molded from the dust by God's hands, not the result of a development untold ages in length. Evolution was also thought to impugn Christ's divinity. In Darwin's hypothesis there seemed to be no room for a supernatural being, no toleration for biological miracles. William Jennings Bryan expressed the opposition to evolution in words beyond the abilities of other fundamentalists: "Christ has made of death a narrow, star-lit strip between the companionship of yesterday and the reunion of tomorrow; evolution strikes out the stars and deepens the gloom that enshrouds the tomb." The center of antievolution agitation in Texas was Fort Worth, the home of J. Frank Norris, a firebrand Baptist minister. Norris early became the belligerent champion of a movement to expose unsound instruction in the University of Texas and Baylor University, and by his excoriations won many converts to his views. By 1925 his church was the largest Baptist church in the nation. He was generally credited with having brought about the dismissal of six Southern professors because of their religious beliefs. In view of the mounting demand for a state antievolution law, two state representatives, J. T. Stroder of Navarro County and S. J. Howeth of Johnson County, introduced a bill designed to add censorship of textbooks to the usual prohibition against teaching evolution in the public schools. The House passed the bill, 71 to 34, but the Senate let the measure die without a vote. Although a similar bill proposed in 1925 did not secure favorable action in the House, state officials decided to act upon their own initiative. Governor Miriam Ferguson was the leading force in the adoption of a ruling by the State Textbook Commission that the state would select only works on biology that contained no mention of evolution and "that all objectionable features in science texts shall be revised or eliminated to the satisfaction of the revision committee." "I am a Christian mother who believes Jesus Christ died to save humanity and I am not going to let that kind of rot go into Texas textbooks," Mrs. Ferguson declared. However, although five Southern states passed antievolution laws during the 1920s, Texas did not; and in time the fundamentalist crusade in the state lost much of its force.

Prohibition was basically a reform of the middle class, which in

Baptizing in the San Pedro Park Swimming Pool. Photograph by E. O. Goldbeck. San Antonio, 1925. Goldbeck Collection, HRHRC. A fundamentalist movement swept Texas in the 1920s, as religious leaders fought against inclusion of Charles Darwin's theory of evolution in school textbooks. J. Frank Norris, pictured here baptizing converts, was a firebrand Baptist preacher and opponent of evolution.

both country and city was predominantly native, old-stock, and Protestant. In *Progressives and Prohibitionists: Texas Democrats in the Wilson Era* (1973), Lewis L. Gould showed that in Texas statewide prohibition became a major goal of progressive Wilson Democrats "because it spoke directly to most of the perceived social problems of the state"; it was also "the major divisive element" in state politics. After the ratification of the Eighteenth Amendment in 1919, the prohibitionists seemed to have won their fight, but it soon became apparent that many otherwise good citizens did not intend to abide by the law. The tenuousness of the dry victory was nowhere more transparent than in the South, both a major prohibition stronghold and a major producer and distributor of illicit whiskey. In his *Recollections of Farm Life* (1965) Robert L. Hunt, Sr., recalled that "There was always some making of moonshine liquor in the area of Northeast Texas, but people were not so bad about drinking it until the 18th Amendment shut off the supply of good liquor." When Hunt returned from France in 1919, "The moonshiners had become rather common in the area. In fact so much moonshine was hauled out of the area that some places had quite a reputation for liquor making. Farms were left idle in some places and farmers turned to making liquor as a more profitable occupation."

During the early 1920s the second Ku Klux Klan dominated the politics of the Southwest. The organization capitalized on the hate generated by war propaganda and the hysteria of the Red Summer of 1919, when race riots flared across the country. Anti-Catholicism, white supremacy, hatred of Jews, antiradicalism, opposition to immigration—these were the salients of Klan ideology. Membership in the secret order was principally confined to the lower middle class. However, men prominent in business and politics donned white robes and hoods, and many clergymen welcomed the Klan as an agency of moral censorship. A close observer remarked, "There is a great 'inferiority complex' on the part of the Klan membership—due in part to lack of education—Dallas and Fort Worth (where the Klan is especially strong) being largely populated by men and women reared in obscure towns and country places where public schools are short-termed and scarce." The revived Klan made its first appearance in Texas at Houston in the fall of 1920, taking advantage of the sentiment for the past rekin-

dled by the annual reunion of the United Confederate Veterans. Simmons was there, along with a companion and aide, Nathan Bedford Forrest III, grandson of the "imperial wizard" of the Reconstruction-era Klan. Sam Houston Klan No. 1 was the first chapter to be established in Texas. By 1922 state membership was between 75,000 and 90,000. The "Realm of Texas" had been organized under its first "grand dragon," an Episcopalian priest, Dr. A. D. Ellis of Beaumont, and divided into five provinces, with their headquarters in Fort Worth, Dallas, Waco, Houston, and San Antonio. The "grand titan" of Province No. 2 was a plump, affable dentist, Hiram Wesley Evans, who had been "exalted cyclops" of the state's largest "klavern," No. 66, in Dallas. After becoming national secretary of the Klan, Evans was elected "imperial wizard" in November 1922, thereby seizing control from the Simmons–Clarke faction. From 1922 to 1924 the secret order was the chief issue in Texas politics; it elected sheriffs, attorneys, judges, and legislators. The Klan probably had a majority in the House of Representatives of the Thirty-eighth Legislature, which met in January 1923. Perhaps as many as 400,000 Texans belonged to the Klan at one time or another.

According to historian Charles Alexander, the "distinctive quality" of the Klan in the Southwest was "its motivation, which lay not so much in racism and nativism as in moral authoritarianism." In the Southwest "the Klan was, more than anything else, an instrument for restoring law and order and Victorian morality to the communities, towns, and cities of the region. Its coercive activity and its later preoccupation with political contests make vigilantism and politics the main characteristics of Klan history in the Southwest." Only a relatively small part of the Klan's defense of morality and society was directed at blacks. Its campaign of systematic terrorism—beatings and tar-and-featherings—was aimed mostly at bootleggers, gamblers, wayward husbands and wives, wife beaters, and other sinners. The Klan in Dallas was credited with having flogged 68 men in the spring of 1922, most of them at a special Klan whipping meadow along the Trinity River bottom.

Some Texans were alarmed by these outrages and attempted to take preventive measures. A number of outspoken district judges ordered investigations. Some sheriffs and city officials attempted to prevent Klan parades. The mayor of Dallas, Sawnie Aldredge,

Ku Klux Klan Parading, Beaumont, November 10, 1922. Courtesy Spindletop–Gladys City Boomtown Museum, Beaumont. The Texas branch of the Ku Klux Klan elected sheriffs, attorneys, judges, and legislators, and counted between 75,000 and 90,000 members in 1922.

demanded that the Klan disband. Forty-nine members of the state legislature petitioned a silent Governor Neff for a law against masks. American Legion posts, the Daughters of the American Revolution, the State Bar of Texas, chambers of commerce, the Masons, and others denounced the Klan. The most serious threat to Klan political activity in the Dallas area was the Dallas County Citizens' League, formed on 4 April 1922 at a mass meeting of 5,000 citizens. This organization chose Martin M. Crane, attorney general of Texas during the Culberson administration, as chairman and adopted resolutions deploring the existence of a secret order that engaged in terrorism. However, all but one of the Klan-backed candidates for Dallas County office won election despite the opposition of the Citizens' League; the following year (1923) anti-Klan mayor Aldredge and the rest of his ticket were defeated in the election by a margin of almost three to one.

During the 1920s the Klan was as intensely active in Texas politics on the state level as it was on the local. In 1922 it made its influence felt quite dramatically in the race for United States senator. In the Democratic primary, which took place on 22 July, seven candidates sought the seat held by Charles Culberson, who was old and ill after a quarter century of service. The Klan backed an avowed "knight," Earle B. Mayfield of Austin, a member of the Railroad Commission who received a plurality of the ballots cast. The runner-up was former governor Jim Ferguson. Culberson finished a poor third. Mayfield won the second primary on August 26 by a vote of 273,308 to 228,701 over Ferguson. A substantial group of Democrats, taking the position that Mayfield was the Klan and not the Democratic nominee, turned to the Republicans with the sug-

gestion of a fusion candidate. The Republican nominee, E. P. Wilmot of Austin, a banker, was withdrawn, and Democrat George E. B. Peddy, a young assistant district attorney in Houston, was substituted as the Republican and Independent Democratic candidate. In the general election on 7 November 1922, Mayfield won easily, 264,260 to 130,744. Peddy charged that Mayfield had won the race through gross irregularities, and a subcommittee of the Senate Committee on Privileges and Elections heard the case from May to December 1924. Peddy introduced more than 30 witnesses from Texas, including Klan officials; Mayfield introduced but two witnesses. The committee decided that there were no grounds for unseating Mayfield.

On the national scene in the 1920s, Texas was a pivotal state in the transitional struggle between the prohibitionist, native-stock, Protestant Southern and western wing of the Democratic party and its urban, wet, new-immigrant northeastern faction. "Romantic in history, powerful in Democratic politics, Texas provides more interest for those watching political developments than almost any other State in the South," editorialized the New York *Times* in April 1928. "Ever since the 'Immortal Forty,' under the unit rule, stood by Woodrow Wilson at Baltimore until the nomination was won, an importance attaches to the Texas delegation out of proportion to the size of its vote or the state's geographical and industrial significance." In the spring of 1924 a three-man race developed in Texas to control the state's delegation to the Democratic national convention. First, Senator Oscar W. Underwood of Alabama, an antiprohibitionist, was supported by former senator Joseph W. Bailey, A. S. Burleson, Wilson's postmaster general, and former governor Oscar B. Colquitt, who was treated to the enmity of Klansmen and prohibitionists. Next, there was William Gibbs McAdoo, Wilson's son-in-law, whose candidacy was championed by the Wilson leader in Texas, Thomas B. Love of Dallas, and supported by the State Democratic Executive Committee. And finally, there was Governor Neff, a prohibitionist who was opposed to the selection of a pledged delegation and favored one instructed only to uphold dry principles in the party platform. Neff had some hopes that political lightning might strike for him as a dark-horse candidate at the New York convention, if the convention deadlocked between McAdoo and the other leading candidate, Al Smith of New York.

It was rumored during the campaign that the Klan had agreed to support McAdoo in return for Tom Love's support of the Klan candidate for governor, Judge Felix D. Robertson of Dallas. Subsequent events made it apparent that some form of understanding was reached. Love, however, forcefully denied any formal bargain, though he readily admitted that he had freely worked with any group willing to support McAdoo. In any case, on the eve of the precinct conventions, secret orders went out to all Klansmen to vote for McAdoo delegates. McAdoo's overwhelming victory in Texas stimulated his flagging campaign and gave it the impetus to drive on to New York City, where it was halted by a 103-ballot debacle in Madison Square Garden. The Texas delegation was widely characterized around the convention as a "klan dominated delegation from a klan dominated state." Love was preparing to carry Texas for McAdoo in 1928 when the Californian withdrew from the race, on 17 September 1927.

In the 1924 gubernatorial race in Texas, the Klan suffered a decisive setback. The hooded order campaigned actively for Judge Robertson. One of his opponents was Miriam Ferguson. Her husband was prohibited from running because he had been impeached as governor in 1917 and declared permanently ineligible to hold a state office. He remained the idol of the dirt farmers, the "boys at the forks of the creeks," and other rural voters. Mrs. Ferguson was his proxy. She based her campaign in part on a fight for the vindication of her husband at the hands of Texas voters and in part on opposition to the Klan. No candidate received a majority in the first primary, and Robertson, who had a large plurality, and Mrs. Ferguson contended against each other in the runoff. In the offing was one of the most heated political campaigns in Texas history. The group supporting Mrs. Ferguson adopted as campaign slogans "Me for Ma, and I aint got a durn thing against Pa," "A bonnet and not a hood," and "Two governors for the price of one." The Robertson camp countered with, "Not Ma for me. Too much Pa." Ferguson directed his wife's campaign and made the most of her political addresses. His opposition to the Klan, however, revealed no advanced social wisdom. He averred that "ex-Gizzard Simmons and Clarke were whore lovers and the present Grand Dragon [Evans] is a nigger lover." Throughout the state large numbers of politicians and voters flocked to Mrs. Ferguson's support in the second primary, not because they were for her, but because they were against the Klan-backed Robertson. Robertson was defeated in the second primary by nearly 100,000 votes. At the state Democratic convention in Austin on 2–3 September, the Klan was given a merciless political drubbing. The convention inserted in its platform an anti-Klan plank that began: "The Democratic party emphatically condemns and denounces what is known as the Invisible Empire of the Ku Klux Klan as an un-democratic, un-Christian and un-American organization." Mrs. Ferguson's Republican opponent in

the general election was George C. Butte, dean of the University of Texas law school. Pa Ferguson attacked him as "a little mutton-headed professor with a Dutch diploma," who was taking orders from the "grand dragon" of the "Realm of Texas," Z. L. Marvin, "the same as Felix Robertson did." According to the New York Times, the 4 November election signified "the greatest political revolution that ever took place in Texas." Tens of thousands of rock-ribbed Democrats cast a ballot for a Republican candidate for the first time. Klansmen deserted wholesale to Butte, who was not in sympathy with the organization, as did a number of anti-Ferguson Democrats, outraged that Ferguson should return to power through his wife. Under the leadership of Tom Love they formed an association called the Good Government Democratic League of Texas, the purpose of which was to defeat the Fergusons. However, Butte was defeated by more than 127,000 votes. These developments signaled the demise of the Klan as a force in Texas politics. "It was all over," recalled a former Klansman. "After Robertson was beaten the prominent men left the Klan. The Klan's standing went with them." By the end of 1924 Texas was no longer the number-one state in Klandom. The following year Ferguson persuaded the legislature to pass a bill making it unlawful for any secret society to allow its members to be masked or disguised in public.

During Mrs. Ferguson's first administration, according to historian Rupert N. Richardson, "reform took a holiday." Ma's first term was marked by behind-the-scenes domination by her husband, favoritism in the granting of highway contracts to firms that had advertised in the Ferguson Forum, and an extremely liberal pardon policy. In two years she granted 1,318 full pardons and 829 conditional pardons. "Jim's the governor, Ma signs the papers," one insider noted. In February 1925 came vindication day for Jim Ferguson, when the legislature voted to restore his political rights. On 31 March a radiant Mrs. Ferguson signed the amnesty bill with a gold pen given her by friends in Temple. (In 1927, however, the legislature passed a resolution declaring that the previous legislature had no authority to annul Ferguson's impeachment trial.) In 1926 Mrs. Ferguson sought reelection and was opposed by the youthful and able attorney general of Texas, Daniel J. Moody, Jr. During the race the Fergusons, in an effort to use the Klan issue as in 1924, attempted to link Moody with the Invisible Empire. Ferguson charged in the opening rally of the campaign at Sulphur Springs: "Moody's campaign was daddied in the evolved monkey end of the Baptist church and boosted by the Ku Klux Klan and supported by the big oil companies opposed to the gasoline tax." However, since Moody had a consistent anti-Klan record as a public official, the charge did not stick. Moody replied by referring to Ferguson's impeachment. He charged that Mrs. Ferguson was governor in name only, that her husband was the actual chief executive, and that the only real issue in the campaign was "Fergusonism." This political label covered a host of real or merely alleged sins of which the Fergusons were guilty. An interesting sidelight of the campaign was Mrs. Ferguson's challenge to Moody in her brief opening speech at Sulphur Springs: "I will agree that if he leads me by one vote in the primary . . . I will immediately resign without waiting until next year if he will agree that if I lead him 25,000 in the primary on July 24th he will immediately resign." Against the advice of some of his managers, Moody accepted the wager, but Mrs. Ferguson reneged when Moody led her by 126,250 votes in the first primary. Moody won the run-off, 495,723 to 270,595; he went on to win by a 191,537 vote majority over his Republican opponent, Harvey H. Haines, in the general election.

The dominant theme of state politics in the South in the 1920s was business progressivism, a doctrine that emphasized the old progressive themes of public services and efficiency. "The Business class political philosophy of the new South is broad enough to include programs of highway improvement, educational expansion, and health regulation," political scientist H. C. Nixon noted in 1931. "But it does not embrace any comprehensive challenge to laissez faire ideas in the sphere of relationship between capital and labor, and the section is lagging in social support of such matters as effective child labor regulation and compensation legislation." In some states, business-progressive governors failed to win the support of rural-dominated state legislatures—among them Pat Neff and Dan Moody in Texas. In his messages to the legislature, Neff (1921–25) advocated reorganization of the state's administrative system in order to eliminate extravagance and duplication of effort, laws to halt the rising crime rate, a constitutional convention, and fundamental changes in the state tax system. Although some offices were eliminated or consolidated, the legislature refused to modify greatly the organization of the state administration, no constitutional convention met, and there were no fundamental changes in the state tax system. Neff thought the chief cause of the worst crime wave in Texas history was the suspended-sentence law, and he asked for its repeal, without result. Neff himself issued only 92 pardons and 107 conditional pardons during his entire four years in office. He deserves some credit for improving the highway system, and the state park system had its beginning in 1923 with the establishment of a nonsalaried park board. The legislature did not provide one dollar with which to buy parkland, and Neff had to solicit private donations of land suitable for public purposes. Somewhat later he wrote: "As I now look back on my four years in the Governor's office, it is difficult to know just how much worthwhile service was rendered. Early in my administration I discovered that it was impossible to do the things that I had dreamed I would do. Many things hindered. Numberless contending and opposing forces had to be reckoned with. Frequently a Governor is helpless to do the things that, as a matter of fact, should be done. At times he feels that about all he can do is to write proclamations that no one reads, and give advice that no one heeds."

Governor Moody (1927–31) was also more progressive than the legislature. In his initial message, he proposed the correction of existing evils and abuses by the development of a scientific system of taxation, reform of the judicial system and court procedure, the enactment of a classified civil-service law, a unified system of accounting for all state departments, laws against indiscriminate pardoning of criminals, the efficient and economical development of a system of correlated state highways, adequate revenues for the highway department, improvement of the election laws, amendment of the libel law, improvements in the state penitentiary system, coordination of educational institutions to eliminate duplication, provision of a stable income for public schools based on the state's taxable wealth, and further development of Texas ports. Historian Ralph W. Steen wrote in 1937: "The Moody recommendations were in keeping with the best thought in political economy, and if adopted would have replaced the present government with a more modern government." But the legislature carried out only half or less of the ambitious "Moody Program," and few of the major organizational changes that Moody proposed were adopted. The determined opposition of state officials to any change in the status quo had a tremendous influence upon the solons. There was a natural hesitancy on the part of the legislature itself to deal with the complex problem completely. And the voters rejected necessary constitutional amendments. The greatest difficulty, however, was the argument that administrative reorganization would concentrate too much power in the governor's hands. No genuinely constructive reforms were achieved in the tax system, no fundamental changes were made in the cumbersome judiciary, civil service based on merit was turned down, no unified system of accounting was imposed, the prison system was incompletely reorganized, and money was not appropriated for a modern state highway system. During his four years in office, Moody had 8 legislative sessions, vetoed 15 bills during the sessions, and used the postadjournment veto 102 times. Only one of his vetoes was overridden.

His record as governor was more noteworthy for its administrative than for its legislative endeavors. He reversed the Fergusons' liberal pardon policies, corrected the state textbook situation, and reformed the highway department—three areas subject to much criticism during the previous administration. Shortly before Moody left office, the Dallas *Morning News* noted that his record fitted well into the circumstances of his first election. "His candidacy for Governor was not a response to the call for great legislative enterprise needing a leader. . . . His candidacy was primarily, and almost exclusively, a pledge to rescue public services from the grievous state into which they had been brought by maladministration." When Dr. John C. Granbery wrote Moody commending his 1929 message to the legislature, Moody replied: "Some parts of it, as you would imagine, have not met with any great amount of enthusiasm at the hands of the Legislature, and likely will not be enacted into law. I have sometimes felt that our attitude in Texas is a little too reactionary, and that we were not ready to accept progressive measures which worked successfully in other states." Moody's failure to mediate the bitter fight between Al Smith and anti-Smith Democrats in Texas in the election of 1928 left both factions dissatisfied with his leadership and embittered his relations with the Forty-first Legislature. "All the time the Legislature was in session, a crazy 'wild' group, and Dan sweating so hard to put over constructive measures," Moody's wife, Mildred Paxton Moody, wrote in her diary on 25 May 1929. "Reactions were deadly, to the recent Smith–Hoover fight, with Dan the 'goat,' both sides." Jim Ferguson was "still working his hate" at the Capitol.

Business progressivism in Texas had little to offer African Americans or Mexican Americans. A law passed during the Neff administration barring blacks from Democratic party primaries—the "white primary"—was declared unconstitutional by the United States Supreme Court in *Nixon v. Herndon* (1927). The Fortieth Legislature responded by giving political parties authority to determine their own membership, providing no one was excluded because of former political party affiliations or views. There was some criticism of the corrupt South Texas machines, such as the Parr organization in Duval County, which routinely delivered huge majorities for favored candidates, but no serious effort was made to break up the power that rested on economic and political manipulation of Mexican Americans through boss rule.

After the cause of woman suffrage achieved its ultimate triumph with the ratification of the Nineteenth Amendment to the United States Constitution in 1920 the Joint Legislative Council, or "Petticoat Lobby" of the 1920s, a coalition of women's groups, became one of the most successful public-interest lobbying groups in Texas history. The organization backed legislation dealing with education, prison reform, prohibition enforcement, maternal and child health, the abolition of child labor, and other social reforms.

Beginning in 1918 Annie Webb Blanton served four years as state superintendent of public instruction—the first Texas woman to win a state office. Jane McCallum was a lobbyist, journalist, publicist, Democratic party worker, and Texas secretary of state under two governors, Dan Moody and Ross Sterling. In 1922 Edith Wilmans of Dallas became the first woman elected to the Texas House of Representatives. Four years later Margie E. Neal of Carthage became the first woman to be a Texas state senator.

In the 1928 Texas Senate race, Senator Mayfield claimed that he had long since broken with the Klan, which in Texas was said by Governor Moody to be "as dead as the proverbial doornail." Mayfield politically championed Al Smith and pulled support away from Jim Ferguson, his 1922 run-off opponent; but Congressman Thomas T. Connally went to the Senate instead. Minnie Fisher Cunningham, a former president of the Texas Equal Suffrage Association, ran a poor fifth, polling just 28,944 votes in a total of 675,038. She later wrote in an article, "Too Gallant a Walk," in *Woman's Journal*: "When, before opening my campaign, I called on certain leading men of the state with whom I have cooperated in various other campaigns to ask support and advice in mine, every one of them in his own way assured me that I would be defeated, and when asked why, replied 'Because you are a woman.'" The consensus was that it was "too gallant a walk for a lady to take."

In 1928 the national Democratic party stretched the loyalty of the South to the breaking point by nominating the Catholic Al Smith for president at its Houston convention. The party, in effect, asked the rural, Protestant, and prohibition-minded South to support a candidate diametrically opposed to most things close to Southern hearts. Complained Cone Johnson, a dry Texas delegate, "I sat by the central aisle while the parade passed following Smith's nomination and the faces I saw in that mile-long procession were not American faces. I wondered where were the Americans." Here and there party professionals yielded to the strain. Senator Furnifold Simmons of North Carolina, Senator Tom Heflin of Alabama, and Tom Love in Texas, among others, bolted to the Hoovercrats, Southern Democratic supporters of Republican Herbert Hoover. But most party leaders remained regular. In Texas, ultradry Democrats organized as the "Anti–Al Smith Democrats of Texas" and selected Alvin Moody of Houston as chairman. The group resolved that the "purpose of the organization shall be the defeat of Gov. Alfred E. Smith for President and the wrestling of Democracy from the grip of Tammany Hall." A fusion electoral ticket was arranged with the Republican party. The Republicans and Anti–Al Smith Democrats flooded the state with literature. Smith's Catholicism was an important issue. J. D. Cranfill admitted to Hoover, "Quite unhappily the Catholic question obtrudes itself here constantly and perhaps more persistently than any other part of the United States." On election day the combined Republicans and Hoovercrats gave Hoover 26,004 more votes than Smith and put Texas into the Republican column for the first time in a presidential election.

The contest between Texas Hoovercrats and party regulars continued into the 1930 gubernatorial race. Former congressman James Young of Kaufman, who had been the leader of the Smith Democrats, and Tom Love, the leader of the Hoovercrats, were candidates. The state Democratic executive committee tried to keep Love off the ballot as a "bolter," but he appealed to the state Supreme Court and was allowed to have his name appear. Governor Moody intended to run for a third term, but he was unwilling to oppose the chairman of the Highway Commission,

Thomas Delashwah (right), proprietor of Delashwah's Drug Store, Austin, ca. 1920s. Delashwah's Drug Store Photographs and Receipts Collection, CAH; CN 02962. Although blacks enjoyed fewer economic opportunities than whites, some, like Delashwah, prospered as the state's economy expanded in the 1920s.

Ross Sterling, a Houston millionaire and former president of Humble Oil Company. Sterling's platform included a call for a large state bond issue to build highways and to relieve the counties of payments on highway bonds. He promised to operate the government on a business basis. Someone said of him: "As a person, Ross Shaw Sterling is a Horatio Alger hero come to life." Jim Ferguson again attempted to secure a place on the ballot, contending that the 1925 amnesty act had removed the disqualification from state officeholding placed upon him in 1917, and that the 1927 repeal of this act had had no effect. The Texas Supreme Court ruled that the amnesty act was unconstitutional, and that the legislature could not remove a penalty imposed by the Senate sitting as a court of impeachment. Mrs. Ferguson then filed for a place on the ballot. Pa's campaign speeches indicated that Ma was running primarily against Dan Moody, who was not even a candidate. Mrs. Ferguson led an 11-candidate field in the first primary with 242,959 votes; Sterling was second with 170,754 votes; and Senator Clint C. Small, who ran on a "let's adjourn politics" platform, was a surprising third with 138,934 votes. Love trailed badly in fourth place with 87,068 votes, and Young was fifth with 73,385 votes. In the run-off, "Fergusonism" was again the main issue. Most of the defeated candidates gave their support to Sterling. The portly Sterling lacked color and was a poor speaker, but he was aided on the stump by such capable speakers as Dan Moody, Walter Woodward, Clint Small, Pink Parrish, and James Young. In the words of Gen. Jacob F. Wolters, one of Sterling's managers, "The issue now was HONEST AND RESPONSIBLE GOVERNMENT VERSUS DISHONEST AND PROXY GOVERNMENT. With that the battle cry, the great moral forces of the state arose and Mr. Sterling was on August 23rd triumphantly nominated." Sterling received 473,371 votes to Mrs. Ferguson's 384,402. The New York *Times* was pleased that the people of Texas, "in a time of economic discontent and even distress, refused to follow adroit and popular demagogues."

By 1932, however, as the depression deepened, Texas voters were ready for a change; and Mrs. Ferguson narrowly defeated Sterling by less than 4,000 votes in the run-off. The Sterling camp charged that voter fraud in East Texas had given her the victory, but Sterling supporters were unable to overturn the result. When Mrs.

Ferguson decided not to seek another term in 1934, the newspapers described the gubernatorial contest (won by Attorney General James Allred) as the quietest in more than 20 years. *Texas Weekly* explained the public's apathy: "It takes a mob-rousing issue like that of Ku Kluxism, prohibition as it used to be, Fergusonism, or something of that kind—a single issue which divides the people into sheep and goats, according to one's point of view—to get the voters excited during the heat of summer. Fortunately, we think, no such issue looms at present." Thus, the three main issues in Texas politics during the 1920s—the Ku Klux Klan, "Fergusonism," and prohibition—had passed away and were replaced by problems arising out of hard times, especially the issue of state old-age pensions, which dominated Texas politics for the remainder of the decade.   *Norman D. Brown*

Great Depression. Texans were optimistic about the future in January 1929. Over the past decade the state population had increased to 5,824,715, representing a gain of more than a million people, or almost 25 percent. Although geared to one crop—"Cotton is King"—the economy was somewhat diversified. In East Texas the Piney Woods accounted for a substantial lumber industry; in the lower Rio Grande valley, with the introduction of irrigation, both truck and citrus farming had proved extremely profitable; on the Edwards Plateau and in West Texas, livestock had established the state as the nation's number-one producer of hides and wool and mohair; and at such sites as Desdemona and Wink, wildcatters pursued the legacy of Spindletop by producing vast amounts of oil and gas. In fact, Texans prided themselves on their situation, in being the largest state—indeed bigger than any western European nation—and in maintaining the American frontier traits of rugged individualism, fierce competitiveness, unblushing patriotism. At the same time they had solidified and strengthened their economic position through political action: the brilliant Dan Moody had been reelected governor, and anti-Catholic Texas Hoovercrats had made their voice heard nationally in the 1928 presidential election.

But on "Black Tuesday," 29 October 1929, 16 million shares of stock changed hands and the New York *Times* industrial average plunged nearly 40 points, thus marking the worst day in Wall Street history to that point. Over the next few weeks stocks on the New York exchange fell by 40 percent, a loss of $26 billion. Concerned and apprehensive, President Hoover reasoned that since the stock market was responsible for the collapse, the way to recovery was to correct the weaknesses within that institution. Having fashioned United States domestic policy over the past nine years, both as secretary of commerce and as president, he could not conceive that the entire economy was unsound. He therefore inundated the news media with expressions of confidence, with continual testimonials by cabinet members and business leaders. For instance, on 4 November 1929, Henry Ford announced that "things are better today than they were yesterday." To keep up the prevailing tempo Hoover also resorted to numerous meetings and conferences at the White House, time and again predicting that the depression was at an end or soon would be. Almost to a person Texans agreed. Through 1930 they persisted in their optimism, in their belief that the depression affected only those moneyed "gamblers" in the stock market, and in their denunciation of greedy easterners who tried to undermine the sound United States economy. They therefore readily supported Hoover's morale crusade. After all, they relied upon the land of their forefathers as well as cattle and oil—

and fortunately the 1929 cotton crop had already been harvested and sold at a healthy price. Besides, New York and financial chaos were far away; and, if need be, Texans could always produce enough from their farms to keep from going hungry.

Even in urban Texas this mindset prevailed, with both community leaders and news media indulging in unrealistic logic and provincial pride. In Fort Worth the *Record–Telegram* and *Star–Telegram*, until the spring of 1931, pointed to increased construction, railroad traffic, oil production, and cattle and poultry sales as stabilizing, if not propitious, influences. "As a matter of fact, in America, we don't know what hard times are," a 1930 *Star–Telegram* editorial asserted. In Austin both university expenditures and state government employment bolstered the economy, while the political activities of the Forty-first Texas Legislature occupied much of the newspaper space. Even though swarms of insects had devastated a bumper crop and the stock market crash had the sobering effect of sweeping away "paper profits and some cash," local merchants, fearing that pessimistic headlines might have deleterious consequences in the economy, boomed the city through advertisements. Typical of their rhetoric was a paid plea to "talk Austin, write about Austin, work for Austin, and live for Austin." In Dallas, the construction business was flourishing in 1930; recent arrivals the year before had seen to that. The East Texas oil boom, centering around Kilgore, lessened thoughts of depression until the summer of 1931, when overproduction and falling prices affected the city economy. In Houston optimism was equally high. Although fear of depression was widespread during the first months following the crash, the *Post–Dispatch* offered a continual salve. "More and more it appears," the editor asserted on 17 November 1929, that "the changes in stock prices are purely an affair of and for stock speculators." Again in March 1930, after the mayor had dismissed a number of city employees and 600 demonstrators had marched in protest, the *Post–Dispatch* announced that "Houston is comparatively free of discontent due to economic conditions." Besides, with proceeds from a busy port nourishing the local economy, with oil refineries being constructed to meet increasing needs of production, and with financier–banker Jesse H. Jones as their leader, Houstonians temporarily ignored harsh realities. And in San Antonio, business leaders seemed afraid to admit depression, especially in the *Express*, even though unemployment and bleak economic conditions were omnipresent. An October 1930 front-page article in the *Express* reported that San Antonio was "one of five cities . . . to which men of billions . . . [were] looking to invest their money"; another on October 5 debunked the "talk of 'depression' and 'money shortage'"; and still another on September 28 noted that economists were predicting "better times . . . in store for San Antonio and the rest of the United States."

As depression worsened across the United States in 1931 and 1932 Texans eventually had to recognized its existence, then attempt to combat its devastating effects. Since the Hoover administration seemed incapable of meeting the people's needs, private charities shouldered the burdens of the poor and desperate until funds were exhausted, whereupon city governments and community leaders intervened. At Temple, after two banks folded in 1931 and cotton dropped between five and six cents a pound, the Retail Merchants Association issued scrip—as did the San Antonio School Board—in denominations of 25 cents, 50 cents, and one dollar. In Midland, Dallas, and Fort Worth the chambers of commerce sponsored gardening projects, either donating land and seed or encouraging people to plant vegetables. In turn, businessmen in

Customers wait to gain access to safety-deposit boxes at City–Central Bank and Trust, San Antonio, October 1, 1931, the first day patrons were granted access to their boxes after the bank failed to open on September 28. San Antonio *Light* Collection, ITC. City–Central Bank and Trust was one of 298 U.S. banks that suspended operations in September 1931.

Fort Worth and San Antonio pledged to hire laborers on a part-time or weekly basis but at the same time passed ordinances not to hire transients; hobo concentrations, soon to be called "Hoovervilles," alarmed Texans. To obtain more money for relief, to provide soup kitchens and breadlines as well as shelter for the hapless, any number of cities—Houston, Dallas, Fort Worth, Austin—sponsored plays or musicals, the proceeds of which went to charity. In rural Texas economic conditions during 1931 and 1932 also deteriorated. But farmers, many of whom were sharecroppers and tenants, were already accustomed to some poverty and therefore did not always realize the degrees of hardship. Yet, as prices plummeted, as drought exacerbated their plight, as debts rose and foreclosures mounted alarmingly, they sought relief from their worsening situation. Nor did Governor Ross Sterling or the Hoover administration, although funneling some funds to farmers through the Reconstruction Finance Corporation, reverse this dire trend. The depression had, indeed, overwhelmed them.

Consequently, Texans sought new solutions to their problems. President Hoover, whom they had ardently supported for over two years, was now a villain of huge proportions, a betrayer of capitalism and democracy, the man who was responsible for their eco-nomic calamity. With grim satisfaction they readily endorsed the debunking of their hero by calling—sometimes laughingly, sometimes savagely—armadillos "Hoover hogs" and pants pockets turned inside out "Hoover flags." So when Democrats nominated Governor Franklin D. Roosevelt of New York for president and John Nance Garner of Uvalde for vice president in the summer of 1932, the election choice was evident. Texans agreed that a "New Deal for the forgotten man" required their backing; the Democratic ticket garnered 88.6 percent of the state vote. Residents of the state, hoping for immediate returns on their political decision, were not disappointed. The state representation in Washington was powerful and influential. Garner performed the "role as liaison man between the administration and Congress" until 1937 and was considered by some to be "the most powerful Vice President in history." Sam Rayburn of Bonham also figured prominently. In the House he chaired the Interstate and Foreign Commerce Committee; as Garner's acknowledged protégé, he was in line for majority leader and, eventually, speaker. Six other Texans also held House chairmanships, including James P. Buchanan of Brenham on Appropriations, Hatton W. Sumners of Dallas on Judiciary, and Marvin Jones of Amarillo on Agriculture;

Salome Rodriguez (left) with a caravan of Mexican repatriates, October, 1931. San Antonio *Light* Collection, ITC. As the United States economy deteriorated, falling wages, loss of jobs, and ineligibility for relief forced several hundred thousand Mexican workers and their families to return to Mexico.

omy in 1933 by aiding passage of the Emergency Farm Mortgage Act, the Farm Credit Act, and the Agricultural Adjustment Act as well as providing drought-relief funds for the Panhandle and West Texas. In 1934 he aided Texas ranchers with the Jones–Connally Act and sugar producers with the Jones–Costigan Sugar Act. The Texas delegation, overall, supported the National Industrial Recovery Act and emergency unemployment, ever mindful that a good deal of federal aid would find its way to Texas.

Officials on the state level during FDR's first term were not nearly as effective. In November 1932 former governor Miriam Ferguson defeated incumbent governor Sterling, who was a victim of depression politics as well as election fraud in East Texas. After her inauguration in January, Mrs. Ferguson tried to deal with the state's pressing economic problems. To avert a financial panic she boldly—and with questionable constitutional authority—declared a bank moratorium on 2 March. Three days later Roosevelt sustained her decree by proclaiming a national bank holiday and promising to reopen all suspended banks within a short time, but under federal guidelines. At the same time, with estimates that the state debt was in the $14 million range, Governor Ferguson repeatedly but unsuccessfully proposed to the legislature both state sales and income taxes. Except for the passage of a two-cent-a-barrel tax on oil, she could reduce deficits only by cutting appropriations. An even more important issue for her administration was unemployment and relief—a problematic matter that led to scandal. The Fergusons were delighted when, late in 1932, the RFC made substantial funds available to the governor, who was to dispense money to counties through three regional chambers of commerce. Here was an excellent opportunity to build an even more powerful political machine with federal money. By executive order, therefore, Mrs. Ferguson established the Texas Relief Commission and selected Lawrence Westbrook as director. Immediately she and her husband and Westbrook brought local relief administrations into their organization and placed the funds in pet banks. Then in May 1933, after Congress passed the Federal Emergency Relief Act, they had an even greater windfall to administer, with the Texas Rehabilitation and Relief Commission specifically instituted by the legislature to oversee and distribute federal money through a system of county boards. Jim Ferguson, at the behest of his wife, became the commission chairman, although without a legal right to do so. Together with Westbrook and several appointees, he filled county boards with constituents and friends.

To keep their political machine well oiled, the Fergusons needed money, and lots of it. Consequently they pressured the legislature to approve a $20 million relief bond issue in the form of a constitutional amendment upon which the electorate would vote. Then they used every possible maneuver to get it adopted. They padded payrolls with supporters, paid poll taxes for "their voters," and financed the campaign, partly with federal funds. The situation in Bexar County exemplified their tactics. The county had 252 people on its payroll with monthly salaries as large as $300, whereas the average county had about 50 employees and sometimes paid them very little. Of course, the Fergusons also appealed to basic greed as well as human compassion. "We told them [social workers] if they wanted more money to give out that they had better vote with us," Bexar County relief administrator Tex Alsbury testified, "and we got them to get the precinct vote. The people . . . were out of work and money. They were hungry and they lined up to vote." As a final coup de grace, the Fergusons persuaded FERA administrator Harry Hopkins to join the campaign. In a radio address three days before

while in the upper house Morris Sheppard headed the Military Affairs Committee and Tom Connally chaired Public Buildings and Grounds. Equally if not more impressive was the position of Jesse Jones. As head of the RFC he managed an economic empire within the government. By 1938 he had disbursed $10 billion to financial institutions, agriculture, railroads, and public works—and, remarkably, practically all of the money was later repaid.

The conservative Texas delegation members, Congressman George H. Mahon candidly stated, were "Democrats first and New Dealers second." But more than anything else they were Texans interested in economic recovery for the United States, hence for their state. Philosophically most of them agreed during Roosevelt's first term with Jones, who bluntly told a convention of resentful bankers in 1933 to be smart, for once, and take the government into partnership. They therefore figured prominently in New Deal legislation. In banking, Garner and Jones—over Roosevelt's opposition—helped incorporate the Federal Deposit Insurance Corporation into the Glass–Steagall Banking Act. To correct many weaknesses in the stock market, Rayburn was instrumental in passing the Truth in Securities Act and the Securities Exchange Act. He was also important in such legislation as the Emergency Railroad Transportation Act, the Federal Communications Act, the Rural Electrification Act, and the Public Utility Holding Company Act. In Agriculture, Marvin Jones helped restructure the agrarian econ-

the election he announced that "the federal government has no intention of continuing to pay 95 percent of the Texas relief bill after the bond election on Saturday." Hence on 26 August 1933, Texans approved of relief for the unemployed. But the Fergusons' ambitious tactics brought questions of corruption, and both legislative chambers called for an investigation. During the fall of 1933 a Senate investigating committee heard conflicting testimony. Yet the issue was soon resolved after Westbrook, director of the Texas Relief Commission, admitted under oath, "I know that in some instances outright fraud has been committed, forgeries, misapplication of funds." As a result, A. R. Johnson, the Austin city manager, replaced Westbrook on 12 February 1934, thus destroying the Ferguson relief machine.

Still another issue during the Ferguson years was the lack of law and order, a problem involving the Texas Rangers, who, during the Democratic primary late in July 1932 supported Governor Ross Sterling—a grave error politically, especially in the Ferguson stronghold of East Texas. In January 1933 the new governor fired every ranger, 44 in all. The results were disastrous. The legislature reduced new ranger salaries, eliminated longevity pay, slashed travel budgets, and limited the force to 32 men. Mrs. Ferguson then appointed new officers, many of whom "by any standard," historian Steve Schuster candidly asserted, "were a contemptible lot." In less than a year one private was convicted of murder; several others in Company D, after having raided a gambling hall in Duval County, were found to have set up their own establishment with the confiscated equipment; and still another, a captain, was arrested for theft and embezzlement. But even worse, the governor began using special ranger commissions as a source of political patronage. Within two years she enlarged the group of special rangers to 2,344 men, thus prompting the Austin *American* to comment that "about all the requirements a person needed . . . to be a Special Ranger was to be a human being." The effects of the rangers' becoming a source of patronage, corruption, and ridicule directed toward state law enforcement were catastrophic. During the Ferguson years crime and violence became widespread, bank holdups and murder commonplace. Soon few states could claim a more vicious assortment of gangsters or provide a safer sanctuary for the criminal element. For instance, residents in the Dallas–Fort Worth area alone included George "Machine-Gun" Kelly, Raymond Hamilton, and "mad-dog killers" Bonnie and Clyde. Who besides Ma Ferguson was responsible for this breakdown in the public defense? To most Texans the answer was obvious. As one newspaper sarcastically remarked, "A Ranger commission and a nickel will get . . . a cup of coffee anywhere in Texas."

Since Mrs. Ferguson decided not to seek reelection in 1934 (she honored the two-term tradition, having first served as governor from 1925 to 1927), the Democratic primary was wide open. Then James Allred stepped into the breach. Clean-cut and personable, the 35-year-old Allred was easily the front runner in the lackluster gubernatorial campaign. As Texas attorney general for the past four years, he had the greatest name recognition of the candidates; he received powerful support from such men as Vice President Garner, Jesse Jones, and former governor Ross Sterling; and he had a well-financed campaign to help him tout the virtues of the New Deal as well as stricter enforcement of the law. Allred led the field of six candidates in the Democratic primary and then defeated wealthy oilman Tom Hunter of Wichita Falls by 40,000 votes in the primary runoff. In November he was the victor over Republican D. E. Wagonner. Once elected, Allred ensured his tenure as governor

Woman of the High Plains [Nettie Featherston]. Photograph by Dorothea Lange. Near Childress. Library of Congress; USF 34-18294-C. At the time of this picture Featherston and her husband, migrant farmworkers with three children, had been out of work for three months. They had sold their car in order to eat and when it last snowed had burned beans to keep warm.

for four years by bringing New Deal money to Texas. He immediately sought permission to issue the remaining $3.5 million from the $20 million relief bonds passed in August 1933, hinting that the federal government might give matching funds for old-age pensions. He next decided to replace the dole to the unemployed with direct work relief. Hence, he focused on the CCC, WPA, NYA, and PWA. As a consequence Texas received, one report stated, more than $166 million by 31 August 1936, of which Washington proffered more than $96 million; another source estimated the total to be $350 million by the end of the year.

The CCC was very active in Texas. At its peak in 1935 the corps had 27 camps in Texas constructing recreational parks and an additional 70 camps for work in forest and soil conservation. Because assignment to states was random, many Texans participated in other states' CCC camps, joining some 2,500,000 men across the country. In addition to economic aid, the CCC left an architectural legacy in Texas, seen today in buildings in 31 state parks and several city and county parks. The NYA also greatly benefited Texans, specifically those of ages 16 to 25. Under the leadership of 27-year-old Lyndon Baines Johnson, the state program provided support for high school students in 248 counties as well as for young people in 83 colleges and universities. For two years, beginning in the summer of 1935, Johnson employed 10,000 to 18,000 students a month

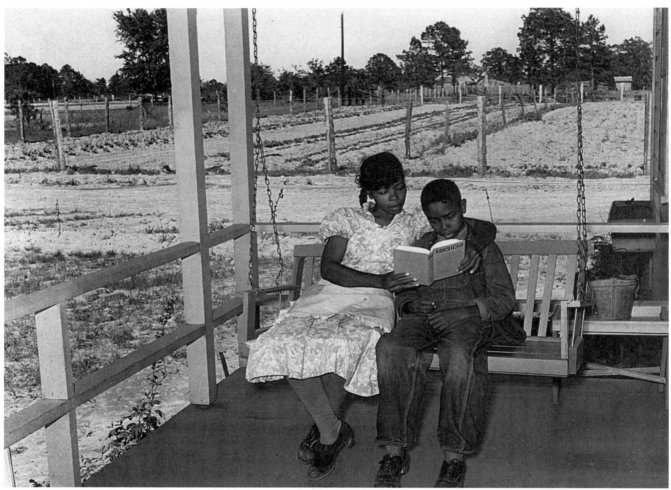

Sabine Farms, a Farm Security Administration project for Negroes, by Russell Lee. Twelve miles south of Marshall, 1939. Library of Congress; USF 34-33107-D. Sabine Farms was one of 11 community projects launched in Texas under New Deal legislation. This East Texas project comprised 120 farm units of 80 acres each, and offered tenants a cooperative store, community center, and crafts building.

"at various part-time clerical or maintenance jobs earning a maximum $6.00 per month in high school and $15.00 in college." In out-of-school work programs he hired more than 12,000 young Texans who, in turn, constructed 250 roadside parks, graveled the shoulders of 2,000 miles of highway, improved or built recreational facilities in 76 state parks, and refurbished the playgrounds of public schools. Because of Johnson, NYA programs helped 19,000 young African Americans, the primary requisite for selection being that of "need." But the emergency public employment programs of the PWA and WPA were equally if not more helpful to the state economy. In Fort Worth, for example, these federal agencies expended $15 million on a variety of projects. From 1935 to 1938 they "completely modernized the entire school system," historian John McClung asserted, "making it one of the best in the state." The PWA constructed 13 school buildings and made additions to 13 more, while rehabilitating most of the existing structures. In conjunction with these projects, the agency "landscaped and beautified fifty-four of the existing sixty-three school grounds." These agencies also provided funds for red-brick roads, some of which are still in existence, the 12,000-seat concrete high school stadium named Farrington Field, Will Rogers Memorial Coliseum and Auditorium, John Peter Smith City–County Hospital, a new city

hall and jail, a new public library, and the Fort Worth Rose Garden. Together with the Federal Writers' Project, whereby scholars were hired to index newspapers and record local history, the Federal Theater Project and the Federal Art Project provided money for artists and thespians to develop their crafts.

Another aid to the state's economy at this time was the Texas Centennial celebration in 1936. Despite the depression, the Texas Centennial Commission was formed in September 1934 to plan the celebration, and the legislature passed an appropriations bill for the effort in April 1935. With additional federal assistance, the state centered its activities on Dallas, where a $25 million effort was put into transforming Fair Park into a world's fair with permanent buildings. Work proceeded quickly, and with a very positive effect on the local economy. In June 1936 President Roosevelt joined Governor Allred, who was campaigning for his second term, in visiting the grounds. In addition to the Dallas festivities, the celebration included a program of permanent monuments, markers, museums, and restorations, as well as a highly successful publicity and advertising campaign.

Allred was a willing conduit for massive amounts of federal funds. At the same time, however, he dealt with a number of state problems that greatly affected his constituency. In both regular and special sessions the legislators, at his behest, authorized a state planning board, appropriated $11 million for higher education, and set aside $10 million for rural relief. Allred also established the Texas Department of Public Safety, which brought the famed Texas Rangers and the uniformed Highway Patrol under one aegis, thereby fulfilling one of his major campaign promises—better law enforcement. After Congress passed the National Social Security Act in August 1935, he pushed through complementary legislation having to do with old-age pensions, unemployment compensation, teacher retirement, and aid for needy children and the blind. At the same time he increased the state deficit to $19 million. Because he made needed reforms and provided governmental service, Jimmie Allred, as the New Deal governor of Texas, governed popularly and reasonably well.

Yet in 1937–38, despite great political influence in Washington, ready access to federal money, and Allred's leadership, a number of Texans began to harbor grave reservations about the New Deal and, particularly, the power of the president. After the November elections of 1936, in which Roosevelt carried all but two states (the electoral vote was 523 to 8), Vice President Garner appeared to be more and more alienated. With increasing frequency he openly criticized New Deal spending programs, while abhorring labor's newest tactic against management, the sit-down strike. Texans were further distanced from the president when, on 5 February 1937, FDR announced his plan to reorganize the judiciary, including a proposal to increase the membership of the Supreme Court. This controversial "court-packing" recommendation, which would allow the president to add a justice (up to six) to the court each time an incumbent member turned 70 but did not retire, was Roosevelt's attempt to overcome the high court's rulings against various New Deal laws. Garner, together with Sam Rayburn, Hatton Sumners, Tom Connally, and most of the Texas delegation, was firmly opposed. The plan ultimately failed in Congress. Then, in the midyear elections of 1938, Roosevelt committed the ultimate political sin, as far as they were concerned; he tried to purge the Democratic party of those who had opposed New Deal programs. On his hit list were eight Texas congressmen—Martin Dies, Richard M. Kleberg, Fritz (Frederick G.) Lanham, Joseph J. Mansfield, Milton H. West, Clyde L. Garrett, Nat Patton, and Sumners—all of whom won against Roosevelt men in the primaries, while New Deal incumbents Maury Maverick and W. D. McFarlane lost. These political events, coupled with the formation of a vitriolic anti-Roosevelt group who called themselves the Jeffersonian Democrats (led by J. Evetts Haley, Joseph W. Bailey, Jr., and J. M. West), nurtured opposition throughout the state against the New Deal.

But in the spring of 1938 a political phenomenon took place in Texas that overshadowed these party struggles and allowed Texans to focus upon one central figure—"Pappy" O'Daniel. O'Daniel was a Fort Worth businessman and radio personality who sold Hillbilly Flour with the use of a three-man band known as the Light Crust Doughboys. He announced his candidacy for governor on 1 May 1938, after receiving more than 54,000 letters in one week "begging" him to run. He then proceeded to dumbfound political analysts and stun his opponents. Using campaign techniques that resembled the old-fashioned revivalism of camp meetings, he stumped the state in a bus, playing traditional songs and Gospel music before passing collection plates in the form of barrels labeled "Flour—not Pork." Texans had not seen anything like him, not even Pa Ferguson. For what could opponents say about a man whose platform was the Ten Commandments and motto the

Golden Rule, who pledged a pension of $30 a month for every Texan over 65, and who recited to attentive, enraptured audiences such poems as "The Boy Who Never Got Too Old To Comb His Mother's Hair"? When newsmen and opponents pointed out that O'Daniel had not been civic-minded enough to pay a $1.75 poll tax in order to vote, he damned the professional politicians, declaring that "no politician in Texas is worth $1.75." In a field of 13, which included Attorney General William McCraw of Dallas, Railroad Commissioner Ernest O. Thompson of Amarillo, and Tom Hunter of Wichita Falls, O'Daniel soon became the front runner, and in the July Democratic primary he won by a majority of 30,000 votes.

For almost three years the O'Daniel aura held sway in state politics, although without much legislative impact. After his inauguration in January 1939, at which 100,000 people jammed into Memorial Stadium at the University of Texas, the new governor quickly demonstrated his inability to lead, his ineptness in dealing with the legislature, and his lack of understanding of the art of government. To support his pension plan and provide money for a state budget, O'Daniel proposed a 1.6 percent tax on business transactions, actually a well-concealed multiple sales tax, which the legislature promptly rejected. He then campaigned for a constitutional amendment whereby the electorate would vote upon the merits of a state sales tax; however, a militant minority in the House, the "56 Club," prevented its passage. Consequently, to cut costs as well as retaliate against hostile legislators, Pappy line-item-vetoed a number of appropriations that were important to the well-being of Texans: for new state-hospital buildings; beds for epileptics, orphans, and the feeble-minded; and funds for the Texas Department of Public Safety and State Highway Department. This last economy resulted in the Texas Rangers having, at times, "to borrow ammunition from highway patrolmen." Equally inappropriate, if not laughable, were many of his appointments. For example, as state labor commissioner he selected a desk worker at Southwestern Bell Telephone Company who was not even an officer in his own union and whose only qualification was a letter he wrote praising one of O'Daniel's radio addresses. For the state highway commission O'Daniel chose oilman J. M. West of Houston, a leading Jeffersonian Democrat; the Senate, fearing the possible loss of federal road funds, immediately rejected this nomination.

Despite this carnival in Austin and his lack of accomplishment, O'Daniel remained strong with the people. In the Democratic primary of 1940 he proved that his first election was not a fluke, that his vote-getting powers were a reality. Against a fairly strong field, including Ma Ferguson, Railroad Commissioner Jerry Sadler, Highway Commissioner Harry Hines, and Ernest O. Thompson, he polled a majority of a little more than 102,000 votes. In the spring of 1941 the stalemate between the governor and the legislature therefore continued—that is, until circumstances dictated a political realignment—and O'Daniel staged an accompanying farce. On 9 April, United States senator Morris Sheppard died, and O'Daniel, although himself desiring the position, had to appoint a "suitable and qualified" interim replacement. So on San Jacinto Day, 21 April, he selected someone who would never be a threat to his own candidacy, 87-year-old Andrew Jackson Houston, the only surviving son of Sam Houston. One veteran politician observed, "That old man probably couldn't tell you whether the sun was up or had gone down." At any rate, Houston was sworn in on 2 June and filled this prestigious position until his death later in the month. In the meantime O'Daniel geared himself for the June special election to fill Sheppard's seat. The competition was formidable. Besides

Congressman Martin Dies and Attorney General Gerald Mann, the young congressman Lyndon Johnson, who received the support of FDR as well as most of the moneyed people in Texas, announced against him. A number of people actually wanted to get O'Daniel out of Texas, however, by sending him to Washington. Reputedly Jim Ferguson, who "had been very friendly with the liquor interests for close to three decades," feared that the governor would appoint "good clean honest Christian dry citizens" to the state Liquor Control Board and was thus campaigning for his election to the Senate. But more important for O'Daniel was the tremendous support from the friends of Lieutenant Governor Coke Stevenson, who would inherit the governorship if O'Daniel went to the Senate. After a hard-fought, expensive campaign O'Daniel once again proved his resiliency by receiving a plurality of votes over LBJ of 175,590 to 174,279. In August 1941, with O'Daniel's resignation, Stevenson became governor. The turbulent rivalry between the executive and legislative branches subsided, and none too soon. Within four months, on 7 December, the Japanese attacked Pearl Harbor and the United States entered World War II.

Ben H. Procter

World War II. *Stateside.* On the home front during World War II Texans sacrificed whatever was necessary to support "our boys overseas." Rationing became a way of life; stamp books for meat, sugar, coffee, shoes, rubber, auto parts, and eventually gasoline became a necessity. At increasingly frequent intervals communities held scrap-iron drives; adults bought war bonds; school children had time allotted during class periods to buy, then paste, savings stamps in bond books; and many a family, as in World War I, planted "victory gardens" to conserve food for the war effort. During these years the war conquered the Great Depression, which became only a memory. Along the Gulf Coast from the Beaumont–Port Arthur area southward to Corpus Christi, the greatest petrochemical industry in the world was built to refine fuel for the American war machine. Farmers, with prices high, cultivated the soil to its maximum, thereby helping the United States become the granary for the Allied nations. And wartime industries mushroomed throughout Texas: steel mills in Houston and Daingerfield, the largest tin smelter in the world in Texas City, enormous aircraft factories in Garland, Grand Prairie, and Fort Worth, extensive shipyards in Beaumont, Port Arthur, Houston, Galveston, and Corpus Christi, a revitalized paper and wood-pulp industry in East Texas, and munitions and synthetic rubber factories in different parts of the state. As a result manufacturing increased fourfold, from $453 million in 1939 to $1.9 billion in 1944. Labor was therefore at a premium, especially with men in the service, with defense contracts readily available, and with wages escalating. Consequently, 500,000 Texans moved from rural areas to job markets in nearby cities, as did thousands of people from other states. Women entered heretofore male occupations as punchpress operators, assemblyline workers, and riveters—hence a popular song of the day, "Rosie the Riveter."

While the state government cooperated with federal authorities to sustain an allout war effort, Governor Coke R. Stevenson seemed to epitomize a dual role, that of cooperation as well as representation of Texas interests. Because of his relaxed demeanor— he was a pipe smoker with a calm expression that seldom betrayed his thoughts—this staunchly conservative man received the appellation "Calculating Coke" from Capitol correspondents. Although he accepted rationing in 1942, Stevenson denounced gas rationing

Two 18 year old boys waiting for their physical exams prior to induction into the army. Photograph by John Vachon. San Augustine, Texas, April 1943. Library of Congress; LC-USW3 25296-D. Hundreds of thousands of Texans entered the United States armed forces in World War II. Many were barely of age, like the two pictured here, seated under a notice that encouraged them to join up.

in Texas, where gasoline was as much a necessity, he asserted, as "the saddle, the rifle, the ax, and the Bible." He also negotiated a nostrike agreement with labor, an arrangement that pleased Texans. He received high approval ratings from his constituency for raising departmental budgets, while eliminating the $42 million debt that had accrued since the depression. During these war years Stevenson improved the state highway system, raised public school salaries, initiated a building program for the University of Texas, and emphasized the necessity of soil conservation.

During the Stevenson administrations a number of trends developed that greatly affected Texas in postwar years. After 1937 the Jeffersonian Democrats gained adherents, and with each passing year their disaffection hardened. In 1940 they were appalled when Roosevelt ran for a third term; four years later he repeated this desecration, which, they believed, was leading the nation toward dictatorship. Besides, he was far too liberal for them, first in his support of labor unions, then in New Deal spending programs, and, most devastating of all, in replacing Vice President John Nance Garner of Texas in 1940 with leftwinger Henry A. Wallace of Iowa. And if price-fixing of Texas oil was not enough, then the president's "Communist" wife Eleanor surely was. Many Texans deplored her outspoken support for black equality under the law, together with the Supreme Court decision in *Smith v. Allwright* (1944), by which blacks obtained the right to participate in white primaries. Consequently in 1944 the Jeffersonian Democrats formed a new political organization named the Texas Regulars. In the November election they polled 135,000 votes for president, even though no one headed the ticket. They caused tremendous difficulties in postwar Texas for the dominant Democratic party.

Many Texas Regulars and those of like ilk also concerned themselves with higher education as represented at the University of Texas. Under Governors W. Lee O'Daniel and Coke Stevenson they became a majority in the University of Texas board of regents and then attempted to rectify what they considered to be the evils of academia. In the spring of 1942 the regents, by a fourtotwo vote, fired three liberal economics instructors. Over the course of the next two years they tried to abolish the tenure system, but University of Texas president Homer Price Rainey obstinately blocked their efforts. After they proscribed John Dos Passos's novel *USA* from a supplemental reading list of the English Department, declaring it to be obscene and perverted, Rainey dramatically denounced the regents at a general faculty meeting on 12 October 1944. Three weeks later they fired him. Such threats to academic freedom and the growth of higher education were of utmost concern to Texans in August 1945, especially since Rainey decided to run for governor in 1946.

In turn, conditions emanating from World War II motivated minorities to demand equal partnership in Texas. Blacks, suffering from segregation under the "separate but equal" clause of *Plessy v. Ferguson* (1896), saw no change in attitude by Governor Stevenson. In Texarkana on 13 July 1942, a mob dragged black Texan Willie Vinson from a hospital bed and hanged him after he was identified by a white woman as the man who had victimized her; the governor, however, took no action on the matter, reasoning that "even a white man would have been lynched for this crime." Again on the night of 15 June 1943, when a riot exploded in Beaumont, where three people were killed and hundreds injured, Stevenson ordered the president pro tem of the Senate to handle it since both he and Lieutenant Governor John Lee Smith were at that time out of the state. Then in 1944 came the *Smith v. Allwright* decision and in August 1945 the end of the war.

Since 257,798 African Americans from Texas had registered under the selective service system and approximately onethird had served in segregated units usually commanded by white officers, they returned home after being discharged more militant in their demands for equal rights under the law. Mexican Americans were also discriminated against, but usually in less obvious ways. In 1945 thousands of Hispanics, upon returning home from service to their country—five had won the Medal of Honor—were determined to seek equality under the law. By 1948 the American G.I. Forum had formed to protest discrimination against Mexican-American veterans and soldiers. Women too increased their demands for equality,

Mother who works in the shipyard calling for her son at the nursery school at 6 p.m. Photograph by John Vachon. Orange, Texas, May 1943. Library of Congress; LC-USW3 27980-D. Texas women did their share during World War II, not only taking over men's jobs in factories and in shipyards, but continuing with their traditional work. Children also had to adjust to new living conditions.

having been placed in the same category, one writer stated, "with minors and idiots." Although having the right to vote, they could not serve on juries and grand juries until 1 January 1955. Nor could a woman buy a car or house or stocks and bonds, make contracts, agree to promissory notes, sue if injured, or sign a bail bond without her husband's signature. In fact, she could not establish a business without the court's permission and, even then, could not have a credit rating. And besides suffering salary discrimination both in public and private sectors, women had to endure a double standard under the law. As much as anything else, however, in 1945 Texas women had to combat "tradition and custom," Judge Sarah T. Hughes insightfully asserted, as well as being "satisfied with their role" or "too humble about their abilities."

Yet during World War II the most obvious changes in Texas were demographic and economic. Because of wartime demands people migrated to the state in increasing numbers, as many as 450,000 in less than four years. Since industrial jobs were plentiful in or near such cities as Houston, San Antonio, Austin, Dallas, and Fort Worth, Texans saw rapid urbanization, along with its accompanying benefits and evils. In turn, oil became the dominant resource and commodity in the state. Cotton and cattle were no longer "king," and the petrochemical industry along the Gulf Coast stimulated the economy. Texans, however, had instituted a more diversified approach in productivity during the war years. In West Texas, from El Paso to the Pecos River to the Panhandle, farmers depended more and more on irrigation and scientific agriculture; in East Texas a number of people shifted to the dairy industry and cattle ranching, while maintaining a prosperous lumber industry; and, from Brownsville to Laredo, the Rio Grande valley continued its development as a lush truckfarming and citrus

General Dynamics aircraft factory, 1943. Courtesy Lockheed Martin. With the outbreak of World War II, the aviation industry came to Fort Worth. The General Dynamics Fort Worth division manufactured B-24 and C-87 cargo aircraft.

country. With better roads connecting all parts of the state, with rural electrification touching even the most remote areas, and with more than 600,000 veterans returning home in anticipation of enjoying greater freedoms and the benefits of a victorious war, Texas in 1945 was moving to a more diversified, urban status.

Military installations of every type were located in Texas during World War II. Some of these, such as at Fort Sam Houston at San Antonio and Fort Bliss at El Paso, existed before the war and served as headquarters for various army commands. Others, such as Camp Wolters near Mineral Wells, Camp Fannin near Tyler, Camp Howze near Gainesville, Camp Bowie near Brownwood, and Camp Hood near Killeen, were opened immediately before or during the war. Twenty combat divisions comprising more than 1,200,000 troops trained at the 15 major army camps in Texas between 1940 and the end of 1945. Texas was the center for training army and naval airmen during the war. Randolph Air Field at San Antonio, dedicated in 1930, was known as the "West Point of the Air" and served as a major base for pilot instruction. Kelly and Brooks Fields, located nearby, were enlarged, and Ellington Field near Houston was reactivated. The national headquarters of the Air Force Training Command was located at Carswell Field in Fort Worth. The largest naval flight-training center in the world was opened at Corpus Christi just before Pearl Harbor. An estimated 200,000 airmen, including 45,000 pilots, 12,000 bombardiers, 12,000 navigators, and thousands of aerial gunners, photographers, and mechanics, were trained at the 40 military airfields in Texas.

More prisoners of war were housed in Texas during World War II than in any other state. More than 50,000 prisoners, mainly Germans but also 3,000 Italians and 1,000 Japanese, were held in 21 prisoner base camps and more than 20 branch camps located throughout the state. The largest camps were at Mexia, Hereford, Hearne, and Huntsville. Early in the war maximum security for the prisoners was maintained but gradually this was changed to allow utilization of prisoners as badly needed agricultural workers. Many prisoners replaced American personnel at military bases as clerks, bakers, carpenters, electricians, groundskeepers, machinists, and mechanics. In addition to the POW camps there were three camps opened in Texas to house Japanese Americans removed from the West Coast by the Western Defense Command. Operated by the Immigration and Naturalization Service, the World War II internment camps were located at Seagoville, Kenedy, and Crystal City. By the end of the war 5,000 Japanese were housed in these camps.

Ben H. Procter

Texans in service. The Japanese attack on American military installations in Hawaii on 7 December 1941 brought the United States into World War II. Although the aerial bombardment of Pearl Harbor was a surprise, American entry into the war raging in Europe and Asia was not totally unexpected. The United States had opposed the expansionistic moves of Japan in the Far East, and Germany and Italy in Europe and Africa, throughout the 1930s. The invasion of Poland in 1939, followed by the fall of France in the summer of 1940, increased American concerns for national security. While the majority of American people opposed direct involvement in the foreign conflict, they supported efforts to aid those nations opposing aggression and to strengthen our own defenses. Texans strongly supported Roosevelt's steps to aid the British, French, and Chinese and to strengthen national defense. Texas congressmen, with the exception of Martin Dies and Hatton W. Sumners (who abstained), voted for the Burke–Wadsworth Selective Service Act of 1940, which instituted the first peace-time

draft in American history. Texas congressmen, particularly Senator Tom Connally, who chaired the Senate Foreign Relations Committee, played leadership roles in the debate over the Lend Lease bill to provide war supplies to nations resisting aggression. The entire Texas delegation, except Joseph Mansfield, voted for the bill, which passed the House by 260 to 165 and the Senate by 60 to 31 in early 1941.

Texans reacted quickly to the attack on Pearl Harbor. Connally introduced the joint resolution for a declaration of war with Japan on December 8. Several days later he introduced similar resolutions for war with Germany and Italy, Japan's allies who had declared war on the United States. Texas governor Coke Stevenson urged support for the war effort, denouncing the "cowardly Japanese attack." He predicted accurately that Texans would respond enthusiastically to defend their country. Long lines of men gathered at recruiting stations to volunteer for military service. Although Texas had 5 percent of the United States population, it provided 7 percent of those who served in the armed forces. Secretary of the Navy Frank Knox later declared that Texas had contributed a larger percentage of men to the armed forces than any other state. By the end of the war 750,000 Texans, including 12,000 women, served in the armed forces. The majority were in the army and the air force, but nearly onefourth served in the navy, marines, or coast guard. During the war 22,022 Texans were killed. One-third of these fatalities were in the navy, marines, or coast guard.

Texans served with distinction in various theaters of operations in World War II. Among the first to see action were members of the Second Battalion, 131st Field Artillery of the Thirty-sixth Infantry Division, the Texas National Guard. Detached from the division in the fall of 1941, the battalion was rushed to the Far East, where artillery was badly needed. The battalion was captured on Java when the Japanese overran the Dutch East Indies. Together with captured survivors of the cruiser *Houston*, sunk in the Sundra Strait on 1 March 1942, members of the unit came to be known as the Lost Battalion because for a year no one at home knew what had happened to them. The men of the battalion spent the rest of the war in Japanese prison camps. The 112th Cavalry Regiment, another Texas unit to see service in the Pacific, was stationed at Fort Bliss and Fort Clark before the war. The regiment, made up mainly of Texans, was the last American unit to serve on horseback in the war. After being sent to New Caledonia to guard an air base, the 112th took part in heavy fighting in New Britain, Leyte, and Luzon, along with the First Cavalry Division, another regular army unit stationed in Texas before the war. The First Cavalry, dismounted for jungle fighting, captured Los Negros in the Admiralty Islands group in February 1944. A year later the First Cavalry was the first American division to reach Manila in the reconquest of the Philippines. The 103d and 144th Infantry regiments were other Texas units to see extensive action in the Pacific.

Texans also played an active role in the war in Europe. The Thirty-sixth Division was the first American division to invade Europe. Mobilized at Camp Bowie (Brown County) on 25 November 1940, the division trained in Texas, Louisiana, and Florida before landing in North Africa in April 1943. The division stormed ashore at Salerno on 9 September 1943, participated in the ill-fated and controversial attempt to cross the Rapido River, and took part in the liberation of Rome, the invasion of southern France, and fighting in Alsace and the Ardennes. When the war ended the division was in Austria. In all, the Thirty-sixth was in

Coke Stevenson speaking at Washington-on-the-Brazos, 1946. Prints and Photographs Collection, Coke Stevenson file, CAH; CN 08123. Governor from 1941 to 1946, the deeply conservative Coke Stevenson supported American entry into World War II and forced state agencies to cut their budgets drastically as a patriotic measure. He feuded with federal bureaucrats, however, over rationing of beef and gasoline.

combat 19 months, fought in 5 major campaigns, engaged in 2 amphibious assaults, and captured more than 175,000 prisoners. The division suffered among the highest casualties for any American unit: 3,717 killed, 12,685 wounded, and 3,064 missing in action, or 19,466 total. Men from other states served in the division as the war went on, but it continued to be identified as a Texas unit. Displaying the Lone Star flag and wearing the famous T-patch on their shoulders, men of the Thirty-sixth were proud to be known as the "Texas army." The Ninetieth Division, composed originally of national guardsmen and draftees from Texas and Oklahoma, also saw much action in Europe. The division was activated at Camp Barkeley near Abilene in March 1942. It landed on Utah Beach on D day, 1944. As a part of Gen. George Patton's Third Army, the Ninetieth took part in Operation Cobra, the Allied breakout in northern Europe. The Ninetieth drove across France in the summer of 1944, participated in heavy fighting at Metz and in the Saar, and played a role in relieving besieged American forces in the Ardennes. The division was in Czechoslovakia when the war ended. Like the Thirty-sixth Division, the Ninetieth sustained heavy casualties, especially in the savage struggle in the Bocage hedgerow country of Normandy. The Second Infantry, a regular army division, was another unit that had strong ties with Texas. The division was headquartered at Fort Sam Houston in San Antonio before the war. Identified by its Indian-head shoulder patch, the Second Division landed at Omaha beach the day after the initial American assault. It formed a part of the United States First Army, first under Omar Bradley and later under Courtney Hodges. Like the Ninetieth Division, the Second fought its way across France in the summer and fall of 1944. It crossed the Rhine at the Remagen bridgehead in March 1945 and was in Leipzig when the war ended.

Individual Texans distinguished themselves in various theaters of the war. Thirty-three Texans won the Medal of Honor—twenty-five in the army or air force and eight in the navy or marines. One of these, Lt. Audie L. Murphy, was the most highly decorated

American in the war. Commander Samuel D. Dealey of Dallas, another Texas recipient of the Medal of Honor, was the most highly decorated man in the United States Navy. James Earl Rudder was decorated for his service as commander of the Second Ranger Battalion at D-day. More than 150 generals and 12 admirals were either natives or residents of Texas. Dwight D. Eisenhower, the supreme Allied commander in Europe, was born in Denison and was stationed at Fort Sam Houston when the war began. Chester W. Nimitz, appointed commander of the Pacific Fleet after the Pearl Harbor disaster, was a Fredericksburg native and descendant of a pioneer Texas German family. William Simpson, commanding general of the Ninth Army, which fought its way across France and Germany under Eisenhower's command, was the son of a Confederate veteran and a native of Weatherford. Jonathan M. Wainwright, who surrendered American forces at Corregidor after Douglas MacArthur's departure to Australia, was a native of Washington but spent much of his military career stationed in Texas and made his home in Texas after the war. Walter Krueger, a native of Germany who became commanding general of the Sixth Army, which served under MacArthur in the liberation of the Philippines, considered San Antonio his home. Commerce native Claire L. Chennault, former high school teacher and fighter pilot, organized the American Volunteer Group, the legendary Flying Tigers, which fought with the Chinese against the Japanese before Pearl Harbor. He was recalled to active duty when the United States entered the war and commanded army air forces in China. Oveta Culp Hobby, wife of former Texas governor William P. Hobby, was appointed to develop and command the United States Women's Army Corps.

Many of the Texans who fought in World War II were members of minority groups. Doris Miller, a black man from Waco, served on the USS *West Virginia* and courageously manned a machine gun under attack, with unknown results. His vessel, the USS *Liscome*, was lost with all hands two years later. Another black mess attendant from Texas, Leonard Roy Harmon from Cuero, received the Navy Cross posthumously for bravery in caring for the wounded while his ship, the USS *San Francisco*, was under attack in the

Sherman tanks of the Second Armored ("Hell on Wheels") Division roll through a German city, spring 1945. Courtesy Fourth Infantry Division Museum, Fort Hood, Texas. Fort Hood was used as a training center for tank destroyers in World War II. By late June 1943, more than 95,000 soldiers were in camp there.

Cleto Rodríguez. Courtesy U.S. Department of the Army, Office of the Chief of Information, Washington. Photograph courtesy ITC. Rodríguez was one of 33 Texans who were awarded the Medal of Honor for service during World War II.

Solomon Islands. When the Japanese attacked Pearl Harbor, Hispanics from across the state responded to the nation's call for military service. Five Tejanos, Lucian Adams of Port Arthur, Macario García of Sugar Land, José M. López of Brownsville, Silvestre S. Herrera of El Paso, and Cleto L. Rodríguez of San Antonio, received the Medal of Honor. Another Mexican Texan, Dr. Hector García, won the Bronze Star and six battle stars while serving in North Africa and Italy. After the war García founded the American G.I. Forum of Texas to help Hispanic veterans.

Ralph A. Wooster

Since World War II. The last five decades of the twentieth century witnessed the further transformation of Texas from a rural and agricultural state to an urban, industrial one. The changes caused new problems and exacerbated old ones for a population grounded in agrarian values. Two-party politics emerged as the state's electorate turned from a near absolute allegiance to its Southern Democratic heritage to one that frequently elected Republican officeholders. The changing demography of the state intensified political rivalries. The high birthrate among Hispanics and their increased migration into Texas made them the state's largest minority ethnic group. Mexican Americans joined African Americans in demanding a more positive political response to the needs of minorities. The federal government abetted their cause through court decisions and legislation that struck down legal segregation. The sex ratio of the population changed, as women out-

numbered men in Texas by 1960. Many women renounced their traditional political, social, and economic roles. Interstate migrations also shaped a different Texas. The state's location in the Sun Belt and its economic boom during the 1970s and early 1980s brought newcomers from outside the rural and Southern traditions. These joined with intrastate migrants in population centers that increasingly forced the legislature to address the needs of an urban society.

Population statistics testified to the emergence of an industrial state. The census of 1950 recorded 7,711,194 Texans, a 20.2 percent increase over 1940. The population grew further over the next several decades, to 9,579,677 in 1960, 11,198,655 in 1970, 14,229,191 in 1980, and 16,986,510 in 1990. Texas was the third most populous state in 1990, after California and New York, having moved past Ohio and Illinois in the sixties and Pennsylvania in the seventies. The economic boom in the late seventies and early eighties brought some of the spectacular growth; 500,000 immigrants moved to Texas between 1970 and 1975, 1,000,000 more came over the next five years, and nearly 1,000,000 more came in the early eighties. Texans were predicted to outnumber New Yorkers by 1990, but an economic downturn in the eighties prevented this. The net immigration dropped to 32,000 in 1986 but increased thereafter.

The dominant migration pattern in postwar Texas was movement from the countryside to the city. Statisticians reported in 1945 that some 500,000 Texans left 200 rural counties to join the wartime industrial workforce in the 54 urban counties. The 1950 census failed to show an expected return of the workers to the farms but reported that, for the first time in the state's history, more Texans lived in the city than in the country. More than 80 percent of the state's population resided in urban areas in 1990, a figure that exceeded the national average. Houston grew from 384,514 inhabitants in 1940 to 1,630,553 in 1990, Dallas from 294,734 to 1,006,877, and San Antonio from 253,854 to 935,933. If one linked Fort Worth to Dallas, about half of the state lived in the metropolitan areas of these four cities.

The declining agricultural population marked a change in the nature of farming both in Texas and in the nation. Most Texans would have identified farm bankruptcies, farm tenancy, and depressed crop prices as the major economic weaknesses besetting the state before World War II. New Dealers argued that raising agricultural prices through planned scarcity would be the best method both to produce a disposable income for the population and to combat the Great Depression. Congress enacted legislation designed to establish parity prices by reducing overproduction and bringing supply more in line with demand. This general policy, although with much political contentiousness, has remained the cornerstone of federal farm policy. One of its results was to drive marginal farmers and tenants off the land and into the city. State agencies and agricultural colleges endorsed the government's position and encouraged efficiency and mechanization as solutions for farm woes. Agricultural statistics reflected the move from country to city and from small farms to agribusinesses. The farm population declined from 1,500,000 in 1945 to 215,000 in 1980, the number of farms from 384,977 to 186,000, and farmworkers from 350,000 (including parttime workers in the cottonfields) to 85,000. During this period the average farm size almost doubled to more than 700 acres, and the value of buildings and land per farm increased from $9,286 to $275,047. Even if inflation skewed the latter figures, they still revealed that the modern Texas farmer no longer tilled the small family farm that characterized the very recent history of the state. In 1986 fewer than 2 percent of Texans were producers on farms and ranches.

Although agriculture no longer dominated the Texas economy, farming remained an essential ingredient for prosperity. Some 20 to 25 percent of the population supplied, processed, or marketed agricultural products in the eighties, and their activities in 1990 put $40 billion into the Texas economy. The sources of income recalled the past. In value, cattle ranked first among agricultural products in 1986. They had held this position for most of the postwar years, with cotton holding the second spot and edging into first place only during the drought years 1954 and 1955. In the era of family farms, corn usually trailed cotton in acreage planted, but in the 1980s grain sorghum and wheat vied for that distinction. In 1986 their combined value almost totaled that of cotton. Overall the state placed either second or third among states in the value of agricultural products during most of the period. But like all other agricultural states, Texas faced a farm crisis in the late 1980s. Farm income peaked in 1979. Afterward, increasing global agricultural competition and the high interest rates of the early eighties squeezed the American farmers. The resulting agricultural depression stimulated both state and national governments to reevaluate their farm policies. No clear-cut solutions have yet emerged.

World War II launched industrialization in Texas. The state's climate, its powerful leaders in the Democratic party, and its abundance of petroleum encouraged the location of military posts, the growth of the construction business, the rise of defense industries, and the expansion of petrochemical facilities within its boundaries. Per capita income in the state more than doubled during the war, to $1,234, or 85.2 percent of the national average, and the value added by manufacturing more than tripled, to $1,727,476,000. Six northern states accounted for more than 50 percent of the nation's manufacturing value, and Texas was a distant twelfth. In 1950 Texans, 5.1 percent of the nation's population, produced 2.3 percent of its goods. Industrial growth modified that. In 1986 Texas had 7 percent of the population of the United States, accounted for 7.4 percent of the gross national product, and employed one of every 11 of the country's workers. A 1987 profile of the industry of the state mirrored that of the nation. Trades and services provided almost 50 percent of the workforce. Government employed more people than manufacturing; together the two hired nearly a third of the state's workers. Finance, insurance and real estate, transportation and public utilities, construction, and mining filled out the business base of Texas. Although the rate of inflation in the postwar economy confounded any simple method of calculating the state's real economic growth, the value added by manufacturing in 1984 stood at $55,556,000,000, when Texas was fourth among the states. The per capita income of Texans matched the national average in 1981 for the first time, but the downturn in the state's economy reversed the upward trend temporarily.

The comptroller of public accounts described the Texas economy of the late 1980s as being in a period of transition. The oil and gas industry, which had been probably the most important key to Texas economic growth, could no longer be counted upon to dominate future prosperity. Oil production rose from 754,710,000 barrels in 1945 to a high of 1,301,685,000 in 1972. Even though wells pumped at near capacity after that, production figures declined for several years. The Organization of Petroleum Exporting Countries agreed to limit the supply of oil in 1973, and the price per barrel skyrocketed, overriding the impact of falling production. Nine

years later OPEC collapsed, the price of oil fell, and unemployment crept up. Oil and gas production accounted for 28 percent of the state's revenue in 1981 and 15 percent at the close of 1986. Energy-related industries—rigging, drilling, refining—employed 500,900 persons, or one out of every 12 non-farm workers in 1982. After that, those industries lost 282,000 jobs. Economists estimated that for every job lost in the oil industry another 3.7 disappeared in other economic sectors. The 1986 slump in construction, rise in office vacancies, decline in housing starts, and general economic gloom verified their judgments during the late eighties.

Despite estimates that the state still had 1.263 billion barrels of proven and 7.9 billion barrels of unproven oil reserves, or 25 percent of the nation's total, state leaders such as the comptroller warned that never again would petroleum products lead automatically to economic growth. No one discounted the value of oil or denied that the state might still attract new industries and settlers. But by stressing a diversified economy, the leaders of Texas seemed to turn away from the historic practice of encouraging prosperity through raw-material production. They now looked to building upon the industries that oil and defense spending helped produce. That meant that the "Gone to Texas" booms based on cotton in the 1870s and oil in the 1970s had likely been replaced with the slow, gradual growth of the service and trade sectors that characterized other urban, industrial states.

African Americans were 11.6 percent of the state's population in 1990, down somewhat from the percentage recorded in 1945. Duplicating national migration trends, the majority of blacks left farms and settled in urban areas. They soon constituted more than 20 percent of the population of such cities as Houston, Dallas, Fort Worth, Beaumont, and Waco. The urban environment allowed more freedom for civil-rights groups to demand that the Jim Crow

Sweeny Refinery, Texas Gulf Coast, 1956. Courtesy Phillips Petroleum Company, Bartlesville, Oklahoma. Natural gas, which this refinery produced, has been a major industry in modern Texas.

African Americans in the "Colored Waiting Room" at a bus station. Photograph by R. C. Hickman. Dallas, ca. 1950s. R. C. Hickman Photograph Collection, CAH; CN 08024. Integration of blacks became an important political topic after Heman Sweatt was admitted to the law school at the University of Texas in 1950. The last bills supporting segregation passed the Texas legislature in 1957.

system end. In 1951 and 1953 the federal courts extended the *Smith v. Allwright* decision to include local primaries, and black people who paid the poll tax could vote in all Texas elections. The Voting Rights Act of 1965 and the Supreme Court decision in 1966 that struck down the poll tax eliminated barriers to suffrage. Black voter registration in Texas rose from 35.5 percent of the voting-age population in 1960 to 59.1 in 1984. The Supreme Court's "one man, one vote" ruling, which forced state legislatures to redistrict, aided voters in 1966 in electing Barbara Jordan of Harris County to the state Senate and Curtis Graves of Houston and Joseph Lockridge of Dallas to the House. They were the first blacks since 1898 to serve in the Texas legislature. In 1985, 260 blacks held elective office in Texas, including a United States congressman (Mickey Leland), a state senator, and 13 members of the state House. The struggle for black social equality went handinhand with the demand for suffrage. The NAACP undertook a campaign in 1945 to challenge separate school systems in the federal courts. Heman M. Sweatt of Houston agreed to sue the University of Texas School of Law for admission on the grounds that the state offered no professional training for its black citizens. The state's leadership answered by broadening the educational programs at Prairie View A&M, by starting an all-black law school in Austin, and by incorporating Texas State University for Negroes into the state school system. Sweatt v. Painter case went to the United States Supreme Court, which ruled in 1950 that the black law school could not compare to the University of Texas and ordered the admission of Sweatt. Integration of the other public colleges soon followed.

In *Brown v. Topeka Board of Education* (1954) the Supreme Court ruled that segregated public schools were intrinsically unequal and consequently unconstitutional. Governor Allan Shivers announced his opposition to the decision, but his rhetoric did not embody much of the bitter racism that characterized many of the other Southern states. He used the Texas Rangers at Mansfield in 1956 to prevent black students from entering the school and supported the segregation laws that the legislature

passed the next year. But his successor, Price Daniel, Sr. did not enforce these laws, and the massive resistance and violence that marred Southern history and later erupted in such places as Massachusetts did not sweep Texas. The move to integrate the public school system was, however, a slow and painful process. Many communities evaded integration through redefining school-district boundaries and appealing court desegregation orders. By 1964 only 18,000 of the state's 325,000 black students attended predominantly white schools. The Civil Rights Act of 1964 allowed the withdrawal of federal funds from segregated school districts, however, and the rate of integration increased. Further Supreme Court decisions in 1969 and 1971 instructed school districts to stop evading real compliance with the *Brown* decision and approved busing as a means of achieving the desired racial mix.

Black Texans also fought to bring down other barriers that existed after World War II. Aided by federal court decisions, they gained the use of such publicly owned facilities as golf courses, restrooms, and beaches in most Texas cities by the midfifties. In 1954 and 1956 the Interstate Commerce Commission and the Supreme Court ruled against segregation on buses. Cafeterias in bus stations, airports, and federal and municipal agencies were desegregated by the end of the decade. The concept of nonviolent sitins that began in Greensboro, North Carolina, in 1960 soon spread across the South. Students at Wiley and Bishop colleges in Texas staged demonstrations that year. Protests, boycotts, and picketing at restaurants and theaters by blacks and their white allies in Austin, Houston, San Antonio, and other cities caused voluntary desegregation by 1963 of most private businesses. The Civil Rights Act of 1964, supported by President Lyndon B. Johnson and Senator Ralph Yarborough, and five state acts that dismantled Jim Crow legislation in 1969 ended legal segregation in Texas. Though the peaceful demonstrations of the early civil-rights movement turned to Black Power protests that hardened the attitudes of some whites against the civil-rights movement, the riots and violence that occurred elsewhere were largely missing in Texas. In 1967 at Texas Southern University and in 1970 at the People's Party II headquarters in Houston, blacks clashed with the police over the issue of harassment in the ghettos. Much of the energy that went into ending legal barriers in the fifties and sixties turned to demands for more minority officials and a larger share of the nation's economic riches. Though the number of minority members of police forces, including a black chief of police in Houston, had grown by the late 1980s, blacks had not achieved equal income. The median income of black families was $14,818 in 1985, or three-fifths that of whites.

Hispanics replaced blacks as the largest minority group in the state and by 1990 constituted 25.6 percent of the population. The overwhelmingly Hispanic agricultural counties of South Texas remained one of the poorest regions of the nation, while industrialization attracted Mexican Americans from their traditional location along the border into the major metropolitan areas. Houston led the state in 1990 in the number of Hispanics concentrated in Metropolitan Statistical Areas with 707,536, followed closely by San Antonio with 620,290. Dallas, Fort Worth, and Arlington recorded a total of 518,917, El Paso 411,619, McAllen–Edinburg–Mission 326,972, and Brownsville–Harlingen 212,995. Sizable Mexican-American minorities lived in cities such as Austin, Lubbock, and Odessa, and smaller numbers were scattered throughout the sheep and cattle sections of West Texas. Mexican Americans were urbanized, bicultural, acculturated, and heterogeneous. The political climate after 1945 offered more opportunities to them than ever before. Shortly after the war Dr. Hector García of Corpus Christi organized the American G.I. Forum of Texas, which won national notoriety in 1948. That year, a mortician at Three Rivers refused the use of his chapel for services for Félix Longoria, who was killed in the battle of the Philippines. Although more radical than the older League of United Latin American Citizens, the G.I. Forum joined with the league in voter drives. When Henry B. Gonzalez, a state senator from San Antonio and later a United States congressman, ran for governor in 1958, his losing campaign mobilized Mexican-American voters. Many of his staff joined other organizations in promoting the 1960 Viva Kennedy campaign, which crystallized into the Political Association of Spanish Speaking Organizations. Working with the Teamsters Union in 1963, PASSO elected an all-Hispanic slate to the city council of Crystal City.

Tejanos had social problems similar to those of blacks. Hispanic lawyers succeeded in *Delgado v. Bastrop ISD* (1948) in persuading a federal court to declare segregation of Mexican Americans unconstitutional. Six years later Gustavo C. García won a United States Supreme Court case, *Hernández v. the State of Texas*, that outlawed exclusion of Mexican Americans from juries. Henry Gonzalez joined Abraham Kazen of Laredo and white allies in the legislature in fighting segregation in the fifties. Federal actions that ended the poll tax, passed the Civil Rights Act and Voting Rights Act, and forced legislative reapportionment aided Mexican Americans as well as black people. Nevertheless, for many young Hispanics the struggle seemed too slow. They took the name Chicano and joined movements of direct confrontation. The Starr County Strike in June 1966, which led to a march from the Rio Grande valley to the Capitol, was a catalyst for the movement. Governor John Connally refused to meet the marchers in Austin but met them instead at New Braunfels and announced his opposition to both a special session of the legislature to address farmworkers' grievances and a Labor Day rally for worker solidarity.

The 490-mile march and the governor's rebuff encouraged the brown-power militancy that lasted until the mid-seventies. This militancy took several forms. The older, more middleclass organizations, while more outspoken, still worked within the system. They founded MALDEF (the Mexican American Legal Defense and Educational Fund) in 1968 to desegregate the schools. Chicano groups such as the Mexican American Youth Organization (MAYO) and the Raza Unida party stressed separatism and opposition to racism. José Ángel Gutiérrez, the party founder, and two other party members won seats on the Crystal City school board in 1970. Two years later the Raza Unida candidate, Ramsey Muñiz, garnered 6 percent of the popular vote in the gubernatorial election, thus almost enabling Republican Hank Grover to upset Democrat Dolph Briscoe. The successes of the early seventies encouraged local Hispanics to announce for public office and break white political control of the Valley. Most of the separatism that characterized the civil-rights movement had faded by the mid-seventies. Pressures from state and federal agencies and infighting within the movements dissipated much of their reform energies. Nevertheless the movements galvanized many of the young into political action and helped train them in politics. Later successes of the Mexican American Democrats, organized in 1975, and the Mexican American Legislative Caucus were built upon the lessons taught in the political wars of the previous decade. In 1987 Hispanic voter registration was 47.2 percent of the voting-age population, or slightly more than 15 percent of the state's registered voters. That year 1,572 of the nation's 3,314 Hispanic officeholders were in Texas.

Paul Eggers, George Bush, John Tower, and Richard Nixon campaigning in Texas. Photograph by Charles Pantaze, 1970. Courtesy John R. Knaggs, Austin. Democratic control of the state began to collapse in the early 1960s, and the elections of 1966, in which Republican John Tower was elected to his first full-length term as U.S. senator, signaled the emergence of Texas as a two-party state.

Their number included 25 state legislators, 4 congressmen, and Mayor Henry Cisneros of San Antonio, later a member of William J. Clinton's cabinet. Hispanic family median income of $17,435 was about three-quarters of Anglo family income.

The postwar years also brought significant changes in male–female relationships in Texas. In 1987 women made up 50.7 percent of the Texas population. Industrialization and urbanization continued the trend begun in World War II of multiplying jobs for women outside the home; 3,111,000, or 56.6 percent, of Texas women were employed in 1984, as compared to 720,531, or 26.8 percent, in 1950. Duplicating national trends, Texas families included more two-income households, as the majority of married women were employed, and more working mothers. The 1980 census reported that almost 50 percent of women with children under 6 and more than 60 percent of those with children 6 to 17 were in the labor force. Of these women 467,362 were single parents. Texas women continued to dominate such occupations as teaching, nursing, dietetics, and library work. Although household occupations remained overwhelmingly women's work, they employed fewer than 2 percent of working females. Women had moved increasingly into sales and clerical occupations; about a third of all working women were employed in the latter category. Opportunities for women in professional and managerial positions had expanded. But men still by far outnumbered women in higher paying jobs; in 1984 women earned 64 percent of men's median income. In the fifties President Eisenhower appointed Houstonian Oveta Culp Hobby the first secretary of the Department of Health, Education and Welfare. Women won the right to serve on juries in 1954. Feminists joined other allies in the sixties, and the National Organization for Women established chapters in the state. In 1971 women's-rights advocates formed the Texas Women's Political Caucus to promote political activism and party participation. The efforts of the TWPC and women's business and professional clubs aided the successful campaigns in 1972 for the Texas Equal Rights Amendment to the state constitution and the 1973 legislature's approval of the Equal Rights Amendment to the federal constitution (though the latter eventually failed to be ratified). Frances Farenthold ran an unsuccessful but spirited campaign for the 1972 Democratic gubernatorial nomination. Women won 698 public offices in Texas in 1982. State Treasurer Ann Richards, the first woman elected to statewide office in more than 50 years, was elected governor in 1990 but lost her reelection bid to George W. Bush in 1994. In 1987, 3 women served in the state Senate and 13 in the House. In 1991 woman mayors headed three of the largest Texas cities: Kathy Whitmire, Houston, Annette Straus, Dallas, and Kay Granger, Fort Worth.

The political wars that followed World War II took place in the changing social and economic environment that turned Texas into an urban state. Governor Coke Stevenson enjoyed immense popularity during the war, but opposition to the New Deal signaled deep divisions within the Democratic party. The schism between liberal and conservative Democrats became apparent in the 1946 gubernatorial campaign. Homer Rainey, whom the UT regents, dominated by Texas Regulars, had fired from the presidency of the University of Texas, announced for governor. Attorney General Grover Sellers counted on the support of conservatives. As the campaign progressed, Beauford Jester, a member of the Railroad Commission and an oilman from Corsicana, emerged as the front runner. He put together a moderate and conservative alliance that defeated Rainey in the runoff. The affable governor went on record as opposing any new taxes. He also promised to restrict the growing power of labor unions, which had begun organizing campaigns on the Gulf Coast in the war years, to fight Communism, and to uphold states' rights. In 1947 the rural-dominated legislature passed a spate of laws that clearly defined Texas as an antiunion state. The restrictions were broadened in 1951, and Texas has never developed a strong union movement. In 1948 the governor worked for party harmony by endorsing Harry S. Truman, who carried the state easily in the presidential election despite a Dixiecrat bolt that former Texas Regulars supported. Jester won reelection that year without campaigning. Much state political attention was focused upon the United States Senate seat that "Pappy" O'Daniel abdicated. Congressman Lyndon Johnson, who had lost a narrow election to O'Daniel in 1942, and Coke Stevenson waged an acrimonious campaign that still may be the most famous in Texas history. Johnson won the seat in a highly controversial election after a federal court ordered his name placed on the Democratic ballot. The new senator joined with Congressman Sam Rayburn to form one of the most effective legislative teams in recent times.

When the Fifty-first Legislature convened in January 1949, Jester and Lieutenant Governor Shivers surprised the lawmakers with an agenda that for the first time addressed the problems of urban Texas. The legislation included improvements in eleemosynary institutions, a law against lynching, reform of the prison system, and minimum requirements for persons engaged in health services. The Gilmer–Aikin Laws, possibly the most important accomplishment of the session, reorganized the funding and administration of Texas public schools and formed the basis for the current school system. Nevertheless the legislature refused to pass new taxes.

When Jester died of a heart attack in 1949 the 41-year-old Shivers succeeded him. The new governor presided over a special session of the legislature, which had failed to appropriate funds for needed state services. He called for new taxes in a famous "goat speech" that characterized Texas as "first in oil and forty-eighth in mental hospitals" and "first in goats and last in care for state wards." The result was an increase in already existing taxes and new appropriations for colleges and hospitals. Shivers easily won reelection in 1950. The legislature passed the first bill that expanded taxes in 16 years. The new taxes concentrated on consumer levies, but they included a gathering tax on natural-gas pipelines that was later declared unconstitutional. Laws enacted included the first redistricting bill in 30 years and more money for roads, schools, prisons, and the mentally handicapped. Yet by 1950 Shivers was drifting away from the national Democratic party. Truman's administration had come under increasing conservative fire. Conservatives accused the president of being soft on Communism and too committed to fighting a "no win" war in Korea. These criticisms dovetailed in Texas with the more volatile issue of control of the tidelands, adjacent undersea lands that were thought to be rich in oil deposits. The Tidelands Controversy dominated the 1952 presidential election in Texas. The Democratic party split when the governor, who controlled the party organization, refused to support Adlai Stevenson. Instead, Shivers endorsed both Dwight Eisenhower and a 1951 law that permitted candidates to cross-file on both parties' tickets. The alliance of "Shivercrats" and Republicans carried the state for Eisenhower, and the conservatives continued their control over the Democratic party, as Shivers defeated Ralph Yarborough and Attorney General Price Daniel beat a Truman supporter, Congressman Lindley G. Beckworth, for the spot vacated by Thomas T. Connally in the United States Senate.

Eisenhower signed a quitclaim bill in spring 1953 that gave the states control over the tidelands, which included recognition of historic state claims in Texas and Florida of a three-league boundary. Republicans hoped that Ike's successes would lead to an exodus of conservatives from the Democratic party into theirs, but such was not to be. Eisenhower's election was more of a personal than a party triumph. Moreover, his administration faced other problems that affected Texas Republicans. The party lost control of Congress in 1954, and the president's legislative program depended upon the good will of Johnson, the majority leader in the Senate, and Rayburn, the speaker of the House. If Eisenhower tried to build the Republican party in the state through appointments and patronage, he would alienate those two powerful Democrats. His policies also were more moderate than those of some Texas Republicans, who objected to such measures as the Civil Rights Act of 1957 (guided through the senate by Johnson) and the sending of federal troops to Little Rock. When Eisenhower defeated Stevenson in 1956, he carried Texas by a larger margin than in 1952. Shivers endorsed the president, and cross-filing, to the chagrin of local Republicans, protected conservative Democratic candidates. The lone Republican victory in 1956 was that of Congressman Bruce Alger of Dallas, who had first won in 1954 in a campaign in which liberals refused to vote for Wallace Savage, the state party chairman of the 1952 Democrats for Eisenhower organization.

A sharpening division between liberals and conservatives characterized Democratic politics in the mid1950s. Governor Shivers announced for an unprecedented third term in 1954, when he seemed to be at the height of his political popularity. The legislature responded that year to his demands for increased taxes to support education and expanded state services. He pushed through legislation that made membership in the Communist party punishable by a jail sentence of 20 years and a $20,000 fine, thus augmenting earlier acts that outlawed the party and required loyalty oaths of state employees and public college students. Shivers's actions were in part an attempt to defuse Yarborough's campaign to replace him as governor. In the bitter 1954 contest Yarborough sought to link the governor's administration to the lax state laws that allowed insolvent insurance companies to operate in Texas and accused Shivers of shady real-estate transactions. The governor in turn charged that his challenger was controlled by Communist-dominated unions and that Yarborough endorsed the *Brown* integration decision. The vituperative campaign ended with a runoff victory for the governor. But his power diminished in his last term in office. Insurance scandals rocked the state for the next two years. The failure of the United Services Trust and Guaranty Company brought new regulatory laws and exposed an unseemly connection between some legislators and corporations. Reporters exposed irregularities in the operation of the Veterans' Land Board that ended with the sentencing of the commissioner of the General Land Office, James Bascom Giles, to six years in the penitentiary. Since the governor and attorney general were members of the board, they were linked in the public's mind to the scandal. Shivers chose not to run in 1956.

That year the moderate conservative Price Daniel became governor by narrowly defeating Yarborough, who won the special election for the vacated Senate seat. Much of Yarborough's support was generated by the newly organized Democrats of Texas, liberal political clubs that operated outside state party machinery, by organized labor, and by the *Texas Observer*. Frankie Randolph of Houston financed this liberal paper and participated in the organization of the DOT. Yarborough defeated William Blakley in the 1958 Democratic primary and Republican Ray Wittenburg in the general election. His triumph gave hope to the liberal forces, an inchoate group in the late fifties that loosely advocated corporate taxes, civil rights, expanded state services, and loyalty to the national Democratic party. Despite liberal expectations, however, the moderate–conservative wing of the Democratic party controlled politics in the sixties. Daniel defeated the liberal Henry B. Gonzalez in the 1958 primary and the conservative Jack Cox two years later. His three terms in office were more popular with the voters than with the legislature. The governor's major accomplishments included a water-development program, regulation of lobbyists, a code of conduct for state officials, a statewide safety program, and the reorganization of the state insurance board. The issue of taxing took up much of his administration's energies. Although Daniel strongly opposed a general sales tax, the refusal of the legislature to consider alternate taxing sources brought in a 2 percent sales tax in 1961.

In the sixties politics centered on the career of Lyndon Johnson. He persuaded the legislature in 1959 to move the primary to May so that he could be a candidate both for the Senate and for the presidency. In the general election Johnson fought back a surprising Republican challenge from John Tower, a little-known teacher at Midwestern University. Johnson continued to campaign for the presidential nomination, but he lost to John F. Kennedy at the Democratic convention in Los Angeles and then astounded supporters and detractors by accepting the second slot on the ticket. Johnson's vice-presidential nomination confused Democratic politics in the state, as conservatives disliked the national party platform and liberals harbored suspicions because Johnson supported the moderate–conservative wing of the state party. In November 1960 Texans voted for Kennedy and Johnson over Republicans Richard M. Nixon and Henry Cabot Lodge III by a mere 26,000 votes. Tower defeated the conservative Democrat Blakley in the 1961 special election to fill Johnson's vacated Senate seat. The refusal of liberals to support a conservative nominee of the Democratic party may well have precipitated the election of the first Republican senator from Texas since Reconstruction. Tower's election raised the Republicans' expectations and unified the GOP. The Democrats, on the other hand, were racked with dissension between the Johnson and Yarborough contingents. In the Democratic primary of 1962, John Connally, considered a Johnson protégé, ran ahead of Don Yarborough and Price Daniel, who tried for a fourth term. Connally won the runoff, but Yarborough claimed 49 percent of the vote. In November Connally defeated Jack Cox, who had turned Republican. The Republicans, however, added a congressmen and won eight state legislative races, while Cox garnered almost 46 percent of the vote in the governor's race. The Texas GOP looked forward to a 1964 presidential contest that they anticipated would pit the conservative Republican senator from Arizona, Barry Goldwater, against John Kennedy.

In Dallas, however, on 22 November 1963, Lee Harvey Oswald killed Kennedy and seriously wounded Connally. Johnson succeeded to the presidency, and Connally became unbeatable. With the aid of Johnson, Connally secured control of the state's Democratic party machinery. The presidential campaign of 1964 annihilated Republican candidates. Johnson skillfully portrayed Goldwater as a right-wing extremist, and by inference a like label was applied to Texas Republicans. The Democrats swept the state. Goldwater received fewer than a million votes of the 2,588,000 cast. Ralph Yarborough defeated George H. W. Bush for the Senate, and Connally trounced Don Yarborough in the primary and Republican Jack Crichton in the general election. The lone survivor of the Republican victories of 1962 was a state representative from Midland.

Connally, who easily won reelection in 1966, dominated Texas politics during his three terms in office. Although closely identified in many voters' perceptions with Johnson, he carefully distanced himself from the Great Society. His moderate conservatism, much like the business progressivism of the 1920s, stressed economic growth through long-range government planning, improved higher education, increased tourism, and attraction of out-of-state industries. Thus he pressured the legislature to increase faculty salaries and university building programs, to strengthen the Texas Commission on Higher Education, to institute a fine-arts commission, and to fund tourist and industrial commissions. New intergovernmental agencies to coordinate and plan the activities of the various subdivisions of state and local governments were organized. Liberals maintained that Connally tried to expand the economy at the expense of the needs of the poor and minorities, and the legislature turned down some of his requests, such as legalizing horse racing and liquor by the drink, four-year terms for governors and annual legislative sessions, and a revision of the constitution. Yet few would deny his attraction to Texas voters. Connally could probably have been elected senator if he had wished it. The attraction of the strong and dynamic governor to mainstream and conservative voters retarded both the growth of liberalism and a two-party Texas. The latter was ironic because Connally changed parties in the seventies and contended unsuccessfully for the Republican nomination for the presidency.

Both President Johnson and Governor Connally announced that they would not seek reelection in 1968, and the Democrats nominated Vice President Hubert Humphrey to oppose Republican Richard Nixon for the presidency. Humphrey carried Texas by fewer than 40,000 votes and lost the national election. Although cheered by Nixon's victory, Republicans failed to gain as much as expected. Tower won reelection in 1966, when liberals refused to support his Democratic opponent, Waggoner Carr. Tower and three congressmen, including George Bush, constituted the party's national congressional delegation. The party elected eight members to the Texas House and two state senators. Results were more disappointing for liberals. The elimination of the poll tax and oneman, onevote court rulings did not produce the anticipated new liberal constituency. Lieutenant Governor Preston Smith defeated Don Yarborough in the Democratic gubernatorial primary and Republican Paul Eggers in the general election. Smith claimed an easy reelection victory in 1970, a year that brought further disappointments to liberals and Republicans, when Lloyd Bentsen, Jr., supported by conservative Democrats and business interests, unseated Ralph Yarborough in the primary and turned back the challenge of George Bush in the general election.

The conservative Democrats controlled politics as the seventies began. Smith, a not very dynamic governor, did not push his legislative program with the intensity of the articulate and colorful Connally. The governor proposed a state minimum wage, a lower voting age, a water plan for West Texas, and additional taxes. The voters turned down the water plan, and the legislature vetoed higher taxes. The legislature, ruled by Speaker Gus Mutscher, was opposed to reform and identified closely with large financial interests. Most political observers thought that Lieutenant Governor Ben Barnes, a Connally protégé, was destined for the governorship and possibly national office. But rumors of scandal erupted in 1971. The Federal Securities and Exchange Commission began a probe of state officials, charging that in 1969 Mutscher and some of his supporters had received loans from Sharpstown State Bank in Houston to purchase stock in the National Bankers Life Insurance Company. Frank Sharp owned both of these enterprises. Investigators alleged that in exchange for quick profits Mutscher had guided two bills through the legislature that would have allowed the tycoon's bank to avoid federal regulation. A "Dirty Thirty" coalition of liberals, Republicans, and others unhappy with Mutscher's highhanded rule led a legislative revolt to oust the speaker and to institute reform measures, but the speaker had enough votes to thwart them and to draw a redistricting plan that he hoped would defeat the Dirty Thirty in the coming election. A federal district court overturned the Mutscher plan in January 1972, and, after a series of court battles, in 1975 all 150 House members represented single-member districts.

The year 1972 was not good for incumbents. Mutscher was defeated and later convicted on charges of bribery and conspiracy. Barnes and Smith announced for governor. Although they were never charged in the Sharpstown scandal, their executive duties linked them to the original bill, and they ran third and fourth respectively in the Democratic primary. Conservative Dolph Briscoe defeated Frances Farenthold, a member of the Dirty Thirty, in the second primary, and Republican Hank Grover in the general election. The Republicans profited from the new single-member House districts and won 17 seats. Nixon trounced his Democratic opponent, George McGovern, and Tower won a third term in the Senate. But the defeat of the incumbents did not bring substantive changes to Texas politics. Governor Briscoe continued conservative Democratic policies. His programs stressed no new taxes and support for strengthening law-enforcement agencies and enforcement of criminal law. Despite a comfortable reelection in 1974 to a recently approved four-year term, he never exercised strong executive leadership. The legislature passed ethics legislation that included a financial-disclosure law and the filing of lists of campaign supporters. The reform atmosphere generated by the Sharpstown scandal encouraged the public to authorize a revision of the Constitution of 1876. A legislative constitutional convention, with Speaker of the House Price Daniel, Jr., presiding, met in January 1974. After much wrangling, the legislature refused to approve of its own work. Public indignation forced the 1975 legislature to reconsider the issue of constitution revision. Eight amendments were submitted to the voters in the November elections that would have amounted to a new state constitution, but they were turned down by a three-to-one vote. The impulse for reform had waned by the mid-seventies.

The decade ended with surprises for seasoned political observers, in spite of the long shadow of the Watergate scandal that fell over the Republican party. Texans and the nation elected Democrat James E. Carter over President Gerald Ford in 1976. The state Democratic party rallied in support of its candidates, and the harmonious effort sent Bentsen back to the Senate. Intraparty fighting between supporters of Ronald Reagan and those of Ford and Tower seemed to forecast ill for future Republican gains. Briscoe announced for a third term in 1978—not unusual in Texas politics, except that reelection would have accorded him an unprecedented 10 years as governor. His opponent, the moderately liberal attorney general John Hill, won the primary. Dallas oilman William Clements, who had close ties to Ronald Reagan, challenged Hill in the general election and, after a well-organized and lavishly funded campaign, astounded a complacent Democratic party with an upset victory. Not only had the GOP elected the first Republican governor of the state in more than a hundred years, but Tower withstood a strong challenge by Congressman Robert K. Krueger for the Senate, and the GOP increased its state legislative strength to 4 senators and 23 House members. Republicans claimed that two-party politics had come to Texas. Texas voters overwhelmingly supported Ronald Reagan in 1980 and in 1984. When Tower chose not to run for reelection, Republican Phil Gramm, formerly a Democratic congressman, won the 1984 race for the United States Senate. The attraction of the top of the ticket that year helped the party to send 10 congressman to Washington and 55 representatives and 6 senators to Austin. Republican strength also appeared in county and district races; the party's local officeholders increased from 278 in 1980 to 494 in 1986.

Observers attributed Republican successes to several factors. The eighties were simply more conservative than the sixties and seventies, they claimed, and much of the conservatism came from the Sun Belt cities, which lacked the tradition of liberalism of their northeastern counterparts. Court rulings that ordered redistricting and urban growth therefore increased the Republican constituency. The popularity of the party in the suburbs led state GOP chairman George Strake to predict that Republicans would be the majority party with the mandated 1992 legislative redistricting.

But state politics did not immediately verify Strake's optimism. Clements's first term in office was only a moderate success for

Republicans. His relations with his own party were generally quite good, but his somewhat abrasive and outspoken manner may have alienated prospective voters. He ran as a political outsider, and his somewhat cool relationship with the Democrats led to the rejection of most of his agenda in the first legislative session. His promise to cut governmental expenses and reduce the number of state employees failed. In the second session the governor proposed more limited goals and succeeded in passing most of his anticrime package. His vigorous support for Reagan gave him national visibility, and that, combined with the state prosperity of the early eighties, encouraged supporters to expect the governor's reelection. But the 1982 gubernatorial campaign once again confounded political prognostications. The Democrats nominated Mark White for governor. He had worked in Briscoe's 1972 campaign, was appointed secretary of state, and upset Price Daniel, Jr., in the 1978 race for attorney general. Observers classified him as a conservative. Other Democratic nominees for public office represented the broad perspective of the party. Bentsen announced for reelection, as did Lieutenant Governor Bill Hobby. They campaigned vigorously for a ticket that included progressives Jim Hightower for commissioner of agriculture, Ann Richards for state treasurer, Jim Maddox for attorney general, and Gary Mauro for land commissioner. White won with 54 percent of the vote, and the Republicans failed to gain any downballot statewide offices. White's victory was credited to high voter turnout in the Hispanic and black communities, support from rural areas, and disenchantment of schoolteachers with the Clements administration.

White's victory amplified some of the changes that had occurred over the last 40 years in the Democratic party. The fierce divisions between conservative and liberal factions had subsided since the Yarborough–Shivers shootouts and the volatile sixties. Democrats needed high turnouts in minority and low-income precincts to win statewide elections. This necessity, along with the desertion of conservative Democrats to the Republicans, had moderated the party's economic and social views. Success depended on turning out voters in a period of increasing political apathy to support a ticket that represented a broad political appeal and that had attractive statewide candidates.

Governor White's administration soon encountered political difficulties. The economic troubles of the eighties caused a shortage of state revenue, while demands for improved education and higher teachers' salaries, a court-required expansion of the prison system, and a needed improvement of the highway system necessitated more money. In addition, the governor tied a teacher pay raise to an upgrading of public education. The legislature responded with the Education Reform Act of 1984, which included an appointed school board, competency tests for students and teachers, and the "no pass–no play" rule for extracurricular student activities. This controversial measure offended some teachers, students, and parents. Like all governors since Connally, White promised no new taxes. Yet to pay for the needed state services, the legislature raised revenues slightly in 1984. Two years later, as oil prices dropped, the governor called a special session that temporarily increased taxes, deferred revenue payments, transferred special money into the general-revenue fund, froze state employee raises, and cut expenditures. The bill was a compromise, marked by acrimonious debates, and clearly a stop-gap solution. Both White and Clements announced for governor in 1986. The tax and "no pass–no play" issues seemed to dominate the campaign, in which

Ann Richards giving the keynote address at the 1988 Democratic national convention, Atlanta. Photograph by Ralph Barrera. Courtesy Austin *American–Statesman*. Ann Richards became a player on the national political scene after television viewers' favorable response to her keynote address.

the bitter political rhetoric recalled the fifties. Clements beat White, who received 36,000 fewer votes than he had four years earlier. Analysts credited low turnouts in Hispanic and rural areas, the economic depression, and doubt about White's leadership abilities as the reasons for his defeat. Democrats once again won the downballot elections in the statewide races, however.

Shortly after he assumed office, investigations linked Clements to a football scandal at Southern Methodist University, where as the head of the governing board he had authorized the paying of athletes. Temporary revenue measures forced the legislative session of 1987 to pass a new tax bill in violation of the governor's promise. The $5.7 billion tax increase was the largest approved by any state at any time ever. Clements's popularity plummeted in opinion polls as Texas geared up for the 1988 elections. Though Lloyd Bentsen was easily able to secure his reelection to the Senate, Republican George Bush captured Texas in the presidential election; the Republicans also finally demonstrated their ability to win seats at the local level, where they increased from 494 district and county level offices in 1986 to 616 in 1988.

In 1990 Governor Clements announced he would not seek a third term, and the Republicans put forward West Texas newcomer Clayton Williams. Ann Richards defeated Mark White and Jim Maddox in the Democratic primary, and narrowly squeaked to victory in the governor's race. Williams's "Good Old Boy" campaign, initially attractive to conservative Republican voters, suffered from a series of unguarded crude remarks that alienated many Republican women and independent voters. Phil Gramm easily defeated Hugh Parmer for reelection to his Senate seat. William P. Hobby, Jr., chose not to run for lieutenant governor again in 1990, thus ending his 16 years in that office, the record to date. He was succeeded by Democrat Bob Bullock. Texan Ross Perot's third-party candidacy in the 1992 presidential election helped split

Democratic support in Texas; George Bush carried the state, though Democrat William J. Clinton won the national election. When Lloyd Bentsen was chosen as secretary of the treasury by Clinton, Kay Bailey Hutchison won the special election in 1993 to take his Senate seat. In 1994 Texas voters handed the Democratic party a significant defeat and continued the trend to parity between the parties. Hutchison defeated Richard Fisher in 1994 to win a full term. Republican George W. Bush defeated incumbent governor Ann Richards by a substantial majority, winning more than 53 percent of the vote. As a result, Texas had two Republican senators, Gramm and Hutchison, and a Republican governor for the first time since Reconstruction. The Republicans also retained the office of agricultural commissioner, gained all three seats on the Railroad Commission, gained a Republican majority on the State Supreme Court, and picked up two congressional seats. The Democrats still retained control of the state legislature after the election of 1994, with 17 Senate seats to the Republicans' 14, and 88 seats in the House of Representatives to the Republicans' 62. Party politics was in a state of flux as the century neared its end. Polls reported that Texas may have become a "no party" state, since roughly one-third of the voters called themselves Democrats, one-third Republicans, and one-third independents. The majority party, whichever it is, will have to address the ongoing problems of an urban Texas: water shortages, transportation difficulties, economic changes, educational challenges, and an embattled taxation system.

Robert A. Calvert

A. H. Belo Corporation. Pioneering media corporation, the oldest continuously operated business in Texas. Samuel Bangs published the first edition of the Galveston *Daily News* on 11 April 1842. Under a successor editor, Willard Richardson, the company originated the *Texas Almanac*. Alfred Horatio Belo, of North Carolina, became owner in 1876 and sent George B. Dealey to Dallas to establish the Dallas *Morning News* in 1885. Dealey opened WFAA, the first network radio station in Texas, in 1922, and the company remained in the radio business until 1987. In 1963 Belo bought seven Dallas–Fort Worth area newspapers, which form a wholly owned subsidiary, DFW Suburban Newspapers, Inc. In 1950 the company acquired its principal television station, WFAA–TV (ABC); in 1984 it purchased four more TV stations and in 1994, one. Belo stock went public in 1981. *Judith M. Garrett and Michael V. Hazel*

Abilene, Texas. In the northeast corner of Taylor County. Founded as a shipping point for agricultural products on the Texas and Pacific Railroad in 1881, the town was named for the Kansas cattle town. Abilene incorporated and became the county seat in 1883. It had a population of 3,194 by 1890. Additional railroad connections and the impoundment of several lakes nearby ensured the city adequate transportation links and water resources in the early twentieth century. Abilene's population jumped from 3,411 in 1900 to 9,204 in 1910, and reached 23,175 in 1930. World War II brought military bases at Camp Barkeley and Tye Field to Abilene; the recommissioning of Tye Field as Dyess Air Force Base after the war ensured a continued military presence in the community. The local oil industry expanded significantly after the war. The city population grew rapidly in the 1940s and 1950s, reaching 90,638 in 1960. In 1990 Abilene had a strong economy based on manufacturing, oilfield service industries and retail businesses, and a population

Circa 1947 view of the Abilene Christian College Administration Building at a time of great growth for the college. L.L. Cook Postcard Company, Milwaukee, Wisconsin. Courtesy TSL.

of 106,654, partly in Jones County. Abilene has numerous churches and three church-related universities, Hardin–Simmons, McMurry, and Abilene Christian; Cisco Junior College also offers courses in the community. The Abilene Philharmonic Orchestra gave its first concert in 1950, and the Abilene Civic Center and the Taylor County Coliseum were constructed in the 1960s. Nearby historic sites include Fort Phantom Hill and Buffalo Gap Historic Village. *Fane Downs*

Abilene Christian University. A private institution originally known as Childers Classical Institute; founded in 1906 in West Abilene, renamed Abilene Christian College in 1920, and moved to a new campus in northeast Abilene in 1929. When threatened by depression-era financial reverses, the college was rescued by John G. Hardin (1934). The originally "ungraded" institution

Bird's eye view of Abilene, ca. 1910. Courtesy TSL. This real photo postcard graphically shows the platted streets and homesites that typified the turn-of-the-century growth of Abilene.

became a junior college in 1912, was augmented to a four-year college in 1919, and added a graduate school in 1953. For its first 45 years, ACC was unaccredited; it achieved full accreditation in 1951. It adopted its present name in 1976. The institution is governed by a board of trustees who are members of the Church of Christ. Though it offers degrees in many fields, it emphasizes study of the Bible. Enrollment surpassed 4,000 in the 1990s.

John C. Stevens

Ab Initio Question. The question was whether all laws and transactions based on laws passed from the beginning (*ab initio*) of Confederate Texas in 1861 and the Constitutional Convention of 1866 were null and void. The Radical Republicans, led by Morgan C. Hamilton, argued affirmatively. The opposition, led by Andrew J. Hamilton and others, prevailed.

Seymour V. Connor

Acequias. The Spanish brought to the New World an already old method of irrigation by ditches, or acequias. The first acequias in Texas were constructed near Ysleta (post-1680). Later, an elaborate system of acequias was built in San Antonio, where the five missions depended upon them for farming and stock raising. The oldest acequia in San Antonio, the Concepción (1729), was in public use until 1869. Other public acequias in San Antonio conveyed water to the elite Canary Islanders. Numerous private acequias were also built to irrigate ranches and farms in South Texas.

Christopher Long

Adams, Carleton W. Architect; b. Alma, Nebraska, 26 November 1885; d. Devine, 20 November 1964; m. Marcia Booth (1909); 3 children; ed. Columbia University (B.Arch., 1909). The Adams family moved to San Antonio in 1890. In his architectural firm there, Adams worked in several styles: Mediterranean (e.g., the Santa Gertrudis Ranchhouse, King Ranch, 1917), Beaux-Arts (Kerr County Courthouse), Spanish Colonial revival (Jefferson High School, San Antonio, 1930–32), Art Deco (Hall of State, State Fair of Texas, Dallas, 1936; Alamo Cenotaph, San Antonio, 1936, with sculptures by Pompeo Coppini). Among many other buildings, Adams designed the Texas State Archives building in Austin (1962).

Christopher Long

Adelsverein. The Adelsverein (Society of Nobles) was provisionally organized in 1842 by 22 German noblemen who wished to offer surplus German workers a place to settle in the New World. The group first founded Nassau Farm, then reorganized as a joint-stock company (1843) and subsequently formally constituted as the Society for the Protection of German Immigrants in Texas (1844). Under commissioner Prince Carl of Solms–Braunfels the Adelsverein founded New Braunfels. Afterward, under commissioner John O. Meusebach, it founded Fredericksburg and several other German settlements. By 1847, however, the society was facing bankruptcy, and in September 1853 all its properties and colonization rights went to creditors. The Adelsverein brought 7,000 German settlers to Texas and, just as importantly, established Texas as a major goal of subsequent emigration from Germany.

Louis E. Brister

Ad Interim Government. The "interim" was from March 16 to October 22, 1836—between the composition of the Constitution of the Republic of Texas and the inauguration of Sam Houston as president. The advance of the Mexican army delayed ratification and implementation of the new charter, and this government-on-the-move, authorized by the Convention of 1836 and headed by David G. Burnet, deliberated while fleeing from site to site.

Adjutant General. A state office quartered at Camp Mabry in Austin. The adjutant general serves as the governor's aide in supervising the military department of the state, which comprises the Texas State Guard, the Texas Army National Guard, and the Texas Air National Guard.

Dick Smith and Laurie E. Jasinski

Adobe Walls, Battles of. (1) On 26 November 1864, Col. Kit Carson led the First Cavalry, New Mexico Volunteers, in an attack on the Kiowa village of Chief Dohäsan before moving on to the ruins of William Bent's abandoned adobe fort near the Canadian River in what is now Hutchinson County. Gen. James H. Carleton had commanded Carson to seek out and eliminate the raiders who were harassing wagontrains bound for Santa Fe. The abandoned fort, known as Adobe Walls, turned out to be within a mile of a Comanche village with 3,000 to 7,000 inhabitants. These Indians attacked throughout the day and were discouraged only by Carson's two mountain howitzers. By late afternoon, low on supplies and facing vastly larger numbers of Indians than expected, the cavalry decided to withdraw. The Comanches torched the grass near the river, the expected route of retreat, but Carson rode to higher ground and lit his own fires between the Indians and the soldiers and so made his escape. The next day, in order to provide security for Lt. Col. Francisco P. Abreu's infantry, which was following the cavalry with water and supplies, Carson ordered a general withdrawal. General Carleton lauded the action. Indian casualties were estimated at 100 to 150, and 176 Kiowa lodges were destroyed, along with Dohäsan's winter provisions. Though the battle was a clear victory, it decided little. Carson estimated that 1,000 troops would be required if Adobe Walls were to be reoccupied.

(2) The second battle of Adobe Walls began on 27 June 1874. Buffalo hunters who built a camp about a mile from Adobe Walls were attacked by 700 Plains Indians, mostly Cheyennes, Comanches, and Kiowas, under the leadership of Quanah Parker and Isa-tai. The defenders holed up in a saloon and two stores and were able to repel the charge. The Indians conducted a desultory siege for a few days without attacking again. Billy Dixon shot a Cheyenne off his horse at a distance of seven-eighths of a mile—a famous feat. Hunters in the vicinity came to help, and before the official rescue party had arrived the Indians were gone. The fight is significant because it led directly to the Red River Indian War, which resulted in the final relocation of the Southern Plains Indians to reservations in Indian Territory.

H. Allen Anderson

African Americans. People of African descent are some of the oldest residents of Texas. Beginning with the arrival of Estevanico in 1528, African Texans have had a long heritage in the state and have worked alongside Americans of Mexican, European, and indigenous descent to make the state what it is today. The African-American history of Texas has also been paradoxical. On the one hand, blacks have worked with others to build the state's unique cultural heritage. But on the other hand, African Americans have been subjected to slavery, racial prejudice, and exclusion from the mainstream of state institutions. Their contributions to the state's development and growth in spite of these obstacles have been truly remarkable.

From the beginning of European settlement in Texas, people of African descent were present. In 1528 Estevanico, a Moor, accompanied Spanish explorer Cabeza de Vaca across the territory known today as Texas. Estevanico was an important member of Cabeza de Vaca's mission because he could interpret the languages of many of the Indians that the expedition encountered. Along with the other members of the expedition he was captured by Indians and enslaved for five years. After escaping, Estevanico and the surviving members of the expedition made their way to Mexico. In 1539 he accompanied a second expedition into the Southwest. This time he was murdered by the Zuñi Indians and the mission failed. Other pioneer Africans accompanied the Spanish into the Southwest, and some settled with them in the region known today as Texas. By 1792 Spanish Texas numbered 34 blacks and 414 mulattoes. Some of them were free men and women.

Unlike Estevanico and some of the Africans who inhabited the province prior to settlement by Anglo-Americans, most African Americans entered the area as slaves. The first Anglo-Americans who settled in Texas came from the southern United States and were accustomed to using African slaves as an important source of labor. During the first 15 years of white settlement in Texas, from 1821 to the Texas Revolution of 1836, slavery grew very slowly. On the eve of the revolution only about 5,000 blacks were enslaved in Texas. With independence from Mexico, however, whites made African slavery an integral part of the state's economic development, and the institution grew rapidly. By 1840, 11,000 African Americans were enslaved in Texas. By 1850, 58,000 were enslaved, and by 1860, 182,000—30 percent of the Texas population. According to historian Randolph Campbell, slavery in Texas was similar to that in other parts of the American South. The records gathered by Campbell as well as the testimony of African Americans enslaved in Texas attest to the fact that black slaves in Texas had as harsh and as easy a lot as slaves in other parts of the South. Two cases illustrate this fact. In 1861 a Canadian newspaper published the story of Lavinia Bell, a black woman who had been kidnapped at an early age and sold into slavery in Texas. She escaped from bondage and told of being forced to work naked in the cottonfields near Galveston. She also told about how after her first escape attempt, she was mutilated and beaten severely by her owner. Other African Americans who were enslaved in Texas told similar stories of violence and cruelty by their owners. Hundreds sought escape, especially to Mexico. But there were also cases such as that of Joshua Houston, one of the slaves of Sam Houston. Joshua, owned initially by Houston's second wife, became an important member of Houston's family. He was treated well, taught to read and write, and prepared well for his eventual emancipation by the Houston family. After the Civil War Joshua became a politician in Huntsville, and, as if to underscore his loyalty to his former owners, on one occasion he offered to lend money to Sam Houston's widow when she faced financial difficulties.

Though the treatment of African Americans enslaved in Texas may have varied, it was clear that white Texans in general accepted and defended slavery. Moreover, slavery in Texas had all of the characteristics that had made it successful in other parts of the South. For instance, slaveholders dominated the state's

S. B. Hill,   Austin, Texas.

Hal and Jane Mason. Photograph by Samuel B. Hill. Austin, ca. 1895–1900. Andrew W. George Papers, CAH; CN 02926. Hal and Jane Mason began their lives as slaves. By the mid-1880s Hal Mason was assistant jailer at the Travis County Jail.

economic and political life. The government of the Republic of Texas and, after 1845, the state legislature passed a series of slave codes to regulate the behavior of slaves and restrict the rights of free blacks. The census counted about 400 free blacks in 1850, although there may have been close to 1,000. White Texans also restricted the civil liberties of white opponents of slavery in order to suppress dissent about the institution. When rumors of a slave insurrection circulated in the state in 1860, Texans virtually suspended civil liberties and due process in the state. Suspected abolitionists were expelled from the state, and one was even hanged. A vigilante group in Dallas lynched three black slaves who were suspected of starting a fire that burned most of the downtown area. Other slaves in the county were whipped.

The Texas vote for secession in February 1861 hastened the end of slavery and set in motion the eventual liberation of the state's African-American population. For blacks in Texas, freedom did not come until Juneteenth, June 19, 1865. In contrast to other parts of the South, where the approach of the Union Army encouraged thousands of enslaved blacks to free themselves and run away, Texas blacks remained enslaved until the end of the

Republican county convention, Fayette County, 1904. Courtesy Fayette Heritage Museum/Archives, La Grange; 81.83.58. About 200 black delegates attended the convention. In this photograph, convention chairman Charles Gates sits in the judge's chair and secretary Charles Toney speaks from the stand.

Civil War. Few were able to run away and enlist in the Union Army, as black men did in other parts of the South.

The Reconstruction era presented black Texans another challenge. Many had to rebuild their lives, locate lost family members, and begin to live as free men and women. The establishment of the Freedmen's Bureau in the state aided this transition from slavery to freedom. But given the continuing racial animosity that separated blacks and whites after the war, this was not an easy task. The state legislature and several Texas cities passed Black Codes to restrict the rights of blacks, to prevent them from having free access to public facilities, and to force them back to the rural areas as agricultural laborers. The use of the political and legal system to regulate black behavior was accompanied by outbreaks of terrorism. From 1865 to 1868 white Texans committed over 1,500 acts of violence against blacks; more than 350 blacks were murdered by whites. These were attempts to reestablish white supremacy and to force blacks back into their "place." Only the intervention of Congress and the imposition of military rule in the state after 1867 eliminated the Black Codes and brought a modicum of safety to African Americans. The arrival of military and Congressional efforts to protect black rights ushered in the second phase of Reconstruction in the state. In this period African Americans made a substantial contribution to the transition of Texas from a slave-labor state to one based on free labor. Ten black delegates at the Constitutional Convention of 1868–69 helped to write a constitution that protected civil rights, established the state's first public education system, and extended the franchise to all men. Between 1868 and 1900, 43 African Americans served in the state legislature, and they helped to move the state toward democracy. Such black Reconstruction leaders as George T. Ruby and Norris Wright Cuney became important members of the Republican party and, along with other blacks, dominated state Republican politics through the turn of the twentieth century. During the course of the Reconstruction period, many African Americans moved from the state's rural areas to cities such as Dallas, Austin, Houston, and San Antonio. On the outskirts of these cities they established "freedmantowns," which became the distinct black neighborhoods that still exist today. Black labor also contributed substantially to the economic development of these cities and helped the state to begin the transition from its near-total dependence on agriculture to industrialization. In 1879 a few thousand black Texans moved to Kansas seeking greater opportunities. Other black Texans participated in the postwar cattle boom, while the presence on the frontier of black soldiers, called Buffalo Soldiers by their Indian foes, exemplified the desire of many blacks to enter into the military responsibilities of citizenship.

As in other parts of the South, Reconstruction lasted only a short time in Texas. Democrats regained control of the state in 1873 and proceeded to reverse many of the democratic reforms instituted by black and white Republicans. Between 1874 and 1900 the gains that African Americans had made in the political arena were virtually lost. In the 1890s, for example, more than 100,000 blacks voted in Texas elections. But after the imposition of a poll tax in 1902 and the passage of the white primary law in 1903, fewer than 5,000 blacks voted in the state in 1906. In addition, segregation was established in all facets of public and private life in Texas for African Americans. In Dallas, Houston, and San Antonio, public transportation and accommodations, schools, and, eventually, neighborhoods were segregated by law. Blacks in Houston and San Antonio challenged segregation on public transportation by forming their own bus and jitney companies. Dallas blacks won a case in 1916 that overturned a residential segregation ordinance. But nothing succeeded in reversing segregation until much later. The victims of lynching, which did not end until the 1940s, were predominantly black. Riots destroyed black neighborhoods. African Americans became disfranchised, second-class citizens, denied the basic human rights other citizens in the state took for granted. As a result, several thousand black Texans moved out of the state to the North and West in the twentieth century. Although the percentage of blacks in Texas fell to 20 percent of the population by 1900 and declined further in the twentieth century, their numbers grew to more than 600,000 in 1900 and 900,000 in 1940.

Despite their second-class status, African Americans still built viable and progressive communities throughout the state. Almost immediately after Civil War, they established churches, schools, and other social organizations to serve their own needs. They established newspapers (the Dallas *Express*, Houston *Informer and Texas Freeman*, and San Antonio *Register*), grocery stores, funeral homes, and other business establishments that served a predominantly black clientele. In the late nineteenth century black farmers formed a cooperative to encourage black land ownership and to raise crop prices. From 1900 to 1940 a majority of black Texans remained in farming, with about 20 percent owning their land while most rented farms as tenants. The Great Depression of the 1930s hastened a trend toward urbanization. In the same period blacks in Dallas organized a cotton-processing mill, but it failed in less than five years. These self-help and economic development efforts by black Texans indicate that they did not allow the oppression of white racism to deter them from striving to build successful communities. After the Civil War, African Americans also developed their first educational institutions. Black colleges such as Bishop, Paul Quinn, and Wiley were founded by several religious denominations, primarily Baptist and Methodist organizations. African-American churches such as Boll Street African Methodist Episcopal in Dallas also started the first schools in that city for black children. The city of Houston provided schools for its black citizens beginning in 1871. By 1888 the city government in Dallas followed suit.

African Americans also contributed to the state's social and cultural heritage in the late nineteenth and twentieth centuries. Musicians such as Blind Lemon Jefferson, Huddie (Leadbelly) Ledbetter, Eddie Durham, Scott Joplin, Bobbi Humphrey, and many others became innovators in blues, jazz, and ragtime. Singers such as Julius Bledsoe and Osceola Mays sang songs from the African-American folk tradition as well as their own contemporary compositions. Such writers as Maude Cuney–Hare, J. Mason Brewer, and Sutton Griggs wrote biographies and novels and recorded the folklore of black Texans. Artist John Biggers of Houston became one of the nation's most important mural painters and an internationally recognized artist. In sports, such black Texans as Charlie Taylor, Ernie Banks, Jack Johnson, and George Foreman earned national fame

Sharecroppers picking cotton in the Dallas area, ca. 1907. Stereograph. Prints and Photographs Collection, Cotton file, CAH; CN 01281. At the turn of the century relatively few who farmed, whether black or white, owned the land they worked.

The Bronze Peacock nightclub, Houston, ca. 1950. Courtesy Galen Gart/Big Nickel Publications, Milford, New Hampshire. The Bronze Peacock, a highly successful dinner and dance club in the business district of the Fifth Ward, Houston, opened in 1945. Its founder, Don Deadric Robey, promoted the careers of many important black artists through his record companies and talent-booking agency.

in football, baseball, and boxing. After the integration of the state's universities, black Texas athletes such as Earl Campbell of the University of Texas at Austin, Elvin Hayes of the University of Houston, and Jerry Levias of Southern Methodist University had outstanding college athletic careers.

One of the most significant achievements of blacks in the state was their participation in the Texas Centennial of 1936. This event was important because it allowed African Americans to highlight the contributions that they had made to the state's and the nation's development. Through the efforts of A. Maceo Smith of the Dallas Negro Chamber of Commerce and Samuel W. Houston of Huntsville, the Hall of Negro Life was built at Fair Park in Dallas to bring to the state the works of Harlem Renaissance painter Aaron Douglass as well as to exhibit the paintings of Texas artists Samuel A. Countee of Houston and Frank Sheinall of Galveston. More importantly, the Negro Day event at the Centennial celebration proved to be an important opportunity for black Texans to meet and plan strategy to end the segregation and discrimination that they faced. Three organizations emerged from Negro Day, 1936: the Texas State Conference of Branches of the National Association for the Advancement of Colored People, the Texas State Negro Chamber of Commerce, and the Texas Negro Peace Officers Association (now the Texas Peace Officers Association). All three organizations had as their objective to improve the lot of blacks in Texas. The Texas Centennial was indeed a watershed event for

African Americans. After it they launched a campaign to win the citizenship rights that the state's segregation laws denied them. Texas blacks won two of the nation's most significant civil-rights cases. They renewed challenges to the state's white primary system four times, and eventually won a Supreme Court decision in *Smith v. Allwright* (1944), which declared the white primary unconstitutional. This landmark case opened primaries for blacks throughout the South. In 1950, black Texans also won one of the major legal cases that eliminated segregation in the South's graduate and professional schools. *Sweatt v. Painter*, filed by Thurgood Marshall and local NAACP attorney William J. Durham of Dallas, forced the University of Texas law school to admit black students. Although *Sweatt* was one of several cases that the NAACP filed to gain entry for black students into graduate and professional schools, it also became one of the cases that laid the groundwork for the NAACP's challenge to segregation in pubic schools in the famous *Brown v. Board of Education* case.

Despite the notion among some historians that Texas did not need a civil-rights movement to end its legacy of racial discrimination, African Americans had to use both the courts and direct action in the 1950s and 1960s to win access to public services throughout the state. Using a variety of methods, black citizens won the right to sit on juries, equal pay for equal work for black teachers, the elimination of residential segregation in the state's major cities, jobs on the police forces of Dallas and Fort Worth, and open seating on public transportation throughout the state.

They also used sit-ins in Houston and Marshall to end segregation in public accommodations. By the mid-1960s, only one area of citizenship rights continued to elude black Texans: serving in elective office. In 1958, Houstonian Hattie White became the first African American to win an elective office in the state since Reconstruction by winning a seat on the school board. But many citizens thought that she was white and voted for her in error. She served 10 turbulent years on the Houston school board, fighting constantly to force other members of the board to implement court-ordered desegregation of the school system. After Mrs. White's election black Texans did not win another elective office until 1966, when several black candidates throughout the state won political races. Among the pioneers were Joe Lockridge of Dallas, who won a seat in the state house of representatives, and Barbara Jordan of Houston, who won a seat in the Texas Senate. In 1971, Judson Robinson became Houston's first black city councilman since Reconstruction. A year later Barbara Jordan was elected to the United States House of Representatives, thus becoming the first African American in Texas history to represent the state in Congress.

Her election symbolized the progress that blacks had made in the state after over 100 years of racial segregation and exclusion. Afterward, blacks won elective office on the city, county, and statewide levels. In 1992, for example, Morris Overstreet of Amarillo became the first African American to win a statewide office when he was elected a judge on the Texas Court of Criminal Appeals. Employment opportunities also increased significantly for black Texans, especially in the larger urban areas such as Dallas and Houston. In 1983, for instance, Dallas was named "one of the ten best cities for blacks" because of the social, political, and economic opportunities available there for African Americans. In addition, black Texans continued to participate in the state's social and cultural life and to add their creative talents to the state's as well as the nation's artistic development. Two of many examples are the works added to American literature by Houston playwright and author Ntozake Shange and short story writer J. California Cooper of East Texas. Shange's work *for colored girls who have considered suicide when the rainbow is enuf* played on Broadway and toured the country for several years. Her novels *Sassafras, Cypress, and Indigo* (1982) and *Betsey Brown* (1985) were national best-sellers. Cooper's short stories in *A Piece of Mine* (1984) and *Family* (1991) also earned her national acclaim.

African Americans have lived in the area known as Texas as long as any other ethnic group except American Indians. Throughout their history in the state, they have contributed their blood, sweat, and hard labor to make Texas what it is in the 1990s. Although the 2,000,000 black Texans in 1990 formed only 12 percent of the state's population, blacks had made major contributions to Texas history and culture. The previous thirty years of African-American history in Texas had been quite eventful. During that period black citizens had taken major steps toward reversing the negative aspects of the previous 100 years. Yet, they had only begun to reap the benefits of their labor and persistence.
W. Marvin Dulaney

Agreda, María de Jesús de. Spanish nun, mystic; b. Agreda, Spain, April 1602; d. there, 24 May 1665. As a young Franciscan nun, María de Agreda fell into trances and dreamed of being transported to a distant land, where she taught the Gospel to pagans. At the same time, a mysterious Lady in Blue was said to have appeared in Texas and New Mexico to the Jumanos and other Indians and taught them. In 1629, 50 Jumanos appeared at a convent south of Albuquerque asking for instruction; they already had rudimentary knowledge of Christianity, acquired from the Lady in Blue. When interviewed by Alonso de Benavides in Spain in 1631, Sor María claimed 500 bilocations to New Spain and admitted that she was the Lady in Blue. The story of the miraculous events was current for many years, and was echoed as late as World War II. María de Agreda, who also wrote a long life of the Blessed Virgin Mary, has been declared venerable by the Catholic Church—the first big step on the way to canonization.
Donald E. Chipman

Agriculture. Modern Texas agriculture evolved from the agriculture of prehistoric Texans and agricultural practices transferred from Europe, Asia, and Africa. Crops native to North America included the food staples corn, beans, and squash, and such diverse vegetables as tomatoes, "Irish" potatoes, chili peppers, yams, peanuts, and pumpkins. Spanish colonists introduced wheat, oats, barley, onions, peas, watermelons, and domestic animals, including cattle, horses, and hogs. Prior to European settlement, most of Texas was occupied by nomadic hunting and gathering groups for whom agriculture was peripheral. When

Jaranames (Aranamas), by Lino Sánchez y Tapía, after a sketch by Jean Louis Berlandier. Near Goliad, ca. 1830. Watercolor. From the Collection of Gilcrease Museum, Tulsa, Oklahoma; accession no. 4016.336, plate XI. Some Indians, such as the Caddos, farmed in Texas before the arrival of Europeans. The Aranamas probably took up agriculture as mission Indians. By 1843 they were extinct.

African-American man plowing on a farm. Photograph by Henry Stark. Cherokee County, ca. 1895–96. Courtesy Dallas Historical Society. At the turn of the century almost two-thirds of employed blacks worked in agriculture. Most were sharecroppers and tenant farmers; only 31 percent owned the land they worked.

Europeans first arrived, however, advanced agriculture existed among the Caddo Indians in the east and in the pueblo cultures concentrated in New Mexico. The Caddos lived in permanent villages and depended for food primarily on the cultivation of corn, beans, and squash, with hunting and gathering to supplement the crops. They prepared fields for planting by burning and girdling, and cultivated with wooden hoes, stones, and sharpened sticks. In extreme west Texas, pueblo cultures also depended heavily on corn, beans, and squash, raised cotton for fiber, and practiced irrigation.

Livestock industries, predominantly for cattle, sheep, goat, and hog production, developed in Spanish Texas. Farming was largely limited to small garden plots adjacent to missions and settlements—San Antonio, El Paso (Ysleta), and Nacogdoches, for instance. By 1727 a 2½-mile acequia was watering fields and gardens in San Antonio. Ranching and farming expanded only slightly in Texas over the next 100 years, since Comanches, Apaches, and other nomadic and warring tribes dominated the land.

After its independence from Spain in 1821, Mexico encouraged settlement in its vast provinces north of the Rio Grande. Moses Austin secured the first empresario or colonial grants from Spain. His son, Stephen F. Austin, initially led 300 families from the United States into an area extending from the Gulf Coast into Central Texas. Settlers received a sitio or square league of land (about 4,338 acres) for grazing, and a labor (177

acres) of farming land. The American settlers quickly introduced the slavebased cotton-plantation system, expanded commercial livestock production, and developed concentrations of small, nonslaveholding family farms. Extensive Anglo-American colonization led to the Texas Revolution, the independence of Texas, and the subsequent annexation and Mexican War.

The plantation system, small family farming, and the range cattle industry expanded rapidly between 1836 and the Civil War. Annual cattle drives were being made from points in south central Texas south and east along the Opelousas Trail to New Orleans, and on the Old Government Road to Little Rock and Fort Smith, Arkansas; and on other trails or extensions to Alexandria and Shreveport, Louisiana, or Natchez and Vicksburg, Mississippi. In 1846 Edward Piper drove a herd of Texas cattle to Ohio. In the 1850s Texas herds were being driven to Chicago and Illinois markets, to California, and to railheads in Iowa. The value of livestock on Texas farms rose from about $10.5 million to $43 million between 1850 and 1860. The cotton-plantation system, concentrated in Southeast Texas on the lower Colorado, Brazos, and Trinity rivers, generated much of the state's agricultural production before the Civil War. Cotton production rose from 58,000 bales in 1850 to over 431,000 bales in 1860. Numbers of slaves grew from 58,161 to 182,566 in the same period, while the total population approximately tripled, from 212,592 to 604,215. The primary export was cotton; cattle were second.

Most agriculture before the Civil War involved small, subsistence family farms. The great majority of people were nonslaveholders. Germans established small farms and communities such as New Braunfels, Brenham, and Boerne. Czechs settled heavily in Fayette and Brazos counties. Other settlers streamed in from the South and Midwest and spread across the Blackland Prairies and Cross Timbers of north central Texas by 1860. Agricultural practices on the small farm, which typically ranged in size from 120 to 160 acres, varied from purely pastoral to a combination of pastoral, crop, and garden farming. Hunting and gathering provided an important supplement to family food provisions. In Washington County a farmer with 120 acres might be expected to use 100 acres for unfenced cattle and hog raising, firewood gathering, and hunting. Of the remaining 20 acres, 10 to 12 would ordinarily be devoted to corn, a staple for both human beings and farm animals. An acre or less might be used variously for sweet sorghum or sugarcane, a fruit orchard, home garden and herb plot, and tobacco. Cash income, always minimal, came from the cultivation and harvest of two or three acres of cotton. Farms and plantations primarily utilized teams of oxen for plowing, and occasionally horses or mules. Mules became much more prevalent after the Civil War. Plows were fabricated locally, or, when cash was available, farmers might import farm equipment such as the Eagle plow through New Orleans and Galveston. Commerce generally depended on wagons to and from the port of Galveston; some produce was floated down the rivers. Although steamboat transportation and railroad construction began in Texas before the Civil War, river steamer and rail transportation were generally postwar developments.

After the war the traditional cotton-plantation system continued, but with tenant farmers in place of slaves. Tenants were both black and white, but the latter far outnumbered the former by 1880. As the economy became more of a moneybased system, small farmers increasingly slipped into tenancy or left farming. Generally, in tenant farming the landlord or planter contracted with the tenant for the cultivation of a small plot of land (usually in the range of 16 to 20 acres) on which the tenant was expected to raise as much cotton as possible. The planter ordinarily received one-third of the income from the crop for supplying the land and one-third for provisioning the farmer with tools and housing, while the tenant received one-third for the labor. Credit was extremely expensive and scarce for the planter and disabling for the tenant, who commonly ended a year more deeply in debt than before. But despite the difficulties, the number of farms in Texas rose from about 61,000 in 1870 to 174,000 in 1880 and 350,000 by 1900. Stimulated largely by the extension of railroads throughout Texas between 1870 and 1900, farm and ranching enterprises expanded rapidly as emphasis on commercial production and marketing grew. Subsistence farming and small farm operations declined. Cattle and cotton production dominated farming operations through the remainder of the nineteenth century, but wheat, rice, sorghum, hay, and dairying became important.

Under the terms of the Morrill Land Grant College Act (1862), Texas established Texas A&M, which began operation near Bryan in 1876. A&M College established the Texas Agricultural Experiment Station in January 1886 and sponsored instructional farmers' institutes throughout Texas beginning in 1889. Dr. Mark Francis, the veterinarian for the experiment station, initiated research that helped lead to the eradication of Texas fever in

Kiyoaki Saibara (fourth from left) standing with workers in a rice field owned by his father, Seito Saibara. Webster, Texas, 1904. Courtesy ITC. Seito Saibara brought about 70 Japanese families to the area around Webster in Harris County beginning in 1902. Around the turn of the century, the first attempt to cultivate rice using irrigation was made. Many Japanese immigrants were rice farmers.

cattle and greatly improved livestock production everywhere. He also headed efforts to establish a school of veterinary medicine, which opened under the auspices of A&M with Francis as dean in September 1916.

A&M sponsored the organization of a Texas Farmers' Congress, which met annually on the campus between 1898 and 1915. The congress, in turn, sponsored a Farm Boys' and Girls' Progressive League (1903), which became the predecessor of the 4H Club. In cooperation with Seaman A. Knapp, a special agent of the U.S. Department of Agriculture Bureau of Plant Industry, Texas A&M established a demonstration farm program at Greenville and Terrell in September 1903. In 1905 the college assumed responsibility for the greatly expanded demonstration program and appointed special agents to direct demonstration farm work. This activity became the impetus for the development of formal cooperative extension farm programs, entered into by agreements between the college and the U.S. Department of Agriculture. Cooperative extension work became a national farm program under the terms of the Smith–Lever Act of 1914, which established the Agricultural Extension Service. Advanced cultivation practices, improved plant varieties, the mechanization of agriculture, and the greater availability of capital contributed to both higher yields and increased acreage in cultivation. Bonanza farming and largescale cattle operations, often funded by foreign investors, developed in Texas in the 1880s. Many ventures failed in the depression of the 1890s, and new corporate operations developed intermittently after 1900.

After the Civil War falling prices, high credit and transportation costs—and after 1893 a national depression—precipitated farm organization and revolt. Although some farmers in the state joined the Grange, Texas participation in that group was weak. The Grange sought to impose state regulation on railroad freight rates and grain-elevator charges, to lower credit costs and put more money in circulation, and to reduce tariffs on nonfarm products. Texas farmers began to seek these measures through their own association, the Farmers' Alliance, which originated in Lampasas County in 1872. Under the leadership of Charles W.

Macune, the Alliance embraced the Grange objectives and stressed the development of farm cooperatives. The merger of the Texas Farmers' Alliance and the Louisiana Farmers' Union in January 1887 yielded the National Farmers' Alliance and Industrial Union of America (better known as the Southern Alliance). This organization grew rapidly throughout the South and into the Midwest. The independent Colored Farmers' Alliance and Cooperative Union was organized in Houston in 1886. These organizations, like the northern Farmers' Alliance, advocated paper money as legal tender, the unlimited coinage of silver, government control or ownership of railroads and telegraph systems, lower tariffs, a graduated income tax, the Australian or secret ballot, and the direct election of U.S. senators, as well as expanded public education. The Alliance movement, in turn, led to the organization of a national farmers' political party called the People's party of America or Populist party. Although the party generally failed to achieve its objectives, by the time of its demise after 1896 Populism had began to influence the programs of the major political parties.

Prosperity returned to Texas farmers in the first two decades of the twentieth century. As both rapid urbanization in the United States and the advent of World War I increased the demand for agricultural commodities, their prices rose more rapidly than those of nonfarm goods and services. Because of the resulting favorable economic position for farmers, between 1900 and 1920 the number of cultivated acres on Texas farms grew

from 15 million to 25 million. Cotton production expanded from 3.4 to 4.3 million bales, and corn stabilized at approximately 100 million bushels, though it declined afterwards. The value of livestock more than doubled, from $240 to $590 million. Rice farming, which had been introduced in the 1880s on the Coastal Plain, produced nine million bushels annually by 1910. Wheat, introduced to Texas near Sherman in 1833, had emerged as a major export by 1900; production and milling centered in the north central area, around Fort Worth, Dallas, and Sherman. Such favorable conditions brought further expansion to the state's agricultural system. In South Texas land promoters launched campaigns to attract investors to the lower Rio Grande valley and the Winter Garden Region. With mild winters and water from the Rio Grande, the area became one of the state's most prolific farm sections. By first planting sour orange rootstocks in 1908, Charles Volz and others such as John H. Shary launched the citrus fruit industry in Cameron, Hidalgo, and Willacy counties, where, by 1929, 85 percent of the five million citrus trees were grapefruit. Furthermore, those same counties, with the Winter Garden area to the north, became a major site for commercial truck farming of such vegetables as onions, cabbage, lettuce, carrots, beets, and spinach. During the same period the High Plains also emerged as a major area for crop production. As cattlemen placed their large ranches on the market, cheap land prices in an area without the boll weevil made the region particularly attractive to cotton farmers. With the

Sugarcane harvesting, Rio Grande valley, ca. 1986. Courtesy Texas Department of Transportation/Bill Reaves. The sugarcane being harvested in this picture was crushed at a mill in Santa Rosa (Cameron County), one of the most modern in the country. The truck shown here on the right accommodated ten tons of cane, which could be unloaded at the mill in two minutes.

Estate surrounded by citrus trees. Young trees surround the landscaped grounds—two miles north of Weslaco. Photograph by Russell Lee, 1948. Standard Oil (New Jersey) Company Collection, Photographic Archives, University of Louisville; Neg. no. SONJ 57267. This photograph was taken in one of the peak years in Texas citrus production, after which freezes killed most Texas citrus trees.

development of cotton types adapted to the plains by scientists at the Texas Agricultural Experiment Station at Lubbock, the planting of hard red winter wheat, and the widespread adoption of the tractor, the oneway disk plow, and the combine, the High Plains became one of the state's premier areas for both cotton and wheat production by the end of the 1920s.

By that time the basic structure of the state's modern farming system appeared to be in place. While livestock producers focused upon raising cattle, sheep, and goats on the grazing areas that covered approximately 70 percent of the state's acreage, farmers grew crops on 17.5 percent of the land. Cotton, planted on 60 percent of the state's cultivated acreage, outdistanced all other commodities as a cash crop. Though it was grown in most areas of the state, the heaviest concentration was on the Blackland Prairies, the Coastal Plain around Corpus Christi, and the southern High Plains. Acreage devoted to corn was usually second to cotton in the eastern half of the state, while sorghum was the leading livestock feed in the western half. Wheat, which was produced most extensively on the northern High Plains and in the counties along the Red River, led the small grains and

ranked second to cotton in cash-crop receipts. Besides the citrus and vegetable industries in South Texas, such truck-farming goods as tomatoes, watermelons, and peas were marketed in northeastern Texas. On the Coastal Plain rice was raised, and timber was important in the Piney Woods of East Texas. In most areas of the state cropland was interspersed with pastureland; stock farming was therefore more common than other farming.

Texas farmers like those throughout the nation experienced hard times during the 1920s. The decade began with the agricultural crisis of 1920–21, when postwar commodity surpluses caused a sharp decline in crop prices. Instead of making efforts to curb production, farmers turned to various panaceas to remedy their plight. Some joined marketing cooperatives such as the Texas Wheat Growers Association or the Texas Farm Bureau Cotton Association, in which producers pooled their harvests with the hope of forcing processors to negotiate prices. Others sought to cut costs by replacing draft animals with tractors and increasing their crop acreage. Yet the imbalance in the marketplace continued until the end of the decade, thus contributing to the economic catastrophe of the Great Depression. The number of farms in Texas increased from 436,038 in 1920 to 495,489 ten years later, while cropland harvested grew by 3.5 million acres. Despite the surpluses, the acreage planted in wheat virtually doubled, from 2.4 million to 4.7 million, and cotton acreage increased from 12.9 million to 16.6 million. As wheat prices plunged from $2.04 to 334 a bushel, income declined from $41 million in 1920 to $9.4 million in 1932; cotton sales receipts dropped from $376 million to $140 million between 1920 and 1932, as the price fell from 174 to less than 64 a pound. The farmers' plight grew even worse when a drought accompanied by high winds brought about the Dust Bowl, which was particularly severe on the High Plains, where crop production virtually halted. With these developments rural poverty spread across Texas.

The implementation of Franklin D. Roosevelt's New Deal farm programs had both an immediate and long-range impact upon the Texas agricultural system. The Agricultural Adjustment Act of 1933 launched a series of programs designed to control surpluses and maintain minimum income. For such basic commodities as cotton, corn, wheat, rice, hogs, and milk, farmers accepted acreage allotments and marketing quotas and engaged in soil-conservation practices, in exchange for receiving payments or guarantees of parity prices through nonrecourse loans. In addition, the availability of credit through agencies of the Farm Credit Administration made money more accessible. Furthermore, the Soil Conservation Service was established to awaken farmers to the need of protecting their land through such techniques as terracing, contour listing, strip cropping, and the maintenance of vegetative cover. The combination of the government programs and the nation's involvement in World War II laid the basis for a major shift in the structure of Texas agriculture. First, farm tenancy declined from 60 percent of the state's farm operators in 1930 to 37.6 percent 15 years later, as some landowners took advantage of government checks and cheap credit to replace tenants with machines. Furthermore, the rapid growth of good industrial jobs in urban areas during the war years contributed to a decrease in farm population from 2.16 million to 1.52 million and a loss of approximately 115,000 farm units in the 10 years following 1935, when farms had numbered a half million. Yet farm income grew from approximately $500 million to $1.1 billion as wartime demand forced prices higher. The improved economic situation for Texas farmers, along with a guarantee of 90 percent of parity prices for at least two years after the war, set the stage for the modernization of the Texas agricultural system.

A major step towards the transformation of Texas farm life occurred with increased mechanization. Foremost in this change was the emergence of the tractor. Though steam tractors had been introduced at the turn of the century and gasoline tractors had appeared before World War I, mules and horses remained a common source of power until the 1940s. Then, both the growth in farm income and the enhanced versatility of the allpurpose tractor contributed to the virtual elimination of draft animals from Texas farms. The increase in tractor horsepower in subsequent years from 40 to as much as 200 or more permitted the use of larger auxiliary equipment. The one and two row implements of the World War II era were replaced with breaking plows, listers, tandem disks, rotary hoes, grain drills, and other tools that could cover up to 16 rows, thus enabling a farmer to till or seed as much as 200 acres in a day. In addition, major innovations in

harvesting equipment further transformed Texas farming. By the 1920s the general acceptance of the combine, capable of doing the work of a binder or header and a thresher, spurred the expansion of wheat production in the state. Whether owned by individual farmers or itinerant custom cutters, the combine underwent a series of technical improvements after World War II that ranged from the replacement of the tractor-drawn models with selfpropelled machines to the enlargement of the header size from six feet to 30 feet and the development of attachments that allowed for cutting grain sorghum, corn, and similar commodities, all of which increased the farmers' efficiency and versatility. In addition, machines for harvesting hay, spinach, potatoes, beans, sugar beets, pecans, peanuts, and other commodities reduced labor requirements. The marketing of mechanical cotton harvesters in the 1940s represented a major breakthrough in production. Almost immediately the use of spindle-type pickers and roll or finger strippers reduced the labor requirements for producing and gathering an acre of cotton from an average of 150 to 6.5 man hours. Once engineers had refined some of the technical problems with harvesting and gin equipment and scientists had developed cotton varieties that could be gathered more easily, as well as herbicides and defoliants that eliminated much of the weed and leaf trash prior to ginning, farmers acquired enough machines that by the late 1960s cotton production was almost fully mechanized. Furthermore, as a reduction in the number of gins delayed processing, during the 1970s inventors developed the module, which by compacting the crop in the field postponed the ginning without causing damage. By the 1990s most Texas cotton was machine harvested and processed, with approximately onefourth gathered by spindle pickers, threefourths collected by strippers, and 70 percent ginned from modules.

While advances in mechanization allowed farm operators to handle more land with less labor, the expansion of irrigation after World War II greatly enhanced the state's agricultural productivity. Although approximately 900,000 acres was being watered in 1939, primarily from surface sources in the lower Rio Grande valley, the Winter Garden, the Coastal Prairie, and the TransPecos regions, the major thrust for crop irrigation developed when farmers of the High Plains who had suffered through the Dust Bowl began tapping the Ogallala Aquifer extensively. The availability of financial resources and equipment technology initially spurred the drilling of wells and the installation of furrow systems utilizing drainage ditches and plastic, rubber, or aluminum siphon tubes in the shallow-water belt south of the Canadian River. However, after operators north of the river observed how irrigation enhanced yields by 50 or 60 percent, permitted greater crop diversification, and provided production stability even in the drought years of the 1950s, they too drilled wells and installed ditches or center-pivot sprinkler systems. In 1979, when the state's irrigated acres reached a high of 7.8 million—a third of all of the Texas land in production—87 percent of the watered land was located on the High Plains, where farmers received approximately 40 percent of the state's cash crop receipts.

In conjunction with such capital investments, Texas farmers who recognized that profitability depended upon achieving higher crop yields at reduced labor costs readily incorporated the application of chemicals in their agricultural programs. The use of fertilizers, particularly ammonia-based and nitrogen prod-

Women packing broccoli in the Vahlsing shed, Elsa, 1947. Standard Oil (New Jersey) Company Collection, Photographic Archives, University of Louisville; Neg. no. SONJ 57121. Hidalgo County produces many winter vegetables, including broccoli. Since the 1940s many farm workers in the area have been migrant workers from Mexico.

ucts, generally enhanced commodity returns. Furthermore, the introduction of herbicides at the preplanting, preemergence, or postemergence of the crops usually reduced weed growth and cut labor expenses. In addition, insecticides applied by tractor-mounted equipment or by aircraft helped lessen damage inflicted by insects and diseases.

As farming became more complex after World War II, the role of research scientists and advisors from the state and federal agricultural experiment stations, the colleges of agriculture, and the cooperative extension services expanded. Besides supplying operators with information about effective methods or discoveries, the researchers' success in developing higher-yielding crop varieties had an immense influence upon the state's production. By the 1980s their efforts contributed to the rise of average wheat yields from 10 to 30 bushels an acre; irrigated semidwarf winter varieties exceeded 100 bushels per acre, corn production grew from 15 to 120 bushels per acre, rice from 2,000 pounds to 4,600 pounds per acre, and cotton from approximately 200 pounds to 400 pounds per acre on dry land and 500 pounds on watered acreage. A prime example of the impact of agricultural research was demonstrated with the emergence of grain sorghum as a major Texas commercial crop. Sorghum varieties such as hegari

and kafir, originally planted in the state's more arid western areas due to their drought-resistant qualities, were grown for livestock forage; hand-cut milo maize was fed as a grain. Marketing sorghum as a feed grain began in the late 1940s, when breeders succeeded in reducing the plant's height so as to permit harvesting with a combine and farmers with irrigation discovered the prolific nature of the crop when watered. Yet this was only a beginning, for after several years of experimentation researchers introduced hybrid grain sorghum, which was first distributed for planting in 1957. Immediately, average yields of 1,200 pounds an acre doubled, and as improved varieties were bred farmers of irrigated milo maize frequently harvested as much as 5,000 pounds per acre. Though production centered on the High Plains initially, the lower Rio Grande valley, the Coastal Bend, the Blackland Prairies, and the Rolling Plains also started growing sorghum.

Grain sorghum hybridization supplied the impetus for the rise of the cattle-feeding industry on the High Plains. In the area where cattle raising thrived and the locally produced feed grain supply was greater than the demand by the 1960s, entrepreneurs and promoters conceived the idea of combining the two resources to prepare beef animals for slaughter. By the end of the decade large feedlots capable of handling several thousand animals had been erected and expanded to the extent that in the early 1970s more than three million head were being marketed annually. With 70 percent of the cattle being fattened on the High Plains, Texas became the leader of fed-cattle production in the nation. In turn, the cattle-feeding industry stimulated the resurrection of corn as an important commodity in Texas. Though corn was a major household-food and livestock-feed crop from the time of initial settlement of the state, acreage devoted to its production declined after World War II as reliance upon animal power dwindled. However, when skyrocketing sorghum prices threatened the profitability of the cattle-feeding industry after a trading agreement with the Soviet Union in 1973, High Plains irrigation farmers turned to corn hybrids. With normal yields in excess of 100 bushels of grain per acre plus the silage, growers found that they could achieve a good return on their investment and meet the requirements of the feeders. Besides serving as a cattle feed, corn was valuable as a sweetener, starch, and fuel. The lower Rio Grande valley, the Coastal Plains, and the Blackland Prairies also became centers for corn production.

Just as scientific and technological achievements had influenced corn raising, they gave farmers a greater flexibility in crop selection. Along with the introduction of commercial vegetable and sunflower production on the High Plains, sugar beets emerged as a valuable crop there during the 1960s, following the construction of the Holly Sugar Company plant at Hereford, Deaf Smith County. Soybeans, which normally were grown in the humid region of the upper Coastal Plain, fared well in Hale County on the High Plains as well as in Northeast Texas. In addition to the vegetable and citrus industries in the Valley, sugarcane reemerged as a crop in the late 1970s. The Spanish and, after 1973, the Florunner varieties of peanuts, the production of which had been centered in such north central Texas counties as Comanche and Eastland for decades, flourished in sandy soils on the High Plains, while commercial orchards in thirty counties of Central and West Texas propelled the state to second place in the production of pecans. By the 1980s wineries had appeared in West Texas as vineyards added an additional commercial crop.

The move towards crop diversification often occurred in reaction to restraints imposed by federal governmental policies. Continuing the goals established in the 1930s of attempting to prevent the accumulation of price-depressing surpluses and to provide stable incomes, such instruments as acreage allotments and marketing quotas remained in use, while such other approaches as set-aside or diversion programs were tried as a means of maintaining control over the production of the basic commodities grown in Texas—wheat, feed grains, cotton, rice, and peanuts. Further long-term limitation efforts included the Soil Bank program of 1956, the 1965 Cropland Adjustment Program, and the Conservation Reserve Program in 1985, by which cropland was removed from production and replaced with grasses or hay. The rewards for participating in such programs came in the form of income or price-support policies that varied from benefit payments for idling acreage to nonrecourse loans for commodities placed in storage. In the 1970s those who cooperated became eligible to receive disaster payments when emergencies caused crop losses or deficiency payments for those farmers whose average cash receipts for cotton, wheat, corn, sorghum, and oats were less than the target price that political

authorities deemed acceptable. After 1940 annual federal governmental payments to Texas farmers ranged from a low of $25 million in the 1950s to a high of $1.4 billion in 1987.

Though the governmental restriction programs applied primarily to crop production, the livestock industry maintained a significant role in Texas agriculture, for cash receipts from livestock and livestock products exceeded crop sales continuously after 1970. In a state where twothirds of the space is pastureland, beef-cattle enterprises, which normally furnished more income than any other agricultural endeavor, operated in every Texas county. On farms and ranches the basic cow–calf operations, including the breeding of registered animals, prevailed. Though some calves were maintained on the pastureland, others were either sent to graze on winter wheat from late fall to late winter or went directly or indirectly to feedlots for fattening before slaughter. Another aspect of cattle production, dairying, grew as urbanization spread in the state. With 95 percent of the milk produced east of a line from Wichita Falls to Corpus Christi, large dairy farms often consisted of herds in excess of 100 cows, which gave an average of 15,000 pounds of milk per animal annually. Sheep and goat ranching, with its wool and mohair harvest, continued to be centered on the Edwards Plateau. Along with raising hogs for pork, poultry operations provided income through the sale of eggs and broilers; Angelina and Camp counties in East Texas and Gonzales County in south central Texas were the leading producers.

With the convergence of technological, scientific, economic, and political factors after World War II, large commercial farms and ranches became dominant in the Texas agricultural system. As their operators acquired sophisticated machines that allowed them to handle more acreage with less labor, began to use chemicals and improved seed varieties that enhanced their crop productivity, and introduced livestock and poultry breeding techniques to develop more marketable goods, large numbers of poorly capitalized marginal farmers found the costs beyond their capability and left the profession. Consequently, between 1945 and 1990 the farm population fell from 1.52 million to about 245,000, or 1.1 percent of the state total, and the number of farms declined from 385,000 to 185,000. Yet the average value of farm assets, including land and buildings, rose from approximately $9,000 to $475,000, and the cash receipts from crop and livestock marketing jumped from $1.1 billion to $11.8 billion as the average farm size grew from 367 acres to 700 acres. Though approximately three-fourths of the farms in the state were smaller than 500 acres by 1990, 80 percent of the commodity sales came from 8.7 percent of the farm units, an indication of the impact of the large commercial operations upon agricultural production. Four areas—the High Plains, the lower Rio Grande valley, the upper Coastal Prairie, and the Blackland Prairies—had become the primary centers for large commercial units by the 1980s. With the exception of the Blackland Prairies, where diversified dry-land stock farms were prevalent, the other regions included heavily capitalized operations with extensive irrigated acreage. In the upper coastal region of Southeast Texas, rice and soybeans generated the most income. The mild winters of the Valley allowed for a great variety of produce, ranging from citrus fruits and vegetables to cotton, grain sorghum, and corn. On the northern High Plains, where large farms averaged more than 2,000 acres, wheat, grain sorghum, and corn were raised in fields adjacent to mammoth cattle feedlots. A more intensive cropping system in the southern High Plains counties made the area the state's leader in cotton production. In most of the remaining farm areas of the state, stock farming, which usually combined cattle raising and dry-land raising of wheat, sorghum, or cotton, continued, with variations dependent upon the land and climate. However, major changes did occur in some regions such as East Texas, where the expense of modernization and federal controls upon production caused a shift from small cotton farms to an emphasis upon cattle raising, with hay as the primary crop.

Yet, whether they produced livestock, raised crops, or operated stock farms, Texas agriculturalists found themselves a part of an infrastructure that influenced their actions and decisions. Increasingly, loan officers at such lending institutions as commercial banks, federal land banks, production credit associations, and insurance companies offered advice on planning. Often the ability of an array of agribusinessmen from private enterprises or cooperatives to supply such goods and services as implements, seeds, fertilizers, chemicals, fuel, repair facilities, and other necessities affected their decision making. In addition, representatives from federal agencies supervised their compliance with production programs or counseled them on conserving their land. Information gathered by researchers at federal and state agricultural experiment stations, universities, or private firms became available through county agents, farm magazines, radio and television broadcasters, and other sources. Most farmers belonged to a general organization such as the American Farm Bureau Federation, the National Farmers Union, or the American Agriculture Movement, and perhaps to more than one commodity association; both the general organizations and the commodity associations became the farmers' instruments for promoting their interests in political arenas or in marketing their produce.

Marketing also changed. Instead of sending their crops and livestock to distant terminal points on railroads, farmers and ranchers profited from the introduction of motor vehicles, particularly trucks, in the 1920s and the subsequent improvement in roads, which gave growers more options for delivering their produce directly to nearby gins, elevators, packing sheds, or livestock auctions for sale through cooperatives or to private buyers. Some producers engaged in futures trading through commercial brokers as a hedge against possible price declines. Though much of the produce went to fresh fruit and vegetable markets or cottonseed mills, flour mills, textile mills, meat-packing plants, canneries, or other processors both within the state and outside, the Texas Gulf ports as well as those on the Atlantic and Pacific coasts became the debarkation points for Texas crops sent to all areas of the world. With rice, cotton, cottonseed oil, peanuts, and livestock products as the leading export goods, the annual $2.5 billion international sales of Texas commodities by the 1990s represented approximately 20 percent of the state's cash receipts from crop and livestock marketing.

The manner of living for Texas farm families changed significantly after World War II. As electricity became available through rural cooperatives, farmers began enjoying the same household conveniences as those who lived in the city. In addition, the construction of farm roads and improved roadways made areas beyond the immediate community more accessible. Besides virtually eliminating the small country stores, the roads made shopping at supermarkets in nearby towns easy; milk cows and laying hens disappeared from many farmsteads. As consoli-

dation programs led to the closing of rural schools, children were bused to larger educational facilities, which usually offered access to more programs than such groups as 4H Clubs or Future Farmers of America. From the towns young men and women increasingly went to colleges and universities, either to pursue careers in urban areas or to return to their home communities trained in agricultural practices. Though some farmers chose to live in nearby towns and commute to their farms, by the 1980s a majority of Texans residing on farms earned their principal income elsewhere. Along with the advent of radio and television, which both entertained and kept farmers aware of world events and the latest crop and livestock market quotations, such devices as twoway radios and computers became helpful management tools, particularly at large commercial operations.

Even as changes came in the Texas agricultural system, several challenges existed with which farmers and livestock producers had to deal. Regardless of where farming and ranching occurred, environmental or climatic problems had always arisen. In some years there was little rain and in others too much. Crops still suffered from diseases and insects. Though the application of scientific and technological practices could ameliorate some of these difficulties, plains farmers felt a sense of hopelessness when their crops were destroyed by hail, for instance; citrus growers in the lower Rio Grande valley saw their orange and grapefruit orchards frozen on four occasions between 1950 and 1990. In addition, the fear of being caught on the wrong side of the cost–price squeeze was ever present. As commercial operators became dependent upon agribusiness suppliers, any variations in costs or slippage in prices placed them in jeopardy. For example, the rapid rise in natural gas prices during the 1970s forced both Upland and Pima irrigated cotton producers in Pecos and Reeves counties to reduce their acreage by twothirds. Besides the costs, irrigation farmers on the High Plains faced the threatened depletion of the Ogallala Aquifer, which had made the region one of the most prolific in the state. Despite such remedial efforts as the organization of water-conservation districts, the return of substantial watered acreage to dry land, the institution of minimum tillage techniques, and the installation of more efficient equipment such as the center pivot sprinkler or the low-energy pressure-application systems, the concern remained. Furthermore, though farmers and ranchers recognized that both national and international incidents could influence their livelihood, an element of insecurity existed when political leaders assumed the authority to render decisions affecting agriculture. Yet even with these and other issues, Texas agriculture remained a vital industry both in the state and the nation at the end of the twentieth century. By the 1990s crop and livestock cash receipts continued to grow. Agricultural receipts of approximately $12 billion combined with agribusinesses to add about $40 billion to the state's economy, thus making Texas one of the leading farm states.

Henry C. Dethloff and Garry L. Nall

Aguayo, Marqués de San Miguel de. Spanish governor; birth name José de Azlor y Virto de Vera; b. Spain, 16–?; d. Coahuila, New Spain, 7 March 1734; m. Ignacia Xaviera de Echevers. Aguayo received his title through his marriage to the daughter of the first Marqués de Aguayo. Aguayo and his wife lived on their one of their haciendas, Patos, which included almost half of Coahuila. Aguayo was perhaps the most important governor of

Spanish Texas. In 1719 the French invaded East Texas and forced the abandonment of missions and presidios. The same year, after offering to drive the French out of territory claimed by Spain, Aguayo was appointed governor of Coahuila and Texas. The next year the viceroy sent him on his most significant mission, which came to be known as the Aguayo expedition (1721). The expedition traveled to East Texas, where they met Louis Juchereau de St. Denis, the French commander, who agreed to withdraw to Natchitoches, Louisiana. When Aguayo entered Texas the province had only one presidio and two missions, one of which, San José y San Miguel de Aguayo, had been established only a few months earlier under his patronage. When he left, Texas had four presidios and ten missions, six of which were East Texas missions reestablished by the expedition. On its return southwestward, the expedition established a third mission in San Antonio, as well as Loreto Presidio and Espíritu Santo Mission in La Bahía. The Aguayo expedition established so definite a Spanish claim to Texas that it was never again disputed by France or the French in Louisiana. Aguayo was also responsible for the beginnings of colonization in Texas. He recommended that steps be taken to settle 400 families between San Antonio and the East Texas missions, one-half of the settlers to be recruited from Galicia, the Canary Islands, and Havana and the other half to be composed of loyal Tlaxcalán Indians. He resigned the governorship in ill health in 1722.

Lewis W. Newton

Aikin, A. M., Jr. Legislator; b. Red River County, 9 October 1905; d. Paris, Texas, 24 October 1981; m. Welma Morphew (1929); ed. Paris Junior College and Cumberland University, Lebanon, Tennessee (LL.B., 1932). In his 46 years (1932–79) as a representative and senator in Austin, Aikin missed only 2½ legislative days. Education was his focus and legacy. He supported all-weather farm roads, for instance, on the grounds that good schools were useless if they were inaccessible. The "father of modern Texas education" is best remembered for his sponsorship of the Gilmer–Aikin Laws (1949, with Rep. Claud Gilmer), which established a centralized state education system, and the Minimum Foundation school program; the latter set minimum teachers' salaries and other funding requirements. Aikin also sponsored an amendment for minimum teacher-retirement compensation (1956). He served as acting governor for 14 days in 1943 and was dean, then dean emeritus, of the state Senate. Two education chairs were established at the University of Texas at Austin in Aikin's name in 1985. His archives are at Paris Junior College.

Daisy Harvill

Ailey, Alvin. Black dancer; b. Rogers, 5 January 1931; d. New York City, 1 December 1989. Ailey and his mother, deserted by his father, lived in poverty and moved to the West Coast. In Los Angeles, under the influence of choreographer Lester Horton, Ailey turned to professional dance. He took over Horton's company in 1953, made his Broadway debut in 1954, and in the next four years appeared in a number of New York musicals (e.g., the Broadway production of *Tiger Tiger, Burning Bright*, 1962, and Langston Hughes's off-Broadway song-play *Jericho Jim Crow*, 1964); he also worked in movies and choreographed Samuel Barber's *Antony and Cleopatra*, the first production at the new Metropolitan Opera in Lincoln Center. In 1958 he began his own dance company, which was sent by the State Department on sev-

eral foreign tours beginning in 1962. More than 15 million people around the world saw his performances. After Ailey retired from dancing in 1965, he devoted himself to choreography and his company, which continued with a splendid worldwide career. The company was all black until 1963, when it was integrated and Ailey found himself criticized—a victim, in his words, of "reverse racism." He received many honors, among them the Kennedy Center Honors from President Ronald Reagan (1988).

Kharen Monsho

Air-conditioning. The importance to Texas of air-conditioning could hardly be overstated. Before refrigerated air, attempts at keeping people or such products as milk cool by cooling the air included the use of well water, ice, dry ice, and various evaporative cooling methods such as forcing air through wet blankets. The revolution began when the Rice Hotel cafeteria (Houston) was air-conditioned by refrigeration in 1922. By the 1940s Texas was a manufacturing center for air-cooling machines and inventions, including the heat pump and car air-conditioners. The industry continued to grow. Just as important, however, was the fact that air-conditioning made factories and residences more comfortable and therefore was, some believe, a *sine qua non* of the industrial boom in modern Texas. *Willis R. Woolrich*

Alabama Trace. An Indian road that ran from the Old San Antonio Road near the site of San Augustine to Colita's Village on the Trinity River and passed through four Alabama Indian villages. The trace was used by illegal immigrants and contraband traders who entered Spanish Texas by such alternate routes in order to avoid Nacogdoches. Part of the trace was later a stagecoach road. *Howard N. Martin*

Alamo. San Antonio de Valero Mission in San Antonio was abandoned by 1793, and its archives were taken to San Fernando Church. The Second Flying Company of San Carlos de Parras, from Álamo de Parras, Coahuila, occupied the mission in 1803. The name Alamo came either from this association or from a grove of cottonwoods (*álamos*) growing beside the mission's acequia. The Alamo was occupied by Spanish, then Mexican, forces almost continuously from 1803 to 1835, when Gen. Martín Perfecto de Cos surrendered it to Texas revolutionary forces after the siege of Bexar. William B. Travis entered the Alamo on 23 February 1836 with a force that was annihilated at the battle of the Alamo on 6 March. The Republic of Texas gave the ruined mission back to the Catholic Church in 1841. After annexation the establishment was variously claimed and/or used by the U.S. government, Confederate forces, and the church. In 1883 Texas bought the Alamo property from the church and stipulated that it be cared for by a custodian under the direction of San Antonio. In 1905, however, the legislature was obliged to evict a business from the fortress. At that time the Daughters of the Republic of Texas were given custody. Disputes about who should manage the Alamo are ongoing. *Amelia W. Williams*

Alamo, Battle of the. The siege and the final assault on the Alamo in 1836 constitute the most celebrated military engagement in Texas history. The battle was conspicuous for the large number of illustrious personalities among its combatants. These included Tennessee congressman David Crockett, entrepreneur–adventurer James Bowie, and Mexican president Antonio

Ruins of the Church of the Alamo, San Antonio de Bexar, by Edward Everett, 1847. Pen and ink, watercolor, and gouache on paper. 6" × 9⅜". Courtesy Amon Carter Museum, Fort Worth; gift of Mrs. Anne Burnett Tandy in memory of her father, Thomas Loyd Burnett, 1870–1938. Edward Everett, noted scientific draftsman, made several views of the Alamo.

López de Santa Anna. Although not nationally famous at the time, William Barret Travis achieved lasting distinction as commander at the Alamo. For many Americans and most Texans, the battle has become a symbol of patriotic sacrifice. Traditional popular depictions, including novels, stage plays, and motion pictures, emphasize legendary aspects that often obscure the historical event.

To understand the real battle, one must appreciate its strategic context in the Texas Revolution. In December 1835 a Federalist army of Texan (or Texian, as they were called) immigrants, American volunteers, and their Tejano allies had captured the town from a Centralist force during the siege of Bexar. With that victory, a majority of the Texan volunteers of the "Army of the People" left service and returned to their families. Nevertheless, many officials of the provisional government feared the Centralists would mount a spring offensive. Two main roads led into Texas from the Mexican interior. The first was the Atascosito Road, which stretched from Matamoros on the Rio Grande northward through San Patricio, Goliad, Victoria, and finally into the heart of Austin's colony. The second was the Old San Antonio Road, a *camino real* that crossed the Rio Grande at Paso de Francia (the San Antonio Crossing) and wound northeastward through San Antonio de Béxar, Bastrop, Nacogdoches, San Augustine, and across the Sabine River into Louisiana. Two forts blocked these approaches into Texas: Presidio La Bahía (Nuestra Señora de Loreto Presidio) at Goliad and the Alamo at San Antonio. Each installation functioned as a frontier picket guard, ready to alert the Texas settlements of an enemy advance. James Clinton Neill received command of the Bexar garrison. Some 90 miles to the southeast, James Walker Fannin, Jr., subsequently took command at Goliad. Most Texan settlers had returned to the comforts of home and hearth. Consequently, newly arrived American volunteers—some of whom counted their time in Texas by the week—constituted a majority of the troops at Goliad and Bexar. Both Neill and Fannin determined to stall the Centralists on the frontier. Still, they labored under no illusions. Without speedy reinforcements, neither the Alamo nor Presidio La Bahía could long withstand a siege.

At Bexar were 21 artillery pieces of various caliber. Because of his artillery experience and his regular army commission, Neill was a logical choice to command. Throughout January he did his best to fortify the mission fort on the outskirts of town. Maj. Green B. Jameson, chief engineer at the Alamo, installed most of the cannons on the walls. Jameson boasted to General Houston that if the Centralists stormed the Alamo, the defenders could "whip 10 to 1 with our artillery." Such predictions proved excessively optimistic. Far from the bulk of Texas settlements, the Bexar garrison suffered from a lack of even basic provender. On 14 January Neill wrote Houston that his people were in a "torpid, defenseless condition." That day he dispatched a grim message to the provisional government: "Unless we are reinforced and victualled, we must become an easy prey to the enemy, in case of an attack."

By 17 January, Houston had begun to question the wisdom of

maintaining Neill's garrison at Bexar. On that date he informed Governor Henry Smith that Col. James Bowie and a company of volunteers had left for San Antonio. Many have cited this letter as proof that Houston ordered the Alamo abandoned. Yet, Houston's words reveal the truth of the matter:

> I have ordered the fortifications in the town of Bexar to be demolished, and, *if you should think well of it*, I will remove all the cannon and other munitions of war to Gonzales and Copano, blow up the Alamo and abandon the place, as it will be impossible to keep up the Station with volunteers, the sooner I can be authorized the better it will be for the country [italics added].

Houston may have wanted to raze the Alamo, but he was clearly requesting Smith's consent. Ultimately, Smith did not "think well of it" and refused to authorize Houston's proposal.

On 19 January, Bowie rode into the Alamo compound, and what he saw impressed him. As a result of much hard work, the mission had begun to look like a fort. Neill, who well knew the consequences of leaving the *camino real* unguarded, convinced Bowie that the Alamo was the only post between the enemy and Anglo settlements. Neill's arguments and his leadership electrified Bowie. "I cannot eulogize the conduct & character of Col. Neill too highly," he wrote Smith; "no other man in the army could have kept men at this post, under the neglect they have experienced." On 2 February, Bowie wrote Smith that he and Neill had resolved to "die in these ditches" before they would surrender the post. The letter confirmed Smith's understanding of controlling factors. He had concluded that Bexar must not go undefended. Rejecting Houston's advice, Smith prepared to funnel additional troops and provisions to San Antonio. In brief, Houston had asked for permission to abandon the post. Smith considered his request. The answer was no.

Colonel Neill had complained that "for want of horses," he could not even "send out a small spy company." If the Alamo were to function as an early-warning station, Neill had to have outriders. Now fully committed to bolstering the Bexar garrison, Smith directed Lt. Col. William B. Travis to take his "Legion of Cavalry" and report to Neill. Only 30 horsemen responded to the summons. Travis pleaded with Governor Smith to reconsider: "I am unwilling to risk my reputation (which is ever dear to a soldier) by going off into the enemy's country with such little means, and with them so badly equipped." Travis threatened to resign his commission, but Smith ignored these histrionics. At length, Travis obeyed orders and dutifully made his way toward Bexar with his 30 troopers. Reinforcements began to trickle into Bexar. On 3 February, Travis and his cavalry contingent reached the Alamo. The 26-year-old cavalry officer had traveled to his new duty station under duress. Yet, like Bowie, he soon became committed to Neill and the fort, which he began to describe as the "key to Texas." About 8 February, David Crockett arrived with a group of American volunteers.

On 14 February, Neill departed on furlough. He learned that illness had struck his family and that they desperately needed him back in Bastrop. While on leave, he labored to raise funds for his Bexar garrison. He promised that he would resume command when circumstances permitted, certainly within 20 days, and left Travis in charge as acting post commander. Neill had not intended to slight the older and more experienced Bowie, but Travis, like Neill, held a regular army commission. For all of

his notoriety, Bowie was still just a volunteer colonel. The Alamo's volunteers, accustomed to electing their officers, resented having this regular officer foisted upon them. Neill had been in command since January; his maturity, judgment, and proven ability had won the respect of both regulars and volunteers. Travis, however, was unknown. The volunteers insisted on an election, and their acting commander complied with their wishes. The garrison cast its votes along party lines: the regulars voted for Travis, the volunteers for Bowie. In a letter to Smith, Travis claimed that the election and Bowie's subsequent conduct had placed him in an "awkward situation." The night following the balloting, Bowie dismayed Bexar residents with his besotted carousal. He tore through the town, confiscating private property and releasing convicted felons from jail. Appalled by this disorderly exhibition, Travis assured the governor that he refused to assume responsibility "for the drunken irregularities of any man"—not even the redoubtable Jim Bowie. Fortunately, this affront to Travis's sense of propriety did not produce a lasting breach between the two commanders. They struck a compromise: Bowie would command the volunteers, Travis the regulars. Both would cosign all orders and correspondence until Neill's return. There was no more time for personality differences. They had learned that Santa Anna's Centralist army had reached the Rio Grande. Travis did not believe that Santa Anna could reach Bexar until 15 March, but the Mexican army's arrival on 23 February convinced him otherwise. As Texans gathered in the Alamo, Travis dispatched a hastily scribbled missive to Gonzales: "The enemy in large force is in sight. We want men and provisions. Send them to us. We have 150 men and are determined to defend the garrison to the last." Travis and Bowie understood that the Alamo could not hold without additional forces. Their fate now rested with the General Council in San Felipe, Fannin at Goliad, and other Texan volunteers who might rush to assist the beleaguered Bexar garrison.

Santa Anna sent a courier to demand that the Alamo surrender. Travis replied with a cannonball. There could be no mistaking such a concise response. Centralist artillerymen set about knocking down the walls. Once the heavy pounding reduced the walls, the garrison would have to surrender in the face of overwhelming odds. Bottled up inside the fort, the Texans had only one hope—that reinforcements would break the siege.

On 24 February, Travis assumed full command when Bowie fell victim to a mysterious malady variously described as "hasty consumption" or "typhoid pneumonia." As commander, Travis wrote his letter addressed to the "people of Texas & all Americans in the world," in which he recounted that the fort had "sustained a continual Bombardment and cannonade for 24 hours." He pledged that he would "never surrender or retreat" and swore "Victory or Death." The predominant message, however, was an entreaty for help: "I call on you in the name of Liberty, of patriotism & everything dear to the American character, to come to our aid, with all dispatch." On 1 March, 32 troops attached to Lt. George C. Kimbell's Gonzales ranging company made their way through the enemy cordon and into the Alamo. Travis was grateful for any reinforcements, but knew he needed more. On 3 March he reported to the convention at Washington-on-the-Brazos that he had lost faith in Fannin. "I look to the colonies alone for aid; unless it arrives soon, I shall have to fight the enemy on his own terms." He grew increasingly bitter that his fellow Texans seemed deaf to his appeals. In a let-

Battle of Bexar—Heroism of Col. Crockett, anonymous, 1837. Wood engraving. From *Davy Crockett's Almanack of Wild Sports in the West, Life in the Backwoods, and Sketches of Texas,* Vol. 1, No. 3 (Nashville: Published by the heirs of Col. Crockett, [1836?]). Courtesy Huntington Library, San Marino, California. This woodcut appeared in one of the popular "Crockett almanacs," which claimed that Crockett killed 17 men in his final moments.

ter to a friend, Travis revealed his frustration: "If my countrymen do not rally to my relief, I am determined to perish in the defense of this place, and my bones shall reproach my country for her neglect."

On 5 March, day 12 of the siege, Santa Anna announced an assault for the following day. This sudden declaration stunned his officers. The enemy's walls were crumbling. No Texan relief column had appeared. When the provisions ran out, surrender would remain the rebels' only option. There was simply no valid military justification for the costly attack on a stronghold bristling with cannons. But ignoring these reasonable objections, Santa Anna stubbornly insisted on storming the Alamo. Around 5:00 A.M. on Sunday, 6 March, he hurled his columns at the battered walls from four directions. Texan gunners stood by their artillery. As about 1,800 assault troops advanced into range, canister ripped through their ranks. Staggered by the concentrated cannon and rifle fire, the Mexican soldiers halted, reformed, and drove forward. Soon they were past the defensive perimeter. Travis, among the first to die, fell on the north bastion. Abandoning the walls, defenders withdrew to the dim rooms of the Long Barracks. There some of the bloodiest hand-to-hand fighting occurred. Bowie, too ravaged by illness to rise from his bed, found no pity. The chapel fell last. By dawn the Centralists had carried the works. The assault had lasted no more than 90 minutes. As many as seven defenders survived the battle, but Santa Anna ordered their summary execution. Many historians count Crockett as a member of that hapless contingent, an assertion that still provokes debate in some circles. By eight o'clock every Alamo fighting man lay dead. Currently, 189

defenders appear on the official list, but ongoing research may increase the final tally to as many as 257.

Though Santa Anna had his victory, the common soldiers paid the price as his officers had anticipated. Accounts vary, but best estimates place the number of Mexicans killed and wounded at about 600. Mexican officers led several noncombatant women, children, and slaves from the smoldering compound. Santa Anna treated enemy women and children with admirable gallantry. He pledged safe passage through his lines and provided each with a blanket and two dollars. The most famous of these survivors were Susanna W. Dickinson, widow of Capt. Almaron Dickinson, and their infant daughter, Angelina. After the battle, Mrs. Dickinson traveled to Gonzales. There, she reported the fall of the post to General Houston. The sad intelligence precipitated a wild exodus of Texan settlers called the Runaway Scrape.

What of real military value did the defenders' heroic stand accomplish? Some movies and other works of fiction pretend that Houston used the time to raise an army. During most of the siege, however, he was at the Convention of 1836 at Washington-on-the-Brazos and not with the army. The delay did, on the other hand, allow promulgation of the Declaration of Independence, formation of a revolutionary government, and the drafting of a constitution. If Santa Anna had struck the Texan settlements immediately, he might have disrupted the proceedings and driven all insurgents across the Sabine River. The men of the Alamo were valiant soldiers, but no evidence supports the notion—advanced in the more perfervid versions—that they "joined together in an immortal pact to give their lives that the spark of freedom might blaze into a roaring flame." Governor Smith and the General Council ordered Neill, Bowie, and Travis to hold the fort until support arrived. Despite all the "victory or death" hyperbole, they were not suicidal. Throughout the 13-day siege, Travis never stopped calling on the government for the promised support. The defenders of the Alamo willingly placed themselves in harm's way to protect their country. Death was a risk they accepted, but it was never their aim. Torn by internal discord, the provisional government could not deliver on its promise to provide relief, and Travis and his command paid the cost of that dereliction. As Travis predicted, his bones did reproach the factious politicos and the parade-ground patriots for their neglect. Even stripped of chauvinistic exaggeration, the battle of the Alamo remains an inspiring moment in Texas history. The sacrifice of Travis and his command animated the rest of Texas and kindled a righteous wrath that swept the Mexicans off the field at San Jacinto. Since 1836, Americans on battlefields over the globe have responded to the exhortation, "Remember the Alamo!" *Stephen L. Hardin*

Alarcón, Martín de. Spanish governor, founder of San Antonio; vital statistics unknown. Alarcón was appointed governor of Texas by Viceroy Marqués de Valero on 9 December 1716. He entered with 10 families (72 persons) in April 1718 and the next month, with Padre Antonio de San Buenaventura y Olivares, founded San Antonio de Valero Mission (the Alamo) and San Antonio de Béxar Presidio. The Villa de Béxar formed around the mission and presidio. Alarcón visited the six previously established East Texas missions, returned to San Antonio in January 1719, and in the fall of that year was relieved of his duties as governor. *Donald E. Chipman*

Alavez, Francita. The "Angel of Goliad"; vital statistics unknown. She accompanied Capt. Telesforo Alavez to Texas in March 1836 but was not married to him. At Copano Bay she persuaded Mexican troops to loosen the bonds of Maj. William P. Miller's captured men and give them food. She went then with Alavez to Goliad, where she is credited with saving Miller's men from the Goliad Massacre and hiding several prisoners to save their lives. She subsequently aided Texan prisoners in Matamoros. She was later abandoned in Mexico City by Alavez. Doctors Joseph Barnard and John Shackelford, two Goliad prisoners spared by the Mexicans, publicized Francita's saintly behavior, for which she gained her nickname and was recognized as a heroine of the Texas Revolution. *George O. Coalson*

Alcalde. The *alcalde ordinario*, usually designated by *alcalde* alone, was the head of the ayuntamiento or town council in a Spanish or Mexican municipality. He was usually chosen by the council, but could be appointed by the governor or elected. He was a judge in local civil matters, a maker of laws, and the chief administrator of the town. His decisions could, however, be appealed to the ayuntamiento, to the governor, or to the governor's aide, the *alcalde mayor*. The office of alcalde lasted without much change from the beginning of Spanish Texas to the Texas Revolution. *Geoffrey Pivateau*

Alguacil. The municipal policeman of a Spanish or Mexican municipality, who carried out the orders of the alcalde and belonged to the ayuntamiento. His office combined those of sheriff and bailiff. The alguacil was elected or appointed, could hold no other office, and was often paid a percentage of judgments from the alcalde's court. *Geoffrey Pivateau*

Allen, Augustus Chapman. Cofounder of Houston; b. Canaseraga, New York, 4 July 1806; d. D.C., 11 June 1864; m. Charlotte Baldwin (1831); ed. Polytechnic Institute, Chittenango, New York. Allen taught mathematics and engaged in business with his brother John K. Allen before the two moved to Texas in 1832. They contributed a vessel to the Texas cause during the Texas Revolution. In 1836 they bought land on Buffalo Bayou and decided to establish a town named for Sam Houston there. In 1837 other family members—mother, father, four brothers, and a sister—arrived in Texas. The brothers all became prominent. The Allens contrived to make Houston grow by, among other measures, helping to get Sam Houston elected president of the Republic of Texas and building a capitol in the town, which became one of the Texas capitals as a result. In addition to their investment in Houston, the brothers owned more than 100 leagues of land, held shares in the Galveston City Company, and were partners of Thomas F. McKinney and Samuel May Williams. John Allen died in 1838, the parents died by 1841, and the other four brothers demanded from Augustus their share of the complex estate. Much of John and Augustus's money had come from Augustus's wife, Charlotte Allen, who left her husband in 1850 over the handling of the estate (without divorce). Allen got sick, went to Mexico, hobnobbed with Benito Juárez, and became United States consul for the ports of Tehuantepec and Minotitlán (1852 and 1858), offices that gave him considerable importance. His new businesses thrived until, gravely ill, he traveled to Washington to resign his consulships and there died. *Amelia W. Williams*

Allen, Richard. Black political leader; b. a slave in Richmond, Virginia, 10 June 1830; d. Houston, 16 May 1909; m. Nancy——; 5 Children. Allen, trained as a carpenter, was active politically and in civic affairs from Reconstruction to 1896. He was a Freedmen's Bureau agent (1868) and supervisor of voter registration, helped organize the Republican party in Harris County, and took part in the nomination of Radical Republican Edmund J. Davis for governor (1869). He was elected to the legislature in 1869 and may have been reelected in 1873, though his Democratic opponent was seated instead. Allen was a vice president of the Union League (1871). He was a delegate to Republican national conventions through 1896 and to the National Colored Men's Convention in 1872 and 1879. In Houston he was elected street commissioner in 1878. The same year he was nominated for lieutenant governor, thus becoming the first black man to seek statewide office in Texas. He was a customs inspector in the early 1880s. Though a crusader for civil rights, he often broke with other black leaders—for instance, by supporting the Exodus Movement of blacks to Kansas and urging peaceful protest in a labor dispute (1890). He was a Masonic leader and Baptist Sunday school superintendent.

Alwyn Barr and Cary D. Wintz

Allred, James Burr V. Governor; b. Bowie, 29 March 1899, d. Wichita Falls, 24 September 1959; ed. Cumberland University, Lebanon, Tennessee (LL.B., 1921); m. Joe Betsy Miller (1927); V was a name, not an initial. Allred was appointed DA for the

Governor James Allred presents Alabama–Coushatta chief Ti-ca-i-che with a Texas flag at the centennial celebration of the signing of the Texas Declaration of Independence. Washington-on-the-Brazos, 1936. Courtesy Star of the Republic Museum, Washington, Texas.

Thirteenth Texas District in 1923, a post in which he opposed the Ku Klux Klan. He ran unsuccessfully for attorney general in 1926 and won the office in 1930. He was elected governor in 1934 after building a reputation for distrust of large corporations, a trait he further exhibited during two terms in the Governor's Mansion. He worked for ending the Great Depression through taxing businesses progressively and introduced many measures—a teacher-retirement system, an enlarged welfare program, and higher salaries for state employees, for instance—that became part of the liberal Democratic tradition. Many of his programs were approved by the Texas legislature but not funded. While still governor, Allred was appointed a federal judge by Franklin D. Roosevelt. He resigned the position in 1942 to run for the United States Senate, but was defeated by Pappy O'Daniel. Harry Truman returned him to the bench in 1949, and he remained a federal judge until his death. Allred was named the "Outstanding Young Man in America" for 1935.

Floyd F. Ewing

All-Woman Supreme Court. Appointed by Governor Pat M. Neff in 1925 to hear a case that turned on whether trustees of the Woodmen of the World were entitled to two tracts of land in El Paso. When the case made its way to the Texas Supreme Court in 1924, all three justices were Woodmen and were therefore legally disqualified from hearing the case. State law required the governor to appoint special justices at once. Neff, however, found after numerous attempts that every prominent male attorney he approached was also a Woodman, so he decided to appoint women attorneys. On 1 January 1925, shortly before his term ended, the governor named three women to serve on the special court: Nellie Robertson of Granbury (named special chief justice), Edith Wilmans of Dallas, and Hortense Ward of Houston. Apparently, however, Neff had not verified that each of his appointees had seven years' legal experience, a requirement stipulated by the state constitution for any Supreme Court justice. After several resignations and reappointments, the special court was finally set with Hortense Ward as chief justice and Ruth V. Brazzil of Galveston and Hattie L. Henenberg of Dallas as associ-

ate justices. These were all well-established lawyers. The appointments were finalized one day before the first hearing in the case. The all-woman court met in the state Capitol on 8 January 1925 to hear court procedure reviewed by Chief Justice C. M. Cureton and to determine if a writ of error would be granted in the case. The women agreed to review the decision of the El Paso Court of Appeals. The special court announced its ruling on 23 May, upholding the El Paso appeals court and allowing the Woodmen of the World full title to the two tracts. The novelty of an all-woman court, believed to have been the only such court to exist in the country, and the contemporaneous election of a woman (Miriam A. Ferguson) to the state's highest office, gave some distinction to the role of women in Texas politics. It was some 30 years later, however, before Texas women were allowed to serve on juries. And it was not until 1982 that a woman was named to serve full-time on the state Supreme Court, when Governor William Clements appointed a woman to fill an unexpired term on the court.   *Debbie Mauldin Cottrell*

Almonte, Juan Nepomuceno. Mexican official; b. Necupétaro, Michoacán, 15 May 1803; d. Paris, 21 March 1869. Almonte, an enemy of Spain, supported Mexico during the Mexican War of Independence and negotiated a commercial treaty with England, Mexico's first treaty with a major power. In 1834 he was sent to Texas on an inspection tour that resulted in the important report for which he is chiefly remembered, the "Statistical Report of Texas." The government's purpose in the mission was to promise reforms to the restive Texans, who looked as if they might try for independence. Almonte was captured at San Jacinto by Edward Burleson. Afterward, he hobnobbed with Antonio López de Santa Anna and served as a diplomat. While minister plenipotentiary to London, he promoted schemes that led to the French intervention in Mexico; he returned to Mexico with the French troops. Emperor Maximilian appointed him envoy to France, where he died.   *Winifred W. Vigness*

Álvarez de Pineda, Alonso. Explorer; birth date and place unknown; d. Mexico, 1520. Álvarez de Pineda commanded a Spanish expedition sent by Francisco de Garay, governor of Jamaica, in 1519, to explore the coast of the Gulf of Mexico. The expedition sailed along the Gulf coastline from Florida to Cabo Rojo, Mexico. Álvarez and his men were the first Europeans to explore and map the Gulf littoral between the areas previously explored by Juan Ponce De León and Diego Velázquez. The voyage ended when he encountered Hernán Cortés, who perceived him as a rival and arrested the messengers he sent ashore. Subsequently, Álvarez started a settlement on the Pánuco River, where he was killed by Indians. No original report of his voyage is extant, though a report is summarized in a royal *cédula* of 1521. Álvarez discovered that Florida is not an island, as previously reported, and was the first European to see the Mississippi. When his men returned to Jamaica without him in 1519, they presented Garay the first known map of the Gulf.

Robert S. Weddle

Amarillo, Texas. Commercial center of the Panhandle, in southern Potter County; extends into Randall County. When the Fort Worth and Denver City Railway began building across the Panhandle in 1887, a group of Colorado City merchants chose the site to establish stores. In April 1887, J. T. Berry platted the new town, choosing a well-watered section of school land, located along the railroad in Potter County, which included a large playa known as Amarillo, or Wild Horse, Lake. On 30 August 1887, Berry's townsite was elected county seat for Potter County. The settlement was originally called Oneida but was renamed Amarillo after the nearby lake and creek. These natural features had been named by New Mexican traders and *pastores*, probably for the yellow soil along the creek banks or the yellow wildflowers that were abundant during the spring and summer. The railroad arrived shortly after the county election, and by October 1887 freight service was made available. Amarillo boomed as a cattle-marketing center. Holding grounds, complete with pens, were built near the tracks to corral the numerous herds that came from ranches in the Panhandle, South Plains, and eastern New Mexico for shipment. A lumberyard and a 25-room hotel were established, and the town's first weekly newspaper, the Amarillo *Champion*, began publication on 17 May 1888. Arguing that the townsite was on low ground that would flood during rainstorms, Henry B. Sanborn, part owner of the Frying Pan Ranch, and his partner, Joseph F. Glidden, began buying land to the east to move Amarillo out of its "mudhole." They purchased four sections and offered to trade lots in the new location for those in the original site and contribute to the expense of moving buildings. Businesses began to move to Polk Street in the new commercial district. Sanborn built the elegant 40-room Amarillo Hotel, which became the town's social center and the unofficial headquarters of area cattle buyers. He also donated a half block for Amarillo's first union church. In the spring of 1889, when heavy rains almost flooded "Old Town," the railroad embankment prevented effective drainage and prompted more people to move to Sanborn's higher location. The depot and courthouse remained at the old site, since the law decreed that they could not be moved until five years after the 1887 election. In 1893 another county-seat election officially transferred the title to Sanborn's town, and the records were housed in a newer building there. In the meantime the FW&DC had installed a second depot at the Polk Street crossing for the convenience of passengers. Ellwood Park, the first of Amarillo's many city parks, was established in the 1890s.

On 18 February 1899 the citizens voted to incorporate and elected Warren W. Wetzel mayor. However, the inauguration of city government was restrained by injunctions, and municipal administration was carried on by county officials and Texas Rangers for a while. The first annual Tri-State Fair was held in Amarillo in the fall of 1899. The population grew from 482 in 1890 to 1,442 by 1900. Construction of the Southern Kansas, the Pecos and Northern Texas, and the Chicago, Rock Island and Gulf railroads by 1903 added to the shipping facilities and helped to increase the population to 9,957 by 1910. In 1902 the two-story St. Anthony's Hospital, the first hospital in the Panhandle, was constructed; it served the entire area. Electrical service also came that year with the establishment of the Amarillo Light and Water Company, precursor to Southwestern Public Service. The Amarillo Independent School District was formed in 1905, and by the following year a new stone courthouse and jail were completed. The Amarillo Street Railway Company began operating its electric streetcar lines in January 1908. Increasing production of wheat and small grains made Amarillo an elevator, milling, and feed-manufacturing center during the early 1900s. Gas was discovered in 1918 and oil three years later. In 1928 the discovery

of the Cliffside gas field, with its high helium content, led to the establishment of the United States Helium Plant by the Federal Bureau of Mines four miles west of town. Lee Bivins, W. E. Fuqua, and others promoted the aviation industry, and in 1929 the Panhandle Air Service and Transportation Company was established; at one time Amarillo had five airfields, including the Municipal Airport. In 1926 Eugene A. Howe and Wilbur Clayton Hawk bought the Amarillo *News* and merged it with the *Globe* to form the Amarillo *Globe–News*. J. Lawrence Martin started Amarillo's first radio station, WDAG, in 1922. A municipal auditorium was completed in 1923, a 12-piece Philharmonic Orchestra was formed in 1925, and the Amarillo Little Theater was organized in 1927. The Bivins addition became the first suburban extension in southwest Amarillo.

The 1930s brought drought and black dusters to Amarillo. However, the city was a regional center for numerous federal relief programs, especially the WPA, whose funds helped improve the streets, water, and sewerage facilities. The popularity of Art Deco architecture was reflected in several new public buildings, including the Santa Fe Building, headquarters of the Panhandle and Santa Fe Railway, and the new Potter County Courthouse. Howe made news with his "Tactless Texan" column and merged the competing WDAG and KGRS radio stations as KGNC. In 1934 Cal Farley founded the Maverick Club for underprivileged boys; from that program later grew Kid, Incorporated. Four U.S. highways—60, 87, 287, and the fabled Route 66—merged at Amarillo, making it a major tourist stop with numerous motels, restaurants, and curio shops. By 1940 Amarillo's population numbered 51,686. A United States veterans' hospital was built west of the city. During World War II Amarillo Army Air Field was a school for basic pilot training, and the nearby Pantex Ordnance Plant produced bombs and ammunition. The influx of servicemen and their families and the new jobs ended the city's depression and boosted its chamber of commerce. On 15 May 1949 a tornado killed seven people and caused damage estimated at $2.5 million. Between 1950 and 1960 Amarillo grew 85 percent, from 74,443 to 137,969. In 1951 the city's first television station began broadcasting. S. B. Whittenburg published the Amarillo *Times*, which he merged with the *Globe–News* when he and his associates bought the company in 1955. During the late 1960s a municipal building, a civic center, a branch library, a corporation court building, High Plains Baptist Hospital, and a multimillion-dollar medical center were built.

The closing of Amarillo Air Force Base in 1968 contributed to a decrease in population to 127,010 by 1970. In September 1970 the Texas State Technical Institute opened a campus on the former base grounds. The 1970s saw the opening of the Amarillo Art Center on the Amarillo College campus, the establishment of the Amarillo Copper Refinery of ASARCO, Incorporated, and the opening of the Donald D. Harrington Discovery Center, which includes the first computer-controlled planetarium in the nation. Iowa Beef Processors and Owens–Corning Fiberglass also built plants at Amarillo. By 1980 Amarillo had a population of 149,230 and encompassed in its city limits more than 60 square miles in Potter and Randall counties. Between 1969 and 1986 new oil companies were formed; Mesa Petroleum Company, headed by T. Boone Pickens, Jr., became one of the nation's largest oil firms. Gas, petroleum, agriculture, and cattle are Amarillo's principal sources of income. In the 1980s local businesses included petrochemicals, grain storage, processing, meat packing, clothing, feed, leather goods, and cement manufacture. The Helium Monument, located near the Harrington Discovery Center and containing time capsules, designates Amarillo the "Helium Capital of the World." New housing developments and shopping centers in south and west Amarillo followed the completion of Interstate Highway 40, and during the 1980s Interstate 27 was constructed from Lubbock to Amarillo. Amarillo is the home of the world's largest feeder-cattle auction and headquarters of the American Quarter Horse Association. Amarillo was home for such celebrities as country music pioneer Alexander C. (Eck) Robertson and Thomas A. Preston, Jr., better known among card players as Amarillo Slim. The city is celebrated in song by George Strait's "Amarillo by Morning." In 1990 the population was 157,615.

H. Allen Anderson

American Airlines. Headquartered in Fort Worth; founded in 1929 by the Aviation Corporation of New York, which counted among its initial acquisitions 85 small airlines. The next year, routes were redrawn, management reorganized, and the pieces incorporated to form American Airways. Three years later the company introduced flight attendants. A further reorganization followed the reapportioning of airmail contracts by the government, and in 1934 American Airways became American Airlines. Credited with the firm's early success was Cyrus Rowlett Smith (president, 1934–68), a former Texas Air Transport and Southern Air Transport executive, who was named secretary of commerce by President Lyndon B. Johnson. The new company inaugurated the air-traffic-control system administered by the government and later adopted by all airlines. Between 1936 and 1942 AA began flights between Chicago and New York, became the nation's major domestic carrier in revenue passenger miles (a revenue passenger mile equals one passenger flown one mile), and established service to Mexico. Domestic freight service began in 1944, and in 1945 European service began with a transAtlantic division called American Overseas Airlines. After the war, during which AA turned over almost half its fleet to the Air Transport command, the company pioneered nonstop transcontinental and cargo service, and in 1959 began its first jet service with Boeing 707 aircraft. AA's computerized reservation system, known as SABRE, was established in 1959, and by the 1990s it served 25,000 travel agencies. Robert L. Crandall became president and chief operating officer in 1980, and chairman and chief executive officer in 1985, after working at Eastman Kodak, Hallmark Cards, Trans World Airlines, and Bloomingdale's; he was known for his use of computers and advanced technology to achieve efficiency and cost control. Taking advantage of the Airline Deregulation Act (1978), Crandall invented strategies for adapting the airline to a new economic environment. Among the innovations that he helped develop were Super-Saver fares, frequent-flyer programs, loyalty fares, participatory employee-relations policies, and the establishment of a system of hubs in Dallas–Fort Worth, Chicago, Miami, Nashville, Raleigh–Durham, and San Juan. This system began with the opening of the D–FW hub in 1981. The hub system enabled the airline to increase its daily flights from 100 to 300 and, despite the strike of air-traffic controllers, to report profits for that year of $47 million.

AMR Corporation, headquartered in Fort Worth, was established in 1982 when AA stockholders approved a reorganization plan and established a holding company. AMR comprises American Airlines (its principal component) and a number of other subsidiaries: AMR Eagle owns American Eagle carriers; American Airlines Decision Technologies provides decision-support systems for industry worldwide; AMR Information Services offers information-management services; AMR Investment Services provides investment management; AMR Services Corporation provides aircraft handling services, cargo handling, warehousing, and distribution services; and the AMR Training and Consulting Group offers consulting services in airline-related businesses. American Airlines divisions include AA Cargo, which provides freight and mail service; SABRE (Semi-Automated Business Research Environment) Travel Information Network and SABRE Computer Services, which provides travel information services from the world's largest privately owned real-time computer network; and SABRE Development Services, which offers information and computer services, including risk assessment. An additional unit, American Airlines Television or AATV, provides video-production services at the airline's television facilities. In 1987 the airline completed underground facilities to house its computer equipment and software in Tulsa, Oklahoma, and merged with a West Coast airline known as Air Cal. By the early 1990s the airline employed over 96,000 workers. In the 1990s AA saw a major expansion of its facilities at Dallas–Fort Worth International Airport, and the American Airlines C. R. Smith Museum opened. By 1994 the company was operating a fleet of 681 aircraft, which flew a daily average of more than 269,000,000 revenue passenger miles and provided air service to 201 cities worldwide. The company served 361 cities through its American Eagle domestic service. Crandall retired in 1998.

Diana J. Kleiner

American G.I. Forum. Originally a Texas Hispanic organization, later a national one. In 1948, 700 Mexican-American veterans, led by Hector P. Garcia, met in Corpus Christi and organized the forum, a civil-rights organization devoted to securing equal rights for Hispanic Americans. The first issue the forum dealt with was the failure of the Veterans Administration to deliver earned benefits through the G.I. Bill of Rights of 1944. After securing those benefits, the forum addressed other veterans' concerns, such as hospital care and Mexican-American representation on draft boards. The Felix Longoria affair (1949) gained national attention and established the forum as an effective civil-rights advocate for Hispanics. The organizational structure promoted this goal. The local chapter was the basic unit; the membership of each local chapter had to be 75 percent veterans. Beyond the local chapter were the district, state, and (after 1958) national governing bodies. In some areas, auxiliary (female) and junior G.I. forums developed. The charter of each unit emphasized loyalty and patriotism. The forum also prohibited direct official endorsement of a political party or candidate. This sanction blunted possible charges of bloc voting. In 1954 forum lawyers, in conjunction with attorneys for LULAC, successfully argued before the Supreme Court in *Hernandez v. the State of Texas* that Mexican Americans, although technically classified as Caucasian, suffered discrimination as a class and were entitled to the protection of the Fourteenth Amendment. In 1957 the Texas forum ended a 10-year struggle when a federal court agreed that school segregation of Mexican-American children in Texas schools was unjustified. In the same decade the forum helped thousands of Mexican Americans in the Rio Grande valley to register to vote, and incidents of police brutality were confronted in forum efforts. In 1958 the American G.I. Forum became a national organization, and its members led Mexican Americans into national politics. In the 1960 presidential campaign Viva Kennedy–Viva Johnson clubs, administered by forum and LULAC leaders, helped to win Texas and New Mexico for John Kennedy. Although the Kennedy administration did not reciprocate with much federal aid, the Johnson administration did. The G.I. Forum played a significant role in the application of Great Society programs in the barrios, and for the first time Latin Americans were appointed to influential positions and agencies. When Johnson established the first cabinet-level office for Hispanic issues, he selected a former national chairman of the G.I. Forum, Vicente Ximenes, for the position. The American G.I. Forum continued its work through the 1970s with such efforts as the first application of the due-process clause of the Fourteenth Amendment to de facto Mexican-American school segregation in Corpus Christi. In 1983 Garcia received an award for distinguished accomplishment from President Ronald Reagan.   *V. Carl Allsup*

American Legion. A nonpolitical and nonpartisan organization whose principal mission is to secure legislation to benefit veterans, including adequate hospitalization, physical and vocational rehabilitation, and preference in public jobs. The Texas Department was founded under the name Texas Division of World War Veterans in San Antonio on San Jacinto Day (21 April), 1919. Col. Claude V. Birkhead was elected first chairman. The name was changed a short time later to Texas Department, American Legion, to conform to the national organization. Among the most important concerns was the need for adequate hospitals for former servicemen. Donations were collected from posts and individuals throughout the state, and within a short time more than $500,000 was raised. In 1921–22 the department built the American Legion Memorial Hospital at Legion, Texas, with funds raised through Legion activities, supplemented by state aid. The hospital was sold to the United States in 1925 and became a Veterans Administration facility. While rehabilitation for veterans remained the number-one goal of the Legion through the early 1920s, the agenda was soon expanded to include employment, legislation, and the care of needy families, widows, and orphans of veterans. In 1920 the American Legion Auxiliary, composed of the wives and widows of veterans, was formed, with the purpose of augmenting and supporting the organization's activities. During the early 1920s the Legion also turned its attention toward fighting what it perceived as a growing tide of anti-Americanism. The Americanism committee at the 1923 convention called for "vigilance against teaching in public or private schools in Texas false or 'doctored' history, or subversive doctrine." It also endorsed a measure adopted at the national convention calling for the "total cessation of immigration until assimilation shall catch up with immigration."

The Legion also sponsored a variety of civic projects. Some posts erected community Christmas trees or made donations to the needy; others sponsored parks and playgrounds, built swimming pools, and equipped lighted baseball parks. After 1923 most of the posts in the state also sponsored local Boy Scout troops and took part in scouting activities. During the 1920s and early 1930s Legion posts throughout Texas also began to sponsor base-

ball teams and oratorical contests. Beginning in 1938 the Americanism program organized the annual Boys State convention, held each summer in Austin, to promote citizen education for young men. Between 1919 and 1942 membership in the Legion ranged from 10,540 to 37,709. In 1942 veterans of World War II were made eligible, and after the war large numbers of returning soldiers joined the organization. Black Texas veterans were made eligible in 1945. Just after World War II, when the demand for veterans' services exploded, the Legion lobbied for additional hospitals, rehabilitation facilities, and other benefits. Korean War veterans began joining the organization in large number in the mid-1950s, and in 1979 Vietnam veterans were made eligible for membership. By the early 1990s the statewide membership was 90,000. Subsequently, the Legion continued its earlier charitable activities and added new ones, including programs for abused children, the mentally retarded, missing children, and drug-abuse prevention. The state organization has been headquartered in Austin since 1927.

Carrie Wilcox and Christopher Long

American Party. The political branch of the American Order or Know-Nothing movement, an antiforeign, anti-Catholic secret society, which reached Texas by the mid-1850s. The numerous Texans who joined were those who feared "foreign ideas," especially the antislavery views often attributed to Mexican Americans and Germans in the state, or those who believed that the Democratic party was drifting toward secessionism and hoped that the new party might save the Union. Still others were Whigs who, realizing that their party was dying, did not want to join the Democrats. Some Texans were attracted by the secret character of the movement. Texas Know-Nothings, like those elsewhere, pledged to vote only for native-born Protestants for public office and to work to increase the residence requirement in the federal naturalization law from 5 to 21 years. In December 1854, Know-Nothing candidates swept the San Antonio municipal election. In March 1855 Galveston elected a Know-Nothing mayor. In the summer of 1855, Texas Know-Nothing leaders launched a plan to gain political control of the state by subverting the Democratic party. By that time they had secretly won over several Democratic leaders, including Rip Ford, chairman of the state Democratic committee, and Lt. Gov. David C. Dickson. The party, in supposed secrecy, nominated candidates for state offices and Congress. Dickson was pitted against Democratic governor Elisha Pease. The Democrats responded by formally condemning secret political factions and the imposition of tests for voting or officeholding. United States senator Sam Houston endorsed the principles of the American Order. Throughout the campaign Dickson and his supporters criticized Pease's unpopular proposal to pay for railroads with state funds, while the Democratic leadership hammered away at Dickson's defection to the American party. On 6 August Pease defeated Dickson by a vote of 26,336 to 17,968. The American party succeeded in electing Lemuel D. Evans to Congress from the eastern district, Stephen Crosby as land commissioner, and about a dozen members of the legislature.

In 1856 the American party of Texas, abandoning secrecy, met in open convention in Austin. Participants elected delegates to the national convention, nominated candidates for several state offices, and adopted resolutions endorsing the party's nativism and calling for the preservation and perpetuation of the federal

Union, a strict construction of the United States Constitution, the preservation of states' rights, and the denial of the right of Congress to legislate on the issue of slavery in the states.

In February two Texans, Lemuel Evans and Benjamin H. Epperson, attended the party's national convention in Philadelphia, which nominated Millard Fillmore for president. The failure of the party to include any statement in its platform about protecting the institution of slavery disappointed many Texas Know-Nothings and may have discouraged them from active participation in the campaign. At any rate, the American party candidates suffered local and national defeats in the general election. The movement then declined as it split nationally over slavery. In Texas the opposition of the Democrats was very effective. By 1857 the American party had virtually disappeared in Texas, though many of its former members supported Houston's unsuccessful bid for the governorship that year. In its short life, the American party made its mark on the Texas political scene by forcing the Democratic party to organize effectively throughout the state and by focusing on Unionist, nationalist, and nativist issues that perdured long after the movement's demise. *Roger A. Griffin*

Ames, Jessie Harriet Daniel. Suffragist and antilynching reformer; b. Palestine, Texas, 2 November 1883; d. Austin, 21 February 1972; ed. Southwestern University (B.A., 1902); m. Roger Post Ames (1905); 3 children. In 1916 Jessie Ames organized and became the first president of the Georgetown Equal Suffrage League and began to write weekly "Woman Suffrage Notes" for the *Williamson County Sun*. As the protégé of Minnie Fisher Cunningham, she was elected treasurer of the Texas Equal Suffrage Association in 1918; as such, she helped to make Texas the first Southern state to ratify the Nineteenth Amendment. In 1919 she became the founder and first president of the state League of Women Voters. She represented the national LWV at the Pan American Congress in 1923 and served as a delegate-at-large to the national Democratic conventions of 1920 and 1924 and as an alternate delegate in 1928. She also was president of the Texas branch of the AAUW and an officer of the Women's Joint Legislative Council, the Board of Education (Women's Division) of the Methodist Church, the Texas Committee on Prisons and Prison Labor, and the Texas Federation of Women's Clubs. In 1924 she became director of the Texas Council of the Commission on Interracial Cooperation, based in Atlanta. In 1929 she moved to Atlanta to become the national director of the CIC Woman's Committee; a year later, financed primarily by the CIC, she founded the Association of Southern Women for the Prevention of Lynching. Mrs. Ames directed the Association of Southern Women until 1942, when the CIC was replaced by the Southern Regional Council. In 1985 a lecture series was inaugurated in her honor at Southwestern University.

Jon D. Swartz

Anderson, Monroe Dunaway. Philanthropist; b. Jackson, Tennessee, 29 June 1873; d. Houston, 6 August 1939. Anderson was treasurer and partner in Anderson, Clayton and Company, the world's largest cotton merchandiser. He moved to Houston about 1907 and retired in 1938. He is chiefly known for the University of Texas M. D. Anderson Cancer Center at the Texas Medical Center in Houston. This leading hospital was initially funded by a gift from the M. D. Anderson Foundation.

Jesse Daniel Ames. Courtesy Austin History Center, Austin Public Library; Photo no. E.4 D (20).

Anderson, a bachelor, lived most of his later life in a succession of Houston hotels. *Thomas D. Anderson*

Angelina. Indian guide and interpreter for Spanish expeditions; vital statistics unknown. Angelina or Angelique, who had been baptized and had learned Spanish, perhaps at San Juan Bautista, was mentioned in the reports of four early-eighteenth-century expeditions to East Texas. The Angelina River was named for her by 1768. She was called "learned" and "sagacious" on the Aguayo expedition and has been much romanticized.

Diane Lu Hughes

Angelo State University. In San Angelo; founded downtown in 1928 as San Angelo College, a junior college program in the San Angelo ISD. In 1945 a county junior college district was established. In 1947 the first building was built on the present campus. The name was changed to Angelo State College in 1965 by a legislative act that made the college a four-year institution. The first baccalaureate degrees were awarded in 1967. In 1969 the name was changed to Angelo State University. A graduate school was initiated in 1971. In 1975 ASU became a member of the Texas State University System. The university's Management, Instruction, and Research Center is located at O. C. Fisher Lake on 4,645 acres leased from the United States Army Corps of

Engineers. The center supports instructional programs in animal science and other fields. The university offers a large scholarship program through the Robert G. Carr and Nona K. Carr Scholarship Foundation. ASU offers baccalaureate degrees in 33 major fields and graduate programs in 17.   *Sangeeta Singg*

Anglo-American Colonization. Anglo-American colonization in Mexican Texas took place between 1821 and 1835. Spain had first opened Texas to Anglo-Americans in 1820, less than one year before Mexico achieved its independence. Its traditional policy forbade foreigners in its territory, but Spain was unable to persuade its own citizens to move to remote and sparsely populated Texas. There were only three settlements in the province of Texas in 1820: Nacogdoches, San Antonio de Béxar, and La Bahía del Espíritu Santo (later Goliad), small towns with outlying ranches. The missions near the latter two, once expected to be nucleus communities, had been or were being secularized (i.e., transferred to diocesan administration from that of the Franciscans), while those near Nacogdoches had been closed since the 1770s. Recruiting foreigners to develop the Spanish frontier was not new. As early as the 1790s, Spain invited Anglo-Americans to settle in Upper Louisiana (Missouri) for the same reason. The foreigners were to be Catholic, industrious, and willing to become Spanish citizens in return for generous land grants. Spain expected the new settlers to increase economic development and help deter the aggressive and mobile Plains Indians such as the Comanches and Kiowas. Mexico continued the Spanish colonization plan after its independence in 1821 by granting contracts to empresarios who would settle and supervise selected, qualified immigrants.

Anglo-Americans were attracted to Hispanic Texas because of inexpensive land. Undeveloped land in the United States land offices cost $1.25 an acre for a minimum of 80 acres ($100) payable in specie at the time of purchase. In Texas each head of a family, male or female, could claim a headright of 4,605 acres (one league—4,428 acres of grazing land and one labor—177 acres of cropland) at a cost about four cents an acre ($184) payable in six years, a sum later reduced by state authorities.

Beginning in 1824 when the Republic of Mexico adopted its constitution, each immigrant took an oath of loyalty to the new nation and professed to be a Christian. Because the Catholic Church was the established church, the oath implied that all would become Catholic, although the national and state colonization laws were silent on the matter. Religion was not a critical issue, however. The church waited until 1831 to send a resident priest, Michael Muldoon, into the Anglo-Texan communities. This was inconvenient for those wishing to marry because there was no provision for civil ceremonies, and only priests had authority to perform nuptial rites. Anglo-Texans unwilling or unable to seek a priest in Catholic communities received permission from the authorities to sign a marriage bond, a practice common in the non-Anglican foothills of Virginia and the Carolinas before 1776, promising to formalize their union when a priest arrived.

Two other reasons brought Anglo-American settlers to Texas. Through the 1820s, most believed that the U.S would buy eastern Texas from Mexico. Many thought this part of Texas had been part of the Louisiana Purchase and that the United States had "given" it away to Spain in exchange for Florida in the 1819 Adams–Onís Treaty, which established the Sabine River bound-

ary. The Texas pioneers expected annexation would stimulate immigration and provide buyers for their land. A second attraction was that Mexico and the United States had no reciprocal agreements enabling creditors to collect debts or to return fugitives. Therefore, Texas was a safe haven for the many Mississippi valley farmers who defaulted on their loans when agricultural prices declined at the end of the War of 1812 and bankers demanded immediate payment. Faced with seizure of their property and even debtors' prison in many states, men loaded their families and belongings into wagons and headed for the Sabine River, where creditors could not follow and there was opportunity to start over.

Against this background, Moses Austin traveled from Missouri to San Antonio in 1820 to apply for an empresario grant to bring American families to Texas. Like so many others, he had suffered losses in banking failures and hoped to restore his family's fortunes by charging small fees—12½ cents an acre—for land within his assigned area. He had become a Spanish citizen in 1798, when he moved from Virginia to the St. Louis area and acquired an empresario grant to develop a lead mine and import workers. The Spanish governor at San Antonio gave tentative approval to Austin's plan, subject to review by his superiors, to bring 300 moral, hardworking, Catholic families from the former Spanish territory of Louisiana. Although the authorities wanted him to settle close to San Antonio, Austin opted for a still-to-be-defined area along the lower Colorado River, where he hoped to establish a port. He became ill on his return trip to Missouri and died at home in June 1821, leaving the plan with his eldest son, Stephen F. Austin.

Austin's advertisements for colonists coincided with Mexican independence and the presumption that a republic would be organized. Stimulated by these events, some families began moving immediately to the Red River near the site of future Texarkana and across the Sabine along the old Spanish road leading to Nacogdoches. There they remained as squatters, some with intentions of joining the Austin colony, but others engaged in trading with the Indians and Mexicans.

The younger Austin visited San Antonio in mid-1821 as his father's heir and received permission to explore the lower Colorado for a site for the colony. His roaming convinced him that the Brazos River watershed should be added to his grant. Upon returning to Texas in early 1822, Austin discovered he must go to Mexico City to confirm the contract with the national government, even though his first settlers were on their way with only vague instructions about where to settle. Soon after he reached the capital, a coup established an empire, and the resulting turmoil delayed Austin for a year. In April 1823 he finally received a contract under the Imperial Colonization Law, which had been passed in January. Because the empire collapsed in April and the republic was reestablished, Austin's empresario contract was the only one issued under this law. The reinstated republican Congress immediately approved the imperial contract, and Austin rushed back to Texas to organize his colony.

The Imperial Colonization Law specified that colonists must be Catholic, so Austin's first 300 families were affected. The 1824 National Colonization Law and the 1825 Coahuila and Texas State Colonization Law said only that foreigners must be Christian and abide by the laws of the nation, thereby implying they would be members of the established church. Protestant preachers occasionally visited Texas, but they seldom held public services. In 1834 the state decreed that no person should be molested for political or religious beliefs as long as he did not disturb public order. This was as close as Texans came to freedom of religion and speech before 1836.

Slavery was also an issue. Mexicans abhorred slavery as allowed in the United States, but pragmatic politicians shut their eyes to the system in their eagerness to have the Anglos produce cotton in Texas. National and state laws banned the *African* slave trade, but allowed Anglo-Americans to bring their family slaves with them to Texas and buy and sell them there until 1840. Grandchildren of those slaves would be freed gradually upon reaching certain ages. The state inferred in 1827 that it might emancipate slaves earlier, and the immigrants took the precaution of signing indenture contracts with their illiterate servants binding them for 99 years to work off their purchase price, upkeep, and transportation to Texas. Mexican officials recognized the subterfuge as debt peonage, and black slaves continued to arrive in Texas. The most serious threat to slaveholders occurred when President Vicente Ramón Guerrero emancipated all slaves on 15 September 1829 in commemoration of independence. Austin's Mexican friends quickly secured an exemption from the law for Texas.

Austin, the most successful Texas empresario, made four six-year contracts between 1823 and 1828 for a potential 1,200 families. They were to be settled between the watersheds of the Brazos and Colorado rivers and as far as the Lavaca River below the Old San Antonio Road, as well as eastward to the San Jacinto River (but not including Galveston Island) and a small area around the site of present-day Austin. A fifth contract issued in 1831 for 800 families to be settled along the Brazos above the old Spanish road was challenged by Sterling Clack Robertson, who had an expired prior claim. The ensuing conflict made accurate tallies difficult.

Empresarios did not own the land within their grants, nor could they issue titles; the state appointed a land commissioner to give deeds only after 100 families had been settled. Surveyors laid off leagues and labores along the watercourses and roads, after which colonists could choose vacant tracts. The settlers paid fees to the state, the surveyor, the land commissioner, and the clerk, who wrote the deeds on stamped paper and recorded the payments. Austin's plan to restore his family's well-being by selling land was denied because empresarios could not receive fees. The state gave them a bonus of 23,000 acres for each 100 families settled. By 1834, at the virtual end of the empresario system, Austin had settled about 966 families and earned 197,000 acres of bonus land that he could locate where he chose. He could sell the land, but only to those willing to live in Texas.

Austin, as the pioneer empresario in Texas, was burdened with more duties than later contractors. With no published compendium of the Mexican laws, administrative and judicial authority rested with Austin, and the result was a mix of Mexican decrees with pragmatic Anglo-American implementation. Local settlements within his colony elected alcaldes, similar to justices of the peace, and constables. Austin sat as superior judge until 1828, when sufficient population permitted the installation of an ayuntamiento at San Felipe, the capital of the colony. This council, with elected representatives from the settlements, had authority over the entire Austin colony and acted like a county government. As population grew, other settlements within the colony qualified for ayuntamientos. These councils

settled lawsuits, regulated the health and welfare of the residents by supervising doctors, lawyers, taverns, and ferries, surveyed roads, and sold town lots. Capital cases were referred to authorities in Monterrey and later Saltillo. The remoteness of the court disturbed settlers, who wanted accessible courts.

Austin also commanded the local militia to defend the colony against Indians and to keep the peace. His contract area had only a few small Indian villages belonging to such sedentary groups as the Bidais and Coushattas, who wanted only to trade. Less friendly were the seasonally migrant remnant coastal tribes of Karankawas or the inland Tonkawas, who foraged for game and targeted the settlers' livestock. Pioneers along the Colorado River suffered most. Austin led several punitive expeditions between 1823 and 1826; he also negotiated moderately successful treaties with these declining tribes. North and west of the Austin colony Indians continued to resist the flow of immigrants well beyond the colonial period.

Other men besides Austin wanted empresario contracts in Texas, and a few were in Mexico City in 1822. Because of the changing political scene and the slow passage of the colonization laws, they had to wait until 1825, after the passage of national and state colonization laws passed in August 1824 and March 1825. The national law prohibited foreigners from settling within 26 miles of the Gulf of Mexico or within 52 miles of the Sabine River border without special executive permission. To encourage immigration, settlers were free from national taxes for four years. Land ownership was limited to 11 leagues. Owners had to be residents of Mexico. Preference was given to native Mexicans in the selection, and the national government could use any portion of land needed for the defense and security of the nation.

The state colonization law detailed how to apply for land, how much would be given to heads of families (including females and single persons), and the fees to be paid. The law granted freedom from tithes and the *alcabala*, an internal excise tax, for 10 years. Within three weeks four contracts were signed: Haden Edwards could settle 800 families in the Nacogdoches area, Robert Leftwich 800 along the Brazos valley above the Old San Antonio Road, Green DeWitt 400 on the Guadalupe River, and Frost Thorn 400 north of Nacogdoches. DeWitt, who developed the area around Gonzales, was the second most successful empresario in Texas. He settled 189 families before his contract expired in 1831. His colony suffered Indian attacks and also controversy with his neighbor, empresario Martín De León.

De León, a native of a small town 100 miles southwest of the site of present Matamoros, moved his family north across the Nueces River and into the province of Texas in the early 1800s. He lived by catching mustangs and wild cattle and raising mules, then selling the animals in San Antonio or even trailing them to Louisiana. In April 1824, before the passage of the national colonization law, he received permission from the provincial deputation in San Antonio to establish a town for 41 families about 20 miles northeast of La Bahía on the banks of the Guadalupe River. No boundaries were mentioned. By October, De León and 12 families had arrived at a cypress grove, the site of the town of Guadalupe Victoria (now Victoria).

Unaware of the colonization grant to De León in San Antonio, the state assigned the same area of the Guadalupe valley with specific boundaries to DeWitt in April 1825. When DeWitt's settlers arrived, trouble was inevitable. Because the colonization laws gave preference to native Mexicans, De León petitioned the state for redress, and the authorities told DeWitt in October 1825 to respect De León's prior claims but failed to establish boundaries. The state named land commissioners for both De León's and DeWitt's colonies. The commissioners issued titles in 1831, the year DeWitt's six-year contract expired permanently. The boundaries remained unresolved. Eventually 16 non-Hispanic families, some of whom were Anglo-Americans with Irish roots, received headrights in De León's otherwise Hispanic community. De León also quarreled with neighboring empresarios James Power and James Hewetson, natives of Ireland and residents of the United States and Mexico. They received a state contract in June 1828 to settle 200 families—half Mexican and half Irish—in the 26-mile coastal reserve between the mouth of the Guadalupe and the mouth of the Lavaca River, an area that received approval from the president. In 1829 their boundary was extended south to the Nueces River. Two hundred titles were issued to Europeans, but because many were single men the colonial contract was left incomplete, since the law specified families. Nearby, two other Irish natives, residents of Matamoros, secured a contract in 1828 to bring 200 European families to the Nueces above the Power–Hewetson grant. John McMullen and James McGloin's colony was known as the Irish Colony; most of its residents clustered around San Patricio, where the land commissioner issued 84 titles.

Of more importance to the development of Anglo-Texan communities were the large grants made in 1825 to Edwards and Leftwich that were adjacent to the Austin colony on the east and north. Edwards's contract specified land for up to 800 Anglo-American families in a large area of East Texas from northwest of Nacogdoches, including the forks of the Trinity, west to the Navasota River, thence southeast along the Trinity River valley to upper Galveston Bay. The tract did not include Galveston Island or the coastal reserve forbidden to foreigners. The eastern boundary was the 52-mile-wide border reserve along the Sabine River running north from the Gulf of Mexico to the thirty-second parallel. The state instructed Edwards to respect the property of long-time residents in the Nacogdoches area, some of whom had been there since the 1780s. Edwards, insensitive to Hispanic culture, reached Nacogdoches in October 1825 and threatened to dispossess those who had no proof of ownership unless they paid him for the land. The Spanish process to acquire land on the remote frontier was lengthy and expensive, and almost nobody had deeds. But besides Hispanics, there were a number of Anglo-American hunters and traders who had moved there in the 1790s, as well as new squatters who had arrived since 1821. Although local alcaldes were authorized for the scattered settlements, there was no ayuntamiento until 1828, so all official business had to be conducted in San Antonio. In general, Hispanics and old-time Anglos opposed Edwards and complained to the political chief in San Antonio; some newcomers supported the empresario, while others remained aloof. Tensions mounted during 1826, and in response to complaints against Edwards the state abrogated his contract in October and banished him from Texas. Anglo-Texans, even those not involved in the controversy, were disturbed that a contract, almost sacred in Anglo culture, could be canceled. Did that mean that the provisions of the colonization laws might change regarding slavery? Were other empresario contracts vulnerable?

At the time of the cancellation, Haden Edwards was recruiting colonists in Mississippi, but his brother, Benjamin W.

Edwards, rallied supporters to protest the order. In November they seized the alcalde (an Anglo old-timer) and tried others at a drumhead court; after a few days all were released. The following month the insurgents declared independence from Mexico by decreeing the Republic of Fredonia. Benjamin Edwards forged an alliance with some disaffected Cherokee leaders who were unable to secure titles to their villages northwest of Nacogdoches, and Edwards promised to divide Texas between the red men and the whites. The Indians reconsidered, however, and failed to support Edwards, who fled towards Louisiana in January 1827, when soldiers from San Antonio accompanied by Austin's militia approached Nacogdoches. Thus ended the quixotic Fredonian Rebellion, which aroused fears of widespread Anglo-Texan revolt among Mexican leaders. The state banished the ringleaders, promised to send a land commissioner to issue titles to families who had settled the area in good faith, and established a permanent garrison at Nacogdoches to guard against ruffians and filibusters from the United States.

Almost as troublesome was the Leftwich contract, which, unknown to the authorities, was intended as a profit-making undertaking for the benefit of stockholders. This empresario grant eventually was known as Robertson's colony. Leftwich, who was in Mexico City when Austin was there, represented 70 Tennessee investors called the Texas Association. The land assigned was in the upper Brazos valley just north of Austin's grant and touching that of Edwards on the east. When Leftwich returned to Nashville in 1825 with the empresario contract in his name instead of the company's, the investors had to buy out his interest. They sent several agents to Coahuila–Texas to get the contract in their name, but the suspicions raised by the Fredonian Rebellion deterred their efforts. With Austin's help, the Nashville Association (as it was now called) was finally recognized as successor to Leftwich in October 1827. But the stockholders failed to send settlers until October 1830, only six months before the end of their contract. Shareholder Sterling C. Robertson and six others reached the garrison at Fort Tenoxtitlán, one of the new military posts established in 1830; Tenoxtitlán guarded the old Spanish road crossing on the Brazos River. Nine families trailed Robertson, and when they reached Nacogdoches the commandant detained them. The newly passed Law of April 6, 1830, prohibited the entrance of Anglo-Americans into Texas unless they had a passport to Austin's or DeWitt's colony. Austin had quickly secured an exemption from the restriction for his and DeWitt's colonies when he discovered an ambiguous phrase seeming to allow immigration to "established" colonies. This he interpreted as those with more than 100 families in residence. The authorities acquiesced. The Law of April 6 also forbade the immigration of slaves, but even the authorities admitted that this restriction was impossible to enforce.

Passage of the restrictive law was the result of heightened suspicions that the United States intended to seize Texas. Between 1825 and 1829 the United States minister to Mexico, Joel R. Poinsett, unsuccessfully pressured the new nation to sell eastern Texas, and his successor, Anthony Butler, had similar instructions. Mexican leaders feared a rebellion of Anglos and annexation to the United States, just as Spain had lost Baton Rouge and Mobile in the early 1800s. Thus the Fredonian Rebellion inspired an official inspection tour in 1828 from San Antonio to Nacogdoches which revealed that Anglos greatly outnumbered native Mexicans in Texas. Although there was no obvious subversive activity, the Anglos continued to speak only English and conducted legal matters primarily in Anglo tradition. The authorities concluded that Mexico might lose Texas if more Anglo-Americans were allowed to enter and that native Mexicans must be encouraged to settle in the frontier state to "Mexicanize" it. The government dispatched troops to strategic entrances to Texas in late 1830 to enforce the law and also to aid the newly installed customs collectors in levying national import duties. The special exemption from the tariff for Texas pioneer settlers had expired. It was hoped that the new garrisons would produce native Mexican communities and that the tariff would pay for the troops needed to preserve Texas. However, this understandable response to save Mexican hegemony irritated Anglo settlers, who had inherited their grandfathers' distaste for standing armies and troops billeted in residential communities, and who had come to believe that their exemption from tariffs was permanent.

Robertson's colonists surreptitiously passed Nacogdoches and reached the Brazos in November. Amid a flurry of letters to officials, Austin offered the unlucky settlers sanctuary, a step approved officially in September 1831. Meanwhile, Robertson asked Austin, who was leaving to take his seat in the state legislature at Saltillo, to intercede for an extension of the six-year contract. Austin agreed, although he believed the case dead—the six years was up, the Law of April 6, 1830, prevented Anglo settlement, and a French immigration company had already applied for the old Leftwich grant. In early February, however, Austin asked the state for a contract in his name and that of his associate, Samuel May Williams, to settle 800 European and Mexican families on the former Nashville grant, plus some additional land north and west. The application was approved on 25 February 1832.

This action caused trouble with Robertson, who felt betrayed. Austin defended his action by saying that Robertson's cause was hopeless. Austin wanted, he stated, a more dependable frontier neighbor than a French company on his northern frontier, which was still exposed to Indian raiders. Robertson appealed to the ayuntamiento in San Felipe for relief in November 1833 by offering testimony from various persons that the Nashville company had sent 100 families before the expiration of the contract in 1831. The council, influenced by anti-Austin sentiment, agreed that Robertson should be reinstated, and he left for Saltillo, where he presented his documents on 2 April 1834. In May the governor returned the contract to Robertson despite arguments by Austin and Williams's attorney. Robertson's land commissioner began granting titles immediately. Sam Williams attended the 1835 session of the state legislature and won back the colony in May. Austin and Williams's new land commissioner began issuing deeds, while Robertson's commissioner continued to act until the end of the year. The resulting overlapping claims kept lawyers employed past midcentury.

The most controversial of all of the empresario grants, however, were those of David G. Burnet, Joseph Vehlein, and Lorenzo de Zavala, who sold their respective contracts to New York and Boston speculators. This action was contrary to the intent of the national and state colonization laws. The sale was not only illegal, but also deleterious to the purchasers. As a result of it, small and large investors and innocent colonists lost their promised land and sometimes their lives. Burnet, a native of

New Jersey and resident of Ohio, had traded with the Indians in Spanish Texas about 1818 but soon returned to Ohio. In December 1826 he received a contract to settle 300 families in the northwestern area of the former Edwards grant near Nacogdoches. At the same time, Vehlein, a Mexico City merchant, contracted through agents to settle 300 families in the southern portion of the canceled Edwards grant. Neither man visited the land and neither sent a single colonist. Burnet, a younger son of a prominent family, tried to recruit antislavery settlers in Ohio, but lacked the financial means to succeed. In 1829, with time running out, he unsuccessfully offered half of his future bonus land to wealthy and powerful individuals if they would send 300 families to his grant. Finally, in October 1830, he negotiated the sale of his grant to the Galveston Bay and Texas Land Company, as did Vehlein's agent. Joining in the sale was Zavala, a native of Yucatán, a prominent politician and currently a political refugee in New York City. He had acquired the long 52-mile-wide border reserve on the Sabine River as his empresario grant in 1828, when he agreed to settle 500 European or Mexican families. He, too, never saw his Texas land nor sent a colonist.

The Galveston Bay company issued stock entitling investors to scrip in denominations of leagues and labores. Some investors, such as James Prentiss, used their scrip for separate ventures such as the Union Land Company and the Trinity Land Company. Those companies dispatched two schooners to Galveston Bay in January 1831 with a few European settlers recruited in New York City. Though the Law of April 6, 1830, prohibited sending Anglo-Americans, some American workmen accompanied the settlers. John Davis Bradburn, the commandant at Anahuac, allowed the unfortunate immigrants to land briefly. A few stayed and farmed, but most returned to the United States as best they could. The entire undertaking was extortionate. Upon landing, each immigrant was to apply for a headright, of which he would receive 177 acres after three years of labor. The remaining 4,428 acres was signed over to the company. The company employed agents in Mexico to lobby for revocation of the restrictive law of 1830, a step that succeeded in 1834. Moreover, those squatters who had lived in East Texas since 1821 without titles discovered they were now colonists of the three empresarios. Although the state had approved naming a land commissioner in 1828, politics delayed implementation. Finally, in 1834, land commissioners arrived to give deeds to those long-time squatters and also the newcomers. One called himself the agent of the empresario and tried to collect fees until complaints to the state ended the illegal practice.

There were a number of lesser empresarios, including Benjamin R. Milam, Arthur G. Wavell, John Cameron, Stephen Julian Wilson, John Charles Beales, and Richard Exeter, as well as a few native Mexicans. All failed to complete their contracts within the allotted time. Most of their grants were located on the southwestern and northern perimeters of Texas.

Settlers continued to arrive in the established colonies and the area claimed by the Galveston Bay Company until the land offices were closed by the General Council on 27 October 1835 and confirmed by the Consultation the next month. By this time most residents, except in Robertson's colony on the northern frontier, no longer thought of themselves as colonists dependent on an empresario. De León was dead, DeWitt died in 1835, Austin was a sort of elder statesman, and few people in the

Burnet, Vehlein, or Zavala grants were acquainted with the phantom empresarios. By 1834 Texas was divided into three departments: Bexar, the Brazos, and Nacogdoches, each with its own political chief reporting directly to the governor and each having more than one town with an ayuntamiento. This gave the residents a feeling of self-government. Their main goal was achieving separate statehood from Coahuila. The old Austin colony continued to attract newcomers, including some of those unable to secure titles in other colonies. Its stability, its guaranteed deeds, and its easy accessibility by water from New Orleans through Galveston Bay and the Brazos river were drawing cards.

The Anglo-American settlers imported their culture to Texas and resisted Mexicanizing even after 1830, when purchase by the United States was increasingly unlikely. Rich or poor, Anglo immigrants were independent-minded, self-sufficient republicans suspicious of the traditional deferential society of Hispanic culture, even though Mexican reformers were struggling to build a republic. The spirit of Jacksonian democracy pervaded even those not admiring President Andrew Jackson. Moreover, collecting national tariff duties in Texas in 1830 coincided with the growing anti-tariff movement in South Carolina, which resulted in the Nullification Crisis. Texans, like other agrarians, manufactured nothing and disliked import duties on necessities. It was not surprising, then, that American ship captains, supported by Anglo-Texan merchants, refused to pay the new duties and exchanged fire with the fort at the mouth of the Brazos River in December 1831. At this same time, Colonel Bradburn, charged with enforcing Mexican laws regarding immigration and the tariff at Anahuac, arrested civilians and held some without bail for trial before the commandant general at Matamoros. Anglo-Texans believed Bradburn was acting arbitrarily. They did not understand that his actions were required under Mexican law, which lacked anything like a Bill of Rights. Angry men from the Brazos marched to confront Bradburn at Anahuac, while others loaded illegal cannons on a ship to join them. At the mouth of the river, the Anglo-Texans forced the surrender of the fort. The first of the Anahuac Disturbances and the battle of Velasco took place in June 1832, just as the Federalist party's army defeated that of the conservative administration, thus ending a four-year-old civil war. The Texans claimed to be helping the Federalists, who were led by Antonio López de Santa Anna, and convinced authorities sent to investigate that they were not revolutionaries against Mexico. Their action resulted in the departure of all Centralist troops and customs collectors from Texas.

Wanting to capitalize on their support of Santa Anna, who was to be the new president, the Anglo-Texans drafted petitions for separate statehood, a better judicial system, and similar reform measures. In April 1833 Austin took the requests to Mexico City, where most were approved except for separate statehood. In a moment of despondency, Austin wrote an incriminating letter urging the leaders at San Antonio to act unilaterally on separation. For this act of sedition he was arrested in January 1834 and incarcerated in Mexico City until July 1835. Texans remained relatively quiet during Austin's absence, fearing for his life. After Santa Anna's installation as president in 1833, he left governing to his vice president, a Federalist and reformer. By 1835, however, Santa Anna reversed himself, became a Centralist dictator, and sent the army to punish his political enemies. Garrisons and customs collectors returned to Texas in January 1835 and the Anglo-Texan response was predictable. A second

attack recaptured Anahuac in June, and when Austin reached Texas in September he surprised many by endorsing the resistance movement against the oppressive administration. Though at first supporting reform of the Mexican government, public opinion moved quickly toward independence.

There are no accurate figures detailing the number of Anglo-Americans who settled in Texas between 1821 and 1835. Although Mexican law required an annual census of all residents, the colonists resisted such bureaucratic demands. Existing tallies reveal that in 1826 Austin had 1,800 people, including 443 slaves; DeWitt counted 159 whites and 29 slaves; and the lower Trinity River, then outside of any empresario grant, was populated by 407 settlers with 76 slaves. Subsequent extant records show Austin's colony with 2,201 people in 1828, 4,248 in 1830, and 5,565 in 1831, while DeWitt had only 82 persons, including 7 slaves, in 1828. In 1834 the English-speaking Col. Juan N. Almonte made an official inspection of Texas and estimated that 4,000 people lived in the Department of Bexar, 2,100 in the Department of the Brazos (Austin's colony), and 1,600 in the Department of Nacogdoches. The 3,000 decrease in Austin's colony suggests that Almonte's figures were wrong. A few lists of residents in the Nacogdoches area in 1834–35 and scattered other records are extant, but such incomplete records only hint at the Texas population. Anglo-American colonization in Texas was obviously a success, although not what Mexican leaders envisioned. Neither side worked to understand, appreciate, nor resolve the cultural differences intrinsic to the union proposed by Mexico and accepted by Anglo-American immigrants.

Margaret Swett Henson

Anti-Saloon League of Texas. Formed in 1907 with headquarters in Dallas; Benjamin Franklin Riley, a Baptist clergyman, was superintendent. The national league had been formed in 1895. It was modeled on the Ohio Anti-Saloon League, which was founded in 1893 to fight for prohibition laws. The spread of the league to Southern states was slowed by the national officers' objections to segregation. Prohibition organizations, including the WCTU, were already active in Texas, although none adhered to the league's principles of continual attention to the single issue. The Texas league quickly embroiled itself in the state's prohibition politics by taking credit in 1907–08 for winning local-option elections to ban the liquor trade in 12 counties. However, it remained an informal organization with only loose ties to the national office, and it was unable to command the state's prohibition forces. Joel H. Gambrell led the league after 1910. Quarrels among Texas drys hurt the cause at the polls, and in 1915 the national office reorganized the Texas league and installed new officers. Under the leadership of Arthur James Barton the Texas league aggressively raised funds and pursued the prohibition cause. The national league assumed the debt of *Home and State* and turned the paper into the league's voice in Texas. In 1916 the league campaign to initiate state prohibition succeeded with a majority of voters, only to meet defeat in the legislature. The league took credit for adding 12 more counties to the dry column in 1917. Once national prohibition was won, the Anti-Saloon League in Texas and elsewhere withered, in spite of leaders' pleas to supporters to maintain vigilance. Nationally the league was divided over the question of emphasizing enforcement or education in a dry America. Barton, who was replaced by Atticus Webb in 1918, advocated education. In fact, in 1927 the state saw an intensive educational campaign begin. The next year the Texas league, like its Southern counterparts elsewhere, opposed the presidential candidacy of the Catholic Alfred Smith, an outspoken wet. Although prohibition remained popular through the 1920s, after the onset of the Great Depression it quickly lost favor. By 1933 the Anti-Saloon League in Texas and elsewhere stood helplessly by as the repeal movement succeeded. In 1991 the direct descendant of the Texas League was Drug Prevention Resources, Incorporated, based in Dallas. *K. Austin Kerr*

Antone. Alabama Indian chief; b. near Lafourche, Louisiana, ca. 1780; d. Texas, ca. 1870. Antone, the first Alabama chief in Texas, was elected about 1806 and led his people as they moved from site to site in East Texas looking for a home. In 1853 he applied to the Texas legislature for a permanent reservation, and the state granted the Alabamas 1,110.7 acres in Polk County. Two years later Antone and his subchiefs requested an agent to assist in tribal business matters, in contacts with government officials, and in relations with their white neighbors. In 1858 the state tried unsuccessfully to move the Alabama–Coushatta Indians to the Lower Brazos Reserve; with Indian agent James Barclay, Antone rode to the reserve and, upon seeing it, rejected the proposed move. In 1862, when 19 Alabama–Coushattas joined the Confederate cavalry, he also tried to enlist (at the age of 82), but evidently without success. *Howard N. Martin*

Archer, Branch Tanner. Republic of Texas official; b. Fauquier County, Virginia, 13 December 1790; d. Brazoria, 22 September, 1856; m. Eloisa Clarke (1813); 6 children; ed. William and Mary College, University of Pennsylvania (M.D., 1808). Archer moved to Texas in 1831 and was active in the cause of Texas independence. He represented Brazoria at the Convention of 1833, fought in the battle of Gonzales (1835) and was chairman of the Consultation. He, Stephen F. Austin, and William H. Wharton served as commissioners to lobby the United States for funds; they borrowed $250,000 in New Orleans but failed to get help in Washington. Archer was in the First Congress of the republic (speaker in the 2d session) and secretary of war under President Mirabeau B. Lamar. He was grand master of the Masonic Grand Lodge of the Republic of Texas in 1838–39. Archer County was named for him. *David Minor*

Architecture. Texas architecture reflects a remarkable variety of cultural influences, physiographical conditions, and technological advancements. Over a long period of colonization and settlement, people of different nationalities with ingrained customs and taste erected a variety of buildings in forms recalling their social backgrounds. These were situated in regions with character ranging from arid West Texas, largely treeless, to semitropical East Texas, heavily forested. In the beginning, materials of construction naturally came from the locale of buildings, although eventually technology and taste produced certain similarities of design throughout the state. For analysis, historic Texas architecture can be organized into six periods: Indian or precolonial (to 1682), Spanish colonial–Mexican (1682–1835), Republic–antebellum (1835–61), Victorian (1861–1900), Early twentieth century (1900–1941), and Modern (1941–90).

Indian or precolonial. The earliest residents of what is now Texas were nomadic peoples. They erected no permanent structures, but made use instead of such natural shelters as caves and rock overhangs, or lived in temporary structures made of animal hides, wood, or grasses. Anthropological findings of later Indian peoples reveal that before the Europeans arrived at least four basic cultural groups had evolved in the future Texas, each reflecting its particular geographic and environmental setting. The Coahuiltecan and Karankawan peoples, who inhabited the coast of southern Texas and the Trans-Nueces, lacked formal political organization and, like their more ancient ancestors, did not erect permanent structures. By contrast, in the Trans-Pecos the Jumanos and Patarabueyes inhabited villages consisting of houses with mud-plastered pickets and roofs of adobe, probably placed over saplings, grass, and bark. Farther north in the Panhandle a pueblo culture, similar to those in Arizona and New Mexico, flourished between A.D. 1200 and 1500. These peoples constructed one-story pueblos with walls of horizontal masonry and double rows of stone slabs set on edge, oriented to the cardinal points of the compass. Dramatically different were the peoples of the Plains region, the Comanches, Lipan Apaches, Kiowas, and Tonkawas. Their culture, based on buffalo hunting, required them to wander throughout the vast expanses of Central and Northwest Texas in search of the great herds. They relied for shelter on hide-covered tepees that could be readily disassembled and transported. In Northeast Texas, Indians of the Mississippi valley culture flourished, among them the various Caddo groups. A sedentary, agricultural people, they constructed large, round, thatched shelters, some up to fifty feet in diameter. They also built large earthen mounds typical of the Mississippi culture.

Spanish colonial–Mexican. From the end of the seventeenth century through the eighteenth century, Spanish missionaries and soldiers brought to Texas building types and construction techniques they had known at home. On a remote and sometimes dangerous frontier, they established missions with chapels, convents, apartments, and various service structures; presidios with fortifications, chapels, barracks, and storerooms; ranches with dwellings and, in some instances, defensive works; and towns with plazas, commons, churches, and dwellings—all according to Spanish traditions and laws. Spanish colonists employed familiar methods in the construction of shelters and buildings. In heavily forested East Texas, palisado walls of wooden pickets, well known for centuries in Spain and throughout Europe, enclosed rooms roofed with thatch in both missions and presidios. Chapels, apartments, and other spaces of San Francisco de los Tejas Mission, for instance, had walls of posts planted vertically in the ground. Meanwhile, in West Texas, the jacal, a building indigenous to Mexico, sheltered countless families. Its walls were formed with brush or branches contained between pairs of posts spaced several feet apart and plastered with mud. Roofs were either thatched or covered with hides. Particularly in arid and semiarid regions, adobe construction also was common. Walls were made of sunbaked mud bricks laid up in thick beds of mud with openings spanned by wooden lintels. Roofs were either gabled and thatched, or were flat and covered with earth or lime concrete carried upon beams, sometimes hewn. These types of construction, indigenous to the land, remained in use well into the twentieth century, when shingles and other types of roofing replaced thatch and earth. When stone was available, masonry walls enclosed numerous cubical houses, roofed with either thatch or earth. Often, slightly inclined, earthen roofs were surrounded with parapets and drained through *canales*, projecting channeled troughs. In several instances, on locations exposed to attack, loopholes were used instead of windows. Commonly, houses were oneroom structures, although on occasion two or more rooms were situated end-to-end. In some instances, as in Spain, rooms and walls enclosed a court. A beehiveshaped *horno*, or oven, made of mud and grass and located outdoors, was employed for cooking.

Numerous mission chapels were hastily thrown up with a variety of building techniques. Jacals, palisados, or small adobe rooms containing altars were among the first shelters set up at any mission. Although missionaries certainly intended to replace these with more durable works, in many instances the mission was abandoned before large permanent structures could be built. Near El Paso and San Antonio, durable chapels were constructed. The chapel of Nuestra Señora de la Concepción de Socorro Mission, adjacent to the Rio Grande, was executed with thick adobe walls. Both the nave and transepts, which were added much later, were spanned with vigas bearing upon corbel blocks. Each of the five missions at San Antonio eventually built a stone chapel with a design based upon customs in Mexico. San Antonio de Valero Mission (the Alamo) established in 1718, has an incomplete chapel executed between 1744 and 1756, with a Baroque portal similar to a number of Mexican examples. The Chapel of Nuestra Señora de la Purísima Concepción de Acuña Mission (established in 1731), the best preserved of the Texas missions, has a portal with Plateresque details. A beautiful Ultra-Baroque portal with niche pilasters was completed at San José y San Miguel de Aguayo Mission (established in 1720), called the "Queen of the Missions." At both San Juan Capistrano (1731), and San Francisco de la Espada (1731), durable chapels were built, but with little ornamentation.

During the Mexican period (1821–35), relatively little architectural progress was made beyond the construction of dwellings and some military work, although several new towns were established, including Bastrop (laid out in 1830), Liberty (founded in 1831), and Gonzales (founded in 1832). A poor economy, along with religious and political turmoil, precluded noteworthy undertakings and, for that matter, even maintenance of existing buildings.

Republic–antebellum period. During the Republic of Texas and the years that followed until the Civil War, other cultural traditions were brought to Texas by Anglo-Americans and European immigrants, both seeking land and opportunities. New towns were populated, farms developed, and military posts established, all reflecting the traditions and previous customs of the builders. In regions where trees were available, log cabins were common to Anglo-American settlements as well as those of some European immigrants. They required few tools for construction and were used for virtually every type of building, including dwellings, churches, courthouses, schools, jails, barns, and forts. Both single-crib and double-crib houses were common. In the latter, known as dog-trot or dog-run houses, the rooms were separated by a breezeway. Ordinarily, log cabins had only a single story, but occasionally attics were included. In any instance, porches ordinarily extended along the south side of dwellings; porch roofs shaded the walls and provided a protected space. A fireplace was usually placed at a gable end of dwellings. Regardless of type, cabins were assembled with horizontal logs, sometimes hewn or partially hewn. Logs were notched together at corners utilizing several types of joints.

Spaces between them were filled with wooden chinks, rocks, or moss and mud. Roofs were finished with boards, shakes, or shingles. Though no type of log construction can be specifically attributed to any particular ethnic group, *Fachwerk* structures were peculiar to German settlements. *Fachwerk* consisted of hewn frameworks joined with mortise and tenon joints, secured with treenails (wooden pegs). Panels formed by the framework were infilled with either brick or stone nogging, but some openings were framed for doors and windows. Porches were the adaptation of European custom to the hot Texas climate.

As the country and economy developed in antebellum Texas, neat wooden, brick, and stone buildings also appeared in various communities and on numerous farms. Texans, like people in other regions of America, yearned for order and cultural refinement reflected in tidy houses and public buildings. Both were considered important to the development of communities as desirable places to live and raise families. Sophisticated architecture, critics believed, refined public taste and positively influenced people's attitudes. Numerous frame and masonry buildings were plain, but others were distinguished by historic styles, including the Greek Revival style, which dominated Texas architecture from 1840 to 1870. Though often referred to as Southern Colonial, the Greek Revival Style is neither southern nor colonial, since it first appeared in the East in the early nineteenth century. It was introduced into Texas by both experienced builders and authoritative publications. It featured geometric order, formal balance, and decorative details. Its principal feature was derived from the classic temple form of ancient Greece, the temple portico or porch with a roof supported by a row of columns. These columns were of three types or orders: Doric, Ionic, and Corinthian. The Greek Revival style is formal in character, the building being arranged symmetrically about a central axis, the hall, which is flanked by rooms of the same width that give the desired balance. The doorway is flanked by an equal number of windows on each side, and centered on the front of the house is a porch that features columns of one of the classical orders. The Greek Revival style marked numerous houses, school buildings, some courthouses and churches, and even an occasional commercial building. Nationally, its simplicity and dignity seemed to make it appropriate for a country with limited means but with needs for refined architecture. Symmetrical porticoes commonly distinguished houses and some churches and courthouses. Dignifying the exteriors of these, pilasters, columns, and entablatures, ordinarily fashioned from wood, were based upon examples found in pattern books, although builders freely innovated upon these. A number of noteworthy plantation houses, as well as city houses, represented these developments. The simple frame house of the Anglo-American settler, however, continued to be the principal type of house built in Texas until the Civil War. But even frame houses were often given a few classic details, such as a cornice, capped posts on the porches, and multipaned, double-hung sash windows, all of which gave them a resemblance to the larger Greek Revival houses. As the farthest extension of the Old South, Texas possesses some of the most recently built Greek Revival homes, which can be seen in San Antonio, Austin, Waco, Jefferson, and Marshall. The Governor's Mansion (1854–56), in Austin, built by Abner Cook, is one of the most representative examples of the Greek Revival style in Texas. Greek Revival forms and details also marked many other important public buildings. The old Capitol

(1852–54; burned 1881) was a monumental work with an Ionic portico. The Galveston Post Office and Custom House (1858–61), designed by the Treasury architect, Ammi B. Young, displays both Doric and Ionic orders. On a smaller scale, the Methodist Episcopal Church, South (1860), in Marshall is a templetype edifice with square columns and a simplified Doric order.

While the Greek Revival, along with straightforward designs, was common in evangelical churches, Gothic Revival styles marked a number of Catholic and Episcopal churches. Pointed arches, steeply pitched roofs, and buttresses were basic, but a number of variations of Gothic appeared, in some instances reflecting the backgrounds of the builders. Several Catholic Churches, including St. Mary's Cathedral, Galveston (1847), were designed by French émigré architects. Builders in Fredericksburg, a German community, recalled in St. Mary's Church (1861–63) the Gothic of their homeland. Episcopal houses of worship featured characteristics ultimately derived from rural English churches and disseminated in America through publications and the work of English immigrants.

Adjacent to the public square of Anglo-American communities, a typical spatial form brought west, commercial buildings were executed with masonry fronts, either one or two stories high. Ordinarily, street-level openings were spanned by semicircular arches with French doors and fanlight transoms; when a second story was included, it often had segmental arches and doublehung windows. Ornamentation of parapets with a wide variety of brick or stone patterns is a distinguishing feature—characteristics that continued to mark many commercial buildings during the Victorian period.

Victorian. Following the Civil War, from 1870 to 1900, Texas caught up with the mainstream of American architectural fashion, which was the Victorian, so called in the absence of a better name to encompass the multitude of stylistic expressions of that complex period. The exuberance of the Victorian style reflects a period of rapid expansion and new fortunes. In Texas, as elsewhere in America, the Victorian period was marked by revolutionary changes. Numerous new towns were founded, railroads were rapidly extended, and the westerly regions were progressively opened to farming and ranching. At the same time, in large cities outside investment was solicited and new industries were established, contributing to the prosperity essential to opulent architecture. Meanwhile, such buildings as libraries, opera houses, schools, hospitals, and public markets all improved the life of communities. Evolving technology favored the development of cities and architecture within them. During the last two decades of the nineteenth century, waterworks, sewerage systems, electric-light companies, gas works, ice plants, telephone systems, and rail transportation all improved sanitation and afforded numerous conveniences in many towns. Meanwhile, organized fire departments reduced the amount of damage caused by fires in various cities, virtually every one of which had over time been devastated by one or more incendiaries. Building construction and comfort were facilitated by mass production of building components, both wooden and metal. For interior comfort, ventilation devices were introduced, steam heat was developed, and electrical lighting was installed in many buildings. Economical railroad transportation made building materials and products manufactured elsewhere readily available in Texas, although many were still produced at home.

In the wake of Reconstruction, turreted mansions began to spring up in cities and towns all over the state. In contrast to the restrained classicism of the Greek Revival style, the Victorian style was rich in detail, exceedingly ornate, and designed to achieve a romantic and picturesque effect. The buildings were seldom symmetrical, but were characterized by the offcenter tower and projecting bay. The whole was intended to be a balanced composition. Many materials were now available to the builder; these were often combined to achieve greater richness. Sawmills had become widespread, and frame houses were given elaborate gingerbread trim made possible by the jigsaw. Architectural motifs from many historic styles were combined in an eclectic fashion, with the Medieval Romanesque and Gothic vying with the Renaissance for popularity. New views on architecture influenced building aesthetics. Appreciation of beauty of proportion and details—characteristic of the antebellum period—was replaced by admiration of character and opulence. In part achieved with historic forms and styles, character denoted the particular purpose of a building combined with a distinctive image. Associations with the historical development of particular styles made function evident. For instance, general knowledge of medieval European cathedrals and churches readily associated the Gothic Revival with churches. Opulence along with picturesqueness was achieved by the use of a variety of materials, and historic styles were characteristic and much admired. The features of various styles sometimes were mixed into eclectic, original compositions, albeit sometimes without unity. Polychromy and patterns achieved through combinations and treatments of materials were characteristic. These attributes were evident in countless houses in picturesque styles, with fanciful towers, porches, chimneys, bay windows, dormers, spindlework, punch work, shingle patterns, and decorative glass. At the beginning of the Victorian period, these were simply applied to traditional plans, but eventually asymmetrical, picturesque forms prevailed. Numerous historic and novel styles appeared in Texas Victorian houses. The Queen Anne, characterized by turrets and picturesque massing, distinguished numerous large dwellings throughout the state. The Eastlake style, with its spindlework and gingerbread, enriched numerous other houses on various scales. The so-called Stick Style, identified by the articulation of exterior wall surfaces of frame buildings into panels, added further variety. Distinguished by Italian Renaissance details, the Italianate style also dignified numerous large dwellings. The Mansard-roofed Second Empire Style and the Roman-arched Romanesque Revival mode lent imposing images to yet others.

Many Texas cities and towns preserve a rich legacy of Victorian architecture. Among the impressive surviving monuments of the era are the Driskill Hotel (1880), Austin, by Frederick E. Ruffini, the Turn-Verein Building (1892), San Antonio, by James Wahrenberger, and the Albert Maverick Building, San Antonio (1881), by Alfred Giles. Of all the cities in Texas, Galveston was undoubtedly the richest in its collection of Victorian architecture. One of the state's first professional architects, Nicholas J. Clayton, practiced there and added many fine buildings, including the Gresham house, now known as the Bishop's Palace. During the Victorian era civic and commercial architecture became important, and many handsome courthouses, banks, opera houses, and hotels were constructed. The most significant building to be built during this period was the

Capitol, completed in 1888. This impressive red-granite structure was designed by Elijah E. Myers of Detroit in the Renaissance Revival style and inspired by the national Capitol in Washington. The building was originally intended to be of limestone. However, there was not a sufficient supply of the quality required to be found in Texas, so granite was used. The ruggedness of the granite gives the building a unique character, and the tall castiron dome has become symbolic of the state's most important building.

Many towns took pride in their public buildings, which were collectively viewed as signs of progress. Situated prominently on public squares, county courthouses were commonly the most imposing buildings of a county, reflecting their importance as both a social and governmental center. They were designed in a variety of styles and laid out to facilitate cross-ventilation, often with central clock towers and four similar fronts. They frequently had such technological improvements as iron and wrought-iron structural systems. Among the numerous noteworthy examples are the Hill County Courthouse, Hillsboro (1889), a large edifice in eclectic style with a lofty tower designed by W. Clarke Dodson, and the Renaissance Revival–style Ellis County Courthouse, Waxahachie (1894–1896), designed by James Riely Gordon. Usually standing nearby on the public square was the county jail. Architects and clients occasionally favored the medieval castellated style, which gave the impression of strength, although other styles also were used. Surrounding the courthouses and lining main streets leading to the public square were various types of commercial buildings, also considered as signs of progress. Large plateglass windows, castiron supports, and sheet-metal cornices and window hoods—the products of technology—superseded the all-masonry fronts of antebellum days, although brick and stone were still extensively employed for visual interest. In such large cities as Dallas, Fort Worth, and Houston, commercial buildings of three to six stories incorporating technological advances became sources of considerable pride. Among the best examples of these is the Cotton Exchange in Houston (1888), designed by Eugene T. Heiner, which, like other buildings, employed a variety of styles and mixture of details and materials to produce an individuality and opulence appealing to the public.

Ordinarily standing at the corners of street intersections and reflecting prosperity, banks and opera houses were particularly prominent, a situation well represented by the Sealy Bank Building (1895–97) and Tremont Opera House (1870), both in Galveston. Houses of worship, prominently situated in neighborhoods adjacent to commercial districts, accented the skylines of most communities. Many churches were built during the last two decades of the nineteenth century, with the Medieval styles, Romanesque and Gothic, being favored by the liturgical religions such as Catholic and Episcopal. For example, St. Mark's Episcopal Church, San Antonio (1875), designed by Richard Upjohn, the architect of Trinity Church in New York and the leading Gothic Revival architect in America, was inspired by the Perpendicular Gothic of England; the old San Fernando Cathedral in San Antonio, extensively remodeled by François P. Giraud between 1868 and 1878, was based on French medieval models; and St. Mary's Cathedral, Austin (1870), designed by Nicholas Clayton, was executed in the High Victorian Gothic style. In numerous instances, evangelical churches were distinguished from liturgical edifices by broad auditoriums and cor-

ner entrances, evident in the First Baptist Church, Dallas (1890), designed by Albert Ullrich. Moorish styles, on the other hand, projecting associations with Near Eastern architecture, characterized a number of nineteenth-century synagogues. Among the other noteworthy Victorian buildings were the railroad depots, which formed gateways to towns. Scaled according to the size of communities, these were linear structures, with both passenger and freight facilities, stretched along the tracks. Various stylistic and decorative devices emphasized their importance, a tendency evident in the Union Depot, Fort Worth (1899). Such service structures as roundhouses—other products of technology—were also numerous, although most are now gone, along with numerous depots.

Early twentieth century. The years following the turn of the century witnessed continuing immigration and growth of towns and cities throughout the state. Cotton, lumber, cattle, and oil aided a growing economy that fostered cultural development. Meanwhile, new industries and trade pumped up the economies of metropolitan areas, facilitating the building of pretentious edifices, both public and private. During this period, architecture throughout the United States embodied new aesthetic ideals aimed at achieving noble images reflecting cultural advancement. Influenced by the École des Beaux Arts in Paris, design principles called for formal compositions and classical vocabularies. The impressive effects attainable with unified classical design based upon monumental Renaissance architecture were well demonstrated by the overall plan and official buildings of the 1893 World's Columbian Exposition in Chicago. This impressive achievement profoundly influenced taste throughout the country. The architecture of the first half of the twentieth century reflects the growing unity of architectural expression throughout the United States. Regional characteristics rapidly disappeared as a result of the spread of popular taste and the uniformity of architectural fashion.

During the first 30 years of the twentieth century eclecticism was the accepted form of architectural expression. While subscribing to formal principles, numerous critics and architects advocated architecture that reflected some characteristics of its locale. One approach to regional design called for historic styles associated with particular ethnic groups that had settled in an area. Another viewpoint advocated styles that had evolved abroad in certain countries or terrains as types for buildings in regions of Texas with comparable physiographical conditions. A Spanish-inspired mode, the NeoPlateresque style, of the first buildings of Texas Tech University, for instance, was intended to recall the Hispanic heritage of Texas. The Bhutanese style of the Texas School of Mines and Metallurgy, located at the foot of the Franklin Mountains in El Paso, was inspired by a Tibetan monastery in the Himalayan Mountains. These motifs, along with a variety of others, are displayed in Texas houses. At the turn of the century, some of the picturesqueness of the Victorian period still prevailed, but compositions of forms were bilaterally balanced, and classical details soon replaced Eastlake and other features. Eventually, large houses projected stately images through a variety of Classical styles in formal compositions. Monumental pedimented porticoes and extensive balustraded porches contributed to their stately yet residential character. Small houses featured a variety of styles, including Tudor, Spanish Colonial, Colonial, Georgian, and Italian Renaissance, as well as Mission Revival and Pueblo Revival.

By the early years of the twentieth century another influence was being felt in Texas, an attempt to break free of historical precedents, and to forge a new, wholly modern style. The most important of these influences was what became known as the Prairie style. It originated with Frank Lloyd Wright and a group of creative Chicago architects, and rapidly spread through the new suburbs of Texas. Pure examples of the Prairie style, such as the Trost residence (1909), El Paso, by Wright protégé Henry C. Trost, are rare, but vernacular examples, spread widely by pattern books and popular magazines, appeared throughout the state between 1905 and 1915. Even more influential was the Craftsman or Bungaloid style, inspired primarily by the work of Charles S. and Henry M. Greene in California. Like the vernacular examples of the contemporaneous Prairie style, the Bungaloid style was spread through pattern books and popular magazines. The one-story Craftsman house or bungalow became one of the most popular designs for small houses, and numerous examples were constructed in the state between 1905 and the late 1920s.

While regional or early modern designs appeared in many residential edifices after the turn of the century, civic buildings generally were either Beaux-Arts Classical, a massive, heavy, monumental style, or Neo-Classical Revival, a graceful, dignified mode. The Harris County Courthouse, Houston (1911), a massive work, crowned with a dome designed by the firm of Lang and Witchell, exemplifies the former, while the Museum of Fine Arts, Houston (1924), a handsome work with an Ionic colonnade designed by William Ward Watkin, represents the latter. In small towns, commercial buildings largely conformed to Victorian standards, but in the cities office buildings formed new skylines. Houston, Dallas, Fort Worth, San Antonio, and Waco all built noteworthy skyscrapers rising boldly above their surroundings. Such achievements were made possible by technology that had been developed in such cities as Chicago and New York, including methods of structural framing and fire protection of beams and columns. These developments were well represented by the Southwestern Life Insurance Company Building, Dallas (1911–13), a 16-story work with a clearly expressed skeletal structure consistent in design with Chicago School work. Like other types of buildings, both churches and schools echo a variety of motifs. Indicating associations with an important chapter in the history of Christianity, a number of Catholic edifices were built in the Italian Renaissance Revival style, which recalls Renaissance Rome, while others were either in Gothic or a Mexican Colonial style, the latter echoing cultural roots in Texas. Reflecting origins in the Church of England, Episcopal churches were mostly in some variation of the English Gothic, consistent with earlier buildings. Classical styles, Gothic modes, and regional variations all marked Protestant churches, although Presbyterians showed a predilection toward the Romanesque Revival. The Palladian Revival, based upon ecclesiastical work of Italian Renaissance architect Andrea Palladio, distinguished yet others, particularly a number of Baptist churches. Similarly, a variety of stylistic features characterizes schools, both public and private. Catholic and Episcopal schools usually reflected their affiliations through Gothic styles. College, university, and high school buildings, often on a large scale, all appeared in a variety of modes, including Neoclassical Revival and Georgian Revival. Among the important developments during this period was the evolution throughout the state of the public high school into a dominant building type. Housing classrooms, auditorium, gymnasium, shops, offices, and other facilities, the high school became a complex entity that accommodated large numbers of students. Spaces were organized into formal yet functional compositions contained within forms juxtaposed to facilitate efficient crossventilation and admit high levels of light. On the exteriors, patterns of openings and solids suggested function, while various decorative features, both geometric and stylistic, enriched the buildings, reflecting importance and projecting character. Among the best examples of such educational facilities is El Paso High School (1914–16), designed by Trost and Trost.

The period between 1920 and 1940 also witnessed the emergence of the Art Deco or Moderne style. As its name suggests, Art Deco was inspired by the 1925 Paris Exposition des Art Décoratifs et Industriels Modernes. Much like the Prairie style that flourished a decade earlier, it represented an attempt to come to terms with the dramatic changes brought on by industrialization and modernization, and sought to break free of historical precedents and to forge a modern expression. Early Art Deco buildings, such as the Gulf Building in Houston (1927–29), designed by Alfred C. Finn, and the State Highway Building (1932), Austin, designed by Carleton W. Adams, made use of ornate geometric motifs. After 1930 a more stripped-down variant of the style, sometimes called Moderne, or Streamlined Moderne, became popular. Numerous Moderne shops, gas stations, movie houses, and roadside diners featuring characteristic smooth surfaces, glass blocks, and curved corners were constructed before World War II. Hybrid versions of the two styles, such as the remarkable Conoco station on Route 66 in Shamrock (circa 1936), were also common. Unfortunately, these developments were hindered by the Great Depression. After the crash of 1929, building activity slowed within the state. Although numerous public-works projects were undertaken during the 1930s under the aegis of such federal as the PWA and the WPA, private building was considerably retarded until after World War II. Numerous public works during the 1930s displayed features of the Art Deco, among them the Texas Centennial Park, Dallas (1936), planned by George L. Dahl, the San Jacinto Monument (1936), Houston, designed by Alfred C. Finn, and the Houston City Hall (1939), designed by Joseph Finger.

Modern. Though World War II brought an upturn in the economy that eventually stimulated the construction industry, much of the new activity initially served the war effort. Upon conclusion of hostilities, construction of houses and public buildings resumed; inflation, however, reduced the return on expenditures. During the postwar years, many clients demanded economical buildings with functional designs based upon historic traditions. The beauty and associations resident in the Georgian Revival and the Gothic Revival still made these styles attractive for numerous types of building, including houses and churches. A number of other institutions, among them colleges and universities, also built conservatively. Southern Methodist University, for example, continued to construct buildings in the Georgian Revival style, maintaining the theme of the institution's earlier buildings. Numerous church buildings were still designed in both the Georgian and Gothic Revival styles. After 1945, however, the so-called International Style increasingly influenced design throughout the state. Calling for the elimination of applied decoration and the rejection of historical styles, architects of the postwar era advocated straightforward, functional planning, machine-produced building components, and asymmetrical composition. Incorporating these characteristics, the International Style featured skeletal structural systems with curtain walls treated as skins "stretched" over them, emphasizing geometrical patterns. Buildings were viewed as compositions of volumes, rather than masses. Plain boxes with large areas of transparency became hallmarks of modernity. Particularly notable examples of this trend include the Tenneco Building, Houston (1963), and One Shell Plaza, Houston (1971), both designed by Skidmore, Owings, and Merrill. In a number of instances, modern appearances were achieved by simplifying traditional forms and the application of new technology. Churches, for instance, still were planned according to traditional spatial requirements, but were designed with laminated wood, steel, and concrete structural systems free of historic stylistic decoration. In numerous instances, the demand for progressive, modern images resulted in the remodeling of old structures, particularly commercial buildings and public edifices. Typically, historical details were either removed or covered, and aluminum, glass, and plastic components were added, all echoing new technology.

During the Modern period, developing technology had a phenomenal impact upon architecture. Innovative steel and concrete structural systems made possible unprecedented spans of space, as well as new means of architectonic expression. The Astrodome, Houston (1965), and Texas Stadium, Irving (1971), are impressive technological achievements. Another important trend in the post–World War II era has been the growth of massive suburban developments on the periphery of the state's larger cites. Tract housing, frequently designed by contractors rather than trained architects and repeated serially, has come to dominate residential building throughout the state, and entire communities, such as Richardson, Plano, and Clear Lake City, have grown up as a result.

At midcentury, several leading modern architects from outside the state executed important works in Texas that were certainly inspirational if not influential. In 1958, Ludwig Mies van der Rohe completed a major addition to the Museum of Fine Arts, Houston, a steel and glass work with a clearly articulated structure illustrating his idea that "less is more." Shortly thereafter, Philip Johnson, who earlier had executed a number of works in International Style, designed the Amon Carter Museum, Fort Worth (1960), a clearly ordered work with the stateliness of a Greek temple. At about the same time (1959), Frank Lloyd Wright oversaw the completion of the Kalita Humphreys Theatre, Dallas, a monolithic concrete work exemplifying his concept of organic architecture. And Louis I. Kahn conceived the design for the Kimbell Art Museum (1972), Fort Worth, a sublime work with post-tensioned concrete cycloidal vaults, symbolizing a perception of permanence. Such Texas architects as David R. Williams, who developed the Texas ranchstyle house; O'Neil Ford, who designed the Trinity University campus, San Antonio, and the Texas Instruments Semi-Conductor Building, Dallas (1958); Caudill, Rowlett, and Scott, who designed the Jesse H. Jones Hall for the Performing Arts, Houston; and Howard R. Meyer and Max Sandfield, who associated with W. W. Wurster of California to design the Temple Emanu-El, Dallas (1953–59), are among those who have achieved national recognition. Noteworthy technological advances in all phases of life brought increasingly large and complex building functions. Massive shopping malls, large medical complexes, new college campuses, and expansive airports all were complex products of growth and technological advances, requiring a teamwork approach to design and construction. Representative is Dallas–Fort Worth International Airport (1973), an entity architecturally determined by the need to handle complex traffic patterns.

Eventually, the simplicity and lack of poetic content of Modern architecture attracted considerable criticism. Modernity had failed to satisfy the need for decoration and meaning. Consequently, Texas architects, like those elsewhere, searched for new types of expression that included both current technology and references to the past. In the design of Herring Hall (1986) for Rice University, Houston, for instance, East Coast–based architect Cesar Pelli drew upon features of the first campus buildings, yet through technology and spatial organization produced a noteworthy work indicative of its time. Houston-based Taft Architects created a colorful, jazzy, postmodern idiom that brought the firm wide recognition.

After the disastrous destruction of numerous buildings in central business districts under "urban renewal" programs during the 1950s and 1960s, the preservation movement became a significant force in Texas architecture. As a result of the leadership of such agencies as the San Antonio Conservation Society and the Texas Historical Commission, protective legislation was passed and various programs were implemented to assist the preservation and restoration of historic buildings. Among the most significant restoration projects undertaken is the restoration of the Capitol (late 1980s to middle 1990s). Throughout the latter half of the century, much architecture was noted for originality of design. Unique forms and patterns were employed to produce distinctive images, particularly in commercial work. Particularly noteworthy are the skyscrapers of such cities as Dallas, Houston, and San Antonio. At the same time, a revival of interest in regional design character occurred. Such attributes as climate, local traditions, and local materials were viewed as significant informants of design, tying buildings to their locale. Our Lady of Guadalupe Catholic Church, Helotes (1991), a work recalling traditional forms and materials of the Hill Country by Clovis Heimsath Architects, well represents modern regionalism. Such contrasts between hightech and vernacular design illustrate the rich diversity of Texas architecture. Variety contributes to the cultural richness of cities, towns, and rural areas, reflecting particular attributes of the people and the land to which they belong.   *Willard B. Robinson*

Archive War. When Rafael Vásquez "conquered" San Antonio in the first of the Mexican invasions of 1842, Pres. Sam Houston called an emergency session of Congress, to meet in Houston. Austin citizens, thinking that the president wanted to make Houston the capital, threatened to prevent the removal of state papers with armed resistance. From Washington-on-the-Brazos, Houston sent rangers to get the papers. Their mission succeeded, but the Austin vigilance committee commandeered a cannon, caught up with the wagons of papers, and forced their return; the rangers relinquished the archives in order to prevent bloodshed.   *Claudia Hazlewood*

Arlington, Texas. Halfway between Dallas and Fort Worth in east Tarrant County; founded in 1876 on the Texas and Pacific

Railway as a market town for the surrounding farms and ranches, which shipped livestock, cotton, hay, and other crops. The community, known at first as Hayter, received a post office named for Arlington, Virginia, the home of Robert E. Lee, in 1877. By 1910 Arlington had electricity, city water, telephones, and natural gas lines. The population was 4,240 in 1940. In the next two decades the town grew tenfold, to over 44,000 in 1960, and became a manufacturing center. Arlington continued to expand—to more than 122,000 inhabitants in 1978 and 261,721 in 1990. Arlington is the home of the Texas Rangers baseball team, Six Flags Over Texas, and two institutions of higher learning, the University of Texas at Arlington and Arlington Baptist College.

Gayla Weems Shannon

Armadillo. The nine-banded armadillo (*Dasypus novemcinctus*), the only armadillo that occurs in North America, is very common in Texas and has become a major figure of popular art and reference. Thousands of businesses (e.g., a delicatessen called the Armadeli, Armadillo Tours, the Armadillo Candy Company) are named for this mammal, which is frequently seen, dead or alive, along Texas roads. The armadillo is about the size of a large cat. Mature females mate in late summer and autumn and give birth to identical quadruplets the following spring. The armadillo's diet consists chiefly of insects, grubs, and spiders, though it also eats such foods as earthworms, small amphibians, and reptiles. Frequently, the animal's hunts leave tell-tale holes in suburban lawns. Before the mid-1850s the armadillo was known only along the lower Rio Grande, but it had spread throughout most of Texas and into Louisiana and Oklahoma by 1940. Human beings contributed significantly to its spread. Some armadillos were captured or purchased as curious pets and later escaped or were intentionally released. In these ways breeding populations were initially established in Mississippi, Alabama, and Florida. Some people may have carried armadillos into new territory for human consumption. The armadillo has long been considered a game animal in Mexico, and the practice of eating armadillos was adopted by residents of South Texas when the animal migrated there. During the Great Depression, East Texans stocked their larders with armadillos, which they called "Hoover hogs" because of the animal's supposed pork-like flavor (some say chicken-like, and others say worse things) and because they considered President Herbert Hoover responsible for the depression. Currently, barbecued armadillo and armadillo chili are popular foods at various festivals in parts of Texas, Arkansas, and the southeastern United States.

Armadillos have been promoted as a Texas souvenir since the 1890s. Charles Apelt, inventor of the armadillo-shell basket, first displayed his wares at the New York World's Fair in 1902. His family operated the Apelt Armadillo Company near Comfort until 1971. In addition to baskets, Apelt's catalog listed lamps, wall hangings, and other curios fashioned from armadillo shells. The Apelt farm was also a principal supplier of live armadillos to zoos, research institutions, and individuals. Armadillo racing became a popular amusement in Texas during the 1970s. Several organizations, notably from San Angelo, began promoting races throughout the United States, in Canada, and even in Europe. As a result, the animal is strongly associated with Texas. Armadillo World Headquarters in Austin, a rock and country music establishment decorated by the "Michelangelo of armadillo art," Jim Franklin, was from 1970 to 1980 a monument to the association

Grand Opening of the Armadillo World Headquarters, by Jim Franklin, 1970. Poster. 11³⁄₁₆" × 16¹³⁄₁₆". Texas Poster Art Collection, CAH; CN 02889. Sam Lewis of San Angelo made the familiar nine-banded armadillo into a "folk critter" and emblem of Texas. Austin artist Franklin turned Armadillo World Headquarters into what one reporter called the "Sistine Chapel of armadillo art."

between Texans and the armadillo. In the late 1970s the Texas legislature voted down attempts to make the armadillo the official state mammal, but in 1981 it was declared the official state mascot by executive decree.

Larry L. Smith

Armadillo World Headquarters. A music performance hall in Austin. During the 1970s AWH was the focus of musical activity that brought national recognition to the capital. The "Armadillo" was a converted national guard armory that provided an alternative venue to the municipal auditorium across the street. It capped several years of searching by young musicians and artists for a place to perform. Its name evoked the image of a peaceable native critter, the armadillo, often seen heels-up on Texas highways. The AWH opened in August 1970 and quickly became the focus for much of the city's musical life. With an eventual capacity of 1,500, the hall featured a varied fare of blues, rock, jazz, folk, and country music in an informal atmosphere. AWH brought to Austin a variety of musical groups that smaller clubs might never have booked— Frank Zappa, the Pointer Sisters, Bruce Springsteen, the Grateful Dead. Since local artists often opened the shows, the Armadillo also gave vital exposure to such future stars as Joe Ely, Marcia Ball, and Stevie Ray Vaughan. The most dramatic fusion in the Armadillo's eclectic calendar mixed traditional country-music culture with that of urban blues and rock to produce a Texas hybrid character known as the "cosmic cowboy" and a hybrid music called "progressive country" (or "redneck rock"). The acknowledged godfather of this movement was Willie Nelson, who made his Armadillo debut in 1972. To promote its concerts, AWH maintained a staff of poster and mural artists, including Jim Franklin, who contributed to the flowering of poster art in Austin. But the Armadillo operated on a shoestring budget and much volunteer labor, on a month-to-month basis in an atmosphere of perpetual financial crisis. In 1980 the demand for downtown real estate ended the venture. As their lease expired, managers of the hall held a final blowout (31 December 1980), then closed its doors to await demolition.

John Wheat

Armstrong, George Washington. Lawyer and industrialist; b. Jasper County, 26 January 1866; d. Natchez, Mississippi, 1 October 1954; m. Jennie May Allen (1887; d. 1930); 3 children; m. Mary Cozby (1933); ed. University of Texas (LL.B., 1886). Armstrong practiced law and served as county judge of Tarrant County (1894–98), whence his nickname, "Judge." In 1903 he left the practice of law and went into banking and oil production in South Texas. His numerous successful business concerns included development of the Batson and Petrolia oilfields and ownership (or part ownership) of four banks, grain elevators, cotton ginning and exporting enterprises, and steel mills. He farmed and ranched as an "expensive" hobby. He founded the Texas Chamber of Commerce, ran unsuccessfully for Congress in 1902 and lieutenant governor in 1932, and wrote numerous tracts that expressed his frequently controversial views, which included opposition to the Federal Reserve System, advocacy for the repeal of the Fourteenth and Fifteenth amendments, anti-Zionism, anti-Communism, and strong support for segregation and the doctrine of white supremacy. He also established the Judge Armstrong Foundation and the Texas Educational Association to propagate his views. He attracted national attention in 1949 when he offered to provide Jefferson Military College of Washington, Mississippi, with a large endowment on the condition that the school exclude blacks, Jews, and Asians.

Leon B. Blair

Arnold, Hendrick. Texas revolutionary spy; birthdate unknown; d. Bexar County, 1849; m. Martina—. Arnold, though evidently half black and half white, held his own daughter Harriet, child of a slave, as a slave. He had another daughter who may have been the child of his wife. During the Texas Revolution he served in Deaf Smith's spy company at the siege of Bexar and the battle of San Jacinto. He was given land after the revolution in compensation for his "important service" to the Texas cause, though he did not live on the grant, which was part of a wild tract northwest of the site of present Bandera. Arnold lived on the Medina River, operated a gristmill in San Antonio, and died in the cholera epidemic of 1849.

Nolan Thompson

Arnold, Ripley Allen. United States Army officer; b. Hancock County, Mississippi, 17 January 1817; d. Fort Graham, 6 September 1853; m. Catherine Bryant (1839); 5 children; ed. West Point (grad. 1838). Arnold was promoted to first lieutenant in 1839. He was brevetted captain in 1842 for gallant service in the Seminole War, and major in 1846 for his role in the battles of Palo Alto and Resaca de la Palma. His other Mexican War service was extensive. In 1849, while stationed at Fort Graham, he established Camp Worth (later Fort Worth). He was detached to duty in Washington in 1852 and returned to command Fort Graham the next year. In a preemptive strike, his company pursued and defeated a Comanche war party in the future Palo Pinto County. Arnold was killed in a gunfight with Josephus Murray Steiner, who was acquitted by both a court-martial and a civil jury. Arnold had been procuring government horses and selling them for his own profit, and Steiner may have intended to expose him.

Thomas W. Cutrer

Arredondo, Joaquín de. Commandant of the eastern Provincias Internas in Spanish Texas; b. Barcelona, 1768; d. Havana, 1837.

Arredondo suppressed Miguel Hidalgo y Costilla's revolt and criollo-related revolts in Nuevo Santander (1812–13). He utterly defeated an army of rebels in the battle of Medina (18 Aug. 1813), appointed Cristóbal Domínguez governor of Texas, and crushed the filibustering expedition of Francisco Xavier Mina in Soto la Marina (Oct. 1817). He approved Moses Austin's petition (1821) to bring settlers to Texas, however, and swore allegiance to the new Mexican nation before retiring to Cuba.

Robert H. Thonhoff

Arrington, George Washington. Lawman and rancher; b. John C. Orrick, Jr., Greensboro, Alabama, 23 December 1844; d. Canadian, 31 March 1923; m. Sarah Burnette (1882); 9 children. When he arrived in Texas in 1870, after an adventurous start as a Confederate guerrilla and subsequently as an outlaw, John Orrick changed his name to escape his past. He worked for a railroad, farmed, and in 1875 joined the Texas Rangers, in which he had a distinguished career. As a ranger, Captain ("Cap") Arrington led a major charting expedition in the Panhandle and eastern New Mexico. He left the rangers in 1882 in order to begin ranching and was elected sheriff of Wheeler County, a post in which he represented the law for 15 counties. He and his family lived in the county jail in Mobeetie. While sheriff, he acquired ranchland and, through his strict treatment of cattle rustlers and other outlaws, maintained his reputation as the "iron man of the Panhandle." In 1882 he moved to a dugout, built two cabins, and registered his CAP brand. The next year he was appointed manager of the Rocking Chair Ranch, a post he held until 1896. He lived in Canadian for seven years so his children could attend school; while there, he was active in civic affairs. He later started a school on his ranch. To the end of his life he had plenty of enemies and usually carried a gun. His wife (d. 1945) remained active in the Canadian WCTU and First Baptist Church. As the 20th century neared its end, Cap's heirs still ran the Arrington Ranch.

H. Allen Anderson

Ashby, Harrison Sterling Price. Politician; b. Cariton County, Missouri, 18 May 1848; d. Octavia, Oklahoma, May 1923; m. Sara Sophia Wisdom (1871; d. 1876); 4 children; m. Amanda Elizabeth Ray (1879); 5 children. "Stump" Ashby was a licensed Methodist preacher from 1872 to 1888. He was one of the first Farmers' Alliance organizers and speakers in Texas. He led an independent political movement that achieved the election of a Fort Worth mayor (1886). Ashby organized the convention that led to a state Union Labor party convention in July 1888. With Thomas Gaines and William R. Lamb, he organized the founding state People's party convention (1891) and continued as state party chairman in 1892 and 1894. He was a delegate to the organizing convention of the national Populist party in St. Louis (1892). He ran unsuccessfully for lieutenant governor on the Populist ticket in 1896. While he was a delegate to the Populist convention in 1902, he fought a prohibition plank in the party platform. Shortly thereafter he moved to Indian Territory, became president of his local farmers' union, and supported Democrat William H. (Alfalfa Bill) Murray. As a member of the First, Third, and Fourth Oklahoma legislatures, Ashby maintained the reputation for public speaking that had earned him his nickname.

Bruce Palmer

Ashworth Act. An act pertaining to the residence of "free persons of color" in Texas; passed by the Texas Congress in December 1840, in response to an act passed in February of the same year. Although the Ashworths themselves, the original subjects of the law, were not of African origin, the act seems to have been applied also to persons of African ancestry; historically, it has been understood as applying to free persons with varying admixtures of African-American blood. The earlier act prohibited the immigration of free persons of color and ordered all of them to vacate the Republic of Texas within two years or be sold into slavery. It repealed all laws contrary to its provisions and nullified the act of 5 June 1837 that permitted the residence of free persons of color living in Texas before the Texas Declaration of Independence. Immediately after the passage of the February act, influential whites from around the republic had begun to prepare petitions for exemptions. Three petitions submitted were on behalf of several families named Ashworth, who resided in Jefferson County. The first of the petitions, signed by 60 citizens, requested exemptions for four Ashworth immigrants and a family relative. The second petition, which accompanied the first, addressed only the plight of two of the Ashworths, William and Abner, apparently because they were early immigrants and had a stronger case; it was signed by 71 citizens. It claimed that William and Abner had been residents for six years and stated that they had contributed generously to the Texan cause during the revolution. It argued that the law of 5 February 1840 would "operate grievously" if enforced against them. Sixty-one citizens signed the third petition supporting Elisha Thomas, who had served in the army immediately after the battle of San Jacinto. In all three cases the petitions were signed by prominent officials in Jefferson County.

On 5 November 1840, Joseph Grigsby of Jefferson County presented the three petitions to the Texas Congress. The petitions were referred to a special committee, of which Grigsby was named chairman. The committee reported favorably on them, and a bill for the relief of the Ashworths passed its first reading without recorded contest.

Many congressmen had received one or more petitions from their constituents. House member Timothy Pillsbury of Brazoria offered a resolution, adopted by the House, instructing the Committee on the State of the Republic to consider legislation allowing the continued residence of free persons of color who were in the country when the constitution was adopted. Such legislation would rule favorably on petitions for most of the persons involved. Pillsbury himself carried unpresented petitions supporting Samuel H. Hardin and James Richardson. When the Committee on the State of the Republic ignored Pillsbury's resolution, he presented the Hardin and Richardson petitions to the House. James Richardson, of Brazoria County, had served in the garrison at Velasco in the revolution, although he was 60 years old. Samuel H. Hardin's petition requested relief for him and his wife, reporting their long residence, industriousness, and good conduct.

The Hardin and Richardson petitions were referred to the Committee on the State of the Republic. A bill exempting Samuel McCulloch, Jr., and some of his relatives passed its first reading. On 10 November the Ashworth bill passed the House and the McCulloch bill was read a second time. At this reading attempts were made to amend the bill by adding the names of William Goyens, who was supported by Thomas J. Rusk, and two other parties. The amendments lost, but the original bill passed. The Ashworth bill came up in the Senate the same month. A successful amendment inserted the words "and all free persons of color together with their families, who were residing in Texas the day of the Declaration of Independence" after the names of the original beneficiaries. The bill thereby addressed the case of all such free persons who had immigrated to Texas before the Declaration of Independence and conferred residency on David and Abner Ashworth, who had immigrated afterward. The House accepted the Senate's amendment, and on 12 December 1840, President Lamar signed the bill. David and Abner Ashworth became the only free persons of color to immigrate subsequent to the Declaration of Independence who were given congressional sanction to remain in Texas.   *Nolan Thompson*

Association of Texas Colleges and Universities. Formed as the Association of Texas Colleges from the college section of the Texas State Teachers Association in 1916. C. A. Nichols, of Southwestern University, was the first president. In the 1960s the organization changed to its present name and relinquished its power to accredit colleges. The group promotes higher education to the public and serves as a forum for college presidents. Its charter prohibits political lobbying. To join, a school must be fully accredited by the Southern Association of Colleges and Schools. Affiliate memberships are available to schools that are candidates for accreditation. Member institutions numbered 121 in 1994.   *Tracé Etienne–Gray*

Atascosito Road. A route fixed by the Spanish by 1757 as a military highway from Goliad and Refugio in South Texas to the Trinity River in East Texas; named for a settlement on the Trinity. The eastward extension of the Atascosito Road is called the La Bahía Road. In the mid-nineteenth century the Old Atascosito Road was used by cattle drovers en route to New Orleans.   *L. W. Kemp*

Aten, Ira. Lawman; b. Cairo, Illinois, 3 September 1862; d. Imperial Valley, California, 5 August 1853; m. Imogen Boyce (1892); 5 children. Aten and his brothers Calvin and Edwin were all Texas Rangers. Aten served with the Frontier Battalion and attained the rank of sergeant. He and John R. Hughes tracked down and killed a crony of Butch Cassidy in 1887. Subsequently, Aten was drafted as sheriff by citizens of Castro County; Imogen was the jailer. Aten helped organize the first bank at Hereford. When the XIT Ranch began to break up, he moved to California, where he developed an irrigated farm. In 1923 he was elected to the Imperial Valley District Board, which helped bring water and electricity to the area. Late in life he compiled his Wild West memoirs, which were published in *Frontier Times* by J. Marvin Hunter. Aten, the "last of the old Texas Rangers," could still ride and shoot straight at age 90.   *H. Allen Anderson*

Attwater, Henry Philemon. Naturalist and conservationist; b. Brighton, England, 28 April 1854; d. Texas, 25 September 1931; m. Lucy Mary Watts (1885), a widow with 2 children; ed. St. Nicholas Episcopal College, Shoreham, Sussex. Attwater collected natural-history specimens in Texas from 1884 on; he contributed specimens to the Smithsonian and other distinguished

Canis Lupus, Linn, Var Rufus. Red Texan Wolf. Male. After John Woodhouse Audubon. Lithography firm of John T. Bowen, lithograph (hand colored), 1845. Courtesy Amon Carter Museum, Fort Worth. The red wolf once ranged widely in Central and East Texas. In the mid-1990s it was extinct in the wild in Texas and listed by the federal government as an endangered species.

exhibit venues and wrote significant scholarly contributions, particularly in ornithology. He worked for passage of the Model Game Law (1903, reenacted 1907), which set a precedent for financing game management with hunting-license fees. Several species are named for Attwater, including a famous but rare prairie chicken. Attwater contributed his collection to the Witte Museum in San Antonio. *Stanley D. Casto*

Audubon, John James. Naturalist and painter; b. Les Cayes, Santo Domingo, 26 April 1785; d. on the Hudson River, New York, 27 January 1851; m. Lucy Bakewell (1808). The famous naturalist made an expedition to the Republic of Texas in 1837 and included Texas species in both of his great works, *The Birds of America* and *The Viviparous Quadrupeds of North America.* When he and his son John arrived at Galveston Bay, they were officially greeted by the secretary of the Texas Navy, Samuel Rhoads Fisher. They next visited the capitol at Houston, where they met with President Sam Houston in his dogtrot cabin. While in Texas they observed a large number of previously

known birds including bluewinged teals, blacknecked stilts, least terns, roseate spoonbills, skimmers, ivorybilled woodpeckers, blackthroated buntings, and varieties of sandpipers, ducks, and herons. *Quadrupeds* contains more plates drawn from Texas specimens than does *Birds of America.* *Ben W. Huseman*

Aury, Louis Michel. Pirate; b. Paris, ca. 1788; d. Florida, probably 30 August 1821. In the cause of Mexican independence, French sailor Aury harassed Spanish shipping in the Gulf of Mexico and was made resident commissioner of Galveston, which he proclaimed a port of the "Mexican republic" (1816). He built a settlement of shacks on Galveston Island and cruised the Gulf looking for prizes. Henry Perry, sent by the New Orleans associates who had sent Aury, refused to recognize Aury's authority. After the New Orleans group decided against invading New Spain, it severed relations with Francisco Xavier Mina, who had also been sent to Galveston. While Aury accompanied Mina to the Santander River, Jean Laffite and his brother Pierre gained a following in Galveston. When Aury returned, he resigned his commission as ruler of the island (1817). He sailed to the Florida coast, joined Gregor McGregor, the authorized agent of various rebel colonies in Latin America, and attacked the mainland from Amelia Island. He captured Old Providence Island on 4 July 1818, and from headquarters there tried unsuccessfully to aid the republican cause. Some sources state that he was living in Havana in 1845.   *Harris Gaylord Warren*

Austin, Moses. Pioneer promoter of the Anglo-American colonization of Texas; b. Durham, Connecticut, 4 October 1761; d. Herculaneum, Missouri, 10 June 1821; m. Mary Brown (1785); 5 children. Austin was the "father" of the American lead industry and the father of the "father" of Texas. His contract to roof the Virginia capitol in lead was but a step on the way to his control of virtually all smelting in Spanish Upper Louisiana, where he established a settlement in 1798 (later Potosi, Missouri) and another in 1808 (Herculaneum, Missouri). Severe financial losses led him to develop a plan in 1819 for settling an American colony in Spanish Texas. He traveled to San Antonio and was spurned by Governor Antonio María Martínez. Then, accompanied by the Baron de Bastrop, whom he had previously met and now fortuitously met again, he returned to the governor's office. This time, the governor endorsed the colonization plan and forwarded it to higher authority. On his way home, Austin contracted pneumonia. He learned before reaching home that his plan had been approved. His health failed, however, and on his deathbed, as recounted by his wife in a letter to their son, Stephen F. Austin, he enjoined his son to pursue the "Texas venture." Mrs. Austin wrote, "he beged me to tell you to take his place tell dear Stephen that it is his dieing fathers last request to prosecute the enterprise he had Commenced."

David B. Gracy II

Austin, Stephen Fuller. Leading empresario, the "father of Texas"; b. southwestern Virginia, 3 November 1793; d. 27 December 1836; ed. Transylvania University, Lexington Kentucky (2 years). Austin worked with his father, Moses Austin, before coming to Texas. He arrived in San Antonio in 1821 and, authorized by Governor Antonio María Martínez to colonize under his father's grant, sought a colony site on the coastal plain between the San Antonio and Brazos rivers. He arranged with Martínez to offer land to settlers in quantities of 640 acres to the head of a family, 320 acres for his wife, 320 acres for each child, and 80 acres for each slave. Austin was to collect 12½ cents an acre for his services. He was responsible for the colonists' good conduct. He returned to New Orleans to advertise the offer, and the first colonists began to arrive in Texas in December 1821. When Martínez informed Austin that the Mexican government refused to approve the Spanish grant to Moses Austin, preferring to regulate colonization by a general immigration law, Austin hastened to Mexico City and, by unremitting attention, succeeded in getting Agustín de Iturbide's rump congress to pass a law (1823) that offered heads of families a league and a labor of land and provided for empresarios to promote immigration. An empresario was to receive 67,000 acres for each 200 families he introduced. Immigrants were not required to pay fees to the government, a fact that shortly led some of them to deny Austin's right to charge 12½ cents an acre for services. The law was annulled when Iturbide abdicated, but in April 1823 Austin induced congress to grant him a contract to introduce 300 fami-

Stephen F. Austin, by William Howard, 1833. Watercolor on ivory. 5⅜" × 4⅝". James Perry Bryan Papers, CAH; CN 01436. This portrait, the larger of two miniatures of Austin painted by British artist William Howard in Mexico City in 1833, shows Austin, a slender man with an unruly mop of hair, gazing pensively. Soon after these portraits were completed, Austin was arrested on his way back to Texas. He had the pictures sent to his sister, Emily Austin Perry, and brother-in-law.

lies in accordance with its terms. In August 1824 a new congress passed an immigration law that vested the administration of public land in the states, with certain restrictions, and authorized them to make laws for settlement. In March 1825 the legislature of Coahuila and Texas passed a law conforming in general to the previous act approved by Iturbide. It continued the empresario system and offered to each married man a league of land (4,428 acres), for which he was obligated to pay the state $30 within six years. In the meantime, Austin had substantially fulfilled his contract to settle the first 300 families—the "Old Three Hundred." He obtained three additional contracts (in 1825, 1827, and 1828) to settle a total of 900 more families in the area of his first colony, besides a contract in partnership with his secretary, Samuel M. Williams, for the settlement of 800 families in western Texas. Unfortunately, this partnership contract led to a disagreeable controversy with Sterling C. Robertson.

Austin had nearly complete authority over his colonists until 1828. He allowed them to elect militia officers and local alcaldes and drew up legal forms and a simple civil and criminal code. As lieutenant colonel of militia, he planned and sometimes led campaigns against Indians. When population increased and appeals from decisions of individual alcaldes promised to become a burden, he instituted an appellate court composed of all the alcaldes—ultimately seven. When the Constitution of Coahuila and Texas went into effect (1827) Austin gave responsibility for the details of local government to the ayuntamiento. Aside from attracting immigrants to his colonies, Austin's greatest labor was devoted to the land system, which involved surveying and allocating land to applicants without overlapping and with a minimum of conflict. The Mexican practice of issuing titles on loose sheets without a permanent record invited confusion, and Austin asked and obtained permission to record titles in a bound volume having the validity of the original. The costs of government—directing surveyors, allocating grants, preparing titles and records, entertaining prospective colonists, corresponding with state and federal officials, punishing hostile Indians and rewarding friendly ones—were high, and Austin's only resource was the colonists. Some of them, who refused to pay after empresarios began receiving grants of land, appealed to the political chief at San Antonio, and he ruled that Austin could not collect. At the same time, however, he proclaimed a fee bill that allowed the land commissioner (the Baron de Bastrop in the first colony) to charge $127 a league for signing titles, and Austin made a private arrangement with Bastrop to split this fee. The state law of 1825 allowed empresarios to reimburse themselves for costs, and under this law Austin charged a per-league fee. But costs still outran revenue, and Austin had to make up the difference. He wrote shortly before his death that his wealth was merely prospective, consisting of the uncertain value of land acquired as compensation for his services as empresario.

Austin strove for conditions conducive to the settlers' prosperity, and in general the government helped. By a law of 1823, colonists were relieved of paying tariffs for seven years. The status of slavery, however, was always a difficult problem, with regard to which Austin's convictions yielded to the current need of Texas. Many colonists had fled creditors in the United States. Austin secured a state law that closed the courts to potential debt plaintiffs for 12 years and permanently exempted land and farm implements from their efforts. It furthermore stated that Texas debtors who lost in court could not be hurt in "their families . . . husbandry, or art." In effect, it was a sweeping homestead exemption law. Aware of the importance of external trade, Austin urged the establishment of ports and the temporary legalization of coasting trade in foreign ships. Congress legalized the port of Galveston after a survey of the pass by Austin in 1825, and the government winked at the use of the Brazos and other landing places, but the coasting trade in foreign vessels was not established. As a result, external trade was confined to the United States. Austin clearly realized that harmony with government authorities was indispensable. He never allowed the settlers to forget the benefits that they received through the liberal colonization policy or their obligation to obey the laws and become loyal Mexican citizens. He led the militia to assist Mexican troops in putting the Fredonian Rebellion down. Before 1832 he took no part in Mexican party convulsions. "Play the turtle," he urged, "head and feet within our own shells."

By 1832 Austin's colonies comprised 8,000 persons, and other empresarios had brought in more. Reconciling them to cautious leadership became more difficult. Furthermore, as the United States made persistent efforts to buy Texas, the anxiety of Mexican leaders increased and led to the anticolonization Law of April 6, 1830, which applied in effect only to Texas and the United States. Austin ingeniously secured the exemption of his own colonies and the colony of Green DeWitt from the law, which he got repealed in 1833. In the meantime, however, military measures to enforce the 1830 law and imprudent administration of newly applicable tariff laws led to the first of the Anahuac Disturbances. Austin might have averted the uprising if he had not been in Saltillo. After it was put down he abandoned his policy of aloofness from partisanship and adopted the cause of Antonio López de Santa Anna against the administration of President Anastasio Bustamante. Santa Anna won, and the colonists sought reward for their support. The Convention of 1832 met to ask the government for repeal of the prohibition against immigration from the United States, extension of tariff exemption, separation from Coahuila, and authority to establish state government in Texas—petitions that were never presented to the government. Though Austin was president of the convention, he feared that it would make the colonists look disloyal, especially because the old Mexican inhabitants of San Antonio had sent no delegates. Austin may have hoped to persuade the San Antonians to take the lead in asking for reforms in a later convention. At any rate, he was in San Antonio engaged on this mission when the ground was cut from under his feet by publication of a call for a second convention to meet at San Felipe on 1 April 1833. Again Austin acquiesced and served in the convention, hoping in some measure to moderate its action. This convention repeated petitions of the previous one and went further in framing a constitution to accompany the request for state government. Austin, though he thought the movement ill-timed, was sent to Mexico City to deliver the petitions. He persuaded the government to repeal the Law of April 6, 1830, and to promise reforms in Texas local government. But Santa Anna, increasingly a Centralist tyrant, would not approve state government for Texas. Austin was arrested in Saltillo (January 1834) under suspicion of trying to incite insurrection in Texas, and taken back to Mexico City. No charges were made against him, no court would accept jurisdiction of his case, and he remained a prisoner, shifting from prison to prison, until December 1834, when he was released on bond and restricted to the Federal District. He was freed by a general amnesty law in July 1835 and at the end of August returned to Texas by way of New Orleans.

Upon his return after this 28-month absence, he learned that an unofficial call had been issued for a convention, or consultation, to meet in October. Probably he could have quashed this call, but in a notable speech at Brazoria on 8 September he gave it his sanction, and election of delegates proceeded. The Consultation was organized on 3 November. In the meantime, during September and early October, Austin had been in effect civil head of Anglo-American Texas, as chairman of a central committee at San Felipe. War began at Gonzales on 1 October. Austin was elected to command the volunteers gathered there and led them against the Mexican army at San Antonio. In November the provisional government elected him to serve, with William H. Wharton and Branch T. Archer, as commissioner to the United States. He arrived in New Orleans in January 1836 and returned to Texas in June. The commissioners were to solicit loans and volunteers, arrange credit for munitions and equipment, fit out warships, and do whatever they could to commit the government of the United States to recognition and eventual annexation if Texas should declare independence. They got most of what they wanted, but not the long-term assurances they sought from President Andrew Jackson and Congress. Austin

Train depot, Austin, Texas, 1884, by Austin photographer S. B. Hill. Courtesy TSL. In 1871, with the arrival of the Houston and Texas Central Railway, Austin became the westernmost railroad terminus in Texas and was transformed into an important trading center.

was convinced that Congress would have voted for recognition in May, after the battle of San Jacinto, if acting president David G. Burnet had cooperated with the commissioners by sending them official reports of conditions in Texas. Somewhat hesitantly, Austin ran for the presidency, was defeated in the election of September 1836, but accepted the office of secretary of state.

Although his policy of caution was criticized by some, judged by historical standards, Austin did a great work in fostering the Anglo-American colonization of Texas. He wrote in July 1836, "The prosperity of Texas has been the object of my labors, the idol of my existence—it has assumed the character of a *religion*, for the guidance of my thoughts and actions, for fifteen years." After his untimely death, his body was transported on the *Yellow Stone* to Peach Point Plantation for burial, then reinterred in 1910 in the State Cemetery. *Eugene C. Barker*

Austin, Texas. The capital of Texas, county seat of Travis County, and home of the University of Texas at Austin; bisected by the Colorado River. The city is at the eastern edge of the Hill Country and the Edwards Plateau. It was established by the young Republic of Texas in 1839 to serve as its permanent capital, and named in honor of the founder of Anglo-American Texas, Stephen F. Austin. A site-selection commission appointed by the Texas Congress in January 1839 chose a site on the western frontier, after viewing it at the instruction of President Mirabeau B.

Lamar, a proponent of westward expansion who had visited the sparsely settled area in 1838. Impressed by its beauty, healthfulness, abundant natural resources, promise as an economic hub, and central location in Texas territory, the commission purchased 7,735 acres along the Colorado River comprising the hamlet of Waterloo and adjacent lands. Because the area's remoteness from population centers and its vulnerability to attacks by Mexican troops and Indians displeased many Texans, Sam Houston among them, political opposition made Austin's early years precarious ones. Surveyors laid out the new town, working under the direction of Edwin Waller, who was appointed by Lamar to plan and construct Austin. Out of the 7,735 acres they chose a 640-acre site fronting on the Colorado River and nestled between Waller Creek on the east and Shoal Creek on the west. The plan was a grid, 14 blocks square, bisected by Congress Avenue, and extending northward from the Colorado River to "Capitol Square." Determined to have Austin ready by the time the Texas Congress convened in November 1839, Waller opted for temporary government buildings at temporary locations. The one-story frame Capitol was set back from Congress Avenue on a hill at what is now the corner of Colorado and Eighth streets. During October, President Lamar arrived, government offices opened for business, Presbyterians organized the first church, and the Austin *City Gazette*, the town's first newspaper, made its appearance. Congress convened in

November, Austin was incorporated on 27 December, and on 13 January 1840, Waller was elected the town's first mayor. By 1840 Austin had 856 inhabitants, including diplomatic representatives from France, England, and the United States.

Austin flourished initially but in 1842 entered the darkest period in its history. Lamar's successor as president, Sam Houston, ordered the national archives transferred to Houston for safekeeping after Mexican troops captured San Antonio on 5 March 1842. Convinced that removal of the republic's diplomatic, financial, land, and military-service records was tantamount to choosing a new capital, Austinites refused to relinquish the archives. Houston moved the government anyway, first to Houston and then to Washington-on-the-Brazos, which remained the seat of government until 1845. The archives stayed in Austin. When Houston sent a contingent of armed men to seize the General Land Office records in December 1842, they were foiled by the citizens of Austin and Travis County in an incident known as the Archive War. Deprived of its political function, Austin languished. Between 1842 and 1845 its population dropped below 200 and its buildings deteriorated. But during the summer of 1845 a constitutional convention meeting in Austin approved the annexation of Texas to the United States and named Austin the state capital until 1850, at which time the voters of Texas were to express their preference in a general election. After resuming its role as the seat of government in 1845, Austin officially became the state capital on 19 February 1846, the date of the formal transfer of authority from the republic to the state. The town recovered gradually, its population reaching 854 by 1850, 225 of whom were slaves. Austin entered a period of accelerated growth following its decisive triumph in the 1850 election, which determined the site of the state capital for the next 20 years. For the first time the government constructed permanent buildings, among them a new Capitol at the head of Congress Avenue, completed in 1853, and the Governor's Mansion, completed in 1856. State-run asylums for deaf, blind, and mentally ill Texans were erected on the fringes of town. Congregations of Baptists, Episcopalians, Methodists, Presbyterians, and Catholics erected permanent church buildings, and the town's elite built elegant Greek Revival mansions. By 1860 the population had climbed to 3,546, including 1,019 slaves and 12 free blacks. In February 1861 Austin and Travis County residents voted against the secession ordinance 704 to 450, but Unionist sentiment waned once the war began. By April 1862 about 600 Austin and Travis County men had joined some 12 volunteer companies serving the Confederacy. Like other communities, Austin experienced severe shortages of goods, spiraling inflation, and the decimation of its fighting men. The end of the war brought Union occupation troops to the city and a period of explosive growth of the African-American population, which increased by 57 percent during the 1860s. During the late 1860s and early 1870s the city's newly emancipated blacks established the residential communities of Masontown, Wheatville, Pleasant Hill, and Clarksville, organized such churches as First Baptist Church (Colored), started businesses, and patronized schools. By 1870 Austin's 1,615 black residents composed 36 percent of the 4,428 inhabitants.

On December 25, 1871, a new era opened with the coming of the Houston and Texas Central Railway, Austin's first railroad connection. By becoming the westernmost railroad terminus in Texas and the only railroad town for scores of miles in most directions, Austin was transformed into a trading center for a vast area. Construction boomed, and the population more than doubled in five years to 10,363. The many foreign-born newcomers from Germany, Mexico, Ireland, and Sweden gave Austin's citizenry a more heterogeneous character. For the first time a Mexican-American community took root in Austin, in a neighborhood near the mouth of Shoal Creek. Accompanying these dramatic changes were civic improvements, among them gas street lamps in 1874, the first streetcar line in 1875, and the first elevated bridge across the Colorado River about 1876. Although a second railroad, the International and Great Northern, reached Austin in 1876, the town's fortunes turned downward after 1875 as new railroads traversed Austin's trading region and diverted much of its trade to other towns. From 1875 to 1880 the city's population increased by only 650 inhabitants, to 11,013. Austin's expectations of rivaling other Texas cities for economic leadership faded.

Austin solidified its position as a political center during the 1870s and 1880s and gained a new role as an educational center. In 1872 the city prevailed in a statewide election to choose once and for all the state capital, turning back challenges from Houston and Waco. Three years later Texas took the first steps toward constructing a new Capitol that culminated in 1888 in the dedication of a magnificent granite building towering over the town. In 1881 Austin emerged as a seat of education. In a hotly contested statewide election, the city was chosen as the site for the new University of Texas, which began instruction two years later. Tillotson Collegiate and Normal Institute, founded by the American Missionary Association to provide educational opportunities for African Americans, opened its doors in 1881. The Austin public school system was started the same year. Four years later St. Edward's School, founded several years earlier by the Holy Cross Fathers and Brothers, was chartered as St. Edwards College. In 1888 civic leader Alexander P. Wooldridge proposed that Austin construct a dam across the Colorado River and use water power to attract manufacturing. Proponents of the dam won political control of Austin in 1889. Empowered by a new city charter in 1891 that more than tripled Austin's corporate area from 4½ to 16½ square miles, the city fathers implemented a plan to build a municipal water and electric system, construct a dam for power, and lease most of the waterpower to manufacturers. By 1893 the 60-foot-high Austin Dam was completed, impounding Lake McDonald behind it. In 1895 dam-generated electricity began powering the four-year-old electric streetcar line and the city's new water and light systems. Civic pride ran strong during those years, which also saw the city blessed with the talents of sculptor Elisabet Ney and writer William Sydney Porter (O. Henry). But it turned out that the dam produced far less power than anticipated, manufacturers never came, periodic power shortfalls disrupted city services, Lake McDonald silted up, and, on 7 April 1900, the dam collapsed.

Between 1880 and 1920 Austin's population grew threefold to 34,876, but the city slipped from fourth largest in the state to tenth largest. The state's surging industrial development, propelled by the booming oil business, passed Austin by. The capital began boosting itself as a residential city, but the heavy municipal indebtedness incurred in building the dam resulted in the neglect of city services. In 1905 Austin had few sanitary sewers, virtually no public parks or playgrounds, and only one paved street. Three years later, voters overturned the aldermanic form of government, by which the city had been governed since 1839, and replaced it with commission government. A. P. Wooldridge headed a reform group voted into office in 1909 and served a decade as mayor, during which the city made steady if modest progress toward improving residential life. In 1918 the city acquired Barton Springs, a spring-fed pool that became the symbol of the residential city. Upon Wooldridge's retirement in 1919 the flaws of commission government, hidden by his leadership, became apparent as city services again deteriorated. At the urging of the Chamber of Commerce, Austinites voted in 1924 to adopt council–manager government, which went into effect in 1926 and remained in the 1990s. Progressive ideas like city planning and beautification became official city policy. A 1928 city plan, the first since 1839, called upon Austin to develop its strengths as a residential, cultural, and educational center. A $4,250,000 bond issue, Austin's largest to date, provided funds for streets, sewers, parks, the city hospital, the first permanent public library building, and the first municipal airport, which opened in 1930. A recreation department was established, and within a decade it offered Austinites a profusion of recreational programs, parks, and pools. By 1900 segregation of blacks and whites characterized many aspects of city life, and the lines of separation hardened in the early twentieth century. Despite a two-month streetcar boycott organized by blacks, the city implemented an ordinance in 1906 requiring separate compartments on streetcars. While residences of blacks had been widely scattered all across the city in 1880, by 1930 they were heavily concentrated on the east side of town, a process encouraged by the 1928 city plan, which recommended that East Austin be designated a "Negro district." Municipal services such as schools, sewers, and parks were made available to blacks in East Austin only. At midcentury Austin was still segregated in most respects—housing, restaurants, hotels, parks, hospitals, schools, public transportation—but African Americans had long fostered their own institutions, which included by the late 1940s some 150 small businesses, more than 30 churches, and 2 colleges. Between 1880 and 1940 the number of black residents grew from 3,587 to 14,861, but their proportion of the overall population declined from 33 percent to 17 percent. Austin's Hispanic residents, who in 1900 numbered about 335 and composed just 1.5 percent of the population, rose to 11 percent by 1940, when they numbered 9,693. By the 1940s most Mexican Americans lived in the rapidly expanding East Austin barrio south of East Eleventh Street, where increasing numbers owned homes. Hispanic-owned business were dominated by a thriving food industry.

During the early and mid-1930s Austin experienced the harsh effects of the Great Depression. Nevertheless, the town fared comparatively well, sustained by its twin foundations of government and education and by the political skills of Mayor Tom (Robert Thomas) Miller, who took office in 1933, and United States Congressman Lyndon Johnson, who won election in 1937. Its population grew at a faster pace during the 1930s than in any other decade during the twentieth century, increasing 66 percent from 53,120 to 87,930. By 1936 the PWA had provided Austin with more funding for municipal construction projects than any other Texas city during the same period. The University of Texas nearly doubled its enrollment during the decade and undertook a massive construction program. Johnson procured federal funds for public housing and dams on the Colorado River. The old Austin Dam, partially rebuilt under Mayor Wooldridge but never finished due to damage from flooding in 1915, was finally completed in 1940 and renamed Tom Miller Dam. Lake Austin stretched 21 miles behind it. Just upriver the much larger Mansfield Dam was completed in 1941 to impound Lake Travis. The two dams, in conjunction with other dams in the Lower Colorado River Authority system, brought great benefits to Austin: cheap hydroelectric power, the end of flooding that in 1935 and on earlier occasions had ravaged the town, a plentiful supply of water without which the city's later growth would have been unlikely, and recreation on the Highland Lakes that enhanced Austin's appeal as a place to live. In 1942 Austin gained the economic benefit of Del Valle Army Air Base, later Bergstrom Air Force Base, which remained in operation until 1993. Between the 1950s and 1980s ethnic relations in Austin were transformed. First came a sustained attacked on segregation. Local black leaders and political-action groups waged campaigns to desegregate city schools and services. In 1956 the University of Texas became the first major university in the South to admit blacks as undergraduates. In the early 1960s students staged demonstrations against segregated lunch counters, restaurants, and movie theaters. Gradually the barriers receded, a process accelerated when the United States Civil Rights Act of 1964 outlawed racial discrimination in public accommodations. Shut out of the town's political leadership since the 1880s, when two blacks had served on the city council, African Americans regained a foothold by winning a school-board seat in 1968 and a city-council seat in 1971. This political breakthrough was matched by Hispanics, whose numbers had reached 39,399 by 1970—16 percent of the population. Mexican Americans won their first seats on the Austin school board in 1972 and the city council in 1975.

From 1940 to 1990 Austin's population grew at an average rate of 40 percent per decade, from 87,930 to 465,622. The city's corporate area, which between 1891 and 1940 had about doubled to 30.85 square miles, grew more than sevenfold to 225.40 square miles by 1990. During the 1950s and 1960s much of Austin's growth reflected the rapid expansion of its traditional strengths—education and government. During the 1960s alone the number of students attending the University of Texas at Austin doubled, reaching 39,000 by 1970. Government employees in Travis County tripled between 1950 and 1970, to 47,300. University of Texas buildings multiplied, with the Lyndon Baines Johnson Library opening in 1971. A complex of state office buildings was constructed north of the Capitol. Propelling Austin's growth by the 1970s was its emergence as a center for high technology. This development, fostered by the Chamber of Commerce since the 1950s as a way to expand the city's narrow economic base and fueled by proliferating research programs at the University of Texas, accelerated when IBM located in Austin in 1967, followed by Texas Instruments in 1969 and Motorola in 1974. Two major research consortiums of high-technology companies followed during the 1980s, Microelectronics and Computer Technology Corporation and Sematech. By the early 1990s, the Austin Metropolitan Statistical Area had about 400 high-technology manufacturers. While high-technology industries located on Austin's periphery, its central area sprouted multistoried office buildings and hotels during the 1970s and 1980s, venues for the burgeoning music industry, and, in 1992, a new convention center. But the rapid growth generated strong resistance by the 1970s. Angered by proliferating apartment complexes and retarded traffic flow, neighborhood groups mobilized to protect the integrity of their residential areas. By 1983 there were more than 150 such groups. Environmentalists organized a powerful movement to protect streams, lakes, watersheds, and wooded hills from environmental degradation, resulting in the passage of a series of environmental-protection ordinances during the 1970s and 1980s. A program was inaugurated in 1971 to beautify the shores of Town Lake, a downtown lake impounded in 1960 behind Longhorn Dam. Historic preservationists fought the destruction of Austin's architectural heritage by rescuing and restoring historic buildings. City election campaigns during the 1970s and 1980s frequently featured struggles over the management of growth, with neighborhood groups and environmentalists on one side and business and development interests on the other. In the 1990s Austin was still seeking to balance the economic development it had long sought with the kind of life it had long treasured.

David C. Humphrey

Austin *American–Statesman*. Began as the *Democratic Statesman* (1871), a semiofficial organ of the state executive committee of the Democratic party, which advocated "straight out Jacksonian Democracy" during Reconstruction and Republican control. In 1914 the *Democratic Statesman* took over the Austin *Tribune* (founded 1889), a competitor that in 1904 had absorbed the smaller Austin *Daily News*. The combination was called the *Statesman and Tribune*. In 1916 this paper became the *Evening Statesman*. The Austin *American* began in 1914 under the direction of Henry Hulme Sevier. In 1919 Charles E. Marsh and E. S. Fentress bought the *American*, and in December 1924, the Austin *Evening Statesman*, by then one of the oldest dailies in Texas. The two papers were merged into one company but published as independent newspapers—the *American* in the morning and the *Statesman* in the afternoon. Early in 1948 all of the Marsh–Fentress newspapers became a part of Newspapers Incorporated. The *American* joined the Associated Press, subscribed to the daily wire services of the United Press International News Service, and acquired comics and other news features on an independent basis from the Chicago *Tribune* and other syndicates. In November 1973 the Austin *American* and the Austin *Statesman* combined to become an all-day newspaper issued in four daily editions as the Austin *American–Statesman*. In 1976 Cox Enterprises purchased the paper, which in April 1987 switched from all-day publication to mornings only.

Curtis Bishop and R. L. Schroeter

"Austin City Limits." A country music television program begun in 1974 by the Public Broadcasting Service affiliate in Austin; carried by 280 stations in 1990. The program usually produces 13 live weekly shows a season. It has contributed to the rise of several major country performers. The program, known particularly for its "redneck rock" or "progressive country" music, resulted from the desire of Bill Arhos, then program director at KLRN television, to develop locally produced programming that could attract national attention. Over a couple of years Arhos managed to gain acceptance on PBS. Videotaping began in September 1975 with a reunion of Bob Wills's Original Texas Playboys. The 1976 season defined the show's unique style, a combination of traditional country music with folk and rock influences that flourished in Austin. The show drew on the growing Austin music scene, challenged the dominance of Nashville, and later competed with other network music productions such as Country Music Television. Although "progressive country" and mainstream country have been staples of the program, it has also featured an eclectic mix of American music: jazz, blues, and folk. Program highlights have included the return of Willie Nelson's album *Red-Headed Stranger* to the *Billboard* charts for 48 weeks after his performance on the show (1977), appearances by Ray Charles and Chet Atkins (1979), and the three-hour special "Down Home Country Music," which won Best Network Music Program in the New York International Film and Television Festival (1982). After losing Budweiser as an underwriter in 1990, "Austin City Limits" faced a declining PBS budget and network demands that the series raise more than a quarter of its own funding. By the mid-1990s, "Austin City Limits" was focusing more on songwriters and the "new folk movement," and had introduced a variety of new formats to supplement its traditional stage-show settings.

Damon Arhos

Austin College. Founded at Huntsville (1849) by the Presbyterian Church, named for Stephen F. Austin, and largely led by Daniel Baker. The original board of trustees included Sam Houston, Anson Jones, and Henderson K. Yoakum. With occasional struggles the college survived the Civil War and Reconstruction and was moved in 1876–78 to Sherman. Although a fire lit by a student arsonist set the school back in 1913, the institution has generally flourished with the help of Sherman citizens and consolidation with Texas Presbyterian College for Girls (1929). It became co-ed in 1918. The greatest growth in enrollment and physical plant has occurred since 1950.

J. D. Fuller

Austin State Hospital. The oldest hospital in Texas for the mentally ill; authorized as the State Lunatic Asylum in 1856 and opened in May 1861 with 12 patients. Initially, asylums in Texas were operated under individual boards of five members. In 1913 the legislature placed its mental hospitals under individual boards of managers. In January 1920 state hospitals were placed under the Board of Control. The Austin institution was renamed Austin State Hospital in 1925. In 1949 control of the hospital was transferred to the Board for Texas State Hospitals and Special Schools. In 1993 it was operated by the Texas Department of Mental Health and Mental Retardation. In 1940 the hospital was designated an independent school district and began providing education for school-age psychiatric patients. In 1942 a state dairy and hog farm was established near Austin to provide milk and meat for state mental institutions, and some Austin State Hospital patients were housed there. By 1961 the hospital had a capacity of 2,608 patients, and service had been expanded by outreach clinics and follow-up services for furloughed and discharged patients. In 1964 it expanded, within its own grounds, to incorporate patients from the Texas Confederate Home. The hospital provided surgical services for residents and for persons from the Austin State School, the Travis State School, and the Texas Confederate Home. It operated an adult outpatient clinic and made referrals to county health centers around the state. Admissions of younger patients, alcoholic patients, and drug abusers increased by 1970, when the average daily census was

1,994. By 1986–87, after considerable deinstitutionalization of patients, the hospital averaged only 711 in patients, while the Austin Mental Health and Mental Retardation center served 7,100. By 1992–93 residents had decreased to 450, and the MHMR center served 9,000. In 1990 the hospital served 34 counties in Central Texas and had a daily average patient census of 518. In the 1990s the original administration building, the third oldest state building in Texas, was renovated.

John G. Johnson

Austin State School. A residential and training facility for mentally retarded adults, administered by the Texas Department of Mental Health and Mental Retardation. In 1915 the Texas legislature passed a bill to establish the state's first facility for the retarded, some of whom had been housed at the Austin State Lunatic Asylum until then. Two years later the State Colony for the Feebleminded opened with an initial admission of 65 females, ages 6 to 49. In 1925 it was renamed Austin State School. Dr. John Bradfield, superintendent from 1917 to 1936, faced severe shortages in dormitory space and trained personnel, but he worked to build a residential training program. By 1927 a school building had been added to the facilities. Capable residents were assigned to domestic or farming chores. Beginning in 1930, adult clients also manufactured mattresses and brooms and assisted in the butcher shop, which provided meat for state institutions in the area. In 1934 many male residents of Austin State School were moved to the school's new farm on the eastern edge of Travis County, to work in dairy, poultry, and truck farming. This farm, originally called Austin State School Farm Colony, was separated from the Austin school and renamed Travis State School in 1957. With the farm serving only men and boys until 1973, Austin State School continued to house mostly women and children. During the 1930s and early 1940s the "colonies" were managed restrictively. Buildings generally were kept locked, employees lived on-site, and residents' families had minimal access during visits.

The postwar period witnessed changing treatment outlooks. Texas public schools began offering special-education classes, allowing some disabled youths to remain in their home communities. As the National Association for Retarded Citizens urged a shift from custodial care in isolated settings to social, occupational, and life-skills training for community integration, Austin State School administrators worked to improve facilities and programs for residents during the 1950s and 1960s. Yet overcrowding and understaffing limited the number of residents receiving such training. Despite the establishment of four more Texas training schools between 1946 and 1963 and acquisition of a 75-acre annex campus for the Austin State School in 1960, in 1958 only 400 employees provided 24-hour service for 1,900 individuals at the school. By 1965, 765 employees supervised 2,500 residents and hundreds still awaited admission. In 1963 the school implemented racial integration in its hiring and admission policies. In 1965 the Texas Mental Health and Mental Retardation Act authorized county-based training centers for moderately retarded persons, so Austin State School increasingly served those with more severe retardation or multiple disabilities. To assist the school's residents preparing to move into the community, teachers from the Texas Commission for the Blind established training for blind children and the Texas

Rehabilitation Commission helped to form specialized vocational workshops at the campus in 1967. In the 1970s federal requirements for intermediate-care facilities mandated higher state allocations for the school to provide residents with better housing, staffing ratios, and residential and vocational skills training. In 1972 the ASPEN residential unit began offering specialized training for aggressive residents. By 1974 the entire facility had 1,400 residents and 1,100 staff members.

During the 1970s crowding was eased by new construction at the school and the opening of several new state schools. The school also added more trainers and initiated special services for the hearing impaired at the annex campus. Vocational training services were extended to include 450 residents. By 1977 the school's Community Services division had set up developmental training centers in Kerrville, San Marcos, Seguin, and New Braunfels and had launched its first community-based center for infant training. Such programs enabled people with developmental disabilities to stay in their home communities and increased the normalcy of their lives. In 1983 residents and future residents of Austin State School were included in the *Lelsz v. Kavanaugh* settlement, which brought about many changes during the next decade to help residents achieve as normal a life as possible. As more residents were able to move to community placements, school administrators reorganized and retrained most residential staff to educate and care for those who required more intensive supervision. By 1993 the vocational services staff had moved the school's sheltered workshops from the annex campus to a local commercial site. Meanwhile, Austin State School began routinely admitting individuals transferred from Travis State School in preparation for the latter school's closing. In 1991 the school had a staff of 1,505, more than two-thirds women, which served about 460 individuals at the west Austin campus and 615 in a 14-county region extending south and west of Travis County; about 315 of the off-campus population were under age three. Most campus residents had severe or profound retardation or multiple disabilities. *Sherilyn Brandenstein*

Available School Fund. This fund, which represents state revenue set aside since the 1880s for support of the public school system (now including textbook purchases), comprises earnings from the Permanent School Fund and 25 percent of fuel-tax receipts. It is prorated to school districts according to scholastic population. The fund grew from $95 million in 1950 to $1.3 billion in 1994.

Aviation. The first people in Texas to fly, in the 1860s, were airshow balloonists and their passengers, although several inventors were also busy with plans for winged flying machines. An alleged flight of Jacob F. Brodbeck in 1865 has become a Texas legend. After the Wright brothers' controlled airplane flights in 1903, aeronautical progress generally was slow until 1909—10, when European aviation made rapid strides and the U.S. government acquired its first aircraft. Aerial demonstrations proliferated at sites across America, including Houston, where a Frenchman, Louis Paulhan, made the first airplane flight in Texas on February 18, 1910. Flights in other Texas cities soon followed, and some Texans began building their own airplanes. Although records of many of these projects are often imprecise, one of the earliest Texans to fly appears to have been L. L. Walker of Houston. He apparently flew his aircraft, a Bleriot monoplane, during October and November 1910. Several airplanes and fliers were active around the state before World War I, and at least two women, Marjorie and Katherine Stinson of San Antonio, became well-known pilots.

Military aviation had already begun to develop in Texas. Lt. Benjamin Foulois, a colorful pioneer pilot, arrived at Fort Sam Houston in February 1910, assembled the army's recently purchased Wright biplane, and took to the air on March 2. Three years later the newly established First Aero Squadron, with nine airplanes, was assigned to Texas City. After serving in other states, the First Aero returned to Texas in 1916 to support Gen. John J. Pershing in his pursuit of Francisco (Pancho) Villa into Mexico. In 1917 American entry into World War I brought the first of many military flight schools to Texas, where students appreciated the level terrain and year-round flying weather. In addition to Kelly and Brooks fields in San Antonio, facilities throughout the state trained thousands of fliers, mechanics, and other aviation personnel and established a legacy of military aviation. Texans such as Wiley Post, Howard Hughes, and Douglas "Wrong Way" Corrigan posted records and made headlines during the 1930s. These events dramatized the role of aircraft in reducing time and distance and made Texans more inclined to utilize airplanes in a state where distances were vast and centers of population were far removed from each other and from other urban areas of the United States.

The first commercial line to serve Texas was National Air Transport, one of the private companies incorporated to take advantage of the Air Mail Act of 1925. On May 12, 1926, a National plane left Love Field in Dallas and headed for Chicago with the first air mail; passenger service was added in the fall of 1927. Braniff Airways, a regional carrier started by Kansas native Thomas Elmer Braniff, made Love Field its principal operations and maintenance base in 1934 and in 1942 moved its home office from Oklahoma to Love Field. Under the guidance of Cyrus R. Smith of Austin, American Airlines routes through Dallas not only bolstered the area's reputation but also offered Texans rapid transportation to commercial centers on both coasts. Pan American offered international service from Brownsville to Latin America.

As a major agricultural state, Texas became a lively area of activity for crop dusters. Many operations such as rice culture used aerial seeding, fertilizing, and dusting against insects. The rapid growth of surveying for oil leases in the booming Texas oilfields propelled Tobin Aerial Surveys of San Antonio into early prominence in the new industry of aerial photogrammetry. Around the "oil patch," with widely scattered operations and a lack of convenient all-weather roads, planes became standard tools of the trade for both corporations and wildcatters in a business noted for its aggressiveness.

During World War II geography and climate again made Texas a center for aeronautical training. The base at Corpus Christi became the world's largest naval air-training station; Randolph Field was the army air force's "West Point of the Air." At Avenger Field in Sweetwater, the air force carried out training for WASPS, the Women's Airforce Service Pilots, who flew thousands of warplanes from factories to airfields, towed aerial targets, and performed other functions. Some forty military fields in Texas turned out 45,000 pilots, 25,000 bombardiers, and

12,700 navigators. Moreover, the state became a major aircraft manufacturer; new plants employed thousands of workers. During the war years, two companies in Dallas and Fort Worth alone employed some 70,000 men and women who built 50,000 aircraft. Refineries in Texas were principal suppliers for high-octane gasoline used by Allied aircraft in every combat theater of the world.

In the postwar years, the general aviation sector (agricultural, business, and personal flying) rapidly developed throughout the state. As Texas industry grew, many businesses saw the need for rapid air travel to distant business centers from coast to coast. Scheduled air transport did not always offer convenient and timely schedules; for these reasons, business and corporate flying rapidly increased. In agriculture the long growing season and broad fields favored the development of such specialized agricultural aircraft as the trend-setting AG-1 at Texas A&M University, and Texas became a world leader in the design and production of such airplanes. Along the Gulf Coast, dozens of helicopters made their runs to offshore oil rigs, carrying relief crews, mail, groceries, repair parts, and myriad other cargos. In sprawling cities, especially in rush hours when accidents frequently occurred, the versatility of helicopters as ambulances was invaluable.

However, it was the growth of scheduled air travel that necessitated new urban airports. Houston Intercontinental opened in 1969; Dallas–Fort Worth International opened in 1974. The convenience of air travel attracted much new business to the state. The airlines serving Dallas–Fort Worth, Houston, and other major cities reflected the revolution in aeronautics since 1945. Piston-engined transports gave way to jets in the 1960s, including long-range jumbo jets capable of nonstop flights to Europe from both DFW and Houston. In times past, when a European visit required at least two or three weeks of sailing on ocean liners, only the very wealthy could afford such luxuries of time and expense. The jets, with rapid travel and lower fares, brought a democratization of foreign and domestic travel.

In the mid-1980s Texas listed some 60,000 licensed pilots and 25,000 registered aircraft. There were 250 airline aircraft based in Texas, and 55 different airline companies served the state. But these numbers represented only a small part of the aeronautics and aerospace industry in Texas. Numerous military air bases annually pumped billions of dollars into the state's economy. The United States Air Force Air Training Command, headquartered at Randolph Air Force Base in San Antonio, trained more Air Force pilots than any other facility. The Naval Air Station at Corpus Christi was the second-largest naval aviation center in the free world. After 1945 the Dallas–Fort Worth area, a major military complex, turned out bombers, fighters, and helicopters, as well as missile components and advanced electronics. Because these products played such a significant role in world affairs, such as the multinational production and sales agreements for the General Dynamics F-16 fighter, the aerospace industry helped keep Texans attuned to international economics and politics.

Roger Bilstein

Ayres, Atlee Bernard. Architect; b. Hillsboro, Ohio, 12 July 1873; d. San Antonio, 6 Novemmber 1969; m. Olive Moss Cox (1896; d. 1937); 2 children; m. Katherine Cox (1940); ed. Metropolitan School of Architecture, New York (grad. 1894). The Ayres family moved to San Antonio in 1888. Ayres formed a partnership with his son Robert M. Ayres in 1924, and the firm designed numerous residences in the Spanish Colonial Revival style (e.g., the Atkinson house, 1928, now the Marion Koogler McNay Art Museum), as well as in other styles such as Colonial Revival and English Tudor. As state architect (1915–) Ayres designed the Blind Institute and other state buildings in Austin. He designed buildings at the University of Texas, courthouses in Kingsville, Alice, Refugio, Del Rio, and Brownsville, and numerous buildings in San Antonio, including the Municipal Auditorium (1923), the Plaza Hotel (1927), and the Administration Building at Randolph Air Force Base (1931), known as the "Taj Mahal," with a tower that conceals a 500,000-gallon water tank. Ayres wrote a book, *Mexican Architecture* (1926), was a charter member of the Texas Society of Architects, and was one of three architects instrumental in securing passage of state legislation for the licensing of architects (1937).

Ayuntamiento. The ayuntamiento, or town council of the Spanish and Mexican periods, comprised the alcalde, one or more regidors, and a *síndico procurador* (city attorney). Though it had broad local powers, it was answerable to a higher authority such as the governor or viceroy; it also represented citizens' needs to the authorities. Membership was originally lifelong and quasi-hereditary, but the Constitution of Cádiz (1812) changed this feature by requiring elections. Despite minor changes through the years, the ayuntamiento remained essentially the same from the founding of Spanish Texas to the Texas Revolution.

Geoffrey Pivateau

B

Bailey, Joseph Weldon. United States senator; b. Joseph Edgar Bailey, Crystal Springs, Mississippi, 6 October 1863; d. Sherman, 13 April 1929; m. Ellen Murray (1885; d. 1926); 2 children; m. Mrs. Prudence Rosengren (1927). Bailey attended five colleges before completing his law studies in Lebanon, Tennessee, in 1883. In 1884 he was called to testify before a United States Senate committee investigating violence used by Mississippi Democrats in the local elections of 1883. Charged with being one of the leaders of the Democratic faction that initiated the violence, he did not appear because he refused to perjure himself. No action was taken against him. He moved to Gainesville in 1885, was elected to Congress in 1890, and served from 1891 to 1901, when he became a senator. In the House he favored free silver and opposed expansionism. He also acquired a reputation as a parliamentary tactician and an orator. He was a lifetime friend and hero of the young Sam Rayburn. In the Senate he advocated regulation of railroad rates and service and the 1909 tax on corporations. Charges were made that he had illegally represented the Waters–Pierce Oil Company, which was expelled from Texas for violating the antitrust laws because of its connections with the Standard Oil trust. Bailey damaged his early promise as a potential leader of the Democratic party in 1902 when, after a heated debate, he physically assaulted Senator Albert Beveridge. In 1906 *Cosmopolitan* magazine charged that Bailey was one of the senators who controlled the Senate to protect private interests at the expense of the public. He was, nevertheless, reelected and was eventually exculpated by the Texas House and Senate investigations. Nevertheless, these investigations revealed that as a corporate attorney he had received large fees for his work. An additional and perhaps even more damaging event was the revelation that Waters–Pierce had never broken its ties to Standard Oil, contrary to claims that it had severed relations in 1900. Bailey was never elected to public office again. Facing a stern challenge in 1912 and disillusioned by the progressive movement within the Democratic party, he resigned from the Senate in September 1911 and established a lucrative law practice in Washington. He returned to Texas in 1920 and ran for governor. After his defeat, he established a law office in Dallas. *Bob C. Holcomb*

Bailey, Mollie Kirkland. "Circus Queen of the Southwest"; prob. b. near Mobile, Alabama, 2 November 1844; d. Houston, 2 October 1918; m. James A. (Gus) Bailey (1858; d. 1896); 2+ children; m. A. H. Hardesty (1906). With her first husband and others, Mollie Bailey performed in several states with the Bailey Family Troupe. She was a Confederate spy during the Civil War. Her husband, who was bandmaster for a company of Hood's Texas Brigade, wrote the words of "The Old Gray Mare," inspired by a horse that almost died after eating green corn. In 1879 the troupe acquired a small circus that became the Bailey Circus, "A Texas Show for Texas People." After Gus died, his wife built up Mollie Bailey's Circus, which gave free tickets to Civil War veterans, performed widely, and entertained such major Texas figures as James S. Hogg and Joseph W. Bailey. Mrs. Bailey is said to have shown the first motion pictures in Texas. She con-

tinued to run the circus by mail from home after she became unable to travel. *Diana J. Kleiner*

Baker, Cullen Montgomery. Outlaw, the "Swamp Fox of the Sulphur"; b. Weakley County, Tennessee, probably 22 June 1835; d. Cass County, Texas, 6 January 1869; m. Mary Jane Petty (1854; d. 1860); m. Martha Foster (1862; d. 1866). Hard-drinking, quarrelsome, mean-spirited young Cullen killed his first man a few months after his first marriage. He murdered another man before serving in two Confederate cavalry units. He deserted from the first, and the second left him "sick on the Arkansas River," after which he received a disability discharge. He and his second wife briefly settled in Cass County, where Baker attempted to earn a living in the ferry business. Two months after she died, he proposed to her sister Belle, who refused him and married Thomas Orr, a schoolteacher and later a prominent community activist and politician. Orr and Baker became bitter enemies. When the Union Army and the Freedmen's Bureau came to the area, Baker focused his attention upon harassing and killing employees of the bureau and their clients. In December 1867 he also wrought havoc upon Howell Smith's family because of their alleged "unorthodox" relations with their black employees. He was wounded but escaped. Baker returned to the Reconstruction scene again in mid-1868 as the leader of various outcasts and killers. He and his group are credited with murdering two Freedmen's Bureau agents, one in Texas and another in Arkansas, and numerous black men and women, all the time eluding the army. When his gang disbanded in December 1868, Baker returned to his home in Cass County. There a small group of neighbors led by Orr, whom Baker had earlier attempted to hang, killed him and a companion. Orr collected some of the reward offered for Baker, who had helped the Ku Klux Klan to rise to prominence. Baker even drew the notice of the New York *Tribune*. Although he was not the quickdraw artist some have maintained, writers have made much of Baker's prowess with a sixgun, his harassment of the United States Army, and his defense of "Southern honor" during and after the Civil War. Others see him as a mean, spiteful, alcoholic murderer. Louis L'Amour memorialized Baker in his novel *The First Fast Draw*. *Barry A. Crouch*

Baker, Moseley. Soldier, legislator, and journalist; b. Norfolk, Virginia, 20 September 1802; d. Houston, 4 November 1848; m. Eliza Ward; at least one child. Baker evidently fled Alabama after forging a check. Though the time of his arrival in Texas is uncertain, he was in Liberty by 1835. As a leading advocate of Texas independence, he recruited men for the revolutionary army and was a member of the Consultation, where his long antagonism for Sam Houston began. Baker fought in several engagements of the Texas Revolution, including the battle of Gonzales, the Grass Fight, the siege of Bexar, and the battle of San Jacinto. He held San Felipe during Houston's retreat to East Texas, then burned the town to prevent its capture by the enemy—an act that drew Houston's ire. Baker was elected twice (1836, 1838) to the

Spectators at Mollie Bailey's Circus watch a performer walk a toght-rope stretched from the main tent top. Photograph by Cecil Bouldin James. Hamilton, ca. 1913. Courtesy Maxine Havens, Hamilton.

Congress of the Republic of Texas, where he tried unsuccessfully to have Houston impeached. In 1839 the Congress appointed him a brigadier general in the militia of the republic for a campaign against the Indians on the Brazos. He ran again for Congress but was defeated (1841). In 1842 he was reappointed brigadier general and raised a company in response to Gen. Adrián Woll's seizure of San Antonio. In 1844 Baker wrote an open letter criticizing Houston's policies and calling the president "the greatest curse that Providence in its wrath could have sent upon the country." After his wife's death Baker began preaching. He had started a newspaper, the Montgomery (Alabama) *Advertiser*, early in life; now he published the somewhat heterodox *True Evangelist*, which continued to appear even after the Methodist Church enjoined him to silence. He died of yellow fever, was buried in Houston, and was reinterred in the State Cemetery in 1929. *Thomas W. Cutrer*

Ballí, José Nicolás. Catholic priest; b. Reynosa, Nuevo Santander (now Tamaulipas), ca. 1770; d. 16 April 1829. Padre Island was named for Padre Ballí, an original grantee of the island, to whom clear title was granted posthumously. In addition to his life as a priest, Ballí came from a wealthy, landed family and followed in their footsteps. He offered the sacraments in all the villas and haciendas in the lower Rio Grande valley, lived in Matamoros, and served at Nuestra Señora del Refugio Mission as a secular priest from 1804 to 1829. In 1830 he began building the present Church of Nuestra Señora del Refugio in Matamoros. Ballí

became the official collector of building funds for the churches of the villas on the Rio Grande. He was well known in South Texas and officiated in more than 500 baptisms, marriages, and funerals between 1800 and 1829. He owned the La Feria grant, the Las Castañas grant, part of the Llano Grande grant, the Guadalupe grant, and the Isla de Santiago grant, known as Padre Island. The island had been granted to his grandfather, Nicolás Ballí, by King Carlos III of Spain in 1759, and Padre Ballí requested a clear title to the property in 1827. He was the first to have the island surveyed and was the first settler on the island who brought in families. He also built the first church on the island, for the conversion of the Karankawa Indians and for the benefit of the settlers. On the island he founded El Rancho Santa Cruz de Buena Vista (later known as Lost City), where he kept cattle, horses, and mules. *Clotilde P. García*

Ballinger, Betty Eve. Cofounder of the Daughters of the Republic of Texas; b. Galveston, 3 February 1854; d. Galveston, 23 March 1926. Betty Ballinger's grandfather, William H. Jack, fought in the battle of San Jacinto and served as a Republic of Texas congressman. In 1891 she and her cousin Hally Bryan Perry formed an organization dedicated to the perpetuation of the memory of the heroes of San Jacinto. After reading Henderson K. Yoakum's *History of Texas*, the cousins solicited support from other women of Texas whose husbands or ancestors had served the republic. Hally's father, Guy M. Bryan, introduced the women to Mary Smith (Mrs. Anson) Jones, widow of the last president of the Republic of Texas, and to Mary Harris Briscoe, widow of a Texas patriot. On 6 November 1891, 17 women assembled in Houston to form the Daughters of the Lone Star Republic. The first annual meeting of the Daughters took place in 1892 in Lampasas. In the next year's keynote address, Miss Ballinger proclaimed that the future of Texas "is in the hands of her sons [who] . . . have forgotten the heroic deeds and sacrifices of the past. But it is not so with woman . . . . Daughters of the Republic of Texas, our duty lies plain before us. Let us leave the future of Texas to our brothers, and claim as our province the guarding of her holy past." Ironically, the DRT encouraged women themselves to participate in the future of Texas through emphasis on education and the maintenance of historic sites such as the Alamo. Betty Ballinger subsequently organized and presided over the Galveston chapter of the DRT. She served from 1895 to 1899 as DRT chairman of the Stephen F. Austin Statue Fund, the purpose of which was to commission Elisabet Ney to produce statues of Sam Houston and Stephen F. Austin for Statuary Hall at the Capitol in Washington. By 1912 she had become a staunch supporter of woman suffrage. That year she served as the first vice president of the Galveston Equal Suffrage Association.

Betty, her sister Lucy, and Mrs. Maria Cage Kimball had founded the Wednesday Club (1891), one of the first women's literary clubs in Texas. Although initially organized for the study of Shakespeare, Balzac, Hugo, and other literary giants, the club turned by 1912 to "sociological" topics: "Women in Industry," "Modern Educational Movements," and "Woman Suffrage." Miss Ballinger was an active member from the club's inception through 1929. She was delegate to the first state general convention of women's clubs in Waco in 1897 and served as president of the Wednesday Club from 1909 to 1911. The Galveston hurricane of 1900 brought terrible social disorder and increased the gravity of the club scene in the city. The Women's Health Protective Association, in which Betty Ballinger was active, was organized to give decent burial to the victims of the storm who were not cremated. Afterward the WHPA remained active from 1901 to 1920 as a progressive reform association. Its members worked to revegetate the island, to enact updated city building ordinances, to institute regular inspection of dairies, bakeries, groceries, and restaurants, to eliminate breeding grounds for flies and mosquitoes, and to establish medical examinations for schoolchildren, hot-lunch programs, public playgrounds, and wellbaby and tuberculosis clinics.

Elizabeth Hayes Turner

Banister, Emma Daugherty. Early female sheriff; b. Forney, 20 October 1871; d. Brownwood, 4 June 1956; m. John R. Banister (1894); 4 children + 5 from John's previous marriage. Emma Daugherty taught school before marrying her lawman husband, who was elected sheriff of Coleman County in 1914. Mrs. Banister lived at the jail, cooked for the prisoners, and served as office deputy. When Banister died in 1918, the county commissioners appointed her to finish his term as sheriff. As probably the first woman sheriff in the United States, she made national news. Under the heading "Woman a Sheriff!" the New York *World* classed her among "a stock of westerners that does not know fear." Though invited, she declined to run for a full term. The Banisters' collection of Indian artifacts and law-enforcement trophies is housed at Fort Concho in San Angelo.

Margaret White Banister

Banking. The first institution designated a bank in Texas and authorized to conduct banking activity was the Banco Nacional de Texas, established by decree of a Mexican governor of Texas, José F. Trespalacios, in 1822, shortly after Mexico won its independence from Spain. Its primary function was to issue banknotes, but in 1823 the Mexican government repudiated the redemption of the notes in specie and closed the institution. This bank has been referred to as the "first chartered bank west of the Mississippi." In 1835 the legislature of Coahuila and Texas chartered the Banco de Commercia y Agricultura. This, the first commercial bank in Texas, provided a variety of banking services. The principals of the bank, which was based in Galveston, were merchants Samuel May Williams and Thomas F. McKinney. This bank helped arrange loans for the Texas Revolution and for funding the republic. No banks were chartered in the Republic of Texas. Several banking projects were authorized, but the promoters were unable to raise funds to begin operations. The Constitution of the republic contained no provisions for banks, but the Texas Congress apparently contemplated the establishment of a banking system. President Mirabeau B. Lamar, in his message to Congress on 31 December 1838, urged the organization of a National Bank of Texas, but the proposal was not approved. Private firms carried on banking activities for both businessmen and for government. The most prominent was the mercantile firm of McKinney, Williams and Company, based in Galveston, which issued paper money.

The state Constitution of 1845 prohibited the incorporation of banks and the private issuance of paper money. Merchants increasingly performed limited banking functions, as commission merchants, factors, insurance agents, and bankers. Financial agents flourished first in Galveston, but other agencies opened offices as agricultural development spread to the interior. In time, moneylenders could be found in most towns and many villages; in 1859 they numbered more than 3,000, with loans in excess of $3 million. The Commercial and Agricultural Bank opened in 1847 in Galveston, and was the only chartered bank in Texas before the Civil War. Both the republic and the state of Texas recognized its Mexican charter (1835), but the investors had difficulty raising the $100,000 in specie required to operate. The bank could establish branches, but a branch at Brownsville was the only one that opened. The bank issued notes, underwritten by deposit currency, and engaged in various types of lending. It catered to customers in the mercantile business, but also provided exchange and other financial services to the public. After a decade of activity, an adverse state court decision prohibited the bank from issuing circulating notes, and it closed in 1859. The constitutions of 1861 and 1866 prohibited state-chartered banks. Under the Reconstruction government the Constitution of 1869 omitted this feature, and during the next four years several state banks were established by special acts of the legislature. Ten additional banks were authorized under a general banking law in 1874. The Constitution of 1876 again prohibited state-chartered banks.

From 1865 to 1900, state banks, national banks, and private banks flourished in Texas. Private banks dominated the financial scene immediately after the Civil War. They were built around cotton exporting and other trade and mercantile businesses, and were unregulated and unsupervised. Between 1869 and 1876, only a few state-chartered banks opened for business. The first nationally chartered bank was the First National Bank of

Galveston, established in 1865. Partly because of the $50,000 capital requirement, only 13 national banks were organized up to 1880. The number grew to 68 in 1885, 189 in 1890, and 440 in 1905. Expanding agricultural, commercial, industrial, and mining activities produced a need for additional financial facilities. A movement for a state banking system began in the 1890s, supported by public officials, the private sector, and the Texas Bankers Association. In 1904 the state constitution was amended to permit state banks, and under the leadership of Thomas B. Love, the system was established in 1905. State banks numbered more than 300 by 1908 and two years later exceeded the number of national banks in the state.

National money and banking panics focused attention on the need for banking reform. The Panic of 1907 saw the establishment of the National Monetary Commission to address money ills. Laws guaranteeing deposits in state-chartered banks were enacted in Texas, Oklahoma, Kansas, Nebraska, Mississippi, South Dakota, North Dakota, and Washington. As many Texas banks restricted cash withdrawals during the panic, agitation grew for a system to protect depositors. In the fall of 1907 the Dallas *Morning News* campaigned for a depositors' guaranty-fund law, and the state banking commissioner proposed a guaranty bill in his biennial report. Robert R. Williams and Thomas M. Campbell, both candidates for governor in 1908, endorsed the idea. When the legislature failed in 1909 to pass a guaranty act, Governor Campbell called a special session. William Jennings Bryan addressed the legislators, urging immediate passage of the bill; in a second special session, they voted approval. The guaranty law took effect in January 1910 and empowered Texas state banks to secure deposits by a guaranty-fund system or by a bond security system. Most bankers chose the guaranty-fund option. By this arrangement banks contributed a percentage of their average daily deposits during the preceding year to the fund. If a bank failed, assessments could be levied on other guaranty banks up to 2 percent of their average daily deposits in any one year. Under the bond security system, banks had to furnish bond, policy of insurance, or other guaranty of indemnity equal to the capital stock of the bank. The amount of the bond could be increased as deposits rose above a specified ratio to capital.

The guaranty fund appeared successful. The number of state banks increased from 515 in 1910 to 1,035 in 1920, while the number of national banks remained at about 500. Paid-in capital of the state banks tripled, while total resources increased sixfold. Guaranty-fund receipts easily covered operating expenses. But the depression of 1921 changed the situation. An epidemic of bank failures prompted heavy calls on the fund, and it became de facto insolvent by 1925. An amendment to the banking law in 1925 destroyed its effectiveness, and the guaranty-fund system was abolished two years later. By that time many state banks had become national banks to escape assessments under the fund system. The Federal Reserve Bank of Dallas was established in 1914 and soon began operating branches in El Paso, Houston, and San Antonio. All national banks were required to be, and the large state-chartered banks were encouraged to become, members of the Federal Reserve System and the Federal Deposit Insurance Corporation. State banks responded favorably to the new system. In 1933 Texas embarked on an alternative plan to insure state bank deposits, but it attracted only 17 banks and was abolished in 1937.

The Texas banking scene preceding World War II was turbu-lent. Downturns in the business cycle, chartering of too many banks, dishonest and incompetent bank managers, and an ill-conceived state deposit-insurance system all contributed to failures that prompted efforts to strengthen the supervisory and statutory frameworks of bank operation. More responsible bankers emerged to steer their institutions toward better service for business and the general public. Texas banking operations expanded during the postwar years. Commercial banks, savings and loan institutions (more than 150 by the early 1950s), federal and state credit unions, investment banks that issued and distributed securities of local corporations, and brokerage houses connected with firms in New York and other financial centers all appeared. A variety of federal lending agencies emerged to fill in gaps and improve existing facilities, particularly those for agricultural credit. Lending policies and funding practices changed. As interest rates rose in the mid-1950s, there was an increased emphasis on consumer services. Credit cards came into vogue.

By the early 1970s, multibank holding-company systems had developed in Texas—particularly in metropolitan areas—encouraged by the state prohibition of branch banking. These "group banking systems," about a dozen of which were multibillion-dollar statewide entities, became the dominant organizational form. By the summer of 1985, some 130 such systems controlled almost half of the more than 1,800 separately incorporated banks and held nearly three-quarters of the bank deposits of the state. The remaining banks, principally independent, generally were located in the smaller cities and towns; about 500 became one-bank holding companies, mainly for federal income tax reasons. Beginning in the mid 1970s, the largest group banking organizations reduced the reliance of major Texas-based companies on out-of-state capital (especially money centers in New York and Chicago) for financing. In so doing, they facilitated capital formation and hastened economic growth in the state. Innovations in the Texas banking industry followed. Included were electronic payment systems (such as the South Western Automated Clearing House in Dallas, which serves Texas and adjoining states), ATM networks, and evolving point-of-sale fund-transfer facilities in retail establishments. These technological advancements enhanced the integration of Texas industries with national commercial banking and financial services. Politically and otherwise, the Texas Bankers Association and, to a lesser degree, the Independent Bankers Association of Texas, promoted these ties.

During the late 1980s the Texas banking industry experienced a traumatic downturn. This was caused by an overextension of bank credit and by loose lending to energy and energy-related industries and to the commercial real estate field. These lending policies, principally by major statewide multibank holding companies, coincided with declining world petroleum prices and rising speculation in commercial real estate. Excessive real estate lending caused more damage to the Texas banking system than did lending in the energy and energy-related areas. Commercial and industrial loans to oil and gas producers, unsecured by real estate, followed the pattern of oil-price changes. On the other hand, secured construction and land-development loans of 60 months or less to developers and oil and gas producers did not follow the changes in the real estate or oil-price sphere. Texas banks churned out loans through 1987, despite increasing rates of vacancy in offices and declining crude-oil prices. They soared substantially above the national average from 1978 to 1987. By the mid-1980s commercial real estate markets in the major metropolitan areas in Texas were overbuilt. As commercial real estate returns and values declined, banks were unable to shift financing from completed projects to long-term, nonbank financiers. Nonperforming assets increased from 1.75 percent in 1982 to 6.6 percent in 1987. The Texas banks that failed had a nonperforming-assets ratio of 10.4 percent. As a result the Texas commercial banking industry suffered net losses every quarter from 1986 to 1990.

Seven of the 10 largest commercial banks in Texas failed between 1987 and 1990. Only Texas Commerce Bancshares and Allied Bancshares survived. They merged with major out-of-state banks and were recapitalized without governmental assistance. Seven other banks adjudged insolvent were absorbed by out-of-state interests and recapitalized with assistance from the FDIC. These included the First RepublicBank Corporation, the largest commercial banking institution in Texas, founded when RepublicBank Corporation merged with InterFirst Corporation, both in Dallas. First RepublicBank was absorbed by NCNB Texas National Bank with generous federal aid. It became the largest bank in the state, and a subsidiary of NCNB Corporation, headquartered in Charlotte, North Carolina. Other failed institutions included MCorp, Texas American Bancshares, National Bancshares Corporation of Texas, BancTexas Group, and First City Bancorporation of Texas. The FDIC consolidated 20 MCorp banks into a branch banking system and sold them to Banc One Corporation of Columbus, Ohio. The institution subsequently became Bank One, Texas (National Association), and second in size to NCNB Texas National Bank (renamed NationsBank of Texas, National Association, in January 1992). Texas American Bancshares (Fort Worth) became the Team Bank statewide branch system. In June 1990 the FDIC closed 9 of the 12 subsidiary banks of National Bancshares Corporation of Texas and sold them to NCNB Texas National Bank as branches.

First City Bancorporation experienced financial problems by the end of 1986. In April 1988 the FDIC injected about $1 billion in "note capital" into the restructured bank holding company. This facilitated the raising of over $500 million of new equity by an investor group headed by A. Robert Abboud, who became board chairman and chief executive officer. The Abboud administration proved inefficient, however, and federal and state regulators closed First City and its 20-bank system in October 1992. Texas Commerce Bancshares was the first major statewide commercial bank to seek acquisition in the late 1980s by an out-of-state organization. CEO Ben F. Love earlier had pushed legislative changes in Texas to allow regional banks to operate across state boundaries within the Southwestern–Mountain State area. Because Love and his supporters thought the Texas economy could no longer be tied to the petroleum industry, they sought to remove state legal obstacles to external capital infusions. Major Texas banks, with state banking-industry support, persuaded the governor to call the Texas legislature into special session in the summer of 1986. The legislature passed an interstate banking law and approved a public referendum in the November election to amend the state's constitution to permit limited branch banking. The interstate banking law took effect on 1 January 1987. Despite the depressed energy industry and collapsed commercial real estate markets in Texas, major out-of-state bank holding companies responded favorably. Texas Commerce Bancshares merged with Chemical New York Corporation (renamed Chemical Banking Corporation), and Allied Bancshares merged with First Interstate Bancorp, of Los Angeles. These combinations occurred before federal aid for distressed banks began. The first massive federal assistance bailed out the First RepublicBank Corporation in late July of 1988 and supported its merger with NCNB Corporation. In sum, "statewide" banking giants in Texas tried to seek more efficient formats via branching systems authorized in late 1986; to secure intrastate mergers with holding company systems; and to attract external capital without losing control to outside interests.

The banking crisis in Texas in the 1980s was affected by problems in the savings and loan industry, which had grown rapidly and irresponsibly since the 1970s. Both industries suffered from inadequate federal regulation and supervision. Because of widespread fraud and incompetent management the S&L industry collapsed in Texas—and in the nation generally. Congress passed a law entitled the Financial Institutions Reform, Recovery and Enforcement Act of 1989, by which the government established the Resolution Trust Corporation to address S&L failures. Federal deregulation had played a crucial role in S&L operations in the early 1980s, particularly "thrift" institutions or savings associations. The Depository Institutions Deregulation and Monetary Control Act of 1980 was an effort to improve the efficiency of depository institutions by encouraging competition among institutions and pushing the phaseout of time-deposit interest-rate ceilings (completed in 1986). This legislation also increased the service powers of depository institutions, particularly thrift institutions, with relation to commercial banks. Further deregulation followed under the Garn–St. Germain Depository Institutions Act of 1982, which permitted thrifts to make nonresidential real estate loans up to 40 percent of their portfolio assets. Since S&Ls had been mostly residential mortgage lenders, they surprisingly expanded rapidly, substantially, and haphazardly into construction, real estate development, and other real estate lending—credit areas where commercial banks had been prominent since World War II. The thrifts mounted aggressive competition for deposits and exploited their new character and lending activities, thus prompting more competitive behavior within the commercial banking industry as well. The 1980 law produced a disincentive to fund management in federally insured depository institutions by increasing the insurance coverage in a single account from $40,000 to $100,000.

These statutes, plus other factors, caused a deterioration of bank-loan-portfolio quality, bank operating losses, and erosion of capital. These results occurred first in Texas and the Southwest, because the region entered a recession earlier than other parts of the nation. The 1980–82 deregulatory legislation occurred when the market environment was shifting from an inflationary to a disinflationary situation, a movement that most banks and financiers failed to perceive. Hence there was an overchartering of new banks in Texas during the first half of the 1980s, a development that compounded banking difficulties. Infrequent, lax, and limited governmental regulatory supervision hastened the excessive growth and unsound behavior in the banking world. Federal examination of bank supervision in Texas and the Southwest was limited. In fact, there were fewer examinations in the state than elsewhere in the nation. The federal lowering of S&L capital requirements in the early 1980s was indiscreet and poorly timed, and exacerbated other problems that brought down the S&L industry and magnified the collateral effects on commercial banking.

In the late 1980s federal bank authorities, spearheaded by the FDIC, made a strong effort to alter the control, management, and behavior of the major Texas banks. The economy began a slow, protracted recovery. Additional large banking consolidations and restructurings began. In late 1992 the Federal Reserve Board approved the merger of Team Bancshares into Banc One Corporation, the parent company of Bank One, Texas. During the turbulent decade that began in the mid-1980s, the Texas commercial banking industry shrank significantly. The number of banks declined from 1,800 preponderantly small institutions at the end of 1985 to slightly over 1,100 still mainly small entities in 1992. There were approximately 470 failures, some of which led to mergers with sound banking firms. The decline also saw many conversions to branches. Fewer statewide organizations now existed. With the exception of Texas Commerce Banchares and First City–Texas, these organizations are large branch-banking networks owned by major out-of-state multibank holding-company organizations. In 1993 the approximately 2,500 commercial banking offices operating in Texas (1,100 banks plus more than 1,400 branch offices) varied in size, ownership, and control. As bank assets fell from $209 billion at the end of 1985 to around $170 billion at the end of 1991, Texas banks tightened their lending policies. Like their counterparts elsewhere in the nation, they began selling existing loans and other assets in secondary markets. By the end of 1993 the Texas banking scene was definitely improving. Only 10 banks failed during the year, the lowest since 6 failed in 1984. None of the state's 63 S&Ls failed—for the first year since 1985. Of the 433 state-chartered banks, fewer than 17 had problems. This was a far cry from the preceding decade, when more than 470 banks and 200 thrifts were closed in Texas. And as the nineties progressed, banking prospered along with the rest of the Texas economy.

Lawrence L. Crum

Barbed Wire. Barbed wire made practical the agricultural development of the West by providing an effective means of enclosing cattle so they could not destroy crops. The first and most successful of hundreds of barbed wires was patented by Illinoisan Joseph Glidden in 1874; Glidden sold his interests to Washburn and Moen, a Massachusetts wire manufacturer, in 1876. John Warne (Bet-a-Million) Gates effectively promoted the Glidden wire at a demonstration in San Antonio in 1878, reportedly with the claim that the wire was "light as air, stronger than whiskey, and cheap as dirt." Panhandle rancher Charles Goodnight foresaw the end of the open range and fenced his lands. The process was not without conflict, however, for it brought the fence-cutting wars of the 1880s. Barbed wire is still a staple of the ranching industry. Papers of the Texas Barbed Wire Collectors Association are housed at the Panhandle–Plains Historical Museum in Canyon. *Frances T. McCallum and James Mulkey Owens*

Barbier Infant. In the fall of 1688 a child was born to Gabriel Minime, Sieur de Barbier, and his wife in the Texas colony founded almost four years previously by La Salle. This infant, of whom neither the given name nor the sex is known, was the first child of record born in Texas of European parents and the off-

Eugene C. Barker, Austin, 1937. Prints and Photographs Collection, Eugene C. Barker file, CAH; CN 02350. When the University of Texas started using the title distinguished professor in 1937, Barker was one of the first three chosen for the honor.

spring of the first recorded European marriage there. Like Virginia Dare of the Roanoke colony, the first English child born in America, the infant Barbier suffered an early and cruel fate. Three months old when Karankawa Indians destroyed the French settlement of Fort St. Louis, the infant and its mother, like the Talon children, were spared by the native women and taken to their village. When the Indian men returned from the massacre, however, they first killed Madame Barbier, then her babe, "which one of them dashed against a tree while holding it by a foot." *Robert S. Weddle*

Barker, Eugene Campbell. Historian; b. Walker County, 10 November 1874; d. Austin, 22 October 1956 (buried in Oakwood Cemetery); m. Matilda LeGrand Weeden (1903); ed. University of Texas (B.A., 1899; M.A., 1900), Harvard University (Ph.D., 1908). In his youth Barker was a blacksmith and night mail clerk for the Missouri Pacific Railroad. At UT he served the history department as tutor (1899–1901), instructor (1901–08), adjunct professor (1908–11), associate professor (1911–13), professor (1913–51), and professor emeritus (1951–56). On the death of George P. Garrison in 1910, Barker became chairman of the UT history department, a position he held until 1925. When the title of distinguished professor was inaugurated in 1937, he was among the first three distinguished professors chosen. His first major research project, inherited from Lester G. Bugbee and Garrison, was on the life of Stephen F. Austin. Before finishing the standard biography of Austin (1925), Barker collected, edited, and published *The Austin Papers* (American Historical Association, 1924–28; University of Texas Press, 1927). His other major publications include *Mexico and Texas, 1821–1835* (1928); *Readings in Texas History* (1929); *The Father of Texas* (1935); *The Writings of Sam Houston* (1938–43, with Amelia W. Williams); and a series of public school textbooks for Row and Peterson done in collaboration with William E. Dodd, Henry S. Commager, and Walter Prescott Webb. Barker served as managing editor of the *Southwestern Historical Quarterly* and director of the Texas State Historical Association from 1910 until 1937.

Through his numerous articles he showed the effect that Texas history had on the history of the American West and exploded some myths. He corrected the "conspiracy theory" of the conquest and annexation of Texas and the war with Mexico and abolished the misconception that the Texas Revolution and Mexican War were solely the fault of the Mexicans. Barker was a longtime member of the American Historical Association. With Clarence V. Alvord and others, he helped establish the Mississippi Valley Historical Association (now the Organization of American Historians, publishers of the *Journal of American History*). During his later years he challenged Professor Charles A. Beard's economic interpretation of the Constitution of the United States. Barker was instrumental in the origin of the Nettie Lee Benson Latin American Collection at UT and the Littlefield collection of source materials on the history of the South. After the controversy between UT and Governor Jim Ferguson (1917–18), Barker exercised influence as a leader of the university faculty. When the university named the Barker Texas History Center for him (1950), it was the first time that such an honor had been accorded a living member of the faculty.

William C. Pool

Barker Texas History Center. Popular name of the Eugene C. Barker Texas History Collections; since 1991 a division of the Center for American History at the University of Texas of Austin; named for Eugene C. Barker and opened 27 April 1950. The center brought together for the first time two departments of the university library: the Archives department and the Texas Collection Library, as well as the offices of the Texas State Historical Association. It originally occupied the Old Library Building (now called Battle Hall). It moved in 1971 to Sid Richardson Hall, near the Lyndon Baines Johnson Library and Museum. The Barker collections house more than 130,000 books and periodicals about Texas, published in Texas, or produced by writers strongly associated with Texas; some 3,500 collections of personal papers and official records of individuals, families, groups, and businesses significant to the history of Texas; an extensive newspaper collection; approximately 750,000 photographs documenting Texas persons, places, scenes, and events; 30,000 phonographs relating to Texas music and musicians; and more than 30,000 printed and manuscript maps depicting Texas from the era of exploration to the present.

Katherine J. Adams

Barthelme, Donald. Writer; b. Philadelphia, 7 April 1931; d. Houston, 23 July 1989. At the University of Houston Barthelme edited the college paper, the *Cougar*, worked for a news service, edited the faculty newspaper, *Acta Diurna*, and founded *Forum*, a university literary magazine. He served during the Korean War at Fort Polk, Louisiana, in Japan, and in Korea. In 1955–56 he worked for the Houston *Post* as an entertainment editor and critic. He was director of the Contemporary Arts Museum in Houston (1961–62) before moving in 1963 to Manhattan, where he began his writing career as managing editor of *Location*. He published his first story in 1961 in the *New Yorker* and his first novel, *Come Back, Dr. Caligari*, in 1964. He received a Guggenheim fellowship in 1966 and continued to receive honors throughout his years in New York. By the time he returned to Houston in the early 1980s his published books included *Snow White* (1967), *City Life* (1970), *The Dead Father* (1975), *Amateurs*

(1976), and several other short-story collections. He began teaching creative writing at the University of Houston in the early 1980s. At his death, he had written 15 books and contributed many stories to the *New Yorker*. He won a National Book Award in 1972 for a children's book, *The Slightly Irregular Fire Engine* (1971), and a PEN/Faulkner Award in 1982 for *Sixty Stories* (1981).

Lisa C. Maxwell

Barziza, Decimus et Ultimus. Soldier, politician, and lawyer; b. Virginia, 4 September 1838; d. Houston, 30 January 1882; m. Patricia Nicholas (1869); one adopted son; ed. William and Mary College (grad. 1857), Baylor University (grad. 1859). Barziza practiced law in Owensville until the Civil War. He served in the Fourth Texas Infantry, which became part of Hood's Texas Brigade, was promoted to captain, and led Company C into the battle of Gettysburg. He was wounded at Little Round Top (2 July 1863) and left behind. After a year in federal hospitals and the prison camp at Johnson's Island, Ohio, he managed to escape by diving through the open window of a train near Huntingdon, Pennsylvania. In Canada he was one of the first escapees to use a network set up by Rebel agents and Canadians to send escaped Confederates back to the South via Nova Scotia and Bermuda. Barziza arrived at Wilmington, North Carolina, in April 1864, and was allowed to return to Texas to recover from the hardships of his escape. In February 1865 he published his war memoirs anonymously in Houston under the title *The Adventures of a Prisoner of War, and Life and Scenes in Federal Prisons: Johnson's Island, Fort Delaware, and Point Lookout, by an Escaped Prisoner of Hood's Texas Brigade*. Barziza established a law practice in Houston and entered politics as a Democratic opponent of Reconstruction. He joined other prominent Texans in calling for a "conservative state convention," which was held in the Harris County Courthouse on 20 January 1878. That year he served on a statewide committee that organized the state Democratic convention at Bryan. Barziza was instrumental in removing scalawag governor Edmund J. Davis from office and in 1873 was elected as a representative from Harris County to the Fourteenth Legislature. In 1875 he was reelected but subsequently lost the speakership of the House, by a vote of 45 to 43, to Thomas R. Bonner of Smith County. After resigning from the House on 2 August 1876 he returned to Houston, where he helped found the Houston Land and Trust Company, the state's first trust company.

Jeffrey William Hunt

Bass, Sam. Outlaw; b. near Mitchell, Indiana, 21 July 1851; d. Round Rock, 21 July 1878. He ran away in 1869 and worked in a sawmill at Rosedale, Mississippi, before traveling to Denton (1870), where he found cowboy life a disappointment. He worked at various jobs until 1874, when he went into horse racing with a fleet mount that became known as the Denton Mare. In 1876 he and Joel Collins gathered cattle to take up the trail for their several owners. After selling the herd and paying the hands, they had $8,000 in their pockets, but instead of returning to Texas, where they owed for the cattle, they squandered the money in gambling in Ogallala, Nebraska, and Deadwood, South Dakota. In 1877 Bass and Collins tried freighting, without success, then recruited several hard characters to rob stagecoaches. On stolen horses they held up seven coaches without recouping their fortunes. Next, in search of bigger loot, a band of six, led by Collins and including Bass, rode south to Big

Springs, Nebraska, where they held up a Union Pacific passenger train. They took $60,000 in newly minted $20 gold pieces from the express car and $1,300 plus four gold watches from the passengers. After dividing the loot the bandits decided to go in pairs in different directions. Within a few weeks Collins and two others were killed. Bass, disguised as a farmer, made it back to Texas, where he formed a new outlaw band. He and his gang held up two stagecoaches and, in the spring of 1878, robbed four trains within 25 miles of Dallas. They did not get much money, but the robberies aroused citizens, and the bandits were the object of a spirited chase across North Texas by posses and a special company of Texas Rangers headed by Junius Peak. Bass eluded his pursuers until one of his party, Jim Murphy, turned informer. As Bass's band rode south intending to rob a bank in Round Rock, Murphy wrote to Maj. John B. Jones, commander of the Frontier Battalion. In Round Rock on 19 July Bass and his men got into a gun battle, and Bass was mortally wounded. After his death two days later he was buried in Round Rock and soon became the subject of song and story. *Wayne Gard*

Bastrop, Baron de. Colonizer and legislator; b. Philip Hendrik Nering Bögel (later Hispanicized to Felipe Enrique Neri), Paramaribo, Dutch Guiana, 23 November 1759; d. Coahuila, 23 February 1827; m. Georgine Wolffeline Françoise Lijcklama à Nyeholt (1782); 5 children. Bögel lived in Holland until 1793, when, accused of embezzlement, he left the country and began styling himself the Baron de Bastrop. By April 1795 he had arrived in Spanish Louisiana, where he represented himself as a Dutch nobleman. He received permission from the Spanish government to establish a colony in the Ouachita valley and engaged in several business ventures in Louisiana and Kentucky. After Louisiana was sold to the United States in 1803, Bastrop moved to Spanish Texas and was permitted to establish a colony between Bexar and the Trinity River. In 1806 he settled in San Antonio, where he had a freighting business. In 1810 he was appointed second alcalde in the ayuntamiento of Bexar. Most importantly, he interceded with Governor Antonio María Martínez on behalf of Moses Austin's colonization project in 1820. Bastrop subsequently served as intermediary with the Mexican government for Stephen F. Austin, who would have encountered many more obstacles but for his assistance. In July 1823 Luciano García appointed Bastrop commissioner of colonization for the Austin colony with authority to issue land titles. In 1823 the settlers elected Bastrop to the provincial deputation at Bexar, which in May 1824 chose him as representative to the legislature of the new state of Coahuila and Texas. At the capital, Saltillo, Bastrop sought legislation favorable to immigration and settlers; he secured passage of the colonization act of 1825; and he helped pass an act establishing a port at Galveston. Even in his last will he maintained his spurious nobility. Some of his contemporaries believed him to be an American adventurer; some historians once thought him to be a French nobleman or a Prussian soldier of fortune. Only within the last half century have records from the Netherlands been found to shed light on Bastrop's mysterious origins. Although his pretensions to nobility were not universally accepted at face value even in his own lifetime, he earned respect as a diplomat and legislator. Bastrop, Texas, and Bastrop, Louisiana, as well as Bastrop County, Texas, were named in his honor. *Richard W. Moore*

Bastrop, Texas. County seat of Bastrop County; 30 miles southeast of downtown Austin. The site was first occupied in 1804, when a fort was established at the Colorado River crossing of the Old San Antonio Road and named Puesta del Colorado. The Baron de Bastrop's plan to colonize the area with Germans in the 1820s failed to prosper, but Stephen F. Austin chose to use the Baron's name for the town when he obtained permission in 1827 to found a "Little Colony" of 100 families on the site. Indian raids hindered settlement, so that the community was not platted until 1832. In 1834 the Coahuila and Texas legislature changed the name of the community to Mina, for Mexican hero Francisco Xavier Mina. At the outbreak of the Texas Revolution, Mina had approximately 400 inhabitants and served as the business, commercial, and political center for a wide area. Mina citizens actively participated in the revolution. The town was destroyed by Mexican troops during the Runaway Scrape. The community incorporated in 1837 and changed its name back to Bastrop. It was an important source of lumber until the Civil War. The introduction of slaves to the area after 1839 made cotton an important part of the local economy as well. Fire destroyed much of the downtown in 1862. Floods plagued the place until dams were built in the 1930s. By the 1880s Bastrop was developing a varied manufacturing base. The town had a population of 1,707 in 1910, and it hovered around 2,000 inhabitants during the early decades of the century. Lignite mining, oil, and a revival of the lumber industry sustained the town from 1910 to 1940. Bastrop reached a peak population of about 5,000 during World War II, after the establishment of nearby Camp Swift, but fell to 3,158 in 1950 after the base closed. The 1980s brought new challenges for the community as Austin grew eastward. In 1990 Bastrop had 4,044 residents, some of whom commuted to Austin. Land values had soared. Bastrop remained a center for agribusiness, with industries including oil-well supply and furniture manufacturing. *Paula Mitchell Marks*

Bay City, Texas. County seat of Matagorda County, 90 miles southwest of Houston; named for its location on Bay Prairie. The town was established in 1894 when the Bay City Town Company purchased land and promoted the location as a new site for the county seat. That year, county voters replaced Matagorda with Bay City as county seat. In 1901 the Cane Belt Railroad reached Bay City, the first of several lines to serve the town, and in 1902 the city, which had some 2,000 inhabitants, incorporated. By 1914 Bay City had 3,156 residents, was served by three railroads, and was at the center of the largest rice-producing area in the country. A system of levees and dams was constructed in the 1920s to limit flooding from the Colorado River. The town had a population of 9,427 in 1940. In the 1960s an airport was built, the manmade port of Bay City was completed, and a barge canal linked Bay City to the Gulf Intracoastal Waterway. Oil was discovered in the area early in the century, and by the 1960s and 1970s Bay City emerged as an important petrochemical center. Between 1980 and 1990 the city's population grew from 14,291 to 19,684. Still served by two railroads in the 1990s, the city was a shipping center for the county oil industry. *Diana J. Kleiner*

Baylor, John Robert. Soldier and Indian fighter; b. Paris, Kentucky, 27 July 1822; d. Montell, Texas, 6 February 1894; m. Emily Hanna (1844); 10 children. Baylor served as a volunteer under John H. Moore and Nicholas M. Dawson but managed to

Bay City Rice Mills. Courtesy TSL. Bay City Rice Mills completed construction on its rice warehouse in 1901, and the next year it opened the town's first rice mill. By 1914 Bay City was the center of the largest rice-producing area in the nation.

avoid the Dawson Massacre. After teaching school for a while in Indian Territory, he was implicated as an accomplice in a killing and returned to Texas, where he farmed until he was elected to the state legislature (1851). In 1853 he was admitted to the bar. Two years later he was made an Indian agent but was dismissed in 1857 after quarreling with his superior, Robert S. Neighbors. Baylor then traveled widely, preaching hatred of the Indians. He organized a large vigilante force and edited an anti-Indian newspaper, the *White Man*, in Weatherford. He also led a raid against Indians who had murdered and scalped a white boy. In the Civil War he won a Confederate victory in the battle of Mesilla, established the Confederate Territory of Arizona, and proclaimed himself military governor. After promotion to colonel, he so vigorously pursued the extermination of the Apaches that President Jefferson Davis relieved him of civil and military command, after which Baylor fought as a private in the battle of Galveston (1 January 1863). He was subsequently elected to the Second Confederate Congress and restored to the rank of colonel. After the war he moved to San Antonio and ran unsuccessfully for governor (1873). He moved to Montell in 1878; there he ranched and continued to be involved in violent confrontations, including killings, into his old age. *Jerry Thompson*

Baylor, Robert Emmett Bledsoe. Baptist leader; b. Lincoln County, Kentucky, 10 May 1793; d. Washington County, 30 December 1873. Baylor studied law and was elected in 1819 to the Kentucky legislature, then moved to Alabama, where he again served as a legislator and was elected to Congress (1829). In 1839 he was ordained a Baptist minister and moved to Texas. His efforts contributed significantly to the organization of the Baptist Church in Texas. In 1841 he was elected judge of the Third Judicial District of the Republic of Texas and consequently became an associate justice of the Supreme Court. He was a del-

egate from Fayette County to the Convention of 1845, where helped to write the first state constitution and favored the exclusion of clergy from the legislature. In 1846 Governor James P. Henderson appointed Baylor judge of the Third Judicial District, an office he held until 1863. With William M. Tryon and J. G. Thomas, Baylor prepared the petition that led to the establishment of Baylor University in 1845. He may have donated the first $1,000 to the university; he served as a member of the board of trustees and taught law at the university without pay. While traveling through his judicial districts on horseback to enforce the law, he held court by day and preached in the evenings. He presided at the first district court held in Waco and perhaps delivered the first sermon ever preached there. Baylor was chaplain of the Grand Lodge of Texas Masons in 1843, 1845, and 1847. *Travis L. Summerlin*

Baylor College of Dentistry. Ignoring the opposition of Dallas dentists who feared additional competition and favored apprenticeship as a means for dental training, two dentists from St. Louis, David E. Morrow and T. G. Bradford, received a charter from the state in 1905 to establish State Dental College, the forerunner of Baylor College of Dentistry. The college occupied the second floor of the Juanita Building on Commerce Street, later the location of the entrance to the Adolphus Hotel. By August 1907 the degree of doctor of dental surgery had been granted to seven students, most of whom had begun their work at other dental schools. The college moved in 1907 and again before 1912. In 1916 the owners agreed to transfer control to an advisory board. J. J. Simmons, president of the newly organized Dallas District Dental Society, also served as president of the advisory board. Enrollment grew, but the school remained a proprietary one. In the early years of World War I, when the War Department considered drafting students of unrecognized professional schools, the board sought a new arrangement that would enhance the school's status—absorption by Baylor University Medical College, which was then located in Dallas. In 1918, after graduating 26 dentists, Bradford and Morrow sold their interest to Baylor University, and State Dental College formally became Baylor Dental College, with Bush Jones as dean.

When Baylor College of Medicine moved to Houston in 1943, the dental school was left to rebuild its basic science curriculum without the help of professors from the medical college and in overcrowded postwar conditions. By 1950, when the enrollment had reached 241, a new clinic building was completed that eased overcrowding and provided the college with its first quarters built specifically for dental education. During the fiftieth anniversary year of the college in 1955, the Caruth School of Dental Hygiene was opened, the result of a gift from Dallas philanthropist Walter W. Caruth and the Caruth Foundation. Patricia A. Clendenin served as first director of the Caruth School, where in May 1957 the first class of dental hygienists ever to graduate in Texas received diplomas. Graduate programs in basic sciences and clinical fields were added to Baylor's curriculum beginning in the early 1950s. In 1971, Baylor Dental College became Baylor College of Dentistry, and its association with Baylor University ended. The college became a private, nonprofit, nonsectarian educational corporation. At the same time, the college entered into an agreement with the Texas Higher Education Coordinating Board, whereby Baylor agreed to increase the number of Texas residents in its undergraduate classes so that it would receive state financial support. Between 1974 and 1977 a combined program of new construction and renovation of the existing building more than doubled the classroom, clinic, and laboratory space. By 1980 undergraduate enrollment had grown to 522, and graduate enrollment stood at 48. In 1995 the college trustees voted to merge Baylor College of Dentistry with Texas A&M University.   *James E. Makins*

Baylor College of Medicine. In Houston; the only private medical school in the Southwest and the first institution to locate in the Texas Medical Center (1947). The school was founded in Dallas in 1900, when Texas had only two other schools of medicine—the University of Texas Medical Branch at Galveston (1891) and the Fort Worth School of Medicine (1894). Baylor was the first of eight medical schools to be organized in Dallas during the first decade of the twentieth century. With three physicians as incorporators and a charter filed with the Texas secretary of state, this proprietary school was named the University of Dallas Medical Department, even though this "University of Dallas" did not exist. Having leased the former Temple Emanu-El, the school enrolled 81 students for its opening in November 1900. In 1903 the University of Dallas Medical Department became Baylor University College of Medicine. Over time, other "Baylor units in Dallas" evolved around the College of Medicine—schools of pharmacy and nursing and a college of dentistry—all associated with Baylor University Hospital (now Baylor University Medical Center). Baylor College of Medicine and the University of Texas Medical Branch in Galveston were the only medical schools in Texas to survive Abraham Flexner's stern criticisms of low standards of medical education in his harsh and famous report of 1911. Between 1903 and 1943 Baylor awarded M.D. degrees to 1,670 graduates.

In the latter year a conflict arose between civic leaders and physicians in Dallas and Baylor administrators over the Baptist character and governance of the college. Baylor faced unpalatable alternatives: in exchange for fiscal support and new quarters in a proposed new medical center in Dallas, the medical college was expected to relinquish administrative control and denominational affiliation. Otherwise it would be excluded from the envisioned medical center in favor of a newly founded nonsectarian medical school. Baylor extricated itself by accepting an invitation from the M. D. Anderson Foundation and other Houston benefactors to move to Houston. The other Baylor units in Dallas continued to operate in that city. Shortly after Baylor moved, the newly organized Southwestern Medical College was formed by the physicians and community leaders who were displeased with Baylor's denominational affiliation. The relationship between the Baptist General Convention of Texas and the Baylor College of Medicine was terminated, however, by a mutual agreement in 1969, and the school became a freestanding corporation, nonsectarian and nonprofit, governed by a selfperpetuating board of trustees. With "University" dropped from its name, and with Dr. Michael E. DeBakey occupying its presidency from 1969 to 1979, Baylor College of Medicine was positioned to appeal as a non-Baptist institution for support. Despite its private status, since 1971 Baylor has annually received state appropriations from the Texas legislature, which enabled the college to double the size of each entering class to 168, of whom no fewer than 70 percent are Texans. These students pay tuition fees no higher than those levied by state medical schools. In 1993 Baylor stood first among Texas medical schools and third among the state's universities for receiving federal funds for research and development. Since its founding Baylor has trained more than 11,251 physicians and residents. In 1993 almost 4,400 of this number were in practice in Texas, more than 2,000 of them in the Houston area. One of every seven physicians now practicing in Texas was trained at Baylor.

Baylor's graduate school enrolls students in Ph.D. programs in the biomedical sciences and an M.S. program in nurse anesthesiology. About 835 resident physicians receive training in 22 medical specialties offered jointly by Baylor and its 8 primary affiliated teaching hospitals. Other students are either postdoctoral fellows or students in allied health programs. In 1972 Baylor and the Houston ISD started the nation's first high school for health professions, and between 1983 and 1990 the college developed similar programs for high school students in Mercedes and Corpus Christi. Since occupying the Roy and Lillie Cullen Building in 1947, Baylor has expanded its physical plant considerably. Together with Methodist Hospital of Houston it has administered the Neurosensory Center of Houston since 1977, and with Texas Children's Hospital and the United States Department of Agriculture it has operated the Children's Nutrition Research Center since 1988. A Woodlands campus, north of Houston, is the site of the Baylor Center for Biotechnology, which is dedicated to marketing products of research done by Baylor scientists. Baylor research gives special priority to studies of the molecular basis of genetic ailments.   *Charles T. Morrissey*

Baylor University. In Waco. Robert E. B. Baylor, James Huckins, and William Milton Tryon organized an education society in the Texas Union Baptist Association with the purpose of establishing

Panoramic view of Baylor University campus at the turn of the century. Prints and Photographs Collection, Baylor University file, CAH; CN 10368.

a Baptist university (1841). Baylor University was chartered by the Republic of Texas in 1845 and opened in 1846 at Independence. Professor Henry F. Gillette directed the school until the arrival of its first president, Henry Lee Graves (1847), who organized a collegiate department and in 1849 added lectures in law. Graves resigned in 1851 and was succeeded by Rufus C. Burleson, who, during his first year as president announced a course of study leading to graduation. The university granted its first degree in 1854. In 1861, as a result of continued disagreement with the board of trustees, Burleson and the entire faculty of the male department resigned. George W. Baines, Sr., became president and in 1863 was succeeded by William Carey Crane, during whose presidency the curriculum was broadened and the female department became a separate institution, Baylor Female College. From 1866 to 1886 Baylor University was a male school. After Crane's death in 1885, Reddin Andrews, Jr., an alumnus, was made president. In 1886 the Baptist General Association of Texas and the State Convention, under the control of which Baylor had been operating since 1848, were combined to form the Baptist General Convention, and as a result Baylor University and Waco University, which Burleson had headed since he left Baylor, were consolidated and rechartered as Baylor University in Waco. The university was established on the Waco campus by the end of 1887. Burleson was made president emeritus in June 1897. President Oscar Henry Cooper (1899–1902) secured two new buildings and raised academic standards. Samuel Palmer Brooks succeeded Cooper in 1902 and served as president until his death in 1931. Brooks added new departments and organized the schools of education, law, business, and music. In addition, Baylor acquired four professional schools in Dallas: the College of Medicine (1903), the School of Nursing (1909), the School of Pharmacy (established in 1903 and discontinued in 1930), and the College of Dentistry (1918). The Texas Baptist Memorial Sanitarium in Dallas became Baylor Memorial Hospital in 1919 and was a part of the School of Medicine until 1943, when the school was transferred to Houston. Baylor Theological Seminary, established in 1905, became a separate institution, Southwestern Baptist Theological Seminary, in 1908 and was moved to Fort Worth in 1910. After Brooks's death, W. S. Allen, dean of the college, served as acting president until June 1932, when former governor Pat Neff, alumnus and president of the board of trustees, became president. Under Neff's direction the endowment was increased and salaries were raised; the campus was enlarged and landscaped; the departments of home economics, drama, and radio were added; library and laboratory facilities were improved and extended; four new buildings were built; and the Union Building was begun.

In 1945, despite difficulties incident to World War II, Baylor celebrated her centennial. During the war the university instructed students for the army and navy. With the influx of veterans the enrollment reached 4,589 in the fall of 1947. Neff resigned in 1947. Under President William Richardson White (1948–62) the university made unprecedented growth in both capital assets and academic standards. Eleven new buildings, including the Armstrong Browning Library, were added. In 1962 Abner McCall was named president and White became Baylor's first chancellor. McCall's administration was characterized by an emphasis on scholastic excellence with efforts to upgrade faculty, students, and facilities and to extend the graduate program. By 1965 enrollment reached 6,432—considered the maximum figure consistent with available facilities. In 1994 Baylor was organized into the College of Arts and Sciences (founded in 1919), the Hankamer School of Business (organized in 1923 and renamed in 1959), the School of Education (organized in 1919), the Graduate School (organized in 1947), the School of Law (organized in 1857, closed in 1883, reopened in 1920), the School of Music (organized in 1919 as the College of Fine Arts and renamed in 1921), the School of Nursing (reorganized in 1950 to offer the B.S.N.), the University School (organized in 1987), and the Allied Graduate Program at Baylor College of Dentistry in Dallas and the United States Army Academy of Health Science in San Antonio. The University School operated the honors program, the university scholars program, and interdisciplinary-study programs, as well as programs in American studies, Asian studies, Latin-American studies, Slavic studies, museum studies, and university studies. The campus library facilities include the Armstrong Browning Library; the Baylor Collections of Political Materials, which houses the manuscript collections of several former members of Congress and the Texas legislature; the Moody Memorial Library, which houses general collections, public services, circulation, government documents, music, periodicals, and reserves; the Jesse H. Jones Library, which houses the public service departments of the reference services and the science and engineering collections; and the Texas Collection Library and Archives.

Lillie M. Russell and Lois Smith Murray

Baylor University Medical Center. Began in 1903 as Good Samaritan Hospital, a two-story brick house converted into a private hospital. A year later, after being purchased by the Baptist General Convention of Texas, the hospital became Texas Baptist Memorial Sanitarium. In 1943 the hospital faced a severe blow when its medical school (now Baylor College of Medicine), moved to Houston. The tradition of medical education continued at Baylor University Medical Center. Each year medical residents and fellows as well as nursing students complete their education there, and more than 300 individuals are trained in allied health sciences. In addition to liver transplants, Baylor surgeons perform kidney, heart, lung, and bone marrow transplants. In 1987 the National Institutes of Health named Baylor's program one of only five "centers of excellence." The Baylor Research Institute underwrites much of the funding available for study of digestive diseases, photobiology, transplantation biology, oncology, immunology, biomedical science, metabolic diseases, radiology, and surgical research. BUMC is the hub of the Baylor Health Care System, a nonprofit network founded in 1981. The system includes several North Texas hospitals: BUMC, Baylor Institute for Rehabilitation, and Baylor Medical centers at Ennis, Garland, Grapevine, and Waxahachie. BUMC comprises five connecting patient hospitals and a cancer center. Licensed for 1,509 beds, Baylor is now the second largest nonprofit private hospital in the United States. It is a major referral center for treatment of cancer, heart disease, diabetes, digestive diseases, alcohol and drug abuse, and other ailments. *Susan Hall*

Baytown, Texas. A highly industrialized municipality of refining, rubber, chemical and carbon black plants, located in southeastern Harris and western Chambers counties 30 miles east of downtown Houston. Nathaniel Lynch established a ferry near the site in 1822 and a small settlement called Bay Town grew up around the home of Old Three Hundred colonist William Scott. The area was mostly isolated and undeveloped until the Goose Creek oilfield was developed in 1908. The towns of Pelly and Goose Creek developed near the oilfield and in 1917 Ross S. Sterling and his associates founded the Humble Oil and Refining Company to build a refinery on the William Scott survey. They called the site Baytown and began construction in 1919. The city grew up around the refinery, primarily laid out and managed by Humble. Due to the paternalist policies of Humble the town never incorporated and was annexed as "contiguous and unincorporated" by Pelly in 1945. In 1947 Pelly and Goose Creek consolidated and chose Baytown as the name for the new city, which was formally established in January of 1948. Baytown grew from 20,958 in 1948 to 67,117 in 1990, and in area from 7½ square miles to more than 32. Exxon, still a major employer, runs one of more than 10 major petrochemical plants in the Baytown area. The city is served by two railroads and an interstate highway. The Baytown–La Porte Tunnel, completed in 1953, crossed the Houston Ship Channel until the mid-1990s, when it was replaced by a suspension bridge. *Buck A. Young*

Beales, John Charles. Land speculator; b. Alburgh, Norfolk County, England, 20 March 1804; d. New York City, 25 July 1878; m. María Dolores Soto y Saldaña (1830); 4 children + a daughter from his wife's first marriage; ed. St. George's Hospital, London. Beales traveled as a company surgeon with a mining organization to the Mexican state of Michoacán (1826), then practiced medicine privately in Mexico City. He also practiced in New York City until the 1870s. By 1833 he was developing empresario contracts in Texas. His wife was the widow of Richard Exter, an English land speculator who had left his widow his interests in two empresario contracts encompassing some 48 million acres in eastern New Mexico, the Texas and Oklahoma panhandles, and southeastern Colorado; Exter had held these contracts

Female laboratory worker, Baytown Refinery, Baytown, Texas, 1944. Standard Oil (New Jersey) Collection, Special Collections: Photographic Archives, University of Louisville. Since the founding of the first refinery in 1917, the petrochemical industry has been the basis of the area's economy.

jointly with Stephen Julian Wilson. With these new resources Beales entered the empresario sweepstakes on a grand scale. In 1832 he persuaded officials of the state of Coahuila and Texas to grant him and three different sets of partners three empresario contracts for an estimated 55 million acres of land north of the Rio Grande, on which he was to settle 1,450 families. He appears subsequently to have masterminded the actions of his wife and eight other Mexican citizens, each of whom purchased in fee simple an 11-league tract of "unoccupied land" in the Department of Monclova. In the week after acquiring title, each of the purchasers gave Beales a power of attorney granting him the authority to sell or transfer ownership of the land. Beales then ceded parts of his various holdings to New York speculators, via different land companies and partners. He also tried without much success to attract colonists to the village of Dolores, in what is now Kinney County. After the Texas Revolution, Beales was unable to uphold most of his land titles, though his heirs retained title to the 11-league grants in Southwest Texas. The records being lost, no one knows how much money he received from the prodigious tracts that he once held. Beales was a member of the Royal College of Surgeons of England and a fellow of the New York Academy of Medicine. He became an American citizen in 1850. *Raymond Estep*

Bean, Roy. A frontier justice of the peace known as the "Law West of the Pecos"; b. Mason County, Kentucky, date unknown; d. Langtry, 16 March 1903; m. Virginia Chávez (1866); four children. Bean was taken by his brother Sam down the Santa Fe Trail to Chihuahua, where the brothers set up shop as traders—an arrangement that lasted only a short time before Bean got into trouble with the law and went to San Diego, where his brother Joshua was mayor. Roy was jailed for dueling in February 1852 but broke out and moved on to San Gabriel, where Joshua by this time had established himself as owner of the Headquarters Saloon. Roy inherited the property when Joshua was murdered in November 1852, but made another hasty departure after a narrow escape from hanging in 1857 or 1858. His next stop was Mesilla, New Mexico, where Sam was sheriff of a county that stretched all the way across Arizona. Roy arrived destitute, but Sam took him in as partner in a saloon, and he prospered until the Civil War reached the Rio Grande valley. Bean moved to San Antonio. In an area on South Flores Street that soon earned the name of Beanville, he became locally famous for circumventing creditors, business rivals, and the law. Early in 1882 he left home, probably at the suggestion of his friend W. N. Monroe, who was building the "Sunset" railroad toward El Paso and had almost reached the Pecos River. Moving with the grading camps, Bean arrived at the site of Vinegarroon, just west of the Pecos, in July. Crime was rife at the end of the track. The claim was, "West of the Pecos there is no law; west of El Paso, there is no God." The Texas Rangers were called in, but they needed a resident justice of the peace in order to eliminate the 400-mile round trip to deliver prisoners to the county seat at Fort Stockton. The commissioners of Pecos County officially appointed Roy Bean justice in 1882. He retained the post, with interruptions in 1886 and 1896, when he was voted out, until he retired voluntarily in 1902.

By 1884 Bean was settled at Eagle's Nest Springs, some miles west of Vinegarroon, which acquired a post office and a new name, Langtry, in honor of the English actress Lillie (Emilie Charlotte) Langtry, whom Bean greatly admired. Bean's fame as an eccentric and original interpreter of the law began in the 1880s. There was, however, a sort of common sense behind his unorthodox rulings. When a track worker killed a Chinese laborer, for example, Bean ruled that his law book did not make it illegal to kill a Chinese. Since the killer's friends were present and ready to riot, he had little choice. And when a man carrying $40 and a pistol fell off a bridge, Bean fined the corpse $40 for carrying a concealed weapon, thereby providing funeral expenses. He intimidated and cheated people, but he never hanged anybody. He reached the peak of notoriety on 21 February 1896, when he staged the Fitzsimmons–Maher heavyweight championship fight on a sandbar just below Langtry on the Mexican side of the Rio Grande, where Woodford H. Mabry's rangers, sent to stop it, had no jurisdiction. Fitzsimmons won in less than two minutes. Bean died in his saloon of lung and heart ailments and was buried in the Del Rio cemetery. His shrewdness, audacity, unscrupulousness, and humor, aided by his knack for self-dramatization, made him an enduring part of American folklore. *C. L. Sonnichsen*

Beauchamp, Jenny Bland. Temperance reformer; b. 1833; death date unknown; m. S. A. Beauchamp. As second president of the WCTU in Texas, Mrs. Beauchamp brought local unions into being in more than 20 counties, led in the defense of children against the evils of alcohol, initiated the WCTU practice of petitioning the legislature for reforms, organized a rescue home for girls in Fort Worth, and, as a result of a petition drive to separate juvenile offenders from adults, was instrumental in the establishment of the Gatesville State School for Boys. Like her Baptist-minister husband, she fought for prohibition. She also wrote two religious books and contributed to *The History of Woman Suffrage* (1887). *Judith N. McArthur*

Gusher burning, ca. 1901, by F. J. Trost. Courtesy TSL. The Spindletop oil gusher of 1901 marked the birth of the Texas petroleum industry and produced a boom that left Beaumont with a growing population and great wealth. During the first year of the oil boom three major oil companies were formed in Beaumont.

Beaumont, Texas. County seat of Jefferson County, on the west bank of the Neches River. With nearby Port Arthur and Orange, it forms the Golden Triangle, a major industrial area on the Gulf Coast. A community called Tevis Bluff or Neches River Settlement grew up on the site in the 1820s. Together with nearby Santa Anna, it became the site of the new community of Beaumont in 1835, when Henry Millard, Joseph Pulsifer, and Thomas B. Huling purchased the site and named it for Millard's wife's maiden name. Beaumont became county seat in 1838 and, after several false starts, successfully incorporated in 1881. Though the town was initially a retail center for ranchers and farmers, the advent of railroad service in the late 1800s made it an important lumber and rice shipper, and its population jumped to 9,427 by 1900. The oil strike at Spindletop produced a boom that again transformed Beaumont, giving it a population of 20,640 in 1910 and an extensive oil industry. The Texas Company, Gulf Oil Corporation, and Humble were all formed in Beaumont during the first year of the boom, and the Magnolia (Mobil) Refinery became the city's largest employer. Beaumont also became an important seaport after the Neches was channelized to Port Arthur. Dramatic growth in the 1920s, with the town's population increasing from 40,422 in 1920 to 57,732 in 1930, was accompanied by a brief period of local control by the Ku Klux Klan, and was followed by stagnation in the Great Depression and renewed growth during World War II. The economy grew with petrochemicals and synthetic rubber in the postwar period. The city had a peak population of 119,175 in 1960 and was the sixth largest city in Texas in 1964. The automation of the petrochemical industry and depressed markets led to fluctuations in population in the 1970s and 1980s; Beaumont had dropped to twelfth largest city in 1980 and had the highest unemployment rates on the Gulf Coast in the following decade. In 1990 the population was 114,323. The city includes the main campus of Lamar University and several museums, including the Texas Energy Museum and the Gladys City Boom Town Museum; local events include the South Texas State Fair and the Neches River Festival. *Paul E. Isaac*

Bedichek, Roy. Naturalist and folklorist; b. Cass Co., Illinois, 27 June 1878; d. 21 May 1959; m. Lillian Lee Greer (1910); 3 children; ed. University of Texas (B.S, 1903; M.A, 1925). Bedichek did newspaper work and, at the University of Texas, worked for registrar John A. Lomax. He worked for the University Interscholastic League from 1917 to 1948. Urged by J. Frank Dobie and Walter Prescott Webb, he spent a year in seclusion at Webb's Friday Mountain Ranch, where he wrote *Adventures with a Texas Naturalist* (1947). His other books were *Karánkaway Country* (1950), *Educational Competition: The Story of the University Interscholastic League of Texas* (1956), and *The Sense of Smell* (1960). He twice won the Carr P. Collins award for the best Texas book of the year. *Wilson M. Hudson*

Bell, Peter Hansborough. Governor; b. Spotsylvania County, Virginia, 12 May 1812; d. Littleton, North Carolina, 8 March 1898, and buried there; reinterred in State Cemetery, 1930; m. Mrs. Ella R. E. Dickens (1857), and moved to her home in NC. Bell fought at San Jacinto. During the republic he was assistant adjutant general (1837), inspector general (1839), and a Texas Ranger (1840); he served as a major in the Somervell expedition (1842). After statehood, he fought for the United States Army at Buena Vista during the Mexican War. He was elected governor in 1849 and 1851, but resigned during his second term to fill a vacancy in the United States Congress caused by the death of David S. Kaufman. He refused a commission in the Confederate Army. He received several land grants for his service in the Texas Revolution and, for his service to the state, was voted a donation and a pension in 1891. Bell County is named for him. *Anne W. Hooker*

Belo, Alfred Horatio. Newspaper publisher; b. Salem, North Carolina, 27 May 1839; d. Asheville, North Carolina, 19 April 1901; m. Nettie Ennis (1868); 2 children; ed. University of North Carolina. Belo served in every major engagement of Robert E. Lee's Army of Northern Virginia from Manassas to Appomattox. After the Civil War he rode to Texas, joined the staff of the Galveston *News*, and soon entered a partnership with publisher Willard Richardson. When Richardson died (1875), Belo became principal owner of the newspaper. He established the Dallas *Morning News* (1885) and directed its policy for decades. The Galveston and Dallas papers set a standard for others. After they passed into other hands, the Dallas *Morning News* perpetuated Belo's name under its corporate designation, A. H. Belo Corporation. *George B. Dealey*

Belton Woman's Commonwealth. A commune based on religious perfectionism, celibacy, and Wesleyan sanctificationism. In the late 1860s a group of Protestant women formed under the leadership of Martha McWhirter, who professed to have been sanctified. The women increasingly sought religious and financial autonomy from their husbands, and gradually developed an alternative communal life. In the 1870s the Sanctificationists formed an environment for idiosyncratic religious practices. Members believed themselves to be the recipients of direct revelations from God. One such revelation, for which Mrs. McWhirter claimed Pauline scriptural authority, was that sanctified wives were to live in their homes and perform their household duties, but with no sexual and as little social contact as possible with their unsanctified husbands. The women began to make money by selling eggs and dairy products and by taking in laundry, hauling wood, and working as domestic servants and home nurses. Much of the work was collective, and in 1879, having become financially independent, the women started a common treasury. Because some of the husbands reacted angrily or violently, the McWhirter home began to fill with sanctified sisters seeking refuge. Mr. McWhirter moved into rooms over his store, and the women began to live communally in their various homes or in houses they built. Individual members educated themselves in such useful trades as dentistry, blacksmithing, and shoemaking. Authority was shared in principle, although in practice Mrs. McWhirter exerted much influence. At first the property owned and inherited by various women served only to provide them with shelter. Eventually it became the basis for more ambitious economic efforts; one home became a boardinghouse, one a commercial laundry. In 1886 the women bought one hotel and began building another by expanding the boardinghouse. Title to property was held in individual names for some time, but in 1891 the group incorporated as the Central Hotel Company. By this time they owned a large amount of property in town as well as three farms. Belton citizens, however, blamed Martha McWhirter and the Sanctificationists for separations and divorces. When two immigrant Scottish brothers sought out the group for religious reasons they were kidnapped, whipped, warned to leave town, and briefly committed to the state asylum. No other males tried to join. But by 1887 the hotel had become successful, and hostility gradually dissipated. The sisters' book collection, housed in a small room in their hotel, became so popular that it was moved to a larger facility outside the commune, and in 1903 it formally became the city's public library.

In 1898 or 1899 the women decided to retire from business and move to Washington, D.C., so that they might pursue their growing interest in cultural activities. Using their savings, they bought a house in Mount Pleasant, Maryland. In Washington, where they incorporated in 1902 as the Woman's Commonwealth of Washington, D.C., they became more visible to the national press, and a number of articles were published describing their history and life. In both the Belton and Washington communities membership averaged about 30, most of whom were women and their children. After Martha McWhirter died in 1904, Fannie Holtzclaw took over as leader. By 1906 only 18 adult women were left in the Commonwealth, but they continued to be successful in operating a farm in Maryland and a boardinghouse in Washington. The Woman's Commonwealth gradually expired as death reduced its numbers, but some members continued to live at the Maryland farm as late as 1918. *Mary Ann Lamanna and Jayme A. Sokolow*

Benavides, Plácido. Victoria pioneer and Texas revolutionary soldier; b. Reynosa, Tamaulipas, date unknown; d. Opelousas, Louisiana, 1837; m. Agustina De León (1831). As secretary to Fernando De León, Benavides played an important part in the settlement of Victoria. He married a daughter of empresario Martín De León. During the early stages of the Texas Revolution he served the revolutionary army with distinction in important operations, including the Goliad Campaign of 1835 and the siege of Bexar. He was afterward instrumental in warning James W. Fannin of Antonio López de Santa Anna's plans. Though Benavides was an ardent foe of Santa Anna, he did not support

Texas independence. Like many Tejanos, he was ostracized after the battle of San Jacinto. He fled to Louisiana with the De León family and there died, though members of his family later returned to Texas.
Craig H. Roell

Benavides, Santos. Confederate Army officer and Laredo political leader; b. Laredo, 1 November 1823; d. Laredo, 9 November 1891; m. Augustina Villareal (1842); 4 adopted children. Benavides's uncle, Basilio Benavides, had been a political leader in Laredo, and the younger Benavides continued the family's involvement in local government. He was *procurador* (1843–) and mayor (1856–) of Laredo, then chief justice (i.e., county judge) of Webb County (1856–). His anti-Centralist sentiment brought a traditionally isolated region closer to the mainstream of Texas politics while preserving a sense of local independence. He supported the forces of Mirabeau B. Lamar, which occupied Laredo during the Mexican War, but joined his uncle in opposing annexation of the Laredo area by the United States, as called for by the Treaty of Guadalupe Hidalgo, because he feared it would compromise the independent character of northern Mexico. During the Civil War, Benavides became the highest ranking Mexican American to serve the Confederacy. He and his brothers found Confederate states'-rights principles close to their regionalism. He was commissioned a captain in the Thirty-third Texas Cavalry (or Benavides' Regiment) and assigned to the Rio Grande Military District, where he quickly won accolades as a fighter. He drove Juan Cortina back into Mexico in the battle of Carrizo on 22 May 1861, and quelled other local revolts against Confederate authority. In November 1863 he was promoted to colonel and authorized to raise his own regiment of "Partisan Rangers," for which he used the remnants of the Thirty-third. His greatest military triumph was his defense of Laredo on 19 March 1864, with 42 troops against 200 soldiers of the First Texas Cavalry, USA, commanded by Col. Edmund J. Davis, who had earlier offered Benavides a Union generalship. Perhaps Benavides's most significant contribution to the South came when he arranged for safe passage of Texas cotton along the Rio Grande to Matamoros during the Union occupation of Brownsville in 1864. After the war he served in the state legislature (1879–84) and twice as Laredo alderman. Mexican dictator Porfirio Díaz appointed him Mexican envoy to the United States during the reciprocity controversy in 1880, a role that did not prevent him from being Texas delegate to the World Cotton Exposition in 1884.
Jerry Thompson

Benson, Nettie Lee. Historian and librarian; b. Arcadia, Galveston County, 15 January 1905; d. Austin, 23 June 1993; ed. University of Texas (baccalaureate degree, 1929; master's degree, 1935; Ph.D., 1949). Nettie Benson is best known as the director of the Nettie Lee Benson Latin American Collection at UT. She grew up in Sinton and maintained her membership in the Sinton Presbyterian Church all her life; in later years she was a benefactor of the Presbyterian Children's Home and Service Agency. In 1925 she took a course on Spanish North America from Charles W. Hackett that became her prime motivation for studying Mexico. She moved to Monterrey, Nuevo León, and taught from 1925 to 1927 at the Instituto Inglés–Español, a school run by the Methodist Church. She taught at Ingleside High School, near Sinton, for nearly 10 years (1932–41), during which she sponsored field trips to Monterrey for the senior class. She was also instrumental in gaining admittance of Hispanic students to the previously all-white high school. She returned to UT on a leave of absence in 1941 to take what she thought would be refresher courses, but stayed to complete her doctorate. In 1942 she began her lifelong association with the library that now bears her name. Miss Benson quickly became an authority on Latin-American library acquisitions and bibliography. She began an aggressive acquisition program for the library that included trips to Mexico, South America, and the Caribbean, and developed innovative acquisition methods adapted to conditions in the Latin-American book-publishing trade. From a respectable 30,000 volumes in 1942, the Latin American Collection grew to 305,000 volumes by 1975, the year of her retirement. The Benson Collection became one of the most comprehensive and distinguished Latin-American libraries in the world.

Miss Benson was chosen as the representative for the Latin American Cooperative Acquisitions Project, a consortium of major United States research libraries, for which she collected books in South America and Central America from 1960 to 1962. In 1962 she began to teach Mexican and Latin-American history for the UT history department, and in 1964 she initiated with Ford Foundation funding a Latin-American library-studies program in the Graduate School of Library Science. After she retired from teaching in the library school (1975), she continued her popular graduate seminars in Mexican history until 1989. One of her first history seminars resulted in a classic book of essays written by her students, *Mexico and the Spanish Córtes, 1820–1834* (1966; reprinted in Spanish by the Mexican congress in 1985). Miss Benson directed numerous master's and doctoral theses. She presented countless papers and published many articles and books. A Spanish translation of her doctoral dissertation, *The Provincial Deputation in Mexico: Precursor of the Mexican Federal State*, was published in Mexico in 1952 and again in 1980. An expanded English version was published by the University of Texas Press in 1992. The January 1987 issue of the *Southwestern Historical Quarterly* was dedicated to her. Nettie Benson was a founding member of the Seminar on the Acquisition of Latin American Library Materials in 1956 and of the Latin American Studies Association in 1966. She was elected to the editorial board of the *Hispanic American Historical Review* (1974–79). In 1992 she was elected an honorary life member of the Texas State Historical Association. The Latin American Collection was renamed in her honor in 1975. Upon retirement, she began the endowment of the Nettie Lee Benson Library Fund for the purchase of rare materials for the Benson Collection. Miss Benson was also president of the Fourth International Conference of United States and Mexican Historians (1973) and a recipient of the Order of the Aztec Eagle (1979), the highest official decoration given to non-Mexicans by Mexico. She received other honors from the Southwestern Council on Latin American Studies (1968–69), the UT–Austin Institute of Latin American Studies (1973), the Casa de Cultura Americana (1974), the Conference on Latin American History (1976), the Seminar on the Acquisition of Latin American Library Materials (1977), the Texas House of Representatives (1977), the UT–Austin Ex-Students' Association (1981), the UT–Austin Graduate School (1984), the office of the UT president (1986), and the UT College of Liberal Arts (1990).
Laura Gutierrez–Witt

The Johnsons, Humphreys, Connallys, and Yarboroughs arriving at Bergstrom Air Force Base. Photograph by Russell Lee. Near Austin, 1964. Russell Lee Photograph Collection, CAH; VN RY9 64 4.

Bergstrom Air Force Base. Near Austin; activated in 1942 as Del Valle Army Air Base and constructed on 3,000 acres leased from the city of Austin. The Chisholm Trail ran through the tract. The base was renamed Bergstrom Army Air Field in 1943, in honor of Capt. John A. E. Bergstrom, the first Austinite killed in World War II. The name became Bergstrom Field in November 1943 and Bergstrom Air Force Base in 1948. Initially, Bergstrom was the home of troop-carrier units. It was declared a permanent base after World War II and was at various times assigned to the Strategic Air Command and the Tactical Air Command. After July 1966 it was under the control of the Tactical Air Command and housed the headquarters for the Twelfth Air Force, which was responsible for all Tactical Air Command reconnaissance, fighter, and airlift operations west of the Mississippi River. The economic contribution of the base in fiscal 1989 in a 50-mile radius was estimated to be $343 million and in Central Texas, $533 million. On 30 September 1993 Bergstrom was officially closed. The base is now the site of Austin–Bergstrom International Airport. *Art Leatherwood*

Berlandier, Jean Louis. Naturalist; b. France or Switzerland, ca. 1805; d. near Matamoros, Tamaulipas, 1851; ed. in Geneva. Berlandier early proved his scholarship with his article on goose-

berries (1824), which was later included in a book on plants of the world, the *Prodromus* of Auguste Pyrame DeCandolle. DeCandolle selected Berlandier to make botanical collections in Mexico, where he arrived in 1826. He joined the Mexican Boundary Commission as botanist and collected specimens around Laredo, San Antonio, Gonzales, and San Felipe. He accompanied various other expeditions to Texas with the commission, which was dissolved in 1829. He settled then in Matamoros, married, and became a physician. He made a collecting trip to Goliad in 1834. During the Mexican War he was in charge of the hospitals in Matamoros and served as an interpreter. He and Rafael Chovell published *Diario de viaje de la Comisión de Límites* (1850). Berlandier drowned in the San Fernando River. *Clinton P. Hartmann*

Bexar, Siege of. The first major campaign of the Texas Revolution (October–December 1835). After the battle of Gonzales on 2 October, the Texan army grew to 300 men and elected Stephen F. Austin commander. The Texans advanced on 12 October toward San Antonio (Bexar), where General Cos recently had concentrated Mexican forces numbering 650 men. Cos fortified the town plazas west of the San Antonio River and the Alamo. By the time the Texans camped along Salado Creek east of San Antonio in mid-October their numbers had grown to over 400 men, including James Bowie and Juan N. Seguín, who brought with him a company of Mexican Texans. Bowie and Fannin led an advance to the missions below San Antonio in late October, while Cos brought in 100 reinforcement men. On 25 October the democratic Texans conducted a debate over strategy. Sam Houston, who had come from the Consultation, urged delay for training and for cannons to bombard the fortifications. Austin and others won support to continue efforts at capturing the town. From Espada Mission on 27 October, Austin sent Bowie and Fannin forward to Mission Concepción with 90 men to locate a position nearer the town. The next morning Cos sent Col. Domingo de Ugartechea with 275 men to attack the advance force. The Texans drove off the assault from a position along the bank of the river, inflicting more than 50 casualties and capturing a cannon. Austin arrived after the battle of Concepción to urge an attack on San Antonio but found little support among his officers. Cos then resumed defensive positions in San Antonio and the Alamo, while the Texans established camps on the river above and below the town and grew to an army of 600 with reinforcements from East Texas led by Thomas J. Rusk. After discussion among the Texan officers produced little support for an attack, some volunteers went home for winter clothes and equipment. Yet the arrival of more East Texans in early November offset the departures.

Travis led the capture of 300 Mexican mules and horses grazing beyond the Medina River on 8 November. Four days later Ugartechea left San Antonio with a small cavalry force to direct the march of reinforcements from below the Rio Grande. Austin sent cavalry to intercept him, but the Mexican troops evaded them. Both armies suffered morale problems as a result of colder weather and limited supplies. When three companies with over a hundred men arrived from the United States in midNovember, Austin again planned an attack. Officers still expressed doubts, however, and it was called off. Austin then left to assume diplomatic duties in the United States. The Texas troops selected

Edward Burleson as their new leader. When Deaf Smith reported approaching Mexican cavalry on 26 November, Burleson ordered out troops to cut them off. The ensuing engagement became known as the Grass Fight. After debate and internal dissension on the Texas side, a Mexican officer surrendered with news of declining Mexican morale, whereupon Ben Milam and William Gordon Cooke gathered more than 300 volunteers to attack the town, while Burleson and another 400 men scouted, protected the camp and supplies, and forced Cos to keep his 570 men divided between the town and the Alamo. James Neill distracted the Mexican forces with artillery fire on the Alamo before dawn on 5 December, while Milam and Francis W. Johnson led two divisions in a surprise attack that seized the Veramendi and Garza houses north of the plaza in San Antonio. That night and the next day the Texans destroyed some buildings close to them and dug trenches to connect the houses they occupied. On the seventh the Texans captured another nearby house, but Milam was killed. Johnson then directed another night attack that seized the Navarro house.

On December 8 Ugartechea returned with over 600 reinforcements, but only 170 were experienced soldiers. The other 450 men were untrained conscripts without enough supplies. Burleson sent 100 men into town to join the Texan force, which captured the buildings of Zambrano Row in hand-to-hand fighting. Cos ordered his cavalry to threaten the Texan camp, but they found it well defended. That night Cooke with two companies seized the priest's house on the main plaza, but they seemed cut off from the Texas army.

When Cos sought to concentrate his troops at the Alamo, four companies of his cavalry rode away rather than continue the struggle. Cos then asked for surrender terms on the morning of 9 December. Burleson accepted the surrender of most Mexican equipment and weapons, but allowed Cos and his men to retire southward because neither army had supplies to sustain a large group of prisoners. Texas casualties numbered 30 to 35, while Mexican losses, primarily in the Morelos Infantry Battalion, totaled about 150; the difference reflected the greater accuracy of the Texans' rifles. Most of the Texas volunteers went home after the battle, which left San Antonio and all of Texas temporarily under their control.   *Alwyn Barr*

Bexar Archives. The Spanish and Mexican records of Texas, assembled in San Antonio (Béxar) during its long history as the capital and principal community of Texas; the single most important source for the history of Texas to 1836. The archives, housed at the University of Texas since 1899, constitute more than 80 linear feet of materials in a quarter million pages. The documents are rich in sources about the administrative, legal, military, religious, economic, and social life of Texas and surrounding areas from the founding of the San Antonio de Béxar Presidio in 1718 to Texas independence in 1836. The earlier documents deal with the affairs of the Canary Islanders and relations among the military, civil, and missionary communities that constituted San Antonio. Major topics during the eighteenth century include Indian policy and relations, military affairs, cattle raising, trade, legal proceedings, and exploration and communications. After 1803 the documentation also reflects a growing Anglo-American presence, the development of trade and colonization, and currents of political unrest and revolution. As the

affairs of Texas and the region grew in complexity, so does the volume of documentation in the Bexar Archives. Fully half of the collection represents the Mexican period (1821–36).

UT received the archives in 1899 through the efforts of university history professor Lester G. Bugbee. By agreement with the Bexar County Commissioners Court, the university undertook to house, organize, calendar, and translate the collection. Certain land and legal documents were retained in San Antonio for use in county business. Much of the original order of the Bexar Archives had been disturbed over the years. UT librarians and historians arranged all the documents into chronological order in the following series:

1. Coahuila y Texas Official Publications, 1826–35
2. General Governmental Publications, 1730–1836
3. Nongovernmental Publications, 1778, 1811–36
4. General Manuscript Series, 1717–1836
5. Undated and Undated Fragments

The physical arrangement and a corresponding calendar provided easy access to the Bexar Archives for such scholars as Eugene C. Barker and Carlos E. Castañeda. By the 1930s a systematic translation program had also begun. In the mid-1990s, translations existed for the following portions of the archives:

Series I: 1717–90 (162 volumes)
Series II: 1804–08 (38 volumes)
Series III: Printed Decrees, 1803–12 (4 volumes)

UT greatly expanded access to the Bexar Archives when it microfilmed the entire collection between 1967 and 1971. That project produced 172 reels of film and a corresponding set of published guides. Copies of the microfilm are now available at major educational institutions nationwide. Translations done to date are also available on microfilm. Adán Benavides has compiled a comprehensive name guide to the Bexar Archives, based on all substantive documents as they are entered in the microfilm edition.   *John Wheat*

Bible, Dana Xenophon. Football coach; b. Jefferson City, Tennessee, 8 October 1891; d. Austin, 19 January 1980; m. Rowena Rhodes (1923; d. 1942); 2 children; m. Dorothy Gilstrap (1952); ed. Carson–Newman College, Tennessee. Bible was recruited by Texas A&M in 1916 and promoted to head coach in 1917. The Aggies won five Southwest Conference championships under him, and under him the "Twelfth Man" tradition—in observance of which A&M students stand throughout football games to show their willingness to play if needed—was started. In 1929 Bible went to the University of Nebraska, where he achieved a superb record. In 1936 he went to the University of Texas. There, he initiated the "Bible Plan" for recruitment and support of native Texas players and raised the team from the cellar to championship in five seasons. Again, his win–loss–tie record was excellent (63–31–3). UT won the Southwest Conference in 1943 and 1945. Subsequently, Bible worked as athletic director at the university (1947–56). He also published a book, *Championship Football: A Guide for Player, Coach and Fan*, in 1947. After he left football he and his wife, Dorothy, operated Camp Mystic, a summer camp for girls. Bible was a charter member of the National Football Hall of Fame and the 1954 recipient of the Amos Alonzo Stagg Award. In 1959 he was elected to the Texas Sports Hall of Fame. During the 1960s each of the three of the schools where he had coached enrolled him in

Dana Bible. Courtesy Cushing Memorial Library, Texas A&M University.

its hall of fame. Bible was on the National Collegiate Football Rules Committee for 25 years and served as a president of the American Football Coaches Association. *David S. Walkup*

Big Bend National Park. The first national park in Texas; 1,250 square miles in the Big Bend of the Rio Grande, a land of "killing heat and freezing cold; deadly drought and flash flood; arid lowland and moist mountain woodland; and a living river winding its way across the desert." The Rio Grande flows for 107 miles on the park's southern boundary, through Santa Elena, Mariscal, and Boquillas canyons, the deepest gorges on the river. In 1978 the United States Congress designated a 191-mile section of the Rio Grande a Wild and Scenic River, 69 miles of which lie on the park boundary. Most Big Bend acreage is arid alluvial plains, the most representative example of the Chihuahuan Desert in North America. The Chisos Mountains, the southernmost range in the continental United States and completely enclosed in the park, rise over 7,800 feet above sea level. They support relict forests from the late Pleistocene era. The popular Chisos Basin offers visitors a cool respite from the desert heat and spectacular panoramic vistas. The National Park Service considers the Big Bend "one of the outstanding geological laboratories and class-

rooms of the world." Recovered fossil forms of ancient plants and animals include a bivalve three feet wide and four feet long, the largest known pterosaur (a flying dinosaur), and the skull of a chamosaurus, a horned dinosaur. The topographical and climatic extremes provide habitats for a varied flora and fauna, including over 1,000 species of plants, 78 mammals, 56 reptiles, 10 amphibians, 35 fish, and 434 birds (more than half the species of birds in North America). Endangered species found at Big Bend are the peregrine falcon, black-capped vireo, Mexican long-nosed bat, and Big Bend gambusia (a tiny fish found only in the park). Several species in the United States can be found only in the park: Del Carmen white-tail deer, colima warbler, Mexican drooping juniper. The Chisos agave lives nowhere else in the world. In 1976 the United Nations Educational, Scientific, and Cultural Organization designated Big Bend a "Man and the Biosphere" international reserve, one of only 28 in the United States. Cooperative research and educational programs subsequently began with Mexico. Although human beings came late, the park contains archeological and historical sites representing more than 10,000 years of inhabitants, including Indians, Spanish explorers and missionaries, and farmers, ranchers, miners, and soldiers of the last two centuries.

In 1933 the Texas legislature inaugurated Texas Canyons State Park on 15 sections of land. Later that year the name was changed to Big Bend State Park and the Chisos Mountains were added to the park acreage. The National Park Service investigated the site in January 1934 and recommended establishment of both a CCC camp and a national park. The Park Service regarded Big Bend as "decidedly the outstanding scenic area of Texas." President Franklin Roosevelt took a personal interest because of a proposed companion park in Mexico (still being discussed decades later). The United States Congress passed the enabling legislation in 1935. By 1942 most of the land was purchased with a $1.5 million appropriation from the Texas legislature. Although several thousand acres remained in private hands, the park opened to the public in 1944, when only 1,409 visitors came. In 1972 the Congress appropriated money to purchase the last private land in the park. In the early 1990s the park had more than 100 full-time staff positions supplemented by temporary employees, interns, and volunteers. Although it has visitor centers, restaurants, and other accommodations, the park is managed to "remain largely unaltered by human activity." *John Jameson*

Big Die-Up. During the 1880s Panhandle ranchers built "drift fences" to keep their own cattle from straying southward during the winter and to keep those from farther north out of their ranges. The broken, though very extensive, lines of barbed wire proved catastrophic during a series of blizzards in 1885–87, when cattle jammed against the fences died by the thousands. Wheeler County ranchers, for instance, had cooperatively built a fence along Sweetwater Creek near Mobeetie, and 75 percent of their cattle died against the barrier. The "Big Die-Up" was followed, Texas style, by prolonged summer droughts that wiped out many cowmen. *H. Allen Anderson*

Big Spring, Texas. Big Spring, the county seat of Howard County, is located in the southwest central part of the county in a rocky gorge between two high foothills of the Caprock escarpment. Its name is derived from the nearby spring, a campsite for various

Panoramic photograph of dog and pony circus parade in Big Spring, ca. 1898. Courtesy TSL. In the 1880s Big Spring was located at the site of the Texas and Pacific Railroad line and station and became the county seat.

Indian groups and for early expeditions across West Texas. In the 1870s the community grew up by the spring as a buffalo hunter supply point, and in 1880 the Texas and Pacific Railway built through the area and Big Spring relocated along the railroad. The town became the county seat in 1882, and had a population of 1,255 in 1900. Big Spring incorporated in 1907, and grew to 4,273 inhabitants in 1920. Oil was discovered nearby in 1926, and the town experienced an oil boom for the next ten years, growing to 13,375 inhabitants by 1930 and with 810 wells in production in the vicinity in 1936. The city's growth was halted briefly in the late 1930s, and its population fell to 12,604 in 1940, but the building of Big Spring Army Air Corps Bombardier School led to renewed growth during World War Two. During the 1950s the community flourished as a petrochemical and banking center, and with the reopening of the military facility as Webb Air Force Base, and Big Spring reached a peak population of 31,230 in 1960. Thereafter the community experienced a slow decline. Webb closed in 1977 and the town's population fell to 23,093 inhabitants in 1990. In the 1990s Big Spring remained an important agribusiness and petrochemical center.

Claudia Hazlewood and Mark Odintz

Big Thicket. In Southeast Texas. Though it is ill-defined, early explorers thought of it as the heavily wooded area south of the Old San Antonio Road, east of the Brazos, north of the coastal prairie and the La Bahía Road, and west of the Sabine. The Big Thicket National Preserve comprises 12 protected units scattered through Hardin, Liberty, Polk, Tyler, and Jasper counties. Oldtimers restrict the name Big Thicket to the bear-hunters' thicket, which is about 40 miles long and 20 miles across at its widest. Before the incursion of the lumber industry and oil and gas industry, this heart of the thicket was characterized by dense vegetation and by large numbers of deer, bear, panthers, and wolves, as well as the common varieties of mammals, birds, reptiles, and amphibians. The shoreline that supported the primeval thicket rose above the waters of the Gulf of Mexico during the Ice Age, and was built up by silt washed down and by an ancestral Trinity River. Ten thousand years ago the thicket dwellers included mastodons, elephants, the American horse, Taylor's bison, camels, tapirs, giant sloths, beavers, and armadillos. Preying on these animals were the saber-toothed tiger and the dire wolf. Their day ended around 8,000 years ago. The time of the glaciers established varieties of soils and vegetation in the thicket that remained after the glaciers retreated, and produced a

unique biological crossroads of at least eight different plant communities. The Big Thicket is possibly the most biologically diverse area in the world. Cactus and ferns, beech trees and orchids, camellias and azaleas, and four carnivorous plants all occupy what is called the thicket, along with the pines, oaks, and gums common to the rest of East Texas. The thicket also supports a wide variety of animal life and is especially noted for the 350 species of birds that either live in the area or visit annually. The abundant rainfall and the long growing season ensure that vegetation and all the animal life that depends on it thrive.

Three groups of Indians are historically associated with the early history of the thicket—the Atakapas, the Caddos, and the Alabama–Coushattas. The mound-building Caddos occupied the fertile rolling hills to the north, and the cannibalistic Atakapas bounded the thicket on the Gulf Coast and on the Trinity bottoms. At the end of the eighteenth century the Alabamas and Coushattas began to settle on the northern and western fringes of the thicket, and the woods became theirs. The first man to lay a personal claim to the area was Lorenzo de Zavala (1829), but the first settlers to move into the thicket were Anglo-Americans (1830s) whose WASP descendants still predominate. The thicket did not lend itself to plantation farming and its accompanying slavery. There are a few Cajuns on the southwestern edge. A few Slavonians remained after the days of tie cutting and stave making, and some other foreigners stayed behind after they drifted in to work for the big sawmills or during the oil boom. The economic history of the thicket is much the same as that of the rest of East Texas. Until the 1880s the inhabitants dwelt scattered through the woods and lived off what they raised on subsistence farms. In the 1880s the lumber industry opened up more land to farming and grazing. The Sour Lake oilfield in 1901, then the Saratoga and other thicket oilfields, brought about a period of frantic activity. After the booms, life settled back to its rural pace and remained so through the 1930s. World War II and the shipyards of the Gulf Coast brought about the major change in the thicket way of life. Many of those who went to war or the shipyards never returned. After the war the increasing number of paved roads and cars and power lines funneled in massive doses of the outside world. Except for the most confirmed woodsmen, the bulk of the population is now located in Kountze, Honey Island, Sour Lake, Saratoga, and Batson.

Formal efforts to save the Big Thicket from industrial devastation began with the founding of the East Texas Big Thicket Association by R. E. Jackson in 1927. Early conservationists joined the association, which hoped to preserve 400,000 acres as a national forest. One result was a biological survey in 1936 by H. B. Parks and V. L. Cory of the Texas Agricultural Experiment Station. The East Texas Big Thicket Association gained considerable political support during the thirties, but the war economy at the end of the decade demanded pine lumber and hardwoods, and the conservation movement flagged. In the early 1960s conservationists again began their drive to save parts of the thicket for a state park. They were led by Lance Rosier, a long time thicket guide and naturalist, and Dempsie Henley, mayor of Liberty, who in 1964 founded what became the Big Thicket Association. By 1966 the association had decided to push for national-park status. Senator Ralph Yarborough was its most powerful proponent in Congress. In 1974 a bill by Charles Wilson and Bob Eckhardt to establish the 84,550-acre Big Thicket National Preserve was passed by Congress and signed by President Gerald Ford. *Francis E. Abernethy*

Birds. No other state in the United States has such a remarkable variety of birds as Texas. By 1991 the number of species recorded from the state totaled 594, including extinct, extirpated, and introduced species. An additional 6 species were listed as historical, and 11 species were hypothetically considered to occur in Texas. There are several reasons for the great number of species; aside from being the largest state in the contiguous states, Texas is also one of the most diversified topographically and climatically. It extends north into the Great Plains, east into the humid lowlands of the southeastern United States, south into the subtropical lower Rio Grande region, and west into the desert. Thus the state has attracted species from east and west, north and south, from the sandy gulf coastal islands, the wide open plains of the north, the deserts and desert mountains of the west. This situation applies not only to the permanently resident birds, of which Texas has a greater proportion than any other state with the possible exception of California; but it also means that migrants from other areas of the United States visit Texas. Perhaps the greatest variety of birds is to be found along the coast and in the lower Rio Grande.

In the humid, heavily forested riverbottoms of East Texas one of the most spectacular as well as most famous of birds, now extirpated from Texas, was the ivory-billed woodpecker. Its retiring habits, even where it was in the more inaccessible swamps, made it difficult to study this bird in its native haunts. Its nest, an excavation in a tall tree, was watchfully guarded by the parent birds. This woodpecker is sometimes confused with another inhabitant of the lowland forests, the pileated woodpecker, which, however, is somewhat smaller, has less white on the wing, and lacks also the conspicuous whiteness of bill that suggested the name ivory-billed woodpecker. The pileated woodpecker is much more numerous, although it is shy and at times difficult to approach. It, too, lives in the forest and rears its young in a similar hole in a large tree. The mortise-like holes that it makes in the trees in search of insect food are a good means of identification. When employed in digging these holes it makes the chips fly, and sometimes the noise that results resembles not a little that of a distant woodchopper. Some of the humid bottomlands and forests attract an almost unbelievable population of small birds, among which one of the most beautiful is the yellow-trimmed hooded warbler. This warbler is an inhabitant chiefly of the lower parts of the trees and of the undergrowth, where, particu-

Whooping Crane, by John James Audubon, 1834. Engraving with aquatint (hand-colored). 38⅛" x 25¼". Courtesy Stark Museum of Art, Orange, Texas. Audubon was an international celebrity by the time he arrived in Texas in April 1837 to seek additional species for *The Birds of America* (1827–38). He later concluded that more than two-thirds of the birds of America were native to the republic.

larly in the canebrakes, its song is one of the outstanding bird melodies.

The upland park-like forests do not have so many bird inhabitants as the deciduous areas of the stream valleys. These fragrant pineries, however, attract several interesting birds that are found much less frequently, if at all, in other kinds of country. Among these is the appropriately named pine warbler. It is an inconspicuous olive-green bird which behaves somewhat like an injured creeper and entertains its mate with a monotone song singularly suggestive of that of the chipping sparrow. Another characteristic inhabitant of the pine forests is the brown-headed nuthatch, a cousin of the common white-breasted nuthatch and a smaller, much less conspicuous bird with a voice that sounds like a miniature cracked tin horn. In cultivated lands, and particularly about human dwellings, one of the most conspicuous of all the birds is the Texas state bird, the mockingbird. Its almost unlimited vocal repertoire is famous. Around the lakes of the interior of Texas are the snowy egret and the great egret, the white pinions of which make them conspicuous features of the landscape.

Other herons, particularly the great blue heron, together with the elusive king rail, inhabit the marshes and borders of these bodies of water, while the surface is frequently dotted with various kinds of ducks, particularly in the region of the Great Plains. On the prairies of the interior, as well as on the coast and in other bushy areas, the scissor-tailed flycatcher is conspicuous. This bird, one of the best known of all the land birds of Texas, has gray, black, and white plumage with a dash of red and pink, together with long tail feathers.

The Llano Estacado has a relatively sparse bird population. The slate-gray Mississippi kite is one of the most characteristic; its soaring flight makes it an attractive bird. It nests in the trees of the narrow fringe of vegetation along streams, as well as in the tall bushes of the chaparral. Another bird of the high open areas is the burrowing owl, so called because it makes its nest in a hole in the ground, often adapting to its use an abandoned prairie dog burrow; its choice of home has given rise to the story that it lives with the prairie dog and rattlesnake, a story long since disproved. In the mesquite and other chaparral of the southern and middle parts of Texas, one of the most conspicuous and intriguing birds is the greater roadrunner, or "paisano." Its habit of running to escape its enemies, and the many stories that are told of its prowess in fighting rattlesnakes, have made it almost a legendary character in folklore. Its speed on foot is really remarkable, although often exaggerated. On the coastal prairie lives one of the state's most attractive game birds, Attwater's greater prairie chicken. Unfortunately, this bird has been greatly reduced in relatively recent years, since over-shooting and lack of proper protection caused it to be practically exterminated from many of its former haunts.

In the marshes of the Gulf coast one finds blackbirds and grackles of various kinds in abundance. Their great flocks sometimes resemble swarms of gnats. Hidden away in the grass, reeds, or grain are the long-billed marsh wren, the wary clapper rail, and the brilliantly colored purple gallinule, along with other water and shore birds. On the coastal beaches, both of the islands and the mainland, one of the outstanding birds is the black skimmer, which has received its name from its habit of flying close to the water and dipping its bill frequently into the surface. It sometimes appears in large flocks that range themselves along the sand or on the mud flats like great platoons of soldiers. Another inhabitant of the shores is the red-billed, black and white plumaged American oystercatcher. Perhaps the most conspicuous bird, as it is the largest along the shore, is the brown pelican, which breeds in sometimes extensive colonies not far back from the Gulf of Mexico. This bird, clumsy on land, is marvelous on the wing, for not only can it soar indefinitely, but it has an uncanny ability to skim close over the Gulf waves without touching the water. To obtain its food it dives from on high with a great splash into the water and disappears, soon coming up again but facing in the opposite direction. Perhaps the most spectacular of the state's birds on the wing is the magnificent frigatebird, or, as it is sometimes called, the man-o'-war bird, so named because it is a pirate and obtains a large part of its food by robbing the gulls and other waterbirds. Its black or black and white plumage makes it a conspicuous figure as it sails for long periods with wings and long forked tail expanded, and with very little or no motion of the wings.

In the lower Rio Grande region are many birds that are found practically nowhere else in the United States, these being tropical species that range up from northeastern Mexico. Among them no bird is more bizarre than the northern jacana. This bird, with a peculiar comb-like fleshy appendage on top of its head and bright yellow-green wings, is a strange apparition as it flies low over the water, or with its long, slender, unwebbed toes stalks about over the lily pads. Out on the edge of the arid region in the deep canyons, the remarkable black-capped vireo lives. In addition to its own regular song, it has notes which in many respects remind one of the mockingbird. Like many of the other vireos it inhabits the bushes along the canyons, and, like them, builds a pendant nest in the horizontal fork of a bush. The canyon wren also holds a high place among the songsters of the west. Its remarkable melody, starting high and descending through more than an octave, resounds from the canyon walls until it seems to come from a bird two or three times its size. It lives in the crevices of the rocky walls of the canyons, where it is easily completely hidden from sight. The dry regions of central western Texas harbor such birds as the black phoebe, which places its nest on a little shelf of rock in a canyon or even in an abandoned well. Here, too, lives one of the most remarkable birds of all Texas, the white-throated swift. It is well-named, because it is one of the most rapid fliers in the world. When it really is in haste, it dashes down through the canyons at such speed that the eye finds it difficult to follow. There are also in the desert area other attractive birds, such as the vermilion flycatcher, which draws attention not only because of its brilliant plumage but also because of its intriguing nesting and other habits. Here, too, is the cactus wren, well named because it is so fond of building its coconut-shaped nest in the most forbidding cacti as well as in other bushy vegetation, leaving only a very small opening at the side for an entrance. The tiny verdin, although barely half the size of the cactus wren, sometimes builds a thorny castle almost as large with the entrance being from below at one end, which effectively keeps out most of its enemies.

So many remarkable birds occur in the picturesque Chisos Mountains that it is difficult to pick out the most important. The gray-breasted jay, which is common throughout this range, is found in no other area in the United States and is a noisy, conspicuous inhabitant of the woodland. Here, also, lives the Colima warbler, a very small bird whose color makes it obscure. It breeds in these mountains but nowhere else in the United States. In the Chisos, as well as in other mountains, there are also many birds that have come down from the more northern Rocky Mountains. Such are the zone-tailed hawk, a marvelous flyer that lives in canyons and the forests of the mountains; the Hutton's vireo; the mountain chickadee, which is similar in appearance to the Carolina chickadee of eastern Texas; and the noisy, mischievous Seller's jay.

In addition to the great variety of remarkable birds that are to be found in Texas, there are two famous birds that were formerly common in the state, but which now unfortunately, have been exterminated throughout their ranges in the United States. These are the well-known Carolina parakeet, whose taste for food runs to cockleburs, and the still more widely known passenger pigeon. This bird was at one time so abundant at certain seasons of the year in parts of eastern Texas that it broke down the branches of the trees in some of its roosts.

Harry C. Oberholser

Bird's Creek Indian Fight. Occurred on 26 May 1839 near the site of present Temple. A ranger force of 34 men under the command of Capt. John Bird came in contact with more than 200 Caddo, Kickapoo, and Comanche Indians. The Texans were victorious but suffered several casualties, including Captain Bird. A Comanche chief was killed in the fight. The creek on which the battle was fought became known as Bird's Creek.

Bird's Fort. Built at the northwest corner of the Texas frontier after the battle of Village Creek in May 1841 by order of Gen. Edward H. Tarrant. The fort, constructed by a hundred volunteers of the Fourth Brigade of Texas Militia under Maj. Jonathan Bird in September and October 1841, consisted of a blockhouse and several smaller buildings enclosed in a picket stockade. Bird's company and that of Capt. Alexander W. Webb occupied it until March 1842, when it was apparently abandoned. The Sniveley expedition was disbanded at Bird's Fort in August 1843, and in September the fort housed a council of the Republic of Texas with nine Indian groups. It subsequently became the site of the Tarrant County community of Birdville, now part of northeast Fort Worth.   *Thomas W. Cutrer*

Black, William Leslie. Businessman and goat rancher; b. New Orleans, 1843; d. 11 May 1931; m. Camilla Bogert (1869); 10 children. Black left school at an early age to work for his father, joined the Confederate Army, and was wounded at Shiloh. After his recovery he served in the Confederate Navy, in which he ran cotton through the Union blockade to England. He was also part of an expedition against the Union Navy on the Pacific coast, was captured and imprisoned at Fort Alcatraz, and was sentenced to be hanged as a pirate but was pardoned. After the Civil War he lived in the Bahamas and New York, grew wealthy, helped to found the New York Cotton Exchange, traveled extensively, married, and in 1875 moved to St. Louis. The next year he purchased a ranch near Fort McKavett. He remained in St. Louis for several years, however, as an absentee landlord. Annually he made a trip to West Texas to inspect his cattle and sheep. When he learned that his herders preferred goat meat to mutton, he purchased goats to supply his men. By 1884, when with his family he moved permanently to the ranch, he had discovered the value of Angoras, a better breed that brought more money than the "Spanish" goat. After a few years of Angora breeding, he began shearing the animals for mohair. By the mid-1890s he became the nation's leading authority on Angoras. One of his business enterprises was the Range Canning Company, which canned goat meat and produced tallow and hides on the side. Black studied the Angora and wrote a booklet about the breed. The spirited response to this publication induced him to write *A New Industry—or Raising the Angora Goat* (1900), which remained a favorite manual for more than 40 years. Black's contributions to the industry helped to make the Edwards Plateau an economically productive region. In addition to this more important work, Black invented a cotton picker, patented a "special guide" for windmills, invented his Little Wonder Nut Sheller for use especially on his home-grown pecans, and secured with others a futures market for wool trading.   *Paul H. Carlson*

Black Bean Episode. An infamous aftermath of the Mier expedition. While the Mier prisoners were being marched to Mexico City, many of them escaped at Salado, Tamaulipas (11 February 1843); 176 were recaptured within about a week. A decree that all who participated in the break were to be executed was modified to an order to kill every tenth man. Col. Domingo Huerta was in charge of the decimation. The victims were chosen by lottery, each man drawing a bean from an earthen jar containing 176 beans, 17 black beans being the tokens signifying death. Commissioned officers were ordered to draw first; then the enlisted men were called as their names appeared on the muster rolls. William A. A. (Bigfoot) Wallace decided that the black beans were the larger and drew a white bean. Observers of the drawing later described the dignity, the firmness, the light temper, and general courage of the men who drew the beans of death. Some left messages for their families with their companions; a few had time to write letters home. The doomed men were unshackled from their companions, taken to a separate courtyard, and shot at dusk on 25 March. The victims of the lottery were James Decatur Cocke, William Mosby Eastland, Patrick Mahan, James M. Ogden, James N. Torrey, Martin Carroll Wing, John L. Cash, Robert Holmes Dunham, Edward E. Este, Robert Harris, Thomas L. Jones, Christopher Roberts, William N. Rowan, James L. Shepherd, J. N. M. Thompson, James Turnbull, and Henry Walling. Shepherd survived the firing squad by pretending to be dead; he escaped but was recaptured and killed. In 1848 the bodies were returned from Mexico to be buried at Monument Hill, near La Grange.

Blanton, Annie Webb. Suffragist; b. Houston, 19 August 1870; d. Austin, 2 October 1945; ed. University of Texas (grad. 1899; M.A., 1923), Cornell University (Ph.D., 1927). Annie Blanton, sister of

Annie Webb Blanton, ca. late 1920s. Prints and Photographs Collection, Annie Webb Blanton file, CAH; CN 03545.

U.S. Representative Thomas L. Blanton, taught English at North Texas State Normal College (1901–18), where she established herself as a suffragist and was elected president of the Texas State Teachers Association. In 1917 Texas suffragists found a sympathetic leader in William P. Hobby. They supported him in his 1918 bid for the Democratic gubernatorial nomination and asked Annie Blanton to run for state superintendent of public instruction. She was accused of being an atheist and of running as a tool for others, but she countered that the incumbent, Walter F. Doughty, was closely associated with impeached former governor James Ferguson and the beer interests. In the July 1918 primary, the first in which Texas women voted, Blanton won by a large margin. Her victory in the general election in November made her the first woman in Texas elected to statewide office. While she was state superintendent a system of free textbooks was established, teacher-certification laws were revised, teachers' salaries were raised, and efforts were made to improve rural education. She was reelected in November 1920, when voters also passed the Better Schools Amendment, which she had proposed as a means of removing constitutional limitations on tax rates for local school districts. In 1922 she did not seek a third term but ran unsuccessfully for Congress from Denton County. She taught in the UT education department until 1926, then took a leave of absence for Ph.D. work. After returning to UT in 1927, she remained a professor of education there for the rest of her life. Her works include *A Handbook of Information as to Education in Texas* (1922), *Advanced English Grammar* (1928), and *The Child of the Texas One-Teacher School* (1936). In 1929 she founded the Delta Kappa Gamma Society. She was a vice president in the National Education Association in 1917, 1919, and 1921. Public schools are named for her in Austin, Dallas, and Odessa, and a women's dormitory at the University of Texas at Austin bears her name. *Debbie Mauldin Cottrell*

Blocker, Dan. TV actor; b. Bobby Don Blocker, DeKalb, 10 December 1928; d. 13 May, 1972; m. Dolphia Lee Parker (1952); four children; ed. Hardin–Simmons University (B.A.), Sul Ross State Teachers College (M.A.), UCLA. Blocker, who was 6' 4" tall and weighed over 275 pounds, played football in college, where he became interested in acting. He turned down offers of professional careers in both football and boxing, acted in summer stock in Boston, and served in Korea. He taught school in Sonora and Carlsbad, New Mexico, before moving to California in 1956 to work on a Ph.D. at UCLA. He began his career as a professional actor in Los Angeles. In 1959 he was cast in the role of "Hoss" Cartwright on the NBC production "Bonanza," one of the longest-running and most popular TV series. Blocker was an enormously popular actor and successful businessman. He was co-owner of a nationwide chain of steakhouses called Bonanza. He received the Texan of the Year Award in 1963 from the Texas Press Association, and in 1966 he served as honorary chairman of the Texas Cancer Crusade. He played Hoss for 13 seasons on national television; "Bonanza" was terminated soon after his death.

Bluebonnet. The Texas state flower, *Lupinus subcarnosus*; adopted in 1901 by the state legislature, which in 1971 amended the law to include all varieties of bluebonnet. *L. subcarnosus* and *L. texensis* are native to Texas. At least four other species grow in the state. The flower usually blooms in late March and early April and is found mostly in limestone outcroppings from north central Texas to Mexico. In the 1930s the Highway Department began a landscaping and beautification program and extended the flower's range. Due largely to that agency's efforts, bluebonnets now grow along most major highways throughout the state, more or less profusely in accord with the amount of spring rain. *Jean Andrews*

Blue Norther. The term *blue norther* denotes a weather phenomenon common to large areas of the world's temperate zones—a rapidly moving autumnal cold front that causes temperatures to drop quickly and that often brings with it precipitation followed by a period of blue skies and cold weather. What is peculiar to Texas is the term itself. The derivation of *blue norther* is unclear; at least three folk attributions exist. The term refers, some say, to a norther that sweeps "out of the Panhandle under a blue-black sky"—that is, to a cold front named for the appearance of its leading edge. Another account states that the term refers to the appearance of the sky after the front has blown through, as the mid-nineteenth-century variant "blew-tailed norther" illustrates. Yet another derives the term from the fact that one supposedly turns blue from the cold brought by the front. Variants include *blue whistler*, used by J. Frank Dobie, and, in Oklahoma, *blue darter* and *blue blizzard*. Though the latter two phrases are found out-of-state, *blue norther* itself is a pure Texasism. The dramatic effects of the blue norther have been noted and exaggerated since Spanish times in Texas. But that the blue norther is unique to Texas is folklore. *Roy Barkley*

Board of Control. Established in 1919; composed of three members appointed by the governor for six-year, overlapping terms; replaced in 1979 by the State Purchasing and General Services Commission. The Board of Control purchased supplies for the state departments and eleemosynary and educational institutions, controlled the state's public buildings and grounds, rented extra buildings and offices for state agencies, prepared the biennial appropriation budget and submitted it to the governor, and controlled the state historical parks. It was responsible for the eleemosynary institutions until 1949, when administration was transferred to the new Board for Texas State Hospitals and Special Schools. In 1951 the Budget Division of the Board of Control was transferred to the governor's office. In 1953 the board was reorganized to comprise only three part-time gubernatorial appointees. The agency served as the chief purchasing office for state departments and institutions, audited and certified to the comptroller of public accounts all claims for goods sold to the state, and operated and maintaining the Capitol and other state buildings, the State Cemetery, and other state property in Austin. After the State Building Commission was established in 1954, that agency assumed the duties carried out by the Engineering Section of the Board of Control. The legislature later abolished the State Building Commission and transferred duties back to the board. In the 1970s the board's responsibilities included managing a system of telecommunications services for state agencies. It maintained a central office-supply store, messenger service, and telephone service, as well as an office-machine repair service. *Dick Smith*

Boatright, Mody Coggin. Folklorist; b. Mitchell County, 16 October 1896; d. Abilene, 20 August 1970; m. Elizabeth Reck

(1925; d. 1929); one daughter; m. Elizabeth Keefer (1931); 1 son; ed. West Texas State Teachers College (bachelor's degree, 1922), University of Texas (M.A., 1923; Ph.D., 1932). Boatright taught at Sul Ross State Teachers College before moving to UT (1926), where, except for a year at the College of Mines and Metallurgy in El Paso (1934–35), he stayed until retirement (1968). At UT, Boatright was associated with J. Frank Dobie and the Texas Folklore Society. Unlike many of his contemporaries, he retold stories in an unadorned and concise style close to true folk narration and recognized that in oral performance the tales were molded by the immediate situation. His work stressed the importance of studying folklore in its total cultural context. He also taught that folklore may arise out of conflict between different social groups, a view at variance with the then-common notion that folklore was the result of the shared experiences of an isolated "folk." His major works include *Tall Tales from Texas Cow Camps* (1934), *Big Morgan: Minstrel of the Oil Fields* (1945), *Folk Laughter on the American Frontier* (1949), *The Family Saga and Other Phases of American Folklore* (with others, 1958), *Folklore of the Oil Industry* (1963), and *Tales from the Derrick Floor*, a pioneer work in oral history (with William A. Owens, 1970). Three years after his death *Mody Boatright, Folklorist*, a collection of his essays, was published. Boatright was a member of the Texas Institute of Letters and the Writers Guild.

Ernest B. Speck

Boll Weevil. One of the most devastating pests in American agriculture; a snout beetle (*Anthonomus grandis*) first named by Carl H. Boheman, a Swedish systematist. Ancient specimens have been found from the earliest times in the Valley of Mexico. American entomologists became aware of the boll weevil as a cotton pest as early as 1880, but its first introduction to Texas seems to have been announced by Charles W. DeRyee, a druggist of Corpus Christi, in a letter dated 3 October 1894. The insect is about one-fourth inch long and changes from white to black as it matures. The beetles are susceptible to winter freezes, and those that survive hibernation emerge in the spring to feed for five or six weeks on the tender growth of young cotton plants. They eat and lay eggs in the cotton buds and new bolls. Each punctured bud or boll falls to the ground and becomes food for the eggs, which hatch in two or three days. The boll weevil migrated across the Rio Grande and had spread from the Valley to the north and east boundaries of the state by the beginning of the twentieth century. By 1903 it covered all of eastern Texas to the Edwards Plateau, and by the 1920s it had reached north and west to the High Plains, encompassing all the areas of Texas cotton culture. The infestation caused a steady drop in cotton yields for 30 years. In the South Texas fields in 1904 the loss was estimated at 700,000 bales, worth $42 million. A 6 percent yield reduction in 1910 leaped to a 34 percent reduction in 1921; 53 years later the per-acre yield reduction due to boll weevils still hovered at 7 percent and cost an estimated $260 million a year. The boll weevil was resistant to conventional insecticides and antipest practices. Its spread from Mexico depended on a combination of appropriate weather and cultivation practices, coupled with a shortage of cotton gins. Cotton bolls with seed were often transported from the lower Rio Grande valley to gins as far north as Alice, and this practice may have contributed to the spread of the weevil.

C. H. Tyler Townsend, one of the many colorful personalities involved in the early fight against the boll weevil, traveled through southern Texas in 1894 and reported as much as 90 percent crop damage. In 1899 the state appointed entomologist Frederick W. Mally to direct state efforts to combat the insect. Mally launched a cultivation plan intended to produce crops early, before the weevils multiplied. But record freezes that delayed early planting, heavy rainfall, and the great Galveston hurricane of 1900 all combined to help spread the boll weevil in spite of Mally's brilliant but underfunded labors. E. Dwight Sanderson, who succeeded Mally (1901), continued many of Mally's programs. The Texas legislature offered a $50,000 prize for discovery of a way to rid Texas of the weevil (1913), and the governor appointed a Boll Weevil Commission to judge the contest. This episode made the legislature and the boll weevil a figure of fun for newspapers throughout the nation, a putative illustration of the foolishness of lawmaking bodies. Meanwhile, on Walter C. Porter's demonstration farm at Terrell, Seaman A. Knapp led the work that later served as a model for the National Extension Service. The boll weevil continued to spread year by year—through Louisiana, Arkansas, Mississippi, Alabama, the Carolinas, Tennessee, and Virginia. By World War I calcium arsenate had been found reasonably effective in poisoning the insect, and during the 1920s fluorides were introduced. Mally's cultivation practices continued to be a sensible and important way to manage infestations. Organic pesticides and traps dependent on synthetic pheromones have not been so effective with the boll weevil as they have been with other insects. The possibility of eradication of the organism simply by suspending cotton culture for two or more years over a broad region has not been disproved, but neither has it been fully tested. Since the boll weevil does not survive well on the High Plains, this region seems to be more favorable to future cotton production than the coastal areas.

Frank Wagner

Bolton, Herbert Eugene. Historian; b. Wilton, Wisconsin, 20 July 1870; d. Berkeley, California, 30 January 1953; m. Gertrude James (1895); 7 children; ed. University of Wisconsin (bachelor's degree, 1895) and University of Pennsylvania (Ph.D., 1899). Bolton studied under Frederick Jackson Turner and John Bach McMaster. In 1901 he went as instructor of history to the University of Texas, where he remained until 1909. Though he taught medieval and European history at UT, he soon developed a lively interest in the history of Spanish expansion in North America. Beginning in the summer of 1902, he made a series of pioneering forays into archives in Mexico. At the invitation of the Carnegie Institution he prepared a report on materials for United States history in Mexican archives (1913). Bolton was an associate editor of the *Quarterly of the Texas State Historical Association* (now the *Southwestern Historical Quarterly*). In 1904 he and his colleague Eugene C. Barker published a textbook, *With the Makers of Texas: A Source Reader in Texas History*. Beginning in 1906 Bolton studied the history of Indians in Texas for the United States Bureau of Ethnology and wrote more than 100 articles for the *Handbook of American Indians North of Mexico*. His interest in Texas history was reflected in more than a dozen learned articles as well as in his published volumes on *Athanase de Mézières and the Louisiana–Texas Frontier, 1768–1780* (1914), and *Texas in the Middle Eighteenth Century: Studies in Spanish Colonial History and Administration* (1915). Bolton declined the presidency of the University of Texas in 1914.

From 1909 to 1911 he was professor of American history at Stanford University, and from 1911 until his retirement in 1940 he was professor of history at the University of California, Berkeley. From 1919 to 1940, except for two years, he served as chairman of the history department, and for the same 22 years he was director of the Bancroft Library. At the University of California he inaugurated a course called "History of the Americas," in which he emphasized the need to study the Americas as a whole. He outlined this thesis in his presidential address to the American Historical Association at Toronto in 1932. His bibliography consists of 94 entries, including nearly two dozen books written or edited. His concept of the Spanish Borderlands, the crescent-shaped area from Georgia to California, as a fruitful field for study and interpretation was an important addition to historical thought. More than 300 master's theses and 100 doctoral dissertations were written under his supervision.   *John Haskell Kemble*

Bone Business. The best years of the Texas bone business were 1870 to 1937. Freighters returning to Kansas from Texas forts loaded their empty wagons with buffalo bones and piled them along the right-of-way of the Atchison, Topeka and Santa Fe Railway. A good report on their industrial use reached Kansas at about the same time that the AT&SF rails arrived. The railroad therefore set off a boom of bone picking, hauling, and shipping in 1872. As this business died down in 1874, the slaughter of the Texas buffalo herd began. When it ended in 1878, it had added many thousands of fresh bones to the old from the Cross Timbers to the upper Panhandle to below the Colorado River and up the Pecos River and other streams into New Mexico. Half a dozen bone roads ran northward to points along the AT&SF and other lines, and at least as many went eastward to the rail heads built in Northeast and Central Texas in the 1870s. As many as 100 bone wagons traveled together. A king-sized wagon drawn by oxen or mules, plus its two trailers, could carry 10,000 pounds of bones. When the panic of 1873 stopped rail construction, bone pickers rushed into the field and raised hundreds of "little mountains" of bones along the right-of-ways. Freighters hauled out army, merchant, and ranch supplies and brought back bones. Agents, brokers, buyers, and speculators bought piles, and freighters hauled them to the rails or to intermediate points. San Antonio shipped 3,333 tons between July 1877 and November 1878. Resumption of rail construction brought new opportunities for marketing, and for several years in the early 1880s Texas led the world as a source of bones. Prices climbed from $3 to $4 a ton in the early seventies to as high as $23 briefly in the eighties, then settled around $8 by the end of the century. Texas bones went to Baltimore, Boston, Detroit, Harrisburg, New Orleans, New York, Philadelphia, St. Louis, and Europe. Old bones were ground into meal, fresh ones supplied refineries with calcium phosphate to neutralize cane-juice acid and decolor sugar, choice bones went to bone-china furnaces for calcium phosphate ash, and firm bones went to button factories.

Abilene, Sweetwater, and other towns had their great bone piles. Several stretched a half mile along the tracks and were 30 feet wide and 16 high. Colorado City became the largest Texas and Pacific shipping point. Hundreds of families beat droughts, debts, and famine by picking and selling bones. Huge piles of bones were built by men like James Kilfoile and his crews, who worked ahead of the rail gangs laying tracks. One picker piled up 80 tons at Big Spring and sold the heap for $4,000. To avoid "bone wars" pickers recognized the unwritten law of right of discovery, preemption, and priority to a reasonable area. Cattle bones supplanted buffalo bones before 1900. By the 1920s each county had several bone men, who would keep pastures clean of bones. In the 1930s "boning" temporarily returned to popularity to ease woes of the Great Depression. But with economic recovery and the discovery of a new process of making bone meal, it declined permanently. The bone business had contributed greatly to the freight and rail business and saved many families from being forced back East in the early days. One source estimates that Texas alone shipped out a half million tons of buffalo bones, worth $3 million at $6 a ton.   *Ralph A. Smith*

Bonham, James Butler. Officer of the Alamo garrison; b. Red Banks (now Saluda), South Carolina, 20 February 1807; d. San Antonio, 6 March 1836; ed. South Carolina College (never graduated). Bonham, something of a martinet, was expelled from South Carolina College for leading a protest against the school's poor food; later, as an attorney, he was sentenced to 90 days for threatening to tweak a judge's nose. In 1832, during the Nullification crisis, he was an aide to South Carolina governor James Hamilton, a position that brought him the rank of lieutenant colonel of the militia. At the same time he served as captain of a Charleston artillery company. By October 1834 he was practicing law in Montgomery, Alabama. On 17 October 1835 he led a rally of support for the Texan cause at the Shakespeare Theater in Mobile. Three days later he was elected by citizens of Mobile to carry their resolutions of support to Sam Houston. In another two weeks he was organizing a volunteer company, the Mobile Grays, for service in Texas. Bonham reached Texas in November 1835 and quickly involved himself in political and military affairs. On 1 December he wrote to Houston from San Felipe volunteering his services for Texas and declining all pay, lands, or rations in return. On 20 December he was commissioned a second lieutenant in the Texas cavalry, but apparently was not assigned to any specific unit. He had time to set up a law practice in Brazoria and was advertising in the *Telegraph and Texas Register* by 2 January 1836. He and Houston quickly developed a mutual admiration. Houston recommended to James W. Robinson that Bonham be promoted to major, for "His influence in the army is great—more so than some who 'would be generals'." Bonham probably traveled to the Alamo with James Bowie and arrived on 19 January. He was appointed one of a committee of seven to draft a preamble and resolutions on behalf of the garrison in support of provisional governor Henry Smith. On 1 February he was an unsuccessful candidate in the election of delegates to represent the Bexar garrison at the Texas constitutional convention. He was sent by Col. William B. Travis to obtain aid for the garrison on or about 16 February and returned to the Alamo on 3 March, bearing through the Mexican lines a letter from Robert M. Williamson assuring Travis that help was on its way and urging him to hold out. Bonham died in the battle of the Alamo (6 March 1836), probably while manning one of the cannons in the interior of the chapel. His life and role in the siege and battle have been romanticized more than those of any other defender. He has often been portrayed as a colonel and one of the commanders of the Alamo garrison, although Travis's reference to him as "Colonel" is a mere honorific dating back to Bonham's days with the South Carolina militia. His

Cotton compress and workers, ca. 1910. Courtesy TSL. Bonham was an agricultural and commercial center from the time of the Civil War. The Bonham Cotton Mill, once the largest west of the Mississippi, was chartered in 1900.

actual rank was second lieutenant, and he had no standing in the Alamo chain of command. Bonham is wrongly remembered as bringing the news that Fannin was not coming to Travis's aid, when he actually brought the message from Williamson that help *was* coming. In 1936 the Texas Centennial Commission placed a statue of Bonham on the courthouse square in Bonham, the town named in his honor.   *Bill Groneman*

Bonham, Texas. County seat of Fannin County; 12 miles south of the Red River on the northern edge of the Blackland Prairie. Early settler Bailey Inglish built Fort Inglish on the site in 1837, and he and John P. Simpson donated land for the town of Bois d'Arc. The town was declared the county seat of Fannin County in 1843 and was renamed Bonham, in honor of Alamo hero James B. Bonham, in 1844. Bonham incorporated in 1848 and became a supply point and agricultural center for North Texans. A succession of colleges made the town an educational center in the second half of the nineteenth century. During the Civil War, Confederate headquarters for the northern subdistrict of Texas was located in the town. In 1873 Bonham was a division point on the Texas and Pacific railroad, and in 1887 the Denison, Bonham

and New Orleans connected Bonham to Denison. By the 1880s Bonham was shipping row crops including grain and cotton, and in 1900 the Bonham Cotton Mill, once the largest west of the Mississippi, was chartered. The city benefited from public works projects during the Great Depression. World War II brought an airbase and a POW camp. After the war livestock replaced row crops as the principal shipment and light industry developed. In 1990 Bonham had a population of 6,686. The Sam Rayburn House and Sam Rayburn Library commemorate the town's most famous citizen; a replica of Fort Inglish, Bonham State Recreation Area, and Lake Bonham are local attractions. Bonham hosts the annual Fannin County Fair.   *Diana J. Kleiner*

Bonnie and Clyde. Outlaws: Bonnie Parker (b. Rowena, Texas, 10 October 1910) and Clyde Barrow (b. near Telico, Texas, 24 March 1909). This infamous couple got together in 1930. Clyde, who had a burgeoning career as a burglar and convict, went back to jail soon after he met Bonnie, a pint-sized "honor student." She smuggled a pistol to him in jail. After his escape, the two started the trail of murders and robberies for which they are notorious. First with Raymond Hamilton, then with Clyde's

Gail Borden, Jr., and son John. Courtesy Rosenberg Library, Galveston.

members of the San Felipe de Austin committee of correspondence. In the Convention of 1833 he represented the Lavaca District . He also assumed many of the duties of colonial secretary for Austin in the absence of Samuel M. Williams. In 1835 he began publishing the *Telegraph and Texas Register* with his brother Thomas and Joseph Baker. He made the first topographical map of Texas. He served as collector for the Department of Brazos (1835–37) and helped lay out the site of Houston (1836). In 1837 he sold his partnership in the *Telegraph* to Jacob W. Cruger and became the first collector of the port of Galveston under the Republic of Texas. His first period as collector lasted until President Lamar removed him for political reasons (December 1838); he was again collector from December 1841 to April 1843, when he resigned after a dispute with President Sam Houston. From 1839 to 1851 Borden was secretary and agent for the Galveston City Company, which owned most of Galveston Island and for which he helped sell 2,500 lots. He invented a "locomotive bath house" for women who wished to bathe in the Gulf of Mexico. As an alderman he helped to rid the island temporarily of gamblers. He and his first wife reputedly became the first Anglo-Americans to be baptized in the Gulf west of the Mississippi River. Borden was a trustee of the Texas Baptist Education Society, which founded Baylor University, as well as an officer in the local temperance society and deacon and clerk of the local Baptist church. In 1842 he directed insular defenses against an expected Mexican invasion.

In the middle 1840s he began inventing. He is supposed to have experimented with large-scale refrigeration as a means of preventing yellow fever and with a "terraqueous" machine, a sort of prairie schooner that would go on land or water. In 1849 he perfected a meat biscuit, made of dehydrated meat compounded with flour, which he tried to market worldwide in partnership with Ashbel Smith. Although this project left him deeply in debt, for seven years Borden struggled to sell meat biscuits and moved to New York in 1851 to be nearer trade centers. In 1853 he sought a patent on a process for condensing milk in vacuum, but it was 1856 before he received American and British patents. He opened a factory in Connecticut in 1856 but failed, then tried and failed again in 1857. Through Jeremiah Milbank, a New York financier, he received new backing and opened another factory in Connecticut in 1858. When the Civil War intensified the demand for condensed milk, sales grew so much that the Borden Company's success was assured. He opened factories in Connecticut, New York, and Illinois and licensed other concerns in Pennsylvania and Maine. He also invented processes for condensing various fruit juices, for making extract of beef, and for condensing coffee. After the Civil War he established a meat-packing plant at Borden, Texas, twelve miles west of Columbus, and a sawmill and copperware factory at Bastrop. After 1871 he spent his winters in Texas because of the milder climate. In 1873 he built a freedmen's school and a white children's school, organized a day school and a Sunday school for black children, aided in constructing five churches, maintained two missionaries, and partially supported numerous poorly paid teachers, ministers, and students. After his death his body was shipped by private car to New York to be buried in Woodlawn Cemetery.

Joe B. Frantz

brother Buck and Buck's wife Blanche, Bonnie and Clyde robbed banks and killed people, mainly lawmen, for three years of generally uninterrupted hell-raising. On 24 May 1933 a group of lawmen, led by former Texas Ranger Frank Hamer and FBI special agent L. A. Kindell, exterminated the two near Gibsland, Louisiana. The bodies were taken to Arcadia and later put on public display in Dallas before being buried. In later years Clyde and Bonnie were sometimes characterized as latter-day Robin Hoods. Their exploits became the basis of more than a half dozen movies, most notably *Bonnie and Clyde* (1967), starring Warren Beatty and Faye Dunaway. The originals were often compared with the other criminal figures of the Great Depression era, including John Dillinger and Al Capone. Bonnie and Clyde, like these famous sociopaths, were both ruthless killers who displayed no conscience or remorse. (According to a witness, for instance, Bonnie remarked about a policeman whom she had just shot in the head that "his head bounced just like a rubber ball.") But in marked contrast to the legendary gangsters of the era, the Barrow gang were failures—small-time hoods whose largest haul was only $1,500.

Christopher Long and Kristi Strickland

Borden, Gail, Jr. Inventor, publisher, and surveyor; b. Norwich, New York, 9 November 1901; d. Borden, Texas, 11 January 1874; m. Penelope Mercer (1828); 7 children; m. Augusta Stearns (1845); m. Emeline Eunice Church (1860). Borden surveyed and taught school in Mississippi before moving to Texas (1829), where he farmed and raised stock in upper Fort Bend County. By February 1830 he had succeeded his brother Thomas as surveyor for Stephen F. Austin's colony. In 1832 he was named one of three

Borger, Asa Phillip. Town builder; b. near Carthage, Missouri, 12 April 1888; d. Borger, 31 August 1934; m. Elizabeth Willoughby (ca. 1907). When World War I broke out in Europe, "Ace" Borger and his brother Lester (nicknamed Pete) began selling real estate in Picher, Oklahoma, a town that profited from its lead production during the war. In 1917 the Borgers and noted wildcatter Tom Slick laid out the oil town of Slick near Bristow, Oklahoma. At each town the Borgers and their associates built hotels, filling stations, and lumberyards, sold real estate, and pushed for the building of railroad lines to the sites. In 1922 they successfully launched Cromwell, Oklahoma, as a boomtown. Attracted by the Panhandle oilfield, Borger bought 240 acres from rancher John Frank Weatherly and obtained a grant from Texas secretary of state Emma Grigsby Meharg to organize the Borger Townsite Company. The company laid out the town and opened the sale of lots in 1926. By the end of the first day, it had grossed between $60,000 and $100,000, and after six months Borger sold out completely. He established a lumberyard in the town named for him and opened its first bank. Often he took out full-page ads in area papers promoting settlement in Borger and other oil-rich sites in which he had bought an interest. He also owned a string of Panhandle wheat elevators and 19,000 acres of farmland in Hansford County. In 1927 Ace and Pete Borger, in association with Albert S. Stinnett, established the towns of Stinnett and Gruver. In 1929 Borger built his wife the first brick residence in Borger. From the beginning he had set aside building sites for churches and schools. The Borgers became known for hospitality, but their manner of living inspired hatred in county treasurer Arthur Huey, particularly after failure of the bank of which Borger was president. Borger was convicted of receiving deposits in the insolvent bank and assessed a two-year prison term, a judgment that he appealed. Meanwhile, Huey was jailed for embezzlement and reportedly asked Borger to help bail him out. After Borger refused, Huey shot him to death at the post office. At his trial, which was held in Canadian, Huey claimed that Borger had been gunning for him and that he had shot in self-defense. The jury acquitted him. Three years later, however, he was sent to the state penitentiary for theft of county funds. Borger was buried in the family plot at Carthage, Missouri. The Borger house is now a Texas historical landmark. *H. Allen Anderson*

Boss Rule. During the second half of the nineteenth century and the first part of the twentieth, boss rule became a prevalent pattern of political organization in the big cities of the United States. Typically, a clique of politicians dominated the political life of a city by manipulating the votes of large numbers of immigrants. The bosses resorted to bribery and coercion, but they also won the support of hard-pressed newcomers by providing informal welfare services and limited opportunities for upward mobility. Businessmen as well often embraced the systems to secure special favors from city government. Some historians have argued that the centralization of authority resulting from boss rule was an essential step in solving social problems growing out of rapid urban growth. Such concentration of political power in the hands of a few has not been uncommon in Texas cities during the twentieth century. In cities like Dallas and Houston, powerful business interests prevailed. Their candidates usually carried the city elections. The corporate leaders also directly decided such basic social issues as the pace of racial integration in Dallas.

Nevertheless, the basic features of Texas boss rule are somewhat different from this business-oriented model. The truest and most notorious form of machine politics took root in South Texas during the closing decades of the nineteenth century and was still visible in some counties 90 years later. Stephen Powers and James B. Wells, Jr., oversaw the establishment of a Democratic political machine in Cameron County during the 1870s and 1880s. The ring retained control of Cameron County politics until 1920 and contributed to the formation of similar organizations in Hidalgo, Starr, and Duval counties. All of the South Texas Democratic machines followed the same pattern of operation. While manipulating the vote of the Hispanic majority and engaging in varying degrees of graft, the bosses and their cohorts served the interests of their constituencies. In the courts and the state legislature, lawyer-politicians defended the ambiguous and sometimes suspect land claims of local ranchers. The politicos held land taxes to a minimum and lobbied for the deployment of Texas Rangers to maintain order and intimidate the Mexican masses, who had shown signs of rebelliousness against white domination during an earlier era. The bosses catered to the needs of land speculators, developers, bankers, and merchants by promoting the extension of railroad lines to this remote section of the state. To the Mexican-American laborers the South Texas politicians offered paternalistic services modeled after the feudalistic obligations of Mexican *patrones* to their *peones*. In return for relief during hard times and the financing of weddings, funerals, and other special occasions, lower-class Mexican Americans submitted to the political control of the bosses. Anglo politicians also reached an accommodation with the well-to-do Hispanic families who were able to retain their lands and businesses in the face of the American onslaught after the Civil War. Manuel Guerra was the political boss of Starr County from 1905 until his death in 1915.

Thousands of white settlers came to South Texas, especially when large-scale irrigation was introduced in the lower Rio Grande valley. Racial hatred intensified during the border violence accompanying the Mexican Revolution. These influences fueled a widespread rebellion against boss rule in South Texas after 1900. The white challengers to the Democratic machines expressed both a commitment to honest, businesslike public administration and a racist contempt for Hispanic involvement in politics. Still the machines displayed remarkable resilience. Although the Wells machine of Cameron County collapsed in 1920, the Hidalgo County organization under John Closner and later Anderson Baker survived until 1930. The Guerra family continued to rule Starr County until 1946, when another Hispanic-controlled organization established its dominance. The most notorious of all the South Texas rings, the Duval County structure headed by Archer Parr from 1908 until his death in 1942 and then by his son George Parr, lasted until 1975. The rule of the Parrs weathered public outcries over apparent political murders, repeated state and federal investigations into blatant acts of graft and election fraud, and even the imprisonment of George Parr in 1936 for income-tax evasion. The Parr machine gained nationwide attention in 1948 when late and allegedly fraudulent election returns from Duval County and neighboring Jim Wells County gave Lyndon Johnson a narrow primary victory over Coke Stevenson in the United States Senate race. At different times, political machines dependent on Hispanic support have existed in Corpus Christi, Laredo, and El Paso, but Texas-style boss rule left its most enduring imprint on the rural counties of South Texas. Not even the suicide of George

Parr and the collapse of his organization in 1975 brought this political phenomenon to an end. *Evan Anders*

Boundaries. In the middle of the twentieth century the boundaries of Texas were 2,845.3 miles long, counting the great arc of the Gulf Coast line and only the larger river bends. If the smaller meanderings of the rivers and the tidewater coastline were followed, the boundary was 4,137 miles long and enclosed 263,644 square miles of land and 3,695 square miles of water surface. The location of Texas boundaries has been the subject of international and interstate conflict resulting in treaties, litigation, and commissions from 1736 to the present. Controversy over details continues, as the Tidelands Controversy and the Chamizal Dispute illustrate. In 1995 the state legislature authorized a Red River Boundary Commission to fix the boundary between Oklahoma and Texas, where the still-shifting Red River has frequently changed course and muddied the issue for two centuries.

The eastern boundary was the first to become the subject of controversy and the first to be marked definitely. Both Spain and France claimed the area of present Texas, and by 1716 Spanish presidios at Los Adaes and French trading posts at Natchitoches were separated by only a few miles. In 1736 the commanders at the two outposts agreed on the Arroyo Hondo, a Red River tributary between the Sabine River and Natchitoches, as the boundary between Louisiana and New Spain. After Louisiana was ceded to Spain in 1762, the Arroyo Hondo continued to be regarded as the boundary between the province of Louisiana, a subdivision of the captaincy-general of Cuba, and the province of Texas, a subdivision of the commandancy-general of the Provincias Internas. When the United States purchased Louisiana in 1803, the boundary of the purchase was not defined, but early in 1804 President Jefferson decided that the territory extended to the Rio Grande. To refute this claim Spain began to investigate her historic claim to the Texas area. Father Melchor de Talamantes and later José Antonio Pichardo made detailed studies of the limits of Louisiana and Texas. While they made academic investigations of the historic boundaries, Spanish forces, in 1806, moved east of the Sabine River to repel an anticipated invasion by Aaron Burr. In order to avert a clash, James Wilkinson and Simón de Herrera, the United States and Spanish military commanders, entered into an agreement that established the Neutral Ground, the area between the Arroyo Hondo and the Sabine River, as a buffer. The makeshift arrangement lasted until 1819, when the Adams–Onís Treaty between Spain and the United States defined the eastern boundary of Texas as beginning at the mouth of the Sabine River, continuing along the west bank of the river to its intersection with the thirty-second parallel, and running due north from that intersection to the Red River. Spain delayed ratification of the Adams–Onís Treaty until 1821. By that time Mexico had declared her independence of Spain and refused to recognize the treaty boundary line. In 1828, after repeated efforts by the United States, the Mexican administration agreed to a survey of the 1819 line, but the Mexican congress refused to confirm the survey treaty until 1832, and then the line remained unsurveyed. Meanwhile, between 1819 and 1836 the Neches River was occasionally advanced as the eastern boundary of Texas. In 1840–41 a survey was made of that portion of the line between the Republic of Texas and the United States from the Gulf of Mexico to the Red River by a joint commission representing the two countries.

On 5 July 1848 the United States Congress passed an act giving its consent to the state of Texas to move its eastern boundary from the west bank of the Sabine River (including Sabine Pass and Sabine Lake) to the middle of that stream, and on 21 November 1849 the Texas legislature enacted a law to that effect. The boundary was unchallenged from that time until 1941, when Louisiana governor Sam Jones wrote Texas governor Coke Stevenson, asserting that Louisiana's western border was the west bank of the Sabine River. Louisiana's claim rested on United States treaties of 1819 with Spain, 1828 with Mexico, and 1838 with the Republic of Texas, all of which designated the west bank of the Sabine as the boundary of the United States. However, the boundary of the United States at the west bank of the Sabine River was not identical to that of the Louisiana boundary, which extended only to the middle of the river. The state of Louisiana contended that the United States was negotiating on Louisiana's behalf and consequently had no authority to grant Texas the western half of the river in the act of 1848. It was more than 27 years after Governor Jones's letter to Governor Stevenson before Louisiana participated in any legal proceedings. United States district judge Robert Van Pelt, special master for the United States Supreme Court, heard the claims and recommended to the court, in a report filed in May 1972, that the boundary between Texas and Louisiana should be the geographic middle of the Sabine River, Sabine Lake, and Sabine Pass. He also recommended that Louisiana be awarded all islands that existed in the river on 8 April 1812 (the date Louisiana was admitted to the Union), subject, however, to any claims that Texas might make to any such islands by reason of acquiescence and prescription; that all islands formed in the eastern half of the Sabine River since 1812 be awarded to Louisiana; and that all islands formed in the western half of the river since 1812 be awarded to Texas. Sixty-one square miles of the river and lake was involved in the dispute; at stake were land measuring more than 35,000 acres, four producing oil wells, and $2.6 million in oil-lease bonuses collected by Texas. Both states filed exceptions to the recommendations by the special master in July 1972, and after answers to each state's exceptions the Supreme Court was to rule on the master's report. The case was argued before the court in December 1972; the court's ruling came early in March 1973, saying, in effect, that the boundary was the geographic middle of the Sabine River. However, the case was sent back to the special master for further study in regard to the ownership of islands and also to determine the extension of the boundary into the Gulf of Mexico.

Except for the possible claim of the Rio Grande as the western boundary for the Louisiana purchase, the western boundary of Texas had no significance in international relations and practically no mention in Mexican interstate relations before Texas independence (1836). In 1721 the Medina River was considered the boundary between Texas and Coahuila; in 1811 the Nueces River was the boundary between Texas and Tamaulipas. Provisions of the secret treaty of Velasco, which bound the Mexican army to retreat beyond the Rio Grande and Texas not to claim land beyond that river, was the beginning of the Texas claim to the Rio Grande as the western boundary. On 19 December 1836 the First Congress of the republic declared the southern and western boundary of Texas to be the Rio Grande from its mouth to its source and thence a line due north to the fortysecond parallel. The Texan Santa Fe expedition of 1841 was an unsuccessful attempt to assert Texas authority in the New Mexico area embraced in that land claim. Texas claimed the same western limits after annexation. The Treaty of Guadalupe Hidalgo (1848) affirmed the Rio Grande boundary to El Paso as the international boundary, but the Texas claim to New Mexico, then occupied by United States troops, remained in dispute. Texas decreed a county, Santa Fe County, to include the area, but the people of New Mexico protested the Texas claim. After prolonged debate in Congress and the Texas newspapers and near-armed dispute, an adjustment was reached in the Compromise of 1850. The compromise line ran the Texas western boundary from El Paso east along the 32d parallel to the 103d meridian, up that meridian to 36°30" latitude, and along that line to the 100th meridian, thence down the 100th meridian to the Red River. The 36-30 line was chosen since Texas was a slave state and that line had been established in 1820 as the Missouri Compromise line between slave and free territory in the Louisiana Purchase. After 1850 the line was apparently fixed, but the boundary was not. An error in the surveying of the western line gave Texas a strip about two miles wide west of the 103d meridian, and Congress confirmed the boundary, as surveyed, in a joint resolution of 11 February 1911. But shifts in the channel of the Rio Grande necessitated other changes. In 1929 the Supreme Court assigned to Texas 25,000 acres of former New Mexican land lying on the western side of the channel of the river. The Rio Grande Rectification Project, authorized in 1933, provided for the exchange of 3,500 acres of land, part of it in the El Paso area, between the United States and Mexico. The International Boundary and Water Commission is a permanent agency with jurisdiction over the boundary questions on the Rio Grande.

As defined in the Adams–Onís Treaty of 1819, the northern and northwestern boundary of Texas followed the course of the Red River westward to the 100th meridian and north along that meridian to the Arkansas River, the whole line as depicted in the Melish map of 1818. Then the Compromise of 1850 placed the north line of the Panhandle at 36°30". No problem arose over this boundary until 1858, when A. H. Jones and H. M. Brown, who had been employed to locate the 100th meridian in making surveys of grants to various Indian tribes, discovered that the Melish map had erroneously located that meridian 100 miles too far east. In 1852 Randolph B. Marcy discovered that there were two main branches of the Red River lying between the Melish line and the 100th meridian. The supposedly correct meridian was surveyed in 1860, the same year that the Texas legislature decreed Greer County. Because of the Civil War and Reconstruction, Greer County was not organized until 1886 and was in process of being settled when the United States land commissioner protested the Texas claim to the land north of the Prairie Dog Town Fork of the Red River. The controversy went to the United States Supreme Court, which ruled on 16 March 1896 that the Texas boundary was the south or Prairie Dog Town Fork of the Red River and the astronomical 100th meridian.

The northern boundary again became controversial in 1919, when Texas drillers discovered oil in the bed of the Red River just north of Burkburnett. Oklahoma claimed the bed of the river and sued Texas for title in the Supreme Court. The Greer County case had defined the Texas boundary as the south bank of the Red River, but Texas claimed that the south bank in 1919 was not the same as the south bank at the time of the Melish map and the treaty of 1819. The contest became a three-cornered suit, with Oklahoma claiming the entire riverbed, Texas claiming title to the south half, and the United States disputing both claims and asserting ownership of the south half as trustee for the Indians. The decision in the four-year suit was rendered on 15 January 1923. In it the Supreme Court defined a riverbank as the bank cut by the normal flow of water, or where vegetation stopped, gave Oklahoma the north half of the bed and political control of the entire bed, and gave the United States the south half of the bed as trustee for the Indians, but allowed Texas to retain control of the oil wells in the floodplain between the riverbanks. To prevent further dispute, the court ordered a survey of the south bank as it was in 1819 and the placing of concrete markers along the survey line. The report of Arthur Kidder and Arthur H. Stiles, the commissioners who made the survey, was accepted in 1927.

In the meantime, in 1920 Texas sued Oklahoma on the grounds that the surveys of the 100th meridian made in 1858 and 1860 had erroneously placed that meridian a half mile too far west. Surveys made in 1892 and 1902 had not solved the problem of ownership of an area 134 miles long and between 3,600 and 3,700 feet wide. One Oklahoma resident complained that she had not moved a foot in 45 years but had lived in one territory, two states, and three counties. In 1927 the Supreme Court ordered Samuel S. Gannett to survey the meridian. He worked from 1927 to 1929, largely at night to avoid the aberrations of heat waves, and placed concrete markers at every two-thirds of a mile. The court ruled in 1930 that the Gannett line was the true meridian. Oklahoma tried unsuccessfully to buy back the strip that the Texas legislature incorporated in 1931 in Lipscomb, Hemphill, Wheeler, Childress, and Collingsworth counties. Higgins was the only town in the ceded area.

Bourland, James G. Soldier and state senator; b. South Carolina, 11 August 1801; d. Texas, 20 August 1879; m. Catherine Wells; m. Nancy Salina; total of 7 children. Bourland traded in slaves and horses in Kentucky and Tennessee before moving to the future Lamar County in 1837. He fought against Indians and in the Mexican War, served as a deputy surveyor and collector of customs, and was elected to the Senate of the First and Second state legislatures. In 1851 he invested in a mercantile enterprise and founded a plantation on land now in Cooke County, where he again led a volunteer company against Indians. During the Civil War he served as provost marshal and in that role directed the investigation that climaxed with the Great Hanging at Gainesville in 1862. Afterward, he was eventually given control of all troops on the northwestern frontier. He was accused of atrocities, but Confederate officials ignored the accusations. After the war ended he received a presidential pardon and was acquitted by a civil court.   *Richard B. McCaslin*

Bowie, James. Alamo hero; b. Logan (now Simpson) County, Kentucky, probably 10 April 1796; d. San Antonio, 6 March 1836; m. Ursula de Veramendi (1831); 2 (?) children. In 1800 the family moved to Madrid, now in Missouri, and the next year they settled in Louisiana and swore fealty to Spain. In his teens Bowie worked in Avoyelles and Rapides parishes, where he floated lumber to market. He invested in property on the Bayou Boeuf and traded in 1817–18 at what is now Bennett's Store, south of Cheneyville. He and his brother Rezin participated in the War of 1812. Afterward, they traded in slaves bought from Jean Laffite. When they had $65,000 they quit the business. They also dabbled in land speculation and developed friendships with local wealthy planters. James became engaged to Cecelia Wells, who died in 1829, two weeks before their wedding was to take place. After James had a near-deadly quarrel with Norris Wright, Rapides parish sheriff and local banker, Rezin gave his brother a large butcher-like hunting knife to carry. On 19 September 1827, near Natchez, Bowie participated in the Sandbar Fight, where he was seriously wounded and where he wielded the first "Bowie knife" to good effect. Reports of Bowie's prowess and his lethal blade captured public attention, and he was proclaimed the South's most formidable knife fighter. Men asked blacksmiths and cutlers to make a knife like Jim Bowie's. During the late 1820s Bowie speculated on land in southern Louisiana and lived in New Orleans. He and his brothers Rezin and Stephen established Arcadia, a sugar plantation, in Terrebonne Parish, where they set up the first steam-powered sugar mill in Louisiana. Rezin was elected to the Louisiana state legislature. James traveled to the East as well as to Arkansas and Mississippi. In 1831 the brothers sold Arcadia.

When Bowie first entered Texas is unknown. He possibly was recruited in 1819 in New Orleans with Benjamin R. Milam and others for James Long's filibustering expedition, but if so, he was not among those captured. On 1 January 1830 he and a friend left Thibodaux for Texas. They stopped at Nacogdoches, at Jared Groce's farm on the Brazos River, and in San Felipe, where Bowie presented a letter of introduction to Stephen F. Austin from Thomas F. McKinney, one of the Old Three Hundred. Bowie and his friend Isaac Donoho took the oath of allegiance to Mexico. Bowie, age 34, was at his prime. He was well traveled, convivial, loved music, and was generous. He also was ambitious and scheming; he played cards for money, and lived in a world of debt. He reached San Antonio with William H. Wharton and Mrs. Wharton, Isaac Donoho, Caiaphas K. Ham, and several slaves. They carried letters of introduction to two wealthy and influential Mexicans, Juan Martín de Veramendi and Juan Seguín. Bowie's party continued on to Saltillo, the state capital of Coahuila and Texas. There Bowie learned that a law of 1828 offered Mexican citizens 11-league grants in Texas for $100 to $250 each. He urged Mexicans to apply for the grants, which he purchased from them. He left Saltillo with 15 or 16 of the grants, and continued to encourage speculation in Texas lands. His activities irritated Austin, who hesitated to approve lands Bowie wanted to locate in the Austin colony but eventually allowed the tracts there. In San Antonio Bowie posed as a man of wealth, attached himself to the wealthy Veramendi family, and was baptized into the Catholic Church, sponsored by the Veramendis, whose daughter he married. In 1830 in Saltillo he became a Mexican citizen, a privilege contingent on his establishing wool and cotton mills in Coahuila. Through his friend Angus McNeill of Natchez, he purchased a textile mill for $20,000. He had appeared before the mayor, falsely declared his age as 32, and pledged to pay Ursula a dowry of $15,000. He valued his properties at $222,800. But the titles to his 60,000 arpents of Arkansas land, valued at $30,000, were fraudulent. Walker and Wilkins of Natchez owed Bowie $45,000 for his interest in Arcadia, and had given McNeill $20,000 for the Saltillo mill. Bowie borrowed $1,879 from his father-in-law and $750 from Ursula's grandmother for a honeymoon trip to New Orleans and Natchez. The Bowies settled in San Antonio.

Veramendi family tradition says Bowie spent little time at home. He apparently became fascinated by tales of the "lost" Los Almagres Mine. He obtained permission from Mexican authorities for an expedition into Indian country financed by the Veramendis, and on 2 November 1831 he left San Antonio with his brother Rezin and nine others. Six miles from the San Sabá Mission site they fought a large war party for 13 hours, during which Bowie lost one man killed and several wounded. The party returned to San Antonio. On 23 January 1832, now wearing the title "colonel" of citizen rangers, he left Gonzales with 26 men to scout the headwaters of the Colorado for Tawakonis and other hostile Indians. After a fruitless search of 2½ months, he returned home. In July, in Natchez, he learned that José de las Piedras, Mexican commander at Nacogdoches, had visited the towns of Anahuac and Velasco to quiet the antagonisms between the government and the mainly Anglo citizens. Upon his return, Piedras demanded that all citizens in his jurisdiction surrender their arms. The colonists rejected the demand. Bowie hurried to Nacogdoches, and the battle of Nacogdoches ensued. On 9 March 1833, Monclova replaced Saltillo as the state capital. When the two towns raised small armies to contest the change, Bowie favored Monclova. On one occasion when the forces confronted each other, he rode out and tried to precipitate a battle. He believed that the fortunes of Texas land speculators lay with Monclova. In September, Veramendi, his wife Josefa, and Ursula Bowie died of cholera at Monclova. Bowie was ill with yellow fever in Natchez and unaware of the deaths. On October 31 he dictated his last will, in which he bequeathed half of his estate to his brother Rezin and half to his sister Martha Sterrett and her husband.

Mexican laws passed in 1834 and 1835 opened the floodgates to wholesale speculation in Texas lands, and Texas–Coahuila established land commissions to speed sales, since the state treasury was empty. Bowie was appointed a commissioner to promote settlement in John Mason's purchase. The governor also was empowered to hand out 400-league parcels for frontier defense. The sale of these large tracts angered some colonists, who also resented a rumored plan by speculators to make San Antonio the capital. They questioned Bowie's handling of Mason's 400-league purchase. One traveler met Bowie and Mason en route from Matamoros to Monclova with $40,000 in specie to pay the last installment on Mason's land. Bowie also sold Mason land certificates to his friends in Natchez. In May 1835, however, Santa Anna abolished the Coahuila–Texas government and ordered the arrest of all Texans doing business in Monclova. Bowie fled the capital for Texas. On 22 June he wrote a friend in Nacogdoches that all communication between Mexico and Texas had been cut, that troops were boarding ships at Matamoros for the Texas coast, and that Mexican forces were en route from Saltillo toward the Rio Grande. In July, Bowie and others in San Felipe and Nacogdoches were beating the drum for war. Bowie led a small group of Texas "militia" to San Antonio and seized a stack of muskets in the Mexican armory there. On 31 July 1835, Travis wrote Bowie that Texans were divided and that the Peace Party appeared the stronger. Travis was a leader of the War Party. Bowie had hired Travis as early as 1833 in San Felipe to prepare land papers, and in June 1834 Travis represented Bowie and Isaac Donoho in a case filed by Francis W. Johnson. Travis also did legal work for Bowie's friend Jesse Clifft, a blacksmith who is often credited with making the first Bowie knife. The War Party sought military support among the Indian tribes in East

Texas. On 3 August, Bowie reported on a recent tour of several villages where he found many of the Indians drunk and all reluctant to cooperate. On 1 September Austin arrived home from a long imprisonment in Mexico City. Two days later Santa Anna abolished all state legislatures in Mexico. After being elected to command the volunteer army, Austin issued a call to arms. On 16 October his forces camped on Cibolo Creek 20 miles from San Antonio. Bowie arrived with a small party of friends, and Austin placed him on his staff as a colonel. Travis and others joined the army. General Houston, in command of the Texas regular army, arrived and condemned the idea of attacking Bexar. He maintained that Austin's army, weak and ill-trained, should fall back to the Guadalupe or Colorado river. Bowie and Fannin, at Austin's orders, scouted south of Bexar for a new campsite. On their way Bowie drove off a Mexican patrol. On 26 October Austin moved 400 men to Espada Mission. Bowie took 92 horsemen and inspected the area of Concepción Mission, near Bexar. At dawn on the twenty-eighth, in a heavy fog, the Mexicans attacked Bowie with 300 cavalry and 100 infantry. Bowie fought for three hours in the battle of Concepción, where he proved himself "a born leader," in Noah Smithwick's words.

Three days after the battle Austin sent Travis and 50 men to capture some 900 horses being driven south to Laredo, and asked Bowie to create a diversion to cover the escape of Mexican soldiers who wanted to desert. Bowie made a display of force, yet the soldiers failed to come out. On 31 October he notified General Cos that he would join Austin in an attack on Bexar. The next day, Austin demanded that Cos surrender, but the Mexican general refused. Austin hesitated. On 2 November, his officers voted 44 to 3 against storming Bexar. Bowie did not vote. He asked the same day to be relieved of command and again tried to resign on 6 November. He apparently had little interest in a formal command. Provisional governor Henry Smith and Houston wanted him to raise a volunteer group and attack Matamoros, but the General Council declared that Bowie was not "an officer of the government nor army." Bowie left the army for a brief trip to San Felipe in mid-November. He was back in San Antonio on 18 November, and on the twenty-sixth he and 30 horsemen rode out to check on a Mexican packtrain near town, while Burleson followed with 100 infantry. Bowie met the train and charged its cavalry escort, in what came to be called the Grass Fight. Bowie subsequently proceeded to Goliad to determine conditions there. During his absence, Burleson attacked Bexar on 5 December and forced the Mexican garrison to surrender and retire to the Rio Grande. The volunteers left for home. Bowie received a letter from Houston dated 17 December, suggesting a campaign against Matamoros. If that was impossible, Houston suggested, Bowie could perhaps organize a guerrilla force to harass the Mexican army. The Matamoros expedition was approved, but the issue of command was muddied by the political rivalry between Governor Smith and the council, and Houston soon found another assignment for Bowie.

On 19 January 1836 Bowie arrived in Bexar from Goliad with a detachment of 30 men. He carried orders from Houston to demolish the fortifications there, though some historians believe these orders were discretionary. The situation was grim. Col. James C. Neill, commander of a contingent of 78 men at the Alamo, stated that his men lacked clothing and pay and talked of leaving. Mexican families were leaving Bexar. Texas volunteers had carried off most of the munitions and supplies for the

James Bowie, after George P. A. Healy. Courtesy TSL.

Matamoros expedition. On 2 February Bowie wrote Governor Smith, urging that Bexar be held because it was a strategic "frontier picqet guard." Travis, promoted to lieutenant colonel, arrived with 30 men on 3 February. Crockett rode in with 12 men on the eighth. The garrison had some 150 men. On 11 February Neill gave his command to Travis and left. The volunteers preferred Bowie as commander and insisted on holding an election on 12 February. The volunteer vote placed Bowie in command, and he celebrated by getting drunk. While under the influence he ordered certain prisoners set free and paraded the volunteers under arms in Bexar. Travis took his regulars from the Alamo to the Medina River to escape implication in the disgraceful affair. On 13 February Bowie and Travis worked out a compromise giving Travis command of the regulars, Bowie command of the volunteers, and both men joint authority over garrison orders and correspondence. On 23 February the two learned that some 1,500 Mexican cavalrymen were advancing on Bexar, and sent a dispatch to Goliad asking Fannin for help. Within hours the Mexicans marched into Bexar and requested a parley. Without consulting Travis, Bowie asked for and received terms: the Texans must surrender. These terms were rejected. On 24 February Bowie, who was suffering from a disease "of a peculiar nature," which has been diagnosed as pneumonia or typhoid pneumonia but probably was advanced tuberculosis, collapsed, ending his active participation in commanding the garrison. Most historians no longer believe that he fell from a platform

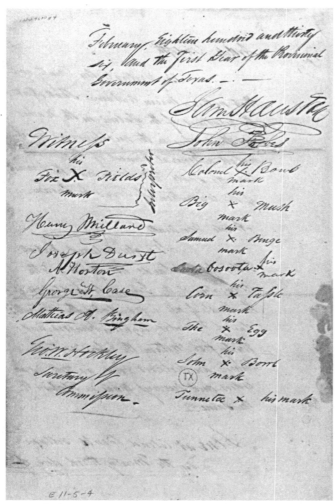

Treaty of February 23, 1836, signed by Sam Houston, Cherokee Chief Bowl, and others at Bowl's village on Caney Creek, about nine miles north of Henderson. Courtesy TSL. This treaty gave Bowl's tribe and others the right to live and farm between the Angelina and Sabine rivers.

---

while attempting to position a cannon. He was confined to a cot and urged the volunteers to follow Travis. He was occasionally carried outside to visit his men. After the battle of the Alamo on 6 March, Santa Anna asked to see the corpses of Bowie, Travis, and Crockett, and Bexar mayor Francisco Ruiz identified the bodies. Bowie lay on his cot in a room on the south side. He had been shot several times in the head. During his lifetime he had been described by his old friend Caiaphas K. Ham as "a clever, polite gentleman . . . attentive to the ladies on all occasions . . . a true, constant, and generous friend . . . a foe no one dared to undervalue and many feared." *William R. Williamson*

Bowl. Cherokee chief; b. North Carolina, ca. 1756; d. Texas, 16 July 1836. Bowl (also known as Duwali, Diwal'li, Chief Bowles, Colonel Bowles, Bold Hunter, and the Bowl), principal chief of the Cherokees in Texas, was the son of a Scottish father and a full-blooded Cherokee mother. He was leader of a village at Little Hiwassee, in western North Carolina. In 1791 he signed the Treaty of Holston, and in 1805 he signed an unauthorized cession treaty, a move that proved unpopular with the majority of Cherokees. In early 1810, to obtain better hunting ground and to escape growing pressures of white settlement, he and his band moved across the Mississippi River and settled in the St. Francis River valley, near New Madrid, Missouri. In 1812–13 his people moved into northwestern Arkansas, south of the Arkansas River, and in 1819 they once more moved on, stopping briefly in southwestern Arkansas and at the three forks of the Trinity River before settling north of Nacogdoches. In Texas, Chief Bowl became the primary "civil" or "peace" chief of a council that united several Cherokee villages. In 1822 he sent diplomatic chief Richard Fields to Mexico to negotiate with the Spanish government for land in East Texas. In 1827 he cooperated with the Mexican government in putting down the Fredonian Rebellion. In 1833 he made another attempt to secure from the Mexican government land on the Angelina, Neches, and Trinity rivers, but negotiations were interrupted by political unrest in Texas. In February 1836 Sam Houston negotiated a treaty with Bowl's council, guaranteeing the tribe possession of lands occupied in East Texas. After the Texas Revolution, however, the treaty was invalidated by the Senate of the republic. In desperation, Bowl briefly allied with agents soliciting allies for a Mexican reinvasion of Texas. Shortly thereafter, President Lamar ordered him and his people to leave Texas. After negotiations failed, Bowl mobilized his warriors to resist expulsion. On 16 July 1839 he was killed in the battle of the Neches. *Dianna Everett*

Bowman, Sarah. The Great Western, a legendary camp follower in the Mexican War; b. Sarah Knight, Tennessee or Missouri, 1812 or 1813; d. Fort Yuma, date unknown. Sarah acquired several husbands during the course of her travels, many without benefit of clergy, so there is considerable confusion about her surname. She is variously called Mrs. Bourjette, Bourget, Bourdette, Davis, Bowman, Bowman–Phillips, Borginnis, and possibly Foyle. She stood six feet two inches tall and was probably nicknamed for a contemporary steamship noted for its size. John Salmon Ford wrote that she "had the reputation of being something of the roughest fighter on the Rio Grande and was approached in a polite, if not humble, manner." In 1845 she accompanied her husband, a soldier in the Eighth United States Infantry and a member of Zachary Taylor's army of occupation, to Corpus Christi. At that time the wives of enlisted men could enroll with the army as cooks and laundresses and follow their husbands into the field. Sarah first distinguished herself as a fighter at the crossing of the Arroyo Colorado in March 1846, when she offered to wade the river and whip the enemy singlehandedly if Gen. William Jenkins Worth would lend her a stout pair of tongs. During the bombardment of Fort Brown in May 1846 she refused to join the other women in an underground magazine but calmly operated her officers' mess uninterrupted for almost a week, despite the fact that a tray was shot from her hands and a stray shell fragment pierced her sunbonnet. Her fearlessness during the siege earned her another nickname, the Heroine of Fort Brown. She traveled with the army into the interior of Mexico and opened a hotel in Saltillo, the American House, where she again demonstrated her bravery during the battle of Buena Vista by loading cartridges and even carrying some wounded soldiers from the battlefield to safety.

During this period she was married to her second husband, known variously as Bourjette, Bourget, and Bourdette, a member of the Fifth Infantry. Sarah apparently remained in Saltillo as

The "Great Western" as Landlady, by Samuel E. Chamberlain. From Chamberlain's manuscript "My Confession," in the West Point Museum, United States Military Academy. Courtesy Summerlee Foundation, Dallas. This is the only known likeness of Sarah Bowman, the "Great Western."

a hotelkeeper until the end of the war, but in July 1848 she asked to join a column of dragoons that had been ordered to California. By this time her husband was probably dead, and she was told that only married women could march with the army. Whereupon she rode along the line of men asking, "Who wants a wife with fifteen thousand dollars and the biggest leg in Mexico? Come, my beauties, don't all speak at once. Who is the lucky man?" After some hesitation a dragoon named Davis, probably David E. Davis, stepped forward, and the Great Western once again marched with the army. In 1849 Sarah arrived in El Paso and briefly established a hotel that catered to the flood of Forty-niners traveling to the gold fields. She leased the hotel to the army when she left for Socorro, New Mexico, with a new husband, Albert J. Bowman, an upholsterer from Germany. When Bowman was discharged in 1852, the couple moved to Fort Yuma, where Sarah opened another restaurant. She lived first on the American, then the Mexican, side of the river, to protect her adopted children. By the mid-1860s she was no longer married to Bowman, but she served as company laundress and received an army ration. In 1856 she traveled to Fort Buchanan to set up a hotel 10 miles below the fort. She had returned to Fort Yuma by 1861. Although Sarah was well known as a hotelkeeper and restaurateur, she probably had other business interests as well. One chronicler referred to her as "the greatest whore in the West," and Lt. Sylvester Mowry, a soldier stationed at Fort Yuma in 1856, wrote of Sarah that "among her other good qualities she is an admirable 'pimp'." She reportedly died from a tarantula bite, some say in 1863. She was buried in the Fort Yuma post cemetery on 23 December 1866 with full military honors. In August 1890 the Quartermaster's Department of the United States Army exhumed the 159 bodies buried at the cemetery, including that of the Great Western, and moved them to the presidio at San Francisco, California.

Regina Bennett McNeely

Bradburn, John Davis. Mexican military officer; b. Virginia, 1787; d. Matamoros, Tamaulipas, 20 April 1842 (buried in Hidalgo County); m. María Josefa Hurtado de Mendoza. Bradburn lived in Kentucky (1810–), then Tennessee. He was probably a member of the Gutiérrez–Magee expedition (1812). Subsequently, he and Henry Perry joined Luis Michel Aury on Galveston Island. He accompanied Francisco Xavier Mina's successful attack on Soto la Marina, Tamaulipas, where he joined Mexican guerrillas (1817). Upon joining the patriots at Fort Sombrero in Guanajuato in July, Bradburn became second in command of the American volunteers. A successful siege by the royalists forced the insurgents to evacuate, and Bradburn was one of the few to escape. He managed to join Vicente Ramón Guerrero near Acapulco and served the cause until December 1820, when he defected to Agustín de Iturbide, commander of the Spanish army. Iturbide, a native Mexican, was secretly planning a coup to expel the Spaniards, and Bradburn apparently served as intermediary between Iturbide and Guerrero in uniting the diverse Mexican factions in order to defeat the Spanish. The union of the two allowed the promulgation of the Plan de Iguala in February 1821, and the Spanish soon admitted defeat. After independence, Bradburn remained in the Mexican army as a lieutenant colonel and an aide to Iturbide. He survived the numerous political changes of the 1820s and in 1830 was appointed commander of a new garrison on Galveston Bay. Commandant Gen. Manuel de Mier y Terán ordered him to locate a site for the fort, a military town, and a customhouse, to be named Anahuac. Bradburn chose Perry's Point, overlooking the mouth of the Trinity River.

Bradburn encountered hostility from his fellow Anglo-Americans, who were already irritated by the restrictive immigration Law of April 6, 1830. His duties included inspecting land titles, issuing licenses to Anglo lawyers, and enforcing the customs laws. The exemption from paying tariffs granted to Stephen F. Austin's colonists had expired, and the federal government expected the resumed tariff revenue to pay for the six new military posts guarding the entrances to Texas. William B. Travis violated the military laws governing the post by words and deeds calculated to stir a rebellion. When Bradburn arrested him and other leaders of the movement, thus precipitating the first of the Anahuac Disturbances (1832), a force marched to attack Anahuac. The insurgents, in the Turtle Bayou Resolutions, explained their action in light of news that the Federalist faction under Santa Anna was defeating the Centralist administration supported by Bradburn. An uneasy peace lasted while the rebels sent to the Brazos for cannons and Bradburn appealed for help from other military commanders in Texas. Col. José de las Piedras marched from Nacogdoches, but fearing that he was outnumbered he met with Anglo insurgents near Liberty and agreed to their demands: remove Bradburn from command and free Travis and the others. After Bradburn was relieved of command on 2 July he feared plots against his life and fled to New Orleans. He returned to the Rio Grande and continued his career with the waning Centralist army until its defeat in December 1832. He then lived in retirement at his home near Matamoros until 1836, when he was ordered against his wishes to join José de Urrea's command of the port of Copano, where he saw none of his old adversaries. After the battle of San Jacinto the Mexican army retreated. Bradburn made his way back to Matamoros and retirement. He was briefly called back to duty

Thomas Braniff, Fort Worth, 1935. Courtesy Braniff Collection, History of Aviation Collection, University of Texas at Dallas. The new Lockheed L-10A had just arrived at Meacham Field in Fort Worth when Tom Braniff posed with it in 1935.

during the Federalist Wars, but ill health prevented him from attacking San Antonio in the Mexican invasions of 1842. His only son, Andrés, became a priest. The widow Bradburn sold the ranch, which eventually became La Lomita Seminary near Mission. *Margaret Swett Henson*

Braniff Airways. Once the world's sixth largest airline; grew out of the Oklahoma City–Tulsa Airline, founded in 1928 by Thomas Elmer Braniff and four friends. Universal Air Lines, a St. Louis conglomerate, bought the company in 1929 and renamed it Braniff Air Lines. In 1930 Braniff Airways was incorporated and went public as a subsidiary of the Universal Air Lines System, which subsequently sold the Braniff division to Aviation Corporation, the holding company that later became American Airlines. Braniff soon called itself "The World's Fastest Airlines" and began using Lockheed Vega aircraft to add routes to Chicago, Kansas City, St. Louis, and Wichita Falls. Braniff was close to insolvency when it acquired an airmail route between Dallas and Chicago in 1934, the year Braniff moved its operations to Love Field. At the time, airmail routes were the lifeblood of many small airlines. In 1935 the company bought Long and Harmon Air Service and gave it mail contracts connecting

Dallas–Fort Worth and the Panhandle with Mexico through connections in Brownsville. During World War II, Braniff surrendered over half its fleet to the United States military and trained military pilots, radio operators, and mechanics. At the same time it continued to expand and in 1942 moved its administrative offices from Oklahoma City to Dallas. The Civil Aeronautics Board granted approval to serve South America in 1943, and the company was renamed Braniff International Airways. By 1948 Braniff routes were opened to Ecuador, Panama, and Cuba. In 1952 Braniff International merged with Mid-Continent Airlines, thus adding 32 routes to the 29 domestic and 9 international routes the company operated at the time. Tom Braniff was killed in a private plane crash near Shreveport, Louisiana, in 1954, and Charles E. Beard became president of the airline. By 1957 Braniff's annual payroll had increased to over $22 million, and the company operated maintenance facilities in Dallas, Minneapolis–St. Paul, Chicago, Kansas City, San Antonio, and Lima, Peru. The company moved into a new headquarters in Dallas and new terminal facilities at Love Field in 1958. Revenue passenger miles increased from 550 million in 1953 to 1.5 billion in 1964; during the same time the company's one-cent-per-share earnings increased to $2.03.

In 1964 the Dallas-based Greatamerica Corporation, an insurance company, acquired 57.5 percent of Braniff stock, after Troy Post, Greatamerica chairman, determined that Braniff was poorly managed. Post recruited Harding L. Lawrence, former executive vice president of Continental Airlines, to lead Braniff. Lawrence replaced Beard as president and CEO in 1965 and reincorporated Braniff Airways in Nevada in 1966. From that time until 1990, despite subsequent changes, Post and his administration dominated the firm. Lawrence brought a flamboyant style to the airline and oversaw Braniff's greatest period of growth. Declaring that "sameness is boring," he announced an "end of the plain plane" by painting company aircraft in seven bright solid colors, hiring an interior decorator to redesign cabins and terminals, and having Italian fashion designer Emilio Pucci design revealing uniforms for flight attendants. In November 1967 Post sold Greatamerica and a controlling interest of Braniff stock to Ling–Temco–Vought, Incorporated. Braniff executives blamed LTV for bleeding the airline of cash during the late 1960s to finance other acquisitions. In 1971, on the orders of the Department of Justice, LTV was forced to divest itself of Braniff to purchase a steel company. Braniff International Corporation was formed in 1972 as a holding company with Braniff Airways. By 1969 the company had become an exclusively jet airline using the advertising slogan, "If You've Got It, Flaunt It!" After his "Jellybean Airline" acquired South American competitor Panagra Airways in 1967, Lawrence commissioned artist Alexander Calder to paint a DC-8 "to focus international attention on South America as a vacation destination." Calder also painted a Braniff Boeing 727 red, white, and blue in 1976 to commemorate the United States Bicentennial. By 1978 the airline was flying to Hawaii, South America, London, Paris, Frankfurt, and Amsterdam.

The Airline Deregulation Act of 1978 prompted Lawrence to embark on what was then the greatest expansion in airline history. Convinced that survival in a deregulated environment was dependent on size, he added 31 destinations to Braniff service over the next two years. Long-term debt increased, however, and a countrywide recession led to decreased air travel. Braniff began to lose money, while interest payments increased. The company's net worth fell by nearly four-fifths. In 1979 Braniff withdrew from 10 unprofitable routes. The company began selling its more modern planes and relying on older, less fuel-efficient ones. Layoffs increased. In 1980 the company withdrew from its unprofitable routes in the Far East. That year Braniff lost $131 million, an industry record at the time. In December 1980 Lawrence resigned, and in January 1981 John J. Casey, executive vice president since 1968, took over. Casey refocused the company on its shorter routes and obtained a 10 percent pay-cut agreement from union employees, but he was unable to stop the red ink and was shortly forced to lay off another 1,000 employees and discontinue all routes to Europe except the London route. In late 1981 Casey hired Howard D. Putnam, former president and CEO of Southwest Airlines, to assume similar duties at Braniff. Putnam and Philip Guthrie, the executive vice president of finance, reduced the number of fares from 582 to 15 and removed first-class seats from domestic flights. By the end of 1981 Braniff had a negative net worth estimated at $90 million. Unable to meet its payroll, the line ceased operations in May 1982, recalled its 62 aircraft, fired all but 225 of its 9,000 employees, and filed for Chapter 11 protection from creditors.

In 1983 the Pritzker family of Chicago obtained bankruptcy-court approval for a $70 million offer to revive the airline. The next year a new Braniff, Incorporated, launched its first flight with a fleet of 30 planes under the direction of president William Slattery, formerly chief of European operations for TWA. Of the company's 2,200 employees, 98 percent had worked for the old Braniff and agreed to return to work for lower wages. The low-cost airline, headquartered in Dallas, operated routes out of Dallas–Fort Worth International Airport to 21 cities. In 1988 Philadelphia investors Jeffrey W. Chodorow and Arthur G. Cohen bought the company, but increased price competition forced the airline to declare bankruptcy again in 1989 and ground its jets. Chodorow and Cohen started flights again under the Braniff name in 1991, using the assets of Emerald Airlines, a Houston charter airline they had purchased in 1990. Under new chief executive officer Gregory B. Dix, the company attempted to carve a niche for itself in the leisure-travel market by offering $79 one-way fares from D–FW to Newark and Los Angeles. In 1992 the company ceased operations, again citing increased fare wars. By 1993 all that remained of the former airline was Dalfort Aviation, a training enterprise associated with Love Field in Dallas. *Jon Kutner, Jr.*

Brazos Indian Reservation. Twelve miles south of Fort Belknap; one of two reservations in Texas established in 1854 by Gen. Randolph B. Marcy, under orders from the federal government; originally four leagues (18,576), later doubled to accommodate western Indians. The main building was three miles east of the site of Graham. Under the direction of Maj. Robert S. Neighbors, Capt. Shapley P. Ross was made the Brazos agent. J. J. Strum was agriculturist, and Zachariah Ellis Coombes was educational instructor. About 2,000 Indians took up life on the Brazos Reservation; Caddo, Anadarko, Waco, and Tonkawa Indians had their own villages, and these shrinking groups were glad to have protection from the Comanches. Contracts were made with ranchers for beef, and on an average 34 cattle were delivered each week. The federal government had control of the reservation and a 10-mile surrounding area to prevent the sale of liquor to the Indians. Texas, however, reserved the right of jurisdiction over persons other than Indians. The Indians cultivated about 600 acres. They were good farmers, and many white settlers recognized and respected the reservation dwellers, did not interfere with them, and were not molested by them. Rangers and military officers enlisted the Indians as scouts against the warring tribes. Between fifty and 100 were on regular duty. However, this pleased neither the anti-Indian white men nor the wild Indians. It also incited a spirit of envy among the friendly Penateka Comanches on the Upper Reserve, who were not permitted to fight against other Comanche groups. The situation grew worse. Small depredations took place and were always attributed to reservation Indians, so that a lone Indian off the reserve was not safe. A little newspaper published in Jacksboro called the *White Man* added fuel to the flame of hatred. By 1858 feeling ran so high that Governor H. R. Runnels and Sam Houston appealed to the federal government to move the Indians out of the state.

The government ordered a survey of land in Indian Territory, but before a suitable location could be secured two incidents brought the issue to a climax. Choctaw Tom and a hunting party were attacked on 26 December 1858, and seven were killed. After

A busy day at the courthouse in Brenham, ca. 1870. Stereograph. Lawrence T. Jones III Collection, Austin. In the late nineteenth century, Brenham was the county seat of a prosperous agricultural area and a railroad-shipping center for the state's interior.

investigation, the governor warned the whites and ordered Col. John Henry Brown to the frontier with 100 men. No indictments were made. On 23 May 1859 several hundred whites led by John R. Baylor appeared at the reservation in search of certain Indians. Baylor defied the United States troops and killed an Indian woman and an old man. Indians pursued Baylor to the Marlin Ranch, beyond federal jurisdiction. There Baylor made a stand. Chief John Hatterbox was killed, two of Baylor's men lost their lives, and others were wounded. The Baylor men were buried on the ranch, and the next morning the wounded were taken to Fort Belknap. Thereupon Neighbors ordered the removal of the Indians from both reservations to Indian Territory. As there was no land allotted there for Texas Indians, they were placed with the Wichitas in the Washita valley. The Brazos reservation was abandoned in 1859.   *Carrie J. Crouch*

Brazosport, Texas. Sixty miles south of Houston in southern Brazoria County, where the Brazos River meets the Gulf of Mexico. It is a 214-square-mile industrial and port area. The name may date back to eighteenth-century nautical charts. Port facilities, sulfur mines, and the chemical industry were largely responsible for rapid growth in the community after Dow Chemical Company arrived in 1939. By 1990 Dow employed almost 11,000 local people. The Brazos River Harbor was opened in 1954, and the nation's first seawater conversion plant was established in Brazosport in 1959. The population of the city grew from 23,000 in 1945 to 52,258 in 1990. Brazosport has an extensive resort industry, including beaches, fishing spots, and a number of annual events. Brazosport College opened in 1968.
Diana J. Kleiner

Brazos River. The longest river in Texas; rises at the confluence of its Salt Fork and Double Mountain Fork in Stonewall County and runs 840 miles to the Gulf of Mexico in Brazoria County.

The two forks emerge from the Caprock 150 miles above the confluence, thus forming a continuous watershed 1,050 miles long, which extends from New Mexico to the Gulf of Mexico and comprises 44,620 square miles, 42,000 of which are in Texas. It traverses a varied landscape, from the plains "draw" drainage through canyons at the breaks of the Llano Estacado, the West Texas rolling plains, and the Grand Prairie hill region, to its meandering course through the Coastal Plain. The Brazos has seven principal tributaries, including the Salt and Double Mountain forks. The others are the Clear Fork, the Bosque and Little rivers, Yegua Creek, and the Navasota River. The Brazos is probably the river that Indians of the Caddoan linguistic group called Tokonohono. It is widely identified as the river that La Salle named the Maligne. The name Brazos was probably first applied to the Colorado River, and there is considerable evidence that some early explorers confused the two. In 1716 Espinosa and Domingo Ramón probably called the Brazos "la Trinidad." The present names, however, were established well before the end of the Spanish period. The full name of the river, often used in Spanish accounts, is Los Brazos de Dios, "the arms of God." The earliest of several legends about this name is that Vázquez de Coronado and his men were about to perish from lack of water when the Indians guided them to a small stream, which the Spaniards named Brazos de Dios. Although the Brazos was well known to Spanish explorers and missionaries who described the Indians along its banks, the first permanent settlements on the river were made by Anglo-Americans. John McFarland, one of the Old Three Hundred, founded San Felipe de Austin at the Atascosito Crossing of the Brazos. The town became the colonial capital of Texas. The river acquired further significance as being, at Velasco, the scene of the first colonial resistance to Mexican authority, and, at Columbia and Washington-on-the-Brazos, the site of two of the first seats of government of the republic. Cotton and sugar plantations established along the Brazos in pre–Civil War days were showplaces of Texas and homes of some of the wealthiest men in the state. Originally, the Brazos was navigable for 250 miles from the Gulf to Washington. It was an important waterway before the Civil War, and efforts to improve it for navigation continued until the early twentieth century. The water of the Brazos basin is administered by the Brazos River Authority, established by the legislature in 1929. In later years the Brazos has maintained its importance as a source of water for power, irrigation, and other services. The river has been dammed in several places to form reservoirs for flood control, municipal use, and recreation, the most important of these man-made lakes being Possum Kingdom and Whitney Reservoir. In *Goodbye to a River* (1960), John Graves gave a notable account of his journey in a canoe down the Brazos in 1958, with historical sketches of Indians and pioneers. *Kenneth E. Hendrickson, Jr.*

Brenham, Texas. County seat of Washington County, 72 miles northwest of Houston. Hickory Grove changed its name to Brenham in 1843 to honor physician and Army of the Republic veteran Richard Fox Brenham. The town became county seat in 1844 and was incorporated in 1858. With the construction of the Washington County Railroad in 1860, Brenham, the rail terminus, served as a distribution point for the state's interior until the Houston and Texas Central was extended to Austin in 1871. Brenham prospered despite the 1867 yellow fever epidemic, a destructive riot by federal troops during Reconstruction, and fires in 1873 and 1877. Germans came in the 1870s and 1880s and founded Mission Institute (now Blinn College) in 1883. The Gulf, Colorado and Santa Fe Railway arrived in 1880, and by the 1890s local industries included mattress manufacturing, food and fiber processing, and metal fabrication. Brenham's population doubled every decade between 1860 and 1900, then grew slowly until the 1950s. New industries contributed to the town's growth from 7,740 inhabitants in 1960 to 11,952 in 1990. Local festivals include the annual Maifest and Juneteenth celebrations. Bluebell Creameries, the largest ice cream producer in the state, is located in Brenham. *Carole E. Christian*

Brinker, Maureen Connolly. Tennis champion; b. San Diego, California, 17 September 1934; d. Dallas, 21 June 1969; m. Norman E. Brinker (1955); 2 daughters. In 1944 Maureen began playing tennis in San Diego. She eventually dominated women's tennis worldwide. She won the United States Women's Singles Championship in 1951, 1952, and 1953; the French Singles Championship in 1953 and 1954; and Wimbledon in 1952, 1953, and 1954. In 1953 she became the first woman to win the grand slam of tennis, with victories at the national championship tournaments of Australia, France, Great Britain, and the United States. She earned her nickname, "Little Mo," from sportswriters who likened her explosiveness on court to the battleship USS *Missouri.* During her time of tennis stardom she also worked occasionally as a copy girl and columnist for the San Diego *Union.* Her amateur tennis career was cut short in July 1954, when she injured her right leg in a horse-riding accident. In 1963 she and her equestrian husband moved to Dallas, where they started a restaurant chain called Steak and Ale. In Dallas, in an effort to acknowledge the assistance she had received as a junior player, Mrs. Brinker and Mrs. Frank Jeffet established the Maureen Connolly Brinker Tennis Foundation to advance

Maureen Connolly Brinker. Courtesy Maureen Connolly Brinker Tennis Foundation, Dallas.

achievement among junior tennis players in Texas. This foundation supports junior tennis through tournaments, awards, and financial support. In 1968 the city honored Maureen Brinker as Woman of the Year for her work with its youth, and in that same year she was elected to the International Tennis Hall of Fame. The year before her death an annual tennis tournament was started in Dallas in her honor. An award in her name was established shortly after her death by the foundation and the United States Lawn Tennis Association to honor outstanding junior girl players. The foundation has since established many other programs and awards bearing Maureen Brinker's name.

Debbie Mauldin Cottrell

Brinkley, John Romulus. Medical charlatan; b. Jackson County, North Carolina, 8 July 1885; d. San Antonio, 26 May 1942 (buried in Memphis, Tennessee); m. Sally Wike (1908; divorced 1913); 3 daughters; m. Minnie Telitha Jones; 1 son. Brinkley attended school at Tuckasiegee, North Carolina, but never earned a diploma. After dallying at several diploma mills such as Eclectic Medical University of Kansas City, he was somehow licensed by the state of Arkansas and set up a medical practice in Milford,

Kansas. In 1918 he began performing his famous "goat gland operation," designed to restore male virility and fertility by the implantation of goat glands. Before long more than 100 customers a week were receiving the $750 rejuvenation operation. As a result of the operations and a large patent-medicine business, "Doc" Brinkley became extremely wealthy. In 1923 he constructed the first radio station in Kansas, KFKB, which carried country music and fundamentalist preaching. In 1928, AMA executive secretary Dr. Morris Fishbein attacked Brinkley for diagnosing illnesses and prescribing medicines over the radio. In 1930 the Kansas State Medical Board revoked Brinkley's medical license and the Federal Radio Commission refused to renew his broadcasting license. Brinkley responded by running for governor, hoping to appoint new members to the medical board. Running as an independent, write-in candidate, he came extremely close to winning—his loss coming only because thousands of votes were thrown out on technicalities. Subsequent bids for the governorship in 1932 and 1934 also failed. In 1931 he received authority from Mexican officials to build a powerful transmitter at Villa Acuña, Coahuila, across the river from Del Rio. In 1933 he moved his entire medical staff and facilities to the Roswell Hotel in Del Rio. He used his station, XER, to entice his listeners to visit his clinic or buy an array of gimmicks, among them ampules of colored water, at a price of six for $100. In Texas he rarely implanted goat glands, but substituted what he described as "commercial glandular preparations." He also performed numerous prostate operations and instituted the use of Mercurochrome shots and various pills to help restore youthful vigor. Estimates are that he earned $12 million between 1933 and 1938. During this period his conspicuous display of wealth—a lavish mansion, expensive cars, planes, yachts, and diamonds—was second to none. In 1938 he moved his medical activities to Little Rock, Arkansas, but maintained his residence in Texas. About that time he lost a libel suit against Fishbein, fought numerous malpractice suits, and battled the IRS over back taxes. In 1941 he was forced to file for bankruptcy.

Keith D. McFarland

Bronté Club. The oldest women's literary club in Texas; started by Viola Case in 1855. The organization, originally named the Victoria Literary Club, was a literary society for the girls of Mrs. Case's school, Victoria Female Academy. The members collected books that were lent to the girls on a weekly basis. This embryonic lending library eventually became the Victoria Public Library. Until 1975, when it was placed under the management of the city and county of Victoria, the library was governed by the Library Committee of the Bronté (sic) Club. During the 1860s the club is said to have devoted more time to war relief than to literary study. The founding in New York City of the Sorosis Club (1868)—in protest against the all-male Press Club, which gave a banquet for the visiting Charles Dickens and invited no women—gave impetus to women's clubs across the country. Though started as a school society, the Bronté Club was reorganized as a community club in 1873, became a school society again in 1878, and in 1880 was changed to a community club again. In 1880, because the club needed new members and wanted a more distinctive name, it accepted older girls and young married women and changed its name to Bronté Literary Club, in honor of Charlotte Brontë. When the national movement for federation of women's clubs began, the club sent a delegate, Mrs. Alfred

B. Peticolas, to the first meeting of the Texas Federation of Women's Clubs, held in Tyler in 1898. The club's calendar for that year shows it as a member of this state organization, which joined the national General Federation of Women's Clubs in 1899. The Bronté Club dropped "literary" from its title in its *Year Book* of 1901–02. The *Year Book* of 1905–06 stated that the club's objectives were to promote the "mental and social culture of its members," an "altruistic spirit," and philanthropic endeavors, as well as "the interests of State and Fifth District Federation." The club offered a wide variety of programs through the years. Among its civic projects was the sponsorship of a lecture by Eleanor Roosevelt in December 1940, an event that Mrs. Roosevelt later wrote about. The club continued to contribute both funds and books to its original civic work, the Victoria Public Library. It was made an honorary member of the library, and an appointed club member serves on the library's advisory board.

Geraldine F. Talley

Brooke Army Medical Center. At Fort Sam Houston in San Antonio. Activities at Brooke cover almost every aspect of health care, postgraduate medical education, medical training, and medical research. Located within Brooke is the Army Burn Center, operated by the United States Army Institute of Surgical Research. In 1870, when the Post of San Antonio was established on the Texas frontier, Brooke began as a small medical dispensary in a log cabin. Two temporary buildings served as the post hospital until 1886, when the first permanent hospital was built. That structure is now used as quarters for visiting dignitaries. In 1907 the army completed a new hospital with 84 beds. During the next decade an additional 1,000 beds were added in 50 temporary wooden structures, but after World War I these buildings fell into disuse. During ensuing years Brooke was called the post hospital and was housed in a variety of buildings, all of which led up to the construction of the main hospital, opened in 1938. The facility was named Brooke General Hospital in 1942 in honor of a previous commander, Brig. Gen. Roger Brooke. Other units—a convalescent facility and psychiatric hospital—were later added. Brooke has been a medical center since 1946 and at one time was responsible for all of the medical training in the army. A new Brooke Army Medical Center began construction in 1987. As part of its mission Brooke supports the Army Burn Center, the Fort Sam Houston Dental Activity, and the Area Dental Laboratory, all at Fort Sam Houston.

Ray Dery

Brooks Air Force Base. Seven miles southeast of San Antonio; established as a Gosport System training facility during World War I and originally named Gosport Field. In the Gosport method, developed by the Royal Air Force, an instructor spoke to a student pilot through a tube and corrected him in flight. The field was renamed Signal Corps Aviation School, Kelly Field No. 5, on 5 December 1917. On 4 February 1918, after the death of Cadet Sidney Johnson Brooks, Jr., in a training accident, the army renamed the facility Brooks Field. By the end of that year the field had 16 hangars. Hangar 9, now the Edward H. White II Memorial Museum, is a national historic landmark and is reputedly the oldest existing hangar in the U.S. Air Force. In 1919 the army replaced the pilot school with a balloon and airship school. Following a series of accidents, however, the army closed this school (1922). From 1922 until 1931 Brooks served as the primary flying school for the army air corps; more than 1,400 pilots were trained there. Notable instructors and students included such aviation figures as Charles Lindbergh, Claire Chennault, Lester Maitland, and Jimmy Doolittle. The School of Aviation Medicine was transferred from Hazlehurst Field in New York to Brooks in 1926. In 1928 Brooks began training paratroopers. On Thanksgiving Day, 1929, the first mass paratroop drop in United States Armed Forces history took place at Brooks. The experiments at Brooks confirmed the practicality of tactical paratrooper warfare, which was used on many occasions during World War II. Both the flying school and the aviation medicine school were moved to nearby Randolph Field (now Randolph Air Force Base) in 1931. Brooks served as a center for aerial-observation training in the 1930s. A special school for combat observers was begun there in 1940. The army established an Air Corps Advanced Flying School at Brooks in 1941 to teach pilots of single-engine aircraft aerial-observation skills. Observation training was discontinued in 1943, when Brooks began training pilots of the new B-25 bomber for use in World War II. Brooks's training function ceased in 1945 when a tactical unit under the Third Air Force joined the facility. In 1948, after the air force was separated from the army, the Department of Defense changed the name of the base to Brooks Air Force Base. From 1949 until 1958 operating units at the base included the 259th Air Base, the 2577th Air Force Reserve Flying Training Center, the 2577th Air Base Group, and the 3790th Air Base Group.

Starting in the summer of 1959, Brooks began a transition from a flight-training base to a center for medical research, development, and education. The School of Aviation Medicine returned to Brooks from Randolph, and the base became headquarters for the Aerospace Medical Center on 1 October 1959. In 1960 all flying at the facility ceased. With the growth of the space program, the aviation medicine school received the new title United States Air Force School of Aerospace Medicine (1961). In November 1961 the center and school became part of the Aerospace Medical Division, which was renamed Human Systems Division in 1987. The medical center developed the capsule that carried the monkey Sam into outer space on 4 December 1959. President John Kennedy's final official act was the dedication of four buildings in the complex that housed the Aerospace Medical Division headquarters and the School of Aerospace Medicine. Researchers at Brooks continued in the 1990s to study space medicine and have contributed to the advancement of manned flight. Brooks also houses the Air Force Human Resources Laboratory, the Air Force Occupational and Environmental Health Laboratory, the Air Force Drug Testing Laboratory, and the Air Force System's Command Systems Acquisition School. In November 1987 Sidney J. Brooks, Jr., Memorial Park was dedicated on the base. In 1995 the Department of Defense decided to close the base.

Edward B. Alcott

Broussard, Joseph Eloi. Rice grower and miller; b. Jefferson County, 18 December 1866; d. 6 October 1956; m. Mary Belle Bordages (1889); at least 9 children. In 1889 Broussard moved with his bride to Beaumont and bought one-third interest in a gristmill, which he converted to a rice mill in 1892. The result, Beaumont Rice Mills, became the first commercially successful rice mill in Texas. Less than 1,500 acres was planted with rice in Texas in 1892. To foster rice production, in 1898 Broussard cofounded the Beaumont Irrigation Company, whose initial

canal led to the formation of the Lower Neches Valley Authority. The system is now capable of irrigating 50,000 acres of rice while supplying the area's industrial requirements for water. Through family landholdings and the advancement of credit to farmers, the mill, under Broussard's management, farmed some 10,000 acres of rice in peak years. On this acreage rice growing was rotated with cattle raising, a lifelong interest of Broussard. At the time of his death, acres planted with rice in Texas annually reached well over 400,000, and production had spread to 23 counties. From 1907 to 1918 Broussard was president of the Rice Millers' and Dealers' Association, forerunner of the present Rice Millers' Association of America. In 1909, when the industry faced a financial crisis, Broussard was a member of a two-man team that successfully marketed American rice in Europe. In 1950 the International Rice Festival at Crowley, Louisiana, was dedicated to him. As an exemplary Catholic, Broussard was knighted in 1938 by Pope Pius XI.

Gerry Doyle

Brown, Henry Stevenson. Early settler and Indian fighter; b. Madison County, Kentucky, 8 March 1793; d. Columbia (now West Columbia), 26 July 1834; m. Mrs. Margaret Kerr Jones (ca. 1814). In 1810 Brown moved to St. Charles County, Missouri, where he was later sheriff. He volunteered for the War of 1812 and participated in the battle at Fort Clark, Illinois, in 1813. He moved to Pike County, Missouri, in 1819, and carried on trading via flatboat between Missouri and New Orleans. In December 1824, accompanied by his brother John (Waco) Brown, he landed at the mouth of the Brazos River equipped to trade with the Mexicans and Indians. In 1825 he was in command of a party of settlers that attacked and destroyed a band of Waco Indians at the site of present Waco. Brown was in Green DeWitt's colony in 1825 and in 1829 was in command of a company from Gonzales on a 32-day campaign against Indians. From 1826 to 1832 he engaged in the Mexican trade from headquarters in Brazoria, Gonzales, and San Antonio. At the time of the Anahuac Disturbances of 1832, Brown carried the information on the Turtle Bayou Resolutions from Gonzales to the Neches and Sabine River settlements and under John Austin commanded a company of 80 men in the battle of Velasco. He was a delegate from Gonzales to the Convention of 1832 at San Felipe de Austin and in 1833 was a member of the ayuntamiento of Brazoria. Brown County was named for him.

John Q. Anderson

Brownsville, Texas. County seat of Cameron County; across the Rio Grande from Matamoros, Tamaulipas, at the southern tip of Texas. In 1765 the community of San Juan de los Esteros (present-day Matamoros) was established across the Rio Grande. In 1781 Spanish authorities granted 59 leagues of land on the northern bank of the river, including all of the site of Brownsville, to José Salvador de la Garza, who established a ranch about 16 miles northwest of the site. During the early nineteenth century a small number of squatters, mostly herders and farmers from Matamoros, built huts in the area. A small settlement had formed by 1836, when Texas declared her independence from Mexico, but the region was still only sparsely settled when United States troops under Gen. Zachary Taylor arrived in early 1846. Taylor's forces constructed Fort Texas, which was renamed Fort Brown a short time later. After the Mexican War, at the signing of the Treaty of Guadalupe Hidalgo in 1848, the area became part of the state of Texas and fell within the jurisdiction

Miller Hotel, Brownsville, ca. 1865–1866. Photograph attributed to Louis de Planque. Courtesy Lawrence T. Jones III Collection, Austin. An early social center in Brownsville, the Miller Hotel offered a barroom and a noted restaurant and served as a terminus for several stage lines.

of San Patricio County. The same year Charles Stillman purchased a large part of the Garza grant north and northwest of Matamoros, including part of the city's common landholdings, from the children of the first wife of José Narciso Cavazos. Cavazos had remarried, however, and the heirs of his second wife, led by the eldest son, Juan N. Cortina, had been given legal title to the property, a fact that later led to a long series of legal battles over ownership. Stillman and his partner, Samuel Belden, laid out the town of Brownsville. In December 1848, Stillman, Belden, and Simon Mussina formed the Brownsville Town Company and began selling lots. Brownsville was made county seat of the new Cameron County on 13 January 1849, and a post office went into operation on 3 February. Within a short time the town's population—swollen by refugees from Matamoros and Forty-niners taking the Gila route to the gold fields of California—had increased to more than 1,000. Despite a cholera epidemic in the spring of 1849 that reportedly killed nearly half the population, the town continued to boom. Brownsville soon replaced Matamoros as the leading trade center for northern Mexico. Merchants on both sides of the border quickly recognized the advantage of shipping goods to Brownsville and then smuggling them across the Rio Grande to avoid paying high Mexican duties. During the Mexican War, Richard King, Mifflin Kenedy, and Charles Stillman had set up a transport company to haul American troops and supplies up the river. After the war the three men managed to establish a virtual monopoly on Rio Grande transportation, thus ensuring the Anglo dominance of trade in the area and helping to spur the town's growth. Numerous stores sprang up along the riverfront. A city market opened in 1850, when the town had a population of 519. Efforts were made to incorporate the town in the early 1850s, but a protracted series of legal battles over who had actually owned the land—Stillman or Cavazos's heirs—complicated matters. The title issue was not completely settled until 1879, when the United States Supreme Court ruled in favor of the Stillman group.

Despite recurring epidemics of cholera and yellow fever, Brownsville prospered and grew. The first Catholic church was founded by the Oblates of Mary Immaculate in 1854, and by 1856 the Episcopalians, Methodists, and Presbyterians had established churches. The Civil War years were a period of prosperity for Brownsville and Matamoros. After the Union Navy succeeded in blockading most Southern ports, the Confederates

looked for other avenues to ship cotton to Europe in return for ammunition, medicines, and other war supplies. After Union forces captured Port Isabel the trade was moved inland to Brownsville. In November 1863 federal troops under Gen. Nathaniel P. Banks marched on Brownsville seeking to interrupt the trade. The outgunned Confederates abandoned Fort Brown, blew it up with 8,000 pounds of explosives, and withdrew. Confederate troops commanded by John S. (Rip) Ford reoccupied the town on 30 July 1864 and held it until May 1865. On 13 May 1865, they fought a skirmish with Union troops just outside of Brownsville—the battle of Palmito Ranch, the last battle of the Civil War. After the war Union armies reoccupied Brownsville and launched a massive construction effort to repair Fort Brown. By 1869 army engineers had completed 70 new buildings at the fort and stationed army, infantry, and cavalry units there. The Brownsville economy, which had been buoyed up by the smuggling trade during the war years, however, was slower to recover. The narrow-gauge Rio Grande Railroad was constructed from Brownsville to Port Isabel in 1872, and by 1884 the town had two banks, three churches, two ice houses, a cotton gin, and a population of nearly 5,000.

In 1904 the St. Louis, Brownsville and Mexico Railway reached the town. Northern farmers began arriving in the lower Rio Grande valley in large numbers after the turn of the century. The new settlers built extensive irrigation systems and roads, and introduced large-scale truck farming. In 1904 H. G. Stillwell, Sr., planted the first commercial citrus orchard in the area, thus opening the way for one of the Valley's leading industries. In 1908 work on a city-owned electric-lighting system, waterworks, and sewerage system was launched, and in 1910 the first international car bridge connecting Brownsville and Matamoros was completed. The Brownsville Raid of 1906 involved black troops stationed at Fort Brown. Relations between persons of Mexican descent and the Anglo populace also began to deteriorate; the animosities grew even worse during the Mexican Revolution, when border raids by Mexican bandits wrought havoc among the Valley's populace. Before the arrival of the farm settlers, politics in South Texas was dominated by cliques of merchants, lawyers, and large landowners. In Brownsville the political scene was controlled by Democratic political boss James B. Wells. He welcomed the participation of Mexican Americans in his political organization and the municipal government, and he provided modest, informal support for his most impoverished constituents, much like a Mexican patrón or big-city boss. As a new Anglo elite, made up mostly of recent arrivals, emerged, Wells lost control of Brownsville in 1910, and a new social order, based on de facto segregation, became the rule for the next half century. During the 1920s Brownsville underwent a new period of prosperity as the area experienced a prolonged land boom. Agents went to the Midwest and North boosting the abundant cheap land in and around Brownsville. The population of Brownsville, which was just over 6,000 in 1900, reached 22,021 in 1930. During the Prohibition years Brownsville became a popular port of entry into Mexico, attracting numerous tourists who wanted to have a drink in Matamoros. Smuggling, always an important industry, had a brief heyday as the town became an important crossing point for illegal liquor. The 1920s also witnessed a series of civic improvements: roads were paved, a new international bridge was opened, and the first airport was constructed.

In December 1928 voters approved a measure establishing the Brownsville Navigation District and provided $2 million in bonds to build a ship channel from Brazos Santiago Pass, so that deepwater vessels could dock in Brownsville. The work initially went slowly, but after a major hurricane hit the area in 1933 the PWA lent money to the district to complete the 17-mile-long channel. The port of Brownsville, located five miles northeast of the city, was officially opened on 15 May 1936. State Highway 48 runs alongside the channel, which connects the port to the Gulf Intracoastal Waterway. By 1980 the port had 48 piers, wharves, and docks, with 17 facilities in the Brownsville Ship Channel, 17 in the fishing harbor, and 14 on the Brownsville Turning Basin. The port was connected by rail to the Missouri Pacific Railroad, the Southern Pacific Transportation Company, and the National Railways of Mexico. The completion of the port made Brownsville the shipping center for the lower Rio Grande valley and northeastern Mexico and helped the city to weather the worst effects of the Great Depression. During World War II Fort Brown served as training base for the 124th Cavalry, and large numbers of servicemen passed through the town. The fort was deactivated in 1945, and the grounds were eventually turned over to the city. After the war, shrimpers from Texas and Louisiana moved into the area and established the town as one of the leading shippers of shrimp in the country. The port of Brownsville also saw a growing volume of agricultural produce as vegetable and citrus farming in the Valley expanded. In 1949 the Gulf Intracoastal Waterway was extended to Brownsville and the ship channel was expanded to accommodate larger vessels. Cotton, introduced to the area on a large scale in the late 1940s, saw a marked upswing in the early 1950s, and for a time the port of Brownsville became the world's leading exporter of cotton. Union Carbide began construction of a plant near Brownsville in 1959. The same year, an immigration and customs building was constructed at the International Gateway Bridge. Between 1950 and 1960 the population increased from 36,066 to 48,040, and by 1970 the town had 52,522 inhabitants.

In 1966 the Industrial Development Council was formed to encouraged new industries, and the following year the Border Industrialization Program was instituted by the Mexican government to attract Mexican businesses and laborers to the border area. Major industries in the early 1990s included petrochemicals, frozen foods, canned fruits and vegetables, and the manufacture of paper bags, beverages, mill work, garments, mattresses, hats, and metal products. From the 1970s to the mid-1990s Brownsville grew rapidly. Much of the population growth came from immigration from Mexico, but the area has also seen growing numbers of retirees from the North and Midwest. In 1980 the population of the city was 84,997; by 1990 it had increased to 98,962; approximately 80 percent of the population in the early 1990s was of Mexican decent. After considerable lobbying from local leaders the University of Texas System took over Pan American University at Brownsville and renamed it the University of Texas–Pan American in 1989. In September 1991 the name was changed to the University of Texas at Brownsville, and at that time the institution began a partnership with Texas Southmost College. Points of interest in and around Brownsville include Fort Brown, the Charles Stillman home, the sites of the battles of Palo Alto, Resaca de la Palma, and Palmito Ranch, the Gladys Porter Zoo, South Padre Island, and Matamoros.

Alicia A. Garza and Christopher Long

Brownsville Raid. An alleged attack by soldiers from companies B, C, and D of the black Twenty-fifth United States Infantry stationed at Fort Brown (13–14 August 1906); resulted in the largest summary dismissals in the annals of the United States Army. When black soldiers arrived in Brownsville, they encountered some racial discrimination. After a reported attack on a white woman (August 12), Maj. Charles W. Penrose declared an early curfew the following day. Around midnight someone shot and killed a bartender and destroyed the arm of a policeman. Residents claimed they saw soldiers running through the streets shooting. Ensuing investigations presumed the guilt of the soldiers without identifying individual culprits. The conflict grew until on 5 November President Theodore Roosevelt summarily discharged "without honor" all 167 enlisted men previously garrisoning Fort Brown. Roosevelt had served with black troops in the Spanish-American War and conspicuously appointed African Americans to government posts. The Constitution League, a civil-rights organization, decried the lack of due process accorded the soldiers and impugned the timing of the order, which followed the congressional elections. Amid signs of alienation that could jeopardize the presidential ambitions of Secretary of War William Howard Taft, Senator Joseph B. Foraker (R–Ohio) urged a Senate investigation. Foraker, a nemesis of Roosevelt and an aspiring presidential candidate in his own right, kept the issue alive through speeches and writings over the next several years. He and Roosevelt clashed in addresses to the Gridiron Club in 1907 and hired private detectives to enhance their investigations. The Senate Military Affairs Committee, which included Foraker, conducted hearings while courts-martial cleared Penrose and officer-of-the-day Capt. Edgar A. Macklin of alleged negligence. The majority report, issued in March 1908, concurred with the official White House decision, while a minority of four Republicans found the evidence inconclusive. Yet another minority report, submitted by Foraker and Morgan G. Bulkeley (R–Connecticut), asserted the soldiers' innocence. Submitting to pressure, the administration appointed a board of retired army officers to review applications for reenlistment. After interviewing somewhat over half the applicants, the Court of Military Inquiry in 1910 inexplicably approved only 14 of the men. The decision, in conjunction with Taft's presidential victory, Roosevelt's retirement, and Foraker's failure to win renomination, effectively closed the matter for more than 60 years. In 1972, convinced by recent research critical of the government's handling of the affair, Representative Augustus Hawkins (D–California) urged reparations for the debarred soldiers. The Nixon administration concurred and awarded honorable discharges without back pay. Still maintaining the battalion's innocence, Dorsie Willis, the only surviving veteran, received a $25,000 pension. *Garna L. Christian*

Brownwood, Texas. County seat of Brown County; named for Henry S. Brown. The area was settled by farmers and cattle ranchers in the 1850s, and when the county was organized in 1857 the hamlet of Brownwood was chosen as the seat. Early developers included Greenleaf Fisk and John Y. Rankin. After the Civil War, Brownwood lay on a feeder line of the Western Trail. In the 1880s and 1890s the town became the center of a farming district. The population increased from 725 in 1880 to 2,176 in 1890 and 3,965 in 1900. Railroads were built through the town in 1885 and 1891. Cotton became the dominant crop by 1900, and by 1920 the

Bird's eye view of Brownwood, ca 1907. Postcard published by S. Langsdorf & Co., New York and Germany. Courtesy TSL. This view shows a thriving community built on cotton and shipping.

city was the largest cotton-buying center west of Fort Worth. Oil production became significant in the 1920s, when the town's population leaped from 8,223 to 12,789. Growth slowed during the Great Depression, though the town benefited from the completion of Lake Brownwood in 1933. Camp Bowie was built nearby in 1940 as the United States geared up for World War II, and overcrowded Brownwood may have had a population in excess of 50,000 during the war years. After the base closed the town's population fell to 20,140 in 1950 and 16,974 in 1960, and then remained relatively static over the next 30 years; it was 18,387 in 1990. In the 1990s important businesses included meat packing, commercial printing, a Superior Cable factory, and a 3M plant. Local attractions include Lake Brownwood State Recreation Area, and the Brown County Museum of History. Howard Payne University is in Brownwood. *Mark Odintz*

Bryan, John Neely. Founder of Dallas; b. Fayetteville, Tennessee, 24 December 1810; d. Austin, 8 September 1877; m. Margaret Beeman (1843); 5 children. After being admitted to the Tennessee bar, Bryan moved to Arkansas (ca. 1833), where he became an Indian trader. He made his first trip to the future site of Dallas in 1839, then settled there in 1841. In 1842 he persuaded several families who had settled at Bird's Fort to join him. He was a postmaster in the Republic of Texas and operated a ferry across the Trinity River where Commerce Street crosses the river today. In 1844 he persuaded J. P. Dumas to survey and plat the site of Dallas and possibly helped him with the work. Bryan was instrumental in the organizing of Dallas County in 1846 and in the choosing of Dallas as its county seat in August 1850. He donated the land for the county courthouse. He joined the California gold rush in 1849 but returned to Dallas within a year. In January 1853 he was a delegate to the state Democratic convention. In 1855, after shooting a man who had insulted his wife, Bryan fled to the Creek Nation. The man recovered, but Bryan did not return to his family in Dallas for about six years. He traveled to Colorado and California, apparently looking for gold, and returned to Dallas in 1860 or early 1861. He joined Col. Nicholas H. Darnell's Eighteenth Texas Cavalry in the winter of 1861 and served with that unit until late 1862, when he was discharged because of his age and poor health and returned to Dallas. In 1863 he was a trustee for Dallas Male and Female Academy. In 1866 he was prominent in efforts to aid victims of a flood. He also chaired a citizens' meeting that pressed for the completion

of the Houston and Texas Central Railway and presided at a rally seeking full political rights for all former Confederates. In 1871–72 he was one of the directors of the Dallas Bridge Company, the company that built the first iron bridge across the Trinity. He was also on the platform at the welcoming ceremonies for the Houston and Texas Central train when it pulled into town in mid-July 1872. By 1874 Bryan's mind was clearly impaired. He was admitted to the State Lunatic Asylum in Austin in 1877 and died there. *Cecil Harper, Jr.*

Bryan, Texas. County seat of Brazos County; forms, with adjoining College Station, the urban center of the county. In 1859 William Joel Bryan donated land for a townsite to the Houston and Texas Central Railroad, and the town was named in his honor. Even though the Civil War delayed construction of the line until 1867, the town replaced Boonesville as county seat in 1866. The first courthouse was built in 1871 and the city incorporated in 1872. Texas A&M College opened in College Station in 1876. By 1889 the city had electric lighting and a waterworks, and in 1900, when Bryan had a population of 3,589, a second railroad, the International–Great Northern, was built through the community. Bryan became an important cotton-shipping center in the early decades of the twentieth century. The town grew to 6,307 inhabitants in 1920 and 11,842 in 1940. The completion of State Highway 6 in 1936, Bryan Army Air Field during World War II, and most of all, the continued growth of Texas A&M University, helped stimulate Bryan's growth. Since the 1960s Bryan, in partnership with College Station, has developed vari-

John Neely Bryan and his wife, Margaret Beeman Bryan. Courtesy Dallas Historical Society.

ous university-related businesses, including defense electronics and high-tech manufacturing. The city's population has increased dramatically in recent decades, from 27,542 in 1960 to 55,002 in 1990. Local attractions include the Brazos Valley Museum of Natural Science, the Messina Hof Winery, and many turn-of-the-century homes. *Mark Odintz*

Bucareli. Spanish settlement on the Trinity River, probably near the Robbins Ferry crossing of the river in Madison County, north of Midway. Dissatisfied Spanish colonists ordered from their East Texas homes as a result of the report of the Marqués de Rubí lived for a brief time in San Antonio until they could persuade Viceroy Antonio María de Bucareli y Ursúa to permit them to return to East Texas. Permission was granted for a settlement at the site where the Old San Antonio Road crossed the Trinity. The settlement, named Nuestra Señora del Pilar de Bucareli, was founded in September 1774, and soon had a plaza, a church, a guardhouse, twenty houses of hewn wood, and numerous huts. It was to be exempt from civil taxation and church tithes for ten years. For a time the community prospered, reportedly because of illicit trade with the French, but an epidemic in 1777 was followed by Comanche raids in 1778. Led by Antonio Gil Ibarvo, the settlers, without official permission, deserted Bucareli and moved back to East Texas, where, before April 1779, they established the settlement that became Nacogdoches.

Buck, Frank. Hunter and author; b. Gainesville, 17 March 1884; d. Dallas, 25 March 1950; m. Amy Leslie (early 1900s; separated 1911); m. Muriel Riley (1928); 1 daughter. In Dallas, Buck's father was a Studebaker carriage dealer. Buck left home at the age of eighteen and in 1911 made his first expedition to South America. He eventually also traveled to Malaya, India, Borneo, New Guinea, and Africa. From these and other expeditions he brought back many exotic species that he sold to zoos and circuses. He was the author of *Bring 'Em Back Alive* (with E. Anthony, 1930), *Wild Cargo* (with Anthony, 1931), *Fang and Claw* (with F. L. Fraser, 1935), *Jim Thompson in the Jungles* (1935), *On Jungle Trails* (with Fraser, 1937), *Animals Are Like That!* (with C. Weld, 1939), and his autobiography, *All in a Lifetime* (1941). He was a contributor to the *Saturday Evening Post* and *Colliers,* and for some time he had a radio program. He was president of Frank Buck Enterprises, Incorporated, and Jungleland, Incorporated, and produced several motion pictures, including *Bring 'Em Back Alive, Wild Cargo,* and *Fang and Claw* (made from his books), and *Jungle Menace, Jungle Cavalcade,* and *Jacare.*

Buffalo. The first reports of the animals popularly called buffalo (a genus of American bison) in Texas were written by Cabeza de Vaca in his description of his journey from Florida to Mexico (1528–36). The buffalo once occupied about a third of the North American continent, from Canada to Mexico, and from the Blue Mountains of Oregon to western New York, Pennsylvania, Virginia, and the Carolinas. Authorities disagree about their range in Texas because of the migratory nature of the animals and the shifting of the herd during the period of buffalo hunting by white men, but it is generally agreed that they roamed the western and central plains of Texas in great numbers. The four main herds in Texas migrated from northern Montana and

entered Texas between the 99th and 101st meridians on established trails. The main buffalo trails in Texas were east of the Trans-Pecos and Llano Estacado and west of the Western Cross Timbers. At the height of the buffalo population in Texas these trails could be several miles wide. The buffalo usually did not range farther than the Concho River valley, but during certain seasons they migrated as far east and south as the Coastal Plain. The "great slaughter" took place in the early 1870s, and by 1878 the so-called southern herd was practically exterminated. There have been several attempts to protect the buffalo. In 1875 the Texas legislature considered a measure to protect the animals from wholesale slaughter, but Gen. Philip H. Sheridan protested the bill, contending that peace with the Indians could be maintained only if their food supply was eliminated. The bill failed. Preservation of a few animals was due to the efforts of such men as rancher Charles Goodnight and Charles J. (Buffalo) Jones, who preserved small herds on their ranches. In 1949 buffalo were found in several city zoos in Texas and on a few ranches in Armstrong and Nolan counties. In the late twentieth century various ranches throughout Texas continued to maintain buffalo herds, and the animal was fairly common from the Midwest to the Southwest and West.

Buffalo Hump. Penateka Comanche chief; d. 1870. His name is evidently a euphemism for a name with several variants (including Pochanaquarhip) that had phallic significance. Outraged by the Council House Fight (1840), he led nearly 400 warriors and an equal number of women and children on the Linnville Raid of 1840. Texas militiamen intercepted his party and administered it a stinging defeat in the battle of Plum Creek (12 August 1840), but most of the Comanches and their leader escaped to their camps on the upper Colorado River. In 1844 Buffalo Hump met with Sam Houston and demanded that the white men remain east of the Edwards Plateau. Houston tacitly agreed to this proposal, but the government was unable to stem the flood of settlers, and so the Indians resumed their raids. In response, Texas Rangers struck at Penateka camps, but Buffalo Hump managed to hold his own for some time. Finally, in May 1846 he led the Comanche delegation at Council Springs that signed a treaty with the United States. As war chief of the Penatekas, Buffalo Hump dealt peacefully with American officials throughout the late 1840s and 1850s. In 1849 he guided Rip Ford's expedition part of the way from San Antonio to El Paso, and in 1856 he led his people to the newly established Brazos Indian Reservation. His band's lack of freedom and food forced Buffalo Hump to move his band off the reservation in 1858. While camped in the Wichita Mountains, the Penatekas were attacked by United States troops under the command of Maj. Earl Van Dorn, who, unaware that Buffalo Hump's band had recently signed a treaty at Fort Arbuckle, killed 80 of them. In 1859 Buffalo Hump settled his remaining followers on the Kiowa–Comanche reservation near Fort Cobb, Indian Territory. There, in spite of his distress at the demise of the Comanches' traditional way of life, he asked for a house and farmland so that he could set an example for his people. *Jodye Lynn Dickson Schilz*

Bullis, John Lapham. United States Cavalry officer; b. Macedon, New York, 17 April 1841; d. San Antonio, 26 May 1911; m. Alice Rodríguez (1872; d. 1887); m. Josephine Withers (1891); 3 daughters. In 1862 Bullis enlisted as a corporal in the 126th New York

Volunteer Infantry. He was wounded and captured at Harper's Ferry (September 1862). After exchange, he was again wounded and captured at the battle of Gettysburg and spent the following 10 months in the notorious Libby Prison in Virginia. After again being exchanged for Confederate prisoners (1864), he joined the 118th United States Infantry, Colored, as a captain. Bullis reenlisted in the regular army as a second lieutenant in 1867 and returned to Texas, where his Civil War regiment had been stationed for Reconstruction duty. In 1869 he was transferred by request to the new Twenty-fourth United States Infantry, composed of white officers and black enlisted men. Although the initial years of service along the lower Rio Grande border proved fairly routine, Bullis participated in a number of operations against small Indian raiding parties and cattle rustlers. More important, while stationed at Fort Clark in 1873, he received command of a special troop of Black Seminole scouts that had been mustered three years earlier. Because of their intimate knowledge of the terrain in Coahuila, the scouts were assigned to Col. Ranald Mackenzie's expedition in 1873 against renegade Kickapoo camps at Remolino. Bullis and his 20 scouts distinguished themselves in battle and played an important role in Mackenzie's withdrawal to Texas. They served again with Mackenzie during the Red River Indian War of 1874. Sixteen years later Bullis received brevet citations for his "gallant service" at Remolino and in subsequent fighting. Upon his transfer in 1882 from command of the Black Seminole scouts to new duties in Indian Territory, the people of Kinney County presented him with two ceremonial swords in appreciation of his efforts to protect the border. The swords were later donated by his daughters to the Witte Museum in San Antonio. The Texas legislature likewise passed a special resolution in his honor.

After service at Camp Supply in Indian Territory from 1882 to 1888, Bullis joined his old regiment in Arizona and served as agent for the Apaches at San Carlos Reservation. In 1893 he was transferred to Santa Fe to act as agent for the Pueblos and Jicarilla Apaches. Four years later he returned to Texas with the rank of major and was appointed paymaster at Fort Sam Houston. During the Spanish-American War and Philippine Insurrection he saw service in Cuba and the Philippines. In 1904 President Theodore Roosevelt promoted him to the rank of brigadier general, and on the following day Bullis retired from service. Drawing upon knowledge from his experiences across West Texas, he purchased numerous tracts of land as investments. In 1885 he also entered into a lucrative partnership with fellow officer William R. Shafter and rancher John W. Spencer to open mines in the Shafter Mining District. The investments made Bullis a wealthy man and helped promote the settlement of West Texas. He received a final, posthumous, honor when, on the eve of American entry into World War I, the new military training base near San Antonio was named Camp Bullis, a component of Leon Springs Military Reservation.

Michael L. Tate

Burleson, Edward. Soldier and statesman; b. Buncombe County, North Carolina, 15 December 1798; d. Austin, 26 December 1851; m. Sarah Griffin Owen (1816); 9 children. Burleson fought in the War of 1812 under command of his father. In 1817 he was appointed a captain of militia in Howard County, Missouri; he was commissioned colonel in 1821 in Saline County, and was colonel of militia from 1823 to 1830 in Hardeman County,

Tennessee. He arrived in Texas on 1 May 1830 and received title for land in April 1831. In 1832 at San Felipe de Austin, he was a member of the ayuntamiento governing Austin, Bexar, Goliad, and Guadalupe counties. Late that year he was elected lieutenant colonel of the militia of Austin Municipality. In 1833 he was elected a delegate to the Second Convention in Mina. He fought in many engagements defending settlers against hostile Indians. In May 1835 in Bastrop he was elected to the committee of safety and was therefore unable to attend the Consultation, although he had been elected a delegate. In October 1835 in Gonzales he was elected lieutenant colonel of the infantry in Gen. Stephen F. Austin's army. On 24 November he became general of the volunteer army and replaced Austin. On 26 November with his father he fought in the Grass Fight during the siege of Bexar. On 1 December, Burleson was commissioned commander in chief of the volunteer army by the provisional government. On 6 December he entered Bexar and, with Ben Milam, wrote a report to the provisional government. On 14 December he reported on the success at Bexar to the provisional governor, Henry Smith. The volunteer army disbanded on 20 December, and Burleson raised a company and rode to Gonzales in February 1836. By 10 March, in Gonzales, he was officially elected colonel of the infantry, First Regiment. At the battle of San Jacinto (21 April 1836) he commanded the First Regiment, which was placed opposite Mexican breastworks and was the first to charge them. Burleson accepted the sword and surrender of Gen. Juan N. Almonte.

Subsequently, he served as brigadier general of the Republic of Texas militia, built roads, served in the Congress of the republic, and defeated Mexican insurgents in the Córdova Rebellion. President Lamar made him commander of the Frontier Regiment (1839), and in that role he defeated Cherokee chief Bowl. The next year he commanded troops in the battle of Plum Creek. In 1841 he was elected vice president of the republic. In the spring of 1842, when the Mexican army under Rafael Vásquez invaded Texas, Burleson was elected commander. Houston, who had been deeply offended by Burleson's handling of the Cherokees, sent Alexander Somervell to take over, and Burleson yielded the command to him. Burleson then made his famous speech before the Alamo: "though Thermopolae had her messenger of defeat, the Alamo had none." In the fall of 1842 Mexican general Adrián Woll invaded Texas. Burleson raised troops for defense and again yielded the command to Somervell, sent by Houston. In 1844 Burleson made an unsuccessful bid for the presidency against Anson Jones. In December 1845 he was elected senator from the Fifteenth District to the First Legislature of the state of Texas. He was unanimously elected president pro tem. During the Mexican War, Burleson and Governor James P. Henderson went to Monterrey, Nuevo León; Burleson was appointed senior aide-de-camp, held the rank of major, and served as a spy during the siege of Monterrey and at Buena Vista. In 1847 he, Eli T. Merriman, and William Lindsey surveyed and laid out the town of San Marcos. In 1848 Burleson, still president pro tem, introduced a resolution to establish Hays County and donated the land for the courthouse. He chaired the Senate Committee on Military Affairs, which awarded a $1,250,000 grant to the state for Indian depredations. Burleson County is named for him, and the site of the State Cemetery was purchased in his honor in 1854.

Helen Burleson Kelso

Burnet, David Gouverneur. President and vice president of the Republic of Texas; b. Newark, New Jersey, 14 April 1788; d. Galveston, 5 December 1870; m. Hannah Este (1830); 4 children, only one of whom survived childhood. Burnet came from a distinguished family—which included a surgeon general, a Supreme Court justice–U.S. senator, and a mayor of Cincinnati—whose accomplishments he strove to equal. He studied law in Cincinnati. He wrote in 1859 that he deplored the course of the "ignorant popular Sovereignty." His attitude and politics did not make him popular in Texas, and his entire life was a string of disappointments. He worked at a commission house in New York (1805) and went on an unsuccessful filibustering expedition to Venezuela before returning to New York at the end of 1806. About 1817 he moved to Natchitoches, Louisiana, and for the next two years traded with the Comanches near the headwaters of the Brazos with John Cotton. After returning to Ohio, in 1826 he received an empresario grant that authorized him to settle 300 families near Nacogdoches, part of the area recently replevined from Haden Edwards, within six years. He was to receive 23,000 acres from the state of Coahuila and Texas for every 100 families settled. Burnet spent 1827 in Texas and then returned to Ohio, where he fruitlessly sought colonists and financial backing. In desperation he and refugee Lorenzo de Zavala sold the rights to their colonization contracts in October 1830 to a group of northeastern investors, the Galveston Bay and Texas Land Company. Burnet received an undisclosed sum of money and certificates for four leagues of land from the new company. Unfortunately, he was not allowed to locate the leagues because of the Law of April 6, 1830. He used the money to buy a steam sawmill, which he placed on the San Jacinto River. There he made his home. But the mill lost money, and he sold it in June 1835.

The articulate Burnet impressed local residents, and though he took no part in the first of the Anahuac Disturbances (1832), they chose him to represent the Liberty neighborhood at the convention at San Felipe in 1833. He helped draft the plea to sever Texas from Coahuila and made an earnest statement against the African slave trade. He hoped to become chief justice of the newly established Texas Supreme Court in 1834 but was only named to head the Brazos District Court. Instead of his $1,000 per annum allotment, Burnet wanted a handsome stipend in land like that which Chief Justice Thomas J. Chambers received. He was against independence for Texas in 1835, although he deplored the tendency of the national government toward a dictatorship. His more radical neighbors did not choose him as a delegate to either the Consultation or the Convention of 1836. Nevertheless, he attended the session on 10 March, where he gained clemency for a client sentenced to hang. The delegates, who were opposed to electing one of their number president of the new republic, elected Burnet. His ad interim presidency of the republic lasted from 17 March to 22 October 1836, and was very difficult. His actions angered Sam Houston, the army, the vice president, many cabinet members, and the public, and he left office embittered, intending never to return home, where a number of neighbors had turned against him. He lacked legal clients and was forced to turn to subsistence farming. In 1838 he entered the race for vice president and rode Lamar's coattails to victory. Forced to serve part of the time as secretary of state and acting president, Burnet became more out of step with public opinion. His bid for the presidency in 1841

David G. Burnet. Prints and Photographs Collection, David G. Burnet file, CAH; CN 00450.

against his old enemy, Houston, resulted in defeat after a vitriolic campaign of name-calling. Burnet was against annexation to the United States in 1845 but nevertheless applied for the position of United States district judge in 1846. Even with the Whig influence of his brothers, however, he lacked enough political influence. He was named secretary of state by Governor James P. Henderson in 1846 and served one term. An application to the Whig administration in 1849 for a position as Galveston customs collector also failed. His only other public office was largely symbolic, a reward for an elder statesman. In 1866 the Texas legislature named Burnet and Oran M. Roberts United States senators, but upon arrival in Washington they were not seated because Texas had failed to meet Republican political demands. Although intellectually opposed to secession, Burnet had embraced the Southern cause when his only son, William, resigned his commission in the United States Army and volunteered for Confederate service. The son was killed in a battle at Mobile in 1863, a crushing blow to Burnet, who had lost his wife in 1858.

After Hannah's death Burnet had to rent his farm to pay for room and board in Galveston. He and Lamar intended to publish a history of the republic to expose Sam Houston, and though Burnet furnished Lamar with many articles, Lamar was unable to find a publisher. Burnet burned his manuscript shortly before his death. He outlived all of his immediate family, died without money, and was buried by friends. His remains were moved from the Episcopal Cemetery to the new Magnolia Cemetery and finally to Lakeview Cemetery in Galveston, where the Daughters of the Republic of Texas placed a monument to him and his friend Sidney Sherman in 1894. Burnet County is named for him. In 1936 the state put a statue of him on the grounds of the high school in Clarksville.

Margaret Swett Henson

Burnett, Samuel Burk. Rancher and oilman; b. Bates County, Missouri, 1 January 1849; d. 27 June 1922; m. Ruth B. Lloyd (1869; divorced); 3 children; m. Mary Couts Barradel (1892); 1 son. In the late 1850s the family moved to Denton County, Texas. Burnett's first trail drive occurred in 1866. The following year he served as trail boss for his father. In 1868 he became a partner with his father, and in 1871 he acquired his own brand and began building what became one of the largest cattle empires in Texas history—the Four Sixes Ranch. He weathered the panic of 1873 by holding over the winter the 1,100 cattle he had driven to Kansas. The following year he sold this stock for a profit of $10,000. He was one of the first ranchers in Texas to buy steers and graze them for market. At first his herd consisted of longhorn cattle, but later he introduced Durhams and then Herefords into the herd, thus producing a fine breed. In 1874 Burnett bought and moved cattle from South Texas to the area of Little Wichita, now Wichita Falls, where he established his ranch headquarters in 1881. The move was partly prompted by an agreement drawn up between Burnett and Quanah Parker, Comanche chief and friend of Burnett. Through Parker's assistance over a period of years Burnett leased 300,000 acres of Kiowa and Comanche land in Indian Territory for 6½ cents an acre. He grazed 10,000 cattle on this land until 1902. After 1898 cattlemen were told to surrender their lease agreements to allow the opening of Oklahoma Territory to homesteaders. Burnett again called on a friend for assistance—Theodore Roosevelt—who helped him get an extension so that he could purchase land to offset the loss of grazing rights in Oklahoma. Between 1900 and 1903 Burnett bought 107,520 acres in Carson County and the Old "8" Ranch, of 141,000 acres, in King County. Ultimately, he owned ranches in Oklahoma and Mexico in addition to his holdings in Texas and ran 20,000 cattle under the Four Sixes brand.

In 1905, in return for Roosevelt's assistance, Burnett helped organize a wolf hunt for the president. During the president's visit, Roosevelt influenced the changing of the name of Nesterville, on the Four Sixes spread in Wichita County, to Burkburnett. Five years later Burnett discontinued personal direction of his ranch. He leased the Four Sixes to his eldest son, Tom, so that he could concentrate his attention on other business. After the discovery of oil on land near Burkburnett in 1921, Burnett's wealth increased dramatically. He had already expanded his business interests by buying property in Fort Worth, where he had maintained a residence since 1900. By 1910 the city had become headquarters for his financial enterprises and he had become the director and principal stockholder of the First National Bank of Fort Worth and president of the Ardmore Oil Milling and Gin Company. He continued his interest in ranching through his association with the Stock-Raisers Association of North-West Texas. He was also president of the National Feeders and Breeders Association and in 1896 of the Fort Worth Fat Stock Show. At the time of his death his wealth was estimated at $6 million, part of which, through the efforts of his widow, became an endowment for Texas Christian University.

David Minor

Butterfield Overland Mail. Also Southern Overland Mail; a semiweekly mail and passenger stage service from St. Louis and Memphis across northern Texas to San Francisco; operated from 1858 to 1861. The routes from the two eastern termini united at Fort Smith, Arkansas. From St. Louis to San Francisco the distance was 2,795 miles, probably the longest route of any system using horsedrawn conveyances in the history of the United States. An act of Congress, effective on 3 March 1857, authorized a mail contract calling for the conveying of letter mail twice weekly, in both directions, in fourhorse coaches or spring wagons suitable for carrying passengers; it was further specified that each trip should be completed within 25 days. The contract, awarded to John Butterfield and associates, provided for a compensation of $600,000 a year in addition to receipts for passengers and express. As of 1858 the route extended from San Francisco to Los Angeles, thence by Fort Yuma, California, and Tucson, Arizona, to Franklin, Texas (present El Paso); thence across Texas and across the Red River at Colbert's Ferry, eight miles below Preston. The mail went through almost without exception in the 25 days allowed. The postage rate of 10 cents a half ounce resulted in receipts in 1860 of $119,766.77. Early in 1859 Sherman was made a distribution point through which Texas settlements were given postal service. In addition to mail and express the Concord coaches had room for five or six passengers, and at times more were crowded in. The fare averaged $200 one-way. Passengers, with firearms ready to meet attacks by Indians, generally endured the ordeal of the trip without rest; for if a traveler laid over, he forfeited his seat, and he might be marooned for a month before he could secure another. Stage service on the Southern route was terminated in March 1861, when an agreement was made to modify the contract and move the route northward out of Texas.

Rupert N. Richardson

Bywaters, Jerry. Artist; b. Williamson Gerald Bywaters, Paris, 21 May 1906; d. Dallas, 7 March 1989; m. Mary McLarry (1931); ed. Southern Methodist University (grad. 1926 in comparative literature). After college, Bywaters traveled for two years in France, Spain, Mexico, and New England and studied at the New York Art Students League. When he returned to Dallas he found that his contemporaries had similar interests in expressing their native region in art. He became a central figure and spokesman for a group of young artists including Alexandre Hogue, Otis Dozier, William Lester, Everett Spruce, and others who found inspiration in the Texas landscape. In 1933 *Art Digest* announced that Bywaters had "arrived." He produced a significant body of landscape, still-life, and portrait paintings, as well as lithographic prints and public murals. Stylistically and aesthetically, his work paralleled the national movement known as the American Scene. He produced most of his important paintings and murals between 1937 and 1942. His paintings in museums include *Self-Portrait* (1935), *Sharecropper* (1937), and *On the Ranch* (1941) at the Dallas Museum of Art; *Where the Mountain Meets the Plains* at SMU; and *Oil Field Girls* (1940) at the Archer M. Huntington Art Gallery in Austin. Other important paintings include *Texas Subdivision* (1938), *Century Plant, Big Bend* (1939), *Autumn Still Life* (1942), and *Houses in West Texas Big Bend* (1942). His original lithographs include *Gargantua* (1935), which won a prize in the 1935 Allied Arts Exhibition; *Ranch Hand and Pony* (1938), exhibited at the 1938 Venice Biennial Exposition; *Texas Courthouse* (1938), purchased by the Dallas Museum of Fine Arts in 1938; and *False Fronts, Colorado* (1939), which received a prize from the Dallas Print Society in 1941. Bywaters was a founding member of Lone Star Printmakers, a group of artists in Texas who produced and published editions of original prints and circulated touring exhibitions of prints from 1938 to 1941.

During the 1930s and early 1940s, Bywaters successfully competed in federally sponsored post office mural competitions and completed six projects in Texas. He was art critic for the Dallas *Morning News* from 1933 to 1939. He served from 1943 to 1964 as director of the Dallas Museum of Fine Arts while teaching art and art history at SMU. During his 20-year tenure as director of the Dallas Museum of Fine Arts, Bywaters recognized the educational possibilities of the art museum and produced such ambitious and excellent exhibitions as Religious Art of the Western World (1958) and The Arts of Man (1962). In the mid-1950s he and the museum's board of trustees weathered accusations that the museum was exhibiting works by communists. Bywaters wrote and produced catalogues for art exhibitions, published an art magazine, and edited books on art. He was long associated with the *Southwest Review*. After retirement from SMU he served as regional director of the Texas Project of the Archives of American Art, Smithsonian Institution, and he continued to curate exhibitions. In 1981 he gave SMU his papers on the art and artists of the region to form the Jerry Bywaters Collection on Art of the Southwest. He was elected a life member of the Dallas Art Association (1972); received the Distinguished Alumni Award from SMU (1978); was recognized by the Texas Arts Alliance for distinguished service to the arts in the state (1980); and received an honorary doctorate from SMU (1987).   *Francine Carraro*

C

CCC. The Civilian Conservation Corps, proposed by President Franklin Roosevelt, operated nationwide between 1933 and 1942. It provided outdoor employment for 2.5 million young men working out of nearly 3,000 camps. The camps of 200 men each were supervised by the army and the work projects by the departments of agriculture and interior, in cooperation with the states. At individual camps the CCC hired LEMs ("locally experienced men") to work as craftsmen and teachers, and professional architects and engineers to provide design assistance and construction supervision to enrollees. To be an enrollee, a young man was required to be 17 to 25 years old and from a family on relief. The pay was $30 a month, of which $25 dollars was sent directly to the family. Veterans of World War I were also eligible and were housed in separate camps. At its peak in Texas the CCC operated camps with a capacity of 19,200. Assignment to states was random, so workers in Texas came from all over the country. Although most camps were devoted to soil-conservation and erosion-control projects, about 25 were responsible for the development of state parks. Participants performed heavy, semi-skilled, outdoor labor; most worked on seeding, sodding, planting trees, banking slopes, or building roads and small dams. Although the enacting statute for the CCC forbade discrimination based on race, color, or creed, black enrollees were often segregated. The CCC offered participants a variety of activities in addition to work. The young men could enroll for classes in camp or in local high schools or colleges and earn educational credits from the elementary to the college level. They could also participate in a sports program that often included baseball, football, and track. In Texas the CCC left behind significant physical improvements to forest and farmland and passed on soil-conservation information to more than 5,000 farmers. Of the 56 state parks established through CCC efforts, 31 are still in existence, including Bastrop, Davis Mountains, Garner, Goliad, and Palo Duro Canyon. Several CCC city and county parks also remain. The CCC declined as the economy recovered. The advent of World War II brought prosperity and new priorities, and in the summer of 1942 the program ended.

Kenneth E. Hendrickson, Jr.

Caballo, Juan. Black Seminole leader; also known as Juan Coheia, Juan Cavallo, Gopher John, and John Horse; d. 1882; m. Susan July; 1 son. He was a successful farmer and stockman in Florida in the early 1800s. His parents are believed to have been of mixed race (African, Spanish, and American Indian). Like many of the Black Seminole Indians (also called maroons), he began his life as a slave of the Seminoles. In 1843, after he helped a group of Seminoles reach Indian Territory, he was granted his freedom. Throughout his life he served the interests of Black Seminoles, including negotiations with whites. He was fluent in at least four languages. Caballo first achieved prominence during the Second Seminole War as a negotiator and military leader. Between 1838 and 1842 he traveled between Florida and Indian Territory helping Indians and maroons to relocate. During the last two years of the war, he was responsible for convincing at least 535 belliger-

ents to surrender. As in the Seminole homeland, once the groups arrived in Indian Territory, Black Seminoles established autonomous communities adjacent to their Seminole masters. Caballo's band settled on the Little River in Oklahoma at a place he named Wewoka, the "Village of Refuge." Life in the territory was extremely difficult for both Seminoles and Black Seminoles due to the domination of the Creek Indians. Seminoles allowed their slaves to own weapons and to control their own labor, but the Creeks put intense pressure on the Seminoles to adopt the more stringent Creek slave codes. By 1849 Caballo, in conjunction with Seminole leader Coacoochee, induced a group of dissatisfied maroons and Indians to leave the territory and settle in Mexico, where slavery was outlawed. Mexican authorities provided them with land and supplies in exchange for their promise to patrol the area and subdue renegade Comanches and Apaches. For his service to Mexico in fighting Indians, Juan Caballo was given the title of captain in the Mexican army.

By 1870, the internal problems of Mexico forced the Moscogos, as the Mexicans called them, to abandon their lands and return to the United States. Many of the Black Seminoles entered the United States Army as scouts ("buffalo soldiers"), on the army's promise that they and their families would eventually be allowed to move to their own land in Oklahoma. Always skeptical of the white man's promises, Caballo refused to join the Black Seminole scouts, though he served them as an unofficial interpreter at times. In December 1873, John Kibbetts, Caballo's longtime second-in-command, beat out the elder leader in a vote for civil chief. Despite the loss, Black Seminoles continued to rely on Caballo's diplomatic skills. Dissatisfied with the delays of the government in giving the Black Seminoles a permanent home, Caballo returned to Mexico in 1876 with a band of followers. He died on a mission to Mexico City to secure previously issued government land grants. Some say he was murdered by outlaws; others believe that he died in a Mexico City hospital of pneumonia. During his life the chief had survived four assassination attempts—a fact that gives some credence to the murder theory.

E. Douglas Sivad

Cabeza de Vaca. Early Spanish explorer; b. Álvar Núñez, Jérez de la Frontera, ca. 1490; d. Spain, mid-1550s. As a young man he campaigned in Italy with the army of Charles V. His service to the crown probably earned him the position of treasurer in the 1527–28 expedition of Pánfilo de Narváez, who obtained a royal patent to found a colony in "Florida"—i. e., the Gulf Coast from Pánuco to the Florida peninsula. Narváez landed on the west coast of Florida in April 1528 and, despite protests from Cabeza de Vaca (an adopted surname), separated 300 men from his support vessels to reconnoiter the land. He was soon permanently separated from his ships and stranded on the Florida coast, which he believed to be only a few leagues from the Pánuco River in Mexico. The expedition then marched up the interior coast to northwestern Florida, where it remained for three months. Faced with hostile natives and food shortages, Narváez crowded his remaining 250 men into five improvised barges and

Title page of Cabeza de Vaca's *Relación* (Valladolid, 1555). Courtesy CAH; CN 00835a. Cabeza de Vaca's book, also known as *Los Naufragios* or *Shipwrecks,* is the first published eyewitness account of Texas. This title page, a hand-colored woodcut, appeared in the second edition.

set sail for Pánuco. A storm near the Mississippi River drove the barges apart, after which two of the battered craft were beached on an island (probably Follets Island) off the Texas coast (November 1528). Among some 80 survivors were Cabeza de Vaca, Andrés Dorantes de Carranza, his African-born slave Estevanico, and Alonso Castillo Maldonado. These men, known as the "four ragged castaways," were among the first non-Indians to set foot on Texas soil, and they were the only survivors of the Narváez expedition. Most of the others succumbed to disease, injuries, drowning, or violence at the hands of hostile coastal Indians.

After Cabeza de Vaca became separated from the other survivors, all but two of them proceeded down the coast. Cabeza de Vaca recovered from a near fatal illness and later became the first European merchant in Texas. He ranged inland as well as along the coast, carrying sea shells and mesquite beans to the interior and returning with skins and red ochre. He also had success as a medicine man; his treatment consisted of blessing the afflicted, breathing on injuries, and praying. His reluctance to leave the Galveston area was influenced by a single surviving countryman, Lope de Oviedo, who refused to leave the initial landfall island. In 1532 Cabeza de Vaca persuaded the reluctant Spaniard to

accompany him along the coast toward Pánuco, the route the other survivors had taken in 1529. On the way Lope de Oviedo turned back and disappeared. Cabeza de Vaca eventually rendezvoused with three astonished colleagues at what they called the "River of Nuts," probably the Guadalupe. There the four castaways, who were made slaves of the Mariame Indians, plotted their escape to Mexico. Not until 1534, however, did they start for Pánuco. They arrived at Culiacán, an outpost near the Pacific Coast of Mexico, in early 1536.

Their path has been the subject of historical controversy for more than a century, and the Texas portion of the odyssey has received the most attention. The *Relación* of Cabeza de Vaca reported the experience, and the joint report, a cooperative account, was written by the three surviving Spaniards. Both accounts were composed shortly after the trek ended in 1536. Biotic, enthnographic, and physiographic information contained in these narratives provides clues as to where the four men spent nearly seven years in Texas and what they saw. Their reports of their experiences provide valuable data on Texas Indians, landforms, flora, and fauna. The data, when correlated with the established goal of reaching Pánuco, strongly suggest a southern route along the inner Texas coast and a crossing of the lower Rio Grande into Mexico near the site of International Falcon Reservoir. Ultimately, the castaways' successful flight on foot brought them back to Texas at the junction of the Rio Grande and the Río Conchos near the site of present Presidio. On that portion of the trek, Cabeza de Vaca removed an arrow from the chest of an Indian—said to be the first surgical operation in Texas, which earned him remembrance as the "patron saint" of the Texas Surgical Society. He also deserves recognition as the first geographer, historian, and ethnologist in Texas. He was the only Spaniard to live among the coastal Indians of Texas and survive to write about them. As a result he, along with Dorantes de Carranza and Castillo Maldonado, may be remembered for producing the first Texas literature. In the early 1540s Cabeza de Vaca again served the Spanish crown as a governor in what is now Paraguay. He was, however, charged with misrule there, recalled to Spain, tried, and temporarily banished to North Africa. Later he was cleared of charges and permitted to return to Spain.   *Donald E. Chipman*

Cabildo. In Spanish Texas the cabildo was the building that housed meetings of the ayuntamiento, though colonists generally used the term to refer to the council itself. *Ayuntamiento* was used more frequently in late Spanish Texas, but the two terms were interchangeable.   *Geoffrey Pivateau*

Cacti. More than 100 species of cacti grow in Texas, the widest assortment found in any state in the U.S. Many are best known by such nonscientific names as blind pear, cow-tongue cactus, night-blooming cereus, Texas rainbow, tree cactus, early bloomer, and devil's head, so-called because its rigid spines are dangerous to the hoofs of horses and cattle. Numerous other varieties are commonly called strawberry cactus, pincushion, and jumping jack. Cacti are used in Texas for foods, for landscaping, and for commercial and private botanical collections. The tunas, or seed pods, of the prickly pear are used in making salads, wines, and jelly; the pads, or *nopalitos,* with their spines singed off, make a substantial food for cattle and form a minor staple in Tex-Mex foods. Other cacti are used to make food col-

Cactus Flowers, by Dawson Dawson–Watson, 1929. Oil on canvas. 26" × 21". Courtesy Witte Museum, San Antonio. Dawson–Watson was to cacti what Julian Onderdonk was to bluebonnets. He was attracted to Texas by the Texas Wildflower Competition that oilman Edgar B. Davis sponsored, and he continued to paint different versions of cacti thereafter. One of Dawson–Watson's cactus paintings won the 1927 contest.

orings, medicines, and candy. The climatic adaptability of cacti and their ease of culture make them useful in gardens and as shrubbery; their unusual forms and multicolored flowers, which vary in shade from green and white to magenta and purple, attract many collectors. The sizes of cacti range from the minute button cactus, smaller than a dime, to the barrel or fishhook cactus, which weighs up to half a ton or more.

The cacti of Texas represent 10 genera:

Echinocereus. Echino- ("spiny") refers to the very thorny covering of this genus, and *cereus* ("wax candle") comes from the stately appearance of its upright species. *Echinocerei* are oval, conical, or cylindrical cacti, always with ribbed stems. The flowers are usually large and beautiful, though a few have small and inconspicuous greenish flowers. The fruits are always fleshy and thin-skinned and often edible; they are also spiny, but the spines loosen as the fruits mature and may be easily brushed off. The *Echinocerei* grow mostly in exposed places on dry slopes and hills in full sun.

Wilcoxia. Five species in this genus are usually recognized, four in Mexico and one in South Texas. The cacti have slender stems of about five-eighths inch or less diameter. The spines are very short, a quarter inch or less long. The flower is large and

beautiful, bell-shaped or funnel-shaped, reddish to purplish, and diurnal. The ovary surface is scaly, wooly, and covered with bristly or hairlike spines that remain on the fruits.

Peniocereus. The "thread cereus" cacti all have slender stems and an extremely large, fleshy taproot, from which grow stems that are ribbed at first but become round. All have fragrant nocturnal flowers produced from within the spine areole, and all have very short spines on the stems and rigid spines on the fruits.

Acanthocereus. There are about a dozen species in the "acanthus candle" genus. These are more or less shrubby plants that grow upright but cannot support their own weight for long and depend on some support, usually other plants. Supported stems may grow to 20 feet tall. All stems are from one to four inches in diameter, and mature stems have from three to seven conspicuous ribs. The flowers are nocturnal, large, and white, and the ovary is usually spiny. These tropical lowland cacti are never found far from a coast and seem to thrive best on semiarid coastal plains. They tolerate much more moisture than most cacti and when water is adequate grow very rapidly. A light frost will kill the tips of the stems, and 32° F will kill all of the plant above the ground, though the roots may sprout again. In the U.S. the *Acanthocerei* have a precarious existence along the coast in South Texas and Florida.

Echinocactus. Most members of this genus, known as the barrel cacti, have strong, rigid, numerous spines. A few have more slender and flexible spines, and the genus includes a some spineless members. The barrels range in size from several hundred pounds to miniature forms only a few inches high. The exterior exhibits from eight to more than 20 vertical or spiraling ribs. Flowers are produced at or near the apex of the plant and have no distinct floral tube; the ovary bears scales and sometimes wool but not spines.

Lophophora. The members of this genus, the "crest-bearers," are small, globose, or depressed globose cacti that grow from comparatively large, carrot-shaped taproots. The stem is about three inches in diameter but stands no more than two inches above the ground. Stems may be single or may branch from the base to form large clusters. Surfaces are blue-green and often glaucous. The plants have no spines after the early seedling stage. The ribs are broad and flat. The areoles are small and round with long white to yellowish wool that often persists, and the flowers are small, bell-shaped, and varied in color. In this genus the ovary and fruit are entirely naked, and the fruit remains always fleshy. The stems are ribbed. Monomorphic areoles produce the flowers from the apexes of young tubercles rather than from the axils. Peyote belongs to this genus.

Ariocarpus. This is a small genus with only one species in Texas and the others in Mexico. The body of the plant consists of one or occasionally a cluster of low flattened stems ranging from two inches in diameter to 10 inches across. The smaller species may not project above the surface of the ground, whereas the larger ones reach five inches tall. The stem sits on top of a large carrot-like taproot. The surface of the stem is divided into very distinct, usually imbricated but noncoalescent tubercles. There are no spines after first seedling growth. This genus is unusual in that it flowers in the fall. Flowers open widely, are diurnal, and are white, yellowish, or purplish. The ovary and fruit are both naked. The fruit is fleshy at first, becomes dry at maturity, and disintegrates, leaving the seeds in the wool at the center of the plant.

Epithelantha. Although a number of species of this genus grow in Mexico, only one grows in the U.S. The whole stem is covered with very many, very tiny tubercles, apparently the smallest tubercles of any U.S. cactus. These are hidden almost entirely from view by many tiny spines. The growing tip of the stem is a distinct depression filled with a great deal of hairlike wool and covered over by the converging, later deciduous, tips of the longer spines; this covering makes it difficult to observe the formation of the tubercles, areoles, and flowers. Also unusual about this cactus is the fact that it produces its flowers not in the axil of the tubercle but at the top of it. This cactus does not produce its flower from within a monomorphic spine areole as previously believed. The blossom is produced after a division of the meristem into a determinate spiny portion and a separate, indeterminate, floral or vegetative meristem.

Mammillaria. Members of this genus are small or very small. The stems vary in different species from depressed and almost flat to globular or sometimes columnar and are often referred to as heads. In some species these remain single, but in many others they multiply from the base to become caespitose; one individual sometimes forms a large clump of heads. In a few species branches may occasionally grow from higher up on the stem. Each stem is entirely covered by a system of nipple-like projections called tubercles. These are usually arranged in spiral rows but in a few cases are more loosely organized. The tubercles are usually cylindrical or conical but sometimes have more or less quadrangular bases.

Opuntia. This large genus is generally regarded as more primitive than the others. In more than half of the states of the United States opuntias are the only cacti found; it is this genus that allows the claim that cacti grow over almost the entire U.S. Characteristics are jointed stems, cylindrical or conical leaves on young stems, the presence of glochidia (barbed hairs or spines), and the production of spreading, rotate flowers with more or less sensitive stamens and with areoles that often produce glochidia and spines on the ovaries. The fruits have thick rinds.

John G. Johnson

Cal Farley's Boys Ranch.

Cal Farley's Boys Ranch was founded in 1939 by former professional wrestler and Amarillo businessman Cal Farley on the site of Old Tascosa in Oldham County. Land was donated by Panhandle Rancher Julian Bivins, and the old county courthouse was used as the first dormitory. The ranch was to provide "the boy nobody wanted" with "a shirttail to hang to." Celebrities like Roy Rogers, Jack Dempsey and J. Edgar Hoover were among the friends of the ranch, and an MGM movie, *Boys Ranch* (1946), provided much needed publicity. An annual rodeo was introduced in 1944. By 1973, the facility had cared for and educated 2,500 boys. In 1987 Girlstown, U.S.A., with campuses at Borger and Whiteface, merged with Cal Farley's Boys Ranch. In 1994 the resident population at Boys Ranch was 412, and it was a co-ed facility *H. Allen Anderson*

Callahan Expedition.

An expedition into Mexico in October 1855, ostensibly for punishment of Lipan Apaches who raided in Texas and retreated into Mexico; the real purpose, however, may have been to recover runaway slaves. James Hughes Callahan was authorized by Governor Elisha M. Pease (July 1855) to lead the expedition. Governor Santiago Vidaurri of Nuevo León y Coahuila rebuffed an emissary sent by slaveholders to gain the Mexicans' cooperation, and the slaveholders agitated for punishment of the Mexicans as well as the Indians—and perhaps for the return of slaves. Callahan, who kept the real purpose of the expedition secret even from his own men, left Bandera Pass on 18 September, crossed the Rio Grande on 1–3 October, skirmished with a Mexican force, then returned to Piedras Negras and took the town. As the Mexican force approached on 5 October, Callahan ordered his men to set fire to houses to cover their retreat, and on the evening of the next day Maj. Sidney Burbank, commander of the American forces across the river at Fort Duncan, turned four cannons to cover the Texans as they recrossed the river. Callahan defended his invasion of Mexico, claiming that he had received permission from the Mexican authorities to cross the river in pursuit of the Lipans. Pease said that the burning of Piedras Negras was justified because the Mexicans had deceived Callahan by leading him into an ambush. Quartermaster Edward Burleson, Jr., alluded to a different purpose, however, in a letter to newspaper editor Rip Ford about a slave who had escaped to Piedras Negras: The "Mexicans took him up and sent him back to this side immediately. We can guess why they did it." Historians have argued for years over the purpose of the expedition, but there was little misunderstanding at the time by those who were there. Even Bvt. Maj. Gen. Persifor F. Smith, who had encouraged Pease to appoint a company of rangers to help defend the frontier, reported to the adjutant general's office that the Texans were organizing a party to retrieve runaway slaves. "I presume," Smith wrote, "that the party of Captain Callahan was the one alluded to." The claims originating with this invasion of Mexico were not officially settled until 1876, when the Claims Commission of 1868 awarded approximately 150 Mexican citizens a total of $50,000 in damages. *Ron Tyler*

Camels.

In 1836 Maj. George H. Crosman urged the United States War Department to use camels in Indian campaigns in Florida because of the animals' ability to keep on the move with a minimum of food and water. Facing the need for transportation and military action against Indians in the "Great American Desert," which was considered virtually uninhabitable, Secretary of War Jefferson Davis urged Congress to appropriate money to test the value and efficiency of camels in the Southwest. In 1855 Congress made $30,000 available for "the importation of dromedaries, to be employed for military purposes." Maj. H. C. Wayne received the special presidential assignment. The naval storeship *Supply*, commanded by Lt. D. D. Porter, trafficked down the North African coast and arrived at Indianola in April 1856 with 33 camels, three Arabs, and two Turks. On June 4 Wayne started the caravan westward. They stopped near Victoria, where the animals were clipped and Mrs. Mary A. Shirkey spun and knitted for the president of the United States a pair of camel-hair socks. The animals were taken to Camp Verde, where several successful experiments were made to test their utility in chasing Indians and carrying loads. Wayne reported that camels rose and walked with as much as 600 pounds without difficulty, traveled miles without water, and ate almost any kind of plant. One camel trek was made to the unexplored Big Bend. A second load of 41 camels was also quartered at Camp Verde. In 1857 Secretary of War John Floyd directed Edward Beale to use 25 of them in his survey for a wagon road from Fort Defiance, New Mexico, across the 35th parallel to the Colorado River. After this survey, the drive continued to Fort Tejon, California, where the camels were used to transport supplies and dispatches across the desert for the army. Eventually some of the animals were turned loose, some were used in salt pack-trains, and others even saw Texas again after Bethel Coopwood, Confederate spy and Texas lawyer, captured 14 from Union forces. During the Civil War, 80 camels and two Egyptian drivers passed into Confederate hands. The animals soon were widely scattered: some were turned out on the open range near Camp Verde; some were used to pack bales of cotton to Brownsville; and one found its way to the infantry command of Capt. Sterling Price, who used it throughout the war to carry the whole company's baggage. In 1866 the federal government sold the camels at auction; 66 of them went to Coopwood. Some in California had been sold at auction in 1863, and others escaped to roam the desert. The failure of the camel in the United States was not due to its capability; every test showed it to be a superior transport animal. It was instead the nature of the beasts that led to their demise—they stank, frightened horses, and were detested by handlers accustomed to mules.

Two private importations of camels followed the government experiment. On 16 October 1858 Mrs. M. J. Watson reported to Galveston port authorities that her ship had 89 camels aboard, and claimed that she wanted to test them for purposes of transport. One port official, however, suspected that she was using the camels to mask the odor typically associated with a slave ship and refused her petition to unload the cargo. After two months in port, Mrs. Watson sailed for the slave markets in Cuba after dumping the camels ashore in Galveston, where they wandered about the city and died from neglect and slaughter around the coastal sand dunes. A second civilian shipment of a dozen camels arrived at Port Lavaca in 1859, where it met a similar fate.

Chris Emmett and Odie B. Faulk

Camp Barkeley. Eleven miles southwest of Abilene. It was originally planned as a temporary camp for infantry and supply troops, but during World War II it became one of the state's largest military installations. At its peak it had a total population of 50,000. The camp was named for David B. Barkley, a native Texan who was awarded the Medal of Honor in World War I. A clerical error apparently caused the discrepancy in spelling. Construction began in December 1940 on land leased by the government. The first unit to occupy the camp was the Forty-fifth Infantry Division, consisting of 19,000 men under the command of Maj. Gen. William S. Key. The *45th Divisional News* was published at Camp Barkeley. One member of the paper's staff, William Mauldin, became a famous war cartoonist during World War II. Other units in addition to the Forty-fifth trained at Camp Barkeley, among them the Ninetieth Division (infantry) and the Eleventh and Twelfth Armored divisions. A medical officer candidate school was established at Barkeley in May 1942, and from it 12,500 candidates eventually graduated. A POW camp at the post housed 840 prisoners in 1945. On 30 April of that year Camp Barkeley was deactivated. It was officially closed in September 1945 and dismantled. At the time it closed, it encompassed one-ninth of Taylor County—77,436 acres—of which the government owned 18,976. After the camp was abandoned, the leased land reverted to its owners. Camp Barkeley had long-term local effects. Construction and army payrolls helped the local economy, and the community demonstrated an

ability to maintain satisfactory relations with a large military population that influenced the government's decision in the 1950s to locate Dyess Air Force Base in Abilene.

James M. Myers

Campbell, Thomas Mitchell. Governor; b. Rusk, 22 Apr. 1856, d. Galveston, 1 April 1923; m. Fannie Irene Bruner, 1878; 5 children. After home study of law, Campbell was admitted to the bar (1878). He practiced law in Longview before becoming court-appointed receiver for the International–Great Northern Railroad (1891) and moving to Palestine, where his efforts on behalf of the railroad brought him into conflict with the machinations of the road's owner (and Campbell's boss), Jay Gould. At the urging of former governor James S. Hogg, and with the support of Senator Joseph Weldon Bailey, Campbell ran successfully for governor in 1906. Reformist legislation characterized his two terms (1906–11): railroad regulation, antitrust measures, pure food and drug laws, equitable taxation, the Robertson Insurance Law (1907), which required insurance companies to invest policy reserves in Texas, and, perhaps most important, prison reform, including the end of the convict-lease system. New state agencies instituted under Campbell included the forerunners of the departments of banking, licensing and regulation, and health, as well as the Texas State Library. After his gubernatorial terms ended, Campbell practiced law in Palestine and ran unsuccessfully for the U.S. Senate (1916).

Janet Schmelzer

Camp Bowie. Texas has had three Camp Bowies, all of which were named for James Bowie:

1 (Brown County). Established September 1940 as an infantry and artillery training center for the Thirty-sixth Infantry Division, Texas National Guard; the first major defense construction project in Texas in World War II. The camp was occupied by the end of December 1940 by the 111th Quartermaster Regiment of the Thirty-sixth Division, commanded by Maj. Gen. Claude V. Birkhead. By October 1942 the camp had expanded from an original 2,000 acres to a total of 120,000 acres and was occupied, in addition to the Thirty-sixth Division, by the 113th Cavalry of the Iowa National Guard, the Eighth Army Corps with its headquarters, and troops of the Third Army under Gen. Walter Krueger. The Third Army personnel at Camp Bowie comprised special troops of the Seventh Headquarters Detachment of the Third Army, medical units ranging from the Second to the Seventeenth, some engineer companies, signal battalions, and chemical companies. The Eighth Corps included the 174th and 142nd Field Artillery groups. The Eighteenth Field Artillery Brigade, the Fourth Armored Division, and the Seventh Headquarters Special Troops of the Fourth Army were also stationed at Camp Bowie at various times. A WAC contingent was attached to the Tank Destroyer Group and the Service Command Unit. A rehabilitation center to serve all posts and camps of the Eighth Service Command was set up in January 1942, and in August 1943 a POW camp with a capacity of 3,000 prisoners was established within the post for German prisoners of war. The camp was declared surplus by a War Department order, effective August 31, 1946.

2 (Jackson County). On the east side of the Navidad River a mile below Texana; principal encampment of the Army of the Republic of Texas from April 22 through the middle of June 1837. The first commander, Gen. Albert Sidney Johnston, was succeeded by Col. Joseph H. D. Rogers and Col. H. R. A. Wiggington. At this camp, on the night of 5 May 1837, Col. Henry Teal was murdered, after which President Sam Houston issued indefinite furloughs to almost all of the men of the dangerously undisciplined and mutinous army. In the latter part of May, Secretary of War William S. Fisher issued furloughs and travel orders to 1,200 troops—two-thirds of the army. By the third week in June the 200 men remaining at Camp Bowie had been transferred to Camp Crockett, and the post was abandoned.

Thomas W. Cutrer

3 (Tarrant County). In the Arlington Heights neighborhood of Fort Worth; a World War I installation established for training of the Thirty-sixth Infantry Division; 2,186 acres. The First Texas Cavalry guarded the camp during its raising. Although classified as a tent camp, it required much construction to accommodate a division of men. Camp Bowie was opened officially on 24 August 1917 with Maj. Gen. Edwin St. John Greble of the regular army as commander. The division remained at Camp Bowie for ten months. Training dragged, partly because of epidemics and equipment shortages, but morale never flagged, thanks in part to the cooperation of Fort Worth in tending to the social needs of the troops. Relations between town and camp were remarkably good, though the February 18, 1918, issue of *Pass in Review* announced a base-mandated "purity crusade" designed to close down the brothels that thrived in Hell's Half Acre. Camp Bowie's greatest average monthly strength was recorded in October 1917 as 30,901. On April 11, 1918, the Thirty-sixth went on parade in the city for the first time. The four-hour event drew crowds estimated at 225,000, making it possibly the biggest parade in Fort Worth history. For about five months after the departure of the Thirty-sixth for France in July 1918, the camp functioned as an infantry replacement and training facility, with monthly population ranging from 4,164 to 10,527. A total of more than 100,000 men trained at the camp. Greble's retirement in September 1918 began a fairly rapid turnover of commanders that did not end until the camp ceased operation. Shortly after the Armistice on 11 November 1918 Camp Bowie was designated a demobilization center. By 31 May 1919 it had discharged 31,584 men. The heaviest traffic occurred in June, when it processed thousands of combat veterans of the Thirty-sixth and Ninetieth Texas–Oklahoma divisions. The demobilization having been concluded, Camp Bowie was closed on 15 August 1919. After the camp closed it was quickly converted to a residential area, as builders took advantage of utility hookups left by the army. *Lonnie J. White*

Camp Ford. A Confederate conscript-training camp four miles northeast of Tyler; established in 1862 and named for Rip Ford. In 1863 the Trans-Mississippi Department established a prison camp at Camp Ford and transferred the prisoners of war then located at Shreveport, Louisiana, to Tyler for confinement. These and other POWs sent to Tyler encamped in the open under guard until November 1863, when reports of a plan to escape caused alarm among the local citizenry and the Confederates in charge. Accordingly, a stockade was built enclosing an area of two to four acres. A large spring ran along the south wall of the stockade and served as a water supply for the prison camp. The prisoners were required to improvise their own shelter, which they fashioned out of logs and other primitive building materials. Until the spring of 1864, morale among the prisoners at Camp Ford was passable, and the ranking fed-

eral officers maintained a decent sense of order. Enterprising prisoners made goods for use and sale, including crude furniture, clay dishes, woven baskets, brooms, clothing, and other useful articles. Some of these were traded or sold to local citizens for food and clothes. Living conditions became deplorable in April 1864, however, when the population was suddenly tripled by the addition of about 3,000 prisoners captured at the defeat of the Union Army in Arkansas and in the Red River campaign. The stockade area was doubled in size in an effort to accommodate this influx. The 4,725 inmates were overcrowded and critically short of food, shelter, and clothing. Their plight was desperate for several months, until major exchanges of prisoners in July and October 1864 alleviated somewhat the shocking conditions that had prevailed.

For the rest of the war the Confederates encountered great difficulties in supplying adequate rations to both prisoners and guards at Camp Ford. Sometimes the standard daily pint of meal and pound of beef per prisoner was down to a quarter pound of each, depending upon the supply available to the Confederate commissary department. Beginning with the overcrowding in April 1864, the quality of the shelters deteriorated. Nearby timber was less plentiful, and shelters had to be constructed quickly. The prisoners improvised all sorts of crude shelters ranging from brush arbors to blanket tents. Some simply dug holes in the ground for protection from the cold winds. A popular form of shelter was called a "shebang," a burrow into a hillside covered by a crude A-shaped framework made of poles, sticks, and clay to protect the entrance. The majority of the prisoners required the clothes that they were wearing when captured to see them through their captivity. The acute shortage of clothing was due to a lack of manufacturing in the South and to the federal blockade. In response to a letter from the ranking Union officers at Camp Ford, at least two shipments of clothes from the United States government were received by and distributed among the prisoners. Escapes were common, but no reliable estimate of the number is available. Postwar accounts of escape attempts, some successful, were abundant among the members of the former inmates. After the war the former prisoners charged the Confederates with mistreatment and failure to provide humane living conditions at Camp Ford. However, the published accounts present many conflicting stories and viewpoints among the former prisoners. Nothing came of the charges. About 6,000 prisoners were confined at Camp Ford over the two years of its existence, making it the largest Confederate prison camp west of the Mississippi River. Of this number, 286 died there. Following the surrender of the Confederate Trans-Mississippi Department, the 1,200 remaining prisoners left Camp Ford, on 17 May 1865, bound for Shreveport. The remains of the prison compound were destroyed in July by a detail of the Tenth Illinois Cavalry. *F. Lee Lawrence*

Camp Henry E. McCulloch. A Confederate training camp four miles north of Victoria; named for a commanding general of the Department of Texas. Its commanding officer was Col. Robert R. Garland. Ten infantry companies from Calhoun, Victoria, Bell, Matagorda, Bexar, Gonzales, DeWitt, Travis, and Guadalupe counties, as well as two cavalry companies, were assembled at Camp McCulloch. The camp rented Victoria Male Academy to use as a hospital. Wearing uniforms manufactured at the Texas State Penitentiary at Huntsville, the raw recruits were drilled until they became adept at marching with military precision. In December 1861 units of the regiment were ordered to Indianola and Saluria to ward off a Union attack that never occurred. The troops broke camp on 22 May 1862 and left for Arkansas. *Charles D. Spurlin*

Camp Howze. A United States Army infantry-training camp northwest of Gainesville in central Cooke County; established in 1942 on a 59,000-acre tract purchased from local landowners beginning in December 1941 and named for Maj. Robert E. Lee Howze, a Medal of Honor winner who had seen action in the Indian campaigns of the late nineteenth century, the Philippine Insurrection, and World War I. With a troop capacity of 39,963 men, the camp served as the training ground for several hundred thousand men between 1942 and 1946. Among the units prepared for action in World War II were the 84th, 86th, and 103d divisions. The camp provided employment for hundreds of area civilians. In addition, the $20 million spent by the national government on Camp Howze fueled the local economy. In 1946 the camp was declared surplus, disbanded, and leveled.
Brian Hart

Camp Hudson. On San Pedro Creek, a tributary of the Devils River, 21 miles north of Comstock in Val Verde County; established in 1857 and named for Lt. Walter W. Hudson, who had been killed by Indians; one of several posts built between San Antonio and El Paso to protect travelers on the so-called Chihuahua Trail. Zenas R. Bliss, who was stationed at Camp Hudson for two years, reported seeing only four or five people during that time who were not related to the army. In 1859 one of the experimental caravans of camels from Camp Verde passed through Camp Hudson. The troops left in 1861 for service in the Civil War. In 1866 the post office closed. In October 1867 a stage from Camp Hudson to Fort Stockton was ambushed by Indians, and two military escorts were killed. Two companies of cavalry were ordered to Camp Hudson, and by April 1868 other troops had returned to the area. In 1876 Lt. Col. George P. Buell arrived at Camp Hudson from Fort Concho with two companies of cavalry. Under his leadership, the post was to be used as a summer camp to protect newly arrived settlers. The troops at Camp Hudson fought with Indians on several occasions and sometimes followed them into Mexico. In January 1877 the installation was permanently closed because the threat of Indian attacks no longer existed. *Julia Cauble Smith*

Camp Hulen. Originally Camp Palacios; just west of Palacios; established as a summer training camp for the Thirty-sixth Infantry Division after the Palacios Campsite Association donated the land to the state in 1926. It reached its peak use as an army training center during World War II. Some 6,500 men came to the first training session in the summer of 1926, when the camp newspaper, the *Camp Palacios T-Arrow Daily* began. In 1930 the camp was renamed Camp Hulen, after John Augustus Hulen, state militia commander and World War I hero. By 1934 some 1,886 concrete tent floors had been laid for the trainees. Because the surrounding bays provided a safe range for target practice, in 1940 the United States War Department began to use the base for antiaircraft training for national guard units from across the country (the Thirty-sixth Division had moved to

Camp Bowie in Brown County). In January 1941 the first draftees arrived, and the following month saw the first printed issue of the weekly *Camp Hulen Searchlight*, of which a few 1943 copies are housed at the Barker Texas History Center. Civil contractors and the WPA constructed additions to the camp, which eventually included some 400 semipermanent buildings and 2,825 floored, framed, and screened tents, as well as a tent theater, fire station, bakery, weather station, library, dental clinic, post office, and 500-bed hospital. At its height the installation's troop capacity was 14,560. Housing for soldiers' families and other newcomers was limited in nearby Palacios, and the town, a fourth of which did not even have proper sewerage facilities, was temporarily overloaded by the sudden rise in population. At one time the Texas Rangers were called in to help maintain order. In January 1944 Camp Hulen was converted to a prisoner of war camp; the Germans housed there were farmed out to help with agricultural work in the county. On 31 May 1946 the War Department declared Camp Hulen surplus and returned it to the Texas National Guard. The guard slowly dismantled it for scrap. In 1965 the site was sold to developers hoping to construct an industrial park, which was unbuilt decades later. The army air base associated with the camp became the Palacios Municipal Airport. *Rachel Jenkins*

Camp Liendo. On Leonard W. Groce's Liendo Plantation, 2½ miles east of Hempstead; probably established in 1862 to house Union soldiers captured by Confederate forces at the battle of Galveston. Most of the prisoners stayed temporarily before being taken to Camp Ford. Camp Liendo was also a recruiting station for the Confederate Army and a refugee center for women and children fleeing from other Southern states. At the end of the Civil War it was a rallying point; the Twenty-ninth Texas Cavalry disbanded there. Afterward, a federal division under the command of Gen. George Armstrong Custer camped at Liendo for four months. Groce lent a rocking chair to Mrs. Custer, who accepted his family's invitation to stay in the plantation house while recovering from an illness.
Clinton P. Hartmann

Camp Mabry. In Austin; headquarters of the Texas National Guard; established in the early 1890s and named for Woodford H. Mabry, adjutant general of Texas. In 1909 the United States government contributed 200 acres, and the camp comprised 400 acres by 1911. It was a mobilization site during the Spanish-American War. The state arsenal building was built there in 1915. During World War I the U.S. Army used the camp as a training site and engine-rebuilding station. When the Texas National Guard was called into federal service during World War II, Camp Mabry served as headquarters for the Texas Defense Guard, the remaining state militia. It was also a training ground for the Texas Department of Public Safety and the Texas Rangers until 1953. The state adjutant general's office was moved to Camp Mabry in 1954, and the Texas National Guard State Officer Candidate School was established there in 1959. The Texas National Guard Academy opened at Camp Mabry in June 1984. Also located on the post are the headquarters of the Texas Air National Guard, the Texas State Guard, the United States Property and Fiscal Office, the Texas National Guard Armory Board, the Headquarters Armory of the 49th Armored Division, a clinic, and a parachute packing and storage facility. The camp's 100th anniversary included an informal opening of the Texas Military Forces Museum. *Vivian Elizabeth Smyrl*

Camp Maxey. A World War II infantry-training camp 10 miles north of Paris; activated in 1942 and named for Confederate general Samuel Bell Maxey. The first division to be trained at the camp, the 103rd Infantry Division, was organized and activated on 15 September 1942. In addition to the army ground forces trained at Camp Maxey, army service forces and army air forces had a part in the development of camp activities. The varied terrain provided facilities for working out problems of infantry training to meet modern battle conditions. An artillery range, obstacle course, infiltration course, and "German Village" were included in training maneuvers. Troop capacity was 44,931. The camp was put on an inactive status on 1 October 1945 and thereafter served as a training center for the Texas National Guard. Most of the original buildings were demolished or sold and removed. In 1990 the camp sewage-treatment plant was used by the city of Paris. When Pat Mayse Lake was constructed, parts of the northern edge of the base were inundated.

Camp Peña Colorado. A United States Army post on Peña Colorado Creek four miles southwest of the site of Marathon. A nearby bluff, Peña Colorada ("red rock") gave the creek and post their name, though the army was not fastidious about Spanish grammatical gender. In historical times the site had been a major stopping place on the Comanche Trail to Mexico. It was first occupied by United States infantry in 1879. The post, on the road connecting Fort Clark and Fort Davis, was also on the prospective southern route of the transcontinental railroad, and was within practicable supporting distance of Fort Stockton to the northeast and Fort Davis to the northwest. It was likely established as part of a larger army strategy to increase pressure on the Apaches living in the Trans-Pecos. The outpost was founded the same month that Victorio and his Warm Springs Apaches escaped confinement on the Mescalero reservation. The primary mission of the garrison at Camp Peña Colorado, as it turned out, was to provide escort through the region, perform scout duty, and pursue bandits. In July 1880 the garrison was relieved by two companies of the Twenty-fourth United States Infantry, which remained for four years. During this time the spartan post consisted of several crude huts made of stone and mud and included two long, narrow buildings, one to serve as enlisted men's barracks and the other as a storehouse. Other buildings included two smaller huts for officers' quarters and a stone granary. The coming of the Southern Pacific Railroad in 1882 just to the north, however, brought commodities from the East. After July 1884 the garrison was principally composed of units of the Tenth United States Cavalry. Among the Tenth's famous "buffalo soldiers" who served at Camp Peña Colorado was Lt. Henry O. Flipper. The Third Cavalry replaced the Tenth in the summer of 1885, when Geronimo and his band were causing trouble in Arizona and New Mexico. Units of the Third Cavalry made up the garrison until relieved by a temporary detachment of the Eighteenth Infantry. Camp Peña Colorado was abandoned in 1893. By that time the settling of the country around the post was well along, and the need for United States Army troops in the Big Bend had shifted closer to the border. The site of the camp is located on Post Ranch, part of the Combs Cattle Company. The company's founder, David St. Clair Combs, early trail driver and prominent Texas rancher, donated the land around Peña Colorada Springs for a park in 1935. The park is still enjoyed by residents of the area, among whom the spot is commonly known simply as the Post. *Richard A. Thompson*

Camp Swift. Seven miles north of Bastrop; built in 1942 on 55,906 acres; initially had 2,750 buildings designed to accommodate 44,000 troops. The camp was named after Eben Swift, a World War I commander and author. During World War II it reached a maximum strength of 90,000 troops and included, at different times, the 95th, 97th, and 102nd Infantry divisions, the 10th Mountain Division, the 116th and 120th Tank Destroyer battalions, and the 5th Headquarters, Special Troops, of the Third Army. Swift was the largest army training and transshipment camp in Texas. It also housed 3,865 German prisoners of war. After the war much of the site was returned to former owners. The government retained 11,700 acres as a military reservation. That land housed parts of the Texas National Guard, a medium-security federal prison, and part of the University of Texas Environmental Science Park. Environmental-impact studies and development plans for the mining of extensive lignite deposits under Camp Swift began in the 1970s. Opposition by environmentalists and former landowners resulted in decades of litigation. *Art Leatherwood*

Camp Travis. Originally Camp Wilson; five miles northeast of downtown San Antonio abutting Fort Sam Houston. In May 1916 it became the mobilization point for the Texas National Guard during the Mexican border crisis. In 1917, after its selection as the training site for the Ninetieth Division of the army, it was renamed Camp Travis, in honor of Alamo hero William B. Travis. The camp comprised 18,290 acres, of which 5,730 were on the main campsite adjoining Fort Sam Houston. The Ninetieth Division was organized at Camp Travis in September and October of 1917. The ranking officers, including Maj. Gen. Henry T. Allen, the division and camp commander, were regular army officers. The junior officers were primarily Texas and Oklahoma graduates of the officer-training camp at Camp Funston. The enlisted personnel consisted of Texas and Oklahoma draftees. Hispanics and Indians were intermixed with Caucasians in the new draft division, but blacks were assigned to the camp depot brigade. By mid-October 1917 the Ninetieth Division numbered more than 31,000 officers and men. Equipment shortages, illness, and transfers to other commands interfered with training, however. At the time the division departed for Europe in June 1918 it was composed in considerable part of recent conscripts, many from states other than Texas and Oklahoma. During the summer of 1918 Camp Travis served as an induction and replacement center, with an average strength in July of about 34,000 white and black troops. In August and September the Eighteenth Division was formed of old and new units at the post under the command of Brig. Gen. George H. Estes. The Eighteenth was still in training when the war ended on 11 November. On 3 December Camp Travis was named as a demobilization center. In 1919 it was also designated a local recruiting station and a regional recruit depot. Some 62,500 troops were discharged at Camp Travis in about eight months. The camp then became the home station of the Second Division. Its service as a separate entity was terminated, however, upon its absorption by Fort Sam Houston in 1922.

Lonnie J. White

Canadian River Expedition. An 1868 Indian campaign; the westernmost prong of Gen. Philip H. Sheridan's winter campaign undertaken to chase down Cheyennes and Arapahos who had fled south of the Arkansas River after raiding white settlements in northwestern Kansas; the goal was to force the Indians to move to the reservations set up under the Medicine Lodge Treaty of 1867. The main force was led by Gen. Alfred Sully and included Lt. Col. George A. Custer's Seventh Cavalry. Maj. Andrew Wallace (Beans) Evans—a distinguished Civil War veteran recalled as a "melancholy, philosophically inclined officer, devoted to literature, suffering from an old wound, and having, to all appearance, registered a vow never to smile"—led a two-column western action to retrieve stragglers after Custer's victory in the battle of the Washita (Oklahoma). Evans led a southern column along the Canadian River, endured a blizzard, and engaged the Comanches at Soldier Spring, now in Greer County, Oklahoma, on Christmas Day, with devastating loss to the Indians. He turned back toward New Mexico on 3 January 1869. Maj. Eugene A. Carr led the northern column, which located no Indians.

Upon returning, Evans's troops were famished and suffering from exposure. Nevertheless, as it turned out, the village he and his men had destroyed at Soldier Spring was that of Horseback's Nokoni Comanche band, which had committed several depredations in Texas the previous summer and fall. At the height of the engagement the Nokonis had been reinforced by Kiowa braves under Woman's Heart, but to no avail. Afterward, several Nokonis and Kiowas surrendered to the authorities at Fort Cobb (Oklahoma), while others came in at Fort Bascom (New Mexico) in such haste that they arrived even ahead of Evans, who had returned there by 7 February. By the end of December 1868 most of the Kiowa and Comanche bands, except for the isolationist Quahadis, had been consolidated at Fort Cobb. The following spring, after the establishment of Fort Sill as the new headquarters for the Comanches and Kiowas, Custer made a sortie into the eastern Panhandle and induced several recalcitrant Cheyenne and Arapaho bands to report to Camp Supply for assignment to their new reservation. Although lasting peace was not effected for almost another decade, the raiders of the southern plains realized that the winter season was no longer a safeguard against campaigns by white horse-soldiers. Evans, who was brevetted colonel for his action at Soldier Spring, received a brigadier general's brevet in 1890 for his gallantry in an engagement against Apaches at the Big Dry Wash in Arizona on 17 July 1882.

H. Allen Anderson

Canary Islanders. In 1729 the Marqués de Aguayo proposed to the king of Spain that 400 families be transported from the Canary Islands, Galicia, or Havana to populate the province of Texas. His plan was approved, and notice was given the Canary Islanders to furnish 200 families. The Council of the Indies suggested that 400 families should be sent from the Canaries to Texas by way of Havana and Veracruz. By June 1730, 25 families had reached Cuba, and 10 had been sent on to Veracruz before orders from Spain to stop the movement arrived. Under the leadership of Juan Leal Goraz, the group marched overland to San Antonio de Bexar Presidio, where they arrived on 9 March 1731. The party had increased by marriages on the way to 15 families, a total of 56 persons. They joined a military community that had been in existence since 1718. The immigrants formed the nucleus of the villa of San Fernando de Béxar, the first regularly organized civil government in Texas. Several of the old families of San Antonio are descended from the Canary Islanders.

Capitals. Valladolid, Madrid, and Paris could be considered capitals of Texas under the competing claims of Spain and France. Mexico City could also be considered the first capital, since at the beginning of Spanish Texas there was no intermediate provincial capital. Ysleta, said to be the first settlement in Texas, had Santa Fe, New Mexico, as its capital. Monclova, Coahuila, became the first provincial capital of Texas in 1686. In 1721 the Marqués de Aguayo established headquarters at Los Adaes (present Robeline, Louisiana), which remained the capital of Texas for half a century. From 1772 until 1824 San Antonio was the seat of government, although acting governor Manuel Antonio Cordero y Bustamante made his headquarters in 1806 in the Old Stone Fort in Nacogdoches; in 1810 Manuel María de Salcedo had his headquarters there for three months. After the Mexican War of Independence Texas was united with Coahuila, with Saltillo as the provincial capital. On March 9, 1833, Monclova was made capital of Coahuila and Texas. The Department of Texas had become a subdistrict of the province, and San Felipe de Austin was named its capital in 1824. Therefore the conventions of 1832 and 1833 met at San Felipe, as did the Consultation (1835). The Convention of 1836, which declared Texas independent, met at Washington-on-the-Brazos. Harrisburg and Galveston were both occupied by President David G. Burnet as temporary capitals, and after the battle of San Jacinto Burnet and the cabinet met at Sam Houston's headquarters near the battlefield. The government then returned briefly to Galveston before moving to Velasco, which served as the seat of government through the end of September 1836.

Columbia (now West Columbia) became the first capital of an elected government of the Republic of Texas in October 1836 and remained capital for three months. Houston was then selected as a temporary capital, and President Sam Houston ordered the government to move there on December 15, 1836. Houston was capital from April 19, 1837, until 1839. A capital-site commission selected a site near La Grange in 1838, and Congress passed a bill to build the capital there, but Houston vetoed it. Waterloo, soon renamed Austin, was approved as the capital on January 19, 1839.

President Mirabeau B. Lamar and his cabinet arrived there on October 17, 1839. Fearing an attack on Austin by the Mexicans, President Houston ordered the government to return to Houston on March 13, 1842. Washington-on-the-Brazos became capital again by executive order in September of that year, and the order spawned the Archive War when President Houston attempted to move the archives from Austin. The Constitution of 1845 provided that Austin be capital until 1850, when a vote was required to choose the permanent capital. Austin received 7,674 votes, a majority. Another election was scheduled for 20 years later and held in 1872. Austin won with 63,297 votes, compared to Houston's 35,188 and Waco's 12,776.

John G. Johnson

Capitol. The present Capitol building (constructed 1882–88), is the fourth one in Austin. The Constitution of 1876 set aside three million acres of land—the XIT Ranch— in the Panhandle to fund construction. After a competition in which 8 architects entered a total of 11 designs, the Capitol Board approved the design entered by Elijah Myers of Detroit (1881). Mathias Schnell of Rock Island, Illinois, received the building contract but assigned it to Taylor, Babcock and Company, a Chicago firm that included Charles and John Farwell. Abner Taylor became the chief contractor but subcontracted the work to Gustav Wilke, a young Chicago builder. Although specifications called for native limestone, all of the limestone found near Austin contained discoloring iron particles. Taylor proposed using limestone from Bedford, Indiana, but the Capitol Board and Governor Ireland wished to use Texas stone, specifically red granite from Granite Mountain in Burnet County. The owners of the mountain, George Lacy, William Westfall, and Nimrod Norton, offered to give the state enough granite for the building. After some controversy about the cost of using granite, Wilke signed a supplementary contract (1885) in which he agreed to use red granite for the Capitol if the state would supply it free of charge, share the "extra cost," construct a narrow-gauge railroad from Burnet to Granite Mountain, and furnish convict labor to quarry the stone. Taylor also agreed to pay the state for the use of the convicts and to provide room and board for them. After labor difficulties arose in 1886, stemming from the use of convict labor to quarry the granite, Wilke imported granite cutters from Scotland, in violation of the Contract Labor Act of 1885. In spite of a subsequent boycott, work began on the Capitol dome in mid-1887, and the Goddess of Liberty was hoisted to the top of it in February 1888. The Capitol first was opened to the public on the evening of 21 April 1888, before its completion. The structure was dedicated during a week-long celebration the next month. But the Capitol Board refused to accept the structure because of a leaky roof and other problems. After corrections, the Capitol Board received the building in December 1888. In 1882 the three million acres of land in the Capitol reservation was valued at $1.5 million. The total cost of the Capitol was $3,744,630.60, of which the state assumed about $500,000. A hundred years later, the lands exchanged for the Capitol had a tax valuation of $7 billion. In February 1983 a fire badly damaged the east wing of the Capitol and provided the impetus for a restoration of the building and construction of an underground annex, which was carried out at a cost of $200 million by early 1995. The restored structure, which is open for tours, was rededicated on San Jacinto Day, 21 April 1995. *William Elton Green*

Carbajal, José. Soldier and politician; b. San Fernando de Béxar, date unknown; d. Soto la Marina, Tamaulipas, 1874; m. María del Refugio De León Garza (ca. 1830); 2 children. Carbajal renounced Catholicism under the influence of Alexander Campbell and became an ardent Protestant. Nevertheless, aided by Stephen F. Austin, he was made the official surveyor for Martín De León, laid out the town of Victoria, and married De León's daughter. In 1831 he accompanied José Francisco Madero to survey and issue land titles in East Texas and was arrested by John Davis Bradburn, but was soon released. He acted as ad interim secretary for the ayuntamiento of Bexar and in February 1835 was elected deputy from Bexar to the legislature of Coahuila and Texas, where he acted as secretary. In the spring of 1835 the legislature authorized him to publish the laws and decrees of the state in English and Spanish. The laws were published in Texas in

Convict laborers with granite blocks for construction of the state capitol, ca. 1885. Courtesy Austin History Center, Austin Public Library; Photo no. PICA 06359. The use of convict labor on the construction of the Capitol precipitated a boycott of the job by the granite cutters' union.

The Goddess of Liberty was raised to her position on the dome of the Capitol in 1888. Prints and Photographs Collection, Capitols—present file, CAH; CN 01225.

1839. Domingo de Ugartechea ordered him arrested for attempting to stir up rebellion, and Carbajal left for New Orleans, where in November 1835 he joined Peter Kerr and Fernando De León in chartering the *Hannah Elizabeth* to supply the Texas forces. The vessel was captured by Mexicans, and Carbajal was imprisoned at Brazos Santiago and then at Matamoros. While preparations were underway to transfer him to San Juan de Ullóa, he escaped and returned to Texas, where he or possibly his brother Mariano, who was with Fannin in 1835, signed the Goliad Declaration of Independence (2 December 1835). Carbajal was elected to the Convention of 1836 at Washington-on-the-Brazos but did not attend. In 1839, in command of a group of American volunteers, he defeated a Mexican Centralist army near Mier but was wounded in the engagement and lost the use of his left arm. As an advocate of an independent republic in northern Mexico, he commanded a division of the Mexican army against the United States in 1846. From 1850 to 1853 he led American merchants and filibusters in the border engagements known as the Merchants' War. Although he was arrested twice by United States authorities, he was released both times. He was living in Piedras Negras in 1855, when his house was destroyed by the Callahan expedition. In 1861 Carbajal was commander in chief of state troops of Tamaulipas and was defeated at Matamoros while supporting the *de jure* government of Jesús de la Serva. In 1862 he joined the Mexican liberal army to serve against the French. He was governor of Tamaulipas and San Luis Potosí in 1865, when he was commissioned financial agent to negotiate a loan from the United States. Some time later he moved to Hidalgo County. From there he moved in 1872 to Soto la Marina.

Carnegie Libraries. The public library movement was late in coming to Texas. Before the building program financed by Andrew Carnegie began, the state had only a handful of public libraries; some of the larger were the Galveston Public Library, the Houston Lyceum Library, the El Paso Public Library, and St. Mary's Church Library in San Antonio. Carnegie defined the public library as one that not only served the public but was supported by public funds. The cities that received his gifts were told they must make themselves responsible for the maintenance of the gifts. He asked that they pledge an amount equal to 10 percent of the grant, to be made available annually for the library, and that the city also provide a suitable site for the building. Between 1898 and 1917 Carnegie gave 34 gifts totaling $645,000 to various Texas communities. These donations were responsible for the construction of 32 public library buildings. Pittsburg, a mining town of fewer than 1,500 inhabitants, was the first Texas community to receive a Carnegie building grant. In 1899 and 1900 gifts were awarded to the Dallas, Fort Worth, and San Antonio public library associations and the Houston Women's Club. The El Paso Public Library Association received a grant of $37,500 in 1904. Grants to such smaller communities as Clarksville, Waco, Belton, Tyler, Gainesville, and Sherman often resulted from applications from women's clubs, many of which had already started their own subscription libraries. Typically, the buildings were constructed with two stories and a basement. Club rooms and auditoriums were included in the early buildings to provide rental fees to help defray operating costs. Later the Carnegie Corporation refused to approve plans that included rooms for nonlibrary use. The libraries in smaller communities were located wherever land was made available to them. Usually this property was adjacent to the business section of town, and frequently the development of a park around the library was planned, if one did not already exist. Construction on the last Texas library built by Carnegie funds began in May 1915 in Vernon. On its completion, the Vernon Library Committee found that it had no money with which to buy books, a problem frequently encountered in small communities. However, two years later the library was able to open with 4,000 volumes provided through the efforts of the city commission and the women's library club.

In many small communities the libraries functioned as the educational institutions they were intended to be. For example, Gainesville expanded service to the entire county, the second Texas library to do so. Sulphur Springs, Tyler, Sherman, and Waco enhanced support of their successful libraries with increases in funding and use. But in some of the smaller communities, interest declined due to the lack of good books and professional guidance. By 1914 fourteen communities were defaulting on the agreements made with the Carnegie Corporation, despite efforts by the Texas State Library and his-

torical commission to remedy the situation. In 1916 Alvin S. Johnson of Columbia University reported to the Carnegie Corporation that Texas libraries were poorly stocked and badly run and suggested that funds might better have been used for both books and buildings, with a provision for competent librarians for the initial period. He recommended that the corporation's attention be directed to education for librarianship. Shortly thereafter, the building grants were discontinued. Although the libraries were not successful in some small communities, the program stimulated interest in the public library movement and supplied a means by which many library buildings were built. In Texas the program resulted in the construction of libraries in five of the largest cities, thus permitting local resources to be spent entirely for staff and book collections. The resulting institutions are among the largest libraries in Texas.

Anne H. Jordan

Carroll, Benajah Harvey. Baptist leader; b. near Carrollton, Mississippi, 27 December 1843; d. Fort Worth, 11 November 1914; m. Ellen Virginia Bell (1866); 9 children; m. Hallie Harrison (1899); 1 child; ed. Baylor University. Carroll was ordained a Baptist minister in 1866 and preached at rural churches until he assumed the pastorate of First Baptist, Waco, where he stayed for more than 20 years and became known for eloquence, vigor, and orthodoxy, proclaimed a "new giant in Israel." He published voluminously and led in the consolidation of regional associa-

Reading room at the new Carnegie Library, Dallas Public Library, 1903. Dallas Public Library. The Carnegie donations for construction of public libraries stimulated interest in the public library movement and supplied the only means by which many libraries could have been built.

tions into the Baptist General Convention of Texas. He taught at Baylor (1872–1905) and was a statewide prohibition leader. After finally leaving the First Baptist Church he served as corresponding secretary for the Educational Commission, which was dedicated primarily to securing financial stability for Texas Baptist schools. He served as chairman of the Baylor University Board of Trustees (1886–1901) and as a trustee of Southern Baptist Theological Seminary (Louisville, Kentucky). In 1905 he organized Baylor Theological Seminary, which became Southwestern Baptist Theological Seminary in 1908. Carroll taught at the new school, which moved to Fort Worth in 1910, and served as its president until his death. His largest work is *An Interpretation of the English Bible* (1973), a commentary in 17 volumes. Baptist leader George Truett called Carroll "the greatest preacher our State has ever known." *Charles Chauncey Carroll*

Carrollton, Texas. Fourteen miles north of downtown Dallas in Dallas, Denton, and Collin counties; established in the early 1840s and probably named for Carrollton, Illinois, the hometown of many of the early settlers in the area. The first church in the agricultural community was built in 1846, the first school 10 years later. In 1878 the Dallas and Wichita, which soon after became part of the Kansas and Texas, built through the town, and in 1888 the Cotton Belt line crossed the Katy at Carrollton. The community flourished as a shipping center. In 1913 the town incorporated, and a gravel industry grew up around the same time; by the 1940s Carrollton was a "grain and gravel" town. After World War II Carrollton was caught up in the development of the Dallas metropolitan area, and grew from 1,160 inhabitants in 1950 to 13,855 in 1970, 40,595 in 1980, and 82,169 in 1990. In the 1980s the major area industries included auto-parts distribution, food packing, light manufacturing, and manufacturing of computers, semiconductors, and electronic components. Carrollton is part of the area called Metrocrest, a group of four northwest Dallas County cities (including Addison, Coppell, and Farmers Branch) served by a single chamber of commerce.

Joan Jenkins Perez

Carswell Air Force Base. At Fort Worth; called Tarrant Field (1932–43), Fort Worth Army Air Field (until January 1948), Fort Worth Air Force Base (in January 1948), Griffiss Air Force Base (for a few days in January 1948), and Carswell Air Force Base (from 1948). The base is named after Maj. Horace S. Carswell, Jr. The site of the base was selected in 1941 as a Consolidated Vultee factory for the production of B-24 bombers. A separate contract was let for a landing field, Tarrant Field, to be built to support the aircraft factory. The construction of an air force base on the east side of Tarrant Field was authorized after the Japanese attack on Pearl Harbor (7 December 1941), and Tarrant Field Airdrome was assigned to the Army Air Forces Flying Training Command in July 1942. The base became one of the first B-24 transition schools to begin operation. After more than 4,000 students were trained in B-24s at the base, its mission was changed to B-34 transition because of the nearness to the Consolidated factory. In 1945 the mission was changed from B-34 to B-29 aircraft training. The base was assigned to the newly formed Strategic Air Command in March 1946. In June 1948 the first B-36 was delivered to the Seventh Bomb Wing at the base. The six-engine, heavy bomber, later augmented by four jet engines, was phased out beginning in August 1957. In February 1949 the B-50, a later-

Amon Carter, Sr., seated with Harry Truman in Fort Worth during Truman's presidential campaign, September 27, 1948. Texas Governor Beauford Jester is seated to the left and Margaret Truman is seated behind Harry Truman. Sam Rayburn Photograph Collection, CAH; CN10462

model B-29, took off from Carswell for the first nonstop flight around the world. After mid-air refueling and 23,108 miles in 94 hours and one minute, the *Lucky Lady* landed at Carswell. The Seventh Bomb Wing became operational with the all-jet B-52 and KC-135 in January 1959. The unit was deployed to Guam in June 1965, flew more than 1,300 missions over Vietnam, and returned to Carswell in December 1965. In the 1980s the base received several new weapons systems, including modified B-52H aircraft and cruise missiles. By 1984 Carswell was the largest unit of its kind in the Strategic Air Command. The base contributed personnel and recruits to Operation Desert Storm in the Middle East in 1991. *Art Leatherwood*

Carter, Amon G., Sr. Newspaperman and entrepreneur; b. Giles Amon Carter, Crafton, Texas, 11 December 1879; d. Fort Worth, 23 June 1955; m. Zetta Thomas; 1 child; m. Nenetta Burton (divorced 1941); 2 children; m. Minnie Meacham Smith. Carter changed his name as an adult, named his son Amon Gary Carter, Jr., and was widely known as Amon Carter, Sr. He quit school at 11, did odd jobs in Bowie, and later worked in Oklahoma and California. He moved to Fort Worth in 1905, became advertising manager of the Fort Worth *Star*, bought the paper, and merged it with the Fort Worth *Telegram*. In 1925 he bought the rival Fort Worth *Record*, which was published by William Randolph Hearst. In 1922 he established WBAP, Fort Worth's first radio station; it became the first television station in the South and Southwest in 1948. Carter was chairman of the first board of directors of Texas Tech (1924–27). He was the youngest president of the Fort Worth Chamber of Commerce. When oil was discovered in North Texas in the 1920s he helped persuade oilmen to move to Fort Worth and encouraged construction of skyscrapers; he later served as director of the American Petroleum Institute. In 1911 he headed a committee that brought the first airplane to the Fort Worth area; by 1928 he was a director and part owner of the company that became American Airlines. Carter helped bring to Fort Worth a huge Convair complex, later to become General Dynamics. In 1952 he persuaded Bell Aircraft Corporation to locate a helicopter plant in nearby Hurst. Amon G. Carter Field was named for him in 1950. Carter's philanthropy was fueled by wealth from the oil business. His first successful well was drilled in New Mexico in 1935, and in 1945 the Amon G. Carter Foundation was established for cultural and educational purposes. Carter was named Range Boss of West Texas in 1939 and Ambassador of Good Will in 1941 by the Texas legislature. He received the Exceptional Service Medal from the United States Air Force and the Frank M. Hawks Memorial Award from American Legion Post 501 of New York City. He was an organizer and director of the Southwestern Exposition and Livestock Show, president of the Fort Worth Club for 35 years, and a contributor to Fort Worth hospitals and civic centers. Under the terms of his will the Amon Carter Museum was established in Fort Worth from his collection of Remingtons and Russells.

Ben H. Procter

Cart War. A "war" of 1857 between white and Hispanic carters. By the mid-1850s, Mexicans and *Tejanos* had built a successful business of hauling food and merchandise from the port of Indianola to San Antonio and elsewhere. Mexican carters moved freight more rapidly and cheaply than their competitors, who retaliated by harassing them so severely that a "campaign of death" seemed under way. Although public opinion in some counties between San Antonio and the coast ran heavily against the carters, who were regarded as an "intolerable nuisance," some newspapers spoke out against the violence—the Austin *Southern Intelligencer* and the San Antonio *Herald*, for instance. The news reached the Mexican minister in Washington, who protested to Secretary of State Lewis Cass. Cass urged Texas governor Elisha Pease to end the hostilities. Pease, concerned that "there is no security for the lives of citizens of Mexican origin engaged in the business of transportation, along the road from San Antonio to the Gulf," asked the legislature for a special appropriation for the militia, and the legislators approved with little opposition. Though some citizens who wanted the "peon Mexican teamsters" out of business were angry at the arrival of armed escorts for *Tejano* carters, the "war" subsided in December 1857. *David J. Weber*

Carvajal y de la Cueva, Luis de. Governor, slave trader, and the first Spanish subject to enter Texas; b. Mogodorio, Portugal, ca. 1540; d. Mexico, 23 February 1590; m. Guiomar de Ribera (ca. 1565). Carvajal sprang from Jewish converts to the Christian faith. As a young man he spent three years at Cape Verde as the king's accountant and treasurer in the black slave trade. Then he emigrated to Spain, traded in grain and wines at Seville, and married the daughter of a Portuguese royal slave factor. Two years later, driven by financial losses and marital discord, he sailed for New Spain with his own ship as admiral (second in command) of the Spanish Indies fleet. Upon arrival he was accorded the viceroy's appointment as *alcalde ordinario* of Tampico. In that capacity, in the fall of 1568, Carvajal rounded up 77 defenseless Englishmen marooned on the Tamaulipas shore by master John Hawkins, who had lost some of his ships in a shootout with the Spanish fleet at Veracruz. Impressed by this deed, which seems to have grown with each telling, Viceroy Martín Enríquez de

Almanza commissioned Carvajal a captain and sent him to open a road between Pánuco province and the Mazapil mines, then to chastise hostile Indian bands at the mouth of the Río Bravo (Rio Grande). In carrying out the latter assignment, Carvajal claimed to have punished the natives responsible for the massacre of 400 castaways from three ships wrecked on the coast while en route to Spain—doubtless the Padre Island Spanish shipwrecks of 1554. During the campaign, he crossed the lower Rio Grande into what is now Texas, thus becoming the first Spanish subject to do so. In 1578 Carvajal was summoned to Mexico City to answer charges that such exploits were but a thin disguise of his traffic in Indian slaves. Witnesses at the hearing generally upheld his probity, but the affront hastened the plan that may have been in his mind from the beginning.

He soon embarked for Spain, where in March 1579 he presented to the Council of the Indies one of the most sweeping proposals it had ever seen. He sought authority to develop all the ports from the Río Pánuco to Santa Elena on the Atlantic coast; to settle the area between Tampico and the mines of Mazapil and Zacatecas; and to extend exploration and settlement across Mexico "from sea to sea." So fervently did the council recommend the plan that the king approved it, in substance, without consulting the viceroy. For his life and that of his heir, Carvajal was granted the title of governor and captain-general with authority to "discover, pacify, and settle" a new province to be called the Nuevo Reyno de León. The jurisdiction was defined as extending west from the port of Tampico to the borders of Nueva Galicia and Nueva Vizcaya and northward into undiscovered lands. Within five years Carvajal was to reconnoiter the interior, convert the Indians, and settle all the ports from Tampico to St. Joseph Bay, which bordered the Florida jurisdiction of Pedro Menéndez de Avilés. North of Nueva Galicia and Nueva Vizcaya, he might "discover" from sea to sea, but no farther than 200 leagues of latitude and the same of longitude, without infringing on prior rights. Implicit in such a description was the crown's profound ignorance of the territory it claimed; the distance from Tampico to St. Joseph Bay was far greater than 200 leagues. After buying a ship and recruiting 100 families— many of them his wife's kin or his own—Carvajal again sailed for New Spain in June 1580, in the same fleet that carried a new viceroy, Conde de la Coruña. A bit heady over his success, the governor found Coruña an irritant. In a grave strategic blunder, he complained to the king. Although no details are found, Carvajal claimed to have reconnoitered his grant, the northern limits of which extended almost to the site of Austin. Sixty leagues northwest of Tampico, by his estimate, he discovered silver mines and founded, at the site of present Cerralvo, Nuevo León, a village pretentiously called Ciudad de León. His claims consistently exceeded his accomplishments. He established a village called San Luis at the site of present Monterrey and another called Almadén at that of Monclova. But litigation in the next century discredits many of his purported achievements, establishing that virtually all the places he occupied had been settled previously under authority of the governor of Nueva Vizcaya.

Indeed, charges of usurpation were brought against Carvajal in his own time. To these were added allegations that the governor made a habit of slave raiding on the Río de las Palmas (present Soto la Marina) and the Río Bravo and was selling Indian captives into slavery by the hundreds. In January 1587 he was brought again before the royal *audiencia* in Mexico City to face an inquiry. His renewed complaint to the crown brought an order for his recall to Spain. Carvajal, however, had already disappeared into his wilderness jurisdiction to resume his slave raiding. The viceroy's agent sent to arrest him found in the New Kingdom of León only two meager settlements of four or five huts each, distant from each other by 15 to 20 days' march. Carvajal finally was overtaken at Almadén, which he had established with "renegades who acknowledged neither God nor king," to carry on his slaving operation among peaceful Indians. Arrested and taken to Mexico, Carvajal left Gaspar Castaño de Sosa in charge of the Almadén settlement.

While in prison awaiting disposition of the viceroy's charges, Carvajal was accused by the Inquisition of heresy. He remained Catholic, but members of his extended family had reverted to Judaism—notably his niece, Isabel Rodríguez. It became apparent that the governor had known of Isabel's leanings and had failed in his obligation to denounce her. As a result, he was sentenced on 23 February 1590 to a six-year exile from New Spain. Before the year was out, while still awaiting execution of the sentence, Carvajal died in the Mexican prison. In the years that followed, the Inquisition indicted other members of the family. In 1596 charges were brought against Luis de Carvajal the younger, the governor's nephew and heir. Luis broke under torture and implicated up to 120 other practicing Judaists among the Carvajal colonists, including his own mother, brothers, and sisters. Many of them were subjected to the rack and burned on Mexico City's main plaza on 8 December 1596.

Robert S. Weddle

Casas Revolt. One of the many challenges to imperial authority that convulsed New Spain after Miguel Hidalgo y Costilla's initial action to achieve Mexican independence from Spain in September 1810. The royalist governor of Texas, Manuel María de Salcedo, found that Mexican revolutionaries seeking to overthrow Spanish rule hoped to get aid from the United States via Texas. In late 1810 Salcedo discovered two revolutionary agents from Nuevo Santander, militia lieutenants Francisco Ignacio Escamilla and Antonio Saenz, working among his troops. After ordering their imprisonment in San Antonio de Valero Mission, Salcedo decided to take preemptive action. Aware that the viceregal authorities could not spare forces to protect Texas, he tried in January to muster his men to crush the rebellion on the Rio Grande. Members of the garrison were unhappy at the prospect of leaving their families unprotected against Indians and other dangers. Equally disconcerted were the alcaldes, led by Francisco Travieso, who would be faced with mounting a citizen guard during the militia's absence. Along with a militia representative, Travieso called upon Capt. Juan Bautista de las Casas to assume command of the San Antonio troops. The next morning, 22 January 1811, Casas, leading the rebellious militia, arrested Governor Salcedo and the garrison commandant and ordered the release of Saenz and Escamilla. Casas and his supporters declared themselves against government by European-born Spaniards, *gachupines*, in accordance with Hidalgo's declaration. Casas ordered the arrest of all *gachupines* in the province and the confiscation of their property. The revolutionary leadership in Coahuila, upon word of Casas's success, appointed him ad interim governor of Texas. Meanwhile, Casas sent Saenz and alcalde Gavino Delgado, at the head of 80 troops, to establish the revolutionary government in Nacogdoches, where they arrived

on February 1. There they arrested *gachupines*, confiscated property, and set up a provisional government before returning to San Antonio with prisoners in tow.

When the successful Nacogdoches expedition returned, Casas had Saenz arrested for pocketing some of the confiscated wealth. The charges were dropped, but neither Saenz nor Delgado received recognition for the mission. The slighted revolutionaries made common cause with the remaining royalists. The two groups found a leader in Lt. Col. Juan Manuel Zambrano, a scandalous churchman and Bexar native who had long been out of favor with local authorities. Delgado persuaded leading townsmen to support Zambrano's efforts at undermining Casas, while Saenz agitated among the militia. Events soon came to a head. Ignacio Aldama, Hidalgo's ambassador to the United States, arrived at Bexar with a retinue and a substantial sum of money and silver to solicit arms and troops. After determining that Aldama would not remove Casas from the governorship, Zambrano and his fellow conspirators spread the rumor that Aldama was actually a Napoleonic agent. Fear of the French cemented the support of the populace for the counterrevolutionaries. In a predawn movement on 2 March, Zambrano's forces captured and arrested Casas and Aldama. Casas was sent as a prisoner to Monclova for court-martial as a traitor. On 3 August 1811 he was demoted, shot in the back, and beheaded. The body was buried at Monclova, and the head was sent to San Antonio to be publicly displayed. With the troops loyal to the new junta, royal authority was soon reestablished throughout the province of Texas. Salcedo was restored to the governorship.

Laura Caldwell

Castañeda, Carlos Eduardo. Historian. b. Ciudad Camargo, Tamaulipas, 11 November 1896; d. Austin, April 3, 1958; m. Elisa Ríos (1921); 3 children; ed. University of Texas (A.B., 1921; M.A., 1923; Ph.D., 1932). Castañeda moved to the United States in 1906 and graduated as valedictorian from Brownsville High School in 1916. He taught Spanish in Beaumont and San Antonio and from 1923 to 1927 was associate professor at the College of William and Mary in Virginia. He became librarian of the Genaro García Collection at UT (1927) and served as associate professor of history from 1939 to 1946. During World War II he took a leave of absence to serve as regional director of the President's Committee on Fair Employment Practice. In 1946 he became professor of Latin-American history, a position he held until his death. Castañeda's scholarly interests centered on the history of the Catholic Church in the Spanish Borderlands. His principal work was the sevenvolume *Our Catholic Heritage in Texas, 1519–1936*, with a *Supplement* that brought the story to 1950. He translated Juan Agustín Morfi's *History of Texas, 1673–1779* (1935) and (with Jack A. Dabbs) compiled *Guide to the Latin American Manuscripts in the University of Texas Library* (1939). He was president of the American Catholic Historical Association (1939), a Knight of the Equestrian Order of the Holy Sepulchre of Jerusalem (1941), and Knight Commander of the Order of Isabel the Catholic (1950). He received honorary doctorates from St. Edward's University (1941) and the Catholic University of America (1951), as well as the Junípero Serra Award of the Americas from the Academy of American Franciscan History in Washington (1951). The main library at the University of Texas at Austin is named for him and Ervin S. Perry.

Félix D. Almaráz, Jr.

Carlos Castañeda, ca. 1941–1948. Eleuterio Escobar Papers, Benson Latin American Collection, University of Texas at Austin.

Castro, Henri. Empresario; b. department of Landes, France, July 1786; d. Monterrey, Nuevo León, 31 November 1865; m. Amelia Mathias (1813). Castro was descended from Portuguese Jews who fled the Spanish Inquisition and later occupied a position of wealth and status in southwestern France. At 19 Castro was appointed by the governor of Landes to a committee to welcome Napoleon during a visit to the province, and in 1806 he served as a member of Napoleon's guard of honor when the emperor installed his brother Joseph as king of Spain. Castro's wife brought him a dowry of 50,000 francs. After the fall of Napoleon, he immigrated to the United States and in 1827 became a naturalized citizen. He returned to France in 1838 and became a partner in the banking house of Lafitte and Company. While with that firm he tried to negotiate a loan for the Republic of Texas and thus became interested in the young republic. Out of gratitude for his influence and kindness to Texas, President Sam Houston appointed him consul general for Texas in Paris. In 1842 Castro entered into a contract with the Texas government to settle a colony on the Medina River. After great expense, labor, and vexing delays, between 1843 and 1847 he succeeded in chartering 27 ships, in which he brought to Texas 485 families and 457 single men. His task was more difficult because the French government was trying to colonize Algeria and because the Mexican War often made Texas ports unsafe. Castro was able, however, to settle his first shipload of families at Castroville in September 1844; he also established the communities of Quihi

(1845), Vandenburg (1846), and D'Hanis (1847). Castro was learned, wise, and humane. He spent his own money freely—more than $200,000—for the welfare of his colonists, furnishing them cows, farm implements, seeds for planting, medicines, and other needs. He had unbounded faith in the capacity of intelligent men for self-government. Among his duties Castro found the time to publish his memoirs. He made many maps of his colonial grant and of the area bordering on it and circulated them throughout the Rhine districts of France to induce colonists to join his settlements. After he died on his way to France, his interests were carried on by his son, Lorenzo. Castro County was named in his honor.   *Amelia W. Williams*

Castroville, Texas. The "Little Alsace" of Texas; on the Medina River 25 miles west of San Antonio in eastern Medina County. The town was named for its founder, Henri Castro, whose land grant began four miles west of the Medina River and comprised frontier lands in Comanche territory. Wanting to locate his first settlement on the Medina River, Castro purchased the sixteen leagues between his grant and the river from John McMullen of San Antonio. He arranged transport for mostly Catholic Alsatian farmers to the Texas coast, from where the colonists were escorted overland to San Antonio. On 2 September 1844 Castro set out from San Antonio with his colonists, accompanied by Texas Ranger John C. Hays and five of his men, to decide upon a site for settlement. The company chose a level, park-like area near a sharp bend of the Medina River covered with pecan trees. Subsequently, the colonists endured raids by Comanches and Mexicans, droughts in 1848 and 1849, an invasion of locusts, and a cholera epidemic in 1849. Castro patterned his town after European villages in which small town lots were surrounded by individual farming plots. The town was surveyed by John James. Its streets were named in honor of Castro's relatives and friends and the capitals of Europe. In 1844 citizens of Castroville built St. Louis Catholic Church, the first church in Medina County. By 1856 Castroville supported three large stores, a brewery, and a water-powered gristmill. Castroville architecture and style were distinctly European. The houses were not arranged along parallel lines but were spread out over many acres. The house builders used rough-cut stone or stone and timber combinations and smoothed over the exterior with lime plaster. The European method of building ground floors of stone and second floors with vertically placed timbers was characteristic of two-story construction. A cross was set up on Mount Gentilz.

The first post office in Medina County opened in Castroville in 1847. In 1848 the Texas legislature established Medina County and designated Castroville its county seat. In 1853 Castro donated two lots for the site of the new courthouse, which when completed in 1855 served as a school. During the Civil War wagontrains loaded with freight stopped at Castroville on their way to Mexico, and the town thrived. By the mid-1860s Castroville was the twelfth largest city in Texas. In 1884 the town had a population of 1,000, a weekly newspaper, a steam gristmill and cotton gin, a brewery, Catholic and Lutheran churches, a convent, and a public school. The principal marketable goods produced at this time were cotton, hides, and grain. By 1890 pecans were being marketed, and a telephone system had been installed. In 1880 the Southern Pacific Railroad, extending its line to the west, passed south of Castroville because the town refused to grant the railroad a bonus. Hondo became the county seat in 1892.

Castroville citizens voted that year to disincorporate their town, and it remained unincorporated until 1948. In 1915 the old courthouse was converted into a school with three large classrooms. The population dropped to 500 during the 1920s, bottomed out at 325 in 1930, then began to grow again, reaching 865 in 1940 and 1,508 in 1960. In 1963 the Castroville Public Library, the first public library in Medina County, opened. In the 1980s agribusinesses in Castroville included a plant processing whole-grain corn for local tortilla and corn-chip manufacturers, feed mills, and irrigation, tractor, and farm-implement dealers. Castroville is also a center for applied research in genetics and artificial breeding of livestock. In 1990 the population was 2,159. Many of the structures built in Castroville's earliest days continued to house people and businesses in the 1990s. Castroville has been recognized as a national and a Texas historic district. Many of the 97 Historical American buildings in Castroville can be seen on a walking tour, including the Landmark Inn State Historic Site, the St. Louis Catholic and the Zion Lutheran churches, the Moye Formation Center, the Tarde Hotel, and Henri Castro's original homestead. Castroville celebrates St. Louis Day on August 22 each year. *Ruben E. Ochoa*

Cattle Trailing. The principal method of getting cattle to market in the late nineteenth century. Cattle trailing provided Texans with a practical, economical means of marketing livestock. It also achieved mythological stature as an aspect of the American frontier. Although their heyday was from 1866 to 1890, organized livestock drives to market in the U.S. date to the seventeenth century, especially in the Carolinas, Massachusetts, New York, and Pennsylvania. Easterners, however, often afoot and aided by shepherd dogs, herded relatively tame animals, whereas Texas drives during the nineteenth century usually featured mounted riders tending decidedly wilder beasts, at first mostly longhorn cattle and very often mavericks. As early as the 1830s, opportunists drove surplus Texas cattle from Stephen F. Austin's colony eastward through treacherous swamp country to New Orleans, where animals fetched twice their Texas market value. After statehood, during the 1840s and 1850s, some cattlemen drove Texas cattle northward over the Shawnee Trail to Illinois, Indiana, Iowa, Missouri, and Ohio, where they were sold mostly to farmers who fattened them for local slaughter markets. The first recorded large cattle drive occurred in 1846, when Edward Piper herded 1,000 head from Texas to Ohio. Outbreaks of "Texas fever" during the mid-1850s caused both Missouri and Kansas legislatures to quarantine their states against "southern cattle." The California gold rush brought substantial demand for beef, and during the early to middle 1850s some adventurous Texans herded steers westward through rugged mountains and deserts to West Coast mining camps, where animals worth $14 in Texas sold for $100 or more. During the Civil War most animals were left untended at home, where they multiplied, though some Texans drove cattle to New Orleans.

At the war's end, Texans had three million to six million cattle, many of them unbranded mavericks worth locally as little as two dollars each. However, the same beasts were potentially far more valuable elsewhere, especially in the North, which had been largely denuded of its livestock by wartime demand and where longhorns commanded $40 or more a head. As early as 1865 a few Texans reportedly tested export markets by trailing cattle to Mexico and Louisiana, but most cattlemen waited until the spring of 1866 to mount large trail drives, especially to the North. That year Texans drove more than 260,000 cattle to assorted markets. Some went eastward to Louisiana, where many animals were shipped by boat to Cairo, Illinois, and St. Louis, Missouri. In search of possible sales among Rocky Mountain miners, veteran cattleman Oliver Loving and his young partner Charles Goodnight that year drove a herd of cattle westward through dangerous Indian country to New Mexico and sold them profitably at Fort Sumner, New Mexico, and at Denver, thereby inaugurating the famed Goodnight–Loving Trail. Yet the vast majority of Texans who drove cattle to market in 1866 apparently followed the familiar and safer Shawnee Trail through Indian Territory either to Kansas City or to Sedalia, Missouri, both of which possessed railroad facilities for transshipment eastward, especially to meatpackers at Chicago. While many drovers found profitable markets and sold cattle for as much as $60 a head, others encountered armed, hostile farmers, especially in Missouri, where new outbreaks of Texas fever engendered much anger. Therefore, many cattlemen reportedly resolved not to drive cattle northward again. A number of states, including Colorado, Nebraska, Kansas, Missouri, Illinois, and Kentucky, either barred or severely restricted the trailing of Texas cattle across their borders. The restrictions included fines up to $1,000, and in some areas herds were either impounded or killed.

Postwar cattle trailing might have ended had not Illinois cattle buyer Joseph G. McCoy established a marketplace away from settled areas. Selecting Abilene, Kansas, near the center of the mostly uninhabited Great Plains—then a veritable sea of grass—McCoy enticed Kansas Pacific Railroad executives to provide sidings and other facilities and even to pay him a commission on each carload of cattle it shipped from Abilene. He also persuaded Kansas officials not to enforce the state's quarantine law at Abilene in order to attract trail herds; he later successfully lobbied the Illinois legislature to revise its restrictions to allow entry of Texas cattle that had been "wintered" in Kansas, documentation of which soon accompanied every shipment eastward. McCoy advertised his facilities with handbills and by word of mouth, attracting drovers and an estimated 35,000 head of cattle in 1867. Thereafter, until closed to southern cattle by renewed quarantine in 1873, Abilene, Kansas, was the principal railhead-market for Texas cattle. The most important cow path from Texas to Abilene was the Chisholm Trail. Between the Civil War and 1873 more than 1.5 million Texas cattle were driven over it to Abilene, as well as to Wichita and Ellsworth, rival Kansas cattle towns along the trail.

This enormous traffic gave rise to contract drovers, who, for a fee (usually $1 to $1.50 per head) walked Texas animals to market for their owners, large and small cattle raisers alike who mostly remained at home, tending their breeding stock. Railroads to northern and eastern markets, available in Texas after 1873, did not immediately diminish trail traffic because freight rates were two to three times more expensive than drovers' fees. Numerous Texans, mostly young former Confederates, became contract drovers. The most active of these was probably John T. Lytle, who, in association with at least three partners between 1871 and 1886, delivered about a half million cattle to Kansas markets. Also important were John R. and William B. Blocker, George W. Littlefield, Ike (Isaac Thomas) Pryor, Moses Coggin, Eugene B. Millett, Charles Goodnight,

William H. Jennings, and numerous others, most of whom also became substantial ranchers. In addition to contract deliveries, they often included their own livestock on drives, as well as animals they bought cheaply in Texas and drove to market for speculation. However, most of their profits derived from volume and efficient use of manpower. All told, contract drovers accounted for as much as 90 percent of total trail traffic between 1866 and 1890, the rest being moved by those who had actually raised the animals.

A herd delivered by contract drovers typically consisted of as many as 3,000 head and employed about 11 persons. An estimated two-thirds of these individuals were white—"cowboys" mostly, youths aged 12 to 18 who were readily available for seasonal work as "waddies," the appellation often given trail hands then. Trail bosses and ramrods—also usually whites—were somewhat older. The rest were members of minorities—blacks, Hispanics, or Indians—mature men usually, who often served as cooks and horse wranglers. A few adventurous young women rode the trail, frequently disguised as boys. Wages ranged from $25 to $40 a month for waddies, $50 for wranglers, and $75 for cooks and ramrods, to $100 or more for trail bosses, who often also shared the profits. With chuck and equipment wagons leading the way toward suitable campsites, followed closely by horse wranglers and remudas (herds of spare horses), drives were herded by a couple of waddies on "point," two or more on "flank," and two or more on "drag," that dusty rear position often reserved for greenhorns or meted out as punishment to enforce discipline. Little of the work was glamorous. Most days were uneventful; a plodding, leisurely pace of 10 to 15 miles a day allowed cattle to graze their way to market in about six weeks. Drudgery was occasionally punctuated with violent weather, stampedes, dangerous river crossings, and, rarely, hostile Indians. Even so, few trail bosses allowed youthful waddies to carry pistols, which were prone to discharge and stampede cattle. The gun-totin' image of cowboys owes more to Hollywood than to history.

About 1876 most northern cattle drives shifted westward from the Texas Road (or Chisholm Trail) to the Western (Dodge City or Ogallala) Trail. By then much of the eastern trail in Texas traversed settled country, and farmers vigorously objected to cattle being driven through their fields. Civilized tribes in Indian Territory increasingly demanded grazing fees from the drovers who crossed their reservations. And, after 1873, Texas herds capable of carrying Texas fever were quarantined from Abilene, Ellsworth, and Wichita, forcing drovers who continued to use the Chisholm Trail westward to Hays. Looking for an alternate route and market, in 1874 contract drover John Lytle blazed the Western Trail to Dodge City, but few of his contemporaries immediately followed his path. Most of them waited until the Comanches and Kiowas had been disarmed and forced onto reservations after the Red River Indian War (1871–76). Thereafter, until Kansas and other northern states and territories totally quarantined themselves against Texas fever in 1885, the trail to Dodge was the principal thoroughfare over which between 2.7 million and 6 million Texas cattle were moved to market. To forestall the end of trailing, contract drovers and South Texas cattlemen sought to circumvent quarantines by asking Congress to establish a National Trail, a federal highway for cattle that would have departed the Western Trail south of the Kansas border, run westward through the Oklahoma Panhandle, and then turned northward to pass through Colorado, Nebraska, Wyoming, and Montana, ending at the international boundary. But the bill died in the House of Representatives. By then the Western Trail had been blocked in innumerable places with barbed wire fences, legally erected and not, both in Texas and north of the Red River. With the movement of cattle thus greatly impeded by quarantines and barbed wire, Texas cattlemen increasingly shifted to railroads to transport their animals to market. *Jimmy M. Skaggs*

Cayuga. A small river steamer; the first commercially successful steamboat in Texas. The vessel, an 88-ton side-wheeler, was built in 1832 in Pittsburgh, Pennsylvania. She was 96'11" long, 17'4" wide, and 5'4" deep. The *Cayuga* had one deck, two boilers, a high-compression engine, a cabin on deck, a plain head, and a pointed stern. Her first owners were Pennsylvanians who sold her to Mississippi interests; they in turn sold to J. F. Aisles of New Orleans. William P. Harris and Robert Wilson, Texas entrepreneurs and partners, bought the vessel in 1834 from Aisles. Having been in the Mississippi steamboat trade, Harris and Wilson knew the virtues of river transportation. In order to finance their purchase they secured pledges from Texas investors for 5,000 acres of land and $800. The *Cayuga* cleared New Orleans for Galveston Bay on 1 August 1834, under Capt. John E. Ross. She was the only steamer in Texas at this time. She operated on the Brazos River during the fall of 1834 under the command of Capt. William P. Harris and ascended the river as high as Washington-on-the-Brazos. The necessity of waiting for three different rises of the river in running upstream and three in going downstream gave Harris the opportunity to clear and plant corn on 300 acres of the pledged land. On 8 January 1835 a ball was given in San Felipe in honor of the arrival of the *Cayuga*. The steamer left San Felipe on 15 January and ran aground downstream. Throughout 1835 she continued to ply the Brazos River, Galveston Bay, and Buffalo Bayou, where Harris and Wilson maintained a store, warehouse, and sawmill at Harrisburg.

In April 1836 David Burnet, ad interim president of the new Republic of Texas, impressed the Cayuga for public service. The ship began transporting provisions to the Texas army and rescuing officials and citizens fleeing the advancing Mexican armies. On 15 April Captain Harris, in command of the steamer, evacuated Harrisburg just ahead of General Santa Anna and his troops. The refugees included President Burnet, his cabinet, and all the inhabitants of the town. After stopping at Lynch's Ferry and New Washington the *Cayuga* preceded to Anahuac and Galveston, where the passengers disembarked. The cabinet members remained aboard and on April 19 were rejoined by Burnet, who had left the steamer at Lynch's Ferry to get his family and had narrowly escaped being captured by the Mexicans at New Washington. The business of the republic was conducted through April 26 on the *Cayuga*, the temporary capitol. During this time the republic bought the steamer for $5,000 from Harris. The Republic of Texas spent $300 for repairs on the vessel and by the end of the year authorized the secretary of the navy to sell it. The steamer was sold at auction on 15 December 1836 at Lynch's Ferry. The new owners refitted her and renamed her the *Branch T. Archer*; she was thus one of two Texas ships named after Archer. The *Archer* remained in the Houston–Galveston trade during 1837 and 1838. In June 1838 she was reported to have ascended the Trinity River as far as the Coushatta Indian Village. John E. Ross was captain of the vessel during these years.

The last mention of the little steamer was in the notice for a Liberty County sheriff's sale on 4 September 1839, advertising all the right, title, and interest of John Huffman in the steamboat *Pioneer*, the late *Branch T. Archer*, together with the tackle and furniture. The vessel lay near the residence of Robert Wiseman in the Old River. The sale was to settle claims of John E. Ross and Robert Adkinson. *Jean L. Epperson*

Cazneau, Jane McManus. Author, journalist, and unofficial diplomat; pseudonyms Montgomery, Cora Montgomery, Corrine Montgomery; b. Troy, New York, 6 April 1807; d. at sea, 10 December 1878; m. William F. (or Allen B.) Storms (1825, divorced 1831); 1 son; m. Texas entrepreneur and politician William Leslie Cazneau (1849). In 1830 Jane Storms was named as Aaron Burr's mistress in a divorce suit brought against Burr. With her brother Robert she traveled to Texas—the first of nine trips between 1832 and 1849. She applied to S. F. Austin for a headright and a league of coastal land. By one account, the Mexican government granted her 11 leagues of land for an empresario project, but since she lacked the money to move her German settlers from the Texas coast to the designated colony the enterprise broke up at Matagorda. She speculated in Texas land from 1834 to 1851. Apparently in 1833, her brother Robert and her parents moved to Matagorda. She supported the cause of Texas independence, and in the mid-1840s her columns in the New York *Sun* helped swing American opinion toward annexation of Texas. She contributed "The Presidents of Texas" to the March 1845 issue of the *Democratic Review*. That same year her *Texas and Her Presidents, With a Glance at Her Climate and Agricultural Capabilities* was published in New York. She and her husband lived for a time at Eagle Pass, where he founded a town, opened a trade depot, and investigated mining opportunities. Jane recounted her experiences there in *Eagle Pass; or Life on the Border* (1852), in which she charged that Mexicans had been kidnapping Texas residents into peonage in Mexico. Her complaints induced the State Department to broach the issue with the Mexican government and led Frederick Law Olmsted to investigate the matter. Olmsted reported in *A Journey Through Texas* that he found no evidence to corroborate Mrs. Cazneau's accusations. Throughout the antebellum period Jane Cazneau maintained close ties to Mirabeau B. Lamar, who dedicated a volume of poetry to her (*Verse Memorials*, 1857).

She participated in United States diplomacy almost a century before the first woman was appointed to the American Foreign Service. During the Mexican War she played an important, if unofficial, part in the unsuccessful secret peace mission of *Sun* editor Moses Yale Beach to Mexico City (1846–47), an assignment authorized by President James K. Polk. During that mission she became the only female war correspondent and the only American journalist to issue reports from behind enemy lines. Between 1847 and her death she also promoted "Manifest Destiny" in Latin America. She resided for much of the 1850s in the Dominican Republic, where her husband was serving as United States secret agent and commissioner, diplomatic missions which she helped initiate. It is difficult to separate ideology from self-interest when it comes to her expansionist advocacy; she and her husband made substantial investments that promised profit if the U.S. government implemented her policies. To promote these causes as well as her opinions on domestic political issues, she wrote letters to presidents and demanded and received presidential audiences. She socialized with and sent letters to politicians and journalists, including James K. Polk, James Buchanan, Jefferson Davis, Horace Greeley, Thurlow Weed, and William H. Seward. She contributed pieces to city newspapers in the East, including the New York *Sun*, the Philadelphia *Public Ledger*, the Washington *States*, and the New York *Tribune*, as well as magazines such as *Hunt's Commercial Magazine* and the *Democratic Review*. She bought into the New York *Morning Star* so that she could use its press to publish her own expansionist journal, the short-lived *Our Times*. Between 1848 and 1853 her column "The Truth," regularly published in the Spanish and English language newspaper *La Verdad*, advocated the annexation of Cuba to the United States. Her books, particularly *The Queen of Islands* (1850) and *Our Winter Eden: Pen Pictures of the Tropics* (1878), conveyed her expansionist message.

The Cazneaus purchased Esmeralda, an estate in the Dominican Republic, in 1855. Though Abraham Lincoln's administration terminated Cazneau's diplomatic appointment to that country in 1861, he and his wife remained at their estate. When Spanish troops destroyed Esmeralda in October 1863, they fled to Keith Hall in Jamaica, another of their properties. After Spanish evacuation of the Dominican Republic in 1865, they returned and became involved in both the project of President Andrew Johnson to acquire a United States coaling station at Samaná Bay and President Grant's attempt to annex the Dominican Republic to the United States. William Cazneau died in 1876. Jane died in the sinking of the steamship *Emily B. Souder*, bound from New York to Santo Domingo. Her will left her property to Ann S. Stephens, a New York writer. *Robert E. May*

Chabot, Frederick Charles. Historian; b. San Antonio, 11 May 1891; d. Mexico, 18 January 1943 (buried in San Luis Potosí); ed. Sorbonne, University of Berlin, and George Washington University. In Texas, between his European education and his study in Washington, Chabot had a brief career as a concert pianist and organist. He got a job at the Library of Congress in 1917, and the same year he embarked upon the diplomatic career for which he had prepared. It took him to Paris, Athens, Sofia, Rio de Janeiro, San Salvador, San José, and finally, in 1923, Caracas. He was not a successful diplomat and was asked to resign (1924), though he claimed to be a victim of Republican politics. After returning to Texas he published his first book, *The Alamo, Altar of Texas Liberty*, in 1931. Through the auspices of the Yanaguana Society, founded by Chabot in 1933 and devoted to promoting the study of Texas history, he published and edited a number of brief books on a variety of topics. His most notable works are *With the Makers of San Antonio* (1937); *Excerpts from the Memorias for the History of Texas, by Father J. A. Morfi* (1932), a translation of those parts of Juan A. Morfi's work that dealt with Indians in Texas; and *Texas in 1811*, a translation done in 1941. He also contributed articles dealing with the history of Texas to the San Antonio *Light*. His other contributions include his locating 13 original paintings by Théodore Gentilz, which were later placed in the Alamo, helping in the restoration of La Villita and San José Mission in San Antonio, and compiling an album entitled *Pictorial Sketch of Mission San José* (1935). Chabot died of uremic poisoning while on a research trip to Mexico.

Michael L. Krenn

Chambers of Commerce. The first two chambers of commerce in Texas were chartered by the Republic of Texas—Houston (1840) and Galveston (1845). After the Civil War several other municipalities organized commercial associations—Austin (1877), Fort Worth (1882), Gainesville (1888), Hillsboro (1890), Dallas (1893), San Antonio (1894), Marlin (1898), Waco (1899), and Port Arthur (1899). The commercial-organization movement gained full momentum during the first decade of the twentieth century as urban populations grew. Realizing the advantages of organized effort, businessmen in every city in Texas organized chambers of commerce before 1910. While vigorously building their own communities, Texas business interests moved rapidly into a program of statewide cooperation. Chamber of commerce executives organized their statewide association in 1906. Two years later the Texas Business Men's Association was founded. It functioned successfully as the first statewide chamber of commerce until 1914, when the state attorney general obtained a temporary injunction to close it on grounds that it engaged in politics. The charge was never proved, and the lawsuit was dismissed five years later. Local chambers of commerce had not been included in the injunction. Upon recommendation of the post–World War I Readjustment Conference, the Texas Chamber of Commerce was formed in April 1919. It was dissolved four years later because Texas businessmen preferred regional organizations. The powerful West Texas Chamber of Commerce was founded in February 1919. Although rudimentary commercial associations existed in other sections, additional regional chambers of commerce were not founded until 1926, when the present East Texas Chamber of Commerce and the South Texas Chamber of Commerce were organized. The Lower Rio Grande Valley Chamber of Commerce began in 1944. Chambers of commerce have been the propelling force in promoting highways, transportation, industry, business, agriculture, tourism, and new community facilities and services. In 1988 the regional chambers of commerce merged to form the Texas Chamber of Commerce.

Carl A. Blasig

Champ d'Asile. A colony of Bonapartist refugees founded on the Trinity River in 1818. Although it endured barely six months, its impact on the future of Texas was strong. The concern aroused among United States and Spanish diplomats over this intrusion into disputed territory caused two immediate results. United States pressure forced Jean Laffite, who had assisted the French colonists, to leave Galveston. And French presence at Champ d'Asile precipitated the Adams–Onís Treaty of 1819, which eliminated the Neutral Ground agreement and established the Sabine River as the Louisiana–Texas boundary and the border between the United States and New Spain. The body of thought, art, and literature evoked in Paris around Champ d'Asile also had important long-term effects on Texas. Bourbon Spain still ruled Mexico in 1818, and the Mexican army marched against the colony. In Restoration France, therefore, artists and the liberal press could represent the failure of Champ d'Asile as a Bourbon attack against the remains of France's imperial glory. A legendary Champ d'Asile stirred French attachment to Texas, intermit-

tently rekindled by journalists, which two decades later resulted in France's becoming the first European power to recognize the Republic of Texas. Champ d'Asile, the Bonapartist refugees, and Laffite the pirate persist as themes in French literature.

In February 1818 Gen. Charles Lallemand brought an armed expedition to Galveston, where the Frenchmen were the guests of Pierre and Jean Laffite, special agents of the Spanish government. The Laffites provisioned and transported the filibusters while reporting their activities to the Spanish consul in New Orleans. On 10 March, with the aid of their hosts, the French left for the Texas mainland in small boats and ascended the Trinity River to a locale now unknown, near the site of Liberty. There they built their fortress, Champ d'Asile. What Lallemand and his officers intended to do in Texas remains an open question. Lallemand had offered his services to Spain, but the viceroy had turned him down. At the same time an emissary of Lallemand's claimed to have made an arrangement to train insurgents in a remote part of Texas, a project to have been financed by Mexican mine owners. One deserter from Champ d'Asile reported that the general spoke of the wealth and power the mines would give the filibusters, perhaps to be used to free the captive Napoleon; other deserters called the expedition mysterious. Lallemand issued a manifesto claiming that his men, although organized into military units, were peaceable colonists dedicated to tilling the soil. However, there is no evidence of their having undertaken agriculture, and lack of food was one cause that led finally to the breakup of the encampment. In any case, the officers primarily dedicated themselves to building a fortress and manufacturing munitions. Their pretension to agriculture masked Lallemand's aggressive intent, though the objective of the aggression is not known. There probably were never many more than 100 officers at the encampment at one time. The roster of all those whose names are known amounts to 149. In addition there were four women and four children, three enlisted orderlies, several servants and laborers, and a few others. Most of the men were French, and the rest were former Grande Armée officers of other nationalities. The latter formed the most discontented and unstable element of the expedition, and most of the desertions were from their ranks. The French themselves were divided, some partisans of Lallemand and others of Antoine Rigaud, the second in command, who was in charge during Lallemand's frequent absences. Learning while away that Spanish troops had been dispatched from San Antonio to expel the filibusters, Lallemand ordered the camp abandoned. By 24 July the retreating invaders were at Galveston Bay waiting to be returned to the island in the Laffites' boats. In August George Graham, a United States special agent, arrived at Galveston to inform Lallemand that the American government wanted the French to leave Texas. When Graham left, Lallemand and a few others went with him and Rigaud remained in command. In September a hurricane inundated the island, destroying the refugees' shelters and supplies. In October a Spanish officer arrived and commanded the French to leave. With aid of the Laffites, most of the filibusters were in New Orleans by the end of November.

The myth of Champ d'Asile took over after the collapse of the colony and the withdrawal of all the colonists. In Paris, artists and the liberal press opposed to Louis XVIII seized the image of Charles Lallemand and the unfortunate half-pay veterans depicted as soldiers of the plow. Led by Benjamin Constant, the newspaper *Minerva* raised funds to send veterans to Texas, then to bring them back to France after the colony dispersed. Jean Pierre Béranger composed a touching song, and Louis Garneray, Charles Aubry, Charles Abraham Chasselat, and other artists prepared highly sentimental engravings and lithographs. Even wallpaper and labels on liqueur bottles represented an imaginary Champ d'Asile. Three books on the subject were published in 1819: Hartmann and Millard, *Le Texas, ou Notice historique sur le Champ d'Asile*; L. F. L'Heritier, *Le Champ d 'Asile*; and *L'Héroine du Texas*, a fictionalized version of the love story of two real colonists. Although it was probably written in Paris, *L'Héroine* may be the first novel set in Texas. Philippe Brideau, the archvillain of Balzac's novel *La Rabouilleuse* (1842; translated as *A Bachelor's Establishment*), was a colonist at Champ d'Asile. The most popular book featuring Champ d'Asile was first published in French in 1878: *Adventures of a French Captain, at Present a Planter in Texas, Formerly a Refugee of Camp Asylum*, whose author uses the pseudonym Girard Roy Just. In 1985, after extensive research in Texas, French novelist Jean Soublin published *Le Champ d'Asile*, in which the Comanches play an expanded role. In this novel some of the survivors form a utopian colony, an imaginative conclusion that telescopes the Franco-Texan experience of the entire nineteenth century.

Kent Gardien and Betje Black Klier

Chennault, Claire Lee. Aviator and air force general; b. Commerce, 6 September 1893; d. New Orleans, 27 July 1958 (buried in Arlington National Cemetery); m. Nell Thompson (1911; divorced 1946); 8 children; m. Anna Chan (1947); 2 children; ed. Louisiana State University and Louisiana State Normal College. Chennault grew up in Louisiana and taught school before serving in World War I as a flight instructor with a lieutenant's commission. Subsequently, he was with the border patrol (1919–23), the Hawaiian Pursuit Squadron (1923–26), and the U.S. Pursuit Development Board (1930–36) as leader of the Air Corps Exhibition Group, nicknamed "Three Men on a Flying Trapeze." Deafness and disagreements with his superiors over tactics forced his retirement in 1937. In the same year he became advisor to Chiang Kai-Shek and the Chinese Air Force. In 1941 he organized the American Volunteer Group (Flying Tigers) in China. In March 1943 Chennault was promoted to major general and to command of the Fourteenth Air Force. His tour was marked by conflicts with the theater commander, Lt. Gen. Joseph Stilwell. Chennault was retired against his will in July 1945, since air corps strategists thought the defensive tactics he favored were obsolete. He then organized and was chairman of the board of Civil Air Transport. He maintained homes in Taipei and near Monroe, Louisiana. He was the author of an autobiography and several works on fighter tactics. Among his many decorations were the Distinguished Flying Cross with cluster; Army and Navy Air Medal with cluster; Chinese Army, Navy, and Air Force Medal; Commander of the British Empire; Legion of Honor; Croix de Guerre with Palm; and Chevalier Polonia Restituta. Monuments were erected to him in Taipei, on the grounds of the Louisiana Capitol at Baton Rouge, and at Chennault Air Force Base, Lake Charles, Louisiana.

James W. Pohl

Cherokee War. The culmination of friction between white settlers in Northeast Texas and the Cherokee, Kickapoo, and Shawnee Indians. The Indians, who had obtained squatters' rights to the land from Spanish authorities, were promised title to the land by the Consultation. On 23 February 1836 a treaty made by Sam Houston and John Forbes, who represented the provisional government, gave title to the lands between the Angelina and Sabine rivers and northwest of the Old San Antonio Road to the Cherokees and their associated bands. The treaty was declared null and void by the Texas Senate in December 1837, despite Houston's insistence that it be ratified. The Córdova Rebellion in August 1838 caused T. J. Rusk to march on the Cherokees in an effort to intercept Vicente Córdova; but Córdova did not seek shelter among the Cherokees, and Rusk returned to the settlements. On 16 October 1838, Rusk and 230 troops pursued a band of Kickapoos, destroyed their village, and killed 11 warriors, including a renegade Cherokee. There were sporadic raids by the Indians during the fall of 1838 and spring of 1839.

After the discovery, in May 1839, of a letter in the possession of Manuel Flores exposing plans by the Mexican government to enlist the Indians against the Texas settlers, President Lamar, supported by popular opinion, determined to expel the East Texas Indians. In July 1839 Kelsey H. Douglass was put in command of approximately 500 troops under Edward Burleson, Willis H. Landrum, and Rusk, and was ordered to remove the Indians to Arkansas Territory. The army camped on Council Creek, six miles south of the principal Cherokee village of Chief Bowl, and dispatched a commission to negotiate for the Indians' removal. The Indians agreed to sign a treaty of removal that guaranteed to them the profit from their crops and the cost of the removal. During the next two days they insisted they were willing to leave but refused to sign the treaty because it provided them an armed escort out of the republic. On 15 July the commissioners told the Indians that the Texans would march on their village immediately and that those willing to accept the treaty should display a white flag. Landrum was sent across the Neches to cut off possible reinforcements, and the remainder of the army marched on the village. The battle of the Neches occurred a few miles west of Tyler, in what is now Henderson County. By sundown 3 Texans had been killed and 5 wounded; the Indians had lost 18. The Indians fled, and Douglass made camp. Pursuit was begun the next morning. A scouting party under James Carter engaged the Cherokees near the headwaters of the Neches River at a site now in Van Zandt County. The Indians sought shelter in a hut and the surrounding cornfields but were forced to abandon them after Carter was reinforced by the arrival of Rusk and Burleson. After 30 minutes of fighting the Indians were forced to the Neches bottom, where Chief Bowl was killed and a number of warriors were lost. After the last fighting near Grand Saline, it was estimated that more than 100 Indians had been killed or wounded. On 21 July the Texans marched toward the headwaters of the Sabine River along the route taken by the fleeing Indians. Numerous huts and fields were destroyed that afternoon, and several villages and more than 200 acres of corn were burned the next day. The destruction continued during the pursuit, which was not abandoned until 24 July. Most of the Indians fled to Cherokee lands outside the republic. During the winter a small group under Chief Egg and John Bowles, son of Chief Bowl, attempted to reach Mexico by skirting the fringe of white settlements. Burleson, on a campaign against the Plains Indians, intercepted the Cherokees and attacked them near the mouth of the San Saba River on 25

December 1839. Egg and Bowles and several warriors were killed, and 27 women and children were captured. This was the last important action against the Cherokees in Texas.

Chicken Ranch. The brothel in La Grange made famous by the Broadway musical *The Best Little Whorehouse in Texas*, traced its lineage to 1844, when a widow, "Mrs. Swine," brought three young prostitutes from New Orleans. By the end of the nineteenth century, prostitution had moved out of the hotels and into a red-light district on the banks of the Colorado River. There Miss Jessie Williams (born Faye Stewart) operated her business (1905–) until news of an impending crackdown persuaded her to move outside the city limits. As America entered the twenties, automobiles made her establishment accessible to many more customers. New prostitutes came and necessitated more rooms and new furniture. The rooms were simply built onto the main house in a haphazard fashion as needed. Miss Jessie stayed on good terms with the sheriff, Will Lossein, who visited every evening to pick up gossip and get information on criminals who had visited the whorehouse. While the sheriff kept a tight grip on criminals, Miss Jessie ruled the house with a firm hand. Nothing exotic was allowed, and none of the bedroom doors had locks on them. Miss Jessie would walk the halls, and if she heard a customer giving one of her girls a hard time she would chase him out of the house with an iron rod and perhaps never admit him again. In the Great Depression Miss Jessie, whose numerous customers now had no money, began the "poultry standard" of pricing—"one chicken for one screw." Hence the term Chicken Ranch. Miss Jessie supplemented the income by selling chickens and eggs. As the CCC began construction of Camp Swift and the military moved in, the ranch recovered. Miss Jessie, though confined to a wheelchair by arthritis, ruled the house with her iron rod even into the 1950s, when she was confined to her bed and cared for by a longtime nurse. She spent her last few years with her wealthy sister in San Antonio and died in 1961 at the age of eighty.

Edna Milton had arrived at the Chicken Ranch from Oklahoma in 1952 at the age of 23. When she bought the place from Miss Jessie's heirs for the inflated price of $30,000 she already had a good relationship with the new sheriff, T. J. Flournoy, who had been elected in 1946 and had immediately put in a direct line to the Chicken Ranch, so he could replace the nightly visits of his predecessor with nightly calls. Edna also interacted with the community in the same ways Jessie had: social contact between the girls and the residents of La Grange was forbidden; girls saw the doctor weekly and shopped with local merchants; and commodities and supplies were bought from local stores on a rotating basis. Edna also continued Jessie's custom of giving money to local civic causes and became one of the town's largest philanthropists. During the 1950s the ranch reached its 16-girl maximum. On some weekends there was a line of students and soldiers at the door. No cursing or drinking was allowed. The going rate for a whore was $15 dollars for 15 minutes. After giving an estimated 75 percent to Edna, the prostitutes still made $300 a week and had no expenses. Even before profits from the Cokes, cigarettes, and jukebox, the ranch probably had an income of more than $500,000 a year. All new employees were fingerprinted and photographed by Sheriff Flournoy before they could start work, and a criminal record of any kind prevented their employment.

The Chicken Ranch continued operating successfully until mid-1973, when Marvin Zindler from KTRK–TV in Houston ran a week-long exposé on it. He claimed that his motive was inaction on the part of the Texas Department of Public Safety and local law officers to combat organized crime and corruption. All of the attention drawn to the ranch forced Governor Briscoe to meet with the head of the DPS, the state attorney general, and Zindler. At the meeting it was disclosed that the DPS had run a two-month surveillance on the Chicken Ranch and had failed to find evidence of connection with organized crime. However, the pressure on the governor was such that he scheduled a meeting with Flournoy and ordered the house closed. Most of the ranch's employees headed for Austin or Houston. Edna attempted to buy a house in La Grange, but her downpayment was returned. She subsequently got married and moved to East Texas. But customers showed up for more than two years looking for the Chicken Ranch. Zindler also came back for a follow-up story and in the midst of an argument with Sheriff Flournoy was pushed down, after which he sued the sheriff for $3 million. Many local people contributed to Flournoy's cause by selling T-shirts and bumper stickers, and Flournoy settled out of court for much less than $3 million. The musical about the ranch was very successful. Edna had a silent role in the Broadway production, which was later turned into a movie. Two lawyers from Houston bought the ranchhouse and land and in 1977 moved part of the building to Dallas to open a restaurant named the Chicken Ranch. It opened in September 1977 with Miss Edna as the hostess, the building and furniture in their original condition, and a menu of mainly chicken dishes. The restaurant closed in January 1978. Sheriff Flournoy resigned in 1980, saying that he and his wife were sick of hearing about the Chicken Ranch. When he died in October of 1982, his funeral was attended by Lieutenant Governor Bill Hobby and nearly 100 lawmen. He was credited with solving every murder and bank robbery in Fayette County during his 34-year term, partly because of those telephone contacts with the Chicken Ranch. *Walter F. Pilcher*

Chicken War. The Texas manifestation of the War of the Quadruple Alliance in Europe; caused abandonment of the Spanish missions in eastern Texas in 1719. With news that Spain and France were on opposing sides in the conflict, Lt. Philippe Blondel at the French post of Natchitoches, Louisiana, struck in June 1719 at the nearest Spanish target: San Miguel de Linares de los Adaes Mission, at a site near that of present Robeline, Louisiana. Finding only a lay brother and one soldier at the mission, Blondel and his detail of seven gathered up the sacred vestments and provisions, then raided the henhouse. As he mounted his horse after tying the chickens to the pommel of his saddle, the chickens flapped their wings, the horse reared, and the lieutenant was spilled in the dirt. His companions rushed to his aid. Taking advantage of the confusion, the lay brother dashed off into the woods. After reaching Nuestra Señora de los Dolores Mission (at the site of presentday San Augustine, Texas), he informed Fray Antonio Margil de Jesús of what he had been told by Blondel: Pensacola had been captured by the French, and a hundred soldiers were on their way from Mobile with the East Texas settlements as their objective. Lacking confidence in the Spaniards' relationship with the Indians, Father Margil viewed retreat as the only alternative. He packed his vestments and headed for Nuestra Señora de la Purísima Concepción Mission (in the area of present Nacogdoches County) to spread the alarm. Capt. Domingo Ramón of Nuestra Señora de los Dolores de los Tejas Presidio, heeding the clamor of his soldiers and their wives, gathered citizens and livestock to withdraw toward San Antonio and await reinforcements. Margil, Isidro Félix de Espinosa, and two soldiers remained at Mission Concepción for 20 days "consoling" the Indians, who were reluctant to let them leave. They received word on 14 July that Ramón was withdrawing farther than agreed upon, and they set out to overtake the caravan at the border of Hasinai (Tejas) country. There they encamped until the end of September, when Espinosa resolved to go personally to San Antonio de Béxar and San Juan Bautista to seek help. After traveling 20 leagues he encountered a volunteer relief expedition from San Juan Bautista and learned that no military support would be forthcoming. On 3 October the entire camp marched for San Antonio. While Margil and the seven other friars took residence at San Antonio de Valero Mission, Espinosa went on to San Juan Bautista to make a personal appeal for military aid in recovering the missions. There he learned of the appointment of the Marqués de Aguayo as governor of Coahuila and Texas and of the military campaign Aguayo was mounting to reclaim eastern Texas for Spain. Despite Espinosa's urging, the Aguayo expedition was delayed a year and a half. In the meantime the war ended, and the operation, planned as one of reconquest, became merely one of reoccupation. The Chicken War represented a costly overreaction by Spanish religious and military men to a feeble French gesture. The French made no aggressive move against Texas after Blondel's comical fiasco. Aside from causing a two-year hiatus in the Spanish missionary effort, the episode also disrupted the commercial aims of the French Company of the West. Directors of the company sent word to Jean Baptiste Benard de La Harpe, who had just established a trading post on the Red River in the area that is now Bowie County, that he was not to make war on the Spaniards but to pursue trade with them. The Spanish withdrawal following Blondel's raid left no one with whom he might trade.

Robert S. Weddle

Chihuahua Expedition. A trading trip undertaken by a caravan from Chihuahua City (1839–40) that sought direct trade with the United States by way of a shorter trail than the circuitous route through El Paso, Santa Fe, and St. Louis. In response to Mexican interest in trade after the opening of the Presidio del Norte entry to Texas in 1830, Henry Connelly, a Missouri physician and Chihuahua merchant, organized a party of more than 100 men accompanied by 50 Mexican dragoons that left Chihuahua with $200,000 or $300,000 in specie on 2 April 1839. They traveled northeast to the Rio Grande, crossed at the site of present Presidio, then went on to the headwaters of the Colorado and Brazos rivers. Moving northeast, the party initially mistook the Canadian for the Red River, then proceeded to the Red, traveled downriver, and crossed at the mouth of the Wichita River into Indian Territory. There, a Delaware Indian band directed them to Fort Towson. Connelly proceeded east, reached the post in June, and presented the commandant, Maj. Henry Wilson, a passport issued at Chihuahua on 1 April by Governor Simón Elías Gonzales, authorizing him to pass with his party through the Republic of Mexico to the state of Arkansas. Connelly next took a steamboat to Louisiana to buy merchandise, then

returned to Fort Towson in early September. He left Fulton, Arkansas, in April 1840 with 60 to 80 new wagons loaded with merchandise and a company of American equestrian circus performers carrying tents and equipment to entertain in Mexico. Residents of the northern Texas settlements were eager for the trade and dealt generously. The route passed through what became Red River, Lamar, Fannin, Grayson, Cooke, Montague, Clay, and Archer counties. The expedition passed the sites of Paris and Bonham, swung south of Sherman through Whitesboro, north of Gainesville and Muenster, and into the city limits of St. Jo in Montague County. Some six miles west, the travelers veered northward into the Cross Timbers between Montague and Nocona, where the caravan spent five weeks cutting through and traversing the muddy prairies. The remainder of the route passed northwest of the site of Montague, north of Brushy Mound, and northwest of Bowie. The traders eventually hit their incoming route near Archer City and marched west past Seymour before turning south. After fording the head branches of the Brazos, they found another part of their path near the site of modern Snyder, and crossed the area of Big Spring. The route then ran southwest to the Pecos River. From near McCamey it passed near Comanche Springs at Fort Stockton, traveled a mile north of Alpine, then moved on through Paisano Pass to the west and down the course of Alamito Creek to the site of Presidio on the Rio Grande. On arrival, the traders spent 45 days reaching a compromise on duty payments. Governor José Irigoyen, who had promised lower tariffs, had died, and full duties were now threatened. Eventually, the caravan crossed the Rio Grande, passed down its original trail along the Río Conchos, and arrived at Chihuahua City (27 August 1840). Because of the tariff increases and unfavorable reports on the trail, the trip was not repeated, and use of the route was curtailed until the late 1840s. Connelly's route is sometimes called the Chihuahua Trail, though the principal Chihuahua Trail was west of Texas.

Roy L. Swift

Childress, George Campbell. Author of the Texas Declaration of Independence; b. Nashville, Tennessee, 8 January 1804; d. Galveston, 6 October 1841; m. Margaret Vance (1828); 1 son; m. Rebecca Stuart Read Jennings (1836); 2 daughters; ed. Davidson Academy (grad. 1826). Childress practiced law and edited the Nashville *Banner* and Nashville *Advertiser* before making his first trip to Texas (1834), where his uncle, Sterling C. Robertson, was organizing a colony. After raising money and volunteers in Tennessee for the Texas army, Childress left permanently for Texas. He reached Robertson's colony on 9 January 1836. He and his uncle were elected to represent Milam Municipality at the Convention of 1836. Childress called the convention to order and subsequently introduced a resolution authorizing a committee to draft a declaration of independence. Upon adoption of the resolution, he was named chairman of the committee and is almost universally acknowledged as the primary author of the document. On March 19, President David G. Burnet sent Robert Hamilton and Childress, whose family was on friendly terms with President Andrew Jackson, to Washington as diplomatic agents for the Republic of Texas. In late May 1836 they were replaced by James Collinsworth and Peter W. Grayson. Childress returned to Texas in 1837, 1839, and 1841. Unsuccessful in law practice, he slashed his abdomen with a Bowie knife and died

George Childress, by unknown artist, ca. 1830. Watercolor on ivory. Courtesy CAH; CN 01094. An attorney and former newspaper editor from Tennessee, Childress arrived in Texas in January 1836 and was immediately elected to represent Robertson's colony at the convention at Washington-on-the-Brazos. He is generally considered the author of the Texas Declaration of Independence.

soon thereafter. Childress County was named for him. After his death, his sister Sarah married James K. Polk.   *Joe E. Ericson*

Chinese. The Chinese were the first of the Asian immigrants to come to Texas, and until the influx of the Vietnamese in the 1970s they were also the most numerous. The Chinese first came to Texas, in two contingents, with the railroads. The first group, 250 contract laborers from California, arrived in January 1870 with the Houston and Texas Central, whose railhead was then at Calvert. Although their labor on the Houston–Dallas line was abruptly terminated after less than a year and most of them soon left the state, a few nevertheless remained in Robertson County. In 1880 these 72 were 53 percent of the 136 Chinese living in Texas. The second contingent, also from California, came in 1881 with the Southern Pacific, whose 3,000-man workforce was, except for 400, all Chinese. When the line was completed in 1883, some of them, too, stayed in Texas. By 1890 the number of Chinese statewide had jumped to 710, of whom 225 (32 percent) were in El Paso County. After reaching a peak of 836 in 1900, the Chinese population in Texas began to decline as a delayed reaction to the congressional enactment in 1882 of the Chinese exclu-

sion law, which for the next six decades barred practically all further immigration from China. The decline would have been more precipitous than it was but for one of the rare occasions when the exclusion law was set aside. In 1917, when General Pershing returned to the United States from Mexico, after his fruitless pursuit of Pancho Villa, he was permitted to bring with him 527 Mexican Chinese who had assisted his troops during the invasion. Most of these "Pershing Chinese" settled in San Antonio and thereafter replaced those in El Paso as the largest Chinese community in Texas. Even with this infusion, the statewide Chinese population in 1930 was only 703, of whom 321 (46 percent) were in Bexar County. The Chinese exclusion act was repealed in 1943, and American immigration laws were greatly liberalized in the following decades. As a result, the Chinese population in Texas boomed. From 1,031 in 1940 the statewide population soared to 25,461 in 1980, of whom 12,048 (47 percent) were in Harris County. In the 1950s Houston surpassed San Antonio as the center of Chinese life in the state.

These postwar immigrants from China were in several respects very different from their predecessors—so much so that the two groups and their descendants often have little to do with each other. Whereas the old immigrants had originated almost exclusively in the Canton region of south China and spoke only Cantonese, the new immigrants were generally from north and central China (though often by way of Taiwan or Hong Kong) and spoke Mandarin. Furthermore, the old immigrants were originally of peasant stock and had come to the United States initially as unskilled and illiterate contract laborers, such as railroad workers. Once in Texas, however, they had carved out for themselves niches in the service and commercial sectors of the urban economy—notably hand laundries, which required little capital and posed no economic threat to Caucasian males; chop houses and restaurants that served American food as well as ersatz Chinese food like chop suey; and retail groceries that often catered to Hispanics or blacks. The descendants of these older immigrants, though upwardly mobile, usually stayed in the business world. The new immigrants, on the other hand, have generally been products of China's elite culture and have tended toward professional careers in the sciences and engineering. Finally, the old immigrants had come to America not as permanent settlers. They were nearly all men—in 1910 only 13 of the 595 Chinese in Texas were women—and their primary purpose in coming to America was to earn money to support the families they had left behind in China and hoped eventually to rejoin. Because of this "sojourner" attitude on their own part as well as because of the exclusion law, which barred them from bringing their wives, a normal conjugal family society did not emerge among the Chinese Texans until the late 1920s or 1930s, long after they first arrived in the state. The new immigrants, on the other hand, usually came with their families as permanent residents.

Except in the 1870s, when most of the Chinese in Robertson County were sharecroppers and field hands on the cotton plantations near Calvert and Hearne, the Chinese Texans have always been overwhelmingly an urban population. As noted, they were successively drawn to El Paso, San Antonio, and Houston. Around the turn of the century in El Paso they were numerous enough to form a small but compact Chinatown. Socially, the Chinese in Texas have always been a close-knit, inward-looking community, bound by their own awareness of the distinctiveness of their original Chinese culture as well as by a long history of discrimination in the United States. They have looked to themselves and their own institutions for support and protection. The foremost institution among all Chinese has been the patriarchal family, on whose behalf, for example, the old immigrants endured long periods of separation during the era of exclusion. Among both old and new immigrants it is not unusual for three generations to be under one roof, with the aged parents living with their adult children and their grandchildren. Aside from the family, other social groups have also played an important role, though probably more among the old immigrants and their descendants than among the new. These include the clan or family association (usually defined by a common surname), the district association (defined by a common county of origin in China), and the merchant association (descended from a secret society of an earlier era, e.g., the Hip Sing and On Leong associations). These organizations, either individually or collectively, have looked after the general well-being of all Chinese; they claim, for example, to have kept the Chinese Texans off the welfare rolls during the Great Depression. Politically, the Chinese have similarly kept to themselves. Until the end of exclusion, they were classified as aliens ineligible for citizenship and thus, except for the few who had been born in the United States, were denied the right to vote. In 1937 they successfully lobbied against an amendment to the Texas alien land law that would have driven the Chinese groceries out of business. They were not, however, otherwise active in Texas politics. They preferred to involve themselves instead in the politics of their native land. They contributed generously to China's struggle against Japanese aggression in the 1930s and early 1940s, when branches of the Chinese Nationalist party, or Kuomintang, were established in San Antonio and El Paso. Since the repeal of the exclusion act in 1943 and the triumph of the Communists in China in 1949, however, their ties to China have loosened considerably. In 1964 Tom. J. Lee of San Antonio became the first Chinese Texan to be elected to the state House of Representatives. More recently, others have been elected to local office in Houston.

Culturally, Chinese Texans have retained, to varying degrees, some of the distinctive elements of the old-world ways. Many prefer Chinese food to American, though the proliferation of Chinese restaurants since the 1970s has been due more to the changing tastes of the general public than to any Chinese demand. Most celebrate the Chinese (lunar) new year. And, under the influence of Confucianism, they tend to emphasize family solidarity and the value of education more than most other ethnic groups do. They have also attempted to pass on to the younger, American-born generation some knowledge of Chinese languages and culture. A Chinese school operated in San Antonio for more than 20 years beginning in 1928; another was founded in Houston in 1970. But such efforts have been of only limited success. By and large, the Chinese, despite an adherence to traditional values and practices, have assimilated into the mainstream of American life. In religion, many are Baptists.

Edward J. M. Rhoads

Chisholm Trail. The major Texas cattle trailing route. Although it was used only from 1867 to 1884, the longhorn cattle driven north along it provided a steady source of income that helped the impoverished state recover from the Civil War. Youthful trail hands on mustangs gave a Texas flavor to the entire range cattle industry of the Great Plains and made the cowboy an enduring folk hero. Missouri and Kansas had closed their borders to Texas cattle in the 1850s because of Texas fever, but the demand for beef in the East was growing. In 1867 Joseph G. McCoy of Illinois persuaded Kansas Pacific officials to lay a siding at the hamlet of Abilene, Kansas, on the edge of the quarantine area. He began building pens and loading facilities and sent word to Texas cowmen that a cattle market was available. That year he shipped 35,000 head; the number doubled each year until 1871, when 600,000 head glutted the market. In 1864 Scot–Cherokee Jesse Chisholm had marked a trail from the North Canadian River, near Oklahoma City, to Kansas. Although originally applied only to the trail north of the Red River, Chisholm's name was soon attached to the entire trail from the Rio Grande to central Kansas. The herds followed the old Shawnee Trail by way of San Antonio, Austin, and Waco, where the trails split. The Chisholm Trail continued on to Fort Worth, then passed east of Decatur to the crossing at Red River Station. From Fort Worth to Newton, Kansas, U.S. Highway 81 follows the trail. It was, Wayne Gard observed, like a tree—the roots were the feeder trails from South Texas, the trunk was the main route from San Antonio across Indian Territory, and the branches were extensions to various railheads in Kansas. The Chisholm Trail led to the new occupation of trailing contractor. Although a few large ranchers such as Capt. Richard King and Shanghai Pierce delivered their own stock, trailing contractors such as John T. Lytle, George W. Slaughter, the Snyder brothers, and the Blocker brothers handled the vast majority of herds. The Chisholm Trail was finally closed by barbed wire and an 1885 Kansas quarantine law; by 1884, its last year, it was open only as far as Caldwell, in southern Kansas. In its brief existence it had been traversed by more than five million cattle and a million mustangs, the greatest migration of livestock in world history.

Donald E. Worcester

Chisos Mining Company. A major quicksilver producer in southern Brewster County. Howard E. Perry founded the company in 1903; for 30 years production increased as production methods improved. A major ore discovery in 1915 coincided with World War I, which greatly increased the need for mercury and consequently led to the mine's greatest period of prosperity. The community of Terlingua, now a virtual ghost town *cum* tourist attraction, grew up around the Chisos Mine. Residents had access to a company-owned commissary and hotel, several excellent employees' dwellings, a school, a company doctor, telephone service, a dependable water supply, and thrice-a-week mail delivery. Prior to the advent of mechanized vehicles in the early 1930s, the mule-drawn wagontrains that delivered the quicksilver to the railroad at Alpine and Marathon supplied the settlement. Production declined during the late 1930s, and in 1942 the company went bankrupt. The Esperado Mining Company purchased the Chisos assets and operated the mine unsuccessfully until the end of World War II. At that time most of the surface installations were demolished and sold for scrap. On December 6, 1944, Howard E. Perry died in his sleep in a Boston hotel en route to a Florida vacation.

Kenneth B. Ragsdale

Chisum, John Simpson. Cattleman; b. Hardeman Co., Tennessee, 16 August 1824; d. Eureka Springs, Arkansas, 22

December 1884. His family moved to Red River County, Texas, in 1837. His father, probably the earliest settler in Paris, was public-spirited and wealthy. John worked at various jobs, accumulated land, and served as clerk of Lamar County (1852–54). With Stephen K. Fowler, a New Orleans investor, he entered the cattle business in Denton County. By 1860 he was running 5,000 head of cattle valued at $35,000, owned six slaves, and was considered a major cattleman. In the Civil War he was exempted from service and placed in charge of several herds in his district. He took a herd to the Confederate forces at Vicksburg in 1862 but thereafter exhibited little interest in the Southern cause. In the fall of 1863, suffering from Indian raids and drought, he and other cowmen in the Denton area started moving herds to Coleman County. He terminated ties with Fowler and received cattle for land. Chisum and his partners soon had 18,000 head grazing along the Colorado. In 1866 he joined Charles Goodnight and others driving cattle to feed the 8,000 Navajos on the Bosque Redondo Reservation near Fort Sumner, New Mexico. Chisum eventually arranged to supply Goodnight, now ranching in Colorado, with Texas cattle. For three years he delivered 10,000 head annually to Goodnight crews at Bosque Grande, for a dollar a head over Texas prices. In 1872 he established his headquarters at Bosque Grande; he claimed a range extending more than 100 miles down the Pecos. In 1874 he won a contract to provide beef to several Apache reservations in New Mexico, only to have his operations crippled by Indian raids. His total stock losses from 1868 to 1874 reached $150,000, the largest in the nation. In November 1875 he transferred his livestock holdings, estimated at over 60,000 cattle, to Hunter, Evans, and Company, a St. Louis beef-commission house, which assumed his indebtedness, mostly for Texas cattle, of over $200,000. Chisum settled at South Springs, near Roswell.

As he helped Hunter and Evans gather cattle for markets, horse thieves and renegade Indians struck branding crews and horse herds. Lincoln County authorities and the army at Fort Stanton offered little help. Simultaneously, Chisum was drawn into the Lincoln County range war of 1878 by festering difficulties generated by his attorney, Alexander A. McSween, and rancher John H. Tunstall, who defied Judge Lawrence G. Murphy's economic stranglehold on the county. In 1878, with both Tunstall and McSween dead and the county in chaos, Chisum and Hunter and Evans cleared their cattle from the Pecos. The next year Chisum and his brothers adopted the U brand and returned to South Springs, where they built a comfortable ranchhouse, improved their cattle, and became active in local and territorial livestock associations. Chisum was a major figure in the southwestern cattle industry for nearly 30 years, 18 of which (1854–72) were in Texas. He primarily was a cattle dealer who traveled in search of markets. His colorful and eccentric life epitomized the adventurous world of open-range cattle operations that set the tone for the industry after the Civil War. He died of cancer and was buried in Paris.

Harwood P. Hinton

Ciboleros. Mexican buffalo (*cíbolo*) hunters who operated on the Llano Estacado. Although they were often associated with the Comancheros, they were a distinct group. Like the Indians, the ciboleros considered the thrill of the chase as much a part of the hunt as the kill. Most of them operated out of Taos, Santa Fe, or the El Paso area, and they were an important factor in the even-

tual demise of the buffalo herds on the southern plains. Since pre-Columbian times sedentary Pueblo Indians from the upper Rio Grande had ventured onto the plains to supplement their vegetable diet with buffalo meat. The acquisition of horses from the Spaniards made these annual journeys faster, easier, and more successful. Early Spanish expeditions into West Texas, beginning with that of Vicente de Zaldívar in 1598, hunted and even tried to capture and domesticate buffalo. Though the Pueblos and Spanish colonists of New Mexico obtained most of their meat and hides through barter with the plains nomads, they soon mastered many buffalo-hunting techniques. By the late seventeenth century ciboleros had begun to venture out in force onto the Llano Estacado. They generally hunted in October, after they had harvested the crops at home and when the weather was still good. Buffalo hides were in prime condition that time of the year, and the animals had migrated into the Canadian River breaks from their summer grazing ranges farther north. The ciboleros soon became legendary for their hunting prowess, their main weapons being bows and arrows or, more commonly, lances. They often dressed gaudily and sometimes rode their agile Spanish ponies bareback to prevent entanglement in gear. Racing to the side of a running buffalo, the cibolero drove the razor-sharp lance point into the animal's heart, quickly dismounted, often at great risk, to pull out the lance, and then remounted to continue the chase and kill as many animals as he could. A skilled lancer could bring down as many as 25 buffalo during a single chase, which often covered two or three miles. The ciboleros traveled in groups numbering as many as 150 men, accompanied on occasion by their women and children. Even before the lancers finished their job, the other members of the party went to work skinning fallen animals, loading the meat onto horses or into wooden *carretas* and hauling it back to their campsite, where they cut it Indian fashion into thin strips that they hung out to dry. The jerked slices were then beaten or kneaded with the feet, a process thought to help preserve them, and packed into the carts. The fat was made into tallow for cooking and candles. The cracklings that remained were a favorite treat among the children. Hides were tanned into rugs and robes by scraping and kneading with repeated applications of buffalo brains. Horns were made into utensils and decorative objects, and the long hair from the neck and shoulders was made into coarse cloth or used as mattress stuffing. To avoid conflict with Plains Indians who were also after buffalo, the ciboleros brought along homemade bread, beads, and other trinkets to use as barter. Sometimes Indian hunting parties were given flour, sugar, coffee, and other provisions when they called on the cibolero camps. Hence the similarity to the Comancheros. On the return trip to the Rio Grande settlements with their carts laden with meat and other products, successful hunters rode proudly through villages in a triumphal procession. In their hometowns they received a hero's welcome and on the first night were treated to a fandango. Although most of their products were subsequently sold, they kept some of the meat for themselves.

By the beginning of the nineteenth century the ciboleros had become an important economic factor. They supplied food for the New Mexico settlements and hides for the rich Santa Fe–Chihuahua trade. Their jerky found ready markets throughout northern Mexico, while delicacies like dried buffalo tongues were hauled as far south as Mexico City, where they sold for as much as two dollars apiece. The expedition of Francisco Amangual in June 1808 encountered hunting parties in West Texas, and in the 1840s Josiah Gregg described their colorful manner of life in detail. The ciboleros also gained a thorough knowledge of the trackless prairies and inspired the Comancheros to begin their lucrative trading expeditions to the breaks and canyons of the Llano. As early as 1832 ciboleros were reported to have killed between 10,000 and 12,000 bison each year. Such butchery resulted in increased antagonism on the part of the southern plains tribes by the 1850s. In southeastern Colorado skirmishes broke out between the ciboleros and Cheyennes, compelling the former to restrict their hunts largely to the Comanchería in the Texas Panhandle. Further serious Indian opposition was avoided until after the Civil War. By that time the ciboleros had begun replacing their flimsy carts with larger, more durable wagons each capable of holding the jerked meat of 45 buffalo. They were thus capable of depleting the herds even more. In addition, military officials in New Mexico and Indian Territory attempted to close the Llano Estacado to all native New Mexicans in an effort to curb the illicit activities of the Comanchero trade. Even so, many ciboleros managed to continue their activities until the decimation of the buffalo herds in the late 1870s by white hide hunters with their long-range rifles.   *H. Allen Anderson*

Civil-Rights Movement. Civil-rights campaigns in Texas are generally associated with the state's two most prominent ethnic minorities: African Americans and Mexican Americans. Mexican Americans have made efforts to bring about improved political circumstances since the Anglo-American domination of Texas began in 1836. African Texans have fought for civil rights since their emancipation from slavery in 1865. Organized campaigns, however, were not launched until the early twentieth century.

In the aftermath of the Texas Revolution, Hispanic Texans were largely dispossessed. In the 1850s they faced expulsion from their Central Texas homes on the accusation that they helped slaves escape to Mexico. Those in the Goliad area suffered during the Cart War of 1857, as others did in South Texas in 1859 after Juan N. Cortina's capture of Brownsville. Following the Civil War, both newly freed slaves and Tejanos were harassed. In the 1880s, lynching was used in East Texas used violence as a method of political control. Extralegal executions became common and, although sometimes committed against whites, were more often perpetrated against blacks, for alleged rapes of white women or for other charges. Mexican Americans of South Texas experienced similar forms of brutality. The Ku Klux Klan, the White Caps, and some Texas Rangers harassed both Mexican Americans and black Texans.

De facto segregation followed emancipation. Freedmen found themselves barred from most public places and schools and, as the nineteenth century wore on, confined to certain residential areas of towns. By the early twentieth century, such practices had been sanctioned by law. Whites never formulated these statutes with Tejanos in mind, but they enforced them through social custom nonetheless. By the 1880s and 1890s, furthermore, minority groups faced legal drives to disfranchise them, though Anglos turned to a variety of informal means to weaken their political strength. African and Mexican Americans faced terrorist tactics, literacy tests, the stuffing of ballots, and accusations of

incompetence when they won office. Political bosses in South Texas and the El Paso valley, meantime, attempted the Mexicans' domination through the controlled franchise.

In 1902 the legislature passed the poll-tax law, and the next year Texas Democrats implemented the white primary. These mechanisms disfranchised blacks, and Mexican Americans for that matter, for white society did not regard Tejanos as belonging to the white race. Progressive reformers of the age viewed both minority groups as having a corrupting influence on politics. By the late 1920s, Texas politicians had effectively immobilized black voters through court cases that defined political parties as private organizations with the right to exclude members. Some scholars have estimated that no more than 40,000 of the estimated 160,000 eligible black voters retained their franchise in the 1920s.

Newer Jim Crow laws in the early twentieth century increased the segregation of the races, and in the cities, black migrants from the rural areas joined their urban compatriots in ghettoes. The laws ordinarily did not target Mexicans, but were enforced on the premise that Mexicans were an inferior and unhygienic people. Thus Tejanos were relegated to separate residential areas or designated public facilities. Hispanics, though mostly Catholic, worshiped in largely segregated churches. Blacks and Hispanics attended segregated and inferior "colored" and "Mexican" schools. As late as the mid-1950s, the state legislature passed segregationist laws directed at blacks (and by implication to Tejanos), some dealing with education, others with residential areas and public accommodations. Governor Allan Shivers went so far as to call out the Texas Rangers at Mansfield in 1956 to prevent black students from entering the public school. Although Price Daniel, Sr., Shivers's successor, was more tolerant, the integration process in Texas was slow and painful. Supreme Court decisions in 1969 and 1971 ordered school districts to increase the number of black students in white schools through the extremely controversial practice of busing.

Violence in the era leading to the Great Depression years resembled that of the nineteenth century. In the 10-year period before 1910, about 100 black men were lynched, at times after torture. Between 1900 and 1920, numerous race riots broke out, with black Texans often witnessing their homes and neighborhoods destroyed in acts of vengeance. Similarly, Tejanos became victims of Anglo wrath for insult, injury, or death of a white man, and some Anglos applied lynch law to Tejanos with the same vindictiveness as they did to blacks.

African and Mexican Americans criticized segregationist policies and white injustices via their newspapers, labor organizations, and self-help societies. Black state conventions issued periodic protests in the 1880s and 1890s. On particular occasions during the nineteenth century, communities joined in support of leaders rising up against perceived wrongs or in behalf of those unjustly condemned. Tejanos, for one, rallied behind Juan Cortina and Catarino Garza, and contributed to the Gregorio Cortez Defense Network, which campaigned for the defense of a tenant farmer named Gregorio Cortez, who killed a sheriff in self-defense in 1901.

The period between 1900 and 1930 saw continued efforts by minorities to break down racial barriers. In 1911 Mexican-American leaders met at the Congreso Mexicanista in Laredo and addressed the common problems of land loss, lynchings, ethnic subordination, educational inequalities, and various

African-American college students protest segregation at the University of Texas, Austin, April 27, 1949. UT Texas Student Publications, Inc., Photographs, CAH; CN 02653. Although UT admitted African Americans to some graduate and professional programs in 1950, it continued to exclude black undergraduates until 1956.

other degradations. In 1919 the Brownsville legislator J. T. Canales spearheaded a successful effort to reduce the size of the Texas Ranger force in the wake of various atrocities the rangers had committed in the preceding decade. La Agrupación Protectora Mexicana, founded in 1921, had as its intent the protection of farm renters and laborers facing expulsion by their landlords.

Much of the leadership on behalf of civil rights came from the ranks of the middle class. Black leaders established a chapter of the NAACP in Houston in 1912, three years after the founding of the national organization; by 1930 some 30 chapters existed throughout the state. The association pursued the elimination of the white primary and other obstacles to voting, as well as the desegregation of schools, institutions of higher education, and public places. Tejanos established their own organizations to pursue similar objectives, among them the Orden Hijos de America (Order of Sons of America). The order was succeeded in 1929 by LULAC, which committed itself to the same goals of racial equality.

Mexican Americans and Black Texans continued their advocacy for equality during the depression era. In San Antonio, Tejanos founded La Liga Pro-Defensa Escolar (School Improvement League), which succeeded in getting the city's school board to build three new elementary schools and make improvements in existing facilities. Mexican Americans in the Gulf Coast area near Houston and in El Paso organized the Confederación de Organizaciones Mexicanas y Latino Americanas in the late 1930s, also for the purpose of eradicating racist policies. The black movement, for its part, won increased white support in the 1930s from the ranks of the Association of Southern Women for the Prevention of Lynching and from such prominent congressmen as Maury Maverick.

After World War II, Tejano war veterans founded the American G.I. Forum, and by the 1950s, LULAC and the Forum became the foremost Mexican-American groups using the legal system to remove segregation, educational inequities, and various other discriminatory practices. In 1961 the politically oriented Political Association of Spanish Speaking Organizations joined LULAC and the G.I. Forum to pursuing the goal of mobilizing the Texas-Mexican electorate in an effort to prod mainstream politicians to heed the needs of Hispanics. African Americans, meantime, undertook poll-tax and voter-registration drives through the Democratic Progressive Voters League; the white primary had been declared illegal in 1944. During the 1960s the Progressive Voters League worked to inform black people about political issues and encouraged them to vote.

During the 1960s both African Americans and Mexican Americans took part in national movements intended to bring down racial barriers. Black Texans held demonstrations within the state to protest the endurance of segregation. They also instituted boycotts of racist merchants. In conjunction with the National March on Washington in 1963, approximately 900 pro-

roup, which included
low pace of desegre-
ally's opposition to
v the latter half of
ity flocked to the
as a means of
rty and life in
ates. In a sim-
ement of the
ment's mil-
eparatism
aded the
ty, Raza Unida
y addressed by reformist
ne G.I. Forum. Members used
oycotts and confrontational approaches,
or significant magnitude seldom materialized. The
ement declined by the mid-1970s.

During the same period, the federal government pursued an agenda designed to achieve racial equality, and Texas Mexicans and black Texans both profited from this initiative. The Twenty-fourth Amendment, ratified in 1964, barred the poll tax in federal elections, and that same year Congress passed the Civil Rights Act outlawing the Jim Crow tradition. Texas followed suit in 1969 by repealing its own separatist statutes. The federal Voting Rights Act of 1965 eliminated local restrictions to voting and required that federal marshals monitor election proceedings. Ten years later, another voting-rights act demanded modification or elimination of at-large elections.

After the 1960s several organizations joined LULAC and the G.I. Forum in the cause of equality for Mexican Americans. The Mexican American Legal Defense and Education Fund, founded in 1968, emerged as the most successful civil-rights organization of the late twentieth century. It focused on the state's inequitable system of financing schools, redistricting, and related problems. Working to see the increasing political participation of Tejanos was the Southwest Voter Registration Education Project. Groups at the city level that sought to help out barrio residents included COPS in San Antonio, and EPISO in the El Paso area. The struggle for civil rights also produced a number of favorable court decisions. Black Texans won a judicial victory in 1927 when the Supreme Court ruled in *Nixon v. Herndon* that the white primary violated constitutional guarantees. When the state circumvented the decision by declaring political parties to be private organizations that had the right to decide their own memberships, blacks again turned to the courts. Not until the case of *Smith v. Allwright* (1944) did the Supreme Court overturn the practice.

The post–World War II era brought increased successes for civil-rights litigants. The case of *Sweatt v. Painter* (1950) integrated the University of Texas law school, and in its wake several undergraduate colleges in the state desegregated. The famous case of *Brown v. Board of Education* (1954) produced the integration of schools, buses, restaurants, and other public accommodations. Mexican Americans won similar decisions that struck at discriminatory traditions. The decision in *Delgado v. Bastrop ISD* (1948) made it illegal for school boards to designate specific buildings for Mexican-American students on school grounds. *Hernandez v. Driscoll CISD* (1957) stated that retaining Mexican-American children for four years in the first two grades

amounted to discrimination based on race. *Cisneros v. Corpus Christi ISD* (1970) recognized Mexican Americans as an "identifiable ethnic group" so as to prevent the subterfuge of combining Mexicans and blacks to meet integration requirements. And *Edgewood ISD v. Kirby* (1989) held that the system of financing public education in the state discriminated against Mexican Americans. In another significant case, *Hernandez v. State of Texas* (1954), the United States Supreme Court recognized Mexican Americans as a class whose rights had been violated by Jim Crow practices.   *Arnoldo De León and Robert A. Calvert*

Clark, Edward. Governor, Confederate soldier; b. New Orleans, 1 April 1815, d. Marshall, 4 May 1880; m. Lucy Long (1840), who died without children; m. Martha Melissa Evans, July 1849; 4 children. Clark was a delegate to the Texas Constitutional Convention of 1845. He fought with distinction in the Mexican War and became secretary of state (1853–57), state commissioner of claims (1858), and lieutenant governor under Sam Houston (1859). When Houston refused the oath of allegiance to the Confederacy, the Texas Secession Convention made Clark governor. In this office, Clark raised taxes for the war, mustered forces to protect the frontier, and enacted measures to supply troops to the Confederacy. He ran for governor against Francis R. Lubbock (1861) but was defeated. Clark subsequently fought for the Confederacy and was wounded, promoted to brigadier general, and discharged. After living briefly in Mexico at the end of the war, he returned to Marshall, where he practiced law until his death.   *Ralph A. Wooster*

Clark, Thomas Campbell. U.S. attorney general and Supreme Court justice; b. Dallas, 23 September 1899; d. New York City, 13 June 1977; m. Mary Ramsey (1924); 3 children; ed. Virginia Military Institute (1917–18) and UT (A.B., 1921; law school degree, 1922). Clark was civil district attorney of Dallas County from 1927 until 1937. He became assistant to the United States attorney general in 1937 and the department's chief of West Coast offices in 1940. In 1942 he directed the internment of Japanese Americans, a project he later considered a big mistake. In 1942 he was appointed head of the War Frauds Unit of the Justice Department, where he prosecuted frauds uncovered by Senator Harry Truman. He became assistant attorney general in 1943 and headed the antitrust and criminal divisions until he became attorney general to President Truman in 1945. As attorney general, Clark worked for a strong central government. He vigorously enforced the government's antitrust laws while successfully prosecuting the United Mine Workers Union and labor leader John L. Lewis for violating a federal no-strike injunction. In *United States v. California* (1947) he successfully argued before the Supreme Court that the U.S. and not the individual states owned off-shore oilfields (*but see* Tidelands Controversy). He also helped develop Truman's national civil-rights policy in opposition to some of the states. Clark's support of a strong national government also extended to the defense of loyalty oaths and opposition to domestic dissent. He issued the first attorney general's list of subversive organizations and initiated prosecution of the leaders of the American Communist party under the Smith Act.

In 1949 he replaced Frank Murphy on the United States Supreme Court, where he served for 18 years. He was generally considered a liberal member of the Vinson court and a more conservative justice during the years of the Warren court. He usually voted to uphold McCarthy-era prosecutions—a stand that put him in the minority in *Watkins v. United States* (1957), for instance, which curbed the investigations of the House Committee on Un-American Activities; and in the majority in *Barenblatt v. United States* (1959), which upheld a contempt conviction of a professor who refused to answer the committee's questions. Clark consistently voted in favor of integration. In *Sweatt v. Painter* (1950) his support of the majority opinion was particularly important. He wrote the opinion in *Terry v. Adams* (1953), which struck down the white primary in Texas. A decade later he wrote an opinion for the unanimous upholding of the 1964 Civil Rights Act in *Heart of Atlanta Motel, Inc. v. United States*. Clark helped extend federal authority in other areas. He wrote the opinion striking down prayer and Bible reading in public schools in *School District of Abingdon v. Schempp* (1963). In 1967, when his son William Ramsey Clark was appointed attorney general by President Lyndon Johnson, Clark retired from the bench to avoid charges of conflict of interest. He was replaced by Thurgood Marshall. Afterward, Clark served on eleven of the United States circuit courts of appeals and in 1968 was appointed the first director of the Federal Judicial Center, where he studied the judicial system and worked for improvements in its administration.   *Paul Finkelman*

Clarksville *Standard*. The first and for many years most important newspaper in Northeast Texas; in Clarksville. The *Northern Standard* was founded in 1842 by Charles DeMorse, who ran the paper until his death in 1887. It was renamed the *Standard* in 1852. In 1854 DeMorse built a two-story brick building to house the paper and installed new equipment, including a cylinder press. The only other such press in Texas at the time was that of the Galveston *News*. In the following years the *Standard* was second in circulation among Texas newspapers and had agents as distant as Philadelphia, New York, and Boston. While DeMorse was away during the Civil War, the *Standard* was managed by John R. Woolridge. In 1874 DeMorse closed the office and retired; but, persuaded by his friends, he purchased a Campbell press, installed it in the old building, and in 1879 resumed publication. After his death in 1887 his daughter continued the publication of the paper for about a year. The nearly complete files of the paper in the University of Texas at Austin library constitute a valuable source for the study of the economic, social, and political life of Texas during the republic and early statehood.
Ernest Wallace

Clayton, Nicholas Joseph. Architect; b. Cloyne, County Cork, Ireland, 1 November 1840; d. Galveston, 9 December 1916; m. Mary Lorena Ducie (1891); 5 children. Clayton moved in 1872 to Galveston to serve as supervising architect of the First Presbyterian Church. He subsequently designed so many of the major public, commercial, and residential buildings in Galveston (1870s to 1900) that Howard Barnstone described this period in the city's history as the "Clayton Era." Major concentrations of his buildings are in the Strand Historic District and the East End Historic District. Clayton was a High Victorian architect whose works were exuberant in shape, color, texture, and detail. He excelled at decorative brick and iron work. His designs were distinguished by a compositional order underlying picturesque shapes and rich ornament. His religious architec-

ture accounted for the broadest geographical distribution of his work outside Galveston. His major extant works include St. Mary's Cathedral and St. Edward's University in Austin. He designed many churches and other institutional buildings in the Catholic dioceses of Galveston, Dallas, and Alexandria, Louisiana. His foremost public buildings include the University of Texas Medical Department Building in Galveston. Clayton served on an advisory board for the construction of the dome of the Capitol in Austin and was responsible for specifying furnishings for the building. He designed numerous commercial buildings, most of which have been demolished, and many houses, the most notable of which is the Gresham House, Galveston, also known as the Bishop's Palace. He was a fellow of the American Institute of Architects and a member of the Catholic Knights of America and the Knights of Columbus. His architectural drawings and office records are in the Rosenberg Library, the Galveston County Historical Museum, the Barker Texas History Center (UT Austin), and the Architectural Drawings Collection (UT Austin).   *Robert A. Nesbitt and Stephen Fox*

Coahuila and Texas. Provinces closely associated in Spanish and Mexican Texas, and at times combined into one province. In 1689–90 Alonso De León, governor of the Spanish province of Coahuila, extended his authority to include Texas. Early in 1691 he was succeeded by Domingo Téran de los Ríos, who was appointed governor of Coahuila and Texas. In 1693, however, Spain withdrew the Catholic missions from East Texas, and it was not until 1716 that Martín de Alarcón, who had been appointed governor of Coahuila in 1702, reextended his control over Texas. Alarcón was succeeded by the Marqués de Aguayo, whose activities resulted in the separation of the two provinces around 1726, during the time of his successor, Fernando Pérez de Almazán. The provinces were governed separately, with the capital of Texas at Los Adaes and that of Coahuila at Monclova.

By the Constitution of 1824 the Mexican provinces of Nuevo León, Coahuila, and Texas were united as one state. Nuevo León was detached on 7 May 1824. A constituent congress was elected and assembled at Saltillo in August 1824, and a provisional governor was named for the state. A provisional chief was appointed for Texas in August 1824. In December the Department of Texas was legally established as a subdivision of the state of Coahuila and Texas. The Constitution of Coahuila and Texas was adopted on 11 March 1827. The state was at first divided into three departments, but the number was eventually increased to seven: Saltillo, Parras, Monclova, Rosas, Bexar, Brazos, and Nacogdoches. After some agitation Monclova replaced Saltillo as the capital of the state in March 1833. The legislature at Monclova passed several acts beneficial to Texas, creating new municipalities, dividing Texas into three departments, permitting the use of English in schools and public affairs, and allowing an additional representative from Texas. Also the Monclova government attempted to revise the judicial system, which had been particularly troublesome to Texans, by appointing Thomas J. Chambers superior judge of a three-district judicial circuit established for Texas, and by providing within this new system for trial by jury. Chambers was prevented from organizing the court system, however, by difficulties in Coahuila.

When the Monclova legislature closed its session in April 1834, Coahuila lapsed into confusion. A rump meeting of the Monclova deputation in June declared against Santa Anna's Plan of Cuernavaca. In July, Saltillo formed a state government in opposition to the Monclova faction, annulled the acts of the previous legislature, and appointed José María Goribar as military governor. The time for elections arrived amid growing party hostility, but before any serious collision occurred, the rival governments submitted their case to Santa Anna for arbitration. The president ordered that Monclova remain the seat of government and that a new election should be held for the entire state. The elections took place, but trouble arose almost immediately, and in protest against a decree providing for the wasteful sale of public land in Texas the Saltillo faction withdrew from the newly elected legislature. The national government was petitioned to nullify the election, which, it was alleged, had been conducted illegally. Martín Perfecto de Cos, military commandant for the eastern division of the Provincias Internas, supported the Saltillo faction in a stand against the Texas land sales and ordered a company of federal troops to disband the legislature at Monclova. After decreeing that the governor had the authority to change capitals, the legislature hastily adjourned on 21 April 1835. Agustín Viesca then called out the militia with the object of reducing Saltillo and, when threatened by General Cos, resolved to make Bexar (San Antonio) the capital of the department. In this he was supported by a number of Texans, and on 25 May, accompanied by about 150 militiamen and 20-odd Texans, he left Monclova with the archives. The military was ordered to prevent his crossing the Rio Grande, and he returned to Monclova to attempt a secret withdrawal to Texas aided by Ben Milam and John Cameron. The party was captured and imprisoned, but most of the men escaped and eventually reached Texas. Viesca and the remaining members of the legislature were arrested in Coahuila. José Miguel Falcón, who was appointed governor, was replaced on 8 August by Rafael Ecay Músquiz, but neither man served. Ramón Músquiz, the vice governor under Viesca, took over the governorship on 28 June 1835. This overthrow of constitutional government, together with the arrest of the incendiary Viesca, precipitated long-smoldering resistance in Texas and led to the Texas declaration against Santa Anna. In November 1835 the Consultation declared Texas a separate state under the Constitution of 1824 and formed a provisional government. The severance of Texas and Coahuila was made final by the Texas Revolution and the Mexican War.

Cohen, Henry. Jewish leader and historian; b. London, 7 April 1863; d. Galveston, 12 June 1952; m. Mollie Levy (1889); 2 children; ed. Jews' Hospital and Jews' College, London. When Cohen graduated from college in 1884, he was ordained a rabbi. He served first in Kingston, Jamaica, where Sephardic Jews composed a significant portion of the congregation. In 1885 he began serving at Woodville, Mississippi, where he taught romance languages at the female seminary, wrote poetry, and developed a strong community. In 1888 he moved to Galveston as rabbi for Temple B'nai Israel, then comprising 175 families. After the Galveston hurricane of 1900 Cohen served as a member of the Central Relief Committee, which kept law and order with the help of shotguns and ministered to people of all religions. He became nationally known for his work. He helped immigrants who arrived at the port of Galveston to find homes in less populated areas and families in the New York slums to move to various regions of the South and Midwest. He helped to establish Galveston's Jewish Immigrant Information Bureau in 1907 and

Rabbi Henry Cohen, with his wife, Mollie Levy Cohen, and their children, Ruth and Henry. Galveston, after 1889. Courtesy Temple B'nai Israel Archives, Galveston. Photograph courtesy ITC.

later distributed relief for Mexican immigrants. During World War I he served as a lieutenant of the American Expeditionary Force in France and was responsible for getting Congress to provide Jewish naval chaplains. During the 1920s he battled the Ku Klux Klan, and in 1926 Governor Moody appointed him to the Texas Prison Board. Cohen won statewide recognition as a prison reformer. In 1924 he received an honorary doctor of Hebrew law degree from Hebrew Union College, in 1939 an honorary doctor of divinity from the Jewish Institute of Religion, and in 1948 an honorary doctorate from Texas Christian University. He was a recognized authority on the Talmud and was proficient in more than 10 languages. Cohen wrote *Talmudic Sayings* (1894) and did a study for the American Jewish Historical Society; published a number of monographs, including *Settlement of the Jews in Texas* (1894), *Henry Castro, Pioneer and Colonist* (1896), and *The Galveston Immigration Movement, 1907–1910* (1910); and coauthored *One Hundred Years of Jewry in Texas* (1936?). In the 1890s he wrote articles for the *Texas Journal of Education*, along with translations and poems. Among his roles he was a member of the advisory board of Hebrew Union College and the Jewish Publication Society, president of the Texas Historical Society of Galveston, and one of seven charter members of the Galveston Equal Suffrage Association. His papers and library are housed at the Barker Texas History Center, University of Texas at Austin.   *James C. Martin*

Coke, Richard. Governor, United States senator; b. near Williamsburg, Virginia, 13 March 1829, d. Waco, 14 May 1897; ed. William and Mary College (civil law diploma, 1848); m. Mary Evans Horne (1852); 4 children. Coke moved to Texas in 1850, practiced law in Waco, and was a delegate to the Secession Convention (1861). He served as a captain in the Civil War. Governor A. J. Hamilton appointed him a state judge in 1865. Coke was elected to the state Supreme Court but removed by Gen. Philip H. Sheridan. He defeated Republican gubernatorial incumbent Edmund J. Davis in 1873. As governor (1874–76), Coke presided over the end of Reconstruction and led a Democratic reaction against four years of Republican rule that had been plagued by disorder attendant upon the end of the war. During his tenure the Constitution of 1876 was adopted, public education was reorganized, and Texas A&M was founded. Though overwhelmingly reelected in 1876, Coke ran for the Senate in May of that year, resigned the governorship in December, and replaced Morgan C. Hamilton in the Senate in March 1877. As a senator (1877–95), "Old Brains" Coke generally opposed extensions of federal power. Meanwhile, in Texas, he supported the gubernatorial bid of James S. Hogg and fought prohibition. *John W. Payne, Jr.*

Coleman, Bessie. The world's first licensed black pilot; b. Atlanta, 26 January 1892; d. near Jacksonville, Florida, 30 April 1926 (buried in Lincoln Cemetery, Chicago). She spent the early years of World War I working as a manicurist at the White Sox Barbershop in Chicago. She then operated a chili parlor. Apparently in early 1917 she married Claude Glenn, but she never publicly acknowledged the marriage and the two soon separated. In 1920 she went to aviation school in Le Crotoy, France, after she discovered that no American school would accept African Americans. Robert S. Abbott, editor of the Chicago *Weekly Defender*, assisted her in contacting schools abroad. After studying for 10 months she was issued a license (1921) by the Fédération Aéronautique Internationale. She returned to the United States with the goal of opening a flying school for black students. In 1922 she made a second trip to Europe and during her studies took lessons from the chief pilot for the Fokker Aircraft Company in Germany. Bessie Coleman's first American air show was at Curtiss Field, near Manhattan, on 3 September 1922. She subsequently made exhibition flights all over the country, many of them in the South. After several years of touring the East and West coasts, she traveled back to Texas and established her headquarters in Houston in 1925. Her first performance in Texas took place in that city on 19 June 1925. Her daredevil stunts and hairraising maneuvers earned her the nickname "Brave Bessie." She primarily flew Curtiss JN4D planes and army-surplus aircraft. During her trips she often gave lectures to schools and churches to encourage young black men and women to enter aviation. On one occasion in Waxahachie she refused to give an exhibition on white school grounds unless blacks were permitted to use the same entrance as whites. The request was granted, although the races remained segregated once inside. Early in her career she was presented a loving cup for her achievements from the cast of *Shuffle Along*, a black Broadway

Bessie Coleman, 1921–1926. Courtesy National Air and Space Museum, Smithsonian Institution; SI neg. no. 92-13721. Known as "Queen Bess," Coleman gained great fame as a stunt flier.

musical. By 1926 she had become one of America's most popular stunt fliers. She had her first major accident in 1924 while barnstorming in California, and she took a year off to recover. She died during a test flight before a show sponsored by the Negro Welfare League of Jacksonville. Although her dream of establishing a flying school for black students never materialized, the Bessie Coleman Aero groups were organized after her death. On Labor Day, 1931, these flying clubs sponsored the first allblack air show in America, which attracted 15,000 spectators. In 1977 a group of black female student pilots in Indiana organized the Bessie Coleman Aviators Club. In 1990 a street in Chicago was renamed Bessie Coleman Drive, and 2 May 1992 was declared Bessie Coleman Day in Chicago. In 1995 the United States Postal Service issued a 32-cent commemorative stamp in her honor. *Roni Morales*

College of St. Thomas More. Founded as St. Thomas More Institute (1981) by parishioners of St. Patrick Cathedral, Fort Worth, "to make accessible the great tradition of learning that celebrates language and literature, history, philosophy, and theology as the philosophic forms of the soul, seeking to give these an ordered existence and to make them accessible to every student." In 1983 the institute moved into a donated building in Fort Worth. By 1985 an annual budget had been established and the basic courses of a two-year curriculum leading to the associate of arts degree had been developed. The college bought a building on Merida Street and subsequently acquired a building on Lubbock Street. In 1986 St. Thomas More's Oxford Studies Program, initiated at the Oxford suburb of Littlemore, England, was started. In 1988 the school applied to the Texas Higher Education Coordinating Board to become a degreegranting institution. In January 1989 the school became a college under Texas law and began its Rome term. In 1994 it began sponsoring conferences and lectures throughout North Texas. In June 1994 the College of St. Thomas More was granted full accreditation as a two-year college by the Southern Association of Colleges and Schools. *Patrick Foley*

College Station, Texas. Home of Texas A&M University, just south of Bryan in southwest central Brazos County. The Houston and Texas Central Railway built through the area in 1860, and in 1871 the site was chosen as the location of the proposed Texas A&M College, which opened in 1876. In 1877 a post office, College Station, opened near the railroad tracks, and the town took its name from the post office. The community had a population of 391 in 1900. In the 1920s and 1930s, as the college grew, the community expanded in all directions. College Station incorporated in 1938; it had a population of 2,184 inhabitants, not including students, in 1940. Ernest Langford, called by some the "Father of College Station," was elected mayor in 1942 and held the office for 26 years. Texas A&M initiated a major expansion program in the 1960s, and the city continued to grow with the school, reaching a population of 11,396 in 1960 and 52,456 in 1990. Through its ties with the university, College Station has developed high-tech manufacturing industries and become a major research center. *Mark Odintz*

Colony of Kent. A shortlived British settlement on the Brazos River in what is now Bosque County. Its founders envisioned Kent as the commercial center of an elaborate colonization pro-

Roy Inks Dam on the Colorado River, between Llano and Burnet counties, 1936–38. Courtesy Texas Department of Transportation/Randy Green. Inks Dam was one of several dams built on the Colorado in the 1930s for flood control and the generation of electricity.

ject of the Universal Emigration and Colonization Company of London. The colonists planned to sell cooperatively produced grain to nearby Fort Graham as well as in an expected export market. In addition, they imagined Kent as a "Philadelphia on the Brazos," a manufacturing center with a navigable link to the Gulf of Mexico, and thence to world markets. Unfortunately, their plans were totally inadequate to the demands of farm life in nineteenth-century Texas. In 1850, 30 families sailed from Liverpool to Galveston. Others left later. They included people of the middle class such as shopkeepers, bank clerks, bakers, and tailors. Sir Edward Belcher was to be in charge of overseeing the settlement, and Lt. Charles Finch MacKenzie was to be an on-site leader in charge of government. The colonists, on their way to "New Britain," were discouraged by cold, wet weather, and some turned back. Kent was officially founded in January 1851 at the foot of a hill called Solomon's Nose. Belcher returned to England, from where he foresaw Kent "at no very distant period" as the "*chief city* in Texas." The project reflected not only the general English emigration impulses of midcentury but constant promotion by George Catlin, the preeminent American painter of Indians. Catlin had shown his work since 1840 throughout Britain and the continent, but without financial success. He then turned to a new career as colonization expert, building on his reputation as one who knew the West. He mortgaged his gallery in order to promote the proposed project in Texas, but after two years of intensive, unremunerated promotion, he resigned as

Texas superintendent of the company. After the company refused Catlin his anticipated per capita recruitment fees, he continued to borrow in order to repay earlier creditors. When the Texas project failed and with it the company, Catlin faced creditors demanding several times the gallery's value, and the gallery passed in 1852 to an American industrialist, Joseph Harrison. The Catlin Indian Gallery eventually reappeared in the Smithsonian. The Colony of Kent did not survive 1851. Many of the settlers died before summer from exposure. In the summer of 1852 only one immigrant remained in the colony; the other survivors had departed for more developed areas. The land reverted to its sellers. Catlin had painted an image of Texas frontier life that emphasized the glories of a presumed natural life, not the requisite hardships and hard work.   *Richard H. Ribb*

Colorado River. Rises in Dawson County and flows to Matagorda Bay on the Gulf of Mexico. Important reservoirs on the Colorado include Lake Colorado City, Lake J. B. Thomas, Buchanan Lake, Inks Lake, Lake Lyndon B. Johnson, Lake Travis, and Town Lake in Austin. The Colorado is probably the river called Kanahatino by Indians of the Caddoan linguistic family and Pashohono by some of the other Indian groups. It has also been identified as the stream that Domínguez de Mendoza and Nicolás López called San Clemente in 1684, and as the one La Salle named La Sablonnière ("Sand-Pit") in 1687. The name Colorado, Spanish for "red," is evidently a misnomer, for the water of the stream is clear and always has been. The name Colorado was first applied by Alonso De León in 1690, not to the present stream but to the Brazos. The Colorado was used as a route inland by early colonists, including several of the Old Three Hundred who settled on its banks. Austin became the capital of the Republic of Texas in 1839. In 1844, when both England and France were working to prevent the annexation of Texas by the United States, the British minister in Mexico secured a written avowal from Antonio López de Santa Anna to recognize the independence of Texas with the Colorado as its boundary. Principal tributaries include the Pedernales, Llano, San Saba, and Concho rivers and Pecan Bayou, the most westerly "bayou" in the nation. With the exception of the bayou, the tributaries flow into the river from the Edwards Plateau and are spring-fed.

Although the Colorado has a relatively small annual run-off with relation to its watershed, it has presented some of the most serious drainage problems in Texas. Early in the nineteenth century its slow current caused the formation of a raft, or log jam, which gradually grew upstream so that the river was navigable in 1839 for only 10 miles above its mouth. By 1858 the situation in Matagorda and Wharton counties had become so bad that the state appropriated funds to dig a channel around the raft. The United States Army Corps of Engineers opened the channel in the mid-1800s, but since it was not maintained the raft filled it up. Teamsters unloaded vessels above the raft and carried the cargo to other teams that loaded it on other boats for shipment to Galveston and other Gulf ports. Shallow-draught vessels were at times able to ascend the Colorado to Austin. After the Civil War the Colorado ceased to be a factor in transportation. The delta that developed after removal of the log jam (1925–), reached across Matagorda Bay as far as Matagorda Peninsula by 1936; that year a channel was dredged through the new delta from the Gulf of Mexico to the town of Matagorda, thus forcing the river to deposit its flotsam and sediment directly into the Gulf. With removal of the raft, the community of Matagorda, formerly a major Texas seaport, gradually became landlocked. The present Caney Creek channel was the channel of the Colorado until about a thousand years ago, when the river cut into a wide estuary in the present Caney Creek area and redirected its flow to the west. The need for a steady flow of water to irrigate rice in Wharton and Matagorda counties, combined with the necessity for flood-control measures, has presented more recent challenges. These have been met largely by the construction of Lake Travis and Lake Buchanan. Three smaller reservoirs in Burnet County—Inks, Johnson, and Marble Falls—produce power from water running over the Buchanan Dam spillway. The dam at Lake Austin, which is largely filled with silt, produces power from water flowing from the lakes above. Town Lake, a recreation site that divides north and south Austin, is the last impoundment in this section of the river. Town Lake and the lakes above Austin are known as the Highland Lakes. Conservation and use of the Colorado are overseen by three agencies established by the state legislature, the Lower, Central, and Upper Colorado River authorities, and formerly the Colorado River Municipal Water District.

Comer Clay and Diana J. Kleiner

Colquitt, Oscar Branch. Governor; b. Camilla, Georgia, 16 December 1861, d. Dallas, 8 March 1940; m. Alice Fuller Murrell. (1885); 5 children. Colquitt founded the Pittsburg *Gazette* (1884) and published the Terrell *Times–Star* (1890–97). He was a state senator from 1895 to 1899, during which time he wrote delinquent-tax laws, served as state revenue agent, and functioned as tax expert of a special commission. He was admitted to the bar in 1900. He worked as a lobbyist for corporations in the 1899 and 1901 legislatures and succeeded John H. Reagan as railroad commissioner. He ran unsuccessfully for governor in 1906 but was elected to the office in 1910 as an antiprohibitionist. During his terms (1907–15), he fostered prison reform, education, and measures to help laborers. He supported Germany early in World War I and tried without success to get the German government to help him buy the New York *Sun*, which he planned to edit as a pro-German organ. He ran for the United States Senate in 1916 and was defeated in a runoff election by the incumbent, Charles A. Culberson. Colquitt headed a Dallas oil firm for the next decade, split with most of the Democratic party to head the Hoover Democrats of Texas in 1928, served as a member of the United States Board of Mediation from 1929 to 1933, and was a field representative of the Reconstruction Finance Corporation from 1935 until his death. He was renowned as a stump speaker.

George P. Huckaby

Columbus, Texas. County seat and second largest town in Colorado County, 65 miles west of Houston, on a small rise south and west of a lazy horseshoe bend in the Colorado River. Members of Stephen F. Austin's Old Three Hundred began arriving in the area in 1821; in late December Robert H. Kuykendall, his brother Joseph, and Daniel Gilleland moved from a newly established settlement on the Brazos River, later known as Washington-on-the-Brazos, to a site on the Colorado River near that of present Columbus. By 1823 a small community had developed. It became known as Beeson's Ferry or Beeson's Ford, named for Benjamin Beeson, one of the original settlers, who operated a ferry across the Colorado. In 1835 it was renamed Columbus, allegedly at the suggestion of a former resident of Columbus, Ohio. The town began as a river crossing and became the seat of local government in 1822, when Austin's colony was divided into two autonomous districts by Mexican governor José F. Trespalacios. Trespalacios had the Baron de Bastrop travel to the Colorado River District to supervise local elections. Gathering at Beeson's Crossing, the residents elected John J. Tumlinson, Sr., alcalde, Robert Kuykendall captain, and Moses Morrison lieutenant. Austin had intended to locate his headquarters here and even laid out a town the following year, but finally opted for a more promising location on the Brazos River. By the time of the Texas Revolution, Columbus was home to over 25 families. The community had a ferry, a cotton gin, a gristmill, a sawmill, and a small inn or boardinghouse for travelers. Sam Houston camped on the east bank of the Colorado River at Columbus from 19 to 26 March 1836, during the Runaway Scrape. Although Houston had Columbus burned when he departed, a traveler noted in 1837 that the refurbished town had two public houses, two stores, half a dozen shanties, and quite a bit of gambling. Columbus was designated the county seat of Colorado County when the county was established in 1836; the county was organized the following year. The first of its three courthouses was constructed in 1847. In 1839 Col. Robert Robson moved to Columbus from Dumfries, Scotland, and built a castle, complete with a drawbridge and moat, on the south bank on the Colorado River north of town. It was three stories high and had

Street scene with sleet on ground, 1877. Stereograph half. Prints and Photographs Collection, Columbus, Texas, file, CAH; CN 10370

a large ballroom and roof garden. The foundations of the castle were undermined by a flood in 1869, and it was torn down in 1883. Columbus was incorporated in 1866. The latter half of the nineteenth century was marred by almost continual violence. A fresh wave of killings in 1906 prompted the citizens of Columbus to petition the mayor and city council to reestablish the office of city marshal, abolished in 1903. The council voted three to two against the measure. Incensed by the council's lack of responsiveness, the citizens then approached county judge J. J. Mansfield, who ordered an election to decide the fate of the city charter. By a vote of 99 to 35 Columbus was disincorporated, and the county commissioners' court took over city government. Columbus remained unincorporated until 1927, by which time the population had risen to 3,100. The population declined during the Great Depression and did not climb above 3,000 again until the mid-1950s. The town had 3,751 residents in 1995. Industries that have flourished in the town at different times include a cigar factory, cottonseed oil mills, meat packing plants, and gravel pits. Columbus grew steadily after World War II, as the local economy became increasingly focused on recreation. In 1961 a group of civic leaders organized the Magnolia Homes Tour; tours include the Stafford Opera House, the Senftenberg–Brandon House Museum, the Alley Log Cabin Museum, the Dilue Rose Harris House Museum, and the Mary Elizabeth Youens Hopkins Santa Claus Museum. Other historic buildings in the area include the Confederate Memorial Museum in the brick-based Water Tower (1883), the Brunson Building (1891), the Raumonda house (1887), the Gant house (ca. 1870), and the Colorado County Courthouse (1891). *Don Allon Hinton*

Comanche Trail. Though the Comanche Trail has long been named in the historical literature of the Southwest, only an occasional reference is made to it in contemporary records and documents. A map of West Texas made by J. H. Young in 1857 shows such a trail. The lower portion had two prongs, one crossing the Rio Grande about the vicinity of Boquillas and the other at Presidio. The two converged at Comanche Springs, near the site of Fort Stockton. From this point the trail extended north to cross the Pecos at or near Horsehead Crossing and continued northeasterly across the sand hills to the site of present Big Spring. From Big Spring it extended east of the Caprock past watering spots on Tobacco Creek, Mooar's Draw, and Gholson Spring. From this point there were two routes across the Staked Plains. One was up Yellow House Canyon by Buffalo Spring to the forks of the canyon in what is now Mackenzie State Recreation Area in Lubbock, thence up the north fork of the Double Mountain Fork of the Brazos, where there was running water just west of the site of present Abernathy. From there this branch extended to Sod House Spring, north of the site of present Littlefield. From this point it ascended Blackwater Draw to Portales Spring, to Tiban Spring, and thence to the Pecos near Fort Sumner. The alternative route from Gholson Spring extended southeast to Blanco Canyon and thence up that canyon and Running Water Draw, past the site of present Plainview about 20 miles, at which point the route left the draw and extended west to Spring Lake. From there it continued to Blackwater Draw, where it intercepted the Yellow House route 15 miles east of the site of present Muleshoe. Young's map indicated that water could be had daily from Big Spring northward and northwest to the site of Fort Sumner, New Mexico. The upper portion of the trail from Plainview westward was possibly used by Francisco Vásquez de Coronado on his return to the Pecos.

William Curry Holden

Comancheros. Natives of northern and central New Mexico who traded with the nomadic Plains Indians, notably the Comanches, often at designated areas in the Llano Estacado. They cut trails followed by traders and later ranchers and settlers. The term *Comanchero*, unknown in Spanish documents, was popularized during the 1840s by Josiah Gregg. Initially, the Comancheros' lucrative practices were considered legitimate. Increased demand for cattle in New Mexico, however, led them to trade stolen cattle to the Indians. The resulting hostility between Indians and settlers led to army intervention in 1874 and the Comancheros' eventual demise. Comancheros ranged east to the Wichita Mountains of Oklahoma, southeast as far as the Davis Mountains in Texas, and north to the Dakotas. Their trade began with a treaty of 1786 between the Spanish governor of New Mexico, Juan Baptista de Anza, and the Comanche Indians of the plains, allowing trade between New Mexico and the Indians in return for Indian protection of Texas against intruders on Spanish territory. At first many Comancheros used burros to transport their merchandise into the trackless Comanchería. But by the 1840s Gregg, James Abert, and other American mapmakers found evidences of broad cart trails leading into the Canadian River valley. Randolph Marcy described the "old Mexican cartroad" in his 1849 survey. Abert met with some Comancheros at Bent's tradinghouse on the Canadian in September 1845, and in 1853 the New Mexico traders helped guide Lt. Amiel W. Whipple across the Panhandle. During the first decades of the Comancheros' trade, their merchandise consisted largely of beads, knives, paints, tobacco, pots and pans, and calico and other cloth; foodstuffs such as coffee, flour, and bread; and the metal spikes that Indians came to prefer over flint points for their arrows.

From about 1840 on, Comanches stole horses and cattle to trade to the Comancheros. Because of the rising demand for cattle in New Mexico, between 1850 and 1870 thousands of animals stolen by Indians were traded by Comancheros to merchants in New Mexico and Arizona who had contacts with government beef contractors. The addition of firearms, ammunition, and whiskey to the list of trade items from New Mexico likewise added to the trade's declining reputation. Although the territorial governors of New Mexico attempted to regulate the trade by requiring licenses, Comancheros mainly neglected the law. Many American officials, particularly federal Indian agents, believed that trading was merely a cover-up for the New Mexicans' real purpose of inciting resentment against Anglo-Texans. Certainly the traders and their Comanche customers shared a common dislike of white settlers, and their victims returned the favor. As business grew, the Comancheros sought remote places for consummating their deals, and many sites in the Texas Panhandle–South Plains proved to be ideal. Probably the most controversial aspect of the Comancheros' operations was the ransoming of captives, a practice dating back centuries. At first enterprising New Mexicans had bought only captive Indians for use as mine workers or servants, but as time went on they began accepting Mexican prisoners as well. Many traders reportedly made large profits from highborn captives they had ransomed from Comanches by holding them for a suitable "reward" from relatives in the settlements of Texas or northern Mexico or from American government officials.

The Civil War momentarily left the Texas frontier practically defenseless and allowed the Indian raiders free access to livestock in the Cross Timbers and Hill Country. Comancheros profited handsomely from this stock, much of it left unbranded as well as unattended, which they frequently traded to army posts, government Indian reservations, and ranchers for guns, ammunition, and whiskey to trade to the Indians. Noted traders like José P. Tafoya maintained crude rock and adobe shelters at places like Las Lenguas or Tecovas Springs during the 1860s. Comancheros often accompanied Comanches on cattle raids into Coleman County and environs in the 1870s. The days of the Comancheros were numbered, however, as Texas Rangers and army patrols mounted increasing pressure on their Indian customers. Col. Ranald Mackenzie and other army commanders often enlisted, or perhaps conscripted, Comancheros to guide them to the camps of the Indians with whom they had traded. The final defeat of the Comanches and their allies in the Red River Indian War, along with the extermination of the buffalo by hunters, ended the Comanchero trade. In the late 1870s Casimero Romero, José Tafoya, Juan Trujillo, and others who had sometime engaged in the Comanchero trade settled for a time in the western Panhandle as peaceful *pastores*.

H. Allen Anderson

Comisario. A Spanish elected official who served under the ayuntamiento in districts of around 500 inhabitants for a term of one year; though a *comisario* might be reelected, he could not be compelled to serve more than one year in three. He could attend ayuntamiento sessions, where he could speak but not vote. His duties were to take the census of the district, record new arrivals, assist tax collectors, arrest disturbers of the peace, and report undesirable persons to the alcalde.

Compromise of 1850. The results of the Mexican War (1846–48) brought Texas into serious conflict with the national government over the state's claim to a large portion of New Mexico. The claim was based on efforts by the Republic of Texas, beginning in 1836, to expand far beyond the traditional boundaries of Spanish and Mexican Texas to encompass the land extending the entire length of the Rio Grande. Efforts to occupy the New Mexican portion of this territory during the years of the republic came to naught with the ignominious Texan Santa Fe Expedition. In the early months of the Mexican War, however, federal troops, commanded by Gen. Stephen W. Kearny, easily occupied New Mexico. Kearny quickly established a temporary civil government. When Texas governor J. Pinckney Henderson complained to United States secretary of state James Buchanan, the latter replied that, though the matter would have to be settled by Congress, Kearny's action should not prejudice the Texas claim. By the provisions of the Treaty of Guadalupe Hidalgo, Mexico relinquished all claim to territory north and east of the Rio Grande. The treaty did not, however, speak to the issue of the Texas claim to that portion of New Mexico lying east of the river. By this time New Mexico and all other lands ceded to the United States by Mexico had become embroiled in the slavery controversy. Southern leaders insisted that all of the new territory be opened to slaveholding. Northern freesoilers and abolitionists were determined to prevent this and so resisted the claims of Texas to part of the area in question. Texas attempted to further its claim by organizing Santa Fe County in 1848, with boundaries including most of New Mexico east of the Rio Grande. In New Mexico military and civilian leaders then petitioned the federal government to organize their area into a federal territory. Texas governor George T. Wood responded by asking the legislature to give him the power and means to assert the claim of Texas to New Mexico "with the whole power and resources of the State." Soon afterward his successor, Peter H. Bell, made a more moderate request, asking only for authority to send a military force sufficient to maintain the state's authority in that area. Bell then sent Robert S. Neighbors west to organize four counties in the disputed area. Although he was successful in the El Paso area, Neighbors was not welcomed in New Mexico.

Publication of the report of Neighbors's mission in June 1850 led to a public outcry in Texas. Some advocated the use of military force; others urged secession. Bell reacted by calling a special session of the legislature to deal with the issue. Before the session began, the crisis deepened. New Mexicans ratified a constitution for a proposed state specifying boundaries that included the territory claimed by Texas. Also, President Millard Fillmore reinforced the army contingent stationed in New Mexico and asserted publicly that should Texas militiamen enter the disputed area he would order federal troops to resist them. Southern political leaders responded by sending Governor Bell offers of moral and even military support. Meanwhile, Congress was grappling with the issue. On 16 January 1850, Senator Thomas Hart Benton of Missouri introduced a bill that would have had Texas cede all land west of 102° longitude and north of the Red River to the United States for $15 million. The bill would also divide Texas into two states. Soon afterward, Senator John Bell of Tennessee offered a resolution that would have divided Texas into three states. Then a Senate committee, chaired by Henry Clay of Kentucky, reported a bill that would have given Texas an unspecified sum in exchange for ceding all lands northwest of a straight line from the El Paso area to that point on the 100th meridian that intersects the Red River. None of these efforts proved successful.

Finally, Senator James A. Pierce of Maryland introduced a bill that offered Texas $10 million in exchange for ceding to the national government all land north and west of a boundary beginning at the 100th meridian where it intersects the parallel of 36°30', then running west along that parallel to the 103d meridian, south to the 32d parallel, and from that point west to the Rio Grande. The bill had the support of the Texas delegation and of moderate leaders in both the North and South. Holders of bonds representing the debt of the Republic of Texas lobbied hard for the bill, for it specified that part of the financial settlement be used to pay those obligations. The measure passed both houses of Congress in the late summer of 1850 and was signed by President Fillmore. Though there was some opposition in Texas to accepting the proffered settlement, voters at a special election approved it by a margin of three to one. The legislature then approved an act of acceptance, which Governor Bell signed on 25 November 1850. The boundary act and four additional bills passed at about the same time, all dealing with controversial sec-

tional issues, came to be known collectively as the Compromise of 1850. *Roger A. Griffin*

Comptroller of Public Accounts. Superseded an office established in 1835, made part of the Treasury Department of the Republic of Texas in 1836, and constitutionally continued since. The comptroller is elected and serves for four years in the tasks of keeping accounts of state funds, acting as tax administrator and collector for the state, and furnishing research and statistics for estimating revenue. The office submits financial reports to the governor and the legislature with statements on the previous fiscal year, outstanding appropriations, and estimates of anticipated revenue. *Laurie E. Jasinski*

Concepción, Battle of. The opening engagement in the siege of Bexar, 28 October 1835. After the battle of Gonzales (2 October) the Texas army under Stephen F. Austin grew to 400 men as it advanced on San Antonio. Gen. Martín Perfecto de Cos, with a Mexican army that peaked in size at 750 men in late October, fortified the plazas in San Antonio and the Alamo. On 27 October Austin ordered James Bowie and James W. Fannin, Jr., to lead 90 men from San Francisco de la Espada Mission to locate a protected position closer to the town. The four companies of Andrew Briscoe, Robert M. Coleman, Valentine Bennet, and Michael Goheen explored the other missions and briefly engaged Mexican scouts before reaching Concepción. There the officers decided to camp for the evening rather than return to the main army as Austin had directed. The Texans occupied a wooded bend in the San Antonio River protected by an embankment, and sent out pickets to warn of a Mexican attack. A few cannon shots from the town failed to inflict losses. Cos seized the opportunity to attack the separate force the next day, sending out Col. Domingo de Ugartechea with 275 men and two cannons before dawn. The 200 Mexican cavalry drove in the Texan guards in early morning fog and formed on the west side of the river. Lt. Col. José María Mendoza led the smaller infantry and artillery forces across the stream to attack from the east. Mexican volleys crashed through the trees overhead, but inflicted no casualties among the Texans until Bowie moved Coleman's company to meet the advance. Then one man fell mortally wounded. The Texans responded with accurate rifle fire that drove back three Mexican charges and killed or wounded most of the infantry and artillerymen in about 30 minutes. Then the Texans counterattacked and captured one of the cannons. Mexican cavalry covered the retreat of the infantry and cannoneers who survived. Austin and his other troops rushed to the field when they heard firing, but arrived too late to do more than hurry the Mexican withdrawal. Austin urged an assault on the town, but most of his officers believed San Antonio too well fortified. Mexican losses included 14 killed and 39 wounded, some of whom died later. Texas losses included one killed and one wounded.

Alwyn Barr

Concordia University at Austin. The fourth, and first successful, institution founded by the Missouri Synod Lutherans to train young men for the ministry; originally a secondary school modeled on the German *Gymnasium* and named Concordia College of Texas; renamed Concordia Lutheran College (1965). The college joined nine other Missouri Synod institutions to

Entrance, Kilian Hall, completed 1926. Prints and Photographs Collection, Concordia Lutheran College file, CAH; CN 10371. The administration building was named in honor of John Kilian, pastor of the Wendish settlers at Serbin, Texas.

form the Concordia University System in 1993 and was given its present name two years later. It is two miles north of the Capitol, at a site deemed beautiful by the first president, Henry Studtmann. Kilian Hall, the first building, won an award from the Architects' Guild of Texas. This structure was named after Rev. John Kilian, who led 500 Lutheran Wends to America from Prussia and Saxony in 1854. After classes began in this building in 1926, 26 students slept on the second floor on rented army cots until permanent beds arrived, read from a library furnished with donated books, cleared the campus of underbrush, and cut out their own baseball field.

Enrollment slumped during the Great Depression but recovered after World War II. Concordia added junior college curriculum in 1951, admitted women in 1955, discontinued high school classes in 1967, was accredited by the Southern Association of Colleges and Schools in 1968, and became a four-year institution in 1979.   *Louann Atkins Temple*

Confederate Air Force. The "Ghost Squadron," headquartered in Midland; a nonprofit educational organization dedicated to preserving and flying a complete collection of World War II air-

craft. It provides museum buildings for the permanent display of the aircraft as well as nonflying artifacts from the same period. In 1951 a group of former military pilots around Mercedes began to acquire surplus fighter aircraft. They realized that the 300,000 airplanes produced by the United States during World War II were about to be melted down for scrap metal. The group's first plane, a P40 Warhawk, was acquired in 1951 by Lloyd Nolen, a flight instructor during World War II. In 1957 the group bought a surplus P51 Mustang, upon which someone painted "Confederate Air Force." The airfield at Mercedes became Rebel Field, and every member became a "colonel." The airplane collection has grown to include military aircraft from all the nations engaged in World War II. By 1967 the force had participated in two movies depicting air battles of World War II. In a British film entitled *The Battle of Britain*, the CAF was commissioned to do the flying in return for two British "Spitfires" and three German ME-109s to go into the flying museum. *Tora, Tora, Tora* was a story depicting the Japanese bombing of Pearl Harbor. By 1968 the group had outgrown the small airfield at Mercedes, and they moved to the old Harlingen Aerial Gunnery School facility at Harlingen. They renamed their new facility Rebel Field and remained there until 1991, when they moved to the dryer climate and more central location of Midland. In 1983 the American Airpower Heritage Foundation, Incorporated, was formed to develop financial support for the CAF. In 1990 two additional corporations were established: the American Airpower Heritage Flying Museum, to obtain and maintain legal title to CAF aircraft, and the American Airpower Heritage Museum, responsible for the acceptance, preservation, and display of all nonflying artifacts, relics, and documents, as well as on-site display of aircraft. The Confederate Air Force remains the flying organization. In 1993 the CAF was composed of some 10,000 members, organized into 90 units called Wings, Squadrons, and Detachments, located throughout the United States and in France, England, New Zealand, and Australia. The corporation holds title to 140 aircraft. Most are in flying condition and are regularly flown in air shows throughout the country.

Art Leatherwood

Confederate Woman's Home. Near Austin; opened in 1908 to care for widows and wives of honorably discharged Confederate soldiers and other women who aided the Confederacy; cared for more than 3,400 indigent women over a period of 55 years. Many of these women were related to men at the Texas Confederate Home in Austin. Residents were required to be at least 60 years old and without means of financial support. The home was conceived in 1903, opened in 1908, and initially owned by the United Daughters of the Confederacy, who operated it until 1911. That year, the third attempt to transfer ownership to the state was successful. The home opened with three women and 15 bedrooms, was expanded to 39 bedrooms in 1913, and added a hospital in 1916 and a hospital annex in 1919. The Board of Control took it over in 1920. The home housed between 80 and 110 residents from 1920 through 1935. By the late 1930s new admissions were decreasing and most residents were in poor health. From 1938 to 1945, the population of the home fell from 87 to 55. In 1949 the home fell under the jurisdiction of the Board of Texas State Hospitals and Special Schools. During the late 1950s the nine remaining residents were consolidated into one hospital wing.

Governor John Connally and President Lyndon Baines Johnson aboard *Air Force One*. Photograph by Yoichi R. Okamoto, September 28, 1967. Courtesy Lyndon Baines Johnson Library, Austin. Connally and Johnson are shown here during a trip to inspect flood damage in South Texas and the Rio Grande valley in the wake of Hurricane Beulah.

In 1963 the last three residents were moved to private nursing homes at state expense, and the facility was closed. The state sold the property in 1986. The home was popular in Austin and was the site of many community events over the years.

Barbara Stocklin–Steely

Connally, John Bowden, Jr. Governor, attorney; b. near Floresville, 27 February 1917, d. Houston, 15 June 1993 (buried in State Cemetery); m. Idanell (Nelly) Brill (1940); 4 children. Connally fought heroically in World War II and subsequently became a major political figure. He began in politics as secretary to Congressman Lyndon B. Johnson (1938), with whom he worked until Johnson's death (1973). With LBJ and Sam Rayburn he fought for control of the state Democratic party against Allan Shivers, who supported Republican Dwight D. Eisenhower for president (1952, 1956). But he also feuded with liberal Democrat Ralph Yarbrough. Connally was secretary of the navy in John F. Kennedy's cabinet (1961–). He was elected governor in 1962, with the help of his oil-rich legal client Sid Richardson. After being wounded in the Kennedy assassination (22 November 1963), he was reelected governor in 1964 and 1966. He emphasized education, sought to increase tourism to Texas, and worked for establishment of the state fine arts and historical commissions as well as the University of Texas Institute of Texan Cultures. In 1969 he joined the Houston legal firm Vinson and Elkins. He subsequently became a major advisor of President Richard Nixon, whom he served as secretary of the treasury (1971–). Connally spearheaded Democrats for Nixon (1972), became a Republican in 1973, and was a strong contender to replace Vice President Spiro Agnew, who resigned that year. After Nixon himself resigned (1974), Connally returned to Vinson and Elkins. He was acquitted of bribery and conspiracy allegations in a "milk-price" scandal. He ran briefly for president in 1980 but was hurt by his "wheeler-dealer" image, the impression that he was a political "chameleon," and other damaging perceptions. Considering himself a victim of the Watergate scandal, he quit politics. He

retired from Vinson and Elkins in 1982, after entering the real estate business with an old protégé, Ben Barnes, in 1981. The two were seriously overextended financially when the oil price plummeted in the mid-1980s. Connally declared bankruptcy, and he and his wife sold their possessions in a famous auction. Connally was a member of the board of many major corporations and belonged to four bar associations. *Walter H. Gray*

Connally, Thomas Terry. U.S. senator; b. McLennan County, 19 August 1877; d. 28 October 1963; m. Louise Clarkson (1904; d. 1935); one son; m. Lucile Sanderson Sheppard, the widow of Senator Morris Sheppard (1942); ed. University of Texas (law degree, 1898). Connally was elected to the state House unopposed in 1900 and 1902. He was opposed monopolies and the powerful Senator Joseph Weldon Bailey. After declining to run for a third term, he was Falls County prosecuting attorney from 1906 to 1910. He was elected to Congress in 1916. In 1928 Connally ran successfully against Senator Earle B. Mayfield, a Klansman who had been elected during the heyday of the Ku Klux Klan. In his first term he fought President Herbert Hoover's efforts to raise the tariff, levy a national sales tax, and aid business and mortgage holders at the evident expense of homeowners. During Franklin D. Roosevelt's first term as president, Connally was a stalwart New Dealer. His main accomplishment, the Connally Hot Oil Act of 1935, effectively outlawed the interstate shipment of oil produced in violation of new state quotas and was fiercely resisted by many independent drillers and processors.

Connally split with Roosevelt on the court-packing plan of 1937, and the measure failed in the Senate. Also in 1937 Connally led the filibuster against the antilynching bill and fought diligently for the southern differential in the wage and hour law. He was a traditional southern internationalist who resisted the isolationist tide and the neutrality acts of the middle and late 1930s. He led the Senate battle for the arms-embargo repeal in 1939 (the Cash and Carry Act) and for the Lend Lease Act of 1941. As chairman of the Senate Foreign Relations Committee from 1941 to

Tom Connally (left) speaks to fellow Texas senator Morris Sheppard (second from right). Prints and Photographs Collection, Morris Sheppard file, CAH; CN 08126. First voted into public office in 1900, Connally never lost an election.

1947, he was one of the handful of Americans who devised the UN and its charter. Together with Arthur Vandenburg, he helped to determine bipartisan foreign policy during Harry Truman's administration, including the establishment of NATO. During the war years Connally and his fellow Texas senator, W. Lee O'Daniel, supported the Republican–Southern Democratic coalition more often than any other southern duo. In 1942 Connally led the 10-day filibuster against the repeal of the poll tax. The Smith–Connally Act of 1943 extended the power of the president to seize strike-bound war plants, a measure that Connally believed helped the war effort. In his years of prominence in the 1930s and 1940s Connally was the best showman in the Senate. A contemporary politician, describing the 200-pound, white-haired Connally, decreed him to be "the only man in the United States Senate who could wear a Roman Toga and not look like a fat man in a nightgown." By the early 1950s, however, he had lost some of his effectiveness. Moreover, his notions of party loyalty were distasteful to the powerful tidelands oil lobby. The lobby wanted a strong leader who would support whichever 1952 presidential nominee embraced state ownership of offshore oil lands. After they found their candidate in state attorney general Price Daniel, Sr., whose speeches effectively linked Connally with the unpopular Truman administration, Connally retired.   *George N. Green*

Conroe, Texas. County seat of Montgomery County, seven miles southeast of Lake Conroe. In 1881 Houston lumberman Isaac Conroe established a sawmill on Stewarts Creek two miles east of the International–Great Northern Railroad's Houston–Crockett line. A small tram line connected the mill to the I–GN track, but Conroe soon transferred his operations down the track to the rail junction, where his new mill became a station on the I–GN. In January 1884 a post office was established at the mill commissary, and, at the suggestion of railroad official H. M. Hoxey, the community took the name Conroe's Switch, in honor of the Northern-born, former Union cavalry officer who founded it and served as its first postmaster. Within a decade the name was shortened to Conroe. In the mid 1880s the Gulf, Colorado and Santa Fe Railway extended its Navasota–Montgomery spur eastward through the town. A lumber boom beginning in the late nineteenth century in the Piney Woods of eastern and central Montgomery County attracted scores of settlers to Conroe. By 1889 the population had climbed to an estimated 300. In that year Conroe replaced Montgomery as county seat. A residence donated by Isaac Conroe served as a temporary courthouse until a permanent brick structure was built in 1891. By 1892 the community had become a shipping center for lumber, cotton, livestock, and bricks, and had five steam-powered saw and planing mills, several brickyards, a cotton gin, a gristmill, several hotels and general stores, and a population of 500. In 1902 the town's first high school class graduated. In April 1903 a private coeducational vocational school for blacks was founded by Dr. Jimmie Johnson in northeast Conroe and quickly began to attract students from around the state. Conroe incorporated in 1904 with a population of 1,009, and its first mayor and city council were elected the following year. In 1906 the first electric lighting appeared in the town when an electrical generating plant was constructed on nearby Stewarts Creek.

The prosperity of the local agriculture and timber industries in the early twentieth century enabled Conroe to continue its rapid early growth despite severe fires in 1901 and 1911, which destroyed much of the business district near the courthouse square. Southwest of town in 1913 the Delta Land and Timber Company established one of the most extensive milling operations in the South; the company eventually employed 700 people. A sanitarium was established in Conroe in 1920. The community acquired its first fire truck in 1921, and two years built its first fire station. In 1922 the courthouse grounds became the scene of communal violence when a black mill worker accused of rape was lynched. In the mid-1920s the Dr Pepper Company opened a soft-drink plant in the community. The population continued to climb, reaching 2,457 by 1930. After years of sustained growth, the town's prosperity was threatened in the late 1920s by the dwindling of the improperly managed local timber supply. In 1930 the Great Depression drastically curtailed lumber production and forced many mills to close. Conroe's only bank abruptly failed and pushed many residents and institutions into financial doldrums that lasted many years. But the community's fortunes began to improve on 13 December 1931, when George W. Strake discovered oil seven miles southeast of town, thus marking the opening of the Conroe oilfield and triggering an oil boom in the county. Within weeks many petroleum wholesalers, retailers, and service companies and thousands of workers entered the town. By 1933 the population was an estimated 5,000. The Conroe school district, rescued from financial distress by oil, became one of the wealthiest in the state, and its enrollment began to grow rapidly. A community center and a swimming pool were completed by the district in the early 1940s. During the early 1930s streets were paved for the first time and U.S. Highway 75 was extended through the town. The 37-room State Hotel was completed in 1933. The ornate Crighton Theater was built on the courthouse square in 1935. In 1936 a new courthouse was constructed, and two years later a county hospital was completed not far from the courthouse square. That year the population surged to an estimated 10,000, but it soon began to subside as production in the Conroe oilfield crested and began a gradual decline. By 1941 the population stood at an estimated 4,624.

The town's lumber industry briefly revived during World War II, but it lapsed into a steady decline after 1950. Its former position was increasingly assumed by chemical firms, including a carbon black factory and a recycling plant, established after the oil discovery. The Montgomery County Airport, three miles northeast of town on Farm Road 1484, was constructed during the war as a military facility but since 1945 has served as a local airfield. In 1946 the Montgomery County Library was established in Conroe. Conroe's population climbed to 7,313 in 1950, 9,192 in 1960 and 11,969 in 1970. With the construction of Interstate Highway 45, increasing numbers of Houstonians took up residence on the margins of Conroe. Lake Conroe, impounded in the late 1960s and early 1970s seven miles northwest on the West Fork of the San Jacinto River, further stimulated growth. In the 1980s Conroe had two hospitals, a nursing home, 10 medical clinics, 19 churches, 3 radio stations, a television station, a cab company, and a new sewage treatment plant. The population was 27,610 in 1990.

Charles Christopher Jackson

Considerant, Victor Prosper. Founder of La Réunion, a colony near Dallas; b. Salins, France, 12 October 1808; d. Paris, 27 December 1893; m. Julie Vigoureux. Considerant devoted himself to applying the utopian ideas of Charles Fourier and became the international leader of the Fourierist movement during the volatile revolutionary period of 1830–50. After the abortive insurrection of 13 June 1849 against Louis Napoleon Bonaparte, he was forced to flee to Brussels. There he was contacted by Albert Brisbane, an American Fourierist, who interested him in colonization efforts in Texas. After visiting Texas in 1852–53, he established the European Society for the Colonization of Texas upon his return to Belgium. In two books—*Au Texas* (Paris, 1854) and *The Great West* (New York, 1854) Considerant presented plans for a joint European–American colony, La Réunion, and proposed the ultimate establishment of a network of colonies throughout the Southwest. Early in 1855 his agents bought 2,500 acres on the Trinity River near Dallas. Before adequate provision had been made for them, however, nearly 200 colonists made their way to La Réunion. When Considerant and his wife arrived with more colonists later that year, the settlement was completely disorganized. It never recovered. Departing from orthodox Fourierism, Considerant planned for La Réunion to be a loosely structured commune administered by a system of direct democracy. The participants would share in the profits according to a formula based on the amount of capital investment and the quantity and quality of labor performed. When La Réunion collapsed in 1859 due to financial insolvency, Considerant moved to San Antonio, where he unsuccessfully attempted to raise funds for another commune. He became an American citizen and farmed in Bexar County until 1869, when he and his wife returned to Paris. There he lived as a teacher and socialist sage of the Latin Quarter until his death.

Rondel V. Davidson

Constitutional Convention of 1974. A futile attempt to rewrite the ponderous Constitution of 1876. Recognizing the need for a new state constitution, the Sixty-second Legislature passed a resolution in May 1971 that called for the establishment of a constitutional revision commission and for the convening of the Sixty-third Legislature as a constitutional convention in January 1974. The proceeding was to be a limited convention, meaning that the Bill of Rights could not be changed. Voters approved the resolution as a constitutional amendment (7 November 1972). In 1973 the legislature duly established a commission to "study the need for constitutional change." Robert W. Calvert, former speaker of the Texas House of Representatives and former chief justice of the Texas Supreme Court, was named chairman of the commission, and Mrs. Malcolm Milburn, former president of the Texas Federation of Republican Women, was named vice chairman. Other members of the commission included Peter Flawn, Clotilde Garcia, Leon Jaworski, Page Keeton, Janice May, and Ralph Yarborough. After holding 19 public hearings across the state, the commission presented its recommendations for a new constitution to the legislature on 1 November 1973. The proposed document represented the first thorough attempt to draft a new constitution for Texas since the Constitutional Convention of 1875. On 8 January 1974, the legislature convened as a constitutional convention, meeting as a unicameral body with Lieutenant Governor Hobby presiding as temporary chairman. Speaker Price Daniel, Jr., of Liberty County, was elected president of the convention, and State Senator A. M. Aikin, Jr., of Lamar County, was elected vice president. The delegates were appointed to 13 committees. James F. Ray, executive director of

the commission, was appointed executive director of the convention. Upon the completion of its work the convention was to submit a proposed new constitution to the voters of Texas for their approval or rejection. The convention was originally planned to adjourn on 31 May 1974, but members soon voted by a two-thirds majority to extend that time for 60 days, the maximum allowed, to 30 July. With the legislators as delegates, divisive politics became a major obstacle to completing the task at hand. The most controversial issue was a right-to-work provision in the constitution. Unionized labor groups strongly opposed the measure. An election primary in May 1974 also served as a political distraction for many legislators campaigning for reelection. More than $3 million in appropriations was spent on the convention. When the convention ended on 30 July, it had failed by three votes to produce a document to submit to the voters. In 1975, in a further effort, the legislature approved a new constitution in the form of eight amendments approved by the normal amendment process. The Bill of Rights remained unchanged, but the eight amendments went before the voters on 4 November 1975 in a special election. All were defeated. One legacy of the 1974 constitutional convention was a large body of written material on the Texas constitution.

Mary Lucia Barras and Houston Daniel

Constitutional Union Party. An antebellum political party. After the demise of their party in the mid-1850s Whigs searched for another organization that could win elections. For a time some drifted into the American (Know-Nothing) party, but its nativism cost it votes and alienated some of the more prominent former Whigs. By 1859 a new party, generally called the Opposition party, was attracting disaffected Democrats worried about the growing radicalism of their former party, as well as most ex-Whigs and unconditional Unionists. The Opposition party, led by its gubernatorial candidate, the former Democrat Sam Houston, swept the majority of the statewide elections that year. Another member of the party and another former Democrat, Andrew Jackson Hamilton, was elected to Congress. In 1860 the Opposition party, minus much of its Democratic support, became the Constitutional Union party, and a state organizational meeting was held at Marshall, Texas. Starting in the spring of 1860 members of the Opposition began to call for the nomination of either Millard Fillmore or Sam Houston for president. Houston had much more appeal to the Democratic strain of the party than the former Whig president, but neither candidate had much support outside of the lower South. On April 27 a small group of Governor Houston's East Texas friends, who were supporters of the new party, assembled in Tyler to elect four delegates to the national convention, to be held at Baltimore in May—Anthony Norton, Abram Gentry, Benjamin Epperson, and Lemuel Evans. In Baltimore the Texas delegation worked for the nomination of Houston, but John Bell, an ex-Whig from Tennessee, defeated Houston.

In 1860 four viable candidates ran for the presidency: Abraham Lincoln, the Republican; John C. Breckinridge, the Southern Democrat; Stephen A. Douglas, the Northern Democrat; and Bell. In Texas, Republicans were so disliked that Lincoln was not even on the ballot. Douglas had a few supporters, but the Texas campaign was really between Bell and Breckinridge. Two weeks after being rejected at Baltimore, Houston accepted a presidential nomination offered him at a

San Jacinto celebration in April. Eventually, however, as former Whigs who were not already allied with the other parties began to rally to Bell, Houston lost his out-of-state newspaper support, and in August he withdrew his candidacy and became a backer of the Constitutional Union party. Even before Houston's withdrawal, Whig Unionists in East Texas were organizing for Bell. They had support from many newspapers. Elsewhere in the state, Union clubs sprang up—in Galveston, Texana, Austin, San Antonio, Corsicana, Waco, Georgetown, and in a number of counties between the San Antonio–Austin area and Galveston, including Colorado and Fayette counties. Until August 1860 the race much resembled earlier contests between the Democrats and the Whigs. Partisan accusations, not concern for the Union, held center stage. Fear that the election of Lincoln might precipitate a crisis changed the tone of the Constitutional Unionists, however. The party lost heavily to the regular Democrats in a statewide election on 6 August, and party leaders began to call for fusion with the Douglas Democrats. Constitutional Unionists repeatedly described themselves as the party most capable of saving the Union. The hybrid nature of the party was reflected in the election in early September of two Unionist Democrats, George W. Paschal of Travis County and John H. Robson of Colorado County, and two old-line Whigs, William Stedman of Rusk County and Benjamin Epperson of Red River County, as presidential electors. Unionist campaigners, however, faced militant opposition motivated by the suspicion of abolitionist plots in Texas, as well as by a growing belief in the need for Southern solidarity. Attempts at fusion that might have restored the effective coalition of 1859 failed. Democrats voted for the Democratic candidate, and Breckinridge swept the state, with only three counties—Bandera, Gillespie, and Starr—voting for Bell.

In the 1860 election, calls to save the Union could not overcome party loyalty and party history. Germans and Mexican Texans well remembered that many of the leaders of the Constitutional Union party had been Know-Nothings. Democrats saw the nomination of Bell and the failure to focus clearly on Unionism early in the campaign as signs that the Constitutional Unionists were simply Whigs in new garb. Even the last-minute attempt to combine with the Douglas Democrats and the claim that only they could keep Abraham Lincoln out of the White House failed to broaden their appeal significantly. Lincoln won the 1860 election, although he received no votes in Texas, and his victory caused a popular movement for secession across the South. But the Constitutional Union party had already split along former partisan lines before the election, and with the growth of secession sentiment the fragile coalition collapsed entirely. *Walter L. Buenger and James Alex Baggett*

Constitution of 1876. The Constitution of 1876 is the sixth constitution by which Texas has been governed since independence from Mexico was achieved in 1836. It was framed by the Constitutional Convention of 1875 and adopted on 15 February 1876 by a vote of 136,606 to 56,652, and it remains the basic organic law of Texas. The constitution contains some provisions that are uniquely Texan, many of which are products of the state's unusual history. Some, for example, may be traced to Spanish and Mexican influence. Among them are sections dealing with land titles and land law in general, debtor relief, judicial procedures, marital relations and adoption, and water and other mineral rights. Other atypical provisions may be attributed to the twin influences of Jacksonian agrarianism and frontier radicalism—both prevalent when Texas first became a state and both widely supported by the bulk of immigrants to Texas before the Civil War. Those influences produced sections prohibiting banks and requiring a stricter separation of church and state than that required in older states. Reconstruction, under the highly centralized and relatively autocratic administration of Governor Edmund Davis and his fellow Radical Republicans, prompted provisions to decentralize the state government. Upon regaining control of both the legislative and executive branches of the government, the Democrats determined in 1874 to replace the unpopular Constitution of 1869. They wanted all officials elected for shorter terms and lower salaries, abolition of voter registration, local control of schools, severely limited powers for both the legislature and the governor, low taxation and state expenditures, strict control over corporations, and land subsidies for railroads.

Early in 1874 a joint legislative committee reported an entire new constitution as an amendment to the Constitution of 1869. Because the document had not been prepared by a convention and because of the possibility that its adoption might antagonize the federal government, the legislature rejected the proposal. On the advice of Governor Richard Coke, the next legislature submitted the question of a constitutional convention to the voters, who, on 2 August 1875, approved the convention and elected three delegates from each of the 30 senatorial districts. In the convention, which convened on 6 September, 75 members were Democrats and 15, including 6 blacks, were Republicans. Not one had been a member of the Convention of 1868–69, 41 were farmers, and no fewer than 40 were members of the Grange, the militant farmers' organization established in response to the Panic of 1873. In the convention the Grange members acted as a bloc in support of conservative constitutional measures. To assure that the government would be responsive to public will, the convention precisely defined the rights, powers, and prerogatives of the various governmental departments and agencies, including many details generally left to the legislature.

The Constitution of 1876 began with a lengthy bill of rights. It declared that Texas was a free and independent state, subject only to the Constitution of the United States, that all free men have equal rights, and that the writ of habeas corpus could not be suspended or unduly delayed. The article also forbade religious tests for office, unreasonable searches, and imprisonment for debt, and it guaranteed liberty of speech and press, the right of the accused to obtain bail and to be tried by a jury, and the right of citizens to keep and bear arms. The legislative article defined the powers and limitations of the legislature in great detail. The legislature was to be composed of two houses, a Senate to consist of 31 members and a House of Representatives never to exceed 150 members. Senators and representatives were to serve terms of four and two years, respectively. Legislators were to receive mileage allowance and not more than five dollars a day for the first 60 days of each session and two dollars a day thereafter. The legislature, which was to meet biennially, could incur no indebtedness greater than $200,000 and could establish no office for longer than two years. It was required to levy taxes on all property in proportion to its value and to hold its sessions in Austin. The executive article provided for seven officers—governor, lieutenant governor, secretary of state, comptroller of public accounts, treasurer, commissioner of the land office, and attorney general. All except the secretary of state were to be elected by the voters for a term of two years but with no limitations on eligibility for new terms. All salaries were reduced, that of the governor from $5,000 to $4,000. The governor was empowered to convene the legislature in special sessions, to call out the militia to execute the laws, to suppress insurrections, to protect the frontier against hostile Indians, and to veto laws and items in appropriations bills; his veto, however, could be overridden by a two-thirds vote of both houses. The governor was also empowered to make certain appointments, fill vacancies, and cause the laws to be faithfully executed, but was given no control over local or other elected state officials. The judicial article provided for a supreme court, a court of appeals, district courts, county courts, commissioners' courts, and justices of the peace. All judges were to be elected by popular vote, with terms of six years for the supreme and criminal appeals courts, four years for the district courts, and two years for all other courts. The number of district courts was placed at 26, but the legislature was authorized to establish others as needed. The Texas Supreme Court, composed of three judges, was vested with appellate jurisdiction in civil cases only, and the court of appeals, composed of three judges, was vested with appellate jurisdiction over all criminal cases and certain classes of civil cases. The district courts received original jurisdiction (in criminal cases) over felonies and over misdemeanors involving official misconduct and (in civil cases) over a long list of classes of suits. The district courts were given appellate jurisdiction over the county courts in probate matters. The article also mandated a court in each organized county with original jurisdiction over misdemeanors not granted to the courts of justices of the peace and certain civil cases and appellate jurisdiction in cases originating in the justice of the peace courts. The courts of the justices of the peace, not fewer than four or more than eight in each county, were granted jurisdiction in civil and criminal matters involving not more than $200 in controversy or in penalties. The commissioners' court was to consist of the county judge and four elected commissioners, one from each commissioner's precinct.

The article on education drastically changed the system established by the Republicans in 1869. In the first section the framers ordered the legislature to establish and make provision for the support and maintenance of an efficient system of public free schools but then added provisions that made that directive impossible. To support the system the article authorized the legislature to levy a poll tax of one dollar on all male inhabitants between the ages of 21 and 60 and to appropriate not more than one-fourth of the general revenue. In addition, it set aside as a perpetual fund all proceeds from lands previously granted to the schools, including all the alternate sections of land already reserved for the state or afterwards reserved out of land grants to railroads or other corporations (as specified in the Constitution of 1866), and the proceeds from the sale of one-half of all other public lands (as prescribed by an act of the legislature in 1873). The document abolished the office of state superintendent, founded a board of education composed of the governor, comptroller, and secretary of state, eliminated compulsory attendance, provided for segregated schools, and made no provision for local school taxes. The Constitution of 1876 provided for the establishment of the University of Texas and made Texas A&M, which had been founded by the legislature in 1871, a branch of it. The

constitution further required the legislature to establish an institution of higher education for the instruction of the black youth of the state. To support the university and its branches the constitution set aside one million acres of the public domain, with all sales and proceeds therefrom to be placed in a Permanent University Fund. It also provided that proceeds from the lands previously granted for the establishment and maintenance of the university (including the 50-league grant by the legislature in 1858 but not the one-tenth of the alternate sections of land granted to railroads) and all future grants would permanently belong to the university.

The constitution also provided for precinct voting. It provided for homestead grants of 160 acres to heads of families and 80 acres to single men 18 or more years of age, and for protection against the forced sale of a homestead for debt. It declared railroads to be common carriers, forbade their consolidation and further aid in grant of money or bonds, and authorized the legislature to enact regulatory laws, including maximum freight and passenger rates. To promote the construction of new track, the document authorized the legislature to grant the railroads 16 sections of public land for each mile of road constructed. It prohibited the state from chartering banks but mandated the legislature to enact general laws for the establishment of private corporations other than banks, that would provide fully for the adequate protection of the public and individual stockholders.

Overall, the Constitution of 1876 complied with public opinion. It provided for biennial sessions of the legislature, low salaries for public officials, precinct voting, abolition of the road tax, and a return to the road-working system; for a homestead exemption clause, guarantees of a low tax rate, a less expensive, locally controlled, segregated school system, and a less expensive court system; for county and justice of the peace courts; and for popular election of officers. It also prohibited the registration of voters and grants of money or bonds to railroads. The document was adequate for a rural people engaged principally in subsistence farming, but not for an urban-industrial-commercial society. Very few changes were made during the first half century of the constitution's existence, but since then it has been changed at a steadily increasing rate. Changes are made through constitutional amendments submitted to the voters by consent of two-thirds of the members of each house of the legislature and approved by a majority of those voting. Of 99 amendments submitted by September 1928, only 43 were adopted, but by 1980 the voters had approved 235 proposals. No provision was made in the constitution for calling another constitutional convention. On several occasions there has been considerable agitation for a new document, but the voters defeated a proposal for a constitutional convention in 1919, and in 1975 they rejected an extensive revision prepared by the legislature. The constitution's more than 63,000 words make it one of the most verbose of state constitutions. Its wealth of detail causes it to resemble a code of laws rather than a constitution. Its many requirements and limitations on both state and local governments make it one of the most restrictive among state constitutions. Some of its passages are so poorly drafted as to need clarification for understanding, and others have been declared by the Texas Supreme Court to be beyond interpreting. Finally, since many of its provisions relating to the same subject are scattered widely throughout the text, a detailed index is necessary.

Most of the numerous amendments have dealt with the legislature, the judiciary, public education, and state finances. Those relating to the legislature have generally removed existing limitations on legislative action. Changes in the article on the judiciary have been so sweeping that the article has been almost completely rewritten. Alterations in provisions relating to public education have also removed original limitations and permitted expansion of the public school system. Provisions relating to the state's financial system have been altered to permit adoption of new expenditure programs and use of new sources of revenue. Other constitutional changes have relieved some of the burden of detail imposed on the governor's office in 1876, revamped the basic suffrage requirements, altered the method of chartering municipal corporations, lengthened the term of office for many state and local officials, and established an ever-growing number of specifically allocated funds in the state treasury. In spite of its cumbersomeness, of its need for frequent amendment, and its occasional obscurity, however, Texans have continued to hold on to the Constitution of 1876.

Joe E. Ericson and Ernest Wallace

Consultation. A meeting in revolutionary Texas; grew out of a proposed meeting of Texas representatives to confer on the pre-revolutionary quarrel with Mexico. The idea was first advocated by opponents of revolution. A meeting in Columbia on 15 August used the term *consultation*, perhaps to avoid the revolutionary connotations that the word *convention* implied in Mexican politics. There was not complete agreement on the power of this body. Though originally set for 15 October, the Consultation was delayed until 1 November by the eruption of war earlier in the month. On 16 October 31 members assembled at San Felipe and recognized the legitimacy of a Permanent Council for an impermanent two-week period. Delegates gathered on 1 November and chose Branch Archer to preside. None came from the war zone districts of Bexar, Goliad, Refugio, Victoria, or San Patricio, and fewer than half of those elected attended from Bevil, Mina, and Matagorda. A total of 58 of the 98 credentialed delegates attended the Consultation. These factors weakened the influence of Stephen F. Austin, who remained with the Texas army, because several of the absent delegates had strong affiliations with him. John A. Wharton and Henry Smith directed the faction opposed to the Austin group, headed by Don Carlos Barrett. Each group had the support of about a third of the delegates; the resulting balance of power led the Consultation toward compromise.

Three issues dominated Consultation deliberations–the purpose of the war, the power and structure of government, and the virtues of different leaders. Barrett favored endorsement of the Constitution of 1824; there was still hope that Mexican liberals might rally to support Texas. The Wharton–Smith group sought an immediate declaration of independence. On 7 November the Consultation, by a vote of 33 to 14, endorsed establishment of "a provisional government upon the principles of the Constitution of 1824." Yet, at the same time, the delegates declared that Antonio López de Santa Anna had already dissolved the social compact and that Texas had the right to declare its independence. Smith chaired the committee on the provisional government. The Consultation approved an interim structure called the Organic Law on 13 November. This law abolished Mexican political titles, but otherwise reflected a spirit of balance and hesitation. It established an executive along with a general council,

made up of a representative from each municipality chosen by his delegation, to assist the governor. Its members had no legislative authority unless "in their opinion the emergency of the country requires" it, and could levy import duties but no other taxes. The governor was to have "full and ample" executive authority, including being head of the military forces, and could be given additional powers that the council thought necessary. The Organic Law also provided for judiciary and treasury departments. But the Organic Law embodied the rash assumption that the governor and council could share powers and work together. The delegates chose the disputatious Smith as governor over Austin by 30 to 22. The Consultation designed a land policy to reassure the soldiers who feared that while they sacrificed, the speculators would carry off the spoils. In three separate articles the Organic Law nullified the "fraudulent" grants made by the last state legislature, reaffirmed the benefits of earlier emigration policies to citizens who had not yet received their land, and ended all transactions for the duration of the war. The Consultation also provided for land grants of unspecified amounts for each volunteer.

On 13 November the Consultation passed both the Organic Law and a measure concerning the military. It provided for militia organization but also established a regular army with two-year enlistments and United States Army regulations; Sam Houston won unanimous election as commander, with the rank of major general. However, the Consultation made no attempt to assert its will over existing bodies of volunteer troops who elected their own officers, had little discipline, and served for unspecified enlistments. As a result, a regular army was not recruited. The Consultation refused to reconsider this arrangement on 14 November, the day of its adjournment. The focus on moderation and compromise held the Consultation together but left Texas without a clear course to its future in terms of leadership, purpose, structure of government, or military authority.

Paul D. Lack

Cook, Abner. Austin master builder; b. near Salisbury, North Carolina, 15 March 1814; d. Austin, 22 February 1884; m. Mrs. Eliza T. Logan (1842); 4 sons. He arrived in Texas in 1839 and with a partner, carpenter Heman Ward, filled private commissions for houses and furniture. Ward left Texas. In October 1839 Cook and five others founded the first church in Austin, a Presbyterian church. Cook later built the congregation's first log building with his own hands. In 1847 he built a large residence for Thomas William Ward, commissioner of the General Land Office and one of the wealthiest men in Austin. Ward's was a two-story frame house with a single-story portico, late Federal in style and not unlike the Lewis Utzman House in Salisbury. Several years later Cook built a singlestory brick house in the Federal style for his friend Dr. William Copeland Philips (1854), and a twostory frame house in the same style for another friend, Dr. Samuel G. Haynie. Cook soon bought the latter house to live in. He supervised the construction of the Texas State Penitentiary at Huntsville (1848–50). In Austin he was contractor for woodwork on the 1852 Capitol, built to the designs of his partner and fellow carpenter John Brandon, who seems to have had no experience in the planning of large public buildings. Early in the 1850s Cook built his own brick kiln on the banks of Shoal Creek and became part owner of another lumber mill near Bastrop. He seems to have purchased Minard Lafever's *The Beauties of*

Modern Architecture (1835), a volume that deeply influenced Cook's subsequent projects. The earliest work to show the change was a farmhouse for William S. Hotchkiss, later owned by Beriah Graham, which, though a single story, is prefaced by a box-columned portico with a weighty entablature. The Hotchkiss–Graham House also seems to have been the first of Cook's houses to feature an X-and-stick balustrade, a Federal motif that became one of Cook's trademarks. Next was a house for John Milton Swisher, which was two stories, brick, with two sets of paired columns, Greek Ionic in detail and proportion.

In 1854 Cook began three great brick houses with Greek Ionic porticoes stretching across their front. These were houses for state treasurer James H. Raymond and state comptroller James B. Shaw, and the Governor's Mansion. Governor Pease, first occupant of the mansion, later bought Shaw's place and named it Woodlawn Mansion. In 1856–57 Cook switched to the Greek Doric for houses for Washington L. Hill and Mary and Reuben Runner, now known as the Neill–Cochran House and Westhill, respectively. For the door frames, window frames, and mantels of these houses Cook designed simplified, abstracted versions of the shouldered architraves illustrated in Lafever's book. During Reconstruction professionally trained architects moved to Austin, and Cook began to leave design to the architects and to concentrate on construction. He was contractor for the North Building at the State Lunatic Asylum (1874—75), for the First National Bank Building (also known as Cook's Corner) at Sixth and Congress (1875–76), and three stores in a business block, 912, 914, and 916 Congress (1875–76), all built to the Victorian designs of architect Jacob Larmour. Cook's largest residential project of the postwar era was a twostory Italianate house for cattle baron Seth Mabry at Twelfth and Lavaca (1876). His last great work was the construction of the west wing of the main building of the newly founded University of Texas. This High Victorian Gothic building, designed by Frederick E. Ruffini, was dedicated in September 1883. Like many of Cook's works, Old Main has been demolished, but most of his Greek Revival houses of the 1850s remain. Cook was the most significant designer of Greek Revival buildings in antebellum Texas. His works combined a monumentality of form and a sophistication of detail rarely seen in Texas since the days of the Franciscans. *Kenneth Hafertepe*

Coppini, Pompeo Luigi. Sculptor; b. Moglia, Mantua, Italy, 19 May 1870; d. San Antonio, 26 September 1957; m. Elizabeth di Barbieri (1898); ed. Accademia di Belle Arte, Florence, under Augusto Rivalta (grad. *summa cum laude*, 1889). In 1896 Coppini immigrated to the U.S. After hearing of Frank Teich's search for a sculptor, he moved to Texas in November 1901. He became an American citizen in 1902. He was commissioned to model the statue of Jefferson Davis and other figures for the Confederate monument (1901–03) subsequently erected on the Capitol grounds in Austin. Other Texas commissions included the Littlefield Fountain Memorial (1920–28) at the University of Texas, seven bronze statues along the south mall of the university grounds, a statue of Rufus C. Burleson at Baylor University (1903), the monument to Sam Houston at Huntsville (1910), a monument at Gonzales in commemoration of the first shot fired for Texas independence (1910), a statue of a Confederate soldier at Victoria (1911), busts of Albert Sidney Johnston, Robert E. Lee, Jefferson Davis, and Stonewall Jackson for the Confederate monument at Paris (1903), and a group statue called *The Victims of*

Pompeo Coppini working on the central figure for the Alamo cenotaph, San Antonio, 1938. San Antonio *Light* Collection, ITC.

the Galveston Flood (1903–4), which was given to the University of Texas. Coppini also modeled the equestrian monument to Terry's Texas Rangers (the Eighth Texas Cavalry) on the Capitol grounds (1905–07), the Charles H. Noyes Memorial in Ballinger (1918–19), the John H. Reagan Memorial in Palestine (1911), and the bronze doors of the Scottish Rite Cathedral in San Antonio (dedicated 1926). One of his best-known works is a statue of George Washington in Mexico City (1911). Coppini lived and worked in San Antonio until 1916, when he moved to Chicago for financial reasons. Three years later he moved to New York City to facilitate the production of the Littlefield Fountain Memorial. He was assisted on this and other major projects by sculptor Waldine Tauch, who began studying with Coppini in 1910 and continued to work with him as his colleague and foster daughter until his death. In 1937 Coppini established a studio in San Antonio in order to work on a major commission for the Texas Centennial, the cenotaph to the heroes of the Alamo (1937–39) on Alamo Plaza in San Antonio. Other Centennial commissions awarded to him were the commemorative half–dollar (1934) and the Hall of State bronze statues of Stephen F. Austin, Thomas J. Rusk, William B. Travis, James W. Fannin, Mirabeau B. Lamar, and Sam Houston (1935–36).

Coppini is represented elsewhere in the U.S. by 36 public monuments, 16 portrait statues, and about 75 portrait busts. He often criticized modernism, which he attributed to a general lack of screening of pupils in art schools. He thought that art training should be a regular branch of learning in a university, with strict standards that would assure adherence to classic and academic artistic traditions. From 1943 to 1945 he was head of the art department of Trinity University in San Antonio. In 1945 he and Tauch cofounded the Classic Arts Fraternity in San Antonio (renamed Coppini Academy of Fine Arts in 1950). Coppini was buried in Sunset Memorial Park in a crypt of his own design. His San Antonio studio now serves as a museum of his and Tauch's work. In 1931 he was decorated "Commendatore" of the Crown of Italy for his contribution to art in America. In 1941 he was awarded an honorary doctorate by Baylor University.

Córdova Rebellion. A rebellion against the Texas government borne of a conspiracy in 1838. Former citizens of the United States, now citizens of the Republic of Texas, lived in constant fear of retaliation from the Mexican government. Before 1836 Hispanics had made up the largest segment of the population of Nacogdoches. After the Texas Revolution, many remained loyal to Mexico. Indians, principally Cherokees, were aggrieved that they still had no clear title to their lands, a reward promised them by the republic for their neutrality in the Texas Revolution and abrogated by Texas officials in 1837. In late 1836 several sources reported to President Sam Houston that the Cherokees had concluded a treaty with Mexico for a combined attack on Texas. It would be a war of extermination, and the Indians would receive title to their land in return for their allegiance. Vicente Córdova, a financially comfortable Nacogdochian who had served his community as alcalde, judge, and regidor, maintained contact with agents of the Mexican government during this period. On 4 August 1838, a group of Nacogdochians searching for stolen horses was fired upon by a party of Hispanics. Finding evidence that suggested the presence of a large assembly of people, they returned to Nacogdoches and reported their discovery. After being informed that at least 100 Mexicans led by Córdova were encamped on the Angelina River, Thomas J. Rusk called up the Nacogdoches squadron and sent a call to nearby settlements for reinforcements. On 8 August, Houston issued a proclamation prohibiting unlawful assemblies and carrying of arms and ordered all assembled without authorization to return to their homes in peace. Two days later the leaders of the rebellion replied with their own proclamation, signed by Córdova and 18 others. They claimed injuries and usurpations of their rights, and proclaimed themselves ready to die in defense of those rights. On the same day Rusk learned that the insurrectionists had been joined by local Indians, who brought their number to approximately 400.

After ascertaining that the rebellious band was moving toward the Cherokee nation, Rusk sent Maj. Henry W. Augustine with 150 men to follow them. Rusk, ignoring Houston's orders not to cross the Angelina River, took his remaining troops and marched directly toward the Cherokee village of Chief Bowl. En route Rusk learned that the rebellious army had been overtaken near Seguin and defeated. After communicating with local Indians, who disavowed any knowledge of the uprising, Rusk and his volunteer army returned to Nacogdoches. Houston remained in Nacogdoches throughout the insurrection, writing letters of reassurance to his friend Bowl, and issuing orders to Rusk. Houston trusted the Cherokees' loyalty and hoped to keep peace with Bowl. Rusk, on the other hand, distrusted the Cherokee leadership and thought that a show of force was necessary. Rusk disobeyed Houston's orders and often bypassed him completely by sending reports to Vice President Lamar, who was in closer agreement with Rusk's views.

The leaders of the insurrection escaped arrest and went into hiding. Córdova eventually made his way to Mexico. Thirty-three alleged members of the rebellion, all with Spanish surnames, were arrested and indicted for treason in the Nacogdoches District Court. Because of the "distracted state of public feeling" a change of venue to neighboring San Augustine County was granted to all but one of the defendants. José Antonio Menchaca, one of those tried in San Augustine County, was found guilty of treason and sentenced to hang, while the remaining defendants were found not guilty or had their cases dismissed. After several former jurors claimed to have been pressured in their decisions, President Lamar pardoned Menchaca, only four days before his scheduled execution. About 20 August, Julián Pedro Miracle was killed near the Red River. On his body were found a diary and papers that indicated the existence of an official project of the Mexican government to incite East Texas Indians against the Republic of Texas. The diary recorded that Miracle had visited Chief Bowl and that they had agreed to make war against the Texans. On 18 May 1839 a group of Texas Rangers defeated a party of Mexicans and Indians, including some Cherokees from Bowl's village. On the body of Manuel Flores, the group's leader, were found documents encouraging Indians to follow a campaign of harassment against Texans. Included were letters from Mexican officials addressed to Córdova and Bowl. Although Bowl denied all charges against his people and Houston maintained his belief in their innocence, Lamar became convinced that the Cherokees could not be allowed to stay in Texas. The Cherokee War and subsequent removal of the Cherokees from Texas began shortly thereafter.

Rebecca J. Herring

Corona, Leonora. Operatic soprano; b. Lenore Cohron, Dallas, 14 October 1900. Lenore, considered a child prodigy, gave piano recitals in Dallas. After moving to Seattle, she the Chicago Grand Opera and the Scotti Opera Company perform and became increasingly drawn to singing. She wrote a brief opera "The Egyptian Tragedy," which was performed in Seattle. She studied voice in New York and Italy and made her operatic debut around 1924 in Naples, where she changed her name to Leonora Corona. In Italy she sang in five operas under Tullio Serafin and performed at La Scala in Milan. She sang in more than 25 European theaters before signing a contract with the Bracale Opera Company and touring in Havana and Puerto Rico. She signed a long-term contract with the Metropolitan Opera in 1927 and made her debut there in November of that year in the role of Leonora in Verdi's *Il Trovatore*. Corona sang at the Met for 8 seasons, performing in 12 operas during this time, including the leading roles in *Tosca*, *Aïda*, and *Don Giovanni*. She also performed at Carnegie Hall and at the Opéra Comique in Paris. Critics praised both her vocal and dramatic powers and her picturesque beauty. Her tenure with the Met overlapped with that of two other Texans, Etheldreda Aves of Galveston and Rafaelo Diaz of San Antonio, and followed the career of Texan Lillian Eubank. Corona returned to Dallas occasionally for concerts. After her career with the Met concluded in 1935, she sang with such regional opera companies as the San Carlo Opera of Chicago, and presented recitals at both Town Hall and Carnegie Hall in New York. She appeared in a performance of *Cynthia Parker* at North Texas State Teachers College in 1939. Despite her fame as a singer, virtually no information is available on Leonora

North Beach. McGregor Collection, Corpus Christi Museum. In the 1930s the population of Corpus Christi more than doubled. The crowds at the North Beach amusement park testified to the city's affluence.

Corona after the late 1930s. No obituary for her appeared in Dallas or New York papers, and it is not certain that she remained in this country in her later life.

Debbie Mauldin Cottrell

Corpus Christi, Texas. At the mouth of the Nueces River on the west end of Corpus Christi Bay; county seat of Nueces County and the largest city on the South Texas coast. In prehistoric times the area was inhabited by various tribes of the Karankawa Indian group, which migrated up and down the Coastal Bend. The area remained uninhabited by Europeans until September 1839, when Henry Lawrence Kinney and his partner, William P. Aubrey, established a trading post on the west shore of Corpus Christi Bay. Kinney and Aubrey quickly developed a brisk illegal trade with Mexico. In 1841 Capt. Enrique Villarreal, a rancher from Matamoros who had been granted the land by the Mexican government, led a force of 300 men to reclaim his property and seize the arms stored at Kinney's stockade. Kinney, who at the time reportedly had only eight men under his command, managed to negotiate an agreement to purchase the land. Attacks by Mexican bands forced the abandonment of the post in 1842, but Kinney returned a short time later and reestablished his business. A post office opened the same year with Aubrey as post-

master. By the mid-1840s the settlement—now known as Corpus Christi ("the Body of Christ")—was a small village. In 1846 the town became county seat of the newly formed Nueces County. It was incorporated the same year, but because no public officials were elected, the corporation was repealed, and the town was not reincorporated until 1852. In September 1845 Gen. Zachary Taylor's army encamped nearby, and in the late 1840s numerous fortune-seekers passed through to join wagontrains headed for California, but few settlers put down permanent roots. In 1852 Kinney organized a state fair—reportedly the first in Texas—in an attempt to put Corpus Christi on the map, but it proved to be a failure and did little to spur the town's growth. A yellow fever epidemic decimated the population in 1854. Difficulty in obtaining fresh water plagued the city throughout the 1850s. The chief impediment to growth, however, was the lack of a deepwater port, a problem that occupied the town's leaders for the next 70 years. Large ships, unable to enter Corpus Christi Bay, were forced to anchor offshore where supplies were offloaded onto lighters, shallow-draft vessels capable of navigating the narrow, twisting channels of the bay. Some immigrants came and the population grew slowly, but the town continued to reflect something of a frontier character through the early 1850s. Public drunkenness and lawlessness were common. For many years there was no effective city government. By the middle of the decade, however, the situation began to change. The first schools opened around 1854, and by the eve of the Civil War the town had several established churches and several fraternal lodges. During the 1850s steamships of the Morgan Lines began making regular stops, and the volume of trade through the city gradually increased. By 1859 it was reported that some 45 vessels carried on trade between Corpus Christi and Indianola alone. In 1860 the population reached 1,200; nearly one-third of the residents were foreign born.

During the early years of the Civil War, Corpus Christi served as an important crossroads for Confederate commerce. In defiance of the Union blockade, small boats sailed inside the barrier islands transporting goods from the Brazos River to the Rio Grande or delivering them for overland transport to Mexico. In an effort to halt the trade, Union forces seized Mustang Island in September 1863 and bombarded Corpus Christi on two occasions. They did not occupy the town until the end of the year. Military occupation continued until the early 1870s, but the town's economy quickly recovered, in large measure due to the growth in sheep and cattle ranching in the surrounding region. Between 1870 and 1880 Corpus Christi was the center of a wool market. But the growth of the cattle industry had the greatest impact on the town's economy in the postbellum period. During the great cattle boom of the 1870s Corpus Christi emerged as an important shipping point for cattle from the South Texas plains, and in the 1880s packing houses, stockyards, and markets for

hides, tallow, and other cattle by-products flourished. As the city grew in importance as a shipping center, efforts were made to improve access to the ocean. In 1874 the main sea channel was dredged to a depth of eight feet to allow large steamers to navigate. The Corpus Christi, San Diego and Rio Grande Narrow Gauge Railroad was organized in 1875, and by 1881 it was extended to Laredo as the Texas Mexican Railway. In 1885 Corpus Christi was a city of some 4,200 residents, with three banks, a customhouse, railroad machine shops, an ice factory, carriage factories, several hotels, Episcopal, Presbyterian, Methodist, Catholic, and Baptist churches, and two newspapers. Many of city's streets were paved for the first time in the 1880s, a street railway system was built in 1889, and a public water system opened in 1893.

By 1914 Corpus Christi was served by four railroads—the Texas Mexican, the San Antonio and Aransas Pass, the St. Louis, Brownsville and Mexico, and the San Antonio, Uvalde and Gulf. Rail agents promoted the city as a tourist center, billing it as an all-year resort "where the weary can come to rest, the invalid can come for health, and the gay devotee come for pleasure." During the teens, the Texas State Epworth League of the Methodist Church held its annual encampment in the city, and some 5,000 to 8,000 visitors each year took advantage of excursion rates to spent several weeks on the shore. Many others also came to the city, fueling a construction boom for hotels, cottages, and boardinghouses. A city administration elected in 1913 and headed by mayor Roy Miller adopted an aggressive program of

The Navy's oldest ship, *USS Constitution*, on tour, Port of Corpus Christi, 1932. Photography Collection, HRHRC.

modernization. In three years it paved 12 miles of streets, laid 26 miles of storm and sanitary sewers, installed a modern water system, organized a paid fire department with two "triple-motor" pumpers, and constructed a new city hall and municipal wharf. The efforts, however, all seemed to come to naught on 14 September 1919, when the city was hit by a powerful hurricane that destroyed much of the North Beach and the central business district and killed 350 to 400 people. The tremendous economic loss convinced civic and business leaders that for the city to recover and prosper it would be necessary finally to build a deepwater port. Various city and local organizations lobbied the federal authorities to build a 30-foot-deep channel from the gulf to a protected harbor in the city. In 1922 President Harding approved a rivers and harbors act that authorized construction of the ship channel. Dredging and construction began the following year. In 1926, seven years to the day after the hurricane hit, the jubilant city celebrated the opening of its deepwater port. The impact on Corpus Christi was immediate. In just ten years, from 1920 to 1930, the city's population more than doubled, growing from 10,522 to 27,741. The town's new-found prosperity was also apparent in other ways: in 1927 the first "skyscraper," the Nixon Building, was finished, and by 1930 two other modern office buildings and a large hotel, the Plaza, dotted the central business district.

Growth slowed during the years of the Great Depression. The number of businesses fell from 920 in 1931 to 710 in 1933, but the discovery of oil in the county in 1930 and the continued development of the port of Corpus Christi helped to offset the depression's worst effects. Between 1931 and 1941 the population more than doubled again, climbing from 27,741 to 57,301. In the years after World War II Corpus Christi continued to grow rapidly. By 1952 the city had 108,053 residents and 2,845 businesses. Already in 1948 the port was twelfth in volume of business in the United States, and it ranked ninth in the United States and second in Texas in 1969, when it handed more than 29 million tons of cargo. A new system of channels 40 feet deep and 400 feet wide was completed in 1965, assuring entry of the latest supertankers into the port. Corpus Christi exports cotton, grain sorghums, and wheat. Its coastal shipments include fuel oils, gasoline, crude petroleum, and natural gas. Other major contributors to the income of the area are petroleum and natural gas, manufacturing, agriculture, fishing, Truax Field, and tourism. The region has become the center of a large petroleum and petrochemical industry. Its six oil refineries are located in close proximity to 1,500 oil wells. Short-distance pipelines connect Corpus Christi to one of the nation's largest supplies of natural gas. Other manufactured goods of importance are metals, stone products, glass, chemicals, and gypsum products. In addition to its port facilities for agricultural products, the city also has some food processing, meat packing, and cottonseed oil manufacturing. Corpus Christi and nearby Aransas Pass are the commercial fishing headquarters of the area, and the city is a seafood-processing center. Truax Field, formerly the Corpus Christi Naval Air Station, adds more than $40 million annually to the economy. The Corpus Christi metropolitan area offers numerous recreational facilities. Opportunities for boating, swimming, fishing, camping, and birdwatching are provided by Padre Island National Seashore, Aransas National Wildlife Refuge, the Rob and Bessie Welder Foundation and Refuge, Goose Island State Park, and Lake Corpus Christi State Recreation Area. The region includes historic Fort Lipantitlán, Fort Marcy, the San Patricio cemetery, and a number of historic homes. Annual events include Buccaneer Days, the All-Texas Jazz Festival, the Navy Relief Festival, the New Year's Day Swim, and the Cinco de Mayo celebration. Major cultural attractions include the Corpus Christi Museum, the Art Museum of South Texas, a symphony orchestra, and a little theater. Del Mar College and Texas A&M University at Corpus Christi provide higher education. Del Mar Technical Institute, a branch of Del Mar College, and the University of Texas at Austin Marine Science Institute in nearby Port Aransas offer specialized training. In recent years the city has continued to grow steadily. In 1968 the number of residents topped the 200,000 mark for the first time, and it reached 250,000 in 1990, when 50 percent of the population was Hispanic.

Christopher Long

Corsicana, Texas. County seat and largest town in Navarro County; 58 miles southeast of Dallas. It was established in 1848 to serve as the county seat of the newly established county. José Antonio Navarro, a hero of the Texas Revolution after whom the county was named, was given the honor of naming the new town; he suggested Corsicana after the island of Corsica, the birthplace of his parents. David R. Mitchell, an early area settler, donated 100 acres for a townsite, and with the assistance of Thomas I. Smith, platted the land and began selling lots. The new town was centered near a log tavern built in 1847 and owned and operated by Rev. Hampton McKinney. The first courthouse, a two-room log structure, was constructed in 1849, and was replaced by a frame building in 1853. Within a few years, a large number of mercantile establishments opened on and around the courthouse square, and a new brick courthouse was erected in 1858. By 1850 Corsicana's population had already grown to some 1,200. At outbreak of the Civil War in April 1861 townspeople held a mass demonstration on the courthouse square in favor of the Confederacy, and appeals were made for volunteers to serve in the Confederate Army in Virginia; five companies were raised by 1863. After the war, Union soldiers commanded by Capt. R. A. Chaffee occupied the town. The economy suffered a serious setback during the war and the early Reconstruction years, but by the beginning of 1870s business had begun to recover. In 1871 the town's first bank opened, and in 1874 Union troops were withdrawn. In November 1871 the Houston and Texas Central Railroad built through the town. The coming of the railroad brought numerous settlers and new merchants, among them the Sanger Brothers, the Padgitts, and others, who established stores near the new depot on East Collin Street. The construction of the Texas and St. Louis Railway (later the Cotton Belt) in 1880 prompted further commercial development, and by the mid-eighties Corsicana had become the leading trading and shipping center for a large area of the northern blacklands. In 1872 the town was incorporated with a mayoral form of government, and in 1880 a public school system was organized. The eighties also saw the establishment of a city fire department, a municipal waterworks, the installation of the first telephone system, and the construction of the State Orphans Home and the Odd Fellows Orphans Home. By 1885 Corsicana had a population of approximately 5,000.

By the early 1890s the rapidly expanding town had outgrown its water supply, and the following year civic leaders formed the Corsicana Water Development Company with the aim of tapping a shallow artesian well in the area. Drilling began in the spring of 1894; but instead of water, the company hit a large pocket of oil and gas. The find—the first significant discovery of oil west of the Mississippi River—led to the state's first oil boom: within a short time nearly every lot in the town and in the surrounding area was under lease, and wells were being drilled within the city limits—5 in 1896 and 57 the following year. The first oil refinery in the state was built at Corsicana in 1897, and by 1898 there were 287 producing wells in the Corsicana field. The oil find attracted numerous oil men from the East, among them Edwy R. Brown, H. C. Folger, W. C. Proctor, C. N. Payne, and J. S. Cullinan, founder of the Cullinan Oil Company, which later evolved into the Magnolia Oil Company. Oil transformed Corsicana from a regional agricultural shipping town to an important oil and industrial center, spawning a number of allied businesses, including the Johnston–Akins–Rittersbacher shops (later known as American Well Prospecting Company), producer of the newly invented rotary drilling bits. In 1900 Corsicana had grown to 9,313 inhabitants. A new courthouse was completed in 1905, and in 1917 the Corsicana Chamber of Commerce was founded. The Corsicana Transit Company converted from mule-drawn cars to electric trolleys in 1902; in 1912 the Trinity and Brazos completed a line between Corsicana and Houston; and in 1913 the Texas Electric Railroad instituted service to and from Dallas. In 1923 a second, even larger oil deposit, the Powell oilfield, was discovered, unleashing a new oil boom. Within a few months Corsicana's population swelled to unprecedented heights; some estimates placed the number of residents as high as 28,000 during the peak months of the oil frenzy. New construction transformed the face of the city, and street lights were installed for the first time to control the increased traffic. During the height of the Powell field boom 550 wells in and around the city produced an estimated 354,000 barrels per day. As the boom subsided, the population dropped to 15,202 in 1930.

With the onset of the Great Depression in the early 1930s many Corsicanans found themselves out of work. Particularly hard hit was the cotton wholesale and processing industry, which suffered from the combined effects of falling prices and the boll weevil. The oil industry helped to mitigate the worst effects of the depression, however. In 1942 Air Activities of Texas opened a large flight-training center where thousands of pilots received basic training, and in 1942 Bethlehem Steel took over the American Well Prospecting Plant, expanding the production of rotary drills. Corsicana's leading industries during the 1950s included the Texas–Miller Products Company, a leading producer of hats; the Oil City Iron Works; the Wolf Brand Company, producer of chili and tamales; several textile plants; the Bethlehem Supply Company; and the Collin Street Bakery, a leading producer of fruitcakes. Huge oil profits fostered great wealth in Corsicana. During the early 1950s there were said to be at least 21 millionaires in the town. In 1956 a new oilfield was discovered in East Corsicana, and within months 500 wells had been drilled. Since that time Corsicana has experienced steady, if not spectacular, growth. The population reached 20,750 in 1965 and 25,189 in 1990. The leading industries in 1990 included oil and gas extraction, meat packing, fruit and vegetable canning, the printing of business forms, and manufacture of prepared foods, furniture, chemical and rubber products, and oil field machinery.   *Christopher Long*

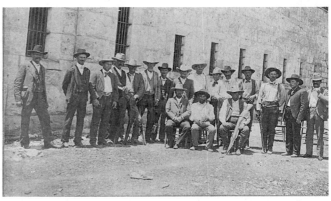

Gregorio Cortez (seated, center) and his guard, ca. 1901. Photography Collection, HRHRC. Gregorio Cortez became a folk hero when, perhaps in self-defense, he killed the Karnes County sheriff. Newspapers considered his subsequent flight—which involved posses of hundreds of men—front-page material.

Cortez, Gregorio. Mexican-American folk hero; b. near Matamoros, 22 June 1875; d. 28 February 1916; m. Leonor Díaz (1890; divorced 1903); 4 children; m. Estéfana Garza (1904); m. again in 1916, perhaps to Ester Martínez. In 1887 the family moved to Manor, near Austin. Cortez and some of his relatives may have been involved in horse theft, an act that Hispanic historians have typically interpreted as resistance to racial oppression. On 12 June 1901, Karnes county sheriff W. T. "Brack" Morris sought Cortez out as a horse-theft suspect. After a dispute that resulted partly from mistranslations on the part of an interpreter, a gunfight erupted. Cortez killed the sheriff, perhaps in self-defense, and fled the scene. He was caught ten days later. His evasion of the gringo police became legendary and was celebrated as early as 1901 in *corridos* (ballads). More lawmen, including Sheriff Glover of Gonzales County, were killed in the pursuit. At least nine persons of Mexican descent were killed, three wounded, and seven arrested. The incidents were publicized widely in the press. Cortez was considered an "arch fiend" by some writers, while others touted his "remarkable powers of endurance and skill in eluding pursuit." The posses searching for him involved hundreds of men, including the Texas Rangers. Once he was captured, a legal-defense campaign began and a network of supporters developed. A series of trials followed, the last in 1904. By the time Cortez began serving life in prison for the murder of Sheriff Glover, he had been in 11 jails in 11 counties. While in prison he worked as a barber. His jailers provided him the entire upper story of the jail as a "honeymoon suite" when he married Estéfana Garza. Attempts to pardon him began as soon as he entered prison and led eventually to Governor Colquitt's issuance of a conditional pardon in 1913. Cortez went to Nuevo Laredo and fought with Victoriano Huerta in the Mexican Revolution. He died of pneumonia. "El Corrido de Gregorio Cortez" was similar to those that depicted Juan N. Cortina and Catarino Garza. Folklorist Américo Paredes popularized the story of Gregorio Cortez in *With His Pistol in His Hand: A Border Ballad and Its Hero* (1958). A movie called *The Ballad of Gregorio Cortez* was produced in 1982.

Cynthia E. Orozco

Cortina, Juan Nepomucena. Mexican outlaw and folk hero; b. Camargo, Tamaulipas, 16 May 1824; d. Atzcapozalco, 30 October 1894. His mother was an heiress of a large land grant in the lower Rio Grande valley, including the area that surrounded Brownsville. The family moved to that land when Cortina was still young. In the Mexican War he served in an irregular Mexican cavalry unit. Afterward he returned to Texas, where he was indicted at least twice by a Cameron County grand jury for stealing cattle. Although he frequently appeared in public, his political influence among Mexicans prevented him from being arrested. In the decade following the Treaty of Guadalupe Hidalgo, he came to hate a clique of judges and Brownsville attorneys whom he accused of expropriating land from Mexican Texans unfamiliar with the American judicial system.

The incident that ignited the first so-called Cortina War occurred on 13 July 1859, when Cortina saw the Brownsville city marshal, Robert Shears, brutally arrest a Mexican American who had once been employed by Cortina. Cortina shot the marshal in the impending confrontation and rode out of town with the prisoner. On 28 September he rode into Brownsville at the head of 40 to 80 men and seized the town. Five men, including the city jailer, were shot during the raid, as Cortina and his men raced through the streets shouting "Death to the Americans" and "Viva Mexico." Many of the men whom Cortina had sworn to kill, however, escaped or went into hiding. When several of the town's leading citizens appealed to Mexican authorities in Matamoros, the influential José María Carbajal crossed the river to negotiate with Cortina. Cortina agreed to evacuate the town and retreated to the family ranch at Santa Rita in Cameron County, where he issued a proclamation asserting the rights of Mexican Texans and demanding the punishment of anyone violating these rights. Tensions remained high in Brownsville. A town posse captured Tomás Cabrera, one of Cortina's men. About 20 citizens of the town formed a group called the Brownsville Tigers, and, assisted by a militia company from Matamoros, moved against Cortina, who was reported to be at his mother's ranch some six miles upriver. With two cannons the Brownsville–Matamoros force launched a half-hearted attack, which Cortina easily repulsed; the "Tigers" lost their cannons and retreated in complete disarray. Cortina was idolized by many of the poorer Mexicans on both sides of the river, and his small army grew as recruits joined his ranks. He demanded that Cabrera be released and threatened to burn the town. In the first part of November an undisciplined company of Texas Rangers commanded by Capt. William G. Tobin arrived. Cabrera was hanged the next day, and an unsuccessful attack was launched against Cortina. Cortina issued a second proclamation on 23 November asking Governor Sam Houston to defend the legal interests of Mexican residents in Texas. By early December a second company of rangers, commanded by Rip Ford, arrived, as did Maj. Samuel P. Heintzelman with 165 regulars. Cortina, who was reported to have over 400 men by this time, retreated upriver, laying waste to much of the lower Valley. On 27 December Heintzelman engaged Cortina in the battle of Rio Grande City; Cortina was decisively defeated, losing 60 men and his equipment. He retreated into Mexico and next appeared at La Bolsa, a large bend on the Rio Grande below Rio Grande City, where he attempted to capture the steamboat *Ranchero*, owned and operated by two of his antagonists, Richard King and Mifflin Kenedy. With the approach of the steamboat, Major Ford and his

rangers crossed into Mexico, secured the south bank, and forced Cortina to retreat. Col. Robert E. Lee, now in command of the Eighth Military District, arrived in the lower Valley determined to restore peace and threatening to invade Mexico if necessary. Cortina, however, had retreated into the Burgos Mountains, where he remained for more than a year.

With the secession of Texas from the Union, Cortina appeared on the border again and started the second Cortina War. In May 1861 he invaded Zapata County and attacked the county seat, Carrizo. He was defeated by Confederate captain Santos Benavides and retreated into Mexico; Cortina lost 7 men in the fray, while 11 others were captured by Benavides and hanged or shot. On 5 May 1862, during the period of French intervention in Mexico, Cortina helped to defend San Lorenzo at Puebla. He saw action at Matamoros and, envisioning himself as an independent and powerful caudillo, briefly cooperated with the imperialists. Later he fought in central Mexico and was at Querétaro at the execution of Maximilian. In 1863 he proclaimed himself governor of Tamaulipas and was promoted to general of the Mexican Army of the North by President Benito Juárez. Cortina appointed himself governor again in 1866 but immediately relinquished the office to General Tapia. He returned to the border in 1870, and 41 residents of the Valley, including a former mayor of Brownsville, signed a petition asking that he be pardoned for his crimes because of his service to the Union during the Civil War. The petition failed in the Texas legislature on its second reading, in 1871. In subsequent years, stockmen in the Nueces Strip accused Cortina of leading a large ring of cattle rustlers. Subsequent American diplomatic pressure was largely responsible for his arrest in July 1875 and his removal to Mexico City.

Jerry Thompson

Cos, Martín Perfecto de. Mexican general; b. Veracruz, 1800; d. Minatitlán, Vera Cruz, 1 October 1854. Cos became a cadet in the Mexican army in 1820, a lieutenant in 1821, and a brigadier general in 1833. In September 1835 he was sent by Santa Anna to investigate the refusal of Texans at Anahuac to pay duties imposed after Santa Anna had established himself as president of Mexico with centralized powers. General Cos dispersed the legislature of Coahuila and Texas, then in session at Monclova, landed 300 men at Matagorda Bay, established headquarters in San Antonio, and declared his purpose of ending resistance in Texas. He intended to arrest several Texas critics of Santa Anna. A force of Texans under Stephen F. Austin and Edward Burleson held the Mexican troops in the siege of Bexar until Cos surrendered after an attack led by Ben Milam in December 1835. Cos and his men were released on their pledge not to oppose further the Constitution of 1824. Texans believed the pledge was broken when Cos returned in the spring of 1836 to command a column in the attack on the Alamo. At San Jacinto he was taken prisoner. After his release he returned to Mexico and in the Mexican War commanded a post at Tuxpan. He died while serving as commandant general and political chief of the Tehuantepec territory.

Claudia Hazlewood

Council House Fight. A battle that erupted in a peace council at San Antonio (19 March 1840). Penateka Comanches, driven by fear of Cheyenne and Arapaho attacks along the northern frontier of Comanche territory, sought in January 1840 to make peace with their Texan adversaries. Government representatives

General Cos, possibly after William H. Croome, ca. 1848. Engraving. 2¼" × 2". From John Frost, *Pictorial History of Mexico and the Mexican War . . .* (Philadelphia: Charles DeSilver, 1869), p. 169. Courtesy Benson Latin American Collection, University of Texas at Austin.

demanded the return of all captives held by the Penatekas and insisted that the Comanches abandon Central Texas and avoid white settlements. At the arranged council on 19 March the prominent peace chief Muk-wah-ruh headed the Indian delegation, which brought only a few prisoners, namely several Mexican children and 16-year-old Matilda Lockhart. Matilda, who had been captured with her sister in 1838, claimed that her captors had physically and sexually abused her. Burn scars and a mutilated nose supported her stories. She also said that 15 other captives remained in Comanche hands and that the tribe's leaders intended to ransom these hostages one at a time. When the Texans demanded the release of the other captives, Muk-wah-ruh replied that these prisoners were held by Comanche bands beyond his authority. The uncomprehending commissioners rejected the chief's explanation. Texas soldiers entered the Council House, where the peace talks were being held, and the commissioners informed the assembled chiefs that they were to be held as hostages until the remaining captives were released. In response to these threats, the Comanche chiefs attempted to escape and called to their fellow tribesmen outside the house for help. In the ensuing melee, Texans attacked several Indians while soldiers killed many of the Comanches who remained in the Council House courtyard. A Comanche woman was freed by Texas authorities and ordered to secure the release of the white captives in exchange for 27 Comanches captured in the fight. The Penateka leaders refused to respond to Texas demands, and most of the Texans' captives escaped. Thirty Comanche leaders and warriors, as well as some five women and children, had been killed. Comanche hatred of the Texans was inflamed. Led by Buffalo Hump, the Penatekas retaliated with increased violence.
Jodye Lynn Dickson Schilz

County Commissioners' Court. Also known as county board. During the Republic of Texas the county board was composed of the chief justice (county judge) and the justices of the peace of the county; under the constitutions of 1845, 1861, and 1866, it was composed of the chief justice and four elective commissioners; and under the Constitution of 1869, it was made up of any three of the five county justices of the peace. The commissioners' court as established by the present constitution (1876) comprised the county judge and four commissioners elected from precincts for two-year terms. A constitutional amendment adopted in 1954 changed the term of office to four years. The commissioners' court has none of the functions of a court but is the general governing body of the county. It locates the courthouse and jail, appoints numerous minor officials such as the county health officer, fills vacancies in the county offices, lets contracts in the name of the county, builds and maintains roads and bridges, administers the county's public welfare services, performs numerous duties in regard to elections, sets the county tax rate, issues bonds, adopts the county budget, and serves as a board of equalization for tax assessments. *Dick Smith*

County Organization. The origin of the Texas county is found in the municipality, the unit of local government under Spanish and Mexican rule. Municipalities were rather large districts embracing one or more settlements and the surrounding rural territory. There were 23 of them by 1836, when Texas won her independence from Mexico. The government of the municipality was vested in an ayuntamiento (council), composed of at least one alcalde (judge), a varying number of regidors (aldermen), a *síndico procurador* (attorney), an alguacil (sheriff), and an *escribano* (secretary). Under the Republic of Texas the municipalities became counties, but the Spanish–Mexican influence on their government was negligible. The new local governments were based on the county as found in the southern United States. The chief governing body of the county during the republic was a county board, composed of the chief justice of the county court (appointed by Congress) and elective justices of the peace, although in 1845 four elective commissioners were substituted for the justices of the peace. The other officers were the sheriff, coroner, and clerk (all elected), a tax assessor (appointed by the county board), and a surveyor (appointed by Congress). New counties could be established if 100 free male inhabitants living in an area containing at least 900 square miles petitioned the government. By 1845 Texas had 36 regular counties. County government under the Constitution of 1845 varied only slightly from that under the republic, the major changes being the election of all officials and the establishment of a few new offices. By the end of 1860 the number of organized counties had increased to 122. When Texas entered the Confederacy in 1861 and adopted a new state constitution, no changes were made in county government, nor were any really significant ones made by the Constitution of 1866. The government set up by that constitution lasted only a short while because of the passage of the Reconstruction Acts in 1867. Under the military rule that followed, many local elected officials were removed indiscriminately and either were not replaced or were replaced by appointees. This constitution lasted until 1870, when the government was reorganized under the Constitution of 1869. By the end of 1870 the state had 129 organized counties. Under the Constitution of 1869 the government of the county was again in the hands of an elected county board and several other elected officers, but actual administration, up to 1873, when the radical element was overthrown, was virtually a continuation of the Reconstruction government.

No real changes were made until the adoption of the Constitution of 1876. This constitution contains much detail about the organization of county government. The chief governing agency continued to be a county board, the county commissioners' court, but provision was also made for a county judge, county attorney, county tax assessor, county surveyor, and county treasurer, as well as for the offices of constable, sheriff, justice of the peace, and clerk of the county court. In addition, there were several statutory officers, the most important of which were the county superintendent of schools and the county auditor. The constitution was also specific about the establishment of new counties: no new county from unorganized territory could be smaller than 900 square miles and should be square if possible; new counties formed from established counties should contain not less than 700 square miles. Early responsibilities of county governments included road construction and maintenance, law enforcement, and tax collection. As populations increased, however, county operations expanded to include such additional programs as health and social welfare, solid-waste management, and housing and community development. Environmental protection and floodplain-development controls have also become concerns of county government. Texas has had 254 counties since the organization of Loving County in 1931. Voters adopted a home-rule provision in 1933, but the measure proved to be unworkable and was repealed in 1969. *Dick Smith*

Coushatta Trace. A road from Louisiana into Texas that was used by the Coushatta Indians in their hunting and trading activities. It was an important middle road between the better-known and Spanish-patrolled Atascosito Road along the Texas coast and the Old San Antonio Road farther inland. The Alabama Indians opened a path from their village on the Sabine River southwestward to La Bahía and perhaps farther, known to early American settlers as the Coushatta Trace. The narrow route led to the best crossings of streams or rivers and proceeded straight across the country. Gen. Sam Houston chose the route at its crossing of the Brazos in his retreat in 1836. It probably was a favorite route of contraband traders, for trains of packmules loaded with merchandise in transit from Louisiana to Mexico used the route, and field notes for some of the surveys along the Coushatta Trace refer to it as the "contraband trace." Also, the trail was used by several early settlers coming into Stephen F. Austin's colony. Jared E. Groce moved to Texas in 1821 and established a settlement in the area that is now Waller County at the crossing of the Coushatta Trace and the Brazos River. Francis Holland also traveled the Coushatta Trace from Louisiana to Austin's colony in 1822 with a large party of relatives. In organizing the Austin colony government, the ayuntamiento of San Felipe used portions of the Coushatta Trace to establish boundaries of the Bastrop and Viesca precincts. Titles or grants to land, beginning in 1821, frequently refer to the Coushatta Trace to establish location. The trail became so traveled that the Mexican government built Fort Terán in 1831 at the Coushatta Trace crossing of the Neches River as a means of controlling the movement of settlers into Texas. Later, stagecoach and horse mail

routes were established along sections of the trace. When new counties were organized in Texas after 1845, one of the principal responsibilities of the commissioners' court in each county was to "view" and establish new roads, and these new roads gradually replaced the Coushatta Trace. Only a few sections of the trail remained in use in the 1990s; an example is the paved tenmile section of Farm Road 350 west of Moscow in central Polk County. Although the Coushatta Trace and the Atascosito Road were the most important trails through Austin's colony, the actual route of the Coushatta Trace has been discovered only recently, by Howard N. Martin. *Howard N. Martin*

Craft, Juanita. Civil-rights leader; b. Juanita Jewel Shanks, Round Rock, 9 February 1902; d. 6 August 1985; m. Johnny Edward Craft (1937; d. 1950); ed. Prairie View State Normal and Industrial College (certificate, 1921) and Samuel Huston College (teaching certificate). Juanita Shanks taught kindergarten in Columbus, was in an unsuccessful marriage in Galveston, and worked as a hotel maid and dressmaker in Dallas before her marriage to Johnny Craft. Joining the NAACP (1935) began her civil-rights activity. She was appointed Dallas NAACP membership chairman in 1942 and in 1946 was promoted to Texas NAACP field organizer and made Youth Council Advisor. She and Lulu Belle White of Houston organized 182 branches of the NAACP in Texas over 11 years. In 1944 Mrs. Craft became the first black woman in Dallas County to vote. In 1946 she was the first black woman deputized in the state to collect the poll tax. Her youth unit became a prototype for other NAACP youth groups throughout the country. In 1955 she attempted to enroll the first black student at North Texas State College, thus precipitating a battle that was eventually won through litigation. That same year her youth group spearheaded the picketing of the State Fair of Texas to protest the policy of admitting blacks only on Negro Achievement Day. From 1961 through 1964 she led the Youth Council in picketing lunch counters, restaurants, theaters, and public transportation to protest segregation. In 1967 she initiated an investigation of fraudulent trade-school practices in black communities in Dallas; it resulted in the passage of legislation establishing rules for such schools.

Juanita Craft was a Democratic precinct chairman from 1952 to 1975 and served two terms on the Dallas City Council between 1975 and 1979. She was a member of the Munger Avenue Baptist Church, the Democratic Women's Club, the YWCA, the League of Women Voters, and the National Council of Negro Women. She participated on numerous local, state, and national boards, including those of the Urban League of Greater Dallas, Goals for Dallas, Dallas United Nations, the Governor's Human Relations Committee, and the NAACP. During her 50 years of public service she received the Linz Award, Dallas's highest civic award (1969), the NAACP Golden Heritage Life Membership Award (1978), and the Eleanor Roosevelt Humanitarian Award for public service (1984). She visited the White House on invitations from presidents Kennedy, Johnson, and Carter. In 1985 she was one of 72 black women featured in Women of Courage, a traveling photographic exhibit sponsored by the Arthur and Elizabeth Schlesinger Library at Radcliffe College. The Dallas Parks and Recreation Department dedicated the Juanita Jewel Craft Recreation Center to celebrate Mrs. Craft's seventy-second birthday in 1974. The Juanita Craft Foundation was established

State and national leaders of the National Association for the Advancement of Colored People (top row, left to right: John J. Jones, M. T. Blanton, Thurgood Marshall; bottom row, left to right: unidentified, Juanita Craft, Walter White, Peyton Medlock), Dallas, 1948. Juanita Jewel Shanks Craft Collection, CAH; CN 00674. Juanita Craft helped organize 182 NAACP branches in Texas.

in 1985 to further her ideals. The Craft Foundation donated her home to the Dallas Parks and Recreation Department. She had no children but claimed to have "adopted the world."

Mamie L. Abernathy–McKnight

Crash at Crush. A train wreck staged as a publicity stunt 15 miles north of Waco on 15 September 1896. In 1895 William George Crush, passenger agent for the Missouri, Kansas and Texas Railroad, proposed to Katy officials that the company stage a train wreck. He planned to advertise the event months in advance, sell tickets to transport spectators to and from the site on Katy trains, and then run two old locomotives head-on into each other. The officials agreed. Throughout the summer of 1896 bulletins and circulars advertising the "Monster Crash" were distributed throughout Texas. Many newspapers in Texas ran daily reports on the preparations, and some papers outside the state carried the story. As Crush had predicted, the Katy offices were flooded with ticket requests. The engines, Old No. 999, painted a bright green, and No. 1001, painted a brilliant red, were displayed in towns throughout the state. Thousands turned out

to look at them. As the arena for his spectacle, Crush selected a shallow valley conveniently located close to Katy's Waco–Dallas track. In early September 500 workmen laid four miles of track for the collision run and constructed a grandstand for "honored guests," three speaker's stands, two telegraph offices, a stand for reporters, and a bandstand. A restaurant was set up in a borrowed Ringling Brothers circus tent, and a huge carnival midway with dozens of medicine shows, game booths, and lemonade and soft-drink stands was built. Workmen built a special depot with a platform 2,100 feet long, and a sign was painted to inform passengers that they had arrived at Crush, Texas.

Two dollars bought a round-trip ticket on one of 33 excursion trains from anywhere in the state, and some passengers were obliged to ride on top of the cars because there was no room left inside. Although Crush told a reporter that he expected a crowd of around 20,000, by 3:00 P.M. on September 15 more than 40,000 people were on the grounds picnicking, listening to political speeches, and waiting for the great crash. At 5:00 P.M. the engines squared off at opposite ends of the track. Crush appeared on a white horse, trotted to the center of the track, raised his white hat, and after a pause whipped it sharply down. A great cheer went up from the crowd as they pressed forward for a better view. The locomotives jumped forward, and with whistles shrieking roared toward each other. Then, in a thunderous, grinding crash, the trains collided. The two locomotives rose up at their meeting and erupted in steam and smoke. Almost simultaneously, both boilers exploded, filling the air with pieces of flying metal. Spectators turned and ran in blind panic. Two young men and a woman were killed. At least six other people were injured seriously by flying debris. Katy trains moved in to remove the larger wreckage, and souvenir hunters carried off the rest. People began to leave for home, the tents, stands, and midway booths came down, and by nightfall Crush, Texas, ceased to exist. The Katy quickly settled all damage claims brought against it with cash and lifetime rail passes. The railroad fired Crush that evening but rehired him the next day. He continued to work for the Katy until his retirement. In the early twentieth century Scott Joplin commemorated the event in his march "Great Crush Collision."　　　　*Allen Lee Hamilton*

Crawford, Joan. Movie actress; b. Lucille Fay LeSeur, San Antonio, 23 March 1906; d. New York City, 10 May 1977; m. Douglas Fairbanks, Jr. (1929; divorced), Franchot Tone (1935; divorced), Phillip Terry (1942; divorced), and Alfred N. Steele (1955). She suffered several miscarriages and adopted four children who later claimed that she treated them harshly. Her father deserted the family before she was born, and her life was marked by numerous hardships, including periods of near-poverty that lasted for years. In Oklahoma as a child Lucille adopted the stage name Billie Cassin and began dancing in her stepfather's music hall. Later, after winning a Charleston contest in a Kansas City café, she moved to Chicago with $46 in her pocket and hopes of hitting the big time. She won a part with a traveling dance company and performed as a chorine in some of the more reputable theaters in the Midwest. J. J. Schubert saw her work and hired her for a show he was producing in New York. Lucille subsequently caught the eye of a Metro–Goldwyn–Mayer talent scout, who invited her to take a screen test. She passed the test, signed a six-month contract with MGM for $75 a week, and moved to Hollywood in early 1925. She made such a positive impression during her early film career that MGM head Louis B. Mayer launched a fan-magazine contest to find her a new name. The result was "Joan Crawford," a name she claimed she never liked. Her career with MGM stretched from 1925 to 1942, and she became one of that company's biggest stars. Theater owners voted her among the top 10 money-making stars from 1932 to 1936, and by the late 1930s she was one of Hollywood's highest paid actresses. Joan's rise to the top of the Hollywood heap was marked by tenacity, hard work, and a protean adaptability. In the 1920s she frequently played flappers and other "wild youth" roles common to the period. In marked contrast, during the 1930s she often portrayed depression-era working women struggling to survive. No matter what roles she played, audiences flocked to her movies. Despite her successes, Joan Crawford believed that MGM was giving its meatiest roles to other actresses, and in 1942 she asked the studio to release her from her contract. MGM obliged, believing her popularity was waning. Her career then saw new life with Warner Brothers, and she began playing strong-willed maternal figures, such as the waitress-turned-restauratrice alienated from her daughter in *Mildred Pierce*

(1945), the film for which she won the Academy Award for best actress. Though she was considered a has-been by the late 1950s, she made a surprising comeback in the highly successful *What Ever Happened to Baby Jane?* (1962), which cast her with her old rival Bette Davis. Similar roles in the handful of low-budget horror movies that followed rounded out a film career that spanned more than 40 years and included performances in more than 80 films. She made her last movie in 1970. Her last husband was chairman of the board of Pepsi-Cola, a firm with which Crawford was associated after his death (1959). The terms of her will suggested the depth of the animosity that had developed between her and her children. Twins Cynthia and Cathy each received $77,500, but Christina and Christopher were cut off without a cent "for reasons which are well known to them." A year after Joan Crawford's death Christina published *Mommie Dearest*, a scathing autobiography of growing up as an abused child. The book was turned into a Hollywood movie in 1981, starring Faye Dunaway.　　　　*Martin F. Norden*

Criollo. A person born in New Spain to Spanish-born parents; socially one step lower than a *peninsular*, since it was difficult to distinguish between pure criollos and the still-lower mestizos. In Spain it was widely believed that exposure to the sun in the New World retarded the development of children born there. On the frontiers, criollos held important positions in the colonial administration because of the scarcity of *peninsulares* and their reluctance to serve in remote regions. The highest offices, however, were usually reserved for the Spanish-born. Criollos and mestizos shared the other military and civil appointments and generally fared well in church positions because of their connections with parishes. Social fluidity promoted miscegenation on the frontier, and the lines between criollos and mixed bloods quickly eroded.　　　　*Joan E. Supplee*

Crockett, David. Alamo hero; b. Greene County, East Tennessee, 17 August 1786; d. San Antonio, 6 March 1836; m. Mary (Polly) Finley (1806; d. 1815); 3 children; m. Elizabeth Patton (1815). Crockett had considerable military experience—including service under Andrew Jackson in the Creek Indian War—before winning election to the Tennessee legislature (1821). In 1827 and 1829 he was elected to Congress, but he was defeated in his bid for a third term. Meanwhile, his reputation as a sharpshooter, hunter, and yarn-spinner brought him into national prominence. He was the model for Nimrod Wildfire, the hero of James Kirke Paulding's play *The Lion of the West*, which opened in New York City on 25 April 1831. Mathew St. Clair Clarke's *Life and Adventures of Colonel David Crockett of West Tennessee* was published in 1833 and reprinted the same year under a different title, *Sketches and Eccentricities of Colonel David Crockett of West Tennessee*. Much of the same material spilled over into the first few issues of a series of comic almanacs published under Crockett's name from 1835 to 1856 that constituted a body of outrageous tall tales about the adventures of the legendary Davy rather than the historical David Crockett. Building in part upon his growing notoriety, Crockett won reelection to Congress in 1833. The following year he published his autobiography, written with the help of Thomas Chilton, *A Narrative of the Life of David Crockett of the State of Tennessee*, the only work that he actually wrote. It was intended to correct the portrayal given by Clarke and to deny Crockett's authorship of that account, which did not bear Clarke's name. The *Narrative* was also a campaign biography of sorts, for Whig politicians were touting Crockett as an anti-Jackson candidate for the presidency in 1836. On 25 April 1834 he began a three-week triumphal tour of the eastern states, and his "campaign swing" was recorded in the first of two Whig books published the next year under his name, *An Account of Colonel Crockett's Tour to the North and Down East.* The second, a negative *Life of Martin Van Buren,* was issued less than three months later. Crockett apparently thought himself a serious presidential candidate, but he was likely only a convenient political tool to the Whigs, an independent frontiersman with a national reputation perhaps the equal of Jackson's who opposed Jackson on key political issues. The point became academic, however, when Crockett lost his 1835 congressional campaign to Adam Huntsman, a peg-legged lawyer supported by Jackson and by Governor Carroll of Tennessee, by 252 votes.

Disenchanted, Crockett departed for the West with William Patton, Abner Burgin, and Lindsey K. Tinkle (1 November 1835). On the way, at a bar in Memphis, he offered his now famous remark, "Since you have chosen to elect a man with a timber toe to succeed me, you may all go to hell and I will go to Texas." Crockett traveled on the Mississippi and Arkansas rivers to Little Rock, overland to Fulton, Arkansas, and up the Red River, then to Clarksville, Nacogdoches, San Augustine, and on to San Antonio. At San Augustine the party evidently divided. Burgin and Tinkle went home. Crockett and Patton signed the oath of allegiance to the "Provisional Government of Texas or any future republican Government that may be hereafter declared." Crockett inserted the word *republican.* In his last extant letter (9 January 1836) he wrote,

> I must say as to what I have seen of Texas it is the garden spot of the world. The best land and the best prospects for health I ever saw, and I do believe it is a fortune to any man to come here. There is a world of country here to settle. . . . I have taken the oath of government and have enrolled my name as a volunteer and will set out for the Rio Grand in a few days with the volunteers from the United States. But all volunteers is entitled to vote for a member of the convention or to be voted for, and I have but little doubt of being elected a member to form a constitution for this province. I am rejoiced at my fate. I had rather be in my present situation than to be elected to a seat in Congress for life. I am in hopes of making a fortune yet for myself and family, bad as my prospect has been.

Crockett arrived at San Antonio de Béxar in early February; General Santa Anna arrived on 20 February. The Americans in Texas were split into two political factions that divided roughly into those supporting a conservative Whig philosophy and those supporting the administration. Crockett chose to join Travis, who had deliberately disregarded Sam Houston's order to withdraw from the Alamo, rather than support Houston, a Jackson sympathizer. What was more, he saw the future of an independent Texas as his future, and he loved a good fight. He got a mortal one in the battle of the Alamo. The manner of his death was uncertain, however, until the publication in 1975 of the diary of Lt. José Enrique de la Peña. Susanna Dickinson said Crockett died on the outside, one of the earliest to fall. Joe, Travis's slave and the only male Texan to survive the battle, reported seeing Crockett lying dead with slain Mexicans around him and stated

David Crockett, by John Gadsby Chapman. Oil on canvas. 24½" × 16½". Courtesy Art Collection, HRHRC. This painting is a copy of a life-sized portrait executed by Chapman in 1834 and since lost in a fire at the Texas Capitol. It features Crockett as his legend portrays him, with his rifle and coonskin cap.

that only one man, named Warner, surrendered to the Mexicans (Warner was taken to Santa Anna and promptly shot). When Peña's eyewitness account was placed together with other corroborating documents, Crockett's central part in the defense became clear. Travis had previously written that during the first bombardment Crockett was everywhere in the Alamo "animating the men to do their duty." Other reports told of the deadly fire of his rifle that killed five Mexican gunners in succession, as they each attempted to fire a cannon bearing on the fort, and that he may have just missed Santa Anna, who thought himself out of range of all the defenders' rifles. In evident fact, Crockett and five or six others were captured when the Mexican troops took the Alamo, even though Santa Anna had ordered that no prisoners be taken. The general, infuriated when some of his officers brought the Americans before him to try to intercede for their lives, ordered them executed immediately. They were bayoneted and then shot. Crockett's reputation and that of the other survivors was not, as some have suggested, sullied by their capture. Their dignity and bravery was, in fact, further underscored by Peña's recounting that "these unfortunates died without complaining and without humiliating themselves before their torturers." Coincidentally, a work mostly of fiction masquerading as fact put the truth of Crockett's death before the American public in the summer of 1836. Despite its many falsifications and plagiarisms, Richard Penn Smith's *Col. Crockett's Exploits and Adventures in Texas . . .Written by Himself* gave a reasonably accurate account of Crockett's capture and execution. Many others thought the legendary Davy deserved better, and they provided it, from thrilling tales of his clubbing Mexicans with his empty rifle and holding his section of the wall of the Alamo until cut down by bullets and bayonets, to his survival as a slave in a Mexican salt mine. Finally, however, no matter how fascinating or outrageous the fabrications were that gathered around him, the historical David Crockett proved a formidable hero in his own right and succeeded Daniel Boone as the rough-hewn representative of frontier independence and virtue. In this regard, the motto he adopted and made famous epitomized his spirit: "Be always sure you're right—then go a-head!"

Michael A. Lofaro

Crockett State School. A school for delinquent black girls; founded under the Board of Control at a disused POW camp in McCulloch County under the name Brady State School for Negro Girls (1947); renamed Colored Girls Training School and moved to a farm near Crockett, Houston County, in 1950, under the auspices of the State Youth Development Council. The institution was placed under the administration of the Texas Youth Council in 1957 and integrated in 1966, when it was renamed Crockett State School for Girls. Its educational program included academics, sewing, housekeeping, child care, and cooking, as well as vocational courses in cosmetology and janitorial work. The school had an enrollment of 209 in 1972 but closed in 1973. Its name was changed to Crockett State Home on December 13, 1973, and the facility was used as a home and educational center for dependent and neglected children until 1975. In 1975 Crockett State School reopened as a correctional institution for boys and had a capacity of about 100 students. Its accredited education program included academic courses and work in horticulture, auto mechanics, and shop. In the late 1980s the legislature appropriated funds to expand the facility in order to provide relief for overcrowded conditions at other schools.

Vivian Elizabeth Smyrl

Crouch, Hondo. Humorist; b. John Russell Crouch, at Hondo, 4 December 1916; d. Blanco, 27 September 1976; m. Helen Ruth (Shatzie) Stieler, daughter of the 1945 "Goat King of the World," Adolf Stieler of Comfort; four children; ed. University of Texas (grad. 1941), where he was an All-American swimmer. After training as a navigator in the Air Corps at Garner Field in 1942, Crouch settled down to raise livestock near Fredericksburg. He was swimming coach at various Texas children's camps from the 1930s until the 1970s. In 1964 he was president of the Hall of Fame for UT athletes and in 1975 was influential in persuading the university to build the Texas Swim Center. From 1963 to 1975, under the pen name Peter Cedarstacker, Crouch wrote about 600 "Cedar Creek Clippings" for the Comfort *News*, in which he satirized politics (he was a Republican), environmentalists, deer hunters, and other targets. In 1971 he bought the community of Luckenbach. There he presided as mayor over a population of three and a single parking meter. As "clown prince" he brought to life the town's motto, "Everybody's Somebody in

Luckenbach." He held zany celebrations, such as the Luckenbach World's Fair, the first Texas "women only" chili cook-off, Return of the Mud Daubers, and no-talent contests. Crouch participated in a Folklife Festival for Texas at the Smithsonian Institution in 1964. On July 4, 1976, Luckenbach received national attention for celebrating the Non-Buy Centennial, protesting the commercialization of the national Bicentennial of the Declaration of Independence.

Becky Crouch Patterson

Crowell, Grace Noll. Poet; b. Grace Noll, Inland, Iowa, 31 October 1877; d. Dallas, 31 March 1969; m. Norman H. Crowell (1901; d. 1953); three sons; ed. German–English College, Wilton, Iowa (B.A., 1901). The Crowells moved in 1917 to Wichita Falls and two years later to Dallas. Grace Crowell's poems appeared in major magazines throughout the U.S. and abroad. Her first book of poetry, *White Fire* (1925), was awarded first prize by the Texas Poetry Society. In 1935 she was designated state Poet Laureate. In 1938 she was awarded the Golden Scroll Medal of Honor as National Honor Poet, and the Golden Rule Foundation named her American Mother of the Year, while and *American Women,* a biographical publication, selected her as one of 10 Outstanding American Women. Baylor University awarded her an honorary doctorate in 1940. Among many subsequent honors, she was selected honorary chancellor of the National Federation of State Poetry Societies in 1965. In the early 1940s Mrs. Crowell was called "the most popular writer of verse in America." Her husband quit his job to manage her career, in which she published over 35 books. Her *Songs for Courage* underwent 25 printings. In 1977 a reprint of her 1965 collection of poems appeared as *The Eternal Things: The Best of Grace Noll Crowell.*

Betty S. Flowers

Crystal City, Texas. County seat of Zavala County. In 1905 Carl F. Groos and E. J. Buckingham purchased the 10,000-acre Cross S Ranch, sold off most of the land as farms, and platted the townsite of Crystal City, named for the clear artesian water of the area. The town received a post office in 1908, the same year the Crystal City and Uvalde Railway provided the first rail service to the community and the first school building was built. Crystal City was incorporated in 1910, when it had an estimated 530 inhabitants. By 1914 the community had a bank, three general stores, and the weekly *Chronicle*. In 1928 the county voted to make Crystal City the county seat, and that same year the community added a city manager to its mayor–council government. As soon as the railroad reached Crystal City, the community became a major shipping point for winter vegetables. At first onions were the major crop, but by the 1930s the city developed a reputation as the "Spinach Capital of the World." In 1936 the first annual spinach festival was held, and the following year a statue of the cartoon character Popeye, that mighty consumer of spinach, was placed across from the city hall. Carrots, tomatoes, peppers, and other vegetables were also marketed, and a vegetable cannery was opened in 1932. Under the stimulus of agricultural growth the population rose from an estimated 800 in 1920 to 6,609 in 1930, then fell slightly to 6,529 in 1940. The majority of residents in the 1930s were Mexican or Mexican-American migrant laborers who followed a seasonal cycle of spinach in the winter, onions in the spring, and beet or cotton work in the summer and fall. Making Crystal City their home base, most of these workers

Turkey Trot, Cuero, ca. 1912. Parks Photo, Port Lavaca. Louis Lenz Collection, CAH; CN 08007. The Turkey Trot was organized in 1912 to promote the area turkey industry, a principal source of revenue in DeWitt County throughout most of the twentieth century.

lived in slum conditions with poor services and limited educational opportunities. During World War II an alien internment camp, primarily for Japanese, was built on the site of a prewar labor camp on the edge of town. After the camp closed in 1947, the area was converted to low-rent housing, and the schools built there became part of the Crystal City ISD. In 1945 the California Packing Corporation, later the Del Monte Corporation, built an extensive canning plant just northwest of Crystal City. Since that time it has been the largest single employer in the area. The company added a can-manufacturing plant in 1958 and expanded its Crystal City facilities several times in the 1970s and 1980s. The employment opportunities offered by Del Monte helped increase the population of the community to 7,195 in 1950 and 9,101, a probable all-time high for Crystal City, in 1960. The 1960s were a period of dramatic political change for the town. In spite of the fact that Mexican Americans had formed 80 percent or more of the city's population since the 1930s, the Anglo minority had kept a tight hold on city government and school administration. Frustration over several controversial attempts at urban renewal in the late 1950s and over continuing educational discrimination led to the increasing politicization of Crystal City's Hispanics. In 1963 and much more successfully in 1969, they sought to gain control of key city and school-board positions in the "Crystal City Revolts." Among the important outgrowths of this political movement was the formation of the Raza Unida party in 1970, which soon assumed statewide importance. From 1971 through the 1980s, the town's

city managers and school superintendents were all Hispanic. The population declined somewhat during the 1960s, to 8,104 in 1970, and remained relatively static through the 1980s. In 1990 Crystal City had 8,263 residents. The annual November spinach festival, which was halted by World War II, was resumed in 1982.

Mark Odintz

Cuero, Texas. County seat and largest town in DeWitt County. The first post office in the county was established in May 1846 in Daniel Boone Friar's store, four miles north of the present site; it was also called Cuero (later Old Cuero). Cuero is named after Cuero Creek, which the Spanish had called Arroyo del Cuero, or Creek of the Rawhide, in reference to the Indians' practice of killing wild cattle that got stuck in the mud of the creekbed. When the Gulf, Western Texas and Pacific Railway was extended from Indianola to San Antonio, the Cuero site was chosen as a midway stopping point in the construction of the line. Although the tracks were not completed to Cuero until January 1873, construction of business establishments and homes was begun as early as November 1872. Gustav Schleicher, who surveyed the railroad, platted the new town for his Cuero Land and Immigration Company, and Robert J. Kleberg surveyed the site in January 1873.

The city government was organized in the summer of 1873; the town was incorporated in 1875 and replaced Clinton as county seat in 1876. Cuero grew as Clinton declined, and after the great hurricanes of 1875 and 1886 people came from

Indianola. Among the significant early businesses were Otto Buchel's bank, J. R. Nagel's hardware, and H. Runge and Company, a branch of Henry Runge's Indianola-based store and bank, which was operated in Cuero by Edward Mugge, Sr. Mugge was joined by William Frobese, Sr., and Emil Reiffert, Sr., when the firm moved its operating base to Cuero after the hurricane that destroyed Indianola in 1886. These men are credited with much of Cuero's early expansion. Professor David W. Nash opened Guadalupe Academy (also known as Nash's School or Cuero Institute), a coeducational private school, in September 1873; it operated until about 1910. The Cuero ISD was formed in 1892. Among its German social associations were the Sons of Hermann and a turnverein. Cuero prospered despite a period of lawlessness and a disastrous fire in April 1879. Citizens organized the Home Protection Club, which drilled regularly as a military unit and aided law officers when necessary. Shipping opportunities increased in 1886 when the San Antonio and Aransas Pass Railway connected Cuero to Houston. By 1887 Cuero recorded a population of 2,500, mostly Anglos and Germans. Truck farming became an important industry, as did cotton, poultry, and livestock. Cuero had an estimated population of 3,671 by the mid-1920s, at which time the town had an assessed value of $3.7 million. The power dam on the Guadalupe River, which formed part of the community's privately owned hydroelectric plant, was the largest in the state. Cuero pioneered the turkey-raising industry in south central Texas and became one of the largest poultry markets in the Southwest. The Cuero turkey industry was already shipping processed birds nationwide by 1906, though the renowned Turkey Trot did not begin until 1912. The city also supported large cattle, dairy, and meat-packing industries and produced pecans, cottonseed products, and feeds. Its Crescent Valley Creamery was one of the largest independent creameries in the South in 1935. Oil speculation began in 1919, although a successful well was not hit until after 1929. The city's population rose to 5,474 by the mid-1940s and reached 7,498 in the next decade. By 1949 the broiler-chicken industry had passed turkeys as the second most important source of livestock income. Cuero's population peaked about 1969 at 7,800 and had declined to 6,920 by the mid-1970s. Agribusiness still dominated the local economy, though the turkey and cotton industries had declined in significance. The county courthouse, built in 1895–96, was restored in 1955–57. The DeWitt County Historical Museum was established in Cuero about 1974. The population in 1990 was 6,700. *Craig H. Roell*

Culberson, Charles Allen. Governor, senator; b. Dadeville, Alabama, 19 June 1855; d. Washington, D.C., 19 March 1925; ed. Virginia Military Institute (grad. 1874) and University of Virginia law school; m. Sally Harrison (1882); one child. Culberson moved in 1887 from East Texas to Dallas and practiced law there. He was twice elected attorney general (1890, 1892) and twice elected governor (1894, 1896). As attorney general, he defended the Railroad Commission. As governor, he fought the People's party and populist measures. In order to prevent a ballyhooed prizefight between James J. Corbett and Bob FitzSimmons sponsored by his political enemies, Culberson pushed through the legislature a law making prizefighting illegal. Helped by Edward M. House, Culberson succeeded Roger Q. Mills in the Senate and held the office for 24 years. He was Democratic minority leader (1907–10) and chairman of the Judiciary Committee

The Texas Hercules Tackles the Trust Monster, by Elmer Burruss. Original published in *Texas Sandwich,* January 27, 1895. Texas Newspaper Collection, CAH; CN 08522. Reproduced from Maury Forman and Robert A. Calvert, *Cartooning Texas: One Hundred Years of Cartoon Art in the Lone Star State* (College Station, Texas: Texas A&M University Press, 1993), p. 14. Governor Culberson is portrayed here as Hercules, taking on insurance, cottonseed, coal, and oil trusts.

(1913–19). His senatorial career was erratic, marred by alcoholism and associated ill health. The legislative activity required of him during World War I led to a decisive breakdown. He lost the election of 1922 because of his poor health and his opposition to the Ku Klux Klan, which was in the ascendant. The aloof, conservative, talented Culberson exhibited many talents that remained only partly developed at his death.

Robert L. Wagner

Cullen, Hugh Roy. Oilman and philanthropist; b. Denton County, 31 July 1881; d. Houston, 4 July 1957; m. Lillie Cranz (1903); five children. At the age of 16 Cullen worked for a cotton broker; he later went into that business for himself and also dealt in real estate. He moved to Houston in 1911 and entered the oil business in 1918. His policy of drilling deep wells was so successful that he became known as the "king of the wildcatters." He made major discoveries in the Houston area, notably at Pierce Junction, Blue Ridge, Rabb's Ridge, Humble, and the O'Connor field. He owned half of the South Texas Petroleum Company and later formed the Quintana Petroleum Company. He was firmly dedicated to states' rights and spent much energy opposing the New Deal. He promoted W. Lee O'Daniel for governor in 1938 and 1940 and for senator in 1941. Although Cullen aided the Dixiecrat movement in 1948, he normally supported Republican candidates, particularly Dwight D. Eisenhower in 1952. He gave more than $11 million each to his favorite projects, the University of Houston and Houston hospitals. In 1947 he established the $160 million Cullen Foundation to provide for continual aid to education and medicine. By 1955 he had given away an estimated 90 percent of his fortune. Cullen served in many capacities during his career, including chairman of the board of regents of the

University of Houston, vice president of the Texas World Fair Commission in 1939, and director of the Boy Scouts of America. He received honorary degrees from the University of Pittsburgh in 1936, Baylor University in 1945, and the University of Houston in 1947. He was an honorary member of the American Hospital Association and a member of the Sons of the Republic of Texas.

Rita Crabbe

Cuney, Norris Wright. Politician; b. to a white planter and slave mother near Hempstead, 12 May 1846; d. San Antonio, 3 March 1898. Cuney attended George B. Vashon's Wylie Street School for blacks in Pittsburgh, Pennsylvania, from 1859 to the beginning of the Civil War, then wandered on riverboats and worked at odd jobs before he returned to Texas and settled in Galveston. There he met George T. Ruby, president of the Union League. He studied law and by July 18, 1871, was appointed president of the Galveston Union League. Cuney supported Radical Republican governor Edmund J. Davis. In 1873 he was appointed secretary of the Republican State Executive Committee. He was defeated in the race for mayor of Galveston in 1875 and for the state House and Senate in 1876 and 1882 respectively. From his appointment as the first assistant to the sergeant-at-arms of the Twelfth Legislature in 1870, he went on to serve as a delegate to every national Republican convention from 1872 to 1892. In 1873 he presided at the state convention of black leaders at Brenham. He became inspector of customs of the port of Galveston and revenue inspector at Sabine Pass in 1872, special inspector of customs at Galveston in 1882, and finally collector of customs of the

Norris Wright Cuney. From Maud Cuney Hare, *Norris Wright Cuney, A Tribune of the Black People* (New York: Crisis Pub. Co., 1913), frontispiece. Prints and Photographs Collection, Norris Wright Cuney file, CAH; CN 01074.

port of Galveston in 1889. In 1883 Cuney was elected alderman on the Galveston City Council from the Twelfth District. He was also a contracting stevedore. In 1886 he became Texas national committeeman of the Republican party, the most important political position given to a black man of the South in the nineteenth century. One historian of the Republican party in Texas characterizes the period between 1884 and 1896 as the "Cuney Era." In order to lead Texas blacks to increased prosperity, in 1883 Cuney bought $2,500 worth of tools and called together a group of black dockworkers, which he eventually organized into the Screwmen's Benevolent Association. He was appointed a school director of Galveston County in 1871 and supported the black state college at Prairie View. He was first grand master of the Prince Hall Masons in Texas (1875–77) and also belonged to the Knights of Pythias and the Odd Fellows.

Merline Pitre

Cunningham, Minnie Fisher. Suffragist; b. near New Waverly, 19 March 1882; d. 9 December 1964; m. Beverly Jean (Bill) Cunningham (1902; d. 1927). After having been educated by her mother, Minnie passed a state examination to earn a teaching certificate when she was 16. She taught for a year before enrolling in the University of Texas Medical Branch at Galveston. In 1901 she became one of the first women to receive a degree in pharmacy in Texas; she worked as a pharmacist in Huntsville for a year, but later claimed that inequity in pay "made a suffragette out of me." Her lawyer husband's successful race for county attorney as a reform candidate was her first taste of political campaigning. The Cunninghams moved to Galveston in 1907. By 1910 Mrs. Cunningham was elected president of the Galveston Equal Suffrage Association and toured Texas to speak for the cause. In 1915 she was elected to the first of four annual terms as president of the Texas Woman Suffrage Association (subsequently the Texas Equal Suffrage Association). The number of local auxiliaries quadrupled during her first year in office, largely because of her leadership. In 1917 she moved to Austin, opened state suffrage headquarters near the Capitol, and began a campaign that culminated in legislative approval for woman suffrage in state primary elections in 1918. In 1919 Carrie Chapman Catt, president of the National American Woman Suffrage Association, persuaded Minnie Cunningham to lobby Congress for the Nineteenth Amendment. That same year, she helped organize the National League of Women Voters and became its executive secretary. In 1928 she became the first Texas woman to run for the United States Senate. She lost to Earle B. Mayfield in the primary, then campaigned for Tom Connally, who edged out Mayfield in the runoff. From 1930 to 1939 Cunningham worked in College Station as an editor for the Texas A&M Extension Service. She returned to Washington in 1939 to work as an information specialist for the Women's Division of the Agricultural Adjustment Administration. President Franklin Roosevelt is credited with having given her the nickname by which she later became widely known, "Minnie Fish." She resigned in 1943 to protest a rule impeding the flow of information to farmers.

In 1944, at the Democratic state convention, anti-Roosevelt forces elected "uninstructed" delegates to the national convention. Outraged, Roosevelt supporters elected their own slate of delegates at a rump convention. When a coalition of liberal Democrats failed to draft J. Frank Dobie as a candidate for governor, Minnie Fish ran herself. Angry that the incumbent governor, Coke Stevenson, did not take a public stand on the split, she

Minnie Fisher Cunningham (right) campaigning for the United States Senate, 1928. Courtesy Austin History Center, Austin Public Library; Photo no. PICA 16817. In 1928 Minnie Cunningham became the first woman from Texas to run for the United States Senate.

ran an outspoken campaign, calling on Stevenson to declare his views, and prevented his leading the anti-Roosevelt delegation to the national convention. Stevenson won the primary by a landslide. Nevertheless, in a field of nine candidates, Cunningham finished second. In 1946 she retired to Fisher Farms in New Waverly to raise cattle and pecans, but continued to campaign for liberal Democrats. She played a pivotal role in founding the *Texas Observer* in 1954 and helped start Democrats of Texas, an organization of liberals. In 1960, at the age of 78, she managed the campaign headquarters for John F. Kennedy in New Waverly.

Patricia Ellen Cunningham

Custer, George Armstrong. Cavalry officer; b. New Rumley, Ohio, 5 December 1839; d. Little Bighorn River, Dakota Territory, 25 June 1876; m. Elizabeth Bacon (1864); ed. West Point (grad. 1861). Custer finished the academy at the bottom of his class but won distinction in the Civil War as a cavalry officer. At 23 he was made brigadier general of volunteers, and at 25 was brevetted major general. With his long blond hair set off by a red tie, a sailor's blouse, and a blue jacket agleam with gold, the "boy general" cut a dashing figure. Admired by some, envied and disliked by others, he captured the public's imagination and became a popular hero in the North. At the end of the war he

was assigned to duty in Texas as part of General Sheridan's effort to prevent Confederate retrenchment in Mexico under the emperor Maximilian. During an uneventful five-month stay in Hempstead and Austin, which ended when he was mustered out of the volunteers on 1 February 1866, Custer alienated many in his command by strict enforcement of regulations prohibiting foraging, lawlessness, and destruction of private property; by the same enforcement he won the gratitude of many Texans, who found him a generous and courtly soldier. Effective September 1866, Custer, whose regular army rank was captain, was appointed lieutenant colonel of the newly formed Seventh United States Cavalry. He served on the southern plains against the Cheyennes, Comanches, Kiowas, and Arapahos. Controversy followed him—he was court-martialed in 1867—but he gained a reputation as an Indian fighter in November 1868, when the Seventh Cavalry destroyed a Cheyenne village on the Washita River in what is now Oklahoma. After Reconstruction duty in the South, he returned to the plains, this time to Dakota Territory, and led the Seventh Cavalry on the Yellowstone expedition in 1873, the Black Hills expedition in 1874, and the fateful Sioux expedition in 1876, when he and his men were annihilated. There is controversy about where the blame for the massacre lies—on Custer or on his battalion commanders. There was also contemporary controversy, which began as soon as the news of disaster reached the East. The Centennial year, 1876, was a year of vigorous discussion and appraisal of America. It was also a presidential election year. Custer was championed in the Democratic press as a martyr to Republican mismanagement, and Democratic Texans chose to remember him as a friend, "the Stuart of the North . . . once our foe, but a generous and manly one." Papers throughout the state clamored for the right to raise a volunteer force: "Texas deserves the honor of attempting to wipe out the Sioux," the Austin *State Gazette* insisted. Resolutions passed at a public meeting in Dallas, and a reunion of Hood's Texas Brigade in Bryan praised Custer as "a rare and magnanimous officer." The state legislature passed a resolution of condolence, subsequently published as a congressional document, noting that Custer had "endeared" himself to Texans by his frontier service. Custer's wife lived to the age of 91, wrote three books about him, and was buried beside him at West Point (1933). Her *Tenting on the Plains* (1887) presents a charming picture of their stay in Texas. Custer's headquarters building in Austin, the Blind Asylum, located on the "Little Campus" of the University of Texas, has been restored.   *Brian W. Dippie*

Czechs. A Slavic people from Bohemia, Moravia, and parts of Silesia. Among the first Czechs to arrive in Texas were the writer Carl Postl (Charles Sealsfield), who may have visited the Texas-Louisiana borderland as early as 1823; Frederick Lemsky, who arrived in 1836 and played the fife in the Texas band at the battle of San Jacinto; Bohumir Menzl, a Catholic priest who moved to New Braunfels in 1840; and Anthony M. Dignowity. Rev. Josef Arnošt Bergman, however, can best be described as the "father" of Czech immigration to Texas. Soon after arriving at the Austin County community of Cat Spring, he began writing to his friends in Europe about the opportunities that awaited future immigrants. His letters stimulated Bohemian and Moravian immigration. The first immigrants were chiefly poor laborers from northeastern Bohemia. On August 19, 1851, headed by Josef Šilar, they began the long, circuitous journey that took them to Hamburg, Liverpool, New Orleans, and eventually Galveston. Dangerous and unhealthful traveling conditions reduced the group's numbers by half. Two years later, a second group of immigrants from the same geographical area came to Texas. Their leader, Josef L. Lešikar, who had been influenced by Bergman's letters, had helped organize the first group. In the following years many groups of immigrants came from Moravia, particularly the eastern part of that province. The transatlantic voyage grew less dangerous, and Galveston became established as the preferred port of entry. Cat Spring continued to be the point of dispersal for the immigrants. The Central Texas counties of Austin, Fayette, Lavaca, and Washington had early Czech settlements, and Fayette County in particular became established as the center of Czech population in Texas. About 700 Czechs had established themselves in Texas by the time of the Civil War. By 1900 the number of foreign-born Czechs in the state had climbed to 9,204, and by 1910 to 15,074. After this time, however, Czech immigration decreased; foreign-born Czechs numbered 14,781 in 1920, 14,093 in 1930, and 7,700 in 1940, although the number of Czech "foreign white stock" (defined by the United States Bureau of the Census as those who spoke Czech at home during childhood) had climbed to 62,680 by that year.

During the years of greatest immigration before World War I the abundance of good, relatively inexpensive farmland in Texas undoubtedly provided the chief motivation for the immigrants, most of whom had been small landowners who saw little chance for economic achievement at home. Political and religious oppression and military conscription in the Austrian Empire also encouraged emigration. By the twentieth century approximately 250 Czech communities had been founded in Texas, especially in Blackland Prairie areas where farming looked promising. The greatest concentration was found in Lavaca and Fayette counties, though Czech settlement extended into Washington, Burleson, and Brazos counties. North of this strip was a larger belt of Blackland Prairie, where more scattered Czech communities were located in an area running northeast from Williamson County through Bell County and into McLennan County, with smaller offshoots to the north in Hill, Ellis, and Kaufman counties. Most of the other Czech communities were in the Coastal Plain, with concentrations in Wharton, Fort Bend, Victoria, and a few South Texas counties.

Two basic characteristics of the Czechs in Texas lie at the heart of their social structure: the extremely close-knit family unit and the attitude toward land. The typical Czech farm family was a largely self-contained economic and social unit whose main purpose was to cultivate the land. Farming was a way of life not clearly separated from other life goals and not seen merely as a way of making money. The rural Czech settlements were characterized by such cooperative institutions as the beef club, designed to provide each member family with a supply of fresh beef weekly during the spring and summer. Settlements also often had an egalitarian social structure, a characteristic that helps to explain the Czechs' pronounced enthusiasm for American democratic ideals. Communities became established, and social clubs and organizations began to proliferate, first on a local, then on a state, level. The result was the establishment of fraternal organizations such as the SPJST (known in English as the Slavic Benevolent Order of the State of Texas) in 1897; and the KJT in 1888 and the KJZT in 1897, Czech Catholic organizations for men and women, respectively. Each of these organizations grew out of a national Czech fraternal order but split away to become a Texas institution.

Perhaps as many as 90 percent of the Czech immigrants were Catholics in their homeland, and the majority of these maintained an allegiance to the Catholic Church in Texas. Their first church, a small log structure, was built at Ross Prairie in 1859. A significant minority of the immigrants were Protestants, however. Several independent congregations (the first had been established at Wesley in 1864) were organized into the denomination known as the Unity of the Brethren in 1903. Members of this group considered it to be a continuation of the traditional Czech religious movement of the same name, which had been suppressed by the Austrians in the seventeenth century. The Czechs in Texas also included freethinkers, who openly challenged all religious authority, but in general the freethinking movement among the Czechs was much less significant in Texas than it was in other parts of the United States, especially in the Midwest, where it often dominated Czech-American culture.

Organized education in the Czech language began early in Texas. Bergman was conducting lessons in both Czech and German at Cat Spring as early as 1855. In 1859 Josef Mašík became perhaps the first formal Czech teacher in the United States when he opened his school at Wesley. The Catholic school he built in 1868 in Bluff (later Hostyn), with Terezie Kubálová as the first teacher, may have been the first of its kind in the United States. Czechs were also especially active in establishing schools in Lavaca County late in the nineteenth century. The first school to offer instruction in both Czech and English was established at Praha in 1870. Although instruction in Czech in the public schools declined rapidly in the late nineteenth century, Czech-American clubs and organizations continued to advocate study of the language, particularly at the college and university level. The continued promotion of such study in the late twentieth century is significant, for language is the most important indicator of Czech ethnic identity.

Because the majority of Texas immigrants came from Moravia, the Czech spoken in Texas is largely characterized by Moravian dialects, which vary to some extent from the Bohemian dialects spoken by most Czech Americans. Czech-language journalism has been very active in the state over the years. Thirty-three newspapers and periodicals have been published. In the 1990s a weekly newspaper published at Granger and a monthly published at West were still being published entirely in Czech. Other periodicals such as *Vestnik* and the *Brethren Journal* contained sections printed in Czech. A wealth of oral literature has also been preserved in Texas, including stories, proverbs, and especially folk songs. Singing and dancing were the most popular forms of folk art maintained in Texas, but other forms, such as certain games and elaborate wedding rituals, have been preserved. In addition, some ethnic foods have become well known to virtually all Texans.

In spite of the development of such ethnic institutions as the fraternal organizations and the ethnocentric Brethren Church and efforts to preserve the Czech language and folklore, Czech-American leaders have generally argued for full participation in the political and economic life of the state and nation. Community leader Augustin Haidušek, in the late nineteenth and early twentieth centuries, articulated assimilationist ideals most prominently and influentially. Friction between Czechs and Anglo-Americans was most pronounced during the Civil War. Many recent immigrants did not fully understand the conflict between North and South, and at the same time they were suspect as foreigners. Most significantly, virtually none of them had any allegiance to the institution of slavery, not only for moral reasons, but also because the concept of slavery was alien to their system of intensive family farming. Ethnic pride among Czechs in Texas perhaps reached its height during World War I and immediately afterwards, for it was spurred by popular enthusiasm for the newly founded free state of Czechoslovakia. Such groups as the Czech National Alliance, which identified with the Czech cause in Europe, found support among the Czechs in Texas. As measured by the widespread use of Czech in churches, fraternal organizations, journalism, and books, as well as the preservation of ethnic music and other folk arts, Czech ethnicity remained strong in the state until World War II. Beginning in the 1960s, as part of a national interest in ethnic awareness, Czech ethnic festivals and celebrations became increasingly popular, although the use of the language continued to decline.

In the mid-1980s a Czech society known in English as Texans of Czech Ancestry was formed to organize a celebration of the Texas Sesquicentennial and the role of Czechs in Texas history. Related projects included compiling community histories, pioneer registries, family histories, and information on Czech cemeteries, schools, and churches. In the early 1990s the SPJST had more than 140 lodges statewide and maintained the Czech Heritage Museum in Temple. The Fayetteville Museum also contained many items on Czech history and culture. The Czech Heritage Society had at least twelve chapters in Texas. A number of Czech festivals were held in the state annually, including Czech Fest in Rosenberg, Czhilispiel in Flatonia, Westfest in West, and the National Polka Festival in Ennis. Several radio stations in Central Texas regularly played Czech music. As of the 1990 census, 168,023 people in Texas were of at least partial Czech descent.

Clinton Machann

D

Dallas, Texas. On the Trinity River in the center of Dallas County; founded by John Neely Bryan, who settled on the east bank of the Trinity near a natural ford in November 1841. Bryan had picked the best spot for a trading post to serve the population migrating into the region. The ford, at the intersection of two major Indian traces, provided the only good crossing point for miles. Two highways proposed by the Republic of Texas soon converged nearby. Unknown to Bryan, however, he had settled on land granted by the republic to the Texan Land and Emigration Company of St. Louis, headed by William S. Peters. Bryan eventually legalized his claim, and the extensive promotional efforts of the Peters colony attracted settlers to the region. In 1844 J. P. Dumas surveyed and laid out a townsite comprising a half mile square of blocks and streets. The origin of the name Dallas is unknown. Candidates include George Mifflin Dallas, vice president of the United States, 1845–49; his brother, Commodore Alexander J. Dallas, United States Navy; and Joseph Dallas, who settled near the new town in 1843. When Dallas County was formed in 1846, Dallas was designated as the temporary county seat; in 1850 voters selected it as the permanent county seat over Hord's Ridge (Oak Cliff) and Cedar Springs, both of which eventually came within its corporate limits. The Texas legislature granted Dallas a charter in 1856. Dr. Samuel Pryor, elected the first mayor, headed a town government consisting of six aldermen, a treasurer–recorder, and a constable. Dallas quickly became a service center for the rural area surrounding it. By the 1850s it had dry-goods stores, groceries, a drugstore, an insurance agency, a boot and shoe shop, brickyards, and saddle shops, as well as a weekly newspaper, the Dallas *Herald*, founded in 1849. In 1852 French immigrant Maxime Guillot established the first factory, manufacturing carriages and wagons. Alexander and Sarah Horton Cockrell, who purchased Bryan's remaining interest in the townsite in 1852, built a three-story brick hotel, a steam sawmill, and a flour mill. With the breakup of the nearby La Réunion colony in the late 1850s, skilled European craftsmen and artists moved into Dallas, including brickmakers, cabinetmakers, tailors, milliners, brewers, and musicians. By 1860 the population was 678, including 97 African Americans as well as French, Belgians, Swiss, and Germans. On 8 July 1860 a fire that originated in the W. W. Peak Brothers Drugstore spread to the other buildings on the square and destroyed most of the businesses. Suspicion fell on slaves and Northern abolitionists; three slaves were hanged, and two Iowa preachers were whipped and run out of town. In 1861 Dallas voters voted 741 to 237 to secede from the Union. Dallas was selected as one of 11 quartermaster and commissary posts in Texas for the Trans-Mississippi Army of the Confederacy. After the war, freed slaves flocked to Dallas in search of jobs and settled in freedmen's towns on the periphery of the city. By 1870 the population was about 3,000.

The arrival of the Houston and Texas Central in 1872 and the Texas and Pacific in 1873 made Dallas one of the first rail crossroads in Texas. Like Atlanta, Dallas found itself in a strategic geographical location for the transport of abundant regional products to northern and eastern manufacturing plants. Cotton became the region's principal cash crop, and Elm Street in Dallas was its market. Dallas became the world center for the leather and buffalo-hide trade. Merchants who opened general stores along the railroad route as rail construction crept north settled in Dallas and founded their flagship stores there. By 1880 the population had more than tripled, to 10,385. During the last quarter of the nineteenth century, banking and insurance emerged as major industries under the leadership of such men as William Henry Gaston, William L. Cabell, and J. T. Trezevant. With their close involvement in civic affairs, Dallas businessmen launched the State Fair of Texas, organized a board of trade, and founded a merchants' exchange to promote the city's favorable business climate. Dallas acquired telephones (1881), electricity (1882), and several daily newspapers, principally the Dallas *Morning News* (1885) and the Dallas *Times Herald* (1888). After annexing the neighboring town of East Dallas (1890), Dallas ranked as the most populous city in Texas, with 38,067 residents. Three years later, in the wake of a national financial panic, five Dallas banks and several industries failed. Cotton prices dropped to less than five cents a pound. Only 62 new manufacturing firms were established in Dallas during the 1890s. The panic also affected unionized labor, which had just begun to organize: the American Federation of Labor granted a charter to the Trades Assembly of Dallas in 1899.

By the turn of the century the economy had recovered, and Dallas was the leading book, drug, jewelry, and wholesale liquor market in the Southwest. It was the world's leading inland cotton market, and it still led the world in manufacture of saddlery and cotton-gin machinery. Its population stood at 42,638. In 1905 businessmen formed the 150,000 Club, aimed at increasing the city's population to 150,000 by 1910. Although the numerical goal was not met until 1920, the population did increase to 92,104 by 1910, and the city doubled in area to 18.31 square miles, partly through the annexation of Oak Cliff in 1904. Dallas built its first steel skyscraper, the 15-story Praetorian Building, in 1907. In the second decade of the twentieth century Dallas began to implement the city plan commissioned from George E. Kessler after a disastrous flood in 1908. Oak Cliff and Dallas were connected by the Houston Street Viaduct, at the time the longest concrete structure in the world; the Union Terminal Company consolidated six downtown railroad depots; and the railroad tracks were removed from Pacific Avenue. Dallas was selected as the site for a federal reserve bank in 1914, and Ford opened an auto assembly plant in the city. A wave of immigrants from Mexico helped swell the population to 158,976 by 1920, when Dallas ranked as the forty-second largest city in the nation. The post–World War I era was marked by the reemergence of the Ku Klux Klan. With 13,000 members, the Dallas chapter was the largest in Texas, and the national "imperial wizard" was a Dallas cut-rate dentist named Hiram Wesley Evans. Some 75,000 citizens greeted Evans on "Klan Day" at the 1923 State Fair. The Dallas *Morning News* led the attack on the Klan, helping Ma Ferguson defeat Dallas judge Felix Robertson, the Klan candi-

City Hall and Market House, 1877. Stereograph by Stamper & Paxton. Prints and Photographs Collection, Dallas, Texas, file, CAH; CN 01232.

date, in a Democratic runoff for governor in 1925. Dallas women were in the forefront of movements in Texas for reform in child-welfare practices, pure food and drink legislation, sanitation, and other causes. By 1920 they were also entering the workforce in increasing numbers. In 1927 the local chapter of the National Association of Business and Professional Women estimated that there were 15,000 women working in 125 occupations, trades, and professions in Dallas. Dallas was also a major center for the textile industry, which employed many women as dressmakers. Minority businessmen also began to organize. The Dallas Negro Chamber of Commerce (later renamed the Dallas Black Chamber of Commerce) was organized in 1925, and the Mexican Chamber of Commerce (now the Hispanic Chamber of Commerce) was formed in 1940.

The Great Depression put 15,000 Dallasites on the relief roles by 1933, and retail sales and bank deposits plummeted. The population, which had soared to 260,475 by 1930, climbed only to 294,734 in 1940. The pain of the depression was eased somewhat for Dallas by the discovery of oil in East Texas in 1930. Dallas bankers such as Nathan Adams of the First National Bank were the first in the nation to conceive of the idea of lending money to oil companies with oil reserves in the ground as collateral. Dallas soon became a center for petroleum financing. In a massive engineering effort begun in 1930, the channel of the Trinity River was moved, straightened, and confined between levees to prevent future flooding. Dallas businessmen also succeeded in making Fair Park the site of the Texas Centennial celebration, thus providing work for local builders, contractors, advertisers, concessionaires, and construction workers. The city hosted 10 million visitors, including President Franklin D. Roosevelt. One of the premier suburbs in Texas, Highland Park, developed within Dallas during the early part of the twentieth century. In it was built the first large-scale shopping center in the nation, Highland Park Village, in 1931. Highland Park incorporated, and its battles with Dallas over annexation lasted into the 1940s. Until World War II, Dallas ranked as a minor manufacturing center in the

nation. Its three leading industries were food processing, apparel manufacturing, and printing and publishing. Subsequently, war-related industries such as North American Aviation pushed industrial employment in Dallas to more than 75,000 in 1944. Dallas businesses experienced a boom after World War II comparable to that following the coming of the railroads. In 1949, 5 new businesses opened each day and 13 new manufacturing plants opened every month. In 1950 the population stood at 434,462. During the 1950s and 1960s, Dallas became the nation's third-largest technology center, with the growth of such companies as Ling–Tempco–Vought and Texas Instruments. In 1957 two developers, Trammell Crow and John M. Stemmons, opened a Home Furnishings Mart that grew into the Dallas Market Center, the largest wholesale trade complex in the world. The opening of Dallas–Fort Worth International Airport in 1974 attracted numerous corporate headquarters to Dallas and consolidated the city's reputation as a national financial and business center. The population grew from 679,684 in 1960 to 844,401 in 1970, 904,078 in 1980, and 1,006,877 in 1990. The 1990 census reported the ethnic groups in the city as white, 47.67 percent; black, 28.88 percent; Hispanic, 20.88 percent; and Asian, 2.18 percent. Racial integration of public facilities began on 15 August 1961, when a carefully orchestrated plan sent African Americans to lunch counters and businesses throughout the city for equal service. This plan, which proceeded without incident, was the work of a biracial committee appointed by the Dallas and Negro chambers of commerce, which devised a publicity campaign and notified business owners in advance.

Catastrophe struck the city on 22 November 1963, when President John Kennedy was assassinated in Dealey Plaza, only yards from the site where John Neely Bryan had settled in 1841. Two days later, his alleged assassin, Lee Harvey Oswald, was killed before television cameras by a Dallas nightclub owner, Jack Ruby. In 1989, after 25 years of debate about how the city should commemorate the event, the Sixth Floor, a museum, opened in the former Texas School Book Depository, from where Oswald had shot Kennedy. In 1993 Dealey Plaza was declared a National Historic Landmark District, the city's second after Fair Park.

The religious composition of Dallas has changed considerably over the years. The first Episcopal parish was organized in 1856. Catholics celebrated the first Mass in Dallas in 1859. Permanent places of worship were built as the city began to grow: Lamar Street Methodist (later First Methodist), City Temple Presbyterian, and First Baptist, all in 1868. Early black churches included Bethel African Methodist Episcopal (1869–72), New Hope Baptist (1872), and St. Paul Methodist (1873). The first Jewish synagogue, Temple Emanu-El, was built in 1873, and the first Catholic parish was established in 1872, when Dallas was still in the Diocese of Galveston. Congregationalists organized in 1875, Seventh Day Adventists in 1876, Lutherans in 1878, Unitarians in 1889, Christian Scientists in 1894, and Mormons in 1897. The variety of communions helped to make Dallas a religious stronghold by the turn of the century, and the continued growth of churches marked Dallas as a city of churchgoers. In the early 1980s, Dallas had six churches among the nation's 100 largest: First Baptist, Lovers Lane United Methodist, Cliff Temple Baptist, Beverly Hills Baptist, First United Methodist, and East Grand Baptist. Three more on the list were in suburbs: Highland Park United Methodist, Highland Park Presbyterian, and Park Cities Baptist. Subsequently, as the population has diversified, so have the religious faiths. Buddhists, Eastern Orthodox, Hindus, Muslims, and Sikhs are now found in Dallas. Southern Baptists have the largest representation in the Dallas area, followed by Catholics, black Baptists, and United Methodists.

The Art Saloon of Adolph Gouhenant (actually a photograph gallery), located on the south side of the courthouse square in the 1850s, was an early expression of artistic interest in Dallas. An 1857 diary reference to a visit "to the court house to look at the paintings of the Hudson schollars" may mark the earliest art exhibit in Dallas. Art shows at the annual state fairs after 1886 presented art to the public, while plans for the Carnegie Library, which opened in 1901, included an upstairs art gallery. The success of early shows there, which featured such regional artists as Frank Reaugh and Edward G. Eisenlohr, led to the organization

Main Street, ca. 1900. Prints and Photographs Collection, Dallas, Texas, file, CAH; CN 00756. By the turn of the century Dallas was the most populous city in Texas and had active markets and manufacturing plants. This photograph shows signs of a modern affluent society—telephone and electric poles, streetcars, and automobiles.

of the Dallas Art Association, which began assembling a permanent collection. After several moves and name changes, the Dallas Museum of Art now occupies a building designed by Edward Larrabee Barnes in the Dallas Arts District. By 1873 Dallas had a theater, Field's Opera House, where the first performance of an opera in the city took place in February 1875. The influx of German immigrants with the railroads led to the formation of the Dallas Frohsinn, a male singing society and member of the Texas State Sängerbund, which hosted statewide singing meets in 1883, 1892, 1904, and 1914. The Dallas Symphony Orchestra traces its roots to performances in 1900, and the Dallas Opera was launched in 1957. By the early 1920s Dallas was home to one of the earliest radio stations in Texas, WFAA. During the 1920s and 1930s popular music was centered in the Deep Ellum district on the eastern edge of downtown, close to one of Dallas's original freedmen's towns. Major black jazz and blues musicians such as Huddie Ledbetter and Blind Lemon Jefferson performed at Ella B. Moore's Park Theater, Hattie Burleson's dance hall, and other local clubs. Today Dallas has a wide variety of popular music and entertainment venues including the Summer Musicals, Starplex, and productions by the Dallas Jazz Orchestra, the Classical Guitar Society, the Dallas Chamber Orchestra, the Dallas Black Dance Theater, and the U.S.A. Film Festival. Dramatic productions in the nineteenth century were available as early as 1872 in Thompson's Variety Theater. The Little Theater of Dallas was established in 1921 and won the national Belasco Cup several times; it was followed by such other companies as the Civic Theater, the New Theater League of Dallas, and the critically acclaimed Margo Jones company. The Dallas Theater Center was founded in 1955 and is housed in a building on Turtle Creek designed by Frank Lloyd Wright. Other groups include Theatre Three, Teatro Dallas, the Dallas Children's Theater, and the Dallas Shakespeare Festival. Institutions of higher learning in the city include Southern Methodist University, founded in 1911; Paul Quinn College, a formerly black private institution that moved from Waco in 1990; Bishop College, another historically black institution founded in Marshall in 1881; and the University of Texas Southwestern Medical School, founded in 1943. Several campuses of Dallas County Community College, established in 1965, are located within the city.

Sporting events and teams in Dallas have their roots in the nineteenth century, when horse racing was popular enough to support a Dallas Jockey Club, founded in 1869. Horse racing was a major attraction at the State Fair of Texas from 1886 until 1909. The national bicycling craze inspired the formation of the Dallas Wheel Club in 1886, and races were held at Cycle Park from its construction in 1896 until its conversion to an open-air theater. Baseball was played in Dallas as early as 1877, when a touring team played a local team. By 1882 Dallas had its first semiprofessional team, the Brown Stockings, which won the league championship in 1883 and 1884. The Dallas Hams, a professional team, won the Texas League pennant in 1888. Dallas continued to field minor league teams until 1970. Football made its first appearance in Dallas with the organization of a Dallas Football Club in 1891. A team formed at Dallas High School in 1900 is thought to have been the first high school team in Texas. SMU sent a team to the 1935 Rose Bowl, and Doak Walker drew crowds to the Cotton Bowl in the late 1940s. Two professional teams, the Dallas Cowboys and the Dallas Texans, competed for fans in the early

1960s, until owner Lamar Hunt moved the Texans to Kansas City in 1963. The Dallas Cowboys (who now play in Irving) won Super Bowl titles in 1972, 1978, 1993, and 1994. Dallas's first professional basketball team, the Chaparrals, was moved to San Antonio, but the new franchise, the Dallas Mavericks, was organized in 1980. Dallas also hosts a professional soccer team, the Sidekicks, and an NHL hockey team, the Dallas Stars.

In 1907 Dallas voters adopted the commission form of city government to replace the aldermanic system. In 1930 the Citizens Charter Association won voter approval for the council–manager form of city government; an amendment in 1949 provided for direct election of the mayor. The CCA and the Dallas Citizens Council, a small group composed of business leaders, dominated local government until a 1971 lawsuit forced election by districts rather than at large. A 1992 amendment expanded the council to 14 single-member districts, with the mayor elected at large. Dallas purchased Fair Park from its owners in 1904 and continues to maintain this National Historic Landmark through a contract with the State Fair of Texas. Other municipal facilities include the City Hall, designed by I. M. Pei; the Dallas Convention Center, the Dallas Public Library, the Dallas Zoo, Union Terminal, and Love Field. The city also owns the Dallas Museum of Art, the Morton Meyerson Symphony Hall, the Dallas Zoo, and the Dallas Arboretum. Most of the cultural institutions are operated by private, nonprofit entities under contracts with the city.

Bryan's original survey for Dallas used the Trinity River as the western boundary, with streets laid out at right angles to the river. A competing survey drawn by Warren A. Ferris, done for John Grisby, was laid out at 45 degrees off cardinal directions. A third survey made for the Peters colony laid out sections using cardinal directions. The results are an odd series of doglegged streets downtown. Annexation of adjacent communities added another layer of surveying patterns to the Dallas street map. Although the first residential subdivision, the Cedars, was built south of downtown in the 1880s, most residential development has been toward the north and east. Segregated housing confined African Americans to a few overcrowded areas. Violence occurred as blacks began to integrate neighborhoods in South Dallas during the 1950s. Freedman's Town, the oldest of the freedmen's towns, in the State–Thomas area northeast of downtown, virtually disappeared with commercial development in the 1980s except for a historic cemetery that was literally unearthed during the widening of Central Expressway. The principal Hispanic barrio, immediately north of downtown, has also been displaced by commercial development. The building boom of the 1970s and 1980s produced a distinctive contemporary profile for the downtown area, influenced by nationally prominent architects. At the same time, the establishment of the West End Historic District in the 1980s preserved a group of late-nineteenth-century brick warehouses that have been adapted for use as restaurants and shops. Similar efforts have been made in Deep Ellum, where the 1920s-era storefronts now house clubs and restaurants. The Dallas Park Department oversees some 406 parks that comprise 50,000 acres. White Rock Lake, Bachman Lake, and Lake Cliff are surrounded by parks. City-owned greenbelts follow the waterways in the city, including White Rock Creek, Turtle Creek, and the Trinity River. Modern historic preservation efforts began in the 1970s with the formation of the Historic Preservation League. The city's Landmark

"Texas Baptist University." Courtesy TSL. This postcard shows an early view of the school building.

Commission has designated numerous buildings and several neighborhoods as landmarks, including Swiss Avenue, Munger Place, South Boulevard–Park Row, and State–Thomas. Fair Park is the largest Art Deco art and architecture district in the world. Old City Park, a museum of architectural and cultural history on the site of Dallas's oldest public park, is located just south of downtown. *Jackie McElhaney and Michael V. Hazel*

Dallas Baptist University. In southwest Oak Cliff; successor of Decatur Baptist College, founded as Northwest Texas Baptist College in Decatur (1891). In 1897 the Baptist General Convention of Texas purchased the institution and renamed it Decatur Baptist College. From 1898 to 1965 the institution was a church-affiliated coeducational junior college that prepared students for Baylor University. It was controlled by a board of trustees elected by the Baptist General Convention of Texas. DBC was accredited by the Southern Association of Colleges and by the Texas Education Agency. Its policy was "distinctly Christian and unswervingly Baptistic." Students were expected to attend church services and chapel regularly and were required to take two Bible courses before graduation. By 1959 the college also offered courses in fine arts, business, languages, and vocational training. DBC typically employed twelve faculty members and enrolled an average of 150 students, most of whom came from within a 50-mile radius of Decatur. Of the college's six presidents J. L. Ward, who held the office from 1900 to 1907 and 1914 to 1950, was most influential in the development and expansion of the institution. By 1958 DBC was the oldest junior college in the world. In 1965 the college was moved to its present location in Dallas and renamed Dallas Baptist College. In 1968 it became a four-year institution. It was renamed Dallas Baptist University on January 1, 1985, and began offering graduate degrees in education, religion, and business administration. The Decatur property was purchased at auction by a local resident, Coke L. Gage, who donated the administration building and an acre of land to the Wise County Historical Association. The building houses the Wise County Heritage Museum and provides auditorium facilities for the local Little Theater group. *B. Jane England*

Dallas Christian College. A four-year coeducational college of the Christian church, located on a 22-acre campus in Farmers Branch. Vernon M. Newland called a meeting in 1949 to plan the founding of a college that would recruit and train a "Bible-believing, evangelistic ministry." DCC opened in 1950 with 34 students in facilities shared by Cole Park Christian Church in Dallas. Newland was president. The college moved twice to larger locations. The second move, in 1967, was to the present location in Farmers Branch. Between 1974 and 1985 DCC operated a 12-grade school, Heritage Christian Academy, on the campus. In 1986 the college had an enrollment of 120. The institution is accredited by the American Association of Bible Colleges. It offers both bachelor's and associate degrees. *Cecil Harper, Jr.*

Dallas Cowboys. Founded in 1960, when the National Football League awarded its thirteenth franchise to Clint Murchison, Jr., and Bedford Wynne for $600,000. In 1952 another NFL franchise had played in Dallas, but it later moved to Baltimore. Because the new franchise was sold after the college draft, Murchison, Wynne and the general manager, Tex Schram, were forced to select their players from the existing NFL teams. The owners selected native Texan Tom Landry as coach. Because of missing the college draft, the team did not win a single game the first year. The Cowboys were also beset by poor attendance. In 1966, however, Dallas won its first championship, taking the Eastern Conference title with a 10–3–1 mark and losing to the Green Bay Packers 34–27 in the NFL championship game. That game repeated itself the following season when the Cowboys again fell to the Packers, dropping a 21–17 decision in the game that became known as the Ice Bowl because of the temperature—13 degrees below zero. The Cowboys won the NFC championship in 1970 and repeated in 1971. They lost to Baltimore in the Super Bowl after the 1970 season, but behind quarterback Roger Staubach won their first Super Bowl the next year with a decisive (24–3) victory over the Miami Dolphins. In 1971 Dallas also moved from the Cotton Bowl to Texas Stadium in Irving. Under the direction of the innovative Tom Landry, who was coach until 1989, the Cowboys reached the playoffs for eight years in a row (1966–73) to break their own NFL record. That string was broken in 1974 when the team finished 8–6. The Cowboys reached the Super Bowl again in the 1975 season, after beating Minnesota on Staubach's historic 50-yard pass to Drew Pearson and destroying Los Angeles. However, they lost Super Bowl 10 to Pittsburgh 21–17. Dallas won its second Super Bowl by defeating the Denver Broncos 27–10 on 15 January 1978. That year, Bob Ryan, the editor in chief of NFL Films, dubbed the Cowboys "America's Team." The Cowboys' fourth appearance in the Super Bowl tied Minnesota for the most times ever, and their second win equaled the records of Green Bay, Miami, and Pittsburgh. Dallas reached the Super Bowl for a record fifth time the next season, but dropped a 35–31 thriller to Pittsburgh.

In 1984 the Murchison family sold the Cowboys to an 11-member limited partnership headed by Dallas banker H. R. "Bum" Bright. The following year Dallas running back Tony Dorsett became only the sixth player in NFL history to have a career record of 10,000 rushing yards. That season the Cowboys extended their NFL-record streak of consecutive winning seasons to 20, the third longest in professional sports history, behind only the baseball New York Yankees (39 straight) and hockey Montreal Canadians (32). The Cowboys had difficulty in sustaining their winning power in the late 1980s. Despite Landry's career record of 250–162–6, the team went 3–13 in 1988. Arkansas oil-and-gas investor Jerry Jones purchased the club from Bright in 1989, fired Landry, and hired Jimmy Johnson as head coach. Jones also signed UCLA quarterback Troy Aikman for a rookie record six-year salary of $11.2 million. Despite the influx of cash and personnel, the Cowboys were 1–15 in the first year of new ownership and only 7–9 in the second. But Jones and Johnson rebuilt the team, which won back-to-back Super bowls over the Buffalo Bills after the 1992 and 1993 seasons to become one of just three NFL teams to claim four world championships. Aikman, most valuable player in Super Bowl 27, renegotiated his contract in 1993 for an NFL record of $50 million for eight years. Following Super Bowl 28 Johnson stepped down in March 1994 and was replaced as coach by Barry Switzer. The next season the Cowboys lost the NFC championship to their archrivals, the San Francisco 49ers. In 1995–96 the Cowboys had a spectacular season capped by a victory in the Super Bowl. They had a winning season the next year, but in 1997 lost more games than they won. The team's executive offices are at Valley Ranch in Irving.

Kirk Bohls

Dallas–Fort Worth International Airport. One of the largest airports in the world; at the site where the towns of Euless, Irving, and Grapevine meet between Dallas and Fort Worth. The present facility developed after a longstanding airport rivalry between the two cities. Realizing that expanding Meacham Field in Fort Worth and Love Field in Dallas was impractical, representatives of the cities collaborated in a regional airport, Midway Airport. When development was stymied by disagreement over which way the terminal was to face, Midway was turned over to the city of Arlington (1943). It was renamed Greater Fort Worth International Airport when the city of Fort Worth decided to develop it as its major airport (1947). Fort Worth annexed the site (1950) and renamed the airport Amon G. Carter Field. The rivalry between Carter Field and Love Field was so bitter that Fort Worth mayor Amon G. Carter refused to eat in Dallas restaurants. Carter Field was renamed Greater Southwest International Airport in 1960 and purchased by the city of Fort Worth. But traffic there declined to less than 1 percent of the Texas total, while traffic at Love Field increased to 49 percent. In 1964 the corresponding congestion at Love Field led the Civil Aeronautics Board to order the two cities to come up in less than 180 days with a voluntary agreement on the location of a new regional airport, or the federal government would do it for them. CAB examiner Ross I. Newmann served as a mediator between the two cities. Both cities appointed committees, and by 1965 plans were set for a Dallas–Fort Worth Board, to consist of 11 members—7 from Dallas and 4 from Fort Worth. The board named Thomas M. Sullivan executive director of airport construction and operations. The site for the facility, originally called Dallas–Fort Worth Regional Airport, was chosen, and the plan received broad support. In December 1968 ground was broken. Dallas–Fort Worth International Airport was dedicated in September 1973 and became operational on January 13, 1974, replacing Love Field. In 1988, under the threat of increased noise and reduced property values, the three cities that meet at the site began a legal battle against planned expansion of the airport, but the Supreme Court sided with the airport in 1994. The airport has continued to expand. D–FW contributes $5 billion annually to the local economy and provides 25,000 jobs.

Art Leatherwood

Dallas Historical Society. Founded by George B. Dealey and 100 others in 1922; focuses on collecting, preserving, and interpreting materials relating to the history of Dallas, Dallas County, the state of Texas, and the Southwest. The society office was originally in the library of Southern Methodist University, but moved to the Hall of State at Fair Park in 1938. Membership is open to the public. The society provides school tours of the Hall of State to school children. Its outreach specialist travels to area schools and uses artifact reproductions and slides to illustrate talks. In addition, the society presents exhibits from its own archival and museum collections and hosts traveling exhibitions. The DHS operates the George B. Dealey Library at the Hall of State, which is open to the public by appointment. The collection contains rare books and manuscripts on the founding of the Republic of Texas, Texas since 1845, and Dallas and North Texas. Large archival collections include the papers of local, state, and national leaders as well as the Texas Centennial Commission papers. The museum has over 15,000 items pertaining to the social, economic, and political history of Dallas and Texas. Rare items include General Santa Anna's spurs and James W. Fannin's watch. In recent years the society has made strong efforts to acquire items documenting the different cultures living in Dallas and North Texas. Society publications include *Dallas Rediscovered: A Photographic Chronicle of Urban Expansion, 1870–1925* (1978); *When Dallas Became a City: The Letters of John M. McCoy, 1870 to 1881* (1982); and *Legacies: A History Journal for Dallas and North Central Texas*, which is published with the Dallas County Heritage Society.

Guy C. Vanderpool

Dallas *Morning News*. One of the leading newspapers in Texas; developed from the Galveston *News*. By 1879 Alfred H. Belo, who had acquired control of the Galveston paper, wanted a paper in North Texas. When efforts to purchase the old Dallas *Herald* failed, Belo sent George B. Dealey to launch the Dallas *Morning News*, which began publication on October 1, 1885. Linked across 315 miles by telegraph, and sharing a network of correspondents across the state, the Dallas and Galveston papers were the first two newspapers in the country to publish simultaneous editions. From its parent paper, the Dallas *News* inherited the concept of being a state paper and of refraining from becoming the organ of any political party. Beginning with a circulation of 5,000, the Dallas *News* soon absorbed its major competitor, the *Herald* (not to be confused with the Dallas *Times Herald*). It immediately leased a special train on the Texas and Pacific Railway to carry papers to Fort Worth, and in 1887 it engaged a special train on the Houston and Texas Central to deliver papers to McKinney, Sherman, and Denison on the morning they were printed. This expedient enabled the paper to meet the threat of the St. Louis newspapers, which in 1885 had a larger circulation in North Texas than did any Texas paper. By 1888 the *News* was printing an 8 to 12 page edition daily and 16 pages on Sunday. Its circulation reached 17,000 by 1895. In 1914 the *News* launched an evening paper, the Dallas *Journal*, which was sold in 1938. It also published the *Semi-Weekly Farm News* from 1885 until 1940. During the 1890s the *News* stood firmly against the agrarian wing of the Democratic party, as represented in the state by James Stephen Hogg and nationally by William Jennings Bryan. The paper supported both Grover Cleveland and William McKinley, especially as to hard-money views. Beginning about

1900 it avoided controversy and name-calling in political attack, with the exception of its vehement opposition to the reelection of Joseph Weldon Bailey as senator in 1906. In that year circulation climbed to 38,000. In a courageous move, the paper condemned the Ku Klux Klan in the early 1920s. Another step it took in the face of financial loss was its decision in 1920 not to accept any advertising for oil stock because of the difficulty of distinguishing between fraudulent and honest firms. Adolph Ochs of the New York *Times* stated in 1924, "I received my ideas and ideals from the Galveston *Daily News* and the Dallas *Morning News.*"

The *News*, which had initially supported Franklin D. Roosevelt and his New Deal, found itself disagreeing with Roosevelt's domestic policies as the president's tenure in office stretched to include a fourth term. However, it backed Roosevelt's foreign policies, including unreserved support of America's participation in World War II after Pearl Harbor. The paper supported Republican Dwight D. Eisenhower for president over Adlai Stevenson in 1952 and 1956, and Richard M. Nixon over John F. Kennedy in 1960. It was neutral in the contest between Lyndon B. Johnson and Barry Goldwater in 1964, but endorsed Richard Nixon in 1968 and 1972, Gerald Ford in 1976, Ronald Reagan in 1980 and 1984, and George Bush in 1988 and 1992. The paper's circulation, which stood at 150,000 in 1950, grew to 276,000 (Sunday) and 346,273 (daily) by 1968. In 1994 the circulation of the *News* was 814,400 (Sunday) and 527,300 (daily). Two long-time programs supported by the Dallas *Morning News* have been city planning for Dallas and encouragement of enlightened farming practices in North Texas. In addition, it has backed campaigns to clean up the city and make it more attractive, to build levees for flood control on the Trinity River, to construct a union railroad station, and to adopt first the commission form of government and later the city manager form. The *News* has published several special editions that have contributed to state and local history, including the Fiftieth Anniversary Edition of October 1, 1935; the Texas Centennial Edition of June 7, 1936; an edition of April 11, 1942, marking the 100th anniversary of its parent paper, the Galveston *News*; and the Texas Unlimited Edition of May 22, 1949. It subsequently published special editions celebrating its own 100th anniversary on October 1, 1985, and the 150th anniversary of the A. H. Belo Corporation on April 11, 1992. The Dallas *Morning News* received Pulitzer prizes in 1986, 1989, 1991, 1992, 1993, and 1994.

Judith M. Garrett and Michael V. Hazel

Dallas Nine. A group of painters, printmakers, and sculptors active in Dallas in the 1930s and early 1940s, who turned to the land and people of the Southwest for artistic inspiration. "Nine" is somewhat misleading, as the group expanded and contracted. The artists most closely identified with the name seem to have been the men who lobbied the Texas Centennial Commission unsuccessfully for the privilege of decorating the walls of the Hall of State, the main building of the Centennial Exposition in Dallas (1936). They were Jerry Bywaters, Thomas Stell, Jr., Harry Carnohan, Otis Dozier, Alexandre Hogue, William Lester, Everett Spruce, John Douglass, and Perry Nichols. Other artists closely associated with the group were Charles Bowling, Russell Vernon Hunter, Merritt Mauzey, Florence McClung, Don Brown, and Lloyd Goff. The sculptors Dorothy Austin, Michael

Owen, Allie Tennant, and Octavio Medellín also participated in the Dallas Regionalist movement. The Dallas Nine flourished during a period when critics and theorists such as John Dewey, George Santayana, Constance Rourke, and Holger Cahill exhorted American artists to draw inspiration from their surroundings instead of following European trends. At the local level critics such as Henry Nash Smith, David R. Williams, and Alexandre Hogue promoted the Regionalist aesthetic in the pages of the *Southwest Review*. In his role as art critic for the Dallas *Morning News* and editor of the short-lived *Southwestern Arts*, Bywaters emerged as the leading spokesman of Regionalism in Dallas.

A number of changes and new organizations in Dallas stimulated the development of the Dallas Nine. John S. Ankeny's arrival in 1929 as the first professional director of the Dallas Art Association invigorated what had become a somewhat stodgy organization. Ankeny and his successor, Lloyd Rollins, presented exhibitions of early Italian painters, Mexican muralists, and contemporary American lithographers, all of which had a strong effect on the young artists in the area. The museum-sponsored annual competitive Allied Arts Exhibition functioned as an important source of encouragement and public recognition for the Regionalist artists. The Dallas Artists League, an informal discussion group active from 1932 to 1936, provided a forum for the exchange of ideas and heightened the public profile of its artist members with the popular annual Alice Street Art Carnivals. Organizations such as the Dallas Art Institute, the Highland Park Society of Arts, the Dallas University Club, the Klepper Sketch Club, the Lawrence Art Galleries, and the Joseph Sartor Galleries further stimulated the Dallas artistic climate by exhibiting young artists' work. Members of the Dallas Nine received much-needed financial support with the beginning in 1933 of the federal Public Works of Art Project, which awarded mural commissions to many Regionalist artists. New Deal patronage of artists continued into the early 1940s under the auspices of the WPA and the Treasury Section federal art project. The Centennial Exposition of 1936 was perhaps the most influential event in forging a group identity among the Dallas Regionalists. Although the Nine failed to secure the mural commissions for the Hall of State, they dominated the Texas section of the Dallas Museum of Fine Arts exhibition, and were praised in the national as well as the local press.

For the most part, the Dallas Regionalists eschewed the abstraction of School of Paris artists in favor of naturalistic representation. Most of the painters in the group used tight brushwork and an earthy palette, working in a hard-edged style that broke away from the misty Impressionism of the Bluebonnet School of painters that had dominated Texas art in the early twentieth century. The Dallas Regionalists focused on the people, land, and wildlife of the Southwest. Positive evocations of the region can be seen in works such as Mauzey's *Neighbors* (1938) and McClung's *Squaw Creek Valley* (1937). More characteristic of the group was Hogue's grim *Drouth Stricken Era* (1934). Such contemporary Mexican painters as Diego Rivera and José Clemente Orozco were major influences on the Dallas Regionalists, particularly in their use of murals and inexpensive prints as populist tools to increase regional pride and political awareness. Italian primitive painting of the Quattrocento and American folk art also influenced the composition and drafts-manship of many of the Dallas Regionalists. Members of the Nine were familiar with the work of Thomas Hart Benton and other nationally known Regionalists, but they rejected the nativism of the American-scene movement led by Benton and critic Thomas Craven. Indeed, Harry Carnohan and several other members of the group traveled and studied in Europe and shared their experiences with their colleagues upon their return. A Surrealist influence can be detected in certain works by Carnohan, Dozier, Lester, Nichols, and Bywaters; Dozier also experimented with the contradictory perspective schemes of Cubism in his award-winning *Still Life With Striped Gourd* (1935).

Sculptors associated with the Dallas Regionalists experimented with direct carving, a modernist rejection of traditional processes that frequently required technical assistance, thus distancing the artist from his materials. Dorothy Austin, Michael Owens, and Allie Tennant worked in a blocky, robust style, although Tennant also produced such streamlined figures as the *Tejas Warrior* (1936), placed above the entrance to the Hall of State. Octavio Medellín developed a powerful style inspired in part by the art of the Maya and Toltec Indians, and exerted considerable influence over young artists through his teaching posts at the Witte Museum, North Texas State Teachers College, Southern Methodist University, and the Dallas Museum of Fine Arts.

In the later 1930s printmaking, particularly lithography, became an important medium for the Dallas Regionalists. Initially spurred by the establishment of the Dallas Print Society in 1934 and its Print Center, which opened in 1937, experimentation in that medium accelerated after Bywaters and other members of the Dallas Nine formed the Lone Star Printmakers in 1938. About 15 artists contributed prints to a traveling exhibition in which impressions were offered for sale. Hogue, Bywaters, and Dozier were the most experienced printmakers when the group was formed, but by the time of the last circuit in 1942 Bowling and Mauzey had emerged as the outstanding talents in the group. Lone Star Printmakers prompted the establishment of the Printmakers Guild of Dallas, a group of printmakers originally limited to women, which operated a print circuit from 1940 to 1965.

The influx of European émigrés to the United States during World War II produced a ferment of art activity that culminated in the Abstract Expressionist movement of the late 1940s and early 1950s. Regionalism, sullied by its association with American Scene jingoism, became dated. Dozier, Spruce, Lester, and other Dallas artists injected new life into the Regionalist aesthetic by experimenting with a semiabstract style still rooted in Southwestern subject matter. Although the Dallas Nine ceased to operate as a group after its members scattered to pursue careers throughout the state and beyond, artists from that circle continued to do meaningful work and exerted a powerful influence over a new generation of artists through their positions as teachers and museum administrators. Their achievements as artists and teachers were celebrated in an exhibit at the Dallas Museum of Art in 1985.   *Kendall Curlee*

Dallas Symphony Orchestra. Inaugural concert conducted by Hans Kreissig at Turner Hall on 22 May 1900. The 32-member ensemble played music by Franz Joseph Haydn, Gioacchino Rossini, Richard Wagner, Pietro Mascagni, and Kreissig and continued sporadically with one or two concerts per season for the following 10 years. In 1911 Walter J. Fried reorganized the Kreissig orchestra into the 40-member Beethoven Symphony Orchestra. Two years later Carl Venth moved to Dallas from the Kidd–Key Conservatory in Sherman and placed the Dallas Symphony Orchestra on a professional basis, with Fried as concertmaster. Economic reverses caused the orchestra to founder in 1914–15, but Fried kept the group together and presented a four-concert series annually on a modest scale from 1918 to 1924. Fried died in 1925 and was succeeded by Paul van Katwijk, dean of music at Southern Methodist University, who conducted the expanded orchestra until 1937. At that time the orchestra was taken over by Jacques Singer, whose spirited tenure ended in 1942, when he and a third of the orchestra's personnel entered military service. Under Antal Dorati, who conducted the reconstituted DSO from 1945 to 1949, the orchestra rose to major status. Dorati was succeeded by Walter Hendl, who conducted until 1958. At that time Paul Kletzki was hired and introduced a sense of Central European solidity to the programs. The Dallas Symphony engaged Georg Solti for the 1961–62 season, and the following year Donald Johanos, a young American conductor, was appointed music director. During his nine-year tenure, the Dallas Symphony received favorable national reviews and a recording contract. The 1970–73 tenure of Anshel Brusilow and the brief one-year appointments of Max Rudolf and Louis Lane were a period of waning community support, but the popularity of the orchestra was restored in 1977 when Eduardo Mata, a Mexican conductor, was hired as music director and Kurt Masur as principal guest conductor. The orchestra developed a brilliant image and prospered. From the 1930s until 1989 the Dallas Symphony performed in McFarlin Auditorium at Southern Methodist University and at the Fair Park Music Hall, which became its home in 1973. A fund drive for a new hall was launched in 1982, and the new Morton H. Meyerson Symphony Center opened in September 1989. In 1985 the Dallas Symphony under Mata made its first European tour, to London, Paris, Berlin, Stuttgart, Frankfurt, Madrid, and Barcelona, performing to appreciative audiences and good reviews. The orchestra has made records with RCA Victor, which produced performances by Dorati, Hendl, and Mata; Turnabout–Candide, which produced the Johanos concerts; and both Telarc Records and Angel–EMI, which produced recordings of Eduardo Mata. Mata, who was succeeded as conductor in September 1994 by Andrew Litton, was killed in a plane crash in Mexico on 4 January 1995.   *Theodore Albrecht*

Dallas Texans. A professional football team. In the late 1950s Lamar Hunt sought to obtain a professional football franchise for Dallas. When the National Football League told him that there would be no expansion in the foreseeable future, he set out to form a new league. He found other men to join him, and in 1959 Hunt formed the American Football League. He named his team the Dallas Texans and hired Hank Stram, an assistant coach at the University of Miami, as head coach. The AFL made its professional debut in 1960. The Texans placed second in the AFL Western Division. The 1960 Texans had the league's most exciting player, Abner Haynes, a rookie from North Texas State University, who won the league rushing title, was chosen the AFL's first Player of the Year, and became the symbol of the new league. In 1962 Stram won the championship; the Texans, bolstered by the addition of quarterback Len Dawson and rookie fullback Curtis McClinton, swept to the Western Division title with a spectacular 11-win and 3-loss season. Stram was named Coach of the Year, Dawson Player of the Year, and McClinton Rookie of the Year. The Texans beat the Houston Oilers in the 1962 championship game. Two minutes and 54 seconds into the second overtime period rookie Tommy Brooker kicked a field goal to give the Texans a 20 to 17 victory in the longest football game ever played. But in 1963, under the pressure of competition at home from the NFL's Dallas Cowboys, Hunt moved his team to Kansas City, Missouri. *Jim Schaaf*

Dallas Theological Seminary. A nondenominational, premillenialist Protestant school that opened in 1924 as Evangelical Theological College with twelve students who proposed to study under Lewis Sperry Chafer. By 1929, thanks to gifts, the five-acre campus on Swiss Avenue was complete. The seminary pioneered in offering a fouryear course for the master of theology degree. Under the name Dallas Theological Seminary and Graduate School of Theology (1936–), it continued to grow and add to its physical plant. By 1976, with a student body of 1,000, DTS was one of the five largest Protestant seminaries in the world. In 1980 it began offering a doctor of ministry degree. It also instituted programs in Philadelphia and San Antonio. Chafer was president from 1924 to 1952, and John F. Walvoord served from 1952 to 1986.

Dallas *Times Herald*. Founded in 1888 with the merger of the *Daily Times* and the *Daily Herald*; the first Dallas newspaper to use electricity. The *Daily Times–Herald* joined the Associated Press in 1890 and advanced such causes as street paving, improved sanitation, and water facilities in Dallas. In the gubernatorial election of 1892 it supported the reelection of James S. Hogg but subsequently suffered major financial setbacks and went into receivership. Under Edwin J. Kiest's direction (1896–) the paper recovered. By 1903 it included sections on the arts, entertainment, agriculture, and sports. In 1926 Kiest bought KRLD radio. In 1929 circulation reached 64,063 for the daily edition, and the paper occupied new headquarters at Pacific, Griffin, and Patterson streets. In 1941, the year Kiest died, circulation reached 95,432 for the daily edition. Tom C. Gooch was president of the *Daily Times–Herald* until 1952, when John W. Runyon secured the office. In 1954 the paper was redesigned and *Daily* was dropped from its name, which was henceforth unhyphenated. In 1964 photographer Bob Jackson received a Pulitzer Prize for his photograph of the slaying of Lee Harvey Oswald. Three years later James F. Chambers, Jr., took over as publisher of the paper, which in 1969 was sold to the Los Angeles–based Times Mirror Company. The new owner expanded the paper's coverage of local news and began printing a morning edition. In 1973 W. Thomas Johnson became the executive editor and vice president, and two years later he replaced Chambers as publisher, a position he held from 1975 to 1977, when Lee Guitar succeeded him. Guitar served until 1981, when Thomas R. McCartin became publisher. Under the leadership of these last three publishers the paper reached the peak of its success. In 1975 *Newsweek* ranked it in the top five newspapers in the South, and in 1977 the Sunday edition of the *Times Herald* slightly outsold the more conservative Dallas *Morning News*. Additional Pulitzer prizes went to photographers Erwin H. Hagler (1980) and Jay

Dickman (1983). The paper also had nine Pulitzer Prize finalists, four Picture of the Year awards, two George Polk awards, and two Overseas Press Club awards. In 1986 William Dean Singleton and the Media News Group bought the paper from Times Mirror for $110 million. Two years later a majority of the paper's stock was purchased from Media News Group by John H. Buzetta and the newly formed DTH Media, with MediaNews Group remaining as a minority stockholder.

By the late 1980s the *Times Herald* was in the middle of a decline that eventually ended in its demise. A number of factors contributed to the paper's decline. Afternoon newspapers suffered from TV news competition. Times Mirror failed to provide significant reinvestment in the paper, while the rival *News* aggressively reorganized its activities. Times Mirror also failed to recognize the growing trend away from city issues and towards suburban needs, while suburban delivery became inadequate and many subscribers failed to receive their papers. The paper's suburban circulation fell far behind that of the *News*. A number of conflicts occurred within the *Times Herald*'s management. The last blow came in 1989, when the rights to 26 Universal Press Syndicate features that the *Times Herald* had been running were bought by the A. H. Belo Corporation, publisher of the *News*. The *Times Herald* filed an antitrust lawsuit against Belo, but lost in both the trial and the appeal. On 8 December 1991, Belo bought the *Times Herald* for $55 million. Like many other major cities Dallas became a one-newspaper town. The Dallas *Times Herald* printed its final edition on 9 December 1991. *Matthew Hayes Nall*

Daniel, Marion Price, Sr. Governor, senator; b. Dayton, 10 October 1910; d. 25 August 1988; ed. Baylor University (law degree, 1932); m. Jean Houston Baldwin; 4 children. Daniel held more offices of public trust than anyone else in Texas history. He was elected in 1939 to the state legislature, where he opposed a state sales tax; in 1943 he was unanimously elected speaker of the House. After service in World War II as a judge advocate general, he was elected state attorney general, the youngest in the United States. In that office he defended the University of Texas in *Sweatt v. Painter*, fought organized gambling, and defended the state in the Tidelands Controversy. This conflict extended into Daniel's tenure in the Senate, to which he was elected in 1952 as a supporter of Eisenhower. He resigned from the Senate when he was nominated for Texas governor in 1956; he won the election and was reelected in 1958 and 1960. His governorship was replete with legislation in many areas, including highways, prison reform, water conservation, teachers' salaries, care for the mentally impaired, and the founding of the Texas State Library. Against his wishes, the legislature passed a state sales tax (1961), which Daniel allowed to become law without his signature so that the government would not go broke. Blamed by the electorate for this tax, he lost his reelection bid in 1962. He subsequently practiced law in Austin and Liberty until 1967, when President Lyndon B. Johnson made him head of the Office of Emergency Preparedness. Governor Preston Smith appointed him to fill an unexpired term in the Texas Supreme Court in 1971, after which Daniel was elected to the position in 1972 and 1979. Before retiring during his second term, he especially influenced groundwater law and laws dealing with uranium, oil, and gas. He was a devoted Baptist, the recipient of many honors including an honorary doctorate from Baylor, and a member of

Price Daniel, Sr., and his family, during his 1952 campaign for the United States Senate. Price Daniel Papers, Sam Houston Regional Library and Research Center, Liberty.

several honorary organizations. His son, Price Daniel, Jr., was speaker of the Texas House and president of the Constitutional Convention of 1974.   *Daniel Murph*

Darnell, Linda. Actress; b. Monetta Eloyse Darnell, Dallas, 16 October 1923; d. Cook County, Illinois, 10 April 1965; m. J. Peverell Marley, Philip Liebmann, and Merle Roy Robertson; divorced all three; one adopted daughter (with Marley). As a teenager, Linda Darnell modeled for Southwestern Style Shows, was a "Texanita" during the Texas Centennial, and won the regional Gateway to Hollywood contest. In 1938 talent scout Ivan Kahn arranged for her to have a screen test that led to an eventual contract with Twentieth Century–Fox. She starred in her first film, *Hotel for Women*, in 1939. Darryl Zanuck, head of production, immediately cast her in a series of motion pictures opposite Tyrone Power, including *Daytime Wife* (1939), *Brigham Young—Frontiersman* (1940), *The Mark of Zorro* (1940), and *Blood and Sand* (1941). In 1944 *Look* magazine proclaimed her one of the four most beautiful women in Hollywood. After reshaping her celluloid image from that of a sweet young thing into that of a sultry vixen, she reached international stature in the title role of the screen spectacle *Forever Amber* (1947) and further demonstrated her skill as an actress in such films as *Hangover Square* (1945), *Fallen Angel* (1945), *Unfaithfully Yours* (1948), *A Letter to Three Wives* (1948), *Slattery's Hurricane* (1949),

and *No Way Out* (1950). After leaving Twentieth Century–Fox in 1952, she made three pictures at RKO: *Blackbeard the Pirate* (1952), *Second Chance* (1953), and *This Is My Love* (1957); two in Italy; and low-budget productions for Paramount and Republic. She never again equaled her earlier success. Darnell made a Broadway debut in the unsuccessful *Harbor Lights* in 1956, appeared frequently in television dramas, toured with tenor Thomas Hayward in a nightclub act, and performed regularly in regional theaters across the country in such plays as *Tea and Sympathy*, *A Roomful of Roses*, and *Janus*. She worked for numerous charities, including the National Kidney Foundation, and helped raise funds to preserve the battleship *Texas* as a public shrine. She died of burns received in a house fire in Glenview, Illinois.   *Ronald L. Davis*

Daughters of the Republic of Texas. The original Texas patriotic women's organization; founded by Betty Ballinger and Hally Bryan. The organizational meeting was held on 6 November 1891 in the Houston home of Mary Jane Briscoe. Mary S. M. Jones, widow of Anson Jones, agreed to serve as president. The group called itself Daughters of Female Descendants of the Heroes of '36, then Daughters of the Lone Star Republic, and, by the first annual meeting in April 1892, Daughters of the Republic of Texas. The DRT was planned as a companion to the Texas Veterans Association, and the two groups held joint meetings until the veterans disbanded in 1907. The objectives of the association are to perpetuate the memory and spirit of the people who achieved and maintained the independence of Texas and to encourage historical research into the earliest records of Texas, especially those relating to the revolutionary and republic periods. The DRT encourages the preservation of documents and relics, the publication of historical records and narratives, and the celebration of important days in the state's history. It also encourages the teaching of Texas history in public schools and sponsors historical markers. Members are required to be women who can prove lineal descent from a man or woman who served Texas before annexation (1846). As of 1994 more than 6,500 members were organized into 108 chapters. Local chapters also sponsor chapters of the Children of the Republic of Texas, a junior association organized in San Antonio in 1929. Members must be under the age of 21 and must prove the same lineal descent as DRT members.

One early DRT project was to persuade the Texas legislature to purchase the land on which the battle of San Jacinto was fought. The Daughters placed battlefield markers on the important sites pointed out by members of the Veterans Association. A more recent and continuing project is the placement of bronze medallions on the graves of citizens of the Republic of Texas. The Daughters were instrumental in the state's decision to purchase life-size statues of Stephen F. Austin and Sam Houston sculpted by Elisabet Ney for the rotunda of the Capitol in Austin. The DRT also used its influence to place a monument at Washington-on-the-Brazos, where the Texas Declaration of Independence was signed. In 1905, through the combined efforts of the association and two of its members, Clara Driscoll and Adina de Zavala, the Daughters became custodians of the Alamo. Their library there is open to all researchers. In Austin the DRT maintains the French Legation, built in 1840 for the French diplomatic mission to the Republic of Texas and open to the public. The DRT was instrumental in saving the Old Land Office Building, on the Capitol grounds in Austin. For many years the organization used this building as a museum. The United Daughters of the Confederacy had a museum on the lower floor. The DRT purchased its own building in Austin to house the museum and headquarters, opened to the public in 1991. The DRT also owns and maintains the Cradle, a building in Galveston where Betty Ballinger and Hally Bryan made plans to organize the association. In 1961 the legislature adopted the Daughters' design for the reverse side of the Great Seal of Texas. Sarah Roach Farnsworth of San Antonio produced the design, which incorporates the six flags of Texas, the Alamo, the Gonzales "Come and Take It" cannon, and Vince's Bridge, destroyed by Deaf Smith on orders from Sam Houston at the battle of San Jacinto. The original watercolor painting of the design, by Joy Harrell Carrington of Medina, hangs in the office of the Texas secretary of state. In 1986 the Daughters buried a time capsule containing memorabilia of the Sesquicentennial celebration at the Cradle in Galveston. The capsule is to be opened during the Texas Bicentennial in 2036.

The DRT has sponsored the publication of several volumes of Texas history and biography and has published the lineages of its members in the multivolume *Founders and Patriots of the Republic of Texas* (1963–). Since 1928 the DRT has sponsored an annual fellowship, named for Clara Driscoll in 1930, awarded to a University of Texas student doing research on the state's his-

tory. In 1986 the association established the Texas Sesquicentennial Fellowship under the same guidelines.

Mrs. Grady Rash, Jr.

Davis, Edmund Jackson. Governor; b. St. Augustine, Florida, 2 October 1827; d. Austin, 7 February 1883; m. Anne Elizabeth Britton (1858); 2 sons. Davis moved to Texas in 1848 and was admitted to the bar the next year. He worked as a customs inspector in Laredo (1849–53), as district attorney in Brownsville (1853–), then as judge of the same (Twelfth) district (ca. 1856–). He left the Whig party for the Democratic party, opposed secession, fled the state in 1862, then raised and commanded the First Texas Cavalry, USA during the Civil War. After capture, release, and promotion to brigadier general, he commanded Gen. Joseph J. Reynolds's Union cavalry in the Division of Western Mississippi. He joined the Republican party after the war, served in two constitutional conventions (1866, 1868–69), and upheld the *ab initio* theory, which stated that state laws made in the Confederacy were invalid. He was elected governor in 1869. While in office he combated lawlessness with the State Police and upheld various other measures of Radical Republican rule, which were vehemently opposed by the Democrats and often by Republicans. He lost the next gubernatorial election (1873) to Richard Coke by a vote of two to one. Blaming the national Republican administration for his defeat, he stayed in office until

Edmund J. Davis. Courtesy Massachusetts Commandery, Military Order of the Loyal Legion, and the U.S. Army Military History Institute, Carlisle, Pennsylvania.

removed by Democrats. He subsequently headed the state Republican party, ran again for governor and lost (1880), then ran for Congress and lost (1882). He was offered the job of collector of customs in Galveston (1880) but refused it.

Carl H. Moneyhon

Dawson Massacre. An episode of the second of the Mexican invasions of 1842. Capt. Nicholas M. Dawson raised a company of 53 men to respond to Mathew Caldwell's call for troops to fight Adrián Woll's Mexican invaders. While possible reinforcements were occupied elsewhere, Dawson's men met 500 Mexican troops in a mesquite thicket where Fort Sam Houston now stands. The Texans repelled a charge, only to be battered with artillery until, beaten, Dawson tried to surrender. The Mexicans, disregarding the proffered surrender, continued to fire. Heroic in the fight was Griffin, a slave of Samuel A. Maverick, who, his rifle shattered, fought on with a mesquite limb until he was killed. Thirty-six Texans died on the field, fifteen were taken prisoner, and two escaped. The prisoners were marched away to Perote Prison in Mexico. Of these men, only nine survived to return to Texas. Two days after the massacre the Mexican army retreated toward the Rio Grande, and the Dawson men were buried in shallow graves where they fell. *Thomas W. Cutrer*

Dealey, George Bannerman. Newspaperman, civic planner; b. Manchester, England, 18 September 1859, d. Dallas, 26 February 1946; m. Olivia Allen (1884); 5 children. Dealey worked for the Galveston *News*, then for the Dallas *Morning News*, and in 1926 acquired the latter and affiliated publications founded by Alfred H. Belo. He was vitally involved in Dallas civic life and, through the *News*, opposed the Ku Klux Klan, boosted the city, and supported social agencies. He belonged to many press and charitable organizations, as well as the Philosophical Society of Texas. He received three honorary doctorates and is commemorated by the name of Dealey Plaza in Dallas. *Joan Jenkins Perez*

Declaration of November 7, 1835. A declaration of causes for taking up arms against Mexico preliminary to the Texas Declaration of Independence; adopted by the Consultation at San Felipe. Since hostilities had already begun and troops were marching against San Antonio, the Consultation had to justify the war. The peace party, however, feared that Mexican Federalists would interpret the movement as secession and unite with other Mexicans against them. The declaration had to be a strategic document that would justify Texas action in the eyes of the rest of the world and at the same time convince the Federalists that the Texans desired only to preserve the Constitution of 1824. Consultation president Branch T. Archer called for a committee of twelve to draft a declaration and named John A. Wharton as chairman. Preliminary plans by Daniel Parker, Don Carlos Barrett, Robert M. Williamson, and Stephen F. Austin were used in framing the declaration. As adopted, in eight parts, the document declared that the Texans had taken up arms in defense of their rights and liberties and the republican principles of the Constitution of 1824. It stated that Texas was no longer bound by the compact of union but that Texans offered their support to such members of the Mexican confederacy as would take up arms against military despotism, that they would not cease to carry on war against the Centralist authorities while their troops were in Texas, that in the meantime they held it to be

their right to establish an independent government, that Texas was responsible for the debts of her armies in the field and pledged to pay debts contracted by her agents, and that she would reward with lands and citizenship those who volunteered their services in the struggle. Despite some dissatisfaction, the ambiguous declaration was unanimously adopted, and 1,000 copies were ordered printed and distributed.

Defunct Counties. At least 32 legally established Texas counties no longer exist. They fall into five categories: (1) judicial counties, (2) counties established by declaration of the Constitutional Convention of 1868–69, (3) counties established by legislative act but never organized and later abolished by legislative act, (4) counties established outside the present boundaries of Texas, and (5) counties that were renamed. The so-called judicial counties had the same status as constitutional counties except that they were not represented in the Congress of the Republic of Texas. County seats were established; county courts were organized; county judges, surveyors, and land commissioners were appointed. In 1842 the Texas Supreme Court declared judicial counties unconstitutional, principally because the Constitution of the Republic of Texas specified that each county was entitled to at least one member in the House of Representatives. At its first session after the decision, the Congress accepted the invalidity of the judicial counties but passed a law on July 18, 1842, that validated the acts of the surveyors and land commissioners of the defunct counties. The judicial counties were Burleson, Burnet, DeWitt, Guadalupe, Hamilton, La Baca, Madison, Menard, Neches, Panola, Paschal, Smith, Spring Creek, Trinity, Waco, and Ward. The Constitutional Convention of 1868–69, by declaration, attempted to organize Delta, Richland, Webster, and Latimer counties. Probably because of Texas opposition to the Radical Republican convention, the legislature never organized or legalized the counties, and three of them were never more than names. Delta County was reestablished by legislative act in 1870. The five counties authorized by the legislature but never organized were Buchel, Dawson, Encinal, Foley, and Wegefarth. Counties established outside the present boundaries of Texas were Greer, Worth, and Santa Fe, which were formed in areas that became parts of Oklahoma and New Mexico. Renamed counties include: Harrisburg (changed to Harris in 1839), Navasoto (changed to Brazos in 1842), Davis (changed from Cass in 1861 and back to Cass in 1871), Buchanan (changed to Stephens in 1861), and Cibolo (changed from Wilson to Cibolo and then back to Wilson).

DeGolyer, Everette Lee. Geophysicist and petroleum geologist; b. in a sod house near Greensburg, Kansas, 9 October 1886; d. Dallas, 14 December 1956; m. Nell Virginia Goodrich (1910); four children; ed. University of Oklahoma (B.A., 1911). "Mr. De" lived in Missouri mining districts, then in Oklahoma, before working (1906–09) as a cook and then field assistant for the United States Geological Survey in Wyoming, Colorado, and Montana. In 1909 he became head of the exploration staff of El Águila (the Mexican Eagle Oil Company) in Tampico, and the next year he located the Potrero del Llano No. 4 well in the Mexican Golden Lane, one of the world's largest oilfields. He returned (1914) to Oklahoma to run his own consulting office, then in 1916 moved his office to New York. For owner Lord Cowdray, he negotiated the sale of El Águila to the Royal Dutch Shell Company in 1918.

Everette Lee DeGolyer (seated) and Leon Russ at the Potrero del Llano No. 4 oil well, near Tuxpan, Mexico, ca. 1915. Courtesy DeGolyer Library, Southern Methodist University; Ag83.283.2. DeGolyer located this well, one of the most famous in the history of the petroleum industry, when he was 24.

Cowdray then commissioned him to organize the Amerada Petroleum Corporation for exploration in the United States and Canada and the Rycade Oil Company for exploration of salt-dome lands bordering the Gulf of Mexico. In 1926 DeGolyer became president and general manager of the corporation and its affiliates. In 1922, through Rycade, he instigated a torsion balance survey at the Spindletop oilfield, the first geophysical survey of an oilfield in the United States. At Nash in 1924, Rycade located what became the first oilfield discovered by geophysical methods. In May 1925 DeGolyer organized a subsidiary of Amerada, the Geophysical Research Corporation, which located a record 11 Gulf Coast salt domes in 9 crew months and perfected a reflection seismograph that has become the principal tool for geophysical oil exploration worldwide. This technology inaugurated the modern age of oil exploration with the 1930 discovery of the Edwards oilfield in Oklahoma.

In 1932 DeGolyer resigned from all Amerada enterprises, moved to Dallas, and initiated a number of prospecting concerns, such as Atlatl Royalty Corporation (1932), the Felmont Corporation (1934), and, with John Clarence (Karch) Karcher and Eugene B. McDermott, Geophysical Service, Incorporated, a seismic contracting company. He also established Core Laboratories, Incorporated (1932), and Isotopes, Incorporated (1956), to adapt radioactive isotopes to industrial use. He reorganized his consulting practice in 1936 with Lewis MacNaughton. DeGolyer served as a director of a number of companies, including Transwestern Oil Company, Texas Eastern Gas Transmission Corporation, Southern Pacific Railroad Company, Dresser Industries, and the United States and Foreign Securities Corporation. During World War II he served as director of conservation in the Office of the Coordinator for National Defense (1941–42). As assistant deputy administrator of the Petroleum

Administration for War, he headed its mission to Mexico in 1942 and the Petroleum Reserve Corporation's mission to the Middle East in 1943–44. He was chief of the technical advisory commission to President Roosevelt at the Teheran Conference. His continued government service after the war included membership on the National Petroleum Council and the National Security Resources Board, and advisory functions for the Atomic Energy Commission and the International Scientific Conference on Conservation and Utilization of Resources.

DeGolyer was director of the American Petroleum Institute for more than 20 years and a founder of the American Association of Petroleum Geologists. He received the association's highest honor, the Sidney Powers Gold Medal, in 1950. He was also a fellow of the Geological Society of America, the American Association for the Advancement of Science, the British Institute of Petroleum, and other professional societies. He was an honorary member of the National Research Council, the National Academy of Sciences, the Society of Exploration Geophysicists, Sigma Xi, Phi Beta Kappa, the Texas Academy of Science, and the Texas Institute of Letters. He was also a trustee of the Texas Research Foundation. He became the first "oilman" president of the American Institute of Mining and Metallurgical Engineers (1927) and was awarded its Anthony F. Lucas (1941) and John Fritz (1942) medals. In 1939 he received the Distinguished Service Award of the Texas Mid-Continent Oil and Gas Association and, in 1948, the Distinguished Service Citation of the University of Oklahoma. He was inducted into the Oklahoma Hall of Fame in 1952.

DeGolyer contributed prolifically to the literature of his own science and assembled one of the world's best libraries for the history of science, which he donated to the University of Oklahoma. He was also associate editor of the *New Colophon* and the *Southwest Review* and chairman of the editorial board of the *Saturday Review of Literature*, of which he gained controlling interest in 1948. He was a student of the early Spanish exploration of the Southwest and wrote the 1930 *Encyclopaedia Britannica* biographical entry on General Santa Anna. He donated his collection of first and rare editions of modern American and English writers to the University of Texas (Austin), where he served as distinguished professor of geology in 1940. His collection of works on oil and gas law and western and Mexican history makes up part of the DeGolyer Library holdings at Southern Methodist University. DeGolyer is recognized as the "father" of American geophysics and was for a long time the world's leading oil consultant. His unorthodox acceptance of the European plastic-flow theory of the origin and nature of salt domes and his consequent development of the tools capable of subterranean prospecting revolutionized oil exploration, though he was convinced of the role of luck in his own success. Viewing science and technology as the key to wealth with its political ramifications, DeGolyer believed that the function of science was to serve the economy. He held seven honorary doctorates, lectured at MIT and Princeton, and was a regent of the Smithsonian Institution. He was a Congregationalist, a Republican, and a Mason. After seven years' suffering from aplastic anemia, he committed suicide.

Joan Jenkins Perez

De León, Alonso. Spanish explorer and governor; b. Cadereyta, Nuevo León, 1639 or 1640; d. Coahuila, 20 March 1691; m.

Agustina Cantú; survived by 6 children. At the age of 10 De León, whose father was also named Alonso, was sent to Spain, where he enrolled in school and prepared for a naval career. He joined the Spanish navy in 1657, but his service as a naval cadet was brief, for he had returned to Nuevo León by 1660. Over the next two decades he led a series of entradas that traversed the northeast coast of New Spain as well as the banks of the Río de San Juan. By the 1680s De León had become a seasoned outdoorsman and successful entrepreneur. In 1682 he petitioned the viceroy of New Spain for a franchise to work salt deposits along the Río de San Juan, open trade with neighboring settlements, and search for mines. Those efforts netted a 15-year concession. When news that the French had founded a settlement on the northern Gulf Coast reached New Spain in the mid-1680s, De León was a logical choice to lead overland efforts aimed at finding the foreign interlopers and extirpating their colony. In all, he led four expeditions between 1686 and 1689. His initial reconnaissance followed the Río de San Juan to its confluence with the Rio Grande. After striking the larger river, Don Alonso marched along the right bank to the coast and then turned southward toward the Río de las Palmas (the Río Soto la Marina). This effort yielded no conclusive evidence that Frenchmen had visited the region. His second expedition set out in February 1687. This entrada forded the Rio Grande, probably near the site of present Roma–Los Saenz, and followed the left bank to the coast. De León then marched up the Texas coast to the environs of Baffin Bay but again found no evidence of Frenchmen. The third expedition, launched in May 1688, was in response to news that a white man dwelled among Indians in a *ranchería* (temporary settlement) to the north of the Rio Grande. That effort resulted in the capture of Jean Jarry, a naked, aged, and confused Frenchman. The fourth expedition left Coahuila on 27 March 1689, with a force of 114 men, including chaplain Damián Massanet, soldiers, servants, muleteers, and the French prisoner, Jarry. On 22 April De León and his party discovered the ruins of the French settlement, Fort St. Louis, on the banks of Garcitas Creek. In 1687 De León became governor of Coahuila. Three years later he and Massanet cooperated in founding the first Spanish mission in East Texas, San Francisco de los Tejas, at a site in the environs of present Augusta, Texas. De León, an honest soldier and an early pathfinder in Spanish Texas, left the future Lone Star State for the last time in July 1690. He is credited with being an early advocate for the establishment of missions along the frontier, and he blazed much of the Old San Antonio Road on his expeditions. His descendants still reside in the Mexican state of Nuevo León. *Donald E. Chipman*

De León, Martín. Empresario; b. Burgos, Nuevo Santander, 1765; d. Texas, 1833; m. Patricia de la Garza (1795); 10 children. The De Leóns were an aristocratic family of great wealth; members were educated in Madrid, Paris, and London and were acquainted with European rulers. Martín, however, declined his father's offer to complete his education in Monterrey and Europe, choosing instead to become a merchant and supplier of provisions to the miners of Real de San Nicolás. In 1790 he joined the army to fight Indians in Nuevo Santander. He was promoted to captain, thus achieving the highest rank available to a criollo. Ten years after his marriage, he established a ranch in Texas between Chiltipin Creek and the Aransas River, stocked it with cattle, horses, mules, and goats that he brought from Mexico, and enclosed several leagues of land with a brush fence in an effort to corral and domesticate mustangs. In 1807 and 1809 he petitioned Governor Manuel María de Salcedo for the right to establish a colony, but was refused both times as a result of rising political troubles in Mexico and rumors that the De Leóns were not loyal to Spain. De León then established a new ranch on the east bank of the Nueces River near the site of present San Patricio, where he enclosed another pasture. He had by this time driven several herds of livestock to market at New Orleans, thus becoming one of the earliest traildrivers in Texas. Texas presidio garrisons were moved as a result of the Hidalgo uprising in September 1810. Because the frontier then became vulnerable to hostile Lipans and Comanches, De León removed his family to the safety of San Antonio, where he joined the Republicans in resisting the Royalists under Joaquín de Arredondo and Ignacio Elizondo. After a respite in Burgos in 1816 De León returned to his ranch and cattle, now numbering about 5,000 head. In 1823 he drove a large herd of livestock to New Orleans and became interested in settling a colony on the lower Guadalupe River.

Mexican independence from Spain brought a more open colonization policy. In 1824 De León successfully petitioned the provincial delegation at San Fernando de Béxar to settle 41 Mexican families on the lower Guadalupe and founded the town of Nuestra Señora Guadalupe de Jesús Victoria. Patricia De León contributed $9,800 and cows, horses, and mules valued at $300, which she inherited from her father. De León was the only Mexican empresario in Texas, and his colony was the only one populated mainly by Mexicans. As a Mexican citizen he received legal preference in the numerous border disputes with American settlements encircling Guadalupe Victoria. Indians called him "Capitán Vacas Muchas" ("Captain Plenty of Cows") since he often placated raiding parties by feeding them beef. His five-league (22,140-acre) ranch was located on Garcitas Creek in what is now southeastern Victoria County and probably included the site of Fort St. Louis. His thousands of cattle carried the first brand in Texas, an E and J connected, signifying "Espíritu de Jesús." De León registered the historic brand in 1807; Jesuits had used it for hundreds of years before the royal De León family in Spain adopted it. De León's ranchland, though considerably less extensive than that of later cattlemen, provided a foundation for Texas ranching. As a devout Catholic, De León was planning to build a church without rival in Texas when he became a victim of the cholera epidemic of 1833 and died.

In addition to dominating Guadalupe Victoria, the family of Martín De León controlled the ayuntamiento of Goliad; sons-in-law José Miguel Aldrete and Rafael Manchola each served as alcalde, and Manchola was also commandant of the La Bahía garrison. The family was intimately involved with the Texas cause against Antonio López de Santa Anna as well. Gen. José M. J. Carbajal and Capt. Plácido Benavides were sons-in-law of De León. Martín's sons contributed horses, mules, cattle, military equipment, and provisions to the Texas army and offered the safety of their ranches to colonists needing refuge. Not surprisingly, the Mexican army of occupation under Gen. José de Urrea singled out the De León family as traitors and arrested two of De León's sons. After the Texas victory at San Jacinto, the De Leóns fell victim to the prejudice directed against Texans of Mexican descent. Agapito De León, Martín's son, was murdered by Mabry B. (Mustang) Gray, who was rustling De León cattle. Son Fernando was wounded in a similar affray. The De León,

Benavides, and Carbajal families were forced to abandon their lands, cattle, and most possessions and flee to Louisiana for their lives. The De Leóns remained in New Orleans for about three years before moving to Soto la Marina (now in Tamaulipas), the childhood home of Patricia de la Garza De León, where her daughter Agustina De León Benavides died in 1841. Soon thereafter, Patricia and her family returned to Texas to recover their property, but they were largely unsuccessful. In April 1972 the De Leóns were honored with Texas state historical markers in Evergreen Cemetery, Victoria. Among the dignitaries attending the dedication were Patricia De León, great-granddaughter of the empresario, and Dr. Ricardo Victoria of Mexico, great-grandson of President Guadalupe Victoria, for whom Victoria, Texas, is named.   *Craig H. Roell*

Dell Computer Corporation. Originally PC's Limited; designs, manufactures, sells, and services IBM-compatible personal computers. The company was founded in 1984 by Michael S. Dell, then an 18-year-old freshman at the University of Texas at Austin. Intrigued by computers during his teens, Dell turned a hobby of building customized computers into a company that pioneered the marketing and sale of personal computer systems by telephone. In 1984 he purchased an Austin business license and incorporated PC's Limited. In 1985 the company introduced an IBM-compatible PC clone called the Turbo. By selling computer components and kits by telephone and advertising in trade magazines, Dell built a clientele of businesses and experienced computer users. His familiarity with the marketing potential of telephone sales gave Dell a competitive advantage over larger rivals IBM and Compaq, who, like the vast majority of computer makers, sold their products through high-markup retail outlets. By building computers only to order, the company lowered inventory costs. By the end of the company's first fiscal year, sales totaled $6 million. Following a low-price leader strategy, PC's Limited grew exponentially. In 1987 the company took its founder's name and became Dell Computer Corporation. Dell next opened its first sales office in Great Britain, printed its first catalog, began selling application software, and established a support center to handle customer inquiries. The company further differentiated itself from IBM, Compaq, and other mail-order rivals by introducing next day on-site service free for a period after purchase through such third-party service companies as Honeywell Bull, along with unlimited telephone technical support and a money-back guarantee. In 1988 Dell Computer Corporation made an initial public offering of common stock and subsequently opened wholly owned subsidiaries in Canada and West Germany. By late 1989 the company had 1,600 employees worldwide, had introduced its first 316LT laptop computer, and had opened a French subsidiary. In 1990 the company announced an agreement with Soft Warehouse, Incorporated (Comp USA), then the largest computer superstore chain in the United States, to sell Dell products. In 1991 the firm opened a manufacturing plant in Limerick, Ireland. As competitors began to imitate its telephone-sales strategy, Dell became the first PC manufacturer to offer free installation of applications software with the purchase of a computer. In 1992 Dell entered into a third-party maintenance agreement with BancTec Service Corporation and announced Critical Care, a new and even more rapid response system for customer service problems. Michael Dell dedicated the Michael S. Dell Computer Lab at the University of Texas at Austin, was appointed to the board of directors of the Foundation for the National Technology Medal, and was named Man of the Year by *PC Magazine*. In 1992 the company was named to the Fortune 500 list of the country's largest manufacturers. By 1993 the company was listed among the Fortune 500, owned 14 international subsidiaries, employed more than 4,800 workers, sold computer products in more than 70 countries, generated sales of over $2 billion dollars, and was the world's fourth-largest computer maker.   *Jon Kutner, Jr.*

De Luxe Show. In Houston in 1971; one of the first racially integrated exhibitions of contemporary artists in the United States. The show occurred in the remodeled De Luxe Theater in the Fifth Ward, 22 August to 29 September. The Menil Foundation sponsored the exhibition. In 1968 the Black Emergency Cultural Coalition had been formed to lobby for exhibitions using works of black artists, after the Metropolitan Museum of Art (New York) organized the exhibition Harlem on my Mind with only limited input from Harlem artists. In 1971 the coalition called for a boycott of the Whitney Museum's exhibition Contemporary Black Artists in America because black participation in its organization was limited. Critical response centered on black political reaction, with little discussion of the art itself. Two exhibitions organized by the Menil Foundation in 1971 for the Institute for the Arts at Rice University provided the immediate backdrop for the De Luxe Show. Some American History (February–April 1971), an exhibition on slavery and black life in America, was criticized in the national press for focusing on the work of white artist Larry Rivers; the six black artists who assisted Rivers were dissatisfied with their role in the project. The Menil Foundation subsequently decided call on black leaders to coordinate the De Luxe Show. For Children (May–August 1971), a popular exhibition that encouraged playful interaction with paintings and sculpture, prompted the idea of exhibiting black art in one of Houston's poor neighborhoods.

John De Menil approached painter Peter Bradley, an associate director of the Perls Galleries in New York, and Bradley agreed to curate the show after the decision was made to include artists of both races. Menil also enlisted the aid of two instructors from Texas Southern University: Jefferee James, who publicized the show, and community leader Mickey Leland, who helped to select the site and coordinate the exhibition. The De Luxe Theater had provided a safe, family-oriented alternative to other black neighborhood movie theaters when it opened in April 1941. It had fallen into decay after movie theaters were integrated and was closed in 1969. With the help of Rice University Institute for the Arts, Jones and Bynam Construction Company transformed the old theater into an exhibition space in just three weeks. To emphasize the historical significance Bradley left the façade, lobby, and balcony intact. The balcony was walled off so that old westerns and horror movies could be shown there, and the rest of the interior was gutted, sheetrocked, and coated with two layers of white paint for an exhibition area measuring approximately 50 by 80 feet. Two rows of theater seats, the only other remnant of the past, were left in the center of the exhibition space to facilitate relaxed viewing.

Bradley selected 40 abstract works by 19 contemporary artists, some well known and some not. Artists Sam Gilliam and Kenneth Noland, critic Clement Greenberg, other community organizers and neighborhood members, and Institute for the

Arts staff assisted Bradley. Huge posters depicted the exterior of the De Luxe in black and gray, and flyers, bumper stickers, and newspaper, radio, and television advertisements publicized the event as "hard art at the De Luxe Show." When the show opened, more than 1,000 people attended to view abstract works by such painters as Peter Bradley, Virginia Jaramillo, Ed Clark, Larry Poons, Jules Olitski, and William T. Williams. Sam Gilliam's sensuously draped canvas *Rather* (1970) and Alvin Loving's untitled arrangement of brightly colored cubes vied with the minimalist constructions of Richard Hunt and Anthony Caro for sculptural interest. The exhibition was hailed by critic Eleanor Freed as a "challenging social and visual experiment" that brought painting and sculpture to a part of Houston "better known for urban decay than aesthetics." By the time the exhibition closed, more than 4,000 people had seen it. The gallery–theater remained open as a display location for African art from the Menil collection and, until 1976, for the Black Arts Center.   *Kendall Curlee*

Democratic Party. State laws dictate formal party organization in Texas and provide for both temporary and permanent organs. The temporary party organs consist of a series of regularly scheduled (biennial) conventions beginning at the precinct level and limited to persons who voted in the party primary. The chief function of the precinct convention is to choose delegates to the county convention or the senatorial district convention held on the second Saturday after the first primary. When a county has more than one senatorial district because of its large population, a separate senatorial district convention is held for each Senate district in the county. The delegates who gather at the county and the senatorial district conventions are likewise chiefly concerned with choosing delegates to the state convention held biennially in June for the purpose of formally choosing the state executive committee, adopting a party platform, and officially certifying the party's candidates to be listed on the general election ballot. In presidential election years the state convention also chooses delegates to the national presidential nominating convention. Until 1984 two state conventions were held in gubernatorial years, one for state affairs in September and one for sending delegates to the national Democratic convention. The permanent organs of the party are largely independent of the temporary ones. Voters in the Democratic primary in each precinct elect for a two-year term of office a chairman or committee person who is formally the party's agent or spokesman in that precinct. A few of these precinct chairmen work diligently for the party and its nominees; some do very little. Normally the precinct chairman will be in charge of the conduct of the primary in his precinct, and, perhaps less assuredly, will serve as chairman of the precinct convention and of the delegation to the county convention. The party's county executive committee consists of the precinct chairmen plus a county chairman who is elected in the primary by the Democratic voters in the county as a whole. The county committee determines policy in such matters as the conduct and financing of the primary, and officially canvasses its results. It also serves as a focal point for party organizing and campaigning efforts.

The State Democratic Executive Committee includes one man and one woman from each of the 31 state senatorial districts, plus a chairman and a vice-chairman, formally chosen by the state convention but informally chosen by a caucus of the delegates from each senatorial district. Occasionally a governor

and his advisers will decide that a caucus nominee is simply unacceptable and then will substitute his own choices. By law the state committee is responsible for overseeing the party primary and for canvassing the returns. It also undertakes fund-raising and campaign work for the party. Before Republican Bill Clements' election as governor in 1978, the committee's role was to serve as an adjunct of the governor's office, designed to help the governor as best as it could with political and policy problems. However, after Clements was elected, the party and its machinery developed a new degree of independence from the governor.

The Democratic party has played a central role in the political development of Texas since white Americans settled the region. The majority of early settlers came from the American South and brought their past political allegiances with them. Texas Democrats evolved over the years from a very loose association into an organized party. This evolution was slow because the lack of a second party in Texas throughout much of the state's history caused Democrats to be less concerned with developing a unified, centralized party organization and more inclined to engage in factional strife. Throughout much of its existence, the Democratic party has been protective of the status quo.

The history of the party in Texas can be divided into two major periods. In the first period, from independence in 1836 through the presidential election of 1952, the Democratic party in Texas was the only viable party in the state. It dominated politics at all levels. In the second major period, after 1952, the party faced a growing challenge to its control of state affairs from the once ineffective Republican party. Both of the major periods, however, can be subdivided. The years 1836 through 1952 divide into six subsections: from independence in 1836 through the Civil War, Reconstruction, the late 19th Century, the Progressive Era, the 1920s, and the New Deal–World War II era. The latter period divides into three subsections: the 1950s, the 1960s, and the 1970s and 1980s.

Several crucial events marked the years 1836–65 in Texas political history, including the independent nationhood of the Republic of Texas, entrance into the Union, and secession and the Civil War. During these years the Democratic party officially formed in Texas and consequently shaped, and was shaped by, these events. Even before Texas gained its independence from Mexico the Democratic party in the United States influenced the politics of the region. As early as 1822, with the formation of the Texas Association in Russellville, Kentucky, individuals interested in land speculation came together to secure land grants in Texas. The Texas Association drew its membership from professionals—merchants, doctors, and lawyers—in Kentucky and Tennessee. Many of these men were also close friends of Andrew Jackson and had strong ties to the Democratic party. Likewise, most of the settlers in Texas were either from the Upper South or the Lower South and held strong allegiances to the Democratic party. Elections in the Republic of Texas demonstrated competition among rival factions or strong individuals. Despite sympathy for the Democratic party in the United States, as yet there was no strong party tradition in the Republic of Texas. Before 1848, elections in Texas were conducted without organized political parties. Personality was the dominant political force. Contests between factions evolved into a more defined stage of competition with the development of the Democratic party in Texas as a formal organ of the electoral process during the 1848 presidential campaign. Even so, it was some time before Democrats adopted any sort of a statewide network or arranged for scheduled conventions.

Nevertheless, between annexation and 1861 partisanship developed slowly but steadily. Men who governed the state generally reflected the views of the burgeoning Democratic party. However, personal loyalty such as that found in the factions supporting and opposing Governor Sam Houston (1859–61) still heavily influenced state politics. Competition for the Democrats came from various sources at different times and included first the Whig party, then the American (Know-Nothing) party, and finally the Opposition or Constitutional Union party. The mid-1850s witnessed rapid growth of the formal mechanisms of party discipline. For example, delegations from 12 counties attended the state Democratic convention in 1855, yet the following year, with the Know-Nothing threat still seemingly viable, more than 90 percent of Texas counties were represented. During these years the convention system became the chief method of recruiting candidates for office in the Texas Democratic party. In the years after 1854 the ongoing upheaval in national politics influenced the party. In the process Texans moved away from an earlier identification with Jacksonian nationalism and became closely associated with the states'-rights goals of the lower South. Yet the election of Houston as governor in 1859 demonstrated the divisions within the state's political structure, since he represented the Opposition in the contest against the Texas Democratic party. During the Civil War, the Democratic party in Texas became closely associated with the extreme proslavery wing of the Democratic party in the Confederacy, and partisan activity came to a halt.

In the immediate aftermath of the Civil War, during the period of presidential Reconstruction, the split between Unionist and Secessionist Democrats reemerged. During the war the strongest Unionists had disappeared from the political scene or moved north. Of those who stayed active, many reluctantly supported the Confederacy. After the war the Unionists continued to support a more egalitarian distribution of power in the state, while working to reduce the influence of former planters. But they split also. Their positions on freedmen ranged from supporting full civil and political rights to opposing anything beyond emancipation. In part as a result of the split among Democrats but more as a result of congressional Reconstruction nationally, Republicans captured both the governor's office and the state legislature in 1869. By 1872 Democrats regrouped and overturned the Republican government in the Texas legislature, charging that the administration of Governor Edmund Davis (1870–74) was corrupt and extravagant. Much of the money appropriated during Republican control had in fact gone to frontier defense, law enforcement, and education. Davis had two more years in office, but he could do little with a Democratic legislature pledged to austerity. In the gubernatorial election of 1873, the Democratic campaign theme included support for states' rights, loyalty to the Confederacy, and an attack on freedmen and Republicans. The final Democratic measure to overturn all Republican influence in Texas came with the passage of the Constitution of 1876, which severely constrained the powers of the state government, cut back on state services and limited the amount of money that could be raised in taxes.

The Democrats' return to power at the end of the Reconstruction era did not mean an end to factional divisions within the state. Like the rest of the nation, Texas faced various third-party challenges during the Gilded Age, a fact that reflected a growing uncertainty about economic conditions. In 1876, however, the state Democratic party continued to focus its attention on the concerns of the Civil War era. In fact, the majority of the delegates to the state Democratic convention were Confederate veterans. Democratic voters were often white landowning agrarians, manufacturers, lumbermen, bankers, shippers and railroad men, and Protestants. Indeed the conservative political moods of the state through the late 1880s can be attributed to the growing cult of the Confederacy throughout the South. Against this backdrop a vote against the Democratic party became a vote against the cultural legacy of the "Lost Cause." Party organization also encouraged more Southern loyalist candidates through the convention process. After 1878 Texas Democrats had trouble adjusting to the various third-party challenges of the late nineteenth century, as demonstrated by conflicting responses to the Greenback party. At times Democrats endorsed even more drastic inflationary measures, but at other times they bitterly attacked financial views that encouraged printing of additional paper money. In the end the Greenback challenge forced Texas Democrats to pay attention to the economic problems of the state. By the 1880s the issue of prohibition also began to cause problems for Texas Democrats, who initially sought to dodge the question by calling for local-option elections. Nevertheless, prohibition politics evenly split the party and laid the ground for bigger battles in the early twentieth century.

In the 1880s and 1890s Texas Democrats faced an even bigger challenge, first from the Farmers' Alliance and then from the People's (Populist) party. Maintaining an official posture apart from organized politics, the Farmers' Alliance sometimes worked with the state Democratic party. By the late 1880s Texas Democrats recognized the agrarianists' demands and adopted a platform supporting the abolition of national banks, issuance of United States currency, and the regulation of freight rates and businesses. The election of James Stephen Hogg as governor in 1890 temporarily allied the agrarian protest with the Democratic party. Hogg's efforts on behalf of the newly constituted Railroad Commission divided the Democratic party into three factions: businessmen who sought to limit the commission's impact, leaders of the Farmers' Alliance who sought to dominate the commission, and farmers, businessmen, and politicians who supported Hogg. Alliancemen soon split further away from Hogg and the majority of Texas Democrats over the idea of subtreasuries. By the 1890s Texas Democrats had given their support to silver coinage. In the years after 1896 most Populists in Texas returned to the Democratic party because Democrats had incorporated portions of the Populist platform and economic conditions for farmers had improved, while segregationism discouraged economic cooperation with African Americans.

In the first two decades of the twentieth century the party split into a "progressive" wing that increasingly identified with the demands of prohibitionists and a stand-pat wing opposed to progressivism. The reality of one-party politics in Texas and the South paved the way for factional splits, such as the one over the prohibition issue during the first third of the twentieth century. Personality also played a key role in the split in the Democratic party when the progressive forces within the party banded together to squelch the influence of United States senator Joseph Weldon Bailey in state politics. The "Bailey question" became associated with the perceived evils of corporate power and swollen private interests in the public domain. Yet reforms during the 1890s and early 1900s had reduced the influence of railroads, out-of-state corporations, and insurance companies in state politics, leaving moral and cultural problems to consume the attention of Progressive Era reformers. During the presidential election of 1912 a common thread connecting the progressive Democrats supporting Woodrow Wilson and the advocates of prohibition became apparent. In the immediate aftermath of Wilson's election Texas Democrats—including Albert S. Burleson, Thomas Watt Gregory, Edward M. House, David F. Houston, and Morris Sheppard—established an important precedent for Texas Democrats by taking a significant role in national political affairs that continued throughout the twentieth century. In 1914 personality again ruptured the Democratic party in Texas with the election of James Ferguson as governor. Ferguson sought to avoid the liquor question entirely, although his sympathies and his big contributors were wet. His official actions as governor, including an ongoing battle with the state's cultural and intellectual elite at the University of Texas, eventually united progressive Democrats in their opposition to him. After Ferguson was impeached, dry, progressive Democrats aligned with the new governor, William P. Hobby, Sr. (1917–21), and enacted their agenda of liquor reform, woman suffrage, and reform of the election laws.

For Texas Democrats the decade of the 1920s was a bridge between the ethnocultural issues of the Progressive Era and the economic concerns of the Great Depression and the New Deal. During World War I, Texas Democrats had addressed many issues of the Progressive Era and found legislative solutions, leaving Texans to argue over the results of Prohibition for the next decade. But Texas Democrats, like their counterparts throughout the South, soon shifted their goals for reform away from a social and cultural agenda toward what can best be described as business progressivism, or an increased concern for expansion and efficiency in government. Yet they did not limit their attention to issues such as highway development, economic growth, and education improvement, but also joined numerous intraparty battles revolving around the enforcement of prohibition, the Ku Klux Klan, and "Fergusonism." Despite the fact that Pat Neff's gubernatorial administration (1921–25) fostered the cause of business progressivism with such measures as government consolidation, prison reform, education reform, highway construction, and industrial expansion, the legislature was not willing to accept all of Neff's ideas. The result was a mixed record on business progressivism. The state elections in 1924 quickly evolved into a fight over the Klan issue. Furthermore, the presence of Ma Ferguson as the leading anti-Klan candidate further weakened the progressive Democratic forces in the state. However, electing Mrs. Ferguson did have one ameliorative affect on Texas politics, namely the elimination of the Klan as a political force. The other major political development in Texas during the 1920s centered around the 1928 presidential election. In Texas, as in the rest of the nation, the contest served to heighten the tensions between wet and dry Democrats. In the fall of 1927 several young Democrats who opposed Prohibition organized to fight the entrenched dry progressive wing of the state Democratic party and to work for an uninstructed delegation to the national convention that eventually endorsed Al Smith. They regarded Governor Dan Moody (1927–31) as their leader. The

selection of Houston as the host city for the Democratic national convention further enlivened Texas politics as Smith's backers and the bone-dry forces maneuvered for control of the state's delegation and Moody's support.

In the spring of 1928 the dry progressive Democrats formed the Texas Constitutional Democrats to gain control of the state's party machinery and to work for a presidential ticket that reflected their views. Governor Moody led a third group, the Democrats of Texas or the Harmony Democrats, that eventually organized to prevent a bitter feud between the warring factions of the party and to try to develop a common program. These factional divisions within the party resulted in a bitter division both among delegates at the Houston convention and within the state Democratic party. Some of the state's most ardent Democratic supporters of Prohibition put principles above party and worked for the Republican nominee Herbert Hoover in the general election rather than support the Catholic wet candidate, Al Smith. The Klan faction of the Democratic party, although waning in influence, also informally supported Hoover. Dry voters in rural North and West Texas and urban voters influenced by the Klan and Republican prosperity in Harris, Dallas, and Tarrant counties account for most of the Democrats who went with Hoover. The Republicans also did well among fundamentalists. Hoover was the first Republican presidential nominee to carry Texas, but it was all for naught. The depression, the New Deal, and World War II put Republican ascendancy in Texas on hold for 24 years.

Economic crisis followed by recovery dominated the period 1932–52 in Texas politics. The early New Deal years yielded a period of political harmony within the state's Democratic party, but by the late 1930s conservative forces had regrouped and regained control of state politics. At the same time liberal factions began to exert pressures on the political process that did not subside for the remainder of the twentieth century. In the years immediately following the stock-market crash in 1929, controversies surrounding the oil and gas industry, the agricultural depression, the return of Fergusonism, and the rapid passage of New Deal legislation that overshadowed state and local efforts to combat the depression paralyzed state government and the Democratic party in Texas. At the same time, Texas Democrats in Washington, including Jesse H. Jones, John Nance Garner, Tom Connally, Marvin Jones, James P. Buchanan, Hatton W. Sumners, Wright Patman, and Sam Rayburn, exerted significant influence after the election of Franklin D. Roosevelt. By the mid-1930s the depression became the single most important issue in state politics. As yet, little conservative opposition to New Deal reforms had coalesced in Texas. In 1934 Texas voters elected James Allred governor. His administration attempted to deal with the impact of the depression on the state by reorganizing state law enforcement, putting a state tax on chain stores, increasing assistance to the elderly, starting a teachers' retirement system, and increasing funding to public schools. Allred's advocacy of these measures earned him the respect and admiration of the liberal wing of the state Democratic party.

By 1936 conservative reaction to the national Democratic party erupted in the formation of the Jeffersonian Democrats. This national organization received significant aid from several prominent conservative Texas Democrats including John Henry Kirby, Joseph Weldon Bailey, Jr., and J. Evetts Haley. Though the Jeffersonian Democrats had little impact on the 1936 election, they did foreshadow political trends of the 1940s and 1950s.

Indeed the election of "Pappy" O'Daniel as governor in 1938 signaled the return to power of the conservative wing of the Democratic party in Texas. Though O'Daniel's campaign rhetoric appealed to impoverished Texans still suffering the effects of the depression, his financial supporters and policy advisors were generally drawn from the state's business and financial leaders. The battle over a third term for Roosevelt also divided the party. When many Texas Democrats encouraged the unsuccessful presidential candidacy of Vice President John Nance Garner, the party split between Garner Democrats, including many of the old Jeffersonian Democrats, and the New Deal Democrats. The 1940 fissure remained throughout the coming decade as conservatives and liberals fought for control of the party. But attention to foreign policy during World War II temporarily slowed the battles between the factions.

The politics of race, however, renewed tensions within Texas when the Supreme Court overturned the state's white primary law in *Smith v. Allwright* (1944). The success of the white primary as a method of controlling access to the ballot box was closely tied to the fortunes of the Democratic party. The device went through several changes throughout its existence, but it relied heavily on a solid Democratic dominance that made a Democratic primary victory tantamount to election. In 1927 in *Nixon v. Herndon* the United States Supreme Court had struck down a Texas law preventing blacks from voting in the Democratic primary. The Texas legislature then authorized the Democratic State Committee to exclude blacks, and, when the Supreme Court overturned this law in *Nixon v. Condon* in 1932, Texas repealed the law and left control of the primary entirely with the Democratic party. Since no state action was now involved in the committee's decision to exclude blacks from the Democratic primary, in 1935 the court held the new Texas arrangement valid in *Grovey v. Townsend*. Then came *Smith v. Allwright*. Though it initially opposed the decision, the Texas Democratic party came to rely on black voters.

More important at the time, however, the presidential election of 1944 heightened tensions between the Roosevelt and anti-Roosevelt wings of the party. FDR's renomination for a fourth term led conservative Texas Democrats to join with the American Democratic National Committee, an organization formed to defeat the president. Texas conservatives received support from the same individuals who had aided the Jeffersonian Democrats a decade earlier. Wealthy Texas conservatives with an interest in the increasingly powerful oil and gas industry funded the conservatives, who controlled about two-thirds of the delegates to the state Democratic convention in May 1944. National convention delegates from Texas thus supported the conservative anti–New Dealers, but angry liberals rejected the actions of the state convention and sent their own delegation to the national convention. The New Deal Democrats in Texas barely regained control of the state party's machinery at the governor's convention in September. However, conservative Texas Democrats organized into the Texas Regulars and arranged for the placement on the November ballot of an independent slate of electors who would never vote for FDR. The Texas Regulars received less than 15 percent of the state vote; they and their conservative backers learned that a strong voice in state politics would not translate directly into influence on national politics. Despite the persistent loyalty of the majority of the state's voters to the Democratic party, the widening schism between the fac-

tions indicated that a growing number of Texans were receptive to more conservative politics both within and outside the traditional Democratic party. Indeed actions including the appointment of conservative businessmen to state boards and commissions and the passage of a right-to-work law that Texas governors, all Democrats, implemented during the 1940s reflected the dominant conservatism of the state.

The 1948 Senate race in Texas exemplified many of the tensions within the state party. Lyndon B. Johnson, who eventually defeated Coke Stevenson in an election fraught with charges of wrongdoing on both sides, represented the difficulties liberal New Dealers faced when they attempted to campaign statewide. To appeal to a conservative but Democratic electorate required pragmatic compromise. By the end of the 1940s the Democratic party in Texas had split at least three ways—into a conservative wing that usually controlled state politics, a liberal wing that had supported the New Deal and that later championed the rights of women, the working class, and ethnic minorities, and a group in the middle that shifted back and forth between the two extremes. By the middle twentieth century the Texas Democratic party was riven by factional strife. The liberal–conservative Democratic split also aided the development of a viable state Republican opposition. In the years after the 1952 presidential election a two-party system began to emerge. The gubernatorial administration of Allan Shivers (1949–57) and the efforts of the liberal opposition to reclaim power within both the state party machinery and the state government dominated state Democratic politics during the 1950s. During the 1950s Texas Democrats also wielded significant power in Washington, with Sam Rayburn as speaker of the House and Lyndon Johnson as Senate majority leader. Texas Democrats Oveta Hobby and Robert Anderson held cabinet appointments during the Eisenhower administration. After becoming governor, Shivers took control of the party machinery by instituting a purge of the State Democratic Executive Committee, an organization with two members from each state Senate district, and stacking its membership with his supporters. Shivers also engineered a change in the election laws that permitted cross-filing for both the Democratic and Republican primaries in the 1952 election. As a result of the change, conservative Democrats, termed "Shivercrats" because of their allegiance to the governor, also filed in the Republican primary, thus reducing the number of Republicans that ran for office.

The ongoing struggle with the federal government over control of the Texas Tidelands further complicated the 1952 election in the state. Though federal ownership of the submerged oil-rich lands would benefit Texas in terms of royalty payments, oil and gas interests in the state stood to profit more if the state retained possession of the Tidelands. Conservative Democrats took the lead in championing native interests, which were backed by most Texans as well. Liberal and moderate Democratic politicians, who had stronger ties to the administration of President Harry S. Truman and the national Democratic party, found themselves in a more precarious position and either carefully balanced their support for Texas ownership of the Tidelands with the larger national interests or opposed Texas ownership altogether.

Following the triumphs of Eisenhower and Shivers in 1952, liberals in the Texas Democratic party decided to organize and increase their influence on party politics. In May 1953 the short-lived Texas Democratic Organizing Committee was formed. By

January 1954 this group became part of the newly constituted Democratic Advisory Council. The DAC participated in Texas politics for two years before the Democrats of Texas organized in 1956. The DOT, the most successful of the three groups, lasted through 1960 before disbanding. Each of these groups received support from the liberal weekly journal of political information, the *State Observer* and its 1954 successor, the *Texas Observer*. Each of these liberal organizations also received support from labor and a number of women activists. The goals of the groups focused on taking control of the official machinery of the Texas Democratic party away from the Shivers forces. In 1956 Johnson and Rayburn battled Shivers, the nominally Democratic governor who had helped deliver the state's votes to Eisenhower in 1952, for control of the Democratic party machinery. Three main groups—the Shivercrats or conservative Democrats, moderate Democratic backers of LBJ, and the liberals—engaged in this intraparty battle that featured mistrust, mudslinging, shifting alliances, and ultimately a deeper division within the party. The Republicans, with the help of Shivers, managed to carry Texas for Eisenhower again in 1956. The following year liberal Democrats in Texas fought back against the strength of the Shivercrats, and Ralph Yarborough's narrow victory in the 1957 special United States Senate race gave the liberal wing of the Texas Democratic party a new elected voice in national politics.

Factional infighting in the Democratic party declined during the 1960s. First Johnson's presidential ambitions and then his presidency dominated Texas politics in that decade. In 1959 the state legislature authorized a measure moving the Democratic primary from July to May and permitting candidates to run simultaneously for two offices, thus allowing Johnson to run for the Senate and the presidency. (This measure, dubbed the LBJ law, also benefited Lloyd Bentsen's dual run for the vice-presidency and the Senate in 1988.) Despite efforts by the Democrats of Texas to secure the support of state convention delegates and power within the party machinery, conservative Democrats retained control. Through the work of LBJ and the Viva Kennedy–Viva Johnson clubs, the Democrats narrowly carried Texas in 1960, reversing the direction of the 1952 and 1956 presidential elections in Texas. Similarly, the 1961 special election to fill Johnson's Senate seat had a lasting effect on Democratic party organization in Texas.

After Yarborough's unexpected victory in the 1957 special election, conservative Democrats in the state legislature amended the election laws to require a run-off in special elections when no candidate received at least 50 percent plus one vote. In 1961, within a field of 72 candidates, 3 individuals made a strong claim for the liberal vote, thus dividing liberal strength and opening the way for a runoff between William A. Blakley, the interim senator and a conservative Texas Democrat, and John Tower, the only viable Republican candidate in the race. Liberal Democrats thought Blakley as conservative as Tower and opted either to "go fishing" during the run-off or support Tower, thinking it would be easier to oust him in 1966 with a more liberal Democratic challenger. Tower, however, easily won his next two reelection bids and eked out a third in 1978. Liberals also hoped that a Republican victory would encourage the development of an effective Republican party in the state and allow moderates and liberals to gain control of the state Democratic party. Indeed, Texas Democrats statewide remained divided between liberals who supported Yarborough and moderates who

backed LBJ. The two factions waged war over the gubernatorial contest in 1962, when John B. Connally, a moderate to conservative Democrat associated with the Johnson wing of the party, was elected. As governor, Connally concentrated his efforts on economic development but received criticism from liberals who thought he neglected minorities and the poor. The Kennedy assassination on 22 November 1963, which traumatized the citizens of Texas, also deeply shook the state Democratic party since it propelled Johnson into the White House and compelled a greater degree of accommodation between moderate and liberal Texas Democrats. In the 1964 presidential race Johnson carried his home state with ease. In the middle to late 1960s, however, Connally's iron rule of the State Democratic Executive Committee further weakened the liberal forces within the state Democratic party. The results of the 1968 presidential election in Texas also emphasized the sagging fortunes of the Democratic party in Texas, as Hubert Humphrey barely managed to carry the state.

Liberals in the Texas Democratic party reached a low point in 1970 with the defeat of their spiritual leader, Ralph Yarborough, in the Democratic primary by conservative Democrat Lloyd Bentsen, Jr. Bentsen successfully employed a strategy that conservative Democrats in Texas later used against the increasingly viable Republican party, namely, developing a base of support among middle to upper income voters in the primaries, then drawing from the traditional Democratic constituencies of lower income people, labor unions, and minorities in the general elections.

The 1972 gubernatorial election marked the culmination of a gradual transition in Texas Democratic party politics from an era when elite leaders fighting behind closed doors over a conservative or liberal agenda dominated party politics to an era of moderation and greater toleration for differing views. This contest took place against the backdrop of the Sharpstown Stock Fraud Scandal in the Texas state legislature. The scandal ended the political careers of Governor Preston Smith, Lieutenant Governor Ben Barnes, and Speaker of the House Gus Mutscher, all of whom were closely tied to the old Democratic establishment. The two front-runners in the race, Frances (Sissy) Farenthold and Dolph Briscoe, benefited from the public backlash against incumbents. The contest between Farenthold and Briscoe also reflected the nature of the transition at work in the Democratic party. Farenthold drew her strength from liberals and college students. But in his victory the politically conservative Briscoe effectively split the liberal coalition by securing the neutrality of organized labor. The trend was toward more moderate, establishment-backed Democratic candidates.

In the 1972 presidential election the GOP again demonstrated that it could carry Texas in national contests. In fact, from 1976 through 1992 Democratic presidential candidates failed to win Texas. Republicans also proved they could successfully challenge Democrats for control of state politics when Bill Clements won the governor's race in 1978. His victory further sparked the ascendancy of the moderates in the Democratic party, and in 1982 a new generation of Democrats came to power in Texas. The warchests of incumbent United States senator Lloyd Bentsen and incumbent lieutenant governor William P. Hobby, Jr., aided the election bids of challengers Mark White for governor, Jim Mattox for attorney general, Ann Richards for state treasurer, Gary Mauro for land commissioner, and Jim Hightower for

✦VIEWS OF DENISON, TEXAS, AND VICINITY✦

Verkin & Enos, Photo. View and Crayon Artists, 103 Main St.

An orderly collection of businesses on Main Street, ca. 1889–1890. Stereograph by Verkin & Enos. Lawrence T. Jones III Collection, Austin. By 1889 Denison was a retail and shipping center for North Texas.

agricultural commissioner, all of whom won in the general election. These candidates benefited from and represented the more moderate to liberal position of the state Democratic party.

In the 1970s and 1980s the Democratic party in Texas also appeared more open to the interests of women and minorities. Groups such as the Mexican American Democrats and Texas Democratic Women gained a greater voice in party affairs. Also, women and members of minorities could now be found in elected positions from the governor down. Nevertheless, the state GOP continued to gain strength into the early 1990s, demonstrating its ability to compete not only in gubernatorial and senatorial races but in such down-ballot offices as state treasurer, agriculture commissioner, state Supreme Court justice, and railroad commissioner, as well as in various county and local posts. By 1990 Republicans also held about a third of the seats in both houses of the state legislature.

In the early 1990s the GOP also successfully gained control of about a third of the Texas congressional delegation. Before the 1950s, Democrats had controlled the entire delegation. In 1993 the GOP held both United States Senate seats in Texas after Lloyd Bentsen became secretary of the treasury. The growing strength of the Republican party among the Texas delegation served to dilute the power of Texas Democrats in Washington. Compared with the 1950s, when Rayburn and Johnson controlled the House and Senate as speaker and majority leader, Texas Democrats in the 1980s and 1990s managed to retain only a few key chairmanships in Congress. However, after the election of William J. Clinton as president in 1992 Texas Democrats played a role in the executive branch, with Bentsen at the Treasury Department and

Henry Cisneros as secretary of housing and urban development, despite the fact that Clinton did not carry Texas. Previously, Democrats had to win Texas in order to win the presidency; no Democrat had won the White House since Texas entered the Union in 1845 without carrying the state. But Clinton was elected, and Texas Democrats' political clout in Washington declined.

The Republican lock on about a third of the state's electorate by the early 1990s had a double impact on the Democratic party. It encouraged the development of a more moderate leadership for party machinery and pushed some individual Democratic candidates to try to appear more conservative than their Republican challengers. Thus, even though the fledgling GOP in the 1950s and 1960s developed on the political right, the hopes of liberal activists in the 1950s and 1960s for establishing a liberal Democratic party in Texas were at best only partially successful, since the revamped moderate Democratic party had difficulty retaining control of elected offices in the state. In 1994 Republicans regained the governor's office, retained the office of agricultural commissioner, gained all three seats on the Railroad Commission, and picked up two congressional seats.

Nancy Beck Young

Denison, Texas. Seven miles north of Sherman in northeastern Grayson County. In the early 1870s William Benjamin Munson, Sr., and R. S. Stevens bought land in the area in anticipation of the arrival of the Missouri, Kansas and Texas Railroad. The townsite was laid out in 1872 and named for the vice president of the railroad, George Denison. The town incorporated the following year, when it had 3,000 inhabitants. Additional rail links were added between 1875 and 1900, and the town became a major retail and shipping point for North Texas. Denison's population passed 10,000 in 1900, was 13,850 in 1936, and reached 21,505 in 1990. During the twentieth century industrial and manufacturing plants provided a diversified economic base for the city; electronic parts, clothes, furniture, and a variety of plastic goods are among the products manufactured in Denison. The Eisenhower Birthplace State Historic Site commemorates the Denison birthplace of Dwight Eisenhower. *David Minor*

Deno, Lottie. Gambler; b. Warsaw, Kentucky, 21 April 1844; d. Deming, New Mexico, 9 February 1934; m Frank Thurmond (1880); probably named Carlotta J. Thompkins at birth. Her wealthy father, a planter, took her with him abroad and entertained her at the finest gambling casinos. After he was killed in the Civil War, Lottie was sent Detroit to find a proper husband, accompanied by her nanny, a seven-foot-tall black woman named Mary Poindexter. In Detroit, Lottie met a Jewish jockey, Johnny Golden, who had ridden for her father. The two went gambling together down the Ohio and Mississippi. Lottie's Christian mother disowned her. In 1863 Lottie and Johnny parted with plans to meet in San Antonio. Lottie and Mary arrived there in 1865, but Johnny did not show up for five years. During that time Lottie became a house gambler at the University Club, where she worked for the Thurmond family and was smitten with Frank Thurmond. Lottie was known in San Antonio as the "Angel of San Antonio." In 1869 she followed Frank to West Texas—leaving the newly arrived Johnny behind—after Frank supposedly killed a man in a gambling altercation. She gambled at Fort Concho, Jacksboro, San Angelo, Denison, Fort Worth, and eventually Fort Griffin. Johnny Golden, jilted in San Antonio, killed a man there and became an outlaw. In Fort Concho, Lottie had been called Mystic Maud. In Fort Griffin she began to call herself Lottie Deno, a name supposedly derived from a card game she was suspected of cheating; one player suggested she should call herself "Lotta Dinero." Golden followed Lottie to Fort Griffin and was killed there within a day after finding her. Frank Thurmond was there under the alias Mike Fogerty. Lottie's gambling opponents included Doc Holliday and other well-known western figures. She left Griffin in May 1877 to join Frank in Kingston, New Mexico. There the two ran a small gambling room on the rear of the Victorio Hotel. Later Lottie owned the Broadway Restaurant in Silver City, where Lottie and Frank were married. In 1882 they moved to Deming, where they lived as respected citizens. Frank became a miner and eventually vice president of the Deming National Bank. Lottie became a founding member of St. Luke's Episcopal Church. Frank and Lottie were immortalized as Faro Nell and Cherokee Hall in a series known as the Wolfville books, written by Alfred Henry Lewis. Lottie was also the prototype for Miss Kitty in the television series "Gunsmoke" and for Laura Denbo in Leon Oris's movie *Gunfight at the OK Corral* (Paramount, 1957). *Cynthia Rose*

Denton, Texas. County seat of Denton County, less than 40 miles north of the Dallas–Fort Worth metropolitan area. The community was founded as the county seat in 1857 and named, like the county, for John B. Denton. Denton incorporated in 1866 and slowly grew to a population of 1,194 in 1880. The following year

the Texas and Pacific and the Missouri, Kansas and Texas railroads provided rail connections between the city and Dallas, Fort Worth, and Sherman, and Denton's population more than doubled by 1890. Lack of east–west rail connections hindered the city's development into a major manufacturing and wholesale center, but Denton became a college town when North Texas Normal College (now the University of North Texas) was established in 1890 and the Girl's Industrial College (now Texas Woman's University) was established in 1903. By the 1980s, with a total enrollment of almost 25,000 students, the two universities provided half the city's population and greatly influenced its cultural and economic life. In 1960 the Denton State School, a school for the mentally retarded, was established. Denton has grown rapidly in recent decades, increasing from 26,844 in 1960 to 66,270 in 1990. Proximity to Dallas–Fort Worth, the expansion of the two universities, the increasing diversity of Denton's industrial concerns in the 1960s and 1970s and the presence of nearby Dallas–Fort Worth International Airport since 1974 explain much of the city's growth. *E. Dale Odom*

Denton State School. A facility for the mentally retarded on a 200-acre tract four miles south–southeast of Denton; managed by the Texas Department of Mental Health and Mental Retardation; serves 22 counties. After a vigorous lobbying effort by the Denton Chamber of Commerce, MHMR chose Denton as the site for the state school because of the city's proximity to Dallas and Fort Worth and because of its universities—Texas Woman's University, which at that time (1957) had the largest nursing program in the state, and North Texas State University, which had the largest teacher-training facility in Texas. The city also donated land purchased by residents' contributions. Construction was completed in July 1960. Originally, the school accepted only citizens of Texas between the ages of 6 and 21 with IQs of 70 or below. By 1980, however, the age restriction had been removed. E. W. (Ed) Killian, the school's first superintendent, had a 20-year tenure. In 1994 the school had more than 60 buildings and 2,000 employees serving 670 residents and a large number of off-campus clients. School programs included vocational services and early childhood intervention. The school also directed outreach community service in 12 counties. A foster-grandparent program enabled senior citizens to give one-to-one attention to residents at the school. The state has provided more than 90 percent of the school's funding; the United States departments of Health and Human Services, Agriculture, and Education have also contributed. *David Minor*

DeWitt, Green. Empresario; b. Lincoln County, Kentucky, 12 February 1787; d. Monclova, Coahuila, 18 May 1835; m. Sara Seely (1808); at least six children. DeWitt served in the Missouri state militia in the War of 1812 and was for a time sheriff of Ralls County, Missouri. Inspired by Moses Austin, in 1822 he petitioned the Mexican government for an empresario contract but was unsuccessful. He journeyed in 1825 to Saltillo, where he petitioned the state government for a land grant. Aided by the Baron de Bastrop, he was awarded an empresario grant to settle 400 Anglo-Americans on the Guadalupe River and was authorized to establish a colony adjacent to Stephen F. Austin's, subject to the Colonization Law of 1824. DeWitt brought to Texas his wife, two sons, three of four daughters, and three other families (1826). The group joined those already in the colony, who eventually settled at Gonzales. For almost the next decade DeWitt worked to develop the colony. Noah Smithwick later said that DeWitt "was as enthusiastic in praise of the country as the most energetic real estate dealer of boom towns nowadays." Because the Mexican government had inadvertently included the earlier colony of Martín De León within DeWitt's grant, the two empresarios had numerous disputes involving boundaries and contraband trade. DeWitt represented the District of Gonzales in the Convention of 1833 but never held an elected office in the colony's government. He was unable to fulfill his contract by the time it expired in 1831. He spent his last years engaging in some limited commercial investments and improving his own land on the right bank of the Guadalupe across from the Gonzales townsite. Having apparently invested all his family's resources in his struggling colony, he endorsed his wife's petition in December 1830 to the ayuntamiento of San Felipe de Austin asking for a special grant of a league of land in her maiden name "to protect herself and family from poverty to which they are exposed by the misfortunes of her husband." The Mexican government complied in April 1831. DeWitt issued a handwritten land-scrip currency to his colonists, one of the earliest examples of Texas paper currency. He journeyed in 1835 to Monclova, where he hoped to buy unlocated 11-league grants from the governor, but he failed to acquire any land. He probably died of cholera, and was buried in an unmarked grave. His wife and daughter, Naomi, cut up Naomi's wedding dress to make the "Come and Take It" banner that his fellow colonists adopted as their battle flag early in the Texas Revolution. *Edward A. Lukes*

Diamond Bessie Murder Trial. A sensational nineteenth-century Texas trial. A well-dressed man and woman calling themselves "A. Monroe and wife" got off a train and registered at the Brooks House in Jefferson on 19 January 1877. A. Monroe was really Abraham Rothschild, the traveling-salesman son of Meyer Rothschild, a Cincinnati jeweler. He had met Bessie Moore at a brothel in Hot Springs, Arkansas, several years before. Although they traveled together as husband and wife, there is no evidence that they ever married. Two days before, they had arrived in Marshall by train and registered at the Old Capital Hotel as A. Rothschild and wife. On the Sunday morning after their arrival in Jefferson, Abe bought two lunches for a picnic from Henrique's Restaurant, and the couple were seen disappearing into the fog as they crossed the footbridge over Big Cypress Creek. Abe returned to town that afternoon by another path and was seen casually going about his affairs. When asked about his wife, he replied that she was in the country visiting friends and that she would meet him Tuesday morning to leave town. But on Tuesday morning the staff of the Brooks House found room 4 empty and "A. Monroe" gone. Witnesses later stated that Rothschild had left town alone on Tuesday morning on the eastbound train with the couple's luggage. A week of snow and bad weather followed this, and after it began to warm up, Sarah King found the body of a well-dressed woman, without jewelry, near a twisted oak. The remnants of a picnic lunch were also found near the tree. The coroner ruled that the woman was killed by a gunshot wound in the head. The citizens of Jefferson took up a collection and buried the unidentified body at Oakwood Cemetery. An initial warrant was issued for the arrest of A. Monroe on suspicion of murder. After determining that Monroe had left on an eastbound train and that in Marshall he

and Bessie had registered as A. Rothschild and wife from Cincinnati, Ohio, a new warrant was issued for Abraham Rothschild of Cincinnati, and the victim was identified as Bessie Moore. Meanwhile, in Cincinnati, Rothschild had been drinking heavily and swore someone was following him, after which he walked into the street and attempted to kill himself, but only succeeded in blinding his right eye. While he was in the hospital he was arrested, and Texas and Marion County officials were sent to Cincinnati to identify and extradite him. Rothschild's family put up a fight, but on March 19 extradition was approved.

The trial was notorious. Most of the lawyers in East Texas tried to become involved either on the side of the state for prestige or on that of the defense for the Rothschild money. The governor of Texas personally sent a letter to two attorneys, Campbell and Epperson, appealing for aid with the prosecution, and two Texas assistant attorney generals were involved. The defense had an impressive array of legal talent including a future governor of Texas, Charles Culberson, and a United States senator, David B. Culberson. The jury in the first trial found Rothschild guilty of first-degree murder and sentenced him to hang. Tradition says that during jury deliberation over the verdict, jury foreman C. R. Weathersby drew a noose on the wall, signed it, and stated that that was his verdict. On appeal to the Seventh Texas Court of Appeals, the trial was deemed unfair, and Judge J. Clarke declared a mistrial. The state issued another indictment against Rothschild on 2 December 1880, and the second trial began on 14 December in Jefferson. The defense focused on the testimony of Isabelle Gouldy, one of the women who had prepared the body of the victim for burial, who claimed to have seen the victim in the company of a man who was not the defendant on Saturday, 20 January, and Thursday, 25 January. Although the prosecution attacked Gouldy's credibility, the defense managed to plant a seed of doubt in the jurors' minds. Also, Rothschild's lawyers argued that the body was too well preserved to have been in the woods for 15 days and that the murder must therefore have happened after their client left town. On 30 December 1880, the jury found Rothschild not guilty.

There the actualities of the case ended and the rumors began. Many stories about the case and Rothschild circulated during and after the trial, and some of them became part of the folklore surrounding the trial. Several rumors concerning the jury were heard. It was said, for instance, that 12 $1,000 bills were lowered into the jury room during deliberations, and that all 12 jurors met violent deaths within a year of the trial. The rumor that a hack was waiting outside the door of the courthouse and that the verdict was not announced until after the train whistle blew has not been substantiated; nor has the rumor that Rothschild was later imprisoned on a 20-year sentence for grand theft. The popular rumor that Bessie was pregnant when she died has also never been proved. In the 1890s a handsome, elderly man wearing a patch over his right eye asked to be shown the grave of Bessie Moore. Upon seeing it, he laid roses on it, knelt in prayer, commented on the goodness of the citizens to provide a decent burial, and gave the caretaker money for the care of the grave. Folklore asserts that this was a repentant Rothschild visiting the grave. In the 1930s a headstone mysteriously appeared on the grave where none had been before. In 1941, E. B. McDonald admitted putting up the stone because he had thought it wrong for Diamond Bessie to sleep in an unmarked grave. In the 1960s the Jessie Allen Wise Garden Club built an iron fence around the grave. The case, still officially listed as unsolved, attracts many investigators and lawyers to this day. Since 1955 a courtroom drama relating the story has been presented each spring as part of the Jefferson Historic Pilgrimage. *Walter F. Pilcher*

Dickinson, Susanna Wilkerson. Alamo survivor; b. Tennessee, ca. 1814; d. Austin, 7 October 1883; m. Almaron Dickinson (1829); one daughter. The Dickinsons moved from Tennessee to Green DeWitt's colony. Susanna and her daughter may have joined other families hiding in the timber along the Guadalupe River during the battle of Gonzales (October 1835). Almaron left to fight the Mexicans, and Susanna joined him in San Antonio; there she lodged in Ramón Músquiz's home, opened her table to boarders (among them David Crockett), and did laundry. On 23 February 1836 the family moved into the Alamo. After the battle of the Alamo on 6 March, Mexican soldiers found her and took her and her daughter, Angelina, along with the other women and children, to Músquiz's home. The women were interviewed by Santa Anna, who gave each a blanket and two dollars in silver before releasing them. Legend says that Susanna displayed her husband's Masonic apron to a Mexican general in a plea for help and that Santa Anna offered to take Angelina to Mexico. Santa Anna sent Susanna and her daughter, accompanied by Juan N. Almonte's servant, Ben, to Sam Houston with a letter of warning dated 7 March. On the way, the pair met Joe, William B. Travis's slave, who had been freed by Santa Anna. The party was discovered by Erastus (Deaf) Smith and Henry Wax Karnes. Smith guided them to Houston in Gonzales.

Susanna probably followed the army eastward in company with the other Gonzales women. Illiterate, without family, and only 22 years old, she petitioned the government meeting at Columbia in October 1836 for a donation, but the proposed $500 was not awarded. She needed a male protector, and by June 1837 she was cohabiting with John Williams, whom she married that year. He beat her and Angelina, and she petitioned in Harrisburg (later Harris) County for a divorce, which was granted on 24 March 1838—one of the first divorces in the county. By 1839 Almaron Dickinson's heirs had received rights to 2,560 acres for his military service; they sold the land when Angelina reached 21. Subsequent requests to the state legislature in November 1849 were turned down. Susanna tried matrimony three more times before her union with Francis P. Herring (1838), who died in 1843. In 1847 she married Pennsylvania drayman Peter Bellows. In 1850, 16-year-old Angelina was living with them. By 1854 Susanna had left Bellows, who charged her with adultery and prostitution when he filed for divorce in 1857. She may have lived in the Mansion House Hotel of Pamelia Mann, which was known as a brothel, before marrying Bellows. Nevertheless, Susanna received praise from Baptist minister Rufus C. Burleson for her work nursing cholera victims in Houston, where he baptized her in Buffalo Bayou (1849). Susanna married Joseph William Hannig in Lockhart in 1857. They soon moved to Austin, where Hannig became prosperous with a cabinet shop and later a furniture store and undertaking parlor; he also owned a store in San Antonio. Hannig buried Susanna in Oakwood Cemetery. Even though he married again, he was buried next to her after his death in 1890. *Margaret Swett Henson*

Dies, Martin, Jr. Congressman; b. Colorado City, 5 November 1900; d. Lufkin, 14 November 1972; m. Myrtle Adams (1920); three sons; ed. National University, Washington (law degree, 1920). Dies was elected to his father's old seat in Congress in 1930; he was the youngest member of Congress. He achieved fame as the first chairman of the House Un-American Activities Committee, established in 1938 to investigate subversion. The Texas Senate established a similar committee to ferret out communists at the University of Texas in 1941 but could not discover any. Dies ran unsuccessfully for the United States Senate in 1941, finishing last in a four-way race won by Lyndon B. Johnson. In 1944 he announced his retirement after the CIO launched a vast voter-registration drive and found a candidate to oppose him. In 1952 he won election to a new congressman-at-large seat, but he was not allowed to return to the HUAC, which believed that he had damaged the cause of anticommunism. When he ran for the Senate in the special election of 1957, state leaders such as Johnson and Sam Rayburn, believing that Dies was too conservative to defeat liberal challenger Ralph Yarborough, attempted to pressure him out of the race in favor of Lt. Gov. Ben Ramsey. Their effort failed, however, and Dies lost to Yarborough. Dies practiced law in Lufkin between terms in Congress and after declining to run for reelection in 1958. He continued to warn that the United States was succumbing to communism. He wrote *Martin Dies' Story* (1963) and was the putative author of *The Trojan Horse in America* (1940), actually written by J. B. Matthews. From 1964 to 1967 Dies was a popular writer in *American Opinion* magazine. *George N. Green*

Diga Colony. A self-help community established at San Antonio in 1932 by Maury Maverick. It started as a city-sponsored relief effort for destitute World War I veterans, many of whom had returned from the unsuccessful Bonus March on Washington, D.C. As the tax collector of Bexar County, Maverick witnessed firsthand the ravages of the Great Depression. He was especially concerned about veterans because he was a disabled veteran himself. He became involved in "Grocery Balls" and other efforts to provide relief for the destitute. When the veterans moved into a municipal park in San Antonio, the city began to provide limited help. Maverick was appointed by the mayor as director of the War Veterans Relief Camp. Even though the veterans were moved to the fair grounds at Exposition Park, it soon became apparent that facilities in the city were neither large enough nor appropriate for the growing number of homeless people. Maverick secured land about five miles from the city from the Humble Oil Company for a dollar a year. He was able to get discarded railroad boxcars from the Missouri Pacific Railroad; these he had moved to the site and remodeled into living quarters. Maverick's name for the colony was made up from the words "Agricultural and Industrial Democracy." The new site developed quickly into a community organized along military lines with a commander, daily orders, and regular military-type reports. Residents numbered 171 in January 1933. R. R. Rogers, the camp commander, reported directly to Maverick, who did not live in the community. Property was held in common, and people had to give up their possessions to join—a relatively small sacrifice, since few of them had anything to give up. Members were required to give a portion of their earnings from outside employment to the community treasury. During the short existence of the community, Maverick did all he could to make it successful and well-known. He even had a medal struck to commemorate the venture. A library was set up, and various liberal and radical publications, some of which Maverick wrote, were made available to the residents. Maverick later bemoaned the fact that the residents were not really susceptible to radicalization. He said they were more concerned about jobs and food in their stomachs than about changing the world. By late April 1933, Maverick's poor health forced him to give up his association with the community, and he left the state for medical help. After Franklin D. Roosevelt took office in 1933 and launched the New Deal, direct federal relief programs replaced some of the aid that people received through the community; Diga had received some government funds from the Reconstruction Finance Corporation. The exact date of the end of the experiment is not known. After Maverick's association ended, internal squabbling and bickering became more serious. Camp commander Rogers became very unpopular and a center of controversy. The community was still in existence in October 1933, but nothing beyond that date can be ascertained for certain.

Donald W. Whisenhunt

Dimmitt, Philip. A hero of the Texas Revolution; b. Jefferson County, Kentucky, ca. 1801; d. Saltillo, August 1841; m. María Luisa Lazo. His last name is spelled several different ways. Dimmitt traveled to Texas about 1823 with a letter of introduction to Stephen F. Austin. He settled in La Villita at Bexar and for several years was commissary contractor to the Mexican garrison there. His wife's father was a De León colonist and kinsman of Martín De León. By his marriage Dimmitt received a three-league headright in De León's colony. He acquired a fortune by operating trading posts on the Guadalupe River near Victoria, at Goliad, and at Dimitt's Landing on Lavaca Bay, where he established a wharf and warehouse. He also fought Indians on the Nueces River. In 1835 he purchased land from an original member of the Power and Hewetson colony, but hostilities with Mexico interrupted his family's resettlement. When George M. Collinsworth's Matagorda volunteers arrived at Guadalupe Victoria en route to capture Goliad, Plácido Benavides, Silvestre De León, José M. J. Carbajal, Dimmitt, and some 30 Mexican rancheros joined the expedition, though most did not sign the "Compact of Volunteers" drafted on 9 October 1835. At Victoria, Dimmitt received word that Mexican general Martín Perfecto de Cos had left La Bahía with only a skeleton garrison and was en route to Bexar. Collinsworth's force then attacked and captured Goliad, and soon La Bahía was reinforced with additional volunteers, who elected Dimmitt captain. He commanded Goliad from about 14 October 1835 to about 10 January 1836. He was particularly well informed about activities in northern Mexico through various members of the De León family and his brother, who lived in Zacatecas. Though the capture of Goliad gave the Texas army needed provisions, Dimmitt supplied the army as well from his own warehouses.

On 21 October 1835, he issued an "Appeal to the Inhabitants of Texas Residing East of the Guadalupe" for support. To show his allegiance to the Mexican Federalists, he designed the green–white–red tricolor flag that later became the traditionally recognized banner of the Texas force in the battle of the Alamo. In time, however, he came to support Texas independence—but not without conflict with Austin, who held out longer for support of the Constitution of 1824. About 6 December 1835 Dimmitt and a small force proceeded to Bexar and participated in the final assault against Cos that ended the siege of Bexar. He

returned to Goliad about 14 December and designed what has been called the first flag of independence, depicting a bloody arm holding a bloody sword on a white field, which was raised on 20 December 1835 at La Bahía to commemorate the Goliad Declaration of Independence. Dimmitt's garrison was an independent command composed of volunteers who captured and garrisoned La Bahía. It received great praise from acting governor James W. Robinson for gathering provisions, arms, and horses, which were supplied to the revolutionary army and to refugees at Refugio, Goliad, and Victoria. When Francis W. Johnson and James Grant arrived at Goliad with a force en route to capture Matamoros, in the Matamoros Expedition of 1835–36, both men, being loyal to the Constitution of 1824 and antagonistic toward Dimmitt, and each thinking himself to be commander of the Texas army, demanded that the bloody-arm flag of independence be lowered and seized the garrison's transportation stock and many supplies. These actions induced Dimmitt to resign his command on or about 10 January 1836 and discharge his men, many of whom subsequently served with Francis W. Thornton, who assumed command of Goliad.

Dimmitt arrived at Bexar about 24 January with about 30 volunteers to reinforce the Alamo and was appointed army storekeeper; his warehouse at Dimmitt's Landing then served as a depot for government stores landed at Lavaca Bay. Though many of the volunteers returned home upon the arrival of William B. Travis and his men on 3 February, Dimmitt remained in San Antonio scouting for Travis and Bowie until 24 February. He was with B. F. Nobles when the two were cut off by the arrival at Bexar of the Mexican army. Dimmitt retreated to the vicinity of Victoria, where until early March he operated a station to recruit volunteers to relieve the Alamo. On 12 March Sam Houston ordered Dimmitt to join him at Gonzales, and though he had recruited but 21 volunteers, rumors spread that he headed a force of 200 to relieve Fannin at Goliad or Travis at Bexar. Dimmitt arrived at Gonzales to find it occupied by the Mexican army. After a fight on Kerr Creek, his force retreated down the Guadalupe River to Victoria. The men arrived on 19 March exhausted and without food and learned the next day of Fannin's surrender. Mexican general José de Urrea entered Victoria on the twenty-first, and Dimmitt apparently helped with evacuations and joined the refugees in the Runaway Scrape. After 15 April he arrived on Matagorda Island to bring recruits to General Houston's army, which was then moving to San Jacinto, and with John J. Linn he arrived on 22 April 1836, bringing the first supplies and reinforcements to Houston's victorious army after the battle of San Jacinto.

After the revolution Dimmitt settled in Refugio, where he became a justice and continued in business. On 4 July 1841 he and some comrades were captured by Mexican troops who were looting in the area. The Centralist government in Mexico had issued a warrant for Dimmitt's arrest for his role in the Texas Revolution, particularly for the Goliad Declaration of Independence. He was taken to Matamoros. Mass meetings held at Aransas City, Lamar, Refugio, and Victoria demanded that the Texas government obtain the hero's release and threatened private retaliation. In September President Lamar sent Henry Lawrence Kinney to Mexico to petition for Dimmitt's release, but he was unsuccessful. Dimmitt and his comrades, together with 19 other Texans, were put in irons and marched to Monterrey in August 1841 en route to prison in Mexico City. At

Saltillo the Texans tried to escape by drugging their guards with alcohol laced with morphine. Eighteen escaped, but 11 were overtaken and shot. Dimmitt, separately confined and unable to escape, overheard that he would be shot if the fugitives did not surrender. Facing either execution or interminable imprisonment, he chose to take his own life by morphine overdose, remarking: "I do not fear death but dread the idea of ending my life in a loathsome dungeon. Tell them I prefer a Roman's death to the ignominy of perpetual imprisonment, and that my last wish is for my country's welfare." His regard for his country was evident even in his children's names, which included Antonio Alamo Dimmitt and Texas Philip Dimmitt. In 1858 Dimmit County was established and named in his honor.

Craig H. Roell

Dirt Farmers' Congress. On invitation by the Texas legislature, farmers and stock raisers met in Austin in February 1939 to counsel the legislature. This meeting, known as the "Dirt Farmers' Congress," was made up of representatives of more than 100 counties. It stressed a closer relationship between the producers and industry and requested the legislature to consider such problems as insect and rodent control, conservation of forests and wildlife, soil erosion, and compulsory dog vaccination. The Dirt Farmers' Congress met again with the House of Representatives in 1949, but afterward no more references to it appeared in House journals.

J. C. Conradt

Dixon, Billy. Frontier scout; b. William Dixon, Ohio County, West Virginia, 25 September 1850; d. Cimarron County, Oklahoma, 9 March 1913 (buried at Texline, reinterred at Adobe Walls in 1929); m. Olive King (1894); 7 children. Dixon was orphaned at 12 and lived with an uncle in Missouri for two years, then worked in woodcutters' camps along the Missouri River until he got a job from government freight contractors in Kansas as a bullwhacker and muleskinner. He became a skilled marksman and occasionally scouted for eastern excursionists brought out by the railroads for buffalo hunting. In 1869 he joined a venture in hunting and trapping on the Saline River northwest of Fort Hays. Buyers gave a dollar each for buffalo cow hides and two dollars for bull hides, so Dixon's marksmanship paid off. He invested in a supply store that was successful until 1871, when, during Dixon's absence, the store manager, Billy Reynolds, sold out and took off with the money. At one time Dixon probably had as many as four or five skinners in his employ. He had scouted Texas as far south as the Salt Fork of the Red River when the buffalo hunters moved into the Panhandle in 1874. He and his group hunted along the Canadian River and its tributaries near the new Adobe Walls, not far from the old Adobe Walls built by William Bent around 1843. It was said that after the spring migrations occurred, Dixon could shoot enough buffalo to keep 10 skinners busy, and he found Adobe Walls a convenient place to store his hides. He was one of the 28 men who with one woman participated in the second battle of Adobe Walls in 1874, fighting from inside James Hanrahan's saloon. The story of his famous "long shot"—with which he knocked an Indian off a horse nearly a mile away—may be exaggerated. Dixon himself never claimed credit for it.

He did no more hide hunting after the battle. In Dodge City in August 1874, Gen. Nelson Miles enlisted him as a scout in the detachment commanded by Lt. Frank Baldwin. After his hero-ism in the Buffalo Wallow Fight, Dixon was among the five survivors awarded the Medal of Honor. He was present at the rescue of the German sisters from the Cheyennes in 1874 and was with the party that selected the site of Fort Elliott in 1875. Dixon was attached to that post for duty when he saved the command of the Nolan expedition by leading the men to water (1877). He returned to civilian life in 1883, worked on the Turkey Track Ranch, built a home near the site of the original Adobe Walls, planted an orchard and 30 acres of alfalfa that he irrigated from Bent's Creek, and became postmaster at Adobe Walls, a position he held for 20 years. In 1901 he was elected the first sheriff of the newly formed Hutchinson County but resigned in disgust at the political strife surrounding county organization. In addition, he served as a state land commissioner and justice of the peace. He and S. G. Carter operated a ranch-supply store. For three years after her marriage to Billy, Olive King Dixon was the only woman living in Hutchinson County. The family moved to Plemons in 1902 to provide schooling for their children, but Dixon found small-town life irksome and in 1906 went to homestead in the open spaces of Oklahoma. During his last years he reportedly lived near poverty; friends tried to obtain a pension for him. Dixon Creek in southern Hutchinson County is named for him, as is the Billy Dixon Masonic Lodge in Fritch. Personal artifacts from his scouting days are housed in the Hutchinson County Museum in Borger and the Panhandle–Plains Historical Museum in Canyon.

T. C. Richardson

Dobie, James Frank. Folklorist and writer; b. Live Oak County, 26 September 1888; d. 18 September 1964 (buried in the State Cemetery); m. Bertha McKee (1916); ed. Southwestern University (grad. 1910), Columbia University (M.A., 1914). He moved to Alice at 16, worked two summers as a reporter (for the San Antonio *Express* and then the Galveston *Tribune*), and got his first teaching job in 1910 in Alpine, where he was also the principal, play director, and editor of the school paper. He taught in Georgetown, 1911–13. In 1914 he joined the University of Texas faculty and the Texas Folklore Society. He served in the field artillery in World War I. He resigned his position at the university in 1920 to manage his uncle Jim Dobie's ranch, where his interest in folklore became paramount. Dobie returned to Austin and the university in 1921. In 1922 he became secretary of the Texas Folklore Society and immediately began a publication program. *Legends of Texas* (1924) carried the seeds of many of his later publications. Dobie served as the society's secretary and editor for 21 years and built the society into a permanent professional organization. When the university would not promote him without a Ph.D., he accepted the chairmanship of the English department at Oklahoma A&M, where he stayed from 1923 to 1925. During these two years he began writing for the *Country Gentleman*. With considerable help from his friends on the UT campus, he was able to return in 1925 with a token promotion. Showing the people of Texas and the Southwest the richness of their culture and traditions became his purpose in life. He began writing articles on Texas history, culture, and folklore for magazines and periodicals and soon started to work on a book. His *Vaquero of the Brush Country* (1929) established him as a spokesman of Texas and southwestern culture. It articulated the struggle of the individual against social forces, in this case the battle of the open-range vaquero against barbed wire. Two years later Dobie published *Coronado's Children* (1931), the tales of free

J. Frank Dobie at a barbecue given by Austin writer and publisher Joe Small. Photograph by Russell Lee. Wimberley, ca. 1957. Russell Lee Photograph Collection, CAH; CN 03130.

spirits who abandoned society in the search for gold, lost mines, and various other treasures. It won the Literary Guild Award for 1931 and, combined with his continuing success as a popular writer in *Country Gentleman*, made Dobie a nationally known literary figure. He was promoted in 1933 to professor, the first Texan non-Ph.D. to be so honored at the university. In 1942 he published the *Guide to Life and Literature of the Southwest*, an annotated reading list. As head of the Texas Folklore Society and author of *On the Open Range* (1931), *Tales of the Mustang* (1936), *The Flavor of Texas* (1936), and *Apache Gold and Yaqui Silver* (1939), Dobie was the state's leading spokesman and literary and cultural figure during the Texas Centennial decade, the 1930s. He began writing for the *Southwest Review* in 1919, when it was the *Texas Review*, and continued the association throughout his life. The *Southwest Review* published his *John C. Duval: First Texas Man of Letters* in 1939. His first period of writing ended with the publication of *The Longhorns* in 1941.

Dobie spent World War II teaching American literature in Cambridge. After the war he returned to Europe to teach in England, Germany, and Austria. He said of his Cambridge experience in *A Texan in England* that it gave him a broader perspective, that it was the beginning of his acceptance of civilization, but a civilization enlightened and free of social and political

rigidities and with full respect for individuality. The University of Texas regents, critical of liberal professors, had fired President Homer Rainey in November 1944. Dobie, a liberal Democrat, was outraged and vociferous, and Governor Coke Stevenson said that he was a troublemaker and should be summarily dismissed. Dobie's request for a continuation of his leave of absence after his European tour in 1947 was denied by the regents, and he was dismissed from the UT faculty under what became known as the "Dobie Rule," which restricted faculty leaves of absence to two years except in emergencies. After this separation he devoted all of his time to writing and anthologizing. The next decade saw the publication of *The Voice of the Coyote* (1949), *The Ben Lilly Legend* (1950), *The Mustangs* (1952), *Tales of Old Time Texas* (1955), *Up the Trail From Texas* (1955), and *I'll Tell You a Tale* (1960). Before he died he published *Cow People* (1964) and almost finished the manuscript for *Rattlesnakes*, which Mrs. Dobie later edited and published in 1965. Dobie wrote a Sunday newspaper column from 1939 until his death, and as an outspoken critic of the Texas scene he was a popular subject of newspaper stories. His most celebrated targets were professional educationists ("unctuous elaborators of the obvious"), state politicians ("When I get ready to explain homemade fascism in America, I can take my example from the state capitol of Texas"), Pompeo Coppini's Alamo cenotaph ("From a distance it looks like a grain elevator or one of those swimming pool slides"), and inappropriate architecture (the University Tower "looked like a toothpick in a pie"). His war against bragging Texans, restraints on individual liberty, and the mechanized world's erosion of the human spirit was continual. Four days before his death, President Johnson awarded him the nation's highest civil award, the Medal of Freedom.   *Francis E. Abernethy*

Dr Pepper. The Dr Pepper Company, incorporated in 1923 in Dallas, markets fountain syrups and sells soft-drink concentrates to independent franchised bottlers, who add sweeteners and carbonated water, package the result, and sell the varied finished products. The original beverage was first made in Waco in 1885 by a pharmacist named Charles Courtice Alderton, who was employed by Wade Morrison. Morrison named Alderton's most popular concoction after Dr. Charles T. Pepper, a physician and pharmacist for whom Morrison had worked in Rural Retreat, Virginia. The trademark employed a period after *Dr* until 1950. As demand increased, Morrison and Waco beverage chemist Robert S. Lazenby started the Artesian Manufacturing and Bottling Works (1891). In 1898 the Southwestern Soda Fountain Company of Dallas purchased the rights to produce and sell Dr Pepper fountain syrups. In 1902 Southwestern Soda Fountain changed its name to Dr Pepper Company. Circle "A" Corporation, which purchased Artesian Manufacturing and Bottling Works in 1920, was the only bottler of Dr Pepper concentrate. In 1923 Circle "A" went bankrupt. The same year, the remnants of the old Dr Pepper Company and Circle "A" incorporated as the Dr Pepper Company. The company expanded after the U.S. Fifth District Court of Dallas declared in 1963 that Dr Pepper was not a cola, a ruling that allowed independent bottlers to carry Dr Pepper along with Pepsi-Cola or Coca-Cola; they could now produce Dr Pepper without violating their franchise contracts, which state that bottlers are not permitted to bottle competing brands. Between 1968 and 1977, under CEO Woodrow Wilson Clements, sales increased from $41.9 million to $226.8 million.

However, the company incurred tremendous debts in its acquisition of bottling plants and purchase of Canada Dry in 1982. As market growth leveled off, the soft drink industry became increasingly competitive, and Dr Pepper struggled against increased advertising of Coca-Cola, PepsiCo, and Seven-Up. Market share and rate of growth declined, while the rapid proliferation of brands begun in 1982 by Seven-Up with Like Cola pushed Dr Pepper off the grocer's shelves. In an effort to meet the challenge Dr Pepper concentrated primarily on nation-wide advertising and ignored independent bottlers' needs. Independent bottlers thus no longer pushed Dr Pepper with the same zeal. In 1983 Dr Pepper sought a buyer, preferably a large conglomerate, to increase its competitiveness, but because of the company's poor cash position few companies showed interest. In February 1984 shareholders accepted an offer from Forstmann and Little, a New York investment-banking firm, and the company went private. Subsequently, the company sold a majority of its fixed assets—Canada Dry and all 10 company-owned bottling plants. Nevertheless, Dr Pepper ended its centennial year (1985) with a 7½ percent share of the market as the third-largest soft drink. Dr Pepper merged with Seven-Up in 1986 and soon thereafter moved its manufacturing operations to St. Louis, while keeping its corporate headquarters in Dallas. A collection of Dr Pepper memorabilia forms the core of the Dr Pepper Museum, which opened in Waco in 1991. *Patrick Farl*

Domínguez de Mendoza, Juan. Spanish explorer; b. 1631; death date and place unknown. Domínguez de Mendoza went to New Mexico at age 12. In 1654 he accompanied the expedition of Diego de Guadalajara from Santa Fe to the juncture of the three branches of the Concho River near the site of present San Angelo. On this expedition and a longer one from El Paso del Norte (1683–84), he probably saw more of the Texas plains than any previous Spanish explorer. As lieutenant general and *maestre de campo* in New Mexico, he played a prominent part in countering the Pueblo Indian revolt of 1680 before the Spaniards finally were forced to withdraw to the El Paso area. In 1681 a group of Indian chiefs led by the Jumano Juan Sabeata came to the Paso del Norte settlement requesting the Spaniards to establish missions among the Jumanos. the governor sent Domínguez and Fray Nicolás López to Jumano country to explore, found missions, and establish trade. The expedition left the El Paso area on 15 December 1683 and descended the Rio Grande to La Junta de los Ríos, near the site of present Presidio. Leaving Fray Antonio de Acevedo in charge of new missions there, fathers López and Juan de Zavaleta continued with Domínguez de Mendoza on a journey that extended beyond the Pecos River to the Edwards Plateau. There, on a river that Domínguez called "the glorious San Clemente," the Spaniards spent six weeks. They built a bastion for protection against Apaches and hunted buffalo for the hides, as well as to feed the thousands of friendly natives who surrounded the camp. The two priests baptized many of the Indians. Both the location of San Clemente and the route that Domínguez took to reach it have been the subject of controversy in the works of scholars, including Herbert Eugene Bolton (1908), Carlos E. Castañeda (1936), Jesse W. Williams (1962), and Seymour V. Connor (1969). The matter remains unsettled. Domínguez and López returned to the Paso del Norte full of hope for establishing missions, and even a colony, among the Jumanos of the Texas plains. The spreading Indian revolt, however, continued to sap Governor Petriz de Cruzate's resources. Not easily discouraged, the explorers journeyed to Mexico City to urge the Jumano settlement as a barrier against the Apache onslaught. A combination of factors doomed their proposal: the revolt raging across the northern frontier and the invasion of Spanish territory by the Frenchman La Salle, who had landed at Matagorda Bay early in 1685. La Salle caused a shift of the missionary focus from western to eastern Texas.

Robert S. Weddle

Dove Creek, Battle of. A battle between Confederate troops and Kickapoo Indians. On 8 January 1865 about 160 Confederates and 325 state militiamen attacked a large encampment of migrating Kickapoo Indians 20 miles southwest of the site of present San Angelo. The Texans were routed after a desperate fight. The previous month, a Confederate force discovered an abandoned Kickapoo camp 30 miles up the Clear Fork of the Brazos River from the ruins of old Fort Phantom Hill. A militia force of about 325 men gathered under Capt. S. S. Totten (Totton), and state Confederate troops of the Frontier Battalion were dispatched under Capt. Henry Fossett. From the beginning the two forces neglected to cooperate fully or agree upon a unified command. After waiting two days at Fort Chadbourne for a rendezvous that never took place, Fossett impatiently set out on 3 January with 161 men and followed a broad trail to the North Concho River and beyond. Four days later his scouts found the Indians, whom they assumed to be hostile Comanches or Kiowas, encamped in timber along Dove Creek. As Fossett prepared to strike, Totten's delayed militia arrived (8 January). Without much previous cooperation, and operating on the frontier assumption that all Indians were dangerous, the two commanders hastily formed an awkward battle plan that produced a correspondingly poor attack. Fossett later estimated the Indian force at between 400 and 600. Totten said 600 and charged that Union jayhawkers were among them. The Indians' position in a heavy thicket was superior, for it gave the well-armed defenders cover, high ground, and a good field of fire. The militiamen were slowed by the creek, heavy briars, and brush. Participant I. D. Ferguson later recounted the fatal wounding of three officers and 16 enlisted men in the opening minutes. The militia was soon routed and out of the battle.

Although Fossett's mounted force captured the Indian horses, his attack was repulsed and the Confederate troops were caught in a crossfire and separated into three groups as the Indians closed in under cover. An Indian counterattack early in the afternoon was repulsed, and the battle continued until almost dark before ending in disorder and confusion. The Indians recaptured their horses and inflicted additional casualties on the Confederates retreating toward Totten's militia, which was tending to the wounded three miles away on Spring Creek. The battered veterans spent a miserable night, drenched by chilling rain that turned to heavy snow. They remained the next day, cold and hungry, forced to eat some of the horses in order to survive. A casualty count showed 22 dead and 19 wounded. An exact number was never known because many militiamen deserted. Indian casualties were less certain. Totten said they numbered more than 100. Fossett gave a body count of 23. The Indians, after crossing the Rio Grande near Eagle Pass, said they had lost 12 in the fight and 2 more who died after arrival in Mexico. Carrying their wounded on crude litters strapped between pairs

Richard W. (Dick) Dowling. Albumen *carte de visite* by Harvey R. Marks. Houston, ca. 1865. Courtesy Lawrence T. Jones III Collection, Austin. For this portrait Major Dowling wore his Confederate uniform and the medal he was given for his victory at Sabine Pass on 8 September 1863.

of horses, the Texans retreated eastward on 11 January, after retrieving their dead. They found shelter and food at John S. Chisum's ranch near the confluence of the Concho and the Colorado rivers. The Kickapoos had been on their way to Mexico to escape the dissension and violence of the Civil War. The battle embittered this peaceful tribe and led to vengeful border raiding from the sanctuary given them by the Mexican government near Santa Rosa, Coahuila. White settlers along the Rio Grande paid heavily for the misjudgments that led to the Texans' defeat on Dove Creek. Col. Ranald S. Mackenzie finally led 377 men of the Fourth United States Cavalry from Fort Clark on a punitive expedition across the Rio Grande in May 1873. Hostilities declined thereafter.   *Elmer Kelton*

Dowling, Richard William. Civil War hero; b. Galway County, Ireland, 1838; d. Houston, 23 September 1867; m. Elizabeth Ann Odlum (1857); at least two children. After 1846 the family immigrated to the United States and settled in New Orleans. Dowling eventually settled in Houston, where he successfully pursued business in saloons, banking, and liquor importing. In 1861 he joined the Jefferson Davis Guards as first lieutenant and conducted raids on U.S. Army outposts on the Mexican border. With the First Texas Heavy Artillery, under the overall command of Col. J. J. Cook, he participated in the battle of Galveston. Subsequently, as artillery commander aboard the steamer *Josiah*

A. Bell, he took part in a naval battle on 21 January 1863 with two Union vessels. The Confederate forces achieved a victory in part because of Dowling's accuracy with the eight-inch Columbiad gun, which he commanded. He was singled out for making some of the "prettiest shots" and for saving the *Bell'*s magazine from flooding. By August 1863 Dowling was commanding Company F, which consisted of 47 men armed with six cannons, at Fort Griffin on Sabine Pass. On September 8 in the battle of Sabine Pass he disabled two U.S. gunboats, the *Clifton* and the *Sachem*, and forced the remaining enemy vessels to withdraw. As a result of federal ineptitude and Dowling's leadership, Dowling and his men captured two ships and 350 prisoners and routed the invasion without a single casualty. After the war Dowling returned to business in Houston, where he died of yellow fever.

James R. Ward

Dreissiger. A collective term ("Thirtiers") for some of the intellectual refugees of the German liberal movements of the 1830s, which, in the wake of the French July Revolution of 1832, included the Hambacher Fest of 1832 and the Frankfurter Putsch of 1833. In opposition to official repression of academia and the media, some of the liberals subsequently known as the Dreissiger organized the Giessen Emigration Society under Paul Follenius and Friedrich Münch to direct German migration to a "new and free Germany in the great North American Republic." Others continued the resistance in Germany until the failure of the Frankfurter Putsch temporarily broke the liberal backbone. The exiles included several interesting early Texas Germans, among them Ferdinand J. Lindheimer, a New Braunfels botanist and editor, and Dr. J. E. F. Gustav Bunsen, a leader of the Frankfurter Putsch who, like Lindheimer, was a teacher in Frankfurt before his exile to the United States. Bunsen and Lindheimer first settled in 1834 at the "Latin" village of Belleville, Illinois, across the river from St. Louis. From there, with others, they traveled to New Orleans and eventually to Texas. Bunsen fought under Sam Houston and died at the battle of San Jacinto. Lindheimer, having missed the battle due to a storm at sea, remained in Texas as a botanical collector for George Engelmann and Asa Gray of Harvard; he also founded and edited the New Braunfels *Herald–Zeitung*. Some primary accounts of the Dreissiger were written by later Forty-eighters, notably Friedrich Kapp. Secondary studies of the Forty-eighters, a numerically more significant group, often include overviews of the Dreissiger as predecessors of the later liberals.   *Glen E. Lich*

Driscoll, Clara. The "Savior of the Alamo"; b. St. Mary's, Texas (near the site of present Bayside), 2 April 1881; d. Corpus Christi, 17 July 1945; m. Henry Hulme Sevier (1906); ed. in private schools in Texas, New York City, and France. Clara Driscoll returned to Texas from study abroad at the age of 18, imbued with an appreciation of the importance of preserving historic sites. She was shocked to discover the disrepair of the plaza and barracks adjoining the Alamo, and to learn that the property might soon be converted into a hotel. She worked with the Daughters of the Republic of Texas to acquire and preserve the old mission, and personally paid most of the purchase price. She subsequently wrote a novel, *The Girl of La Gloria* (1905), a collection of short stories, *In the Shadow of the Alamo* (1906), and a comic opera, *Mexicana*, the production of which she financed on Broadway in 1906. After her marriage at St. Patrick's

Clara Driscoll, San Antonio, 1931. San Antonio *Light* Collection, ITC. Clara Driscoll Sevier, as she was then called, examines plans to beautify Alamo Plaza, almost 30 years after she helped save part of the Alamo property from commercialization.

Cathedral, she stayed in New York with her husband. Hal was financial editor of the New York *Sun*. Clara was president of the Texas Club and entertained extensively at their opulent villa on Long Island. After her father, a rich rancher, died in 1914, the Seviers returned to Austin to be near her family's financial interests. Hal established the Austin *American*, and his wife became active in the Austin Garden Club and Pan American Round Table and served as president of the DRT. She also directed construction of Laguna Gloria, a fine Italianate mansion located on the Colorado River. At the death of her brother, Robert Driscoll, Jr., in 1929, Mrs. Sevier closed Laguna Gloria and moved with her husband to her family's Palo Alto ranch headquarters to manage extensive land and petroleum properties and to serve as president of the Corpus Christi Bank and Trust Company. Under her astute leadership the financial dominion almost doubled in value. After a two-year residence in Santiago, Chile, while her husband served as U.S. ambassador there, the Seviers returned to Texas in 1935 and shortly thereafter legally separated. When the childless, 31-year marriage was dissolved, Clara legally resumed her maiden name and was thereafter officially known as Mrs. Clara Driscoll.

She assisted the Texas Federation of Women's Clubs in liquidating the mortgage on its Austin clubhouse, served as vice chairman of the Texas Centennial Exposition executive board,

and presented Laguna Gloria to the Texas Fine Arts Association to be used as a museum. To memorialize her brother and to improve the economic life of Corpus Christi, she constructed the lavish 20-story Hotel Robert Driscoll, where she occupied the large penthouse apartment. She was elected the Democratic national committeewoman from Texas in 1922 and served in that position for an unprecedented 16 years. In 1939 she promoted the candidacy of her friend John Nance Garner for president. After Franklin D. Roosevelt was reelected for a third term, however, she remained loyal to what she considered the best interests of her party and supported Roosevelt's fourth-term efforts during a bitter battle at the 1944 state convention. She died suddenly of a cerebral hemorrhage. Although Catholic, after her body had lain in state at the Alamo chapel, she was interred at the Masonic Cemetery in San Antonio. She bequeathed the bulk of her family fortune to establish the Driscoll Foundation Children's Hospital in Corpus Christi.
Dorothy D. DeMoss

Droughts. Recorded as a problem in Texas since Spaniards explored the area. Cabeza de Vaca found a population of soil tillers near the site of present-day Presidio, where it had not rained for two years. Regarding the white man as a god, they begged him to tell the sky to rain. In 1720 a summer dry spell in Coahuila killed 3,500 of the 4,000 horses that the Marqués de

Aguayo was prepared to bring to Texas. A drought in Central Texas dried up the San Gabriel River in 1756, forcing the abandonment of a settlement of missionaries and Indians. Stephen F. Austin's first colonists also were hurt by drought. In 1822 their first corn crop died from lack of moisture. Each decade since then has been marked by at least one period of severe drought. Associated with dry times are grasshopper plagues, brush and grass fires, sand and dust storms, crop failures and depression, livestock deaths, disease resulting from insufficient and impure drinking water, and migrations of citizens from parched territory. Information concerning pioneer-day droughts is sketchy because of the absence of official statistics; but data on some droughts, especially those during the nineteenth century, can be compiled from individual complaints recorded in newspapers, diaries, and memoirs. In 1883 Texas opened its western school lands, drawing thousands of immigrant farmers to the area. One of the worst droughts in Texas history, 1884–86, caused most of the farmers to fail and to return to the East. In later years official detailed recordkeeping makes possible a better understanding of the geographical distribution of droughts. Drought occurs when an area receives, in a given year, less than 75 percent of its average rainfall. The number of drought years in each of 10 geographical areas of Texas in the 100 years between 1892 and 1992 was as follows: Trans-Pecos, 16 years; lower Rio Grande valley, 17; Edwards Plateau, 17; South Central, 15; Southern, 15; North Central, 12; Upper Coast, 13; East Texas, 10; High Plains, 10; and Low Rolling Plains, 8.

There has been at least one serious drought in some part of the state every decade of the twentieth century. The most catastrophic one affected every part of the state in the first two-thirds of the 1950s. It began in the late spring of 1949 in the lower Valley, affected West Texas by fall, and covered nearly all of Texas by the summer of 1951. By the end of 1952 the water shortage was critical; Lake Dallas, for instance, held only 11 percent of its capacity. Spring rains in 1953 gave some brief respite to Northeast Texas. In the Trans-Pecos, however, only eight inches of rain fell the entire year of 1953, and the drought grew worse from 1954 to 1956. Streams only trickled or dried up completely. The drought ended abruptly in the spring of 1956 throughout Texas with slow soaking rains. There were several less severe and shorter droughts in the 1970s. Most were ended by rain from tropical storms. A massive heat wave in 1980 started a severe drought that blistered most of Texas during the early 1980s. This gradually worsened until it reached extreme proportions in the Pecos River valley during 1983. Even mesquite trees withered. This drought was ended in the western half of the state by the residue of a north Pacific cyclone, which moved across Mexico. The drought shifted eastward in 1984, inflicting hardship on central and southern Texas; some towns ran out of water and others enforced rationing. On occasion, attempts to make rain artificially have been instituted by both private individuals and public organizations, but these have met with little success. Constant improvement in moisture conservation and utilization, however, has aided Texans in their struggle with drought.

Roy Sylvan Dunn

Dubois de Saligny. French diplomat in the Republic of Texas; b. Jean Pierre Isidore Alphonse Dubois, Caen, Normandy, 8 April 1809; d. St. Martin du Vieux Bellême, Normandy, 1888; m. María de Ortiz de la Borbolla (ca. 1860 in Mexico); one son. Dubois

entered on a diplomatic career in 1831 and became, successively, secretary of the French legations in Hanover, Greece, and the U.S. Sent by the French government to Texas to investigate the new republic, in 1839 he visited Galveston, Houston, and the coastal area as far west as Matagorda. His reports influenced the French government to recognize Texas in a treaty of friendship, navigation, and commerce. Appointed to head the new legation with the rank of chargé d'affaires, "A. de Saligny," as he now signed himself (he was not in fact a member of the French nobility), returned to Texas in January 1840. He established his residence in Austin, bought 21 acres of land, and began building the house known today as the French Legation. As a strong supporter of the Catholic Church, he worked effectively in this period with Fr. John Timon and Jean Marie Odin for the restoration of church property taken at the revolution. Pope Gregory XVI later awarded him the Order of Saint Gregory the Great. Dubois was drawn into Texas politics and backed the controversial Franco-Texan Land Company, became identified as a supporter of Sam Houston, and was a bitter enemy of the Mirabeau B. Lamar faction. His personal and political troubles culminated in the Pig War and in his withdrawal in April 1841, without instructions from the French foreign minister, to Louisiana. Dubois had sold his still unfinished house and property to Bishop Odin, and he never again returned to Austin. Somewhat tardily, Secretary of State Anson Jones apologized to Dubois and paved the way for his return to Galveston in April 1842. Dubois resumed cordial relations with the Houston administration, but poor health caused him to depart for France in July. During his absence Viscount Jules de Cramayel served as chargé d'affaires.

Though he was disappointed in his hopes for promotion to a more prestigious post, Dubois returned in January 1844 to serve as the French representative until the annexation of Texas. Now, however, he evinced a marked preference for Louisiana over Texas as a place of residence and traveled only infrequently to Galveston to fulfill his duties. With a British colleague, Capt. Charles Elliot, he tried to stave off annexation, but, constrained by his instructions, he could offer only the good offices and moral support of France in seeking to obtain Mexican recognition of the Texas republic. Dubois withdrew to Louisiana in April 1845. In 1849–50 he served as French minister plenipotentiary to the Hague and in 1856 represented France on a commission to verify the Russo-Turkish border in Asia. Emperor Napoleon III appointed him plenipotentiary to Mexico in 1860. His urging of French intervention helped the emperor decide to place Maximilian and Carlota on their Mexican thrones. In 1862 Dubois was promoted to grand officer in the Legion of Honor. After being accused of dishonest financial operations and too close an association with the clerical party in Mexico, he was recalled in 1863 and the next year returned to France in disgrace. Despite repeated attempts to vindicate himself, he was unable to obtain another assignment from the foreign ministry.

Nancy N. Barker

Dubuis, Claude Marie. Second Catholic bishop of Texas; b. Teche, France, 8 March 1817; d. Vernaison, France, 21 May 1895; ed. St. Irenaeus Seminary, Lyons; ordained 1844. At Lyons in 1846 he met Jean Marie Odin, vicar apostolic of Texas, who had returned to France to find priests and nuns for work in Texas. Dubuis and other recruits were sent first to the Barrens, a Vincentian Seminary in Perryville, Missouri, to learn English, after which they arrived in Texas in winter 1847, about six months after Pope Pius IX elevated the state of Texas to a diocese with Odin as bishop. Dubuis served first at Castroville, where his ministry included D'Hanis, Vandenburg, Quihi, New Braunfels, and Fredericksburg. He often had to ride through hostile Comanche territory and was captured four times by Indians. In 1851 he was assigned to San Fernando Cathedral in San Antonio. He is credited with developing the architectural style distinctive to Castroville, which resembles that of Alsatian structures. In 1852 he was sent to France to seek volunteers for the Texas missions; 14 students and priests responded. When he returned to Galveston, Dubuis was appointed vicar general and again sent to San Antonio. There he completed work on the Ursuline convent as well as the church that became St. Mary's Cathedral. When Odin was made archbishop of New Orleans, Dubuis was appointed bishop of Galveston—i.e., of the whole of Texas. During his tenure he brought 66 religious into the state, many of them members of the Sisters of Charity of the Incarnate Word of Lyons. Building upon the foundation laid by the Franciscans, the Vincentian Fathers, and others, Dubuis restored a church ravaged by the Civil War. He directed the building of hospitals, schools, and orphanages. At his request Pope Pius established the Diocese of San Antonio in 1874. In 1880 Dubuis returned in ill health to France and Bishop Nicholas A. Gallagher took over administration of the diocese, though Dubuis remained ordinary of Galveston until 1892. In 1949 Bishop Lawrence J. FitzSimon visited Dubuis's grave at Coutouvre, France, and discovered that Dubuis's name on the stone was unreadable and that his tenure as bishop of Texas was not mentioned. By 1951 FitzSimon had had the body removed to a crypt inside the parish church, where a suitable monument was erected.   *Patrick Foley*

Dugout. A temporary rude shelter dug into the ground by pioneers in the West and roofed with sod or occasionally some other material; used until the owner could build a house. Until the dugout itself could be built the settler lived in a wagon or tent, which sometimes blew away. Dugouts were quite common on the Texas prairies, where wood was scarce. After houses were built, dugouts commonly became cellars or storage bins. The dugout was made tolerably comfortable in both summer and winter by the temperature of the ground. The Texas plains dugout consisted of a rectangular pit 5 to 7 feet deep, 8 or 10 feet wide, and of variable length. If wood was available, short extensions of the walls aboveground were built around the pit, allowing the construction of windows for light and ventilation; these were closed with either shutters or sashes. The roof was often fashioned from log beams that supported saplings or branches placed side by side and covered with grass, weeds, or towsacks, all finally covered with dirt. In some instances the roofs were framed with sawed lumber—which was expensive to transport—and covered with shingles. Access to the interior was down a stair dug into the ground. Dugouts were occasionally flooded. For the half dugout, favored in areas of broken terrain, a rectangular excavation was made into the side of a hill. This style drained better. Walls with doors and windows were placed at the open end of the pit and along the sides with the use of sod, stone, or logs. Openings also were sometimes made in the sides. Occasionally stone was used to line the sides of the excavation. Regardless of the type of dugout, floors generally were tamped earth, although in some instances wooden flooring eventually

was installed. Often rugs were placed over the earth floors. Walls were sometimes whitewashed or covered with domestics, and ceilings might be lined with canvas. Commonly, iron stoves were used in full dugouts, and occasionally fireplaces were built at the ends of partial dugouts, with flues dug through the earth. Although dugouts provided vital shelter, they were not pleasant places of abode. Uninvited residents included snakes, spiders, and salamanders. On occasion a cow stepped through the roof. Dirt constantly fell from the walls and roof into food or whatnot. Examples of both types of dugout are preserved at the Ranching Heritage Center in Lubbock.   *Willard B. Robinson*

Dust Bowl. The drought, wind erosion, and appalling dust storms that plagued the southern plains in the latter half of the 1930s; also, the place and time where these occurred. Some of the storms rolled far eastward, darkening skies all the way to the Gulf and Atlantic coasts. The areas most severely affected were western Texas, eastern New Mexico, the Oklahoma Panhandle, western Kansas, and eastern Colorado. According to the federal Soil Conservation Service, the bowl covered 100 million acres in 1935. By 1940 the area had declined to 22 million acres. It disappeared in the forties. A prolonged drought, combined with unusually high temperatures and strong winds, caused the normally semiarid region to become for a while a veritable desert. During some growing seasons the soil was dry to a depth of three feet. Lack of rain plagued the northern plains states too, though less severely. In historic times there is no record of such wind erosion as accompanied the drought in the thirties. In 1932 there were 14 dust storms of regional extent; in 1933, 38; in 1934, 22; in 1935, 40; in 1936, 68; in 1937, 72; in 1938, 61; in 1939, 30; in 1940, 17; and in 1941, 17. In Amarillo the worst year for storms was 1935, when they lasted a total of 908 hours. Seven times, from January to March, the visibility in Amarillo declined to zero; one of these complete blackouts lasted 11 hours. In another instance a single storm raged for 3½ days. Some of the storms afflicting the plains were merely "sand blows," produced by the low sirocco-like winds that came from the Southwest and left the sandier soils drifted into dunes along fencerows and ditches. Less frequent but far more dramatic were the "black blizzards," which appeared with a sudden, violent turbulence, rising like a long wall of muddy water as high as 7,000 or 8,000 feet. The most notorious of these occurred on 14 April 1935. Like the winter blizzards to which they were compared, these storms were caused by the arrival of a polar continental air mass; the atmospheric electricity they generated lifted the dirt higher and higher in a cold boil, sometimes accompanied by thunder and lightning and at other times by an eerie silence. Such "dusters" were not only terrifying to observe but immensely destructive to the region's fine, dark soils.

Repeatedly in those years dirt and sand destroyed crops, property, and mental and physical health. The misery of the era was widely chronicled and eloquently captured in such books as John Steinbeck's *The Grapes of Wrath* (1939). People shoveled the dirt from their front yards and swept up bushel basketfuls inside their houses. Automobile and tractor engines were ruined by grit. The human costs were even harder to calculate and bear. Old people and babies were the most vulnerable to eye and lung damage, as were those with respiratory ailments like asthma. The medical remedies available to them were primitive and makeshift. The Red Cross furnished light gauze masks, and peo-

Dust storm in the Panhandle, April 14, 1935. Prints and Photographs Collection, Panhandle—sandstorm file, CAH; CN 02655. In 1935 the Dust Bowl covered 100 million acres across the western United States. Visibility in Amarillo that year dropped to zero seven times during the first three months, with one blackout lasting eleven hours.

ple stuffed rags around windows and door cracks. Domesticated and wild animals often suffocated or were blinded. As the agricultural base of the region was buried under dust, extreme hardship loomed over the southern plains. In May 1934 dust fell from a massive storm on the Mall and the White House in Washington, D.C., and helped focus federal attention on the desperate situation. The Soil Erosion Service of the U.S. Department of Commerce established the Dalhart Wind Erosion Control Project in 1934 under the direction of Howard H. Finnell. That year $525 million was distributed to cattlemen for emergency feed loans and as payment for some of their starving stock; farmers were provided with public jobs such as building ponds and reservoirs or planting shelter-belts of trees. Seed loans were provided for new crops, and farmers were paid to plow lines of high ridges against the wind. In 1935 the Soil Conservation Service of the USDA replaced the Soil Erosion Service and opened the Region Six office in Amarillo. There Finnell supervised the conservation work for the entire Dust Bowl. With the cooperation of the CCC, the WPA, the Agricultural Adjustment Administration, and other agencies, the Soil Conservation Service made efforts to limit the worst effects of wind erosion. Also in 1935 the Texas legislature established conservation districts for wind-erosion control in nine Panhandle counties, where local authorities were given power to force farmers to institute measures to halt blowing dust. Between 1935 and 1937 over 34 percent of the farmers in the area left.

The Dust Bowl was not only the result of bad weather but also of human actions that exacerbated the drought. Immediately before the thirties men had entered the plains fired with enthusiasm to make them yield abundant wealth, and, in a few short years, they had destroyed much of the native grass holding the dirt in place. Some of them had overstocked the land with cattle and reduced its ability to survive a time of severe drought. Others had come intent on transforming the area into row-crop agriculture. Both sorts of settler ignored the hard-won experience of their predecessors on the plains as well as available scientific data and thereby put at risk a vulnerable environment.

In the boom years of the twenties, from 1925 to 1930, the time of what one writer has called "the great plow-up," farmers tore up the vegetation on millions of acres in the southern plains, an area nearly seven times the size of Rhode Island. They introduced new gasoline tractors, which allowed them to plow faster than ever before. Some "suitcase farmers" had no more responsible plan than speculating on a quick crop or two. More grandiosely, the movie mogul Hickman Price arrived in Plainview, Texas, in 1929 to establish a factory farm covering over 54 square miles in Swisher, Castro, and Deaf Smith counties. To every part of the region came similar pacesetters who fervently believed in the twenties' creed of unlimited economic expansion and who were convinced that modern methods of industrial capitalism, so apparently successful elsewhere in the economy, were what the plains needed. Even traditional conservative agriculturists were induced to follow these entrepreneurs' lead and try to cash in on a period of good weather and high market demand. Most of the freshly plowed ground went into wheat, so that during the twenties wheat production jumped 300 percent, creating a severe glut by 1931. When the black blizzards began to roll, one-third of the Dust Bowl region—33 million acres—lay ungrassed and open to the winds. The origin of the Dust Bowl was therefore related to the near-simultaneous collapse of the American economy. Both catastrophes revealed the darker side of entrepreneurialism, its tendency to risk long-term social and ecological damage in the pursuit of short-term, private gain. The New Deal was elaborated partly to prevent such disasters in the future. Some argue that plains agriculture was chastened by the Dust Bowl years and has, with government help, reformed itself adequately so that the thirties nightmare will not recur. Others, less sanguine, point to the dust storms of the mid-1950s and 1970s as evidence that the old Dust Bowl can be reborn, if and when weather and market forces collide again.

Donald Worster

Duval, John Crittenden. Writer; b. Bardstown, Kentucky, 14 March 1816; d. Fort Worth, 15 January 1897; ed. St. Joseph College, Bardstown, and the University of Virginia. In 1835 he left college to join a small company organized by his brother Capt. Burr H. Duval to fight with the Texans against Mexico. Burr died in the Goliad Massacre (1836), but John escaped and moved to Virginia to study engineering. He returned to Texas by 1840 and became a land surveyor. In 1845 he and Bigfoot Wallace were members of Jack Hays's company of Texas Rangers. Duval fought in the Confederate Army and was a captain at the end of the Civil War. His writings justify his being called the first Texas man of letters. *Early Times in Texas* was published serially in *Burke's Weekly* at Macon, Georgia, in 1867 (book form, on execrable paper, in 1892). The story of Duval's remarkable escape from the Goliad Massacre and of his more remarkable adventures before he rejoined human society became a Texas classic. Of all personal adventures of oldtime Texans it is perhaps the best written and the most interesting. *The Young Explorers* (189?), a semifictional book for boys, is a sequel to *Early Times in Texas*. His most artistic and most important book is *The Adventures of Bigfoot Wallace, the Texas Ranger and Hunter* (1870).

J. Frank Dobie

Dyess Air Force Base. Four miles west of Abilene; established in 1942 as Tye Field; subsequently renamed for William Edwin Dyess, a distinguished World War II pilot (d. 1943). The base was deactivated after the war. In 1947 it was deeded to the city of Abilene as surplus and used as a municipal airport. It was reactivated during the Korean War as Abilene Air Force Base, under the Strategic Air Command. In December 1946 it became Dyess Air Force Base. The 341st Bombardment Wing was the first SAC wing assigned to Dyess. It was equipped with B-47 aircraft, and they were supported by KC-97s. By 1961 the army had installed Nike Hercules missiles, and SAC had Atlas F ICBMs installed in nearby silos. Both missile units were deactivated by the mid-1960s. In 1965, Dyess AFB came under the control of the Second Air Force, which brought the 96th Strategic Aerospace Wing, with its supporting units, to the base in 1967. The wing was equipped with B-52 aircraft and was supported by the 917th Air Refueling Squadron, using KC-135 aerial tankers. Between 1965 and 1973 both B-52s and KC-135s from Dyess were engaged in combat activities over Southeast Asia. The 96th was reequipped with supersonic B-1B aircraft in June 1985. Through the years, improvements and modernization have continued. Dyess contributes substantially to the Abilene economy.

Art Leatherwood

E

Eagle Pass, Texas. County seat of Maverick County; on the Mexican border. During the Mexican War a company of Texas Mounted Volunteers under the command of Capt. John A. Veatch established an observation post on the Rio Grande opposite the mouth of the Río Escondido and beside an old smuggler's trail that crossed the river at this point. The crossing, known as El Paso del Águila, was so named because of frequent flights of Mexican eagles from the wooded grove along the Escondido. Though abandoned by the military at the end of the war, the site remained a terminus and crossing point for trappers, frontiersmen, and traders. In 1849 Fort Duncan was established two miles upstream, and its proximity caused a rudimentary settlement to spring up at the crossing below the post. In 1850 San Antonio merchant James Campbell opened a trading post there. He was soon joined by William Leslie Cazneau and his bride, Jane Cazneau. The village name, derived from that of the river crossing, was translated to Eagle Pass as the Anglo presence grew. Concurrent with the growth of Eagle Pass below the fort, emigrants bound for the California gold fields via Mazatlán established a staging area above the post known as California Camp. The resulting trade and traffic brought a shift in the settlement of Eagle Pass from the old crossing downstream to its present location above the fort. John Twohig, owner of the land, surveyed and laid out a townsite, which he named Eagle Pass. Friedrich W. C. Groos contracted to haul supplies for the military and brought some 70 Mexican families to settle near the fort. A stage line between Eagle Pass and San Antonio was estab-

lished in 1851. The settlement and adjoining fort were frequently attacked by Lipan Apache and Comanche Indians. Piedras Negras, established in 1850 across from Eagle Pass in Mexico, became a haven for fugitive slaves, and both banks of the river were infested with outlaws. In 1855 the Callahan expedition crossed into Mexico at Eagle Pass with three companies of volunteer rangers in pursuit of Lipans and Kickapoos. After a fight with Mexican forces on the Escondido, Callahan fell back on Piedras Negras and set the village afire as he crossed back into Eagle Pass. During the Civil War, a party of renegades crossed from Piedras Negras and overran the Confederate garrison at Fort Duncan. The townsmen, fighting from behind a barricade of cotton bales, successfully drove off their assailants. Following federal occupation of Brownsville in 1863, Eagle Pass became an important shipment point for Confederate cotton. After the war the last Confederate force in the field, the Shelby expedition, crossed the Rio Grande at Eagle Pass and in a ceremony buried in the river the last flag to fly over Confederate troops.

Maverick County, which had been formed from Kinney County in 1856, was finally organized in 1871, and Eagle Pass became the county seat. St. Joseph's Academy, a Catholic school for girls, was opened in 1872. By 1875 the population numbered 1,500; their principal occupation was mercantile business and stock raising. Following the war years, bands of cattle thieves and fugitives led by John King Fisher dominated Eagle Pass through the 1870s. Law and order was restored with the coming of the railroad in the next decade. In 1882 the Galveston, Harrisburg

Ferry crossing Rio Grande from Eagle Pass to Piedras Negras, Mexico. Stereograph by A. V. Latourette. Lawrence T. Jones III Collection, Austin. The area around Eagle Pass has been a terminus and crossing point for early trappers, frontiersmen, and traders; for emigrants bound for the California gold fields; for Confederate shippers of cotton; and for twentieth-century tourists.

and San Antonio Railway built from Spofford to Eagle Pass, connecting the isolated community to the rest of the country. The railroad was continued into Mexico at Piedras Negras as the Mexican National Railway, and the community became an important international center. By 1884 Eagle Pass had an estimated population of 2,000. A new courthouse was built the following year. Eagle Pass grew slowly in the early decades of the twentieth century, reaching 2,729 inhabitants in 1900, 5,765 in 1920, and 7,247 in 1950. Irrigated farming techniques strengthened the agricultural economy of the region in the 1930s and 1940s, and Eagle Pass Army Air Field was constructed twelve miles north of Eagle Pass during World War II. From the 1950s to the 1980s the town grew dramatically, reaching 12,094 inhabitants in 1960, 15,364 in 1970 and 21,407 in 1980. Always a community with a large Hispanic majority, Eagle Pass was 94 percent Hispanic in 1980. With the completion of Highway 57 the town became a major gateway to Mexico and, along with Piedras Negras, developed a substantial tourist trade. Retailers on both sides of the border served Mexican and American tourists and for years enjoyed a flourishing business. In the late 1960s Eagle Pass embarked on a "Model Cities Program" to modernize city services. Government grants funded the construction of new water and sewerage plants, new schools, and an industrial park. Several manufacturers located in the area in the 1970s and 1980s, and significant oil finds boosted the local economy during those years. In 1982 the devaluation of the peso led to economic depression in Eagle Pass as Mexican shoppers stopped coming to the town. Later in the decade maquiladoras began to prop up the local economy. Five industrial plants were located in Eagle Pass and 19 in Piedras Negras by 1987. Textile and arms manufacturing were the leading employers. In 1990 the population had dropped a bit to 20,651, but Eagle Pass remained a center for county government, tourism, and varied manufacturing.

Ben E. Pingenot

Eaker, Ira Clarence. Aviation pioneer and U.S. Air Force general; b. Field Creek, Texas (Llano County), 13 April 1896; d. Andrews Air Force Base, Maryland, 6 August 1987 (buried at Arlington National Cemetery); m. Leah Chase (ca. 1930; divorced almost immediately); m. Ruth Huff Apperson (1931); ed. Southeastern State Teachers College, Durant, Oklahoma. Eaker was commissioned a second lieutenant in the Infantry Section, Officers Reserve Corps, on 15 August 1917, and assigned to the Sixty-fourth Infantry at Fort Bliss. He received a similar commission in the regular army on 26 October 1917. His aviation experience began in March 1918, when he was directed to attend ground school at the University of Texas in Austin and flight training at Kelly Field, San Antonio. After training, he was sent to Rockwell Field, California, where he met Col. H. H. "Hap" Arnold and Maj. Carl A. "Tooey" Spaatz, two men with whom he had a close military relationship for the rest of his life. In July 1919 he was appointed commander of the Second Aero Squadron and sent to the Philippines for a two-year tour. In 1920 he was reassigned as commander of the Third Aero Squadron and promoted to captain. Upon return to the United States in 1921 he was assigned to Mitchel Field, New York; while there, he attended Columbia Law School. He subsequently spent three years on the staff of Maj. Gen. Mason M. Patrick, chief of air service, in Washington, D.C.

Captain Eaker was one of 10 pilots chosen to make the Pan American Goodwill Flight in 1926. During the flight both members of one crew died in a crash. Eaker and his copilot were the only team to complete the entire 23,000-mile itinerary, which included stops in 23 countries. The flight left San Antonio on December 21 and ended at Bolling Field, D.C., where President Coolidge presented the pilots with the Distinguished Flying Cross, a new award authorized by Congress just a few months earlier. In 1929 Eaker, with Tooey Spaatz and Elwood R. Quesada (both of whom were later generals), flew a Fokker tri-motor named the Question Mark for 150 hours, 40 minutes, and 15 seconds, shuttling between Los Angeles and San Diego, refueling with a hose lowered from a Douglas C-1. They set an endurance record that endured for many years. In 1930 Eaker flew the first transcontinental flight that depended solely on aerial refueling. He was promoted to major in 1935. In 1936 he flew blind under a hood from Mitchel Field, New York, to March Field, Riverside, California. Maj. William E. Kepner (who also became a general) flew alongside in this experiment in instrument flight as a safety observer. He stated that Eaker "was under the hood and flying blind" the entire time except for eight take-offs and landings.

During the 1930s Eaker attended the Air Corps Tactical School at Maxwell Field, Alabama, and the Army Command and General Staff School at Fort Leavenworth, Kansas. He also served on the Air Staff in Washington. He was promoted to full colonel in December 1941 and to brigadier general in January 1942, when he was assigned to England to form and command the Eighth Bomber Command. He was instrumental in the development and application of daylight precision bombing in the European Theater. This tactic was a major factor in the defeat of the Germans. In December 1942 Eaker became commander of the Eighth Air Force in England. On 13 September 1943 he received promotion to lieutenant general, and on 15 October he assumed overall command of both American air forces in the United Kingdom, the Eighth and the Ninth. He took over as commander of the joint Mediterranean Allied Air Forces on 15 January 1944. With 321,429 officers and men and 12,598 aircraft, MAAF was the world's largest air force. On 22 March 1945, Eaker was transferred back to Washington to become deputy chief of the army air force under General Arnold. In that position, representing the air force, he transmitted the command from President Truman to General Spaatz, who was then commanding the Pacific Air Forces, to drop the atomic bomb on Japan. Eaker retired in 1947 and was associated with Hughes Aircraft until 1957. That year, he became a corporate director of Douglas Aircraft Company, a post he held until 1961, when he returned to Hughes as a consultant, with the freedom to pursue a long-desired goal of being a journalist. He had already coauthored three books with H. H. Arnold: *This Flying Game* (1936), *Winged Warfare* (1941), and *Army Fliers* (1942). In 1964 he began a newspaper column in the San Angelo *Standard Times* that continued for 18 years and was syndicated by Copley News Services in 700 newspapers. In 1974 he transferred to the Los Angeles Times Syndicate. He wrote on security matters from the point of view of a military man. Between 1957 and 1981, 329 of his articles appeared in military periodicals. In 1972 he became the founding president of the United States Strategic Institute. Among his more than 50 decorations were the Congressional Gold Medal, the Distinguished Flying Cross with Oak Leaf Cluster, the Distinguished Service Medal with Oak Leaf Cluster, the Order of the Partisan Star (First Class), the Silver Star, and the Wright

Trophy; he was also made a Knight of the British Empire. He was promoted from lieutenant general to general by an act of Congress in 1985.   *Art Leatherwood*

Earthquakes. No Texas earthquake has exceeded a magnitude of 6.0, and most have been fairly small and have caused little or no damage. Between 1847 and 1994 there were more than 110 recorded earthquakes of magnitude three or greater in Texas. Damage occurred in at least 25 of them, and one death has been attributed to a Texas quake. Almost all of the earthquakes in Texas have resulted from one of two causes. The major cause is relief of tectonic stress along fault lines. Quakes so originating are most common in the Rio Grande rift belt, the Panhandle, the Ouachita Belt, and the Coastal Plain. Small earthquakes have also been attributed to well injections associated with oil and gas field operations. The largest earthquake in Texas occurred on 16 August 1931 in Jeff Davis County; it measured about 6.0 on the Richter Scale. Many of the other West Texas earthquakes have occurred in El Paso, one of which caused a death in Ciudad Juárez (7 March 1923). Some of the larger earthquakes in the Panhandle occurred in 1917, 1925, and 1936, and 1948. No earthquake in the Panhandle has exceeded a magnitude of 5.0. Earthquakes in East and Central Texas have been fairly small. Some notable ones have occurred at Seguin (1847), Manor (1873), Paige (1887), Creedmore (1902), and Trout Switch (1934). In April 1993 an earthquake of magnitude 4.2 that took place in Atascosa County damaged homes and a gas pipeline.

Erika Murr

East, Sarita Kenedy. Philanthropist; b. Corpus Christi, 19 September 1889; d. New York City, 11 February 1961; m. Arthur Lee East (1910); attended H. Sophie Newcomb Memorial College, New Orleans. Her wealthy rancher father, son of Mifflin Kenedy, named the town of Sarita after her around 1904. Sarita made her debut in New Orleans, then returned to the family ranch, La Parra. After Arthur East died in 1944, Mrs. East and her brother John G. Kenedy, Jr., were in charge of the 400,000-acre Kenedy ranch. Upon her brother's death in 1948, Sarita and her sister-in-law Elena Suess Kenedy became the sole heirs to the ranch. Sarita East also owned the San Pablo Ranch near Hebbronville and Twin Peaks Ranch in Colorado. She served as a county commissioner of Kenedy County and was on the board of directors of Alice National Bank. In addition to her business dealings she engaged in philanthropy, especially to Catholic charities. In 1952 she received the Ecclesia et Pontifice medal and membership in the Ladies of the Holy Sepulchre of Jerusalem from Pope Pius XII for her service to the church. She was also named an honorary member of the Franciscans and the Oblates of Mary Immaculate. In her 1948 will she bequeathed La Parra Ranch headquarters and 10,000 acres of land to the Oblates and 13,000 acres to the Diocese of Corpus Christi. The rest of her vast estate was divided among relatives and ranch kin. In 1948 Mrs. East met Christopher Gregory, a Trappist monk who had taken the name Brother Leo. Two years earlier Brother Leo had been released from his vow of silence and assigned to raise funds for new Trappist monasteries. He was on a fund-raising trip through South Texas when he met Sarita East, and over the next few years he became her advisor and traveling companion. In the 1950s Mrs. East allowed oil and gas exploration on her ranch, which up to that time had largely been an untapped resource.

During that time she gave money to the Trappist monks and visited monasteries throughout the world. In 1959, with other family members and Brother Leo, she went on a South American tour and donated $300,000 to build a mission in Chile. That same year Brother Leo introduced her to J. Peter Grace, chairman of the board of W. R. Grace and Company, in New York. In 1960 the three established the John G. and Marie Stella Kenedy Memorial Foundation, with Sarita Kenedy East as sole member. Mrs. East also wrote another will leaving the bulk of her estate to the foundation. Over the next few months she wrote a series of codicils to her will that increasingly gave more control of the foundation to Brother Leo and Grace. Just before her death she named Brother Leo sole member of the foundation. Within months after her death a group of South Texans, including Elena Kenedy, members of the Turcotte family, and the Diocese of Corpus Christi, filed a lawsuit disputing Brother Leo's control of the foundation, charging that Leo and Grace exerted undue influence over Mrs. East while she was disoriented by medication. Other relatives also contested her 1960 will and wished to reinstate her 1948 will. Over the course of the battle more than 200 people claimed to be legitimate heirs. In 1964 a settlement regarding the foundation resulted in the splitting of assets. Grace and the New York group relinquished control of the foundation, over Brother Leo's objections. The bulk of the funds, approximately $100 million, went to the control of the South Texans, but Grace received oil royalties (not to exceed $14.4 million) from the estate and established a smaller foundation in New York, the Sarita Kenedy East Foundation. In 1966 Brother Leo filed an appeal against the decision, but the Supreme Court finally refused to overturn the Texas Supreme Court, which had ruled against the monk. The ranch headquarters went to the Oblate Fathers. The estate was finally turned over to the foundation in 1982. In 1984, the first year that the foundation officially operated, it had $100 million in assets and was the largest charitable foundation in South Texas. It was stipulated that at least 10 percent of the income go to the Corpus Christi diocese, with a total of 90 percent of funds going for religious activities and the other 10 percent going to secular agencies.   *Laurie E. Jasinski*

Eastland, Texas. County seat of Eastland County. In 1875 Jacamiah S. Daugherty and Charles U. Connellee platted a townsite that the voters chose as county seat; Merriman, the older county seat, was farther from the center of the county. The new community was named Eastland. A stone courthouse was built, and the county commissioners' court held its first session in September 1875. In 1880 the Texas and Pacific Railway was paid a number of town lots to induce the railroad to build through the community. A second courthouse of red stone was constructed in 1883, and by 1884 Eastland had three churches, a school, a flour mill, two cotton gins, and an estimated 500 inhabitants. Eastland was incorporated in 1891 and reincorporated in 1897. The second courthouse was destroyed by fire in 1896, and a third courthouse was built the following year. A horned lizard, later to become famous as "Old Rip," was supposedly placed in the cornerstone. When the third and final courthouse was built in 1928, the cornerstone was opened, and the lizard was found alive. Eastland's population slowly increased to 596 in 1900 and 855 in 1910. The local economy was heavily dependent on cotton. Eastland County experienced a dramatic oil boom from 1917 to 1922, and the city of Eastland grew rapidly, reaching 3,368 inhabitants in 1920, though some estimates claim that there were as many as 10,000 people in the town during the height of the boom in 1919. The town's prosperity in the 1920s helped fund city improvements like the new courthouse, a new high school, and the paving of city streets. The community reached its peak census population in 1930 with 4,648 inhabitants. Thereafter Eastland began a slow decline, falling to 3,849 inhabitants in 1940, 3,606 in 1950, and 3,178 in 1970. The community experienced renewed growth in the 1970s, and the population increased to 3,747 in 1980. In 1990 Eastland had a population of 3,690. The local economy depended on county government, agribusiness, printing, and several manufacturing plants.

Mark Odintz

East Texas Baptist University. An undergraduate university at Marshall with a background in liberal arts and Christian teaching; originally the College of Marshall, chartered in 1912 as a result of the work of W. T. Tardy; opened as a junior college in the summer of 1917. In 1944 the name was changed to East Texas Baptist College and the institution was reorganized as a fouryear school. In 1945 the first eight baccalaureate degrees were granted. In 1949 the plant consisted of seven buildings on a campus of 100 acres. Enrollment was 643. In 1972 the college received accreditation from the Southern Association of Colleges and Secondary Schools; it offered a program of teacher education as well as a four-year liberal-arts curriculum. The Baptist General Convention approved organizing the college as a university in November 1982 and in 1984 renamed it East Texas Baptist University.

Nancy Beck Young

East Texas Historical Association. The name of two organizations: (1) W. F. Garner, chairman of the Department of History at Stephen F. Austin State Teachers College, invited members of his faculty and of the faculties at Sam Houston State Teachers College and East Texas State Teachers College to form an organization to promote the study of East Texas history. The group met in Nacogdoches for 10 days in April 1927, and annually thereafter on campuses in Huntsville, Commerce, and Nacogdoches, until it disbanded because of the Great Depression in 1932. An annual issue of papers read at the meetings was published. Historical papers were read at its meetings by such historians as Eugene C. Barker and Rev. George L. Crocket, who served as the first president of the association. (2) In 1962 the second ETHA resulted from the work of Ralph Steen and C. K. Chamberlain, respectively president and history-department chairman at Stephen F. Austin State College, and attorneys F. I. Tucker of Nacogdoches and F. Lee Lawrence of Tyler. Historians in East Texas received invitations to a meeting held on the SFA campus in Nacogdoches on 29 September. They wrote a new constitution (revised in 1981), calling for an annual meeting each fall in Nacogdoches and a spring meeting elsewhere in East Texas; the publication of the semiannual *East Texas Historical Journal*; and the collection and deposit of archival material in the library at Stephen F. Austin State College. Because charter membership was left open for many months, the association claims 425 charter members. Its officers are alternately lay and professional historians. The association meets on the campus of Stephen F. Austin State University in Nacogdoches and continues to publish two issues of its journal annually. After 1971 the ETHA established new programs to encourage the study of East Texas his-

tory and to honor those who do so. It also sponsors in-service workshops for teachers in partnership with the Texas State Historical Association and provides a clearinghouse for information about the history of East Texas. *Archie P. McDonald*

Eberly, Angelina Belle Peyton. Frontier innkeeper; b. Angelina Belle Peyton, Sumner County, Tennessee, 2 July 1798; d. Indianola, 15 August 1860; m. her first cousin, Jonathan C. Peyton (1818; d. 1834); 3 children; m. Jacob Eberly (1836; d. 1841). In 1822 the Peytons sailed to Texas from New Orleans. They settled in San Felipe de Austin in 1825 and there operated an inn and tavern. After Jonathan died, Angelina continued to operate the hotel until residents destroyed the town to prevent its falling into Mexican hands. In Columbia she married again. She and Jacob settled in Austin (1839), where she ran the Eberly House. On 18 October 1839 Angelina served dinner to President Mirabeau B. Lamar and his cabinet. President Sam Houston chose to live in her house rather than occupy the president's home. In the Archive War (1842), alarmed at the removal of government records from Austin, she roused the town by firing a six-pound gun that officials kept loaded with grapeshot in case of Indian attack. In 1846 Angelina leased Edward Clegg's Tavern House in Lavaca (later Port Lavaca). By 1851 she was running a hotel in Indianola. She left an estate of $50,000.

C. Richard King

Ector's Brigade. A Civil War brigade formed during the reorganization of Gen. Braxton Bragg's command in November 1862, which resulted in the Army of Tennessee. Gen. Mathew D. Ector, the original commander, served until he was wounded in July 1864. The original units of the brigade were the Tenth, Eleventh, and Fourteenth Texas Dismounted Cavalry, and the Douglas Battery. The Fifteenth Texas Dismounted Cavalry (the Thirty-second Texas Cavalry) joined the brigade soon after it was formed. Other units, from Texas, North Carolina, Alabama, Mississippi, and Arkansas, served at various times with the brigade. At Murfreesboro, Ector's Brigade took part in the initial assault on the Union right (31 December 1862) and suffered 38 killed and 308 wounded. The brigade marched to Mississippi and joined Gen. Joseph E. Johnston's forces in an attempt to relieve the besieged Confederates at Vicksburg. After the surrender of that city they participated in the siege of Jackson (July 10–17), before returning to the Army of Tennessee and fighting in the battle of Chickamauga, Georgia, on 19–20 September 1863. At this battle the brigade had 59 killed, 239 wounded, and 138 missing. In September 1863 Ector was again ordered to march his brigade to Mississippi, and after reaching General Johnston's army it joined Gen. Samuel French's division in the Army of Mississippi. After Johnston assumed command of the Army of Tennessee, Gen. Leonidas Polk took command of the Mississippi army and assembled his forces at Meridian to contest Gen. William T. Sherman's. When the federals moved, Polk transferred his troops to Demopolis, Alabama, where they remained until they joined the Army of Tennessee in Georgia in May 1864.

Ector's brigade reached Rome, Georgia, in time to defend the town from Union troops on 16 May before joining Johnston's army at Kingston, Georgia. It participated in the long retreat toward Atlanta, taking part in numerous skirmishes and being lightly engaged at Dallas before seeing action at the Lattermoure House and then at Kennesaw Mountain and Smyrna. After Gen.

John Bell Hood took command of the Army of Tennessee on July 17, Ector's troops remained in their trenches at Atlanta until they were lightly engaged in the battle of Peach Tree Creek on July 20. Once Hood had abandoned Atlanta, French's division was ordered to attack the federals at Allatoona, Georgia, where Ector's brigade saw heavy fighting. In this action the brigade had 43 killed, 147 wounded, and 11 missing out of about 400 troops and did not reach Hood's army until after the battle of Franklin, 30 November 1864. The brigade marched north with the Army of Tennessee and participated in the battle of Nashville (15–16 December) before retreating to Mississippi. During the retreat the brigade formed part of the rear guard that ambushed a federal force at Sugar Creek on Christmas Day. After Johnston resumed command of the Army of Tennessee, Ector's Brigade was detached and ordered to Mobile, Alabama, where it joined other Confederate soldiers defending Spanish Fort (March–April 1865). It was forced to evacuate the city and finally surrendered at Meridian, Mississippi, on 4 May 1865.

David V. Stroud

Edinburg, Texas. County seat of Hidalgo County; part of the McAllen–Pharr–Edinburg metropolitan area. Hidalgo, on the Rio Grande, was the county seat until 1908, when John Closner and William Briggs, who had land-development projects in the vicinity of Chapin, 17 miles north of Hidalgo, made Chapin county seat. The townsite was named after Dennis B. Chapin, another of its promoters. In 1911 the name was changed to Edinburg, in honor of the birthplace in Scotland of John McAllen and John Young. The town grew to some 800 inhabitants by 1915 and incorporated in 1919. During its early years it served a ranching community, but after the arrival of irrigation in 1915 Edinburg quickly became a center for buying and processing cotton, grain, and citrus produce. After World War II the economy diversified further to include peach and melon production, food-processing plants, cabinetry, oilfield equipment, concrete products, agricultural chemicals, and corrugated boxes. The first railroad service in 1909 was a spur line, extending from the one connecting Brownsville and San Juan. Seventeen years later the city received direct rail connections with Corpus Christi and San Antonio. After highways and trucks replaced rail service, Edinburg benefited from its location on a major highway intersection. It has been called the "gateway city" to the Rio Grande valley. Hispanics constitute 80 percent of the population. The University of Texas–Pan American at Edinburg was founded in 1927 as a junior college, and in 1946 the local Rio Grande Bible Institute began training Protestant ministers for Latin America. In 1976 the city became the home of the South Texas Symphony Association, which sponsors the Valley Symphony Orchestra, the Valley Symphony Chorale, and the South Texas Chamber Orchestra. The major historical landmark of Edinburg is its city hall, built in 1909; in 1990 it housed the county historical museum. The population was 29,885 in 1990.

Hubert J. Miller

Education. Education in Spanish Texas was designed to Christianize and domesticate the Indians and to provide the rudiments of learning for the children of garrison troops and Spanish colonists. Mission schools were established for the Indians, the first being at San Francisco de los Tejas Mission in East Texas in 1690. The mission schools taught Christianity, the Spanish language, and practical arts, but they achieved few permanent results for many reasons, including the difficulty in getting supplies, illness, and indifference or hostility of some of the Indians. A nonmission school was in operation at San Fernando de Béxar (San Antonio) as early as the 1740s, but it, as well as all other schools started during the period, proved transitory. Legislative proclamations were issued as early as 1802 to compel parents to send their children to school. Settlements and military posts with large enough populations were called upon to provide salaries for teachers, but apparently the effort failed. Sometime after 1812 a public school was established at San Antonio. It was to be supported by public funds, but the school had a precarious existence and did not last. A private soldier, José Galán, taught school at La Bahía in 1818. The military nature of the Texas colony, the frontier conditions, the sparseness of the population, the poverty of the people, and the failure of the central government to provide financial support contributed to the failure of the few attempts at general education in the Spanish period.

The Constitution of 1824, ratified by the new Republic of Mexico, delegated control of education to the states. The Constitution of Coahuila and Texas provided for the establishment of elementary schools and seminaries in the principal towns of the state but did not include any means of support. In 1829 action was taken to provide a plan for free instruction for pupils whose parents were unable to pay tuition. The establishment of these "Lancastrian schools," which had arisen in England and were popular in the northern United States, was well received in other parts of Mexico, but none was established in Texas. In 1830 six primary schools were projected; at least one of these opened in Nacogdoches, but, overall, plans for education in Mexican Texas never materialized. Neither the towns nor the state had funds with which an educational system could be established. One of the grievances listed in the Texas Declaration of Independence was that Mexico had "failed to establish any public system of education." During the colonial period, however, several private schools operated, and some of them occasionally were subsidized by local funds. Among the Mexican towns, Bexar had the best school facilities. In 1828 the community established the Public Free Primary School, supported by private subscriptions and a municipal subsidy. Instruction was given in religion, morals, and the Three Rs. Plagued by lack of funds, supplies, and competent teachers, however, the school closed sometime during or after 1834. In the American settlements, the wealthier colonists sent their children to the United States for schooling. "Old field schools" and academies, similar to those in the South, sprang up as early as 1823. Largely because of Stephen F. Austin's interest, his colony retained educational leadership throughout the period. Thomas J. Pilgrim opened both an academy and a Sunday school in the colony around 1829. Frances Trask Thompson operated a boarding school at Coles Settlement as early as 1834, and by 1836 more than a score of private schools had been established among the Anglo-American colonists.

The Texas Declaration of Independence condemned the Mexican regime for failing to establish a system of public education; the Constitution of the Republic of Texas therefore compelled Congress to provide such a system. During Sam Houston's administration several private schools were chartered, but problems demanding the attention of the new government

Public School House, Teacher and Pupils, in Live Oak County, Texas, 1887. Photograph by Asa A. Brack. Courtesy Western History Collections, University of Oklahoma Library. Many rural schools remained small and primitive more than 30 years after the state instituted a public school fund. Here a teacher meets fewer than a dozen pupils under a brush arbor.

prevented public education from receiving much consideration. The first definite action toward a system of public education was taken during the administration of Mirabeau B. Lamar, who requested Congress in 1838 to establish and endow an education system. As a result of his message, Congress passed bills in 1839

A. M. Aikin, Jr., 1941. Courtesy Aikin Regional Archives, Paris Junior College, Paris, Texas. As a state senator, Aikin helped to enact the Gilmer–Aikin Laws of 1949, which established the Texas Education Agency and a multifaceted program to improve the quality of public education.

and 1840 that adopted a plan for a school system ranging from the primary to the university level, delegated control over this system to the counties, and granted 17,712 acres to each county for the support of schools. The plan failed to produce the desired results immediately because land prices were too low for this endowment to provide revenue. There was also some popular indifference on the county level to the establishment of schools, as evidenced by the fact that by 1855, 38 counties had made no effort even to survey their school land. In spite of these setbacks, however, Lamar's vision later earned him the nickname "Father of Education in Texas." Private schools and academies of the type prevalent before the Texas Revolution continued to operate, and in the republic several institutions of higher education were chartered.

With the annexation of Texas to the United States, the state provided under the Constitution of 1845 for the establishment of free schools. The constitution further stipulated that it should be the duty of the legislature to set apart not less than one-tenth of the annual revenue of the state derived from taxation as a perpetual fund for the support of such schools. The actual foundation for the present Texas school system was laid in 1854 under a school law that called for the organization of common schools, provided a system for payment of tuition for indigent and orphaned children, allowed for the convertibility of private schools to common schools, and, perhaps most importantly, set aside $2 million of the $10 million received by Texas from the sale of lands to the United States for schools. In 1858 New Braunfels was reported to be the first town in Texas where resi-

Heman Sweatt registering for courses at the University of Texas law school, Austin, 1950. Prints and Photographs Collection, Heman Sweatt file, CAH; CN 00323B. Sweatt won admission to the University of Texas law school as a result of *Sweatt v. Painter,* which went to the United States Supreme Court.

During the latter half of the nineteenth century the educational system in Texas still operated on a sporadic and localized basis. Some Texans regarded education as a private matter and resented any state involvement. Private and church schools continued to play key roles in the educational development of Texas and in some areas offered the only choice of formal schooling. Schools short of funds often faced problems of low supplies, inadequate facilities, and poorly trained teachers. Since the days before the republic some government officials had called for guidelines specifying the qualifications of teachers. By the 1870s the Peabody Fund, established by wealthy New England merchant George Peabody, began to have some positive impact on schools in the state. The fund was to be used to establish tax-supported public schools. In Texas Peabody agents promoted city schools and teacher training, and instigated a campaign to enlighten the public about education and its benefits. The Constitution of 1876 provided that "all funds, lands, and other property heretofore set apart and appropriated for the support of public schools, all the alternate sections of land reserved by the state of grants heretofore made or that may hereafter be made to railroads or other corporations of any nature whatsoever, one-half of the public domain of the state, and all sums of money that may come to the state from the sale of any portion of the same shall constitute a perpetual public school fund." The constitution allotted more than 42 million acres of Texas public domain to school purposes and reestablished the separation of funding for white and black schools. It also provided for a poll

dents citizens voted for a tax to support a "free" school, New Braunfels Academy. After the Civil War the Constitution of 1866 incorporated most of the features of the Constitution of 1845 and further made provision for the education of African Americans through taxation of their property. The Freedmen's Bureau brought in teachers from the American Missionary Association, primarily from the North, to teach in black schools. Later, some white Southerners and educated blacks taught, but the early African-American schools were often the subject of controversy and suffered discrimination and intimidation. The Constitution of 1866 was soon supplanted by the Constitution of 1869, which eliminated the separation of taxation for the white and black populations and reaffirmed the provisions of the fund for public education. This constitution set compulsory school attendance at four months a year and provided that the legislature should set aside one-fourth of the general revenue for public schools, assess a poll tax of one dollar, and commit all money from the sale of public land to the school fund. In 1871 Governor Edmund J. Davis signed a bill initiating a public school system in the state. Its measures included the establishment of a state board of education consisting of the governor, attorney general, and superintendent of public education. The bill became the subject of partisan politics, however, as Democrats in their efforts to regain political power tried to discredit the actions of the Republican government.

President Lyndon Baines Johnson signs the Elementary and Secondary Education Act. Photograph by Yoichi R. Okamoto. Johnson City, April 11, 1965. Courtesy Lyndon Baines Johnson Library, Austin. Johnson's grade-school teacher, Kate Loney, sat at his side as he signed this landmark legislation.

Summer English class for pre-school Spanish-speaking children, with teacher Iva Nelda Blohm. Austin Elementary School, Corpus Christi, 1959. E. E. Mireles Papers, Benson Latin American Collection, University of Texas at Austin. After a successful pilot project sponsored by LULAC, the state began offering English instruction to pre-school Spanish-speaking children in the 1959–60 school year.

tax of a dollar and a commitment of one-fourth of the occupation taxes for school support. Some legislators thought that one-fourth was too high, and later in a special session the amount was cut to one-sixth. Provision was further made for local taxation. Beginning in 1883 a constitutional amendment added a 20-cent state ad-valorem school tax. The rate was raised to 35 cents in 1918, when the state began supplying textbooks.

Around the turn of the century a growing movement in vocational education began, the result of increasing national awareness for the need to teach technical and trade skills to youth. Early training programs included courses in agriculture, carpentry, and industrial trades for both black and white boys and home economics for girls. Vocational education continued to evolve and play an important educational role throughout the twentieth century. In 1910 a scholastic census recorded 625,917 children attending school in country school districts. The numbers were broken down to 501,806 whites and 124,111 blacks. Many of the rural schools consisted of one-room schoolhouses with one teacher instructing a number of grade levels. That same year there were 342,552 children (272,075 whites and 70,277

blacks) attending school in independent school districts across the state. These districts included some 670 communities of all sizes. In 1920 Texas voters passed the Better Schools Amendment, which allowed the amount of local taxation for education to increase. The law was designed to ease the state's burden of school financing. The measure had some positive results, though some counties were slow to increase their school funding. The problem of financial inequality also contributed to inadequate funds and facilities for some schools. Sparsely settled counties, racial and linguistic differences presented by large percentages of African-American and Mexican-American students, and a wide variance in the distribution of natural resources made for considerable lack of uniformity in the state school system. In 1930 *Del Rio ISD v. Salvatierra* attempted to show the inferior quality of educational facilities for Mexican Americans and helped launch a movement against segregated schools, though the plaintiff, Jesús Salvatierra, lost. Advocates of desegregation gained some ground in the case of *Delgado v. Bastrop ISD* in 1948 when a district judge ruled against the segregation of Mexican-American children in the public school system. In 1949 the Fifty-first Legislature passed the Gilmer–Aikin Laws in an effort to raise the general level of school standards and to eliminate inequalities. Important measures of the bill included the increasing of teacher salaries, establishment of the foundation school program, and the establishment of the Texas Education Agency.

In the school year 1950–51 disbursements for the public education system in Texas totaled $199,527,347. Of this amount $95,225,919 was provided from the available school fund, $59,056,428 from the foundation school program fund, $250,000 from vocational funds supplied by the federal government, and $44,500,000 from city and $495,000 from county funds. In 1950–51 the scholastic population numbered 1,566,610, and the state had 2,505 school districts. The ensuing two decades saw major changes in education in Texas. *Sweatt v. Painter* (1950) challenged the previous "separate but equal" doctrine of *Plessy v. Ferguson* (1896) and laid the groundwork for integration in schools. With the United States Supreme Court decision in *Brown v. Board of Education* in 1954, states were compelled to end school segregation for African Americans. San Antonio was one of the first districts to comply. School districts across the state began the implementation of integration, though some discriminatory practices continued well into the next decade. The 1954 decision was finally extended to Mexican Americans, for whom segregation had not been universal, in *Cisneros v. Corpus Christi ISD* in 1970. The federal government continued to enlarge its role in education in the 1960s. The Elementary and Secondary Education Act of 1965, signed by President Lyndon B. Johnson, offered government assistance to underfunded school districts. By 1965 approximately 98 percent of Texas public school teachers had college degrees and about 40 percent had graduate degrees. The Permanent School Fund totaled more than one-half billion dollars; annual earnings were used to defray current expenses of public schools. Earning power of the fund increased through legislative authorization permitting investment in corporate securities, in addition to investments previously authorized in federal, state, and municipal bonds. In the 1964–65 school year the state had 1,253 school districts with an enrollment of 2,535,381. Countywide day schools for the deaf and special classes for non-English-speaking preschool children, emotionally dis-

First grader on a school bus. Photograph by Mike Fluitt. Austin, 1974. Courtesy Austin History Center, Austin Public Library; Photo no. PICA 10721. Desegregation plans often called for students to be bused to schools in neighborhoods other than their own.

JOSHUA AT THE WALLS OF JERICHO HIGH

Joshua at the Walls of Jericho High, by Bob Taylor. Original published in Dallas *Times Herald,* October 18, 1984. Courtesy Bob Taylor, Auburn, California. As chairman of a governor-appointed committee to study Texas schools, H. Ross Perot lobbied successfully for a measure known as "no pass–no play." This cartoon portrays Perot as Joshua, heralding the 3 R's and bringing down the walls of Tradition, within whose precincts individuals are worshipping a giant football.

turbed children, minimally brain-injured children, and the educable mentally retarded were initiated. In the middle 1960s a few schools in the state experimented with a longer school day and shorter school term in an attempt to educate the children of migratory workers.

By the 1970s some new major issues faced the Texas public school system. In 1970 in *United States v. Texas* a federal judge called for the integration of all Texas schools. Previous federal investigations had uncovered discriminatory practices in some Texas public school districts. The changing of school-district boundaries, reassessment of extracurricular activities, and increased busing of students to other schools were among some of the measures taken to enforce integration. Another issue that sparked controversy in the public school system was bilingual education. Throughout most of the twentieth century an English-only teaching requirement had been imposed. In 1973 the state legislature enacted the Bilingual Education and Training Act, which mandated bilingual instruction for all Texas elementary public schools that had 20 or more children with limited English-speaking skills. In the 1970s as the scholastic

population and the cost of education increased, the number of school districts decreased. Small school districts in thickly populated areas were consolidated into larger units in order to effect a lower cost per pupil and to increase educational opportunities through providing better school facilities. Two factors then slowed the rate of consolidation. First, in many sparsely settled areas of Texas, further consolidation was difficult because of the time and distance involved in transporting children sometimes as far as 125 miles daily. Second, more than 100 small Texas schools joined forces to improve their educational programs through sharing resources and working together in a statewide small-schools project. A few schools built all or large parts of their plants underground to avoid noise, to reduce costs of construction and maintenance, and to provide less expensive, year-round climate control. Also in the 1970s much experimental work was underway in classrooms. More audiovisual aids were in use, and new approaches to learning enabled pupils to progress at their own rate of speed. Closed-circuit television, team teaching, nongraded schools, accelerated classes, and electronic laboratories were some of the innovations. School taxes were the subject of considerable controversy as school population increases necessitated more buildings, more supplies, more teachers, and more textbooks. In 1977 the state legislature formed the School Tax Assessment Practices Board to determine the property wealth of school districts. The state had 1,099 school districts and a scholastic population of 3,012,210 during the 1979–80 school year.

During the second half of the twentieth century church schools and other private schools also continued to play an important role in education. Some parents viewed them as attractive alternatives to the public school system, where classes were too big, standardized-test scores were declining, and drugs and violence were increasing. Many private schools focused more on academics and the teaching of deportment and moral discipline through religious courses than on extracurricular activities and peripheral matters. In the 1980s the Texas Education Agency examined the possibility of regulation for church and private schools—a move that some advocates of private schools saw as an infringement on religious freedom.

During the 1980s citizens, educators, and politicians raised concerns about declining test scores and literacy among public schoolchildren. This resulted in a call for major public school reform. Dallas billionaire H. Ross Perot was appointed to head a select committee to manage the effort. In 1984 House Bill 72 placed stringent guidelines on teacher certification and initiated competency testing. Teachers' salaries were directly tied to performance. Stricter attendance rules were enacted, and the reforms also adopted the "no-pass, no-play" rule, which prohibited students who scored below 70 in any class from participating in any extracurricular activities. National norm testing was also implemented, as were equalization formulas for state financial aid. That same year the case of *Edgewood ISD v. Kirby* was filed. The plaintiffs charged that public school financing discriminated against students in poor school districts. MALDEF (the Mexican American Legal Defense and Educational Fund), which filed on behalf of the Edgewood ISD, came out against House Bill 72. For the next several years the case was involved in a series of appeals that ultimately led to a ruling for the Edgewood ISD. During this time the state legislature attempted to reach a plan for a more equitable system of school financing. In 1990 a "Robin Hood" plan was devised by which money from wealthy school districts would be redistributed to poorer ones. This measure was defeated by voters, but similar proposals were made in an effort to avoid court deadlines for an acceptable plan. Failure to find an equitable alternative plan would result in the loss of federal education money. In 1993 the state legislature passed another school-financing plan, which gave school districts a number of options to choose from in order to distribute funding more equally. Afterward, various factions still argued that school financing needed more equalization.

In 1992–93 there were 1,060 school districts in Texas. In the 1990s a popular movement sought to increase the length of the school year or possibly to implement year-round school. A few school districts had already established the latter policy by 1995, when computers had become standard teaching tools in many classrooms. Parents continued to explore other educational options, including private and church schools, educational kindergartens, education vouchers, and home schooling.

Max Berger and Lee Wilborn

Edwards Plateau. In south central Texas east of the Pecos River and west of the Colorado; the southernmost part of the Great Plains. The plateau is an erosional region with thin soil over beveled Comanchean limestone exposures that extend as limestone beds to constitute the underpinning of the High Plains, lying above the Permian and Triassic beds and beneath the more recent unconsolidated Pliocene and Pleistocene deposits, the latter forming the constructional surface of the High Plains. If any such loose cover ever mantled the Edwards Plateau, it has long since been carried away by erosion, although remnant summit areas in the northwest portion of the plateau, in the transition zone adjacent to the High Plains, are characterized by a cover of unconsolidated silty materials. On such areas a deep black soil occurs. By and large, however, the Edwards Plateau is erosional with the margins of the region frayed rather deeply so that the plateau as a whole is perceptibly higher than adjacent areas. Its distinctive physical features, especially its lack of deep soils suitable for farming, cause the Edwards Plateau to be an outstanding grazing region of Texas. Its cattle, sheep, and goat industries are of national importance. The distribution of livestock in the region serves to indicate the various types of the natural environment, particularly as reflected in the different kinds of natural vegetation. Cattle, for instance, are grazed on the typical mesquite-shrub, short-grass areas, characterized by deeper soils. Such areas are the best grazing lands of the region. The next best grazing areas support large numbers of sheep, while the poorest support large numbers of goats. Limited farming is carried on in the deeper soil areas along the broader valleys in the northeast quarter of the Edwards Plateau, as well as in the black-earth soil district on a remnantal summit area in the vicinity of Eldorado. Although some cotton is grown, much of the agriculture is devoted to grain sorghum production as an adjunct to the predominant livestock enterprises.

Along the northeastern edge of the plateau occurs a distinctive district unlike any other part of Texas. This is the Llano country, from which the radically dipping Comanchean limestones and older sedimentaries have been removed by erosion, thereby unroofing the pre-Cambrian rocks that form the central and higher portion of the area. The Llano country is a circumscribed basin, rimmed in by interior-facing escarpments, particularly of the Comanchean limestones. The inner portion is underlain by granitic and metamorphosed pre-Cambrian rocks; the outer portion, rimming the granitic outcrops, is underlain by Paleozoic sedimentaries that dip beneath the surrounding and geologically younger Comanchean limestones. Though structurally an uplifted area, the rough and broken Llano district is topographically a basin threaded by the Llano and Colorado rivers. It is timbered, but grasses are practically absent on the rougher portions of the granitic central section. The Edwards Plateau as a whole, like the High Plains, offers limited permanent supplies of surface water. Before modern transportation and the means of tapping underground water were developed, travel across the Edwards Plateau country was difficult. *E. H. Johnson*

Edwards, Haden. Pioneer settler and land speculator; b. Stafford County, Virginia, 12 August 1771; d. Nacogdoches, 14 August 1849; m. Susanna Beall (1820); 13 children. Edwards's father was a landowner and United States senator. With his bride Edwards moved to Mississippi, where he and his brother Benjamin acquired a plantation. After hearing of Moses Austin's coloniza-

Haden Edwards. Daguerreotype. Ca. 1845. Courtesy East Texas Research Center, Ralph W. Steen Library, Stephen F. Austin State University.

tion plans, Edwards traveled to Mexico City (1823), where he joined Stephen F. Austin, Robert Leftwich, and others in a three-year attempt to persuade various Mexican governments to authorize American settlement in Texas. Because of his wealth Edwards was often called upon to finance Austin. Their efforts resulted in the colonization law of 1824 in Mexico City and of 1825 in Saltillo, which allowed empresarios to introduce settlers to Texas. Edwards suffered more than he profited from his relationship with Austin, at least in his own mind, since he believed that Austin claimed the best lands and tried to push his boundaries in every direction at the expense of other empresarios. Edwards received a grant near Nacogdoches on which to settle 800 families. Like other empresarios he agreed to honor preexisting grants and claims made by Spain or Mexico. Of all empresarios, Edwards probably had the most such claims, some over a century old. In 1825 he posted notices to inform all potential claimants that they must come forward with proof of their claims or he would consider the land his and sell it to new settlers. This angered the older settlers, who opposed Edwards until he was expelled two years later.

Edwards also became involved in an election dispute between the representative of the older settlers, Samuel Norris, and Chichester Chaplin, Edwards's son-in-law. As empresario, Edwards certified the election of Chaplin. Norris then protested to Governor José Antonio Saucedo in San Antonio, and Saucedo upheld Norris's claim to office. However, Chaplin continued to hold the position until Norris requested aid from the local militia. Continued complaints from the area caused Edwards to come under suspicion, and his brother Benjamin, who handled business affairs while Haden was absent from Texas in 1826, addressed such strident correspondence to government officials that it resulted in the revocation of the Edwards grant in October of that year. Edwards was shocked by this turn of events. He had invested more than $50,000 to secure and launch the grant, and he did not willingly surrender it. Additionally, the cancellation of his grant resulted in the forfeiture of the claims of all settlers who had moved onto his lands. Thus, when the events known as the Fredonian Rebellion, which the Edwards brothers eventually headed, began the following month, the Edwards grantees were most supportive. The Fredonians dispersed in 1827, and Edwards fled to Louisiana for safety. He returned to Texas during the Texas Revolution and lived in Nacogdoches, engaged in the land business, until his death. Edwards was the first worshipful master of Milam Lodge No. 2 when it was organized in 1837, a fact that indicates his social status.   *Archie P. McDonald*

Eighth Texas Cavalry. A group of Texas volunteers for the Confederate Army popularly known as Terry's Texas Rangers; assembled by Benjamin Franklin Terry in August 1861. Each man was required to furnish a shotgun or carbine, a Colt revolver, a Bowie knife, and a saddle, bridle, and blanket. The army would provide the mounts. The regiment was mustered into Confederate service at Houston on 9 September 1861. Terry was elected colonel, Thomas S. Lubbock lieutenant colonel, and Thomas Harrison major. After Terry died at Woodsonville, Kentucky (8 December 1861) and his successor, Lubbock, died of an illness, John Austin Wharton was elected colonel and John G. Walker lieutenant colonel. When Wharton was promoted to brigadier general in the fall of 1862, Harrison became the regimental commander; he served in that post until the end of the war. Although the regiment had been promised duty in Virginia, it was diverted to Bowling Green, Kentucky, at the request of Gen. Albert Sidney Johnston, who was in command of the army headquartered there. Terry's Rangers distinguished themselves at the battles of Shiloh, Perryville, Murfreesboro, Chickamauga, and Chattanooga; in the Atlanta campaign; and as raiders in Kentucky and Tennessee under Lt. Gen. Nathan Bedford Forrest. The rangers were also part of the inadequate force under Gen. Joseph E. Johnston that attempted to slow Sherman's inexorable "march to the sea." Terry's Rangers delivered what was probably the last charge of the Army of Tennessee at the battle of Bentonville (March 19–20, 1865). Rather than surrender with the rest of Johnston's army at Durham Station, North Carolina, on 26 April 1865, 158 of the reported 248 survivors of the regiment slipped through Union lines to join other Confederates yet in the field. With the total collapse of the Southern cause, however, the Terry Rangers drifted home as individuals and in small groups, having never officially surrendered. With the exception of Hood's Texas Brigade, the Eighth Texas Cavalry was probably the best-known Texas unit to serve in the Civil War. It earned a reputation that ranked it among the most effective mounted regiments in the western theater of operations.   *Thomas W. Cutrer*

Eighth Texas Infantry. Organized as battalion of the Confederate States Army by Alfred Marmaduke Hobby in Refugio County on 14 May 1862; later known as Hobby's Eighth Texas Infantry Regiment. It began as three companies under captains Robert E. Jones, William E. McCampbell, and P. H. Breeden. A fourth company under Edwin E. Hobby was added in June 1862, and a fifth, under José M. Peñaloza, completed the battalion. The unit trained at Camp Charles Russell near Banquete until 19 July 1862, when it was ordered to defend Corpus Christi as a part of the Twenty-ninth Brigade. There it was joined by various other units of light artillery and mounted rifles and in February 1863 became the Eighth Texas Infantry Regiment, with a staff including John Ireland. As a battalion, the force prevented a federal invasion at Corpus Christi in August 1862 and in September captured J. W. Kittridge of the federal fleet. In 1863, after organization of the regiment, the Eighth guarded Fort Esperanza on Matagorda Island, kept a battery on Mustang Island, and in May drove Union troops off St. Joseph Island. In the fall of 1863 superior Union forces under Nathaniel P. Banks were able to force Hobby's troops back to the San Antonio River. After December 1863 the regiment was ordered transferred to East Texas, but many entered Waul's Legion instead. Part of the Eighth regiment was stationed on Galveston Island in the winter of 1863; other units in the area of Indianola and Lavaca engaged in skirmishes with the federals as late as February 1864. Most of the units fought under Thomas N. Waul to repel the Red River campaign in April 1864, and from then to the end of the war were employed in coastal defense in Texas. The regiment was mustered out of service on 22 May 1865.   *Hobart Huson*

Eighth United States Infantry. Regiment formed in 1838. It served briefly on the Canadian border and was transferred to Florida, where it participated in the Second Seminole War. On the eve of the Mexican War the Eighth was transferred to Texas with Zachary Taylor's army of occupation. It fought with Taylor in his drive to Monterrey and gained recognition for its role in eight engagements. After the war the regiment was deployed in Texas and New Mexico against the Apache Indians, and gradually assumed responsibility for protecting the trail between San Antonio and Santa Fe in the 1850s. In February 1861 Gen. David E. Twiggs surrendered federal posts in Texas to officials of the state Secession Convention. Though some of its officers resigned their commissions and joined the Confederate Army, almost all of the enlisted personnel of the Eighth remained loyal to the Union, and many were held in Texas as prisoners of war until exchanged for Confederate prisoners in February 1863. During the Civil War elements of the old Eighth were reconstituted as part of the Fifteenth Infantry, which fought for the Union in the eastern theater. Subsequently, the Eighth Infantry fought in Indian campaigns in Montana (1872) and Arizona (1876, 1886), participated in the Spanish-American War, and served in the Philippine Insurrection. As part of the Fourth Infantry Division it participated in World War II and later saw combat in Vietnam.   *Robert Wooster*

Electrical Power. The first electric power plant in Texas was built at Galveston in the early 1880s, and thereafter industrial development was slow. By 1900 there were numerous small, privately owned generating systems, some steam, some hydroelectric. The next decade brought a few larger developments, of which perhaps the best example was the hydroelectric plant established at a dam built across the Colorado River in 1891–92 to serve Austin. Though expected to provide 14,000 horsepower, the system, it was found, would produce only 900 horsepower during the summer months of minimum flow. The dam was destroyed by a flood in 1900. In 1912 a high-voltage transmission line was built from Waco to Fort Worth with a branch line from Hillsboro to Ferris, whence it branched north to Trinity Heights (near Dallas) and south to Corsicana. In 1920 the state consumed 679,000,000 kilowatt-hours, evidence of a marked expansion of the power industry. By 1925 consumption reached a total for the year of 1,268,000,000 kilowatt-hours, and in 1930 the total was 2,922,000,000. The only drop occurred in 1935, when only 2,538,000,000 kilowatt-hours was consumed. In 1945 more than 6,780,874,000 kilowatt-hours was sold to about a million customers. The average cost per kilowatt-hour to the consumer in 1945 was about half what it was in 1925. Although rural electrification began with the first cross-country transmission lines, it was not until the organization of rural electric cooperatives in 1936 under the Rural Electrification Administration that rural electrification began to be widespread. In 1946, 71 co-ops served 146,000 rural homes, and privately owned lines served approximately 118,000.

By 1950 the transmission lines in Texas of all power producers were coordinated into the Texas Grid System. By 1954 the total generating capacity of Texas power plants was 5,521,180 kilowatts, four times as much as in 1944. Of the 192 plants, 72 were powered by steam and produced 4,971,400 kilowatts; 101 were powered by internal combustion engines and produced 196,990 kilowatts; and 19 were hydroelectric and produced 352,790 kilowatts. By 1963 the 176 electrical power plants in Texas increased their total generating capability to 11,990,392 kilowatts, more than twice the 1954 figure. Although by 1970 the number of electric power plants had decreased to 171, their generating capability had risen to 25,117,928 kilowatts, almost five times the 1954 capacity. Of the total number of plants, 82 were steam-powered and had a capability of 23,955,741 kilowatts, 68 were powered by internal-combustion engines or gas turbines and had a capacity of 644,727 kilowatts, and 21 were hydroelectric plants with a capability of 517,460 kilowatts. Seventy-seven distribution cooperatives of the Rural Electrification Administration served 97 percent of the total Texas farms in 1970. In 1992 there were 132 electric power plants serving Texas (14 were not located in the state) with a combined capacity to generate 67,806 megawatts. Sixty-seven percent of the power plants were fueled by natural gas, 30 percent by coal and lignite, 7 percent by nuclear power, and 1 percent by water flow. Electric power in Texas was supplied by municipally owned systems, rural electric cooperates, federal and state financed projects, and 10 investor-owned electric utility companies. In 1992 Texas electric utilities employed more than 40,000 people and received $14 billion in revenues.

El Orcoquisac. A Spanish outpost north of the site of present Wallisville, consisting of San Agustín de Ahumada Presidio and Nuestra Señora de la Luz Mission. Indians, including Orcoquisacs, attracted French traders to the region as early as the 1720s, and rumors of French incursions reached Governor

Jacinto de Barrios y Jáuregui at Los Adaes. Alarmed, the governor in 1754 dispatched Lt. Marcos Ruiz and 25 soldiers, who arrested Joseph Blancpain of Natchitoches and others. Blancpain's log trading post was dismantled, and the lumber was given to the Orcoquiza Indians. The prisoners were marched to Mexico City, where Blancpain died (1756). Barrios decided to establish an outpost on the site of the French trading post. Ruiz marched again to the Trinity with 31 men, 151 horses, guns, swords, saddles, supplies, and other military equipment and took possession of the site. The presidio was named San Agustín de Ahumada in honor of the viceroy. Temporary structures were completed by 12 July 1756. Two missionaries from Zacatecas were assigned to the new Nuestra Señora de la Luz Mission. Both priests quickly fell ill, and the older one died and was replaced. By the fall of 1759 the mission had been rebuilt on a hill east of the presidio. In 1763 Capt. Rafael Martínez Pacheco was appointed commander of the presidio, to replace the unsatisfactory Lt. Domingo del Río (1756–63), who left the garrison demoralized. Although Martínez maintained cordial relations with the Franciscans and the Indians, the soldiers regarded his command as cruel and arrogant. All but five deserted and fled to Natchitoches. Upon hearing this, Governor Ángel de Martos y Navarrete suspended Martínez and ordered Ruiz and a small force to El Orcoquisac to arrest the commander. Refusing to surrender, Martínez and a few men fortified themselves within his quarters. After three days of unsuccessful negotiations, Ruiz and his men set fire to the presidio on 11 October 1764 in an effort to flush them out. But the wily commander slipped out of a secret passage in the chimney of his quarters and fled to San Antonio. Ruiz was briefly installed as commander of the outpost and served until his arrest in November 1765 on charges of burning a royal presidio. He was replaced by Melchor Afán de Rivera. Ironically, the command of the presidio was restored to Martínez Pacheco, who had been cleared of responsibility for the fire. The mission and presidio were ravaged by hurricanes in 1762 and 1766, and the presidio was moved to a low hill about a quarter league from its original location. The Marqués de Rubí and a capable engineer, Nicolás de Lafora, made a formal inspection of the outpost in 1767. Rubí concluded that the post was of little strategic importance to Spain. His report, along with a comedic series of attempts to relocate the outpost over the course of its history, led to its abandonment in 1771. Two centuries later the site was found and archeologically verified. An area including the mission, presidio, Blancpain's trading post, and about 200 Indian sites, named the El Orcoquisac Archeological District, was added to the National Register of Historic Places in Texas in 1972.   *Kevin Ladd*

El Paso, Texas. At the far western tip of Texas, where New Mexico and the Mexican state of Chihuahua meet in a harsh desert environment around the slopes of Mount Franklin on the Rio Grande. As they approached the Rio Grande from the south, Spaniards in the sixteenth century viewed two mountain ranges rising out of the desert with a deep chasm between. This site they named El Paso del Norte (the Pass of the North), the future location of two border cities—Ciudad Juárez on the south or right bank of the Rio Grande, and El Paso, Texas, on the opposite side of the river. Since the sixteenth century the pass has been a continental crossroads; a north–south route along a historic *camino real* prevailed during the Spanish and Mexican periods, but traf-

fic shifted to an east–west axis in the years following 1848, when the Rio Grande became the international boundary. The El Paso area was inhabited for centuries by various Indian groups before the Spaniards came. The first party of Spaniards that certainly saw the Pass of the North was the Rodríguez–Sánchez expedition of 1581. This was followed by the Espejo–Beltrán expedition of 1582 and the historic colonizing expedition under Juan de Oñate, who, on 30 April 1598, in a ceremony at a site near that of present San Elizario, took formal possession of the entire territory drained by the Río del Norte (the Rio Grande). This act, called La Toma, or "the claiming," brought Spanish civilization to the Pass of the North and laid the foundations of more than two centuries of Spanish rule over a vast area. In the late 1650s Fray García founded the mission of Nuestra Señora de Guadalupe on the south bank of the Rio Grande; it still stands in downtown Ciudad Juárez. The Pueblo Indian Revolt of 1680 sent Spanish colonists and Tigua Indians of New Mexico fleeing southward to take refuge at the pass, transplanting the names of New Mexico river pueblos, including La Isleta and Socorro, to the El Paso area. On 12 October 1680, midway between the Spanish settlement of Santísimo Sacramento and the Indian settlement of San Antonio, the first Mass in Texas was celebrated at a site near that of present Ysleta, which was placed on what is now the Texas side by the shifting river in 1829; Ysleta thus has a claim to being the oldest town in Texas. By 1682 five settlements had been founded in a chain along the south bank of the Rio Grande—El Paso del Norte, San Lorenzo, Senecú, Ysleta, and Socorro. By the middle of the eighteenth century about 5,000 people lived in the El Paso area—Spaniards, mestizos, and Indians—the largest complex of population on the Spanish northern frontier. A large dam and a series of acequias (irrigation ditches) made possible a flourishing agriculture. The large number of vineyards produced wine and brandy said to have ranked with the best in the realm. In 1789 the presidio of San Elizario was founded to help in the defense of the El Paso settlements against the Apaches.

With the establishment of Mexican independence from Spain in 1821, the El Paso area and what is now the American Southwest became a part of the Mexican nation. Agriculture, ranching, and commerce continued to flourish, but the Rio Grande frequently overflowed its banks, causing great damage to fields, crops, and adobe structures. In 1829 the unpredictable river flooded much of the lower Rio Grande valley and formed a new channel that ran south of the towns of Ysleta, Socorro, and San Elizario, thus placing them on an island some 20 miles in length and two to four miles in width. Of the various land grants made by the local officials in El Paso del Norte, the best known and most successful was given to Juan María Ponce de León, a Paseño aristocrat, in what is now the downtown business district of El Paso. By this time a number of Americans were engaged in the Chihuahua trade, two of whom—James W. Magoffin and Hugh Stephenson—became El Paso pioneers at a later date. After the outbreak of hostilities between the United States and Mexico in May 1846, Col. Alexander Doniphan and a force of American volunteers defeated the Mexicans at the battle of Brazito, entered El Paso del Norte, and invaded Chihuahua in December. The Treaty of Guadalupe Hidalgo, which officially ended the Mexican War, fixed the boundary between the two nations at the Rio Grande, the Gila River, and the Colorado River, thence westward to the Pacific. Thus El Paso del Norte, the future Ciudad Juárez, became a border town.

Plaza and Church of El Paso, by Augustus de Vaudricourt, 1857. Chromolithograph by Sarony Major and Knapp, New York. 6" × 8⁵⁄₁₆". Prints and Photographs Collection, El Paso file 2, CAH; CN 09227. When the final boundary between the U.S. and Mexico was drawn, the Mexican town of El Paso (now Ciudad Juárez) remained in Mexico and the American village of Franklin became the new El Paso.

By late 1849, aided by the gold rush to California, five settlements had been founded along the left bank of the Rio Grande: Frontera, the northernmost, established by T. Frank White; the flour mill known as El Molino, founded by Simeon Hart; the mercantile store of Benjamin Franklin Coons, located on the ranch he purchased from Ponce de León; Magoffinsville, built by the veteran Chihuahua trader; and the property of Hugh Stephenson, later called Concordia, an estate that had belonged to his wife's family. In addition, the three Mexican towns of Ysleta, Socorro, and San Elizario were declared to be in the United States; thus by 1850 the bicultural, bilingual foundations of the future El Paso were clearly established. A number of important developments during the 1850s shaped the character of the area north of the river. A settlement on Coons' Rancho called Franklin became the nucleus of El Paso. El Paso County was established in March 1850, with San Elizario as the first county seat. The United States Senate fixed a boundary between Texas and New Mexico at the thirty-second parallel, thus largely ignoring history and topography. A military post called Fort Bliss was established in 1854. And the Butterfield Overland Mail arrived in 1858. A year later pioneer Anson Mills completed his plat of the town of El Paso, a name that resulted in endless confusion until the name of the town across the river, El Paso del Norte, was changed to Ciudad Juárez in 1888. During the Civil War most of the El Paso pioneers were overwhelmingly sympathetic to the South. Although Confederate forces occupied Fort Bliss in 1861, the tide began to turn in favor of the Union cause

the following year, and in August the Stars and Stripes was raised once again over Fort Bliss. The local Southern sympathizers eventually received presidential pardons, but some, such as Simeon Hart, battled for years before they recovered their property. In 1877 the region had its own civil war, the Salt War of San Elizario, a bloody racial conflict that had little to do with salt, but that set Texan against Mexican, strong man against strong man, faction against faction, and the United States against Mexico. Bad blood, personality conflicts, and intense personal rivalries characterized the affair, and mob violence, rape, robbery, and murder went unpunished with the breakdown of law enforcement. At length Fort Bliss, which had been shut down, was reestablished, and six months of bloodshed was brought to a halt. The arrival of the railroads in 1881 and 1882 transformed a sleepy, dusty little adobe village of several hundred inhabitants into a flourishing frontier community that became the county seat in 1883 and reached a population of more than 10,000 by 1890. As El Paso became a western boomtown, it also became "Six Shooter Capital" and "Sin City," where scores of saloons, dance halls, gambling establishments, and houses of prostitution lined the main streets. In the 1890s reform-minded citizens conducted a campaign to curb the most visible forms of vice and lawlessness, and in 1905 the city finally enacted ordinances closing houses of gambling and prostitution.

After 1900 El Paso began to shed its frontier image and develop as a modern municipality and significant industrial, commercial, and transportation center. The city grew from

Public School House, ca. 1890. Photograph by Charles B. Turrill. Southern Pacific Sunset Route Photographs, CAH; CN 02967. The arrival of the railroads in 1881 and 1882 transformed the "adobe village" of El Paso into a flourishing, respectable frontier community.

15,906 in 1900 to 39,279 in 1910 and 77,560 in 1925. The exodus of refugees fleeing the disruption of the Mexican Revolution contributed heavily to the city's growth during this period. Factors making this rapid development possible included El Paso's geographic location as a gateway to Mexico; its proximity to the mining areas of Mexico, New Mexico, and Arizona; its plentiful natural resources; and an abundant supply of cheap Mexican labor. The Kansas City Smelting and Refining Company constructed a large smelter at El Paso in 1887 and merged with several smaller companies in 1899 to become the American Smelting and Refining Company (ASARCO), which continued to be a major local employer into the 1980s. The completion of Elephant Butte Dam in 1916 in New Mexico ensured a steady water supply for agricultural development and helped make cotton the predominant local crop. Standard Oil Company of Texas (now Chevron USA), Texaco, and Phelps Dodge located major refineries in El Paso in 1928 and 1929. Prohibition provided a boost to the local economy by stimulating a growing tourist trade with the drinking and gambling establishments across the border in Juárez. For more than 130 years Fort Bliss has played a significant role in local, national, and international affairs, and the relationship between the city and the post has always been close. The military establishment was responsible for much of El Paso's growth during the 1940s and 1950s, when El Paso absorbed the town of Ysleta and greatly increased its municipal area. In 1986 military personnel made up one-fourth of the city's population and accounted for one out of every five dollars flowing through El Paso's economy. Textiles, tourism, the manufacture of cement and building materials, the refining of metals and petroleum, and food processing were El Paso's major industries

in the 1980s; prominent local brands included Tony Lama boots, Farah slacks, and Levi's. Public education in El Paso began with the establishment of an elementary school in 1884 and a high school in 1885. The State School of Mines and Metallurgy opened in 1914, held its first commencement in 1916, changed its name to Texas Western College in 1949, and became the University of Texas at El Paso in 1967. El Paso has had several junior colleges, beginning with the College of the City of El Paso, which held classes for two years starting in 1918 and was followed by El Paso Junior College from 1920 to 1927 and the current El Paso Community College, established in 1972. The El Paso Symphony Orchestra, one of the oldest in the state, traces its roots back to 1893. The El Paso Museum of Art, established in 1947 as El Paso International Museum, houses a collection of works by European Old Masters. El Paso's two major newspapers, the *Times* and the *Herald Post*, date from the early 1880s. The city has operated a public transportation system since 1882.

A major characteristic of El Paso is its special relationship with Mexico in general and Ciudad Juárez in particular. In 1983 El Paso–Juárez was the largest binational urban area along the Mexican border. Historic developments—the Taft–Díaz meeting of 1909; the taking of Ciudad Juárez by the revolutionary forces of Francisco I. Madero in 1911; the activities of Pancho Villa, particularly the raid on Columbus, New Mexico, followed by Gen. John J. Pershing's punitive expedition of 1916; the immigration of Mexican families, rich and poor, during and after the Mexican Revolution; the smuggling and bootlegging activities during the Prohibition era; the Chamizal Dispute and its settlement in 1964; and the growing interdependence of the two cities—all attest to the unique relationship existing between El

Paso and Ciudad Juárez. The rapid growth that characterized El Paso during the first quarter of the twentieth century slowed somewhat during the 1930s. After reaching 102,421 in the 1930 census the population declined to 96,810 by the 1940 census. Postwar development brought the number of residents up to 130,003 in 1950. Fueled by rapid military and commercial expansion, El Paso's population more than doubled during the next 10 years, reaching 276,687 in 1960. Slower but steady growth continued throughout the 1960s, with the population reaching 339,615 in 1970. Despite a period of sluggishness from 1971 to 1974, El Paso's population grew by 32 percent during the 1970s, to 425,259 in 1980. The population has always been predominantly Hispanic. In 1980 it was 62.5 percent Spanish-surnamed, and the interaction between the Spanish–Mexican North and the Anglo-American Southwest continued to be the dominant feature of El Paso's culture. In 1990 the population was 515,342.

W. H. Timmons

Emory, William Hemsley. Army officer and boundary surveyor; b. Queen Anne's County, Maryland, 7 September 1811; d. D.C., 1 December 1887; m. Matilda Wilkins Bache (1838); three children; ed. West Point (grad. 1831). Emory resigned from the army in 1836 to work as a civil engineer but returned to the service in 1838. Subsequently, as a lieutenant, captain, and major in the topographical engineers, he specialized in exploration and boundary surveys along the Texas–Mexican border (1844), the United States–Canadian border (1844–46), the United States–Mexican border (1848–53), and the Gadsden Purchase (1854–57). In 1844 he served on an expedition that produced a new map of Texas showing Texas claims westward to the Rio Grande. He came to public attention as the author of *Notes of a Military Reconnaissance from Fort Leavenworth in Missouri to San Diego in California*, published by Congress (1848). This report described terrain and rivers, cities and forts, pueblos and prehistoric ruins, animals and plants, and Indians and Mexicans, primarily in New Mexico, Arizona, and Southern California. It was one of the important chronicles and descriptions of the Southwest. Emory, a reliable cartographer, drew dozens of maps of the West. His accurate rendering of the topography usually made other maps obsolete. He acquired his greatest fame as supervisor of the United States–Mexican boundary survey between 1848 and 1853. That survey included an exploration of the Big Bend region of the Rio Grande. He became the foremost authority on the trans-Mississippi Southwest. During the Mexican War he served in the Southwest and in California as chief engineer in the Army of the West under Gen. Stephen W. Kearny. His Civil War service included command of a division in the Red River campaign. After the war Emory held a number of posts, most importantly commander of the Department of the Gulf, a demanding and dangerous Reconstruction assignment. General Sheridan removed Emory from command and saw to it that he was retired in 1876. *Joseph G. Dawson III*

Empresario. A land agent or land contractor who operated under the Mexican colonization laws. Outstanding Texas empresarios included Stephen F. Austin, Samuel May Williams, Green DeWitt, Martín De León, Sterling C. Robertson, James Power, James Hewetson, John McMullen, James McGloin, and Arthur G. Wavell.

English. The first Englishmen in Texas, according to an early written account, were not settlers, but three seamen set ashore by John Hawkins in Mexico in the sixteenth century near Tampico, after a battle with the Spanish at Veracruz on Hawkins's third expedition to the Indies. The three seamen, David Ingram, Richard Twide, and Richard Browne, allegedly walked across lower Texas on their way north in 1568, and Ingram's brief account was included by the younger Richard Hakluyt in his publication in 1589 of *The Principall Navigations, Voiages and Discoveries of the English Nation* (though Hakluyt's doubts about the authenticity of the story caused its omission from subsequent editions). Scattered English farmers and businessmen may have settled in Texas by 1800. At least six Englishmen were awarded empresario contracts in the 1820s, though none was successful in bringing in families; in the 1830s attempts at colonization began on a much larger scale, though again with limited success. John Charles Beales's Rio Grande colony included a few English families, and the contract granted by the Republic of Texas to the Peters colony in 1841 eventually resulted in the scattered settlement of large areas in North Texas, covering parts of 26 future counties. William Kennedy failed to fulfill a contract to bring 600 families to Texas, but he did attract a good deal of attention with his book, *Texas: The Rise, Progress, and Prospects of the Republic of Texas* (1841); William Bollaert, who published some of his own accounts of traveling in Texas in English magazines, was attracted to the new republic by Kennedy's book. A later colonization attempt, the Colony of Kent, was made in Bosque County in 1850.

Ranching and land-investment interests in the Panhandle undoubtedly reflected the greatest intercourse between England and Texas, especially in the boom years of 1880–87. By the end of 1886 the English had invested about $25 million in western ranches and directly controlled more than 20 million acres of Panhandle land. The largest investor, the Capitol Freehold Land and Investment Company, showed nominal capital of 31,532,226 in 1885. Concerned that Texas lands were becoming monopolized by foreign control, many Texans sought protection from the large corporations. In 1891 Governor James S. Hogg approved the Alien Land Law, which prohibited aliens from holding lands unless they became United States citizens. Even though the law was later changed and did not prohibit land ownership by alien corporations, British investments declined in the following decades. The benefits that British investors and managers conferred upon the land and economy of Texas are not easily measured. They helped to introduce barbed wire, steel windmills, deep wells, and better breeds of cattle into Northwest Texas, and they also made attempts to attract more settlers.

The considerable English influence upon diplomacy and law in Texas during its years as a republic resulted in several treaties and mediations. English culture in Texas through the nineteenth and twentieth centuries, mostly mediated by the settlement of Anglo-Americans, became so pervasive that it is difficult to isolate various contributions. In the twentieth century the largest influx of English into the country occurred when soldiers returning home after World War II were accompanied by their English brides. In 1953 the Anglo-Texan Society was formed in London to foster the establishment of closer cultural ties; Graham Greene, the British novelist, served as the first president. In the latter part of the twentieth century, Renaissance festivals and the Texas Folklife Festival in San Antonio celebrated

English culture. The 1990 census listed 2,024,001 persons of English descent in the state.   *John L. Davis and Phillip L. Fry*

Episcopal Theological Seminary of the Southwest. In Austin; founded by John E. Hines, coadjutor bishop of the Diocese of Texas. The church had a lease on a residence near the University of Texas in which Bible classes were being taught by Rev. Gray M. Blandy, instructor at the Canterbury Bible Chair and chaplain of Episcopal students at the University of Texas. Two other clergymen, Rev. Lawrence Brown, Bible Chair instructor at Texas A&M, and Rev. John M. Holt, vicar of the mission church at Mexia, assisted Blandy. Classes began in 1951, under the auspices of Austin Presbyterian Theological Seminary. The seminary received a bequest from the estate of Ann Laird of Kilgore and was given the library of the former De Lancy Divinity School of Buffalo, New York. It received a charter from the state of Texas in 1951 and was recognized as an agency of the Diocese of Texas in January of 1952. At the same time it was recognized by two other dioceses in Texas, West Texas and Dallas, which had sent students to it and shared in its board of trustees. Dr. and Mrs. Ernest Villavaso and Frederick Duncalf donated five acres for a campus. After Bishop Hines was elected presiding bishop of the Episcopal Church and resigned as chairman of the trustees, he was succeeded by Bishop E. H. Jones of West Texas. In 1998 the seminar had an enrollment of 118 students and a faculty of 18.   *Lawrence L. Brown*

Escandón, José de. South Texas colonizer; b. Soto la Marina, Santander, Spain, 19 May 1700; d. Mexico City, 10 September 1770; m. Dominga Pedrajo (1727; d. 1736); m. María Josefa de Llera (1737); 7 children. Escandón is known as the colonizer and first governor of Nuevo Santander. He founded over 20 towns or villas and a number of missions in the colony, including Camargo, Reynosa, Mier, and Revilla south of the Rio Grande and Laredo and Nuestra Señora de los Dolores Hacienda north of the Rio Grande. For his colonization efforts Escandón is sometimes called the "father" of the lower Rio Grande valley. At the age of 15 he arrived at Mérida, Yucatán, where he served as a cadet in the Mounted Encomenderos Company. In 1727 he subdued an Indian uprising in Celaya and received the rank of sergeant major of the regiment at Querétaro. In 1740 the viceroy of Mexico named him colonel of the military companies of Querétaro, since he had been successful in pacifying the Indians. In 1746 Escandón was commissioned to inspect the country between Tampico and the San Antonio River. In January 1747 he sent seven divisions into the area, and in October he presented a colonization plan. After delays by the Spanish bureaucracy, Escandón was made governor and captain general of Nuevo Santander in 1748. In 1749 he was made Count of Sierra Gorda and Knight of the Order of Santiago by Fernando VI, and began establishing his settlements along the Rio Grande. Laredo was the largest and most successful permanent Spanish settlement in Southwest Texas. After the appointment of a royal commission in 1767, the settlers of Nuevo Santander were assigned the land grants that Escandón had promised them. Grants were made to residents of the colonies of the Rio Grande, thus starting the colonization of South Texas from the Rio Grande to the San Antonio River. Escandón was accused by Diego Corrido of maladministration, and he had to travel to Mexico City to defend himself. He died during his trial. In 1773 his son Manuel Ignacio de Escandón y Llera petitioned the court for a settlement; the court completely exonerated Escandón.   *Clotilde P. García*

Espejo–Beltrán Expedition. Followed upon the Rodríguez–Sánchez expedition, which had left two Franciscan priests in danger in New Mexico. Concern for their safety, combined with glowing accounts of new discoveries made by the earlier expedition (1581–82), led another Franciscan in Santa Bárbara, Bernardino Beltrán, to seek authority to send a rescue mission to New Mexico. Antonio de Espejo, a wealthy fugitive from justice accused of murder, who had taken refuge on the frontier and was looking for an opportunity to exonerate himself, offered his services and finances to Fray Beltrán. The expedition, consisting of 14 soldiers, their servants, 115 horses and mules, arms, munitions, and provisions, left San Bartolomé, a mining outpost nine leagues north of Santa Bárbara, on 10 November 1582. A month later the travelers reached the juncture of the Río Conchos and the Rio Grande, which Espejo named the Río del Norte. Up the river was a nation Espejo called the Jumanos, who lived in large pueblos with flat roofs, gave the Spaniards food, and told them that some years before three white men and a Negro had passed through the area. In January 1583 the expedition approached the El Paso area, inhabited by the Suma and Manso Indians. They followed the Río del Norte upstream, through a "mountain chain on each side of it, both of which were without timber," a possible reference to El Paso del Norte, as Spaniards later named it. In late January 1583 Espejo and his companions reported "a large black rock," a possible reference to Elephant Butte, and on 1 February they arrived at the southernmost pueblos of New Mexico. Here they learned that both Rodríguez and López had been killed by the Indians. Beltrán therefore proposed that the expedition return since the fate of the two missionaries had been determined, but Espejo, whose leadership was unchallenged by this time, insisted on further explorations in the hope of finding riches. From March to July 1583 the party explored extensively in what is now Arizona. Although he found no riches, Espejo remained convinced that the reports of wealth were true. Meanwhile, Beltrán and several others had left the expedition and returned to Santa Bárbara. In June 1583 Espejo and his companions turned eastward. They entered the Pecos valley, followed the Pecos River southward into the land of the Jumanos, and on 22 August reached the juncture of the Rio Grande and the Conchos. The little band finally arrived in San Bartolomé on 10 September. Espejo's report of rich silver mines and natives of an advanced cultural level who would be receptive to conversion aroused widespread interest and a strong desire among Spanish officials to occupy and colonize the lands that he had visited. In the succeeding years there were numerous applicants, including Espejo, for the necessary official authorization to conquer and colonize New Mexico, but all were denied. Not until 1595 was a candidate found with the necessary qualifications to gain the approval of the Spanish crown for this important assignment. His name was Juan de Oñate.   *W. H. Timmons*

Espinosa, Isidro Félix de. Missionary; b. Querétaro, 26 November 1679; d. Querétaro, 14 February 1755. He entered the Franciscan missionary College of Santa Cruz de Querétaro as a novice in 1696, was ordained a priest in 1703, and was assigned to San Juan Bautista. In 1709 accompanied by Father Antonio de San Buenaventura y Olivares, Capt. Pedro de Aguirre, and 14 soldiers, Espinosa traveled to the site of future San Antonio. There the padres were much impressed by the availability of water and the prospects for Spanish settlement. The Espinosa–Olivares–Aguirre expedition probed beyond the San Antonio River to the Colorado, where it hoped to make contact with the Tejas Indians, who were rumored to have moved there. After finding no Tejas but learning that those Indians were still ill-disposed toward the Spanish, the expedition returned to San Juan Bautista. Espinosa soon returned to Querétaro and remained there until he was named president of the new missions to be established in Texas by his college. In 1716 he accompanied the expedition of Domingo Ramón, which established three missions in East Texas: Nuestro Padre San Francisco de los Tejas, Nuestra Señora de la Purísima Concepción, and San José de los Nazonis. Espinosa participated in two more Texas expeditions, those of Martín de Alarcón (1718) and the Marqués de Aguayo (1721). His contributions as a chronicler of early Texas history are without peer. Dubbed "the Julius Caesar of the Faith in New Spain" because he worked by day and wrote all night, Espinosa left a remarkable body of literature. It includes a biography of his friend Antonio Margil de Jesús and *Crónica de los colegios de propaganda fide de la Nueva España*, called "the most important contemporary account of the Franciscans in Texas." He was recalled from Texas in late 1721 to serve as guardian of his missionary college and never returned to the province. In 1733 he was named president of the future Hospicio de San Fernando in Mexico City. In late life he returned to the college of Santa Cruz in Querétaro. *Donald E. Chipman*

Estevanico. Slave; also known as Estevan, Esteban, Estebanico, Black Stephen, and Stephen the Moor; b. Azamor, Morocco; d. New Mexico, March 1539. In Spain before 1527 Estevanico became the personal slave of Andrés Dorantes de Carranza. Though he is usually referred to as a Negro or African black, a Spaniard, Diego de Guzmán, who saw him in Sinaloa in 1536, described him as "brown." Estevanico accompanied his master as a member of the Narváez expedition, which landed in mid-April 1528 near what is now called Tampa Bay. Narváez, after a futile attempt at marching along the Gulf Coast, elected to slaughter the horses and to build five makeshift barges. The boat containing Estevanico was placed under the joint command of Dorantes and Alonso Castillo Maldonado. After a month at sea, the craft was wrecked on or near western Galveston Island. On foot Estevanico, Dorantes, and Castillo reached Matagorda Bay. Their continued safety among hostile coastal Indians hinged on the success of faith healing, first introduced to them by Castillo Maldonado. After six years of precarious existence, a fourth survivor, Cabeza de Vaca, joined them. Subsequently, the castaways escaped to the interior of Texas. Estevanico was the first African-born slave, and the first black Catholic, to traverse Texas. In the company of his master, he traveled a west-by-northwest route from the site of San Antonio to that of Pecos. In March 1536 the four survivors were reunited with their countrymen north of Culiacán in Nueva Galicia, where Dorantes sold Estevanico to Viceroy Antonio de Mendoza. The viceroy assigned the slave to a Franciscan, Fray Marcos de Niza, who had been ordered to Nueva Galicia. In early March 1539 Niza and Estevanico arrived at the Río Mayo in what is now Sonora. Estevanico, restless over the slow progress of the friar and his support party, was sent ahead as an advance scout. Separated by several days' travel from

Niza, he approached Cíbola, thought today to be the pueblo of Hawikuh, and announced his intentions to make peace and heal the sick. He told the villagers that he had been sent by white men who would soon arrive and instruct them in divine matters. The village elders, suspicious of his claims that he came from a land of white men and resentful of his demands for turquoise and women, killed him when he attempted to enter the village. Hawikuh, the southernmost of the seven pueblos known as the Seven Cities of Cíbola, was 15 miles southwest of the site of present Zuni, New Mexico. *Donald E. Chipman*

Examining Boards. State licensing boards, generally appointed by the governor. They examine applicants and issue licenses for the practice of a particular profession or trade. They can investigate and revoke licenses. Members must have professional licenses and usually at least five years' experience. Some other government agencies also administer licensing: the Texas State Library and Archives Commission, 1909; Texas Education Agency, 1949; Texas Department of Aviation, 1989; State Board of Insurance, 1957; State Bar of Texas, 1936; and Texas Department of Health, 1879.

The examining boards, with their dates of establishment, are as follows:

Texas State Board of Acupuncture Examiners, 1993
Texas Appraiser Licensing and Certification Board, 1991
Texas Board of Architectural Examiners, 1937
State Board of Barber Examiners, 1929
Texas State Board of Chiropractic Examiners, 1949; an earlier board established in 1943 was declared unconstitutional in 1944
Texas Cosmetology Commission, 1971; replaced State Board of Hairdressers and Cosmetologists, 1935
Texas Court Reporters Certification Board, 1977
Texas State Board of Dental Examiners, 1919 (six-member), 1971 (nine-member), 1981 (twelve-member)
Texas State Board of Examiners of Dietitians, 1983
Texas Board of Examiners in the Fitting and Dispensing of Hearing Aids, 1969
Texas Funeral Service Commission, 1987; replaced State Board of Morticians
Texas Board of Irrigators, 1979
State Board of Law Examiners, 1919
Texas State Board of Marriage and Family Therapists, 1991
Texas State Board of Medical Examiners, 1907
State Board of Nurse Examiners, 1909
Texas Board of Licensure for Nursing Home Administrators, 1969
Texas Optometry Board, 1969; replaced Board of Examiners in Optometry, 1922
Texas State Board of Perfusion Examiners, 1994
Texas State Board of Pharmacy, 1907
Texas State Board of Physical and Occupational Therapy Examiners, 1993; included functions of Texas State Board of Physical Therapy Examiners
Texas State Board of Plumbing Examiners, 1947
Texas State Board of Podiatry Examiners, 1923; formerly known as the State Board of Chiropody Examiners
State of Texas Board of Polygraph Examiners, 1965
Board of Private Investigators and Private Security Agencies, 1969

Texas State Board of Examiners of Professional Counselors, 1981

State Board of Registration for Professional Engineers, 1937

Texas Board of Professional Land Surveying, 1979; replaced Board of Examiners of Land Surveyors, 1919, and State Board of Registration for Public Surveyors, 1955

Texas Board of Licensure for Professional Medical Physicists, 1991

Texas Board of Examiners of Psychologists, 1969

Texas State Board of Public Accountancy, 1945

Texas Real Estate Commission, 1949

Texas State Board of Examiners of Social Workers, 1993

State Committee of Examiners for Speech Pathology and Audiology, 1983

Texas Structural Pest Control Board, 1971

Board of Tax Professional Examiners, 1977

State Board of Veterinary Medical Examiners, 1911

State Board of Vocational Nurse Examiners, 1951

Dick Smith

Exodus of 1879. A migration of Texas freedmen to Kansas, where a homestead act offered free land to settlers willing to meet occupancy and improvement qualifications. Between 1875 and 1880 Kansas became the "promised land" and "Kansas fever" spread, as black Texans left the Democratic South. The heaviest migration from Texas occurred in 1879–80. In 1879 African Americans from Washington, Burleson, Grimes, Nacogdoches, Walker, and Waller counties, tired of share-cropping and limited influence under the Black Codes, boarded the Missouri, Kansas and Texas Railroad or traveled by wagon to Parsons, Kansas. Kansans called them "Texodusters." Their number can only be estimated, but it is known that around 1,000 left Texas in November 1879 and 3,000 to 4,000 by March 1880. As many as 12,000 are estimated to have made the journey. Before 1879 those leaving North Texas, only about 300 miles from Kansas, found the trip relatively easy. Benjamin "Pap" Singleton, a former Tennessee slave, promoted the migration. But as he inspired travelers, unscrupulous men began selling them bogus railway tickets and fictitious travel amenities. Richard Allen urged a planned, gradual movement out of the state. A convention held in Houston in 1879 to discuss the journey warned against any hasty move and against swindlers at both ends of the journey. As a result, later travelers had better success. Although hardships abounded in Kansas, few Texodusters returned home. Most remained in Kansas and by 1900 found themselves improved economically and politically. The exodus caused hardship for white Texas landowners, however. In some regions only a sparse labor force remained to work fields. In Washington County white farmers tried to retain black workers by offering not only the traditional one-year rentals on farms at five dollars an acre, but three-year terms at an annual reduction to three dollars an acre. Because these new contracts benefited workers choosing to remain, the exodus was generally beneficial for Texas blacks. *Peggy Hardman*

Exotics. The term *exotic* is commonly applied in Texas to foreign big game acquired by private landowners and released within fenced enclosures or allowed to range free. Although exotics are not distributed statewide, several species have become prominent in certain regions. The most popular and numerous are species of deer, antelope, and sheep. Though less popular as a game animal, the European wild swine is among the most numerous introduced species. Most of the more successful free-ranging exotic species in Texas come from the Asian continent. Axis deer, nilgai antelope, and blackbuck antelope were originally from India; the sika deer was imported from Southeast Asia. The mouflon sheep was from Sardinia and Corsica, the fallow deer from Asia Minor and southern Europe, and the European wild swine from Europe. The aoudad sheep was brought to Texas from North Africa. Texans have acquired exotics to observe for pleasure, to substitute for depleted native big game, to increase the variety of game for hunting, to increase production and income from rangelands by using combinations of animals that have varied food habits, and to sustain populations of species that are endangered on their native ranges. Most of the original exotic brood stock in Texas came from zoos. Subsequent stocking has mainly been with animals purchased from private landowners, zoos, and animal dealers. Exotics are not protected by the regulations that cover native game animals, and they are hunted at the prerogative of the landowner. Exceptions are the axis deer in Bexar and Kendall counties and aoudad sheep in counties contiguous to Palo Duro Canyon, where they are under state game regulations.

Perhaps the earliest releases of exotics were of nilgai antelope acquired by the King Ranch between 1930 and 1941 from the San Diego Zoo. During the same decade blackbuck antelope and axis (also called chital and spotted) deer, sika deer, and sambar deer were released. From the late 1930s through the 1950s mouflon sheep, eland antelope, red deer, swamp deer (barasingha), and other species were released. Today, more species and greater numbers of exotic big game are in Texas than anywhere else in North America. The first statewide census of exotics by the Texas Parks and Wildlife Department in 1963 found 13 species and 13,000 animals. The 1984 survey revealed about 75 species and 120,000 animals. Some species, such as the nilgai, are probably more numerous in Texas than they now are in their native habitats. Exotics are found in about half of the 254 Texas counties; 55 percent are concentrated in the Edwards Plateau. South Texas has 18 percent, and most of the remaining number are in localized areas of North, central East, and far West Texas. About 70 percent are confined on pastures by game-proof fences. The remaining 30 percent range free. The most numerous species have developed substantial free-ranging populations. Hybridization or intergradation has occurred between some species and subspecies through planned breeding and by chance; consequently, there are free-ranging individuals that are atypical of the species. Because exotic populations are localized and are found on private lands where their availability is limited, the general public is not aware of their numbers. Most exotics have been released without regard for their chances for survival, their compatibility with native biota, and their roles in the introduction and spread of diseases. Principal studies on exotics in Texas have been done by the Texas Parks and Wildlife Department, Texas A&M University, and Texas Tech University. The most studied species have been the axis, nilgai, blackbuck, sika, fallow, and aoudad; little is known about the ecology of other species.

Generally, though Texas exotics have fared well and ecological complications have been few, even successful free-ranging populations have occasionally had difficulty with their Texas habitat. Nilgai, blackbuck, and axis evolved in warm climates and are not physiologically adapted to withstand severe cold. Some have died in winter. Aoudad have died from infestations of liver flukes, endoparasites for which the sheep are new hosts. Studies indicate that axis, sika, fallow, and nilgai are dominant competitors with native deer for food, and on some heavily populated ranges, native deer are declining as the exotics increase. A major need is proper control of their numbers where prolific free-ranging populations exist. Favorable economic methods of control are to harvest them by sport hunting and for meat. New management changes have begun to emphasize the husbandry of exotics, not just stocking and hunting. The new commercial enterprise involves the production of brood stock, meat, and body parts such as antlers (which are sold as aphrodisiacs in Asia). Exotic meat for human food is gaining attention in the United States, and exotic game dishes are becoming popular in restaurants. Because of the large number of foreign animals and the ecological backlashes they have often caused, many people are opposed to having exotics free-ranging in this country. In Texas, however, where large numbers of exotics are firmly established, the concern now is understanding their ecological roles and practicing sound management. *William J. Sheffield*

Exxon. Traces its descent from the Humble Oil Company, which was chartered in Texas in February 1911, reorganized in 1917, and incorporated the same year as the Humble Oil and Refining Company. The original company resulted from the collaboration of Ross S. Sterling and Walter William Fondren with Robert L. Blaffer and William Stamps Farish and others. In 1919 Humble sold 50 percent of its stock to Standard Oil Company of New Jersey. This initiated Humble's long-term connection with the company that eventually absorbed it. In 1917 Humble had 217 wells and a daily crude oil production of about 9,000 barrels. The company was the largest domestic producer of crude oil during World War II and afterward, with 9,928 operating wells in 1949. Humble established the first production of crude oil in Florida in 1943 and by 1949 had production in Louisiana, New Mexico, Mississippi, Alabama, and California. In 1917 the company had three miles of gathering lines at Goose Creek. In 1949 the Humble Pipe Line Company, a subsidiary, had 3,233 miles of gathering lines and 5,776 miles of trunk lines. These facilities served all important producing areas in Texas and southeastern New Mexico, and the Humble Pipe Line Company was the largest transporter of crude oil in the United States. In the postwar period, the company built a pipeline from Baytown to the Dallas–Fort Worth area and in June 1950 completed an 18-inch direct line from West Texas to the Gulf Coast. When it was first organized, the company owned a small refinery at Humble, Texas. Over the years it operated refineries in San Antonio, Ingleside, and other sites. During World War II, Humble refineries produced high-octane aviation gasoline, toluene for explosives, Butyl rubber, and butadiene for synthetic rubber. The Baytown Ordnance Works produced nearly half of the toluene for explosives for World War II and was subsequently purchased by the company from the government. Humble continued to operate the government-owned butadiene and Butyl rubber plants at Baytown after the war. In the 1940s Humble products were retailed only in Texas, where retail sales had increased from 7 million gallons of refined products in 1917 to 540 million gallons in 1949. Humble's first home office was in Houston. Publications by the company included *The Humble Way, The Humble Bee, The Humble Sales Lubricator,* and the *Farm Family.* Early in 1963 the company moved into a new 45-story building,

at the time the tallest building west of the Mississippi River. It is still a Houston landmark and is the headquarters office of Exxon Company, U.S.A.

In 1958 Standard increased its holdings to some 98 percent of Humble's stock, and the following year Humble and Standard Oil of New Jersey consolidated domestic operations. In September 1959 Humble received a new charter from the state of Delaware. By the end of the year Esso Standard and the Carter Oil Company, other affiliates of Standard of New Jersey, were incorporated into Humble, and in 1960 they were joined by other affiliates including Enjay Chemical, Pate Oil, Globe Fuel Products, and Oklahoma Oil. The restructuring allowed the new Humble company to reduce duplication and costs and to coordinate all of its domestic activities more effectively. The Humble workforce dropped by a quarter in the first five years after the merger, while its profits doubled. In the 1960s Humble had more than 21,000 square miles of land under lease in the United States. The company operated 24,000 producing wells in 21 states with a daily production of 600,000 barrels of crude. Humble-operated wells also produced 2.6 billion cubic feet of natural gas daily. Six Humble refineries and plants processed about 800,000 barrels of crude oil daily and produced from that volume a great variety of products. In 1960 Humble constructed one of the world's largest gas-processing systems near the King Ranch, with extensive storage facilities for natural gas. In 1961 Humble Pipe Line Company and Interstate Oil Pipe Line Company merged to form a wholly owned affiliate of Humble Oil and Refining Company with a combined network of more than 12,000 miles of gathering and trunk lines. Aided by some chartered vessels, Humble's fleet of 19 ocean-going tankers delivered 400,000 barrels of crude oil and products to the eastern seaboard daily. Tows and barges of Humble's Inland Waterways system moved 300,000 barrels a day over the nation's rivers and other inland waterways. Humble began to increase its retailing outlets in the 1950s and 1960s. By 1961 it reached markets in 21 states. Humble was the first gasoline company to issue plastic gasoline credit cards in Texas. In 1961 the company began to sell its gasoline as Enco gas in 19 states, but retained the old brand name Humble in Texas and Ohio. Esso, the brand name of Standard of New Jersey, continued to be used on the east coast. In 1964 the popular "Put A Tiger In Your Tank" advertising campaign was instituted. In the 1960s Humble donated part of its West Ranch to Rice University; the land became the site of the Lyndon B. Johnson Space Center. In 1962, Humble joined forces with the Del E. Webb Corporation to develop 15,000 acres of the ranch; the agreement led to formation of the Friendswood Development Company, which soon began development of the residential part of Clear Lake City. Humble was involved in a number of other Houston-area real estate developments.

In 1972 Humble and Standard of New Jersey announced that their gasoline products were to be marketed as Exxon, that Standard of New Jersey was changing its name to Exxon Corporation, and that, as of 1 January 1973, Humble was changing its name to Exxon Company, U.S.A. The company, which operates only in the United States, is a division of Exxon Corporation, which operates also in foreign countries. Under its new name, it embarked on a renewed search for oil sources in the continental United States. By the mid-1970s most of Exxon's Middle Eastern oil suppliers had nationalized Exxon properties and, with the exception of Saudi Arabia, had become increasingly uncertain sources of crude oil. Exxon's attempts at increasing the domestic supply met with mixed success. In the early 1980s the company unsuccessfully attempted to develop shale oil from the Western Slope of Colorado as a significant source. A more productive, though also more controversial, new source of oil for the company was the development of the Prudhoe Bay field in Alaska. Humble's interest in Alaskan oil dated back to the late 1950s, when the company joined with Shell Oil in a costly drilling attempt that ended in failure. In partnership with Arco, Humble resumed its drilling in Alaska in the 1960s and in 1968 discovered the Prudhoe Bay field, the largest oilfield discovered in North America. Development of the field had to wait for nine years, as environmentalists fought the construction of an oil pipeline through Alaska to the port of Valdez. The pipeline was finally completed in 1977, and Exxon began shipping oil by tanker from Valdez to world markets. By 1985 the Prudhoe Bay field had produced some 800 million barrels. In March 1989 the supertanker *Exxon Valdez* ran aground and spilled almost a quarter of a million barrels of oil in Prince William Sound,

Alaska. Exxon organized a $2.5 billion cleanup and became involved in extended litigation over the damage caused by the spill. Exxon Company, U.S.A., was heavily involved in offshore drilling in the Gulf of Mexico from the 1950s and off the coast of Alaska and California from the late 1960s. It discovered and developed major gas reserves in Mobile Bay, Alabama, as well as an inland source of natural gas at LaBarge, Wyoming. Along with successive expansions of the Exxon refinery system at Baytown, new refineries were opened in Baton Rouge, Louisiana, Benecia, California, and Billings, Montana. In 1990 Exxon Corporation moved its corporate headquarters from New York City to Irving, Texas. In 1994 Exxon had the largest hydrocarbon reserve base in the United States. Its domestic fields produced 562,000 barrels of oil and 2,021 million cubic feet of natural gas a day. Its annual income from exploration and production in the United States totaled $852 million, 30 percent of the corporate total, and its income from domestic refining and marketing was $243 million, 17 percent of the corporate total. *James A. Clark and Mark Odintz*

F

Fannin, James Walker, Jr. A leading Texas revolutionary officer; b. Georgia, probably on 1 January 1804; d. Goliad, 27 March 1836; m. Minerva Fort; 2 daughters; ed. West Point (withdrew after two years). Fannin moved to Velasco in 1834 and became an agitator for the Texas Revolution. The town of Columbia appointed him to use his influence for the calling of the Consultation. On 27 August he wrote to an army officer in Georgia requesting financial aid for the Texas cause and West Point officers to command the Texas army. In September he became active in the volunteer army and subscribed money to an expedition to capture the *Veracruzana*, a Mexican ship at Copano. But the expedition did not materialize, and Fannin went to Gonzales, where, as captain of the Brazos Guards, he participated in the battle of Gonzales (2 October 1835). On 6 October he was one of a committee urging Stephen F. Austin to bring all possible aid to Gonzales, and when Austin brought up the whole Texas army and moved toward Bexar, James Bowie and Fannin were sent as scouts to determine conditions between Gonzales and Bexar and to secure supplies. On 27 October, Bowie and Fannin selected a campsite near Concepción Mission and the next day led the Texas forces in the battle of Concepción. On 10 November, Fannin was ordered to cut a Mexican supply route from Laredo to San Antonio but returned to headquarters when he was not joined by a supporting force. On 13 November Sam Houston, commander in chief of the regular army, offered Fannin the position of inspector general, but Fannin received an honorable discharge from the volunteer army on 22 November and began an urgent campaign for a larger regular army. On 5 December the General Council, acting on Fannin's advice, established an auxiliary volunteer corps. Houston commissioned Fannin as a colonel in the regular army on 7 December, and on 10 December the council ordered him to enlist reinforcements for the army and to contract for war supplies in the campaign against Bexar. Bexar had surrendered the day before, however, so the accumulated supplies were used in the 1836 campaign.

Continuing as an agent of the provisional government, Fannin began recruiting volunteers for the Matamoros expedition. After Houston withdrew from the expedition, Fannin was elected colonel of the Provisional Regiment of Volunteers at Goliad on 7 February 1836 and from 12 February to 12 March acted as commander in chief of the army. When he learned that the Mexicans under José de Urrea had occupied Matamoros, Fannin went no further with plans for the expedition and fell back to strengthen defenses at Goliad. Other elements of the expedition, under James Grant and Francis W. Johnson, were destroyed by Urrea, who then proceeded to attack Goliad. On 12 March Fannin dispatched most of his force to aid Texans near Refugio. Two days later, he received Houston's order to retreat to Victoria, which rescinded a previous order to relieve the Alamo. Waiting for the forces under Amon B. King and William Ward to return from Refugio, Fannin unwisely delayed retreating until he heard of their capture. On 19 March he began his retreat, but he and his men were surrounded and forced to surrender at the battle of Coleto. The Texans were imprisoned by the Mexicans at Goliad and subsequently massacred by order of Antonio López de Santa Anna in what became known as the Goliad Massacre. Fannin, who was already wounded, was shot separately at the mission. In his final weeks, he had written repeatedly asking to be relieved of his command. Most historians now agree that he made many serious mistakes as a commander. Nevertheless, he held out bravely until the end. Fannin County was named in his honor, as were the town of Fannin in Goliad County and Camp Fannin.
Clinton P. Hartmann

Farmers' Alliance. A major nineteenth-century organization. In September 1877, hurt by the falling price of cotton, farmers gathered in Lampasas County—a meeting that began the National Farmers' Alliance and Industrial Union, more commonly referred to as the Southern Farmers' Alliance. This organization eventually claimed a membership of almost three million, one of the largest protest organizations in American history. After slow initial growth, alliance president W. L. Garvin appointed S. O. Daws a full-time, salaried lecturer and ordered him to vitalize the movement, a task at which he was largely successful. The farmers subsequently looked at their plight in terms of the purchasing system, stressing the excessive prices on supplies; and of the marketing system, stressing the falling price of cotton and the exactions of middlemen. The first attempt to address problems in the purchasing system was the trade-agreement strategy. Each county alliance appointed a committee to ask merchants for the lowest prices in return for a guarantee of the alliance members' cash business. Trade agreements marginally improved purchasing conditions for hundreds of alliance farmers. Another strategy was alliance-owned cooperative stores, which reported annual sales ranging from $5,000 to $36,000. Cooperative flour, cottonseed oil, and corn mills, as well as cotton gins, were also established. The co-ops, however, failed to address the problem of declining cotton prices. Nor did they help the poor farmer who did not have the ready cash to participate. Consequently, some alliance farmers demanded political action to address their economic problems.

Tensions between political insurgents and political conservatives within the alliance climaxed at the August 1886 alliance convention in Cleburne, where the insurgents passed a series of political demands. The most controversial of these related to monetary reform. Believing that relief from declining crop prices required the expansion of the currency supply, alliance farmers demanded that the government immediately use silver in addition to gold as legal tender in order to ease the contracted currency supply. They argued, however, that significant relief required a more radical revamping of the existing monetary system than entailed by "free silver"—the establishment of a fiat currency system wherein the government would issue "greenbacks" based on a predetermined per capita circulation volume, rather than on an inflexible metallic standard. Political conservatives within the alliance condemned the Cleburne demands and maneuvered to establish a rival alliance that would be strictly a business organization dedicated to economic self-help. Andrew

Dunlap, a "strictly business" advocate, resigned from the alliance presidency. The chairman of the state executive committee, Charles William Macune, assumed the powers of president pro tem and called a special convention in January 1887. He proposed a central, statewide alliance exchange to coordinate the marketing of the cotton crop of the state membership and to act as a central purchasing house. He also called for the mobilization of the entire Cotton Belt under the alliance banner and set forth plans for a nationwide organizing effort. The "strictly business" advocates were pacified by the scope of his plans, and unity once more prevailed.

In its attack on the purchasing system, the alliance exchange attempted to bypass both retail and wholesale merchants. Most importantly, a cooperative credit program was established as an alternative to the existing crop-lien credit system. In its attack on the cotton-marketing system, the exchange plan instituted statewide bulking of cotton. Each county alliance bulked its members' cotton and sent bale samples to exchange headquarters in Dallas. There they were displayed in a sample room, where textile manufacturers examined them. Having eliminated the middlemen, alliance members received a larger proportion of the profit from cotton production and trade. The enthusiasm for the exchange plan among farmers was evident in the dramatic growth of the alliance from 75,000 in early 1887 to 150,000 by the following year. But by May 1888 the exchange was in a serious financial struggle, and in 1889 creditors foreclosed. A significant decline in state membership ensued; active, dues-paying members dropped from an alleged high in early 1888 of 225,000–260,000 to 142,000 by 1889. The crisis was abated momentarily by a boycott on jute bagging, which held together cotton bales. Jute had dramatically jumped in price in 1888 because of a price-fixing agreement among eight American companies. The boycott reduced the price of jute, but the proposed alternative—a cotton-bagging trust—failed to develop.

In 1889 a major redirection of alliance strategies was provided by Macune. He argued that the root cause of the agricultural depression was an insufficient currency supply, a problem for which the "subtreasury plan" was proposed. This entailed a governmental commodity-loan program and later a land-loan program. Under this plan, federal warehouses would be established for storage of nonperishable crops to wait for higher crop prices, and farmers would be allowed to borrow up to 80 percent of the local market price on the products deposited. The annual interest rate on these loans would be 2 percent, with additional nominal charges for handling, storage, and insurance. The program would be funded with newly printed money until the volume of circulating currency reached $50 per capita, a volume associated with the prosperous war years.

In Texas, a subtreasury educational campaign was begun. The *Southern Mercury*, the state alliance's newspaper, routinely included educational articles on the subtreasury. Scores of lecturers visited local alliances to explain the plan. Grand alliance encampments were centered around the idea of the subtreasury. This shift toward political action was decisive. In Texas the alliance played a major role in the 1890 victory of gubernatorial nominee James Stephen Hogg, a reform Democrat, who was a strong advocate of an intrastate Railroad Commission. However, since neither Hogg nor the state Democratic party platform had supported the subtreasury plan, delegates to the 1890 state alliance convention voted to make future support of the Democratic party contingent on its support of the subtreasury. Some loyal Democrats in the alliance were alarmed and attempted to mobilize an anti-subtreasury faction. In March 1891 they issued their "Austin Manifesto," which claimed that the subtreasury plan was merely a scheme of third-partyites trying to undermine the Democratic party. The manifesto was signed by eleven alliance members, eight of whom were state legislators. It caused tempers to flare; one of its signers got in a fist fight in the corridors of the Capitol with a prominent subtreasuryite. A special alliance convention was called to discuss the manifesto, and a resolution denouncing it passed easily.

In May 1891 a third party became a reality with the establishment of the People's party, whose platform was identical to the national platform of the alliance. The Democratic party's increasing hostility to the subtreasury plan led Texas alliance leaders to begin campaigning for the People's party; the national alliance formally endorsed that party in February 1892. Thereafter, the fate of the alliance was intricately linked with that of the People's party, which abandoned the subtreasury plan in 1896. By that time, however, the alliance had diminished radically. Since the People's party had endorsed the alliance platform in 1891, most alliance members saw no further need to continue paying alliance dues and attending alliance meetings. Consequently, the monetary resources of the alliance were not sufficient to fight the People's party betrayal of its cherished principles. *Donna A. Barnes*

Faulk, John Henry. Humorist and author; b. Austin, 21 August 1913; d. Austin, 9 April 1990; m. Hally Wood (1940; divorced); 1 daughter; m. Lynne Smith (divorced); 3 children; m. Elizabeth Peake (1965); 1 son; ed. University of Texas (B.A., M.A.). Under the guidance of J. Frank Dobie, Walter P. Webb, and Roy Bedichek, Faulk collected folklore and, for his M.A. thesis, recorded and analyzed 10 sermons from black churches in Travis and Bexar counties. He became convinced that African Americans and others were gravely deprived of their civil rights. Faulk taught an English course at UT (1940–42) in which he used mimicry and storytelling to illustrate the best and worst of Texas societal customs. Often made to feel inferior at faculty gatherings, he increasingly told unbelievable tales and bawdy jokes. His ability both to parody and to praise human behavior led to his entertainment and literary career. When the army refused to admit him because of a bad eye, he joined the United States Merchant Marine for a year of trans-Atlantic duty, followed by a year with the Red Cross in Cairo. By 1944 relaxed standards allowed the army to admit him for limited duty as a medic, and he served the rest of the war at Camp Swift. Radio provided Faulk an audience. Through his friend Alan Lomax, who worked at CBS in New York, Faulk became acquainted with industry officials. During Christmas 1945, Lomax hosted a series of parties to showcase Faulk's yarn-spinning abilities. When he was discharged from the army in April 1946, CBS gave Faulk his own weekly radio program, entitled "Johnny's Front Porch"; it lasted a year. Faulk began a new program on suburban station WOV in 1947 and the next year moved to another New Jersey station, WPAT, where he established himself as a raconteur while hosting "Hi-Neighbor," "Keep 'em Smiling," and "North New Jersey Datebook." WCBS Radio debuted the "John Henry Faulk Show" on 17 December 1951. The program, which featured music, political humor, and listener participation, ran for six years.

John Henry Faulk, New York City, 1947. John Henry Faulk Papers, CAH; CN 05869.

It ended in 1957, a victim of the Cold War and the blacklisting of the 1950s. In 1955 Faulk had earned the enmity of a blacklist organization, AWARE, and was branded a Communist. After losing his job, he sought redress. With financial backing from Edward R. Murrow, Faulk engaged New York attorney Louis Nizer. Attorneys for AWARE, including McCarthy-committee counsel Roy Cohn, managed to stall the suit, which was originally filed in 1957, for five years. Eventually, in 1962, the jury awarded Faulk the largest libel judgment in history to that date—$3.5 million. An appeals court reduced the amount to $500,000, and legal fees and accumulated debts erased the rest of the award. Despite his vindication, CBS did not rehire Faulk—indeed, years passed before he worked again as a media entertainer. He returned to Austin in 1968. From 1975 to 1980 he appeared as a homespun character on the television program "Hee-Haw." During the 1980s he wrote and produced two one-man plays. In both *Deep in the Heart* (1986) and *Pear Orchard, Texas*, he portrayed characters imbued with the best of human instincts and the worst of cultural prejudices. In 1974 CBS Television broadcast its movie version of *Fear on Trial*, Faulk's 1963 book that described his battle against AWARE. Also in 1974, Faulk read the dossier that the FBI had maintained on his activities since the 1940s. Disillusioned and desirous of a return to the country, he moved to Madisonville. He returned to Austin in 1981. In 1983 he campaigned for the congressional seat abdicated by Democrat-turned-Republican Phil Gramm. Although he lost the three-way race, he had spoken his mind. During the 1980s he traveled the nation urging university students to be vigilant regarding their constitutional rights and to take advantage of the freedoms guaranteed by the First Amendment. The Center for American History at the University of Texas at Austin sponsors the John Henry Faulk Conference on the First Amendment. The city of Austin named the downtown branch of the public library in his honor. *Page S. Foshee*

Felix Longoria Affair. A watershed civil-rights event that provided a successful case for the American G.I. Forum to fight discrimination against Mexican Americans. In 1948 the remains of Private Felix Longoria of Three Rivers were recovered from the Philippines, where Longoria had been killed during the last days of World War II. His body was shipped home for burial in the Three Rivers cemetery, where the "Mexican" section was separated by barbed wire. The director of the local funeral home would not allow the use of his chapel because of previous disturbances at Hispanic funerals and because the "whites would not like it." Longoria's widow and her sister discussed the refusal with Dr. Hector Garcia, founder of the Forum. On 11 January 1949, Garcia called a meeting of the Corpus Christi Forum, which he had organized as the first G.I. Forum chapter in March 1948; he also sent many telegrams and letters to Texas congressmen. Senator Lyndon Johnson responded with support and an offer to arrange the burial at Arlington National Cemetery. The funeral took place on 16 February 1949. Afterward, the Texas House of Representatives authorized a five-member committee to investigate the incident. Four members of the committee originally concluded that there was no discrimination, but the fifth demurred. Another member withdrew his name from the majority report and filed his own account, which stated that the actions of the director were on "the fine line of discrimination." The report was never filed. Nevertheless, the Felix Longoria Affair became a reference point in the struggle for civil rights. *V. Carl Allsup*

Fence Cutting. One of the defenses open-range cattlemen employed against ranch enclosers and sodbusters in nineteenth-century Texas. Landless cattlemen wanted to retain practices of the open range. More domestic souls bought barbed wire to fence the land. A fence war was precipitated by the drought of 1883, which made it all the harder for the cowman without land of his own to find the grass and water necessary for his herds. Some ranchers enclosed public land when they enclosed their own, and others strung their wire about farms and small ranches belonging to other persons. Often the fences blocked public roads; in some instances they cut off schools and churches and interfered with the delivery of mail. This unwarranted fencing led some men whose land was not actually fenced in to join in the nipping. As the cutting continued, it became less discriminant and attracted rougher elements; soon no fence was safe. Wrecking of fences was reported from more than half the Texas counties and was most common in a belt extending north and south through the center of the state, the ranchman's frontier of 1883. Much of the cutting was done at night by armed bands with names like Owls, Javelinas, or Blue Devils. Often those who destroyed fences left warnings against rebuilding, but these were usually disregarded. In some instances, pastures of the fencers were burned. Some owners defended their property, and at least three men were killed in clashes between fence cutters and ranchmen. Texas newspapers generally condemned the cutting but indicated that not all the fencers were free of blame. Few attempts were made to reconcile the embittered groups. Atypically, at Henrietta spokesmen for the fence cutters met with Clay County ranchmen, and the two groups agreed that fences would be removed from across public roads and land not owned or leased by the fence builders, that gates would be provided for farmers' use, and that wire cutting would end.

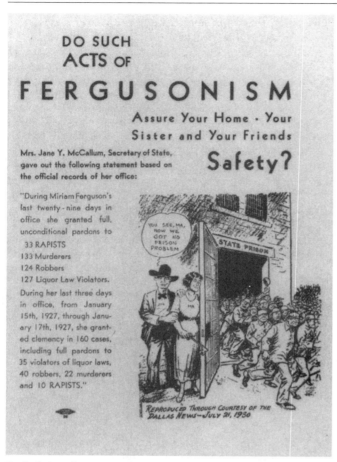

Do Such Acts of Fergusonism Assure Your Home, Your Sister and Your Friends Safety?, 1930. Broadsides Collection, CAH; CN 08010. This broadside, published during the gubernatorial race of 1930, reminded voters of the extremely liberal pardon policy candidate Miriam Ferguson had endorsed when she was governor.

Ferguson, James Edward. Governor; b. near Salado, 31 August 1871; d. 21 September 1944; m. Miriam Amanda Wallace (1875); 2 children. "Gentleman Jim" Ferguson is known mainly for his demagoguery, for his battle with the University of Texas, and for being the only Texas governor to be impeached. He branched out from law practice to engage in the banking and insurance businesses, and lent a hand to politicians seeking election. In his first run for the governorship (1914) he was elected as an antiprohibitionist. During his first term, taxes soared as legislation was passed to benefit rural education, establish teachers' colleges, and enlarge the landholdings of the prison system. During his second term (1916–) the highway department was instituted. Ferguson's hostility to the university, however, led to his loss of office. When the university regents refused to fire certain professors whom Ferguson did not like, he vetoed the university's appropriation. The ensuing conflict led to investigations after which he was indicted on several charges, mainly related to misapplication of funds. Ferguson, unrepentant, posted bond and announced his candidacy for a third term, whereupon the legislature impeached him by an overwhelming vote. Though forbidden to hold state office, he still sought, but failed to obtain, the nomination for governor in 1918; ran for president in 1920; and lost a bid for the United States Senate in 1922. He then decided to govern by spousal proxy. He served as his wife's campaign manager in the gubernatorial election of 1924, when Miriam A. Ferguson beat Felix Robertson, the candidate supported by the Ku Klux Klan. New scandals arose, and Ma Ferguson lost the election of 1926. Jim ran Miriam's gubernatorial campaigns in 1930, when she lost, and in 1932, when she won. He persisted in his political involvement by campaigning again for his wife in 1940, though without much effect.

Ralph W. Steen

Ferguson, Miriam Amanda Wallace. Governor; b. Bell County, 13 June 1875; d. Austin, 25 June 1961; m. James Edward Ferguson (1899); 2 children. After being impeached, James Ferguson implemented his policies through his wife, "Ma" Ferguson, the first woman governor of Texas. She was elected in 1924. Though she fought prohibition and the Klan, her first term was riddled with charges of corruption, and she was further weakened in public opinion for pardoning an average of 100 convicts a month. Daniel J. Moody beat her at the polls in 1926. She ran again, unsuccessfully, against Ross Sterling in 1930. Sterling, blamed for failures during the Great Depression, lost to Mrs. Ferguson in 1932. Her second term was quieter than her first, being largely characterized by depression-era fiscal restraint. She ran again in 1940—promising taxes to support the elderly, measures to aid organized labor, and increased education funding—but lost to "Pappy" O'Daniel, whose demagoguery was flashier than that of the Fergusons.

John D. Huddleston

By the fall of 1883 damage from wrecking of fences in Texas was estimated at $20 million—more than $1 million in Brown County alone. The Fort Worth *Gazette* asserted that fence troubles had caused tax valuations to decline $30 million. The clashes discouraged farming and scared away some prospective settlers. Politicians generally shied from the explosive issue, but on 15 October Governor John Ireland called a special session of the legislature to meet in January 1884. After a deluge of petitions and heated debates, the legislature made fence cutting a felony punishable by one to five years in prison. The penalty for malicious pastureburning was two to five years in prison. Fencing of public lands or lands belonging to others was made a misdemeanor, and builders of such fences were to remove them within six months. Ranchers who built fences across public roads were required to place a gate every three miles and to keep the gates in repair. These measures ended most of the fence troubles, although sporadic outbreaks of nipping continued for a decade, especially during droughts. Texas Rangers were sent after fence cutters in Navarro County in 1888, and for several years the rangers had occasional fence cases in West Texas.

Wayne Gard

Feuds. Although the feuds of Texas have received less general attention and publicity than have the Kentucky variety, they were probably even more numerous and bitter. Half a dozen of the worst ones have become fairly well known, but dozens of others, big and little, have raged in practically every county in the state. Only one important feud broke out in Texas before the Civil War: the Regulator–Moderator War, which raged in Shelby County and adjacent regions from 1839 to 1844, involved several hundred men on each side, and caused much bloodshed and violence. Like many of the later feuds, this trouble was at first a contest between organized outlaws and a group of vigilantes. Typically, the Regulators went to such extremes in their attempts to break up the outlaws that a group of countervigilantes came into existence to "moderate" the Regulators. Typically also, both sides drew in friends, relatives, and sympathizers from many miles away, and a war of extermination would have been the inevitable result if Sam Houston and the militia had not marched in.

Great outbursts of the feuding spirit were part of the aftermath of the Civil War. Feeling against Union authorities and their local supporters touched off several explosions in the 1860s. An example of this type of disturbance was the Early–Hasley feud, which occurred in Bell County from 1865 to 1869. John Early, a member of the Home Guard, abused an old man named Drew Hasley. When Hasley's son Sam came home after service in the Confederate Army, he took the matter up. Early had become a supporter of the Yankee officials, and they backed him. Hasley soon became the head of a party of friends and relatives, including, notably, Jim McRae, a fearless and possibly a desperate man. Early and his crowd accused the Hasley party of all sorts of thievery and depredation and brought in soldiers to clean them out. On 30 July 1869 McRae was ambushed and killed. The Hasley party broke up after that, though one of them pursued Dr. Calvin Clark, an Early supporter, into Arkansas and killed him shortly thereafter. The Lee–Peacock feud, which took place from 1867 to 1871 in the contiguous corners of Fannin, Grayson, Collin, and Hunt counties, followed the same pattern. Bob Lee, a former Confederate officer, fell out with the Union authorities and aroused the enmity of Lewis Peacock, one of their supporters. There was killing on both sides, and Lee was waylaid and killed in 1869. A systematic hunt for his friends and supporters was then begun, and several were killed. Peacock himself was shot on 13 June 1871, and the feud ended. The Sutton–Taylor feud, the biggest of the feuds rooted in the war, began in 1869 and continued to cause litigation until 1899, though most of the bloodshed was over by 1876.

The 1870s saw more lawlessness and more feuding than did any other period in Texas history. Most of the disturbances were the result of depredations by outlaw bands, and the typical pattern of vigilantes and countervigilantes was repeated many times. The war had left Texas comparatively undamaged, and this fact attracted many settlers from ruined communities in the older states, while the frontier offered a refuge to lawless characters. Many good people moved to Texas at this time, but the bad ones, combining forces with homegrown scoundrels, caused an outbreak of desperadoism that was hard to put down. Capt. Leander H. McNelly's special force of Texas Rangers and Maj. John B. Jones's Frontier Battalion gradually got control of the situation, but large groups of outraged citizens felt obliged to take the law into their own hands until life and property were comparatively safe. Many of the cattle feuds of this period occurred in such frontier outposts as Mason, Lampasas, and Shackelford counties. The Horrell–Higgins feud in Lampasas County in 1877, the Hoodoo War or Mason County War of 1875, and the trouble over the Shackelford County mob are typical. Cattle and horse stealing in Shackelford County led to the forming of a secret vigilante society that was responsible for several midnight lynchings. Former sheriff John M. Larn and his henchman John

Selman eventually incurred the suspicion of this "mob," and great enmity grew up between them and some of their neighbors. Larn was surprised and arrested, but in June 1878 his enemies broke into the jail and shot him before he could be tried. Organized highway robbery and cattle theft brought on a lynching feud in Bastrop County. Not long after the Civil War a gang of thieves had gotten a foothold in the county, and by 1874 a vigilante organization was at work. There were fights and extralegal executions in 1876. On 27 June 1877, four of the supposed outlaws were taken from a dance and hanged. This did not stop the gang from killing and robbing their opponents, and on Christmas Eve, 1883, three more men thought to be in sympathy with the thieves were escorted from a store at McDade, taken out into the woods, and lynched. Friends and relatives of the dead men came to town on Christmas Day and staged a battle in the main street of McDade that resulted in three more deaths. The hanging of Pete Allen in 1884 and of Frank Renault in 1886 are supposed to have been the final acts in this feud.

The Salt War of San Elizario in El Paso County in 1877, a different sort of disturbance, involved bitter political divisions and was complicated by a desire to exploit the salt deposits at the foot of Guadalupe Peak. Unusual also was the Mitchell–Truitt trouble, caused by a land dispute that began at Granbury in Hood County in 1874. The two parties fought along the highway after their case had been called in court. Two of the Truitts were killed, and as a result whitebearded Nelson (Cooney) Mitchell, the patriarch of the clan, was hanged at Granbury on 9 October 1875. His son Bill held a grudge against James Truitt, a young minister whose testimony had sent the elder Mitchell to his death. On 20 July 1886 Truitt was shot in his home in Timpson. Mitchell was hunted for years as the killer and captured in New Mexico in 1905, but no conviction against him was obtained until 1910. He did not go to the penitentiary until 1912, and even then the state could not hold him, for he escaped after serving a little more than two years. He was not heard of again.

By the mid-1880s the worst of the feuding was over, and only a handful of fresh disturbances occurred. One of these was the trouble at Graham, Young County, in 1888. A family of brothers named Marlow was accused of mishandling cattle and horses, though the brothers contended that they were victims of the desire of the big cattlemen to own everything. They killed Sheriff Marion D. Wallace when he tried to arrest them. Boone Marlow got away, but Alfred, George, Epp, and Charley were jailed. They broke jail once, were recaptured, and stood off an attempt by a local mob to kill them in their cell. The mob tried again the next day when the prisoners were being moved to Weatherford. The Marlows, though chained, seized guns from their guards and killed three of the mob before the others ran away. Alf and Epp Marlow were killed; Charley and George, each chained to a dead brother, cut off the feet of the corpses with pocketknives and got away. Boone Marlow was later killed in Oklahoma, and the feud subsided into litigation, which was finally dropped. Mob trouble was also at the root of the killings in San Saba County, where organized stealing became unbearable in the late 1880s. A vigilante group led by some religious people began to function, and there were hangings and ambushings. In 1893 a young man named Jim Brown was killed by a mob as he was going home from church. In 1896 there were two more mob executions. Public sentiment turned against this sort of Klanlike work, and District Attorney Linden joined forces with ranger sergeant W. J.

L. Sullivan to work up a case that broke the power of the mob and sent its leaders into exile, though the last suits were not dismissed until 1903. The worst of the troubles of the period was the Jaybird–Woodpecker War of 1889 at Richmond, Fort Bend County. The control of the black vote was the main issue. Family divisions helped to bring on a terrible fight in front of the courthouse on 16 August. In the 1950s the Jaybird Democratic Association still existed. Another political feud was the clash between the Botas and Guaraches at Laredo, which ended in a street riot on 7 April 1886, during which the Guaraches used an old cannon, the only documented case in which Texas feudists made use of artillery.

During the 1890s feuds again grew numerous, but they were neither so big nor so bloody as the feuds of the 1870s. The killing of Sheriff Andrew Jackson Royal at Fort Stockton on 21 November 1894 was the result of a small but bitter feud. Jim Miller and Sheriff Bud Frazer fell out at Pecos, and several people lost their lives. Frazer was shot in a saloon at Toyah on 13 September 1896. Somewhat bigger than these disturbances was the Broocks–Border–Wall feud in San Augustine just before and after 1900. The Wall boys were enemies from boyhood of Curg (Lycurgus) Border, a relative of the powerful Broocks family. The Walls themselves had numerous kin with plenty of backbone. In April 1900 Border shot and killed Sheriff George Wall on the streets of San Augustine. Eugene Wall retaliated by killing Ben Broocks on 2 June. On 4 June a battle around the courthouse resulted in the deaths of Sid and Felix Roberts. Later, two more of the Wall boys were ambushed, and many of their friends and supporters left the country. The feud was not really ended until Sheriff Sneed Nobles killed Curg Border. As bitter as any other were the feuds at Columbus, Colorado County. Two great clans of cattlemen, the Staffords and the Townsends, had trouble that culminated in the killing of R. E. and John Stafford in front of a Columbus saloon on 7 July 1888. Larkin and Marion Hope were accused of the deed. In the 1890s the Townsend family divided against itself. Former Sheriff Sam Reese, who had married a Townsend, grew bitter against the local political machine led by lawyer Marcus Townsend and Sheriff Lite Townsend. On 3 August 1894 Marcus Townsend's follower Larkin Hope was murdered. Reese himself was assassinated in a street battle in 1899. Numerous engagements and killings followed, the last being another general shooting on 30 June 1906.

Probably a hundred smaller feuds could be listed. A book could be written on the political feuds in the lower Rio Grande valley between the Reds and Blues in such places as Brownsville and Rio Grande City. There were three small feuds at Hallettsville in the 1890s. The death of William Cowper Brann, the "Great Iconoclast," at Waco in 1898 was the result of a feud-like action. Even after 1900 feuding went on. Trouble between a ranger detachment and the Mexican-American population of Brownsville in 1902 assumed the proportions of a feud. In 1905 two flareups over prohibition, one at Groveton and the other at Hempstead, brought feud motives into play. The Black, Johnson, and Echols families feuded at Coahoma in 1910. The Boyce–Sneed feud at Amarillo in 1912 and the Johnson–Sims unpleasantness at Snyder in 1916 were brief but bloody feuds. As late as the 1940s Texas papers carried items that reminded one of feuding episodes that cropped up more frequently 50 years before.

C. L. Sonnichsen

Fifty Cent Act. Advocated by Governor Oran M. Roberts and approved by the Texas legislature on 14 July 1879; provided for selling Texas public lands at fifty cents an acre, one-half the proceeds to be used to pay the public debt and the other half to go into the Permanent School Fund. The act opened to settlement about 52 West Texas counties, out of which the state sold 3,201,283 acres for $1.6 million. On 22 January 1883 the act was repealed as a public necessity resulting from fraudulent speculation in the land.

Alice Gray Upchurch

Film Industry. The origins of the film industry date to the first public demonstrations in 1891 of Thomas Edison's Kinetoscope, a "peep" cabinet in which the viewer saw moving images generated from a continuous roll of celluloid film. Three years later the industry began in Texas. In its earliest stages the activity of making films in Texas was not so much an industry as an entrepreneurial phenomenon. Individuals and small companies were involved in introducing a new medium to an audience unfamiliar with cinema. One of the state's first Kinetoscope parlors opened in Austin in 1894. By 1900 technical improvements made possible the projection of film onto a screen or wall, transforming movies into a mass medium. Interest spread quickly; the first public screenings of projected film in the southern United States were held in Virginia and Atlanta, Georgia, in 1895 and in New Orleans in 1896. Although the fact cannot be definitively established, public demonstrations of Thomas Edison's Vitascope in Dallas on 1 and 2 February 1897 were probably the first instances of projected film in Texas. The program at the Dallas Opera House consisted of scenes of a Mexican duel, a lynching, a fire rescue, and Niagara Falls. In Austin, projected film debuted at a tent show in 1900.

The first motion pictures made in Texas did not tell stories, but recorded events and simple activities. The earliest documented and extant moving film shot in Texas is of the aftermath of the Galveston hurricane of 1900. Cameraman G. W. "Billy" Bitzer of the New York–based Biograph Company arrived at Texas City on 13 September, and in the following days shot eight scenes of the destruction. Other short scenes made in Texas at that time, probably by Bitzer, include a passing train and oil wells at Beaumont. Excluding entities that did not apply for incorporation through the office of the Texas secretary of state, the earliest documentable company established in Texas for the purposes of making and distributing motion pictures was the Wheelan–Loper Film Company of Dallas and San Antonio, incorporated in 1908 as the J. D. Wheelan Film Company. The enterprise was started by John D. Wheelan, exclusive Texas representative of the monopolistic Motion Picture Patents Company, and, later, the General Film Company and the Mutual Film Corporation of Texas. Although the enterprise was formed primarily to distribute the films of a number of domestic and foreign companies, part of the capital stock is listed in the company's charter records in terms of equipment and supplies, including cameras, lighting apparatus, and reels of unexposed film. The Wheelan–Loper Film Company ceased doing business after the teens but was not dissolved until 1950. Another early film production company, and the earliest non-Texas production company to operate in Texas, was Star-Film, established in 1910 in San Antonio and operated by Gaston Méliès, brother of pioneer French filmmaker Georges Méliès. Méliès's choice of Texas, based upon its favorable climate, variety of geographical settings, and history, is an early example of outside interest in the state's unique qualities for filmmaking. At the Star Film Ranch, Mélies made approximately 70 titles before moving operations to California in 1911. Also in 1910, brothers Paul W. and Wesley Hope Tilley started the Satex Film Company in San Antonio. The business was moved to Austin in 1911 and produced several features and shorts, some released nationally. Production ceased in July 1913.

Other studios operated briefly in the San Antonio area. Patrick Sylvester McGeeney (lawman, Western genre novelist, and actor) organized the Lone Star Company in 1915 and produced several films. The company was abandoned briefly, then reorganized in May 1917 as the Shamrock Photoplay Corporation. It produced numerous feature films and serials, many of which achieved national distribution. Its production facilities were also leased to out-of-state companies conducting on-location shoots in San Antonio. Production ceased in early fall 1923. Also operating for a brief period in San Antonio were the Neal Hart Production Company (1921–22) and the Sunset Corporation, a studio and processing laboratory branch of a New York–based company. Other attempts at establishing studios in Texas included one by character actor and San Antonio native Maclyn Arbuckle, financed by William Clifford Hogg, and National Pictures' Kier–Phillips Productions, which produced numerous features between 1926 and 1956. The Jamieson Film Company was founded in Dallas in 1916 and became an established film-production company in the Southwest. In 1972 it was absorbed into the Masters Film Company of Houston. Sack Amusement Enterprises, of San Antonio and later Dallas, was formed in 1920 by Alfred N. Sack. The business, a combination theater chain and production company, was a major producer and distributor of features and short subjects starring and produced for African Americans between 1937 and 1945. Sack Amusement Enterprises was declared an inactive corporation in 1979.

Despite fitful but encouraging beginnings, Texas could not compete as a base of film production with the East and West coasts. By the middle teens, centers of film production had become firmly established in the Hollywood–Los Angeles area in California, and in the New York–New Jersey area on the East Coast, thus lessening the likelihood of studios establishing permanent residence in Texas. Instead, the film industry of the state for many years consisted of Hollywood and East Coast–based companies using various Texas locales for location shootings. This trend began in Spring 1918, when Samuel Goldwyn filmed *Heart of the Sunset* in the San Antonio area for the Rex Beach Pictures Company of New York. Much more publicized was a larger production in November 1923, when the Fox Film Company shot exteriors for *The Warrens of Virginia*, also in San Antonio. Clever use of existing sites and structures, natural surroundings, and local extras reduced production costs for the studios and encouraged several to film in the state. The army and air force bases of the San Antonio area, for example, provided locations for *The Big Parade* (1925), *The Rough Riders* (1927), *Wings* (1927), which won the first Oscar award for best picture, *West Point of the Air* (1934), *I Wanted Wings* (1940), and *Air Cadet* (1951).

Film production in Texas was sporadic from the 1920s through the 1960s. A true industry did not begin to mature in the state until the 1970s. Approximately 5 major productions were shot in Texas during the 1920s, only 5 in the 1930s, 14 in the 1940s, 9 in the 1950s, and 11 in the 1960s. Although Texas would seem a logical place to make movies in the popular Western movie genre, only a handful were shot on location within the state. Authentic Texas landscapes provided the backdrop for several notable Westerns, such as *North of 36* (1924), the progenitor of cattle-drive movies, which was filmed at a ranch near Houston; one of its two remakes, *The Texans* (1938), was filmed in South Texas. Other noteworthy Westerns of this period shot in Texas included *Sundown* (1924) and *The Big Show* (1936). In a smaller but vastly popular genre, the story of the battle of the Alamo has been filmed 10 times in Texas, beginning with Gaston Mélies's *The Immortal Alamo* (1911), which was shot in San Antonio. Several versions, including *The Alamo* (1959), *Seguin* (1981), *Lone Star* (1984), *The Alamo: Thirteen Days to Glory* (1986), and *Alamo . . . The Price of Freedom* (1988), have made use of a historically accurate replica of the chapel–fortress in Brackettville.

The turning point in on-location filming in Texas occurred during the 1950s and after, when the major motion picture projects *Viva Zapata!* (1952), *Giant* (1956), John Wayne's *The Alamo* (1959), *Hud* (1962), and *Bonnie and Clyde* (1967) attracted national attention and cultivated an interest that has not waned. By the 1970s the film industry outside the state coordinated location shooting within the state through the Texas Film Commission, an office established in 1971 by Governor Preston Smith. More than 100 movies were filmed in Texas during the 1970s; in the 1980s the number more than doubled to 247. In 1992, 28 films were shot in Texas. A boom in Texas filmmaking occurred in the late 1970s and 1980s and carried over into the 1990s as a number of Hollywood-established Texans, especially writers and directors, reintroduced Texas as a shooting location. L. M. "Kit" Carson, Horton Foote, Warren E. Skaaren, William Whitliff, and others, responsible for *Barbarosa* and *Raggedy Man* (1980), *Places in the Heart* (1983), and *Lonesome Dove* (1988), helped attract film and video crews that bring many millions of dollars in revenue to the state. Other movies shot in Texas include *Arrowhead* (1952), *State Fair* (1962), *The Last Picture Show* (1971), *Leatherface: Texas Chainsaw Massacre* (1974), *Outlaw Blues* (1977), *The Best Little Whorehouse in Texas* (1981), *Silkwood* (1984), and *JFK* (1991). In 1992, total gross budgets were estimated at $143,207,800. Foreign and independent directors have also capitalized on Texas. Their films include Louis Malle's *Alamo Bay* (1984), Wim Wenders's *Paris, Texas* (1983), Paul Verhoven's *Robocop* (1987), and Richard Linklater's cult film *Slacker* (1990).

Because an estimated 50 percent of a production's budget is spent in the location filming area, filmmaking boosts local economies. Film production puts money in circulation as film and tape professionals, local talent, properties, sound stages, rentals, and facilities are utilized. Dollar figures reflecting the impact of film production in Texas before the mid-1970s are elusive and not readily available. In 1977 at least $40 million was spent on film and videotape–related goods and services in the state, and the following year the figure increased by about $20 million. More complete records are available for the 1980s, based on gross sales and gross receipts as reported by the Texas comptroller of public accounts. Film and tape–related goods and services are defined by a classification scheme known as the Standard Industrial Code. In 1984 gross sales reached just over $128.8 million; four years later they totaled over $244 million.

During the first two quarters of 1992 more than $151 million was earned in gross sales for film and tape–related businesses in the state, and since that time the figures have grown exponentially.

John H. Slate

First Regiment, Texas Mounted Riflemen. The first Texas regiment to be mustered into Confederate service in 1861; raised and commanded by Henry McCulloch. The regiment was to protect the Texas frontier between the Red River and the Rio Grande. By mid-April it entered Confederate service. At San Antonio, McCulloch was elected colonel, Thomas C. Frost lieutenant colonel, and Edward Burleson, Jr., major. By the following month the 10 companies of the regiment occupied a line of forts from Camp Jackson, at the confluence of the Red River and the Big Wichita, southwestward to Fort Belknap, Camp Cooper, Fort Phantom Hill, Fort Chadbourne, Camp Colorado, Camp Concho (at present San Angelo), Fort McKavett, and Fort Mason. McCulloch's patrols covered the regiment's 400-mile line, to which were added regular expeditions of two to three weeks into suspected haunts of hostile Indians northwest of the line of forts. The summer and fall of 1861 saw diminished Indian activity. McCulloch returned to San Antonio in September to take temporary command of the Department of Texas, and in December he accepted command of the Western Military District of Texas. As his attention turned to defense of the Texas coast, his regiment on the Indian frontier was commanded for a time by his adjutant and senior officers. The enlistment for the regiment was to run out in the spring of 1862. Rumors spread that Confederate officials planned to remove it from the frontier. The regiment mustered out in mid-April 1862 at Fort Mason, and the state-financed Frontier Regiment replaced it on the frontier. Some of the men returned to frontier service, but most enlisted in the Eighth Texas Cavalry battalion, which later became part of the First Texas Cavalry regiment.

David Paul Smith

First Texas Cavalry, U.S.A. During the Civil War, Texas contributed two regiments and two battalions of cavalry to the federal army. A total of 1,915 men from Texas served the Union; of these, 141 died, 12 of them in action. The First Texas Cavalry Regiment was organized at New Orleans in November 1862, under the command of Edmund J. Davis. Serving primarily in Louisiana, the regiment took part in the Sabine Pass expedition in September 1863, and in October of that year was sent to the South Texas coast as part of the Rio Grande expedition. They occupied Brownsville in November and recruited heavily over the next few months. The Second Texas Cavalry Regiment was formed at the same time in Brownsville. Both regiments returned to Louisiana in July of 1864, leaving behind two companies of the First in Brownsville which rejoined the regiment six months later. In November the two regiments were merged into one. In June 1865, after the war, the regiment was ordered back to Texas, and was mustered out of service on 4 November 1865.

Eugene M. Ott, Jr., and Glen E. Lich

First United States Volunteer Cavalry. Better known as the Rough Riders; one of three cavalry regiments authorized to supplement the regular army at the onset of the Spanish-American War. Nominally commanded by Leonard Wood, the unit was in fact led by Lt. Col. Theodore Roosevelt. This legendary aggrega-tion of cowboys, Indian fighters, outlaws, Eastern aristocrats, and Ivy League athletes assembled and trained at San Antonio in May 1898 and moved on to Tampa, Florida, as part of the cavalry division of the Fifth Corps to embark for the Cuban campaign. Lack of transport forced them to abandon their horses in Florida. They fought through the battles of Las Guasimas and San Juan (actually Kettle) Hill as infantry. On 7 August, following the capitulation of Santiago de Cuba, the regiment, suffering from malaria and yellow fever, was evacuated from Cuba with the rest of the Fifth Corps. The fame of the Rough Riders catapulted Roosevelt to the vice presidency and later the presidency of the United States. In San Antonio, Roosevelt Park, Roosevelt Street, and the Roosevelt Bar of the Menger Hotel, a favorite watering place of the regiment, are named in memory of their sojourn in Texas.

Thomas W. Cutrer

Fisher, John King. Outlaw and lawman; b. Collin County, 1854; d. San Antonio, 11 March 1884; m. —— (1876). In 1869 Fisher borrowed a horse without telling the owner, was arrested, and escaped. He went to Goliad, where he was arrested for housebreaking, and was sent to prison. After being pardoned four months later, he moved to Dimmit County and established a ranch in the Nueces Strip, a lawless area where cattle rustling was the major industry. Fisher became a leader there, and his ranch became a haven for drifters, criminals, and rustlers. Texas Ranger N. A. Jennings said that Fisher wore an ornamented Mexican sombrero, a black Mexican jacket embroidered with gold, a crimson sash, and two silver-plated, ivory-handled Colt revolvers. In the Strip a road bore the sign "This is King Fisher's road. Take the other." In addition to ranching, Fisher was evidently engaged in cattle rustling in Texas and Mexico, and his escapades led more than once to violence. He was arrested at various times by the famous Texas Ranger captain Leander McNelly and his successor Lee Hall. Charged with murder and horse and cattle theft, he managed to avoid conviction, but his legal ordeals took their toll, and Fisher decided to live a quieter life. After marrying, he bought a ranch near Eagle Pass and in 1881 was appointed deputy sheriff of Uvalde County. He became acting sheriff in 1883 after the sheriff was indicted. He turned out to be an efficient and popular lawman and made plans to run for the office in 1884. These plans ended in the Vaudeville Variety Theater in San Antonio, where Fisher and gunman Ben Thompson got in a shootout with the theater's owners and were both killed.

Paul Adams

Fisher–Miller Land Grant. A huge grant made by the Republic of Texas in 1842 and renewed in 1843, as a result of a petition made by Henry Francis Fisher, Burchard Miller, and Joseph Baker to be permitted to settle 1,000 immigrant families of German, Dutch, Swiss, Danish, Swedish, and Norwegian ancestry in Texas under the auspices of the San Saba Colonization Company. The grant included more than three million acres between the Llano and Colorado rivers. The original contract allowed the introduction of 600 families and single men. Fisher and Miller did not succeed in colonizing the grant within the allotted time and took advantage of a legislative amendment of 1844 that extended the deadline. The amendment also increased the number of settlers to 6,000 families and single men. After seeking and obtaining the title of Texas consul to Bremen, Fisher went to Germany to promote colonization. In 1844 he sold an interest in the contract to the Adelsverein. The next year, he and Miller sold their rights in the grant to the society. As a stipulation of the sale Fisher was appointed to the society's colonial committee. Along with the rights to the grant, the society had the responsibility to settle the area and take over any expenses accrued by the San Saba Colonization Company. The grant actually received few colonists from the society, which made only five small settlements; of the five, only Castell survived. Many of the settlers moved to New Braunfels or Fredericksburg and subsequently sold the grants they had received in the Fisher–Miller tract.

Rudolph L. Biesele

Flipper, Henry Ossian. Engineer, the first black graduate of West Point (1877); b. a slave, Thomasville, Georgia, 21 March 1856; d. Atlanta, 3 May 1940. Flipper attended school at the American Missionary Association and, as a freshman at Atlanta University, was appointed to the United States Military Academy (1873). Although he was the fifth black accepted at West Point, he was the first to graduate. He wrote of his successful struggle at the academy in *The Colored Cadet at West Point* (1878). As an officer in the Tenth United States Cavalry, Flipper served at Fort Elliott, Fort Concho, Fort Quitman, and Fort Davis, Texas, and at Fort Sill, Indian Territory. In Texas on his way to Fort Sill he supervised the drainage of malarial ponds. Flipper's Ditch is now a national historic landmark. He later constructed a road from Gainesville to Fort Sill, installed a telegraph line from Fort Elliott to Fort Supply, Indian Territory, scouted on the Llano Estacado, and assisted in the return of Quanah Parker's band from Palo Duro Canyon to the Fort Sill reservation in the winter of 1878–79. During the Victorio campaign of 1880 he fought in two battles at Eagle Springs, Texas. For his service in the field Flipper was made acting assistant quartermaster, post quartermaster, and acting commissary of subsistence at Fort Davis. Col. William Shafter relieved Flipper as quartermaster (1881) and planned to relieve him as commissary. Flipper suspected what he later called a systematic plan to drive him out of the army. The following year, when he discovered post funds missing from his quarters, he attempted to conceal the loss until he could find or replace the money. Shafter filed charges. A divided court-martial acquitted Flipper of charges of embezzlement but pronounced him guilty of "conduct unbecoming an officer and a gentleman." He was dismissed from the service on 30 June 1882. Flipper maintained his innocence until his death and waged a lifelong battle for reinstatement in the army.

He worked as a surveyor in Mexico until 1887, when he opened an engineering office in Nogales, Arizona. He helped settle a dispute over title to the San Juan de las Boquillas y Nogales Mexican land grant in Cochise County, Arizona (1893) and in so doing saved the property of hundreds of landowners. Flipper's activity in the community led to his appointment as a special agent for the U.S. Court of Private Land Claims. In 1895 the government published his translation of *Spanish and Mexican Land Laws: New Spain and Mexico*. Flipper also briefly edited the Nogales *Sunday Herald* and published articles in *Old Santa Fe*, which later became the *New Mexico Historical Review*. He became a member of the Association of Arizona Civil Engineers, the National Geographic Society, and the Southwest Society of the Archaeological Institute of America. He offered to serve in the Spanish-American War in 1898, but bills in the United States House of Representatives and in the Senate to

Henry O. Flipper, ca. 1878. Taken by Peak Photographer, New York. Courtesy Texas Memorial Museum; Acc. 160-2.

restore his rank both died in committee. He served in the court of private land claims until 1901, then spent 11 years in northern Mexico as an engineer and legal assistant to mining companies. The story of Flipper and the Lost Tayopa Mine, based on events of these years, appears in J. Frank Dobie's *Apache Gold and Yaqui Silver*. In 1912 Flipper moved to El Paso, and in 1913 he began supplying information on conditions in revolutionary Mexico to Senator Albert B. Fall's subcommittee on Mexican internal affairs. Flipper drew national attention when he was reported to be in league with Pancho Villa and denied the rumor in a letter to the Washington *Eagle* dated 4 May 1916. Flipper published an article, "Early History of El Paso," and also reputedly wrote a pamphlet about Estevanico. In 1916 he wrote a memoir of his life in the Southwest, which was published posthumously as *Negro Frontiersman: The Western Memoirs of Henry O. Flipper* (1963).

In 1919 Senator Fall called Flipper to Washington as a translator and interpreter for his subcommittee. Upon his appointment as secretary of the interior in 1921, Fall appointed Flipper his assistant. In that position Flipper became involved with the Alaskan Engineering Commission. He served in the Department of the Interior until 1923, when he went to work as an engineer for William F. Buckley's Pantepec Petroleum Company in Venezuela. In 1925 Pantepec published Flipper's translation of

Col. John Salmon (Rip) Ford. *Carte de visite* by Louis de Planque, Brownsville, Texas, and Matamoros, Mexico. Ca. 1865. Courtesy Lawrence T. Jones III Collection, Austin.

Venezuela's *Law on Hydrocarbons and other Combustible Minerals.* Flipper worked in Venezuela until 1930 and retired in 1931. He lived out his life at the Atlanta home of his brother, Joseph S. Flipper, a bishop of the African Methodist Episcopal Church. In December 1976, when a bust of him was unveiled at West Point, the Department of the Army granted Flipper an honorable discharge, dated 30 June 1882. Two years later his remains were removed from Atlanta and reinterred at Thomasville, Georgia. An annual West Point award in honor of Flipper is presented to the graduate who best exemplifies "the highest qualities of leadership, self-discipline, and perseverance in the face of unusual difficulties while a cadet."

Bruce J. Dinges

Ford, John Salmon. Known as Rip Ford; soldier, elected official, and newspaper editor; b. Greenville District, South Carolina, 26 May 1815; d. San Antonio, 3 November 1897. Ford moved to Texas in June 1836 and served in the Texas army under Jack Hays. He settled in San Augustine in 1838 and practiced medicine until 1844, when he was elected to the House of the Ninth Congress, where he introduced the resolution to accept the terms of annexation to the United States. In 1845 he moved to Austin and became editor of the Austin *Texas Democrat;* he was later in partnership with Michael Cronican. During the Mexican War, Ford was adjutant of Hays's regiment and in command of a spy company; he was commended for gallant service by Gen. Joseph Lane. When officially sending out notices of deaths he wrote R.I.P. (*requiescat in pace,* "may he rest in peace") at the top, and thus acquired his nickname. In 1849, with Robert S. Neighbors, Ford made an exploration of the country between San Antonio and El Paso and published a report and map of the route, which came to be known as the Ford and Neighbors Trail. Later in 1849 he was made captain in the Texas Rangers and was stationed between the Nueces and the Rio Grande, where he had numerous Indian fights (1850–51). In 1852 he was elected to the Texas Senate. Again he became an editor and, in partnership with Capt. Joe Walker, established the *State Times,* which was published in Austin until 1857. In 1858 he accepted a commission in the state troops and defeated the Indians in two major battles on the Canadian River. In 1859 he was sent to the Rio Grande, where he commanded operations against Juan N. Cortina. In 1861 Ford served as a member of the Secession Convention, commanded an expedition to Brazos Santiago, initiated a trade agreement between Mexico and the Confederacy, and was elected colonel of the Second Texas Cavalry, with a command in the Rio Grande district. Between 1862 and 1865 he discharged the duties of commandant of conscripts, while at various times he was engaged on border operations protecting Confederate–Mexican trade. In May 1865 he led Confederate forces in the battle of Palmito Ranch, the last battle of the Civil War.

In 1868 Ford moved to Brownsville to edit the Brownsville *Sentinel.* In 1872 he was a delegate to the Democratic convention in Baltimore. He was a special sergeant-at-arms when Richard Coke was inaugurated governor in 1873 and quelled a riot of Austin citizens who were aroused against the radicals and Edmund J. Davis. In 1873 Ford served as a cattle and hide inspector of Cameron County, and in 1874 he was mayor of Brownsville. He was a member of the convention that wrote the Constitution of 1876 and served in the Texas Senate from 1876 to 1879, when he was appointed superintendent of the state Deaf and Dumb School. While in the Senate he urged the promotion of immigration to Texas and popular education, supported in part from the sale of public lands. Ford spent his later years writing reminiscences and historical articles and promoting an interest in Texas history. As a charter member of the Texas State Historical Association, he contributed one of the first articles published in its *Quarterly.*

Seymour V. Connor

Ford, O'Neil. Architect; b. near Sherman, 3 December 1905; d. San Antonio, 20 July 1982; m. Wanda Graham (1940); 4 children. In Denton, after his father died, Neil assumed the responsibilities of breadwinner at 12. He obtained jobs for himself and his younger brother, Lynn Ford, who gained fame as a woodcarver and cabinetmaker, and sister Authella (Mrs. Roland Hersh), skilled in working with copper. After poverty forced him to withdraw from the university in Denton, Ford enrolled in an architecture course from the International Correspondence Schools of Scranton, Pennsylvania. In 1924 he and an uncle traveled through the Alsatian and German communities of

Texas Instruments Semi-Conductor Building during construction, Dallas, ca. 1958. O'Neil Ford, architect. Photograph by N. Bleeker Green. Reprinted by permission of Texas Instruments. This structure united manufacturing, labs, and offices under one roof, and provided interior courtyards to facilitate collegial exchange.

Castroville, Brackettville, and Fredericksburg and were deeply impressed by the simplicity and beauty of the German vernacular architecture; the experience decisively influenced Ford's later work. In 1926 he entered the office of Dallas architect David R. Williams, a leading spokesman for Texas vernacular architecture, where he served his apprenticeship. Flamboyant, extravagant, and often outrageous, Williams became Ford's role model. Together they produced a number of fine regional houses of native brick, wood, and stone in north central Texas. Ford was deeply influenced by the tradition of the English Arts and Crafts Movement and the works of Greene and Greene in California, especially their attempt to synthesize architecture and visual arts. In an attempt to carry on this tradition he enlisted the help of his brother, Lynn, to carve doors, mantels, and beams. Artists Jerry Bywaters and Thomas M. Stell, Jr., also collaborated on many projects, stenciling walls and making mosaics. During the Great Depression Ford worked on WPA projects and with the Rural Resettlement Administration. He formed his first partnership in 1937 with Arch Swank in Dallas. Their major job was the Little Chapel in the Woods on the campus of Texas Woman's University.

The restoration of La Villita by the WPA precipitated Ford's move to San Antonio, where he took Jerry Rogers as his partner (1939–53). Their research into building systems was put to the test in 1949, when they received the commission to design a new campus for Trinity University, along with Bartlett Cocke and Harvey P. Smith. From 1953 to 1965 O'Neil Ford and Associates did a number of projects for burgeoning Texas Instruments, both in Texas and abroad. Among the firm's best-known works for TI was the Semiconductor Building in Dallas (1958). In 1967 Ford formed a partnership with Boone Powell and Chris Carson. Bright young people fresh out of architecture schools were eager to work in this innovative office, and Ford's best work was accomplished in collaboration with talented youth. Campuses for Skidmore College in New York and the first phase of the University of Texas at San Antonio are notable examples of the firm's work during Ford's final years. During World War II Ford was an air force flight instructor. In later years he was often called upon for advice on historic preservation, the environment, aesthetics, and quality education. In 1968 he was appointed by President Lyndon Johnson to the National Council on the Arts. David Rockefeller, Jr., invited him to serve on the American Council for the Arts in Education (1975). His honors included election in 1960 to the College of Fellows, American Institute of Architects, and honorary doctoral degrees awarded by Trinity University (1967), Southern Methodist University (1973), the University of Dallas (1976), and Skidmore College. The first endowed chair in the School of Architecture at the University of Texas at Austin was named for Ford. Wanda Ford served as president of the San Antonio Conservation Society (1955–57).   *Mary Carolyn Hollers George*

Forests. To early explorers and settlers, the forests of East Texas must have been an awesome sight. On dry hills in Southeast

Texas, longleaf pines towered to 150 feet and had bases four to five feet in diameter. The woods were open and easily accessible. Mesic uplands and creekbottoms in other parts of eastern Texas also contained large trees. Magnificent open forests of white oak, beech, elm, water oak, and magnolia occurred in creekbottoms, as did thick clumps of switch cane. In bottomlands, tree trunks stood far apart and sometimes were so big that three men could not touch hands around them. Giant cypress trees grew in swamps and sloughs. As settlers increased in numbers, they cut trees for houses, barns, and furniture and cleared forests for farmland. Thus the numbers of large trees began to decline. By 1830 sawmills began to dot the East Texas landscape. As the mills increased in size and were modernized, and as more people settled in East Texas, the primeval forest was manipulated until few remnants of the original forest, if any, remained. Therefore, most forests in East Texas are in younger stages of plant succession. In addition many are still being managed for the production of pine. Pine plantations are commonplace over the East Texas landscape. On the other hand, several sites in eastern Texas contain old-growth stands that remind us of how the primitive forest might have looked. Such forests can be found, for example, in Caddo Lake State Park and Turkey Hill Wilderness Area.

Texas has approximately 22,032,000 acres of forest. There are five principal forest and woodland regions in the state: pine–hardwood, located essentially in East Texas in the Pine Belt or "Piney Woods"; post oak, associated primarily with the Lost Pine Forest at the state parks in Bastrop County; the Eastern and Western Cross Timbers, centered around the northern part of the state near the Red River; cedar brakes, found primarily on the Edwards Plateau; and scattered coastal forests, found near the Gulf of Mexico. There are four national forests in Texas: Angelina (153,176 acres), in Angelina, Jasper, Nacogdoches, and San Augustine counties; Davy Crockett (161,841 acres), in Houston and Trinity counties; Sabine (160,609 acres), in Jasper, Newton, Sabine, San Augustine, and Shelby counties; and Sam Houston (161,508 acres), in Montgomery, San Jacinto, and Walker counties. The five Texas state forests are the E. O. Siecke State Forest, I. D. Fairchild State Forest, W. Goodrich Jones State Forest, John Henry Kirby State Forest, and Paul N. Masterson Memorial Forest. All the state and national forests are located in East Texas, the primary and most important forest area in Texas. The East Texas Pine Belt extends over 43 counties and accounts for almost all the state's commercial timber. East Texas forests are also a part of the Eastern Deciduous Forest Formation and display an affinity to those forests eastward.

General descriptions of the forests of East Texas were initiated by William L. Bray in 1906 and by Benjamin C. Tharp in 1939. They found that the great variation in topography in East Texas resulted in accompanying vegetational change. For example, dry upland, creekbottom, riverbottom, and swamp forest communities are quite different from each other in species composition. Until 1970 only a smattering of additional information was provided to aid in our understanding of these communities. Since then, mainly through the efforts of E. S. Nixon, P. A. Harcombe, and C. A. McLeod and their graduate students, forest stands have been analyzed in greater detail, and thus there is presently a better understanding of forest structure and composition.

Elray S. Nixon

Fort Anahuac. In a Chambers County park a mile south of Anahuac; site of the first armed confrontation between Anglo-Texans and Mexican troops, on 10–12 June 1832; named Anáhuac after the ancient home of the Aztecs. In November 1830 Col. John Davis Bradburn chose the site for the fort on a bluff overlooking the entrance to the Trinity River. The installation was one of six new outposts located at strategic entrances to Texas and designed to enforce the Law of April 6, 1830. The garrison lived temporarily in a fortified wooden barracks a half mile north of the bluff in the center of the site of modern Anahuac. The barracks was later used as the jail that held William B. Travis and others. Bricks for the permanent fort were made by convict soldiers on-site, beginning in March 1831. A Masonic and military ceremony marked completion of the foundation in May. The exterior walls measured 100 by 70 feet and enclosed two redoubts diagonally opposite on the southwest and northeast corners. Inside the perimeter was a reinforced-brick building about 50 by 35 feet. The southwest redoubt, overlooking Trinity Bay, was named Fort Davis (for Bradburn); it was manned by a maximum of 50 men and defended by a six-pound cannon, while its twin on the northeast guarded the land approach. The cavalry tethered its horses between the two redoubts. An excavated passage connected the enclosure with the powder magazine on the east side, where two bulwarks named Hidalgo and Morelos (for martyrs of the Mexican independence movement) near the sites of the brick kilns, each with a 16-pound cannon, guarded the compound. The garrison grew from 40 men and 4 officers in November 1830 to a maximum of 285 men and 10 officers in May 1832. After March 1832 about 100 of the men were stationed at Velasco, at the mouth of the Brazos, under Col. Domingo de Ugartechea.

Texan insurgents under Col. Francis White Johnson attacked the fort on June 10–12, 1832, to rescue Travis. They dismantled the fort when they left the next month, and a fire gutted the wooden parts in November. The wooden calaboose was burned in December 1832, and settlers took the bricks. In January 1835 Capt. Antonio Tenorio arrived with about 40 troops to reopen the fort; it was in such disrepair that he had to ask his superiors for wood to make repairs. The wood arrived in May but was burned by irate Texans. Tenorio had no artillery when Travis and his volunteers attacked on 29 June, so his troops fled into the woods. He capitulated the next day, and the small garrison sailed to Harrisburg and retreated to Bexar. The fort was never used again. The land became private property. In 1938 the county surveyor made field notes of the existing foundations. Erosion caused by rechanneling the Trinity River sometime after the 1930s caused the remains of the southwestern redoubt to fall into the water. Chambers County acquired the site for a park in 1946, and officials ordered it cleared and the rubble buried to prevent accidents and vandalism. An amateur excavation was made in 1968 before preservation laws went into effect, but no in-depth archeological study has been made of the site.

Margaret Swett Henson

Fort Belknap. The northern anchor of a chain of United States forts founded to protect the Texas frontier from the Red River to the Rio Grande; established in 1851 at the site of present Newcastle, Young County, by Bvt. Brig. Gen. William G. Belknap. After the commanding officer, Capt. C. L. Stephenson, found no water in shafts dug 66 feet deep at the location of the

Photo postcard by H. H. Horne Co., El Paso. Courtesy TSL. In 1915 when this photograph was taken, Fort Bliss, under the command of Gen. John J. Pershing, was the largest cavalry post in the United States.

water tower now in Newcastle, he moved the fort two miles south, where adequate water was found in springs by the Brazos River. The present well was dug in 1857. The first buildings were jacals. Some were later replaced with stone. Fort Belknap was a four-company post. Companies from the Fifth United States Infantry, the Second United States Dragoons, the Seventh United States Infantry, the Second United States Cavalry, and the Sixth United States Cavalry were stationed there at various times. Among the commanding officers were majors George H. Thomas and Samuel H. Starr. Fort Belknap was a post without defensive works. From it troops pursued raiding bands of Indians; on occasion mounted expeditions from the fort carried the war to the enemy on the plains as far north as Kansas. The fort gave confidence to citizens, who came in such numbers that surrounding counties were organized. The fort became the hub of a network of roads stretching in every direction, the most notable of which was the Butterfield Overland Mail route from St. Louis to San Francisco. Although it was abandoned before the Civil War, Belknap was occupied from time to time by state troops of the Frontier Regiment under Col. James M. Norris. Major Starr, with troops of the Sixth United States Cavalry, reoccupied the fort on 28 April 1867. When Fort Griffin was founded (1867), Belknap was abandoned for the last time.

During the Texas Centennial, Senator Benjamin G. Oneal and local citizens restored and rebuilt some of the buildings. During the 1970s officials of the Fort Belknap Archives, with some assistance from the Young County Commissioners Court, rebuilt Infantry Quarters Number Four to house the records of North Texas. Since its restoration Fort Belknap has become a cultural and recreational center. Senator Oneal and others orga-

nized the Fort Belknap Society to supervise its maintenance. The county supports it financially. Professional and learned societies, as well as family groups, use the facilities. Around 30,000 visitors register their attendance annually. *Kenneth F. Neighbours*

Fort Bliss. A large military installation in El Paso and New Mexico; founded after the Mexican War to defend the new border, to maintain law and order, to protect settlers and California-bound migrants from Indian attacks, and to survey for a new transcontinental railroad. The War Department posted troops in the El Paso area in 1848, but withdrew them to Fort Fillmore, 40 miles north, in 1851. A new military post was established on the Rio Grande in January 1854 at Magoffinsville, a hacienda three miles east of Coons' Rancho. The same year, the post was named Fort Bliss, in memory of Lt. Col. William Bliss, Gen. Zachary Taylor's chief of staff during the Mexican War. Lt. Col. Isaac V. D. Reeve was in command of the fort on 31 March 1861, when it was surrendered to Confederate authorities. Confederate lieutenant colonel John Robert Baylor occupied the post with elements of the Second Regiment of Texas Mounted Rifles. Brig. Gen. Henry Sibley used Fort Bliss as a base from which to invade New Mexico. Elements of the California Volunteers commanded by Col. James Carleton reoccupied Fort Bliss for the Union. Under Carleton's protection Mexican president Benito Juárez survived in El Paso del Norte in 1865–66 and received supplies from north of the border before driving the French from Mexico. In 1867 the post at Magoffinsville was swept away by a Rio Grande flood. The troops moved three miles north in 1868 and named their post Camp Concordia. The next year, the camp was renamed Fort Bliss. The War

Department closed the post in January 1877, just before the Salt War of San Elizario flared. A military board, however, was convened to investigate the reopening of the post as a result of the violence; the board recommended in 1878 that Fort Bliss be reestablished, and the post was moved to downtown El Paso, which soldiers called Garrison Town. In late 1879 the government purchased land at Hart's Mill, three miles west of downtown El Paso, and Fort Bliss became a way station for troops pursuing renegade Indians. After Geronimo surrendered in 1886, the government began to abolish small, isolated posts and to replace them with new facilities near railroads. Fort Bliss was almost supplanted by Fort Selden, 18 miles north of Las Cruces, New Mexico, but was kept in El Paso by community leaders, who contributed about $7,000 for the purchase of land on Lanoria Mesa, five miles east of town. Congress then committed $300,000 for new facilities. Fort Bliss moved to its sixth and present home in late 1893.

After the Mexican Revolution started in 1910, the army gradually increased its troop strength at Fort Bliss. Eventually 50,000 men, mostly national guardsmen, were based at the facility. Fort Bliss also changed from an infantry station to the largest cavalry post in the United States. Gen. Hugh Scott commanded briefly in 1914, and Gen. John J. Pershing took charge from 1914 through much of 1916. When Pancho Villa attacked Columbus, New Mexico, in March 1916, Pershing led a punitive expedition south, and Fort Bliss became Pershing's primary supply base. The First Cavalry Division was activated in 1921. With the arrival of the Eighty-second Field Artillery Battalion in 1921, Fort Bliss hosted its first artillery unit. During the 1940s the fort grew from a few thousand acres to more than a million, becoming roughly 75 miles long and 54 miles wide. Most of it is in New Mexico. By June 1943 Bliss had phased out horses, and the cavalry had become mechanized. With the First Cavalry Division's departure in 1943, the fort became primarily an artillery post. William Beaumont General Hospital opened at Fort Bliss in 1921. In 1972 the hospital dedicated a 12-story facility, and in 1973 the hospital became the center of a three-state government medical complex known as William Beaumont Army Medical Center. In 1919 the Fort Bliss Flying Field was established. In 1925 it was renamed Biggs Field, an army flying field used by the Border Air Patrol; in 1947 it became Biggs Air Force Base. During its service, the base handled blimps, DH4s, B-17s, B-29s, B-50s, B-36s, B-47s, and B-52s. In July 1966 the air force base reverted to Fort Bliss and became Biggs Army Air Field. Fort Bliss became an antiaircraft training center in September 1940. German rocket experts, including Wernher von Braun, lived and worked there shortly after World War II. In 1946 Fort Bliss became the United States Army Anti-aircraft Artillery and Guided Missile Center and later the United States Army Air Defense Center. The base hosted in succession Nike–Ajax, Nike–Hercules, Hawk, Sprint, Chaparral, and Redeye missiles and other antiaircraft weapons. The fort played a significant role in training international military students after World War II. Approximately 10 percent of Fort Bliss Air Defense School graduates were from foreign countries. The Third Armored Cavalry has been stationed at Fort Bliss since 1972. In the 1990s Fort Bliss personnel comprised about 20,000 military people and 8,000 civilians. The fort contributed more than $500 million annually to the El Paso economy. In addition, retired service people and their dependents in El Paso numbered in the thousands. From 1977 until his death in 1981 Omar N.

Bradley, latest five-star general of the United States Army, lived and worked at Fort Bliss. A cluster of adobe buildings representing the original 1848 post was built and donated to the post by the city of El Paso during the Fort Bliss centennial in 1948. The replica serves as the post museum.   *Leon C. Metz*

Fort Brown. At the site of Brownsville; originally called Fort Texas; established when Gen. Zachary Taylor arrived to establish the Rio Grande as the southern boundary of Texas (1846). Taylor built an earthen fort of 800 yards perimeter, with 6 bastions, walls more than 9 feet high, a parapet of 15 feet, and the whole surrounded by a ditch 15 feet deep and 20 feet wide. Armament was four 18-pound guns. The Seventh Infantry, with Company I of the Second Artillery and Company E, Third Artillery, commanded by Maj. Jacob Brown, garrisoned the fort. Mexican troops led by Mariano Arista intercepted U.S. troops as they brought supplies from Fort Polk to Fort Brown, leading to the opening battles of the Mexican War, 8–9 May 1846. Brown was killed and the post was named for him.

In 1848 quarters for officers and enlisted men and a permanent post were built a quarter mile north of the first site on a purchased tract of a Spanish land grant. A brick wall, called the Quarter Master's Fence, divided the fort and the community that became the city of Brownsville. Although rumors that the fort was to be abandoned started circulating in 1848, Indian raids in 1852 made it a necessary fortification for the town for protection from Indians and possible invasions from Mexico. In 1859 Juan N. Cortina occupied the fort as a refuge. In 1860 Robert E. Lee was stationed at Fort Brown on assignment to quell border disturbances. The post was abandoned by federal troops in March 1861 and occupied by Texas state troops. It was garrisoned by a small force of Confederates until November 1863. On the approach of Union forces, the Confederates retreated and burned all stored cotton and the fort buildings. Union forces occupied the site until July 1864, when it was again taken by Confederates forces, who held it until November 1865. During Confederate occupation the fort was described as a field work of six bastion fronts with a defense line of 950 yards garrisoned by 2,000 men with an armament of guns of different calibers. The fort was reoccupied by federal forces after the Civil War, again as a protection against Mexican invasion. Fort Brown was rebuilt with brick buildings starting in 1869. Among the buildings were the post hospital, an administration building, a large officers' quarters, and the chapel. In 1882 Dr. William Crawford Gorgas was sent to the post in response to the last and worst yellow fever epidemic at Fort Brown.

After the Brownsville raid of 1906, President Theodore Roosevelt transferred the fort from the War Department to the Department of the Interior. This department converted the place into an experimental garden for spineless cacti. In 1914, because of increased racial and economic tensions in the lower Rio Grande valley, Fort Brown was reactivated and made headquarters for the Brownsville Military District under Gen. James Parker. Within a few months 50,000 state guards were mobilized in the district. The first wireless station there was established about 1916. From World War I to February 1941 Fort Brown was headquarters of the Twelfth Cavalry. That unit was replaced by the 124th Cavalry, which trained there until May 1944, when the fort was deactivated. Official deactivation was declared by the War Department in 1945, at which time the fort was turned over

Fort Brown, Brownsville. *Carte de visite* by R. H. Wallis. Courtesy Lawrence T. Jones III Collection, Austin. This building is probably one of those constructed by the U.S. Army after it reoccupied Fort Brown in 1867.

to the army engineers; it was certified to the War Assets Administration for disposal on 15 May 1946 and assigned to the Federal Works Agency on 7 July. The agency then turned the land over to the Federal Land Bank for farming purposes. On 22 July 1948 the front 162 acres of Fort Brown was deeded to the city of Brownsville, and the old post hospital was granted to the Brownsville schools for the use of Texas Southmost College. The fort buildings were sold or donated to various organizations and schools in the Brownsville area. In the early 1990s much of what was left of the Fort Brown buildings and land was used by the University of Texas–Pan American and Texas Southmost College.

Another Fort Brown, a civilian settlers' fort, was built around 1834 in the future Houston County by the Daniel Parker family.

Elizabeth Pettit Davenport

Fort Clark. At Brackettville; established as Fort Riley in 1852. The site, Las Moras Springs, had long favored by various Indians and was recommended in 1849 by Lt. W. H. C. Whiting as a fort location. The post was renamed in 1852 in honor of Maj. John B. Clark, who had served in the Mexican War. Lt. Col. D. C. Tompkins signed an agreement with Samuel A. Maverick, who owned the land, for a period not to exceed 20 years. The fort's purpose was to guard the Mexican border, to protect the military road to El Paso, and to defend against Indian depredations arising from either side of the Rio Grande. A neighboring settlement, Las Moras, came into existence when Oscar B. Brackett established a supply village for the fort. The town's name was changed to Brackett in 1856 and later to Brackettville. The stage from San Antonio to El Paso ran through the settlement, and for almost a century the town and the fort remained closely identified. In 1854 Gen. Persifor F. Smith, the department commander, made a requisition to Governor Pease for six companies of Texas Rangers to conduct a campaign against Indian raiders. Two of these companies were sent to Fort Clark, where they assisted the regulars in patrolling the road. On 19 March 1861 Capt. W. H. T. Brooks surrendered Fort Clark to a small company of the (Confederate) Provisional Army of Texas. Confederates garrisoned the fort from June 1861 to August 1862, then withdrew. During the war, Indian depredations in the area multiplied. The dilapidated fort was regarrisoned (1866) by Troop C, Fourth United States Cavalry, with the task of protecting the road to El Paso. Repair and construction were sporadic at first. Between 1873 and 1875 most of the buildings, still in use in the historic district in the 1990s, were built of quarried limestone in an ambitious rebuilding project. The government did not receive a deed to the fort property until 1884, when Mary A. Maverick was paid $80,000 for the 3,965-acre tract.

Especially significant during the Indian campaigns in the last half of the nineteenth century were the Black Seminole scouts, who served at Fort Clark from 1872 until 1914. Under Lt. John L. Bullis from 1873 to 1881, the scouts played a decisive role in the Indian campaigns. Four were awarded the Medal of Honor. Attempts by federal troops to curtail Indian raiders from Mexico met with little success until early 1873, when Col. Ranald Mackenzie and the Fourth United States Cavalry were ordered to Fort Clark. The Remolino Raid and other actions by Mackenzie dramatically reduced Indian forays. In 1876 Mackenzie was succeeded by Lt. Col. William Shafter, one of the most successful of Fort Clark's Indian-fighting commanding officers. Under Shafter, Fort Clark became the garrison for the Tenth United States Cavalry and the Twenty-fourth and Twenty-fifth United States Infantry regiments. These mounted regiments of blacks "buffalo soldiers" left a distinguished record of service. As the lesson of Remolino dimmed, violence once more came to the Rio Grande border area. In the fall of 1875 department commander Gen. Edward O. C. Ord established the District of the Nueces, with Fort Clark as headquarters and with Shafter in control. When, in April and May 1876, Lipan warriors killed 12 Texans in an unusually bloody raid, Ord authorized Shafter to go after the offenders in their Mexican villages. Shafter took five companies of cavalry, along with Bullis's scouts, and established a base camp near the mouth of the Pecos River. For two years Shafter's determined thrusts into Mexico in pursuit of the marauding Indians and their chief, Washa Lobo, aroused Mexican animosity and caused tensions between the United States and Mexican governments. Shafter's extensive campaign on the Texas borderlands frontier not only earned him the sobriquet "Pecos Bill" but boldly implemented the army's aggressive policy toward hostile Indians, which was one of removal or extermination. By the end of the decade the Indian problem along the border had finally been brought under control.

As the country became settled, the role of the fort was reduced to a routine of garrison duty and border patrol. Despite the fact that General Sherman declared the fort obsolete in 1882—a railroad was under construction nine miles south—the War Department launched a new program of construction and expansion. During the late 1880s and early 1890s the fort was home for the Third Cavalry, the Eighteenth and Nineteenth Infantry, and occasional elements of the Seventh United States Cavalry. After the fort was again threatened with closure, it revived briefly during the Spanish–American War, when it was garrisoned by the Third Texas Infantry. With American entrance into World War I in 1917, a period of reconstruction and enlargement was begun that continued after the war ended. Many infantry regiments and practically all of the cavalry regiments were stationed at Fort Clark at various times. From 1920 to 1941, Fort Clark was home of the Fifth Cavalry. The regiment, first organized in 1855 as the Second United States Cavalry, had been associated with the fort as early as 1856. Col. George S. Patton, Jr., served at Fort Clark in 1938 as its regimental commander. At the outbreak of World War II the 112th Cavalry Division of the Texas National Guard, under command of Col. Julian Cunningham, was assigned to Fort Clark, where it trained until it was deployed for combat in the Pacific. Just before the 112th Cavalry left, the black Ninth United States Cavalry arrived at Fort Clark from Fort Riley. Elements of the regiment had first served at Fort Clark in 1875, when the fort was a frontier outpost. In 1942 Col. William C. Chase and the 113th Cavalry spent a short stay guarding the Southern Pacific Railroad. In 1943 the Second Cavalry Division, the army's last horse-mounted unit, was activated at the fort under command of Maj. Gen. Harry H. Johnson. More than 12,000 troops were stationed there until their deployment in February 1944 to Europe. During World War II German prisoners of war were incarcerated at the fort.

In June 1944, after full mechanization of the cavalry, the government ordered the closure of Fort Clark. The fort was officially deactivated in early 1946, and later that year it was sold to the Texas Railway Equipment Company of Houston, a subsidiary of Brown and Root, for salvage and later use as a "Guest Ranch." In 1971 Fort Clark was purchased by North American Towns of Texas and developed into a private recreation and retirement community. The historic district of the fort remains much as it was planned and built in the 1870s, with the old parade ground now a well-groomed golf course. Much of the fort's military history is on display in the Old Fort Clark Guardhouse Museum, maintained by the Fort Clark Historical Society. The Seminole–Negro Indian Scout Cemetery, where the four Medal of Honor recipients have specially marked graves, may be visited on Farm Road 3348. In 1979 Fort Clark was entered on the National Register of Historic Places.

Ben E. Pingenot

Fort Concho. In San Angelo; one of a number of United States military posts built to establish law and order in West Texas as settlers began to move in after the Civil War. The site at the juncture of the Main and North Concho rivers was selected in November 1867 for a new post to replace Fort Chadbourne, which lacked an adequate water supply. Company H of the Fourth United States Cavalry arrived there in December. The post was called Camp Hatch, then Camp Kelly, then (1868) Fort Concho. The commissary storehouse (today the oldest building in San Angelo) and its twin, the quartermaster storehouse, were constructed in 1868. Subsequent construction progressed slowly because building materials had to be hauled from the Gulf Coast by oxcart. An official report in 1876 stated that "a flat, treeless, dreary prairie" surrounded the fort, but Capt. Robert G. Carter recalled Fort Concho in the 1870s as "one of the most beautiful and best ordered posts on the Texas border." Civilian stonemasons and carpenters from the Fredericksburg area were employed in the early years of construction, and soldiers built the later buildings. The government did not buy the land on which the fort was built but leased it from private owners. By 1879 Fort Concho was an eight-company post with some 40 permanent structures and a number of temporary frame buildings. The fort was not stockaded, but stone walls surrounded the hospital and the backyards of the officers' quarters. A belvedere on the post hospital afforded a distant view in every direction. Food from the commissary was sometimes supplemented from the post garden at nearby Bismarck Farm or purchased from the sutler's store. Grain and meat were contracted from local suppliers. Hunting parties killed buffalo and turkeys when possible. Drinking water came from a clear-running spring three miles south.

Fort Concho was commanded by such famous officers as William R. Shafter, Ranald S. Mackenzie, Benjamin H. Grierson, John P. Hatch, and Wesley Merritt. While in command of Fort Concho, Colonel Grierson also commanded the District of the Pecos throughout the existence of that military jurisdiction in far western Texas (1878–81). Fort Concho served as regimental headquarters for the Tenth United States Cavalry, a unit of Buffalo Soldiers, from 1875 until 1882. The Fourth Cavalry headquarters was at Fort Concho for several brief periods between 1868 and 1873. The Eleventh Infantry was headquartered at Fort Concho in 1870 and the Sixteenth Infantry from 1882 until 1887. Units of the Third, Eighth, and Ninth United States Cavalry regiments and of the Tenth, Eleventh, Nineteenth, Twenty-fourth, and Twenty-fifth United States Infantry regiments also served the garrison. Soldiers from Fort Concho mapped large portions of West Texas; built roads and telegraph lines; escorted stagecoaches, cattle drives, and railroad survey parties; and served generally as a police force. At times Fort Concho troops were stationed at semipermanent subposts at Grierson's Spring, Camp Charlotte, and the head of the North Concho. Among the numerous temporary field camps were several former Butterfield Overland Mail stops such as Johnson's Station, Grape Creek Station, and old Fort Chadbourne. In the early years of the fort's existence, its soldiers skirmished with numerous small parties of Indians. Fort Concho also furnished personnel and supplies for three major Indian campaigns: Mackenzie's 1872 campaign, the 1874 Red River Indian War, and the Victorio campaign of 1879–80. In 1872–73 more than 100 Indian women and children captured by Mackenzie were imprisoned in a stone corral at Fort Concho for six months. Other important Fort Concho events include the 1875 exploration of the Llano Estacado by Colonel Shafter and the Nolan Expedition (1877).

In 1870 a town, which later became San Angelo, began to form across the river from the fort. As civilian law enforcement improved, Fort Concho ceased to be of any value as a military post; from 1882 to 1889 it was mainly a holding point for soldiers awaiting reassignment. The army abandoned the fort in 1889. Most of its buildings escaped demolition by being converted into civilian housing and commercial storage space. The restored fort is now the focus of Fort Concho National Historic Landmark. *Wayne Daniel and Carol Schmidt*

Fort Croghan. A United States military post originally at the site of a frontier post known as McCulloch's Station, three miles south of the site of present Burnet. Henry E. McCulloch and his rangers were stationed there when the place was chosen for the fort in 1849. On 18 March of that year the site officially became a federal post. On 12 October a new location was chosen, across Hamilton Creek and three miles above the first site. The post was known as Camp Croghan, then Camp Hamilton, and finally as Fort Croghan, in honor of Col. George Croghan. The buildings were of oak covered with shingles; officers' quarters were four log houses, each with two rooms separated by a hall. The hospital was a large four-room log house. The fort became headquarters of the Second Dragoons in 1852, but the government started removing its troops in 1853, and only a small guard remained when orders were issued to abandon the fort in 1855. The buildings were used as residences; the old hospital, long the home of W. P. Fry, was torn down in 1922. In 1940 only the foundations remained. During the late 1950s and early 1960s the Burnet County Historical Society began the reconstruction of Fort Croghan.

Fort D. A. Russell. Originally Camp Albert, then Camp Marfa; founded in 1911 to protect against banditry attendant upon the Mexican Revolution. The cavalry post at Marfa was also the base for Signal Corps biplanes that patrolled the Rio Grande during the crisis. From 1913 to 1916 cavalry units from Fort Bliss rotated to Marfa for garrison and field duties. During World War I, Camp Marfa was expanded to accommodate numerous units, including federal, state, and national guard troops. In 1920 the post was designated as headquarters for the Marfa Command, which replaced the Big Bend District. Between 1923 and 1936 the War Department took advantage of the remote location to con-

duct simulated combat maneuvers on a large tract of land made available by local ranchers. In 1930 the post was renamed Fort D. A. Russell, in honor of Gen. David Allen Russell, a native New Yorker who served in the Mexican War and Civil War. A Wyoming fort that had previously borne the name had been renamed Fort Warren. When the government began to consider abandoning the fort in 1931, Marfa leaders objected. The 650 officers and men, maintenance for 400 horses and mules, and payroll of $480,000 a year added greatly to the Marfa economy during the Great Depression. Nevertheless, in 1933 Fort Russell was left in the hands of caretakers. In 1935 the post was regarrisoned by 700 men of the 77th Field Artillery. In 1938 the first group scheduled for officer training arrived. Training continued at the fort for several years. During the prewar and World War II years, Fort Russell added 2,400 acres donated by the citizens of Marfa, planted 1,000 trees, improved existing buildings, and built new ones. By this time 1,000 men were stationed at the fort. In 1944 the first woman officer was assigned to the post, and civilian women replaced soldiers as drivers of cars and trucks. During the war a camp for prisoners of war was established at Marfa. Fort D. A. Russell was deactivated in 1945, closed on 23 October 1946, and transferred from the army to the Corps of Engineers in preparation for transfer to the Texas National Guard. In 1949 most of the fort area and facilities were sold to civilians. *Lee Bennett*

Fort Davis. Now the focus of Fort Davis National Historic Site, on the northern edge of the town of Fort Davis in Jeff Davis County. The fort was founded in response to War Department interest in a route through the Southwest with available water. It was established by order of Secretary of War Jefferson Davis in 1854. The army post guarded the Trans-Pecos segment of the southern route to California as the key member of a line of forts reaching from San Antonio to El Paso, and played a significant role in the defense and development of West Texas. Westward expansion to the Pacific was assured with the end of the Mexican War in 1848, when a vast territory comprising the present states of New Mexico, Arizona, and California was added to the United States, and with the discovery of gold in California in 1849. Thousands of migrants and, later, mail and freight wagons avoiding the snows and mountainous terrain of northerly routes pushed their way west over southern trails. The San Antonio–El Paso road was an important part of the most southern of these routes. Indian trails leading southward to Mexico intersected the El Paso road, however, and Apache and Comanche raiders preyed on travelers until the Civil War. By 1854 military authorities found it necessary to construct a fort in West Texas. In October 1854 Bvt. Gen. Persifor F. Smith, commander of the Department of Texas, personally selected the site of Fort Davis for its "pure water and salubrious climate." Smith named the post after Jefferson Davis. Six companies of the Eighth United States Infantry under Lt. Col. Washington Seawell, ordered to build and garrison the post, arrived at Painted Comanche Camp on Limpia Creek on October 7 of that year. With the beginning of the Civil War, United States troops evacuated Fort Davis under orders from Brig. Gen. David E. Twiggs, commander of the Eighth United States Military District, and were quickly replaced by Col. John R. Baylor's Confederate cavalry forces in April 1861. Confederate troops occupied the post for almost a year, then retreated to San Antonio after failing to take New Mexico. For

Canyon, Fort Davis–1, by Capt. Arthur T. Lee, Eighth U.S. Infantry, ca. 1855. Watercolor. 4¾" × 7⅝". Department of Rare Books and Special Collections, University of Rochester Library. The federal military presence in Texas was increased when Fort Davis was established in 1854. Captain Lee, one of the founding officers, documented his service there with a number of watercolors.

the next five years Fort Davis lay abandoned, and Indians used the wood from its buildings for fuel. Federal troops, led by Lt. Col. Wesley Merritt, reoccupied the fort in June 1867 and began construction of a new post. By the mid-1880s Fort Davis was a major installation with quarters for more than 600 men and more than sixty adobe and stone structures. From 1867 to 1885 the post was garrisoned primarily by units composed of white officers and black enlisted men of the Ninth and Tenth United States Cavalry regiments and the Twenty-fourth and Twenty-fifth United States Infantry regiments, who compiled a notable record of military achievements against the Apaches and Comanches. In September 1879 Apache chief Victorio and Mescalero Apache warriors began a series of attacks in the area west of Fort Davis. Col. Benjamin H. Grierson led troops from Fort Davis and other posts against the raiders. After the Victorio campaign, life at Fort Davis settled into a quiet routine, and large numbers of cattlemen moved into the area. The soldiers were kept busy drilling on the parade ground, patrolling the surrounding area, and repairing roads and telegraph lines. The military usefulness of Fort Davis had come to an end, however, and the post was ordered abandoned in 1891.

Fort Davis National Historic Site was authorized by Congress in 1961 and established as part of the national park system on 4 July 1963. The 460-acre site includes more than 20 original stone and adobe structures of early Fort Davis, now restored to their 1880 appearance. A visitors' center and museum, lieutenant's quarters, and post hospital are open daily, and audio programs, a slide show, and self-guided tours of the grounds are among services provided year-round. Summer seasons are highlighted by costumed employees and volunteers who explain the refurnished quarters and present cavalry and infantry demonstrations. A picnic grove and extensive nature-trail system are located on the site. Camping, motel, restaurant, and shopping facilities are available nearby.

Another Fort Davis, a civilian stronghold for defense against Indians, existed in Stephens County during the Civil War.

Douglas C. McChristian

Fort Duncan. On the east side of the Rio Grande above Eagle Pass; established by order of Maj. Gen. William J. Worth in 1849 when Capt. Sidney Burbank occupied the site with three companies of the First United States Infantry. John Twohig owned the 5,000-acre site. At the start of the Mexican War in 1846 a temporary post called Camp Eagle Pass had been established at the site. Roads ran from there to Fort Inge and Fort McIntosh, and mail was received from San Antonio. In 1889 the post was named Fort Duncan, after James Duncan, a hero of the Mexican War. It consisted of a storehouse, two magazines, four officers' quarters, and a stone hospital, in addition to quarters for enlisted men. The fort was significant because of the trade crossing into Mexico at Eagle Pass, its location on the California Road, and its position for scouting against Indians in the 1850s. Fort Duncan became involved in the Callahan expedition of 1855 when Callahan seized and burned Piedras Negras, and the commanders at the fort ultimately refused to help him recross the Rio Grande into the United States. Secretary of War John B. Floyd ordered the post abandoned in May 1859, and troops were transferred to Camp Verde on June 18. Because of Juan N. Cortina's disturbances on the Rio Grande, Robert E. Lee ordered the fort regarrisoned in March 1860, and in August 1860 Maj. D. H. Vinton leased the site from Twohig. With the outbreak of the Civil War the post was again abandoned, and John C. Crawford received the property as agent for the state of Texas. During the war the post was known as Rio Grande Station and served the Frontier Regiment. It was also an important customs point for Confederate cotton and munitions trade with Mexico. On June 19, 1864, Duncan was attacked by a force of about 100 Mexicans, but they managed only to take a few horses.

Federal troops reoccupied Fort Duncan on March 23, 1868. In 1870 Seminole Indians were attached to the command as guides. The post was abandoned in 1883, when the government could not secure its purchase. Fort Duncan was renamed the Camp at Eagle Pass that year and served as a subpost of Fort Clark. In 1894, however, the government finally bought the site. From 1890 to 1916 the fort had a skeleton caretaking detachment. In 1916, however, when disturbances in Mexico took national guard units to the river, the number of troops at the fort was increased to 16,000. The fort served as a training facility during World War I, but by 1920 only a small detail remained. In 1933 the city of Eagle Pass began maintaining the old fort as a public park on the condition that the federal government could reclaim the post for military or other reasons. The city formally acquired the property in 1935 and converted it into Fort Duncan Park. In 1942 the mayor offered the fort to the military for use during World War II. The government accepted and used the Fort Duncan Country Club as an officers' club and the swimming pool for commissioned personnel stationed at Eagle Pass Army Air Field. The site was listed in the National Register of Historic Places in 1971. Seven of the original buildings were extant and had been restored. The old headquarters building became a museum.

Fort Elliott.

The United States Army outpost in the eastern Panhandle from 1875 to 1890. Though never involved in a major military engagement, it helped transform the Panhandle into an area of settlement. In 1874, after the second battle of Adobe Walls, the army undertook a major offensive to clear the Panhandle of Indians. By command of Col. Nelson A. Miles in 1874, a temporary post was established on the North Fork of the Red River under the command of Maj. James Biddle. After the end of the Panhandle campaign, Biddle was ordered to select a site for a permanent post. His choice, a low plateau overlooking Sweetwater Creek 27 miles west of the 100th meridian, was confirmed and occupied in June. At first known simply as Cantonment on the Sweetwater, the post was renamed Fort Elliott the following February, in honor of Maj. Joel A. Elliott, who had died at the battle of the Washita. Construction of permanent facilities began in July 1875 and was largely finished by 1878. Enclosing the post within a stockade was not considered necessary. Except during its first months, when more than 400 troops were stationed there, Fort Elliott's strength was normally slightly fewer than 200 men. After 1883 a company of 40 Indian scouts was also stationed at the post. In 1879 a company of the black Tenth United States Cavalry was assigned to the garrison, and between 1880 and 1888 other black units, companies of the

Twenty-fourth United States Infantry and Ninth United States Cavalry, served there. From November 1881 until February 1884 all of Fort Elliott's troops were black. The commissioned officers were all white, however, with the exception of Lt. Henry O. Flipper.

Troops from Fort Elliott patrolled both the Panhandle and western Indian Territory. Their main task was to stop Indian hunting parties from entering the Panhandle, but on several occasions during the late 1870s they pursued bands seeking to escape the reservation. By the mid-1880s the garrison's attention had shifted to policing the range cattle industry, keeping Panhandle stock off the reservation, and supervising southern Texas herds being driven north toward Kansas. The fort provided for the Panhandle not only security but also economic stimulation. Under its protection, numerous large ranches were quickly established, and by 1880 nearly 300,000 cattle grazed the Panhandle. Settlement was clustered near Fort Elliott. Civilians were employed in the fort's construction and thereafter as teamsters or skilled laborers. Post supplies were, whenever possible, purchased locally. Sweetwater City, a hide dealer's trading post one mile from the fort, grew into Mobeetie, with a population of 150 by 1880. Wheeler County, in which the post office stood, was the first among the 25 Panhandle counties to have a large enough population to organize its own government, and for several years it administered the other counties as well. The census of 1880 showed 512 of the Panhandle's 1,379 residents in Wheeler County. In 1887, when the first railroad to enter the Panhandle bypassed Fort Elliott 18 miles to the north and provided a new source of security and prosperity, the post's function ended. In 1890 the army decided to close the fort, and an outbreak of typhoid that summer speeded its abandonment. During the next 16 years the Interior Department sold the buildings and land.

David E. Kyvig

Fort Esperanza.

A Civil War earthwork fortification on the eastern shore of Matagorda Island constructed (1861–62) to guard Cavallo Pass, the entry to Matagorda Bay; also known as Fort DeBray, in honor of Col. Xavier Blanchard DeBray, commander of the Sub–Military District of Houston. Because Fort Washington, a small fort on the extreme southeast corner of the island, was too exposed, Col. R. R. Garland chose a new position farther up the pass and ordered Capt. Dan Shea to begin the construction. Additional fortifications were added by Maj. Caleb G. Forshey in February 1862. Fort Esperanza, armed with eight 24-pound guns and one 128-pounder, was out of range of the guns of large federal vessels in the Gulf but had the same command of the channel as the older Fort Washington. The Confederates thought that the shallow water on the bar would prevent vessels larger than gunboats from attempting to enter the bay. Nevertheless, on 25 October 1862, less than a month after capturing Galveston, William B. Renshaw, captain of the USS *Westfield*, sailed past Fort Esperanza. Much impressed by the federals' gunnery, the defenders of the fort retreated to Indianola before they could be cut off. The Union forces seized Indianola after a brief battle. Port Lavaca was extensively bombarded, but a Confederate battery of two guns put up a determined resistance. In early November the Union fleet withdrew from Matagorda Bay, and since they had no ground forces to leave behind to secure their gains, the Confederates reoccupied Indianola and Fort Esperanza. After the Union debacle in the battle of Sabine

Pass (September 1863), the federal invasion plans for Texas shifted south. The federals invaded the Rio Grande valley in early November. Corpus Christi and Aransas Pass fell in the middle of the month. Union troops advanced up St. Joseph Island. Their crossing to Matagorda Island was unsuccessfully challenged, and a battle took place on 23 November at Cedar Bayou, which separates the two islands. After Union forces under Gen. T. E. G. Ransom reached Fort Esperanza on 27 November and dug in, a two-day battle followed. On the night of 29 November the Confederates, outnumbered and outflanked, evacuated the fort after spiking the guns, firing their stores, and blowing up their magazines. The fort was occupied and repaired by the Union forces, who used it as their base for further campaigns. In the spring of 1864 the Union troops were withdrawn from Matagorda Bay to participate in a proposed invasion of Texas from northeast Louisiana. After the last of the federals left Matagorda Island on 15 June, Fort Esperanza was reoccupied by the Confederates and held until the end of the war. The eastern walls were destroyed by shore erosion in a storm of 1868. By 1878 the rest of the nine-foot-high, 20-foot-thick, turf-covered walls had eroded away. The outlying emplacements and rifle pits can still be traced in some areas.   *J. Barto Arnold III*

Fort Fisher. On the west bank of the Brazos River at a site now within the Waco city limits; built in February 1837 by Capt. Thomas H. Barron's company of Maj. William H. Smith's battalion of Texas Rangers. In 1837, wrote ranger George B. Erath, "Waco was in the possession of buffalo, and only a short time before had been vacated by the Waco Indians." The rangers "built some shanties for barracks near the big spring of the river" and named the post for Secretary of War William S. Fisher. The fort was garrisoned first by Barron's men and later by other rangers. The men "were too far out to do good service," however, and so the fort was abandoned in June 1837 or soon thereafter. The post was reconstructed in 1968 as a home for the Colonel Homer Garrison Museum and serves as headquarters for a company of Texas Rangers. The reconstructed fort displays works of contemporary Western artists and maintains an excellent collection of weapons connected with the history of the Texas Rangers. The Texas Ranger Hall of Fame and Museum is located nearby.   *Thomas W. Cutrer*

Fort Graham. A United States Army post established in 1849 and occupied initially by Maj. Ripley A. Arnold and troops of the Second Dragoons under command of Bvt. Brig. Gen. William S. Harney, commander of the Frontier District of Texas. The site was 14 miles west of the site of present Hillsboro. The post was named either for James D. Graham of the Corps of Topographical Engineers or for Lt. Col. William M. Graham of the Second Dragoons, who was killed in 1847 at the Mexican War battle of Molino del Rey. Territorial gains made by the United States as a result of the Treaty of Guadalupe Hidalgo had given the army the responsibility for frontier defense in the Southwest. Fort Graham was intended to help anchor the northern-frontier defense line between the Towash Indian village and Fort Washita. Arnold's orders directed him to provide escorts for supply trains and travelers, to patrol the countryside as far as the forks of the Trinity, to protect citizens from attacks by hostile Indians, and to attempt to conciliate the local Indians. Construction and patrol duties were hindered by a lack of ade-

quate manpower—a situation that did not improve until the fall of 1849, when Gen. George M. Brooke, the new commander of the Eighth Military Department, was able to send troops of the Eighth United States Infantry under command of Bvt. Lt. Col. James V. Bomford to the northwestern posts. In October 1849 Brooke ordered Lt. W. H. C. Whiting of the corps of engineers to make a general reconnaissance of the frontier posts. According to Whiting, Fort Graham was one of the most important posts on the upper frontier. The post was near a recognized council spot and close to the villages and camps of many Indian groups. It was thus in an excellent position to serve as a frontier "listening post" in the Northwest. It also served as headquarters for Indian agents during their missions to the upper Brazos and provided escorts for the agents during councils and periodic visits to the Indian camps. Moreover, it was located near George Barnard's trading post, a target for criticism from Indian agents and departmental commanders, who accused the traders of selling liquor and firearms to the Indians. Thus Fort Graham's position, both geographically and militarily, was so important that Whiting recommended, and Brooke concurred, that about 200 men should be stationed there. Unfortunately, Brooke did not have such forces. Bomford's arrival brought the strength of the post up to 5 officers and 75 men, however, and during 1850 and 1851 the garrison was able to carry out patrol and escort duties and complete further building. During June 1851 troops from Graham under command of Maj. Henry H. Sibley provided escorts for acting adjutant general Samuel Cooper's inspection of the upper Brazos Indian villages. During the fall the post served as a base for Indian agent Jesse Stem's meetings with various tribal delegations in the region.

By 1853 the line of settlement had advanced far to the west, and Graham's location ceased to be strategic. In August 1853 Bvt. Maj. Gen. Persifor Smith ordered Fort Graham closed and the troops moved to other posts. Before the order could be carried out, the post surgeon, Josephus Steiner, shot and killed Major Arnold, who had returned to Graham to help close it. Despite this disruption the troops began leaving Fort Graham in October, and the post was closed by 9 November 1853. By offering protection against Indian raids, Fort Graham helped open the Hill County area to settlement. It also provided a market for local goods and labor, stimulated economic growth, and helped attract settlers to the region. The post was not in existence long enough, however, to build up a large community in the immediate vicinity. Although a hamlet called Fort Graham developed near the post, attempts to develop a major townsite there after 1853 were unsuccessful. By 1890 the population of the settlement had dropped to 250, and it soon disappeared. In 1936 the Texas Centennial Commission arranged for the state to buy the site, place a historical marker, and reconstruct the barracks, though it is doubtful that a reconstruction was ever built. The site was inundated by Lake Whitney in the 1970s.   *Sandra L. Myres*

Fort Griffin (1). In Shackelford County on the Clear Fork of the Brazos River; a strategic United States unit in the string of frontier posts defending Texas settlers against hostile Indians and outlaws; established in 1867 by the Sixth Cavalry. In 1868 companies of the 17th Infantry joined the garrison. The new post was first called Camp Wilson but was soon renamed after Gen. Charles Griffin. Stone buildings were planned to replace the original picket, log, and frame structures, but soldiers' quarters, stables, and even the hospital were always temporary, some mere canvas-covered shelters. The older forts Belknap, Phantom Hill, and Chadbourne became subposts of the new Fort Griffin, which supplied garrisons for the first two. The subposts furnished escorts for stagecoaches, wagontrains, and surveying parties. In time, Griffin became the nucleus of the border-defense line from Fort Richardson at Jacksboro to the Big Bend country. Law enforcement was strengthened in 1877 by the arrival of Texas Rangers under Capt. G. W. Campbell, who was replaced in July 1878 by Lt. George W. Arrington. By 1879 the southern buffalo herd was depleted, and the fort and its outposts were within a settled area. In 1881 Fort Griffin was closed, and the town surrounding it soon disappeared. The ruins of Fort Griffin stand in Fort Griffin State Historical Park, 15 miles north of Albany.

Vernon Lynch

(2) In Jefferson County; a Confederate fort at Sabine Pass, 15 miles south of Port Arthur. Hoping to block Union threats to the upper Texas Gulf Coast, Gen. John B. Magruder dispatched Maj. Julius Kellersberg to build a fort at the pass in March 1863. With 30 engineers and 500 slaves, Kellersberg constructed a triangular fort on an eminence overlooking the Sabine River. The installation housed six gun emplacements and bombproofs built into a sawtooth front. Timber and railroad iron reinforced the earthwork position. The fort was named for the commander of the 21st Texas Battalion, Col. William H. Griffin. In September 1863 four Union gunboats, leading a strong amphibious invasion force, attacked Fort Griffin. At the battle of Sabine Pass, Lt. Richard Dowling and a 46-man garrison, with two of their six guns put out of action, disabled two of the attacking vessels and scattered the remainder of the Union ships. In anticipation of another possible federal assault, Fort Griffin was strengthened with several captured Parrott rifles and temporarily reinforced. By 1 January 1864, however, the garrison, one of the last coastal positions remaining in Southern hands, had been reduced to 268 men. Confederate troops spiked the five remaining cannons and abandoned the fort by 24 May 1865. Erosion and the channelization of Sabine Pass have removed evidence of the fort's exact location. A statue and a plaque at Sabine Pass Battleground State Historical Park mark what is thought to have been the site.

Robert Wooster

Fort Hancock. Originally (1881) Camp Rice, a subpost of Fort Davis established six miles northwest of Fort Quitman to defend against Indians and Mexican bandits; moved in 1882 to a site on the Southern Pacific Railroad and the next month to higher ground nearby. Commanding general William T. Sherman believed the fort would be permanent because of its proximity to the railroad, and it was one of the few Texas forts to be purchased by the U.S. War Department (for $2,370 in 1883). For efficiency, it became independent of Fort Davis in 1884, when it received $47,000 for major improvements. In 1886 the camp was renamed in honor of Maj. Gen. Winfield Scott Hancock. Capt. Theodore A. Baldwin and Company I, Tenth United States Cavalry, formed the first garrison of the independent post. Thereafter, it was generally garrisoned by mixed detachments of infantry and cavalry rarely numbering more than 60 men. These troops patrolled the Rio Grande to prevent illegal crossings by smugglers, bandits, or insurrectionists. Post commanders included ethnologist and author Capt. John G. Bourke. Fort Hancock suffered at various times from the ravages of both water

and fire. Under Bourke, soldiers of the Third Cavalry constructed dikes to protect the post from overflow from the Rio Grande. Nevertheless, in May and June of 1886 the entire post was flooded to a depth of as much as three feet. A plague of fires in 1889 destroyed several buildings. By this time Fort Hancock had virtually outlived its usefulness. It was turned over to the Department of the Interior on 1 November 1895 and abandoned by the army on 6 December. A marker on U.S. Highway 80, 52 miles southeast of El Paso, marks the site. *Bruce J. Dinges*

Fort Hood. One of the largest military installations in the world; 218,000 acres in southwestern Bell and southeastern Coryell counties. The base, owned by the United States Army, was established as a World War II tank-destroyer tactical and firing center under command of Gen. Andrew D. Bruce. Its first major unit, the 893d Tank Destroyer Battalion, came from Fort Meade, Maryland. Camp Hood, named for John Bell Hood, was officially opened on 18 September 1942 and has been continuously used for armored training ever since. Its mission was almost immediately expanded to include a replacement and basic training center at North Fort Hood. At times as many as 100,000 soldiers were in training there during the war. Some 4,000 German prisoners of war were interned at Camp Hood. After the war the post's population dropped to about 1,700. By 1950 the temporary camp was given the permanent designation Fort Hood. The demands for training brought about by the Korean War accelerated military activities. The installation acquired additional land in the 1950s and 1960s. Major army units stationed at one time or another at Fort Hood included the First, Second, and Fourth Armored divisions. In 1954 Fort Hood was the nation's only two-division installation, and the Third Corps was transferred there from Camp Roberts, California. In 1990 the installation was headquarters of the Third Corps under United States Army Forces command. Fort Hood was located in the Fifth United States Army area. The two active army divisions, the Second Armored Division ("Hell on Wheels") and the First Cavalry Division, were stationed there. Other commands at Fort Hood included the Sixth Cavalry Brigade (Air Combat), Corps Support Command, the Third Signal Brigade, and several tenant organizations including MEDDAC (Medical Department Activity), Test and Experimentation Command, and more than a dozen other smaller support or tenant commands including two major airfields. Reserve units such as the Forty-ninth and Fiftieth Armored divisions and the Thirty-sixth Airborne Brigade of the Texas National Guard and other smaller regular and reserve units of the army, air force, and marine corps used the Fort Hood facility.

The current primary mission of Fort Hood is to maintain a state of readiness for combat missions, and the dominant activity is the training of the Third Armored Corps. A significant part of the combat-ready air and ground forces of the United States Army is stationed at Hood. The combat readiness of the Third Armored Corps distinguishes Fort Hood from installations that lack the same rapid and massive military-response capability. With the end of the Cold War, military cutbacks became common throughout the United States. The Second Armored Division was deactivated for a short period, during which time the Fifth Infantry Division (Mechanized) was assigned to Fort Hood. However, operations Desert Shield and Desert Storm in 1990–91 halted this deactivation, and more than 25,000 troops were sent from Fort Hood to the Middle East. Of these, 17,000 were from the Second Armored Division and the First Cavalry Division. On 12 April 1991, after the Gulf War, the Department of Defense labeled Fort Hood a top fighting installation and stationed 12,000 additional troops there. The installation has also been a critical social and economic reality in Central Texas. Before it was established, the region was cotton and cattle country. The shift from a low-population agrarian environment to a densely populated cosmopolitan environment has had both positive and negative features. On the one hand, Fort Hood has stimulated the growth of educational institutions, commercial conveniences, and professional services such as health care. Local communities have benefited from a military population with a pool of experienced teachers and professionals not found in most rural areas. On the other hand, the large number of transitory personnel has brought a sense of impermanence. Fort Hood is the largest solely federally owned Texas landholding and has taken an initiative in the stewardship of cultural resources on public lands. It includes more than 2,000 recorded archeological sites dating from the Ice Age to historic times. The sites are protected by federal law, and their records provide resources for anthropological research and public appreciation.

Frederick L. Briuer

Fort Inge. Part of the first federal line of frontier forts in Texas; on the east bank of the Leona River a mile south of Uvalde. The site is dominated by Mount Inge, a 140-foot volcanic plug of Uvalde phonolite basalt. Archeological evidence indicates the place has been intermittently occupied since the Pre-Archaic period, about 6,000 B.C. On 13 March 1849 frontier artist Capt. Seth Eastman and troops of the First United States Infantry established Camp Leona. In December the post was renamed Fort Inge in honor of Lt. Zebulon M. P. Inge, United States Second Dragoons, who was killed at the Mexican War battle of Resaca de la Palma. Fort Inge was to serve as a base of operations for army troops and Texas militia. The missions of the soldiers included security patrols for the construction of the San Antonio–El Paso military road, escorts for supply trains and mail, protection for frontier settlements from bandits and Indians, and guarding the international boundary with Mexico. The fort was a typical one-company, 50-man post for most of its history. For a brief period in 1854 it was the regimental headquarters for the United States Mounted Rifle Regiment, with a garrison of 200. One staff inspector reported that Fort Inge "is justly regarded as one of the most important and desirable positions in Texas . . . . [It is in] a state of constant warfare and constant service." Army units and officers of the post included the First Infantry Regiment (1849); Capt. William J. Hardee and Company C, Second Dragoons (1849–52); Bigfoot Wallace's Texas Ranging Company (1850); the United States Mounted Rifle Regiment, under Col. William Wing Loring and captains Gordon Granger and John G. Walker (1852–55); and the Second United States Cavalry, with Capt. Edmund Kirby Smith and lieutenants Fitzhugh Lee, Zenas R. Bliss, and William B. (Wild Bill) Hazen (1856–61). During the Civil War the post was occupied by Confederate and state units including Walter P. Lane's rangers; Company A, C.S.A. Cavalry; and John J. Dix's company, Norris Frontier Regiment. The fort was reoccupied by federal troops in 1866, and its final garrisons included Company K, Fourth United States Cavalry (1866–68);

Company L, Ninth United States Cavalry; and Lt. John L. Bullis and Company D, Forty-first Infantry (1868–69).

The establishment of the post soon attracted a number of farmers to the area. Reading Wood Black bought land a mile upstream in 1853 and began the settlement of Encina in 1855. The community was renamed Uvalde in 1856. Fort Inge was closed for federal service on 19 March 1869, and the garrison was transferred to Fort McKavett. In 1871 United States troops returned to tear down some of the buildings and recover the timber and stone to be used in construction at Fort Clark. The site was used as a camp by the Texas Rangers until 1884. It was subsequently farmland until 1961, when it became Fort Inge Historical Site County Park. From 1980 to 1982 the Uvalde County Historical Commission and local donors sponsored archival research and an archeological project to establish an accurate and detailed history of Fort Inge.

Thomas T. Smith

Fort Lancaster. Now the focus of a state historic site 10 miles east of Sheffield in Crockett County; established as Camp Lancaster in 1855 by Capt. Stephen D. Carpenter and manned by companies H and K of the First United States Infantry. Camp Lancaster became Fort Lancaster in 1856. The post was occupied from December 1861 to April 1862 by Walter P. Lane's Confederate rangers. After the war the fort was vacant until 1871, when it was reoccupied as a subpost by a company of infantry and a detachment of cavalry. It was apparently abandoned in 1873 or 1874, and much of its masonry was used for buildings in Sheffield. Fort Lancaster protected the lower road from San Antonio to El Paso in the years following the discovery of gold in California. The duties of the men stationed there were to escort mail and freight trains, pursue Mescalero Apaches and Comanches, and patrol their segment of road to keep track of Indian movements. The Butterfield Overland Mail changed its route west from the upper road between San Antonio and El Paso to the lower road in August 1859. Mail on the lower road had previously been contracted to George H. Giddings and John Birch. Three coaches per month passed over the road. In June of 1860 Lt. William E. Echols and his camels visited the fort. The fort site was deeded to Crockett County in 1965 and donated to the Texas Parks and Wildlife Department in 1968, after which archeological investigation occurred sporadically for several years. The excavations produced large numbers of artifacts and a great deal of architectural information. Much of this material is presented at the visitors' center at Fort Lancaster State Historic Site and in state archeological reports. Because of a budget shortfall the state yielded management of the site to Texas Rural Communities, Incorporated, in 1993.

John W. Clark, Jr.

Fort Leaton. A private fort five miles southeast of Presidio on a bluff overlooking the Rio Grande and the route of the Chihuahua Expedition. Fort Leaton was listed as the first seat of Presidio County in 1850. It was the citadel of Ben Leaton, a Chihuahua freighter and the first Anglo-American farmer in Presidio County. Leaton built on the ruins of a Spanish fort founded in 1773 and known as El Fortín de San José. After El Fortín was abandoned in 1810, the structure stood unoccupied until Juan Bustillos took it as his home in 1830. By August 1848 Leaton had bought El Fortín from Bustillos and established Fort Leaton as his home, trading post, and private fort. During that month an expedition led by Jack Hays to find a practicable road from San Antonio to Chihuahua via El Paso spent 10 days at Fort Leaton. The adobe fort was built in an L-shape with the long side running east and west for 200 feet, parallel to the river. Because of its desolate location and the constant threat of Indian attack, it offered much-needed frontier defense. The private bastion was the only fortification on the American side of the Rio Grande between Eagle Pass and El Paso before and during the building of Fort Davis, and the army made Fort Leaton its unofficial headquarters. Even after the completion of Fort Davis, 80 miles to the north, the army used the private fort as an outpost for military patrols. Military maps of the 1850s listed Fort Leaton along with official army posts. There is no record of any Indian attack on Fort Leaton, perhaps because Leaton may have traded guns to Indians for horses they had stolen in Mexico. He died before any such charge could be brought against him (1851). His farm, with eight to ten American workers and a gravity irrigation ditch, produced vegetables, wheat, and livestock to supply the fort's inhabitants and needy travelers. Eventually, the fort was acquired by John Burgess, who had held the mortgage. Burgess lived there until Leaton's son Bill killed him in 1875. The fort then fell into disuse. In 1934 and 1935 some restoration work was completed there under a government project. In 1967 the state acquired a five-acre tract around the old fort, and the partially restored structure became Fort Leaton State Historic Site.

Julia Cauble Smith

Fort Lincoln. A mile north of the site of D'Hanis; one of eight federal forts that formed the first line of permanent frontier defense in Texas from Eagle Pass on the Rio Grande to Coffee's Bend on the Red River; named for Capt. George Lincoln, an officer of the Eighth Infantry who died in the Mexican War battle of Buena Vista. In 1848 a Texas Ranger company commanded by Charles S. DeMontel established a camp where the next year Fort Lincoln was established. The site was a 1,476-acre plot patented to the heirs of Milton Anderson in 1846. The fort was built on high, open ground that provided a commanding view of the surroundings. Companies E and G of the Eighth United States Infantry, commanded by Maj. James Longstreet, were stationed at Fort Lincoln to protect settlers and the property transported on the Woll Road, an important trade route from San Antonio to Fort Duncan on the Rio Grande. Longstreet's second in command, Lt. Richard Irving Dodge, was the man for whom Dodge City, Kansas, was named. Water for the post was hauled from Seco Creek, at that time no more than a succession of standing pools. The builders of the fort used local gray limestone in construction. In 1851 the installation had permanent buildings for two companies, a commissary store, a storehouse for company property, a storehouse for the quartermaster's depot, and a hospital. Officers and men stationed at the fort usually numbered between 90 and 120. Fort Lincoln was abandoned in 1852 after the frontier line had advanced westward. The Texas Rangers made headquarters at the site. The barracks were torn down and transformed into residences at D'Hanis after being purchased by Irishman Richard Reily, who lived in the hospital building. None of the buildings remains. On 26 May 1936 a dedication ceremony was held for the unveiling of a marker placed by the Texas Centennial Commission at the site. *H. E. Haass*

Fort Lipantitlán. A Mexican-Texas fort whose name mean "Lipan Land"; conceived about 1825 by José M. J. Carbajal. The site, now in northwestern Nueces County, was that of camping grounds of the Lipan Apaches, on the west bank of the Nueces River three miles upstream from the old town of San Patricio. There, a number of ancient trails beaten by game animals, Indians, and explorers crossed. An old presidio was also reportedly there as early as 1734 but had completely vanished. Mexican general Manuel de Mier y Terán, acting on orders to restrict Anglo immigration into Texas, commissioned the fort and placed Capt. Enrique Villareal in command. Villareal was relieved by Capt. Nicolás Rodríguez in 1835. John J. Linn wrote, "The fort was a simple embankment of earth, lined within by fence-rails to hold the dirt in place, and would have answered tolerably well, perhaps, for a second-rate hog pen." After its construction it was putatively garrisoned with 80 to 120 men, though often far fewer were present. Each of the four parapets was designed for one cannon, but it is doubtful if the fort was ever fully armed. Evidently several buildings and at least one barracks were built surrounding the embankments. During the Texas Revolution the Mexican armies, coming north toward Goliad, Refugio, and East Texas, crossed the Nueces at either the De Leon Crossing at Fort Lipantitlán or Paso de Santa Margarita near San Patricio. During this period Mexican troops were in almost constant occupancy of the fort. Captain Rodríguez was in command when Capt. Ira J. Westover and a force of about 70 Texans defeated the Mexicans at the battle of Lipantitlán, 4 November 1835. Since the Texans did not occupy the fort after their victory, Mexican forces continued to use the old fort on occasion.

Fort Lipantitlán played an important role in the years immediately after the war, when Federalist forces under Gen. Antonio Canales sought refuge on the Nueces River to regroup and to seek assistance from Americans. Gen. James Davis repulsed Mexican troops under Canales at Lipantitlán on 7 July 1842. After the Mexican War put an end to Mexican armies in Texas, Lipantitlán was abandoned and grew up in brush. In the mid-1980s digs on private land uncovered a number of artifacts in a rather large camp adjacent to the old fort where families and army women lived. A population of 300 or more in the camp is considered likely. The site of the old fort is a state park, but no traces of the earthen embankments remain. The archeological digs confirmed Indian presence before the Spanish and Mexican eras, as well as occupancy by Texas forces in 1842. Aboriginal ceramics, Indian artifacts, all types of military buttons and ordnance (Spanish, Mexican, and Texan), money, and miscellaneous hardware were among the hundreds of artifacts recovered.

Keith Guthrie

Fort Marcy. Probably established when Zachary Taylor moved United States forces to Corpus Christi from St. Joseph Island on 15 August 1845; named for William L. Marcy, secretary of war under President James Buchanan. The engineers laid out Bay View Cemetery that month, and the first burials were probably those of eight soldiers killed en route from the island to the mainland. Taylor proposed abandoning the Corpus Christi area in February 1846 and began moving his troops to the Rio Grande on 11 March. There may have been no other federal troops at the site until June 1849, when part of a company of dragoons was stationed there. A depot for military supplies was set up at Corpus Christi in August 1849; Gen. Persifor Smith moved the army headquarters there in 1853 and may have used the name Fort Marcy. The supply depot was probably abandoned in 1857. Whether or not defense works were ever erected at Corpus Christi is not certain, but in 1863 Confederate troops were reported to be positioned behind Taylor's old earthworks.

J. E. Conner

Fort Martin Scott. An installation two miles southeast of Fredericksburg on Barons Creek; one of the first United States Army posts on the western frontier of Texas. The post was established as Camp Houston in 1848 by Capt. Seth Eastman and troops of the First United States Infantry. It served the Fredericksburg–San Antonio road and the local region as part of the army's effort to protect Texan settlers and travelers from Indian depredations. Eastman left in 1849 to establish Fort Inge. Because the Germans in Fredericksburg had established a lasting treaty with the local Comanches in 1847, Indian depredations were initially limited. The Eighth Military Department renamed the camp in 1849 for Maj. Martin Scott (Fifth United States Infantry), who was killed at the Mexican War battle of Molino del Rey in 1847. Fort Martin Scott served as a first line of defense, keeping the peace and minimizing possible friction caused by an active trade between the Comanches and German settlers. The soldiers were also the one constant source of hard cash for businessmen in this rural community. The influx of new settlers, soldiers, and other whites traversing the range led to the brink of open warfare in 1850, when several tribes of Indians met near the San Saba River. Indian agent John Rollins, under escort by Capt. Hamilton W. Merrill and troopers of the Second Dragoons from Fort Martin Scott, met with the Indians. This meeting culminated in the Fort Martin Scott Treaty, which improved the situation enough to prevent open hostilities. As the settlers pushed farther west, Martin Scott lost its significance and economic justification. In 1852–53 it assumed the role of forage depot. The Eighth Military Department ordered it closed in December 1853. Fort Martin Scott was not significant during the Civil War. In September 1866 Gen. Philip Sheridan ordered elements of the Fourth United States Cavalry to the fort to secure the frontier once again from possible Indian depredations. By the end of 1866 the fort was finally abandoned by military units. Many commanders of Fort Martin Scott fought in the Civil War, including William R. Montgomery, Eugene B. Beaumont, William Steele, Edward D. Blake, James Longstreet, and Theodore Fink. The Fredericksburg Heritage Association now leases the site of the fort from the city of Fredericksburg. The association has developed the property as a park and historic site and continues with archeological projects and historic renovations.

Paul R. M. Brooks, Jr.

Fort Mason. At the site of Mason; established in 1851. After annexation, settlement of Texas was hampered by Indians, who controlled the majority of the state. In 1848 the United States War Department authorized a line of army forts from the Rio Grande to the Red River. Fort Mason, one of these, was situated on Post Oak Hill near Comanche and Centennial creeks, then in the northern part of Gillespie County. It was most likely named either for Lt. George T. Mason, who was killed at Brownsville during the Mexican War, or for Gen. Richard Barnes Mason, who died a year before the fort was established. Fort Mason played an important part in settlement of the area. Settlers at first stayed close to it, but as the aggressive attitude of the military became apparent, additional newcomers located farther from the post. The Indians—Kiowas, Lipan Apaches, and Comanches—were driven farther away and began making fewer raids into the settlements. The fort was closed several times during its first decade. It reached its maximum population in January 1856, when the headquarters and six companies of the Second United States Cavalry were stationed there, with Col. Albert Sidney Johnston in command. In 1861 Fort Mason passed into Confederate hands. Twenty officers stationed there before the Civil War became generals—12 Confederate, 8 Union. Among them were Earl Van Dorn, Fitzhugh Lee, E. Kirby Smith, George H. Thomas, Robert E. Lee, John Bell Hood, William J. Hardee, and Philip St. George Cooke. For a short period during 1862 the Confederate Army held 215 men prisoner, mostly civilians accused of being Union sympathizers, in the fort. During August 1862 they were marched to Austin. Indian depredations during the Civil War and immediately afterward were worse than they had ever been. The area was terrorized by killings, thefts, and nuisance raids. Elements of the Fourth United States Cavalry under Gen. John P. Hatch reoccupied the fort in 1866. Fort Mason was repaired and improved by civilian artisans and military labor. Reconstruction lawlessness affected military personnel; a large number of desertions and courts-martial were reported. Cavalry were replaced with soldiers from the Thirty-fifth Infantry over a period of time. The last inspection of the fort occurred on 13 January 1869. The report listed 25 buildings, mostly vacant and in need of repair, and only 69 men. The order to close the fort was carried out three months later. During 1870 the state of Texas organized several companies of frontier forces. Fort Mason was reopened in September of that year as headquarters for Companies A and B, Frontier Forces. Capt. James M. Hunter, later county judge of Mason County, was in command for most of that year. During the next year the forces were disbanded or moved, and for the last time the fort was closed. Although the fort buildings and land became private property, the rock buildings were gradually dismantled by local citizens. Many early homes in the town of Mason incorporated material from the fort. In 1975 a local group of citizens began reconstructing officers' quarters at the site. Many people contributed and assisted in the building. Today, this building belongs to the Mason County Historical Society.

Julius E. Devos

Fort McIntosh. On the Rio Grande near Laredo; established in the aftermath of the Mexican War. American occupation of the former Spanish presidio dates from the arrival in November 1846 of Capt. Mirabeau B. Lamar, former president of the Republic of Texas, with the Laredo Guard of the Texas Volunteers. In 1849 Lt. Egbert L. Viélé and a company of the First United States Infantry set up a camp on a bluff west of Laredo. They named the post Camp Crawford, in honor of Secretary of War George W. Crawford. In January 1850 the site became Fort McIntosh, in tribute to Lt. Col. James S. McIntosh, killed in the battle of Molino Del Rey. The fort was initially a star-shaped earthwork built by army engineers and troop labor. It formed a key link in the dual chain of forts that lined the Rio Grande and the western frontier. The heat and aridity made the location undesirable, but the post nevertheless provided the area needed military and economic security. Comanches and Lipan Apaches harassed the region; the adjacent river ford was popularly known as Indian Crossing. An inspection by Col. J. K. F. Mansfield in 1856 confirmed McIntosh's strategic value, and the temporary removal of the garrison three years later depressed the local economy. The Indian problem expanded the normally small garrison at times to over 400 men, including officers Philip Sheridan and Randolph B. Marcy and Texas Ranger John S. Ford. The Civil War brought Confederate occupation of the fort. During the war Fort McIntosh sustained several unsuccessful Northern assaults. In 1865 federal soldiers returned and inaugurated a period of stability. Permanent construction began three years later, and within the next decade the installation was greatly enhanced. In 1875, after a series of leases, Laredo ceded to the federal government 208 acres adjoining the considerably larger original site. Infantry, cavalry, field artillery, an engineer squadron, and national guard units operated in turns from the premises. Black troops garrisoned McIntosh without notable incident in the 1870s, but their return after the Spanish-American War started a racial conflict that presaged later outbursts at Brownsville and Houston. Complaining of police brutality, an undetermined number of soldiers from Company D of the Twenty-fifth Infantry beat a peace officer in October 1899. Governor Joseph Sayers responded to the public outcry by demanding the removal of all black troops from the state. The furor subsided with the arrest of several infantrymen and the growing alarm of the citizenry that Washington might close the post altogether. The Mexican Revolution and two world wars prolonged the utility of Fort McIntosh long after transportation improvements rendered most of the old frontier posts obsolete. The war department discontinued the installation on 31 May 1946, when the Boundary Commission acquired the northern half of the property and the city of Laredo reclaimed the remainder. Laredo Junior College occupies a portion of the latter.

Garna L. Christian

Fort Milam. (1) On the west bank of the Brazos River four miles southwest of the site of Marlin; built in 1834 and called Fort Viesca; renamed for Benjamin R. Milam in 1835. The fort was built for the protection of the settlers of Sarahville de Viesca at the Falls of the Brazos. It was abandoned during the Runaway Scrape in March 1836. As settlers began to return to the area in the spring, Col. Edward Burleson organized three ranger companies to garrison the fort and provide protection to that exposed region. From Fort Milam detachments were sent to construct Little River Fort in 1836 and Fort Fisher and Fort Henderson in 1837. After the ranger enlistments began to expire during the late summer of 1837 the garrison evaporated, and the fort soon stood vacant.

Thomas W. Cutrer

(2) The other Fort Milam was on the east bank of the Brazos a few miles east of the old Fort Milam. It was built in January and February 1839 in response to a devastating Indian attack and temporarily garrisoned by Capt. Joseph Daniels's company of Milam Guards from Houston. The structure was "150 feet square, built of Cedar pickets doubl[e] banked, eleven feet high with bastions at each angle." Daniels's men departed in mid-February and were replaced by two companies that remained through the spring and summer. The post was renamed Fort Burleson on 26 August 1839, in honor of Edward Burleson, and manned by Company D of the regulars until late 1840. After the

company was moved to Camp Chambers the fort passed into private hands and was maintained by local citizens until danger of Indian attack had passed.

Thomas W. Cutrer

Fort Parker. A private installation built by Silas M. and James W. Parker between Old Springfield and the present site of Groesbeck in 1834 or 1835. Its cabins, to be occupied by families in case of Indian attack, had outer walls that were part of a surrounding stockade perforated with loopholes for defense. On 19 May 1836 the fort was attacked by 500 to 700 Caddo and Comanche Indians. Silas was killed, and his nine-year-old daughter, Cynthia Ann, and six-year-old son, John, Mrs. Rachel Plummer and her son James, and Mrs. Elizabeth Kellogg became Indian captives.

Fort Parker State Recreation Area is on State Highway 14 six miles south of Mexia. The park features a replica of the fort and a 750-acre lake on the Navasota River. The land was donated to the state by the city of Mexia and three property owners in 1935 and 1936. The CCC constructed the dam and the park's other structures in the mid-1930s. Facilities include a hiking trail, a dining hall, camping and picnicking areas, and playgrounds.

Art Leatherwood and Christopher Long

Fort Phantom Hill. One of the second line of forts laid out in the early 1850s to protect the westward-moving frontier of Texas settlement. In 1849 the federal government sent Capt. Randolph Marcy to explore and mark the best route through "Comanchería," the vast region to the north and west of Austin inhabited by the warlike Comanche Indians. This was meant to protect immigrants headed for the California gold fields. The advanced cordon of forts, including Fort Phantom Hill, was established as a result of Marcy's recommendations. Acting on orders from Gen. Persifor Smith, commander of the Eighth Military District, Lt. Col. John J. Abercrombie arrived at the Clear Fork of the Brazos in the area of present Jones County with five companies of the Fifth Infantry on 14 November 1851. The site, not the one originally envisioned by Smith's predecessor, Gen. William Belknap, lacked adequate water and timber. The fort was constructed of locally quarried rock and logs brought from as far away as forty miles. Oddly enough, Fort Phantom Hill was never officially named; military records usually refer to it as the "Post on the Clear Fork of the Brazos." There are several legends about the origin of the unofficial designation Phantom Hill, one of which is that from a distance the hill on which it was built rises sharply from the plains but seems to level out as it is approached, vanishing like a phantom. Life at the fort was difficult. Elm Creek was often dry, and the waters of the Clear Fork were brackish. A well dug near the guardhouse was not always reliable. More often than not, it was necessary to haul barrels of water in wagons from a spring about four miles upriver from the post. Although the isolated fort was vulnerable to attacks, its garrison had only peaceful encounters with Indians. Certainly, it would have been a tactical blunder to match infantry against the Comanche horsemen of the plains. A band of Penateka Comanches led by Buffalo Hump occasionally came calling, as did groups of Lipans, Wichitas, Kiowas, and Kickapoos. Jim Shaw and Black Beaver were among the noted Delaware scouts employed by the garrison as interpreters and guides.

Abercrombie was succeeded as commander by Lt. Col. Carlos A. Waite (1852), Maj. Henry Sibley (1853), and Lt. Newton

C. Givens (1854). Givens was in command for only 12 days—until the fort was abandoned on 6 April 1854. The decline in rank of its commanders shows the fort's decline in importance. At the time of its evacuation, the purpose of curbing the Indian menace had momentarily been attained by the establishment of the reservations on the upper Brazos and the Clear Fork to the northeast near Fort Belknap. Shortly after the soldiers left Phantom Hill, the fort buildings mysteriously burned to the ground, an event variously attributed to everyone from an irate officer's wife to Indians and later to Union sympathizers. The scanty evidence points inconclusively to members of the departing garrison as the arsonists. In 1858 the remaining structures of the fort were repaired and utilized as Way Station Number 54 by the Butterfield Overland Mail. The station was managed by a man named Burlington, whose wife prepared meals for the stage passengers. Most travelers agreed with New York *Herald* correspondent Waterman L. Ormsby that Phantom Hill was "the cheapest and best new station on the route." During the Civil War, when the frontier was patrolled by Texas Ranger companies and subsequently by the Frontier Battalion, Col. Buck Barry or some of the units under his command used Fort Phantom Hill as a base of field operations. Beginning in 1871, the post served as a subpost of Fort Griffin. Gen. William T. Sherman made an overnight stop here during his inspection tour of the Department of Texas. Capt. Theodore Schwan led a column of Col. Ranald Mackenzie's raiders from the post in the first series of Indian campaigns into West Texas between January and March 1872.

After the Indian wars subsided, a town grew up around the fort ruins. In 1876–77 it was a buying and shipping point for buffalo hides. By 1880 the community had a population of 546. It was made county seat of Jones County in May 1881 but lost that distinction to Anson later the same year. The Texas and Pacific Railway routed its tracks through Abilene, 14 miles to the south. A letter written to the San Antonio *Express* in 1892 commented that the Fort Phantom community was nothing but "one hotel, one saloon, one general store, one blacksmith shop, and 10,000 prairie dogs." Fort Phantom Hill is on private land. The owners have improved it and made it available to the public. Three stone buildings and more than a dozen chimneys and foundations remain. Only two miles south of the fort is a man-made reservoir, Fort Phantom Hill Reservoir, which supplies the water for about 100,000 people in Taylor and Jones counties. The remains of Fort Phantom Hill have been celebrated in verse by the cowboy poet William L. Chittenden and in the prose of other Western writers. *H. Allen Anderson*

Fort Polk. On the Rio Grande opposite Matamoros; established by Gen. Zachary Taylor in 1846. Taylor's army drove the Mexican garrison at Brazos Santiago back across the Rio Grande while converting the Mexican installation to an arsenal. On 6 March his men established a military depot near the Brazos Santiago arsenal and named it Fort Polk, in honor of the president of the United States. The fort was also known as Fort Brazos Santiago. Fort Polk was garrisoned from 1848 until 1850, although by January 1849 the buildings were being moved to different locations on the Rio Grande. On 9 February 1850 the post was abandoned. The location was used as a transit depot for materials for Fort Brown in 1852, and on 21 February 1861 it was seized by a Confederate artillery company from Galveston. Long afterward,

the U.S. Army Corps of Engineers straightened the channel and installed jetties in the pass, obliterating the site of both the Mexican fort at Brazos Santiago and Fort Polk.

Thomas W. Cutrer

Fort Quitman. Twenty miles southeast of the site of present-day McNary and 400 yards east of the Rio Grande in far southern Hudspeth County; established in 1858 by Capt. Arthur T. Lee and companies C and H, Eighth Infantry, to protect travelers and mail along the route from San Antonio to El Paso. The fort was named for Mexican War general John A. Quitman. During the Civil War it was intermittently garrisoned by Confederate and Union detachments and quickly fell into disrepair. Capt. Henry Carroll and Company F, Ninth United States Cavalry, reoccupied the crumbling adobe buildings in 1868. Over the next decade, Quitman garrisons of black soldiers from the Ninth Cavalry and the Twenty-fifth United States Infantry guarded the mails and scouted for hostile Indians. Fort Quitman had a reputation as one of the most uncomfortable military installations in Texas. Lydia Spencer Lane described it in 1869 as "forlorn and tumble-down" and was surprised to observe a sergeant, in full-dress uniform, jumping rope outside the guardhouse. "If any one at Quitman could feel cheerful enough to enjoy so innocent a pastime," she concluded, "he was to be congratulated." Surgeon John Culver (1870) found Fort Quitman "entirely unworthy of the name of fort, post, or station for United States troops." The poor soil and dry, hot climate frustrated attempts to cultivate a post garden. Milk and fresh vegetables had to be hauled in at exorbitant prices from San Elizario, El Paso, or San Ignacio, Chihuahua. Soldiers at Fort Quitman spent considerable time repairing the buildings. Fort Quitman was vacated in 1877 but was regarrisoned in 1880–82, during the Victorio campaign, as a subpost of Fort Davis. The post was abandoned partly because it was not on a railroad, and Fort Hancock was established in 1882 at a better site nearby. Today only a cemetery remains near the site of Fort Quitman. *Bruce J. Dinges*

Fort Richardson. One-half mile south of the site of Jacksboro; established in February 1868 to provide protection against Comanche and Kiowa Indians on the North Texas frontier and named for a Union general, Israel Bush (Fighting Dick) Richardson. The unstockaded reservation occupied some 300 acres on Lost Creek, a tributary of the Trinity River. Eventually 55 stone, picket, and cottonwood buildings were constructed at an estimated cost of $800,000. Located 70 miles from Indian Territory and 120 miles from Fort Sill, Richardson was the northernmost army outpost in Texas and the anchor of a defensive line of fortifications that included Fort Griffin and Fort Concho. From 1868 to 1873 Richardson was strategically the most important post in Texas, and in 1872 it had the largest garrison (666 officers and men) among military installations in the United States. During its 10-year history the fort was the regimental headquarters for the Sixth United States Cavalry (1868–71), the Fourth United States Cavalry (1871–73), and the Eleventh Infantry (1873–76), as well as home for various elements of the Tenth United States Cavalry and Twenty-fourth United States Infantry. Richardson soldiers helped local law officers keep the peace, pursued criminals and deserters, escorted wagontrains, oversaw elections, protected cattle herds, and, most importantly, patrolled for Indians. During the prime raiding months of April through September, scouting parties were in the field constantly. Although most excursions were fruitless, occasionally the soldiers had bloody encounters; in July 1879, for instance, Capt. Curwin B. McClellan and 56 officers and men of the Sixth Cavalry were ambushed near the Little Wichita River by some 250 Kiowas and Comanches led by the Kiowa chief Kicking Bird. After a desperate fight McClellan and his men were able to hold off the Indians and retreat to safety. Thirteen men of the Sixth won the Medal of Honor for gallantry in action in the battle of the Little Wichita. In May 1871 General Sherman visited Fort Richardson and received word of the Warren Wagontrain Raid. The Kiowa chiefs Satanta and Big Tree were held in custody at Fort Richardson and in July 1871 had the dubious honor of becoming the first Indians to be tried in a Texas civil court. Subsequently, Sherman authorized Fort Richardson's commanding officer, Col. Ranald S. Mackenzie, to begin offensive operations against any Indians not on the reservation. Over a 15-month period Mackenzie led four major expeditions from Richardson into the Panhandle. In late 1871 he fought a running battle with the Quahadi Comanches, led by their famous war chief, Quanah Parker. In the summer of 1872 Mackenzie explored the unmapped Llano Estacado, and late that year, on the North Fork of the Red River, he located and attacked the encampment of the Comanche chief Mow-way, killing 50 warriors and capturing 130 women and children. During the Red River Indian War (1874–75) Fort Richardson served as a major staging base for the columns of cavalry and infantry that swept the plains and inflicted final military defeat on the Comanche and Kiowa Indians. With the North Texas frontier secure, there was no longer any need for a military presence in Jack County, and in May 1878 the army abandoned the post.

Fort Richardson is now the focus of Fort Richardson State Historical Park. After the army left in 1878 the buildings were left to the elements, and many of the structures collapsed. The city of Jacksboro acquired title to the fort and deeded it to the Texas Parks and Wildlife Department in 1968. The department purchased the adjoining 347 acres in 1970 and 1974. The fort hospital now serves as a museum; it and several other buildings have been restored. The ruins of many of other structures can also be seen. Facilities include a hiking trail, camping and picnicking areas, and restrooms.

Allen Lee Hamilton and Christopher Long

Fort Ringgold. The southernmost installation of the western tier of forts constructed at the end of the Mexican War. The fort, known initially (1848) as the Post at Davis Landing, bore the names Camp Ringgold and Ringgold Barracks before being named Fort Ringgold in the year the government purchased the site from heirs of Henry Clay Davis (1878). The name was in honor of Bvt. Maj. Samuel Ringgold, killed in the battle of Palo Alto. The military chose the site to protect the area from Indian and Mexican attacks. The 96-year occupancy of the post was interrupted when the government considered it redundant, then resumed when the region was threatened. Major periods of occupation were from 1848 until 1861; from 1865 until military exigencies in the Philippines closed it in 1906; and from 1917 to 1944. The army declared the fort surplus and disposed of the property in 1944. The installation was of flimsy construction until after the Civil War. Construction began on new buildings in 1869, and by the mid-1870s the fort's frame and brick struc-

tures along a palm-lined parade ground had made Ringgold one of the most attractive posts along the border. Congress appropriated additional funds for improvements in 1917. In the nineteenth century Ringgold hosted a number of prominent military figures, including Robert E. Lee, John J. Pershing, and possibly Jefferson Davis. In 1875 Capt. Leander H. McNelly and a contingent of Texas Rangers garrisoned the post. Fort Ringgold assured the survival of isolated Rio Grande City and socially and economically affected the life of the community while it safeguarded the citizenry from border violence. The post housed the area's first telegraph office, fueled the local economy through federal appropriations, and warred against abundant smugglers, rustlers, and insurrectionists. The Cortina War and the unrest along the border during the Mexican Revolution particularly emphasized the importance of the garrison. Ringgold troops under the command of Maj. Samuel P. Heintzelman ended the threat of the former by joining forces with John S. Ford and the Texas Rangers to rid the area of Juan N. Cortina in 1860.

The most serious rift between Fort Ringgold and Rio Grande City occurred in 1899 when Troop D of the Ninth United States Cavalry briefly garrisoned the installation. The black troops, returning triumphantly from the Cuban campaign, quickly grew impatient at racial restrictions and harassment. Tensions heightened amid conflicting reports of impending attacks on the fort and town. On the night of 20 November post commander 2d Lt. E. H. Rubottom responded to a presumed assault on the garrison by ordering Gatling gunfire on the area between the post and town. Only one minor injury resulted, but Rubottom's action succeeded in quelling the disturbance. Ensuing federal, state, and grand jury investigations failed to specify culpability or motivation, although many townspeople and other Texans insisted that the soldiers feigned an attack on the fort in order to wreak havoc on the community. Lt. Col. Cyrus S. Roberts of the United States Army and Thomas Scurry, adjutant general of Texas, concluded that Rubottom had acted unwisely but recommended no charges against him or others. Governor Sayers favored the locals' demand that the Ninth Cavalry be moved, and the residents requested that a white garrison be retained. In 1947 remains from the abandoned Fort Ringgold cemetery were reinterred at Fort Sam Houston National Cemetery in San Antonio. The Rio Grande Consolidated ISD purchased the fort property in 1949. The district maintains the standing buildings, the most renowned of which is the Lee House, where Robert E. Lee resided in 1860 while he was investigating Cortina's intrusions.

Garna L. Christian

Fort Sabine. A dirt and timber earthwork overlooking the Sabine River 15 miles south of Port Arthur; built by residents of Sabine Pass during the Civil War. The post was garrisoned by local militia, the Sabine Pass Guard, and later by the Sixth Texas Infantry Battalion. On 24 September 1862 it was shelled by Union gunboats and severely damaged. When yellow fever broke out among the remaining troops, Maj. Josephus S. Irvine ordered the guns spiked and the position abandoned. The following March, Maj. Julius Kellersberg inspected the remains of Fort Sabine and determined that the site was no longer useful. Consequently, he ordered the construction of a new fort, several miles away, which became Fort Griffin (Jefferson County).

Robert Wooster

World War I infantry transport truck and troops at Fort Sam Houston, 1916. Courtesy TSL.

Fort Sam Houston. A major military installation in San Antonio. As early as 1846 the city was vying to get a permanent federal military installation. During the Mexican War the United States Army established a quartermaster depot at San Antonio and a training camp at San Pedro Springs. In 1849 San Antonio was named headquarters of the United States Army Eighth Military District, with forces at Concepción Mission and San Pedro Springs. The Alamo was taken on lease from the Catholic Church and used for storage. The Vance house, a two-story stone house where the Gunter Hotel now stands, was leased for army headquarters. The city made several offers of free land, but all were refused except for a small parcel on Flores Street, which was used for an arsenal.

A formal proposal for a permanent army post was made in 1870, but it met with political opposition in Washington. Secretary of War W. W. Belknap illegally held up funding until 1875. He resigned in 1876 rather than face impeachment, partly over his refusal to fund congressional appropriations for the San Antonio base. On 7 June 1876 construction was finally begun on 93 acres of city-donated land known as Government Hill. The contract was with the Edward Braden Construction Company. Construction of the quadrangle included a one-story north wall 624 feet long, east and west walls 499½ feet long, and a two-story south wall with the only entry gate. Work was completed in February 1873. In 1870 the Texas Department of the U.S. Army had moved to San Antonio. In 1879 the depot that had been in the Alamo moved to the new post. Almost immediately expansion began with the construction of officers' quarters, a huge commander's home later named the Pershing House, and a tent hospital, which was replaced by a permanent post hospital in 1885. Between 1885 and 1891, 43 acres and 60 buildings were added to what was to become the infantry post. In 1890 the military post at San Antonio was designated Fort Sam Houston. Geronimo was held there in 1886 before his exile to Florida, and Theodore Roosevelt stopped with his men at the base to receive provisions before leaving for Cuba in 1898 with the First United States Volunteer Cavalry.

In 1907 the first chapel was built, with donated funds, and nicknamed "Gift Chapel." A new hospital was built in 1908 and enlarged in 1910 and 1915 to 1,000 beds. On 15 February 1910 Lt. Benjamin Foulois brought the army's first airplane to Fort Sam Houston. There he learned to fly with instruction through correspondence with the Wright brothers. He instigated the first experimental flights in United States military aviation and gave the first public demonstration flights on 2 March. Because of a crash that day, the aviation program was temporarily suspended at the post. Foulois's airplane, United States Army Aeroplane Number One, is in the National Air and Space Museum in Washington, D.C. By 1912 the military units at Fort Sam Houston included an infantry regiment, a regiment of cavalry, two batteries of field artillery, and signal and engineer troops. By 1917 the installation had been raised to general depot status and was supplying the Mexican frontier, including General Pershing's pursuit of Pancho Villa. Camp Travis, 1,280 acres adjoining the fort, became part of Fort Sam Houston in 1922. In 1928 $6 million was appropriated for some 500 permanent buildings at the fort. They were built in Spanish Colonial style and still provided a Moorish atmosphere in the 1990s. By 1933 Fort Sam Houston was supporting the CCC. In 1937 the largest maneuvers since World War I were held at the fort, and many of the tactical principles used during World War II were developed, including the "Triangular Division." The Eighth Corps and the Eighth Service Command were organized at Fort Sam Houston, which was also headquarters for the Southern Defense Command. In 1940 the fort was the largest army post in the United States. It was a major internment center for prisoners of war during World War II. By 1949 it had 1,500 buildings on more than 3,300 acres of land and was headquarters for the Fourth United States Army. Some of the great military strategists and commanders of World War II came from Fort Sam Houston. Among them were Lt. Gen. Walter Krueger, United States Third Army; Lt. Gen. Courtney Hodges, who took the Third Army to England; Lt. Gen. William Simpson, United States Fourth Army; and Gen. Dwight Eisenhower, a native Texan who became the commander of Allied Forces in Europe and later president of the United States. After the war Gen. Jonathan Wainwright commanded the Fourth Army at Fort Sam Houston.

In the mid-1930s $3 million was appropriated to build a new base hospital. It opened in 1938 and was named for Gen. Roger Brooke. In 1946 the Institute of Surgical Research, which specialized in trauma surgery, was moved to Fort Sam from Halloran General Hospital in New York. The Burn Center was established in 1949. During the Korean conflict Fort Sam Houston became a major training center with its Medical Field Service School. In 1973 the fort acquired a major military command devoted to medical service, known as the Health Services Command. In the early 1990s Fort Sam Houston comprised the headquarters of the Fifth United States Army, the Health Services Command, the Academy of Health Services, Brooke Army Medical Center, the Institute of Surgical Research, the United States Army Dental Laboratory, the 902nd Military Intelligence Group, and the Joint Military Readiness Center, among other organizations. In addition the fort hosts the real estate projects office of the Fort Worth District, United States Army Corps of Engineers, the West Point Admissions Office, and the United States Army Medical Department Museum and Fort Sam Houston Museum. The fort is the site of Fort Sam Houston National Cemetery. It also supports all of the national guard and army reserve units in Texas, as well as the Texas high school and college ROTC units.

Art Leatherwood

Fort St. Louis. On the right bank of Garcitas Creek "a league and a half" from its mouth in Lavaca Bay, in what is now Victoria County; established by La Salle in the summer of 1685. The previous February the French explorer, seeking the mouth of the Mississippi River, had landed 280 colonists, including 100 soldiers, at the mouth of Matagorda Bay in Spanish-claimed territory. He made a temporary camp on Matagorda Island while he sought a more secure location farther up the bay. After staking the site on an eminence overlooking the "Rivière aux Boeufs"—so named for the numerous buffalo on the surrounding prairie—in April, he put men to felling timber. Early in June, La Salle sent word for the colonists to proceed overland to the new site. The bark *Belle* plied between the temporary camp and a supply dump at Indian Point (now in Calhoun County), bringing supplies and timbers from the storeship *Aimable*, which had been wrecked in Cavallo Pass between Matagorda Bay and the Gulf of Mexico. The cargo was transshipped to canoes for the rest of the journey. During the building of the fort, disease and overwork took a heavy toll. By the end of July the colony had been reduced by more than half. La Salle saw the building well under way, then set out in autumn 1685 to explore the surrounding country. When he departed in January 1687 on his last journey, he left at the fort scarcely more than 20 men, women, and children in the charge of the Sieur de Barbier.

With La Salle assassinated, the end came for Fort St. Louis in late 1688 or early 1689, when the Karankawa Indians gained entry under guise of friendship and murdered all the occupants but five children. These were kept by the tribe until rescued later by the Spanish expeditions of Alonso De León and Domingo Terán de los Ríos. One of the Talon children, nine-year-old Jean-Baptiste, gave the only eyewitness account. The best description of the fort comes from the De León expedition, which found the ruins on 22 April 1689. Of six buildings, the one nearest the creek served as the fort. Solidly built of ship timbers, it had a gabled roof covered with planking and stood four varas high, with an attic storeroom above the four rooms at ground level. The other houses, "not very large," were built of poles plastered with mud and roofed with buffalo hides. A picket fence enclosed a corn patch and herb garden. In 1721 the Marqués de Aguayo claimed to have built Nuestra Señora de Loreto de la Bahía Presidio on the same site, where he turned up various French artifacts while digging the foundation. *Robert S. Weddle*

Fort Stockton. A United States Army post at Comanche Springs, now in the city limits of Fort Stockton; established in 1859 for the protection of the mail service, travelers, and freighters; constructed of adobe and named for Robert Field Stockton. Comanche Springs was on the Comanche war trail into Mexico, the upper and lower San Antonio–El Paso–San Diego roads, the Butterfield Overland Mail route, and the San Antonio–Chihuahua Trail, and near the Pecos River–New Mexico road. Federal troops abandoned the post in April 1861. It was reoccupied by Confederates, then abandoned in August 1862 after Gen. Henry H. Sibley's defeat in New Mexico. In 1867 the fort, in ruins after the Civil War, was reoccupied by Gen. Edward Hatch, who made it the headquarters for the black Ninth United States Cavalry. Hatch built a new post nearby at a cost of $82,000 on land the federal government neither owned nor had leased. Except for the stone guardhouse, the buildings had stone foundations, adobe walls, and dirt roofs. The troops quartered at the post were used for patrols, escorts, and scouts, largely against the Apaches. In 1882, after the Apaches had been defeated, the army began withdrawing. The last contingent left in June 1886. By pro-

viding protection to travelers and settlers, a market for stockmen, irrigation farmers, and merchants, and employment for freighters, mechanics, and laborers, Fort Stockton promoted the establishment and development of a thriving community. Since their abandonment by the military, some of the officers' quarters have been used continuously for residences. *Ernest Wallace*

Fort Tenoxtitlán. One of a chain of Mexican military garrisons designed to stanch immigration from the United States pursuant to the Law of April 6, 1830; at a site now in northeastern Burleson County; constructed in 1830 and named Tenoxtitlán ("Prickly Pear Place"), the Aztec name for Mexico City. On 25 June 1830, Lt. Col. José Francisco Ruiz was dispatched from Bexar in command of 100 cavalrymen of the Second Flying Company of San Carlos de Parras by General Mier y Terán to establish a fort at the strategic point halfway down the Old San Antonio Road where the thoroughfare crossed the Brazos River en route to Nacogdoches. Ruiz reached the Brazos on 13 July and established temporary headquarters on the east bank about a half mile below the road. In October the garrison moved to a high bluff on the west bank of the Brazos 12 miles above the San Antonio crossing, opposite the spot where the present Brazos–Robertson county line strikes the river. Although Mier y Terán, who envisioned Tenoxtitlán as a future capital of Texas, issued elaborate instructions from Matamoros for the design of the fort, most were eventually disregarded; the fortifications themselves were likely of conventional log construction. One of the garrison's most important duties was to assist in the transportation of military funds from Bexar to Nacogdoches. Despite the ban on American settlement, the nearby farming community included an undetermined number of American immigrants; as early as July 1831, for example, Francis Smith operated a thriving general store at the fort, trading manufactured goods to the Indians for beaver pelts and buffalo robes. On 31 December 1830 the ayuntamiento of San Felipe de Austin, acknowledging the importance of the garrison, established a commission to construct a road from San Felipe to Tenoxtitlán.

In late October 1830 Maj. Sterling C. Robertson of the Texas (or Nashville) Association, appeared at Tenoxtitlán requesting permission to select a settlement site for 50 American families accompanying him, as stipulated by the colonization contract that his group had made with the province of Coahuila and Texas. Three months later official announcement of the provincial government's invalidation of this contract reached the fort. Colonel Ruiz, Texas-born himself and sympathetic to the American settlers, evaded orders to apprehend the colonists and take them to Nacogdoches, thus permitting them to scatter into various parts of Texas. On 13 July 1832, despondent over the failure of his grand scheme to settle Mexicans in the Texas wilderness, Mier y Terán committed suicide. Thereupon the demoralized Ruiz decided to abandon Tenoxtitlán. He began evacuation of the garrison and entire Mexican settlement to Bexar in August 1832. By December the only occupants of the site were a handful of Americans. A trading post and settlement continued in the vicinity for many years but disappeared after 1860.

Charles Christopher Jackson

Fort Terán. A Mexican military post on the Neches River; established in 1831 to control the flow of smugglers and illegal immigrants into Texas and named for Gen. Manuel de Mier y Terán, who observed on his inspection tour of East Texas in 1829 that immigrants and smugglers were entering Texas from Louisiana on such unguarded trails as the Coushatta Trace, the Alabama Trace, and the Nacogdoches–El Orcoquisac Road, all of which crossed the Neches at the future site of Fort Terán. The general helped to draft the Law of April 6, 1830, which forbade American immigrants to settle in Mexican territory. Responsibility for enforcing the law was assigned to a "director of colonization," an office first held by Terán. His program included establishing garrisons on the Neches and several other rivers. In 1831 he chose Peter Ellis Bean, a colonel in the Mexican army, to build the fort. Apparently construction proceeded very slowly, since the military commandant at Nacogdoches, José de las Piedras, reported on 19 April 1832 the need for additional carpenters and other craftsmen. The completed project consisted of about 10 wooden cabins for Bean and his small garrison. The Mexican government, however, found itself unable to support its Texas forts adequately, and later in 1832 transferred most of the troops. After Fort Terán was abandoned in 1834, the population in the immediate area was about a dozen. Samuel T. Belt opened a trading post at the fort site and operated a ferry there. When Texas counties were organized after 1845, Fort Terán was used as a point of reference in marking the boundaries of Angelina and Jasper counties. A post office operated there from 1856 to 1866, and the small community, sometimes called Fort Turan, continued as a trading and shipping point until the railroads came to Tyler and Angelina counties in the 1880s. Until 1878 steamboats continued to land near the fort, which was at the head of navigation on the Neches. Stagecoaches used Belt's ferry crossing for many years. The ferry operated, first as Belt's Ferry, then Boone's Ferry, then Duncan Ferry, until the completion of a state highway through Rockland in 1917.

Howard N. Martin

Fort Travis. (1) On the eastern end of Galveston Island; the first fort established by the Republic of Texas in 1836 to protect the Galveston harbor entrance. It was an octagonal structure mounted with 6 and 12 pound guns from the *Cayuga* and was commanded by James Morgan. The fort, originally called Fort Point, was renamed for William B. Travis, commander at the Alamo. When building began in April 1836, the nearby construction camp was called Camp Travis. The garrison was withdrawn in 1844. Two other installations, the earthworks of James Long and later fortifications of the Civil War and Reconstruction period, were west of the fort site. Neither is still standing today.

Maury Darst

(2) The later Fort Travis was across the harbor entrance at the southern end of Bolivar Peninsula. There the federal government purchased a 97-acre site in 1898 for $36,000; other parcels were added later. Federal construction began in 1898 and ended in 1943. The fort was turned over to the coast artillery in 1899. It was defended by four batteries: Ernst and Davis, completed in 1898; Kimball in 1925; and No. 236, finished in 1943. Its firepower ranged from two 12-inch guns mounted on barbette carriages to three-inch rapid-fire guns. There were 27 buildings, all now demolished. After the Galveston hurricane of 1900, a 17-foot seawall was constructed on the Gulf side of the fort. Fort Travis was occupied by troops in both world wars, and a number of German prisoners of war were interned there during World War II. In 1949 the reservation was declared war surplus and sold to the M and M Building Corporation, a private developer, with the

stipulation that the former batteries would be made available to the public during hurricane emergencies. In 1960 the fort was designated an official civil-defense shelter and sold to C. Pat Lumpkin Associates of Houston. In 1973 the Galveston County Commissioners Court purchased the site for a public park.

Maury Darst

Fort Waul. One of the few remaining Confederate earthwork fortifications in Texas; on Waldrip Hill, a high, wide hill on the northern edge of Gonzales. The fort was intended to be a supply depot as well as a defensive post on the Guadalupe River. Its site was chosen because of its central location between Austin, San Antonio, Houston, and Victoria. In addition, it is at the confluence of the Guadalupe and San Marcos rivers, both of which could be used to transport goods and supplies. Col. Albert Miller Lea, chief engineer for the Confederate Army, and Capt. H. Wickeland, topographical engineer, were responsible for the construction of the fort, which was designed to have outside walls 8 feet high, 4 to 6 feet thick at the top, and 12 feet thick at the bottom. The entire compound was to have a defensive entrenchment, 8 feet wide by 4 feet deep, surrounding it. A large, square bastion for cannons was to be situated on each of the four corners, with a redan in the middle of the western wall. The blockhouse was designed to be underground in the center. Construction began in December 1863 and continued throughout 1864, but as the threat of a Union invasion declined, so did the need for the post. Construction had ceased by November 1864, and the fort was soon abandoned. It had never been completed or officially named. It fell into decay, and the stones from the blockhouse were used to rebuild the Gonzales College dormitory. Not until the late 1870s was the site named Fort Waul, in honor of Confederate general Thomas N. Waul, who had lived in the area. The city of Gonzales currently owns the site but has made no use of it. Most of the land has been put under the protection of the Gonzales County Historical Committee. The outer walls of the original fort and a portion of the defensive ditch along the western wall are still plainly visible. In 1991 an unofficial attempt was made to rebuild the northern part of the fort.

James B. McCrain

Fort Wolters. A national guard summer training site four miles east of Mineral Wells; established in 1925 and named Camp Wolters, for Brig. Gen. Jacob F. Wolters. Mineral Wells donated 50 acres, leased 2,300 acres, and in World War II provided land to increase the camp's area to 7,500 acres. The camp became an important infantry-replacement training center with a troop capacity that reached 24,973. Six months after the end of the war the camp was deactivated. Local businessmen purchased the land and facilities and converted them to private use. The Cold War, however, brought the reopening of the camp in early 1951, under the authority of the U.S. Air Force. At the installation, then named Wolters Air Force Base, was housed the newly formed Aviation Engineer Force. Special-category army and air force personnel were trained there. In September 1956 the base became the Primary Helicopter Center, directed by the army. In 1963 it was renamed Fort Wolters. At the time all army rotary-wing aviators received basic and primary flight training there. The Vietnam War increased the need for pilots, and the base became the home for training not just army personnel but also helicopter pilots, for the marines in 1968 and for the air force in

1970. By 1970 Fort Wolters covered 8,500 acres and leased an additional 1,700 to help handle its 1,200 helicopters. By 1 January 1973, 40,000 students had completed the 20-week training program. In 1975 orders deactivating the base were issued. Part of the land and facilities became the property of the city and private businessmen; 90 acres and 13 buildings became the Education Center of Weatherford College. Part of the base is now in Lake Mineral Wells State Park. *David Minor*

Fort Worth. Originally Camp Worth; established at the end of the Mexican War when Gen. Winfield Scott sent 42 men of Company F of the Second Dragoons under command of Maj. Ripley Arnold to North Texas to establish a post to guard East Texas settlements from the Indians. Acting on the advice of scouts who had camped there during the winter of 1848, Arnold chose a position on the south side of the confluence of the Clear Fork and West Fork of the Trinity River. The camp was established in 1849, and named for Brig. Gen. William Jenkins Worth. Its designation was changed to Fort Worth the same year. The project was successful, for there were no Indian raids east of Parker County after the establishment of the camp. The only threat to the post came from a band of Taovaya warriors who were dispersed by a shot from a howitzer, the camp's only artillery. In 1851 Capt. J. V. Bamford of the Eighth Infantry replaced Arnold. The post was abandoned on 17 September 1853, and troops who had been stationed there were sent to Fort Belknap. No permanent fort had been erected, and the abandoned barracks were used as store buildings by the early merchants of the new city of Fort Worth.

Fort Worth, Texas. On the Clear Fork of the Trinity River in central Tarrant County. In January 1849 United States Army general William Jenkins Worth, hero of the Mexican War, proposed a line of 10 forts to mark the western Texas frontier from Eagle Pass to the confluence of the West Fork and Clear Fork of the Trinity River. When Worth died, Gen. William S. Harney assumed the command and ordered Maj. Ripley A. Arnold to find a new fort site near the West Fork and Clear Fork. This site was suggested by Middleton Tate Johnson, who once commanded a detachment of Texas Rangers and founded Johnson Station, just southeast of what is now Fort Worth. On 6 June 1849, Arnold established a camp on the bank of the Trinity River and named the post Camp Worth. In August 1849 Arnold moved the camp to the north-facing bluff that overlooked the mouth of the Clear Fork. The United States War Department officially named the post Fort Worth in November. Although Indians were still a threat in the area, pioneers were already settling near the fort. When relocating the camp, Arnold found George "Press" Farmer living on the bluff and allowed him to open the first sutler's store. Other early settlers were Ephraim M. Daggett, George W. Terrell, Ed Terrell, and Howard W. Peak. When a new line of forts was built further west, the army evacuated Fort Worth, on 17 September 1853. Settlers then took uncontested possession of the site. John Peter Smith opened a school in 1854. Henry Daggett and Archibald Leonard started department stores. Julian Feild ran a general store and flour mill in 1856, and the Butterfield Overland Mail and the Southern Pacific Stage Line used the town as a stop on the way to California. In 1855 a county seat war erupted. Since 1849 the county seat had been Birdville, but in 1855 Fort Worth citizens decided that this honor

Advertisement for Texas & Pacific Railway. Prints and Photographs Collection, Fort Worth, Texas, file, CAH; CN 00802. By the 1890s Fort Worth, the "Queen of the Prairies," was known as a leading meat-packing center.

belonged to their town. In April 1860, after a long bitter fight, Fort Worth became the county seat and construction began on a stone courthouse. After a delay due to the Civil War the courthouse was finished in the 1870s. It burned in 1876.

During the 1860s Fort Worth suffered from the effects of the Civil War and Reconstruction. The population dropped as low

The Dr Pepper Bottling Plant, completed in 1938, is an excellent example of Fort Worth's International or Moderne Style architecture by architect Hubert Hammond Crane. Courtesy W. D. Smith, Inc. Commercial Photography Collection, University of Texas at Arlington Libraries.

as 175, and money, food, and supply shortages burdened the residents. Gradually, however, the town began to revive. By 1872 Jacob Samuels, William Jesse Boaz, and William Henry Davis had opened general stores. The next year Khleber M. Van Zandt established Tidball, Van Zandt, and Company, which became the Fort Worth National Bank in 1884. Barrooms such as Tom Prindle's Saloon and Steele's Tavern welcomed many travelers. Weekly newspapers were prominent, including the Fort Worth *Chief* and the *Democrat*. It was the developing cattle industry, however, that really began the community's economic boom. Known as Cowtown, Fort Worth offered cowboys a rest from the cattle drives to Abilene, Kansas. Northern cattle buyers established their headquarters in the town, and new businesses included Pendery and Wilson's Liquor Wholesale, B. C. Evans dry goods, and Martin B. Lloyd's Exchange Office. In 1873 the city was incorporated with a mayor–council government and W. P. Burts became the first mayor. During this time the *Democrat*, owned by Van Zandt and under the editorial leadership of Buckley B. Paddock, successfully campaigned for a fire department and other civic improvements. In 1874 the first westbound stage arrived, and in 1878 the Yuma Stage Line made Fort Worth the eastern terminus to Yuma, Arizona. The Texas and Pacific Railway designated Fort Worth as the eastern terminus for the route to San Diego, California. After a delay caused by the panic of 1873 the Texas and Pacific was finally completed to Fort Worth on 19 July 1876; by 1900 the Missouri, Kansas and Texas (the "Katy"), the Santa Fe, the Fort Worth and New Orleans, the Fort Worth and Brownwood, the Fort Worth and Rio Grande, the Fort Worth and Denver City, the Fort Worth, Corsicana and Beaumont, and the St. Louis Southwestern (the "Cotton Belt") served the town. The Fort Worth Street Railway Company ran a mile-long route down Main Street. Early newspapers were the Fort Worth *Standard* (1873–78), the *Greenback Tribune* (1878–89, later the Fort Worth *Tribune*), the *Democrat* (1876), the *Democrat–Advance* (1881), the *Gazette* (1882–98), and the Fort Worth *Star–Telegram* (1909–).

The Texas Spring Palace, an agricultural exhibition hall built in 1889 and destroyed by fire in 1890, brought not only entertainment but also an important boost to commercial expansion. On the shady side, Hell's Half Acre provided saloons and bawdy houses for cowboys and havens for desperadoes. By 1876 Fort Worth residents were demanding that the lawlessness be controlled, and they elected Timothy I. "Longhair Jim" Courtright as marshal. By the 1890s the Queen City of the Prairie, as Fort Worth called itself, was becoming a beef center. In North Fort Worth businessmen founded the Texas Dressed Beef and Packing Company, the Union Stockyards Company, and the Fort Worth Stockyards Company. When Swift and Company and Armour and Company began to look for Texas sites for branch plants, Fort Worth citizens pledged a bonus of $100,000 for the two companies if they would locate there. Because of this incentive, and because the town was served by railroads, Armour and Swift decided to build a meat-packing plant in Fort Worth. The venture was successful and, combined with the stockyards, helped Fort Worth become a leading packing-house center. In 1903 the first livestock was slaughtered in the new plants. The rise of the stockyards and packing plants stimulated other livestock-related businesses. J. B. Buchanan and C. E. Lee issued the *Livestock Reporter* and the North Fort Worth *News*. In 1896 the first Fat Stock Show was held, and in 1908 the Northside Coliseum was built to house the Southwestern Exposition and Fat Stock Show (later the Southwestern Exposition and Livestock Show). The city decided to begin the construction of new county courthouse in 1893. The leaders of Fort Worth also caught the reform spirit of the Progressive era, and in 1907 the city government was restructured to the commission form. In 1909 a devastating fire motivated the construction of a dam on the West Fork; the resulting Lake Worth provided a reliable water supply. The city limits were expanded to 16.83 square miles in 1909.

During World War I the United States Army established Camp Bowie in the Arlington Heights area. The camp trained 100,000 men, and the United States Army Air Force converted three local airfields into centers of aviation training. With the discovery of oil in Texas, refinery and pipeline companies such as Sinclair Refining Company, Texaco, and Humble Oil and Refining Company converged on Fort Worth, which also developed into a center for oil stock exchanges. In 1927 Meacham Field opened, offering commercial and passenger service from locally operated Braniff Airways and American Airlines. Medical care was provided by several hospitals—Fort Worth Children's, St. Joseph's, John Peter Smith, and Harris. In 1924 the city government was changed to the council–manager form, and the city limits were expanded to 61.57 square miles. The major additions were Arlington Heights, Riverside, Niles City, and Polytechnic. During the Great Depression of the 1930s Fort Worth was able to secure federal money for many construction projects, including the Will Rogers Memorial Coliseum and Auditorium, as well as the renovation and building of public schools. With the outbreak of World War II the aviation industry came to Fort Worth. Consolidated Vultee Aircraft Corporation, the largest manufacturer in Fort Worth, was later bought by General Dynamics Corporation. Next to the bomber factory the Army Air Force located the Tarrant Field Air Drome, which in 1948 became Carswell Air Force Base, a part of the Strategic Air Command and a station for the B-36. Because the Trinity River had flooded severely in 1922 and 1949, Fort Worth residents secured federal money to build the Trinity River Floodway. The project was completed in 1956. Texas Christian University, Texas Wesleyan College, and Southwestern Baptist Theological Seminary provided higher education. By the 1950s the downtown area had deteriorated, however, and in 1956 the Gruen Plan was introduced. This plan called for a freeway loop around the central business district, the construction of underground tunnels, and the elimination of vehicular traffic inside the loop. Although the plan was never accepted, it emphasized the necessity of planning for the city's future needs. During the 1960s and 1970s Fort Worth was filled with economic activity. The Tarrant County Convention Center, Dallas–Fort Worth International Airport, the Amon Carter Museum, and the Kimbell Art Museum were constructed. Amon Carter, Sr., publisher of the *Star–Telegram*, worked hard to publicize the city and secured government installations and projects. During this time the city limits expanded to 272 square miles. Over the past century the city population has boomed; it was 6,663 in 1880, 26,668 in 1900, 277,047 in 1950, 385,164 in 1980, and 447,619 in 1990. But in spite of increasing urbanization Fort Worth has retained its western flavor as the city "Where the West Begins." *Janet Schmelzer*

Fort Worth Star–Telegram. Grew out of two Fort Worth papers, the *Star* (1906) and the *Telegram*, which merged in 1909. The *Telegram* dated back to the *Evening Mail*, the *Mail Telegram*, and other papers beginning around 1879. Founders of the *Star* included Col. Louis J. Wortham (as publisher) and Amon Carter (as advertising manager). In 1909, when the *Star* was in financial difficulty, Carter and Wortham decided to buy the rival *Telegram*. The *Star–Telegram* was identified in the 1920s by the motto "Where the West Begins" on its masthead. It stressed local news and served 84 counties. It had a preelectronic distribution area of 350,000 square miles, and daily home delivery as far as 700 miles west of Fort Worth. Copies were delivered in the Panhandle by stagecoach. The paper successfully resisted takeover attempts by William Randolph Hearst, who sold the Fort Worth *Record* to the *Star–Telegram* in 1925. In 1922 the paper began the first Fort Worth radio station, WBAP ("We Bring A Program"). The *Star–Telegram* established the first television station in the southern United States in 1948 and did a remote broadcast of President Harry Truman's whistle-stop campaign visit to Fort Worth. In 1954, WBAP–TV also did the first color broadcast in Texas; there were no more than 100 color television sets in Fort Worth and Dallas. Carter was majority owner and publisher of the paper until his death in 1955, when he was succeeded by Amon G. Carter, Jr., who died in 1982. The *Star-Telegram* supported numerous local causes as well as efforts to establish Big Bend National Park and Texas Technological College. It was sold in 1974 to Capital Cities Communications, Incorporated. The circulation at that time was 235,000 daily papers and 224,000 on Sundays. Under Capital Cities, which became Capital Cities/ABC, Incorporated, when it purchased the ABC television network in 1986, the *Star-Telegram* won two Pulitzer Prizes—for photographer Larry Price's photos of Liberian officials being killed by a firing squad (1981) and for a news series about a flaw in Bell helicopters that had been a factor in numerous crashes (1985). In the 1980s the *Star-Telegram* pioneered an electronic information service. StarText, an "electronic newspaper" begun in 1982, complemented the printed newspaper with updated news and information available on computer via a local telephone call in the Fort Worth and Dallas area. In 1986 the newspaper opened a new printing plant. In the early 1990s, under publisher Richard L. Connor, circulation climbed above 290,000 daily and more than 350,000 on Sundays. *Diana J. Kleiner*

Forty-eighters. Supporters of the European revolutions of 1848–49, which in Germany culminated in the meeting of a constitutional parliament in March 1848 and the Frankfurt National Assembly (1848–49). A prominent Forty-eighter in Germany and the first president of the National Assembly was Prince Carl of Leiningen, a half-brother of Queen Victoria and promoter of the Adelsverein, the society which directed the settlement of New Braunfels and Fredericksburg and five other colonies. In addition to thousands of Forty-eighters like Leiningen who stayed in Europe, about 4,000 came to the United States. Of these at least 100 moved to Texas. Many settled in Sisterdale, Kendall County, and others stopped temporarily in larger German towns and in San Antonio before moving on to American cultural and political centers. In Germany, the Forty-eighters favored unification, constitutional government, and guarantees of human rights. In the United States they provided the leadership to oppose nativism and to support a continental foreign policy. They almost universally opposed slavery. Several Forty-eighters, including Friedrich Kapp, who lived briefly in Texas, supported the new Republican party. Many were subsequently prominent during the Civil War, most as Unionists and several as military leaders, and even larger numbers took active public roles during Reconstruction. Throughout the second half of the nineteenth century Forty-eighters in the United States supported improved labor laws and working conditions. They also advanced the country's cultural and intellectual development in such fields as education, the arts, journalism, medicine, and business—notably insurance. Forty-eighters in Sisterdale included Ottomar von Behr, the son of a German prime minister and a published agricultural theorist regarding Texas; Carl Daniel Adolph Douai, introducer of the kindergarten system to the United States; Julius Froebel, mineralogist and educator; Ernst Kapp, geographer and early philosopher of environment and technology; and August Siemering, writer, journalist, and editor. In addition to settling in Sisterdale, Comfort, New Braunfels, and San Antonio, Forty-eighters dispersed as well to many other settlements in the two German areas of Central Texas, where, after a period of activism during the 1850s, Civil War, and Reconstruction, they lived in relative obscurity as teachers, civil servants, merchants, farmers, and ranchers. A few of these wrote memoirs, most of which have apparently been identified, translated, and published. Some Texas Forty-eighters and their sons died at the battle of the Nueces. The most vocal and prominent—and intolerant—Forty-eighters who passed through Texas soon moved to more liberal parts of the country, where they had better prospects as teachers, scientists, winters, and speakers. *Glen E. Lich*

Fourth Texas Infantry. One of the three Texas Civil War regiments in the Texas Brigade of Gen. Robert E. Lee's Army of Northern Virginia. In 1861 Governor Edward Clark established a camp of instruction on the San Marcos River in Hays County. The first units that later formed the Fourth Texas Infantry enlisted there in April 1861. Originally the Texans planned to enlist for a year, but after the outbreak of war (12 April 1861) the Confederate government announced that it would accept only regiments enlisted for the duration of the war. In July 1861, 20 companies of Texas infantry were transferred to a camp near Harrisburg and promptly shipped to Virginia. Soon after their arrival in Richmond the Texas units were officially organized into regiments. Ten companies made up the Fourth Texas. The first commander of the regiment was Robert T. P. Allen, former superintendent of Bastrop Military Academy, who because of his harsh discipline was extremely unpopular and was forced to resign his position in October. He was replaced by Col. John Bell Hood. John F. Marshall, editor of the Austin based *Texas State Gazette* and one of the principle organizers of the regiment, was appointed to the post of lieutenant colonel, and Virginian Bradfute Warwick was given the rank of major. The Fourth was formally assigned to Brig. Gen. Louis T. Wigfall's Texas Brigade shortly after Hood assumed command and was stationed at Dumfries, Virginia, in November 1861. As the regiment drilled and prepared for active duty it was plagued with a great deal of sickness, a typical ordeal for Civil War units. In October 1861 the chaplain of the Fourth, Nicholas A. Davis, reported that more than 400 of the regiment's original 1,187 men were sick. This served to weed out many who were unfit for service and reduce the unit to a fighting trim.

The regiment saw combat at Eltham's Landing (7 May 1862), Gaines' Mill (27 June 1862), Second Manassas (30 August 1862), South Mountain (14 September 1862), and Sharpsburg or Antietam (17 September 1862). After May 1863 the regiment took part in every major action of the Army of Northern Virginia during the rest of the war. At Gettysburg on 2 July 1863 the Fourth Texas participated in the attack against the Union left flank and in the fighting for Little Round Top. At Chickamauga, Georgia, on 19 and 20 September 1863, the regiment, now under the command of Lt. Col. John P. Bane, was part of the rebel force that broke the federal line on the second day of fighting and helped to rout the Union Army of the Cumberland. At the battle of Wauhatchie (28 October 1863), the Fourth was routed by the enemy for the only time during the war. Upon the unit's return to Virginia in April 1864 with the rest of Longstreet's corps, the Texans plugged a gap torn in the Confederate line at the Battle of the Wilderness (7 May 1864). Here the regiment took part in the famous "Lee to the rear" episode. Subsequently, the Fourth was marginally involved in the fighting at Spotsylvania and helped to repel the Union attack at Cold Harbor on 3 June 1864. During the fall and winter of 1864–65 the regiment fought around Petersburg and Richmond before taking part in the Southern retreat that ended in the surrender of Lee's army at Appomattox Court House (9 April 1865).

Throughout its existence 1,343 men were assigned to the Fourth Texas Infantry. Of that number 256 (19 percent) were killed in battle. Another 486 men (35.9 percent) were wounded, many more than once, for the total number of wounds suffered by the regiment in four years of fighting amounted to 606. The total number of battle casualties suffered by the Fourth Texas Infantry was 909 (67.7 percent). The number of prisoners lost by the regiment was 162 (12 percent). Of the regiment, 161 died of diseases (11.9 percent), 251 (18 percent) were discharged due to sickness, wounds, or other causes, and 51 deserted (3 percent). At the time of its surrender the Fourth Texas mustered only 15 officers and 143 men. Despite such heavy losses, or perhaps because

of them, the Fourth Texas Infantry and its parent Texas Brigade won a reputation as one of the hardest fighting and most reliable units in the Confederate Army of Northern Virginia.

Jeffrey William Hunt

Fourth United States Cavalry. Organized in 1855 at Jefferson Barracks, Missouri, as the First Cavalry Regiment; redesignated the Fourth United States Cavalry in 1861. Its first commanders were Col. Edwin V. Sumner and Lt. Col. Joseph E. Johnston. From 1855 to 1865 the regiment served against hostile Plains Indians, sought to keep peace between the opposing factions in Kansas, and fought against Confederates. In August 1865 it was sent to Texas, where it operated for 13 years. Before 1871 the tasks of the regiment were limited to guarding the mail and settlements against Indians and to desultory attempts to overtake bands of Indian raiders. Col. Lawrence Pike Graham never led a major campaign, and none of the regiment's 14 early skirmishes with Indians was of major significance. In December 1870 Col. Ranald S. Mackenzie was given command of the Fourth Cavalry, with orders to put a stop to Comanche and Kiowa raids along the Texas frontier. In February he took command of the regiment at Fort Concho. A month later he moved the headquarters to Fort Richardson, near Jacksboro; companies of the Fourth remained at Fort Griffin and Fort Concho. In May, the Fourth was instrumental in ending the careers of Satanta, Satank, and Big Tree. In August Mackenzie led an expedition into Indian Territory against the Comanches and Kiowas who had left the agency, but he was later ordered to return to Texas. He then led eight companies of the Fourth Cavalry and two companies of the Eleventh Infantry, about 600 men, in search of Quahadi Comanches—who had refused to go onto the reservation and were plundering the Texas frontier—without much success. The following summer, with six companies of the Fourth Cavalry, Mackenzie renewed his search for the Quahadis with better effect. On 29 September he surprised and destroyed Chief Mowway's village of Quahadi and Kotsoteka Comanches on the North Fork of the Red River about six miles east of the site of present Lefors. For almost a year both the Kiowas and Comanches remained at peace. In March 1873 Mackenzie and five companies of the Fourth Cavalry were transferred to Fort Clark with orders to put an end to the Mexican-based Kickapoo and Apache depredations in Texas. This expedition culminated in the Remolino Raid (18 May 1873), which, with an effective system of border patrols, brought temporary peace to the area. In the Red River Indian War (1874) the Fourth Cavalry played a major role. On 26–27 September it staved off a Comanche attack at the head of Tule Canyon, and on the morning of 28 September it descended by a narrow trail to the bottom of Palo Duro Canyon. There it completely destroyed five Comanche, Kiowa, and Cheyenne villages, including large quantities of provisions, and captured 1,424 horses and mules, of which 1,048 were slaughtered at the head of Tule Canyon. Afterward, Mackenzie, with detachments of the regiment, made two other expeditions onto the High Plains. On 3 November the regiment engaged in its last fight with the Comanches. In spring 1875 Mackenzie and the units of the Fourth Cavalry from various posts in Texas were sent to Fort Sill to take control of the Southern Plains Indians. Meanwhile, the Indians in Mexico had renewed their raiding in Texas. In 1878 General Sherman, at the insistence of the Texans, transferred Mackenzie and six companies of the Fourth Cavalry to Fort Clark. This time Mackenzie led a larger and more extensive expedition into Mexico, restored a system of patrols, and reestablished peace in the devastated region of South Texas.

Outside Texas, Mackenzie and the Fourth Cavalry administered and controlled the Kiowa–Comanche and the Cheyenne–Arapaho reservations for several years, and after the annihilation of George A. Custer's command on the Little Big Horn in June 1876 forced Red Cloud and his band of Sioux and the Northern Cheyennes to surrender. In the autumn of 1879 Mackenzie with six companies of the Fourth Cavalry subdued the hostile Utes in Southern Colorado without firing a shot and in August 1880 forced them to move to a reservation in Utah. Immediately thereafter, the Fourth Cavalry was transferred to Arizona, where Mackenzie was to assume full command of all military forces in the department and subdue the hostile Apaches. Within less than a month the Apaches had surrendered or fled to Mexico, and on 30 October Mackenzie and the Fourth Cavalry were transferred to the new District of New Mexico. By 1 November 1882, when W. B. Royall replaced Mackenzie as colonel, the Fourth Cavalry had forced the White Mountain Apaches, Jicarillas, Navajos, and Mescaleros to settle down peacefully on their reservations. From 1884 to 1886 the Fourth Cavalry operated against the Apaches in Arizona. In 1890 the regimental headquarters was moved to Walla Walla, Washington. During World War I the Fourth Cavalry remained in the United States in case hostilities should erupt along the Mexican border. In 1942 the unit was reorganized and redesignated the Fourth Cavalry Mechanized and sent to Europe, where it participated throughout the remainder of World War II. Afterward in Vietnam the unit served with undiminished valor.   *Ernest Wallace*

Franco-Texan Land Company. Chartered under the laws of Texas in 1876; owned about 600,000 acres in Parker, Palo Pinto, Stephens, Callahan, Shackelford, Mitchell, Taylor, Nolan, Jones, and Fisher counties. The state initiated a huge land grant to the Memphis, El Paso and Pacific Railroad in 1856 that authorized the building of a railroad from the eastern state line to the Rio Grande at or near El Paso. By 1861 the railroad directors had surveyed the center line of the road as far as the Brazos River and graded 55 miles on which they were ready to lay the track. The Civil War halted all operations, and the company could do no more than retain its corporate form through the war. In 1866 the legislature extended the limitations on the company's contract for 10 years. Interest revived, and the Texas directors, in search of capital, brought John Charles Frémont into the company. Frémont, envisioning a transcontinental road on the thirty-second parallel, beginning at San Diego and connecting with the East at Memphis, took control and executed three mortgages secured by the road itself and the land yet to be received from the state of Texas. He sold his securities in France and collected some $5 million after he had succeeded, by highly questionable methods, in getting his "puffed-up" bonds quoted on the Paris Bourse. Because the "French Bond Scandal" was widely publicized at home and abroad, and because little of the money was spent on the railroad, Congress refused to grant Frémont a transcontinental charter. He therefore compromised with the rival Texas and Pacific Company, which, since it had to have the Memphis, El Paso and Pacific to get across Texas, agreed to buy the embryonic railroad and take over its liens. Ultimately Frémont was frozen out of the T&P, but the French bondholders

did become the owners of the Texas land that secured their bonds, subject, however, to rules and regulations imposed by John A. C. Gray, the agent who put the Memphis, El Paso and Pacific into receivership and sold it to the Texas and Pacific.

The French bondholders received 13 acres of land for each $100 bond, and this land constituted the capital stock of the Franco-Texan Land Company. The incorporators were H. E. Alexander and S. Pinkney Tuck of New York, and Claiborne S. West and Harry C. Withers of Austin. Tuck, the company's secretary, traveled to Weatherford and began the sale of land in 1878. Henry P. du Bellet, vice secretary residing in Paris, staged a coup in which the New York officers were ousted and Sam H. Milliken of Weatherford was elected president. Du Bellet then came to Texas and had a hand in the company's affairs until he too was ousted. Successive presidents were from Texas and France. With the gradual increase in the value of Texas land, the Franco-Texan Land Company developed into something of a bonanza for the French and American directors, who bought stock certificates for a few cents on the dollar and conspired to loot the company's coffers. The losers were the French peasants who had invested their life savings in the Memphis, El Paso and Pacific bonds. In 1896, after years of local rivalry and dissension, the charter of the company expired by limitation. The legislature allowed the company three additional years to liquidate its assets and conclude its business.   *Virginia H. Taylor*

Fredericksburg, Texas. County seat of Gillespie County, 70 miles west of Austin. The town was one of a projected series of German settlements from the Texas coast to the land north of the Llano River, originally the ultimate destination of the German emigrants of the Adelsverein. In August 1845 John O. Meusebach left New Braunfels with a surveying party to select a site for a second settlement en route to the Fisher–Miller Land Grant. He eventually chose a tract of land 60 miles northwest of New Braunfels, where two streams met four miles above the Pedernales River; the streams were later named Barons Creek, in Meusebach's honor, and Town Creek. Meusebach was impressed by the abundance of water, stone, and timber and upon his return to New Braunfels arranged to buy 10,000 acres on credit. The first wagontrain of 120 settlers arrived from New Braunfels on 8 May 1846. Surveyor Hermann Wilke laid out the town, which Meusebach named Fredericksburg after Prince Frederick of Prussia, an influential member of the Adelsverein. Each settler received one town lot and 10 acres of farmland nearby. The town was laid out like the German villages along the Rhine, from which many of the colonists had come, with one long, wide main street roughly paralleling Town Creek. The earliest houses in Fredericksburg were built simply, of post oak logs stuck upright in the ground. These were soon replaced by *Fachwerk* houses, built of upright timbers with the spaces between filled with rocks and then plastered or whitewashed over. Within two years Fredericksburg had grown into a thriving town of almost 1,000, despite an epidemic that spread from Indianola and New Braunfels and killed between 100 and 150 residents in the summer and fall of 1846. The first two years also saw the opening of a wagon road between Fredericksburg and Austin; the signing of the Meusebach–Comanche Treaty, which effectively eliminated the threat of Indian attack; the opening of the first privately owned store by J. L. Ransleben; the construction of the Vereins-Kirche, which served for 50 years as a church, school, fortress,

Sketch of a theatrical production in Fredericksburg by Friedrich Richard Petri. Texas Memorial Museum. German-trained Petri arrived in Central Texas in the summer of 1852. He often sketched and painted scenes of pioneer life in and around Fredericksburg.

and meeting hall; the formal organization of Gillespie County by the Texas legislature, which made Fredericksburg the county seat; the founding of Zodiac, a nearby settlement, by a group of Mormons under Lyman Wight; the construction of the Nimitz Hotel; and the establishment by the United States Army of Fort Martin Scott, which became an important market for the merchants and laborers of Fredericksburg, two miles east of town. After the signing of the Treaty of Guadalupe Hidalgo in 1848, Fredericksburg also benefited from its situation as the last town before El Paso on the Emigrant or Upper El Paso Road. Like many of the German communities in south central Texas, Fredericksburg generally supported the Union in the Civil War. Still, despite widespread opposition to slavery and secession on philosophical grounds, a number of Fredericksburg residents supported the Confederacy. Charles H. Nimitz organized the Gillespie Rifles for the Confederate Army and was later appointed enrolling officer for the frontier district. The Fredericksburg Southern Aid Society subscribed more than $5,000 in food and clothing for Confederate soldiers in 1861. In general, however, the people of Fredericksburg and Gillespie County suffered under Confederate martial law, imposed in 1862, and from the depredations of such outlaws as James P. Waldrip. Waldrip, the leader of a notorious gang, was shot by an unknown assassin beneath a live oak tree outside the Nimitz Hotel in 1867. The German settlers held to their traditions and language: the first newspaper in the county was the German-language Fredericksburg *Wochenblatt*, established in 1877, and not until after 1900 were the first purely English-speaking teachers employed in Fredericksburg's public schools. The first Gillespie County Fair was held in 1881 at Fort Martin Scott and moved to Fredericksburg in 1889. The fair, celebrated as the first in Texas, soon attracted relatively large numbers of visitors to Fredericksburg.

The town got its first electric-light company in 1896 and its first ice factory in 1907; by 1904 the estimated population had risen to 1,632. The San Antonio, Fredericksburg and Northern Railway reached Fredericksburg in 1913. Residents were reluctant to pay city taxes and the town held off on incorporation until 1928, when it was the largest unincorporated town in the country. The 1930 census gave the population as 2,416. Thereafter the number of residents grew slowly but steadily, reaching 3,544 in 1940, 3,847 in 1950, 4,629 in 1960, 5,326 in 1970, and 6,934 in 1990. As Fredericksburg grew it became the principal manufacturing center of Gillespie County. At various times it has had a furniture factory, a cement plant, a poultry-dressing plant, granite and limestone quarries, a mattress factory, a peanut-oil plant, a sewing factory, a metal and iron works, and a tannery. As early as 1930, however, the town was also becoming known as a resort center, with a tourist camp and hunting and fishing opportunities; a significant part of the town's economy continues to depend upon its ability to attract the tourist trade. One of the organizations that has helped make Fredericksburg an important tourist center is the Gillespie County Historical Society, founded in 1934 to preserve local history and traditions. Its immediate goal was the completion, with the help of the Civil Works Administration, of a replica of the Vereins-Kirche, which had been torn down in 1897. When it was completed in 1936 for the Texas Centennial celebration, the structure became the home of the Pioneer Museum. After the museum was moved in 1955 the new Vereins-Kirche became the home of the Gillespie County archives. Another local structure of some historical significance is the Admiral Nimitz Center in the old Nimitz Hotel, commemorating native son Adm. Chester W. Nimitz, a hero of World War II. In the 1980s Fredericksburg had 38 restaurants, 13 motels, a resort farm, a campground, 3 art galleries, and 20 antique stores. In addition, the town was the site of a number of annual events, including the Wild Game Dinner (for men only) in March and the Damenfest (for women only) in October, both of which benefit the Fredericksburg Heritage Foundation; the Easter Fires Pageant; the Founders Day celebration, on the Saturday nearest 8 May, which benefits the Gillespie County Historical Society; A Night in Old Fredericksburg, in July; Oktoberfest; and the Kristkindl Market and Candlelight Homes Tour, both in December. The Gillespie County Fair is held in Fredericksburg on the third weekend in August; the fairgrounds are also the site of racing meets on Memorial Day and the Fourth of July and a hunter–jumper horse show in June.

Martin Donell Kohout

Fredonian Rebellion. A rebellion against the Mexican government. Haden Edwards's empresario grant entitled him to settle as many as 800 families in a broad area around Nacogdoches. When he arrived there in September 1825, he posted notices on street corners to all previous landowners that they would have to present evidence of their claims or forfeit to new settlers. The number of previous grants was small, partly because the area had its drawbacks. To the east was the Neutral Ground, inhabited mostly by fugitives; to the north and west were Indians; to the south was Austin's colony; and in Nacogdoches itself were the remnants of filibustering expeditions that had failed. Nevertheless, Edwards's threatening behavior polarized the old inhabitants against the new. An alcalde election in December pitted Samuel Norris, the candidate of the old settlers, against Chichester Chaplin, Edwards's son-in-law. After the voting Edwards certified Chaplin's election to political chief José Antonio Saucedo in San Antonio. Norris's supporters charged that Chaplin's support had come from unqualified voters. Saucedo reversed the election in March 1826, but the controversy did not settle down. Mexican authorities became convinced that Edwards was unwilling to abide by their terms, so in mid-year

1826 the grant was declared forfeit. The outraged Edwards found support in the settlers he had brought. On 22 November 1826, Martin Parmer, John S. Roberts, and Burrell J. Thompson led a group of 36 men from the Ayish Bayou to Nacogdoches, where they seized Norris, Haden Edwards, José Antonio Sepulveda, and others and tried them for oppression and corruption in office. Edwards was released; in fact his inclusion in the group may have been to cover up his participation in the attack. The others were tried, convicted, and told they deserved to die but would be released if they relinquished their offices. Parmer turned the enforcement of the verdict over to Joseph Durst and proclaimed him alcalde.

As soon as Mexican authorities heard of the incident, Lt. Col. Mateo Ahumada, principal military commander in Texas, was ordered to the area with 20 dragoons and 110 infantrymen. It was clear to Edwards that his only chance to make good the time and estimated $50,000 he had already expended on his colony was to separate from Mexico. He and Parmer began preparations to meet the Mexican force in the name of an independent republic they called Fredonia. Since they planned to include the Cherokees in their move for independence, the flag they designed had two parallel bars, red and white, symbolizing Indian and white. In fact, although a treaty was signed with the Indian leaders, Richard Fields and John Dunn Hunter, that support never materialized. The flag was inscribed "Independence, Liberty, Justice." The rebels signed it and flew it over the Old Stone Fort in Nacogdoches. Their declaration of independence was signed on 21 December 1826. Haden Edwards designated his brother Benjamin commander in chief and appealed to the United States for help. Ahumada enlisted Stephen F. Austin, who sided with the government. Peter Ellis Bean, the Mexican Indian agent, headed for Nacogdoches. When the Mexican soldiers and Austin colonists reached town on 31 January 1827, the revolutionists fled and crossed the Sabine River. The Indians killed Hunter and Fields for involving them in the venture.

Archie P. McDonald

French. France had a claim to Texas through the explorations of La Salle and his establishment, in 1685, of Fort St. Louis. In 1700 Louis Juchereau de St. Denis made an expedition up the Red River, and in 1714 he crossed Texas from Natchitoches, Louisiana, to San Juan Bautista on the Rio Grande in an attempt to open an overland trade route with the Spanish in Mexico. Later at Natchitoches he traded with Indians of the Red River and East Texas area. In August 1718 Jean Baptiste Bénard de La Harpe established a trading post among the Caddo Indians in the area of present Red River County. He and his party entered a bay on 27 August 1721, which they thought to be San Bernardo but was probably Galveston Bay. Hostile Indians forced La Harpe to withdraw. Another French trader at Natchitoches, Joseph Blancpain, also engaged in trade with the Indians of Texas until his capture in 1754. In April 1817 the French pirate Jean Laffite set up a "republic" on Galveston Island. His settlement grew to more than 1,000 persons, reached its peak of prosperity in 1818, and was abandoned early in May 1820. In 1818 a group of Napoleonic exiles under Gen. Charles Lallemand attempted to make a settlement at Champ d'Asile, on the Trinity River near the site of present Liberty, but the settlement had to be abandoned because of food shortages and threats from Spanish authorities.

On 14 February 1840 a commercial treaty was made between France and the Republic of Texas, and French interest in Texas increased. A French *chargé* or minister was sent to the republic, and plans were made for sending French colonists to Texas. One such plan, the Franco-Texian Bill, proposed sending 8,000 French soldiers to the Texas frontier. The bill was introduced in the Texas Congress in 1841 but failed because of popular opposition. Snider de Pellegrini, director of a French colonization company, arrived with 14 immigrants at Matagorda in July 1842, but his efforts to found a colony failed. The most successful of French colonization projects was that of Henri Castro, who in September 1844 founded Castroville, west of the line of the frontier. From 1843 to 1846 Castro brought a few more than 2,000 immigrants to Texas and was instrumental in establishing Quihi, Vandenburg, and D'Hanis. Victor Prosper Considérant founded, near the site of present Dallas, a socialistic colony named La Réunion, which flourished briefly in the middle 1850s but ultimately failed because of poor soil, inexperienced farmers, poor financing, and too much unsocialistic individualism.

The French who came to Texas in search of better social, political, and economic conditions contributed to the state in extending the frontier and in encouraging cultural development. The census of 1850 showed 647 French-born men in Texas; that of 1860 listed 1,883. In 1930 the census showed 10,185 persons of French nationality in the state. In 1990 there were 571,175.

Frizzell, Lefty. Country musician; b. William Orville R. C. Frizzell, Corsicana, 31 March 1928; d. Nashville, 19 July 1975. His father's occupation was listed as "roustabout" on Lefty's birth certificate, and the family lived in Texas, Oklahoma, and Arkansas as they followed the oilfields. In the late 1930s Lefty had a featured spot on a children's radio program. In his teens he worked country fairs, dances, bars, and clubs throughout North Texas and married a girl named Alice. By the time he was 16, he was making frequent appearances in the Eldorado, Arkansas, area, and he was only 22 when he made his first recordings for Columbia Records in 1950. By 1951 Frizzell was an established recording star, with four songs on *Billboard*'s Top Ten chart. Jimmie Rodgers was an early and lasting influence, even though Frizzell did not imitate him. He did, however, record an album called *Lefty Frizzell Sings the Songs of Jimmie Rodgers*. After 1952 Frizzell's career hit a slump due to the emergence of rock-and-roll. His lack of hit records during this time did not hurt him, however, on the country-fair and package-show circuit, where he remained a popular attraction well into the 1960s. He got on the charts again with the single "Long Black Veil" in 1959. In 1953 he moved to Los Angeles and became a regular on "Town Hall Party," a radio and TV show. In 1964 Frizzell recorded "Saginaw, Michigan," another number-one national hit. His career total of Top Ten songs was 13, three of which were number one. His most successful recordings include "If You've Got the Money, Honey, I've Got the Time," "I Love You in a Thousand Ways," "Always Late," and "I Want to be with You Always." His unique style and musical phrasing carried Frizzell's popularity into the decades following his death, and his influence can be heard in the inflections of such singers as Willie Nelson and George Jones.

Phillip L. Fry

Frontier Battalion. Composed of six 75-man companies of Texas Rangers; organized in 1874 after Governor Coke recommended that Texas organize its own force to protect the frontier. John B. Jones was commissioned major of the force, which established camps along the entire frontier line. Jones himself visited all of the companies, enforcing discipline, and, to tie the command together, established a line of couriers to ride from camp to camp to carry information and pick up Indian signs. By 8 October 1874 he reported the battalion in good working order. During the first 17 months of its organization, the battalion had 21 fights with Indians; from September 1875 to February 1876 no Indians appeared on the border guarded by the battalion, and a new feeling of security resulted. The Frontier Battalion was also established to control ordinary lawbreakers—a particularly necessary measure in the period of lawlessness and social collapse following the Civil War and Reconstruction. The situation was aggravated by the proximity of Texas to Mexico and the conflict that developed as the farm frontier began to encroach on the ranching area. Men of the battalion made arrests, escorted prisoners, guarded jails, and attended courts; hundreds of lawless men were arrested; thousands fled. Among the special tasks assigned to the group were settling the Mason County War, cleaning outlaws out of Kimble County in 1877, ending the Horrell–Higgins Feud in Lampasas County, terminating the Salt War of San Elizario, and capturing Sam Bass. The breakup of the Frontier Battalion began with the death of Major Jones and the resignation of the principal captains in 1881. A court ruling in 1900 destroyed the authority of the force by allowing only commissioned officers to execute criminal process or make arrests. The work of the Frontier Battalion in making Texas "a fairly safe place in which to live" made the designation "Texas Ranger" legendary.

Frontier Regiment. Established in December 1861 by the Texas legislature to replace the (Confederate) First Regiment, Texas Mounted Riflemen. The next month, Governor Lubbock appointed the ranking officers of the regiment: Col. James M. Norris, Maj. James E. McCord, and Lt. Col. Alfred T. Obenchain. The new law directed that the companies of the Frontier Regiment be divided into detachments of at least 25 men each, stationed 25 miles apart and just west of the line of settlements from the Red River to the Rio Grande. In March and April 1862 Norris and his officers rode along the proposed line and established 16 camps. Eventually, only nine companies of the regiment entered the service, as a Confederate regiment under John S. Ford occupied the line from Fort Brown to Fort Bliss. In its first six months on duty the regiment, 1,050 men strong, established patrols from each adjacent camp at two-day intervals. The Indians soon learned the routine and during the

winter of 1862–63 began to make more numerous and bolder raids. In January 1862 the Confederate Congress authorized the secretary of war to receive the Frontier Regiment into Confederate service for the protection of the Indian frontier of Texas. President Jefferson Davis vetoed the bill because it withheld the control of the executive of the Confederate States over the troops. Texas wished to absolve itself of the expense of maintaining the regiment but insisted that the regiment be kept under state control. In early 1863 Lubbock attempted once more to transfer the regiment to Confederate service. To meet Confederate Army regulations he disbanded the regiment and reorganized it into a full complement of 10 companies with the new title of Mounted Regiment, Texas State Troops, although Texans continued to call it by its original name. At the reorganization McCord was elected colonel and James Buckner Barry lieutenant colonel. Once more President Davis refused to accept the regiment if hampered by the condition that it remain under Texas control; it remained on the frontier still funded by Texas authorities.

Detachments of the regiment now occupied a number of other posts in addition to the original 16 camps, including abandoned United States Army forts. Colonel McCord, with evidence before him that the patrol system was breaking down, ordered it discontinued. In its place larger numbers of rangers swept to the west and northwest of their camps. Finally, state authorities transferred the regiment to Confederate control, but only after the legislature approved the establishment of the Frontier Organization to ensure protection of the frontier. The transfer took place officially on 1 March 1864. At the same time the 10 companies were reduced in number to only 80 men each so that two additional companies could be formed. Two months later the six southern companies moved to the interior to replace troops stripped from the coast. In August 1864 Barry received orders to transfer his four companies from the Fort Belknap region to Harrisburg, near Houston, leaving only a two-company battalion at Camp Colorado on the frontier. Barry's men returned to the northwest frontier in October, but the six southern companies remained for the rest of the war chiefly in the central subdistrict.

The Frontier Regiment's six companies were joined by two other organizations to cover the northwestern settlement line. During the last 18 months of the war the regiment found that its frontier-defense function was often overshadowed by use of the frontier units to enforce Confederate conscription laws, arrest deserters, and track down renegades and outlaws.

David Paul Smith

G

GTT. The initials GTT ("Gone to Texas") came into use in the first half of the nineteenth century, when Texas had the reputation for producing and harboring outlaws. The letters were found chalked on the doors of houses in the Southern states to tell where the occupants had gone. The exact date at which they came to be a synonym for "at outs with the law" is not known. Frederick Law Olmsted, in his *Journey Through Texas* (1857), says that residents of other states appended the initials to the name of every rascal who skipped out, and that in Texas many newcomers were suspected of having left home for some "discreditable reason." In 1884, Thomas Hughes, in the preface of his book *G.T.T.*, observed, "When we want to say that it is all up with some fellow, we just say, 'G.T.T.' as you'd say, 'gone to the devil,' or 'gone to the dogs.'"

Gaceta de Tejas. Said to be the first newspaper written in Texas; published by William Shaler and José Álvarez de Toledo y Dubois, whose press was brought to Texas in May 1813, then moved back to Louisiana because of a quarrel between Toledo and José Bernardo Gutiérrez de Lara. The type was already set and dated at Nacogdoches. The paper was actually printed in Natchitoches sometime after 13 May 1813. The paper was written in Spanish and carried the motto "La Salud del Pueblo es la Suprema Ley" ("The Safety of the People is the Supreme Law"). Probably only one issue of the *Gaceta* ever appeared. The first page carried "Reflections," a sort of essay on Spanish-American independence. The second page was devoted to foreign news, with emphasis on aid from America for Texas independence. Whether or not any copies of the *Gaceta* ever reached Texas is uncertain, but its publication is a part of the story of the Gutiérrez–Magee expedition, and the paper was addressed to Texans and devoted to Texas affairs.

Gainesville, Texas. County seat of Cooke County, about 67 miles north of Dallas. Peters colony settlers arrived in the area in the 1840s. The town was established in 1850 and named for Gen. Edmund P. Gaines. It became a stop on the Butterfield Overland Mail route and was the site of the notorious Great Hanging at Gainesville during the Civil War. After the war the town prospered as a supply point for cowboys driving herds to Kansas. Gainesville incorporated in 1873 and got rail connections when the Santa Fe line arrived in 1886 and the Gainesville, Henrietta and Western Railway was constructed in 1887. Unlike some other cattle centers in North Texas, Gainesville continued to prosper after the cattle trailing era. Cotton became the leading area product, and the discovery of oil in the 1920s further aided the town's growth. In the 1930s, when Gainesville had a population of over 9,000, the Gainesville Community Circus acquired a national reputation. Camp Howze, an infantry training center, temporarily more than doubled the local population during World War II. Gainesville's population grew to 10,000 in the 1950s and 14,587 in 1990. In the 1980s Gainesville was home to Cooke County Community College, a municipal airport, Gainesville State School for Girls, and Camp Sweeney for diabetic children. Local businesses include an aircraft firm and a fishing-lure company; sand and gravel are shipped from the town. *David Minor*

Gainesville Community Circus. Originally a fund-raising project of the Gainesville Little Theatre, May 1930. A. Morton Smith, editor of the Gainesville *Register* and an authority on circuses, organized the first two performances, which were so popular that the performers gave a third. Earnings totaled $420. By the spring of 1931 the circus was performing in the main exhibit building at the Cooke County fairgrounds. Citizens from Denton asked that the circus appear the next year at the Denton County Fair. Thus began the Gainesville Community Circus road shows. Several characteristics distinguished the Gainesville Community Circus. It was presented almost entirely by amateurs who had full-time jobs and were residents of Gainesville. Performers had no professional circus experience, received no remuneration, and provided their own costumes and most of the rigging. The circus had three rings with bareback riders, trapeze artists, acrobats, tightwire performers, jugglers, and clowns. Trained animals included lions, chimpanzees, an elephant, and Shetland ponies. Through the years, the equipment grew to include seven tents, a big top that covered 22,000 square feet and seats for an audience of 2,500, six ornamental tableau wagons, hundreds of costumes, a calliope, and much other paraphernalia. Statistics compiled for the 1953 official program showed that from 1930 to 1952 the circus troupe gave 359 performances in 57 cities and canceled only one performance, after a tornado destroyed the big top in 1939 in Ardmore, Oklahoma. In 25 years at least 1,500 Gainesville citizens took part in performances, and spectators totaled 500,000. In 1954, shortly after its twenty-fifth anniversary performance, the tent and equipment were destroyed by fire. Although the entire show made a formal comeback in Odessa in 1958, that year also marked the organization's demise. According to former circus president and chief clown Frank E. Schmitz, "Television and air conditioning killed" the circus, which had "just got too big." *Libby Barker Willis*

Gainesville State School for Girls. Near Gainesville; established in 1913 as the Texas State Training School for Girls, a home for delinquents between eight and 17. Under the direction of its first superintendent, Dr. Carrie Weaver Smith (1916–25), the school sought to rehabilitate delinquent girls and stressed "character building, formation of habits of self-control and stability, better understanding of spiritual values and . . . an ability to cope with present social conditions," as well as providing a vocational education. The school began with four dormitories and a superintendent's residence. By 1948 it had been renamed. At that time the campus included seven brick cottages for 198 students, five frame houses for the families of staff members, and a number of other buildings including a gymnasium, a hospital, a school building with a cafeteria and an auditorium, a beauty parlor, and a laundry. From the beginning the school has been relatively self-sufficient; food for the girls and staff is grown on school land. The Fifty-fifth Legislature transferred control of the school from the Board of Control to the Texas Youth Council. In the early 1990s the school housed more than 250 students. *Brian Hart*

Gallagher, Nicholas Aloysius. Third Catholic bishop of Galveston; b. Temperanceville, Ohio, 19 February 1846; d. Galveston, 21 January 1918; ed. Mount St. Mary's of the West Seminary, Cincinnati. Gallagher was ordained to the priesthood on Christmas Day 1868, the first seminarian to receive Holy Orders in the newly established Diocese of Columbus. He served as an assistant pastor, pastor, seminary president, and diocesan vicar general before the Holy See appointed him administrator of the Galveston diocese (1882). One of his first concerns was to increase ministry to African Americans. In 1886 he opened a school for black children, in cooperation with the Dominican Sisters, in Galveston, the first school of its kind in Texas. The project was so successful that Gallagher had to erect a new building two years later in order to accommodate the number of applicants. As an outgrowth of this school Holy Rosary Church, one of the first black parishes in Texas, was established in 1888. Since San Antonio and Galveston were the only two dioceses in Texas at the time, and the latter covered 150,000 square miles, Gallagher pressed Rome to erect a new diocese in North Texas. Thus, in 1890, the Holy See established the Diocese of Dallas and appointed Thomas F. Brennan its first bishop. Gallagher finally succeeded to the See of Galveston in 1892, when Bishop Dubuis was given a titular archbishopric in France. During his 36-year tenure in Galveston, Gallagher brought to his diocese the Sisters of Charity of the Incarnate Word of San Antonio, the Jesuits, the Basilian Fathers, the Paulist Fathers, the Sisters of the Third Order of St. Dominic of Ohio, and many other religious congregations, which founded churches, schools, and hospitals throughout the diocese. To encourage priestly vocations for Texas, he established Saint Mary's Seminary in La Porte (1901), now the oldest Catholic seminary in the South in continual existence. Gallagher also established Good Shepherd Home for Delinquent Girls in Houston in 1914. As a result of growing migration from Mexico, he established churches for Mexican immigrants in Austin and Houston. From these parish centers, priests traveled all over his diocese caring for Spanish-speaking people. Gallagher initiated parish churches for blacks in Houston, Beaumont, and Port Arthur. One of his most unusual projects was the establishment of a trade school for blacks in Independence in the old building of Baylor University, which had recently moved to Waco. The bishop established a diocesan school board and sponsored teachers' institutes as early as 1911. He witnessed the Galveston hurricane of 1900, which destroyed three churches and St. Mary's Orphanage, and saw that all were reconstructed. He outlived all of the priests who were in the diocese when he was consecrated. He was entombed on the St. Joseph side of St. Mary's Cathedral, Galveston.

Mary H. Ogilvie

Galveston, Texas. On Galveston Island two miles offshore in the Gulf of Mexico, in Galveston County. It is 50 miles from Houston and is the southern terminal point of Interstate Highway 45. The island is a part of the string of barrier islands along the Texas coast. On its eastern end where the city stands the currents of Galveston Bay maintain a natural harbor that historically provided the best port site between New Orleans and Veracruz. Karankawa Indians used the island for hunting and

Galveston Wharf Scene, by Julius Stockfleth, 1885. Oil on canvas. 21½" × 31". Courtesy Rosenberg Library, Galveston. Galveston was the leading port and most sophisticated city in Texas when Stockfleth depicted the wharf, the source of its wealth, from the east side of Twenty-first Street looking west. The railroad, the link with the mainland, is shown running along the wharf. At the peak, approximately 4,000 immigrants entered the United States through Galveston each month.

fishing, and it was the probable location of the shipwreck landing of Cabeza de Vaca in 1528. José de Evia, who charted the Texas coast in 1785, named Galveston Bay in honor of Bernardo de Gálvez, the viceroy of Mexico. Later mapmakers applied the name Galveston to the island. Louis Aury established a naval base at the harbor in 1816 to support the revolution in Mexico, and from this point Aury, Francisco Xavier Mina, and Henry Perry launched an unsuccessful attack against the Spanish in Mexico. When Aury returned with his ships after leaving Perry and Mina on the Mexican coast he found Galveston occupied by Jean Laffite, who had set up a pirate camp called Campeachy to dispose of contraband and provide supplies for the freebooters. In 1821, however, the United States forced Laffite to evacuate. Mexico designated Galveston a port of entry in 1825 and established a small customhouse there in 1830. During the Texas Revolution the harbor served as the port for the Texas Navy and the last point of retreat of the Texas government. Following the war Michel B. Menard and a group of investors obtained ownership of 4,605 acres at the harbor to found a town. After platting the land in gridiron fashion and adopting the name Galveston, Menard and his associates began selling town lots on 20 April 1838. The following year the Texas legislature granted incorporation to the city of Galveston with the power to elect town officers.

Galveston grew on the strength of the port; cotton moved outward, and farming supplies and immigrants came in. The city served as a transfer point for ocean-going vessels and coastal steamers that ran through Galveston Bay and Buffalo Bayou to Houston. The construction of the Galveston, Houston and Henderson Railroad, which built a bridge to the island in 1860, strengthened the link between the two towns. Business collapsed, however, when the Civil War brought a blockade of the port by Union ships and a brief occupation of the town by Union troops. The dramatic battle of Galveston (1 January 1863) ended the occupation, but the port remained isolated and served mainly as a departure point for small blockade runners. Following the war Galveston quickly recovered; northern troops were stationed in the city, and a depleted state demanded the

View showing present and former grades of the city of Galveston, ca. 1910. Photographic postcard. Courtesy TSL. After the devastating hurricane of 1900, for future protection the city and county raised the grade level.

trade goods denied by the blockade and the war effort. With so many susceptible people present, however, the city in 1867 suffered one of its worst onslaughts of yellow fever, which affected about three-fourths of the population and killed at a rate of 20 a day. This disease, a malady of most southern ports, did not cease to be a threat until the institution of rigid quarantines after 1873. Galveston nonetheless surged ahead and ranked as the largest Texas city in 1870 with 13,818 residents and in 1880 with 22,248. It had the first structure to use electric lighting, the Galveston Pavilion; the first telephone; and the first baseball game in the state. The Galveston *News*, founded in 1842, is the state's oldest continuously published daily newspaper. The Galveston buildings, especially those designed by architect Nicholas J. Clayton, were among the finest of the time; in 1881 a statewide election chose Galveston as the site of the state medical school; the Grand Opera House, built in 1894 and known for the high quality of its theatrical productions, was restored as a modern performing-arts hall in the 1980s.

In spite of efforts to maintain trade supremacy by improving port facilities and contributing to the construction of railroads to the city, Galveston business leaders saw their town slip to fourth place in population by 1900. Galveston acquired a coast guard station in 1897 that still operated in the 1990s and a small military base, Fort Crockett (1897–1957), but other cities such as Dallas acquired transcontinental rail connections and a growth

in manufacturing establishments. At a time when Houston, Beaumont, and Port Arthur benefited from the oil discoveries of the early twentieth century, Galveston had to put its energy into recovery from the nation's worst natural disaster, the Galveston hurricane of 1900. The island lay in the pathway of hurricanes coursing across the Gulf; at least 11 of these hit the town in the nineteenth century. The Galveston hurricane of 1900, with wind gusts of 120 miles per hour, flooded the city, battered homes and buildings with floating debris, and killed an estimated 6,000 people. Another 4,000 to 6,000 people died on the nearby coast. For future protection the city and county constructed a 17-foot seawall on the Gulf side of the island, raised the grade level, and built an all-weather bridge to the mainland. The development of other ports by means of the ship channels, alternative sites for business and manufacturing provided by other modes of transportation, and notoriety because of hurricanes restricted the Island City to medium size. In 1991 it had a population of 60,472.

Around 1900, business leaders redesigned the city government into the first commission form in the country. Their idea was to have the governor of the state appoint a mayor and four commissioners. Each commissioner would control a specific function of government—finance, police and fire control, water and sewerage, streets and public improvements. Since the original plan was patently undemocratic, it was subsequently revised to provide for the election of the officers. The commission plan was somewhat popular in the years before World War I but faded in the 1920s in favor of the city-manager plan. Galveston, however, continued with the commission government until 1960, when it too changed to a city-manager form. During the years between the world wars Galveston, under the influence of Sam and Rosario (Rose) Maceo, exploited Prohibition and laws against gambling by offering illegal drinks and betting in nightclubs and saloons. This, combined with the extensive prostitution that had existed in the port city since the Civil War, made Galveston the sin city of the Gulf. Many citizens tolerated the illegal activities and took pride in belonging to "the free state of Galveston." In 1957, however, Attorney General Will Wilson with the help of Texas Rangers shut down bars such as the famous Ballinese Room, destroyed gambling equipment, and closed many whorehouses. Between 1985 and 1988 Galveston voters in nonbinding referenda defeated proposals to legalize casino gambling, although proponents argued that gambling could promote the local economy. Pursuant to a law enacted by the Texas legislature, however, gambling on board cruise ships embarking from Galveston was allowed beginning in September 1989. Galveston has survived on its port, tourism, and the University of Texas Medical Branch. The Galveston Historical Foundation has encouraged historic preservation of the old business area, the Strand, and various Victorian homes. The famous Rosenberg Library serves as a circulating library as well as an important repository for archival materials pertaining to the history of Galveston and Texas. The restoration of the nineteenth-century square-rigged vessel *Elissa* (1975–82) gave Texans their own "Tall Ship" to sail into New York harbor for the celebration of the centennial of the Statue of Liberty.   *David G. McComb*

Galveston Movement. Operated between 1907 and 1914 to divert Jews fleeing the pogroms of Russia and eastern Europe away from congested communities of the Atlantic coast to the interior of the U.S. The Jewish Immigrants' Information Bureau directed the movement as a means of preventing an anticipated wave of anti-Semitism on the Eastern seaboard, which might lead to immigration restrictions. Several benevolent groups tried to find a southern port of entry to disperse the burgeoning population, and Galveston was chosen because it provided access to job opportunities in the West and was a passenger port for Lloyds Shipping Company. Lloyds served the German city of Bremen, the traditional port of departure from the Continent for East European Jews. Jacob Schiff presided over the "Galveston Committee" in New York City, which coordinated the recruiting efforts of the London-based Jewish Territorial Organization and the Jewish Emigration Society of Kiev with the reception and relocation activities of the Jewish Immigrants' Information Bureau, based in Galveston. David Bressler, honorary secretary of the JIIB, administered the program from his New York office. The first refugees—54 men and two women—arrived in 1907. Two days before the ship docked, a warehouse remodeled as a reception center burned down, raising questions about the welcome likely to be afforded the newcomers. Mayor Henry Landes, however, spoke to the immigrants, and a schoolteacher from southern Russia answered with a grateful speech on behalf of the group. Rabbi Henry Cohen of Temple B'nai Israel met almost all of the ships that carried Jewish immigrants and helped direct them to new homes in the interior. The main territory to which the bureau directed immigrants was between the Mississippi River and the Rocky Mountains. The members of the first group were distributed among cities and communities throughout the western states and as far north as Fargo, North Dakota. Four of them settled in Fort Worth; none remained in Galveston, in keeping with the movement's policy.

Despite the economic depression 900 immigrants passed through Galveston before the end of 1907. The following year only 106 came, and Jewish organizations worked hard to stimulate interest in absorbing the immigrants among the smaller communities across the U.S. Within Texas the focus was on Tyler, Texarkana, Marshall, and Palestine, since the railroad fare from Galveston to these towns, at the half-price charity rate, was only four or five dollars. Recruiters stipulated that immigrants should be able-bodied laborers and skilled workers under 40. The number of Hebrew teachers and kosher butchers was restricted in the belief that strict religious adherence would limit the immigrants' ability to be assimilated. Teachers were deemed unskilled, though some entered, as did others, on the pretense that their skills or training met job needs. In 1909, 773 Jews landed at Galveston, and by the following year 2,500 had sailed to the port. In 1911 some 1,400 arrived, only 2 percent of the total Jewish immigration to the U.S. in that year. By 1913 the situation had worsened. Merchants had become concerned about competition from immigrants, and an increasing number of Polish Jews who would not work on Saturday reduced the waning enthusiasm of American Jewish communities further. Three communities declined to take more; the representative from Cleburne complained about the immigrants' "exactions, faultfinding, and refusal to abide by the labor conditions upon which they come." The movement's chances of success were handicapped by continual infighting among the cooperating organizations on both sides of the Atlantic, by the unfavorable condition of the American economy, and by the restrictive attitudes and behavior of Galveston immigration authorities. Further, European Jews did not recognize Texas and the Southwest as the America of their dreams; the area satisfied no religious or nationalistic expectations. Between 1907 and 1914, when it ceased operation, the Jewish Immigrants' Information Bureau brought 10,000 immigrants through Galveston, approximately one-third the number who migrated to the Holy Land during the same period. In 1983 a documentary film about the movement, *West of Hester Street*, was made with assistance of the Texas Committee for the Humanities.   *Jane Manaster*

Galveston News. One of the most important Texas newspapers. The facts of its founding are not clearly established. In June 1843 Wilbur H. Cherry and Michael Cronican leased equipment from Samuel Bangs and began publication of the semiweekly *News*. Willard Richardson assumed editorship of the newspaper the next year and in 1845 became its sole owner. Under his guidance the *News* became a major voice in the Republic of Texas and later a critic of the policies of Sam Houston as both United States senator and governor. In 1858 Richardson had a four-story building constructed for the paper. During the Civil War the *News* published its editions in Houston. It returned to Galveston Island in 1866. Alfred Horatio Belo, a Confederate veteran, joined the staff in 1865 and by 1875 was the newspaper's principal owner. In 1876 he linked the *News* building and his home with the state's first telephone connection. The Dallas *Morning News* was founded in 1885 as a satellite publication. The Belo interests sold the *News* in

1923 to William Lewis Moody, Jr., a Galveston banker and insurance man. In 1927 Moody also acquired the Galveston *Tribune*, an afternoon newspaper. Both were published from a central printing plant designed by architect Nicholas J. Clayton and located on Mechanic Street in downtown Galveston. In 1963 both newspapers were sold to the William P. Hobby family of Houston. The *Tribune* was abandoned in favor of an evening *News* published five days a week and Sundays. A mainland newspaper, *Today*, was printed at the same facility. In June 1967 the Hobbys sold the newspapers to a corporation of southern newspaper interests headed by Carmage Walls and Les Daughtry, who soon restored the *News* to daily morning publication.

Maury Darst

Gammel, H. P. N. Bookseller, publisher, and compiler of the laws of Texas; b. Karl Hans Peter Marius Neilsen, Grenå, Denmark, 24 September 1854; d. Austin, 11 February 1931; m. Anna Marie Andersen (d. 1888); 1 daughter; m. Josephine Matilda Ledel; 8 children. Gammel immigrated to Chicago in 1874, then to "gold fields in the West," before arriving in Galveston in 1877 and walking to Austin. He built a shelf between two chinaberry trees, at Eighth Street and Congress Avenue, where he bought books for five cents and sold them for ten cents, reading and learning from them in the meantime. His business became one of the first bookstores west of the Mississippi to carry a large assortment of miscellaneous literature, law books, and Texana. When Gammel became a publisher, his first title was John C. Duval's *Early Times in Texas* (1892). Other notable titles were C. W. Raines's *Bibliography of Texas* (1896), Noah Smithwick's *Evolution of a State* (1900), and a reprint in 1906 of *Journal of the Continental Convention of the State of Texas* (1875). Gammel was still a newcomer to Texas when, in 1881, the old Capitol in Austin burned. From the debris he gathered wet papers and charred documents, loaded them in a wagon, and took them to his home. He and his wife gradually dried the pages on clotheslines and stored them with their belongings. Years later he sorted and edited the crinkled papers, then published them beginning in 1898 as the famous first 10 volumes of *Gammel's Laws of Texas, 1822–1897*. This work won immediate acclaim, and with the addition of other volumes in later years the set came to be a basic item in Texas law libraries.

Dorothy Gammel Bohlender

Garland, Texas. Fifteen miles northeast of downtown Dallas in northeastern Dallas County. Duck Creek runs through the city, and Lake Ray Hubbard lies on its eastern border. Duck Creek, a station on the Missouri, Kansas and Texas Railroad, and Embree, a station on the Atchison, Topeka and Santa Fe, competed for a post office for several years, until, in 1887, Congressman Joseph Abbott solved the problem by submitting a bill to Congress to move the post office to a place between the two towns; the new site was named Garland after President Cleveland's attorney general, Augustus H. Garland. By 1890 Garland had a population of 478, four churches, three gristmills, three steam cotton gins, a roller flour mill, and several hotels. During the 1880s the town received gas lighting, and Garland was incorporated in 1891. In 1899 a fire destroyed 28 of its 30 businesses. The town rebuilt around a town square. Eventually, plank sidewalks and a fountain for watering horses were added. In 1904 the population was 819. By the mid-1920s the population was more than 1,400. A bond was voted in the 1920s to finance a

2,300-foot well and an overhead storage tank to provide running water. On 9 May 1927 a tornado destroyed much of the city and killed 17 people, including a former mayor, S. E. Nicholson. Six years later the Nicholson Memorial Library opened in his honor. In the late 1930s the Craddock food company, which manufactured pickles, and the Byer–Rolnick hat factory, which in the 1990s made Resistol hats, moved to town. During World War II several aircraft plants operated in the Garland area. After the war, Kraft Foods bought the Continental Motors Plant to retool for its manufacture. The city has experienced dramatic growth in recent decades, growing from 10,571 in 1950 to 72,000 inhabitants in 1969 and 180,650 in 1990. By the 1990s Garland had a variety of industries, including electronics, steel fabrication, oilfield-equipment manufacture, aluminum die casting, hat manufacture, dairy products, and food processing. The city features the Garland Civic Chorus, Ballet Classique, Texas Baroque Ensemble, and Northview Observatory. The Wet 'N Wild Water Recreation facility and Firewheel Golf Park attract visitors from throughout the Dallas–Fort Worth area. The Landmark Museum presents the history of Garland, and Octoberfest is a yearly event.

Lisa C. Maxwell

Garner, John Nance. Vice president of the United States; b. near Detroit, Texas, 22 November 1868; d. Uvalde, 7 November 1967 (buried in Uvalde); m. Mariette (Ettie) Rheiner (1895); 1 son. Except for a semester at Vanderbilt University, Garner's higher education was his own private project. He read law in Clarksville and was admitted to the bar in 1890. After an unsuccessful run for the office of city attorney he moved to Uvalde, where he joined the law firm of Clark and Fuller and was appointed to fill a vacancy as county judge. When he ran for the regular term in 1893 his opponent was his future wife. Garner was county judge from 1893 to 1896. He served in the state legislature, 1898–1902. There he had the opportunity to establish a new Fifteenth Congressional District and at 34 was elected its representative. He entered the Fifty-eighth Congress as a Democrat on 9 November 1903 and served continuously for 15 terms, until 4 March 1933. He was reticent at first. It was 5 January 1905 before he uttered a word in the House, and eight years before he made his first speech. His main efforts appear to have been devoted to obtaining a federal building for Eagle Pass and a new post office in his district. During his early years in Congress he adhered to his number-one rule for success: get elected, stay there, and gain influence through seniority. By 1909 Garner had become party whip. During World War I he was recognized as a leader and became the liaison between President Wilson and the House of Representatives. He served as minority floor leader in the Seventy-first Congress, and when the Democrats organized the House in 1931 he became speaker. With William Randolph Hearst's backing, Garner became a serious candidate for president in the spring of 1932. Although he did not pursue his campaign vigorously, as convention time approached he acquired the 90 Texas and California votes, which a candidate had to have to be nominated. When he gave his votes to Franklin D. Roosevelt on the fourth ballot, Roosevelt became indebted to Garner and to the state of Texas. As a result Garner was offered the vice-presidential nomination, which he reluctantly accepted. On 8 November 1932 he was simultaneously elected to the vice presidency and reelected to Congress. He resigned from Congress on 4 March 1933.

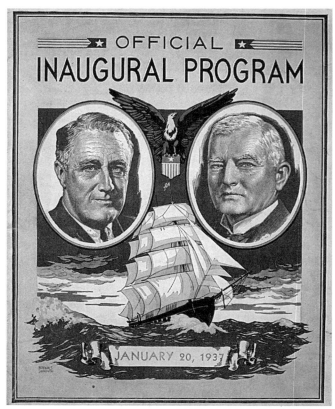

Official Inaugural Program, January 20, 1937. Courtesy Lyndon Baines Johnson Library, Austin. John Nance Garner, shown here (right) with Franklin D. Roosevelt, served as vice president of the United States from 1933 to 1941.

Next to the president Garner was the single most important man in the New Deal because of his experience, friends, and political knowledge. Because of his knowledge of the legislative process the president made him his liaison with Congress, where he had great influence with the Texas congressional delegation, especially Sam Rayburn. This Texas delegation probably had no peer in congressional history. From 1933 to 1938 no fewer than eight Texans held regular committee chairmanships, and two chaired special committees. Also, Rayburn became House majority leader in 1937. With this force behind him Garner was ready to add a new dimension to the office of vice president. Because he knew the strengths and weaknesses of both houses he was able to push bills through quietly or bury them. He was, as one writer stated, "a mole rather than an eagle." A master at circulating on the Senate floor or buttonholing a friend, he was the "wise old man of Congress." On most evenings after a legislative session Garner would hold court over bourbon and branch water and counsel reluctant congressmen in his "Board of Education," or, as some called it, his "Dog House." Most of his contemporaries agreed that his persuasive tactics made him the most powerful vice president in history. In the course of the "Hundred Days," the special session of the legislature called by Roosevelt to inaugurate New Deal programs, Garner was extremely effective in helping to push through the legislation that characterized this phase of the Roosevelt program.

It was inevitable that Garner would split with the president, however, for his view of the Democratic party differed consider-

ably from Roosevelt's. As an old-line Democrat with Progressive Era background, Garner distrusted Wall Street, and so he championed New Deal legislation aimed at correcting the putative excesses of the financial markets. But as the New Deal drifted toward welfare-state concepts, he demurred. In the spring of 1934 he had warned the president to slow down. By 1935 he began to refer to some programs as "plain damn foolishness." The sit-down strikes that closed 1936 marked a breaking point in the Garner–Roosevelt relationship. Garner thought the strikers had violated property rights, and he became furious because he thought that Roosevelt gave tacit support to the unions. Afterward, Garner believed that Roosevelt preferred the suggestions of liberal advisors rather than his own or those of congressional leaders. Therefore, he began to oppose the president in the cloakrooms. The event that sealed the split between Garner and the president was the Court-Packing Plan of 1937, whereby the president was to assume unprecedented powers in the appointment of Supreme Court justices. The shock waves split the Democratic party. Garner, whose loyalty was first to the party, vehemently opposed the plan. In the midst of the struggle he went on vacation to Uvalde, an act that publicized the rift between him and the president. As 1937 drew to a close Garner was the leader of a group of conservative Democrats and Republicans dedicated to retard, change, or scuttle various phases of the New Deal. One commentator called Garner the "conniver-in-chief" of the opposition. Now almost anything that did not meet with Garner's approval was in trouble. Secretary of the Interior Harold Ickes said that Garner was "sticking his knife into the President's back." The final blow to the fast-fading Garner–Roosevelt friendship was the proposed purge of conservative Democratic congressmen by the president. Garner used all his influence to prevent the action. With him at the head, an opposition bloc now began to vote against almost everything the president desired. Though Garner never openly acknowledged his split with Roosevelt, their mutual hostility continued, and the president grew to despise "Cactus Jack."

Opinions about Garner's vice presidency vary widely. John L. Lewis characterized him as a "labor-baiting, poker-playing, whiskey-drinking, evil old man," but the New York *Times* praised his "political miracles." James Farley thought Garner was "more responsible than anyone" for implementing Roosevelt's programs, yet it is realistic to state that Garner prevented completion of the New Deal. In spite of his age Garner's political stature made him a prominent Democratic candidate in the 1940 election. As early as 1938 the Texas state Democratic convention endorsed him as a candidate. By March 1939 both houses of the Texas legislature followed suit, and in June a Garner-for-president committee was formed. The polls said that Garner would be the leading candidate if Roosevelt did not run. Even though Garner declared in December 1939 that he would accept the nomination, his actions indicate he did so primarily because he opposed a third term for Roosevelt. The president's machine, however, was too powerful, and Garner was handily beaten in the primaries he entered. After the convention he packed his belongings and returned to Uvalde, where he lived in relative seclusion. In the late 1940s his wife burned his public and private papers, leaving only his scrapbook collection, which is housed in the Barker Texas History Center at the University of Texas at Austin.

Lionel V. Patenaude

Garza Falcón, Blas María de la. Colonizer of South Texas and Tamaulipas and the first settler of Nueces County; b. Real de las Salinas, Nuevo León, 1712; d. Camargo, Nuevo Santander (Tamaulipas), 1767; m. Catarina Gómez de Castro (1731); three children; m. Josefa de los Santos Coy. By 1734 Garza Falcón was a captain at Presidio de San Gregorio de Cerralvo in Nuevo León. In 1747 José de Escandón, colonizer of Nuevo Santander, chose Garza Falcón to explore the south bank of the Rio Grande. The captain was to establish seven settlements along the river— Revilla, Camargo, Mier, Dolores, Reynosa, Laredo, and Vedoya. In 1749 he settled 40 families from Nuevo León at what became Camargo, the first settlement founded on the Rio Grande. Escandón named him captain and chief justice of the villa. In 1752 Garza Falcón established a ranch, Carnestolendas, now the site of Rio Grande City. After two unsuccessful attempts to colonize land near the Nueces River, Escandón gave the assignment to Garza Falcón, who by 1766 established Santa Petronila five leagues from the Nueces in what is now Nueces County. He took his family and employees there and started a ranch that served as an outpost and way station. In 1767 he returned to Camargo, where he died and was buried in his private chapel, Nuestra Señora de Guadalupe. After his death his land grants were distributed to the settlers; his family received land extending from the Rio Grande to the Nueces River in South Texas and perpetuated his name.

Clotilde P. García

Garza War. An abortive effort in 1891–92 to organize a Texas-based revolution against the Mexican regime of Porfirio Díaz. Catarino E. Garza was a Mexican journalist living in Texas who had for many years launched editorial attacks against Díaz. He and his allies recognized no official border, considered themselves Mexicans, and were active in the internal politics of Mexico. On 3 February 1891, Garza's friend Ignacio Martínez was killed by Díaz agents on a Laredo street. Garza became convinced that he had to take up arms. On 15 September 1891 he led 26 armed men across the Rio Grande at Mier, Tamaulipas, and proclaimed the "Plan Revolucionario." The group returned to Texas after nine days and a brief engagement with Mexican forces. Over the following months, the Garcistas made at least two more incursions into Mexico. According to Garza's own records, by the end of 1891 his army had 63 commanders, 186 officers, and 1,043 soldiers. In response, the Mexican government sent to the border Gen. Lorenzo García, who so brutally suppressed anti-Díaz dissent that his cruelties caused a pro-Garza reaction in Texas. Fearing border war, influential Texans urged fellow citizens to remain neutral and petitioned the governor for special rangers to drive out the revolutionaries. By December 1891 United States Army troops had been sent to patrol the border; one short skirmish occurred, at Retamal Springs. The army generally was ineffective, but the Garcistas soon left the area as newly appointed special rangers proved effective and potential recruits did not sign up. In 1892 Garza reportedly learned that he was wanted by the special rangers and fled Texas.

Joe R. Baulch

Gates, John Warne. Businessman, known as "Bet-a-Million" Gates; b. Winfield, Illinois, 18 May 1855; d. Paris, 9 August 1911; m. Dellora Baker (1874); one son. After meager success in the hardware business Gates went to work for the Washburn–Moen Company as a barbed wire salesman in Texas. He arrived in San Antonio in 1876. Inspired by Doc Lighthall's medicine show, he rented Military Plaza, constructed a barbed-wire corral, filled it with longhorn cattle, and successfully demonstrated the holding power of the wire. His demonstration resulted in orders for more wire than the factory could produce. When Washburn –Moen failed to make him a partner, he went to St. Louis and with Alfred Clifford built the Southern Wire Company into the largest manufacturer and distributor of unlicensed "moonshine/non-patented" barbed wire. He later owned or controlled Consolidated Steel and Wire Company, Illinois Steel Company, American Steel and Wire Company of Illinois, and Republic Steel Company. He invested in the building of the Kansas City, Pittsburgh and Gulf Railroad from Kansas City to Sabine Lake; the road later became the Kansas City Southern Railway, which Gates controlled. When Patillo Higgins applied to Gates for financing of an oil well at the Spindletop oilfield Gates formed the Texas Company (now Texaco), in which he owned 46 percent of the stock. After Spindletop blew in (10 January 1901), Gates urged construction of pipelines and a refinery and furnished $500,000 for the purpose. He constructed new docks; built the First National Bank in Port Arthur, the Port Arthur Light, Power, and Ice Company, and the Plaza Hotel; and contributed $60,000 to build Port Arthur Business College. Gates also gambled at poker, the stock market, and horse races. In 1900 in England he bet $70,000 on Royal Flush with 5½-to-1 odds and won $600,000. Rumor said that he had bet a cool million and won more than $2 million, a fabrication that gave him his nickname. In 1911 he developed throat cancer and went for surgery to France, where he died. His funeral was held in the grand ballroom of the Plaza Hotel in New York City. Gates's contributions to charity included Mary Gates Memorial Hospital in Port Arthur and St. Charles Home for Boys. Mrs. Gates later gave funds to establish Gates Memorial Library in Port Arthur, the forerunner of Lamar University at Port Arthur.

Sidney A. Brintle

Gatesville State School for Boys. Three miles northeast of Gatesville; the first juvenile reform school in the southern United States; opened in January 1889 as the House of Correction and Reformatory, a division of the prison system. The original 68 inmates had formerly been incarcerated with adult felons. The legislature changed the school's name to State Institution for the Training of Juveniles in 1909 and established a five-member board of trustees to administer the institution. A 1913 law changed the school's name to State Juvenile Training School, and in 1919 the new Board of Control assumed management. The legislature renamed the facility Gatesville State School for Boys in 1939. By 1940 the school housed 767 males under the age of 17 when committed. Residents attended academic and vocational classes and farmed on a 900-acre tract of state land and 2,700 acres of leased land. A parole system that rewarded good behavior permitted the release of inmates to private sponsors. The State Youth Development Council began administration of the school in 1949. In 1957 the Texas Youth Council replaced the Youth Development Council. By 1970, 1,830 young male offenders were housed at the five separate units of the institution; the council operated a separate maximum-security unit, Mountain View School for Boys. In 1974 federal judge William Wayne Justice ruled that a number of routine practices at Texas Youth Council facilities violated the national Constitution. He also ruled that the school's staff failed to protect inmates from violence, ordered the state to close the Gatesville and Mountain View schools, and required that community alternatives to large juvenile penal institutions be developed. In 1979, Gatesville State School closed and the offenders were placed in smaller schools at Brownwood, Crockett, Gainesville, Giddings, and Pyote, as well as at a number of foster and group homes, halfway houses, and residential treatment centers. Three Gatesville units became the Gatesville Unit for female inmates of the Texas Department of Corrections in 1980, and the other two became the Hilltop Unit for male felons of the Texas Department of Corrections in 1981.

James W. Markham and William T. Field

General Council. A temporary governing body in revolutionary Texas. Between the adjourning of the Consultation on 14 November 1835 and the opening of the Convention of 1836 on 1 March, Texas was governed, after a fashion, by a provisional government, which operated under a document written by the Consultation and known as the Organic Law. The members of this government were chosen by the Consultation. Henry Smith was elected governor and James W. Robinson lieutenant governor. The General Council was made up of one member from each municipality of the state. The council convened at San Felipe de Austin on 14 November 1835. Fourteen or fifteen members were usually present during November and December, but in January the number began to decline, and the council was soon without a quorum; by 26 February 1836 there were only two members attending. The council moved to Washington-on-the-Brazos in mid-February 1836, after the Convention of 1836 was called. Although the provisional government failed, the council deserves credit for much hard work and for some achievement. It prepared instructions for Stephen F. Austin, Branch T. Archer, and William H. Wharton, who had been chosen by the Consultation as agents to the United States. It devoted some attention to a postal system already in operation and appointed some judges, but organized no effective court system. The body spent much time on a discussion of the land problem but in the end followed the instructions of the Consultation and kept the land offices closed. The council devoted some thought to the problem of finance. It passed several tax laws, but collected little revenue. It also borrowed, issued paper money, collected some land fees due the Mexican government, and received a few gifts, but its fiscal policy was, on the whole, ineffective. Of more importance were its acts calling the Convention of 1836, prohibiting the residence of free blacks in Texas, and appointing Sam Houston and John Forbes to treat with the Cherokees. The council devoted much time to military and naval problems, passed detailed acts that provided for the organization of a regular army, and appointed several officers. The regular army, however, never became large enough to merit much attention. The council aided as best it could the volunteer army at Bexar and enthusiastically supported the proposed Matamoros expedition of 1835–36. It also passed the acts that brought into being the first Texas Navy and issued some letters of marque.

In January 1836 the provisional government was disrupted by a quarrel between Governor Smith and the council. Smith was an outspoken advocate of independence, while the council consistently followed the majority opinion of the Consultation as expressed in the Declaration of November 7, 1835. On 10 January 1836 Smith sent the council an intemperate letter in which he demanded that the body adjourn. The council answered by impeaching him and recognizing Robinson as acting governor, but Smith continued to claim the office. Soon thereafter most members of the council went home, and for all practical purposes the government ceased to exist.

Ralph W. Steen

General Land Office. Established in 1836 by the First Congress of the Republic of Texas. John P. Borden, the first commissioner, opened the office in Houston the next year. He was enjoined by law to "superintend, execute, and perform all acts touching or respecting the public lands of Texas." The Constitution of the Republic of Texas honored all grants made by Spain and Mexico that were deemed valid by the republic; later, the state followed suit. The commissioner assembled from the archives of the former governments a record of valid land grants and translated them. The Spanish archives section of the Land Office is the depository of records of 4,200 Spanish and Mexican land grants, which cover 26,280,000 acres in Texas. Some of these grants received special confirmation by the state legislature, but most of them stand on the original titles from Spain or Mexico. Borden also began to survey and register the new grants that the republic was issuing. These eventually brought the total number of acres granted to 75,647,668. Sales for the purpose of paying the public debt added 2,990,136 acres. For internal improvements to the Capitol, irrigation, drainage, iron works, and transportation facilities, including grants to railroads, grants totaled 32,153,878 acres. For education (the University of Texas, A&M, county schools, eleemosynary institutions, and the public school fund) grants totaled 49,530,334 acres. The individual grants, patents, and surveys by which the public domain has been disposed of are on file in the General Land Office in Austin, and a representation of each, surveyed by metes and bounds, appears on the original grantee map of the county in which the land is located. Although the financial potential of Texas public land was generally limited to surface properties, over the years mineral resources became financially important. In December 1960 the state resumed mineral development of the Gulf area, after Texas ownership was confirmed by the Supreme Court in the Tidelands Controversy judgment (12 December 1960). The mineral revenues were consigned to the Permanent School Fund. New departments and equipment became necessary to manage the increased volume of business resulting from these modern trends.

Texas is the only public-land state with complete control over its public lands and over the proceeds resulting from the administration and sale of lands. As of 1992 the General Land Office was the management agency for 20.5 million acres of state lands and mineral-rights properties, including submerged lands out to 10.3 miles in the Gulf of Mexico. Most of the money from agency leases, trades, and sales goes to the Permanent School Fund. More than $700 million a year is earned from public lands to help finance public school education. The General Land Office is headed by the land commissioner, who is elected. In 1893 the Texas House of Representatives impeached commissioner W. L. McGaughey, who was, however, acquitted in the Texas Senate. Commissioner James Bascom Giles, first elected in 1938, resigned in 1955 and was later convicted in a scandal involving the Veterans' Land Board and sentenced to six years' imprisonment. William S. Porter (O. Henry) was employed as a draftsman at the land office from 1887 to 1891 and used it as a setting

Corrida de la sandía (Watermelon Race), by Theodore Gentilz, 1890[?] copy of 1848 painting? Oil on canvas. 9" × 12". Courtesy Daughters of the Republic of Texas Library; gift of the Yanaguana Society. Gentilz came to Texas in 1844 and became the visual historian of the Tejano community. Here he depicts the watermelon race, in which the object of the game was to cross the finish line with the melon.

for two of his stories. The Old Land Office Building, on the Capitol grounds, was first used in 1857 and has been restored to house historic exhibits. *John G. Johnson*

Gentilz, Théodore. Painter; b. Paris, 1819; d. San Antonio, 4 January 1906; m. Marie Fargeix (1849); ed. as draftsman, painter, and engineer at the Imperial School of Mathematics and Drawing, student of "my master, [Eugène Emmanuel] Viollet-le-Duc." Gentilz was engaged in 1844 by Henri Castro to serve as surveyor, artist, and promotion agent for Castro's projected colony in Texas. With John James, Charles DeMontel, and others, he laid out the village of Castroville and its satellites—Quihi, Vandenburg, New Fountain, and D'Hanis—known collectively as the Castro colony. During the ensuing years, he carried his painting gear and surveying instruments over far-flung trails from the western reaches of El Paso del Norte to the Gulf Coast and deep into Mexico. In 1849, returning from one of his journeys to France on behalf of Castro, Gentilz brought back his French bride and his sister Henriette. They settled in San Antonio, where, in 1852, Henriette married Gentilz's close friend Auguste Frétellière (author of "Reminiscences of a Castro Colonist, 1843–44"). Both families were active participants in the

life of their Catholic parish, and Gentilz was a founding member of the French Mutual Relief Society, a fraternal and insurance organization. Gentilz focused his artistic vision on the Southwest. Indians, Mexican ranchers and villagers, street scenes on both sides of the border, and Spanish missions all captured his attention. Typical of his paintings are the *Camp of the Lipans*, *Comanche Chief*, *Sobre la Huella*, *Ranchero*, *Tamalero*, *Corrida de la Sandía*, *San Antonio*, *Fandango*, *San José de Aguayo*, *El Convite para el Baile*, and *Horse Racing at San Pedro Springs*. In addition to his painting and surveying, for many years Gentilz taught painting at St. Mary's College and in his home (where Marie taught music). Dedicated to history as well as to art, Gentilz tempered his somewhat rigid painterly style with considerable drafting skill to produce a valuable record of events, characters, customs, architecture, and landscapes of his place and time. He also attempted to recreate contemporary events to which he was not actually a witness, as in his *Battle of the Alamo*, *Death of Dickinson*, and *Shooting of the 17 Decimated Texians at El Salado, Mexico*. Most of his works are in such permanent collections as the San Antonio Museum of Art and the Daughters of the Republic of Texas Library at the Alamo.

Dorothy Steinbomer Kendall

Geological Surveys of Texas. The Bureau of Economic Geology, the oldest and one of the largest research units at the University of Texas at Austin, has filled the role of state geological survey since 1909. Before 1909 the Texas legislature established and funded state geological surveys, beginning in 1858 with the Geological and Agricultural Survey of Texas. The first survey was sustained by annual appropriations and was independent of any other institution. Benjamin Franklin Shumard was named state geologist. After four years, the legislature suspended the survey until the end of the Civil War. It was reestablished in 1866 and continued for one more year. In 1870 the legislature formed the second geological survey, with John W. Glenn as state geologist. Like the first, the second survey was surrounded by political turmoil. It finally began work in 1873 and survived only three years. The third survey of the nineteenth century, the Geological and Mineralogical Survey, was established in 1888 by the Twentieth Legislature as part of the Commission of Agriculture, Insurance, Statistics, and History. It received state appropriations for six years and continued without funding for an additional five years before it officially ended in 1901. Under the direction of Edwin T. Dumble, the third survey produced the scientific work that laid the foundation of Texas geological research. The annual reports of the survey contained studies of the regional geology of the state as well as special papers on mineral resources, including lignite, which was one of the most important commodities of the time. Despite its accomplishments, the survey was the subject of a fight in the Twenty-third Legislature and was denied funding by Governor Hogg in 1893. When funding was reconsidered in 1895, Governor Culberson also vetoed the budget. During the disputes over the survey, the legislature transferred the library, records, and collections of the survey to the University of Texas.

In 1901, when it established the University of Texas Mineral Survey, the legislature began to shift responsibility for the survey to the university. The mineral survey was directed by William Battle Phillips and reported to the UT board of regents. Its specific mission was to survey public school and university lands and assess their mineral value. In its four years of existence, the survey studied mineral districts, commodities, and state mining laws and produced eight publications and maps.

The transfer of the geological survey to the university became complete in 1909, when the UT regents founded the Bureau of Economic Geology. The board recognized the usefulness of the mineral survey to the state and its practical role in providing scientific information to the public through the university. Phillips was the bureau's first director, 1909–15. In 1911 the organization was renamed Bureau of Economic Geology and Technology. A reorganization in 1915 established separate heads for a Division of Economic Geology, a Division of Engineering, and a Division of Chemistry. In 1925 these divisions became independent, together called the Division of Natural Resources.

The Bureau of Economic Geology was housed on campus for many years and moved to new facilities at the Balcones Research Center in 1984. For decades the bureau was a small organization with a staff of not more than a dozen professional scientists. With the increasing demands on Texas resources, the bureau grew to a staff of 150 by the mid-1980s. The research staff of 80 included geologists, chemists, biologists, engineers, and computer scientists supported by a staff of 70 in administration, editing, cartography, word processing, public information, curator-

ial work, and rock analysis. At that time the bureau had published more than 600 reports and nearly 400 maps covering nearly every aspect of the geology and resources of Texas. About 1.5 million reports and maps had been distributed or sold to help inform individuals, public agencies, and private organizations about the development and utilization of the state's energy, mineral, and land resources.   *William L. Fisher*

Geology. The geologic history of Texas is recorded in rocks found in outcrops throughout the state and in rocks penetrated by boreholes drilled primarily in the search for oil and natural gas. These rocks indicate that Texas has undergone a long and dynamic history of igneous activity, structural deformation, and sedimentary processes. Study of the origin of these rocks by geoscientists has made possible documentation of the state's changing landscape, which was formed by a process that started several billion years ago in the Precambrian Era and continues to the present. Uplift of mountains, inundation by vast inland seas, river transport of large volumes of eroded sediment, volcanic eruption, and earthquake activity are all processes that have been active throughout the geologic development of Texas. Petroleum resources, lignite, metal ores, groundwater, salt, limestone, granite, ceramic clays, and fertile soils are the legacy of the changing face of Texas.

Precambrian rocks more than 570 million years old underlie much of Central and West Texas. These complexly deformed volcanic, intrusive igneous, and metamorphic rocks occur at the surface in the Llano Uplift of Central Texas and in more isolated outcrops in the mountainous Trans-Pecos region. Other Precambrian rocks are found in the subsurface in Trans-Pecos Texas, Central and West Texas, and the Panhandle. Knowledge of Precambrian rocks and their deformation in the state is much less complete than that of the state's younger rocks, partly because of the relative scarcity of exposure. However, as a result of deep borehole sampling, enough has been discovered about the oldest rocks that major tectonic events or cycles (episodes of largescale deformation of the earth's surface) can be defined. Geologic processes associated with the Sierra Grande–Chaves tectonic cycle (probably a composite cycle) formed the oldest known rocks in Texas, which include extensive granitic, volcanic, and volcano–sedimentary rock suites as much as 1.4 billion years old. These rocks are buried beneath younger strata, mostly in the northwestern part of the state. About 1.2 billion years ago, the metamorphism, igneous activity, and uplift that occurred during the Llano tectonic cycle affected a wide area from the Trans-Pecos to the Llano Uplift. The Llano tectonic cycle corresponds temporally to the Grenville orogeny (episode of mountain building) of eastern North America. Many of the resulting faulted and folded Precambrian rocks contain mineral deposits that formed when the rocks were subjected to extremely high temperature and intense pressure. Geologists continue to search these ancient basement rocks of Texas for commodities of economic importance such as talc, graphite, and granite.

During the Paleozoic Era, which lasted from about 570 million to 245 million years ago, many of the major structures, which are now buried basins and uplifts, and sedimentary accumulations that contain the state's large petroleum reservoirs were formed. During the early phase of the Ouachitan tectonic cycle in the Cambrian Period of the early Paleozoic, rifting of the southern margin of the ancient North American continent led to

Robert T. Hill (second from left) with members of his United States Geological Survey party shortly after they left the Rio Grande near Langtry, 1899. Courtesy U.S. Geological Survey, Denver; R. T. Hill #2. Hill's extensive field work in the service of Texas geology included this 1899 expedition, which explored 350 miles of the Big Bend section of the Rio Grande.

the development of a marine basin to the southeast, along with several failed rift basins, which are elongated troughs extending inland from the continental margin. After this Cambrian activity ceased, the rifted continental margin subsided and shallow seas advanced landward. During the Cambrian and Ordovician periods, widespread carbonateplatform (limestone and dolomite) sediments were deposited over the Texas Craton, which included Precambrian igneous and metamorphic terranes of West and Northwest Texas, as well as much of North America. This was followed by carbonate and terrigenousclastic (sandstone and shale) deposition until the Late Devonian Epoch. Lower Paleozoic rocks are now exposed around the Llano Uplift and in far West Texas near Van Horn and El Paso. They also exist in the subsurface throughout most of West and North Texas.

In the late phase of the Ouachitan tectonic cycle, beginning in the Mississippian Period of the late Paleozoic, compressional (collisional) tectonics became dominant. At the time of the Ouachitan tectonic cycle, a long, deepmarine basin called the Ouachita trough bordered the Texas Craton on the east and south. Collision of the North American tectonic plate with the European and African–South American plates uplifted the thick Ouachita trough sediments to form the Ouachita Mountains before the Middle Pennsylvanian. Today, remnants of this mountain chain are exposed only in southeastern Oklahoma, southwestern Arkansas, and the Marathon region of the Big Bend area of Texas. But in most of Texas the ancient Ouachitas are now buried by younger rocks.

During the Pennsylvanian Period, the Ouachita highlands bordered the eastern margin of several inland marine subbasins, including the Midland, Delaware, and Palo Duro basins, which now collectively compose the oilrich Permian Basin of West Texas. Extensive limestone reefs rimmed the deeper subbasins, and today these reef rocks contain some of the most productive oil reservoirs in the state. Rivers flowing westward from the Ouachitas into the subbasins during the Pennsylvanian fed major delta systems. The resulting fluvial, deltaic, and shallow-marine deposits formed the exposed rocks in north central Texas. By the Permian Period, at the end of the Paleozoic Era, the inland seas were gradually withdrawing from the West Texas subbasins, leaving behind shallow basins rimmed by extensive tidal flats and containing highly evaporative bodies of water in which salt, gypsum, and red muds accumulated in a hot, dry climate. These characteristic Permian "red beds" presently crop out along the eastern edge of the Panhandle as far east as Wichita Falls, as far south as Concho County, and in the TransPecos.

During the early Mesozoic Era (Late Triassic Epoch), about 220 million years ago, the focus of major geologic events in Texas shifted from West and Central Texas to the eastern part of the state. The European and African–South American plates, which had collided with the North American plate to form the Ouachita Mountains, began to separate from North America. This was the initial stage of the Gulfian tectonic cycle, the period during which much of the Coastal Plain of Texas developed. The whole Gulfian cycle consisted of several periods of continental

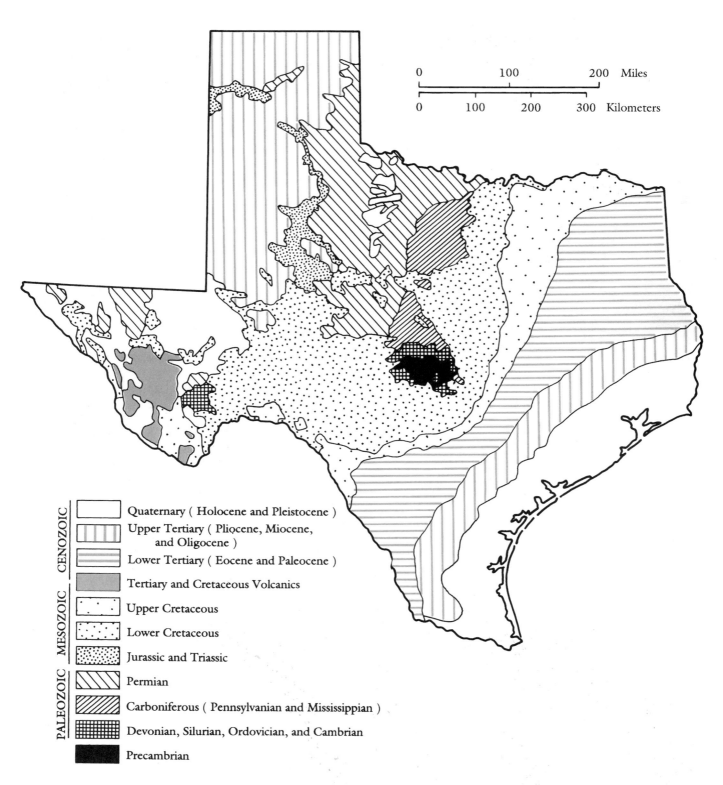

Quaternary (Holocene and Pleistocene)

Upper Tertiary (Pliocene, Miocene, and Oligocene)

Lower Tertiary (Eocene and Paleocene)

Tertiary and Cretaceous Volcanics

Upper Cretaceous

Lower Cretaceous

Jurassic and Triassic

Permian

Carboniferous (Pennsylvanian and Mississippian)

Devonian, Silurian, Ordovician, and Cambrian

Precambrian

CENOZOIC

MESOZOIC

PALEOZOIC

Geologic map of Texas. Drawn by John Cotter. Adapted from original map in Darwin Spearing, *Roadside Geology of Texas* (2nd ed., Missoula, Montana: Mountain Press, 1991, p. 12.

extension (rifting) and compression and is still in progress. In the Triassic, a series of discontinuous rift basins, generally oriented parallel to the edge of the developing ocean basin and extending from Mexico to Nova Scotia, formed as the plates began to separate. As continental separation continued, the rift basins in Texas were eventually buried by thick deposits of Middle Jurassic marine salt in the newly formed East Texas and Gulf Coast basins. Igneous oceanic crust formed in the Gulf Coast Basin during the Late Jurassic; the boundary between oceanic and continental crust probably lies beneath the present-day Texas continental shelf or slope, but its exact location is unknown. Jurassic and Cretaceous deposits formed broad carbonate shelves that were periodically buried in places by deltaic sandstones and shales at the edge of the widening Gulf of Mexico. With increased accumulation of sediments above the Middle Jurassic salt, the salt became unstable and deformed by migrating upward toward depths of lower confining pressure, forming a variety of structures collectively known as salt domes. These structures, which are prominent subsurface features of the Texas Gulf Coast region, formed significant oil and natural gas traps in the tilted and faulted sedimentary rocks that immediately surround them.

By the Early Cretaceous, the shallow Mesozoic seas extended inland, covering much of the state—as far west as the TransPecos region and north almost to the state line. Best exposures of Early Cretaceous rocks are found in the steep canyon walls of the Rio Grande in Big Bend National Park and in the canyons of the Edwards Plateau, as well as in Central Texas from San Antonio to Dallas. During most of the Late Cretaceous, much of Texas lay beneath marine waters that were deeper than the Early Cretaceous seas. The Austin chalk, which crops out from Eagle Pass on the Rio Grande northeastward to the Texarkana area, is a prominent example of the deeper water deposits of the Late Cretaceous. Delta and strandline sandstones of the Woodbine Formation originated in nearshore areas and are the reservoir rocks of the most prolific oilfield in Texas. When discovered in 1930, the East Texas oilfield contained recoverable reserves estimated at 5.6 billion barrels. The Upper Cretaceous rocks dip southeastward beneath the East Texas and Gulf Coast basins. Late Cretaceous volcanoes were widespread in a band roughly parallel to and south and east of the buried Ouachita Mountains. Pilot Knob (Travis County), located southeast of Austin, is the eroded remnant of one of these.

The Late Cretaceous was the time of the last major seaway across Texas. At the end of the Mesozoic Era and the beginning of the Cenozoic Era, major uplift and mountain building in the western United States during the Laramide Orogeny affected the southwestern and western border regions of Texas. This regional uplifting formed the Rocky Mountains, and large river systems draining from the young Rockies southeastward across Texas toward the Gulf of Mexico buried the older marine deposits. Major deltas fed by these rivers prograded the early Cenozoic coastline more than 100 miles seaward into the Gulf of Mexico. Among the effects of this major increase in sediment volume moving into the Gulf of Mexico was renewed upward migration of thick Mesozoic marine salt and the formation of salt domes in the coastal plain area near the site of Houston and in South Texas. Additionally, rapid deposition of deltaic sands over older marine muds resulted in a mechanically unstable sediment column, leading to displacement of the sediments by growth faults

ERA	PERIOD	EPOCH	M.Y.
C E N O Z O I C	Quaternary	Recent	0
		Pleistocene	0.1
			2
	Tertiary	Pliocene	
			5
		Miocene	
			24
		Oligocene	
			37
		Eocene	
			58
		Paleocene	
			66
M E S O Z O I C	Cretaceous		
			144
	Jurassic		
			208
	Triassic		
			245
P A L E O Z O I C	Permian		286
	Pennsylvanian		320
	Mississippian		360
	Devonian		408
	Silurian		438
	Ordovician		505
	Cambrian		570
PRE-CAMBRIAN	Proterozoic		2500
	Archean		4500

Geologic time scale. From Darwin Spearing, *Roadside Geology of Texas* (2nd ed., Missoula, Montana: Mountain Press, 1991), p. xiv. Reproduced by permission.

(large, curved faults that form during sediment accumulation and continue to grow with increasing depth of burial). Linear zones of growth faults of various ages extend from northeastern Mexico into Louisiana and compose traps for large oil and gas fields in offshore Texas. Regional uplift of the western United States beginning in the Miocene Epoch also elevated the Central Texas area. At the boundary between this uplifting plateau and the subsiding Gulf Coast area, a series of normal (extensional) faults formed farther inland than did the extensive growth faults. Examples include the northeast-trending Balcones Fault Zone (forming the Balcones Escarpment near Austin and San

Antonio), which separates the Texas Coastal Plain from the Hill Country in Central Texas.

During the middle Tertiary Period of the Cenozoic Era, TransPecos Texas underwent a period of volcanism and regional deformation that produced much of the rugged landscape in this picturesque part of the state. Volcanic activity there, which occurred from the Eocene through the Miocene Epochs some 47 million to 17 million years ago, produced about 14 volcanic centers (calderas) and associated thick lava and ashflow deposits. Most of the TransPecos volcanism probably occurred during the waning stages of the Laramide Orogeny. The transition from the Laramide compressional regime to a tensional (rift) structural environment, which took place about 30 million years ago, marked the beginning of the period of basin and range deformation in Texas. During this major episode in the geologic development of TransPecos Texas, a series of elongated, north and northwest trending, faultbounded basins formed along with intervening highlands (ranges), such as the Hueco Basin near El Paso and the Salt and Presidio basins farther east and south. Recent fault activity is evident along the margins of the larger basins. The 1931 Valentine earthquake, the largest of earthquakes in historical times in Texas, was produced by sudden rupture along one of these faults.

During the middle to late Cenozoic Era, streams originating in the recently elevated Rocky Mountains to the west transported large volumes of sand and gravel into the Texas Panhandle, which accumulated in large alluvial fans. Vast amounts of finegrained, windblown sediments were also deposited along with the alluvial material. These fans were deposited on older Paleozoic and Mesozoic rocks and occurred from Texas into what is now Nebraska. Between one and two million years ago, the fans in Texas were cut off from their Rocky Mountain source, and the eastern edge of the alluvial sheet began to retreat westward as rivers draining into the Gulf of Mexico caused headward erosion. The resulting bluff that extends in a north–south line in West Texas and the Panhandle is the Caprock Escarpment. The alluvial and windblown deposits have been designated the Ogallala Formation, which is a major aquifer (waterbearing rock unit) throughout the central and southern High Plains of the United States.

Expansion of the polar ice caps during the latest Cenozoic produced the great Ice Age in North America, during which, for more than two million years, thick sheets of glacial ice successively advanced and retreated. Although the continental glaciers never reached as far south as Texas, the state's climate and sea level underwent major changes during each period of glacial advance and retreat. Sea level during glacial advances was 300 to 450 feet lower than during the warmer interglacial periods because so much sea water was contained in the ice sheets. The climate was both more humid and cooler than that of today, and the largest Texas rivers carried more water and sediment to the Gulf of Mexico than they do today. These deposits underlie the outer 50 miles or more of the Gulf Coastal Plain. Approximately 3,000 years ago, sea level reached its modern position, and the coastal features that are present today, such as the deltas, lagoons, beaches, and barrier islands, have formed since that time.

Tucker F. Hentz

Georgetown, Texas. County seat of Williamson County, on the San Gabriel River. It was founded in 1848 and named for George Washington Glasscock, who, with his partner, Thomas B. Huling, donated land for the site. Pioneers were attracted by the abundance of timber and good water, as were the Tonkawa Indians, who had a village there. The first wave of settlers was from Tennessee, Kentucky, North Carolina, Arkansas, Illinois, and other states. Swedish settlers came by the 1850s; after 1870 German, Austrian, and Swiss settlers began arriving and after 1880 Moravian and Czech. A few blacks came with early Anglo families, and migration from Mexico began about 1910. The establishment of Southwestern University in 1873 and construction of a railroad in 1878 contributed to the town's growth and importance. A stable, healthy economy was based largely on agriculture, and a major tributary cattle trail led through the heart of Georgetown to the Western, Chisholm, Dodge City, and Shawnee trails. The *Williamson County Sun*, founded in 1877, continued publication in the 1990s. Industry prior to 1900 included limestone quarries; grist, flour, planing, and woodworking mills; cotton gins; brick, flue, chair, and mattress factories; tin, pewter, blacksmith, saddlery, and shoe shops; a knitting mill, bakeries, and confectioneries; and the Texas Chautauqua Assembly, a bottling works, and an old mill. Well known among cattlemen of Texas and the nation were Dudley Hiram Snyder, John Wesley Snyder, and John Sparks, residents of Georgetown in the years of cattle trailing. Cotton production was dominant in the area from the 1880s to the 1920s, after which crop diversification was practiced. The Georgetown and Granger Railroad was completed to Austin in 1904. Extensive loss from a 1921 flood led Georgetown to seek flood control, an effort that culminated in the building of a dam to impound Lake Georgetown, which opened in 1979. An unlicensed radio station appeared briefly in the 1930s, and KGTN opened in 1962. Population growth and industrial expansion continued modestly in the twentieth century until about 1960, when residential, commercial, and industrial development greatly accelerated. Since then adaptive restoration has been widely practiced, with special emphasis on a Main Street program and private restoration of older homes. Also since then Georgetown has added several heavy manufacturing plants, light and cottage industry, and crushed-stone quarries; parks at Lake Georgetown and in the center of town; retirement and nursing homes; a new hospital; low-cost housing that has been a model for similar projects over Texas; Mood–Heritage Museum; a public library; and Inner Space Cavern. The population in 1980 was 9,468, and 4,500 more lived in the area. In 1990 the population was 14,842.

Clara Stearns Scarbrough

Germans. The largest ethnic group in Texas derived directly from Europe was persons of German birth or descent. As early as 1850, they constituted more than 5 percent of the total Texas population, a proportion that remained constant through the remainder of the nineteenth century. Intermarriage has blurred ethnic lines, but the 1990 United States census revealed that 1,175,888 Texans claimed pure and 1,775,838 partial German ancestry, for a total of 2,951,726, or 17_ percent of the population. By this count, Germans rank behind Mexican Americans and form the third-largest national-origin group in the state. Most persons of German descent do not regard themselves as ethnic Germans. Nevertheless, from their first immigration to Texas in the 1830s, the Germans tended to cluster in ethnic enclaves. A majority settled in a broad, fragmented belt across the south central part of the state. This belt stretched from Galveston and Houston on the east to Kerrville, Mason, and Hondo in the west; from the fertile, humid Coastal Plain to the semiarid Hill Country. This German Belt included most of the Teutonic settlements in the state, both rural and urban.

The German Belt reflects concepts and processes well known to students of migration, particularly the concept of "dominant personality," the process called "chain migration," and the device of "America letters." Voluntary migrations generally were begun by a dominant personality, or "true pioneer." This individual was forceful and ambitious, a natural leader, who perceived emigration as a solution to economic, social, political, or religious problems in his homeland. He used his personality to persuade others to follow him in migration. In the case of the Texas Germans, Friedrich Diercks, known in Texas under his alias, Johann Friedrich Ernst, was the dominant personality. Ernst had been a gardener in the Grand Duchy of Oldenburg in northwestern Germany. He immigrated to America intending to settle in Missouri, but in New Orleans he learned that large land grants were available to Europeans in Stephen F. Austin's colony in Texas. Ernst applied for and in 1831 received a grant of more than 4,000 acres that lay in the northwest corner of what is now Austin County. It formed the nucleus of the German Belt.

Ernst wrote lengthy letters to friends in Germany, and through these he influenced other prospective migrants. He described a land with a winterless climate like that of Sicily. It had abundant game and fish, was fertile and rich, and awaited the impress of German labor to make it produce abundantly. Taxes were virtually nil, and large tracts of land were available for only a surveyor's fee; hunting and fishing required no licenses. Texas was an earthly paradise. Like other writers of "America letters," Ernst stressed the positive aspects of the new land and downplayed or omitted the negative. One of his letters appeared in a newspaper in northwestern Germany and also in an emigrant guidebook and greatly magnified his role in promoting the migration. As a result of Ernst's letters, a small, steady stream of migrants left northwestern Germany for Texas. Within 10 years they had established a number of rural communities in the vicinity of Ernst's grant in south central Texas. The chain migration process was a natural result of dominant personalities and their use of emigrant letters. In the process people moved in clusters from confined districts to settle similarly confined colonial areas overseas. In this manner, people from small rural parishes in Germany settled a county or part of a county in Texas. Typically, their neighbors had been neighbors in the Fatherland. The influence of dominant personalities moved easily among people who knew each other, and the decision to emigrate spread quickly through a population by personal contact. The migration set in motion by Friedrich Ernst drew principally from districts in Oldenburg, Westphalia, and Holstein.

In the late 1830s German immigration to Texas was widely publicized in the Fatherland. The publicity attracted a group of small noblemen who envisioned a project to colonize German peasants in Texas. The nobles hoped the project would bring them wealth, power, and prestige. It could also, they thought, alleviate overpopulation in rural Germany. Their organization, the Adelsverein, began work in the early 1840s. They chose Texas as the site for their colony, in part because of the favorable publicity surrounding the Ernst-inspired migration and perhaps because Texas was an independent republic where the princes might exercise some political control. Though the Mainzer Adelsverein was a financial disaster, it transported thousands of Germans, mostly peasants, to Texas. Between 1844 and 1847 more than 7,000 Germans reached the new land. Some of the immigrants perished in epidemics, many stayed in cities such as Galveston, Houston, and San Antonio, and others settled in the rugged Texas Hill Country to form the western end of the German Belt. The Adelsverein founded the towns of New Braunfels and Fredericksburg.

Most of the German immigrant clusters came from west central Germany, particularly Nassau, southern Hanover, Brunswick, Hesse, and western Thuringia. The nobles focused their advertising and recruitment on these provinces, their home districts. John O. Meusebach, for example, entered Texas as one of the leaders of the Adelsverein, and some 34 villages in his home county, the Dillkreis in Nassau, contributed to the migration. The chain-migration process in the Adelsverein movement drew on both the local and provincial levels. Some farm villages lost a large part of their population to the Texas project. The Hanoverian village of Gadenstedt, for instance, sent at least 73 people during the years 1844 to 1847. Twenty other places near Gadenstedt also contributed settlers to the Adelsverein undertaking.

At about the same time, another colonization project was launched. The Frenchman Henri Castro directed a project that moved more than 2,000 German-speaking settlers, mainly from clusters in the Upper Rhine Plain of Alsace, to Medina County, west of San Antonio. Castroville, founded in 1844, became the nucleus of the Alsatian colony, though many of the immigrants settled in San Antonio because of better economic opportunities there. The German settlers who immigrated to Texas because of Friedrich Ernst, the Adelsverein, and Castro generally were solid middle-class peasants. They were land-owning families, artisans, and, in a few cases, university-educated people. The majority were farmers with a modest experience in trade. The Germans were ambitious farmers and artisans who believed their futures were cramped by the social and economic system at home. They were not poverty-stricken and oppressed. Indeed, they were able to afford the substantial cash investment required in overseas migration.

By 1850, when the organized projects ended, the German Belt in Texas was well established. America letters and chain migration continued through the 1850s but stopped with the Union blockade of Confederate ports. During the 1850s the number of German-born persons in Texas more than doubled, surpassing 20,000. As the German Belt expanded, settlements entered the sandy post oak woods in Lee County, where some 600 Wends from Oberlausitz planted a colony centered on the community of Serbin. The Wends, many of whom spoke German and Sorbian, considered Pastor John Kilian their leader. After the Civil War ended, ships loaded with German immigrants once again unloaded at the Galveston wharves. From 1865 to the early 1890s more Germans arrived in Texas than during the 30 years before the war. The number probably reached 40,000. Many of them settled in the rural areas and towns of the German Belt. Interestingly, the postbellum immigrants generally avoided the Hill Country.

Germans also settled elsewhere in Texas. By the 1880s German ethnic islands dotted north central, northern, and western Texas. Such islands failed to develop in East Texas, the Trans-

Pecos, and the Rio Grande valley, however. As early as 1881, Germans founded the colony of Marienfeld (later Stanton) on the High Plains of West Texas. It was one of the first agricultural settlements in that part of the state. There the German settlers planted splendid vineyards, only to see them destroyed by drought. Most of the postbellum German colonies thrived, however. The families generally came from areas of the Fatherland that had supplied the prewar colonists. Chain migration, aided by America letters, clearly played a role. However, during these years, larger numbers of colonists from the eastern provinces of Germany began arriving in Texas. Also by the 1890s German immigrants who had earlier come to the midwestern states of Illinois, Minnesota, Iowa, and neighboring states moved to Texas. For example, Germans from Iowa and nearby states, sponsored by the Catholic Church and the Flusche brothers, founded a German colony at Muenster in North Texas. By the 1890s sizable German elements had appeared in Texas cities, particularly in San Antonio, Galveston, and Houston. As late as 1880 the population of San Antonio was one-third German. By then a greater percentage of Germans lived in towns and cities than was true of the Texas population at large. German immigration to Texas tapered off during the 1890s. Germans formed new ethnic islands as late as the 1920s, but they were peopled from other areas in Texas, particularly the German Belt. Second and third generation German Texans looking for cheap land flocked westward until the Great Depression halted the movement. Since 1930 the extent of the German-settled area has changed very little, though a considerable post–World War II German immigration was directed to Texas cities.

The Germans who settled Texas included peasant farmers and intellectuals; Protestants, Catholics, Jews, and atheists; Prussians, Saxons, Hessians, and Alsatians; abolitionists and slaveowners; farmers and townsfolk; frugal, honest folk and ax murderers. They differed in dialect, customs, and physical features. A majority had been farmers in Germany, and most came seeking economic opportunities. A few dissident intellectuals fleeing the 1848 revolutions sought political freedom, but few, save perhaps the Wends, came for religious freedom. The German settlements in Texas reflected this variety. Even in the confined area of the Hill Country, each valley offered a different kind of German. The Llano valley had stern, teetotaling German Methodists, who renounced dancing and fraternal organizations; the Pedernales valley had fun-loving, hardworking Lutherans and Catholics who enjoyed drinking and dancing; and the Guadalupe valley had atheist Germans descended from political refugees. The scattered German ethnic islands included Lindsay in Cooke County, largely Westphalian Catholic; Waka in Ochiltree County, Midwestern Mennonite; Hurnville in Clay County, Russian German Baptist; and Lockett in Wilbarger County, Wendish Lutheran. Because of their variety, Texas Germans had a varied influence. They distinguished themselves in many professions and activities—Chester W. Nimitz in the military, Robert J. Kleberg in ranching (see King Ranch), Gustav Schleicher in politics, and Charles A. Schreiner in retail business. Many German settlements had distinctive architecture, foods, customs, religion, language, politics, and economy. In the Hill Country the settlers built half-timbered and stone houses, miles of rock fences, and grand Gothic churches with jagged towers reaching skyward. They spoke a distinctive German patois in the streets and stores, ate spiced sausage and sauerkraut in cafes, and drank such Texas German beers as Pearl and Shiner. They polkaed in countless dance halls, watched rifle competition at rural *Schützenfeste*, and witnessed the ancient Germanic custom of Easter Fires at Fredericksburg. Neat, prosperous farms and ranches occupied the countryside.

German cultural influence in Texas reached a peak in the 1890s. The settlers had survived the difficult years of pioneering, and their relative isolation had preserved much that was German. In the years that followed, acculturation took a heavy toll. Two world wars and the associated anti-German prejudice damaged the interest in German folkways and curtailed the use of the German language. After the early 1900s the rural German communities received no additional immigrants from German Europe, and Anglo-Texan culture increasingly penetrated the Teutonic rural world. Rural depopulation, intermarriage, and modern communications increasingly obliterated rural German Texas. In the twentieth century, German immigration was directed almost exclusively to the cities of Texas. In these urban areas, German culture declined rapidly. The older German ethnic sections in such cities as San Antonio broke up as prosperous third and fourth generation Texas Germans flocked to the suburbs. King William Street, once the most affluent German neighborhood of San Antonio, lost most of its German-American residents. German-language schools also went into decline. In the early 1950s the thriving German-language press, vital to cultural survival in a literate society, fell silent, signaling the end of an era.
Terry G. Jordan

German Sisters. Indian Captives Catherine, Sophia, Julia, and Addie German; b. Fannin County, Georgia, 1850s and 1860s. The family moved after the Civil War to Missouri and Kansas. In the latter state they were attacked by Cheyennes avenging themselves after the second battle of Adobe Walls (27 June 1874). The parents, their son, and two daughters were killed and scalped. The other four sisters—aged 17, 12, 7, and 5—were captured and eventually taken to the Panhandle. They were subjected to exposure, malnutrition, and other maltreatment as their captors traveled southward. Catherine, in particular, recalled instances of gang rape by young "dog soldiers" and indignities at the hands of Cheyenne women, particularly Medicine Water's obnoxious wife, Mochi (Buffalo Calf Woman). Eventually Julia and Addie were traded to Grey Beard's band, who for the most part neglected them. Grey Beard steered his following down the east side of the Llano Estacado, while Medicine Water joined with other groups and moved down the west side, probably crossing at several points into eastern New Mexico. By November 1874 Grey Beard had set up camp north of McClellan Creek, about ten miles south of the site of present-day Pampa. On the morning of 8 November, Lt. Frank D. Baldwin's column charged the Indian encampment. So complete was the surprise that the Cheyennes abandoned the village and left most of their property intact. Riding through the deserted camp, Billy Dixon and other army scouts noticed movement in a pile of buffalo hides; they were astonished to find Julia and Addie German, both emaciated and near starvation. Dixon later recalled how hardened scouts and soldiers turned aside to hide their emotions as the little girls sobbed out their story. At the main supply camp on the Washita River, Col. Nelson Miles placed Julia and Addie in the care of an army surgeon, who took them to Fort Leavenworth, Kansas. In January Miles and Col. Thomas H. Neill sent out friendly Kiowas as messengers to find the Cheyennes and induce them to surrender. When Kiowa chief Stone Calf was told that peace was dependent upon the safety of Catherine and Sophia German, he had them moved into a lodge next to his own. They were released in March, after Stone Calf, Grey Beard, Red Moon, and other chiefs brought in their bands to surrender at Brinton Darlington's agency. The sisters identified the individuals who had murdered their family and those who had abused them, including Medicine Water and Mochi. These, along with others singled out for various crimes, were placed in irons and sent to Fort Marion, Florida, for incarceration. Catherine and Sophia were subsequently reunited with Julia and Addie at Fort Leavenworth, and Colonel Miles was designated their guardian. Congress set aside $10,000 from Cheyenne annuities as an endowment for the girls' support and education. On reaching the age of 21, each sister received $2,500. Reared by Mr. and Mrs. Patrick Corney in Kansas, all four girls eventually married and settled in Kansas, Colorado, and California. In 1936 a Texas Centennial marker was placed near the site of Baldwin's attack on Gray Beard. In October 1952 Julia German Brooks was guest of honor at Gray County's fiftieth anniversary celebration in Pampa.

H. Allen Anderson

Gibbons, Euell. Natural food publicist; b. Clarksville, 8 September 1911; d. Sunbury, Pennsylvania, 29 December 1975; m. Anna Swanson (1935; divorced); 2 sons; m. Freda Fryer (1949). Gibbons and his siblings learned about wild foods from their mother. He concocted menus and wrote about foraging. In 1922 the family moved to a New Mexico farmstead, which Gibbons provisioned by foraging, hunting, and trapping whenever his father was away. At 15 he left home, working towards California and the Pacific Northwest, where, by 1933, he lived in bum camps, foraged, and did manual labor. Gibbons joined the Communist party sometime during the 1930s but left it about 1940 and later called himself a "left-wing Democrat." In Hawaii during World War II he worked in a shipyard. With the war over, Gibbons, a divorcé and conscientious objector, turned to beachcombing. He completed high school and attended the University of Hawaii from 1947 to 1950; he earned money by composing crossword puzzles in Hawaiian. He and Freda taught on Maui until 1953, joined the Quakers, and then left Hawaii and taught at various schools in the eastern and midwestern United States before moving to a midwestern cooperative community. In 1955, while employed at Pendle Hill School near Philadelphia, Gibbons began writing about edible plants. Freda promised to support them while he wrote full-time, and they moved nearby to Tanguy Homesteads. Gibbons had written verse and short stories; now he completed a novel, but his editors advised him, "Take the novel out. Leave the wild food in." He did so, and McKay published *Stalking the Wild Asparagus* in 1962, after which Gibbons was established as the master of his field. In 1963 the Gibbonses moved to a farm named It Wonders Me at Troxelville, Pennsylvania. Gibbons wrote six more books "lauding nature's harvests" and taught foraging. With a voice something like that of Will Rogers, he became famous doing Grape-Nuts television commercials. He helped mold environmental thought, condemned wastefulness and reliance upon technology, and urged life in harmony with nature like that attributed to American Indians. Susquehanna University awarded him an honorary degree in 1972. He died of atherosclerosis. *John Sunder*

Gilmer–Aikin Laws. Bills that restructured public education in Texas in 1949. They consolidated 4,500 school districts into 2,900, supplemented local taxes with state funds, initiated higher salaries, augmented school staffs with education specialists, and provided an incentive to increase attendance by making state funding dependent on enrollment. The statutes also instituted the State Department of Education (now the Texas Education Agency) and guaranteed Texas children minimum public-schooling opportunities for 12 school years of 9 months with a minimum of 175 teaching days a year. Later debates over education in Texas have all been conducted within the framework of the Gilmer–Aikin Laws. The 50th Texas Legislature, deadlocked over a minimum-salary law for teachers, appointed a committee later named the Gilmer–Aikin Committee, after Representative Claud Gilmer and Senator A. M. Aikin, Jr. In 1949 the state Senate readily adopted the three bills containing the Gilmer–Aikin Committee proposals. Passage in the House, however, required careful maneuvering to overcome stiff opposition. Opponents, who characterized the measures as both Communist and Fascist, objected to replacing the elected state superintendent of public instruction with an appointed commissioner of education, and to forbidding the use of school buses by private schools. The House Education Committee hearings on the bills included the first all-night committee hearing in the Texas legislature's history. *Oscar Mauzy*

Girlstown, U.S.A. Nine miles south of Whiteface; originally a temporary shelter for girls, but subsequently developed to provide a stable, longterm home environment for abused and neglected girls; expanded in the later twentieth century to include predelinquent, delinquent, troubled, and disturbed children. Girlstown was the idea of Amelia Anthony, who took in six homeless girls at Buffalo Gap in 1939. In July of that year Lubbock attorney Tom Duggan gave 1,425 acres of ranchland near Whiteface for a campus. An affiliate was opened at Borger in 1967, followed by another at Austin in 1970. The three facilities were governed by a 30member board of directors drawn from throughout the United States. Generally, girls were accepted if the facility could meet their needs and space was available. Children with learning disabilities were often placed on the Borger campus because of the special-education program available in the Borger school district. Because of the urban setting and mental-health resources available in Travis County, the Austin campus accepted girls who were more emotionally disturbed than those generally found on the other campuses. In addition to treatment for residents by a qualified staff, consultants from a variety of community agencies and private practices were utilized. The Whiteface campus was home to girls from across the country and Canada. Farm animals, including a stable of horses, helped provide a country-living atmosphere. The campus had a dining hall, a chapel, a gym, a swimming pool, tennis courts, a game room, and a country store where residents could purchase incidentals. In 1984 a new Career Center was opened where job skills were taught. In 1987 Girlstown merged with Cal Farley's Boys Ranch. Shortly afterward the Austin campus was closed. The facility at Borger was changed to provide a home for elementary schoolchildren, both boys and girls, under Cal Farley's Family Program. The Girlstown Whiteface campus continued to provide a home for girls and had a housing capacity of 75. *Jeanne F. Lively*

Edna Gladney. Courtesy Gladney Center, Fort Worth.

Gladney, Edna. Child-welfare advocate; b. Edna Kahly, Milwaukee, 22 January 1886; d. Fort Worth, 2 October 1961 (buried in Rose Hill Cemetery); m. Sam Gladney (1906; d. 1935). Her mother brought Edna to Fort Worth in 1903 for the girl's health. After marriage, the Gladneys stayed a few months in Havana before moving to Wolfe City, where Sam built the Gladney Milling Company, which manufactured Gladiola flour, and Edna started a crusade to clean up the Grayson County poor farm. Especially distressed at the treatment of children at the institution, she arranged to have the youngsters transferred to Rev. I. Z. T. Morris's Children's Home and Aid Society in Fort Worth. By 1910 she had joined the society's board of directors and had dedicated herself to caring for homeless and underprivileged children. After a trip to New York and Chicago to study settlement work and child welfare, Mrs. Gladney established a free day nursery in Sherman for the children of poor working families. She financed the nursery from her own pocket and from donations to collection boxes that she placed in local businesses. After the flour mill failed, the couple moved to Fort Worth in 1924, and while her husband rebuilt his fortunes Edna Gladney devoted her time to the Texas Children's Home and Aid Society. By 1927 she had been named superintendent. Childless, and widowed in 1935, Mrs. Gladney made the welfare of unwanted children the center of her life. She continued Morris's original work of placing abandoned children with adoptive families and expanded the society's activities to focus on the care of unmarried mothers and an adoption service for their babies. She successfully lobbied the Texas legislature to have the word *illegitimate* kept off birth certificates and urged the passage of legislation to give adopted children the same inheritance rights as other children. As a result of her efforts the state instituted the policy of issuing second birth certificates in the names of adop-

tive parents. Mrs. Gladney acquired a national reputation for her work after the release of the 1941 film *Blossoms in the Dust*, a fictionalized account of her life, starring Greer Garson. In 1950, after acquiring the West Texas Maternity Hospital, which it had operated since 1948, the society changed its name to Edna Gladney Home (now the Gladney Center). Mrs. Gladney was awarded an honorary doctor of laws degree by Texas Christian University in 1957. She placed over 10,000 babies with adoptive parents during her career, and she continued to direct the home until ill health forced her into semiretirement in 1960. She remained active as an advisor and reviewed plans for a new nursery and additional dormitory only a few days before her death.

Judith N. McArthur

Glenn Spring Raid. An attack by Mexican raiders on the settlements of Glenn Spring and Boquillas in southern Brewster County, 5 May 1916. It confirmed the fears of Texas residents living along the Rio Grande during the chaotic early years of the Mexican Revolution. Rumors of attacks by bandits or followers of Pancho Villa and Venustiano Carranza had been common. In June 1915 Governor James E. Ferguson asked the federal government to station troops in the Big Bend to protect citizens, but Maj. Gen. Frederick Funston answered that combating banditry was a state responsibility. Events soon caused a revision of that policy. In January 1916 Villistas stopped a train near Santa Ysabel, Chihuahua, and shot 18 American mining engineers. On 9 March 1916, 485 rebels attacked Columbus, New Mexico, on Villa's orders, killing 17 Americans. President Wilson sent a punitive expedition of 6,000 men under Brig. Gen. John J. Pershing across the border, but Villa escaped.

The raiders at Glenn Spring greatly outnumbered the nine cavalry soldiers stationed there, who took shelter in an adobe building and for several hours exchanged gunfire with the Mexicans. Eventually the raiders set fire to the roof. When the soldiers fled, three of them were killed and four were wounded. Also killed was the young son of storekeeper C. G. Compton. The raiders themselves suffered few losses. Meanwhile, another party raided Boquillas, 12 miles east of Glenn Spring on the Rio Grande. Although their leader, Natividad Álvarez, was captured, his men took storekeeper Jesse Deemer and his assistant hostage before fleeing back across the river. The raiders also robbed the Puerto Rico Mining Company of its payroll. The army believed that Villa was behind these latest outrages and organized another punitive expedition, under the joint command of Col. Frederick W. Sibley and Col. George T. Langhorne. On 11 May, Sibley sent Langhorne across the Rio Grande with 80 men, 2 wagons, and Langhorne's chauffeur-driven Cadillac. Sibley and the rest of the force followed two days later. The Mexicans, at their base in El Pino, Coahuila, sent Langhorne a note from Deemer indicating that the bandits would return the two Americans in exchange for Álvarez and others. Langhorne piled 12 sharpshooters into his Cadillac and headed for El Pino, but the bandits scattered, leaving Deemer and his helper behind in the care of a local rancher. The troops returned to Texas on 21 May with the two hostages, but without having caught the raiders themselves.

The raid led to the reorganization of the American military in the Big Bend. Wilson ordered troops of the national guard mobilized to reinforce the army, and by the end of July 1916 an estimated 116,957 guardsmen were stationed along the border from California to Texas. In addition, permanent cavalry camps were established at more than a dozen locations in the Big Bend, including Glenn Spring and La Noria, near Boquillas. In August 1920, however, the Big Bend Military District was discontinued and the camps abandoned; the threat of banditry had ended. W. D. Smithers, a former muleteer for the troops at Glenn Spring, said that after 1916 there was little for the soldiers to do except "watch for bandits and play baseball." Construction of the permanent barracks at Glenn Spring was never completed.

Martin Donell Kohout

Goat Ranching. Commercial goat ranching in Texas primarily involves the raising of Angora goats for mohair. The United States ranks as the second leading producer of mohair in the world, and as much as 97 percent of the domestic product is grown in Texas. The majority of Texas mohair originates on the Edwards Plateau,where wool and mohair production is a major part of the economy. In 1992 Texas Angora raisers produced 14.2 million pounds of mohair. Spaniards first brought domesticated goats to Texas, though the shorthaired goat was generally raised only for subsistence milk and meat. After the Civil War, when livestock raisers began looking for increased profits from wool and mohair, Angora goats were introduced. William Walton Haupt of Hays County brought the first Angora goats to Texas in 1857–58, when he purchased eight of the animals and began crossbreeding them with the shorthaired Spanish goat. Other ranchers began raising Angoras, most of them located in the hilly country along the Balcones Escarpment, where steep canyons offered brushy vegetation, water, and protection. California and Oregon took the lead in mohair production during the 1860s and 1870s. Increasing land prices in California, rising mohair prices, and a growing awareness of the stock-raising

potential of the Edwards Plateau led to increased Texas production in the early 1880s. By mid-decade almost 200 Texas ranchers were raising Angora goats. In 1886 the American Mohair Growers Association was formed in San Antonio.

Declining mohair prices in the late 1880s slowed the enthusiasm for Angoras, however, and by 1891 the AMGA was defunct. Nevertheless, the pioneer goat raisers who formed the organization played an important role in developing the breeding stock from which future Angora operations were built, since Turkish authorities placed severe limits on the export of Angoras. The limited number and high cost of purebred animals meant that commercially viable mohair operations had to be developed from crossbred goats. Between 1860 and 1880 Texas raisers had demonstrated that marketable mohair could be produced by crossing Angoras with shorthaired goats, and that Angoras could adapt to the semiarid, brushy environment of the Edwards Plateau. As a result, when mohair prices began to rise again in the 1890s, Texas had a base of high-quality breeding stock to use in developing commercial herds. William Leslie Black of Fort McKavett, a retired stockbroker from New York who spent his later years in raising and praising the Angora goat, played a major role in reviving local interest in goat ranching. Encouraged by rising prices, Texas raisers enlarged their herds and began to sell large numbers of goats to stock raisers in other states. By 1900 Texas raisers led the nation in mohair production. About 1895 the Sultan of Turkey prohibited any further exportation of Angoras, but American breeders had already improved their stock so much that it was self-sustaining. Of 117 Angoras brought to the U.S. from South Africa, many went to Texas flocks, helped to improve the American product further, and initiated cooperative ventures between the world's two leading

Angora goats at the Cody Dutton Ranch near Rocksprings, ca. 1991. Courtesy Texas Department of Transportation/Jack Lewis. These goats, sheared in late winter or early spring, retain a "cape" to protect them from the elements.

centers of mohair production. By the 1920s Texas ranchers were raising two million Angora goats and producing more than 80 percent of the American mohair clip. The National Association of Angora Breeders, originally formed and headquartered in Missouri, moved its headquarters in 1925 to Rocksprings, Edwards County, in recognition of the overwhelming predominance of Texas raisers in the mohair industry. The Texas association coined the term *chevon* as a genteel Gallic name for goat meat. Its efforts in the meat trade, however, were not wholly successful. Angoras have been used in the Cross Timbers and East Texas forests as a first step in pasture clearance. On the Edwards Plateau ranchers raise a mixture of cattle, sheep, and goats that fully utilizes the varied vegetation. The number of Angora goats in Texas reached a record high of more than 4.5 million in 1965, when mohair production was 31,584,000 pounds. Herd sizes and mohair production declined steadily afterwards, however, as demand fell, and reached a low of 1,270,000 animals in 1976. The industry began rebounding in 1981.

Goliad, Texas. County seat of Goliad County; originally one of the oldest Spanish colonial municipalities in the state. The town, on the San Antonio River, was established in October 1749, when Nuestra Señora del Espíritu Santo de Zúñiga Mission and its royal protector, Nuestra Señora de Loreto de La Bahía del Espíritu Santo Presidio (Presidio La Bahía), were moved from the Guadalupe River to a site named Santa Dorotea, on the San Antonio River. A new presidio, La Bahía, was built on a hill near the river, where sand, limestone, and timber were abundant. Around the presidio walls grew the settlement of La Bahía, and on the opposite bank stood Mission Espíritu Santo. The fort supplied Spanish men-at-arms to the army of Bernardo de Gálvez in the American colonists' war against the British between 1779 and 1782, garrisoned Spanish troops throughout the 1810–21 Mexican war of independence, and after 1812 saw four separate attempts to establish Texas independence. In the longest siege in American military history, the Gutiérrez–Magee expedition captured La Bahía and held it for the first "Republic of Texas" from November 1812 until February 1813. In June 1817 Henry Perry and 40 companions tried to capture the presidio but were repulsed. James Long, who surprised the occupying garrison in 1821 and met with little resistance, was unseated by deception after three days when 700 Spanish Royalist troops arrived from San Antonio. Early in 1829 La Bahía resident Rafael Antonio Manchola, recently elected to the Coahuila and Texas state legislature, petitioned the governor to change the town's name to Goliad, an anagram of the name of Father Hidalgo, the priest who instigated the Mexican independence movement. By decree on 4 February 1829, La Bahía became Villa de Goliad. At the time, the town had a number of stone houses belonging to wealthy citizens. In one of these, on 24 March 1829, was born Ignacio Seguín Zaragoza, who became one of Mexico's greatest military heroes. Flanking the stone structures stood dozens of jacals, huts of post and mortar construction that sheltered most of the villa's inhabitants. In 1834 a cholera epidemic nearly destroyed the settlement, but it survived. The fourth and most noted effort originating in Goliad to establish Texas independence, known as the Goliad Campaign of 1835, began in October after an armed confrontation called the battle of Gonzales. Texans under Ben Milam and George Collinsworth captured the Goliad fort and its stores of arms and ammunition from the 24-

"Town of Goliad, Formerly La Bahia." Prints and Photographs Collection, Goliad, Texas, file, CAH; CN 01529.

man Mexican garrison. On 20 December Goliad citizens and South Texas colonists met in the presidio chapel to sign a document known as the Goliad Declaration of Independence, the first such declaration for Texas, and afterwards hoisted the first flag of independence, designed by Capt. Philip Dimmitt, above the walls. James W. Fannin, Jr., took command of the post in February 1836 and evacuated it on Sam Houston's orders on 19 March. He and nearly 500 men were returned as prisoners to the presidio after the battle of Coleto and spent a week of captivity there before they were murdered in the Goliad Massacre.

After the battle of San Jacinto the old town was largely deserted, as many Hispanic citizens fled to Mexico and Anglo-Americans moved north of the river to the present townsite. The building of a new town resulted from complications in land titles; people feared purchasing old-town property since it was doubtful that appropriate Spanish or Mexican titles could be obtained. Goliad County, named for the city, was established in 1836; Goliad became county seat and three years later was incorporated under the Republic of Texas. A four-league grant offered to La Bahía during the Mexican era was validated and signed by Houston in 1844, and a post office opened in 1847. Paine Female Institute was founded in 1852, began accepting males in 1873, added a military academy in 1877, and eventually became Goliad College. The Goliad *Advance Guard* has been published continuously since 1855. Goliad was the scene of the Cart War in 1857. The Cart War Oak, or Hanging Tree, still standing on the north lawn of the courthouse lot, saw both court-approved hangings and unauthorized executions during the conflict, which was halted by Texas Rangers. The railroad arrived in 1885–86, and Goliad grew to a population of 2,500 by 1890. A new courthouse was constructed in 1894. Local farmers raised cotton and later cattle, but the town lost population as cotton farming declined. On 18 May 1902 a tornado destroyed more than 100 buildings, killed 115 people, and injured 230. Goliad had 1,261 residents in 1904, grew to 2,500 by 1925, fell to 1,400 during the Great Depression, and grew slowly afterward. In 1940 the town had two cotton gins, a gristmill, a poultry-packing plant, a broom factory, and 50 businesses, but in 1942 another disastrous storm damaged the area and destroyed the courthouse clock tower and turrets. La Bahia Downs, a racetrack, began drawing visitors to horse races in 1961. In 1984–85 the Main Street Project renovated downtown buildings. In 1990 the population was 1,946, and the major industries included oil, cattle ranching and other agribusiness, and tourism. *Jeri Robison Turner*

Goliad Declaration of Independence. Drafted by Ira Ingram; read to the citizens of Goliad assembled at Nuestra Señora de Loreto Presidio on 20 December 1835. The document was enthusiastically ratified and received 91 signatures, the signers including Hispanics José Miguel Aldrete and José María Jesús Carbajal. Philip Dimmitt was a major participant. The enacting clause resolved that the former Department of Texas ought to be a "free, sovereign, and independent State," and the signers pledged their lives, fortunes, and honor to sustain the declaration. The meeting struck off several copies of the document to be sent to various parts of Texas, and the copy that reached Brazoria was printed and widely distributed. A committee including John Dunn, William S. Brown, William G. Hill, and Benjamin J. White carried the original copy to San Felipe and delivered it to the General Council. The council referred the declaration to the Committee on State and Judiciary. The arrival of the document caused some embarrassment because negotiations with José Antonio Mexía and Julián Pedro Miracle were then pending in San Felipe to ascertain whether the true intentions of the Texans were independence or cooperation with the Federalists in northern Mexico. Members of the council warned the Goliad messengers not to circulate the declaration further, and the committee report on the declaration said that it had been inconsiderately adopted. The document was to remain in the files of the secretary without further action. The declaration anticipated by two days Stephen F. Austin's pronouncement favoring independence made at Velasco on 22 December, and preceded the Texas Declaration of Independence by 73 days. The chief importance of the Goliad Declaration was its alienation from Texas of the support of the Federalists of northern Mexico. *Hobart Huson*

Gonzales, Battle of. A skirmish generally called the first battle of the Texas Revolution. When Domingo de Ugartechea, military commander in Texas, received word that the American colonists of Gonzales refused to surrender a small cannon that had been given that settlement in 1831 as a defense against Indians, he dispatched Francisco de Castañeda and 100 dragoons to retrieve it. The troops reached the Guadalupe River opposite Gonzales on 29 September 1835 and found their path blocked by high water and 18 militiamen (later called the "Old Eighteen"). Castañeda announced that he carried a dispatch for alcalde Andrew Ponton but was informed that Ponton was out of town and that the Mexican dragoons would have to wait on the west side of the river until he returned. Unable to proceed, Castañeda pitched camp 300 yards from the ford. Meanwhile, the men of Gonzales summoned reinforcements. After a Coushatta Indian informed Castañeda that the Texan volunteers now numbered at least 140, the Mexican officer left the ford and sought another place not so well defended, where he could "cross without any embarrassment." Around sundown on 1 October he ordered his dragoons to pitch camp seven miles upriver from the contested ford on land belonging to colonist Ezekiel Williams. The Texans marched upriver toward Castañeda's new camp and on 2 October attacked the Mexicans. Castañeda ordered his men to fall back to a low rise behind their camp. During a lull in the

fighting Castañeda arranged a parley with the Texan commander, John Henry Moore, who stated that the Texans were fighting to keep their cannon and to uphold the Constitution of 1824. Castañeda then assured Moore that he was himself a Federalist and opposed to the policies of Santa Anna. He added that he had no wish to fight colonists, but had orders to reclaim the cannon. Castañeda declined Moore's invitation to join the Texans in their fight. When the battle resumed, Castañeda, finding himself outnumbered and outgunned, ordered a withdrawal toward Bexar. In his report to Ugartechea, he stated that "since the orders from your Lordship were for me to withdraw without compromising the honor of Mexican arms, I did so." The "battle" marked a clear break between the American colonists and the Mexican government. *Stephen L. Hardin*

Gonzales, Texas. County seat of Gonzales County; at the confluence of the Guadalupe and San Marcos rivers. The site was surveyed by James Kerr as the capital of DeWitt's colony in 1825 and named for Rafael Gonzales, governor of Coahuila and Texas. It was abandoned in July 1826 after two Indian attacks and was rebuilt on the Guadalupe River in 1827. Gonzales was surveyed a second time, by Byrd Lockhart in August 1832, when it was given 16 leagues of land for town development. As the westernmost point of Anglo-American settlement and the closest town to San Antonio de Béxar, it was the center of much Texas revolutionary activity. On 2 October 1835, Texans led by John H. Moore resisted Mexican dragoons sent to retrieve the town cannon. Challenging the Mexicans to "come and take it," the Texans rallied around the gun and fought the battle of Gonzales, the first skirmish of the Texas Revolution. On 11 October, Stephen F. Austin took command of the volunteer army that had concentrated at Gonzales and there made preparations for the siege of Bexar. The following February the Gonzales Ranging Company of Mounted Volunteers rode to the aid of Travis's command during the battle of the Alamo, where the 32 men of the Gonzales contingent perished on 6 March 1836. On 13 March of that year Susanna W. Dickinson, widow of one of the Alamo defenders, and Joe, Travis's slave, arrived in Gonzales with news of the Alamo slaughter. Sam Houston, who was there attempting to organize the Texas army, had the town burned and ordered a

"View of courthouse, Gonzales, Texas," from *A Description of Western Texas*, compiled by M. Whillden, published by Galveston, Harrisburg & San Antonio Railway Company, Galveston, 1876. Courtesy TSL. The description in this immigrant's guide to Texas reads: "Gonzales, the county seat of Gonzales County, is situated on the Guadalupe river, a short distance below its junction with the San Marcos. The town has about fifteen hundred inhabitants."

retreat, thus precipitating the Runaway Scrape. After the battle of San Jacinto many citizens remained in exile. In 1837 the Republic of Texas incorporated Gonzales and established Gonzales County, but the city council did not have its first meeting until March 1839. A post office opened in January 1839. By the early 1840s rebuilding of the town was concentrated on the original townsite near the Guadalupe River. Many Gonzales volunteers, responding to the Comanche foray known as the Linnville Raid of 1840, rushed to join the battle of Plum Creek. In 1841 a Baptist church, the first in Gonzales, was built. In 1850 Gonzales had a population of 300. In 1851 Gonzales College opened in the town's first permanent school building. This was the first college in Texas to award diplomas to women. The Gonzales *Inquirer* was established in 1853 and was one of the six oldest county papers still operating in Texas in 1995. In 1860 the town had a population of 1,703. Gonzales was incorporated in 1880 and in 1884 had six churches, four schools, a courthouse, two banks, a 500-seat opera house, a library, gas and water works, several lodges, gristmills, cotton gins, several stores, and a population of 2,900. Though bypassed by the Galveston, Harrisburg and San Antonio Railway in 1874, the community was connected by a rail spur to Harwood; on the railroad the community shipped cotton, wool, hides, cattle, horses, cottonseed, and pecans. In 1885 the San Antonio and Aransas Pass Railway began service to Gonzales. The town declined from 4,297 inhabitants in 1900 to 3,139 in 1910, then recovered to 4,722 in 1940. In 1947 the Texas A&M Poultry Experiment Station was established in Gonzales. That same year the town's first radio station, KCTI, went on the air. In 1949 the community staged the first Fryer Frolic, a county-wide celebration that emphasized development of the poultry industry, one of the mainstays of the Gonzales economy. The town's population reached 5,630 in 1950 and 6,527 in 1990. The Gonzales Museum, established in 1936, houses a collection of historical artifacts and weapons. The Eggleston House, a restored dog-trot cabin maintained by the town, is perhaps the finest example of its type. The old 1887 jailhouse is also preserved and serves as headquarters of the Gonzales Chamber of Commerce. Special events include the annual Come-and-Take-It Days, a commemoration of Gonzales as the "Lexington of Texas."

Stephen L. Hardin

Goodfellow Air Force Base. Two miles south of San Angelo. San Angelo Field was designated as a site for U.S. Army Air Corps pilot training in June 1940 and opened in August as the home of the San Angelo Air Corps Basic Flying Training School. It was renamed in 1941 in honor of John J. Goodfellow, Jr., who was killed in France in World War I. The first class of aviation cadets arrived for basic flight training in BT-13 aircraft in January 1941. Members of the Women's Airforce Service Pilots began duty in June 1943. In September 1945 the mission was changed to primary flight training. The base was deactivated in May 1947. Goodfellow Field was reopened in December 1947 as Goodfellow Air Force Base, a basic pilot-training school of the newly independent U.S. Air Force. In June 1954 the base mission was changed to multi-engine flight training in B-25 twin-engine Mitchell light bombers. In February 1956 Goodfellow was made a permanent military installation. When its flight-training mission ended in 1958 with the graduation of the last pilot class, almost 20,000 officers and cadets had been trained at the Texas base. On October 1, 1958, under control of the U.S. Air Force

Security Service, Goodfellow began providing cryptological training to students from all four United States military services. Although its mission remained the same, Goodfellow AFB was returned to the Air Training Command on July 1, 1978. After several threats during the 1970s to deactivate the San Angelo installation, the base was removed from the closure list in 1981 and assigned an additional mission as part of the phased-array radar-warning system, a nationwide network of radar protection against sea-launched ballistic missiles. The actual site of the weapons system, one of only four such systems in the continental United States, was to be a 130-acre tract in the northeast part of Schleicher County, south of San Angelo.

In 1985 the base was designated a technical training center. During the next three years the center brought to Goodfellow advanced imagery training from Offutt Air Force Base, Nebraska, electronic-intelligence-operations training from Keesler Air Force Base, Mississippi, and targeting-intelligence applications and general-intelligence training from Lowry Air Force Base, Colorado. In July 1993 the 17th Training Wing was activated at Goodfellow. Its history of combat operations goes back to World War I. In World War II it conducted the "Doolittle Raid" on Tokyo. Under the designation 17th Bombardment Wing it participated in the Korean War. During the Vietnam period the wing conducted B-52 refueling. After being redesignated the 17th Reconnaissance Wing in October 1982, it operated TR-1 high-altitude reconnaissance aircraft during Desert Shield and Desert Storm on the Persian Gulf. The wing was deactivated in 1991, then was reactivated as the training wing at Goodfellow, after which it provided cryptological and general-intelligence training for air force, army, navy, and marine personnel as well as students from Allied countries. In the 1990s Goodfellow AFB underwent extensive modernization.

Sangeeta Singg and William A. Allen

Good Neighbor Commission. A state agency established in 1943 to handle social, cultural, and economic problems of Mexican Americans in Texas and to strengthen political ties with Latin America. The wartime demand for field hands and other laborers in the Southwest led to the 1942 *bracero* agreement between Mexico and the United States, but in June 1943 the Mexican government placed a ban on the movement of laborers into Texas because of discrimination against Mexicans. Franklin D. Roosevelt's Office of Inter-American Affairs dispatched field representatives to Texas and California in 1943. Governor Coke Stevenson appointed the six-man Good Neighbor Commission, funded by the OIAA. The commission emphasized education, the improvement of housing and health measures for migrant workers, and the solution of human-relations problems. The GNC was placed on the state payroll in 1945. In 1947 Mexico lifted the ban on Texas, but GNC executive secretary Pauline R. Kibbe reported that despite the new agreement, discrimination and poor housing were still prevalent. In 1948 commission chairman Bob Smith avoided the migrant labor issue but continued to carry out antidiscrimination work through Tom Sutherland, the new executive secretary, who helped in desegregating the Texas public schools in favor of Mexican Americans. After the Felix Longoria affair in 1949, under oilman Neville Penrose the GNC turned its discrimination issues partly over to the newly founded Texas Council on Human Relations, and the commission became involved in counseling and information services, translating for other agencies, and publicity and liaison between the Texas government and Mexican agencies. Its executive directors developed close ties with LULAC and the American G.I. Forum. In 1965 the Texas Council on Migrant Labor was abolished and its work transferred to the commission with an increased staff and budget. The GNC, however, could not compete with the newly founded federal Office of Economic Opportunity, which took over many of the problems originally handled by the state agency. In 1977 the commission survived sunset review as an agency responsible for overseeing migrant problems, developing national and international cooperation, and supporting educational exchange programs with Mexico. During the next 10 years the duties of the GNC were gradually absorbed by other agencies, however, and budget cuts in 1987 resulted in its abolition.

George N. Green

Goodnight, Charles. Rancher; b. Macoupin County, Illinois, 5 March 1836; d. Phoenix, 12 December 1929; m. Mollie Dyer (1870); m. Corinne Goodnight (1927). The family moved to Milam County in 1845. With John Wesley Sheek, Goodnight started raising and trailing cattle. He helped Oliver Loving send a herd to the Rocky Mountain mining camps during the gold rush. Goodnight and his neighbors joined Capt. Jack Cureton's rangers, with whom he served as a scout and guide and took part in the recapture of Cynthia Ann Parker. In the Civil War, Cureton's rangers, including Goodnight, were attached to the Frontier Regiment. After his service Goodnight sought out a new range in Throckmorton County, where Indians ran off nearly 2,000 head of his cattle in September 1865. In 1866 he and Loving organized the drive that resulted in the Goodnight–Loving Trail. At the end of their third trip to Fort Sumner in 1867, Loving died from wounds he received in a fight with Indians. In the winter of 1869 Goodnight established his Rock Cañon Ranch on the Arkansas River five miles west of Pueblo. Around that time people started calling him "Colonel." After he married Mollie in Hickman, Kentucky, the newlyweds returned to the Rock Cañon. In 1871 Goodnight trailed cattle with John Chisum to clear a profit of $17,000. In addition he farmed with irrigation, planted an apple orchard, and invested heavily in farmlands and city lots in Pueblo. Among other services he helped found the Stock Growers' Bank of Pueblo and was part owner of the opera house, a meat-packing facility at Las Animas, and other businesses in the area. Along with neighboring cattlemen such as Hank Cresswell, he formed Colorado's first stock raisers' association in November 1871 and in 1875 laid out the Goodnight Trail from Alamogordo Creek in New Mexico to Granada, Colorado.

But overstocked ranges and the panic of 1873 caused a financial loss that led Goodnight to seek a virgin grassland. After sending his wife to relatives in California, in the fall of 1875 he moved his remaining 1,600 longhorn cattle to the upper Canadian River at Rincón de las Piedras, New Mexico, for the winter. With a Mexican cowhand named Panchito, he investigated the vast Panhandle of Texas, recently cleared of hostile Indians, and decided on Palo Duro Canyon as the ideal spot for a ranch. With borrowed money he moved his herd to a range near the future site of Tascosa. He had made a pact with Casimero Romero in which the *pastores* of New Mexico agreed to limit their operations to the Canadian and its tributaries, while Goodnight would have exclusive use of the headwaters and

Charles Goodnight. Courtesy Western History Collections, University of Oklahoma Library.

canyons of the Red River. On 23 October 1876 the Goodnight company, the first cattle outfit in the Panhandle, reached the edge of the canyon in Randall County and set up camp. Within the bounds of the present Palo Duro Canyon State Scenic Park, Goodnight constructed a dugout with abandoned Comanche lodge poles as rafters. Subsequently, farther to the southeast in Armstrong County, he built a house. In Denver, where he went to secure more capital and arrange to fetch Mollie, he struck an agreement with John Adair to expand the ranch into a large-scale operation. In May 1877 the Goodnights and Adairs, along with four cowboys, arrived at the Home Ranch with 100 Durham bulls and four wagons loaded with provisions. On 18 June they drew up the five-year contract that launched the JA Ranch, with Goodnight retaining one-third interest and an annual salary of $2,500 as resident manager. During his 11 years with the JA, Goodnight devoted his time and energy to expanding the range, building up the herd, and establishing law and order in the Panhandle. In the summer of 1878 he took the first JA trail herd north to Dodge City, the nearest railhead, over the route that became the Palo Duro–Dodge City Trail, well-used in subsequent years by Panhandle ranchers. Late that fall, when destitute Indians from the reservations came to hunt the now-scarce buffalo, Goodnight made his famous treaty with Quanah Parker in which he promised two cattle every other day for Parker's followers provided they did not disturb the JA herd. In 1879 Goodnight moved the JA headquarters to its present location. Although he strictly enforced his rules against gambling, drinking, and fighting, he usually was able to hire the cowboys he needed. In 1880 Goodnight helped organize and served as first president of the Panhandle Stock Association in Mobeetie. Two years later he bought the Quitaque (Lazy F) Ranch and reportedly became the first Panhandle rancher to build fences of barbed wire. By the time of Adair's death in 1885, the JA had reached its maximum of 1,325,000 acres, on which grazed more than 100,000 head of Goodnight's carefully bred cattle. In addition, Goodnight was a pioneer in the use of artificial watering facilities and the ownership of permanent ranges in fee. As an early believer in improvement through breeding, he developed one of the nation's finest herds through the introduction of Hereford bulls. With his wife's encouragement, he also started a domestic buffalo herd, sired by a bull he named Old Sikes, from which he developed the "cattalo" by crossing bison with polled Angus cattle. He also invented the first practical sidesaddle, with an additional horn to rest the left knee, for his wife.

In 1886 Goodnight, with two big-city partners, began investing in the Inter-State Land Company, for which he sold shares in land along the Texas–New Mexico border purchased from the Beales–Royuela grant, an old Spanish land grant. At the same time he became involved in the Grass Lease Fight, from which he emerged as a leader for the big cattlemen's interests, but was accused by the press of robbing money from the schoolchildren of Texas. Feeling the need to downsize, he sold his interest in the JA after the second contract expired in 1887. He retained interest in the Quitaque Ranch, half of which he sold to L. R. Moore of Kansas City. Even so, Mrs. Adair retained his services as manager of the JA until 1888, when John C. Farrington succeeded him. Soon after his exit from the JA ownership, Goodnight bought 160 sections in Armstrong County near the Fort Worth and Denver City line, including the Sacra–Sugg Ranch on the Salt Fork and some school land. Near the town that bears his name he built his spacious, two-story ranchhouse, into which he and his wife moved in 1887. After selling his remaining interest in the Quitaque to Moore in 1890, Goodnight invested heavily in a Mexican gold and silver mining venture in Chihuahua; that enterprise proved a failure. Furthermore, his investments in the Inter-State Land Company reduced his fortune considerably after federal courts declared the Beales–Royuela grant invalid. In 1893 he was among the cowmen compensated in part for losses they suffered to the Comanchero trade during the 1860s. As civic leaders and promoters of the higher education he was denied, the colonel and his wife opened Goodnight College at Goodnight in 1898. After 1900 Goodnight limited his ranching activities to 60 sections surrounding his house and near the railroad. There he continued his experiments with buffalo and also kept elk, antelope, and various other animals in zoo-like enclosures, as well as different species of fowl. The Goodnight Ranch became a major Panhandle tourist attraction and featured buffalo meat on its menus. Buffalo from the Goodnight herd were shipped to zoos in New York and other eastern cities, Yellowstone National Park, and even to Europe. As a friend of Quanah Parker and other Plains Indian leaders in Oklahoma, Goodnight staged occasional buffalo hunts for former braves. In addition, he grew Armstrong County's first wheat crop and conducted other agricultural experiments with the encouragement of the pioneer botanist Luther Burbank. The colonel was often called the "Burbank of the Range."

The Goodnights reared a foster child, Cleo Hubbard. After his wife's death in April 1926, Goodnight fell seriously ill but was soon nursed back to health by Corinne Goodnight, a young nurse and telegraph operator from Butte, Montana, with whom he had been corresponding because of their mutual surnames. He celebrated his 91st birthday by marrying her. Shortly afterward they sold the ranch, with the stipulation that he could live there for the rest of his life, and bought a summer house in Clarendon. Goodnight spent his last winters in Phoenix, Arizona, where he was often interviewed by Western authors, journalists, and historians, including J. Evetts Haley. Laura V. Hamner published a biographical novel of Goodnight, *The No-Gun Man of Texas* (1935), but Haley's monumental *Charles Goodnight: Cowman and Plainsman* (1936) remains the standard scholarly work. Goodnight's papers are housed at the Panhandle–Plains Historical Museum. Streets in several Panhandle towns bear his name, as do the Charles Goodnight Memorial Trail and the highway to Palo Duro Canyon State Scenic Park, which includes a restored dugout thought to have been his first 1876 quarters. The Goodnight ranchhouse, owned since 1933 by the Mattie Hedgecoke estate of Amarillo, still stands near U.S. Highway 287. In 1958 Goodnight was one of the original five voted into the National Cowboy Hall of Fame in Oklahoma City. *H. Allen Anderson*

Goodnight–Loving Trail. Also Goodnight Trail; named for Charles Goodnight and Oliver Loving; extended from Young County, Texas, southwest to Horsehead Crossing on the Pecos River, up the Pecos to Fort Sumner, New Mexico, and north. In 1866 Goodnight and Loving drove the first two herds of longhorns over the southern extent of the trail. Later that year Loving blazed the first northern extension of the trail. It ran north from Fort Sumner up the Pecos to Las Vegas, then followed the Santa Fe Trail to Raton Pass and around the base of the Rockies via Trinidad and Pueblo to Denver. In the fall of 1867 Goodnight rerouted the trail 50 or 60 miles to the east before swinging back northwestward to Raton Pass. At the head of Apishapa Canyon, 40 miles northeast of Trinidad, he set up a ranch and cattle-relay station. In 1868 Goodnight entered into a contract to deliver his cattle to John W. Iliff at the Union Pacific Railroad town of Cheyenne, Wyoming. From the Arkansas valley near Pueblo, Goodnight and his men struck out due north, passing east of Denver, to the South Platte River. They crossed that stream at the site of present Greeley and followed a tributary, Crow Creek, to Cheyenne, where the delivery was made. Afterward, Goodnight and his men went back to New Mexico to buy more cattle from John S. Chisum at Bosque Grande. Returning north, Goodnight further "straightened out" the trail by leaving the Pecos north of Fort Sumner and traveling north to Alamogordo Creek and across the plains via Cuervo Creek and its tributaries to a spot on the Canadian River twenty miles west of Fort Bascom. From there he proceeded to the Cimarron Seco west of Capulin Mountain. In order to avoid "Uncle Dick" Wootton's toll station at Raton, Goodnight opened a new, easier passageway through Tinchera Pass into Colorado. The Goodnight–Loving Trail was thus routed, and although Goodnight himself made only one more delivery at Cheyenne, many cattle concerns from Texas, New Mexico, and Colorado used all or portions of the trail extensively until they gained access to railroads in the early 1880s. *T. C. Richardson*

Ellis County Courthouse, Waxahachie, by J. Riely Gordon, ca. 1894–96. Watercolor. Courtesy Architectural Drawings Collection, University of Texas at Austin. This Romanesque Revival courthouse, built of pink granite and red sandstone, features a tower with tournelles and a clock.

Gordon, James Riely. Architect; b. Winchester, Virginia, 2 August 1863; d. Pelham Heights, New York, 16 March 1937; m. Mary Lamar Sprigg (1889); 1 daughter. The family moved to Texas in 1874, and Gordon learned applied engineering by working with the International–Great Northern Railroad. He studied architecture with W. C. Dobson and J. N. Preston and worked in the office of the supervising architect of the United States in Washington. He worked in San Antonio from 1884 to 1900 and Dallas from 1900 to 1902. During his period of practice in Texas he designed hundreds of buildings. He maintained several offices in Texas, one in Shreveport, and another in Phoenix. His first major job was to supervise the construction of the Federal Courthouse and Post Office in San Antonio (1886–89). His design for the Texas Building at the World's Columbian Exposition in Chicago (1892–93) won a medal of merit. Remembered primarily for his courthouses, Gordon designed no fewer than 18 in Texas. In the later twentieth century 12 were still standing, in Bexar, Comal, Ellis, Erath, Fayette, Gonzales, Harrison, Hopkins, Lee, McLennan, Victoria, and Wise counties. Ten were still serving their original purpose. His most important structure built outside Texas is the Arizona Capitol, done for the territorial government (1898–1900). Although most of Gordon's commercial buildings have not survived, the fronts of the Staacke and Stevens buildings in San Antonio have been saved by the San Antonio Conservation Society, and the Riverside Building has been adapted to modern needs. Of many important examples of Gordon's work in Dallas, only the John Deere structure remains. The best preserved of all is probably

the Nolte National Bank in Seguin (1896). Among his fine homes, the most splendid was that for Mrs. Henrietta King in Corpus Christi (demolished). One of the most handsome surviving residences was built for George Kalteyer (1892–93) at 425 King William Street in San Antonio. It has been restored with sympathy and care. During his career in the state, Gordon progressed from a charming and eclectic style in the Moorish manner into a highly effective Romanesque style somewhat like that of Henry Hobson Richardson. His version of this style is seen at its best in the courthouses of Wise, Ellis, and several other counties. During his last years in Texas he worked in a Classical or Beaux-Arts style. The Harrison and McLennan county courthouses are outstanding examples. In 1903 Gordon transferred his center of operations to New York. There he had a distinguished career, which included 13 terms as president of the New York Society of Architects. His records, plans, and other papers are at the University of Texas at Austin.   *Glenn N. Patton*

Government. When Texas was annexed by the U.S. in 1845, Texas government had been shaped largely within the Anglo-American tradition. The Constitution of the Republic of Texas (1836) clearly rested on Anglo-American principles, as did the proposed constitution drafted in 1833 for a separate state within the Mexican Federal Republic. Spanish and Mexican influences were apparent also, however. Major legacies reflected in Texas constitutions were the merger of law and equity, community property, and protection of certain personal property from forced seizure for debt. An extension from the latter was similar protection for the homestead, an innovation claimed by Texas.

1845–61. The first Texas state constitution, framed in 1845 as a condition of admission to the U.S., was based on constitutional principles common in the U.S., among them the concept of a written constitution itself, whose source of authority was the people (popular sovereignty), guarantees of individual rights, a republican form of government, and separation of powers. One state constitutional principle of enduring significance is that state legislatures, as representative of the people, have all powers not denied by the state constitution, the U.S. Constitution, or other valid federal laws. Included is the police power by which public health, safety, morals, and welfare are promoted. Although sharing common principles, state constitutions also differ from one another, influenced by their state and regional politics and culture. The protection of slavery in early Texas constitutions was obviously a product of Southern regionalism.

The Texas statehood constitution, the Constitution of 1845, established a governmental structure that with modifications and supplementation has been carried forward in all subsequent charters. The legislative article provided for a bicameral legislature whose House members served two-year terms and whose senators served four-year staggered terms; for biennial regular sessions; for election of the speaker by the House and the lieutenant governor, who was president of the Senate, by the voters. Legislative powers included the power of the purse, with sole power to initiate revenue measures vested in the House. Debt was strictly limited, but such general principles as equality and uniformity governed taxation, and only the legislature could authorize appropriations. Longstanding concerns about land titles, public lands (Texas was the only state to retain its public land upon admission to the Union), and education, including a precursor of the Permanent School Fund, were addressed. The judicial article, which followed the legislative, provided for a hierarchical structure of courts composed of the state Supreme Court, district courts, and "inferior courts" to be established by legislation. Supreme Court and district judges were appointed by the governor with Senate consent for six-year terms. The attorney general, designated a judicial officer, was also a gubernatorial appointee, but district attorneys were selected by the legislature. Trial by jury was protected "in all cases of law or equity." The executive article was the only one in five Texas state constitutions to provide for the popular election of only two executive officers, the governor and the lieutenant governor, and this was changed in 1850. The governor was given a two-year term, but eligibility was limited to four years in any six. Gubernatorial powers included the veto (subject to override by two-thirds of the legislature), sending messages to the legislature, adjourning the legislature if the houses could not agree, and calling special sessions. The governor could grant clemency and served as commander in chief of the state's military forces. Appointment power was extended to the secretary of state (carried forward in all subsequent state charters), judges, and the attorney general, but the legislature selected the two major fiscal officers, the state treasurer and the comptroller of public accounts, and district attorneys, a unique feature of the 1845 constitution.

The statehood constitution, in common with all Texas constitutions, provided only partially for the state's administrative structure, leaving for legislation the necessary legal framework and financial support of the officers and agencies receiving constitutional recognition and adding others not of constitutional stature. In the early years of statehood, the General Land Office (continued from the republic constitution), the adjutant general, state asylums (eleemosynary institutions) for the insane, deaf, and blind, and the Texas Rangers were among the few agencies and officers established by the legislature in addition to the constitutional officers already named. The county, a political subdivision of the utmost importance in Texas government since independence from Mexico, was the only local government referred to in the Constitution of 1845. Provision was made for the establishment of counties and for several elective county officers, including the sheriff, justice of the peace, constable, and coroner. Other officers were added by legislation, which also required counties to build roads, jails, and county courthouses. Municipalities were established by statute, at first by special act, until in 1858 the first general law providing for incorporation was passed. A basic legal principle governing state-local relations is that the legislature, unless restricted by the state constitution, has the power to form, alter, or abolish local governments, regarded as "creatures of the state."

The 1845 Constitution incorporated a rigid amending process that required two legislative approvals by a two-thirds vote with an intervening election at which a majority of all voters voting for representatives had to approve. The rigidity was retained until the Constitution of 1876 except for substituting a majority of voters on the amendment in the next three charters. The statehood charter was amended only once. The 1850 amendment established a "plural executive" whereby the governor must share power with other popularly elected executives, in this case the lieutenant governor, state treasurer, comptroller, general land commissioner, and attorney general (designated an executive officer in 1869 and 1876). It also provided for popular election of judges and district attorneys.

The right to vote was liberal for the times, based on universal white manhood suffrage without property qualifications. One exception was the absolute disqualification of members of the U.S. armed forces (soldiers, sailors, and marines), an exclusion retained until 1954. The Bill of Rights (Article I) contained rights, many from the Republic of Texas charter, traditional in the U.S., such as freedom of speech, press, assembly, and religion, equality expressed in social-contract terms, property rights, rights of persons accused of crime, trial by jury in civil and criminal cases, and a general proviso that the rights "shall forever remain inviolate." The statehood constitution protected slavery, since slaves were not considered "persons" in the full sense.

1861–75. As momentous as were the Civil War and its aftermath, continuity outweighed change in the fundamental structure of Texas government provided for in the four constitutions from 1861 to 1875. Constitutionally speaking, Texas was adjudged (in *Texas v. White*) never to have left the Union. The Constitution of 1861 approved after secession and the 1866 charter drafted under presidential Reconstruction were actually amendments to the 1845 constitution. The 1861 amendments, which were never submitted to the voters, were minimal with respect to structure. A new provision expressly authorizing the legislature to call a constitutional convention had no lasting effect, but the requirement that amendments be proposed only at regular legislative sessions was not altered until 1972. The 1866 revisions introduced some important provisions, the most significant of which was the governor's power to veto items of appropriation bills, a reform that originated with the Constitution of the Confederate States of America. The document was also the first to confer constitutional status on the county courts as integral parts of the judicial system and to set up the county commissioners' court in its present form. Moreover, the constitution for the first time directed the legislature to organize a university, to educate black children (in separate schools), and to include a constitutional structure for state administration of the public schools. Although approved by the voters, the constitution was rejected within a few months by the newly elected Radical-dominated Congress.

The Constitution of 1869, drafted under congressional Reconstruction by a convention meeting in 1868–69, was within Texas constitutional traditions with some important exceptions unique to the document, among which were annual legislative sessions and six-year overlapping terms for senators. Gubernatorial appointment powers, augmented considerably by the legislature and the necessity of filling numerous vacancies, were not without precedent in the 1845 and 1866 documents. Four-year executive terms originated in 1866. It is of interest that the governor actually lost power in 1869, the power to adjourn the legislature granted in the earlier charters. Although much of local government was retained, county courts were abolished and in general power was more centralized. The 1869 charter also gave unprecedented support for public education under centralized administration.

The voters ratified the new constitution and elected officers to the new government at the same election in 1869. The Republican party won control of the legislature for the first and, to date, the only time. A few months later, normal relations were restored between Texas and the U.S. Although much of benefit occurred under the 1869 constitution and Republican leadership, particularly in education and other public services, the regime was unpopular with the white majority for many reasons, such as the establishment and deployment of the State Police, martial law, high taxes and debt, and the new public-education system. But the most basic problem was the legitimacy of the political order, government having been organized under federal military rule (*see* Fifth Military District) and approved in an election fraught with irregularities. After the Democrats regained governmental control in 1872–73, it was a foregone conclusion that a new constitution would be adopted. Following rejection by the legislature of a proposed document prepared by a joint legislative committee in 1874, a constitutional convention call was referred to and accepted by the voters, who elected delegates at the same election.

The Constitution of 1876, drafted by the Constitutional Convention of 1875, is still in effect. The convention, at which the Democrats dominated but the Grange was the most important interest group, restored most of the earlier structural features changed by the 1869 charter, such as biennial legislative sessions, four-year terms for senators, two-year terms for governor (but without term limits), election of the attorney general and judges, and inclusion of a county court. But there were new provisions as well. The House was scheduled to reach a maximum of 150 members as population grew, and the size of the Senate was fixed at 31. The governor could veto bills after the session ended and was given more time to consider bills during sessions before taking action. Also, for the first time, the chief executive was empowered to specify legislation to be considered at special sessions. A new court, the Court of Appeals, vested with appellate jurisdiction in criminal and some civil cases, was established, and the Supreme Court's jurisdiction was limited to civil cases only. Municipalities with populations of 10,000 or fewer had to be chartered by general law, while larger cities might have their charters granted and amended by special (local) law. Compensation for legislators, the governor, the attorney general, and certain other officers was set in the constitution and could not be changed without amending the constitution.

Most attention has been paid the onerous fiscal restrictions placed on the legislature by the new charter. Of enormous importance were limits on property-tax rates, the first in a Texas constitution, and the flat ban on financial assistance from state and local governments to individuals, associations, or corporations, exceptions to which required constitutional expression. The limit on state debt, although severe, was not as restrictive as that of the 1845 charter. Other restrictions included a prohibition against state bank corporations, carried over from the first three constitutions, and a long list of subjects on which the legislature could not enact a special or local law. The convention even tried to turn the legislature into one of limited rather than plenary powers by enumerating subjects on which it could legislate, but the provision was never enforced by the courts. The articles on railroads, the regulation of which was a major goal of the Grangers, and private corporations also included some restraints on the legislature by mandates or prohibitions. Suffrage provisions were liberal, the convention having defeated the proposal for a poll tax. Aliens who had indicated their intention of becoming citizens were eligible to vote, a continuation from the 1869 charter. For the first time, voting in municipal tax and bond elections was limited to property owners. The Bill of Rights was retained, with some revisions and additions from preceding constitutions. Of particular significance were new provisions prohibiting appropriations for sectarian purposes and a requirement that officeholders "acknowledge the existence of a Supreme Being." As a direct result of Civil War and Reconstruction experiences, there was an absolute ban on the suspension of the writ of habeas corpus. In sharp contrast to all the other Texas constitutions, the amending article provided for an easy amending process. A proposed amendment required a two-thirds vote of the legislature in regular session and the approval of a majority of voters. The process was used frequently in the years ahead.

1876–99. The most significant developments in governmental organization during the last quarter of the nineteenth century were in administration and the judiciary. There were no constitutional changes by amendment in the legislature, the governorship, or cities and counties, only minor changes in the suffrage, and none in the Bill of Rights. The establishment of the Railroad Commission by the legislature in 1891 was a major event. A constitutional amendment authorizing the legislature to establish a railroad regulatory agency was the main issue in the gubernatorial election of 1890. Four years later another amendment changed the agency from an appointive to an elective body whose three members serve six-year staggered terms. A second change of lasting importance was the restructuring of the state's appellate courts by an amendment ratified in 1891. The Court of Appeals was transformed into the Texas Court of Criminal Appeals, which has jurisdiction over criminal cases only; this arrangement left civil cases to the Supreme Court and established the bifurcated Texas judiciary with two courts of last resort. The amendment also set up new intermediate courts of appeals with jurisdiction limited to civil cases. The courts of civil appeals remained without criminal jurisdiction until 1980. A development at the lowest level of the judicial system was the establishment by statute in 1899 of corporation courts (renamed municipal courts in 1969) in every incorporated municipality in the state.

During this period the state's system of higher education finally took shape. The University of Texas was established more than 40 years after the Congress of the Republic of Texas had set aside land in 1839 for such an institution (actually for two, one in the east and one in the west). In pursuance of a mandate in the 1876 Constitution, the legislature enacted laws in 1881 providing for a board of regents, fees, and other needs, and the university was formally opened in 1883. In an election in 1881 the voters had selected Austin as the site. A primary source of funding was the Permanent University Fund, continued in the Constitution of 1876 from its 1858 origins but denied the rich railroad lands originally assigned. The legislature substituted arid lands in West Texas that in the next century proved rich in petroleum. Texas A&M, supported by land grants under the Morrill Act of 1862 and state funds, preceded the University of Texas by accepting students in 1876. Although the 1876 constitution made it a "department of the University of Texas," A&M has always operated under its own board of regents. The 1876 constitution also provided for a general college for "colored youth," but it was never built; in its stead the legislature established Prairie View State Normal School, which began operation in 1885. The University of Texas Medical Branch at Galveston opened in 1891.

Texas State College for Women in Denton did not accept students until 1903, after its establishment in 1901. At the public-school level a constitutional amendment in 1883 authorized the legislature to form school districts empowered to levy property taxes for the support and maintenance of public schools. The amendment also increased state funding for public education.

1900–29. During the first 30 years of the twentieth century there were virtually no significant constitutional changes in the three branches of state government, although serious attempts were made to revise the constitution by the convention method. The legislature, with Progressive support, adopted two resolutions to place on the ballot a convention call, but in 1917 the governor vetoed the first and in 1919 the voters rejected the second. Also, though the governorship did not change by amendment, Governor James E. Ferguson was impeached and removed from office in 1917, the first and only time that a Texas governor has been forced by this method to leave office. Legislative sessions took on a peculiar cast from 1909 to 1930, explained largely by constitutional provisions that paid legislators $5 a day for the first 60 days of a regular session but only $2 thereafter, and $5 a day for special sessions. Regular sessions were short, all but one ending in March. They were followed by an average 2.7 special sessions every legislature (five in 1929–30). The pattern was broken by the passage of a constitutional amendment increasing legislative pay. Governmental changes in the executive branch were primarily administrative. As Texas became more urban and industrial, governmental regulations and services increased correspondingly. A more specialized organization developed as agencies were separated from multifunctional boards and commissions; others were abolished (23 in 1919), and new agencies were instituted. Among the highlights were the establishment of a separate banking department in 1923 (an amendment in 1904 had repealed the constitutional prohibition against state bank corporations), enforcement of labor laws by the Bureau of Labor Statistics set up in 1909 and of the 1913 workers' compensation law by the Industrial Accident Board in 1917, establishment of the state highway department also in 1917 as a condition of federal aid, and separate insurance and agricultural agencies in 1927. (The agricultural commissioner was made a separate elective officer in 1907.) In 1928 a constitutional amendment permitted the legislature to determine the method of selection and the composition of the state board of education. The board was changed from a three-member body (comptroller of public accounts, secretary of state, and governor) to a nine-member board appointed by the governor with Senate consent. The Railroad Commission acquired regulatory power over pipelines in 1917 and over the conservation and production of petroleum and natural gas in 1919; the latter power made it a leading influence in national and international oil and gas markets. It also regulated buses and trucks. In 1929 the Texas Civil Judicial Council (renamed the Texas Judicial Council in 1975) was formed by statute to conduct a continuous study of the Texas judicial system. The council has been a major judicial agency from its inception. A second important change was the division of the state into nine administrative judicial regions to provide management of district courts on a regional basis, authorized by statute in 1927.

Local government was enormously affected by the passage in 1912 of the "Home Rule Amendment," which allows municipalities of more than 5,000 population to adopt their own charters and to pass ordinances of their own choosing, subject only to the Texas constitution and general laws. By another amendment (1909), cities with 5,000 or fewer residents are chartered by general law only, although cities operating under special charters are allowed to continue to do so. With respect to forms of city government, Galveston attracted national attention in 1901 by the adoption of the commission form after the disastrous Galveston hurricane of 1900. Local government was also affected by the "Conservation Amendment" of 1917, which permitted the formation of special districts with unlimited borrowing and taxing power to conserve and develop water resources. Special districts eventually became the most numerous units of local government in Texas.

Changes of considerable magnitude occurred in election and suffrage law beginning with the 1902 constitutional amendment that made payment of the poll tax a requirement for voting. The administration of the poll-tax system also served as a statewide voter registration system, hitherto prohibited by the 1876 constitution. The Terrell Election Law of 1905 was the first to require a statewide direct-primary system for political parties polling a given number of votes (100,000 in the first law), a threshold that in effect applied only to the Democratic party because only rarely did the Republicans win enough votes to qualify. Attempts to exclude African Americans from the Democratic primary (the "white primary") were held unconstitutional in two U.S. Supreme Court cases (*Nixon v. Herndon* [1927] and *Nixon v. Condon* [1932]) but upheld in *Grovey v. Townsend* (1935), before being struck down in *Smith v. Allwright* (1944). Before the Nineteenth Amendment to the U.S. Constitution was ratified in 1920, the Texas legislature in 1918 allowed women to vote in the Democratic party primaries. In 1921 the Texas constitution was amended to provide for woman suffrage but it also required U.S. citizenship as a voter qualification, thus disqualifying aliens, who had been permitted to vote since 1869.

1930–59. During the years of the Great Depression, the New Deal, World War II, postwar prosperity, and rising Texas urbanization, change in Texas government foreshadowed the contemporary state. A dominant characteristic of the period was the growth of state administration, including the implementation of new welfare and other social-service programs, which owed much to the influence of the federal government, the emerging dominant partner in the federal system. In the 1950s federal aid was the largest single source of Texas state revenue. Texas government was also changed by the U.S. Supreme Court decision holding racial segregation in the public schools unconstitutional, as well as by other rulings. The Texas legislature became a more modern institution. A small step was taken when a constitutional amendment adopted in 1930 raised the pay of legislators for the first time since 1876, to $10 a day for the first 120 days of a regular session and $2 thereafter. In 1954 an amendment allowed $25 for the first 120 days but terminated pay after that period. An attempt was made by the "Split Session Amendment" of 1930 to encourage a more efficient management of the legislative process by setting deadlines for various stages, mainly bill introduction, committee study, and floor consideration. Changes of lasting significance in state budgeting occurred in the 1940s and 1950s. The "Pay-As-You-Go Amendment" of 1942 required a balanced budget, and in 1949 and 1951 the legislature instituted for the first time a modern budgeting process. It was based on a novel dual budgeting approach whereby both the legislature and the governor prepare budgets. The Legislative Budget Board, composed of 10 legislative leaders, was formed to make budget recommendations and prepare general appropriation bills for introduction in the legislative process. The governor was also directed to prepare a budget and given the assistance of an executive budget officer. Earlier, in 1943, the office of state auditor had been transferred from the executive to the legislative branch, in conformance with modern budgetary principles. Other moves toward modernity included the establishment of the Texas Legislative Council in 1949 to serve as a research and bill-drafting agency. When Texas constitutional revision was on the agenda in 1957, the legislature directed the council to study the constitution and make recommendations, with the help of a citizens' group. In 1957, in the aftermath of scandals of the time, a legislative code of ethics was enacted, one of only a few in the nation during the period, and a law requiring lobbyists to register, the first for Texas, was adopted.

Resistance by rural and small-town legislators to urban growth was behind the adoption of a constitutional amendment in 1936 that limited the number of representatives from the most populous counties. Failure to redistrict as required by the Texas constitution led to a 1948 amendment that provided for the Legislative Redistricting Board, composed of five officials serving ex officio, to draw legislative districts when the legislature failed to do so. The governor's position was, on balance, probably weakened, despite a gain in compensation by a 1954 amendment that allowed the legislature to set the salary, provided it was at least $12,000 annually, a new budget role, and an increased number of administrative appointments as the administration grew. The governor clearly lost clemency powers by a 1936 amendment that instituted a three-member Board of Pardons and Paroles whose recommendation was required before the governor could grant clemency, except for one 30-day reprieve in any capital case. Moreover, the new budget system was a far cry from the "executive budget" recommended by reformers and was in fact dominated by the legislature. Of most importance, the lieutenant governor had gained so much power as to overshadow the governor as a legislative leader. As chairman of the Legislative Budget Board, the key agency in state budget decision making, and chairman or member of other important legislative agencies, the lieutenant governor was also the real presiding officer of the Senate under Senate rules. The administrative branch took on many new responsibilities during the period. Probably the most dramatic change was the addition of welfare programs, most of which originated with the Social Security Act of 1935 and were financed largely with federal grants. The Department of Public Welfare (renamed the Texas Department of Human Services in 1985) was formed in 1941 to administer the programs. Welfare became the third-largest state expenditure, behind only education and highways. Other new programs included the Veterans' Land Program, which helped veterans to purchase farmland, administered by the Veterans' Land Board; loans to local governments for development of water-supply projects, administered by the Texas Water Development Board; and college building funds administered by the universities and colleges named in the 1947 constitutional amendment authorizing the program. In 1946 the first of many constitutional amendments to allow the state to issue general-obligation bonds to finance new programs was adopted. In 1931 the legislature appointed the Joint Legislative Committee on Organization and Economy to study the Texas administration, but none of the reforms recommended in its comprehensive report became law. The most significant reorganization of the time was in education, part of the historic Gilmer–Aikin Laws of 1949, which established the Minimum Foundation School Program. The new law set up the Texas Central Education Agency, composed of the state department of education, a state board of education whose members were elected from congressional districts, and a commissioner of education appointed by the board. Central management of the administration was improved by modern budgeting, but no central personnel office or statewide merit employment system (civil service) was in place. Civil service was limited to agencies required to adopt it as a condition of federal aid, such as the Department of Public Welfare and the Texas Employment Commission, and to any that used it voluntarily. Public employees' and teachers' benefits were upgraded by the introduction of retirement systems and workers' compensation.

Changes in the judiciary included an increase in the membership of the Texas Supreme Court to nine (its present number), stricter legal eligibility requirements for district judges and more legislative discretion over district courts, the establishment of the State Bar of Texas as an arm of the judiciary (the "integrated bar"), judicial pensions, and jury service for women. A far-reaching reform of local government was promised by passage of the County Home Rule Amendment of 1933 but did not materialize. Lesser changes included four-year terms for county and district officers, municipal and county retirement systems, and workers' compensation. To provide medical services primarily to the indigent to be financed independently of city and county property taxes, the first of many hospital districts was formed. During the 1930s large regional river authorities (also special districts) were set up by statute; among the best known is the Lower Colorado River Authority.

1960–95. An extraordinary number and variety of governmental reforms were adopted during the last decades of the twentieth century, but comprehensive constitutional revision failed in 1975 and various other major changes considered important by some, such as state tax restructuring, have not occurred. Legislative reapportionment, a significant factor in the modernization of state government across the nation, dominated Texas legislative reforms in the 1960s. Following U.S. Supreme Court decisions, a federal district court in 1965, in the first of several cases, ordered both houses of the Texas legislature reapportioned on the basis of equally populated districts ("one person, one vote"), a momentous gain for urban and suburban areas. In the 1970s the emphasis shifted to fair representation of ethnic and racial minorities, one solution for which was single-member districts. These districts were imposed judicially in some Texas metropolitan counties (beginning with Dallas and Bexar counties) and then required of all House seats in 1975 by state law. (Single-member Senate districts had been mandated by the 1876 constitution.) Reapportionment remained a contentious political and legal issue after each federal census for the rest of the century. In 1971 and 1981, for only the first and second times, drawing of legislative districts fell to the Legislative Redistricting Board. Owing much to reapportionment, the Texas legislature has become a more representative institution as increasing numbers of African Americans, Mexican Americans, women, and Republicans have been elected. There is a greater diversity of occupations as well, one change being the decline in the number of lawyer members. Among other legislative reforms in the 1960s were the passage of the Legislative Reorganization Act of 1961, which emphasized continuous use of legislative resources by such means as interim committee meetings, the first constitutional limit on regular sessions (140 days), the first annual legislative salary, and the first constitutional-revision commission (1967).

The 1970s might well be remembered as the decade of legislative reforms. The Texas legislature supported a host of changes, frequently of a liberal cast, such as the Texas Equal Rights Amendment and the first state minimum wage, and by reforming itself took on its modern shape. The Sharpstown Stock-Fraud Scandal, which broke in 1971, led directly to the adoption of a package of reforms by the Sixty-third Legislature (1973–74) on ethics, lobby regulation, campaign finance (the speaker's race was included in the regulations for the first time), and, to ensure easier citizen access to government and enforce accountability, open-record and open-meeting laws. Though never as effective as reformers desired, the changes continued on the agenda in the 1980s and 1990s. The legislature reorganized its committee structure (the House instituted limited seniority for committee selection), added research and other staff, and improved computer technology. In 1975 a constitutional amendment increasing the annual legislative salary to $7,200 was ratified. The Sixty-third Legislature formed the Texas Constitutional Revision Commission in 1973 and served, uniquely, as a constitutional convention in 1974, on authority of a constitutional amendment ratified in 1972. Although the Constitutional Convention of 1974 failed to adopt any proposals, the Sixty-fourth Legislature (1975–76) referred to the voters eight constitutional amendments that contained a new constitution except for the Bill of Rights, which was retained in full; but all eight were rejected at the polls in November 1975. In addition to serving as a convention, the legislature impeached and convicted a district judge (O. P. Carrillo of Duval County) in 1975–76 and began proceedings in 1977 to remove Supreme Court justice Donald B. Yarbrough, whose resignation terminated the process.

In the 1980s the legislature, in addition to demands for public-education reform, massive prison construction, a new workers' compensation law and other changes, was faced with a severe fiscal crisis brought on by a deep recession, in which oil prices and state revenue based on oil production fell sharply. To cope with continuing revenue shortfalls, the legislature passed and the governor signed the largest tax increases in Texas history, authorized unprecedented amounts of borrowing, and adopted a policy of encouraging economic development. The latter required constitutional amendments to ensure that the fiscal restrictions in the 1876 charter did not prevent government assistance to the private sector. To manage its business the legislature was forced to meet in 16 special sessions, the most of any decade, and for 6 sessions in 1989–90, the most of any legislature. The lawmakers also proposed a prodigious number (108) of constitutional amendments, of which 91 were approved by the voters, another decade record. New trends in legislative leadership were also apparent. New records were set for length of service by the speaker and the lieutenant governor. Speaker Bill Clayton (1975–82) held the office for 8 years, and his successor, Gibson "Gib" Lewis (1983–92), for 10. Lieutenant Governor William Hobby (1973–90) was in office for 18 years. With experience came added power. Hobby was regarded as the most powerful lieutenant governor in the U.S. Of several legislative reforms in the 1990s, an ethics commission was established in 1991 as a constitutional agency for the first time. Among its duties was to set per diem pay of legislators and to recommend, subject to voter approval, legislative salary increases, including larger amounts for the presiding officers, who had been receiving the same pay as members.

In 1993, under Speaker James E. "Pete" Laney, the House rules were revised to meet members' demands for reform. One striking result was the end of the usual hectic, last-minute rush in the House to pass bills. The historic renovation of the Capitol, completed in 1995, expanded and improved the physical facilities used by the legislature and coincided with new computer and media services. Representatives were given laptop computers to use at their desks on the floor for the first time, and citizens gained access to government documents by their home computers. During the regular session in 1995, the House experimented briefly with TEX-SPAN, which televised House floor proceedings live and was modeled on C-SPAN. One of the most important developments was the rise of the Republican party. By 1995 the number of Republican legislators had increased to within reach of majority status in both houses. To date, however, neither chamber has organized along political party lines, as does Congress and most state legislatures. And though there are House and Senate party caucuses, legislative proceedings have with important exceptions usually been bipartisan. Nevertheless, the Republican presence, particularly with a Republican governor in 1995, no doubt helped to swing the ideological balance to the conservative side. Most policy reforms in the Seventy-fourth Legislature (1995–96) were regarded by observers as conservative.

Overall, the governor's position as chief executive improved during the last decades of the century. In 1974, four-year unlimited terms for governor and other high elective executives went into effect. Other constitutional changes, though dependent on the legislature, were budgetary execution power (1985), limits on midnight appointments by lame-duck governors (1987), and removal of a given governor's appointees with Senate consent (1980). The governor lost power over paroles in 1983 but was able, by statute, to appoint all members of the enlarged Board of Pardons and Paroles. Also by statute, gubernatorial appointment power was extended to other reorganized and new agencies and, in a departure from tradition, to a few agency heads, such as the commissioner of education and the executive director of the Texas Department of Commerce (both in 1991), as well as to a few board chairmen. In addition to changes in powers, there has been a significant shift in partisan control that began with the election in 1978 of William P. Clements, the first Republican governor since Reconstruction. Of five gubernatorial elections from 1978 to 1994, Republican candidates won three. Republican governor Clements served longer—eight years—than any other governor since 1876. Also, for the first time since Reconstruction, Republicans won "down-ballot" executive races, namely (by 1995), for treasurer, agricultural commissioner, and all three railroad commissioners. The presence of Republicans and Democrats in executive offices raises questions about the future of the plural executive and the election of the governor and lieutenant governor independently of one another.

The Texas administration was subjected to unprecedented

scrutiny between the 1960s and the 1990s in response to concerns about the increasing number of agencies, their accountability and efficiency, and cost savings to avoid tax increases. One result was new methods for legislative oversight of the administration. "Sunset review" originated with the Constitutional Convention of 1974 and was adopted by statute in 1977, one of the first such laws in the nation. By the 1990s the process of periodic review of state agencies and their automatic termination unless renewed by law had extended to more than 200 agencies. One structural reform was the appointment of public members to professional and occupational regulatory boards. In the 1980s the legislature provided limited supervision of administration spending after the adoption of the budget under its newly acquired budget-execution authority (1985) and by statute set up two legislative-oversight boards, one to review implementation of education policy (abolished in 1993) and the other to review policy on criminal-justice law. Other such boards were established in the 1990s. Also in the 1990s a major innovation that received White House recognition was the introduction of "performance reviews" by the comptroller at the request of the legislature. The goal was to review all state agencies for ways to eliminate mismanagement and inefficiency and to reduce administrative costs. The comptroller has recommended numerous changes, many of which have been adopted with considerable savings effected. Changes in Texas administration included the addition of agencies to implement new regulatory and service functions. Among the agencies was the Public Utility Commission, set up in 1975 to administer the Public Utility Regulatory Act, which for the first time required state regulation of intrastate telephone, electric, water, and sewer utilities. An indication of new directions was the Texas Commission on Human Rights, instituted in 1983 to enforce legislation against discrimination in employment; enforcement extended to housing in 1990.

Reorganization of administrative structure by combining existing agencies with common missions into larger departments or commissions was one method employed to improve administration. Three of the four largest agencies (by number of employees) in 1995 were the products of consolidation: the Texas Department of Mental Health and Mental Retardation, the Texas Department of Transportation, and the Department of Criminal Justice (see Prison System). In 1993 several agencies merged to form the Texas Natural Resources Conservation Commission to facilitate more centralized enforcement of environmental laws. Other changes included reorganization of state public-school administration, one of the reforms of H.B. 72, a landmark law on public education enacted in 1984. For a few years, the state board of education was a nine-member board appointed by the governor; in 1989, by a statewide referendum, it returned to elective status but in a new form, as a board of fifteen members elected from as many districts. Reorganization to provide for a central executive office to administer personnel policies was not among the changes of the period, however. The legislature provided for some uniformity in matters of job description and pay scales by the 1961 Position Classification Act, and federal laws on nondiscrimination and affirmative action apply to all agencies. Retirement benefits for state employees and teachers improved after a 1975 constitutional amendment was ratified. Governor Ann Richards (1991–95) appointed a record number of women, blacks, and Hispanics to state positions. Richards herself, the second elected woman governor of Texas

(after Miriam A. Ferguson), exemplified the rise of women to high state government offices. By 1995 the approximate number of state agencies was more than 200, the number of state employees was 236,000, and the two-year budget (1995–96) was $80 billion. Although the overall trend in Texas government has been one of administrative growth, by some measures, such as the number of state employees per capita, a decline occurred in the late 1980s. Texas has always ranked low on state spending, and in 1992 was fiftieth among the states as measured by per capita expenditures.

The major developments in the judicial branch have concerned judicial administration. By statute and constitutional amendment, the Texas Supreme Court has become the administrative head of the Texas judicial system, with power to promulgate administrative rules and rules of civil procedure to promote the efficient and uniform administration of justice. In 1977 the Office of Court Administration was established by statute to provide for management of state courts. The director is appointed by the Supreme Court and answers to it and the chief justice. The director is also executive director of the Texas Judicial Council. The chief justice, by statute, is directed to deliver a "state of the judiciary" speech at the beginning of each regular legislative session. Two other administrative agencies, both mandated by the Texas constitution, are the State Commission on Judicial Conduct (originally named the Judicial Qualifications Commission in 1965) as a disciplinary body and the Judicial Districts Board, authorized in 1985 to redraw judicial districts for the district courts if the legislature failed to do so. The principal change in court organization occurred in 1980, when by constitutional amendment the courts of civil appeals became the courts of appeals after they were given jurisdiction over criminal cases. Other important changes were the increase in 1977 in the membership of the Texas Court of Criminal Appeals to nine (its present size), a new constitutional formula for determining the number of justices of the peace in each county, and a substantial increase in the number of statutory county courts (often called county courts-at-law). In contrast to the county judge, who presides over the constitutional county court (one in each of the 254 Texas counties), the judges of the statutory courts must be attorneys. The method of selecting Texas judges, a long-standing topic of controversy, has not been changed, although the at-large system has been challenged unsuccessfully in federal court. In 1995, however, the first state law limiting the size of contributions in judicial races and the time in which they are permissible was enacted by the Seventy-fourth Legislature (1995–96). Voluntary spending limits were also included in the new law. The issue of retaining partisan elections has taken on new significance as Texas has become a two-party state. In 1995 the Supreme Court majority was Republican, and in several cities, including Dallas and Houston, most judges were Republicans.

Significant changes in state-local relations occurred between the 1960s and the 1990s with the establishment of new state agencies and policies to assist local governments. In 1965 regional councils of governments were authorized by state law as a mechanism for resolving problems of governance in areas characterized by economic, social, and physical interdependence but lacking any areawide government with power to act on common concerns. The situation was particularly acute in the metropolitan areas, where independent units of government with limited jurisdiction proliferated. The Harris County Metropolitan Statistical Area, for instance, has more than 500 such units. The councils of governments, voluntary associations of governments, provide planning in their respective areas, cooperation and coordination, and some services. In 1971 two state agencies that provide state assistance to local governments were established: the Department of Community Affairs (merged with the Texas Housing Agency in 1991 and renamed the Texas Department of Housing and Community Affairs) and the Texas Advisory Commission on Intergovernmental Relations (abolished in 1989), which included among its responsibilities a continuous study of state-local relations.

Long-standing barriers to the right to vote, including the poll tax, were removed in the 1960s and 1970s, mostly by federal action. In 1971 the legislature enacted a modern permanent voter-registration law and in 1988 a new law permitting any qualified voter to vote early without stating a reason. The Texas Equal Rights Amendment, ratified in 1972, prohibited discrimination on the grounds of sex, race, color, creed, or national origin. In a number of cases the Texas courts have interpreted the TERA and other Texas constitutional provisions in such a way as to provide greater protection of rights than guaranteed under the U.S. Constitution. Providing this protection based on state charters has been called "the New Judicial Federalism" and is nationwide. Of enormous importance was *Edgewood ISD v. Kirby*, in which the Texas Supreme Court held unconstitutional the Texas laws on public school finance although the U.S. Supreme Court had ruled in 1973 in *Rodríguez v. San Antonio ISD* that they did not violate the U.S. Constitution.

As the twentieth century drew to a close, Texas government, despite many changes, retained structural features specified by the Constitution of 1876. Unlike most states, Texas continues to function with biennial regular legislative sessions and a low legislative salary fixed in the constitution, with a relatively weak governor, with a nonunified judiciary whose judges are elected by partisan ballot, and with unreformed county government. Moreover, no major state tax restructuring to provide financial support for government has occurred since the sales tax was adopted in 1961.

Janice C. May

Governor. The office of chief executive in Texas is older than the union of the American states and earlier by almost a century than the presidency of the United States. Although most historians settle for the year 1691 and the appointment of Domingo Terán de los Ríos as the beginning of Texas as a political entity, several support the year 1523, when the royal governor from Spain was Francisco de Garay. The long list of *gobernadores*, presidents, and governors provides a colorful index to the history of the state, and even though the basic duties of the chief executive have changed little since the Constitution of 1876, the personalities and politics of these officials have left their imprint on both the form and the function of state government. The following list of governors since the state was annexed to the United States, with dates of tenure in office, shows that most served more than the two-year term set by the Constitution of 1876. In 1972 voters approved the extension of the office to a four-year term that took effect in 1975.

The office of governor as it exists today was established by Article IV, Section 1 of the Constitution of 1876. As a state office it was first established by the Constitution of 1845 and superseded

the office of president of the Republic of Texas. The governor was elected and served for two years. His salary was set by the constitution at $4,000 yearly, and since 1856 the governor has had the use of the Governor's Mansion. To be elected governor, a person had to be at least 30 years old, a United States citizen, and a resident of Texas for at least five years preceding the election. The major executive powers of the governor are to execute the laws of the state, extradite fugitives from justice, serve as commander in chief of the military forces of the state, declare martial law, appoint state officials (with the consent of the Senate), fill vacancies in state and district offices (except vacancies in the legislature), call special elections to fill vacancies in the legislature, fill vacancies in the United States Senate until an election can be held, submit the budget to the legislature, and serve as ex-officio member of several state boards.

The legislative powers of the governor are to call special sessions of the legislature and submit the topics for legislation at such sessions, recommend measures, and submit emergency matters for consideration of the legislature at any time, sign or veto legislative acts, and veto specific items in itemized general appropriation bills. The governor's judicial powers are to grant or deny recommendations for clemency and remissions of fines and forfeitures made by the Board of Pardons and Paroles; to revoke a parole or conditional pardon or grant one 30day reprieve in a capital case at his own discretion; and, with the consent of the legislature, to grant reprieves, commutations of punishment, and pardon in cases of treason.

Of the governors since statehood, only three—Edmund J. Davis, William P. Clements, Jr., and George W. Bush—have been elected as Republicans. W. Lee O'Daniel was the only governor who was not a voter at the time of his election, having refused to pay the required poll tax. James E. Ferguson was the only governor to be impeached, although Sam Houston was removed when he refused to take the oath of allegiance to the Confederacy, and James W. Throckmorton was removed by the military. The youngest has been Dan Moody, who was 33 when elected. Two were born north of the Mason–Dixon line: Lawrence S. Ross (Iowa) and O'Daniel (Ohio). A large number of early governors were soldier-statesmen from the South. Houston had served as governor of Tennessee and president of the Republic of Texas (twice). Miriam A. Ferguson was the state's first female chief executive, and she and Clements were the only governors elected to nonconsecutive terms (Elisha Pease was appointed provisional governor almost 10 years after serving two elective terms). Ann W. Richards, the second woman to be elected governor, was elected in 1990 and soundly beaten in the 1992 election by George W. Bush.

Although the state's highest executive office often has been regarded as a steppingstone to high national offices, few former governors have actually been successful in gaining them. Since 1876 only three, Coke, Culberson, and O'Daniel, have served in the United States Senate after their governorships; Ireland, Campbell, Moody, Allred, and Stevenson failed in bids for the United States Senate, while James Ferguson was defeated for the United States Senate as well as for nomination as president on the American (Know-Nothing) party ticket. Houston had already served in the United States Senate before becoming governor, and Price Daniel, Sr., resigned his seat in the United States Senate to become governor. Connally, secretary of the navy before his election and was secretary of the U.S. treasury after he

Governors of the State of Texas

NAME	TENURE OF OFFICE	COMMENTS
James Pinckney Henderson	Feb. 19, 1846–Dec. 21, 1847	
Albert Clinton Horton	May 19, 1846–Nov. 13, 1846	Acted as governor while Henderson was at war in Mexico.
George Tyler Wood	Dec. 21, 1847–Dec. 21, 1849	
Peter Hansborough Bell	Dec. 21, 1849–Nov. 23, 1853	Resigned to enter U.S. Congress.
James Wilson Henderson	Nov. 23, 1853–Dec. 21, 1853	Became governor when Bell entered Congress.
Elisha Marshall Pease	Dec. 21, 1853–Dec. 21, 1857	
Hardin Richard Runnels	Dec. 21, 1857–Dec. 21, 1859	
Samuel Houston	Dec. 21, 1859–Mar. 16, 1861	Deposed when he refused oath of allegiance to Confederacy.
Edward Clark	Mar. 16, 1861–Nov. 7, 1861	
Francis Richard Lubbock	Nov. 7, 1861–Nov. 5, 1863	Retired to serve as advisor for Confederate Army.
Pendleton Murrah	Nov. 5, 1863–Jun. 17, 1865	Administration ended with fall of Confederacy.
Fletcher S. Stockdale	Jun. 17, 1865–Jul. 21, 1865 Removed by U.S. authorities.	Served as acting governor when Murrah fled to Mexico.
Andrew Jackson Hamilton	Jul. 21, 1865–Aug. 9, 1866	Provisional governor.
James Webb Throckmorton	Aug. 9, 1866–Aug. 8, 1867	Removed by U.S. military.
Elisha Marshall Pease	Aug. 8, 1867–Sep. 30, 1869	Provisional governor (appointed); resigned, leaving state without governor until Jan. 8, 1870.
Edmund Jackson Davis	Jan. 8, 1870–Jan. 15, 1874	Elected, then appointed provisional governor.
Richard Coke	Jan. 15, 1874–Dec. 1, 1876	Resigned to enter U.S. Senate.
Richard Bennett Hubbard	Dec. 1, 1876–Jan. 21, 1879	
Oran Milo Roberts	Jan. 21, 1879–Jan. 16, 1883	
John Ireland	Jan. 16, 1883–Jan. 18, 1887	
Lawrence Sullivan Ross	Jan. 18, 1887–Jan. 20, 1891	
James Stephen Hogg	Jan. 20, 1891–Jan. 15, 1895	First Texas-born governor.
Charles Allen Culberson	Jan. 15, 1895–Jan. 17, 1899	
Joseph Draper Sayers	Jan. 17, 1899–Jan. 20, 1903	
Samuel Willis Tucker Lanham	Jan. 20, 1903–Jan. 15, 1907	Last Confederate veteran to be governor.
Thomas Mitchell Campbell	Jan. 15, 1907–Jan. 19, 1911	
Oscar Branch Colquitt	Jan. 19, 1911–Jan. 19, 1915	
James Edward Ferguson	Jan. 19, 1915–Aug. 25, 1917	Impeached.
William Pettus Hobby	Aug. 25, 1917–Jan. 18, 1921	
Pat Morris Neff	Jan. 18, 1921–Jan. 20, 1925	
Miriam Amanda Ferguson	Jan. 20, 1925–Jan. 17, 1927	Second woman elected governor in the United States.
Daniel James Moody, Jr.	Jan. 17, 1927–Jan. 20, 1931	
Ross Shaw Sterling	Jan. 20, 1931–Jan. 17, 1933	
Miriam Amanda Ferguson	Jan. 17, 1933–Jan. 15, 1935	
James Allred	Jan. 15, 1935–Jan. 17, 1939	
Wilbert Lee O'Daniel	Jan. 17, 1939–Aug. 4, 1941	Resigned to enter U.S. Senate.
Coke Robert Stevenson	Aug. 4, 1941–Jan. 21, 1947	
Beauford Halbert Jester	Jan. 21, 1947–Jul. 11, 1949	First governor to die in office.
Robert Allan Shivers	Jul. 11, 1949–Jan. 15, 1957	First governor to be elected to three consecutive terms.
Marion Price Daniel, Sr.	Jan. 15, 1957–Jan. 15, 1963	Three terms.
John Bowden Connally, Jr.	Jan. 15, 1963–Jan. 21, 1969	Three terms.
Preston Smith	Jan. 21, 1969–Jan. 16, 1973	
Dolph Briscoe	Jan. 16, 1973–Jan. 16, 1979	First governor elected to a four-year term (1974).
William P. Clements	Jan. 16, 1979–Jan. 18, 1983	First Republican governor since Reconstruction.
Mark White	Jan. 18, 1983–Jan. 20, 1987	
William P. Clements	Jan. 20, 1987–Jan. 15, 1991	
Ann W. Richards	Jan. 15, 1991–Jan. 17, 1995	
George W. Bush	Jan. 17, 1995–	

George W. and Laura Bush saluted by a Texas A&M University saber guard at the gubernatorial inauguration at the Capitol in Austin, January 17, 1995. Photograph by David Woo. Courtesy Office of the Governor.

left office, was the only Texas governor to hold high national office both before and after his term. He switched to the Republican party after serving as governor and unsuccessfully ran for nomination to the presidency in 1980. For the most part, Texas governors returned to their previous occupations after stepping down, content to accept posts at the state level when they stayed in public life; several retired into obscurity.

No definite pattern is discernible in the political experience, educational background, or occupation of those attaining the office of governor. Among those who had previously held elective office, several had served as state attorney general or as a county attorney or district attorney. Former legislators and others who served in some capacity in state or local law enforcement or regulatory agencies were also successful. Most governors of Texas received at least some higher education from Texas institutions, while several held degrees from such schools as Harvard University, the College of William and Mary, Virginia Military Institute, and the University of Virginia. In occupation or profession, the largest number have been lawyers, most of whom received legal training in Texas. No college professor or small-town merchant has ever been elected, but the occupations of those outside the legal profession have ranged from newspaper editor to flour manufacturer to housewife. Although the Catholic Church is now the largest Christian communion in the

state, all Texas governors since annexation have been Protestants, mostly Baptists and Methodists, and only a very few have not been Masons. More governors have come from East and Central Texas than any other geographic area; in the 1960s and 1970s Smith (Northwest), Connally (South), and Briscoe (Southwest) were the first governors to come from their respective areas. Near the turn of the century the city of Tyler was the state's political stronghold. For many years the official residences of governors and other state officials at the time of gaining office were in East Texas, but by midcentury Central Texas claimed a higher percentage.

By general acceptance the governor has been the party leader in the state. The convention of rank-and-file delegates in each party, often called the "Governor's Convention" and held in September, gives the party's nominee an opportunity to put his own campaign promises into the state platform, as well as to secure control of the party machinery. Exceptions to the governor's control of the party have been few, and mostly since 1920, when Pat M. Neff gave the convention a free hand in writing a platform and selecting the state executive committee for the Democrats. Ross Sterling lost control to the opposing Ferguson-dominated convention in 1932, which put Ma Ferguson back in office. Another example of weak party leadership was O'Daniel, who seemed indifferent to party matters. By 1944 a large split had separated the Democrats, with former governors Moody and Allred each heading opposing forces that clashed over national and state Democratic policies. Moody, leader of the "Texas Regulars," and Allred, a "New Dealer" supporting President Franklin D. Roosevelt, clashed first at the national convention, with Governor Stevenson trying to restore some unity by appeasing both factions. Allred and his forces won control at the state convention, severing the governor's hold almost completely. Stevenson's separation from party control was a clear warning for future governors, however. Beauford Jester was able to steer his administration through a middle-of-the-road era that in effect gave leadership in the party back to the chief executive, a leadership all governors have enjoyed since. Allan Shivers demonstrated his control by leading a successful bolt from the Democratic ticket that supported Adlai Stevenson in the general election of 1952. He was supported in this remarkable move by his attorney general, Price Daniel, who ruled that Texans could write in the names of Eisenhower and Nixon "without losing status as Democrats." Not coincidentally, Daniel later pursued the Tidelands Controversy to its conclusions during the administration of Eisenhower, who had been noncommittal about the Tidelands before the election, while Adlai Stevenson was against the Texas position. Daniel was aided at his convention in 1956 by Lyndon B. Johnson, who undercut liberal party activists to bring the divided Democratic party under Daniel's control.

Many governors have enjoyed long tenure and fairly strong party control. The Sharpstown Stock Fraud Scandal possibly kept Preston Smith from the third term that his three predecessors had received, however, and the rise of the Raza Unida party as a political force large enough to draw votes away from the Democratic contender in 1972 almost threw the election to the Republican candidate. In 1978 William P. Clements, Jr., became the first Republican to be elected governor in over 100 years; he had some difficulty working with the largely Democratic legislature. The office of governor is probably not as strong in Texas as in some other states. Legally, at least, the governor has little power over certain administrative functions and has no removal power over important elected officials. His legislative veto may be his strongest executive weapon. Politically, however, the governor has been an influence on the decisions of state government at almost all levels. *Phillip L. Fry*

Governor's Mansion. The official residence of the governor of Texas; built 1854–56. Previously, the only specified executive residence in Texas had been a two-story frame "President's House" occupied by President Lamar from 1839 to 1841. Sam Houston probably lived at the Bullock Hotel before he made Washington-on-the-Brazos capital in 1842. Austin became capital again in 1845, but apparently no provision was made for an official residence for the governor. Instead, the legislature authorized $500 a year to rent a place for the governor. The first four state governors lived in either hotels or boardinghouses when the legislature was in session. In 1854 the legislature appropriated $17,500 ($2,500 of which was to be for furnishings) to build a suitable residence for the chief executive. The sale of Austin city lots donated to the state provided money for the building. The original plans called for the residence to be located where the General Land Office building is. Governor Pease, however, picked a lot nearer the Capitol. Abner Cook supervised the construction of the two-story, Greek Revival mansion. The bricks were made in

Austin, and the pine logs used for the pillars were hauled in from Bastrop. Pease, the first governor to occupy the mansion, moved in in June 1856. Since then, the Governor's Mansion has undergone several major improvements and renovations. Gas lighting was added in the 1870s, telephones and indoor plumbing in the 1880s, and electricity in the 1890s. In 1914 Governor Colquitt had a family dining area added and replaced the original kitchen facilities. During the administration of Governor Shivers in the 1950s, a new roof was built and the first air-conditioning and heating system was installed. The most recent, and in some ways the most extensive, renovation took place between 1979 and 1982, during the administration of William Clements, who had to live in other quarters for more than half his term while the house received a complete refurbishment.

Generally, supervision of changes has been by committee. The Board of Mansion Supervisors (1931–) was constituted for the purpose. Its duties were transferred to the Texas Fine Arts Commission in 1965. In the early 1980s the Friends of the Governor's Mansion was established to help finance and oversee the restoration efforts. An endowment was established to assure ongoing maintenance of the Mansion Collection. The position of administrator was established to handle the daily operation of the mansion and maintenance of the building. The 1989–90 legislature officially transferred supervision of the mansion to the Texas Historical Commission. Governors may decorate the private rooms to their taste but are not allowed to change the rooms open to the public or to alter the physical layout of the building. The Governor's Mansion is a nationally recognized house–museum and was recorded as a Texas Historical Landmark in 1962. It was placed on the National Register of Historic Places in 1974. *Vivian Elizabeth Smyrl*

Goyen, William. Writer; b. Trinity, Texas, 24 April 1915; d. Los Angeles, 30 August 1983; m. Doris Roberts (1963); ed. Rice Institute. After teaching at the University of Houston (1939–40) and serving in the navy during World War II, Goyen moved numerous times. From 1954 on, he lived principally in New York. His first novel, *The House of Breath* (1950), and first book of short stories, *Ghost and Flesh* (1952), received much acclaim and won him two Guggenheim fellowships. His work was translated into German by Ernst Robert Curtius and into French by Maurice Coindreau and was soon established in Europe, where it remains in print in several languages. In the early 1950s, in addition to publishing another novel (*In a Farther Country*, 1955) and more short stories, Goyen began to write dramatic works and adaptations of his fiction for the stage. The success of his theatrical work won him a Ford Foundation Grant for Theater Writing. Six of his plays were eventually produced. In later years he taught as a visiting professor at Brown, Columbia, Princeton, the University of Southern California, and other universities. He began work as an editor at McGraw–Hill in 1966 but resigned in 1971 to return to his writing. He published a nonfiction book, *A Book of Jesus*, perhaps his most popular work, in 1973. He subsequently published a novel, *Come, The Restorer* (1974), and his *Collected Stories* (1975). In 1977 he received the Distinguished Alumnus Award from Rice University. He moved to Los Angeles in 1975 and lived there most of the rest of his life. The work of his last years included an unfinished autobiography, short stories (collected posthumously), and a novel, *Arcadio*, published a few weeks after his death. As a writer, Goyen strove to combine spiritual inquiry about the nature of man with the elements of humble daily life. His early childhood left his writing marked by the rhythms of rural speech and the Bible. His father was a lumber salesman, and despite Goyen's absorption with European writers, nearly all of his fiction is permeated with the atmosphere of the East Texas woods and small towns.

Reginald Gibbons

Granbury's Texas Brigade. A Confederate Army brigade formed in November 1863 just before the battle of Missionary Ridge as a part of Maj. Gen. Pat Cleburne's division, with Brig. Gen. James Argyle Smith in command. At Missionary Ridge the brigade quickly established a record for valor. Smith was wounded there and was succeeded in command by Col. Hiram Bronson Granbury of the Seventh Texas Infantry. Granbury was subsequently promoted to brigadier general. In the ensuing retreat of the Army of Tennessee, Cleburne's division, including Granbury's Brigade, probably saved the army by its rearguard stand at Ringold Gap, for which it received the thanks of the Confederate Congress. The brigade fought in Gen. Joseph E. Johnston's army throughout the entire Atlanta campaign, participating in countless skirmishes and the battles of Resaca, New Hope Church, Kenesaw Mountain, Peachtree Creek, Atlanta, and Jonesboro. Cleburne's official report on New Hope Church recorded, "The piles of dead on this front was but a silent eulogy upon Granbury and his noble Texans." After the Atlanta campaign the brigade participated in Gen. John B. Hood's disastrous invasion of Tennessee and was devastated in November 1864 at the battle of Franklin; Granbury and Cleburne were killed in action. At the battle of Nashville, the brigade was commanded by a colonel. What was left of it joined the remnants of the Army of Tennessee in North Carolina in the spring of 1865 and surrendered at Greensboro in April. Granbury's Texas Brigade established a reputation for stark fighting ability unsurpassed by any other brigade in the Confederate Army of Tennessee.

Palmer Bradley

Grand Prairie, Texas. Thirteen miles west of downtown Dallas in western Dallas and eastern Tarrant counties. The townsite comprises 73 square miles surrounded by Dallas, Arlington, Irving, and Cedar Hill. Settlers arrived in the area before the Civil War and built several stores, including the M. M. Miller store and the Phillip Goetsell store. The community was not organized, however, until 1863, when A. M. Dechman's wagon broke down on his trip from Jacksonville, Texas, to Fort Belknap. He was carrying supplies for the army commissary. He traded his broken wagon, ox team, and $200 of Confederate money for a 239-acre tract. The community that grew up became known as Dechman or Deckman when it received a post office in 1874. By that time a daily stage ran through Deckman on its way from Dallas to Fort Worth. The Valley Church, built by 1875, was the first church in the area. This log building served as both a nondenominational church and a school. In 1876 Deckman grew when the Texas and Pacific Railway was built to the site from Eagle Ford, just east of Dallas. The post office continued to call the community Deckman until 1877, when it changed the name to Grand Prairie to agree with the railroad, which had called the town Grand Prairie since 1873. The community was supposedly so named because a woman stepped off the train and said, "What a grand prairie!" By 1890 the town had a population of 300, two

churches, a public school, a steam gristmill–cotton gin, a broom factory, a wagon factory, and general stores. The first telephone was installed in 1900. Grand Prairie incorporated in 1902 with S. R. Lively as mayor. By 1907 the North Texas Traction Company, better known as the Interurban, began service to Grand Prairie, and the Dallas–Fort Worth Pike, later U.S. Highway 80, was graveled. An electrical plant and a volunteer fire department were established before 1920. The Little Motor Kar Company manufactured the "Texmobile" until it went out of business in 1920. In the 1920s the city streets were paved and Highway 80 was macadamized. In 1921 the first Grand Prairie Stock and Poultry Show was held; it continued every year until the 1940s.

The future of the community was changed when Dallas built Hensley Field on 300 acres two miles east of Grand Prairie's city limits in 1928. The field, named for William H. Hensley of San Antonio, became the site for all army operations in Dallas, which were moved from Love Field. Improvements to the field as well as school construction in Grand Prairie took place under the PWA in the 1930s. Mountain Creek Lake was completed just east of the city limits in 1931. The Curtis–Wright Airport of Fort Worth–Dallas was built west of Grand Prairie in 1929. After failing as a flight school operated by the Curtis Flying Service Corporation, it served as the Grand Prairie municipal airport from 1930 until 1940, when it was purchased by the Lou Foote Flying School. During World War II the field was used as a training school for the navy. Because it was too small for jets, it was bought by the city and turned into an industrial park. The population of Grand Prairie increased from 1,263 in 1925 to 1,595 by World War II. The first wartime-era addition was the Naval Reserve Aviation Base, built in 1940 on 30 acres of Hensley Field to be used by the army and navy for flight training. After Pearl Harbor was bombed a $1.5 expansion was implemented. The area just east of Grand Prairie was chosen as the site for a federally operated defense plant, North American Aviation, Incorporated. By 1941 the plant had 5,000 employees. The city rushed to provide services and expanded utilities, built new schools, increased fire protection, and implemented city mail service. At its peak production the airplane plant employed 38,500 workers. Between 1940 and the end of the war the population of Grand Prairie grew from 1,595 to 18,000. On August 14, 1945, there was a complete shutdown of the airplane plant, and the remaining 15,000 employees lost their jobs. Grand Prairie feared a collapse of its economy, but it was able to recover by encouraging the development of such businesses as furniture, boat, and chemical manufacturing. The town had another setback in 1947, when the city of Dallas annexed the industrial area to the east of Grand Prairie, including the aircraft plants, Hensley Field, and Mountain Creek Lake. In 1948, however, United Aircraft Corporation moved to the site of the old aircraft plant with 1,500 employees.

In 1948 Grand Prairie began annexing land around it in order to keep Dallas from taking it. To facilitate annexation Grand Prairie voted in a new home-rule city charter with a city manager. Over the years communities near Grand Prairie had been annexed, including Dalworth Park in 1943 and, by the 1980s, Burbank Gardens, Florence Hill, Freetown, Idlewild–Mountain Creek, and Shady Grove. By 1960 the population of Grand Prairie was 30,000. Through the next several decades the town continued to grow, and by 1990 the population was 99,616. Of this number, 81,527 lived in Dallas County, 18,086 in Tarrant

County, and the rest in Ellis County. Industries produced aircraft and aircraft parts, plastics, machine parts, and mobile homes. Tourism became another important business because of the city's proximity to such attractions as Six Flags Over Texas. Grand Prairie hosts a Cinco de Mayo celebration, the Prairie Dog Chili Cookoff, the National Championship Indian Pow-wow, the Oktoberfest, and the Western Days Rodeo. Nearby Joe Pool Lake and Mountain Creek Lake provided water recreation.

Lisa C. Maxwell

Grange. A major farmers' organization in the late nineteenth and early twentieth centuries; also known as the Patrons of Husbandry. This nonpartisan, agrarian order offered to farm families a four-fold plan for cooperation in business, happier home lives, more social contacts, and better educational opportunities. R. A. Baird of the national Grange organized the first Grange in Texas at Salado in July 1873. In October delegates organized the Texas State Grange at Dallas. In 1876 the Texas Grange, including Indian Territory, claimed 40,000 patron, matron, and juvenile members in 1,275 lodges. Thereafter the Grange slowly declined and by 1950 had little influence. Several elements contributed to the shrinkage: opponents told alien settlers that its secrecy made the Grange another American (Know-Nothing) party, professional men misconstrued its attack upon "all middlemen," merchants plotted destruction of its cooperatives, and ranchers instinctively feared "nesters." The drought of 1885–87 and the rival Farmers' Alliance also contributed. Nevertheless, the Grangers did achieve victories. Half of the members of the Constitutional Convention of 1875 were Patrons. Articles providing low salaries for public officers, homestead protection, railway regulation, and restrictions on taxing power show their influence on the convention. Laws encouraging immigration, restricting speculative land companies, setting maximum interest rates, regulating railways by a commission, and requiring a six-month school term and the election of public weighers originated with the state Grange. The Texas Grange supported the national Grange in demanding free trade, an interstate commerce commission, a department of agriculture, a pure food and drug law, inflation, popular election of senators, and reduction of express and postage rates.

The Grange also did important work in education and business. The bimonthly Grange hall meeting was a school for the whole family; there they established libraries, sang songs, read essays, and developed speakers. They worked for free and uniform textbooks, nine-month school terms, consolidation of rural schools, capable teachers, and vocational courses. Granges organized schools under the "school community system." Some sold stock in cooperative associations to operate the first secondary schools in Texas. When Texas A&M College opened, the Grange was already working toward a cooperative college and experiment farm at Austin. The Grange for two decades considered itself the special guardian of A&M; from 1889 to 1896 a Granger, Archibald J. Rose, was president of the A&M board. The Grange also contributed to the early growth of Texas Woman's University. In business the Grangers used the Rochdale cooperative plan. In 1875 they organized the Texas Grange Manufacturing Association in Marion County to process iron and farm equipment; in 1878 they opened the Texas Cooperative Association at Galveston to market farm commodities and to purchase goods wholesale for their 150 cooperative stores. Their

cooperative textile mills for making rough cloth and twine were a failure. More successful were the Texas State Grange Fair Association, which operated a 400-acre experiment farm and exhibition hall at McGregor, and the Texas Grange Mutual Fire Insurance Association. The Texas Farmer Publishing Association printed the *Texas Farmer,* the eight-page organ of the Grange.

Ralph A. Smith

Grasslands. In Texas before European settlement, grasslands—areas dominated by grasses, with tree or shrub canopies covering less than 25 percent—occupied about two-thirds of the landscape and ranged from desert and semidesert grasslands of the mountains and foothills of the Trans-Pecos to midgrass prairies of the Rolling Plains and Edwards Plateau to tallgrass or true prairies of the Blackland and Upper Coastal prairies. More than 470 native grass species live in Texas. With over 570 species, subspecies, and varieties of grasses, Texas leads the United States in numbers of grasses. The rich agricultural lands of Texas are so in large part due to the grasses that they once supported. The gentle topography and fertile soils of former grasslands today support most of the state's row crops, for most of the grasslands of the Coastal and Blackland prairies and High Plains have been converted to cropland. In fact, less than 1 percent of the original Blackland Prairie remains approximately as it once was. The fertile soils and mild climate of the Blacklands were responsible for the development of the cotton economy in Central Texas in the mid-1800s. More recent technological advances have allowed irrigation of the High Plains, and hence exploitation of the rich soils and gradual slopes of the region for cotton and small-grain production.

In general, grasslands of the Blackland Prairie and Coastal Prairie are southern extensions of the true prairie, the Rolling Plains and Edwards Plateau are southern extensions of midgrass Great Plains grassland, and the High Plains are a southern extension of the shortgrass prairie. The grasslands of Texas comprise seven geographic regions: (1) the Blackland Prairies (including the Grand, San Antonio, and Fayette), (2) the Coastal Prairie (including the Sand Plain), (3) the Rolling Plains (including the Rolling Red Prairie), (4) the Edwards Plateau, (5) the High Plains, (6) the South Texas Plains, and (7) the Trans-Pecos.

Blackland Prairie. As defined, the Blacklands consist of about 12.6 million acres. In Texas before European settlement, uplands were dominated by little bluestem (*Schizachyrium scoparium*), big bluestem (*Andropogon gerardii*), Indian grass (*Sorghastrum nutans*), and tall dropseed (*Sporobolus asper*). The lowlands throughout and the typical clayey Vertisol soils in the northeast (where precipitation is highest) were dominated by eastern grama grass (*Tripsacum dactyloides*) and switch grass (*Panicum virgatum*). Also in the northeast, over loamy Alfisol, are unique communities dominated by Silvenus dropseed (*Sporobolus silveanus*), mead sedge (*Carex meadii*), and switch grass. Included within the Blacklands were expansive, virtually open grasslands along with areas of scattered trees and shrubs or mottes of woody vegetation. Numerous wooded stream bottoms crossed the prairies, and these were dominated by sugarberry, elm, cottonwood, pecan, and oak trees. The Lampasas Cut Plain, which separated the main belt of the Blacklands and the Grand Prairie, also supported junipers, oaks, and elms. Most of the main belt of the Blacklands has been converted to cropland or tame pasture. In addition, the cities of San Antonio, Austin, Temple, Waco, and Dallas cover large areas of former grassland. Most of the areas that have not been plowed have been abusively grazed by domestic livestock. The largest areas of native sod are within the Grand Prairie, but overall the Blacklands represent the most completely altered of all Texas grasslands and their remnants are in need of conservation.

Coastal Prairie. The Coastal Prairie extends from Baffin Bay to the Louisiana border, forming a crescent that comprises about 6.35 million acres. Also included here are the 1.75-million-acre Coastal Sand Plain, which extends south from Baffin Bay to the subtropical zone, and the barrier-island grasslands. Grasslands of the Upper Coastal Prairie, north of San Antonio Bay, are dominated by little bluestem, brownseed paspalum (*Paspalum plicatulum*), Indian grass, and low panic (*Dichanthelium species*). The lower coastal prairie supports little bluestem, cane bluestem (*Bothriochloa barbinodis*), tall dropseed, and a variety of midgrasses. The Coastal Prairie was never a broad, expansive open grassland, but rather is dissected by numerous wooded stream bottoms. Furthermore, without periodic fire the Coastal Prairie is quickly invaded by woody species. The barrier-island grasslands were dominated by little bluestem, sea oats (*Uniola paniculata*), and fimbry (*Fimbristylis* species). Many fresh and brackish marshes are included within the barrier islands, and much variation exists with dune stability. The Coastal Sand Plains of South Texas were dominated by little bluestem, cane bluestem, Indian grass, Pan American balsamscale (*Elyonurus barbiculmis*), silveusgrass (*Trichoneura elegans*), and other grasses, along with live oak mottes and individual trees. Most of the Coastal Prairie has been plowed and converted to row crops or tame pasture, especially Bermuda grass (*Cynodon dactylon*) and King Ranch bluestem (*Bothriochloa ischaemum*). In addition, overgrazing and fire suppression have led to invasion or increase of the most diverse assemblage of native and introduced woody species of any Texas grassland. Included are Macartney rose (*Rosa bracteata*), Chinese tallow tree (*Sapium sabiferum*), mesquite (*Prosopis glandulosa*), and huisache (*Acacia farnesiana*). Overgrazing and fire suppression in the Sand Plain have led to an increase in mesquite, live oak, and shrubs more characteristic of the brush country to the northwest.

Rolling Plains. The Rolling Plains extend westward from the Western Cross Timbers to the Caprock at the edge of the High Plains and from the Edwards Plateau northward to the Texas–Oklahoma border. This diverse, 30-million-acre area was historically midgrass prairie with scattered mesquite or, on rough, broken ground, grassland with numerous junipers and oaks. Important grasses include sideoats grama (*Bouteloua curtipendula*), little bluestem, Texas wintergrass (*Stipa leucotricha*), and common curly mesquite (*Hilaria belangeri*). On sandy soils, species such as sand bluestem (*Andropogon gerardii* var. *hallii*) and switch grass were also important, along with sand sagebrush (*Artemisia filifolia*). Many of the deeper, more fertile soils of the Rolling Plains have been converted to row crops, but the majority of the area consists of native sod that has a long history of overgrazing by domestic livestock. Native grasses such as hairy grama (*Bouteloua hirsuta*), three-awns (*Aristida* species), and sand dropseed (*Sporobolus cryptandrus*) have replaced climax native grasses, and woody species such as mesquite, lotebush, and red-berry juniper have increased in importance.

Edwards Plateau. The Edwards Plateau comprises about 17 million acres in Central Texas. It is circumscribed by the Balcones Fault zone on the south and east, the Rolling Plains on the north, and the Pecos–Devils River divide on the west. The southern and western third is heavily dissected, with the slopes and canyons dominated by oak forests and Ashe juniper–live oak woodlands. The relatively flat, deep-soiled uplands were historically open woodlands or grasslands with scattered mottes or individuals of live oak and cedar elm. Grasslands were dominated by little bluestem, Texas cup grass (*Eriochloa sericea*), common curly mesquite, cane bluestem, and sideoats grama. Most of the Edwards Plateau surface still consists of native sod, though there has been a long and continuing history of heavy, abusive grazing by domestic livestock. Grasses such as three-awns, Texas grama, and hairy tridens (*Erioneuron pulchellum*) have replaced climax dominants. Ashe juniper, mesquite, agarita, lotebush, live oak, and other shrubs have increased due to suppression of fire and overgrazing.

High Plains. The High Plains include 19.4 million acres of west Texas, including most of the Panhandle. The area was primarily shortgrass prairie in pre-European settlement times, dominated by blue grama (*Bouteloua gracilis*) and buffalo grass (*Buchloe dactyloides*). Most of the flat landscape of the central and northern High Plains has been converted to irrigated cropland, which utilizes water from the Ogallala Aquifer. The sandier soils of the southern High Plains were historically dominated by sand dropseed, little bluestem, plains bristlegrass, cane bluestem, and short grasses along with scattered mesquite and sand sage. This same midgrass–sand sage community also occurs in the northern Panhandle, north of the Canadian River. Also in this area are deep, stabilized dunes that support an unusual tallgrass–Havard shin oak community. Dominant grasses include sand bluestem, little bluestem, switch grass, sand dropseed, and sand lovegrass. These sandier soils have generally not been plowed. However, overgrazing has caused an increase in annual three-awn, gramas, sand dropseed, tridens species, and sand sagebrush.

South Texas Plains. The South Texas Plains have such a long history of overgrazing by feral and, later, domestic, livestock that reconstruction of presettlement vegetation is nearly impossible. However, much of the northern and central part of the area was probably grassland with scattered mesquite and other shrubby species. Climax grasses included cane bluestem, *Chloris* species, and *Bouteloua* species, but no relicts of this type have been quantitatively sampled, and perhaps none remain. The current vegetation is characterized by mostly dense shrubland of mesquite, blackbrush, and spiney hackberry. Some areas have been mechanically cleared and planted with buffel grass (*Cenchris ciliaris*).

Trans-Pecos. In the Trans-Pecos, semidesert grassland generally occurs from about 3,500 to 4,500 feet elevation in the foothills of mountains, especially the Davis, Guadalupe, and Chisos mountains. These shortgrass communities grade into midgrass Piedmont grasslands at higher elevations, and tobosa (*Hilaria mutica*) occurs on run-on clay flats within a matrix of desert shrublands at lower elevations. Climax dominants of the semidesert and Piedmont grasslands include black grama (*Bouteloua eriopoda*), sideoats grama, chino grama (*Bouteloua breviseta*), California cottontop (*Digitaria californica*), and blue grama, plus, at higher elevations, Texas bluestem (*Schizachyrium cirratum*), cane bluestem, and bull muhly (*Muhlenbergia emersleyi*). Much of these grasslands has been severely overgrazed, especially near perennial springs or wherever water has been artificially made available to domestic livestock.

Two less extensive grassland areas occur in West Texas. Havard shin oak–tallgrass dunes occur in Ward, Crane, and Winkler counties. These are similar to dune areas in the Panhandle, but are more open and contain a greater variety of xeromorphic shrub species such as catclaw acacia, mesquite, and lotebush. Also, within the salt basin of Hudspeth and Culberson counties and scattered throughout West Texas are saline flats dominated by alkali sacaton (*Sporobolus airoides*). Such areas are often converted to four-wing saltbush shrubland by overgrazing.

David D. Diamond

Great Hanging at Gainesville. The hanging of 40 suspected Unionists in October 1862. Two others were shot as they tried to escape. Although the affair reached its climax in Cooke County, men were killed in neighboring Grayson, Wise, and Denton counties. Most were accused of treason or insurrection, but evidently few had actually conspired against the Confederacy, and many were innocent of the abolitionist sentiments for which they were tried. Tension leading to the event had built for years. The completion of the Butterfield Overland Mail route through Gainesville brought many new people from the Upper South and Midwest into Cooke County. By 1860 fewer than 10 percent of the heads of households owned slaves. The slaveholders increasingly feared the influence of Kansas abolitionists in every unrest. In the summer of 1860 several slaves and a Northern Methodist minister were lynched in North Texas. Cooke and the surrounding counties voted against secession and thus focused the fears of planters on the nonslaveholders in the region. Rumors of Unionist alliances with Kansas Jayhawkers and Indians along the Red River, together with the petition of E. Junius Foster, editor of the Sherman *Patriot*, to separate North Texas as a new free state, brought emotions to a fever pitch. Actual opposition to the Confederacy in Cooke County began with the Conscription Acts of April 1862. Thirty men signed a petition protesting the exemption of large slaveholders from the draft and sent it to the Congress at Richmond. Brig. Gen. William Hudson, commander of the militia district around Gainesville, exiled the petitioners' leader, but others who remained used the petition to enlist a nucleus for a Union League in Cooke and nearby counties. The members were not highly unified, and their purposes differed with each clique. Most joined to resist the draft and provide common defense against roving Indians and renegades. Rumors began to circulate, however, of a membership of over 1,700 and of plans for an assault when the group had recruited enough men. Fearing that the stories of Unionist plots to storm the militia arsenals at Gainesville and Sherman might prove to be true, Hudson activated the state troops in North Texas in late September 1862 and ordered the arrest of all able-bodied men who did not report for duty.

Texas state troops led by Col. James Bourland arrested more than 150 men on the morning of 1 October. In Gainesville he and Col. William C. Young of the Eleventh Texas Cavalry, home on sick leave, supervised the collection of a "citizen's court" of 12 jurors. Bourland and Young together owned nearly a fourth of the slaves in Cooke County, and seven of the jurors chosen were slaveholders. Their decision to convict on a majority vote was a bad omen for the prisoners, all of whom were accused of insurrection or treason and none of whom owned slaves. The military

achieved its goal of eliminating the leadership of the Union League in Cooke County when the jury condemned 7 influential Unionists, but an angry mob took matters into its own hands and lynched 14 more before the jurors recessed. Violence in Gainesville peaked the next week when unknown assassins killed Young and James Dickson. The decision already made to release the rest of the prisoners was reversed, and many were tried again. Nineteen more men were convicted and hanged. Their execution was supervised by Capt. Jim Young, Colonel Young's son. Brig. Gen. James Throckmorton prevented the execution of all but five men in Sherman, but in Decatur, Capt. John Hale supervised a committee that hanged five suspects. A Southern partisan shot a prisoner in Denton.

Texas newspapers generally applauded the hangings, disparaged the Unionists as traitors and common thieves, and insisted they had material support from Kansas abolitionists and the Lincoln administration. The state government condoned the affair. Governor Lubbock, an ardent Confederate, praised Hudson for his actions, and the legislature paid the expenses of the troops in Gainesville. Articles from the Texas press were reprinted across the South. President Jefferson Davis, embarrassed, abandoned his demand for an inquiry into a similar incident involving Northern troops in Palmyra, Missouri, and dismissed Gen. Paul Octave Hébert as military commander of Texas for his improper use of martial law in several instances, including the hangings. The Northern press heralded the story as another example of Rebel barbarism. Andrew J. Hamilton, a former congressman from Texas and a Unionist, had been speaking in the North warning of the danger to loyal citizens in Texas. Reports of the Great Hanging and other incidents lent support to his campaign and led to his appointment as military governor of Texas and the disastrous Red River campaign of 1864.

The unrest did not end with the hangings in North Texas. Albert Pike, Confederate brigadier general in charge of Indian Territory, was implicated in testimony and arrested. Although later released, he continued to be regarded with suspicion and served the rest of the war in civilian offices. Capt. Jim Young killed E. Junius Foster for applauding the death of Young's father. He also tracked down Dan Welch, the man he believed to be his father's assassin, then returned with him to Cooke County and had him lynched by some of the family slaves. The Union League was powerless to exact revenge; many members fled along with the families of the slain prisoners, leaving bodies unclaimed for burial in a mass grave. A North Texas company of Confederate soldiers in Arkansas learned of the executions and almost mutinied, but tempers were defused by Brig. Gen. Joseph Shelby, their commander. Several men later deserted to return home, but Shelby prevented a mass assault on Gainesville. The half-hearted prosecution of those responsible for the hangings after the war, resulting in the conviction of only one man in Denton, increased resentment among the remaining Unionists in North Texas, but the failure of a Union League march on Decatur indicated the futility of further attempts at retaliation.

Richard B. McCaslin

Greenback Party. An agrarian party of the late nineteenth century. At the first convention of the Texas Greenback party in Austin on 12 March 1878 the delegates did nothing more than state the aims of the party. A convention at Waco on 7 August nominated a full ticket for state offices, with Gen. William H.

Hamman of Robertson County as candidate for governor. The platform, which closely followed that of the national Greenback party, denounced the law making greenbacks only a partial legal tender and the acts establishing the national bank system, exempting national bonds from taxation, and resuming specie payment for greenbacks. The platform urged the national government to issue greenback money as full legal tender and to redeem treasury notes and bonds with such greenbacks. Other planks provided that tariffs should be levied for revenue only and demanded the repeal of the "smokehouse" tax law, the convict labor law, the abolition of useless offices, a decrease in public salaries, the establishment of a tax-supported school system, and the curbing of the power of the railroads. In the election of 1878 the Greenback party replaced the Republicans as the second party in Texas by winning 12 seats in the legislature and electing George W. Jones of Bastrop to Congress. The 1880 convention was held at Austin with 140 delegates, including 20 African Americans. The platform was similar to that of 1878. Hamman was nominated again for governor, but the party had lost strength and he finished third. Only four representatives were returned to the legislature. Jones was reelected to Congress. The 1882 Greenback state convention met at Fort Worth in June but took no definite action. The delegates met again at Corsicana on 31 August; attendance was small. Though no candidates were nominated, the convention called on all Greenbackers to support independent candidates. The Republicans also supported George W. Jones as an independent candidate, and he polled 102,501 votes against John Ireland, who received 150,891. When the Greenback convention met at Waco on 26 August 1884, only 20 delegates were present. No candidates were nominated, and again the Independents were supported. No convention was called in 1886, and with no effort made to revive it the Greenback party passed out of Texas politics. Its membership of dissenting Democrats and Republicans soon went back to their old parties. Tenants, heavily indebted farmers, and smaller numbers of organized laborers and businessmen interested in specie speculation or expansion of their businesses had formed the bulk of the party's voters. Despite their defeat, the Greenbackers popularized a number of reform issues that gained national attention at the end of the nineteenth and beginning of the twentieth centuries, as the crusade of the farmer and the laborer was soon taken over by the People's party.

Jack W. Gunn

Greenville, Texas. County seat of Hunt County, a commercial and manufacturing center 60 miles northeast of Dallas. The community was founded in 1846 when Hunt County was established; the county seat was called Greenville to honor Gen. Thomas J. Green. The location was decided by county residents, who chose a 640-acre site donated by McQuinney Howell Wright, a surveyor, land speculator, and early settler. A post office opened in 1847; it was the only one in the county until 1849. Greenville's first school opened in the county courthouse in 1847. By 1850 a one-room building had been built to house the Greenville Institute, a private primary school. Greenville incorporated in 1852. During the Civil War the town raised and supported a company of soldiers that saw action in Arkansas and eastern Tennessee. During Reconstruction a federal garrison was stationed in Greenville from 1868 to 1870 to maintain peace in the area, which was the scene of a violent feud between former Confederates led by Capt. Bob Lee of Fannin County and

Unionists led by Lewis Peacock of Grayson County. The Missouri, Kansas and Texas Extensions Railway arrived in Greenville in the fall of 1880, constructed through from Whitewright in Grayson County, and the East Line and Red River Railroad arrived in February 1881, the Dallas and Greenville Railway in 1886, the St. Louis Southwestern Railway in 1887, and the Texas Midland line in 1896. Greenville was a leading cotton market by the mid-1880s. In 1891 the municipal government purchased and began operating an electricity-generating plant, the first such municipally owned utility system in Texas. By 1892 the city, described as the "principal city of . . . one of the richest blackland counties" in the state, reported a population of 5,000, and shipped over $1 million worth of cotton annually. In 1895 Burleson College, a Baptist junior college, began operations in Greenville; it closed in 1931. Texas Holiness University was established on the northern outskirts of Greenville in 1889 and moved in 1920 to Bethany, Oklahoma. Greenville witnessed the rise and decline of a small red-light district before 1910. A notorious incident of the period occurred in 1908, when a Greenville mob killed a black man accused of raping a white woman.

The population of Greenville climbed from 8,500 in 1900 to 12,384 by the mid-1920s. Wesley College, a private primary school and junior college, moved from Terrell to Greenville in 1912 and remained in operation until 1938. By 1914 Greenville reported a population of 14,000 and the largest cottonseed oil mill in the South. Natural gas was piped into the city from Dallas in 1926. During 1941 and 1942 the municipal government issued bonds to purchase and improve 760 acres outside of the city for a federally funded wartime airfield named Majors Field, for Lt. Truett Majors of Greenville, the first Hunt County man killed in World War II. In February 1951 Texas Engineering and Manufacturing Company leased a portion of Majors Field for the purpose of overhauling aircraft, generally for the armed services. By 1960 TEMCO employed 2,200 in Greenville; by the late 1960s, following a 1961 merger, Ling–TEMCO–Vought employed 4,600 and was the city's largest employer. Other local industries included the Henson–Kickernick and Shirey lingerie and sleepwear companies, the Electric Supply Company, and Mary of Puddin' Hill, Incorporated, bakers and retailers of fruitcakes. The community's population increased from 19,200 in the mid-1960s to 23,650 by 1976. During the mid-1970s LTV sold its Majors Field facilities to E-Systems Corporation, a major electronics and defense contractor, which has remained the city's largest employer. In 1990 the city had a population of 27,750 and 422 rated businesses. Buildings of interest include the post office, which is on the National Register of Historic Places, and the Ende–Gaillard House museum. Greenville is also the site of the Hunt County Fair in August and the Cotton Pickin' Arts and Crafts Jubilee in November.

Brian Hart

Greer County. A would-be Texas county that wound up in Oklahoma; formed by state legislative act in 1860, with boundaries "beginning at the confluence of Red River and Prairie Dog Town River; then running up Red River, passing the mouth of the South Fork [Elm Fork] and following main or North Red River to its intersection with the twenty-third degree of west longitude (the 100th meridian); thence due south across the Salt Fork to Prairie Dog River, and thence following that river to the place of beginning." Because of the Civil War little was done immediately to get the county going. In 1884, however, 144,000 acres of land was patented to the Day Land and Cattle Company, which also leased 203,000 additional acres. By 1885 there were in the county some 10 families and 60,000 cattle belonging to 7 or 8 firms that employed 100 men. The Francklyn Land and Cattle Company owned 40,000 cattle there. In July 1886 the settlers met at Mobeetie and organized Greer County on the authority of the act of 1860. Mangum was named the county seat, and provision was made for a county government. County commissioners began building a county jail, post offices were established at Mangum and Frazier, and a school system was set up. But the rapid development was disturbed by a dispute between Texas and the United States over the ownership of the area. The controversy had its origin in the Adams–Onís Treaty (1819), which designated the boundary between Spanish territory and the United States. Part of the treaty provided that the boundary should follow "the course of Red River westward to the degree of longitude one hundred west . . . then crossing the said Red River and running thence by a line due north to the River Arkansas." Accompanying the treaty was the Melish map, on which the boundary line had been drawn. This map, as was later discovered, depicted the 100th meridian at 90 to 100 miles farther east than the true meridian; and the Red River, in its upper course, divides into two major branches instead of having only one as shown on the Melish Map.

The United States took the position that the treaty involved the true 100th meridian, and that the South Fork was the main Red River, and therefore that the boundary was along the South Fork of the Red River to the true 100th meridian and thence northward. The acceptance of this position would make Greer County United States territory, since the true 100th meridian was near the western boundary of Greer County. Texas held that the 100th meridian of the Melish map was the boundary intended by the framers of the treaty and that the North Fork was the main Red River and therefore the boundary. In 1886 the Texas Boundary Commission met on the matter in Galveston, then Austin, but accomplished little. In 1890 President Harrison approved an act providing for the organization of Oklahoma as a territory and the prosecution of a suit against Texas for a final settlement of the dispute over the ownership of Greer County. The suit was taken up in the Supreme Court in October 1895. After hearing the arguments, the court ruled that the true 100th meridian was intended, that the South Fork of the Red River was the boundary between the United States and Texas, and that Greer County was under the jurisdiction of the United States. The county thus became a territory of the United States and, in 1906, part of Oklahoma.   *Webb L. Moore*

Gregory, Thomas Watt. United States attorney general; b. Crawfordsville, Mississippi, 6 November 1861; d. 26 February 1933 (buried in Austin); m. Julia Nalle (1893); 4 children; ed. Southwestern Presbyterian University, Clarksville, Tennessee (grad 1883), University of Texas (law degree, 1885). Gregory championed UT and was on its board of regents (1899–1907). His success as a lawyer in Austin, in partnership with Robert L. Batts and Victor L. Brooks, led him to politics. From 1891 to 1894 he was an assistant city attorney. He declined appointments as an assistant state attorney general in 1892 and as a state judge in 1896. Although he used the Progressive rhetoric condemning "plutocratic power," he was part of Edward M. House's essen-

tially conservative Democratic coalition. He established his credentials as a progressive reformer with his attacks against Senator Joseph Weldon Bailey, the symbol of political corruption in the eyes of Texas progressives, and with his service as a special prosecutor for the state in a series of antitrust suits, including the famous Waters–Pierce Case. In 1911–12 Gregory joined other Texas reformers and erstwhile conservatives such as House in promoting Woodrow Wilson for president. The contributions of the Texas delegation to Wilson's victory at the 1912 Democratic national convention and House's growing influence upon Wilson led to Gregory's appointment as a special assistant to the United States attorney general to conduct antitrust litigation against the New York, New Haven and Hartford Railroad in 1913. In 1914 he became attorney general. In 1916 Wilson wanted to appoint Gregory to the Supreme Court, but the attorney general declined. Despite his commitment to progressive reform, Gregory's performance as attorney general provoked enormous controversy because of his collaboration with postmaster general Albert S. Burleson and others in orchestrating a campaign to crush domestic dissent during World War I. Gregory helped frame the Espionage and Sedition Acts, which compromised the constitutional guarantees of freedom of speech and press, and lobbied for their passage. He encouraged extralegal surveillance by the American Protective League and directed the federal prosecutions of more than 2,000 opponents of the war. After resigning on 4 March 1919 he played a brief role at the Paris Peace Conference and then served on Wilson's Second Industrial Commission (1919–20), studying the social effects of industrial development. He also practiced law in Washington and Houston, where he lived from 1924 until his death. He campaigned for Franklin Roosevelt in 1932. He died during a trip to New York to confer with Roosevelt.   *Evan Anders*

Griffenhagen Report. A depression-era report on Texas government, authorized by the state legislature in 1931. An appointed committee of legislators (senators H. Grady Woodruff and Carl C. Hardin and representatives Harry N. Graves, Phil L. Sanders, and J. Turney Terrell) met in June 1931 under the name Joint Legislative Committee on Organization and Economy and employed Griffenhagen and Associates, specialists in public administration, to make a survey and act as consultants. The Griffenhagen staff made a comprehensive examination of all phases of state administration and compiled a report of more than 2,000 pages, covering fiscal and administrative agencies, highways, law enforcement, the judiciary, welfare programs, prisons, health, and education. The committee submitted *The Government of the State of Texas* to the 43d Legislature in due time, it thought, for the recommendations to be considered in the budget for 1933–35. The letter of transmittal stated that the recommended reforms might save over $6 million a year without curtailing the services of the government. The recommendations included reducing the executive branch from its 131 departments to 19, consolidating special funds, and appointing an independent auditor. The committee called for a shorter ballot by which only the governor, lieutenant governor, and attorney general would be elected; the governor's powers would be increased to include the right to appoint other major officials. The report proposed to establish departments of finance and administrative services and taxation and revenue. It advocated a pay plan for state employees based on job requirements rather than fixed salaries. Inertia and political expediency, however, prevented the legislature from taking any effective action on the recommendations. The net result of this rather expensive if unfulfilled project was to leave a document of considerable value to students of Texas history and government.   *J. Horace Bass*

Guadalupe College. A black college in Seguin, founded in 1884 by members of the Guadalupe Baptist Association. Association trustees bought property that had been the site of several other schools and is now the campus of Joe F. Saegert Middle School. The college opened in 1887 with J. H. Garnett as president, and in 1888 the state granted a charter. The purpose of the school was to awaken educational interest among the African Americans of Texas and to train teachers and religious leaders. Like white institutions of the time, the college department offered four years of classical courses that led to a B.A. degree. Preparatory, primary, theological, musical, and industrial departments offered a variety of courses and certificates. The State Board of Education endorsed Guadalupe College as a school of the first rank from 1902 until 1906, when it was the only black Baptist institution of higher learning in South Texas. Annual enrollment during the first 12 years averaged more than 200 and reached a high of more than 450 in 1907. Black Baptists contributed most of the support. Philanthropist George W. Brackenridge of San Antonio donated generously to the operation and development of the college. Students maintained the grounds and buildings and built all new structures. David Abner, Jr., succeeded Garnett as president in 1891, and the college flourished during his 15-year tenure. After conflict with trustees forced Abner's resignation in 1906, the institution underwent considerable turmoil with lawsuits, financial crises, declining enrollment, and loss of state endorsement.

Supporters of the school decided to begin anew and in 1914 moved the facility to Guadalupe River farm property. Brackenridge, who favored expansion of the vocational program, contributed funds for construction of two brick buildings. The administration, convinced that a liberal arts education was more important, continued to maintain a traditional college department, as well as an academy and grammar school, with only incidental training in agriculture and trades. Students were required to give evidence of good moral character and to attend weekly prayer meetings and Sunday school. They also worked a specified number of hours each day for the college. Gradually the institution regained its former stature. Enrollment in college-level courses increased after the Texas Department of Education classified Guadalupe College as a standard junior college in 1926 and accepted its credits in granting teacher certification. The institution was officially designated a senior college in May 1929. Students in the early 1930s averaged 60 in the college division and 125 in the academy. Hard-pressed financially by the Great Depression, however, Guadalupe College returned to junior college status in 1931 and suffered a fatal blow when fire destroyed the main building on 9 February 1936. Although the Missionary Baptist General Convention eventually built another building and conducted classes for ministers and lay leaders in the 1940s, efforts to reestablish a fully accredited college failed. The secretary of state issued a new charter to the College of the Guadalupe Baptist Association in 1971, but no regular classes resulted. The history of Guadalupe College paralleled that of many black institutions throughout the South and, though

marked by inexperienced leadership and financial difficulty, pointed the way toward permanent advancement.

Anne Brawner

Guadalupe Mountains National Park. In Hudspeth and Culberson counties on the New Mexico border; preserves some of the exposed remnants of the Capitan Reef, one of the world's finest examples of ancient barrier reefs. The Guadalupe Range slopes upward from New Mexico to its highest peak within the park. The park comprises 76,293 acres and includes the four highest peaks in Texas. Plants and animals combine in the park in a mixture of species native to Mexico, the Rocky Mountains, and the eastern United States. The park includes a small segment of the Chihuahuan Desert and protects several desert species. The cliffs of McKittrick Canyon harbor an oasis of spring-fed streams, porcupines, mule deer, and lush stands of gray oak, velvet ash, bigtooth maple, and alligator juniper. Wild turkeys, elk, mountain lions, and black bears roam forests of conifers and aspens at higher elevations. Many species of birds, ranging from hummingbirds to golden eagles, may be found in the park. Aoudad sheep that were introduced into the Guadalupes from North Africa by hunting-lease operators have taken over the ecological niche once occupied by desert bighorn sheep, which were killed off in the Guadalupes by 1910. Hunter-gatherer groups left pictographs and cooking pits in the Guadalupes as early as 12,000 years ago; some Indian rock art sites are now accessible by park trails. Mescalero Apaches claimed the Guadalupes as one of their last strongholds after Comanche horsemen and subsequently the United States Army pushed them from the plains below. As early as 1680 the Apaches raided the small community of El Paso del Norte (Ciudad Juárez), 100 miles to the west, and for nearly two centuries harassed Comanches and whites alike from the Guadalupe highlands. A troop of United States Cavalry, led by Lt. Howard B. Cushing, devastated a Mescalero encampment at Manzanillo Springs in 1869. A company of Texas Rangers attacked the remaining Guadalupe Apaches in 1881 at Hueco Tanks. The first Butterfield Overland Mail stagecoaches to leave St. Louis and San Francisco met just west of Guadalupe Pass in 1858. The Pinery stagecoach station near Pine Springs was once a regular stop, and its stone foundations remain near the park entrance. Most of the land within the park was once the Guadalupe Mountain Ranch, sold to the federal government by J. C. Hunter, Jr., whose father had purchased the ranch in 1924. Texas senators and congressmen introduced bills in Congress in 1963 and 1965 to establish Guadalupe Mountains National Park, but opposition surfaced to the purchase of more Texas land while approval was pending for Padre Island National Seashore and Big Thicket National Preserve. In 1966 President Lyndon Johnson signed the act establishing the park. The park was established in 1972. An 80-mile network of trails offers the best means to see the park, either on foot or horseback. The hardwood trees of McKittrick Canyon turn to brilliant colors in late October and early November. High winds usually blow in the spring, and severe storms may produce flash floods in the summer. The National Park Service maintains the Frijole Visitor Center at the park entrance on U.S. highways 62 and 180, a visitor center at the entrance to McKittrick Canyon, and a ranger station in Dog Canyon accessible by New Mexico Highway 137.

Mark Maliszkiewicz

Hill Country Landscape, by Hermann Lungkwitz, 1862. Oil on canvas. 18¼" × 24⅛". Museum of Fine Arts, Houston; Bayou Bend Collection, gift of Miss Ima Hogg. German immigrant Lungkwitz saw the Texas Hill Country in the same Romantic terms that dominated the vision of European and American landscapists of the day. Here the distant cave on the Guadalupe River evokes mystery in natural beauty.

Guadalupe River. Rises in two forks in Kerr County, then flows southeast for 230 miles to its mouth on San Antonio Bay. Its principal tributaries are the Comal and the San Marcos rivers. The upper Guadalupe flows across part of the Edwards Plateau. The Balcones fault line, which the river crosses near New Braunfels, marks the transition to the coastal plains. The name Guadalupe, or Nuestra Señora de Guadalupe, has been applied to the present river, at least in its lower course, since 1689, when the stream was so named by Alonso De León. Domingo Terán de los Ríos, who maintained a colony on the river from 1691 to 1693, renamed it San Agustín, but the name Guadalupe continued to be used. Most of the early explorers, including Father Isidro Félix de Espinosa, Domingo Ramón, and the Marqués de Aguayo, called the Guadalupe River the San Ybón above its junction with the Comal, and referred to the Comal River as the Guadalupe. Above the mouth of the Comal the name Guadalupe was applied to the present river at least as early as 1727, when Pedro de Rivera y Villalón so referred to it. Artifacts dating from the Archaic era have been found in the Guadalupe River valley, suggesting that the area has supported human habitation for several thousand years. The peoples encountered by early explorers belonged to the Tonkawa, Waco, Lipan Apache, and Karankawa Indians. These early inhabitants were gradually displaced by settlers from Mexico, Europe, and the United States. European settlement along the Guadalupe began as early as the 1720s, when the Spanish established several missions above the site of present Victoria. In 1755 the short-lived San Xavier Mission was established near San Marcos Springs. For a brief time in 1808 a settlement grew up at the intersection of the Guadalupe River and the Old San Antonio Road, but flooding and the threat of Indian raids made the site untenable. Settlements of a more permanent nature along the Guadalupe were not long in coming, however. Martín De León established Victoria near the mouth of the river in 1824, and in 1825 James Kerr founded Gonzales 60 miles upstream, where on the south bank a historical marker has been placed to commemorate the firing of the first shot for Texas independence in the battle of Gonzales (2 October 1835). During the 1830s some 30 or 40 families homesteaded along the banks of the lower Guadalupe, which was an early boundary of the Power and Hewetson colony. Settlement farther upriver increased in the late 1830s. Seguin (then called Walnut Springs) was surveyed by Ben McCulloch in 1839, and New Braunfels was founded in

1845 by a group of German settlers led by Prince Carl of Solms–Braunfels. In 1856 Kerrville was established on the upper Guadalupe. The construction of railroads through the middle and upper Guadalupe valley in the 1880s brought large numbers of new residents to the area. Kerrville, Comfort, Luling, and Cuero were among the small communities on the Guadalupe that prospered with the arrival of the railroads.

Projects to make the Guadalupe navigable were approved by the Mexican government in the late 1820s and early 1830s, but these were interrupted by the Texas Revolution. Some improvements to the lower reaches of the river were authorized by the Republic of Texas in the 1840s and by the Texas legislature in the 1850s. Large snags in the Guadalupe above Victoria made travel upriver impossible, but commercial routes were developed from Victoria to ports on the Gulf of Mexico. River traffic declined after the completion of the San Antonio and Mexican Gulf Railway from Victoria to Port Lavaca in 1861. Interest in the river's potential navigability was renewed in the early 1900s, but a 1935 study by the United States Army Corps of Engineers pronounced such a project economically unfeasible. Instead, the corps proposed a canal paralleling the river to connect Victoria with the Gulf Intracoastal Waterway. The proposal was reviewed in 1950, and construction began soon thereafter. The 35-mile Victoria Barge Canal was opened to commercial traffic in the mid-1960s, thus eliminating the need to improve the Guadalupe itself for such a purpose. The steady flow from the springs that feed the Guadalupe and its tributaries have made the river an attractive source of waterpower. The Guadalupe Waterpower Company was established in 1912, and by 1920 the company had built a series of dams between New Braunfels and Seguin in an effort to harness the river's power. Flooding, however, continued to be a problem. In 1933 the state legislature established the Guadalupe–Blanco River Authority to oversee the control, storage, and distribution of water from the Guadalupe and Blanco rivers. In 1958 the corps of engineers, in cooperation with the river authority, began construction of the dam at Canyon Lake, several miles upriver from New Braunfels. After its completion in 1964, the dam provided the first effective flood control for areas downstream. During the early 1990s the Guadalupe River continued to play a critical role in providing the surrounding area with power, water, and recreation. At least six power stations in the middle and lower portions of the river depended on a steady release of water from Canyon Dam, and the construction of several more such stations was under consideration. Recreation on the river, which included canoeing and inner-tubing as well as water parks and the facilities available at Canyon Lake and Guadalupe River State Park, attracted large numbers of people to the vicinity and contributed heavily to the area's economy.

Vivian Elizabeth Smyrl

Gulf Intracoastal Waterway. A coastal canal from Brownsville to the Okeechobee waterway at Fort Myers, Florida. The Texas portion of the canal system extends 426 miles, from Sabine Pass to the mouth of the Brownsville Ship Channel at Port Isabel. The idea of building a massive system of canals gestated for many decades before Congress authorized a survey for a system to connect inland waterways from Donaldsonville, Louisiana, to the Rio Grande (1873). By 1875 the army engineers had submitted the first plan for a waterway east of the Mississippi. Fierce opposition from railroads, together with wars and the magnitude of the task, slowed progress on the intracoastal waterway until after World War II. The state of Texas had already dredged a shallow channel through part of the West Bay inside Galveston Island. In 1892 Congress authorized enlargement and extension of that channel to Christmas Point in Oyster Bay, and in 1897 authorized purchase from the Brazos Navigation Company of an 11-mile canal that connected Oyster Bay to the Brazos River. The purchase was completed in 1902. The discovery of oil and the development of the Spindletop oilfield near Beaumont provided a major impetus for further canal development. In 1905 the Rivers and Harbors Act authorized a second major survey of inland waterways. The subsequent growth of the oil and gas industry along the Texas coast produced a great demand for cheap transportation of bulk materials. In 1905 the Interstate Inland Waterway League (now the Gulf Intracoastal Canal Association), a grass-roots organization, was founded by Clarence St. Elmo Holland and others. The league pledged support for a continuous 18,000-mile water transportation system extending from the Great Lakes through the Mississippi River and all its tributary systems and along the Texas and Louisiana coast. By 1905 Congress had provided authorization and money to tie the various existing canal segments into a continuous channel 9 feet deep and 100 feet wide from New Orleans to Galveston Bay. By 1941 the canal had been extended to Corpus Christi Bay; by 1949 it had been enlarged to 12 feet deep and 125 feet wide and extended to the Brownsville Ship Channel. The waterway was financed and constructed by the federal government through the United States Army Corps of Engineers. In 1975 the Texas legislature assumed sponsorship of the main channel of the Texas part, administered by the Texas State Highway and Public Transportation Commission. Disposal of materials from dredging the canal—a part of maintenance—has at times caused conflict. Some method of cost recovery for the operation of the nation's waterways has been debated since the 1930s. In 1978 Congress enacted the Inland Waterway Revenue Act, which levied a fuel tax on commercial users. Although the tax has increased in steps, the ultimate goal of a 100 percent user-supported canal seemed remote.

This commercial trade link with inland consumers through the Mississippi River system, and with world commerce through the Gulf of Mexico, is of major economic significance to Texas and the United States. The canal is directly linked to 10 deep-draft ports (ports with water 25 feet or more deep) and 26 shallow-draft channels. An average of 65 million tons of goods moved along the canal each year between 1968 and 1984. A record 72 million tons was carried over the canal in 1986. The principal commodities transported are crude petroleum and petroleum products, iron and steel, building materials, fertilizers, liquid sulfur, and other bulk products. The Texas Department of Transportation estimated that $35.5 billion worth of goods was moved over the waterway in 1986, by a work force of 145,000 people. Additionally, the canal is used extensively for recreation. In 1980 an estimated 2.4 million boat trips originated in Texas waters, and 79 percent of them used the Gulf Intracoastal Waterway. *Art Leatherwood*

Gulf of Mexico. For 624 miles, from the Rio Grande delta to Sabine Pass, the Gulf of Mexico washes the Texas shore. This partially landlocked body of water, an indentation in the southeastern coast of North America, served as an avenue for discovery, exploration, and settlement of the southern and western sectors of what is now the United States as well as Mexico: the initial approach to the mainland continent. It brought the Spanish conquerors to Mexico and Texas, French colonists to Louisiana, and, somewhat later, settlers of numerous other nationalities to the republic and state of Texas. Today, the Gulf serves a vital commerce. It links the ports of five southern states and Mexico with the larger ocean and forms the basis of the various marine resources of Texas, which include navigation, recreation, oil and gas, commercial fisheries, oysters, and shell. The Gulf is open to the Atlantic Ocean through the Straits of Florida and to the Caribbean Sea through the Yucatán Channel. These passages, approximately 100 and 125 miles wide respectively, lie on either side of the island of Cuba, which extends into the Gulf's mouth "like a loose-fitting bottle cork." The United States and Mexico form the Gulf's mainland shore, which extends more than 4,000 miles from the Florida Keys to Cabo Catoche, the northwestern promontory of the Yucatán Peninsula. Sharing the Gulf coast are Florida, Alabama, Mississippi, Louisiana, and Texas, as well as the Mexican states of Tamaulipas, Vera Cruz, Tabasco, Campeche, Yucatán, and Quintana Roo.

The Gulf's waters cover 500,000 square miles and plunge to a depth of 2,080 fathoms (more than 12,000 feet). This deepest part is Sigsbee Deep, an irregular trough more than 300 miles long, sometimes called the "Grand Canyon under the sea." Its closest point to the Texas coast is some 200 miles southeast of Brownsville. The cooler water from the deep stimulates plankton growth, which attracts small fish, shrimp, and squid. These and other sealife that feeds on plankton attract larger fish to make this a prime fishing ground. Biologists have counted more than 300 fish species off the Texas shore. Drainage of some 1,250,000 square miles is brought to the Gulf by the various rivers that discharge into it. Its water volume is calculated as 559,000 cubic miles. Through the Gulf courses the Caribbean Current, which enters from the Caribbean Sea through the Yucatán Channel and makes a circuit of the Gulf. The dominant feature of a complex system of currents in the Gulf, it flows out through the Straits of Florida and the Bahama Channel, where it joins the Antilles Current to form the Gulf Stream. As early as 1519, Spanish navigators recognized this flow as an aid to navigation into and out of the Gulf. The current, in combination with the prevailing wind, determined the course of the Spanish fleets, aiding them on their entire round-trip voyage from Europe. Ships entered the Gulf through the Yucatán Channel and rode the prevailing wind and current westward to the port of Veracruz. These forces, changing directions against the Mexican coast, favored ships returning to Spain by carrying them north and east into the Straits of Florida and the Bahama Channel. Not all aspects of the intricate system of currents are understood, even today; it is still the object of scientific study. Tides—ocean waters' response to gravitational pull by the moon and the sun—help to keep the waters in motion. The Gulf of Mexico, under ordinary conditions, has tides of two feet or less, but on the wide and shallow shelf such a variation is quite noticeable.

The Gulf's geologic origin remains uncertain. Various theories pose that it is a foundered and ocean-flooded continental crust, an ocean basin that has been subjected to rifting, or an ancient sea that has existed since the various continents formed a single land mass. Scientific drilling of the sea floor had not been able by 1994 to provide a complete answer. The longterm international Ocean Drilling Program, headquartered at Texas A&M University, seeks solutions to such riddles of oceanic geology by taking cores from ocean bottoms. It also gathers information on the origin and evolution of life in the sea, the shifting of the earth's continental plates, and other data pertinent to the Gulf, as well as the world's oceans at large.

The Texas shoreline is characterized by seven barrier islands: Galveston, Follets, Matagorda, St. Joseph (San José), Mustang, Padre, and Brazos. Padre Island is the longest barrier island in the world. These islands, formed 5,000 to 8,000 years ago, are the survivors of several sets of barriers that have existed along the northwestern Gulf Coast during the last million years, formed and destroyed by fluctuating sea level (usually related to glaciation) and the resultant shoreline alteration. During the four major glacial periods that covered North America with ice, the sea level was lowered by some 100 meters, exposing the continental shelf. Consequently, rivers emptying into the Gulf deepened their channels and carried sediment seaward. In the warmer interglacial periods, when the sea level rose, estuarine sediments and fossils were left on the shelf. Corral reefs, known to fishermen as "snapper banks," were formed from hard shale forced up by salt domes. These banks are found in the northwestern Gulf west of 91° west longitude. The Flower Garden Banks, the northernmost coral reefs on the North American continental shelf, lie about 110 miles southeast of Galveston. More than 50 feet under the surface, "flowers"—actually, brightly colored corals and other marine animals and plants that attract both sport divers and scientists—blossom in brilliant hues. The two banks, resting atop salt domes and encompassing areas of about 100 and 250 acres, were designated a marine sanctuary in 1992 (under the Marine Sanctuary Program established by the United States Congress in 1972) by the National Oceanic and Atmospheric Administration.

Credit for the first European discovery of the Gulf belongs to Sebastián de Ocampo, a Spaniard who circumnavigated Cuba in 1508–09 and returned to Santo Domingo (Hispaniola) with news of the body of water that lay beyond. Thereafter, the Gulf served as a primary approach to the North American mainland. Before that, and after Columbus's discovery of the Antilles, several maps portrayed what latter-day interpreters have assumed to be the Gulf, thereby disputing the actual discovery date. The basis for such cartography, however, is uncertain. It may be considered either hypothetical (as the 1500 map of Juan de la Cosa) or as representing the coast of Asia in keeping with Columbus's concept (as the 1502 prototype known as the Cantino map). The first known mainland landing within the Gulf of Mexico by Europeans was Juan Ponce De León's on the Florida peninsula in 1513. The next three voyages to penetrate the "hidden sea"—those of Francisco Hernández de Córdoba, Juan de Grijalva, and Hernán Cortés, 1517–19—focused on the southern Gulf. Shortly after Cortés's departure from Cuba early in 1519, destined for the conquest of Mexico, Alonso Álvarez de Pineda sailed from Jamaica to probe the Gulf's northern shore and western perimeter, seeking a strait to the Pacific Ocean. This voyage provided the "Pineda map," the first cartographic representation of any part of Texas, as well as of the Gulf itself. Álvarez de Pineda's crew were the first Europeans to glimpse the Texas coast. Although Álvarez's sketch provided no place names along the Texas shore, descriptive terms that still apply began appearing on Spanish maps: words that suggest a low-lying coast subject to flooding and lack of a secure anchorage. The Gulf itself remained nameless until the early 1540s, being considered a part of the Atlantic Ocean or "North Sea." The Spanish name most often applied to it was Seno Mexicano (*seno* = "gulf" or "bay"), although it was occasionally referred to in maps and documents as Golfo de Nueva España, Golfo de México, or a variant. For more than a century and a half after its discovery, it remained a sacrosanct "Spanish sea," forbidden to other nations.

Almost all European contact with Texas during this early period was through the Gulf of Mexico. Visitors included the expedition of Pánfilo de Narváez (1528); the remnant of the Hernando De Soto entrada, led by Luis de Moscoso Alvarado, in 1543; salvagers of the Padre Island Spanish shipwrecks of 1554; and Guido de Lavazares, who landed at Matagorda Bay in 1558. Such expeditions advanced the Spanish mapping of Texas and began the study of the Gulf's hydrology, which continues today. The practically oriented Spanish pilots compiled a rudimentary bottom profile of coastal waters with no more advanced technology than the sounding lead. With this primitive but effective device, they determined not only the water depth "within soundings" but also a description of the bottom material. This latter information, recorded in sailing instructions kept in the Casa de Contratación in Seville, helped establish the identity of a given location by the nature of the sediment. It also provided a clue to the bottom's suitability for holding an anchor. These early expeditions accomplished nothing toward the occupation of Texas. In that sense, the more meaningful exploration followed the Texas landing of the La Salle expedition (1685). Spanish voyages seeking La Salle's settlement included the first complete circumnavigation of the Gulf (by the Rivas–Iriarte expedition, 1686–87) and brought forth names for Texas and Louisiana coastal features that graced European maps for years to come. Whereas the French intrusion motivated Spanish interest in the middle Texas coast, the intractable Karankawa Indians, holding the barrier islands from Galveston Bay to Aransas Pass, forestalled Spanish control. Aided by forbidding geography, they prevented the opening of a Gulf port, the lack of which imposed a severe handicap on Spanish activities in Texas.

Although the Mexican coast was explored and much of it settled in the sixteenth century, some segments remain inaccessible by motor vehicle in the twentieth. The last area to be subdued and occupied during colonial times was the coastal strip known as Nuevo Santander, or Costa del Seno Mexicano, which comprises what is now the Mexican state of Tamaulipas and that part of Texas between the lower Nueces River and the Rio Grande. Since the first Europeans sailed the Gulf of Mexico, the body of water and its littoral have been severely affected by man and nature. River deposits contribute to nature's work, but storms and hurricanes claim a greater share of the consciousness of coastal residents. With seeming regularity, hurricanes—spawned either in the eastern Atlantic Ocean, the Caribbean Sea, or the Gulf itself—regularly ravage some part of the Gulf shore during the months of June to November. Although most often viewed in terms of their destructive force, the high winds and accompanying storm surge have played a large part in sculpting the shore. Hurricanes and storms, while destroying one island, may build another. Their beneficial effects for the Gulf and its littoral include reviving drought-stricken wetlands, balancing the salinity and stirring up nutrients in coastal estuaries (the

spawning areas and nurseries for commercial fisheries), and moderating the atmosphere.

From the beginning of European settlement in the Gulf, human beings have placed themselves at odds with these natural forces and have often paid the price. On 29 April 1554 an equinoctial storm drove three Spanish treasure ships aground on Padre Island with heavy loss of life and cargo. In early September 1766 a hurricane scattered a Spanish fleet crossing the Gulf, driving ships aground in Louisiana and Texas and destroyed the Spanish mission (Nuestra Señora de la Luz) and presidio (San Agustín de Ahumada) on the lower Trinity River. The list goes on. The more intense the coastal development, the greater the potential for destruction by hurricanes. Developers, vacationers, and condominium owners often assume an uncompromising attitude in facing the killer hurricanes, refusing to acknowledge that the Gulf beaches and barrier islands actually belong to the sea. A case in point is the intensive development of South Padre Island, a part of the 113-mile stretch of barrier sand between Corpus Christi and the Rio Grande. This development, with apartments and condominiums built on bulldozed dunes, has been built since Hurricane Beulah sliced the island into 31 segments in September 1967. Considering the pitfalls of predicting a hurricane's path and timing, forecasters cringe at the thought of the loss that a Beulah-like storm might cause in the same area today.

Population along the Texas Gulf coast is becoming increasingly dense. The more people, and the greater the demands placed on the Gulf's environs, the more critical becomes the effect on the natural balance. Various studies and government reports note that 225 Texas acres of topsoil wash into the Gulf each year. Louisiana is similarly plagued, losing more than 50 square miles of topsoil a year to erosion. The United States Army Corps of Engineers estimates that 60 percent of the Texas shore is eroding, 33 percent stable, and 7 percent advancing. One factor contributing to beach erosion is the impoundment behind large dams of river water that would normally supply beach-building materials. The reduced river flow results in the formation of settling basins that trap sediments before they reach the Gulf. Other "high-tech" engineering projects also contribute to the problem by curtailing the free exchange of sediments. "Manmade sand traps" along the shore now include six deep channels and several long jetties. Additionally, the Gulf and its beaches are being polluted by hundreds of thousands of gallons of oil and hazardous materials that spill into the water annually. More than 500 tons of trash washes ashore each year. Under state or federal protection are Aransas National Wildlife Refuge, wintering ground of most of the world's whooping cranes in the wild; Padre Island National Seashore, the nation's longest stretch of undeveloped beach; and several other shoreline segments. The preserves stand in contrast to "dream homes" and amusement parks built on fragile stretches of barrier sand.

The Gulf coast is the center of the state's oil refining and petrochemical industries. They are served by the Gulf Intracoastal Waterway, which extends 1,200 miles from Brownsville to Carrabelle, Florida, its course passing within the Texas barrier islands and thence mostly through channels dredged inside the coast. The waterway traverses the heart of the endangered whooping cranes' refuge with hazardous cargos of crude oil, benzene, carbon tetrachloride, hydrochloric acid, and other caustic chemicals; a mishap could be disastrous. The waterway must be dredged to remain open. Disposal of spoilage—some 400 million cubic yards of silt a year—gives rise to environmental threats, which must be balanced against the economic benefits. Environmentalists are generally opposed to expanding the waterway to accommodate more traffic and larger vessels, claiming that wetlands would be endangered by resultant incursion of salt water. Yet the waterway is credited with reducing the hypersalinity of the Laguna Madre (enclosed by Padre Island), which resulted in large fish mortalities in the 1930s and 1940s. From an economic standpoint, the waterway has proved highly cost-effective. It moves some 80 million tons of cargo along the coast each year. The waterway and the industries that depend on it provided more than 145,000 jobs in 1986.

The Gulf itself is one of the world's most concentrated ocean-shipping areas. Cargo received and shipped through Texas ports in 1990 totaled more than 335 million tons, of which 321 million tons was handled by 13 major ports. Eighty percent of this tonnage in 1986 was made up of oil and petrochemical products. Because of its location on the Gulf of Mexico, Texas is economically linked to Latin America, especially to Mexico, with which it maintains an important trade relationship. Texas port facilities have generally been closely linked to offshore drilling for oil, a situation somewhat altered by a downturn in the oil and gas industry in the mid-1980s. Refuse from both ships and oil rigs, which punctuate the continental shelf of both the United States and Mexico, has contributed to the Gulf's being labeled the "dumping ground for a hemisphere's trash." An international treaty known as MARPOL now makes such trash dumping in the Gulf illegal, but the measure is considered unlikely to bring a complete solution: the same ocean current that aided sailing ships entering the Gulf from afar also brings trash from afar. Detritus from near the equator has been known to wash up on Padre Island National Seashore, where the shore current seems to "suck in" debris, and sometimes shipwrecks. The prevailing southeasterly wind produces wave trains that strike the beach at a slight angle, generating a longshore drift on the upper coast. In the coastal-bend area, this shore current meets a north-flowing current driven by opposing winds; the impeded flow deposits its flotsam upon the shore. This effect is perhaps most noticeable on North Padre's Big Shell Beach, which offers a constantly changing array of sea-borne debris, as well as a kaleidoscopic assortment of shells. MARPOL is but one manifestation of the growing concern for the Gulf environment. With some 1,000 oil spills, major and minor, occurring each year on the Texas coast, the Texas legislature has improved the state's response system. Responsibility for the effort is assigned to the General Land Office, which has pushed for oil-spill reforms, beach and shoreline erosion programs, better beach access, and protection of coastal habitats. That protection of Texas beaches and wildlife does not rest solely upon state solutions, however, is demonstrated not only by the debris-laden current from outside the Gulf but also by episodes like the 1979 blowout of a Mexican oil well in the southern Gulf. The well, Ixtoc 1 in the Bay of Campeche, for a time spewed some 30,000 barrels of oil a day into the sea. Borne across the Gulf by the current, a resulting oil slick reached the Texas barriers two months later; birds sickened, beaches blackened, and tourists departed. The state braced for a major disaster, which it was spared only by a seasonal change in

wind and current. Nevertheless, a two-month clean-up effort was required on the 125-mile stretch from Port Isabel to Port Aransas, and lumps of Ixtoc tar were still washing ashore years later with each springtime warming. A scientist of the University of Texas Marine Science Institute at Port Aransas has predicted that the effects may last as long as 30 years; others believe they will last twice that long.

The Marine Science Institute, along with the Sea Grant College program of Texas A&M University, is concerned with understanding the Gulf of Mexico and attacking its problems. Since the institute was founded in 1941, following a massive fish kill resulting from a "red tide" in 1935, it has studied the phenomenon—which recurred in the Gulf in 1986—and its causes. It also studies the role of seaweeds and seagrasses in aquatic food chains, circulation and exchange processes in the oceans, and the physical properties of seawater in bays and estuaries of the Gulf of Mexico and the world's oceans. The institute is looking into the feasibility of natural spawning of saltwater fish and shrimp in captivity for commercial production. The Texas A&M Sea Grant program participates in the Institute of Marine Life Sciences, which has headquarters in Galveston. The focus is on protection of coastal waters from pollution by industrial and human waste, ships, and recreational boating.

In recent years a sharp decline has been observed in the Gulf shrimp catch. Though overfishing is considered the primary culprit, freshwater runoff in the heavy rainfall years has hindered shrimp development and contributed to a decline in the harvest. In 1994 the Texas Shrimp Association and the Texas Parks and Wildlife Department were attempting to hammer out regulations to ease the shrimpers' plight. Industry spokesmen note that the shrimping industry constitutes 94 percent of all reported commercial fishing in Texas and provides 30,000 jobs with annual payrolls of $326 million. This dominance results from a number of causes, including the fact that the public favors sport fishing and tourism over commercial fishing.

The Gulf of Mexico today is a far cry from the pristine sea discovered by Spanish navigators almost half a millennium ago. Though nature continues to revise its own creation, human endeavor in the Gulf and its environs exerts its own impact, much of it deleterious: on fish and wildlife, the beaches, inlets and estuaries, and the atmosphere. Parallel to efforts to preserve the whooping crane is concern for other endangered species such as the manatee (in eastern Gulf waters) and Kemp's ridley sea turtle. The latter, which often becomes enmeshed in shrimp nets and drowns, exemplifies the conflict that often occurs between human industry and nature. As both these factors have altered the Gulf of Mexico and its environment in the past, they will continue to do so in the future. Scientists are constantly trying to fathom the direction and effect of that change. Among the concerns is the so-called "greenhouse effect," which some people believe will bring a rise in global temperatures that will melt polar ice caps and raise sea levels. In the Gulf, that could mean inundation of large areas of low-lying coastal lands. On the basis of an Environmental Protection Agency report, a Louisiana scientist has projected a twelve-foot rise in the sea level by the year 2040. Such a rise would flood a fourth of Louisiana and seriously affect not only Louisiana but Texas and all the lands bordering the Gulf. The Corps of Engineers, meanwhile, wages a battle to keep the Mississippi River from hastening its race for the Gulf by taking over the Atchafalaya River and bypassing New Orleans. It's all a part of the contest between transient humankind and the eternal forces of the cosmos. *Robert S. Weddle*

Guthrie, Woody. Singer and song writer; b. Woodrow Wilson Guthrie, Okemah, Oklahoma, 14 July 1912; d. New York City, 3 October 1967 (cremated); m. Mary Jennings (1933; divorced); 3 children; m. Marjorie Greenblatt Mazia (divorced); 4 children, including Arlo Guthrie; m. Anneke Marshall; 1 child. After his mother was committed to a mental hospital, Woody lived in Pampa, 1929–37. He dropped out of high school but found a spiritual mentor in the Lebanese poet Kahlil Gibran. He supported himself by odd jobs, especially sign painting. Performing with bands at night clubs and radio stations in the Panhandle, Guthrie found his calling. With his first wife he experienced the pain of the Dust Bowl and the Great Depression, inspiration of many of his songs. The most memorable song of the Pampa years, "So Long, It's Been Good to Know You," was a response to the great dust storm of 14 April 1935, which led some Pampans to think the world was ending. Guthrie left for Los Angeles in 1937 and worked at radio station KFVD, where, to fill hours of air time, he turned out lyrics at stream-of-consciousness speed, usually setting them to someone else's music. His listeners were often Okies, Arkies, and Texans who had fled to the West Coast, where, Guthrie told them, they would find the American dream if they had brought "Do Re Mi." Some longed nostalgically for "The Oklahoma Hills" and all listened knowingly while Guthrie sang "Dust Bowl Refugee" and "I Ain't Got No Home in this World Anymore." Thrilled by the hydroelectric power flowing from massive New Deal dams on the Columbia River in Washington and Oregon, Guthrie composed "Roll On, Columbia," which celebrates the New Deal, and "Pastures of Plenty," which celebrates the nobility of nearby migrant laborers. "This Land Is Your Land" was written in 1940 to tell countrymen that America belongs to the many and not the few. After 1940 Guthrie usually called New York City home. Although he wrote children's songs, he wrote others that displayed a populist rage against Eastern rich men, each with his "Philadelphia Lawyer," who allegedly drove farmers from their land. During the 1940s Guthrie taped his songs for the Library of Congress, performed on CBS radio shows, and published the first of several books, *Bound for Glory*, which was later made into a movie. He survived two German torpedoes in the United States Merchant Marine. After Mary divorced him he married a beautiful Jewish dancer from the Martha Graham company. By the early 1950s his period of great productivity—he wrote perhaps a thousand songs—was over. In 1953 Huntington's disease put him in a hospital where he spent nearly all of his last 14 years. The protest singers of the 1960s, including Bob Dylan, idolized him. Pampans held their first annual Tribute to Woody Guthrie on 3 October 1992. *Richard B. Hughes*

Gutiérrez–Magee Expedition. An early (1812–13) filibustering expedition against Spanish Texas, carried out against the background of growing unrest in Mexico under Spanish rule. In January 1811 a former militia captain named Juan Bautista de las Casas, inspired by the Diez y Seis revolt in Guanajuato, led an insurrectionist movement against the royalists in San Antonio, seizing Governor Manuel María de Salcedo and his military

staff. In March, royalists staged a successful countercoup against the Casas Revolt, captured Casas, and executed him. In December 1811 an envoy of the rebels, José Bernardo Gutiérrez de Lara, traveled to Washington in the hope of securing United States support for the antiroyalist cause. Conferences with American officials brought only vague promises of aid, but Gutiérrez was led to believe that the United States would not hinder the organization of the expedition against Texas. After discussing his plans with José Álvarez de Toledo y Dubois, Gutiérrez sailed for New Orleans with a letter of introduction to Governor William Claiborne, who introduced him to William Shaler, a consular officer seeking to enter New Spain as an observer for President Monroe. Shaler became the principal adviser of the expedition. Many adventurers, some of whom hoped to win Texas for the United States, assembled at or near Natchitoches, Louisiana, to form the nucleus of an invading army. Shaler enlisted the aid of Lt. Augustus Magee and helped Gutiérrez send propaganda into New Spain. After crossing the Sabine with some 130 men on 8 August 1812, Magee scattered royalist frontier detachments and entered Nacogdoches on 12 August. American and Mexican recruits, attracted by possibilities of booty and encouraged by merchants of Natchitoches, increased Magee's strength to about 300 men before he marched against Santísima Trinidad de Salcedo on 13 September. Governor Salcedo concentrated his forces on the Guadalupe River to protect San Antonio, but Magee changed the direction of his attack and entered La Bahía (present Goliad) on 7 November with almost no opposition. Salcedo, pursuing the invaders with fewer than 200 men, laid siege to La Bahía on 13 November. When reinforcements increased this force to about 800, Magee asked for terms of surrender. Salcedo's offer was so unsatisfactory that the filibusters decided to fight. Before any decisive action had taken place, Magee died (6 February) and Samuel Kemper succeeded to the command. Under Kemper's leadership, the expedition won its greatest success. Salcedo, defeated in attacks on 10 and 13 February, retreated toward San Antonio on 19 February. Kemper moved out in a belated pursuit a month later with 800 men, including volunteers from Nacogdoches and deserters from the Spanish army, and on 29 March 1813 defeated a royalist army of 1,200, commanded by Simón de Herrera, in the battle of Rosillo. Salcedo surrendered San Antonio unconditionally on 1 April. Gutiérrez, nominally commander-in-chief of the expedition, began to assume a greater role in its affairs. On 3 April he reportedly permitted the execution of Salcedo and 14 royalist officers, including Herrera. This act caused many Americans to abandon the enterprise at once. A few days later, having lost confidence in Gutiérrez and his provisional government, Kemper led more than 100 Americans back to Louisiana on "furlough."

Organization of the Spanish effort to recover Texas fell to Col. Ignacio Elizondo and Gen. Joaquín de Arredondo. Acting more or less independently, Elizondo laid siege to San Antonio with 900 men. Reuben Ross, successor to Kemper in command of the Americans, advised a retreat; but, when a council of war refused to support him, he resigned and was followed by Henry Perry. In the battle of the Alazán (20 June 1813), Perry routed Elizondo's troops in a dawn attack and returned to San Antonio with considerable booty. While Elizondo was rallying his scattered forces and Arredondo was marching to join him, Shaler guided an intrigue by which he replaced Gutiérrez in command. Most of the Americans supported the new commander; but several Mexicans, led by Col. José Menchaca, attempted to sabotage the expedition by preventing Toledo from moving promptly against Arredondo's advancing forces. With a small army badly demoralized by intrigues, Toledo succeeded in moving from San Antonio on 15 August, too late to prevent a junction between Arredondo and Elizondo. Three days later, in the battle of Medina, the royalists annihilated the republicans and filibusters.

Arredondo then entered San Antonio and proceeded with the harsh pacification of Texas. In San Antonio royalists shot 327 persons, and in Nacogdoches one of Arredondo's lieutenants carried out a similarly bloody purge. Despite the victory of the royalists, however, the Gutiérrez–Magee expedition so intensified interest in Texas that complete peace could not be restored. The province remained the center of plots or the object of invasion until Agustín de Iturbide finally brought the revolution to an end.

Harris Gaylord Warren

H

H-E-B. A Texas-based supermarket chain, among the largest private companies in the United States. In 1905 Florence Thornton Butt, with a $60 loan, started a one-room grocery store on the ground floor of the family home. In 1919 she turned management of the business over to her youngest son, Howard Edward Butt, who introduced low-cost distribution innovations that eliminated middlemen and maximized profits. In 1922 he replaced his credit-and-delivery system with a policy of self-service cash-and-carry, thus increasing the turnover of goods and heralding a new era of shopping. Butt established a successful enterprise at Del Rio in 1926, followed in 1927 by the purchase of three grocery stores in the lower Rio Grande valley. By specializing in low-priced goods the company survived the Great Depression so successfully that he was able to introduce employee picnics and a group life-insurance policy, move company headquarters to the Valley, and expand to nearly 20 stores in Southwest Texas, with a gross business of $2 million in 1931. The company began advertising with free gifts—dispensed in one case by throwing tagged live chickens, good for free groceries, and handfuls of nickels off a store roof—and later gave away cars, mink stoles, trading stamps, and cash prizes. Butt moved into manufacturing by acquiring the Harlingen Canning Company and opening a bakery in Corpus Christi in 1936. In 1940 company headquarters moved to Corpus Christi to centralize distribution. In 1942 Butt installed air-conditioning in his stores, introduced frozen foods, and opened the first store under the name H-E-B, in San Antonio.

During World War II the Harlingen Canning Company produced food for the armed forces, and won a War Food Administration "A" award for its food processing. Women managed some stores. H-E-B became known for its interest in personnel development. A store that opened in Austin in 1944 became the fiftieth H-E-B. The grocery stores grew into supermarkets in the 1950s. During that decade H-E-B introduced in-store fish markets, butcher shops, drugstores, and bakeries. Since Butt was a traditional Baptist deacon, the stores carried no beer or wine until his son took over in the 1970s. The Texas Gold Stamp Company, a subsidiary, was organized in 1955 to produce consumer trading stamps, and the first retail support center, a manufacturing and distribution center, was opened in San Antonio in 1964. In 1971 Charles C. Butt took over his father's position as president and CEO. Under his administration, the firm restructured its management and introduced generic goods. A milk plant opened in San Antonio in 1976, and the company introduced Futuremarkets, a further diversification that added in-store pharmacies, photo processing, and video rentals. During the 1980s, H-E-B stores began offering bulk foods and fresh flowers. The company headquarters moved to the renovated army arsenal on the San Antonio River in 1985. The introduction of H-E-B Pantry Foods in 1988 took H-E-B to East and North Texas, as the company expanded across the state. In 1995 the company ran 224 stores, all in Texas. Throughout H-E-B's history, about 5 percent of all pre-tax earnings have been donated to civic and charitable organizations as part of the firm's commitment to the community. *Diana J. Kleiner*

Haley, J. Evetts. Historian, rancher, and political activist; b. Belton, 5 July 1901; d. Midland, 9 October 1995; m. Mary Vernita Stewart (1928; d. 1958); 1 son; m. Rosalind Kress Frame (1970); ed. West Texas Normal College (grad. 1925) and the University of Texas (M.A., 1926), where he studied under Eugene C. Barker. Haley championed individualism and personal freedom, the study and preservation of history, and a principled conservatism, all of which are reflected in his published works and his life as a rancher. He was editor and writer of official publications as a student in Canyon and Austin. He was commissioned to write *The XIT Ranch of Texas and the Early Days of the Llano Estacado* (1929), a critically acclaimed work that got its author sued for libel. Other historical works followed: numerous articles in periodicals as varied as *Southwestern Historical Quarterly* and *Ranch Romances*; *Charles Goodnight: Cowman and Plainsman* (1936); *George W. Littlefield, Texan* (1943); *Charles Schreiner, General Merchandise* (1944); *Jeff Milton, A Good Man With a Gun* (1948); *Fort Concho and the Texas Frontier* (1952); and *Rough Times— Tough Fiber: A Fragmentary Family Chronicle*. In addition, Haley, often embroiled in controversy, wrote polemics that reflected his political views. He sided with the regents of the University of Texas in their controversy with Homer Rainey and argued his points in *The University of Texas and the Issue*. His scathing *A Texan Looks at Lyndon* was published during the 1964 presidential election campaign. Haley ran unsuccessfully for governor in 1956 on a platform that endorsed segregation and states' rights and opposed labor unions and federal price controls on natural gas. The following year he and other conservative Texans formed the political action group Texans for America with Haley as state chairman. During this same period the federal government charged him and his son with violating the Agricultural Adjustment Act of 1936 by exceeding their wheat acreage allotment on their Oklahoma ranch. The Supreme Court eventually heard the case and overturned a lower court ruling favoring the Haleys. Haley's library and personal papers became the cornerstone of the Nita Stewart Haley Memorial Library in Midland. Haley received many honors, including investiture in the Knights of the Order of San Jacinto by the Sons of the Republic of Texas in 1978, an Award of Merit from the American Association of State and Local History in 1981, induction into the Hall of Great Westerners at the National Cowboy Hall of Fame and Western Heritage Center (Oklahoma City) in 1990, and similar recognition by the Heritage Hall of Fame at the State Fair of Texas in 1994. *B. Byron Price*

Hamer, Frank. Lawman; b. Francis Augustus Hamer, Fairview, 17 March 1884; d. Austin, 10 July 1955; m. Gladys Johnson (1917); two sons, plus Gladys's two daughters from a previous marriage. Hamer joined the Texas Rangers in 1906 after working as a cowboy. He was marshal of Navasota (1908–11), then returned to the

Frank Hamer. Walter Prescott Webb Papers, CAH; CN 03116.

Hamilton, Andrew Jackson. Governor; b. Huntsville, Alabama, 28 January 1815; d. Austin, 11 April 1875; m. Mary Bowen; 6 children. Hamilton, an attorney, joined his older brother, Morgan, in Texas in 1846. In 1849 Governor Peter H. Bell appointed him acting attorney general. He represented Travis County for one term (1851–53) in the state House of Representatives. He was a member of the "Opposition Clique" in Texas, a faction of the regular Democratic party that opposed secession and other Southern extremist demands. In 1859 he won election to the Congress from the Western District of Texas. He served on the House committee formed during the secession winter of 1860–61 to try to solve the sectional crisis. When he returned to Texas in 1861 he won a special election to the state Senate, and he remained in Austin until July 1862, when alleged plots against his life forced him to flee to Mexico. Hamilton became a hero in the North and delivered speeches in New York, Boston, and other Northern cities. His rhetorical targets included slavery, disunionists, and the "slave power," which he believed was trying to subvert democracy and the rights of nonslaveowners. After he met with President Abraham Lincoln in November 1862, he accepted a commission as brigadier general of volunteers and an appoint-

rangers. He patrolled the South Texas border from the Big Bend to Brownsville when arms smuggling, bootlegging, and banditry were rampant. The rangers, including Hamer, were criticized for their tactics; notably, legislator José T. Canales accused Hamer of threatening him in 1918. Hamer was transferred to Austin in 1921 and attained the rank of senior captain. Subsequently he restored order in oil-boom towns such as Mexia and Gander Slu in 1922 and Borger in 1927, and he participated in numerous fights with lawbreakers. In 1928 he was credited with exposing a banking "reward ring" in which the Texas Bankers' Association publicly announced a standing reward of $5,000 for any dead bank robber. Hamer charged that some people were tracking down small-time hoods just to kill them and collect the money. In 1932 he retired from active duty but retained his commission. In 1934 Marshall Lee Simmons, head of the prison system, asked Hamer to take the new position of special investigator for the system and assigned him the task of tracking down Bonnie and Clyde; with others, Hamer killed the infamous couple near Gibsland, Louisiana, on 23 May 1934. Congress awarded him a special citation. During the late 1930s Hamer worked for various oil companies and shippers as a private agent preventing strikes and breaking up mobs. In 1948 he again was called to duty as a ranger by Governor Coke Stevenson to accompany him and help check the election returns in Jim Wells and Duval counties in the controversial United States Senate race. Hamer retired in 1949 and lived in Austin until his death. He had been wounded numerous times and had killed an undetermined number of felons. *John H. Jenkins*

Brig. Gen. A. J. Hamilton. *Carte de visite* by E. Jacobs & Co., New Orleans, ca. 1863–65. Courtesy Lawrence T. Jones III Collection, Austin.

ment as military governor of Texas. Hamilton accompanied an unsuccessful federal expedition into South Texas in late 1863 and spent most of the rest of the war in New Orleans, where his family joined him late in 1864.

His career during Reconstruction was stormy and frustrating. As provisional governor from the summer of 1865 to the summer of 1866, he tried to limit officeholders to former Unionists, sought ratification of the Thirteenth Amendment, and advocated granting economic and legal rights (although not the vote) to freedmen. When the Constitutional Convention of 1866 refused to enact most of Hamilton's suggestions, he rejected presidential Reconstruction and promoted the harsher program of the Radical Republicans. He then endorsed black suffrage and helped organize the Southern Loyalists' Convention in Philadelphia in September 1866. For a time he served as a bankruptcy judge in New Orleans, but in 1867 he returned to Texas as an associate justice on the state Supreme Court. Hamilton played a leading role in the Texas Constitutional Convention of 1868–69 and served on the Republican National Executive Committee. His political views changed again, however; he once again came to favor a quick reconstruction of Texas. He opposed the Radicals' scheme for turning West Texas into a separate, Unionist state and withdrew his support for black suffrage. As a result, although his brother Morgan H. Hamilton was a leading Radical spokesman and United States senator, Hamilton became one of the state's leading moderate Republicans and ran against Radical Edmund J. Davis in the 1869 governor's race. Davis won, but Hamilton remained a vocal opponent of Radical policies. Hamilton never sought public office after this defeat. In 1871 he was a leader in the Tax-Payers' Convention. He practiced law and worked on his farm near Austin.   *James A. Marten*

Hardin, John Wesley. Outlaw; b. Bonham, 26 May 1853; d. El Paso, 19 August 1895; m. Jane Bowen; 3 children. His father was a Methodist preacher. Hardin's violent career started in 1867 with a schoolyard squabble in which he stabbed another youth. At 15, in Polk County, he shot and killed a black man as a result of a chance meeting and an argument. With the Reconstruction government looking for him, he fled to his brother's house, 25 miles north of Sumpter, where in the fall of 1868 he claimed to have killed three Union soldiers who sought to arrest him. Within a year, he killed another soldier at Richard Bottom. In 1871 Hardin went as a cowboy up the Chisholm Trail. He killed seven people en route and three in Abilene, Kansas. After allegedly backing down city marshal Wild Bill Hickok, who may have dubbed him "Little Arkansas," Hardin returned to Gonzales County, Texas, where he got into difficulty with Governor Davis's State Police. He then settled down long enough to marry. He added at least four names to his death list before surrendering to the sheriff of Cherokee County in September 1872. He broke jail in October and began stock raising but was drawn into the Sutton–Taylor Feud in 1873–74. He aligned himself with Jim Taylor of the anti-Reconstruction forces and killed the opposition leader, Jack Helm. In May 1874 he started two herds of cattle up the trail; while visiting in Comanche he killed Charles Webb, deputy sheriff of Brown County. From that time, Hardin was constantly pursued in Texas. He went with his wife and children to Florida and Alabama, adding one certain and five possible names to his death list before the Texas Rangers captured him in Pensacola on 23 July 1877. He was tried at Comanche for the murder of Charles

John Wesley Hardin, Abilene, 1871. Courtesy Robert McCubbin Collection, El Paso.

Webb and sentenced in 1878 to 25 years in prison. During his incarceration he made repeated efforts to escape, read theological books, was superintendent of the prison Sunday school, and studied law. He was pardoned on 16 March 1894 and admitted to the bar. In 1895 he went to El Paso to appear for the defense in a murder trial and to establish a law practice. He took as his lover the wife of one of his clients, Martin Morose, and when Morose found out about the affair, Hardin hired a number of law officials to assassinate him. Constable John Selman, one of the hired killers, shot Hardin in the Acme Saloon, possibly because he was not paid for the murder of Morose. Hardin's autobiography, completed to the beginning of his law studies in prison, was the subject of some litigation and was published in 1896. Hardin considered himself a pillar of society, always maintaining that he never killed anyone who did not need killing.   *Leon C. Metz*

Hardin–Simmons University. Coed; in Abilene; established in 1891 as Abilene Baptist College by the Sweetwater Baptist Association; renamed Simmons College in 1892 (in honor of donor James B. Simmons), Simmons University (1925), and Hardin–Simmons University (1934, in honor of donors John G. and Mary Hardin). HSU was at first an academy—that is, most of its students were in high school. Between 1902 and 1909, under the presidency of Oscar Henry Cooper, three additional years of study were added to the curriculum, allowing the school to offer bachelor's degrees. The first graduate program was introduced in 1926, and in the mid-1980s HSU had a master's degree program in six fields. The institution has been accredited by the Southern Association of Colleges and Secondary Schools since 1927. Jefferson Davis Sandefer, president from 1909 to 1940, was succeeded by Rupert N. Richardson. Since 1940 the university has been under the control of the Baptist General Convention of Texas. From the end of World War II to the 1990s, annual enrollment stayed at around 2,000 students. In the 1960s President Elwin L. Skiles launched a building campaign that produced a new library, a science center, and a physical education and health complex. President Jesse C. Fletcher subsequently restructured the university into schools, including, in addition to the graduate school, schools of art and science, business and finance, education, music, nursing, and theology. A western motif predominates at HSU, as the Cowboy Band attests. The athletic teams are called the Cowboys and Cowgirls. Football was discontinued in the 1960s, though the university continues to participate in intercollegiate athletics. *Kenneth R. Jacobs*

Harlingen, Texas. Harlingen's strategic location at the intersection of U.S. highways 77 and 83 in northwestern Cameron County fostered its development as a distribution, shipping, and industrial center. In 1904 Lon C. Hill envisioned the Arroyo Colorado as a commercial waterway. He named the town he founded on the north bank after a city in Holland. The town's post office was established that year. Harlingen was incorporated in 1910, when the population was 1,126. The local economy at first was almost entirely agricultural, with vegetables and cotton as the major crops. World War II military installations in Harlingen caused a jump in population to 23,000 in 1950 and 41,000 by 1960. Harlingen Army Air Field preceded Harlingen

Air Force Base, which closed in 1962. The city's population fell to 33,603 by 1972, then climbed to 40,824 by 1980. Local enterprise, focused on the purchase and utilization of the abandoned base and related housing, laid the groundwork for continuing progress through a diversified economy. In the 1990s income from tourism ranked second only to citrus fruit production, with grain and cotton next in order. The addition of wholesale and retail trade, light and medium manufacturing, and an array of service industries has broadened the economic base. Large-scale construction for multifaceted retirement communities is a new phase of industrial development. The city of Harlingen operates a busy industrial airpark where bombers used to land. At Valley International Airport the Confederate Air Force once occupied hangar and apron space. Development and appreciation of the fine arts are encouraged by organizations such as the Rio Grande Valley Art League, the Art Forum, and the Rio Grande Valley Civic Association, which stages its winter concert series at the 2,300-seat Harlingen Municipal Auditorium. Each March Harlingen is the site of the Rio Grande Valley International Music Festival. The city has two newspapers—the Harlingen *Press*, a weekly paper established in 1951, and the *Valley Star*, a daily established in 1911. Harlingen had 48,735 residents in 1990 and was named an All-American City in 1992. *Minnie Gilbert*

Hatteras. A United States Navy vessel sunk by the Confederate *Alabama* on 11 January 1863. The wreck lies in 60 feet of water about 20 miles south of Galveston. The site is one of the few shipwreck sites in the National Register of Historic Places. The steel-hulled, side-wheeled steamship represents the transition between the wooden sailing ship and the modern steamship. She is comparatively intact since she sank very rapidly and, unlike the majority of Texas shipwrecks, lies in deep water away from the destructive surf. The *Hatteras* was a converted merchant ship

Onion harvest near Harlingen, Texas, ca. 1949. Courtesy TSL. Traditionally the local economy of Harlingen has depended upon agriculture—primarily vegetables and cotton.

formerly named the *St. Mary*. She was acquired by the United States Navy from Harland and Hollingworth of Wilmington, Delaware, on 25 September 1861. She was armed and fitted out at the Philadelphia Naval Yard and commissioned in October 1861. The ship and her crew of 126 first saw duty with the South Atlantic blockading squadron and subsequently with the Gulf of Mexico blockading squadron. She carried out raids on the Confederate coastline, engaged a Confederate warship, CSS *Mobile*, in an inconclusive action, and captured a number of blockade runners. The *Hatteras* was sunk by Confederate captain Raphael Semmes after a short battle. Commercial treasure hunters filed a suit claiming to be the salvors and owners of the wreck, but because the *Hatteras* was a United States naval vessel, the federal government was able to keep control of the site and preserve it for scientific investigation. This is one of the few cases in which the courts have found in favor of historic preservation and against commercial exploitation of a historic shipwreck site. The New Orleans Outer Continental Shelf Office of the Bureau of Land Management, as the responsible federal agency, has undertaken various investigations of the wreck.

J. Barto Arnold III

Hays, John Coffee. Texas Ranger; b. Little Cedar Lick, Wilson County, Tennessee, 28 January 1817; d. California, 21 April 1883; m. Susan Calvert (1847); 6 children. Jack Hays, Rip Ford, Ben McCulloch, and Samuel H. Walker established the Texas Ranger tradition. Hays traveled to New Orleans in 1836 and entered Texas at Nacogdoches in time to join the troops under Thomas J. Rusk and bury the remains of victims of the Goliad Massacre. Houston advised him to join a company of rangers under Deaf Smith for service from San Antonio to the Rio Grande, under the orders of Col. Henry W. Karnes. In this role Hays took part in an engagement with Mexican cavalry near Laredo, assisted in the capture of Juan Sánchez, and rose to the rank of sergeant. After appointment as deputy surveyor of the Bexar District, Hays combined soldiering and surveying for several years. The more he learned about Indian methods of warfare, the better he protected surveying parties against Indian attack. In the three-way struggle among Anglo colonists, Hispanic settlers, and Indians, Hays proved to be an able leader and fearless fighter (called "Devil Yack"), who gained the respect of the rank and file of the Texas Rangers. From 1840 through 1846 Hays, at first a captain, then a major, and his ranger companies, sometimes with Mexican volunteers and such Indian allies as Lipan chief Flacco, engaged the Comanches and Mexican troops in small skirmishes and major battles. Important military actions took place at Plum Creek, Cañón de Ugalde, Bandera Pass, Painted Rock, Enchanted Rock (where Hays made a lone stand that enhanced his reputation as an Indian fighter), Salado Creek, and Walker's Creek. In these battles Hays and his rangers were usually outnumbered, and their effective use of revolvers revolutionized Western warfare. In the Mexican War the rangers were transformed into mounted irregular troops celebrated in song and story throughout the United States. This metamorphosis in fact and fiction started with the formation of the First Regiment, Texas Mounted Riflemen, under Colonel Hays. Serving with the army of Gen. Zachary Taylor, the rangers marched, scouted, and took part in the attack on Monterrey in 1846. The next year Hays formed another regiment that participated in keeping communication and supply lines open between Veracruz and Mexico

City for the troops under the command of Gen. Winfield Scott. In doing so, Hays's rangers fought Mexican guerrillas near Veracruz and at such places as Teotihuacán and Sequalteplán. Controversy between the rangers and the Mexican people still lingers, for they robbed and killed each other off the battlefields. In the years that followed the Mexican War, Hays pioneered trails through the Southwest to California and became a prominent citizen of that state. In 1848 he tried unsuccessfully to find a route between San Antonio and El Paso, and the following year he received an appointment from the federal government as Indian agent for the Gila River country. In addition, he was elected sheriff of San Francisco County in 1850, appointed United States surveyor general for California in 1853, became one of the founders of the city of Oakland, and ran successful enterprises in real estate and ranching. Though he was neutral during the Civil War, he was prominent in Democratic politics in California; he was a delegate to the Democratic national convention in 1876. Hays County, Texas, is named in his honor.

Harold J. Weiss, Jr.

Health and Medicine. Long before trained physicians offered medical services to Texans properly so-called, Indian "medicine men" and Spanish explorers and padres responded to the sick and injured in the future Texas. Apache Indians mashed poison ivy leaves to prepare a remedy for ringworm. Comanches skillfully treated fractured limbs and gunshot wounds. The Karankawas, who lived along the Gulf Coast, used various plants to control diarrhea. In November 1528 Cabeza de Vaca and a few other shipwreck survivors waded to the shores of Galveston Island and encountered a band of Karankawas. For six years, the Spaniard traveled throughout the future state and acquired a reputation as a lay healer because he removed an arrow from the chest of a Karankawa and attended others when they were ill. But infectious diseases were endemic in the missions, presidios, and ranchos established by Spanish settlers during the eighteenth century. Smallpox epidemics afflicted San Antonio (1739), Nacogdoches (1759), and other towns. Measles, influenza, malaria, and venereal diseases occurred regularly. In addition to prayer, the Spanish priests utilized herbal remedies brought from Europe and some others that were popular with the Indians. A few soldiers became renowned as lay surgeons, and some presidios acquired trained surgeons. Federico Zerván, a military surgeon, accompanied the bishop of Monterrey on a visit to San Antonio de Béxar in October 1805. Governor Cordero y Bustamante agreed to designate a room in San Antonio de Valero Mission (the Alamo) as a military infirmary that could accommodate 20 patients. Zerván administered the infirmary for three years.

Attracted by the empresario system, many immigrants settled in Texas during the 1820s and 1830s, including professionally educated doctors whose beliefs and practices were rooted in centuries of European tradition. Although scientific beliefs about health and disease had changed significantly since Greco-Roman antiquity, the military surgeons and civilian doctors who treated Texans during the years of Mexican rule and afterward still used ancient treatments subsequently discarded, such as bloodletting and purging. Anglo-American settlers utilized Anglo physicians, such as Irishborn James Hewetson, who accompanied Moses Austin in June 1821. On November 14, 1829, the ayuntamiento of San Felipe de Austin granted Robert Peebles

Bird's-eye View of Texas State Tuberculosis Sanatorium. Sanatorium, Texas, 1924. From *The Texas State Sanatorium, Located at Sanatorium . . . 1924* (n.p., 1924?). Courtesy Chester R. Burns, Galveston. The state located this tuberculosis colony in an isolated area. Improved treatment of tuberculosis led to the closing of the facility, then known as the McKnight State Tuberculosis Hospital, in 1969.

a professional license; two years later he became one of three physicians appointed to the first board of health in San Felipe. These and others treated the colonists, especially during epidemics, but female neighbors, relatives, and midwives usually delivered babies born during these years. Mothers nursed their infants and attended their sick children and husbands.

Immigrant physicians played leading roles during the Texas Revolution. Seven of the 59 men who signed the Texas Declaration of Independence were physicians. Numerous doctors served as soldiers. George M. Patrick fought at Anahuac, Asa Hoxey served at Bexar, and John Shackelford led the company of Red Rovers from Alabama in the disastrous Goliad campaign of 1836. After the battles, doctors bandaged wounds, amputated damaged limbs, and administered calomel, quinine, opium, ipecac, and other drugs to combat fever and relieve pain. Joseph H. Barnard estimated that more than 500 Mexican soldiers were treated after the battle of the Alamo. Alexander W. Ewing attended Sam Houston, whose right leg had been fractured by a gunshot during the battle of San Jacinto. Two military surgeons, Ashbel Smith and Anson Jones, became prominent political leaders in the new Republic of Texas. Other physicians came to Texas. A native of Kentucky, Jerome B. Robertson, received a medical degree from Transylvania University in 1835 and practiced at Washington-on-the-Brazos and Independence. Samuel G. Haynie, a native of Tennessee, settled at Independence in 1837 and later practiced in Austin, where he served as mayor for four terms. Hill County was named for George W. Hill, a Tennessean who practiced at Spring Hill until his death in 1860. George Cupples, a Scottish doctor, moved to San Antonio in 1844, hoping that South Texas would be a good environment for his sickly

wife. These and fellow doctors set broken bones, delivered babies, prescribed drugs, and comforted the dying. John S. Ford charged $15 for delivering a baby in San Augustine in 1844, $7 for bloodletting, and 75¢ for an "itch ointment."

Bloodletting was a common form of treatment, especially for those afflicted with the fevers associated with infectious diseases. People who rejected bloodletting or who could not afford a doctor utilized various home remedies, including green gourd tea as an emetic and willow-bark pills as a cathartic. Wives of plantation owners frequently ministered to slaves. In 1848 Rutherford B. Hayes visited a plantation near Freeport and noted that Mrs. Emily M. A. Perry was "the nurse, physician, and spiritual advisor of a whole settlement of careless slaves." Medicinal teas were made from many substances, including watermelon, catnip, sage, sassafras, butterfly weed, and corn shucks.

Reputable doctors were general practitioners who cared for the medical needs of an entire family and sometimes traveled great distances on horseback to render their services in the homes of the sick. Some became very busy in the larger communities, such as Galveston. In 1851, Samuel Hurlbut contracted with the Galveston aldermen to become the physician for the city's hospital, the first civilian hospital in the state. He rented the building for $20 a month and charged the city 75¢ a day for each patient he attended. Hurlbut could earn as much as $1,000 a year from this source alone, as the hospital's census ranged between 250 and 500 patients annually during the 1850s. Conditions were quite good in the hospital, where the mortality rate ranged between 5.8 and 7.7 percent.

The mortality rate for the United States Army soldiers who garrisoned the frontier forts in Texas between 1849 and 1859 was less (about 3.5 percent), but the living conditions were miserable and the soldiers suffered numerous bouts of disease (66,846 cases were reported among 20,393 soldiers). There were more than 20,000 cases of fevers, 14,000 cases of gastrointestinal diseases, and 7,000 cases of wounds and injuries. The young recruits built forts, escorted wagontrains, scouted new territories, and battled Indians, blue northers, and stifling heat. They drank alcohol heavily, though only 771 cases of drunkenness were reported. Most of the hospital facilities at the forts were fairly good, though not all forts had attending army surgeons. As for steady income, Hurlbut and the army doctors were exceptions, since most doctors competed privately with each other and with midwives, quacks, patent-medicine vendors, and mothers who cherished home remedies. By the 1860s citizens drank gallons of proprietary medicines, as physicians abandoned bloodletting but offered few proven remedies in its stead. Vendors provided many choices, including Daly's Aromatic Valley Whiskey for Medicinal Purposes and Old Sachem Bitters and Wigwam Tonic. As more women allowed male doctors to deliver their babies, the doctors charged more: $20 for obstetrical attendance in natural labor and twice that amount for difficult labors.

Although many doctors served as army surgeons, the chaos of the Civil War did not remove the economic competition among health-care providers. Conditions during the war were similar to those on the frontier: more soldiers died from diseases than from battle wounds. There were, for example, 44 deaths (mostly from typhoid fever and pneumonia) among the 910 soldiers treated at a Confederate hospital in Columbus between 15 October 1862 and 12 January 1864. Because there were many wounds, however, doctors learned much about surgical care. Greensville S. Dowell, a graduate of Jefferson Medical College in Philadelphia (1846) and a surgeon in the Confederate Army, remained in Galveston after the war. He became the City Hospital physician and admitted poor patients authorized by the city or county of Galveston, sailors and foreign nationals authorized by the customhouse and foreign consuls, African Americans sent by the Freedmen's Bureau, and a few private patients. In 1866 he admitted 773 patients, including 47 women, 76 blacks, and 470 persons of foreign birth. As Galveston rapidly became the state's largest city during the 1870s, Galvestonians proudly supported the opening of a new City Hospital in 1875 and a large addition to St. Mary's Infirmary in 1876.

Although the other substantial cities established similar facilities during the 1860s and 1870s, vast areas of the state were seldom served by educated doctors. In November 1877, Henry F. Hoyt, a partially trained doctor from Minnesota, entered the Llano Estacado and wandered through the Panhandle. In Tascosa, the only American village west of Fort Elliott, Hoyt made a paste of water and gunpowder and smeared it over the skin of the 15-year-old daughter of Casimero Romero, the wealthiest of the *pastores* in that town. Piedad's body was covered with the pustules of smallpox. She recovered, and Hoyt's reputation was quickly established; but he did not settle there. The frontier stirred wanderlust among doctors and patients. Dreams of a new start in a warmer, drier climate attracted thousands to Texas throughout the nineteenth century, many in search of better health. Sherman Goodwin, afflicted with tuberculosis, moved his family in 1849 from Burton, Ohio, to Victoria, where he recovered and practiced medicine until his death in 1884.

Texas-bound invalids, many with tuberculosis, settled in the south central Texas towns of Boerne, Fredericksburg, and Luling Springs. San Antonio became the "Sanitarium of the West." To support his sick wife, Jerome D. Stocking moved to Clarendon in 1885 and became the first doctor to reside permanently in the Panhandle. On railroad tracks that measured 583 miles in 1870 and 10,000 miles in 1900, trains carried "lungers" to such health-resort towns as Mineral Wells and Wooten Wells. Jay Gould, railroad tycoon and consumptive, rode a Pullman car to El Paso in 1892, hoping to improve his health.

Traditional health care prevailed during the years of expansion and settlement between 1870 and 1900. Mothers used home remedies, *curanderos* advised loyal clients, chuckwagon cooks ministered to drovers, army surgeons attended soldiers wounded by Indians, midwives delivered babies, general and drug stores sold thousands of dollars' worth of proprietary medicines and tonics, and general practitioners traveled by horse, buggy, boat, and train to attend families and neighbors suffering from the miseries of infections, injuries, and chronic diseases. Arrows, barbed wire, knives, and guns produced many wounds. But important new features in health services also developed: more custodial care for those with chronic conditions, organized efforts to improve sanitation and public health, more successful outcomes from more surgical operations, more hospitals with greater acceptance by the public, more organizations of doctors and others involved in health care, and the establishment of schools to educate the professionals needed by the citizens of an everexpanding state.

Institutionalized care of those believed to be permanently disabled began before the Civil War. In 1856 legislators authorized the establishment of asylums in Austin for the insane, blind, and deaf. The institutions for the deaf and blind opened in 1857; the one for the mentally ill opened in 1861. Legislators allocated at least $600,000 for the maintenance of these three institutions between 1856 and 1873. The number of those admitted to the asylums increased during the late nineteenth century, but not as fast as the number of tuberculars migrating to Texas. Between 1892 and 1925, 12 private sanatoria for these patients opened in El Paso alone, while 50 beds were also set aside for consumptives at Hotel Dieu between 1894 and 1914. The state established a sanatorium in Tom Green County in 1911 the Bexar County Tuberculosis Sanatorium opened in San Antonio in 1912, and more indigent patients with tuberculosis were admitted to the county hospital in El Paso after the city began sharing ownership in 1925. After thirty years the Carlsbad asylum had expanded to 36 buildings with 17 dormitories that could accommodate about 950 patients. To care for the growing number of mentally ill, the Terrell State Hospital opened in 1885 and the San Antonio State Hospital opened in 1892.

After 1870, public authorities developed stable institutions for supervising sanitation, quarantine, water sources, and food inspection. Galvestonians organized a board of health in 1877 and appointed Cary Wilkinson as health physician. Eighteen months later Galveston received special praise as "one of the cleanest cities in the United States." In 1879 the state assumed responsibility for coordinating quarantines and authorized the construction of quarantine stations in five coastal cities. The state built new stations at Galveston in 1885, 1892, and 1902. Artesian wells provided better drinking water for Dallas, Houston, and Galveston at the turn of the century, but many infants and children still succumbed to infectious diseases caused by impure milk. Slowly and reluctantly, public authorities adopted ordinances that improved the quality of milk and food supplies and significantly reduced infant mortality. Mortality from surgical operations decreased after 1880 as doctors adopted antiseptic and aseptic techniques. For the first time, patients could have hernias repaired, broken bones reunited, and ovaries removed during painfree procedures and not die of blood poisoning or gangrene.

After X rays were discovered in 1895, surgeons needed machines that would not fit in their saddlebags or grips used for home visits. Private and public hospitals sprouted throughout the state to house the equipment and provide the personnel needed for conscientious care of Texans, including those who suffered serious accidents in the railway, lumber, and mining industries. Several hospitals originated as railway institutions. In 1891, the Gulf, Colorado and Santa Fe Railway established a hospital in Temple for its employees. Arthur Carroll Scott moved from Gainesville to Temple in 1892 to become chief surgeon. In 1904 Scott and Raleigh R. White established the Temple Sanitarium, later named Scott and White Memorial Hospital. Railroads also contracted with surgeons who admitted patients to private hospitals. In January 1900, for example, 13 Santa Fe Railway patients were among the 80 patients admitted to St. Mary's Infirmary in Galveston. Between 1870 and 1930, the lumber industry employed more workers than any other industry in Texas. Logging, coal and lignite mining, and sawmilling were the industries with the highest injury rates. Between 1 January and 1 June of 1914, on average, four workers at the Kirby Lumber Company were hospitalized daily, usually with injuries to the fingers, hands, and feet. Deductions from each worker's paycheck were used to pay the costs of medical care given by the company doctors. To feed locomotives and the furnaces of homes and industries, Texans needed the coal that was taken from 14 mines in the vicinity of Thurber, a town owned by the Texas and Pacific Coal Company. By 1900 more than 3,000 persons lived in Thurber, which was seventy miles west of Fort Worth. In 1904, John Thomas Spratt moved from Pecos to Mingus, a settlement on the Texas and Pacific Railway two miles north of Thurber. Spratt was the only private physician serving Mingus and Thurber. Though he sometimes had conflicts with the company doctors, he became quite skillful in treating diseases of the lungs and did not lose a patient during the influenza epidemic of 1918.

To share clinical experiences and scientific knowledge, and to exert some political and economic influence, private doctors organized professional societies. The Galveston Medical Society began in July 1865. Ten doctors organized the Waco Medical Society in April 1866. In June 1869, 28 doctors met in Houston to reorganize the Texas State Medical Association. A Travis County Medical Society was reactivated in 1870. San Antonio doctors organized the Western Texas Medical Association in 1876. Numerous county and regional societies appeared during the 1880s and 1890s, usually small in size but large in spirit. After a realignment with county societies and the American Medical Association in 1903, the state society grew much larger and much more powerful. It also established sections to accommodate the slowly growing number of specialists. Radiologists (1914) and surgeons (1915) were the first groups to organize separate professional societies. Displaying remarkable skills in diagnosis and

Dr. Frances Daisy Emery Allen and Dr. James Walter Allen, 1905. Courtesy Frances M. Allen, Fort Worth. Dr. Frances Allen was the first woman to graduate from a Texas medical school, finishing second in a class of 17 at the Fort Worth University School of Medicine in 1897.

treatment, these early specialists supported the extraordinary growth of new hospitals as workplaces essential for modern medical care.

A few hospitals became centers for training doctors and other health professionals. John Sealy Hospital opened in Galveston in 1890, and two months later initiated a training school for nurses. The hospital, built with donations from the Sealy family, was given to the city, which gave it in turn to the state to be used as the teaching hospital for the first university medical school in Texas, now known as the University of Texas Medical Branch. The medical school began instruction in October 1891. Because UTMB standards were high and students poorly prepared, only 12 of the first group of 22 medical students eventually graduated. A pharmacy school was added in 1893. By 1900 these schools had graduated 182 men and 4 women as doctors, 44 men and 6 women as pharmacists, and 33 women as nurses. In 1903 the University of Dallas Medical Department (founded three years earlier) became the Baylor University College of Medicine, and in 1909 the new Texas Baptist Memorial Sanitarium became the primary teaching hospital for this medical school. UTMB and Baylor were the only two medical schools in Texas between the second decade of the century and 1949. Their graduates settled in many areas of the state. Twenty-five-year-old William Leo Baugh, a graduate of UTMB, moved in 1906 to Lubbock, where he was the only doctor for two years. A. C. Surman graduated from UTMB in 1913 and served a sanitarium in Post. LaRied Steven Oates, a graduate of Baylor, moved to Center in 1929 to begin a practice that continued more than 50 years. Another graduate of Baylor, C. C. McDonald, began a long career at Tyler in 1931 and rallied support for the Mother Frances Hospital, which opened in 1937.

Before 1940 most doctors were general practitioners, including those who moved to Texas from other countries. Some became specialists, particularly in urban areas. George Bond established the radiology departments at John Peter Smith Hospital and St. Joseph Hospital in Fort Worth. In Dallas Joseph W. Bourland, Sr., practiced obstetrics and gynecology, William B. Carrell became an orthopedic surgeon, and Alfred Folsom became a urologist. Hugh L. Moore moved from Van Alstyne to Dallas in 1908 and became the first doctor in Texas to specialize in pediatrics. Sofie D. Herzog settled in Brazoria and became chief surgeon for the St. Louis, Brownsville and Mexico Railway. Claudia Potter served as head of the anesthesiology department at Scott and White Hospital in Temple from 1906 to 1947. Julian T. Krueger became a highly respected surgeon at the Lubbock Sanitarium. Many of these physicians taught the students who attended the hospital nursing schools. The state had 85 accredited training schools by 1923. Students served as ward nurses in their respective hospitals. The job was rigorous. One ward nurse, for example, began her three-year program in Lubbock's West Texas Hospital in September 1930 at the age of 16. She lived with 10 other pupils in an old house near the hospital and was forbidden to marry while a student. Regulations were strict; once she was disciplined because she allowed a patient to wash her own face. Ward nurses worked 12-hour shifts. Private nurses, however, would sometimes work 20 hours, with occasional breaks for rest on a cot beside a patient's bed. During the 1920s and 30s, women working in hospitals also became medical technicians, hospital social workers, occupational therapists, physical therapists, and dietitians.

With midwives, school and public-health nurses, pharmacists, dentists, osteopathic doctors, optometrists, chiropractors, podiatrists, and others offering their services during the early decades of the twentieth century, health care outside of hospitals became as complex as that within. Trained veterinarians attended the livestock of farmers and ranchers, and in 1903 organized the Texas Veterinary Medical Association. *Curanderos* continued their ministries, some vendors of proprietary medicines became very wealthy, quack healers persistently bilked dollars and hope from gullible Texans, owners of mineral wells and hot springs touted their healthrestoring properties, and mothers faithfully continued to use home remedies. Midwives still delivered many babies, maybe half of all those born in the state, as late as 1900. At least 4,000 midwives were practicing in Texas during the early 1920s, many serving rural blacks in East Texas and Mexican Americans in South Texas. Midwives almost disappeared in the cities, however. In Galveston, midwife-attended deliveries dropped from 35 percent in 1910 to 2 percent in 1923. General practitioners continued to deliver babies in homes. During the early years of the century, most nurses worked in hospitals or homes, but some functioned in schools, industrial plants, and public-health clinics. A few public-health nurses pro-

vided services in the homes of invalids, the elderly, or the impoverished. The two world wars stimulated the training and deployment of nurses. The American Red Cross supported 58 county nurses in Texas by 1922, and the industries of the Gulf Coast, which burgeoned during the World War II, hired nurses and doctors to attend employees and their families. The Texas Graduate Nurses Association, a statewide professional society organized in 1907, was renamed the Texas Nurses Association in 1964. Pharmacists offered much advice, sold tons of overthe-counter medicines, and filled thousands of prescriptions. They established the Texas Pharmaceutical Association in 1879. More than 1,500 druggists and guests attended the association's fortyfourth annual meeting at Galveston in June 1923. Dentists extracted thousands of teeth and filled thousands more. The Austin Dental Association and the Texas Dental Association consolidated as the Texas State Dental Association in 1881. Its twentysixth annual meeting at Galveston in June 1906 drew 125 dentists. Two private dental schools began in 1905: Texas Dental College in Houston and the State Dental College in Dallas. The Texas Osteopathic Medical Association and the Texas Optometric Association were organized in 1900. Chiropractors established their state association in 1914, and podiatrists (then called chiropodists) organized the Texas Chiropodist Society in 1917.

Texans could support all of these professionalized and specialized health-care practices because residents of the state had more money than ever after the oil boom that began at the Spindletop oilfield in 1901. As 80 refineries transformed oil into gasoline and other petroleum products by 1928, Texas became the leading oil-producing state. Houston attracted industries that needed water and cheap fuel for maximum production; more than 50 companies had located in or near the Bayou City by 1930, when it became the state's largest city. Oil drilling, petroleum refining, and chemical manufacturing caused hundreds of accidents and injuries. Fires and explosions were major dangers in the refining and processing plants. More insidious, however, were the diseases caused by air and water pollution from the state's industries. Accidents, cancers, and cardiovascular diseases replaced infectious diseases as the leading causes of death in urbanizing and industrializing Texas during the first half of the twentieth century. With improvements in the sanitary production of milk and other foods, infant mortality declined drastically. Of 670 individuals who died in Galveston between April 1, 1875, and March 31, 1876, 36 percent were under the age of one year. In 1915 only 17 percent of those who died in the entire state were infants. There was a 41 percent drop in infant mortality rates between 1935 and 1949, from 71.7 to 42.5 per 1,000 live births. With further improvements in public health, nutrition, preventive vaccinations, and drug therapy, this trend continued. The number of infant (under one year) deaths per thousand of Texas children decreased from an average of 68.3 in 1940 to 25.9 for whites and 43.9 for blacks in 1959.

The differences between whites and blacks reflected the impoverished conditions among minorities, modes of living that sustained poor health practices, and segregated institutions. A separate Negro Hospital opened at UTMB in 1902, to be replaced by a more modern facility in 1937. But black doctors could not admit patients to these hospitals. In 1903 two black physicians, husband and wife James D. and Mary Susan Moore, established the 40-bed Hubbard Sanitarium in Galveston, which functioned into the mid-1920s. As solo practitioners, some blacks achieved considerable status. Benjamin J. Covington, born to former slaves near Marlin, practiced in Houston from 1903 to 1961. Black doctors, usually members of the Lone Star State Medical, Dental, and Pharmaceutical Association, encouraged families to improve their health-related practices. During the 1920s and 1930s the Galveston Volunteer Health League sponsored a Negro Health Week every year that included parades, rallies, picnics, and speeches about health promotion. Health conditions for many Hispanic Texans were also dismal in the early twentieth century. In 1900, 76 percent lived in rural areas, though many crowded together in the barrios of El Paso and San Antonio. In 1926 the tuberculosis death rate for Hispanics in San Antonio was 343 per 100,000 persons, 275 percent higher than that for Anglos. Conditions at the Bexar County Tuberculosis Sanatorium were particularly gruesome during the 1930s and 1940s. Health conditions were somewhat better for those who worked as farm laborers in West Texas, in the mines at Thurber, and as railway laborers. Before 1930, charitable organizations among the Hispanics themselves, such as Cruz Azul Mexicana, responded to the health needs of the impoverished. Social and health conditions gradually improved as Hispanic leaders, including such prominent physicians as Alberto Gonzalo García, José Antonio García, and Hector P. García, successfully challenged prejudices.

Between 1900 and 1925, in response to the obvious needs of citizens and the reformist values of a growing middle class of professionals, the Texas legislature adopted many policies that affected health and medical care. New laws increased safety standards for railroad employees and improved conditions for women and children who labored in large companies. A new law permitted workers to be compensated for work time lost because of injuries. The state established a unified board for licensing physicians (1907) and the first board of health for the entire state (1909). The new state Board of Control exercised authority over all eleemosynary institutions (1919). The state expanded its services for the chronically ill by establishing a hospital for epileptics at Abilene (1904) and other hospitals for the mentally ill at Abilene, Rusk (1919), and Wichita Falls (1922). Cities and counties established public-health departments and built hospitals. The Great Depression slowed developments and produced even poorer health conditions for some, but the federal government's New Deal programs rekindled institutional improvements in health care. The PWA contributed about 45 percent of the cost of a Negro Hospital and about 42 percent of the cost of a Children's Hospital, both of which opened at UTMB in 1937. Franklin D. Roosevelt observed both buildings under construction when he visited Galveston in May 1937. Other federal funds flowed into Texas during the 1940s for support of an extensive array of medical institutions serving military personnel and veterans and for support of biomedical research at academic institutions.

More than a million troops trained at 15 army bases in Texas during World War II, and hundreds of pilots received their training at 40 air bases in the state. William Beaumont General Hospital at Fort Bliss opened in July 1921. A post hospital constructed at Fort Sam Houston in 1886 became Brooke General Hospital in 1942. It was one of the three largest army hospitals in the U.S. at that time, with beds for 3,200 patients. During the war years, the army also operated hospitals at Longview, Temple, and McKinney. Ashburn General Hospital in McKinney became a VA hospital in 1946; six other veterans' hospitals functioned by

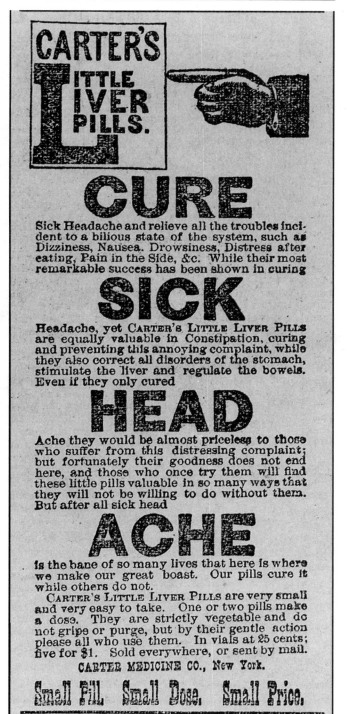

Carter's Little Liver Pills. Newspaper advertisement. Courtesy Rosenberg Library, Galveston. As the twentieth century began, Texans resorted widely to patent medicines and home remedies.

1950. When it was transferred from Carlisle Barracks, Pennsylvania, to Fort Sam Houston in 1946, the Army Medical Service School was already becoming the largest military school for health professionals in the world and the site of steadily expanding biomedical research programs. Though some important experimental projects had been conducted before 1940 by a

Cruz Azul Mexicana. Photograph by Jno. P. Trlica. Granger, 1929. Photography Collection, HRHRC. The Cruz Azul Mexicana, established in San Antonio in 1920, later expanded its activities into other parts of the state.

few individuals in Galveston and Dallas, events during the early 1940s signaled a major change in attitude toward biomedical research. In 1942 the University of Texas regents selected Chauncey Leake (an experimental pharmacologist, not a physician) to be the top administrative leader at UTMB, an institution that received no federal funds for research that year. By 1955, when Leake resigned, UTMB scientists had received more than $600,000 of U.S. Public Health Service grants for a variety of research endeavors. Baylor University College of Medicine moved from Dallas to Houston in 1943 because the M. D. Anderson Foundation offered the school a million dollars for a new building and a million dollars to support research projects. By 1955, Baylor scientists had received more than $400,000 in research grants from the U.S. Public Health Service. In February 1944, Leake and other dignitaries participated in dedication ceremonies in Houston for the newly established M. D. Anderson Hospital for Cancer Research. By 1955, biomedical scientists at this hospital had received almost $300,000 of United States Public Health Service grants for their research projects. Subsequently, academic, military, and aerospace institutions in Texas have received millions of federal dollars for biomedical research.

Aerospace institutions have become one of the most prominent features of the state's biomedical culture. The Air Service Medical Research Laboratory of the United States Army at Hazelhurst, New York, was renamed the School of Aviation Medicine in 1922, the same year that Brooks Field in San Antonio became a primary center for army flight training. The School of Aviation Medicine moved to Brooks in 1926, later to Randolph Field, then back to Brooks Air Force Base when a new Aerospace Medical Center opened in 1959. In planning the Mercury series of manned space flights, scientists and officers conducted many experiments at this center. In 1962 NASA assumed primary responsibility for United States space flights and founded the Manned Spacecraft Center in Houston, now known as the Lyndon B. Johnson Space Center. Collaborative projects between NASA scientists and those at the state's universities were common between 1961 and 1985, as NASA agencies awarded more than $200 million to 39 colleges and universities for support of education and research programs in the space sciences.

University health science centers also developed collaborative relationships with private organizations. One of the earliest occurred in Galveston during the mid-1960s, when the Shriners of North America located one of their three burn hospitals on the UTMB campus. The affiliation agreement between the Shriners and the University of Texas was signed in July 1963, and the Shriners Burns Institute opened in March 1966. Thousands of burned children have been treated there. After 1970, academic health science centers assigned foremost priority to the support of researchers, including the establishment of specialized research centers. UTMB established a Marine Biomedical Institute (1969), an Institute for the Medical Humanities (1973), and the John Sealy Center for Molecular Science (1991). The University of Texas Southwestern Medical Center at Dallas organized the Cecil H. and Ida Green Center for Reproductive Biology Sciences (1974) and the Harold C. Simmons Arthritis Research Center (1983). Baylor College of Medicine organized an AIDS Research Center in 1991.

The number of physician–specialists and biomedical scientists increased significantly during the century's middle decades, and some became nationally and internationally renown. Beginning in 1919 Dudley Jackson, Sr., devoted 40 years to the care of cancer patients in San Antonio and worked with his cousin Maury Maverick, Jr., to establish a national institute devoted to cancer research. Willard R. Cooke of Galveston was a founder of the American Board of Obstetrics and Gynecology and its director from 1935 to 1955. During the 1950s and 1960s, Michael DeBakey, Denton Cooley, and their surgeon colleagues in Houston displayed extraordinary courage and technical expertise as they established the world's standards for heart surgery in newborn infants, for replacing diseased arteries with artificial and venous grafts, and for replacing diseased heart valves with artificial ones during openheart operations. A prominent Dallas internist, Milford Owen Rouse, became president of the American Medical Association in 1967. For extraordinary accomplishments in molecular biology, Joseph L. Goldstein and Michael S. Brown, faculty members at the UT Southwestern

Medical School in Dallas, received the 1985 Nobel Prize in Physiology and Medicine.

Federal, state, and private dollars made possible a tremendous expansion of health and biomedical institutions after 1970. In 1995 Texans supported 8 medical schools, 75 nurse-training programs, 3 pharmacy schools, 3 dental schools, 7 schools of allied health sciences, 8 graduate schools of biomedical sciences, 1 school of optometry, and 2 schools of chiropractic. Texans receive medical treatment in more than 550 hospitals. In responding to the health needs of the populace and the priorities of political authorities and professional leaders, these institutions compete for available monetary resources and collaborate in mutually supportive ways.

Improvements in drugs and medical technology, and the steadily increasing number of professional personnel employed by hospitals and health centers, led to dramatically increased costs for medical and health care during the last half of the century. A general surgeon in Galveston charged $150 for an appendectomy and $250 for removal of a gallbladder when he began practice in 1961. In 1993 his fees for these same procedures were $1,200 and $1,900 respectively. In 1946 the average cost of a private room at John Sealy Hospital in Galveston was $14; in 1981 it was $148. The costs of health-care services and supplies in Texas

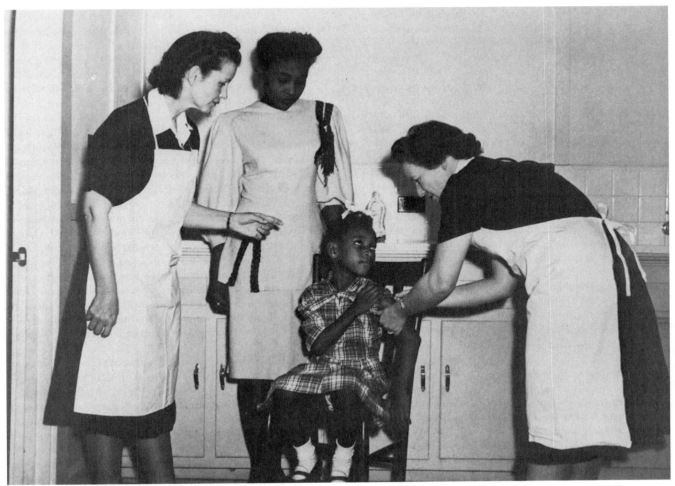

Child receiving inoculation at Austin–Travis County Health Department immunization clinic, ca. 1940s. From Eleanor McElheny Crowder, *Nursing in Texas: A Pictorial History* (Waco: Texian Press, 1980), p. 110. The number of local public health departments increased from 15 in the 1938–40 biennium to 47 in 1946–48, when they served about 60 percent of the population.

Dr. Michael DeBakey. Photograph by Michael Allen Murphy. Houston, 1984. Courtesy Michael Allen Murphy, Austin. During the 1950s and 1960s, surgeon Michael DeBakey and colleagues established new frontiers in heart surgery.

increased threefold between 1975 and 1983, from slightly more than $6 million to more than $18 million, and led to a variety of health-insurance programs. Blue Cross, one of the earliest, originated at Baylor University Hospital in Dallas in 1929. Since then hospitals, insurance companies, governmental agencies, and health-maintenance organizations have developed health-insurance packages that provide benefits to some, but not all, people in the state. Of the more than 20,000 patients who visited the Galveston County 4C's Clinics during 1992, 64 percent had no health insurance.

The most outstanding feature of health care during the twentieth century has been the remarkable increase in longevity resulting from improvements in public health, medical treatment, and ways of life. A white male Texan born in 1905 had a life expectancy of 47.5 years, and a female, 50.2 years. By 1929 the rates were 59.7 years and 63.5 years respectively; by 1958, 67.2 years and 73.7 years. By 1989, Texas ranked fifth among the states in the total number of persons aged 65 years or more. The growing number of elderly Texans is stimulating the development of home-health agencies, adult day-care centers, more long-term-care beds in community hospitals, and more care homes and nursing homes. Professionals and scientists are also investigating ways to help the elderly make better health-promoting choices during their senior years.

Texans have made countless historical choices about ways to prevent disease and promote health. José Joaquín Ugarte, a commander stationed at San Antonio in 1805, ordered soldiers to comb their hair daily and change their clothes "at least every week, in order to prevent their infection with sores and other diseases which are becoming prevalent." Military authorities provided smallpox vaccinations to residents of Bexar. Many proprietary medicines were marketed as preventives as well as curative remedies. Using Radway's Ready Relief or Radway's Ready Regulators, Texans were told, "will in all cases instantly stop pains, quickly cure diseases and always prevent sickness." Newspapers contained admonitions about diet, sleeping, exercise, clothing, and other aspects of daily regimen. Greensville Dowell believed that six hours of sleep was sufficient for most persons; "to sleep longer makes one stupid," he declared. During

a meningitis epidemic in Mingus before World War I, citizens wore bags of asafoetida around their necks or carried Bermuda onions in their pockets. Pediatricians and general practitioners urged vaccinations for children, and physical education teachers and coaches lauded games and sports. In 1923 some of these teachers organized the Texas Association for Health, Physical Education, Recreation, and Dance, an organization that championed physical exercise for all ages. As degenerative and chronic diseases assumed their prominence in the century's middle decades, more Texans started jogging, walking, swimming, golfing, or playing tennis. Throughout the nineteenth and twentieth centuries Texans, like others, longed for health and searched for ways to understand, cure, and prevent diseases, as well as ways to sustain persons suffering from chronic or incurable diseases. Characteristic measures at any given time were determined by the kinds of disease then prevalent, the scientific knowledge and technical expertise available, and the societal conditions that enabled or hindered quests for health by individuals and groups. More was accomplished during the twentieth century than ever before, and many Texans contributed to this progress. As Texans face the health challenges of the twenty-first century, perplexing choices about prevention and cure will be ever present. The extraordinary complexity of health-care institutions will not disappear. *Chester R. Burns*

Hedgcoxe War. A "war" also known as the Peters colony rebellion. Colonists rose in protest against what they viewed as an attempt by the land company to invalidate their land claims. After the state legislature passed a compromise law, the colonists, concerned over the possible sale of some of their claims and angered over government generosity toward the land company, continued their protest and demanded that the law be repealed. In May 1852 the agent of the land company, Henry Oliver Hedgcoxe, published a supposedly explanatory proclamation that was viewed by the company's opponents as arrogant and autocratic. The colonists were further aroused when the attorney general, Ebenezer Allen, issued an opinion upholding the law. At a mass meeting of colonists in Dallas on 15 July, Hedgcoxe was accused of fraud and corruption by an investigating committee. The next day John J. Good led about 100 armed men from the mass meeting to Hedgcoxe's office in Collin County. The agent's files were seized and removed to the Dallas County Courthouse. No violence was done, but Hedgcoxe, ordered to leave the colony, fled to Austin. The chastened land company henceforth adopted a conciliatory tone towards the settlers. On 7 February 1853 an amendment to the compromise law, satisfactory to both sides, was passed. *Victoria S. Murphy*

Helium Industry. Helium was first produced in Texas from the natural gases of the Petrolia oilfield, in Clay County, during World War I. The U.S. Bureau of Mines, with funds from the army and navy, sought nonexplosive helium as a replacement for the explosive hydrogen used in observation balloons and airships. Later, the navy built a large-scale plant in Fort Worth, operated for the government by the Linde Air Products Company. In 1925 the government assumed control of all helium production in the nation. In 1927 the Bureau of Mines began negotiations for control of gas rights on a 50,000acre, helium-bearing natural gas structure known as the Cliffside Field, in Potter County near Amarillo. The government then built a helium-extraction plant near Amarillo, which began production in April 1929. In that same year the Fort Worth helium plant closed because Petrolia supplies had been depleted. In 1934 the Bureau of Mines completed negotiations for the Cliffside helium field, and for a number of years the plant at Amarillo was the sole producer of commercial helium in the world. Texas produced 96,884,410 cubic feet of helium valued at $619,345 in 1944.

Beginning in 1937 the Bureau of Mines was authorized to sell helium to private concerns for medical, scientific, and commercial use. In addition to its main use in floating balloons and airships, helium has been used in a mixture with oxygen to relieve asthma and other respiratory diseases, for welding magnesium, aluminum, and stainless steel, and in radio tubes, electrical searchlights, and deep-sea diving equipment. In 1964 an estimated 95 percent of the world's recoverable helium was produced within a 250mile radius of Amarillo. Three new plants, which began operating in that year, doubled existing capacity. In 1968 helium was extracted from natural gas at federal plants in Amarillo and Exell in Moore County, and at two Phillips Petroleum plants in Moore and Hansford counties. Crude, unrefined helium was placed in underground storage for conservation purposes at the government's Cliffside gas field near Amarillo. By the time the helium industry celebrated its centennial at Amarillo in 1968, Potter County was the "Helium Capital of the World." In 1970 the federal plant at Amarillo shut down, but the Exell plant was modernized. In 1980 Texas produced 38,000,000 cubic feet of refined helium. In 1990, when helium was used in cryogenics, leak detection, and synthetic breathing mixtures, production estimates were no longer recorded, as output and value of crude helium plummeted, and helium in Texas was recovered chiefly by Air Products and Chemicals, Incorporated, in Hansford County. *Diana J. Kleiner*

Hell's Half Acre, Fort Worth. Among the various Hell's Half Acres (red-light districts) that dotted the frontier, none was more infamous or more rambunctious than that in Fort Worth. Although the name first appeared in the local newspaper in 1874, the district was already well established on the lower end of town, where it was the first thing the trail drivers saw as they approached from the south. They saw a collection of saloons, dance halls, and bawdy houses, interspersed with empty lots and a sprinkling of legitimate businesses. The usual activities of the Acre, which included brawling, gambling, cockfighting, and horse racing, were not confined to indoors but spilled out into the streets and back alleys. As the importance of Fort Worth as a crossroads and cowtown grew, so did Hell's Half Acre. It was originally limited to the lower end of Rusk Street (renamed Commerce Street in 1917) but spread out in all directions until by 1900 it sprawled across four of the city's main north–south thoroughfares: Main, Rusk, Calhoun, and Jones. From north to south, it extended from Seventh Street to Fifteenth (or Front) Street. The lower boundary was marked by the Union depot and the northern edge by a vacant lot at the intersection of Main and Seventh. Occasionally, the Acre was also referred to as "the bloody Third Ward" after it was designated one of the city's three political wards in 1876.

In 1876 Longhair Jim Courtright was elected city marshal with a mandate to tame the Acre's wilder activities. He sometimes jailed as many as 30 people on a Saturday night, but still allowed the gamblers to operate unmolested. After learning that such robbers as the Sam Bass gang were using the Acre as a hideout, authorities intensified law-enforcement efforts. Businessmen argued that legal restrictions in Hell's Half Acre would curtail the legitimate business activities there. Despite this tolerance from business, however, the cowboys began to stay away and the businesses began to suffer. Courtright lost support of the Fort Worth *Democrat* and consequently lost the election in 1879. Throughout the 1880s and 1890s the Acre continued to attract gunmen, highway robbers, card sharks, con men, and shady ladies, who preyed on out-of-town and local "sportsmen." At one time or another reform-minded mayors like H. S. Broiles and crusading newspaper editors like B. B. Paddock declared war on the district, but with no long-term results. The Acre meant income for the city—all illegal—and excitement for visitors. Some longtime Fort Worth residents claimed the place was never as wild as its reputation. Suicide caused more deaths than murder, and the chief victims were prostitutes, not gunmen. But no matter how much its reputation was exaggerated, the real Acre was bad enough. The newspaper claimed "it was a slow night which did not pan out a cutting or shooting scrape among its male denizens or a morphine experiment by some of its frisky females." After two events in the late 1880s Mayor Broiles and county attorney R. L. Carlock started a major reform campaign. On February 8, 1887, Luke Short and Jim Courtright had a shootout on Main Street that left Courtright dead and Short the "King of Fort Worth Gamblers." Although the fight did not occur in the Acre, it focused public attention on the city's underworld. A few weeks later a prostitute known only by the name of Sally was found murdered and nailed to an outhouse door in the Acre. These events, combined with the first prohibition campaign in Texas, helped to shut down the Acre's worst excesses in 1889.

But more than any other factor, urban growth began to improve the image of the Acre. New businesses moved into the south end of town. Excluded from the business end of town and the nicer residential areas, Fort Worth's black citizens, who numbered some 7,000 out of a total population of 50,000 around 1900, also moved there. Though some joined in the profitable vice trade (to run, for instance, the Black Elephant Saloon), many others found legitimate work and bought homes. The Acre was no longer attracting cowboys and out-of-town visitors. By 1900 most of the dance halls and gamblers were gone. Cheap but lucrative variety shows and prostitution became the chief forms of entertainment. In 1911 J. Frank Norris began his long offensive against vice and prostitution. His pulpit attacks on businessmen with interests in the Acre led to a bitter fight. In 1917 a new city administration and the federal government, which was eyeing Fort Worth as a potential site for a major military training camp, joined forces with the Baptist preacher to bring down the curtain on the Acre. The police department compiled statistics showing that 50 percent of the violent crime in Fort Worth occurred in the Acre, a shocking confirmation of long-held suspicions. After Camp Bowie (Tarrant County) came (1917), martial law was brought to bear against prostitutes and barkeepers of the Acre, who found themselves facing fines and stiff jail sentences. By the time Norris held a mock funeral parade to "bury John Barleycorn" in 1919, the Acre was history. The name, nevertheless, continued to be used for three decades thereafter to refer to the depressed lower end of Fort Worth. *Richard F. Selcer*

HemisFair '68. A world's fair held in San Antonio from 6 April through 6 October 1968; the first officially designated international exposition in the southwestern United States; commemorated the 250th anniversary of the founding of San Antonio. In 1959 local business leaders started discussing a fair to celebrate the cultural heritage shared by San Antonio and the nations of Latin America—a "HemisFair." In 1962 San Antonio Fair, Incorporated, a nonprofit organization, was formed. Accreditation came from the Bureau of International Expositions in Paris in 1965, when Governor John Connally was named commissioner general. HemisFair was financed by both public funding and private underwriting. Though it was strongly supported by San Antonians, the project had its share of detractors, who objected to destruction of existing "old city" buildings on the 92.6-acre site. To receive federal funding, HemisFair officials were required by an amendment proposed by Texas senator Ralph Yarborough to preserve as many as possible of the historic structures on the site; 22 survived.

With the "Confluence of Civilizations in the Americas" as its overall theme, HemisFair capitalized on San Antonio's ethnically mixed cultural heritage and placed particular emphasis on the city as a probable future center of international commerce and cultural exchange between the United States and Latin America. More than 30 nations participated, many with exhibit pavilions in the international area, named Las Plazas del Mundo. Canada, Mexico, Italy, Spain, France, and Japan hosted large pavilions; other exhibiting nations included Belgium, Bolivia, the Republic of China, Colombia, West Germany, Korea, Panama, Portugal, Switzerland, Thailand, and Venezuela. With less than a month before opening day, and concerned about the small number of Central and South American pavilions, officials arranged for various sponsorships through the Kampmann Foundation in San Antonio, the Good Neighbor Commission in Austin, and the Pan American Forum of Texas to support a Bolivian pavilion; a five-nation Central American pavilion, representing Nicaragua, Honduras, Guatemala, El Salvador, and Costa Rica; and special pavilions of the Organization of American States, representing eleven more Latin-American countries, including Brazil, Argentina, and Peru. The United States Pavilion, on a 4.59-acre site adjacent to the international area, echoed the fair's theme with "Confluence USA"—a two-building complex featuring an exhibit structure and a massive circular theater. With additional construction, this was subsequently converted to serve as the Federal Courthouse. The largest pavilion, that of the state of Texas, was called the Institute of Texan Cultures, now part of the University of Texas.

The HemisFair theme structure, the 622-foot Tower of the Americas, remained after the fair as well, as did the Convention Center and Arena. The Paseo del Rio was extended into the Convention Center complex. Cultural events included theme exhibits, such as "El Encanto de un Pueblo," which displayed 5,000 toys and miniatures from the Alexander Girard Folk Art collection in a series of miniature "views" of Latin-American village life. The fair sponsored a lavish production of Giuseppe Verdi's *Don Carlo*, an exhibit of major works from the Prado in Madrid, and appearances by such groups as the Ballet Folklórico de México and the Bolshoi Ballet from Russia. Major corporate exhibitors with pavilions included Eastman Kodak, Ford Motor

J. Pinckney Henderson. Photograph by H. R. Marks. Austin. Prints and Photographs Collection, Mr. and Mrs. J. Pinckney Henderson file, CAH; CN 00909.

Company, General Electric, General Motors, Gulf Oil Corporation, Humble Oil, IBM, RCA, and Southwestern Bell. Frito Lay–PepsiCola presented a spectacular outdoor event, "Los Voladores de Papantla" ("The Flying Indians"), and the CocaCola pavilion featured the Krofft puppets. Institutional exhibitors included the Mormon Church. Attendance, however, never matched expectations, and the fair lost a reported $7.5 million, despite Mayor Walter McAllister's pledge that the exposition would not cost San Antonio taxpayers "a thin dime." On the other hand the fair attracted more than 6.3 million visitors and focused international attention on the city and state. The structures that were left permanently altered the appearance of downtown San Antonio. *Frank Duane*

Henderson, James Pinckney. Governor; b. Lincolnton, North Carolina, 31 Mar. 1808; d. Washington, D.C., 4 June 1858; m. Frances Cox (1839). After admission to the bar (1829) and service in the North Carolina militia, Henderson moved to Texas (1836). David G. Burnet commissioned him brigadier general and sent him to the United States to find army recruits. He was attorney general of the Republic of Texas (November 1836) and secretary of state (December 1836). As Texas minister to England (1837–40), he negotiated trade agreements with England and France. He practiced law in San Augustine (1840–44), then went to Washington with Isaac Van Zandt to work for annexation. He was a member of the Convention of 1845, was elected governor in November of that year, and took office in 1846—the first governor of the state of Texas. With permission of the legislature, he led troops in the Mexican War. Without seeking a second term as governor, he returned to private law practice and was chosen by the Texas legislature to succeed Thomas J. Rusk in the U.S. Senate, where he served from 9 November 1857, until his death. He was buried in the D.C. Congressional Cemetery, then reinterred in the State Cemetery (1930). *Claude Elliott*

Henderson, James Wilson. Governor; b. Sumner County, Tennessee, 15 August 1817; d. Houston, 30 August 1880; m. Laura A. Hooker (1848; d. 1856); 2 sons; m. Saphira Elizabeth Price; 3 children. Henderson was county surveyor of Harris County, an attorney, a member of the Somervell expedition (1842), and a legislator in the Republic of Texas. He lost the race for lieutenant governor in 1849 and won it in 1851. When Governor Peter H. Bell resigned, Henderson became governor (23 November 1853); he served less than a month (until 21 December). He was elected to the Texas legislature in 1857. He served as a captain in the Civil War, as a delegate to the Constitutional Convention of 1866, and as an officer at Democratic party conventions in 1868 and 1871. *L. W. Kemp*

Henry, O. Writer; b. William Sydney Porter, Greensboro, North Carolina, 11 September 1862; d. New York City, 5 June 1910; m. Athol Estes (1887; d. 1897); 2 children, one of whom died almost immediately; m. Sara Lindsay Coleman (1907). Porter moved to Texas for his health in 1882. While he lived on a ranch in La Salle County for two years with Betty and Richard Moore Hall, he gained a knowledge of ranch life that he later incorporated into many of his short stories. In 1884 the Halls moved to a new ranch in Williamson County, and Porter moved to Austin and lived as a house guest of the Joseph Harrell family for three years. During this time the first recorded use of his pseudonym appeared, allegedly derived from his habit of calling "Oh, Henry" to the family cat. In 1887 he began working as a draftsman in the General Land Office. Porter is believed to have illustrated J. W. Wilbarger's *Indian Depredations in Texas* in 1889. He resigned from the General Land Office in 1891 and became a teller at the First National Bank of Austin. In 1894 he founded a humor weekly, the *Rolling Stone*, a venture that failed within a year. Between October 1895 and June 1896 he wrote a column for the Houston *Daily Post*. In the meantime the First National Bank was examined, and when certain irregularities were discovered Porter was indicted for embezzlement. He left Houston, supposedly to return to Austin, but fled instead to New Orleans and later to Honduras, leaving his wife and daughter in Austin. In January 1897 he returned because of Athol's continued ill health. In February 1898 Porter was declared guilty and sent to serve five years in a federal penitentiary in Ohio. He emerged from the prison three years later reborn as O. Henry, a pseudonym now used to conceal his true identity. He had written at least 12 stories in jail. After leaving prison he went to New York City, where he published more than 300 stories and gained fame as America's favorite short-story writer. Many editions of the stories have been published since his death, and his stories have been translated all over the world. In *The Heart of the West* (1907) appear many of his Texas tales. His years in Texas enabled him to write about cowboys, Texas Rangers, Mexicans, and pioneers with realistic detail. His stories are noted for their unexpected endings and for their sympathetic portrayal of human nature. *Connie Patterson*

Hereford Cattle. The red-to-dark-yellow, whitefaced cattle, with short horns or none, that replaced longhorn cattle as the dominant Texas breed. Durham or shorthorn cattle proved less successful than Herefords, which were better adapted to the open range. Herefords probably originated from aboriginal animals known to be in the Herefordshire area of western England as early as the fifth century. They were first brought to America by Henry Clay in 1817; in 1876 the Ikard brothers of Henrietta brought the first Herefords to Texas. Ranchers—notably Charles Goodnight and Robert J. Kleberg (of the King Ranch)—began raising Herefords. The Texas Hereford Association originated in San Antonio during the International Livestock Exposition in 1899. In the early 1990s there were about 150 Hereford breeders and about 180 polled (hornless) Hereford breeders in Texas. *Art Leatherwood*

Hidalgo County Rebellion. A rebellion against boss rule that helped lead to the founding of LULAC. Anticipating a fraudulent election in 1928, Republican newcomers to Hidalgo County formed the Good Government League. They protested after all the ballots from Weslaco were thrown out, supposedly because the box was not sealed. In 1930 a federal grand jury indicted Anderson Y. Baker, political boss and protégé of James B. Wells, and other area politicos, all of whom were found not guilty. Baker engineered other corrupt elections—one bond election, for instance, for a "Nickel Plated Highway to Hell" that benefited Baker and his henchmen. When LULAC was founded as a result of such activities, Baker responded by proclaiming himself "superior chief" of the "Mexican" people in his area. Along with other publicity, an article by Owen White in *Collier's* referred to Baker and his cronies as the "Texas Tammany boys" and exposed their "system of handling the Mexican voters." When Baker died in November 1930, boss rule allegedly ended in the county. *Cynthia E. Orozco*

Hide and Tallow Trade. Hide and tallow factories flourished on the Texas coast, particularly in Aransas County, from 1840 to 1880, but chiefly from the Mexican War to 1875. During the Mexican War and the Civil War herds of cattle and horses roamed untended upon the coastal prairies. By 1865 they represented the war-ravaged Southwest's only negotiable medium, but transportation difficulties and lack of markets made shipment of stock unprofitable. The cattlemen discovered the eastern market for hides, bones, tallow, and horns, items then far more valuable than the animal on the hoof. No shipping difficulties were involved, since transportation was by water. Every cattleman of any importance soon built a factory to process not only his own herds but those of smaller ranchers. Rockport and Fulton were the centers of greatest activity.

Carcasses of hundreds of thousands of cattle and mustangs were reduced to tallow in the great boilers. Hides were cured and shipped east with the bones and horns. Occasionally attempts were made to preserve some of the meat, but lack of refrigeration made this part of the business impractical, although factories, at times, were referred to as packeries. By 1870 the factories were slaughtering thousands of head of stock every month, and newspapers carried warnings to cattlemen that their herds were in danger of depletion. The winters of 1872 and 1873 were of unprecedented severity, and thousands of cattle died. Hide peelers added to the destruction by despoiling the diminishing herds. The slaughter continued unabated, however, until 1875, when it was apparent that there were no more heavy cattle to supply the boilers. Many factories were abandoned and left to fall into ruin, though some continued operation on a small scale until 1880. More than a century later, in 1991, production had revived. That year Texas exported tallow and lard valued at $68.6 million. Cowhides were included in the $237 million earned in the hide and skin export business. *Hortense Warner Ward*

Highway Development. The earliest roads in Texas included Indian trails and the marked trails of early Spanish explorers. The first subsequent roads developed as the result of the necessity for travel from Mexico to San Antonio, Goliad, and the East Texas missions. The Old San Antonio Road is perhaps the oldest known highway. Another early highway was the La Bahía Road, and in East Texas Trammel's Trace was a frequently traveled route. The Republic of Texas government approved a Central National Road that aided entry for many immigrants, though it never played the international role that planners originally envisioned. Early Texas law called for the establishment of first-class roads between county seats. These roads were 40-foot-wide cleared paths. Stumps less than eight inches in diameter were cut off at the ground, and larger stumps were rounded off so that wagon wheels could more easily roll over them. Second-class roads were 30 feet wide, and third-class roads were 22 feet wide. In 1883 the state government adopted a constitutional amendment that provided for a 15-cent county road tax for every dollar valuation. At that time the county commissioners' court had the power to choose routes and construct roads. Citizens could petition for a new road or for improvements to an existing one, after which the court appointed a jury of view to decide on the matter. In nineteenth-century Texas and even into the early twentieth century, water lanes were also important to road development, since they allowed landowners access to the nearest body of water. Work on roads was conducted at the county level. The county commissioners appointed overseers to supervise workers, who were often landowners on the route under construction. Landowners could pay substitutes. Generally, all able-bodied men aged 18 to 45 were required to donate several days a year to roadwork.

Roads were often named for their termini—Blanco–San Antonio Road, for instance. Early roads often were mere rocky trails or mud streams. They skirted hills, large trees, and boulders. The early roads zigzagged, had right-angle turns, and held water. At the beginning of the twentieth century very few roads in the United States had any kind of hard surface. Probably the most dramatic change in attitude toward highway development in the nation and in Texas occurred with the use of the automobile, which forced drivers to recognize the need for road improvements. In 1903 citizens formed "good roads" associations in Texas in order to promote better roads. The groups organized events like auto tours and set aside special days to do volunteer roadwork. As early as 1903 there were calls to establish a bureau of highways in Texas, but no action was taken at that time. In 1916, however, the Federal Aid Road Act provided for the establishment of state highway departments. That year—the first year of registration—Texas had 194,720 autos registered. The State Highway Department, now known as the Texas Department of Transportation, was established in 1917 by act of the Thirty-fifth Legislature and was originally charged with the

primary responsibility of granting financial aid to counties for highway construction and maintenance. In 1921 the Federal Aid Road Act was amended to offer matching federal funds to supplement state money for road building, and Texas counties applied for their share. In 1923 the state imposed a gasoline tax of one cent per gallon, three-fourths of which went to the state highway fund. The Texas Highway Department assumed responsibility for maintaining state highways in 1924, but not until the next year did the department have clear-cut authority for constructing the state highway system.

During the late 1920s the legislature adopted the pay-as-you-go or debt-free concept advocated by Representative Leonard Tillotson of Sealy. The department devised the first statewide marking system in the 1920s, and in 1929 it placed state and federal route signs including mileages and directions on designated highways in Texas . That same year Texas had 18,728 miles of main highways, 9,271 miles of which was hard-surfaced. The period of the 1930s was marked by the Great Depression and the efforts of the department to provide employment through road construction. Planning and constructing a highway involved four principal objectives: safety, convenience, comfort, and aesthetic appeal. Road crews endeavored to shorten routes, smooth dangerous curves and deep culverts, provide adequate drainage, clear weeds and shrubbery to eliminate blind spots, and plant trees, flowers, and shrubbery to help prevent erosion of the road shoulders and beautify the landscape. Greater highway development led to increased mobility and an emerging tourism industry. In preparation for tourists traveling the state for the Texas Centennial the highway department instituted the Office of Landscape Architect in 1933. The purpose of this office was to incorporate both aesthetics and safety into landscaping. The department appointed Mrs. Frank W. Sorrell to lead a Texas citizens' highway-beautification organization to encourage local groups to seek and promote highway improvement in their areas. The department also planned the building of roadside parks. Because of low funds, local groups were encouraged to help by donating time, labor, and supplies. The NYA provided some federal assistance by constructing roadside parks. Women's groups played a pivotal role in promoting the parks and also lobbied for the restriction of billboard advertising and livestock grazing along highways. In 1936 there were 1,525,579 registered vehicles in Texas, and the state highway system comprised more than 21,000 miles of roads. As the department was emerging from the depression, World War II necessitated a curtailment of road construction because of the scarcity of labor and material.

The most dramatic years in the history of highway development in Texas came after the war. The greatest changes in this period included the development of the farm-to-market and interstate highway systems. As early as 1945 the highway commission authorized the construction of 7,500 miles of rural roads to be financed on a fifty–fifty basis with federal and state funds. The first contracts for construction were let in January 1946 in Randall County. Once the program got started, it became popular, and the demand for rural paved roads grew. The law that really got Texas farmers "out of the mud" was the Colson–Briscoe Act of 1949, which appropriated $15 million a year to the highway department from the Omnibus Tax Clearance Fund to be used in the construction of local roads that did not have sufficient traffic volume to pay for their construction and maintenance. In 1962 the legislature increased the appropriation so that not less than $23 million a year would be available for the construction of new farm roads. In the same year the commission increased the size of the farm-road system from 35,000 to 50,000 miles. By 1989 the Texas FM system included 41,755 miles of pavement and was the most extensive network of secondary roads in the world. The interstate highway system began in 1956, when Congress established the National System of Interstate and Defense Highways, which was to consist of 41,000 miles linking nearly every major population center in the nation. The system was later expanded to 42,000 miles. The law established a trust fund under which the federal government would pay 90 percent and the states 10 percent of the cost of the system. The states were to pay for the construction and be reimbursed by the federal government. As of 31 March 1989, Texas had completed 3,234 miles of interstate highways, and its share of the system was nearly completed. All routes of the network have been constructed as controlled-access arteries with no stop signs or stop lights and no grade crossings. In some densely populated metropolitan areas the department has also developed high-occupancy vehicle lanes to aid in the flow of traffic. The Texas portion of the interstate system is longer than any other state's.

Private contracting has been an important factor in highway construction in Texas. Texas highways are designed by the department, but the actual construction is performed by private contractors who offer competitive bids. In 1988 some 500 prequalified contractors were bidding on highway-construction contracts in Texas. An additional 500 contractors qualified to do specialty work such as making signs, lights, and signals, offered bids on contracts. As of mid-1989, the department had 901 contracts totaling $3,674,777,952 under way, with 59.55 percent of the construction completed. Generally the Texas Department of Transportation has been able to build and maintain highways more cheaply than the national average. In addition to the farm-to-market and interstate highway, in 1990 Texas also had approximately 12,500 miles of U.S. highways and 14,500 miles of state highways. The entire Texas highway system comprised more than 72,000 miles of highways. Additionally, about 30,000 bridges spanned Texas highways.

Texas highways are financed by revenue from a state gasoline tax, vehicle registration fees, and federal assistance. In 1946 Texas voters approved a good-roads constitutional amendment that provides a guaranteed income for state highways by prohibiting the diversion of receipts from gasoline taxes and vehicle registration to non-highway purposes. The amendment reserved a quarter of the revenues for the Available School Fund and set the remainder aside permanently for state highways. In 1988 voters approved another amendment to ensure that federal funds reimbursing the state for highway work also are dedicated to highway purposes.   *Kirk Kite*

Hilton, Conrad Nicholson. Hotel magnate; b. San Antonio, New Mexico, 25 December 1887; d. Santa Monica, California, 3 January 1979 (buried at Calvary Hill Cemetery, Dallas); m. Mary Barron (1925; divorced 1934); 3 sons; m. Zsa Zsa Gabor (1942; divorced 1946); m. Mary Frances —— (1976); 1 daughter. Hilton's first experience in hotels came in 1907, when his father converted part of the family general store into a hotel. After various other jobs and service in the Quartermaster Corps during World War I, he bought his first hotel, the Mobley, in Cisco, Texas (1919; now restored). He afterward built his hotel empire

Conrad Hilton. Courtesy Hilton Hotels Corporation, Beverly Hills, California. Photograph courtesy ITC.

in three stages: first, by leasing and renovating old hotels; next, by building new hotels on leased land, primarily in Texas; and, third, by buying existing hotels at low prices. Hilton opened a new Texas hotel every year between 1925 and 1930 and by the onset of the Great Depression owned eight. He was close to bankruptcy by 1931, however, and was forced to close his El Paso hotel in 1933. He recovered, with the help of Shearn and William L. Moody, Jr., of Galveston and a number of other investors, and subsequently merged his hotels with the Moodys' operations to form the National Hotel Company, of which he was one-third owner and general manager. But the merger failed, and in 1934 Hilton resumed his independent operation with five hotels. He was chairman of the Hilton Hotels Corporation, formed in 1946, and of Hilton International Company, organized in 1948, which became a subsidiary of Trans-World Airlines after 1967. In 1954 he assumed the mortgage and operation of the Shamrock Hotel in Houston and acquired the Statler hotel system. The action resulted in an antitrust suit brought by the Justice Department. In all, Hilton eventually owned 188 hotels in 38 United States cities, including the Mayflower in Washington, the Palmer House in Chicago, and the Plaza and Waldorf–Astoria in New York City, and 54 hotels abroad. He later purchased the Carte Blanche Credit Company and an interest in the American Crystal Sugar Company, as well as other enterprises. After 1965 he was chairman of Hilton–Burns Hotels Company, Incorporated. He received numerous honorary degrees. In 1957 he published his autobiography, *Be My Guest*, and in 1963,

Inspirations of an Innkeeper. His prayer, "America on Its Knees," was first published in 1952 and later placed in every Hilton hotel. Despite his record of marital failure, Hilton was a Catholic who supported charitable causes, including Loretto Academy in El Paso. He received many awards from the United States and overseas governments. He bought his principal residence, Casa Encantada, in the Bel Air section of Los Angeles in 1950. After a succession of 35 separate wills, he gave the bulk of his estate, estimated at a half billion dollars, to charity through his Los Angeles–based Conrad N. Hilton Foundation, established for the purpose of promoting world peace, helping children, and supporting Catholic nuns in their work with the poor.

Diana J. Kleiner

Hinojosa de Ballí, Rosa María. The first "cattle queen" of Texas; b. in the future Tamaulipas, 1752; d. Reynosa, 1803; m. Capt. José María Ballí; 3 sons, one of whom was José Nicolás Ballí. Her aristocratic father was alcalde of Reynosa. Captain Ballí and his father-in-law applied jointly for a large land grant in the La Feria tract, but both men had died by the time the grant was approved in 1790. Ballí's will specified that Rosa María was to inherit his share of 12 leagues (55,000 acres). When Doña Rosa took over the estate it was heavily encumbered with debts; by the time of her death 13 years later, she had doubled the property and made extensive improvements to the La Feria grant. Skillfully and deliberately, she built up her landholdings. In the name of her brother Vicente she financed an application for 35 leagues in the Las Mesteñas tract. When the grant was approved, Vicente transferred title to 12 leagues to her, and she named the property Ojo del Agua. The city of Harlingen is situated on it today. She applied in the name of her son Juan José for 72 leagues in the San Salvador del Tule grant and bought the Las Casteñas tract from the original grantees for her son José María. She made a joint application with her son Padre Nicolás, who eventually became her business associate, for 11 leagues of what is now Padre Island. When reapplication was required in 1800, Doña Rosa withdrew her name in favor of her grandson. She oversaw her lands from her La Feria ranch headquarters, La Florida, in what is now Cameron County. She amassed large herds of cattle, horses, sheep, and goats, and her ranches were territorial landmarks. Doña Rosa was perhaps the most influential woman of her time and place. She took full advantage of the opportunities that only widows could enjoy in Spanish society. Devoutly Catholic, she built and maintained a family chapel and endowed churches in Reynosa, Camargo, and Matamoros. At the time of her death she owned more than a million acres of land in the lower Rio Grande valley, and her holdings extended into the territories of present-day Hidalgo, Cameron, Willacy, Starr, and Kenedy counties.

Clotilde P. García

Hitchcock Naval Air Station. A World War II naval air station for blimps; at Hitchcock, 35 miles south of Houston and 15 miles northwest of Galveston. The mission of the lighter-than-air craft at Hitchcock was to protect shipping facilities and ship traffic along the Texas coast from possible Axis submarine attacks. The construction of the $10 million blimp hangar, which was designed to hold six of the giant airships, was begun in 1942. The hangar was 1,000 feet long, 300 feet wide and more than 200 feet high; it had more than 300,000 square feet of unobstructed floor space. Other necessary buildings included warehouses, dormito-

ries, shops, vehicle garages, administration and office buildings, and a recreation building. All of the buildings were of wood and painted gleaming white. The station was commissioned on 22 May 1943 by navy captain Arthur D. Ayrault. At the time 143 officers and men were attached to it. The base was struck by a hurricane in June but suffered only minimal damage. As the Axis powers were brought toward their ultimate defeat, the threat of U-boat attack on the Texas coast subsided, and the blimp stations were closed down. Hitchcock was redesignated a naval air facility, to be used primarily for the storage of inactive aeronautical material. In 1949 the General Services Administration sold the installation to H. L. Harvey for $143,777. The Commodity Credit Corporation used the hangar for storing rice; it has been noted that the entire rice harvest of Texas could have been stored there. In 1950 the site was sold to John W. Mecom. In 1951, during the Korean War, the facility was leased to Bowen–McLaughlin, Incorporated, and the hangar was converted to remanufacture halftracks and army tanks. The hangar suffered such major damage from Hurricane Carla in 1961 that it was considered too expensive to repair and was demolished in 1962. John Mecom continued to use the site for his various business interests in the early 1990s. The station had a lasting impact on the community of Hitchcock. Many of the civilians and military personnel who came to live and work there either stayed or later returned to the area.

Art Leatherwood

Hobby, Oveta Culp. First commander of the Women's Army Corps and first secretary of the Department of Health, Education, and Welfare; b. Killeen, 19 January 1905; d. Houston,

Oveta Culp Hobby. Cover of *Time* magazine, January 17, 1944. Copyright ©1944 Time Inc. Reprinted by permission.

Governor William Pettus Hobby signs a resolution giving women voting rights on the same terms as men, Austin, February 5, 1919. Prints and Photographs Collection, William Pettus Hobby file, CAH; CN 01024. This resolution, voted upon as a constitutional amendment on 24 May 1919, was defeated since it also called for the disfranchisement of noncitizens, who voted against it *en masse*.

16 August 1995 (buried in Glenwood Cemetery); m. Governor William P. Hobby (1931; d. 1964); 2 children. Oveta Culp evinced a strong interest in politics and history at an early age, worked as a newspaper reporter, and ran unsuccessfully for the state legislature at the age of 25. The next year she married "Governor." The Hobbys pursued interests in radio stations, newspapers (notably the Houston *Post*), and numerous aspects of civic life. Mrs. Hobby was head of the Women's Interest Section, War Department Bureau of Public Relations, in 1941–42. At the request of Gen. George Marshall, she undertook the formation and oversight of the new Women's Army Corps and within three years, with considerable struggle, built it to a completely accepted part of the army. She resigned as a colonel—the first woman to achieve such rank—in 1945. That year she was awarded the Distinguished Service Medal. She resumed her career as director of KPRC radio and television and executive vice president of the Houston *Post*. In 1953, after campaigning in the Democrats for Eisenhower movement, she became the first secretary of HEW. She resigned in 1955 to care for her sick husband, and returned to the *Post* as president and editor. She received many honorary degrees and served on numerous advisory boards. When she died she was one of the richest women in the country.   *William P. Hobby, Jr.*

Hobby, William Pettus. Governor; b. Moscow, Texas, 26 March 1878; d. Houston, 7 June 1964; m. Willie Cooper (1915; d. 1929); m. Oveta Culp (1931); 2 children. Hobby pursued an early interest in newspapers to become managing editor of the Houston *Post*; he left the *Post* in 1907 to manage, and subsequently to own, the Beaumont *Enterprise*. He won the lieutenant governorship in 1914 and 1916. When James E. Ferguson was removed from the governor's office in 1917, Hobby became the youngest governor (at 39) of Texas. During World War I, he guided the immensely important military effort of this state, where half the country's military camps and most of its airfields were located. After decisive reelection (1918), Hobby secured the passage of laws for oil conservation, for the establishment of the Board of Control and of the oil and gas division of the Railroad Commission, and for state-provided textbooks. Subsequently, back in East Texas, he bought the Beaumont *Journal* and became president of the Houston *Post*, which he acquired in 1939 and built into a media empire including radio station KPRC and television station KPRC–TV.   *William P. Hobby, Jr.*

Hofheinz, Roy Mark. Politician and developer; b. Beaumont, 10 April 1912; d. Houston, 22 November 1982; m. Irene Cafcalas (1933; d. 1966); 3 children; m. Mary Frances Gougenheim (1969);

business ventures, among them the building of the Astrodome, the world's first domed stadium. Though several Harris County bond issues funded most of the $31.6 million for the stadium, the Houston Sports Association had a long-term lease on the building. The Astrodome became the home of the Houston Colt 45s (renamed the Houston Astros) and the Houston Oilers. Building on this success, Hofheinz developed the South Loop by adding Astroworld, Ringling Brothers and Barnum and Bailey Circus, and the four "Astrodomain" hotels. In 1970, however, he suffered a stroke that left him confined to a wheelchair, and in 1975 his empire, burdened by high interest rates, came to an end. Astrodomain had accumulated a $38 million debt, and control passed from Hofheinz to two credit companies. Later Hofheinz sold his remaining stock to the companies. Eventually John McMullen and Dave LeFevre purchased the Astros, Servico Incorporated bought the hotels, and Six Flags Over Texas took over Astroworld. *Jill S. Seeber*

Hogg, Ima. Philanthropist and patron of the arts; b. Mineola, 10 July 1882; d. London, England, 19 August 1975 (buried in Oakwood Cemetery, Austin). "Miss Ima," the daughter of Governor James S. Hogg, spent much of her early life in Austin. She attended Coronal Institute in San Marcos and the University of Texas. She studied music in New York, Berlin, and Vienna, then taught piano in Houston, where she helped found the Houston Symphony Orchestra (1913) and was an officer in the Houston Symphony Society (president, 1917–18). Oil struck on the Hogg property near West Columbia enabled her to undertake a wide range of philanthropic projects. In 1929 she founded

Roy Hofheinz (left) and K. S. (Bud) Adams promoting voter approval of a bond issue to complete the Astrodome, Houston, December 1962. Copyright ©1962 Houston *Chronicle* Publishing Company. Reprinted with permission. All rights reserved.

Ima Hogg, Winedale, 1967. Copyright ©1967 Houston *Chronicle* Publishing Company. Reprinted with permission. All rights reserved. In the 1960s Miss Ima restored a nineteenth-century stagecoach stop and several other buildings, which she gave to the University of Texas as part of the Winedale Historical Center.

ed. Rice University, University of Houston, and Houston Law School (grad. ca. 1931). Hofheinz served from 1934 to 1936 in the Texas House of Representatives and from 1936 to 1944 as a county judge in Houston. After losing the election for his third term as county judge, he turned to advancing his career in private-sector law and business. He returned to public life in 1952, when he was elected to the first of two terms as mayor of Houston. His administration was marked by controversy. In 1954, for example, Hofheinz had four city council members arrested for boycotting a special meeting he had called to consider a proposed bond issue. Contention among the council members increased, and in 1955 the council voted to impeach him. Hofheinz, however, publicly announced his refusal to recognize the impeachment, and the council backed down. In an attempt to parade his public support, Hofheinz initiated a city-charter amendment to recall all city officials a year early and hold a new election. The public passed the amendment referendum, but Hofheinz's victory was temporary, as Oscar Holcombe won the mayoral election. Hofheinz returned to law and business. He and his partner, Robert Everett Smith, founded the Houston Sports Association, which evolved into several lucrative

the Houston Child Guidance Center. In 1940, with a bequest from her brother Will, she established the Hogg Foundation for Mental Hygiene, which later became the Hogg Foundation for Mental Health at the University of Texas. In 1943 she was elected to the Houston school board, where she worked to establish symphony concerts for schoolchildren, to get equal pay for teachers regardless of sex or race, and to set up a painting-to-music program in the public schools. In 1946 she again became president of the Houston Symphony Society, a post she held until 1956, and in 1948 she became the first woman president of the Philosophical Society of Texas. Since the 1920s she had been studying and collecting early American art and antiques, and in 1966 she presented her collection and Bayou Bend, the River Oaks mansion she and her brothers had built in 1927, to the Museum of Fine Arts in Houston. The Bayou Bend Collection, recognized as one of the finest of its kind, draws thousands of visitors each year. In the 1950s Miss Ima restored the Hogg family home at Varner Plantation near West Columbia, and in 1958 she presented it to the state of Texas as Varner–Hogg Plantation State Historical Park. In the 1960s she restored the Winedale Inn, a nineteenth-century stagecoach stop at Round Top, which she gave to the University of Texas. The Winedale Historical Center now serves as a center for the study of Texas history and is also the site of widely acclaimed fine arts and Shakespeare festivals. Miss Hogg also restored her parents' home at Quitman, and in 1969 the town of Quitman established the Ima Hogg Museum in her honor. In 1953 Governor Shivers appointed her to the Texas State Historical Survey Committee, and in 1967 that body gave her an award for "meritorious service in historic preservation." In 1960 she served on a committee appointed by President Eisenhower for the planning of the National Cultural Center (now Kennedy Center) in Washington, D.C. In 1962, at the request of Jacqueline Kennedy, she served on an advisory panel to aid in the search for historic furniture for the White House. She was also honored by the Garden Club of America (1959), the National Trust for Historic Preservation (1966), and the American Association for State and Local History (1969). In 1968 Ima Hogg was the first recipient of the Santa Rita Award, given by the University of Texas System to recognize contributions to the university and to higher education. In 1969 she, Oveta Hobby, and Lady Bird Johnson became the first three women members of the Academy of Texas, an organization founded to honor persons who "enrich, enlarge, or enlighten" knowledge in any field. In 1971 Southwestern University gave Miss Hogg an honorary doctorate in fine arts, and in 1972 the National Society of Interior Designers gave her its Thomas Jefferson Award for outstanding contributions to America's cultural heritage. She died after a traffic accident while she was vacationing. The major beneficiary in her will was the Ima Hogg Foundation, a charitable nonprofit organization she established in 1964.

Virginia Bernhard

Hogg, James Stephen. Governor; b. near Rusk, 24 March 1851; d. Houston, 3 March 1906; m. Sallie Stinson (d. 1895); 4 children. Hogg was the first native Texan to become governor of Texas and one of the most effective governors. After his father, a Confederate brigadier general, was killed (1862) and his mother died (1863), he and two of his brothers were left with two older sisters to run the family plantation. Hogg studied for a year in Alabama, continued study and worked as a typesetter in Rusk,

"By Gatlins, I'll See that Uncle Sam Don't Send Any Troops to Texas."

Hogg: *"By Gatlins, I'll See that Uncle Sam Don't Send Any Troops to Texas,"* by William Sydney Porter. From Maury Forman and Robert A. Calvert, *Cartooning Texas: One Hundred Years of Cartoon Art in the Lone Star State* (College Station: Texas A&M University Press, 1993), p. 8. When Governor Hogg criticized President Cleveland's sending troops to Chicago during a railroad strike without their having been requested by the Illinois governor, Hogg's opponents seized upon the incident to portray him as a boorish, truculent demagogue.

and improved his language skills. Gradually, the family estate had to be sold to pay taxes and buy necessities. While helping the sheriff at Quitman, Hogg earned the enmity of a group of outlaws, who lured him over the county line, ambushed him, and shot him in the back. He recovered and turned again to newspaper work in Tyler, after which he ran his own papers in Longview and Quitman from 1871 to 1873, fighting subsidies to railroads, the corruption of the Grant administration, and local lawlessness. He served as justice of the peace at Quitman from 1873 to 1875. He studied law and was licensed in the latter year. Hogg received his only defeat in a contest for public office in 1876, when he ran against John S. Griffith for a seat in the Texas legislature. He was elected county attorney of Wood County in 1878 and served from 1880 to 1884 as district attorney for the old Seventh District, where he became known as the most aggressive and successful district attorney in the state. In the national campaign of 1884 he succeeded in winning enough black votes from the Republicans to make Smith County a Democratic stronghold. Despite a popular move for Hogg to go to Congress, he declined to run for public office in 1884 and entered private practice in Tyler.

In 1886 he was elected attorney general. In this office he encouraged new legislation to protect the public domain set aside for the school and institutional funds, and instituted suits that finally returned over a million and a half acres to the state. He sought to enforce laws providing that railroads and land corporations sell their holdings to settlers within certain time limits and succeeded in breaking up the Texas Traffic Association, which was illegally formed by the railroads to pool traffic, fix rates, and control competing lines. He forced wildcat insurance companies to quit the state and aided legitimate business generally. He helped to write the second state antitrust law in the nation and unsuccessfully defended the Texas Drummer Tax Law before the United States Supreme Court. He managed to regain control of the East Line and Red River Railroad, despite Jay Gould's delaying actions, by making use of federal receivers. Hogg forced the restoration to Texas of railroad headquarters and shops, as a result of which depots and road aids were repaired or rebuilt, and he gradually compelled the railroads to respect Texas laws. Finally, seeing that neither the legislature nor his small office force could effectively carry out the laws to protect the public interest against powerful corporate railway interests, he advocated the establishment of the Railroad Commission and was elected governor on this platform in 1890. While governor (1891–95), Hogg did much to strengthen public respect for law enforcement, defended the Texas claim to Greer County, and championed five major pieces of legislation. The "Hogg Laws" included (1) the law establishing the Railroad Commission, (2) the railroad stock and bond law cutting down on watered stock, (3) the law forcing land corporations to sell off their holdings in 15 years, (4) the Alien Land Law, which checked further grants to foreign corporations in an effort to get the land into the hands of citizen settlers, and (5) the act restricting the amount of indebtedness by bond issues that county and municipal groups could legally undertake. In order to encourage investment in Texas, Hogg traveled to New York, Boston, and Philadelphia explaining to businessmen and chambers of commerce the laws and advantages of the state. He was ever solicitous for the welfare of the common schools, the University of Texas, and Texas A&M. He also paid earnest attention to the normals and to appointments to teacher-training scholarships. Always interested in the history of Texas, he succeeded in obtaining financial aid for a division of state archives and appointed C. W. Raines to supervise the collection and preservation of historical materials.

Without any real difficulty Hogg could have become a United States senator in 1896, but he was content to return to private law practice. After his wife died, he invited his older sister, Mrs. Martha Frances Davis, to come to his home to help rear his children. Though he was in debt when he relinquished the governor's chair to his attorney general, Charles Culberson, Hogg was able to build up a sizable family fortune by his law practice and wise investments in city property and oil lands. He inculcated in his children an interest in individual and public welfare. He aided William Jennings Bryan in the 1896 and 1900 campaigns and spoke on Bryan's behalf before Tammany Hall in 1900. In public appearances he effectively championed Progressive reforms in Texas: "Let us have Texas, the Empire State, governed by the people; not Texas, the truckpatch, ruled by corporate lobbyists." After the oil boom at Spindletop and a trip to England in connection with his expanding business interests in South Texas, Hogg gave up his partnership with Judge James H. Robertson in Austin and moved to Houston, where he formed the firm of Hogg, Watkins, and Jones. One of his last public addresses was at a banquet in honor of President Theodore Roosevelt at Dallas (5 April 1905).

Robert C. Cotner

Oil Man's Christmas Tree, by Alexandre Hogue, 1941. Lithograph. Photograph by George Holmes. Jack S. Blanton Museum of Art, University of Texas at Austin. Gift of the Still Water Foundation, 1992.

Hogue, Alexandre. Painter; b. Memphis, Missouri, 22 February 1898; d. Tulsa, 22 July 1994; m. Maggie Joe Watson (1938); 1 daughter. Hogue, one of the Dallas Nine, is best known for his paintings of the Dust Bowl era. He took classes at the Minneapolis College of Art and Design (1918), worked as an illustrator for the Dallas *Morning News,* and left in 1921 for New York City, where he worked for advertising firms. His summer trips back to Texas often included sketching trips with Frank Reaugh. The theme of natural balance, and the disasters that accompany a failure to respect that balance, is found throughout his work. His ideas are expressed mainly in landscape paintings, but they can also be traced through abstract and even nonobjective works later in his career. Other subjects that appear in Hogue's work are Indian life of the Southwest, the oil and gas industry, farm and ranch life, and the Big Bend area. During the depression era he produced murals in Houston and Graham that dealt with local history. When he returned to Dallas in 1925, he began to paint full-time. He also taught summer classes at the Texas State College for Women from 1931 to 1942, and was head of the art department at Hockaday Junior College from 1936 to 1942. During the 1920s and 1930s he also spent much time in Taos. In 1937 Hogue's Dust Bowl series was featured in *Life* magazine. Works such as *Drouth Survivors* (1936) and *Drouth*

Stricken Area (1934) became well known for their accuracy in depicting the Dust Bowl environment and for the compelling message of the artist. From 1939 to 1941 Hogue painted murals for the Treasury section of the Federal Art Project. With the coming of World War II, he devoted himself to defense work at North American Aviation in Dallas until 1945, when he was named head of the art department at the University of Tulsa, a position he held until 1963. In addition to his teaching and administrative duties, Hogue maintained an active exhibition schedule after the war. He continued in a realist style but now also included abstract and nonobjective elements in his work. Series such as *Atomic* (1950–51), *Alphabeticals* (1960–64), *Calligraphic One-Liners* (1970–74), and *Moon-Shot* (1971–74) all showed a range of styles that the artist assimilated in his later career. His series *Big Bend* (1970s forward) comprises pastels and oils inspired by the space and geologic forms of that natural preserve in southwestern Texas. Hogue retired from the university in 1968, and in 1976 the university established the Alexandre Hogue Gallery. In 1984 a retrospective of his career was organized by the Philbrook Art Center in Tulsa. Hogue helped form the Dallas Artists League in 1932 and was a charter member of the Lone Star Printmakers in 1938. He also wrote various articles on art, mostly for the *Southwest Review*. His works are found in corporate and private collections and in a number of public collections, including those of the Philbrook, the Dallas Museum of Art, the National Collection of Fine Arts (Washington, D.C.), and the Musée National d'Art Moderne (Paris).

Lea Rosson DeLong

Holden, William Curry. Historian; b. Coolidge, 19 July 1896; d. Lubbock, 21 April 1993; m. Olive Price (1926; d. 1937); 1 daughter; m. Frances Virginia Mayhugh (1939); ed. Stamford Junior College (teacher's certificate, 1914), West Texas Normal College (1917–18), and the University of Texas (B.A., 1923; M.A., 1924; Ph.D., 1928). Holden taught at rural schools and was principal at Rotan High School. He served in the Eighty-sixth Infantry at San Antonio (1918–19). Eugene C. Barker was his mentor at UT. His doctoral dissertation was published in 1930 as *Alkali Trails*. In 1923 he organized and chaired the history department at the newly established McMurry College in Abilene. He also launched a course in archeology and with students inspected sites on the Canadian River. In 1929 he joined the faculty of Texas Technological College to teach history and anthropology. In 1936 he became the chairman of the history and anthropology department; in 1938 he was named dean and director of anthropological, historical, and social-science research. Holden built the Museum of Texas Tech University. As dean of the graduate school, 1945–50, he initiated an accredited graduate program in four doctoral fields, including history. In field work, he conducted numerous excavations at important archeological sites across the Panhandle and far west Texas. His most significant archeological discovery occurred near his home in Lubbock. In 1937 in Yellow House Canyon two students found a flint point that Holden recognized as of Paleo-Indian age. He played a crucial role in the 50-year struggle to preserve and investigate the site, which became Lubbock Lake National Historic and State Archeological Landmark in 1989. His *Studies of the Yaqui Indians of Sonora, Mexico* (1936) is based on an ethnohistorical expedition of 1934. Holden also collected a substantial legacy for Texas Tech in the fields of southwestern art history and indigenous culture. In 1955 he and other supporters organized the Southwest Collection and Archives at Tech. Holden authored or coauthored more than 12 books and 42 articles and pamphlets in professional and commercial journals. Four works focused on the Yaqui Indians. *Hill of the Rooster* (1956), his only novel, treats the life of a woman called Chepa during the Yaqui rebellion of 1926–27. *Teresita* (1978) describes the life of Teresa Urrea, a Mexican folk healer. Holden's Yaqui interpreter, Rosalio Moises, recounted his life for *A Yaqui Life* (1971), which Holden and his daughter, Jane Holden Kelley, coauthored. Other books written by Holden include *Rollie Burns* (1932) and *Spur Ranch* (1934). In 1965 he was named distinguished director emeritus of the Museum at Texas Tech University. When he retired in 1970 he received the Distinguished Faculty Emeritus Award of the College of Arts and Sciences. In 1972 Texas Tech named the first museum building Holden Hall, the first such honor accorded a living member of the faculty.

Frances Mayhugh Holden

Holley, Mary Austin. Writer; b. New Haven, Connecticut, 30 October 1784; d. Louisiana, 2 August 1846 (buried in St. Louis Cemetery, New Orleans); m. Horace Holley (1805; d. 1827); 2 children. After her husband's death at sea, Mrs. Holley prepared notes for a memorial book on her husband, *A Discourse on the Genius and Character of the Reverend Horace Holley* (1828). In April 1829 she became governess to the Hermogene Labranche family in Louisiana. After her brother, Henry Austin, settled in Texas, she communicated with him and with her cousin Stephen F. Austin concerning possibilities that she had long considered of gathering her family around her in Texas. The empresario made arrangements to reserve lands for her on Galveston Bay, and in October 1831 she visited the Austin colony. As a result she

Mary Austin Holley. Prints and Photographs Collection, Mary Austin Holley file, CAH; CN 00165.

wrote *Texas: Observations, Historical, Geographical, and Descriptive, in a Series of Letters Written during a Visit to Austin's Colony, with a View to a Permanent Settlement in That Country in the Autumn of 1831*, which was published in Baltimore in 1833. During her first Texas visit she also planned a book to be called "Travels in Texas" and composed a "Brazos Boat Song," illustrated with a vignette of Bolivar House, her Texas residence. Back in Louisiana, Mary Holley continued her teaching, made plans for a future in Texas, and planned a biography of Stephen F. Austin. In 1833 she returned to Lexington, Kentucky, to provide a home for Henry Austin's children; she did not get back to Texas until May 1835, and subsequently remained only a few months. Her manuscript diary of that trip, like her charming family letters, is a valuable picture of the Texas scene. She continued to give good publicity to Texas and to arouse sympathy for the colony during the period of the Texas Revolution. The ladies of Lexington met in her home to sew for volunteers for the Texas army. Her book *Texas*, a history, was at the press by May 1836 and on the market by November 1836. It was the first known history of Texas written in English. After its publication, Mrs. Holley began to work for Texas annexation. Despite her sorrow over the death of Stephen F. Austin and worry over Henry Austin's financial losses, she hoped to be able to derive some income from her Texas lands and in December 1837 was on her way back to Galveston, where she wrote letters to her daughter describing the changes made with the establishment of the Republic of Texas. On this trip she made a number of pencil sketches of the Houston area, thus providing the earliest pictorial documentation of the first Capitol building, the homes of several prominent citizens, and the Long Row. She made a trip to the North in 1838–39, was back in Galveston in November 1840, and then for the third time returned to Lexington. On her last Texas visit in 1843 she interviewed old settlers and secured material for a biography of Stephen F. Austin to go into a new edition of the *History of Texas*. In 1845 she decided to return to her teaching in the Labranche family. She died of yellow fever.

Curtis B. Dall

Holly, Buddy. Rock-and-roll musician; b. Charles Hardin Holley, Lubbock, 7 September 1936; d. near Mason City, Minnesota, 3 February 1959; m. Maria Elena Santiago (1958). In fall 1953 Holly and two friends earned a regular spot on Lubbock radio station KDAV's "Sunday Party" program. In the next two years the group made a few demonstration recordings in Wichita Falls, hoping to land a recording contract, but in 1956 Decca offered Holly a solo contract. He failed to succeed as a country singer, however, and returned to Lubbock. In February 1957 he and a partly new group went to independent producer Norman Petty's studio in Clovis, New Mexico, and adopted the name the Crickets. Brunswick Records signed the group, while Holly signed a solo contract with Brunswick's Coral subsidiary. All of the records included Holly's unmistakable vocal style, which incorporated hiccups, nonsense syllables, a wide range, and abrupt changes of pitch, and was described by one critic as playfully ironic and childlike. The first Crickets single, "That'll Be the Day" (1957), reached number three on the pop charts and number two on the rhythm and blues charts. At first many listeners assumed that Holly and his band were black. In July 1957, when the Crickets flew east, they discovered that they had been booked on various package tours with black artists at such theaters as the

Buddy Holly, on the guitar, and Joe B. Mauldin at the Paramount in New York City, 1957. Prints and Photographs Collection, Buddy Holly file, CAH; CN 04821.

Apollo in New York and the Howard in Washington, D.C. Their reception at the Apollo was chilly, until they launched the third day's show with a wild version of "Bo Diddley." In the next few months Holly and his band appeared on "American Bandstand," "The Arthur Murray Dance Party," and "The Ed Sullivan Show" and in a number of package tours and concert bills with some of the most famous rock-and-rollers of the day. In late December Holly's second solo single, "Peggy Sue," reached number three on the pop and R&B charts. The Crickets' second single, "Oh Boy!," was released in October 1957 and sold close to a million copies. Over the next few months the Crickets toured Australia, Florida, and Great Britain. Their third single, "Maybe Baby," backed with "Tell Me How," also cracked the Top 100. In October 1958, after the group faltered, the Crickets broke up. In New York Holly took acting lessons and recorded several songs with strings and orchestral backing. In January 1959 he agreed to go on tour again with the "Winter Dance Party." Holly, Ritchie Valens, and J. P. (the Big Bopper) Richardson were killed in a plane crash early in the morning of 3 February. Holly's last single, "It Doesn't Matter Anymore," had been released on 5 January and entered the Top 100 on the day of his death. Holly's influence extended to the Beatles, the Rolling Stones, Bob Dylan, the Grateful Dead, Linda Ronstadt, Bruce Springsteen, and Elvis Costello. Not until the release of the movie *The Buddy Holly Story* in 1978 did the city of Lubbock begin to realize Holly's tourism potential. An 8½-foot-tall bronze statue of the singer, by Grant Speed, was unveiled in 1980 near the Lubbock Memorial Civic Center, after which celebrating Holly became a Lubbock specialty.

Martin Donell Kohout

Home Demonstration. Originally a movement to teach rural girls homemaking and social skills. In 1912, Edna Westbrook Trigg accepted the Department of Agriculture's request to work with girls' "tomato clubs" in Milam County. The program was modeled on federally initiated agricultural demonstrations. In 1914, Congress passed the Smith–Lever Act, which required each state to establish a Cooperative Extension Service through its land-grant universities. Texas established the Texas Agricultural

Black women working in a canning house, Beulah Community (Anderson County). Photograph by George W. Ackerman (?), 1933. Courtesy Cushing Memorial Library, Texas A&M University. Although rural white Texas women seem to have owned their own canning equipment, most rural black women apparently worked with cooperatively owned equipment. The women in this picture built their canning house with prize money they won at local fairs.

Extension Service at Texas A&M. State and local governments were required to match federal funding. Mrs. Trigg's initial work was followed by the appointment of other female county agents to work with farm girls in such projects as vegetable gardening, poultry and livestock raising, meat canning, and bread making. By the time the Smith–Lever provisions were in place, a state superintendent for girls' clubs had been appointed and home demonstration work included assistance in clothing, home improvement and management, and family living. By 1917 rural women had joined girls in all phases of home demonstration work in Texas. Early statewide leaders who aided in this expansion and growth included Bernice Carter and Maggie Barry. Because food production and preservation were the initial focus of home demonstration, the program was utilized in the food-conservation programs of World War I. In 1924 county home demonstration councils were established, and in 1926 the Texas Home Demonstration Association was formed to coordinate further statewide activities. The association provided scholarships for girls in Four-H clubs. Home demonstration agents also began using radio broadcasts in conjunction with home visits to teach domestic techniques. Membership grew from 1,725 women in 152 clubs in 1917 to 48,712 women in 2,268 clubs in 1934. Mary

Evelyn V. Hunter was the longtime (1915–31) statewide home demonstration agent for black women in Texas. Jeffie O. A. Conner, also prominent in home demonstration efforts for rural black families, served as agent in McLennan County and as a supervisor for several East Texas counties from the 1920s through the 1940s. In 1937 more than 14,000 rural black women were home demonstration participants.

The work peaked in the 1940s. During World War II the movement was again enlisted for such causes as "victory gardens" and "victory canning." In their demonstrations and teaching, the agents emphasized production and a sense of accomplishment achieved through happy homes and prosperous communities. Home demonstration began to change in the 1950s as more women were employed and fewer families lived in rural areas. Club membership was more than 40,000 in 1951, when the emphasis was still on giving scholarships to deserving Four-H Club girls and on enabling women to develop leadership and parliamentary skills. Clothing making was taught to help families extend their incomes. In 1960 home demonstration clubs were represented at the White House Conference on Children and Youth called by President Eisenhower. The Texas Home Demonstration Association donated $3,000 to assist in building the Texas Four-H Center at Brownwood in 1970, and the 1972 national meeting was held in Dallas. The name of the program was changed to Texas Extension Homemakers Association in 1979, and local clubs were renamed Extension Homemaker clubs. That same year the state president was a representative to the White House Conference on Families of President Carter. In the 1980s programming focused on how policies and legislation affected families. In 1984 two adult career scholarships were initiated to help members who were seeking further education. Membership was 28,686. Members worked to pass legislation on children's car seats and seat belts. Volunteers supported the "War on Drugs." The Family Community Leadership program was initiated to train women to assume leadership roles and then teach other women. In the 1990s club work continued to focus on families. In 1994 the program changed its name again, to Texas Association for Family and Community Education. Its mission was "to work with the Texas Agricultural Extension Service to strengthen and enrich families through educational programs, leadership development and community service." Programs focused on environmental and family topics. Four-H scholarships were presented to nine deserving youths, and adult career scholarships were presented to members. Members included men.   *Debbie Mauldin Cottrell*

Homestead Law. Many Americans who settled in Texas in the early nineteenth century were pursued by their creditors, and for their protection Stephen F. Austin recommended a moratorium on the collection of the colonists' foreign debts. In response to that recommendation the legislature of Coahuila and Texas enacted Decree No. 70 of 1829 to exempt from creditors' claims lands received from the sovereign as well as certain movable property. Although that act was repealed in 1831, the principle remained alive in Texans' minds and was a model for the Texas act of 1839, which protected the home of a family from seizure by a creditor. This was the first act of this sort, and the principle of homestead exemption is therefore deemed Texas's particular contribution to jurisprudence. The homestead principle was embodied in the Constitution of 1845 and all constitutions thereafter. Under the Constitution of 1876 the homestead was defined as the family home on up to 200 acres of rural land or urban land worth up to $5,000 (at the time of homestead designation) with its improvements and used as a family home or place of business. In 1970 the maximum value of the urban land was raised to $10,000. In 1983 the urban homestead was redefined as a maximum of one acre. The legislature has defined the homestead in terms of the maximum amount allowed by the Constitution with the exception of the rural homestead for a single adult, which is limited to 100 acres. In 1973 a homestead was made available to single adults. The Constitution also provides that the homestead cannot be encumbered by a lien except for its purchase price, cost of improvements thereon, or taxes assessed against the property. A Texas homestead is not, however, secure from seizure for a debt owed to the federal government. An encumbrance existing on land prior to its dedication as a homestead is also enforceable. Designation of a homestead is achieved by actual use and no recorded claim to the right is required. Either separate or community property may constitute a homestead. A homestead owner's spouse must join in any transfer or encumbrance of a homestead, and neither spouse can effect an abandonment of the homestead without the consent of the other. In addition to the reduction of taxes made for all homesteads, the Texas Constitution authorizes local governmental units to give further reductions for the aged and disabled. A surviving spouse is entitled to the sole occupancy of a homestead for life, though the owner may have devised ownership rights in the property to someone else.   *Joseph W. McKnight*

Hood, John Bell. Confederate general; b. Owingsville, Kentucky, 1 June 1831; d. New Orleans, 30 August 1879 (buried in the Army of Tennessee Memorial at the Metairie Cemetery, New Orleans); m. Anna Marie Hennen; at least 11 children; ed. West Point (grad. 1853). Philip Sheridan was a classmate of Hood at West Point. Hood served in Missouri and California and was subsequently assigned to Company G of the elite Second United States Cavalry, with which he served on the Texas frontier. He was promoted to first lieutenant in 1858, but resigned from the army on 16 April 1861. Dissatisfied with his native Kentucky's neutrality, he declared himself a Texan. He was commissioned a captain in the regular Confederate cavalry on 16 March 1861, and on 30 September was appointed colonel of the Fourth Texas Infantry. In March 1862 he was promoted to brigadier general and given command of what became known as Hood's Texas Brigade, perhaps the finest brigade of Robert E. Lee's Army of Northern Virginia. The brigade displayed remarkable courage at the battle of Gaines Mill, Virginia (27 June 1862); Hood's superiors noticed and promoted him to major general. He commanded his division at Second Manassas (Second Bull Run), Sharpsburg (Antietam), Fredericksburg, and Gettysburg. At Gettysburg Hood received a severe wound to his left arm, which was incapacitated for the rest of his life. In the autumn of 1863 he and his division accompanied Gen. James Longstreet's First Corps of the Army of Northern Virginia to Tennessee, where the corps played a crucial role in the battle of Chickamauga. At that battle Hood was shot in the upper right thigh, a wound that necessitated the amputation of his leg. In 1864, after a period of convalescence, he was promoted to lieutenant general and transferred to the Army of Tennessee, where he was given command of a corps that he managed aggressively during the Atlanta campaign. On 18 July 1864 he was given command of the Army of Tennessee, superseding Joseph E. Johnston, and a temporary promotion to the rank of full general. This promotion, however, was never confirmed by the Confederate Congress. Sherman forced the evacuation of Atlanta on 1 September 1864, and Hood, hoping to force him back out of Georgia, moved his army onto the Union line of communications in Tennessee. Sherman responded to this threat to his rear by detaching Gen. George H. Thomas's command to deal with Hood while he led the rest of his army toward Savannah, Georgia, and the sea. Strapped to his saddle, Hood led his men, but met disastrous defeats at Franklin (30 November) and Nashville (15 and 16 December). As the remains of the Army of Tennessee retreated it sang, to the tune of "The Yellow Rose of Texas," "You can talk about your Beauregard and sing of General Lee, but the Gallant Hood of Texas played Hell in Tennessee." Relieved of command at his own request on 23 January 1865, Hood was attempting to make his way to Edmund Kirby Smith's army in Texas when the Confederacy collapsed. Accordingly, he surrendered to federal authorities at Natchez, Mississippi, on 31 May 1865. After the war he moved to New Orleans, where he was

General John Bell Hood hit during the battle of Chickamauga, 1863. By permission of the Houghton Library, Harvard University; shelfmark pfMS Am 1585. Hood led the Confederate attack at Chickamauga that broke the Union line. In the fray he received a wound to his right leg, which had to be amputated.

involved in merchandising, real estate, and insurance businesses. He died there of yellow fever. His memoir, *Advance and Retreat* (1880), is one of the classics of Confederate literature. Hood County is named in his honor, as is Fort Hood.

Thomas W. Cutrer

Hopkins, Lightnin'. Blues musician; b. Sam Hopkins, Centerville, 15 March 1912; d. Houston, 30 January 1982; m. Antoinette ——; 4 children. After Hopkins's father died in 1915, the family moved to Leona. By the age of 10, Sam was playing music with his brothers, his cousin, Alger (Texas) Alexander, and Blind Lemon Jefferson, who encouraged him to continue. By the mid-1920s he had started jumping trains, shooting dice, and playing the blues anywhere he could. He served time at the Houston County Prison Farm in the mid-1930s, and after his release he returned to the blues-club circuit. In 1946 he had his big break and first recording—in Los Angeles for Aladdin Recordings. On the record was a piano player named Wilson (Thunder) Smith, who combined well with Sam to give him his nickname, Lightnin'. Aladdin was so impressed with Hopkins that the company invited him back for a second session in 1947. He eventually made 43 recordings for the label. Over his career he recorded for a total of close to 20 different labels, including

Gold Star Records in Houston. He settled in Houston in 1950 but continued to tour the country periodically. Though he recorded prolifically between 1946 and 1954, it was not until 1959, when Hopkins began working with legendary producer Sam Chambers, that his music began to reach a mainstream white audience. Hopkins switched to an acoustic guitar and became a hit in the folk–blues revival of the 1960s. During the early 1960s he played at Carnegie Hall with Pete Seeger and Joan Baez and in 1964 toured with the American Folk Blues Festival. By the end of the decade he was opening for such rock bands as the Grateful Dead and Jefferson Airplane. On a tour of Europe in the 1970s he played for Queen Elizabeth II at a command performance. Hopkins also performed at the New Orleans Jazz and Heritage Festival. In 1972 he worked on the soundtrack to the film *Sounder.* He was also the subject of a documentary, *The Blues According to Lightnin' Hopkins,* which won a prize at the Chicago Film Festival for outstanding documentary in 1970. Some of his biggest hits included "Short Haired Women / Big Mama Jump!" (1947); "Shotgun Blues," which went to number five on the *Billboard* charts in 1950; and "Penitentiary Blues" (1959). His albums included *The Complete Prestige/Bluesville Recordings, The Complete Aladdin Recordings,* and the *Gold Star Sessions* (two volumes). Hopkins recorded a total of more than 85 albums

Sam (Lightnin') Hopkins at a recording session, early 1960s. Courtesy ITC.

and toured around the world. After a 1970 car crash, many of his concerts were on his front porch or at a bar near his house. He had a knack for writing songs impromptu, and frequently wove legends around a core of truth. His autobiographical songs made him a spokesman for Southern blacks. He died of cancer of the esophagus, and his funeral was attended by more than 4,000 people. *Alan Lee Haworth*

Horned Lizard. Popularly known as the horned toad. Three types of horned lizard can be found in Texas: the Texas horned lizard (*Phrynosoma cornutum*), the mountain short-horned lizard (*P. douglasii hernandesi*), and the round-tail horned lizard (*P. modestum*). The Texas horned lizard is the most widely known and the most prevalent in the state, and in 1993 was officially designated the state reptile by the Texas legislature. The Texas "horny toad" is typically 2½ to 4 inches long and has a short, pointed snout, a broad, flat body, and a short tail. It has a prominent crown of spines at the back of its head, with two enlarged spines in the center giving the appearance of horns. There are rows of enlarged spines on either side of the throat. The Texas horned lizard also has two rows of spiny scales on each side of its body, which distinguishes it from the mountain short-horned lizard (which has only one row) and the round-tail horned lizard (no rows). The horned lizard's color varies from light brown to tan or gray to help it blend in with its habitat. Distinctive markings include dark brown spots with rims of yellow or white just behind the head. The horned lizard has several other defense mechanisms in addition to camouflage. It can puff up to twice its normal size, and its spines make it difficult for a predator to swallow. In addition, from ducts in its eyes it can squirt blood for a distance of several feet. The three horned lizard species found in Texas range from central Kansas through Oklahoma, Texas, and eastern Colorado and New Mexico. The Texas horned lizard can be found everywhere in Texas except for the piney woods region in East Texas. Its diet consists principally of the harvester ant of the genus *Pogonomyrmex*. It also feeds on grasshoppers, isopods, small beetles, and beetle larvae.

The invasion of Texas by the fire ant (*Sclerosises invicta*) and the consequent extensive use of insecticides in an attempt to control them, has reduced the population of harvester ants,

greatly diminishing the food supply for the horned lizard. Field surveys conducted in 1992 by the Texas Parks and Wildlife Department indicated reduced populations of horned lizards in those areas where there is extensive agriculture and where the use of chemicals continues. Populations of Texas horned lizards are expected to remain stable in South and far West Texas unless major changes are made in how the land is used. Originally, protection for the Texas horned lizard was sought because it was being overcollected for the pet and curio trades and for trading by the Boy Scouts at national jamborees. By the 1980s protective legislation had reduced the problem of overcollection, though the species remained threatened by the ongoing destruction of its habitat by agriculture and urban development. The most famous horned lizard in Texas, Old Rip, supposedly lived 30 years in the cornerstone of the courthouse in Eastland County. When freed, he became a celebrity, visiting President Calvin Coolidge in the White House in 1928. The increase in the capture and use of horned lizards as pets is often attributed to the fame attained by Old Rip. In the early 1990s the Horned Lizard Conservation Society was founded in Austin. *Art Leatherwood*

Horse Marines. A volunteer ranger group, 1836. Anticipating Mexican troop landings, Gen. Thomas J. Rusk sent mounted rangers to patrol the coast under Maj. Isaac Watts Burton. On June 2, Burton learned of a suspicious vessel in Copano Bay. By daylight next morning he had his men in ambush nearby. Lured ashore by Mexican signals of distress, the captain and four sailors were seized, and 16 of the rangers took their places in the boat and rowed out to the vessel, the schooner *Watchman*, loaded with provisions for the Mexican armies. The crew, mistaking the rangers for their comrades, permitted them to come aboard without resistance. Burton prepared to send the *Watchman* to Velasco as a prize of war, but unfavorable winds delayed immediate departure. On 17 June, two more vessels were sighted off the bar. These schooners, the *Comanche* and the *Fanny Butler*, were also loaded with supplies for the Mexican army. The captain of the *Watchman* was made to decoy the captains of the two vessels aboard the *Watchman*. The officers were seized, and their ships and cargoes fell into the hands of the rangers without struggle. The three prizes were first taken to Velasco and then sent to Galveston, where the cargoes were condemned, but the vessels, being American owned, were eventually returned to their owners. Col. Edward J. Wilson of Lexington, Kentucky, wrote of the capture of three Mexican vessels by a troop on horses and said that he supposed they would be called "Horse Marines." *Hobart Huson*

Horton, Albert Clinton. Governor; b. Hancock County, Georgia, 4 September 1798; d. Matagorda, 1 September 1865; m. Eliza Holliday (1829); 6 children. In Alabama, Horton was a legislator. He recruited the Mobile Grays for the Texas Revolution and outfitted them at his own expense; he later retreated from James W. Fannin's fatal predicament at Coleto Creek. He was a senator in the Republic of Texas Congress, chaired the committee that chose Austin as the Texas capital (1839), and served against Rafael Vázquez's invasion of Texas (1842). His election as the first lieutenant governor of Texas positioned him to take over as governor pro tem while James P. Henderson led troops in the Mexican War (May–November 1846). After his term ended he retired from public life except for attending a

Democratic national convention (Charleston, South Carolina, 1860) and the Secession Convention (1861) of Texas. As a planter he became very wealthy, though he lost much in the Civil War. He was on the board of trustees that established Baylor University. *Matthew Ellenberger*

Horton, Johnny. Country singer; b. Tyler, 3 April 1929; d. Milano, Texas, 5 November 1960; m. Billie Jean Jones, who was formerly married to Hank Williams. After spending his childhood picking cotton in East Texas, he attended junior college in Jacksonville and Kilgore. He earned a basketball scholarship to Baylor University in Waco and went from there to the University of Washington in Seattle. After college, Horton worked in Alaska and California in the fishing industry. In 1950 he began singing country music in Pasadena on KXLA, and then proceeded to Cliffie Stone's "Hometown Jamboree" on KLAC–TV. He joined the Louisiana Hayride in 1955 and performed under the name the Singing Fisherman. Companies he recorded with included Mercury, Dot, and Columbia. Horton was known for his versatility, but his specialty was honky-tonk. In 1956 he had his first hit, "Honky Tonk Man." His first number-one recording in country was "When It's Springtime in Alaska," released in 1959. At that time both country and popular-music radio stations began playing his music. He became famous primarily for his "saga songs," including "The Battle of New Orleans" and "Sink the *Bismarck*." He died in an automobile accident. *Jill S. Seeber*

Hot Oil. Production of petroleum in violation of state or federal regulations or in excess of quotas. Hot oil became a serious problem, particularly in Texas, as soon as attempts were made to stem the overproduction and consequent price decline that followed the development of the vast East Texas oilfield, discovered in October 1930. Adoption of a proration plan by the principal oil states in 1931 caused such a frantic rush of drilling that the governors declared martial law in the Oklahoma and East Texas fields and sent national guardsmen to shut down the wells. To evade the state proration laws and the federal regulation of interstate oil transportation imposed under the National Recovery Act, many independent producers resorted to trickery to increase their output. Their methods included tapping underground pipes or reservoirs, loading trucks by moonlight, disguising oil trucks as moving vans, piping oil to moonshine refineries, and using dummy refineries that shipped oil labeled as gasoline. One producer kept a lookout on a derrick and shut off the illegal flow whenever investigators approached; another built a concrete blockhouse over his controls; several provided guns and cash for private guards delegated to deal with state agents, or cheerfully paid the $1,000 fines that represented only a fraction of a day's profit. The flow of hot oil reached its peak in late 1934 and early 1935. In this period illegal production from the East Texas field alone was estimated at 55,000 barrels a day by the Railroad Commission, at 90,000 to 150,000 barrels by some oil-men and federal officials. Throwing excess oil on the market brought a congressional investigation. Enforcement of quotas was achieved gradually after a new interstate compact, drawn in Dallas in February 1935, was ratified by the legislatures of the oil states and strengthened by passage of the Connally Act, which reimposed federal control of interstate oil shipments after court invalidation of that provided in the recovery act. *Wayne Gard*

House, Boyce. Humorist; b. Piggott, Arkansas, 29 November 1896; d. Fort Worth, 30 December 1961; m. Golda Fay Jamison (1927). House moved to Texas alone, attended school in Brownwood, Uvalde, Taylor, and Alpine, and also lived in San Antonio and Del Rio. He worked for several years on the staffs of the two newspapers in Memphis, Tennessee, where his mother had settled after his father's death. In 1920 he moved again to Texas. He worked at newspapers in Eastland, Ranger, Cisco, Olney, and Fort Worth, and developed a reputation for carrying on the fight for honesty and decency in rough-and-tumble oil towns. He gained a national reputation as the reporter of such curiosities as "Old Rip," the famous horned toad that apparently survived a 30-year entombment in the Eastland County Courthouse, and the Santa Claus bank robbery in Cisco (23 December 1927). House wrote several books on Texas oil and the history of boomtowns. His knowledge of oil towns led him to Hollywood as technical advisor to the production *Boomtown* (1940), starring Clark Gable, Spencer Tracy, Claudette Colbert, and Heddy Lamar. Afterward, he returned to Texas and began to write humorous columns and books. His weekly column eventually appeared in 130 newspapers, and his weekly radio show brought him celebrity status in Texas and an established national reputation. House was twice a losing candidate for lieutenant governor of Texas in the Democratic primary. He was a great admirer of William Jennings Bryan and wrote a number of scholarly articles about Bryan. He was a powerful writer and could capture dramatic, spectacular, and moving events on paper. J. Frank Dobie called him "a poet as well as historian and wordwielder." While he was working on *Boomtown*, House wrote several hundred letters to persons living in Wichita Falls and Burkburnett, attempting to learn every possible detail about the Burkburnett oilfield. As a result he left a large amount of correspondence for future researchers. His papers are now housed at the Fort Belknap Archives. *Harry P. Hewitt*

House, Edward Mandell. Businessman and kingmaker; b. Houston, 26 July 1858; d. New York City, 28 March 1938 (buried at Glenwood Cemetery, Houston); m. Loulie Hunter (1881). House, whose father was a wealthy Texas business leader, attended exclusive Eastern schools but was an indifferent student, though he developed an early interest in politics. After his father's death House supervised the family's extensive landholdings scattered throughout Texas. In 1885 he moved to Austin in order to escape the Houston climate and to be closer to his cotton plantations. He became a prominent member of Austin society and, in the late 1880s and early 1890s, pursued a variety of business activities, including farming and land speculation. In June 1892 he completed a great mansion at 1704 West Asylum Avenue, designed by the New York architect Frank Freeman, one of the finest examples in Texas of the Shingle style of residential architecture (razed in 1967). House was drawn into state politics through his friendship with James Stephen Hogg, who in 1892 faced a formidable challenge for renomination and reelection. House directed Hogg's campaign, established a network of contacts with influential local Democratic leaders, manipulated the electoral machinery, and bargained for the votes of African and Mexican Americans. Hogg triumphed in a bitter three-way race and rewarded House in 1893 with the honorary title of "lieutenant colonel." The press soon shortened the title to "colonel." Fascinated more with the process of politics than with the sub-

433

stance, House proceeded to build his own faction—"our crowd," as he called it—which became a powerful force in Texas politics. He was an ambitious political operator, skilled in organizing and inspiring others. He worked largely behind the scenes, developing ties of loyalty and affection with his close associates and using patronage to rally party workers behind his candidates. From 1894 to 1906 House's protégés served as governors of Texas. He and his associates managed the gubernatorial campaigns of Culberson, Sayers, and Lanham. House was especially close to Culberson, whose elevation to the United States Senate in 1898 the colonel directed. House served as a political counselor, often dispensing advice and controlling patronage for all three governors.

Bored with Texas politics, he entered the oil business after the Spindletop discovery and formed the Trinity and Brazos Valley Railway Company. He also felt the pull of the East. For years he had spent the summers on Boston's North Shore, and gradually he began to winter in New York, severing most of his ties with Texas and only occasionally visiting the state. After 1904 he was

Edward M. House, ca. 1895. Courtesy Charles E. Neu, Providence, Rhode Island.

never again involved in a gubernatorial campaign. As a youth House had dreamed great dreams, yearning for a place on the national political stage. A conservative, sound-money Democrat, he disliked William Jennings Bryan and in 1904 supported Alton B. Parker. Discouraged by the prospects of the Democratic party after Parker's defeat in 1904 and Bryan's in 1908, House found solace in leisurely tours of Europe and in spiritualism. He continued his search for a Democratic presidential candidate and, on 25 November 1911, met Woodrow Wilson. House used his influence to secure the 40 votes of the Texas delegation and the approval of William Jennings Bryan for Wilson's candidacy. After Wilson's victory House refused any official appointment, but was responsible for the appointment of several Texans to cabinet positions. He quickly established himself as the president's trusted adviser and confidant, especially on foreign affairs. After the outbreak of World War I, House undertook several important European missions for the president. When the United States became involved in the war, he won British and French acceptance of Wilson's Fourteen Points as the basis for the peace. House was appointed one of the five American commissioners at the peace conference and served as Wilson's second in command. When the president temporarily returned to the United States during the negotiations, House took his place at the head of the American delegation. After signing the Treaty of Versailles on 28 June 1919, Wilson appointed House to represent him at London in the drafting of provisions for operation of the mandate system set up by the treaty. The relationship between the two men deteriorated after Wilson was incapacitated by a stroke in the fall of 1919, and during the Republican party's ascendancy in the 1920s House ceased to exercise direct influence on public affairs. *Charles E. Neu*

Houston, Margaret Lea. Wife of Sam Houston; b. near Marion, Alabama, 11 April 1819; d. Independence, Texas, 3 December 1867. In Mobile, Margaret Moffette Lea was introduced to Houston at a party held by her sister (1839). Despite an age difference of 26 years and Houston's well-known difficulties with drink, they were married on 9 May 1840. Margaret's kin apparently opposed the marriage. Margaret, a beautiful young woman, was utterly devoted to Houston through their 23-year marriage. She led him to declare total abstinence, which, with some difficulty, he maintained for the rest of his life. She and Rev. George W. Baines persuaded him join the Baptist Church; on 19 November 1854, Houston was baptized by Rev. Rufus C. Burleson in Rocky Creek, near Independence. Margaret's chronic asthma prevented her from following Houston in his journeys; while he was in the Senate she never once went to Washington, nor did she travel his nearly endless campaign trails. Staying at home, she created a domestic circle on which he looked increasingly as a haven. Their large household ultimately included eight children. The Houstons had numerous houses in Texas. Only one of these they kept continuously, Cedar Point, on Trinity Bay. Of their homes only the house at Huntsville (greatly remodeled), the rented Steamboat House nearby, and the Governor's Mansion in Austin are still standing. Raven Hill, Cedar Point, and the house in Independence, near old Baylor College, are gone. Surprisingly few of the Houstons' personal possessions survive. While Houston was in the Senate, they had money and did not have to rely upon farming or land speculation, at which Houston was never successful. When Houston was in Texas the family was not likely to remain long in one place, but traveled about from house to house in a big horse-drawn carryall enclosed in canvas. Nearly every summer they spent time at Cedar Point. Autumn found them in Huntsville or Independence. Before 1853 Margaret's mother lived regularly with them and managed the household, a job that held no interest for Mrs. Houston. Margaret's inquiring mind led her by the late 1840s wholly away from reading novels and plays into religious studies. Her letters to Sam contained long passages on religion and reflected her great insecurity about the beliefs she professed. The unhappy climax of Houston's long political career in 1861 and his subsequent removal from the office of governor of Texas were followed by his two final years in retirement and relative obscurity. Living between Huntsville and Cedar Point, Mrs. Houston was with her husband constantly. Sustained by religion and her children, she saw Houston decline rapidly and gave him support where she could. After his death (1863), the widow was in serious financial straits. She moved to Independence to be once again near her mother, rented a house, and labored to hold her family together. Her condition eventually eased when the state legislature voted to pay her the unpaid balance of Houston's salary as governor. While preparing to move to Georgetown she was stricken by yellow fever and died. Because of the health laws she was buried at once at Independence. *William Seale*

Houston, Sam. One of the most illustrious Texans; b. Rockbridge County, Virginia, 2 March 1793; d. Huntsville, 26 July 1863; m. Margaret Moffette Lea (1840); 8 children. Houston was of Scots–Irish ancestry and reared Presbyterian. He acquired rudimentary education during his boyhood by attending a local school for no more than six months. When he was 13 years old his father died; some months later, in the spring of 1807, he emigrated with his mother, five brothers, and three sisters to Blount County in Eastern Tennessee, where the family established a farm near Maryville. Houston went to a nearby academy for a time and reportedly fed his fertile imagination by reading classical literature, especially the *Iliad*. Rebelling at his older brothers' attempts to make him work on the farm and in the family's store in Maryville, he ran away from home in 1809 to dwell among the Cherokees, who lived across the Tennessee River. Between intermittent visits to Maryville, he sojourned for three years with the band of Chief Oolooteka, who adopted him and gave him the Indian name Colonneh, or "the Raven." Houston viewed Oolooteka as his "Indian Father" and henceforth maintained great sympathy toward Indians. At age 18 he left the Cherokees to set up a school, so that he could earn money to repay debts. After war broke out with the British, he joined the United States Army as a private (24 March 1813). Within four months he received a promotion to ensign of the infantry; in late December he was given a commission as a third lieutenant. As part of Andrew Jackson's army, he fought at the battle of Horseshoe Bend on the Tallapoosa River on 26 March 1814. During the engagement he received three near-fatal wounds. One of them, from a rifle ball in his right shoulder, never completely healed. For his valor at Horseshoe Bend, Houston won the attention of General Jackson, who thereafter became his benefactor. Houston, in return, revered Jackson and became a staunch Jacksonian Democrat. While convalescing, he was promoted to second lieutenant and traveled extensively—to Washington, New Orleans, New York, and points between. While stationed in Nashville, he was

Samuel Houston, ca. 1845. Daguerreotype by L. W. Whitehurst. Courtesy Chicago Historical Society; ICHi-10751.

detailed in late 1817 as sub–Indian agent to the Cherokees. In that capacity, he assisted Oolooteka and his clan in their removal to Indian Territory west of the Mississippi River, as stipulated by the Treaty of 1816. Houston, by then first lieutenant, resigned from the army on 1 March 1818, and shortly thereafter from his position as subagent, following difficulties with Secretary of War John C. Calhoun.

Still in poor health, he read law in Nashville for six months during 1818 in the office of Judge James Trimble. He subsequently opened a law practice in Lebanon, Tennessee. With Jackson's endorsement, he became adjutant general (with the rank of colonel) of the state militia through appointment by Governor Joseph McMinn. In late 1818, Houston was elected attorney general (prosecuting attorney) of the District of Nashville, where he took up residence. After returning to private practice in Nashville by late 1821, he was elected major general of the state militia by his fellow officers. He was likewise prominent in the Nash Masonic order by the early 1820s. His rapid rise in public office continued in 1823, when, as a member of Jackson's political circle, he was elected to the United States House of Representatives from the Ninth Tennessee District. As a member of Congress he worked mightily though unsuccessfully for the election of Andrew Jackson to the presidency in 1824. In 1825 he was returned to Congress for a second and final term. In 1827, ever the Jackson protégé, Houston was elected governor of Tennessee. He was 34 years of age, extremely ambitious, and in the thick of tumultuous Tennessee politics. Standing six feet two inches tall and handsome, he cut a dashing figure wherever he went. In 1829 he married 19-year-old Eliza Allen of Gallatin, Tennessee and subsequently announced his bid for reelection to the governorship. After 11 weeks the marriage ended, however, and the distraught Houston abruptly resigned from his office on 16 April and fled west across the Mississippi River to Indian Territory. His exit brought the Tennessee phase of his career to an end. As a possible heir apparent to Andrew Jackson, he may well have given up an opportunity to run eventually for president of the United States.

He made his way to the lodge of Oolooteka in what is now Oklahoma to live once again in self-imposed exile among the Cherokees, this time for three years. Among the Indians he tried to reestablish his tranquility. He dressed Indian-style and, although he corresponded with Jackson, initially secluded himself from contacts with white society. Initially, too, he drank so heavily that he reportedly earned the nickname "Big Drunk." He quickly became active in Indian affairs, especially in helping to keep peace between the various tribes in Indian Territory. He was granted Cherokee citizenship and often acted as a tribal emissary. Under Cherokee law he married Diana Rogers Gentry, a woman of mixed blood. Together, they established a residence and trading post called Wigwam Neosho on the Neosho River near Fort Gibson. Gradually reinvolving himself in the white world, Houston made various trips East—to Tennessee, Washington, and New York. In December 1831, while on the Arkansas River, he encountered Alexis de Tocqueville, the latter on his famous travels in the United States. Houston impressed the Frenchman as an individual of great physical and moral energy, the universal American in perpetual motion; he undoubtedly served as an example for Tocqueville's composite description of the "nervous American," the man-on-the-make so pervasive in the United States during the Age of Jackson.

On the evening of 13 April 1832, on the streets of Washington, Houston thrashed William Stanbery, United States representative from Ohio, with a hickory cane. The assault resulted from a perceived insult by Stanbery over an Indian rations contract. Houston was soon arrested and tried before the House of Representatives. Francis Scott Key served as his attorney. The month-long proceedings ended in an official reprimand and a fine, but the affair catapulted Houston back into the political arena. Leaving Diana and his life among the Indians, Houston crossed the Red River into Mexican Texas on 2 December 1832 and began another, perhaps the most important, phase of his career. His "true motives" for entering Texas have been the source of much speculation. Whether he did so simply as a land speculator, as an agent provocateur for American expansion intent on wresting Texas from Mexico, or as someone scheming to establish an independent nation, Houston saw Texas as his "land of promise." For him, it represented a place for bold enterprise, rife with political and financial opportunity. He quickly became embroiled in the Anglo-Texans' politics of rebellion. He served as a delegate from Nacogdoches at the Convention of 1833 in San Felipe, where he sided with the more radical faction under the leadership of William H. Wharton. He also pursued a law practice in Nacogdoches and filed for a divorce from Eliza, which was finally granted in 1837. As prescribed by Mexican law, he was baptized into the Catholic Church, under the name Samuel Pablo. In September 1835 he chaired a mass meeting in Nacogdoches to consider the possibility of convening a consultation. By October, Houston had expressed his belief that war

between Texas and the central government was inevitable. That month he became commander in chief of troops for the Department of Nacogdoches and called for volunteers to begin the "work of liberty." He served as a delegate from Nacogdoches to the Consultation of 1835, which deliberated in Columbia in October and at San Felipe in November. On 12 November the Consultation appointed Houston major general of the Texas army. During February 1836 Houston and John Forbes, as commissioners for the provisional government, negotiated a treaty with the Cherokees in East Texas, thus strategically establishing peace on that front. In March Houston served as a delegate from Refugio to the convention at Washington-on-the-Brazos, where, on his birthday, the assembly adopted the Texas Declaration of Independence. Two days later Houston received the appointment of major general of the army from the convention, with instructions to organize the republic's military forces.

After joining his army in Gonzales, Houston and his troops retreated eastward as the Mexican army under Gen. Antonio López de Santa Anna swept across Texas. This campaign caused Houston much anguish because the Texan rebels suffered from a general lack of discipline. He likewise fretted when the citizenry fled in the so-called Runaway Scrape. Despite these problems, Houston and his men defeated Santa Anna's forces at the decisive battle of San Jacinto on the afternoon of 21 April 1836. During this engagement, his horse, Saracen, was shot beneath him, and Houston was wounded severely just above the right ankle. The capture of Santa Anna the next day made the victory complete. At San Jacinto, Sam Houston became forever enshrined in the pantheon of Texas heroes.

Riding the wave of popularity as "Old Sam Jacinto," Houston defeated Stephen F. Austin to become the first regularly elected president of the Republic of Texas. During his two presidential terms he successfully guided the new ship of state through many trials and tribulations. His first term lasted from 22 October 1836 to 10 December 1838. The town of Houston was founded in 1836, named in his honor, and served as the capital of the republic during most of his first administration. During this term Houston sought to demilitarize Texas by cannily furloughing much of the army. He also tried, with limited success, to avoid trouble between white settlers and Indians. One of his biggest crises came with the Córdova Rebellion, an unsuccessful revolt in 1838 by a group of Kickapoo Indians in league with Mexican residents along the Angelina River. In late 1836, Houston sent Santa Anna, then a prisoner of war, to Washington to seek the annexation of Texas to the United States. Although Houston favored annexation, his initial efforts to bring Texas into the Union proved futile, and he formally withdrew the offer by the end of his first term. After leaving office because the Constitution of the Republic of Texas barred a president from succeeding himself, Houston served in the Texas House of Representatives as a congressman from San Augustine from 1839 to 1841. He was in the forefront of the opposition to President Lamar, who had been Houston's vice president. Houston particularly criticized Lamar's expansionist tendencies and harsh measures toward the Indians. After marrying Margaret Lea, Houston succeeded Lamar for a second term as president, 12 December 1841 to 9 December 1844. During this administration he stressed financial austerity and drastically reduced government offices and salaries. He and the Congress even tried to sell the four-ship Texas Navy, an effort forcibly prevented by the people of

Galveston. Houston reestablished peace with the Indians by making treaties with the bands that still remained in Texas. Although many Texans clamored for action, Houston deftly managed to avoid war with Mexico after the two Mexican invasions of 1842. After the first incursion he directed that the government archives be moved from Austin, an order that resulted in the "Archive War." After the second invasion Houston authorized a force under Gen. Alexander Somervell to pursue the enemy to the Rio Grande and, if conditions warranted, to attack Mexico. Part of Somervell's legion became the disastrous Mier expedition, an escapade that Houston opposed. In 1843 Houston approved of the abortive Snively expedition, which sought to interdict trade along the Santa Fe Trail. In 1844 Houston found it necessary to send the militia to quell the Regulator–Moderator War in Shelby County, an East Texas feud that presented one of the most vexing problems of his second administration. Houston was succeeded in the presidency by Anson Jones, whom the electorate viewed as a "Houston man." Texas politics during the republic had been largely a struggle between Houston and anti-Houston factions. Sam Houston's name had become synonymous with Texas.

When Texas joined the union, Houston became one of its two United States senators, along with Thomas Jefferson Rusk. Houston served in the Senate from 21 February 1846 until 4 March 1859. Beginning with the 1848 election he was mentioned as a possible candidate for president. A biography published in 1846 by Charles Edwards Lester, *Sam Houston and His Republic*, amounted to campaign publicity. As senator, Houston emerged as an ardent Unionist, true to his association with Andrew Jackson, a stand that made him an increasingly controversial figure. He stridently opposed the rising sectionalism of the antebellum period and delivered eloquent speeches on the issue. As a supporter of the 1820 Missouri Compromise, which banned slavery north of latitude 36°30', Houston voted in 1848 for the Oregon Bill prohibiting the "peculiar institution" in that territory, a vote proslavery Southerners later held against him. Although he was a slaveowner who defended slavery in the South, Houston again clashed with his old nemesis who led the proslavery forces when he opposed John C. Calhoun's Southern Address in 1849. Houston always characterized himself as a Southern man for the Union and opposed any threats of disunity, whether from Northern or Southern agitators. He incurred the permanent wrath of proslavery elements by supporting the Compromise of 1850, a series of measures designed to ensure sectional harmony. In 1854 Houston alienated Democrats in Texas and the South even further by opposing the Kansas–Nebraska Bill because it allowed the status of slavery to be determined by popular sovereignty, a concept he saw as potentially destabilizing to the nation. He likewise embraced the principles of the American (Know-Nothing) party as a response to growing states'-rights sentiment among the Democrats. In 1854, he accommodated his wife by joining the Baptist Church, no doubt in partial response to the troubles of this period of his life. His career in the Senate was effectively ended when, in 1855, the Texas legislature officially condemned his position on the Kansas–Nebraska Act.

As a lame-duck senator, Houston ran for governor of Texas in 1857. He was defeated in a rigorous campaign by the state Democratic party's official nominee, Hardin Runnels. Predictably, the state legislature did not reelect Houston to the Senate; instead, in late 1857, it replaced him with John Hemphill. The replacement took place at the end of Houston's term, in 1859. So concerned was Houston about sectional strife that during his final year in the Senate he advocated establishing a protectorate over Mexico and Central America as a way to bring unity to the United States. Out of the Senate, he ran a second time for governor in 1859. Because of his name recognition, a temporary lull in the sectional conflict, and other factors, he defeated Runnels in the August election and assumed office on 21 December. As governor he continued to pursue his fanciful plans for a protectorate over Mexico, and envisioned the use of Texas Rangers and volunteers to accomplish that end. He likewise tried to enlist the aid of Robert E. Lee, Benjamin McCulloch, and some New York financiers for his scheme. Because of his staunch Unionism, Houston was nearly nominated for the presidency in May 1860 by the National Union party convention in Baltimore, but narrowly lost to John Bell. His possible candidacy received favorable mention by people in many regions of the nation who longed to prevent sectional strife.

When Abraham Lincoln was elected president of the United States, the clamor of discontent in Texas prompted Houston to call a special session of the state legislature. Adamantly opposed to secession, Houston warned Texans that civil war would result in a Northern victory and destruction of the South, a prophecy that was soon borne out. The Secession Convention, however, began a series of actions that withdrew Texas from the Union. Houston acquiesced to these events rather than bring civil strife and bloodshed to his beloved state. But when he refused to take the oath of loyalty to the newly formed Confederate States of America, the Texas convention removed him from office on 16 March 1861 and replaced him with Lieutenant Governor Edward Clark two days later. Reportedly, during these traumatic days President Lincoln twice offered Houston the use of federal troops to keep him in office and Texas in the Union, offers that Houston declined, again to avoid making Texas a scene of violence. Instead, the Raven—now 68 years old, weary, with a family of small children, and recognizing the inevitable—again chose exile.

After leaving the Governor's Mansion, Houston at least verbally supported the Southern cause. Against his father's advice, Sam Houston, Jr., eagerly joined the Confederate Army and was wounded at the battle of Shiloh. Houston moved his wife and other children in the fall of 1862 to Huntsville, where they rented a two-story residence known as the Steamboat House, so called because it resembled a riverboat. Rumors abounded that Houston, though ailing and aged, harbored plans to run again for governor. But after suffering from pneumonia for several weeks, he died in the downstairs bedroom of the Steamboat House at age 70. Dressed in Masonic ceremonial trappings, he was buried in Oakwood Cemetery. *Thomas H. Kreneck*

Houston, Texas. In 1990 Houston, covering 540 square miles, ranked as the fourth largest city in the United States with a population of 1,630,553. The city passed Philadelphia in 1984 to take a position behind New York, Los Angeles, and Chicago. The consolidated metropolitan population of Houston, which encompassed Galveston, Fort Bend, Harris, Brazoria, Liberty, Waller, and Montgomery counties, amounted to 3,711,000, ranked tenth in the nation, and was second in Texas to Dallas–Fort Worth.

THE TOWN OF HOUSTON.

SITUATED at the head of navigation, on the West bank of Buffalo Bayou, is now for the first time brought to public notice because, until now, the proprietors were not ready to offer it to the public, with the advantages of capital and improvements.

The town of Houston is located at a point on the river which must ever command the trade of the largest and richest portion of Texas. By reference to the map, it will be seen that the trade of San Jacinto, Spring Creek, New Kentucky and the Brazos, above and below Fort Bend, must necessarily come to this place, and will at this time warrant the employment of at least ONE MILLION DOLLARS of capital, and when the rich lands of this country shall be settled, a trade will flow to it, making it, beyond all doubt, the great interior commercial emporium of Texas.

The town of Houston is distant 15 miles from the Brazos river, 30 miles, a little North of East, from San Felipe, 60 miles from Washington, 40 miles from Lake Creek, 30 miles South West from New Kentucky, and 15 miles by water and 8 or 10 by land above Harrisburg. Tide water runs to this place and the lowest depth of water is about six feet. Vessels from New Orleans or New York can sail without obstacle to this place, and steamboats of the largest class can run down to Galveston Island in 8 or 10 hours, in all seasons of the year. It is but a few hours sail down the bay, where one may take an excursion of pleasure and enjoy the luxuries of fish, foul, oysters and sea bathing. Galveston harbor being the only one in which vessels drawing a large draft of water can navigate, must necessarily render the Island the great naval and commercial depot of the country.

The town of Houston must be the place where arms, ammunitions and provisions for the government will be stored, because, situated in the very heart of the country, it combines security and the means of easy distribution, and a national armory will no doubt very soon be established at this point.

There is no place in Texas more healthy, having an abundance of excellent spring water, and enjoying the sea breeze in all its freshness. No place in Texas possesses so many advantages for building, having Pine, Ash, Cedar and Oak in inexhaustible quantities; also the tall and beautiful Magnolia grows in abundance. In the vicinity are fine quarries of stone.

Nature appears to have designated this place for the future seat of Government. It is handsome and beautifully elevated, salubrious and well watered, and now in the very heart or centre of population, and will be so for a length of time to come. It combines two important advantages: a communication with the coast and foreign countries, and with the different portions of the Republic. As the country shall improve, rail roads will become in use, and will be extended from this point to the Brazos, and up the same, also from this up to the head waters of San Jacinto, embracing that rich country, and in a few years the whole trade of the upper Brazos will make its way into Galveston Bay through this channel.

Preparations are now making to erect a water Saw Mill, and a large Public House for accommodation, will soon be opened. Steamboats now run in this river, and will in a short time commence running regularly to the Island.

The proprietors offer the lots for sale on moderate terms to those who desire to improve them, and invite the public to examine for themselves.

A. C. ALLEN, for
A. C. & J. K. ALLEN.

August 30, 1836.—6m

The Commercial Bulletin, of New Orleans, Mobile Advertiser, the Globe, at Washington, Morning Courier and New York Enquirer, New York Herald, and Louisville Public Advertiser are requested to make three insertions of this advertisement, and forward their bills to this office for payment.

Advertisement for "The Town of Houston," published in the *Telegraph and Texas Register*, Columbia, Texas, August 30, 1836. Texas Newspaper Collection, CAH; CN 10375. The city of Houston began when Augustus Chapman Allen and John Kirby Allen ran this advertisement.

When first formed in 1949 the Houston Standard Metropolitan Statistical Area covered only Harris County and had a population of 806,701 people. Over 100 ethnic groups now shape the population; the major components in 1987 were 56 percent white, 17 percent black, 17 percent Hispanic, and 3 percent Asian. This spectacular growth developed as a result of the construction of transportation systems, the fortuitous nearby location of useful natural resources, and an entrepreneurial spirit. The city began on 30 August 1836, when Augustus Chapman Allen and John Kirby Allen ran an advertisement in the *Telegraph and Texas Register* for the "Town of Houston." The townsite, which featured a mixture of timber and grassland, was on the level Coastal Plain in the middle of the future Harris County. The brothers claimed that the town would become the "great interior commercial emporium of Texas," that ships from New York and New Orleans could sail up Buffalo Bayou to its door, and that the site enjoyed a healthful, cool seabreeze. They noted plans to build a sawmill and offered lots for sale at moderate prices. In the manner of town boomers the Allens exaggerated a bit, however. The 43-inch annual rainfall and temperatures that averaged from a low of 45° F in the winter to 93° in summer later inspired

Houston to become one of the most air-conditioned cities in the world. Moreover, in January 1837, when Francis R. Lubbock arrived on the *Laura*, the small steamship that first reached Houston, he found the bayou choked with branches and the town almost invisible.

The Allen brothers named their town after Sam Houston and persuaded the Texas Congress to designate the site as the temporary capital of the new Republic of Texas. The promoters offered lots and buildings to the government. On 1 January 1837 the town comprised 12 residents and one log cabin; four months later there were 1,500 people and 100 houses. Gail and Thomas H. Borden surveyed and mapped the town in typical gridiron fashion, with broad streets running parallel and perpendicular to the bayou. The Republic of Texas Congress first met in Houston on 1 May 1837, and, despite the efforts of Masons who greeted one another in 1837 and the Presbyterians and Episcopalians who formed churches in 1839, the town remained infamous for drunkenness, dueling, brawling, prostitution, and profanity. Congress granted incorporation on 5 June 1837, and James S. Holman became the first mayor. The same year, Houston also became the county seat of Harrisburg County, which was renamed Harris County in 1839. During the nineteenth century, aldermen elected by wards directed the city government. In 1905 the city began to use a modified commission form with aldermen elected at large. Houston switched to a city manager government from 1942 to 1947, and then subsequently to a strong mayor and city council. A 1979 United States Justice Department ruling led to nine city council members elected from districts and five elected at large. Voters selected the first African American for the council in 1971 and the first Mexican American in 1979.

The early settlers used lumber to build frame houses, ditches for drainage, and pigs to clean the streets. Yellow fever struck periodically—in 1839, 1844, 1847, 1848, 1854, 1858, 1859, 1862, and 1867—until it was controlled by quarantine of the coastline. In 1839 the disease killed about 12 percent of the population. Since many of the first Houston settlers were from the South, they endorsed the slavery–plantation system and used urban slaves for menial tasks. This started Houston on the same bifurcated pathway as other Southern towns, where the black minority developed a subordinated and separate social structure. The slaves lived scattered through the neighborhoods, were subject to an 8:00 P.M. curfew, and could not take employment without their owners' permission. There were few free blacks in the city. After the Civil War, separation of the races continued with segregated schools and dissociated churches, clubs, bands, businesses, and sports teams. Segregation by law began with separation on trollies in 1903. It continued through the first half of the twentieth century, during which blacks were excluded from or had only limited access to white parks, depots, schools, drinking fountains, buses, restrooms, and restaurants. Though residential segregation never became part of the legal code, it did operate as part of the social code. Separate residential areas developed for African Americans and Mexican Americans by the end of the century. Despite occasional outbursts such as the Houston Riot of 1917, when a black army unit shot up the town and left 19 people dead, nothing changed the legacy of slavery until the civil-rights movement of the 1950s and 1960s.

Although Houston started as a political boomtown in the nineteenth century, its livelihood depended upon cotton and

Market Place and Gaol, Houston, Texas, March 20th, 1852, by Thomas Flintoff, 1852. Watercolor. Courtesy Houston Metropolitan Research Center, Houston Public Library. Flintoff's are the earliest images of Houston known to have been made at the scene by a professional artist. This view shows the market building and the city hall, surmounted by a cupola.

commerce. The Texas government left Houston for Austin in 1839, and the city settled into the rhythm of agriculture. Businessmen such as William Marsh Rice, Thomas M. Bagby, Charles Shearn, William J. Hutchins, Paul Bremond, and A. S. Ruthven established trade connections. Activity was greatest during harvest and marketing times, and the rest of the year was spent in sending supplies to farmers. Oceangoing ships brought to Galveston cargoes of cloth, flour, whiskey, gunpowder, iron castings, lead, coffee, sugar, nails, books, and hundreds of small items. Small river steamships took the goods from Galveston to Houston. The merchants then sent them by ox wagon to the farmers in the hinterland. In the reverse direction came cotton, corn, and hides through Houston to Galveston and on to New Orleans, New York, and Europe.

From the beginning, Buffalo Bayou was difficult to navigate. After the Civil War, businessmen mounted various efforts to dredge a better channel by forming the Houston Direct Navigation Company, the Houston Ship Channel Company, and the Buffalo Bayou Ship Channel Company. Charles Morgan, a Gulf Coast shipowner, eventually took over and in 1876 opened a 12-foot-deep waterway to Clinton, a port town below Houston. The United States government assumed Morgan's work in 1881 and after delays dug a ship channel through Galveston Bay and Buffalo Bayou to a turning basin above Harrisburg. The

Houston Ship Channel opened in 1914 and has been since widened and deepened. It made Houston a deepwater port variously ranked second or third largest in the United States, with access to the shipping of the world. Complementing this facility, Houstonians worked to build railroads into the countryside. Paul Bremond, a Houston merchant, began a slow northwestward construction of the Houston and Texas Central Railroad in 1853. This line started as the Galveston and Red River, changed its name in 1856, and reached Hempstead in 1858. Meanwhile, the Houston Tap and Brazoria, a seven-mile railway, joined the Buffalo Bayou, Brazos and Colorado Railway at Pierce Junction in 1856. This linked Houston with the sugar plantations of the Brazos valley. Other roads were started, and by 1861 Houston was the rail center of Southeast Texas with five lines stretching 50 to 100 miles south, southeast, west, east, and northwest. The Civil War interrupted construction, but building revived afterwards. When the Houston and Texas Central reached Denison in 1873, Houston joined the national rail network. The railroads efficiently spanned the muddy bogs of the coastal prairie. The city's first expressway, the Gulf Freeway, connected Houston and Galveston in 1952 and later became a part of the interstate highway system. Houston opened its first airport in 1928, Houston International Airport in 1954 (renamed William P. Hobby Airport in 1967), and Houston Intercontinental Airport in 1969.

Houston skyline, ca. 1990. Courtesy Texas Department of Economic Development/Richard Reynolds. Innovative buildings designed by masters such as Philip Johnson and I. M. Pei distinguish Houston's skyline, here photographed looking east from the hike-and-bike trail along Buffalo Bayou.

The various transportation systems, along with the communication systems of mail, telegraph (built 1853–54) and telephone (1878–95), allowed Houston to develop as a cotton and lumber market in the nineteenth century. The discovery of oil at the Spindletop oilfield dramatically changed the Houston economy in the twentieth century. Oil companies built refineries along the Houston Ship Channel, where they were safe from Gulf storms. By 1929, 40 oil companies had located offices in the city. The most important were the Texas Company (now Texaco), Humble Oil and Refining Company (now Exxon), and Gulf Oil Corporation. Sinclair Oil Company built the first major refinery in 1918.

World War II brought a demand for synthetic rubber, gasoline, materials for explosives, and ships from the area. Concrete barges, steel merchant vessels, and warships were built along the ship channel. Houston Shipbuilding Corporation, a subsidiary of Todd Shipbuilding Corporation, for example, built Liberty Ships and employed 20,000 workers by July 1942. The Brown Shipbuilding Company pioneered broadside launching and produced more than 300 war vessels by the end of the war. Nearby coastal deposits of salt, sulfur, and natural gas supplied the ingredients for petrochemicals, and the United States government provided the contracts for war materials. On this foundation after the war Houston developed one of the two largest petrochemical concentrations in the United States with such companies as Dow, Du Pont, Shell, Sinclair, Monsanto, and Goodyear. In 1990 a complex of some 250 interrelated refineries extended from Corpus Christi along the coast to the Louisiana border. The main exports and imports of the port of Houston, consequently, were petroleum or petroleum-related products. Houston thus became a world energy capital in the 1970s, expanded with the rise in oil prices, and suffered with the downturn during the 1980s. In the mid-1980s, for the first time in its history, Houston lost population.

The developments of the twentieth century, however, made Houston the largest city in Texas in 1930, when the population was 292,000. At this time Houston had three newspapers—the Houston *Post* (founded 1880), the Houston *Chronicle* (1901), and the Houston *Press* (1911)—and four radio stations—KPRC (1925), KTRH (1930), KTLC (1930), and KXYZ (1930). Facilities for urban living had to develop along with the growth. Merchants and others complained about the city streets from the beginning. Efforts to rise out of the mud and dust featured experiments with cypress blocks, gravel, planks, shell, limestone blocks, and later cement and asphalt. In 1915 Houston had almost 196 miles of paved streets. In 1922 the municipal government began to replace wooden bridges with steel and concrete. Electric streetlights appeared in 1884 and an electric streetcar system in 1891. Automobiles came at the beginning of the century and caught on fast; there were 1,031 in Harris County in 1911 and

97,902 in 1930. This growth led to traffic regulations on speed (15 miles per hour in 1907), one-way streets in 1920, and traffic signals in 1921. The increasing use of automobiles also led to the building of expressways in the 1950s that extended over 200 miles by 1990, as well as air pollution, urban sprawl, and huge traffic jams. The most important urban necessity, the water supply, improved in the late 1880s after several citizens discovered artesian water by drilling shallow wells. Well water thus replaced the contaminated bayou water used by the private water-supply company. The city took over the company in 1906. Continued pumping from the aquifer, however, resulted in subsidence of the land in southeastern Houston in the 1960s. To avoid further sinking, the city turned to the Trinity and San Jacinto rivers for most of its water. The paving of land and consequent quick runoff of rain resulted in a flood problem. Severe floods in 1929 and 1935 led to the formation of the Harris County Flood Control District, but storm flooding in parts of the metropolitan area has continued. Water pollution has been a long-standing problem. Surges of rainwater into the bayous have flushed the contamination of the ship channel into Galveston Bay and caused fish kills. While building the channel, the United States Army Corps of Engineers forced the city to construct a sewage-disposal system that, when completed in 1902, was among the best in the nation. Urban growth and neglect, however, overcame the advance.

Land developers inspired the spread of the city when they built suburbs such as Pasadena (1892), Houston Heights (1892), Deer Park (1892), Bellaire (1911), and West University Place (1919). The most famous, because of its wealth, was River Oaks (1922–24), started by Mike and William Clifford Hogg and Hugh Potter. There, architect John F. Staub designed tasteful homes to match the curved streets and large green lawns. Suburbs have since spread out in the metropolitan region. An important example is The Woodlands, a new town built by oilman George T. Mitchell between 1964 and 1983 north of Houston in southern Montgomery County. Mitchell blended homes, business places, and recreation facilities into the pine woods with minimal environmental disturbance. In 1948–49, to avoid encirclement by incorporated suburbs, the Houston City Council under Mayor Oscar F. Holcombe used its annexation power to envelop the older suburbs. As a result the city doubled in size. In 1956 the council voted more annexation, and in 1960, while fighting with neighboring towns, the council threatened to annex all unclaimed land in Harris County. Compromises finally brought the annexation war under control. Part of the dispute involved the rich and prestigious land around Clear Lake to the south, where in 1961 NASA built the Johnson Space Center. Houston was able to control the land.

In the ordering of urban space Houston politicians and voters have rejected the use of zoning. The administration of Mayor Kathy Whitmire in the 1980s brought the subject up for review, but Houston remained infamous as the largest unzoned city in the United States. The lack of zoning has not affected development to any great extent, however, since heavy industry concentrated in the area of the ship channel and subdivisions controlled construction through deed restrictions. This casual attitude toward land use encouraged business expansion. The greatest Houston city builder in the first half of the twentieth century was banker Jesse H. Jones. By the mid-1920s he had constructed about 30 commercial structures, and in 1956 he controlled 50

buildings. He brought the 1928 Democratic convention to the city and later served as Franklin D. Roosevelt's secretary of commerce. His most impressive structure was the 37-story Gulf Building, completed in 1929. The prosperity after World War II brought the world famous Galleria shopping mall with its interior ice-skating rink in 1970; Pennzoil Place, a startling black-glass downtown building in 1976; and the Astrodome in 1965. The Houston skyline became a showcase of modern architecture. In 1992 Houston hosted the national Republican convention.

The city meanwhile matured culturally and socially. The Texas Medical Center, with its 14 hospitals, emerged as a global focal point for heart and cancer treatment. The center was the largest employer in Houston in 1990 and was famous for heart transplants. In 1971 Dominique and John de Menil built the Rothko Chapel, which became a place of religious pilgrimage, and in 1987 Dominique de Menil constructed a gallery to house the Menil Collection of modern art. This added to the collections of art that began with the opening of the Museum of Fine Arts in 1924. A free secondary school system began in 1877 and became the Houston ISD in 1924. This district is now one of the largest in the nation. Rice University started in 1912, financed by a bequest from William Marsh Rice, who made his fortune in Houston in the nineteenth century. The University of Houston began as a junior college in 1927 and was supported by oilman Hugh Roy Cullen in its early years, until it became part of the state system of higher education in 1963. KUHT–TV, which started in 1953 at the university, was the first educational television station in the United States. Texas Southern University began in 1934 as part of the University of Houston. The University of St. Thomas began in 1945 and Houston Baptist University in 1963. In 1914 George H. Hermann donated Hermann Park, where a 30-acre zoo was established in 1922. Memorial Park, the other major Houston park, developed from land purchased in 1924. The Houston Symphony Orchestra was formed in 1913, the Houston Grand Opera in 1956, the Alley Theatre in 1947, and the Houston Ballet in 1969. The Houston Public Library opened in 1904 with the help of Andrew Carnegie. Television began in 1949 with broadcasts from KLEE–TV, which became KPRC–TV in 1950. Seven other stations followed. Professional sports teams arrived—the Houston Astros baseball team in 1962 (called the Colt .45s until 1964), the Houston Oilers football team in 1959, and the Houston Rockets basketball team in 1971.

David G. McComb

Houston Astros. A National League baseball team founded as the Houston Colt 45's in 1962 when Roy Hofheinz, with the help of wealthy oilman Robert Everett Smith, gained control of the Houston Sports Association. Former mayor Hofheinz controlled the Astros until the 1979 season. In their first season, the Colt 45's finished a surprising eighth in the National League. The next two years saw identical ninth-place finishes, with the only highlights being no-hitters thrown by Don Nottebart in 1963 and by Ken Johnson in 1964. When the Astrodome opened in 1965, the team changed its name to Astros. The 1965 season was a financial success, drawing 2,151,470 fans to the new building, but the team once again finished in last place. Despite Don Wilson's no-hitter in 1968, the team still had not finished higher than ninth place since its inaugural season. The quality of play over this stretch was poor, but Judge Hofheinz always made sure the fans were entertained with various promotions and stunts. In 1972 the

Astros finished with their best record yet, 84–65. But the mid-1970s saw a sharp decline in the Astros' records and in fan attendance; 1975 was the first time since 1964 that the club drew sold fewer than a million tickets. In 1978 the Astros finished with a .500 record, but the fans were still not coming out. Hofheinz relinquished control of the Houston Sports Association before the 1979 season, and Ford Credit Corporation acquired a majority interest in the Houston Sports Association and the Astros. The team still drew fewer than a million fans in 1979, but finished just 1½ games out of first place in the National League West. In 1980 the Astros signed free agent and Texas native Nolan Ryan to the first million-dollar contract in baseball, and they also reacquired Joe Morgan. The team finished in a tie with the Los Angeles Dodgers for first place and won a one-game playoff for their first-ever division title. They lost an exciting league championship series to the Philadelphia Phillies. The 1981 strike-shortened season also went well, ending in a playoff loss to the Dodgers. The Astros hovered around a .500 winning percentage until 1986. Seemingly out of nowhere they then finished with a 96–66 record, the best in franchise history by far, once again winning the National League West. Pitcher Mike Scott was named Most Valuable Player of the National League. The team lost a dramatic league championship series to the heavily favored Mets, however, and did not approach a division championship for many years. Drayton McClain became owner of the Astros in 1993, and the team started to become competitive once again. In 1998, when the team had a 102–60 record, the division title again became a reality.   *Eric M. Pfeifle*

Houston Baptist University. In southwest Houston; chartered in 1960 by the Baptist General Convention of Texas as Houston Baptist College, a Christian fouryear liberal arts college. The institution opened in September 1963 with a freshman class of 191 students; a new class was added each year through 1966. Initially the curriculum included five academic divisions: Christianity, languages, fine arts, science and mathematics, and social studies. In the following years three new divisions were added: education and psychology, business and economics, and nursing. During the 1970s endowed chairs were established in business, the humanities, and evangelism. William H. Hintor served as first president of the institution, and in 1987 Edward Douglas Hodo became the second. In 1973 when the college became a university the eight academic divisions were reorganized into five colleges. In 1978 the College of Fine Arts and Humanities was subdivided into the College of Fine Arts and the College of Humanities. In 1991 the College of Sciences and Health Professions became the College of Nursing and the College of Science and Mathematics. In 1977 graduate degrees in business and nursing were added. Two years later a master's degree in education was implemented. During the 1980s advanced training in psychology and the liberal arts was added. In 1981 the college began offering off-campus instruction at Bergstrom and Reese Air Force bases and at sites in Belton and Plainview.   *Nancy Beck Young*

Houston *Chronicle*. Founded in 1901 by Marcellus E. Foster, a young reporter for the Houston *Post* who was assigned to cover the Spindletop oil drilling. He gambled $30 on the well and sold his stake for $5,000 the next week. With this money and the help of friends he founded the *Chronicle* in a squalid three-story building on Texas Avenue in downtown Houston. The paper, which sold for two cents a copy, had a circulation of 4,378 at the end of its first month of publication. By 1904 its circulation had grown so well that Foster started a Sunday edition with 44 pages of news and advertising and a revolutionary feature, four pages of comics in color. By 1908 Houston's growth was attracting national attention and the newspaper had outgrown its modest home. Foster struck a buy–sell deal with the young Jesse H. Jones under which Jones would build a 10-story plant and office building for the *Chronicle* and receive a part interest in the paper. Subsequent additions produced the granite and glass offices and printing plant that now occupy the entire block where Jones first built. In the early 1920s the *Chronicle* stood tall in the front ranks in the fight against the Ku Klux Klan, to the detriment of circulation. As time went by, Jones became enamored with the newspaper business and the opportunity it gave him to help guide the growth of Houston. Under the terms of the buy–sell agreement he became the sole owner of the paper. Foster then joined the Houston *Press* as editor and continued his journalistic fervor until his death in 1938. The *Chronicle* became the voice that helped Jones accomplish great things for his adopted city. When he died in 1956, he and his wife, Mary Gibbs Jones, left the Houston Endowment with resources that have financed scores of living memorials to the Joneses' affection for Houston, one of them the Houston *Chronicle*. In March 1964 the *Chronicle* purchased the assets of the Houston *Press*, its evening competition. Under the leadership of president Richard J. V. Johnson (1972–) the paper made its greatest gains in circulation and in plant automation. When the Houston Endowment had to divest itself of the profit-making paper under new state laws, the *Chronicle* was sold to the Hearst Corporation in 1987 for $415 million, at that time the highest price ever paid for an American newspaper. In April 1995 the Houston *Post* folded and Hearst purchased the *Post*'s assets from the Media News Group, making the *Chronicle* the only major daily in Houston. In 1995, with a circulation of 541,478 morning daily and 743,689 Sunday papers, the *Chronicle* was the ninth-largest daily and Sunday newspaper in the nation.   *John H. Murphy*

Houston Oilers. A professional football team that belonged to the Central Division of the American Conference of the National Football League. The club began play in 1960 as one of the original six franchises in the newly formed American Football League. K. S. "Bud" Adams was the team's original owner and longtime president. With Heisman Trophy winner Billy Cannon as quarterback and Lou Rymkus as coach, the 1960 team won the first AFL championship. The Oilers played home games in a renovated high school stadium, since Rice University refused the use of its stadium. The club won the AFL championship again in 1961, and Houston fans regularly filled Jeppesen Field. The next year was also very successful, but the Oilers' bid for a third straight championship ended with a double overtime loss to the Dallas Texans. Subsequently, the club slumped to last place in 1966, then rebounded to win the AFL Eastern Division title in 1967. After this the club moved into the Astrodome. By the end of the 1973 season the Oilers had experienced their second straight 1–13 record and attendance was sagging. In 1975 Adams hired O. A. "Bum" Phillips as the team's tenth head coach in its 15 seasons. The club finished with a 10–4 record for the 1975 season, barely missing the playoffs, and set a new home attendance record. Billy "White Shoes" Johnson was named most valuable player of the Pro Bowl, played in New Orleans. After another losing season, the club drafted its second Heisman Trophy winner, Earl Campbell. The Oilers again won in regular seasons, but could not win in the playoffs. Phillips was fired after the 1980 season despite a 59–38 record over the previous six seasons. The mid-1980s saw Warren Moon become the team's quarterback and Jerry Glanville the team's fourteenth head coach. Moon's quarterbacking once again made the Oilers successful. Jack Pardee became the team's fifteenth head coach, but they still suffered in the post-season. In fact, the Oilers gave up the biggest playoff comeback in NFL history to the Buffalo Bills in 1992, turning a 35–3 third quarter lead into a 41–38 loss. After that devastating loss a major coaching staff change resulted in the hiring of Buddy Ryan as defensive coordinator. During the next season, after initial losses, the Oilers had an unprecedented 12-game winning streak, but still suffered an early loss in the playoff. During and after the 1993 season internal strife had been apparent among the coaching staff, especially between defensive coordinator Ryan and offensive coordinator Kevin Gilbride. Also a breakdown in contract talks resulted in the trading of Moon to the Minnesota Vikings, and backup Cody Carlson took over. Early in the 1994 season Pardee was fired, and staff member Jeff Fisher was hired as the team's sixteenth head coach. Quarterback Steve McNair, the NCAA's all-time leader in passing yardage, was drafted. That year the team finished in last place in their division. Subsequently, a conflict that arose when Adams sought to get a new domed stadium. The city of Nashville lured the team to Tennessee after the 1997 season. *Eric M. Pfeifle*

Houston Post. The first *Post* was established in 1880 by Gail Borden Johnson, who in 1881 combined it with the Houston *Telegraph*. This paper was sold and closed down in 1884. The next year the Houston *Morning Chronicle* and the Houston *Evening Journal* combined, with J. L. Watson as business manager and Rienzi M. Johnston as editor, to establish the present Houston *Post*. Threatened by a strike in 1890, Watson found an alternative to typesetters in Linotype machines, the use of which made the *Post* a modern pioneer. He subsequently bought out other stockholders to gain control of the paper. After his death in 1897, Johnston, G. J. Palmer, and Henry F. MacGregor controlled the business in trust until Watson's son, Princeton graduate Roy Watson, assumed control in 1918. This Christian Scientist banned advertisements for patent medicines, wildcat oil stock, liquor, wine, beer, and yeast. The paper soon lost advertising revenue, and Watson sold the *Post* in 1924 to Ross Sterling, who merged it with the Houston *Dispatch* to form the Houston *Post–Dispatch*. In the 1930s Sterling sold the paper to Jackson E. Josey, who represented Jesse H. Jones. Josey changed the name back to *Post* and operated the paper until 1939, when William P. Hobby acquired a controlling interest. Among workers on the *Post* were O. Henry, W. C. Brann, Judd Mortimer Lewis, and Marcellus E. Foster, founder of the Houston *Chronicle*. The *Post* continued to grow in prestige and circulation. As the Houston *Post–Dispatch*, the company operated radio station KPRC in the 1920s. In 1949 the paper had a paid circulation of 165,667 daily and 177,913 on Sundays. By the early 1950s the Houston Post Company had acquired television station KPRC, and in January 1955 the company opened a new $4 million office building. In August 1955 Hobby became chairman

of the board of directors and his wife, Oveta Hobby, became president and editor. In 1963 the company purchased the News Publishing Company, a transaction that involved the sale of the Galveston *News*, the Galveston *Tribune*, and the Texas City *Sun*. When Hobby died in 1964, the *Post* remained under the management of Mrs. Hobby, assisted by their son, William P. Hobby, Jr., who served as executive editor and executive vice president. In 1967 the Houston Post Company sold the Galveston area papers. In 1969 William H. Gardner was named chief editorial writer and editor, and in the 1970s the paper again became a pioneer with its use of computer-set type. By 12 October 1975, Oveta Hobby was editor and chairman of the board, William P. Hobby, Jr., was executive editor and president (and also lieutenant governor of Texas), and Edwin D. Hunter was vice president and managing editor. In the early 1990s the paper was purchased by a Toronto newspaper, which sold it subsequently to the Media-News Group and William Dean Singleton. In 1991 the *Post* had a daily circulation of 335,000. In April 1995, however, it ceased publication. *Diana J. Kleiner*

Houston Symphony Orchestra. Founded in 1913, when Ima Hogg marshaled her forces to sponsor a concert on 21 June. Julien Paul Blitz directed a 35-member ensemble that played, among other pieces, Mozart's *Jupiter Symphony* and "Dixie." The concert built enthusiasm for continuing activity. Blitz was succeeded in 1916 by Paul Bergé, who remained until the orchestra disbanded in 1918 because of World War I. In 1931 the HSO was reconstituted under Uriel Nespoli, whose programs displayed his loyalty to Italian music and his enthusiasm for Wagner. Unfortunately, the orchestra was not yet up to the latter. There was a brief rivalry during this period with the newly organized Philharmonic Society, and Nespoli's unfamiliarity with the English language and the workings of Houston society made his tenure a rocky one. Frank St. Leger then conducted the orchestra for three seasons. The orchestra at this time was hampered by the unevenness of talent among its members, some of whom were amateurs, and the poor quality of some of the instruments, which resulted from the orchestra's low budget. In the spring of 1936 the symphony society amended its charter and became officially the Houston Symphony Society. Ernest Hoffmann, St. Leger's successor, began the 1936 season with renewed community support. Realizing the orchestra's limitations, he made moderate demands on it initially, but during his tenure he built the ensemble to major status. He was a model of thoroughness and extremely partial to the music of Richard Strauss. During World War II he organized numerous concerts for nearby army camps. On 22 February 1947 the orchestra played on NBC's national radio program "Orchestras of the Nation." Despite these achievements, in 1947 the society asked Hoffmann to resign, a move that caused a rift in the society.

During the following season, the orchestra played under a number of guest conductors, among them Leonard Bernstein. Effrem Kurtz, the next conductor, served seven seasons, through 1953. He was allocated a much more generous budget, and under his direction the orchestra performed with more gloss and virtuosity, especially in the string and woodwind sections. However, the ensemble was not yet performing as a unit, and Kurtz received some less-than-enthusiastic reviews. Despite a brilliant procession of guest artists in 1949, among them Igor Stravinsky as guest conductor, audience attendance slipped throughout the early 1950s. Ferenc Fricsay brought with him a potential Deutsche Grammophon Gesellschaft recording contract in 1954, and conducted with great intensity but with uneven results. Because of his numerous demands, including plans for a new concert hall, he was released in mid-season, to be replaced by the ebullient and prestigious Sir Thomas Beecham. In 1955 Leopold Stokowski arrived, loaded with charisma, exotic tastes, and exciting plans for several premieres each season, at which he often had the composers present. The orchestra bloomed under his direction. Although a segment of the audience did not appreciate his programming and some players resented his demands, under Stokowski the orchestra gained a new sense of its position and widened its coverage of new music. He left it more polished and confident, with a sharpened stylistic facility. Stokowski also made a number of recordings with the orchestra. Sir John Barbirolli, who took the baton in 1961, maintained the orchestra's discipline, constructed stimulating programs, and built an enthusiastic audience, although his programs, like Stokowski's included a fair percentage of modern music. Under his guidance the orchestra's playing grew richer and more imaginative in blend, yet he made few revisions to the ensemble. During the 1963–64 season, Barbirolli took the orchestra on an anniversary tour of the eastern seaboard, passing through Washington, D.C., and culminating with a triumphant performance in New York that garnered unanimously good reviews, which rated the Houston Symphony among the major orchestras of the country. Barbirolli returned to an audience with renewed enthusiasm for the orchestra. After decades in City Auditorium or the Music Hall, the HSO moved into the visually and acoustically fine Jesse H. Jones Hall for the Performing Arts in 1966. The new building brought a surge in audience attendance, but the more expensive hall also necessitated more frequent touring to generate income. With his health declining, Barbirolli became conductor emeritus in 1967; he continued as a guest conductor until his death in 1970.

André Previn brought youthful vigor from 1967 to 1969, with evenings almost equally divided between traditional and modern music. During his tenure, an annual young artists' competition was organized under the Houston Symphony Society's supervision. More and more, the orchestra came to be regarded as a regional, as well as a city, treasure. However, new younger concertgoers were not attracted by the orchestra's young conductor as had been hoped, and the attendance of older patrons began declining. Antonio de Almeida served as principal guest conductor before Lawrence Foster took directorship in 1971. Foster had high standards and was bent on enhancing and polishing the quality of the ensemble, although his detractors claimed he was moody, stiff, and even power-hungry. He expanded the company's repertoire and acquired an exclusive five-year recording contract. The 1970s, however, brought funding problems; deficits grew while audiences shrank, as the Houston Grand Opera and Houston Ballet rivaled the symphony. The first Houston Symphony Marathon was held in 1977 on KLEF–FM, a fund-raiser designed to revive the orchestra's fortunes. Sergiu Comissiona became artistic advisor in the early 1980s and music director in 1984. In Houston's sagging economy, the orchestra continued to experience debt and labor problems until the symphony was broke and near collapse, despite a successful East Coast tour that included a performance at Carnegie Hall. However, a five-year planning effort by the Houston Symphony Society and Comissiona's leadership helped bring the orchestra out of debt; by 1985 the deficit had been greatly reduced and the orchestra once more promised to be a thriving major artistic force. Comissiona claimed his goal was to make music part of the daily life of the population. Christoph Eschenbach became music director of the orchestra in 1988. He and the Houston Symphony recorded for Virgin Classics and Pickwick International. In addition to its tours in the United States, the orchestra performed in the Singapore Festival of Arts in 1990, the Pacific Music Festival in Japan in 1991, and in Germany, Switzerland, and Austria in 1992. In 1993 Eschenbach and members of the orchestra formed a chamber ensemble called the Houston Symphony Chamber Players. In 1994 attendance exceeded 300,000. The season included 54 classical concerts, 24 pops concerts, holiday concerts, children's concerts, and educational concerts.

Theodore Albrecht

Howard, Robert Ervin. Fantasy writer; b. Peaster, 22 January 1906; d. Cross Plains, 11 June 1936. While Howard attended Howard Payne College in Brownwood, he wrote stories for the school newspaper and for the Daniel Baker College newspaper and sold his first story to *Weird Tales*, a popular pulp magazine. Encouraged by his entry into the pulp market and by his friend Tevis Clyde Smith, who had printed Howard's earliest "published" works on a small portable press, Howard resolved to support himself by writing. He produced all sorts of formula fiction including fight stories, ghost stories, historical adventures, and heroic fantasies. In Cross Plains his neighbors complained that his typewriter kept them awake at night while he churned out stories for a penny a word. He reportedly earned $500 in one month during the Great Depression, when the local bank president earned less than a third that amount. Howard bought a new Chevrolet for cash in 1935, supposedly the only person in Cross Plains who could afford to do so. Despite his success he was an unhappy young man with few friends and with a neurotic dependence on his mother. When she slipped into a coma and the nurse told Howard that she would never regain consciousness, he went out to his car and shot himself through the head. Although none of Howard's works was published in book form during his lifetime, novels serialized in pulp magazines, in addition to collections of short stories and poetry, have since been published as books. His most influential achievement lies in his characters. Among the most famous were Solomon Kane, a somber English Puritan who fought all manner of ghosts and vampires in Elizabethan England and Africa, Bran Mak Morn, a savage Pict who battled the iron legions of Rome as well as supernatural menaces, and King Kull, a warrior of fabled Atlantis. Conan the Barbarian, Howard's most popular character, appeared in some 18 stories. Decades later, Howard's works, and pastiches based on his works and characters, sold more copies than the works of any other fantasy writer except J. R. R. Tolkien. Conan lived on in a monthly comic book and in movies, while studies of Howard's life and work multiplied.

Charlotte Laughlin

Howard Payne University. A Baptist institution in Brownwood; founded at Indian Creek by the Pecan Valley Baptist Association in 1889, with J. D. Robnett, pastor of the First Baptist Church in Brownwood, as president of the first board of trustees. Robnett secured a large gift from his brother-in-law, Edward Howard Payne. The first session at Howard Payne College opened in 1890. A. J. Emerson was president. A separate preparatory

The Surrender of Santa Anna, by William Henry Huddle, 1886. Oil on canvas. 71" × 113". Courtesy TSL.

department furnished instruction below the freshman level. The school granted its first academic degree in 1895 and continued as a degree-conferring institution until 1900, then operated as a junior college from 1900 to 1914, when it again became a senior college. In 1974, upon approval of the Baptist General Convention of Texas, Howard Payne College was renamed Howard Payne University. The campus covers 10 square blocks. The defunct Daniel Baker College, a few blocks away, became part of Howard Payne in 1953. The main building of the former Daniel Baker College was remodeled for the Douglas MacArthur Academy of Freedom, which houses a museum depicting the concept of freedom throughout history and facilities for study in social sciences. The school joined the Lone Star Conference in 1956 for intercollegiate athletics. HPU education programs offer flexible meeting places, including a center in Corpus Christi. Besides its liberal arts program, the university offers preprofessional dentistry, medicine, and medical-technology programs.

Jeanne F. Lively

Huddle, William Henry. Painter; b. Wytheville, Virginia, 12 February 1847; d. Austin, 23 March 1892 (buried in Oakwood Cemetery); m. Nannie Zenobia Carver (1889). Huddle served under generals Joseph Wheeler and Nathan Bedford Forrest in the Confederate cavalry. After the war, he moved with his family to Paris, Texas, and worked in his father's gunsmith shop. He soon returned to Virginia to study painting under his cousin, Flavius Fisher, who became a well-known portraitist in Washington, D.C. In 1874 Huddle moved to New York to study

at the National Academy of Design. Along with Henry A. McArdle and Robert J. Onderdonk, he was among the 123 students who formed the Art Students' League during the academy's temporary closure in 1875. The next year Huddle returned to Texas and took up residence in Austin. During these years, he became acquainted with other members of the state's nascent artistic community. He began to concentrate his artistic energies on Texas history and politics, subjects that became his artistic trademark. Gradually, he found his specialty in executing portraits of Texas political and military figures. In 1884, possibly with encouragement from Hermann Lungkwitz, Huddle sailed to Europe for a year of study in Munich. He intended to improve his technique in order better to fulfill a commission from the Texas legislature to paint portraits, to be hung in the state Capitol, of Texas presidents and governors. (When he died, he had completed portraits of all the presidents and the first 17 governors.) When he returned in 1885 he also showed a new interest in historical painting, quite possibly influenced by exposure to this type of art in Munich and his instruction at the academy. He painted *The Surrender of Santa Anna* (1886) to commemorate the fiftieth anniversary of the battle of San Jacinto, and the painting has attained the stature of an icon of Texas history. In 1891 the legislature appropriated $4,000 for the purchase of the painting, which now hangs in the state Capitol, as does Huddle's portrait of Crockett. His painting of Hood's Texas Brigade at the battle of the Wilderness was destroyed in the 1881 Capitol fire.

Sam D. Ratcliffe

Howard Hughes with his H-1 racer, ca. 1935. Jesse Holman Jones Papers, CAH; CN 08132. The H-1 racer led to the development of the radial-engine-powered fighter planes flown in World War II.

Hughes, Howard Robard, Jr. Eccentric tycoon; b. Houston, 24 December 1905; d. 5 April 1976; m. Ella Rice (1925; divorced 1929); m. Jean Peters (1957; divorced 1970). As a youth "Sonny" Hughes tinkered with mechanical things, developed a love of aviation, had only one friend, Dudley Sharp, attended exclusive schools desultorily, and under the tutelage of his mother developed a lifetime phobic regard for his health. At age 18 he inherited a large part of the family estate. His uncle Rupert Hughes agreed to supervise Howard's part of the estate and interests in the Hughes Tool Company until he was 21. Howard quarreled with the family, however, and had company lawyers buy out his relatives. He was granted legal adulthood in 1924, the year he and Ella went to Hollywood. After a first movie-making flop, he hired Noah Dietrich to head his motion-picture subsidiary of Hughes Tool Company and Lewis Mileston as director. In 1928 Mileston directed *Two Arabian Nights* and won an academy award. Hughes worked next on his epic movie *Hell's Angels*, a story about air warfare in World War I. He wrote the script and directed it himself. He acquired 87 World War I airplanes, hired ace pilots, took flying lessons, and obtained a pilot's license. But he crashed and injured his face, and, since he spent little time at home, Ella divorced him. Because talkies had become popular,

Hughes added dialogue scenes to *Hell's Angels* that included actress Jean Harlow. The movie, released in June 1930, cost $3.8 million, the most expensive movie to that date. Though *Hell's Angels* was a box-office smash, Hughes actually lost $1.5 million on it. He was now accepted by the Hollywood establishment, however, and went on to produce *Scarface* (1932), which was decensored after he sued the censorship agency. His later film *The Outlaw* (1941) also was controversial because of promotional publicity.

In 1932 Hughes acquired a military plane through the Department of Commerce and converted it for racing. When the costs rose, he formed the Hughes Aircraft Company as a division of Hughes Tool Company. Since Charles Lindbergh's license number had been 69, Hughes (whose number was 4223) badgered the Department of Commerce to lower his number to 80 in 1933. He signed on with American Airways as a copilot under the name Charles W. Howard, but the deception was immediately discovered and Hughes resigned, thus leaving the only job he ever had. In 1934 he entered his converted Boeing in the All-America Air Meet in Miami and won. Afterward, he gathered a group of engineers and technicians to work on the H-1, the most advanced plane of its time. He personally test-flew the plane himself and precipitated a power struggle in the Hughes empire when he placed Dietrich in control of his holdings. Meanwhile, on 13 September 1935 Hughes set a new land-speed record of 352 miles per hour with his H-1, the *Winged Bullet*. In 1936 he set a new transcontinental record, and the next year he shortened the record to 7 hours 28 minutes. Hughes was now immensely popular and was hosted by the president at the White House. He next converted a special Lockheed 14 for an around-the-world flight. He studied weather patterns and installed an autopilot and four radios to make contacts along his route. He and a four-man crew left New York on 10 July 1938 and cut Lindbergh's record time to Paris in half. Hughes piloted the plane, which landed in New York on 14 July 1938, having circled the globe in 3 days, 19 hours, and 17 minutes. He was honored with parades all over America. Houston renamed its airport in his honor.

Hughes now decided to invest in military aircraft, and sought to sell his planes and ideas to the government. But he veiled his plans in secrecy and ignored regulations and protocol. He also insisted on building planes out of plywood using a "duramold" process, although the industry standard was aluminum. When the Army Material Command declared that the airplanes could not be made combat ready, Hughes used friends in Washington in an attempt to go over their heads. Shipbuilder Henry J. Kaiser convinced the government that a fleet of gigantic flying boats was needed to ferry men and supplies across the ocean, and in 1942 Hughes Aircraft won a contract to build three flying boats in 10 months at a cost of up to $18 million. But Hughes declared the goal impossible to meet and the contract was canceled. In 1944, after Hughes's lobbying in Washington, he received a contract for one flying boat. Only one HK-1, which the public called the "Spruce Goose" (a name Hughes hated), was built. He successfully flew the craft on 2 November 1947. In 1943 Hughes had also received a contract for 101 of his D-2 (XF-11 reconnaissance) planes. The XF-11 was an aluminum redesign of the wooden D-2. At the end of World War II in 1945, Hughes won permission to complete the two prototypes under construction. In 1946, in his first flight of the XF-11, he crashed in Beverly Hills—his fourth crash (in November 1943 he had hit Lake Mead in a crash that killed two people). He successfully flew the second prototype on 5 April 1946. In 1947 a Senate war investigating committee questioned him at length about his failure to deliver on wartime contracts. In 1948 Hughes purchased the movie studio RKO, and in 1955 he sold it to the General Tire Company for profit. He also invested in Trans World Airways, and in 1956 pushed the company into the jet age by purchasing 63 jets. He quarreled with engineers at Hughes Aircraft in 1953, causing a shakeup that imperiled contracts with the Pentagon. That same year, he founded the Hughes Medical Institute in Delaware, thus funding the medical center he earlier had designated as the main recipient of his will. In 1957 he again shook the Hughes empire by firing his long-time associate Noah Dietrich.

During the 1930s in Hollywood Hughes had squired many actresses and socialites, particularly Katherine Hepburn. In his second marriage Hughes remained in Los Angeles until 1966, then began traveling and eventually rented a penthouse in the Desert Inn in Las Vegas. When lawsuits were filed against TWA, he sold his stock in 1966 for $546 million. The next year he began buying properties to build a business empire in Nevada. In 1970 he took over Air West. By this time he was becoming increasingly reclusive and conducted most of his business through memos. He now had little control over his empire. Chester Davis, Raymond Holliday, and Bill Gay, Hughes Tool Company executives, ran his Nevada properties. In 1972, Hughes sold Hughes Tool Company stock to the public and renamed his holding company Summa Corporation. This ended his role as a businessman and entrepreneur. In poor health and accompanied by a squadron of personal aides, he went to Panama, Canada, and London, then to Acapulco. He was indicted in a case relating to the Air West takeover, but it was dismissed. Hughes allowed a CIA ship, the *Glomar Explorer*, to work through one of his companies to recover a sunken Soviet sub. In Los Angeles a break-in occurred at the Hughes headquarters, and many of his personal papers were stolen. With his health rapidly deteriorating, he boarded a plane en route to a hospital in Houston, but died on the way. Since no one knew what he looked like anymore, the Treasury Department made fingerprints to confirm his identity. More than 40 alleged wills and 400 prospective heirs emerged to grasp at part of Hughes's estimated $2 billion. In 1983 the estate was settled among 22 cousins on both sides of his family. For eight years Texas and California pursued inheritance-tax claims, although Hughes executives insisted that Nevada (which has no estate taxes) was Hughes's home. The Supreme Court reviewed the case three times before it was settled. Howard Hughes Medical Institute was given ownership of Hughes Aircraft and sold it to General Motors in 1985 for $5 billion. Hughes's Summa Corporation emerged with four hotels and six casinos in Las Vegas and Reno.   *Walter F. Pilcher*

Hughes, Sarah Tilghman. Federal judge; b. Baltimore, 2 August 1896; d. Dallas, 23 April 1985 (buried at Hillcrest Mausoleum and Memorial Park); m. George Ernest Hughes (1922); ed. Goucher College (A.B., 1917) and George Washington University Law School (LL.B., 1922). George Hughes was from Palestine, Texas. After marrying, the couple moved to Dallas, where he began a private law practice. Mrs. Hughes worked with the firm of Priest, Herndon, and Ledbetter (1923–35) and served three terms in the Texas House of Representatives. In 1935 Governor Allred appointed her to the bench of the Fourteenth District Court in Dallas. She was the first woman state district judge in Texas. She was elected in her own right in 1936 and was reelected on six subsequent occasions, the last in 1960. She was among the first women elected to the legislature after the granting of woman suffrage and was active in debates over major issues of the day—oil proration laws, penal-system reform, and public school land usage. In 1933 newspaper reporters in Austin named her the state's most effective representative. In 1946 she was beaten in the Democratic primary when she ran for Congress. In 1952 she received a token nomination for the vice presidency of the United States at the Democratic national convention but withdrew her name before the vote was taken. At the time, she was national president of the Business and Professional Women's Club. She was also defeated when she ran for the Texas Supreme Court in 1958. In 1961 she asked Senator Ralph Yarborough and Vice President Lyndon Johnson to recommend her for the federal judgeship of the northern district of Texas. Her age, 65, caused the American Bar Association and Attorney General Robert Kennedy to oppose her selection. At her request, the Business and Professional Women's Club undertook a letter-writing campaign in support of her candidacy, and Yarborough, Johnson, and Rayburn lobbied for her. When President John

Sarah T. Hughes at her swearing in as federal district judge, with Sen. Ralph Yarborough (far left), U.S. district judge Joe E. Estes (between Yarborough and Hughes), and Vice President Lyndon B. Johnson (far right), Dallas, October 17, 1961. Reprinted with permission of the Dallas *Morning News*. Photograph courtesy University of North Texas Library, Denton.

Kennedy appointed her in October 1961, she became the first woman to serve as a federal district judge in Texas. While serving the Fourteenth Judicial District of Texas, Judge Hughes played an important part in the construction of Dallas's first juvenile detention center (1950) and in securing an amendment to the Texas constitution allowing women to serve as jurors (1953). Among her most well-known decisions as a federal judge were *Roe v. Wade*, 1970 (the legalization of abortion), *Shultz v. Brookhaven General Hospital*, 1969 (equal pay for equal work for women), and *Taylor v. Sterrett*, 1972 (upgrading prisoner treatment in the Dallas County jail). She was also involved with several cases related to Billie Sol Estes and to the Sharpstown stock-fraud scandal. She became a national figure after the Kennedy Assassination, when she administered the oath of office to Johnson. *Robert S. La Forte*

Hunt, H. L. Oil tycoon; b. Haroldson Lafayette Hunt, Fayette County, Illinois, 17 February 1889; d. 29 November 1974. In 1921 Hunt joined the oil boom in El Dorado, Arkansas, where he became a lease broker and promoted his first well, Hunt–Pickering No. 1. He claimed to have attained a "fortune of $600,000" by 1925, the year he bought a whole block in El Dorado and built a three-story house for his family. His El Dorado investments and a venture called Smackover taught him lessons about the cost of wasteful practices and excessive

drilling, for both fields were depleted rapidly. He also lost money on the Florida land boom, and by the time he got interested in the East Texas oilfield in 1930, he seems to have been broke again. He managed to acquire the well Daisy Bradford No. 3 and surrounding leases from Columbus M. "Dad" Joiner. By 1 December 1930, Hunt had his own pipeline, the Panola Pipe Line, to run oil from the East Texas field. By 1932 the Hunt Production Company had 900 wells in East Texas.

In 1935 H. L. Hunt, Incorporated, was superseded by Placid Oil Company, and the shares were divided into trusts for Hunt's six children. In 1936 Hunt acquired the Excelsior Refining Company in Rusk County and changed the name to Parade Refining Company. It was residue gas from this company's lines that caused the New London School Explosion (18 March 1937). Most of the people involved in that disaster were employees of H. L. Hunt. In 1937 or 1938 the family moved to Dallas. On 5 April 1948, *Fortune* printed a story on Hunt that labeled him the richest man in the United States. It estimated the value of his oil properties at $263 million and the daily production of crude from his wells at 65,000 barrels.

In 1914 Hunt married Lyda Bunker in Arkansas. They had six children. On Armistice Day 1925 a Franklin Hunt married Frania Tye (probably short for Tiburski) in Florida. They had four children. In 1975, after H. L. Hunt had died, Mrs. Frania Tye Lee filed a civil complaint against Hunt in which she revealed the history of their relationship. They had married in 1925 and lived together in Shreveport until 1930, when they moved to Dallas. In May 1934 "Franny" had discovered Hunt's other marriage. Hunt apparently shipped her off to New York and in 1941 provided trusts for each of the four children. A friend of his, John Lee, married her and gave his name to the children. Lyda Bunker Hunt died in 1955. In November 1957 Hunt married Ruth Ray and adopted her four children, who had been born between 1943 and 1950. Ruth Hunt admitted in an interview that H. L. Hunt had, in fact, been their real father. H. L. and Ruth Hunt became Baptists. In his later life Hunt supported two radio shows, "Facts Forum" and "Life Line." In 1952 the former endorsed Senator Joseph McCarthy. In 1960 Hunt published a romantic utopian novel, *Alpaca*, and in 1968 he began to process aloe vera cosmetics.

Jerrell Dean Palmer

Hunter, John Dunn. Cherokee leader; b. ca. 1796; d. February 1827. He claimed that as a child he had been captured by the Cherokees before they came to Texas. He adopted the name of an English benefactor, John Dunn, and later added the name "Hunter" given by the Indians because of his prowess in the chase. Although he lived with the Cherokees until about 1816, he received a fairly good education and traveled through the United States and England. In England he wrote *Memoirs of a Captivity among the Indians of North America* (published in London, 1824). Dr. Hunter, as he was often called, returned to the Cherokees at one of their East Texas villages in 1825. In December of that year he was sent by Richard Fields to renew negotiations with Mexico for land for a Cherokee settlement in Texas. He arrived in Mexico City on 19 March 1826 and was promised land to be granted to individual Indian settlers but was

unsuccessful in getting a tribal grant with the right of selfgovernment. He returned to the village and, with Fields, began negotiations with Martin Parmer and his associates for the movement that resulted in the Fredonian Rebellion. The conspirators made arrangements for dividing Texas between the Indians and the Anglo settlers. At this juncture Peter Ellis Bean arrived in East Texas as an agent of the Mexican government. Through Bean's influence the Cherokee council repudiated the agreement and refused to send men to assist the rebels. Richard Fields and John Dunn Hunter fled after their trial by the Cherokee Council and were caught and executed.

Robert Bruce Blake

Huntsville, Texas. County seat of Walker County. It was founded in 1835 or 1836 by Pleasant and Ephraim Gray as an Indian trading post and named for Huntsville, Alabama, former home of the Gray family. The town originally lay within the northeast section of Montgomery County, which was organized in 1837. It was designated the seat of Walker County when the county was organized in 1846. Huntsville acquired a post office on 9 June 1837. The Grays' trading post was well situated to trade with the Bidai, Alabama, and Coushatta Indians. As trade along the Trinity River grew and colonists arrived to exploit the timber and rich alluvial bottomlands, Huntsville became a center of increasing activity. The 1840s and 1850s saw the arrival of a few relatively well-to-do families from the Carolinas, Alabama, Mississippi, and Tennessee, along with larger numbers of yeomen. Huntsville was also the home of many prominent early Texans, including Sam Houston, Henderson Yoakum, and Samuel McKinney. A number of academies served the community, and in 1879 Sam Houston Normal Institute, the first teacher-training institution in Texas, opened in Huntsville. Although Huntsville

"Outside of Walls West of Penitentiary," ca. 1900, Huntsville. Courtesy TSL. Huntsville was the site of the state's first enclosed penitentiary for convicted felons. The Texas legislature passed a bill to establish the prison on 13 March 1848.

failed to become the site of Baylor University in the mid-1840s, the town succeeded in attracting Austin College, which opened there in the early 1850s. In 1877, when Austin College was moved to Sherman, the Methodist Church bought its building in Huntsville for the use of Mitchell College, a short-lived boys' school. Bishop Ward Normal and Collegiate Institute for Negroes, a coeducational school founded by the Methodist Church, opened in Huntsville in 1883 and operated for seven years. It was the fifth college established for blacks in Texas. Sam Houston Industrial and Training School, located five miles west of Huntsville in Galilee, was a noted East Texas school for black youths. At the end of its first decade, Huntsville also became the site of the new Texas State Penitentiary, established by the legislature in 1847. The prison received its first convict in 1849. The following year Huntsville lost out to Austin in an election to choose the state capital. Perhaps the oldest continuous business in the state is the Huntsville firm of Gibbs Brothers and Company, begun as Gibbs and Coffin in 1841. According to one account, most of the manufacturing in Huntsville before the Civil War was carried on by slaves, who made shoes and other leather goods and cigars. During the war cloth produced at the penitentiary was made into uniforms for Confederate soldiers, and the town contributed several companies to the Confederate forces.

During Reconstruction Walker County was one of three Texas counties put under martial law. Incidents in Huntsville—the murder of a freedman nearby in January 1871; a gun battle at the subsequent trial of the four suspects, during which Leander McNelly and another member of the State Police were wounded and two of the prisoners escaped; willingness of only two citizens to join in pursuit; and the attempted assassination of the trial judge—led to the imposition of martial law on 15 February. It was lifted 60 days later. Economic development suffered considerably from a yellow fever epidemic in 1867, which reportedly killed 10 percent of the town's population. In 1872 the Houston and Great Northern Railroad bypassed Huntsville to the east. The town acquired a rail connection that same year, however, when the eight-mile Huntsville Branch linked it to the H&GN at Phelps. Highway development in the late 1920s and early 1930s enhanced Huntsville's position as a trade center for a significant rural area of East Texas. The population rose from 939 in 1860 to 2,485 in 1904, 5,028 in 1931, 11,999 in 1960, 23,936 in 1980, and 27,925 in 1990. Lumbering, farming, livestock raising, and the tourist trade have constituted the economic base of the city. In recent years substantial lignite deposits have been found in the county. The growth of the penitentiary system and of Sam Houston State University, the expansion of metropolitan Houston, and the development of Lake Livingston and similar attractive living areas revitalized the local economy in the 1970s and 1980s. In 1991 the city had two newspapers and two radio stations. The Joe G. Davis School of Vocational Nursing, at Huntsville Memorial Hospital, opened in 1966. In 1936 the Texas Centennial Commission placed markers in Huntsville for Austin Hall, the original building of Austin College, and for the Steamboat House, the house in which Sam Houston died. The commission also authorized the construction of the James Gillaspie Monument and the Sam Houston Memorial Museum. The homes of Sam Houston and author and soldier John W. Thomason, Jr., are both on the National Register of Historic Places, and Houston's law office has also been preserved. Other tourist attractions include the nearby Huntsville State Park and

Sam Houston National Forest. The Texas Prison Rodeo, formerly held each Sunday in October, was discontinued after the 1986 season. *Charles L. Dwyer and Gerald L. Holder*

Hurricanes. The largest and most destructive storms affecting the Texas coast are the tropical cyclones that occur seasonally from late June through October. From 1818 to 1885 at least 28 hurricanes struck Texas, and from 1885 through 1964, 66 tropical storms were recorded, about two-thirds of which were of hurricane force (with winds of more than 74 MPH). Two major hurricanes occurred in the five years from 1965 to 1970. Frequently these storms rush inland, causing destruction and flooding in the interior, but the heaviest damage has always been to population centers along the coast.

A hurricane spoiled Jean Laffite's pirate encampment on Galveston Island in 1818, and "*Racer's* Storm" passed over the same area in 1837. This strong wind, named for the *Racer*, a British sloop-of-war that encountered the storm in the Yucatán Channel, reached Brownsville about 4 October, curved up the coastline over Galveston, and then moved eastward to the Atlantic Ocean near Charleston, South Carolina. *Racer's* Storm wrecked nearly every vessel on the coast and blew away all the houses on Galveston Island. It sent floodwaters inland 15 to 20 miles over the coastal prairies. Five years later, in September 1842, Galveston was again prostrated. No lives were lost, but parts of the city were tossed about like "pieces of a toy town." Damage to ships and buildings amounted to $50,000. Another September storm struck Texas in 1854 between Galveston and Matagorda. Matagorda was leveled, Houston sustained a $30,000 loss, and heavy damage was reported at Lynchburg, San Jacinto, Velasco, Quintana, Brazoria, Columbia, and Sabine Pass.

The entire Texas coast felt the hurricane of 1867, which entered the state south of Galveston on 3 October. Bagdad and Clarksville, at the mouth of the Rio Grande, were flattened, while Galveston was flooded and raked for a loss of $1 million. On September 16, 1875, a hurricane washed away three-fourths of the buildings in Indianola, Calhoun County, and killed 176 people. Five years later, on October 12–13, 1880, many lives were lost and Brownsville was nearly destroyed by a tropical wind. A second hurricane in Indianola on 19–20 August 1886, struck the town, destroying or damaging every structure.

The Galveston hurricane of 1900, on 8–9 September, is known as the worst natural disaster in United States history. Although the wind was estimated at 120 miles per hour, flooding caused most of the damage. The island was completely inundated. Property loss amounted to about $40 million, and an estimated 6,000 to 8,000 persons perished. On 16–19 August 1915, Galveston again received the brunt of a vicious hurricane. Damage amounted to $50 million, but only 275 lives were lost because of the protection afforded by a new seawall built after the catastrophic 1900 storm.

At Corpus Christi a storm on 18 August 1916 inflicted over $1.5 million damage and took 20 lives. Three years later, on 14 September 1919, the center of a hurricane moved inland just south of the city. Tides were 16 feet above normal, the wind rose to 110 miles an hour, and damage was estimated at $20,272,000. Some 284 persons perished.

The center of a hurricane passed near Brownsville on 4–5 September, 1933. The wind velocity was measured at 106 miles an hour before the anemometer blew away, and wind gusts were estimated at 125 miles an hour. Most of the citrus crop of the lower Rio Grande valley was ruined. Forty persons were killed and 500 were injured.

On June 27, 1957, Hurricane Audrey swept across the Gulf Coast near the Texas–Louisiana line. Nine lives were lost and 450 persons were injured. Property damage, particularly extensive in Jefferson and Orange counties, amounted to $8 million. The effect was more serious across Sabine Lake in Cameron Parish, Louisiana, where hundreds of people died.

Hurricane Carla, the largest hurricane of record in Texas, occurred on 8–14 September 1961. During the storm a tornado ravaged Galveston Island; at Port Lavaca, Carla's wind gusts were estimated at 175 miles per hour. The total damage to property and crops amounted to over $300 million, with the heaviest losses sustained in the area between Corpus Christi and Port Arthur. Because 250,000 persons were evacuated from the coastal region, only 34 were killed; 465 were injured.

Hurricane Beulah, the third largest hurricane of the twentieth century, swept across South Texas on 20–21 September 1967. The storm, which had previously ravaged the Yucatán Peninsula in Mexico, moved inland from the Gulf just south of Port Isabel early on the morning of the twentieth. It struck Brownsville with winds estimated at 140 miles an hour, moved northwest across South Texas to the vicinity of Alice, then turned southwest, crossed the Rio Grande between Zapata and Laredo, and finally blew itself out in Mexico. Advance warnings permitted the evacuation of Port Isabel, Port Mansfield, and Port Aransas, but winds and rain caused considerable property damage there as well as in the resort areas of Padre Island. In the port of Brownsville tides and high winds damaged a large portion of the shrimp fleet, and in the lower Rio Grande valley the citrus crop was ruined. Beulah spawned 115 separate tornadoes, several of which occurred in populated areas. Tornadoes struck New Braunfels, Fulton, and Sweet Home and were sighted as far north as Austin. Rains of up to 30 inches accompanied the storm, and these in turn caused floods that inundated a large part of South Texas for more than two weeks. Three Rivers, Sinton, Victoria, and Pleasanton were hit especially hard. In Harlingen rampaging water from the Arroyo Colorado threatened the entire city. Floodwaters on the Rio Grande put large portions of Camargo and Reynosa, Tamaulipas, under water, and some 9,000 refugees crossed the border to Rio Grande City. On 28 September President Johnson declared 24 counties in South Texas disaster areas. Official estimates in these counties set the number of dead at 18, the injured or sick at 9,000, and the number of homes destroyed or heavily damaged at 3,000. Property damage was estimated at $100 million, crop damage at $50 million. Some 300,000 people were evacuated during the storm and subsequent flooding.

Hurricane Celia, reported to be the costliest in the state's history, ravaged Corpus Christi on 3 August 1970. Before the storm the weather was deceptively calm, with no heavy rains or gusty winds. Preliminary reports indicated the approach of a relatively mild storm. Celia, formed as a tropical depression in the Gulf of Mexico, first hit land at Port Aransas, Ingleside, and Aransas Pass. The eye of the storm moved inland just north of Corpus Christi, then moved successively in several directions, swept that city, Portland, Taft, Bayside, Gregory, Fulton Beach, Rockport, and Key Allegro, and went on through Odem, Edroy, Sinton, Mathis, Agua Dulce, Robstown, Sandia, Orange Grove, and

George West. Winds up to 161 miles an hour and gusts to 180 miles an hour were reported. President Nixon declared seven counties a major disaster area. An estimated 13 persons died near Corpus Christi. Officials estimated damage to commercial buildings, automobiles, and homes at more than $500 million. Crop losses and damage to farm equipment were estimated at more than $100 million. More than 3,500 people left Corpus Christi, and the lowlying regions of entire cities were evacuated. Celia ended on 5 August in a series of thunderstorms near El Paso and the New Mexico border. Hurricane Celia did not produce the torrential rains and flooding that so often accompany storms of this magnitude, however. The heaviest rainfall was 6.38 inches in Corpus Christi, and at Pearsall and Jourdanton, 30 to 40 miles north of the hurricane center, there was no rain. Studies of the Bureau of Economic Geology at the University of Texas at Austin indicated that Celia differed significantly from previous storms that have struck the coast in that it was much narrower and correspondingly more intense in the affected area.

South Texas was hit by Hurricane Allen on 9–11 August 1980. Padre Island and Corpus Christi sustained the worst damage. The southernmost part of the region received 20 inches of rain, and 250,000 residents had to be evacuated. Hurricane Allen spawned 29 tornadoes, one of the worst hurricane-related outbreaks. Three people died, and property damage reached $650 million to $750 million. Another major hurricane to hit Texas in the early 1980s was Hurricane Alicia, which occurred on 15–21 August 1983. Damage, primarily in the Galveston and Houston areas, was estimated at $3 billion. Thirty-two tornadoes resulted from the 130 MPH winds, 18 people were killed, and 1,800 were injured. On 16–18 September 1988, Hurricane Gilbert struck Cameron County. It produced 6 to 10 inches of rain and around 29 tornadoes. One tornado-related death was reported. Damages were estimated at $3 million to $5 million.

Other significant storms include those at Galveston Bay, 1776; Brazos Santiago, 1884; Sabine, 1886; Port Arthur, 1897; Velasco, 1909; near Freeport, 1932; near Seadrift, 1934; near Matagorda, 1941; Matagorda Bay, 1942; near Galveston, 1943; in the Aransas–San Antonio Bay area, 1945; Freeport, 1949; west of Port Arthur, 1963; the Coastal Bend area, 1971; near Port Arthur, 1980; between High Island and Sabine Pass, 1986; and in Harris, Galveston, and Brazoria counties, 1989. Though it is true that hurricane-inflicted damage to property has increased through the years, the death rate has not, because of the implementation of various precautionary measures. *Roy Sylvan Dunn*

Huston–Tillotson College. In Austin; a historically black, coeducational college operated jointly under the auspices of the American Missionary Association of the United Church of Christ and the Board of Education of the Methodist Church. It was formed by the merger of Samuel Huston College and Tillotson College in 1952. Mary E. Branch and William H. Jones, last presidents of Tillotson College, and Karl E. Downs, Robert F. Harrington, and Willis J. King, past presidents of Samuel Huston College, had undertaken cooperative sponsorship of several academic activities beginning in 1945. Matthew S. Davage served as interim president during the transition period. He retired in 1955 and was succeeded by J. J. Seabrook, the first permanent president of Huston–Tillotson. The college, which has no racial requirements, is fully accredited. It grants bachelor's degrees in 15 areas.

Icarian Colony. A utopian colony founded in Texas in 1848 by French immigrants; location unknown, though some sources place it near the site of present-day Justin. Icaria lasted less than a year, and no more than 70 inhabitants were there at any given time. The French socialist Étienne Cabet organized the experiment. In 1839 he published a novel, *Voyage en Icarie*, which set forth his fictional paradise—a centralized state that provided complete freedom and material wealth, with private property and capital abolished. Cabet's ideas became so popular that he soon found himself at the head of one of the most influential socialist movements in France in the tumultuous decade of the 1840s. From May 1847 until February 1848 he concentrated his efforts on establishing a communal experiment in Texas. Deviating from his fictional utopia, he organized the commune as an investment adventure that required an original contribution of 600 francs for each participant and gave Cabet dictatorial powers. He called for 10,000 to 20,000 immigrants and predicted that the venture would ultimately attract a million participants. Subsequently, he negotiated a contract with the Peters Land Company for what was announced to the public as a million acres of Texas land. Much opposition developed within the Icarian movement, however, and in February 1848 only 69 immigrants made their way from France, by way of New Orleans, to the site in Texas. Cabet's land agreement with Peters was not what the settlers had been led to believe, and it contained impossible, almost farcical, restrictions that Cabet had inexplicably kept to himself. For example, the colonists were led to believe that the land was located along the river and thus easily accessible. They were not told that the lots were in unconnected half-mile squares that added up to far less than the expected million acres. A settler could lay claim to a square only if he had built a cabin by 1 July 1848.

Nevertheless, the handful of tenacious Icarians set out to build as many cabins and claim as much land as possible. They were sustained by an often repeated promise from Cabet that a "second advanced party" of 1,500 immigrants was on its way. But the rocky land was unsuited for cultivation, and they did not have enough equipment or horses to produce a crop. Within a few months 12 colonists died, most from malaria; five left the project; and malaria incapacitated everyone. The "reinforcement" arrived in midsummer—10 sick and disillusioned immigrants. The colonists abandoned the Texas site and returned to New Orleans in the winter of 1849. There they were greeted by Cabet himself, who had just arrived from France with about 450 new immigrants. During the fiasco in Texas, he had been caught up in the February Revolution and the effort to establish the Second French Republic. By the summer of 1848, however, he had been discredited in France and had decided to come to America and join the colony. He had arrived in New Orleans in January 1849. A dispute erupted among the Icarians as to what course they should now pursue, and about 200 returned to France in disgust. In March 1849, after deciding against a renewed effort in Texas, some 280 Icarians followed Cabet to Nauvoo, Illinois, where they established a colony on land owned by Mormons. The Icarian colony at Nauvoo survived until 1857.

Rondel V. Davidson

Iconoclast. A widely read nineteenth-century magazine published mainly by William Cowper Brann, who was known as a vitriolic editorialist; published first in Austin (1891–94); originally a monthly, then a quarterly. In 1894 Brann sold the *Iconoclast* to O. Henry. He subsequently regained rights to the publication and moved it to Waco, where he called it *Brann's Iconoclast*. It presented Brann's views on social, economic, political, and religious issues. The *Iconoclast* was the only magazine of its type published west of the Mississippi River. It was also the earliest and most successful of the small periodicals containing highly personalized opinion. By 1897 national and foreign circulation had climbed to 98,000. Much of the magazine's popularity came from the publisher's notoriety. Brann took obvious relish in directing his stinging attacks upon institutions and persons he considered to be hypocritical or overly sanctimonious. He directed his attention generously to Baptists, Episcopalians, anything British, women, and, perhaps with the greatest harshness, blacks. Among his targets was Baylor University, a Baptist institution that he scourged as "that great storm-center of misinformation." On 2 October 1897 Brann was kidnapped by students and taken to the Baylor campus, where he was asked to retract his statements about the university. On 6 October he was beaten by a Baptist judge and two other men. On 1 April 1898 in Waco, Brann was shot in the back by a brooding supporter of Baylor University named Tom E. Davis. Before he died he drew his own pistol and killed his assailant. Editorial supervision of the May *Iconoclast* was assumed by W. H. Ward, Brann's business manager. He was succeeded as editor by G. B. Gerald. The publication was sold in 1898 by Brann's widow and moved to Chicago.

W.W. Bennett

Independent Colleges and Universities of Texas. A trade association; formed by college presidents at the instigation of McGruder E. Sadler, chancellor of Texas Christian University, in 1964 and incorporated the next year. The founders invited nonprofit, private, accredited institutions of higher education to membership, and by the first annual meeting (1965) 26 institutions were paying dues. Since 1969 all eligible institutions—about 40—have joined ICUT. In 1984 the members stipulated that only multipurpose independent institutions where a majority of students pursue associate or baccalaureate degrees are eligible for membership. Until 1982 the organization was heavily dependent upon volunteer leadership. Beginning in 1967, officers served as an advisory committee to the Texas Higher Education Coordinating Board. They contributed to the first master plan for Texas higher education a comprehensive study on the private colleges and universities, *Pluralism and Partnership: The Case for the Dual System of Higher Education* (1968). To implement a legislative program, in 1970 ICUT hired

Robert D. Hunter, a vice president of Abilene Christian College. A result of that program was the enactment in 1971 of the Tuition Equalization Grant, which provided funds to students with need who met residency requirements and wanted to attend a Texas private college. Hunter, who retained his position at Abilene Christian College, was executive vice president part-time for ICUT from 1971 to 1981. He established headquarters in Abilene except during legislative sessions, when activities centered in Austin. The ICUT Research Foundation, formed in 1976, assisted in public policy research. One study, *Advancing Partnership: A Study of Governmental Policy for Student Financial Aid in Independent Higher Education in Texas*, contributed to 1979 modifications of the Tuition Equalization Grant. In 1982 ICUT hired a full-time executive, Carol L. McDonald, who centralized staff functions and established offices in Austin. During the 1970s, seeking appropriations for the Tuition Equalization Grant was ICUT's specific focus. Advocating increased student financial aid for all Texas students has continued. After McDonald became president, the organization addressed a wider range of issues to protect the autonomy of independent institutions and to promote equity with public institutions. The *ICUT Report*, a quarterly newsletter, began in 1973, and an annual booklet describing member institutions, *Your Guide to Independent Higher Education in Texas*, first appeared in 1975. Other organizations with which ICUT maintains cooperative relations include the Association of Texas Colleges and Universities, the state legislature, the Texas Independent College Fund, and the National Association of Independent Colleges and Universities.

Connie S. Andes

Indian Captives. The practice of captive-taking among North American Indians goes back to prehistoric times. Centuries before white men came to these shores, captives were taken from neighboring tribes to replenish losses suffered in warfare or to obtain victims to torture in the spirit of revenge. When warfare developed between Europeans and Indians, white captives were taken for the same reasons or to hold for ransom. The earliest European captives in Texas were Cabeza de Vaca and three companions, survivors of the expedition of Pánfilo de Narváez in 1528. During the next three centuries numerous Spanish and Mexican captives remained many years in the camps of Apache, Comanche, Kiowa, and Wichita raiders. During the succeeding half century after Indian warfare broke out with whites in the 1830s, many settlers underwent Indian captivity.

The life of a captive was fraught with perils and hardships. Survival frequently depended upon the whim of the captor and the fortitude displayed by the captive. Mature males who fell into Indian hands were as good as dead. Captive white women were usually compelled to serve their captors as concubines and menials (the roles of most Indian women). Their ordeals frequently led to early deaths, before or after redemption. The experiences of Rachel Plummer dramatically illustrate the horrors of female captivity among the Plains Indians. Some women, however, were treated with unexpected respect. Indian raiders killed captive children who lagged behind when the Indians were pursued. Children who arrived safely at the Indian village, however, usually were adopted as replacements for deceased relatives and thereafter treated as true sons or daughters. Many of these youngsters enjoyed the wild, free life of the Indians and became

so completely assimilated that they resisted attempts to redeem them. Some youths became fierce warriors who raided the settlements. Among the most formidable "white Indians" were Clinton and Jeff Smith, Herman Lehmann, Adolph Korn, Rudolph Fischer, and Kiowa Dutch. White girls captured before the age of puberty usually became assimilated and married chiefs or warriors. The most famous of these, Cynthia Ann Parker, married the Comanche chief Peta Nocona and became the mother of Quanah Parker, last war chief of the tribe. Millie Durgan lived happily to old age as the wife of a Kiowa warrior. On the other hand, girls taken at childbearing age hated their captors and sometimes risked their lives to escape. Martina Díaz, one of many captives redeemed by the Indian agent Lawrie Tatum, hid in his house from threatening warriors. Matilda Lockhart, 13 years old when captured and treated brutally by the Comanches, precipitated the Council House Fight in San Antonio in 1840 when she revealed that the Indians were hiding other captives.

Many Texas captives were rescued or ransomed by relatives, Texas Rangers, soldiers, Indian agents, or traders. Britton Johnson, a black rancher, traded goods for his own wife and children, for the sister of Millie Durgan, and several other captives. Sam Houston purchased Mrs. Elizabeth Kellogg, seized in the Comanche raid on Fort Parker in 1836, from friendly Delaware Indians. Two young boys taken in the same raid, John Parker and James Plummer, were ransomed by Gen. Zachary Taylor in 1842. Gen. Albert Sidney Johnston rescued Rebecca Jane Fisher and her brother, William Gilleland, captured by Comanches who killed their parents near Refugio in 1842. Sul Ross redeemed a young white girl in 1858 during an attack on a Comanche village. She had forgotten her name, and her identity was never established. She was raised as a member of his family and given the name Lizzie Ross. When the Comanches and Kiowas were driven onto reservations north of the Red River and compelled to release their prisoners, many captives had become so completely assimilated that they chose to remain with their captors. Most of these had married Indians. It is estimated that 30 percent of Apaches, Comanches, and Kiowas had European blood in their veins.

J. Norman Heard

Indianola, Texas. A port town on Matagorda Bay, Calhoun County; founded in August 1846 as Indian Point by Sam Addison White and William M. Cook. In 1844 a stretch of beach near the point had been selected by Carl, Prince of Solms–Braunfels, commissioner general of the Adelsverein, as the landing place for German immigrants bound for western Texas under the sponsorship of the society. One immigrant, Johann Schwartz, built the first house in the area in 1845. Indian Point became firmly established as a deepwater port during the Mexican War. For thirty years its army depot supplied frontier forts in western Texas. Anglo-American landowners in the area had the site surveyed in 1846 and began selling lots. The post office was opened in September 1847, and stagecoach service to the interior began in January 1848. Mrs. Angelina Belle Eberly, heroine of the Archive War in Austin, moved to Indian Point in 1848 and operated hotels there until her death in 1860. In February 1849 the name of the growing town was changed to Indianola. Indianola was the county seat of Calhoun County from 1852 to 1886. The town grew rapidly, expanding three miles

View of Main Street looking west, 1873. Courtesy TSL. From 1852 to 1886, during the time Indianola was the county seat of Calhoun County, the town grew rapidly.

down the beach to Powderhorn Bayou, following its selection by Charles Morgan as the Matagorda Bay terminus for his New York–based steamship line. In a short time, Indianola achieved the rank of the second port of Texas, a position it held until the catastrophic hurricane of 16 September 1875 devastated the low-lying city and caused great loss of life. Indianola was the eastern end of the southern Chihuahua Trail, the military road to San Antonio, Austin, and Chihuahua, Mexico, as well as the road to San Diego, the shortest overland route to the Pacific. It became the chief port through which European and American immigrants flowed into western Texas. The town was incorporated in 1853, the year in which City Hospital began operation. In 1856 and 1857 two shiploads of camels were landed at Indianola. Under the direction of Secretary of War Jefferson Davis, the animals were used in one of the most extraordinary experiments in the history of the department—the use of camels in the transportation of military supplies in the southwestern United States. Indianola was bombarded by Union gunboats on 26 October 1862, then occupied and looted. The Union forces withdrew the following month but returned in November 1863, seized the city again, and remained until 1864. The world's first shipment of mechanically refrigerated beef moved from Indianola to New Orleans on the Morgan steamship *Agnes* in July 1869, opening a new era in the transportation of perishable goods. Railroad service from Indianola to the interior began in 1871. With a population of more than 5,000, Indianola was at the peak of her prosperity when the 1875 hurricane struck. The town rebuilt on a smaller scale and then was almost obliterated by the hurricane of 20 August 1886 and the accompanying fire. By 1887 the site had been abandoned.

Brownson Malsch

Pier, 1880. Photograph by J. G. Hyde, from *Our Indian Summer in the Far West*, by Samuel Nugent Townshend (London, printed by C. Wittingham, 1880). Courtesy TSL. Indianola was an important port for cargo and entry into Texas for European immigrants until it was devastated by the hurricane of 1875.

Indian Rock Art. Pictographs (drawings or paintings) and petroglyphs (carvings) made by Indians are extant in more than 250 known sites in Texas. The rock art is usually found on cave walls, in natural rockshelters beside rivers or streams, or on ledges and cliff faces. There are probably a great number of sites that have not been discovered, but those examined represent a wide variety of styles and many Indian cultures. Vandalism, natural weathering, and reservoir impoundment have taken their toll on the sites. The earliest organized studies of rock art in Texas began in the 1930s. Archeologist A. T. Jackson studied the subject throughout the state for eight years and published an extensive record titled *Picture-Writing of Texas Indians* (1938). Between 1934 and 1942 artist Olea Forrest Kirkland and his wife Lula visited about 80 sites and copied in watercolors various examples of rock art. Rock-art sites have been found near known Indian campgrounds; others have been found in isolated, remote areas, seemingly far from ancient or modern settlements. The artwork ranges in size from one inch to eighteen feet in height and is found anywhere from the ground level to many feet above ground. Some paintings were drawn in places that could only have been reached with the use of scaffolding. Pigments were made from powdered minerals, sometimes mixed with animal fats, and consisted largely of earth tones. Black and red were the most commonly used colors, but white, yellow, orange, and brown were also used, sometimes singly but most often in combination. Subjects ranged from the whole human figure or just hands or feet, to animals of all kinds—deer, mountain lions, buffalo, snakes, and birds. Sun symbols, various kinds of weather, trees, weapons, and geometric shapes were also drawn. In later times Spanish and other non-Indian figures were pictured. The purposes or meanings in the drawings cannot be positively determined, but some are clearly religious or ceremonial in nature, depicting what appear to be images of shamans. Some obviously show events occurring in a tribe or in the life of an individual, often hunting or warfare. Maps, dancing scenes, and tallies of some sort are recorded, as are stories or myths, and a few scenes appear to be intentionally humorous.

Only one region in Texas exemplifies a rock-art tradition among one group of Indians over an extended period of time—the area of the mouths of the Pecos and Devils rivers on the Rio Grande in Val Verde County. The paintings show a beginning and development, a slow refining in style, and an eventual dying out—all in a geographically limited area that was seemingly isolated from outside artistic influences. Evidences of human habitation in the area date back perhaps 10,000 years. It is estimated that the rock art along the lower Pecos was done ca. 3000–2000 B.C. to about A.D. 1880. The Pecos River style per se falls in the period 2000–1000 B.C. These pictographs are considered to be among the finest in the world and constitute possibly the largest collection of pictographs in North America. The Archaic-age Pecos River style generally consists of scenes incorporating several colors and depicting stylized figures as well as humans. The Red Linear style of the Late Archaic Period is characterized by very small dark red pictographs, often depicting humans as stick figures. The Red Monochrome style of the Late Prehistoric Period incorporates red, reddish-orange, and yellow colors and depicts solid human and animal figures. The Historic style shows European influence.

Farther west, in El Paso County, the rock art in Hueco Tanks State Historical Park reflects a different culture. Though not unified in a distinctive style, these paintings, found in centuries-old natural cisterns, show the influence of the forebears of the Puebloan Indians (who lived in Arizona and New Mexico, but whose influence reached into far western Texas). Paintings similar to those at Hueco Tanks can be found in the Panhandle in at least three locations: at Alibates Flint Quarries, near Palo Duro Canyon, and around the Canadian River valley at Rocky Dell in Oldham County. Characteristic subjects of paintings at these sites are masks, shield figures, and blanket designs, probably painted by the Mescalero Apaches between A.D. 900 and 1500, though influenced by the older Puebloan culture.

There are numerous other rock-art sites across Texas, but the work seems not to be the result of any consistent rock-art heritage such as that found in the Pecos River and Puebloan pictograph sites. Many works are more recent and are possibly influenced by the ancient art. Paintings are found throughout the Big Bend area, for instance, that are not related to the Pecos River style. Among the Big Bend sites are Rock Pile Ranch, Fort Davis, Lewis Canyon (the one site that is mostly petroglyphs, but nearly inaccessible), Study Butte, and Comanche Springs. Other places where rock paintings have been found include Nolan County, Winkler County, Paint Rock, and Lehmann Rock Shelter (northwest of Fredericksburg).

In 1967 *The Rock Art of Texas Indians* presented the first opportunity for the interested public to see Forrest Kirkland's watercolor renditions of the rock art, now curated at the Texas Memorial Museum. Subsequently, *Ancient Texans: Rock Art and Lifeways along the Lower Pecos* (1986) offered a sampling of photographer Jim Zintgraff's massive collection of color prints from the Pecos area. Zintgraff and Solveig Turpin then collaborated on *Pecos River Rock Art: A Photographic Essay* (1991), in which Turpin interpreted the art in the context of a widespread religious tradition. This hypothesis is further developed in *Shamanism and Rock Art in North America*, edited by Turpin and published by the Rock Art Foundation. The burgeoning interest in rock art has seen an increase in volunteer participation in its preservation, including the formation of a recording task group within the Texas Archeological Society. The Witte Museum in San Antonio has a permanent exhibit devoted to rock art and its contexts. Guided tours are available at Seminole Canyon, Hueco Tanks, Devils River State Natural Area, and Big Bend Ranch State Natural Area, all managed by the Texas Parks and Wildlife Department. *Melinda Arceneaux Wickman*

Indians. Ethnologists have identified hundreds of groups of Texas "Indians," as the first European explorers to arrive called the peoples they found. Some of these were true tribes, accumulations of families or clans with social customs, traditions, and rules for order; these were occasionally quite large. At the opposite extreme, some were merely small family groups whose names or ethnic designations were taken for tribal names by the Spanish and French and in subsequent secondary literature. The extant names of Texas Indian groups present a dazzling array of variants, partly because the Spanish, French, and English heard the newly "discovered" peoples differently and recorded their names differently. Some names in the historical records are mistakes for groups that never existed.

Spanish period. The variety of the peoples and cultures whom Europeans first found in Texas and the different histories of each group make generalizations about Indians hazardous.

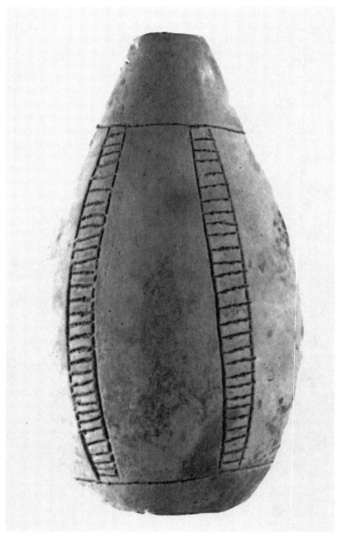

Earthenware Caddo bottle with ladder design, Cherokee County, ca. A.D. 1600 (or earlier)–1700. 8" × 4½". Courtesy Texas Archeological Research Laboratory (neg. no. 41CE12-39), University of Texas at Austin. Caddo pottery, influenced by techniques used farther east, predominated in Northeast Texas after A.D. 700–900.

Texas was not simply a Spanish–Indian or Anglo-Indian frontier, but rather a multisided frontier, a Spanish–Anglo–Comanche–Wichita–Apache–etc. frontier, where multiple groups acted for their own reasons. A few generalizations, however, apply to all Texas Indian groups. First, diseases introduced by the Europeans greatly reduced them, especially after mission and military institutions brought people in contact so that they could be infected. More broadly, anthropologist John C. Ewers has identified no fewer than 30 major epidemics—mainly of smallpox and cholera—between 1528 and 1890 that wiped out perhaps 95 percent of Texas Indians.

Texas also became a "horse-and-gun" frontier for Indians located between competing European powers. French and English traders from the East introduced firearms to the Indians in order to purchase peltry from them and win them as allies in both trade and war. The Spanish introduced horses. Groups able to obtain these two important items had a powerful advantage

over others. The introduction of the horse, especially, produced nothing less than a cultural, technological, and economic revolution, enabling groups to move their habitats, intensify their raiding and trading activities, and hunt buffalo more effectively. When the French gun trade met the Spanish horse trade in the late 1600s, the situation impelled the Spanish to settle Texas in order to block French efforts to move southward and westward toward the Spanish provinces of Mexico and New Mexico. Texas, in effect, was of little importance except as a buffer to be occupied for the protection of more important Spanish possessions.

In the late 1680s, Spanish soldiers and missionaries ventured far beyond existing Spanish settlement to the woodland home of the Caddos. These were 25 to 30 distinct groups that shared the same language, political structure, and religious beliefs and ceremonies. In the 1690s they assembled themselves into three loose confederacies—the westernmost Hasinai Indians (including the Tejas Indians or Tay-sha, from whom Texas got its name) settled on the Angelina and Neches rivers, the Kadodachos along the bend of the Red River at what is now the Texas–Louisiana–Arkansas border, and the eastern Natchitoch Indians. The Caddos were an agricultural people who lived in stable villages and were not especially warlike except for their traditional conflicts with Osages to the north and Tonkawa bands to the west over hunting grounds. Franciscans and Spanish soldiers settled among the Hasinais in 1689. Caddos resisted Spanish efforts to "reduce" them to compact towns; instead, they preferred to live in small clusters stretching through fertile river valleys. The missionaries had little success in converting them to Christianity, and resorted in frustration to ridicule of Caddo beliefs in the effort. A smallpox epidemic swept through the area in the winter of 1690–91, killing 3,000 Caddos, whose religious leaders blamed the friars for the pestilence. Aside from disease, Caddo tenacity in holding onto their religion, and the disrespect offered by the missionaries, other problems smoldered as well. The Caddos invited the Spanish into their villages mainly to get trade advantages, especially a steady supply of firearms with which to defend themselves against Osage raids, but trade was meager and the Spanish refused to supply weapons. Furthermore, Spanish soldiers committed such outrages as molesting Caddo women. Finally, in 1693 a *caddi* (chief) informed a soldier that "all of his people were very annoyed with the Spanish and it would be better if the Spanish went and left his lands"; then he told a priest ("with much ridicule," the priest said) that his people often spoke of throwing out the Spanish. When the Spanish left the next year, four soldiers deserted and joined the Hasinais. Although the Spanish reestablished their presence among the Caddos 20 years later, few Caddos accepted Christianity, and the Spanish never supplied goods with the quality and regularity that the French provided. Caddo agriculture thrived and, combined with the hunt and a strong trade with other tribes, enabled them to withstand Spanish efforts to control them.

The Spanish entry into Texas altered regional trade networks and led the Apaches, Comanches, and Kiowas to migrate into the South Plains to be nearer the supply of Spanish horses. The Spanish also established missions among smaller groups that needed protection from more powerful northern invaders. The Jumanos, who lived on the western tributaries of the Colorado River and along the Pecos River and the Rio Grande, were targets of Spanish slave raids (forbidden by the church) to obtain laborers for mines in Chihuahua. By the mid-1600s, however, they had positioned themselves as middlemen, trading Pueblo Indian textiles and turquoise, Caddo bows, Spanish metals and horses, and their own buffalo hides. This advantageous situation ended with the entrance onto the South Plains of the Apaches, who cut off the Jumanos from the New Mexico pueblos. Many small tribes sided with the Spanish in campaigns against the aggressive Apaches, but by the decade after 1710 the Jumanos had been so severely defeated that they lost their distinct cultural identity. Some merged with their former enemies, the Apaches, while others became wage laborers in Chihuahua and gradually blended into the Mexican populace.

A similar fate befell the Coahuiltecans, who lived in small bands between the San Antonio River and the Rio Grande and along the Balcones Escarpment. Their only defense against Apache attacks was to congregate in the newly formed Spanish missions. San Antonio was founded primarily as a cluster of missions with a presidio serving the small Coahuiltecan, Jumano, and other bands who needed protection from the Apaches. By the early nineteenth century, these peoples had intermarried and become so acculturated among the Spanish Mexicans that their ethnic identity as "Indians" was lost and they entered the lower strata of Hispanic society. San Antonio was a mixed blessing to both the Indian bands and the Spanish. While affording some protection from Apaches, the growing settlement also attracted Apache raids. In 1723 Spanish forces battled a large Apache camp in what is now Brown County, killing 34 warriors, including the chief. Such decisive victories were rare, however, and San Antonio and nearby missions continued to be plagued by Apache raids.

The Apaches themselves had a problem more severe than the Spanish. Just as they had displaced weaker bands from the South Plains, they too resisted dislocation at the hands of a more powerful newcomer to the region—the Comanches. Since the Apaches practiced some agriculture, their seasonal settlements were ripe targets for the completely nomadic Comanches. Eventually, the Comanches ousted the Apaches from the South Plains buffalo range. Some Apache groups moved westward into New Mexico, but others—Lipans—moved southeasterly to the area between the Nueces River and the Rio Grande. Relations with the Spanish were strained. On the one hand, the Apaches needed to ally with them against the Comanches; on the other, Lipan Apaches continued to raid San Antonio, and their recent displacement had brought them closer to the town. The Comanche sweep into the area was facilitated, like the Apache migration earlier, by the horse. Horses not only gave greater mobility and revolutionized Indian culture; they also became the primary measure of wealth and status. At the time the Comanches decisively defeated the previous South Plains inhabitants, they also established connections with French gun traders through Caddo and Wichita bands and thus became the most formidable opponents the Spanish ever faced.

The term *tribe* should be used with caution in regard to the Comanches. Though they had a common language and way of life, they had no political institutions or social mechanisms by which they acted as a unit. Comanche families formed bands that acted autonomously from each other. Bands have generally been delineated geographically—as "northern," "middle," "southern," and "Llano Estacado"—but Comanche bands did not really adhere to any distinct territorial boundaries. Furthermore, Comanche bands were not fixed institutions; they

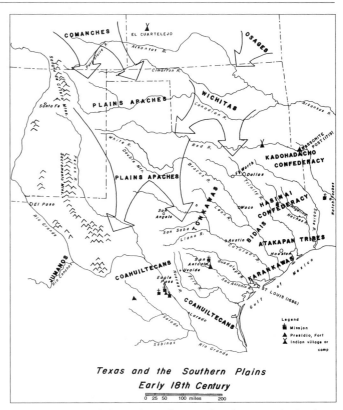

Texas and the Southern Plains Early 18th Century

Hal Story, *Texas and the Southern Plains, Early 18th Century*, in Curtis Tunnell and W. W. Newcomb, *A Lipan Apache Mission: San Lorenzo de la Santa Cruz, 1762–1771* (Austin: Texas Memorial Museum, 1969), p. 142. Courtesy Texas Memorial Museum.

broke apart, re-formed, and merged over the years. A man's connection to a band was one of free association, and he moved from one to another at will. Band populations fluctuated with the popularity of their leaders, mainly based on success at procuring horses and defeating enemies. Because of this type of social organization, no band leader could really control the behavior of individuals, as the Spanish (and later the Americans) learned. Comanche rank and social status were determined by war honors and the accumulation of horses taken from enemies. Horses were the most important type of property, a medium of exchange, and the measure of one's worth. Horse culture promoted decentralized and nomadic living arrangements because of the pasture needed by large horse herds. Horse raiding and trading characterized the Comanche role in Texas. It was not in the Comanches' interest to destroy or drive away Europeans; by using the margins of Spanish (and later Mexican and Anglo) settlement as sources of plunder, they enriched themselves while retarding colonial expansion into their region. In their middleman role, Comanches supplied horses and goods derived from buffalo hunting in exchange for the agricultural surplus of other groups, such as the Wichita bands, and firearms from European-American traders.

A similar maximization of power through the horse-and-gun trade occurred for the Wichitas, another group that migrated from the north in the early 1700s. A confederation of several linguistically related bands (Tawakoni, Taovaya, Iscani, Wichita, Towash), these people moved southward to get away from the more powerful and European-armed Osages. The Wichitas eventually lived on both sides of the Red River, a prime location where they stood between the Comanches and the French and profited accordingly. The Wichita bands subsisted by farming and hunting buffalo. They traded surplus crops to the Comanches for horses, then supplied horses to the French and Caddos living to the east. This trade system—from the French through the Caddos through the Wichitas to the Comanches—defined the diplomacy, economy, and general issues of war and peace from the early 1700s until the early years of Anglo-American settlement near the South Plains. The Wichitas originally made peace overtures to the Spanish in San Antonio, but the Spanish could not compete with the French trade. Also, the Spanish had established amicable relations with the Lipans in the early 1750s, much to the dismay of the Wichitas and everyone else who fought the Lipans in competition for hunting grounds.

The Spanish were seen as protectors of the Lipans, for whom they established Santa Cruz de San Sabá Mission on the San Saba River. The Lipans could not settle at San Antonio because the mission Indians and Spanish settlers feared them. Spanish officials believed San Sabá Mission would serve as a buffer between the Comanches and San Antonio and perhaps begin a chain of settlements between San Antonio and Santa Fe. They had not realized, however, that the mission would also become an attractive target for enemies of the Lipan Apaches. In March 1758, 2,000 warriors surrounded the mission, firing their French muskets into the air. This force, a conglomeration of Comanches, Wichitas, Tonkawas, Caddos, and others, told the Spanish soldiers not to fear them, that they only wished to attack some Apaches who had been raiding them. At the end of the day, 35 Apaches and Spaniards lay dead as the warriors looted and burned the mission. The meager Spanish military force, numbering fewer than 60, had no choice but to remain barricaded in the nearby presidio. The destruction of the mission was a severe blow to the Spanish and Lipans, but the larger meaning of the event swept fear through the province—2,000 warriors representing several groups had united in a concerted attack, displaying large quantities of firearms and notable skill in using them. The Spanish forces scattered through the various presidios of Texas were no match for such formidable opponents. Mission Indians in San Antonio fled southward to escape a predicted onslaught.

Col. Diego Ortiz Parrilla, commander of San Sabá Presidio (San Luis de las Amarillas), organized a punitive campaign against the attackers with more than 600 men, including Lipans, the next year. The objective Ortiz chose was a cluster of Wichita villages on the Red River anchored by the Taovayas. The Indians had constructed a split-rail fort with spaces between the rails for warriors inside to fire their guns. Outside the stockade (for which present-day Spanish Fort is named, although it was actually a Taovaya fort) they made a steep embankment, and beyond that dug a deep moat to prevent horsemen from nearing the walls of the fort. Inside the 130-by-80-yard fortress, the Taovayas had dug four large underground rooms to shelter noncombatants. Ortiz encountered this imposing structure in October 1759. The Taovayas, who had skirmished with Ortiz earlier, protected themselves in the fort, laughing at the Spanish and daring them to try to enter. Indians opened fire from behind the walls, and mounted warriors charged out of the fort at the Spanish line. The battle lasted four hours before Ortiz fell back after nightfall.

The fort's defenders obviously had unlimited ammunition, and Ortiz's Apache scouts could find no approach to the walls. The Taovayas showed greater discipline under fire than his own militiamen and outnumbered them as well, as other Wichita groups sent warriors to aid their kinsmen. Ortiz left the battlefield so quickly that he abandoned two pieces of artillery, which the Wichitas kept as trophies.

The failed assault on the Taovaya fortress demonstrated the limits of Spanish power on the frontier. The Spaniards could make isolated forays into the South Plains and inflict light damage, but they could never get the upper hand against Wichitas and Comanches and had to treat them practically as diplomatic equals. The battle also represented the high point of Wichita strength. Within a few years the Wichitas made peace with the Spanish, mainly because the Seven Years' War between France and Great Britain caused the French in Louisiana to cut back on the trade goods sent to western tribes. Likewise, at least one Comanche band, under a chief named Povea, made peace in San Antonio in 1772, but the chief reminded the Spanish that he could speak only for his own band, not for all Comanches. Spanish relations with the Lipans, never good, deteriorated after the San Saba–Wichita campaign fiasco. Lipans abandoned the missions for good and increased their stock raids on San Antonio. Trade and common enemies influenced Spanish efforts to establish friendly relations with Comanches, Wichitas, and Caddos, who were encouraged by Spanish officials in the early 1770s to finish off the Lipans. Although by 1779 the Lipans had once again made peace with San Antonio, hostilities between them and the other tribes continued for decades.

The Lipans sought allies, but found few. One group, the Tonkawas, formed an alliance with them that lasted more than a century, during which both groups dwindled. The Tonkawas were another small group shoved out of the South Plains buffalo range by the Comanches. Unlike the Lipans, they practiced no agriculture. Though originally known to the Spanish as four distinct bands, the Tonkawas unified in the mid-1700s as a response to epidemics and war losses. They were despised by other Indians not just for their raiding and competition for hunting grounds but also because of their cannibalism. Tonkawa warriors ceremonially cut off the hands and feet of slain enemies and ate them; this practice, described by a few white eyewitnesses (such as Rip Ford in the 1850s), led enemies to seek even greater vengeance for the desecration of their dead kinsmen's bodies. The Tonkawas were even more outcast than the Lipans. The Lipans also allied briefly in the 1780s with groups of East Texas Indians, mainly to establish a source for guns and ammunition other than San Antonio. They made contacts with the small Atakapa bands on the lower Trinity River, who had been given two meager Spanish missions in an attempt to block French expansion. The missions never successfully reduced these hunter–gatherers, who had French contacts through the Caddos. At a trade fair held on the Guadalupe River in 1782, Lipans met Tonkawas, Atakapas, and Caddos and traded 1,000 Spanish horses for 270 guns. Such trade continued for four years, and the Caddos, although friendly to the Spanish, were oblivious to Spanish warnings to end it. By the end of the decade, the Caddos were forced to abandon the trade with the Lipans, as the Spanish again turned all the other tribes (including the Tonkawas, briefly) against the Lipans.

The Spanish policy of Indian alliances depended upon trade.

Their failure to supply goods, especially firearms and ammunition, regularly or in abundance caused peaceful relations to stop and start and never be firmly established. The Spanish colonial bureaucratic structure also contributed to Wichita and Comanche disillusionment, as the viceregal authorities in Mexico City did not adequately understand the situation on the northern margins and communication was slow. Finally, increased Comanche raids led Mexico City to conclude that peace treaties were useless. Only one or two bands of Comanches had actually made peace with the Spanish, and their social structure had no way of preventing bold young men from going off to attain wealth and war honors. Raiding enabled the Comanches and other groups to circumvent Spanish attempts to control trade and regulate access to horses. Spanish power in Texas further raveled in the beginning of the nineteenth century due to events elsewhere in the empire. The Napoleonic Wars in Europe made Spain and Portugal battlegrounds for several years, and the crown had to attend to matters on its doorstep. At the same time, the wars of independence swept through the Americas, including Mexico. In 1821, the Republic of Mexico became independent after the 11-year Mexican War of Independence, and Texas was included within its boundaries. In the end, the Spanish were no longer able to supply adequate trade to Indians or to station a respectable military presence on the frontier. Always an area of marginal importance in the large imperial scheme, Texas was the neglected fringe of a collapsing empire.

Republics of Mexico and Texas. The problems associated with the final years of Spanish rule and Indian relations were inherited by the government of the new Republic of Texas. Most missions had been abandoned; the only active ones were in the vicinity of San Antonio and Goliad. Political upheavals in Mexico City caused virtually annual changes of government and contributed to the neglect of the frontier. As during Spanish rule, the frontier communities of Texas had little to attract settlers from other parts of Mexico. Raids by Comanches, Apaches, and others also checked Mexico's frontier development, and the increase in such raids reflected the changing conditions of the region. At the time of Spanish decline and Mexican independence, traders from the United States began to venture onto the Plains and establish contacts with Santa Fe and the Indian groups between the United States and New Mexico. Mexico was unable to repair broken trade alliances or impose order militarily. Because the American trade gave the Indians a new, strong market and a steady source of firearms, raiding increased in the northern states of Mexico. The Republic of Mexico responded to these changes on its frontier by encouraging immigration from elsewhere.

Most significantly for the Indians of Texas, two new types of immigrant entered the province—Indian bands from the eastern United States and Anglo-Americans. Indian migration from the east began in the 1790s as Choctaw, Chickasaw, Alabama–Coushatta, and Creek hunting parties, reacting to the decline of game in their traditional homelands, seasonally and temporarily entered Texas. Over time, eastern bands found it more convenient to trade deerskins locally than to carry them back east. Expanding white settlement also pushed them westward. By the first decade of the 1800s, the Alabama Indians had established a town on the Neches River above its junction with the Angelina River, and the Coushattas had settled on the Trinity. Relations between the Caddos and these newcomers were generally friendly, although the Caddos occasionally clashed in the early years with Choctaw hunting parties. For the most part, however, the Caddos welcomed the immigrants as allies against the Osages. A second and larger wave of Indians from the east occurred after the War of 1812, as the United States removed the British influence on its frontier and established its unilateral control over frontier tribes. Several tribes, such as the Shawnee and Delaware Indians, had sided with the British in the war, and individual bands moved into Texas. The Creek confederacy had been badly splintered by a civil war during the War of 1812. One faction was soundly defeated by Gen. Andrew Jackson at the battle of Horseshoe Bend in Alabama in 1814, and many of its refugees moved west. Even some groups that had peaceful relations with the United States, such as the Cherokees, moved because of their role in the fur trade and the pressure of white expansion on their traditional lands. By 1820, the concept of "removing" eastern Indians westward began to be discussed by United States politicians; although the policy was not enacted until 1830, many groups understood the implications and left the United States by moving to Texas. The Mexican government welcomed the immigrants and promised them land titles in East Texas, but no titles were ever formally secured.

The Indian migration into East Texas in the 1820s coincided with another important influx—that of Anglo-American immigrants, both legal and illegal. During the Texas Revolution the independence forces sought conciliation with nearby Indians to keep them from allying with the Mexican army. Most bands were neutral, and some, such as the Shawnees, were willing to join in the fight against Gen. Antonio López de Santa Anna. Sam Houston planned to raise a 300-man force of Cherokees, Delawares, Shawnees, and Kickapoos with payments of cash and plunder, but this plan never materialized. The fear that Indians might side with Santa Anna seems to have been greatest during the period between the fall of the Alamo and the Texas victory at San Jacinto. It does not appear to have been grounded in the Indians' behavior but on a general fear that the entire rebellion was falling apart. Nevertheless, the specter of potential Indian hostility remained even after the crisis had ended, and it remained important in the new republic's policies. Certainly, the tribes did listen to Mexican agents who visited them, but on the whole they remained neutral out of doubt about which side would win. The Indian scare had one very significant effect on Texas independence: the widespread rumors of Indian hostility persuaded United States troops from Louisiana to cross into Texas and occupy Nacogdoches in 1836, thus ending the Texans' eastward flight at the same time as the battle of San Jacinto.

In an effort to maintain good relations with the Indians, the provisional government declared in November 1835 that the East Texas bands had just claims to their land and that definite boundaries should be drawn for them. Indian land rights would be respected, explained the General Council,"so as not to compromise the interest of Texas." In February 1836, Houston made a treaty with the Quapaw, Choctaw, Biloxi,Alabama, Coushatta, Cherokee, Shawnee, Delaware, and Kickapoo Indians and with various Caddo bands, which established a reservation where all would live, bounded by the Angelina, Neches, and Sabine rivers and the Old San Antonio Road. According to the treaty, the land could not be sold or alienated to any entity but the Republic of Texas, Indians could have their own laws as long as they were not contrary to Texas law, and the republic would regulate all Indian trade. This first treaty of the Republic of Texas was never ratified by either the provisional government or the Texas Senate. Later, the Texas government realized that no Indians had been granted land titles by the Mexican government, and used this as justification for expelling most of them from Texas.

Texans knew little about the Indians within the borders they claimed, and they had to figure out the proper policies to be followed. The Senate Committee on Indian Affairs tried to delineate the various groups in October 1837 by identifying bands, estimating their length of residency in Texas, and evaluating their relations to others. The Coushattas, Alabamas, Biloxis, and Creeks were identified as living near Nacogdoches and resident in Texas for 50 years. The Choctaws were reported to have lived in Texas for only 10 years and thus to have "no pretensions to the soil." The committee distinguished several Caddo bands, identifying them as friendly to the hostile "Prairie Indians" (the confederacy of Wichita bands that had raided white settlements since the establishment of Stephen F. Austin's first colony). The "Prairie Indians" were described as hunters and horsemen living high up the Brazos and Trinity rivers and friendly with the Comanches. Since the Comanches did not live near the white settlements of East Texas, members of the new government knew little about them except that they were "the natural enemies of the Mexicans whom they contemptuously denominate their stock keepers and out of which nation they procure slaves." The committee believed a treaty of friendship—and alliance with them against Mexico—was possible. Other groups were identified as current residents of Texas but not the government's responsibility. The "Northern Indians" (Kickapoos, Shawnees, Delawares, and Potawatomis) had migrated a decade earlier from the United States and consequently were deemed that nation's responsibility. The Lipans and Tonkawas, on the other hand, were considered by the committee to be part of the Mexican nation, even though the Tonkawas' tenure in Texas predated the Europeans' and the Lipans had arrived a century and a half before Texas independence. The committee made a few errors in its analysis of Texas Indians, as indicated by its description of the Tonkawas and Lipans, but it did trace the Caddo–Wichita– Comanche connection and the Comanches' raiding activities against Mexicans. It also identified and located most of the bands that had migrated from the United States and tried to establish their length of residency in relation to the arrival of Anglo-Americans. Generally, the committee identified as "native" any group that lived in Texas before Stephen Austin; the Alabama and Coushattas, for example, were considered natives of Texas despite their migration from Alabama because they predated Austin's colony. The Shawnees, on the other hand, were classed as "emigrants" for having moved to Texas at approximately the same time as Austin. In reality, the "native–emigrant" division was fluid and inconsistent, and it meant relatively little in terms of the republic's policies and actions.

The Indian policy of the Republic of Texas was for the most part defined by the president, especially Houston and Mirabeau B. Lamar,whose divergent policies defined the spectrum of debate about how to handle the Indians. Houston advocated a policy of fairness and friendship toward the Indians because "natural reason will teach them the utility of our friendship," he explained in his 1836 presidential inaugural address. He believed Indians, as rational human beings, would find it in their best interests to maintain peace with Texans. On a more practical level, Houston understood that trade connections and the recognition of reservation lands were less costly than war, that they would gradually foster Indian dependency on the government, and that the more mobile equestrian tribes would be very difficult to find and defeat decisively. Lamar took a far more bellicose position. "The proper policy to be pursued towards the barbarian race, is absolute expulsion from the country," he said in 1839. "The white man and the red man cannot dwell in harmony together. Nature forbids it." The republic's Indian policy was greatly influenced by considerations of how the various Indian groups figured into the ongoing conflict between Texas and Mexico. The apprehension that they would join the Mexicans so permeated public attitudes and government policy that this fear was exploited to justify dispossession of the Indians. The Mexican forces in Matamoros did hope to win Indian alliances and to reoccupy Texas, but they were ultimately unsuccessful. Texans, however, saw the hand of Mexico in several violent clashes between whites and Indians, and this fed the popular belief that Houston's conciliatory policy was a failure.

The campaigns against East Texas Indians in the late 1830s are illustrative. When some Mexican residents of Nacogdoches led by Vicente Córdova rebelled in 1838, individual warriors of several tribes joined them. Córdova first camped on Cherokee land, and although Cherokee chief Duwali (commonly known as Bowlor Bowles) never cooperated with him, the chief held discussions with both sides, an astute move unappreciated by Texans. Gen. Thomas J. Rusk led troops into Cherokee country and chased Córdova to the Kickapoos, who had already been suspected of frontier raids. Rusk assured the Kickapoo chief that he had no intention of attacking the Indians, but he privately believed that an opportune moment had come to expel them. Several weeks later he attacked the Kickapoo village and, after a sharp fight in which 11 Indians were killed, burned it. Days later, Texans destroyed a Caddo village on the West Fork of the Trinity, killing six, even though they had no apparent connection to Córdova.

Aside from the fear of Indian alliance with Mexico, questions of national sovereignty also made Texans want to erase Indian enclaves in regions filling up with white settlers. Recognition of Indian land rights, Lamar insisted, would be "parcelling out our territory to strangers and intruders, and introducing into the very viscera of the body politic an alien, independent and innately hostile people." Most Texans agreed with Lamar that whites and Indians could not live as neighbors, although Houston maintained that a reservation with well-defined and enforced boundaries could exist peacefully surrounded by whites.

Examples of skirmishes in East Texas abound in this period. Whites did suffer from raids, and they sought retribution. In some cases, Texans did not bother to discern which Indians had committed offenses and punished any Indians they found. In 1840, for example, a small party of Indians killed two whites near Nacogdoches; a white party in pursuit found the raiders' camp, but the culprits had fled. Instead of continuing the pursuit, reported a Houston newspaper, "the party fell back upon a village of Choctaws, and after killing eleven of them returned home." Two years earlier, a man who had lost some horses believed Caddos had taken them, so he went to their village and attempted to kidnap several women and children; three Indians and two whites were killed in the skirmish. The man later found

Ko-Rak-Koo-Kiss, a Towoccono Warrior, by John Mix Stanley, 1844. Oil on canvas. 25" x 30¼". Courtesy National Museum of American Art, Smithsonian Institution; gift of the Misses Henry, 1908. The Tawakonis, a Wichita group, harried white settlements in Texas in alliance with the Comanches. Stanley noted that this man "won the name and standing of a warrior" for a "daring attempt" to steal horses one night from Fort Milam in Falls County.

his horses, which had only strayed from his farm. These skirmishes occurred at a time when East Texas was filling up with both white settlers and Indian refugees from the United States. At the time of the Texas Revolution, the Caddos living in Louisiana had signed a treaty agreeing to move out of the United States—so they crossed the border to join their kinsmen in Texas and greatly alarmed white settlers. During this tense period the Texas Senate renounced the treaty Houston had made in 1836, thus provoking encroachment on Indian land by surveyors and squatters and retaliatory raids by exasperated Indians. As always, the fear of an Indian alliance with Mexico was prevalent.

The impetus for offensive action against the Cherokees and others came in 1839, when Texas Rangers killed Manuel Flores,a Mexican agent sent to recruit East Texas Indians. Among his effects was found a letter from a Mexican general proposing an alliance. Since the courier had been killed before delivering the message, obviously the Indians had not seen it; nevertheless, this

incident was all Lamar needed to link the Cherokees to the Mexicans. He offered to pay the Cherokees for any improvements they had made on their land but not for the land itself, in accordance with his position that they had no title. As General Rusk succinctly told Cherokee, Shawnee, and Delaware leaders, "The wild Indians and Mexicans & we are enemies. It is impossible for you to be friendly to both of us . . . . You are between two fires & if you remain will be destroyed." Chief Bowl agreed to leave, but insisted on remaining until his people's corn could be harvested. He also refused to surrender his warrior's gunlocks, perhaps because the Cherokees had no consensus for removal and he did not want to cause dissent among his people. He declined a Texan escort to the Red River, stating he "had come to this Country by himself and wished to return in the same way." These negotiations accomplished nothing, however, because Texans believed the Cherokees were only stalling until the Mexicans invaded. So they attacked the Cherokee town, destroyed it and the cornfields, killed Duwali, and sent the refugees north of the Red River. Two weeks after the Cherokees' defeat, the Shawnees and Delawares, who had been among the friendliest Indians to the whites and had not been implicated in the documents found on Flores, agreed to virtually the same removal terms. Unlike the Cherokees, they surrendered their gunlocks and accepted the escort out of the country. Pecan, a Shawnee leader, "apprehended that times could be worse" and said "he did not like a fuss[,] that he was going away to avoid it."

The campaigns chased the Caddos westward onto the prairies, wiped out the Kickapoo and Cherokee settlements, and intimidated the Shawnees and Delawares into leaving the republic. Caddos, Shawnees, Delawares, and others had been so splintered by warfare and dislocation that they combined into one multitribal town near the Three Forks of the Trinity. There they traded buffalo robes, tended livestock, and planted 300 acres of corn until 1841, when a force of Texas Rangers destroyed the town, burned the fields, and took the buffalo robes and cattle as prizes. Viewed as a whole, the Republic of Texas waged a successful campaign to clear East Texas of Indians, to rid the area of an undesirable race, and to open it to economic development. The Alabamas and Coushattas, however, present an exception. Though subjected to the same treatment as other Indian groups, they did not retaliate (and thus provoke more white attacks) and looked instead to the government for satisfaction. The fact that they rendered aid to the cause of independence in 1836 worked in their favor; at that time, Alabamas and Coushattas helped retreating white families cross the Trinity River and cared for them while Texans under Houston met Santa Anna at San Jacinto. In recognition of this, the republic assigned the Alabamas and Coushattas two leagues of land along the lower Trinity River.

The republic's relations with the Comanches changed drastically in the late 1830s. As mentioned earlier, whites knew relatively little about them at first; Anglo-American settlers lived far enough away from them not to be victimized by Comanche raids but close enough to be considered by the Comanches as a market for buffalo robes and horses taken from Mexico. But the relentless advance of white settlement, the new government's refusal to recognize Comanche territorial sovereignty, and the fact that white Texans took a much harder line against the Comanches than the Mexicans previously had taken resulted in unyielding warfare by 1840.

With the westward advance of white settlement, the Comanches had new communities to raid. In the summer of 1836, Comanches took more than 100 horses from settlements, taking advantage of the unstable state of affairs during the war for independence. The first serious counterblow occurred in February 1839, but with mixed results. A company of rangers assisted by the Comanches' Lipan Apache enemies penetrated the Comanche heartland, something that had never been done before. The Lipans, who originally proposed the expedition, found a Comanche camp on a creek in the San Saba valley, and they and the rangers charged into it at dawn, "throwing open the doors of the wigwams or pulling them down and slaughtering the enemy in their beds," reported the commander, Col. John H. Moore.The Comanches regrouped and counterattacked as the Texans reloaded their weapons, and Moore was forced to pull back. Soon the Texans found themselves surrounded by hundreds of Comanches, who rode up with a white flag and pro-

posed a prisoner swap. Later, as the rangers rode toward home, the Comanches stole their horses, and they had to walk home the last 100 miles, carrying their wounded.

The incident that most irreparably altered Texan–Comanche relations was the Council House Fight (1840). The Comanches went to San Antonio to negotiate a land treaty and return white captives. Secretary of War Albert Sidney Johnston, however, instructed negotiators not to make any promises that would compromise the republic's ability to decide unilaterally the conditions of residence of any Indian tribe, and further to hold the Comanche delegation hostage until all "American Captives" were surrendered. At the Council House in San Antonio, a traditional meetingplace for Indian negotiations, the Comanches delivered up a teenage girl, who told the Texans that she had seen many other white captives in the large Comanche camp outside of town. Muke-war-wah, the main Comanche spokesman, claimed, "We have brought in the only one we had; the others are with other tribes." Given the decentralized Comanche society, the girl may indeed have been the only captive in Muke-war-wah's band, and he had no authority to deal in captives held by others. Whatever the truth may have been, the Texans assumed he was lying and told the Comanche delegation that they were going to be hostages until more whites were brought in. The delegation rushed the door, stabbing soldiers, and all 12 Comanches in the Council House were shot to death. The gunfire prompted the warriors outside the building to take up the fight, and a general melee ensued through the streets of San Antonio. When the battle ended, 35 Comanches and 7 whites had been killed, 100 horses and a great number of buffalo hides had been taken by the whites, and some 29 Comanche women and children had been taken prisoner. In turn, the fight provoked the largest Indian raid since the attack on the San Sabá Mission 82 years earlier. In the Linnville Raid, 500 Comanches sacked Victoria and Linnville and raided all the way to the Gulf of Mexico. On their return to their own territory, however, they were cut off by militia companies from the Colorado River counties and defeated at the battle of Plum Creek.

Later that year, Colonel Moore conducted another campaign well into Comanche territory, much more successful than his attack a year earlier. Once again, he took his troops far from white settlements and attacked a Comanche camp discovered by his Lipan allies. The villagers fled the attack by running into the river, but the steep banks on the other side proved difficult to climb. Texan marksmen killed them as they slipped and scrambled on the banks. Twice as many Indians were killed in the river than in the initial attack on the village, and approximately 120 bodies littered the site.

The Council House Fight loomed in the memories of Comanches; government officials often found themselves negotiating with men who had lost family members in the battle. Comanches were leery of sending representatives to meetings because they did not want prominent leaders to be taken hostage. They declined to send a delegation to one council unless four whites were sent to them as hostages guaranteeing the safety of the four chiefs who would attend. Though bitter warfare seemed unavoidable, Houston, upon regaining the presidency in 1841, continued to pursue peace overtures. He wanted to establish territorial boundaries for the Comanches, but Congress always voted down such provisions. The 1844 treaty of Tehuacana Creek, for example, drew a line from the Cross

Kiowa camp near the Canadian River, 1869. Photograph by Will Soule. Courtesy Huntington Library, San Marino, California; Album 189 (04).

Timbersto Comanche Peak (now in Hood County) to the ruins of the San Sabá Mission, then southwesterly to the Rio Grande, but this boundary provision was deleted from the ratified version. Even when treaties were made, the Republic of Texas learned what had plagued Spain and Mexico earlier—that an agreement with one Comanche band had no bearing on the half dozen or so others that continued to raid. The Comanches learned that white settlers would continue to encroach on their territory, and that the government could not stop them even if it was so inclined.

Unlike the other groups discussed earlier, the Tonkawas and Lipans allied early with the Republic of Texas. They did so for the same reasons they had previously sought the friendship of Spain, Mexico, and the Caddos—they were small, shrinking groups, and they needed allies to defend themselves against the Comanches when they ventured onto the buffalo range west of San Antonio. They resided between the Colorado and San Antonio rivers in the 1830s and 1840s. They assisted Texans in retrieving horses taken by Wichitas and Caddos, and they joined Texas Rangers in campaigns against the Comanches, as noted earlier. Unfortunately for them, such assistance did not make the Texans treat them differently from other Indians. In one case, a group of Texans and Mexicans in Goliad stole horses from a Tonkawa camp while the warriors were serving with the Texas army on the Nueces frontier. Though many Texans recognized the injustice of the incident, too many potential jurors in the

Goliad area were involved in it for the authorities to prosecute the thieves. The Tonkawas responded by robbing and killing some whites, thus arousing residents of Goliad to talk of exterminating them. Thereupon the Tonkawas moved and by the 1840s were living near Bastrop, begging for food, hiring out as cotton-pickers during the harvest season, and buying liquor from unscrupulous storekeepers. Members of the Texas Congress attempted to recognize their service to the republic by reserving for them two 14-square-mile reservations on the Brazos and Colorado rivers beyond white settlement, a location where they could serve as a buffer against Comanche raids; this proposal, however, was defeated, as were all other similar measures.

Statehood. When Texas entered the United States in 1845–46, the situation for Indians was altered. For one change, raiders such as the Comanches, Kiowas, and Wichitas had to learn that the Americans and Texans were one people now, and that they could not rob one and sell the loot to the other, although unscrupulous frontier traders did this for a while. For another, the United States was obligated by the Treaty of Guadalupe Hidalgoto block Indian raids into Mexico, a part of the agreement that the Comanches did not respect because they had not been consulted. The United States army built forts along the border and tried to maintain a forceful presence in the area. Ecological and demographic changes also took place in the late 1840s and 1850s. With entry into the Union, immigration to Texas rose considerably. The state's population tripled between

1850 and 1860, the country west of San Antonio, Austin, and Dallas filled up with settlers, and the new army forts attracted settlements that sprang up near them. The influx of newcomers and the passing caravans of Forty-niners on their way to the goldfields of California also brought a new wave of disease that laid waste the Indians. The Comanches were hit by smallpox in 1848 and cholera in 1849, when by some estimates half their population died, including such leaders as Santa Anna and Mopechucope (Old Owl), who had been influential advocates of peaceful relations. If this were not enough, the buffalo population began declining during the same period. Partly, the expansion of white settlement and the federally sponsored "Indian removal" program that put 50,000 eastern Indians on the margins of the South Plains reduced available buffalo range and increased the number of people hunting them. But the Indians' hunting style also contributed. They preferred to hunt buffalo cows because their meat was more tender and their hides easier to process into finer robes; the overhunting of breeding-age females contributed to the decline of the buffalo. As the herds shrank, Comanches took to eating their horses, and this depletion of their most important form of property impelled them to increase their cattle raids on both sides of the Rio Grande. They also attack outsiders who hunted buffalo.

The most important change affecting Indians when Texas joined the United States, however, had to do with relations between the state and federal governments. The federal government, constitutionally mandated to be in charge of Indian affairs, took over that role in Texas, but the new state retained control of its public lands. In all other new territories, Washington controlled both public lands and Indian affairs and so could make treaties guaranteeing reservations for various groups. In Texas, however, the federal government could not do this. The state adamantly refused to contribute public land for Indian reservations within the boundaries of Texas, all the while expecting Washington to bear the expense and responsibility of Indian affairs. Since federal Indian agents in Texas understood that guaranteeing Indian land rights was the key to peace, no peace could be possible with the intransigent attitude of state officials on the land question. Furthermore, Texans in the decade before the Civil War were highly critical of the inability of the army to defeat the Indians decisively and prevent raids; many believed that Texas protected its white citizens better when it was independent. This attitude regarding frontier policy became important when Texas seceded from the union in 1861.

Only once did the Texas legislature relent in its opposition to reservations. In 1854 state officials gave in to federal requests and established two small reservations on the Brazos River near Fort Belknap. On the Brazos Indian Reservation, remnants of Caddo and Wichita bands and the Tonkawas, with a few Shawnees and Delawares who had married into the Caddos, established themselves. On the other the Comanches were supposed to settle. Only a small group of Comanches, elements of the Penateka band, went to the reservation, while their kinsmen continued to live freely and raid the frontier. The reservation plan might have worked had the area not filled up with white settlers almost immediately. Since the whites established horse and cattle ranches, the area naturally became a target for Comanche, Kiowa, and Kickapoo raids. Whites believed the proximity of the reservations had something to do with the raids, and blamed the

reservation population for either conducting or abetting them. There may be some justification for accusing the reservation Comanches, since they entertained nonreservation Comanche visitors and their social structure could not prevent young men from leaving the reservation to live with other bands. The Indians of the Brazos reservation, however, had also been the victims of stock raids. They even contributed to two important Texan victories north of the Red River. In May 1858, Rip Ford led a force of Texas Rangers and Brazos reservation warriors to the heartland of Comanche country, and the reservation Indians supplied more men than the rangers. The reservation Indians found a Comanche trail, hunted buffalo along the way to feed the expedition, and found two large Comanche camps. In the ensuing battle, 76 Comanches, including the celebrated chief Iron Jacket, were killed. A year and a half later, Indians of the Brazos reservation participated in a similar campaign led by Maj. Earl Van Dorn of the United States Army. Waco and Tawakoni scouts learned the location of a Comanche camp through their Wichita kinsmen and attacked the Comanches, killing 56 and burning 120 lodges. "If it had not been for [the Indians' help], Major Van Dorn would not have seen a Comanche, nor would Captain Ford," explained army lieutenant William Burnet.

Regardless of their service on the frontier, however, the reservation people continued to be accused of stock thefts by frustrated ranchers in Jack, Palo Pinto, and Young counties. A few days after Christmas 1858, a party of Caddos with official permission to hunt off the reservation were attacked in their sleep by a group of whites; seven were killed. Federal Indian agents insisted that state authorities prosecute the killers, but nothing came of these requests. An organized movement led by John R. Baylor and others formed to expel the reservation Indians from the state; armed parties of citizens patrolled the reservations' boundaries, and in a few instances killed Indians found outside the line. The United States Army entered the reservations to defend the Indians from vigilante violence, a move that enraged Texans and further fed their belief that the federal government's frontier policies were detrimental to the state. At one time, Baylor led armed citizens onto the reservation to force the Indians' expulsion, but the Indians (armed by the United States Army) fought back and chased the Texans away. In August 1859 federal officials negotiated the removal of the reservation Indians to new land north of the Red River on the Wichita reservation. Feeling ran so high against the Indians and their white defenders that federal Indian agent Robert S. Neighbors was murdered by a local white man near Fort Belknap after having removed the Indians from the state.

The expulsion of the reservation Indians did nothing to lessen the frequency or intensity of Comanche and Kiowa raids. Beginning in 1861, Texans had their opportunity to prove Texas could defend the frontier and pacify Indians better than the United States could. But the Confederate state of Texas accomplished little more than federal efforts had, although it must be admitted that the needs of the Civil War took priority in manpower and spending. Raids continued as before and even increased in some counties. The growth of cattle ranching added a new target for raiders, who drove off cattle for resale to the Comancheros, traders from New Mexico who ventured onto the Llano Estacado to buy from the Comanches.

With the defeat of the Confederacy and the length of time it took United States troops to return to the frontier, Indians noticed the unorganized status of the frontier and increased their raids in late 1865. Federal officials tried to settle frontier affairs in the traditional manner—with a land treaty. In October 1865 the Kiowas and a few Comanche bands signed the treaty of the Little Arkansas, in which the federal government promised them a large reservation comprising the Panhandle and most of West Texas (from the southeastern corner of New Mexico to the junction of the North and South forks of the Red River). But the war had not changed the unique legal situation of Texas or the attitudes of its officials. The state still controlled its own public land, and even Republican lawmakers in the Reconstruction state government, heavily influenced by military occupation, refused to cede any land to Indians. In 1867 the Kiowas and Comanches negotiated another reservation treaty at Medicine Lodge Creek, which secured for them less land in the Indian Territory. Although 10 Comanche chiefs signed the treaty, as was customary, they spoke only for the people they represented (less than half of all Comanches) and could not speak for all bands. Therefore, even with the establishment of a reservation, the government still had to use force on the recalcitrant bands.

The final subjugation of the South Plains Indians involved a combination of economic and military measures, in which the destruction of the Indians' trade and subsistence base became primary to their acceptance of reservation life. The suppression of the Comanchero trade in the early 1870s removed an important market for raiders. The arrival of increasing numbers of white buffalo hunters all but destroyed the great South Plains herds; the newly constructed railroads not only brought more hunters but sent hides to eastern markets faster. Furthermore, William T. Sherman,commander of the United States Army, and Philip H. Sheridan,commander of United States troops in Texas, understood from their experiences in the Civil War (Sherman's march through Georgia and Sheridan's campaigns in the Shenandoah valley of Virginia) that victory comes not just from the defeat of enemy armies but from breaking the people's will to resist by destroying their ability to feed and supply themselves. With this strategy in mind, the generals looked to the buffalo. Sheridan encouraged commercial hunters and even tourists to hunt buffalo, and he trained new recruits in marksmanship with buffalo targets. Buffalo meat also supplemented the poor food at many army posts. These attacks on the Indians' economic base coincided with inducements to get them to accept reservation life. The government promised to provide food and shelter. Food shipments to the reservation, however, were sporadic, and on one occasion bureaucrats in Washington ordered the reservation agent to withhold food until the Comanches surrendered some suspected raiders to authorities. The uncertainty of rations therefore failed to make the reservation as attractive as the government would have liked, and actually provoked some Comanches to leave the reservation and continue raiding for subsistence.

Militarily, the army conducted winter campaigns, something not previously done. The Indians learned they had no sanctuary and could find their tepees and food stocks destroyed during the harshest time of the year. Frequently this was done with the help of Indians working for the government, most notably Tonkawas and Lipans working out of Fort Griffin. They received pay and rations as regular cavalrymen while on duty and were allowed to live near the fort for their own protection. The Tonkawas benefited from this relationship because they had nowhere else to go—all other Indian groups except the Lipans despised them for helping the whites and for their ritual cannibalism. Their arrangement with the military was mutually advantageous; they could be safe only with army protection, and the army needed their scouting skills. A great breakthrough for the army came in 1872, when Col. Ranald S. Mackenzie, with a captured Comanchero from New Mexico leading the way, crossed the Llano Estacado, the final redoubt of the Comanche resistance. He noted the trails and areas with abundant grass, wood, and fresh water to support cavalry movements through the area. He put his new knowledge to work immediately by locating and destroying a Comanche camp on McClellan Creek in October 1872; more than 20 Indians were killed, and 124 women and children were captured and subsequently held prisoner at Fort Sill to induce others to surrender. Mackenzie tried to return to his fort with the Indians' 3,000 horses, but the Comanches harassed him so severely while he was driving them off that afterward his policy was to shoot all captured horses. In this additional way, more a result of exasperation than planning, the Comanches found their ability to survive outside the reservation fading away. The next year, Mackenzie's focus turned to the Mexican border, the scene of raids by Kickapoos and others who took advantage of the international boundary to live in Mexican territory and raid in the United States. With 400 troops he crossed the Rio Grande and destroyed three villages of Kickapoos, Potawatomies, and hostile Lipans; Black Seminole Scouts supplied important scouting work. Mackenzie took Indian captives back to the United States to force the rest of the Indians to move from Mexico to the Indian Territory. Eventually, 250 Kickapoos and all the Potawatomies agreed to return to the United States. Communities of Kickapoos and Lipans, however, remained in Coahuila and live there today; some Kickapoos received a reservation in Texas in the 1980s.

The last large military campaigns, and the Comanches' last sustained effort to continue their old way of life without government dependency, occurred in 1874. In the early summer, a medicine man named Isa-tai had a vision in which he learned that Comanches must resist whites or else be reduced to the dependent state of nearby groups like the Wichitas and Caddos. The performance of a Sun Dance was to be the means by which Comanches would be delivered from white domination. Comanches from all bands attended the dance, a ceremony previously unknown to the Comanches and probably learned from the Kiowas. It took place at the time when women and children were being held prisoner to compel good behavior by Comanche men, and when rations at the reservation were being withheld as punishment. At the gathering, the Comanches determined to take action. Their two main problems were military pressure and the destruction of the buffalo herds. First they considered attacking the Tonkawas at Fort Griffin to make an example of them that might compel the government to renegotiate the conditions under which the Comanches would live, but this idea was rejected in favor of an attack on buffalo hunters. These were a far more important target, given the economic crisis the Comanches found themselves in with the loss of trade opportunities, the loss of customary subsistence, and the specter of dependency on the government. As the Kiowa leader Kicking

Bird explained, "The buffalo was their money[,] their only resource with which to buy what they needed and did not receive from the government. The robes they could prepare and trade. They loved them just as the white man does his money, and just as it made a white man's heart feel to have his money carried away, so it made them feel to see others killing and stealing their buffalo." In June 1874 the Comanche war party, led by Quanah Parker,chose to assault a gathering of buffalo hunters encamped at Adobe Walls, the ruins of an abandoned trading post in the Panhandle. The hunters managed to get behind the walls before the attackers could inflict serious damage and return fire with their new, long-range rifles. The Comanches charged repeatedly but could not breach the walls or withstand the hunters' accurate marksmanship. At the end of the day, the Comanches withdrew, having killed 3 hunters and lost 13 warriors.

This second battle of Adobe Walls slowed only temporarily the ingress of commercial buffalo hunters. After it, events were increasingly determined by the army rather than any initiative on the part of the Comanches. Military pressure on the bands outside the reservation increased during the summer and fall of 1874 and caused greater destruction of the Indians' subsistence base. On the Salt Fork of the Red River cavalrymen burned 500 Comanche lodges, and although only one Indian was killed, the destruction of their supplies compelled many Comanches to turn themselves in at Fort Sill. Colonel Mackenzie led his command into Palo Duro Canyon in late September and destroyed five Comanche villages; although there were few casualties on either side, the cavalry captured 1,400 horses, which Mackenzie ordered shot (after his Indian scouts selected some as prizes). Most Comanches off the reservation surrendered by the onset of winter, and by 1875 the last small bands came in. The Lipans and Tonkawas who assisted the government in the final subjugation of the groups resisting reservation life were themselves moved out of the state and put on reservations in the early 1880s.

Texas had been a cultural crossroads where varied groups of Indians met, traded, and fought long before the arrival of Europeans. Spanish settlement and French trade greatly altered the trade networks, alliances, and demography of the area. Some native groups lost their distinct cultural identity through population loss and intermarriage with other groups; others thrived, taking advantage of new opportunities to strengthen their positions in regional diplomacy and trade. The Spanish, though influential, were unable to dominate the Indians of Texas or dictate to them. Spanish immigration to Texas was slight, and politically the province was a marginal, neglected backwater of the empire. The Indians' ability to secure goods, especially guns, from French and later United States sources—and thus play European and American powers off against one another—strengthened their relative independence until the early years of the nineteenth century. The Anglo-American migration into Texas changed trade and diplomacy, to the Indians' detriment. Texas filled up with immigrants who threatened tribal hunting prerogatives and land bases. Attempts to keep the settlers in check, such as stock raids and murder, not only failed to stop the spread of white settlement but angered the newcomers into effective retaliatory strikes. As a result, the Indians were destroyed or chased out of the state.

Today in Texas there are only three reservations, populated, ironically, by Indians who migrated to Texas after European colonization. Though many older historical narratives of Texas portray the Indians as enemies and obstacles, the reality was far more complicated than the civilization-versus-savagery schema so frequently employed in the past. In 1995 the Alabama–Coushatta reservation in East Texas near Livingston, the Tigua Reservation in El Paso, and a projected 125-acre Kickapoo reservation near Eagle Pass were all that remained of any organized Indian settlement in Texas.   *George Klos*

In re Ricardo Rodríguez. A civil-rights case that legally affirmed the right of Mexican Americans to become citizens and vote. Rodríguez, who had resided in San Antonio for 10 years, came before the federal district court of Judge Thomas S. Maxey in May 1896 to request final approval of his application for United States citizenship, which would naturally confer on him the right to vote. Maxey ruled in Rodríguez's favor on 3 May 1897. Rodríguez's request for citizenship focused attention on the fact that most Tejanos were born in Mexico and could not vote unless they had applied for naturalization. Opposition to Rodríguez had centered on his legally indeterminate racial status—he was not "a white person, nor an African, nor of African descent, and is therefore not capable of becoming an American citizen." An 1872 federal statute specified that only Caucasians and Africans could become citizens, but at the same time did not specifically deny Mexicans that right. Despite Rodríguez's acknowledged ignorance of United States government, Maxey stated that since 1836 both "the Republic of Texas and the United States had by various collective acts of naturalization conferred upon Mexicans the rights and privileges of American citizenship." He declared that the Fourteenth Amendment granted citizenship to all people born or naturalized in the United States, regardless of color or race.   *Teresa Palomo Acosta*

Institute of Nautical Archeology. Headquarters near College Station as of 1976; incorporated in 1973 as the American Institute of Nautical Archaeology in Philadelphia. It was founded as a nonprofit organization to gather and disseminate knowledge of man's past from the physical remains of his maritime activities. Funding has come from a number of sources, including the National Geographic Society, the National Endowment for the Humanities, and 20 supporting universities, museums, and archeological organizations. All artifacts recovered belong to the nations in whose waters they are found. Among other regions the institute has interested itself in the eastern Mediterranean, the American War of Independence, and the water off Mombasa, Kenya. An affiliation with Texas A&M University in the summer of 1976 gave the institute a permanent base and enabled Texas A&M to offers M.A. and then a Ph.D. in anthropology with a nautical archeology specialization. In 1978 the institute shortened its name to the Institute of Nautical Archaeology. Field projects by that time encompassed both the New and Old worlds, and institute staff frequently served as consultants to foreign governments. The Institute of Nautical Archaeology owns extensive equipment in Turkey and Jamaica, including a 65-foot steel vessel, *Virazon*, with a double-lock recompression chamber, a darkroom, and compressors and diving equipment; the institute also owns a complete conservation laboratory and camping equipment for 50 people. Its research continues year-round in the Museum of Underwater Archaeology in Bodrum, Turkey (founded 1960). In the late 1970s institute work in Turkey concentrated on the excavation of the "Glass Wreck." Its cargo is one of the finest collections of medieval Islamic glass ever found, and its hull marks the transition in shipbuilding technology from "shell-first" to "frame-first" construction. In the early 1990s the ship and its exquisite cargo were on display in a spectacular exhibit in Bodrum. Since 1984 institute field work in Turkey has focused on the oldest shipwreck known, the 3,400-year-old Bronze Age ship off Ulu Burun. The finds from this ship, including the world's oldest book, are revolutionizing concepts about the Bronze Age in the Eastern Mediterranean. In the New World, work beginning in 1981 at the sunken city of Port Royal, Jamaica, has revealed much about colonial life in the seventeenth century. Texas A&M University Press publishes an INA Monograph series. In the early 1990s reports on INA projects were published in a variety of places, including the quarterly *INA Newsletter* for members and the *International Journal of Nautical Archaeology*.

George F. Bass

International Boundary and Water Commission. Succeeded three earlier international commissions designed to establish the boundary between the United States and Mexico. The first, established in accordance with the Treaty of Guadalupe Hidalgo, surveyed the California–Baja California boundary and then skipped across the desert to establish the New Mexico–Chihuahua boundary. After beginning the survey of the section of the boundary near El Paso, the commission soon encountered difficulty in interpreting the treaty, which was solved only when abolished by the Gadsden Purchase treaty. A second boundary commission reported, informally, the completion of the entire survey in 1855, and produced William H. Emory's elaborate report. In time many of the markers placed by the Emory commission became obliterated, and in order to reestablish the line and settle some disputed territory, a third commission was established through a series of treaties in 1882, 1885, 1889, and 1894, and submitted a report on the relocation of markers in 1896. The functions of the commission were defined and extended through various treaties in 1905, 1933, and 1945. The Water Treaty of 1944 transformed the commission into the International Boundary and Water Commission. Over the years, the commission was charged with the elimination of cut-offs, or *bancos*, flood control, and river-rectification problems. Its biggest achievement was in the peaceful settlement of the Chamizal Dispute (1963). In addition to settling boundary disputes, the present commission was charged with the planning, construction, and operation of three international dams, as well as additional hydroelectric-power and flood-control projects to benefit both countries. To date, two reservoirs, International Falcon and Amistad, have been completed. In addition to the functions outlined by treaties dealing with the water boundary, the permanent commission took on the functions of the previous land commissions. Because of its permanence and unusual character and function, the commission occupies a unique place in international arbitration.

Ireland, John. Governor; b. near Millerstown, Kentucky, 21 January 1827; d. Seguin, 15 March 1896; m. Mrs. Matilda Wicks Faircloth (1854; d. 1856); m. Anna Maria Penn (1857); 3 children, + an adopted grandchild. Ireland was a law officer in Kentucky, became a lawyer in 1852, and moved in 1853 to Seguin, where he served as mayor. At the Secession Convention (1861) he voted for secession. After service in the Civil War he was a member of the Constitutional Convention of 1866 and a district judge (1866–67). Philip H. Sheridan removed him from office. Ireland was elected to the state House, then the state Senate, where he opposed subsidies to railroads. After service on the Texas Supreme Court (1875–76), he ran unsuccessfully for the United States Senate (1876) and House (1878). He was twice elected governor (1882, 1884). During his terms occurred the fence-cutting war (1883) and strikes by the Knights of Labor (1885, 1886); the University of Texas was established; and the cornerstone for the Capitol was laid. Ireland subsequently lost a U.S. Senate bid to John H. Reagan (1887). He practiced law in Seguin after retirement.

Claude Elliott

Irish. Natives of Ireland were among the first settlers in Spanish Texas, and the story of the Irish in Texas is in many ways coincident with the founding of the republic and the development of the state. The heritage of the Irish seems in retrospect to have peculiarly suited their migration to a new land, for the English dominance of Ireland must have been to the new colonists in Texas a close parallel to the oppression they eventually found in the new country. It is not surprising that as many as 25 Irishmen probably signed the Goliad Declaration of Independence, that 4 signed the actual Texas Declaration of Independence, and that 100 were listed in the rolls of San Jacinto—one-seventh of the total Texan force in that battle. Probably the first Irishman in Texas was Hugo Oconór, who became governor *ad interim* of Texas in 1767. Though his national origins are uncertain, Oconór was almost certainly Irish, as his name suggests. His success in reinforcing San Antonio against raiding Apaches was a notable contribution to the further settlement of that region. Philip Nolan, a native of Belfast, was said to be the first Anglo-American to map Texas. James Hewetson and James Power, along with John McMullen and James McGloin, were the first Irishmen to receive empresario contracts from Mexico. They successfully settled the areas now comprising Refugio and San Patricio counties. Hewetson accompanied Stephen F. Austin to Texas on his first trip in 1821, and many Irishmen were counted in Austin's Old Three Hundred. Martín De León's colony at Victoria also included several Irish families, and it should be noted that all of these contracts, except that to McMullen and McGloin, called for the settlement of Mexican as well as Irish families, specifically Catholics. Some writers have maintained that the southern grants were made only to the Irish to form a buffer zone of devout Catholics between Mexico and the northern Anglo settlements, but it now seems clear that the McMullen–McGloin colony was adjacent to the Power and Hewetson colony only by sheer coincidence. During the days of the republic the two colonies were on the frontier that saw the worst possible hardships for settlers. In the Texas Revolution such Irishmen as Francis Moore, Jr., John Joseph Linn, Thomas William Ward, and the four empresarios named above all played important roles. James Power used his influence to seat Sam Houston at the Convention of 1836. Eleven Irishmen died at the battle of the Alamo, and 14 were among those with Fannin at the Goliad Massacre. Appropriately, Refugio and San Patricio counties were among the first established in Texas after the revolution; the date was 17 March 1836, Saint Patrick's Day.

The 1850 census listed 1,403 Irish in Texas; 10 years later the number was 3,480. Notable Irish-born Texans in the nineteenth century included William Kennedy, whose book *The Rise, Progress and Prospects of Texas* (1841) encouraged immigration to the new republic; Richard W. Dowling, whose company of all-Irish Confederates repulsed the Union fleet at Sabine Pass; Peter Gallagher, a Texas Ranger and later an organizer of Pecos County; Samuel McKinney, an early president of Austin College; and John William Mallet, first chairman of the University of Texas faculty. Irish colonists in Texas endured the same problems in education, farming, and economic hardship as did other settlers, though perhaps with better success, considering their proximity to hostile forces. The descendants of generations who had long fought and died for their civic and religious liberties, the Irish were quicker than most to recognize incursions upon their rights and to defend against them. In 1980, 572,732 Texans described themselves as of Irish descent. The Irish were third among those claiming European ancestry, following the English and the Germans.

Phillip L. Fry

Irving, Texas. Twelve miles west of Dallas in west central Dallas County. It began as a settlement called Gorbit (Gorbett, Torbit) and had a post office under that name from 1889 to 1894. In 1894 the name of the settlement and post office was changed to Kit, and the location was shifted to anticipate the route of a railroad. The line did not follow the original survey, and in 1902 Julius Otto Schulze and Otis Brown promoted a third townsite, called Irving, possibly after Washington Irving, Mrs. Brown's favorite author. The post office was moved to Irving in 1904. By 1912 the town had a population of 500, a bank, a newspaper, and 20 businesses. Irving was incorporated in 1914. In 1925 the population was only 357, but by the 1930s a steady increase began. The number of residents more than doubled between 1925 and 1945; businesses exceeded 200. In the 1940s Irving became the center of a consolidated school district. In 1963 the city had a population of 45,000, 730 businesses, 70 churches, 16 public schools, 3 banks, and 2 hospitals. Manufacturing plants produced paint, cement blocks, aluminum products, millwork, roofing, chemical supplies, petroleum, and electronic components. In 1964 the world's largest trucking terminal was built in Irving. By the end of the 1970s the population was well over 100,000, and the number of businesses close to 2,000. The University of Dallas in Irving was founded in 1956, and the North Lake campus of Dallas Community College opened in 1977. Mayor Robert Power brought the Dallas Cowboys to Irving and built Texas Stadium, which is municipally owned. It was financed by revenue bonds and completed in 1971. Irving is also the home of the Las Colinas Urban Center, a totally planned, privately funded, 7,000-acre commercial development that houses a number of regional and national businesses, as well as the headquarters of the Boy Scouts of America and the Irving Film Commission. In 1990 Irving had a population of 155,037 and 3,004 rated business.

June Rayfield Welch

Isa-tai. Quahadi Comanche warrior and medicine man; details of birth and death unknown. His name means "Coyote Anus." He gained prominence as a prophet and "messiah" in 1873–74, when he temporarily succeeded in uniting the autonomous Comanche bands as no leader had ever done before. He also organized what was said to be the first Comanche sun dance, a Plains Indian ritual that his tribe had not previously adopted. Isa-tai claimed to

have ascended above the clouds, where he had conversed with the Great Spirit and been granted the ability to cure the sick, raise the dead, control the weather and other natural phenomena, and make the white man's bullets fall harmlessly to the ground. He claimed to have belched up a wagonload of cartridges and then swallowed them. He also correctly predicted the disappearance of a comet in 1873 and a drought later that year, prognostications that supported his vatic claims. At the sun dance in May 1874 he preached a war of extermination and promised the warriors that they would be invincible against their enemies. After discarding a plan to annihilate the Tonkawas, who were believed to be cannibals and who had long served as scouts for the whites, the Comanches decided to attack the hunters in the Panhandle, who were destroying the buffalo at a frightening rate. On 27 June, with Kiowas and Cheyennes, they attacked the buffalo hunters' headquarters, Adobe Walls, on the South Canadian River. During the battle, led primarily by Quanah Parker, Isa-tai remained on a distant hill, apparently unwilling to trust his own medicine. The whites fought off the Indians and finally compelled them to withdraw. About fifteen warriors were killed and a larger number wounded. Isa-tai tried to absolve himself by saying that his magic had been weakened before the battle when one of the Cheyennes violated a sacred taboo by killing a skunk. Several Cheyennes responded by beating him, and with that he was totally discredited and publicly humiliated. Although not a major historic engagement, this second battle of Adobe Walls was a crushing spiritual defeat for the Southern Plains Indians, who had come to believe fully in the supernatural powers of the medicine man. The event marked the beginning of their steep decline as military powers. Isa-tai was eventually forgiven but remembered only as a comical figure. He was still alive in the 1890s.

Gaines Kincaid

Italians. The few Italians who entered Texas during the seventeenth, eighteenth, and early nineteenth centuries were mainly explorers, adventurers, or missionaries. Between 1880 and 1920, however, the immigration to Texas increased from a trickle to a flood as Italians journeyed to the state to escape the deplorable social and economic conditions in their native land. In 1870 there were 186 Italians resident in Texas. By 1920 their numbers had swelled to 8,024. The immigration was part of a movement of Italians to the wider region; many others also settled in and around New Orleans, and the Gulf Coast formed one of the principal centers for Italian immigrants. The immigrants' primary goal was to provide a higher standard of living for themselves and their families. Sicilians settled in the lower Brazos valley and on the Galveston County mainland, while Piedmontese established homes in Montague County. Meanwhile, Modenese, Venetians, and Piedmontese worked the rich coal mines at Thurber, and Lombards helped to construct the New York, Texas and Mexican Railway, the "Macaroni Line," between Victoria and Rosenberg. Eventually, Italian settlements developed in Houston, Galveston, and San Antonio.

A few men provided the initial direction or focus of the immigration, and other pioneers acted upon their advice. Later, railroad and steamship advertisements and notices published in the Italian-language press supplemented letters and word-of-mouth information. Italian Texans learned to grow cotton and corn on Texas soil, to speak English, and to adapt to their new environment. They purchased land, opened businesses, and acquired a degree of geographic mobility. Virtually all were farmers, miners, or unskilled laborers. A majority of the earliest migrants were males between the ages of 14 and 44. The largest concentration was located in the Brazos valley. The initial Sicilian settlements expanded along the river, and then fanned into the surrounding communities.

Most of the Italians living in Thurber and in Victoria County returned to Italy or moved to other places in America when their services were no longer needed in the coal mines or in railroad construction. The pillars supporting the Italian communities that remained in Texas were the immigrant Catholic Church, the Italian-language press, and the benevolent–fraternal organiza-

tions. Each of these institutions had its origins in Europe. Yet each was formed and then constantly changed in Texas. Italian settlers mined coal, worked to construct railroad networks, opened small businesses in urban areas, and contributed to the agricultural development of the state. Among them were gifted artists—sculptor Pompeo Coppini, for instance. Parks, airports, streets, and communities bear the names of prominent Italian immigrants, among them Bruni Park in Laredo, named for Antonio Mateo Bruni; Varisco Airport in Bryan, named for Biagio Varisco; Liggio Street in Dickinson and Laneri Street in Dallas; and Varisco and Bruni, Texas. In the late twentieth century around 200,000 residents of Texas claimed Italian descent.

Valentine J. Belfiglio

J

J. J. Pickle Research Campus. A campus of the University of Texas at Austin, formerly the Balcones Research Center; in northwest Austin. As an industrial research park, the campus has been instrumental in the development of such Central Texas firms as Texas Nuclear, Tracor, and Radian Corporation. It provides a center for civil, electronic, aerospace, mechanical, petroleum, and environmental-health engineering research, along with scientific research in botany, zoology, paleontology, nuclear physics, chemistry, psychology, atmospheric science, and archeology. Over the course of its history, it has been home to as many as 70 laboratories, a training site for scientists and engineers, and a place where chemists, physicists, and engineers are encouraged to conduct interdisciplinary research. The current facility developed from a magnesium plant built by the federal government during World War II and operated by International Minerals and Chemical Corporation. After the war the government declared the plant surplus. In 1945 electrical engineering professor C. Read Granberry and civil engineering professor J. Neils Thompson, acting together on behalf of UT, obtained a lease agreement with an option to purchase the plant from the War Assets Administration. The resulting agreement, completed in 1946, committed the university to use of the original 402 acres and 29 buildings, representing a total of 216,000 square feet of space. The first component of the facility emerged from a National Defense Research Committee laboratory originally known as the War Research Laboratory or War Physics Laboratory, established at UT in 1942. Its original purpose was to develop the means for testing aiming devices in airborne flexible gunnery systems and to improve aircraft gunsights for the B-29 bomber. Out of this project grew the Military Physics Research Laboratory, which was moved to the Balcones Research Center in 1946. In 1949 the university negotiated a contract with the help of Congressman Lyndon Johnson to purchase the property over time. Initially designated the Off-Campus Research Center, the property was renamed Balcones Research Center in 1953 by Judge James P. Hart, first chancellor of the university. In 1964 the Military Physics Research Laboratory merged with the Defense Research Laboratory, which had been developed on campus to work on radar, underwater acoustics, and surface-to-air guided missiles for the navy, and in 1968 the two were retitled the Applied Research Laboratories. With over 500 employees, this facility represented the largest activity at the center. Other early components included the Electrical Engineering Research Laboratory, which investigated the angle of arrival of radio waves for the national Office of Scientific Research and Development during wartime, and the Nuclear Physics Research Laboratory, designed to study atomic structure and properties of matter, which later operated an atom smasher at the site. The Radiobiological Laboratory, a forerunner of the Air Force School of Aerospace Medicine, evaluated the performance of animals under conditions of space flight. It is best remembered for raising and training a Rhesus monkey which, as the first animal in space in 1959, contributed to the study of long-term effects of exposure to radiation in space.

In 1971 the university obtained clear title to the property. The regents subsequently purchased an additional 83 acres adjacent to the west tract in 1974, and additional acreage that brought the total to 475 acres. The campus subsequently developed unique features for research and development, including a power supply exceeding that of the entire campus of the University of Texas in a single building. At various times the campus has employed up to 1,000 people, comprised 100 buildings, and housed everything from energy research laboratories and earth sciences, water resources, structural research, and archeological research projects to art studios. The institution has worked on technology-transfer projects with a wide range of corporate and public interests, including Motorola, Texas Instruments, Sandia National Laboratories, and Sematech. Later planning included buildings to house the Bureau of Economic Geology and centers for energy studies, electromechanics, and fusion engineering. In the 1990s the campus housed the research facilities of Microelectronics and Computer Technology Corporation, a collaborative research effort of 20 computer and electronics firms involved in development of materials for semiconductors and optoelectronic devices. In 1994, in honor of his ongoing efforts on behalf of the facility, the Balcones Research Center was renamed the J. J. Pickle Research Campus. Jake Pickle included support for the center as a plank in his first congressional campaign and later served as chairman of the House Science, Space, and Technology Committee. *Diana J. Kleiner*

Japanese. The Japanese first moved to Texas in significant numbers after a factfinding tour of the Gulf Coast by a consular official, Sadatsuchi Uchida, in 1902. Local officials and businessmen told Uchida that rice farmers from Japan would be especially welcome in Texas. Soon thereafter, various Japanese made at least 30 separate attempts to grow rice in different parts of the state. The two most successful sites were at Webster, near Houston, founded by Seito Saibara in 1903 and in Orange County, established by Kichimatsu Kishi in 1907. By 1910 the Japanese population in Texas numbered 340, in contrast to 13 in 1900. Saibara and Kishi, each of whom had been quite well off in Japan, traveled to Texas to settle. Saibara, a lawyer and a party politician, had been president of Doshisha University in Kyoto before immigrating to the United States; Kishi attended Hitotsubashi University in Tokyo. Both brought families and tenants to help work the land; the tenants in time sent for their wives or, if single, arranged for "picture brides" to join them in Texas. As the two settlements prospered they attracted other Japanese, who purchased and operated rice farms nearby. After World War I, however, the rice market collapsed, nearly ruining the Japanese along the Gulf Coast. Some, like Kishi, switched to truck farming; others operated plot nurseries; still others left Texas. Meanwhile, in the second two decades of the twentieth century, another group of Japanese came to Texas. Many were fleeing from the anti-Japanese agitation in California. They too farmed, but they generally settled in Cameron and Hidalgo counties, in the lower Rio Grande valley, and grew citrus fruit and vegetables. In 1914 Japanese geographer Shigetaka Shiga erected a monument at the Alamo in San Antonio and a similar one in Okazaki, Japan, to draw parallels between the battle of the Alamo and similar battles in Japanese and Chinese history.

Though initially welcomed, the Japanese faced increasing hostility both locally and nationally. The American Legion post in Harlingen in 1920 warned Japanese newcomers to stay away from the Valley. The Texas legislature in 1921 passed an alien land law that prohibited foreignborn Japanese from purchasing or leasing additional farmland. Three years later the Unites States Congress banned Japanese immigrants and barred foreign-born Japanese from acquiring American citizenship. Finally, when the United States went to war with Japan in 1941, there were widespread doubts about the loyalty of the Japanese Americans. Many Japanese men in Texas were rounded up by federal authorities for interrogation, though the detention of Japanese in Texas was brief and not universal. In San Antonio the Jingu family, who for two decades had been entrusted by the city with the care of the Japanese Tea Garden, were forcibly evicted, and the site was renamed Chinese Tea Garden. Suspicions of the Japanese Americans, however, proved unwarranted. Many Japanese men joined the armed forces, and some served in Europe with the famous all-*Nisei* 442nd Regimental Combat Team.

A large new group of Japanese arrived in Texas during the war, but their stay was brief. Of the 5,000 to 6,000 aliens sent to the three federal internment camps set up in Texas, a majority were Japanese, some from the West Coast of the United States and others from Central and South America (*see* World War II Internment Camps). Few, however, remained in the state after the war. Among the exceptions was Isamu Taniguchi of California, an internee at Crystal City, who settled as a farmer near Harlingen and later retired to Austin, where he designed and built the Japanese Garden in Zilker Park.

Up to the 1940s the Japanese in Texas were mostly an agricultural population scattered across the state. One-third were living in Harris County, mostly near Houston. Other counties with a sizable number of Japanese in 1940 were Bexar, Cameron, and El Paso, which together accounted for another third of the Japanese population. By this time a second generation of Japanese, known as *nisei*, had been born and reared in Texas; 41 percent of the 458 Japanese in Texas in 1940 were women, and 63 percent had been born in the United States. Both because they were residentially dispersed and because their children had attended American schools, the Japanese were relatively well assimilated into the mainstream of American life. Kichimatsu Kishi's son, for example, played halfback for the Texas A&M in the mid-1920s. Many Japanese families joined local Christian churches. Urban Japanese often operated restaurants.

In 1950 the Japanese in Texas totaled 957; of this number 56 percent were still rural. But after 1950 the Japanese population in Texas changed greatly, both in size and in composition. By 1980 Japanese residents numbered 10,502, a tenfold increase. Even so, they composed less than .1 percent of the state's total population. Some of the increase, particularly in the early 1950s, was a result of an influx of war brides of United States servicemen stationed in Japan during the American occupation and the Korean War; they were so numerous that among the Japanese in the state women have greatly outnumbered men in recent decades. The ban on Japanese naturalization was lifted in 1952. Unlike other Asians, however, Japanese did not immigrate to the United States in significant numbers in the 1950s and 1960s, despite liberalization of immigration laws.

The more recent increase is a result of growing trade with Japan. Many Japanese have been posted temporarily to Texas to represent their home companies. In Houston, where more than 100 branches of Japanese firms are located, representatives of such firms constitute the largest group of Japanese in the city. Most of these temporary Japanese Texans, however, do not interact much with the Americans, including Japanese Americans. Meanwhile, the second and third generation (*sansei*) descendants of the original Japanese settlers in Texas have left farming, entered the professions, and joined the move to the cities. Whereas in 1950 the Japanese in Texas were still predominantly rural, by 1970 they had become overwhelmingly urban; half of them are concentrated in the Houston, Dallas, and San Antonio areas.

Edward J. M. Rhoads

Jarvis Christian College. At Hawkins; originally (1912) known as Jarvis Christian Institute. Since its founding, JCC has been affiliated with the Disciples of Christ. By 1988 it was the only historically black college that remained of the 12 such black colleges originally founded by the church. The school is modeled after the Southern Christian Institute in Edwards, Mississippi. In 1904 the Negro Disciples of Christ in Texas and the Christian Woman's Board of Missions began collaborating to raise money. At around the same time, Virginia Hearne, state secretary for women's work, contacted Ida Van Zandt Jarvis, who with her husband, Maj. James Jones Jarvis, deeded 456 acres to the Christian Woman's Board of Missions for the school (1910). In 1912 construction began. The first classes were held in January 1913 with 12 elementary-level students. James Nelson Ervin of Johnson City, Tennessee, became the school's first president in 1914. That year the school began officially teaching high school courses; until 1937 it was the only accredited high school exclusively for blacks in the area. The school began regularly offering junior college courses in 1927 and was incorporated as a college the next year. Senior college courses were offered beginning in 1937. In 1938 high school classes were eliminated. In 1939 the college was granted its charter by the state of Texas, and in 1950 JCC was included by the Southern Association of Colleges and Schools on its "Approved List of Colleges and Universities for Negro Youth," the only regional accreditation available at that time for black colleges in the South. In 1958 an independently elected board of trustees began governing the college, replacing a board that had been appointed by the Department of Institutional Missions of the United Christian Missionary Society. The independent board, however, still included representation from the church. In 1964 the college became affiliated with Texas Christian University, a relationship that was discontinued in 1976. In 1966 Dr. James Oliver Perpener, Jr. became the first Jarvis alumnus to serve as president of JCC. The next year JCC affiliated with the Texas Association of Developing Colleges, a consortium of black colleges, and also gained accreditation from the Southern Association of Colleges and Schools. The Texas Education Agency approved the school's teacher-education program in 1969. The alumni associations of Jarvis Christian College and the Southern Christian Institute merged in 1979. In 1981 the title of the original land donation was transferred to the college from the United Christian Missionary

Society. Oil wells discovered on the property in the early 1940s were still providing some revenue in the early 1980s, when the college owned about 1,000 acres. In the early 1980s the school began systematically compiling an archive of materials related to Jarvis Christian College, Southern Christian Institute, and the Black Christian Church (Disciples of Christ). JCC is now a fully accredited four-year institution. *Rachel Jenkins*

Jaworski, Leon. Lawyer; b. Waco, 19 September 1905; d. near Wimberley, 9 December 1982 (buried in Houston); m. Jeannette Adam (1931); 3 children; ed. Baylor University law school (grad. 1925), George Washington University (LL.M., 1926). Jaworski moved to Houston in 1930 and practiced in the firm of Dyess, Jaworski, and Strong until April 1931, when he joined the firm of Fulbright, Crooker, Freeman, and Bate. He became a partner in 1935 and managing partner in 1948; his name was added to the firm's in 1954. Twenty years later, the firm name was shortened to Fulbright and Jaworski. By the time Jaworski retired in 1981 the firm ranked among the largest in the nation; it maintained offices in Houston, Austin, San Antonio, Dallas, Washington, and London. Jaworski held the presidencies of the American College of Trial Lawyers (1961–62), the State Bar of Texas(1962–63), and the American Bar Association (1971–72). He served in the United States Army judge advocate general's department during World War II and conducted investigations of several hundred cases concerning German crimes against persons living in the American zone of occupation. He also personally tried two cases—the first having to do with the murder of American aviators shot down over Germany in 1944 and the second involving the doctors and staff of a German sanatorium where Polish and Russian prisoners were put to death. He later wrote about his wartime experiences in *After Fifteen Years* (1961).

Jaworski successfully represented Lyndon B. Johnson in the case that allowed Johnson to run for both the Senate and the vice presidency in 1960. After Johnson became president in 1963 he appointed Jaworski to important positions on the President's Commission on the Causes and Prevention of Violence, the International Centre for Settlement of Investment Disputes, and the Permanent International Court of Arbitration. Jaworski's most widely remembered public service occurred in 1973 and 1974 when he headed the Watergate special prosecution force charged with uncovering the facts surrounding the Republican break-in at the national Democratic party headquarters during the presidential campaign of 1972. In July 1974 he argued the case of *United States v. Nixon* before the United States Supreme Court and won a unanimous decision ordering President Richard Nixon to turn over to the district court magnetic audiotapes that implicated him and members of his staff in a conspiracy to obstruct justice. Shortly thereafter, President Nixon resigned from office. Jaworski published his account of the Watergate prosecution as *The Right and the Power* (1976). In 1977 he was called back to Washington to serve as special counsel to the United States House of Representatives Committee on Standards of Official Conduct. In what the press referred to as "Koreagate," he developed cases of misconduct in an influence-buying scandal that resulted in disciplinary action against six members of Congress and two private citizens.

Jaworski became a trustee of the M. D. Anderson Foundation in 1957 and was later on the boards of the Texas Medical Center and the Baylor College of Medicine. He was the president of the

Blind Lemon Jefferson. Prints and Photographs Collection, Lemon Jefferson file, CAH; CN 01028.

Houston Chamber of Commerce in 1960 and a director of the Bank of the Southwest; Anderson, Clayton, and Company; Southwest Bancshares; and Coastal States Gas Producing Corporation. Among his many other activities, Jaworski promoted the building of the Astrodome, belonged to the Philosophical Society of Texas, and received many honorary degrees, including an LL.D. from Baylor in 1960. He coauthored two autobiographical volumes, *Confession and Avoidance: A Memoir* (1979) and *Crossroads* (1981). He was a member of the First Presbyterian Church of Houston.

Newton Gresham and James A. Tinsley

Jefferson, Blind Lemon. Blues musician; b. Coutchman, Texas, July 1897 (?); d. Chicago, December 1929 (buried in Wortham). He was born blind and was known all his life as Blind Lemon Jefferson. He traveled from town to town in the Wortham area, playing his guitar and singing songs, most of which were his own compositions. He later moved to the Dallas–Fort Worth area and became a well-known figure in the Deep Ellum district. There he met Huddie Ledbetter (better known as "Leadbelly"), and for a time they played together in brothels. Jefferson was discovered by a talent scout for Paramount Records while in Dallas and was taken to Chicago. He made 79 records for Paramount in the 1920s, each estimated to have sold 100,000 copies; he also made two recordings under the "Okeh" label. He recorded spirituals under the pseudonym Deacon L. J. Bates. Jefferson is recognized as one of the earliest representatives of the "classic blues" field, considered to be one of the best folk blues singers of the 1920s, and said to have influenced such artists as Louis Armstrong, Bessie Smith, and Bix Beiderbecke, and to have encouraged "Lightnin'" Hopkins. Jefferson was inducted into the Blues Foundation's Hall of Fame in 1980.

Marilynn Wood Hill

Jefferson, Texas. County seat of Marion County, on Big Cypress Creek and Caddo Lake. It was named for Thomas Jefferson when it was founded in the early 1840s by Allen Urquhart and Daniel Alley. In the late 1830s Urquhart, who immigrated to Texas from North Carolina, received a headright on a bend in the creek; he laid out a townsite there around 1842. At about the same time Alley obtained a 586-acre parcel adjacent to Urquhart's survey and laid out additional streets that became known as Alley's Addition. As the westernmost outpost for navigation on the Red River, Jefferson quickly developed into an important riverport. The first steamboat, the *Llama*, reached Jefferson in late 1843 or early 1844. A post office was established in 1846, and the town was incorporated in March 1848, though because of various delays a city charter was not adopted until 1850. In the same year the town adopted the aldermanic form of city government. Jefferson became the county seat of Cass County in 1846 and served as such until Linden became county seat in 1852. The first newspaper, the Jefferson *Democrat*, was printed in 1847, and the following year the *Jimplecute*, the town's longest-running and most influential paper, made its appearance. During the late 1840s efforts were made to clear Big Cypress Creek for river navigation. Within a few years steamboats were regularly making the trip from Shreveport and New Orleans, transporting cotton and other produce downstream and returning with supplies and manufactured goods, including materials and furnishings for many of the early homes. By the late 1840s Jefferson had emerged as the leading commercial and distribution center of Northeast Texas and the state's leading inland port. In 1860 Jefferson became county seat of the newly established Marion County. Jefferson men volunteered for military service in large numbers, and during the Civil War a meat cannery was established in town, as were factories for boots and shoes. After the war the town's economy recovered quickly. A fire destroyed practically the entire business section in 1866, but it was rebuilt within a few years. In 1867 Jefferson became the first town in Texas to use gas for lighting, and ice was first manufactured on a commercial scale there in 1868. By 1870 Jefferson, with a population of 4,180, was the sixth largest city in Texas; in the late 1860s it was shipping more than 75,000 bales of cotton annually. By 1870 only Galveston surpassed Jefferson in volume of commerce. The town reached its peak in 1872, when a supplementary census reported 7,297 inhabitants.

But in 1873 two events occurred that eventually spelled the end of Jefferson's importance. The first was destruction of the Red River Raft, a natural dam of logs and debris on the river above Shreveport. In November nitroglycerin charges were used to remove the last portion of the raft, which had previously made the upper section of the river unnavigable. The demolition reopened the main course of the river, but significantly lowered the water level of the surrounding lakes and streams, making the trip to Jefferson difficult, particularly in times of drought. Even more important to Jefferson's decline was the completion of the Texas and Pacific Railway from Texarkana to Marshall, which

bypassed Jefferson. Although another line of the T&P reached Jefferson the following year, the development of rail commerce and the rise of Marshall, Dallas, and other important rail cities brought an end to Jefferson's golden age as a commercial and shipping center. By 1885 the population had fallen to some 3,500. During the late 1870s the town's attention was briefly diverted from its economic woes by the sensational Diamond Bessie murder trial. Jefferson's economy rebounded briefly in the late 1930s after the discovery of oil in the county. In 1940 it reported some 3,800 residents and 150 businesses. Subsequently the town slowly declined—to 3,203 in 1970 and 2,199 in 1990. In 1971 a 47-block area containing 56 historic structures was listed in the National Register of Historic Places. In addition, some 10 other buildings have been accorded National Register status, including the antebellum Excelsior Hotel and Planters Bank and Warehouse. Every year Jefferson sponsors a three-day spring historic pilgrimage to view these sites. Since 1955 the festivities have also included a reenactment of the Diamond Bessie trial. *Christopher Long*

Jeffersonian Democrats. A group of Democrats opposed to the New Deal. Although in 1936 relief from the Great Depression was being widely attributed to the Roosevelt administration, some business and professional groups were discontent. During the presidential campaign, the Jeffersonian Democrats attempted to capitalize on this unrest. They constituted the first serious, organized effort among disenchanted Democrats and Republicans to oppose the New Deal. In August 1936 W. P. Hamblen, a lawyer from Houston, issued a call for a statewide meeting in Dallas of people who were disillusioned with the New Deal. Twenty-eight attended the gathering at the Hotel Adolphus, where, under the sponsorship of Hamblen, John Henry Kirby, and former congressman Joseph W. Bailey, Jr., the organization known as Constitutional Democrats of Texas was founded. Within a few days Kirby, Bailey, and J. Evetts Haley, chairman of the new group, attended a meeting in Detroit, where a national organization known as the Jeffersonian Democrats was formed. The national chairman was Senator James A. Reed of Missouri, and the national secretary was Sterling Edmunds, an attorney from St. Louis. The Texans, whose quandary was similar to that of disaffected Democrats elsewhere, played a prominent part in starting the national organization. Since the election was only three months away, a third party movement was out of the question, but the Jeffersonians from the South feared to support Republican Alf Landon because that would make it difficult to support local Democratic candidates. The meeting finally agreed that the methods for opposing Roosevelt would be left entirely to the states. As a result of the Detroit meeting, the Constitutional Democrats of Texas changed their name to that of the national movement. By the end of August they opened state headquarters in Austin. The stated objective of the Jeffersonians was to turn the Democratic party back to the people. The Texas membership was composed largely of lawyers, followed by businessmen, farmers, and ranchers. Their theme was that the New Deal was un-American and a threat to the institutions that Texans cherished and respected. In all, there were probably not more than 5,000 members. The Jeffersonians' main publicity vehicle was a paper, the *Jeffersonian Democrat*, which was aimed primarily at farmers. The Jeffersonian Democrats attempted to identify the Roosevelt administration with communism and made extreme charges against the president and his family. They also used religion, white supremacy, and prohibitionism in their appeals. They expected to deflect at least a third of the Texas votes from Roosevelt, but their opposition turned out to be ineffective. Nevertheless, many Jeffersonians belonged to organizations that opposed the New Deal in later campaigns.

Lionel V. Patenaude

Jester, Beauford Halbert. Governor; b. Corsicana, 12 January 1893; d. en route to Galveston, 11 July 1949; m. Mabel Buchanan (1921); 3 children; ed. Harvard and University of Texas (LL.B., 1920). Jester, son of a lieutenant governor of Texas, had an impressive law career and a stint on the UT board of regents (1929–35; chairman, 1933–35), as well as a period of service on the Railroad Commission, before becoming governor in 1947. As a regent he supported a major building program at UT. During his two terms as governor the legislature passed laws relating to prison improvement, educational reform, and the building of rural roads and state parks. Jester supported an antilynching law and repeal of the poll tax, as well as the foundation of a major university for blacks. His labor legislation, including a 1947 right-to-work law that abolished the union shop, gave him an anti-union reputation. Jester was the first Texas governor to die in office.

Tommy W. Stringer

Jews. Jews have been a part of the warp and woof of the Lone Star State since the period of Spanish Texas. To the untamed future state came Jewish seekers of fortune and freedom. Heirs to the Spanish and European forms of Jewish ritual practice, the Jews of Texas adapted their seminal faith to the new ambience without damaging the integrity of a 5,000-year-old tradition. Though some abandoned their roots, most were tenacious in the nurturing of their heritage. Before 1821, Jews who openly practiced their religion could not legally live in Texas, a Spanish colony where only Catholics could take up residence. Samuel Isaackshad settled on the Brazos River by December 1821, however, Adolphus Sternemoved to East Texas in 1826, and by 1838 Jews were living in Velasco, Bolivar, Nacogdoches, Goliad, San Antonio, and Galveston. Their settlement pattern was repeated numerous times: first the formation of a cemetery–benevolent society, followed by a synagogue, formal or informal. Jewish cemeteries were established in Galveston in 1852, Houston in 1854, San Antonio in 1856, Victoria in 1858 and Jefferson in 1862. The first chartered Jewish congregation in Texas was Congregation Beth Israel, Houston,founded in 1859. It began as an Orthodox synagogue, but became a Reform congregation some 15 years later. The oldest Reform congregation, Temple B'nai Israel, Galveston,was established in 1868. By the turn of the century, numerous congregations had been organized: Hebrew Sinai Congregation of Jefferson in 1873, Beth El of San Antonio in 1874, Temple Emanu-El of Dallas in 1875, Beth Israel of Austin in 1876, Rodef Shalom of Waco in 1879, United Hebrew Congregation of Gainesville in 1881, Shearith Israel of Dallas in 1884, B'nai Abraham of Brenham in 1885, Beth El of Tyler in 1887, Temple Moses Montefiore Adath Israel of Marshall in 1887, Tiferet Israel of Dallas in 1890, Mount Sinai Congregation of Texarkana in 1890, Ahavath Sholom of Fort Worth in 1892, and Beth El of Corsicana in 1898. Beth El of Fort Worth followed in 1902 and Ahavath Achim of Tyler in 1903.

In addition to cemeteries and synagogues, beginning in the 1870s various Jewish communities organized benevolent associations such as chapters of the International Order of B'nai B'rith, aid societies with predominantly female members, literary societies, community lecture series, Sunday schools, and afternoon schools. M. N. Nathan of New Orleans possibly became the first rabbi to officiate in Texas when Rosanna D. Osterman brought him to dedicate the Galveston Jewish Cemetery in 1852. In 1860 the first resident rabbi, Zachariah Emmich, began service at Beth Israel in Houston. Of all the rabbis to serve in Texas, Henry Cohen of Galveston's B'nai Israel left the most well-known legacy; his service began in 1888 and lasted 62 years. In the late 1800s, Rabbi Cohen's first colleagues included Aaron Suhler (Dallas, Emanu El, 1875), Nehemiah Mosessohn (Dallas, Sherith Israel, 1893), Moses Sadovsky (San Antonio, Agudas Achim, 1889), Tobias Schanfarber (Austin, Beth Israel, 1884), Abraham Levy (Waco, Rodef Shalom, 1887), Heinrich Schwarz (Hempstead, 1875), and Hyman Saft (Marshall, 1887).

The earliest Jews, who arrived with the conquistadors, came from Sephardic (Spanish–North African–Israel) communities. After the Mexican period, Jewry in Texas essentially comprised immigrants from Germany, eastern Europe, and the Americas. The same broadsides that attracted their non-Jewish fellow immigrants from other countries and from other states attracted the Jews. Texas was a land of promise with seemingly limitless potential. For many Jews, Texas and the United States also offered more religious freedom than Europe. The movement of Jewish settlers followed the standard patterns of movement throughout the state. Trade routes, railroad lines, new towns, established communities, and relatives who had already arrived drew Jewish settlers to diverse areas of Texas. As a result, the Jewish population remained heterogeneous, geographically scattered and stronger for it.

No aspect of nineteenth-century Texas history is without the involvement of committed Jewish Texans. Adolphus Sterne of Nacogdoches served as alcalde,treasurer, and postmaster in 1826, Albert Moses Levy was surgeon in chief in the revolutionary armyin 1835, Jacob and Phineas De Cordova sold land and developed Waco, Simon Mussina founded Brownsville in 1848, Henri Castro founded several towns, Michael Seeligson was elected mayor of Galveston in 1853, Rosanna Osterman funded significant religious and charitable activities through her will, Sid Samuels and Belle Doppelmayer were in the first graduating class at the University of Texas in 1881, Olga B. Kohlberg started the first private kindergarten in Texas in 1892, and Morris Lasker was elected to the state Senate in 1895. Jews also established themselves in Beaumont, Brenham, Corsicana, Gainesville, Hempstead, Marshall, Palestine, Texarkana, Tyler, Port Arthur, Wichita Falls, Baytown, Corpus Christi, Brownsville, New Braunfels, McAllen, Alice, Amarillo, Columbus, Wharton, Giddings, Navasota, Crockett, Lubbock, Longview, Jefferson, San Angelo, and Schulenburg.

With the turn of the century the Jewish population began to increase more rapidly in response to new outbreaks of anti-Semitism in Russia and the significant movement of Eastern European Jewry to the United States. Leo N. Levi framed the famous Kishinev petition, cabled by President Theodore Roosevelt to the Russian czar to protest massacres of Jews. Between 1900 and 1920 estimates of the Jewish population of Texas grew from 15,000 to 30,000. In particular the major cities, Houston, Dallas, Fort Worth, and San Antonio, saw mushrooming populations of Jews. This growth resulted in a concomitant increase in the membership of religious, educational, and social-service organizations, as well as the building of synagogues. The *Jewish Herald Voice* began publication in Houston in 1906, and was eventually followed by the *Jewish Journal* and *Jewish Record* of San Antonio and the *Texas Jewish Post* of Dallas–Fort Worth. Many new immigrants came through the port of Galveston. From 1907 to 1914, the Galveston Movement, locally spearheaded by Rabbi Henry Cohen, settled some 10,000 Jewish immigrants. Though the plan called for them to settle in the middle states of the country, most remained in the Southwest.

A number of the great Jewish mercantile establishments date from the early years of the twentieth century. Many of the Jewish immigrants who settled in the state began as backpack peddlers of goods they acquired by selling their possessions at the port of entry. If the community to which such a peddler traveled was hospitable, and if the potential for earning a livelihood was optimal, the new immigrant usually set down roots, opened a small store, and established a chain linking him to his supplier at the port of entry. In turn, as relatives arrived, they were sent out as peddlers from the new location to newer areas, where they opened stores. In this way the chains were extended. This entrepreneurial spirit gave rise to small businesses and larger ones that became well known. A small but diverse sampling includes Joseph Weingarten, Schwarz, Proler, Weiner, Aronoff, Abraham M. Levy, Finger, Farb, Schnitzer, Simon and Tobias Sakowitz, and Axelrod of Houston; Roger's Texas State Optical and Edwin Gale of Beaumont; Zale Jewelry Corporation, Neiman–Marcus, the Lorch Company, Bernard Gold, Pearle, Elsie Frankfort, and Sanger Brothers of Dallas; Schwarts of El Paso; Levines of Lubbock; Bettins and Lacks of Victoria; Kanes of Corpus Christi; Avigael of Laredo; Roosth and Genecov of Tyler; Appel and Brachman of Fort Worth; Michael Riskind of Eagle Pass; Harris and Isaac Kempner, Seinsheimer, and Morris Lasker of Galveston; Smith of Austin; Rapoport and Smith of Waco; Louis Kariel of Marshall; Wolens and Goldens of Corsicana; and Arons, Moskowitzs, and Wilkenfelds of Baytown.

Immigration ended for a time with the 1920s immigration-quota acts. In that decade Texas Jews opposed the rise of the Ku Klux Klan, and in the 1930s they watched with growing concern the growth of anti-Semitism in Germany and elsewhere. Organizations were founded in the national Jewish community before World War II to respond to the needs of persecuted Jews in Europe, and branches of these were established in Texas. Houston established its Jewish Community Council in 1936 under the presidency of Max Nathan and enhanced its Jewish Family Service under Ruth Fred. Dallas was well organized by Jack Kravitz. After the war the Jews of Texas became involved in the resettlement of Holocaust survivors who sought refuge in the United States. Their memory has been carefully preserved by the Dallas Memorial Center for Holocaust Studies. The number of Jews in the state continued to grow after the war, from an estimated 50,000 in 1945 to 71,000 in the mid-1970s and 92,000 in 1988. This population was increasingly concentrated in the larger urban areas of the state, as the small-town Jewish communities faded away. Texas Jews continued to demonstrate significant concern for the welfare of Jews outside the state and around the world. Perhaps the most significant community effort since World War II was support for the establishment of the state of Israel, though not initially with unanimity. The belief of some

Jewish immigrants just landed at Galveston. Courtesy TSL. Galveston grew on the strength of the port; cotton moved outward, and farming supplies and immigrants came in.

Jews elsewhere that such an establishment was unwise was echoed in Texas. Concerns beyond a regional level have led to national service, as exemplified by Helen Smith of Austin, past international president of B'nai B'rith Women, and Dolores Wilkenfeld of Houston, past president of the National Federation of Temple Sisterhoods. In addition to these community activities in the international arena, local and regional efforts have included youth camps such as Echo Hill Ranch, Camp Bonim, Camp Young Judea, and Greene Family Camp. On the college campuses the Jewish presence is found at Hillel foundations, Chabad houses, fraternities such as Tau Delta Phi, Sigma Alpha Mu, Alpha Epsilon Pi, Zeta Beta Tau, and sororities such as Alpha Epsilon Phi, Delta Phi Epsilon and Sigma Delta Tau.

The freedom experienced by Jews in Texas encouraged them to become active in many fields. Among those who served as mayors were Isaac H. Kempner and Adrian Levy, Sr., of Galveston. Some of their more recent counterparts include Barbara Crews and Eddie Schreiber of Galveston, Adlene Harris and Annette Strauss of Dallas, Ruben Edelstein of Brownsville, Abe Lichtenstein of Corpus Christi, Minnie Solomonson of Padre Island, Bayard Friedman of Fort Worth, Jeff Friedman of Austin, and Veta Winick of Dickinson. Other names of prominence include Ambassador Robert Strauss, state senator Babe Schwartz, Billy Goldberg, and Congressman Martin Frost. Hermine Tobolowsky was a leading figure in the campaign for the Texas Equal Rights Amendment in 1972. Jewish federal judges have included Irving Goldberg, Norman Black, and David Hittner; Hattie Heneberg and Ruby Sondock were state justices. The Texas Jewish community has also been home to more eclectic souls, including such military men as Samuel Dreben and Maurice Hirsch, 1930s wrestler Abe Coleman, and country–western singer Kinky (Richard) Friedman, who not only made headlines with his Texas Jew Boys but also wrote a series of mysteries. Prominent Texas Jewish authors and journalists have included Fania F. Kruger, John Rosenfield, Jr., and Rosella H. Werlin. In the later part of the twentieth century the expansion of Texas universities and the development of high-tech industries drew Jewish academics and professionals to Texas from other parts of the country. Outstanding Texas rabbis who have achieved national recognition in the twentieth century

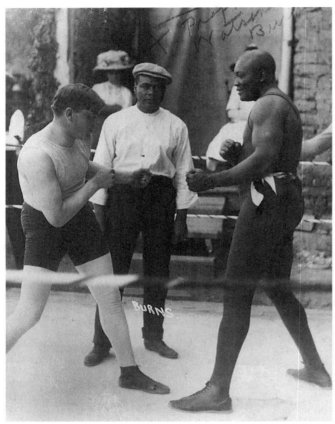

Jack Johnson (on the right). Las Vegas, New Mexico. Courtesy Denver Public Library, Western History Department. Johnson reigned as world heavyweight boxing champion from 26 December 1908 to 5 April 1915.

include Robert Kahn and Samuel Karff of Houston and Levi A. Olan and David Lefkowitz of Dallas, all of whom served as presidents of the Central Conference of American Rabbis, and Hyman J. Schachtel of Houston, who delivered the invocation at the inauguration of President Lyndon Johnson.

The formal preservation of the history of Texas Jewry goes back to Rabbi Henry Cohen of Galveston and Rabbi David Lefkowitz of Dallas, who set out to interview as many early settlers and their families as possible. They produced a historical account for the Texas Centennial in 1936. Rabbi Floyd Fierman of El Paso and Rabbi Harvey Wesel of Tyler collected and recounted much of the history of their area. Through the efforts of Rabbi Jimmy Kessler of Galveston, the Texas Jewish Historical Society came into existence in 1980. The society has established an archive at the Barker Texas History Center in Austin. The entrepreneurial and pioneer spirit that pervaded Texas, a reflection of some of the major teachings of Jewish tradition, has been part of the impetus for the involvement and achievements of Jewish residents. Though Judaism is a religion, it is also clearly a way of life that calls upon its adherents to be actively involved in the community within which they live. Texas is a case in point.

Rabbi James L. Kessler

Johnson, Jack. Boxer; b. Arthur John Johnson, Galveston, 31 March 1878; d. near Raleigh, North Carolina, 10 June 1946; also known as Lil' Arthur; m. Etta Terry Duryea (1911; committed sui-

cide 1912); m. Lucille Cameron (1913; divorced 1924); m. Irene Marie Pineau (1925). Johnson began his fighting career as a sparring partner and participated in so-called battles royal, in which black youths fought each other and white spectators threw money to the winner. He started fighting in private clubs in the Galveston area, and became a professional prizefighter in 1897. The Galveston hurricane of 1900 destroyed his family's home, and the next year he was jailed for boxing—at that time it was illegal in Texas. He subsequently wandered the country fighting. As his career took off he turned to white women, fast cars, and expensive jewels, defying an antagonistic press and public. He was known "for his arrogance, his golden smile, and his white wives." In 1903 he won the Negro heavyweight championship. Jim Jeffries, the reigning white heavyweight champion, refused to fight him. In 1908 Johnson defeated Tommy Burns in Australia, to win the world heavyweight boxing championship; even then he was not officially recognized as the champion. The actual title was bestowed on him in 1910 in Las Vegas, when he defeated Jim Jeffries, who had stepped out of retirement to become the first in a series of recruited "white hopes." Race riots erupted after the match. After his victory, Johnson continued to fight and also appeared in several vaudeville skits. In 1913 he fled a contrived conviction for a violation of the Mann Act, which forbade the transportation of white women interstate for the purpose of prostitution. Facing a year in prison and a $1,000 fine if he remained in the United States, he toured Europe, Mexico, and Canada and hoped for a pardon. He lost his championship to white Jess Willard in Cuba in 1915. In 1920 he returned to the United States and was jailed in Leavenworth Prison, where he was appointed the athletic director of the penitentiary. After his release he returned to boxing, but his professional career was over. By 1928 he was only taking part in exhibition fights. He also gave speeches to sell war bonds during World War II. He died in an automobile crash.

James W. Byrd

Johnson, Lyndon Baines. President of the United States; b. near Stonewall, Texas, 27 August 1908; d. 22 January 1973 (buried on the Johnson Ranch, near Johnson City); m. Claudia Alta "Lady Bird" Taylor (1934); 2 daughters; ed. Southwest Texas State Teachers College (teacher's certificate, 1928; B.A., 1930). Johnson's year of teaching poor Hispanic students in Cotulla (1928–29) had an important effect on his attitude toward poverty and the role of government. In 1931 he became secretary to Congressman Richard M. Kleberg of Texas. During the four years he held the position he gained valuable contacts in Washington. Mrs. Johnson proved to be an effective political partner. Her business acumen was an important element in the success of the radio station that they acquired in Austin in 1943. Johnson's first important political position was as director of the NYA in Texas (1935–37). When the incumbent congressman of the Tenth Congressional District died in 1937, Johnson entered the race as a devoted supporter of Franklin D. Roosevelt and the New Deal. He spent 11 years in the House and became intimately familiar with the legislative process. He was a supporter of Roosevelt's programs and policies and a close ally of Sam Rayburn. He was the chairman of the Democratic Congressional Campaign Committee in 1940 and helped the Democrats retain control of the House. In 1941 he ran for the Senate from Texas but was narrowly defeated in a special election. In World War II Johnson saw combat during an inspection tour of the South

Pacific in 1942. He left the navy when President Roosevelt directed that congressmen should remain in Washington. He made another race for the Senate in 1948 against popular former governor Coke Stevenson. Texas had lost its earlier affection for the New Deal, and Johnson stressed his own conservatism in the election. The runoff primary in August 1948 was very close. Amid charges of ballot-box stuffing and other fraudulent practices, Johnson was declared the Democratic nominee only after extended legal battles. He easily defeated his Republican opponent in the general election. He was an effective senator who mastered the organization and rules of the upper house. His Democratic colleagues elected him majority whip in 1951, and in 1953 he was chosen to be minority leader—the youngest such leader in the history of the Senate. He won a second term in 1954. The Democrats regained control of Congress that same year, and in January 1955 Johnson became majority leader.

In his rush to power, however, he had neglected his health. In 1955 he had a severe heart attack. He returned to his duties in the Senate late that year. He followed a strategy of cooperation with the Republican administration of Dwight Eisenhower. As majority leader, Johnson was instrumental in the passage of the first civil-rights acts for more than 80 years in 1957 and 1960. He also pushed hard for an expanded United States role in space. His presidential ambitions during the 1950s shaped his attitude toward Texas politics during the decade. In 1956 he waged a heated battle against Governor Shivers for control of the Texas delegation to the Democratic national convention, a contest in which Johnson prevailed. The Texas legislature also passed a measure to allow Johnson to run simultaneously for the presidency and reelection to the Senate in 1960. Despite these maneuvers, his bid for the White House in 1960 failed, and he settled for being John F. Kennedy's vice president. Johnson campaigned hard across the South; his ability to put Texas and other Southern states in the Democratic column helped Kennedy gain his narrow victory. Johnson's elevation to the vice presidency left his Senate seat vacant in 1961, and Republican John Tower won a special election to succeed him. During the vice presidential years (1961–63), Johnson's national power faded. In Texas his former aide John B. Connally, Jr., won election as governor in 1962. Feuding between Connally and Texas senator Ralph Yarborough imperiled the unity of the party in the 1964 election and brought President Kennedy to Dallas in November 1963 to heal the intraparty wounds. The Kennedy assassination thrust Johnson into the White House.

On the domestic side, Johnson's presidency brought significant changes in how the government functioned, most notably the Civil Rights Act of 1964, the Voting Rights Act of 1965, and the Great Society program. In the 1964 election Johnson carried Texas by an overwhelming margin, swept Senator Yarborough to reelection against the Republican candidate, George H. W. Bush, and slowed the emergence of the GOP as a serious challenge to Democratic supremacy in Texas. In foreign policy, Johnson inherited the commitment that Kennedy had made to the preservation of South Vietnam. He decided in late 1963 not to withdraw from Southeast Asia. By 1965 his escalation of the war against North Vietnam brought protests from Democrats on the left, who saw the conflict as misguided, while Republicans attacked the president for not prosecuting the war with sufficient vigor. Antiwar protests, racial unrest, and expanded government programs turned Texas voters against the Johnson

Lyndon Johnson campaigning by helicopter for the United States Senate, 1948. Photograph by Jimmie Dodd. Jimmie Dodd Photographic Collection, CAH. LBJ brought modern campaign techniques, including the helicopter, to his 1948 Senate race.

administration during the mid-1960s. Senator Tower won reelection in 1966, as the political fortunes of the Johnson White House soured. By 1967 Johnson's political base had eroded. The president had difficulty in traveling around the country because of protesters who followed him. Social upheaval in the form of urban riots and racial tension became associated with the Johnson years. Within the Democratic party nationally, efforts went forward in 1967 to find an alternative to Johnson. Liberals in Texas, long unhappy with Johnson's leadership, echoed this unhappiness. Through Connally and other associates such as Austin attorney Frank C. Erwin, Jr., Johnson controlled the state Democratic party against these insurgent forces. The war in Vietnam seemed stalemated as 1967 ended. The Tet offensive, which began on 30 January 1968, was a defeat for North Vietnam militarily but a blow to Johnson's weakened standing at home. Faced with political challenges from Eugene McCarthy and Robert Kennedy in his own party, Johnson also worried about what would happen to his own health if he ran again. On 31 March 1968 he announced that he was limiting the bombing of North Vietnam and was seeking negotiations. In a political surprise, he also announced that he would not be a candidate for reelection.

After retiring to the ranch, Johnson wrote his memoirs, *The Vantage Point: Perspective of the Presidency, 1963–1969*, published in 1971. He also supervised the construction of the Lyndon

Baines Johnson Library and Museum at the University of Texas at Austin. Despite his withdrawal from national politics, Johnson exercised continued influence in Texas affairs. His friends helped Vice President Hubert Humphrey carry Texas in the fall of 1968 against former vice president Richard Nixon and Alabama governor George Wallace. Johnson also supported Lloyd Bentsen, Jr., in 1970 in a race against Bush for the United States Senate. The ailing former president offered less encouragement to the Democratic presidential candidate in 1972, Senator George S. McGovern, who lost Texas in the Nixon landslide of that year. Johnson was a significant force in Texas for almost four decades. His Senate race against Coke Stevenson in 1948 remains one of the most controversial episodes in the history of American elections. His relationships with such men as Rayburn, Connally, and Bentsen affected the direction of state politics for a generation. On the other hand, Johnson's feud with Yarborough was an important factor in the relative weakness of Texas liberalism during the 1950s and 1960s. Johnson also had a large effect on the Texas economy during his political career, as he steered congressional appropriations to the state in the form of military bases, crop subsidies for farmers, government facilities, and jobs for federal workers. The Lyndon B. Johnson Space Center, headquarters of the NASA space program in Houston, is a symbol of Johnson's impact on Texas and the Sunbelt. Unfriendly biographers have depicted Johnson as driven only by a lust for power. His personality could be abrasive, and his methods were often crude. Nonetheless, the impulse that he displayed to improve the lives of Texans and all Americans reflected genuine conviction on his part. Despite his foreign-policy failure in Vietnam, Johnson was one of the most important presidents during the period after World War II. His ambitious Great Society program embodied the expansive policies of American liberalism. The reaction to this program laid the basis for the conservative trend that followed him. The war in Vietnam called into question the ability of the United States to exercise its influence where it chose in the world. Johnson tried to be a great president and achieved some impressive results. He also demonstrated the limits of the government and the presidency to produce social change and to succeed in an activist foreign policy. No Texan has left a greater mark on the history of the United States.

Lewis L. Gould

Johnson Space Center. At Clear Lake, south of Houston. The current United States space program came into being to compete with the Soviet Union, which launched its first satellite into orbit in 1957. NASA was established in 1958, Project Mercury put Alan Shepard into orbit in 1961 as a rejoinder to the Soviet Yuri Gagarin's space flight, and President Kennedy subsequently set the goal of putting a man on the moon by 1970. Central to the plan was the construction of a manned-space-development aggregation, including the rocket launch facilities at Cape Canaveral, Florida; the Marshall Space Flight Center, Huntsville, Alabama; a planned rocket assembly and test plant on the Pearl River in southeastern Mississippi; and a new space-management, crew-training, and flight-control center, for which the Texas site was selected during the vice presidency of Lyndon Johnson. The center was originally called the Manned Spacecraft Center. In 1963 it was renamed the Lyndon B. Johnson Space Center. Over the succeeding years, houses, apartments, motels, and shopping centers were built on prairies in the Clear Lake

area. A highlight of the center's complex history occurred when *Apollo 11* landed on the moon (20 July 1969) and Neil Armstrong made his historic walk. The Skylab program, which comprised the first United States space-station missions, began in 1973. Skylab reentered the earth's atmosphere on 11 July 1979. Altogether nine Skylab astronauts spent a total of 171 days in space. The first international space mission, the Apollo–Soyuz Test Project, began in 1975 as a cooperative venture between the United States and the Soviet Union. The project tested an international docking system and joint space-flight procedures, but is remembered most for the first space handshake between crews from different nations.

The massive space-shuttle program began when the Johnson Space Center designed, developed, produced, and tested its first shuttle, *Enterprise*, after the project was approved by President Nixon in 1972. The *Columbia* STS-9 Spacelab mission (1983) put into orbit a scientific workshop built by the European Space Agency. On 28 January 1986 a leak in a solid rocket booster seal caused the shuttle *Challenger* to explode shortly after liftoff. All the crew died, including Judith Resnik. After being grounded for 32 months, astronauts reentered space on 29 September 1988 as part of a *Discovery* mission, and subsequent shuttle launches carried major interplanetary and astronomical payloads. *Atlantis* launched the Magellan spacecraft to Venus in May 1989, and *Galileo* began a six-year journey to orbit Jupiter in October 1989. The Hubble Space Telescope was deployed by *Discovery* in April 1990, and a second Great Observatory, the Gamma Ray Observatory, was launched by *Atlantis* in 1991 to make images of objects at high energy wavelengths. By 1993, when Ellen Ochoa on *Discovery* became the first Hispanic woman in space, the shuttle fleet had launched 54 successful missions, traveled more than 130 million statute miles, and flown 161 individuals in space, including 16 non–United States astronauts from 10 countries. In 1984 President Reagan committed the nation to developing a permanently staffed space station within a decade, and in 1988 a formal international agreement was reached among Japan, Canada, and nine European Space Agency members to participate in the Space Station Freedom program.

The Space Center Houston visitor center, designed by Walt Disney Imagineering, opened in 1992. Visitors can tour Mission Control and astronaut-training facilities at the Johnson Space Center, view historical spacecraft and displays, watch movies including IMAX film shot in space, and explore a museum of the American space program. Space Center Houston is owned and operated by the nonprofit Manned Space Flight Education Foundation, Incorporated. No NASA funds were used for the visitor-center construction or operations.

Charles C. Alexander and Diana J. Kleiner

Johnston, Albert Sidney. Army officer; b. Washington, Kentucky, 2 February 1803; d. battle of Shiloh, 6 April 1862 (buried in New Orleans; by special appropriation, in January 1867 the Texas legislature had his remains transferred to the State Cemetery); m. Henrietta Preston (1829; d. 1835); m. Eliza Griffin (1840); ed. Transylvania University and West Point (grad. 1826). Because of his wife's illness Johnston resigned his commission in 1834. In 1836 he moved to Texas and enlisted as a private in the Texas army. He was appointed adjutant general by Thomas Jefferson Rusk and in 1837 became senior brigadier general in command of the army to replace Felix Huston. A duel with

Huston resulted; Johnston was wounded and could not take the command. In 1838 President Lamar appointed him secretary of war for the Republic of Texas, and in December 1839 he led an expedition against the Cherokees in East Texas. After his second marriage he settled at China Grove Plantation in Brazoria County. During the Mexican War he was colonel of the First Texas Rifle Volunteers and served with W. O. Butler as inspector general at Monterrey, Nuevo León. In 1849 he became paymaster in the United States Army and was assigned to the Texas frontier. He went with William S. Harney to the Great Plains in 1855,and in 1856 was appointed colonel of the Second Cavalry. From 1858 to 1860 Johnston acted as brevet brigadier general in an expedition to escort the Mormons to Salt Lake City. He was sent to the Pacific Department and stationed at San Francisco in 1860. At the beginning of the Civil War he resigned his commission in the United States Army, refused the federal government's offer of a command, and returned overland to Texas. Jefferson Davis appointed him a general in the Confederate Army and assigned him command of the Western Department. Johnston took Bowling Green, Kentucky, issued a call for men, and formed and drilled an army. In February 1862 he moved his line of defense to the vicinity of Nashville, and later to Corinth, Mississippi. In 1905 a stone monument executed by Elisabet Ney was placed at his grave in Austin. *Jeanette H. Flachmeier*

Jones, Anson. Last president of the Republic of Texas; b. Seekonkville, Great Barrington, Massachusetts, 20 January 1798; d. Houston, 19 January 1858; m. Mrs. Mary Smith McCrory (1840). Jones practiced medicine in various locations in Virginia and Pennsylvania, lived in Venezuela for two years, and in October 1832 renounced medicine and became a commission merchant in New Orleans. Success still eluded him. In October 1833, at the suggestion of Jeremiah Brown, he drifted to Texas. He had engaged passage back to New Orleans when John A. Wharton and other citizens of Brazoria urged him to "give Texas a fair trial." Jones soon had a practice at Brazoria worth $5,000 a year. As tension between Texas and Mexico mounted, he counseled forbearance and peace until the summer of 1835, when he joined in signing a petition for the calling of the Consultation, which he visited. At a mass meeting at Columbia in December 1835 he presented resolutions for calling a convention to declare independence but declined to be nominated as a delegate. When war came he enlisted in Robert J. Calder's company and during the San Jacinto campaign was judge advocate and surgeon of the Second Regiment. Nevertheless, he insisted upon remaining a private in the infantry. On the field of San Jacinto he found Juan N. Almonte's Journal and Order Book, which he sent to the New York *Herald* for publication in June 1836. After brief service as apothecary general of the Texas army, Jones returned to Brazoria, evicted James Collinsworth from his office with a challenge to a duel, and resumed practice.

During the First Congress of the republic, Jones became increasingly interested in public questions and critical of congressional policies. He was elected a representative to the Second Congress as an opponent of the Texas Railroad, Navigation, and Banking Company. As chairman of the Committee on Foreign Relations, he advocated a withdrawal of the Texas proposal for annexation to the United States. He was also chairman of the committee on privileges and elections and the committee on ways and means. He helped formulate legislation to regulate

medical practice and advocated a uniform system of education and an endowment for a university. At the end of his congressional term, President Sam Houston appointed him minister to the United States (June 1838) and authorized him to withdraw the annexation proposal. Jones's purpose as minister was to stimulate recognition from and trade relations with Europe in order to make the United States desire annexation, or to make Texas strong enough to remain independent. Thus early he hit upon the policy of alternatives that characterized his management of foreign relations until Texas joined the Union and that gave him the sometime nickname "Architect of Annexation." He was recalled by President Lamar in May 1839 and resolved to retire from politics, but when he arrived in Texas he found that he had been elected to finish William H. Wharton's term in the Senate. As senator he criticized the fiscal policies of the Lamar administration and the Texan Santa Fe expedition. Jones was chairman of the committees on foreign relations and the judiciary and was president pro tem of the Senate during the Fifth Congress. After marrying, he returned to practice in Brazoria. He declined candidacy for the vice presidency in the election of 1841, in which Houston again became president. Houston appointed Jones secretary of state, and from 13 December 1841 until 19 February 1846, Jones managed the foreign relations of Texas through a series of crises. Both Houston and Jones later claimed to have devised the foreign policy followed by Texas after 1841, and it is impossible to determine which man originated its leading features. In the main they agreed on the purpose of getting either an offer of annexation from the United States or an acknowledgment of Texas independence from Mexico. They preferred getting both proposals simultaneously, so that an irrevocable choice might be made between them.

Jones was elected president of Texas in September 1844 and took office on 9 December. He had made no campaign speeches, had not committed himself on the subject of annexation, and did not mention the subject in his inaugural address. After James K. Polk was elected president of the United States on a platform of "reannexation of Texas" and President John Tyler proposed annexation by joint resolution, Jones continued his silence. But the Texas Congress declared for joining the Union. Before Jones received official notice of the joint resolution, the charges of England and France induced him to delay action for 90 days. He promised to obtain from Mexico recognition of Texas independence and delayed calling the Texas Congress or a convention. Meanwhile, public sentiment for annexation and resentment against Jones mounted. He was burned in effigy, and threats were made to overthrow his government, but he remained silent until Charles Elliot returned from Mexico with the treaty of recognition. On 4 June 1845, Jones presented to the people of Texas the alternative of peace and independence or annexation. The Texas Congress rejected the treaty with Mexico, approved the joint resolution of annexation, and adopted resolutions censuring Jones. The Convention of 1845 considered removing him from office. He subsequently retained his title, though his duties were merely ministerial. On 19 February 1846, at the ceremony setting up the government of Texas as a state in the Union, Jones declared, "The Republic of Texas is no more." Then he retired to Barrington, his plantation near Washington-on-the-Brazos.

Jones hoped to be elected to the United States Senate, but Houston and Rusk were chosen. For 12 years Jones brooded over his neglect while he became a prosperous planter and accumu-

Jesse Jones with President Franklin D. Roosevelt at the opening of the Texas Centennial, Dallas, 1936. Jesse Jones Papers, CAH; CN 08130. As chairman of the Reconstruction Finance Corporation, Jones was a champion of government–business cooperation and one of the most powerful men in the nation.

lated a vast estate. After an injury that disabled his left arm in 1849, he became increasingly moody and introspective, and his dislike for Houston turned into hatred. While in this frame of mind he edited his *Republic of Texas,* which contained a brief autobiography, portions of his diaries, and annotated selections from his letters. The book was published in New York in 1859, after his death. In 1835, with four other persons, Jones had established the first Masonic lodge in Texas, originally Holland Lodge No. 36 at Brazoria. He was its first head. He called the convention that organized the Grand Lodge of Texas in 1837 and was elected first grand master. He was a charter member and vice president of the Philosophical Society of Texas in 1837 and in 1853 helped found the Medical Association of Texas. In 1857 he believed that the legislature would send him to Washington as senator, but he received no votes. He committed suicide and was buried in Glenwood Cemetery, Houston. The Texas Centennial Commission placed a statue of him in Anson, Jones County, both of which were named after him. His plantation home is preserved in Washington-on-the-Brazos State Historical Park.

Herbert Gambrell

Jones, Jesse Holman. Businessman and New Deal official; b. Robertson County, Tennessee, 5 April 1874; d. Houston, 1 June 1956 (buried in Forest Park Cemetery); m. Mary Gibbs (1920). Jones worked his way up to manager of his uncle's lumber company in Dallas. In 1898, after his uncle's death, he went to Houston as general manager. There he established his own South Texas Lumber Company. He then began to expand into real estate, commercial buildings, and banking. In a few years he was the largest developer in the area and was responsible for most of Houston's major prewar construction. He also built structures in Fort Worth, Dallas, and New York City. Gradually he began to concentrate on real estate and banking. In 1908 he bought part of the Houston *Chronicle,* which he later (1926) purchased *in toto.* Between 1908 and 1918 he organized and became chairman of the Texas Trust Company and was active in most of the banking and real estate activities of the city. By 1912 he was president of the National Bank of Commerce (now Texas Commerce Bank). During this period he made one of his few ventures into oil as an original stockholder in Humble Oil and Refining Company (later Exxon). As chairman of the Houston harbor board he raised money for the Houston Ship Channel. During World War I, President Woodrow Wilson asked Jones to become the director general of military relief for the American Red Cross. He remained in this position until he returned to Houston in 1919. Jones served as director of finance for the Democratic National Committee, made a $200,000 donation, and promised to build a hall. These actions were instrumental in bringing the 1928 Democratic national convention to Houston. At the convention Jones was nominated as a "favorite son."

On the recommendation of John Nance Garner, President Herbert Hoover appointed Jones to the board of the RFC, a new government entity established to combat the Great Depression. President Franklin Roosevelt appointed Jones chairman of the RFC, a position he held from 1933 until 1939. In this capacity, Jones became one of the most powerful men in America. The RFC became the leading financial institution in America and the primary investor in the economy. The agency also facilitated a broadening of Texas industry from agriculture and oil into steel and chemicals. Jones's success in Washington was closely associated with Roosevelt and Garner. Garner and Jones were conservatives, however, and did not always approve of the politics of the New Deal. During Roosevelt's regime, these two were undoubtedly the second and third most influential men in Washington. Jones's tough business acumen made the RFC the most powerful and successful agency in the Roosevelt administration. In 1939 Roosevelt appointed Jones to head the Federal Loan Agency. Jones resigned as head of the RFC, but as federal loan administrator continued overall control of the RFC. He also had general supervision over the Federal Housing Authority and the Home Owners Loan Corporation. After flirting with the vice-presidential nomination in 1940, Jones was offered the post of secretary of commerce. With congressional approval, he was allowed to retain his post as FLA chief during the war years, when he supervised more than 30 agencies that received federal money. Jones's relationship with the president and some members of his cabinet, however, deteriorated. In 1944 Roosevelt believed that Jones was allied with Republican Thomas E. Dewey against him. On 20 January 1945, Jones received a letter from the president asking him to resign so that the post could be given to Henry Wallace, his former vice president. Jones was offered other positions but declined and returned to Houston. From this time to his death he occupied himself with his business ventures and philanthropy. He also broke with the Democratic leadership and supported the Republican ticket in 1948 and 1952. The Jesse H. Jones Hall for the Performing Arts in Houston was named for him. Houston Endowment, which he established in 1937, was the nation's fifteenth largest charitable foundation by 1979. A graduate scholarship in business is named for Jones and his wife and funded by Houston Endowment. Collections of Jones's papers and memorabilia are housed at the Barker Texas History Center, at the Library of Congress, and at Houston Endowment.

Lionel V. Patenaude

Jones and Plummer Trail. From Texas to Kansas; established in the fall of 1874, when Charles Edward (Dirty Face) Jones and Joseph H. Plummer started a store at the head of Wolf Creek, just east of what is now U.S. Highway 83. They had seen the need for a convenient place for buffalo hunters to sell hides and obtain supplies after Quanah Parker's raid had persuaded the Dodge City merchants to abandon Adobe Walls. Jones marked the trail, and the partners' trips to and from Dodge City to deliver hides and buffalo meat and to purchase goods cut ruts into the sod deep enough for others to follow. The route to Wolf Creek extended about 160 miles. The trail was extended farther south to Mobeetie but kept its original name. During the late 1870s Jones and Plummer's store gained a reputation as a safe place for outlaws to hide and replenish their supplies. In the winter of 1878 Bat Masterson and a posse from Dodge City pursued a gang of train robbers along the trail, only to lose them at the store. During the peak freight years of 1880 to 1886 the Jones and Plummer trail provided a crucial conduit for the materials needed to sustain such important projects as the building of Fort Elliott. Charles Rath shipped 150,000 pounds of freight a week to Mobeetie in 1878. Eventually five towns were established along the trail, which served as their primary artery for commerce and travel. After 1879 the trail was used by mail contractors, and in 1886 P. G. Reynolds made it a major stagecoach route from Dodge City to Mobeetie. Though primarily a freighting trail, the Jones and Plummer Trail was also used by cattlemen driving herds north. The trail's usefulness ended when rail lines were built into the region. Pulling into Panhandle City on 1 January 1888, an Atchison, Topeka and Santa Fe locomotive rang its bell, signaling the end of yet another frontier trail.

C. Robert Haywood

Joplin, Janis Lyn. Blues and rock singer; b. Port Arthur, 19 January 1943; d. 5 October 1970. By the time Janis graduated from Jefferson High School in Port Arthur in 1960, her vocabulary of four-letter words, her outrageous clothes, and her reputation for sexual promiscuity and drunkenness caused her classmates to call her a slut. She responded with defensive contempt. In her junior year she found acceptance in a small group of Jefferson High beatniks who read Jack Kerouac and roamed the nightspots from Port Arthur to New Orleans. Janis did not read music, but at the roadhouses or at home listening to records of Odetta, Bessie Smith, or Willie Mae Thornton, she had an uncanny ability to imitate the sounds she heard. Out of imitation she slowly developed her distinctive style. She fled to the University of Texas in 1962 to study art. Indifferent to classwork, she found soulmates at the "Ghetto," a counterculture enclave, and got gigs around Austin, most importantly at Threadgill's, a converted filling station and late-night hangout. The proprietor, country singer Kenneth Threadgill, offered Janis encouragement and lifelong friendship. She craved such acceptance, but her nonconforming behavior often provoked rejection, as when university fraternity pranksters nominated her as their candidate in the annual Ugliest Man on Campus contest. Characteristically, she laughed to cover the hurt, and dreamed of San Francisco, where Beats and Hippies were not outsiders. She spent 1963 to 1965 in the Bay area and won attention from local audiences, until drugs became more important than singing and reduced her to an emaciated 88 pounds. Her friends passed the hat and gave her a bus ticket home. Parental care restored her health, and fear of relapse produced a period of sobriety. Subsequently, however, she received an invitation to audition for a new rock band, Big Brother and the Holding Company, and headed west in May 1966. Janis's belting of rock gathered huge swaying, clapping, shouting, and dancing audiences. She stopped the show at the Monterey Pop Festival in 1967 with "Ball and Chain." That triumph and the album *Cheap Thrills* (1968) elevated her to

Janis Joplin with Kenneth Threadgill at the Newport Folk Festival. Photograph by David Garth. Newport, Rhode Island, 1968. Courtesy Threadgill's Archive Collection, Austin. Threadgill remembered Janis as a rather shy girl who didn't sing the first time she visited his Austin roadhouse.

national stardom. A new manager, Albert Grossman, whose stable of stars included Peter, Paul and Mary and Bob Dylan, urged Janis to dump Big Brother for more versatile and disciplined support. The Kosmic Blues band was never satisfactory; the FullTilt Boogie band was. Joplin's career now surged forward full tilt, driven by Southern Comfort booze, heroin, bisexual liaisons, compulsive work, and the hope that fame would bring inner peace. She performed in Madison Square Garden, Paris, London, Woodstock, and Harvard Stadium; was written up in the New York *Times*; and appeared on the "Ed Sullivan Show." For some reason she attended her tenth-anniversary class reunion in Port Arthur and left it feeling further alienated from her classmates, her parents, and her hometown than before. She died two months later of an accidental overdose of heroin and alcohol, and her ashes were strewn over California. She has been called "the best white blues singer in American musical history" and "the greatest female singer in the history of rock 'n' roll." *Pearl*, a album recorded just before her death and featuring "Me and Bobby McGee," shows that Janis was growing musically almost to the moment of her death. The film *The Rose* (1979), starring Bette Midler, is not faithful in detail to Janis's life, but it captures her mesmerizing power on stage, in contrast to her offstage inability to halt her descent to self-destruction.

Richard B. Hughes

Joplin, Scott. The "King of Ragtime"; b. probably at Caves Springs, near Linden, 24 November 1868; d. New York City, 1 April 1917 (buried in St. Michael's Cemetery, New York); m. Belle Hayden (ca. 1902); m. Lottie Stokes (ca. 1909); 1 daughter (died in infancy). His father, a former slave with rudimentary musical ability, moved the family to Texarkana by about 1875. By age 7 Scott was proficient in banjo and began to experiment on a piano owned by a neighbor for whom his mother did domestic work. At about age 11, he began free piano lessons with Julius Weiss, who lodged as family tutor for lumberman Col. R. W. Rodgers. The second-hand square piano that Joplin's father bought him probably came from the Rodgers home. After Rodgers died (1884) and Weiss left, Joplin may also have left Texarkana. After several years as an itinerant pianist in brothels and saloons, he settled in St. Louis about 1890. A type of music known as "jig-piano" was popular there, and the bouncing bass and syncopated melody lines were later referred to as "ragged time," or simply "ragtime." During 1893 he played in sporting areas adjacent to the Columbian Exposition in Chicago, and the next year moved to Sedalia, Missouri, whence he toured with his eight-member Texas Medley Quartette as far east as Syracuse, New York, and in 1896, into Texas, where he possibly witnessed the Crash at Crush. In 1897 he enrolled in Sedalia's George R. Smith College for Negroes to study piano and theory. During this time he was an "entertainer" at the Maple Leaf Club and traveled to Kansas City, where in 1899 Carl Hoffman issued Joplin's first ragtime publications, including his best-known piece, *Maple Leaf Rag.* The sheet music went on to sell over a million copies. Thereafter Joplin entered into an on-and-off arrangement with John Stark, a publisher in Sedalia and later in St. Louis and New York.

In addition to his output of increasingly sophisticated individual rags, Joplin began to integrate ragtime idioms into works in larger musical forms: a ballet, *The Ragtime Dance* (1899), and two operas, *The Guest of Honor* (1902–03) and *Treemonisha* (1906–10). The orchestration scores for both the operas are lost. A piano–vocal score and new orchestration for *Treemonisha* were later published. When he moved back to St. Louis in 1901, Joplin renewed an acquaintance with Alfred Ernst, conductor of that city's Choral–Symphony Society, and possibly took theory lessons from him. Joplin had a strong conviction that the key to success for African Americans was education, and this was a common theme in his works. He followed Stark to New York in 1907, used the city as a base for his East Coast touring, and settled there permanently in 1911 to devote his serious energies to the production of *Treemonisha,* mounted unsuccessfully early in 1915. Joplin had contracted syphilis some years earlier, and by 1916 his health had deteriorated considerably, as indicated by his inconsistent playing on the piano rolls he recorded. He was projecting a ragtime symphony when he entered the Manhattan State Hospital, where he died. Joplin's other works include *The School of Ragtime* (1908) and many works for piano: rags, including *Maple Leaf, The Entertainer, Elite Syncopations,* and *Peacherine;* marches, including *Great Crush Collision* and *March Majestic;* and waltzes, including *Harmony Club* and *Bethena.* His collected works were published by the New York Public Library in 1971, and his music was featured in the 1973 motion picture *The Sting,* which won an Academy Award for its film score. In 1976 Joplin was posthumously awarded a Pulitzer Prize for *Treemonisha,* the first opera by an African American.

Theodore Albrecht

Jordan, Barbara Charline. Politician; b. Houston, 21 February 1936; d. Austin, 17 January 1996 (buried in the State Cemetery); ed. Texas Southern University (grad. 1956) and Boston University (law degree, 1959). After teaching at Tuskegee Institute for a year, she returned to Houston in 1960 and practiced law. She registered black voters for the 1960 presidential campaign and twice ran unsuccessfully for the state Senate in the early 1960s. In 1967 redistricting and increased registration of black voters secured her a seat in the Texas Senate, where she was the first black state senator since 1883. Her career was endorsed and facilitated by Lyndon Johnson. In the legislature she worked for minimum-wage laws and voter registration and chaired the Labor and Management Relations Committee. In 1972 she was unanimously elected president pro tem of the Senate. The following year she was elected to the United States House of Representatives from the Eighteenth Texas District. She was the first black woman from a Southern state to serve in Congress, and, with Andrew Young, was the first of two African Americans to be elected to Congress from the South at that time in the twentieth century. She was a famous public speaker. Impressed with her eloquence in the Watergate hearings, the Democratic party chose her to deliver the keynote address at the 1976

Candid portrait of Barbara Jordan at the Lyndon Baines Johnson Library, Austin, October 18, 1976. Photography by Frank Wolfe. Courtesy Lyndon Baines Johnson Library, Austin.

Democratic national convention; she was the first woman to do so. Her speech helped rally support for James E. Carter's presidential campaign. In 1979, after three terms in congress, Jordan retired from politics to accept the Lyndon Baines Johnson Public Service Professorship at the LBJ School of Public Affairs, University of Texas at Austin. She published her autobiography, *Barbara Jordan: A Self Portrait,* in 1979. She served as ethics advisor to Governor Ann Richards in the early 1990s. In 1992 she once again delivered the keynote address at the Democratic national convention. She served as chairwoman of the United States Commission on Immigration Reform in 1994. Among her many honors were induction into the National Women's Hall of Fame in 1990 and a Presidential Medal of Freedom in 1994. She suffered from a number of ailments in her later years, including a form of multiple sclerosis, and was confined to a wheelchair. She survived a near-drowning incident at her home in 1988. Her papers are housed in the Barbara Jordan Archives at Texas Southern University.

Mark Odintz

Judiciary. Three characteristics of the judicial system in Texas distinguish it from the national norm: it has two appellate courts of last resort, its trial courts do not have uniform jurisdiction of subject matter, and its judges are chosen in partisan elections.

Constitutional history. Stephen F. Austin's appointment of Josiah H. Bellas provisional justice of the peace for the province of Texas in 1822 was supplanted by the Mexican provisional governor's institution of three positions for elected alcaldes. The alcalde, who had both administrative and judicial duties, applied Spanish law, both civil and criminal, in Austin's colony. The system did not please the Texans, but attempts to reform it were made moot by the revolution.

In 1836 the Constitution of the Republic of Texas established a judicial department that was predominantly Anglo-American. The judicial power was vested in one Supreme Court, which had jurisdiction over appeals only, and such inferior courts as the Congress might establish. Congress might divide the republic into judicial districts, each having a judge, who served as trial judge and member of the Supreme Court. The chief justice and district judges were elected by joint ballot of both houses of

Congress. Each county had a county court and justice of the peace courts; the judges of these lower courts were elected by popular vote.

The state constitutions of 1845, 1861, 1866, and 1869 all retained the structure of the judicial system established in the constitution of the republic. The role of the district judges in the Supreme Court was eliminated in 1845, and two associate justices were provided for. In the first years of statehood, the justices of the Supreme Court and the district judges were nominated by the governor with the advice and consent of the Senate, but in 1850 the constitution was amended to make the offices elective, and they have remained so (except under the Reconstruction Constitution of 1869). The revival of the economy after Reconstruction increased the business of the courts, and the Supreme Court fell behind in its docket of civil and criminal appeals. To relieve it, the Constitution of 1876 established another appellate court of last resort—the Court of Appeals, which was given jurisdiction of appeals in criminal, probate, and county court cases. The Supreme Court neither had nor desired jurisdiction to review the decisions of the Court of Appeals, which was the court of last resort for its classes of cases. The intent was to leave the Supreme Court free to decide the civil appeals from the district courts. The Court of Appeals failed to rescue the Supreme Court, which continued to fall behind in its work. The second plan to relieve the Supreme Court was to establish an intermediate level of appeals courts for civil cases. This was done by constitutional amendment in 1891. The new courts of civil appeals were given jurisdiction over most civil appeals from the district and county courts; further review by the Supreme Court was discretionary with that court. The system of intermediate appellate courts made it possible for the Supreme Court to regulate its docket by exercising its discretion to deny review of most appeals. Another advantage of the new courts was that the capacity of the civil appellate system could be expanded by the formation of more courts of civil appeals; originally 3 in number, the courts of civil appeals had increased to 14 by 1980.

Despite its failure to rescue the Supreme Court, the Court of Appeals was not abolished in 1891 but was renamed the Texas Court of Criminal Appeals.It has jurisdiction over appeals in criminal cases from district and county courts. The Supreme Court has no jurisdiction in such matters; the Court of Criminal Appeals is the court of last resort in criminal cases. Though several states have intermediate appellate courts whose jurisdiction is limited to criminal cases, only Texas and Oklahoma have separate courts of last resort in civil and criminal cases. As the population of Texas grew, so did the caseload of the Court of Criminal Appeals. Since the Court of Criminal Appeals had neither the discretion to deny review of appeals nor the assistance of intermediate courts of appeal, the only way for it to cope with more cases was to add more judges. Constitutional amendments increased the number of judges from three to five in 1966 and to nine in 1978, but the court was still unable to stay current with its caseload. In 1980 the constitution was amended to give the legislature the same tools to manage the criminal docket that it had acquired over civil cases in 1891. The courts of civil appeals (renamed courts of appeals) were given original jurisdiction of appeals in noncapital criminal cases, and the Court of Criminal Appeals was given jurisdiction for discretionary review of the decisions. The legislature increased the number of justices on the

intermediate courts of appeals. The Texas Supreme Court and Court of Criminal Appeals are careful to remain within their respective jurisdictions and to avoid issuing conflicting interpretations of the same laws. This policy prevents the confusion caused in 1911 when the two courts rendered conflicting decisions on the validity of a provision for initiative and referendum in a city charter.

Organization of courts. The Texas judicial system has been called one of the most complex in the United States, if not the world. The state has three levels of trial courts—district, county, and inferior—and there is no uniformity of jurisdiction among the courts at each level. To be sure of a trial court's jurisdiction, one must examine the statute that established it. There are two levels of appellate courts: the courts of appeals and the two courts of last resort, the Court of Criminal Appeals and the Supreme Court.

The inferior courts are the justice courts and the municipal courts. They come closest to having uniform jurisdiction throughout the state. Most of their cases are traffic offenses. Their collection of fines in traffic and criminal cases makes them net revenue producers for the jurisdictions that fund them. Justice of the peace precincts are required in each county; the least populous counties may have one precinct, but counties of 30,000 or more population must have from four to eight precincts. Each precinct has one justice of the peace, who serves a term of four years. The justice courts are not courts of record, which means that appeals from them to the county-level courts are *de novo* proceedings: they are tried again. Justice of the peace courts have jurisdiction over criminal offenses that are punishable by fine only, and over civil cases in which the amount in controversy is small (not more than $5,000 in 1995). In at least 60 counties the county-level courts have been given concurrent jurisdiction with the justice of the peace courts. Justices of the peace have important functions as magistrates who can issues warrants to arrest or search in felony and misdemeanor cases, and as coroners in counties that do not have medical examiners.

Municipal courts have been established by the legislature in each of the approximately 840 incorporated cities of Texas; large cities usually have more than one judge. Though most judges of municipal courts are appointed by the governing body of the city, a few are elected by the voters of the city. Most municipal courts are not courts of record, which means that a case is retried on appeal to a county-level court, but the legislature has formed municipal courts of record in at least 23 cities. Appeal from conviction in such courts is on the record to a county-level court. Municipal courts have exclusive jurisdiction over violations of city ordinances, as well as jurisdiction over the lowest class of state misdemeanors, which are punishable by fine only. They have virtually no civil jurisdiction.

The county-level courts are the constitutional county courts and the statutory county courts. Each of the 254 counties has a constitutional county court. In addition to its jurisdiction over appeals from the inferior courts, the constitutional county court has criminal jurisdiction over the higher range of misdemeanors, general jurisdiction of probate matters, and jurisdiction (concurrent with the justice court) on civil matters in which the amount in controversy is from $200.01 to $5,000. The office of county judgeis reminiscent of the colonial alcalde's: the county judge presides over the county commissioners' court, which exercises powers over all county business. This legislative and executive function is by far the most important role of the constitutional county judge, whose term of office was increased from two to four years by constitutional amendment in 1954. In at least 74 counties the constitutional county court's judicial duties have been given, in whole or in part, to statutory county courts (which may be called county courts at law, probate courts, county criminal courts, or other designations). The civil, criminal, family-law, and probate jurisdictions of the statutory courts vary greatly from county to county, depending on the decisions of the county. Some of them exercise jurisdiction over matters that are usually reserved for district courts, but others have concurrent jurisdiction with justice courts. There were 185 statutory county courts operating in state fiscal year 1994. The populous counties may have many statutory courts; there were 23 in Harris County, for example. Each court has one judge, who serves a four-year term.

District courts are the trial courts of general jurisdiction in law and equity. This classification includes criminal cases of the grade of felony and misdemeanors involving official misconduct, divorce, cases of title to liens to land, election contests, and civil actions where the amount in controversy is at least $200. A constitutional district court's jurisdiction cannot be reduced by the legislature, though the legislature has established some nonconstitutional courts (such as criminal district courts or domestic-relations courts) that have limited jurisdiction. Most district courts exercise criminal and civil jurisdiction, but in the metropolitan areas there is a tendency for the courts to specialize in either civil, criminal, or family-law cases. A few district courts also exercise the subject-matter jurisdiction exercised by county courts. In state fiscal year 1994 the state had 386 district-level courts. The geographic area of most judicial districts is one county, although a populous county has many district courts; Harris County, for example, had 59. No judicial district is smaller than a county. Some judicial districts in sparsely populated areas comprise more than one county. Each court has one judge, who serves a four-year term.

The appellate level courts are the courts of appeals, the Texas Court of Criminal Appeals, and the Supreme Court. An appeal to these courts is based on the written record of a trial. The appellate courts do not hear witnesses. Courts of appeals hear most appeals from the county and district trial courts (the biggest exception being death-penalty cases, which go directly to the Court of Criminal Appeals). The state is divided into 14 court of appeals districts; in each is a court of appeals that has a chief justice and at least two other justices, who serve four-year terms. The decisions of the courts of appeals may be reviewed by the Court of Criminal Appeals (in criminal law matters) or the Supreme Court (in other kinds of cases), except that the decisions of the courts of appeals on questions of fact are conclusive. The Court of Criminal Appeals hears appeals from death-penalty convictions and denials of bail. It has discretion to review the decisions of the courts of appeals in other criminal cases, although it may refuse to review any decision without explanation. Its determinations in criminal cases are final unless they involve a question of federal constitutional law reviewed by the United States Supreme Court. There is no appeal from the Court of Criminal Appeals to the state Supreme Court. In addition to its appellate jurisdiction, the Court of Criminal Appeals has exclusive jurisdiction to grant habeas corpus relief from a final felony conviction, and each year it receives thousands of petitions from inmates of Texas prisons. In 1981 the court was given authority to make rules of appellate procedure in criminal cases, and in 1986 to make rules of evidence for the trial of criminal cases. The legislature has not relinquished its authority to make the other laws for criminal procedure before and during trial. The court administers grants for judicial education. The court comprises a presiding judge and eight other judges, who serve six-year terms. It sits in Austin.

The Supreme Court of Texas exercises the judicial power of the state. Its authority to do so was made explicit by a constitutional amendment in 1980, which gave the court a basis to regulate the legal profession of the state. (The State Bar of Texas, a quasi-public agency to which every licensed attorney must belong, had been at risk of being abolished or radically reformed by the legislature in the late 1970s.) The court has statutory authority to supervise the operations of the state bar and the rules for admission, discipline, and disbarment of attorneys, for approving the law schools in the state, for promulgating the rules of evidence and the rules of civil procedure and appellate procedure for the conduct of civil litigation, for promulgating the rules of the Commission on Judicial Conduct and for disciplining or removing judges, for promulgating rules of administration for the judicial system, for equalizing the dockets of the courts of appeals by transferring cases among them, and for promulgating the rules of the Court Reporters Certification Board. The court's judicial jurisdiction includes a small class of appeals from injunctions and a general discretion to review the decisions of the court of appeals in cases other than criminal-law matters. It may deny review without explanation. The court comprises a chief justice and eight other justices, who serve six-year terms. It sits in Austin.

Judges. Except for some municipal judges, the judicial officers of Texas are chosen in partisan elections by the voters of the geographical jurisdiction that the court serves. For a hundred years after Reconstruction, during which the Democratic party dominated the elections, judicial races were often uncontested. Two-thirds of judges gained office by appointment when a bench became vacant, and most appointees retained their seats at the next election. The emerging strength of the Republican party in the 1980s led to contested elections, and straight-ticket voting swept many incumbent judges from their benches. Judicial races do not attract as much attention or funding as do the campaigns for other offices, and it is sometimes doubtful that the voters are well-acquainted with the qualifications of the candidates. In 1976 Donald B. Yarbrough, a lawyer who was distinguished only by the similarity of his name to that of a better-known politician, was elected to the Supreme Court; he resigned during impeachment proceedings after being indicted for a felony offense of aggravated perjury before a grand jury, and he was convicted and sent to prison. Stephen W. Mansfield was elected to the Court of Criminal Appeals in 1994 despite having made false claims about his experience and personal background, for which he was later reprimanded by the State Bar of Texas. After the Constitutional Convention of 1974 voters did not adopt a new state constitution that would have permitted nonpartisan election of judges. The legislature has rejected many proposals for the appointment or nonpartisan election of judges, and the topic is still hotly debated.

The qualifications required of judicial officers, other than having been elected, increase with the level of the court. Justices

Part of the fair parade held in Bonham, ca. 1910. Photograph by Erwin E. Smith. The Erwin E. Smith Collection of the Library of Congress on deposit at the Amon Carter Museum, Fort Worth; LC S611-790. Black Texans have celebrated Juneteenth, commemorating the date the Emancipation Proclamation was first read in the state, since at least 1867.

of the peace are not required to have special qualifications; only about 5 percent of the state's 885 justices of the peace were lawyers in state fiscal year 1994. The compensation and qualifications of municipal judges vary, except that all statutes establishing municipal courts of record require the judges to be licensed to practice law in Texas. The judge of the constitutional county court is required by the constitution to be "well informed in the law of the State." The requirement has not been interpreted to include a law license or formal study of law, and about 85 percent of county judges are not lawyers. Judges of the statutory county courts must be licensed to practice law in Texas and (beginning in 1991) must be at least 25 years old and must have practiced law for four years preceding election. The county judge is a state official, whose minimum salary must be $1,000 less than the salary of a district judge. The law does not set a maximum salary; the judges of some statutory county courts have higher salaries than that of the chief justice of the Texas Supreme Court. A district judge must be a citizen of the United States and of Texas, be licensed to practice law in Texas, and have been a practicing lawyer or a judge for four years before election. Justices of the courts of appeals, judges of the Court of Criminal Appeals, and justices of the Supreme Court must be licensed to practice law in Texas, be citizens of the United States and of Texas, have attained the age of 35 years, and have been practicing lawyers or judges of

courts of record for at least 20 years. The justices of the court of appeals are elected by the voters in their court of appeals district. Court of Criminal Appeals and Supreme Court elections are conducted statewide.

In 1965 retirement and removal provisions were added to the constitution. Judges of the district courts and judges and justices of the appellate courts must retire when they reach age 75; the legislature may reduce that age to as low as 70. Judges may be removed from office, suspended, censured, or disciplined by the State Commission on Judicial Conduct (which comprises five judges from all levels, two lawyers, and four citizens) for incompetence, willful violation of the Code of Judicial Conduct, willful or persistent violation of rules promulgated by the Supreme Court, or conduct that is clearly inconsistent with the performance of judicial duties or that casts public discredit upon the judiciary or the administration of justice. A judge may be removed or involuntarily retired for permanent disability that seriously interferes with the performance of duties.

Paul Womack

Juneteenth. June 19, the anniversary of Gen. Gordon Granger's announcement in 1865 to the slaves of Texas that they were free; long celebrated as a holiday by African Americans, and now a state holiday. The first celebrations of Juneteenth were political rallies where freedmen were taught their voting rights. Shortly, however, Juneteenth was marked by festivities throughout the state, often at "Emancipation Parks." In Austin, Juneteenth was first celebrated in 1867 under the direction of the Freedmen's Bureau. Limestone County has a notable Juneteenth celebration. The holiday declined in popularity in the early 1960s under the influence of the push for integration. Subsequently, blacks' renewed interest in celebrating their cultural heritage led to the revitalization of the holiday throughout the state. Juneteenth became a state holiday in 1979 under Republican governor William P. Clements, Jr. Black Texans who have moved to Louisiana and Oklahoma have taken the celebration with them. In 1991 the Anacostia Museum of the Smithsonian Institution sponsored "Juneteenth '91, Freedom Revisited," featuring public speeches, African-American arts and crafts, and other cultural programs. *Teresa Palomo Acosta*

Junior Historians of Texas. The oldest of several student educational programs conducted by the Texas State Historical Association; founded in 1939 by Walter Prescott Webb. The idea for the participation of secondary students in the work of state historical organizations appears to developed in two places. The Indiana Historical Society organized the Indiana Junior Historical Society in 1938, and in Texas the Junior Historian movement took place independently the next year. Webb, director of the TSHA, introduced the idea of a young persons' branch of the association in the *Southwestern Historical Quarterly* in October 1939. The program was designed to encourage students in grades 6 through 12 to study their state and local history. In almost all instances the program operates within, but independent of, public school systems. Most club sponsors are history teachers. As conceived by Webb and H. Bailey Carroll, the first director of the Junior Historian program and its guiding hand from 1939 until his death in 1966, the original objective of the program was to develop future historians. Consequently the Texas program was originally centered around the writing of history by young people, and in January 1940 the association began publishing the *Junior Historian* magazine. This unique publication, the first published magazine in which the writing was done both by and for young people, changed its name to *Texas Historian* in September 1970. Most of the essays published have won awards in the Junior Historian or Texas History Day writing contests. Ken Ragsdale, the director of the association's educational division from 1966 to 1977, introduced a historical-exhibits component to the annual meetings of the Junior Historians. He also encouraged integrating local Junior Historian chapter work with that of local historical societies and history museums. Annual competitions in history-related performances and media displays were established under David De Boe, the next director of the program. In 1981 members of the Junior Historians were able for the first time to compete with students from other states, through the Texas History Day and National History Day programs. In the 1994–95 school year there were about 110 active chapters of Junior Historians. *Texas Historian* was published four times a year and had a subscription list of 1,800. *David De Boe*

K

Katayama, Sen. Founding member of both the American and Japanese Communist parties; b. Sugataro Yabuki, Japan, 1859; d. Soviet Union, 5 November 1933 (buried in the Kremlin); m. Fude —— (d. 1903); 2 children; m. Hari Tama (1907); 1 child; ed. Grinnell College (grad. 1892) and Yale Divinity School. In Tokyo, Katayama formed a lifelong friendship with Iwasaki Seikichi, whose uncle was one of the founders of the Mitsubishi company. Iwasaki was beginning to learn English, and he inspired Katayama to do the same. After Iwasaki went off to Yale, Katayama worked his way to America. During his studies he became a Christian and a socialist. He returned to Japan in 1896, became the director of a settlement house called Kingsley Hall, and was soon immersed in social causes, which came to include labor organizing and antiwar activities. Iwasaki urged him in 1903 to return to America to look into rice-planting opportunities. Katayama had kept up his interest in America, teaching English and publishing a "Student's Guide to America." He accepted Iwasaki's offer of financial assistance. On the way, he attended the Second International Socialist Congress in Amsterdam and an American Socialist Party convention in 1904 in Chicago. However, his main business had become rice growing in Texas, where he lived and worked most of the time from February 1904 to January 1907. In Houston he became friends with a Japanese restaurant owner, Tsunekichi Okasaki, in whose restaurant he worked for a time as a waiter and cook. There were already Japanese farmers at Garwood, but they disapproved of his attending socialist conventions, so after the conventions he decided to settle down at Aldine, where he purchased a 160-acre farm in October 1904. After a crop failure, Katayama and Okasaki formed a partnership. Okasaki purchased 10,202 acres of land in Live Oak and McMullen counties, and in December 1905 he and Katayama returned to Japan to get money from Iwasaki and recruit laborers. Iwasaki provided $100,000, formed the Nippon Kono Kabushiki Kaisha (Japan Farming Company) to develop the Texas project, and appointed Katayama managing director on condition that he "promise to stop working publicly as a socialist." Katayama seems to have agreed, with the thought that he would leave the socialist cause in other hands for the time being, and he returned to Texas. Okasaki remained in Japan to recruit workers. When he returned to Texas he found that Katayama had violated his pledge by bringing some of his American socialist friends into the directorship of the company. (Texas law required that the majority of the company stockholders be American citizens.) The result was a bitter quarrel. Okasaki complained to Iwasaki, and Iwasaki recalled Sen Katayama to Japan and dissolved the company. Katayama returned in 1906 to Japan, where he remained active in the Socialist movement and pursued a career in journalism. His participation in the Tokyo Streetcar Strike of 1912 resulted in his imprisonment, and after his release he left Japan for good. He returned to the United States and resided mostly in California. Disillusioned with socialism and attracted by the success of the Bolshevik revolution of 1917–18, he became a communist. In his capacity as an officer for the Comintern he was sent to Mexico in 1921 and later that year was called to Moscow, where he was hailed as one of the leaders of the Japanese Communist movement.   *F. Hilary Conroy*

Kelly Air Force Base. In San Antonio; at the time of its closing, the oldest continuously operating flying base in the United States Air Force and the largest single employer in San Antonio. Capt. Benjamin Foulois, the "father of military aviation," selected the site in November 1916 to expand the activities of the fledgling Aviation Section of the U.S. Army Signal Corps from Fort Sam Houston. The field was named for Lt. George E. Kelly, who was killed in a crash at Fort Sam Houston on 10 May 1911, the first American military aviator to lose his life while piloting a military aircraft. Flying activities began on 5 April 1917 and with America's entry into World War I grew rapidly. The base served as a reception and testing center for recruits as well as a training center for almost all the skills required to operate an air force. Almost all of the combat aviators of World War I earned their wings at Kelly Field. At some point of their training most of the future leaders of the air force passed through Kelly Field. They included the later air force chiefs of staff Carl "Tooey" Spaatz, Hoyt Vandenberg, and Curtis LeMay; Charles Lindbergh earned his wings at Kelly Field, as did the famous "Flying Tiger" Claire Lee Chennault. In 1928 the Academy Award–winning film "Wings" was filmed at the base. During World War II a part of Kelly became the Aviation Cadet Reception Center, later to become Lackland Air Force Base. All pilot training was transferred to other installations, and Kelly became the base for the San Antonio Air Materiel Area, which stored and distributed materiel and modified or repaired aircraft, engines, and related equipment. Kelly Field was renamed Kelly Air Force Base when the air force achieved autonomy in 1947. The base continued to expand and had worldwide logistic responsibilities for such aircraft as the B-29, B-50, B-36, B-47, and B-58 bombers; F-102 and F-106 fighters; and various cargo aircraft, including the huge C-5 transport. All of the remaining World War I hangers were removed, and a million-square-foot hanger was constructed. It was the largest structure in the world without center columns. In keeping with developing technology, mechanized central receiving operations, underground fuel and defuel systems, modern data-processing systems, and an automated air-freight terminal were installed at Kelly. In addition to the logistical mission, Kelly AFB was host to the Electronics Security Command, the Air Force News Service, and national guard and reserve units. The base was placed on the base-closure list in 1993, after which a public outcry got it removed. It was again designated for closure in 1995, after which it began to close down its operations. Final closure was scheduled for 1 September 2001.   *Art Leatherwood*

Kelly Plow Company. The only full-line plow factory in the Southwest; began in 1843, when John A. Stewart began making crude plows in a shop near Marshall. In 1848 Stewart moved his work to Four Mile Branch, a popular campsite for wagoners, four miles west of Jefferson. There he and his brother-in-law,

Zachariah Lockett, made plows and operated a general repair shop, where they melted iron in a pocket furnace heated by charcoal. In 1852 George Addison Kelly joined the company, which became Kelly and Stewart in 1858 and subsequently added cast-iron stoves, cooking utensils, machinery castings, and andirons to its products. Kelly bought full ownership in 1860, the same year that he developed the Blue Kelly Plow, which later became so widely used in Texas that "Kelly" became a household word and "Blue Kelly" was synonymous with "plow." During the Civil War the Kelly Plow Company was a part of the Confederate arsenal. By 1866 the enlarged business began to manufacture its own iron by smelting East Texas ores in a furnace two miles west of Kellyville. It produced a new "pony plow" during Reconstruction. The coming of railroads and the decline of Jefferson as a commercial center decreased the value of Kellyville as a factory location. The plant burned in 1880, and Kelly transferred the salvage to Longview in 1882. General agricultural implements were added to the line of products in 1882, and in 1907 the plant produced a full line of steel plows and tillage implements. The Kelly family continued to run the business until the 1960s. As late as the 1970s George A. Kelly, Jr., was engaged in banking and investing activities and used the name Kelly Plow Company to refer to his investment company.

Kennedy Assassination. On the morning of 22 November 1963, President John F. Kennedy addressed a breakfast sponsored by the Fort Worth Chamber of Commerce, flew to Dallas, and began a motorcade trip in an open car with his wife, Governor John Connally, and the governor's wife through town toward the Dallas Trade Mart, where Kennedy was to speak at a luncheon. At 12:30 P.M., as the car started down the Elm Street hill leading beneath a railroad overpass in Dealey Plaza, several shots were fired, and Kennedy and Connally were hit. They were rushed to Parkland Memorial Hospital, where the president was pronounced dead at 1:00 P.M. from wounds in the neck and head. Connally eventually recovered. At 2:38 P.M. Lyndon Johnson was sworn in as president. Between 1:45 and 2:00 P.M. of the same day, Lee Harvey Oswald was arrested in the Texas Theatre in the Oak Cliff section of Dallas and charged with the murder of policemen J. D. Tippit. The next day, Oswald was charged with murdering Kennedy with a rifle fired from the sixth floor of the Texas School Book Depository. On 24 November Oswald was shot and killed by Jack Ruby, a Dallas lounge operator, in the basement of the city jail while being transferred to the county jail. Ruby was convicted of murder in March 1964. The conviction was appealed, and in November 1966 a new trial with a change of venue was ordered. Ruby died (3 January 1967) before the second trial could begin. On 29 November 1963 Johnson established the President's Commission on the Assassination of President John F. Kennedy, also known as the Warren Commission, which consisted of seven men representing the United States Supreme Court, Senate, House of Representatives, the public, and the CIA. Chaired by Chief Justice Earl Warren, the commission met first on 1 December 1963 and submitted its multivolume report on 24 September 1964. From the moment of publication the report was both criticized and defended vigorously. Hundreds of books and articles have been written on the subject. Skeptics are critical of the commission's inquiry or offer alternate theories about the circumstances and events connected with the assassination. Conversely, many defenders of the Warren report have debunked a number of conspiracy theories. Although the commission concluded that Oswald acted alone, they also noted that it was impossible to prove conclusively that no conspiracy existed. In February 1975, Congressman Henry B. Gonzalez introduced a resolution to convene a House select committee to reexamine the assassinations of John Kennedy, Robert Kennedy, and Martin Luther King, Jr. The committee concluded in its final report (July 1979) that JFK "was probably killed as the result of a conspiracy" but admitted that "the Committee was unable to identify the other gunman or the extent of the conspiracy." In 1992, as a result of increased public interest in the assassination, a law was passed ordering the further release of classified documents relating to the assassination. In June 1999 the Russian government made public its files regarding the assassination.

Kenney's Fort. Sixteen miles north of Austin; built in 1839 by San Jacinto veteran Thomas Kenney to protect the outermost settlement on the Colorado River frontier. The small fort was ordinarily defended by five or six armed farmers. It consisted of a single blockhouse and three or four log cabins surrounded by an eight-foot stockade. In 1839–40 government soldiers were stationed at nearby Camp Caldwell, but generally the settlers had to see to their own defense. In August 1840 Joseph Weeks and other settlers successfully defended the fort against Comanche Indians. A retaliatory expedition was planned against the Indians by Felix Huston, major general of the militia, and the fort was renamed Fort Dunnington for Lt. William M. Dunnington, who was killed in the Council House Fight at San Antonio. By November, however, these plans were abandoned, and Fort Dunnington again became Kenney's Fort. In 1841 the Texan Santa Fe expedition assembled at Camp Cazneau, which was located next to the fort. During the Archive War, the state records were surrendered near Kenney's Fort. The only known remnant of the fort is a part of the flagpole. In 1936 the Texas Centennial Commission placed a historical marker a half mile north of the site. *Clara Stearns Scarbrough*

Kerrville, Texas. County seat of Kerr County, 62 miles northwest of San Antonio. Geography has always been important in the Kerrville area—from prehistoric times, with archeological evidence suggesting human habitation as early as 10,000 years ago, to the present, when the town has achieved a national and international reputation for its karstic landscapes, scenic roadways, river and streams, lakes, caves, biological diversity, ranches, architecture, and popular culture. The original settlement, named for James Kerr and situated on a bluff north of the Guadalupe River in the eastern half of the county, grew from a successful shinglemakers' camp into a mercantile and shipment center for the Hill Country. One of the earliest shinglemakers was veteran and explorer Joshua D. Brown. Pioneers built permanent homes at what they called Brownsborough in the early 1850s. From this settlement, Kerrsville, later Kerrville, was platted after Kerr County was organized in 1856. It was voted county seat by a narrow margin, and its claim was tenuous until 1862, when rival Comfort was included in newly formed Kendall County. In 1857 German master miller Christian Dietert and millwright Balthasar Lich started a large grist and saw mill on the bluff. This mill, with a permanent source of power and protection from floods, became the most extensive operation of its kind in the Hill Country west of New Braunfels and San

Camp Waldemar, ca. 1948. Courtesy TSL. Kerrville has a national reputation for its beautiful landscape and scenic recreational areas.

Antonio. Related mercantile and freighting enterprises led to the foundation of Charles A. Schreiner's family empire of retail, wholesale, banking, ranching, marketing, and brokering operations—which during the next five decades became the catalyst of Kerrville's and the area's early prosperity and growth. The Civil War slowed this development, but with the start of Reconstruction Kerrville's economic boom continued anew as demand in San Antonio for lumber, produce, and craftsmen combined with the cessation of Indian raids and the expansion of cattle, sheep, and goat ranching into the upper Hill Country and Edwards Plateau. Cattle drives punctuated the boom years of the late 1880s and the 1890s. In 1887 the San Antonio and Aransas Pass Railway reached Kerrville, and in 1889 the town incorporated. The Kerrville Water Works Company began to provide water for town dwellers in 1894, telephone service was introduced in 1896, and the city began to pave streets in 1912. Kerrville grew steadily throughout the twentieth century, increasing from 1,423 residents in 1900 to 2,353 in 1920, 5,572 in 1940, 8,901 in 1960, and 15,276 in 1980. Its economic has diversified and broadened through business, farming, light manufacturing, health care, transportation, services, education, the arts, and tourist attractions. By 1995 the city's official population was still under 18,000, with another 20,000 people in relatively affluent residential areas south of the river and in the rest of the county. Public and private schools, Schreiner College, several university extension programs, and an unusually large public library served the town. Two museums preserved cowboy art and the history of the Schreiner family. The Kerrville music festivals, sports competitions, arts and crafts fairs, working ranches, wildlife, and exotic game preserves have been widely known in the state since the early 1900s. Businesses in the early 1990s ranged from clinics, sanatoria, summer camps, convention centers, hotels, restaurants, and three hospitals, to an aircraft-manufacturing facility, a major silversmith, a regional bus company, an airport, banks, radio and television stations, newspapers, retail stores, and services. The city also had a large number of artisans, painters, writers, and musicians.   *Glen E. Lich*

Kicking Bird. Kiowa chief; also Tene-Angopte, Striking Eagle; b. ca. 1835; d. Fort Sill, Oklahoma, 4 May 1875; best known as a proponent of peace and accommodation with whites. After the

death in 1866 of Dohäsan, paramount chief of the united Kiowa bands, Kicking Bird assumed the leadership of the tribe's "peace faction." With Satanta, Satank, and others, he represented his people at the Medicine Lodge Treaty Council in 1867 and in 1869 helped to gain the release of Lone Wolf and Satanta from army captivity. Yet peace was elusive, and as conditions on the reservation worsened, Kicking Bird's close relationship with white men made enemies among his own people. At the same time, the ranks of such war chiefs as Satanta and Lone Wolf swelled as hostile Kiowas continued raiding settlements in Texas. By early 1870 Kicking Bird, his influence diminished by accusations of cowardice, had joined the fray and put together his own raiding party. In July his group, some 100 strong, crossed the Red River. Several warriors broke away from the group and robbed a mail stage at Rock Station, near the site of present Jermyn, Jack County. Capt. Curwin B. McClellan led the Sixth Cavalry in a retaliatory attack near the site of Seymour (12 July 1870) and was defeated. The victory in the battle of the Little Wichita River marked the end of Kicking Bird's military career. Expressing regret that tribal divisions forced him to adopt violence, he devoted the rest of his life to reestablishing his contacts with whites and securing peace for his people. In 1871, after the Warren Wagontrain Raid, Kicking Bird acquiesced in the arrest of Satanta, Satank, and Big Tree and worked to calm his tribesmen after the three chiefs were transferred to Fort Richardson. However, in late 1873 he skillfully negotiated the release of Satanta and Big Tree, a diplomatic coup that earned him the loyalty of some two-thirds of his tribesmen. At the same time he worked to further the cause of assimilation among his people by inviting Rev. Thomas Battey to live among the Kiowas as a teacher and counselor.

Even Kicking Bird's considerable abilities were not enough to quell a rising sense of dissatisfaction over reservation conditions, however, and, by late 1873 the war faction went on a raid in Texas and Mexico. During this expedition two young warriors, one the nephew and the other the son of paramount chief Lone Wolf, were killed. Stimulated by a desire for revenge and angered by the continued slaughter of the buffalo, Kiowa warriors again took to the warpath. Though Kicking Bird was successful in keeping his followers on the reservation, a number of Kiowas, including Bird Bow, White Shield, White Horse, Howling Wolf, and perhaps Satanta and Lone Wolf, joined with Quanah Parker's Quahadi Comanches in the unsuccessful attack in the second battle of Adobe Walls (27 June 1874). Afterward, Kiowa military power was utterly destroyed. When Satanta stepped down as war chief in late 1874 and Lone Wolf surrendered early the next year, Kicking Bird was left as the only leader with a sizable following. Consequently, in an effort to influence Kiowa affairs, the United States Army named Kicking Bird principal chief in early 1875. The majority of the tribe, essentially leaderless, acquiesced. As chief and principal intermediary between the tribe and federal authorities, Kicking Bird was placed in charge of those hostile Indians captured during the 1874–75 uprising. Though this position allowed him to shield many of his tribesmen from possible danger, it also placed him under the influence of army authorities. Consequently, when it was decided that some of the hostile Kiowas would be incarcerated in Florida, Kicking Bird was required to choose which of his tribesmen would go. He chose White Horse, Maman-ti, Lone Wolf, and a number of obscure Kiowas, Comanches, Cheyennes, Arapahoes,

Kicking Bird (also known as Striking Eagle and Tene-Angopte). Photograph by Will Soule. Courtesy Seaver Center for Western History Research, Natural History Museum of Los Angeles County; photo Soule #3. A Kiowa chief who tried to secure peace for his people by acquiescing to demands made by the United States Army, Kicking Bird died under mysterious circumstances at about the age of 40.

Joseph S. Key in 1892, she became Lucy Ann Kidd–Key, and the school became North Texas Female College and Conservatory of Music. The college eventually grew to include seven brick buildings, several cottages, and a gymnasium, after taking over the property of Mary Nash College (across the street) in 1905. Peak enrollments of more than 500 were reached before World War I. By 1910 the school owned 120 pianos. With teachers imported from Europe, Mrs. Kidd–Key extended the reputation of the music school far beyond Sherman. By the eve of World War I, however, the policy of off-campus chaperonage, compulsory church attendance, and strict regulations about dress and demeanor appealed to fewer and fewer students and parents. The steady decline in enrollment was exacerbated by hard economic times and the opening of Southern Methodist University in 1915, with the consequent reduction of Methodist support for smaller schools. North Texas Female College officially became Kidd–Key College and Conservatory in 1919, three years after Mrs. Kidd–Key's death.

Edwin Kidd succeeded his mother as president and served until 1923, when E. L. Spurlock took on the duties. When, in 1928, ill health forced Spurlock to resign, Kidd resumed the presidency with reluctance and made a last attempt at expanding the college. Despite a new administration building and auditorium, completely refurbished facilities, and heavy expenditures for new furniture, equipment, and landscaping, enrollments failed to rise. In 1930 Kidd–Key and neighboring Austin College attempted to weather the oncoming depression by coordinating programs and sharing facilities. Kidd–Key eliminated its junior college and taught only home economics, religion, fine arts, and women's physical education. The cooperative venture prolonged the institution's existence by a few years, but complete withdrawal of Methodist support forced the college to close in 1935. The property reverted to creditors and was sold to the city of Sherman in 1937 as a site for a municipal center. Nothing remains of the original buildings. *Larry Wolz*

and Mexican captives, some 70 prisoners in all. Not surprisingly, Kicking Bird's acquiescence to the demands of the army was interpreted as treason by many Kiowas. When officials from Fort Sill presented him with a gray horse, the image of Kicking Bird as a collaborator was strengthened further. Consequently, when he died suddenly after drinking a cup of coffee, it was widely assumed, but never proved, that he had been poisoned. Several Kiowas claimed that he was killed by witchcraft. He was given a Christian buried at Fort Sill, even though he had never been converted. His grave was marked only with a wooden cross, and when that decayed the location of his remains was forgotten. *Brian C. Hosmer*

Kidd–Key College. At Sherman; founded in the late 1860s as Sherman Male and Female High School by Rev. William R. Petty under the patronage of the North Texas Methodist Conference. The institution became North Texas Female College in 1874 but was forced to close in 1886. Two years later Methodist bishop G. D. Galloway persuaded a stalwart widow, Lucy Ann Thornton Kidd, who was teaching at Whitworth College in Brookhaven, Mississippi, to move to Texas and reopen the school. North Texas Female College reopened in September 1888 with 100 students. From the beginning Mrs. Kidd's curriculum emphasized the fine arts, especially music. Upon her marriage to Bishop

Kilgore, Texas. In south central Gregg County. The area was first settled before the Civil War by planters from the Old South, but the city was not founded until 1872, when the International–Great Northern Railroad built a line between Longview and Palestine. The railroad bypassed New Danville, and the company platted a new town, which they named for Constantine Buckley Kilgore, who sold the townsite to the railroad and urged many of the businesses of New Danville to move there. A post office opened in 1873, and by 1885 Kilgore had two steam gristmill–cotton gins, a church, and a district school; the estimated population was 250. The town had a reported population of 700 by 1914 and reached a population of 1,000 in 1929. But the combined effects of the Great Depression and the decline of cotton, on which the town's economy had largely depended, brought a steep population decline. By the middle of 1930 the number of residents dropped below 500 and many businesses had been forced to close. The discovery of the surrounding East Texas oilfield in the fall of 1930 transformed Kilgore from a declining rural community into a boomtown. Within days thousands streamed into the town, putting up tents and shacks in every vacant space. Honky-tonks sprouted around the town; schools and other public institutions were overwhelmed. By 1936 the town's population had swelled to 12,000. To deal with the

Street scene with railroad ties, ca. 1902–1908. Courtesy East Texas Research Center, Ralph W. Steen Library, Stephen F. Austin State University. Constantine Buckley Kilgore sold a 174-acre townsite (later named Kilgore in his honor) to the Great Northern Railroad in 1872. The railroad provided transportation for the growing lumber industry.

onslaught, the city incorporated in February 1931. Kilgore, located near the geographic center of the oilfield, became an important production, processing, service, and supply hub. Numerous wells were drilled in the city itself, and at the height of the boom there were over 1,100 producing wells within the city limits. On part of one downtown block in the early 1930s stood the greatest concentration of oil derricks in the world; the area came to be known as the "World's Richest Acre." But the huge increase in production caused oil prices to fall precipitously, and in August 1931 Governor Ross Sterling ordered martial law to control production and bring order to the area. The boom began to subside in the mid-1930s. Major oil companies gradually bought out most of the independents, and by the eve of World War II the boom was largely over, although oil production in the area continues. In 1990 the population was 11,066. In the early 1990s the town housed a major office of the Oil and Gas Division of the Railroad Commission and the headquarters of various branches of the oil and gas industry. The East Texas Oil Museum and Kilgore College, the home of the Kilgore Rangerettes, are also in Kilgore, the hometown of Van Cliburn.

Kilgore Rangerettes. The first women's precision drill team in the world; started in 1940 by Gussie Nell Davis, a physical-education teacher at Kilgore College. The team was organized to attract female students, to provide half-time shows during the football season, and to promote women's physical education. Davis enlisted the help of local oil millionaire Liggett Crim to pay for the Rangerettes' initial costs. Within a year the Ranger-

ettes had traveled to New Orleans to represent the region's oil business at the Lions International convention. The Rangerettes began appearing throughout East Texas in "bond shows" in support of the war effort. They have continued to perform for the college and have also participated in many other events, including the Macy's Thanksgiving Day Parade and the American Bar Association Convention. Since the 1970s they have taken six world tours, to South America, the Far East, Romania, France, Canada, and Japan. The troupe thrived under the direction of Gussie Davis for almost four decades, until her retirement in 1979. She turned the Rangerettes into a company that executed perfect routines by holding to the concept that the Rangerettes "don't make mistakes." The Rangerette costume—a blouse, arm gauntlets, a belt, and a short circular skirt, in red, white, and blue, with white hat and boots—has remained unchanged, except for a slight shortening of the skirt. Since the Kilgore Rangerettes became so popular, all-female drill teams have proliferated. Kilgore College opened a Rangerette Showcase on its campus in 1979.   *Teresa Palomo Acosta*

Killeen, Texas. In western Bell County about 40 miles north of Austin. In 1881 the Gulf, Colorado and Santa Fe Railway, planning to extend its tracks through the area, bought 360 acres some 2 miles southwest of a community known as Palo Alto, which had existed since about 1872. Soon afterward the railroad platted a 70-block town on its land and named it after Frank Killeen, the assistant general manager of the railroad. The first train passed through in May 1882, and by the end of the year the town included the railroad depot, several stores, a saloon, and a school. By 1884 the population was about 350, served by five general stores, two gristmills, two cotton gins, two saloons, a lumberyard, a blacksmith shop, and a hotel. As it became an important shipping point for the cotton, wool, and grain produced on local farms, Killeen continued to expand. Some 780 people lived there by 1900, virtually all of them white Protestants, since the community openly discouraged blacks and Catholics from moving there. The First National Bank of Killeen was incorporated in 1901, and the town's first electric-light system and power plant was installed in 1904 and 1905. About that same time local boosters helped to persuade the Texas legislature to build bridges over Cowhouse Creek and other streams, effectively doubling Killeen's trade area. A public water system began operating in 1914. By that year the town had two banks and a population of about 1,300. Until the 1940s Killeen remained a relatively small and isolated farm trade center. During the Great Depression local economic problems were offset to some extent by New Deal programs that helped to provide jobs and sustenance. By 1939 projects funded by the WPA had helped to improve the community by paving its streets, by installing a new water and sewage system, and by widening a number of local bridges. During the depression federal funds also constructed U.S. Highway 190 through the area.

Killeen was permanently altered in 1942, when Camp Hood (recommissioned as Fort Hood in 1950) was established nearby. Construction workers, soldiers, and their families moved into the area by the thousands, and Killeen became a military boomtown with an acute housing shortage; some newcomers found themselves paying rent to sleep in henhouses, and at one time about 1,000 workers lived in a tent city raised to deal with the unexpected influx. The opening of Camp Hood also forced a fundamental change in the nature of the local economy, since the sprawling new military base covered almost half of Killeen's trade area. The loss of business from about 300 closed-down farms and ranches led to the demise of Killeen's cotton gins and other businesses related to farm supply, while new businesses were started to provide services to the military camp. Killeen became a boom-or-bust town that expanded and contracted depending on the size of the military presence in the area. A severe recession occurred when Camp Hood was all but depopulated after the end of World War II, but when Fort Hood was established as a permanent army base in 1950, the city boomed again. Its population increased from about 1,300 in 1949 to 7,045 in 1950, and by 1955 Killeen had an estimated 21,076 residents. In 1955 the municipal government drew up a master plan for the city in response to public demand for more amenities, such as street improvements, parks, and recreation centers. Troop cutbacks and transfers in the mid-1950s led to another recession that lasted until 1959, when the First Armored Division was returned to Fort Hood. The town continued to grow through the 1960s, especially after the Vietnam War led to increased activity at Fort Hood. By 1970 Killeen had developed into a city of 35,507 inhabitants and had added a municipal airport, a new municipal library, and a junior college (Central Texas College). Though the cycle of booms and busts continued into the early 1990s, the city continued to grow, as Fort Hood survived periodic cutbacks and transfers. By 1980, when the census counted 49,307 people in Killeen, it was the largest city in Bell County. In the late 1980s the city launched a public-relations campaign

designed to entice tourists to the area by redefining the popular image of a military town: "Tanks for the Memories" became the official slogan. By 1990 the population had increased to 63,535, and 255,301 people lived in the area. In addition to shaping local economic development after 1950, Fort Hood also changed the city's racial, religious, and ethnic composition. By the 1980s Killeen had a heterogeneous population including whites, African Americans, Mexican Americans, Koreans, and a number of foreign nationals.   *John Leffler*

Killough Massacre. Probably the largest single Indian depredation in East Texas; occurred on 5 October 1838 in what is now northwestern Cherokee County. The victims, principally the extended family of Isaac Killough, Sr., had immigrated to Texas from Alabama the year before. Their land was part of a larger tract originally granted to the Cherokees by treaty in 1836. The treaty, however, was nullified by the Republic of Texas Senate in December 1837, and portions of the land were sold to the Killoughs and other settlers. The rescinding of the treaty and the growing incursions of new settlers from the Old South provoked bitter resentments in the Indians and laid the basis for the uprisings in 1838. The Córdova Rebellion, although suppressed by Gen. Thomas J. Rusk, raised the fears of settlers, who fled the area. Killough and his group returned in the fall. On the afternoon of October 5 a hostile band attacked their settlement and killed or carried off 18 people. The survivors, including Killough's wife, Urcey, eventually made their way to Lacy's Fort, forty miles to the south. Rusk and his militia found the band, attacked, and killed 11 of them, including a renegade Cherokee named Tail. Gen. Hugh McLeod later wrote that the band included Caddos, Coushattas, runaway slaves, Mexicans, and possibly Keechis. The survivors of the massacre claimed that they saw a white man dressed as an Indian among the attackers, but the claim was never substantiated. The Killough Massacre and its aftermath represent a final chapter of the Córdova Rebellion, but the deep-seated resentments aroused by the abrogation of Sam Houston's treaty and the incursions of new settlers led to the Cherokee War the following year.   *Christopher Long*

King Ranch. The most famous Texas ranch; now 825,000 acres, in Nueces, Kenedy, Kleberg, and Willacy counties. In 1852 Richard King and Gideon K. Lewis set up a cattle camp on Santa Gertrudis Creek in Nueces County. The next year they bought the surrounding Spanish land grant, Rincón de Santa Gertrudis, of 15,500 acres. In the following years, first in partnership with Lewis and afterward with James Walworth, King acquired more land. In 1860 Mifflin Kenedy, with whom King had been associated in a steamboating business, bought interest in the ranch. When Walworth died in 1865, King and Kenedy bought his interest from his widow. The two dissolved their partnership in 1868, and King retained Santa Gertrudis; other acreage was added later. During the early days of the ranch King tried raising cattle, horses, sheep, and goats. His first officially recorded brand was the HK (1859). The Running W was registered in 1869 as the official brand for the King Ranch and is still used today. When the ranch began, King employed a number of Mexican hands, and it is said that in 1854 he moved the inhabitants of an entire drought-stricken Mexican village to his ranch and employed them. His workers came to be known as *kineños*, "King's men." King became associated with Robert Justus Kleberg in a lawsuit and later hired him as legal adviser on the ranch. Upon King's death (14 April 1885), Mrs. King retained Kleberg as manager of the ranch. Kleberg later married Alice King, the youngest daughter. Kleberg's greatest contribution to the management of the ranch and to the Texas cattle industry as a whole was his work in eradicating Texas fever. Because of his father's fading health, Robert Justus Kleberg, Jr., became ranch manager in 1933. In 1935, after the death of Mrs. King, the ranch came under the control of King Ranch, Incorporated, with Kleberg as manager and the King–Kleberg descendants as stockholders. The foundation stock of the King Ranch was the longhorn. In 1874 King bought several Brahman bulls. In the 1880s shorthorns and Herefords were brought to the ranch. Brahmans, which were especially adapted to the South Texas climate, were crossbred with the shorthorns to produce the famous Santa Gertrudis cattle, officially recognized as a breed in 1940.

During the first part of the twentieth century the King Ranch became a diversified enterprise. In the early 1940s the ranch began breeding and racing both quarter horses and English thoroughbreds. In 1947 the ranch had 2,900 quarter horses and 82 racehorses. After Assault won the Triple Crown in 1946 and became for a time racing's all-time money winner, the ranch expanded its horse-breeding operations. It bought a 680-acre bluegrass farm called Idle Hour Stable in Kentucky in 1946. Subsequently, King Ranch horses became regular winners. In 1954 and 1955, for example, High Gun won $486,025, and in 1955 Rejected entered 40 races, won 10, placed second in 10, and won a total of $544,000. The ranch employed Valgene W. Lehmann as a conservationist in 1945 and placed strict game restrictions on its properties. Some sections of the ranch are wildlife preserves for deer, quail, ducks, wild turkeys, and antelope. More than 2,000 miles of fence have been built on its four divisions—Santa Gertrudis, Laureles, Norias, and El Sauz. In 1989 the ranch had 300 water wells. Formerly, most wells had been run by windmills, but in 1980 Hurricane Allen destroyed many of them, and most of the windmills were replaced with electric pumps. During the 1920s and early 1930s the King Ranch was in serious financial difficulties resulting from a poor beef markets. Oil was its salvation. As early as 1919 the ranch had a lease with Humble Oil and Refining Company, which drilled a few dry holes. The lease expired in 1926, and throughout the 1920s the ranch and Humble negotiated for oil and mineral rights on the property. Agreement was not reached until 1933 because Humble's top management was uncertain about the oil potential of this part of Texas. Company geologist Wallace E. Pratt finally convinced Humble to gamble on the largest oil-lease contract negotiated in the United States. Its subsequent leases with neighboring ranches gave Humble nearly two million acres of mineral rights between Corpus Christi and the Rio Grande. The first well on the King Ranch was completed in 1939. Drilling was minor until 1945, when the Borregas oilfield was discovered. After that, several major oil and gas discoveries were made on the ranch, where in 1947 Humble operated 390 producing oil wells. Humble constructed a large refinery in Kingsville to handle its South Texas production. In 1953 the ranch had 650 producing oil and gas wells. In 1980 a subsidiary, King Ranch Oil and Gas, was formed to conduct exploration and production of oil and gas in five states and the Gulf of Mexico. Louisiana and Oklahoma holdings were sold to Presidio Oil in 1988 for more than $40 million. In 1992 King Ranch Oil and Gas was one among several compa-

nies to discover natural gas off the coast of Louisiana. By 1994 the King Ranch had received oil and gas royalties amounting to more than $1 billion since World War II. The King Ranch entered the lumber industry in 1967, when it purchased 50,340 acres of timberland in Harris, Montgomery, Liberty, and San Jacinto counties for $17.6 million.

Cattle operations of the King Ranch have become worldwide. King Ranch, Incorporated, bought a 4,300-acre fattening range in Chester County, Pennsylvania, in 1946. The experiment proved its value because of its proximity to the market and good grass, and an additional purchase increased the Pennsylvania spread to 10,500 acres. In 1947 the ranch in Chester County was expanded to about 17,000 acres. In 1952 the King Ranch bought ranches in Cuba and Australia. The Cuban ranch, more than 38,000 acres, was lost to the communist revolution (1959). The Australian ranch was expanded in 1958, with the help of Australian businessmen, into a three-million-acre range in the northwest region. By 1958 the King Ranch also had cattle ranges of 147,000 acres in Brazil (operated in conjunction with Swift and Company) and 22,000 acres in Argentina. All of these ranges, like those of the home ranch itself, were devoted to the development and promotion of Santa Gertrudis cattle.

After Kleberg died in 1974, James Clement became CEO. He retired in 1988, and Darwin Smith took over. He was the first head who was not related to Richard King by blood or marriage. In 1989 Roger Jarvis assumed the position of CEO, and corporate headquarters were moved to Houston. During the 1990s the King Ranch had approximately 60,000 head of cattle and had ranching operations in Texas, Arizona, Kentucky, Florida, and Brazil. The ranch's farming operations included the cultivation of grain sorghum, cotton, sugarcane, and wildflowers. The ranch was ranked 175th out of the top 500 businesses in Texas. The King Ranch has long held significant banking and mercantile interests in Kingsville, a town located in the heart of the ranch. It has long supported the agricultural educational programs of Texas A&M University, both at College Station and Kingsville. During the 1980s and 1990s the ranch became more involved in tourism. By the later 1980s visitors could tour the ranch along a 12-mile driving loop. In the 1990s tourists could also visit the King Ranch Museum in Kingsville, which features historic ranch items and photographs. Also located in Kingsville is the King Ranch Saddle Shop, which offers a variety of leather goods. *John Ashton and Edgar P. Snead*

Kinney, Henry Lawrence. Land speculator; b. near Shesequin, Pennsylvania, 3 June 1814; d. Matamoros, 3 March 1862; m. Mrs. Mary B. Herbert (1850). In 1838 Kinney appeared in Texas and settled near the site of present-day Brownsville. He began using the title "Colonel," which he claimed to have earned during the Seminole War in Florida, but there is no evidence that he took part in that conflict. In 1841, in partnership with William P. Aubrey, he began ranching and trading near Corpus Christi, a city that Kinney helped to found. Some of his business allegedly involved illegal trading with Mexico. His practice of buying out small ranchers and traders in the area developed considerable opposition, particularly from another merchant, Philip Dimmitt. When Dimmitt and several others were captured by a Mexican raiding force and taken back to Mexico, Kinney was accused of being an informant for the Mexicans and was indicted and tried for treason. He was eventually acquitted and resumed his activities. He was elected as a senator to the Ninth Texas Congress and served as a delegate to the Convention of 1845. James Pinckney Henderson appointed him to his staff for the campaign in northern Mexico at the beginning of the Mexican War. At the end of the war Kinney returned to Corpus Christi and began trading with a number of Central and South American countries. He also operated a fleet of prairie schooners that transported freight from Corpus Christi to the interior of Texas. He served in the Senate for the First, Second, Third and Fourth legislatures of the new state of Texas. He also became increasingly involved in buying large tracts of land and selling them to new immigrants. In 1852 he organized the Corpus Christi Fair in an effort to promote the region. But though the fair itself was a success, Kinney was less successful in luring settlers, and he began to lose a great deal of money. In order to recover some of his losses, he went to Washington in an attempt to persuade the government to invest in several schemes, including the use of camels to transport goods from Corpus Christi to San Francisco and an army hospital in Corpus Christi. None of the ideas ever materialized, and Kinney embarked on a new venture to establish a colony in Nicaragua. Financed by New York speculators, he contracted for 30 million acres along the Mosquito Coast. But he faced stiff opposition from the United States government, and when his largest financial backer died Kinney was forced to abandon his plans. His marriage proved unhappy—in part because of Kinney's decision to legitimize his illegitimate daughter—and Mrs. Kinney took her children and settled in Galveston. After the failure of the Nicaraguan venture, financially ruined and distraught, Kinney returned to Texas. He was elected to the Eighth Legislature. He was opposed to the secession movement, however, and in March 1861 he resigned his seat and moved to Matamoros. He was apparently killed in a gunfight between two local factions. *Amelia W. Williams*

Kirby, John Henry. Businessman; b. near Peach Tree Village, Tyler County, 16 November 1860; d. Houston, 9 November 1940; m. Lelia Stewart (1883); 1 daughter. Kirby learned law from state senator Samuel B. Cooper and was calendar clerk of the Texas Senate (1882–84). In Houston, at Cooper's recommendation, a group of Boston investors engaged Kirby's legal services. His business career wildly fluctuated. The Texas and Louisiana Land and Lumber Company and the Texas Pine Land Association, formed with his Boston associates to speculate in East Texas timberlands, provided him with a small fortune. Those successes led him, in company with Bostonians Nathaniel D. Silsbee and Ellington Pratt, into the building of the Gulf, Beaumont and Kansas City Railway in 1896. The profitable sale of the railroad to the Atchison, Topeka and Santa Fe nearly coincided with the organization by Kirby and Patrick Calhoun in 1901 of the Houston Oil Company of Texas and the Kirby Lumber Company. Mutual distrust and charges of misrepresentation by Kirby and Calhoun led to receivership for both companies and prolonged litigation. Nonetheless, at one time the Kirby Lumber Company controlled more than 300,000 acres of East Texas pinelands and operated 13 sawmills. Kirby was a founder and five-time president of the Southern Pine Association, served two terms as president of the National Lumber Manufacturers' Association (1917–21), and briefly during World War I was southern lumber director of the United States Shipping Board Emergency Fleet Corporation. He also served two terms in the

John Henry Kirby. Courtesy Houston Metropolitan Research Center, Houston Public Library.

Texas legislature and was a delegate to the 1916 Democratic national convention. He shared the conviction of many contemporary entrepreneurs that power naturally followed wealth, and he guarded against any social or political force that threatened the prerogatives of wealth. He was a paternalistic, rigorous, but often generous employer, who considered labor unions anathema because he believed they inflamed the passion of otherwise contented and relatively prosperous workers. Personally convinced that the New Deal would destroy the very fabric of American life, Kirby cofounded the Southern Committee to Uphold the Constitution and contributed his money and energies to other anti–Roosevelt organizations. Financial bankruptcy in 1933 ended his control of his lumber company and of the Kirby Petroleum Company, which he had organized in 1920, although he continued to serve as chairman of the boards of both companies until his death. *George T. Morgan, Jr.*

Kleberg, Robert Justus, Jr. Rancher; b. Corpus Christi, 29 March 1896; d. Houston, 13 October 1974; m. Helen Campbell (1926); 1 daughter. This scion of one of the state's leading ranching families was the grandson of Richard King, founder of the King Ranch. In spite of his name, he was the third rather than the second Robert Justus Kleberg. He began his ranching career at the King Ranch in 1916 and managed the ranch after his father's death in 1932. He was named president of the operation when it became a family corporation in 1935. In addition to the King Ranch, Kleberg also managed holdings in Florida, Kentucky, and Pennsylvania, and in Brazil, Argentina, Spain, Morocco, and Australia. He is credited with developing the first United States breed of beef cattle, the Santa Gertrudis, perfected over 30 years. He became known in agriculture with his development of grazing grasses. He received honorary doctorates in agricultural science from Texas A&M (1941) and in science from the University of Wisconsin (1967), where he had done under-

Robert Justus Kleberg, Jr., ca. 1960s. Courtesy Belton Kleberg Johnson, San Antonio. Print courtesy ITC; 83-277.

graduate work. Under Kleberg's direction, the King Ranch developed thoroughbred racetrack winners that averaged $825,000 a year in purse money. The best known was Assault, the Triple Crown winner in 1946; Middleground and Bold Venture both won the Kentucky Derby. Kleberg had other business, banking, and railroad interests.

Knights of the Golden Circle. A secret antebellum organization that sought to establish a slave empire encompassing the southern United States, the West Indies, Mexico, and part of Central America—the "Golden Circle." The Knights hoped to control the commerce of the area and have a virtual monopoly on the world's supply of tobacco, sugar, and perhaps rice and coffee. The association was organized in 1854 by George W. L. Bickley, a Virginia-born doctor, editor, and adventurer living in Cincinnati. It grew slowly until 1859 and reached its height in 1860. The membership, scattered from New York to California, was never large. Like other secret societies, the Knights had an elaborate ritual, but the organization was poorly financed and even more poorly led. Bickley's main goal seems to have been the annexation of Mexico. Hounded by creditors, he left Cincinnati in the late 1850s and traveled through the East and South promoting a filibustering expedition to seize Mexico and establish a new domain for slaveholders. He found his greatest support in Texas and managed within a short time to organize thirty-two "castles," or local chapters, in cities that included Houston, Galveston, Austin, San Antonio, Jefferson, and La Grange. Among his prominent Texas supporters were Alfred M. Hobby,

Elkanah Greer, George Cupples, Trevanion Teel, and Capt. John B. Lubbock. Bickley received some favorable newspaper coverage in the Texas papers, and for a time courted Governor Sam Houston, who was reportedly initiated into the group. Houston, however, was opposed to the KGC's anti-Union stand and ultimately refused to throw his support behind it.

In the spring of 1860 the group made the first of two attempts to invade Mexico from Texas. A small band reached the Rio Grande, but Bickley failed to show up with a large force he claimed he was assembling in New Orleans, and the campaign dissolved. In April some KGC members in New Orleans, disgusted by Bickley's inept leadership, met and expelled him, but Bickley called a convention in Raleigh, North Carolina, in May and succeeded in having himself reinstated. He attempted to mount a second expedition to Mexico later in the year, but with Abraham Lincoln's election he and most of his supporters turned their attention to the secessionist movement. Bickley served for a time as a Confederate surgeon and was arrested for spying in Indiana in July 1863. He was never tried but remained under arrest until October 1865 and died, broken and dispirited, in August 1867. The KGC quietly dissolved during the war. Some at the time claimed that the organization operated as a fifth column in the North, and in the 1864 political campaign Republicans accused some antiwar Democrats of being secret members of the group. The charges, however, were largely unfounded. Although KGC forms and symbols were sometimes used by other groups, the Knights evidently had no organization in the Northern states; they did operate in Kentucky, a "border state." After the war sporadic reports of KGC activities cropped up, some of them as far west as West Texas and Oklahoma Territory, but by that time, practically speaking, the organization had ceased to exist.   *Christopher Long*

Knights of the Order of San Jacinto. In a letter to William Henry Daingerfield dated 28 January 1843, President Sam Houston stated that Daingerfield and Ashbel Smith would be made Knights of the Order of San Jacinto. Houston's intent was that diplomats of the Republic of Texas would not have to appear titleless and ribbonless among the aristocratic diplomats of Europe. In the letter Houston described the ensign of the order as a green ribbon, worn on the left breast or buttonhole of the coat. Along with the diplomats, Houston wished to honor others who distinguished themselves in service to Texas. The actual awards were probably never made, and besides the letter to Daingerfield there is no mention of the award in contemporary papers. In 1939, however, at the suggestion of Hobart Huson, the Sons of the Republic of Texas revived the honorary title. Huson suggested that the award be given to living men and women who had made a distinguished contribution to Texas, but at the next annual meeting, members nixed giving the award to women. The award was given from 1941 through 1945 and then discontinued, as some members felt that several men not worthy of the order had been nominated. The honor was reinstated in 1952. A nominee had to be an active or honorary member of the Sons of the Republic of Texas and a white male over age 18. Racial qualifications were later abolished, though as of 1990 all of the 137 knights had been white.   *John G. Johnson*

Knights of Pythias. A charitable and fraternal order established in Texas with the installation of Lodge No. 1 in Houston in 1872, eight years after the first lodge of the order had been established in Washington, D.C. The Grand Lodge of Texas was instituted at Houston in 1874, with 10 lodges participating. The order expanded rapidly, but since many lodges were hastily organized, 15 of the first 20 ceased to exist by the end of 1877. After 1878 the Grand Lodge began to rebuild on a firmer basis. In 1895 the Knights of Pythias was granted a charter by the state. The zenith in number of lodges was attained in 1910 with 378, and in number of members in 1922 with 30,507. In 1942 there were 105 lodges with 9,553 members. Since 1909 the organization has maintained the Pythian Widows and Orphans Home, three miles east of Weatherford. An auxiliary order, the Grand Temple Pythian Sisters, has been in operation since the mid-1890s. Throughout the twentieth century the order continued to operate halfway houses and other community facilities. In Dallas, for example, the Knights of Pythias operated a senior citizens' home and a credit union. In the early 1990s there were approximately 53 lodges across the state with an estimated total of 1,700 members.

Helen B. Frantz

Knights of the White Camellia. A short-lived secret Southern organization of white supremacists in the Reconstruction period; opposed racial amalgamation and carpetbaggers and sought to restore white control of the government. The order was organized in New Orleans in May 1867 by Col. Alcibiade DeBlanc and soon reached as far west as Central Texas and as far east as the Carolinas. Though similar in some respects to the Ku Klux Klan, the White Camellias denied any Klan connection. The Camellias operated with less publicity but with perhaps more effectively than Klansmen, although they did not employ such violent methods. They are thought to have been even more numerous than Klansmen, and their secrets were better kept. They were typically better organized than the Klan, and their membership, which was generally from a higher social stratum, included newspaper editors, physicians, lawyers, law-enforcement officials, public figures, and even a few former officers of the Union army. Many of the members freely admitted their membership; officers sometimes identified themselves as members before congressional or legislative committees and detailed their organization and some of their activities. Though some renegade members committed atrocities, many others left the order because of its lack of militancy. Like the Klan, the Knights had an elaborate secret ceremony and ritual, and their customs included signs, grips, and passwords. The constitution of the order, adopted at a convention in New Orleans in June 1868, provided for an organizational structure similar to that of the Klan, albeit with more conventional nomenclature. In Texas the membership of the Knights appears to have been concentrated particularly along the Louisiana border, though councils were found as far west as Waco. The order generally shunned the activities of outlaw gangs such as those of Ben Bickerstaff and Cullen Baker. By 1869 the Camellias were on the decline. They held a convention in New Orleans that year, but many of the councils had already disbanded. Some of the more strident members joined the Klan or the White Leagues.

Christopher Long

Koreans. Koreans in Texas are an important part of the fast-growing immigration from East Asia. Except for wives of American servicemen who fought in the Korean War (1950–53) or were sta-

tioned in South Korea afterwards, few Koreans lived in Texas until the late 1960s. As late as 1970 the census recorded only 2,090 Koreans in the state. Twenty years later the Korean population had increased 15-fold to 31,775. In 1990 Koreans ranked fifth in population among Asians and Pacific Islanders, behind the Vietnamese, Chinese, Asian Indians, and Filipinos, but ahead of the Japanese. This extraordinary increase in the number of Koreans was due largely to the 1965 liberalization of United States immigration laws, which previously had denied entry to all but a few Asians. Many of these post-1965 immigrants originally came to the United States and to Texas in search of economic opportunities; others came later to join relatives who were already here. Almost half of the Koreans in Texas in 1990 were evenly divided between Dallas (7,290) and Harris (6,571) counties; other counties with a sizable Korean population were Bell, Bexar, Travis, Tarrant, and El Paso.

The Koreans in Texas, as elsewhere in the United States, are largely made up of three groups: wives of American servicemen previously stationed in Korea, small business entrepreneurs, and professional people. Because of the ongoing presence of many American troops in South Korea, war brides have continued to arrive in large numbers, accompanying their husbands as they are transferred home. They are scattered across the state, particularly among various military bases such as Fort Hood in Bell County and others in Bexar and El Paso counties. Because of the preponderance of the war brides, the Koreans in Texas—as in the whole country—are, unlike the Vietnamese, Chinese, and Asian Indians, a predominantly female population. In 1990, among the Koreans, women outnumbered men three to two.

The operations of Korean entrepreneurs in Texas are generally small and thus do not need much in the way of startup capital; they are run almost entirely by family members who work long hours and pool their resources. Such "mom-and-pop" businesses include gas stations, convenience stores, liquor stores, and restaurants, most of which require only a limited knowledge of English. Korean entrepreneurs also operate ethnic businesses like groceries and restaurants that sell Oriental produce and serve a mixture of Korean, Chinese, and Japanese cuisine. These businesses sometimes feature signs written in Hangul, the distinctive phonetic writing system of Korea. There is some clustering of Korean businesses, such as in the Spring Branch area of Houston. But because they cater mostly to the general public, they are not so concentrated anywhere in Texas as to form "Koreatowns."

Many of the professional Koreans came originally as students and then remained after their graduation. For example, Sung Kwak, who was born in Seoul, arrived in the United States in the mid-1960s, graduated from a music school in New York, and was appointed the conductor of the Austin Symphony Orchestra in 1982. A number of Korean professionals are college teachers. Wendy Lee, who earned a Ph.D. in economics from Northwestern University, came in 1970 to teach at Texas A&M University, where she married her colleague, Phil Gramm. When her husband was elected in 1978 to the United States House and later to the Senate, Mrs. Gramm joined him in Washington, where she worked as an economist and from 1988 to 1993 chaired the Commodity Futures Trading Commission.

The three main groups of Koreans in Texas generally have little to do with each other. The war brides, in particular, tend to be dispersed and isolated; moreover, they often differ in educa-

Fania Feldman Kruger, ca. 1910. Courtesy Bert Kruger Smith, Austin.

tion and socioeconomic origins from the entrepreneurs and the professionals. Even though the latter two groups are generally well educated and come from the upper middle class of Korean society, their occupations in the United States lead them in separate directions. Nevertheless, the two principal centers of Korean social activity are the Christian Church and the Korean Association. Unlike other East Asians except Filipinos, the vast majority of Koreans arrive in the United States already as Christians, usually Protestants. In Texas cities with a large Korean population, a number of different denominations offer services in Korean as well as English; in Austin in the early 1990s, for example, there were eight Korean churches, seven Protestant and one Catholic. Typically, as in Austin, the largest of the Korean churches in each city is Presbyterian. There is generally only one Korean Association in each city. It sponsors communitywide celebrations, assists new arrivals, and speaks for the local Korean community in its dealings with the outside world.

Edward J. M. Rhoads

Kruger, Fania Feldman. Poet;. b. Sevastopol, 8 March 1893; d. Austin, 16 July 1977 (buried in Temple Beth Israel Cemetery); m. Sam Kruger (1912); 2 children. Her father was a rabbi. Because of the family's faith, Fania was denied entrance to the *Gymnasia* three times before she was admitted. As a child she witnessed a murder committed by Cossack troops and saw her father after they had beaten him. She and her sister became partisans in the political underground during the revolution of 1905, and out of fear for their safety the Feldmans immigrated to the United States in 1908. They settled in Fort Worth, where Fania learned to speak English. In 1913 Sam and Fania Kruger moved to Wichita

Falls, where Sam opened a jewelry and antique store and Fania became active in a Jewish women's group and the local literary society. After Sam died in 1952, Fania moved to Austin. Her experiences in Russia inspired her poetry and were the basis for a lifelong commitment to human rights. She published three collections of poems, *Cossack Laughter* (1938), *The Tenth Jew* (1949), and *Selected Poems* (1973). Her poetry was also published in *Southwest Review, Crisis, American Guardian, American Hebrew, Texas Quarterly,* and the *Year Book* of the Poetry Society of Texas. Her "Peasant's Pilgrimage to Kiev" was translated into Russian and published in Moscow. A short story, "To a Young Mother," was published in the October 1960 issue of *Redbook* magazine and was produced and repeatedly televised in Austin between 1965 and 1970. Fania Kruger narrated and appeared in the film. In 1969 the University of Cincinnati commissioned violinist, conductor, and composer Frederic Balazs, director of the Philharmonia Orchestra, to set "The Tenth Jew" to music. Among Kruger's awards were first place for the best poem of the year from the Poetry Society of America for "Passover Eve" in 1946, the Lola Ridge award from the same society in 1947 for "Blessing the New Moon," and first place for poetry in 1956 from the New York City Writer's Conference. She was a member of the poetry societies of England, America, Texas, and Austin and of the Texas Institute of Letters. In 1959 she returned to the Soviet Union for the first time in 50 years and visited Moscow and Yalta, but was not permitted to go to her birthplace, Sevastopol, probably because it had become the site of a Soviet naval base. She was surprised by her reception in Russia as a celebrity.

Nancy Baker Jones

Ku Klux Klan. In addition to persistent low-level infestation of society, this racist, nativist, anti-Catholic organization has afflicted Texas seriously in two historic eras—Reconstruction and the 1920s. The original organization was founded in Pulaski, Tennessee (1866) and decked out with grandiose and often illiterately derived titles. Its name reportedly derived from the Greek word *kuklos*, meaning circle or band; "Klan," though redundant, was appended to the name for alliteration. The founders adopted elaborate secret rituals patterned after the Kuklos Adelphon, a college fraternity of the antebellum South. Officers consisted of a "grand cyclops" or president, a "grand magi" (plural *sic*) or vice president, a "grand Turk" or marshal, and a "grand exchequer" (*sic*) or treasurer. Local chapters were called dens. In its early years the Klan's regalia included a white mask with holes for the eyes, a high, conical, cardboard hat, and long flowing robes. Initially the organization existed solely for amusement, but as it spread through the Southern states it became more and more associated with racist vigilantism and opposition to Republican rule. By the late 1860s the Klan became one of the principal forms of opposition to Reconstruction, and members were pledged to support white supremacy, to oppose racial mixing, to resist carpetbaggers, and to restore white control of the government. The Klan of the Reconstruction era was not a single organization or even a loose confederation of local and state groups. Several different Klan-like organizations coexisted in various parts of the South; they included the Knights of the Red Hand, the Pale Faces, the White Brotherhood, the Constitutional Union Guards, and, in Texas, the Knights of the Rising Sun and the Knights of the White Camellia. Evidence that the Klan had spread to Texas was first noted in March 1868. At first the group's activities consisted of parades, publications of cryptic newspaper notices, and midnight meetings at graveyards. Republican newspapers satirized these happenings, but by May, when the Klan began to resort to murder and acts of intimidation directed at freedmen and white Republicans, the light-hearted notices ended.

Despite its outward appearance of unity, the Klan in Texas was loosely organized. Roger Q. Mills, a former secessionist and later a congressman, coordinated activities in the state, but often the local groups acted autonomously. Members came from every social stratum, though the upper crust usually shied away from acts of violence. In addition to harassing or killing African Americans, local groups of the Klan or bands posing as Klansmen sometimes used terrorist acts such as stealing horses or burning crops merely to gain economic advantage, in which case most of their victims were Republicans. Generally, Klan violence closely followed politics. Most of the Klan's activities were focused in Northeast Texas, and at least 20 counties, extending from Houston north to the Red River, suffered some form of Klan terror. By late 1868, however, authorities began to gain the upper hand throughout the state. Between October 1868 and September 1869, 59 cases were tried before military courts in Texas, resulting in 29 convictions. In 1870 Republican governor Edmund Davis called on the legislature to form a State Police and a militia, and the measures were passed in June and July. The following year the legislature passed another law making it illegal to be armed and disguised. The Texas Klan began to wane in 1869. In March of that year, the chief executive, or "grand wizard," proclaimed a disbanding of the group. Many of the local chapters followed the lead of the statewide organization, but isolated pockets of Klan activity were still observable in the early 1870s. Such incidents, however, became less common after mid-1870, and the organization in general ceased to exist after Congress passed the Ku Klux Klan Act of April 1871, which permitted the president of the United States to suspend the writ of habeas corpus in cases of secret conspiracy. Although federal efforts played a role in the dissolving the Klan, just as important was the growing reluctance of the Southern white leadership to tolerate violence.

Around the time of World War I a new Ku Klux Klan, patterned after the original one, made its appearance. It flared up in Georgia, where William J. Simmons dedicated it at a cross-burning on Stone Mountain (1915). The success of D. W. Griffith's epic film of the same year, *Birth of a Nation*, based on Thomas Dixon's novel *The Clansman* (1905), with its vivid portrayals of Radical Republican excesses, had helped to fan the flames of racial animosity, which had smoldered since Reconstruction. Also fueling the fire was a growing American nativist movement with its concomitant distrust of Catholics, Jews, blacks, and other "foreign" elements. At first the new Klan grew slowly, but in the aftermath of World War I the organization spread rapidly, not only in the South and Southwest, but also through the Midwest and to both coasts. At its height in the early 1920s the new Klan boasted some two million members. As before, its members or those posing as Klansmen perpetrated acts of violence, and although atrocities were committed across the nation, they were generally concentrated in the South. Some Texans were receptive to the Klan's angry and insular message, and by the early 1920s membership in the state organization numbered in the tens of thousands. Hooded legions paraded in Texas cities

and towns, and cross-burnings, intended to show the power of the "invisible empire," became all too common. The revived Klan's main public appeal was as a fraternal lodge, a refuge for white, Protestant America. It promised to reform politics, to enforce Prohibition, and to champion traditional morality. The preponderance of the membership was concentrated in small towns, but the organization also spread to Dallas, Houston, San Antonio, and the other large cities. Members were drawn from all sectors of society, and many civic leaders, politicians, and law-enforcement officials either belonged or deferred to the Klan. Many officials, however, opposed it. Growing violence attributed to the Klan caused wide resentment, and by 1922 a number of anti-Klan organizations had formed across the state. Recognizing the threat to the organization's growth, Dallas dentist Hiram Wesley Evans, who was elected "imperial wizard" at the organization's first national convention in November 1922, sought to reform the Klan and change its image. He placed strict controls on local groups, which were, for instance, no longer allowed to wear Klan regalia except at Klan-sponsored events, and sought to extend Klan power by working to get members elected to important political posts.

The strategy was especially successful in Texas. With a membership of perhaps as many as 100,000, the Klan used its united voting block to elect state legislators, sheriffs, judges, and other local and state officials. Its greatest success, however, was in securing the election of Earle Mayfield to the United States Senate in 1922. The following year the Klan established firm control of city governments in Dallas, Fort Worth, and Wichita Falls, and the order probably had a majority in the House of Representatives of the Thirty-eighth Texas Legislature, which met in January. By the end of 1922 the paid membership swelled to as many as 150,000, and Kluxers looked forward to even greater triumphs. The year 1923, however, was the high-water mark for the Klan. Its candidate for governor, Felix D. Robertson, a member of the Dallas Klan, was defeated in 1924 by Miriam Ferguson, and dissension within the organization and growing anti-Klan sentiment combined to weaken its influence greatly. By 1928 the membership had declined to around 2,500, and most prominent supporters had left the fold. During the Great Depression, Klan strength waned even further. The fraternity continued its attack on blacks, Jews, and Catholics, but added New Deal politicians and labor organizers to its list of enemies. In 1939 Evans sold ownership of the Klan to James A. Colescott, a veterinarian from Terre Haute, Indiana, but Colescott was soon forced to dissolve the organization because of problems with back taxes and protests over the Klan's association with the German–American Bund.

After World War II the Klan became increasingly fragmented. During the civil-rights era of the late 1950s and early 1960s, Klan activity in Texas again increased, but because of new anti-Klan laws and FBI pressure, the organization remained small and politically impotent. Subsequently, the Klan fractured into numerous small cells that still exist. During the early 1980s the Klan gained new notoriety for its attacks on Vietnamese shrimpers along the Gulf Coast, and in the early 1990s it was again in the news because of assaults on black residents in Vidor. In the waning years of the twentieth century various Klan groups forged links with skinheads and other neo-Nazis and, despite numerous legal actions, continued to be an irritant.

Christopher Long

L

La Bahía. "The Bay," a term with multiple meanings in Texas history. Various sites on the Gulf Coast were so designated. The Spanish came to use the name as a short form of La Bahía del Espíritu Santo, or Bay of the Holy Spirit, now called Matagorda Bay and Lavaca Bay. (In 1519 Álvarez de Pineda called the Mississippi River the Río del Espíritu Santo, and others extended the name to the bay.) The official application of the name to Matagorda and Lavaca bays occurred during the Spanish search for the French colony planted by La Salle. The name La Bahía subsequently referred both to the bay and to entities associated with it. During the Aguayo expedition, a detachment under Domingo Ramón occupied La Bahía del Espíritu Santo and in April 1721 founded a presidio, popularly called Presidio La Bahía, upon the ruins of La Salle's Fort St. Louis. In 1722 the Marqués de Aguayo authorized Father Agustín Patrón y Guzmán to establish Mission La Bahía across the creek from this presidio. Thus the bay, as well as the presidio and the mission because of their location on the bay, were all commonly called La Bahía. Although the presidio and mission were at least twice moved farther inland, the names, including La Bahía, were retained. La Bahía presidio and mission were reestablished in 1726 on the Guadalupe River near the site of present Mission Valley in Victoria County. In 1749 the mission was moved to the north bank of the San Antonio River near the site of present Goliad in Goliad County, and the presidio to the south bank. The missions of Nuestra Señora del Rosario and Nuestra Señora del Refugio, 27 miles away at the site of modern Refugio, were sometimes grouped with Nuestra Señora del Espíritu Santo, and all three were called the La Bahía missions.

In time a civic settlement grew up around the presidio, and it, too, was known as La Bahía. This village became commercially important because it was on the Atascosito Road, the La Bahía Road, and roads from San Antonio de Béxar and El Cópano. La Bahía, Bexar, and Nacogdoches were the most important areas of Spanish settlement in Texas. The importance of La Bahía continued after Mexico won independence from Spain in 1821 and during the period of Anglo-American colonization. In 1829, after a successful petition submitted to the Coahuila and Texas state legislature by Rafael Manchola, who argued that the name La Bahía had become meaningless because neither mission nor presidio had been located on "the bay" since 1726, the Mexican government proclaimed the settlement a villa—a chartered town with municipality jurisdiction—and changed its name to Goliad. During the Texas Revolution the town was called both La Bahía and Goliad, though the old Spanish term was used primarily to mean the presidio and was often corrupted by Anglo-Americans to "Labadee." During the period of the Republic of Texas and after annexation, the old mission and presidio fell into ruin, but the presidio chapel remained intact and was used first as a residence and then for church services after the Catholic Church regained possession of it about 1853. This chapel was commonly referred to as "La Bahía Mission," a designation that led to confusion with the actual La Bahía mission, Espíritu Santo, which lay in ruins until reconstructed as a public-works

project in the 1930s. Presidio La Bahía and its chapel were restored in the 1960s by the Kathryn O'Connor Foundation. Both are now in Goliad State Historical Park. *Craig H. Roell*

Labor. A Spanish land unit measuring 177 acres (pronounced *lahbór*). Under the Mexican colonization act by which the first settlers entered Stephen F. Austin's colony, heads of farm families were to receive a labor of land each. Cattle raisers received a sitio or league. Most of the original settlers combined ranching and farming and received a league and a labor.

Labor Organizations. Short-lived labor unions were established by printers and carpenters in Houston during the Republic of Texas, and "Workingman's" or "Mechanic's" associations, more along the lines of benevolent societies, were constituted in Houston, Galveston, Austin, and New Braunfels before 1860. A local of the National Typographical Union was active in Galveston in antebellum Texas. It sent Joel Miner as a delegate to the meeting of the International held at New Orleans in 1857. Galveston was the earliest center of union activity in the state; the Carpenter's Local No. 7, organized there in 1860, has a nationally recognized claim to a longer history uninterrupted by reorganization than any other local in the United States. Locals of the Typographical Union were organized at Houston in 1865, at Austin in 1870, and in San Antonio about the same time. Most of the building trades in Galveston and Houston organized in the early 1870s, and railway unions developed there and in Austin and Fort Worth. Several of these participated in the great wave of labor unrest in 1877. In 1866 an organization of longshoremen was chartered as the Screwmen's Benevolent Association, and in 1870 a Negro Longshoremen's Association was chartered. Members of these organizations cooperated with the longshoremen in Mobile, Alabama, to form a Southern Association. During the Civil War and Reconstruction many other craft-union locals were formed, but the attempts of the unions of the northeastern United States to form a national organization left Texas untouched.

In the turbulent decade of the 1880s labor organization in the state and nation was dominated by the Knights of Labor. Five district assemblies of the order operated in Texas. The state District Assembly No. 78, with headquarters at Fort Worth, reported 1,901 locals and 8,900 individual members. District Assembly No. 145, which covered the lumbering area and maintained headquarters at Texarkana, had 550 members. District Assembly No. 101, made up of employees of Jay Gould's Southwest system of railways, most of which were in Texas, had 3,300 members. District Assembly No. 211 was chartered for the city of Galveston. District Assembly No. 135, organized for mineworkers with headquarters at Columbus, Ohio, had large locals in Texas at Strawn, Thurber, Bridgeport, Lyra, Gordon, and other places. A report in the Dallas *Morning News* in 1885 estimated the total membership of the Knights in Texas as 30,000. The unsuccessful strike of District Assembly No. 191 against the management of the Gould system, from March to

International Typographical Union members celebrate Labor Day in Wichita Falls, 1910. Courtesy Special Collections Division, University of Texas at Arlington Libraries.

May 1886, seriously affected the area from St. Louis south to Waco and west to El Paso. Although the strength of the Knights was broken by failure of this strike, its repercussions led to the first official investigation of industrial relationships by a congressional committee, which held hearings in Fort Worth, Marshall, Palestine, and other towns. The Knights also assisted the International Granite Cutter's Union in their successful boycott against the contractors who were building the Capitol in Austin with convict-quarried stone. The resulting trial and fining of the contractors for importing Scottish granite cutters was the first and most important prosecution by the federal government for violation of the Alien Contract Labor Law.

With the passing of the Knights, unions became more focused in the larger towns, where the AFL craft unions and streetcar workers predominated, and among railway workers. But exceptions did exist, as illustrated by the almost totally unionized mining town of Thurber and considerable organizing activities among Hispanic workers along the Rio Grande. As the Knights disintegrated, the craft unions attempted to form a state organization in 1891, but were at first unsuccessful. The Texas State Labor Union, organized in 1895, was not craft but agriculturalindustrial in base and lasted for four years only. In 1900 six city-central trade councils—at Austin, Sherman, Corsicana, Dallas, Gainesville, and Hillsboro—were given charters by the AFL. In the same year at a state meeting held at Cleburne, seven cities, with a membership of 8,475, were represented. Since 1903 the Texas State Federation of Labor has held annual meetings and published proceedings. In the early years, the largest voting strength of the state federation was in the Carpenters Union and the United Mine Workers. Membership grew steadily to a peak of 512 locals in 1918. Declining membership through the 1920s brought a low of 135 locals in 1931. There was steady yearly growth for half a century, although membership in the TSFL does not include all members of the American Federation of Labor. In 1943 Texas had about 1,400 locals, with a membership of 225,000, affiliated with the national body.

The International Oil Workers Union, which has at some periods had a significant membership in the state, was one of the original groups that formed the Committee for Industrial Organization, later the CIO. The growth of the CIO in the state has been steady in the cities and the industrial areas that developed rapidly after 1940. In 1944 union membership was found in 115 local bodies: 30 in the Oil Workers International; 12 in the United Steel Workers of America; 8 in the United Automobile Workers; 5 in the American Newspaper Guild; 4 each in the United Cannery, Agricultural Packing and Allied Workers, the National Maritime Union, the American Communications Association, and the Amalgamated Clothing Workers; and 3 in the Mine, Mill, and Smelter Workers; 23 miscellaneous unions; and 18 local industrial unions. There were 5 county organizations. All of these groups composed the Texas State Industrial Union Council (later the Texas State CIO Council), which served as a coordinating agency on legislation and organization. The membership of all labor organizations in the state in 1944 would probably represent about 10 to 12 percent of the total labor force.

Rapid industrialization of Texas during and immediately after World War II increased the number of nonagricultural workers and thereby the potential union membership. Organizational drives by several national unions proved quite successful in the immediate postwar period. By 1946 about 350,000 Texans were union members, of whom about 225,000 were in unions affiliated with the AFL and 60,000 were in CIO-affiliated unions; the remainder were in such unaffiliated unions as the railroad brotherhoods and the Southwestern Telephone Workers (the two largest independent groups), or in such company unions as that of the Humble Oil Company's employees. During the decade following the war, union membership grew faster in Texas than in the nation as a whole. Yet the increase was primarily a result of rapid economic and population growth, for the percentage of nonagricultural workers unionized remained relatively stable at a little below 20 percent, compared to a national average of about 30 percent. Total union membership in the state reached about 375,000 by the mid1950s, or approximately 17 percent of the nonagricultural labor force. The vigor of CIO organizational efforts was demonstrated by an increase in membership in affiliated unions to something over 100,000, while membership in the AFL unions had remained stable and the membership in unaffiliated unions had actually declined to about 40,000. Much of the union growth was in the larger industrial establishments. More than 60 percent of manufacturing plants employing more than 250 workers were organized in 1955, but less than 10 percent of those with fewer than 250 workers had unions. In addition, most labor union strength was in new industries: more than 75 percent of the workers in transportation, communication, and the manufacture of transportation equipment were union members; two-thirds of employees of paper, primary metals, and chemical manufacturers were unionized; and more than half of those working in the petroleum industry were organized. The older industries—lumber, textiles, food, and agricultural processing—remained less than 25 percent unionized. Union membership was therefore both numerically and proportionately strongest in geographic areas where new industry flourished. Almost half of the state's union members were in the Houston–Beaumont area and about onethird in Dallas–Fort Worth. Yet the character and size of the industrial establishment seemed more critical than the location. Wherever large heavy industry was found, unions appeared. There were, for example, large locals of steelworkers in Daingerfield, auto workers in Greenville, rubber workers in Bryan, and oil workers in Tyler, Borger, and Dumas, all towns where few other union members lived. On the other hand, most small industries in Houston, Dallas, and especially San Antonio were not organized.

In July 1957 the 21-year split between the AFL and the CIO in Texas was bridged when, after 18 months of negotiation, the Texas State Federation of Labor and the Texas State CIO Council merged into the Texas State AFL–CIO. The agreement was delayed primarily by differences over representation in and leadership of the new body; jurisdictional disputes between former AFL and CIO unions; and disagreement over the role, scope, and power of the state organization, which was more philosophical than a reflection of the craft–industrial union conflict. Disagreement over policy between the chief officers of the state AFL–CIO, one of which represented the old AFL group and the other the old CIO unions, flared into a floor fight between their supporters for control of the 1961 state convention. That dissension, which threatened to split Texas labor again, involved personalities as well as the craft–industrial union conflict. With the magnanimity of the winners and the grace of the losers, however, a split was avoided, although the ill will between craft and industrial unions that has divided American labor throughout its history remained strong in Texas labor in the 1960s. The dissension helps to explain the continued decline of affiliation of local unions with the state organization. By 1966 only a few more than half the members of AFL–CIO unions were affiliated with the Texas State AFL–CIO, compared to about 60 percent affiliated at the time of the merger. Equally if not more responsible for disaffiliation was the dissatisfaction over the growing assessments by the state AFL–CIO on local unions to finance increasing social and political activities.

Only after World War II did organized labor emerge as a political and social force in Texas. The CIO, through its Political Action Committee, contributed greatly to the 1944 presidential campaign in Texas and gave support to Homer Rainey in the 1946 Democratic gubernatorial primary. The state AFL did not openly enter politics until 1948, when it endorsed Coke Stevenson over Lyndon Johnson in the senatorial primary and supported Roger Evans for governor. Ralph Yarborough's several statewide races received extensive support in the 1950s, and his election as United States senator marked unionized labor's first important political victory. Although in the 1950s there was reason to think that unionized labor's support was more to be avoided than sought in Texas, where antiunion attitudes are strong, by the time of the merger the unions' endorsement was being sought by both local and statewide candidates. In 1958 the state AFL–CIO began to rate members of the legislature and to work actively in legislative races, with little success except in areas of great union strength, where a considerable number of laborsupported candidates were being elected by the mid-1960s. Organized labor also began to play a growing role in other areas. Representatives of organized labor were being regularly placed on local charity committees, social service committees, planning committees, and the like. In 1954 the Texas State Federation of Labor began to grant several college scholarships, and organized labor provided extensive support for the Warm Springs Foundation, which operated a rehabilitation hospital at Gonzales for the physically impaired. A youth conference was sponsored annually by the Texas AFL–CIO, and the state organization entered several court cases relating to insurance rates, the poll tax, and other issues with implications for all Texans, not just union members. Unions in Texas likewise were active in the civil-rights movement. Although there was some internal dissatisfaction with this involvement, integration within most unions was accomplished smoothly.

Increased activity outside the sphere of wages, hours, and working conditions grew in an era when labor was losing strength in the nation and in Texas. Internal division, along with a variety of other factors, retarded union growth. Exposés of labor racketeers in the mid-1950s had a great impact on public opinion, already hostile in Texas, although none of the malfea-

CIO packing-house workers, Dallas, 1930s. Courtesy Special Collections Division, University of Texas at Arlington Libraries.

sance directly involved Texas unions. Automation, with the accompanying loss of jobs, struck hard at several unions. Unions continued to grow slowly until about 1960, when they peaked at something over 400,000 members, of whom about 375,000 were in AFL–CIO affiliates. By 1964 members had declined to 370,000 total—320,000 in AFL–CIO unions, 39,000 in national unions outside the AFL–CIO, and the remainder in local unaffiliated, mostly company, unions.

The massive demographic and socioeconomic changes that began in Texas in the 1960s have had a dramatic negative impact on the role of organized labor. The state's population increased by almost 90 percent between 1960 and 1995. Since a good portion of this growth was a result of adult immigration, the labor force grew at a slightly higher rate than the general increase. The movement of women, many of whom were not prime breadwinners, into the labor force, together with the fact that half the population growth in the 1980s was Hispanic, brought a need for different organizational strategies that have been slow to develop. A successful effort to unionize the new workforce occurred at the four Fojtasck plants in the Dallas area. The Amalgamated Clothing and Textile Workers merged with the International Ladies' Garment Workers' Union in 1995 and successfully organized the workforce, which predominantly consisted of legal immigrants from Mexico and El Salvador, at the Fojtasck plants. The eventual results were better minimum wages, better benefits, and better working conditions for the plant employees.

Another cause of the decline of organized labor, equally difficult to evaluate with precision, has been the increasing conservative bent of the state and national social and political climates. Little doubt exists that the influence of unionized labor in Austin has weakened. Though unions no longer have the political clout they once wielded in areas of former strength, such as Beaumont–Port Arthur and Houston, other factors have been at work. The National Labor Relations Board, under Republican administrations and those of Democrats James E. Carter and William J. Clinton, has been a less than vigorous supporter of unionization. In numerous cases where unions won initial representative elections, for example, the NLRB has allowed companyinitiated appeals and legal proceedings to drag on for months and even years. In industries with highly mobile employees such as poultry processing and retail trade, the end result has often been decertification after the original prounion workers have moved on. Perhaps more basic to the decline of union influence have been the fundamental changes that began in the 1970s and greatly accelerated in the early 1980s. During the troubled decade following 1982, employment in sectors of the economy with few union members (wholesale and retail trade, finance, service, and government) grew by a little over 1.25 million. Workers in those sectors where unions have been traditionally strong (mining and oil, construction, manufacturing, and transportation), on the other hand, declined by about 370,000. By the early 1990s only 21 percent of the labor force worked in highly unionized industries, compared to 47 percent 20 years before.

Organized labor began responding to these changing conditions in the 1970s. The state AFL–CIO and several of the established unions provided logistical and financial support for organizing efforts. Communication workers, for example, supported membership activities by the Texas State Employees Union, which claimed something like 25,000 members by the 1990s, although the laws forbidding collective bargaining by public employees have limited the union's effectiveness. Other white-collar public-sector unions, such as the American Federation of Teachers and the American Federation of State, County and Municipal Employees, have also made significant gains since the 1970s. The Teamsters helped retail clerks organize both as Teamsters and in the United Food and Commercial Workers. But even though initially successful—about 32,000 retail workers had union contracts in 1990—locals often suffered a fate similar to that of the Kroger workers in San Antonio and the lower Rio Grande valley, where in 1993 the company simply closed its stores, or of Apple Tree employees the year before, who saw the company declare bankruptcy and a judge void the union contract. Similarly, the efforts to organize farmworkers, which began in the 1960s, have had little success. In some of the rapidly growing sectors of the economy, unionization has been practically nil. The many new computer-manufacturing establishments, for example, remain unorganized. Texas Instruments has been especially unreceptive to union attempts to organize its employees.

These compromising conditions for organized labor, when combined with such management practices as downsizing, contracting out, permanently replacing strikers, and moving to other countries, resulted in a reduction of the number of union members by about a third in the dozen years after 1982. Members of those unions affiliated with the state AFL–CIO, for instance, usually about 70 percent of total union members, dropped from 289,065 to 196,439. Isolated areas of union strength still exist, however. Almost all 33,000 nonsupervisory workers for the Bell Telephone companies are unionized, as are those in oil refining (20,000 members), maritime trades (12,000 members) and rubber workers (15,000 members). But in each of these, while the percentage of union workers has remained high, the number of workers in the industry has decreased. Unions outside the state body have suffered similar declines. The Teamsters (with about 35,000 members in the nineties) were hit hard in 1978–79 by the deregulation of interstate carriers, which drove many companies out of business. The United Auto Workers has seen a decline to about 15,000 members as a result of a shift from cars to trucks at the General Motors plant and reductions of defense spending that have affected Northrup Grumman. Even if the highest estimates of total union membership (about 400,000) are accepted, fewer than 6 percent of nonagricultural workers were union members in the mid-1990s, the least since the 1920s.

Even as the unions were forced onto the defensive by changing conditions, they also strengthened their efforts in such areas as combating environmental hazards and achieving safe working conditions. The Oil, Chemical and Atomic Workers' Union sought compensation for workers afflicted with asbestosis after working at the Pittsburgh Corning Corporation plant in Tyler in the 1960s. A landmark strike was called in 1973 against Shell Oil Company, allegedly America's first environmental strike, in a dispute over whether the union could have some say in monitoring the workplace environment through periodic medical exams and access to mortality statistics. Although the strike brought the oil workers into alliance with environmental groups that were also concerned about toxic wastes, the workers were eventually forced to accept a severely watered-down monitoring system. Texas industries have also been plagued by unusually high rates of work-related cancer and on-the-job accidents. In 1979, for example, there were 2.66 on-the-job deaths for every 10,000 employees in Texas, compared to a national average of .86. In the oil and gas industry, unions opposed unsafe working conditions associated with poorly designed facilities, the bypassing of safety procedures in the interest of greater production, and the replacement of trained union workers with poorly trained contract labor. The 1989 explosion and fire at Phillips Petroleum in Pasadena, which killed 23 workers and injured 314, brought investigations by the Occupational Safety and Health Administration and by the Oil, Chemical and Atomic Workers' Union and led to massive fines for safety violations levied against Phillips and against Fish Engineering and Construction, a contractor. However, unions have been able to achieve little more than token opposition to corporate control of the workplace.

Ruth A. Allen, George N. Green, and James V. Reese

Lackland Air Force Base. At San Antonio; originally part of Kelly Field. In June 1942 it was separated from Kelly and became the San Antonio Aviation Cadet Center. It provided classification and preflight training for aspiring pilots, bombardiers, and navigators. It was also known as "Kelly on the Hill." By 1945 the base was training personnel for almost every air corps need, including fiscal officers, nurses, dentists, medical technicians, and chaplains. Departments included chemical warfare, equipment maintenance, personnel and budget, and psychological research. In 1946 the base was renamed Lackland Army Air Field for Gen. Frank A. Lackland, an early commander of Kelly Field, and after separation of the air force from the army in 1948 it became Lackland Air Force Base. It was also known as the "Gateway to the Air Force," as all personnel entering the air force were processed and trained at Lackland.

After World War II, training programs were introduced for women entering the air force and for officers entering the force with direct commissions. After the Korean War a language school was established at Lackland. In 1957 Wilford Hall, the largest medical facility in the air force, was completed. By 1958 the air force marksmanship school and the sentry-dog training program had been established at Lackland. In 1966 the air force acquired 3,500 acres from the Atomic Energy Commission, which doubled the size of Lackland and provided the establishment of the Department of Cryptographic Training. Among other major construction, a new wing was added to Wilford Hall Medical Center. As part of the realignment caused by closing bases, Lackland in 1993 had a net gain of 492 jobs. The base lost 109 jobs when the officers' training school was moved to Maxwell Air Force Base, Alabama, after 34 years at Lackland. It gained 151 jobs with the transfer of the Inter-American Air Forces Academy to Lackland, and 450 jobs were gained as technical training course instructors from two closing bases were transferred to Lackland. *Art Leatherwood*

Laffite, Jean. Pirate; b. Bayonne, France, probably in 1780 or 1781; d. Mexico, ca. 1825. Jean and Pierre Laffite (Lafitte) were the sons of a French father and a Spanish mother. The family migrated to Española. By 1804 the brothers were in New Orleans, where they soon began smuggling. They held shares in many privateers that sailed the Gulf and the Caribbean and took their prizes to Barataria. While defying Governor William Claiborne's weak efforts to dislodge them, the Laffites became involved in a farflung plot to attack Texas and Tampico; but the approach of a British fleet to attack New Orleans enabled Claiborne to break up Barataria in September 1814, and the plot against Mexico and Texas was suspended for a while. During the War of 1812, in September 1814, the British, attempting to gain a foothold in the lower Mississippi valley by seizing New Orleans, asked Laffite for help. Laffite, however, hoping to gain a pardon for his illegal activities and the restoration of his confiscated goods, opted instead to fight on the side of the United States. He supplied men, weapons, and his knowledge of the region, and during the battle of New Orleans (8 January 1815) his followers helped the forces led by Andrew Jackson to secure an overwhelming victory. After the battle, Laffite and his brother attempted to regain the property they had lost at Barataria. Jean Laffite went to Washington and Philadelphia in the winter of 1815–16 to lay their case before President Madison, but in March 1816 he returned to New Orleans without success. His brother in the meantime had pledged their services to the Spanish government. Jean Laffite's first assignment was to accompany Arsène Lacarrière Latour on a mapping expedition west of Arkansas Post. He returned from this trip in November 1816. During his absence the New Orleans plotters had broadened their plan to open a port on the Texas coast that would serve as a haven for privateers and as a base for an attack against Texas.

Louis Michel Aury had escaped from Venezuela to Haiti, where the New Orleans plotters communicated with him early in 1816. Aury had established himself at Galveston Island in July 1816. The subsequent struggle for control of the island lasted a year, after which Laffite returned to make Galveston a center for smuggling and privateering. When the expedition of Charles Lallemand arrived from Champ d'Asile in January 1818, the Laffites plotted to betray the French refugees to Spain. This plot failed, and Galveston went on with its illicit activities. Lallemand's men were at Galveston when George Graham arrived in August 1818 to investigate affairs in Texas. Graham suggested that Jean Laffite should take possession successively of points on the coast as far as the Rio Grande and surrender them to the United States after faked attacks. Nothing came of this scheme, which apparently was Graham's idea, although James Monroe may have suggested it. Jean cooperated halfheartedly with James Long during the latter's invasion of Texas, but his principal interest lay in the privateering business, while his brother managed the intrigues with Spanish officials and took care of the New Orleans business arrangements. Finally, with nothing to hope for from Spain and confronted with the American government's determination to end the Galveston establishment, the Laffites decided the game was up. Laffite abandoned Galveston early in May 1820 and sailed to Mugeres Island, off the coast of Yucatán. There he continued his illegal activities until, mortally ill, he went to the mainland to die. Although his brother was the leader in all their affairs, Jean Laffite, more colorful than his older brother, has become the center of many romantic tales.   *Harris Gaylord Warren*

La Grange, Texas. County seat of Fayette County; 63 miles southeast of Austin. It is at the site where La Bahía Road crossed the Colorado River. Aylett C. Buckner settled in the vicinity about 1819, and in 1826 John Henry Moore built a twin block-house, Moore's Fort, at the site. Area settlers sought shelter there from Indian attacks, and by 1831 a small community had developed around the fort. A town was platted in 1837. When Fayette County was established that year, La Grange became its seat of government. The county had been named after the Marquis de Lafayette, and the county seat took its name from his château. A post office was established there in 1838. That same year the Texas Congress passed a bill to place the capital of the Republic of Texas on a site contiguous with La Grange, but the bill was vetoed by Sam Houston. La Grange grew as a trade center for the area's developing plantation economy. La Grange was incorporated in 1850, and by 1855 it had at least four schools. The ethnic composition of La Grange began to change during the 1840s and 1850s, as increasing numbers of Germans and Czechs immigrated to Fayette County. In 1859 the Casino Association of La Grange opened the area's first German Free School, and in 1860 Heinrich Kreische, a German immigrant from Saxony, established in La Grange one of the state's first commercial breweries. Though many of the German immigrants in the area were against slavery, the plantation economy of Fayette County influenced many La Grange residents to support the South in the years leading up to the Civil War. When the war began a number of militia companies were organized at La Grange to aid the Confederate cause. Some of the Germans in La Grange fled to Mexico or returned to Germany; still others formed the La Grange German Company, organized as a State Reserve unit in July 1861. Though La Grange was untouched by fighting during the Civil War, during Reconstruction the town was torn by conflict and disorder. Local peace was disrupted in May 1865 as returning Confederate veterans robbed local German businesses, provoked arguments and fights, and, on one occasion, threatened to burn down the town. La Grange was occupied by federal troops in 1866, and an agency of the Freedmen's Bureau was established there to protect the rights and welfare of the many freed slaves in the surrounding area. Friction between the federal authorities and ex-Confederates in the town led to a number of altercations. From August to December 1867 La Grange was ravaged by a deadly yellow fever epidemic that killed 240 people—about 20 percent of the population.

La Grange began to grow again as a trade center after the Galveston, Harrisburg and San Antonio Railway began service there in 1880 and the city's first bridge was built across the Colorado River in 1883. By 1884 the town had a population of 1,800. A three-story stone county courthouse was completed in 1891. By 1896 La Grange had electric service and a waterworks, and by 1900 some 2,392 people lived in the community. The population dropped to 1,960 by 1910, then revived in the 1920s to reach 2,350 in 1930. After World War II the traditional economic base was threatened by declining cotton production in the area. During the 1950s La Grange civic leaders attempted to attract more industries. In 1960 the city had a mattress factory, a furniture-manufacturing plant, 2 banks, 2 cotton gins, 3 hatcheries, 7 feed mills, and more than 100 retail establishments. By 1969 it also included a bottling plant, a structural-steel fabricator, and a business that built laminated beams; that year the city devised a comprehensive plan for its future development. Nevertheless, by

Julius Meyenberg's Farm, by Louis Hoppe, 1864. Watercolor on paper. 8¼" × 11¾". Courtesy Witte Museum, San Antonio. Farmer Meyenberg, who built his house on a high bluff in Fayette County, is shown in his garden with his wife and six of his eight children and numerous farm animals. Little is known of Hoppe, who was obviously self-taught and might have been an itinerant laborer.

the early 1970s all but one of the cotton gins in La Grange had closed. The population of La Grange varied from 2,729 in 1950, to 3,623 in 1960, 3,092 in 1970, and 3,951 in 1990. The town received national attention during the late 1970s and early 1980s when the story of the Chicken Ranch was publicized through the Broadway production and Hollywood movie *The Best Little Whorehouse in Texas*. Just outside of the city is Monument Hill, where Nicholas Mosby Dawson and other members of the ill-fated Dawson Massacre of 1842 are interred.

La Isla. When Mexico became independent in 1821 a chain of six towns stretched along the southern bank of the Rio Grande in the El Paso area. In the early 1830s the capricious river formed a new channel south of the old one, thus placing three of them—Ysleta, Socorro, and San Elizario—on an island 20 miles long and 2 to 4 miles wide. By 1848 water had ceased to flow in the Río Viejo, or old riverbed. A flourishing agriculture existed on the Island. The wine and brandy produced by its vineyards ranked with the best to be found in the viceroyalty of Spain, according to almost every official who visited the area. Most of the land—haciendas, ranches, and farms—with the exception of the ejidos (communal holdings of the mission Indians), was owned by the wealthy Paseños of El Paso del Norte (Ciudad Juárez) across the river, the largest town and political capital of the area. Supplementing the Island's agricultural base was the Chihuahua trade along the Old San Antonio Road, a natural extension of the

Santa Fe trade with Missouri that began a decade earlier. Ysleta and Socorro were established as missions by refugees from the Pueblo Revolt in New Mexico in 1680—Ysleta for the Tiguas and Socorro for the Piros. Both missions were swept away by the flooding river in the early 1830s, but they were at length replaced by the present structures, Socorro in 1843 and Ysleta in 1851. San Elizario, a presidio that was moved upriver to the El Paso area in 1879, became the nucleus of a town. According to a census of 1841 the total population of the three Island settlements was 2,850. Each town was governed by an alcalde appointed by the ayuntamiento of El Paso del Norte, which was controlled by the landowning and mercantile aristocracy. Most heads of families on La Isla were farmworkers or servants. Indians were dependents, and poverty was widespread. The two-room adobe structure was the general pattern for all.

During the Mexican War Col. Alexander Doniphan's force brought the El Paso area under United States control. The Treaty of Guadalupe Hidalgo (2 February 1848) provided that the new international boundary was to be "the Rio Grande . . . following the deepest channel . . . to the point where it strikes the southern boundary of New Mexico." American officials declared the Island to be United States territory, and in November 1848 Col. John M. Washington, military governor of New Mexico, appointed T. Frank White president and directed him to extend his jurisdiction over all of the territory east of the river that had formerly been a part of Chihuahua. In February 1849 Mexican officials reported that an armed force of the United States had occupied Ysleta, Socorro, and San Elizario and had taken possession of all the lands, including ejidos. Mexican protests proved futile. Meanwhile, by mid-1849 the discovery of gold in California had brought into the El Paso area hordes of immigrants, many of whom decided to remain. By late 1849 five settlements had been established by Anglo-Americans—Frontera, Hart's Mill, Coon's Ranch, Magoffinsville, and Stephenson's Ranch. These five, together with the three Mexican settlements on the Island, constituted a bilingual, bicultural complex at the Pass of the North. That the Mexican town of San Elizario should become El Paso County's first county seat is significant.

W. H. Timmons

La Junta de los Ríos. A historic farming and trading area at the junction of the Rio Grande (called Río del Norte by the Spanish) and the Río Conchos. At the center of La Junta are Presidio, Texas, on the north bank of the Rio Grande, and Ojinaga, Chihuahua, on the south bank. The limits of the district may have extended as far as 35 miles upriver to Ruidosa, 18 miles downriver to Redford, and 18 miles north of the river to Shafter. The southern boundary reached to Cuchillo Parado, Chihuahua. La Junta is considered the oldest continuously cultivated farmland in Texas. Corn farmers of the Cochise culture settled there about 1500 B.C., attracted by abundant water, fertile farmland, and bountiful game. Mountains on the north and south edges of the area and several hot springs offered protection from winter. The area was located on an ancient and heavily traveled north–south trade route, where settlers exchanged ideas as well as goods with those who passed through. The Cochise culture was replaced by the Mogollón about A.D. 900. The Mogollones were potters, weavers, and carvers, as well as farmers. They encountered the Anasazi culture probably through trade and adopted some of their ideas to form a new culture. The Mogollón–Anasazi culture was replaced in turn by a culture unlike the previous ones. Before the Spanish appeared in La Junta, this culture was supplanted by the Patarabueyes (later called Julimes) and the Jumano Indians.

The first Spaniards reached La Junta in December 1535 with Cabeza de Vaca, who erected a cross on the mountainside and named the place La Junta de las Cruces. He described the natives as strong and energetic. These Indians lived in permanent houses and raised large crops of corn, beans, squash, pumpkins, and melons. Both the Patarabueyes and Jumanos succumbed to Spanish influence, however. The former vanished in an attempt to remain aloof from the Spaniards, while the Jumanos became dependent subjects of the Spanish crown. Three additional Spanish expeditions came to La Junta—those of Fray Agustín Rodríguez (1581), Antonio de Espejo (1582), and Juan Domínguez de Mendoza (1683–84). Domínguez's expedition may have established about five missions at La Junta, including several on the Texas side of the Rio Grande. Fray Nicolás López, who traveled with the Domínguez entrada, celebrated the first Christmas Eucharist in Texas at La Junta. The first two priests left the area by the end of 1684 because of a rebellion by the Conchos Indians. In 1686 Fray Agustín de Colina and Fray Joaquín de Hinojosa came to La Junta, and in 1687 they heard of La Salle's colony from Cíbolo and Jumano Indians. The priests abandoned the area in 1688 due to regionwide unrest among the Indians. In 1715 Juan Antonio de Trasviña Retis escorted two Zacatecan missionaries back to La Junta, but they were withdrawn in 1717. Renewed efforts began again in 1730. In 1747 three military expeditions visited La Junta in order to make recommendations regarding the area—entradas led by Pedro de Rábago y Terán, Fermín Vidaurre, and Joseph de Ydoiaga. Ydoiaga recorded the life and geography of the region during 1747–48 in a report that historians have relied on. Although the Spanish clergy worked to convert the Indians to Christianity, other Spaniards wanted to enslave them in the silver mines. Spanish slavers raided La Junta from 1563 until 1760, leading to Indian protests that periodically closed the missions. The Presidio de la Junta de los Ríos Norte y Conchos was completed on 22 July 1760 for the protection of the missionaries. The presidio and missions were abandoned in 1767. By 1794 the Spanish Missions and presidios declined. The surviving missions of La Junta and the presidio were deserted with the coming of the unsuccessful Hidalgo revolution in 1810. La Junta de los Ríos resumed its ancient role as a trade and cultural junction in 1839, when Dr. Henry Connelly opened what is sometimes called the Chihuahua Trail. Traders hauled goods in carts between Independence, Missouri, and Chihuahua by way of La Junta. After the Mexican War Anglos settled on the north side of the Rio Grande and accepted La Junta's opportunities for trading, farming, and ranching.

Maria Eva Flores, C.D.P., and Julia Cauble Smith

La Llorona. "The Weeping Woman," a ghostly woman who wanders at night crying for her missing children; although found in many cultures and regions, she is perhaps the best-known ghost among Texas Hispanics. As tradition has it, after having borne a child to Hernán Cortés, his mistress, called La Malinche, was replaced by a highborn Spanish wife. Her Aztec pride and her jealousy drove her to acts of vengeance against the intruders from across the sea. Another story relates that a young hidalgo fell in love with a lowly girl, usually named María, who bore him two or three children before he gave in to his parents' urging that he marry a suitable lady. At the wedding María stood veiled at the back of the church, then returned home in a crazed state, killed the children, threw them into a nearby body of water, and then drowned herself. Refused entry into heaven without her children, La Llorona wanders along streams at night, crying out, "*Ay, mis hijos!*" According to some, she has been known to take revenge on men she meets. She usually dresses in black. Her face is sometimes that of a horse, but more often horribly blank, and her long fingernails gleam like polished tin in the moonlight. The most frequent use of the story is to warn teenage girls against falling for boys who are too far above them to consider marriage. In the Cortés variant, La Llorona's loss is compared to the demise of indigenous culture after the conquest of Mexico by the Spanish.

John O. West

Lamar, Mirabeau Buonaparte. President of the Republic of Texas; b. near Louisville, Georgia, 16 August 1798; d. Richmond, Texas, 19 December 1859 (buried in the Masonic Cemetery, Richmond); m. Tabitha Jordan (1826; d. 1830); 1 daughter; m. Henrietta Maffitt (1851); 1 daughter. Lamar was a painter in oils and a poet. He had experience as a Georgia state senator and twice ran unsuccessfully for Congress. He also was a newspaper publisher. In 1835 he followed Fannin to Texas to collect historical data, and decided to stay. Characteristically, he immediately

Mirabeau Buonaparte Lamar, ca. 1850s. Courtesy San Jacinto Museum of History, Houston.

declared for Texas independence, helped build a fort at Velasco, contributed three poems to the Brazoria *Texas Republican*, and hurried back to Georgia to settle his affairs. At the news of the battle of the Alamo and the Goliad Massacre, he rushed back to Texas and joined the revolutionary army as a private. At San Jacinto he was instrumental in saving the lives of Thomas J. Rusk and Walter Paye Lane. As the battle was about to start, he was verbally commissioned a colonel and assigned to command the cavalry. Ten days after the battle, having become secretary of war in Burnet's cabinet, he demanded that Santa Anna be executed as a murderer. A month later Lamar was major general and commander in chief of the Texas army, but the unruly Texas troops refused to accept him and he retired to civilian life.

In September 1836, in the first national election, he was elected vice president, an office in which he had leisure to augment his historical collections and study Spanish. He spent most of 1837 in Georgia being feted as a hero and publicizing the new republic. Upon his return to Texas, he organized the Philosophical Society of Texas and found that his campaign for the presidency of Texas was already under way, sponsored by opponents of President Sam Houston, who by law could not succeed himself. The other candidates, Peter W. Grayson and James Collinsworth, both committed suicide before election day, thus assuring Lamar's election by an almost unanimous vote. At his inauguration on 10 December 1838, he declared the purposes of his administration to be promoting the wealth, talent, and enterprises of the country and laying the foundations of higher institutions for moral and mental culture. His term began with Texas in a precarious situation, however: only the United States had recognized her independence, she had no commercial treaties, Mexico was threatening reconquest, the Indians were menacing, the treasury was empty, and currency was depreciated. It was characteristic of Lamar to divert the thoughts of his constituents from the harassments of the moment toward laying the foundations of a great empire. He thought Texas should remain a republic and ultimately expand to the Pacific Ocean. For Houston's conciliatory Indian policy, Lamar substituted one of sternness and force. The Cherokees were driven to Arkansas in 1839; in 1840 a campaign against the Comanches quieted the western Indians at a cost of $2.5 million. Lamar sought peace with Mexico first through the good offices of the United States and Great Britain, then by efforts at direct negotiation. When it was clear that Mexico would not recognize Texas, he made a quasiofficial alliance with the rebel government in Yucatán and leased to it the Texas Navy. He proposed a national bank, but instead of establishing the bank Congress authorized additional issues of paper money in the form of redbacks, which were greatly depreciated by the end of his administration. Receipts for his administration were $1,083,661; expenditures were $4,855,213. At Lamar's suggestion, the new capital city of Austin was built on the Indian frontier beside the Colorado River and occupied in October 1839. Another step in his plans for a greater Texas was the Texan Santa Fe expedition, undertaken without congressional approval in the last months of his administration. If it had succeeded, this botched venture might have solved many of the problems of Texas; its failure was proof to Lamar's enemies that he was "visionary." Lamar's proposal that the Congress establish a system of education endowed by public lands resulted in an act of 1839 that set aside land for public schools and two universities. Although it was decades before the school system was established, Lamar's advocacy of the program earned for him the nickname "Father of Texas Education." A dictum in one of his messages to Congress, "Cultivated mind is the guardian genius of democracy," became the motto of the University of Texas.

As the national election of 1841 approached, Lamar's popularity was at its lowest ebb, and Texas was at the verge of bankruptcy. The blame cannot be assessed against the president exclusively, however, for most of his policies were implemented by acts of Congress, and economic and political conditions in the United States and abroad blocked measures that might have temporarily stabilized the Texas currency. Forces that neither Lamar nor his enemies fully understood or controlled brought failure to his grandest projects. Smarting under criticism, he retired to his home near Richmond at the end of 1841 and busied himself with his plantation and with the collection of historical materials. After his daughter's death in 1843, he was plunged into melancholia and sought relief in travel. His poem "On the Death of My Daughter" was later published in the *Southern Literary Messenger*. At Mobile in 1844 he fell in with a literary coterie that encouraged his interest in poetry. He received callers at the City Hall in New York and was given a courtesy seat in the United States Senate at Washington. Though he had formerly opposed annexation, he had been convinced that Texas statehood was necessary to protect slavery and prevent the state from becoming an English satellite; he therefore lobbied for annexation while in Washington. With the outbreak of the Mexican War, he joined Zachary Taylor's army at Matamoros as a lieutenant colonel and subsequently fought in the battle of Monterrey. Later he was captain of Texas Mounted Volunteers on the Rio Grande. He organized a municipal government at Laredo and in 1847 represented

Nueces and San Patricio counties in the Second Texas Legislature.

After 1848 Lamar traveled much and began writing biographical sketches for a proposed history of Texas. He denounced the Compromise of 1850, which convinced him that the interests of the South could be protected only by secession. In 1857 he was appointed United States minister to Nicaragua and Costa Rica, a post he held for 20 months. His *Verse Memorials* appeared in September 1857. Lamar had great personal charm, impulsive generosity, and oratorical gifts. His powerful imagination caused him to project a program greater than he or Texas could actualize in three years. His friends were almost fanatically devoted to him; though his enemies declared him a better poet than politician, they never seriously questioned the purity of his motives or his integrity. Lamar County and the town of Lamar in Aransas County were named for him. In 1836 the Texas Centennial Commission placed statues of him in the Hall of State in Dallas and in the cemetery at Richmond. The commission also marked the site of his home near Richmond and the place of his residence as president in Austin, and built a miniature replica of his home on the square at Paris. The *Telegraph and Texas Register* eulogized him as a "worthy man." *Herbert Gambrell*

Lamar University at Beaumont. Originated as South Park Junior College in 1923. The first classes were held on the third floor of the new South Park High School. The institution was renamed Lamar College almost immediately, in honor of Mirabeau Lamar. A building program begun in 1933 gave the college almost entirely separate facilities. In 1940 the Lamar Union Junior College District was established and Lamar College was separated from the South Park district. Bonds for construction of a new campus were approved, and in June 1942 classes were held on the present campus on the Port Arthur highway, three blocks east of South Park High School. As enrollment increased rapidly after World War II, a movement was launched to make Lamar a four-year institution. In June 1949 the Texas legislature passed a bill approving Lamar State College of Technology, effective on 1 September 1951. The bill specified that Lamar would emphasize engineering, technology, and science, but left to the board of regents discretionary authority to establish whatever educational programs were deemed proper. Under the leadership of Dr. F. L. McDonald, president from 1952 until his death in 1967, Lamar expanded rapidly. Enrollment increased to 9,000 students, 25 additional buildings were constructed, and many new academic programs were begun. Graduate work was authorized in 1960, when master's degrees were offered in several fields. The doctorate of engineering was authorized in 1971, the year the college officially became Lamar University. In 1969 an extension center opened in Orange, and another opened in 1975 when the private Port Arthur College became Lamar University at Port Arthur. The Lamar University System was established in 1983. It comprises the Beaumont campus, Lamar University at Orange, Lamar University at Port Arthur, and the John Gray Institute, a privately funded, state-operated, nonprofit research center located on the southern edge of the Beaumont campus. *Ralph A. Wooster*

Lamar University at Orange. Established as a lower-division extension center in 1969 and designated a component of the Lamar University System in 1983. The branch comprises a main campus and the Brown Center, the former mansion of Edgar W. Brown, Jr. The mansion is used for conferences and as a cultural and educational center. In 1991 the university received status from the Texas legislature as an independent degree-granting institution. In the early 1990s it offered associate degrees in academic and technical programs as well as certificates of completion in several technical and occupational fields. Renovation of the main building and a student building was completed in 1992. Lamar University at Orange is accredited by the Southern Association of Colleges and Schools. *Diana J. Kleiner*

Lamar University at Port Arthur. Originated as Port Arthur College, founded in 1909 by John Warne Gates. The college was a city-owned, nonprofit school that offered training in stenography, secretarial work, bookkeeping, accounting, and radio. By 1925 it owned a 15-acre campus. In 1933 its radio station, KPAC, was established. In 1947 the school had 25 faculty members and an average annual enrollment of 800. Port Arthur College joined Lamar University in 1975 and was designated a component of the Lamar University System in 1983. It received degree-granting status from the Texas legislature in 1991. It offers associate degrees, courses preparatory to pursuit of a baccalaureate degree, and vocational and technical courses. *Diana J. Kleiner*

Land Fraud Board. Established in 1883 to investigate purchases of state land that violated the land acts of 1879 and 1881 and to investigate the operation of the General Land Office; three members, appointed by the governor. These agents were sent separately to counties where fraud was deemed likely. Agent Charles DeMorse wrote in August 1883 that he had unearthed more than enough irregularities in sales, forged titles, and destroyed records to cover the cost of the board. The board's report of 3 January 1884 stated that 750,000 acres of land had been secured by illegal or improper means and could be recovered by due diligence on the part of the state. Lack of time and appropriations prevented complete investigation, but the board did recommend several suits to the attorney general, and some state land was recovered in resulting court action. *Curtis Bishop*

Land Grants. The history of land grants in Texas is a long and complex one. The earliest grant was made by the Spanish crown to establish a mission and presidio in East Texas in 1716. In 1731 town lots in San Antonio de Béxar were granted to Canary Islanders, and by the mid-1700s larger livestock grants were being made along the San Antonio River valley. In later years, the titles were issued by the governor of the province, who received a small fee, as did the local officials who participated in the process. Ranching lands farther away from the town were generally held informally in the early years of Spanish Texas, and only regularized in later years. Private land grants in what is now South Texas did not begin until the mid-eighteenth century. Settlers in the colonies founded by José de Escandón in South Texas requested individual land allocations as early as 1753, but not until 1767 did a Spanish royal commission began the work of surveying and granting possession of land to individual colonists at the Rio Grande *villas* of Laredo, Mier, Camargo, Revilla (later Guerrero), and Reynosa. The commissioners, Juan Armando de Palacio and José de Ossorio y Llamas, were instructed to survey the various settlements and jurisdictions, distribute the land to individual settlers, and record all transactions. The land was to be divided on the basis of merit and seniority, with the colonists divided into three categories: original, old, and recent settlers. Due to the shortage of water and the importance of irrigation for agriculture in the region, the commissioners surveyed long, thin strips of land, each with narrow frontage on a watercourse. These elongated quadrangles were known as *porciones*. The *porciones* in each of the five settlements was assigned a number. Many of the grants, especially the larger ones, also acquired names, usually derived from saints' names, physical or natural characteristics of the region, or events. The grants were finalized by an act of juridical possession several months later. The transactions were recorded in documents known as *Acts of the Visit of the Royal Commissioners* (*Autos de la General Visita*). Some 170 *porciones* granted in what is now Texas are entered in the five *visitas*. In addition to the grants with water frontage, the royal officials also made larger grants at the back of the *porciones* or along the Gulf of Mexico. Most of these grants, which were intended for grazing, went to influential citizens of Camargo and Reynosa. They often covered large expanses of land, the largest being the 600,000-acre Agostadero de San Juan de Carricitos grant to José Narisco Cabazos. The small number of grants initially made to women usually went to recipients whose husbands had died after the grants were initiated and before they were perfected, or to women who were heads of households. A few women, particularly from wealthy or influential families, were in possession of large parcels of land by the end of the colonial period.

Land grants in other regions followed somewhat different patterns. Along the upper Rio Grande few formal grants were made. In Nacogdoches and other areas along the northern frontier, families usually received land through oral agreements with local officials. With the beginning of American incursion into the Nacogdoches area in the 1790s, however, many families sought to formalize these grants in order to preserve their rights. Despite the granting of large areas of land in the north, the number of inhabitants of the region remained small. In an effort to populate the area, Spanish officials experimented with a policy to entice settlers from the American frontier with promises of land, religious tolerance, and special privileges. In 1820 the Spanish government passed a measure to open Texas to foreigners who would respect the laws and constitution of the country. In January 1821, Moses Austin was promised a contract to land on the Brazos River in exchange for bringing 300 Catholic families from Louisiana. After his death in June of that year his son, Stephen F. Austin, assumed the contract. Though the grant was declared void after the Mexican War of Independence, Austin succeeded in negotiating a new contract under President Agustín de Iturbide's colonization law of 1823. After Iturbide's downfall in March 1823, the new Mexican government passed the state colonization law of 24 March 1825, which opened the way for Americans to settle in the northern province of Coahuila and Texas. In exchange for a small fee, heads of families could obtain as much as a league or sitio (4,428.4) acres of grazing land and a *labor* (177.1 acres) of cropland. Under the provisions of the decree foreigners had to take an oath promising to obey the federal and state constitutions, practice Christianity, and prove their morality and good habits. Upon agreeing to these conditions and establishing residence, foreigners became Mexican citizens. The wording of the decree as it pertained to slavery was vague and did not immediately prohibit the importation of

slaves. Individuals could petition for grants directly, but more often applications were handled by immigration agents, or empresarios. An empresario selected colonists, allocated land, and oversaw the enforcement of Mexican law. In compensation he was entitled to five leagues and five *labores* for each 100 families he settled. Between 1821 and 1835, 41 empresario grants were made, the majority going to emigrants from the United States. In addition to Austin, among the most important empresarios were Green DeWitt, Ben Milam, and Sterling C. Robertson. Other important empresarios included Haden Edwards, Robert Leftwich, Frost Thorn, Martín De León, James Power and James Hewetson, John McMullen, James McGloin, Lorenzo de Zavala, David G. Burnet, and Joseph Vehlein.

Officials of Tamaulipas, which included much of what is now South Texas, also sought to encourage colonization of its vacant lands through the colonization law of 1825. Grants were made to Mexican ranchers, but the attempts to attract large numbers of settlers proved unsuccessful. In 1836 the first Congress of the Republic of Texas declared that the Texas boundaries extended to the Rio Grande, but the state of Tamaulipas continued to issue land titles in the trans-Nueces region until the Mexican War ended in 1848. As a provision of the Treaty of Guadalupe Hidalgo, which ended the boundary dispute with Mexico, the new state of Texas officially recognized the land grants made under Spanish and Mexican rule as valid. To quell confusion, in 1848 Governor Peter H. Bell called on the legislature to conduct an investigation of claims arising from the Tamaulipan and Chihuahuan cession. In 1850 the legislature instituted a board of commissioners to oversee the process and appointed William H. Bourland and James B. Miller as commissioners. The recommendations of the commissioners are contained in a document known as the Bourland and Miller Report, now in the archives of the General Land Office. In February 1860 the legislature passed a measure that gave the responsibility for confirming Spanish and Mexican titles to the district courts.

The Republic of Texas made many *headright* grants, that is, grants given on the condition that specified requirements be met by the grantees. Under the Constitution of 1836 all heads of families living in Texas on 4 March 1836, except blacks and Indians, were granted "first class" headrights of one league and one *labor* (4,605.5 acres), and single men aged 17 years or older, one-third of a league (1,476.1 acres). By later laws "second class" headrights of 1,280 acres to heads of families and 640 acres to single men were granted to those who immigrated to Texas after the Texas Declaration of Independence and before 1 October 1837, and who remained in the republic for three years and performed the duties of citizenship. "Third class" headrights of 640 acres for heads of families and 320 acres for single men went to recipients who immigrated to Texas after 1 October 1837 and before 1 January 1840. In 1841 "fourth class" headright certificates of 640 acres for family heads and 320 acres for single men were granted conditionally to residents who immigrated to Texas between 1 January 1840 and 1 January 1842. A total of 36,876,492 acres was granted by the republic in headright certificates. In order to attract settlers, the Republic of Texas also made colonization contracts with various individuals to establish colonies in the republic and receive payment in land. In addition to large grants made directly to the contractors, settlers in such colonies were granted 640 acres each, if heads of families, or 320 acres, if single. Land grants made under colonization contracts amounted to

4,494,806 acres. As a further inducement to settlers, in 1845 the Congress of the republic passed the first Pre-emption Act, which gave to persons who had previously settled upon and improved vacant public lands, or who might thereafter settle upon and improve them, the right to purchase (pre-empt) up to 320 acres. Pre-emptors, or homesteaders, were required to cover their locations with valid certificates within three years. Under the state government this period was extended to 1 January 1854. By an act of 1853 homestead grants of not more than 320 acres were made available to those who had settled under the Pre-emption Act. This act was replaced by the Homestead Act of 1854, which reduced homestead grants to 160 acres and required a residence of three years. The policy of homestead grants was continued under acts of 1866 and 1870 and under the Constitution of 1876. The amount of land disposed of under the pre-emption and homestead laws of Texas is recorded at 4,847,136 acres.

Both the republic and state granted lands for military service in the form of bounty and donation grants. An act of 21 December 1837 provided for donation certificates of 640 acres each to all persons involved in the battle of San Jacinto, to all who were wounded the day before, and to all who were detailed to guard the baggage at Harrisburg; by the same act bounty warrants were granted to those who had participated in the siege of Bexar, the Goliad campaigns of 1835 and 1836, and the battle of the Alamo, or to their survivors. By an act of 1879 certificates for an additional 640 acres were granted under stringent restrictions to indigent veterans of the Texas Revolution. An act of 1868 granted warrants to Texans who had fought in the Union Army, but no land was ever claimed under this law. In 1881 the state voted to issue bounty warrants for 1,280 acres to Confederate veterans who had been permanently disabled in service. Bounty and donation grants for military service amounted to a total of 3,149,234 acres.

Vast areas of Texas lands were also granted in return for making internal improvements: building railroads, canals, and irrigation ditches, constructing shipbuilding facilities, clearing river channels, and, during the Civil War, manufacturing firearms and munitions and constructing highways. Lands granted to railroads amounted to 32,153,878 acres, or nearly one-fifth of the total area of the state. For other internal improvements a total of 138,640 acres was granted.

Finally, special education land grants totaling 172,319 acres were made by the Republic of Texas to private colleges and seminaries. Other lands were subsequently set aside for state educational and eleemosynary institutions, but they are more appropriately classified as land appropriations for education rather than grants. *Aldon S. Lang and Christopher Long*

Land Scrip. In 1836 the Republic of Texas was rich in lands but poor in money. In an effort to convert the public domain into cash the republic authorized the issuance of land scrip for sale in the United States at not less than 55¢ an acre, the proceeds of the sale to be applied to the public debt. The scrip was often called Toby Scrip, for Thomas Toby of Toby and Brother Company of New Orleans, the chief scrip agent. Under the Confederate Soldier's Bill of 1881 the state issued scrip certificates to wounded Confederate soldiers, their servants, or their widows. Those having property valued at $1,000 or more were ineligible. Most recipients of the certificates sold them, and the bill was repealed in 1883. The state, to raise money and pay off debts, in 1879

offered for sale scrip for certain western lands at 50¢ an acre and in 1889 at two dollars an acre. Certificates issued for internal improvements were also called land scrip. *Manuel Guerra*

Lanham, Samuel Willis Tucker. Governor; b. Spartanburg District, South Carolina, 4 July 1846; d. Weatherford, 2 July 1908; m. Sara Beona Meng (1866); 8 children. Lanham served the Confederacy with distinction. He moved to Texas in 1866 and taught school at various places before being admitted to the bar in Weatherford (1868). As a district attorney (1871–76) appointed by Edmund J. Davis, he prosecuted Kiowa Indian chiefs Satanta and Big Tree for their part in the Warren Wagontrain Raid. Lanham was a presidential elector in 1880, was elected to Congress in 1882, and served until March 1893. After losing a bid for the Democratic gubernatorial nomination to Charles A. Culberson in 1894, he was again elected to Congress in 1896 and served until 1903. In Washington he represented the interests of cattlemen and victims of Indian depredations, worked on boundary questions, and helped secure a federal court at El Paso. With the support of Edward M. House, Lanham was nominated for governor in 1902 without opposition; he was reelected in 1904. He was the last Confederate veteran to serve as governor. Because the Terrell Election Law, which provided for party-primary elections, was passed during his tenure, he was the last Democratic gubernatorial candidate chosen by the party-convention method. He received an honorary doctorate from Baylor University (1905). After retirement he spoke often at Confederate veterans' camps and was appointed a regent of the University of Texas (1907). He and his wife died in the same month. Congressman Frederick Garland Lanham was their son, and Texas novelist Edwin M. Lanham, Jr., was their grandson. *Lawrence A. Landis*

Laredo, Texas. On the Rio Grande in southwestern Webb County, 150 miles southwest of San Antonio; a major port of entry for international trade and tourism between the United States and Mexico. Laredo was established in 1755, when Tomás Sánchez de la Barrera y Garza was granted permission by José de Escandón to form a new settlement about 30 miles upriver from Nuestra Señora de los Dolores Hacienda in what is now Zapata County. Laredo was the last town established under the authority of Escandón, who had been given responsibility for settling the province of Nuevo Santander. Altogether Escandón saw to the founding of twenty towns and eighteen missions in an attempt to thwart French incursion into Spanish territory and to propagate the Christian faith among the various Indian tribes of the region. Sánchez chose a site downriver from a ford later called El Paso de los Indios but known at that time as El Paso de Jacinto (after Jacinto De León of the San Juan Bautista garrison, who noted it in a report of 1745). About eight miles downriver from Laredo was another crossing, called the Don Miguel or Garza ford (after Miguel de la Garza Falcón). Tienda de Cuervo, who inspected the community in 1757, reported that Laredo was the usual crossing place for those traveling to Texas from Nuevo León and Coahuila. The initial settlement at Laredo was made by Sánchez and three families from Dolores. They soon found that lack of rain restricted farming to the riverbottoms; the rest of the land lay too high above the river for irrigation. The raising of livestock—chiefly goats, sheep, and cattle—thus became their principal livelihood. In 1760 Laredo received a resident priest,

Street scene with *carretas*, ca.1900–1910. Courtesy TSL. Ox-drawn carts were the primary means of transporting commercial goods between Mexico and Texas.

becoming the second oldest parish (after San Fernando de Béxar) to be administered by secular clergy in what is now the southwestern United States. Until Laredo was accorded the status of a villa in 1767, Sánchez, who held the title of "captain," exercised authority over both civil and military matters. During this period the 15 leagues granted to the community were held in common. The communal system mandated by Escandón was intended to forestall disputes and the formation of land monopolies that would discourage immigration. Colonists, however, proved reluctant to make improvements without holding private title. In 1767 the viceroy appointed a commission to oversee the partitioning of lands in Nuevo Santander. In Laredo this commission supervised the laying out of San Agustín Plaza and the common areas of the village, as well as 89 *porciones*, each having a river frontage of a half mile and a depth of about 15_ miles. Though no Indians lived at Laredo initially, bands of Carrizo, Borrado, and Lipan Indians would occasionally come to trade after the community had become established. Allowing for the possibility that Indians might one day congregate there, the commissioners set aside a place for them on the right bank, across the river from the town. In 1767 or 1768 Father Gaspar José de Solís, while on a visit to the Texas missions, sent a group of Indians to Laredo for religious instruction. In addition to seeing to the distribution of land, the commissioners raised Laredo to the status of a villa, a town with a governing body. The first election for local officials was held in 1768. Laredo grew steadily: its population rose from 85 in 1757, two years after its founding, to 185 in 1767 and 708 in 1789. The latter figure included 111 Carrizo Indians. As the surrounding ranchos became more prosperous, raids by Comanches and some Apaches became a concern. A military garrison was established at Laredo in 1775. Raiding increased in the last several decades of the 1700s, and Laredo implored authorities for more soldiers, especially the effective *compañías volantes* (cavalry), for protection. The threat from Indian raids was compounded between 1810 and 1820, when troops from Laredo were called away to combat insurgents and filibusters along the Rio Grande. Laredo itself remained one of the few islands of Royalist sentiment in a sea of pro-independence activists on the northern frontier. The political alignment of the town has been attributed to the dependence of the propertied classes there upon the Laredo presidio, which remained loyal to the Spanish crown.

During the Texas Revolution Laredo served as a concentration point for the forces of Antonio López de Santa Anna. After the war, Texas leaders generally considered the Rio Grande to be the southern boundary of the new Republic of Texas, but they made no effort to extend jurisdiction over the border region. The residents of Laredo continued to consider themselves citizens of the Mexican state of Tamaulipas. Though Laredoans identified with Mexico, they felt their needs had been neglected for decades by the central government. In late 1838 the rancheros of this region revolted, and in January 1840 insurgents proclaimed the Republic of the Rio Grande, with Laredo as the capital. It was not long, however, before Centralist forces arrived to crush this Federalist-inspired rebellion, headed by Antonio Canales Rosillo and Antonio Zapata. Laredo continued to witness the marching of troops during the period of hostilities between Texans and Mexicans in the 1840s. During the 1842 Somervell expedition a revenge-seeking army of Texans sacked the town. The looted goods were ordered returned to the citizens by an outraged Gen. Alexander Somervell, and some were restored, but Laredoans claimed that Texans kept other goods worth 12,674 pesos. No effort was made to place Laredo under the jurisdiction of Texas until the Mexican War. In March 1846 Texas Ranger captain Robert Addison Gillespie raised the United States flag over the city, and the next November an American garrison, under the command of former Republic of Texas president Mirabeau B. Lamar, occupied the town. In 1848 Laredo became the county seat for newly established Webb County. The establishment of the Rio Grande as the international boundary divided the town of Laredo, many of whose residents had homes and ranchos on the right bank (in Mexico). A number of other families who did not wish to live under the American flag chose to move across the river to what became the village of Nuevo Laredo, Tamaulipas. Fort McIntosh was established a mile west of Laredo in 1849. The post, originally called Camp Crawford, became critical in the protection of the community and the Rio Grande frontier, and saw almost continuous service until 1947, when the facilities were turned over to the newly established Laredo Junior College.

During the Civil War the Union blockade of the southern coast caused Confederate shippers to send their cotton to Mexico, from where it could be exported. In the early years of the war much of the cotton passed through Brownsville, but in 1863 the fear that Union troops might capture Brownsville drove the trade farther west. Laredo was one of the towns to receive this redirected trade. In March 1864 Union troops advanced on Laredo with orders to destroy all the bales of cotton that were stored around San Agustín Plaza. Col. Santos Benavides and his Laredo Confederates repulsed the federalists at Zacate Creek in the battle of Laredo. Laredo's modern era began in 1881, a watershed year that saw the establishment of the Laredo *Times*, the arrival of the Texas Mexican Railroad from Corpus Christi, and the completion of Jay Gould's International and Great Northern Railroad from San Antonio to the border. In 1882 the Rio Grande and Pecos Railway was completed to the cannel coal fields along the Rio Grande above Laredo. Laredo was the first Texas bordertown below Eagle Pass to secure a rail connection, and it remained the only one until Brownsville, near the mouth of the Rio Grande, acquired rail service in 1904. By 1887 the Mexican National railway linked Nuevo Laredo with Mexico City. The arrival of the railroads produced marked social as well as economic changes. Anglo-Americans had settled in Laredo during and after the Mexican War and Civil War, but their numbers were small compared to the influx brought by the railroads. As the numbers of Anglo residents grew, intermarriage declined and a separate Anglo society developed alongside the original Mexican community. In 1882 the principal streets were improved by grading and graveling and a city hall and courthouse were constructed. In 1883 water mains were laid and telephone service inaugurated. The last 20 years of the 1800s witnessed economic growth stimulated variously by the railroads, coal mining some 20 miles upriver, and the introduction of onion farming in 1898, which opened the area north of the city to irrigated farming.

The population rose from 3,521 in 1880 to 13,429 by 1900. This period also witnessed a memorable political confrontation, which took place the day after a hotly contested city election in April 1886. The two political factions—the Botas, representing the new commercial class that had arrived with the railroads, and the Guaraches, representing the older elite—engaged in a shootout on San Agustín Plaza. Estimates of the dead range from more than a dozen to 60. Out of the violence later emerged the Independent Club, a Democratic party machine that tightly controlled city and county elections until 1978. Laredo was also a hotbed of activity for anti–Porfirio Díaz activist exiles between 1890 and 1910. After the Mexican Revolution of 1910 and the subsequent political instability in Mexico, Laredo became a refuge for thousands of Mexican citizens seeking a stable, peaceful, and more economically secure environment. Rich oil and gas finds in the area surrounding Laredo in the first quarter of the 1900s gave an added boost to the economy. During World War II, Laredo Army Air Field served as an important tactical training base for fighter pilots. After the war the field was deactivated, and the property reverted to the city of Laredo, which made it a municipal airport in 1950. The base was reactivated and renamed Laredo Air Force Base in April 1952; it was closed permanently in 1973. The population of Laredo increased from 22,710 in 1920 to 39,274 in 1940, 60,678 in 1960, and 122,899 in 1990. In spite of periodic economic instability, Laredo by the early 1990s had become one of the state's most active centers for import and export trade with Mexico. The development of maquiladoras along the border during the 1970s and 1980s, as well as the North American Free Trade Agreement of the early 1990s, ensured that Laredo would continue to be at the forefront of social and economic activity along the border. *Carlos E. Cuellar*

La Sal del Rey. A shallow, mile-long salt lake on private property 28 miles northeast of McAllen; sometimes ungrammatically called El Sal del Rey and also known as La Purificación. The crystalline bed consists of 99.0897 percent sodium chloride. The large salt deposit, the depth of which is undetermined, has no connection with any other body of water, and how it was formed is not known. Salt blocks removed from any spot in the lake are quickly replenished, often in two or three days, as the water is shifted by the predominantly southeastern winds of the area. Engineers estimate that the lake holds four million tons of salt. The water may dry out completely or, in periods of much rainfall, be more than ten feet deep. Spanish explorers claimed the lake for the king of Spain and declared it open for public use. In 1798 the lake became part of a land grant to Capt. Juan José Ballí. Tracks from wooden carts used in Spanish days can still be found

around the lake. Rock salt from La Sal del Rey was the first export out of the lower Rio Grande valley. During the Mexican War the amount of salt mined and exported from the lake declined. During the Civil War a huge increase in the demand for salt caused the state government to take over control of its mining and export. Governor Francis R. Lubbock appointed Antonio Salinas of Brownsville as controlling agent, and, after allowing Jesús Cárdenas, owner of the lake, to sell the salt already mined, the Confederate government rushed salt to designated points by camel caravan, each camel carrying 600 pounds. Freight thefts, however, caused so many problems that the project was abandoned. In addition to its value as a source of salt, the lake has been used as a therapeutic wading pool to cure arthritis and to decorated such items as branches, which when thrown into the lake can be recovered a day or two later encrusted in sparkling crystals. *Eloise Campbell*

La Salle, Sieur de. Explorer; b. René Robert, St. Herbland parish, Rouen, France, 22 November 1643; d. Texas, 19 March 1687. The title La Salle, which René Robert assumed, was the name of a family estate near Rouen. La Salle, educated at the Jesuit College in Rouen, later entered the Society of Jesus as a novice, an act requiring him to give up his inheritance. Finding himself unsuited for priestly life, he severed his connection with the order at age 22. He sailed in 1666 for Canada, where his brother Jean, a priest of St. Sulpice, had gone the previous year. The Sulpicians granted him land near La Chine rapids, above Montreal, where he began a fortified village, acquired a substantial interest in the fur trade, and sought to learn Indian languages.

His imagination was fired by reports of a great river system, which he thought must flow into the Gulf of California and provide passage to China. La Salle sold his holdings in 1669 and undertook his first major exploration. He discovered the Ohio River, but desertion of his followers forced him to turn back short of the Mississippi, leaving that discovery to the Joliet–Marquette expedition of 1673. On trips to France in 1674 and 1677, La Salle received a patent of nobility and a seigneurial grant that included the Fort Frontenac site (Kingston, Ontario), then a trade concession to the western country. He built and launched the first sailing vessel to ply the Great Lakes, then began in earnest to carry out his plan of establishing a chain of trading posts across the Illinois country and down the Mississippi. Convinced by this time that the Mississippi emptied into the Gulf of Mexico and not the South Sea (the Pacific Ocean), he envisioned a warm-water port—fortified against Spanish and English incursion—on the Gulf to serve his commercial empire. La Salle devoted the next three years to laying the cornerstones of his visionary plan. Consolidating Indian alliances, he built an entrepôt at Niagara and a fort among the Illinois. In the winter of 1682 he sledded down the frozen Illinois River to the Mississippi and, after the river was free of ice, descended it by canoe to reach the mouth of the eastern passes on 7 April 1682. Claiming for France all the lands drained by the river, La Salle named the territory La Louisiane in honor of the French King, Louis XIV.

He returned to France late in 1683 and obtained royal support for a voyage to the Mississippi through the Gulf of Mexico, there to establish a colony "a secure distance" from the river. The voyage, which sailed from La Rochelle on 24 July 1684, was attended by numerous misfortunes. La Salle missed the mouth of the Mississippi and landed his colonists at Matagorda Bay on 20 February 1685, believing the Mississippi near. From his Fort St. Louis, on Garcitas Creek in what is now Victoria County, he explored westward possibly as far as the Pecos River and eastward beyond the Trinity River, in an effort to establish his location. On his second eastward journey, intended to reach his post on the Illinois River, La Salle was murdered by Pierre Duhaut, a disenchanted follower, "six leagues" from the westernmost village of the Hasinai (Tejas) Indians. This description indicates a point east of the Trinity River, some distance from either the Grimes County or the Cherokee County locations most often mentioned. Although La Salle's projects ended in failure, his explorations were landmarks. He was responsible for opening the Mississippi valley for development, and his entry into the Gulf of Mexico sparked a renewal of Spanish exploration in the entire Gulf region. His abortive colony gave the French a claim to Texas and caused the Spaniards to occupy eastern Texas and Pensacola Bay. Because of La Salle the United States was able to register a claim to Texas as part of the Louisiana purchase; the boundary question between Spain and the United States was complicated until the Adams–Onís Treaty of 1819. Yet history's judgment of the man is clouded by his ineptness as a leader; of the 200 colonists he landed in Texas in 1685, barely 15 remained alive five years later. *Robert S. Weddle*

Latin Settlements. Five communities in Texas where most of the settlers were highly educated immigrants from Germany. In the German culture of the time, knowing Latin was a prerequisite for higher learning and a sign of educational attainment. The Latin Settlements, established during the late 1840s, included Millheim in Austin County, Latium in Washington County, Bettina in Llano County, and Sisterdale and Tusculum in Kendall County. Many of the residents of these settlements, who were sometimes referred to as *Lateiner* ("Latins"), were political refugees who had fled Germany in the wake of the abortive 1848 revolution. A number of them later attained prominence in medicine, education, law, journalism, and politics. *Rudolph L. Biesele*

La Villita. A historic community in the heart of San Antonio, at the site of a Coahuiltecan Indian village. The first huts in the community were probably built about 1722. Families of soldiers attached to San Antonio de Béxar Presidio lived on the east side of the San Antonio River, which separated them after 1731 from the more aristocratic Canary Islanders. In 1773 La Villita was opened to refugees from East Texas. Events of the Casas Revolt occurred in the village. By 1819 a fairly exclusive residential area had grown up beside the humble homes of the soldiers. On 10 December 1835, Martín Perfecto de Cos capitulated to Texas soldiers at 515 Villita Street. John Coffee Hays lived in the area in 1838. By the 1840s Germans had given a European flavor to the section; they were later joined by Swiss and French. The Indian, Spanish, Mexican, and Anglo history of the section is preserved in the street and house names: Guadalupe Street, Bolivar Hall, Juarez Plaza, Cos House, Canada House, and McAllister Corner. La Villita was restored as a result of a city ordinance of 1939, and is owned by the city and operated as a craft and recreational center. The NYA assisted in the two-year restoration. San Antonio architect O'Neil Ford and others contributed to the project.

During World War II La Villita was used as a Red Cross Center. At the end of the war it was returned to the purpose of preserving early Texas and Spanish culture, fostering arts and crafts, and providing a community center. In 1948 artists and master craftsmen taught apprentices in some 15 shops in the village. In 1972 the 27 buildings in the area were added to the National Register of Historic Places. The authenticity of even small details has made the restoration project a demonstration of the development of Southwestern architecture. La Villita is the site of the annual Night in Old San Antonio celebration, as well as numerous other festivals, meetings, and fairs. *Lydia Magruder*

Law. The law of Texas is much like that of other parts of the United States. The government of the state is defined by a written constitution, which institutes the judicial system for the resolution of disputes. Adjudicating disputes between citizens and between citizens and governmental authorities is the principal function of the judiciary. The law applied for this purpose is an amalgam of traditional principles (mostly derived from English and Anglo-American law) and of statutes enacted by the Texas legislature, as well as statutes enacted by the United States Congress and principles embodied in the United States and Texas constitutions. Like most other states and the federal government, Texas has civil and criminal courts at the trial level and intermediate appellate courts. Unlike the federal government and all other states except Oklahoma, Texas has two higher appellate courts, the Supreme Court of Texas for civil matters and the Texas Court of Criminal Appeals for criminal cases. Rules of civil evidence and procedure are promulgated by the state Supreme Court and sometimes supplemented by legislative act. Most rules of criminal procedure are provided by statute, although rules of criminal evidence and criminal appellate rules are judicially promulgated. Rules of administrative law are those governing the administrative agencies of Texas government (such as the Railroad Commission). By legislative authority administrative rules of both a substantive and a procedural nature are promulgated in writing by the administrative agencies for the conduct of matters before them. Alongside the state courts the federal courts in Texas function under the United States Constitution to adjudicate disputes between Texans and non-Texans as well as disputes raising federal questions under United States law, including bankruptcy and admiralty matters.

In 1836 the Republic of Texas adopted the Anglo-American common law of crimes with jury trial. Those rules were the basis of the Penal Code of 1856, and criminal law has since been governed by statutes along with the safeguards of the United States and Texas constitutions. The nonstatutory, civil common law of Texas has been developed since the republic adopted "the common law of England as the rule of decision" in 1840. "Common law" was understood to include such matters as obligations arising by agreement (contracts) and those arising by injury (torts), as well as claims to property (lands as well as chattels), the status of citizens (such as marriage, divorce, welfare of children, corporations, and partnerships), and that body of legal doctrine embraced within the English concept of equity. Many of those rules have been put in an authoritative form by act of the legislature, while others have not. If codification has occurred, the legislative rules are interpreted by the courts and amplified by judicial decisions. Principles of law that are not codified are found in judicial decisions and learned writings. Only decisions of appellate courts designated to be published are looked to as sources of common law, and only about 20 percent of appellate decisions are so designated by the appellate courts deciding them.

Before the adoption of Anglo-American law, Spanish (Castilian) law prevailed in Texas. Spanish rules were not altered in any significant degree in Mexican Texas (1821–36). The records of Hispanic towns in the San Antonio River valley (San Fernando and La Bahía) and Nacogdoches in East Texas show the effective operation of Spanish law, also apparent in the records of El Paso del Norte and Laredo, which were outside the territorial boundaries of Spanish Texas. During the Spanish regime, however, there were no legally trained judges in Texas or practicing lawyers in the modern sense. The only legal professional who functioned in Texas during the entire Spanish period was the self-taught notary of San Fernando, Francisco de Arocha. Despite a lack of legal professionals and a small European population that rarely had recourse to legal rules, Spanish law was maintained through the use of a few law books referred to by administrators and citizens in the preparation of legal instruments and in trials to settle disputes. This state of affairs was little changed under the Mexican regime except in one important particular: among the Anglo-American colonists of the 1820s and 1830s there were a few lawyers from the United States who rendered legal services to their fellow colonists and developed a familiarity with the prevailing principles of Hispano-Mexican law. As a consequence some rules of Spanish law became established and were maintained by legislation of the republic. Although some of these principles have survived in other areas of Texas law, their chief significance today is in family property law.

Much of the legislation of the republic was of a governmental nature or was passed for the benefit of particular citizens. Because of the unsettled state of defense and government at that time, however, neither the legislature nor the courts functioned very effectively. Apart from a few civil statutes of the republic and early statehood that perpetuated Hispanic legal institutions, most of the general civil and criminal laws were borrowed from the statutes of various American states. Since annexation in 1845–46 some civil rules deemed of particular and lasting importance have been embodied in constitutional provisions so that they will not be subject to easy legislative tampering. The concepts of separate property, community property, and homestead law are among the doctrines given constitutional protection. During the republic the use of the jury was carried well beyond its common-law scope, and a broad adherence to jury trial has been maintained. A statute of 1846 allowed a jury to pass sentence in criminal convictions except in capital cases or when the penalty was fixed by law, and the first restriction was removed in 1857. In 1846 the legislature also abolished some of the most archaic elements of the English procedural law, but not until 1871 were all interested parties made competent to testify in civil disputes, and not until 1889 was a person accused of crime allowed to testify under oath on his own behalf. During the first 12 years of statehood the Supreme Court of Texas continually consisted of three men of very considerable ability and experience—John Hemphill, Abner S. Lipscomb, and Royal T. Wheeler. They laid a firm foundation for the common law of Texas for the rest of the century.

With the coming of the Civil War, legislative attention shifted from other matters to those of the war. Though the Supreme Court continued to function to a limited extent during the war, for a decade thereafter the tenure of judges was short, as one brief government followed another and ties with the legal past were broken. Although the government was returned to the Texas electorate with the election of 1874 and the Constitution of 1876, the rift with the past was never fully mended. Texas law, like Texas politics, then took on a tone of populism that lasted through most of the twentieth century. Until after the Civil War, Texas substantive civil law and procedure had maintained some elements of the Spanish law, most particularly the simple system of quasi-Hispanic civil procedure that had prevailed among the Anglo-Americans in Mexican Texas. But the new learning at the state law school established in 1883 produced a new type of Texas lawyer trained in the nuances of civil procedure derived from the old English system, which was beginning to be replaced with more modern rules elsewhere in the United States. The preoccupation of Texas law with great procedural formality lasted until the mid-twentieth century. Although a great many lawyers continued to be educated wholly by apprenticeship, the quality of the bar (and thus the judiciary) was much enhanced by formal legal training. Private law schools had been established before the Civil War but perished soon thereafter. The availability of public legal education at a modest price and with good instruction did much to restore continuity in Texas law.

From 1846 until the adoption of the 1876 constitution, various authors published annotated collections of the statute law as commercial ventures. In these compilations the laws were typically arranged alphabetically, but no effort was made toward a systematic codification. The Constitution of 1876 provided that every 10 years the legislature would revise the general-statute law. The first compilation by legislative act was made in 1879. By appointing a commission of three lawyers to revise the laws and then reenacting their revision, the legislature achieved a reordering of the statutory laws and suppression of some inconsistencies in 1895, in 1911, and finally in 1925. The legislature failed, however, to comply with the constitutional directive to revise the statutes every decade. Under the 1876 constitution (as under other constitutions except that of 1869) the legislature meets biennially for 4½ months and at such other special sessions as the governor may call, but with an increasing population and new problems of government it was easy to postpone statutory revision as a subsidiary function of legislative responsibility.

An attitude of Jacksonian democracy adverse to banks achieved a prohibition of legislative grants of banking charters in the Constitution of 1845, and an effort to operate a bank under a Mexican charter of 1835 was successfully put down by a criminal prosecution concluded in 1859. From the end of the Civil War to World War II, Texas continued to be dominated by noncommercial interests. The majority of the population remained on the land and in towns with a population of fewer than 20,000. The laws reflected this limited commercialism. From the time of the republic there was a strong public feeling against the centralization of capital and a resulting antagonism to banks and some other commercial pursuits. Until after the Civil War banking activities were carried out by mercantile houses. The state Grange was organized in 1873 and was largely responsible for adoption of constitutional restraints on the railroads. Many Texans questioned the wisdom of making grants of land for railroad building, and laws controlling railroad rates of the 1870s and 1880s reflected antirailroad sentiment. The Railroad

Commission was instituted by a constitutional amendment in 1891. Though the United States Supreme Court had invalidated an earlier attempt at business-control legislation in 1888, this effort to control railroads survived constitutional challenge.

Like the rest of the country, toward the end of the nineteenth century Texans were much alarmed by the growing power of the business trusts, and almost a year before the enactment of the federal antitrust act of 1890 the Texas legislature passed a similar measure that had little effect but indicated the attitude toward increasing financial power in a few hands. Although some banking charters had been granted by the Reconstruction legislatures in the early 1870s and a number of federally chartered (national) banks were also established, much of the state did business without chartered banks until 1905, when the law was changed to allow the issuance of state banking charters. The state constitution, however, continued to prohibit branch banking until 1986. In 1893 the Stock and Bond Act sought to control the issuance of public securities by railroads, and the Insurance Act of 1907 required that insurance companies invest three-quarters of all premiums in Texas. Like the railroads, the banks were closely regulated by a state commission, and in the decade immediately preceding World War I statutes were enacted to regulate the issue of securities generally.

At the same time that banking was being tightly constrained, the insurance companies were less closely controlled. This development was in many respects fortuitous. Investment in life insurance was a popular form of saving to provide for the needs of a family left without its principal provider, and the accumulation of insurance capital was not seen as an acute economic danger because the insurance companies were not engaged in making small loans. As a result of lax incorporation laws and less than vigorous regulation of insurance companies, Texas attracted the formation of insurance companies that in turn assured their own political power.

After the Civil War and well into the twentieth century the legislature gave little attention to specific rules of private law that regulated dealings and disputes between citizens. When changes were made in private law, they occurred as a means of bringing about social and economic reform, as in the introduction of the workers' compensation system in 1913. This scheme of injury insurance had originated in Germany in the late nineteenth century and had been enacted elsewhere in Western Europe and the United States. As a means of prompt settlement of injury claims of employees against employers within fixed limits of financial liability, the state instituted an insurance system to which employers subscribed. Workers benefited by being freed from the three common-law impediments to recovery: the doctrine of contributory negligence, the fellow-servant doctrine, and the principle of assumed risk. Neither employers nor employees accepted the system without some resistance. After a time, however, the scheme functioned effectively within the judicial system as an alternative to common-law recovery.

The woman-suffrage movement, which was particularly strong in Texas during the early years of the twentieth century, produced a reform in family-property law even before voting rights for women were achieved. In 1911 the legislature gave married women the right to seek judicial approval to conduct business affairs without their husbands' participation. Two years later the legislature gave married women sole control of the income of their separate property. In subsequent legislative ses-

sions the property rights of married women were further increased. In the decade immediately following World War I, however, the Texas Supreme Court declared some of these statutes unconstitutional, and the new property rights attained by married women were thereby curtailed. National women's suffrage rights, as well as national prohibition of liquor sales had been achieved in the meantime. The latter reform put a heavy burden on criminal-law enforcement, as did the social turmoil engendered by the collapse of the national economy in the early 1930s. Prison reform had been undertaken with some success before World War I, but attention to the criminal law was diverted by other matters. Nor was Texas civil law much affected by the economic crisis beyond a substantial broadening of types of moveable property exempt from creditors' claims.

The most significant legal reform that occurred in the years immediately preceding World War II was a general revision of the rules of civil procedure designed to remove some of the pitfalls and delays to proceedings that had previously barred claimants from bringing their claims to trial. This change, which involved much work on the part of the judiciary and the professorate, was heavily influenced by similar reform in the federal courts and evidenced a revival of external influences on Texas law. The receptivity of Texans to new ideas reflected the widespread national openness to reform and experimentation, which was particularly popular in the law schools. Texas enacted two laws in 1951 promulgated by the Commissioners for Uniform State Laws and subsequently has enacted more than 30 other uniform laws.

The process of legal reform that followed World War II was enhanced by a broadened general outlook as a result of the war and economic prosperity. The State Bar of Texas has been a very active force in this process. The bar's initial involvement was the preparation of the Probate Code (1955) and Business Corporation Act (1955, amended in 1961), followed by reform of nonprofit corporate law in 1959 and partnership law in 1961. The process was quickened by legislative realization that the constitutionally mandated decennial revision of the statutory law had not been undertaken since 1925, though some significant consolidation of laws had already been achieved in the fields of insurance (1951) and succession (1955). In 1963 the legislature instituted a new scheme of statutory revision by which large individual legal topics would be recompiled as independent codes. The bar was heavily involved in this process of statutory legal restatement: revision of criminal procedure (1965), commercial law (1967), family law (1967–73), water law (1971), penal law (1973), and civil procedure and practice (1985). In the course of these developments the legislature abolished the common-law doctrine of contributory negligence and substituted the principle of comparative negligence in tort recovery (1973). The process of statutory revision nevertheless continued to depend on the existence of a common-law framework to which the statutory codification was merely ancillary. The codes do not constitute an exclusive body of legal rules except with regard to criminal law. As a consequence of the contagion of the notion of "Legal Realism" imparted by the University of Texas law school during the 1920s and 1930s and the ideology of judicial activism elsewhere in the country, the Texas Supreme Court participated in the process of law reform during the two decades after the 1960s, particularly in the field of tort law. The legislature also took up the implementation of tort-law reform with the enactment of a statute on deceptive trade practices (1973). The political nature of the Supreme Court changed markedly in the late 1980s and early 1990s. In 1995 there was a Republican majority on the court for the first time since Reconstruction.

In the Constitution of 1876 final appellate review of criminal decisions at the behest of a prisoner was vested in a Court of Appeals, which also heard appeals of some civil cases. In 1891 the constitution was amended to put appellate review of all criminal cases in a Court of Criminal Appeals, and civil appeals were heard in regional Courts of Civil Appeals with further appeal to the Supreme Court. Because the single court for criminal appeals had become inadequate to handle the volume of appeals, the courts for civil appeals were transformed in 1980 into regional courts of appeals, which hear both civil and criminal appeals, with further civil appeals to the Supreme Court and criminal appeals to the Court of Criminal Appeals. The state was also allowed to take appeals in criminal prosecutions in 1989.

To encourage settlement and development during the eighteenth and nineteenth centuries, prior sovereignties and the state have disposed of a prodigious quantity of land at very low prices. Land grants were limited by prevailing rules of law as to formalities and extent, but irregularities in acquisition were not ordinarily asserted except by a subsequent government. Grants were usually defined by their own terms, and these terms have occasionally been brought into question, as in the Valmont Plantations case (1962), in which water rights to Spanish grants along the lower Rio Grande were defined. Spanish and Mexican grants often had a watercourse as one of their boundaries, and their shapes were irregular. After 1840 most land grants followed a more geometrical configuration and were later made in blocks in the North American manner. The seaward boundaries of coastal grants approach the sea more closely than grants made before Texas independence because of a difference between Spanish and English law in this regard. In the Constitution of 1866 the state's claim to minerals (preserved from the Spanish regime) was given up in favor of surface owners of land. As public lands shrank, the legislature began to have a change of mind with respect to their disposition. In 1895 the policy of not including water rights in subsequent land grants was adopted. In 1901 it was decided that the state would dispose of mineral interests for fixed terms only, and the surface rights were thereafter sold without the underlying minerals. The changed attitude toward disposition of minerals was influenced by discovery of large quantities of oil and the decision that this resource underlying public lands should be exploited for the public interest. The development of oil and gas deposits with large financial interests at stake also produced a new subject of Texas law, developed as disputes arose. This body of law as enunciated by the courts took on a peculiarly Texan content: the mineral "lease" is not a mere contractual right to use the land for a term of years but a right of ownership of the subterranean minerals.

When Texas entered the Union, her public lands did not pass to the national government; therefore, federal landholdings in Texas (confined mostly to military and naval facilities) are much smaller than those in most western states. Although the United States Supreme Court ruled in the Tidelands Controversy (1950) that the seabed of the Texas Gulf coast was not subject to state sovereignty, a congressional act of 1953 relinquished to Texas an area of more than 10 miles in breadth as claimed under Hispano-Mexican law. The general land law, however, had remained largely unchanged except for instances when general social policy or particular interests were at stake. Thus, some large landowners were able to convince the legislature to relinquish the state's title to streambeds when a landowner owned both sides of the stream (1929). Overcoming constitutional arguments with heavy reliance on legislative authority, the Supreme Court in 1981 approved the shift of water-rights regulation from judicial to administrative supervision. With the emergence of federal control of environmental concerns, basic policy is laid down by the federal government, but administration of environmental programs has been delegated to the state in most cases. The control of land use, both rural and urban, has generally continued under the state. In disputes between private owners of land, common-law rules have mostly remained unchanged. Whether the transfer of a land interest is that of absolute ownership (a fee simple) or of a lesser interest or claim, transfers are ordinarily made by a formal written instrument (a deed), which is recorded in the county where the land is located in order to give any prospective purchaser of the land notice of the status of title to the land. Although many citizens often seem unaware of the rules, title to land may be lost through long occupancy by a person without a deed or by a person holding a deed from someone other than the owner, particularly when the claimant has paid annual state taxes on the land. A claim to a right-of-way or other easement may also be established by adverse use as well as by a grant from the owner of land. A claim of adverse possession may not be asserted against the state, however. The number of years of adverse possessions or use required to alter title to land varies with the circumstances of open occupancy or use. In order to protect himself against a claim that may be later asserted against him, the seller of land ordinarily supplies the buyer with a policy of insurance against that eventuality. Although claims of title to land may be proved in various ways, the most formal mode is the common-law process of ejectment, ordinarily known as trespass to try title.

The Texas laws of contracts, commerce, and business institutions are virtually identical to those in the rest of the United States, with some modest variations. As in other states the assertions of tort claims in the later twentieth century is sometimes thought to put an undue burden on professionals and nonprofessionals alike in the conduct of their activities. The cost of insurance against such claims has so increased along with the number of tort recoveries that many regard the cost of insurance as beyond their means. It is also sometimes asserted that the verdicts of some juries are well beyond a reasonable valuation of loss and that attorneys for plaintiffs negotiate too high a portion of injury awards for their fees.

Texas family property and succession laws differ significantly from those of most other states in that Texas maintains a system of community property between husband and wife. Texas law is also far from identical to that of any one of the other eight community-property states, though a 1987 change in the law so that the surviving spouse more frequently takes the deceased spouse's share of the community property on intestacy has brought Texas law into closer harmony with that of other community-property states. Although Texas allows an equitable (and hence unequal) division of community property between spouses on divorce, no post-divorce award of support (alimony) for an ex-spouse is allowed. The Texas law of marriage is similar to that of most other states except that Texas maintains the principle of informal

Bobby Layne, ca. 1947. Courtesy Sports Information Office, University of Texas at Austin.

(or common-law) marriage and the majority of American states do not. With respect to rules governing the relationship of parents to their children, however, Texas law is similar to those of most other states, although the Texas law of adoption is somewhat more sophisticated than that of most other states.

Joseph W. McKnight

Law of April 6, 1830. Initiated by Lucas Alamán y Escalada, Mexican minister of foreign relations, in response to recommendations by Manuel de Mier y Terán; stimulated the Texas Revolution as the Stamp Act did the American Revolution. Mier y Terán had encouraged counter-colonization of Texas by Mexicans and Europeans. Article 11 of the new law, which the Texans found most objectionable, originated with Alamán and was intended to prohibit or limit immigration from the United States. Mier became federal commissioner of colonization despite his doubts concerning the wisdom of Article 11 and of other articles concerning slavery and passports. Texas colonists were greatly troubled by news of the law. Stephen F. Austin tried to allay the disturbance but protested the law to Mier y Terán and to President Anastasio Bustamante. By his manipulation of the interpretation of articles 10 and 11, Austin secured exemption from the operation of the law for his contract and for that of Green DeWitt, but the measure shook his belief in the good will of the Mexican government. Subsequently he was able to secure the repeal of Article 11. Application of the law slowed immigration, voided contracts that had been awarded but not carried toward fulfillment, and suspended two active enterprises—

Sterling C. Robertson's colony and the Galveston Bay and Texas Land Company. Enforcement of the customs provisions of the law resulted directly in the Anahuac Disturbances of 1832 and indirectly in the battle of Velasco, the conventions of 1832 and 1833, and the accumulation of grievances that helped lead to the revolution.

Curtis Bishop

Layne, Bobby. Football player; b. Robert Lawrence Layne, Santa Anna, Texas, 19 December 1926; d. Lubbock, 1 December 1986; m. Carol Krueger (1946); 2 sons; ed. University of Texas (grad. 1948). At Highland Park High School in Dallas, Layne was a teammate of Doak Walker, another future member of the Pro Football Hall of Fame. At UT he garnered every major school passing record, including most attempts, most completions, most passing yards, most total yards, and most touchdowns. As a UT baseball player he compiled a record of 39 wins and 7 losses as a pitcher; his 1946 Southwest Conference record of two no-hitters and 84 strike-outs stood for 30 years thereafter. After graduating he joined the Lubbock Hubbers baseball team of the Class C West Texas–New Mexico League, but ultimately decided that his future lay in football. After his senior season he had been drafted by the Pittsburgh Steelers, who immediately traded the rights to his services to the Chicago Bears. The Baltimore Colts of the rival All-American Football Conference offered Layne a three-year contract worth $77,000, but he opted to sign with the better-established NFL for less money. He spent the 1948 season in Chicago as a backup before Bears coach George Halas traded him to the lowly New York Bulldogs for $50,000 and two first-round draft choices. Later Halas called the trade "the worst deal I ever made." Before the 1950 season the Bulldogs sold Layne to the Detroit Lions, with whom he spent the next eight seasons. Reunited with his old friend Walker, Layne led Detroit to NFL championships in 1952, 1953, and 1957, and to the title game in 1954, when he was named All-Pro quarterback. He gained even more notoriety, however, for his off-field carousing. Once he was arrested for driving while intoxicated, but a sympathetic judge let him off, ruling that the arresting officer had simply been unable to understand Layne's drawl. On the following day, a sign appeared in the Lions' locker room reading, "I'm not drunk, I just speak Texan." In 1957 Layne joined the Steelers. He spent five seasons in Pittsburgh, but the Steelers had fewer quality players than the Lions, and Layne won no more championships. His autobiography, *Always on Sunday* (1962), contained a number of anecdotes about his exploits on and off the field; in the book he denied that he had been drunk during a notorious collision with a parked Pittsburgh streetcar early one morning. Layne was called "the best all-around quarterback who ever played," and by the time he retired before the 1963 season, he held the NFL records for passing attempts, completions, touchdowns, yards, and interceptions. During the 1950s he entered the oil business in Lubbock. After his retirement he served briefly as an assistant coach with the Steelers and then in the 1960s with the St. Louis Cardinals. He also tried unsuccessfully for the head coach position at Texas Tech University in 1980. He devoted most of his time to his business interests in Texas. He was elected to the Texas Sports Hall of Fame in 1960, to the Longhorn Hall of Honor in 1963, and to the Pro Football Hall of Fame in 1967. In November 1986, days before his death, he traveled to Michigan to present the Hall of Fame ring and plaque to Doak Walker.

Martin Donell Kohout

Ledbetter, Huddie. Musician, known as Leadbelly; b. near Mooringsport, Louisiana, 21 January 1888; d. New York City, 6 December 1949; lived with Margaret Coleman (1905–); 2 children; m. Eletha Henderson (1916; divorced); m. Martha Promise (1935). Ledbetter lived on a farm in East Texas beginning when he was ten. Having learned to play the sixstring guitar, he left home in 1901 to make his way as a minstrel, first on Fannin Street in Shreveport, and later in Dallas and Fort Worth. He spent summers working as a farmhand. While working in Dallas, he met Blind Lemon Jefferson, and it was as his partner that Leadbelly first began to play the 12-string guitar. In 1918, under the name of Walter Boyd, Ledbetter was convicted of murder and sentenced to 30 years in the Texas penitentiary. Pardoned in 1925 after having written a song in honor of Governor Pat Neff, he did odd jobs until 1930, when he was imprisoned at Angola, Louisiana, for assault with intent to murder. There his music attracted Texas folklorist John Avery Lomax and his son Alan. As a result of Lomax's intervention, Leadbelly was released from prison, and for several months he toured with the Lomaxes, giving concerts and assisting them in their efforts to record the work songs and spirituals of black convicts. Soon after their arrival in New York City, Leadbelly's singing and his unconventional background combined to bring him national prominence. Despite his growing reputation as an entertainer, he was again briefly incarcerated for assault in 1939 on Riker's Island. He was more popular among whites than blacks. His associates included Woody Guthrie, Pete Seger, and Sonny Terry. Leadbelly's most popular composition, "Goodnight Irene," achieved its greatest success in the early 1950s after his death. He died of Lou Gehrig's disease. In 1988 Louisiana erected a historical marker at his gravesite. In 1980 the Nashville Songwriters Association inducted him into their International Hall of Fame. That honor was followed in 1986 with membership in the Blues Foundation Hall of Fame, and in 1988 his work was honored by the Rock and Roll Hall of Fame. *Christine Hamm*

Lee, Harper Baylor. Matador; b. James Harper Gillett, Ysleta, 5 September 1884; d. Bexar County, 26 June 1941; m. Roxa Dunbar (1915). Gillett's mother was the daughter of ranger colonel George Wythe Baylor. She and her husband were divorced in 1889, and after she married Samuel M. Lee (1895), Gillett began to sign himself Harper Baylor Lee. His schoolmates called him El Gringo Harper. He showed early promise in bullfighting games and received invitations to bull ranches, where he attended the breeders' testings of their young fighting stock and showed exceptional talent. After graduation from high school (1904) he worked for his stepfather's firm on railway construction jobs in central Mexico and took time off frequently to appear as an *aficionado* in amateur corridas. Under the tutelage of his friend Francisco (El Chiclanero) Gómez, a retired matador from Spain, Lee quit his job to try his hand as a professional *torero*. He made his first appearance as a *novillero*, or apprentice matador, at the bullring in Guadalajara on 28 July 1908. In 1910 in the Plaza de Toros at Monterrey he was awarded his *alternativa* in a formal ceremony that made him a full-fledged *matador de toros*, the first North American to earn such rank. The public cheered him as "Opper Li." He was excellent in all three parts of the bullfight: with the cape, especially with the banderillas, and with the muleta and sword. Behaving with respect for the technical tenets and traditions of Spanish bullfighting, he demon-

Huddie Ledbetter, better known as "Leadbelly," ca. 1940s. Prints and Photographs Collection, Huddie Ledbetter file, CAH; CN 04111. The son of a black tenant farmer, Huddie Ledbetter learned to play the sixstring guitar as a child and left home at about age 13 to make his way as a minstrel.

strated valor, spirit, skill, and art. He appeared as a professional matador in 52 corridas in 24 Mexican cities and killed 100 bulls. Twice he suffered nearly fatal gorings. When his career was cut short by the chaos of the Mexican Revolution and its accompanying anti-American feelings, he "cut the pigtail" in the formal ceremony of retirement on 3 December 1911. After 24 years of estrangement, Lee was reconciled with his father in 1914, and after his mother and stepfather died he changed his name to Harper Baylor Gillett. He had met his wife before a bullfight in San Luis Potosí. After his retirement, they owned and operated a poultry farm on the outskirts of San Antonio. *Tom Lea*

Lee, Nelson. Literary charlatan; b. Brownsville, New York, 1807. In *Three Years Among the Camanches* [sic]: *The Narrative of Nelson Lee, the Texas Ranger, containing a Detailed Account of His Captivity* . . . (1859), Lee depicted himself as having been a Texas Ranger, a soldier, and an Indian captive. Unfortunately, nothing is known of his activities except through this book. His claims have often been taken seriously. Walter Prescott Webb stated that "there is no better description of the life of the Texas Rangers than that of Nelson Lee." Lee's book has since been a source for several writers about Comanche culture. But in 1982 anthropologist Melburn D. Thurman called Lee's account of Comanche ceremonies "blatantly erroneous" and demonstrated that Ernest Wallace and E. Adamson Hoebel's discussion of the "Comanche" Green Corn Ceremony in *The Comanches: Lords of the South Plains* (1952) employed questionable data from Lee's book. Though noted Indian scholars have long identified the Comanches as a nonsedentary and therefore nonagricultural people, Lee narrated to his New York editors that Comanches planted corn, beans, and tobacco. Other wildly erroneous claims abound. Lee said that the Comanches wrote hieroglyphics on tree bark; built villages with central squares, streets, and houses of important men located on the squares; and resolved irreconcilable differences between two adversaries by lashing them together with a cord and requiring them to fight to the death. Accordingly, Thurman and other specialists of Plains Indians disputed Lee's captivity claims and, by extension, other claims he makes concerning his exploits. Indeed, Nelson Lee's name does not appear on muster rolls, in newspapers, or other documents that would support his stories of serving in various battles and with the Texas Rangers. His near-death escapes—surviving a shipwreck by clinging to rigging, remedying a rattlesnake bite by applying snake flesh to his wound, outswimming a 14-foot alligator that pursues him across a stream, avoiding death by Comanche captors when his alarm watch goes off as they search him—place Lee's work firmly in the realm of literary hoax. The book is one of several Indian captivity narratives of the early nineteenth century whose "chief concern," wrote one critic, "was neither accuracy of sensation nor fidelity to the hard facts of frontier life, but rather the salability of pulp thrillers." Lee himself gave hints. His tales were, the editors admitted, "not precisely in his own words," and Lee hoped the book would "be the means of improving, in some measure, his present impoverished condition." The book does, however, suggest that Lee was quite a raconteur who put himself in the ranks of other larger-than-life heroes prominent in Texas folklore.   *Richard Allen Burns*

Leland, Mickey. Congressman; b. Lubbock, 27 November 1944; d. Ethiopia, 7 August 1989 (buried in Golden Gate Cemetery, Houston); m. Alison ——; twin sons; ed. Texas Southern University. In the 1960s Leland, a pharmacist, pressured Houston health officials to set up community clinics and, as a member of the black Community Action team, worked for other reform measures. In 1972, supported by philanthropist John de Menil, he was elected to the Texas House of Representatives. He was reelected twice. He is especially remembered in the Texas House for promoting legislation that allowed for the prescription of generic drugs and fostered state employment opportunities for members of minorities. In 1978 Leland constructed the National Black–Hispanic Democratic Coalition that drew attention at the Democratic midterm convention in Memphis. Later that year, he took the congressional seat vacated by Barbara Jordan. He served for more than 10 years in Congress—at first flamboyantly wearing a dashiki and eccentric hats and sporting an Afro haircut, and later abandoning such fillips in order to establish bipartisan relationships. He chaired the Congressional Black Caucus; served as a member of the Energy and Commerce Committee; and in 1984 helped establish the Select Committee on Hunger, which pushed Congress to approve $8 million annually for a Vitamin A program in the Third World that is believed to have reduced child mortality. The committee also fought to feed impoverished neighborhoods in the United States. Leland's trip to the Sudan in the spring of 1989 marked the beginning of efforts to aid Sudanese refugees in Ethiopia. On his sixth visit to Africa, his plane crashed into a mountainside on the way to the Fugnido refugee camp, where 300,000 Sudanese had fled from famine and war. Leland was honored at services throughout Texas and in Washington. Mrs. Leland was pregnant at his death. In January 1990 she gave birth to their twins.   *Jill S. Seeber*

Leon Springs Military Reservation. A U.S. Army camp off I-10 northwest of San Antonio; established to supply increasing military needs after the Spanish–American War, which brought unprecedented growth to Fort Sam Houston; comprises Camp Stanley and Camp Bullis. In 1906 and 1907, 17,273 acres near Leon Springs was acquired, and the reservation was established. In 1908 the first military maneuvers were held involving both regular army and national guard units. These training exercises included units of the Third Cavalry, First Field Artillery, and Ninth and Nineteenth infantries, as well as signal and hospital units. The first recorded artillery firing at the reservation occurred in 1909. The first use of aircraft took place in 1911 when Benjamin Foulois and Phillip O. Parmalee delivered a message from Fort Sam Houston to the reservation. In February 1917 Maj. Gen. Frederick Funston, commanding general of the Southern District, died in San Antonio, and facilities at the Leon Springs Reservation were named Camp Funston in his honor. But another camp in Funston's native Kansas was also named for him, so Leon Springs was redesignated Camp Stanley, after Brig. Gen. David S. Stanley, former commander of the Department of Texas. In May 1917 the First Officers Training Camp was established at Camp Stanley. Its purpose was to provide in 90 days most of the junior officers for newly formed divisions. The trainees became known as "90-day wonders." Lt. Dwight Eisenhower was among the officers of the Fifty-seventh Infantry, which moved to the camp in 1917. Lt. Walton H. Walker, who later commanded the United States Eighth Army in Korea, was also a member of this unit. In the spring of 1917 a remount station was established at Leon Springs to process and maintain horses used by the mounted arms of the military services. The old San Antonio Arsenal, originally built in 1859, was poorly located and by 1919 had been surrounded by the downtown area. It was moved to Camp Stanley and by 1937 required an area of 1,760 acres. At this time Camp Stanley was devoted to storage and testing of ordnance materials, and all other military activities at the Leon Springs Military Reservation were conducted at Camp Bullis.

Events beginning in 1916, when Pancho Villa crossed the United States border, and extending into World War I, greatly accelerated the build-up of facilities at Fort Sam Houston and Leon Springs. In September 1917 an additional 16,000 acres was leased, extending the Leon Springs Reservation to the south. A new camp was established there to provide maneuver areas and rifle ranges for troops from Fort Sam Houston and named for Brig. Gen. John L. Bullis. After the war the camp was used for demobilization. Between 1918 and 1940 the army built permanent facilities there. In 1926 two motion pictures, *The Rough Riders* and *Wings*, were made at Bullis, with suitable sets and soldiers as extras. During the 1920s and 1930s Camp Bullis provided facilities for training the Civilian Military Training Corps, the CCC, the ROTC, and the Officer Reserve Corps. With World War II looming, a reception center was established at Camp Bullis in September 1940 to process and train draftees. After the attack on Pearl Harbor (7 December 1941) the camp served for activation and training of infantry divisions, service schools, a reception center, a prisoner of war camp, and a test bed for tactics and organizational units. In 1942–43 the Second, Ninety-fifth, and Eighty-eighth Infantry divisions used Camp Bullis. Smaller units continued to use the camp until 1944. After the war

500,000 soldiers were processed out through the separation centers at Fort Sam Houston and Camp Bullis.

The changing medical needs of the army during and after World War II brought major changes to Fort Sam Houston and Camp Bullis. By 1944 a school for enlisted medical technicians and a basic training course for army nurses was added. The greater portion of Fort Sam Houston became hospital wards and a convalescent center, Brooke Army Medical Center. Camp Bullis provided field training for small arms and a stretcher obstacle course to train combat medics in the handling of wounded on the battlefield. Camp Bullis was largely on stand-by status until the invasion of South Korea by North Korea in June 1950. At Camp Bullis the Army Food Service School established a field site, the Detroit Arsenal a tire-testing facility, and the Fourth Army a chemical defense school. The growth of San Antonio and commercial aviation increased air traffic over the camp, making it necessary to restrict the firing of mortars and artillery. By 1955 Camp Bullis was providing ranges and training areas for medical units of the regular army, reserve component units, ROTC, and United States Army Reserve schools. Trainers conducted field exercises under realistic conditions, including survival techniques, map reading, and escape and evasion. The trainee loads increased significantly when 40,000 medical personnel prepared for Vietnam duty. The Forty-fifth Medical Unit, Self Contained, Transportable, was the first of these units sent overseas. The unit was a modular facility of inflatable shelters developed at Fort Sam Houston and field-tested at Camp Bullis. A mock Vietnam village was constructed at Camp Bullis to help prepare soldiers for service in Vietnam. In 1965 the air force was conducting weapons training for trainees, air police, and the security service at Camp Bullis. As the war in Vietnam wound down, so did activity at Camp Bullis. The General Services Administration declared 1,140 acres of the reservation excess in 1972. Dwight D. Eisenhower Park opened on 323 acres of the camp transferred to the city of San Antonio in 1988. Another 94 acres was transferred to Bexar County in 1977 to allow the widening of Blanco Road, and 47 acres was turned over to the county for a park near Borgfield Drive. These reductions had little effect on the mission of the camp.

In 1977 an Air Force Security Police Training Site, known as Victor Base, was constructed to accommodate the Air Force Security Police Academy. The air force was subsequently the largest single user of Camp Bullis until 1987. The army began emergency deployment readiness exercises at Camp Bullis in 1973, when elements of the 101st Airborne Division from Fort Hood were air-dropped at Camp Bullis. Other exercises were conducted by the 101st and the Eighty-second Airborne in 1980 and 1981. In 1985 the 307th Medical Battalion and a French army medical unit were air-dropped on Camp Bullis. A combat assault landing strip was constructed at the camp in 1983. The First Marine Amphibious Force conducted landing operations at the strip in 1986 and 1989. Unit training at Camp Bullis for the garrison and tenant organization of the Department of Defense has been vigorous and sometimes innovative. Commanders have taken their administrative, overhead, and garrison troops to practice "real soldiering" at Camp Bullis. Since the Vietnam War the post has undergone organizational changes. In 1990 the camp was under the operational control of the Directorate of Plans, Training, Mobilization, and Security at Fort Sam Houston. It was used for firing ranges, maneuver areas for army, air force, and marine combat units, and for field training of the various medical units from Brooke Army Medical Center. Camp Stanley was largely used for ammunition storage and testing. The total area of the reservation was slightly more than 26,000 acres.

Art Leatherwood

Le Poste des Cadodaquious. A small French fort northwest of the site of Texarkana; founded in 1719 by Bénard de La Harpe as a part of his land concession. The founding was an opportunistic military advance in an area where the Spanish had made similar advances. La Harpe built his stockaded post on the south bank of the Red River near a village of the Nasoni Indians, a Caddoan group. Consequently, the fort was sometimes called Le Poste des Nassonites, for Nasoni Indians, or, more commonly, Le Poste des Cadodaquious, reflecting the French pronunciation of Kadohadacho, a name used by various Caddoan peoples to describe themselves and their homeland. Recent analysis of source material and subsequent related records for the area suggests that the site was on the escarpment near the present site of Everett or Barkman. La Harpe was the fort's first commandant. After his departure in late 1719 the post was garrisoned by a sergeant's detachment from Natchitoches, Louisiana, and Louis Juchereau de St. Denis succeeded La Harpe in command. The trader and interpreter Alexis Grappé was important at the fort. The post had little military significance except in limiting the northward influence of the Spanish and serving as a French station for trade. In 1719 Durivage and Mustel explored the Red River from the post. Later, La Harpe moved on to the northwest and came into contact with various Wichita groups, probably along the lower Canadian River, thereby laying the ground for years of French trade in the region. Early trade ventures involving Francis Harvey (Herve) extended westward to the Kiamichi and Boggy rivers and to the Pani Piques, or Taovaya Indians, after their removal to the Red River around 1757. The post was a supply base for the expeditions of Fabry de La Bruyere in 1742 and Pierre A. Mallet in 1750. Jean Baptiste Brevel left the post for Santa Fe in 1767. A small French settlement developed close to the fort from its earliest days. At least two of Grappé's children were born there. The French abandoned the post shortly after the Louisiana cession. In 1770 Athanase de Mézières attempted to reestablish the post for the Spanish under the name San Luiz de los Cadodachos. The Nasonis deserted their ancestral home shortly thereafter. Archeological studies of Nasoni gravesites have revealed a variety of French trade goods. Thomas Freeman, although aware of the vicinity, failed to locate the fort in 1806. The name Fort St. Louis de Carloretto is an American misnomer.

Morris L. Britton

LeTourneau University. In Longview; a private, nondenominational, evangelical Christian institution founded by Robert Gilmour LeTourneau. With the help of Carl Estes, publisher of the Longview *News*, and others, LeTourneau purchased Harmon General Hospital, a government hospital with 220 buildings on 156 acres, for only one dollar. LeTourneau Technical Institute of Texas was chartered and began classes in 1946. The institute accepted only male students, most of whom were veterans. During its first two years the school was divided into an academy and a college division. Students worked on a plan by which one-half attended classes three days a week while the other half worked at LeTourneau's plant. This work met the laboratory requirements of the industrial courses. The alternate-day scheduling continued until 1961. The institute was accredited in 1947 by the State Board of Education, the Texas Junior College Association, and the American Association of Junior Colleges. From 1946 to 1961 the administrative structures of the school and the plant were unified by LeTourneau, who served as president and chairman of the board of both organizations. He advertised the institute internationally through a periodic newsletter, *LeTourneau Tech NOW*, which eventually reached a circulation of more than 500,000. Some 300 to 400 students enrolled in the institute each year between 1946 and 1961. In 1961 the institute became LeTourneau College, a coeducational, four-year college. Also at this time a master plan was developed, and permanent steel and brick buildings began to replace the old wooden barracks. In 1970 LeTourneau received accreditation from the Southern Association of Colleges and Schools. Enrollment surpassed 1,000 in 1980 and dropped somewhat thereafter. In 1985 LeTourneau joined the Christian College Coalition in an effort to participate in student exchanges and other benefits. President Alvin O. Austin (1986–) changed the name of the institution to LeTourneau University. In addition to the Longview campus, LeTourneau offers courses in Tyler, Dallas, and Houston.

Ken Durham

Liberty–Nacogdoches Road. An important early north–south route established by Spanish authorities as a line of communication between Nacogdoches and El Orcoquisac. The road connecting Nacogdoches and the Trinity River settlement was described by the Marqués de Rubí, whose mapmaker, Nicolás de Lafora, kept a diary of Rubí's tour in 1767. The approximate route of the Liberty–Nacogdoches Road was indicated on a map of Texas prepared by Stephen F. Austin and published by Henry Schenck Tanner of Philadelphia in 1837. In April 1961, Howard N. Martin described his use of surveyors' fieldnotes to trace the road through Nacogdoches, Angelina, Tyler, Polk, Liberty, and Chambers counties. The total length was about 132 miles. In 1771 El Orcoquisac was abandoned, and subsequent attempts to reestablish the mission and presidio were unsuccessful. In 1805 the military post of Atascosito was established, and the Spanish resumed extensive use of the Liberty–Nacogdoches Road, which connected this post and Nacogdoches. The road was also heavily used by members of the Alabama and Coushatta Indian tribes, who began entering Texas in the 1780s. The Alabamas and Coushattas settled along the Neches and Trinity rivers, respectively, and they adopted the Liberty–Nacogdoches Road for trips to Nacogdoches to trade and to receive gifts from the Spanish. White settlers entering East Texas traveled the road. Samuel T. Belt established a ferry at the Fort Teran crossing in the 1830s, and stagecoaches began operating on parts of the road to deliver mail and passengers to Liberty, Nacogdoches, and San Augustine. A succession of ferry operators at the Fort Teran crossing provided ferry service continuously until 1917, when a state highway connecting Woodville and Lufkin was built through this area, crossing the Neches River near Rockland.

Howard N. Martin

Lieutenant Governor. The state office of lieutenant governor was first established by the Constitution of 1845 and superseded the office of vice president of the Republic of Texas. The lieutenant governor was elected and served for two years. In 1972 Texas voters approved an amendment to the Constitution of 1876 to increase the term of office to four years, effective with the election of 1974. The salary, as set by the constitution, is the same as that of a state senator when the lieutenant governor serves as the presiding officer of the Senate, and the same as the governor's when he assumes the governor's duties. He is also provided an apartment in the Capitol. A lieutenant governor must be at least 30 years old, a United States citizen, and a Texas resident for five years prior to the election. Administrative duties of the lieutenant governor are to exercise the powers of the governor's office in case of the governor's death, resignation, removal from office, or absence from the state. Legislative duties are to serve as presiding officer of the Senate, appoint the committees of the Senate, and cast the deciding vote in case of a tie. The lieutenant governor serves as chairman of the Legislative Budget Board and the Legislative Council, as vice chairman of the Legislative Audit Committee and the Legislative Education Board, and as a member of the Legislative Redistricting Board. Since World War II the lieutenant governor has exerted growing influence in lawmaking and in administration and public policy. Before 1894 it was not customary for lieutenant governors to succeed themselves even for a second term. Until that year only John A. Greer, Richard Hubbard, and Thomas B. Wheeler were elected to second terms of office. Beginning with the election of George T. Jester in 1894, however, it became common for the lieutenant governor to seek two terms. The only lieutenant governors not reelected for a second term after Jester were W. A. Johnson, T. W. Davidson, Will H. Mays, and Lynch Davidson. Johnson lost his bid for reelection; the others did not run. The first lieutenant governor to serve three terms was Asbury B. Davidson. In the 1920s Barry Miller followed suit. Subsequently, Ben Ramsey and Preston Smith were elected more than twice. Though Ramsey holds the record of six terms, William P. Hobby, Jr., actually served longer (from 1973 to 1991).

The office of lieutenant governor has been vacant several times. In seven cases the lieutenant governor has succeeded to the governor's office. One lieutenant governor, George W. Jones, was removed from office by Reconstruction forces, and one, James W. Flanagan, was elected to the United States Senate without ever occupying the lieutenant governor's office. The vacancies seem never to have raised problems. The Texas Constitution provides that the president pro tempore of the Senate perform the two constitutional duties of the office without actually succeeding to the office. He presides over the Senate when it is in session and is available to succeed to the governorship if that position should become vacant. At no time in Texas history has succession officially gone beyond the lieutenant governor. On a number of occasions when the lieutenant governor has acted temporarily as governor while the latter was out of the state, the lieutenant governor has also left the state to permit the president pro tem to act as "governor for a day."

Almost all the lieutenant governors have been Democrats. Only during the turbulent years surrounding secession, the Civil War, and Reconstruction have nominees of other parties won. During the first decade of Texas statehood, nominations were generally made by personal announcement or by caucus. Most of the candidates were Democrats, and a person was never elected with a clear majority. The rising competition of the

LIEUTENANT GOVERNORS OF THE STATE OF TEXAS

[Note that election years rather than inauguration years are used in the table; thus, before the Constitution of 1876 the years are odd-numbered, whereas from 1876 to the present they are even-numbered.]

NAME	TERMS SERVED	COMMENTS
Albert Clinton Horton	1846–47	Acted as governor several months while Governor James Pinckney Henderson was at war in Mexico.
John Alexander Greer	1847–49, 1849–51	First to serve two terms.
James Wilson Henderson	1851–53	Succeeded to governorship November 1853, when Governor Peter Hansborough Bell resigned to serve in U.S. Congress.
David Catchings Dickson	1853–55	
Hardin Richard Runnels	1855–57	First to be elected governor (1857).
Francis Richard Lubbock	1857–59	Second to be elected governor (1861).
Edward Clark	1859–61	Succeeded to governorship March 1861, when Sam Houston vacated the office.
John McClannahan Crockett	1861–63	Acted as governor a few weeks when Governor Francis Richard Lubbock entered Confederate Army.
Fletcher S. Stockdale	1863–65	Technically succeeded to governorship when Governor Pendleton Murrah fled after the Civil War. Removed by U.S. authorities.
George Washington Jones	1866–67	Removed from office by U.S. authorities in 1867.
James Winwright Flanagan	1869	Elected but never inaugurated. Selected to serve as U.S. Senator.
Richard Bennett Hubbard	1873–76, 1876	Second to be elected for two terms, but succeeded to governorship in December 1876, when Governor Richard Coke resigned to enter the U.S. Senate.
Joseph Draper Sayers	1878–80	Later elected governor, 1898–02; third lieutenant governor to be elected governor.
Leonidas Jefferson Storey	1880–82	
Francis Marion Martin	1882–84	Ran unsuccessfully for governor and lieutenant governor at later dates.
Barnett Gibbs	1884–86	
Thomas Benton Wheeler	1886–88, 1888–90	Third to be elected for two terms.
George Cassety Pendleton	1890–92	
Martin McNulty Crane	1892–94	
George Taylor Jester	1894–96, 1896–98	
James Nathan Browning	1898–1900, 1900–02	
George D. Neal	1902–04, 1904–06	
Asbury Bascom Davidson	1906–08, 1908–10, 1910–12	First elected for three terms.
William Harding Mayes	1912–14	
William Pettus Hobby	1914–16, 1916–17	Succeeded to governorship after impeachment of Governor James Edward Ferguson (September 1917).
W. A. Johnson	1918–20	First to be defeated for immediate reelection.
Lynch Davidson	1920–22	
Thomas Whitfield Davidson	1922–24	
Barry Miller	1924–26, 1926–28, 1928–30	Second to be elected for three terms.
Edgar E. Witt	1930–32, 1932–34	
Walter F. Woodal	1934–36, 1936–38	
Coke Robert Stevenson	1938–40, 1940–41	Succeeded to governorship when Governor Wilbert Lee O'Daniel resigned to enter U.S. Senate (August 1941).
John Lee Smith	1942–44, 1944–46	
Robert Allan Shivers	1946–48, 1948–49	Succeeded to governorship on death of Governor Beauford Halbert Jester (July 1949).
Ben Ramsey	1950–52, 1952–54, 1954–56, 1956–58, 1958–60, 1960–61	First to serve more than three terms. Resigned when appointed to Railroad Commission (September 1961).
Preston Smith	1962–64, 1964–66, 1966–68	Elected governor in 1968.
Ben Barnes	1968–70, 1970–72	Defeated in race for governor in 1972.
William P. Hobby, Jr.	1972–74, 1974–78, 1978–82, 1982–86, 1986–90	By constitutional amendment approved by Texas voters in 1972, the term of office for lieutenant governor was increased to four years, effective in 1975. Hobby, reelected in 1974, was the first lieutenant governor to assume the four-year term, which began January 21, 1975.
Robert D. Bullock	1990–94, 1994–98	
Rick Perry	1998–	(assumed office January 1999)

American (Know-Nothing) party forced the Democrats to nominate by convention beginning in 1855. In 1859 Sam Houston and Edward Clark, running as independents with Know-Nothing backing, defeated the Democratic incumbents, Hardin Runnels and Francis Lubbock. The Democrats recaptured the offices in 1861 but were ousted from office by the military rule after the Civil War. A Republican governor was then elected, but the lieutenant governor's position remained vacant. The Democrats again captured both offices in 1873 and retained them until William P. Clements was elected governor as a Republican in 1978. Before the late twentieth century, the only other serious challenge to Democratic supremacy came with the rise of the People's party in the 1890s. The first Republican in the history of Texas actually to become lieutenant governor was Rick Perry.

The advent of the direct primary in 1906 and the double primary in 1918 brought about a change in the nomination procedure. The real contest for state office now occurred in the primary; the general election was usually a mere formality in the lieutenant governor's race. As a general rule a candidate who ran to succeed himself had little opposition, but when the office was open the candidates multiplied. Usually the one who led in the first primary would win the nomination and election, but there are several notable exceptions to this rule. The first of these was T. W. Davidson, who came from behind in 1922 to win by a substantial margin in the second primary and the general election. Others who overcame a first primary deficit were Edgar E. Witt in 1930, Coke Stevenson in 1938, Ramsey in 1950, and Preston Smith in 1962. In their bids for reelection all (except Davidson, who chose not to run) won rather easy victories.

The lieutenant governors of Texas have generally been men who were active in state politics before election to that office. Ordinarily they have served in the legislature, particularly in the Senate. They have sometimes sought the office as a climax to a political career, although frequently they have hoped to use the lieutenant governorship as a steppingstone to higher office. The latter aspiration has generally not been fulfilled, however. In the early days of statehood several lieutenant governors entered the governor's race, but few were elected. Of the first eight lieutenant governors seven ran for governor, and two were elected under rather unusual circumstances. In 1857 Runnels defeated Houston, who was running for governor as an independent, while Lubbock was elected lieutenant governor. Two years later Houston defeated Runnels in his bid for reelection, while Clark defeated Lubbock for the lieutenant governor's post. At the next election (1861), both Lubbock and Clark ran for governor, and Lubbock was elected by a margin of 124 votes. Later, former lieutenant governors G. W. Jones, F. Marion Martin, and Barnett Gibbs ran unsuccessfully for governor. Not until 1898 was another former lieutenant governor elected governor. Sayers has the distinction of having served one term as lieutenant governor (1878) and then 20 years later being elected governor. Nor has long tenure in the lieutenant governor's office aided in a later campaign for governor. Three of the four lieutenant governors who have been elected governor without first having succeeded to the office by a vacancy served only one term as lieutenant governor; the exception was Preston Smith, who served three terms as lieutenant governor. On the other hand, several who were elected to two or more terms as lieutenant governor failed miserably in a subsequent race for governor. Seven lieutenant governors have inherited the governor's office without being elected

to it. Three governors resigned to serve in the United States Congress (Bell, Coke, and O'Daniel), one governor resigned at the time of secession (Houston), one governor vacated his office and fled from the country (Murrah), one governor was impeached and removed from office (James Ferguson), and one governor died in office (Beauford Jester). Of the seven lieutenant governors who succeeded to the governor's office, three later ran for the office and were elected to additional terms (Hobby, Coke Stevenson, and Allan Shivers), two ran and were defeated (James P. Henderson and Edward Clark), and two did not run again (Hubbard and Stockdale, who only served technically as governor before being removed by United States authorities).

J. William Davis

Light Crust Doughboys. A famous western swing band. In 1929 Bob Wills moved from West Texas to Fort Worth and formed the Wills Fiddle Band, made up of Wills as fiddler and Herman Arnspiger as guitarist. In 1930 Milton Brown joined the band as vocalist, and in 1931 the Wills Fiddle Band—Wills, Arnspiger, and Brown—became the Light Crust Doughboys. With help from friends and fans in Fort Worth, Wills persuaded Burrus Mill and Elevator Company to sponsor the band on a radio show. The band advertised Burrus's Light Crust Flour. After two weeks, W. Lee O'Daniel, president of Burrus Mill, canceled the show because he did not like "their hillbilly music." A compromise, inspired by Wills's persistence and the demands of thousands of fans who used Light Crust Flour, brought the group back to the air in return for its members' agreement to work in the mill as well as perform. So impressed was O'Daniel with the band's growing following that he became the announcer for the show and organized a network of radio stations that broadcast the Doughboys throughout Texas and most of Oklahoma. The Southwest Quality Network included such radio stations as WBAP and KTAT, Fort Worth; WOAI, San Antonio; KPRC, Houston; and KOMA, Oklahoma City. The show became one of the most popular radio programs in the Southwest. In 1932 the original Doughboys began leaving the band. Brown left the show that year to form the Musical Brownies, and in 1933 O'Daniel fired Wills for missing broadcasts, especially because of drinking. The Doughboys never departed from the fiddle-band style that Wills established. In October 1933 O'Daniel took a new and talented group of Doughboys to Chicago for a recording session with Vocalion Records. O'Daniel continued as manager and announcer until the mid-thirties. In 1935, when Burrus Mill fired him after a series of disputes, O'Daniel formed his own band, the Hillbilly Boys, and his own flour company, Hillbilly Flour. O'Daniel used this band in his successful bid for the governorship in 1938. The years between 1935 and World War II were the most successful in the long history of the Doughboys. By 1937 some of the best musicians in the history of western swing had joined the band. Kenneth Pitts and Clifford Gross played fiddles. The rhythm section consisted of Dick Reinhart, guitar; Marvin (Smoky) Montgomery, tenor banjo; Ramon DeArman, bass; and John (Knocky) Parker, piano. Muryel Campbell played lead guitar. At various times Cecil Brower played fiddle. Doughboys records outsold those of all other fiddle bands in the Fort Worth–Dallas area. By the 1940s the Doughboys broadcast over 170 radio stations in the South and Southwest. Their shows took the listeners' minds off the economic problems of the thirties and added joy to their lives. In the early months of World War II members of the band went into either the armed forces or war-related industries, and in 1942 Burrus Mill ended the Doughboys' radio show. The mill reorganized the band in 1946, but the broadcasts were never as appealing as they had been in the prewar years. The company tried various experiments and even hired Hank Thompson and Slim Whitman in the hope that somehow the radio show could be saved. By 1950 the age of television had begun, however, and the dominance of radio was over. With its passing went the Doughboys. In the early 1990s Burrus Mill still owned the Doughboy name and employed Doughboy great Marvin Montgomery and others to play special events and to make promotional recordings.

Charles R. Townsend

Lily-White Movement. A white faction in the Republican party after the Civil War. As white GOP leaders sought "respectability" among Southern voters and a conviction grew that continued "black and tan" involvement thwarted expansion of the party, the lily-white Republicans began an organized effort to drive blacks from positions of party leadership. Though Texas blacks appealed to Northern party managers to halt the movement, lily-whiteism flourished because Republican presidents after 1865 wanted approval from the Southern white majority. The term *lily-white* apparently originated with black leader Norris Wright Cuney at the 1888 Republican state convention in Fort Worth, when a group of whites attempted to expel a number of black and tan delegates. The term was soon applied to similar groups throughout the South. Though Cuney was reappointed to the national committee at the 1892 Republican national convention, the black–white struggle in Texas resulted in a fractured party and the first GOP state convention without a black and tan delegation in attendance. The 1892 election proved a turning point for both GOP factions as Cuney aligned the black and tans behind George Clark, a conservative Democrat, in his fight with James S. Hogg, and the lily-whites nominated Andrew Jackson Houston for the governorship. Houston, son of Sam Houston, received only 1,322 votes in the November election, while Cuney suffered a dual setback: not only did Clark go down in defeat, but the Democrat Grover Cleveland won the presidency, so that Cuney lost all federal patronage. Southern GOP leaders, black and white, relied upon the dispensation of federal jobs to maintain their state organizations; and when Cuney lost out under Cleveland, the door was opened for a lily-white takeover. Though Cuney was replaced as national committeeman as well as state chairman during the 1896 campaign, other black and tan leaders emerged to lead the state party. Edward H. R. Green (son of multimillionaire Hetty H. R. Green), who arrived in Texas to oversee his mother's railroad empire, captured the party after Cuney's downfall by forming a political alliance with William M. (Gooseneck Bill) McDonald, a black banker from Fort Worth.

The Green–McDonald partnership, however, was unable to stem the lily-white insurgents, and after Green's withdrawal as state chairman in 1902, Cecil A. Lyon, a white businessman from Sherman, took control. Lyon generally spearheaded the party and the movement in Texas until his death in 1915. By 1904 Lyon was Theodore Roosevelt's agent in the state as well as national committeeman and state chairman. Though black and tan delegations appeared at the 1904 and 1908 national conventions, they were pushed aside by Lyon's forces. To avoid criticism, one or two blacks were usually seated with lily-white delegations at the national gatherings. The lily-whites gained new momentum with the adoption of the poll tax and the passage of the Terrell Election Law. The lily-white Republicans appealed to racism to establish their party as a viable alternative for southern Democrats. As a result, blacks increasingly lost influence and power in the Republican party. The Southern Democratic leadership also greatly discouraged black membership, so many blacks felt that they had no political party in which to participate. When the Republican factions split during 1906 and both made gubernatorial nominations to oppose Democrat Tom Campbell, the lily-white candidate, A. C. Gray, outpolled his black and tan challenger, Alexander W. Acheson, by a fourtoone margin. Lyon supported Roosevelt in 1912 during his famous fight with William Howard Taft, and he later organized the Progressive or Bull Moose party in Texas, which resulted in the loss of his party posts to Henry Frederick MacGregor, a Houston businessman. Roosevelt's Bull Moose campaign finished shattering Republican harmony in the state. The lily-whites generally supported the new movement's calls for a white opposition party to the Democrats, and the black and tans allied themselves with Taft. After amalgamation of the GOP for the 1916 presidential campaign, Rentfro B. Creager, a Brownsville lawyer and 1916 gubernatorial candidate, soon became party leader. Though McDonald attempted a comeback in 1920 and proclaimed that color should predominate because "95 percent of all Texas Republicans were Negroes," the lily-whites under Creager retained firm control after the upheavals of 1912–16. They reigned supreme under Republican presidents Harding, Coolidge, and Hoover, despite the threats of blacks throughout the 1920s to bolt the Republican fold for the Democratic party, and despite efforts by Republican congressman Harry Wurzbach to court the black and tans in his fight for ascendancy with Creager. When black and tan factions appeared at the 1920, 1924, and 1928 Republican national conventions, they were shunted aside by Creager and his followers. Lily-white domination of the state GOP ceased to matter for Texas African Americans during the 1930s, when Texas blacks flocked to support of Democrat Franklin D. Roosevelt's New Deal.

Paul D. Casdorph

Limekilns. Lime was used on the frontier for making concrete, mortar, and plaster, for softening water, and for reducing the acidity of butter, cream, milk, and "sour" soil. Cooks used it to make hominy, tacos, and tortillas. Other uses included tanning leather, blowing fish out of water, destroying diseased animal bodies, killing termites and weevils, drying cuts on livestock, whitewashing, sanitizing outhouses, and making sheep-dip. Kilns were important under Spanish and Mexican rule, as well as later. The ruins of at least ten Spanish *caleras* can be seen today near the stone missions and the one stone–lime mortar presidio. Beginning in the 1840s German colonists built the best kilns and made the best lime. Most of their *Kalköfen* were in Bexar, Comal, Gillespie, Kendall, Kerr, Mason, McCulloch, and Taylor counties. Any group of two or three houses was usually accompanied by a limekiln in these German areas. Most kilns for calcining quicklime from limestone in pioneer Texas were built west of the Balcones Escarpment. They were generally dug near the edges of dirt banks and straight down or with inside walls shaped slightly into bowls or jugs. Several had stone curbs. Some families burned rocks on top of the ground under piles of dirt or mixed with logs; others devised sundry other types of kiln. But most American kilns were the creek-bank type. Most common was the family-type kiln, dug about 10 feet deep, 6 feet across, and 2 feet back from the face of a bank with an opening in the lower, outer side. Community and commercial kilns were larger and sometimes entirely under or above ground. Among a score of well-known German kilns still partly standing are the Andreas Lindig kiln, built in 1874 and located in the present Lyndon B. Johnson State Historical Park, several kilns of Conrad Kappmeier in Comal County, and the George H. Kalteyer kilns in San Antonio. The last burned the lime for building the Capitol in Austin from rocks quarried from the site of the Sunken Garden in San Antonio. Among the largest Texas commercial kilns whose ruins remain are the McNett kiln in Lampasas County, the Logan Gap kilns in Comanche County, the Doc Carter kiln in Concho County, and the J. D. Cahill aboveground kiln in San Marcos. One of the largest community kilns was at Lime Spring in Mason County. It was unusual in that it was on level ground and was shaped like a spittoon, being 18 feet across at the bottom, 14 feet across at a man's height, and 16 feet across at ground level. It had no door at the bottom for ventilation or for raking out the ashes and quicklime. The lime from a community kiln, in contrast to the commercial ones, was not sold.

Cooking lime involved an enormous amount of work: digging or building the kiln, gathering rocks, cutting, hauling, and pitching a great amount of firewood down the kiln, maintaining vigilance at the kiln around the clock for about two weeks, and slaking the quicklime. To cook high-quality lime thus required a skilled cook, rocks, fuel, and controlled cooking. The cook wanted the hardest and oldest limestone available. Bluish or grayish, streaked, fist-sized chunks of surface limestone were preferred, particularly weather-exposed pieces obtained from hilltops. For fuel, the cook preferred live oak, post oak, mesquite, or brush, in that order. The heat had to be maintained at 1,800° F or higher. By tapping with a hammer or breaking open a hot stone, the cook could tell when the lime was done. After the kiln had cooled for a week, the quicklime stones and ashes were raked out through the side hole. The stones were slaked, that is, put in water so that they would crumble, and then were used, sold at the kiln, or hauled off to a limehouse and sold for fifty cents to a dollar for a hundred pounds. Early West Texas kilns supplied lime in the 1850s through 1870s for Fort Phantom Hill, Fort McKavett, Fort Lancaster, Fort Griffin, and Fort Concho, where their ruins can be seen. Making lime in pioneer kilns came to an end when railways brought in Portland cement and advanced fuels. A commercial economy developed, and the old-timers who had made the lime began to disappear. Erosion and bulldozing have contributed to destroying the remains of over 130 kilns in 38 counties.   *Ralph A. Smith*

Linnville, Texas. On Lavaca Bay 20 miles from Victoria; the site was in Victoria County and is now in Calhoun County. Linnville was one of the most important ports of entry during the early period of the Republic of Texas. The town, originally called New Port, was established by John J. Linn in 1831. It was in De León's colony on a quarter-league grant belonging to Pedro Gonzales. Like the other ports around Lavaca Bay, Linnville grew up around a core of warehouses holding goods unloaded from ships and destined for inland markets such as Victoria, Gonzales, and San Antonio; eventually the town also became the site of the customhouse for the District of Lavaca. Its population was esti-

mated at 200 about 1839. Linnville was the ordnance arsenal and depot for the Federalist armies of Mexico during their attempt to defeat Centralist forces under Santa Anna; nearby Victoria was the headquarters of the short-lived provisional government of the Republic of the Rio Grande (1840). It was this association, together with the rich stores of merchandise, that prompted the Comanches, incited both by a desire for revenge after the Council House Fight and by Mexican Centralists working to defeat Canales, to attack Linnville and Victoria in 1840. Only one building remained after the Linnville Raid of 1840. Most residents moved to a site called Labbacca (La Vaca), 3½ miles southwest of Linnville near the mouth of Linn Bayou. Labbacca, or Port Lavaca as it is called today, continued to grow in importance as a port, and its prosperity contributed to the final decline and abandonment of Linnville. The deserted site became part of Calhoun County when it was established in 1846. A granite marker was placed there during the Texas Centennial in 1936, and a historical marker in 1964.   *Craig H. Roell*

Linnville Raid of 1840. A notorious Indian attack; the sacking of Victoria and Linnville in what was then Victoria County. The attack originated as an aftermath of the Council House Fight. By August 1840 the Penateka Comanches were able to accept the leadership of their remaining chief, Buffalo Hump, the others having been killed in the Council House Fight. In what became the largest of all southern Comanche raids, Buffalo Hump launched a retaliatory attack down the Guadalupe valley east and south of Gonzales. The band numbered perhaps as many as 1,000, including the families of the warriors, who followed to plunder and make camp. The number of warriors was probably between 400 and 500, though witnesses put the figure higher. The total included a good number of Kiowas and Mexican guides. The raiders appeared at Victoria without warning on the afternoon of 6 August, and upon crossing Spring Creek were mistaken at first for Lipans, members of a friendly group that often traded with settlers around the town. John J. Linn wrote of the attack on Victoria and the burning of Linnville in his *Reminiscences of Fifty Years in Texas* (1883). The Comanches killed a number of slaves working in fields and also some whites who were unable to reach Victoria. They took more than 1,500 horses, some of which belonged to Mexican horse dealers. The Indians surrounded the town, but the settlers' defensive efforts apparently prevented their sacking the town itself. The attackers retired to Spring Creek at day's end and killed a white settler and two black slaves before a group of Victoria men left for the Cuero Creek, Lavaca, and Gonzales settlements for help. The next day the Comanches killed a party of men returning to town, except for Jesse O. Wheeler and a companion, who escaped. With their spoils the Indians then left Victoria and thundered toward the coast. They camped the night of 7 August on the ranch of Plácido Benavides, 12 miles from Linnville. There two wagoners were intercepted, of whom one escaped and the other was killed. Three miles from the small port of Linnville the raiders killed two black men cutting hay. Tradition holds that Daniel Brown warned the citizens of the danger and that Mary Margaret Kerr Mitchell rode horseback across Prairie Chicken Reef with word of the attack on Victoria. Nevertheless, early on 8 August the Comanches surprised the town; most residents took them for Mexican horse traders.

The Indians surrounded Linnville and began pillaging the

stores and houses. They killed three whites, including customs officer Hugh Oran Watts, who delayed escape to retrieve a gold watch; they captured Watts's wife of only 21 days, Juliet Constance, and a black woman and child. The surprised people of Linnville fled to the water and were saved by remaining aboard small boats and a schooner captained by William G. Marshall at anchor in the bay. From their Gulf vantage point the refugees witnessed the destruction of their town. For the entire day the Comanches plundered and burned buildings. They tied feather beds and bolts of cloth to their horses and dragged them about in sport. They herded large numbers of cattle into pens and slaughtered them. One exasperated onlooker, Judge John Hays, grabbed a gun and waded ashore through the shallow water, but the Indians ignored him. When he returned to the schooner his gun was found to have been unloaded. Goods valued at $300,000 were at Linnville at the time of the raid; many items were en route from New Orleans to San Antonio. Linn noted that in his warehouse were several cases of hats and umbrellas belonging to James Robinson, a San Antonio merchant. "These the Indians made free with, and went dashing about the blazing village, amid their screeching squaws and 'little Injuns,' like demons in a drunken saturnalia, with Robinson's hats on their heads and Robinson's umbrellas bobbing about on every side like tipsy young balloons." After loading the plunder onto pack mules the raiders retired in the afternoon with horses now numbering 3,000 and several captives, including Mrs. Watts, and encamped across the bayou near the old road.

Meanwhile, the men of Victoria had recruited reinforcements from the Cuero Creek settlement. On the morning of 7 August the combined forces joined volunteers from the Gonzales and Lavaca settlements under Adam Zumwalt and Ben McCulloch and skirmished with the Comanches kin two encounters. The Indians stole away with their captives and plunder but were defeated by volunteers at Plum Creek, near the site of present Lockhart, on 12 August. When the Indians killed the captives during this final battle, Juliet Watts's corset prevented her arrow wound from killing her. She returned to the Linnville area, married Dr. J. M. Stanton, and opened the Stanton House, the first hotel in Port Lavaca, the new settlement established on the bay 3½ miles southwest by displaced Linnville residents.

Twenty-three settlers are known to have been killed in the Victoria–Linnville raid, including eight blacks and one Mexican. There is evidence that this raid also was part of a scheme among Mexican Centralists to punish the citizens of Victoria and Linnville for providing Mexican Federalists a port and site for the short-lived provisional government of the Republic of the Rio Grande. The captured horses and plunder were evidently received by Centralist generals Valentín Canalizo and Adrián Woll and used in an invasion of Texas. Although this was the last great Comanche raid into the coastal settlements, Linnville never regained prominence and soon vanished in the wake of Port Lavaca's growth. The Victoria battle is commemorated by a historical marker on De León Plaza in downtown Victoria.

Craig H. Roell

Mance Lipscomb playing his guitar on a porch. Photograph by Bill Records. Lipscomb–Myers Collection, CAH; CN 01861. Lipscomb called himself a "songster." Born Bowdie Glenn, he named himself Mance after a friend named Emancipation.

Lipscomb, Mance. Folk musician; b. Bowdie Glenn Lipscomb, near Navasota, 9 April 1895; d. Navasota, 30 January 1976; m. Elnora ——; 1 son and 3 adopted children. Lipscomb was a tenant farmer for most of his life. He dropped his given name and took the name Mance when a friend, an old man called Emancipation, passed away. Lipscomb represented one of the last remnants of the nineteenth-century songster tradition, which predated the development of the blues. Though songsters might incorporate blues into their repertoires, as did Lipscomb, they performed a wide variety of material in diverse styles, much of it common to both black and white traditions in the South, including ballads, rags, dance pieces, and popular, sacred, and secular songs. Lipscomb himself insisted that he was a songster, not a guitarist or "blues singer," since he played "all kinds of music." (He likewise took exception when he was labeled a "sharecropper" instead of a "farmer.") His eclectic repertoire included perhaps 350 pieces spanning two centuries. Lipscomb's father was a fiddler, his uncle played the banjo, and his brothers were guitarists. His mother bought him a guitar when he was 11, and he was soon accompanying his father, and later entertaining alone, at suppers and Saturday night dances. Although he had some contact with such early recording artists as fellow Texans Blind Lemon Jefferson and Blind Willie Johnson and early country star Jimmie Rodgers, he made no recordings until his "discovery" by whites during the folk-song revival of the 1960s. Lipscomb's rendition of "Tom Moore's Farm" was taped at his first session in 1960 but released anonymously (Arhoolie Records, *Texas Blues, Volume 2*), presumably to protect the singer, who had attacked the notorious landlord Moore. Between 1956 and 1958 Lipscomb lived in Houston, working for a lumber company during the day and playing at night in bars where he vied for audiences with Texas blues great Sam "Lightnin'" Hopkins. With compensation from an on-the-job accident, he returned to Navasota and was finally able to buy some land and build a house of his own. He was working as foreman of a highway-mowing crew in Grimes County when blues researchers found and recorded him in 1960. During more than a decade of involvement in the folk-song revival, Lipscomb won wide acclaim and emulation from young white audiences and performers for his virtuosity as a guitarist and the breadth of his repertoire. Admirers enjoyed his reminiscences and observations regarding music and life, many of which are contained in taped and written materials in the Mance Lipscomb–Glenn Myers Collection at the Barker Texas History Center in Austin. Lipscomb appeared at such festivals as the Berkeley Folk Festival of 1961, where he played before a crowd of more than 40,000. In clubs he often shared the bill with young revivalists or rock bands. He was also the subject of a film, *A Well-Spent Life* (1970). Despite his popularity, however, he remained poor. After 1974 declining health confined him to a nursing home and hospitals. Arhoolie Records (El Cerrito, California) has released seven albums of material by Lipscomb. Another was released by Reprise.

John Minton

Literature. *From the beginnings through the nineteenth century.*

In the beginning, Texas literature, though written in Spanish, was formally very much like that of Puritan New England—primarily historical in nature, consisting of narrative, descriptive, and factual prose accounts. The first and most notable work in the early Spanish literature relating to Texas is Cabeza de Vaca's *Relación* (1542). This book, translated into English numerous times, is an American classic, a spiritual odyssey detailing the explorer's experiences among Texas Indians. Other significant early Spanish narratives include Pedro de Castañeda's *Relación de la jornada de Cíbola*, the best account of Vásquez de Coronado's expedition, and Fray Alonso de Benavides's *Memorials* (1630–34). Also of interest is *The Narrative of the Expedition of Hernando de Soto, by the Gentleman of Elvas*, parts of which touch upon areas of Texas as far west as the site of Waco.

Nonfiction accounts also characterized the literature of the revolutionary era. Mary Austin Holley, cousin of Stephen F. Austin and visitor to his colony, produced *Texas* (1833), the first book in English that dealt entirely with Texas. It initially consisted of 12 letters to people back East, and was much expanded in 1836 into *History of Texas*. After David Crockett's death at the Alamo, a book entitled *Col. Crockett's Exploits and Adventures in Texas* (1836) capitalized on the frontiersman's fame in the lively, colorful style of southwestern humor. The Mexican side of the Texas Revolution had its chroniclers as well. For events immediately preceding the Revolution, the best Mexican account is Juan N. Almonte's *Noticia Estadistica Sobre Tejas* (1835). The best contemporary account of the revolution is José Enrique de la Peña's *La Rebelión De Texas: Manuscrito Unédito de 1836, Por un Oficial de Santa Anna.* John H. Jenkins III calls it "one of the most important eye-witness records of the Texas Revolution, and especially of the Siege of the Alamo." It was Peña who first reported that Davy Crockett surrendered before being put to death.

In the years immediately following annexation (1846), several works merit attention in so far as they reflect the pluralistic vigor of early Texas history. Victor Prosper Considerant's *Au Texas* (1854) related the story of the founding and dissolution of the French Utopian community of La Réunion, near Dallas. Viktor F. Bracht's *Texas im Jahre 1848, nach mehrjährigen Beobachtungen dargestellt* (1849) told of German immigrants and agrarian life in early Texas. From the Anglo-American perspective there is Noah Smithwick's *The Evolution of a State; or, Recollections of Old Texas Days* (1900), declared by Jenkins to be "the most fun to read" of all Texas memoirs. John Crittenden Duval, whom J. Frank Dobie called the "Father of Texas Literature," wrote a lively account of his escape from the Goliad Massacre in *Early Times in Texas* (serial form, 1868–71; book, 1892). His *Adventures of Big-Foot Wallace* (1872) contains tall tales, legends, true adventure, satire, and straight history. The chapters on the Mier expedition are among the best published accounts of that episode, rivaled only by William Preston Stapp's *The Prisoners of Perote* (1845). Another failed expeditionary venture of the Texas republic was recorded by George W. Kendall of the New Orleans *Picayune* in his *Narrative of the Texan Santa Fe Expedition* (1844). Although most travelers in early Texas wrote favorably of the inhabitants, one memorable exception was famed urban landscape architect Frederick Law Olmsted, whose *A Journey Through Texas* (1857) painted a grim picture of slavery-ridden East Texas, indicting the people as crude, the food as bad, and the level of civilization as negligible. Not until he reached New Braunfels, recently colonized by Germans, did Olmsted find anything fit to eat or any civilization worthy of the name. Narratives of the Texas Rangers constitute a subgenre of Texas writing. Among those dealing with the immediate post-republic era, the best is James Buckner Barry's *A Texas Ranger and*

Frontiersman: The Days of Buck Barry in Texas, 1845–1906 (1932). In the post–Civil War period, James Buchanan Gillett's *Six Years with the Texas Rangers, 1875–1881* (1921) is a highly readable and useful personal memoir.

Of the many former Confederate soldiers who moved to Texas after the Civil War, one was young Sidney Lanier, a Southern poet of considerable reputation in his day. He recorded his impressions, including a charming essay on "San Antonio de Bexar," in *Retrospects and Prospects* (1899). Also in the wake of the war came federal troops. With Gen. George A. Custer was his young wife, Elizabeth, who felt at first that Texas seemed the "stepping off place" but eventually came to enjoy her stay and wrote a lively account in *Tenting on the Plains* (1887). The cowboy, a subject that dominated Texas literature thereafter, entered the scene in the 1880s. Alex E. Sweet and J. Armoy Knox treated cowboy lore in a humorous, satirical fashion in their *On a Mexican Mustang, Through Texas from the Gulf to the Rio Grande* (1883). Charlie Siringo, a native Texan who rode the range for nearly 20 years, turned author in 1886 with *A Texas Cowboy: or Fifteen Years on the Hurricane Deck of a Spanish Pony*, later revised as *Riata and Spurs* (1912). Siringo's books became required reading for those interested in the cattle industry.

Fiction about Texas, which began very early in the nineteenth century, is of interest today only to the occasional scholar willing to slog through an undistinguished morass of romantic historical novels. The first Texas novel, *L'Héroïne du Texas: ou, Voyage de madame aux États-Unis et au Mexique*, "by a Texian," was published in Paris in French in 1819, but was not available in English until Donald Josep's translation of 1937. Its author is identified only as "F–n. M. G–n." The novel deals romantically, after the manner of Chateaubriand, with the short-lived French colony named Champ d'Asile. Its ideological thrust is characteristic of the strong anti-Catholic bias of early Texas fiction: a Protestant hero marries a Spanish Catholic girl, after which both must flee from ecclesiastical authorities. Timothy Flint's *Francis Berrian; or the Mexican Patriot* (1826), although set only partially in Texas, introduced two motifs that often reappeared in nineteenth-century Texas fiction: the captivity narrative in which white women are captured by and rescued from Indians, and the religious–cultural conflict between Protestant Anglos and Catholic Mexicans, with the hero usually representing the former. *Mexico versus Texas*, the first novel to incorporate seminal historical events such as the Goliad Massacre and the battle of San Jacinto, was published anonymously in 1838; it was reissued in 1842 under the title *Ambrosio de Letinez* and credited to A. T. Myrthe, although its title page lists Anthony Ganilh. The novel's argument is characteristic of the period: the dedication poses the rhetorical question "whether anything could have taken place more conducive to the regeneration and improvement of Mexico than the success of the Texans."

The Travels and Adventures of Monsieur Violet (1843) by Frederick Marryat, a retired British naval officer and prolific author, consists of pure adventure ranging over much of the American West, including the Texas of revolutionary times. Carl Anton Postl, an Austrian former monk who wrote prolifically under the pseudonym Charles Sealsfield, used early Texas as the setting for *The Cabin Book* (1844), in which the hero becomes a general in the Texas army. Frenchman Olivier Gioux, whose pen name was Gustave Aimard, devoted one of his more than 20 novels of the American West to Texas—*The Freebooters, a Story of the Texas War* (ca. 1860). Charles Wilkins Webber, in *Old Hicks the Guide* (1845), added the search for a lost Spanish mine to Texas adventure fiction. And Alfred W. Arrington, writing as Charles Summerfield in *The Rangers and Regulators of Tanaha . . . A Tale of the Texas Republic* (1856), contributed the bandit motif in his novel, which is set among plantation slaveholders in East Texas in 1845–46. Emerson Bennett's *Viola* (1852) also takes place during the republic era. Jeremiah Clemens in *Mustang Gray* (1858) fictionalized the life of Mabry B. Gray, a soldier–bandit of early Texas.

Not surprisingly, the legend of the Alamo proved a popular subject for early novelists. Augusta Evans Wilson's *Inez: A Tale of the Alamo* (1855) pits an Anglo heroine against the unscrupulous wiles of Catholic priests. Amelia E. Barr's *Remember the Alamo* (1888) sums up the anti-Catholic feeling of much fiction from the republic and post-republic era: "the priesthood foresaw that the triumph of the American element meant the triumph of freedom of conscience, and the abolition of their own despotism." Barr's autobiography, *All the Days of My Life: An Autobiography, the Red Leaves of a Human Heart* (1913), which includes a lengthy section on life in late-nineteenth-century Austin, retains more interest today than does her florid fiction. Hostility against Mexicans is also a strong ingredient of novels about the republic. *The Trapper's Bride: or, Love and War: A Tale of the Texas Revolution* (1869), by W. J. Hamilton (pseudonym for Charles Dunning Clark), is peppered with virulent racist epithets, as is Jeremiah Clemens's *Bernard Lile: An Historical Romance, Embracing the Periods of the Texas Revolution and the Mexican War* (1856). Scores of dime novels exploited the subjects of bandits, rangers, and cowboys, but these belong to the vast underthicket of popular culture. The first novel to make use of the trail drive was *Live Boys: or Charley and Nacho in Texas*, written by Thomas Pilgrim in 1878 under the pen name Arthur Morecamp. J. Frank Dobie praised its authenticity.

Anglo Texas had its roots in Southern, not Western, culture. The first settlers were slaveholding planters or would-be slaveowners. The early Texas novel most firmly rooted in Old Southern culture was Mollie E. Moore Davis's *Under the Man-Fig* (1895), which details events in Brazoria County from 1857 to 1880. Even more interesting is her *The Wire-Cutters* (1899), which moves from a Southern plantation context (in Kentucky) to a West Texas ranch and the conflict between open-range cattlemen and small farmers; its theme was reprised in hundreds of Western novels to come.

Early Texas poetry was abundant but undistinguished. That from the republic era usually reflected two themes representative of the attitudes of Southerners in general: a martial spirit coupled with religious sentiment. Poems dealing with contemporaneous history were commonplace. "To Santa Anna," a typical piece, addresses its subject as "thou blood-hound of death." Poems honoring such Texas heroes as Ben Milam, James W. Fannin, and Sam Houston were plentiful. Later in the era, poets turned to more pacific subjects, writing of labor in poems celebrating the "plough" and cattle drives, or of Texas landscapes and natural phenomena, or of cities, or even, as early as 1849, the blue norther. An excellent brief anthology of such poetry is *Early Texas Verse (1835–1850)*, edited by Philip Graham in 1936. Much of the verse in this collection is anonymous. Among the poets whose authors are named, a few deserve mention. Mirabeau B. Lamar, soldier and statesman, is remembered chiefly for two lyrics, "Carmelita" and "The Daughter of Mendoza." His only volume is *Verse Memorials* (1857). The poetic reputations of two of his associates in affairs of state rest on one poem each: "Hymn to the Alamo" by Reuben M. Potter and "All Quiet Along the Potomac" by Lamar Fontaine, son of Mirabeau Lamar's secretary, Edward Fontaine; others have claimed the latter poem. Much better known in the nineteenth century was Mollie E. M. Davis, who, in addition to her fiction, gained renown with Civil War poems published in newspapers. "Lee at the Wilderness" and "Minding the Gap" were widely circulated throughout the South. Davis, known as the "Texas Mocking Bird," published several volumes of verse, including *Minding the Gap, and Other Poems* (1867) and *Poems* (1872).

After the Civil War, with the development of the cattle industry, ballads of the range became popular. Usually sung or recited, these ballads were orally transmitted, and the names of their author–composers were often lost. The same process occurred in Spanish verse along the Mexican border in South Texas, where *corridos* were composed, sung, and passed down from one generation to the next. Collecting cowboy ballads and *corridos* became a major occupation of scholars and folklorists in the twentieth century. Even the skillful and popular recitative piece "Lasca" (1882), at one time the best known of all Texas poems, was passed around and handed down orally. By the time it got into print, lines had been lost and the author identified only as Frank Desprez. Not until the 1950s was anything known about this Englishman, who was for three years "occupied on a Texas ranch" before he returned to England and became a professional writer. Another famous cowboy recitation was "The Cowboys' Christmas Ball" by William Lawrence Chittenden, an Eastern newspaper reporter who became known as the "Poet–Ranchman of Texas." His poem immortalized the Anson ball of 1885, which is still reenacted each Christmas under the title Cowboys' Christmas Ball; dancers in costume come from hundreds of miles away for this celebration. Chittenden's volume *Ranch Verses* (1893) has seen many editions. John P. Sjolander, a young Swede, immigrated to the Texas Gulf Coast in 1871, settled on Bayou Cedar, built boats, farmed, and wrote poems for periodicals. In 1928 his poems were gathered into a volume titled *Salt of the Earth and Sea*. Before his death in 1939 he was called the "Dean of Texas Poets." Except for the cowboy ballads, however, none of the nineteenth-century Texas verse outlasted its day.

The story of theater in Texas is not generally well known. The first edition of the *Handbook of Texas* mentions folk plays in Spanish that were performed orally along the border, but contains no mention of early Texas Anglo drama. There were, however, plays that deserve mention. Again, not surprisingly, the battle of the Alamo was a popular subject. Francis Nona's *The Fall of the Alamo: An Historical Drama in Four Acts* (1879) told its story in verse. Hiram H. McLane's *The Capture of the Alamo: An Historical Tragedy in Four Acts, with Prologue* appeared in 1886. The only play dealing with Texas themes that achieved popular success was A. P. Hoyt's *A Texas Steer* (1890), which traced in a farcical manner the colorful doings of a Texas rancher–congressman named Maverick Brander from Red Dog, Texas, "where men are men and the plumbing is improving." Hoyt's play enjoyed great popularity, was filmed three times including a 1927 version starring Will Rogers, and was still in print as late as 1939.

After 1900. At the turn of the twentieth century historical subjects were much in demand in American fiction, and once

again Texas fiction mirrored the national trend. The republic era proved to be by far the most popular historical subject during the early years of the new century. Indeed the Alamo proved so popular that Stephen Crane, after a visit to San Antonio in 1895, wrote, "Statistics show that 69,710 writers have begun at the Alamo." A partial listing of works includes the following, each of which features the Alamo: William O. Stoddard, *The Lost Gold of the Montezumas: A Story of the Alamo* (1900); Opie Read, *In the Alamo* (1900); Clinton Giddings Brown, *Ramrod Jones, Hunter and Patriot* (1905); Frank Templeton, *Margaret Ballentine; or, The Fall of the Alamo: A Romance of the Texas Revolution* (1907); Eugene P. Lyle, Jr., *The Lone Star* (1907); Edward Plummer Alsbury, *Guy Raymond: A Story of the Texas Revolution* (1908); Everett McNeil, *In Texas with Davy Crockett: A Story of the Texas War of Independence* (1908); and Joseph A. Altsheler, *The Texan Star: The Story of a Great Fight for Liberty* (1912). But the most notable work dealt with the more recent past, the era of the cattle drive, captured vividly in Andy Adams's *The Log of a Cowboy* (1903). Written expressly to counter the romanticism of Owen Wister's immensely popular *The Virginian*, published the previous year, Adams's book, constructed as a novel but without a romantic plot, depicted the cowboy as a worker instead of a dandy. It was instantly regarded as a classic of cattle culture. In a more popular vein, some of the local-color stories of O. Henry were set in Texas. His 1907 collection, *Heart of the West*, is typical.

Literary interest in the past took other forms than the somewhat bloated, over-written historical novels listed above but long forgotten. One of the strongest expressions of this interest occurred in the emerging field of folklore. The Texas Folklore Society, launched in 1909, proved instrumental in locating, collecting, and publishing material of intrinsic interest as well as providing source material for future writers. Francis Edward Abernethy's *The Texas Folklore Society, 1909–1943* and *The Texas Folklore Society, 1943–1971* provide a valuable historical record of the accomplishments of the society. J. Frank Dobie, the foremost figure in the society, mined the past for stories of gold-seekers, legendary hunters, cattlemen, cowboys, and every species of wild critter from mustangs to rattlesnakes. His first book, *A Vaquero of the Brush Country*, appeared in 1929, and his second, *Coronado's Children*, an account of lost mines and legends of fortune-seekers, followed in 1930 and became a Literary Guild selection. Other members of the society made substantial contributions also. John A. Lomax collected songs and ballads from the cattle range; his *Cowboy Songs, and Other Frontier Ballads* (1910) is a major early collection. Emily Dorothy Scarborough, a folklorist with a Ph.D. from Columbia University whose *curriculum vitae* is inscribed on her tombstone in Waco, published a valuable collection of folklore, *On the Trail of Negro Folk Songs*, in 1925. That same year she incorporated folkloric elements into her best-known novel, *The Wind*, published anonymously and famous for its depiction of harsh frontier conditions in late-nineteenth-century West Texas. *The Trail Drivers of Texas* (1923–24), collected and edited by George W. Saunders and J. Marvin Hunter, brought together numerous oral accounts of old-time cattlemen and cowboys that has proved a treasure trove for future novelists such as Larry McMurtry. Among later folklorists, Mody C. Boatright, secretary and editor of the Texas Folklore Society from 1943 to 1964, published several works featuring another major Texas industry, oil, in such books as *Gib Morgan, Minstrel of the Oil Fields* (1945), *Folklore of the Oil*

Industry (1963), and (with William A. Owens), *Tales from the Derrick Floor, A People's History of the Oil Industry* (1970). Ben K. Green earned a reputation as a folk expert on horses and cows. His *Horse Tradin'* appeared in 1967, *Wild Cow Tales* in 1969, and *The Last Trail Drive Through Dallas* in 1971.

In 1943 J. Frank Dobie's influential bibliography, *A Guide to Life and Literature of the Southwest*, mentioned only a handful of fiction titles dealing with Texas. Dobie ignored a good deal of extant fiction, and since then the number of novels written about Texas has increased exponentially to the point where a substantial book-length bibliography would be required to list them all. The following is an attempt to chart the broad outlines of Texas fiction in the twentieth century.

From the 1920s through the late 1960s, much of the best of Texas writing came from the Southern side of the ledger. This is contrary to received myth, but the facts speak for themselves. There were at least as many writers following in the Southern tradition as in the Western, a point most saliently developed by scholar James W. Lee. The Southern-based novels explored the fabric of life on the farms and plantations of East Texas, sometimes looking nostalgically backwards at the past, but more often looking critically at the present. Sue Pinckney's *In the Southland* (1906) was an early attempt to treat East Texas culture as an extension of the Old South. Consisting of two novelettes titled "Disinherited" and "White Violets," *In the Southland* offers a highly romantic portrait of cavaliers, ladies, and plantation customs familiar to any reader of Southern historical fiction. Laura L. S. Krey's *And Tell of Time* (1938), a later effort in the same manner, is a novel marinated in the Confederate worldview and one that, like *Gone With the Wind*, found much of value in the antebellum social order. Among the novelists who explored cotton-plantation culture in East Texas were a number who, instead of idealizing the past, criticized the present, especially the system of farm tenancy. Dorothy Scarborough alone wrote three novels on the subject. The best of them, *In the Land of Cotton*, appeared in 1923; the other two are *Can't Get a Redbird* (1929) and *The Stretchberry-Smile* (1932). Ruth Cross explored similar themes and materials. *The Golden Cocoon* (1924) paints a grim picture of life in the cottonfields and an even grimmer one of the faculty at the University of Texas, "a backwash of incompetents whom life had rejected." In *The Big Road* (1931) Cross produced a melodramatic study of the clash between provincial ignorance (picking cotton) and cosmopolitan values (pursuing a classical music career in Europe).

Several agrarian novels of the thirties and forties deserve mention. Edward Everett Davis's *The White Scourge* (1940) called cottonfields "the great open air slum of the South," an indictment that characterizes much of the fiction written about tenant farming. In *Land Without Moses* (1937) Charles Curtis Munz realistically portrayed the life of an East Texas sharecropping family. John W. Wilson's *High John the Conqueror* (1949) is especially notable for its narrative skill in convincingly portraying the lives of black sharecroppers living on an East Texas farm. Though set in Oklahoma, *The Stricklands* (1939), by Edwin M. Lanham, Jr., of Weatherford, is also a fine contribution to the literature of the tenant farmer. Two other sharecropper novels of the period are Sigman Byrd's *The Redlander* (1939) and John Watson's *The Red Dress* (1949). The most significant of the tenant-farming novels, however, is easily George Sessions Perry's *Hold Autumn in Your Hand* (1941), which won both the Texas

Institute of Letters award and the National Book Award, the first Texas novel to be so honored. Set on a small blackland farm near Rockdale in the late thirties, *Hold Autumn in Your Hand* is a kind of Texas *Georgics*, developing themes put forward by the Roman poet Vergil: "The farmer cleaves the earth with his curved plough,/ This is his yearlong work, thus he sustains/ His homeland, thus his little grandchildren" (*Georgics*, Book II). John W. Thomason's *Lone Star Preacher* (1941) belongs in the Southern tradition as well. It traces the life and times of a fiery Methodist preacher in East Texas during the Civil War era.

On the basis of international reputation, the status conferred by inclusion in major anthologies of American literature, and the respect indicated by academic criticism, Katherine Anne Porter must be judged the most acclaimed Texas literary artist. She, too, belongs indisputably to the Southern tradition. "The Old Order" sequence of stories, contained in *The Leaning Tower and Other Stories* (1944), includes her most widely anthologized masterpiece, "The Grave." These stories, along with the three short novels of *Pale Horse, Pale Rider* (1939), the single greatest artistic work authored by a Texas writer, define a world of fading nineteenth-century moral assurance symbolized by an older generation played off against a younger one, dramatized chiefly in the developing consciousness of Porter's alter ego, Miranda.

In the post–World War II years the Southern tradition in Texas writing informed the careers of three major Texas authors: Charles William Goyen, William Humphrey, and William A. Owens. Goyen's *The House of Breath* (1950) is one of the more daring works of experimental modernist narration by a Texas writer. Told in highly convoluted oral and rhetorical style, it conveys a powerful sense of a provincial East Texas community giving way before the tide of modernity. Today Goyen's work is more highly valued in France than it is in the United States. William Humphrey has produced a number of novels and short stories grounded in the culture and mores of the corner of Northeast Texas where he grew up, in Clarksville, near the Arkansas–Oklahoma border. *Home from the Hill* (1958) is a tale of a legendary hunter and a Gothic marriage, laced with the sometimes too obvious influence of William Faulkner. *The Ordways* (1964) is a comic picaresque tale that rambles across Texas. Perhaps best of all is Humphrey's 1975 memoir, *Farther Off From Heaven*, a book that charts the changes in East Texas from the 1930s to the 1960s. Also of interest is *No Resting Place* (1989), a historical novel that explores the lamentable removal of the Indians from East Texas during Lamar's presidency of the republic. William A. Owens, folklorist, novelist, and memoirist, produced his best work in an autobiographical trilogy that comprises *This Stubborn Soil* (1966), *A Season of Weathering* (1973), and *Tell Me a Story, Sing Me a Song* (1983). *This Stubborn Soil* gives an especially vivid account of the arduous struggle of a youth attempting to obtain an education in dirt-poor rural Texas in the first decades of the twentieth century.

Other recent East Texas writers of note include Bill Brett, whose first-person vernacular narration is reminiscent of Mark Twain. His collection of back-country tales, *Well, He Wanted To Know and I Knew So I Told Him* (1972), reissued as *East Texas Tales* (1972), and his novel, *The Stolen Steers: A Tale of the Big Thicket* (1977), bring the old tradition of Southwestern humor into modern times in rural East Texas. Leon Hale's *Bonney's Place* (1972) captures well the flavor of life surrounding a honkeytonk in East Texas. In his *Half a Look of Cain: A Fantastical*

Narrative (1994) Reginald Gibbons consciously drew upon the example of William Goyen for its East Texas setting and themes. Mary Karr's memoir of a dysfunctional East Texas family, *The Liar's Club* (1995), received glowing reviews in the national press.

Although the history and culture of African Americans have been treated by most of the white writers in the Southern tradition, often very stereotypically, there is one major exception. John Howard Griffin, a Catholic who studied art in France, underwent skin treatments to darken his skin in order to travel in the South as a Negro and recorded his experiences in an influential book during the civil-rights movement, *Black Like Me* (1961). There have as yet been few works by black Texas writers, though there is also some indication recently that things are beginning to change in this regard. The earliest black writer of fiction in Texas was Sutton E. Griggs, whose *Imperium in Imperio: A Study of the Negro Race Problem, a Novel* (1899) was one of several novels that he wrote about race in America. Two important black writers are folklorist J. Mason Brewer and C. C. White, a preacher. In his collections of folk tales, *The Word on the Brazos* (1953) and *Dog Ghosts and Other Texas Negro Folk Tales* (1958), Brewer depicted the humorous side of black life, though at the same time revealing the harshness and unpleasantness of life in a segregated society. C. C. White's *No Quittin' Sense* (1969), told to Adam M. Holland, is the best account in Texas literature of growing up black in East Texas. Albert Race Sample's *Racehorse: Big Emma's Boy* (1984) is a work of raw power that details the life of a black convict in Texas prisons. A promising recent black author who deals with Texas in varying degrees in his short fiction is Reginald McKnight, whose *The Kind of Light That Shines on Texas* appeared in 1992. More recently, Anita Richmond Bunkley in *Black Gold* (1994) combined historical research with a flair for steamy melodrama in a novel about blacks living in a Texas oil boomtown in the 1920s.

In addition to agriculture, East Texas was also the site of several important oilfield discoveries, and several novels have explored the impact of the oil and gas industry on the lives of small communities in that region. Karle Wilson Baker's *Family Style* (1937) describes the changes wrought by the oil boom upon the life of a farm woman. Mary King O'Donnell's *Quincie Bolliver* (1941) also looks at oil-boom days from the perspective of the working class, in this instance a muleskinner's daughter. Jewel H. Gibson's *Black Gold* (1950) humorously examines the rowdy life of roughnecks in the oil patch. William A. Owens's *Fever in the Earth* (1958), set during the boom days following the opening of the Spindletop oilfield, studies the effects of instant wealth upon rural Southerners in the Beaumont area at the turn of the century.

Two other writers round out the picture of the Southern tradition. Madison A. Cooper's *Sironia, Texas* (1952) is a whopping, two-volume, 1,100,000-word portrait of postbellum aristocratic families in Waco. Frederick B. Gipson of Central Texas enjoyed considerable success with novels on agrarian and hunting themes that embodied the flavor of Southern mores. *Hound-dog Man* (1949), *The Home Place* (1950), and *Old Yeller* (1956), a popular juvenile novel set on the frontier, were all made into films.

Despite the accomplishment of Southern writers in the state, those who have written in the Western tradition have dominated the nation's popular conception of Texas. Two seminal writers in this configuration are J. Frank Dobie and Walter Prescott Webb. Dobie's prolific reading and collecting of ranch lore led to such books as *The Longhorns* (1941), *The Mustangs* (1952), and *Cow People* (1964), instant classics in the literature of the cattle culture. Webb, probably the most influential Western historian since Frederick Jackson Turner, is best known for *The Texas Rangers* (1935), a romanticized, celebratory account of the exploits of the state's most famous frontier law-enforcement agency, and *The Great Plains* (1931), a work of lasting impact in the study of the economy and ecology of the arid Western plains states. By ignoring East Texas and cotton culture, the work of Dobie and Webb strongly contributed to promulgating a picture of Texas as a Western state dominated by dust and cattle. Unintentionally, their version of Texas accorded perfectly with the Wild West, shoot-'em-up images being circulated in the works of popular novelists such as Zane Grey and in hundreds of Western movies.

Though other writers in the Western tradition active in the 1930s have been all but eclipsed by the popularity of Dobie and Webb, three deserve to be better known: Edward E. Anderson, Winifred Sanford, and Edwin M. Lanham, Jr. Anderson's *Thieves Like Us* (1937) is a hard-boiled tale of outlaws resembling Bonnie and Clyde that has been filmed twice. Lanham, who produced several serious novels in the 1930s before turning to detective fiction, is the most undeservedly neglected of Texas novelists. His *The Wind Blew West* (1935) is a complex study of the shifting fortunes of a small town bypassed by the railroad. The novel includes a fascinating retelling of the Warren Wagontrain Raid and the subsequent trial of the Indian defendants. *Thunder in the Earth* (1941) is a noteworthy addition to a largely undistinguished body of Texas fiction that deals with the oil and gas industry. Winifred Sanford, a protégé of H. L. Mencken, published a number of excellent stories about women in Texas in the 1930s that were collected in *Windfall and Other Stories* (1988). Another writer of the Great Depression era who has recently resurfaced is Chicago-based Nelson Algren. *The Texas Stories of Nelson Algren*, edited by Betinna Drew, appeared in 1994.

Nonfiction writers following in the wake of Dobie and Webb have produced a number of notable works dealing with Western life in Texas. Edward C. Abbott's rollicking *We Pointed Them North* (with Helena Huntington Smith, 1939) is a wonderfully entertaining account of cattle drives and flesh-and-blood cowboys. Tom Lea's two-volume *The King Ranch* (1957) is a sumptuous history of the state's most famous cattle ranch. Paul Horgan's *Great River: The Rio Grande in North American History* (1954) retells crucial events in Texas history better than any other book. J. Evetts Haley's *Charles Goodnight, Cowman and Plainsman* (1936), the definitive biography of the state's most famous cattleman, is a rich source of information about the cattle kingdom. Sally Reynolds Matthews's *Interwoven: A Pioneering Chronicle* (1936) offers an engaging account of ranching life in West Texas from a patrician woman's point of view.

Dobie's interest in nature, a strong corollary of his devotion to ranch life, influenced the work of subsequent writers. One was his close friend Roy Bedichek, whose *Adventures of a Texas Naturalist* (1948) ranged far and wide in its depiction of natural lore, including memorable chapters on the mockingbird and chickens. Bedichek's letters to Dobie, Webb, and many other correspondents, collected in *Letters of Roy Bedichek* (1985), edited by William A. Owens and Lyman Grant, are one of the real treasures of Texas writing. In the next generation John Graves became the heir of the Dobie–Bedichek vein of natural history and legend. His *Goodbye to a River* (1960), an account of a canoe trip down the Brazos River in the late 1950s, is one of the most honored books in Texas letters. *Hard Scrabble* (1974) and *From a Limestone Ledge* (1980) are substantive additions to the bookshelf of Texas nature lore. More recently, Stephen Harrigan has followed the Dobie–Bedichek line of close observation of man's interaction with his ecological environment in two collections of essays, *A Natural State* (1988) and *Comanche Moon* (1995). His two novels, *Aransas* (1980) and *Jacob's Well* (1985) also pursue ecological themes. Another follower of the naturalist tradition is Rick Bass, whose *The Deer Pasture* (1985) and *Oil Notes* (1989) provide scrupulous examinations of local conditions, of how men and women exploit or revere the earth. Dan L. Flores's *Caprock Canyonlands: Journeys into the Heart of the Southern Plains* (1990) won the admiration of ecologists and nature writers.

In fiction, two Western-oriented novelists of the post–World War II era have consistently mined the Dobie–Webb legacy. Benjamin Capps has written about cattle drives (*The Trail to Ogallala*, 1964), told the story of the settlement of West Texas by a Goodnight-like pioneer (*Sam Chance*, 1965), retold the story of Cynthia Ann Parker (*A Woman of the People*, 1969), portrayed the clash of Comanche and white culture at the turn of the century (*The White Man's Road*, 1969), and recreated the failed Utopian community of La Réunion (*The Brothers of Uterica*, 1967). All these books are narrated in a low-key manner reminiscent of Andy Adams. Elmer Kelton, whose best work has dealt with twentieth-century ranching, began his career by writing for Western pulp magazines and broke into hardcover after a succession of well-researched but formulaic paperbacks. His hardcover publications include novels about the past: *The Day the Cowboys Quit* (1971), based on the "cowboy strike" of the 1880s; *The Wolf and the Buffalo* (1980), a novel of the clash between Indians and United States Cavalry troops on the West Texas frontier that features an Indian warrior and a black soldier; and *Stand Proud* (1984), another frontier saga of a rugged individualist. Kelton's novels about twentieth-century ranch life are probably his best. *The Good Old Boys* (1978) is a comic study of a charming, footloose cowboy who resists the blandishments of the automobile and marriage in favor of a rambling life. Best of all is *The Time It Never Rained* (1973), the portrait of a dogged old rancher named Charlie Flagg, who survives the terrible drought of the 1950s without succumbing to federal assistance. Several of the novels of Capps and Kelton have won awards from Western Writers of America.

Although Capps and Kelton represent an earnestness of spirit and a reliable base of research and experience, their novels are generally characterized by a provincial flatness not unlike the sparse landscapes from which they spring. They are also curiously genteel in language and incident, as mild as Dobie. But flint-hard Protestantism has its limitations when it comes to representing "the way we live now," the goal of all novelists working in the terrain of their own time. The same genteel hands-off tone handicaps the productions of West Texas women novelists of the post–World War II period. Loula Grace Erdman's *The Edge of Time* (1950) and Jane Gilmore Rushing's *Against the Moon* (1968) equally suffer from a tameness of language and vision.

If literary history were as tidy as the historian would like, then Capps and Kelton would have written all of their works in the 1950s, leaving the field open to the iconoclastic Larry McMurtry,

the most important figure in Texas writing since Dobie. But it did not happen that way. In 1961—before Capps, before Kelton—McMurtry published his first novel, *Horseman, Pass By*. It inverted the classic form of the genre (*Shane*) and introduced a level of irony and sexual frankness into the old pastoral world of the courtly cowpoke that made old-timers cringe and made McMurtry for a time the *enfant terrible* of Texas letters. All through the 1960s McMurtry continued to explore the passing of an era and its replacement by a less kind, less gentle way of life, in novels such as *Leaving Cheyenne* (1963), *The Last Picture Show* (1966), and a book of valuable reflections, *In a Narrow Grave: Essays on Texas* (1968). At the end of the decade and into the next, he turned his attention to urban life in Texas in the so-called Houston trilogy: *Moving On* (1970), *All My Friends Are Going To Be Strangers* (1972), and *Terms of Endearment* (1975). No fewer than four of these first six novels were turned into films, three of which won major Academy Awards. Having said all he had to say about Texas, it seemed, McMurtry then wrote several novels set either completely or mostly outside the state. *Cadillac Jack* (1982) is the best of these. Then, in 1985, in a famous reversal of his published animadversions against Texas writers enfeebled by a nostalgic love of the past, he brought out *Lonesome Dove*, a blockbuster novel of epic sweep that drew upon all the old traditions of cattle-drive lore and the Texas Rangers, salted with a healthy and by now familiar dose of sex and ultraviolence. The result was a best-seller that outstripped James Michener's sodden doorstop of a novel, *Texas* (1986), and garnered its author, now transformed into the *éminence grise* of Texas letters, a Pulitzer Prize. Since that high point, McMurtry has continued to produce novels at a rapid rate, though none has achieved the popularity of *Lonesome Dove*. In two novels he turned to other legendary Western materials, the Billy the Kid legend in *Anything for Billy* (1988) and Calamity Jane in *Buffalo Girls* (1990). He also recycled many of his earlier novels in a series of sequels. *Texasville* (1987) comically updated the characters of *The Last Picture Show*; *Some Can Whistle* (1990) reprised the Beat writer Danny Deck from *All My Friends Are Going To Be Strangers*; and *The Evening Star* (1992) was a lackluster sequel to *Terms of Endearment*. *Lonesome Dove* itself spawned two spin-off novels. *Streets of Laredo* (1993), one of McMurtry's darkest works, told the story of Woodrow Call and other survivors from the precursor novel; and *Dead Man's Walk* (1995), a "prequel," placed a young Woodrow Call and Augustus McCrae amid the bloody events of the Mier expedition of 1842.

McMurtry's claim to being the most important Texas writer in the Western tradition has received a very strong challenge from Cormac McCarthy, a Tennessee-based author who, before moving to Texas, had established himself as a writer of impeccable credentials with several novels deeply imbued with the influence of William Faulkner. In the early 1980s McCarthy moved to El Paso and since then has produced three novels of extraordinary merit. *Blood Meridian, or the Evening Redness in the West* (1985) is an elegant and incredibly violent frontier saga of torture, murder, and redemption. *All the Pretty Horses* (1992) won for its author just about every prestigious literary award in the country and, on top of that, was a national best-seller. A coming-of-age story written in beautiful cadences, it was the first in a projected "Border Trilogy"; the second installment, *The Crossing*, appeared in 1994. McCarthy's brooding artistic commitment sets a standard for all Texas writers to emulate.

The brand of realism inaugurated by McMurtry and others in the early 1960s led to a considerable amount of revisionist, post-Dobie-era fiction dealing with the Western side of Texas culture. Though writers in this category are too numerous to mention, some stand out. Russell G. Vliet brought a poet's sensibility to his highly subjective, lyricist fiction in such novels as *Rock Spring* (1974), *Solitudes* (1977), and *Scorpio Rising* (1985). Robert Flynn has displayed a wide fictional breadth, first in his parodic cattle-drive novel, *North to Yesterday* (1967), which anticipated many of the themes of *Lonesome Dove*, and then in the witty, satirical small-town novel *Wanderer Springs* (1987). John Irsfeld's gritty *Little Kingdoms* (1976) adapted multiple-point-of-view techniques to tell a modern outlaw story set in West Texas. Max Crawford produced a wild, exaggerated, stylistically exuberant tale of modern West Texas in *Waltz Across Texas* (1975), then turned to the frontier clash between cavalry and Indians in *Lords of the Plain* (1985), narrated in a quiet period voice of the 1870s. Andrew Jolly, in the underrated novel *A Time of Soldiers* (1976), told a history of a family of soldiers spanning the years from the Mexican Revolution through the Vietnam War. James Lee Burke's *Lay Down My Sword and Shield* (1971), a political novel set in the explosive 1960s, looked back to Texas history and the Korean War. C. W. Smith's *Thin Men of Haddam* (1973) offered a sensitive, carefully wrought story of conflicts between Anglos and Mexicans in South Texas. Edwin Shrake's *Blessed McGill* (1968) possessed an originality rarely seen in historically based Westerns. Clay Reynolds exhibited a great deal of versatility in three novels set in West Texas: *The Vigil* (1986), a town-centered allegory; *Agatite* (1986), released in paperback as *Rage*, a brooding, violent novel; and *Franklin's Crossing* (1992), a big-canvas historical novel about a black frontiersman.

West Texas has also produced a number of essayists. Larry L. King's collections such as *. . . And Other Dirty Stories* (1968) and *The Old Man and Lesser Mortals* (1974) represent the best of his work. A. C. Greene's *A Personal Country* (1979) describes manners and mores in and around Abilene. Allan R. Bosworth's *New Country* (1962) is a lively memoir of growing up in West Texas. Two works set in the brush country and south of there, in the lower Rio Grande valley, are J. Houghton Allen's *Southwest* (1952) and Hart Stilwell's *Uncovered Wagon* (1947). Also of note are three collections of essays. James Ward Lee's *Texas, My Texas* (1993) offers a slumgullion of perceptive comments on Texas popular culture; Gary Cartwright's *Confessions of a Washed-Up Sportswriter (Including Various Digressions about Sex, Crime and Other Hobbies)* (1982) is a consistently lively and entertaining account of subjects ranging from Jack Ruby to newspaper reporting in Fort Worth; Joe Bob Briggs's *A Guide to Western Civilization, or My Story* (1982) is an extremely funny and clever look at Texas from a vernacular redneck perspective. Briggs is the pen name of John Bloom, who achieved national prominence in the 1980s for his comic reviews of drive-in movies.

In 1981 McMurtry, in a controversial essay, "Ever a Bridegroom: Reflections on the Failure of Texas Writing," faulted Texas authors for having ignored the life of the cities. Although no Texas writer could lay claim to having produced a significant body of work about urban life, many had set novels in cities. The best urban novel is unquestionably William Lee Brammer's *The Gay Place* (1961), an elegantly written work set in Austin that depicts the life and times of a larger-than-life governor based closely upon Lyndon B. Johnson. Other notable urban novels include Philip Atlee, *The Inheritors* (1940), Fort Worth; George Williams, *The Blind Bull* (1952), Houston; Al Dewlin, *The Bone-Pickers* (1958), Amarillo; Edwin Shrake, *But Not For Love* (1964), Fort Worth, and *Strange Peaches* (1972), Dallas; Bryan Woolley, *November 22* (1981), Dallas; Laura Furman, *The Shadow Line* (1982), Houston; Peter Gent, *North Dallas Forty* (1973), Dallas; and Peter LaSalle, *Strange Sunlight* (1984), Austin. Shelby Hearon deserves special mention in this context. In a series of novels set variously in Austin (*Hannah's House*, 1975), New Braunfels (*A Prince of a Fellow*, 1978), San Antonio (*Owning Jolene*, 1989), Waco (*Hug Dancing*, 1991), and rural Texas (*Now and Another Time*, 1976, and *Life Estates*, 1994), Hearon has proved herself a shrewd and prolific observer of upper-class manners and mores in modern Texas. Beverly Lowry also contributed two novels about Texas: *Daddy's Girl* (1979) was set in Houston, and *The Perfect Sonya* (1987) caused a minor stir in Texas literary circles for its transparent portrait of an affair between the heroine and the state's most distinguished writer of rural beatitudes. Dan Jenkins has mined his native Fort Worth for humorous Texas stereotypes in a number of popular comic novels, including *Semi-Tough* (1972), *Baja Oklahoma* (1981), and *Fast Copy* (1988). Sarah Bird also treats urban life in comic terms in such novels as *Alamo House: Women Without Men, Men Without Brains* (1986), a very funny look at Austin academic culture, and *The Mommy Club* (1991), set in San Antonio.

Any reckoning of urban literature in Texas should also take into account what is almost a separate type—the true-crime story. Foremost in this genre are Thomas Thompson's *Blood and Money* (1976), which deals with the John Hill murder case in Houston, and Gary Cartwright's *Blood Will Tell* (1979), a study of the Cullen Davis murder case in Fort Worth. Both were national best-sellers. Formulaic detective and crime fiction has also produced a readership for an increasing number of crime-genre novelists, including David L. Lindsey, A. W. Gray, Jay Brandon, Bill Crider, Kinky Friedman, Doug Swanson, and Mary Willis Walker.

In addition to the Southern, Western, and Urban traditions in Texas fiction, a fourth, the Chicano tradition, has had a definite impact in the past 30 years. Americo Paredes's folkloric study of Texas-Mexican culture, *"With His Pistol in His Hand": A Border Ballad and Its Hero* (1958) reconstructed the story of Gregorio Cortez Lira, a Mexican American who killed an Anglo sheriff in a misunderstanding over the ownership of a horse. Cortez's flight from a huge posse of Texas Rangers inspired *corridos* celebrating his courage and tenacity, while attacking the rangers for their racism. Paredes's effort to overturn the romanticizing of the rangers by such Anglo authors as Webb and Dobie made his book a seminal text among Mexican-American intellectuals. Many years later Paredes published a novel written during the late 1930s titled *George Washington Gómez* (1990), which, among other things, satirized the figure of Dobie as a garrulous racist named K. Hank Harvey, the "Historical Oracle of the State." One Anglo writer, Chester Seltzer, writing under the pen name Amado Muro, wrote so well of Mexican life on the El Paso border that for many years he was assumed to be Mexican American. His *Collected Stories* appeared in 1971. Tomás Rivera became the first Chicano author of fiction in Texas to win acclaim. In 1970 his *". . . y no se lo trago la tierra"* [*. . . And the Earth Did Not Part*], a series of 12 sketches developed in an experimental manner, won the Quinto Sol Award. Stories from this collection have appeared in textbook anthologies of American literature. The most prolific Chicano novelist is Rolando Hinojosa, who since 1973 has published a series of interrelated works under the broad title "The Klail City Death Trip." Set mostly in the valley, his novels employ experimental narrative techniques of multiple voices and documents, placing more emphasis on dialogue and nuance than plot and character. *Estampas del valle y otras obras/Sketches of the Valley and Other Works* appeared in a bilingual edition in 1973. This work was later recast by Hinojosa in English as *The Valley* (1983) and is probably his best-known novel. *Klail City y sus alrededores [Klail City and its Surroundings]*, published in 1975, won the Casa de las Americas Prize. *Generaciones y semblanzas* appeared in 1977. *Rites and Witnesses*, in 1982, was Hinojosa's first novel written only in English. His other works include *Dear Rafe* (1950), *Partners in Crime* (1985), and *Becky and her Friends* (1990).

The forgotten Texas Chicano novelist is John Rechy, a native of El Paso who has set parts of much of his fiction in that region. He is known nationally for his long-time association with Los Angeles and his frank advocacy of homosexuality and sensational material. His Texas-related work includes *City of Night* (1964), *This Day's Death* (1969), *The Fourth Angel* (1972), and *Marilyn's Daughter* (1988). Other Chicano novels and short stories include Max Martinez, *The Adventures of the Chicano Kid and Other Stories* (1982), Joseph V. Torres–Metzgar, *Below the Summit*, and Estela Portillo Trambley, *Rain of Scorpions* (1975). Three younger Chicano writers who have received recognition are Lionel Garcia, Sandra Cisneros, and Dagoberto Gilb. Garcia's *Hardscrub* (1990), a novel about a poor Mexican family growing up on a meager West Texas farm, shared the fiction award of the Texas Institute of Letters in 1990. Sandra Cisneros's politically correct vision of Hispanic feminism found a national audience in her collection of stories, *Woman Hollering Creek* (1991). Dagoberto Gilb's *The Magic of Blood* (1993), a strong collection of stories about working-class Hispanics set mostly in El Paso, won the Texas Institute of Letters fiction award.

Short fiction also enjoyed a burst of growth in the postwar era. Traditional stories from O. Henry to Sylvan Karchmer were brought together in *21 Texas Short Stories* (1954), edited by William W. Peery. In 1974 James P. White anthologized both well-known and beginning authors in *The Bicentennial Collection of Texas Short Stories*. A similar mix of established and novice authors appeared in *Texas Stories & Poems* (1978), edited by Walter McDonald and James P. White. The 1980s, however, saw the publication of the most numerous short-story collections, which brought before the public the work of a host of talented writers, including Tom Zigal, Pat Carr, James Crumley, Jan Seale, and others. The principal collections include *Her Work: Stories by Texas Women* (1982), edited by Lou Rodenberger; *South by Southwest: 24 Stories from Modern Texas* (1986), edited by Don Graham; *Prize Stories: Texas Institute of Letters* (1986), edited by Marshall Terry; *New Growth: Contemporary Short Stories by Texas Writers* (1989), edited by Lyman Grant; *Common Bonds: Stories by and about Modern Texas Women* (1990), edited by Suzanne Comer; *New Growth II: Contemporary Short Stories by Texas Writers* (1993), edited by Mark Busby; and *Texas Bound: 19 Texas Stories* (1994), edited by Kay Cattarulla.

Besides anthologies, numerous individual volumes of short stories by Texas writers were published during the 1970s and 1980s. Carolyn Osborn was one of the most productive and artistic; her collections include *A Horse of Another Color* (1977), *The Fields of Memory* (1984), and *Warriors and Maidens* (1991). Mary Gray Hughes's *The Calling* (1980) exhibited a high degree of craft, as did Dave Hickey's resurrection of his stories from the 1960s, *Prior Convictions* (1989). *Afoot in a Field of Men* (1983) by Pat Ellis Taylor (who subsequently changed her name to Pat LittleDog) depicted the down-and-out lives of hippie families living in an unglamorous Dallas. Marshall Terry's *Dallas Stories* (1987) explored the lives of the well-to-do in Dallas, while A. C. Greene's *The Highland Park Woman* (1983) ranged from the rich suburbs of Dallas to West Texas ranches. Robert Flynn's *Seasonal Rain and Other Stories* (1986) brought together stories about West Texas, and a second collection, *Living with the Hyenas* (1995), comprised stories set in West Texas and Vietnam. Annette Sanford's *Lasting Attachments* (1989) exhibited a quiet sureness about the lives of Texas women; Jim Sanderson's *Bit by the Metal* (1993) won the 1992 Kenneth Patchen Prize; Pat Carr's *Night of the Luminaries* (1986) spoke in spare rhythms of modern themes; Janet Peery's *Alligator Dance* (1993) employed an energetic vernacular style; Donley Watt's *Can You Get There From Here?* (1994) used laconism to capture a Texas voice; James Hannah's *Desperate Measures* (1988) offered dark glimpses into the lives of working-class East Texans; Jan Epton Seale's *Airlift and Other Stories* (1992) concentrated on revealing the lives of women in Texas; and James Crumley's *Whores* (1988) brought together the great title story with other quite effective work.

In addition to the proliferation of fiction since World War II, there has been increased activity in organized study and commentary on Texas writing. If the first decades of the century were spent in collecting stories of farm and range, the last decades have been spent in critical classification and commentary. Indeed the 1980s might justly be labeled the Age of Criticism. Two major academic conferences helped point the way. The first, held in 1983 at the University of Texas at Austin, resulted in the publication of *The Texas Literary Tradition: Fiction Folklore History*, edited by Don Graham, James W. Lee, and William T. Pilkington. This book contained essays and an extensive bibliography. A second conference was held at North Texas State University in 1986. Centers for the study of Texas and southwestern literature were established at the University of North Texas and Southwest Texas State University. Monographs and collections of essays devoted to such authors as Katherine Anne Porter and Larry McMurtry were plentiful. Throughout the period much lively debate surrounded the whole question of Texas literature. A useful collection showing all sides is *Range Wars: Heated Debates, Sober Reflections, and Other Assessments of Texas Writing* (1989), edited by Craig Clifford and Tom Pilkington.

There were also several volumes addressing various aspects of Texas writing. William T. Pilkington's *My Blood's Country: Studies in Southwestern Literature* (1973) was a pioneering examination of Southwestern literature from Cabeza de Vaca to Larry McMurtry. Pilkington's *Inventing Texas: The Literature of the Lone Star State* (1981) offered a brief survey of developments in Texas writing. A. C. Greene's *The Fifty Best Books on Texas* stirred up a lot of interest. Later, James W. Lee's *Classics of Texas Fiction* (1987) contained useful commentary on additional Texas books. C. L. Sonnichsen's *From Hopalong to Hud: Thoughts on Western Fiction* (1978) included several chapters highly pertinent to Texas writing. Don Graham's *Texas: A Literary Portrait* (1986) divided the state into literary regions and reported on interesting work about the state by famous visitors such as Graham Greene and Gertrude Stein.

Drama remains a relatively minor genre in Texas writing, although, according to anthologist William B. Martin, "a solid body of respectable Texas plays does exist." This is not a large assertion, however, and the evidence suggests that it is about all that can be claimed. Texas drama in the twentieth century has generally explored the same themes as fiction. Preston St. Vrain Jones's "Texas Trilogy," the best known plays about Texas, depicted in rather pedestrianly realistic terms the lives of small-town West Texas racists, cheerleaders-cum-waitresses, and crotchety old settlers confronting the challenges of time and modernity. Although they achieved widespread popularity in the state, they did not succeed in New York. The three plays composing the trilogy, *The Knights of the White Magnolia* (1973), *Lu Ann Hampton Laferty Oberlander* (1974), and *The Oldest Living Graduate* (1974), rarely rise above stereotypes, and the language mainly sticks to rural idioms heavily sprinkled with clichés. Comparisons with Eugene O'Neill proved premature. The work of Horton Foote poses a similar problem. Best known for the numerous films made from his work, Foote is a solid if unexciting dramatist of low-keyed language, quiet action, and genteel manners. *The Trip to Bountiful* (1954) and *1918* (1974–77) are typical. With roots in early television, Foote may also be remembered for *Harrison, Texas: Eight Television Plays by Horton Foote* (1956). Other notable Texas plays include a number of works of strictly regional interest. L. Ramsey Yelvington's *A Cloud of Witnesses* (1955) tells, for the millionth time, the story of the Alamo, only this time, and not the first, in verse. Exploring small-town Texas life seems to be both a preoccupation and severe limitation for Texas playwrights. Oliver Hailey's *Who's Happy Now?* (1967) and *Kith and Kin* (1986) probe in a comic vein the lives of close-knit small-town Texas families. Jack Heifner's short plays, such as *Vanities* (1977), *Porch* (1977), and *Patio* (1978), combine Texas comic idioms with less sunny appraisals of lives spent in provincial settings. Mary Rohde's *Ladybug, Ladybug, Fly Away Home* (1977) explores feminist themes in a small-town beauty-parlor setting. James McLure exploits good-ol'-boy stereotypes in *Lone Star* (1979), a study of the effect of the Vietnam War on a returning veteran, and in *Laundry and Bourbon* (1980) he examines the women in the lives of the characters of the earlier play. In plays such as *The Night Hank Williams Died* (1989) Larry L. King has tried to tap the same success that he enjoyed with his comic portrayal of life in a small town in *The Best Little Whorehouse in Texas* (1978), co-written with Peter Masterson. This musical play, based upon King's journalistic piece about the closing of the Chicken Ranch, a famous brothel outside La Grange, had a long run on Broadway. Also worth mentioning is John Logan's *Jack Ruby, All-American Boy* (1970). One black playwright who has utilized Texas materials is Ted Shine, whose *Shoes* (1970) examines racial themes against the background of an exclusive Dallas country club. On balance, Texas drama has a long way to go before it produces any work equal to that of such national dramatists as Eugene O'Neill, Arthur Miller, or Tennessee Williams.

Before World War II Texas poetry flourished, but without distinction. There were many local poets of modest ability, and nearly every town counted a local versifier or two among its denizens. State government selected a poet laureate, but in general the poetasters honored with the title were no more distinguished than the politicians who appointed them. Typical is John Lang Sinclair, a representative poet of the day who is remembered only for the song "The Eyes of Texas." Poets in the early part of the century were often influenced by minor poets of the past rather than the more invigorating new poets who were producing the most significant American verse of the century, such as the modernists Ezra Pound, T. S. Eliot, William Carlos Williams, and Wallace Stevens. Instead, Texas poets chose minor nineteenth-century Southern poets as their models, such men as Henry Timrod and Sidney Lanier, or, in the twentieth-century, such backward-looking poets as Rupert Brooke, a British poet killed in World War I, or rhymesters like Joyce Kilmer, author of "Trees." A generous sampling of Texas poetry during the early part of the century appears in Hilton Ross Greer's anthology *Voices of the Southwest: A Book of Texan Verse* (1923). Altogether too many of these poems are cloyed with phony archaic diction—"o'er" and "hath" and "begirt"—and altogether too many invoke Love and such personified abstractions. Few were the poems that actually drew upon the Texas landscape or culture or people in any convincing way. Two more anthologies, *Texas Poets* (1936) and *The Greater Texas Anthology of Verse* (1939), contain hundreds of poems by, as R. S. Gwynn puts it, "stereotypical trinomial poetesses with resonant names" such as Ura Link Eckhardt and Corrie Birdsong Teagarden. Gywnn concludes justly that "a mere recitation of the table of contents of *Texas Poets* surpasses the lyricism of the poems collected in it." Easily the most prolific and best known Texas poet of the late Twenties onward was Grace Noll Crowell, who published 22 volumes between 1928 and 1959. During her stint as poet laureate she published a small book of Texas poems in honor of the Texas Centennial. *Bright Destiny* (1936) contains her best, most concrete work, but most of her poetry was in the inspirational vein and is collected in *Poems of Inspiration and Courage* (1965).

Still, from the 1930s there are a few poets who at least occasionally broke away from the pallid verse of sentimental idealism and Christian bromides and sought to wring poems out of the Texas earth. Karle Wilson Baker, for example, in *Dreamers on Horseback* (1929), tried to capture the differing moods of Texas in her sequence "Some Towns of Texas," and in her poem "Song of the Forerunners" she assessed the differing contributions made to Texas history by men and women. Berta Hart Nance's "Cattle," from *Flute in the Distance* (1935), contains the often-quoted couplet: "Other states were carved or born,/ Texas grew from hide and horn." Another poet of the 1930s, long since ignored, was Lexie Dean Robertson. *Red Heels* (1928) contained some interesting realistic poems about life in oilfield boom-towns, including "Aftermath," which recounts the ravages upon land and spirit following the end of a boom. In *Acorn on the Roof* (1939) Robertson included 12 Texas poems, some in dialect and all in plain, straightforward diction. "Carbon Black," for example, tells in dialect the story of a woman and a community ruined by industrial pollution, an unusual subject for Texas poetry of that era. *I Keep a Rainbow* (1932) also contained some poems dealing realistically with homely Texas subjects. Boyce House, a Fort Worth newspaperman known primarily for his collections of Texas jokes and stories, wrote poems of considerable vitality. *Texas Rhythms* (1936) contained a number of original poems, including "Texas Poets," a prescient analysis of the poetic scene in the Centennial year. House began, "You write about bluebonnets" and urged poets instead to write about the events, past and present, that make Texas unique. He mentions such available subjects as "Clyde and Bonnie" and "Farmer Jim and Ma Ferguson," concluding, "And yet, Texas poets, you swoon when you behold a dew-/ drop enfolded by a rose!" Interestingly, Bonnie Parker, Clyde Barrow's gun moll, wrote ballads that have more verve than the piles of poetry about bluebonnets, mockingbirds, and the Alamo produced by most of the poets laureate of the era.

During the 1940s and 1950s, and increasingly in the following decades, Texas poetry had its greatest period of development. More technically accomplished poets began to publish, with a keener sense of English and American poetic traditions. Several wrote in traditional meters and genres. Arthur M. Sampley, a university-trained poet, brought out *This Is Our Time* in 1943 and *Selected Poems, 1937–1971* in 1971. In such volumes as *Man Now* (1954) and *A Beginning* (1966) William Burford exhibited a technical facility with a willingness to treat, in some poems, specifically Texas materials. Robert Lee Brothers, Jr., displayed a strong affinity with the poetry of Emily Dickinson in tightly disciplined verse in the poems collected in *Democracy of Dust* (1947) and *The Hidden Harp* (1952). William Barney, deeply influenced by Robert Frost, revealed a keen eye for Texas customs and rhythms in *Kneel from the Stone* (1952) and *The Killdeer Crying* (1977), edited by Dave Oliphant. Martin Staples Shockley published a number of clever poems about Texas landscapes and Texas critters that have been collected in *Last Roundup: Selected Published and Unpublished Works* (1994). Joseph Colin Murphey's *A Return to the Landscape* (1979) presented spare, unsentimental, and at times deeply moving portraits of Texas folk. Gene Shuford wrote of gunfighters and other frontier topics in taut verse; his *Selected Poems* appeared in 1972. Vassar Miller's poems began appearing in book form in 1960 and were collected in 1991 in *If I Had Wheels of Love*. Intense, concentrated, and characterized by religious and philosophical themes, Miller's work, which has an audience beyond the state, has little Texas resonance. Novelist R. G. Vliet also wrote poetry of note, including *Events & Celebrations* (1966), *The Man with the Black Mouth* (1970), and a long ballad, *Clem Maverick: The Life and Death of a Country Music Singer* (1983). One of the most prolific of the poets of the seventies and eighties is Dave Oliphant, who adapted the techniques and free-verse rhythms of William Carlos Williams to Texas subjects. Oliphant's volumes include *Lines & Mounds* (1976), *Footprints* (1978), *Maria's Poems* (1987), and *Austin* (1985), a book-length poetic history of the city that is the longest of his series of poems titled "Texas Towns and Cities."

A number of other poets have written verse attempting to come to grips with the specific local facts of Texas culture and history. Charles Behlen's *Perdition's Keepsake* (1978) belongs in this category, as do Sandra Lynn's *I Must Hold These Strengths* (1980) and *Where Rainbows Wait for Rain: The Big Bend Country* (1989); Betsy Colquitt's *Honor Card & Other Poems* (1980); Naomi Sahib Nye's *Different Ways to Pray* (1980) and *Hugging the Juke Box* (1982); Betty Adcock's *Beholdings* (1988); Jerry Bradley's *Simple Versions of Disaster* (1981); and Leon Stokesbury's *Often in Different Landscapes* (1976). Among Chicano poets, Rosemary Catacalos in *Again for the First Time* (1984) writes of Mexican and Anglo lives intertwined in Texas culture, chiefly in and around San Antonio. Ray Gonzalez in *Twilights and Chants* (1987) demonstrates a feeling for land-

scapes and solitudes. Carmen Tafolla's *Sonnets to Human Beings* (1987) probes states of feeling and culture among Mexican Americans. Tino Villanuevo's *Scene from the Movie GIANT* (1993) is a substantial narrative poem that relates the impact of the celebrated Hollywood film upon a young Chicano boy living in San Marcos. Black poets who have contributed their views of contemporary Texas include Lorenzo Thomas and Harryette Mullen. Susan Wood deserves mention for her precisely rendered poems in *Campo Santo*. Albert Goldbarth, a nationally recognized poet who lived in Texas for a number of years, produced one of the most interesting long poems in the state's history, in his *Different Fleshes: a novel/poem* (1979), a richly allusive modernist poem intermingling Paris of the 1920s with Round Rock, from the Sam Bass era forward. Other poets who have been active in chapbook publication include Thomas Whitbread, David Yates, James Hoggard, Paul Woodruff, Rick Sale, J. M. Linebarger, Stan Rice, Paul Foreman, Terry Wiggs, and Karl Kopp. Among the most prolific and award-winning poets of Texas in the 1970s and 1980s is Walter McDonald, whose poems have appeared in many national quarterlies and have been collected in such volumes as *Caliban in Blue and Other Poems* (1976), *One Thing Leads to Another* (1978), *Working Against Time* (1981), and *Rafting the Brazos* (1988). In the mid-1990s McDonald was probably the most Texas-rooted poet with the highest standing in and outside the state.

During the 1980s poetry in Texas underwent the same kind of dialectical debate that surrounded fiction. One group championed the "nativist" position that Texas poets, following in the tradition of William Carlos Williams, should develop a poetry based on local conditions that looked inward and not to Europe or the classical past for inspiration. The other view proposed that poets should draw upon modernist and postmodernist currents to produce a poetry of "otherness" resistant to long-standing traditions of frontier Protestant conservatism and chauvinism. Surveying Texas poetry in 1987, William Lockwood observed that there is "no nationally recognized poetic voice resident in Texas." Although his assessment is correct, there is no dearth of Texas poets trying to find their voice and a larger audience. Poetry continues to be among the liveliest genres of writing in Texas. Small presses, local quarterlies, anthologies, symposia, and local poetry readings constantly spring up to stimulate poetic activity. *Texas in Poetry: A 150-Year Anthology* (1994), edited by Billy Bob Hill, offered Texans a fine opportunity to assess the poetic traditions of the state, ranging from established figures such as William Barney and Walter McDonald to promising newcomers such as Violette Newton and Betsy Berry. A succession of annuals published by the University of North Texas, *New Texas*, continues to bring together the most recent work in short fiction and poetry. These and other publications by regional and small presses ensure a vigorous, ongoing field of poetic production. *Don B. Graham*

Littlefield, George Washington. Cattleman, businessman, and University of Texas regent and benefactor; b. Panola County, Mississippi, 21 June 1842; d. Austin, 10 November 1920; m. Alice Payne Tillar (1863); 2 children, both of whom died as infants; ed. Gonzales College and Baylor University. Littlefield grew to young manhood on the family plantation in Gonzales County, helping his mother to manage the place after his father's death (1853). In the Civil War he fought with Terry's Texas Rangers and

George Littlefield. Prints and Photographs Collection, George W. Littlefield file, CAH; CN 02938.

in adjacent Kimble and Menard counties, a ranch he put under management of half-nephew John Will White. In the 1890s Littlefield assembled acreage that came to be known as the LFD Farm near Roswell. He capped his ranching operation in 1901 with the purchase for two dollars an acre of the 312,000-acre Yellow House (southern) Division of the XIT Ranch in Lamb and Hockley counties. To reach the prevailing wind above the escarpment at the ranch headquarters, Littlefield put up a windmill 130 feet tall to the top of the fan, claimed at the time to be the world's tallest windmill. In 1912 he established the Littlefield Lands Company under Arthur Pope Duggan to sell some 64,000 acres in Lamb County for farms, and founded the town of Littlefield.

Littlefield moved to Austin in 1883 and shortly accepted a position on the board of the State National Bank. In 1890 he organized the American National Bank, which he served as president until 1918, when he relinquished the post to the nephew who had been his mainstay in the bank, Hiram Augustus Wroe. In 1910–11 he built the ornate nine-story Littlefield Building to house the bank. Through the bank Littlefield gained interests in a number of businesses, in particular the Driskill Hotel, in which the bank was first housed. In 1911 Governor Colquitt appointed Littlefield to the Board of Regents of the University of Texas. When Littlefield complained of Northern bias in the textbooks used in teaching American history, historian Eugene C. Barker replied that better history could not be written without adequate archival resources. Littlefield established the Littlefield Fund for Southern History to collect such material in 1914, and during the remaining six years of his life he gave well over $100,000 to the fund. In 1918 he gave $225,000 to purchase the John Henry Wrenn Library. Including benefactions such as the Littlefield Fountain, Alice P. Littlefield Dormitory for freshman women, and his home, Littlefield gave more than any other single individual to the university during its first 50 years.   *David B. Gracy II*

Llano Estacado. The "Staked Plain," one of the largest tablelands on the continent; the southern extension of the High Plains of North America, south of the Canadian River in northwest Texas and northeast New Mexico. The Llano is bounded on the north by the southern escarpment of the Canadian River valley and on the east by the irregular and deeply incised Caprock escarpment. The western boundary is the Mescalero Escarpment east of the Pecos River valley of New Mexico. The southern end of the plateau blends into the Edwards Plateau. The Llano Estacado embraces all or part of 33 Texas and 4 New Mexico counties and covers approximately 32,000 square miles, a larger area than New England. It is part of what was known to early explorers and settlers as the Great American Desert, a sandy, semiarid region with average annual precipitation of 18 to 20 inches. The Llano was first described by Vázquez de Coronado in a letter to the king of Spain (1541): "I reached some plains so vast, that I did not find their limit anywhere I went, although I travelled over them for more than 300 leagues . . . with no more land marks than if we had been swallowed up by the sea . . . . there was not a stone, nor bit of rising ground, nor a tree, nor a shrub, nor anything to go by." Randolph B. Marcy (1852) echoed Coronado's impressions: "It is much elevated . . . very smooth and level . . . without a tree, shrub, or any other herbage to intercept the vision . . . . the almost total absence of water causes all animals to shun it: even the Indians do not venture to cross it except at two or three

achieved the rank of major, a title by which he was later addressed. Back in Texas he "went to work to make the best, as he thought, of a miserable life, having to carry his crutches everywhere." His first years farming after the war ended in disaster caused by three years of worm infestation and flood. Even the road-side store he opened, which prospered because George accepted barter, in particular cattle, could not make up for the losses. In 1871 he gathered a herd of cattle and drove it to Abilene, Kansas, where he sold the animals for enough to discharge all of his debts and leave him with $3,600 "to begin business." Over the next several years he opened a dry-goods store in partnership with J. C. Dilworth in Gonzales, bought and trailed cattle, bought ranches in Caldwell and Hays counties, and developed his plantations. In 1877 Littlefield bought water rights along the Canadian River near Tascosa and established the LIT Ranch, which he sold in 1881 for $248,000. In 1882 he purchased water interests sufficient to control some four million acres of land in New Mexico east of the Pecos River between Fort Sumner and Roswell, on which he established the Bosque Grande Ranch. He bought the site of the first windmill on the New Mexico plains at the Four Lakes north of Tatum (1883) and developed the Four Lakes Ranch with windmills and barbed wire to control access to water and permit upgrading of stock. In 1887 he began acquiring land in Mason County, that soon spread over some 120,000 acres

places." The uplift of the Rockies during the Cenozoic (which began 70 million years ago) provided the materials underlying the Llano Estacado. As rain and snow melt eroded the Rocky Mountains, debris was carried eastward onto the High Plains. As the mountain streams left the canyons of the high mountains and moved out on the plains, they slowed, and unable to carry the vast load of boulders, pebbles, and silt, dropped those materials into their beds. The stream beds were aggraded, and the streams overflowed and found new avenues of descent over ever lower and flatter terrain. This process left large interconnected alluvial fans much like the deltas that form at river mouths. The land surface was made up of aggraded materials, which theoretically stretched all the way to the Gulf of Mexico. Calcium carbonate, which had been carried in solution from the mountains, seeped into the alluvial deposits and through evaporation formed a hard caprock of impervious material, commonly called caliche. Subsequent fracturing of the caliche caprock allowed weathering by wind and water of the more humid east to form the lower plains of Texas but left the more arid Llano Estacado high and dry.

Formations on the east, north, and western boundaries of the Llano Estacado probably account for its name. These steep escarpments of 50 to 300 feet were caused by the slumping of the less resistant beds that underlie the hard, resistant Caprock. To explorers approaching the High Plains from the west the sheer cliffs of the Mescalero Escarpment near the site of present Cuero, New Mexico, appeared to be stockaded or palisaded like a fort. The bluffs were described by Coronado and other early European explorers as "palisades, ramparts, or stockades." Thomas Falconer, in *Letters and Notes on the Santa Fe Expedition* (1844), described the escarpment as "elevated or palisaded much

as palisaded sides of a fort." References to other "stakes" abound. All are associated with finding one's way to water or marking a route on the treeless and featureless high plain. Early travelers used stakes to mark routes, cowboys to tether horses, or Indians to torture enemies. In the sources, however, such stakes are either not defined at all or are variously described—on the Coronado expedition as "piles of bones and cow dung," for instance. Marcy, in his *Exploration of the Red River* (1849), mentions piles of "stones and buffalo dung." J. Evetts Haley in *Charles Goodnight, Cowboy and Plainsman* (1936), tells of finding "mojoneras [landmarks] of stone" marking waterholes. Though these references to the use of markers provide a plausible theory for the origin of the name, the express metaphoric comparison of cliff formations and palisades made repeatedly by explorers argues more convincingly for the geological origin.

A critical shortage of water restricted the early exploration and settlement of the Llano, which is at best a semiarid region with a very high evaporation rate. The gently sloping surface directs most of the sparse rainfall into shallow depressions, where the impervious Caprock inhibits its percolation to the underground. The runoff evaporates. Minerals left behind by the process render most surface water in playas unusable. The only reliable source of groundwater has been the Ogalalla Aquifer, a huge underground reservoir that extends all along the North American High Plains east of the Rocky Mountains. Its southern extension under the Llano Estacado has been cut off and sealed mainly by the drainage of the Pecos River and, to a lesser extent, by the Canadian River and their tributaries. That isolation prevents any recharge from Rocky Mountain runoff, making the groundwater under the Llano Estacado a finite resource that is being rapidly depleted. Development of the

Hay Makers on the Staked Plains, Texas, 1890. Photograph by J. A. Caldwell. Courtesy Lawrence T. Jones III Collection, Austin.

Llano did not begin until the 1870s. By the end of 1886 the area and adjacent lands had at least 30 large ranches recognized by name and cattle brand, grazing thousands of cattle on free grass and water on mostly unappropriated public lands. Some of the largest ranches were the Quarter Circle T, JA, Rocking Chair, LX, Turkey Track, T Anchor, Shoe Bar, Frying Pan, and Matador. The earliest ranches on the Llano Estacado were supported by the pioneer settlements of Tascosa, Mobeetie, and Clarendon. Most of the largest ranches were broken up by 1920, and much of the land came under the control of land developers who promoted campaigns to bring new settlers to West Texas. Innovative farmers learned techniques to make the rich, dry land productive; they also drilled into the Ogalalla Aquifer. Massive irrigation projects led to large production of cotton, corn, wheat, sorghum, and a great variety of melons and vegetables now grown on the Llano. Natural gas was discovered in Potter County in 1917 and oil in Carson County in 1921. These initial discoveries led to the development of the vast West Texas oilfields, which by the 1980s had yielded 47 billion barrels of crude oil. The discovery and development of the oil and gas fields brought large-scale industry to the Llano area in the 1930s. Thus within a relatively short period the Llano witnessed the most rapid development of any section of the state, progressing from an economy based on unfenced public grazing land to a modern industrial economy within half a century. The total population of the Llano in 1880 was only 1,081. By 1980 the total was over 900,000 with approximately 23 percent living in rural areas and 77 percent in urban centers. In 1990 there were four metropolitan statistical areas on the plateau—Amarillo, Lubbock, Midland, and Odessa. *Art Leatherwood*

Llanos–Cárdenas Expedition. A followup to Alonso De León's discovery of the remains of La Salle's Fort St. Louis (1689). The expedition sailed from Veracruz on 12 October 1690 to reconnoiter the fort's site and map its environs, then returned to its home port in early December. Francisco de Llanos, captain of the frigate *Nuestra Señora de la Encarnación* of the Armada de Barlovento, was in overall command of the expedition. Assigned as mapmaker was the engineer Manuel José de Cárdenas y Magaña. This voyage to the Texas coast, says Herbert Bolton, was "of first importance in fixing the location of La Salle's colony." *Robert S. Weddle*

Lomax, John Avery. Folklorist; b. Goodman, Mississippi, 23 September 1867; d. Greenville, Mississippi, 26 January 1948; m. Bess B. Brown (1904; d. 1931); 4 children; m. Ruby R. Terrill (1934); ed. University of Texas (grad. 1897). The Lomaxes moved to Texas when John was two. On the farm, located on a branch of the Chisholm Trail, he heard many cowboy ballads and other folk songs; before he was 20 he began to write some of them down. After graduating at UT, he remained at the university as secretary to the president, as registrar, and as steward of the men's dormitory. In 1903 he taught English at A&M. In 1906 he received a scholarship at Harvard University, where Barrett Wendell and George Lyman Kittredge encouraged him to take up seriously the collection of western ballads he had begun as a youth. He collected by means of an appeal published in western newspapers and through his own vacation travel, financed in part by Harvard fellowships. In the back room of the White Elephant Saloon in Fort Worth he found cowhands who knew

many stanzas of "The Old Chisholm Trail." A Gypsy woman living in a truck near Fort Worth sang "Git Along, Little Dogies." At Abilene an old buffalo hunter gave him the words and tune of the "Buffalo Skinners." In San Antonio in 1908 a black saloonkeeper who had been a trail cook sang "Home on the Range." Lomax's first collection, *Cowboy Songs and Other Frontier Ballads,* was published in 1910. From 1910 to 1925 Lomax was secretary of the Alumni Association, which became the Ex-Students Association of the University of Texas, except for two years, 1917–19, when he was a bond salesman in Chicago. He was active in the fight to save the university from political domination by James Ferguson. From 1925 until 1931 he was vice president of the Republic National Company in Dallas. He was a founder of the Texas Folklore Society and president of the American Folklore Society. In his collecting he traveled 200,000 miles and visited all but one of the states. Often accompanied by his son, Alan, he visited prisons to record the work songs and spirituals of black inmates—notably Huddie Ledbetter, whom Lomax took on a tour and recorded. In 1919 Lomax published *Songs of the Cattle Trail and Cow Camp.* With his son he edited *American Ballads and Folk Songs* (1934), *Negro Songs as Sung by Lead Belly* (1936), *Our Singing County* (1941), and *Folk Song: U.S.A.* (1947). In 1947 his autobiographical *Adventures of a Ballad Hunter* (1947) was awarded the Carr P. Collins prize as the best Texas book of the year by the Texas Institute of Letters. Beginning in 1933 Lomax was honorary curator of the Archive of Folksong at the Library of Congress, which he helped establish as the primary agency for preservation of American folksongs and culture. *Wayne Gard*

Lone Star Army Ammunition Plant. Nine miles west of Texarkana; also known as the Lone Star Ordnance Plant. The plant, next to the Red River Army Depot, was constructed at the beginning of World War II at a cost of $45.5 million and operated for the army by the Lone Star Defense Corporation, a subsidiary of the B. F. Goodrich Rubber Corporation, as an ammunition-loading plant for artillery shells, bombs, fuses, boosters, and other auxiliary ammunitions items. The contract for the plant was let on 23 July 1941; the first small-caliber ammunition was sent out on 27 May 1942. Production of aluminum nitrate was suspended in the spring of 1943, and in April of the same year the depot was consolidated with the Red River Army Ordnance Depot to form the Texarkana Ordnance Center. The plant continued to operate after the war. In the early 1990s the base had a small number of military personnel and some 4,300 Civil Service employees. *Christopher Long*

Long, James. Filibuster; b. Culpeper County, Virginia, probably in 1793; d. Mexico City, 8 April 1822; m. Jane Wilkinson (1815). After service as a surgeon in the War of 1812, Long practiced medicine and engaged in merchandising in Mississippi. In 1819 the Adams–Onís Treaty aroused such strong opposition in Natchez that prominent citizens planned an expedition to conquer Texas and placed Long in command. The Long expedition was the last of a series of early filibustering campaigns that included the Gutiérrez–Magee expedition and the expedition led by Francisco Xavier Mina. It was mounted by citizens in the Natchez area and financed by subscriptions said to total about $500,000. It attracted recruits with a promise of a league of Texas land to every soldier. An advance force of 120 men, led by Eli Harris, crossed the Sabine River on 8 June 1819, and went on to

Nacogdoches, where Long arrived on 21 June. At Camp Freeman, citizens of Nacogdoches met to organize a provisional government with Long as its chief. On June 23 this "government" declared the independence of Texas. Its Supreme Council voted ten sections of land to each private and provided for selling Red River lands at prices ranging downward from fifty cents an acre. By the middle of July, Long had more than 300 men under his command, among them John Sibley, Samuel Davenport, and José Bernardo Gutiérrez de Lara, and had made overtures for assistance to Jean Laffite at Galveston. Failure to receive supplies from Laffite or from the Natchez committee caused Long to scatter his men in an attempt to live off the country. Small parties took possession of strategic points in July and August, and Long continued his plan to bring Galveston into his republic. On 9 October the Supreme Council declared Galveston a port of entry, authorized the construction of a fort at Point Bolivar and made Laffite governor of the island. At the end of September, Governor Antonio María Martínez sent Col. Ignacio Pérez with more than 500 men to eject Long from Spanish territory. By the end of November he had driven the American settlers out of East Texas.

Long escaped and, undeterred, joined forces with José Félix Trespalacios, who was organizing an expedition in New Orleans to support the Mexican liberals. Long established his headquarters at Point Bolivar, where he was joined by his wife. There, beginning in April 1820 he attempted to reorganize his forces. With the aid of Trespalacios, Benjamin R. Milam, Gutiérrez de Lara, and others, Long revitalized the Supreme Council. He later broke with Trespalacios, and the expedition led an uncertain existence at Fort Las Casas on Point Bolivar until 19 September 1821, when Long and 52 men sailed to capture La Bahía. The town fell easily on 4 October, but four days later Pérez forced Long to surrender. Long was eventually sent to Mexico City to plead his case before Agustín de Iturbide, but was shot and killed by a guard. Although the shooting was said to be an accident, there was some evidence that it was instigated by Trespalacios.

Harris Gaylord Warren

Long, Jane. The "Mother of Texas"; b. Jane Herbert Wilkinson, Charles County, Maryland, 23 July 1798; d. Fort Bend County, 30 December 1880; m. James Long (1815). Mrs. Long acquired her nickname before her death because she claimed, mistakenly, that her child born on Bolivar Peninsula on 21 December 1821 was the first white child born in Texas. At Propinquity Plantation near Natchez she met her future husband when he was returning from the battle of New Orleans. Long left for Nacogdoches in June 1819, and Jane, with two daughters and a black maid named Kian, followed him shortly thereafter. Within two months after arriving, she had to flee with the other American families towards the Sabine River when Spanish troops from San Antonio arrived. About March 1820 James took Jane to Bolivar Peninsula. She later claimed to have dined with Jean Laffite on Galveston Island. The Longs returned to Alexandria, Louisiana, for their daughter on their way to New Orleans to seek support for Long's cause. Jane went on to Rodney, Mississippi, to get her daughter Ann, whom she had left with Anne Chesley, Jane's sister. Jane and Ann waited in Alexandria until Warren D. C. Hall came to guide her overland to Bolivar. Jane was not the only woman at Fort Las Casas on the peninsula. Several families remained there when Long left for La Bahía on 19 September

Jane Long. Prints and Photographs Collection, Jane Long file, CAH; CN 01351.

1821. Jane, pregnant, waited for him after the other families left Bolivar. After the birth of her third daughter in December, lonely and near starvation, Jane joined immigrants heading for the San Jacinto River early in 1822. Upon learning that her husband was dead, she traveled to San Antonio to seek a pension from Governor José Félix Trespalacios, her husband's former associate. She arrived on 17 October 1822 and remained 10 months without success before returning to Alexandria.

She returned to Texas with Alexander Calvit's family after the death of her youngest child on 25 June 1824 (another daughter had died previously). She received title to a league of land in Fort Bend County and a labor in Waller County from empresario Stephen F. Austin. She lived in San Felipe until April 1830, when she took Ann to school in Mississippi. In January 1831 Ann married Edward Winston; Jane returned to Texas with the newlyweds. In 1832 she bought a boardinghouse at Brazoria. In 1837 she moved to her league, a portion of which she had sold to Robert E. Handy, who developed the town of Richmond. Jane opened another boardinghouse and developed a plantation two miles south of town. She bought and sold land, raised cattle, and grew cotton with the help of slaves (twelve in 1840). Her plantation was valued at over $10,000 in 1850. By 1861 she held 19 slaves valued at $13,300 and about 2,000 acres. When the war ended, she continued to work the land with tenants and briefly experimented with sheep. In 1870 she lived by herself next door to Ann, who had married James S. Sullivan; Ann died in June, leaving the care of Jane to the grandchildren. By 1877 Jane was unable to manage her diminished estate, valued at only $2,000. She died at the home of her grandson, James E. Winston, and was buried in the Morton Cemetery in Richmond. Folklore and family tradition hold that Jane was courted by Texas's leading men, including Ben Milam, Sam Houston, and Mirabeau B. Lamar, but that she refused them all. Her history depends primarily on what she told Lamar about 1837, when he was gathering material for a history of Texas. *Margaret Swett Henson*

Longhorn Army Ammunition Plant. Beside Caddo Lake in Harrison County; also called the Longhorn Ordnance Works. In December 1941 the Monsanto Chemical Company selected the site for a facility for the manufacture of TNT, and the company began operation of the $22.5 million plant in 1942. By 15 August 1945 the plant had turned out 414,805,500 pounds of TNT. It closed in November 1945 and remained on standby until 1952, when it was reopened. It subsequently produced munitions and a variety of pyrotechnic devices under the management of the Universal Match Corporation until 1956. The Thiokol Chemical Corporation, awarded a contract in 1952 for producing solid-fuel rocket motors for the army, built a facility at Longhorn for that purpose between 1953 and 1955. Rocket motors of various kinds were produced at Longhorn until early 1971. The Vietnam War brought an increased demand for pyrotechnic devices, and the Longhorn plant resumed production of such items as flares and ground signals in the 1960s. In 1987 the plant continued to manufacture illuminating devices for the army under the direction of Thiokol, and employed some 962 workers. In 1989 LAAP was one of the sites selected to fire and destroy Pershing IA and II missiles under the terms of the Intermediate Nuclear Forces Treaty between the United States and the Soviet Union, a project completed in 1991. *Mark Odintz*

Longhorn Cattle. The principal cattle breed in frontier Texas. "A few old-timers," J. Frank Dobie wrote, "contend that both the horns and bodies of the Texas cattle were derived from importations from the States out of Longhorn Herefords of England," but he was convinced that the Texas longhorn was largely Spanish. Spanish cattle had roamed in Texas probably before the eighteenth century. Some cattlemen observed that not only the horns and bodies, but also the colors of many Texas longhorns resembled the English Bakewell stock brought from the Ohio valley and Kentucky. Criollo cattle are of solid color ranging from Jersey tan to cherry red. Black animals are few and brindles rare. Spanish and English cattle mixed on a small scale in the 1830s and after, but by the Civil War the half-wild Texas longhorns emerged as a recognizable type. Old males (four years old and older) had extremely long horns, and the large number of these animals in postwar trail herds produced the popular misconception that all Texas cattle had unusually long horns. In the 1880s, when younger cattle with improved blood were trailed north, the average horn spread was less than four feet.

After the Civil War, millions of Texas longhorns were driven to market. Herds were driven to Indian and military reservations in New Mexico and Arizona, and in 1867 Illinois cattle dealer Joseph G. McCoy arranged to ship cattle from Abilene, Kansas, to the Union Stockyards in Chicago. Over the next 20 years contractors drove 5 to 10 million cattle out of Texas, commerce that helped revive the state's economy. Longhorns, with their long legs and hard hoofs, were ideal trail cattle; they even gained weight on the way to market. After the buffalo herds were slaughtered and the Plains Indians confined in the late 1870s, private and syndicate ranches spread northward to the open range and free grass on the Great Plains. Texas longhorns, accompanied by Texas cowboys, stocked most of the new ranches; the trailing era made the cowboy a folk hero.

The "Big Die-Up" of 1886–87, together with the rapid spread of barbed wire fences, brought an abrupt end to the open-range cattle boom and with it the dominance of the longhorn. Fencing made possible controlled breeding, and with the end of free grass it was economically advisable to raise cattle that developed faster than longhorns. By this time ranchers had begun crossing longhorns with shorthorn Durhams and later with Herefords, thus producing excellent beef animals. Longhorns were bred almost out of existence; by the 1920s only a few small herds remained. In 1927 the Texas longhorn was saved from probable extinction by Will Barnes and other Forest Service men, when they collected a small herd of breeding stock in South Texas for the Wichita Mountains Wildlife Refuge in Oklahoma. A few years later J. Frank Dobie, with the help of former range inspector Graves Peeler and financial support from oilman Sid Richardson, gathered small herds for Texas state parks. After the wildlife-refuge herd had increased to several hundred, the Forest Service held annual sales of surplus animals. Cowmen at first purchased them as curiosities, then rediscovered the longhorn's longevity, resistance to disease, fertility, ease of calving, and ability to thrive on marginal pastures. Its growing popularity in beef herds was spurred by a diet-conscious population's desire for lean beef.

In 1964 Charles Schreiner III of the YO Ranch took the lead in organizing the Texas Longhorn Breeders Association of America, which maintains a registry in order to perpetuate the breed in a pure state. In the 1990s the official state Texas longhorn herd was kept at Fort Griffin State Historical Park. Other herds were located at Possum Kingdom State Recreation Area, Palo Duro Canyon State Scenic Park, Abilene State Park, Dinosaur Valley State Park, and Copper Breaks State Park. *Donald E. Worcester*

Longview, Texas. County seat of Gregg County, 125 miles east of Dallas in eastern Gregg and western Harrison counties. There was no significant settlement of the area until the 1840s and 1850s. What became Longview consisted of mostly hilly land in the southeast corner of Upshur County. Before the Civil War there were two rural communities in the area: Earpville in the east and Pine Tree in the west. Longview was founded in 1871 when the Southern Pacific Railroad extended its track from Marshall in Harrison County westward into Gregg County. The railroad bypassed Earpville and laid out a new town a mile to the west on land purchased from Ossamus Hitch Methvin, Sr. Railroad management called the new settlement Longview, reportedly because of the impressive view from Methvin's house, which was on what is now Center Street. Due to financial problems the Southern Pacific delayed further track construction for two years, and Longview became the western terminus of the railroad. A commercial district, composed of hastily built frame buildings, sprang up around the terminal. In 1871 Longview incorporated. Earpville disappeared from the map, but Pine Tree endured as a community, known successively as Awalt, Willow Springs, and finally as Greggton before being annexed by Longview in the 1960s. In its first years Longview was a rough railroad town; violence was common, and nearly half of the town's businesses were said to have been saloons. In 1872 the International Railroad built a connection between Longview and Palestine. The track joined the Southern Pacific about a mile east of the Longview depot, and the area became known as Longview Junction. A third railroad, the Longview and Sabine Valley, began construction from Longview Junction in 1877. As the railroads furthered the economic transformation of the region, seven new counties were established in northeastern Texas. In 1873 a county centered geographically and politically on Longview was proposed; it was to take pieces from Upshur, Rusk, and Harrison counties. Longview became the county seat. When the Rusk portion turned out smaller than hoped and the Harrison part proved unattainable, Longview was left very near one edge of a small and peculiarly shaped Gregg County. During the 1870s and early 1880s the town grew rapidly. Partly due to a major fire in 1877, the original frame buildings of the commercial center were replaced with structures of brick and stone. By 1882 the estimated population was 1,525.

Longview Junction was annexed to the city in 1904. From 1882 until after World War II the city's main industrial plant was the Kelly Plow Company. By 1910 the town had a population of 5,155. The Longview Electric Light and Power Company began supplying electricity around 1895, the first municipal waterworks was installed in 1904, and a sanitary sewer system was installed around 1910. In 1903 the Graham Manufacturing Company built a large crate and box factory for farm produce. In 1920 Longview was a rural cotton and lumbering center with an estimated 5,713 residents; African Americans made up 31 percent of the population. Racial tension led to the burning of black residences and businesses in the Longview Race Riot of 1919. During the 1920s a paved highway, later known as U.S. Highway 80, was built through the town. The Longview Chamber of Commerce, founded in 1916, promoted the city with an aggressive advertising campaign. A Rotary Club was organized in 1920. In 1926 Longview became the headquarters of the newly founded East Texas Chamber of Commerce. Due to railroad closings, the town's population fell to 5,036 in 1930. The discovery of the rich East Texas oilfield in the early 1930s, however, saved Longview from the severest effects of the Great Depression. Located several miles outside the oilfield, Longview was spared the worst aspects of boomtown chaos but was able to capitalize on its position as the established business center and governmental seat of Gregg County. The population more than doubled during the 1930s, to 13,758 in 1940. Burgeoning tax receipts allowed city and county officials to build numerous new government structures and schools, including a new county courthouse in 1932. In 1942 construction began on the Big Inch pipeline, which originated in Longview. From 1943 to 1945 this pipeline transported more than 261 million barrels of crude oil to the East Coast for refining. Concerted efforts to attract diversified industries to Longview during the war and for 20 years thereafter were led by newspaper publisher Carl Lewis Estes. During World War II the federal government built a large hospital complex, Harmon General Hospital, just outside of Longview. After the war, Robert G. LeTourneau opened a large manufacturing plant for earth-moving equipment, and he acted with other civic leaders to turn Harmon General Hospital into LeTourneau Technical Institute. In 1950 Eastman Kodak Company chose a site near Longview for its new subsidiary, Texas Eastman Company, which became the largest chemical complex in inland Texas. Other area develop-

ments during the immediate postwar period included Gregg County Airport and Lake Cherokee. In 1966 a Schlitz brewery and an associated container factory were built in Longview; the beer plant later became the Stroh Brewery, the largest in Texas, producing 4 million barrels annually. During the 1940s and 1950s the population of Longview grew steadily, from 24,502 in 1950 to 40,050 in 1960. More recently the Longview metropolitan area has spread east into Harrison County. The city population reached 45,547 in 1970 and 62,762 in 1980. In the early 1990s Longview was an important regional industrial and medical center. Its population in 1990 was 73,263. *Eugene W. McWhorter*

Los Adaes. The easternmost establishment in Spanish Texas for more than 50 years. Its primary purpose was to block French encroachment upon Spain's southwestern possessions. Including both San Miguel de Linares de los Adaes Mission and Nuestra Señora del Pilar Presidio, the settlement conformed to the Spanish practice of utilizing these frontier institutions in combination both to serve and to control local Indians. The mission at Los Adaes was founded by Domingo Ramón by 1717 but was abandoned in 1719 when threatened by the French. The reestablishment of the Spanish presence, near the location of present-day Robeline, Louisiana, occurred under the direction of the Marqués de Aguayo. His expedition established the presidio and reoccupied the mission at Los Adaes in 1721. Upon completing his task Aguayo left the continued enactment of Spanish frontier policy to a few Franciscans and 100 cavalry troops. In 1729 two decisions by Spanish authorities further defined the character of Los Adaes: it was designated the capital of Texas, and its garrison was reduced to 60 to lessen the expense of defending the Spanish frontier in North America. The reduction in the number of troops stationed at Los Adaes was encouraged by the absence of a local Indian threat. The Caddoan-speaking groups of the surrounding region, including the nearby Adaes Indians, were friendly. Indeed, these groups were inveterate enemies of the troublesome Lipan Apaches, who posed a constant threat to Spanish settlement farther west in Texas. Despite cordial relations with the local natives, however, the Franciscans at Los Adaes were unsuccessful in their attempt to resettle them at the mission. The ability of these Indians in their scattered hamlets to provide themselves with a constant food supply militated against the missionaries' efforts. In 1768 the Franciscan college in Zacatecas, which directed the missionary activities at Los Adaes, officially abandoned its labors in this region.

Los Adaes and the other Spanish settlements in East Texas composed a pocket of isolated Spanish settlement connected with New Spain only by a slender thread of overland communication. The major trail west, a *camino real*, was nothing more than a path, often blocked by swollen streams and hostile Indians. The Adaesans turned to the French at nearby Natchitoches, on the Red River in Louisiana, for assistance. Foods such as corn, beans, and wheat were supplied to the Spanish in significant quantities from this source. That the Spanish recognized the need for this trade is confirmed by the fact that they constantly relaxed restrictions on commerce in food. Though trade in other goods was prohibited, illicit commerce developed across the frontier in spite of the exertions of Spanish authorities. French trade items, which made up part of this commerce, were important elements in the Indian trade carried on by the inhabitants of Los Adaes. It is ironic that Los

Adaes, established to protect East Texas from French encroachment, found itself dependent upon the French settlement that it confronted. Aside from the military character of the garrison and the religious nature of the mission, a wide diversity of occupations existed at Los Adaes among the civilian populace. Included among these were cattle tending, woodcutting, blacksmithing, and domestic service. Many settlers were also involved in the deerskin trade with the Indians as well. The worst time for the Adaesans came in the mid-1730s. Crop failures, severe weather, and inadequate supplies from New Spain combined to produce a desperate state of affairs. Although the settlers did not experience such severe circumstances again, life at Los Adaes nevertheless continued to remain harsh.

The character of the East Texas borderlands was altered with the transfer of French Louisiana to Spain in 1762. Los Adaes now bordered on Spanish Louisiana. Prompted by these new circumstances, the Spanish government undertook a reorganization of the North American frontier following the design of the Marqués de Rubí. Acting on his recommendation, the Spanish crown issued the Royal Regulation of 1772, a decree by which Los Adaes was ordered abandoned and the capital of the province was transferred to San Antonio de Béxar. The inhabitants of Los Adaes were ordered removed to the San Antonio area. After painfully short notice in June 1773, a population estimated to number nearly 500 found itself uprooted. Despite official instructions, however, the Adaesans did not resettle at San Antonio. Instead, exhibiting an independent spirit nurtured by their experience on an isolated frontier, they returned to East Texas, where, after their disappointing stay in Bucareli, they established the permanent foundations for Nacogdoches.

James L. McCorkle, Jr.

Los Almagres Mine. An expedition seeking a site for an Apache mission in 1753 led to the discovery of Los Almagres Mine in what is now Llano County. Traversing the Central Mineral Region, Lt. Juan Galván heard from Indians of a *cerro de almagre*, a hill of red ocher, indicating the presence of mineral-bearing ores. Upon Galván's return to San Antonio, several men from that settlement were guided to the hill by Apaches in August 1753. No valuable ore was found, but interest in the hill containing gossan refused to die. Governor Barrios y Jáuregui, fearful that the use of Apache guides by unauthorized prospectors would arouse the Comanches, decided to send an official expedition. To lead it, he chose Bernardo de Miranda y Flores, who left San Antonio with 23 soldiers and citizens on 17 February 1756. After locating the *cerro de almagre* (now known as the Riley Mountains, a quarter league from Honey Creek), Miranda's men opened a shaft and found "a tremendous stratum of ore." They named the mine San José del Alcazar. So abundant were the ore veins, Miranda reported, that he guaranteed "a mine to each of the inhabitants of the province of Texas." Following Miranda's return to San Antonio on 10 March, Barrios sent a three-pound ore sample to the viceroy in Mexico City for assay, but the sample was deemed too small for accurate analysis. The assayer suggested that 30 mule-loads of the material be sent to Mazapil for further testing. Miranda sought a subsidy for extracting the thirty *cargas* of ore and for establishing a presidio at the site, with himself as captain, to protect the workers. His bid was not successful. In the meantime, the Apache mission and a presidio were established on the San Saba River near the site of present-day Menard. The presidio captain, Diego Ortiz Parrilla, seeking permission to move his garrison to Los Almagres to work the mine, obtained ore samples and smelted them at his post. He calculated a yield of 1½ ounces of silver from 75 pounds of ore. After destruction of the San Sabá Mission by hostile Indians in March 1758, Ortiz Parrilla was reassigned. The mine was never officially opened. Parrilla's interest, combined with Miranda's report, gave birth to an enduring legend. The slag heap the Spaniards left on the bank of the San Saba River when the presidio was abandoned a decade later fired the imagination of later treasure seekers, who supposed the mine to be in that area.

Interest in the mines continued to surface from time to time throughout the colonial period. Fray Diego Jiménez and Capt. Felipe de Rábago y Terán, Ortiz Parrilla's successor at San Sabá, proposed reestablishing the San Sabá Mission on the Llano River, so that the mineral veins might be worked. The Barón de Ripperdá, as governor, sent an expedition to examine the mines in 1778; ore samples were extracted and sent to the commandant-general of the Provincias Internas, Teodoro de Croix. In 1788–79 a French sojourner, Alexandre Dupont, extracted ore samples from the site and took them to Mexico for assay. He never returned. On the heels of his last visit, six prospectors from San Antonio were attacked at Los Almagres by Apaches. All but one were killed. Indian hostilities thereafter put a damper on such activity. Stephen F. Austin, on his first trip to Texas, heard from Erasmo Seguín that there was a rich silver mine on the San Saba River and a gold mine on the Llano. Hearing again in Mexico City of the unworked ore deposit called Los Almagres "in the territory of Sansava," he sent soldiers to inspect it. They probably went to the wrong place. In 1829 the mythical "lost" silver mine of San Sabá began appearing on Austin's maps. A year later, Henry S. Tanner borrowed Austin's designation for his own famous Texas map. Its wide distribution resulted in "a rash of maps showing silver mines near the old Spanish fort." Austin, doubtless realizing the value of the legend in attracting immigrants, repeated it in an 1831 promotional pamphlet. For years afterward it was mentioned in nearly every book about Texas.

James and Rezin Bowie, on their sallies into the Hill Country, reinforced the legend. Los Almagres was transformed into the "lost San Saba mine," then the "lost Bowie mine." After 1895 some prankster (presumably) appended the word *mine* to the Bowie name on the presidio's stone gatepost at Menard. Today, the legend is the focus of an annual Menard festival called Jim Bowie Days, which, like Austin's pamphlet, has a promotional intent.

The fact is that the Los Almagres mine that inspired the legend was at another location more than 70 miles away. In 1842 two Anglo-Texans found the old Spanish diggings on the *cerro de almagre* but associated them with neither the nearby Arroyo de los Almagres (Honey Creek) nor the legendary San Sabá mine. After the name Almagres was brought forth in a translation of Antonio Bonilla's summary of Texas history in 1904, Herbert Bolton obtained a copy of Miranda's journal from a Mexican archive. Miranda's route description led Bolton, accompanied by J. Farley of Dallas, to what had become known as the Boyd shaft on Honey Creek. Farley formed the Los Almagres Mining Company. In 1909 members of the United States Geological Survey visited the site, which they entered on a geologic map of Llano County. They described the mine as being unproductive. Bolton's claim of having found the lost San Sabá mine has not deterred the romantics. Among those who prefer an imaginative tale to historical fact, the search for the mythical lode goes on—in a region of non-mineral-bearing limestone. Fortunes and lives have been wasted in chasing the chimera. Ortiz Parrilla's slag heap left by the old presidio, coupled with Bolton's discovery, emphasizes the futility of their quest. *Robert S. Weddle*

Lost Battalion. The Second Battalion, 131st Field Artillery; a Texas unit of the Thirty-sixth Infantry Division. The battalion left Camp Bowie, Brown County, on 10 November 1941, and 11 days later boarded the United States Army transport *Republic* at San Francisco, bound for the Philippines. The *Republic* was sailing west of Hawaii on 7 December 1941, when the troops learned of the Japanese attack on Pearl Harbor. The convoy, still proceeding toward the Philippine Islands, which were under attack from another Japanese force, received orders to sail to Brisbane, Australia; the ships arrived there on 22 December. Six days later, the battalion was ordered to board a Dutch ship, the *Bloemfontein*, and sail to Surabaya, Java, to provide ground support for an army air force unit. The Texans arrived on 11 January 1942, the same day the Japanese began invading the Dutch islands. Initially, the battalion acted as ground crew for the Nineteenth Heavy Bombardment Group, which had been forced to leave its original support sections at Clark Field when fleeing the Philippines. When the bomb group was ordered to Australia, the Second Battalion was left in Java to support the morale of the people there. The unit earned the title "Lost Battalion" because they were not evacuated with other military forces. The Dutch surrendered the islands on 8 March 1942. The Japanese imprisoned the Texans, along with 5,500 British and Australian troops, at a camp called Tan Jong Priok, near Batavia. Five weeks later the battalion marched to a new prison known as Bicycle Camp, where they encountered the first of many acts of Japanese brutality. On 2 October 1942, nearly 200 battalion members were marched to a ship and transferred to Singapore. Nine days later most of the remaining members followed, and the group was reunited at Changi Barracks POW camp, formerly a British army post, before being shipped to Moulmein, Burma, on 11 January 1943. The Texans traveled by train to Thanbyuzayat, Burma, and immediately began work on the Japanese "Railroad of Death," which ultimately connected Burma to Bangkok, Siam. The unit labored in various work camps on the railroad, including the one at the famous "Bridge on the River Kwai," and suffered numerous casualties and deaths. Seventy thousand Allied prisoners of all nationalities perished on the railroad project. In 1944 the Japanese transferred some of the Texans to prison camps in Cambodia and Vietnam and others to Bangkok, where the survivors of the Second Battalion remained for the rest of the war. *E. R. Milner*

Lubbock, Francis Richard. Governor; b. Beaufort, South Carolina, 16 October 1815; d. Austin, 22 June 1905; m. Adele Baron (1835), Mrs. Sarah E. Black Porter (1883), and Lou Scott (1903). Lubbock worked in retail business before and after moving to Houston in 1836. He ranched, ran a general store, and served as comptroller of the Republic of Texas and as Harris County district court clerk (1841–57). He was elected lieutenant governor in 1857 but lost the office in 1859. He and other Southern delegates to the 1860 Democratic national convention walked out in protest against the party's nominee, Stephen A.

Governor Francis R. Lubbock. Prints and Photographs Collection, F. R. Lubbock file, CAH; CN 00912.

Douglas; Lubbock chaired the Southerners' convention in Richmond that nominated John C. Breckinridge. In 1861 he was elected governor of Texas by 124 votes. As governor he boosted the Confederacy and worked to improve the state's military capabilities by chairing the state military board (which sought to trade for military goods through Mexico), worked to establish a state foundry and percussion-cap factory, and supported Confederate conscription and the replacement of whites in manual labor by slaves (so that the whites could enlist in the army); he exempted frontier counties from the draft, however, so that their residents could protect against Indian attacks. After his term, Lubbock entered the military and served in several high positions, including aide-de-camp to Jefferson Davis. He fled Richmond with Davis at the end of the war, was captured in Georgia, and was kept in solitary confinement at Fort Delaware for eight months before being paroled. Back in Texas he dropped ranching, went into business in Houston and Galveston, and served as tax collector as well as state treasurer (1878–91). He subsequently remained in Austin. *Louis Mitchell*

Lubbock, Texas. County seat of Lubbock County and largest city on the South Plains; 327 miles northwest of Dallas and 122 miles south of Amarillo. Lubbock was founded as a part of the movement westward onto the High Plains of Texas by ranchers and farmers. More directly it was the result of a compromise between two groups of town promoters, one led by Frank E. Wheelock and the other by W. E. Rayner. In 1890 these groups abandoned their settlements, known respectively as Old Lubbock and Monterey, and agreed to combine into a new settlement. In 1876 the county had been named for Thomas S. Lubbock, former Texas Ranger and brother of Francis R. Lubbock, governor of Texas during the Civil War. As early as 1884 a federal post office called Lubbock existed at George W. Singer's store in Yellow House Canyon, in the northern part of the present-day city. One of the first orders of business of the town promoters was to circulate a petition for county organization. At the resulting election on 10 March 1891, Lubbock was duly elected county seat. Within three years the town had six lawyers and as many stores, a dentist, three land agents, a livery stable, two hotels, including the Nicolett, which had been moved across the canyon from the original settlement, and the county courthouse and jail. The town had little to distinguish it from scores of other rural settlements on the plains until 1909, when the Santa Fe sent its first train south from Plainview. Lubbock incorporated as a city in 1909 and by the census of 1910 had 1,938 residents. The population reached 4,051 by 1920. The first hospitals, West Texas Sanitarium and Lubbock Sanitarium, the predecessor of Methodist Hospital, appeared in 1917. In 1923 the legislature authorized the establishment of Texas Technological College, and Lubbock won the contest for its location. By this time the civic infrastructure was well in place. A city election in 1917 provided for a commission government to replace the mayor and city council. In 1916 the city council authorized the building of a city electrical plant, which in time evolved into Lubbock Power and Light. By 1930 Lubbock had three banks with deposits of more than $5 million. Much of the city's growth and prosperity depended on production from the surrounding rich agricultural area, which during the 1930s was turning increasingly to cotton and sorghum culture as irrigation increased rapidly. In 1930 Lubbock had some 67 wholesale outlets and an increasing number of manufacturing plants. By the 1980s it had 292 industrial establishments, including Texas Instruments, Gould's Pumps, Furr's Cafeterias, and Furr's, Incorporated. Lubbock was the wholesale trade center for 51 counties in West Texas and eastern New Mexico and the retail center for much of the same area. The city was also the world's leader in the cottonseed industry.

Lubbock, in an area once called "a treeless, desolate waste of uninhabited solitude," grew from a population of 1,938 in 1910 to 128,068 in 1960, and during the decade 1940–50 it was the second most rapidly growing city in the country, lagging behind only Albuquerque. In the 1980s Lubbock was the eighth largest city in Texas, with a population of 187,000. Of these 70 percent were Caucasian, 21 percent Hispanic, and 9 percent black. Texas Technological College became Texas Tech University in 1969 and a year later added its medical school, which grew into the Texas Tech University Health Sciences Center. Added to the city's seven hospitals with more than 2,000 beds, the Health Sciences Center made the city a leading medical center. Reese Air Force Base had by the 1980s become an important economic part of Lubbock, though in 1995 it was scheduled to be closed. Lubbock Christian College opened in September 1957 and was restructured and renamed Lubbock Christian University in 1987. Lubbock State School opened in 1969. The Lubbock Symphony Orchestra was founded in 1946, and the Lubbock Civic Ballet was founded in 1969. On 11 May 1970, the city center was devastated by a tornado that took 26 lives and caused more than $135

million damage. The city quickly drew itself together and built a civic center, a library, and other replacements. Lubbock is the home of the Museum of Texas Tech and the Ranching Heritage Center, 62 parks including Mackenzie State Recreation Area, three country clubs, and four public golf courses. An annual arts festival in April attracts large numbers of people, as do Las Fiestas Mexicanas and Juneteenth. The Lubbock Lake Site, an archeological site discovered in north Lubbock in 1936 near the site of Singer's store, has become internationally known for its unique and unbroken 11,000-year-old archeological record of early man. In 1988 it was designated the Lubbock Lake Landmark State Historical Site and subsequently the Lubbock Lake National Historic and State Archeological Landmark.

Lawrence L. Graves

Lubbock Christian University. A private four-year institution in Lubbock; emphasizes academic quality in a Christian environment and offers bachelor's degrees in 26 areas, including preprofessional programs in medicine, law, engineering, and social service. An agreement with Texas Tech University enables students to be enrolled in both schools concurrently. LCU began as a kindergarten in 1954 at the Broadway Church of Christ. After the church had established a Bible chair at Texas Tech, it decided to establish a Christian college by adding a grade a year through the college level. M. Norvel Young, the minister of the Broadway church, accelerated the plan by urging the Broadway elders to serve as the first board of trustees and to establish a junior college to begin in the fall of 1957. Lubbock Christian College first conducted classes in surplus military barracks purchased and moved from air force bases in Lubbock and Clovis, New Mexico. In 1972 the school graduated its first senior class. In 1987 it was renamed Lubbock Christian University. In 1974 the EPA granted $10 million to the university to recover and use Lubbock's sewage water. The university irrigates its own 4,000-acre farm near Wilson, and studies the effects of the water on soil, crops, and people. The project benefits the city of Lubbock, serves as a model for other cities in handling their effluent water, and helps finance the operation of the university. The LCU athletic fieldhouse is a former hangar used by the AEC in Los Alamos, New Mexico. The LCU athletic director took 18 students to Los Alamos and spent a summer disassembling the hangar and hauling it to Lubbock, in more than 150 truckloads. LCU bought the hangar from military surplus for $1,700 but spent about $200,000 to reassemble it. The university primarily enrolls members of the Church of Christ in West Texas and eastern New Mexico, though students from many states and foreign countries and from a variety of religions attend. *Carroll Burcham*

Lubbock State School. A school in Lubbock for the mentally retarded; opened in 1969. Lubbock State School serves a 52-county area in the Panhandle and South Plains. It has special treatment programs including speech therapy for all clients, an extensive recreational program, and a work program on campus for approximately 182 clients. By the early 1970s the school was able to accommodate over 600 students. From the beginning an outreach program was designed and operated to delay or prevent institutionalization of persons evaluated by the school's Diagnostic and Evaluation Center. Six communities aid the school with outreach programs. The school had 660 students in the early 1970s and 440 in 1993.

Lufkin, Texas. County seat of Angelina County, in the heart of the Piney Woods of East Texas. It was founded in 1882 as a stop on the Houston, East and West Texas Railway, when the line built from Houston to Shreveport, Louisiana, and named for Capt. Abraham P. Lufkin, a Galveston cotton merchant and city councilman, who was a close friend of HE&WT president Paul Bremond. Lufkin grew both because of its proximity to the railroad and because of the extensive lumber industry in the surrounding area. Soon after the railroad arrived, the company began to advertise the public sale of town lots. At the same time, many of the business firms and professionals from nearby Homer began to move to Lufkin to be nearer the railroad. Early stores were located on Cotton Square, which soon became the center of activity for the town. Lufkin acquired a post office in 1882 and a telegraph line in 1883. The town was incorporated in 1890. Even before its incorporation, Lufkin had sought to move the county courthouse, still situated at Homer, to the railroad settlement, but by an election in 1885 it stayed at Homer. In November 1891, however, a mysterious fire destroyed the courthouse, and one day later the county commissioners received a petition from Lufkin citizens asking for a new election to decide if the courthouse should be in Lufkin. When the election was held on 2 January 1892, Lufkin won. Much of the economic prosperity of early Lufkin was tied to three lumbering families: the Kurths, Hendersons, and Wieners. In 1890 they organized the Angelina County Lumber Company, which became the forerunner of many innovations in lumber manufacturing and forest management in East Texas. At the height of their activity, the three families were involved in nearly a dozen Texas sawmills, a paper mill, foundries, hotels, movie theaters, railroads, investment companies, newspapers, radio and television stations, insurance firms, banks, hospitals, and many other enterprises. Two of the city's principal industries, Southland Paper Mills (now St. Regis) and Texas Foundries, were begun as hometown companies in the late 1930s and were responsible for much of the city's industrial growth. The largest industrial employer, Lufkin Foundry and Machine Company (now Lufkin Industries), was also founded as a hometown company in 1902 and achieved worldwide fame for its oilfield pumping units. Between 1965 and 1983 Lufkin built a new library, two new museums, a civic center, a new federal building, a junior college, a new country club, and two major shopping malls; the city also made widespread improvements in its ISD and parks. In 1982 Lufkin celebrated its centennial with an extensive beautification effort and by building the largest exposition center between Dallas and Houston. Though the economy was still linked significantly to the harvesting of timber and the manufacture of lumber, paper, plywood, and other forest products, by 1990 the city had also developed a diversified economic base, including the manufacture of oilfield pumping units, machinery and gears, truck trailers and flooring, foundry products, candy, dairy products, and recreational goods. Lufkin also emerged in the 1970s as a regional trade center and developed a significant tourist and convention economy, largely because of its proximity to Sam Rayburn Reservoir and hunting lands. In 1990 the population was 30,206. *Bob Bowman*

LULAC. The League of United Latin American Citizens; a national organization of Texas origin, founded in 1929 at Corpus Christi. LULAC was organized to fight for the civil rights of Mexican Americans. It merged the Corpus Christi council of the Sons of America, the Alice council of the Sons of America, the Knights of America, and the Latin American Citizens League in the Rio Grande valley and Laredo. Its original name, United Latin American Citizens, was changed to League of United Latin American Citizens at the constitutional convention in May 1929. The first president of LULAC was Bernardo (Ben) F. Garza. The major architects of the LULAC constitution were José Tomás Canales, Eduardo Idar, and Alonso S. Perales. Though the 1929 constitution proclaimed English the official language of the league, the organization promoted bilingualism. In 1931 the league obtained its charter. Members were typically skilled laborers and small-business owners, though a handful of lawyers played a crucial role. The 1949 constitution opened membership to Caucasians, and in 1986 any person living in the United States was permitted membership, a change intended to include Mexican immigrants. Mexicans were always honorary members, but, in the case of Felix Tijerina and Raoul Cortez, national presidents. In 1991, LULAC membership typically included government and lower-level corporate employees. Chapters have also been organized by college students. Women have played an important role in LULAC as both members and nonmembers. They attended the 1929 constitutional convention as interested wives and family members, and by 1991 they constituted half of the LULAC membership. Notable women in LULAC have included Alice Dickerson Montemayor, Esther Nieto Machuca, and Adela Sloss Vento. Texas LULAC has no permanent state headquarters because of the lack of a solid financial base and the annual changes in leadership. In 1991 LULAC had a state director, district directors, and autonomous local councils. LULAC has played a role in the formation of several other organizations. It gave rise to La Liga Pro-Defensa Escolar (the School Improvement League) in San Antonio, and formed a veterans' committee to address the rights of G.I.'s before LULAC member Hector P. Garcia organized the American G.I. Forum. LULAC members instituted the Little School of the 400, the model for the federal educational program Head Start. In 1964 LULAC helped start the SER—Jobs for Progress, Incorporated, the largest employment agency for Hispanics in the United States. Later, LULAC members helped secure a grant from the Ford Foundation that started MALDEF (the Mexican American Legal Defense and Educational Fund).

LULAC has been heavily involved in school desegregation efforts as well as other education measures, including scholarship funds. Direct political involvement by LULAC members has included the organization of poll tax drives at the local level from the 1930s until the mid-1960s, when the League advocated abolishing these taxes. League members have fought for appointment of Mexican Americans to important federal and state positions and were also active in Viva Kennedy–Viva Johnson Clubs and in PASSO (the Political Association of Spanish-Speaking Organizations). In immigration matters, LULAC played a major role in the banning of *braceros* from Texas because they were exploited, and supported Operation Wetback (1954). In numerous other ways, LULAC has worked for the advancement of Hispanics. LULAC ideology has historically encompassed liberalism, individualism, and support of free-market capitalism; anticommunism and United States patriotism have also been central. In 1974 the LULAC Foundation was established and LULAC began receiving corporate contributions. The success and longevity of LULAC can also be attributed to effective communication. From

1931 through the 1970s the league published the *LULAC News*, and before 1940 it sponsored the publications *Lulac Notes*, *El Defensor*, *Alma Latina*, and *El Paladín*, all in Texas.

Cynthia E. Orozco

Lumber Industry. Lumber has been manufactured in Texas since the early nineteenth century. Records exist of a number of sawmills, both near the Gulf coast and inland, during the two decades before the Texas Revolution. These were sash mills consisting of a single blade held in a frame and powered by water, animals, or eventually steam, laboriously producing crude lumber one board at a time at a rate of 500 to 1,200 board feet a day. In 1829 John Richardson Harris planned what was perhaps the first steam sawmill in Texas, but he died before completing the project. His brothers William and David, with Robert Wilson, completed the mill, which operated with success at least until 1833. Antonio López de Santa Anna's troops destroyed it in 1836. After the revolution the increasing demand for lumber encouraged the development of sawmills along the Gulf Coast at Houston, Galveston, Beaumont, and Orange. In the interior of the state a number of mills served local needs in Bastrop, Cherokee, Nacogdoches, Rusk, and San Augustine counties. The 1860 census reported some 200 sawmills in Texas with about 1,200 employees, which manufactured lumber valued at $1.75 million annually. A considerable turpentine and barrel-stave industry had also developed in East Texas. At the end of the Civil War a number of operators built larger mills featuring circular saws that could cut more than 25,000 board feet of lumber a day. Yet in comparison to that of leading lumber states, Texas production was small; the state reported less than 100 million board feet in 1869 and only 300 million a decade later. Until this time most of the pine forest of East Texas remained untouched. Travelers remarked on the magnificent pine stands, the parklike, clean forest floor, and the individual trees often growing to 150 feet in height and measuring more than five feet in diameter.

The next 50 years, from about 1880 to the Great Depression, has been called the "bonanza era" in Texas lumbering. The railroad network developed rapidly and provided transportation to every section of East Texas. Entrepreneurs followed closely behind, establishing complete lumber-manufacturing plants and often tram roads to carry the logs to the mills and transport the finished lumber to mainline railroads. To provide for the employees, often numbering several hundred, the owners also built company towns such as Camden, Fostoria, Kirbyville, and Diboll. In the isolated areas of East Texas, the mill owner was like a feudal baron dominating the lives of his workers and their families. In many operations the company paid the workers not in cash but in merchandise checks, scrip, or tokens that were worth face value only at the commissary or company offices. Thus the dependence of the worker upon the company was nearly absolute. These conditions began to change after World War I, as the automobile and improved communications provided mill workers with more links to the outside world.

Lumbermen Henry Lutcher and G. Bedell Moore moved from Pennsylvania to Orange in 1877 and built the first "big mill," with a daily capacity of 80,000 to 100,000 board feet. For the next half century, Lutcher and Moore set a high standard for quality lumber, advanced technology, and leadership in civic projects. Soon afterward, such lumbermen as John Martin Thompson, Joseph H. Kurth, Sr., Thomas L. L. Temple, W. T.

Carter, and W. T. Joyce built complete sawmill plants, supported by thousands of acres of virgin pinelands purchased at bargain prices, and established themselves as major manufacturers. John Henry Kirby, an East Texas farm boy, rose to become the largest lumber manufacturer in Texas by combining some 14 sawmills into the Kirby Lumber Company in 1901. He also organized the Houston Oil Company to hold the mineral, timber, and surface rights to a million acres in Southeast Texas. So widespread were his activities that the press referred to him as "Prince of the Pines." His name became known throughout the nation, and he held a number of important industry and government positions.

For the Texas worker the early lumber industry was one of long hours, low pay, and frequent accidents. The United States census bureau listed logging and sawmilling as among the most hazardous of occupations. Until 1913, when the Texas legislature established a workmen's compensation system, any payment for job-related injuries depended on the personal policy of the mill owner or a successful suit in the courts. Hours of labor averaged 11 a day until about 1900, 10 until World War I, and 9 until World War II. Employers classed most of their workers as common laborers and paid wages averaging $1.50 to $2.50 per day from around 1900 until the early 1920s. Only a few skilled employees—sawyers, edgermen, trimmers, planers, and saw filers at the mill, and fallers, scalers, loaders, skidder operators and railroad personnel in the woods—earned more than common laborers' wages.

Though their grievances were obvious and their wage scale below that of other industries, lumber workers failed repeatedly to organize effective unions to bargain collectively for their advancement. This was partly due to disunity within the workforce. Skilled and unskilled workers failed to cooperate, and racial tensions divided the lumber workers. The mill owners also discouraged labor organization. They formed trade associations such as the Southern Pine Association and the Southern Lumber Operators Association to promote their own interests and block the formation of unions, especially the Brotherhood of Timber Workers. In these goals they were uniformly successful until the era of the New Deal.

Many lumbermen such as Robert A. Long of Long–Bell, Charles Keith of the Central Coal and Coke Company, and W. A. Pickering pursued a cut-out-and-get-out policy, cutting all marketable timber and moving on to a new region, fully expecting that the cut-over area would be converted into farms. Conservationists led by W. Goodrich Jones, a Temple banker, argued that much of the East Texas land was good for growing pine trees and not much else. They demanded that the lumber companies follow a program of selective cutting, sustained yield, and reforestation. To promote these aims, Jones organized the Texas Forestry Association in 1914 and successfully lobbied to have the state legislature establish a state department of forestry the next year. This agency, later renamed the Texas Forest Service, promoted fire prevention and reforestation on public and private lands alike, with increasingly good results.

The Texas lumber industry grew rapidly and in 1907 reported an annual cut of more than 2.25 billion board feet of lumber (third largest in the United States), a figure that has remained a record for the state. During World War I Texas lumbermen cooperated with the United States Shipping Board's effort to build wooden ships for freight transport. The war ended, however, before most of the "pine-built" vessels were completed. In

Thompson and Ford Company's new sawmill, Sour Lake, ca. 1907–08. Courtesy East Texas Research Center, Ralph W. Steen Library, Stephen F. Austin State University. A steam sawmill was in operation in Texas as early as 1829, but lumbering did not reach its peak in the state until 1907, when mills in the state sawed 2,229,590,000 board feet.

the 1920s lumbering declined, as many companies exhausted their timber holdings and ceased operations. The Great Depression accelerated this trend, and production fell to 350 million board feet in 1932, the lowest since 1880. During the 50-year "bonanza" period, lumbermen had logged about 18 million acres of pine timber and produced some 59 billion board feet of lumber. Most of the virgin pine had been cut, and many operators had moved to new locations, often to the Pacific coast, leaving vast cut-over areas behind them.

Under the New Deal program of President Franklin D. Roosevelt, Texas lumbermen participated in the drafting and administration of the National Recovery Administration fair-practice lumber code during the brief life of the NRA. The CCC fought forest fires, cleared underbrush, and planted pine seedlings in the state forests and other public lands. The federal government purchased more than 600,000 acres of cut-over land and established four Texas national forests. On these and other lands the United States Forest Service and the Texas Forest Service began the long-term task of developing a vigorous second-growth forest that would provide timber, recreation areas, and an improved wildlife habitat for the next generation of Texas citizens. Slowly, timber production increased to predepression levels, so that by 1940 the state again reported an annual cut of more than a billion board feet. The same decade saw the first

successful production of newsprint from southern yellow pine. After Georgia chemist Charles Holmes Herty had developed a satisfactory experimental newsprint pulp in his laboratory, he interested Ernest L. Kurth, Arthur Temple, Sr., and others in establishing a commercial venture to produce newsprint for southern newspapers. This group built the Southland Paper Mills at Lufkin, which began operation in 1940. Thus began an important new industry that spread to other parts of the South. Also, timber growers had a profitable new market for their pine trees.

The generation after World War II saw a revolution in the Texas lumber industry. The introduction and widespread adoption of the log debarker opened the door for the production of a variety of wood products and the utilization of much more of the total tree. Texas pine now went into laminated beams and other engineered wood products such as particle boards, fiber boards, and wood flour, plus a myriad of paper products and newsprint. In 1964 Arthur Temple, Jr., of the Southern Pine Lumber Company, and the United States Plywood Corporation joined in producing the first plywood from southern yellow pine. Within 10 years plywood became a major export of the Texas lumber industry. The new diversification of the forest products industry greatly increased the demand for trained foresters. Before 1946 no Texas institution offered a forestry program, although the

Enchanted Rock (Scene near Fredericksburg), by Hermann Lungkwitz, 1864. Oil on canvas. 14" × 20". Courtesy Witte Museum, San Antonio. The "granite mountains" and river valleys of the Texas Hill Country were Hermann Lungkwitz's favorite subjects. He painted in the Romantic tradition of other American landscape artists.

state forester had taught some courses at the Texas A&M before 1921. In 1946 Stephen F. Austin State College organized a department of forestry under the direction of W. Robert Owens, who had been trained at Duke University. The program grew to become the Texas School of Forestry, which offers both undergraduate and graduate training, including the Ph.D. In 1937 Texas A&M again authorized forestry courses to be taught in its College of Agriculture, but not until 1969 did the institution establish a department of forest science. In addition to training young men and women for positions in government and the forest-products industry, the faculties of the two universities conduct valuable research on the problems of Texas forests.

The postwar generation also witnessed a significant change in the pattern of mill and forest-land ownership. Almost without exception, the traditional family-owned lumber company gave way to a national or international multipurpose corporation with no local roots. The International Paper Company took over the holdings of the Frost Lumber Industries, Owens–Illinois acquired the Angelina County Lumber Company, Champion Paper purchased the W. T. Carter and Brother Lumber Company, and a subsidiary of Boise Cascade bought out the Lutcher and Moore Lumber Company. The Kirby Lumber Company became a wholly owned subsidiary of the Atchison, Topeka, and Santa Fe Railway, and the Southland Paper Mills

became part of the St. Regis Paper Company. Temple–Eastex, a consolidation of the Temple properties, merged with the Time–Life Corporation. With the announced retirement of Arthur Temple, Jr., in 1983, the last of the great Texas lumber families passed from active management roles in the industry that they helped found.

The Texas lumber industry continues to be a large and important contributor to the state economy. But relatively, the industry's status is far below its dominant position at the beginning of the twentieth century. Then it was the state's largest manufacturing enterprise, first among Texas industries in generating income, and the largest employer of labor in the Lone Star State. In 1991 loggers cut 460,848,865 cubic feet of pine and 104,527,642 cubic feet of hardwood to produce an estimated 1,134,100,000 board feet of lumber. Employment in 1992 was 31,100 in sawmills, logging camps, lumber, and wood production, 9,700 in planing mills, and 25,200 in paper and allied products.

Robert S. Maxwell

Lungkwitz, Hermann. Painter and photographer; b. Halle-an-der-Saale, a Prussian province of Saxony, 14 March 1813; d. Austin, 10 February 1891; ed. Royal Academy of Fine Arts, Dresden, under Adrian Ludwig Richter. The academy awarded Lungkwitz a certificate of achievement for a view of the Elbe

River in 1843. Thereafter, he made three annual summer sketching tours of the Austrian Salzkammergut and Upper Bavarian Alps. Through the remainder of the 1840s he may have worked as a professional artist in Dresden. He and his family immigrated to the United States in 1850, perhaps as a result of Lungkwitz's involvement in the revolution of 1848–49 and the unsuccessful insurrection against the Saxon king in May 1849. By way of New York City and Wheeling, Virginia (now West Virginia), Lungkwitz and his party, including his artist brother-in-law, Friedrich Richard Petri, reached Texas in 1851. The next year they settled on a farm near Fredericksburg, where Lungkwitz remained until 1864. He and Petri could not support their families by painting, so they resorted to cattle raising and farming on the Hill Country frontier. After Petri's death in 1857, Lungkwitz learned photography, a profession that he followed in San Antonio with Carl G. von Iwonski from 1866 until 1870. He then moved to Austin, where he was photographer for the General Land Office under his brother-in-law, commissioner Jacob Kuechler. He remained at this position until the end of Governor E. J. Davis's Republican administration in 1874. During his tenure in the land office his daughter Martha was appointed clerk and thus became probably the first woman employee of the state of Texas. During the 1870s and the 1880s Lungkwitz taught drawing and painting in the German–English schools run in Austin by his son-in-law Jacob Bickler. He also worked on the sheep ranch of his daughter Eva Klappenbach near Johnson City and gave private art lessons in Austin and Galveston, where he periodically visited the Bicklers after they moved there in 1887.

Of approximately 350 of Lungkwitz's extant works, the majority are pencil and oil studies from Europe. His Texas studies and landscape paintings—of the Hill Country, old San Antonio and its Spanish missions, and Austin—span four decades and provide unexcelled examples of romantic landscape scenes and visual documentation of nineteenth-century Texas. In addition, two pre–Civil War lithographs (*Dr. Ernest Kapp's Water-Cure, Comal County, Texas* and *Friedrichsburg, Texas*) and one postwar lithograph (*San Antonio de Bexar*) have been identified. Lungkwitz first did careful fine-line drawings out-of-doors, then finished the paintings in his studio, often on commission. Enchanted Rock, Bear Mountain, and other promontories north of Fredericksburg, which Lungkwitz called the granite mountains, and the Guadalupe, Pedernales, Llano, and Colorado valleys were his favorite subjects. Luminosity and bright earth colors are typical of his detailed, carefully worked compositions. Romantic in treatment and feeling, his Texas paintings reflect his training at the Dresden academy. Lungkwitz was virtually forgotten for a generation after his death, but his works, along with those of Richard Petri, have been exhibited in Texas museums and universities since the 1930s. Significant examples of their art can be found at the Texas Memorial Museum, University of Texas at Austin; the Museum of Fine Arts, Houston; the Amon Carter Museum, Fort Worth; and the San Antonio Museum of Art.   *James Patrick McGuire*

Lynching. *Lynching* originally denoted illegal punishment generally, though the term was narrowed in time to denote hanging. In the South and Southwest it is hard to estimate the frequency of lynchings before the 1880s. It seems, however, that they occurred only sporadically before 1865, and were usually the result of "frontier justice" dispensed in areas where formal legal systems did not exist. In antebellum Texas, vigilantes perpetrated most lynchings. The captured offender was "tried" before a mock judge and jury. Convictions most often resulted in whipping, followed by expulsion from the community, but at least 17 vigilante organizations resorted to the noose, claiming some 140 lives. The earliest of these groups, the Shelby County Regulators of 1840–44, killed at least 10 people during the Regulator–Moderator War. The San Saba County lynchers, the deadliest of the lot, claimed some 25 victims between 1880 and 1896. Vigilante lynching died out in the 1890s, but other varieties of mobs continued. It is unknown when the first of the non-vigilante lynch mobs appeared in Texas, but certainly they increased in frequency with the approach of the Civil War. In the five years preceding the war, mobs frequently sought out suspected slave rebels and white abolitionists. The most serious outbreak of this sort occurred in North Texas in 1860, when rumors of a slave insurrection led to the lynching of an estimated 30 to 50 slaves and possibly more than 20 whites. The war subsequently inured people to violence, until war-generated tensions produced the greatest mass lynching in the history of the state, the Great Hanging at Gainesville. The use of organized terror by lynch mobs appeared in Texas during Reconstruction as the Ku Klux Klan and similar organizations resorted to violent methods of restoring white supremacy. The humiliation of defeat, increasing idleness and violence, mistrust of all levels of government, alteration of the traditional racial order, and fear of violence by blacks all contributed to an outbreak of lynch-mob activity and instilled in some whites a belief in a "right to lynch."

Immediately after Reconstruction, lynch law evidently declined somewhat, but it soon increased again. Mobs began removing suspects from legal custody, sometimes with the cooperation of legal authorities. In 1885 an estimated 22 mobs lynched 43 people, including 19 blacks and 24 whites, one of whom was female. After this the number of lynching victims generally decreased, dropping to 5 in 1893, but increased again to 26 in 1897. The number of victims continued to decline (to 23 in 1908 and 15 in 1909) until 1915, when there were 32. The 1915 figure, which is probably an underestimate, reflected an increase in racial hostility that accompanied the spread of Jim Crow laws and border troubles growing out of the Mexican Revolution. In 1922, 13 mobs claimed 15 victims. After this there was a sharp decline; 1925 was the first lynching-free year. The Sherman Riot in 1930, however, was a notable example of racial violence committed by a mob. After 1930 there was never more than one mob a year. Six years without a lynching preceded the final clear-cut case, the lynching of accused rapist William Vinson at Texarkana on 13 July 1942. Texas stands third among the states, after Mississippi and Georgia, in the total number of lynching victims. Of the 468 victims in Texas between 1885 and 1942, 339 were black, 77 white, 53 Hispanic, and 1 Indian. Half of the white victims died between 1885 and 1889, and 53 percent of the Hispanics died in the 1915 troubles. Between 1889 and 1942 charges of murder or attempted murder precipitated at least 40 percent of the mobs; rape or attempted rape accounted for 26 percent. Blacks were more likely to be lynched for rape than were members of other groups, although even among blacks murder-related charges accounted for 40 percent of the lynchings and rape for only 32 percent. All but 15 of the 322 lynching incidents that have a known locality occurred in the eastern half of the state.

Texans also made important contributions to the antilynching movement. Part of this was unintentional: the gruesome and widely publicized 1893 torture-burning of Henry Smith before an assembly of thousands at Paris helped galvanize the infant anti-lynching movement into action. Jessie Ames of Georgetown founded and served as president of the Association of Southern Women for the Prevention of Lynching, the most effective anti-lynching group in the country. The legislature passed an anti-lynching law in 1897, governors called out the Texas Volunteer Guard to help defend prisoners on numerous occasions, and local officers sometimes went to great lengths to protect their prisoners. *John R. Ross*

Lynch's Ferry. Located at the site of Lynchburg, where the main land route from South Texas to the Mexican border crosses the San Jacinto River below the mouth of Buffalo Bayou; built in 1822 by Nathaniel Lynch. The ferry, a flatboat hand-pulled by a rope, was one of numerous conveyances on the waterways of southern Harris County. In 1830 Lynch received an operating license from the ayuntamiento of San Felipe. When General Santa Anna hoped to cut off the retreat of the Texas army across Lynch's Ferry in April 1836, local residents fled the approaching Mexican army in the Runaway Scrape. Dilue Rose Harris later recalled waiting three days at the ferry with 5,000 others. Lynch bequeathed the ferry to his family, and it was later sold to a series of operators. In 1837 the Harris County Commissioners Court set ferry rates, and in 1890 the ferry operated free for the first time. In 1949 a ferry operating at the same site across the Houston Ship Channel was called the Lynchburg Ferry. Twenty-five miles below the turning basin, today's ferry connects the Crosby–Lynchburg Road below the San Jacinto River mouth with the midpoint between the Washburn and Baytown–La Porte tunnels, which handle the majority of auto traffic. *Diana J. Kleiner*

Lyndon Baines Johnson Library and Museum. On the campus of the University of Texas at Austin; completed in 1971 and dedicated the next year. It was the nation's fifth presidential library and the first to be located on a university campus. It serves as a center for scholarly research and a historical museum. More than 30 million pages of manuscripts, mostly papers of President Johnson, formed the original core of the research collection. Added to the Johnson papers were those of Lady Bird Johnson and many of Johnson's contemporaries and associates. The library continues to gather these materials. It is operated by the National Archives and Records Administration. The Lyndon B. Johnson School of Public Affairs, established in relation to the library, is under the administration of UT. The school is located in a building beside the library. In the early 1990s the library and museum underwent a major renovation project. At that time the LBJ Library and Museum had more than 400,000 visitors a year. In 1995 the library housed 45 million pages of historical documents.

M

McAllen, Texas. Sixteen miles west of Weslaco in southern Hidalgo County. It is situated on land that was part of *porciones* 63 and 64, granted respectively by Spain to Antonio Gutiérrez and Juan Antonio Villareal in 1767. Gutiérrez and his heirs inhabited the land at least until 1883, and Villareal's heirs lived on his land for at least 50 years prior to 1852. The Santa Anita Ranch was established around 1797 by José Manuel Gómez, who received a grant from Spain in 1800. He raised cattle, sheep, goats, and horses on his ranch and helped to continue colonizing the area. His great-granddaughter Salomé Ballí, who inherited the land in the early 1800s, married John Young, a Brownsville businessman, about 1848. They proceeded to acquire land in the surrounding area, and in 1852 Young applied for *porciones* 64 and 65 in southern Hidalgo County. Young died in 1859, leaving his holdings to his widow and son, John J. Young, with John McAllen, Young's assistant, as manager. McAllen married Salomé Ballí de Young in 1861, and in 1862 they had a son, James Ballí McAllen. They continued adding land to the ranch, which was renamed McAllen Ranch. The site of present-day McAllen was within the ranch's boundaries. By 1903 there were scattered ranches in the area, and in March of that year the Hidalgo Irrigation Company was organized. On 20 August 1904 the Hidalgo and San Miguel Extension (now the Sam Fordyce Branch) of the St. Louis, Brownsville and Mexico Railway reached the Santa Anita Ranch. John McAllen and his son James donated land to have the railroad cross their land. On 5 December the McAllen Townsite Company was formed by Uriah Lott, Leonidas C. Hill, Sr., John McAllen, James Ballí McAllen, and John J. Young. The new community, which was named for John McAllen, had the depot nearest to the county seat, Hidalgo, eight miles to the south. That year the community also had a general store owned by Manuel Samano and a restaurant as well as a cluster of eight or nine tents. In 1907 a post office named McAllen was established. The new community did not grow very rapidly and was endangered by a competing community that was established in 1907 two miles east by William Briggs, O. E. M. Jones, and John Closner. The second town came to be known as East McAllen. By 1908 the Rio Bravo Irrigation Company was finishing a canal to East McAllen and a hardware store and furniture store were under construction there. East McAllen also had five stores, two taverns, and two lumberyards and an estimated population of 300. Around 1909 W. E. Stuart constructed the town's first brick building, the First State Bank building, and the town's first newspaper, the McAllen Monitor, began. By 1911, 5,000 acres was under cultivation in East McAllen with produce consisting of cotton, alfalfa, broom corn, citrus fruits, grapes, and figs. East McAllen had an estimated population of 1,000 that year, and West McAllen had ceased to exist. In 1911 the town applied for and was issued a charter of incorporation under the name McAllen.

In 1916, 20,000 soldiers were stationed at McAllen to help with border disturbances. The resulting economic boom increased the population from 1,200 in 1916 to 6,000 in 1920. As the local economy shifted from a Hispanic-dominated ranching economy to an Anglo-dominated farming economy, Mexican Americans were increasingly segregated. Schools in McAllen were segregated through the fifth grade; Mexican children were not expected to go beyond that level. Not until the late 1920s were segregated junior and senior high schools established. Hispanics were also segregated in the hospital. McAllen adopted a home rule charter in 1927. Canning factories, a winery, tortilla plants, wood-working plants, and some oil exploration increased the population to 9,074 by 1930. In 1936 Hiram Garner opened the Valley Distillery, which produced wines from citrus juices. Between 1937 and 1942 the United States Farm Security Administration and the Farm Placement Service of Texas established a camp in what is now east central McAllen. It was constructed as housing for migrant agricultural workers and to facilitate the hiring of workers by farmers. The town was a petroleum and farm center with a population of 11,877 in 1940, by which time it had adopted the nickname City of Palms. In 1941 a suspension bridge replaced the old bridge to Reynosa, Tamaulipas; the new toll bridge was purchased by the city and was officially called the McAllen–Hidalgo–Reynosa International Bridge. Its construction resulted in an increased tourist trade that made McAllen a winter resort and port of entry to Mexico. Oil discovered in the Reynosa area in 1947 resulted in a large migration of people from the Mexican interior that constituted a new tourist market and cheap labor supply for McAllen. The sister cities were linked as a result of the increased traffic between them. The population of McAllen was 20,005 in 1950 and 32,728 in 1960. McAllen was an agricultural, oil, and tourist center in 1970, when the city had 37,636 residents, a 200-bed hospital and a new air-conditioned high school, the first school in the nation featuring on-site power generated by natural-gas-powered turbines. During the late 1980s the McAllen Foreign Trade Zone was an important general-purpose foreign trade zone. The city remained one of the top three ports of entry to the United States from Mexico in the 1990s. McAllen celebrates several annual events, including the Candlelight Posada, held in Archer Park in early December, the Fourth of July Fajita Cookoff, the Texas Citrus Fiesta, Springfest!, Borderfest, and the Annual Texas Square Dance Jamboree. The population was 84,021 in 1990, when McAllen had more than 2,000 businesses. McAllen is bordered on all sides by colonias of varying sizes, inhabited primarily by agricultural workers.						*Alicia A. Garza*

McCallum, Jane. Suffragist and Texas secretary of state; b. Jane Yelvington, La Vernia, Texas, 30 December 1877; d. Austin, 14 August 1957 (buried in Oakwood Cemetery); m. Arthur Newell McCallum, Sr. (1896); 5 children; ed. Dr. Zealey's Female College, Mississippi (1892–93), University of Texas (1912–15). The McCallums moved around in Texas until Arthur became school superintendent in Austin, a post he held for 39 years (1903–42). Mrs. McCallum entered politics by campaigning for prohibition and woman suffrage. In 1915 the Austin Women's Suffrage Association elected her president. She also teamed with Minnie Cunningham, president of the Texas Equal Suffrage Association,

Secretary of State Jane Y. McCallum (at the podium) presides over the opening of the Texas legislature, Austin, 1933. Courtesy Woman's Collection, Texas Woman's University, Denton. Former "Petticoat Lobby" leader Jane McCallum was the only secretary of state who held the position under two governors and for more than two terms, serving seven years.

in leading statewide campaigns for suffrage. She spoke in public and wrote a suffrage column that appeared in the Austin *American* and later the Austin *Statesman*. During World War I, as women's chairman of the fourth Liberty Loan Drive, she led Austin women in raising nearly $700,000 for the war effort. After suffrage was won she concentrated on political reforms. She was state publicity chairman for the Education ("Better Schools") Amendment to the Texas constitution (1920). She also headed publicity efforts for the League of Women Voters of Texas and served a term as first vice president. From 1923 to 1925 she served as executive secretary of the Women's Joint Legislative Council, a coalition of six statewide women's organizations that lobbied for education bills, prison reform, stronger prohibition controls, maternal and child health funds, and eradication of illiteracy and child labor. Known as the "Petticoat Lobby," the coalition became an important lobbying group of the era. Jane McCallum was also a member of the Texas Committee on Prisons and Prison Labor. In 1926 she led the Petticoat Lobbyists in campaigning for Dan Moody's gubernatorial bid against Ma Ferguson. Moody appointed her secretary of state in January

1927, and she retained the position under Governor Ross Sterling from 1931 to 1933; she was thus the only person in Texas to hold the position under two governors and for more than two terms. Shortly after assuming office in 1927, she discovered in a vault in the state Capitol an original copy of the Texas Declaration of Independence. She considered her role in restoring and displaying the document to be one of her important contributions to the state.

Mrs. McCallum served as a presidential elector in 1940 and as a state Democratic committeewoman for the Twentieth Senatorial District in 1942 and again for the Tenth United States Congressional District in 1944. She also remained active in civic affairs throughout her life. In 1944 she was appointed to the first Austin city planning commission; in January 1945 she led the Women's Committee on Educational Freedom into the Capitol to protest the firing of University of Texas president Homer P. Rainey; and in 1954 she became the first woman grand jury commissioner in Travis County. Her column, "Woman and Her Ways," appeared at intervals in the Austin *American–Statesman* until the late 1940s. She chronicled the history of the Texas suffrage movement for *History of Woman Suffrage (1881–1922)*. She profiled the sculptor Elisabet Ney for the University of Texas literary publication, *Texas Magazine*, and for *Holland's Magazine*. Her collection of biographical sketches of early American leaders, *Women Pioneers*, was published in 1929. During the 1950s *Texas Parade* published some of her works, including a few excerpts from her unpublished manuscript, "All Texians Were Not Males."

Roberta S. Duncan

McCulloch, Benjamin. Indian fighter, Texas Ranger, and soldier; b. Rutherford County, Tennessee, 11 November 1811; d. Arkansas, 7 March 1862. The McCullochs, including Ben's brother Henry McCulloch, moved frequently. Two of Ben's older brothers briefly attended school taught by a close neighbor and family friend in Tennessee, Sam Houston. Also in Tennessee, David Crockett was among their closest neighbors. Ben agreed to follow Crockett to Texas, planning to meet him in Nacogdoches on Christmas Day, 1835. Ben and Henry arrived too late, however, and Ben followed Crockett alone toward San Antonio. After sickness from measles prevented him from reaching the Alamo before its fall, McCulloch joined Houston's army on its retreat into East Texas. At the battle of San Jacinto he commanded one of the famed Twin Sisters and won from Houston a battlefield commission as first lieutenant. He soon left the army, however, to earn his living as a surveyor in the frontier communities of Gonzales and Seguin. He then joined the Texas Rangers and, as first lieutenant under John Coffee Hays, won a considerable reputation fighting Indians. In 1839 McCulloch was elected to the House of Representatives in a campaign marred by a rifle duel with Reuben Ross. McCulloch received a wound that partially crippled his right arm for the rest of his life. On Christmas Day of that year Henry McCulloch killed Ross in a pistol duel in Gonzales. In 1842 Ben chose to return to surveying and the pursuit of a quasimilitary career. At the battle of Plum Creek (12 August 1840) he distinguished himself as a scout and as commander of the right wing of the Texas army. In the first of the Mexican Invasions of 1842 (February) he scouted enemy positions and took a prominent role in the fighting that harried Rafael Vásquez's raiders back below the Rio Grande. In the second invasion (September) McCulloch again did valuable scouting service and joined in the pursuit of Adrián Woll's invading troops to the Hondo River, where Hays's rangers engaged them on 21 September. After the repulse of the second Mexican invasion, McCulloch remained with the ranger company that formed the nucleus of an army with which the Texans planned to invade Mexico. The so-called Somervell expedition was poorly managed, however, and Ben and Henry left it on the Rio Grande only hours before the remainder of the Texans were captured at Mier, Tamaulipas, on 25 December 1842.

McCulloch was elected to the First Legislature after the annexation of Texas. At the outbreak of the Mexican War he raised a command of Texas Rangers that became Company A of Col. Jack Hays's First Regiment, Texas Mounted Volunteers. He was ordered to report to the United States Army on the Rio Grande and was soon named Zachary Taylor's chief of scouts. As such he won his commander's praise and the admiration of the nation with his exciting reconnaissance expeditions into northern Mexico. The presence in his company of George Wilkins Kendall, editor of the New Orleans *Picayune,* and Samuel Reid, who later wrote a popular history of the campaign, *The Scouting*

Expeditions of McCulloch's Texas Rangers, propelled McCulloch's name into national prominence. Leading his company as mounted infantry at the battle of Monterrey, McCulloch further distinguished himself, and before the battle of Buena Vista his astute and daring reconnaissance work saved Taylor's army from disaster and won him a promotion to the rank of major of United States volunteers. McCulloch returned to Texas at the end of the war, served for a time as a scout under Bvt. Maj. Gen. David E. Twiggs, and traveled to Tennessee on family business before setting out from Austin in 1849 for the gold fields of California. Although he failed to strike it rich, he was elected sheriff of Sacramento. His friends in the Senate, Sam Houston and T. J. Rusk, mounted a campaign to put him in command of a regiment of United States cavalry for duty on the Texas frontier, but largely due to McCulloch's lack of formal education the attempt was frustrated. In 1852 President Franklin Pierce promised him the command of the elite Second United States Cavalry, but Secretary of War Jefferson Davis bestowed the command instead on his personal favorite, Albert Sidney Johnston. McCulloch was, however, appointed United States marshal for the Eastern District of Texas and served under Judge John Charles Watrous during the administrations of Franklin Pierce and James Buchanan. In 1858 he was appointed one of two peace commissioners to treat with Brigham Young and the elders of the Mormon Church; he is credited with helping to prevent armed hostilities between the United States government and the Latter-Day Saints in Utah.

When secession came to Texas, McCulloch was commissioned a colonel and authorized to demand the surrender of all federal posts in the Military District of Texas. After a bloodless confrontation at the Alamo on 16 February 1861, General Twiggs turned over to McCulloch the federal arsenal and all other United States property in San Antonio. On 11 May, Jefferson Davis appointed McCulloch a brigadier general, the second-ranking brigadier general in the Confederate Army and the first civilian to be commissioned a general-grade officer. McCulloch was assigned to the command of Indian Territory and established his headquarters at Little Rock, where he began to build the Army of the West with regiments from Arkansas, Louisiana, and Texas. He established vital alliances with the Cherokees, Choctaws, Creeks, and other inhabitants of what is now eastern Oklahoma. On 10 August 1861, he won an impressive victory over the army of Brig. Gen. Nathaniel Lyon at Wilson's Creek, or Oak Hills, in southwest Missouri. McCulloch's continuing inability to come to personal or strategic accord with Gen. Sterling Price, however, caused President Davis to appoint Maj. Gen. Earl Van Dorn to the command of both McCulloch's and Price's armies. Van Dorn launched the Army of the West on an expedition to capture St. Louis, a plan that McCulloch bitterly resisted. The Confederates encountered the army of Union major general Samuel R. Curtis on the Little Sugar Creek in northwest Arkansas. Due largely to McCulloch's remarkable knowledge of the terrain, Van Dorn's army was able to flank the enemy out of a strong position and cut his line of communication to the north. McCulloch, commanding the Confederate right wing in the ensuing battle of Pea Ridge, or Elkhorn Tavern (7 March 1862), overran a battery of artillery and drove the enemy from his original position. As he rode forward through the thick underbrush to determine the location of the enemy line, he was shot from his horse, and died instantly. His command devolved upon Brig. Gen. James M. McIntosh, who was killed a few minutes later while leading a charge to recover McCulloch's body. Col. Louis Hébert, the division's senior regimental commander, was captured in the same charge, and soon McCulloch's division, without leadership, began to fall apart and drift toward the rear. Most participants and later historians attribute to McCulloch's untimely death the disaster at Pea Ridge and the subsequent loss of Arkansas to the Union forces. McCulloch was first buried on the field, but his body was removed to the cemetery at Little Rock and thence to the State Cemetery in Austin. His papers are in the Barker Texas History Center at the University of Texas at Austin.

Thomas W. Cutrer

McCulloch, Henry Eustace. Texas Ranger and Confederate officer; b. Rutherford County, Tennessee, 6 December 1816; d. Seguin, 12 March 1895 (buried in San Geronimo Cemetery); m. Jane Isabella Ashby (1840). Although he played an important role in military affairs in early Texas, he received fewer accolades than his more famous cohorts Rip Ford, Jack Hays, and his older brother, Ben McCulloch. In the 1830s Ben and Henry McCulloch traveled the Mississippi River on log rafts to various markets, and by the end of the decade they had moved to Gonzales to survey and locate lands. In 1839, in the political struggles at Gonzales, Henry shot and killed Reuben Ross, after the latter, intoxicated and obnoxious, drew his pistols. McCulloch joined the Texas Rangers in the heyday of their role as citizen soldiers against Indians and Mexican troops. In the battle of Plum Creek in 1840 against the Comanches, he scouted, fought with distinction, and was wounded. He also served as a lieutenant in Hays's rangers in their military operations against the Comanches and Mexican nationals. During the Mexican Invasions of 1842, McCulloch scouted, infiltrated enemy lines seeking information, and participated in the battle of Salado Creek. In 1843 he was elected sheriff of Gonzales and began a merchandising career there. The following year he moved his business to Seguin. During the Mexican War and afterward, he served as a captain of a volunteer company guarding the Indian frontier. He became especially adept at organizing regular ranger patrols in intervals from different camps to cover a designated area. In the early 1850s he served in the state legislature (both houses) from Guadalupe County, and at the end of the decade he accepted an appointment as U.S. marshal for the Eastern District of Texas. As Texas left the Union, he assumed command of the posts on the northwestern frontier from Camp Colorado to the Red River and used Texas secessionist troops to accept the surrender of federal forces. Given the rank of colonel by the Confederate Congress, McCulloch organized the First Regiment, Texas Mounted Riflemen, in 1861. This unit slowed down penetration of the western frontier by Indians through a system of patrols and smallscale engagements. After promotion to brigadier general, McCulloch commanded the Northern Sub-District of Texas from 1863 to the end of the war. In this role he faced the threats of Indian raids and the movement of Union forces. He also had to deal with the activities of draft dodgers, deserters, and bushwhackers. At one time he tried unsuccessfully to arrest William Quantrill for robbery and murder. With the war ended, McCulloch went home to Seguin with an armed escort for protection against deserters who had sworn to take his life. After the Civil War he remained in the limelight. In 1874 he assisted the newly elected governor, Richard Coke, in removing Edmund J. Davis from the executive offices. Early in 1876, as a reward for his years of service, McCulloch was given the superintendency of the Deaf and Dumb Asylum, but he proved inept at this civilian post and was forced to resign in 1879. *Harold J. Weiss, Jr.*

McGinty Club. A men's fun-making and booster group in El Paso in the "wonderful nineties," named for a song, "Down Went McGinty." A convivial group of El Paso men loved to gather at the assay office of Dan Reckhardt and O. T. Heckleman ("Reck and Heck") on San Francisco Street. Reckhardt, a 300-pounder who had been an oarsman at Columbia in his college years, was the only president the club ever had. Peg Grandover was involved in everything the club did. Without any firm rules and with a constitution that was largely a joke (it stated the club's purpose as "to put down liquor"), the club nevertheless drew to its membership lawyers, three mayors, three prominent bankers, several judges, the manager of Myar's Opera House, a tax assessor, two physicians, and "almost everybody who was anybody." It had over 300 members. It named as its "poet liar-ate" the poet–scout Capt. Jack Crawford, whose daughter later became Mrs. Dan Reckhardt. The club enlisted the aid of the bandmaster from Fort Bliss, and throughout the nineties the McGinty marching band was a part of almost every civic endeavor. The club established "Fort McGinty" on a hill near the downtown area; its booming cannon would wake the town for the next big civic event. Long before El Paso dreamed of a chamber of commerce, the McGinty Club was the town's chief booster organization. Its endless projects included bicycle races made famous by the appearance of Miss Annie Londonderry, who had just completed a world tour by bicycle; the appearance of such theatrical lights as Edwin Booth and Madame Luisa Tetrazzini at Myar's Opera House (Reckhardt bought two seats, both for himself, with the partition removed); the hometown baseball club, the El Paso Browns; a United States Department of Agriculture experiment that used explosives in a valiant attempt to produce rain; a world's heavyweight-championship boxing match; a reception for President Benjamin Harrison; a major railroad convention for the proposed White Oaks Railroad; the volunteer fire department. The McGinty Club was never formally disbanded. It simply died out with the coming of a new and more sophisticated century and by the end of 1902 was a glorious but fading memory.

Conrey Bryson

Mackenzie, Ranald Slidell. Army officer; b. New York City, 27 July 1840; d. Staten Island, 19 January 1889 (buried at West Point); ed. Williams College and West Point (grad. 1862). Mackenzie, first in his West Point class, was commissioned a second lieutenant and rose to brevet major general before the end of the Civil War. In three years he received seven brevets and six wounds. In 1867 he was appointed colonel of the Forty-first Infantry, a newly formed black regiment reorganized two years later as part of the Twenty-fourth United States Infantry. The unit had its headquarters at Fort Brown, Fort Clark, and later at Fort McKavett. In 1871 he assumed command of the Fourth United States Cavalry at Fort Concho and a month later moved its headquarters to Fort Richardson. That summer he began a series of expeditions into the uncharted Panhandle and Llano Estacado in an effort to drive renegade Indians back onto their reservations. In October his troops skirmished with a band of

Northern Cheyennes. After a short tour of duty in Washington, during which he commanded troops mustered to keep the peace in the event of disturbances following the presidential election of 1876, Mackenzie returned to the Black Hills, then to Fort Sill. In late 1877 Indians from Mexico were again raiding in South Texas, and by March 1878 Mackenzie was again at Fort Clark. He began patrols and in June led an expedition into Mexico. His incursion prompted the Mexican government to act, and by October the raiding had ceased. In October 1879 Mackenzie was sent to Colorado with six companies of cavalry to prevent an uprising of the Utes at the Los Pinos agency. The Indian Bureau eventually negotiated a removal treaty, but the chiefs refused to leave until Mackenzie informed them that the only alternative was war. Two days later, the Utes started for Utah. On 21 September 1881 Mackenzie received orders to move his cavalry to Arizona, take field command of all troops there, and subdue the Apaches. After a short and brilliant campaign, despite the opposition of the department and division commanders, Mackenzie was assigned on 30 October to command the District of New Mexico, where the Apaches ignored departmental and international lines and the Navajos were restless. Within a year the army was in control. Mackenzie was promoted to brigadier general but was seriously ill. On 27 October 1883 he was reassigned to command the Department of Texas. He planned to marry and retire soon on land that he had bought near Boerne, but by 18 December he was suffering from "paralysis of the insane." A few days later he was escorted to New York City and placed in the Bloomingdale Asylum. On 24 March 1884 he was retired from the army. In June he went to his boyhood home in Morristown to live. In 1886 he was moved to New Brighton, Staten Island, where he died.   *Ernest Wallace*

Ranald S. Mackenzie. Courtesy National Archives; 111-SC-87407. Career army officer Ranald Mackenzie is remembered as an Indian fighter.

McKinney, Texas. County seat of Collin County, 32 miles north of Dallas. For the first two years of the county's history Buckner, seven miles northwest of McKinney, served as the county seat. Because Buckner was not within three miles of the center of the county as required by law, the legislature called for a special election to select a new site. By a vote of 10 to one McKinney was chosen. Like the county, the town was named for Collin McKinney, signer of the Texas Declaration of Independence and author of a bill establishing counties in North Texas. In 1849 William Davis, who owned 3,000 acres where McKinney now stands, donated 120 acres for the townsite. Ten years later McKinney was incorporated, and in 1913 the town adopted the commission form of government. For the first 125 years of its history McKinney served as the principal commercial center for the county. The county seat provided farmers with flour, corn, and cotton mills, cotton gins, a cotton compress and a cotton-seed oil mill, as well as banks, churches, schools, newspapers, and, from the 1880s, an opera house. Businesses also came to include a textile mill, an ice company, a large dairy, and a garment-manufacturing company. Farmers and manufacturers were able to ship their goods on the Houston and Texas Central Railway, which reached McKinney in 1872, and, beginning in 1881, on the Missouri, Kansas and Texas Railroad. From 1908 to 1948 the Texas Electric Railroad, running from Denison to Dallas and Waco, served McKinney. In 1943 the United States Army built the 1,500-bed Ashburn General Hospital (now the McKinney Job Corps Center) in McKinney. On 3 May 1948 the town was struck by a tornado that killed 3 persons, injured 43,

Comanches in Blanco Canyon, where he was wounded, and on 29 September 1872 they defeated another near the site of the present town of Lefors. In 1873 Mackenzie was assigned to Fort Clark to put an end to the plunder of Texas livestock by Indian raiders from Mexico. On 18 May, in the Remolino Raid, he burned a Kickapoo village near Remolino, Coahuila, and returned with 40 captives. That and effective border patrols stopped the raiding. In July 1874 Lt. Gen. Philip Sheridan ordered five commands to converge on the Indian hideouts along the eastern edge of the Llano Estacado. Mackenzie, in the most daring and decisive battle of the campaign, destroyed five Indian villages on 28 September in Palo Duro Canyon and on 5 November near Tahoka Lake won a minor engagement, his last, with the Comanches. His destruction of the Indians' horses after the battle of Palo Duro Canyon, even more than the battle itself, destroyed the Indians' resistance. In March 1875 Mackenzie assumed command at Fort Sill and control over the Comanche–Kiowa and Cheyenne–Arapaho reservations. On June 2 Quanah Parker arrived at Fort Sill with 407 followers and 1,500 horses. The Red River Indian War was over.

After Custer's troops had been wiped out on the Little Bighorn River in 1876, Mackenzie was placed in command of the District of the Black Hills and of Camp Robinson, Nebraska. In October he forced Sioux chief Red Cloud, who had won a campaign in 1868 against the United States, to return his band to the reservation. On 25 November, Mackenzie decisively defeated the

and destroyed an estimated $2 million worth of property. The population grew from 35 in 1848 to 4,714 in 1912. By 1953 McKinney had a population of more than 10,000 and 355 businesses. The town continued to serve as an agribusiness center for the county until the late 1960s. By 1970 McKinney was surpassed in size by Plano. By the mid-1980s the town had become a commuter center for residents who worked in Plano and Dallas. In 1990 the city had a population of 21,283 and was the home of Collin County Junior College. *David Minor*

McKinney, Williams and Company. An important early mercantile establishment; founded by Thomas F. McKinney and Samuel M. Williams in 1834 at Quintana and moved to Galveston in 1838. As the largest commission-merchant firm in early Texas, it controlled much of the cotton trade at Houston and Galveston. The company held interests in lands, banking, and industrial and town promotion. Though not wealthy, the partners had good enough credit that they could advance the Republic of Texas more than $150,000. The firm was one of the first to open up river navigation in the republic. Before the revolution their steamers, the *Laura* and the *Yellow Stone*, were in operation on the Brazos, Colorado, and Trinity rivers and on Buffalo Bayou, linking Texas plantations and the New Orleans export trade. During the revolution the provisional government used the company's vessels for conveying troops and supplies. In 1837 at Quintana the company began banking functions. In 1841 the Texas Congress authorized the firm to issue its notes for circulation as money, using for security mortgages on real estate, slaves, and a sawmill. The Commercial and Agricultural Bank, finally organized in 1847, was the first legal bank established in Texas. McKinney, Williams and Company continued as a private banking business after its mercantile interests were sold in 1842 to Williams's brother, Henry Howell Williams. Under Arthur Lynn, British consul in Galveston, and H. H. Williams's son, John H. Williams, the firm was subsequently known as Lynn and Williams, and eventually passed to the firm of Wolston, Wells and Vidor, which finally closed. McKinney, Williams and Company remained a partnership business until Williams's death in 1858, although all active partnership ceased about 1853, when McKinney moved to the Austin area. *Curtis Bishop*

McMurry University. In Abilene; founded by the Northwest Texas Conference of the Methodist Church and opened in 1923; named for Bishop William Fletcher McMurry. James Winfred Hunt, a Methodist minister and former president of Stamford College, led in the founding after Stamford College closed. Abilene citizens offered money, land, free water, and streetcar connections to induce the Methodists to locate the college in Abilene. McMurry College opened with Hunt as president, 22 faculty and staff members, and 191 students. The first senior class, of four students, graduated in 1926, the year the school was accredited as a senior college by the Texas Association of Colleges and the Educational Board of the Methodist Church. Though founded as a liberal arts college, McMurry added teacher training and business administration in its first decade. The fine arts division of the college began to offer degrees in 1928. The college has served the Methodist Church by educating potential clergy and laity. Its ties with the United Methodist Church have remained strong. During the rigors of the Great Depression, McMurry survived by stringent economies and fed-

McMurray College, Abilene, ca. 1949. Courtesy TSL. McMurray College opened in 1923 and grew rapidly after World War II.

eral money from the NYA and WPA. The college had a difficult time in the 1940s also because so many male students left to serve in World War II. Afterward, however, enrollment increased, budgets stabilized, and more faculty with doctorates were hired. The college saw a building boom. McMurry is a founding college of the Texas Intercollegiate Athletic Association. It has five intercollegiate sports programs for men and four for women. McMurry operates a branch at Dyess Air Force Base. In the 1980s fewer than half of the students were Methodists. Students could major in fine and applied arts, education, business, humanities, social sciences, science, or mathematics. In the 1980s McMurry joined Hardin–Simmons University, Abilene Christian University, and Hendrick Medical Center to form the Abilene Intercollegiate School of Nursing, which awards the B.S.N. degree. In 1990 McMurry College became McMurry University. *Fane Downs*

Malhado Island. The name ("Isle of Misfortune") applied by Cabeza de Vaca to an island off the Texas coast where and he and approximately 80 Spaniards and an African were shipwrecked in November 1528. Its location has often been the subject of heated debate since the 1920s. In particular, a civil action in 1990 contended that Malhado Island was Galveston Island. But there are compelling arguments that the initial landfall was slightly to the west of Galveston Island, and that Cabeza de Vaca's Malhado was a combination of San Luis Island and Oyster Bay peninsula in the Brazosport area. This revisionist conjecture was first advanced in 1918 by Harbert Davenport and Joseph X. Wells, who contended that silting from the discharge of rivers and the impact of hurricanes turned what was an elongated island in Cabeza de Vaca's time into a peninsula. Furthermore, the dimensions of Malhado, given by Cabeza de Vaca as about one-half league by five leagues (1.3 by 13 miles), are too small for Galveston Island but approximate those of San Luis Island. The Spaniards, as modern-day measurements have confirmed, were amazingly accurate in estimating their travel in leagues. If San Luis Island is accepted as Malhado, then the distances between it and four successive waterways (Oyster Creek, the Brazos River, the San Bernardo River, and Caney Creek), which were crossed by Cabeza de Vaca's men as he made his way down the coast, are consistent with his account and topography. The large island described by Cabeza de Vaca as lying behind Malhado (toward Florida) logically becomes Galveston Island. No one can determine with absolute certainty any portion of Cabeza de Vaca's journey across Texas and large portions of Mexico during the years 1528 to 1536. With his own *Relación* and a *Joint Report* written by Cabeza de Vaca, Andrés Dorantes de Carranza, and Alonso Castillo Maldonado as the sole eyewitness accounts of that odyssey, route interpreters must rely on logic, distances traveled, gross landscape features as described in the narratives, flora, fauna, and ethnographic evidence. These considerations suggest that Isla de Malhado was San Luis Island rather than Galveston Island. *Donald E. Chipman*

Mallet Expeditions. Journeys of the Mallet brothers, Pierre and Paul, eighteenth-century French voyageurs from the "Mizuri" country, in what later became the Louisiana Purchase. In 1739 they made a trip across the plains from the Missouri River to Santa Fe. In 1740 they encountered and descended the Canadian River, crossing the Panhandle of Texas. They continued down the Arkansas and Mississippi rivers to New Orleans. The Sieur de Bienville, governor of Louisiana, commissioned André Fabry de la Bruyère to accompany the Mallets on a return trip and map the route. The party ascended the Arkansas and entered the Canadian in 1741. Because of the river's dry bed, little progress could be made. Fabry returned to Arkansas Post and to Le Poste des Cadodaquious for horses. By the time he returned to the Canadian, the Mallets had pushed on.

Fabry returned to New Orleans via Le Poste des Cadodaquious in 1742. The Mallets made little progress and were forced to return down the Canadian and Arkansas rivers. They continued exploring out of Arkansas Post. In 1750 Pierre and three hired companions ascended the Red River, obtained horses and supplies at Le Poste des Cadodaquious, then traveled overland to the Canadian River and proceeded to Santa Fe, again across the Texas Panhandle. Pierre was arrested and sent to Mexico City and eventually to Havana. Except for Fabry's assignment, the French paid little attention to the Mallets' geographical discoveries. From them the Spanish, through depositions, gained accurate descriptions of the Arkansas River and its tributaries, but the knowledge was protected and forgotten. Fabry apparently failed to leave any evidence of what the Mallets had reported. Zebulon M. Pike, who consulted with the French, shows the course of the Canadian River as too short and southerly. Because neither French nor Spanish cartographers benefited from the Mallets' discoveries, the Río Colorado of New Mexico (the Canadian River) was considered the source of the Red River until around 1820. *Morris L. Britton*

Mammals. Because of its size and ecological diversity, Texas supports a native fauna of about 140 species of terrestrial mammals. In addition to native mammals, some species have been introduced.

Order Marsupialia. Only one marsupial, the Virginia opossum (*Didelphis virginiana)*, occurs in Texas. It is distributed statewide, except for some arid far-western parts of the state.

Order Insectivora. Two families of insectivores, Soricidae (shrews) and Talpidae (moles), are represented in Texas. Four species of shrew occur: two kinds of short-tailed shrew (*Blarina*) in East Texas, the least shrew (*Cryptotis*) in much of East and Central Texas, and the desert shrew (*Notiosorex*) in arid habitats

in West Texas. Of the moles, the eastern mole (*Scalopus*), a species of burrowing mole, is the only one that occurs in the state. It is common over much of eastern Texas and reaches westward to the Panhandle, the eastern edge of the Llano Estacado, and Presidio County.

Order Chiroptera. Four families of bats are represented in Texas: Mormoopidae (mustached bats and allies), Phyllostomidae (leaf-nosed bats and allies), Vespertilionidae (common bats), and Molossidae (free-tailed bats). A single species of Mormoopidae, the ghost-faced bat (*Mormoops*), occurs in Texas and is known as far north as the southwestern and south central regions of the state. Members of the family Phyllostomidae are limited primarily to the American tropics. Three species barely reach Texas. The Mexican long-tongued bat (*Choeronycteris*) has been recorded once in the lower Rio Grande valley, the big long-nosed bat (*Leptonycteris*) is known in the Big Bend, and the hairy-legged vampire (*Diphylla*) has been taken but once from near Comstock. Twenty-two members of the family Vespertilionidae make up an important component of the Texas fauna. All are insectivorous. Some, such as the big brown bat (*Eptesicus*), are nearly statewide in distribution. Others, such as several species of the genus *Myotis*, have more restricted distributions. And some, such as the silver-haired bat (*Lasionycteris*), may be present in the state only during semiannual migrations. Four species of the free-tailed bats or Molossidae—three in the genus *Tadarida* and one in the genus *Eumops*—occur in Texas. Only one, the Brazilian free-tailed bat (*T. brasiliensis*), can be distributed statewide, and only in the warm months.

Order Xenarthra. Of the armadillos (Dasypodidae) and their allies, only one, the nine-banded armadillo (*Dasypus novemcinctus*), occurs in Texas. The armadillo ranges over most of the state, being absent only from the extreme western and southwestern parts.

Order Lagomorpha, family Leporidae. Four species of lagomorphs are found in Texas, the most common and widespread being the black-tailed jackrabbit (*Lepus californicus*), which occurs over most of the state but is abundant westwardly, and the eastern cottontail (*Sylvilagus floridanus*), which is a common inhabitant of all but parts of the extreme southwest. Two other species of *Sylvilagus* are known—the desert cottontail, which occurs in upland habitats in the western half of the state, and the swamp rabbit, which occupies lowland areas in the eastern third of Texas.

Order Rodentia. This order is represented in Texas by members of the family Sciuridae (squirrels and allies), of the family Geomyidae (pocket gophers), of the family Heteromyidae (pocket mice and kangaroo rats), of the family Castoridae (beavers), of the family Cricetidae (New World mice and rats), and of the family Erethizontidae (porcupines).

Because most are diurnal, squirrels are among the best known of native rodents. In the Texas fauna there are two tree squirrels (*Sciurus*), the fox squirrel and the gray squirrel, native to the eastern and central parts of the state and frequently introduced westwardly, and four species of ground squirrels (*Spermophilus*), some of which occur in all but East Texas. Additionally, there are the unique prairie dog (*Cynomys*), once widely distributed in the West and still common in some areas, the antelope ground squirrel (*Ammospermophilus*) of the Trans-Pecos region, a chipmunk (*Tamias*), known only from the

Guadalupe Mountains and the Sierra Diablo, and the nocturnal southern flying squirrel (*Glaucomys*), which occurs in the eastern third of the state.

The mounds of the pocket gophers, burrowing rodents, are typical features of the Texas landscape. Pocket gophers are common, often abundant, in favored soils; at least one type can be found anywhere in the state, but the kinds never coexist with each other. The Texas fauna includes at least five species of brown pocket gophers (*Geomys*), Botta's pocket gopher (*Thomomys*), and the yellow-faced pocket gopher (*Cratogeomys*).

The nocturnal pocket mice and kangaroo rats are typical of the grasslands and semiarid regions of the western and southern parts of the state. The kangaroo rats (*Dipodomys*), frequently seen along roadways at night, are represented by five species in Texas, the spiny pocket mouse (*Liomys*) by a single species that occurs only in the lower Rio Grande area, and the true pocket mouse (*Perognathus*) by six species, the largest of which, the spiny pocket mouse (*P. hispidus*), is the only heteromyid that is nearly statewide in distribution.

The Castoridae are represented in the New World only by the familiar beaver (*Castor canadensis*), which is known from East and Central Texas and westward along the Rio Grande and its tributaries and the Canadian River.

New World mice and rats are represented by more species native to Texas (29) than any other mammalian family. The most conspicuous of cricetids are the semiaquatic muskrat (*Ondatra zibethicus*), because of its wide distribution and commercial value as a furbearer, and the wood rats (*Neotoma*), four species of which occur in the state (at least one of which can be found in any area), because of their frequently conspicuous "houses." The most common and widespread genus contains the white-footed mouse (*Peromyscus*), with nine species. Other native mice and rats include one pygmy mouse (*Baiomys*), two grasshopper mice (*Onychomys*), four harvest mice (*Reithrodontomys*), two rice rats (*Oryzomys*), the golden mouse (*Ochrotomys*), two cotton rats (*Sigmodon*), the woodland vole (*Pitymys*), and the Mexican vole (*Microtus*). The prairie vole (*M. ochrogaster*) once occurred in southeastern Texas, but that population is probably now extinct.

The distinctive porcupine (*Erethizon dorsatum*) is a characteristic mammal of the western half of Texas. It is mostly an animal of coniferous woodlands, but occupies a variety of habitats, some quite distant from forests.

Order Carnivora. Representatives of the families Canidae (coyotes, foxes, and allies), Ursidae (bears), Procyonidae (the raccoon and its allies), Mustelidae (weasels, skunks, and allies), and Felidae (cats) occur in Texas.

Six species of canids are native to Texas. One, the red wolf (*Canis rufus*), evidently now is extinct, and its larger relative, the gray wolf (*C. lupus*), once common, is represented only by an occasional straggler from Mexico in the Trans-Pecos region. The coyote (*C. latrans*) is common and of statewide occurrence. Two small foxes, the desert or kit fox (*Vulpes macrotis*) and the swift fox (*V. velox*), occur only in far western Texas, whereas the gray fox (*Urocyon*) is found nearly all across the state. The red fox (*V. vulpes*), a North American native that was introduced in the 1890s, now is found over most of eastern and central Texas and west to the Panhandle.

The grizzly bear (*Ursus arctos*) once occurred in the mountainous regions of the Trans-Pecos but was long ago extirpated. The black bear (*U. americanus*), once widespread, probably also

is extinct in Texas, though occasional individuals still may be found in the mountains of the Trans-Pecos and in the forests of East Texas.

The raccoon (*Procyon lotor*), one of the most familiar and economically important of Texas carnivores, has a statewide distribution and is of common occurrence. Its smaller and less well-known relatives, the coati (*Nasua narica*) and ringtail (*Bassariscus astutus*), have more restricted distributions, the latter occurring mostly in the western and central parts of the state and the former only in the lower Rio Grande valley and Big Bend.

Eleven mustelids are known in Texas: the long-tailed weasel, mink, and black-footed ferret (*Mustela*), the last probably extinct; the river otter (*Lutra*), now limited to waterways in the eastern part of the state; the badger (*Taxidea*), widespread in the western two-thirds of Texas; and six skunks—two spotted species (*Spilogale*), two hog-nosed species (*Conepatus*), the hooded skunk (*Mephitis macroura*), and the familiar striped skunk (*M. mephitis*), the only species with a statewide distribution.

Of the cats, the mountain lion (*Felis concolor*) once was found throughout Texas but now occurs only in the Trans-Pecos mountains and as an occasional wanderer in forested East Texas. The bobcat (*F. rufus*) is relatively common, widespread, and valuable for its fur. The ocelot (*F. pardalis*) now occurs in some numbers along the lower Texas coast and probably in the Rio Grande valley, whereas the uncommon jaguarundi (*F. yagouaroundi*) is found only in the latter area. Two other felids, the jaguar (*F. onca*) and the margay (*F. wiedii*), evidently no longer occur in the state.

Order Artiodactyla. Representatives of four families of the order of even-toed ungulates occur in Texas: Tayassuidae (javelinas or peccaries), Cervidae (deer and their allies), Antilocapridae (the pronghorn), and Bovidae (bison and allies).

The collared Peccary (*Tayassu tajacu*) or javelina is the only Tayassuid in Texas. It once ranged rather broadly but now is restricted to the southwestern part of the state and the brush country of South Texas.

Two familiar members of the family Cervidae are the white-tailed deer (*Odocoiluse virginianus*), which has a statewide distribution in suitable brushy or wooded habitats, and the mule deer (*O. hemionus*), which occurs in the rough western country. Another cervid, the wapita or American elk (*Cervus canadensis*), has been reintroduced in the Guadalupe Mountains, where it apparently once occurred.

The pronghorn antelope, a readily recognizable species (*Antilocapra americana*), is found in West Texas, from the Panhandle southward to the Trans-Pecos, where it is most common. Its habitat is relatively open rangelands. It once occurred much farther eastward.

The bison (*Bison bison*), popularly called the buffalo, once ranged over much of Texas but now occurs only in captivity. The bighorn sheep (*Ovis canadensis*) once occurred on the desert mountains of the Trans-Pecos, was extirpated, and now has been reintroduced in limited numbers.

Introduced mammals. Aside from several native North American mammals mentioned above that have been introduced or reintroduced in Texas, a number of exotics species have been transported to the state by man, accidentally or on purpose. Among these are four rodents—the house mouse (*Mus*), two species of rats (*Rattus*), and the nutria or coypu (*Myocastor*).

The house mouse and rats, of Old World origin, are commensals of man; they live primarily in and around human habitations. The semiaquatic nutria, a native of southern South America, was introduced into Louisiana in the mid-1930s and has spread over most of the southeastern United States. In Texas it now occurs in aquatic habitats over much of the eastern part of the state.

Several ungulates, or hoofed mammals, have been introduced as game species. Some still occur mostly in at least semiconfinement and are not treated here, but others thrive in the wild state. The Barbary sheep (*Ammotragus*) was introduced in the canyon country of West Texas in the late 1950s and now occurs also in some desert mountains of the Trans-Pecos. The nilgai antelope (*Boselaphus*), blackbuck (*Antilope*), and axis deer (*Cervus axis*) are found in parts of Central and South Texas.

J. Knox Jones, Jr.

Mansfield, Jayne. Screen actress; b. Vera Jayne Palmer, Bryn Mawr, Pennsylvania, 19 April 1933; d. near New Orleans, 29 June 1967 (buried in Fairview Cemetery, Pen Argyl, Pennsylvania); m. Paul Mansfield (1949; divorced 1956); 1 daughter; m. Mickey Hargitay (1958; divorced 1964); 3 children; m. Matt Cimber; 1 son. In 1939 Jayne moved with her mother to Dallas, where she attended high school. She studied dramatics at Southern Methodist University, at the University of Texas, and later at UCLA. She was Miss Photoflash in 1952 and subsequently won many other beauty titles. Though some say she appeared first in *Underwater* (1954), her first film was evidently *The Female Jungle* (1955). She made brief appearances in *Prehistoric Women* (1955), *Illegal* (1955), and *Pete Kelly's Blues* (1955) and signed for her Broadway debut in George Axelrod's play *Will Success Spoil Rock Hunter?* (1955). The following year she emerged in films and became a major sex symbol in the mode of Marilyn Monroe. Jayne was featured in the movie version of *Rock Hunter* opposite Tony Randall (1957), and in *The Wayward Bus* (1957), *Kiss Them for Me* (1957), *The Sheriff of Fractured Jaw* (1958), *The George Raft Story* (1961), *It Happened in Athens* (1962), *A Guide for the Married Man* (1967), and other movies. She made a number of guest appearances on television, formed Jayne Mansfield Productions, posed several times for *Playboy* magazine, performed with nightclub acts in Las Vegas, and, toward the end of her career, starred in a number of low-budget films in Europe. Her second husband was a former Mr. Universe. Her third was a director who had directed her in *Bus Stop* in Yonkers, New York, and later in the film *Single Room Furnished* (1967). She was killed in a motor accident on the way to a television engagement.

Ronald L. Davis

Manufacturing Industries. Manufacturing industries in Texas evolved from frontier enterprises to modern economic entities. The Texas region has had the advantages of rich and varied natural resources, a geographic position encouraging the expansion of population, and the increase of transportation facilities. Utilization of these assets has come, predominantly, by export of the raw materials but increasingly by manufacture in Texas into semiprocessed and consumers' products, as rail lines have been laid and deepwater ports excavated, while the tide of American migration shifted westward. Prior to 1900 Texas industries were of either the kind that had necessarily come to the source of raw materials, such as lumbering, stone cutting, and brick manufacturing, or the kind that produce for the immediate demands of a local market, as the milling of flour and corn meal and the manufacture of harness and saddlery. Much industry was on a toll basis, notably early flour and grist milling. Weaving, ceramics, stonework, and other industries were developed around the Spanish missions at San Antonio, but it was not until the period of Anglo-American colonization that permanent industrial development began. The lumber industry and flour and grist milling were the first permanent industries established in Texas and remained the two leading industries throughout the early period of development. What was probably the first sawmill was built near San Augustine in 1825. One was built on Buffalo Bayou in 1831 and another on Adam's Bayou in 1836. A steam sawmill was constructed at Harrisburg in 1836 and another at Turner's Ferry in 1841. From a small beginning in the colonial period, sawmilling developed rapidly after independence was established, bringing a wave of immigration from the United States with a demand for homes. Probably the first power-driven gristmill in Texas was that at of San José y San Miguel de Aguayo Mission in San Antonio. With Anglo-American colonization small horse and water driven buhrstone mills became numerous. Wine, brandy, rum, and whisky were also produced in Texas during the colonial and republic periods and even during the preceding mission era. As early as 1839 there were makers of natural cement, furniture, tin and sheet-iron products, and saddlery and harness. Galveston was the principal industrial center. There had been quarrying and stonecutting at San Antonio during the Spanish era, and this industry spread northward as the westward tide of immigration reached the limestone-based Blackland and Grand Prairies. Sugar cane was used to manufacture sugar as early as 1844.

The annexation of Texas to the United States in 1845 brought a new wave of immigration and public confidence that stimulated industrial development and pushed it inland from the coast. By 1850 the new capital city of Austin had a saddlery, boot and shoe shops, a wagon factory, tin and sheet-metal works, and other industries. Two casting foundries and a woolen mill were in operation in the state. By 1857 four flour mills were located at Dallas and Lancaster, in Dallas County. Brick was made in Dallas as early as 1850. On Alum Creek, near Bastrop, a stoneware and pottery factory was operated. In Galveston, Hiram Close, M. L. Parry, and James A. Cushman produced steam engines, boilers, sugar mills, kettles, and other iron and brass products. I. F. W. Ahrens of that city manufactured saddles, harness, and furniture. Just prior to the Civil War development of the iron ores of East Texas began with a foundry at Kellyville. The cutting off of the state from industrial supplies brought into existence several war industries, including a woolen mill at Huntsville and a factory to produce cannons, caps, and cartridges at Austin. The economic stagnation during Reconstruction was short-lived. The census of 1860, on the eve of the war, had shown 3,449 wage earners and $3,209,930 total value of manufactured products. That of 1870 showed 7,927 wage earners and $5,244,209 value of products; that of 1880, 12,159 and $7,753,659, respectively.

From the Civil War to the end of the century lumbering and flour and grist milling were the leading industries, except that cottonseed crushing supplanted flour and grist milling in second rank, according to the census of 1900. The rise of the cottonseed oil industry, which began with a small mill at High Hill in Fayette County in 1867, was the most significant development of the period. By 1900 this industry had climbed to second rank among

Texas industries with $14,005,324 value of products, and it has remained among the leading Texas industries in each succeeding census. There was a rapid expansion of building-materials manufacture and also of railroad construction and repair. The first permanent cotton mill was established at Dallas in 1891, and several others were constructed before the end of the century. There had been an earlier flurry of cotton and woolen mill building, growing primarily out of the dire need for fabrics during the Civil War, but these older mills disappeared by 1900. The Bastrop Cotton Mill was in operation in 1867 with 1,100 spindles, and there were cotton mills during this early period at Hempstead, Waco, Houston, Tyler, and Gonzales, while one at New Braunfels produced both cottons and woolens. Between 30 and 40 corporations were formed to manufacture cotton and woolen goods, but most of them never were in operation. The most successful woolen mill prior to 1900 was the Slayden–Kirksey mill at Waco, which began about 1885 producing both cloth and men's suits. It operated successfully for more than a decade. During the 1880s and 1890s there was also considerable development of the iron industry, with blast furnaces at Rusk and New Birmingham in Cherokee County and at Jefferson in Marion County. One of these was state-owned and operated by prison labor. This industry declined later because of lack of a coal adaptable to the production of coke. Several small meat-packing plants were established, though it was not until 1901 that the first two large plants were built at Fort Worth.

The beginning of the twentieth century was for several reasons a point of transition into a different era of industrial development. The discovery of the Spindletop oilfield was the outstanding single factor. This first of a long series of petroleum discoveries marked the beginning of the greatest contribution from a single source to the state's economic expansion. In the preceding 20 years the cultivated acreage of Texas had increased from 12,650,314 to 19,576,076, and barbed wire fences had cut the range into ranches, giving stability to cattle raising. At the same time population had increased from 1,591,749 to 3,048,710, railroad mileage from 3,244 to 9,867, and commerce through the Gulf ports was getting under way. In 1901 two big slaughtering plants were established at Fort Worth by national packing companies, inaugurating an era of interest in Texas industrial opportunity by outside capital.

In the decade following 1900 the number of industrial wage earners almost doubled, and "value added by manufacture" more than doubled. At the same time there was a rapid increase in variety of manufactured products. This development continued until the Great Depression decade of 1930–40, in which there was a slight decline in number of wage earners. It was followed by the war industry boom of 1941–44 with a postwar decline, which, however, readjusted in 1945 to production of civilian goods at a level considerably higher than in 1940. The period from 1900 to World War I was characterized primarily by the development of petroleum refining. Progress was rapid during the 1910–20 decade, and the census of 1920 reported it as the leading industry of the state, with $241,757,313 of products in the preceding year. Slaughtering and meat packing also developed rapidly, standing, with $42,530,000, in first place of products in 1909 and ranking second to petroleum refining in 1919 but with an increased value of $125,191,873. A number of cotton mills were built, and there was a rapid expansion of clothing manufacture, notably in Dallas. There was also rapid development of the

building-materials industries, including brick and tile, Portland cement, and gypsum products, in ice and ice cream manufacture, and in cabinet and millwork and furniture manufacture. World War I did not bring to Texas the new industries nor the decentralization of old ones, but it stimulated temporarily, and permanently in most instances, the development of basic factors favorable to industrial development. Notably, it brought into production hitherto unutilized mineral resources.

The decade of 1920–30 was notable for the establishment of the first cheese, condensed milk, and general dairy-products plants in Texas and also the first poultry packing plants with nationwide markets. The first creamery in Texas was established at Terrell as early as 1885, but there had been only slow development of commercial production for other than local markets until 1925. Several new cotton mills were built during the 1920s. The Great Depression of the early 1930s brought an abrupt decline in industrial payrolls and value of products, as well as a cessation of new industrial development. The decline was less than that in most older industrial areas, however, and the census of 1940 showed a recovery almost to the level of that reported in the census of 1930. The six leading industries in value of products, according to the census of 1940, were (1) petroleum refining—$698,850,077; (2) meat packing (wholesale)—$85,461,048; (3) cottonseed (oil cake, meal, and linters)—$44,406,882; (4) flour and other grain-mill products—$41,250,858; (5) oilfield machinery and tools—$41,149,017; and (6) bread and other bakery products—$32,994,866. From the beginning of the century to World War II the value of manufactured products in Texas increased 1,647 percent, compared with a gain of 480 percent for the country as a whole.

The World War II period in Texas, 1941–45, brought greater industrial developments, as measured in number of wage earners and value and physical volume of products, than in all preceding history. No official census was taken during this period, but data from war agencies indicated that there were 380,000 wage earners in the early part of 1945 against 126,996 reported for 1939. There was a corresponding jump in the total value of products from $1,530,220,676 to $6,500,000,000. This great increase came from federal construction and subsidization of private industry. Airplane building was centered largely at Dallas and Fort Worth; shipbuilding was centered at Houston, Galveston, and Orange; while ordnance was decentralized at smaller inland points, principally at Texarkana, Karnack near Marshall, McGregor near Waco, and Amarillo. There was also a revival of iron and steel industries during the war period both for the purpose of utilizing scrap iron and for consuming Texas ores. The largest of these were the American Rolling Mill blast furnace and steel hearths at Houston, utilizing both scrap and ore, and the coke ovens and blast furnace of the Lone Star Steel Company at Daingerfield, constructed to utilize East Texas ore. A small plant was built at Rusk to smelt iron ores in charcoal furnaces for the production of pig iron and chemical by-products. These industries declined precipitately with the end of the war, but most other industries, including both the new ones and those that had been expanded to meet war needs, continued during the immediate postwar years to operate at capacity. Notable among the new industries were the synthetic-rubber plants at Beaumont, Houston, and Borger. Several large chemical plants closed down or decreased operations, but the net result of the war period was a large permanent expansion of Texas chemical industries, of which the Dow plant at Freeport, producing magnesium and a number of other products from seawater, was probably the largest. Because most Texas industries were primarily producers of basic manufactured products such as cement, flour, petroleum products, cottonseed oil products, lumber, and textiles, there was little problem of retooling either for conversion to war industry or for reconversion to peacetime production, a factor that aided in sustaining the level of Texas production during both critical periods. Notable among developments intended primarily for the postwar period were the construction of the DuPont nylon salt plant at Orange, the Celanese Corporation's chemical plant at Bishop, and the General Tire Company plant and the Owens–Illinois Glass Company factory, both at Waco.

The period after World War II continued the war-stimulated growth in Texas manufacturing. The first postwar census of manufactures gave data for 1947, which showed an increase over 1939 of 93 percent in production workers and 285 percent in value added by manufacture. By 1947 the conversion to peacetime activities was generally complete, so the comparison between 1939 and 1947 census figures reflects the permanent effect of the wartime expansion on Texas manufacturing. The increase in the value added by manufacture between 1939 and 1947 was due in part to the rise in the level of prices. The wholesale price index of the Bureau of Labor Statistics was 92 percent higher in 1947 than in 1939, but even after making allowance for this price increase the output of manufacturing plants doubled. The difference between the percentage increase in employment and in output represented the rise in the productivity of labor. Much of the manufacturing capacity added during the war was highly automated, resulting in increased output per worker. Both measures of manufacturing activity are significant, since a factory not only turns out products, but also provides jobs, which add to the total income in the state. The composition of Texas manufacturing in 1947, as shown by the census of manufactures, differed substantially from that of the prewar years. The greatest relative increase in value added by manufacture was in instruments, primary metals, chemicals, transportation equipment, paper and allied products, electronic machinery, and fabricated metals. The largest industry in 1939, petroleum refining, and the second largest, food processing, showed substantial growth and retained their respective positions in 1947, although their rates of growth were substantially below those registered by the smaller, newer industry groups. The postwar changes in Texas manufacturing in general were a continuation of trends established during the war. The greatest rate of growth between 1947 and 1967 was shown in electronic machinery, which was 41 times as large in 1967 as in 1947. The value added by manufacture compiled by the Bureau of the Census is affected by changes in the level of prices, but during the period 1947 to 1967 the wholesale price index increased only 30.7 percent, so most of the rise in value added by manufacture reflected an increase in the physical volume of output.

The chemical industry, which was the fifth largest in the state in 1939 and third largest in 1947, had advanced to first place in 1967, with value added by manufacture almost nine times the 1947 level. Although the rate of increase in the chemical industry was lower than for electronic machinery, transportation equipment, and primary metals, its size makes the rate of growth it achieved spectacular. Twenty percent of the total increase in value added by manufacture for the entire state was concentrated

in the chemical industry. Food processing dropped from second place in value added by manufacture in 1947 to fourth place in 1967 but continued by a wide margin to employ the largest number of persons of all industry groups in the state. The disparity between the growth in the number of employees and value added by manufacture is the result of the difference in the productivity of labor, which is largely the result of variations in the amount of capital investment required by the industry. In 1967 the petroleum industry produced $75,970 of value added by manufacture per production worker, while the foodprocessing industry produced $22,941 per production worker. The apparel industry showed the lowest productivity per production worker at $7,198. It ranked third in employment in 1967 but tenth in value added by manufacture. Petroleum and coal products, which in Texas consist almost entirely of petroleum products, showed a value added by manufacture per production worker of $12,000 in 1947 and $75,970 in 1967. The number of production workers in the industry decreased 20 percent during the period, while value added by manufacture increased 400 percent. The chemical industry showed almost as high a value added by manufacture per employee as petroleum, $66,348. These two industries in 1967 represented 66 percent of the value added by manufacture in Texas but employed only 11 percent of the production workers.

In 1992 manufacturing represented 16 percent of the state's gross product; it generated $65 million. Manufacturers around the state employed 968,000 people, making them the fourth largest employer after the service industry, wholesale–retail trade industry, and state and local government. The three biggest manufacturing employers were industrial machinery makers with 111,000 employees, the electronics industry with 98,000 people, and food producers with 96,000 employees. The chemical industry continued to be a major employer with 86,000 jobs. The highest paid workers in manufacturing in 1990 were malt-beverage employees, who averaged $20.25 an hour working 45 hours a week. The lowest paid worker in the field was the textile employee, who made an average of $6.12 for a 37-hour work week. Chemical workers maintained high wages with an average of $18 an hour for a 45-hour work week. These figures represent a decline in manufacturing from the early 1980s, but growth in the computer industry has subsequently improved the state of manufacturing in Texas. Defense transportation equipment, oilfield machinery, petroleum refining, and textile and apparel production have slowly declined in importance.

The major concentrations of manufacturing in Texas are in the northern part of the state with a narrow strip across the blacklands to San Antonio and in the southeastern part of the state along the Gulf of Mexico. The Beaumont–Port Arthur–Orange, Houston, and Galveston–Texas City metropolitan statistical areas reported 42 percent of the total value added by manufacture in the state in 1967. The Dallas and Fort Worth MSAs accounted for 28 percent of the total, leaving only 30 percent of the total for the remainder of the state. The MSAs not in the two major concentrations accounted for 15 percent of the total, with 15 percent in smaller cities throughout the state. Individual industries show a considerable degree of geographic concentration. Petrochemicals and refining activity are largely concentrated in the Beaumont–Port Arthur and Houston areas, with smaller concentrations along the Gulf Coast, in the Panhandle, the Permian Basin, El Paso, and East Texas. Apparel plants are concentrated in the Dallas area and to an increasing degree along the Rio Grande and in San Antonio, where a large pool of labor is available. Foodprocessing plants are scattered throughout the state and are the major representatives of manufacturing industry in the lower Rio Grande valley. Aircraft and automobile production is largely concentrated in the Dallas and Fort Worth areas. The aircraft industry came to North Texas during World War II, and the automobile industry is market-oriented. In recent years defense cutbacks have made a major impact on the aircraft industry, with General Dynamics selling its Fort Worth fighter jet production facilities to Lockheed. Marine transportation manufacturing is found along the Gulf Coast, particularly in the Beaumont–Port Arthur–Orange, Galveston–Texas City, and Houston standard metropolitan areas. The leading areas of concentration of the manufacture of electronic machinery and scientific instruments are Dallas, Houston, and Fort Worth. Central Texas, in particular Austin, provides a home for computer hardware and software development in the state.

The future growth of manufacturing in Texas appears to be dominated by the new industries founded on recent advances in science and engineering. This does not mean that all growth will be concentrated in these industries, for other classifications may be expected to continue to expand with the growth of population in the Southwest. The fastest growth rates, however, are likely to be achieved by these science-oriented industries. The upward trend in the industries related to the exploration of space was given substantial support by the location of the Johnson Space Center near Houston, and future historians may find that the location of this facility in Texas will be as important to the industrial history of the state as the discovery of oil at Spindletop, which ushered in the oil industry at the beginning of the century. The first impact of the center was felt by industry in the Houston area, but cities all over the state have benefited from the attraction this facility has for supporting industries. The increased support of the leaders in the state for improvements in education from the elementary schools through the graduate schools is an encouraging sign, for the newer industries are influenced in their location by the quality of research and graduate teaching in the universities. It is also significant that a strong nucleus of science-oriented manufacturing firms in the state has developed. The firms that have developed instruments, the science of oil exploration, the manufacture of petrochemicals, aircraft, and electronic devices for civilian and military uses have attracted other science-oriented concerns. Industries of this type offer the greatest potential for expanding the manufacturing output of the state in the near future.   *Clara H. Lewis and John R. Stockton*

Maps. The cartographic history of Texas can be divided into five overlapping periods, based on the sources and quality of geographic data and the mapmaking technology available in each period. In the early periods prototype maps incorporating the results of recent explorations and discoveries were copied by imitative mapmakers. These copies were often less accurate than the prototype and often were still being published long after improved renditions of the territory were available. The earliest period extends from the beginning of European activity in the New World through the end of the seventeenth century. The maps of this period were based on reports and charts from the earliest expeditions, often supplemented by information received from individual explorers and adventurers. The observations were crude, and the maps were usually compiled by mapmakers in Europe, who attempted to synthesize incomplete, vague, and often contradictory data. The resulting delineations can be related to the actual topography they depict only with great care. Typical maps of this period include those customarily attributed to Alonso Álvarez de Pineda and Alonso de Santa Cruz, as well as those published by Abraham Ortelius and Robert Dudley. These maps generally feature a rough delineation of the Gulf Coast, a few vague rivers and inland features, an indication of the location of Indians, and sometimes a plethora of place names that can only rarely be matched to specific locations.

The second period stretches from about 1700 to 1820 and coincides with Spanish presidial and missionary activity. Maps of this period were based on data from observations made by Spanish officers and explorers using the crude instruments and techniques of the era. Details on these maps are more complete than those of the previous period and can often be identified on modern maps. The place names are those assigned by Spanish colonists, missionaries, and officials and are often based on Indian names. The delineations in these maps remain impressionistic rather than precise, and their accuracy decreases as the distance from established settlements and routes increases. Typical maps of this period are those accompanying the reports of Alonso De León, Pedro Vial, José María Puelles, José Antonio Pichardo, and Francisco Álvarez Barreiro. The reports were rarely published, however; the printed maps of Guillaume Delisle, José Antonio de Alzate y Ramírez, Aaron Arrowsmith, and Alexander von Humboldt were more widely distributed. Maps of this period characteristically offer more accurate renditions of the coast than did those of the previous period; fairly complete and accurate indications of the rivers of Texas and other natural features, particularly those east of the 100th meridian; and the location of Spanish settlements and missions, Indian bands, and the routes of explorations.

In the third period of Texas cartographic history, from roughly 1820 to 1850, accuracy of the maps of the region improved greatly. These maps were the first based on accurate and detailed surveys made for the location of land claims by settlers and performed by experienced surveyors using the most modern instruments and techniques available. The delineations were precise and accurate wherever actual surveys had taken place, but they were still plagued by errors and distortions in the unsettled and incompletely explored areas in the north and west. The archetypal map of this period was that produced and published by Stephen F. Austin in 1830; other maps of note include those by Jacob De Cordova, Henry S. Tanner, William H. Emory, John Arrowsmith, and John Disturnell. They show the progress of colonization in Texas and emerging political divisions, but they also bear witness to the relative lack of knowledge about the area west of the 100th meridian.

This brief period of great change was followed by a longer period in which maps of Texas were constructed from more precise data, derived by geodetic methods. These data resulted from detailed and exhaustive expeditions of long duration and great expense. Most of the resulting maps were products of governmental agencies, ranging from the U.S. Coast Survey of the 1850s through the USGS in the closing decades of the century. The compilation by Robert T. Hill, published by the Geological

Survey in 1900, is the culmination of the new mapping technology. These detailed and accurate maps revealed outlines and features recognizable to the modern observer. They were used as sources by such commercial mapmakers as George Cram and Charles H. Pressler and firms like Rand McNally that fed cartographic products to an increasingly avid market of travelers and immigrants.

The final period extends from 1930 to the present day. It is characterized by the application of modern technology to the problem of map construction. With the advent of aerial photogrammetry in the 1930s, maps became at once more accurate and more easily produced. The evolving technologies of remote sensing, satellite mapping, and computer graphics hold the promise of ever-improved depictions. The maps produced throughout the history of Texas reveal not only the evolution of the process itself but also the results of other activities in the region. Maps therefore illustrate the entire continuum of the Texas past in ways that other documents cannot.

Robert S. Martin

Marcy, Randolph Barnes. Army officer and explorer; b. Greenwich, Massachusetts, 9 April 1812; d. West Orange, New Jersey, 22 November 1887; m. Mary A. Mann (1833); 3 children; ed. West Point (grad. 1832). Marcy was brevetted a second lieutenant in the Fifth Infantry in 1832 and rose to captain in 1846. He spent most of this period on the northwest frontier in Michigan and Wisconsin. During the Mexican War he served with Gen. Zachary Taylor's army at Palo Alto and Resaca de la Palma. He returned to Texas in 1847, and in 1849 he determined the route of the Marcy Trail, from Fort Smith to Santa Fe. In 1851 he commanded Gen. William G. Belknap's escort on the tour that selected the sites for forts on the Texas frontier. In March 1852 Marcy was assigned the command of a 70-man exploring expedition across the Great Plains in search of the source of the Red River and directed to "collect and report everything that may be useful or interesting." Second in command of the Marcy expedition was Capt. George B. McClellan, who later became his son-in-law and during the Civil War his commander. Among Marcy's scouts was Jim Ned, a Delaware Indian whom Marcy called "the bravest warrior and the most successful horse thief in the West." Between 2 May and 28 July 1852, Marcy's party crossed a thousand miles of previously undocumented Texas and Oklahoma territory, discovering numerous valuable mineral deposits as well as 25 new species of mammals and 10 of reptiles. Marcy recorded a prairie dog town that covered 400,000 acres. He reportedly discovered the sources of both forks of the Red River, as well as the Palo Duro and Tule canyons, which he became the first white man to explore. The expedition encountered and documented the little-known Wichita Indians and compiled the first Wichita dictionary. It also returned with information on Cynthia Ann Parker. Eastern newspapers erroneously reported that Marcy died at the hands of the Comanches. Marcy's 1852 expedition has been called "the best organized, best conducted, and most successful" venture into the region to that date. Zebulon Pike, Stephen Long, and Thomas Freeman had all previously searched for the source of the Red River and failed to find it. Marcy's report on his expedition, *Exploration of the Red River of Louisiana, In the Year 1852 . . . With Reports on the Natural History of the Country,* supple-

mented by a handsome collection of lithographs, was published in 1853. It quickly became a classic of Western Americana.

In 1854 Marcy surveyed Indian reservations in northern and western Texas, and in 1856 he explored the headwaters of the Big Wichita and Brazos rivers. His report of the 1856 expedition was published by the Senate. In 1857 he served briefly against the Seminole Indians in Florida and accompanied Gen. Albert Sidney Johnston's expedition against the Mormons. During that campaign he received national fame for a winter march of over a thousand miles to secure relief for Johnston's army, which was stranded without supplies in the Utah mountains. After this adventure Marcy was recalled to Washington to prepare a semiofficial guidebook for the War Department. The result, *The Prairie Traveler* (1859), was an excellent compendium of practical hints for travelers about what equipment to carry, methods of organizing a wagontrain, and techniques of avoiding Indian attacks, as well as detailed notes on 34 of the most important overland trails. On 22 August 1859 Marcy was promoted to major and assigned as regimental paymaster. With the outbreak of the Civil War, he was promoted to colonel and named inspector general of McClellan's Army of the Potomac. He served two stints as acting brigadier general of volunteers. He was brevetted brigadier general in the regular army "for gallant and meritorious service in the field" and major general of volunteers on the same day, 13 March 1865, "for faithful and meritorious service during the war." From 1863 through 1878 he served as inspector general of various departments of the army, and in 1871 he accompanied Gen. William T. Sherman on his fact-finding tour of the Texas frontier. On 12 December 1878 he was promoted to the regular rank of brigadier general and was named inspector general of the army. He wrote two volumes of reminiscences, *Thirty Years of Army Life on the Border* (1866) and *Border Reminiscences* (1872), which contain much Texas material. He retired from the army in 1881.

Thomas W. Cutrer

Margil de Jesús, Antonio. Early missionary; b. Valencia, Spain, 18 August 1657; d. Mexico City, 6 August 1726. As a boy Margil referred to himself by his lifelong sobriquet, "Nothingness Itself." He joined the Franciscans in 1673, was ordained at the age of 25, and soon accepted the challenge of missionary work in New Spain. He arrived at Veracruz on 6 June 1683 and was assigned to the missionary College of Santa Cruz de Querétaro, from where he ranged for several years of missionary service to Yucatán, Costa Rica, and Guatemala. In 1707 he traveled to Zacatecas to found and preside over the missionary College of Nuestra Señora de Guadalupe de Zacatecas. He was to have accompanied Domingo Ramón's expedition of 1716, charged with setting up Franciscan missions in East Texas. However, illness at San Juan Bautista prevented his arrival in East Texas until 1716, after the founding of the first four missions. The next year he supervised the founding of Nuestra Señora de los Dolores and San Miguel de los Adaes, which with the previously established Nuestra Señora de Guadalupe completed the missions under the control of the Zacatecan Franciscans. During the "Chicken War" of 1719 the six missions and a presidio in East Texas were all abandoned, and the entire Spanish population withdrew to San Antonio. In February of the following year Margil founded at San Antonio the most successful of all Texas missions, San José y San Miguel de Aguayo. In 1722 he was recalled to Mexico to serve again as *guardián* of the college he had founded. After three years he resumed missionary work in Mexico. Margil was the most famous missionary to serve in Texas. The cause for his canonization is ongoing. His Zacatecan brethren assumed control of all Texas missions in 1773.

Donald E. Chipman

Marshall, Texas. Thirty-nine miles west of Shreveport, Louisiana, in central Harrison County. The county was marked off in 1839. Two years later, in an effort to influence the commissioners who were choosing a site for the county seat, Peter Whetstone offered land for a courthouse, a church, and a school. The offer was accepted, and the town, named by Isaac Van Zandt in honor of Chief Justice John Marshall, became the county seat in 1842. It was incorporated by the Texas legislature in 1844 and enlarged in 1850 to include an area of one square mile with the courthouse at the center. Marshall was the first town in Texas to have a telegraph; by 1854 the local paper had a telegraph link to New Orleans, which gave it quick access to national news. By 1860 Marshall was one of the largest and wealthiest towns in East Texas, with a population estimated at 2,000. The community had an outstanding group of lawyers and political leaders, including the first and last governors of Confederate Texas, Edward Clark and Pendleton Murrah. The town, encouraged by Robert W. Loughery's ultra-Southern newspaper, the Marshall *Texas Republican*, voted unanimously for secession in 1861. The Confederate government of Missouri located its capitol there during the war. After the fall of Vicksburg split the Confederacy in 1863, the town became a center of operations for Gen. Edmund Kirby Smith's Trans-Mississippi Department. During the spring of 1865 the army of the Trans-Mississippi Department disintegrated, and Marshall was occupied by United States troops on 17 June. Reconstruction after the war was bitterly controversial, as the town became not only the base for occupying forces but the home for an office of the Freedmen's Bureau as well. White citizens angrily opposed federal authority and the influx of blacks who came seeking government protection. The whites were not satisfied until the Citizens party "redeemed" Marshall and all of Harrison County in 1878. The Southern Pacific Railroad, built from Caddo Lake to Marshall before the Civil War, was absorbed by the Texas and Pacific system during the early 1870s. Harrison County offered the T&P a $300,000 bond subsidy, and the railroad located its shops and general offices for Texas in Marshall. The town received an immediate boost from an influx of railroad workers and became a major cotton-marketing center for East Texas, too.

Marshall University, although more of a secondary school than an institution of higher learning, and Marshall Masonic Female Institute attracted hundreds of students from outlying areas during the era of the Civil War and Reconstruction. Higher education for African Americans began locally at Wiley College in 1873 and Bishop College in 1881. The latter moved to Dallas in 1961, but Wiley remained. East Texas Baptist College was founded in 1914. In 1880 the town's population stood at 5,624. It reached 10,000 shortly after 1900 and 20,000 during the 1940s. As Harrison County's cotton economy declined after 1930, the town became increasingly important as a retail center and as the location of industries such as wood and metal working. After 1960, approximately one-half of the county's residents lived there, and retail sales was the most rapidly expanding occupation in the

area. The location of Marshall on Interstate 20, the main route from Shreveport to Dallas, has contributed significantly to the town's growth and prosperity. Public library service began in Marshall in 1970. The old courthouse on the square has housed a local museum since 1965. Numerous homes and buildings in Marshall are listed in the National Register for Historic Places, and scores of historical landmark medallions have been awarded in the city by the Texas Historical Commission. In 1976 the National Municipal League designated Marshall an All American City. The population was 24,921 in 1980 and 23,682 in 1990.

Randolph B. Campbell

Marshall Conferences. Three conferences held at Marshall during the Civil War to address problems of the Confederate states west of the Mississippi. At the suggestion of President Jefferson Davis, the first conference was called by Texas governor Francis R. Lubbock in July 1862, as Union forces threatened to cut off the western Confederacy by taking control of the Mississippi River. Lubbock and Missouri governor Claiborne F. Jackson met at Marshall in late July and prepared three recommendations for Davis: that a commanding general be given jurisdiction over the western states, that a branch of the Confederate treasury be located west of the Mississippi, and that the government alleviate the "most distressing want of small arms on this side of the river." These recommendations were endorsed by Governor Rector of Arkansas and Governor Moore of Louisiana, neither of whom was able to attend the meeting.

The second conference took place in August of the following year, after the Union army had made good its threat by capturing Vicksburg and taking over the entire Mississippi. This action cut the Confederacy almost exactly in half. Gen. Edmund Kirby Smith, appointed commander of the Confederate Department of the Trans-Mississippi, called leaders from each western state to Marshall to discuss the crisis. The conference began on 15 August 1863. Representing Texas were Lubbock (who became chairman of the meeting on August 17), governor-elect Pendleton Murrah, Senator W. S. Oldham, and Confederate special agent Guy M. Bryan. In response to the need for protection of homes and property and for additional armaments, Missouri governor Thomas C. Reynolds's committee gave an overly optimistic report on the region's military strengths. Other committee recommendations endorsed by the full convention included establishing county committees to report disloyalty and putting Smith in charge of all cotton transactions in order to control cotton speculation and aid the economy. However, conference members concluded that Smith should exercise only such powers as leaders in Richmond had been exercising. Finally, the conference strongly endorsed developing diplomatic relations with French and Mexican leaders in Mexico.

The third conference, in May 1865, was precipitated by the surrender of all Confederate land forces east of the Mississippi and the dissolution of the Richmond government. Union authorities asked Smith to surrender on the same terms that Grant had given Lee. Smith refused. Then, with no direction from Richmond and in need of some form of civil authority to back him, he called for a conference of governors. Murrah, who was dying of tuberculosis, sent Bryan in his place. Between 9 and 11 May the conference members produced a plan for surrender that was unrealistically favorable to the Confederacy. Although Smith did his best to persuade the Union to accept this plan, the answer was firmly in the negative. An impasse in peace negotiations followed. Finally, with members of his army deserting in droves, the general directed that the Union terms be met.

Allan C. Ashcraft

Martin, Mary. Musical theater star; b. Weatherford, Texas, 11 December 1913; d. Rancho Mirage, California, 3 November 1990 (buried in Weatherford); m. Benjamin J. Hagman (1930; divorced 1935); 1 son, Larry Hagman; m. Richard Halliday (1940); 1 daughter. After her divorce from Hagman, she left Weatherford to try a performing career under the name Mary Martin. She gained singing spots on national radio broadcasts in Dallas and at Los Angeles nightclubs. Her performance impressed a theatrical producer enough to cast her in a play in New York. Though that production never opened, she got a role in Cole Porter's production *Leave It To Me*. Her rendition of "My Heart Belongs to Daddy" soon endeared her to Broadway audiences and opened her way to Hollywood. Paramount Pictures signed her to appear in *The Great Victor Herbert* in 1939. During the next three years she starred in 10 movies on contract with that company. Between films she performed frequently on NBC and CBS radio programs, including "Good News of 1940" and "Kraft Music Hall." With her husband as her manager, she returned to New York in 1943, cast as Venus in *One Touch of Venus*, for which she won the New York Drama Critics Poll. In 1946 she appeared in *Lute Song*, a Chinese story adapted to showcase her talents. The following year she had the lead role in a touring production of Irving Berlin's *Annie Get Your Gun*. After returning to Broadway in 1949, Mary Martin appeared with Ezio Pinza in the Rodgers and Hammerstein hit *South Pacific*. In 1951 she moved to London for a two-year run of *South Pacific*. For the rest of the 1950s she divided her time between stage and television performances. In *The Skin of our Teeth* and *Annie Get Your Gun*, she made televised portrayals built on her stage experience. Likewise, she took the youthful character of Peter Pan, in the play of the same name, from a brief Broadway run to repeated NBC–TV presentations. She called this her favorite role, perhaps because it featured her own optimism and love of adventure. Mary Martin won Tony Awards for *Peter Pan* and *The Sound of Music*. She also starred in a 1965–66 production of the musical *Hello, Dolly!* on a challenging tour for military personnel stationed in Asia. Later in 1966 she was back on Broadway, appearing with Robert Preston in *I Do, I Do*. Her stage career slowed during the 1970s, as she and her husband spent longer periods on their ranch in Brazil, where he died in 1973. She made a Broadway comeback in 1978 in the comedy *Do You Turn Somersaults?* In 1981 she hosted a public television series on aging, "Over Easy." After a debilitating automobile accident, she joined Carol Channing in a 1986 touring production of *Legends*, portraying an aging actress. Her lifetime achievements brought her an award from the John F. Kennedy Center for the Performing Arts in Washington in 1989. *Sherilyn Brandenstein*

Massanet, Damián. Missionary; b. in Spain, most likely in Majorca; d. probably in Mexico. After ordination, Massanet was among 24 Franciscan priests who crossed the Atlantic in 1683 to help found the missionary College of Santa Cruz de Querétaro. By the late 1680s he had moved to the mining and cattle frontier of northern New Spain. Between Monclova and a mining camp known as Boca de Leones, Massanet had set up Mission San Bernardino de la Caldera near the border of Nuevo León. In 1689 he accompanied Gov. Alonso De León in the successful search for La Salle's Fort St. Louis, and the next year he assisted in founding the first mission in East Texas, San Francisco de los Tejas. Massanet, although placed in charge of missionary work in East Texas, did not remain there. He differed with De León over the size of the military guard left at Mission San Francisco, and from Mexico filed a report that was critical of the veteran commander. Massanet returned to East Texas with Domingo Terán de los Ríos in 1691, and he quarreled once again with civil authority. In this instance, Massanet refused to release horses from San Francisco de los Tejas Mission that were needed by Governor Terán for the return trip to Mexico, and the animals had to be commandeered. Difficulties with the Tejas Indians as well as problems with floods, failed crops, and shortages of necessary supplies, doomed the first missions in East Texas. On 25 October 1693, Massanet and the surviving priests set fire to the remaining mission, San Francisco de los Tejas, and left for Coahuila. The small party lost its bearings for several weeks and did not reach Monclova until 17 February 1694. At that juncture, the viceroy of New Spain requested that Father Massanet suggest additional mission sites to be developed in northern Coahuila, but the padre declined—arguing that he had recommended sites on other occasions, only to see that without necessary supplies and governmental support such plans were futile. Massanet, along with the other missionaries from East Texas, returned to his missionary college in Querétaro, and it seems probable that he spent his remaining years at the College of Santa Cruz.

Donald E. Chipman

Masterson, Bat. Frontier lawman; b. Bartholomew Masterson, Quebec, Canada, 26 November 1853; d. New York City, 25 October 1921 (buried in Woodlawn Cemetery, New York); m. Emma Walters (1889?). As a young man he adopted the name William Barclay (or W. B.) Masterson and used it as his official signature. He hunted buffalo with Billy Dixon and Wyatt Earp, helped construct the Adobe Walls trading post, and took part in the second battle of Adobe Walls. He served as a civilian scout with the U.S. Army under Col. Nelson Miles in the Red River Indian War. In Mobeetie, Texas, on 24 January 1876 he was badly wounded in a gunfight in which Cpl. Melvin A. King and Mollie Brennan were killed. That episode started Masterson's reputation as a hair-triggered gunfighter, although he may not have killed King. He never killed another man. After his recovery, he served briefly as a policeman in Dodge City. In October 1877 he was elected sheriff of Ford County, and early in 1878 he tracked down and apprehended nearly all of the Rourke–Rudabaugh gang, who had attempted to rob trains and raid the depot at Kinsley, Kansas. In October 1878 Masterson led the posse that captured Jim Kennedy, who had killed a well-known stage star, Dora Hand. Early in January 1879 Masterson escorted Henry Born from Colorado to Dodge to be tried for horse stealing. Shortly afterward, he was commissioned a deputy United States marshal. The next month he brought in seven Cheyenne prisoners to stand trial for depredations committed during Dull Knife's flight from Indian Territory the previous fall. Despite his impressive record, Masterson's popularity in Dodge City had waned by the 1879 elections because of his exorbitant spending in the Cheyennes' inconclusive trial and his connection with the "Gang," the town administrators led by Mayor James H. (Dog)

Kelley, who were opposed by the so-called reform element. Consequently, Masterson was defeated in the sheriff's race, after which he left for Leadville, Colorado, where he gambled for a time. In February 1881 he accompanied Wyatt Earp and Luke Short to Tombstone, Arizona, where he assisted Earp at the gaming tables of the Oriental Saloon. He served for a time as a deputy sheriff in Las Animas, Colorado, and in 1883 was instrumental in persuading the governor of Colorado to prevent the extradition of Doc Holliday to Arizona.

Masterson made his first try at the newspaper business in 1885, but his paper, *Vox Populi*, ceased publication after a single issue. In 1886, in a surprising move, he briefly became a prohibitionist and closed the Dodge City saloons after being appointed a special officer. His conversion was short-lived, however. By 1887 he was working with Luke Short at the White Elephant Saloon in Fort Worth, where he witnessed the fatal shooting of Timothy I. (Longhair Jim) Courtright by Short on 8 February. Such excursions were merely visits, however, for after 1880 Masterson considered Denver his hometown. During the 1890s he occasionally wore a badge and in 1892 served as marshal at Creede, Colorado. He spent most of his time, however, in the gambling house. He helped promote prizefighters John L. Sullivan and Jim Corbett and attended the controversial boxing match between Bob Fitzsimmons and Peter Maher staged by Judge Roy Bean near Langtry, Texas, in 1896. As his drinking habit worsened, Masterson fell in with some unsavory gamblers, and in 1902 he and his wife were compelled to leave Denver. Disillusioned with the turn of events in the West, he moved to New York City, where troubles continued to plague him until President Theodore Roosevelt commissioned him a deputy U.S. marshal for the Southern District of New York. Masterson met writer Alfred Henry Lewis, who helped launch his journalistic career. Lewis wrote numerous stories and a novel, *The Sunset Trail* (1905), about Masterson and persuaded him to write a series of sketches about his gunfighter friends for *Human Life Magazine*. In time Masterson became sports editor of the New York *Morning Telegraph* and was noted for his pungent columns.

Gary L. Roberts

Matachines. A traditional religious dance and the dancers, musicians, and elders who participate in it. Its roots go back to a medieval sword dance called a *morisca*, which depicted the battle between Christianity and paganism. The Spanish brought the ritual to the New World, where over time it incorporated Mexican, Indian, and American elements. Most modern versions rely heavily on representations of the Virgin Mary and the Holy Cross. The dance is often performed by 12 to 18 dancers who represent such characters as El Monarca (Montezuma), his bride (Malinche), El Abuelo (the Grandfather), and El Toro. Typically, the story revolves around a young virgin, Malinche, who tries in vain to get someone to slay El Toro. El Toro (paganism) is eventually slain by El Monarca, who symbolizes the acceptance of Christianity. Supporting characters such as El Abuelo and La Vieja (the Old Woman) provide comic relief. The dance is done in a series of scenes and can take an entire day to complete. Brilliant colors and elaborate masks are common to most performances. In Texas, the group Los Matachines de la Santa Cruz de la Ladrillera performs a variation of the traditional *matachín*. The group moved to Laredo from the coal-mining towns of Mexico in 1939 and settled in the barrios that became known as La Ladrillera and Cantarranas. On 12 December in honor of Nuestra Señora de Guadalupe and on 3 May in honor of the Holy Cross, the 50 or so members of the group follow the image of the Virgin and an eight-foot wooden cross adorned with colorful flowers on a procession to Holy Redeemer Church, dancing at stops along the way. In 1987 the group was invited to the American Folklife Festival at the Smithsonian Institution in Washington. It has also received a Texas Folklife Resources apprenticeship grant. The troupe performed at the Texas Folklife Festival in San Antonio in 1988 as well as the Dance Performance program in Houston. Matachines are also performed by other groups in Laredo, in other Texas towns, and as far west as California, as well as in northern Mexico. Some groups such as the Yaquis prohibit women from participating, but for the most part the dance is performed by both men and women.

Norma E. Cantú

Maverick, Samuel Augustus. Land baron, civic leader, legislator, and patriarch of a famous Texas family; b. Pendleton, South Carolina, 23 July 1803; d. San Antonio, 2 September 1870 (buried in City Cemetery No. 1); m. Mary Ann Adams (1836); 10 children; ed. Yale University (grad. 1825); Virginia law license, 1829. Maverick ran for the South Carolina legislature in 1830, but his antisecession and antinullification views contributed to his defeat and led him to leave the state in 1833. He moved to Texas in March 1835 and, as the Texas Revolution heated up, was put under house arrest. Forbidden to leave San Antonio by Martín Perfecto de Cos, he kept a diary that provides a vivid record of the siege of Bexar. He and fellow prisoner John W. Smith were released on 1 December and quickly made their way to the besiegers' camp, where they urged an immediate attack. In the attack on 5 December, Maverick guided Benjamin R. Milam's men. He remained in San Antonio after the siege and in February was elected one of two delegates from the Alamo garrison to the independence convention scheduled for 1 March 1836 at Washington-on-the-Brazos. After the convention, ill and needed for family business, he departed for Alabama about the time of Sam Houston's victory at San Jacinto. In Alabama he was married. In 1837, with their first-born, Samuel Maverick, Jr., and a small retinue of slaves, the couple started for Texas. In June 1838 they established a home in San Antonio. Maverick obtained his Texas law license, speculated in West Texas land, and served as San Antonio mayor in 1839. He followed his term as mayor with a term as treasurer and continued to serve on the city council until the Mavericks joined the "Runaway of '42," a move based on rumors of an impending Mexican invasion. They settled temporarily near Gonzales, but Maverick returned to San Antonio for the fall term of district court and was one of the prisoners taken by Mexican general Adrián Woll. He was released from Perote Prison in April 1843 through the intervention of United States minister to Mexico Waddy Thompson. Upon his return, Maverick, who had been elected to the Seventh Congress of the Republic of Texas, served in the Eighth Congress, where he was a strong advocate of annexation. In 1844 he moved his growing family to Decros Point on Matagorda Bay.

When he returned permanently to San Antonio (1847), Maverick left a small herd of cattle on Matagorda Peninsula with slave caretakers. This herd, allowed to wander, is said to have given rise to the term *maverick*. In 1854 Maverick had the cattle rounded up and driven to his Conquista Ranch, near the site of

The Terry Rangers, by Carl G. von Iwonski, ca. 1862. Oil on canvas. 11½" × 15". Courtesy Witte Museum, San Antonio. Iwonski, a German immigrant and Unionist, painted this portrait of the young Sam Maverick of San Antonio (second from left), who served the Confederacy throughout the Civil War, first in Benjamin Franklin's famous Terry's Texas Rangers (Eighth Texas Cavalry).

Toutant Beauregard, a brother of Confederate general Pierre G. T. Beauregard, on range delivery, which meant the purchasers had to hunt for the animals on the open range. The men covered several counties looking for strays. Any unbranded cattle were claimed as "Maverick's" and branded. By 1857 people around San Antonio were referring to unbranded, weaned cattle as "mavericks." After the Civil War there were numerous unbranded cattle, especially in Southwest Texas and on the coastal plains southeast of San Antonio, and the term became common. In the St. Louis *Republic* of 16 November 1889, George Madison Maverick, Samuel's son, published an article on the origin of the term *maverick*. The Texas legislature passed a law against driving another person's livestock from its accustomed range and theoretically outlawed mavericking, but the practice was not generally considered theft until the late 1880s, after open-range ranching gradually came to an end and cattle ranchers began acquiring grazing land and fencing their property. The Cowboy Strike of 1883 occurred in part as a response to the ranchers' insistence that mavericks were company property and could not be taken by the cowboys as wages. More recently, the term *maverick* came to refer to any living creature, human or otherwise, that goes its own way rather than acting as part of a group or herd.

David Dary

present Floresville, before selling them in 1856. Subsequently, he expanded his West Texas landholdings to more than 300,000 acres. He gained land primarily by buying such land grant instruments as headright certificates and bounty and donation certificates. In the 1850s and 1860s he was one of the two biggest investors in West Texas acreage. Maverick County was named in his honor. Maverick served as a Democrat in the Fourth through Ninth state legislatures (1851–63). There he worked to ensure equal opportunity for his Mexican and German constituents, to foster fair and liberal laws for land acquisition and ownership, to develop transportation and other internal state improvements, to provide protection for the frontier, and to ensure a fair and efficient judicial system. He also worked until the outbreak of the Civil War to stem the tide of secessionism, but, seeing that a conflict was inevitable, threw his support to the Confederacy. He was one of three secession commissioners appointed by the Texas Secession Convention. The three successfully effected the removal of federal troops and the transfer of federal stores in Texas to the state government. During the war he was elected chief justice (county judge) of Bexar County and served a second term as San Antonio mayor. After the war he received a presidential pardon and was active in attempts to combat the Radical Republican regime in Reconstruction Texas. He was an Episcopalian. *Paula Mitchell Marks*

Maverick. Although there are several versions of how unbranded cattle came to be known as "mavericks," nearly all of them involve Samuel A. Maverick. In Matagorda County he accepted a herd of 400 cattle instead of cash repayment for a $1,200 loan. When the family returned to San Antonio, the animals were neglected and many of the calves were not branded. Residents soon were referring to any unbranded cow as "one of Maverick's." In 1854 Maverick moved the cattle he could find to his San Antonio ranch, where they were allowed to roam unchecked. In 1856 Maverick sold his cattle and brand to A.

Maxey, Samuel Bell. Confederate general and United States senator; b. Tompkinsville, Kentucky, 30 March 1825; d. Eureka Springs, Arkansas, 16 August 1895 (buried in Paris, Texas); m. Marilda Cass Denton (1853); ed. United States Military Academy (grad. 1846). Maxey's roommate for a year at West Point was Stonewall Jackson. Maxey fought in the Mexican War battles of Cerro Gordo, Contreras, Churubusco, and Molino del Rey. He was commended for valor, brevetted first lieutenant, and placed in command of one of the five select companies that formed a city police guard in Mexico City. In 1849 he resigned from the army and began practicing law in Albany, Kentucky, with his father. He and his father moved their families to Texas, where they arrived in October 1857 and purchased five acres of prairieland south of Paris. After the state Secession Convention, Maxey, then district attorney of Lamar County, became captain of a company called the Lamar Rifles and accompanied a military force into Indian Territory. Why he ran for the Texas Senate in 1861 is something of a puzzle, for he simultaneously began to write letters to influential Confederate friends to obtain permission to form a regiment. He won the election but sent his father to the Senate in his stead. In January 1862 Maxey's newly formed Ninth Texas Infantry regiment left Camp Benjamin, near Bonham, and marched on orders toward Bowling Green, Kentucky, to join the forces of Gen. Albert Sidney Johnston. Maxey was promoted to brigadier general in March 1862. He fought at Port Hudson, in the Vicksburg campaign, and at Jackson, Mississippi; he often commanded as many as 3,000 men. In December 1863 he was appointed commander of Indian Territory, where he served until February 1865, when he was given a division of cavalry and ordered to report to Beauchamp Springs, near Houston. On 22 May 1865, discouraged at the large-scale desertion from his division, he asked to be relieved of his command. After the war he learned from Texas Confederate senator H. C. Burnett that before his resignation President Jefferson Davis had approved Maxey's nomination to major general and that the Confederate Senate had confirmed it. Maxey was elected to the United States Senate in 1874 and served two terms. He was on the post office committee and did much to develop the postal system in Texas. He also aided in establishing the stage route from Fort Worth to Yuma. He pressed for federal aid for the improvement of Texas harbors, for frontier protection for Texas, and for the extension of the Texas and Pacific Railway. He believed that the war ended at Appomattox and adopted reason and moderation as his guidelines. He was a friend of Sherman and Grant. The Maxey home in Paris, a two-story frame residence completed in 1868, is a combination of Greek Revival and High Victorian Italianate styling; it was listed on the National Register of Historic Places in 1971.

Louise Horton

Mayfield, Earle Bradford. United States Senator; b. Overton, 12 April 1881; d. Tyler, 23 June 1964; m. Ora Lumpkin (1902); 3 sons; ed. Southwestern University (grad. 1900) and the University of Texas law school (1900–01). In 1907 Mayfield began to practice law in Meridian. He served in the Texas Senate from 1907 to 1913 and was a member of the Railroad Commission from 1913 to 1923. He ran for United States senator in 1922 against the elderly Charles A. Culberson's bid for a sixth term. With the endorsement of Senator Morris Sheppard, he obtained the Democratic nomination in a bitter runoff campaign against former governor James E. Ferguson, in which Ferguson was billed as the antiprohibitionist candidate and Mayfield, who supported the Volstead Act, as the Ku Klux Klan candidate. Mayfield avoided the Klan issue and spoke out against federal control of freight rates. In the general election he was opposed by an Independent Democratic–Republican fusion candidate, George E. B. Peddy, whom he defeated by a vote of two to one. Peddy demanded an investigation of the election by the United States Senate, complaining that his name was not printed on the ballot, that Mayfield missed the filing dates, spent too much money in his campaign, and was supported by the Klan. After investigating for two years, the Senate found in favor of Mayfield and permitted him to take his seat. He sought renomination in 1928 and led a field of six candidates in the first Democratic primary, but in the runoff he was defeated by Congressman Thomas Terry Connally. In the 1930 Democratic primary for governor he ran seventh in a field of 11. After leaving the Senate, Mayfield lived in Tyler, where he practiced law and was president of the Mayfield Wholesale Grocery Company. He received an honorary doctorate from John Brown University of Siloam Springs, Arkansas.

Frank H. Smyrl

Medical Quackery. During the days of the Republic of Texas, Texas newspapers regularly advertised Burnham's Drops, Lin's Balm of China, Connel's Pain Extractor, Christie's Galvanic Belt, and many other alleged keys to prolonged and painless life. "Thousands are daily *quacked*, out of comfort, out of temper, out of health, out of money, out of liberty, out of their senses, and finally into their graves," declared one Texan. Humbuggery abounded. The vast territory of Texas made it impossible for trained doctors to serve everyone, and there was no convincing evidence that trained doctors provided remedies better than the cheaper nostrums offered by entrepreneurial quacks. Saddlebags carried pills or bottles of tonics that often contained large amounts of alcohol and, in some cases, morphine. By the time of the Civil War, ads in the Galveston *Weekly News* touted

Hostetter's Stomach Bitters; or Dr. Leroy's French Specific for All Affections of the Urinary Organs, and those Affections Only; or Daly's Aromatic Valley Whiskey for Medicinal Purposes; or Brown's Bronchial Troches; or Sanford's Family Blood Purifying Pills; or Old Sachem Bitters and Wigwam Tonic. Texans imbibed gallons of the tonics and ate tons of the pills.

Indian Medicine shows were popular. During the 1880s Charlie Bigelow, a Bee County farmer, staged one of the greatest. He sold vast quantities of Kickapoo Indian Sagwa as a tonic for indigestion, constipation, rheumatism, and almost any other symptom or disease. His traveling show included Indian dances, trapeze artists, trained dogs, fancy shooting, and a mock Indian marriage ceremony. Those enjoying the free show usually thanked Bigelow's troupe by purchasing a one-dollar bottle of the tonic. William Radam, an Austin gardener, exploited a popular belief that germs cause all diseases; his mixture supposedly exterminated these germs. "I treated all my patients with the same medicine," Radam claimed, "just as in my garden I would treat all weeds alike." Radam made so much money that he left his Austin gardens for a New York City mansion overlooking Central Park. During the twentieth century, Texans spent thousands of dollars in support of three of America's most prominent quacks: John R. Brinkley, Norman Baker, and Harry M. Hoxsey. In 1919 Brinkley acquired a license to practice medicine in Texas. He eventually became famous as the "goat-gland doctor," a self-labeled specialist in sexual rejuvenation. Hundreds of patients flocked to Del Rio to receive "goat-gland" transplants and thereby sustain Brinkley's millionaire manner of living. In Laredo, Norman Baker lured patients to his hospital with boasts of cancer sure-cures. In Dallas, Harry Hoxsey offered similar cures to desperate patients for 25 years.

Chester R. Burns

Medina, Battle of. Occurred 20 miles south of San Antonio in a sandy, oak-forest region then called El Encinal de Medina, 18 August 1813; the bloodiest battle on Texas soil. The conflict between republicans and royalists affected the destinies of Spain, Mexico, the United States, England, and France. At Medina, republican forces of the Gutiérrez–Magee expedition under Gen. José Álvarez de Toledo y Dubois met a Spanish royalist army under Gen. Joaquín de Arredondo. Mexico and Latin America were in revolt against Spain, whose king was Joseph Bonaparte, brother of Napoleon. Napoleon was on a rampage in Europe, and the United States was in a war with England, later to be called the War of 1812. In this cauldron of world events, Gutiérrez and Magee, abetted by the United States, organized an expedition to wrest Texas from Spain. Their effort was crushed at the battle of Medina. After some initial success they proclaimed independence. Their "republic," however, was short-lived, for Arredondo, commandantgeneral of the Provincias Internas, organized an army of 1,830 men to meet the filibusters' force of about 1,400. Outfoxed by Arredondo, the republicans walked into a furious surprise attack. Fewer than 100 survived, and of these no more than 20 have been identified. Arredondo lost 55 men, who were given honorable burial the next day on the way to San Antonio, where he established martial law and severely punished the rebels and their families. One of his subalterns was Lt. Antonio López de Santa Anna, who returned to Texas with another army 23 years later. The bodies of the republicans were left on the battlefield until 1822, when José Félix Trespalacios, the first governor of Texas under the Republic of

Mexico, had the bones buried. So disastrous was *la batalla del encinal de Medina* that its battlefield has become lost, its "Green Flag" has remained largely unrecognized, and its participants have been generally unknown and unsung. Some of its survivors were sons of American revolutionaries, some fought with Andrew Jackson later in the War of 1812, and some fought again during the Texas Revolution in 1835–36.   *Robert H. Thonhoff*

Menken, Adah Isaacs. Actress and poet; also known as Adelaide McCord and Ada Bertha Théodore; probably born Ada C. McCord, Memphis, Tennessee, 15 June 1835; d. Paris, 10 August 1868; m. Alexander Isaac Menken (1856; separated); m. John Carmel Heenan (1859; divorced 1862); m. twice more. Adah's life before her stage career is obscured by her elaborate accounts, which include a variety of names, ethnic backgrounds, birthplaces, and genealogies. Although it has been claimed that she attended Nacogdoches University, the first documented evidence of her presence in Texas appeared in a Liberty *Gazette* advertisement on 8 October 1855, announcing that Ada Bertha Théodore would be giving readings of Shakespeare. Subsequent issues contained poems and essays attributed to her and datelined Austin City and Washington, Texas. She married in Livingston and, after two years of limited engagements at small theaters in New Orleans, Shreveport, and Nashville, urged her husband to take her to his family in Cincinnati. There she embraced Judaism; she occasionally claimed to have been born a Jew. She made her theatrical debut in 1857 as Pauline in *The Lady of Lyons* at Shreveport, and then appeared as Bianca in *Fazio* in New Orleans. In March 1859 she made her New York debut as the Widow Cheerly in *The Soldier's Daughter*. She published a number of poems in the Cincinnati *Israelite*. Her husband's family, however, was not amused by the attention lavished upon Adah in her unorthodox career. The couple secured a rabbinical diploma dissolving their marriage, but Adah continued using Menken as her stage name. Her second husband was a noted Irish prizefighter who divorced her and left her pregnant when he discovered that she was not legally divorced from Menken.

Adah continued to write poetry and to play minor roles until June 1861, when she was called upon to star in *Mazeppa; or The Wild Horse of Tartary*, a melodrama based on a poem by Lord Byron that opened at Albany's Green Street Theatre. Already accustomed to male roles, Adah was game to try strapping herself to a horse for the climax. In flesh-toned tights, under the dimmed stage lights she appeared to be nude. She became an overnight sensation. During the next few years the drama played the major northeastern and midwestern cities, toured the West, then was a great success in Europe. Although she took other roles, she always returned to *Mazeppa*. Meanwhile, she married and divorced two more husbands, Civil War satirist Robert Henry Newell (pseud. Orpheus C. Kerr), whom she married in 1862 and divorced in 1865, and James Paul Barkley, a gambler she married in 1866 and left almost immediately. Always longing for recognition as a poet, Adah associated with many of the literary personages of her time. She admired Walt Whitman, and her posthumously published volume, *Infelicia* (1868), contained an early collection of free verse. In the West she mingled with the young Samuel Clemens, Bret Harte, and Joaquin Miller. In Europe she purportedly had affairs with French novelist Alexander Dumas *père* and with English poet Algernon Charles Swinburne. Adah dedicated her book of verse to Charles

Dickens, and George Sand was godmother at the baptism of Adah's son Louis. Adah abandoned her militant Jewish role after encountering anti-Semitism in Europe. She spent her large earnings from the theater on luxuries and gave generously to friends, struggling actors and artists, and charities, so that she had little left at the end. In the winter of 1867–68 she attempted without much success to revive *Mazeppa*. Afterward, she returned to Paris and went into rehearsal for a revival of her other mainstay, *Les Pirates de la Savane*, but complications arose from an injury she had sustained while performing in London. Her last performance was on 30 May 1868.   *Pamela Lynn Palmer*

Mercer Colony. In north central Texas east and south of the Peters colony. It lay roughly between the Brazos and Sabine rivers, north from Waco to McKinney in Collin County, skirting to the south and east of what is now the Dallas metropolitan area. Its boundaries encompassed portions of 18 future Texas counties. The colony grew out of a statute enacted by the Texas Congress on 4 February 1841 restoring the Mexican policy of granting empresario contracts. In spite of growing opposition to such contracts, President Sam Houston granted Charles Fenton Mercer a contract to settle at least 100 families a year for five years, beginning on 29 January 1844. Mercer soon organized a company, the Texas Association, to advertise and promote colonization, and sold shares at $500 each to investors in Virginia and Florida as well as in Texas. The work of colonization was impeded by the fact that various politicians, land speculators, and squatters, all eager to supplant the empresario system with the Anglo-American land system, questioned both the wisdom and the legality of granting away the republic's vast public lands without financial gain. Mercer himself was also unpopular, for he was known as an abolitionist, a speculator, a monopolist, and an opponent of free immigration for Anglo-Americans. One day after the execution of Mercer's contract the Congress of the republic passed, over Houston's veto, a statute outlawing colonization contracts. Congressional resentment culminated in an investigation during 1844–45 of Mercer's contract and his efforts to fulfill its terms. Meanwhile, squatters moved into the Mercer survey and denied the claims of settlers who held Mercer colony certificates. Settlers also discovered land speculators and holders of bounty and headright certificates already claiming the land for which they had contracted, and Mercer's surveyors reported that Robertson County, joining the colony on the south, was sending its surveyors into the limits of the empresario grant and claiming the land they surveyed. Finally, Mercer surveyors and settlers clashed with both civil and military forces when they attempted to penetrate that portion of the grant lying west of the Trinity River.

Mercer's association initially offered only 160 acres to families and 80 acres to single men. The fact that the adjacent Peters colony promoters were offering 320 acres (later 640) to families diverted many newcomers to that colony before Mercer finally matched the offer. Nevertheless, by the end of the first year of the contract, more than 100 families had complied with the requirements and received land certificates. After the Convention of 1845 instructed the new state of Texas to begin legal proceedings against all colony contracts, Governor Albert C. Horton instituted suit in 1846 against Mercer and the Texas Association in the district court of Navarro County. Judge R. E. B. Baylor of the Third Judicial District declared the contract between Mercer and Houston null and void, but the Texas Supreme Court subsequently upheld the legality of the contract. In 1850 the Texas legislature, seeking to quiet the confusion within the colony, guaranteed all land claims made by settlers in the Mercer colony before 25 October 1848. By virtue of this legislation, 1,255 land certificates were recorded in the General Land Office, but the measure failed to adjust all conflicting land claims, some of which were in process of litigation as late as 1936. In the face of these developments, and in hopes of protecting the investments of his associates in his Texas project, Mercer severed all connection with the grant on 27 February 1852 by assigning his interest in the Texas Association to George Hancock of Louisville, Kentucky. Although settlers recruited by Mercer and the Texas Association were ultimately granted the lands they had settled on, the state of Texas steadfastly refused to legalize any claims of the association itself. The state would not allow the association to sue in state courts and defended with vigor against all claims that it brought. The commissioner of the General Land Office threw open for sale the public lands within the Mercer grant. On 6 March 1875 the chief agent of the association filed an injunction in the United States circuit court at Austin, demanding that the land titles of the association be legalized whether within the area of the Mercer colony grant or elsewhere within the public domain of Texas. The United States Supreme Court settled the issue in 1883 by denying all compensation owed the association that was based on the original empresario contract.

Joe E. Ericson

Mercury Mining. In Texas all mercury mining has been done about 90 miles south of Alpine. The producing area, known as the Terlingua District, is the third-largest mercury-producing area in the U.S. Cinnabar, the brilliant red ore of mercury, was discovered and first worked in Texas by Indians, who probably used it as war paint and certainly used it in rock paintings. Cinnabar was probably an article of commerce among the Plains Indians, for Ferdinand von Roemer, who traversed the Comanche country in 1840, mentions trading a lasso for a small quantity. In 1884 white men took a sample of ore to Alpine for identification. This event led to prospecting and additional discoveries, and the first flask (76 pounds) of mercury was produced in 1886. In 1898 mining was started by what later became the Marfa and Mariposa Mining Company. By 1900 the company had produced about a thousand flasks by means of retorts. The Big Bend and Texas Almaden at Study Butte and the Chisos Mining Company at Terlingua began production in 1903, and the Chisos Company operated continuously for the next 40 years. The Mariscal Mine near Hot Springs operated intermittently from 1916 to 1942. The Fresno Mines at Buena Suerte began production in 1940. Numerous small properties operated when the price of mercury was above normal. Mercury has vital wartime uses. During both world wars, under the stimulus of patriotic endeavor and the inducement of high prices, the U.S. led in quicksilver production. From 1939 to 1945 at least five mines were active, but with the end of World War II supplies from warimpoverished countries, principally Spain, were dumped into world markets and created such an oversupply that Texas mines were abandoned by 1946. After the war Spain and Italy produced 70 percent of the world supplies, and this country produced 20 percent. No reliable records of mercury production in Texas before 1919 are extant. Production from 1919 to 1941 was

55,081 flasks. In 1954 the federal government's price guarantee of $225 per flask and increased national consumption of mercury stimulated further recovery around Terlingua, and the following year two Texas mines produced mercury for the open market. Nevertheless, the heyday of the industry was over. Various companies—notably Diamond Shamrock—recovered mercury from Texas mines sporadically thereafter, but after 1973, because of decreased demand, no further production was reported.

W. D. Burcham and Harris S. Smith

Mesquite. Perhaps the most common leguminous plant occurring naturally in Texas. Four species occur; the variety *Prosopis glandulosa glandulosa* is the most widespread, being found throughout the state. Mesquite ranges from a shrub to a tree and has thorns and pinnately twice-compound leaves. Its flowers are creamy white and turn yellow with maturity. The fruit is a leathery, solid, indehiscent pod several centimeters long. Mesquite is a sprouting plant with numerous dormant buds below-ground that are activated when the aboveground portion is damaged or killed. The plant, native to Texas and the Southwest, originally grew only along streams and rivers and in open groves, but now it occupies about 50 million to 60 million acres of Texas rangelands, excluding the piney woods. Its spread can be attributed to such causes as the cessation of prairie fires, overgrazing, wagontrains traversing the state, trail drives, and drought. Mesquite furnishes shade for livestock and habitat for wildlife. It provides food and cover for such species as quail, dove, raven, turkey, Gambel quail, mallard duck, white-tail and mule deer, wood rat, kangaroo rat, chipmunk, pocket mouse, ground squirrel, prairie dog, cottontail, jackrabbit, skunk, peccary, coyote, and Mexican raccoon. It has many varied uses throughout the Southwest. The mesquite-bean pod was a staple in the Indians' diet and was even considered a luxury by some groups. Pods were also ground into meal and made into bread or mixed with water to form a sweet, nutritious atole, which, when fermented, produced a weak beer. Honey made from the nectar of mesquite flowers is considered a delicacy. Indian women used mesquite bark to make diapers, skirts, and other articles of clothing. They wove baskets, ropes, and twine from mesquite fibers. Mesquite bark was also used to make a poultice for treating wounds and illnesses. The gum exuded from mesquite trunks was used as candy, as a glue for mending pottery, and as a black dye. Unfinished mesquite wood has been used for fenceposts and corrals. It can also be used as boiler fuel, wood chips, wood flakes, meal, feed, mulch, particleboard, insulation batting, and charcoal. The trees have been used as ornamentals in landscaping homes. The wood is very hard and has been successfully made into such articles of furniture as cabinets, game tables, and desks.

Though mesquite has been beneficial to many cultures, it is also a menace because of the amount of water it uses. Sparse stands do not deplete soil water drastically, but dense stands growing along streams and rivers, above shallow water tables, and in deep soil use water extravagantly. In addition to reducing the amount of water that ultimately could be available for agricultural purposes, mesquite reduces the amount of forage available for livestock. Its presence also causes an inconvenience to ranchers working livestock. In the early 1980s mesquite became a popular fuel for cooking in restaurants all over the country.

Ronald E. Sosebee

Mestizo. In New Spain a mestizo was a person born in the New World with one Spanish-born and one Indian parent. Frequently, mulattos passed into this group as racial characteristics blended over centuries of settlement. On the social ladder, mestizos occupied a middle rung below pure bloods, but above Indians, free blacks, and slaves. The legal status of mestizos, like their heritage, was mixed. They paid the same taxes as the upper classes, obeyed the same laws, and owed military service. They were additionally subject to the same sumptuary laws as Indians, although enforcement of these laws was lax. When José de Escandón took colonists across the Rio Grande into Texas in 1748, some areas were already occupied by settlers; among them were mestizos. Many Tejanos were descendants of mestizos. On the frontier this group rapidly became the largest segment of the population. They were eligible for all kinds of lower administrative positions and occasionally rose to positions of power, depending upon their abilities. They also acquired property. In spite of the fluidity of the social structure on the frontier, mestizos remained below peninsulares and criollos.   *Joan E. Supplee*

Metropolitan Statistical Areas. Since 1910 the federal government has issued census information on metropolitan areas, labeled variously as metropolitan districts, metropolitan counties, industrial areas, or labor-market areas. In 1949 the term Standard Metropolitan Areas was introduced. In 1958 "Statistical" was added as an identifying phrase. The concept aided in the collection of comparable statistics so that socioeconomic factors such as labor force, industrial output, and criminal records could be used in analyses. A Standard Metropolitan Statistical Area was officially defined as one or more counties containing a core city of at least 50,000 inhabitants, or two cities with a combined population of at least 50,000, provided the smaller had at least 15,000 persons. The area had to have a "metropolitan character," or at least 75 percent of its labor force in nonagricultural employment, as well as economic and social integration between the central city and its county and outlying counties. An urban region could have more than one SMSA; Fort Worth, Dallas, and Sherman–Denison were separate although contiguous SMSAs. In 1970 Texas had more SMSAs than any other state (24). The designation "Standard" was later dropped, and three area classifications based on population were adopted: (1) the Metropolitan Statistical Area, the basic unit, a freestanding urbanized area with a population of at least 50,000; (2) the Primary Metropolitan Statistical Area, having two or more MSAs and 100,000 or more population; and (3) the Consolidated Metropolitan Statistical Area, having two or more PMSAs with a total population of 1,000,000. In 1990 the United States had 261 MSAs of which 28 were in Texas; 7 of 71 PMSAs in the United States were in Texas, and 2 of 20 United States CMSAs were in Texas—the Dallas–Fort Worth area (population about 4,000,000) and the Houston area (population about 3,750,000). Cities want to obtain the highest possible statistical designation because many congressional appropriations are made according to size. Businesses use population data for market analysis and advertising. Texas MSAs include only 48 of the 254 counties but 80 percent of the population.   *Shirley Chapman*

Meusebach, John O. Founder of Fredericksburg; b. Baron Otfried Hans Freiherr von Meusebach, Dillenburg (now in the German state of Hessen), 26 May 1812; d. Loyal Valley, Texas, 27

John O. Meusebach, 1832. Pencil sketch. Courtesy ITC. This portrait was made when Meusebach was a young man at the University of Bonn, 13 years before he emigrated to Texas to fill the position of commissioner general of the Adelsverein, or Society for the Protection of German Immigrants in Texas.

May 1897 (buried at Cherry Spring); m. Countess Agnes of Coreth (1852); 11 children; ed. University of Bonn, University of Halle. Meusebach could read five languages and speak English fluently. In 1845 the Adelsverein appointed him to succeed Prince Carl of Solms–Braunfels as its commissioner general in Texas. After arriving in Galveston, he rode to New Braunfels in six overnight stops. He served the immigrants in accord with the motto on his family's crest, "*Tenax Propositi*" ("Steadfast in Purpose"). He founded the settlements of Fredericksburg, Castell, and Leiningen. Soon after his arrival in New Braunfels, he adopted the name John O. Meusebach. Convinced that use should be made of the land in the Fisher–Miller Land Grant, he acquired headrights in it on credit. Before surveying and settlement of the site could occur, it was necessary to arrive at an agreement with the Comanche Indians. In December 1846, speaking through Indian interpreter Jim Shaw, Meusebach arranged to meet with 10 Comanche chiefs on the lower San Saba River. Despite current reports that the Comanches were on the warpath, Meusebach and a delegation of German settlers met with the head chiefs—Buffalo Hump, Santa Anna, and Mopechucope (Old Owl)—and their people. He promised them presents worth $3,000 in return for their pledge not to disturb the surveyors or harm the colonists. On May 9, 1847, the Comanche chiefs went to Fredericksburg to sign the Meusebach–Comanche Treaty and collect their gifts. This treaty was one of the most important pioneer works of the Germans in Texas. After it, in July 1847, thinking that his work for the society was complete, Meusebach gave up the office of commissioner general.

Among Meusebach's close associates in Texas were botanist Ferdinand Lindheimer and geologist Ferdinand von Roemer. He also corresponded and exchanged native plants with George Engelmann, founder of the Missouri State Botanical Gardens. With Engelmann as his intermediary, Meusebach annually supplied from his land in Central Texas thousands of cuttings of native black Spanish grapes to replace the phylloxera-ravaged plants of French vineyards. He also supplied Texas yucca plants to the American and foreign markets. At least once Engelmann provided Meusebach with *Catalpa speciosa* seeds. In 1851 Meusebach was elected to the Texas Senate, where he was a member of the committees on state affairs and education. In the latter, he advocated universal and compulsory education. In early 1852 the committee got a bill passed to provide for a system of public schools. In 1854 Meusebach received an appointment as commissioner from Governor Elisha M. Pease to issue land certificates to immigrants of 1845 and 1846 who had been promised them by the Adelsverein. Meusebach lost his first fiancée, Elisabeth von Hardenburg, to typhoid fever. He retired to his 200-acre farm in Loyal Valley in 1869 and spent his remaining years tending his orchard, vineyards, and rose garden. *Cornelia Marschall Smith and Otto W. Tetzlaff*

Mexía, José Antonio. Mexican military officer; b. probably in Jalapa, 1800, but perhaps in Cuba; d. Mexico City, 19 September 1896; m. Charlotte Walker (1823); 2 + children. The deaths of Mexía's father and brother in the Mexican War of Independence forced him to seek refuge in the U.S., where he acquired such proficiency in the English language that in November 1822 Texas governor José Félix Trespalacios named him interpreter for a Cherokee Indian delegation to Mexico City. In 1823–24 he served as secretary of the state congress of Tamaulipas, and from 1825 to 1827 as collector of customs in Tuxpan. In 1825–27 he took an active part in the growth of York Rite Masonry, and, after 1827, in the affairs of the Federalist party. He again entered active service in 1827, when he was named to the staff of Gen. Vicente Guerrero. He was promoted to lieutenant colonel (1828), colonel (1829), and brigadier general (1832). Mexía served in the U.S as secretary of the Mexican legation, 1829–31. There he became an agent for the Galveston Bay and Texas Land Company. In June 1832, after the Anahuac Disturbances, he led the so-called Mexía's expedition to Texas to suppress an apparent rebellion. Stephen F. Austin and other Texas leaders convinced him that the settlers were loyal to Mexico. While a senator from the state of Mexico in 1834, Mexía joined Federalist forces that rose in protest against Santa Anna's assumption of dictatorial powers, was defeated in Jalisco, and was exiled to the U.S. During his exile he led a failed attack on Tampico (1835) and traveled to Cuba and Central America for a New Orleans export–import company of which he was a partner. With the resurgence of the Federalists he returned to Tampico in 1839 and joined Gen. José de Urrea as second in command. When Urrea's undermanned forces were routed by government troops near Puebla, Mexía

was captured and executed by a firing squad. In November 1833 the state of Coahuila and Texas granted Mexía's daughter Adelaida and his son Enrique separate titles to 11-league tracts of land in Limestone, Freestone, and Anderson counties. In 1871 the Houston and Texas Central Townsite Company named the town of Mexia for Enrique and the Mexia family.

Raymond Estep

Mexican Americans. People of Mexican descent in Texas trace their biological origins to the racial mixture that occurred following the Spanish conquest of Mexico in the 1520s. During the Spanish colonial period, population grew as Spanish males mixed with Indian females, begetting a mestizo race. By 1821, when Mexico won its independence from Spain, the mestizo population almost equaled the size of the indigenous stock and that of Iberian-born persons. Mexicans advanced northward from central Mexico in exploratory and settlement operations soon after the conquest, but did not permanently claim the Texas frontierland until after 1710. In the late seventeenth and early eighteenth centuries, the French became increasingly active along the Texas Gulf Coast, and in response, the viceroy in Mexico City made preparations for the colonization of the Texas wilderness. The first expedition in 1716 peopled an area that subsequently became the town of Nacogdoches; a second in 1718 founded San Antonio; and a third established La Bahía (Goliad) in 1721. During the 1740s and 1750s, the crown founded further colonies along both banks of the Rio Grande, including what is now Laredo. At this early time, the crown relied primarily on persuasion to get settlers to pick up and relocate in the far-off Texas lands. Those responding hailed from Coahuila and Nuevo León, though intrepid souls from the interior joined the early migrations. In reality, few pioneers wished to live in isolation or amid conditions that included possible Indian attacks. They feared a setting that lacked adequate supplies, sustenance, and medical facilities for the sick, especially infants. Frontier living inhibited population growth so that at the beginning of the nineteenth century, when Spanish Texas neared its end, the Mexican-descent population numbered only about 5,000.

Between then and the time of the Texas Revolution in 1836, the number of Hispanics fluctuated, but then increased perceptibly, so that the first federal census of Texas in 1850 counted more than 14,000 residents of Mexican origin. Subsequently, people migrated from Mexico in search of agricultural work in the state, and in the last half of the century, moved north due to a civil war in the homeland (the War of the Reform, 1855–61) and the military resistance against the French presence (1862–67). But they also looked to Texas as a refuge from the poverty at home, a condition exacerbated by the emergence of President Porfirio Díaz (1876–1911), whose dictatorial rule favored landowners and other privileged elements in society. The Mexican Revolution (1910–1920) increased the movement of people across the Rio Grande. Mass relocation persisted into the 1920s as agricultural expansion in the southwestern United States also acted to entice the desperately poor. The total Mexican-descent population in Texas may have approximated 700,000 by 1930. The Great Depression and deportation drives undertaken during the 1930s stymied population expansion. Growth resumed during the 1940s, however, as labor shortages in the United States induced common people from Mexico to seek escape from nagging poverty in the homeland. Many

Mexican woman and children looking over the side of a truck that is taking them to their homes in the Rio Grande valley from Mississippi, where they have been picking cotton. Photograph by Russell Lee, 1939. Library of Congress; USF 33-12466-M2. As late as the 1940s, the majority of Tejanos resided in rural areas and worked vegetable or cotton fields.

turned to Texas ranches and farms, but also to urban opportunities, as the state entered the post–World War II industrial boom. Their presence, combined with births among the native-born population, augmented the Spanish-surnamed population to 1,400,000 by 1960. Though economic refugees from Mexico continued to add to the expansion of Tejano communities after the 1960s, the majority of children born since that date have had U.S.-born parents. The 1990 census counted 4,000,000 people of Mexican descent in the state. Fewer than 20 percent of that population were of foreign birth.

In 1836, when Texas acquired independence from Mexico, Tejanos remained concentrated in settlements founded during the eighteenth century, namely Nacogdoches, San Antonio, Goliad, and Laredo. Other communities with a primarily Mexican-descent population in 1836 included Victoria, founded by Martín De León in 1824, and the villages of San Elizario, Ysleta, and Socorro in far west Texas. Spaniards had founded these latter settlements on the west bank of the Rio Grande during the 1680s as they sought to claim New Mexico, but the villages became part of the future West Texas when the Rio Grande changed course in the 1830s. Population dispersals until the mid-nineteenth century occurred mainly within the regions of Central and South Texas. In the former area, Tejanos spread out into the counties east and southeast of San Antonio seeking a livelihood in this primarily Anglo-dominated region. In South

Texas, they pushed from the Rio Grande settlements toward Nueces River ranchlands and still composed a majority of the section's population despite the increased number of Anglo arrivals after the Mexican War of 1846–48. In the years after the Civil War, Mexicans moved west of the 100th meridian, migrating simultaneously with Anglo pioneers then displacing Indians from their native habitat and converting hinterlands into cattle and sheep ranches. By 1900, Tejanos were settled in all three sections. They formed a minority in Central Texas and a majority in South Texas; they held a demographic advantage along the border counties of West Texas, but were outnumbered by Anglos in that section's interior.

The rise of commercial agriculture in the late nineteenth and early twentieth centuries summoned laborers for seasonal and farm work, and both recent arrivals from Mexico and native-born Tejanos answered the call by heading into South and Central Texas fields. During this period, they also made for Southeast Texas and North Texas, searching out cotton lands as well as opportunities in large cities such as Houston and Dallas. Between 1910 and 1929, migrant workers began what became a yearly migrant swing that started in the farms of South Texas and headed northward into the developing Northwest Texas and Panhandle cotton lands. They settled in smaller communities along the routes of migration, and by the 1930s the basic contours of modern-day Tejano demography had taken form. With

Market Plaza, by Thomas Allen, 1878–79. Oil on canvas mounted on panel. 26" × 39½". Courtesy Witte Museum, San Antonio. Although Tejanos were a minority in San Antonio by 1876, their culture continued to make the city one of the most colorful in the country. Allen was an American artist trained in the United States and Europe.

the exception of Northeast Texas, most cities and towns in the state by the pre–World War II era had Tejano populations.

Tejanos relied on a wide spectrum of occupations in the nineteenth century, though most found themselves confined to jobs as day laborers and in other unspecialized tasks. They worked as maids, restaurant helpers, and laundry workers, but the great majority turned to range duties due to the orientation of the economy and their skills as ranchhands and shepherds (*pastores*). A small percentage found a niche as entrepreneurs or ranchers. After the 1880s, Texas Mexicans turned to new avenues of livelihood, such as building railroads and performing other arduous tasks. During the agricultural revolution of the late nineteenth and the early twentieth centuries, many worked grubbing brush and picking cotton, vegetables, and fruits, primarily in the fields of South Texas, but also migrated into the other regions of the state as farmhands. In the urban settlements, an entrepreneurial sector—comprising shopowners, labor agents, barbers, theater owners, restaurateurs, and the like—ministered to Mexican consumers in familiar terms. Even as Texas society experienced increased urban movements following World War I, Tejanos remained preponderantly an agrarian people. In towns, many faced labor segregation and took menial jobs in construction work, city projects, railroad lines, slaughterhouses, cotton compresses, and whatever else availed itself. After World War II, however, increased numbers of Tejanos left agricultural work and found opportunities in the industrializing

cities. Most found improvements in wages and working conditions in unskilled or semiskilled positions, though a growing number penetrated the professional, managerial, sales, clerical, and craft categories. Presently, the great majority of Tejanos hold urban-based occupations that range from high-paying professional positions to minimum-wage, unskilled jobs. An unfortunate minority remain tied to farm work as migrating *campesinos* (farmworkers).

Since the initial settlements of the early eighteenth century, a sense of community has given Tejanos a particular identity. On the frontier, common experiences and problems forced Texas Mexicans to adjust in ways different from those of their counterparts in the Mexican interior. Tejanos fashioned an ethic of self-reliance, wresting their living from a ranching culture, improvising ways to survive in the wilderness expanse, and devising specific political responses to local needs despite directives from the royal government. In barrios (urban neighborhoods) and rural settlements in the era following the establishment of American rule, Tejanos combined tenets of Mexican tradition with those of American culture. The result was a Tejano community that practiced a familiar folklore, observed Catholic holy days and Mexican national holidays, spoke the Spanish language, yet sought participation in national life. But Tejanos faced lynching, discrimination, segregation, political disfranchisement, and other injustices. This produced a community at once admiring and distrusting of United States republicanism. The arrival of thousands of Mexican immigrants in the early years of the twentieth century affected group consciousness as now a major portion of the population looked to the motherland for moral guidance and even allegiance. Recent arrivals reinforced a Mexican mentality, as they based familial and community behavior upon the traditions of the motherland. Many took a keener interest in the politics of Mexico than that of the United States. By the 1920s, however, birth in Texas or upbringing in the state produced newer levels of Americanization. Increasingly, community leaders sought the integration of Mexicans into mainstream affairs, placing emphasis on the learning of English, on acquaintance with the American political system, and acceptance of social norms of the United States. In modern times, a bicultural Hispanic community identifies primarily with United States institutions, while still upholding Mexican customs and acknowledging its debt to the country of its forefathers.

In truth, Tejanos are a varied group, even divided along social lines. During the colonial era, a small, elite group that included landowners, government officials, and ambitious merchants stood above the poverty-stricken masses. Though the American takeover of Texas in 1836 reversed the fortunes of this elite cohort, Mexican Americans devised imaginative responses in their determination to maintain old lands, buy small parcels of real estate, found new businesses, and develop political ties with Anglo-Americans. The nineteenth-century social fragmentation remained into the early 1900s, as even the immigrants fleeing Porfirio Díaz and the Mexican Revolution derived from different social classes. The lot of the great majority of Tejanos remained one of misery. Most Mexican Americans lived with uncertain employment, poor health, and substandard housing. Out of the

newer opportunities developing in the 1920s, however, emerged a petit bourgeoisie composed of businessmen, doctors, lawyers, and other professionals; from this element descended the leaders who called on the masses to accept United States culture during the 1920s. According to the 1930 census, about 15 percent of Tejanos occupied middle-class positions. After World War II, social differentiation became more pronounced as numerous Tejanos successfully achieved middle-class status. By the 1990s, nearly 40 percent of the Tejano labor force held skilled, white-collar, and professional occupations. The majority, however, remained economically marginalized.

Tejanos faced numerous obstacles in their efforts to participate in the politics of the nineteenth century. Anglos considered them unworthy of the franchise and generally discouraged them from voting. Where permitted to cast ballots, Tejanos were closely monitored by Anglo political bosses or their lieutenants to ensure that they voted for specific candidates and platforms. Members of the Tejano landholding class cooperated in this procedure. The status quo for them meant protecting their possessions and their alliances with Anglo rulers. Despite efforts to neutralize Tejanos politically, Texas Mexicans displayed interest in questions of regional and even national concern. Especially along the Rio Grande and in San Antonio, they joined reform movements and attempted to mobilize people behind economic issues that bore on the wellbeing of barrio residents. Some held offices as commissioners, collectors, or district clerks. Moreover, they took stands on the divisive issues of the 1850s, the Civil War, Reconstruction, and Gilded Age politics. During the early decades of the twentieth century and continuing until the late 1940s, political incumbency took a downturn. The Democratic

Chili stand on Military Plaza, San Antonio, ca. 1887–90. Courtesy ITC. At the turn of the century, urban Tejanos generally lived in barrios with limited work opportunities. This man served residents of the city by lantern light after dark.

Alberto and Eva Garcia with their family, Austin, 1922. Courtesy of Martha X. García, Lago Vista. Alberto Garcia was the first Mexican-American doctor in Austin. His practice would probably have been limited to Tejanos, who often found themselves segregated and underserved.

party institutionalized the white primary during this period, the legislature enacted the poll tax, and demographic shifts occurred that diluted the majority advantage held by Tejanos in South and extreme West Texas. The nineteenth-century bosses who had compensated Mexican voters with patronage under the system of boss rule suffered setbacks from the Progressive challenge and were removed from power during the teens. Some Mexican-American politicians in the ranch counties of South Texas—Webb, Zapata, Starr, and Duval—did manage to retain their positions, however.

In the post–World War II years, Anglo political reformers solicited Mexican-American cooperation in efforts to establish improved business climates in the cities. Due to a more tolerant atmosphere and political resurgence in the barrios, Tejano politicians once more gained access to political posts; in 1956 Henry B. Gonzalez became the first Mexican American to win election to the Texas Senate in modern times. In the mid-1960s a liberal–reformist movement spread across Tejano communities, led by youths disgruntled with barriers in the way of Tejano aspirations and inspired by a farmworkers' march in 1966. Anglo society became the object of militant attacks. Out of this "Chicano" movement surfaced the Raza Unida party with a plank that addressed discriminatory practices and advocated the need for new directions in Texas politics. For a variety of reasons, this political chapter in Tejano history ended by the mid-1970s and was succeeded by more moderate politics, led by leaders wanting to forge workable coalitions with liberal Democratic allies. The 1970s and 1980s saw a dramatic rise in the number of Tejano incumbents. Federal legislation and court decisions, a more open-minded Anglo society, and the impact of the Chicano movement brought successes.

Clubs with political leanings existed throughout Texas in the nineteenth century and in the early twentieth century, although no large successful organization appeared on the scene until 1929, when activist members of a small but growing Tejano middle class founded LULAC (the League of United Latin American Citizens). Though the league was nonpolitical, it sought to interest Texas Mexicans in politics (by sponsoring poll tax drives, for

instance) and worked to change oppressive conditions by investigating cases of police brutality, complaining to civic officials and business proprietors about segregation, and working for a sound educational system. Along with the American G.I. Forum of Texas, which was founded in 1948, LULAC utilized the judicial process to effect changes favorable to Mexican Americans. During the Chicano movement of the 1960s and 1970s, these two organizations turned to the federal government to get money for needy Mexican-American communities in the state. Both pursued a centrist political position after the Chicano period. In 1968, civil rights lawyers founded the Mexican American Legal Defense and Educational Fund to fight for legal solutions of problems afflicting Mexican Americans. By the 1970s, MALDEF had gained distinction by winning judicial victories over diluted political rights, employment discrimination, poor educational opportunities, and inequitable school finance.

As descendants of Spaniards who brought their religion to Mexico, the majority of Texas Mexicans belong to the Catholic faith. Generally, Texas-Mexican Catholics have observed doctrine and received the sacraments by marrying in the church and having their children baptized and taught religion, though their adherence to Catholic teaching is far from complete. Close to 60 percent believe themselves to be "good Catholics." Protestants have proselytized among Texas Mexicans with general success. Many barrios in the larger towns featured Protestant places of worship by the 1870s, and newer enclaves in the twentieth century had several "Mexican" Protestant churches. Protestant work among Mexican Americans has been constant in the twentieth century; Evangelicals, Pentecostals, and Jehovah's Witnesses have made special efforts to convert Mexican-American Catholics. Approximately 20 percent of Mexican Americans in the United States belong to Protestant communions.

Anglo-American society in the nineteenth century did not concern itself over the education of Texas-Mexican children, since farmers and ranchers had little need for a literate working class. Where public schooling might exist, however, Tejano families urged their children to attend. Those who could afford it, on the other hand, enrolled their youngsters in private religious academies and even in colleges. Select communities established local institutions with a curriculum designed to preserve the values and heritage of Mexico. Not until the 1920s did government take a serious interest in upgrading education for Tejanitos, but even then, society provided inferior facilities for them. Texas-Mexican children ordinarily attended "Mexican schools" and were discouraged from furthering their education past the sixth grade. Attendance in these schools, however, did have the effect of socializing and Americanizing an increased number of young folks whose parents were either foreign-born or unacculturated. Though Texas Mexicans had protested educational inequalities since the second decade of the century, it was not until the 1930s that they undertook systematic drives against them—namely as members of LULAC, but also through local organizations such as the Liga Pro-Defensa Escolar (School Improvement League) in San Antonio. Before World War II, however, the educational record for Tejanos proved dismal, as poverty and administrative indifference discouraged many from regular attendance. The children of migrant parents, for example, received their only exposure to education when the family returned to its hometown during the winter months. After the war, the G.I. Forum joined in the struggle to improve the education of the Mexican community with the motto "Education is Our Freedom." With LULAC, the forum campaigned to encourage parents and students to make education a priority. Both organizations also worked through the legal system and successfully persuaded the courts to desegregate some districts. During the 1950s, indeed, Tejanos witnessed slight improvement in their educational status, though this may have been partly due to the rural-to-urban transition of the time. City life meant better access to schools, better enforcement of truancy laws, and less migration if heads of families found more stable employment. The gap between Mexican-American and Anglo achievement remained wide, however, and after the 1960s, MALDEF leveled a legal assault on issues such as racial segregation and the inequitable system of dispersing public funds to school districts. Concerned parents and legislators also strove for a better-educated community by supporting such programs as Head Start and bilingual education. In more recent times, however, Mexican-American students still had the highest dropout rate of all ethnic groups. In part, this explained the fact that Mexican-American students average only 10 years in school.

Within the social space of segregated neighborhoods or isolated rural settlements, Tejanos carried on cultural traditions that blended the customs of the motherland with those of the United States. They organized, for instance, an array of patriotic, recreational, or civic clubs designed to address bicultural tastes. Newspapers, either in Spanish or English, informed communities of events in both Mexico and the United States. Tejanos also developed a literary tradition. Some left small autobiographical sketches while others wrote lay histories about Tejano life. Creative writers penned narratives, short stories, and poems that they submitted to community newspapers or other outlets; some were in Spanish, especially those of the nineteenth century, but works were also issued in bilingual or English form. Civic leaders compiled records of injustices or other community concerns, and academicians wrote scholarly articles or books. Among the latter may be listed Jovita González de Mireles, Carlos E. Castañeda, and George I. Sánchez, who published after the 1930s. Painters, sculptors, and musicians have made some contribution to Tejano traditional arts, though not much is known of such contributions before the 1920s. During the 1930s, Octavio Medellín begin a career as a sculptor of works with pre-Columbian motifs. After World War II, Porfirio Salinas, Jr., gained popularity as a landscape artist, and during the 1960s some of his paintings hung in Lyndon B. Johnson's White House. More recent is José Cisneros, known for his pen-and-ink illustrations of Spanish Borderlands historical figures. The workers of Amado M. Peña, a painter from Laredo, and the sculptor Luis Jiménez of El Paso reveal a border influence but go beyond ethnicity. Numerous musicians have established legendary careers in Spanish; several Tejanos have topped the American rock 'n roll charts, and some have earned Grammys. Folklore, much of it based on the folk beliefs of the poor in Mexico, has flourished in Mexican communities in Texas. While reflecting many themes, it has especially served to express feelings about abrasive confrontations between Tejanos and Anglos. *Corridos* of the nineteenth century and early twentieth century, for example, criticized white society for injustices inflicted on barrio dwellers or extolled heroic figures who resisted white oppression.

In the nineteenth century, the dominant language in the bar-

State senator Henry B. Gonzalez filibustering against segregation bills, Austin, 1957. Mexican Americans gained political power in the state after World War II.

rios and rural settlements was that of Mexico, though some Tejanos also attained facility in English. Various linguistic codes characterize oral communications in present-day enclaves, however, due to continued immigration from Mexico, racial separation, and exposure to American mass culture. Some Texas Mexicans speak formal Spanish only, just as there are those who communicate strictly in formal English. More common are those Spanish speakers using English loan words as they borrow from the lexicon of mainstream society. Another form of expression, referred to as "code-switching," involves the systematic mixing of the English and Spanish languages. Another mode of communication is *caló*, a "hip" code composed of innovative terminology used primarily by boys in their own groups.

Friction has characterized relations between mainstream society and Tejanos since 1836. Mechanisms designed to maintain white supremacy, such as violence, political restrictions, prohibition from jury service, segregation, and inferior schooling caused suspicion and distrust within the Mexican community. Repatriation of Mexican citizens during the depression of

Crystal City High School during student boycott, December 1969. San Antonio *Light* Collection, ITC. Beginning in the 1930s, groups like LULAC began a systematic fight against the unequal education provided Hispanic children in Texas. The Mexican-American student boycott of Crystal City High School won fuller representation in student affairs, bilingual education, and Hispanic culture courses.

the 1930s and Operation Wetback in 1954 inflicted great anguish on some of the communities touched by the drives, as Tejanos perceived them to be racially motivated. In more recent times, conflict between the two societies has persisted over such issues as immigration, the right to speak Spanish in schools, and the use of public money to support the Tejano poor. Even as Anglo-American society attempted to relegate Tejanos to second-class citizenry, Mexican Americans have sought to find their place in America. Middle-class businessmen have pursued integration into the economic mainstream, and the politically minded have worked for the involvement of Tejanos in the body politic. These were the objectives of such organizations as LULAC, the G.I. Forum, and MALDEF. Though recent immigrants wrestle with two allegiances, their children have ordinarily accepted the offerings of American life. Indeed, Texas Mexicans have proven their allegiance toward the state on numerous occasions, especially during the country's several wars. Seldom have drives toward separatism gained support across the spectrum of the community. Probably the most prominent movement emphasizing anti-Anglo sentiments was the Chicano movement, but even its rhetoric appealed only to certain sectors of the community. In the Lone Star State, Mexican Americans stand out as one of the few groups having loyalties to the state while simultaneously retaining a binary cultural past.   *Arnoldo De León*

Mexican Invasions of 1842. Two attempts on the part of Mexico to reverse the Texas Revolution. Because of Mexico's refusal to recognize the independence of Texas, the republic was in constant fear of a Mexican invasion. The fear assumed reality on 9 January 1842, when Gen. Mariano Arista issued a statement from Monterrey telling the Texans that it was hopeless for them to

continue their struggle for independence and promising amnesty and protection to all who remained neutral during his planned invasion. Early in March, Goliad, Refugio, and Victoria were occupied, and on 5 March the Mexican troops under Rafael Vásquez appeared before San Antonio. The Texans retreated, leaving the town to the Mexicans, because John C. Hays found it impossible to gather enough men to make a defense immediately. The militia under Alexander Somervell was called out, however, and gathered at San Antonio on 15 March, but the Mexican forces had abandoned the town on 9 March. Edward Burleson, the leader of the volunteers, had no orders to follow the invaders; so the Texan force remained in San Antonio until it was disbanded on 2 April. The most unfortunate result of the raid was the panic that it caused in the western settlements. On 10 March President Sam Houston declared a national emergency and ordered the archives removed to Houston; the quarrel known as the Archive War resulted. Meanwhile Houston had made an appeal to the U.S. for money and volunteers, and Adjutant General James Davis was sent to Corpus Christi to organize volunteers with orders to hold them until the time was opportune for an invasion of Mexico. On 7 June Davis's forces had a skirmish with Antonio Canales Rosillo, but Canales soon retired to Mexico. During the session of the Texas Congress that met on 27 June 10 million acres of land was appropriated to finance a war of invasion against Mexico, but the bill was vetoed by Houston. Davis's forces were dismissed, and Texas was left undefended.

On 11 September 1842 Gen. Adrián Woll, with a force of 12,000 Mexicans, captured San Antonio. By 17 September, 200 Texans had gathered on Cibolo Creek above Seguin and marched under Mathew Caldwell to Salado Creek six miles northeast of San Antonio. On 18 September Caldwell sent Hays and a company of scouts to draw the Mexicans into a fight; the battle of Salado Creek resulted. While the fight was going on, Capt. Nicholas M. Dawson approached from the east with a company of 53 men. These men were attacked a mile and a half from the scene of the battle and killed in what came to be known as the Dawson Massacre. Woll drew his men back to San Antonio and retreated to Mexico by 20 September. The reinforced Texans pursued him for three days and then returned to San Antonio. By 25 September a large number of Texans had gathered at San Antonio, and plans were made for a punitive expedition, the Somervell expedition, which evolved into the Mier expedition. *Jack W. Gunn*

Mexican–United States Boundary Commission. Authorized by the Treaty of Guadalupe Hidalgo. In December 1848 President Polk named Ambrose Sevier the United States commissioner, but Sevier died before he could be confirmed by the Senate. John B. Weller replaced Sevier and traveled to San Diego. On 6 July 1849, the United States commission met formally for the first time with the Mexican commission, headed by Gen. Pedro García Conde. The joint boundary commission ran the portion of the line from the Pacific Ocean to the junction of the Gila and Colorado rivers and met on 15 February 1850 on the Pacific Coast. Weller and García Conde agreed to recess until late that year and to arrange for the survey of the El Paso area, at the other end of the line. Weller left the commission sometime after 15 February 1850, the victim of political intrigues and infighting. John C. Frémont was to be his successor, but Frémont resigned upon his election as the first senator from California. William H. Emory served as temporary commissioner until John Russell Bartlett officially replaced Frémont as the United States commissioner on 15 June. In December the joint commission met in El Paso and resumed its deliberations. Immediately an impasse developed over the location of the southern boundary of New Mexico. The Mexican commissioner caught Bartlett unaware of the fact that there were several serious discrepancies in the official Disturnell Treaty map. The resulting negotiations led to the Bartlett–García Conde compromise in the spring of 1851. This agreement caused a crisis that was not resolved until the Gadsden Purchase was negotiated in 1853. The commission's survey of the Texas portion of the Rio Grande did not produce any major territorial disputes, although the Mexicans were unhappy about a change in the riverbed as a result of an 1850 flood. Both sides were eager to survey channel changes that were beneficial to them, and it was this sort of occurrence that caused the Chamizal Dispute. The first surveys of the Rio Grande north of El Paso to the New Mexico border were carried out by Lt. Amiel W. Whipple and José Salazar early in 1851. In the summer of 1851, with the survey stalled in New Mexico over the Bartlett–García Conde line, the joint commission took steps to begin the survey of the Gila River and the Rio Grande south of El Paso. This latter effort was initially undertaken by Lt. Col. James Duncan Graham and José Salazar. However, Graham had a serious conflict with Bartlett and was subsequently replaced by Emory, who arrived at El Paso in November 1851 and found the Rio Grande survey stalled and the American commission in complete disarray. Salazar, unhappy with the United States suspension of its survey of the Bartlett–García Conde line, began delaying tactics of his own.

The death of García Conde in December 1851 eventually led to Salazar's appointment as Mexican commissioner, and by the spring of 1852 the river survey began in earnest. The American part of the survey reached Laredo in December. Marine T. W. Chandler and Lt. Duff Green worked south of Presidio surveying the Big Bend until forced to abandon the effort. Lt. Nathaniel Michler worked south from Fort Duncan near Eagle Pass to Laredo. Bartlett, who had been absent from this part of the survey since the spring of 1851, arrived in El Paso from California in August of 1852. When he reached Ringgold Barracks in December 1852 and finally met with Emory, he discovered that the United States Congress had shut down the commission until the Bartlett–García Conde dispute was settled. Senator Thomas J. Rusk led the Texas delegation in this effort, but special legislation permitted the completion of the Rio Grande survey in 1853 under Emory with Gen. Robert Blair Campbell serving as the United States commissioner. Lieutenant Michler completed the survey north of Eagle Pass to the point where Chandler had stopped. Arthur Schott, James Radziminski, and G. Clinton Gardner also participated in surveying alternating sections south of Laredo. The Mexican part of the survey was carried out under the direction of José Salazar. Francisco Jiménez surveyed the Matamoros section north to Laredo in the fall of 1852 and spring of 1853, and Agustín Díaz surveyed sections south of El Paso. After this work was completed the only part of the boundary in debate was the Bartlett–García Conde line. With this dispute settled by the Gadsden treaty, Emory was made United States commissioner and joined Salazar in El Paso in the fall of 1854 to complete the final survey. The Mexican–United States Boundary Commission finished its surveying work on 15 October 1855. *Harry P. Hewitt*

Mexican War. The conflict between the U.S. and Mexico in 1846–48. The war had its roots in the annexation of Texas and the westward thrust of American settlers. On assuming the American presidency in 1845, James K. Polk attempted to secure Mexican agreement to setting the boundary at the Rio Grande and to selling northern California to the U.S. What he failed to realize was that even his carefully orchestrated policy of graduated pressure would not work because no Mexican politician could agree to the alienation of any territory, including Texas. Frustrated by the Mexican refusal to negotiate, Polk, on 13 January 1846, directed Gen. Zachary Taylor's army at Corpus Christi to advance to the Rio Grande. The Mexican government viewed that as an act of war. On 25 April the Mexican troops at Matamoros crossed the river and ambushed an American patrol. Polk seized upon the incident to secure a declaration of war on 13May on the basis of the shedding of "American blood upon American soil." Meanwhile, on 8 and 9 May, Taylor's 2,200-man army defeated 3,700 Mexicans under Gen. Mariano Arista in the battles of Palo Alto and Resaca de la Palma.

Initial American strategy called for a blockade of the Mexican coast and the occupation of the northern Mexican states in the unrealistic hope that these measures would lead to an acceptable territorial settlement. Taylor, reinforced by a large body of volunteers including regiments of Texans, seized Monterrey in September and declared an armistice with Arista. Col. John Coffee Hays's Texas Mounted Rifles played a significant role in storming the city's defenses. Polk repudiated the armistice, so Taylor thrust south to Saltillo and east to Victoria. A second

An Available Candidate, by N. Currier (?), 1848. Lithograph. Library of Congress; USZ62-5220. General Zachary Taylor parlayed his Mexican War victories at Palo Alto, Resaca de la Palma, Monterrey, and Buena Vista into a Whig party nomination as president in 1848. Democrats viewed these conquests as his major claim to fame.

force under Gen. John E. Wool marched from San Antonio to threaten Chihuahua but ultimately joined Taylor. Gen. Stephen W. Kearny led another column from Fort Leavenworth to seize New Mexico. During July, while Taylor's forces gathered, the navy's Pacific squadron under Commodore John D. Sloat occupied Monterey and San Francisco, California. They linked up with the American settlers there, who had established their own government at the urging of the explorer John C. Frémont. Although an incursion into southern California in August failed, the area was secured by a joint army–navy expedition under Kearny and Commodore Robert F. Stockton in January 1847.

Neither American success on the battlefield nor the restoration to power of the deposed strongman Antonio López de Santa Anna brought the expected negotiations. The administration prepared a new army under Gen. Winfield Scott to march from the coast to Mexico City. Santa Anna, aware of the American plans, attempted to defeat Taylor's troops in the north before returning to face Scott's force. The Mexican commander's plan failed when Taylor's largely untested 4,600-man army won a closely contested battle against 15,000 Mexicans at Buena Vista

on 22–23 February 1847. The astute reconnaissance work of Maj. Benjamin McCulloch's spy company contributed significantly to the American victory. A naval squadron under Commodore David Conner put Scott's 10,000-man army ashore near Veracruz on 9 March 1847. It was America's first large-scale amphibious assault. After securing the port as a base, Scott led his army inland. At Cerro Gordo on 17–18 April the Americans destroyed Santa Anna's hastily gathered eastern force of nearly 17,000 men. Scott's advance ground to a halt at Puebla in May, when the volunteers who composed over half his force insisted on returning to civilian life. The American army remained at Puebla, cut off from its base at Veracruz, until reinforcements, especially Texas Rangers under Hays, reopened communications in August.

After initiating a notably successful campaign, Scott set out for Mexico City. In the battles of Contreras and Churubusco on 19–20 August his 8,500 men drove possibly three times their number of Mexican defenders into the Mexican capital. When Santa Anna did not sue for peace as expected, Scott resumed the assault on the city with an attack on its outworks at Molino del Rey on 8 September. In the final assault on 13–14 September, Scott's force seized the heights of Chapultepec and breached the inner defenses. Santa Anna abandoned the city but salvaged enough of his army to attack Puebla unsuccessfully later in the month. The Mexicans could not prevent American occupation at will of other cities in central and eastern Mexico. Along the Pacific coast the navy, now commanded by Commodore W. Branford Shubrick, also seized the chief port, Mazatlán, neutralized Guaymas, and eliminated Mexican authority in Baja California. Since no Mexican government functioned after the fall of Mexico City, Scott and State Department agent Nicholas P. Trist had to wait until February 1848 before a government could be formed that would agree to peace. Then, in the Treaty of Guadalupe Hidalgo, the U.S. gained California, Arizona, New Mexico, and the Rio Grande as the boundary of Texas, as well as portions of Utah, Nevada, and Colorado. *K. Jack Bauer*

Midland, Texas. County seat of Midland County, 20 miles northeast of Odessa. Midland Draw runs through the northern part of town. In late June 1881 the Texas and Pacific Railway, which was building its line between Dallas and El Paso, established Midway Station, a section house, halfway between those two cities. The first permanent resident of Midway was Herman N. Garrett, who moved from California with a herd of sheep in 1882. Over the next two years a number of other ranchers moved into the area, and a post office was granted in 1884, when the area was still attached to Tom Green County. Because other towns in Texas were already named Midway, the site was renamed Midland to get the post office. In early 1884 an Ohio real estate firm bought land at the site, established the Midland Town Company, and began to promote the settlement across the Midwest. The company drilled three water wells and held a successful land auction; by early 1885 there were 100 families living at the site. When Midland County was organized in March 1885, Midland became the county seat. A new courthouse was built by January 1886; later that year Baptist and Methodist churches were established in the town and Midland's first school was opened. Before long the Midland *Gazette* was promoting the town as "the Queen City of the South Plains." The First National Bank of Midland was chartered in 1890, and the city began to serve as a regional financial center. By 1890 it had become one of the most important cattle-shipping centers in the state and had an estimated population of 600. The population rose to 1,000 by 1900. A second bank was established in 1903, and in 1905 a new stone courthouse was built. At this time the city's residents obtained their water from wells with windmills; virtually every house had a windmill in its yard, and Midland became known as the "Windmill Town." Local residents approved a charter to incorporate the in 1906. Three major fires swept through the town between 1905 and 1909, however, and the last fire destroyed much of the its central business district. In response, local leaders pushed for a new water system and a fire department; both were in place by 1910, just in time to extinguish another fire downtown. The city charter lapsed in 1910, but after an election in January 1911 Midland was again incorporated. It was governed under an aldermanic system until 1940, when a council form of government was adopted. By 1914 Midland had a population of 2,500, and in 1915 another railroad, the Midland and Northwestern line, was built into the city, linking it with Seminole. Extended droughts and a depressed agricultural economy caused hundreds of Midland County residents to leave, however, and Midland consequently declined. By 1920 the population was only 1,795; the Midland and Northwestern ceased operations in 1921.

The decline was soon reversed, however, by the Permian Basin oil boom, which began in the 1920s. Thousands of investors and workers moved into the area and injected new life into Midland; by 1929, 36 oil companies had offices in the city. Street lighting and paving improvements were under way by 1927, and impressive new structures like the 12-story Hogan Building were soon constructed. In 1929 the county sold its old courthouse for one dollar, a move that was publicized in Ripley's "Believe It Or Not," and by the next year a new, four-story courthouse was in place. By 1930 there were 5,484 people living in Midland, and the town's boosters pointed with pride to the city's new airport and luxurious hotels like the 150-room Scharbauer. The onset of the Great Depression in the 1930s decreased the nation's demand for oil, and petroleum companies in the Permian Basin were forced to cut back their production; meanwhile, new oilfields opening in East Texas helped to glut the oil market and sent petroleum prices spiraling downward. Many of the oil businesses centered in Midland folded, throwing their employees out of work. By 1932 one-third of Midland's workers were unemployed. The local economy began to recover, however, by the mid-1930s, after the Railroad Commission began to regulate oil production and the federal government placed a tariff on foreign oil. As dozens of new oilfields were opened in the Permian Basin during the late 1930s, Midland revived and continued to grow; in 1936, for example, the First National Bank renovated its headquarters and began to build a new eight-story office building. By 1940 there were 9,325 people living in the city. World War II guaranteed a continuing demand for oil. The area also profited from the establishment of Midland Army Air Force Base, one of the largest training bases in the world at the time; the Army Air Force Bombardier School operated there between 1942 and 1945. Oilfield activities and the infusion of cash from the military helped to energize the local economy, and by 1945 Midland had grown to a population of 14,000. When the air base was closed in 1946, its facilities were converted to provide the city airport. As oil and gas production in the Permian Basin rapidly expanded between 1945 and 1960, Midland developed

from an essentially small country town into a city with a skyline that could be seen 30 miles away. In 1950, 215 oil companies had offices in Midland. The Midland Chamber of Commerce worked to encourage growth and development, and in 1950 the city adopted the Midland City Plan, 1950, which established goals and guidelines to shape the city's expansion. Midland Memorial Hospital, which opened in 1950, offered a new standard of medical care for people living in the region, and the Midland Symphony began performing in 1953. (It merged with the Odessa Symphony in 1962.) A new two-story library and museum was constructed by the county. The population, 21,713 in 1950, burgeoned to 62,625 in 1960.

The local economy slumped between 1960 and 1970, however, as the area's petroleum companies struggled against competition from foreign oilfields. A number of companies left the area, and others trimmed their workforces. The population declined to 59,463 by 1970. Meanwhile, city leaders and businessmen worked on plans to revitalize the city's downtown, which had been declining since the 1950s because of competition from new suburban shopping malls. Midland College, a two-year college, began offering classes in 1969. The area's economy began to recover during the early 1970s and then boomed again after the Arab oil embargo led to oil price increases and more relaxed federal regulations. During this period several downtown blocks were razed, and new federal buildings, including a regional post office center, were constructed; a number of new high-rise office buildings also were built. By 1980 the population was 70,525. Though thousands of new apartments and houses were built in the city during the boom, contractors could not keep pace with demand. By 1981, when the price of oil rose to $40 per barrel, newcomers to the city were living in tents, cars, and trailers. A number of cultural and educational buildings were constructed in the city during the 1970s, including the Permian Basin Museum, the Marian Blakemore Planetarium, and a new campus for Midland College. The boom ended abruptly in 1982, when the price of oil unexpectedly tumbled and the drilling-rig count dropped by 50 percent. Financial shocks caused by the oil glut and declining crude prices led to the failure of three banks in the city in 1983; meanwhile, many office buildings were vacant or underutilized and newly constructed houses went unsold. Though the economy had become more diversified by the late 1980s, the area's petroleum industry, a main source of the city's prosperity, continued to labor under relatively low oil prices and declining production. In 1990 Midland had a population of 89,443 with 106,611 in the metropolitan area. The city remained the financial and administrative center for the Permian Basin. Oil, chemicals, plastics, and electronic calculators were important to the local economy. *John Leffler*

Midwestern State University. In Wichita Falls; opened in 1922 as Wichita Falls Junior College, the second municipal junior college in Texas; operated by the Wichita Falls ISD and superintendent Randolph Lee Clark. Its original class of 55 freshmen met in the high school on Broad Street. After two years both high school and college moved to expanded quarters on Avenue H. In 1934 Mr. and Mrs. John J. Hardin, local philanthropists, established the Hardin Foundation to promote a separate campus. Voters approved $200,000 in bonds and a junior college district with the same officers and board as the school district. A PWA grant was secured by President Herbert Fillers (1931–41) and his trustees. W.

B. Hamilton and N. H. Martin donated a 40-acre campus, which opened in 1937 under the name Hardin Junior College. In 1941 the legislature separated the college from the school district. After World War II, Hardin grew considerably—eventually to more than a small regional university. President James B. Boren (1942–55) established vocational programs in such fields as horology and aviation. In 1946 the school began offering junior and senior years and became Hardin College. In 1950 it became Midwestern University, and by 1952 it offered graduate degrees. Under President Travis White (1955–74), MU continued its growth. A drive led by Senator George Moffett to place MU in the state college system succeeded in 1961, and the name became Midwestern State in 1975. By 1992 the campus had grown to 172 acres with 50 buildings. The university is fully accredited. It offers 38 baccalaureate, 7 preprofessional, and 15 master's programs. MSU belongs to the National Association of Intercollegiate Athletes and is the home of Midwestern Press. *Everett W. Kindig*

Mier Expedition. The last and most disastrous of the raiding expeditions from Texas into the area south of the Nueces River during the days of the Republic of Texas. It developed out of the Somervell expedition, which captured Laredo and Guerrero. On 19 December 1842, Alexander Somervell, recognizing that his expedition had been a failure and concluding that a longer stay on the Rio Grande might prove disastrous, ordered his troops to prepare to return home by way of Gonzales. Many of the men were so dissatisfied with the order to return home that they determined to separate from the command, cross the river, and attack the Mexican settlements to secure cattle and horses. Only 189 men and officers obeyed the order to return; five captains and most of the men refused to do so. Constituting what is known as the Mier expedition, they moved down the Rio Grande to a convenient campsite and selected William S. Fisher as their commander. Some wanted revenge and retaliation; many sought adventure; the leaders were nearly all political opponents of Sam Houston. The expedition set out on 20 December. Forty men under Thomas J. Green floated downstream in four vessels captured near Guerrero. A small group of Texas Rangers serving as a spy company under Ben McCulloch operated along the west bank of the river; the main body of men under Fisher went down the east side. On 22 December the 308 Texans reached a point on the east bank of the Rio Grande opposite Mier, and McCulloch's spy company was sent to reconnoiter the town. They found that Mexican troops were assembling along the river, advised Fisher against crossing, and abandoned the expedition when their advice was not heeded. Leaving a camp guard of 45 men, Fisher and the remainder of his men crossed the river on 23 December and entered Mier without opposition. A requisition for supplies levied against the town was fulfilled by late afternoon, but there were no means for transporting the goods to the river. When the alcalde promised to have the supplies delivered the next day to the Texas camp, the Texans withdrew from Mier, taking the alcalde with them to guarantee delivery of the supplies. All the next day the Texans waited in vain for the goods. During the morning A. S. Holderman, who had crossed the river to look for horses, was captured. His journal revealed to the Mexicans the size, character, and organization of the Texan force. On Christmas Day, Fisher learned from a captured Mexican that Gen. Pedro de Ampudia had arrived at Mier and prevented delivery of the sup-

The Mier Expedition: The Drawing of the Black Bean, by Frederic Remington, 1896. Oil on canvas. 20⅛" × 40". Museum of Fine Arts, Houston; Hogg Brothers Collection, gift of Miss Ima Hogg. Depicted is the infamous Black Bean Episode, in which the men of the Mier expedition drew beans to see who was to be executed by the Mexicans. An engraving of this painting accompanied the article in *Harper's Monthly* (December 1896).

plies. The Texans decided to go after their rations. On the afternoon of 25 December a camp guard of 42 men under Oliver Buckman was posted, and 261 Texans crossed the Rio Grande once more, attacked Mier, and fought until the next afternoon, outnumbered almost 10 to one. Ampudia sent a white flag to them and demanded their surrender. The Texans later claimed they had surrendered as prisoners of war, but President Houston stated that the men had acted without authority of the government, leaving the impression that they were not entitled to treatment as POWs unless the Mexican government wished to assume that obligation. The Texan camp guard, with the exception of George W. Bonnell and a man named Hicks, avoided capture and retreated into the settled area of Texas.

The captured Texans were sentenced to execution, but on 27 December Ampudia had the execution decree reversed. The able-bodied prisoners were marched through the river towns to Matamoros, where they were held until ordered to Mexico City. En route to the capital they planned their escape frequently. Finally, at Salado, on 11 February 1843, a successful break was carried out. For seven days the Texans headed towards the Rio Grande, but in trying to pursue a circuitous route through the mountains during the dry season they became separated and lost. After extreme suffering, they surrendered singly and in small groups to Mexican troops sent in pursuit; in the end only three members of the expedition made good their escape to Texas. The 176 recaptured Texans were returned to Salado. Upon learning of the escape, Antonio López de Santa Anna ordered that those who had fled be executed, but Governor Francisco Mexía of the state of Coahuila refused to obey the order, and the foreign ministers in Mexico were able to get the decree modified. The government then ordered that every tenth man be executed. Seventeen men who drew black beans from a mixture of black and white were blindfolded and shot. Ewen Cameron, leader of the break, did not draw a black bean but was later executed by special order of Santa Anna. During June, July, and August 1843, the Texans did road work near Mexico City. In September they were transferred to Perote Prison, where the San Antonio prisoners whom they had set out to liberate were being held. A few of the Mier men escaped while stationed in the vicinity of Mexico City; others tunneled out of Perote and succeeded in reaching home. A few of the wounded who had been left at Mier recovered, bribed the guard, and escaped. Many died in captivity from wounds, disease, and starvation. From time to time a few of the prisoners were released at the request of officials in the United States and others at the request of foreign governments. The last Mier men were released by Santa Anna on 16 September 1844.

Joseph Milton Nance

Milam, Benjamin Rush. Revolutionary and entrepreneur; b. Frankfort, Kentucky, 20 October 1788; d. San Antonio, 7 December 1835. He fought with the Kentucky militia in the War of 1812. In 1818 he was in Texas trading with the Comanche Indians on the Colorado River when he met David G. Burnet. In New Orleans in 1819 Milam met José Félix Trespalacios and James Long, who were planning an expedition to help the revolutionaries in Mexico and Texas gain independence from Spain. Milam joined Trespalacios and was commissioned a colonel. While they sailed to Veracruz, Long marched to La Bahía, which he easily captured, only to discover that the people and soldiers there were revolutionaries, not Royalists. They gave him a hostile reception, and he moved on to San Antonio. In Veracruz and Mexico City, Trespalacios and Milam met with the same reception that Long had received and were imprisoned. Ultimately, with Long, they were able to justify their intentions to the new revolutionary government, which accepted and treated them with respect. Nevertheless, Long was shot and killed by a guard under circumstances that convinced Milam that the killing was plotted by Trespalacios. Milam and several friends then planned to kill Trespalacios. The plot was discovered, however, and Milam and his friends were imprisoned in Mexico City. Through the influence of Joel Poinsett, United States minister, all were released. Mexico adopted the Constitution of 1824 and now had a republican form of government. In Mexico City, Milam met Arthur Wavell, an Englishman who had become a general in the Mexican army. Trespalacios, now prominent in the new government also, made overtures to Milam to renew their friendship, and Milam accepted. He was granted Mexican citizenship and commissioned a colonel in the army in 1824. In 1825–26 he became Wavell's partner in a silver mine in Nuevo León; the two also obtained empresario grants in Texas. Wavell managed the mining in Mexico and leased the most productive mine to an English company, which by 1828 was unable to fulfill the terms of their contract. In 1829 Milam sought to organize a new mining company in partnership with Burnet, but they were unable to raise the necessary capital.

In April 1830 the Mexican Congress passed a law prohibiting further immigration of United States citizens into Texas. This was one reason why Milam, as Wavell's agent for his Red River colony, and Robert M. Williamson, as agent for Milam's colony, were not able to introduce the required number of settlers specified in their empresario contracts, which were due to expire in 1832. During this time Milam removed the great Red River raft, a huge clot of debris that for years had blocked traffic in the upper Red River for all vessels except canoes and small, flat-bottomed boats. He then purchased a steamboat, the *Alps*, the first of its kind to pass through the channel. In 1835 Milam went to Monclova, the capital of Coahuila and Texas, to urge the new governor, Agustín Viesca, to send a land commissioner to Texas to provide the settlers with land titles. Viesca agreed to do this. However, before Milam could leave the city, word came that General Santa Anna had overthrown the representative government of Mexico, had established a dictatorship, and was en route to Texas with an army. Viesca fled with Milam, but both were captured and imprisoned at Monterrey. Milam eventually escaped and headed for the Texas border, which he reached in October 1835. By accident he encountered a company of soldiers commanded by George Collinsworth, from whom he heard of the movement in Texas for independence. Milam joined them, helped capture Goliad, and then marched with them to join the main army to capture San Antonio. While returning from a scouting mission in the southwest on 4 December 1835, Milam learned that a majority of the army had decided not to attack San Antonio as planned but to go into winter quarters. Convinced that this decision would be a disaster for the cause of independence, Milam then made his famous, impassioned plea: "Who will go with old Ben Milam into San Antonio?" Three hundred volunteered, and the attack, which began at dawn on December 5, ended on December 9 with the surrender of Gen. Martín Perfecto de Cos and the Mexican army. Milam, however, was killed by a sniper before the victory occurred. In 1897 the Daughters of the Republic of Texas placed a monument at Milam's gravesite in Milam Park, San Antonio. The marker was moved in 1976, and the location of the grave was forgotten until 1993, when a burial was unearthed that archeologists think is probably Milam's.

Lois Garver

Military History. Military affairs have dramatically shaped the history of Texas. Among the region's Indians, tribal economies and cultures depended heavily upon warfare. Likewise, the Spanish army was a significant factor in early exploration and colonization. Only through force did the Republic of Texas secure its independence from Mexico and see its annexation by the United States assured; military might also allowed the Union to defeat the Confederacy's attempt to establish a separate nation. By sponsoring exploration and building frontier forts, the army encouraged westward migration of European immigrants and ensured the ouster of virtually all of the Indians. Defense and defense-related industries took an increasingly large role in the Texas economy during World wars I and II. By the latter half of the twentieth century, the nation's larger permanent military establishment had become fundamental to the state's economy.

Before the arrival of Europeans, Indians living in Texas often settled their differences through warfare. The Caddoes established defensive confederacies; the scattered tribes of southern Texas and the Rio Grande delta practiced seasonal feuding and smallscale raiding against one another. Fear of inland enemies often kept the Karankawas, tenaciously protective of areas they claimed for their own tribes, near the Gulf Coast. Among these and the other groups that came to dominate the plains of Texas, pre-Columbian warfare generally emphasized personal bravery. The introduction of horses and firearms, along with the greater pressures stemming from the European intrusions, often increased the violence of the culture of warfare. The arrival in large numbers of Apaches and Comanches, groups whose cultures were based on warfare, added further pressure. Raids and guerrilla-style harassment usually characterized these clashes, with the latter emerging during the late 1720s after a long struggle with the Apaches as the dominant military force on the Southern Plains.

The army played a fundamental role in Spain's occupation of what later became the Lone Star State. Armed columns escorted most sixteenth-century explorers, and military detachments guarded the early mission establishments along the Rio Grande. The French colony at Fort St. Louis challenged Spain to step up its activities in Texas. The first missions in East Texas, with but a tiny garrison, failed during the 1690s, but subsequent efforts during the next century included larger armed contingents. Even so, the failure to enlist strong Indian support caused Spain's temporary evacuation of East Texas, in the face of an armed French force of fewer than 10 men, during the Chicken War (1719). Determined to restore Spain's honor, the Marqués de Aguayo reestablished the missions of East Texas, leaving two presidios behind as well. To forestall potential French threats to the coast, he also set up a presidio and mission at La Bahía, and reinforced the burgeoning complex at Bexar. But the costs of such efforts seemed to outweigh the benefits, particularly as the French threat waned. Pressured from the north by the Comanches, the Apaches challenged Spanish expansion into Central Texas and even Bexar itself. As the tribes secured more guns (often from French traders) and grew more accustomed to European military methods, it became increasingly difficult to deliver the punishing retribution upon which Spain's policy depended. In 1758–59, for example, warriors from several tribes destroyed San Sabá de la Santa Cruz Mission, and a subsequent punitive column led by Col. Diego Ortiz Parrilla limped back to San Antonio after an unsuccessful assault on a stockaded Taovaya village.

Defeat in the Seven Years' War (1756–63) led to an overhaul of Spanish defenses. Following the reports of the Marqués de Rubí and José Bernardo de Gálvez Gallardo, the Royal Regulation of 1772 relocated presidios all along the frontiers. The East Texas outposts were abandoned and the northern provinces eventually separated from the viceroyalty of New Spain under a commandant-general, who was given civil, judicial, and military powers. Still, the scattered garrisons were too poorly trained, equipped, or supplied to be truly effective against the more mobile Plains Indians. Spanish attempts to pit either the Apaches or the Comanches against one another failed to duplicate the success generated by Indian alliances in neighboring New Mexico. Though never able to achieve military supremacy in Texas, the army remained a bastion of Spanish settlement. In the 1792 census the 720 soldiers and their families at Bexar and La Bahía made up nearly 20 percent of the entire population of Spanish Texas. And military force delayed unwanted American intrusions. Philip Nolan and about two-score Americans were defeated in 1801. Although in 1813 several hundred revolutionaries and adventurers on the Gutiérrez–Magee expedition briefly drove Spanish authorities from San Antonio, they were in turn crushed at the battle of Medina by Joaquín de Arredondo's royalists. Arredondo swept organized opposition to Spanish rule from Texas, but the empire's continued decline boded ill for the future. In the Adams–Onís Treaty of 1819, the United States recognized the Spanish claims to Texas, only to induce James Long and some 300 American filibusters and Mexican revolutionaries to capture Nacogdoches in protest. Spanish troops crushed

Long's movement, but the American threat had not dissipated. Fearful that American infiltrators would eventually seize Texas, crown officials approved the request of Moses Austin to bring in several hundred new colonists in a desperate hope that a larger population base might help meet defense needs.

In the end, internal turmoil rather than external invasion doomed Spanish Texas. Royal soldiers north of the Rio Grande, though unable to defeat the Indians or prevent armed incursions from the east, retained a precarious foothold. Spanish authority in Texas collapsed upon the establishment of an independent Mexico. Under the leadership of Stephen F. Austin, the American colony in Texas began the military activities that eventually led to Texas independence. The Karankawas were annihilated and the shortlived Fredonian Republic of 1826–27 suppressed. Mexican officials, fearing the growing Anglo influence, attempted to halt further American immigration and reinforce the Mexican garrisons in Texas with the Law of April 6, 1830. Still, the population resisted the army in minor clashes at Anahuac and Nacogdoches. Antonio López de Santa Anna's turn to Centralism and reliance upon the army to enforce policy antagonized Texans and led directly to the Texas movement for independence. In fall 1835, following skirmishes with Mexican regulars at Gonzales and Goliad, several hundred Texans laid siege to San Antonio. In late November, Edward Burleson took command of the "Army of the People" after Austin left to solicit aid from the United States. Engagements at Concepción and at the Grass Fight highlighted the siege until 5 December, when Ben Milam and Frank (Francis W.) Johnson led several hundred volunteers in a successful assault against the Mexican troops. Overconfident Texans dreamed of further conquests. Although Sam Houston, the Consultation's choice to command Texas forces, opposed the move, several groups gathered in South Texas for a proposed march on Matamoros.

Meanwhile, Santa Anna, having routed a rebellion in the Yucatán, turned his attentions toward Texas. Still the Texans dallied, assuming that Mexican troops would wait until spring before moving northward. On 23 February, Santa Anna arrived at San Antonio, where about 150 rebels holed up in the old Alamo mission. Disputes still plagued the Texas military; only the failing health of James Bowie allowed William B. Travis to assume effective command of troops there. Travis's pleas for reinforcements brought only a 32-man delegation from Gonzales. On 6 March, Santa Anna attacked; although his army suffered heavy casualties, the defenders were killed. Protecting Santa Anna's coastal flank, Gen. José de Urrea routed scattered Texas forces under Johnson at San Patricio, Dr. James Grant at Agua Dulce, Amon B. King at Refugio, and William Ward near Victoria. James W. Fannin, who held Goliad with some 300 men, seemed paralyzed throughout the campaign. At first insistent upon defending the site, then convinced that he must go to the aid of the Alamo, and finally attempting to retreat, Fannin allowed his command to be caught on 19 March at Coleto Prairie. Low on water and outnumbered by Urrea's 800 troops, Fannin surrendered the following day. On the 27th, most of those captured in the South Texas campaigns were executed in the Goliad Massacre.

Overconfidence, carelessness, and indecision had heretofore characterized the Texans' military operations. Now only Sam Houston and fewer than 400 men at Gonzales stood between Mexican troops and the Sabine River. Having no other viable options, Houston retreated across the Colorado and Brazos Rivers. Santa Anna pushed ahead, hoping to complete the rout, and caused most of the colonists to join a panicky retreat known as the Runaway Scrape. Some, including ad interim president David Burnet, accused Houston of having no plan, charges fostered by the general's determination to keep his own counsel. As Houston retreated, his army, fired by desire for revenge and having benefited from training exercises conducted during the retreat, developed into a more cohesive military force. Reinforcements from the United States as well as from the older Texas settlements further bolstered his army. And Santa Anna grew progressively weaker. Although several thousand Mexican troops were now in Texas, the dictator's zeal to catch either Houston or Texas leaders had led him to the banks of the San Jacinto River with only a small part of his total force. Houston turned and attacked on the afternoon of 21 April. Taking the exhausted Mexicans by surprise, the Texans fell upon the enemy camp. At the cost of 9 men killed and 30 wounded, Houston listed 630 Mexicans killed and 730 taken prisoner. Among the latter was the Mexican chieftain, Santa Anna. Texas independence was thus assured.

Although San Jacinto had been a decisive battlefield victory, military problems faced the newly declared republic. About 2,000 Mexican troops remained north of the Nueces River, and the composition of the Texas army was changing. Texas residents had dominated the force at San Jacinto. But by summer 1836, the army had swollen to over 2,500, three-quarters of whom had come to Texas after the battle of San Jacinto. To make matters worse, a painful ankle wound had forced Sam Houston, the only Texan who had been able to control large numbers of troops up to this point, to seek medical treatment in New Orleans. The Treaties of Velasco failed to resolve the military crisis. In Mexico, the government annulled them and threatened to continue the war. Although Mexican troops withdrew, the Texas army refused to allow Santa Anna's release. Led by Felix Huston, many within the army called for an offensive campaign against Matamoros. In a flagrant challenge to the shaky ad interim government, the troops refused to accept Mirabeau B. Lamar as their commander. In May 1837, fearful of military insurrection and anxious to reduce government spending, President Houston furloughed most of the army. Defense now rested upon a small detachment of mounted rangers, a disorganized militia consisting in theory of all able-bodied males between the ages of 17 and 50, and volunteers called up to meet emergencies. Violent encounters with Indians and rumors of Mexican invasions continued, but the president's determination to delay military action in hopes of securing annexation by the United States was consistent with his reduced defense budget.

Houston's successor, Lamar, favored an aggressive Indian policy. To protect the frontiers and to provide bases for offensive action, in 1838 Congress provided for a line of military posts along the republic's northern and western frontiers, to be manned by a regiment of 840 men and supported by a military road stretching from the Red River to the Nueces. To the east, the Cherokees, suspected of having allied themselves with Mexico, were driven into what is now Oklahoma after the battle of the Neches. Campaigns against the Comanches proved less decisive, but did cause the withdrawal of most of that tribe farther west and north. Lamar also hoped to force concessions from Mexico. After brief attempts to purchase some sort of set-

tlement on recognition or the boundary, the president encouraged domestic revolt against the Mexican government, going so far as to rent the Texas Navy to rebels in Yucatán. To stake the republic's western claims in summer 1841, he also sent a military force on the Texan Santa Fe expedition, led by Col. Hugh McLeod. Dogged by misfortune and poor leadership, the exhausted Texans surrendered upon reaching Santa Fe, the city they had set out to capture.

After being reelected president in 1841, Houston found himself immersed in the problems resulting from Lamar's policies. Operations against the Indians alone had cost $2.5 million during a three-year period in which government receipts totaled just over $1 million. Houston cut the army to a few companies of rangers, attempted to sell the navy, and signed treaties with several Indian tribes. But Mexico, with Santa Anna again at the helm, retaliated against the recent threats. Gen. Rafael Vásquez and about 500 troops briefly occupied San Antonio in March 1842. Congress declared war, but Houston, still cautious, vetoed this measure. Enraged by the continuing disputes along its northern frontier and by the attempted Texas blockade of its ports, Mexico mounted another offensive. Leading 1,400 men, in mid-September Gen. Adrián Woll seized San Antonio. He withdrew under pressure from Texas militiamen, and Houston dispatched Alexander Somervell with 750 men to show the Lone Star flag along the Rio Grande. Somervell withdrew that December, but about 300 men, led by William S. Fisher, defied orders and crossed the Rio Grande. At Mier, however, the invaders surrendered to a much larger Mexican force.

The Texas military situation changed dramatically upon annexation. Although the United States maintained but a small regular army and navy, its growing population and industrial base gave it a formidable military potential. Such resources were tapped in the Mexican War, which had been triggered by the recent annexation of Texas. About 6,000 Texans saw military service during the conflict; the most visible of the Lone Star units fought with Zachary Taylor and Winfield Scott in northern and central Mexico, respectively. These troops, who called themselves the Texas Rangers, proved superb scouts and hard fighters, but their violent methods and vengeance against the civil population of Mexico left behind a bitter legacy. After the Treaty of Guadalupe Hidalgo, the state, with some assistance from the federal government, continued to employ varying numbers of ranging companies to patrol its western frontiers. But United States regulars assumed the bulk of the defensive duties as well as furthering exploration of the TransPecos and Panhandle regions. Several military posts lined the Rio Grande from Brownsville to Eagle Pass in response to potential Mexican and Indian incursions. Others composed a huge semicircle extending from Fort Worth to Fredericksburg to Corpus Christi; the forts were pushed farther west as nonIndian settlement expanded. To offer protection and succor for the thousands of California-bound migrants and travelers, the army also occupied several positions along the roads from San Antonio to El Paso.

Brief attempts to establish reservations in Texas having failed, the army launched a series of offensives against hostile Indians. In the most significant of these campaigns, Bvt. Maj. Earl Van Dorn led Texas-based detachments, stiffened by allied Indian scouts and auxiliaries, to victory against Comanche encampments across the Red River at Rush Spring (1 October 1858) and Crooked Creek (13 May 1859). But Texans wanted even more action, and a ranger force led by Rip Ford defeated a sizable Comanche encampment on 12 May 1859 near the Antelope Hills in the Indian territory. In February 1861, the secession convention of Texas listed the federal government's inability to protect its citizens from Indian attack as one of the reasons for the state to leave the Union. This must have seemed ironic to War Department officials, for as much as one-quarter of the entire army had been stationed in Texas during the 1850s. In a controversial move, David E. Twiggs, commanding the Department of Texas, surrendered all federal property and forts in Texas in exchange for the safe passage of his troops. Before all the soldiers could embark, however, the outbreak of war led state officials to scrap the agreement. Garrisons from several TransPecos forts, led by Bvt. Lt. Col. Isaac V. D. Reeve, surrendered to Earl Van Dorn just west of San Antonio. Van Dorn had joined the Confederacy.

Relations with the new Confederate government proved a thorny problem for state officials. Although states'-rights doctrine suggested that Texas should retain control over its men and war materiel, Confederate leaders demanded that resources be pooled under a more centralized authority. And while an initial surge of volunteers flocked to the colors, in early 1862 the Confederacy enacted a conscription law that was eventually extended to most nonblack males between the ages of 17 and 50. Of the 100,000 to 110,000 eligible, between 60,000 and 90,000 probably served in the military. Most Texans displayed a strong desire for mounted duty and a fierce independence that limited efforts to enforce discipline. Early in the Civil War, state regiments penetrated into Indian territory and patrolled the western and Rio Grande frontiers. In late 1861 and early 1862, Brig. Gen. Henry H. Sibley and three regiments of Texans marched west into New Mexico, but fell back into Texas after the battle of Glorieta. In October 1862, Union naval forces occupied Galveston Island. John B. Magruder, commander of Confederate forces in Texas, retook Galveston on New Year's Day, 1863. Another federal invasion force, including 26 ships and 4,000 troops commanded by Maj. Gen. William B. Franklin, was checked at Sabine Pass in September 1863 by Lt. Dick Dowling and a single artillery battery. In late 1863, the federals captured Brownsville, thus cutting off the lucrative trade between Texas and Matamoros. Northern troops advanced up the Rio Grande as far as Rio Grande City, and another column pushed north along the coast past Corpus Christi. But the South Texas offensive was then halted; troops were shifted from South Texas to join Gen. Nathaniel P. Banks in Louisiana. Before Banks could reach Texas, however, Richard Taylor defeated his army in the Red River campaign. Although the final major Union threat to Texas had been blunted, the war was not over in the Lone Star State. In July 1864, Rip Ford's Texans recaptured Brownsville, and in the final encounter of the Civil War routed another federal force at Palmito. During the Confederacy, with the withdrawal of federal troops from western posts, Indians struck back against the white intruders. The state's inability to defend its frontiers was exemplified in the battle of Dove Creek (January 1865), in which 140 Kickapoos migrating to Mexico from Indian Territory defeated 370 state troops. The war itself was resolved east of the Mississippi River. In the Army of Northern Virginia, thousands of Texans formed the bulk of Hood's Texas Brigade, named for its first commander, Texan John Bell Hood. Other Texas units, such as the Eighth Texas Cavalry (Terry's Texas

Rangers) and Ross's Brigade, also fought in Arkansas, Mississippi, Georgia, Tennessee, and the Carolinas. Albert Sidney Johnston, former secretary of war for the Republic of Texas, was commander of the Confederate Army of the Mississippi until killed at the battle of Shiloh. In 1864, President Jefferson Davis transferred Hood from Virginia to Georgia, where he commanded Confederate armies in the closing stages of the Atlanta campaign and in the disastrous defeats at Franklin and Nashville. In July 1863, Grant's capture of Vicksburg made direct communications between Texas and Richmond precarious at best. To resolve the administrative impasse, the Confederacy instituted the Trans-Mississippi Department, which encompassed Texas, Arkansas, Missouri, and much of Louisiana, under the command of Edmund Kirby Smith. The department was virtually isolated from the rest of the Confederacy for the remainder of the war. After Robert E. Lee's surrender at Appomattox, Smith attempted to continue the war, but, with support waning, capitulated on 2 June.

Federal troops, some of whom were black, poured into the Lone Star State. To help force the Emperor Maximilian and the French out of Mexico, some 50,000 United States soldiers were assembled near the Rio Grande in 1865–66. With the death of Maximilian, the French quiescent, and Congress having declared military rule over most of the former Confederate states in the Reconstruction Acts of 1867, the army turned to domestic matters. Texas and Louisiana were combined to form the Fifth Military District, commanded by Gen. Philip Sheridan. Determined to establish federal authority, Sheridan ousted newly elected Governor Throckmorton and several other officials. District military commanders generals Charles Griffin and Joseph J. Reynolds used their troops to intervene in state and local elections in support of the nascent Republican party. The army also backed the Freedmen's Bureau, which helped former slaves secure labor contracts, established separate courts, and set up a rudimentary education system. Governor Edmund Davis's declaration of martial law in several counties and use of a State Police force that was 40 percent black further infuriated whites, as did the corruption that plagued efforts to reorganize a state militia. In such towns as Brenham, soldiers openly clashed with civilians. But an uneasy peace characterized most of the state. Conservatives tried to convince army and federal officials that the troops were needed to protect against Indian attacks rather than openly challenging the men in blue. By summer 1867 several companies had returned to the Indian frontiers. Forts Richardson, Griffin, Concho, Stockton, Davis, and Clark soon held substantial garrisons of regulars, who proved invaluable to travelers and local economies.

With the election of Governor Davis, President Grant declared Reconstruction in Texas to be at an end. The army's emphasis thus shifted to Indian service. In late 1868, columns from New Mexico, Indian Territory, and Kansas moved against several Southern Plains tribes. The resulting campaign brought a temporary peace, but as railroads and white settlers pushed west and the slaughter of the buffalo herds began in earnest, violence continued. Texans claimed that many tribes conducted raids into the state, then retreated to the safety of their reservations. To help patrol the frontiers, in 1874 the state legislature mustered two ranger forces: the Frontier Battalion, designed to control Indians; and the Special Force, organized to guard the Mexican border. During the early 1870s, the army stepped up its campaigns on the Llano Estacado. Col. Ranald Mackenzie, the most effective regular commander, routed a large Comanche village near McClellan Creek in September 1872. The Red River Indian War, which involved troops from Texas, New Mexico, Kansas, and Indian Territory, began in summer 1874. From Fort Concho, Mackenzie delivered the most telling blow at Palo Duro Canyon on 28 September 1874. Human casualties were minimal, but Mackenzie's decision to kill nearly 1,500 captured Indian ponies helped force several tribes to surrender the following year. Farther west, several Apache groups had also resisted encroachment. After witnessing futile pursuits of Victorio and the Apaches, Col. Benjamin H. Grierson seized upon an effective tactic in summer 1880. Rather than attempt to overtake the Indians, Grierson stationed his men at strategic waterholes throughout the TransPecos. After several sharp skirmishes, Victorio withdrew across the Rio Grande, where he was killed by Mexican soldiers. Throughout the period, regulars clashed with their rivals, the Texas Rangers, over methods and effectiveness. In their efforts to punish Indian and Mexican raiders, several state and federal officers crossed over the Rio Grande. In 1873 Mackenzie destroyed several Indian villages near Remolino, about 40 miles inside of Mexico. Texas Rangers splashed across the river two years later near Las Cuevas, seeking to stamp out cattle rustlers. Lt. Col. William Shafter led several army sorties in 1877, even as Mexican protests increased. The following year, Mackenzie and a large United States column twice engaged in longrange skirmishing with Mexican troops. The actions of Texas, United States, and Mexican military forces, the slaughter of the buffalo, the expansion of the railroads, and the westward migration of settlers combined to destroy the military power of the Plains Indians in Texas. But the armed forces' influence was far greater than simply that of its military campaigns. Frontier posts stimulated civilian settlement, and army contracts proved a tremendous boon to local businesses and jobseekers. The state militia, organized as the Volunteer Guards upon passage of the Militia Law of 1879, provided supplemental income to another 2,000 to 3,000 guardsmen as well as a lucrative, if sometimes sporadic, source of appropriations.

About 10,000 Texans served in the Spanish-American War. In April 1898, Congress allowed soldiers in existing organized militia units to volunteer for federal service. Under this law, state troops formed the First Texas Volunteer Infantry Regiment, which sailed to Havana in late 1898. Other Texans joined assorted regular and volunteer formations such as the Rough Riders (the First United States Volunteer Cavalry), organized and trained at San Antonio and made famous by their flamboyant lieutenant colonel, Theodore Roosevelt. Texas and the military remained closely linked during the early twentieth century. Although incidents at Brownsville, Houston, Del Rio, El Paso, Waco, San Antonio, and Texarkana between black garrisons and white and Hispanic residents were symptomatic of the racial tensions that divided American society, this relationship was generally amicable. Early Signal Corps experiments in aviation were conducted at Fort Sam Houston, San Antonio. Turmoil within Mexico in 1911 led the War Department to concentrate a "Maneuver Division" at San Antonio. Eighteen months later, the Second Division was mobilized at Galveston and Texas City. By 1914 other regular army forces, totaling some 12,000 men, were also stationed along the border. After Pancho Villa's strike into New Mexico in March 1916, President Wilson called the national guards of Texas and Oklahoma into federal service. The president soon expanded the callup, and by late July, 112,000 national guardsmen from 14 states had massed along the Rio Grande.

As the Mexican crisis cooled, the guardsmen were in the process of demobilizing when in April 1917 Congress declared war on Germany. Most Texas and Oklahoma national guard units formed the Thirty-sixth Infantry Division, a process formalized that fall. Texans also composed most of the Ninetieth Division; several thousand others were funneled into the Forty-second Division, the socalled "Rainbow Division," a unit that comprised men from 26 states. In all, the selective service registered nearly a million Texans for possible duty; of these, 197,389 were drafted or volunteered. Engaging in the patriotic fervor that swept much of the United States, Texas became a major military training center during the First World War. More than $20 million was spent constructing Camp Bowie (Fort Worth), Camp Logan (Houston), Camp Travis (San Antonio), and Camp MacArthur (Waco) for new recruits. Fort Sam Houston (San Antonio) and Fort Bliss (El Paso) also underwent major expansion. Likewise, military aviation found a warm reception in the state, where Fort Worth, San Antonio, Dallas, Houston, Waco, and Wichita Falls housed key flight and service training centers. Most soldiers from Texas never went abroad. However, the Thirty-sixth Division, supplemented by wartime recruiting and the draft, left for Europe in midsummer 1918. Elements of the Thirty-sixth finally saw combat, as part of the Fourth French Army, at St. Étienne and during the Aisne offensive, for which the units earned substantial accolades from an adoring press. The Forty-second Division was one of the most acclaimed American units of the war, and the Ninetieth Division, composed largely of Oklahomans and the "Texas Brigade" (the 180th Infantry Brigade), also fought in the St. Mihiel and Meuse–Argonne operations. In all, more than 5,000 Texans died overseas.

Numerous bases, availability of land, public support for the military, and an increasingly influential congressional delegation made Texas an important military training center in World War II. The Third and Fourth armies, which oversaw basic and advanced training in several southern and western states, respectively, were headquartered at San Antonio. More than 200,000 airmen trained in Texas, which had more than 50 airfields and air stations, including naval air stations at Corpus Christi, Beeville, and Kingsville. Carswell Field, Fort Worth, was home to Air Force Training Command headquarters. Seventy camps in Texas held 50,000 prisoners of war. About 750,000 Texans (roughly 6 percent of the national total) saw military service during the war. Texas claimed 155 generals and 12 admirals, including the supreme Allied commander in Europe, Dwight Eisenhower, and Pacific Fleet admiral Chester Nimitz. Col. Oveta Hobby directed the Women's Army Corps; Walter Krueger commanded the United States Sixth Army. Among units that included large Texas contingents, the Thirty-sixth Infantry, including the famous "Lost Battalion," fought in Java and Italy in some of the war's bloodiest combat. The division suffered heavy casualties in an unsuccessful attempt to cross the Rapido River under enemy fire. This action, ordered by Fifth Army commander Mark Clark to support Allied landings at Anzio, led to an inconclusive congressional investigation in 1946. The First Cavalry, Second Infantry, and Ninetieth Infantry divisions saw extensive duty in the European Theater. In the

Pacific campaigns were the 112th Cavalry and 103rd Infantry. In all, some 23,000 Texans lost their lives overseas. The war had a tremendous impact upon the Texas economy, in which federal and private investments brought massive industrial development. Aircraft production blossomed in Dallas–Fort Worth; shipbuilding boomed in Orange, Port Arthur, Beaumont, Houston, and Galveston. Sprawling industries along the Gulf Coast also formed the world's largest petrochemical center. Munitions plants, steel mills, and tin smelters were built, and increased demand for food, timber, and oil offered new opportunities throughout the state. With labor at a premium, half a million rural Texans moved to the cities, and women and members of minorities took jobs once reserved for white males.

After the war the United States retained a much larger permanent military establishment in Texas than before. Between the active military, the organized and inactive reserves, the national guard, and the selective service, most male Texans of eligible age experienced the military or its bureaucracy in some direct manner. Thousands of Texans served in the Korean conflict, in which native Texan Walton H. Walker held command of all United Nations ground forces from July to December 1950. During the 1960s and early 1970s, the nation's involvement in Vietnam dominated military affairs. More than 500,000 Texans saw service. In addition, several Texas-based units were transferred to South Vietnam. Fort Hood contributed the United States II Field Force Vietnam, assigned to coordinate operations of the III and IV Corps, and the 198th Infantry Brigade, which joined the American (Twenty-third) Division. The Forty-fourth Medical Brigade was dispatched from Fort Sam Houston. More than 2,100 Texans died in Vietnam. Texans and Texasbased forces also remained a major source of the nation's military strength through the 1980s and early 1990s. During the 1980s Texas was second only to California as home of record for both active-duty and retired military personnel. Sprawling military complexes at San Antonio, El Paso, and Fort Hood, as well as defense manufacturing plants in the Dallas–Fort Worth area, had become essential to national defense as well as the state's economy. During the Desert Shield–Desert Storm operations of 1990–91, for example, the Third Armored Cavalry Regiment and Eleventh Air Defense Artillery Brigade were dispatched to the Persian Gulf from Fort Bliss, while Fort Hood contributed the First Cavalry Division, the First Brigade of the Second Armored Division, and the XIII Corps Support Command. Texas National Guard units, which included more than 20,000 members (many of them parttime) during the early 1990s, supplemented the regular forces and were often called out to assist victims of natural disasters. In 1991 the state militia maintained 138 armories in 117 Texas cities and spent about $250 million in state and federal money.

Robert Wooster

Military History of the Southwest. Began in 1961 as a quarterly published in Austin by the National Guard Association of Texas; first published under the title *Texas Military History* and edited by Maj. Jay A. Matthews, Jr. H. Bailey Carroll was an early contributor; associate editors included Alwyn Barr, David Gracy, James Day, and Jimmy Skaggs. The journal was distributed to all units of the Texas National Guard; to historical associations in Texas, New Mexico, Oklahoma, Arkansas, and Louisiana; to history departments of colleges and universities in those states; and to subscribers. In the late 1960s the board of directors of the National Guard Association of Texas assigned all proprietary rights to the publication to the editor, who continued the journal under the title *Military History of Texas and the Southwest* (1971–).With Volume 19 (1981) the journal became *Military History of the Southwest*, a biannual publication of the University of North Texas history department. Issues have featured articles on numerous Texas military topics, although in 1971 the editorial board expanded the focus to include the entire Southwest.

Jay A. Matthews, Jr.

Military Road. A project of the Republic of Texas. In December 1839 the republic Congress passed a law directing military personnel to cut a road between Austin and Fort Inglish (now Bonham). The road was intended to protect and advance the frontier by connecting a series of forts to be erected from San Patricio northward to a point near Coffee's Station on the Red River. Col. William Gordon Cooke, commanding the First Regiment of Infantry, was in charge of the expedition, which set out in the fall of 1840 with instructions to begin the road on the Texas side of the mouth of the "Kiamishua Red" river in what is now northwest Red River County and terminate at the Brazos. The troops followed a route close to that of Interstate Highway 35, angling toward the east from the approximate site of present-day Abbott. Drought, loss of supplies, cold, and a scarcity of game delayed the effort to construct the forts and lay out the road. Cooke ultimately camped on Timber Creek north of Fort Inglish and established Fort Johnston, southwest of Coffee's trading post. He chose not to terminate the road at the mouth of the Kiamichi because of the western settlements that would be left unprotected, and led a westward search for hostile Indians, north of the Red River, past the North Fork and over the Pease River. Cooke returned to Austin in late January 1841. Thereafter, Capt. M. B. Houghton left Timber Creek and established a bivouac, Camp Jordan, near the site of modern Randolph in Fannin County. A few of Houghton's troops from Camp Jordan accompanied engineer William Hudson Hunt when he surveyed and located the Cedar Springs post (within the city limits of present Dallas) near the Trinity River crossing. After the Texas army was disbanded, John J. Holliday, commanding at Fort Johnston, and Houghton departed for Austin in April 1841. They followed the ridge between the Elm and the East forks of the Trinity. This became the historic Preston Road, roughly followed by modern U.S. Highway 289. The troops crossed the Trinity River at the Cedar Springs post and followed the high ground of present-day Cockrell Hill, Duncanville, Cedar Hill, and Midlothian. They joined the original route near the site of Abbott and arrived in Austin on 3 May. Interest in the road diminished after Houston became the capital. However, the road that developed along Cooke's passage became an early thoroughfare, an emigrant road, and the route of the first great Southwest cattle trail, the Shawnee Trail.

Morris L. Britton

Miller, Doris. Black sailor in World War II; b. Willow Grove, Texas, 12 October 1919; d. Gilbert Islands, 24 November 1943. Miller was named by a midwife who expected the baby to be a girl. At 19 he enlisted in the United States Navy in Dallas; after training in Norfolk, Virginia, he was assigned to the USS *West Virginia*. On 7 December 1941, as a mess attendant, second class, he was collecting dirty laundry just before 8:00 A.M. When the first bombs blasted his ship at anchor in Pearl Harbor, he went to the main deck, where he assisted in moving the mortally wounded captain. He then raced to an unattended deck gun and fired at the attacking planes until forced to abandon ship. It was Miller's first experience firing such a weapon because black sailors serving in the segregated steward's branch of the navy were not given the gunnery training received by white sailors. Although later news stories credited Miller with downing from two to five airplanes, these accounts have never been verified and are almost certainly apocryphal. Miller himself told Navy officials he thought he hit one of the planes. Navy officials conferred the Navy Cross upon Miller on 27 May 1942, in a ceremony at Pearl Harbor. Following a Christmas leave in 1942, when he saw his home and family in Waco for the last time, Miller reported to duty aboard the aircraft carrier *Liscome Bay* (or *Liscomb Bay*) as a mess attendant, first class. During the battle of the Gilbert Islands his ship was torpedoed and sunk in the Pacific Ocean, and Miller perished. At that time, he had been promoted to cook, third class, and probably worked in the ship's galley. In addition to conferring upon him the Navy Cross, the navy honored Doris Miller by naming a dining hall, a barracks, and a destroyer escort for him. The USS *Miller* is the third naval ship to be named after a black navy man. In Waco a YMCA branch, a park, and a cemetery bear his name. In Houston, Texas, and in Philadelphia, Pennsylvania, elementary schools have been named for him, as has a VFW chapter in Los Angeles. An auditorium on the campus of Huston–Tillotson College in Austin is dedicated to his memory. The Doris Miller Foundation in Chicago honors persons who make significant contributions to racial understanding.   *Neil Sapper*

Miller County, Arkansas. A county that, as constituted by an act of the territorial legislature of Arkansas on 1 April 1820, included most of what is now Miller County, Arkansas, and also Bowie, Red River, Lamar, Fannin, Cass, Morris, Titus, Franklin, Hopkins, Delta, and Hunt counties, Texas. The area, named for James Miller, territorial governor of Arkansas, was partially taken out of Hempstead County, where Stephen F. Austin had held court in 1820. The original county seat was the Gilliland settlement. In 1831 a fiveman commission located the county seat at the Jonesborough plantation near what is now Clarksville, Texas. In 1836, when Texas became a republic and Arkansas became a state, most of the residents of the county considered themselves Texans; county residents Travis G. Wright, Richard Ellis, and Bailey Inglish were significant figures in the Republic of Texas. For a time the territory was represented in both the Arkansas legislature and the Texas Congress. In 1837 Texas organized Red River County. Arkansas retaliated the next year by making it a misdemeanor for a citizen in Miller County to hold an office in the Republic of Texas. Texas then established and organized Fannin County in 1838. Arkansas failed in an attempt to establish a county court and attach the area to Lafayette County. Annexation of Texas to the United States in 1845 settled the approximate boundary between Texas and Arkansas. In December 1874 Miller County was formed out of the part of Lafayette County lying west and south of the Red River, and Texarkana, Arkansas, was made the county seat.
Seymour V. Connor

Milton Brown and His Musical Brownies. An important western band. In 1930 Milton Brown, of Stephenville, became the vocalist for Bob Wills's band, the Wills Fiddle Band. In 1931 Wills, guitarist Herman Arnspiger, and Brown began playing a radio show as the Light Crust Doughboys, sponsored by the Burrus Mill and Elevator Company. When W. Lee O'Daniel, president of Burrus Mill, ordered the Doughboys to quit playing dances, Brown left the band. In 1932 he organized Milton Brown and His Musical Brownies, perhaps the best of the early Fort Worth bands. According to Durwood Brown, who played guitar with the Doughboys when not in school, his older brother Milton was a cigar salesman with little musical experience when he joined the Wills Fiddle Band. But Milton was a born band leader who learned quickly under the tutelage of Wills and Arnspiger. He took Durwood from the Wills band to play rhythm guitar; he then added Jesse Ashlock on fiddle, Ocie Stockard on tenor banjo, and Wanna Coffman on bass. Shortly after he organized the band, Brown employed pianist Fred (Papa) Calhoun and fiddler Cecil Brower. Milton Brown and His Musical Brownies began broadcasting on KTAT, a Fort Worth radio station, and playing dances at the Crystal Springs dance hall in Fort Worth. The band was highly influential in the Fort Worth and Dallas area. Brown himself, one of the best vocalists western swing produced, influenced Wills's singers and consequently most western swing singers. Since the Brownies was always a fiddle band, the Bob Wills influence indelibly marked Brown's style. Jesse Ashlock, Brown's first fiddler, learned fiddling from Wills and had often gone to Wills's dances, where he would sit "right behind Bob and play real low and learn the tunes he played." In other ways Milton Brown further developed the Wills style. In 1934 he added Bob Dunn, the first, and in many ways the best, steel guitarist in western swing. In the formative years of the music, Dunn strongly influenced men like Leon McAuliffe and other steel guitarists. Brown was also the first to use a piano in western swing.

Between 1934 and 1936 his band made more than 100 recordings for Victor and Decca. The royalties from recordings were so meager that band members thought the record companies were cheating them, but the companies claimed their recordings simply had not sold well. What the band needed was a big-selling recording, but this possibility ended when Milton Brown was killed in an automobile accident in 1936, just as his career was developing. After Milton's death, the popularity of the band declined. Brown and his musicians were among the earliest pioneers of what was later called western swing, a mixture of country, blues, jazz, pop, and other musical forms. Wills and Brown were responsible for making Fort Worth the "Cradle of Western Swing."
Charles R. Townsend

Mina, Francisco Xavier. Filibuster; b. Idocín, Navarre, Spain, 3 December 1789; d. Mexico City, 11 November 1817. As a student at the University of Zaragoza in 1808, when his countrymen rebelled against French control, Mina joined the Spanish liberals and quickly became a leading guerrilla. When Ferdinand VII returned to the Spanish throne and renounced the liberal constitution of 1812, Mina opposed him and was eventually forced to flee. In October 1814 he arrived in England, where he became acquainted with Gen. Winfield Scott of the United States and a priest who encouraged Mina to strike at Ferdinand VII through an invasion of Mexico. Scott also is thought to have encouraged Mina and to have assured him of the support of the United States for an expedition to free Mexico from Spain. In 1816 Mina sailed from Liverpool to Norfolk, Virginia, and proceeded to Washington, then to Baltimore, Philadelphia, and New York, enlisting aid for his cause. By the end of August 1816 he was ready to sail, but complications arose with the Spanish minister in Washington, who was bringing pressure to bear on the United States to prevent the expedition. Two vessels, the *Caledonia* and the *Dolphin*, however, were dispatched to Port-au-Prince on 1 September 1816. The priest, Father Mier, who was with Mina on the expedition, was sent ahead to contact revolutionary forces in Mexico. Mina, in the *Calypso*, sailed from Baltimore to Port-au-Prince, thence to Galveston to join Louis Michel Aury, who was also planning an invasion of Mexico. Father Mier, meanwhile, had been forced by bad weather to land in New Orleans and in early December left for Galveston with the information that assistance could be raised in New Orleans, probably with the proviso that Mina proceed to Pensacola rather than Mexico. Mina went to New Orleans in February 1817 and conferred with his associates there but decided against an attack on Pensacola, deploring the commercial character of such an expedition. On March 16 he was again at Galveston, where he received the 100-man force of Col. Henry Perry. Aury was to be naval commander of the expedition, while Mina was to have command of the military. The invasion point was to be Soto la Marina, Tamaulipas. The expedition captured Soto la Marina without difficulty and proceeded inland. After many small victories over the Spanish, Mina was defeated and captured at Venadito on 27 October. He was taken to Mexico City, tried, and executed at Fort San Gregorio with 25 companions.   *Harris Gaylord Warren*

Mineral Resources. Minerals and mineral products of Texas are presented alphabetically. Counties, place names, and physical features are not cross-referenced.

Aluminum. Three Texas plants produce aluminum oxide from imported aluminum ore (bauxite). Aluminum processing plants are located in Calhoun, Milam, and San Patricio counties.

Antimony. Although antimony ore is not produced in Texas, antimony ores are processed at a smelter in El Paso.

Asbestos. Amphibole asbestos is associated with talc deposits in Hudspeth County. Tremolite asbestos occurs in some of the Precambrian metamorphic rocks of the Llano region. No asbestos is mined in Texas.

Asphalt. Numerous deposits of asphaltbearing rocks occur in Texas. They include asphaltic Cretaceous limestones in Bexar, Burnet, Kinney, Uvalde, and other counties. Large amounts of the asphaltic limestone are quarried in Uvalde County for use chiefly as paving material. Asphaltic Cretaceous sandstones, which are not currently quarried, occur in Cooke, Montague, Uvalde, and other counties.

Barite. Deposits of barite are widely distributed in Texas, but most are minor. They occur in Baylor, Brewster, Culberson, Gillespie, Hudspeth, Jeff Davis, Llano, Taylor, and other counties. During the 1960s barite was mined in the Seven Hart Gap area for use as a weighting agent in rotarydrilling muds.

Basalt. Intrusive masses of basalt are present in several counties along the Balcones Fault Zone and in the TransPecos area of West Texas. It is produced for aggregate, road ballast, and road material in Uvalde County.

Beryllium. Beryllium minerals are present at several localities in the TransPecos area of West Texas. In recent years a beryllium prospect has been located in Hudspeth County near Sierra Blanca where several beryllium minerals are associated with fluorspar, but no production has been reported.

Bismuth. Bismuth occurs in association with molybdenum and gold in a Precambrian pegmatite dike at the Kiam prospect on Honey Creek in Llano County. It was found also in small quantities in the old Heath gold prospect in Llano County. No bismuth has been produced commercially in Texas.

Bleaching clay. Bentonite clays that are commonly used as bleaching clays and fuller's earth occur at numerous localities in Tertiary formations of the Coastal Plain and deposits on the High Plains. Bleaching clays are used for refining petroleum products and to a lesser extent for refining vegetable oils. Texas bleaching clays are currently produced in Fayette and Gonzales counties.

Brines. Brines containing strong concentrations of mineral salts occur in a variety of geological conditions in widely separated areas of Texas. Shallow brines occur in broad shallow basins usually occupied in part by one or more saline playas or alkaline lakes. Surface and seep waters draining into the playas undergo rapid natural evaporation, resulting in the concentration of salts leached from soils and rocks of the drainage area. Shallow brines are produced for sodium sulfate in Gaines and Terry counties. Brine reservoirs containing salts of sodium, calcium, magnesium, potassium, and other elements are present in the Permian Basin. These aquifers lie at considerable depth and have not been tapped commercially for their salts. In TransPecos Texas shallow brines containing mainly common salt and gypsum occur in the Salt Basin in northern Culberson and Hudspeth counties. Highly gypsiferous waters are present in eastern Culberson County and parts of Reeves County. In southern Texas, brines containing sodium chloride and other salts occur in La Sal Vieja and La Sal del Rey in Willacy and Hidalgo counties. No salts are produced from these brines. Local brine areas are known in the vicinity of salt domes in the Texas Coastal Plain. In parts of East Texas, some moderately strong brines occur in saliferous Tertiary formations not related to salt domes.

Bromine. Bromine is extracted from sea water at Freeport in Brazoria County.

Caliche. Caliche occurs abundantly in surface and nearsurface deposits in the semiarid and arid parts of Texas and is particularly abundant in the High Plains and the outcrop belt of the Goliad Formation of South Texas. A large quantity of caliche is produced chiefly for road construction from numerous and widespread localities.

Celestite. Celestite is known at numerous localities, particularly in the Cretaceous Glen Rose Formation and the Upper Permian Whitehorse Formation in North and north central Texas, respectively. These occurrences are small and have no commercial value. Extensive deposits of celestite are present in Brown and Nolan counties. Small quantities of celestite were produced from these counties during the late 1930s and early 1940s. Most of the celestite produced in Texas has been used as a weighting agent in rotary-drilling fluids.

Cement. Limestone and clay are the principal components used in the manufacture of cement. Iron ore and gypsum are also used in smaller amounts. Cement is currently produced in Bexar, Comal, Dallas, Ector, Ellis, El Paso, Harris, Hays, McLennan, Nolan, Nueces, Potter, and Tarrant counties. Portland cement output rose slightly during 1989 to a total of 7.2 million short tons with a value of $286 million. Historically, the state's Portland cement output has accounted for about 10 percent of the annual United States production. Texas usually has been ranked first or second among the 38 producing states. In 1989 Texas was ranked second behind California. Masonry cement continued its five-year downtrend, and output was estimated at less than half of that in 1984. Declines in Texas construction industries generally have caused a decrease in demand for Portland cement. Texas Portland cement production was up 200,000 tons over that of 1988 but was still lower than the 1975 production. The demand for masonry cement has fallen every year since a record high of 291,000 short tons in 1984.

Clay. Texas has an abundance of various types of clays, occurring in many geologic units. Production includes ball clay, bentonite, common clay and shale, fire clay, fuller's earth, and kaolin. Texas is one of the leading producers of clays in the United States. Ceramic products include structural building brick, paving brick, decorative tile, drain tile, and expanded clay for lightweight aggregate. Common clay suitable for the manufacture of cement or common brick is found in many counties. Clays suitable for ceramic and refractory ware contain a high proportion of kaolin and are found primarily in northeastern Texas. Nonceramic clays are used as bleaching or adsorbent clays, fillers, coaters, additives, bonding clays, drilling muds, and catalysts. Most nonceramic products are produced from bentonites that are found primarily in the Coastal Plain. Kaolin clays found in East Texas are used as paper coaters and fillers and rubber fillers. Highpurity kaolin clays have a high alumina content and are a potential source of metallic aluminum.

Coal. Bituminous coal of Pennsylvanian age occurs primarily in Coleman, Eastland, Erath, Jack, McCulloch, Montague, Palo Pinto, Parker, Throckmorton, Wise, and Young counties of north central Texas. Bituminous coal deposits are also found in Cretaceous deposits of the Olmos Formation in Maverick County and in Eocene age cannel coal deposits in Webb County. These coals provided a significant energy source prior to the development of oil and gas in the 1940s. Mines in these areas were inactive from the early 1940s until the 1970s, when high petroleum prices prompted a revaluation of the Texas coal deposits. Limited bituminous coal production in these areas was resumed during the late 1970s. A decline in demand during the late 1980s resulted in the closing of the North Texas coal mines. The mines in Webb County reduced production but were still in operation in 1992. Cretaceous bituminous coals in TransPecos Texas have little potential for development as a fuel. They have been marketed primarily as a soil conditioner (leonardite). Commercial mining for coal and lignite started in the late 1880s. The first year coal production was listed for Texas was 1884, when 125,000 short tons was mined. Production declined from 1885 to 1888. It subsequently climbed at a high rate to 1,107,953 short tons in 1901, then gradually increased to a high of about 2.4 million tons in 1913. After that year, coal and lignite production gradually declined. Annual production fell below one million short tons in 1930 and below 100,000 short tons in 1945. Production of bituminous coal ceased in 1944; production of lignite continued but declined drastically during the early 1950s. Coal and lignite were mined primarily by underground methods until the 1950s. In the mid1950s the industry received a tremendous boost when ALCOA started using char produced from lignite at its plant near Rockdale. In 1954 estimated lignite production exceeded a million short tons. The production of lignite by strip-mining methods and the utilization of lignite to fuel mine-mouth generators for the production of electricity caused Texas to become a major coal (lignite) producer during the 1970s. Coal production in Texas now exceeds 50 million short tons annually.

Copper. Copper deposits in Texas occur in the TransPecos region, in the Permian red beds of north central Texas, and in the Llano region. Mining has been attempted at different times on the deposits in each region. Most of the state's small production has been from the Van Horn–Allamoore mining district, whereas only small shipments of copper have been reported from the North Texas and Llano regions. The last reported copper production was eighteen tons in 1952, valued at $8,712. Most of the ore came from the Old Hazel Mine in Culberson County. During the mid-1950s, however, most of the Texas copper mines were inoperative. Large deposits of ore exist in North Texas but have not been developed because of their low metal content. Copper refineries operate in El Paso and Potter counties. Copper smelters are operating in plants at Amarillo, El Paso, and Texas City. These depend upon imported ore from Arizona, Chile, New Mexico, and Mexico to produce refined copper, copper anode, copper sulfate, and other copper products.

Diatomite. Diatomite, or diatomaceous earth, occurs in the upper Tertiary and Pleistocene lacustrine deposits on the High Plains. No Texas diatomite has been produced.

Dolomite. Dolomite is widely distributed in Texas except in the Coastal Plain and over the greater part of the High Plains. It occurs in beds of varying thickness and extent in rocks ranging from Precambrian to Cretaceous in age. Dolomite was mined from the Ellenburger Formation in Burnet County as an ore of magnesium during the 1940s. It was processed in the Austin plant of International Minerals and Chemical Company and the Mathieson Alkali Works, Lake Charles, Louisiana. The Ellenburger dolomites are now used by Dow Chemical at Freeport in Brazoria County as a part of a process of removing magnesium from sea water. Dolomites from the Edwards Formation are used as a source of crushed stone.

Evaporites. Evaporites, including rock salt, gypsum, potassium minerals, and other similar compounds, occur extensively in Permian deposits that underlie the greater part of the High Plains and parts of adjacent regions. The evaporite compounds of West Texas are not being produced, although potash is mined extensively in the vicinity of Carlsbad, New Mexico. Salt, anhydrite, and gypsum occur in the salt domes of the Coastal Plain. These minerals, except anhydrite, are considered separately.

Feldspar. Feldspar occurs in Precambrian formations in parts of the Llano and TransPecos regions. During the 1950s it was produced from pegmatite dikes in Llano and Culberson counties and used in the manufacture of pottery, ceramics, and glassware. Feldspars are not currently being produced in Texas.

Fluorspar. Fluorspar or fluorite is an important industrial mineral used in the manufacture of steel, aluminum, glass, and fluorocarbons. It occurs at several localities in the TransPecos and Llano regions of Texas. TransPecos deposits are commonly associated with Tertiary volcanics and Cretaceous limestones. Mining operations first started in 1943 at Eagle Mountain in Hudspeth County. Occurrences of fluorspar have also been found in the Quitman Mountains of Hudspeth County, the Chinati Mountains of Presidio County, the Franklin Mountains of El Paso County, and the Christmas Mountains and other areas of Brewster County. The fluorspar in the Llano region occurs in pegmatite dikes and lenses and veins in Precambrian schists and gneisses. None of the deposits in Texas are currently being produced.

Gemstones. Collecting gem rock and mineral specimens has attracted numerous fans ("rockhounds") and has proved quite profitable. Agate, jasper, cinnabar, fluorite, topaz, calcite, opal, petrified wood, and tektites are stones that are commonly collected by lapidarists. No records are available on the quantities of gemstones collected and sold each year.

Gold. Gold mining has not been extensive in Texas since the occurrence of the metal is limited. Main production, confined to the Presidio and Hazel mines in West Texas and the Heath mine in the Llano region, amounted to a total of 8,277 fine ounces by 1942, valued at $233,499. Most of the gold produced has come as the by-product of silver and copper ores, but traces of it occur in the Shafter, Van Horn, Allamore, and Quitman Mountains, and in Howard, Taylor, Irion, Uvalde, and Williamson counties with other rocks and ores. The last reported gold production was from the Presidio mine in 1942.

Graphite. Deposits of fineflake graphite occur in the Precambrian Packsaddle schist in the Llano region. Graphite was previously produced in Burnet County.

Greensand. Greensand or glauconite sand occurs in Upper Cambrian rocks in the Llano region and in the Midway, Weches, and other Eocene formations in the Texas coastal plain. Greensand has been used in the past as a soil conditioner and in purifying water. It is not currently produced commercially in Texas.

Grinding pebbles. Pebbles suitable for use in grinding mills occur in widely distributed surface deposits along the interior margin of the southern and southwestern Coastal Plain. They have been produced in Bastrop, Colorado, Fayette, Frio, and Gonzales counties. However, modern grinding methods have eliminated the demand for grinding pebbles, and there is no current production of these materials.

Guano. Bat guano occurs in numerous caverns in the Edwards Plateau and in the TransPecos region and to a more limited extent in Central Texas. Guano has been produced in Edwards, Medina, Real, and other counties, but is not currently being produced.

Gypsum. Gypsum is widely distributed and extensively developed in Texas. The main occurrences are (1) in the Blaine and other Permian formations that crop out east of the High Plains; current mining from these extensive bedded deposits occurs in Fisher, Hardeman, and Nolan counties; (2) in the Permian Castile gypsum that crops out in large areas between the Delaware and Apache Mountains and Pecos River in Culberson and Reeves counties; (3) in rocks of probable Permian age in the vicinity of the Malone Mountains in Hudspeth County; (4) in the Cretaceous Edwards Formation in Gillespie and Menard counties, mined in Gillespie County; (5) in caprocks of the Gulf Coast salt domes mined at Hockley dome in Harris County and previously at Gyp Hill in Brooks County. Gypsum is used in the manufacture of plaster of Paris, wallboard, and cement.

Helium. Texas is the leading producer of helium, which is extracted from natural gas in the Panhandle at a United States Bureau of Mines plant in Moore County and at two privately owned plants in Moore and Hansford counties. Production is from the Cliffside gas field near Amarillo.

Iron. Deposits of iron ore, including siderite and the limonite-group minerals, are present in the Eocene Weches Formation in northeastern Texas. Deposits are present in Anderson, Camp, Cass, Cherokee, Harrison, Henderson, Marion, Morris, Nacogdoches, Smith, and Upshur counties. Deposits in Cherokee and Henderson counties are mined chiefly as a source of iron for the manufacture of cement. Several deposits of iron ore minerals are present in Central Texas, such as the magnetite deposits at Iron Mountain in Llano County and the hematitic sandstone deposits in Llano, Mason, McCulloch, and San Saba counties. Hematite also is present in the TransPecos.

Lead and Zinc. Lead and zinc are commonly considered together because they are generally associated in mineral deposits. These metals occur in small deposits in Texas, and much of their past production has been as a byproduct in the production of silver. A large part of the lead was obtained as a minor product of silver–lead ores taken from the Presidio mine in Presidio County. Practically all of the state's zinc production and an approximately equivalent amount of lead was produced from the Bonanza and Alice Ray mines in Hudspeth County from ores with a small silver content. Lead and zinc are also present in the Quitman Mountains southwest of Sierra Blanca in Hudspeth County and in the Apache Mountains in Culberson County. Lead deposits are known at several localities in Cambrian strata in Blanco, Burnet, and Gillespie counties in Central Texas. The only reported production from Central Texas was in 1930 from the Pavitte prospect in western Burnet County. Lead and zinc are not currently produced in Texas and have not been mined in the state since 1952. Between 1885 and 1952 the total lead production in Texas amounted to 5,443 short tons and the total zinc production was 837 short tons. Lead was formerly produced as a byproduct of silver mining, mainly from the Presidio Mine in Presidio County and the Bird Mine in Brewster County. Zinc production had come chiefly from the Bonanza and Alice Ray mines in Hudspeth County, with small amounts also from the Chinati and Montezuma mines in Presidio County and the Buck Prospect in Culberson County. Although no longer a producer of lead and zinc, Texas had a primary smelter that produced lead and zinc in El Paso County until the mid-1980s. The ore came from western states and Mexico.

Lignite. Lignite or brown coal occurs in extensive deposits in the Eocene, Wilcox, and Claiborne groups of the Texas Coastal Plain. The Wilcox Group contains the largest reserves and highest quality lignite. The principal resource area is north of the Colorado River in Central and East Texas. Lignite was first mined in Texas during the 1850s and was produced primarily from underground mines. Lignite production declined during the 1940s and early 1950s, when oil and gas supplies became readily available. Recovery of the Texas coal-mining industry began in the 1950s, when stripmining techniques were first used to mine Texas lignite and provide a feed stock to mine-mouth electrical generators. Texas is now the nation's sixth-largest coal producer, with estimated recoverable near-surface reserves (at depths of less than 200 feet and seam thicknesses of three or more feet) of 23 billion short tons. Lignite is currently utilized at electrical generators in Atascosa, Bastrop, Freestone, Grimes, Harrison, Hopkins, Limestone, Panola, Rusk, and Titus counties. It is also produced in Harrison County as a source of activated carbon. Deepbasin lignite resources (200 to 2,000 feet deep) are approximately equal to nearsurface lignite resources. These resources can be developed by the process of *in situ* gasification.

Lime. Limestones, which are abundant in many parts of Texas, are utilized in the manufacture of lime. They are crushed and calcined to drive off the excess carbon dioxide and convert the calcium carbonate to calcium oxide. Uses of lime include soil stabilization, water purification, paper and pulp manufacture, metallurgy, sugar refining, agriculture, construction, and removal of sulfur from power-plant stack gases. Plants for the production of lime are currently operating in Bexar, Bosque, Burnet, Comal, Deaf Smith, Hill, Johnson, Nueces, and Travis counties.

Magnesite. Magnesite occurs in Precambrian deposits commonly associated with marbles. Small-scale mining operations in Llano and Mason counties have extracted magnesite for use as agricultural stone and terrazzo chips.

Magnesium. Magnesium chloride, magnesium sulfate, and other mineral salts are present in Upper Permian brines in Borden County and in shallow brines underlying playas in the High Plains. Magnesium chloride is extracted from sea water at a plant in Brazoria County and is used to produce magnesium compounds and magnesium metal.

Manganese. Manganese is known to occur in residual and surface deposits in Precambrian rocks in Mason and Llano counties, at several localities in Cretaceous and Quaternary deposits in Val Verde County, in Lower Cretaceous deposits in Jeff Davis County, and in Triassic sandstones in Dickens County. Small quantities of manganese have been mined from the deposits in Jeff Davis County, but no production has been reported since the mid1950s.

Mercury. Mercury mineral deposits occur in the Terlingua district of southern Brewster and southeastern Presidio counties, where mining was initiated in 1896. During the early 1930s Texas was one of the nation's leading producers of mercury. The sharp reduction in price and demand after World War II caused the closure of all Texas mercury mines. A rise in price during the 1950s caused sporadic mining activity in the area. Record high prices for mercury in the middle to late 1960s prompted renewed interest in the area that resulted in the reopening of several mines and the discovery of new reserves. All of the mines closed in the early 1970s, when prices again declined. No production has been reported since 1973.

Mica. Mica is present in Precambrian pegmatite dikes on the western side of the Van Horn Mountains in western Culberson County and also in Precambrian schists and pegmatites in the Llano region. Some mica has been produced in the past from the Culberson County area, but production is no longer active.

Mineral water. Water containing high concentrations of salts and bitterns has been extracted from a variety of groundwater horizons. Mineral water has been produced at Mineral Wells in Palo Pinto County, near Marlin in Falls County, at Milford in Ellis County, and at Thorndale in Williamson County. No production of mineral waters is currently reported.

Molybdenum. Deposits of molybdenum minerals have been found in Brewster, Culberson, Hudspeth, Llano, and Presidio counties, but no production has been reported.

Nitrates. Sodium nitrate and potassium nitrate are present in volcanic rocks in the vicinity of Candelaria, but attempts at production have been unsuccessful.

Novaculite. Novaculite, a chertlike, siliceous rock, occurs in the Caballos Formation of Devonian age that crops out in prominent ridges in the Marathon area in Brewster County. It is not produced in Texas.

Opal. Common opal associated with chalcedony occurs in the Catahoula and other Tertiary formations of the Texas Coastal Plain. Opal also occurs as nodules and masses, as cement in sandstones, as vein and cavity fillings, and as a replacement of wood.

Oyster shell. Oyster and clam shells occur in reefs and beds in the bays and lagoons bordering the Gulf of Mexico and in some Quaternary sediments along the seaward margin of the Coastal Plain. Shells from many of these areas were extensively produced until the early 1960s, when production was discontinued because of environmental concerns.

Peat. Peat bogs are widely distributed in the middle and eastern part of the Coastal Plain at localities in Gonzales, Guadalupe, Lee, Milam, Polk, and San Jacinto counties. Peat from some of these deposits has been produced in the past for use as a soil conditioner.

Perlite. Perlite is a glassy igneous rock that expands to a porous lightweight mass when heated. Its uses include filter medium, lightweight aggregate, and horticultural aggregate. Perlite has been produced near Pinto Canyon in Presidio County. No perlite is currently produced in Texas, but imported perlite is processed at plants in Bexar, Dallas, El Paso, Guadalupe, Harris, and Nolan counties.

Phosphate. Small quantities of phosphate rock are present in Paleozoic formations in West and Central Texas. Upper Cretaceous and Tertiary deposits in northeastern Texas also contain lenses of rock phosphate. No phosphate is mined in Texas, but imported phosphate rock is processed at a plant in Brownsville.

Potash. Potash minerals, including polyhalite, are found in extensive deposits in Permian strata in parts of West Texas. After World War I a search for potash sources, conducted by state and federal agencies, resulted in the development of highgrade potash rock containing sylvite and other potash minerals in New Mexico. Texas potash deposits are of a lower grade and have not been developed.

Pumicite. Volcanic ash or pumicite occurs in numerous deposits in some of the Tertiary formations of the Texas Coastal Plain, particularly in the Catahoula and Jackson formations. Other Tertiary ash deposits occur in volcanic rocks in the TransPecos. Pleistocene volcanic-ash deposits occur at several localities in the High Plains and eastward as far as Wichita County. Volcanic ash was formerly mined in Dickens, Gonzales, Lynn, Scurry, and Starr counties.

Rare-earth minerals. Elements of the Lanthanide series are commonly termed rare-earth elements. Yttrium is also commonly included in the group because it is associated with the heavier rare earths. Several of the rare earths have anomalous concentrations in the rhyolitic and related igneous rocks in the Quitman Mountains and the Sierra Blanca area of TransPecos Texas. A deposit containing several rare-earth minerals was exposed at Barringer Hill in Llano County before it was covered by the waters of Lake Buchanan. No rare earths are produced in Texas.

Salt. Salt occurs in large quantities in salt domes in the Texas

Coastal Plain and with other evaporites in the Permian Basin of West Texas. Smaller quantities are present in surface and near-surface brines and in playas and saline springs in West and South Texas. Rock salt is produced from an underground mine at Grand Saline in Van Zandt County. However, most of the salt production in Texas is from brine wells. Texas is one of the leading saltproducing states.

Sand and gravel. Sand and gravel deposits of commercial value are found adjacent to the major rivers that flow across Texas and in the Goliad, Uvalde, and Willis formations in the Texas Coastal Plain. Extensive deposits also occur in Seymour Formation gravels and basal Cretaceous formations in north central Texas, in alluvial fan deposits east of the Caprock, and in the mountain areas of TransPecos Texas. Sand and gravel deposits are mined primarily as a source of construction materials. The principal sand and gravel producing counties in Texas include Bexar, Brazos, Colorado, Dallas, Ellis, Fayette, Hays, Hidalgo, Johnson, Kaufman, Liberty, McLennan, Montgomery, Parker, Pecos, Reeves, Travis, Val Verde, Victoria, and Wise counties.

Sands. Sands used for industrial purposes commonly have unique physical or chemical characteristics that make them suitable for special purposes. Most of these sands have a high silica content. Sands suitable for industrial use occur in Tertiary deposits of the Texas Coastal Plain and East Texas, Cretaceous formations of north central Texas, and Paleozoic rocks of Central Texas. Industrial sands produced in Texas include abrasive, blast, chemical, engine, filtration, foundry, glass, hydraulicfracturing, molding, and pottery sands. These are produced from formations in Atascosa, Bowie, Colorado, El Paso, Gonzales, Guadalupe, Hardin, Harris, Johnson, Liberty, Limestone, McCulloch, Newton, Smith, Somervell, Upshur, and Wood counties.

Silver. The discovery of silver in Texas has been credited by some to Franciscans who discovered and operated mines near El Paso about 1680. Reportedly, these mines were worked periodically, closed down and concealed, and later rediscovered. However, no documentation of these operations is available. Documented silver production started in the late 1880s at the Presidio Mine, near Shafter in Presidio County. About 1885 silver mining began in the Van Horn–Allamoore district in Hudspeth and Culberson counties. Other areas where silver has been produced in Texas include the Shafter district, northern Quitman Mountains district, Loma Plata mine, Altuda Mountain district, Eagle Mountains district, and Van Horn Mountains district. Between 1885 and 1955, Texas produced 32,663,405 troy ounces of silver.

Stone, crushed. Texas is among the nation's leading producers of crushed stone. Crushed stone can be produced from many varieties of igneous, metamorphic, and sedimentary rocks. Most crushed stone produced in the state is limestone. Other stones that provide smaller volumes of crushed stone include basalt, dolomite, granite, marble, rhyolite, sandstone, and serpentine. Crushed stone is used primarily as aggregate for use in concrete and road material. Large tonnages are also used in the manufacture of lime and cement. Relatively small tonnages of crushed stone are used for fillers, filter material, riprap, roofing chips, and terrazzo.

Stone, dimension. Materials suitable for dimension stone or building stone can be found in most parts of the state except the High Plains and the Gulf Coastal Plain. Granite, limestone, and sandstone are the only stones currently being produced as dimension stone. Granites are produced from Precambrian granites in Burnet, Gillespie, Llano, and Mason counties. Limestones are produced from rocks of Permian age in Jones and Schackelford counties and rocks of Cretaceous age in Lampasas, Travis, and Williamson counties. Sandstones are produced from Triassic deposits in Ward County.

Sulfur. Sulfur occurs in the caprocks of salt domes in the Gulf Coastal Plain, in Permianage bedded deposits in TransPecos Texas, and as a constituent of sour gas and petroleum. Mining of native sulfur deposits is accomplished by the Frasch process, which uses superheated water to melt the sulfur so that it can be pumped to the surface. Sulfur is used in petroleum refining and in the preparation of fertilizer and chemicals. Texas is one of the nation's leading producers of sulfur. Native sulfur is produced from one salt dome in Wharton County and from subsurface Permian deposits in Culberson County. Recovered sulfur is extracted from oil and gas at more than 60 plants in about 36 Texas counties.

Talc. Talc deposits are present in Precambrian metamorphic rocks in the Allamoore area of Culberson and Hudspeth counties and in Blanco, Gillespie, and Llano counties of the Llano Uplift area. Deposits in the Allamoore are currently being produced. Talc is used as a filler in the manufacture of roofing materials, paper, plastic, and synthetic rubber and in ceramic materials.

Tin. The tin mineral cassiterite is present in the Franklin Mountains north of El Paso, where small quantities of tin ore were produced during the early 1900s. Minor quantities have also been found in the Streeter area of Mason County. The only tin smelter in the United States is located at Texas City. Imported ore concentrates and other tinbearing materials are processed at this plant. Tin is not currently being mined in Texas.

Titanium. The titanium mineral rutile occurs in association with Tertiary silicified tuffs and kaolin at the Mueller prospect in south central Jeff Davis County. The mineral ilmenite also contains titanium and is present in several counties on the Coastal Plain. No deposits of commercial interest have been discovered.

Topaz. Colorless and light-blue varieties of topaz are found in Precambrian granite in the vicinity of Streeter in Mason County. Topaz is not produced commercially.

Tripoli. Tripoli occurs in several deposits in the Marble Falls limestone in southern Lampasas County. The tripoli, a siliceous incoherent material consisting of particles of sponge spicules, has been produced in small quantities, but there is no current production from the area.

Tufa. Tufa and travertine are freshwater limestone deposits commonly associated with springs and streams in limestone regions. Tufa deposits were previously produced in San Saba County, but no current production is known.

Turquoise. Turquoise occurs in the Precambrian Carrizo Mountain schist in the Van Horn area near the Culberson–Hudspeth county line. Material has been produced from this area in the past, but no production is known at present.

Uranium. Uranium was discovered in Texas in the mid1950s in Karnes County. Deposits were found in Tertiary formations in a mineralized zone that extends from the central Coastal Plain southwestward to the Rio Grande. Uranium mineralization was subsequently discovered in the Trans-Pecos area, the Llano Uplift, and the High Plains. A small amount of uranium was produced from deposits in the High Plains during the 1950s, but most of the Texas production has been from the Coastal Plain. In the past uranium was produced from surface mines in Atascosa, Gonzales, Karnes, and Live Oak counties. These mines are now closed and reclaimed. Current uranium production is by *in situ* leaching. Demand and production of uranium decreased sharply during the 1980s.

Vermiculite. Vermiculite is a micalike mineral that expands when heated. It is used as a horticultural medium, lightweight aggregate, and insulating material. Deposits are present in Precambrian metamorphic deposits in the Llano region. Exfoliation plants at Dallas, Houston, and San Antonio currently process vermiculite mined outside of Texas. Vermiculite is not currently produced in Texas.

Zeolites. Zeolite minerals occur in Tertiary volcanic deposits in TransPecos Texas and in the Coastal Plain. They are used in ionexchange processes, as catalysts, in air and water purification, and other purposes. Deposits in McMullen County are currently being produced. *L. Edwin Garner*

Minute Women of the U.S.A. Founded in 1949 by Suzanne Stevenson of Connecticut to fight communism in government and education and to demand the teaching of the American heritage in schools and colleges. Membership was especially strong in Texas, California, West Virginia, Maryland, and Connecticut. Texas chapters of the organization were formed in 1951 in Houston, Dallas, San Antonio, and Wichita Falls. The most active Minute Women group in Texas was in Houston, where the organization became one of the leading chapters in the nation and one of Houston's most prominent anti-Communist organizations. Approximately 200 men and women attended the first publicized meeting of Houston Minute Women in July 1951; by 1952 the chapter had 500 members. Eleanor Watt was the original chairman of the Houston chapter, but when turmoil developed within the organization concerning its secrecy in the fall of 1951, Stevenson appointed Virginia Biggers to the position. Other leading women within the Houston organization were Virginia Hedrick, Faye Weitinger, and Helen Darden Thomas. The Minute Women organization was officially nonpartisan. Members were drawn to the organization for a variety of reasons: opposition to socialized medicine, support of the oil industry, patriotism, opposition to integration, and concern over new teaching theories. Only United States citizens were eligible for membership, and members were required to pledge to vote in every election and to support the perceived traditional American way of life. Fearing Communist infiltration, Suzanne Stevenson set up the organization with no constitution or bylaws, no parliamentary procedure to guide the meetings, and no option for motions from the floor. Also, all officers were appointed rather than elected. Across the nation the women used a chain-telephoning system to call meetings and convey their opinions to government officials and to their opponents. They waged letter-writing campaigns and heckled speakers. The Minute Women also promoted anticommunist, anti–New Deal, and anti-Semitic literature. Their views could be heard in Houston on "Minute Women Calling for Liberty," a Sunday evening radio program. In 1952 they succeeded in electing Minute Women supporters to the board of the Houston ISD, from where they caused resignations and firings of teachers and school officials, including the deputy superintendent of the Houston public schools. In October 1953 the Houston *Post* published an exposé of the organization that brought about an investigation of the Houston school system in 1954. The National Education Association report indicated no reason to believe the Houston schools were harboring communist teachers and gave a negative view of the Minute Women's activities. This report coincided with a general nationwide decline in the reputation of Senator Joseph McCarthy of Wisconsin and with changing international relations, which somewhat eased American fears of Communist infiltration. Although the Minute Women remained active into the 1960s, the size and influence of the organization steadily diminished. *June Melby Benowitz*

Missouri Compromise. The parallel of 36°30' north latitude, the southern boundary of Missouri, was established by the Missouri Compromise of 1820 as the northern limit of that part of the Louisiana Purchase that could be slave territory. Because of the Adams–Oñís Treaty Texas was not considered a part of the Louisiana Purchase; therefore the annexation resolutions passed by Congress on 29 February 1845 included a restriction that if Texas were to be divided into more than one state, any state established north of the Missouri Compromise line (which was thus extended westward across Texas) would be a free state. As a part of the Compromise of 1850 the northern boundary of the Texas Panhandle was fixed at the Missouri Compromise line, thus averting conflict in interpretations and making Texas clearly a "slave state." *Seymour V. Connor*

Mobeetie, Texas. The "mother city" of the Panhandle; in northwestern Wheeler County. It developed from Charles Rath and Bob Wright's supply store at a buffalo-hunters' camp called Hidetown, established in 1874, and grew to 150 residents the following summer as a trading post for nearby Fort Elliott, which had been opened in May of that year. Bat Masterson, Pat Garrett, and Poker Alice were among the famous visitors to Hidetown, which was so named because residents used buffalo hides in the construction of their dwellings. Henry Fleming, later the first sheriff of Wheeler County, built his rock house across Sweetwater Creek from the camp. The village was located at the southern end of the Jones and Plummer Trail and was a center of activity for the buffalo-hide trade. After the buffalo slaughter waned, many transient hunters stayed. Some made a living catering to the soldiers at the fort, and in 1878 the town was moved a short distance closer to the post. At first the community was called Sweetwater, but when a post office was applied for in 1879, duplication in names caused the Indian word *mobeetie*, possibly meaning "sweet water," to be chosen. Mobeetie was elected county seat when Wheeler County was organized in 1879. Throughout the 1880s it was the commercial center of much of the Panhandle, connected by a mail route with Tascosa, to the west. The main street was jammed with various businesses, including livery stables, wagonyards, a barbershop, a drugstore, a Chinese laundry, a blacksmith shop, two hotels, and boardinghouses. Several saloons—Fleming built the first—were available. Like other open whiskey towns, Mobeetie had its share of gamblers, rustlers, and prostitutes. However, Capt. George W. Arrington and his Texas Ranger company proved an effective deterrent to the lawless element. In 1881 Mobeetie became the judicial center of the Thirty-fifth District, which comprised 15 counties. Several lawyers set up shop, including Temple

Street scene, Mobeetie, ca. 1900. Courtesy Panhandle–Plains Historical Museum, Canyon, Texas. In the decade of the 1880s, Mobeetie was the commercial center for much of the Panhandle. After Fort Elliott was abandoned in 1890, the town steadily declined.

crude flagpole, Fort Elliott's sole surviving remnant, is nearby, and the original rock schoolhouse is now a private residence.

H. Allen Anderson

Mobile Grays. A company of about 30 volunteers organized November 1835 in Mobile, Alabama, by James Bonham, Albert Horton, and S. P. St. John; arrived at San Antonio under command of David N. Burke three days after Cos surrendered. When the army reorganized for the Matamoros expedition of 1835–36 the group, enlarged by transfers from the New Orleans Greys, proceeded to Goliad and, on 12 February 1836, became part of the Second, or LaFayette, Battalion of the Provisional Regiment of Volunteers under Fannin. There may have been as many as 38 Mobile Grays with Fannin at Goliad. If so, one was killed in action on 19 March; 3 escaped, 4 were spared on 27 March, and 30 were killed in the Goliad Massacre that day.

Mockingbird. The Texas state bird, the northern mockingbird (*Mimus polyglottos*); one of more than 30 species called mockingbirds. All 30 live in the New World, but only the northern mockingbird occurs in the United States, where it is represented by two subspecies, *M. p. polyglottos* (eastern United States) and *M. p. leucopterus* (western United States). In Texas the two subspecies intergrade in the Cross Timbers, the eastern part of the Edwards Plateau, the southern portion of the Blackland Prairie, and the central Coastal Plains. The northern mockingbird is robin-sized but is more slender than a robin. It is gray above and gray-white below and has conspicuous white wing patches and white outer tail feathers. The sexes appear almost identical and are rarely separable in the field, but the female is on the average smaller and has slightly darker outer tail feathers. Juvenile birds have brown hair spots on the underparts—a feature suggesting that the mockingbird's ancestors were spotted below, as are many of the other members of the family (Mimidae) that are living today. The western subspecies has a relatively shorter tail and is somewhat more buff-colored below. Partial and total albinism have been reported. Northern mockingbirds occur throughout the United States except in the most northern regions. Their range extends south into Mexico and the West Indies. In Texas the species is a permanent resident from sea level to over 6,000 feet above sea level, and it is particularly common in gardens, parks, brushy areas, and along roadsides. It is rarely seen in deep forests or on prairies devoid of shrubs or small trees. It feeds on insects and other small animals, including lizards, snails, and sowbugs, as well as on fruits and berries. A unique behavior in mockingbirds is called wing-flashing. It is most commonly seen as the bird runs along the ground foraging for insects. The mockingbird stops abruptly and spreads both wings simultaneously, thus briefly exposing the white wing patches. It is generally thought that it does this to flush insects, but the behavior may have other functions as well; it is also seen in young birds when they are exposed to a situation new to them. Mockingbirds build their nests in trees, shrubs, and vines up to a height of 50 feet; they use twigs, leaves, horsehair, grass, cotton, string, and other materials. They lay three to six eggs that vary from blue to green, with reddish, brownish, or purplish spots. Both sexes build the nest and feed the young, but only the female incubates the eggs (for 10 to 13 days). A pair may remain mated for several years, and birds may live 12 years or longer in the wild.

Houston, who served as district attorney before his election to the state Senate. By 1882 the Texas Panhandle, the region's first newspaper, was in operation. A rock schoolhouse, which also served as a union church and community center, was built in 1889. In 1893 the saloons were closed after a revival meeting resulted in 300 conversions. Baptist and Methodist churches were constructed soon afterwards. Mobeetie began a period of quick decline after Fort Elliott was abandoned in 1890, and its attempts to secure a railroad ended in failure. The town's troubles increased on 1 May 1898, when a cyclone took seven lives and leveled many of the buildings. Another blow occurred in 1907 when a controversial election made Wheeler the county seat. Nevertheless, Mobeetie survived, with its school, a bank, a lumberyard, and various other businesses. In 1929 the town suffered a major setback when the Panhandle and Santa Fe Railway built its line from Pampa to Clinton, Oklahoma, across the north end of the county, missing the town by two miles. The post office and most of the businesses moved to the railroad, and the settlement of New Mobeetie was born. Old Mobeetie was subsequently incorporated into the new town. In its heyday, Old Mobeetie's resident population fluctuated from 300 in 1886 to 400 in 1890, 128 in 1900, and 250 in 1910. In the heart of a ranching and agricultural area, New Mobeetie quickly showed promise as a shipping point. During the 1930s modern school facilities, including a gymnasium–auditorium, were constructed. By 1940 the population of the incorporated town of Mobeetie numbered around 500, but it slowly declined to 291 in 1980 and 154 in 1990, mainly because of improved highways and the proximity of Pampa and other towns. Although a few people still resided at the old townsite, many of its houses were abandoned and falling down. The old county jail is a museum. A

The mockingbird's remarkable ability to imitate sounds is the basis for both its common and scientific name (*Mimus*, "mimic"; *polyglottos*, "many-tongued"). The song may continue for more than an hour without pause, and it is not unusual for singing to last through the night. The highly variable song contains not only sounds of other birds, but also such inanimate noises as those of whistles and sirens. Some of the sounds the birds imitate have a frequency higher than the human ear can detect. The male sings more than the female does, apparently to establish a territory and attract a mate. Mockingbirds are among the most capable defenders of their territory and frequently attack hawks and cats, which prey on them and their young. Northern populations are partially migratory, but Texas birds seem to migrate very little if at all. The northern mockingbird is the state bird of Arkansas, Florida, Mississippi, and Tennessee, as well as of Texas. It was adopted as the state bird of Texas in 1927, at the request of the Texas Federation of Women's Clubs. Until the early twentieth century it was a popular caged bird in Texas and the United States, as it is in parts of Mexico even today. It was also used to make bird pie in parts of the state. Like almost all nongame birds, the northern mockingbird has been strictly protected by state and federal laws for more than 70 years.

Kent Rylander

Montezuma Affair. An incident in diplomatic relations between Britain and the Republic of Texas (1842). The Mexican government had contracted with Lizardi and Company of Liverpool and London to build two ironclad warships to be named the *Guadaloupe* and the *Montezuma*. (A former vessel named *Montezuma*, a steam frigate also built by Lizardi and Company for the Mexican navy, had been practically destroyed by the Texas ship *Invincible* in March 1836.) Crews for the two new ships were to be recruited in England, and the vessels were to be delivered to Veracruz under command of English officers. In May 1842, William Kennedy, Republic of Texas consul general in London, and Ashbel Smith, minister to England, protested the building of the vessels for Mexican use against Texas and urged the English government to detain them. Lord Aberdeen of the British Foreign Office decided that arms might be placed on the vessels so long as they were not mounted in English ports, and the *Guadaloupe* sailed in June despite Texas protests. Aberdeen insisted that the English would maintain strict neutrality in the struggle between Texas and Mexico and that no English commissioned officer would be allowed to serve in the Mexican nation against Texas. In July 1842 James Hamilton, then in England, learned that English officers had secured permission of the Admiralty to command the *Montezuma* and that guns were being placed aboard the ship. He presented customs officials with an affidavit to the effect that the *Montezuma* was about to sail in violation of the Foreign Enlistment Act, which provided for confiscation of vessels equipped and armed to make war against a country at peace with England. The customs officials detained the ship, and Hamilton and Lizardi and Company both took the case to the Lords of the Treasury, who decided that the law had been violated technically but not intentionally and decreed that the *Montezuma* was to be released after its large guns were removed and its crew reduced to that of a merchant vessel. Smith protested to Aberdeen that Texas would, if the *Montezuma* were permitted to join the *Guadaloupe*, believe that

Great Britain was trying to aid Mexico. Despite Hamilton's further efforts to have the ships detained in Cuba, both vessels reached Mexico and took part in action against Yucatán, where the Texas Navy was then employed. Commodore Edwin Ward Moore of the Texas Navy attacked the ships off the coast of Yucatán in April 1843, damaging the *Montezuma* and almost disabling the *Guadaloupe*.

Moody, Daniel James, Jr. Governor; b. Taylor, 1 June 1893; d. Austin, 22 May 1966; m. Mildred Paxton (1926); 2 children; ed. University of Texas. Moody's law career was interrupted by service in World War I, after which he became the youngest person elected to several successive offices: county attorney of Williamson County, 1920–22; district attorney of the 26th Judicial District, 1922–25; state attorney general, 1925–27; and governor of Texas (two terms, 1927–31). As attorney general he established a reputation by prosecuting members of the Ku Klux Klan, which generously returned his hostility. Though serving in the gubernatorial administration of Miriam A. Ferguson, he uncovered some of the Fergusons' corruption and opposed Ma Ferguson in 1926. He won on a platform of prohibition and other anti-Ferguson planks. As governor, he was known as a reformer, particularly of abuses that had grown rife under the Fergusons. He reorganized the highway system and cut its costs; he began the office of state auditor. Many of his progressive ideas failed to become law, however. After his terms as governor, he practiced law in Austin and served (1935–) as special assistant to the United States attorney general. He ran unsuccessfully against W. Lee O'Daniel and James Allred for the U.S. Senate in 1942—his only election defeat. He opposed the New Deal and the renomination of Franklin D. Roosevelt, though he did not join the other "Texas Regulars" in walking out of the 1944 Democratic national convention. He represented Coke Stevenson in a legal challenge to Lyndon B. Johnson's controversial narrow victory in the 1948 U.S. Senate election. Subsequently, though remaining a Democrat, Moody supported Dwight D. Eisenhower (1952, 1956) and Richard M. Nixon (1960).

Richard T. Fleming

Moonshining. The unlicensed distillation of whiskey in Texas long precedes the "temperance" movement. The unintended side effect of this movement, which enacted local-option laws in 1876 and 1891, was to boost the moonshine industry, which reached its heyday during the period of national Prohibition (1919–33). Many moonshiners thought that they were unfairly persecuted and resented being treated as common criminals. They occasionally attained the status of folk heroes who beat the system. During the Great Depression some people viewed moonshining as an honorable alternative to the humiliation of employment lines or government relief. Occasionally, the moonshiners' prosperity would irritate law-abiding or less successful citizens, but the whiskey makers frequently operated with the tacit support of the community. Local law enforcers were often motivated by unofficial sympathy or well-placed bribes to turn a blind eye. Moonshine was often made on the "halves" system, in which a bootlegger or distributor would furnish the raw material, kegs, and fruit jars, and the moonshiner would supply the still, distill the liquor, and bear most of the risk of getting caught. A typical recipe for corn whiskey called for 50 pounds of sugar, 50 pounds of steel-cut corn chops, and 35 gallons of water. The mixture was allowed to "rot" for four to seven days. When the sour mash stopped bubbling after a few days and turned sky blue it was ready to be "cooked off" or distilled. An average still could produce 45 to 60 gallons a week. "Charter moonshine," considered the best, was put in charred oak barrels for several days, where it turned dark and absorbed flavor from the charcoal. A variety of ingredients could be added for taste—red oak chips, peaches, apples, caramel, raisins, syrup, rock candy, tobacco, or whatnot. Dr Pepper was a popular additive. Adding lye to the mash accelerated fermentation but caused the consumer's lips to swell painfully. Another shortcut consisted of routing the mixture through an automobile radiator and adding battery acid to the brew. This mixture could be cooked off in one day instead of the usual three or more. But lead absorbed from old radiators or improperly soldered connections could cause lead poisoning, partial paralysis or jake leg, permanent brain damage, or death. In addition to these harmful results, improperly manufactured moonshine might contain additives that tasted bad, even if they were not permanently disabling. Moonshiners and law officers have reported discovering dead raccoons, snakes, frogs, possums, and hogs floating in vats of untended moonshine. Moonshining was often a family operation in which distinctive recipes and techniques were passed down from generation to generation or from one relative to another. Although local authorities often tolerated moonshining, moonshiners and their associates feared the agents of the United States Bureau of Alcohol, Tobacco, and Firearms. A successful raid by these "revenuers" could cost the moonshiners several hundred dollars in lost equipment and supplies, not to mention a loss of income and the possibility of a jail sentence if the moonshiner failed to escape through the woods. Most moonshiners moved their stills frequently to avoid such costly disruptions and minimize losses to small-time pilferers or "beer drinkers," who wandered through the woods sampling the moonshiners' wares.

The repeal of Prohibition greatly reduced the profitability of moonshining. World War II dealt the industry a double blow by sending many consumers overseas while driving up the price of sugar. Though legal competition has ruined most of the market, some moonshining still occurs. Bottled gas has replaced smoky wood fires at the stills, which are sometimes hidden in abandoned urban buildings. Improved law-enforcement techniques and the increased availability of substitutes for bootleg whiskey have reduced the one-time flood of illegally manufactured liquor to a mere trickle. Meanwhile, the dry areas of Texas have radically diminished in number, as citizens have increasingly voted wet in local-option elections. Even in areas that have remained dry, moonshine is not in demand since bootleggers can bring in legally produced liquor from other areas. Treasury Department officials destroyed an average of 25 stills a month in the Southeast Texas–Gulf Coast jurisdiction before World War II. They averaged only 12 to 14 stills a year during the early 1960s. Only six stills were confiscated in 1970, when Texas was described as having a "moderate" moonshine problem, ranking fifth in the nation (behind Alabama, Georgia, North Carolina, and Tennessee). According to the Texas Alcoholic Beverage Commission, in 1993 two stills were seized in Texas with a combined capacity of 35 gallons. Despite the decrease in popularity, a few diehard moonshiners carry on the tradition in the brushy bottomlands of East Texas, and some customers still prefer "white lightning" to anything that can be purchased over a counter. *Bill O'Neal*

Moore Air Force Base. Fourteen miles northwest of Mission; established in September 1941 and named for 2d Lt. Frank Murchison Moore, a native of Houston, who was killed in World War I. The flight school for advanced pilots of single-engine planes trained 6,000 pilots before it was closed on 31 October 1945. In 1950 part of the field was operating as the Weaver H. Baker Memorial Sanatorium, and part was jointly operated by Mission, McAllen, and Edinburg as Tri-Cities Municipal Airport. In 1954, after the closing of the sanatorium and as part of the Cold War military expansion by the United States, the base was reactivated under the name Moore Air Force Base. By December 1960 some 4,000 air force pilots received their primary flight training and academic instruction at Moore. From July 1959 until the base was again deactivated, the six-month training program featured jet-plane flight instruction. In February 1962 about half of the site was turned over to a private industry trying to eradicate the screwworm fly. *Lucy H. Wallace*

Mormon Mill Colony. Site now on Mormon Mills Road in south central Burnet County. A group of 20 Mormon families led by Lyman Wight founded the colony in 1851. Wight's band broke away from the rest of the Church of Jesus Christ of Latter-Day Saints in protest against Brigham Young's leadership after founder Joseph Smith died. Wight, who had been a prominent leader in the church, took his followers to Texas in search of a new Zion. The Mormons established a colony they called Zodiac near Fredericksburg on the Pedernales River, but after a flood and heavy debts drove them out, Wight led the group to a picturesque site on Hamilton Creek, where they established Mormon Mill Colony. Many of the Mormons were highly skilled artisans; they built a wooden dam and a three-story mill building with a 26-foot waterwheel, using materials from the surrounding countryside. Hamilton Creek flowed year-round, providing power for the grain and sawmills, which served the Burnet, Marble Falls, and Austin areas. The colonists farmed and hunted, made willow baskets, spun and wove cloth, and raised gourds for storage of lard and dried fruit. Mormon Mill, with its population of about 250, also supported several blacksmiths and skilled furniture craftsmen. The colony remained apart from the civic affairs of the county. Wight and a board of elders were the sole governing body. Despite the Mormons' industry and ingenuity, the colony once again incurred heavy debts. Plagued by financial problems, mounting resentment of their unconventional theology by local citizens, and frequent Indian raids, the Mormons decided to move on. In December 1853 Wight led most of the group to Bandera County. They sold the Mormon Mill property to Noah Smithwick. Smithwick opened a store and built a school for the remaining Mormons who worked at the mill. He also modified the mill so that only breadstuffs could be processed, thus prompting local farmers to raise more wheat. A post office opened in 1856 with Smithwick's partner and nephew, John R. Hubbard, as postmaster. Smithwick eventually sold out to Hubbard; thereafter, the mill passed through several other owners, including Samuel E. Holland. As new mills opened in the area, business gradually declined. The population dwindled until the post office closed in 1875. In 1901 the mill closed down, and a year later the flume and several surrounding buildings burned. Local farmers tore down the remaining mill buildings and used some of the materials. In 1915 the remaining abandoned residences burned. *Lea Anne Morrell*

Moscoso Expedition. The name given Hernando De Soto's expedition after De Soto's death (on 21 May 1542); the first expedition to explore the future southeastern U.S. De Soto's 600-man army landed on May 30, 1539, near what is now Tampa Bay. When De Soto died in the future Arkansas, command was transferred to Luis de Moscoso Alvarado. The primary goal was to find an overland route back to New Spain (now Mexico). Many attempts have been made to reconstruct the route of the expedition, nearly all of which bring it into Texas in the summer of 1542. Information on the route is found in four primary accounts of the journey. The most exhaustive early attempt to reconstruct the route of the Moscoso expedition, not only in Texas but through the entire southeastern United States, was published in 1939 by the United States De Soto Commission to celebrate the expedition's 400th anniversary. The commission's proposed version of the route through Texas posits that the expedition entered Texas in what is now Shelby County and from there traveled south to a point near the site of modern San Augustine. It then turned west and went as far as the Navasota River in east central Texas. At this point the soldiers decided that they would not be able to find enough food to feed the expedition if they continued farther west, and therefore the expedition retraced its route to the Mississippi River in Arkansas. In 1942 Rex Strickland used historical, archeological, linguistic, and geographical sources to provide a detailed reconstruction of the army's route through Texas. He suggested that the army entered the state near Texarkana and then moved south along a trail that later became known as Trammel's Trace to the vicinity of the future San Augustine. Here the expedition turned westward and traveled as far as the Trinity River. At this point they abandoned their hopes of reaching New Spain by land, and they returned along the same route.

Later, renewed efforts were made to understand the expedition's route through Texas. Charles Hudson, working in cooperation with the De Soto Trail Study authorized by Congress in 1987, suggested that the army entered Texas from northwestern Louisiana and moved west along Big Cypress Creek; it then turned south and traveled down the Neches River into what is now Angelina County. In his theory the expedition then turned back to the north and finally traveled west, reaching the Trinity River before it abandoned hopes of reaching New Spain overland. More recently, James Bruseth and Nancy Kenmotsu reconstructed the Moscoso route by relying heavily upon the location of sixteenth-century archeological sites, and, following the lead of Strickland, upon trails that likely existed at the time of the expedition. Bruseth and Kenmotsu bring the army into Texas from Oklahoma and south along either Trammel's Trace or the Jonesborough-to-Nacogdoches trail. The army moved south to a point near what is now Nacogdoches, then west on a trail that later became known as the Old San Antonio Road. The expedition went as far as the Guadalupe River but turned back toward the Mississippi River in Arkansas. During the winter of 1542–43 the men camped at the Mississippi and constructed boats for a return by water to New Spain. On 2 July 1543 they started down the Mississippi River, and on September 10 some 311 expedition members reached the Pánuco River in Mexico. Although the expedition failed to find the riches that similar Spanish explorations had encountered in Central and South America, it made the first major exploration into the interior of the North American continent and provided some of the earliest observations of American Indians, including the Caddos of Texas. An important map, known as the Soto Map, came out of the expedition. It begins at Punta de Santa Elena (South Carolina) and depicts the Atlantic coast south to the Florida cape and then around the gulf to the Pánuco. The map was the work of Alonso de Santa Cruz. *James E. Bruseth*

Mountains. The principal peaks and mountain ranges of Texas are in the TransPecos region, although sharp hills and small promontories are found in the Burnet–Llano region and along parts of the Balcones Escarpment, while the east-facing Caprock of the Llano Estacado and its outliers, rising in places as much as 1,000 feet, are impressive sights on the north central plains. The eastern ranges of the Rocky Mountain system cross Texas in a general northwest–southeast direction in the TransPecos. The highest, the Guadalupe Mountains, projects into Culberson County from New Mexico and rises to a maximum elevation of 8,749 feet at Guadalupe Peak. Probably the most familiar Texas Mountains are the Davis Mountains in Jeff Davis County, whose highest peak is Mount Livermore (8,206). Other well-known peaks of this range are Sawtooth Mountain (7,748), Blue Mountain (7,835), and Mount Locke (6,781) on which is located the University of Texas at Austin McDonald Observatory. The Chisos Mountains, capped by Emory Peak (7,825) and Lost Mine Peak (7,550) in Big Bend National Park, are the third most prominent Texas range. The Chinati Mountains in Presidio County, Eagle Mountain in Hudspeth County, and the Franklin Mountains in El Paso County are other notable TransPecos eminences. In general the mountains of the TransPecos region, both igneous and sedimentary, and the peaks of the Balcones Escarpment were uplifted. Those along the Balcones Escarpment reflect extraordinary crustal movement, while the promontories of the North Central Plains are plateau remnants, the result of the erosion of the surrounding terrain.

Murphy, Audie Leon. World War II hero and movie actor; b. near Kingston, Texas, 20 June 1924; d. near Christiansburg, Virginia, 28 May 1971 (buried at Arlington National Cemetery); m. movie actress Wanda Hendrix (1949; divorced 1951); m. Pamela Archer (1951); 2 sons. Murphy enlisted in the army in June 1942. After basic infantry training at Camp Wolters, Texas, and advanced training at Fort Meade, Maryland, he was assigned to North Africa as a private in Company B, Fifteenth Infantry Regiment, Third Infantry Division. Murphy later commanded Company B. During his World War II career he received 33 awards, citations, and decorations and won a battlefield promotion to second lieutenant. He received every medal that the United States gives for valor, two of them twice. On 26 January 1945 he was awarded the Medal of Honor for exceptional valor near Holtzwhir, France, where he was personally credited with killing or wounding about 50 Germans and stopping an attack by enemy tanks. After the war's end, Murphy also received several French and Belgian decorations for valor. He fought in eight campaigns in Sicily, Italy, France, and Germany; participated in

"Most decorated soldier." *LIFE Magazine* cover, July 16, 1945. J. F. Laughead, LIFE Magazine ©Time Warner. In World War II, Audie Murphy received 33 awards, citations, and decorations. After the war he became a successful movie actor, author, and song writer.

two amphibious assaults, in Sicily and southern France; and was wounded three times. After the war he was a successful movie actor, a lyric writer for country and western songs, an author, and a poet. He appeared in 45 motion pictures and starred in 39 of them. His best-known films were *The Red Badge of Courage* (1951), *To Hell and Back* (1955), *Night Passage* (1957, with James Stewart), and *The Unforgiven* (1960, with Burt Lancaster). In 1955 Murphy was selected one of the year's most popular Western stars by United States theater owners, and in 1957 he was chosen as the most popular Western actor by British audiences. He wrote the lyrics for 14 songs and collaborated on three instrumentals. Two of his songs, "Shutters and Boards" and "When the Wind Blows in Chicago," were in the top 10 songs on the Hit Parade for several weeks. With David McClure, Murphy wrote the best-selling book *To Hell and Back* (1949), the story of his World War II exploits, which went through nine printings. In 1950 he joined the Thirty-sixth Division of the Texas National Guard as a captain, hoping to fight in the Korean War. The division, however, was not called to active duty. Murphy remained with the Thirty-sixth "T-Patchers" for several more years, eventually attaining the rank of major. In 1957 he was assigned to inactive status. He transferred to the United States Army Reserve in 1966. He died in an airplane crash. Two funeral services were held for him on 4 June 1971, one at Hollywood Hills, California, and the other at the First Baptist Church in Farmersville, Texas.

An Audie L. Murphy Memorial is located at Farmersville, a statue of Murphy stands at the Veterans Hospital in San Antonio, and a collection of Murphy memorabilia is housed at Hill College.   *Harold B. Simpson*

Murrah, Pendleton. Governor; b. probably in Alabama and probably in 1826; d. Monterrey, Nuevo León, 4 August 1865; m. Sue Ellen Taylor (1850); ed. Brown University (grad. 1848). Murrah, who had tuberculosis, moved to Texas for a dry climate in 1850. He was elected to the state legislature in 1857 and withdrew from the 1861 race for the Confederate Congress because of ill health. He beat Thomas Jefferson Chambers for governor in 1863, partly because of Chambers's known dislike for the Jefferson Davis administration. As governor, Murrah squabbled with Confederate generals John B. Magruder and Edmund Kirby Smith, who maintained, *contra* Murrah, that Texas state militiamen were subject to Confederate conscription. Further conflict with Richmond came when Murrah sought to buy Texas farmers' cotton with state warrants, thus relieving them from having to sell to the Confederacy for its dubious currency; the governor reluctantly acceded to Confederate demands. At the end of the war, however, Murrah continued to urge resistance to the Union. When Union occupation of Texas was imminent, he vacated his office to Lieutenant Governor Fletcher Stockdale and fled to Mexico, where he succumbed to his chronic tuberculosis.   *Ralph A. Wooster*

Museums. Museums are a relatively recent development in Texas. Perhaps the first museum was nothing more than the exhibition in a local hotel room of an itinerant limner's portrait samples, such as Thomas Jefferson Wright presented in Houston in 1837. But in 1879 Sam Houston Normal Institute established a museum to preserve materials relating to Sam Houston, hero of the Texas Revolution, president of the Republic of Texas, and senator and governor of the state, and in 1881 Albert Friedrich began the collection of horns that became the Buckhorn Hall of Horns in San Antonio. By the turn of the century the Museum of Human Anatomy at the University of Texas Medical Branch in Galveston(1890), the Strecker Museum at Baylor University in Waco (1893), and the teaching museum at Our Lady of the Lake College in San Antonio (1896) were in operation, and art associations throughout the state had given birth to fledgling art galleries in Houston, Dallas, San Antonio, Fort Worth, and several other cities. A few museums, such as the Texas Confederate Museum (1904), were established during the early twentieth century to honor the state's heroes and war dead, and the Witte Museum in San Antonio dates from 1926. But the 1936 Texas Centennial celebration of Texas independence was the major impetus to museum-building in the state. Several buildings were constructed in Fair Park in Dallas, which was the official headquarters for the celebration, and museums were also built in El Paso, Houston, Austin, Huntsville, and other cities. The Dallas Museum of Art, the Hall of State, the Museum of Natural History, the Aquarium, the Garden Center, and the Health and Science Museum, all in Dallas, the San Jacinto Museum of History in Houston, the Texas Memorial Museum in Austin, the Sam Houston Memorial Museum in Huntsville, the Gonzales Memorial Museum, and the El Paso Centennial Museum all date from this cultural and building boom during the 1930s. The national bicentennial in 1976 inspired even more effort, as local historical societies throughout Texas established museums in old jails, courthouses, railroad depots, and other historic buildings, and museums already in existence added to their space and installed new exhibitions. Museums have been established in the remains of Spanish missions and old forts and in the homes of such famous men and women as writer O. Henry, sculptor Elisabet Ney, and presidents Dwight Eisenhower and Lyndon Johnson. Exhibitions have been set up at the sites of battle-grounds and Indian settlements and on board the battleship *Texas.*

Long famous for its philanthropists, Texas is fortunate that a number of them chose to establish museums. Perhaps the Kimbell Art Museum and the Amon Carter Museum in Fort Worth are the most obvious examples, but the Marion Koogler McNay Art Museum in San Antonio, the Stark Museum of Art in Orange, Bayou Bend and the Menil Collection in Houston, and the Sid Richardson Collection of Western Art in Fort Worth also owe their existence to the inspiration of a single collector or family. The McNay Art Museum opened to the public in 1954, housed in Jessie Marion Koogler McNay's Mexican–Mediterranean style mansion. The Amon Carter Museum followed in 1961, presenting the unexcelled collection of paintings and sculpture by Frederic Remington and Charles M. Russell that Amon G. Carter, Sr., had accumulated in a building designed by New York architect Philip Johnson. In 1966 the Houston Museum of Fine Arts opened Bayou Bend, the mansion that John F. Staub had designed for Miss Ima Hogg and her brothers, with their encyclopedic collection of American furniture, paintings, silver, and china. The Kimbell Art Museum, based on the collection of European and British paintings that Fort Worth businessman Kay Kimbell had acquired during his lifetime, opened in 1972, and in 1978 the Stark Museum of Art, containing H. J. Lutcher Stark's vast assortment of American paintings and sculptures, rare books, letters, manuscripts, prints, American Indian artifacts, Steuben glass, and porcelains, opened its doors. The Sid Richardson Collection of Western Art opened in 1982, the Menil Collection in 1987, and the Michelson–Reves Museum of Art, devoted to the art of Leo Michelson, in Marshall in 1985. Other museums not named for individual donors have benefited from generous gifts. The El Paso Museum of Art received 57 old master paintings and two sculptures from the Samuel H. Kress Foundation in 1961, and the Archer M. Huntington Art Gallery and the Harry Ransom Humanities Research Center at the University of Texas at Austin have been given a large number of paintings, such as James and Mari Michener's collection of twentieth-century American art, C. R. Smith's collection of American western art, a group of Frank Reaugh's paintings, and many more. The Hogg brothers' collection of paintings by Frederic Remington is a perennial attraction at the Museum of Fine Arts, Houston, as is the huge nineteenth-century scene by Frederic Edwin Church entitled *The Icebergs,* given anonymously to the Dallas Museum of Art. Nor have outstanding acquisitions by Texas museums been limited to gifts. The nation perhaps first became aware of Texas museums' serious commitment to quality in 1965 when the Fort Worth Art Museum acquired a major painting by Picasso during a nationally televised benefit auction. With its long list of distinguished purchases, the Kimbell Art Museum has become internationally recognized as a leader in the worldwide quest for masterpieces. The Museum of Fine Arts, Houston, won much publicity for its acquisition of a well-known Picasso, while the Amon Carter Museum continues to enlarge upon the holdings of its original donor in the field of nineteenth and early twentieth century American art with purchases of stunning works by American masters such as Thomas Cole and Thomas Eakins.

Significant exhibitions have also brought Texas museums into the spotlight. The era of "blockbuster" exhibits in Texas dates at least from the 1973 Kimbell exhibition of the French impressionists from the Hermitage Museum in Russia. The Museum of Fine Arts, Houston, followed in 1974 with an exhibition of old masters from Russia, and the Dallas Museum of Art subsequently played host to the exhibition Pompeii A.D. 79. The history and natural science museums joined in the contest for the public eye with exhibitions such as the Russian space program at the Fort Worth Museum of Science and History, the history of horses in North America at the Witte Museum, and a large exhibition of Peruvian gold objects and artifacts at the Houston Museum of Natural Science. The recent exhibition of the French impressionist paintings from the Barnes Collection at the Kimbell drew more than one-half million visitors. College and university art museums have become increasingly important. The largest such museums are the Archer M. Huntington Art Gallery at the University of Texas at Austin, which houses a collection of Greek and Roman art, a large print collection, and a large collection of nineteenth and twentieth century American and Latin-American paintings and sculpture; the Meadows Museum at Southern Methodist University, which specializes in Spanish paintings acquired by Dallas businessman Algur H. Meadows; and the Museum of Texas Tech University, which houses the Diamond M Foundation collection of works by Peter Hurd, N. C. Wyeth, Andrew Wyeth, and other well-known Americans, assembled by Claire and Clarence T. McLaughlin. History and natural history museums include the Panhandle–Plains Historical Museum at West Texas A&M University in Canyon; the Texas Memorial Museum at the University of Texas at Austin; the Strecker Museum at Baylor University; and the John E. Conner Museum at Texas A&M University at Kingsville, among others.

Texas museums have also begun to research and organize some of their own shows. One of the most outstanding bicentennial exhibitions in the nation was organized by the Amon Carter Museum, which has a 35-year record of producing its own exhibitions. The Face of Liberty included the famous Gilbert Stuart portraits of George and Martha Washington as well as portraits of Benjamin Franklin, Thomas Jefferson, and other well-known revolutionary figures. The exhibition of contemporary Hispanic-American paintings at the Museum of Fine Arts, Houston, brought young Hispanic artists to the public's attention, and the internationally known American artist Frank Stella reemerged in an exhibit at the Modern Art Museum of Fort Worth. The Kimbell Art Museum has won international critical acclaim with its series of exhibitions relating to European and Asian art. Museum trustees are also aware of the role of the museum itself as a work of art. The first bold stroke occurred in 1954, when the Houston Museum of Fine Arts commissioned Ludwig Mies van der Rohe, one of the great twentieth-century architects, to design its new wing. Cullinan Hall opened in 1954, and the master plan was finished with the addition of the Brown Pavilion in 1974. Philip Johnson, one of Mies's followers, designed the Amon Carter Museum (1961) and the Art Museum of South Texas (1972) in Corpus Christi, and Louis I. Kahn of Philadelphia designed the Kimbell Art Museum (1972), one of the great museums of the world. The Cambridge Seven, a Connecticut design group, won plaudits for its striking renovation of the old Lone Star brewery for the San Antonio Museum of Art, and the Dallas Museum of Art is now at home in its downtown quarters designed by Edward Larrabee Barnes, the architect of the very successful Walker Art Center in Minneapolis. More recently, Renzo Piano designed the Menil Collection in Houston.

The most numerous group of museums in the state is the history museums, which range from tiny collections of artifacts exhibited in an old log cabin to the massive Panhandle–Plains Historical Museum, the largest state-owned museum as well as the oldest, founded in 1929. Like the Panhandle–Plains Museum, the Dallas Historical Society, which is housed in the Hall of State building at Fair Park, was the beneficiary of the WPA program whereby talented artists painted murals in state-owned buildings.

Two special cities are almost museums in themselves: San Antonio and Galveston. San Antonio has refurbished its downtown section and riverwalk (the Paseo del Rio) to the point that it is one of the most charming in the nation. Within easy walking distance of the winding San Antonio River are several museums unique either in themselves, such as the Alamo, the "shrine of Texas liberty," or in their approach to the history of the state, such as the University of Texas Institute of Texan Cultures, which is organized according to the ethnic groups that settled the state. Other museums that elaborate on San Antonio's heritage and the Hispanic contribution to Texas are located in the same area. Galveston, equally enticing and representative of a totally different era and culture, offers the museums and shops lining the Strand, the "Wall Street of the Gulf," which recall the glory days of the state's major port before the devastation of the Galveston hurricane of 1900. In addition to the Texas Maritime Museum, Galveston hosts the Galveston County Historical Museum, the tall ship *Elissa*, and a new and innovative Center for Transportation. Oil has also left its impression on the state's museums. At least three are devoted exclusively to telling the story of oil and energy development: the East Texas Oil Museum in Kilgore, the Permian Basin Petroleum Museum in Midland, and the Texas Energy Museum in Beaumont. Several of the state's large history and natural history museums, such as the Houston Museum of Natural Science and the Panhandle–Plains Historical Museum, also have exhibitions devoted to the history of oil and its technology. Transportation also claims its share of interest, with the Pate Museum of Transportation outside Fort Worth, the Panhandle–Plains Historical Museum (with a large display devoted to transportation, from the buggies and wagons of pioneer West Texas to the automobile), and perhaps the greatest homage to trains in the state, the Center for Transportation and Commerce in Galveston. Two historic trains still run: the Hill Country Flyer from Austin to Burnet and the Texas State Railroad from Rusk to Palestine. The most unusual museum in the state may well be the Confederate Air Force Flying Museum, a large collection of World War II airplanes that are all in working condition. The CAF, located at the Midland–Odessa airport, puts its more than 100 vintage aircraft through their paces each October, with a few enemy planes thrown in to heighten the drama. The Spitfires, Mustangs, and Flying Fortresses are on exhibit year round.

Even in a state as historically rich as Texas, however, museums are not mired in the past. The Fort Worth Museum of Science and History, with its Omni Theater and laser shows, continually draws large audiences with a taste of the future as well as of the aesthetics of science and technology. Two other sites provide a look into ongoing research as well as a sense of the past: the NASA museum at Clear Lake, outside Houston, and the University of Texas at Austin McDonald Observatory, just outside Fort Davis. Tours and exhibitions are available at both facilities, even though they are both involved in the forefront of research in their respective fields.

In addition to the great variety and quality of museums in the state, the number of museums has also increased significantly. In the 1950s there were several dozen important museums; in 1976 the number was estimated at more than 200. Only two years later the Texas Historical Commission published a directory of 410 museums, which the commission defined as "organized and permanent nonprofit institutions, essentially educational or aesthetic in purpose, which exhibit objects with intrinsic value to science, history, art, or culture, and which are open to the public." The commission estimated the number of museums in Texas in 1995 at 660.   *Ron Tyler*

Music. Music of virtually every Western genre has flourished in Texas, from before the advent of Europeans through the times of colonization, settlement, and revolution, until the present—the outgrowth of a fusion of races and nations. The earliest Texas music was the monophonic song of Indians, of which few accounts survive. The first European music was that of the Catholic Church, which came by way of Mexico City, where a European music school was established in 1525. In the missions around El Paso, in East Texas, and near San Antonio, music attracted Indians and formed an integral part of the liturgy. Spanish folk music and guitars came with soldiers and settlers to the missions; French songs drifted in from Louisiana during the eighteenth century. After 1820 Anglo-Americans introduced music from the United States, especially songs of the English, Scots, and Irish. The first pianos and many other instruments came during the 1830s. At the battle of San Jacinto "Yankee Doodle" and "Will You Come to the Bower?" were played. In the theater opened at Houston in 1838 an orchestra and singers from Europe and the United States performed excerpts from popular operas and other music. Sacred music societies were organized in several towns. Bishop Jean Marie Odin had an organ for his cathedral in Galveston in 1848. Beginning about 1845, the greatest contributors to musical development were the Germans, whose first singing society was organized at New Braunfels in 1850. Beginning in 1853 the Germans of Texas held biennial singing festivals; after 1877 they imported an orchestra and soloists who were replaced by Texas musicians by 1894. Colonies of French and Swiss also included musicians; among those who settled near Dallas was Allyre Bureau, a Parisian composer and director. Among Hispanics, singing and dancing to string orchestras was common in the homes and on the plazas. The German music centers were the beer gardens. At the Casino Club in San Antonio and the Turnverein Hall in Austin, and later at the Scholz Garten under the direction of William Besserer, there were operettas and choral productions. The Anglo-Americans brought visiting concert groups in the early 1840s; a few small opera companies came from New Orleans and Mexico before 1860. Local bands, sometimes military, played in the larger communities before 1850; by 1900 most of the towns had bands.

Music instruction was introduced into the public schools of Galveston in 1845, and most private schools offered music instruction to girls, but no marked progress was made in teaching music, except among the Germans, until introduction of the phonograph and radio. The first powerful broadcasting station was WFAA (established in 1922) at Dallas; after 1936 state networks developed rapidly, and music was widely disseminated. Within a decade entire radio programs were devoted to Texas music, and national programs were given by Texas musicians. With these media of diffusion, other agencies joined. Artist concerts were provided by plans of advanced subscriptions. Opera was encouraged by college and civic groups. After the establishment of the San Antonio Symphony Orchestra (1904), the Dallas Symphony Orchestra (1911), and the Houston Symphony Orchestra (1933), more than a dozen such organizations developed, while the pioneer orchestras attained national distinction. By 1949 there were more than 30 schools of music in Texas colleges. Church music conferences, instituted in 1928, encouraged choirs, sacred concerts, and oratorio performances. Folk music, especially the songs of Mexicans, blacks, and cowboys, has flourished in Texas. John A. Lomax was outstanding as a collector of such material, and his *Cowboy Ballads* (1910) was a pioneer work that received national recognition.

Texas-born composers of distinction include Frank Van der Stucken, Oscar Fox, David Guion, Harold Morris, Radie Britain, Julia Smith, and Don Gillis. Olga Samaroff, born in San Antonio in 1882, was recognized as an outstanding pianist, teacher, and music critic. Composers who have lived in Texas include John M. Steinfeldt, Arthur Claasen, William J. Marsh, Carl Venth, Carl Hahn, Ruben Davies, and Julius Jahn. Texas operatic singers have included Josephine Lucchese, May Peterson Thompson, Rafaelo Diaz, and Mack Harrell. Works by Texas composers were first featured by the Houston Symphony in 1933; in 1948 the orchestra played an entire program of music by native or adventive Texans. The first firm in Texas that published music extensively was that of Thomas Goggan and Brothers, established in 1866.

The history of music in Texas since 1950 is largely a reflection of the cultural boom that has swept the United States since World War II. Musical activities of every type have increased, resident opera and ballet companies have been founded, symphonies have been reorganized and expanded, choral groups have been formed, and all have played to larger audiences and received more financial support than ever before. At the same time each of these groups has suffered from rising costs and, in many cases, general public apathy. Foundation grants, the Texas Commission on the Arts, and generous support from civic-minded individuals and businesses have made possible much of the progress achieved by musical organizations in the state.

In large measure classical music in Texas has come of age during the past fifty years. In 1958 pianist Van Cliburn of Kilgore won the Tchaikovsky Piano Competition in Moscow. The resulting acclaim given to the Texan led to the establishment of the Van Cliburn International Piano Competition in Fort Worth in

Roberta Dodd Crawford, ca. 1920s. Courtesy Texas A&M University—Commerce Archives. Crawford was an African-American opera star who sang in both the United States and Europe, but when she appeared in her home town, Bonham, her family was forced to sit in the balcony of the opera house.

the early 1960s. A number of the state's musical institutions—the Houston, San Antonio, and Dallas Symphony orchestras, for instance—have become internationally renowned. Community orchestras like the Amarillo Symphony have also achieved notable progress. In 1967 the Amarillo orchestra consisted of 85 members, all local talent; although the symphony had not grown in size, its budget in 1995 had risen to almost $800,000. Comparable organizations exist in Fort Worth, Austin, Wichita Falls, Corpus Christi, Beaumont, Lubbock, and other cities. The El Paso orchestra, the oldest continuous symphony orchestra in the state, celebrated its sixty-fifth consecutive season in 1995. Midland and Odessa strengthened their musical resources in 1964 by combining their two symphonies into an interurban orchestra. Each of the state's symphonic groups has played a significant role in bringing live concerts to its area—often with high artistic results and despite sharp financial limitations. In 1995 the Fort Worth Symphony, for instance, under the direction of John Giordano, had an annual budget of $5 million, maintained an active education program, and served as the host orchestra for the Van Cliburn Piano Competition. Suburban orchestras, such as the Richardson Symphony Orchestra and the

Irving Symphony, have increased in number and improved in quality since 1960. The Richardson orchestra began in 1961; 34 years later it consisted of 70 members drawn from Richardson and 15 neighboring communities.

The San Antonio Symphony was the first professional resident opera producer in Texas. In 1945 conductor Max Reiter conceived a plan for extending the symphony season by adding a spring opera festival and launched the venture with *La Bohème*, starring Grace Moore. From 1945 until 1983 the San Antonio Symphony presented an annual season of opera—four different works given each year, one performance each, divided between two successive weekends. While stars from the Metropolitan and New York City operas were imported for leading roles, the chorus was drawn largely from three local colleges. Most of the sets were designed by Peter Wolf of Dallas. With few exceptions the opera festival closed its seasons financially in the black, in part because the San Antonio Municipal Auditorium would seat nearly 6,000 and symphony officials looked upon a audience of 4,500 as a poor showing. Inflation plus a move into less spacious housing forced a termination of the annual opera festival, although the San Antonio Symphony has continued to present concert versions of theatrical works. Fort Worth followed San Antonio's resident opera productions in 1946 with the formation of the Fort Worth Opera Association. One of the company's prime ambitions has been to provide opportunity for gifted local singers, with professionals used only in stellar roles. *La Traviata* launched the organization in November 1946. From 1955 to 1969 conductor Rudolf Kruger, who formerly worked with the Columbia (South Carolina) Symphony and the Chicago Light Opera, served as the Fort Worth musical director and general manager. Under his supervision four operas were performed each season, spaced over fall, winter, and spring; two performances were given of each work, and most productions were in English. Beginning in the late 1960s more of the company's operas were sung in the original language. Economic constraints in subsequent decades forced the company to reduce its number of yearly productions to three. The third Texas resident opera organization, the Houston Grand Opera Association, began in January 1956 with *Salomé*, starring Brenda Lewis. In 1969 the company's musical director was Walter Herbert, who had held similar posts earlier with the New Orleans and Fort Worth operas. Under Herbert's leadership the Houston company presented four or five works annually, usually in the original language. Noted singers were used only for leading roles, and local talent was employed whenever artistically feasible. The Houston company proved dynamic in repertory by presenting such seldom-heard works as Rossini's *La Cenerentola* and *La Donna del Lago*, the Texas premiere of Richard Strauss's *Elektra*, a rare Texas staging of Wagner's *Die Walküre*, Handel's *Rinaldo*, Ralph Vaughan Williams's *Hugh the Drover*, and world premieres of John Adams's *Nixon in China*, Carlisle Floyd's *Willie Stark*, and Thomas Pasatieri's *The Seagull*. In 1987, under general director David Gockley, the Houston Grand Opera moved its productions to the Wortham Center; the company's budget in 1995 exceeded $14 million.

The Dallas Opera, founded in 1957 by Lawrence V. Kelly and Nicola Rescigno, formerly of the Chicago Lyric Theatre, received immediate national and international acclaim. A concert by legendary soprano Maria Callas got the project off to a brilliant start in 1957, followed shortly by a production of Rossini's novelty *L'Italiana in Algeri*, with Giulietta Simionato in the title role. "For a couple of nights running," *Newsweek* reported, "Dallas was the operatic capital of the United States." Afterward, Dallas presented a number of remarkable productions and artists. In 1958 Callas returned for *La Traviata*, in a production designed by Franco Zeffirelli, and highly praised performances of Cherubini's *Medea*, staged by Alexis Minotis of the Greek National Theater—a production later loaned to Covent Garden (London) and La Scala (Milan). The 1960 Dallas season saw the United States debut of Joan Sutherland in Zeffirelli's production of Handel's *Alcina*, an American premiere. Other American premieres for the company have included Monteverdi's seventeenth-century classic *Coronation of Poppea* and Vivaldi's *Orlando Furioso*. The Dallas Opera also staged the state's first complete cycle of Wagner's *Der Ring des Nibelungen* and in 1988 gave the world premiere of Dominick Argento's *The Aspern Papers*. Since the city sampled the Metropolitan Opera's tour in the spring from 1939 until 1984, the Dallas Opera tried not to duplicate the New York company's repertoire and artists. Instead, the resident company's aim was to give Texas a look at European productions; each year manager Kelly borrowed at least one production from abroad—in 1960 *Alcina* from La Fenice (Venice) and *Figlia del Regimento* from Palermo, and in 1961 *La Bohème* from Spoleto. In addition to Sutherland's United States debut, the Dallas company benefited from those of Teresa Berganza, Luigi Alva, Denise Duval, Placido Domingo, Montserrat Caballé, Gwyneth Jones, Jon Vickers, Magda Olivero, Linda Esther Gray, and Ghena Dimitrova. Under general director Plato Karayanis, the Dallas Opera expanded its offering to six productions a year, with most performances attracting capacity audiences. The Austin Lyric Opera was formed in 1985 with Walter Ducloux as artistic director, and within a decade the company had built its season to three productions. In 1995 the annual budget was $2.25 million, and the repertoire included Wagner's *Tannhäuser*. The Austin Lyric Opera employs major international artists, as well as American talent, and stages its productions in the Bass Concert Hall at the University of Texas.

Resident ballet companies exist in Houston, Dallas, Fort Worth, Austin, and Corpus Christi. Musical comedy has also received considerable attention in Texas since World War II. The Starlight Operettas were begun in Dallas in 1941 in an outdoor arena and bandshell on the fairgrounds and were renamed the State Fair Musicals in 1951, when the shows were moved into the Music Hall. Outstanding Broadway and Hollywood talent was imported each summer for musicals of recent vintage, as well as the older "operetta" show. In 1952 the musicals opened with William Warfield and Leontyne Price in Gershwin's *Porgy and Bess*, the premiere of a production that the State Department later sent to Moscow. Each year during the State Fair of Texas the national company of a recent Broadway musical has been brought to the Music Hall. Mary Martin began her tour in Irving Berlin's *Annie Get Your Gun* at the fair in October 1947, and succeeding years saw productions of *South Pacific*, *Guys and Dolls*, *The King and I*, *My Fair Lady*, *The Sound of Music*, *A Chorus Line*, and *Cats*. Houston instituted a summer season of Broadway musicals. Casa Mañana in Fort Worth introduced "musicals-in-the-round" to the Southwest and staged an occasional show not seen elsewhere in the state.

African Americans and Mexican Americans have contributed

significantly to the music of Texas. The state has excelled in jazz, blues, and country and western music.

Lota M. Spell and Ronald L. Davis

Mustangs. Horses famous in Texas history and folklore. The word *mustang* is thought to come from Spanish *mesta*, which denotes a company of graziers; the adjective *mesteño* means "belonging to the graziers." *Mustang* originally referred to the bloodstock imported from the Iberian Peninsula. Horses brought by the Spanish included the Ginete, Arabian, Villano, Berber, and Barb bloodlines. Today the term refers to wild horses on federal lands, but very few wild herds today possess original Spanish blood. The first American Indian horses were bred from stock acquired from the herds of the Spanish missions beginning in the early 1600s. The first Spanish horses on record were brought to Texas in 1542 by the Moscoso expedition. The chronicles of the La Salle expedition also mention them. In 1686 La Salle acquired five horses from Caddo Indians in East Texas. The Caddos had a large supply of them in 1689 when Henri de Tonti was searching for La Salle. Mustangs brought some of the first Americans. In 1785 Philip Nolan visited Texas seeking permission to capture and remove horses. Thomas Jefferson wrote Nolan in 1798 asking for information about the habits of the wild horses of Texas.

Visitors who saw the vast herds of mustangs were enthusiastic. The Little Rock *Arkansas Gazette* of 10 July 1839, for instance, states,

> The mustang or wild horse is certainly the greatest curiosity to those unaccustomed to the sight, that we meet with upon the prairies of Texas. They are seen in vast numbers, and are often times of exceeding beauty. The spectator is compelled to stand in amazement, and contemplate this noble animal, as he bounds over the earth, with the conscious pride of freedom. We still meet with many in the lower counties, and during the summer hundreds were seen in the neighborhood of Houston, darting over the plains, and seeming to dare the sportsman for a contest in the chase.

The numbers of mustangs were impressive. Just before the Mexican War, Lt. Ulysses S. Grant, while with Gen. Zachary Taylor's army on the Nueces River, stated, "I have no idea that they could all have been corralled in the state of Rhode Island, or Delaware, at one time." Artist Frederic Remington remarked, "Of all the monuments which the Spaniard has left to glorify his reign in America, there will be none more worthy than his horse." Many individual horses with unique talents and characteristics could be found among these original Spanish mustang herds. Several became legends in Texas folklore—the Ghost of the Staked Plains, Black Devil, the Pacing White Stallion. Some of the best were eventually captured and either line-bred for specific characteristics or cross-bred to produce hybrids. The original Spanish mustangs became foundation stock for many American breeds, including quarter horses. The many remarkable qualities of the Spanish mustang, particularly its endurance, made it the horse of choice for most frontiersmen and cowboys. Every cattle range in Texas used mustangs. Numerous mustangs remained in Texas in the mid-nineteenth century. J. Frank Dobie claimed the number of wild cattle and horses was nearly a million. A band of 100 palominos ran between Quihi Prairie and Hondo Creek in South Texas.

Some ranchers intentionally released domesticated horses into nearby herds to "breed up," or increase the size, of the horses. This was the beginning of the wild horse that is found on federal lands today. As the Spanish blood was diluted, many of the Spanish mustang's best characteristics were lost. In the 1950s a few individuals who still retained specimens of the original Spanish mustang began to work together to resurrect the breed. Registries developed to keep track of the true Spanish blood and to keep it pure. Fewer than 3,000 purebred Spanish mustangs are left today. At the close of the twentieth century some of the strongest efforts to restore the Spanish mustang were centered in Texas, including the American Indian Horse Registry, headquartered in Lockhart, and the efforts of private ranches such as Karma Farms near Marshall, Blazing Saddles Ranch in Winona, and Las Remudas in Odessa.

Thomas Earl Speir

N

NYA. The National Youth Administration, a New Deal agency (1935–43), was directed in Texas by Lyndon Johnson (1935–37) and Jesse Kellam (1937–43). Its purpose was to provide education, jobs, recreation, and counseling for male and female youth between the ages of 16 and 25. The NYA student-aid program provided financial assistance to students, in exchange for the performance of part-time jobs. An out-of-school work program provided jobs for young people who had dropped out of school or who had graduated and remained employed. Participants worked for the most part on highways and roadside parks, playgrounds and schools, parks, and public buildings. Other out-of-school projects, such as the agricultural training center for men in Luling, or the teaching program in stenography and general office practice for women at Blinn College, included on-site housing and were called resident training projects. Financial need was a criterion for participation in both the student aid and out-of-school programs. Other programs, less successful in Texas, were the Junior Employment Project, which worked through the Texas State Employment Service to place youth in full-time employment, and the Apprentice Training Program, intended to be a direct feeder to private industry. The latter failed in Texas and most other states because of fear that it would antagonize labor unions. After the beginning of World War II, in 11 resident training centers in Texas, young people received instruction in skills vital to the defense effort—welding, sheet-metal work, woodwork, and radio repair. After their training they were sent all over the nation to jobs in private companies with defense contracts. After this program was inaugurated, other aspects of NYA operations were phased out, and financial need was eliminated as a requirement for participation. In Texas the NYA operated a separate program for African Americans, which had its own advisory committee and such projects as the domestic-service training program at the Prairie View A&M resident center. Although the NYA had a better record than other New Deal relief programs, the number of black participants never corresponded to the percentage of black youths on relief. Mexican Americans participated in the NYA in Texas, but unlike blacks they were not listed separately, and it is difficult to determine how many were involved. After lengthy debates in Congress in 1943, the NYA was voted out of existence. Its overall effect in Texas was beneficial. Between 1935 and 1943 more than 175,000 students received assistance that enabled them to complete their education, and more than 75,000 were employed in the out-of-school programs. At such places as Inks Lake State Park and the restored La Villita in San Antonio, Texans continue to benefit from NYA work. *Kenneth E. Hendrickson, Jr.*

Nacogdoches, Battle of. Sometimes called the opening battle of the Texas Revolution; occurred 2 August 1832, when a group of Texas settlers defied an order by Mexican battalion commander Col. José de las Piedras to surrender their arms to him. Tensions had been building since the passage of the Law of April 6, 1830, which halted immigration from the United States to Texas. Manuel de Mier y Terán, commanding the northern provinces,

had stationed garrisons and customs collectors in Texas to implement the 1830 law. The situation also reflected a clash of states'-righters in Texas against the Centralists in power in Mexico. The Texans found support (they thought) from Antonio López de Santa Anna, who declared in 1832 against the Centralist regime. Piedras issued his inflammatory order after investigating the first of the Anahuac Disturbances. He feared a similar problem in Nacogdoches. The ayuntamiento of Nacogdoches resisted the order, organized a "National Militia," and on 28 July sent messengers to Ayish Bayou, Teneha, San Felipe, and outlying settlements requesting military aid. The settlers who responded rendezvoused at Pine Hill, east of Nacogdoches, and elected as their senior captain James W. Bullock, of Attoyac Bayou. On the morning of 2 August Bullock demanded that Piedras rescind his order and declare for Santa Anna, but he refused. Piedras placed soldiers in the Old Stone Fort, in a church, and in his headquarters, the Red House. About 2 P.M. Bullock's militia entered the town from the east, were fired upon, and drew back as Mexican cavalry charged up the main street. About 100 Texans remained, fought house-to-house, and captured the Stone Fort, Sim's Tavern, Thorne's store, and Robert's Store. The Mexicans retreated to the *cuartel* (the main fortification). Texans who had gathered north of town and prepared to march down North Street succeeded in driving off Mexican cavalry near the Red House. Other Texans, Redlanders from St. Augustine, with the help of directions from local settler Nicholas Sterne, moved along Lanana Creek and circled around to approach the town square from the rear. During the night Piedras evacuated his soldiers and headed for San Antonio. The next morning, James Carter and 16 mounted men (including Bowie) pursued the Mexican column, and at Buckshot Crossing on the Angelina River overtook them and began a running fight upriver toward Linwood Crossing. Here Piedras took refuge in John M. Durst's home (near what is now Douglas), where his men turned against him. Capt. Francisco Medina took command and surrendered Piedras and some 300 troops. The Texans escorted the Mexicans back to Nacogdoches. Asa Edwards took Piedras to San Felipe and turned him over to Stephen F. Austin. The colonel was given a parole and left for Mexico. Bowie marched the Mexican garrison to San Antonio, where they were discharged. In the battle, Piedras lost 47 men killed and 40 or more wounded. Three Texans were killed (a fourth died later), and four were wounded. The battle of Nacogdoches is an important lesser-known conflict that cleared East Texas of military rule and allowed the citizens to meet in convention without military intervention.

Archie P. McDonald

Nacogdoches, Texas. County seat of Nacogdoches County, 50 miles west of the Sabine River and 100 miles north of Beaumont. The town was named for the Nacogdoche Indians, a Caddo group. Archeological research has established that mounds found in the area date from approximately A.D. 1250, when the Indians built lodges along Lanana and Bonita creeks, which converge just south of Nacogdoches and continue as a single stream to the Angelina River. The mounds were found to contain human bones and pottery. Louis Juchereau de St. Denis was sent by the French governor Sieur de Cadillac to establish trade with the Indians in Spanish Texas. St. Denis marked a trail through Nacogdoches to the Rio Grande, along part of the route later known as the Old San Antonio Road, and was briefly arrested. In the summer of 1716 he accompanied Domingo Ramón back to East Texas to found Nuestra Señora de Guadalupe de los Nacogdoches and five other missions. Guadalupe Mission was abandoned briefly two years later due to fears of a French invasion but was reestablished by the Marqués de Aguayo in 1721. It operated more or less continuously until 1772, when viceroy Antonio María de Bucareli y Ursúa promulgated the New Regulations for Presidios, which recommended the recall of all missions and settlers to San Antonio. The following year Governor Juan María Vicencio de Ripperdá sent soldiers to force the removal of all Spanish subjects to San Antonio. Antonio Gil Ibarvo, from the Lobanillo Creek area southeast of Nacogdoches, became the leader of the settlers. He petitioned successfully for the group to be allowed to return part of the way to East Texas. They established a community named Bucareli on the banks of the Trinity River, where they remained for four years until floods and Indian raids caused Ibarvo to lead them in 1779 to the abandoned mission site at Nacogdoches, possibly the only building of European origin then standing in East Texas. Later Ibarvo was commissioned commander of the militia and magistrate of the pueblo of Nacogdoches, the first official recognition of civil status for the community.

Nacogdoches became a gateway for trade, mostly illicit, with the French and later the Americans, from Natchitoches and New Orleans, Louisiana. Ibarvo constructed a stone house, later known as the Old Stone Fort, where he conducted business. A replica of the building was constructed on the campus of Stephen F. Austin State University during the Texas Centennial celebration (1936). The location of Nacogdoches also gave it prominence in early military and political activities. During the 1790s the American mustanger and filibuster Philip Nolan often headquartered there. In 1806 Lt. Col. Simón de Herrera headquartered at Nacogdoches while negotiating the Neutral Ground agreement with Gen. James Wilkinson of the United States. In 1812 the Gutiérrez–Magee expedition proclaimed Texas free from Spain while at Nacogdoches, and they published the first newspaper in Texas, the *Gaceta de Tejas*, before going on to meet defeat at the hands of Gen. Joaquín de Arredondo. Arredondo ordered all who collaborated with them to be arrested, and the entire population of Nacogdoches fled into the Texas or Louisiana wilderness for safety temporarily. Arredondo's men almost completely destroyed the town. After the signing of the Adams–Onís Treaty, which fixed the Sabine River as the boundary between Texas and the United States, James Long and 300 followers occupied Nacogdoches in 1819 and again declared Texas independent of Spain. Long remained in Nacogdoches only a short time before attempting another expedition on the coast, which resulted in his death. The empresario grant of Haden Edwards was headquartered at Nacogdoches, as was his abortive Fredonian Rebellion (1825–27). After this movement Col. José de las Piedras commanded a Mexican military garrison at Nacogdoches until driven from the area in August 1832 after the battle of Nacogdoches, one of the events that led to the Texas

Revolution. During that movement several prominent figures, including Hayden Arnold, Adolphus Sterne, and four signers of the Texas Declaration of Independence—John Roberts, Charles Taylor, Thomas J. Rusk, and Robert Potter—claimed Nacogdoches as their home. The town was a seat of unrest and supplied the revolutionary cause with men and money. After the revolution the Córdova Rebellion against the Republic of Texas in 1838 also centered around Nacogdoches.

In antebellum Texas and during the Civil War and Reconstruction, Nacogdoches lost its prominence in state political and business affairs, due to lack of transportation facilities, particularly railroads and navigable rivers. Though once one of the three most important counties in Texas, Nacogdoches County was reduced to 902 square miles as other counties were formed from its territory. Nacogdoches itself had been incorporated in 1837. During the twentieth century it remained a small city with steady if not dramatic growth. When Stephen F. Austin State Teachers College was established in Nacogdoches in 1923, the college became the community's largest attraction to new residents and inducement to cultural activities. The Nacogdoches economy is based on education, agriculture, agricultural services, and manufacturing. The town is the headquarters for Texas Farm Products, manufacturers of fertilizer, animal feed, and animal health products. Several poultry hatcheries, feeders, and processing plants are located in the city. McGraw Edison (electrical equipment), Sun Terrace (lawn furniture), East Texas Canning Company (beverages), Bright Coop Company (chicken coops), Foretravel (recreation vehicles), Herider Farms (processed poultry), Holly Farms and Indian River International (chicks, feed, poultry breeding stock), Mize Brothers Manufacturing Company (women's wear), Moore Business Forms, and NIBCO (valves) are among the local industries. Nacogdoches is a distribution and trade center for East Texas. Tourism is also a major industry. The population was 27,149 in 1980 and 30,872 in 1990. Cultural activities in Nacogdoches center around the university, where local and professional theatrical productions and musical performances are held. Recreation is available at the city parks, at the lake belonging to the park system (primarily intended as a water reservoir), and at nearby Sam Rayburn and Toledo Bend reservoirs. The center of the city, still a viable downtown shopping area, is a mixture of historic and contemporary architecture. Historic preservation is encouraged; among the historic structures are the restored home of Adolphus Sterne, the oldest structure in the city, the Old University Building, the Blount House, Millard's Crossing (a preservation village), and many private dwellings.
Archie P. McDonald

Nacogdoches Archives. The collection of official documents preserved at Nacogdoches during Spanish and Mexican rule. These include communications from the king, the viceroy, and the commandant general to the governor of Texas and relayed by him to the political chiefs of the departments, together with correspondence of the alcaldes, proceedings of the ayuntamiento, military and land records, election returns, census records, and records of other local matters, all accumulated at Nacogdoches in the conduct of the government from 1737 to 1836. In 1850 the documents were transferred to the secretary of state's office and in 1878 to the Texas State Archives, where they have been kept. These documents, presenting the official picture of life on the frontier of Spanish and Mexican Texas, have been transcribed and bound into 89 volumes of about 250 pages each; copies are available in the Barker Texas History Center in Austin and in the Steen Library at Stephen F. Austin State University, Nacogdoches. *Winnie Allen*

Nacogdoches–Neches Saline Road. A relatively unknown road that greatly facilitated the settlement of East Texas between the Neches and Angelina rivers. The ancient Indian trail led from the Caddo villages near the site of present Nacogdoches, crossed the Angelina River east of the site of present Alto, and traveled the length of Cherokee County northwest to the Brooks Saline on the Neches River, seven miles west of the site of present Bullard in Smith County. Stephen F. Austin indicated the salt springs on his 1840 map of Texas. Before recorded history animals and Indians had made a path to the salt licks near the river. The earliest land surveys in Cherokee County use the old trace as a reference point. The old highway, commonly called the Saline Road as noted on the 1851 map, once traveled through Dialville, Jacksonville, Lakeview, and Larissa. In 1765 Spanish Franciscan José Francisco Calahorra y Saenz, with other Spaniards and 100 Indians on a peace mission to the upper Sabine River, traveled the road from the Hainai Indian village on the Angelina River northwesterly. By the 1820s Texans were manufacturing salt at the Saline by boiling salt water in huge iron pots. Cherokee chief Bowl, Martin Lacy, George Bays, and Dr. E. J. Debard were early salt makers. A white settlement was begun at the Neches Saline about 1830. At the beginning of the Texas Revolution about 40 people lived in or near the Saline village, 75 miles northwest of Nacogdoches. During the Runaway Scrape all the residents fled down the Saline Road to Lacy's Fort on the Old San Antonio Road. The Killough clan, including the Williams and Wood families from Talladega County, Alabama, established a settlement southeast of the Neches Saline in what is now Cherokee County in 1837. In 1838, when the Córdova Rebellion occurred, the Killoughs traveled the Saline Road to Nacogdoches to wait out the trouble. Córdova and his renegade forces were chased by Maj. Henry W. Augustine's 150 Texas soldiers up the old road to the Neches Saline, where the trail was lost. The refugee Killoughs returned to their home near the Saline about the first of October to gather their crops. On 5 October 1838, renegades attacked the settlement and killed or captured 18 people. Again survivors of the massacre fled down the Saline Road to Lacy's Fort.

During the Mexican War the First Regiment of Kentucky Volunteer Cavalry marched from the Sabine River to Robbins's Ferry on the Trinity River, part of the way on the Saline Road. The soldiers had to widen the road to allow passage of the large supply wagons. One of the officers, Maj. Pollard Gaines, declared in his diary that the Kentucky regiment built the Texans 60 miles of good road. The Cherokee County Commissioners Court noted the road improvement and authorized the Saline Road, with a new-cut detour to the county seat, as a stage route from Rusk to Tyler in Smith County. Near the Saline Road in Jacksonville was a strong spring. When the International Railroad built through in 1872, the watering hole was enlarged to furnish water for steam locomotives. The spring was used as a recreational area by local residents; a big political rally was held there in 1855, at which some of the state's most able speechmakers, including T. J. Rusk, Louis Wigfall, and Richard Hubbard, were present. In 1874–75 the Rusk Transportation Company

chartered and built a tram railroad from the Cherokee county seat to the International–Great Northern Railroad at Jacksonville. The Rusk Tramway closely followed the Saline Road from south of Dialville to Jacksonville. In 1882 the Kansas and Gulf Short Line Railroad Company (Cotton Belt), building south from Tyler, utilized parts of the tram right-of-way and from Dialville to Rusk faithfully followed the Saline Road. Only two sections of the old highway were preserved by 1989. Farm Road 347 from Dialville north to Jacksonville follows the old trail with little deviation. Farther to the northwest the Larissa Road from near Lake Acker to the Killough Massacre Monument site parallels the Saline Trace to the west.

Bernard Mayfield

Nash's Iron Foundry. The first iron furnace in Texas; 16 miles northwest of Jefferson; built in 1847 on a tributary of Alley's Creek by Jefferson S. Nash, a Cass County planter impressed with the quality of the local iron ore. A foundry was added sometime thereafter, but it was only intermittently operational. In 1857, J. S. Nash and Company reorganized. Short of money for equipment, the company approached the state legislature for help, but without success. In January 1858 the company was incorporated as the Nash Iron, Steel, and Copper Manufacturing Company, and by this time the Nash furnace is reported to have sent more than 10,000 pounds of iron to Jefferson, the nearest shipping point. Still hoping to receive financial assistance from the state legislature, the company expanded and retooled its facilities in 1859–60. The secession crisis and the outbreak of the Civil War ended the possibility of government aid, and the operation found its transportation and equipment difficulties considerably aggravated by the war. In 1861 the company attempted to shift over to the manufacture of cannons, cannon-shot, and rifles for the Confederate Army; it made some cannon-balls but apparently no small arms. In 1863 the company was reincorporated under the name Texas Iron Company. It continued to suffer from shortages of equipment and capital, and was sold to the Kelly Iron Company toward the end of the war. Much of the plant was dismantled and moved to Kellyville, and by the later 1860s all that remained of Nash's enterprise was an abandoned furnace. *Mark Odintz*

Nashville Convention. Helped to pave the way for the Confederacy. When the Mexican War brought new territory in the Southwest, a crisis developed between the minority South and an increasingly determined North. Realizing the importance of unity more than ever before, 69 Southern congressmen, representing every slave state except Delaware, launched a movement for unity in 1848. A few months later a bipartisan convention met at Jackson, Mississippi, and issued the call for a southern convention to meet at Nashville, Tennessee, in June 1850, "to devise and adopt some mode of resistance to northern aggression." Senator John C. Calhoun of South Carolina played a major role in these activities. At first southerners in general responded favorably, but events in Washington pointing toward compromise lessened support for the convention. Democrats supported the convention proposal more than Whigs. Both senators from Texas, Sam Houston and Thomas J. Rusk, as well as most of the state's newspapers, opposed the convention. Nevertheless, the Southern rights movement had strong support in the state. J. Pinckney Henderson, the sole Texas delegate to the convention, was concerned about the boundary dispute with New Mexico. A total of 175 delegates from nine Southern states met at the McKendree Methodist Church from 3 to 12 June 1850. They set forth a platform based on the extension of the 36°30' line and adopted a series of 28 resolutions and a more radical address directed to the people of the slaveholding states, exclusive of Delaware. In this address Robert Barnwell Rhett of South Carolina argued the unacceptability of the compromise being debated in Congress. The Texas boundary bill would transfer from the South to the North territory sufficient for two states. The convention's adjournment was conditional. Should Congress fail to meet their demands, the delegates were to assemble again at Nashville. The passage of the compromise measures took away much of the momentum generated by the first session of the Nashville Convention. When Congress passed the bill giving Texas $10 million and New Mexico most of the disputed land, all the Texas congressmen voted for it. A majority of Texans accepted the new law, and the legislature approved an act of acceptance in 1850. Therefore, it is not surprising that Texas was not represented at the second session of the Nashville Convention, which included 59 delegates from seven Southern states, who met in November 1850. Though the delegates rejected South Carolina's resolution advocating united secession, they approved measures affirming the right of secession, denounced the compromise, and recommended a Southern congress.

Thelma Jennings

National Archives—Fort Worth Branch. One of eleven regional branches; established in 1969 as the Federal Archives and Records Center to preserve records of permanent value that are produced or held by field offices of federal agencies in Arkansas, Louisiana, New Mexico, Oklahoma, and Texas. It received its present name in 1985. In addition to original records, the branch has copies of many National Archives microfilm publications. Research rooms, microfilm-reading equipment, and document-reproduction facilities are available to the public. The branch arranges records, prepares finding aids, performs reference services, mounts exhibits, and works with colleges to aid faculty and students to make effective use of archival resources. Public programs include outreach, internships, teacher workshops, film series, symposia, exhibits, and tours. Holdings include original records of U.S. District courts of Arkansas (1865–1969), Louisiana (1806–1966), Oklahoma (1907–69), and Texas (1846–1975); records of the U.S. Court of Appeals for the Fifth Circuit (1891–1971), which hears appeals from lower federal courts in Georgia, Florida, Alabama, Mississippi, Louisiana, and Texas; records of the Bureau of Indian Affairs from field offices in Oklahoma (1870–1970); and records of the U.S. Army Corps of Engineers from district offices in Albuquerque (1935–43), Galveston (1897–1943), Little Rock (1907–43), New Orleans (1837–1943), and Tulsa (1908–44). Holdings also include records from the War Manpower Administration, the Southwestern Power Administration, the U.S. Park Service, the Federal Highway Administration, INS, Wichita Mountains Wildlife Refuge, EPA, DEA, and other sources. Microfilm holdings include most of the nineteenth-century correspondence of the Department of State, many German records captured during World War II, and federal census population schedules from 1790 to 1910.

Jeanette Ford

National Biological Control Laboratory. Twelve miles northwest of Mission on land that once belonged to Moore Air Force Base; operated by the U.S. Department of Agriculture, the Animal and Plant Health Inspection Service, and Plant Protection and Quarantine. The APHIS also operates biological control laboratories in Niles, Michigan, and Bozeman, Montana. In 1985 the facility was inaugurated in Texas at Moore Air Force Base, where other projects such as a successful screw-worm-eradication program had operated since the mid-1950s. The APHIS laboratory serves all 50 states and some foreign countries in biological control. Its purpose is to find ways to minimize the damage from weeds and insect pests by taking advantage of their natural enemies. Predatory beetles, parasites, and disease organisms that attack agricultural pests are tested for use. Predators that prove to be of value are distributed to areas in need of specific disease or pest control.

Robert E. Norton

National Trail. Proposed by Texas cattlemen in the 1880s in an attempt to thwart proposed northern quarantines against Texas cattle. Texas fever, caused by ticks indigenous to the Southwest, had inflicted heavy losses upon the northern range cattle industry by the early 1880s, and these losses had caused northern cattlemen (roughly all those north of the thirty-second parallel) to lobby for state and territorial quarantines against infected livestock. Since it was much less expensive for Texas cattlemen to trail their herds to northern railheads and ranges and then ship them by rail rather than ship directly from Texas, most Texans saw these proposed quarantines as a threat to their economic well-being. When the cattle industry convention met in 1884 in St. Louis, such prominent Texas cattlemen as Richard King, B. B. Groom, C. C. Slaughter, and John Lytle pushed through a resolution calling upon Congress, "in the interest of cheaper food," to build and maintain a National Trail from Doan's Crossing on the Red River north through the Indian Territory, the present Oklahoma Panhandle, Colorado, Nebraska, Wyoming, South Dakota, and Montana to the Canadian border. Partially in retaliation, the following year Colorado, Kansas, Nebraska, New Mexico, Wyoming, and Canada passed quarantine laws against Texas cattle, seriously restricting northern drives during the regular trailing season. Finally, in 1886, Texas congressman James Francis Miller of Gonzales introduced the National Trail proposal in the United States House of Representatives. The measure was blocked in the House committee on commerce by northern cattle interests and by Texas railroads, which presumably wanted to replace the trail with rails. The failure of the National Trail, the northern quarantines, and the western migration of farmers and barbed wire sounded the death knell of cattle trailing.

Jimmy M. Skaggs

Naval Air Station, Beeville. Also known as Chase Field; formed in 1943 by the conversion of a municipal airport then under construction into a military airfield and named for Lt. Commander Nathan Brown Chase, who was killed on a training mission at Pearl Harbor in 1925. The field was commissioned a naval auxiliary airfield in June 1943. In July 1946, after VJ Day, it was reduced to caretaker status. As a result of the Korean War the field was purchased from the city of Beeville by the navy in August 1952. In November 1953 it was officially designated a naval auxiliary air station. It received almost $13 million under a 1967 military-construction bill. In 1968 its status was elevated to that of full naval air station. It employed approximately 2,500 military and civilian personnel. From its beginning the station trained naval and marine aviators and ground crews. Jet-aircraft training began in 1954. Training Air Wing Three was established at the station on 1 October 1971 and continued into the 1990s. In 1993 the base was decommissioned. *Art Leatherwood*

Naval Air Station, Corpus Christi. The "University of the Air"; founded in June 1940, when President Franklin Roosevelt signed a $25 million appropriation proposal. The base was dedicated by the secretary of the navy in March 1941. Its main station was at Flour Bluff, and its six auxiliary stations were Rodd, Cabaniss, Cuddihy, and Waldron at Corpus Christi, Kingsville Naval Auxiliary Field at Kingsville, and Chase Field at Beeville. The total station covered some 20,000 acres in three counties. By 1945, 997 hangers and other buildings had been constructed, and the cost had run to more than $100 million. The station was initially used to train aviation cadets as pilots, navigators, aerologists, gunners, and radio operators. By 1950 it was training naval aviators in the advanced stages of flying multi-engine land and sea planes. In addition, the United States Naval Hospital, the United States Naval School of All-Weather Flight, the Fleet Logistic Air Wing, Acceptance, Test, and Transfer Unit, and the headquarters for the Corpus Christi Naval Reserve Training Center were operating at the Naval Air Station. After World War II, activity at the station was curtailed. By late 1948 the Naval Air Advanced Training Command had transferred to Corpus Christi from Jacksonville, Florida, and the Naval Air Station, Corpus Christi, became a permanent installation. The Navy's precision flight team, the Blue Angels, made their headquarters at Corpus Christi in 1949 and remained there until 1955, when they moved to Pensacola, Florida. In 1959 the navy shut down a major repair and assembly facility, which had employed the majority of the 4,000 civilians at the base. In 1961 the facility was converted into the Army Aeronautical Depot Maintenance Center. From the 1960s into the 1990s the Naval Air Station continued to provide fully trained naval aviators of multi-engine land and sea planes; its students included many from foreign countries. In 1986 the station's airfield was named Truax Field in honor of Lt. Myron Milton Truax, United States Navy. In the 1990s the station continued to maintain and operate facilities to support operations designated by the chief of naval operations. Three training squadrons were operating aircraft from the station. *Art Leatherwood*

Naval Air Station, Dallas. A shore installation of the commander of Naval Air Reserve Forces, one of 15 major naval-reserve installations in the United States; located at the northwest end of Mountain Creek Lake, just west of Dallas. It was established in August 1929 by the city of Dallas as a training field for reserve pilots and was named Hensley Field for Maj. William N. Hensley, who was on the first trans-Atlantic dirigible crossing in 1919 and was a flying instructor near Dallas in the early 1920s. The site was leased to the United States Army by the city of Dallas for 20 years for $1 a year, and the field became the Air Corps Reserve Base in the Eighth Corps Area. The lease was extended to 40 years at the beginning of World War II. The United States Navy began maintaining operations there in March 1941 and on 15 May of that year established a naval reserve

training base on 160 acres adjacent to Hensley Field. In October 1941, Maj. Thomas D. Ferguson, commander at the field, was made control officer for the Middle West Area of the United States, and in December Hensley became headquarters of the Midwest Area of the Air Corps Ferrying Command. It served as such until the ferry command became the Fifth Ferrying Group and was so expanded that it had to be moved to Love Field. The installation became Naval Air Station, Dallas, on 1 January 1943. Its mission was to provide primary flight training for naval, marine, and coast guard cadets. Enlisted personnel for aviation duty with the fleet were also trained there, and at one time a number of Free French aviators received flight training at NAS Dallas. During World War II the base also served as a radial engine repair station. NAS Dallas handled all air traffic for the adjacent North American Aircraft Company plant. It was also the flight test facility and the receiving station for 4,400 SNJ (Texan) training aircraft manufactured at that plant. In 1946 Congress appropriated funds to establish a naval reserve training program at NAS Dallas, and by March of that year the reserves had taken over the field. The United States Marine Air Reserve Training Command also established itself there at that time. Reservists from Texas, Oklahoma, and eastern New Mexico continued to train at NAS Dallas. Hensley Field passed from the command of the Air Force to that of the Navy in 1949, but the field continued to serve as an air force reserve training center. In 1950 the naval reserve squadron stationed at NAS Dallas was the first air reserve squadron to be called to active service in the Korean War. The station continued to grow with the installation of new and longer runways. Jet aircraft were assigned to NAS Dallas in 1952. In 1963 the base was the first one to fly the F8 Crusader. The 1980s brought to the installation some of the nation's most sophisticated aircraft, including the F-14 (Tomcat) and the C9B. By 1990 there were 2,057 active-duty personnel on the base, with 6,789 reservists assigned to the station. The total economic impact of the base by then was almost $76 million. By the following year, more than 1,700 soldiers, sailors, and marines had been deployed from the base to the Persian Gulf. *Art Leatherwood*

Naval Air Station, Kingsville. Known as the Naval Auxiliary Air Station, Kingsville, until 1968, when it was redesignated a naval air station. When it was commissioned in July 1942 it was one of three advanced air-training bases of the Naval Air Training Command. At that time its facilities were 85 percent complete; the field did not have a name, being officially designated as "P4." During World War II four squadrons taught fighter and bomber tactics at the station as well as gunnery for combat aircrewmen. For a short time the field handled an overflow of basic-training recruits from an Illinois naval-training center. At the end of the war, pilot training at the base dropped sharply. In September 1946 the station was closed and turned over to the city of Kingsville, which leased the base to the Texas College of Arts and Industries as an agricultural station. The base was reactivated in April 1951 as an auxiliary air station under the command of the chief of naval air advanced training located at the Naval Air Station, Corpus Christi. Three training squadrons used the twoseated TF9J and the singleseated AF9J. The station trained 300 men a year during the mid1960s and received $3.8 million under a 1967 military construction bill, which was used to improve operation and maintenance facilities as well as troop housing. In 1986 the airfield portion of the station was named in honor of Adm. Alva D. Bernhard, who had chosen the site. In 1990 the station was the headquarters for Commander Training Air Wing Two, composed of three jet-training wings that trained 170 Navy and Marine Corps aviators each year. The station employed 900 military and 1,100 civilian personnel with an annual payroll of $45 million. The Naval Air Station at Kingsville also operates the Naval Auxiliary Landing Field at Orange Grove, 45 miles northwest of Kingsville.

Neches River. Rises in Van Zandt County and flows southeast for 416 miles to its mouth on Sabine Lake. Except for a few miles near its head, the Neches for its entire length serves as a county line. Two major reservoirs are located on the Neches: Lake Palestine and Lake B. A. Steinhagen. Abundant rainfall makes the Neches a large-volume stream. Major tributaries include the Angelina River, Bayou La Nana, Ayish Bayou, Pine Island Bayou, Village Creek, Kickapoo Creek, and Flat Creek. Tyler is the largest city in the Neches basin; other cities include Beaumont, Lufkin, and Nacogdoches. Archeological excavations reveal long Indian occupation of the Neches basin similar to that of the Sabine basin. When the first Europeans entered the area in the sixteenth century, they found Hasinai Indians living along the upper reaches of the stream, which they called River of Snows. The river is supposed to have been named for the Neches Indians by Spanish explorer Alonso De León (late 1680s). On his fifth and final expedition in 1690 De León was accompanied by Queretaran missionary Damián Massanet, who founded the first mission in Texas, San Francisco de los Tejas. The same year another Queretaran, Francisco Casañas de Jesús María, founded the mission of Santísimo Nombre de María on the banks of the Neches, which he knew as "El Arcángel San Miguel." In 1691 Domingo Terán de los Ríos, while exploring the region, reported that the Neches was a small stream, difficult if not impossible to navigate. In 1721 an expeditionary force led by the Marqués de Aguayo found the river so swollen by rain that they were forced to build a bridge, one of the earliest bridges built in Texas. A Río de Nievas (River of Snows) noted by the Sevillian historian Francisco López de Gamarra in his *Historia General de las Indias* was evidently not the Neches. Spanish maps from the early years of the eighteenth century called the river Río Mexicano, Río de los Tejas, or Río del Arcángel San Miguel. Many maps mislocated the Neches or confused it with the Sabine or other streams. Pichardo wrote that the term Río Mexicano applied properly only to the Neches.

Despite the attempts of the Spanish to colonize the area, large numbers of Europeans did not enter the Neches basin until the 1820s, when Anglo-Americans from the southern United States began to settle there. When Mexican official Gen. Manuel de Mier y Terán was sent to the region in 1828 to report on conditions, he found that the ratio of Americans to Mexicans was nearly 10 to one. Numerous hand-propelled ferries established along the river during the 1830s and 1840s helped open the area for settlement. On his first trip to Texas, Stephen F. Austin recognized the potential of the Neches as a means of transportation, as he recorded in his journal in 1821. During the 1830s and 1840s flat-bottomed barges were used to float cotton and other agricultural produce downriver to Sabine Lake, where it was loaded on larger ships for transport to New Orleans, Galveston, and other ports. The booming river trade on the Neches and the Sabine, which also empties into Sabine Lake, contributed to the rise of Beaumont and Port Arthur. The first steamships began to ply the river in the late 1840s, when Robert and Moses L. Patton purchased the steamer *Angelina*. Because the upper reaches of the Neches were usually too shallow for steamers during the dry season, farmers had to haul their goods to Bunn's Bluff on the lower part of the river. As a result Bunn's Bluff developed into a port with large warehouses and docks. The riverboats continued to navigate the Neches until the 1890s, although by the 1870s railroads had begun to replace them. The last of the large steamers, the *Neches Belle*, operated on the river from 1891 to 1894. During the late nineteenth and early twentieth centuries the upper Neches River basin was the site of intensive logging, and numerous sawmills were built along the banks of the river and its tributaries. Downstream, the broad Neches floodplain became the site of intensive rice culture during the early 1900s. After the Spindletop boom of 1901, the Neches basin also became the site of large-scale oil exploration. The growth of the oil industry led to the development of the Beaumont–Port Arthur–Orange metropolitan area as a major site for oil refining, processing, and shipping. As a consequence of these developments, as well as decaying vegetation from forested land, the once clean waters of the Neches have become increasingly polluted. Although a water-quality plan has been adopted for the area, in the early 1990s the pollution problem continued, especially in the river's lower reaches. *Christopher Long*

Neff, Pat Morris. Governor; b. Coryell County, 26 November 1871; d. Waco, 20 January 1952; m. Myrtle Mainer (1899); 2 children; ed. Baylor University (A.B., 1894; A.M. 1898) and University of Texas (LL.B., 1897). Neff served in the state House (1899–1905) and was speaker—the youngest to that date—in his last term. He was county attorney of McLennan County (1906–12), where he prosecuted 422 defendants and lost only 16 cases. He ran against Joseph Weldon Bailey for governor in 1920 as a prohibitionist and won in a runoff. He intended reforms in education, prisons, public health, law enforcement, and taxation, but because he failed to develop a productive relationship with the legislature much of what he wanted failed to happen. He increased funding to rural schools, established Texas Tech, reorganized the Highway Commission, founded the state park system, and greatly reduced executive pardons. He declared martial law twice, both times in 1922: at Mexia, where lawlessness burgeoned with the oil industry; and at Denison, where a railroad strike threatened commerce. West Texans started the "Sweetwater Secession Movement" when Neff vetoed the bill for West Texas A&M College. He was offered the presidency of the University of Texas in 1923, but declined it. He was mentioned as a presidential candidate in 1924. After his second term as governor ended (1925), he held various government service positions including one on the Railroad Commission (1929–32), which he resigned in order to become president of Baylor University, a position he held until 1947. Baylor thrived under him, though some thought him too rigid and unmodern and some considered him too lax (because he invited Harry Truman, who drank, to receive an honorary degree). Neff was president of the Baptist General Convention of Texas (1926–28), president of the

quently became major hits in the United States. Offers began to pour in from Hollywood, and in 1922 Negri signed a contract with Famous Players–Lasky (later Paramount). Her arrival in New York was greeted with great fanfare. She quickly rose to stardom in such films as *Forbidden Paradise* (1924) and *Hotel Imperial* (1927). Known for her fiery temperament and her exotic looks, she became the prototypical "vamp" of 1920s Hollywood. She was romantically linked with Charlie Chaplin, and carried on a well-publicized affair with Rudolph Valentino, which lasted until his death in 1926. With the advent of talkies in the late 1920s her Hollywood career faltered, and in the early 1930s she returned to Europe. She made one film in France, *Fanatisme* (1934), before signing a contract with German film studio UFA in 1935. She made several well-regarded films in those years, including *Mazurka* (1935), *Moskou–Shanghai* (1937), and *Madame Bovary* (1937). She fled Germany after the outbreak of World War II, settled briefly in France, then sailed for the United States in 1940. Her arrival in New York was clouded by unfounded charges that she had had an affair with Hitler. She eventually cleared her name and attempted to make a comeback in Hollywood, but made only two films thereafter, *Hi Diddle Diddle* (1943) and *The Moonspinners* (1964). In 1957 Negri moved to San Antonio with her longtime friend Margaret West, who was from a prominent family of the city. They lived for a time in a suite in the Menger Hotel and later in a large home in Olmos Park. In her later years Negri lived in semiseclusion. She served on the board of directors for the San Antonio Symphony Orchestra and the San Antonio Little Theater. She donated her library to Trinity University and gave a large collection of memorabilia, including several rare prints of her early films, to St. Mary's University. She also left a large portion of her estate to St. Mary's, which established a scholarship in her name.

Christopher Long

Barbara Apollonia Chalupec, better known as Pola Negri. From New York *Journal–American*, July 1941. Courtesy HRHRC.

Southern Baptist convention (1942–45), and grand master of the Masonic Grand Lodge of Texas (1946). *Thomas E. Turner*

Negri, Pola. Screen actress; b. Barbara Apollonia Chalupec, Janowo, Poland, 31 December 1894 (?); d. San Antonio, 2 August 1987 (buried in Los Angeles); m. Polish count Eugene Domski (before 1920; divorced); m. Prince Serge Mdivani (1927; divorced). Pola was her childhood nickname, shortened from Apollonia; Negri she later took as her stage name after Italian poetess Adah Negri, her girlhood idol. As a youth she attended the boarding school of Countess Platen in Warsaw and studied at the Imperial Ballet School in St. Petersburg before entering the Philharmonia Drama School in Warsaw. She made her stage debut in 1913 in Gerhardt Hauptmann's *Hannele* in Warsaw and appeared the following year in her first film, *Niewolnica Zmyslow*. Her stage work attracted the attention of Alexandr Hertz, a pioneer Polish film producer, who made several of her earliest films. She also starred in Max Reinhardt's pantomime play *Sumurun* in Warsaw, and in 1917, at Reinhardt's urging, she continued the role in Berlin. After World War I she appeared in a series of German films, including *Carmen* and *Madame DuBarry* (*Passion*) both directed by Ernst Lubitsch. The two films subse-

Neighbors, Robert Simpson. Indian agent and legislator; b. Charlotte County, Virginia, 13 November 1815; d. Fort Belknap, 14 September 1859 (buried in the civilian cemetery there); m. Elizabeth Ann Mays (1851); 2 surviving sons. Neighbors arrived in Texas in 1836 and served in the Texas revolutionary army. As a member of John C. Hays's volunteer company he was made prisoner by Gen. Adrián Woll in 1842, taken to Mexico, and released in 1844. Early the next year he began his service as Texas Indian agent. He instituted the field system of Indian control; instead of remaining at the agency headquarters and waiting for the Indians to pay him a visit, as was the common practice, Neighbors dealt with them directly in their home territory. He spent much time far beyond the frontier and exercised greater influence over the Indians in Texas than any other white man of his generation. After annexation he became federal special Indian agent (1847). He took part in a council between commissioners of the United States and the Texas Comanches near the site of Waco in 1846 and one between the Comanches and the German colonists on the San Saba River in March 1847. Since Neighbors was a Democrat, his services as Indian agent were terminated by the national Whig administration in September 1849. As Texas commissioner, sent by Governor Peter H. Bell, he organized El Paso County in 1850 and tried, without success, to organize counties in New Mexico. As a member of the legislature (1851–53) he sponsored a law that opened the way for establishing Indian reservations. He was a presidential elector in 1852, and shortly after the election of Franklin Pierce he was again appointed Indian agent. In 1853 he was made supervising agent for the Texas Indians. In 1854 he joined Capt. Randolph B. Marcy to locate sites in Northwest Texas for Indian reservations. Neighbors alleged that the army officers at Fort Belknap and Camp Cooper failed to give adequate support to him and his resident agents. Many frontier civilians joined in the military's antipathy, and charged that the reservation Indians were committing depredations on the white settlements. In spite of threats against his life, Neighbors never faltered in his determination to protect the Indians. With the aid of federal troops he managed to hold back the white people from the reservations, and in August 1859 he eventually succeeded in moving the Indians without loss of life to a new reservation in Indian Territory. On his return he stopped at the village of Fort Belknap, where he was murdered by one Edward Cornett.   *Rupert N. Richardson*

Neiman Marcus. Established in 1907 as a local specialty store by Herbert Marcus, his sister Carrie Neiman, and Carrie's husband, Abraham (Al) Neiman. The opening took place under unpromising conditions. The country was in the midst of an economic recession known as the Panic of 1907. Both Carrie Neiman and Herbert Marcus missed the opening; Carrie was in the hospital recovering from a miscarriage, and Herbert was at home with typhoid fever. The founders emphasized that Neiman Marcus was not a department store but a specialty store, featuring women's outerwear and millinery. Marcus and the Neimans stressed high-quality, ready-to-wear items in an era when clothing was usually one or the other. The store also developed a reputation for high prices as well as high quality, even though it depended primarily on the sale of medium-priced items. Neiman Marcus grew up along with Dallas and with Texas. After a fire in 1913, Neiman Marcus moved to the corner of Main and Ervay in downtown Dallas. The store's wealthier clientele represented mainly the cotton aristocracy of East and north central Texas. Later the oil-rich of East and West Texas added to Neiman's growing reputation regionally and nationally. Stanley Marcus, Herbert's eldest son, joined the business in 1926; "Mr. Stanley" later assumed leadership of the company. In 1928 a combination of business and personal disagreements led to the end of Al Neiman's association with Neiman Marcus. He sold his interest in the firm for $250,000; shortly afterwards, his marriage to Carrie Marcus ended in divorce. The Great Depression of the 1930s did not hit Neiman's as hard as it did other firms in other parts of the country. The store had just completed a major expansion when the hard times began. Neiman's suffered relatively small losses only in 1931 and 1932 and by 1935 had returned to predepression levels of sales and profits. An important factor in this growth during the depression was the discovery in 1930 of the East Texas oilfield, which produced a new group of millionaires and Neiman's customers. World War II led to a general economic boom in Texas and another expansion of the store. As a family-run operation, Neiman's was much affected by the dislocations of the war. Stanley Marcus served with the War Production Board in Washington while brothers Lawrence, Edward, and Herbert, Jr., also involved in store operations, served in the armed forces. Despite wartime restrictions and shortages, Neiman Marcus retained its reputation for high quality and personal service.

The postwar period led to major changes in Neiman's opera-

tions. In 1950 Herbert Marcus, Sr., died, leaving Carrie as chairman of the board and Stanley as the store's chief executive officer and driving force. In 1951 Neiman's opened its first branch store in Dallas and also expanded its main store. It opened a Houston branch in 1955. The company's growth was interrupted when a major fire struck the downtown Dallas store in 1964—at that time the costliest store fire in history. By the late 1960s Neiman's had four stores in operation—two in Dallas, one in Houston, and one in Fort Worth—but desire for continued growth was blocked by a lack of capital. In 1969 the decision was made to merge with the California-based Broadway–Hale Stores, which later merged with yet another retailing group to form Carter, Hawley, Hale, Incorporated. Neiman's, with outlets across the nation, became part of the specialty-store division of the parent company. Stanley Marcus became a top-ranking executive with Carter, Hawley, Hale, leaving his son Richard as president of Neiman Marcus. In 1987 the company was restructured, and General Cinema became the majority shareholder of Neiman Marcus. In May 1989 Allen I. Questrom succeeded Richard Marcus as president. Neiman's was the first retail store in Texas to mount a major national advertising campaign. The store has always followed a liberal credit policy, dating from the days when cotton farmers were permitted to defer payments until after their crops were harvested. In 1938 Neiman's introduced its annual fashion award, which not only honored outstanding designers but also promoted the store itself. The first of the annual "fortnights," sales featuring merchandise and cultural exhibits from other nations, was held in 1957, the embodiment of Neiman's successful blending of the cultural with the commercial. The store's Christmas catalog is also a widely publicized seasonal event.   *Don M. Coerver*

Neville Ranch Raid. On 25 March 1918; the last serious attack on a Texas ranch by Mexican raiders. Edwin Neville's isolated Presidio County ranch stretched 18 miles along the Rio Grande. The American military stationed in Van Horn had received rumors of an impending raid from across the Rio Grande. Neville, who was in Van Horn for supplies and heard the report, rode eight hours to reach his ranch and found it quiet. He concluded that no danger was imminent. Nevertheless, 50 horsemen approached and opened fire on the house. Seeking protection, Neville and his son Glen ran toward a ditch about 300 yards away. The older Neville reached the ditch uninjured, but Glen was killed. The housekeeper, Rosa Castillo, was also shot and her body mutilated. As Neville wandered in the darkness, the raiders stole horses, clothes, bedding, and supplies. Thirty-one men from Troop G arrived shortly after the attack but waited until Troop A arrived before pursuing the raiders. The soldiers crossed the Rio Grande and fought the bandits in the village of Pilares, where 33 Mexicans were killed and 8 wounded. One American, Private Carl Alberts, was killed. The soldiers destroyed all but one house in Pilares and recovered some of Neville's stolen property. It is likely that the Neville ranch raid was not a simple act of robbery, since Neville had little to steal. Since many of the raiders were associated with nearby Porvenir, the attack on the Neville ranch may have been retaliation for the Porvenir Massacre, which had taken place two months before. It is also likely that the raiders had connections with Pancho Villa. In addition, soldiers found German-made Mauser rifles at Pilares, a fact that may suggest German involvement in the raid.

Landa Mills, ca. 1895–1896. Photograph by Henry Stark. Merchant Joseph Landa erected a complex of water-powered mills at Comal Springs in New Braunfels. Courtesy Dallas Historical Society.

After the raid, Ed Neville sold his ranch and opened the Long Horn Cafe in Marfa. Because he could not forget the death of his son, he carried out a vendetta against Mexicans he suspected of involvement in the raid until his death in 1952.

Julia Cauble Smith

New Braunfels, Texas. County seat of Comal County, is at the confluence of the Guadalupe and Comal rivers 30 miles northeast of San Antonio. It was founded in 1845 when, under the auspices of the Adelsverein, Nicolaus Zink led a German immigrant wagontrain up the Guadalupe River to the ford of the San Antonio–Nacogdoches road. They made camp at a site on Comal Creek (now Dry Comal Creek) chosen by Prince Carl of Solms–Braunfels, the first commissioner general of the Adelsverein, and promptly organized to receive later arrivals. Zink platted preliminary town and farm lots and supervised construction of a primitive stockade, the Zinkenburg, to protect the immigrants against Indians. Within weeks Prince Carl had laid the cornerstone for a more permanent fort and headquarters for the immigrant association, the Sophienburg (now the Sophienburg Museum), made provision for supplying the burgeoning settlement through its first summer on the frontier, and handed leadership of the colony over to John O. Meusebach. By summer the settlers numbered between 300 and 400 and the community had been incorporated under the name Braunfels, after Prince Solms's estate on the Lahn River in western Germany. Taking advantage of the water power afforded by

Comal Springs and the community's position on the road between Austin and San Antonio, the settlers wasted little time establishing the stores, millworks, and craft shops that soon made New Braunfels the commercial center of a growing agricultural area. Within a decade of its founding the town had emerged as a manufacturing center supplying wagons, farm implements, leather goods, furniture, and clothing to pioneers settling the hills of Central Texas. It is reported that in 1850 New Braunfels was the fourth largest town in Texas. Citizens voted unanimously to impose a tax for the support of a public school 18 years before the Constitution of 1876 provided for such local taxation throughout Texas. New Braunfels, Galveston, and Fredericksburg were among the first Texas towns to collect taxes to support schools. The Germans of New Braunfels also organized the Germania Singing Society, the Schuetzen Verein (shooting club), and one of the early Turnvereins or athletic clubs. The Neu Braunfelser Zeitung, which issued its first edition in 1852, was published continuously in German until 1957; it later merged with the English language newspaper, the New Braunfels *Herald.* By the early 1880s, with a population estimated at 2,000, the community was linked by telegraph and rail lines with Austin and San Antonio, and textile factories along the Comal River were shipping cotton and woolen products. The following decade saw the installation of electric streetlights. A permanent county courthouse adjacent to the town square opened in 1898.

By 1900 both the International–Great Northern and the Missouri, Kansas and Texas railroads provided freight and passenger service. Flour mills, textile factories, and processing plants for construction materials provided the basis for steady growth in the twentieth century; from a population estimated at 3,165 in 1912 the town doubled in size to 6,242 by the onset of the Great Depression. The depression and the boll weevil nearly devastated the textile industry, which returned very slowly. New growth during and immediately after World War II brought the population to 12,200 in 1950. To keep pace with such growth and attendant social changes, New Braunfels reorganized its city government twice in the twentieth century, replacing the original aldermanic form in 1920 with the mayor–commission system, and subsequently replacing that with a council–manager form. In 1947 the city incorporated eight suburbs within its limits. In the twentieth century New Braunfels added tourism to its major industries. By 1936 the city had reserved much of the land along the Comal and Guadalupe rivers within the city limits for parks by purchasing Cypress Bend and Landa parks. Landa Park had first opened in 1899 as a private resort area, and, promoted by the International–Great Northern Railroad, had begun to develop as a tourist destination for weekend excursions from San Antonio. Tourist trade accelerated in the decades following World War II, when Interstate Highway 35 was completed and when local merchants and investors began to capitalize on the natural and historic attractions offered by the town and its environs, particularly the recreational potential of the Guadalupe River and, after 1964, of Canyon Lake. The opening of Natural Bridge Caverns and the Wurstfest, a German-heritage celebration, in the early 1960s also facilitated the growth of the tourist industry, which by the mid-1980s supported some 30 hotels and motels, as well as resort condominiums, around the city and Canyon Lake. Proximity to San Antonio also influenced growth; in 1973 Comal County became part of the San Antonio Metropolitan Statistical Area. New Braunfels grew to 17,859 residents in 1970, 22,402 in 1980, and 27,334 in 1990, when the town extended into Guadalupe County. *Daniel P. Greene*

New London School Explosion. A depression-era disaster. In 1937 New London, Texas, had one of the richest rural school districts in the United States. Community residents in the East Texas oilfield were proud of the beautiful, modern, steel-framed, E-shaped school building. On 18 March students prepared for the next day's Interscholastic Meet in Henderson. At the gymnasium, the PTA met. At 3:05 P.M. Lemmie R. Butler, instructor of manual training, turned on a sanding machine in an area which, unknown to him, was filled with a mixture of gas and air. The switch ignited the mixture and carried the flame into a nearly closed space beneath the building, 253 feet long and 56 feet wide. Immediately the building seemed to lift in the air and then smashed to the ground. Walls collapsed. The roof fell in and buried its victims in a mass of brick, steel, and concrete debris. The explosion was heard four miles away. It hurled a two-ton concrete slab 200 feet away, where it crushed a car. Fifteen minutes later, the news of the explosion had been relayed over telephone and Western Union lines. Frantic parents at the PTA meeting rushed to the school building. Community residents and roughnecks from the East Texas oilfield came with heavy-duty equipment. Within an hour Governor Allred had sent the Texas Rangers and highway patrol to aid the victims. Doctors and medical supplies came from Baylor Hospital and Scottish Rite Hospital for Crippled Children in Dallas and from

Nacogdoches, Wichita Falls, and the United States Army Air Corps at Barksdale Field in Shreveport, Louisiana. They were assisted by deputy sheriffs from Overton, Henderson, and Kilgore, by the Boy Scouts, the American Legion, the American Red Cross, the Salvation Army, and volunteers from the Humble Oil Company, Gulf Pipe Line, Sinclair, and the International–Great Northern Railroad.

Workers began digging through the rubble looking for victims. Floodlights were set up, and the rescue operation continued through the night as rain fell. Within 17 hours all victims and debris had been taken from the site. Mother Francis Hospital in Tyler canceled its elaborate dedication ceremonies to take care of the injured. The Texas Funeral Directors sent 25 embalmers. Of the 500 students and 40 teachers in the building, approximately 298 died. Only about 130 students escaped serious injury. Those who died received individual caskets, individual graves, and religious services.

Investigators learned that until 18 January 1937 the school had received its gas from the United Gas Company. To save expenses of $300 a month, plumbers, with the knowledge and approval of the school board and superintendent, had tapped a residue gas line of Parade Gasoline Company. School officials saw nothing wrong—the use of "green" or "wet" gas was a frequent money-saving practice for homes, schools, and churches in the oilfield. The researchers concluded that gas had escaped from a faulty connection and accumulated beneath the building. Green gas has no smell; no one knew it was accumulating beneath the building, although on other days there had been evidence of leaking gas. No school officials were found liable. More than 70 lawsuits followed, but few cases came to trial, and those that did were dismissed by district judge Robert T. Brown for lack of evidence. Public pressure forced the resignation of the superintendent, who had lost a son in the explosion. The most important result of the disaster was the passage of a state odorization law, which required that distinctive malodorants be mixed in all gas for commercial and industrial use so that people could be warned by the smell. The 30 surviving seniors at New London finished their year in temporary buildings while a new school was built on nearly the same site. A cenotaph of Texas pink granite, designed by Donald S. Nelson, architect, and Herring Coe, sculptor, was placed in front of the new school in 1939. *Irvin M. May, Jr.*

New Orleans Greys. Two companies of United States volunteers that served together in the Texas Revolution; organized in New Orleans on 13 October 1835. Nacogdoches alcalde Adolphus Sterne was present at the organizational meeting and offered weapons to the first 50 men who would volunteer for Texas. By the evening's end nearly 120 men appear to have been recruited. Two companies were formed, the first under Capt. Thomas Breece and the second under Capt. Robert Morris. Weapons and equipment were provided, probably from the stores of the Washington Guards. Herman Ehrenberg, who joined Breece's company, indicates that the uniforms were "grey . . . for service on the prairie." Indians around Nacogdoches mistook the Greys for United States regulars. The two companies left New Orleans within two days of each other. Breece's company was welcomed with a public dinner at San Augustine and a dinner of roast bear and champagne at Nacogdoches, where two-thirds of the company were given horses before proceeding to San Antonio.

Morris's 68-man company sailed from New Orleans and arrived at Velasco on 22 October 1835, then proceeded to Brazoria by steamship and marched inland to Victoria, where some of the men were issued horses. The rest secured mounts at La Bahía. In San Antonio Morris was appointed a major and assumed command of a division made up of both companies of Greys; Cooke assumed command of Morris's old company. The Greys took an active part in the siege of Bexar, after which both companies underwent a series of organizational changes as a result of the Matamoros expedition of 1835–36. All but 22 members of Breece's company and one of Cooke's company left San Antonio under Francis White Johnson and James Grant. Those who remained at San Antonio were under the command of Capt. John James Baugh. When Baugh became garrison adjutant, William Blazeby took command of the company, all members of which died in the battle of the Alamo. The company standard was among the flags captured by the Mexicans; it is now the property of the National Historical Museum in Mexico City. The Greys who went south with Grant and Johnson became members of either the San Antonio Greys under Cooke or the Mobile Grays under Capt. David Burke. After Cooke departed with Sam Houston in January 1836, his company was commanded by Samuel Pettus. Though a number of the Greys continued with Grant, including both Morris and Breece, most chose to become part of the garrison at Goliad under Fannin. Nineteen members of Cooke's old company were killed in the Goliad Massacre. Four members of the Greys escaped from the massacre, including William Hunter and Ehrenberg. Three, including Joseph Spohn, were spared. Although the Texan disasters at the Alamo and Goliad destroyed the New Orleans Greys as military units, at least seven Greys were present at the battle of San Jacinto, including William Cooke, the only senior officer of the Greys to survive the Texas Revolution. Thus the Greys are one of the few volunteer units that fought at Bexar, the Alamo, San Patricio, Refugio, Coleto, Goliad, and San Jacinto. *Kevin R. Young*

Newspapers. Early Texas newspapers, usually four pages long, varied in dimensions from 9½ by 12 inches to "blanket" sheets. With the exception of a few dailies, they appeared weekly, semi-weekly, or triweekly. Their content was similar to that of newspapers in other states: foreign news, reprints from other papers, literary features, official notices, and little local news. Editorials were political, civic, or personal in nature. The writing was subjective, diffuse, semihumorous, and often vilifying. The publishers, the editors, and in many instances the printers of early Texas were well-educated and able men who enjoyed the respect of their communities. The press was wholly independent, its guiding principle being the welfare of the people and the country. Editors generally opposed political and sectional influences. They often fearlessly took sides in political campaigns, advocated the election of honest men and, after elections, urged the support of successful candidates. Editors usually took a firm stand against gambling, dueling, intemperance, and all sorts of vices and supported the building of schools and churches. They devoted themselves to the religious, educational, and social improvement of their communities and the state. And most of all they loyally promoted abroad the merits of their country in order to attract settlers.

Between 1813 and 1846 at least 86 different newspaper titles made their appearance in Texas. This figure, however, is larger than the number of newspapers actually published during the period because some papers were planned and advertised in prospectuses but never published. Some were also known by more than one title, for the names changed frequently. The earliest Texas newspaper of record was a small sheet measuring 7 by 13 inches, printed in Spanish on both front and back, called *Gaceta de Texas*. The *Gaceta* was edited by William Shaler and José Álvarez de Toledo in May 1813. This paper, the organ of the Gutiérrez–Magee expedition, was followed a month later by *El Mejicano*, edited by the same men and for the same purpose. Certainly not more than one or two numbers of either paper was ever issued. Until the very eve of the Texas Revolution no newspaper was able to take firm root in Texas. Gen. James Long began publishing the Nacogdoches *Texas Republican* on 14 August 1819. His purpose was to preserve a record of the Long expedition in print, but in October his forces were defeated and the paper stopped. The San Antonio *Texas Courier*, a weekly believed to have been published in San Antonio in April and May 1823, was the next paper in Texas. A prospectus of 9 April is the only record of it. The Nacogdoches *Mexican Advocate* was printed by Milton Slocum at Nacogdoches during the fall of 1829. In the same year Godwin Brown Cotten began the *Texas Gazette*, sometimes called the *Cotton Plant*, at San Felipe de Austin. In January 1831 he sold the *Gazette* to Robert M. Williamson, who had formerly edited it for Cotten. The *Gazette* appears to have changed its title for a time to *Mexican Citizen*. Sometime during the early part of 1832 Cotten moved his press from San Felipe de Austin to Brazoria and published his paper there as the *Texas Gazette and Brazoria Commercial Advertiser*. D. W. Anthony purchased the *Gazette* press and merged it with his *Constitutional Advocate and Brazoria Advertiser*, which began in August 1832 and continued until July 1833. This paper was followed by the Brazoria *Advocate of the People's Rights*, published by Oliver H. Allen and John A. Wharton. The Brazoria *Texas Republican* was published by Franklin C. Gray from July 1834 through 1836.

At least nine papers were established between 1819 and 1836. Of these only one weekly—the *Telegraph and Texas Register*, founded late in 1835, was in operation at the time of Texas independence. Four years later, however, there were more than a dozen newspapers in the Republic of Texas. The first attempt at a daily was made in 1839 with the publication of the Houston *Morning Star*, which appeared triweekly in 1841. The press followed the capital to Austin with the founding in 1839 of the Austin *City Gazette* by Samuel Whiting and George K. Teulon. To keep the people in touch with the government, Jacob Cruger, of the *Telegraph*, with George W. Bonnell, established the Austin *Texas Sentinel* in 1840. The Austin *Daily Texian* (also the *Weekly Texian*), edited by G. H. Harrison, appeared in 1841. At least 10 newspapers were published in Austin during the period of the republic. Others that sprang up in key communities included the weekly Matagorda *Bulletin* (1837–39), the Richmond *Gazette* (1838–41), the *National Vindicator* (Washington-on-the-Brazos, 1843–44), the La Grange *Intelligencer* (1844–46), the San Augustine *Red-Lander* (1838–39, 1841–47), and the Columbia *Planter* (1843–46). Until 1846 there was no newspaper west of the Colorado River. The high attrition rate among publishing ventures is indicated by the fact that seven newspapers, involving 18 publishers in all, were started and failed in Galveston within the four-year period 1838 to 1842. In 1842 the oldest newspaper still functioning, the Galveston *News*, began publication as a semi-weekly. The Galveston *Zeitung*, probably the first German-language newspaper in Texas, was founded in 1847. The first religion-affiliated papers appeared in Houston about the same time.

In 1852 there were 36 newspapers in operation; Houston had four, Galveston three, and Brownsville, Huntsville, Marshall, and San Antonio two each. At least 82 newspapers were being published in 1860, but nearly all had ceased operation within a year after the outbreak of the Civil War. Recovery thereafter, however, was rapid, and by 1868, 73 papers were being printed in the state. Only 8, however, were dailies, and half of those were in Galveston. The number of dailies had increased to 34 by 1890 and to 59 by 1894. In 1910 the state had 89 dailies, 20 semiweeklies, and 768 weeklies, published in 550 towns. The number of dailies was 110 in 1920 and 111 in 1943, but the weeklies dwindled from 679 in 1920 to 604 in 1943. In 1943, 543 Texas towns had some publication, including 235 of the 254 county seats. Between 1910 and 1943 the total number of newspapers in Texas fell from 877 to 731, while the number of other periodicals increased from 73 to 233. Trends that developed before 1950 in the number of daily newspapers and circulation continued to 1965. In 1950 Texas had 115 daily newspapers, 26 semi-weeklies, 562 weeklies, and 300 other periodicals. Thirteen new dailies were started, 11 discontinued publication, and 3 merged with other dailies. Of the 13 new dailies, 7 were suburban, a reflection of population shifts in the state. The notable success of the Southwest edition of the *Wall Street Journal* at Dallas, which began publication in 1948, was indicative of the industrial, commercial, and financial growth in the state and region. Daily newspapers remained almost constant at 114, one fewer in 1965 than in 1950. In the number of dailies per state, Texas ranked third behind California and Pennsylvania. Between 1950 and 1965 daily circulation increased by 26 percent, from 2,439,000 to 3,072,000, a figure slightly larger than the total number of households in the state. About 80 percent of Texas households received one or more daily newspapers in 1965.

The rise and fall of the total number of weekly newspapers provided an indication of the social and economic changes taking place in the state. After a seven-year decline that began in the middle of World War II, weeklies increased for several years until various influences, including the wage-and-hour law, the Korean War, and continued urbanization, reversed the trend in 1951. After a five-year decline total weeklies leveled off largely as a result of the economies afforded by offset printing and central printing plants. Of the 567 weeklies in the state in 1965 more than 200 were printed offset, which largely accounted for the increase of weeklies over a three-year span. Circulation in 1965 was about 1,050,000, of which about 48,000 were free. Paid circulation was about 12.5 percent larger than in 1950. In number of weeklies per state, Texas ranked third behind California and Illinois. Newspapers in the metropolitan statistical areas, which had 83 percent of all daily circulation, increased in size per issue by more than one-third from 1950 to 1965. While the amount of space devoted to news increased, the proportion of news to advertising stayed about the same. The news took approximately 40 percent of total space for smaller papers and 32 percent for larger papers. News content changed to meet the need for greater social responsibility, and more space was devoted to medicine, science, education, economic affairs, mental health, government, civil rights, and international news. Through tem-

perateness and a relatively progressive outlook on racial integration, the Texas press played a significant role in the efforts that brought improvements in racial problems in the state without the violence that occurred in many other states. Chain ownership increased in the state for both daily and weekly newspapers. In 1965, 11 Texas-based chains owned 59 of the 114 daily newspapers, and 3 Texas dailies were owned by out-of-state chains. The growth of multiple ownership can be attributed largely to efforts to cope with the economic problems of newspaper publishing and to the need for suburban dailies in the large metropolitan areas. The largest chain in the state was Harte–Hanks Newspapers (later Harte–Hanks Communications), which owned 13 daily newspapers in Abilene, Big Spring, Corpus Christi, Denison, Greenville, Marshall, Paris, San Angelo, and San Antonio. By 1994, Harte–Hanks owned only 5 dailies and 6 weeklies in the state.

In the 10 years after 1965 the major trends noted for the previous 15 years continued. Daily newspapers increased by 4, to 118, only 27 of which were morning papers. In number of newspapers Texas moved to second state in the nation. Fifty-five dailies used offset printing by 1974, the two largest being the *Wall Street Journal* (Southwest edition) and the Beaumont *Enterprise*. There were 565 weekly newspapers in the state in 1975, 17 of which were published by African Americans. The black papers had circulations ranging from 2,000 to 40,000. By 1994, the number of African-American publications had declined to 11, with circulations ranging from 2,000 to 80,000. Two of the largest were the Dallas *Examiner* and the Houston *Sun*. In 1994 overall, Texas supported 83 daily newspapers, 75 semiweeklies, and 425 weeklies.

In 1994 the functioning newspapers that were founded before the end of the Civil War were the Galveston *News* (founded in 1842), the Bay City *Daily–Tribune* (originally Bay City *Tribune*, 1848), the Seguin *Gazette–Enterprise* (originally the Seguin *Gazette*, 1846), the Victoria *Advocate* (1846), the Rusk *Cherokeean–Herald* (originally the Rusk *Cherokeean*, 1847), the Gladewater *Mirror* (1849), the Huntsville *Item* (1850), the New Braunfels *Herald–Zeitung* (originally the *Neu Braunfelser Zeitung*, 1852), the Bastrop *Advertiser* (1853), the Gonzales *Inquirer* (1853), the *Colorado County Citizen* (1857), the Cameron *Herald* (1860), the Jasper *News-Boy* (1865), the Jefferson *Jimplecute* (1865), and the San Antonio *Express–News* (originally the San Antonio *Express*, 1865).

Louise C. Allen, Ernest A. Sharpe, and John R. Whitaker

Ney, Elisabet. Sculptor; b. Münster, Westphalia, 26 January 1833; d. Austin, 29 June 1907; m. Edmund D. Montgomery (1863); 2 sons; ed. Munich Academy of Art (grad. 1854). After her formal education, Ney studied with Christian Daniel Rauch and developed a classical style in the German tradition, with a tendency toward realism and a faithfulness to accurate scale. Through Rauch she also became acquainted with Berlin's artistic and intellectual elite and sculpted her first works, among them portraits of such luminaries as Jacob Grimm and Alexander von Humboldt. During the late 1850s and 1860s she traveled around Europe to complete portraits of intellectual and political leaders. Among her best-known works from this period are portrait busts of Schopenhauer, Garibaldi, and Bismarck and a full-length statue of King Ludwig II of Bavaria. With her husband, a Scottish physician and scientist, she settled briefly in

Elisabet Ney in her studio with her bust of William Jennings Bryan, Austin, 1900. Prints and Photographs Collection, Elisabet Ney file, CAH; CN 02910. When Ney found out that Bryan was going to visit Austin, she contacted Governor Hogg, his host, and requested that Bryan pose for her.

Thomasville, Georgia (1871). In 1872 the family moved to Texas and purchased Liendo Plantation in Waller County. For much of the next 20 years, Ney managed the plantation while Montgomery busied himself with his scientific work. After visiting Austin at the invitation of Governor Oran Roberts in the 1880s, Ney built a studio (now the Elisabet Ney Museum) in the Hyde Park area of Austin (1892) and began lobbying notable citizens and the state legislature for commissions. During the next 15 years she completed a number of portrait busts as well as statues of Stephen F. Austin and Sam Houston, now in the state Capitol, and a memorial to Albert Sidney Johnston, in the State Cemetery. Copies of the Austin and Houston statues are also in the United States Capitol. One of her few ideal pieces, a depiction of Shakespeare's Lady Macbeth, was also a major project during her Austin years; the marble is now displayed in the Smithsonian's National Museum of American Art. Four years after her death, her supporters founded the Texas Fine Arts Association in her honor. *Emily F. Cutrer*

Nimitz, Chester William. Navy officer; b. Fredericksburg, 24 February 1885; d California, 20 February 1966 (buried in Golden Gate National Cemetery, San Bruno, California); m. Catherine Vance Freeman (1913); 4 children; ed. United States Naval Academy (grad. 1905). After two years on the U.S.S. *Ohio*, Nimitz was commissioned an ensign and given command of the old Spanish gunboat *Panay* in the Philippines. After transfer to the destroyer *Decatur*, he ran the ship aground and was court-martialed, reprimanded, and assigned to a submarine. In four consecutive undersea commands, he became a leading "pigboat" authority. After study of Diesel engines in Germany and Belgium, he went to Brooklyn Navy Yard to supervise the building and installation of the first diesel engine to power a United States Navy vessel. With the rank of commander in World War I, he served as chief of staff to Adm. Samuel S. Robison, commander of the Atlantic Submarine Force, then as executive officer of the battleship *South Carolina*. Afterward, Nimitz went to Pearl Harbor to build the submarine base and command the Submarine Division. At the Navy War College, 1922–23, he dealt with a theoretical Pacific war. He was assigned to the University of California at Berkeley in 1926 to develop the prototype for the Naval Reserve Officers Training Corps; his model was duplicated in 52 colleges. Nimitz left Berkeley with the rank of captain in 1929 and progressed through commands of a submarine division, the San Diego destroyer base, and the cruiser *Augusta*, flagship of the Asiatic Fleet. After service in Washington as assistant chief of the navy Bureau of Navigation and promotion to rear admiral, he commanded first a cruiser division, then a battleship division.

In 1939 he became chief of the Bureau of Navigation. In the aftermath of the attack on Pearl Harbor (7 December 1941), Nimitz replaced Adm. Husband E. Kimmel as commander in chief of the Pacific Fleet. He focused not on American mistakes that led to the attack, but on the enemy's mistakes. With James H. Doolittle's carrier-based raid on Japanese cities in April 1942 and victories in the Coral Sea and at Midway Island, Allied forces seized the initiative. Nimitz was named commander in chief of Pacific Ocean Areas, in addition to his Pacific Fleet command. With authority over the entire Pacific theater except for Gen. Douglas MacArthur's Southwest Pacific sector and the inactive southeast, Nimitz coordinated the offensive that brought the Japanese to unconditional surrender. He signed the peace treaty for the United States aboard the battleship *Missouri* in Tokyo Bay (2 September 1945). He was much decorated by foreign governments and was awarded both the army and navy Distinguished Service medals of the United States. On 15 December 1945, Nimitz succeeded Adm. Ernest J. King as commander in chief of the United States Fleet. He withdrew after two years. Never officially retired, he was assigned to "duty as directed by the

Secretary of the Navy." He served the United Nations as roving ambassador, was a regent of the University of California, and, by appointment of President Harry Truman, became chairman of the Presidential Commission on Internal Security and Individual Rights. After a severe fall in 1963, the admiral moved with Mrs. Nimitz from their home in Berkeley to naval quarters on Treasure Island in San Francisco Bay.   *Robert S. Weddle*

Ninetieth Division. The "Tough 'Ombres," "Texas' Own," or the "Alamo" division; activated at Camp Travis in August 1917 under command of Maj. Gen. Henry T. Allen. Texas and Oklahoma furnished the original division, although all states were later represented. The T-O insignia was adopted in France. In summer 1918 the division set up headquarters at Aignay-le-Duc and saw action in the Villers-en-Haye and Puvenelle sectors of Lorraine and in the St. Mihiel and Meuse–Argonne operations. Total casualties suffered were 310 officers and 9,400 enlisted men. After the armistice in November 1918, the division moved into Germany for occupation duty. It was sent home for demobilization in May 1919. During World War II the Ninetieth was reactivated at Camp Barkeley (1942). Motorized in September 1942, but again designated an infantry division in May 1943, the unit

Chester W. Nimitz accepting the Japanese surrender aboard the USS *Missouri*, Tokyo Bay, September 2, 1945. Olin Culberson Papers, CAH; CN 08127. As commander in chief of the Pacific Ocean Areas, Nimitz coordinated the offensive that compelled the Japanese to surrender on 14 August 1945.

saw action on D-Day (6 June) in Normandy. It participated in campaigns in Normandy, Northern France, the Ardennes, the Rhineland, and Central Europe. Tentative casualty figures compiled late in 1945 reported 2,963 killed, 14,009 wounded, 1,052 missing, and 442 captured. The division was on occupation duty in Germany until November 1945, then deactivated on 27 December at Camp Shanks, New York. It was reactivated at Dallas on 4 August 1947 as a part of the Organized Reserve Corps. With headquarters at Dodd Field, Fort Sam Houston, the Ninetieth Army Reserve Command is composed of approximately 9,000 reservists who in 1994 served in 110 units in 50 communities in Texas and New Mexico. The Ninetieth ARCOM soldiers, still known as the "Tough 'Ombres" or "Texas' Own," were not mobilized during the Vietnam War. They were used in civil affairs and psychological operations in Grenada and in postinvasion humanitarian-relief efforts in Panama. In 1990–91 they played a major role in the Persian Gulf, where 28 units with more than 2,500 soldiers were deployed to provide combat and service support to the Allied coalition. In 1994 the Ninetieth ARCOM was engaged in a comprehensive drug-demand-reduction program in Central America and in the construction of roads, schools, and water wells in Honduras, Guatemala, and Belize. Also in 1994 the unit planned and hosted a series of ceremonies commemorating the fiftieth anniversary of the Normandy invasion in France, culminating in 1995 in events recognizing the fiftieth anniversary of VE Day. *Dorman H. Winfrey*

Ninth United States Cavalry. One unit of the "Buffalo Soldiers." Post–Civil War army legislation (1866), designed in part to recognize service rendered the Union by black troops, provided for six regiments of black regulars, four of infantry and two of cavalry. One of the regiments was the Ninth Cavalry. Until the late 1880s all of the black regiments were commanded by white officers. Col. Edward Hatch was assigned command of the Ninth, and Wesley Merritt was appointed lieutenant colonel. Since cavalry was needed badly on the frontier, the Ninth was organized in great haste at Greenville, Louisiana. Officer procurement proceeded slowly, however, for many officers refused to serve with blacks. By contrast, the enlisted ranks were easily filled, though many of the recruits were as yet unfit for military service. In 1867 the regiment was ordered to Texas, although few officers had reported for duty and the enlisted men had not been properly trained and disciplined. On April 9 a mutiny occurred while 10 companies were undergoing additional training at San Antonio. It was put down with great difficulty, and when the regiment was ordered to stations on the frontier several weeks later, there were doubts regarding the soldierly qualities of the men and the future of the unit. The Ninth was one of only three cavalry regiments in the state. In cooperation with several infantry units, the cavalry was responsible for protecting and defending a vast region of West Texas, as well as hundreds of miles of Rio Grande frontier. It kept the vital San Antonio–El Paso road safe from Indian raiders, cattle thieves, and bandits. The Ninth soon removed doubts about the fighting qualities of its black troopers. With a full complement of officers and greater care in enlistment, training and discipline improved swiftly. Hatch established headquarters at Fort Davis, and companies of the Ninth operated out of stations including Fort Stockton, Fort Clark, Fort McKavett, and Fort Quitman. Constant patrols, pursuits, and frequent bloody clashes turned the Ninth into a tough,

hard-striking, and combat-wise regiment. In the spring of 1870 a member of the Ninth (Sgt. Emanuel Stance) won the unit's first Medal of Honor. In 1874, with the outbreak of the Red River Indian War, a battalion of the Ninth formed the backbone of one of five columns thrown into the field against hostile bands of Kiowas, Comanches, Southern Cheyennes, and Arapahoes. The column, organized at Fort Griffin under Lt. Col. George P. Buell of the Eleventh Infantry, conducted a relentless campaign of three months with little rest. The black troopers received high praise from Buell for their courage, durability, and cheerfulness under extremes of heat and cold and without adequate food and shelter. The Ninth was ordered to New Mexico in 1875 to fight in the seemingly endless Apache wars. In 1877 the unit made a final contribution to peace and order in Texas by bringing the Salt War of San Elizario to an end. In 1880 most of the regiment was ordered to Indian Territory to engage in the distasteful and unrewarding task of repelling Boomer invasions. Subsequently, the Ninth had a period of relative quiet, but at the close of the frontier period, a battalion of the regiment served against the Sioux hostiles after the catastrophe at Wounded Knee. Twenty-four years of continuous service in the American West had made the Ninth Cavalry one of the crack regiments in the United States Army. *William H. Leckie*

Nolan, Philip. Mustanger and filibuster; b., he claimed, in Belfast, Ireland, 1771; d. Texas, 21 March 1801; m. Frances Lintot (1799); 1 son. Through business association with Gen. James Wilkinson in Kentucky, Nolan learned of the opportunities for trade in Texas. In 1791 he secured from Governor Esteban Rodríguez Miró a passport to visit Texas on a trading expedition. His goods were confiscated, however, and after living with Indians for two years he returned to New Orleans with 50 mustangs. By 6 June 1794, Nolan was back in Nacogdoches with a passport from Louisiana governor Baron de Carondelet authorizing him to obtain horses for the Louisiana militia. He visited the provincial capital, San Antonio de Béxar, made the acquaintance of Governor Manuel Muñoz, and through him obtained permission of the commandant general of the Provincias Internas, Pedro de Nava, to export horses to Louisiana. He took 250 animals to Natchez by the end of 1795. He had gained information about the "unknown land" but not without making Spanish officials suspicious about his loyalties. He increased their suspicions by returning to Natchez from a mapping expedition up the Missouri River with the party of Andrew Ellicott, boundary commissioner for the United States. Nolan attempted to mollify Manuel Gayoso de Lemos, governor of Natchez, and went on to New Orleans, where he obtained another passport (1797) from Carondelet. Nolan made a will in which he named his father as heir, gave charge of his affairs to merchant Daniel Clark, and left for Texas, authorized to obtain more horses for the Louisiana regiment. This time he took a considerable load of trade goods, even though trade between Louisiana and Texas was strictly prohibited. He arrived at Bexar in October, presented his credentials, and claimed to have Carondelet's permission to go to Nuevo Santander in search of horses. Nava ordered Muñoz to assist Nolan in fulfilling his Louisiana contract and gave approval for the introduction of 2,000 pesos' worth of goods to defray expenses.

Meanwhile, Gayoso had written to the viceroy of Mexico, warning against foreigners (like Nolan) who were stirring up the Texas Indians against Spanish rule. Nava tried to justify his allowing Nolan to enter Texas but revoked the permission for him to trade. Thinking that Nolan had left the province in the summer of 1798, Nava was alarmed to find him still there almost a year later. Governor Muñoz, in bad health, defended Nolan vigorously and claimed that his delays were unavoidable. With Muñoz's support Nolan left Texas safely. He arrived in Natchez in the latter part of 1799 with more than 1,200 horses and soon became aware of Gayoso's hostility toward him. He intended to meet with Thomas Jefferson, who had written him concerning Texas and its herds of wild horses, but the meeting apparently never took place. Instead, Nolan was soon making plans for another trip to Texas, even though he could not obtain a passport and knew that it would be a dangerous undertaking. He left Natchez with a body of well-armed men in October 1800 and made his way to the area north of Nacogdoches. He then proceeded to a tributary of the Brazos River in the future McLennan or Hill County, where he built a small fortification with corrals and began catching mustangs. He was killed there by troops from Nacogdoches sent out to intercept him. His men were captured and tried, and spent years in prison for their part in Nolan's final expedition, the precise nature of which has not yet been satisfactorily explained. Nolan is recognized as the first of a long line of filibusters that eventually helped to free Texas from Spanish and Mexican rule. He is often credited with being the first Anglo-American to map Texas, but his map has never been found. His observations were passed on to General Wilkinson, however, who used them to produce a map of the Texas–Louisiana frontier around 1804. *Jack Jackson*

Nolan Expedition. The Nolan or so-called "Lost Nigger" expedition occurred in pursuit of marauding Indians whose theft of livestock may have been the last Comanche raid in Texas. The first group, 24 buffalo hunters led by James Harvey, started in May 1877. The second group, Capt. Nicholas Nolan and about 60 black troops of Company A, Tenth United States Cavalry, started from Fort Concho in July. The buffalo hunters had been searching for the Indians over the Llano Estacado for months when they met Nolan on Bull Creek in mid-July. The combined groups set up a supply base at Double Lakes, Lynn County. A party consisting of Nolan's men and some of the hunters began an unsuccessful pursuit of the Indians on 26 July, and when the Indian trails scattered the next day, the men abandoned the chase and started looking for water. The hunters found water on 28 July. Nolan and his men, however, went without water for 86 hours. His casualties were 4 men dead or missing, 25 horses, and 4 pack mules. Eastern newspapers reported that the expedition had been massacred. The buffalo hunters proceeded to the site of present Lubbock, where they found much of the stolen stock and learned that the Indians were returning to Indian Territory.

Norias Ranch Raid. Occurred during the "bandit wars" of 1912–15 on the Texas–Mexico border. At dusk on 8 August 1915 a band of Mexicans rode into the southern end of the sprawling King Ranch and attacked the Norias division headquarters, located on the railroad about 70 miles north of Brownsville. Earlier that afternoon, in response to a call from Caesar Kleberg at Kingsville concerning Mexican horsemen in the Sauz division, Texas Rangers and others, including cavalrymen stationed at Harlingen, arrived at Norias on a special train from Brownsville. They left the soldiers, then hurried by horseback to the Sauz pas-

ture. The regular train reached Norias near sundown with three customs inspectors and Cameron County deputy sheriff Gordon Hill. There were now 16 men at the headquarters. At dusk 50 to 70 Mexican horsemen attacked the ranchhouse. The defenders took cover outside. At nightfall, after two hours of fighting, the raiders suddenly stopped firing and vanished into the darkness. They had broken into the section house and killed Manuela Flores. Four defenders were wounded. Some five or more raiders were killed and perhaps a dozen wounded. A wounded bandit said later that they expected to find only three or four cowboys at the headquarters. They planned to rob the ranch store, derail and loot the night train, and burn the house. The Norias raid provoked outrage in the lower Rio Grande valley. Mexican banditry escalated, and the United States Army promptly increased its presence in the area to curb the violence. *Alicia A. Garza*

Norris, J. Frank. Baptist preacher; b. John Franklin Norris, Dadeville, Alabama, 18 September 1877; d. Jacksonville, Florida, 20 August 1952; ed. Baylor University (1898–1903) and Southern Baptist Theological Seminary, Louisville, Kentucky (M. Theol., 1905). In 1909 J. Frank Norris accepted the pastorate of the First Baptist Church of Fort Worth, a position he held for 44 years. He was involved in numerous social and civic reform activities, including prohibition and gambling reform. He established a ministry to servicemen stationed at Camp Bowie during World War I. He began the first regular radio ministry in the United States in the 1920s and openly supported the Ku Klux Klan. He preached to crowds that numbered up to 10,000 and was pastor of Temple Baptist Church in Detroit and First Baptist in Fort Worth simultaneously in the 1930s—flying back and forth when air travel was in its infancy. When his church was destroyed by fire in 1912, Norris was charged with arson but acquitted. By 1920 he had rebuilt his facilities to include a 5,000-seat auditorium, a gymnasium, and a swimming pool. The revolving electrical sign and the spotlight mounted on the church roof became trademarks of his style. During the 1920s he became the leader of the fundamentalist movement in Texas by attacking the alleged teaching of evolution at Baylor University. As a result, he and his Fort Worth church were denied seats at the annual meeting of the Baptist General Convention of Texas in 1922 and 1923. In 1926, during the height of a controversy involving Norris, Mayor H. C. Meacham, and anti-Catholicism, Norris shot and killed D. C. Chipps, one of Meacham's friends. Norris was indicted for murder on July 29 and acquitted on grounds of self-defense. During 1928, Norris vigorously campaigned against the election of the Catholic Al Smith to the presidency. His anti-Catholic views, voiced from the pulpit, his radio station, and his weekly newspaper, led the Republican party to honor him for his role in defeating Smith. In January 1929 his church burned again and had to be rebuilt during the height of the Great Depression. The new facilities, occupied in 1932, bore little resemblance to the grander edifice of the 1920s. In the late 1930s, Norris organized the World Missionary Baptist Fellowship, a group of independent, premillennialist Baptist churches, to combat socialist, liberal, and "modernist" tendencies in the Southern Baptist Convention. In 1939 he began urging the United States to support and assist her European allies. After the war, when John Birch, a graduate of his seminary in Fort Worth, was killed by the Chinese communists, Norris launched a renewed attack on Communist influences within the United States. His premillennialist views led him to urge President Harry Truman to recognize and support the new state of Israel. Dissension among his leadership led to a major division in his organization in 1950. This split resulted in the formation of a rival group led by his former assistant, Beauchamp Vick, based in Springfield, Missouri. Norris and his group continued to operate from Fort Worth.

C. Gwin Morris

Norwegians. Most Norwegians who came to Texas were from the rural areas of Norway and became farmers in their new homeland. Norwegian settlement in Texas was never as large as that of several other European groups, the census of 1860 listing only 326 persons of Norwegian birth then in Texas. Those Norwegians who did come were seeking economic and social betterment. The first known settler, Johannes Nordboe, was in his seventies when he came to Texas to live with his wife and three sons on a farm a short distance from Dallas in 1841. In 1845 Johan Reinert Reiersen had land for his colony surveyed several miles west of the Neches River in Henderson County. Another group of settlers became part of a small settlement started in Van Zandt, Cherokee, and Kaufman counties between 1846 and 1853. The 1850 United States census listed 105 Norwegian-born persons living in Texas. Cleng Peerson, who had corresponded with Johannes Nordboe, came to Texas with Ole Canuteson and Carl Engebretson Quaestad. The three scouted along the Bosque River, and in 1854, when Bosque County was established, they led the first Norwegian settlers into the area. Among the first settlers were Hendric Dahl and Jens Ringness. Ole Ringness, the son of Jens Ringness, invented the disc plow. Immigration to Texas, particularly to the settlement of Norse, continued until 1872, and old-world customs were maintained until the early years of the twentieth century. The census of 1900 reported 1,356 Norwegianborn persons in Texas; that of 1940 listed 1,169. By 1940, however, the language had all but disappeared, and descendants of the original pioneers had been integrated into the fabric of Texas rural life. Some of the architecture of the Bosque County area showed European influence, and names on mailboxes were still largely Norwegian. An old-world custom that remained in 1970 was the annual smorgasbord held at Our Savior's Lutheran Church, near old Norse in Bosque County. In 1975 the Norwegian Society of Texas was formed to preserve the group's cultural and ethnic heritage. In the 1990 census 94,096 Texans claimed Norwegian ancestry.

W. Phil Hewitt

Nueces River. A stream rich in history; rises in two forks in Edwards and Real counties and runs generally southeast for 315 miles to Nueces Bay. The East Prong forms part of the Real–Edwards county line, then flows through a canyon of remarkable beauty paralleling Ranch Road 335 before joining the West Fork in Uvalde County. The major tributary of the Nueces, the combined Frio and Atascosa rivers, joins the stream near Three Rivers. The Nueces then forms the line between Jim Wells and San Patricio and San Patricio and Nueces counties. Corpus Christi, at the mouth of the Nueces, is the only large city on the stream. Uvalde is the second largest. Major impoundments in the Nueces watershed include Choke Canyon Reservoir and Lake Corpus Christi. The Nueces, the first Texas river to be given a prominent place on European maps, is the Río Escondido ("Hidden River"—i.e., hidden behind its barrier island) that first

appeared on a 1527 map attributed to Diogo Ribeiro. It was to this river that La Salle—confused by inadequate maps—sailed in 1685, believing that it was the Mississippi. Four years later Alonso De León, marching from Coahuila to find La Salle's settlement, crossed the Nueces in what is now Dimmit or Zavala County and named it Río de las Nueces ("River of Nuts") for the pecan trees growing along its banks. In 1691, Domingo Terán de los Ríos acknowledged De León's name for the river, yet gave it a different one—San Diego. Fray Damián Massanet, on the same expedition, called it San Norberto, for having arrived there on St. Norbert's day. In January 1707, Martín de Alarcón, serving his first term as governor of Coahuila, perceived the Nueces as a tributary of the Rio Grande. He planned an expedition to reach the Frio River by descending the Rio Grande to the Nueces mouth and ascending the Nueces. Such a voyage was never attempted, yet Alarcón's erroneous concept endured until 1747. In March 1707, Alarcón sent Capt. Diego Ramón of San Juan Bautista presidio to the Nueces to punish raiding Indians and recruit natives for the missions. Ramón traced out the rivercourse in what is now Dimmit and La Salle counties and fought the hostiles at two locations. Still, while the stream was often crossed in this sector, its connection with the river whose mouth remained hidden away in Nueces Bay was not recognized. The 1747 exploration related to the founding of the Nuevo Santander colony established the link. Capt. Joaquín de Orobio y Basterra, exploring between the San Antonio River and the Rio Grande, reached the lower Nueces and recognized it as an extension of the river crossed farther upstream by the Old San Antonio Road. He gave the name San Miguel Arcángel to the bay system (Nueces and Corpus Christi bays) into which the river empties. The Nueces thereafter became the boundary between the provinces of Texas and Nuevo Santander. A Spanish villa was planned near the mouth, now part of a new colony. Villa de Vedoya, had it become a reality, would have been the first European settlement on the river; but it died aborning, the victim of poor planning and long supply lines. More than a dozen years later, the first Nueces River settlements came into being far upstream, in the rocky canyon of the future Real and Uvalde counties. These were the "El Cañón" missions, San Lorenzo de la Santa Cruz and Nuestra Señora de la Candelaria, founded in 1762 as successors to the failed Apache mission of Santa Cruz de San Sabá. Early in the nineteenth century, a private fort, Ramírez, was built on the south bank of the Nueces in what is now southern Live Oak County, probably on a family land grant from the king of Spain. After 1821 the Mexican government made numerous grants in the Trans-Nueces, reaching to the river itself. In 1830 the Mexican government built Fort Lipantitlán on the Nueces near San Patricio. It served the Republic of Texas for defense against the Mexican invasions of 1842. Later, two frontier posts of the United States Army were built on the right bank, Fort Merrill (1850) and Fort Ewell (1852). The beginnings of Corpus Christi had been made with an 1832 trading post, which got a boost from the arrival of Gen. Zachary Taylor's army in 1845. From the Texas Revolution to the end of the Mexican War, the Trans-Nueces had been disputed territory. Establishment of the international boundary at the Rio Grande by the 1848 Treaty of Guadalupe Hidalgo proved to be a key to development. Still, years of struggle remained before the Nueces Strip—the region between the Nueces and the Rio Grande—was tamed.

The Nueces today flows through a rural region of diverse agriculture. After rising in the Edwards Plateau, noted for wool and mohair production, it descends through the Winter Garden Region. Much of its course lies through the Brush Country, where such species as mesquite and prickly pear—the legacy of over-grazing—have presented a challenge to taming the land. Gradually, the tangled growth has yielded in some areas to modern technology, and diversified farming and ranching enterprises have developed. Every county along the Nueces course except Kinney and Real claims significant mineral production. This consists largely of oil and gas, but Uvalde County is noted for asphalt and stone. The upper Nueces watershed, embracing the Tricanyon area of the Nueces, Frio, and Sabinal rivers, is notable for its scenic beauty and appeal to outdoorsmen, especially for deer and turkey hunting and fishing. It is a favored area also for hiking, camping, and nature study, especially around Lost Maples State Natural Area and Garner State Park. Of importance for water sports are the two lakes, Choke Canyon and Corpus Christi, each with its state park. At the Nueces mouth, Corpus Christi is recognized as a major resort area, especially for fishing and water sports. Mustang Island State Park, on the barrier island enclosing Corpus Christi Bay, is also the gateway to Padre Island National Seashore. Served by the Gulf Intracoastal Waterway, the port of Corpus Christi, which exists because of the Nueces River, is second only to Houston among Texas ports.
Robert S. Weddle

Nuecestown Raid of 1875. Also known as the Corpus Christi raid. between 1871 and 1875 the raiding of South Texas ranches by Mexicans reached a climax. Richard King's ranch was raided twice in the spring of 1875. Some Mexican Texans worked in collusion with the raiders or were intimidated by them. There was a lucrative trade in stolen cattle and horses in Mexico. Skinning wars or "hide-peeling" incidents were also common at the time. In the case of the Nuecestown raid, however, cattle theft was apparently not the raiders' goal. Juan N. Cortina was probably an instigator of the raid, if not actually involved. The Mexican raiders concentrated their efforts on Nuecestown and the surrounding area, but other areas between Nuecestown (in Nueces County) and the Rio Grande were also hit. In late March 1875 a number of men left Mexico in small groups and met about 20 miles from where the raid began. They were joined by others with fresh horses. The raiders subsequently attacked homes, killed men who fought back, took hostages, and looted. When word of the raid reached Corpus Christi, two companies formed to pursue the raiders, one led by Nueces county sheriff John McClane and the other by Pat Whelen. The latter group of 10 caught up with the raiders (who numbered about 35) and attacked them. One of Whelen's men, John Swanks, was shot and killed, and the Anglos retreated when they ran out of ammunition. Subsequently the raiders released the male prisoners. McClane's posse caught a wounded raider, who was lynched a few days later. The Mexican raiders sent two escorted wagons of plunder ahead. Though this should have slowed them down, neither posse made further contact. The raiders passed through Piedras Pintas, shooting and killing a man for his horse. On 2 April they surrounded the town of Roma in Starr County with the intent to rob the customhouse but were stopped by United States troops. It appears also that several people were killed by

the same bandits in Hidalgo County and Laredo. Once back in Mexico, some of the raiders were identified, and Mexican authorities arrested them, but Cortina was able to assist them in avoiding trial.

Anglo residents of South Texas retaliated indiscriminately. Bands of volunteers organized "minute companies" in every county from the Nueces to the Rio Grande. They proceeded to hunt down Mexican outlaws, peaceful rancheros, and merchants; the avengers looted property and burned homes. Since saddles were among the goods stolen by the raiders, Mexicans seen with new saddles were killed. Retaliation extended outside of the immediate geographical area, as well. In Encinal County at La Parra, the jacals of squatter Mexicans were burned. The avengers also killed all the adult males at the Mexican-owned La Atravesada Ranch in what is now Kenedy County. Similar incidents occurred at El Penascal, Corral de Piedra, and El Mesquite. Stores at La Atravesada and El Penascal were also burned down. After the devastation, Mexican rancheros in the area fled in fear for their lives. According to the Corpus Christi *Gazette*, "good Mexicans" were afraid to travel to Corpus Christi. Sheriff McClane requested the assistance of the Texas Rangers, who thereafter disbanded the companies and reported that the acts committed by "Americans" were "horrible." While the Texas Rangers prevented the "minute companies" from further acts of violence, raids and atrocities from across the Rio Grande continued, as often as not against Hispanic Texans.
Cynthia E. Orozco

Nueva Estremadura. Another name for Coahuila, used as early as 1602, when three priests from Zacatecas were assigned to a Saltillo convent. They traveled 25 leagues inland, to a valley abundantly supplied with water. After seeing the pastures and realizing the possibility for the raising of sheep for wool, the priests named the place for the western region of Spain that borders Portugal. The new province was north of the New Kingdom of León, east of Nueva Vizcaya (Chihuahua), and west of the Río Bravo (Rio Grande). Through the center of the province ran the Río de los Conchos. A map in Henderson K. Yoakum's *History of Texas* shows Coquila (Coahuila) or Nueva Estremadura lying below the Medina River and the New Philippines (Texas).

Nueva Vizcaya. The first province of northern Mexico to be explored and settled by the Spanish, the heartland of the northern frontier for some 250 years. In the early years of settlement the name referred to the area north of Zacatecas. The province eventually included most of the modern Mexican states of Chihuahua and Durango, and, at different times, parts of Sinaloa, Sonora, and Coahuila. The area was initially explored by Nuño de Guzmán in 1531, José de Angulo in 1533, and Ginés Vázquez de Mercado in 1552. Francisco de Ibarra explored the region in 1554, and mining and missionary activities began soon thereafter. In 1562, Ibarra was appointed to colonize the region, then regarded as the northernmost part of the province of Nueva Galicia. Ibarra began to establish settlements and organized the region as Nueva Vizcaya, named for his home province of Vizcaya, Spain. The capital of the province, Durango, was similarly named for Ibarra's birthplace. Over the course of the next 250 years, exploratory expeditions and missionary efforts launched from Nueva Vizcaya settled New Mexico, founded

Parras and Saltillo, and helped to develop Sonora and Sinaloa. Nueva Vizcaya remained a separate province after the Mexican War of Independence but was divided into the states of Chihuahua and Durango in 1824.   *Mark Odintz*

Nuevo Santander. A Spanish province that comprised the present Mexican state of Tamaulipas and part of Texas; founded by José de Escandón and named for his native province in Spain. After designation as a province by viceregal order in 1746, the region was explored the following year under Escandón's personal leadership. With actual settlement begun late in 1748, it was the last part of northeastern Mexico to be conquered and effectively occupied. Despite the lateness of its beginning, the Nuevo Santander population reached 30,000 by the end of the century. The colony, initially called Colonia de la Costa del Seno Mexicano ("Gulf Coast Colony"), grew from a series of proposals by Nuevo León governors and others for controlling the hostile Indians who took refuge in the coastal jungle and adjacent mountains. For more than two centuries the territory had been held by "*indios bárbaros.*" These natives, many of whom had suffered at Spanish hands, had resisted the inroads of Christianity and civilization. Not only had they denied Spain the economic benefits of ports, salt deposits, and agricultural lands, but they had forced travelers between Mexico City and La Bahía, on the Guadalupe River in Texas, to take a route twice the shortest distance. The original plan of conquest put forth by the Marqués de Altamira, *auditor de guerra* of the New Spain viceroyalty, called for colonizing both sides of the Rio Grande. The San Antonio River was to be the northern boundary. La Bahía Presidio and Nuestra Señora del Espíritu Santo de Zúñiga Mission were to be moved from the Guadalupe River to Santa Dorotea (the site of present-day Goliad) to serve as the colony's northern anchor. To link Nuevo Santander with the Province of Texas, two civilian settlements were planned: Villa de Balmaceda on the San Antonio and Villa de Vedoya near the mouth of the Nueces River. Before the coastal route could be proved, however, Vedoya's settlers despaired and went elsewhere. Neither Vedoya nor Balmaceda became a reality. Although the mission and presidio were moved in 1749 from the Guadalupe to Santa Dorotea, they remained in the Texas jurisdiction. The Nueces River, rather than the San Antonio, became Nuevo Santander's northern boundary.

From 1748 to 1755 two dozen settlements were made within the colony, most of them below the Rio Grande. Two were in the area of the present state of Texas: Laredo and an impermanent village of 13 families called Nuestra Señora de los Dolores, farther down the Rio Grande. Other towns extended along the right bank of the river toward its mouth. Stockmen from these settlements gradually pushed their herds beyond the river, defying hostile Indians, water scarcity, and great distances to utilize the extensive grasslands. Yet this region received little official attention. José Tienda de Cuervo, visiting the colony as the head of an inspection commission in 1757, interrogated colonists to compile a description of each settlement but barely ventured beyond the Rio Grande. A decade later, the Ortiz Parrilla Gulf Coast expedition explored and mapped the Texas coast below the Nueces, revealing a dearth of knowledge of the entire littoral. At the time, Blas María de la Garza Falcón of Camargo maintained Santa Petronila Ranch "five leagues" south of Corpus Christi Bay. Following the 1786 coastal reconnaissance by José Antonio de Evia, the Nuevo Santander governor proposed separation of the Texas portion of Nuevo Santander to form a new province. Manuel de Escandón, who had succeeded to his father's office and titles, envisioned new settlements at the mouths of the Rio Grande and the Nueces River, opening a river-borne trade to serve the interior. Because of the distance between the proposed new sites, Escandón thought it necessary to separate the area north of the Rio Grande from Nuevo Santander. He believed that such a move would bring about maritime commerce serving these and other northern provinces of New Spain, bring new settlers to the region, and form a link between Nuevo Santander and Texas. Thus, an alternative would be provided to the long overland trail from Mexico. Consideration of the matter, which might have been a step forward for both Nuevo Santander and Texas, was stalled by the death of Viceroy Bernardo de Gálvez. When Félix María Calleja inspected the province in 1795, he took note of the "almost nonexistent" commerce. He viewed the solution much as had Manuel de Escandón: the opening of ports on the Gulf. From Tampico to the Nueces River, he noted, the ports, bays, and river mouths were undeveloped and useless. Even so, the population had passed 30,000.

A frontier ranching province, Nuevo Santander was both more populous and more opulent than the neighboring province of Texas. At this point it had one "city," 25 *villas*, 3 mining districts, 17 haciendas, 437 *ranchos*, and 8 missions. Through a Nuevo Santander blacksmith named José Bernardo Gutiérrez de Lara and its governor Joaquín de Arredondo, the colony extended to Texas its involvement in the Mexican War of Independence. From 1836 to 1845 the part of the colony above the Rio Grande was the focus of a border dispute between Mexico and the Republic of Texas. Upon the annexation of Texas, the dispute erupted into the Mexican War. With resolution of the conflict, Mexican inhabitants of the "Nueces Strip" found themselves living in occupied territory and subject to a strange government and customs they did not readily understand. These displaced persons and their descendants have given the region an enduring cultural legacy.   *Robert S. Weddle*

O.P.Q. Letters. Two letters, dated 28 January and 8 February 1834, intended to incite the colonists in Texas to rise in protest against the imprisonment of Stephen F. Austin in Mexico. They were written anonymously by Anthony Butler, who, as minister of the United States, was trying to buy Texas and believed that insurrection might induce Mexico to sell. The first was addressed to "Don B. T. A."—Branch T. Archer. The second may have been directed to the same address. Both were signed "O. P. Q." Copies were given to Col. Juan N. Almonte, who visited Texas on an inspection trip in the summer of 1834, and he translated and forwarded them to the government. The originals and English copies have disappeared. The letters characterized Austin's arrest as a cowardly act of "an ignorant, fanatical and arrogant race" and described Almonte's mission as a cynical attempt to placate the Anglo settlers in Texas. Despite their shrill tone and the worsening political climate, however, the letters apparently caused little excitement in Texas, largely because leading colonists distrusted Butler and because Austin had written letters urging the colonists to remain tranquil. Although initially skeptical, Almonte became convinced that Butler was the author of the letters and suspected that he might be acting on secret instructions from the United States government. In July Almonte wrote to the secretary of foreign relations in Mexico City recommending that his government request Butler's recall. Mexican authorities, however, failed to take action. Butler was not recalled until the following year, and then only because of President Andrew Jackson's displeasure with his handling of affairs.

Eugene C. Barker

Oblate School of Theology. In San Antonio; founded in 1903 as the San Antonio Philosophical and Theological Seminary by the Oblates of Mary Immaculate, a Catholic missionary congregation of men, at the urging of the bishop of San Antonio. The seminary's purpose was to prepare the candidates of the Oblate missionaries, as well as those from the Diocese of San Antonio and certain other dioceses in the southwestern United States and Mexico, for service as bilingual ministers. From the beginning the students have come from various national backgrounds. With the establishment of the Southern United States Province of the Oblates in 1904, the school became the responsibility of the new province, whose members at that time served in South Texas and Mexico. In 1905 the teaching of the preparatory levels was added, and this new department was known as St. Anthony's College and Apostolic School (the present St. Anthony High School Seminary). In 1911 the Diocese of San Antonio arranged for the training of its students elsewhere. Since the number of Oblate students continued to increase at all levels, in 1920 the school site was given over exclusively to the preparatory department (i.e., the minor seminary). The original school for philosophical and theological studies (major seminary, or scholasticate) was moved to Castroville, a few miles outside San Antonio, where, under the name Sacred Heart Scholasticate, it occupied the former convent of the Sisters of Divine Providence. By this time the Oblates who graduated from the school were ministering throughout Texas, in northeastern New Mexico, and in parts

of Louisiana. The Mexican Revolution had forced their withdrawal from that field several years earlier, but they soon expanded their work into Southern California. Larger facilities were again needed for the school, and in 1927 it was moved to a new campus a few miles north of San Antonio and renamed De Mazenod Scholasticate, in honor of Bishop Charles Eugene de Mazenod, founder of the Oblates (1816). The school has remained at this site, now well within the city limits, as buildings have been enlarged and added. In 1943 Mexico once again became a missionary field for its graduates.

The undergraduate department was affiliated with the Catholic University of America in 1947. The school was chartered by the state of Texas in 1950 to grant academic degrees, and a B.A. in philosophy was instituted in 1951. In 1962, as a result of an agreement with Our Lady of the Snows Scholasticate (an Oblate seminary in Mississippi), the philosophy program in San Antonio began to be phased out. In return, De Mazenod Scholasticate received the candidates from the Southern, Central, and Western United States Provinces of the Oblates into its master of divinity program (the first professional degree in ministry). Later that year the school was renamed Oblate College of the Southwest. In 1968 a new charter was approved, a board of trustees was instituted, and the school was granted accreditation by the Southern Association of Colleges and Schools. The late 1960s and the 1970s saw profound changes in the life of the school, mirroring those occurring in church and society. The number of candidates for the Oblate priesthood began to decline, and the other Oblate provinces gradually withdrew their students. The Oblate presbyteral candidates at the school dropped from 54 in 1967 to 15 in 1972. Assumption Seminary in San Antonio, established for the education of priest candidates from several Southwestern dioceses, was experiencing similar difficulties. Consequently, Oblate College and Assumption entered into a collaborative arrangement in 1970, by which the diocesan candidates receive their theological and pastoral training at Oblate, while continuing to reside at and receive their personal and spiritual formation at Assumption. By fall 1972 the diocesan students constituted half of the 42 presbyteral candidates at Oblate College. That same fall Catholic religious congregations of men began entering into the same collaborative arrangement for their own candidates. In 1970 the first students from Catholic religious congregations of women had been accepted into the school for coursework. Their numbers increased, and they were soon joined by laity. In 1976, to provide graduate theological studies to persons already in ministry, the master of theological studies was instituted; enrollment in this program steadily increased. To reflect more clearly the institution's evolving status, its name was changed to Oblate School of Theology in 1981. The school's degree programs were accredited by the Association of Theological Schools in 1982. During the 1980s new nondegree programs were developed for the ministerial and theological renewal of priests and religious sisters and the solid preparation of laity for ministry. All of these factors contributed to a gradual, if somewhat fitful, increase in enroll-

"Pappy" O'Daniel campaigning for governor, 1938. Photograph by Jimmie Dodd. Jimmie A. Dodd Photograph Collection, CAH; CN 08129. In 1938 W. Lee O'Daniel, unknown in politics and not registered to vote, entered the governor's race late and beat 12 opponents. His campaign featured the Hillbilly Boys musical group and a platform supporting the Ten Commandments, mother love, state pensions for oldsters, and abolition of the poll tax.

ment. The school's library is especially notable for its extensive collection of Catholic theological journals.

Robert E. Wright, O.M.I.

O'Daniel, Wilbert Lee. Known as "Pappy" O'Daniel; Texas governor and United States senator; b. Malta, Ohio, 11 March 1890; d. Dallas, 12 May 1969 (buried in Hillcrest Memorial Park); m. Merle Estella Butcher (1917); 3 children. O'Daniel worked in a flour mill as a youth. He moved to Kansas City in 1919 and to New Orleans in 1921. In 1925 he moved to Fort Worth, where he became sales manager of Burrus Mills. He took over the company's radio advertising in 1928 and began writing songs and discussing religious subjects on the air. He hired a group of musicians and called them the Light Crust Doughboys. O'Daniel served as president of the Fort Worth Chamber of Commerce in 1933–34. He organized his own flour company in 1935. At the behest of radio fans, he ran for governor in 1938. During the campaign he stressed the Ten Commandments, the virtues of his own Hillbilly Flour, and the need for old-age pensions, tax cuts, and industrialization. Under the direction of public-relations men, accompanied by his band, the Hillbilly Boys, and carrying the Bible, he attracted huge audiences. In the primary he smashed the other candidates and eliminated the usual necessity of a runoff. He had pledged to block any sales tax, abolish capital punishment, liquidate the poll tax (which he had not paid), and raise old-age pensions, but he reneged on all these promises. He unveiled a tax plan that amounted to a multiple sales tax, but the legislature voted it down. Solons laughed at the vaudevillian atmosphere of the O'Daniel administration, but most of his legislative opponents were defeated for reelection. O'Daniel won again in 1940, after divulging that he had wired President Franklin Roosevelt that he had confidential information about a fifth column in Texas. No one ever found the traitors. The governor and several Texas business leaders began attacking orga-

nized labor in the spring of 1941, but most of the provisions of the ensuing O'Daniel Anti-Violence Act were eventually discarded by the courts. O'Daniel began packing the University of Texas Board of Regents with members who eventually contributed to firing UT president Homer Price Rainey. As governor, O'Daniel was unable to engage in normal political deal-making with legislators, vetoed bills that he probably did not understand, and was overridden in 12 out of 57 vetoes—a record. But he was able largely to negate his political handicaps with masterful radio showmanship.

O'Daniel ran for the Senate in a special election in 1941 and edged his leading opponent, New Deal congressman Lyndon Johnson, in a flurry of controversial late returns. After taking office in August, O'Daniel introduced a number of antiunion bills, all of which were defeated. In running for reelection the next year, he faced former governors James Allred and Dan Moody. He charged that there was a conspiracy among Moody, Allred, the professional politicians, the politically controlled newspapers, and the "communistic labor leader racketeers" to smear and defeat him. O'Daniel won barely. During the war years he and Tom Connally supported the Republican–Southern Democratic coalition more often than any other Southern duo in the Senate. O'Daniel was the leading campaigner for the Texas Regulars, a third-party effort to siphon off enough Democratic votes in Texas in 1944 to deny Roosevelt a fourth term. With public opinion polls giving him only 7 percent support in 1948, O'Daniel announced that he would not run again since there was only slight hope of saving America from the communists. He bought a ranch near Fort Worth, invested in Dallas real estate, and founded an insurance company. He attempted comebacks in the Democratic gubernatorial primaries of 1956 and 1958. In the campaigns he ranted about blood running in the streets because of the "Communist-inspired" Supreme Court decision desegregating the nation's schools. He failed to make the runoff on both occasions, although in 1956 he carried 66 counties with almost 350,000 votes.

George N. Green

Odessa, Texas. Largest town and county seat of Ector County; the chief shipping point for the surrounding livestock area as well as a center for the oil and gas industry. Located in the heart of the vast oil-rich area known as the Permian Basin, it is 321 miles west of Fort Worth. Odessa traces its founding to the extension of the Texas and Pacific Railway across the South Plains in July 1881, and to a real estate promotion by the Odessa Land and Townsite Company. Odessa was a water stop on the railroad, supposedly named by railroad workers who thought the area resembled their home in Odessa, Russia. A post office opened in 1885 and the city was platted in 1886. Odessa became the county seat when Ector County was formally organized in January 1891. In 1927 it incorporated as a city. Odessa was a sleepy little cowtown until the first producing oil well in the county was brought in on the W. E. Connell ranch, about 16 miles southwest of town, on 28 December 1926. With the opening of Penn Field in 1929 and Cowden Field in 1930, Odessa became an established oil center and grew rapidly. In 1925, just prior to the discovery of oil, the population in Odessa was 750; by 1929 it had risen to 5,000. As the demand for oil grew during World War II the population exceeded 10,000, and Odessa became the world's largest inland petrochemical complex. In the 1950s and 1960s the population rose to over 80,000. The petrochemical complex began operations in 1957–58 as the nation's first privately financed, fully integrated plant for synthetic-rubber manufacture. The plant, a joint venture of El Paso Natural Gas Company and General Tire and Rubber Company, was designed to use waste products from gas and oil production to make the rubber. From this beginning Odessa developed as a major distribution and processing point in the petrochemical industry. The city's economy has long been subject to the boom and bust cycles of the oil patch, linked to fluctuations in world demand for petroleum products. Realizing that petroleum is a nonrenewable resource, Odessa's leadership has begun to look for other means of support for its economy. Efforts to aid in diversifying the economic base include the establishment of the Center for Energy and Economic Diversification by the University of Texas of the Permian Basin in 1990. Higher educational needs are served by Odessa College, a two-year community college founded in 1946 under the guidance of Murry Fly, and by UTPB, which began classes in 1973. Medical care is provided by Medical Center Hospital, a general hospital and teaching facility for Texas Tech Regional Academic Health Center residency programs; Women's and Children's Hospital, a medical facility handling obstetric, gynecologic, and pediatric patients; and the Permian Basin Rehabilitation Center for speech, hearing, and orthopedic therapy. In the 1990s the Odessa population was around 90,000. The municipal water supply comes from lakes on the Colorado River supplemented by wells in Ward and Ector counties. Odessa has a council–manager form of government, with a mayor and five councilmen. The annual Sand Hills Hereford and Quarter Horse Show and Rodeo is the first rodeo of the year for those following the rodeo circuit. Odessa is home to the only museum in the United States devoted exclusively to the office of the presidency (dedicated in 1965) and to an authentic replica of Shakespeare's Globe Theatre, the Globe of the Great Southwest, located on the Odessa College campus. Odessa boasts the world's largest jackrabbit, whose temporary home is in front of the Ector County ISD administration building; the Meteor Crater at Odessa, one of the nation's largest known craters; and the Odessa Chamber of Commerce Chuck Wagon Gang, founded in 1940, which serves as a goodwill ambassador for Odessa. The Permian Basin Oil Show is a biannual event staged at the Ector County Coliseum. Odessa's museums and theaters include the Permian Playhouse, the Art Institute for the Permian Basin, and the White–Pool House.

Bobbie Jean Klepper

Odin, Jean Marie. Catholic bishop; b. Hauteville, Ambierle parish, HauteLoire, France, 25 February 1800; d. Ambierle parish, 25 May 1870; ed. Seminary of St. Irenaeus at Lyon (Sulpician) and St. Mary of the Barrens Seminary (Vincentian), Perryville, Missouri. Odin responded to a plea for French missionaries to serve in the Diocese of Louisiana and the Floridas. After arriving at New Orleans in 1822 he was sent to Missouri to continue his preparation. He was ordained on 4 May 1823. In 1825 he joined the Congregation of the Mission (Vincentian Fathers). Between 1825 and 1840 he served the church in Missouri as a pastor, as professor of theology at the seminary at Perryville, and as a missionary. In order to rebuild the Catholic Church in Texas after its decline attendant upon the Texas Revolution, the Holy See established the Prefecture Apostolic of Texas and placed it under the care of the Vincentians (1839). The new apostolic prefect, Father John Timon, appointed Odin vice

prefect apostolic and charged him with the church's future in Texas. Odin and three fellow Vincentians, all Spaniards, arrived at Linnville on 12 July 1840. In December 1840 Pope Gregory XVI named Odin coadjutor bishop of Detroit, but Odin refused that honor. In 1841 the pope raised Texas to the status of a vicariate apostolic and made Odin vicar apostolic. He rebuilt the church with such success that in 1847 Pope Pius IX established the Diocese of Galveston, which encompassed all of Texas, and named Odin its first ordinary. In 1861 the Vatican nominated Odin to succeed Archbishop Anthony Blanc as archbishop of New Orleans. He died in the parish of his birth, after becoming ill at the First Vatican Council.

Patrick Foley

Oil and Gas Industry. After the Moscoso expedition was forced ashore between Sabine Pass and High Island in July 1543, the explorers observed oil floating on the surface of the water—the first oil sighted by Europeans in Texas. They collected the asphaltic substance and used it to caulk their vessels. Thereafter, settlers in Texas and visitors commonly observed seepages of crude oil. During his visit to Texas in 1854, Frederick Law Olmsted noted "a slight odor of sulphurreted hydrogen" at Sour Lake. The discovery and production of oil occurred sporadically during the second half of the nineteenth century. After the Civil War, encouraged by the growing national market for kerosene and other petroleum products, Lyne T. Barrett drilled and completed a well near Oil Springs in Nacogdoches County, but a decline in prices barred further financing of the venture. In 1886, George Dullnig, a Bexar County rancher, discovered a small quantity while drilling for water, but it was not sufficient to justify additional development. The first economically significant discovery came in 1894 in Navarro County near Corsicana. The Corsicana oilfield developed gradually and peaked in 1900, when it produced more than 839,000 barrels. The first relatively modern refinery in Texas, operated by the J. S. Cullinan Company, opened at the field in 1898. The major importance of the Corsicana field lay in establishing the potential for commercial oil production in Texas. Its success prompted random exploration in various parts of Navarro County, which led to the discovery of the Powell oilfield in 1900. This field rose to 673,221 barrels of oil a year in 1906 and peaked at 33,177,831 in 1924 after the Woodbine sand was found in January of the previous year.

Following the lead of Pennsylvania, the Texas legislature passed its first regulatory statute for oil in 1899, relating to the protection of groundwater, the abandonment of wells, and the conservation of natural gas. Subsequent legislation modified and expanded this statute. Beginning in the upper Gulf Coast area, drillers and producers attempted to establish field rules, relating primarily to fire prevention. According to one operator, "the constant danger of fire was a source of great anxiety." One of the most popular areas for exploration in the upper Gulf Coast was near Beaumont, where drilling began in 1892. Following three shallow failures, the Gladys City Oil, Gas, and Manufacturing Company hired Anthony F. Lucas, who supervised the drilling activity of the Hamill brothers of Corsicana and brought in the first well of the Spindletop oilfield on 10 January 1901. The well produced more than an estimated 75,000 barrels of oil a day.

The success of this prolific new field prompted additional exploration in the Gulf Coast area, especially on similar salt domes. A series of economically significant discoveries followed, beginning with the Sour Lake (1902), Batson–Old (1903),

Tong crew laying an early pipeline. Courtesy American Petroleum Institute Photograph and Film Collection, Washington, D.C. Pipelines supplied Texas oil for the East Coast.

Humble (1905), and Goose Creek oilfields (1908). Like earlier fields in Pennsylvania and West Virginia, Gulf Coast fields typically flourished and declined quickly. During the first decade of development, however, operators produced sufficient crude oil to provide feedstock for several refineries and to provide traffic for a growing pipeline system in the region. The Texas Company, later Texaco (formed in 1902 from the Texas Fuel Oil Company), the J. M. Guffey Company, and the Sun Pipe Line Company connected with most of the fields and carried Texas crude oil for use as an unrefined boiler fuel and to Gulf Coast refineries for processing into fuel oil. In 1904 the total pipeline runs of the Security (Standard Oil of New Jersey), Texas, Guffey, and Sun pipelines was about 18,000,000 barrels. The largest producer in Texas was the J. M. Guffey Petroleum Company, which produced more than a third of the state's oil. Texas was still the province of small producers in 1905, when only three Texas companies produced more than $45,000 worth of crude oil. The Rio Bravo Oil Company (part of the Southern Pacific Railroad) and the Landslide Oil Company were the only other firms to produce more than $45,000 worth of crude during the third quarter of that year.

Small refineries proliferated at Spindletop during the first year of production. In 1902 J. M. Guffey Petroleum Company (renamed Gulf Oil Corporation in 1907), built a larger refinery capable of producing kerosene. In that same year Gulf and the Texas Company built pipelines to connect their refineries with the Glenn pool in Oklahoma. Gulf's processing capacity grew to 50,000 barrels of crude a day by 1916. That year the total capacity of plants in Jefferson County was 154,000 barrels. Other companies, principally Sun and the Houston Oil Company, also built sizable installations. The Security Oil Company, owned by a foreign subsidiary of the Standard Oil Company of New Jersey, lost its plant in 1909, when the state sold it at auction for violations of antitrust statutes; after brief ownership by John Sealy of Galveston, it was acquired by Socony (Standard Oil Company of New York) directors, reopened as the Magnolia Petroleum Company, and expanded to 25,000 barrels in 1916. In 1925 Magnolia merged with Socony-Vacuum. The largest refinery in the area was the Baytown plant of the Humble Oil and Refining

Company (later Exxon), which expanded steadily until 1940, when it was the largest installation in the United States, with a capacity of 140,000 barrels.

All of the activity in the Gulf Coast region expanded the economies of cities and villages, especially after service, supply, and related manufacturing companies located plants and distribution facilities in the Houston–Beaumont–Port Arthur area, thereby diversifying the economy of the region. The Houston Ship Channel opened in 1914 and began to attract refineries after the end of World War I. Employment related to the oil industry in the Houston area continued to grow during the 1920s and 1930s; by 1929, 27 percent of all manufacturing employees in Harris County were employed by refineries. Between that date and 1940, the capacity of all of the installations in the county increased fourfold. Oil production in the upper Gulf Coast area was boosted by numerous discoveries, the most prolific of which were the Orange (1913), Damon Mound (1915), Barbers Hill (1916), West Columbia (1918), Hull (1918), and Blue Ridge (1919) oilfields. Thereafter, though exploration was spread over more of Texas, large discoveries were made in the Pierce Junction (1921), Thompson (1921), High Island (1922), and Sugarland (1928) fields during the 1920s.

During its first two decades, the petroleum industry added to both the folklore of Texas life and to public coffers. New terms and images included the go-for-broke wildcatter, the hardworking and hard-playing roughneck, and the newly rich oilman, all of them fully established in folklore and films by the 1920s and subsumed in Jett Rink, a major character in Edna Ferber's unflattering novel *Giant* later in the century (1952). Beginning in 1905 with taxation on oil production, the industry became increasingly important as a source of public revenue. During 1906, the first full year of taxation, the comptroller of public accounts collected $101,403.25 on the basis of 1 percent of value of product. Thereafter, the sum varied with the volume of production and the tax rate; it exceeded $1 million in 1919 and $5.9 million in 1929.

By the latter date, oil exploration and production had extended beyond the Coastal Plain into North Texas, the central section of the state, and into the Panhandle and Permian Basin of West Texas. In North Texas, from Wichita Falls to Stephens County, wildcatters found numerous fields, including five that rank in the group of four dozen that comprise the major oil plays in Texas. Interest in the region grew from small discoveries near Jacksboro and from modest production found in Archer County and in the Petrolia oilfield of Clay County. Major development began with the Producers Oil Company's discovery well in the Electra field in January 1911. Thereafter, the Burk field followed in 1912, Iowa Park in 1913, and the composite Wichita County Regular field in 1915. Major discoveries followed in the region, including the Ranger field, by the Texas Pacific Coal Company in 1917, Burkburnett Townsite and Desdemona in 1918, and K.M.A. (after the Kemp, Munger, and Allen Oil Company) in 1919. Further developments occurred in Archer, Coleman, and Young counties in 1921 and in Eastland, Stephens, and Shackelford counties in 1922. During this same period numerous smaller fields were discovered and developed and larger fields were extended and completed to greater depths, making the region of increasing importance in the industry. In 1924 about one-third of the new wells in Texas were completed in the Holliday–Archer City area alone. Much as in the Gulf Coast

Cars mired in muddy main street after a heavy rain in Desdemona, 1919. Photograph by Norris. Courtesy Permian Basin Historical Society Archival Collection, University of Texas of the Permian Basin, Odessa. When the Joe Duke oil well was discovered in 1918, Desdemona became a boomtown overnight, with oil rigs all over its downtown.

area, expanded oil production in North Texas brought further industrial development. Service and supply companies opened offices in Wichita Falls and, later, in Fort Worth. Gulf Oil Corporation opened a refinery in Fort Worth in 1911, followed by Pierce Oil Corporation in 1912 and Magnolia Petroleum in 1914. North Texas was integrated into the industry through pipelines constructed by the Texas and Gulf pipeline companies in 1912. The Prairie Pipeline Company extended lines from Ranger to Galveston and from Ranger to Cushing, Oklahoma. Natural gas, produced in most of the fields in the region, was commonly piped to nearby towns and cities. With the construction of a carbon black plant in Stephens County in 1923, the Texas petrochemical industry was born. Wichita Falls, nearer early production, began as the service and supply center in the region; its population grew from 8,200 in 1910 to 40,079 in 1920. However, as production moved southward and the Texas and Pacific Railway extended spur lines to the new areas, Fort Worth, served by the T&P, supported much of the new exploration and development.

Exploration shifted back to Central Texas when A. E. Humphreys found the Woodbine sand in the Mexia field in Navarro County, in 1920. An 18,000-barrel confirmation well triggered a major leasing and drilling boom in the oldest producing section of the state the following year. Thereafter, production was found in the Currie in 1921, and three fields, Deep Powell, Wortham, and Richland, in 1924. Extensive pipeline con-

struction begun in 1922 continued through 1924, as the Gulf, Humble, Magnolia, Prairie, and Texas pipeline companies provided further connections between wells in the area and refineries in the Gulf Coast area. By mid-1925, 1,725 wells were producing oil in the Corsicana area. Magnolia Oil Company operated the largest refinery in the region.

Early exploration in the Panhandle proceeded during developments in North Texas, based initially on water-resource survey work carried out by Charles N. Gould, who began mapping geological formations in the area in 1904. The actual discovery came in 1918, when the Amarillo Oil Company's gas well, Masterson No. 1, was completed with initial production of 10,000,000 cubic feet daily. Additional wells, especially Masterson No. 4, which produced 107,000,000 cubic feet, and Bivins No. 1, which extended the field nearly nine miles, confirmed the presence of a natural gas field of national importance. By 1994 the various sections of the Panhandle gas field had produced about eight trillion cubic feet of natural gas. After the round of early drilling, additional gas wells were drilled for local consumption, and a line was laid to Amarillo in 1923. An oil discovery by Gulf in 1921 spurred activity briefly, but work in the region lagged until 1923, when J. C. Whittington's No. 1 Sanford well in Hutchinson County was completed as a flowing well. By 1926 the Panhandle was a major producing region. Most of the oil came from the Borger area and other parts of Hutchinson and Carson counties, though discoveries had also been made in

Gray, Potter, Moore, and Wheeler counties. Peak production during the era of exploration in the Panhandle was reached in 1927, at 39,431,789 barrels, principally from Hutchinson County. After several years of declining yields, the full development of discoveries in Gray County produced a rebound in production to 32,274,822 barrels in 1930. During 1926, seven oil companies constructed pipelines and storage facilities in the area, some connecting to systems that reached the Gulf Coast and Oklahoma. Related industrial activity began in 1922 with the construction of a gasoline stripper plant, the American Refining company (later the Phillips Panhandle Refinery). Carbon black operations began with the Western Carbon Company operation in Carson County in 1926. Amarillo grew with this activity, from 15,494 in 1920 to 43,142 in 1930, but much of the population growth occurred in such new settlements as Borger and in older shipping points such as Panhandle. The former, founded by Ace Borger in February 1926, grew rapidly during its first year, like boomtowns before and after it. Estimates place its population at between 10,000 and 20,000. After it developed the reputation of being a wide-open settlement sheltering legions of moonshiners, gamblers, prostitutes, and hijackers, the Texas Rangers arrived in force and drove scores of miscreants out of town, much as they had done in other parts of the state; they repeated the performance in Wink in 1929. In the Panhandle, oil and gas activity diversified the regional economy, as it had already done in other sections of the state. Repeating a pattern that began in Beaumont, oil and gas also offered alternative employment to sharecroppers and their sons, many of whom left the land and followed drilling rigs to successive booms over Texas. Model-T and Model-A Fords, with boxes and suitcases strapped to their trunks, rear seats filled with children and household goods, became familiar sights in most parts of Texas during the first three decades of the twentieth century. Ragtowns, tent cities, and shotgun houses were as common in the oil patch as dog-run houses in the countryside and mail-order bungalows in towns. Gushers and forests of drilling rigs replaced herds of longhorn cattle as symbols of Texas life.

With less stir, oil production began in Southwest Texas with a series of small discoveries in McMullen, Calhoun, and San Patricio counties and assumed increasing importance with the opening of the Piedras Pintas field in Duval County and the Mission field in Bexar County in 1907. The Somerset field, discovered accidentally during drilling for a water well in 1913, went into major development in 1920, bringing the first sizable oil production to the area. In the same year, oil was discovered in the Refugio gas field. In random drilling near Laredo, Oliver W. Killam made small commercial discoveries in the Mirando City and Aviator fields beginning in 1921. Killam and his associates operated a medium-sized refinery in the area and built a pipeline to carry crude oil to the Texas and New Mexico Railroad. During the late 1920s, additional discoveries were made in Southwest Texas, including Government Wells in Duval County, adjacent to the Jennings gas field, and smaller gas production in the Agua Dulce, Kohler, and Three Rivers fields. Even after oil prices declined in 1929, exploration continued in the region, leading to the discovery of the Pettus Townsite field in Bee County in 1929. The steady progress of geological mapping led to the discovery in 1929 of the Darst Creek oilfield, the region's first major oilfield. In view of the glut of crude oil, operators in the field negotiated an agreement to limit production, with the cooperation of the Railroad Commission, which supervised the operation of the pact. Natural gas discoveries of importance were made at White Point in 1914, and near Laredo in 1911 and Kingsville in 1920 and 1922. As was common in other areas of natural gas production, service was first extended to communities near the fields, beginning with Laredo in 1911 and San Antonio in 1922. Completion of a gas well that produced 41,000,000 cubic feet per day in the Carolina field confirmed the presence of large quantities of natural gas in and around Webb County. During the 1920s, further important discoveries of gas were made in Southwest Texas. By 1927 natural gas production in the region passed four billion cubic feet a day. Natural gas pipelines were constructed from Live Oak County and from White Point and Refugio to Houston in 1926. Lines were also built from Mirando to the lower Rio Grande valley and from other fields to New Braunfels, Seguin, San Marcos, and Austin. Construction of trunk lines to deliver gas from the region to the Gulf Coast began in 1925 and connected to home and industrial distribution systems in Houston and Baytown during 1926 and 1927. Thereafter, the pipeline system was upgraded and expanded, especially during the 1950s and 1960s, making this region a gas-producing province of great importance to the state. With the completion of these lines and those from the Panhandle to the Middle West, the natural gas industry in Texas was established as an important part of the state's economy. The comparatively modest oil production of Southwest Texas and the absence of sufficient outlets for petroleum products retarded related industrial development until the ship channel was completed in Corpus Christi in 1926. Thereafter, the city became attractive as a site for refinery location. Humble built a small refinery at Ingleside, and a large number of small plants opened in Corpus Christi, Refugio, and Port Lavaca during the 1930s. Of this group, the largest were in Corpus Christi, operated by the Taylor Refining Company, the Pontiac Refining Company, and the Southwestern Oil and Refining Company. The Grayburg Oil Company of San Antonio extended the old Somerset field with deeper drilling and produced about 1,000 barrels of oil a day, which the company ran to its local refinery; products were sold in a dozen Grayburg stations in the area.

Oil and gas production lagged considerably in Central Texas. Though several small wells were completed in the Austin Chalk formation in 1913, the first notable discovery in the region came near Thrall, in Williamson County about 40 miles northeast of Austin, the following year. Compared to production in prolific fields in North Texas, however, wells in this field were modest and did little more than focus attention on the region for a brief period of time. The Luling field, about forty miles south of Austin, was the scene of random drilling during the third decade of the century. The United North and South Oil Company of Edgar B. Davis brought in the first significant production in the Edwards lime formation in 1922. In 1924 Magnolia ran a pipeline to Luling that connected with its refinery at Beaumont. Two years later the Lytton Springs field, 28 miles south of Austin, opened; it sustained interest in the prospects of the region in part because it, like the Thrall field, produced from the "serpentine plug," an altered igneous-rock formation. The first big year for exploration in the region came in 1928, with the discovery of the Salt Flat field, the second major Edwards lime production.

The penultimate section of the state to secure significant oil production was the Permian Basin, a geological province that includes several counties of eastern New Mexico. Despite modest discoveries, including one in Mitchell County in 1920, this region did not attract statewide attention until 1924, when wells brought in by Michael L. Benedum in the Big Lake oilfield, discovered in 1923, proved the presence of commercial quantities of crude oil. Between that date and 1930 highly important discoveries were made, including the Howard–Glasscock (1925), McCamey (1925), East Howard–Iatan (1926), Yates (1926), Hendrick (1926), Kermit (1928), North Ward–Estes (1929), and Fuhrman–Mascho (1930) fields. The cumulative potential production of these fields made the thinly populated region of great importance and led to the growth of Big Spring, San Angelo, Midland, and Odessa and to the establishment of new settlements in Upton, Crane, Howard, and Winkler counties. With declining oil prices and limited pipeline transportation to Gulf Coast refineries, however, the region developed relatively slowly. Thus, producers in the Yates and Hendrick fields negotiated voluntary limitations of production, under the auspices of the Railroad Commission. With increased production from California, Oklahoma, and the Van field of Texas came lower crude oil prices in 1929, and this region settled into relative inactivity by the end of the year.

In the first quarter of 1929, Texas operators produced 69,541,834 barrels of oil. More than half of this amount came from the following 10 companies, listed in declining order of volume: Gulf Production Company, Humble Oil and Refining Company, Southern Crude Oil Purchasing Company (Standard Oil of Indiana), the Texas Company, Shell Petroleum Corporation, Yount–Lee Oil Company, Magnolia Petroleum Company, J. K. Hughes Oil Company, Pure Oil Company, and Mid-Kansas Oil and Gas Company (Ohio Oil Company). Independent operators remained active and important, however, in most sections of the state.

East Texas, the final section of the state to obtain high-volume oil production, had long been an arena for relatively unsuccessful exploration, with the exception of the closely owned Van field, discovered by Pure Oil Corporation in 1929. Further tests of the Woodbine sand in various parts of this large section of the state indicated that it was unlikely that oil would be produced profitably from it. That prognosis was proved grandly erroneous in 1930 by two promoters, Columbus M. "Dad" Joiner, and A. D. "Doc" Lloyd (Joseph I. Durham). Their discovery well, the Daisy Bradford No. 3, brought oil from the Woodbine sand formation in Rusk County on 6 October 1930. The approximate size of the field, about 43 miles long and 12½ miles wide, was largely established during the next four months: in December, Ed Bateman and Associates' Crim No. 1 extended it 9 miles, from the Joiner well to the vicinity of Kilgore; during January 1931, Moncrief–Faring–Arkansas Gas and Fuel Company's Lathrop No. 1 found oil 12 miles from Bateman's well. The giant East Texas oilfield ultimately extended into parts of Upshur, Gregg, Rusk, Smith, and Cherokee counties. The flood of production from the field depressed exploration in West Texas and Southwest Texas until the middle of the 1930s, and the economic impact of the discovery compounded the negative effects of the Great Depression. By May, average daily production from the field reached 303,750 barrels; by June, crude oil in East Texas was selling for 22 cents a barrel, and higher gravity oil in the Mid-Continent area of Oklahoma, Kansas, and North Texas had fallen to 27 cents. The field developed rapidly because more than

Laundry day in an Andrews ragtown, Andrews County, ca. 1930s. Courtesy Standard Oil (New Jersey) Co. Collection, Photographic Archives, University of Louisville; neg. 27380. Women who lived under makeshift conditions in the oil ragtowns near the big fields worked hard to clean oil-stained clothing.

three-quarters of the productive and prospective acreage was owned by independent operators and wells were relatively inexpensive to drill and complete. Operators had drilled 1,100 wells by mid-1931 and more than 2,000 more by the end of the year. By mid-year, 31 refineries had been completed and 6 more were under construction. Taylor Refining Company, of Tyler, the East Texas Refining Company, of Dallas, Central Refining Company, Dallas, and Sinclair Refining Company, Fort Worth, were the largest processors. One hundred one-barrel and two-barrel "cookers" were also manufacturing gasoline and kerosene in the field. Production in the field soared from 109,561,000 barrels in 1931 to 156,109,346 in 1932 and 211,586,118 in 1933. During the latter year, the posted price varied greatly, from $.75 in January to $.10 in April, back to $.75 in August and to $1.00 from September 30 to the end of the year. "Hot oil," a term that meant, variously, oil produced in excess of Railroad Commission orders and oil that was siphoned from pipelines and otherwise dishonestly obtained, was reported as selling for as little as $ .03 a barrel during the year.

State officials and agencies made a number of unsuccessful attempts to curb excess production in East Texas. After reversals in court and numerous heated conferences on the topic, Governor Sterling ordered a field shut-down and sent the Texas National Guard to enforce his decree and the proration rulings of the Railroad Commission that followed. Production in the field resumed, and in February 1932 the state Supreme Court ruled that the governor's decree was illegal. With additional assistance of the Texas Rangers, the commission got significant compliance in the spring of 1933, but was unable to curb the sizable outflows of hot oil to adjoining states. A partial remedy for illegal shipments came in the fall of 1933, when Section 9(e) of the National Industrial Recovery Act authorized federal interdiction of interstate shipments of oil produced in violation of state conservation regulations. Two years later, this provision was made a free-standing statute. In the meantime, continued improvement in production technologies, including instruments for measuring the bottom-hole pressure in oil wells, made it possible for the Railroad Commission to enforce allowable production levels through the legal system of the state. The increasing ownership position of major refiners and the decline of "edge" wells also facilitated limitation of production. At the end of 1935 there were still more than 1,000 operators in the field, producing oil from 19,313 wells. Reported production for the year was 158,599,275 barrels. By 1937 major refiners processed half of the oil from the field, and only half a dozen significant independent refiners remained in the field. The Texas Company operated the largest plants, in Neches and West Dallas.

As the East Texas field settled into stable production patterns, interest in the Permian Basin revived, leading to discoveries north of existing production. The North Cowden (1930), Means (1934), Goldsmith (1935), Seminole (1936), Wasson (1937), Slaughter (1937), and Dune (1938) fields became major fields that supplied distant refineries. Older areas, such as Kermit and South Cowden, were developed more fully with the stabilization of prices and the construction of additional pipeline facilities. By the end of the decade the region had 11 refineries, the largest belonging to the Cosden Petroleum Company, in Big Spring, and the Col-Tex Refining Company, in Colorado City. Two carbon black and 13 natural gasoline plants were also in operation at the time.

In the Panhandle, oil discovered during the 1920s was developed more fully during the next decade, when it supported eight refineries, the largest of which was operated by the Phillips Petroleum Company in Borger in 1938. Thirty-one carbon black plants were in operation in the Panhandle during the same year, along with 42 natural gasoline plants, which stripped liquid from the vast quantity of natural gas produced in the region. Southwest Texas continued to be active during the 1930s, with a relatively large discovery, the Tom O' Connor field, in 1934. Other finds of regional significance included the Greta, Sam Fordyce, Loma Novia, Lopez, Placedo, Plymouth, Flour Bluff, Benavides (or North Sweden), and Premont fields. Additional refineries were constructed, bringing the number to 26 at the end of the 1930s. The largest installation was Humble Oil and Refining Company's expanded refinery at Ingleside. During this period the continued construction of natural gas pipelines tied the growing volume of natural gas production to urban markets and to the growing petrochemical industry on the Gulf Coast. The major find in Central Texas also occurred during the depression, with the discovery of the Pearsall field in the Austin Chalk of Frio County in 1936. East Texas production was supplemented with oil from the Talco field the same year. In 1931 Conroe oilfield set off renewed exploration in the Gulf Coast area. Thereafter, large production was found in the Tomball (1933), Old Ocean (1934), and Anahuac (1935) fields, in addition to smaller finds at Manvel (1931), Hastings (1935), and Webster (1936). Natural gas resources in the region were boosted with major discoveries in the Old Ocean field in 1936 and with the first of a long succession of gas discoveries in the complicated and prolific Katy field in 1938.

In 1939, the beginning of World War II in Europe disrupted European petroleum markets. American exports to Europe fell by nearly a quarter. In Texas the Railroad Commission responded by cutting allowables by one-fifth and by increasing shut-down days. With further curtailments in 1942, Texas was producing less than 60 percent of its potential, and both exploration and field development slowed. In the last year of the war, with the completion of the Big Inch and Little Big Inch pipelines,

which carried Texas oil to Eastern markets, the industry picked up somewhat. During the course of the war, however, shortages of trained personnel and the diversion of steel for war uses continued to hold back areas of known reserves. The wartime system of price controls and rationing lasted until 1946. During the war years, 1939–46, Texas oilmen found 77 new fields or producing horizons. Many of these discoveries, modest by prewar standards, were in older fields, but they made significant additions to reserves in Texas. New development occurred in most sections of the state, except the Panhandle, North Texas, and Central Texas. The Oyster Bayou field in Chambers County went into production in 1941 and was tied to upper Gulf Coast refineries. In the Seeligson field of Southwest Texas (Kleberg and Jim Wells counties), six new producing horizons were discovered; 19C produced nearly 100 million barrels by 1994. In this same region, the TCB 21-B field (Tijerina–Canales–Blucher), brought significant gains in reserves. The discovery of the Hawkins Woodbine field in East Texas was the largest significant find in Texas during the entire period. Quitman Paluxy field also added significantly to the reserves of this region. In West Texas, Wasson 6000' (1940) and 7200' (1941), McElroy (1941), Fullerton (1941), Mabee (1943), Sandhills–McKnight (1944), Anton–Irish (1944), Fullerton 8500' (1944), TXL Devonian (1944), Midland Farms (1945), Fullerton San Andres (1945), Block 31 (Devonian) (1945), Levelland (1945), and Fullerton (Ellenburger) (1945) were important discoveries and continued the development of this prolific region. Old production was extended on the Louisiana border with the Rodessa field. Major additions to natural gas reserves were made with the discovery of the Carthage (Pettit, Lower Gas) and Opelika (Transpeak) fields in East Texas and the Headlee (Devonian) and Brown–Bassett (Ellenburger) fields in the Permian Basin.

Postwar markets for oil and gas expanded so rapidly during the autumn of 1947 that the Texas Railroad Commission ordered no shutdown days for the first time in eight years. With the end of federal regulation of oil and gas production, reversion to well-spacing regulations of the commission brought a surge of drilling. As demand swelled, petroleum prices rose to heights unequaled in almost three decades, beginning as soon as price controls ceased, on 25 July 1946. The posted price of West Texas intermediate-grade crude, for example, frozen at $.92 during the War, jumped to $1.27 by the end of that month, rose another $.10 before the year's end, and went to $1.62 in March 1947, $1.82 in October, and $2.32 in December 1947. Demand for natural gas grew, in part as a result of strikes by Eastern coal miners in 1946. Some of the extraordinary demand for oil products was met with imported crude oil, however, and in 1948, despite peak domestic production, the United States became a net importer of oil. Imports increased 24 percent in 1948–49 alone. Large-scale importation retarded exploration in areas that did not seem to have the promise of large oil reserves; Southwest Texas was especially affected. Nevertheless, by 1948 further pipeline construction connected fields in Southwest Texas and the Permian Basin with regional outlets for oil and gas. By 1950, Texas had 15,010 miles of gas transmission line and 26,409 mile of crude oil trunk lines. Their operation encouraged development of additional gas reserves in the upper Gulf Coast area, in Southwest Texas (especially in Hidalgo and Zapata counties), and in the Permian Basin. Interstate gas shipments more than doubled between 1950 and 1955 as transmission systems reached 46 of the

Fractionators, Phillips gasoline plant, Borger, Texas, November 1942. Photograph by John Vachon. Library of Congress; USW 3-11515-D.

contiguous states. In the Permian Basin, the discovery of high-grade crude oil below the Permian formations encouraged deep tests in both new areas and old fields; it also led to reinvestigation of areas where prospecting had been unsuccessful in the twenties and thirties. Drilling in the region rose 50 percent between 1947 and 1948 and again between 1949 and 1950. Between 1946 and 1951 the number of independents and major oil companies doing business in Midland rose from 135 to 363, as companies such as J. S. Abercrombie of Houston and Rowan Drilling of Fort Worth established local offices. Among the newcomers were growing numbers of young men from other parts of the country; George H. W. Bush and John and Hugh Liedtke, among others, launched oil careers in the Permian Basin during this era. Major finds in this region included new discoveries in the Midland and Delaware basins, on the Central Basin platform and in the multicounty Spraberry trend. Major discoveries during the period 1946–50 included Andector (1946), Goldsmith 5600' (1947), Kelly–Snyder and Diamond M (1948), TXL (Ellenburger) and Cogdell (1949), and Prentice and Salt Creek (1950). By the end of the decade the Permian Basin was the leading oil-producing area in the United States.

The long-standing Tidelands controversy was settled with federal legislation in 1953. Earlier work, including a discovery on State No. 245, had not established the economic importance of these areas, but geophysical work off Brazoria, Chambers, Galveston, Jefferson, and Matagorda counties supported increasing levels of leasing and, in later years, significant discoveries. On-shore discovery of the Neches field in 1953 and West Hastings in 1958 supported declining reserves in the upper Gulf Coast and East Texas areas. The intense exploration of the early 1950s made sizable additions to the estimated known reserves of the state, which peaked in 1952 at 15,314,964,000 barrels. The major on-shore oilfields of Texas had been located by the middle of the 1950s. Though there were annual increases during some years thereafter, the general trend was downward, to 14,859,674,000 barrels in 1960 and 13,063,182,000 barrels in 1970.

During the period of declining oil reserves, natural gas came to occupy an increasingly important place in the petroleum industry of Texas both as a source of energy and as the origin of feedstocks for a growing petrochemical industry. Federal and state governments had important roles in this general development. In 1947, the Railroad Commission ordered well shutdowns where it found operators flaring large quantities of casinghead gas. Its first target was the complex Seeligson field in Southwest Texas, where it required that all oil or gas be put to uses that conformed to conservation orders. The Seeligson order marked the first shot in a series of legal battles over gas conservation from which the commission emerged triumphant. By the end of 1948, 82 projects utilizing casinghead gas had been completed in Texas and 43 more were underway, largely undertaken by major companies and large independents, often acting cooperatively. On 1 April 1953 the commission shut down the 2,268 producing wells in the Spraberry trend of the Permian Basin in its battle to eliminate the conspicuous waste of natural gas. A large measure of control over natural gas passed to the Federal Power Commission in 1954, when the United States Supreme Court ruled that the FPC had jurisdiction over the production of gas sold in interstate commerce (the FPC had set interstate prices since 1939). This decision, and the FPC policy of keeping the price of natural gas low, led to the growth of intrastate gas sales and encouraged the further expansion of the petrochemical industry within the state, as El Paso Natural Gas and other companies invested in sizable gathering and transmission systems.

During the 1950s, oilmen enhanced the gas reserves of Texas with the discovery of two new horizons in the Katy field (1954) and of eight new gas fields: Hansford (Morrow, Upper) in 1953, Emperor (Devonian) in 1954, Dora Roberts (Devonian) in 1955, Fashing and Halley (Devonian) in 1956, Viboras (Brooks) in 1957, and Thompsonville, NE (Wilcox 9500') and the Massive First and Massive Second sands of Viboras in 1959. Oil producers were less fortunate in sustaining reserves, in part because of a persistent cross-pressure of rising costs against constant revenues, largely the consequence of the increasing volume of less expensive foreign crude oil. With the exception of a short break during the Suez crisis of 1956, cheap foreign oil continued to reach American markets in increasing volume. In 1955, when total demand for oil rose 7.6 percent over the previous year, imports increased by 17.2 percent. When domestic demand fell in 1957 and 1958, Texas allowable production was cut in half, but imports continued to rise. Attempts made by the Texas Independent Producers and Royalty Owners Association and other industry associations to restrict imports did not succeed in Washington. By 1960, increased imports prompted the Railroad Commission to lower producing days to eight per month, a level that remained into 1962. The consequence of low prices and severely restricted production was the sale of numerous oil and gas properties and companies during the 1960s. Honolulu Oil, Union Texas Natural Gas, Republic Natural Gas, Monterey Oil, and Plymouth Oil were among the companies acquired by other firms during the decade. In 1969 Michel T. Halbouty of Houston, a leader in petroleum trade associations, estimated that the number of independent producers in the United States had declined by three-quarters during this period; though Texas was less hard-hit, as many as one-quarter of the independents in Midland, one of the state's petroleum centers, went out of business between 1951 and 1969.

The most notable developments in oil during the latter half of the 1950s were the improved management of production, the expansion of the petrochemical industry, and natural gas discoveries. Producers, caught between rising costs and prices depressed by imported crude oil, increasingly implemented efficiency measures, including unitized production of oil from common fields or pools. Scurry County producers formed the Scurry Area Canyon Reef Operators Committee, and the large and complex Seeligson field was unitized, along with fields throughout the state, with the encouragement of the Railroad Commission. The commission also sought and secured the watchdog's role over pollution, confirmed by judicial decision in

1964. The petrochemical industry of Texas grew dramatically as national demand for products grew at a rate of 10 percent a year into the 1960s. New installations appeared along the upper Gulf Coast, along the Houston Ship Channel, in Odessa, and in other locations. New products included styrene, butadiene, polypropylene, and benzene; larger quantities of synthetic rubber and ammonia were also produced in the state.

Expansion of petrochemical production in Texas was a response to the increasingly large quantities of intrastate gas available from Southwest Texas, the Permian Basin, and the upper Gulf Coast area. In Southwest Texas the Wilcox sands yielded new reserves in Bee, Goliad, Webb, and Duval counties, while exploration in Hidalgo County found additional gas in the Frio sands. During the early years of the 1960s, drillers located more than half a dozen new gas fields in Zapata and Zavala counties. In the upper Gulf area, new production was found in the Alligator Bayou (Chambers County) and Chocolate Bayou (Brazoria County) fields. The largest gas discoveries were located in the Permian Basin of West Texas: Oates, N.E. (Devonian), Sandhills, Lockridge (Ellenburger 18600'), Waha, Toro, Sawyer, Block 16 (Devonian), Greasewood, Barstow (Fusselman), Block 16 (Ellenburger), MiVida (Fusselman) Evetts (Silurian), ROC (Devonian), Grey Ranch, War–Wink, Vermejo, and Elsinore. The largest gas discovery since the Panhandle field, the Gomez field in Pecos County, was followed by large additions to the Coyanosa and Ozona fields during the latter half of the decade. In Southwest Texas there were important gas discoveries in the Alazan, North (J-36), Laguna Larga, Zone 21-b trend, Laredo, C. J. Martin, and McMurray fields. In the upper Gulf Coast area the Katy I-B, Katy Cockfield Upper B, and Point Bolivar fields came into production near petrochemical installations. The other major gas fields discovered during the 1960s and 1970s include Trawick (Travis Peak) and Oak Hill (Cotton Valley) in East Texas, Giddings (Austin Chalk, Gas) in Central Texas, Washita Creek (Hunton 19475'), Buffalo Wallow (Hunton 19600'), Buffalo Wallow (Morrow), and Canadian, South East (Douglas) in the Panhandle, and No Word (Edwards) in Lavaca County.

In response to the Permian Basin Rate Case decision by the United States Supreme Court in 1964, which confirmed more extensive Federal Power Commission jurisdiction over the production of gas for the interstate market, the shift of gas to the intrastate market continued, making additional feedstock available to installations within the state. As prices moved up sporadically during the 1960s and early 1970s, hitting $.35 per thousand cubic feet of "new gas" in 1973, exploration for natural gas increased. Oil activity also picked up during 1972, when the Railroad Commission increased allowables to 100 percent of the "maximum efficient rate." In response to the continuing decline of national petroleum reserves, the federal government, which had capped oil prices in 1972, reclassified them according to four categories: old oil (oil produced from properties in production in 1972), released oil (oil from old reservoirs in excess of 1972 production), stripper oil (from wells that produced 10 barrels or less per day), and new oil (not in production in 1972). Price ceilings were removed from all but old oil. Texas achieved record production in 1972 with 1,263,412,000 barrels, but estimated proven crude oil reserves continued to decline from the historical high point of 15,581,642,000 barrels, achieved in 1951. The decline of Texas reserves both affected and reflected the loss of spare capacity in the domestic petroleum industry with the continuing decline of the domestic industry and reserves.

Though the Texas industry had come to accept the fact that the prospects of the oil industry were increasingly determined in Washington, during 1973 it was indisputable that the future of Texas oil was being written in foreign capitals. Renewed warfare between Israel and some Middle Eastern Arab countries brought the United States and the Netherlands to support Israel, thus prompting Mu'ammar al-Gadhafi of Libya to call for an embargo of crude oil shipments from Muslim counties to the two western nations. Though the embargo "leaked" from the time it was proclaimed, the occasion permitted OPEC (the Organization of Petroleum Exporting Countries) to execute a grand shift of economic power: suppliers took control over the price of crude oil from multinational purchasers. Within six weeks of the October onset, the price of Arabian crude rose from $5.40 to $17 a barrel. In the United States the Emergency Petroleum Allocation Act, the federal government's response to shortages, adjusted the ceiling price of "old" oil upward to a national average of $5.05. New, released, and stripper oil was still uncontrolled and rose to $10.82 in December. In Texas the response was a dramatic increase in drilling and exploration. The rig count increased 35 percent in 1973–74 and 26 percent the following year. The increased activity slowed the rate of decline of the state's oil production and crude oil reserves. The impetus lasted until 1976, when new federal classifications and lower price lids were established. Thus, while well completions rose 30.8 percent in 1975, they declined 4.3 percent the following year, in response to federal price regulation. Federal regulation also encouraged an economically risky shift of exploration investment to the Anadarko Basin of Texas and Oklahoma. Producers continued to implement secondary recovery projects in the Seminole and other fields. With improvements in geophysical techniques, offshore exploration for large reserves actually increased and the discovery rate improved, from Galveston to Corpus Christi, with significant discoveries in Galveston Bay and other areas by Pennzoil, Union Oil of Texas, and other companies. Refineries in the state invested largely in energy-saving and pollution-control technologies in response to higher operating costs and more stringent federal regulation. Federal policies changed again in 1976, with the Energy Policy and Conservation Act, which reorganized categories of oil, reduced the price of "upper-tier" oil, and placed ceilings on other categories. Wildcat drilling declined temporarily, but after six months new prices were issued, producing an increase in activity during 1977. During this year a brisk demand in the interstate gas market stimulated additional off-shore exploration and the construction of additional processing projects on the Texas Gulf Coast. Refineries continued to reduce stack-gas emissions and to process waste oil for energy generation. By the end of the following year, the Alaska Pipeline was flowing; it alleviated international shortages until the autumn of 1978.

The second major international shock to the petroleum industry came in late 1978 with the fall of the government of the Shah of Iran. Shortages stemming from that event led to international shortages that lasted into the fall of the following year. With panic buying on new international oil exchanges and a rise in spot prices, crude prices rose by nearly one-third in March alone, while product prices rose by nearly two-thirds. President James E. Carter decontrolled oil prices in the United States, and

Financial Center of Midland, ca. 1940s. Gelatin silver print. Cornell Capa, LIFE Magazine © Time Warner. Although Midland County had no oilfields, it held the headquarters for 150 oil companies. For a time speculators did $50 million worth of business a year in the lobby of the Scharbauer Hotel.

the average price rose from $12.64 in 1979 to $21.59, and to $30 and then to $34 in 1980. In Texas, rig counts jumped from a yearly average of 770 in 1979 to 1,318 in 1981. During these years, old records in bids for state leases were broken. Costs of lease bonuses, royalties, supplies, and services and compliance with federal regulation, especially the Clean Air Act, drove the cost of exploration ever higher. Federal inducements through the Natural Gas Policy Act led oilmen to seek economically risky objectives, notably deep tight-sand gas. The Windfall Profits Tax of 1980 and the Economic Recovery Tax Act of 1981 made it progressively more difficult to raise capital for exploration. Subsequent lowering of the maximum tax rate and the setting of minimum tax standards dried up sources of the risk capital that had funded exploration during the postwar period. Some areas remained active, including edges of the Midland basin, gas exploration in off-shore areas and in South Texas, and the Austin Chalk formation of Central Texas. The latter, long known to contain oil, saw extensive lease play and drilling to 1986. State government received increased tax revenues from the petroleum industry during the boom. In 1983, 28 percent of all tax revenue came from oil and gas operations. With the inclusion of federal payments, income from oil and gas taxes, mineral lease and bonus, and oil and gas royalties still comprised 17.16 percent of the revenues of state government.

As most of Texas on-shore was considered "mature" in terms of geological exploration, producers turned increasingly during the 1980s to costly secondary and tertiary development programs to extract more crude oil from known fields. Shell, Mobil, Amoco, and Gulf undertook expensive carbon dioxide injections in Permian Basin fields. Texaco undertook steam-flood projects in the Sour Lake field; Mitchell Energy and Development Corporation and other operators tested Enhanced Oil Recovery techniques in East and North Texas. Though higher natural gas prices had prompted additional searches for this resource, oil exploration was prompted increasingly by optimistic economic projections of the price of oil. As Daniel Yergin put it, "forecasting blossomed." With the passing of time, however, oilmen realized that the decline of economic activity, especially in Europe during the early 1980s, fuel substitutions, and conservation had reduced demand in developed countries during the Texas boom. Thus, as price balanced demand, the price of crude oil declined and precipitated the initial wave of business failures in oil, finance, and real estate in Texas. In March 1983, OPEC cut its price from $34 to $29 a barrel. In October of that year, distress in Texas business was clearly signaled by the failure of the largest independent bank in the state, the First National Bank of Midland. Further reversals were anticipated in 1985, when declines to $18 to $20 were forecast, but markets rose to $31.75 in late November, prompting buy-outs within Texas. The following year, prices fell as low as $7, triggering additional failures within the industry and the related financial community. The Texas rig count fell by more than half, from 677 to 311 in 1986, the most dramatic proportionate decline since the end of World War II. Drilling permits fell to about one-third of the high point reached in 1981. The rig count, reflecting exploration, fell to 206 in 1989, one-sixth of the record achieved eight years earlier. Austin Chalk–area exploration and development continued in brisk spurts, in response to new technologies such as horizontal drilling, used extensively by Oryx Energy in the area. Natural gas exploration in Southwest Texas and in off-shore areas slowed, but was sustained by finds in the Vicksburg sands and by the application of three-dimensional geophysical modeling of offshore areas. The rig-count in 1991 fell to 315, less than a quarter of its level in 1981. As national oil reserves and production declined sharply—by two million barrels a day between 1986 and 1990—Texas followed the trend. Estimated proven reserves as of 1 January 1992, were 6,797,000,000 barrels, less than half the historical peak achieved 40 years before. Production of 612,692,000 barrels was less than half of the peak reached 20 years earlier.

Texas refineries, still the most active in the nation, processed 1,625,156,579 barrels of fluids during 1992, including 784,805,108 barrels of gasoline, 136,972,276 barrels of home heating oil, and 107,953,913 barrels of kerosene (jet fuel). In that year seven refineries had individual capacities or more than 200,000 barrels of oil a day: Amoco (Texas City), Exxon (Baytown), Chevron (Port Arthur), Mobil (Beaumont), Lyondell Petrochemical (Houston), Star Enterprise (Port Arthur and Neches), and Shell (Deer Park). Beginning in the late 1970s, with the decline of domestic oil production, these installations processed increasing quantities of heavier, higher-sulfur crude oil from Saudi Arabia, Canada, Mexico, and Venezuela that required investments in improved desulfurization techniques.

During the 1970s and 1980s the Texas oil and gas industry had what might well have been its last boom. Subsequently, economic, social, and political life in the state changed greatly. The petroleum industry, more than one-quarter of the state's economy in 1981, fell to half that level 10 years later. Massive losses in energy and real estate lending brought the collapse of the large, home-owned financial institutions that had commonly been at the center of community development; of the large banks, Frost National alone survived. One-third of oil and gas employment was lost between 1982 and 1994. Workers left producing regions as rigs shut down and producers carried through successive reductions in staff; white-collar ranks thinned noticeably from the late 1980s onward, as producers cut technical and managerial personnel in the face of stagnant prices and rising costs. State and local governments found that lower income from production and property taxes necessitated austere budgets, and affected communities launched searches for new revenue and increased efforts to diversify their economies—an effort that was increasingly successful as the century neared its end. The proportion of state government revenue from the petroleum industry declined to 7 percent in 1993, one-quarter of its level 10 years earlier. In the final decade of the twentieth century, a great industry and the aspects of Texas life that were related to it were downsizing. Only petrochemicals gained: lower prices for oil and gas caused facilities to expand and related employment to increase by one-tenth between 1988 and 1991. This sector of the industry remained competitive in international markets, despite pollution control and abatement costs, which approached $1 billion a year in 1994. At a rate governed by international prices and technology, the rest of the petroleum industry in Texas was inching down the road from Spindletop. *Roger M. Olien*

Old Rip. "Old Rip" was a horned lizard, placed in the cornerstone of the old Eastland County Courthouse in 1897, that supposedly emerged alive when the block was reopened in 1928. The animal became something of a national sensation, toured many U.S. cities, and received a formal audience with President Calvin Coolidge; he eventually returned home and died of pneumonia. Old Rip is now on display in a glass and marble case at the courthouse where he lived.

Old San Antonio Road. A Spanish *camino real*, also known as the San Antonio–Nacogdoches Road. The trail, from San Juan Bautista to the missions in East Texas, was blazed by Alonso De León (1690), Domingo Terán de los Ríos (1691), Gregorio de Salinas Varona (1693), and Louis Juchereau de St. Denis (1714). The road served as a lifeline taking freight and military protection to the missions, and it facilitated trade. During the eighteenth century Spanish ranchers conducted cattle drives along the route to the annual fair in Saltillo, Coahuila. The road facilitated immigration. Moses Austin traversed the trail en route to San Antonio in 1820, and many AngloAmerican colonists entered Texas at Gaines Ferry on the Sabine and arrived at Nacogdoches and the interior of Texas over the road. The Old San Antonio Road was only an approximate route, a network of trails that developed over time. Feeder roads branched off the main course, and considerable stretches of the road probably existed as Indian trails before the Spanish arrived. In its later development, the road connecting Bastrop and Crockett did not come into use until after 1790. During the eighteenth century the route gradually shifted southeastward, probably as a result of the Apache and Comanche threat to Spanish travelers. Nor was the

Old San Antonio Road the only *camino real* in the Provincias Internas—or, for that matter, in the future United States.

In 1915 the Texas legislature appropriated $5,000 to survey and mark the route. Professional surveyor V. N. Zivley was commissioned to make the study. He examined river crossings and other topographic features, Spanish land grants, and laws of the Republic of Texas. From the Rio Grande to San Antonio he found little physical evidence of the trail, but by use of Juan Agustín Morfi's diary of 1778, he sought to establish it anyway. The route traced by Zivley followed a southeasterly course. It began at Paso de Francia on the Rio Grande, passed near Cotulla and Poteet, and entered San Antonio, from where it passed between Hays and Caldwell counties and through Bastrop, Lee, and Burleson counties, formed the boundary between Robertson and Brazos and Madison and Leon counties, and passed through Houston, Cherokee, Nacogdoches, San Augustine, and Sabine counties, before crossing the Sabine River at Gaines Ferry. The total distance was 540 miles. In 1929 the Texas legislature designated the Zivley version of the Old San Antonio Road one of the historic trails of Texas. The legislature also directed the highway department to preserve and maintain the road along the route. Save for some temporary deviations and a few locations impractical for a usable road, most of the distance from the Sabine to San Antonio had been opened and paved by 1949. Much of this route is still in use as State Highway 21 and related country roads.

In order to commemorate the route's 300th anniversary in 1991, the legislature authorized the formation of a nine-member Old San Antonio Road Preservation Commission and a supporting advisory committee. It also directed the State Department of Highways and Public Transportation to identify the disposition of the historical trail, to develop a historic preservation plan, and to prepare a comprehensive report. After a yearlong study the project staff, headed by archeologist A. Joachim McGraw, determined that the route that Zivley plotted was only one of several changing historic routes known as the Old San Antonio Road. The study identified no fewer than five different main routes that were used at various times. Researchers determined that the route employed by travelers often depended on season, natural conditions, and Indians. All of the routes began at the Presidio del Río Grande, also known as San Juan Bautista, led across South Texas, and converged in San Antonio. After Texas independence the road fell into disuse as the greater emphasis was on north–south routes. Courses shifted to accommodate the growth of new settlements and new markets, and to provide access to coastal trade. Shortly after the Mexican War, the *camino arriba*, what is now called the Old San Antonio Road, regained some of its former importance as travelers from East Texas hastened to San Antonio and onward toward the West Coast during the Gold Rush. Later, during the Civil War, the road served as a significant route for transportation of cotton from eastern Texas to San Antonio to Laredo and on to Mexico. After the war large segments of the route were abandoned in favor of newer, shorter roads that linked the growing urban centers of the state. In the latter part of the nineteenth century the coming of the railroads significantly changed transportation routes and the development of towns and commerce, thereby causing the abandonment of some of the old roads. The remaining portions of the *caminos* served local transportation needs. After the 1991 highway department study, the state adopted a comprehensive preservation plan, which called for continued efforts to study the road, to preserve existing artifacts, and to develop educational and tourist materials to publicize the road's history.

Old Spanish Trail. A national highway completed in the 1920s from St. Augustine, Florida, to San Diego, California. The Texas part runs through Orange, Beaumont, Houston, San Antonio, and El Paso. The name Old Spanish Trail was chosen by the Old Spanish Trail Association, formed in December 1915 in Mobile, Alabama, to promote the construction of a southern transcontinental highway. By August 1926 the group had distributed 83,000 maps and booklets. In 1919 the association established headquarters at the Gunter Hotel in San Antonio. By 1929 the highway was completed. This road is not to be confused with the Old San Antonio Road, which was sometimes referred to as the Old Spanish Trail. *Will Fossey*

Old Three Hundred. The settlers who received land grants in Stephen F. Austin's first colony. After Moses Austin died, the younger Austin took over his father's Spanish permit to settle 300 families in Texas. By the end of the summer of 1824 most of the Old Three Hundred were in Texas. During 1823–24 Austin and land commissioner Baron de Bastrop issued 272 titles, but Bastrop was called away in August 1824, and the work remained unfinished until 1827, when the new commissioner, Gaspar Flores de Abrego, issued the remaining titles. Since the family was the unit for distribution, Austin permitted unmarried men to receive grants in partnership, usually in groups of two or three. Twenty-two such partnership titles were issued to 59 partners. In all, 307 titles were issued, with nine families receiving two titles each. Thus the total number of grantees, excluding Austin's own grant, was actually 297, not 300. The colonization decree required that all the lands should be occupied and improved within two years; most of the settlers were able to comply with the terms, and only seven of the grants were forfeited. The lands selected by the colonists were along the rich bottomlands of the Brazos, Colorado, and San Bernard rivers, extending from the vicinity of present-day Brenham, Navasota, and La Grange to the Gulf of Mexico. Each family's sitio was to have frontage on the river equal to about one-fourth of its length; thus the east bank of the Brazos was soon completely occupied from the Gulf to what is now Brazos County. Most of the labores were arranged in three groups around San Felipe de Austin, which formed the nucleus of the colony. The majority of the Old Three Hundred colonists were from the Trans-Appalachian South; the largest number were from Louisiana, followed by Alabama, Arkansas, Tennessee, and Missouri. Virtually all were originally of British ancestry. Many had been born east of the Appalachians and were part of the large westward migration of the early years of the nineteenth century. Most were farmers, and many—including the Bell, Borden, Kuykendall, McCormick, McNair, McNeel, Raab, and Varner families—already had substantial means before they arrived. Because Austin wanted to avoid problems with his colonists, he generally accepted only those of "better" classes; indeed, only four of the Old Three Hundred grantees were illiterate. Another indication of the financial stature of the grantees was the large number of slaveholders among them. One of the colonists, Jared E. Groce, had 90 slaves. Though not all of the original grantees survived or prospered, Austin's Old Three Hundred, as historian T. R. Fehrenbach has written, formed "the first Anglo planter–gentry in the province."   *Christopher Long*

Olmsted, Frederick Law. Landscape architect and author; b. Hartford, Connecticut, 26 April 1822; d. New York City, 28 August 1902. Prevented by an eye infection from entering college, he studied surveying for two years and attended scientific lectures at Yale. He worked for a time with an importing firm in New York and from 1844 to 1850 engaged in scientific farming. During this period he traveled extensively in New England, Canada, China, and Europe and wrote his first book, *Walks and Talks of an American Farmer in England* (1852). With a commission to write articles about slavery for the New York *Times*, Olmsted made extensive tours throughout the South from 1852 to 1857. One of the products of this travel was *A Journey through Texas* (1857). On his route via Natchitoches down the Old San Antonio Road, through the German settlements, down to the coastal prairie towns, through San Antonio, Eagle Pass, Houston, and Liberty, Olmsted commented on all phases of town and country life in Texas. He was a fervent opponent of slavery, and his journeys through Texas and the other slave states confirmed this deep-seated antipathy to forced servitude and to the South in general. Comparing the conditions he saw in the South with those of his native New England, he argued that because of the costs of maintaining slaves in bondage, free labor was ultimately cheaper than slave labor. He also argued that the practice of slavery was leading the Southern economy to ruin. He expounded on these views in *The Cotton Kingdom*, which included many of his previous writings on the South, among them his travelogue on Texas. The book, published in the fall of 1861, six months after the Civil War had begun, helped to galvanize antislavery sentiment in the North. From 1857 to 1895 Olmsted was engaged in landscape architecture, superintending Central Park and designing Riverside Park in New York as well as other parks and university campuses.   *Lewis W. Newton*

Oñate Expedition. Reports of great wealth and natives who would be responsive to conversion in the country to the far north in the 1580s brought responsive action from the monarchy of Philip II of Spain in the form of a royal decree authorizing the pacification and settlement of the new land. It was Philip's conviction that as Hernando Cortes had conquered Mexico in 1521, there existed on the northern frontier of the viceroyalty of New Spain a second rich kingdom—another Mexico. With its conquest and colonization, therefore, Spanish fortunes would be restored after the disastrous defeat of its armada by England in 1588. Thus the viceroy of New Spain was instructed to find a suitable leader to organize an expedition. The contest for the position of governor and captain general of New Mexico was spirited, despite the crown's requirement that the candidate chosen would have to bear most of the costs of the expedition. At length, in 1595 the viceroy awarded the contract to Don Juan de Oñate, a wealthy and distinguished man whose father had made a fortune from the silver mines of Zacatecas, and whose wife was the granddaughter of Hernando Cortes and the great-granddaughter of Montezuma. After many delays in getting the expedition assembled, in January 1598 the colony of 400 men (of whom 130 brought families), 83 wagons and carts to carry the baggage and

provisions, and more than 7,000 head of stock began the march northward from Santa Barbara along the upper Río Conchos. Ten Franciscans joined later. Unlike previous expeditions, which followed the Conchos to the Rio Grande, this one headed straight across the sand dunes of the Chihuahua desert. A vanguard, after four days without water, reached the Rio Grande on April 20, and six days later the colony was reunited. In celebration of its survival a great feast was held. The expedition then ascended the river a distance, and on 30 April 1598, a significant date in the history of the El Paso Southwest, Oñate in a formal ceremony took official possession of the entire territory drained by the Rio Grande for his monarch, Philip II of Spain. This event, which took place at a site near that of present-day San Elizario, Texas (the river at that time ran several miles north of its present channel), is called La Toma, "the taking possession of"; it laid the foundation for more than two centuries of Spanish rule in the American Southwest. Ascending the river, the expedition crossed the river to the east side on May 4, at a site just west of present downtown El Paso. Oñate called this operation "El Paso del Río del Norte," an early use of the name El Paso. Near the upper reaches of the river he established his headquarters, founded a church, and formally founded the province of New Mexico. During the next few years Oñate sent out exploring parties in all directions, but the results were extremely disappointing—New Mexico was a distinct contrast to the Mexico that Hernando Cortes conquered. Everywhere the picture was the same—a large Indian population living in adobe houses, some of which were two stories high, but there was no gold, no silver, only a few fertile farms, and tenacious Indian resistance in many areas. Since the new land had failed to measure up to the high hopes and expectations of the colonists, quarreling and dissension increased, food was soon scarce, and desertions mounted. Charges were brought against the governor, accusing him of misconduct and mismanagement, of ignoring the complaints of the colonists, and of misinforming the crown about conditions in New Mexico. At length, in 1607 Oñate resigned his command, retired from the scene, and returned to Spain to defend himself against his alleged misdeeds. The Spanish crown, after some hesitation, decided to maintain its foothold in New Mexico, having received word that if it left it would be abandoning 7,000 converts. In 1609 a new governor, Pedro de Peralta, was appointed, and in the following year Santa Fe was founded as the new capital. With the exception of a 12-year period from 1680 to 1692, when the Spaniards were driven out of New Mexico by the Pueblo Revolt, Spain maintained its control over the frontier province until 1821.   *W. H. Timmons*

Operation Wetback. A project of the United States Immigration and Naturalization Service to repatriate illegal Mexican immigrants ("wetbacks") from the Southwest. During the first decades of the twentieth century, the majority of migrant workers who crossed the border illegally did not have adequate protection against exploitation by American farmers. As a result of the work of the Good Neighbor Commission, Mexico and the United States began negotiating an accord to protect the rights of Mexican agricultural workers. Continuing discussions and modifications of the agreement were so successful that the Congress chose to formalize the "temporary" program into the Bracero Program. In the early 1940s, while the program was being viewed as a success in both countries, Mexico excluded Texas from the labor-exchange program on the grounds of widespread violation of contracts, discrimination against migrant workers, and such violations of their civil rights as perfunctory arrests for petty causes. Oblivious to the Mexican charges, some Texas growers' organizations continued to hire illegal Mexican workers and violate such laws as the requirement to provide workers transportation costs from and to Mexico, fair and lawful wages, housing, and health services. World War II and the postwar period increased the Mexican exodus to the United States, as the demand for cheap agricultural laborers increased. Graft and corruption on both sides of the border enriched many Mexican officials as well as unethical "coyote" freelancers in the United States who promised contracts in Texas for the unsuspecting *bracero*. The Bracero Program increased the number of illegal aliens in Texas and elsewhere. Because of the low wages paid to legal, contracted *braceros*, many of them skipped out on their contracts either to return home or to work elsewhere for better wages as wetbacks. Increasing grievances prompted the Mexican government to rescind the *bracero* agreement. The INS, under pressure from various agricultural groups, retaliated against Mexico in 1951 by allowing thousands of illegals to cross the border, arresting them, and turning them over to the Texas Employment Commission, which delivered them to work for various grower groups in Texas and elsewhere. This action by the federal government, in violation of immigration laws and the agreement with Mexico, caused new problems for Texas. Between 1944 and 1954, "the decade of the wetback," the number of illegal aliens coming from Mexico increased by 6,000 percent. It is estimated that in 1954 before Operation Wetback got under way, more than a million workers had crossed the Rio Grande illegally. Cheap labor displaced native agricultural workers, and increased violation of labor laws and discrimination encouraged criminality, disease, and illiteracy. According to a study conducted in 1950 by the President's Commission on Migratory Labor in Texas, the Rio Grande valley cotton growers were paying approximately half of the wages paid elsewhere in Texas. In 1953 a McAllen newspaper clamored for justice in view of crimes committed by wetbacks.

The resulting Operation Wetback, a national reaction against illegal immigration, began in Texas in mid-July 1954. The Border Patrol, headed by INS commissioner Gen. Joseph May Swing and aided by other law-enforcement authorities and the military, began a quasimilitary operation of search and seizure of all illegal immigrants. Fanning out from the lower Rio Grande valley, Operation Wetback moved northward. Illegal aliens were repatriated initially through Presidio because the Mexican city across the border, Ojinaga, had rail connections to the interior of Mexico by which workers could be quickly moved on to Durango. A major concern of the operation was to discourage reentry by moving the workers far into the interior. Others were to be sent through El Paso. On 15 July, the first day of the operation, 4,800 aliens were apprehended. Thereafter the daily totals dwindled to an average of about 1,100 a day. The forces used by the government were actually relatively small, perhaps no more than 700 men, but were exaggerated by Border Patrol officials who hoped to scare illegal workers into flight back to Mexico. Valley newspapers also exaggerated the size of the government forces for their own purposes: generally unfavorable editorials

attacked the Border Patrol as an invading army seeking to deprive Valley farmers of their inexpensive labor force. While the numbers of deportees remained relatively high, the illegals were transported across the border on trucks and buses. As the pace of the operation slowed, deportation by sea began on the *Emancipation*, which ferried wetbacks from Port Isabel to Veracruz, and on other ships. Ships were a preferred mode of transport because they carried the illegal workers farther away from the border than did buses, trucks, or trains. The boatlift continued until seven deportees jumped ship and drowned, an incident that provoked a mutiny and led to a public outcry in Mexico. Other aliens, particularly those apprehended in the Midwest states, were flown to Brownsville and sent into Mexico from there. The operation trailed off in the fall of 1954 as INS funding began to run out.

It is difficult to estimate the number of illegal aliens forced to leave by the operation. The INS claimed as many as 1,300,000, though the number officially apprehended did not come anywhere near this total. The INS estimate rested on the claim that most aliens, fearing apprehension by the government, had voluntarily repatriated themselves before and during the operation. The San Antonio District, which included all of Texas outside of El Paso and the Trans-Pecos, had officially apprehended slightly more than 80,000 aliens, and local INS officials claimed that an additional 500,000 to 700,000 had fled to Mexico before the campaign began. Many commentators have considered these figure to be exaggerated. Various groups opposed any form of temporary labor in the United States. The American G.I. Forum, for instance, had little sympathy for the man who crossed the border illegally. Apparently the Texas State Federation of Labor supported the forum's position. Eventually the two organizations coproduced a study entitled *What Price Wetbacks?*, which concluded that illegal aliens in United States agriculture damaged the health of the American people, that illegals displaced American workers, that they harmed the retailers of McAllen, and that the open-border policy of the American government posed a threat to the security of the United States. Critics of Operation Wetback, however, considered it xenophobic and heartless.

Fred L. Koestler

Orange, Texas. The "Gateway City," county seat of Orange County; located on Adams Bayou at the junction of the Sabine River and the Gulf Intracoastal Waterway near the Louisiana border in eastern Orange County. The community was originally called Green's Bluff, for Resin (or Reason) Green, a Sabine River boatman who arrived there sometime before 1830. It was renamed Madison in 1840 in honor of President James Madison. It obtained a post office in 1850 and became the county seat upon the 1852 organization of Orange County. To avoid confusion with a community called Madisonville, the town was renamed again when it incorporated in 1858, taking the name Orange from an orange grove owned by George Patillo. Because of its relative isolation on the Louisiana border, the community became a stopping place for outlaws and renegades interested in crossing the Sabine River into Texas. Steam sawmills were established at Orange in the 1840s, and cotton shipments made the town part of the steamboat era from the 1840s until the 1890s, when cotton crops dwindled and railroads replaced river navigation. The Texas and New Orleans Railroad reached the community in

1860, but the track was destroyed during the Civil War and was not rebuilt until 1876. Three companies of Confederate troops were raised at Orange, and nearby Niblett's Bluff served as an important military supply point for the region. During Reconstruction, the Thirty-seventh Illinois Volunteers and a succession of other units occupied the town, but civil officials resumed their jobs in 1867, and the city resumed its charter and reincorporated in 1881. The lumber industry was responsible for Orange's late Victorian "Golden Age," when 17 steam sawmills made the community the center of the Texas lumbering district. Successful businessmen built elaborate mansions, and a rich social life flourished around the town's opera house and hotel. One of the principal firms, the Lutcher–Moore Lumber Company (organized by Henry Jacob Lutcher and G. Bedell Moore), operated from 1877 until the 1930s, using Niblett's Bluff as a log yard and railroad terminal for its Orange mill. By 1902, however, most of the area's smaller lumbermills had been con-

solidated into six major companies. In 1885 Orange had a population of 3,800, served by five churches, the *Tribune*, and five schools. By 1890 the town included two banks, four hotels, a board of trade, a lumber exchange, two cotton gin–gristmills, a waterworks, a fire department, and an electric company. By 1896 a rice mill, an ice factory, and the weekly *Tribune and Leader* were in operation, and the town shipped rice in addition to other products.

The Kansas City Southern line reached the community in 1897, and the Orange and Northwestern Railroad (later part of the Missouri Pacific) was chartered in 1901. The community remained a focal point for racial and other conflicts, however, witnessing, for example, activity by the Ku Klux Klan. By 1914, when its population numbered 7,000, Orange had three banks, a paper mill, a bag manufacturer, a box factory, a shipyard, an oil refinery, and an ironworks. Oil discoveries after 1913 at the Orange field six miles to the west produced little lasting benefit for the community, and the oil wells had largely dried up by 1930. Orange served as a major shipbuilding center during World War I, but its population fell off after the war, as shipbuilding and lumbering decreased and the Great Depression forced many to seek work elsewhere. Completion of a channel in 1916 made Orange a deepwater port; at the same time the community became a center for speakeasies, gambling, and bootlegging. East Orange grew famous for its Silver Slipper and Show Boat nightclubs in the 1920s, establishing an atmosphere of crime and violence that lasted for several decades. Local ferries, which had operated during much of the town's history, were replaced in 1938 by the Rainbow Bridge on Highway 87 across the Neches River between Orange and Port Arthur; at the time of its construction, it was the highest bridge in the South. The population of Orange grew again during World War II, when shipbuilding increased the number of residents of the greater metropolitan area to roughly 60,000, prompting the construction of government housing and other residential developments. Three shipyards were still in operation in 1949, and the United States Navy maintained a "mothball" fleet of more than 140 ships berthed in the Sabine River. Petrochemical industries developed in the postwar period, and U.S. Steel built facilities in the area. The population of Orange numbered 21,100 in 1950. Later, Orange, along with Beaumont and Port Arthur, came to be considered part of an industrial "Golden Triangle" that became a major manufacturing center as well as a seaport. Lamar University at Orange was established in 1971, and the Stark Museum of Art in 1978. The population level remained relatively stable after the war, varying from a low of 21,100 in 1952 to a high of 28,960 in 1976. Orange is credited with pioneering the first black Boy Scout troop in Texas and in 1970 elected its first black city council member. The city was 90 percent white in 1980. As the state's oil-based economy declined in the 1980s, the city's shipyards and oil industry complex suffered major strikes and layoffs. In 1990 the population of Orange numbered 22,525. The town's W. H. Stark House, Lutcher Memorial Church Building, and Sims House were listed in the National Register of Historic Places.

Diana J. Kleiner

"Orange, Texas—Queen of the Sabine," advertisement in *The Southern States*, August 1885 (Baltimore, Maryland). Courtesy TSL. The lumber industry was responsible for Orange's "Golden Age" in the last decades of the nineteenth century.

Orbison, Roy. Rock 'n' roll musician; b. Vernon, Texas, 23 April 1936; d. Hendersonville, Tennessee, 6 December 1988; m. twice; 5 sons. Orbison grew up in Wink, a small West Texas oil town,

Roy Orbison and his rock and roll group, the Teen Kings. Courtesy Chester and Geraldine Frady, Crosby, Texas.

where his father taught him to play the guitar at age six. In high school he formed the Wink Westerners, later the Teen Kings. The group played throughout West Texas and on a number of television shows and recorded "Ooby Dooby," which Sun Records (Memphis) recorded and made a "rockabilly" hit. Nevertheless, without much success on the charts, the Teen Kings dissolved and Orbison left Sun. Most of his early success was as a songwriter. "Claudette," a song written by Orbison and named after his first wife, was a hit of the Everly Brothers in 1958. In 1959 Orbison joined the small Monument label in Nashville, which resulted in a string of international hit records from 1960 to 1966, including such rock 'n' roll melodramas as "Only the Lonely" (1960), "Blue Angel" (1960), and "Running Scared" (1961). Elvis Presley once called Orbison "the greatest singer in the world." Singing songs that featured dark, brooding themes of love, loss, and longing, wearing black clothes, slicked-back hair, and dark glasses, he played around the world. In England in 1963 he headlined a tour that included the Beatles, then on the verge of international popularity. Orbison's time at the top was brief. His wife was killed in a motorcycle accident in 1966, and in 1968 two of his three sons were killed in a fire at his Nashville home. He married his second wife, Barbara, in 1969. Orbison underwent open heart surgery in 1979. In the late 1970s and 1980s his popularity rebounded when artists such as Linda Ronstadt and Van Halen recorded some of his songs. His 1980 recording of "That Loving You Feeling Again" with Emmylou Harris won a Grammy Award, and in 1987 his recording "In Dreams" was featured in the soundtrack of *Blue Velvet*, a popular movie. That same year he was inducted into the Rock 'n' Roll Hall of Fame. In 1988, the year of his death, Orbison's renewed popularity was confirmed in a critically acclaimed television special. He also released an album that year, *The Traveling Wilburys, Volume One*, featuring Orbison and his friends Bob Dylan, George Harrison of the Beatles, Tom Petty, and Jeff Lynne of the Electric Light Orchestra, which was in the top 10 at the time of his death.

George B. Ward

Ortiz Parrilla, Diego. A leading figure in Spanish Texas; b. Villa de Lúcar, bishopric of Almería, Spain, probably ca. 1715; d.

Madrid, by the end of November 1775. After service in Cuba, this son of "persons of distinguished nobility" served as a dragoon captain at the fortress of Veracruz, then was sent in January 1747 to Puebla de los Angeles to put down a native revolt. He was promoted to lieutenant colonel the following June. On 27 March 1749 he was appointed governor and captain-general of Sinaloa and Sonora charged with "reducing and extinguishing" various Indian groups who were disturbing the jurisdiction. In the process of carrying out this mission, he became embroiled in a bitter controversy with the Jesuit missionaries that foreshadowed his strife with the Franciscans of Santa Cruz de San Sabá Mission in Texas. After promotion to colonel in February 1751, Ortiz Parrilla was replaced as governor in 1752 so that he could return to Veracruz as captain of a dragoon company. In January 1756 he received crown permission to go to Spain for a year to claim his late father's estate by primogeniture. Before he could make the trip, he was ordered to Texas to take command of San Xavier Presidio. He was to move the garrison to the San Saba River, then to establish a new presidio to protect the new Apache mission. While spending the winter of 1756–57 in San Antonio, Ortiz Parrilla became a partisan in the personal feud between Fray Mariano de los Dolores y Viana and Fray Alonso Giraldo de Terreros, president of the San Sabá mission enterprise. He made no secret of his belief that the Apaches were faithless and the undertaking foolhardy. The missionary group bound for the San Saba River was split into factions. The colonel was accused repeatedly of causing delays and squandering the funds provided by the mission benefactor, Pedro Romero de Terreros, the mission president's cousin. Ortiz Parrilla arrived on the San Saba River on 17 April 1757, explored the river valley, and chose a site for his presidio on the riverbank a mile west of the site of present Menard. He built a log stockade, explored the area for signs of mineral deposits, and brought ore samples from the Los Almagres Mine for smelting and assay. As signs of an impending Indian attack mounted, he urged the missionaries to move to the presidio for protection. They refused. When the mission was attacked and destroyed on 16 March 1758 the presidio, with its forces dispersed on various assignments, was powerless to intervene. Afterward, the commandant withstood a petition from his company to move the presidio to a safer spot while he submitted alternate proposals to the viceroy. Whether or not the presidio was moved, he advised, a campaign should be made into the country of the *Norteños* to preserve Spanish prestige. The march, with 360 presidial soldiers and volunteers from the presidios and settlements of northern Mexico and Texas and 176 Indians, left San Antonio in mid-August 1759, and proceeded to San Sabá and thence northward. At the Clear Fork of the Brazos River, the force attacked a Tonkawa camp, killed 55 natives, and took 140 prisoners. On the Red River, near the site of present Spanish Fort, the Spaniards on 7 October assaulted a fortified Taovaya village where several of the allied tribes were gathered, including Comanches. Unable to take the village in a four-hour battle, Ortiz Parrilla, after council with his officers, withdrew the following day. On reaching San Sabá, he left Manuel Rodríguez of San Juan Bautista in charge and traveled to Mexico City to explain his defeat and the new set of circumstances on the frontier. He was not allowed to return, for Felipe de Rábago y Terán, exonerated of misconduct while serving as commandant of the San Xavier garrison, was to be restored to command. Ortiz

Parrilla was named captain of Presidio de Santa Rosa María del Sacramento in Coahuila but almost immediately was called to Florida to quell a native uprising. Given 400 men from the garrisons of Veracruz and Havana, he was sent as governor to San Miguel de Pensacola. Settling the Indian problem took two years. By that time Florida had been lost to the British in the settlement of the Seven Years' War. It fell to Ortiz Parrilla to transfer Pensacola to the British Royal American Regiment on 2 September 1763. He removed to Veracruz the Spanish troop and all the converted Florida Indians who were willing to leave their homeland.

After at last assuming command of Presidio de Santa Rosa, Ortiz Parrilla served as interim governor of Coahuila from (1764–65). During that time he authorized for Antonio Rivas, who had once served with him, a sizable land grant that is now part of southern Maverick County, Texas. In 1766 he was commissioned to explore the Texas Gulf Coast in response to a rumored English invasion. After exploring Padre Island, he drew a map of the coast as far as Galveston Bay, on the basis of his own exploration and interviews with persons who knew the coast. The map of his Gulf Coast expedition gave a clearer picture—though still an unclear one—than had previously existed. In December 1767 the viceroy Marqués de Croix finally authorized Ortiz Parrilla's trip to Spain to claim his inheritance. If indeed he left, he was back at Santa Rosa in September 1774, when he asked to be relieved to take a post in Spain, "at the Plaza de Valencia or some other." On 1 October 1774 the crown informed Viceroy Bucareli that the Santa Rosa captain had been assigned to the Valencia post with the rank of brigadier. Ortiz Parrilla was in Madrid by 16 November 1774, and presumably assumed his new duties.

Robert S. Weddle

Oswald, Lee Harvey. Assassin; b. New Orleans, 18 October 1939; d. Dallas, 24 November 1963; m. Marina Nikolaevna Prusakova (1961); 2 daughters. After the loss of his father, Oswald lived in an orphanage and subsequently in several places with his mother. After the two moved to New York in August 1952, he became a chronic truant and was placed under psychiatric care. They moved again to New Orleans in January 1954. In 1955 Oswald left school and tried unsuccessfully to join the Marine Corps. He found a job and used his spare time to pursue his growing interest in communist literature. He returned to Fort Worth with his mother in July of the following year and in October 1956 joined the Marine Corps. He served 15 months overseas, mostly in Japan; later he served in California. After an appeal based on the illness of his mother, he was released early from the service in September 1959. A month later Oswald left for the Soviet Union, entering through Finland. He tried to commit suicide when ordered out of Russia, but while attempting to renounce his U.S. citizenship he was permitted to remain and work in a Russian radio factory. He married in Russia. In June 1962, after prolonged efforts, he was allowed to return with his family to the United States. He lived in Fort Worth until October, when he moved to Dallas. On 10 April 1963 he attempted unsuccessfully to kill Maj. Gen. Edwin A. Walker at the latter's home. In late April, upon his return to New Orleans, Oswald organized a so-called Fair Play for Cuba Committee. He went to Mexico in September in an unsuccessful effort to get a visa to Cuba and the Soviet Union, and he returned in October to Dallas. After his arrest on 22 November 1963 he was charged with the Kennedy assassination and the murder of policeman J. D. Tippit. It was alleged that Oswald positioned himself in a sixth-story window of the Texas School Book Depository and there fired on the motorcade of President Kennedy and Governor John B. Connally. It was also claimed that Oswald killed J. D. Tippit shortly after the assassination while resisting arrest. Oswald was arrested in a movie theater that same day in the Oak Cliff section of Dallas. Two days later, on 24 November 1963, Oswald was shot and killed by Jack Ruby in the basement of the city jail while being transferred to the county jail.

Our Lady of the Lake University. The oldest regionally accredited institution of higher learning in San Antonio. It comprises a College of Arts and Sciences, a School of Business and Public Administration, a School of Education and Clinical Studies, and the Worden School of Social Service. The university's 32 areas of specialization are mostly in the liberal arts and the service professions. Several are offered in the Weekend College for adults. The university developed from an academy for girls established by the Sisters of Divine Providence in 1895. It became a liberal arts college for women in 1911 and received its charter from the State of Texas in 1919. In 1923 it attained membership in the Southern Association of Colleges and Schools. In 1927 it became the third Texas school to be approved by the American Association of Universities. Our Lady of the Lake became a coeducational college in 1969 and a university for men and women in 1975.

In 1895 Mayor Henry Elmendorf deeded 18 acres of land for a school south of Elmendorf Lake to the sisters, on the condition that they spend $75,000 on improvements in ten years. The congregation subsequently acquired a total of 71 acres at the site and constructed 34 buildings, 19 of which are a part of the university complex. Several of these buildings are noted for their architecture, including the Gothic Conventual Chapel, designed by Leo M. J. Dielmann in 1923. In 1958 the administration of the buildings and land was legally divided. A board of trustees administers all that pertains to Our Lady of the Lake University, and the Congregation of Divine Providence administers land and buildings of the Convent of Our Lady of the Lake.

Sister Mary Generosa Callahan, C.D.P.

Our Lady of Victory College. A Catholic women's college in Fort Worth; incorporated into the University of Dallas. In 1885 the Sisters of St. Mary of Namur were invited to establish a school in Fort Worth by Bishop Nicholas A. Gallagher and the pastor of St. Stanislaus Church, Rev. Jean Marie Guyot. The sisters had already founded schools in Corsicana, Denison, and Sherman. St. Ignatius Academy in Fort Worth was quite successful, and by 1908 the sisters had chosen a site for a new and enlarged school on South Hemphill Street. Our Lady of Victory College and Academy opened in 1910 with 72 students. The curriculum included English, German, Latin, and French, science, religion, art, elocution, and physical education. In 1911 the school was chartered by the state of Texas and empowered to grant degrees. Three years later it was affiliated with the Catholic University of America, and in 1921 with the University of Texas. The first college-level courses were offered to the order's novices in 1922, a year after Our Lady of Victory had begun to serve as the location of the motherhouse of the Western Province of the Sisters of St. Mary of Namur. In 1929 the college became affiliated with the Southern Association of Universities and Colleges. In the following year laywomen were admitted, and a regular junior college curriculum was implemented. In 1931 Our Lady of Victory College was approved for membership by the Association of Texas Colleges and Universities. In addition to classics, mathematics, and languages, by 1944 the college offered chemistry, zoology, biology, botany, and bacteriology. St. Joseph's School of Nursing was affiliated with Our Lady of Victory from 1935 to 1956. By the latter year several new buildings had been added to the campus, including a Home Economics Annex and a Campus House with recreational and dining facili-

ties. In 1954 Thomas K. Gorman, bishop of Dallas–Fort Worth, had approved a request by the order's superior, Mother Theresa Weber, to establish a new, enlarged college for women in the Oak Cliff area of Dallas. Within a few months, however, the decision was made to establish an entirely new, coeducational, liberal arts university that would resurrect the title University of Dallas. The new college, which opened on a 1,000-acre site in Irving in September 1956, had four sisters of St. Mary of Namur on its first faculty. The new Our Lady of Victory College remained in operation through the 1957–58 academic year and was then, in effect, incorporated into the new university.

Thomas W. Jodziewicz

P–Q

Padilla, Juan de. Early Spanish missionary; probably d. near Quivira, ca. 30 November 1544. The date of this Franciscan priest's arrival in America is not known. His signature appears on a letter from the New World dated 19 October 1529. He was among the friars selected to sail from Tehuantepec to the Orient as part of an expedition organized by Hernando Cortés, but the ships proved unseaworthy. Subsequently, Padilla labored among the Indians at various sites in Mexico. He was one of the two priests chosen to accompany Fray Marcos de Niza on Vásquez de Coronado's expedition in 1540. After Coronado's capture of Cíbola (or Háwikuh), the westernmost Zuñi pueblo, in July, Padilla, in the company of Pedro de Tovar, visited the Moqui (Hopi) villages in Arizona. In August he accompanied the advance guard under Capt. Hernando de Alvarado to the Cicuye (Pecos) and Taos pueblos and the buffalo plains beyond. Padilla was among the select party that journeyed in 1541 with Vázquez de Coronado to Quivira, the Wichita village in present Kansas. He reportedly conducted a service of thanksgiving in Palo Duro Canyon. When the disillusioned Coronado declared his intention to return to New Spain in the spring of 1542, Padilla chose to return to Quivira to continue missionary efforts among the plains tribes. With him were two lay brothers, Luis de Escalona and Juan de la Cruz, who worked in the New Mexico pueblos and reportedly were martyred. Three blacks, one of whom was accompanied by his family; a Portuguese soldier named Andrés do Campo; and several Indian converts from the monastery of Zapotlán likewise volunteered to remain with Padilla. Leaving Escalona at Cicuye, Padilla and his companions set out for the buffalo plains. Some accounts claim that they followed the Canadian River as far as the area of present Hutchinson and Roberts counties before turning north to Quivira, where they were warmly received by the natives. After working in the area about two years, Padilla, do Campo, and two Tarascan mission Indians named Lucas and Sebastián sought to expand their ministry to neighboring tribes in unexplored territory. On their way they were attacked by a war party of enemy tribesmen. Urging his companions to flee, the account goes, the friar knelt and deliberately sacrificed himself to "the arrows of those barbarous Indians, who threw him into a pit, covering his body with innumerable stones." Do Campo and the two Tarascans were allegedly held captive by the Indians, but later escaped. Afterwards they made their way south to Pánuco and reported the incident. The actual location of Padilla's death is disputed, as are certain details surrounding the episode, such as who was really with him. However, he has been revered by Texas Catholics as the first Christian martyr of Texas, and possibly of the United States. In 1936 a monument commemorating his martyrdom was erected jointly by the state of Texas and the Knights of Columbus in Ellwood Park, Amarillo.   *H. Allen Anderson*

Padre Island National Seashore. Dedicated in 1968 by Mrs. Lyndon Johnson. The national seashore includes 67½ miles of Padre Island, which is 130 miles long, and some of the Laguna Madre. Efforts to establish a state park on the island began in the 1930s. Investment, real estate speculation, and commercial development accelerated during the 1940s and 1950s. In 1955 the United States Park Service issued a publication, *The Vanishing Shoreline*, on the loss of America's natural shorelines. A year later a 10-year plan entitled Mission 66 was unveiled by director Conrad Wirth, who wanted to establish more national parks and seashores. In 1958 Senator Ralph Yarborough introduced a bill to establish a national park on Padre Island. A year later the bill was reintroduced, and committee hearings were held in 1959 and 1960. Texas citizens favored the establishment of a park but were opposed by developers and land investors. Though a similar bill proposing a smaller 40-mile park was introduced, Yarborough was able to guide his bill through Congress in 1962. Five years of condemnation proceedings occurred before Padre Island National Seashore was dedicated. Separate civil suits at Corpus Christi in 1965 and Brownsville in 1966 resulted in larger settlements than had previously been expected. The island's surface land was finally purchased at a cost of nearly $23 million, compared to the initial estimate of $4.5 million. Subsoil and mineral rights still belong to private owners. Nueces County has a park at the northern end of the island, and Cameron County maintains another at the southern end. Areas between the county parks and the national seashore remain under private or corporate ownership. The chief attraction of Padre Island is its wide eastern beach of fine sand and shell fragments that slopes gently into the Gulf of Mexico, making it ideal for swimming and surf fishing. This is the longest beach of its kind in the United States. Along it is a belt of sand dunes that rise to 35 feet. In the interior of the island are numerous deflated basins that become ponds and lakes in wet periods. In addition to these basins there are extensive dune fields of great scenic beauty, particularly early or late in the day. The National Park Service plans to alter the landscape as little as possible, so that visitors can experience the wind, sand, sea, and sky with minimal distraction. Although only a few small land animals live on the island, shore birds and migratory waterfowl abound. A new complex with visitor center, observation deck, snack bar, gift shop, showers, and changing area was completed in 1989.

Thomas N. Campbell and Joseph R. Monticone

Padre Island Shipwrecks of 1554. On 9 April 1554 four Spanish ships set sail from San Juan de Ulúa (Veracruz) bound for Spain. Their combined cargoes had an estimated value of a little over two million pesos or more than $9.8 million (1975 dollars). On 29 April, three of the four vessels were lost in a storm near Padre Island. Of the approximately 300 people on the three wrecked vessels, perhaps twothirds drowned while trying to reach the beach. Upon learning of the disaster, officials in Mexico promptly organized a salvage expedition, which arrived at the wreck sites within two months of the storm. One of the three ships was still visible above the waves, and free-diving salvage workers began recovery operations. The other two wrecks were located by dragging. The expedition raised somewhat less than half of the approximately 1,000,000 ducats lost in the three ships.

When in 1967 a General Land Office field representative officially reported the discovery of a sunken Spanish ship off Padre Island near Port Mansfield, recovery attempts for artifacts from the ship, the *Espíritu Santo*, were already in full operation by a private outofstate salvaging firm; the company, however, did not have a permit to operate within the state, and its activities were stopped by a temporary injunction in 1968. The Indiana company filed suit in a federal court against the state actions, and after 1968 several rulings were handed down verifying federal jurisdiction in the case, and an injunction was filed to halt state proceedings in the original suit. The artifacts recovered from the salvaging company were taken first to the General Land Office, then to the Texas Memorial Museum, and in October 1969 to the University of Texas Balcones Research Center in Austin. The case remained in litigation until 1984, when the state attorney general and the Texas Antiquities Committee settled, awarding the salvage firm $313,000 while Texas kept the artifacts the firm had recovered from the *Espíritu Santo*.

The find was considered a major discovery by most antiquarians and archeologists and at the time was cited as the earliest Spanish material ever recovered from American waters. Among the 400-year-old objects recovered from the wreck were a small solid-gold crucifix, one gold bar, several silver discs, cannons, crossbows, and three astrolabes (navigation instruments, now extremely rare). As a result of the difficulties surrounding the salvaging attempts the Texas legislature passed the Antiquities Bill in September 1969 to fix procedures in artifact-recovery attempts. The bill provided for a committee with the authority for the designation and regulation of archeological landmarks and the protection and preservation of the archeological resources of Texas. On recommendation of the Antiquities Committee, the Institute of Underwater Research, a privately financed nonprofit organization, was formed in 1970 to locate other sunken ships in the same area as the 1967 find. In addition, the organization was to assist artifact recovery by any properly licensed salvaging company. The institute surveyed an area near Port Mansfield, and 16 possible sites of sunken Spanish ships were located and mapped for future investigation. The Texas Antiquities Committee's investigations at the 1554 wreck site tentatively identified the *San Esteban*. Recovery from this ship began in 1972. In addition to extensive excavations at the site, a surface survey of the island opposite the wreck sites was carried out in order to locate evidence of the survivors or salvagers' camps. Encrusted artifacts weighing over 12,000 kilograms were recovered during the two seasons of excavation. Recovered were wrought-iron anchors, cannons, tools, ship's fittings and fastenings, and silver coin and bullion. Of particular interest were several items of aboriginal manufacture, including a mirror made from a polished iron pyrite nodule and prismatic blades of obsidian. The silver coin and bullion and a small amount of gold bullion comprised the greatest part of the fleet's cargo, but such perishable items as cochineal, hides, and wool were also being shipped to Spain. The collection from the *San Esteban* is housed in the Corpus Christi Museum. The third wreck, the *Santa María de Yciar*, was destroyed in the 1950s when the Port Mansfield Channel was dredged.

J. Barto Arnold III and Melinda Arceneaux Wickman

Paleoenvironments. Changes in Texas vegetation during the past 30,000 years offer clues about climatic changes, about the animals that once lived here, and about the hardships the earliest Texans, the Paleo-Indians, had to face in their daily quest for food and shelter. The remains of ancient plants yield the most reliable information about past vegetation. Unfortunately, most soils in Texas are unfavorable to plant preservation. In most of the state the less resistant plant parts decompose quickly after they are buried and leave no visible traces. Through the techniques of phytolith (plant crystal) research, through palynological investigation, and through evidence from other fields, however, we can now assemble a rough conjectural view of the major vegetational changes in Texas during the past 30,000 years.

The years 30,000–22,500 B.C. were an interlude between two major glacial periods in North America. During this time conditions in Texas were stable and favorable. Pollen records from deposits in West Texas reveal that at first most of the area north and west of Austin was covered by a large prairie and few trees. Grasses dominated the land, and pine, juniper, Douglas fir, and spruce trees were restricted mostly to the higher elevations of the Guadalupe, Davis, and Chisos ranges. The prairie of the Edwards Plateau probably supported stands of juniper and piñon in some higher and more protected habitats. The probable climate of West Texas in this period was cooler and wetter than today, with fewer temperature extremes. Pollen evidence suggests that minor climatic fluctuations occurred. These are reflected in the fossil record by cyclical increases and decreases in the proportion of tree pollen to pollen from other plants. Some cycles lasted several thousand years and suggest that at times large islands of pine and juniper invaded the grasslands. Prairie remained dominant in West Texas for this entire period, however, and provided grazing for many species of now-extinct animals. Knowledge about the early vegetation of the same period in Central, South, or East Texas is limited. An extensive oak–hickory–pine forest probably dominated East Texas, but its western limit is unknown. It probably extended as far west as Huntsville. Research indicates that during this early period much of the currently forested regions in the central United States was covered by vast prairies marked with patches of shrubs. It is possible that this vegetation pattern extended through Central Texas as far south as San Antonio. Other research, however, suggests that a vast oak–hickory–pine forest extended across the southern United States and terminated somewhere in East or Central Texas. South Texas from San Antonio west to Del Rio and south to Mexico was probably covered by a mosaic of grassland and prairie interspersed with islands of shrubby oaks. But even minor changes in the amount of rainfall could have changed the vegetation quickly.

Between 22,500 and 8,000 B.C. changes in world climates led to a buildup of large continental ice sheets in North America that reached their maximum size around 20,000 years ago. The disruption of wind patterns and the cooling influence of such large masses of ice in North America affected the vegetation and climate of the whole continent. In Texas the average annual temperature dropped to about five degrees centigrade cooler than it is today. The difference that this made would be equivalent to the difference between the climate in Uvalde, where summers are hot and dry and where it rarely freezes, and that in Lubbock, where summers are cooler, winter days are freezing, and snows are frequent. Pollen records from West Texas suggest that as this period began, the cooling reduced evaporation and led to the formation of large playas in many areas of West Texas. The resultant cooler and wetter climate encouraged existing forests and produced parklands. The spruce, juniper, Douglas fir, and pine forests of the West Texas mountains expanded downward to lower altitudes and spread out onto the mountain flanks, where they mixed with grasslands to form parklands and savannas. These changes produced a perfect habitat for vast numbers of now-extinct giant herbivores, including mastodons, mammoths, horses, Pleistocene bison, and camels. The oak–hickory–pine forests of East Texas probably did not expand significantly during this period. However, the dominant species of trees probably changed somewhat. Pollen records show that from about 22,500 to 12,000 B.C. the cooler-weather oak, elm, spruce, maple, hazelnut, alder, and birch may have dominated the forests. Likewise, atmospheric conditions in East Texas during this period were like those in West Texas. The existing vegetation in South Texas during this period did not change significantly. Areas of oak and juniper parklands expanded in the northern portion of the region just south of San Antonio, and the drier regions near the Mexican border filled with lush grassland. Vegetational variations were caused primarily by cycles of drought and wet years.

During the last few thousand years of this period the large glaciers receded as the North American continent warmed. By 10,000 years ago the ice sheets were gone; the path of the jet stream probably moved northward to bring warmer and drier winds to much of Texas. In West Texas the large playas dried, and the forests of pine, Douglas fir, and juniper contracted until they were again confined only to the protected mountain summits. Spruce disappeared entirely. The pine and juniper trees that once formed the prairie parklands also disappeared. Once again the West returned to a giant, uninterrupted grassland. Around the lower Pecos area of Southwest Texas the canyons and protected hills lost most of their piñons and junipers, and many desert plants presently found in that region, such as cacti, agave, yucca, and sotol, were already becoming quite common.

The vegetation on the rolling hills of the Edwards Plateau in Central Texas changed during the last few thousand years of this period from a dominance of piñon and juniper to a dominance of scrub oak and juniper. East of the Balcones Escarpment the forests lost most of their cool-loving species between 14,000 and 8,000 B.C. Alder, maple, spruce, and hazelnut disappeared entirely from the East Texas forests. Most of the birch species also disappeared from these forests, leaving behind only small patches of the warm-tolerant river birch. Basswood, dogwood, chestnut, and a few other forest species that grow best in cooler, wet habitats did not disappear entirely but were reduced to minor components in the new deciduous forests. Expanding into these forests were the species that now dominate them—new species of oak, hickory, walnut, pecan, sweet gum, and elm. Loblolly pines also may have expanded their numbers around 8,000 B.C. Yet many scientists believe that the dominance of pines in East Texas is fairly recent.

By 8,000 B.C. the vegetation in South Texas probably looked much as it does today and as it had before 30,000 B.C.—a mosaic that changed in wet and dry years. Moisture controlled how much of the region became oak shrubs, grassland, or semidesert.

The fossil pollen record reveals that the Texas climate has become progressively hotter and drier through the last 10,000 years. During that time a number of minor climatic oscillations have occurred. Around 500 B.C. West and Southwest Texas

underwent a notable cooling that allowed the forests of West Texas to expand downslope and also encouraged the southward expansion of the lush grasslands of the Southern High Plains. This expansion reached the Rio Grande and was widespread enough to encourage large herds of buffalo (bison) to range freely as far south and east as Langtry and Del Rio. Like most of the brief climatic reversals of the last 10,000 years, the one in West Texas was probably triggered by changes in the weather such as unusually strong hurricanes, which could have carried large volumes of water farther inland than usual; changes in ocean currents that could have caused phenomena like *el niño* off the coast of Chile; changes in the path of the continental jet stream that could have brought cooler or hotter surface temperatures; or localized weather changes that produced regional droughts. Each climatic oscillation during the last 10,000 years was brief, and most were restricted in area. By 8,000 B.C. West and Southwest Texas vegetation probably consisted of prairies extending in an unbroken wave north of a line running from the site of San Angelo to that of El Paso. South of this line the vegetation consisted of a graded mosaic beginning with mixed scrub and grasslands, then changing to scrublands, and ending with patches of semidesert south of a line from Marathon eastward to the edge of the Edwards Plateau. As today, moisture was the single most critical influence on the vegetation of West Texas.

In South Texas little changed during the last 10,000 years, though various vegetational components expanded or contracted. The scrub oak parklands that for thousands of years had been the dominant vegetation in areas south of San Antonio began to disappear, for example, and soon were restricted to their present moist areas. Scrublands of mesquite, acacia, and cactus expanded into the areas once covered by oaks, and throughout South Texas desert succulents such as agave, yucca, sotol, and cacti became common. Grasses became scarce in some South Texas areas that dried and turned into semideserts.

The forests of East and Central Texas also changed. In Central Texas just east of Austin the oak–hickory forests became more open as fingers of grassland invaded. The fossil pollen records suggest that the forests probably persisted until between 3,000 and 1,500 years ago. After that time all that remained was pockets of oak and pecan isolated in a vast grassy savanna. This contraction of the Central and East Texas forests continued until the forests reached their present westward margin around Huntsville. Loblolly pines probably came to dominate the forests of East Texas at this time. Fossil pollen evidence suggests that even though the early forests of East Texas may have expanded as far west as Austin, they were primarily composed of deciduous trees. Records show that the large relic stands of loblolly pines in Bastrop State Park, in Central Texas, did not expand southward, northward, or westward during the past 15,000 years. They probably did not expand even during the height of the Wisconsin glacial period around 20,000 years ago.

Vaughn M. Bryant, Jr.

Palestine, Texas. County seat of Anderson County, 108 miles southeast of Dallas. It was the early home of Daniel Parker and was named after the Parkers' former home of Palestine, Illinois. It was also the home of John H. Reagan and Governor Thomas M. Campbell. Palestine was established when Anderson County was formed in 1846. A post office opened at the site the next year. By 1848 the town had 210 residents. In 1856 a brick courthouse

Main Street of Palestine, ca. 1875–1880. Stereograph. Courtesy TSL.

was built, and a few years later four acres was donated for the establishment of the Palestine Female Institute. Soon, small business concerns were clustered around the square; in 1866, 12 dry-goods businesses were in operation. Commerce was served by paddle-wheel steamers that during periods of high water plied the Trinity River to Magnolia, the port for Palestine. Arrival of the International–Great Northern Railroad in 1872 led to the demise of local river shipping. The road also changed the face of the town, since the line bypassed the courthouse hill and built its shops, switching yards, and offices on level ground nearly a mile to the west. By 1896 a new depot had been constructed. Large quantities of cotton, lumber, cottonseed oil, and fruit were shipped from Palestine. During the 1880s and 1890s stores, saloons, and lodging houses rapidly formed a new business district by the tracks. By the 1890s Palestine had a population estimated at 6,000. In 1914 the county's fifth courthouse (still standing in the 1990s) was completed, and Palestine had a population estimated at 11,000. The discovery of oil in 1928 at Boggy Creek, east of Palestine, diversified the town's economy and carried Palestine through the Great Depression. Several producing fields were later found in Anderson County, and Palestine became a center for oil-well servicing and supplies. In 1952 the Missouri Pacific line acquired ownership of the International–Great Northern and in 1956 constructed an office building in Palestine. The railroad contracted with the city to base a certain number of railroad employees in Palestine. When the Missouri Pacific sold its lines to the Union Pacific in 1982, many railroad jobs in Palestine ended, though a few railroad employees remained there. In 1990 the town had a population of 18,042, and local industries included oil and gas producers, well servicers, a beef-packing plant, and the railroad. Four state prisons in the county also provided local jobs. Palestine is the site of the NASA National Scientific Balloon Flight Facility. Each spring the town is host to several thousand who visit Texas Dogwood Trails. Palestine is a terminus of the Texas State Railroad, now the focus of a state park that operates steam excursion trains between Palestine and Rusk. Another tourist attraction is Eilenberger's Bakery, established in 1898, which ships cakes throughout the world. City parks include the 900-acre community forest. Engeling Wildlife Management Area is in the northern part of the county. Lake Palestine, a reservoir of 25,500 surface acres on the Neches River, provides water. *Lester Hamilton*

Palm, Swante. Book collector and promoter of Swedish immigration; b. Swen Jaensson, Bästhult, Barkeryd Parish, Småland,

Sweden, 31 January 1815; d. Austin, 22 June 1899; m. Agnes Christina Alm (1854); 1 son, who died in infancy. Jaensson was tutored by the parish clerk and became interested in books and learning at a very early age. He worked as a court clerk and newspaper editor until, influenced by his nephew Swante Magnus Swenson, he immigrated to Texas (1844). Soon thereafter he took the name Swante Palm. In 1853 he went to Panama as diplomatic secretary to United States consul Thomas William Ward. After his return to Austin the next year, Palm continued to be associated with Swenson in various business interests. Proslavery but antisecessionist, he cautiously maintained neutrality during the Civil War. This fact left him in a relatively advantageous political position after the war, and he served in a number of public offices, among them Travis County justice of the peace and member of the Austin City Council. From 1858 to 1860 he participated as a meteorologist in the first Texas Geological and Agricultural Survey. In 1868 he helped organize the Swedish Evangelical Lutheran Gethsemane Church in Austin (later called Gethsemane Lutheran Church). From 1869 to 1872 he was Austin postmaster. In 1866 the Swedish government named Palm vice consul for Norway and Sweden, a position he held the rest of his life. As an agent of the American Emigrant Company in the 1870s, he encouraged Swedes to immigrate to Central Texas and helped them when they arrived. In 1883, on one of Palm's two trips to Sweden, King Oscar II awarded him the Order of Wasa in appreciation of his service as vice consul. As a result of this award, he is often called, incorrectly, Sir Swante Palm. In 1891 Bethany College, Lindsborg, Kansas, awarded him an honorary doctorate. Palm is best known for his library of about 12,000 volumes, collected over a lifetime from all over the United States and Europe. His collection included Scandinavian works, books about Texas, classics, literature, and scientific books. He knew English, French, Latin, German, and various Scandinavian languages. Copious marginalia indicate that he read much of what he collected. He donated most of his books to the University of Texas in 1897, a gift that increased the size of the university library by more than 60 percent. Palm spent his last days as assistant librarian, supervising the cataloguing and use of his collection, which, he stated, "is closely interwoven with my very existence."
Alfred E. Rogers

Palo Alto, Battle of. The first major engagement of the Mexican War, fought north of Brownsville on 8 May 1846 by American forces under Gen. Zachary Taylor and Mexican troops commanded by Gen. Mariano Arista. On 23 April, Mexico had proclaimed a "defensive war" against the United States, which had annexed Texas. The battle at Palo Alto, which began about 2:00 P.M. and lasted until twilight, resulted in a standoff. Darkness ended the action, and both armies bivouacked on the battlefield. Of 3,461 troops that formed the Mexican Army of the North, Arista's commissary reported 102 killed, 129 wounded, and 26 missing, including deserters. Lt. George Meade, who interrogated captured Mexican officers, concluded that Mexican losses numbered 400 men. The American army, which totaled over 2,200 soldiers, reported 5 dead and 43 wounded. Arista's adjutant, Jean Louis Berlandier, however, stated that American casualties were "about 200 dead and wounded." At Palo Alto Taylor tested the superiority of the so-called "flying artillery" developed by Maj. Samuel Ringgold, who was mortally wounded in the battle. Guns were mounted on light carriages drawn by specially trained teams of horses and could be moved quickly for tactical advantage. Although soldiers on both sides clamored for the traditional bayonet charge across the field, the artillery duel dominated the action. The last maneuver at Palo Alto, nonetheless, was a desperate Mexican charge at sunset. To neutralize the American artillery advantage at Palo Alto, the Mexican army moved southward at dawn on 9 May to Resaca de la Palma, where Taylor charged and defeated Arista's army. Shortly, the Americans captured Matamoros, and Arista retreated southward toward Monterrey. Other notables at Palo Alto included Gen. Pedro de Ampudia, Gen. Anastasio Torrejón, Col. José López Uraga, Gen. William J. Worth, Lt. Ulysses S. Grant, and Texas Ranger captain Samuel P. Walker. *Joseph P. Sanchez*

Pampa, Texas. County seat and largest town in Gray County. The site, once owned by the Francklyn Land and Cattle Company (later White Deer Land Company), was designated as a station on the Southern Kansas Railway in 1887. The first resident was Thomas H. Lane, the railroad section foreman, who settled his family in a half-dugout near the boxcar station, which was known initially as Glasgow and then as Sutton. Because of confusion with Sutton County, railroad officials asked George Tyng, manager of the White Deer Land Company, to select a new name for Sutton. Tyng submitted the name Pampa because the place resembled the pampas of Argentina. Tyng constructed Pampa's first frame building, the White Deer Land Company boardinghouse. This building later was leased to the Matador Ranch as a headquarters and then sold to Alfred Ace Holland, who made it the town's first hotel. The plat for the townsite was approved on 14 April 1902, the same day that 152 voters petitioned to organize Gray County. Tyng's successor, Timothy Dwight Hobart and his two associates, Cecil V. P. Buckler and Montague K. Brown, promoted the area to farmers. Pampa soon thrived as a small agricultural and railroad shipping point, populated largely by homesteaders and cowboys. By 1910 the town had a school, a bank, and a drugstore serving an estimated 400 people; by 1926 the population had risen to 987. Alexander Schneider, a Swiss immigrant, bought the Holland Hotel and remodeled it as the Schneider in 1912; he also organized a town band. The town voted to incorporate in 1912, with a commission–manager government. The discovery of oil in 1926 caused Pampa to grow. Its future was assured in 1927, when Godfrey Cabot, head of Cabot Carbon in Boston, established the first of several local carbon black plants. Another victory came in 1928, when Pampa supplanted Lefors as county seat after a special election. In 1931 the town had 10,470 residents. Further railroad service was provided by the extension of the Fort Worth and Denver and the Clinton and Oklahoma Western lines to Pampa in 1932. World War II brought about the establishment of Pampa Army Air Field. More importantly, the war and its aftermath spurred industrial growth; the Columbian Carbon and Coltexo companies and the Celanese Corporation of America built plants in the vicinity, as did the Skelly, Phillips, Shell, and Kerr–McGee oil firms. Dick Hughes and other real estate men quickly relieved the postwar housing shortage. The population in Pampa grew from 12,895 in 1941 to 24,664 in 1960. Pampa's community spirit was demonstrated in the opening of the modern, city-owned Coronado Inn in 1960. By 1967 the city had 34 industrial plants that produced petrochemical products, furniture, industrial machines, sheet-metal products, and heavy machinery. Economic recession and the reorganization of certain industrial firms resulted in a population decrease to 21,726 by 1972. In the 1980s the chamber of commerce and city development board continued to advertise Pampa as the "Friendly City at the Top O' Texas, Where Wheat Grows and Oil Flows." In 1990 the population was 19,959. Annual events include the Junior Stock Show and Hereford Breeders' Show in March, a rodeo in July, and a golf tournament during Labor Day weekend. The White Deer Land Museum contains that company's records and documents, in addition to pioneer relics. *H. Allen Anderson*

Panhandle. The 25,610-square-mile Panhandle of Texas was shaped by the Compromise of 1850, which resolved the state's controverted territorial claims. It is bounded on the east by the 100th meridian, on the north by parallel 36°30', and on the west by the 103d meridian. It comprises the northernmost 26 counties of the state; the line forming the southern boundary of Swisher County in the central Panhandle marks the southern boundary. The elevation declines from about 4,700 feet in the northwest (Dallam County) to about 2,000 feet in the southeast (Childress County). The growing season increases from 178 days a year to 217 days over the same distance. The average annual precipitation ranges from about 21.5 inches in the eastern counties to about 17 inches in the western counties. Thus the dry Panhandle climate ranges narrowly from subhumid to semiarid. The High Plains cover all but the gently undulating southeastern third of the Panhandle, where the Rolling Plains begin. The two are separated by the scenic eastern High Plains escarpment commonly called the Caprock. The upper tributaries of the Red River and the Canadian River drain the region. The Canadian cuts across the High Plains to isolate the southern part, the Llano Estacado, which has little drainage and a reputation as one of the world's flattest areas of such size. Beneath the High Plains lies the enormous store of relict water held by the Ogallala Aquifer—unquestionably the region's most valuable resource. High Plains soils are loamy, clayey, deep, and calcareous; those of the Rolling Plains are loamy and sandy; and those of the canyonlands and river valleys are loamy, clayey, shallow, and calcareous and support woody species including juniper, cottonwood, hackberry, mesquite, elm, willow, and plum. Scrub oak, grape, and stretchberry grow on the escarpments. Grasses found on the uplands include mainly the bluestems, gramas, buffalo grass, and, around playas, western wheat grass. Especially on the Llano Estacado, short grasses have protected the surface from erosion and, along with subhumidity and fire, have inhibited tree growth. In sum, Panhandle physiography produced a primordial grassland that supported the southern buffalo herd and a buffalo-hunting Indian culture, invited a grazing economy introduced by Americans, and eventually gave rise to a farming economy that displaced much of the grassland.

Human presence in the Panhandle dates from the time of Paleo-Indian hunters of Pleistocene animals, whose presence is verified by exquisitely knapped Folsom and Clovis projectile points found in situ with datable materials. Thereafter, occupation ebbed and flowed with environmental variations until the eve of historic times, when an elaborate archeological complex, the Panhandle Aspect, occupied the Canadian River and nearby streams. Panhandle Aspect culture appears to have crested from roughly A.D. 1350 to 1450, but was nowhere to be found when Indians of the Panhandle were first observed by persons who left documentary evidence. The entrada of Francisco Vázquez de Coronado crossed the Llano Estacado in 1541 in a futile quest for wealth, and found a culture of pedestrian, buffalo-hunting nomads whom the Spaniards called "Querechos," identified by modern scholars as Athabaskan ancestors of the Apaches. Apacheans evidently controlled the Panhandle and surrounding territory uncontested until after 1700, when Comanches, now mounted, appeared, challenged the Apaches, and eventually dispossessed them. By 1800, along with their Kiowa and Kiowa Apache allies, Comanches dominated the Great Plains south of the Arkansas River and held Comanchería against all comers for a century and a half. Besides providing the first documented observations of the Llano Estacado, the Coronado expedition established the orientation of the whole region toward the Hispanic Southwest, an orientation reinforced by the expedition of Juan de Oñate, who traveled along the Canadian River in 1601. In subsequent years, Spaniards and Pueblo Indians entered the region for a variety of purposes and regarded it as a part of New Mexico. Commercial ties between the plains and the river valleys of New Mexico were probably the strongest bonds between the two. In time, trade shifted from New Mexico to prearranged sites in West Texas such as Palo Duro and Tule canyons, Tecovas Springs, and Quitaque Creek, while Comancheros emerged as the principal agents of commerce. Though innocent enough in its early days, the Comanchero trade acquired sinister characteristics in the nineteenth century, as it dealt increasingly in stolen livestock and human traffic.

In any event, the southwestern orientation of the Panhandle stood for 180 years after Coronado, until the pivotal year 1821 brought forces reorienting the region toward the United States and introducing a succession of more-or-less separate but overlapping phases through which regional history evolved. In 1821 the successful Mexican War of Independence opened Santa Fe to legal trade with United States citizens and Maj. Stephen H. Long explored the Canadian River valley, thus initiating the Anglo-American exploratory phase of Panhandle history. Between 1821 and the 1853 the Pacific railroad survey of the thirty-fifth parallel, led by Lt. Amiel Weeks Whipple, and expeditions led by United States Army officers explored and described the Canadian valley, the Rolling Plains, and the upper tributaries of the Red River. Only the interior of the Llano Estacado lay beyond the ken of the Americans. Meanwhile, in 1840 Josiah Gregg found the south side of the Canadian an advantageous trade route, and in 1849 Capt. Randolph Marcy, closely following Gregg's tracks, specifically marked the Fort Smith–Santa Fe Trail so that ties of commerce and travel, along with exploration, pulled the Panhandle toward the American orbit.

Until after 1865 the southern Plains Indians remained essentially undisturbed, mainly because of the sectional controversy and the Civil War, but in the early 1870s commercial buffalo-hide hunters entered the Panhandle from western Kansas. Normal Indian resentment toward this incursion was heightened by the Indians' understanding that the Medicine Lodge Treaties of 1867 guaranteed them exclusive hunting grounds south of the Arkansas River. In retaliation, resentful warriors led by Quanah Parker and the charismatic medicine man Isa-tai plotted an attack upon the buffalo hunters' trading post at Adobe Walls in what is now Hutchinson County. The attack failed to overrun the post and cost heavy losses, although it sent both hide men and merchants scurrying for the safety of Dodge City and temporarily interrupted the buffalo-hunting phase of Panhandle history. Most importantly, the second battle of Adobe Walls goaded the government into the climactic campaign against the southern Plains Indians, the Red River Indian War of 1874–75. Earlier efforts to deal militarily with the southern Plains tribes won some battles, but resolved very little. In November 1864 a 500-man force under Kit Carson had engaged several villages in the vicinity of the Bent brothers' old adobe trading post on the Canadian. Doubtlessly the Indians were hurt considerably, but Carson achieved little of strategic consequence. Rather more successful was the Winter War of 1868, in which a strategy contrived by Maj. Gen. Philip H. Sheridan directed four converging columns upon the Indians' haunts to catch them unsuspecting in their winter camps. No column came from the south, however, and many camps simply dropped southward out of the encirclement. The 1874 campaign added a column of the Fourth United States Cavalry led northward by Col. Ranald Mackenzie to complete the encirclement. The Red River Indian War saw some dramatic pitched battles, most famously Mackenzie's victory in the battle of Palo Duro Canyon on 28 September 1874, but mainly it was a campaign of harassment that gave the Indians no rest until, near starvation, they accepted their inevitable move to reservations.

By early 1875 the military phase of Panhandle history was over. The hide men quickly felled most of the remaining buffalo with relatively minor interference from Indians, and the region lay essentially empty, awaiting its next phase. Fort Elliott, placed in Wheeler County as a hedge against Indian outbreaks, supported white settlement with numerous essential services. In 1876 the Texas legislature marked off the 26 Panhandle counties from the Bexar Land District, thereby essentially completing the transformation of the region from a southwestern Hispanic cultural domain to an Anglo-American one. The empty grassland was attractive to the *pastores*, led by Casimero Romero, who initiated the grazing phase of Panhandle history by bringing their sheep to the western Canadian basin, where Charles Goodnight found them when he moved his cattle from Colorado in the spring of 1876. Leaving the Canadian to the New Mexican sheepherders, Goodnight moved on to Palo Duro Canyon where, in partnership with James Adair, he built the JA Ranch. Almost simultaneously, Thomas Sherman Bugbee arrived in Hutchinson County and established the Quarter Circle T Ranch. Other pioneers soon followed, and the towns of Tascosa, Mobeetie, and Clarendon developed as the centers from which settlement, commerce, and political organization emanated. Their counties, Wheeler, Oldham, and Donley, were organized in 1879, 1881, and 1882, respectively. The federal census of 1880 counted 1,607 persons in the Panhandle, including 1,198 Anglos concentrated in Wheeler, Hemphill, and Donley counties; 358 Hispanics concentrated in Hartley, Oldham, and Deaf Smith counties; and 51 African Americans, 36 of whom lived near Fort Elliott. Of adults over age 15, 365 were born in former Confederate states, while 364 were born in Union states or territories. The region's foreign-born represented 11 nations.

Although sheep ranching initiated the grazing phase, its dominance quickly gave way to cattle, which first came in herds of as few as 100 head, owned by cattlemen who took the best grass and water. Few followed Goodnight's lead when he purchased 12,000 acres of JA range. Individual enterprise soon gave way to corporate enterprise because the attraction of low-cost cattle, low labor costs, the subsidy of free grass, and high market prices infused large amounts of capital from both the East and Europe. The first corporate giant was the Prairie Cattle Company of Edinburgh, Scotland. Another, the Capitol Freehold Land and Investment Company, Limited, is best known as the XIT Ranch. Corporate financial resources brought barbed wire, deep wells, and windmills, thus enabling more effective use of pasturage away from surface water and the upgrading of herds through selective breeding. Barbed wire soon enclosed much state-owned land, and the state's insistence on grazing fees bred bitter controversy, which was eventually resolved peacefully. Early corporate ranching contained the seeds of disaster, however, because its very success caused excessive investment, overstocking, bad management, and depressed prices, thereby making the industry vulnerable to any dislocation. The first rather feeble attempts at farming in the region, which came in the early eighties, were equally vulnerable. Both ranches and farms were devastated by unusually severe winters and summer droughts in the mid-eighties. Farming had to wait another generation for a new start. Though many ranches failed, well-managed ones survived, and a far better-organized industry emerged. It became the foundation for a ranching industry that remains integral to the economy and culture of the Panhandle.

Every phase of regional development profited by completion of the Fort Worth and Denver Railway in 1888. In time, the Rock Island and Santa Fe joined the FW&D in providing a region-wide rail network. Because the escarpments of the Staked Plains partly dictated routes, the rails crossed in the central Panhandle at the point where Amarillo was fortuitously located and made the town the center of the region's cultural, social, and commercial life. Railroads determined the location of townsites, ranchers got far easier access to supplies and markets, and promoters of various sorts, especially railroad men, ardently boosted the Panhandle as the new garden for farmers. Not until well into the twentieth century, however, did improved dry-land farming techniques and the first stirrings of modern irrigation, both backed by emerging technology, assure permanence of an agricultural foundation for the region. By 1917 beef, wheat, and cotton emerged as the basics of commercial production. Unusually favorable weather, markets impelled by World War I, and technological improvements blessed the efforts of producers who expanded acreage and increased production. The artificial demand and prices raised by the war, however, encouraged excessive production and cultivation of marginal lands better left to grazing, a fact that portended disaster in the 1930s. Fortunately for the Panhandle, a new and unanticipated industry burst upon the economic scene and permeated the whole fabric of regional life.

Drawing upon the research of geologist Charles N. Gould, a group of entrepreneurs led by grocer Millard C. Nobles organized the Amarillo Oil Company, leased 70,000 acres of ranchland, and began drilling. Their first wells produced only natural gas, but on 2 May 1921, Gulf–Burnet No. 2 produced the first Panhandle oil and encouraged further exploration. In 1925 Dixon Creek Oil Company hit a vast reserve in Hutchinson County that yielded 10,000 barrels a day. Oil spawned numerous collateral industries and towns, of which Borger was surely the most chaotic. The place eventually became so lawless that only martial law brought it stability. Other communities such as Lefors, Pampa, and Dumas profited from oil but avoided such

tumult. Amarillo became the corporate center of major oil companies. Abundant natural gas brought plants for extraction of carbon black, helium, and zinc smelting, while the marketing of petroleum products required construction of refineries and pipelines. The availability of moderately priced automobiles and cheap fuel brought a demand for better roads, and in the 1920s the Panhandle led Texas in the development of highways, including the legendary Route 66. Farm-to-market transportation flourished under the Rural Roads Act, and the combination of gasoline-powered transportation and paved roads strengthened Amarillo's position as the tri-state (Texas, Oklahoma, and New Mexico) trade center.

The arrival of the complex of oil-related industries could scarcely have been more timely, since they provided some economic diversification and activity after the events of September 1929. In fact, during the Great Depression they prospered and the oil counties grew in population. Agriculture, by contrast, had to contend with the economic dislocations of the time as well as an ecological calamity induced by land abuse, unsuitable farming methods, severe drought, and abnormally high winds. The Dust Bowl drove many farmers, especially tenants, from the land. Between 1935 and 1940 both the number of farms and property values declined sharply. Six agricultural counties lost more than 25 percent of their residents between 1930 and 1940; 10 others lost more than 10 percent. The stark reality of human suffering found expression in poignant images recorded by Farm Security Administration photographers, while the environmental crisis was nowhere made more vivid than in the graphic paintings of Alexandre Hogue. Immediate relief for depression victims proved to exceed the resources of localities, despite valiant efforts by such leaders as Mayor Ernest O. Thompson of Amarillo. In the long term, two absolute necessities emerged: stabilization of the agricultural economy and healing of the land. In 1932 Panhandle voters turned to the New Deal of Franklin D. Roosevelt, who carried all 26 counties with 87 percent of the popular vote. Four years later, Roosevelt gleaned 96 percent of the Panhandle vote. Through various New Deal agencies, federal aid came in a variety of projects ranging from multiple agricultural programs to construction of Palo Duro Canyon State Scenic Park, to the building of curbs, streets, and gutters in towns, to documenting and recording regional history, to producing public art. Of enormous advantage to the region was its United States representative, Marvin Jones, who chaired the House Agriculture Committee beginning in 1931 and heavily influenced the New Deal's agricultural legislation. Doubtless through Jones's influence, but also through dire need, the Panhandle was among the first areas in the nation to receive New Deal aid and became something of a proving ground for its programs. Of all programs affecting the Panhandle, and especially rural life, few, if any, could match the depth and permanence of the Rural Electrification Act, which brought electric power first to the rural Panhandle in Deaf Smith County in 1937.

As the "Dirty Thirties" waned and the effects of the Great Depression subsided, Panhandle citizens' attention turned outward toward Europe and Asia. Tangible portents of a new world became evident on 25 November 1940, when units of the Texas National Guard mobilized at Amarillo. Though guard personnel served world-wide, the Second Battalion, formed from the 131st Field Artillery under Col. Blutcher S. Tharp of Amarillo, was immortalized as the Lost Battalion of Java. Two Panhandle men,

John C. "Red" Morgan and Charles H. Roan, won the Medal of Honor, while former representative Jones served throughout the war as war food administrator. Because of the large number of days per year suitable for flying, the Army Air Corps placed training fields at Dalhart, Pampa, and Amarillo. Only the Amarillo installation remained after the war. McLean and Hereford hosted German and Italian prisoners of war. The Pantex Army Ordnance Plant, established in 1942 in Carson County to produce bombs and artillery shells, assumed a conspicuous role in the Cold War as the assembly plant for nuclear warheads. The demands of global war combined with ample rainfall sent Panhandle wheat and beef production soaring; cotton production also significantly increased, though less dramatically. Largely because of the leadership of Ernest Thompson in his position on the Railroad Commission, the Panhandle oil and gas fields had been developed and were poised to fuel and lubricate the machines of war. In March 1943 the Exell Helium Plant in Moore County began extracting helium from natural gas to provide lifting power for the blimps that escorted transoceanic convoys; also, completely without the knowledge of Exell personnel, the plant provided helium for the Manhattan Project. The number of peaceful applications of Helium later increased, although it was Cold War demands for nuclear weaponry that kept the Exell Plant in operation after the armistice.

The post–World War II years sustained the prosperity stimulated by the war, although it still rested mainly upon its traditional foundations, agriculture and petroleum. The Korean War bolstered the demand for both and introduced a pivotal decade in regional history, the 1950s. In the five years following 1952, Amarillo recorded less rainfall than in any comparable period of the 1930s, and emerging dust clouds evoked fears of another Dust Bowl. The happy fact that the worst did not happen may be attributed to expanding irrigation and the soil-conservation practices learned 20 years earlier. During the 1930s, as the number of farms decreased, the size of farms increased. The average of almost 1,000 acres by 1940 reflected advanced mechanization and especially widespread irrigation, the number of irrigation wells having increased from a mere 41 in 1930 to more than 700 in 1940. Recurring drought in the fifties encouraged irrigation all over the High Plains, but especially north of the Canadian River, where the Ogallala Aquifer had previously been considered too deep for feasible irrigation. Technology changed that, however, and over the High Plains the number of wells increased from 14,000 in 1950 to 27,500 in 1954. Irrigated acreage expanded from 1.86 million acres to 3.5 million in the same period. The irrigation boom peaked in the middle 1970s, subsided, and stabilized about 1980. It assured a measure of agricultural prosperity and stimulated a pervasive agribusiness that remains a dominant force in the regional economy—especially in cattle feeding. An explosion of feedlots in northwestern Texas came about through the chance presence of Paul Engler, a Nebraska cattle buyer, in Hereford in 1960. Engler noticed an abundance of components: space, favorable climate, cattle, and massive irrigated hybrid sorghum. Far-sighted bankers, especially Henry Sears of Hereford, provided capital for the infant industry, which quickly grew into an obstreperous, youthful industry. The early 1970s brought a sobering collapse that eventually yielded a more sound, scientifically managed enterprise.

As the hot war in Korea intensified the Cold War, Amarillo Army Air Field reopened as Amarillo Air Force Base in 1951 to train technicians and to base units of the Strategic Air Command. The Atomic Energy Commission claimed the Pantex plant in 1950 and added manufacture of nuclear warheads to the installation's former functions. Operated by private contractors under the Department of Energy, Pantex became the nation's sole assembly plant for nuclear warheads in 1975. As early as 1926, visionary individuals considered harnessing Canadian River water for domestic and industrial use. Austin A. Meredith made a virtual life's work of promoting an impoundment, and his efforts and those of many others led to the formation of the Canadian River Municipal Water Authority in 1953. Eleven Panhandle and South Plains cities joined the authority, secured federal financing, and constructed Sanford Dam. The resulting Lake Meredith impounds up to 821,300 acre-feet of water. Excessive salinity plagues the lake, however. The 1950s also featured a remarkably rapid reversal in the traditional Democratic politics of Panhandle voters who, after overwhelmingly supporting Franklin Roosevelt through four elections, gave President Harry Truman a decisive victory in 1948 and helped Democratic senator Lyndon B. Johnson defeat his Republican opponent. Four years later Republican Dwight D. Eisenhower won 24 Panhandle counties, although he took only 16 in 1956. In 1960 it became evident that the 1950s had witnessed a political transition-in-progress, for Richard Nixon won 22 Panhandle counties and carried the region with 62 percent of the popular vote. Except for Johnson's narrow regional victory in 1964, no Democratic presidential candidate has carried the Panhandle since 1948. The shift has reflected a general conservative trend, for local, state, and congressional Republican candidates have become increasingly successful.

Deactivation of Amarillo Air Force Base in 1968 shook the entire regional economy, but was turned to account when the base facilities were purchased by the state of Texas and made the campus of Texas State Technical Institute, which opened in 1970 and has since supplied skilled labor to the regional workforce. The runways built to accommodate B-52 strategic bombers opened the way for construction of a new air terminal to accommodate an expanding economy. Accordingly, in 1971 a new air terminal opened to serve the three-state area. Because of its exceptionally long runway, Amarillo Air Terminal was designated a port of entry to the United States.

At the end of the Cold War, Pantex turned aboutface and started dismantling nuclear warheads. The plant is promoted as the center of a research consortium for finding peaceful applications for nuclear materials. The possibility implies great economic impact for the region, but also raises concerns among residents who are concerned about potential dangers of plutonium storage, as well as possible contamination of the Ogallala Aquifer. Population trends of the 1980s and 1990s suggest that the Texas Panhandle is in a transitional, and somewhat confusing, phase. Between 1970 and 1980 the regional population grew by nearly 60,000, or about 18 percent. In the 1980s the overall region lost slightly less than 6 percent of its population. Only two counties had statistically significant population gains—Moore County (including Dumas) and Randall County. The latter grew by nearly 20 percent because of Amarillo's southwestward expansion beyond the Potter county line and because of the emergence of Canyon as a virtual suburb of Amarillo. Of the remaining counties, four lost more than 20 percent of their population, and 13 lost from 9 to 19 percent. All of these are agricul-

Cynthia Ann Parker, Austin, February 1861. Courtesy Lawrence T. Jones III Collection, Austin. Comanches captured Cynthia as a child. Her forced reintegration into white society 24 years later failed, and she made several unsuccessful attempts to rejoin her Comanche family.

tural counties or oil and gas producers or both. The decline of formerly reliable industries has compelled a search for alternatives, among which tourism and prisons are promising. The Ogallala Aquifer remains the Panhandle's most precious resource, however, and although the threat of its depletion appears to have subsided, its finitude necessitates earnest consideration and planning if the economic well-being of the region is to endure. *Frederick W. Rathjen*

Paris, Texas. Paris, originally known as Pinhook, is the county seat of Lamar County. It is in the upland separating the tributaries of the Red and Sulphur rivers. Settlements were known to be in the area as early as 1824. The town was founded by merchant George W. Wright, who donated 50 acres of land in February 1844, when the community was also selected as county seat by the voters. It was incorporated by the Congress of the Republic of Texas on 3 February 1845. The community of Pinhook was renamed for the French capital Wright's employees, Thomas Poteet. The Central National Road of the Republic of Texas ran from San Antonio north through Paris to cross the Red River. By the eve of the Civil War, when it had 700 residents, Paris had become a cattle and farming center. The Texas and Pacific reached town in 1876; the Gulf, Colorado and Santa Fe and the St. Louis and San Francisco in 1887; the Texas Midland (later Southern Pacific) in 1893; and the Paris and Mount Pleasant (Pa–Ma Line) in 1910. Paris Junior College was estab-

lished in 1924. In 1877 and 1916 major fires forced the city to rebuild, and in 1982 Paris was hit by a tornado that destroyed more than 1,500 homes and left 8 dead and 3,000 homeless. From 1984 through the early 1990s, local businesses invested nearly $7 million in renovating and revitalizing the downtown area. In the early 1990s Paris was a regional medical center serving northeastern Texas and southeastern Oklahoma. At that time there were two military installations in Paris and nearby: Gaines Boyle Memorial Reserve Center and Camp Maxey. During the early 1990s local residents were involved in agribusiness—including the raising of beef and dairy cattle, hay, wheat, and soybeans—and in numerous industries, among them Babcock and Wilcox (steam generation); Campbell Soup, Incorporated; Flex-O-Lite (reflective glass beads); Kimberly–Clark Corporation (disposable diapers); Merico (Earth Grains and packaging divisions); and Philips Lighting (incandescent-lamp parts). The town has been home to Sam Bell Maxey, John S. Chisum, and A. M. Aikin, Jr. The population of Paris grew from 9,358 in 1904 to 15,649 in 1930, 18,678 in 1940, 20,977 in 1960, 23,441 in 1970, and 25,498 in 1980, before declining to 24,699 in 1990. *Daisy Harvill*

Parker, Cynthia Ann. Indian captive; b. Crawford County, Illinois, 1824 or 1825. She was captured by Comanches on 19 May 1836 at Fort Parker and remained with the Indians for almost 25 years. She became thoroughly Comanche. It is said that in the mid-1840s her brother, John Parker, who had been captured with her and then released, asked her to return to their white family, but she refused, explaining that she loved her husband and children too much to leave them. Other attempts to lure her back occurred, though some may be apocryphal. Indian agent Robert S. Neighbors learned, probably in 1848, that Cynthia was among the Tenawa Comanches. She had married chief Peta Nocona and eventually had three children, including Quanah Parker. On 18 December 1860, Texas Rangers under Sul Ross attacked a Comanche hunting camp at Mule Creek, a tributary of the Pease River, and took three captives. One of them, a non-English-speaking woman with an infant daughter, had blue eyes. Col. Isaac Parker later identified her as his niece, Cynthia Ann. Cynthia accompanied her uncle to Birdville on the condition that military interpreter Horace P. Jones would send along her sons if they were found. While traveling through Fort Worth she was photographed with her daughter at her breast and her hair cut short—a Comanche sign of mourning. She thought that Peta Nocona was dead and feared that she would never see her sons again. In 1861 a sympathetic Texas legislature voted her a grant of $100 annually for five years and a league of land and appointed Isaac D. and Benjamin F. Parker her guardians. But she was never reconciled to living in white society and made several unsuccessful attempts to flee to her Comanche family. After three months at Birdville, her brother Silas took her to his Van Zandt County home. She afterward moved to her sister's place near the boundary of Anderson and Henderson counties. Though she is said in some sources to have died in 1864, the 1870 census enrolled her and gave her age as 45. At her death she was buried in Fosterville Cemetery in Anderson County. In 1910 her son Quanah moved her body to the Post Oak Cemetery near Cache, Oklahoma. She was later moved to Fort Sill, Oklahoma, and reinterred beside Quanah. *Margaret Schmidt Hacker*

Parker, Quanah. Last chief of the Quahadi Comanches; b. about 1845 (?) near the Wichita Mountains in what is now Oklahoma; d. Oklahoma, 23 February 1911. Parker was the son of Peta Nocona and white captive Cynthia Ann Parker. The name Quanah means "odor." In 1860 Peta Nocona was killed defending an encampment on the Pease River against Texas Rangers under Sul Ross. The raid, which resulted in the capture and incarceration of Cynthia Ann and Quanah's sister Topasannah, also decimated the Nocones and forced Quanah, now an orphan, to take refuge with the Quahadi Comanches of the Llano Estacado. By the 1860s the Quahadis ("Antelopes") were known as the most aloof and warlike of the various Comanche bands. Among them Quanah became an accomplished horseman and leader. As a consequence of their refusal to attend the Medicine Lodge Treaty Council or to move to a reservation as provided by the treaty, the Quahadis became fugitives on the Staked Plains. There, beyond the effective range of the military, they continued to hunt buffalo in the traditional way while raiding settlements. For the next seven years Parker's Quahadis held the Texas plains virtually uncontested. Attempts of the Fourth United States Cavalry under Col. Ranald Mackenzie to track and subdue the Indians in 1871 and 1872 failed. Not only was the army unable to find them but, at Blanco Canyon on the morning of 9 October 1871, the troopers lost a number of horses when Quanah

Chief Quanah Parker. Photograph by William S. Soule. Probably at Fort Sill, Indian Territory, ca. 1869. Prints and Photographs Collection, Indians—W. Soule, Photographer file, CAH; CN 01356. Parker was the son of Comanche Peta Nocona and Cynthia Ann Parker. After his mother's return to white society, Quanah remained with the Comanches and became a Quahadi Comanche chief.

and his followers raided the cavalry campsite. Afterward, the Indians seemingly disappeared onto the plains, only to reappear and attack again. Mackenzie gave up the search in mid-1872. But as buffalo hunters poured onto the plains, Parker and his followers were forced to take decisive action. The Quahadis, under the guidance of Quanah and a medicine man named Isa-tai, formed an alliance dedicated to expelling the hunters from the plains. On the morning of 27 June 1874, this army of some 700 warriors—Cheyennes, Arapahos, Kiowas, and Comanches—attacked Adobe Walls. But their planned surprise was foiled, and the hunters' superior weapons repelled repeated attacks. In the end the hunters suffered just one casualty, while 15 Indians died and numerous others, including Parker, were wounded. Defeated and disorganized, the Indians retreated and the alliance crumbled. Within a year Parker and the Quahadis, under relentless pressure from the army and suffering from hunger, surrendered their independence and moved to the Kiowa–Comanche reservation in southwestern Oklahoma.

While most Indians, found adjustment to the reservation life difficult or impossible, Quanah made the transition with such seeming ease that federal agents named him chief. Though this action was outside federal jurisdiction, the leaderless tribe acquiesced. Over the next quarter century, Quanah worked to promote his people's self-sufficiency. To this end, he supported the construction of schools on reservation lands and encouraged Indian youths to learn the white man's ways, promoted ranching, and called on his followers to construct houses of the white man's design and to plant crops. He also served as a judge on the tribal court, an innovation based on county tribunals; negotiated business agreements with white investors; and fought attempts to roll back the changes instituted under his direction. Here, his influence was most keenly felt in his successful attempt to prevent the spread of the ghost dance among his people. He also approved the establishment of a Comanche police force, which he believed would help the Indians to manage their own affairs. Through shrewd investments, including some $40,000 worth of stock in the Quanah, Acme and Pacific Railway, Parker became very wealthy. He was a close associate of several prominent Panhandle ranchers, counted Theodore Roosevelt as one of his friends, and was frequently interviewed by magazine reporters. Yet he did not completely repudiate his past. He rejected suggestions that he become monogamous and maintained a 22-room house for his 7 wives and numerous children. He refused to cut his long braids. He rejected Christianity, even though his son White Parker was a Methodist minister. Quanah was a member of the peyote-eating Native American Church and is credited with introducing and encouraging peyote use among the tribes in Oklahoma. Despite his artful efforts to protect his people and their land base, in 1901 the federal government decided to break up the Kiowa–Comanche reservation into individual holdings and open it to settlement by outsiders. For the remaining years of his life Parker operated his profitable ranch, continued to seek ties with whites, and maintained his position as the most influential person among the now-dispersed Comanches. In 1902 his people honored him by naming him deputy sheriff of Lawton, Oklahoma. At his funeral he was dressed in full Comanche regalia but, befitting his position as a man of two worlds, was reputedly buried with a large sum of money. After robbers plundered his grave four years later, his remains and those of his mother were reburied at Post Oak Mission Cemetery. In 1957 expansion of a missile base forced the relocation of the cemetery and the reburial of Quanah and Cynthia Ann Parker at Fort Sill.

Brian C. Hosmer

Parmer, Martin. Signer of the Texas Declaration of Independence; b. Charlotte County, Virginia, 4 June 1778; d. Jasper County, 2 March 1850; m. Sarah Hardwick (ca. 1798; d. 1826); 10 children, who later spelled their name "Palmer"; m. Margaret Griffin Neal (ca. 1827); 1 daughter; m. Louisa Lout (ca. 1830); 1 son + at least 6 children from Louisa's previous marriage; m. Zina Kelley (ca. 1839); 5 children. Parmer had a political career in Missouri, where, partly as a result of his military service in the War of 1812, he was chosen colonel of the Missouri militia and led four companies against the Indians. In 1825 he moved to Texas, where he joined Haden Edwards and fought for Benjamin Edwards in the Fredonian Rebellion. On 25 November 1826 he presided over the court-martial that tried and convicted Samuel Norris, the alcalde of Nacogdoches, and his attorney, José Antonio Sepulveda. When the rebellion collapsed in defeat, Parmer fled first to Gonzales and later to Louisiana. He attempted to return to Texas in 1831 but was expelled by Mexican authorities. After being pardoned in 1835 he returned to East Texas in time to be elected as a delegate from Tenaha (now Shelby County) to the Consultation of 1835. The same year he was elected to the General Council. The following year San Augustine County selected him as a delegate to the Constitutional Convention of 1836. At Washington-on-the-Brazos he signed the Texas Declaration of Independence and was assigned to the committee to draft the new constitution. In 1839 President Lamar appointed Parmer chief justice (i.e., county judge) of Jasper County. He held this post for less than a year. Parmer was buried 12 miles southeast of Jasper. Later his body was moved to the State Cemetery in Austin. Parmer County is named in his honor.

Joe E. Ericson

Parr, George Berham. The "Duke of Duval"; b. San Diego, Texas, 1 March 1901; d. 1 April 1975; m. Thelma Duckworth (1923; divorced, remarried, and again divorced in 1949); m. Eva Perez. Parr had two daughters. At 13 this son of political *patrón* extraordinaire Archer Parr served as his father's pageboy in the Texas Senate. Despite a disastrous record at several colleges, he entered the University of Texas law school as a special student in 1923 and passed the state bar examination three years later without earning a law degree. The disinclination of his brothers, Givens and Atlee, to pursue political careers paved the way for George to become the political heir to his father, who had ruled Duval County since 1907. Archie chose George to complete Givens's term as Duval county judge (1926). George was soon managing local affairs as the aging boss, already in his late sixties, struggled with various physical ailments and became increasingly preoccupied with state and national matters. George surpassed his father as protector of the impoverished Mexican-American laborers who formed the majority of the county population and served as the mainstay of the Democratic machine. He became far more fluent in Spanish than Archer, tirelessly learned the names of his constituents and their children, and provided help in times of need in return for one concession—absolute loyalty. Under his leadership, both corruption and paternalism flourished in Duval County. Not even a conviction for income-tax

evasion in 1934 and his subsequent imprisonment for nine months in 1936–37 destroyed Parr's growing political power. His handpicked candidates continued to sweep county elections, and by the time of his father's death in 1942, Parr stood as the undisputed political and economic boss of Duval County. He amassed a fortune with income from banking, mercantile, ranching, and oil interests—and from the public treasury. His political influence extended into other South Texas counties as well. With a pardon from President Harry Truman in 1946, he reclaimed the right to run for public office, and later held the posts of county judge and sheriff.

The remainder of Parr's political career was highlighted by a seemingly endless series of spectacular scandals, involving election fraud, graft on the grand scale, and violence. His most celebrated scheme decided the outcome of the United States Senate race between Coke Stevenson and Lyndon Johnson in 1948. With Stevenson the apparent winner, election officials in Jim Wells County, probably acting on Parr's orders, reported an additional 202 votes for Johnson a week after the primary runoff and provided the future president with his 87-vote margin of victory for the whole state. Amid charges of fraud, the voting lists disappeared. Even more sordid controversies followed. As strong challenges from the Freedom party developed in several South Texas counties, two critics of Parr's rule and the son of another met violent deaths. Though denying Parr's involvement in two of the killings, his biographer, Dudley Lynch, concedes that the evidence against Parr in the shooting of the son of Jacob Floyd, an attorney for the Freedom party, was both "highly circumstantial" and "highly incriminating." After this third murder, Governor Shivers, Texas attorney general Shepperd, and federal authorities launched all-out campaigns to destroy the Parr machine. Investigations of the 1950s produced over 650 indictments against ring members, but Parr survived the indictments and his own conviction for federal mail fraud through a complicated series of dismissals and reversals on appeal. Another legal offensive occurred in the 1970s. While appealing a conviction and five-year sentence for federal income tax evasion, Parr committed suicide at his ranch, Los Harcones.

Evan Anders

Parsons's Brigade. A Confederate brigade organized in 1862 to serve as cavalry for the Army of the Trans-Mississippi then forming in Arkansas. For much of the war the brigade was commanded by Col. William Henry Parsons, who had raised the Twelfth Texas Cavalry Regiment in the summer of 1861. In late 1862 Brig. Gen. James M. Hayes briefly commanded the brigade, in 1863 Col. George W. Carter led part of the regiments, in 1864 Brig. Gen. William Steele assumed command, and in 1865 Parsons regained total control. The permanent components of the brigade were Parsons's Twelfth Texas Cavalry Regiment, Nathaniel Macon Burford's Nineteenth Texas Cavalry Regiment, George Washington Carter's Twenty-first Texas Cavalry Regiment, Charles Leroy Morgan's Texas Battalion, and Joseph H. Pratt's Tenth Texas Field Battery. During the Civil War Parsons's Brigade earned the reputation as one of the finest mounted units serving in the Trans-Mississippi Department. The brigade took part in almost 50 battles, although most were too small to rate a name, and the men were responsible for watching federal operations from Memphis to Vicksburg. For three years they provided outposts and scouts for the army headquartered first at Little Rock and later at Shreveport. The brigade rarely mustered in full at any single place; instead, the troops generally fought by detachments or regiments. Much of the brigade's well-deserved reputation resulted from the outstanding fighting record of the Twelfth Texas Cavalry Regiment and the leadership of Colonel Parsons. *Anne J. Bailey*

Pasadena, Texas. Between Houston and Deer Park in southeastern Harris County; founded in 1893 by John H. Burnett of Galveston and named because of its lush vegetation for Pasadena, California. The La Porte, Houston and Northern Railroad was built through the townsite in 1894 and opened the area for development as a farming community. Retired Kansas banker Charles R. Munger and land promoter Cora Bacon Foster were instrumental in organizing the early community. After the Galveston hurricane of 1900 Clara Barton, of the American Red Cross, purchased 1½ million strawberry plants for Gulf Coast farmers. Pasadena quickly established itself as the strawberry capital of the region. By the 1920s all of southeast Harris County was known as "Pasadena Acres." In addition to strawberries, the Pasadena farmers sold cantaloupes, cape jasmine flowers, cucumbers, and other produce. In 1899 Pasadena residents formed the first ISD in Harris County. A four-year high school program was established in 1924 with the construction of Pasadena High School. Both the Genoa and South Houston school districts were consolidated into the Pasadena system in 1935. The citizens of Pasadena voted to incorporate in 1923 to disincorporate the next year. They voted again to incorporate in 1928. The city comprised about half the land Burnett had originally platted for his town. At the time of incorporation, water, electricity, and gas utilities had only recently been brought to the community. Burnett had laid his town out on the southern bank of Buffalo Bayou, which became the Houston Ship Channel. When Joseph Cullinan, founder of Texaco, moved his company to Houston in 1906, he purchased 200 acres in Pasadena. There he operated an experimental farm for 20 years, while he promoted this site and other lands along the ship channel. The Sinclair (now ARCO), Texaco, and Crown oil companies all built refineries in the area by 1920. Transition from a farming economy to an industrial one did not occur until the late 1930s, when the war in Europe spurred a major increase in the ship-channel industries. Pasadena had a population of 3,436 in 1940 and 22,483 in 1950, as the postwar boom continued. It annexed the communities of Deepwater, Middle Bayou, and Red Bluff. From 1.7 square miles in 1893 the community site grew to 58.6 square miles in 1980, when the city had a population of 112,560 people. In 1993 Pasadena had a population of 122,805 and 2,147 businesses. Employment in Pasadena is closely linked to the ship-channel industries, Bayport Industrial District, and the Johnson Space Center in Clear Lake. San Jacinto College and Texas Chiropractic College are located in Pasadena. Musical entertainment ranges from the fare at Gilley's Country and Western Club to performances of the Pasadena Philharmonic Orchestra. The Pasadena Historical Museum, Bay Area Museum, Armand Bayou Nature Center, Pasadena Rodeo, and San Jacinto Strawberry Festival are major tourist attractions. *C. David Pomeroy, Jr.*

Pat Dunn County. A nonexistent county proposed by Duval County political boss Archer Parr. In 1913, as a state senator, Parr came up with a scheme to double the amount of political patronage and revenue sources at his disposal. He proposed dividing Duval County roughly in half and turning the southern portion into a new county. In January 1913 he introduced a bill proposing the formation of Ross County, but protests by Duval County residents and the opposition of powerful Starr County rancher Edward C. Lasater doomed the bill to failure. Later in 1913, however, during a special session of the legislature, Parr caught his opponents off guard and secured the passage of another bill calling for the establishment of Pat Dunn County, named after a Corpus Christi legislator and Parr ally. By gerrymandering in the December 1913 county seat election they deprived Realitos, the ranching town that was Lasater's Duval County headquarters, and Concepcion of their voting boxes in an effort to ensure that Parr's hometown, Benavides, would be chosen. These blatant tactics resulted in an injunction blocking the election. Parr's supporters proposed an alternate precinct plan that was no improvement, with the same result. Before they could try again, it was determined that the legislation authorizing Pat Dunn County violated an obscure provision of the state constitution that requires a distance of at least 12 miles between the boundary of a new county and the seat of an existing county (the town of San Diego, in the case of Duval County). Despite the failure of Pat Dunn County, Parr introduced another county-formation bill in 1914. This one passed the Senate, but failed in the House after Parr offered some injudicious testimony regarding his influence over Duval County politics. He tried again during the May 1915 special session, but this bill also failed in the House. Thereafter Parr concentrated on solidifying his power in Duval County, a task in which he met with conspicuous success. *Martin Donell Kohout*

Patman, Wright. Congressman; b. Cass County, 6 August 1893; d. Bethesda Naval Medical Center, Maryland, 7 March 1976; m. Merle Connor (1919; d. 1967); 4 sons; m. Pauline Tucker (1968); ed. Cumberland University Law School, Lebanon, Tennessee (law degree, 1916). Before his election to the Texas House of Representatives (1920), Patman served as assistant county attorney for Cass County. After two terms in the legislature he was elected district attorney of the Fifth Judicial District and occupied the office for four years. In 1928 he won election as a Democrat to the United States House, representing the First Texas Congressional District, which included Marshall, Paris, and Texarkana. During the Great Depression he was a scathing critic of the economic policies of President Herbert Hoover and Secretary of the Treasury Andrew Mellon. His most noteworthy legislative initiative during the Hoover administration was the Veterans' Bonus (Patman) Bill, which mandated the immediate cash payment of the endowment promised to servicemen of World War I. The bill failed during Hoover's term but eventually passed (1936). Patman favored nearly all of the New Deal. He consistently supported the domestic programs of presidents Truman, Kennedy, and Johnson. He coauthored the Federal Anti–Price Discrimination (Robinson–Patman) Act, a landmark antitrust measure prohibiting retail stores from restraining competition by charging unreasonably low prices. He was also instrumental in the passage of the Federal Credit Union Act of 1934, the Full Employment Act of 1946, the British Loan Act of 1946, the Defense Production Act of 1950, and the Housing acts of 1946, 1949, 1961, and 1965. Patman was chairman of the Select Committee on Small Businesses (1955–63) and the Joint

Patman Brings Industries to Texas, 1962. Courtesy Lone Star Technologies, Dallas, and Lyndon Baines Johnson Library, Austin. Wright Patman became a member of Congress in 1928 and filled the important position of chairman on the Committee on Banking and Currency from 1963 to 1975.

Economic Committee (1957–59, 1961–63, 1965–67, 1969–71, and 1973–75). He wielded his foremost influence, however, as chairman of the Committee on Banking and Currency from 1963 to 1975. He was the first to call for the investigation of Penn Central (1970) and Watergate (1972). Altogether Patman was elected to 24 terms in the House. During his final two terms in the House, he was the senior member of Congress. Notwithstanding the fact that he had compiled a generally liberal voting record, he was considered unsympathetic to the demand that House procedures be modernized. In early 1975 he was removed from his chairmanship of the Banking and Currency Committee by the House Democratic Caucus. One of his sons, William N. Patman, was a state senator from 1961 to 1980 and a congressman from the Fourteenth District of Texas from 1981 to 1985.

Philip A. Grant, Jr.

Paul Quinn College. The oldest black liberal arts college in Texas; founded in Austin in 1872 by circuit-riding preachers of the African Methodist Episcopal Church and named for Bishop William Paul Quinn. The first classes were held in churches and people's homes, but in 1877 the school moved into its own building after moving to Waco. The college received its official state charter in 1881. In 1990 the school moved to Dallas, taking over the campus of the defunct Bishop College. The original purpose of the school was to teach industrial skills such as blacksmithing and carpentry to former slaves. In 1882 the college was housed in one three-story building and offered elementary, secondary, and college courses. Under the leadership of Bishop Richard H. Cain

in the early twentieth century, Quinn began offering students either an industrial or liberal arts education. The school's growth stopped in the 1930s with the onset of the Great Depression. When A. J. Jackson became president in 1932, enrollment had dropped to only 125 and the debt was about $42,000. Jackson enlisted students and staff to restore and maintain the physical plant. He also organized Progressive Clubs, consisting of a combination of alumni and friends of the college, to direct fund-raising efforts. By 1936, $10,500 had been paid on the debt and enrollment exceeded 300. Like many other small private colleges, Paul Quinn College survived the depression through cooperation with other colleges, including Prairie View A&M. The Texas department of education granted accreditation in 1938. By the 1950s the school had three academic divisions—Humanities, Natural Sciences, and Social Sciences. Integration and competition from Baylor University and Waco Community College cut into Quinn's enrollment. The move to Dallas was intended to rejuvenate the institution, which developed cooperative degree programs with Texas State Technical College, Eastfield College, and the University of Texas at Dallas. Paul Quinn College is supervised by a board of trustees chaired by the presiding prelate of the AME Church. *Douglas Hales*

Peace Party. A name given to those who sought reconciliation with and reform of Mexico rather than the independence favored by the War Party. The Peace Party helped to sway public opinion against armed conflict with the rest of Mexico from 1832 to 1835. Both parties surfaced during the Anahuac Disturbances of 1832. The Peace Party, probably representing more Texans throughout the period, loudly criticized the War Party's agitation. Events of 1835, which displayed the increasingly centralized nature of Antonio López de Santa Anna's regime, began to define the lines between the two factions. Contemporary references to "Peace Party" are fairly scarce. Sometimes the term "Tory" was used, but "Tory" was also applied to those who remained loyal to Mexico after the outbreak of the Texas Revolution. Most Peace Party members joined the revolution. Travis used the term for the first time in a letter to Bowie on 30 July 1835, in which he wrote, "The *peace-party*, as they style themselves, I believe are the strongest, and make much the most noise." Those advocating peace from 1832 to 1835 included Stephen F. Austin and David G. Burnet. *Jodella K. Dyreson*

Pease, Elisha Marshall. Governor; b. Enfield, Connecticut, 3 January 1812; d. Austin, 26 August 1883; m. Lucadia Christiana Niles (1850); 3 children. Pease, seeking his fortune in the West, arrived in the Municipality of Mina, Texas, in 1835 and was swept up in the events of the Texas Revolution. He attended the Convention of 1836 and wrote part of the Constitution of the Republic of Texas. He served in several capacities in the republic, including that of first comptroller of public accounts, after which he practiced law in Brazoria. He was elected to the first three state legislatures. After running for governor unsuccessfully in 1851, he won the office in 1853 and 1855. He persuaded the legislature to establish a system of public education, established the Permanent School Fund, encouraged railroad construction, tried to put the state penitentiary on a self-sustaining basis, and urged establishment of reservations and education for Indians. His building campaign eventually led to completion of the Governor's Mansion, the General Land Office Building, the State Orphan's

Elisha Pease. Prints and Photographs Collection, Elisha M. Pease file, CAH; CN 00910.

Home (now the Corsicana State Home), and a new Capitol. He settled the public debt and made available funds for what later became the Austin State Hospital, the Texas School for the Deaf, and the Texas School for the Blind. He quietly supported the Unionist position during the Civil War, ran unsuccessfully for governor in 1866, and in 1867 helped to organize the state Republican party. Gen. Philip H. Sheridan removed Gov. James W. Throckmorton from office and appointed Pease in his place (1867). Bitter conflict ensued, and Pease resigned in 1969 because of Gen. Joseph J. Reynolds's despotic Reconstruction policies. Pease was president of the Tax-Payers' Convention (1871), which opposed many of Gov. Edmund J. Davis's Radical Republican measures. He chaired the Texas delegation to the Liberal Republican convention of 1872 and was appointed collector of customs at Galveston in 1879 by President Rutherford B. Hayes. Pease practiced law in Austin during his declining years.

Roger A. Griffin

Pecos Army Air Field. A World War II training center activated on 11 July 1942, while still under construction; took over Pecos Municipal Airport. It first served in the Army Air Forces West Coast Training Center (later the Western Flying Training Command) as a basic pilot school. After the Japanese attack on Pearl Harbor (7 December 1941) galvanized the army air forces into launching a training program, Pecos was chosen as one of five new training fields. The first commander, Col. Harry C.

Wisehart, arrived on 28 June 1942. At its peak in 1944 the field numbered 4,304 people, including 482 officers, 972 cadets and student officers, 2,218 enlisted personnel (including 200 WACs), and 604 civilian employees, of which 25 were WASPs. This population, nearly as large as that of Pecos itself, placed a great strain on the town's resources. PAAF consisted chiefly of "theater of operations" type buildings—cheap, rapidly constructed, single-story structures covered with tarpaper. It also had two large hangars, extensive maintenance facilities, and barely adequate eating and living quarters. Off-base housing in Pecos and neighboring towns was very limited, for an even larger airfield, Pyote Air Force Station, had been built 20 miles east. In all, PAAF produced 17 classes of basic pilots, a total of 3,367 who finished the course. When basic pilot training ended on 7 January 1944, no time was lost converting to advanced pilot training. Advanced classes ranged in size from 245 to 526, and fewer students were washed out than in basic training. When the last advanced class at PAAF, 45-B, received silver wings and commissions as second lieutenants or appointments as flight officers on 15 April 1945, the active mission of the field ended. Although the city tried to develop a continuing federal use for the field, it was closed on 12 May 1945 and was deactivated on 30 August. A year later it was returned to municipal control. Over the years part of the field was sold off and Interstate Highway 20 cut through it. Pieces were used for the sites of a hospital, zoo, and trailer park. The Pecos Municipal Airport is on the remaining airfield property, where most of the original facilities have been torn down. The last hangar came down about 1986, and the last barracks were torn down about 1987. In the 1990s the airport still used four runways that had been maintained since the 1940s.

James L. Colwell

Pecos River. A major tributary of the Rio Grande and a major cultural and geographical feature of Texas; rises in New Mexico, enters Texas just east of the 104th meridian, and flows to its mouth on Amistad Reservoir, an impoundment on the Rio Grande in Val Verde County. Through most of its more than 900-mile-long course, the Pecos parallels the Rio Grande. Its tributaries are generally small. The topography of its valley varies from irrigated plains to deep canyons. New Mexico towns on the river include Las Vegas, Santa Rosa, Fort Sumner, Roswell, and Carlsbad; in Texas, the main town on the river is Pecos, seat of Reeves County. The Pecos serves as the eastern boundary of the most mountainous and arid region of Texas, generally known as the Trans-Pecos. From below Sheffield in eastern Pecos County to the river's confluence with the Rio Grande, it passes through a deep gorge, which has long constituted a barrier to transportation and which has prevented irrigation from this part of the lower Pecos. Elsewhere along the course of the river, however, the diversion and impoundment of its water has radically altered its character. Early-day travelers described the river as generally 65 to 100 feet wide and 7 to 10 feet deep, with a fast current. It was fordable at only a few places, the most famous of which was Horsehead Crossing. Irrigation from the upper Pecos in New Mexico began in 1877. Completion of Red Bluff Reservoir (in Reeves and Loving counties, 45 miles north of Pecos) and a hydroelectric power plant in 1936 made possible the establishment of water-improvement districts in the lower valley. By the mid-1980s more than 400,000 acres of the Pecos Valley was irrigation, producing cotton, alfalfa, forage, grain sorghums, vegetables, cantaloupes, and other crops. By that time the river was usually a small, shallow, narrow stream with a sluggish current, bordered by desert shrubs. Nonetheless, thunderstorms can still turn the Pecos into a dangerous river.

The earliest-known settlers along the river were the Pecos Pueblo Indians, who arrived about A.D. 800. Supposedly the first European to cross the river was Vázquez de Coronado (1541). In 1583 Antonio de Espejo called the river the Río de las Vacas ("Cow River") because of the number of buffalo in the vicinity. Gaspar Castaño de Sosa, who followed the Pecos northward, called it the Río Salado because of its salty taste, which caused it to be shunned by men and animals alike. According to Adolph F. Bandelier, the name Pecos first appears in Juan de Oñate's reports concerning the Indian pueblo of Cicuye, now known as the Pecos Pueblo, and is of unknown origin. To Mexicans the river was long known as the Río Puerco ("Pig [i.e., dirty] River"). With the Anglo-American occupation of Texas, the middle and upper Pecos valley became the chief western cattle trail to the north and the site of several famous cattle ranches as well as of Fort Lancaster (1855). Water-conservation practices on the Pecos River are overseen by the United States Bureau of Reclamation, along with the state engineer of New Mexico, the Pecos Valley Artesian Conservancy District, and the Carlsbad Irrigation District in the upper river valley. The Red Bluff Water Power Control District oversees water use in the lower valley. For many years the amount of water available for irrigation was a matter of contention between New Mexico and Texas. Around 1948 the two states entered into an agreement known as the Pecos River Compact, which required New Mexico to maintain delivery of water depending on the amount of water reaching the river in New Mexico by natural causes. Texas for years considered New Mexico to be deficient in living up to the terms of the contract and in 1974 filed suit. The United States Supreme Court ruled in June 1987 that New Mexico owed Texas 340,000 acre-feet of water for the period between 1950 and 1983 and repayment over 10 years. *Delmar J. Hayter*

Peerson, Cleng. Facilitated immigration of Norwegians to the United States; b. Tysvær, Norway, 17 May 1782; d. Bosque County, Texas, 16 December 1865 (buried at Norse, Texas). He came to the New World as a result of hardships in his native land, including the high price of farmland, the numerous drownings among fishermen, and drought. He arrived at New York City in 1821 seeking homes for fellow Norwegian Quakers (most later immigrants from Norway were Lutherans). Between 1825 and 1847 Peerson helped establish communities for Norwegian Quakers and their compatriots in New York, Indiana, Illinois, Wisconsin, Minnesota, Iowa, and Missouri. He moved to Texas in 1850 and lived with friends near Dallas until 1854. Then he moved to newly organized Bosque County, urging fellow Norwegians in East Texas to do so as well. In recognition of his service, the Texas legislature granted Peerson 320 acres of land in Bosque County, half of which he gave to Ovee Colwick in exchange for a home. Peerson lived with Colwick until his death. King Olav V of Norway visited Norse in October 1982 in celebration of the 200th anniversary of the birth of Cleng Peerson. *Karen Yancy*

Penick, Harvey Morrison. Golfer; b. Austin, 23 October 1904; d. Austin, 2 April 1995; m. Helen Holmes (1929); 2 children. Penick was a caddy at the Austin Country Club at age eight, an assistant professional at age 13, and head professional of the club at age 19. He claimed that watching Sam Snead persuaded him to concentrate on teaching. From 1931 to 1963 Penick coached, mostly without pay, the University of Texas golf team to 22 Southwest Conference titles. From 1932 to 1934 he was president of the Texas chapter of the Professional Golfers Association. He retired to golf professional emeritus status in 1971, and in 1984 moved with the country club to Lake Austin. A broken back in 1972 resulted in his degenerative arthritis and increasing immobility and pain in later years. Penick was in the first American generation to succeed the English and Scottish professionals who brought the game to the United States. His conversation was flavored with firsthand references to Jimmie N. Demaret, Babe Zaharias, Walter Hagen, and other pioneers of the big-money professional tour. He achieved international fame, however, as a teacher, who mastered and conveyed the fundamentals to beginners, duffers, and tournament professionals, including Texans Ben Crenshaw and Tom Kite and 6 of the 13 members of the Ladies Professional Golfers Association Hall of Fame. In the 1930s Penick began recording observations in a red Scribbletex notebook that eventually became *Harvey Penick's Little Red Book* (1992, written in collaboration with Bud Shrake), the all-time best-selling sports book that remained on the New York Times best-seller list for 54 weeks. There followed two more books (with Shrake), *And If You Play Golf You're My Friend* (1993) and *For All Who Love the Game: Lessons and Teachings for Women* (1995). A teaching facility and three lines of clubs were named for Penick. He was inducted into both the Texas Golf Hall of Fame (1979) and the Texas Sports Hall of Fame (1984), was the PGA's first National Teacher of the Year (1989), and received a posthumous resolution in the Texas House of Representatives (1995). *James A. Wilson*

Peninsular. A resident of New Spain born on the Iberian peninsula. A *peninsular* was favored over an American-born Spaniard (criollo) in administrative, military, and ecclesiastical appointments because the Iberians were more closely tied to the Spanish court. This occupational advantage allowed *peninsulares* to assume higher positions on the social scale, even though criollos were equal to them under the laws of the kingdom of Castile. As a result of competition between the two groups, criollos and mestizos began to refer to *peninsulares* as *gachupines* ("spurred ones") and *chapetones* ("tenderfeet"), both terms of derision. Harsh conditions on the frontier diminished the social distance dividing *peninsulares*, criollos, and mestizos. The crown was forced to rely on criollos and racially mixed groups to fill frontier positions because *peninsulares* eschewed them. In spite of the breakdown of social stratification based on birth and occupation, *peninsulares* automatically held the highest social status. Nevertheless, their influence in frontier society was not great because they were few in number. *Joan E. Supplee*

Pennybacker, Anna J. Hardwicke. Clubwoman, author, and woman suffrage advocate; b. Petersburg, Virginia, 7 May 1861; d. Austin, 4 February 1938; m. Percy V. Pennybacker (1884; d. 1889); 3 + children. As a high school student Anna substituted the unexplained initial *J* for her second given name, McLaughlin. She wrote and published *A New History of Texas* in 1888, and the textbook was a staple of Texas classrooms for 40 years. She

Mrs. Percy V. Pennybacker, by Alphaeus Cole, ca. 1936. Oil. San Antonio *Light* Collection, ITC.

founded one of the first women's clubs in Texas, the Tyler Woman's Club (1894). She was president of the Texas Federation of Women's Clubs (1901–1903), a position in which she raised $3,500 for women's scholarships at the University of Texas and helped persuade the legislature to fund a women's dormitory there. Under her leadership the federation began a traveling library and art collection that resulted in the establishment of many permanent libraries in Texas. She was active in the General Federation of Women's Clubs for decades and was its president from 1912 to 1916. Mrs. Pennybacker was a trustee of the Leslie Woman's Suffrage Committee as early as 1917. She was a principal influence behind the Chautauqua, New York, Women's Club, and was its president from 1917 to 1938. She staved off bankruptcy at Chautauqua in 1935 by persuading John D. Rockefeller, Jr., to match a fund drive. In 1936 she also got President Franklin D. Roosevelt to speak at the Chautauqua Institute's summer camp, thus helping to raise more money. As an associate member of the Democratic National Committee (1919–20), she met Eleanor Roosevelt in 1924, and they had a long friendship based on shared interest in the advancement of women, world peace, and the Democratic party. During World War I, Mrs. Pennybacker was active in the Food Administration of Texas. In 1934 she served on the Texas Centennial Commission. In 1937 she became the first woman in the history of Houston to give the commencement speech to the city's combined high schools. She traveled the country lecturing on such topics as the status of women and immigrants, the activities of the World Court and League of Nations (in which she participated as a special correspondent), and her frequent visits to the White House.

Stacy A. Cordery

People's Party. The party of Populism, an agrarian reform movement, which evolved from the Grange, the Greenback party, and the Farmers' Alliance into the most successful third-party movement in state history. In Texas the party benefited from a grassroots communication structure developed by the largest state Farmers' Alliance in the country. The alliance was born in Texas, and its most innovative and extensive projects were formulated there. Movement toward establishing a third party in Texas began in the late 1880s and culminated with the formal organization of a Texas People's party in Dallas on 18 August 1891. Party organization included Populist clubs, primaries, biennial county conventions, district conventions, and the state convention. There was an executive committee and a campaign committee at each level. An educational campaign to spread Populism made use of printed appeals, reform speakers, and camp meetings similar to revival meetings. Texas politics became more vigorous than at any time since Reconstruction. Populist leaders encouraged the establishment and growth of reform journals. The weekly *Texas Advance* (Dallas) and later the weekly *Southern Mercury* (Dallas) were statewide party organs. In 1895, 70 Texas counties had Populist newspapers; of about 600 papers published in Texas in that year, 75 were Populist. At the height of the movement there were about 100 Populist newspapers.

In 1892 the Populist party was nominating candidates who posed a serious threat to the dominance of the Democratic party. The Democrats attempted to deflect alliance attention from the subtreasury plan demand by advocating a more conservative reform—"free silver." They agreed that the root cause of the economic crisis was an insufficient currency supply. In 1873 the federal government had returned the treasury to the gold standard, which it had temporarily abandoned due to Civil War expenses. This action had contracted the currency supply severely, thereby precipitating a major economic crisis. A return to a bimetallic monetary base of gold and silver would, it was argued, revitalize the economy. Not all Democratic politicians in Texas, however, were supporters of bimetallism. The bimetallists, led by incumbent governor James Hogg, were opposed by the gold-standard, "sound-money" advocates led by George Clark. The latter accused the Hogg faction of a "weak and cowardly surrender" to third-partyism. The Clark supporters bolted at the state Democratic convention in August 1892 and put out an independent ticket. Third-party activists such as Harry Tracy and Stump Ashby, working in large part through alliance-established communication networks, criticized both gold-standard advocates and bimetallists. A fiat monetary system, as entailed in the subtreasury plan, was essential to these men, and consistent with the Omaha platform adopted by the national People's party in 1892. The success of the third-party campaign was limited. The results in the 1892 Texas gubernatorial election placed Populist Thomas Nugent third in a field of five candidates; he garnered about 25 percent of the vote or 108,483 votes, roughly the equivalent of half the Texas alliance membership. The presidential election returns from Texas gave Democrat Grover Cleveland 57 percent of the vote and Populist James B. Weaver 24 percent. The party's failure in this election resulted partly from its attempt to build a coalition of black and white voters. Despite such high-profile black Populists as John B. Rayner, who was on the executive committee, the People's party was unable to persuade the majority of black Texans to abandon the Republican party.

Under the new Cleveland administration, the economic crisis

grew more severe. The rebellious spirit of the people did not go unnoticed. Texas Democrats recognized that another split in the state ticket might be disastrous, and at their 1894 convention they agreed that there would be no bolting. The platform adopted did not include any monetary reform demands. Yet, in an ironic twist, the reform faction won most of the nominations, including that of free-silverite Charles Culberson for governor. As a consequence, the candidates opposed the platform of the party that nominated them. Populists argued in 1894 that voters could not expect reform from a party that had no genuine, unified commitment to reform. Many voters agreed: they elected 22 Populist candidates to the state House of Representatives and 2 to the state Senate. In 8 of the 13 national congressional elections, the Populist candidates polled over 40 percent of the vote. In the gubernatorial election, Culberson won with 49 percent of the vote. Populist Thomas Nugent received about 36 percent of the vote, an 11 percent increase in third-party support since 1892. This increased support occurred despite such electoral illegalities as firing penitentiary employees who refused to pledge support to the Democrats—a move that spread fear among employees. In contrast to Texas, nationally the People's party did very poorly in 1894. It obtained over 40 percent of the vote in only 33 of the 350 congressional races. This was a major blow to the party since a key reform demand—revamping the monetary system—could be accomplished only at the national level.

After national party chairman H. E. Taubeneck recommended that the People's party gather bimetallists under its banner to maximize its chance of winning office, most Texas third-partyites were disgusted. When a well-known Texas Populist, James H. "Cyclone" Davis, sided with him, they were angry. Nevertheless, Taubeneck successfully mobilized a majority faction in favor of his plan. His plan went awry, however, when unexpectedly the national Democratic party endorsed bimetallism and nominated free-silverite William Jennings Bryan for president. It was too late for Taubeneck to change course. Consequently, pro-Bryan sentiment was strong at the national People's party convention, and by a vote of 1,042 to 321 Bryan won the presidential nomination. The Texas delegation, however, cast all 103 of its votes for Bryan's opponent, S. F. Norton. Dallas county Populists had sent a telegram to the convention: "Five hundred Populists say never surrender. Bryan means death." The antifusionists, led by Ashby, were successful in preventing complete fusion of the Democratic and Populist tickets. They rallied support behind Southern Populist Tom Watson for vice president rather than Democratic candidate Arthur M. Sewall. Thus, while the Populists officially supported Democrat Bryan, some states offered the Bryan–Watson ticket as an alternative to complete fusion. At the Texas People's party convention that began a week after the national convention in 1896, wild cheering broke out in support of Ashby and the other "Immortal 103" antifusionists. A committee appointed to contact other state Populist conventions proposed a telegram that read: "No Watson, no Bryan." But Charles H. Jenkins, state party treasurer and chairman of the platform and resolutions committee, argued that the national convention had nominated Bryan and the nomination was binding. He delayed the vote on whether to send the telegram until it made little difference, other state conventions having adjourned. Some Texas antifusionists thought that the Democratic party was attempting to destroy the People's party, and they angrily stated that they would not vote for Bryan.

The Texas press picked up on this and charged that Texas Populists were in collusion with the Republican party; Republican support for the state Populist ticket was allegedly being traded for Populist support of the national Republican ticket. Although the chairman of the state People's party denied the charges, the alleged fusion dominated the news and caused considerable dissention among rank-and-file Populists.

The 1896 election results in Texas placed the Bryan–Watson ticket in third place, with a mere 15 percent of the vote. The ticket carried only one county in Texas—Sabine. Populists in the state attributed the poor performance to the fusionist efforts of the national party leaders. As evidence of the continued viability of the People's party, they noted that the Populist gubernatorial candidate, Jerome Kearby, had garnered 44 percent of the vote. However, Kearby's success was largely due to the fact that the Republicans did not field a gubernatorial candidate; in fact, Republican ballots bore the names of the Populist candidates for state office. The continued wrangling between the antifusionists and fusionists took its toll. In the 1898 gubernatorial election in Texas, Populist Barnett Gibbs received only 28 percent of the vote. In 1900 the split between the two factions became official. Antifusionists bolted and called for a separate national convention in Cincinnati. In Texas, delegates to the state People's party convention voted to send representatives to Cincinnati. Some Texas Populists were angered by the vote, stating that it placed them out of the sphere of influence within the regular party organization. These Populists, who included all three representatives to the national People's party executive committee and most of the members to the state executive committee, bolted from the convention amid hisses and jeers. The delegates at the regular People's party convention in 1900 again nominated Bryan as president and Charles Towne, a free-silver Republican, as vice president. When Towne later resigned, the national executive committee made no move to replace him but instead accepted complete fusion with the Democratic Bryan–Stevenson ticket. The antifusionists fielded a straight Populist ticket, nominating Wharton Barker as president and Ignatius Donnelly as vice president. But the Barker–Donnelly ticket flopped. In Texas it received only 5 percent of the vote. The Populist gubernatorial candidate received only 6 percent of the vote. The People's party had clearly lost its viability as a reform party.

Historians have attributed the demise of the party to various factors, including the demoralization caused by fusion, the return of prosperity after 1896, and the development of a more sympathetic Democratic party platform at this time. Whatever the cause, the party's political effectiveness was over by 1900, although it slated a candidate for governor in Texas through 1904 and a presidential candidate through 1908. Despite its demise, the People's party in Texas represented a successful coalition of Anglo small farmers, African Americans, and labor. Its effectiveness in voicing the concerns of these groups was an important part of Texas politics at the turn of the century and was instrumental in the rise of other reform groups in Texas in the twentieth century.

Donna A. Barnes

Permanent Council. The very impermanent governing body of Texas from 11 October 1835 until a quorum arrived for the Consultation. The council consisted of the committee of safety of San Felipe and representatives from other communities, including Richard R. Royall of Matagorda and Joseph Bryan of

Liberty, two men who answered Stephen F. Austin's request to come to San Felipe to be part of the interim government. Royall was its president and Charles B. Stewart its secretary. The Permanent Council sent supplies and volunteers to the army in the field, commissioned privateers, set up a postal system, ordered the land offices closed and surveying discontinued, authorized Thomas F. McKinney to go to the United States and borrow $100,000, and appealed to the citizens of the U.S. for men, money, and supplies. A journal of the council was kept from 11 October through 26 October, and the group was active until 31 October 1835.

Permanent School Fund. A fund to assist public education, authorized by the state Constitution. The fund provides non-tax money, thus easing the tax burden on the state's citizens. Its predecessor, the Special School Fund, was established by the School Law of 1854 and funded with $2 million in United States Treasury bonds left over from the $10 million settlement the United States government had given Texas in exchange for surrender of land claims on parts of the future New Mexico, Colorado, and Oklahoma, dating from the days of the republic. Although the original purpose of the Special School Fund was to finance a public school system, the legislature found other ways to spend the money—buying railroad stock to encourage railroad construction, building state prisons, acquiring weapons for the Confederacy. When the Democrats regained power and wrote the present constitution, they renamed the remaining fund the Permanent School Fund and restricted its use to disbursement of interest only, to be invested according to strict rules. Before the turn of the twentieth century, school-land sales and leases produced the revenue added to the Permanent School Fund, but more recent years have seen fuel taxes and leases of off-shore oil lands generate the revenue that goes into the fund. Interest is drawn from the Permanent School Fund and paid into the Available School Fund. *Michael E. McClellan*

Permanent University Fund. A public endowment that provides financial support to institutions in the University of Texas System and the Texas A&M University System. The principal, which includes all proceeds from oil, gas, sulfur, and water royalties, all gains on investments, all rentals on mineral leases, and all amounts received from the sale of university lands, may not be spent. The surface income generated by grazing leases on university lands and the net income from interest and dividends for PUF investments make up the Available University Fund, which is divided between the two university systems. The idea for such an endowment began in 1839, when the Congress of the Republic of Texas set aside 50 leagues (221,400 acres) of land to fund higher education. The state legislature passed an act establishing the University of Texas in 1858, acknowledging the 1839 endowment and enlarging it with $100,000 in United States bonds; the act also set aside one of every 10 sections of land that had been reserved for state use under the 1854 Act to Encourage the Construction of Railroads in Texas by Donations of Land. As more of the state began to be settled, however, the agricultural value of the acreage set aside for higher education led the legislature to change its mind about keeping it for a university that as yet existed only on paper. In the Constitution of 1876, the state confirmed the previous university land grants with the exception of the one out of every 10 sections that had been reserved for

the university by the act of 1858. The legislature replaced the railroad sections with a million acres of previously unappropriated land, all of which was located in West Texas and considered less than prime.

When the University of Texas actually opened in 1883, its supporters pushed the legislature to appropriate another million acres for the endowment. The land chosen for this purpose was also in West Texas and was thought to be of little commercial value. The income it generated was primarily from grazing leases and amounted to only $40,000 in 1900. Early regents of the university kept the land in hopes of obtaining a better price through sale at a future date, and their patience paid off. On 28 May 1923, Frank Pickrell and Carl G. Cromwell brought in the Santa Rita oilwell on university property in Reagan County. By 1925 the PUF was growing by more than $2,000 a day. By the late 1950s the market value of the PUF exceeded $283,642,000 and provided investment income of more than $8,513,000 annually for distribution to the two university systems. The PUF and its beneficiary institutions have since grown considerably. *Vivian Elizabeth Smyrl*

Perote Prison. A Spanish castle in Vera Cruz, used as a prison to incarcerate Texans during the republic; originally the Castle of San Carlos; built in the 1770s to guard a trade route and serve as a depository for treasure awaiting shipment to Spain. Texans imprisoned there were chiefly from three sources: the Texan Santa Fe expedition, the Dawson Massacre, and the Mier expedition. Despite the fact that they had surrendered as prisoners of war, the men were forced to perform common labor. They were, however, allowed to communicate with friends, to receive money and gifts, and to purchase supplies from outside the castle. Their plight aroused sympathy in Texas and in the United States, and in April 1843 President John Tyler instructed Waddy Thompson, United States minister in Mexico, to negotiate for their release. The Texas Congress made appropriations for relief of the men at Perote, but the money never reached the prisoners, many of whom came to think that President Sam Houston was not making any effort to secure their release. Groups of the Perote prisoners were released from time to time through the influence of Thompson and the British minister, Lord Packenham. Some escaped. On 16 September 1844 the remaining Texas prisoners, about 105, were released. Accurate records on the number who escaped, were released through influence of friends, died from disease, starvation, or exposure, or were killed by Mexican guards are not available. *Seymour V. Connor*

Perry, George Sessions. Writer; b. Rockdale, 5 May 1910; d. Guilford, Connecticut, 13 December 1956; m. Claire Hodges (1931); attended Southwestern University, Purdue University, and the University of Houston. Sessions was orphaned at 12 and reared by his autocratic maternal grandmother, the model for major characters in his works. In 1937 the *Saturday Evening Post* published one of his stories, and soon thereafter Doubleday published his first book, *Walls Rise Up*, a comic novel about three vagrants living along the Brazos River. In 1941 Perry firmly established his place with *Hold Autumn in Your Hand*, a novel about a year in the life of a tenant farmer, perhaps the best agrarian novel about Texas. The book won the Texas Institute of Letters award in 1941 and, in 1942, became the first Texas book to win the National Book Award. In 1945 Jean Renoir made a

George Sessions Perry writing at home while planes from nearby Randolph Field fly overhead, Schertz, 1942. Courtesy HRHRC. Before World War II, Perry wrote lighthearted fiction about life in rural Texas. He went to Italy as a war correspondent in 1943 and returned "defictionized," able to write nonfiction only.

movie, *The Southerner*, based on it. In 1942 Perry published *Texas: A World in Itself*, an informal guide to the history, traditions, and folklore of Texas. He continued to write short stories for the *Saturday Evening Post* and *Country Gentleman*, and in 1944 he published his last book of fiction, a collection of short stories titled *Hackberry Cavalier*. Although officially medically unfit for service in World War II, Perry served as a war correspondent and went ashore on the Sicily landings in 1943. The death and suffering he witnessed there, he said, "defictionized" him for life. Henceforth he found great difficulty writing about the war or about rural Texas, and so devoted himself to nonfiction and journalism. In 1949 he published *My Granny Van* and in 1951 *Tale of a Foolish Farmer*, an account of his misadventures in buying and trying to run the farm that had been the scene of *Hold Autumn in Your Hand*. He also wrote an official history of Texas A&M University. He and Claire moved to Guilford, Connecticut, but Perry developed a sense of guilt at having abandoned his roots and his first love, fiction, for what he saw as the easier and more lucrative field of journalism. In his terms he had opted for the easy "sandy land farming" instead of the harder, but more satisfying, "black land farming." His unpublished writings in the early 1950s reflect his deepening depression and his worry about his severe arthritis and his drinking problems. In great pain and tortured by hallucinations, Perry walked into the river near his home and disappeared. When his body was recovered two months later, the coroner rendered a verdict of accidental death by drowning. *Maxine Hairston*

Pershing, John Joseph. Army general; b. near Laclede, Missouri, 13 September 1860; d. Walker Reed Army Hospital, 15 July 1948 (buried at Arlington National Cemetery); m. Helen Frances Warren (1905; d. 1915); ed. West Point (grad. 1886). After graduation, Pershing served against Apaches in New Mexico and Sioux at Wounded Knee, South Dakota, before returning in 1897 to West Point to teach. He was nicknamed Black Jack for his service with black troopers of the Tenth United States Cavalry. During the Spanish-American War he rode as a first lieutenant with the Tenth Cavalry in the Santiago campaign in Cuba. Subsequently he rose through the ranks as he fought in the Philippines, served as military attaché to the American embassy in Japan, and observed Japanese forces fighting in Manchuria. President Theodore Roosevelt appointed him brigadier general, a promotion that bypassed 862 officers, thus making Pershing militarily prominent but unpopular. In April 1914 Pershing took command of Fort Bliss, which had been an infantry post. On 16 March 1916 he led a large punitive expedition into Chihuahua to subdue revolutionary forces and capture Pancho Villa. During the campaign the general encountered major transportation problems as his heavy trucks attempted to negotiate dirt roads designed for lighter traffic. Pershing introduced to warfare the use of aerial reconnaissance to search for the best routes through difficult terrain, and he used railroads when possible. Despite heroic efforts in engagements such as that of the Seventh Cavalry at Guerrero on 29 March and a disastrous defeat at Carrizal in June, Pershing returned to the United States in January 1917 without Villa. He had, however, scattered the Villistas.

On 21 February 1917 he assumed command of the Southern Department, which took him to Fort Sam Houston in San Antonio. There he received with enthusiasm the news of Wilson's resolution to enter the European war. In addition to his military duties during the Great War, Pershing advised and assisted San Antonio civilian authorities. He spoke to many audiences on the proper duties of a citizen in wartime. He supported the drafting of all able-bodied men and convinced Governor James Ferguson to argue his case before the Texas congressional delegation. After notification on 2 May 1917 that he would be in charge of the American Expeditionary Forces in Europe, he left for Washington. In Europe he avoided trench warfare and generally fought independently of Allied forces. After the war, Pershing helped frame military terms for the Treaty of Versailles. In 1919 he received the highest rank ever given an American army officer—General of the Armies of the United States. Furthermore, he served as chief of staff from 1921 to 1924, when he retired. In 1915 Pershing's wife and daughters had died in a fire at the Presidio, San Francisco. *Leon C. Metz*

Peters Colony. Name commonly applied to a North Texas empresario grant made in 1841 by the Republic of Texas to 20 American and English investors led by William S. Peters, an English musician and immigrant to Pennsylvania. Influenced by the philanthropic ideas of William Godwin and Thomas Paine, Peters may have wanted to provide opportunities for the English industrial middle class. The headquarters of the colony was in

Louisville, Kentucky, from where Peters and his son-in-law Samuel Browning departed in1839 to seek English support for the colony—the first of several such trips. In 1841 in Austin, Browning signed the first of four contracts with the Republic of Texas. The contract established the boundaries of the colony and required the empresarios to recruit 200 families in three years from outside Texas. The colonists were to be granted 320 acres per single man and a maximum of 640 acres per family. The empresarios were allowed to retain up to one-half of a colonist's grant, however, as payment for services rendered. They also received 10 sections of premium land from the republic for each 100 families. Insufficient unappropriated land within the boundary of the colony led to a request for an extension of the boundary, which was granted in a second contract, signed on 9 November 1841. The boundaries were extended 40 miles southward, but the number of required colonists was increased to 800. On 20 November the Texas Agricultural, Commercial, and Manufacturing Company was formed in Louisville to help offset the absence of financial backing from the London investors. The new company sent the first group of immigrants to the Cross Timbers of Texas by steamboat as early as December 1841, but difficulties in attracting and keeping people in the colony caused the company to request an extension of time and another adjustment of the boundaries. By terms of a third contract, signed by Sam Houston for the republic on 26 July 1842, the company was given a six-month extension for the introduction of the first third of the colonists, and the boundary was extended to enclose a 10-mile-wide strip on the west and a 12-mile-wide strip on the east. In return for these concessions, however, the republic reserved for itself each alternate section of land.

On 3 October 1842 the English investors transferred their interests to three other Englishmen and three Americans, each of whom was scheming for control of the colony—Daniel J. Carroll, Sherman Converse, and Charles Fenton Mercer. Converse, after persuading the Louisville group to assign their rights to him, obtained a fourth contract with the Republic of Texas in January 1843. It gave an extension to 1 July 1848 to fulfill the contract and added over 10 million acres to the west of the colony. When the promises that Converse had made were not fulfilled, the Louisville group, thinking themselves deceived, found additional investors and reorganized as the Texas Emigration and Land Company on 15 October 1844. Under the leadership of Willis Stewart, an astute Louisville businessman and one of the new investors, the company made good its claim to be the true owners of the Peters colony. The confusion over ownership, however, discouraged immigration to the colony, and by 1 July 1844, according to the company's own agent, Ralph H. Barksdale, there were only 197 families and 184 single men in the colony. The company was further hampered in its attempts to attract settlers by an ordinance passed by the Convention of 1845 that required an investigation of all colony contracts on the assumption that they were unconstitutional. The company increased its problems by employing as its agent in 1845 the London-born Henry O. Hedgcoxe, whose foreign and officious manners irritated the colonists and reinforced a commonly held suspicion that the contractors were mere land speculators. An influx of squatters into the colony also complicated the company's task of administrating the colony.

Expiration of the contract in 1848 did not end the company's difficulties. Land within the colony was now legally open for the free laying of certificates that permitted new settlers to obtain grants of 640 acres from the state. Many of the old settlers thought that the company's claim of half their land was intolerable. The settlers demanded that the legislature rectify an unjust situation. Their protest took the form of mass meetings, petitions, and a colony convention, held in Dallas on 21 May 1849. During the controversy John H. Reagan and James W. Throckmorton, neither of whom were colonists, emerged as leaders in the protest movement. In January 1850 the legislature passed a law to secure the colonists' claims. The legislation, which was detrimental to the company's interests, angered the stockholders and led to litigation. A compromise was reached in 1852, when the legislature passed an act granting 1,700 sections of land in floating certificates to the company. The colonists would have until 1 July 1852 to establish their claims, and the company would have 2½ years from that date to lay its certificates. The colonists immediately opposed the compromise law and resolved to continue their fight. The "Hedgcoxe War" resulted. Although the compromise law was amended to extend the deadline for colonists to file their claims to 7 May 1853, it took nearly 10 legislative enactments over nearly 20 years to bring final settlement of the land titles. The colony helped settle North Texas but brought little if any profit to the investors and much disgruntlement among the settlers. *Harry E. Wade*

Philosophical Society of Texas. Founded in 1837 by 26 Texans who met in the capitol of the republic at Houston. The stated purpose was "the collection and diffusion of correct information regarding the moral and social condition of our country; its finances, statistics and political and military history . . . and the thousand other topics of interest which our new and rising republic unfolds to the philosopher, the scholar, and the man of the world." Charter members included Mirabeau B. Lamar (president), Ashbel Smith, Anson Jones (both vice presidents), David G. Burnet (one of the secretaries), Thomas Jefferson Rusk, Sam Houston, and other illustrious figures. Occasional meetings were held during the annual sessions of the Congress of the Republic of Texas, but the society became inactive before annexation. In 1935 the organization was revived by Herbert P. Gambrell, Samuel Wood Geiser, and others. It was chartered the next year as a nonprofit educational corporation, the purpose of which was to perpetuate the memory and spirit of the men who founded the original society and to encourage research and the preservation of historical, literary, and philosophical documents and materials. Membership was by invitation and was limited to persons who were born within or had resided in the geographical boundaries of the Republic of Texas and who had contributed to the achievement of the original aims of the society. Bylaws provided for 100 active members and 50 associate members and permitted the election of not more than 25 non-Texan members. By the 1990s the bylaws allowed for 200 active members and varying numbers of emeritus and associate members. The PSOT had its office in the Hall of State upon its reorganization, but by the 1990s the office was in Austin. Since 1937 the society has published an annual volume of *Proceedings*. Presidents have included George B. Dealey, Ima Hogg, Harry H. Ransom, Rupert N. Richardson, and Leon Jaworski. *Herbert Gambrell*

665

Photography. On 17 April 1839, almost three years after the Texas victory at the battle of San Jacinto, the Telegraph and Texas Register reprinted an article that described (with considerable inaccuracy) the processes then being perfected to produce a permanent image entirely through the action of light and chemistry by Louis J. M. Daguerre in France (on a silver-plated copper sheet) and William Talbot in England (on paper). By 1841 or 1842 photographers in the northeastern United States were producing daguerreotype portraits, but the process apparently did not arrive in Texas until December 1843, when a Mrs. Davis advertised her photographic services in the Houston newspapers. Although she might have remained for "two or three weeks" and was probably the first person to produce a photograph in Texas, none of her work is known to exist. Dozens of transient daguerreotypists followed Mrs. Davis to Texas. They adopted the same procedure that she had used by advertising in the local newspapers and inviting patrons to come by their temporary studios to have their portraits made. B. F. Neal visited Galveston in mid-1844, and Joseph R. Palmer, a New Orleans daguerreotypist, worked in Galveston and Corpus Christi in 1846, while following Gen. Zachary Taylor's army into Mexico. In 1847 C. Asberry appeared in Clarksville, Adolphus Behn in La Grange, and James H. and J. Selkirk in Matagorda. George A. Davis and E. P. Whitfield advertised in Austin in January 1848; Whitfield subsequently sold his equipment to the proprietor of the hotel where he was staying, Alfred Smith, and Smith presumably added photography to his hotel business. A Dr. Whitfield is the first photographer recorded in San Antonio (1849). Perhaps some of the work of these photographers remains, but scholars have not been able to associate them with a single image taken in Texas before 1850.

The earliest extant daguerreotype that was definitely made in the state is an image of the Alamo taken in 1849 that is now in the collection of the Barker Texas History Center at the University of Texas at Austin. At least two early photographers remained in the same locality for an extended period of time. The firm of James H. and J. Selkirk continued in Matagorda until the Civil War, and John H. S. Stanley, an immigrant from England born about 1800, opened a gallery in Houston in 1850 or 1851 and remained there until at least 1870. Photographers often had to pursue other occupations to make a living. James Selkirk, for example, is listed in the 1850 census as a pilot; both Neal and Palmer were active in the newspaper business. Although all early photographers in Texas used the daguerreotype process, there were some who experimented with other methods. Insofar as is known, none used Fox Talbot's calotype process, which produces a negative that can be used to make positive prints, because they would have had to acquire a license. J. H. S. Stanley of Houston apparently experimented with Frederick Scott Archer's wet collodion negative–positive process. In 1851 and 1852 he advertised in the Houston papers that he had succeeded in making photographs on glass and that he would soon offer them to the public. Daguerreotypes were still used, especially for portraits, during the Civil War, after variations of the wet collodion process had produced the ambrotype (a negative on glass, backed by a black surface) and the tintype (with the photographic emulsion on a black-lacquered iron plate).

The light and unbreakable tintype became popular during the Civil War because the images could be inexpensively produced and sent intact to loved ones. Texas photographers produced tintypes for decades. It is impossible to determine when the process was abandoned in the state, but examples produced in the 1890s are common. Despite the fact that almost every Texas photographer could make glass negatives and paper prints after about 1857, actual images of these types are rare in Texas until about 1866. A series of views of San Antonio, probably taken by William DeRyee in 1859 and 1860, is extant, and comparable images may have been made in other important Texas towns before the war. DeRyee also published a set of photographic prints of the members of the Eighth Texas Legislature in 1860. The discovery that collodion could be used to hold photographic salts to glass for the production of negatives was paralleled by the discovery that egg albumen could be used for the same purpose on paper. These two innovations dominated all of photography from the end of the Civil War until practically the end of the nineteenth century. The initial paper prints to prove popular in Texas were called cartes de visite, first popularized by André Disdéri of Paris in 1859. The name refers to the size of the cardboard upon which the albumen print was mounted—the size of a visiting card, approximately 2½ by 4 inches. The carte remained the most popular format until about 1870. Many were made after that date, but by then a new size—the cabinet—had taken the lead in fashionable galleries. The cabinet mount measures about 4½ by 6½ inches; it remained the most popular photographic size until the end of the century. Many Texas photographers also produced stereographic cards, usually of local buildings or scenes. These cards contain two images of the same scene which, when viewed through a stereoscope, appear to converge into a single, three-dimensional picture.

After the Civil War many Texas cities and towns could support permanent photographers. During the last three decades of the century, such practitioners as Harvey R. Marks in Austin, James R. Davis in Dallas, Frederick W. Bartlett in Galveston, Charles J. Wright in Houston, Henry A. Doerr in San Antonio, and William D. Jackson in Waco each worked for at least 15 years. Operators in many small towns also stayed put for long careers in one location. Examples run the alphabet from James A. Arvin in Mexia to Reiner J. Zimmermann in Fayette County. There were still some situations, however, where a traveling photographer could make a living. In the lightly settled ranch country of the Edwards Plateau, McArthur Ragsdale traveled from town to town during the 1870s and 1880s. Many other photographers worked circuits in South and West Texas. Itinerants occasionally set up in cities where, by offering lower prices, they could compete with permanent photographers for short periods. During the nineteenth century a few Texas photographers made notable contributions to the progress of the art. Texans corresponded with the national photographic press and were members of national photographic societies. Such communication was behind the facts that Stanley was experimenting with the wet collodion process the year it was invented, and that William DeRyee produced a book illustrated with tipped-in photographic prints in 1860. C. Conrad Stremme made photographic copies of county maps in the General Land Office in the early 1860s, surely one of the earliest attempts by a government to use technology to make inexpensive copies of documents available to the public.

During the last quarter of the nineteenth century the technical basis for modern black-and-white photography was established. The wet collodion negative was replaced by the gelatin

The Alamo. Daguerreotype, 1849. Courtesy CAH; CN 07471a. This is the earliest known dated photograph made in Texas.

dry plate, which evolved into the cellulose cut and roll films of today, and albumenized printing paper gave way to papers coated with a gelatin-based emulsion. Before these technical advancements individual photographers had to make or sensitize their own negatives and paper, but the modern materials could be mass-produced in factories. These developments, particularly the popularizing of roll-film cameras by Eastman Kodak, not only reduced the work required of the professional, but also made photography easily and cheaply available to anyone who wished to try it. Amateur photography soon became the most significant segment of the photo-supply business. The most important activity for most photographers has always been making studio portraits. During the nineteenth century many photographers advertised making and selling both urban and scenic views and stereographs, but almost all professional photographers made the vast majority of their income from portraits. With the coming of the Kodak era, however, more and more people took their own portraits for all but the most formal occasions.

As the twentieth century progressed, the majority of photog-

raphers increasingly went into commercial work making images for business uses—advertising, promotion, legal proceedings, and so forth. Even so, the most widely recognized professional photographer in the state today, Paul L. Gittings, is known almost entirely for his portrait work. Collections of a few local photographers working before World War II have been preserved in libraries and museums. Examples include Harry F. Annas (Lockhart), Otis A. Aultman (El Paso), Fred Gildersleeve (Waco), Joe Litterst (Houston), Ray Rector (Stamford), and John Paul Trlica (Granger). The Texas Professional Photographers Association was organized in 1898 to encourage cooperation among its members and to provide a means to speak out on issues involving their business. The TPPA, allied with the national association, provides strong support for professional commercial photographers. Though the overwhelming majority of professional photographers in Texas are white males, many women and members of ethnic minorities have made significant contributions to the progress of photography in the state. In addition to the earliest documented Texas daguerreotypist, Mrs. Davis, information is available about more than 100 woman

Year	Photographers			Population	Photographers per 100,000
	Female	Male	Total		
1850		10	10*	212,592**	4.7
1860		61	61*	604,215**	10.1
1870	1	109	110	818,579	13.4
1880	2	197	199	1,591,749	12.5
1890	23	431	454	2,235,527	20.3
1900	64	669	733	3,048,710	24.0
1910	128	915	1,043	3,896,542	26.7
1920	296	908	1,204	4,663,228	25.4
1930	360	1,058	1,418	5,824,715	24.3
1940	279	1,118	1,397	6,414,824	21.8
1950	645	1,811	2,456	7,711,194	31.8
1960	473	2,031	2,504	9,579,677	26.1
1970	677	2,641	3,318	11,198,655	29.6
1980	1,435	4,147	5,582	14,229,191	39.2
1990	2,855	6,226	9,091	16,986,510	53.5

* Includes both "photographers" and "artists." In 1850 only the occupations of males were noted; in 1860 the sex of occupation respondents was not reported.
** Includes free and slave.

photographers working in the state before 1900. Minority men and women have always been active in photography, particularly in large minority communities in urban areas.

Another important outlet for photographic work since World War I has been the increasing number of publications that use photographs to illustrate stories and provide editorial content. Freelancers working in Texas have contributed many important images to both local and national periodicals. In the 1920s Jack Specht was hired as a staff photographer by the San Antonio *Light*, and soon most other newspapers hired photographers. By the end of 1995 photographers working for Texas newspapers had won more Pulitzer Prizes than those from any other state. William Snyder and Larry C. Price both won two Pulitzers at the Dallas *Times Herald*, one each for spot news and one each for feature photography. In 1995 University of Texas graduate Jean Marc Bouju, working for the Associated Press, received a Pulitzer for feature photography. Students of photojournalism teachers such as J. B. Colson at the University of Texas and George Krause at the University of Houston have made significant contributions to publications across the nation. Such statewide magazines as *Texas Monthly* provide local photographers with important outlets for their work. Although from the beginning of photography its practitioners have advertised their work as artistic, in fact the vast majority of photographers have used their skill to make a living, with little concern for commenting on the universal human condition. The early twentieth century provides a few examples of people in Texas who used photography as a medium of expression rather than as a commercial enterprise. Frank Reaugh and Erwin E. Smith made photographs of Texas cattle operations and other Western subjects as artistic expressions or as a basis for paintings. Between the two world wars Wilfred Smithers documented many aspects of West Texas life. Though many of his images were sold to newspapers,

he used some of his most striking negatives to make film positives for lampshades after World War II. Many of the photographers working for the Farm Security Administration during the Great Depression made photographs detailing rural life in Texas. Eugene Goldbeck, a San Antonio photographer who specialized in making panoramic photographs of very large groups, often arranged the subjects to form a living symbol of the organization. In the 1940s and 1950s Carlotta Corpron, an art teacher at Texas Woman's University, produced a remarkable series of abstract photographs while investigating the nature of light.

The 1960s brought a new opportunity for Texas artists to express themselves through photography. Beginning at the University of Texas in Austin with Russell Lee, several universities around the state added photography to their art curricula and gave established photographic artists a forum to teach and influence talented students. Many of these students, and others encouraged by the new climate in the state for photographic expression, have produced notable images that have been exhibited and published nationwide. The most prolific of this new generation of photographers are Jim Bones and Keith Carter. Several of the teachers, notably Geoff Winningham (at Rice University) and Garry Winogrand (at UT Austin), have published collections of Texas photographs. While most photographic artists working in Texas have had to rely on informal and short-lived spaces to exhibit their work, a few commercial galleries have supported photographic expression on a larger scale. Two examples are AfterImage in Dallas and Benteler–Morgan in Houston. Beginning in the late 1970s groups of photographers themselves organized "artists' spaces" in the cities to show the work of contemporary photo artists. Important spaces that have followed the pioneering Allen Street in Dallas include the Houston Center for Photography and, in Austin, the Texas Photographic Society and Women and Their Work. In addition to providing gallery space, some groups produce newsletters and other publications. A few noncollecting museums such as the Galveston Art Center and the Contemporary Arts Museum in Houston exhibit the work of Texas photographers. A unique opportunity for photographic artists has been provided every two years since 1988 by the FotoFest in Houston, a combination of gallery shows, lectures, workshops, and master classes.

Moreover, libraries and museums all across the state hold vast numbers of photographic negatives and prints. Most of these collections concentrate on local or regional material. Collections of statewide interest are maintained by the Amon Carter Museum, the Center for American History, the Harry Ransom Humanities Research Center, the Dallas Historical Society, the University of Texas Institute of Texan Cultures, the San Jacinto Museum, and the Texas State Archives. Major collections of artistic photography (not necessarily from Texas) include those of the Amon Carter Museum, the Museum of Fine Arts, Houston, and the Humanities Research Center. Purchases by these institutions have had a very positive effect on the market for Texas photographers, and scholars working with museum collections have made many important contributions to our understanding of the history of photography and its influence on our society and culture. Though one might assume that the proliferation of videotape and computer-imaging technology (both amateur and professional) would lessen the importance of photography in the years to come, no such prediction can be confidently made. The 1990 census reported the largest number

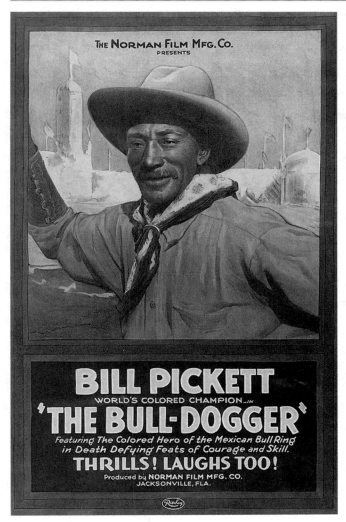

Bill Pickett, ca. 1920. Four-color lithograph poster. 40½" x 26¾". Courtesy Buffalo Bill Historical Center, Cody, Wyoming. The son of former slaves, Pickett became an internationally famous rodeo star traveling with a Wild West show. He subdued huge steers in the ring by biting their upper lips.

of photographers per capita in the state's history, and the art-photography movement is vital and growing. These facts argue that photography will continue to be an important cultural tool for the foreseeable future. *David Haynes*

Pickett, Bill. Rodeo cowboy; b. to former slaves, Travis County, 5 December 1870; d. 2 April 1932; m. Maggie Turner (1890); at least 9 children. Will (later Bill) Pickett became a cowboy after completing the fifth grade. He observed herder dogs subduing steers by biting their upper lips and found he could do the same thing. He perfected this unique method of bulldogging as well as roping and riding and was soon giving exhibitions and passing the hat for donations. In 1888 he performed at the first fair in Taylor, his family's new hometown. The Pickett brothers established a horse-breaking business in Taylor, where Will was a member of the national guard and a Baptist deacon. As the "Dusky Deamon," he exhibited his bulldogging at rodeos and fairs throughout Texas and the West, creating a sensation at the 1904

Cheyenne Frontier Days, then America's premier rodeo. Bulldogging rapidly became a popular cowboy contest that evolved into steer wrestling, one of the standard events of contemporary rodeo. Capitalizing on his fame, Pickett contracted in 1905 to perform at the 101 Ranch in Oklahoma. By 1907 he had become a full-time employee of the ranch, where he worked as a cowboy and performed with the 101 Ranch Wild West Show. He moved his wife and nine children to Oklahoma the next year. With the show he entertained millions in the United States, Canada, Mexico, South America, and England, and was featured in several motion pictures, the first black cowboy star. From his earliest days in Oklahoma through the 1920s, Pickett competed in rodeos large and small and might well have amassed a significant record as a competitor if blacks had not been barred from most contests. He was often billed as an Indian or not identified as black in order to compete against whites. He died after being kicked in the head by a horse. His friend Will Rogers announced on his radio show the funeral at the 101 Ranch. In 1972 Pickett became the first black honoree in the National Rodeo Hall of Fame in Oklahoma City. In 1989, he was also enshrined in the Prorodeo Hall of Fame and Museum of the American Cowboy at Colorado Springs. In 1994 the United States Post Office issued a stamp in his honor, though the stamp accidentally bore a picture of one of Pickett's brothers. *Mary Lou LeCompte*

Pierce, Abel Head. Cattleman; b. Little Compton, Rhode Island, 29 June 1834; d. Texas, 26 December 1900 (buried in Hawley Cemetery, near Bay City); m. Fanny Lacey (1865); 2 children. In 1854, "Shanghai" Pierce stowed away on a schooner bound for Indianola, was discovered, and was put to work handling cargo. At Port Lavaca he met Richard Grimes, for whom he worked splitting rails. Pierce soon began to acquire his own cattle, which he registered and branded AP. He served in Augustus C. Buchel's Confederate cavalry during the Civil War, returned to find his holdings evaporated, but continued in the cattle business, branding on the open range. He and his brother, Jonathan E. Pierce, organized a partnership and established the Rancho Grande in Wharton County in 1871. They later had several other partnerships. After some difficulties in Matagorda County and the death of his wife and infant son, Pierce converted his cattle into gold and went to Kansas for 18 months. Back in Texas, he began buying land until he acquired 250,000 acres and formed the Pierce–Sullivan Pasture Company, of which he was president. The company sent thousands of cattle up the northern trails and shipped thousands by rail. In his efforts to solve the mystery of Texas fever, Pierce experimented in removing ticks and concluded that the ticks caused the fever. He toured Europe in search of a breed of cattle immune to ticks, and returned without a definite solution but with the conviction that Brahmans were most likely. In the early 1890s he commissioned sculptor Frank Teich to make a marble statue of himself. A 6'5" likeness was eventually placed atop a 10-foot granite pilaster which was itself mounted on a 10-foot piece of gray granite. The structure later marked his grave. In 1900 Pierce lost more than $1.25 million in the Galveston hurricane of 1900, in a bank failure, and in the purchase of the Gulf Island Railroad. After his death the Pierce estate imported Brahman cattle from India, which furnished Texas with the base stock from which large herds of Brahmans have grown. *Chris Emmett*

Pig War. The name given to a dispute between Dubois de Saligny, French *chargé d'affaires*, and the Lamar administration that resulted in a temporary rupture of diplomatic relations between France and the Republic of Texas. It originated in 1841 in a quarrel between the Frenchman and an Austin hotelkeeper, Richard Bullock. Dubois de Saligny complained that Bullock's pigs invaded his stables, ate his horses' corn, and even penetrated to his very bedroom to devour his linen and chew his papers. Bullock, charging that the Frenchman's servant had killed a number of his pigs on orders from his master, thrashed the servant and threatened the diplomat himself with a beating. Dubois de Saligny invoked the "Laws of Nations," claimed diplomatic immunity for himself and his servant, and demanded the summary punishment of Bullock by the Texas government. The Frenchman was already on bad terms with the administration, especially acting president David G. Burnet and secretary of state James S. Mayfield, who opposed Dubois's project of a Franco-Texan commercial and colonization company (although Mayfield had originally introduced the Franco-Texian Bill in the House). Dubois may have exploited the pig problem as a means to vent his spleen on the current administration of the republic. When Mayfield refused to have Bullock punished without due process of law, the *chargé d'affaires*, acting without instructions from his own government, broke diplomatic relations and left the country in May 1841. From Louisiana he emitted occasional dire warnings of the terrible retribution that would be exacted by France. The French government officially supported its agent, but disapproved of his highhanded departure from his post and had no intention of resorting to force on his behalf. The "war" ended in a compromise. The Houston administration, which succeeded that of Lamar, made "satisfactory explanations" to the French government and requested the return of Dubois de Saligny. These explanations were less than Dubois had asked for, as they contained neither censure of the previous administration nor promises to punish Bullock. But aware of disapprobation in the French Foreign Ministry, he accepted this peace offering and returned to Texas in April 1842 to resume his official duties.

Nancy N. Barker

Pinckney, Pauline A. Art historian; b. Austin, ca.1889; d. there, 25 October 1982 (buried in Oakwood Cemetery); ed. University of Texas (bachelor's degree, 1917), Columbia University (master's degree). She taught art at Texas Woman's College in Fort Worth (now Texas Wesleyan University), Southern Methodist University, Purdue University, and Kansas State College. She directed research for the *Index of American Design* in Washington, D.C., and served as a consultant on folk arts for the Dallas Museum of Fine Arts. In the 1930s she published articles in the Washington *Post*, New York *Times*, and Dallas *Morning News* on art, architecture, furniture design, and related topics. In 1940 her first book, *American Figureheads and Their Carvers*, was published by W. W. Norton. This work is reputed to give the first survey of the art of decorative ship carving. Pinckney published two articles on ship figureheads in 1941 and in 1948 assembled a photographic exhibit of American figureheads at the Dallas Museum of Fine Arts. Her best-known work, *Painting in Texas: The Nineteenth Century*, was published in 1967 for the Amon Carter Museum. The book, one of the first of its type, emphasized the relationship of Texas artists to their culture. It included biographical sketches of more than 50 artists, more than 100 reproductions, and an introduction by Jerry Bywaters. An exhibit of paintings selected for inclusion in the book was held at the University of Texas at Austin and at the Amon Carter Museum. *Painting in Texas* won an award from the Texas Institute of Letters.

Debbie Mauldin Cottrell

Pinta Trail. Extended 180 miles northwest from San Antonio to the site of Santa Cruz de San Sabá Mission near Menard; has been a transportation route for hundreds of years. Benjamin Enderle, Gillespie county surveyor for more than 60 years, heard about the Pinta Trail from local ranchers and passed on the story to his high school students and friends. Field notes of Republic of Texas land-grant surveys and county maps noted the trail location. The origin of the route was attributed to the historic Plains Indians, mainly Apaches and Comanches. Spanish expeditions in the Hill Country and military campaigns against the Lipan Apaches dating from 1732 to 1756 probably used the trail. Later expeditions from San Antonio to San Sabá Mission (founded 1757) definitely did so. In the 1840s German naturalist Ferdinand von Roemer described the Pinta Trail as an old Indian trail and related its use by German immigrants, especially teamsters. Where the trail crossed the Guadalupe River in Kendall County, John Coffee Hays and a company of Texas Rangers defeated the Comanche chief Yellow Wolf and his warriors in the mid-1840s, in an engagement known as the battle of Walker's Creek. The Pinta Trail was traveled by Forty-niners and later by stagecoach, mail, and freight lines. The development of parallel railroads in the late 1880s and early 1900s signaled the decline of use of the Pinta Trail. From San Antonio, U.S. Highway 87 and Interstate Highway 20 follow the trail to Boerne, Ranch Road 1376 continues along the trail through Sisterdale, U.S. Highway 290 parallels the route from Cain City to Fredericksburg, U.S. 87 proceeds along the trail through Cherry Spring and Mason, and State Highway 29 follows the Pinta Trail from Mason to Menard.

Nina L. Nixon

Plano, Texas. Fifteen miles north of Dallas in central Collin County. Indians killed early settlers McBain Jameson and Jeremiah Muncey in 1844, but settlers from the Peters colony moving into the area the following year met no further violence. Plano developed when Kentucky farmer William Forman purchased land in 1851, built a general store and several enterprises that formed a focal point for the sparsely settled community, and opened a post office in his home. When the town established a post office in 1852, it considered Forman and Fillmore, for President Millard Fillmore, as possible names, but postal authorities approved Plano, Spanish for "level," suggested by Dr. Henry Dye because of the surrounding terrain. Plano was platted and incorporated in 1873 and elected a mayor and board of aldermen that year. The public school system was organized in 1891. Early Plano industries included plumbing and stove plants, a garment factory, and an electric-wire factory. Until 1872, when the Houston and Texas Central Railway connected the community to nearby Dallas, the Shawnee Trail, which crossed western Collin County, served as a conduit for another source of area income, cattle. Though an 1881 fire destroyed 52 buildings and temporarily reduced Plano to a tent city, new markets opened by 1888, when the St. Louis, Arkansas and Texas Railway Company

PLAN OF SAN DIEGO

intersected the Houston and Texas Central, and Plano became a retail outlet for productive blackland-prairie farmers. By 1890 the town had a population of 1,200, two railroads, five churches for whites and one for blacks, two steam gristmill–cotton gins, three schools, and two newspapers. In 1908 Plano became an interurban stop on the Texas Electric Railroad. Between 1900, when the population numbered 1,304, and 1960, when it reached 3,695, the town averaged an increase of just over 600 new residents per decade and remained a farming community. A dramatic increase caused by the growth of Dallas and migration to the Sun Belt during the 1970s led to major public-improvement projects, while a 1970 land reappraisal raised taxes and contributed to the demise of farming in the area. In 1970 the population was 17,872. It had more than doubled five years later, then doubled again by 1980, when the total surpassed 72,000, more than half from outside of Texas. By the mid-1980s Plano had an estimated 1,000 businesses and had overtaken McKinney as the commercial, financial, and education center for Collin County. Plano was the corporate home of Frito–Lay Corporation, a satellite communication system, and computer manufacturers. By 1990 it was a city of 72 square miles with a population of 128,713. The Farrel–Wilson Farmstead Museum (Heritage Museum), which occupies a former sheep ranch, provides the only evidence Plano was once a farming community. Three colleges have made Plano their home: a branch of the University of Texas, formerly the Graduate Research Center of the Southwest, now in Richardson; the University of Plano, no longer in existence; and a branch of the Collin County Junior College system. Each October the city hosts balloon races, for which it is nicknamed the Balloon Capital of Texas. Fans of the "Dallas" television program visit the town's Southfork Ranch, which was used for the series' exterior shots.   *Shirley Schell and Frances B. Wells*

Plan of San Diego. A radical scheme, spawned by the Mexican Revolution, for a new "republic" in the Southwest and West. With the outbreak of revolution in northern Mexico in 1910, federal authorities and officials of the state of Texas feared that the violence might spill over into the Rio Grande valley. The Hispanic population in the Valley far outnumbered the Anglo population, and many residents had relatives in northern Mexico. The revolution caused an influx of political refugees and illegal immigrants into the border region, politicizing the Valley population and disturbing the traditional politics of the region. Some radical elements saw an opportunity to bring about drastic political and economic changes in South Texas. The most extreme example of this was a movement supporting the "Plan of San Diego," a revolutionary manifesto supposedly written and signed at the South Texas town of San Diego on 6 January 1915. The plan, actually drafted in a jail in Monterrey, Nuevo León, provided for the formation of a "Liberating Army of Races and Peoples," to be made up of Mexican Americans, African Americans, and Japanese, to "free" the states of Texas, New Mexico, Arizona, California, and Colorado from United States control. The liberated states would be organized into an independent republic, which might later seek annexation to Mexico. There would be a no-quarter race war, with summary execution of all white males over the age of 16. The revolution was to begin on 20 February 1915.

Federal and state officials found a copy of the plan when local authorities in McAllen arrested Basilio Ramos, Jr., one of the leaders of the plot, on 24 January. The arrival of 20 February produced only another revolutionary manifesto, rather than the promised insurrection. Similar to the original plan, this second Plan of San Diego emphasized the "liberation" of the proletariat and focused on Texas, where a "social republic" would be established to serve as a base for spreading the revolution throughout the southwestern United States. Indians were also to be enlisted in the cause. But with no signs of revolutionary activity, state and federal authorities dismissed the plan as one more example of the overblown rhetoric that flourished along the border. This feeling of complacency was shattered in July 1915 with a series of raids in the lower Rio Grande valley connected with the Plan of San Diego. These raids were led by two adherents of Venustiano Carranza, revolutionary general, and Aniceto Pizaña and Luis de la Rosa, residents of South Texas. The bands used the guerrilla tactics of disrupting transportation and communication in the border area and killing Anglos. In response, the United States Army moved reinforcements into the area.

A third version of the plan called for the foundation of a "Republic of Texas" to be made up of Texas, New Mexico, California, Arizona, and parts of Mississippi and Oklahoma. San Antonio was to serve as revolutionary headquarters, and the movement's leadership continued to come from South Texas. Raids originated on both sides of the Rio Grande, eventually assuming a pattern of guerrilla warfare. Raids from the Mexican side came from territory under the control of Carranza, whose officers were accused of supporting the raiders. When the United States recognized Carranza as president of Mexico in October 1915, the raids came to an abrupt halt. Relations between the United States and Carranza quickly turned sour, however, amid growing violence along the border. When forces under another revolutionary general, Pancho Villa, attacked Columbus, New Mexico, in March 1916, the United States responded by sending a large military force under Gen. John J. Pershing into northern Mexico in pursuit of Villa. When the United States rejected Carranza's demands to withdraw Pershing's troops, fear of a military conflict between the United States and Mexico grew. In this volatile context, there was a renewal of raiding under the Plan of San Diego in May 1916. Mexican officials were even considering the possibility of combining the San Diego raiders with regular Mexican forces in an attack on Laredo. In late June, Mexican and United States officials agreed to a peaceful settlement of differences, and raids under the Plan of San Diego came to a halt.

The Plan of San Diego and the raids that accompanied it were originally attributed to the supporters of the ousted Mexican dictator Gen. Victoriano Huerta, who had been overthrown by Carranza in 1914. The evidence indicates, however, that the raids were carried out by followers of Carranza, who manipulated the movement in an effort to influence relations with the United States. Fatalities directly linked to the raids were surprisingly small; between July 1915 and July 1916 some 30 raids into Texas produced only 21 American deaths, both civilian and military. More destructive and disruptive was the near race war that ensued in the wake of the plan as relations between whites and Hispanics deteriorated in 1915–16. Federal reports indicated that more than 300 Mexicans or Mexican Americans were summarily executed in South Texas in the atmosphere generated by the plan. Economic losses ran into the millions of dollars, and virtually all residents of the lower Rio Grande valley suffered some disruption in their lives from the raids. Moreover, the plan's legacy of racial antagonism endured long after the plan itself had been forgotten.

Don M. Coerver

Plum Creek, Battle of. An engagement between a volunteer Texan army and the Comanches after the Linnville Raid of 1840. After sacking Linnville, the Indians retreated. The Texans, including Gen. Felix Huston, Col. Edward Burleson, Capt. Mathew Caldwell, and Texas Rangers under Ben McCulloch, overtook them at Plum Creek near the site of Lockhart on 11 August 1840. A decisive defeat on the following day pushed the Comanches westward.

Plummer, Rachel Parker. Indian captive; b. Illinois, 22 March 1819; d. Houston, 19 March 1839; m. Luther Thomas Martin Plummer (1833). James W. Parker, Rachel's father and a Baptist minister, brought his family to Texas in 1832. They settled the next year on the Navasota River. Rachel and Luther had a son, James Pratt, in 1835, the year Luther received a large grant of land now in Limestone County. Fort Parker, built the same year, was attacked on 19 May 1836 by a large group of Indians, mainly Comanches. Five inhabitants of the fort were massacred, one was wounded, and five others were taken captive, including Rachel and James Pratt Plummer and Cynthia Ann Parker. When the Comanches learned that James had been weaned, he was taken from Rachel, and she never saw him again. Rachel became a slave to the Comanches and was beaten, burned, and deprived of sufficient clothing. In order to finish her assigned tasks she often had to work all day and most of the night. The Comanche band never stayed more than three or four days in one place except in extremely cold weather. Rachel traveled thousands of miles with the Comanches as they wandered from the headwaters of the Arkansas River to the Wichita Mountains. She was pregnant at the time of her capture; she bore a second son about October 1836 and named him Luther. The Indians thought that the baby was interfering with Rachel's work, so they killed him when he was about six weeks old. Rachel was held captive by the Comanches for 13 months. She was sold to Mexican traders north of Santa Fe on 19 June 1837. Her rescue had been arranged by Col. and Mrs. William Donaho, to whom she was delivered in Santa Fe after a journey of 17 days. Several weeks after her arrival, the Donahos, fearing trouble with the Mexicans, fled some 800 miles to Independence, Missouri, taking Rachel with them. Several months later, Rachel's brother-in-law, Lorenzo Nixon, escorted her back to Texas, where she was reunited with her husband on 19 February 1838. She was emaciated, covered with scars, and in very poor health. She wrote an account of her captivity entitled *Rachael Plummer's Narrative of Twenty One Months Servitude as a Prisoner Among the Commanchee Indians*, published in Houston in 1838. This was the first narrative about a captive of Texas Indians published in Texas. In 1844 James W. Parker published a revised edition as an appendix to his *Narrative of the Perilous Adventures, Miraculous Escapes and Sufferings of Rev. James W. Parker.* Rachel bore a third child in 1839 and died shortly thereafter; the child died two days later. Late in 1842 James Pratt Plummer was ransomed, and in 1843 he was reunited with his family. He married twice and fathered four children. While serving in the Confederate Army he died, on 17 November 1862, at Little Rock, Arkansas, of pneumonia.

Jo Ella Powell Exley

Pocket. A United States merchant vessel involved in a diplomatic incident of the new Republic of Texas. The *Pocket* was contracted in New Orleans to supply Santa Anna in his subjugation of Texas. M. de Lizardi and Company, a mercantile house under purchase instructions from Rubio and Company, a worldwide general agent for Santa Anna, sent the ship to deliver provisions to Matamoros. Lizardi gave Capt. Elijah Howes a signal pennant indicating that the provisions aboard the *Pocket* were to support the dictator's operation. The *Pocket* had as passengers several well-known Mexican naval officers. But it also carried United States citizens. On 3 April 1836, somewhere near the mouth of the Rio Grande, the *Pocket* encountered the Texan armed schooner *Invincible*, mastered by Jeremiah Brown. Brown boarded the *Pocket*, compared the cargo with the manifest, and discovered that the arms and ammunition aboard were not listed. He also found a detailed map of the coastline of Texas and military dispatches written in Spanish and recognized one of the Mexican naval officers. Based on this evidence, he assigned a prize crew to sail the *Pocket* to Galveston Island, where all was turned over to commandant James Morgan. Brown then took the *Invincible* to New Orleans to be refitted. There, news of the capture and return of most of the crew and passengers inflamed the situation. Bad press by New Orleans publications incited the local merchants into a united front with the insurance carriers to do something to protect their commerce in the Gulf of Mexico. Their fierce lobbying forced the hand of local federal officials, who requested Commodore A. J. Dallas, United States Gulf of Mexico squadron commander, to arrest the crew of the *Invincible* on a charge of piracy (1 May 1836). After a hearing they were released because evidence of piracy could not be substantiated. Later Jeremiah Brown made an inflammatory statement to a local port official that again caused consternation among merchants and insurance carriers. The crew would have been arrested a second time, but William Bryan, in cooperation with Toby and Brother Company, temporarily appeased those individuals by purchasing the *Pocket* for $35,000 and settling some additional claims.

However, the *Pocket* affair was not settled by this gesture of good faith. Shortly thereafter, the insurance carrier for the cargo of the *Pocket* filed a civil action to recover the money it had paid to Lizardi and Company. Brown was again arrested and held for $9,000 bond, which William Bryan and Toby and Brother paid to secure his release. This civil action lingered on the court dockets until 1840, and a final disposition of the suit has not been discovered. Several claimants aboard the *Pocket* clamored for redress. Since Texas did nothing regarding a negotiated settlement, the claimants asked the United States government to intercede. Finally, after some controversy, a convention of indemnity was agreed upon between the United States and Texas. The *Pocket* affair officially ended with the signing of this document on 11 April 1838. The *Pocket* incident, coupled with earlier seizures of other American merchant vessels, forced Texas to recognize the rights of other nations upon the seas. Because of the affair Texas had to announce formally a blockade of Mexican ports. Also, Texas established a district court with

4l4l4l4

admiralty jurisdiction to adjudicate prize vessels, a move that had not been contemplated before the capture of the *Pocket*.

Robert W. Kesting

Poet Laureate. Since 1933, appointed biennially by a committee composed of the governor, three senators, and three representatives. Until 1961 a new poet laureate of Texas was appointed every two years; subsequently, the term was reduced to one year. The honorary appointment carries with it no obligations or requirements. The selecting committee, for the most part, chooses those whose poetry can be understood by the average reader. The first ten poets laureate were Judd Mortimer Lewis of Houston (1932–34), Aline T. Michaelis of Austin (1934–36), Grace Noll Crowell of Dallas (1936–39), Lexie Dean Robertson of Rising Star (1939–41), Nancy Richey Ranson of Dallas (1941–43), Dollilee Davis Smith of Cleburne (1943–45), David Riley Russell of Dallas (1945–47), Aline B. Carter of San Antonio (1947–49), Carlos Ashley of Llano (1949–51), and Arthur M. Sampley of Denton (1951–53). Others from 1953 through 1988 have included Mildred Lindsey Railborn of San Angelo (1953–55), Margaret Royalty Edwards of Waco (1957–59), Jenny Lind Porter of Austin (1964–65), Dr. Terry Fontenot of Port Arthur (1971–72), William D. Barney of Fort Worth (1982–83), Ruth E. Reuther of Wichita Falls (1987–88), and Vassar Miller of Houston (1988–89).

Poetry Society of Texas. Organized in 1921 by Tyler poet Therese Lindsey, who called a meeting of interested persons in Dallas. Mrs. Lindsey was chosen corresponding secretary; charter members included Hilton Greer, Karle Baker, Clyde Hill, Jewell Wurtzbaugh, Whitney Montgomery, and Louella Vincent. In 1922 the society published its first yearbook and received its charter under state law. Its aim was to enlist public interest in poetry. Membership was open to anyone in sympathy with this goal. In 1994 the society had 600 members in 25 chapters across the state; headquarters were in Dallas. Active members must be native Texans, residents of Texas, or former residents of Texas who have been active in the society in the past; associate memberships have no geographical qualifications. The annual awards dinner, held in November, distributes 95 awards with prizes ranging from $25 to $350. In June the society presents its Student Awards Festival. The society sponsored an annual book-publication contest from 1925 to 1933. It holds annual and monthly contests with awards for individual poems. It has a permanent collection in the Dallas Public Library comprising several hundred books and pamphlets by Texas poets. Since 1922 the society has annually published a yearbook containing general information, a summary of the year's activities, and the monthly prizewinning poems of members. It also publishes a monthly news bulletin for members.

Sonja Fojtik

Poinsett, Joel Roberts. Diplomat; b. Charleston, South Carolina, 2 March 1779; d. South Carolina, 12 December 1851. He was educated under private instructors, in a Connecticut academy, and in London and Edinburgh, and became proficient in French, Spanish, Italian, and German. He also studied medicine, military science, and law. In early manhood he traveled for eight years in Europe, western Asia, the United States, and Canada. Several years as legislator and state senator helped to fit him for diplomatic service. Poinsett's relation to Texas history grew chiefly from his instructions to buy Texas while he served as first United States minister to Mexico, 1825–29. In spite of his more favorable qualifications for the service, his pronounced republicanism and the turbulence of Mexican politics all but wrecked his hopes. Among other instructions his government told him to try to get the consent of Mexico to readjust the boundary fixed by the Adams–Onís Treaty of 1819 to include land as far toward the Rio Grande as possible. In 1827 he was authorized to agree to pay a million dollars for land bounded by the Rio Grande and the Pecos and by a line from the source of the Pecos due north to the Arkansas River. The sensitiveness of the Mexican government did not permit him to press this offer, and in 1828 he signed a treaty, not ratified by the Mexican Senate until 1832, to accept the treaty boundary of 1819. He believed that the peaceful settlement of Texas by AngloAmericans then going on would make its acquisition easier in the future. Because Mexico forced his recall in 1829, Poinsett did not get to present President Andrew Jackson's instructions to offer $5 million for a line running between the Nueces and the Rio Grande northward to the forty-second degree north latitude. Poinsett was a pronounced Unionist in the South Carolina nullification controversy, served four years as secretary of war under Martin Van Buren, and spent his last days on a South Carolina plantation.

Lewis W. Newton

Poles. The first Polish immigration to America (1608–1775) consisted of only a few adventurers or religious refugees. Not until the period from 1776 to 1853 did political refugees from the Napoleonic Wars, the partitions of Poland, and the Polish Revolution of 1830 influence immigration to Texas. Early in 1818 a group of Polish veterans who had served under Napoleon were among the roughly 400 men of various nationalities who sailed up the Trinity River and founded the military camp of Champ d'Asile near the site of Liberty. This short-lived colony soon dispersed because of famine and the threat of Spanish military opposition. A few Polish veterans fought in the Texas Revolution at Goliad and San Jacinto. The greatest wave of immigration began in 1854 and lasted until the outbreak of World War I in 1914. Partition of Poland by its neighbors had led to deteriorating socioeconomic conditions in the homeland, and Texas offered encouragement to immigrants. Some came as early as 1830, as individuals rather than in groups, and these for the most part were absorbed into the communities where they settled. Simon Weiss was one of the Poles in Texas during the 1830s; he was living in Galveston by 1833, and served as a collector of customs under the governments of both Mexico and the Republic of Texas. Father Leopold Moczygemba, a Polish Franciscan missionary, worked in the areas of San Antonio, New Braunfels, and Castroville beginning in September 1852. Through his influence a group of some 100 Polish families from Pluznica and other villages of the Upper Silesian area of Poland arrived in south central Texas. They sailed on the *Weser*, out of Bremen, and landed in Galveston on 3 December 1854; traveling inland, they founded the town of Panna Maria ("Virgin Mary") in Karnes County on 24 December and offered the first Mass there on Christmas Day. This was the first permanent Polish colony in the United States, and ruins of the first stone buildings remain today. Though the first year in Texas was extremely hard, they persevered, and some 700 of their Polish countrymen followed, arriving in

Galveston on 15 December 1855; 30 additional families arrived the next year. Some chose to remain in the coastal communities, and others continued along the San Antonio and Medina rivers, settling in St. Hedwig, Bandera, San Antonio, and Yorktown. It was at Panna Maria, however, that the first Polish Catholic church (1855) and the first Polish school, St. Joseph's School (1866), in the United States were established.

By 1861 there were about 1,500 Poles in Texas. With the influx of immigrants after 1865, the Texas towns of Cestohowa, Kosciusko, Falls City, Polonia, New Waverly, Brenham, Marlin, Bremond, Anderson, Bryan, and Chappell Hill were either founded or populated by the Poles. Though the Poles settled primarily in South and Central Texas, after the Civil War some immigrants moved to East Texas, where landowners recruited them to replace slave labor. In East Texas the Poles worked primarily as tenant farmers. The earliest Polish colony founded in East Texas was the town of New Waverly (1867) in Walker County. Later in the nineteenth century more Polish immigrants moved to the north and northeastern sections of the United States to settle in the industrialized cities. For many years the Poles did not contribute directly to the political, cultural, or social life of the state; the language barrier was difficult to overcome, and many Poles chose to remain isolated rather than adapt to new situations. They did, however, contribute to the economy, being industrious farmers, artisans, and laborers. Their social life was bound up in the feasts and festivals of the Catholic Church. Native Polish clergy cared for the spiritual welfare of the people, and Polish national churches were founded. There were also small numbers of Polish Jews in some of the communities. Education, at first considered unimportant, became necessary to second and third generation Poles. Thorough "Americanization" of the Poles, however, did not take place until after World War II.

Texas Poles formed some fraternal groups. St. Joseph's Society, the first chapter in Texas of the Polish National Alliance, was established at Bremond in 1889. In the twentieth century the Texas branch expanded to include 12 lodges statewide by the 1970s. The locales included Houston, San Antonio, Panna Maria, Chappell Hill, Bremond, El Paso, and Yorktown, and a popular activity of the fraternal organization was the observance of Polish Constitution Day on 3 May. The Poles did not generally print newspapers in their own language as did other European ethnic groups, and the teaching of the Polish language never developed beyond the primary level. It was not until 1971 that Polish ethnic consciousness in Texas emerged at the statewide level, with the founding of a Texas chapter of the Polish American Congress by Father John W. Yanta.

By the late twentieth century the largest Polish population in Texas was in Houston, but with the exception of the Bryan, Houston, and San Antonio groups, the Polish settlements remained predominantly rural. The customs, traditions, and language of the old country were still in evidence among the older groups of Poles in Texas. In 1966 President Lyndon Johnson presented a mosaic of Our Lady of Czestochowa, also known as the Black Madonna, the patron saint of Poland, to Immaculate Conception Church—the oldest Polish church in the United States—in Panna Maria, honoring 1,000 years of Polish Christianity. In 1984 the Polish Genealogical Society of Texas was formally organized, and a special contingent of Polish descen-

dants from Panna Maria greeted Pope John Paul II, the "Polish pope," during his visit to San Antonio in September 1987.

In the 1990s a number of Polish organizations operated in Texas, including the Polish Arts and Culture Foundation and the Polish National Alliance Lodge No. 2540, both located in San Antonio, and the Polish Genealogical Society of Texas, located in Houston. The Panna Maria Historical Society published the *Panna Maria Newsletter*. The group promoted Polish cultural awareness. The Panna Maria visitors' center and St. Joseph's School Museum displayed artifacts and exhibits depicting Polish pioneer life, and the University of Texas Institute of Texan Cultures in San Antonio had an exhibit on Texas Polish culture. San Antonio was also home to Our Lady of Czestochowa shrine and museum, a grotto commemorating Poland's millennium of Christianity. A number of Texas Historical Commission markers across the state noted Polish towns, individuals, and churches; this included a number of markers in the Panna Maria area, as well as at St. Stanislaus Church in Bandera. Polish-related festivals in the state included an annual Homecoming Turkey Dinner every October in Panna Maria and a Polish food and arts-and-crafts booth at the Texas Folklife Festival every August in San Antonio. In 1990 there were 237,557 Texans of Polish descent. Of that total, 191,069 lived in urban areas and 46,488 lived in rural areas.   *Jan L. Perkowski and Jan Maria Wozniak*

Polignac's Brigade. A famous Texas Civil War unit. Col. Robert H. Taylor's 22d, Col. Trezevant C. Hawpe's 31st, and Col. Almerine M. Alexander's 34th Texas Cavalry regiments were raised in 1861–62 in North Texas. They were ordered into Indian Territory and Arkansas, where they were organized into a brigade with some Indian regiments under Col. Douglas H. Cooper. In the fall of 1862 the brigade fought at Shirley's Ford and at Newtonia, Missouri, before being driven back into Arkansas, where they were dismounted for service as infantry. The brigade was joined by Col. Thomas Coke Bass's 20th Texas Cavalry, served under several commanders, and fought at Prairie Grove, Arkansas, in the late fall and winter of 1862. In January 1863 the 15th Texas Infantry under Col. Joseph Warren Speight joined the brigade, which marched through snow back to Texas under Speight's command, leaving the 20th Texas in Indian Territory. In the spring of 1863 the brigade was sent to Louisiana, where the 22d and 34th were retrained as infantry, while the 15th and the 31st were joined by the 11th Texas Battalion in skirmishes and the battles of Stirling's Plantation and Bayou Bourbeau. In the fall of 1863 the brigade was reunited under Gen. Camille de Polignac, with the addition of the 17th Texas Consolidated Dismounted Cavalry and the later loss of the 11th Texas Battalion. The brigade skirmished at Vidalia and Harrisonburg, Louisiana, in early 1864 before joining Gen. Richard Taylor's army to defeat federal forces in the Red River campaign in April and May. Polignac became division commander after the battle of Mansfield and was succeeded by several brigade commanders, including Robert Dillard Stone (killed at Yellow Bayou), Wilburn Hill King, and Richard E. Harrison. In the fall of 1864 the brigade moved into Arkansas and then back to Texas, where it disbanded in May 1865.   *Alwyn Barr*

Ponce de León Land Grant. Land occupied by most of downtown El Paso; the subject of numerous lawsuits. In 1827 Juan

María Ponce de León received a grant of two *caballerías* that belonged to the city of El Paso del Norte, bounded on the south by the Rio Grande and valued at 80 pesos. He farmed the land and built a house that was washed away in 1830. Because of the flood damage, he petitioned for an additional grant and was awarded the alluvial accretion between the old and new riverbeds. After the Mexican War it became obvious that the United States military would play a part in the area. Recognizing this, Benjamin Franklin Coons offered to purchase the grant for $18,000; fearing that the grant might not be recognized by Texas, Ponce de León accepted the offer. In 1848 the United States government ordered the establishment of a post at or near the pass, and in 1849 the Third Infantry leased the main buildings on Coons' Rancho, plus six acres, for $4,200 a year. In 1851 United States troops were transferred from the area, and this plus other business losses made Coons unable to make payments. Ponce de León repossessed the land and managed it until his death (1 July 1852). Title passed to his wife and daughter, with the property managed by his soninlaw, Mariano Varela. Varela established a freighting business with William T. Smith, who offered to purchase the grant for $10,000. Again fearing that the title would not be recognized by Texas, the owners sold the land. The grant comprised slightly more than 599 acres. From time to time Smith sold small unsurveyed tracts to persons who had settled on the land. Confirmation of the grant was included in the Relinquishment Act passed by the Sixth Legislature, but this was vetoed by Governor Pease. In 1858 Smith and others in the area were able to get a special relief act passed that acknowledged the validity of the grant. For various reasons, mostly attempts by persons with no claim to the land trying to discredit boundary lines because of the land's increasing value, the grant was embroiled in lawsuits throughout the remainder of the nineteenth century. In 1872 the United States Circuit Court for West Texas held that the grant included only the original 215 acres. In a suit filed the next year in the Twentyfifth Judicial District Court of Texas and upheld by the Texas Supreme Court, it was found that the grant was larger because the river had changed course, that the original grant was 247 acres, and that the accretion grant of 1830 was approximately 352 acres. In 1877 a jury in a hearing at the United States Circuit Court agreed. Several later attempts to redefine the grant's boundaries were defeated. In the early 1900s a small portion of the grant became involved in the Chamizal Dispute. The squabble was settled on 28 October 1967, when 7.82 acres of the Ponce de León grant was awarded to Mexico, a ruling that finally settled the southern boundary of the grant.

John G. Johnson

Popeye. The comic-strip Sailor Man, perhaps the most famous native son of Victoria. The Victoria *Advocate* was the first newspaper to run Elzie Crisler Segar's comic strip, originally called "Thimble Theatre," which starred the spinach-eating hero. Segar (1894–1938), born in Chester, Illinois, got a job on the Chicago *Herald* through the influence of "Buster Brown" cartoonist R. F. Outcault. Segar drew "Charlie Chaplin's Comic Capers" for two years, until the *Herald* went out of business; he then worked in 1917 for the Chicago *Evening American*, where he drew "Looping the Loop," a cartoon covering local events. In late 1919 the editor of the *American* sent some of Segar's drawings to the King Features Syndicate in New York; three weeks later Segar moved

there, where, as he recalled, "I met 'Popeye,' 'Castor Oyl,' 'Olive Oyle,' and the members of the cast of 'Thimble Theater.'" The salty sailor was not among the strip's original cast but appeared on 17 January 1929, when Segar was living in Santa Monica, California. The new character was probably inspired by Frank "Rocky" Feigle of Segar's hometown. By 1932 Popeye was the undisputed star of "Thimble Theatre," as evidenced in fan mail, toys, games, novelties, and jokes. The comic strip's cast of characters grew to include Sea Hag, Professor O. G. Watasnozzle, Eugene the Jeep, Brutus, Alice the Goon, J. Wellington Wimpy, Swee'Pea, Granny, and Poopdeck Pappy. Segar himself called the Victoria *Advocate* Popeye's "hometown" and contributed a special cartoon for the *Advocate*'s historic 1934 anniversary issue. In this cartoon, Popeye claims that "Victoria is me ol' home town on account of tha's where I got born'd at." The Austin *Dispatch* wryly noted, in a story headed "President and Popeye Congratulate Texas Paper on Anniversary," that Popeye was among the more famous of the dignitaries to offer their congratulations, others including President Franklin Roosevelt, Vice President Garner, Ma and Pa Ferguson, and Texas senators Thomas Connally and Morris Sheppard. The cartoon series was animated in 1932 under the direction of Max Fleischer. Sammy Lerner composed the words and music to the theme song, "I'm Popeye the Sailor Man." After Segar's death the newspaper series "Thimble Theatre" was written by Tom Sims, then Ralph Stein; the artwork was drawn by Doc Winner, then Bill Zaboly. Joe Musial and Bud Sagendorf later produced the series, and Sagendorf drew the comic-book version until George Wildman and Bill Pearson took over in the 1970s. The spinach industry credited Popeye with the 33 percent increase in spinach consumption from 1931 to 1936, and in 1937 Crystal City, Texas, the "Spinach Capital of the World," erected a statue to honor Segar and his sailor.

Craig H. Roell

Port Arthur, Texas. On the lower west bank of Sabine Lake, 5 miles east of the Neches River Rainbow Bridge and 17 miles southeast of Beaumont in southeast Jefferson County. It was founded by Arthur E. Stilwell, a Kansas railroad promoter, who in 1894 launched the Kansas City, Pittsburg and Gulf Railroad. His intention was to link Kansas City to the Gulf of Mexico, and originally the Gulf Coast terminus was to be Sabine Pass. But Stilwell changed his mind, evidently because he could not reach an acceptable agreement with Luther and Herman Kountze, New York bankers who owned most of the land around Sabine Pass. By December 1895 Stilwell and his backers had acquired land on the western shore of Sabine Lake and begun platting a townsite, which the promoter named for himself and which became a municipality in 1895. Stilwell envisioned Port Arthur as a major tourist resort as well as an important seaport; proximity to the lake and a mild climate convinced him that visitors could be easily attracted to the area. But in his attempt to transform this marshy terrain into a tropical garden, Stilwell never lost sight of his primary endeavor. In June 1896 the Port Arthur Channel and Dock Company was established, and in April 1897 it began cutting a canal along the western edge of the lake to deep water at Sabine Pass. Port Arthur became a port in fact as well as name in March 1899. By the fall of 1897 it had 860 residents, and the following spring it was incorporated. A mayor–council government was established, but it gave way to the commission sys-

Petrochemical plant, ca. 1948. Courtesy TSL. By 1914 Port Arthur was the second largest oil-refining center in the nation, and by 1950 five refineries in the Port Arthur area employed 12,000 workers.

tem in 1911. A city manager–commission system was implemented in 1932. Despite his achievements, Stilwell was replaced as Port Arthur's chief financial backer in the early twentieth century by John W. (Bet-a-Million) Gates, a noted Wall Street plunger. After the Kansas City, Pacific and Gulf went into receivership in the spring of 1899 Stilwell's role in Port Arthur ebbed quickly and ended in 1904. Gates arrived in Port Arthur in December 1899 and was in the city periodically thereafter until his death in August 1911. His major concerns, like Stilwell's, were the port and canal. Port Arthur became an official port of entry in 1906, and by 1908 the Sabine–Neches canal had been deepened and extended up the Neches River to Beaumont and Orange. Extension of the canal was not an unmixed blessing, though, for it cut Port Arthur off from Sabine Lake and thereby diminished the city's prospects as a tourist resort. Aside from business, Gates's legacy included Port Arthur College, a business and radio school founded in 1909 that became a branch of Lamar University in 1975, and Gates Memorial Library, funded by Mrs. Gates in 1918 as a memorial to her husband and son.

The eruption of Spindletop on 10 January 1901 secured the town's future. Major oil companies—Gulf, Magnolia, Humble, and Texaco—all emerged from the Spindletop oilfield boom. Gulf in 1901 and Texaco in 1902 built major refineries at Port Arthur. Pipelines tied the city to Spindletop, and petroleum products soon were shipped through the canal. By 1909 Port Arthur had become the twelfth largest port in the United States in value of exports, and by 1914 it was the second largest oil-refining point in the nation. Development as a major petrochemical center was reflected in population growth. From 900 residents in 1900, Port Arthur expanded to a population of 7,663 in 1910 and 50,902 in 1930. After the late 1960s, when the city had 69,000 residents, the population slightly declined; in 1990 it was 58,724. By 1950 five refineries in the Port Arthur area employed some 12,000 workers. In 1948 the CIO's Oil Workers International had some 8,000 Port Arthur members, while the various craft unions of the AFL had 5,000. Beginning in the mid-1970s union influence declined somewhat. In the 1960s a new bridge called Gulfgate was built over the Sabine–Neches waterway in order to connect Port Arthur with Pleasure Island and offer access to the Sabine Lake Causeway leading into Louisiana.

The Rainbow Bridge, one of the tallest bridges in the South (230 feet with a vertical clearance of 176 feet), crosses the Neches River on State Highway 87 between Port Arthur and neighboring Orange and was completed in 1931.   *John W. Storey*

Porter, Katherine Anne. Writer; b. Callie Russell Porter, Indian Creek, Brown County, 15 May 1890; d. College Park, Maryland, 18 September 1980; m. John Henry Koontz (1906; divorced 1915); m. Ernest Stock (1926), Eugene Pressly (1933), and Albert Erskine (1938). After her mother died (1892), Callie's grandmother, Catherine Anne Porter, took the children to her home in Kyle, where she cared for them until her own death in 1901. Katherine Anne attended school in San Antonio. Subsequently, using her training in dramatic arts, singing, elocution, and dancing, she supported herself and her father by teaching these subjects in a rented room in Victoria. Influenced by her husband's family, she rejected the Methodism of her childhood and entered the Catholic Church in 1910. Except for a stint in Chicago in 1914, Porter lived in Texas until 1918, when she left to take a job on the *Rocky Mountain News* in Denver. After a successful year as a journalist she went to New York and spent the 1920s, in her words, "running back and forth between Mexico City and Greenwich Village." During this period she did what she called "hack work"—publicity work for a film company, journalism, and the ghostwriting of a book, *My Chinese Marriage* (1921, published under the initials M. T. F.). She also began writing short stories and published three children's stories in a magazine, *Everyland*. She was in Mexico for shorter periods than she liked to pretend, although her last period of residence there lasted over a year (1930–31). From Mexico she traveled to Europe on a Guggenheim fellowship and lived in Berlin and Basel and finally in Paris from 1933 to 1936. In 1936 she returned to the United States and lived in Doylestown, Pennsylvania, New York, New Orleans, Houston, and Baton Rouge. During this period she published some of her most important short fiction, including *Noon Wine*, "Old Mortality," and "The Grave," all set in Central Texas. By 1940 she lived in upstate New York. She was periodically a guest at the artists' colony Yaddo, and bought a house near Saratoga Springs. In 1944 she published *The Leaning Tower and Other Stories*. Though her writing brought moderate financial gain, she did not manage to maintain the house by it and, in an effort to earn more, went to Hollywood in 1945 to work as a scriptwriter. She worked only brief stints at this job but settled in California for a time to work on a novel.

In 1948 she began a series of teaching positions, delighted by the idea that she who had never been a university student should be invited to teach in prominent universities. She worked at Stanford, the University of Michigan, briefly at the University of Liège, Belgium, and at Washington and Lee University in Virginia. She also presented a lecture at the University of Texas in 1958. Although Porter often lectured and read in universities, she gave up trying to support herself with full-time positions and settled in 1959 in the Washington, D.C., area in a last-ditch effort to finish her novel. *Ship of Fools* was finished in Boston in 1961 and triumphantly published in 1962. The book brought fame and fortune, though this time critical approval was mixed with adverse criticism. Financially secure at last, she lived in a large house in Spring Valley, near Washington, until ill health made smaller places necessary. Katherine Anne Porter's physical remains were buried beside her mother's grave in the Indian

Creek Cemetery, near Brownwood. Her literary remains, however, were left to the University of Maryland, which had in 1968 established a Katherine Anne Porter Room to house her library, furniture, and personal memorabilia. In the 1950s she had hoped that the University of Texas would honor her by naming a library for her. In return she intended to leave all her papers to UT. But no library or room was named for her, and she looked elsewhere for a deserving recipient of her substantial literary archive. In 1939, when she was receiving national acclaim for *Pale Horse, Pale Rider,* she had been a candidate for the first award given by the recently formed Texas Institute of Letters, but the medal was awarded instead to J. Frank Dobie for *Apache Gold and Yaqui Silver.* Nevertheless, Porter received numerous awards and honorary degrees. Her novel was made into a successful movie. Her works were translated into many languages. *The Collected Stories of Katherine Anne Porter* (1965) won the Gold Medal for Fiction awarded by the National Institute of Arts and Letters, the Pulitzer Prize, and the National Book Award. She was appointed to the American Academy of Arts and Letters in 1966. Texas historical markers were placed in her honor at Indian Creek Cemetery and Kyle.

Joan Givner

Porvenir Massacre. One of a series of clashes between Mexican Americans and the Texas Rangers set off by the Mexican Revolution and accompanying events. In November 1917 ranger captain J. M. Fox attributed the theft of livestock to Carrancistas and Villistas near Presidio County. On 25 December 1917, Mexicans perpetrated the Brite Ranch raid, in which several Mexicans and Anglos were killed, horses were stolen, and the ranch store was robbed. Several days later Company B of the rangers, with some local ranchers, attacked the ranch of Manuel Morales in Porvenir and killed 15 men. Exactly what occurred is unclear. In February 1918 Fox claimed to the adjutant general that the Mexicans were marched to the edge of town and that comrades of the Mexicans fired at the rangers, who then returned fire. He said the Mexicans had been found with pocket knives, soap, and shoes belonging to the Brite Ranch. He also claimed that one dead man had "sent word" some nine months earlier that a raid would be made on "Texas Gringos" and that looting and burning would also occur. According to Walter Prescott Webb, agreement was unanimous among the rangers and ranchers on the "culpability of the Mexicans." Webb based his assessment of the incident on the testimony of Anglos, however, ignoring affidavits by Mexican-descent women. Henry Warren, whose father-in-law, Tiburcio Jáquez, was killed in the incident, later called the incident a "massacre" and blamed it on the rangers. Apparently, the cavalry's role and requests by officials of the Mexican government led to a federal investigation. The father of Felipa Mendez Castañeda, whose husband was killed, owned a newspaper in Pilares, Chihuahua; he asked the Mexican government for assistance, and Mexican ambassador Ygnacio Bonilla asked for an investigation. On 4 June 1918, Governor William Hobby disbanded Company B of the Texas Rangers and dismissed five rangers for their actions. Eulalia Gonzales Sánchez gave Warren power of attorney and sought to recover damages for the death of her husband. In 1919 state legislator José T. Canales highlighted the Porvenir Massacre in his investigation of the rangers. About 140 Porvenir residents abandoned their homes and fled to Mexico, and the community ceased to exist for several years.

Cynthia E. Orozco

Charles William Post. Courtesy Texas State Historical Association, Austin.

Post, C. W. Cereal magnate and town developer; b. Charles William Post, Springfield, Illinois, 26 October 1854; d. Santa Barbara, California, 9 May 1914 (buried in Battle Creek, Michigan); m. Ella Letitia Merriweather (1874; divorced 1904); 1 daughter; m. Leila Young (1904). During his youth in Springfield, Post invented and secured patents on such farm equipment as cultivators, a sulky plow, a harrow, and a haystacker. After a nervous breakdown caused by overwork, he went to Texas in 1886 and in Fort Worth became associated with a group of real estate men who were developing a 300-acre tract in the eastern part of the city, an area now known as Riverside. Other members of the family followed. In 1888 the Posts acquired a 200-acre ranch on the outskirts of the city and began the development of a subdivision on their property; they laid out streets and lots for homes and constructed a woolen mill and a paper mill. In 1891 Post suffered a second breakdown and moved with his wife Battle Creek, Michigan, where he entered a sanitarium. With rest and the ministrations of a Christian Science practitioner came recuperation, and soon he was experimenting with a cereal drink he called Postum. He subsequently developed Grape-Nuts and Post Toasties, breakfast foods that by the end of the century made him millions of dollars. He served as president of the American Manufacturers Association and of the Citizen's Industrial Association. Post was a bitter opponent of labor unions and an advocate of the open shop. In 1906, as a result of his desire to own a farming community in Texas, he purchased some 225,000 acres of ranchland along the Caprock escarpment in Garza and Lynn counties and designated a site near the center of Garza County as the location of his new town, which would be the county seat. In 1907 Post City (now Post) was platted, farms of 160 acres were laid out, shade trees were planted, and a machine shop, a hotel, a school, churches, and a department store were constructed. Post tried various forms of automatic machinery in developing dryland farming techniques and introduced varieties of grain sorghums such as milo and kafir. One of his most spectacular and least successful experiments was his rain-making effort through dynamite explosions detonated at firing-stations along the rim of the Caprock (1911–14). His main contribution to Texas was opening the plains to agricultural development. He probably committed suicide. *William M. Pearce*

Postosuchus. An unusual rauisuchian (rauisuchians were the largest terrestrial carnivores during the Middle and Late Triassic, rivals of dinosaurs) from the Triassic Dockum Formation of Texas; found near Post at a site that has rapidly come into prominence as one of the richest paleontological sites for that period ever discovered in the world. Among findings there are the world's oldest bird, the oldest pterosaur, the earliest planteating dinosaur, various armored archosaurs, labyrinthodonts, lizards, mammallike reptiles, and possibly a mammal. Evidence indicates that these animals perished in a flash flood. Though it is a rocky, dry, and forbidding place today, the South Plains was lush with vegetation and water during the Triassic period, 225 million years ago. *Postosuchus* was the arch-predator in the Triassic forest of the American Southwest. It was about 15 feet long and 8 feet high; it walked on two powerful legs, balancing its body on its strong tail. The skull is very large, equipped with sharp, serrated teeth for cutting flesh. The sharp-clawed front feet were used for seizing and manipulating food. The animal was a smaller version of *Tyrannosaurus rex* but was not as fully developed for hunting and killing as this king of the Cretaceous. Its crocodilelike ankle joint discouraged fast running. *Postosuchus* was probably an ambush predator that captured its prey by stealth and surprise like the modern komodo dragon of Indonesia. In contrast, the dinosaurs acquired refined locomotion and cursorial adaptations and could run faster with longer strides than the rauisuchians. At the end of the Triassic, many forests gave way to more open prairie, where the great speed and endurance of dinosaurs became more advantageous. The ambush hunting strategy of *Postosuchus* and other rauisuchians became less effective in this new environment. They began to decline and soon became extinct at the end of the Triassic, while the dinosaurs proliferated. *Sankar Chatterjee*

Pottery. The history of pottery making in Texas may be divided into prehistoric and historic eras, analogous to the divisions in archeology.

Prehistoric. Five prehistoric pottery regions can be identified in Texas: Northeast (Caddoan area) and North Central, Southeast, Central and South, the High Plains, and West. Central and South Texas pottery was heavily influenced, if not derived from, the first two. The High Plains and West Texas regions were heavily influenced by the Southwest. Pottery in Northeast Texas was derived from the Southeastern United

States and lower Mississippi valley. The earliest Texas pottery (ca. 500 to 100 B.C.) was related to the Tchefuncte tradition from the latter area. This early pottery includes bone, clay, and sand tempered pastes, as well as sandy pasteware. North of the Sabine River, the earliest pottery is primarily clay-tempered, with bone as a minor element, often with clay or sand. Plain bone-tempered pottery in the Sabine drainage and Toledo Bend areas may reveal a relationship to early cultures in Arkansas. Williams Plain (ca. 100 B.C. to A.D. 1000) is the most abundant early pottery type in Northeast Texas. It is absent from the Western Sabine and Neches–Angelina basins. After A.D. 700–900, Caddoan ceramics dominated Northeast Texas, with most Caddoan elements being recognizable as local developments strongly influenced from farther east. Clay and bone tempering continued as the primary technological tradition until its replacement by shell tempering (ca. A.D. 1400 to 1500). Caddoan pottery also occurs as trade ware in east Central, Southeast, and possibly north Central Texas. North Central Texas received influence from several directions. Shelltempered technology may have been present between A.D.. 200 and 700, followed by a sandy paste pottery between A.D. 700 and 900. A more widespread clay, grit, and bone tempered pottery possibly began as early as the sandy paste material, but certainly after A.D. 1000, and continued to the end of the prehistoric period. Southern plains–related shelltempered pottery is found in north Central Texas, dating after A.D. 1300.

The earliest pottery in Southeast Texas is from the Sabine Lake region (ca. 70 B.C.) and includes lower Mississippi valley types and attributes, as well as sandy paste Goose Creek ware and clay tempering. Goose Creek ware became widespread in Southeast Texas after A.D. 500. Similar pottery appears in the Galveston Bay area (A.D. 100–425), while clay tempering appears in this latter area by A.D. 1000. Sandy paste pottery also occurs in Central Texas, but is much less common north of the Sabine River. Pottery along the Lower Texas Coast, including Padre Island, from Baffin Bay to Matagorda Bay, is related to Goose Creek ware and is known as Rockport ware (A.D. 1200–1400 to the Historic period). It may have been made by Karankawanspeakers, as well as other coastal Indians.

In Central Texas, pottery is a late occurrence, with Caddoan trade ware being the earliest pottery in this region. Bonetempered Leon Plain (post A.D. 1200–1300) is a distinctive Central and South Texas ware. It appears to have spread from Central Texas into South Texas, where it began to be made sometime after A.D. 1200 and continued into the sixteenth or seventeenth centuries. Goliad ware, defined from sites of Spanish missions sites, is similar to Leon Plain, but often is thicker and distinctively decorated.

Pottery that appears on the High Plains after A.D. 200 shows influences from both the Southern Plains and the Southwest (plain and corrugated brownwares). This locally made pottery is tempered with coarse crushed rock and bone. Early intrusive pottery includes both Mogollón and Anasazi wares; while after A.D. 1300, tradewares include pottery from North Central, Northeast, and Central Texas. One type of pottery on the High Plains, associated with late Apache sites, consists of locally made utility wares tempered with micaceous sand. Pottery apparently imported from the Southwest in these sites consists of Anasazi glaze paint polychromes and plain utility ware. On the basis of the glazewares, the earliest of these sites may date to A.D.. 1300, while the majority date from A.D. 1450–1500 to A.D. 1700.

The pottery of West Texas is strongly affiliated with that of the Southwest, with a number of intrusive types present. Locally made pottery includes El Paso Brown, which may appear as early as A.D. 100–300, and El Paso Polychrome, which postdates A.D. 1100. El Paso Polychrome is decorated with black and red horizontal geometric designs on the upper third of the vessels.

Historic. Although leadglazed earthenwares occur on Spanish Colonial sites, no definitive manufacturing loci are known for Texas. The first evidence of historic ceramic production dates after 1830, when European immigrants produced a demand for earthenware or stoneware vessels. Limited transportation and prohibitive costs for importing stoneware clays and completed vessels made it necessary to rely on locally produced wares. Although some stoneware potteries produced earthenwares, only the Abraham Babcock Pottery in Jackson County produced them on a regular and largescale basis. The earliest stoneware pottery was established in Rusk County around 1839 by Taylor Brown, who was granted a secondclass headright to land just north of Henderson. The 1850 census of industry and manufacture lists four Texas stoneware potteries with capital over $500—three in Rusk County and one in Montgomery County. By 1860, at least 11 such potteries were operating, in Austin, Bastrop, Denton, Guadalupe, Henderson, Lee, Limestone, Montgomery, Rusk, Titus, and Waller counties.

Over 60 stoneware potteries operated during the nineteenth and early twentieth centuries, in Bastrop, Bexar, Bowie, Cass, Cooke, Denton, Falls, Franklin, Guadalupe, Harris, Harrison, Henderson, Limestone, Montgomery, Nacogdoches, Parker, Rusk, Smith, Titus, Upshur, Wilson, and Wood counties. Archeological evidence has been documented for many of these potteries, including kilns and waster-sherd piles, and a few of these potteries are on the National Register of Historic Places. During the nineteenth century, wares were shipped by wagon or rail within about a 100mile radius of the pottery. After 1915 the demand for stonewares lessened and many potteries ceased operating. A few potteries were active after 1920: for example, the Athens, Ideal, Love Field, and Southern potteries in Dallas; the Guy Daugherty Art Pottery in Denton; the Marshall, Grubbs, and Star potteries in Marshall; the Athens Pottery in Athens; and the San Antonio and Meyer potteries in Bexar County.

Potteries were located near suitable clay outcrops (e.g., the Wilcox Group and the Woodbine Formation) and included both part-time and full-time, rural and urban, kin and non-kin-related individuals. Most early potteries were operated by uncles, brothers, sons, and nephews who immigrated from other parts of the United States or Europe. Several African Americans began as slave potters at the Wilson Potteries in Guadalupe County.

Four stoneware glazes—alkaline, salt, natural clay, and Bristol—were produced in Texas, and their use varied over time and among potteries. Alkaline glazes were used in East Texas, while the other three types were commonly used throughout the state. Salt glaze was the most common glaze prior to 1875, when natural clay slips became popular. Bristol glazes introduced in the 1880s were initially used in conjunction with clay slips. After 1920, most stoneware vessels had Bristol glazes.

A variety of stoneware vessels were produced for household and farm use. Major forms include jugs, churns, large and narrow mouth jars, and bowls. Bottles, pitchers, sieves, water coolers, funnels, animal feeders, spittoons, chamber pots, tobacco pipes, marbles, flowerpots, and grave markers were less common. These vessels were predominantly thrown on a potter's wheel and fired in woodburning kilns. Common kiln types included updraft and downdraft beehive and crossdraft groundhog kilns.

Susan A. Lebo and Maynard B. Cliff

Prairie Dog. A once-multitudinous resident of Texas, a species of squirrel (*Cynomys ludovicianus*). Its name derives from the barks or yipping calls of this sociable, diurnal rodent whose yellow-grey or buffy appearance and noisy, active presence relieved the monotony of traveling over the short-grass plains in the nineteenth century. The typical prairie dog hole descends vertically from a small, volcano-like dirt cone on the ground surface into a number of passages of varying lengths, which may descend three to five meters below ground. The prairie dog carefully tends the dirt pile built up on the surface in order to prevent water from flooding its burrow system, and uses grass to line the nesting cavity in which the young are born. In severe cold the animals become dormant. They feed on grasses and herbs surrounding their burrows, and are subject to predation from hawks, coyotes, skunks, foxes, rattlesnakes, and badgers. They also are a favorite target of "varmint" hunters. Prairie dogs occupy colonies called "towns," often 100 hectares (247 acres) in area or more, which may be divided into "wards" by physical features such as ridges and gullies, and further subdivided into "coteries," or family groups, averaging about eight individuals. In nineteenth-century Texas some of these towns extended over an enormous area. In August 1841 George Wilkins Kendall came upon a "commonwealth" of prairie dogs whose "mercurial and excitable denizens" provided some sustenance for the famished and disoriented members of the Texan Santa Fe expedition. He admired the "wild, frolicsome, madcap set of fellows . . . ever on the move . . . chattering away the time, and visiting from hole to hole to gossip and talk over each other's affairs." Dobie noted that in 1852 a single town of some 50 million animals occupied a million acres of the Llano Estacado. As recently as 1900 a dog town extended 250 miles north from San Angelo to Clarendon and was 100 miles wide, having an estimated 400 million animals. In 1905 biologist Vernon Bailey calculated that the Texas population was 800 million prairie dogs in an area of 90,000 square miles in West Texas.

Researchers suggest that prairie dog numbers increased in Texas during the latter part of the 1800s as stockmen reduced their natural predators and killed off buffalo and antelope that competed for forage. Ranchers and farmers began a war on prairie dogs, which intensified after about 1914, when Donald Gilchrist directed rodent control in the Texas district for the United States Department of Agriculture's Bureau of Biological Survey. The federal government joined forces with county agents and landowners in order to poison prairie dog towns. An effective formula, including strychnine, cyanide, and syrup on a corn or wheat base, was pioneered in 1901. It was used in a modified form in Texas with 200,000 pounds of poisoned grain annually. As a result, dog towns disappeared quickly. In 1918 Bailey noted a decline of more than 90 percent around the San Angelo region, where only about a dozen colonies remained. Control operations persisted, and sizable inroads into West Texas prairie dog numbers occurred in the 1920s. In the mid-1970s, a survey of aerial photographs turned up 1,336 prairie dog colonies extending over 89,987 acres in 89 counties. The species continues to inhabit its ancestral range, but habitat loss through the expansion of cropland and metropolitan areas, plus poisoning, has served to reduce the state population to an estimated 2.2 million animals. The results of attempts at elimination or control of prairie dogs have been both good and bad. Though the animals definitely compete with livestock for forage, some scholars believe that the expansion of brush brought about by the reduction of prairie dogs has caused greater losses of livestock forage than the animals themselves. The poisoned grain and fumigants used to kill prairie dogs also kill other species that inhabit prairie dog towns or eat prairie dogs. Species so affected include the burrowing owl, some hawks, the cottontail rabbit, various reptiles, and, at one time, the black-footed ferret. *Robin W. Doughty*

Prairies. The Prairies in east central Texas, extending from the Red River to the Coastal Plain, developed on outcrops of calcareous clays or chalk. The Black Prairies area in the Inner Lowland forms the interior portion of the Coastal Plain and is underlain by limy clays, marls, and chalk beds of the Upper Cretaceous. The topography is of a round, rolling, or undulating nature, and the soils are generally deep except along the western margin of the Austin chalk, where erosion is particularly active. The Black Prairies comprise several belts, each of which is developed on the outcrops of the major formations composing the Upper Cretaceous section. For instance, the Austin chalk, or White Rock strip, not only forms a belt of slightly higher elevation in the Black Prairies, but also its western portion is well eroded. Through its characteristically shallow soils appear large areas of exposed chalk. The shallow-soil areas afforded good foundations for roads in the early days, particularly in contrast to the deep-soil areas to the east and west of the Austin chalk, which are characterized by deep mud during much of the year. Since the 1880s the Black Prairies have constituted one of the outstanding cotton regions of the United States. With the coming of railroads into the area important commercial centers arose. The flat Coastal Prairies just interior from the Gulf Coast afford examples of two types of prairie soils. Most of the Beaumont clays belt is characterized by heavy black soils; the interior Lissie formation, although characteristically occupied by tall grasses, has light-colored soils. In the middle portion of the Central Dissected Belt of the Coastal Plain is a strip of country underlain by calcareous clays of Tertiary age. These include the Brenham–Schulenburg prairies, which form an important farming region. Although the surface is somewhat more deeply and more intricately dissected than is the case of the Black Prairies, this district has good black soils that form the basis for its prosperous farming operations. On either side of the Brenham–Schulenburg Prairies are woodlands, which occur on dissected areas underlain by non-limy sands and sandy clays. The Coastal Plain is an important oil-producing district. The Upper Gulf or Houston district, which extends into the timbered country along the southern margin of East Texas, is generally designated as the salt dome area. The ordinary salt domes are of the piercement type, which rise nearly to the surface; others are of the seep dome type, of which the Conroe oilfield is considered a good example. *E. H. Johnson*

Prairie View A&M University. A historically black university in Prairie View; authorized in 1876 under the Morrill Land-Grant College Act as an "Agricultural and Mechanical College for the Benefit of Colored Youth," part of the Agricultural and Mechanical College of Texas (now Texas A&M University). A three-man commission bought Alta Vista Plantation, from Helen Marr Kirby for $15,000, and commissioner Ashbel Smith turned the project over to the A&M board. Texas A&M president Thomas S. Gathright hired Mississippian L. W. Minor as the first principal, and in 1878, eight young men enrolled in the short-lived Alta Vista Agricultural College at a tuition of $130 for nine months of instruction, board, and one uniform. Governor Roberts, A&M board chairman, suggested closing the college in 1879 because of the lack of patronage. But Barnas Sears, an agent for the Peabody Fund, persuaded the Sixteenth Legislature to charter two "normal" schools for the training of teachers, one of which was named Prairie View Normal Institute. The A&M board met at Hempstead in August 1879 and founded the coeducational institution. Girls were housed in the plantation house now called Kirby Hall, and boys were housed in a combination chapel and dormitory called Pickett Hall. A destructive storm and financial reversals subsequently forced the governor to solicit money from merchants. In 1887 an agricultural and mechanical department was added. Booker T. Washington made his first commencement address at Prairie View on 4 June 1897. The legislature designated the school Prairie View State Normal and Industrial College. In 1926 Willette R. Banks, new principal of the school, sought funding from private philanthropy, the state government, and federal agricultural agencies. He acquired campus buildings, faculty scholarships, a doubtful "A" rating from the Southern Association of Colleges in 1934, and a graduate school in 1938. Banks also secured law, engineering, pharmacy, and journalism departments "substantially equivalent" to those at the University of Texas. Banks, continually frustrated over funding, retired in 1946. The last principal, first dean, and first president of Prairie View A&M, Edward Bertram Evans, assumed leadership. Formerly the state leader of the Cooperative Extension Service, Evans was a veterinarian well-respected by the A&M system and the federal government. During his tenure he promoted and oversaw a development project for buildings and dormitories. The Fiftieth Legislature added "Agricultural and Mechanical" to the college's name. By 1950 instructional divisions had become schools, and their heads had become deans. Evans was retained as president for seven years beyond his normal tenure. He later became a consultant for the United Nations in northeast Africa and the Middle East.

The school was integrated in 1963, and in 1966 Alvin Thomas, dean of the School of Industrial Education and Technology, became president. Faced, like Evans, with the fact that his campus was an active outpost of the "black revolution" and caught in the controversy regarding the need for separate black colleges after *Brown v. Board of Education of Topeka* (1954), Thomas offered two remedies: the residential college and the idea of "partners in progress." Under the residential college concept, he sought to build an atmosphere where the idea of success in a caste society could grow. He hoped to break the barrier that kept his students isolated from the mainstream of society with programs such as the naval ROTC in 1968, the Centennial Council of 1968 (which recommended a large building program), and the constant effort to make alliances with the business world. In 1973 the legislature changed the institution's name to Prairie View A&M University. In the early 1990s Prairie View A&M offered degrees in agriculture, arts and sciences, engineering, home economics, nursing, and industrial education and technology. It was the largest employer in Waller County.

George Ruble Woolfolk

Presidiales. Soldiers attached to a Spanish presidio; often loosely applied to other military forces. The usual personnel of a presidial company at full strength was a captain, a lieutenant, a first-degree ensign, a second-degree ensign, a chaplain, an armorer, 2 sergeants, a drummer, 4 corporals, 4 riflemen, and 56 soldiers. Spanish soldiers were regarded as employees of the government and were required to provide their own uniforms, horses, arms, and food. Soldiers had to provide personally for the welfare of their families, if any, even on the frontier. *See* Presidios.

Presidio del Norte. The name given to both the eighteenth-century fort and the settlement on the south side of the river at La Junta de los Ríos (the fort was also called Presidio del Norte de la Junta de los Ríos and Presidio de Belén). The fort and settlement occupied the site of present Ojinaga, Chihuahua. In 1747 three Spanish entradas, each with an interest in building a presidio, visited the junction of the Rio Grande and the Río Conchos, at La Junta. On 10 November the viceroy ordered Governor Pedro de Rábago y Terán of Coahuila to reestablish the six abandoned missions and to establish a presidio to protect the missionaries and converts. Capt. José de Idoyaga was also sent to help build the presidio. Capt. Fermín Vidaurre surveyed the needs of La Junta and recommended the building of a presidio and the rebuilding of the missions. Despite the Spanish interest in building a presidio at La Junta in 1747, it was not built until Capt. Alonso Rubín de Celis arrived in December 1759. The presidio, between San Francisco de los Julimes and Nuestra Señora de Guadalupe pueblos, was completed the next year. It was abandoned in 1766 and moved to Julimes on the Río Conchos. In 1772 the king ordered its reestablishment at La Junta, and by 1773 the fort was back at its original site. The name was shortened to Presidio del Norte. In November 1865 the garrison and the settlement were renamed Ojinaga for Manuel Ojinaga, governor of Chihuahua, who was executed by the French.

Julia Cauble Smith

Presidios. When the Spanish frontier expanded northward from central Mexico, the presidio, the mission, and the civil settlement became related frontier institutions for supporting Spanish colonization. Spanish missions generally were accompanied by presidios. Martín Enríquez, fourth viceroy of New Spain (1568–80), is generally credited with originating the presidios of the Southwest. He ordered the construction along the main road from Mexico City north to Zacatecas of *casas fuertes* ("fortified houses"). Eventually the name was changed to presidio (from Latin *praesidium*, "garrisoned place"). The pattern of the early presidios was learned from the Moors and dated from the days of the reconquest in Spain. By the early eighteenth century, when Spaniards settled Texas, it had changed but little.

The presidios in Texas were Nuestra Señora de los Dolores de los Tejas (1716), San Antonio de Béxar (1718), Nuestra Señora de Loreto and Nuestra Señora del Pilar de los Adaes (both 1721), San Francisco Xavier de Gigedo (1751), San Agustín de Ahumada (1756), San Luis de las Amarillas (1757), and San Elizario (1789).

Across the Rio Grande, other presidios important to Texas included Presidio del Norte, San Juan Bautista, and San Gregorio de Cerralvo. Presidio soldiers engaged in military operations from the Pecos River to the Red River, among them the campaigns of Vicente Rodríguez and Diego Ortiz Parrilla. Each presidio had a specific role. Dolores protected the 1716 missions in East Texas and served as a listening post on the French. Loreto (also known as La Bahía Presidio) patrolled the coast against invaders and rescued shipwreck victims. Los Adaes countered the Louisiana French established at Natchitoches. San Agustín curbed French trading activities along the coast. San Luis de las Amarillas (also known as San Sabá Presidio) served as a buffer for San Antonio against raids by northern Indians, including Comanches.

Presidios were constructed of local building materials (sometimes adobe, sometimes log). Where stone was available it was preferred for the permanent structure. The forts were typically square or rectangular with some walls 10 feet high. On two diagonal corners, round bastions (*torreones*) were placed. These rose above the walls of the presidio and were pierced with firing ports, through which soldiers could fire down the length of all four walls at attackers. There were occasional variations, as at Los Adaes in East Texas, which had wooden palisades and diamond-shaped bastions. Buildings were contained by walls 18 feet apart, the roofs of which were high enough to serve as parapets from which men also could fire over the walls. A presidio included storage facilities, a chapel, and quarters for officers and men. The only openings were a main gate, which locked from the inside, and sometimes a rear gate. The two urban presidios on the northern frontier, at San Antonio and Santa Fe, had no walls, no towers, and no barracks, although the presidio at San Antonio was enclosed by a stockade, as Governor Domingo Cabello y Robles reported in 1781. In both cases the residence of the governor–captain was situated on the town plaza, as also were a guardhouse and the chapel, while the soldiers lived in their huts in town. The systems of fortification being developed in Europe during the eighteenth century had only slight influence on frontier Spanish presidios. The Indians of the region had no cannons with which to blast fortress walls, and most officers in frontier service were slaves to tradition. Thus they continued to rely on traditional, inexpensive designs and materials that produced forts little different from the fortresses erected in Spain during medieval days.

Presidio soldiers assigned to protect the Spanish missions also conducted supply trains, escorted missionaries, colonists, and merchants, carried the mail, and explored the country. At the missions, soldiers' aggressiveness and conduct toward Indian women occasionally caused problems. The soldiers usually brought families or else married local Christian natives. Their families constituted a permanent Spanish population in the new land. Conferences with Indians were conducted at presidios, which thus functioned as frontier Indian agencies. The presidios were oases of safety for travelers who camped in their shadows. Around them the soldiers and their families built homes. Merchants came to sell goods, farmers came to plant their crops, and small civil settlements grew. The soldiers in these presidios lived lives of considerable hardship and danger. When the Marqués de Rubí inspected the northern frontier, including Texas, in 1766–68, he found an almost total lack of discipline. Soldiers had not been instructed in using their firearms, most of them were deeply in debt because their salaries were in arrears, and their equipment and arms had badly deteriorated or were lacking altogether. Officers were profiteering by selling inferior goods to the soldiers at inflated prices, and morale was shot through with insubordination. Rubí sought not only to correct abuses, but to withdraw forces from the desired frontier to a real one and take up more defensible positions. He recommended that the presidios of the northern frontier be reorganized into a chain of 15 forts stretching from the Gulf of California to the Gulf of Mexico, each approximately 40 leagues from the next to allow quick communication and the rapid dispatch of help. The soldiers in the garrisons were to be properly equipped, regularly paid, and carefully instructed in their duties.

Despite the efforts of Rubí and other high officers on the northern frontier, soldiers stationed in the 15 presidios and capital cities of San Antonio and Santa Fe were never able to conquer the Comanches, Apaches, Navajos, and other nomadic warring tribes for two reasons. First, the strategy of building forts across the northern frontier was based on concepts of European warfare. In the Old World, armies would advance on a fortified city and halt to invest it. If they failed, they retreated. The Indians in the New World saw no reason to attack a presidio; they preferred to ride around it to attack civilian settlements, ranches, and farms. Second, each Spanish soldier was so burdened with weapons and equipment that he needed some six mounts to undertake a campaign. Presidial compounds were not large enough to hold the horses, which therefore had to be picketed some distance away from the fort—and thus were conveniently gathered for Indians to steal. The presidial soldiers could not pursue the raiders because they were left afoot. For all their shortcomings, however, Spanish presidios served a useful purpose on the northern frontier. Their design was so practical that the Indians of the region never were able to overcome one by frontal assault, although they did penetrate a few by stealth. Many American traders and military leaders of a later date recognized the basic worth of presidios and chose to build their forts in the Southwest on the same pattern. The restored Presidio La Bahía at Goliad stands today as a state monument to the Spanish presidio. *Odie B. Faulk*

Prisoners of War. During World War II Texas had approximately twice as many prisoner-of-war camps as any other state. Twenty-one prisoner base (permanent) camps were located on military installations, and over 20 branch (temporary) camps were constructed throughout the state. More than 45,000 German, Italian, and Japanese prisoners were interned in Texas from 1942 to 1945. As the war continued, a policy of maximum utilization replaced a policy of maximum security for the prisoners, which resulted in the use of over 27,000 prisoners in numerous agricultural tasks, such as picking cotton, pulling corn, and harvesting rice. The prisoners were well treated, and very few escape attempts occurred. After the war almost all prisoners were returned to their native countries, and many expressed their desire to return to Texas. Over 100 prisoners who died of wounds or of natural causes are buried in Fort Sam Houston National Cemetery in San Antonio. *Robert W. Tissing, Jr.*

Prison System. Before a central state penitentiary was established in Texas, local jails housed convicted felons. The Congress of the Republic of Texas defeated bills for a penal institution in 1840 and 1842; in May 1846 the First Legislature of the new state passed a penitentiary act, but the Mexican War prevented implementation of the law. On 13 March 1848 the legislature passed the act that began the Texas penitentiary. The law authorized gubernatorial appointment of three commissioners to locate a site and choose a superintendent and three directors to manage the institution. The commissioners selected Huntsville, in Walker County. Abner H. Cook supervised the construction and was the first superintendent of the prison. In October 1849 the first prisoner, a convicted horse thief from Fayette County, entered the partially completed Texas State Penitentiary at Huntsville. The facility held only 3 prisoners in 1849, but by 1855 it housed 75 convicts, and by 1860, 182. In 1852 the state established the office of financial agent, a position first held by John S. Besser. Texas initially supervised its prisoners under the Auburn System, developed by penologists at the state penitentiary in Auburn, New York. In Auburn penology, prisoners housed behind enclosed walls did day labor and retired in silence to their cells during the evening hours. By 1856 the state had built a cotton and wool mill at Huntsville in order to make the penitentiary self-sustaining. The mill, which could process 500 bales of cotton and 6,000 pounds of wool annually, provided money to the state. During the Civil War the penitentiary sold more than two million yards of cotton and nearly 300,000 yards of wool to both civilians and the government of the Confederate States of America. Wartime production made a profit of $800,000. The end of the war and reduced demand for cotton and wool products, however, resulted in financial difficulties as the prison population grew.

The number of convicts increased from 146 to 264 between the end of the Civil War and the fall of 1866, when the legislature enacted a measure that established a five-member Board of Public Labor to administer the penitentiary. The governor, secretary of state, comptroller, attorney general, and state treasurer composed this body. In February 1867 the board leased 100 prisoners to the Airliner Railroad and 150 to the Brazos Branch Railroad. For most of the next 45 years the state contracted large numbers of Texas prisoners to private employers. From April 1871 to April 1877 the Ward Dewey Company of Galveston leased the entire penitentiary from the state. For six months of 1877 another Galveston firm, Burnett and Kilpatrick, leased the prison. E. H. Cunningham of Guadalupe County and L. A. Ellis of Marion County leased the Huntsville Penitentiary from January 1878 through March 1883, and Morrow, Hamby, and Company leased the new Rusk Penitentiary in Cherokee County from January through March 1883. During the remainder of the leasing era the state contracted many prisoners to railroads, mining companies, and plantations; other convicts remained at the Huntsville and Rusk penitentiaries. Important penitentiary superintendents in this period included James Gillaspie, Thomas Jewett Goree, Jonas S. Rice, Searcy Baker, and J. A. Herring.

During the era of the convict-lease system the prison underwent a number of managerial changes. In 1879 the legislature formalized existing practices by requiring the governor to name three directors, with state Senate approval, to serve two-year terms. Also, pursuant to the 1879 law, a superintendent, appointed by the governor with Senate approval, was to serve as chief executive, assisted by an officer responsible for inspecting prisoner labor camps operated by private employers. The legislature amended this law in 1883 by allowing the governor to appoint two officials, subject to Senate confirmation, who with the governor would constitute a Board of Prison Commissioners. The Rusk Penitentiary, constructed to develop iron-ore deposits in East Texas, began receiving prisoners in 1883. The legislature had also authorized a third penitentiary west of the Colorado River for the production of wool, cotton, and leather, but the state never built it. Between 1885 and 1887 about 500 prisoners quarried granite and limestone for construction of the new Capitol in Austin; prisoners at the Rusk Penitentiary manufactured the building's interior cast-iron features. Convicts also constructed the Texas State Railroad from Rusk to Palestine between 1893 and 1909. The prison system operated the Rusk Penitentiary until 1917 and owned the railroad until 1921. The prison population increased from 489 in 1870 to 1,738 by 1878. It reached 3,199 by 1890 and 4,109 by 1900. The number declined slightly during the remaining years of the convict lease, reaching 3,471 at the end of 1912. During the years 1870–1912, 59 to 60 percent of Texas state prisoners were black, 30 to 40 percent were white, and 10 percent were Hispanic. Female prisoners usually constituted less than 2 percent of the total.

After lengthy discussion and debate, the legislature abolished the convict-lease system at a special session in 1910. A new law imposed a number of reforms and established a three-member Board of Prison Commissioners to administer the prison system. Each commissioner was to be appointed by the governor, subject to Senate confirmation. One commissioner would serve as the prison system's financial agent, another would manage the employees, and the third would direct the convicts. Although the 1910 law permitted existing contracts to run until January 1914, Governor Colquitt canceled the leases before the end of 1912. Notable prison commissioners under this managerial system were Ben E. Cabell, Louis W. Tittle, Robert W. Brahan, W. O. Murray, S. J. Bass, W. O. Stamps, J. A. Herring, S. J. Dean, H. C. McKnight, W. R. Dulaney, S. G. Granberry, and H. W. Sayle.

During the convict-lease period the state entered into some sharecropping arrangements in which prisoners worked the lands of private farm owners. The state also began to purchase large plantations for commercial agricultural production. In 1883, to house disabled or ill prisoners, the prison system bought the 1,900-acre Wynne Farm near Huntsville. Two years later, the system acquired the 2,500-acre Harlem Farm (later Jester State Prison Farm) on Oyster Creek in Fort Bend County; subsequently the state expanded the size of Harlem by purchasing adjoining lands. Texas bought the 5,527-acre Clemens Farm in Brazoria County in 1899 and subsequently added an adjoining plantation that increased the size of Clemens to 8,212 acres. During 1908 the state bought Imperial Farm, a 5,235-acre tract, from the Imperial Sugar Company in Fort Bend County; in the same year the prison system acquired the 7,762-acre Ramsey Farm. By 1911 officials had placed women prisoners on the 1,000-acre Goree Farm, near Huntsville. After the conclusion of the convict-lease system, the state continued to expand prison farmlands, but, except for 1916 through 1918, 1924, and 1927, failed to profit from them. By 1921 state prison farms encompassed more than 81,000 acres. Much of the land was used for cultivation of sugarcane, cotton, corn, feed crops, and vegetables. New farms

Convicts Going to Dinner, Huntsville. Stereograph by A. V. Latourette. Courtesy of Lawrence T. Jones III Collection, Austin. Before the end of the convict lease system in 1912, convicts at both the Huntsville and Rusk penitentiaries manufactured bricks, ice, wagons, railcars, lumber, brooms, paint, iron, clothing, and sheet metal.

included the 6,747-acre Darrington Farm and the 7,428-acre Retrieve Plantation in Brazoria County. The state had also purchased Blue Ridge Farm (5,416 acres) in Fort Bend County, Eastham Farm (13,040 acres) in Houston County, and Shaw Farm (4,688 acres) on the Red River in Bowie County.

The prison system remained a notable public issue despite the end of convict leasing. Repeated financial losses and routine legislative investigations of alleged mismanagement, corruption, and mistreatment of prisoners dogged the system. During the 1920s an organization known as the Texas Committee on Prisons and Prison Labor received authorization from the legislature to conduct an extensive survey of the prison system. As a result of the CPPL study and a series of prison scandals during Governor Miriam Ferguson's administration, voters adopted a state constitutional amendment in 1926 that permitted the legislature to abolish the Board of Prison Commissioners and replace it with a nine-member Texas Prison Board. The new law, which the legislature adopted in 1927, also permitted the board to set policy for the prison and to hire a general manager to direct the system. This administrative structure remained virtually intact until September 1990. Robert Homes Baker served as first chairman of the new board, and W. H. Mead was the first general manager (June 1927–November 1929). Although the prison farms earned a profit in 1924 and 1927, they showed financial losses thereafter. During much of the 1920s the state debated proposals to dispose of most prison properties and to centralize operations in a single penal facility, either in Brazoria County or in Central Texas near Austin. Governor Dan Moody and the CPPL urged the Austin plan, believing that the state should expand industrial training for prisoners and reduce commercial agricultural operations. The legislature refused to approve the relocation, however, but appropriated $575,000 in 1930 to upgrade existing prison properties. By 1931 the state had sold the Shaw Farm and changed the name Imperial Farm to Central Farm, but continued to employ most of a population of 5,000 convicts at the Huntsville Penitentiary and at 11 prison farms covering more than 73,000 acres. Although commercial agriculture and the iron works at Rusk typically had occupied most Texas prisoners, the Huntsville and Rusk penitentiaries also operated modest industrial plants. Convicts at those two facilities manufactured bricks, ice, wagons, railcars, lumber, brooms, paint, mattresses, iron ore, boxes, furniture, shoes, clothing, and sheet metal before the end of the convict-lease system in 1912. Although the iron industries had closed, the prison system added a printing shop, license-plate factory, and a number of food-processing plants by the 1930s to manufacture goods for the prison and other state agencies.

While the prison system continued to incur annual financial losses during the 1930s, Texas governors largely avoided prison issues and granted generous acts of clemency through the Board of Pardons and Paroles. General manager Marshall Lee Simmons, who served from April 1930 to November 1935, proved especially adept at public relations and helped promote a favorable image for the prison system by inaugurating the Texas Prison Rodeo, which was performed from 1931 to 1986 at the Huntsville Penitentiary. Board member Dave Nelson succeeded Simmons in November 1935 but died after only two weeks on the job and was replaced by O. J. S. Ellingson, who served until October 1941. "Thirty Minutes Behind the Walls," a series of weekly radio broadcasts over station WBAP in Fort Worth, began in 1938, featured an all-prisoner cast, and ran for more than five years; it also brought favorable publicity to the prison system. Nevertheless, reports of unsanitary living conditions, atrocities perpetrated by employees, and mysterious deaths of convicts, as well as the system's repeated financial failures, persisted during the decade and ultimately persuaded the Texas Prison Board to dismiss Ellingson, who lacked Simmons's public-relations talent. The prison population increased to almost 7,000 prisoners by 1939. During most of the 1930s, about 50 percent of the prisoners were Caucasian, 40 percent were African Americans, and 10 percent were Mexican Americans. The female prisoners usually numbered around 100, nearly two-thirds of whom were black.

The number of prisoners in Texas declined during World War II. From 6,070 in 1940, the total fell to 3,270 in 1945. However, after the war the inmate population rose to 5,675 in 1947 and 6,424 in 1950. Douglas W. Stakes, who replaced Ellingson in November 1941, resigned under pressure in November 1947 after an investigation by national penal reformer Austin MacCormick. The board replaced Stakes in January 1948 with Oscar Byron Ellis, who persuaded the legislature to appropriate funds to modernize prison facilities and alleviate overcrowding. Ellis expanded mechanization on prison farms and increased the number of prison industries. The state built cell-block units to replace dormitories ("tanks") on many of the farms and increased expenditures for fences, picket towers, flood lights, and other equipment. However, the prison system retained its austere character, and most prisoners continued to be employed in agriculture. Although the farms still did not become completely self-supporting, Ellis's management successfully lowered operating costs.

In 1957 the legislature renamed the state prison agency the Texas Department of Corrections. The Texas Prison Board became the Texas Board of Corrections, and the general man-

ager became the director. In all other respects the administrative structure did not vary from that specified in the 1927 law. By the end of 1953 the inmate population had increased to 7,781, of which white prisoners composed more than 50 percent, blacks 30 percent, and Hispanics nearly 15 percent; only 91 of the prisoners were women. The system's landholdings exceeded 74,000 acres in 1958. After Ellis died in November 1961, George John Beto, a former board member, became the prison system's new director, effective March 1, 1962. Beto largely continued the policies implemented by Ellis but expanded prison industrial operations. Aided by the legislature's enactment of a law in 1963 that required prison industries to sell products to other state institutions, TDC developed a dental laboratory, garment factories, a bus-repair shop, a tire-recapping facility, a coffee-roasting plant, a wood shop, and a record-conversion operation. The prison population increased from 11,890 at the beginning of 1962 to 15,709 by the end of 1972.

During the 1960s TDC designated the Huntsville Penitentiary and prison farms as "units" and opened several new facilities. The state no longer owned the Blue Ridge Farm, and the Ferguson Farm for a number of years acted as a special unit for offenders between the ages of 17 and 21. The system inaugurated a separate Diagnostic Unit at Huntsville in 1964 to evaluate and classify new prisoners, and in 1963 TDC opened the 11,672-acre Ellis Unit north of Huntsville; the 22,640-acre Coffield Unit, near Tennessee Colony in Anderson County, began operating in 1965. In 1969 Windham School, an institution for inmates in all units, became a regular school district eligible to receive state foundation funds. The prison system owned more than 100,000 acres in 1972. W. James Estelle succeeded the retired Beto as director in 1972. During the 1970s the inmate population grew at an accelerated pace as the state's overall population increased and public attitudes toward offenders hardened. The state population increased by 19 percent between 1968 and 1978, while the Texas prison population grew 101 percent. During the middle of the 1970s the state incarcerated felons at a rate of 143.7 per 100,000, compared to a national rate of 86.9 per 100,000. The number of prisoners reached 22,439 by the beginning of 1978. The demographics did not change much, although the percentage of Hispanic prisoners increased slightly to 19 percent.

The 1970s and 1980s were a period of dramatic change in TDC, characterized by a growing population, the opening of new units, and increasing legal challenges of prison management on the part of inmates. In 1980 federal district judge William Wayne Justice issued a ruling in a class action case, *Ruiz v. Estelle*, filed by inmates in 1972. Justice's ruling, which determined that conditions of confinement violated the Eighth Amendment of the United States Constitution (the prohibition of "cruel and unusual punishment"), required the state to reduce overcrowding, improve prisoner rehabilitation and recreational programs, and refrain from practices deemed detrimental to the prisoners' safety and welfare. Ruiz, the longest-running prisoners' lawsuit in United States history, was followed by lengthy litigation as the state of Texas adjusted to the federal court order. Several new prison units opened during the 1980s, and the functions of some older ones changed. The Goree Unit became a facility for male inmates, as TDC transferred its female population to property formerly operated by the Texas Youth Council near Gatesville in Coryell County. The 97-acre Mountain View Unit began receiving females in 1975; by 1980 the

1,244-acre Gatesville unit also incarcerated female felons. The Hilltop Unit, another former Texas Youth Council facility on 1,240 acres in Coryell County, started accepting male prisoners in 1981. Beto Units I and II, comprising 18,000 acres in Anderson County, housed TDC prisoners beginning in 1980 and 1981. Pack Units I and II, 6,000 acres in Grimes County, opened in 1982. The prison system established the Texas Department of Corrections Hospital on one floor of John Sealy Hospital at Galveston in 1983. Additional units opened on existing prison properties. Jester added a third unit in 1983, TDC opened the Ellis II Unit on 7,000 acres north of Huntsville in 1983, and the Michael Unit began operation in 1987 on property shared with the Coffield Unit in Anderson County. TDC was also supervising some prisoners at prerelease halfway houses in various cities by 1987. Beginning in July 1988 the prison system reserved the Skyview Unit for the care of mentally ill inmates at the 58-acre site of the former Rusk State Hospital in Cherokee County.

During the 1980s a succession of directors administered the prison system. After Estelle resigned in October 1983 amid controversy surrounding the Ruiz case and allegations of mismanagement and mistreatment of prisoners, the board selected Dan V. (Red) McKaskle to serve as interim director. Raymond Procunier became the new director in May 1984 and served until June 1985, when he resigned for health and personal reasons. The board then hired Lane McCotter, who occupied the position until January 1987; he resigned due to differences with Governor William Clements. McKaskle, Procunier, and McCotter led TDC during a period of turmoil and heightened inmate violence that followed the demise of an inmate guard system. In May 1987 the board named James Lynaugh, who had been serving as acting director, to the position of director.

The inmate population grew from 36,769 on August 31, 1983, to 39,664 at the end of August 1988. Between August 1987 and August 1988 the prison system received 33,816 new inmates but released 33,428 prisoners through parole or discharge, to mandatory supervision, or after termination of shock probation. TDC initiated construction on several new units in 1988 in order to jail an expanding number of convicted felons. Maximum-security units at Amarillo and Gatesville, as well as prerelease facilities in Snyder, Dayton, Woodville, and Marlin, increased the system's capacity by 10,000. Four 500-bed prerelease centers operated by private contractors were opened in 1989 at Bridgeport, Venus, Cleveland, and Kyle. Other units followed. Prison industrial operations had expanded by 1988 to include factories producing stainless steel, license plates, retreaded tires, and fabricated metal products, as well as garments, mattresses, cardboard boxes, woodwork, shoes, refinished furniture, highway signs, soap, and wax. The prison system managed a print shop, textile mills, and bus-repair and record-conversion facilities. Some prisoners engaged in construction and building maintenance on prison property, while others continued to work in farming and food processing. In the early 1990s TDC employed more than 19,000 regular staff members and had a 1990–91 biennium budget of more than $1.7 billion.

In 1989 the Texas legislature abolished the Texas Corrections Board, the Board of Pardons and Paroles, and the Texas Adult Probation Commission and merged them into one department, the Texas Department of Criminal Justice, supervised by a nine-member Texas Board of Criminal Justice. The board named James Lynaugh executive director, responsible for coordinating the three agencies of the new department. The new law renamed TDC the Texas Department of Criminal Justice, Institutional Division.   *Paul M. Lucko*

Prohibition. The prohibition movement influenced Texas and American politics from the 1840s to the 1930s. In the nineteenth century a movement against alcoholic beverages arose when some Americans, appalled by the social damage and individual wreckage that alcohol consumption caused, sought to persuade citizens to refrain from drinking liquor. This "temperance" movement enjoyed considerable success and continued parallel with the prohibition movement. In the eyes of some reformers a sober America was attainable only under laws that declared illegal the manufacture and sale of liquor. In their view the profit motive led the distilling, brewing, and saloon industries to encourage more people to drink. The destruction of the legal liquor traffic appeared to be the solution of a widespread individual and social problem. Prohibition sentiment found ready partisans among fundamentalist Protestants in Texas. Fundamentalists had long taught that drinking is immoral, and many of them came to believe that state-enforced teetotalism would improve public morality. In this regard, fundamentalists contributed to the extension of state power. Legal prohibition would, they thought, conduce to greater freedom. In subsequent years, however, in spite of this temporary alliance with political liberalism, and in spite of continuing opposition to alcohol sales and consumption, fundamentalists demonstrated a staunch aversion to government control.

Drys, as the reformers were called, first animated Texas politics in the 1840s. They sought measures allowing voters in prescribed areas to declare what was prohibition in effect—so-called local-option laws for neighborhoods, towns, cities, and counties. Eventually the drys sought statewide prohibition and an amendment to the United States Constitution declaring illegal the manufacture and sale of alcoholic beverages. In 1843 the Republic of Texas had passed what may have been the first local-option measure in North America. A Texas law of 1845 banned saloons altogether. The law was never enforced, however, and was repealed in 1856. The prohibition controversy, however, did not disappear in either Texas or the nation. The United Friends of Temperance, the first Texas-wide dry organization, was formed around 1870. In 1883 the state branch of the WCTU was founded. In 1886 the Prohibition party offered candidates for office in Texas. The new Constitution of 1876 had required the legislature to enact a local-option law. In 1887 the drys engineered a state prohibition referendum, which they lost by more than 90,000 votes. Nevertheless, dry sentiment was widespread. In 1895, 53 of the 239 counties were dry, and another 79 counties were partly dry under local option.

In the twentieth century the prohibition movement advanced from the rural counties of North Texas to convert a majority of the state's voters. As before, the liquor industries opposed the measure with well-financed publicity and well-placed financing of political leaders. In 1903 the *Home and State* began to counteract liquor publicity, and the Texas Local Option Association united dry groups. That association merged in 1908 with the state Anti-Saloon League, which had appeared in 1907. In Texas the drys in 1908 and 1911 tried again for a prohibition law but lost the referendum by a close margin. Nevertheless, the number of dry counties was increasing. North Texas was dry;

Sheriff Dan Harston and deputies posing with confiscated stills. Photograph by Frank Rogers. Dallas, ca. 1925. From the collections of the Texas–Dallas History and Archives Division, Dallas Public Library. After Prohibition took effect with ratification of the Eighteenth Amendment in 1919, law-enforcement officers had to contend with the increased production of moonshine liquor.

only areas with relatively large concentrations of African, Hispanic, and German Americans continued to license the liquor industries. With the electorate split on the issue, prohibition continued to divide Texans. In 1913 Morris Sheppard, a dedicated dry, won a seat in the United States Senate and assumed leadership in the national prohibition campaign by his sponsorship of what became the Eighteenth Amendment. In 1916 the drys won enough congressional races to have Congress initiate the national prohibition amendment. The Texas legislature, encouraged by the Anti-Saloon League, ratified the federal amendment in 1918. In 1919 Texas voters approved a state prohibition amendment.

Prohibition was controversial in both national and Texas politics in the 1920s. The Anti-Saloon League was deeply divided over the question of how to use the Eighteenth Amendment: as a measure providing new opportunities to persuade Americans to abstain from liquor, or as a measure demanding strict enforcement. In Texas, Atticus Webb, who assumed leadership of the state league, failed to obtain strict enforcement. In 1925 opponents of prohibition were in control of the Texas government and refused to support enforcement. In the meantime, the drys were unable to obtain funds for a large-scale, sustained educational campaign on behalf of abstinence. Nationally, popular support for prohibition receded dramatically after the onset of the Great Depression in 1929, and in 1933 the Twenty-first Amendment repealed prohibition. In 1935 Texas voters ratified a repeal of the state dry law. Thereafter the prohibition question reverted to the local level, and the drys had available only local-option statutes.

In the 1980s a neoprohibition movement emerged in the United States. The reformers sought not to outlaw the liquor industries but more closely to regulate their marketing campaigns. In 1984, for instance, Congress required Texas and all other states to declare the minimum drinking age to be 21 in order to receive full federal highway funding. Subsequently,

"warning labels" stating the dangers of alcohol consumption were mandated. *K. Austin Kerr*

Provincias Internas. Formally authorized by the king of Spain in 1776s; a huge semiautonomous administrative unit that included Texas, Coahuila, Nueva Vizcaya, New Mexico, Sinaloa, Sonora, and the two Californias (Baja and Alta). The first capital of the Provincias Internas was the town of Arizpe on the Sonora River, equidistant between Nueva Vizcaya and the Californias. The rationale for carving this jurisdiction from the viceroyalty of New Spain sprang from the desire to promote administrative efficiency on a frontier far removed from Mexico City, to stimulate economic development, and to protect Spanish realms from English and Russian designs. It came at a time when Hugo Oconór was in the field as commandant inspector of presidios on the northern frontier. Henceforth, Oconór continued to supervise military matters until his resignation in January 1777, but he was obliged to serve under a commandant general who reported directly to the king, rather than to Oconór's friend Viceroy Antonio María Bucareli y Ursúa. The new official with titles of governor and commander in chief of the Provincias Internas was Teodoro de Croix, nephew of the Marqués de Croix, viceroy of New Spain from 1766 to 1771. Croix's tenure (1776–83) coincided exactly with the years of the American Revolution. In 1783, Teodoro de Croix left northern Mexico to become viceroy of Peru, and at that juncture the Provincias Internas entered an interregnum of 10 years marked by brief tenures for 5 successive commandants general. During that interval the official capital was Villa Chihuahua. In 1786 the viceroy regained control of the Provincias Internas. The restoration of viceregal authority signaled the temporary end of a single administrative unit, and the Interior Provinces were then divided into three military regions. The eastern provinces, which included Texas, Coahuila, Nuevo León, and Nuevo Santander, were placed under the command of Juan de Ugalde. But this arrangement did not last long. In 1787 the three regions were reduced to Eastern and Western provinces, with Ugalde and Ramón de Castro exercising control over Texas for an additional six years. In November 1792 King Charles IV ordered that the two regions be reorganized into a single unit and again removed the Provincias Internas from the control of the viceroy of New Spain. That juncture marked an end to the interregnum and ushered in the administration of Pedro de Nava, which lasted until 1802. In 1804 the king reversed his position and again ordered two separate jurisdictions, but that reorganization was delayed under the administration of Commandant General Nemesio de Salcedo y Salcedo (1802–13) by Napoleon Bonaparte's designs in Spain. The Eastern Division fell under the control of Commandant General Joaquín de Arredondo in 1813 and remained under his heavy hand until Mexican independence (1821). *Donald E. Chipman*

Pueblo. Term generally used in Spanish Texas to designate a purely civil colony, but in its extended meaning applied to towns of every description—Spanish missions with their adjacent Indian villages, villages at presidios, and regularly settled colonies. As used in New Spain, *pueblo* meant a corporate town with certain rights of jurisdiction and administration and generally designated settlements other than mining camps that were not large enough to be called *ciudades*.

Quedlinburg Art Affair. A notorious case centered upon a Texan's possession of priceless medieval art objects belonging to the Lutheran Church of St. Servatius in Quedlinburg, Germany, 30 miles east of Berlin. In June 1945 church authorities reported that objects from their treasury were missing from a mineshaft where the church had hidden them during World War II. Since the Eighty-seventh Armored Field Infantry battalion had recently helped guard the mine, church officials lodged a complaint with the United States Army. However, the whereabouts of the works could not be determined, and subsequent investigation was deemed futile. The objects from the Quedlinburg treasury became the subject of an intense search after one of them, the *Samuhel Gospel*, appeared on the market in Europe in 1987 and was sold in April 1990 to the Cultural Foundation for the States in Berlin, an organization devoted to the repatriation of lost German art. The purchase of the *Samuhel Gospel* led a German investigator, Willi Korte, to search Pentagon records and then led him to Texas. He discovered the remaining objects at the First National Bank of Whitewright, 60 miles north of Dallas, where they had been placed by Jack Meador and Jane Meador Cook, heirs to the estate of Joe T. Meador, their brother, who died in 1980. Joe Meador was a 29yearold lieutenant with the Eighty-seventh when it occupied Quedlinburg in 1945. Fellow soldiers report having seen him enter the mine and leave with bundles; it is believed he sent the items home through military mail. Meador was discharged from the army in 1946. In 1950 he took up permanent residence in Whitewright to assist with running the family's hardware store and to care for his mother, who died in 1978. After Joe's death, his brother and sister began selling the objects.

A civil action filed in 1990 in United States District Court in Dallas, on behalf of the Quedlinburg church, sued for the return of the treasures to Germany. Since the ownership of the objects was contested, both parties agreed to move them from the bank vault to a neutral location. Eight objects from the treasury and other unrelated items were stored at the Dallas Museum of Art during the lawsuit. Because the statute of limitations in Texas is only two years, state law clearly favored the Meadors' claim. For that reason, both sides pursued a negotiated settlement, and in 1991 the parties announced in London that they had reached an agreement: the Germans would pay the Meador family $2.75 million for the return of the treasures to Quedlinburg. That sum included previous payments for the *Samuhel Gospel* sold in 1990. After the announcement, legal negotiations continued until the agreement was finally signed by all parties in 1992. The eight works from the treasury that had been in storage at the museum, as well as the *Evangelistar* (a jewel-covered book of 1513), which was returned from Germany for exhibition, were on public display at the Dallas Museum of Art from 7 March to 26 April 1992. The affair, however, was not over for the Meador family, who still faced the assessments of the Internal Revenue Service, as well as some public disapproval. When the news of the treasures surfaced in 1990, Quedlinburg was in East Germany. Their return to a united Germany appeared to symbolize the recent reunification of a country that had been divided for as long as the treasures were lost.   *Emily J. Sano*

Quivira. Also Cuivira, Quebira, Aguivira; the legendary Indian province first mentioned to Hernando de Alvarado and Francisco Vázquez de Coronado in the fall of 1540 by the Pawnee captive El Turco. According to the Turk's stories, Quivira lay far to the east of the New Mexico pueblos somewhere on the Buffalo Plains. The region was said to contain a large population with much gold and silver. However, when the Spaniards reached the supposed site of Quivira in 1541, they found only villages of grass huts and a partly agricultural, partly bison-hunting economy. El Turco, after confessing that he had told his stories to lure the conquistadors away from the pueblos, was garroted. Nevertheless, the legend of Quivira remained strong; the unsuccessful expedition of Francisco Leyva de Bonilla and Antonio Gutiérrez de Humaña in 1595 and that of Juan de Oñate in 1601 also visited Quivira, with the same disappointing results. Fray Juan de Padilla, who had accompanied the Coronado expedition, was martyred there after attempting to establish mission work among the Indians of Quivira. Quivira has been identified with the Indians later known as Wichita. Frederick Webb Hodge stated that the name was possibly a Spanish version of Kidikwius, or Kirikurus, the Wichitas' name for themselves, or of Kirikuruks, the Pawnee name for the Wichitas. The actual location of Quivira has been a source of controversy and speculation among historians, ethnologists, and archeologists alike. Some, like Carlos E. Castañeda, conclude from Spanish journals that Coronado and Oñate never went beyond the Panhandle of Texas or that of Oklahoma; they thus place the Indian villages above the South Canadian River in what is Hutchinson or Roberts County, or above the North Canadian (Beaver) River, in what is now Beaver County, Oklahoma. However, archeological evidence more readily points toward Hodge's conclusion that the mythical province was actually located north of the Arkansas River, somewhere between the sites of present Great Bend and Wichita, Kansas. Herbert Eugene Bolton and others also demonstrate the plausibility of the Kansas location in their writings.
                                          Margery H. Krieger

R

Radio. Broadcasting emerged in Texas on the campuses of the University of Texas and Texas A&M in College Station. In 1911 J. B. Dickinson constructed wireless facilities at both schools to teach electrical engineering students about radio transmissions. As part of his experiments in high-frequency radio, a physics professor, S. Leroy Brown, built radio equipment and began broadcasting weather and crop reports from a physics laboratory on the UT campus. During World War I, using the call letters KUT, the university's Division of Extension operated Brown's equipment to broadcast reports from the United States Marketing Bureau and Department of Agriculture. By March 1922 the station had combined with a second campus station (call letters 5XY) and with a 500-watt power rating was one of the best-equipped and most powerful stations in the nation. The usual broadcasts were from 8 to 10 P.M. three nights a week; programming consisted of music, lectures, and agriculture and marketing reports. In addition, football games were broadcast in season and a church service was aired on Sunday. In 1919 possibly the first broadcast of a football game in the country aired via call letters 5XB, which is now WTAW. The station operated as a ham relay station at 250 watts. Originally, it was to air the final score of the Texas–Texas A&M Thanksgiving game, but Frank Matejka decided to send a play-by-play account of the game via Morse Code. Student Harry Saunders and assistant coach D. X. Bible designed a set of abbreviations to fit every possible football situation and sent the list to every station that would broadcast the contest. The game aired over the ham relay stations; the Morse Code was decoded and announced to fans over a public-address system. Another early station was WRR of Dallas, owned by the city, which began broadcasting in 1920 with Dad Garrett as announcer. During these early days of broadcasting, many small, homemade radio stations went on the air on a noncommercial basis, primarily for the amusement of the operators and their neighbors. By the end of 1922, the year that commercial radio broadcasting began in Texas and before there was a federal agency to regulate radio broadcasters, 25 commercial stations were in operation in the state. Among them were WBAP, Fort Worth; KGNC, Amarillo; WFAA, Dallas; WOAI, San Antonio; KFJZ, Fort Worth; KILE, Galveston; and WACO, Waco.

Radio Station WBAP in Fort Worth established the country-music format later taken over by Nashville's "Grand Ole Opry" and Chicago's "National Barn Dance" with a program that began on 4 January 1923, featuring fiddler, square-dance caller, and Confederate veteran Capt. M. J. Bonner. WFAA in Dallas, operating on 150 watts, held many firsts in radio broadcasting in Texas. It was the first to carry programs designed to teach; first to produce a serious radio drama series—entitled "Dramatic Moments in Texas History" and sponsored by the Magnolia Petroleum Company; first to air a state championship football game; first to join a national network (1927); and first to air inaugural ceremonies, those of Governor Ross Sterling in 1931. WFAA was the property of the A. H. Belo Corporation, publisher of the Dallas *Morning News*; Adam Colhoun, the first announcer, at times read to his listeners from that newspaper

when there was nothing else to offer. Some early programs carried the voices of the Early Birds, the Cass County Kids, and Dale Evans (then the wife of piano player Frank Butts). The Folger Coffee Company, WFAA's first paying advertiser, sponsored the Bel Canta Quartet.

The first station in South Texas, WOAI in San Antonio, went on the air on 25 September 1922. In 1928 WOAI joined the world's first network, the National Broadcasting Company. It eventually became a clear channel operating on 50,000 watts. WOAI was one of the first stations to employ a local news staff. One of its greatest achievements was a regular Sunday broadcast of "Musical Interpretations," featuring Max Reiter, conductor of the San Antonio Symphony Orchestra. Reiter also conducted the orchestra for NBC's nationwide "Pioneers of Music," originating from San Antonio's municipal auditorium. In Houston an amateur radio club was organized in 1919 for amateur builders and operators of crystal sets, with James L. Autrey as president. The first local commercial station was WEV, owned and operated by Hurlburt Still. On 21 May 1922 the Houston *Post* broadcast a Sunday concert from the radio plant of A. P. Daniel. Later that year the Houston Conservatory of Music sent out programs over station WGAB. In 1924 the Houston *Post–Dispatch* absorbed a station operated by Will Horwitz and established it as KPRC, which made its debut in May 1925. Several new stations were licensed in the next few years. KXYZ, which had first broadcast on 20 October 1930, was taken over by Jesse H. Jones in 1932. It increased its power to 1,000 watts two years later. When stations KPRC and KTRH installed one broadcasting plant for sending out waves simultaneously in 1936, the plant was the second of its kind in the world. Each station increased its power to 5,000 watts. KTRH became the Houston *Chronicle* station in 1937. KNUZ–KQUE hired the first female account executive in radio and the first black disc jockey (1948). Other KNUZ–KQUE firsts include a remote broadcast studio, helicopter reporting, wireless microphones, a computer traffic system, a full-dimensional FM antenna and a solid state AM transmitter.

With the advent of television during the second half of the twentieth century the number of radio stations decreased, and by 1971 there was a combined total of 392 standard radio broadcasting (AM) and frequency modulation (FM) stations. During the next two decades there was an upswing, however, and by 1993 Texas had 311 AM and 420 FM radio stations with valid current operating licenses.

Railroad Commission. A Texas state agency that has been one of the most important regulatory bodies in the nation, through its influence on the supply and price of oil and natural gas; established in 1891 to oversee railroads. Railroad regulation had been a goal of the supporters of James S. Hogg, who won the governorship in 1890. The legislature gave the commission jurisdiction over rates and operation of railroads, terminals, wharves, and express companies. Hogg's first appointments to the agency were John H. Reagan (chairman), Judge William Pinckney McLean, and Lafayette L. Foster. In 1894 the legislature made the agency elective, the three commissioners henceforth serving six-year, overlapping terms in Austin. Despite the fact that the federal Interstate Commerce Commission preempted the regulation of interstate transportation, and despite inadequate funding and occasionally hostile court decisions, the Railroad Commission had some success in restraining intrastate freight rates. In the twentieth century the commission has continued to regulate intrastate railroads, and has had buses and trucks added to its transportation responsibilities. In 1917 the legislature granted the commission the authority to see that petroleum pipelines remained "common carriers"—that is, that they did not refuse to transport anyone's oil or gas. Two years later, commissioners received responsibility for promulgating well-spacing rules. In the early 1920s the agency accepted jurisdiction over gas utilities. This gradually growing responsibility prepared the way for the enormous expansion of commission activity during the next decade. In the early 1930s unrestrained production from the huge East Texas oilfield caused the price of crude to plummet worldwide and created consternation in the industry. To stabilize oil prices and to help conserve the valuable resource, a coalition consisting of parts of the industry, scientists, and public officials attempted to have output regulated. This coalition was soon ably led by Ernest O. Thompson, who was appointed to a vacancy on the commission by Governor Sterling in 1932. After a protracted and occasionally violent political struggle, the Railroad Commission won the authority to prorate, that is, to set the rate at which every oil well in Texas might produce. By limiting production in East Texas and elsewhere, commissioners succeeded both in supporting oil prices and in conserving the state's resources. Under the Connally Hot Oil Act of 1935, the federal government undertook to enforce in interstate commerce the production directives of the Texas commission and its sister state agencies. When the Organization of Petroleum Exporting Countries was organized, the Railroad Commission was used as a model. Because of its ability to prorate Texas oil production and because of this state's crucial role in the petroleum industry, the Railroad Commission was until the early 1970s of vital importance to national and international energy supply. With the decline of Texas oil reserves, the great increase in world demand, and the rise of OPEC, however, the commission's influence over oil has dwindled. Today, its responsibilities in this area consist mainly of enforcing cleanliness in the fields and maintaining equity among producers.

If its influence over oil has declined, however, the commission's responsibility for natural gas has greatly expanded. There were conflicts over gas in the 1930s. Because gas was of relatively lower value than oil, however, commission policies in this area were less developed. Because gas was so relatively valueless, oil operators in that era commonly burned ("flared") the casing-head gas that they inevitably produced with their oil. By the mid-1940s, about a billion and a half cubic feet of natural gas a day was being lost statewide. In 1947, under the prodding of a new member with a petroleum engineering background, William J. Murray, Jr., the commission issued orders that effectively forbade the flaring of casinghead gas. This action not only preserved an irreplaceable natural resource, but, by forcing producers to return gas to reservoirs, sustained their pressure, thus significantly increasing the recovery of oil. Gas acquired considerable importance again in the 1970s. When the Lo-Vaca gathering company became unable to meet its contracts to supply nat-

ural gas to four million South and Central Texas consumers in the winter of 1972–73, the Railroad Commission was handed a political quandary. To allow Austin, San Antonio, and Corpus Christi to run out of gas was unthinkable. Yet further supplies were available only at much higher prices, which would impose higher utility bills on consumers. Amid almost constant bad publicity, and in a context of increasing natural gas prices, commissioners struggled with this problem for seven years. In September 1979 they finally ratified a complex compromise that was acceptable, minimally, to the parties involved. More problems with gas occurred in the 1980s. The federal Natural Gas Policy Act of 1978 imposed a complex regulatory framework on Texas producers, yet required the state to assume responsibility for implementation. Railroad commissioners are consequently faced with the unappealing prospect of enforcing a multitude of ambiguous rules on a resistant state industry, while fending off criticism from Washington. Thus, although the commission's involvement in oil policy has drastically declined, it remains an important actor on the national energy stage. In the early 1990s the commissioners oversaw an agency consisting of four regulatory divisions: Oil and Gas, Transportation–Gas Utilities, Surface Mining and Reclamation, and Liquefied Petroleum Gas.

David F. Prindle

Railroads. Inadequate transportation was a major problem facing early settlers in Texas. As late as 1850 the settled area of the state was largely confined to the riverbottoms of East and South Texas and along the Gulf Coast. Although steamboat navigation was common on the lower stretches of a number of such rivers as the Rio Grande, Brazos, and Trinity, Texas rivers were not deep enough for dependable year-round transportation. Roads were either poor or nonexistent and virtually impassable during wet weather. An oxcart hauling three bales of cotton could travel only a few miles a day, and the cost of wagon transport was 20 cents per ton mile. Many proposals to improve internal transportation were both considered and attempted during the period of the Republic of Texas and early statehood. These included river improvements, canals, and plank roads in addition to railroads. However, it was the railroads that made the development of Texas possible, and for many years railroad extension and economic growth paralleled each other.

On 16 December 1836 the First Congress of the Republic of Texas chartered the Texas Rail Road, Navigation, and Banking Company to construct railroads "from and to any such points . . . as selected." This occurred less than 10 years after the first public railroad was chartered in the United States. Although many leading citizens were included among its incorporators and it had the sanction of Stephen F. Austin and Sam Houston, the scheme aroused the public's suspicions, mainly due to the banking and monopoly provisions attached to the charter. These were bitterly attacked by many Texans, including Anson Jones and Houston newspaper editor Francis Moore, Jr. The charter and the company it would create became a major issue in the second congressional elections. Although the company was still active in mid-1838, it collapsed soon after without making any attempt to build a railroad.

However, the problem of transporting goods to market and travel remained acute. Three additional railroad charters were granted by the Republic of Texas to run from Galveston Bay, from Harrisburg, and from Houston to the Brazos Valley. Two

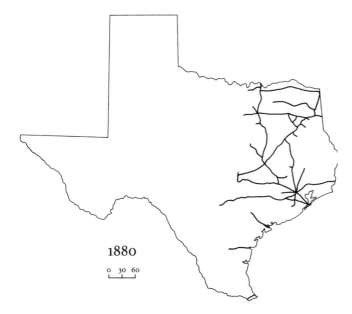

1880

0 30 60

Railroads in 1880. From Charles P. Zlatkovich, *Texas Railroads* (Austin: University of Texas Bureau of Business Research, 1981), p. 109.

of the companies, the Brazos and Galveston Rail-road and the Harrisburg and Brazos Rail Road, were tied to real estate promotion schemes. Although all three companies awarded contracts, none was able to construct a railroad. The Harrisburg and Brazos, subsequently chartered as the Harrisburg Rail Road and Trading Company, with Andrew Briscoe as its first president, graded about two miles and made other efforts to construct a railroad before it, too, ended in failure. However, the Harrisburg project was the precursor for the first successful railroad in Texas. In early 1847 Gen. Sidney Sherman acquired the Harrisburg town lots and surrounding land from Briscoe and his associates, and later that year he was successful in attracting northern capital to his project. This led to the chartering of the Buffalo Bayou, Brazos and Colorado Railway Company on February 11, 1850. Among the other incorporators were William Marsh Rice and John Grant Tod, Sr., from Texas, and Bostonians Jonathan F. Barrett, Elisha H. Allen, and John Angier. Work on this railroad began in 1851, and the first locomotive, named for Sherman, arrived in late 1852. The initial 20-mile segment from Harrisburg (now a part of Houston) and Stafford's Point (now Stafford) opened by 7 September 1853. The Buffalo Bayou, Brazos and Colorado was the first railroad to operate in Texas, the second railroad west of the Mississippi River, and the oldest component of the present Southern Pacific.

In 1848 Ebenezer Allen of Galveston obtained a charter for the Galveston and Red River Railway Company. The project remained dormant until taken over by citizens of Houston and Washington County. On 1 January 1853 Paul Bremond and Thomas W. House broke ground for the Galveston and Red River. Although initial progress was slow the company opened its first 25-mile segment between Houston and Cypress on 28 July 1856. Shortly thereafter, the name of the railroad was changed to Houston and Texas Central Railway Company. Before the end of 1856 the city of Houston completed its seven-mile line, known as the Houston Tap, to a junction with the

Buffalo Bayou, Brazos and Colorado. Other railroads were soon active. By the end of 1861 there were nine railroad companies with about 470 miles of track in Texas. Five of the railroads were centered in the Houston area, and all but one ran from either a seaport or riverport. There had already been a merger between the Houston Tap and the Houston Tap and Brazoria Railroad Company, which occurred in 1858.

Although all of the companies operated for relatively short periods of time, they had caused major improvements in Texas transportation. A writer to the Houston *Tri-Weekly Telegraph* recalled a trip by stage from Houston to the Hockley area in December 1854 following 10 days of rain. The 35-mile trip took nearly 1_ days and included an overnight stop. In May 1857 the writer made a similar trip aboard the Houston and Texas Central in an hour and 40 minutes. In December of the same year the *Telegraph* stated that although there was high water in the Brazos, no boats had been reported on the river as the railroads had already handled all of the business. When State Engineer William Fields inspected the first five miles of the San Antonio and Mexican Gulf Railroad in February 1858, he reported that trains carrying passengers and freight operated two or four times a day over the short section extending from Port Lavaca. Although the terminal was a point on the prairie distant from any settlement or public highway, numerous teamsters sought it out to transship their goods to or from the railroad.

There was insufficient local capital in Texas to finance the early railroads, and eastern and foreign capitalists were hesitant about investing in a frontier state. Incentives were necessary and took three major forms. Between 1850 and 1876, when the practice was prohibited by the state Constitution, individual cities and counties issued about $2.4 million in bonds to aid railroad construction. The state, however, provided the major incentives in the form of land grants and loans. Six of the antebellum railroads borrowed $1,816,500 from the Special School Fund at the rate of $6,000 per mile of track. The railroads repaid $4,172,965 in principal and interest. Only one of the carriers, the Houston Tap and Brazoria, defaulted, and the state was able to recover some of the debt by foreclosing and selling the railroad.

As early as 1852 the charter for the Henderson and Burkville Railroad Company called for a land grant of eight sections of land for each mile of railroad. Other charters received the same provision, but the size of the grant was too small to attract much interest. A general land grant law was passed in 1854 that authorized 16 sections a mile. This law was in effect until the new Constitution of 1869 prohibited land grants. An 1874 Constitutional amendment permitted land grants, and in 1876 a new law, similar to the original 1854 law, was passed. The land grant provision was repealed in 1882, when no unappropriated vacant land remained. Estimates of the amount of land actually granted range from 27,000,000 acres to about 35,780,000 acres. The railroads received a net of about $1.34 an acre when they disposed of the land.

Three railroads, the Texas and New Orleans Railroad Company, the Eastern Texas Railroad Company, and the Washington County Rail Road Company, were completed and opened after the outbreak of the Civil War. Other operating companies, such as the Houston and Texas Central, were forced to suspend their construction efforts. Additional railroads, such as the Memphis, El Paso and Pacific Railroad Company and the Indianola Railroad Company, had graded rights-of-way or had construction materials on hand, but were unable to resume construction until much later. Although most of the Texas railroads did not suffer the depredations inflicted elsewhere in the South, all were in bad physical condition at the close of hostilities. Four years of constant use without materials or manpower for repairs had taken their toll. The Texas and New Orleans was forced to shut down between Beaumont and Orange. In addition, the rails of the Eastern Texas between Beaumont and Sabine Pass had been removed to be used for fortifications and other military needs. General John B. Magruder ordered the destruction of the San Antonio and Mexican Gulf to prevent its falling into the hands of enemy forces. The Southern Pacific Railroad Company (later a part of the Texas and Pacific and not related to the present Southern Pacific) had been required to remove part of its line between Marshall and Swanson's Landing on Caddo Lake and to relay the rails to connect with the Vicksburg, Shreveport and Texas Railway Company near the Louisiana line, thus forming a route between Marshall and Shreveport, Louisiana. Late in the war one short line was constructed in Houston when the Galveston and Houston Junction Railroad built a bridge across Buffalo Bayou, connecting the Galveston, Houston and Henderson Railroad Company with the Houston and Texas Central.

Although it was the decade of the 1870s before any significant new mileage was constructed in Texas, the Houston and Texas Central was able to resume construction in 1867. The company built steadily northward, reaching Corsicana in 1871, Dallas in 1872, and the Red River in 1873. At the same time, the company, having acquired the Washington County, began work on its Western Division, reaching Austin on Christmas Day in 1871. Meanwhile, the Missouri, Kansas and Texas Railway Company reached Denison from the north on 24 December 1872, and with the completion of the Houston and Texas Central to that point the following year, the Texas railroad system was finally connected to the nationwide network. The San Antonio and Mexican Gulf was also rebuilt during the late 1860s by the occupying military forces.

The Houston and Great Northern Railroad Company was the first major new railroad to start construction after the war. After beginning at Houston in December 1870, the company reached Palestine in September 1872. During the same period the International Railroad Company built from Hearne to Palestine and on to Longview. The two companies merged to form the International and Great Northern Railroad Company in 1873. By 1876 the International and Great Northern had completed a line from Hearne to Austin. In northeast Texas the Texas and Pacific Railway Company acquired the Southern Pacific and the Memphis, El Paso and Pacific and finished a line from Texarkana to Dallas and Fort Worth. Other lines constructed during the decade included the extension of the Galveston, Harrisburg and San Antonio Railway Company, formerly the Buffalo Bayou, Brazos and Colorado, from Columbus to San Antonio during the years 1873 to 1877. The Texas and New Orleans, which totally shut down in 1868, briefly reopened in 1870 before discontinuing service again. By 1876 the company had been rebuilt and was again operating between Houston and Orange. Work also began on the Gulf, Colorado and Santa Fe Railway Company as well as on several shorter railroads, including the Houston East and West Texas Railway Company and the East Line and Red River Railroad Company.

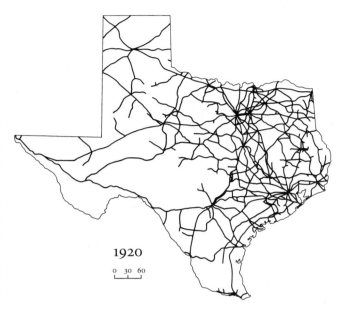

Railroads in 1920. From Charles P. Zlatkovich, *Texas Railroads* (Austin: University of Texas Bureau of Business Research, 1981), p. 113.

By the end of 1879 railroad mileage in Texas had reached 2,440 miles. The railroad system in eastern Texas was becoming well developed, but there was less than 100 miles of track west of a line drawn from Denison through Fort Worth, Austin, San Antonio, and Cuero. All this was about to change as during the next 10 years more than 6,000 miles of railroad was constructed in the state. More than 4,000 miles was built during the years 1881, 1882, and 1887 alone. Between 1880 and early 1883 both the Galveston, Harrisburg and San Antonio and the Texas and Pacific built across West Texas to El Paso, forming two transcontinental routes across the state. Another major line built during this period was the Fort Worth and Denver City Railway Company, which stretched from Fort Worth to the New Mexico border, thus becoming the Texas portion of a line to Denver. Other major additions included the extension of the International and Great Northern to San Antonio and Laredo and the completion of the main line of the Gulf, Colorado and Santa Fe.

During the 1880s the first railroad systems were developed as a number of the independently owned Texas companies were bought by outside interests that controlled railroads in other states. The Southern Pacific acquired an interest in the Galveston, Harrisburg and San Antonio and ownership of the Texas and New Orleans and the Houston and Texas Central, as well as several smaller companies, while the Gulf, Colorado and Santa Fe became a subsidiary of the Atchison, Topeka and Santa Fe Railroad Company. Jay Gould gained control of a number of Texas railroads, including the Texas and Pacific, the International and Great Northern, and the Missouri, Kansas and Texas (Katy). He leased the International and Great Northern to the Katy and both the Katy and the Texas and Pacific to his Missouri Pacific Railroad Company. Although the initial Missouri Pacific foray into Texas was soon to end and the various leases terminated before the end of the decade, all of the railroads, with the exception of the Missouri, Kansas and Texas,

Building of the Railroad, by Clara McDonald Williamson, 1949–50. Oil on panel. 27" × 29½". Courtesy A. H. Belo Corporation, Dallas. Here "Aunt Clara" Williamson portrays the excitement that the community of Iredell felt when the railroad arrived in 1880.

remained firmly in Gould's control until well into the twentieth century.

Despite power given to the state by the Constitution of 1876 to act against railroad abuses, and subsequent laws prohibiting rebates, by the mid-1880s shippers, farmers, and many state and local officials were protesting what they perceived to be high rates, rebates, traffic pools, and other restrictive practices. Railroads, the most powerful industrial force in Texas, were accused of running the state through bribery, hidden monopolies and controls, and favoritism to officials while profits, such as they were, went to outside capitalists. In 1888 Attorney General James S. Hogg filed several lawsuits, mainly against the Gould railroads, alleging that their control by companies chartered outside of the state were in violation of the Texas constitution. He also obtained a court decision against rail pools that set rates and divided available traffic among the larger systems. The success of these suits forced the reshuffling of the Gould empire and led to the termination of the lease of several Texas railroads by outside companies. In 1890 Hogg was elected governor with the establishment of a state Railroad Commission as the main issue in the race. Using rail reform as his key, Hogg won an overwhelming victory in the race despite bitter opposition from several Texas newspapers, notably the Dallas *Morning News*. The Railroad Commission, established in 1891, became one of the most powerful regulatory bodies in the state.

At the beginning of 1900 there was still less than 10,000 miles of railroad in Texas, which represented about 5 percent of the railroad mileage of the United States. Although only 25 percent of the national system, which peaked in 1916, was built after 1899, nearly 45 percent of the Texas mileage was built between 1900 and 1932, when mileage reached 17,078. At the turn of the century the lower Rio Grande valley had virtually no railroad track,

while vast areas of the South Plains, Panhandle, and West Texas were also without railroads. These voids were filled over the next 30 years. New railroads were also constructed in the more developed areas of Texas. Two additional lines were completed between Dallas–Fort Worth and Houston, while a second railroad was built connecting Houston and New Orleans. In 1911 Texas became the state with the most railroad mileage, a position it still maintains.

In 1901 there also began a flurry of construction on electric interurban railways. About 500 miles of electric interurban tracks was constructed in Texas. The first such interurban was the 10-mile Denison and Sherman Railway, which began service between the two cities in May 1901. The largest company was the Texas Electric Railway, with 226 miles centered at Dallas. This company was also the largest interurban between the Mississippi River and the Pacific Coast. The Galveston–Houston Electric was for years the fastest interurban line in America, while the Northern Texas Traction Company, between Dallas and Fort Worth, was considered one of the best-engineered lines. The smallest interurban was the 4½ mile Roby and Northern, which electrified an existing steam railroad in 1923. The last interurban railway developed in the United States was the Houston North Shore, which opened between Houston and Goose Creek and Baytown in 1927. The Houston North Shore became a subsidiary of the Missouri Pacific and, though it offered frequent passenger service, was a major freight carrier from the beginning. It was operated by electricity until 1948 and ran replacement railbuses until 1961. The former Houston North Shore, the last vestige of the Texas interurban system, continues to operate as an important branch of the Missouri Pacific. With the exception of the Houston North Shore, few of the interurbans developed extensive freight operations and were solely dependent on passenger traffic, which made them easily susceptible to competition from private automobiles. Most of the interurbans were abandoned in the 1930s. Only the Roby and Northern, abandoned in 1941, the Texas Electric, which abandoned its last line in 1948, and the Houston North Shore lasted until the 1940s. The Texas Transportation Company, a short switching line at San Antonio, continues to be electrically operated, although it was never a part of the Texas interurban system.

In 1920 there were still a number of major independent railroads in Texas. The Gould system, which in 1900 had controlled several railroads, including the Texas and Pacific, International and Great Northern, and the St. Louis Southwestern Railway Company of Texas, had broken up, and all three companies were now independent. The Gulf Coast Lines, whose major Texas components were the St. Louis, Brownsville and Mexico and the Beaumont, Sour Lake and Western Railway Companies, had been financed by the St. Louis and San Francisco Railroad Company, but had been separated from their parent as a result of the 1914 receivership. The Missouri Pacific, which had no presence in Texas, began to buy stock in the Texas and Pacific in 1918. In the mid-1920s the Missouri Pacific built an extensive system by acquiring the New Orleans, Texas and Mexico Railway Company and through the NOT&M the balance of the Gulf Coast Lines, the International–Great Northern, and a number of smaller companies. The Santa Fe and the Southern Pacific also bought other Texas railroads during the 1920s. In 1932 the Southern Pacific Company acquired the St. Louis Southern Railway Company and its Texas subsidiaries. By the end of 1932 three systems, the Southern Pacific, Missouri Pacific, and Santa Fe, owned or controlled more than 11,700 miles or 70 percent of the railroad mileage in Texas.

When the Texas legislature passed the Law to Regulate Railroads in 1853, it required that the railroads operating in the state be headquartered in Texas. This requirement was later included as part of Article X of the Constitution of 1876. As a result the various railroad systems operating in Texas did so through subsidiary companies. Some, such as the Southern Pacific, Missouri Pacific, and Santa Fe, retained the corporate names of Texas railroads they had acquired. Others, such as the Missouri, Kansas and Texas, chartered separate subsidiaries to operate in Texas. However, the Transportation Act of 1920 gave additional regulatory powers to the Interstate Commerce Commission. In 1934 the Kansas City Southern Railway Company sought to lease the Texarkana and Fort Smith Railway Company lines in Texas. Although the Interstate Commerce Commission gave approval to this lease, the state of Texas fought the case to the Supreme Court of the United States, which upheld the federal agency. The Missouri Pacific and its subsidiaries came out of receivership in 1954, at which time all of the companies in Texas operating as part of the Missouri Pacific Lines were merged into the parent company. The Katy merged its Texas subsidiary in 1960, while the Southern Pacific merged the Texas and New Orleans in 1961. The Santa Fe followed suit in 1965. The last of the separate Texas railroads was the Fort Worth and Denver, which merged into the Burlington Northern Railroad Company in 1982.

The Burlington–Rock Island Railroad Company inaugurated the first Texas streamlined diesel passenger service in 1936, when the Sam Houston Zephyr began operating between Houston and Dallas–Fort Worth. Shortly thereafter the Texas and New Orleans acquired streamlined equipment pulled by a steam locomotive for its Sunbeam between Dallas and Houston. By 1938 both companies were providing double daily streamliner service between Houston and North Texas. In 1940 the Fort Worth and Denver inaugurated the Texas Zephyr between Dallas and Denver, Colorado. In the optimism following the end of World War II, the various railroads ordered new equipment for their major trains. Existing trains such as the Texas Special, operating between St. Louis and San Antonio, and Sunset Limited, running between New Orleans through Texas to Los Angeles, were streamlined, while other railroads added new trains. These included the Texas Chief between Chicago and Houston–Galveston on the Santa Fe and the Texas Eagle of the Missouri Pacific and the Texas and Pacific operating between St. Louis and all of the major Texas cities.

Although these trains were initially well patronized, the improvement in highways, primarily the construction of the interstate highway system, and the inauguration of jet air transportation siphoned off most of the rail passenger traffic. By 1970 only the Santa Fe and Southern Pacific were still operating passenger trains in Texas. On 1 May 1971 the remaining trains were turned over to the National Railroad Passenger Corporation, better known as Amtrak. Amtrak chose to continue the Sunset Limited on a triweekly basis and initially operated the Texas Chief between Houston and Chicago. This train, later renamed the Lone Star, was subsequently discontinued. The only other Amtrak route in Texas at the end of 1995 was the Texas Eagle, operating from Chicago to San Antonio on a triweekly basis.

Unlike several other states, Texas did not fund additional passenger-train service. This, along with the failure of a proposed high-speed railroad connecting the four major cities to obtain financing, meant that additional rail passenger service in Texas was unlikely. However, several operators have attempted to operate excursion trains on a regular basis. These have included runs over the Texas Mexican Railway between Corpus Christi and Laredo, the Texas Limited between Houston and Galveston, and a dinner train operating out of San Antonio. All three have discontinued service. In 1995 three steam passenger trains were in operation. These were the Texas State Railroad State Historical Park between Rusk and Palestine, the Austin Steam Train Association between Cedar Park and Burnet, and the Tarantula Train at Fort Worth.

Texas continues to have more railroad mileage than any other state and the largest number of railroad employees. In 1992 chemicals accounted for 30 percent of the railroad tonnage originating in the state, while agricultural products, the leading category during the early years, accounted for only 7 percent. Coal represented the largest category of rail tonnage terminating in Texas. The state is second only to Virginia, with its extensive coal-shipping piers, in the amount of coal terminated. The passage of the Staggers Act in 1980 deregulating railroads resulted in a new era for the companies, as they were now able to compete on the basis of rates as well as service. In addition, the act also allowed the railroads more freedom in abandoning or selling marginal branch lines. With these changes the major freight railroads have been able to attract additional business and better concentrate their resources, resulting in the best physical plant in their history. At the same time some of the historic Texas lines, such as the Roscoe, Snyder and Pacific Railway Company, no longer had a role to play and were abandoned. This was offset by a number of new companies, such as the South Orient Railroad Company, which were organized to acquire and operate secondary and branch lines no longer wanted by the major companies. These new railroads have attempted to preserve rail service over lines that otherwise might have been abandoned.

In 1992 the Association of American Railroads recognized 40 different railroads operating in the state, of which 17 had been formed since deregulation. These lines operated a total of 11,285 miles of track, which represented a decrease of about 33 percent since the peak reached in 1932. The 40 companies represent the remainder of some 300 railroads that have operated in the state. The merger of Texas railroads that began in 1858 with the combination of the Houston Tap and the Houston Tap and Brazoria continues. Major changes in recent years include the merger of the Texas and Pacific into the Missouri Pacific in 1976 and the merger of the St. Louis–San Francisco Railway Company into the Burlington Northern in 1980. The Union Pacific Corporation acquired the Missouri Pacific in 1982, and the operations of the Missouri Pacific and the Union Pacific Railroad were subsequently consolidated. However, the Missouri Pacific still remains a separate company and in 1989 merged with the Missouri–Kansas–Texas. On 22 September 1995 the Burlington Northern and Santa Fe merged to form the Burlington Northern and Santa Fe Railroad. *George C. Werner*

Rainey, Homer Price. University president; b. Clarksville, 19 January 1896; d. 19 December 1985; m. Mildred Collins (1920); 2 daughters; ed. Austin College (B.A., 1919) and University of

Homer Price Rainey (second from left) at his inauguration as president of the University of Texas, Austin, December 9, 1939. Prints and Photographs Collection, CAH; CN 05741. Rainey's career at the university was short because his disagreements with university regents over such issues as censorship led to his dismissal on 1 November 1944, and to a consequent strike by students.

Chicago (M.A., 1923; Ph.D., 1924). Rainey was ordained a Baptist minister at the age of 19. He served in World War I and taught in Oregon before becoming president of Franklin College in Indiana (1927). From 1931 to 1935 he was president of Bucknell University in Pennsylvania. During four years as director of the American Youth Commission of the American Council on Education, he summarized numerous surveys; the summaries were published as *How Fare American Youth?* (1937). Rainey was named president of the University of Texas by the board of regents in 1939. The complexion of the board soon changed due to appointments by governors W. Lee O'Daniel and Coke Stevenson. By 1941 some regents began exercising a resolve to control faculty and courses. Several on the board pressured Rainey to fire four full professors of economics who espoused New Deal views. In 1942 the regents fired three untenured economics instructors and a fourth who had only a one-year appointment for having attempted to defend federal labor laws at an antiunion meeting in Dallas. Rainey protested in vain. He again displeased the regents when he tried to bring the University of Texas Medical Branch at Galveston into the university proper. He also protested to the board when tenure was weakened and social science research funds were terminated. Regent D. F. Strickland wrote Rainey that the president of the University of Texas had no business suggesting anything to the regents and that if the abolition of tenure would make it more difficult to recruit out-of-state professors, Texas would be better off.

The most significant incident dividing Rainey from the regents was the board's repression of John Dos Passos's *USA* and its efforts to fire the professor who placed the third volume of the trilogy on the English department's sophomore reading list. The regents deemed the work subversive and perverted. Since the selection had been a committee decision no one was fired, but Rainey was outraged at the protest. He made a dramatic public statement of all his grievances to a general faculty meeting on 12 October 1944. The regents seized the opportunity to fire him on

1 November, without citing any reasons. Regent Marguerite Fairchild cast the sole dissenting vote. University students reacted by going on strike, and 8,000 marched from the campus to the Capitol and the Governor's Mansion. Controversy lingered for months. Early in 1945 Governor Stevenson appointed six new regents. They made some amends, such as increasing research funds and offering reemployment to the fired economic instructors, but refused to rehire Rainey. Meanwhile the AAUP, the Southern Association of Colleges and Secondary Schools, and Phi Beta Kappa reprimanded the university. The AAUP censorship lasted nine years, until the organization was convinced that the regents had changed their policies.

In 1946 Rainey ran for governor. Although he was a devout Christian, he was attacked as a dangerous radical. His candidacy was identified with controversial causes—academic freedom, taxes on natural resources, labor unions, and suspected integrationism. Four candidates concentrated their fire on Rainey. After a bitter primary, he was beaten badly in a runoff by Railroad Commissioner Beauford Jester. Rainey was the first candidate to run for state office who was supported by an emerging urban coalition of labor, minorities, and independent progressives. In 1947 he became president of Stephens College in Missouri. He joined the education faculty at the University of Colorado in 1956, received an outstanding teacher award in 1964, and became professor emeritus that same year. In 1971 he published *The Tower and the Dome*, an account of his experiences at UT.

George N. Green

Ramón, Diego. Spanish soldier; b. Querétaro (?), 1641; d.1724. As commandant of the presidio of San Juan Bautista from its establishment in 1703 until his death, Ramón played a key role in the development of Spanish Texas and the founding of missions in both Texas and Coahuila. He had a number of children, but there is no record of his marriage. In 1674 he was a soldier with Francisco de Elizondo's expedition to Fray Juan Larios's Coahuila mission, "fourteen leagues" north of the Río de Sabinas. As a captain in 1687–88, Ramón was left in charge of Santiago de la Monclova during absences of Governor Alonso De León. His first entry into what is now Texas probably occurred in 1688, when he accompanied De León on the expedition to arrest the Frenchman Jean Jarry in the area of present Kinney County. After De León's death in 1691, Ramón served as governor ad interim of Coahuila. Following the ineffectual Texas expedition of Domingo Terán de los Ríos in 1691–92, he reported to the viceroy on the plight of the missionaries in eastern Texas. As a result, Gregorio de Salinas Varona, who had just been named Coahuila governor to succeed Ramón, undertook in the spring of 1693 an expedition to relieve the missionaries' distress. In 1699 Ramón led the founding expedition of Mission San Francisco Xavier, 40 miles northwest of Monclova. The next year, as *sargento mayor*, he officiated in the removal of San Juan Bautista Mission from the Río de Sabinas on the Coahuila–Nuevo León border to the site of present-day Guerrero, Coahuila, five miles from the Rio Grande. In March 1701, on recommendation of the bishop of Guadalajara, Captain Ramón was placed in command of a "flying company" charged with defending the Rio Grande missions. Two years later, the company was given permanent station in Presidio de San Juan Bautista, adjacent to San Juan Bautista Mission, with Ramón in command. In 1706, when smallpox swept through the native population, both in the mission settlement and in the *montes*, the captain and several of his soldiers accompanied a missionary priest into the Texas wilds to baptize dying Indians. The following year he led an expedition to the Nueces River to punish hostile Indians for raiding in Coahuila and Nuevo León, while exploring the country and recruiting Indians for the smallpox-ravaged missions. In 1714 he received the French commercial agent Louis Juchereau de St. Denis, who had journeyed from Mobile seeking an entry to trade with the Spaniards, and sent him on to Mexico City for interrogation. In 1715, following an Indian uprising, Ramón crossed the Rio Grande with Fray Francisco Ruiz to return the rebellious natives to the missions. In 1717, on the basis of complaints by Fray Antonio de San Buenaventura y Olivares, Governor Martín de Alarcón launched an investigation into the Ramón family's involvement in St. Denis's trade scheme. A royal decree dated 30 January 1719 ordered Don Diego's removal from San Juan Bautista Presidio and his reassignment to a distant post. The decree, not acted upon immediately, ultimately was nullified by Diego Ramón's death of natural causes. Many of Ramón's descendants were involved in historic events. *Robert S. Weddle*

State senator Ben Ramsey in his law office. Photograph by John Vachon. San Augustine, Texas, April 1943. Library of Congress; USW 3-25211-D. Ramsey later served as secretary of state and lieutenant governor.

Ramsdell, Charles William. Historian; b. Salado, 4 April 1877; d. 3 July 1942; ed. University of Texas (B.A., 1903; M.A., 1904) and Columbia University (Ph.D., 1910). From 1906 until his death he was a member of the history department at UT. He was a visiting lecturer at many universities. He became such an authority on the Old South that his colleagues commonly referred to him as the "Dean" of Southern historians. His numerous publications include *Reconstruction in Texas*, *A School History of Texas* (in collaboration with Eugene C. Barker and Charles S. Potts), and *Behind the Lines in the Southern Confederacy* (published posthumously). He was coeditor with Wendell Holmes Stephenson in the planning stage of the multivolume *A History of the South*, a joint endeavor of the Littlefield Fund for Southern History at the University of Texas and the Louisiana State University Press. Ramsdell was president of the Mississippi Valley Historical Association (1928–29) and the Southern Historical Association (1936); treasurer of the Texas State Historical Association (1907–42); and an associate editor of the *Southwestern Historical Quarterly* (1910–38). *J. Horace Bass*

Ramsey, Ben. Politician; b. San Augustine, 28 December 1903; d. Austin, 27 February 1985; m. Florine Hankla; 3 children; ed. University of Texas. Ramsey passed the state bar examination before graduation and was licensed to practice law in 1931. He was elected state representative and served two terms. Afterward he returned to San Augustine to practice law with his brother for five years. In 1940 he was elected to the first of two four-year terms as state senator. He became a Senate leader in antideficit legislation and legislation to regulate labor unions. In 1949 Governor Jester appointed him secretary of state. In 1950 Ramsey was elected lieutenant governor. When Governor Allan Shivers's conservative Democrats clashed with the state's more liberal Democrats, led by Senate majority leader Lyndon Johnson and speaker Sam Rayburn, the two factions agreed to support Ramsey as a member of the National Democratic Committee. In fiscal affairs, especially opposition to higher taxes, Ramsey was considered conservative. Despite this, he supported Shivers in raising revenue necessary for higher teachers'

pay, state hospitals, and prisons. Like Shivers he was an enemy of labor unions. He strongly supported rural electrification, water conservation and development, paving of farms roads, and stricter laws regulating what he called "fly-by-night insurance companies." In 1961 Gov. Price Daniel appointed him to an unexpired term on the Railroad Commission, to which he was subsequently elected three times. He served three two-year terms as chairman. Just before his appointment to the commission, Texas was successful in achieving control over offshore oil in the Tidelands Controversy, and Ramsey helped composed the rules for Texas coastal drilling. *Richard M. Morehead*

Ranchería Grande. A name used by several Spanish expeditions to designate any unusually large temporary settlement or encampment of Indians. The Ranchería Grande of the middle Brazos River in the vicinity of what is now Milam County, for example, is not to be confused with the Ranchería Grande on the Nueces River, probably at a site now in Webb County, which was sought by Capt. Diego Ramón on his 1707 campaign from San Juan Bautista. The name Ranchería Grande evidently was used to designate the band of Indians encountered on a Brazos River tributary by Domingo Ramón's mission-founding expedition in 1716. The Spanish caravan camped near the village, which may have had some Tonkawas but also included an Ervipiame chieftain and his following. As the visitors bartered for deer and buffalo hides, men, women, and children appeared in large numbers to take part in the exchange. Ramón placed the number at 2,000; Father Isidro Félix de Espinosa estimated 500 and identified them as Pamayes, Payayes, Cantonas, Mescales, Jarames, and Sijames. While Governor Martín de Alarcón was at San Antonio in January 1719, fear of French activity among the Indians caused him to send "a person of his confidence" to ascertain the state of affairs among the "twenty-three nations of the Rancheria Grande." The Marqués de Aguayo failed to find the Ranchería Grande in 1721, even though he was traveling with one of its chiefs, Juan Rodríguez, who had come to San Antonio to solicit missions for his people. It was said that all the Indians had gone to council with the French. The next year Aguayo established San Francisco Xavier de Nájera Mission at San Antonio for Juan Rodríguez's followers. The mission soon languished, without permanent buildings ever having been constructed. Pressure from the Apaches caused the Indians of Ranchería Grande to move east and perhaps to scatter. Juan Antonio Bustillo y Cevallos, Texas governor from 1732 to 1734, wrote in 1746 that only the name of Ranchería Grande survived in his time. Father Juan Agustín Morfi, nevertheless, relates that the San Xavier missions, begun in 1747, were for the people of Ranchería Grande, as well as for the Deados, Mayeyes, Yojuanes, Cocos, and others.   *Robert S. Weddle*

Ranching. The word *ranch* is derived from Mexican-Spanish *rancho*, which denotes the home (headquarters) of the *ranchero*. In Texas, the word initially denoted an establishment engaged in livestock production using unimproved range pastures as the primary resource, with or without plowland crops. From the beginning, ranching often included raising cattle, sheep and goats, and horses. Cattle ranching has been a major Texas industry for nearly three centuries. As early as the 1690s the Spaniards brought in stock with their entradas. Ranching as such dates from the 1730s, when herds were loosed along the San Antonio River to feed missionaries, soldiers, and civilians in the San Antonio and Goliad areas. As the Spanish missions declined, ranching shifted to private raisers, including Tomás Sánchez de la Barrera y Garza, Antonio Gil Ibarvo, and Martín De León. Modern scholarship places the birth of the Texas ranching industry in the southeast Texas–southwestern Louisiana area, from where cattle raisers drove herds to market in New Orleans. The Spanish government also encouraged the cattle industry in the Coastal Bend, where liberal land grants often developed into feudal estates. Huge tracts were given to those who, like Tomás Sánchez at Laredo, owned seed stock of horses, cattle, and sheep and commanded a following to occupy the land and handle livestock. The Cavazos (San Juan de Carricitas) grant in Cameron County comprised 50 sitios (a sitio was 4,605 acres), and other grants were even larger. Though few are still owned by the descendants of the original grantees, many ranches in South Texas predate the American Revolution. Spanish and Mexican ranches were not usually called by the name of the owner or his brand, as was the American custom, but by such distinctive names as Ojo de Agua, Las Mesteñas, La Parra, and Santa Gertrudis; the last two survive under their Spanish names at the Kenedy Ranch and the King Ranch in Kleberg County.

At first, Spain severely restricted commerce, but during the brief Spanish rule of Louisiana (1763–1803), barriers to trade were relaxed and Texas cattlemen found a wider outlet for their animals to the east. However, Indian raids in South Texas increased in scope and intensity, forcing many rancheros to leave their herds behind and flee to the settlements for protection.

In Mexican Texas, beginning in 1821, conditions improved. Land policies of Mexico and the Republic of Texas were less liberal than those of Spain, but were still favorable to range husbandry. Individual citizens, until crowded out by settlement, had access to vast areas of public land for grazing. American colonists flooding into Texas during the 1830s were primarily farmers and not ranchers, but they quickly saw the significance of lush pastures where cattle could thrive with minimum care. Men who came to Texas to plow and plant became cattle raisers. Cattle raising remained a domestic industry during the republic

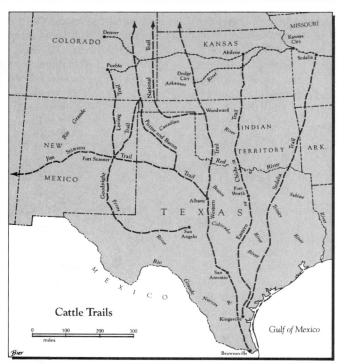

Cattle trails. From *The History of Texas* by Robert A. Calvert and Arnoldo De León, ©1990 by Harlan Davidson, Inc. Reproduced by permission.

and early statehood, supplying the small urban population, immigrants, and the bartering trade. In the 1840s and 1850s ranchers continued to drive small herds to New Orleans. A few hardy souls headed north, principally on the Shawnee Trail, seeking feeder areas in Missouri, Illinois, and Iowa, where they could fatten their cattle and ship them to markets in Philadelphia and New York. In the 1850s Texas cattle were shipped from coastal ports by the Morgan Lines to New Orleans and the West Indies. Herds also were trailed west through hostile Indian country to the California goldfields. By 1860, Texas cattle ranching was shifting from Southeast and South Texas to the north central frontier. The core area lay west of Fort Worth, in Palo Pinto, Erath, and Comanche counties. For the first time cattle brought cash revenue to Texas, although the annual increase in herds far exceeded exports.

During the Civil War, Texas furnished beef to the Confederacy until the summer of 1863, when federal armies closed the Mississippi River to traffic. Cattle multiplied until they were estimated at eight per capita of the population. Mavericks by the thousands roamed the range. At the end of the war, steaks and roasts were selling in eastern markets at 25 to 30 cents a pound, while a mature, fat Texas steer could be bought for $6 to $10. The same steer was worth $30 or $40 at the end of the trail. Texas was cattle poor, but the way to market was through storms, across swollen rivers, and into hostile Indian country. In 1866, Texas trail herds began marching to Montana gold mines, New Mexico Indian reservations, and Kansas railheads. Within two decades more than five million head had been trailed to outside markets. In the late 1870s, after the Indian menace ended in Texas, the cattle industry leap-frogged to fresh pasturage in the Davis Mountains and the Big Bend, and on the plains of West Texas.

Contrary to general views, the Texas cattle industry was not founded entirely on "free grass." Ranch enterprisers such as Thomas and Dennis M. O'Connor, Richard King, Mifflin Kenedy, and scores of other antebellum ranchers operated on their own land from the beginning. Other cattlemen who wisely bought land after the Civil War, while their neighbors were scorning it, included Charles Goodnight, William T. Waggoner, C. C. Slaughter, S. M. Swenson, and William D. and George T. Reynolds. Early Anglo-American ranches generally consisted of a primitive headquarters surrounded by open range. In the earlier-settled part of Texas, ranchers owned the land on which their improvements were built, but as the frontier advanced, stockmen set up quarters without benefit of title or surveyor's lines. When the real owner appeared, the squatter moved farther into the unsettled domain. Before the advent of barbed wire in 1874, few stockmen acquired land on which to graze cattle. Their primary need was a favorable site from which to work cattle and to control the water, which in turn controlled the range. Even foreign capitalists who invaded the range country in the cattle boom of the early 1880s bought only enough watered land to hold the range.

As markets could not absorb surplus Texas cattle, ranchers soon looked north to the unpopulated range that extended to the Canadian border and covered the entire Great Plains east of the Rocky Mountains. While sending mature steers to slaughter markets, they moved breeding stock into New Mexico, Montana, Wyoming, Dakota, Colorado, the Cherokee Outlet, and western Kansas and Nebraska to start new herds. Methods of handling cattle, range terminology, and range practices developed in Texas spread with the herds across the western part of the United States. The Panic of 1873 momentarily crippled the cattle industry, but beef recovered rapidly and zoomed into an unprecedented boom that peaked 10 years later. Pamphlets describing the "Beef Bonanza" flooded Great Britain, and English and Scottish money (at the Matador, Rocking Chair, and other ranches) competed with eastern capital in acquiring herds and range rights. The industry had grown up as individual enterprise, usually managed by the owner; now the corporation entered the field with all the advantages of mobilized capital but with the disadvantages of nonresidence and hired managers. In the late 1880s the change from open range to fenced pastures brought conflict between large and small ranchers, ranchers and farmers (sometimes in the form of fence cutting), and employers and employees as in the Cowboy Strike of 1883.

By the end of the nineteenth century the transformation of ranching to the closed range was practically complete. Open-range drift fences were superseded by a complete enclosure of the ranch holdings. Railroads invaded ranch country, and corporations subdivided their holdings into smaller pastures for better range utilization, improved livestock management, and sale. Panic and drought in 1893 brought hard times, but the men who owned their grass and were free of debt were doing business when the upward tide returned. During World War I the cattle and horse market boomed, but the decade of the 1920s brought deflation and bankruptcies. The owner-operator who resisted the temptation to speculate came through safely. Price recovery from the slump was slow, however, and another setback followed the bursting of the stock-market bubble in 1929. Cattlemen and their financial backers were soon in deep water, and a desperate government, for the first time in history,

extended aid to the cattle industry through agricultural credit agencies. Although the help was of some benefit, prices continued downhill, droughts plagued the land, ranges were overstocked, and grass was scarce. In 1934 the government intervened with a desperate remedy—a program to buy and kill cattle to buoy a depressed market. As the government generally destroyed the culls—sick, crippled, and scrub cattle—many ranchers used the payments to upgrade their herds. After the slaughter, the rains came again and the range grassed over. In addition to slaughter markets and outlets in corn-belt feedlots, a new cattle range developed. Farmers in the southern states suddenly saw cattle as a means of utilizing acreage taken out of cotton farming. Texas herds supplied much of the seed stock from East Texas to Georgia. By the 1950s beef cattle had returned to the major farming regions. Although much of the industry was conducted as a range enterprise, stock farming with small herds increased and became soundly based on a crop–livestock system.

Although the Spanish breed provided the foundation for the Texas cattle industry, a liberal sprinkling of cattle came from the United States with Anglo-American colonists. Some stock may have been derived from British and Dutch breeds. The earliest record of importing purebred cattle to Texas dates to 1848, when Thomas J. Shannon shipped two cows and a bull from Queen Victoria's herd of Durham cattle to New Orleans and hauled them in wagons to North Texas. Livestock improvement in South Texas was handicapped by Texas fever, and despite persistent efforts by Richard King and others of his generation, little progress was made until artificial immunization was developed. The shipment of Texas cattle by railroad began in 1873, when the Missouri–Kansas–Texas Railroad shipped 120,000 cattle to market from Denison and brought in 200 carloads of breeding stock for Texas ranches. In 1876 W. D. and George Reynolds of Shackelford County brought Durham cattle from Colorado to their Clear Fork ranch. Charles Goodnight introduced the same blood in the Palo Duro Canyon that year. William S. Ikard saw Hereford cattle at the Philadelphia Centennial in 1876, bought 10 in Illinois, and shipped them to Denison for his Clay County ranch. Though only two survived the trip, in a few years Ikard

Cornelia Adair (second from left) after a wolf hunt at the JA Ranch, 1890. Courtesy Panhandle–Plains Historical Society, Canyon, Texas. Following the death of her husband, Cornelia Adair came into control of the huge JA Ranch.

Cattlemen and buyers at an auction of prize beef steers and breeding stock at the San Angelo Fat Stock Show. Photograph by Russell Lee, 1940. Library of Congress; USF 342101-35456.

had developed the first fever-immune herd of registered Herefords in the state. Devon blood vied with the Durham in the early upgrading of longhorn cattle. In the 1880s and 1890s ranchers introduced Galloways and Aberdeen Angus, but only the latter persisted. The XIT Ranch was among the first to use Angus bulls. The breed rapidly increased in popularity, and in the 1940s there were over 100 registered herds in Texas. C. C. Slaughter caused a sensation when he paid $5,000 for the prize-winning Hereford bull, Sir Bredwell, for his South Plains ranch. In the early 1900s, O. H. "Bull" Nelson sold more than 10,000 Hereford bulls in the state. In 1950 Texas stood at the head of Hereford producers both in quality and numbers, and the Texas Hereford Association was the strongest organization of its kind in the nation.

Though the first shorthorns (Durhams) were dual-purpose animals, Texans favored the Scottish type, bred primarily for beef. The Loving Ranch, in Jack County, maintained a large herd of shorthorns longer than any other range operator. This breed was popular among stock farmers. Between 1925 and 1945 the dual-purpose type known as milking shorthorns grew in popularity, especially in the Panhandle. Other centers were Kyle (Hays County), Wortham (Freestone County), and the area around industrial centers, especially Fort Worth and Dallas. By

the 1950s Texas had more than 1,500,000 dairy cattle of various breeds and stood first in Jerseys. Through cross-breeding with beef bulls, surplus male calves were sold as veal; cows unprofitable for milk production went to slaughter. After 1925 Texas began exporting high-quality breeding stock to other states and abroad. South Africa and South America secured seed stock from Texas, as did Mexico. Texas-bred registered animals went to most of the states in the Union.

A modern ranch is a highly developed unit with miles of fencing, water supplies accessible to grazing land, permanent corrals, and loading chutes. Corrals have replaced roundup grounds, cutting gates are used instead of cutting horses, and loading chutes and trailer trucks substitute for the dusty trail to market. Ranching involves a heavy capital investment in land and improvements. It requires astute business management, a striking contrast to the 1870s and before, when a "ranch" might be nothing more than a dugout or picket shack as "headquarters" on the open range. There are Texas ranches devoted exclusively to cattle, exclusively to sheep or Angora goats, and solely to horses. Contrary to open-range misconceptions, sheep and cattle can be grazed successfully on the same range. On the Edwards Plateau, where browse is abundant, goat ranching thrives. The combination of cattle, sheep, and goats is not unusual. Horse ranches were numerous around the turn of the century, but by 1946 the industry was usually incidental to other ranch enterprises. Dude ranching has thrived better elsewhere than in Texas. Texas has long been the top-ranking state in cattle numbers. On 1 January 1968, according to a United States Department of Agriculture report, the state reached an all-time high of 10,972,000 head. In 1973 there were 15,350,000 cattle and calves in Texas, with an inventory value of $3.5 billion. Beef-cattle raising was the most widely distributed livestock enterprise in Texas. Dairy cow numbers had declined.

Cattle feeding rapidly developed in many areas of the state. The April 1968 USDA report showed 761,000 cattle and calves on feed in Texas. This figure represented a 250 percent increase over the 1958 figures. The principal reason for the change was the gain in commercial feedlots in the state. In April 1968, 275 feedlots were operating in Texas, with a minimum capacity of 1,000 head each; these accounted for 95 percent of the cattle being fattened for the slaughter market. Marketing from Texas feedlots during 1968 approached 1.8 million head, an increase of 508 percent over the 1958 level. In 1968 Texas was third in cattle feeding in the United States. By the mid-1980s Texas was marketing 4.8 million head annually and led the nation in cattle feeding. In 1990 the feedlot industry contributed $11.2 billion to the Texas economy. Custom yards handled from 2,000 to 50,000 head a year. The main feeding area in the state was the northern Panhandle. The expansion of slaughter facilities paralleled the increase of cattle feeding. From 1966 to 1968 the slaughter capacity of plants in the plains area increased more than 100 percent. There were 321 slaughter plants in Texas in 1984, when six million head were slaughtered; the number of slaughterhouses fell to 224 in 1994. From the 1920s to the 1960s, Swift and Company, Armour and Company, and two or three other slaughtering and meat-packing companies dominated Texas beef, pork, and poultry production. The 1980 drought saw several small packers close down in Brownsville, Garden City, Hereford, and elsewhere, while Iowa Beef Producers and other large facilities surged until by the end of the 1980s they controlled 80 percent of slaughtering. In 1991 IBP constructed one of the nation's largest tanneries in Amarillo, located next to the IBP beef-processing plant. In 1995 IBP increased its Texas holdings by acquiring several smaller plants. Meat packers contracted more and more calves at ranches and kept them in feedlots and slaughter facilities.

In recent years, Texas beef producers have adopted modern technology in their operations. They use electric branding irons and hire "helicopter cowboys" to round up and drive cattle to corrals. Ranchers employ computers to enhance management and to obtain information on prices and markets. Purebred producers, responding to consumer demands for leaner beef, have become interested in genetic engineering. Beef producers vigorously promote their industry. Threats of national boycotts in the 1970s prompted ranchers and processors to increase their voice in Austin and Washington. They have addressed such issues as adulterated imported meat, toxicants for predator control, and price fluctuations. Associations of beef producers include the Texas Beef Council, the Texas Cattle Feeders Association, Texas Cattle Women, and others. The ranching industry promotes Livestock Appreciation Day at the Southwestern Exposition and Livestock Show in Fort Worth, at the Fort Worth Farm and Ranch Club meetings, at meetings of the Texas and Southwestern Cattle Raisers Association, and at many other venues. Some of these organizations give annual awards. The Texas Beef Council funds a traveling exhibit to encourage Texans to eat more beef. Texas cattlemen also serve on numerous national livestock boards.

Ranching has generally been a cyclical industry. Beef prices tumbled in 1979, and the cost of raising feeder calves rose 15 percent in 1980–81. Purchasing power in 1980 was the lowest in 25 years. Shortage of winter pastures, high grain prices, and drought caused worries. Ranchers applying for farm credit were encouraged to initiate "self-help" programs and introduce voluntary "check-offs" against cattle-sale receipts to support such programs. Texas attorney general Mark White ordered that all marks and brands be reregistered with the county clerks between August 1981 and February 1982. By 1988 the cattle market turned around, and seven bullish years followed. The cattle trade then plunged into a bear market; calf prices fell 40 percent by the fall of 1995 before stabilizing. Texas beef producers have been keenly interested in the export market, particularly Mexico, Japan, and Korea, and, more recently, Russia. The North American Free Trade Act (effective 1 January 1994) stimulated interest in upgrading breeding stock on Mexican ranges. The Texas Department of Agriculture operates a computer database to provide information on potential Mexican buyers, cattle imports, and problems of disease (especially brucellosis). The future of NAFTA depends on an improved Mexican economy.

In 1995 the Texas ranching industry sported a grand fact sheet. The state led the nation in cattle and calves (15.1 million), beef cows (6.2 million), calves (5.75 million born in 1994), cattle on feed (2.38 million), total value of cattle and calves ($8.532 billion), and cash receipts ($6.353 billion, 1993 sales). Texas also has been number one in number of farms and ranches (185,000) and total farm and ranch land (129.3 million acres). The Texas ranching industry has changed drastically from its early beginnings. The day of the longhorn and the sprawling King Ranch have been replaced by the rise of commercial feedlots, sophisticated slaughter and meat-packing industries, use of computers, and an intensive search for export markets. On many ranches hunting leases have replaced cattle raising. King, Kenedy, and O'Connor would perhaps think it outlandish, as well as entrepeneurially interesting, that on some ranches, ostriches and zebras are now more plentiful than cattle.

T. C. Richardson and Harwood P. Hinton

Randolph, Frankie Carter. Liberal activist; b. Barnum, Texas, 25 January 1894; d. Houston, 5 September 1972 (buried in Glenwood Cemetery); m. Robert D. Randolph (1918); 2 daughters. Mrs. Randolph was one of the founders of the Houston Junior League and served as its president in the 1920s. She was prominent in equestrian circles, the League of Women Voters, and various charities. During the Great Depression she was a volunteer in the Social Service Bureau. As a backer of President Franklin Roosevelt, she fought for city-manager government, city planning, public housing, and better drainage in low-income areas. In 1952 she donated $1,000 to Adlai Stevenson's presidential campaign and helped organize Houston precincts. She was a leader of opposition to the "Shivercrats," Democrats who followed Governor Shivers in supporting Eisenhower. She later helped form the Democrats of Texas, which fought with the state Democratic executive committee for the rest of the decade. Mrs. Randolph was among the founders of the *Texas Observer* in

1954 and later became its publisher. Throughout the late 1950s and early 1960s she was hostess at the "Wednesday Club" luncheons at the *Observer*'s Houston branch office, sometimes attended by 70 or 80 people. She was elected Democratic national committeewoman from Texas in 1956 despite the opposition of conservative Democrats and United States senator Lyndon Johnson, whom she considered an opportunist. Her Harris County Democrats were one of the major forces behind the election of Ralph Yarborough to the Senate in 1957. Her influence was secured beyond Yarborough's 13-year term by the ascension to the federal bench, under Yarborough's sponsorship, of Woodrow Seals of Houston and William Wayne Justice of Tyler. With the help of volunteers she organized the files of Harris County precincts, making thousands of telephone calls and attending numerous precinct meetings. Her precinct-based urban organizing cast her movement up against old-time boss politics as it was then exemplified in Texas by Johnson and Sam Rayburn. As national committeewoman, Mrs. Randolph led the Harris County Democrats to sweeping victories in the county and legislative elections of 1958. In 1960 she refused to go along with the movement in Texas to nominate Johnson for the presidency and was replaced as national committeewoman.

Ronnie Dugger

Randolph Air Force Base. Fifteen miles northeast of San Antonio; called the "West Point of the Air" when it was dedicated as a flying-training base in 1930. Without the nickname, the base has retained pilot-training as its essential mission. The Air Corps Act of 1926 changed the name of the Army Air Service to the Army Air Corps, provided a five-year expansion program for the under-strength air corps, and placed a general officer in charge of all flying training for the corps. Brig. Gen. Frank Lahm (later known as "the father of Randolph Field"), selected to fill this position, established the Air Corps Training Center at Duncan Field, adjacent to Kelly Field. Soon thereafter he realized that air corps training requirements had become too great for Brooks and Kelly fields, and that another field was needed. After a considerable search for a site, a 2,300-acre tract near Schertz was chosen. First Lt. Harold Clark, trained as an architect, designed the field. At the time, Randolph Field was the largest construction project undertaken by the United States Army Corps of Engineers since the Panama Canal. It took more than five years (1928–33) to construct the base's 500plus Spanish Renaissance–style buildings and 30 miles of roadways. A committee decided to name the base after Capt. William Millican Randolph, a native Texan and graduate of Texas A&M, who was killed on 17 February 1928 when his AT4 crashed on takeoff from Gorman Field, Texas. Captain Randolph had been a member of the committee assigned to select a name for the new airfield. In 1931 the Air Corps Primary Flying School was officially established at Randolph. Primary training continued there until 1939, when the mission was changed to basic pilot training. Cadet training continued until March 1943, when it was replaced with the Central Instructors School. For the next three years the mission at Randolph was training instructors for all three phases (basic, primary, and advanced) of the air corps pilot-training program. During this time, the Central Instructors School trained 15,396 pilots as instructors. In April 1945 the Central Instructors School was replaced by the Army Air Force Pilot School, which specialized in transition training for B29 bomber

pilots, copilots, and engineers. From December 1945 to March 1948 primary and basic pilot training was conducted at Randolph. In March 1948 the primary pilot training program was halted, and in August the 3510th Basic Pilot Training Wing became the host unit at Randolph. In September 1947 the United States Air Force became a separate service, and four months later Randolph Field was renamed Randolph Air Force Base.

In July 1957, Air Training Command moved to Randolph from Scott Air Force Base, Illinois. During 1959 the base saw its Seguin Auxiliary Field open and the School for Aviation Medicine end its 28-year tenure at Randolph when it was moved to Brooks Air Force Base. In 1972 the Twelfth Tactical Fighter Wing was redesignated the Twelfth Flying Training Wing and then activated at Randolph Air Force Base. Since that time, the wing has served as host for headquarters of the Air Training Command, Air Force Military Personnel Center, Air Force Civilian Personnel Management Center, Air Force Recruiting Services, and Air Force Management Engineering Agency, as well as more than 20 tenant organizations. With its activation in May 1972, the Twelfth Flying Training Wing's mission became training pilots to be instructor pilots. Shortly after the Vietnam War, the wing's mission was temporarily expanded to include T37, T38, and T39 pilot requalification training (Operation Homecoming, 1973–76) for more than 150 United States Air Force former prisoners of war. In the early 1990s the wing added two new missions—Undergraduate Navigator Training and Pilot Instructor Training for the T1A (Specialized Undergraduate Navigator Training). Randolph AFB employed more than 8,000 personnel, including more than 3,000 civilian workers, and had an annual payroll of more than $277 million.

Timothy M. Brown

Ransom, Harry Huntt. Chancellor of the University of Texas; b. Galveston, 22 November 1908; d. Dripping Springs, 19 April 1976; m. Hazel Louise Harrod (1951); ed. University of the South (B.A., 1928) and Yale University (M.A., 1930; Ph.D., 1938). In the 1930s Ransom taught at the State Teachers College, Valley City, North Dakota, and at Colorado State College, Greeley. After joining the University of Texas in 1935 as instructor of English, he advanced to professor in 1947. From 1942 to 1946 he was in the United States Army Air Forces. In 1951 he was appointed assistant dean of the Graduate School at the University of Texas. In 1953 he was advanced to associate dean, in 1954 to dean of the College of Arts and Sciences, in 1957 to vice president and provost, in 1960 to president, and in 1961 to chancellor of the University of Texas System. After his retirement from the chancellorship in 1971 as chancellor emeritus, he continued his work in the development of special research collections and prepared materials for a history of UT, a project that was incomplete at the time of his death. He is most noted for expanding library materials throughout the system, especially at the Austin campus, where in 1957 he proposed a program for enlarging the special collections. The vast collections of the Harry Ransom Humanities Research Center include literature, the history of science, iconography, theater arts, photography, and cartography. Because of the HRC the University of Texas at Austin library was cited in 1970 by Anthony Hobson in his book *Great Libraries* as one of the 32 leading libraries in Western Europe and North America. Ransom was coeditor (with J. Frank Dobie and Mody Boatright) of the Texas Folklore Publications (volumes 14–17).

Harry Ransom. Courtesy HRHRC. Ransom, who served as president and first chancellor of the University of Texas and established the splendid Humanities Research Center, first joined the university faculty as an English instructor.

From 1952 to 1957 he was associate editor of the *Southwestern Historical Quarterly* and in 1956 was associate editor of *English Copyright Cases, 1660–1775*. In 1958 he founded the *Texas Quarterly*. His principal research interests were in the fields of copyright law, bibliography, Texas history, and eighteenth and nineteenth century literary history. He organized a research program for the International Copyright League in London in 1939 and was chairman of its historical commission for several years. Among his publications are *Bibliography of English Copyright History* (1948), *Notes of a Texas Book Collector, 1850–1899* (1950), and *The First Copyright Statute* (1956). He also fostered programs to improve teaching and research and strove to attract private support to UT. Among his projects was the Undergraduate Library and Academic Center (now the Peter T. Flawn Academic Center). To commemorate Ransom's own brilliance as a teacher, one of his former students inaugurated a Harry Ransom award for excellence in teaching, given annually to a faculty member in the College of Liberal Arts. Ransom received many honorary doctoral degrees and served on many boards, both private and governmental. *Margaret C. Berry*

Rath, Charles. Frontier merchant; b. near Stuttgart, Württemberg, 1836; d. Los Angeles, 30 July 1902; m. a Cheyenne woman (1860); 1 child; m. Caroline Markley (1870); 3 children; m. Emma Nesper; 1 child. In 1848 most of the Rath family immigrated to Philadelphia. They subsequently moved to Ohio. About 1853 Charles ran away from home, made his way west, and joined William Bent's trading enterprise in Colorado, where he worked as an independent freighter hauling supplies and trade goods across Kansas. He and his brother Chris operated a gristmill for a short while before it was washed away in a flood. The Raths then set up a ranch and stage stand on the military road between forts Hays and Riley, near present Ellinwood. In 1860 Charles Rath took over the trading post of George Peacock on Walnut Creek, near the Great Bend of the Arkansas river, after Peacock and five others were massacred by Kiowa warriors led by Satank. Three years later Rath and several partners formally gained title to the place. In addition, Rath operated a sutler's store at nearby Fort Zarah and in November 1860 was elected constable of Peketon County. Eventually, other Rath family members came out to Walnut Creek and put down roots in Kansas. Rath had established trading contacts with the Southern Cheyennes, who became his favorite customers. His first marriage, to a woman whose name meant Roadmaker, ended in divorce; as tensions between Indians and whites mounted, she allegedly persuaded Rath, for his own safety, to divorce her. Throughout the late 1860s Rath and his teamsters hauled freight for the military posts along the Santa Fe Trail and hunted game for the railroad crews building into Kansas. He also freighted for the troops and government agencies in western Indian Territory and began investing in Kansas real estate. In 1869 he made a return visit to the home of his youth in Ohio, where he married his second wife.

Rath was among the first to take advantage of the growing buffalo-hide trade. Even before moving to Dodge City in September 1872, he had begun hunting, freighting, and marketing the hides for a high profit. Often the hideyard of the Rath Mercantile Company held 70,000 to 80,000 hides. As the buffalo slaughter moved south into the Panhandle of Texas, Rath and a business partner, Robert M. Wright, made plans for a store–restaurant at Adobe Walls, near the site of William Bent's old outpost. In 1874 Rath and several employees freighted some $20,000 worth of goods to the new location, where Rath and Company built a building, mainly of sod. Rath and some of his men were back in Dodge City when the second battle of Adobe Walls occurred. In 1875, after the Red River Indian War, Rath and another associate, Frank E. Conrad, opened a branch store and hideyard near Fort Griffin, in Throckmorton County. At about the same time he and Wright established a trading post on Sweetwater Creek at Mobeetie, originally called Hidetown, the new settlement that had sprung up near Fort Elliott. Here they sold supplies to buffalo hunters and bought and shipped hides. In 1876 Rath, William McDole Lee, and E. E. Reynolds took a wagontrain of merchandise south to the Double Mountain Fork of the Brazos in what is now Stonewall County, where they established a trading post and hide agency in sight of the Double Mountains. Called variously Rath City, Camp Reynolds, and Rath's Store, the post, built of poles and buffalo hides, did a booming business for two years, during which Conrad bought out the Lee and Reynolds interests. In 1878 Rath and Conrad built a new store at Fort Griffin, across the street from the Beehive Saloon. By 1879, however, the buffalo supply was exhausted. Although Rath and his associates profited briefly from the bone business, he finally abandoned Rath City and moved his equipment to Camp Supply in Indian Territory.

There he saw his fortune wane as his debts from unsuccessful land speculations mounted. In 1885 he filed for a divorce, charging Caroline with neglect, abuse, and faultfinding. Although the

Sam Rayburn with reporters the day after Democrats elected him majority leader of the U.S. House of Representatives, Washington, 1937. Sam Rayburn Papers, CAH; CN 07613. A master of the political process, Rayburn wielded considerable power as majority leader and then speaker of the House. He eventually groomed Lyndon Johnson for the presidency.

settlement granted her and the children large sums of money, Rath never was able to support them fully. Soon after the divorce he married the sister of his associate Henry Nesper. Emma left Rath in 1896, since he had failed to produce another fortune, and returned with their son to her home in Philadelphia. There the boy, Morris, grew to manhood; he later won notice as a major-league baseball player and sporting-goods merchant. As Mobeetie gradually declined, Rath's expenses exceeded his income. Finally he sold out his remaining holdings in the Panhandle and Kansas and moved to Los Angeles, where his sister lived. His halfblood Indian daughter, Cheyenne Belle, who married twice, served her mother's people many years as a teacher and interpreter; she produced the only grandchildren Rath ever saw. *H. Allen Anderson*

Rayburn, Sam. Speaker of the House; b. Samuel Taliafero Rayburn, Roane County, Tennessee, 6 January 1882; d. Bonham, 16 November 1961; m. Metze Jones (1927; separated within three months); ed. East Texas Normal College (B.S., ca. 1902) and the University of Texas law school (sporadically; he was admitted to the Texas bar in 1908). In 1887 the family moved to Fannin County, Texas. In 1906, inspired partly by Senator Joseph Weldon Bailey, Rayburn won a seat in the Texas House of Representatives; he was reelected twice, and in his third term was speaker. In 1912 he was elected to the United States Congress as a Democrat from the Fourth Texas District. After the 1912 election he had no Republican opponent at any time during his congressional career of more than 48 years. He was majority leader

(1937–40) and in 1940 was elected speaker of the House to fill the unexpired term of Speaker William B. Bankhead. Rayburn continued as speaker in every Democratic-controlled Congress from the Seventy-sixth through the Eighty-seventh (1940–61). During the two periods of Republican majorities in the House (1947–49, 1953–55), he served as minority leader. On three occasions during his legislative career (in 1948, 1952, and 1956), he served as chairman of the Democratic national convention. Because Rayburn's congressional career spanned the particularly accelerated legislative activity that occurred during the administrations of Woodrow Wilson, Franklin D. Roosevelt, and Harry S. Truman, he was a participant in the passage of most of the significant legislation of the first half of the twentieth century. In his first term he introduced a measure for increasing the power of the Interstate Commerce Commission, and during World War I he sponsored the War Risk Insurance Act.

Rayburn became a close political ally of John Nance Garner and in 1932 served as Garner's campaign manager in the race for the Democratic presidential nomination. Rayburn was a major figure in the negotiations that led to the Roosevelt–Garner ticket in 1932. After Roosevelt was elected president, Rayburn became a leading supporter of the New Deal. As chairman of the Interstate and Foreign Commerce Committee (1931–37), he was instrumental in the passage of the Truth in Securities Act, the bills that established the Securities and Exchange Commission and the Federal Communications Commission, the Public Utilities Holding Company Act, the Emergency Railroad Transportation Act, and, with Senator George W. Norris, the Rural Electrification Act. After 1937, as majority leader and then speaker of the House, Rayburn was responsible for guiding the rest of the basic New Deal through that chamber. During World War II he helped ensure the legislative base and financial support for the war effort, and in the postwar years he opposed what he regarded as reactionary or inflationary legislative proposals, while supporting President Truman's foreign-assistance programs and his basic domestic measures. During the Eisenhower administration, Rayburn worked closely with Senate majority leader Lyndon Johnson. They proved to be a potent team. Rayburn supported his protégé Johnson for the presidency, and his approval was crucial to Johnson's decision to run for vice president with John F. Kennedy in 1960. Throughout Rayburn's career he was a strong supporter of the Democratic nominee for president, a position that often placed him in conflict with the conservative wing of the state Democratic party. That conflict was most intense in the 1950s, when he supported Adlai E. Stevenson for president, even though most state elected officials supported Eisenhower.

Rayburn was regarded in his time as more of a "middle-of-the-roader" than a liberal or "New Dealer." Although he was viewed as a loyal "party man," he exercised an independence of action that occasionally cut sharply across party aims, and though his complete mastery of the political process made him a formidable congressional adversary, his fairness brought him respect from both sides of the aisle. Rayburn's personal integrity was legendary: he accepted no money from lobbyists, he went on only one congressional junket (he paid his own way), and he even refused travel expenses on speaking tours. He brought numerous projects to his Northeast Texas district, including rural electrification, farm-to-market roads, Lake Texoma, Lavon Lake, several smaller lakes, the McKinney VA hospital, the

Bonham Veterans Domiciliary (later named for Rayburn), and air force bases. In 1949 "Mr. Sam" was awarded the $10,000 Collier's award for distinguished service to the nation, and this award became the basis of an endowment for establishing and maintaining the Sam Rayburn Library at Bonham. The library, completed in 1957 and dedicated by former president Truman, housed Rayburn's papers until they were moved to the Center for American History at the University of Texas at Austin. The Rayburn Library is a study center for American government.

Anthony Champagne and Floyd F. Ewing

Reagan, John Henninger. Texas, Confederate, and United States political leader; b. Sevier County, Tennessee, 8 October 1818; d. 6 March 1905 (buried in Palestine); m. Martha Music (1844; d. 1845); m. Edwina Moss Nelms (1854; d. 1863); 6 children; m. Molly Ford Taylor (1866); 5 children. Reagan attended three academies in Tennessee and in 1838 moved to Natchez, thence to Texas. Soon after arrival he became involved in the Cherokee War and, on 15 July 1839, participated in an engagement in which the Indians were routed and their leader, Chief Bowl, was killed. Reagan worked as a deputy surveyor and frontier scout before being elected a justice of the peace and captain of a militia company in Nacogdoches. In 1846 he procured a temporary law license and opened an office at Buffalo on the Trinity River. The same year, he was elected the first county judge of Henderson County. The next year he became a member of the state legislature. He ran unsuccessfully for the state Senate in 1849. In 1852 he won an election called after the judge of the Ninth Judicial District died. After 1855 Reagan became increasingly prominent. In East Texas he helped the Democratic party defeat the surging Know-Nothings. He was reelected judge in 1856. In 1857 the Democrats nominated and elected him United States congressman from the Eastern District of Texas. In Washington he dealt with the controversy over slavery in Kansas and soon feared for the safety of the Union. Thus in 1859 he assumed the awkward position of officially supporting secessionist Democratic candidate Hardin Runnels against Unionist Sam Houston in the state governor's race while campaigning for his own reelection to Congress on a middle-of-the-road, pro-Union platform. Both Houston and Reagan won impressive victories.

As the Civil War loomed, Reagan resigned his congressional seat and returned to Texas. In Austin on 30 January 1861 he attended the state Secession Convention and met with Governor Houston to persuade him to "submit to the will of the people" and recognize the convention. Texas withdrew from the Union on 2 February, and two days later delegates elected Reagan to the secession convention at Montgomery, Alabama. Within a month Reagan was appointed postmaster general of the Confederacy, whereupon he raided the United States Post office of its documents and Southern personnel. Upon the selection of Richmond as the Confederate capital (1861), he began seeking ways to make his department self-sufficient by 1 March 1863, as prescribed by the Confederate Constitution. He therefore abolished the franking privilege and raised postal rates. He also cut expenses by eliminating costly routes, inducing competition for mail runs, and employing a smaller, more efficient staff. He was even able to persuade railroad executives to cut transportation charges in half and accept Confederate bonds in whole or partial payment. Although such stringent measures were necessary, the public became dissatisfied with Reagan, despite the fact that

Union armies had disrupted routes, demolished postal facilities, and interrupted mail with increasing frequency. At the end of the war, on 9 May 1865 near Abbeville, Georgia, Jefferson Davis, Francis R. Lubbock, and Reagan were captured. Reagan and Vice President Alexander Stephens of Georgia were sent to Fort Warren in Boston harbor, where for the next 22 weeks Reagan was in solitary confinement. After reading Northern journals and newspapers that revealed the depth of animosity and bitterness toward the South, he wrote an open letter to the people of Texas asking them to recognize the authority of the United States, renounce secession and slavery, and, if commanded by the federal government, extend the "elective franchise" to former slaves. Otherwise, he predicted, Texas would face the "twin disasters" of military despotism and universal black suffrage. After his return to Texas in December he found himself politically disinherited because of the Fort Warren letter. He retired to Fort Houston, his family home at Palestine, and farmed his neglected fields.

After the events of Reconstruction validated Reagan's warning, however, he became respected for his perspicacity and became known as the "Old Roman," a modern-day Cincinnatus who had sacrificed popularity and political power on behalf of his fellow Texans. He and other Democrats worked to regain power and restore political harmony. Their efforts resulted in the 1873 election of Democrat Richard Coke. Reagan was granted amnesty, and his full citizenship was restored. In 1874 he received the Democratic nomination for the First Congressional

John Henninger Reagan. Library of Congress; BH-832-29190.

Approaching Herd, by Frank Reaugh, 1902. Oil. 23¼" × 48½". Courtesy Panhandle–Plains Historical Museum, Canyon, Texas. Reaugh sketched the open rangeland surrounding his family's home, gained fame as the artist of the Texas longhorn, and painted some 7,000 works.

District and was easily elected. From 1875 to 1887 he served in Congress. In 1875 he was a delegate to the convention that framed the Constitution of 1876. In Congress he chaired the Committee on Commerce, which was responsible for passage of the Interstate Commerce Act in 1887. The law, which represented fulfillment of many years of effort for Reagan, regulated railroads through a five-man commission and included provisions against pooling and rebates. Although the law was an effort to control the railroad industry, Reagan had the support of some railroad groups, as well as independent oilmen, merchants, and farmers across the country who believed that the Interstate Commerce Commission would stabilize rates and end undue competition. As further appreciation for his legislative record Texans elected Reagan to the United States Senate in January 1887. Before the end of his term, Governor James S. Hogg persuaded him to resign his Senate seat and accept the chairmanship of the newly formed Railroad Commission. As Reagan led the Railroad Commission, it served not as a neutral regulator of Texas railroads but more as an institution capable of aiding the state's manufacturers and thus directing the growth of the state's economy. He accomplished this effort by having the commission set rates for Texas railroads that, in effect, created tariff barriers against products from other states and fostered native Texas industries. The commission survived a Supreme Court ruling in 1894 and thereafter became an even more vigorous supervisor of Texas railroads. Reagan ran unsuccessfully for the 1894 Democratic nomination for governor. He remained chairman of the Railroad Commission until his retirement in January 1903. In the latter part of his life Reagan was much concerned about recording history as well as preserving his heritage. In 1897 he helped found the Texas State Historical Association. After retirement he worked for two years to complete his *Memoirs* (published in 1906 and reprinted in 1968). *Ben H. Procter*

Reaugh, Frank. Artist; b. Charles Franklin Reaugh (pronounced "Ray"), Morgan County, Illinois, 29 December 1860; d. Dallas, 6 May 1945 (buried in Terrell). The family's original Irish name was Castlereaugh. In 1876 Frank and his parents settled near Terrell. Reaugh became aware of the writings of naturalists Louis Agassiz and John Burroughs and began sketching for amusement at an early age. His subjects were the open rangeland that surrounded the family homestead and the free-roaming longhorn cattle found there. He also used the family's oxen, Tom and Jerry, as models for detailed anatomy studies. Reaugh studied at the St. Louis School of Fine Arts and at the Académie Julian in Paris (1888–89), where he visited the Exposition Universelle. He went to Holland, probably to see Anton Mauve's work and that of others of the "Hague School." He returned to Texas in the summer of 1889 and immediately set out on a sketching trip. In 1890 he moved with his parents to Dallas, where he opened his first art studio, the Ironshed, sometimes called Old Ironsides, behind his parents' home. During the next two decades, Reaugh exhibited his paintings in Boston, Washington, at the Art Institute of Chicago, the Pennsylvania Academy of the Fine Arts in Philadelphia, the National Academy of Design in New York, and the State Fair of Texas. He also exhibited works at the World's Columbian Exposition in Chicago in 1893 and the Louisiana Purchase Exposition in St. Louis in 1903. Two of the 44 paintings sold at the Chicago Fair were Reaugh's. Beginning in the late 1880s he painted primarily in pastel. He used some of his earlier sketches for pastel studies. One of these, dated 1883, is at the Panhandle–Plains Historical Museum. With this medium, Reaugh was able to capture the subtle shades of color he found in the landscapes and skies of West Texas and New Mexico; these became characteristic of his work. Reaugh's most famous works, the series of seven paintings entitled *Twenty-four Hours with the Herd*, are based on sketches made during the early 1880s on trips to the ranches managed by cattlemen Frank and Romie

Houston. Reaugh probably accompanied them on roundups near Wichita Falls, where he documented the period's cattle drives and thus visually preserved a part of Texas history. He eventually painted some 7,000 works and was hailed as the "Dean of Texas Artists." Reaugh was also an inventor and photographer. He took several hundred photographs as studies for his paintings. In 1904 he patented a "cooling mechanism for explosive engines" and in the following year had several other patents pending. He crafted his own pastels, drawing paper, and pastel board. He designed picture cases, a portable easel (1906), the moldings used to frame many of his paintings, La Cicada (his bus used on numerous sketch trips), and his second Dallas studio, El Sibil. In 1921 he copyrighted a "Classification Chart for Animals of North America." He served as one of three directors of the Limacon Pump and Motor Company of Dallas, for which he designed and patented the rotary pump. He brought exhibitions to Dallas from other parts of the country, sometimes at his own expense, and donated the first painting to establish the Dallas Art Association, now the Dallas Museum of Art. He also founded the Dallas School of Fine Arts. The largest collections of his works are at the Panhandle Plains Museum in Canyon, at the Harry Ransom Humanities Research Center in Austin, and in the Southwest Collection at Texas Tech University in Lubbock. Other paintings are located in the Dallas Museum of Art, the Dallas Historical Society, and private collections.

Stefanie Wittenbach

Red River. The second-longest river associated with Texas; one of two Red Rivers in the nation. The Spaniards sometimes called the salty, reddish river Río Rojo. In frontier times the stream was called the Red River of Natchitoches and the Red River of the Cadodacho (the Caddo Indians). Randolph Marcy and George McClellan identified the Prairie Dog Town Fork as the river's main stream in 1852. If one accepts their judgment the total length of the Red River is 1,360 miles, of which 640 miles is in Texas or along the Texas boundary. In 1944 Denison Dam was completed on the Red River to form Lake Texoma, in Oklahoma and Texas, once the tenth-largest reservoir in the United States. Principal tributaries of the Red River, exclusive of its forks, include the Pease, Wichita, and Sulphur rivers in Texas and the Washita in Oklahoma. The Ouachita is the main tributary downstream. The Red River of Texas heads in four main branches: the Prairie Dog Town Fork, the Elm Fork, the North Fork, and the Salt Fork. Water from the river's source in Curry County, New Mexico, forms a channel, Palo Duro Creek, in Deaf Smith County, Texas, which joins Tierra Blanca Creek northwest of Canyon to form the Prairie Dog Town Fork of the Red River. This main channel flows east through Palo Duro Canyon, then across the rest of the Panhandle. When it crosses the 100th meridian its south bank becomes the boundary between Texas and Oklahoma. Twelve miles northeast of Vernon the North Fork joins the Prairie Dog Town Fork to form the Red River proper. The Elm Fork enters the North Fork in Oklahoma. The Salt Fork joins the Prairie Dog Town Fork 16 miles northwest of Vernon. At this junction an ancient buffalo trail and the Western Trail once crossed the stream. Below the junction of the North Fork and the Prairie Dog Town Fork, the Red River continues to mark with its south bank the state line between Texas and Oklahoma. The river becomes the state line between Texas and Arkansas at the northeastern corner of Texas.

Afterward, it cuts across Arkansas, flows southeast across Louisiana, and enters the Mississippi 45 miles northwest of Baton Rouge. Though the river once emptied completely into the Mississippi, more recently a part of its water at flood stage flows to the Gulf via the Atchafalaya.

In 1541 Vásquez de Coronado explored the upper reaches of the Prairie Dog Town Fork in Palo Duro and Tule canyons. In the summer of 1542 the Moscoso expedition crossed the Red River in Louisiana on its way into East Texas. In 1690 Domingo Terán de los Ríos crossed Texas from southwest to northeast and reached the Red River, possibly as far down as the great raft and the Caddo Indian settlements in the area of present Texarkana. French traders used the river to avail themselves of a lucrative trade with the Caddos and associated tribes by the early eighteenth century. Farther up the river the Taovaya Indians had villages near the site of Spanish Fort in what is now Montague County, villages that in the middle eighteenth century flew the French flag. Diego Ortiz Parrilla, in charge of a Spanish punitive expedition, was defeated at the villages in 1759. In 1769 Athanase de Mézières was appointed lieutenant governor of the Natchitoches District with jurisdiction over the Red River valley. He was to suppress the traffic in stolen horses and Indian captives centered in the Taovaya villages, whose inhabitants by 1772 were trading with Englishmen from the east and Comanches on the High Plains. In 1778 Mézières visited the Red River villages and proposed a Tlaxcalán Indian settlement among them. Neither this proposal nor a suggestion in 1792 that a Spanish mission be built on the Red River was carried out. In 1841 the Texan Santa Fe expedition mistook the Wichita River for the Red River. In 1852 Marcy commanded an exploring expedition to the headwaters of the Canadian and the Red rivers, and a year later published a report on the trip, *Exploration of the Red River of Louisiana in the Year 1852*. The Red River Indian War (1874–75) ended conflict with Indians in the area.

The Red River has been a boundary almost since the first Europeans came to the area. In the 1700s the river was generally regarded as the dividing line between France and Spain, and a royal cedula in 1805 proclaimed it the northern and eastern boundary of the Spanish province of Texas. After the Louisiana Purchase by the United States, several American expeditions were sent up the Red River, and a struggle began between the United States and Spain over where the boundary should be. In 1804–05 William Dunbar explored the river as far up as the mouth of the Washita. In 1805 Dr. John Sibley supplied the United States with a detailed description of the area up the river and westward as far as Santa Fe. The Red River was again formally set forth as the northern boundary of Texas in the Adams–Onís Treaty of 1819. Illegal infiltration continued across the river into Texas until the opening to Anglo-American colonization in 1821, when the river became the thoroughfare by which pioneer settlers moved into Texas. Others came down the military road to Fort Towson and crossed the river at Jonesborough and Pecan Point. Many settlers along the river raised cotton in the rich blackland of Northeast Texas, despite its tendency to overflow, and the Red River County area was sufficiently settled to send delegates to the Convention of 1836. The Republic of Texas recognized the Red River as the national boundary with the United States (1836). In the Greer County case, the U.S. Supreme Court ruled that a disputed 16,000-square-mile strip of land did not belong to Texas (1896). The quarrel in that case was really a dispute about which fork of the river was the main stream. A quarter of a century later another argument between Texas and Oklahoma occurred when oil was discovered in the bed of the river. With the extension of the Burkburnett Townsite pool, known as the Northwest Extension, it was discovered that a part of the pool lay in the bed of the Red River. This brought up the old question of Indian headright titles and caused a controversy that reached the Supreme Court and resulted in fixing the boundary of Texas at the bluff on the Texas side. Militia of both Texas and Oklahoma, together with the Texas Rangers, engaged in several battles. The bridge was burned, oilfield equipment destroyed, and property confiscated.

The Red River has been significant also in commerce and transportation. Though its variable current and quicksands menaced settlers, gateways into Texas were established at Pecan Point and Jonesborough in Red River County, Colbert's Ferry and Preston in Grayson County, and Doan's Crossing in Wilbarger County. Indian trading posts on the river became the termini of important trails. In 1836 Holland Coffee had a post on the Oklahoma side at the mouth of Cache Creek; in 1837 he settled at Preston Bend in what is now northern Grayson County, Texas. Abel Warren had a post in northwestern Fannin County in 1836, one on the Oklahoma side of the river near the mouth of Walnut Creek in 1837, and a later one at the mouth of Cache Creek. The Central National Road of the Republic of Texas was surveyed to reach the Red River six miles above Jonesborough at Travis G. Wright's landing, then the head of navigation on the river. In 1853 Colbert's Ferry was opened across the river in northern Grayson County for the route that was subsequently used by the Butterfield Overland Mail. Early crossings were made at Rock Bluff, Doan's Crossing, and Colbert's Ferry. As far as navigable, the river provided an outlet to New Orleans from Northeast Texas, and it became a highway for cotton, farm products, and eventually cattle boats. Sternwheelers, sidewheelers, and showboats plied the river alongside keelboats and pirogues. Before the railroad era, steamboats regularly navigated the Red River from New Orleans to the site of present Shreveport, but navigation of the upper river was hampered by the "great raft," a mass of driftwood and trees that obstructed the channel for 75 miles. In 1834–35 Capt. Henry M. Shreve removed the raft, but the river was not kept clear, and by 1856 the logjam again obstructed the river for 30 miles above Shreveport, backed up the waters of Big Cypress Creek to form Caddo Lake, and so made Jefferson the principal riverport of Texas until the removal of the raft again in 1874.   *Diana J. Kleiner*

Red River Army Depot. Also known as the Red River Ordnance Depot; activated in August 1941 following government purchase of 116 farms and ranches just west of Texarkana. The base includes 50 square miles and approximately 1,400 buildings and structures. Its mission is to receive, store, and issue gun-motor carriages, ammunition, explosives, supplies, and equipment for combat vehicles and various types of demolition equipment and supplies for the United States Army Corps of Engineers. It also serves as a major army maintenance point for rebuilding vehicles and other types of military ordnance. Construction was initially hampered by housing shortages and lack of equipment, but final construction was permanent. The depot was consolidated with the Lone Star Ordnance Plant to form the Texarkana Ordnance Center in April 1943. From its activation through 1945,

the base received 2,482,189,387 pounds of material and shipped 1,539,954,000 pounds. In the early 1990s the depot had a small number of military personnel and some 4,300 civil service employees.   *Christopher Long*

Red River Campaign. A Union Civil War campaign, March to May 1864. After the fall of Vicksburg and Port Hudson, President Lincoln authorized a campaign against Shreveport, Louisiana, a major supply depot and gateway to Texas. Though the operation was opposed by generals Grant, Sherman, and Banks, it was favored by General in Chief Henry Halleck. Banks, commander of the Department of the Gulf, was engaged in operations against the Confederacy along the Texas Gulf Coast. Under some pressure from Halleck, Banks concentrated his forces on a campaign to secure the area along the Red River to Shreveport. Objectives included preventing a Confederate alliance with the French in Mexico, denying supplies to Confederate forces, and securing cotton for northern mills. By 1863 Confederate general Richard Taylor, with his headquarters in Alexandria, was aware that Union operations up the Red River were under consideration as a means to penetrate the Department of Texas. The river was navigable by steamship for as much as six months of the year and could provide for cooperative army and naval operations. It could support shifting bases as an invading force pressed into the interior. Taylor made his concerns known to Gen. Edmund Kirby Smith, commander of the Trans-Mississippi Department, and through him, to President Davis. Taylor began to establish supply bases up the Red River; this included the rehabilitation by Walker's Texas Division of Fort DeRussy near Simmesport, Louisiana. He began to warn citizens of the impending operations, and to limit the sale of cotton to speculators who were selling to Northern buyers. After failing to stem significantly the sale of cotton, Taylor ordered that all bailed and seeded cotton be burned.

In the spring of 1864 Banks began to gather his forces—an army of about 17,000—for a march to Alexandria, Louisiana, where he was to join a 10,000-member troop detachment from Sherman's Mississippi command and a 15,000-member troop detachment under Gen. Frederick Steele. The detachment from Sherman's Army of the Tennessee was under the command of Gen. Andrew J. Smith. Smith's forces, escorted up the Red River by a fleet of ironclads and gunboats under Adm. David D. Porter, disembarked at Simmesport and captured the partially completed Fort DeRussy on 14 March. Smith and Porter occupied Alexandria two days later. Banks arrived on 25 March, a week late. Steele was delayed and was too late to take part in the campaign. The movement of the Union forces up the Red River was slowed by unseasonably low water levels, which hampered Porter in getting his ships over the rapids. Taylor, in command of the Confederate forces opposing Banks, was retreating upriver as he awaited Confederate troops that were on the way to assist him. Taylor's forces consisted of Maj. Gen. John George Walker's Texas Division, Col. William Vincent's Second Louisiana Cavalry, and William Mouton's Louisianans, with a small brigade of Texans under the command of Brigadier General Polignac; reinforcements of cavalry and infantry were coming from Texas. On 21 March the Federals captured 250 of Vincent's men near Henderson Hill after a small skirmish. Brig. Gen. Thomas Green's Texas cavalry joined Taylor at Pleasant Hill. Green was placed in command of Taylor's rear guard, and Taylor fell back to Mansfield. The Union forces had reached the Natchitoches area by 2 April, and remained there until 6 April, when they took a road toward Shreveport through Mansfield. Banks was unaware that another road followed the river and would have allowed support from the Union gunboats. The column was led by the cavalry, under Brig. Gen. Albert L. Lee; following were a large supply train of some 350 wagons, the Thirteenth Corps, the Nineteenth Corps, and a force under Gen. A. J. Smith. On 7 April, three miles north of Pleasant Hill, Lee's cavalry skirmished with Green's rear guard. The next day, the Union column was strung out single file along some 20 miles of road when it encountered the Confederate force about three miles south of Mansfield. Upon contact with the Confederate forces, General Banks came up the column and assumed command. He ordered reinforcements under Maj. Gen. William B. Franklin from the rear, but they were delayed by road congestion. Before the reinforcements could reach the front, General Taylor, with a total force of 8,800, attacked. The Federals, even with Franklin's arrival, were routed. The battle of Mansfield may have been the most humiliating defeat of the entire war. The Union forces of 12,000 had 700 men killed or wounded and 1,500 taken prisoner; 20 Union artillery pieces and 200 wagons were captured, and almost 1,000 horses and mules were lost. The Confederate army of 8,800 had 1,000 killed or wounded.

Banks fell back to Pleasant Hill. William H. Emory and the Nineteenth Corps moved up and met Taylor's pursuing forces at Pleasant Grove. On the late afternoon of 9 April the Confederate forces attacked. They were repulsed and retired from the battlefield. During the night, Banks gave the order to retire to Grand Ecore, Louisiana. The expedition seems to have been abandoned at this point, as the retreat continued down the Red River. The Union forces, especially those under the command of Gen. A. J. Smith, looted, burned, and destroyed everything in their path as they moved south. Admiral Porter, under harassment, also retreated down the river, and on reaching Alexandria he was once more slowed by low water over the rapids. Army engineer Lt. Col. Joseph Bailey constructed a series of wing dams that permitted Porter and his boats to pass on 13 May. That same day A. J. Smith's troops burned the city of Alexandria to the ground. Taylor continued to harass the retreating Union army, with the final skirmishes of the Red River campaign occurring at Mansura, Louisiana, on 16 May and at Yellow Bayou on 18 May.

Art Leatherwood

Red River Expedition. The first (1806) major scientific probe into the American West to be led by civilian scientists and include an academically trained naturalist. As part of his master plan for the exploration of the West, President Jefferson considered the Red River expedition second in importance only to Lewis and Clark's investigation of the Missouri and Columbia rivers. Though it was billed as a scientific survey, the project had strong commercial and diplomatic overtones and became both an element in the boundary dispute with Spain and a source of embarrassment for the Jefferson administration. By sending an American force up the Red River Jefferson hoped to confirm reports that the Red might provide a commercially viable watercourse to Santa Fe, to woo the region's Indians to the American camp, and to test the Louisiana Purchase's disputed western border with New Spain. Secretary of War Henry Dearborn and Natchez scientist William Dunbar were responsible for directing

the expedition. Planning for the mission, which Jefferson called his "Grand Excursion" to the Southwest, began in 1804. Dunbar made a trial reconnaissance up the Ouachita River during the winter of 1804–05. Extensive personnel searches produced Thomas Freeman, an experienced astronomer and surveyor, as field leader and Peter Custis, a medical student at the University of Pennsylvania and protégé of noted naturalist Benjamin Barton Smith, as naturalist and ethnographer. Capt. Richard Sparks, a 45-man military contingent, and French and Indian guides were employed to escort the civilian scientists in their ascent of the river. Congress appropriated $5,000 for the Red River expedition in 1805, and by late April 1806, when the contingent left Natchez, expenses had grown to $11,000, or three times the original funding of Lewis and Clark.

The dream of tracing a water route to the southern Rockies and winning the Indians to the American side was cut short by political machinations culminating in armed Spanish intervention. Hoping to provoke an international confrontation for personal gain, James Wilkinson had informed Spanish officials of the American designs on the Red River area. While the Americans poled their way up the river, two Spanish military expeditions marched to intercept them. Freeman and Custis entered the Red River on 2 May 1806 and left Natchitoches on 2 June. They were 615 miles up the river on 28 July, when they met a Spanish force under the command of Francisco Viana, who ordered them to turn back. By 1 August the Americans were heading down the river. The expedition's turning point, in what is now Bowie County, Texas, is still known as Spanish Bluff. Though the expedition's failure caused political embarrassment for the Jefferson administration, the bloodless confrontation between American explorers and Spanish troops failed to trigger the war that Wilkinson and Aaron Burr had hoped for. The diplomatic uproar caused Spain to pursue a less confrontational policy, which effectively opened up the Red River country to American traders. Diplomatic tensions resulting from the Red River episode persuaded Jefferson to abandon an excursion up the Arkansas River that had been planned for 1807. The scientific achievement was overshadowed by the more dramatic discoveries of Lewis and Clark and obscured in the controversy over the expedition's premature termination. The principal lasting contributions of the Red River expedition were the documents left by its leaders. As records of nineteenth-century scientific exploration, Freeman's journal and Custis's natural history catalogues provide valuable information on the Indian life and ecology of the region.

Dan L. Flores

Red River Indian War. A series of military engagements fought between the United States Army and Indians of the Kiowa, Comanche, Southern Cheyenne, and southern Arapaho tribes from June 1874 to the spring of 1875. The federal government defaulted on obligations to those tribes specified by the Treaty of Medicine Lodge in 1867. Required rations consistently fell short, gun running and liquor trafficking by white profiteers flourished, and white outlaws from Kansas and Texas rustled cattle in Indian Territory with impunity. Federal Indian agents James Haworth at Fort Sill and John Miles at Darlington, both Quaker missionaries, tried to remedy the situation but received little cooperation from the government. Between 1872 and 1874 white buffalo hunters wiped the herds out on the Cheyenne–Arapaho Reservation. A Comanche medicine man named Isa-tai and

Quanah Parker recruited warriors for raids into Texas to avenge slain relatives. Other Comanche chiefs, notably Isa-Rose (White Wolf) and Tabananica (Sound of the Sun) of the Yapparika band, identified the hide merchants as the real threat to the Indian way of life, and suggested that if Quanah were to attack anybody, he should attack them. A war party headed west into the Panhandle of Texas. The second battle of Adobe Walls occurred between 27 June and 1 July 1874, when a war party of 700 Comanche, Kiowa, Cheyenne, and Arapahoe warriors attacked the buffalo hunters' camp at Adobe Walls on the Canadian River in what is now Hutchinson County. The great majority of the Kiowas stayed away from Adobe Walls and awaited direction at their annual Sun Dance. There, Chief Kicking Bird persuaded most of the Kiowas to return to the agency with him. The principal chief, Lone Wolf, succeeded in recruiting a war party of just 50 men, even with the help of Maman-ti, the only other chief who voted for war. In the "Lost Valley Fight" on 12 July in a shallow draw near Jacksboro, Texas, they confronted a force of Texas Rangers of the Frontier Battalion, commanded by Maj. John B. Jones, and killed two, David Bailey and William Glass. The rangers escaped under cover of night.

After numerous bloody incidents in Texas, Kansas, and the Indian Territory, the federal government organized an attack. The strategy was that of generals Sherman and Sheridan, who commanded the Military Division of the Missouri, in which the trouble had broken out. Peaceful Indians were to be quickly registered at their agencies and confined to the reservation before the hostiles could return. Then, troop columns would enter the field from five different directions, force the warriors into their traditional refuges in the canyons along the Caprock of the Texas Panhandle, and there annihilate them or else force their surrender. This strategy was in force by 25 July. In the battle of Palo Duro Canyon the first column in the field was that of Col. Nelson Miles. His force left Fort Dodge, Kansas, on 11 August 1874. It comprised eight companies of the Sixth Cavalry, four companies of the Fifth Infantry, plus artillery (one Parrott 10-pounder and two 10-barrel Gatling guns), scouts, and Delaware Indian trackers. A number of Miles's scouts were buffalo hunters who had been present at Adobe Walls. Advancing into the Texas Panhandle in a searing midsummer drought, Miles fought a running battle with a force of Cheyennes from 27 to 31 August, before the Indians dispersed and vanished. This was along the Red River in the far lower reaches of Palo Duro Canyon. The battle is sometimes styled the first battle of Palo Duro Canyon, and the subsequent action by Ranald Mackenzie, the second. Miles's and Sheridan's reports depict this action as a significant victory, but later sources indicate that the engagement was at best inconclusive because Miles outran his supply lines and left himself open to attack from the rear.

Confinement of tractable Indians at their agencies resulted in violence at the Wichita Agency at Anadarko, Indian Territory, and caused once-peaceable Kiowas to stampede for the Llano Estacado. On the upper Washita they attacked a wagontrain commanded by Capt. Wyllys Lyman, which was being desperately awaited by Miles (10 September 1874). A scouting party searching for the wagontrain, consisting of Billy Dixon, Camp Supply interpreter Amos Chapman, and four soldiers, was pinned down in a buffalo wallow on the morning of 12 September by the same Indians who had attacked the wag-

ontrain. One of the whites was killed in the Buffalo Wallow Fight and all except Dixon were wounded; all six were awarded the Medal of Honor. The awards of Dixon and Chapman, however, were later revoked because they were not in the regular army. Another of Sheridan's troop columns came east from New Mexico under Maj. William Redwood Price and arrived at the scene on the afternoon of 12 September. Price escorted the wagontrain south, but refused aid to the scouts in the buffalo wallow, an act for which Miles censured him and assumed command of Price's troops. A third column of eight companies of the Fourth United States Cavalry, five companies of the Tenth and Eleventh Infantry, and an assortment of scouts including Seminole, Lipan Apache, and Tonkawa Indians, assembled at a base camp on Catfish Creek, about 150 miles west of Fort Griffin. Under the command of Colonel Mackenzie this group fought a skirmish in Tule Canyon on 26 September. Two days later Mackenzie outwitted a large force of Kiowas under Maman-ti, Comanches under a chief named O-ha-ma-tai, and Cheyennes under Iron Shirt, who had taken refuge, trapping them with their families in their main hideout in upper Palo Duro Canyon. In a daring dawn attack down the steep canyon wall, Mackenzie's troops killed only two or three Indians, but captured and torched several entire villages and slaughtered over a thousand captured Indian ponies.

This action broke the back of much of the Indian resistance. The warriors, dismounted and short of supplies, began drifting back to their reservations. The weather during the fall turned unusually wet, and the Indians still at large referred to the miserable pursuit as the "Wrinkled Hand Chase." On 8 November 1874, Lt. Frank Baldwin led a detachment from Miles's column and destroyed a large Cheyenne camp at the headwaters of McClellan Creek, where he rescued two of the German sisters, Julia and Addie. Numerous smaller actions were fought throughout the autumn and winter of 1874–75, and the troops were joined by others from Fort Sill, commanded by Lt. Col. John W. Davidson, and from Fort Griffin and Fort Richardson, commanded by Lt. Col. George Buell. Surrenders increased in number until the last holdouts, Quahadi Comanches under Quanah Parker, surrendered to Mackenzie at Fort Sill, Indian Territory, on 22 June 1875. Previously, on 28 April 1875, about 72 captured chiefs had been sent by Sherman to Fort Marion, Florida, where they were held until 1878. The Red River Indian War, characterized by supply problems on both sides, saw the virtual extinction of the southern herd of buffalo, the final subjugation of the powerful Comanche, Kiowa, and southern Cheyenne Indians, and consequently the opening of the Texas Panhandle to white settlement. The advent of the ranching era followed swiftly.

James L. Haley

Red River War. An interstate "war" in July 1931, occasioned by the opening of a new free bridge across the Red River between Denison, Texas, and Durant, Oklahoma. On 3 July the Red River Bridge Company, a private firm operating an old toll bridge that paralleled the free span, filed a petition in the United States district court in Houston asking for an injunction preventing the Texas Highway Commission from opening the bridge. The company claimed that the commission had agreed in July 1930 to purchase the toll bridge for $60,000 and to pay the company for its unexpired contract an additional $10,000 for each month of a 14-month period in which the free bridge might be opened, and that the commission had not fulfilled this obligation. A temporary injunction was issued on 10 July, and Texas governor Sterling ordered barricades erected across the Texas approaches to the new bridge. However, on 16 July Governor William (Alfalfa Bill) Murray of Oklahoma opened the bridge by executive order, claiming that Oklahoma's "half" of the bridge ran lengthwise north and south across the Red River, that Oklahoma held title to both sides of the river from the Louisiana Purchase treaty of 1803, and that the state of Oklahoma was not named in the injunction. Oklahoma highway crews crossed the bridge and demolished the barricades. Sterling responded by ordering a detachment of three Texas Rangers, accompanied by Adjutant General William Warren Sterling, to rebuild the barricades and protect Texas Highway Department employees charged with enforcing the injunction. The rangers arrived on the night of 16 July. The next day, Murray ordered Oklahoma highway crews to tear up the northern approaches to the stilloperating toll bridge, and traffic over the river came to a halt. On 20–21 July mass meetings demanding the opening of the free bridge were held in Sherman and Denison, and resolutions to this effect were forwarded to Austin. On 23 July the Texas legislature, which was meeting in a special session, passed a bill granting the Red River Bridge Company permission to sue the state in order to recover the sum claimed in the injunction. The bridge company then joined the state in requesting the court to dissolve the injunction, which it did on 25 July. On that day the free bridge was opened to traffic and the rangers were withdrawn.

Meanwhile, a federal district court in Muskogee, Oklahoma, acting on a petition from the toll-bridge company, had enjoined Murray from blocking the northern approaches to the toll bridge. Murray, acting several hours before the injunction was actually issued, declared martial law in a narrow strip of territory along the northern approaches to both bridges and then argued that this act placed him, as commander of the Oklahoma National Guard, above the federal court's jurisdiction. An Oklahoma guard unit was ordered to the bridge, and Murray, armed with an antique revolver, made a personal appearance in the "war zone," as the newspapers called it. No attempt was made to enforce the Oklahoma injunction, but when the free bridge opened, Murray directed the guardsmen to permit anyone who so desired to cross the toll bridge. On 27 July Murray announced that he had learned of an attempt to close the free bridge permanently, and he extended the martial-law zone to the Oklahoma boundary marker on the south bank of the Red River. Oklahoma guardsmen were stationed at both ends of the free bridge, and Texas papers spoke of an "invasion." Finally, on 6 August 1931, the Texas injunction was permanently dissolved, the Oklahoma guardsmen were withdrawn to enforce martial law in the Oklahoma oilfields, and the "war" was over. The controversial free bridge was dynamited on 6 December 1995, to make room for a new one, which has given rise to no battles so far.

Lonn W. Taylor

Reese Air Force Base. Fourteen miles west of Lubbock; a center for undergraduate pilot training for the United States Air Force. In 1941 the War Department announced that a flying installation would be built on 2,000 acres that had been offered by the city of Lubbock. The base was probably originally named Lubbock Army Air Corps Advanced Flying School. Construction began in August 1941, and in November Lt. Col. Thomas L. Gilbert

arrived to assume command of the base. The first students arrived in February 1942. The base was renamed Lubbock Army Flying School in February 1943 and Lubbock Army Airfield two months later. Aircraft flown from the base during World War II included the T-6 Texan, the AT-17 Bobcat, and the AT-9 Jeep. The base was closed on 31 December 1945, after graduating more than 7,000 pilots. Some barracks were converted to veterans' housing, and national guard, air reserve, and naval reserve units took over other buildings. The base was reactivated in 1949 as a multiengine pilot-training base and called Lubbock Air Force Base. In November of that year it was renamed Reese Air Force Base, in honor of 1st Lt. Augustus F. Reese, Jr., a native of nearby Shallowater, who was killed in action during World War II. The main aircraft used was the TB-25 "Mitchell" bomber, which was used to train student officers and aviation cadets. In 1959 the base was converted to single-engine jet training. The last TB-25 to fly at Reese is on display at the main entrance to the base. Reese has always functioned as a base for training pilots for the United States Air Force. In 1952 international students from Allied nations were added.

Steven G. Gamble and Ruedele Turner

Refugio, Texas. County seat of Refugio County; on the north bank of the Mission River. The site was a favorite camping ground of the Karankawa Indians, who developed a permanent village there known to the Spanish as Paraje de los Copanes (Place of the Copanes, a Karankawan tribe). In 1795 Nuestra Señora del Refugio Mission was moved to the site. The Refugio Mission, the last Spanish mission to be secularized after the area became part of Mexico, operated continuously until February 1830. By then, at least 100 Mexicans lived on ranchos in the immediate vicinity, and a village existed around the mission. In 1831 James Power and James Hewetson acquired the rights to the old mission building and the town that surrounded it, and that same year the villa of Refugio was officially established. The villa became the center of Refugio Municipality in 1834. On 14 March 1836, during the Texas Revolution, the battle of Refugio was fought at the town; most of the inhabitants subsequently fled to Victoria, Goliad, and other areas to avoid retribution. When Refugio County was organized after Texas gained its independence, Refugio became the unofficial county seat, but the population remained depleted until about 1842 because of the continuing threat of Mexican raids. Although Refugio was first incorporated in 1837, it had no government until 1842, when the town was reincorporated, and settlers began to return to the area. A post office was established at Refugio in 1847. In 1859 the ruins of the old mission were still the most distinguishing feature of the town, which by that time included three dry-goods stores, a boardinghouse, three churches, and two schools. The town declined after the beginning of the Civil War. The city council stopped holding meetings in 1861; by the end of the war the town had almost disappeared. Refugio had no government at all until 1868, when Moses Simpson moved in from Copano and performed the role of a town council by himself. In the late 1860s and early 1870s saloons and gambling houses were established in Refugio, giving it a reputation as a "free and easy" place, which attracted gamblers, drifters, and criminals. St. Mary's and then Rockport became county seat in 1869. In 1871, when Aransas County was formed from part of Refugio County, the government of Refugio County returned to Refugio. The town council was reorganized in 1874, and Refugio began to revive as it became a marketing and shipping center for the hides, wool, cotton, and livestock produced in the area. By 1884 the town had grown to a population of about 1,000. Without a railroad Refugio had difficulty competing with other towns in the region, however, and shrank again during the 1890s; in 1900 there were 699 people living there.

About 1902 the St. Louis, Brownsville and Mexico Railway began making surveys of the area, and fearing that the railroad would bypass their town unless paid a $30,000 "bonus," leading citizens organized to raise the money. Ultimately, the town paid the railroad $18,000 in cash and half of the town's common lands for a railroad connection, and by December 1905 the tracks had been laid and a depot built about a mile from the city. The discovery of oil in Refugio County in 1928 led to a population boom in the city and rapid development. In 1925 Refugio had an estimated population of only 933, but by 1930 there were 2,019 people living there. That same year the town contracted for a water and sewer system and built its first town hall since the 1850s. A modern schoolhouse was completed in 1934, and by the next year most of the city's principal streets had been paved. By 1941 the town had 120 businesses and a population of 4,077. Refugio continued to grow in the years just after World War II; between 1946 and 1949 about 100 new houses were built in the subdivisions beginning to appear, and by 1950 there were 4,680 people living in Refugio. New projects to modernize and extend the water and sewerage systems were begun during the 1950s, and the city invested in an extensive school-construction program. In 1960 Refugio had 115 businesses and a population of 4,944. The number of residents began to decline after the late 1960s and early 1970s, however, as local petroleum production declined. It dropped to 4,340 by 1970 and to 3,898 by 1980. In 1990 Refugio remained a center for the area's petroleum and petrochemical industries, but its population had dropped to 3,658.

John Leffler

Regidor. An official of the ayuntamiento or Spanish town council. The number of regidors ranged from 4 to 12, depending on the size of the municipality. Spanish law provided for the annual election of regidors, but elections were often not held. Although some regidors were popularly elected, the offices were often sold to the highest bidder, and the proceeds went to the royal government, not to the municipality. Regulations required regidors to be landholders in the town in which they served. They could not involve themselves in areas where there might be a conflict of interest. Their duties were not formally stated, and tradition played a large role in their activities. In general they acted as town councilmen. One of their prime functions was to select the *alcalde ordinario*, who not only served on the ayuntamiento but also functioned as the town's chief executive and local judge. Although the regidors were subordinate in authority to the alcalde, they shared equal votes on the council. The oldest regidor served as chief assistant to the alcalde and acted in his place during the alcalde's absence. A royal decree of 1793 gave each regidor authority over a distinct aspect of public life, such as prisons or weights and measures. The Constitution of 1812 further formalized the officeholding requirements and set a term of two years, but did not fundamentally change the position. During the latter part of the colonial era and under Mexico,

regidors performed their duties in the traditional manner, relatively untouched by political changes in the central government.

Geoffrey Pivateau

Religion. Although it is beguiling to think of Texas as different from the rest of the nation, the state's religious development does not sustain a claim to uniqueness. The Catholic Church was the established religion of Texas until late in the Mexican era, but then declined after the Texas Revolution and remained at a low ebb until sufficient Catholic immigrants arrived from Germany, Ireland, and elsewhere to revive it; the Catholic Church is now the largest religious body in Texas. Otherwise, beginning with the extensive Anglo-American colonization in the 1820s, Texas has reflected impulses typical of Protestant religion in America at large, such as the desire for a Christian Sabbath, enforced if necessary by Sunday closing laws; an effective educational system that operated in tandem with the churches to promote public morality; "temperance," by which was meant prohibition; and an intense hostility toward Catholicism. But Texas was also an extension of the South, and that too has been apparent in its religious ethos, which has generally placed piety and the need for individual redemption ahead of social ethics and the need for corporate morality. Still, like the Catholic Church, Protestant churches in Texas have by no means been oblivious to social concerns. On the contrary, they have been civilizing influences for both the individual and society. They have brought neighbors together in worship, given purpose to life, contributed to a sense of community, promoted sobriety, supported education, encouraged thoughtful discussion on a wide range of societal interests, and helped establish order.

Although Protestantism has dominated the religious life of Texas since the mid1830s, Catholicism was first to penetrate the region. Franciscans entered Texas to Christianize as well as Hispanicize the Indians. Spanish missions, established over a period of more than a century, numbered about 40 and were scattered from Nacogdoches to San Antonio to near the site of Menard. A few endured for more than 100 years, but many lasted only a year or so; seldom were more than 12 in operation at the same time, and virtually all were in disarray by 1800. An invaluable body of literature about the original tribes of Texas is an important legacy of these early outposts of Christianity.

Until almost the end of Mexican Texas, AngloAmericans seeking permission to settle in Texas had to accept the Catholic faith. Moses and Stephen F. Austin, neither of whom seems to have taken organized religion too seriously, readily complied. Although baptized at birth by a Congregational minister in Durham, Connecticut, the elder Austin assured Spanish authorities in 1820 in San Antonio that he was "a Catholic." The son, actually a Jeffersonian Deist who was never formally affiliated with any religious body, likewise satisfied Mexican officials of his Catholicism. Sam Houston was baptized by a priest in 1833.

Lured primarily by economic opportunity, early American settlers obviously could wear whatever religious garb was required. Col. John Hawkins informed Stephen Austin in 1824, "I can be as good a Christian there [in Texas] as I can here [in Missouri]. It is only a name anyhow." For settlers who took oaths more seriously than Hawkins, there was a solution of sorts: an affirmation of one's Christianity usually sufficed. Austin apparently found it useful to assure Mexican officials that his

A church class at St. Cyril and Methodius Catholic Church. Photograph by Jno. P. Trlica. Granger, Texas, 1937. Photography Collection, HRHRC. The Catholic Church gained many members in late nineteenth-century Texas because of immigration from Germany, Czechoslovakia, Poland, France, and Mexico and vigorous efforts on the part of the church.

colonists were good "Christians," but to his credit he also earnestly sought to obey Mexico's religious laws. He repeatedly reminded prospective settlers of the law and tried to avoid trouble by keeping Protestant missionaries out of his colonies. Of special concern were the aggressively evangelistic members of the Methodist Church, whom Austin called "excited," "imprudent," "fanatic," "violent," and "noisy." Apparently it was the missionary Henry Stephenson who prompted Austin's outburst that "one Methodist preacher" would cause more harm for his colony "than a dozen horsethieves."

Austin was rightly convinced that if Protestant evangelists could be held at bay, Mexican authorities would probably ignore private worship services in the homes of Protestants. In fact, Mexican authorities never rigorously enforced the law proscribing Protestant worship. To be sure, Protestant preachers, such as the Baptist Joseph L. Bays, were sometimes arrested, but the attitude of Col. José de las Piedras, the commandant at Nacogdoches, was typical. When informed of a Methodist–Presbyterian camp meeting in 1832, Piedras retorted that unless the worshippers were stealing horses or killing people they were to be left alone. Furthermore, the shortage of Catholic clergy had left a spiritual vacuum that Protestants were eager to fill. From 1810, when the Mexican War of Independence erupted, to 1830, the number of priests in Mexico declined by about 50 percent, and from 1821 to 1836 there was no bishop in Monterrey, the see that included Texas. As late as 1835 there was only two secular

(i.e., diocesan) priests in Texas. Accordingly, Austin's repeated pleas to Mexico for priests to perform baptisms, marriages, and burials brought little more than sympathetic responses. In 1831 Father Michael Muldoon appeared, but his brief stay in San Felipe perhaps served more to confirm the latent hostility of Protestant Texans toward Catholicism than anything else. Muldoon charged $25 for a wedding and two dollars for a baptism, and administered the sacraments on an assemblyline basis. Protestants who received Catholic baptism merely to conform to the law became known as "Muldoon Catholics."

The scarcity of Catholic priests and the absence of Protestant churches combined to produce religious apathy in colonial Texas. Among Anglos, church membership, whether Catholic or Protestant, was negligible, and Sunday was more an occasion for fun and frolic than a time for contemplating eternal truths. An observer wrote in 1831 that Texans "seem to have forgotten that there is such a commandment as 'Remember the Sabbath day and keep it holy,'" for they spent the day "visiting, driving stock, and breaking mustangs." This secular atmosphere obviously pleased some Texans. In 1830, for instance, one early settler approvingly remarked that the region was free of "the shameless strife and animosities" that ordinarily accompanied "the cause of true religion." He continued: "We hear no ravings, and see no rompings, or indecorous and indecent exhibitions under the cloak of a religious assemblage." Of course, the more appalling the reports about religious conditions in Texas, the greater the excitement of evangelical Protestants in the United States. As one scholar aptly observed, the Texas frontier offered an arena in which the godly could battle "the Devil on his own ground." Here was a rugged country where sinners could be snatched from Satan's grasp, a godless society redeemed, and permanent institutions established to carry the struggle against evil into the future. So in defiance of Mexican law, zealous Protestant missionaries furtively slipped into Texas. Near Pecan Point, the Methodist William Stevenson preached the first Protestant sermon in Northeast Texas in 1815. Five years later Bays crossed the Sabine River into East Texas, followed by Sumner Bacon, a Cumberland Presbyterian, in 1829. John W. Cloud, an Episcopalian, was at Brazoria by 1831. Two groups, similar in many ways—Primitive Baptists and Disciples of Christ—brought congregations organized elsewhere into Texas. The Two-Seed in the Spirit Pilgrim Church of Predestinarian Regular Baptists, formed with seven members in Illinois by Daniel Parker in July 1833, moved to a site near La Grange in 1834. These antimissionary Baptists were intensely Calvinistic and fiercely committed to congregational purity. Led by Mansell W. Matthews and Lynn D'Spain, the first Disciples of Christ congregation arrived at Clarksville by way of Alabama, Mississippi, and Tennessee in January 1836. For these followers of Alexander Campbell who wished to "restore" Christianity to its supposed New Testament unity and simplicity, Texas surely posed a mighty challenge. By 1836, with Methodists far ahead of everyone else, Protestant activity was already fairly common in the areas around Nacogdoches and San Augustine, San Felipe, and Houston–Galveston, and at least 33 ministers were in the field—12 Methodists, 13 Baptists, 3 Cumberland Presbyterians, 3 regular Presbyterians, 1 Episcopal, and 1 Disciple.

Although cited in the Texas Declaration of Independence, religion was not a contributing factor to the Texas Revolution. But Texas independence definitely contributed to the advancement of Protestantism. Suddenly freed of all legal restraints, Protestants rapidly sprawled across the new Republic of Texas. By the late 1840s the state had become a grid of Methodist circuits and conferences, Baptist Church associations and conventions, Presbyterian Church presbyteries, and Episcopal parishes of the Diocese of Texas. Like those "upstart towns" described by historian Daniel Boorstin, these were upstart denominations that busily forged organizational structures and aggressively promoted themselves through camp meetings, newspapers, and schools.

Methodists, Baptists, and Cumberland Presbyterians depended heavily upon protracted camp meetings to kindle spiritual fires. Playing upon the emotions, enthusiastic evangelists graphically contrasted the horrors of hell to the joys of heavenly paradise, and aroused penitents often were overcome by excitement. A Houston meeting in the fall 1845 prompted the criticism that "no pen or tongue could give . . . an adequate description of these riotous scenes—a person must see and hear in order to be convinced of their mad extravagancies . . . . [And] they call it revival." Such disparagement notwithstanding, camp revivals, often lasting two to four weeks, served both religious and social needs. They brought a reprieve from the loneliness and tedium of rural and smalltown Texas life. This was particularly the case for women, for whom the daily routine was monotonous and exacting. To maintain regular contact with scattered congregations, Methodists and Presbyterians used itinerant preachers, or circuit riders. This method had advantages as well as disadvantages. Though it enabled a small number of trained clergymen to minister to numerous isolated communities, thereby significantly extending denominational influence, it also enabled congregations to avoid making the necessary financial arrangements to support resident pastors. By contrast, Baptists encouraged obtaining local pastors, an objective accomplished all too frequently with poorly educated clergymen or even laymen.

Along with camp meetings and traveling parsons, newspapers afforded another means of keeping in touch with the faithful. The religious press added a new dimension to denominational "outreach" in the 1840s and 1850s. One who readily grasped the principle was George Washington Baines, Jr., editor of the *Texas Baptist* from 1855 to 1861. Baines asserted that an "ably edited . . . neatly printed and widely circulated" religious paper allowed one to speak "week after week . . . to twice as many thousands as . . . to hundreds in any other way." With publication of the *Texas Presbyterian* in November 1846, the Cumberland Presbyterians were first into this field. They were followed in 1847 by the Methodists and their *Texas Christian Advocate and Brenham General Advertiser*. The Old School Presbyterians issued *The Panoplist and Presbyterian of Texas* in 1855, the year that Baines printed the first copy of the Baptist paper. Not until 1884 did the Disciples of Christ launch the *Firm Foundation*, which was followed six years later by the Episcopalians' *Diocese of Texas* and the Catholics' *Texas Catholic*. These early religious papers were for the most part privately owned, risky ventures. Many of them failed, others merged and moved to more promising locales, and all served partisan denominational and evangelistic interests. The tie between religious journalism and evangelism in the 1840s and 1850s is exemplified by Methodist efforts among German Catholic immigrants. Fueled it seems as much by patriotic fervor as religious zeal, Methodists embarked upon a concerted effort to Americanize and Christianize these "priest-ridden" newcomers. They established missions at Galveston, the port of entry, Houston, and, eventually, New Braunfels, and in July 1855 began printing *Der Deutsche Christliche Apologete*, Southern Methodism's only German-language paper. Concerns about Christian fidelity and national loyalty clearly coalesced in the *Apologete*. "The only way to make these Germans good American citizens," announced one promoter of the paper, "is to furnish them with sound protestant reading."

Although Texas Protestants, especially Methodists, Baptists, and Cumberland Presbyterians, were interested primarily in evangelism, they also devoted some attention to such social matters as education, slavery, and temperance. That Texas was in dire need of temperance was immediately obvious to Martin Ruter, the superintendent of the Methodist Texas Mission, upon his arrival in 1837. Texans had already acquired a reputation for unruliness, and Ruter believed alcohol was partly to blame. Calling attention to the problem of public drunkenness in 1838, he declared "profaneness, gaming, and intemperance" to be the "prevailing vices against which" Texans had "to contend." Methodist, Baptist, and Presbyterian ministers subsequently took the initiative in the war against John Barleycorn. In February 1839 William Y. Allen, an Old School Presbyterian, joined others in founding the Texas Temperance Society at Houston. A featured speaker on this occasion was Sam Houston, whose drinking was well known. Sam Corley, a Cumberland Presbyterian in Northeast Texas, soon joined Allen. The Sons of Temperance, a national organization, entered the state in 1848 and within a year claimed 3,000 members; almost every small town and many rural communities had a local chapter by 1851. Although the state legislature passed a few bills dealing with alcohol in the 1850s, the temperance crusade was just beginning. Nothing less than total prohibition would be acceptable to many clerics.

All the Texas churches valued learning, and so they began establishing schools at an early date. The Catholic Church had conducted schools at missions from the beginning of Texas mission history. Much later, in 1829, Protestant Sunday schools appeared in Austin's colony. Thomas J. Pilgrim, a Baptist layman from New York, initiated the movement at San Felipe. Although Pilgrim's bold affront to Mexican law brought swift action, he later resumed his efforts. Allen joined the cause, and by 1838 Sunday schools were operating in Houston, San Augustine, Nacogdoches, and WashingtonontheBrazos. The first Catholic schools after the demise of the mission schools began in the early 1840s. Except for the Disciples, all the Protestant bodies operated Sunday schools by 1860. Although primarily religious in purpose, these schools generally contributed to the broader intellectual development of communities. Flourishing Sunday schools generated an interest in libraries and academic institutions in general. The American Sunday School Union, for instance, maintained libraries with more than 1,000 volumes in Brownsville and Austin. As for the academic needs of elementary, secondary, and college students, the churches founded a multitude of academies, institutes, colleges, and universities. Between 1836 and 1845 the republic chartered 19 educational institutions, and between 1845 and 1861 the state authorized 117 more. Credit for the vast majority of these facilities goes to Methodists, Baptists, Presbyterians, Catholics, Lutherans, and Episcopalians. Most of these institutions, which were of varied scholastic respectability, sooner or later failed; many were moved, some were consolidated, and all bore the imprint of their respective denominations. Seeking "to drive away the dark clouds of ignorance and superstition and gild the path of Baptists to a brighter and purer and higher state of excellence," as one report read, Baptists alone founded 14 schools between 1845 and 1860 and added another 25 between 1861 and 1900. In January 1840 the Methodists opened the first Protestant college in Texas, Rutersville College, near La Grange. The college, appropriately named in honor of Martin Ruter, was the state's leading educational center until about 1850. Meanwhile, in 1845 the Baptists established Baylor University at Independence, and by the late 1850s it was granting more degrees than all other Texas colleges combined. In 1886 Baylor was moved to Waco and merged with Waco University, which Central Texas Baptists had founded on a coeducational basis in 1861. The Disciples of Christ did not establish a college before the Civil War; they founded Add–Ran College, forerunner of Texas Christian University, in 1873. Before 1861 the Catholic Church had founded at least two institutions that became universities; after the Civil War, Catholic academies, parochial schools, and institutions of higher learning multiplied rapidly.

Religiously inspired centers of higher education did considerably more than indoctrinate future clergymen. They cultivated civic-mindedness by encouraging students to become involved

Garonzik family seder, Dallas, 1903. Courtesy Dallas Jewish Historical Society. Jews entered Texas before it became a republic. Dallas has long had one of the largest Jewish populations among Texas cities.

in the political process; nurtured, within limits, a spirit of critical inquiry; promoted academic opportunities for women, often as coeds; and increased literacy. By 1860, among the state's whites, illiteracy was under 4 percent for men and just over 5 percent for women.

On the overriding concern of the 1850s, slavery, Texas Protestants as well as Catholics were heirs of the Old South. With few exceptions, they defended servitude, saw African Americans as innately inferior, believed evangelization rather than emancipation fulfilled their spiritual obligations to the slaves, justified secession, and supplied chaplains for the Confederacy. A Cumberland Presbyterian probably spoke for most Texans in 1860. "God in the creation of the Negro," he proclaimed, "I think, designed him for a secondary sphere in society that is a sphere of labor and servitude." He thus restated the essence of the *Dred Scott* decision of the United States Supreme Court. With regard to race, the churches in Texas reflected rather than shaped public opinion. Exceptions caused intolerance. Those German Catholics who adopted a resolution opposing slavery in 1854, for instance, only confirmed the suspicion of AngloTexans that the German Catholics were neither Christian nor loyal to the state. Likewise, when Aaron Grigsby, pastor of the Cumberland Presbyterian Church in Jefferson, voiced abolitionist sentiments on the eve of secession, harassment forced him to flee. And in September 1860, when Anthony Bewley, a Northern Methodist missionary, was lynched near Dallas for allegedly encouraging slave insurrections in North Texas, unrepentant Southern Methodists hinted that he had got what he deserved. Splits over slavery had occurred within all the major religious bodies by 1861 except for the Disciples and Catholics. But this was no sign of opposition to slavery in general by Southern Disciples or Catholics. The Disciples' steadfastness reflected, on one hand, Alexander Campbell's success at preventing slavery from becoming a test of church membership, something Presbyterians had attempted but eventually failed to achieve. On the other hand, it would have been difficult for so loosely joined a group as the Disciples to split.

By 1861, with 30,661 members and 410 church buildings, Methodists still remained far ahead of all other religious bodies in the state. With 500 congregations and 280 buildings, Baptists were a distant second. Next came the Cumberland Presbyterians with 6,200 members and 155 places of worship. The other groups were all considerably smaller. The Disciples, who grew dramatically in the 1850s, now had 39 churches, followed by Catholics (33) and Episcopalians (19). Although their growth was impressive, the churches were barely holding their own in comparison to the increase in the general population. Of the 604,215 Texas residents in 1860, no more than about 12 percent were affiliated with any organized religion. By 1906, however, significant changes had occurred. Baptists now represented some 33 percent of the churchgoing public, and the Methodists had declined to 27 percent. Only slightly behind Methodists were the Catholics, whose extraordinary progress in the latter nineteenth century was due not only to an influx of Germans, Czechs, Poles, French, and Mexicans, but also to vigorous efforts by the church. The Disciples, composing about 7 percent of the state's church members, slipped ahead of the Presbyterians, whose adherents totaled approximately five percent. Lutherans, Episcopalians, and several smaller communions completed the picture.

The resurgence of Catholicism in the latter nineteenth century is particularly noteworthy. The shortage of priests and the enormous influx of Americans after Texas independence had promoted Protestant ascendancy. Already poised at the northern and eastern borders, evangelistic Methodists, Baptists, Presbyterians, and Disciples swiftly entered and claimed the terrain as their own, while the Hispanics who had constituted the Catholic Church in Texas fled or became second-class residents, associated as they were with the Mexican enemy. But Catholics never abandoned the field, although the republic posed a problem for the Vatican. To recognize Texas independence would be to offend Catholic Mexico, while not to recognize it would risk the loss of all influence in the new nation. The Vatican never officially acknowledged the republic, but its continuing interest in the region was apparent. It redirected its oversight through Louisiana instead of Mexico. Father John Timon, a Vincentian from New Orleans, surveyed Texas in 1838. Soon thereafter Jean Marie Odin, also a Vincentian, was given leadership; in the 1840s he assembled a cadre of able priests who labored productively among the growing numbers of Germans and Irish. In 1847 Odin became the bishop of the newly formed Diocese of Galveston, which encompassed all of Texas. By 1861, when he left that post to become the archbishop of New Orleans, the Catholic Church was on the rebound in Texas. It had 40 priests, a college, and a number of resident religious orders. The Ursuline Sisters of Galveston, for instance, earned praise for their care of wounded soldiers during the Civil War.

If the Mexican Americans of Texas have overwhelmingly been Catholics, the state's African Americans have just as overwhelmingly been Baptists. In 1860 blacks constituted slightly more than 30 percent of the Texas population, and in 1900 about 20 percent. For white Christians, this African-American concentration simultaneously represented an evangelistic opportunity and a source of alarm. Although black preachers and separate black congregations could be found in antebellum Texas, slaves had generally attended either white churches, where they usually sat in the balcony or rear, or separate services presided over by whites. These arrangements had satisfied the moral obligation of white Christians to share the Gospel with slaves, while dramatizing the blacks' inferiority. Emancipation brought a problem. Should the former slaves be encouraged to stay in white churches? If so, should they be invited to come down from the balconies, engage in church discussions, and share authority with their former owners? In the event, the white churches of Texas were generally no more willing than those elsewhere in the South to embrace blacks as equals. That would have been far more revolutionary than emancipation. Even so, white congregations were sharply divided during the early Reconstruction years over the retention of blacks, and the ensuing debate disclosed unspiritual motives. The white Protestants feared that if unlettered blacks were removed from white congregations, they would not only slip into scriptural error but also fall prey to the flattery of Northern politicians and Catholic priests. In 1868 a Houston Baptist put the case bluntly: to exclude freedmen from white churches would leave them vulnerable "to the combined evil of ignorance, superstition, fanaticism, and a political propagandism more dangerous and destructive to the best interests of both whites and blacks than Jesuitism itself." Supposed Christian duty as well as selfinterest, then, compelled white congregations to "retain the Negroes . . . and control their action" to a certain extent. Just as the antebellum churches had often effected social control by admonishing slaves to be faithful to their masters, they wanted control after emancipation.

Eager to test their new freedom, however, African Americans quickly rendered the debate moot. They withdrew en masse from white-controlled bodies and forged independent institutions. Illustrative was the Trinity Methodist Episcopal Church, Houston's first black congregation. The first Methodist church in Houston had been organized in 1841 with 68 members, almost half of whom were either slaves or free blacks. By the early 1850s the blacks had begun to worship in a separate structure, albeit under a white pastor. From this situation emerged Trinity Church in 1867. Probably because of Baptist democratic polity and congregational autonomy, the overwhelming majority of blacks became Baptists after the Civil War. By 1890 black Baptists numbered 111,138 statewide, while Methodists totaled only 42,214. In 1916 Baptists constituted almost 72 percent of all black church members. This concentration continued. Of the 351,305 African-American church members in 1926, 234,056 were Baptists and 87,926 were Methodists. There were only a few black Catholics, Presbyterians, and so on.

Though it is generally agreed that religion was vital to African Americans, there is much less agreement among scholars about the precise function of the church in their culture. Was the church basically a vessel for enduring aspects of African culture, with the black minister little more than a modern shaman? Was it an example of folk religion, preserving superstitions and practices which had little basis in historic Christianity? Or was it, by virtue of its service to an oppressed people, a truer reflection of Christian ideals than the prosperous, secularized white churches? Was it an aggressive agency in the quest for freedom? Were Negro spirituals subtle protest songs and ministers freedom fighters? Although historians still wrangle over these questions, they usually acknowledge that the black church, which afforded religious, educational, social, recreational, and political opportunities denied blacks in the nation at large, has certainly been an alternative society of sorts. Black congregations in Houston illustrate the point. Seeking to meet the political, recreational, and educational needs of the city's black population, Antioch Baptist Church, founded in 1866, helped organize the Harris County Republican Club in 1869, and three years later joined hands with Trinity Methodist to buy property for Emancipation Park. In 1885 Jack (John Henry) Yates, pastor at Antioch, worked with white missionaries to establish Houston College. Among individual blacks who attained prominence in the religious community was the former slave Richard Henry Boyd, a cowboy and mill hand turned preacher. As much as possible, he wanted African Americans to control their own religious and educational endeavors. To that end, in 1897 he organized the National Baptist Publishing Board, which printed materials exclusively for blacks. As for fiery evangelists, Texas blacks had their own Billy Sundays in the likes of J. Gordon McPherson and J. L. "Sin Killer" Griffin.

The separation of blacks from white churches was paralleled in the late nineteenth century by an emerging concern over "modernist" influences. Thoroughly conservative in theology, most Texas churches were undisturbed by the winds of intellectual change. Nevertheless, a modest freethought movement had taken root in the state's Protestant churches by the early 1880s, and a popular Methodist minister was at its center. After being accused of heretical notions about the Bible and the basic tenets of Christianity, James D. Shaw, pastor of the Fifth Street Methodist Church in Waco, was stripped of his credentials in 1882. He promptly founded the Religious and Benevolent Association, dubbed the "Hell and Damnation Society" by one critic, and in early 1883 launched the *Independent Pulpit*, whose columns carried "the views of . . . independent thinkers on the moral, intellectual, and social questions of the day." A prominent Baptist preacher from nearby Alvarado, Henry C. Renfro, was drawn to the movement, and he, too, was defrocked in February 1884. By the 1920s, as perceived tension between science and religion reached something of a climax, a rigid, intolerant variety of fundamentalism had arisen. Gripped by a beleaguered-fortress mentality, religionists of this persuasion lashed out at imagined enemies. In this climate, only an overriding concern for denominational harmony saved Lee W. Heaton, an Episcopal minister in Fort Worth, from a heresy trial in 1923. The Presbyterian pastor H. G. Kenny was not so fortunate. Among Methodists and Baptists, the conflict focused on college campuses, and J. Frank Norris, pastor of the First Baptist Church, Fort Worth, and a fundamentalist of national stature, proved his ecumenism by hurling charges at professors in both denominations. Except for McMurry in Abilene, all the Methodist colleges came under attack in the 1920s. At Southern Methodist University in Dallas, Norris joined others in faulting scholar John A. Rice for his book *The Old Testament in the Life of Today*. And at Baylor University, Professor Grove Samuel Dow, head of the sociology department, was assailed for his *Introduction to the Principles of Sociology*. Norris was his principal tormentor. That Texas churches and schools weathered the fundamentalist siege, and that Norris eventually was expelled from almost every Baptist body in the state, attests to the moderate nature of the state's religious leadership. Most church leaders and members, especially Baptists and Methodists, were profoundly conservative in theological and social views, but they were not fundamentalists after the fashion of Norris.

Disputes over "modernism" aside, Norris and moderate Protestants easily agreed on temperance, a movement that had

St. John Missionary Baptist Church. Photograph by R. C. Hickman. Dallas, 1954. R. C. Hickman Photograph Collection, CAH; CN 08047. Beginning as early as 1841, blacks founded most of their own churches in Texas. This church in Dallas also served as headquarters for an NAACP convention.

steadily gained momentum in the latter nineteenth century. By 1901 a prominent Texas Baptist even applauded the hatchetwielding antics of Mrs. Carry Nation of Kansas, rationalizing "that the only way to annihilate the saloon is to meet lawlessness with lawlessness." The failure of the Anglo-Protestant majority to achieve statewide prohibition until 1919, however, and then only after World War I and the national momentum for a constitutional amendment, forces a reconsideration of the alleged homogeneity of Texas religion. Baptist and Methodist pervasiveness notwithstanding, religious homogeneity was increasingly more apparent than real by the late nineteenth and early twentieth centuries. In addition to Catholicism, whose Mexican, German, French, Irish, and Italian adherents represented cultural traditions in conflict with Anglo-Protestants on alcoholic consumption, Protestantism itself betrayed deep internal cleavages. Among Baptists, for instance, there were communicants of differing socioeconomic status and varying opinions on the degree of congregational autonomy and the proper means of achieving prohibition. Primitive and Landmark Baptists often took exception to legislated, statewide prohibition because they considered local option more consistent with Baptist tradition. A cursory examination of Texas Baptist life in the late nineteenth century, moreover, would also suggest that controversy was a hallmark of the faith. Within Methodism the Holiness movement revealed tensions between the church's leaders and a segment of the laity. As for the state's Anglo-Protestant political leaders, some favored prohibition, some opposed it. So despite an overwhelming numerical superiority and a seeming homogeneity, Texas Protestants were divided, as the tardy arrival of prohibition suggests.

Although legal success against John Barleycorn came late, the crusade itself was significant in that it brought many church people to social awareness. By 1908, for instance, the Baptist General Convention of Texas, convinced that the tavern was "interlaced . . . into commerce, politics, society, and the administration of law," challenged the churches to become more active

Joe Sierra and his grandson prepare for the memorial of St. Anthony, Ysleta Mission, 1986. Photograph by Bill Wright, ©1986. Courtesy Bill Wright, Abilene.

politically and alert socially. Accordingly, there were expressions of the social gospel in Texas by the early 1900s. Methodists and Baptists prove the point, but Baptists are particularly instructive, for they demonstrate the fallacy of the popular assumption that social Christianity was a byproduct of Northern liberal theology. Despite their intense evangelism and conservative theological views, Baptists increasingly found ample basis for applying the Good News to society. The best exemplar was Joseph Martin Dawson. This longtime (1915–46) pastor of the First Baptist Church, Waco, delivered the first formal series of sermons by a Texas Baptist on social Christianity in 1914 and went on to engage in public controversy over social problems, including racism, throughout his life. Significantly, Texas Baptists gave institutional voice to Dawson's concerns. In 1915 the General Convention established the Social Service Committee, and two years later this committee justified its social emphasis with the exuberant proclamation that "Jesus [Himself] was the great sociologist." From this modest beginning emerged the Christian Life Commission in 1950. Inspired in large measure by Professor Thomas B. Maston of Southwestern Baptist Theological Seminary, this was an activist body dedicated to applied Christianity. Its interests have been a reflection of modern American society. It objected to universal military training in the early 1950s, regularly defended the desegregation and school-prayer rulings of the Supreme Court in the 1950s and early 1960s, approved abortion under limited circumstances, supported sex education, urged a settlement to the Vietnam conflict, grappled with drug abuse, upheld the principle that people were "more important than profit," encouraged businesses to face the problem of air and water pollution, censured "raw violence" and gratuitous sex on television, endorsed bilingual education, sanctioned tax-supported public schooling for the children of illegal aliens, commended programs to rehabilitate Texas prison inmates, and advocated energy conservation.

Among Texas Catholics, Archbishop Robert E. Lucey of San Antonio (1941–69) was one counterpart to this movement. Though thoroughly traditional on matters of church authority, Lucey consistently placed the church on the side of the poor. He championed labor's right to unionize, and within his archdiocese would not permit the use of nonunion laborers for church construction. In support of desegregation, he integrated parochial schools in San Antonio months before the decision in *Brown v. Board of Education* (1954). And in the 1960s farm workers in the Rio Grande valley absorbed his attention. Catholics institutionalized social action in numerous organizations. In 1969, for instance, the Archdiocese of San Antonio founded the Commission on Church and Society, an agency dedicated to racial justice, equality of economic opportunity, job development, and better housing and health services.

At the beginning of the third millenium of Christianity, both change and continuity are evident in the religious heritage of Texas. Most apparent has been the erosion of the secular milieu appreciated by so many Texans of the 1830s or so. Organized religion has grown steadily stronger, and the major denominations today sustain an impressive array of schools, hospitals, and eleemosynary institutions. The Dallas–Fort Worth area alone hosts several seminaries—Perkins School of Theology at Southern Methodist University in Dallas, Brite Divinity School at Texas Christian University in Fort Worth, Southwestern Baptist Theological Seminary in Fort Worth (the world's largest seminary), and Dallas Theological Seminary, which continues to promote the dispensational premillennial views of Cyrus I. Scofield; the University of Dallas trains Catholic seminarians, partly under the aegis of the Cistercian Fathers. As for individual Texans, they are decidedly more religious than their ancestors. Indeed, Texans today belong to organized religious bodies in greater percentages than Americans at large. Whereas about 55 percent of the national population is churched, the state figure is approximately 65 percent. And quite unlike many of those early settlers, contemporary residents actually take religion seriously, as evidenced by polls since the early 1980s. Although only about 44 percent of the population attend church weekly, with Baptists and Catholics being the most frequent, 70 percent reportedly consider religion very important, 54 percent acknowledge having had a "born-again" experience, and 82 percent would look favorably upon a child entering the clergy. One can only wonder what Col. John Hawkins would make of such religiosity. Most of the state's worshipers, approximately 66 percent, are still Protestants, but the configuration has changed considerably in the past century. Representing 9.2 percent of all churchgoers in 1990, the Methodist Church, which dominated the landscape from the 1830s through the late nineteenth century, slipped to a distant third behind Catholics (32.8 percent) and Baptists (29.9 percent). Numerically, the twentieth century belonged to the Baptist Church until 1990, when it was overcome by Catholics. Numerous other bodies, though considerably smaller, function in the state: the Church of Christ (3.5 percent), the Lutheran Church (3.0 percent), the Pentecostal churches (1.9 percent), the Presbyterian Church, USA (1.8 percent), the Protestant Episcopal Church (1.6 percent); the Christian Church (Disciples of Christ), Mormons, and Jews, 1 percent combined; and a few Muslims, Hindus, and Buddhists. In the new millennium Catholics and Baptists will be sharing the terrain with seekers of many persuasions. *John W. Storey*

Remolino Raid. A decisive retaliatory raid against Indian bandits from south of the Rio Grande (1873). Since the Civil War, Indians striking from Mexico into South Texas had stolen tens of thousands of cattle, burned numerous ranches, and murdered scores of settlers. Most of the raiders were Kickapoos who had migrated to Mexico from the United States during the previous quarter century. In return for land grants and annuities from the Mexican government, they promised to help defend that country's northern frontier against marauding Comanches and Kiowas. This alliance with the Mexicans worked so well that soon many Kickapoos had settled near the Rio Grande in Coahuila. They soon discovered that Texas from San Antonio to the Rio Grande was rich in horses, mules, and cattle, and poor in residents to protect them. Stealing was ridiculously simple, and local Mexican government officials abetted the Indians by steadfastly refusing to allow United States troops to pursue the raiders into Mexico. By 1873 the Kickapoos and other Mexican groups had been responsible for an estimated $48 million in property damages and livestock losses in South Texas. Washington was inundated with letters and petitions from settlers. President Grant and Secretary of State Hamilton Fish attempted to find peaceful solutions to the problem by negotiation with the Kickapoos and then diplomatic pressure on the Mexican government, but they failed. The raids continued, and the outcry grew. Finally, in January 1873, Grant ordered the Fourth United States Cavalry under Col. Ranald Mackenzie to move from North Texas to Fort Clark. In April Secretary of War William Belknap and Gen. Philip Sheridan visited Fort Clark and gave Mackenzie instructions to strike at the base of the depredating Indians, which meant crossing into Mexico. Since such an action could have serious diplomatic consequences, Belknap and Sheridan refused to make the orders official; and without anything in writing, the full responsibility for such an action could come to rest totally upon Mackenzie's own shoulders.

For a month Mackenzie secretly prepared for his dangerous assignment. He dispatched trustworthy civilian scouts to spy on three large Kickapoo, Lipan, and Mescalero villages on the banks of the Río San Rodrigo near Remolino, about 40 miles inside Mexico. On 16 May the scouts reported that most of the warriors of the Kickapoo village had ridden off to the west that morning. By 1:00 P.M. the next day, 360 enlisted men and 17 officers, with 24 Seminole scouts and 14 civilians, began to move slowly toward the Rio Grande, and just after sundown the command crossed the river into Mexico. In the darkness the troopers blindly followed their scouts on a winding, tortuous route that avoided all settlements and even isolated ranchhouses. Surprise and speed were essential. Mackenzie wanted to be in position to attack at daybreak, and he pushed his men unmercifully throughout the night. Shortly before sunup on 18 May, having ridden 63 hard miles since crossing the Rio Grande (23 more than the straight-line distance), the raiders reached the Río San Rodrigo about a mile upstream from the three Indian villages. After a short halt to rest the men and water the animals, Mackenzie's troopers spurred their mounts up the stream bank and without hesitation moved against the Kickapoo village (the largest and nearest of the three). The cavalrymen charged by platoons, volley firing as they went, then wheeling out of the way to reload and prepare to charge again. The rear elements dismounted and began to set fire to the canvas teepees and grass huts. The Kickapoos were taken completely by surprise and with so few of their warriors present stood no chance of successfully defending their homes. Some fought like demons but most fled with the soldiers in close pursuit.

In a matter of minutes it was over, and the troopers rode on to the other villages. The Lipan and Mescalero bands had taken flight at the first sound of shots, and the soldiers moved unopposed among their deserted dwellings and set them afire. In minutes, all three villages (a total of around 180 lodges) were totally destroyed. Mackenzie reported 19 Indians killed and 40 women and children taken prisoner. Costilietos, the principal chief of the Lipans, was also taken. Some 65 ponies were captured. Mackenzie lost one man killed and two wounded. At 1:00 P.M., the Americans and their prisoners started for home over a direct route. They reached the Rio Grande at dawn on 19 May without incident. After a night of badly needed rest, the men marched to Fort Clark at a leisurely pace. The response to the raid was immediate and favorable. Although Mackenzie had technically violated Mexican sovereignty and attacked allies of the Mexican government without official orders, Belknap and Sheridan enthusiastically commended his actions, and the Texas legislature extended to Mackenzie "the grateful thanks of the people of our State." The Mexican government did not want to turn the raid into an international issue and after an exchange of notes dropped the matter. As for the border situation, Indian raids all but stopped. Fearing more retaliatory strikes, many bands divided and moved into the mountains. The Kickapoos, in exchange for their wives and children still held prisoner, agreed to return to the United States. By 1874 over half the tribe had resettled at Fort Sill in Indian Territory.

Allen Lee Hamilton

Reptiles. Texas ranks first among the 50 states in numbers of reptilian species, with 35 species of turtles, 61 of lizards, 68 of snakes, and the American alligator. This abundance results from the diversity of habitats within the state and its location in a region where four distinctive biogeographic regions meet, loosely described as eastern, desert, High Plains, and subtropical. Five species (two turtles, two lizards, and the Harter's watersnake) fit none of these categories.

The turtle fauna, which is dominated by freshwater forms, is richest in eastern Texas. Six saltwater species, five sea turtles and the diamondback terrapin, also occur on the Texas coast. Of these perhaps the best known is the Kemp's Ridley turtle. The ornate box turtle (*Terrapene ornata ornata*) is the common land turtle over most of the state. This species, which perishes by untold hundreds each year on the state's highways, is a frequent backyard pet. The only true tortoise in the state is the Texas tortoise (*Gopherus berlandieri*), a species that ranges into southern Texas from Mexico and is on the list of threatened species and thus protected by state law.

The American alligator (*Alligator mississippiensis*) at one time was widely distributed over the eastern part of the state; sightings were recorded as far west as Dallas, Austin, and San Antonio. Today, spotty breeding populations are confined to eastern Texas east of the Trinity River and to coastal areas; rare sightings occur along the Colorado River. Although the species at one time was severely threatened, protection under state and federal law has led to such a significant increase in numbers that limited harvest has been permitted.

Lizards are well represented throughout the state, although the greatest diversity occurs in the west. Certainly the most popular of all Texas reptiles is the horned lizard. The most ubiquitous and widely distributed Texas lizard is the southern prairie lizard, *Sceloporus undulatus consobrinus*, a little spiny lizard with arboreal tendencies in the east but with ground-living habits in the west. Other conspicuous lizards in the western part of the state include the Great Plains skink (*Eumeces obsoletus*), the collared lizard (*Crotaphytus collaris*), and various species of whiptails (*Cnemidophorus*), several of which are unisexual.

Fifteen of the 68 species of snakes in Texas are poisonous. These include the coral snake (*Micrurus fulvius tenere*), western cottonmouth (*Agkistrodon piscivorus leucostoma*), three copperhead species (*Agkistrodon*), and 10 rattlesnakes. The first three of these species, together with two rattlesnakes, are essentially East Texas forms, although the coral snake and cottonmouth both range westward onto the Edwards Plateau and the copperhead occurs as far west as the Davis Mountains. Certainly the most infamous of Texas snakes is the western diamondback rattlesnake (*Crotalus atrox*). This large, dangerous snake occurs over three-quarters of the state, is responsible for over half the cases of poisonous snakebite, and is the culprit in almost all instances of death due to snakebite in Texas. A rich folklore has grown up around this snake, much of which was recorded by J. Frank Dobie in his book *Rattlesnakes* (1966).

Resource collections of state reptiles include the Texas Natural History Collection (Texas Memorial Museum, Austin), the Texas Cooperative Wildlife Collection (Texas A&M University), and the collection of the Strecker Museum (Baylor University). The Texas Herpetological Society, founded in 1939, includes amateur and professional students of amphibians and reptiles and is the oldest state society of its kind in the United States. As of 1988 the following turtles were classified by the Texas Parks and Wildlife Department as endangered: loggerhead, Atlantic hawksbill, Kemp's Ridley, leatherneck, and Big Bend mud. No lizards were classified as endangered, but five snakes were: the speckled racer, Louisiana pine snake, Concho water snake, western smooth green snake, and northern cat-eyed snake.   *John S. Mecham*

Republican Party. The Republican party of Texas originated in the spring of 1867, as Texans responded to the Congressional Reconstruction Act, passed on 7 March. That act required the former Confederate states to fashion new governments and extend the elective franchise to all adult males without regard to race, color, or previous condition of servitude. The law radically altered the struggle for political power in Texas and the rest of the South by integrating African Americans into the political process. The state's Republicans embraced these Congressional demands and pursued the development of a biracial party. Their efforts led to the party's formal organization and the first state convention at Houston on 4 July. Republican leadership came primarily from among antebellum and wartime Texas Unionists, many of whom were supporters of Sam Houston (these were called scalawags by their opponents), recent immigrants from the North (called carpetbaggers), and newly enfranchised blacks. The Unionists dominated the proceedings. Former governor Elisha Pease chaired the convention, and Col. John L. Haynes, the popular commander of the First Texas Cavalry, USA, became the party's first executive-committee chairman. In its first platform, the party advanced an appeal based on loyalty to the Union and the interests of race and class. The platform endorsed the national Republican party and Congressional Reconstruction, demanding the removal of all civil officials who had participated in the Rebellion or who opposed the policies of Congress. Pursuing black and poor white voters, the convention called for a homestead law that would appropriate parts of the public domain to settlers without regard to race, and for a public school system for all the children of the state.

In the summer of 1867 the party secured many county and state offices when federal military officers removed incumbents as "impediments to Reconstruction" and replaced them with Republicans. At this time Pease assumed James Throckmorton's place as governor. These appointments gave Republicans control over voter registration and placed party loyalists in positions to aid local party development, including forming chapters of the Union League. Elections held on 10 February 1868, when party leaders secured a vote favoring a constitutional convention and Republicans gained a majority of seats for the convention, demonstrated the success of the local activity.

In the Constitutional Convention of 1868–69, however, party unity gave way to bitter internal fighting. One faction, called Conservative Republicans, coalesced around Andrew J. Hamilton, prewar congressman and associate of Governor Pease. The Conservatives supported measures favoring private corporations, usually railroads or manufacturing interests, that promised economic development. Possibly to provide economic stability for investment and growth, they advocated the recognition of state and local government actions taken between 1861 and 1868 not in support of the war (the *ab initio* question). Their opponents, known as Radical Republicans, were led in the convention by Edmund J. Davis and Morgan C. Hamilton, A. J. Hamilton's brother. The Radicals supported declaring all acts of the state government after secession null and void from the beginning (*ab initio*), an act that would have restored the public school fund; they also backed dividing the state. In the party convention of 1868, failure to secure inclusion of their issues in the platform led the Radicals to walk out. In the midst of the split, George T. Ruby, a black teacher from Galveston, gained control of the state Union League and delivered its support to the Radicals. Two rival party organizations developed, and the split remained unrepaired in the 1869 state election, when voters considered a ballot listing Conservative and Radical candidates for state office as well as the ratification of the proposed constitution. A. J. Hamilton led the Conservatives and Davis the Radicals. Hamilton obtained endorsements from leading Democratic party politicians, but this support backfired. Some Conservative Republican supporters moved into the Radical camp, and Democrats did not vote in large numbers. As a result, Radical candidates won most of the offices. Davis became governor, and his faction controlled the state Senate and House. Radical legislative majorities sent James Winwright Flanagan and Morgan C. Hamilton to the United States Senate. William T. Clark, Edward Degener, and George W. Whitmore took three of the state's four congressional seats.

The 1869 election returns showed the sources of the new party's electoral strength. The strongest backing came from counties with large black populations. White support came mainly from the German counties of Central Texas, frontier counties south and west of San Antonio, and some counties in Northeast Texas. The sources of white Republican votes were primarily areas that had shown Unionist strength before the war.

Between 1869 and 1874 the Radicals pushed ambitious economic and social programs. They sponsored and secured railroad development financed by state support of railroad bonds, established a system of free schools, instituted a bureau of immigration, and formed the State Police to combat lawlessness. Despite the party's achievements, higher taxes and Republican racial policies produced strong opposition to the administration from Democrats (supported by Conservative Republicans who had reorganized as Liberal Republicans). The Democrats also charged the Republicans with dictatorial practices and corruption. Ultimately, these issues found a response in the electorate. Democrats captured the legislature in 1872, and in the 1873 gubernatorial election Democrat Richard Coke easily defeated Davis. Subsequently, Davis continued to hold control over the party. Under his leadership the party maintained its historic support of black rights and public education. Increasingly, however, the party assumed a position supporting reforms considered to be agrarian, including government restriction on railroads and soft-money policies. After Davis died in 1883, his position of leadership was taken by Norris Wright Cuney, a black politician from Galveston, who kept the party on the course set by Davis.

During the Davis–Cuney years, Republican election success was restricted primarily to the counties with large black populations, where voters supported Republican state candidates and elected Republican local officials. Statewide, however, the Republican electorate could muster no more than 20 to 30 percent of the vote. To gain state offices, Davis and Cuney promoted coalitions with various groups, particularly agrarian protest movements. In 1878 the Regulars endorsed William H. Hamman, the Greenback party candidate for governor, and in 1882 and 1884 they backed George W. "Wash" Jones, an independent. In 1896, despite opposition from national Populist (People's party) leaders, Texas Republicans and Populists united to support Jerome C. Kearby for governor. Fusion seldom succeeded, however, although Jones polled 40 percent in 1882 and Kearby secured 44 percent in 1896. The only major victory came in 1882, when cooperation with Independents sent Thomas P. Ochiltree to Congress.

Within the party, internal strife persisted through the Davis–Cuney years. Federal officeholders were a nagging problem to state leaders. The party's inability to elect state officials or any but an occasional member of Congress meant that national leaders seldom listened to local party officials in filling patronage jobs. Usually, successful candidates received their appointments because of their loyalty to one national leader or another, and they thus owed little to state Republican leaders. As a result, these federal jobholders not only failed to support but often opposed policies such as fusion, which was designed to expand local support, and frustrated the efforts of Davis and Cuney. Individuals who believed that the party should abandon its biracial and agrarian base and build a party based upon whites who supported the national party's economic and foreign policy positions—particularly a protective tariff, sound currency, and expansionism—also challenged Davis and Cuney's leadership. Governor Pease was one of the early backers of the idea that local support could be based on national policy. The idea of abandoning black voters did not fully mature until 1889, however. That year Andrew J. Houston, son of Sam Houston and president of the state League of Republican Clubs, promoted the Lily-White Movement. The group's strength increased from this period, both in the party's traditional stronghold in the northern counties and also in urban areas. The election of 1896 was a turning point in the struggle between the Regulars and Lily-Whites. Cuney failed to back William McKinley's successful bid for the

presidency, thus opening the way for Dr. John Grant, a Lily-White, to take the position of national committeeman from Texas. In 1898, after Cuney died, Grant and the Lily-Whites took over the state convention. The entire state party apparatus came under their control two years later, when Cecil A. Lyon was named head of the state executive committee.

Although the struggle over the party's racial policies continued, with the Cuney faction persisting under the leadership of Edward H. R. Green and William M. "Gooseneck Bill" McDonald, the Lily-Whites maintained control over the state organization.

From 1901 to 1950, under such notable party chairmen as Lyon (chairman from 1901 to 1916) and Rentfro B. Creager (1920–50), the party sought to enlarge its membership by appealing for support from Texans who were sympathetic with the national party's programs. The domestic agenda changed at times, but generally platforms were pro-business. This position was sustained by policies limiting government regulations and expenditures and reducing taxes, while providing aid to businessmen and farmers through extensions of credits and imposition of tariffs. Regarding foreign affairs, especially after World War I, national Republicans stood for a unilateral policy, often tinged with considerable antiforeign sentiment. These years also saw major changes in party organization, especially under Creager's leadership. He was responsible for the establishment of the first state headquarters, with a professional staff assigned to handle fund-raising, press relations, and liaison between state and county leaders. More systematic efforts also were made to develop grass-roots support, including the 1930 organization of the Texas Young Republicans. During the Lyon–Creager years the party survived, but it gathered few additional voters. At times, concern among the state's traditional Democrats with the course of the national party produced Republican converts in presidential elections. In 1928, when the Democrats ran Al Smith, a Catholic, on a platform endorsing an end to Prohibition, enough switched to Herbert Hoover to place the state in the Republican column for the first time ever. The New Deal of Franklin Roosevelt, with its emphasis upon federal efforts to regulate and order the national economy, also turned some Texans in the oil industry against the Democratic party and towards the Republicans, who promised reduced federal regulation.

At the state level, however, almost no change took place. The state Democratic party remained in the hands of conservatives, whose views of the role of government and fiscal policy were almost indistinguishable from those of Republicans. Although tempted at times to abandon national Democratic candidates, party members showed few signs of revolt against local Democratic leaders. Between 1896 and 1950 Republicans elected no one to the United States Senate and only three congressmen. The latter included George H. Noonan from San Antonio (1895–97), Robert B. Hawley of Galveston (1897–1901), and Harry M. Wurzbach of Seguin (1920–31). In the state legislature Republicans never occupied more than one place in the Senate or more than two in the House in any legislative session. Although support for party candidates did not grow between 1900 and 1950, the sources of Republican votes changed. The party's historic core in the state's black belt virtually disappeared. Geographically, Republican votes now came from the Panhandle and from counties to the south and west of a line from northeast

Midland County to northeast Harris County, a region tied both to the oil and gas industry and to traditional Republican voting. Urban counties, where economic conditions and general prosperity produced a heterogeneous community with middle-class, professional, and business groups to offer support for the party, however, provided the greatest number of Republican votes.

The party entered a transitional era after 1950 that lasted until 1978. These years were marked by increasing strength at the polls, but little growth in the number of Texans who identified with the party at the state level. Presidential elections first showed the increasing strength. In 1952 Eisenhower carried the state with 53.2 percent of the vote, more than doubling Thomas Dewey's 24.3 percent in 1948. Thereafter, except in 1964 and 1968, Republican candidates consistently secured more than 48 percent of the state's popular vote in presidential elections. Although never as strong as the presidential candidates, Republican gubernatorial candidates improved over their pre-1950s predecessors. From a low of only 10 percent of the vote in 1954, support for Republican candidates rose to a high with John Cox's 45.8 percent in his 1962 race against John B. Connally, Jr., and then generally reached at least 40 percent thereafter. The party's greatest success in this period was the election of John Tower to the United States Senate in a special election to fill the place of Lyndon Johnson (1961). Tower's election and subsequent career gave the party strong leadership in this transitional period. During this period, the party's urban and geographic bases remained strong. Dallas sent Bruce Alger to Congress repeatedly from 1954 until 1964. In 1966 the party elected two congressmen for the first time since Reconstruction—George H. W. Bush of Houston and Robert D. Price of Pampa. These were joined by a third, James M. Collins of Grand Prairie, in 1968. In addition, urban centers sent more Republicans to the state legislature after a federal court ruling in 1972 abolished multimember legislative districts in the state's cities, thus ending the ability of conservative Democrats to control county politics.

The party's growing strength was partly a natural result of the urbanization of Texas. As late as 1940 the majority of Texans lived in rural areas, but by 1950 the urban population had expanded to 59.8 percent of the state's population, and by 1980 urban dwellers accounted for 79.6 percent of the total. In the latter year residents of the Austin, Dallas, Houston, Fort Worth, and San Antonio metropolitan areas represented by themselves nearly half of all Texans. As these regular Republican strongholds expanded, the party's power in state elections rose as well. Election results also showed that the party's conservative political philosophy also produced new adherents. Its advocacy of state rather than federal regulation of oil and gas naturally attracted Texas oil interests. In 1952 that issue helped spark a revolt within the state Democratic party in which such prominent Democrats as Governor Shivers backed the Republican candidate for president, Dwight Eisenhower. Events in the Eisenhower administration—the federal government's support of desegregation, for instance—led state Republicans to shift their opposition to stronger federal power to an even more general principle. The 1960 state convention set the party's position when it declared opposition to all encroachment on the rights of states and to the growing role of Washington. The convention singled out aid to education, health-insurance programs, welfare, and economic regulations as specific threats. The 1960 platform also reaffirmed the party's historic support of a unilateral

foreign policy, aimed primarily at limiting the growth of Communism, and endorsed a strong military to back up foreign-policy goals. But despite the gains between 1950 and 1978, these years were unsettled ones in state politics. Though voters demonstrated increasing independence from their traditional ties to the Democratic party, they did not firmly identify with the Republicans. As late as 1978 only 150,000 Texans voted in the Republican primary, compared with 1.8 million who voted in the Democratic primary. Statewide election success was not paralleled at the local level, either in district and county offices or in the state legislature.

The election of 1978 marked a new era in the party's history, in which its growing strength took on a more permanent character. After years of Democratic domination, state elections were even fights. In that year William P. Clements, promising to reduce taxes and cut the size of the state government, became the first Republican governor since Reconstruction. He was defeated in 1982 but regained the governor's seat in 1986. In statewide elections Republicans were consistently successful. Phil Gramm held on to Tower's Senate seat after the latter's retirement in 1984. Republican presidential candidates won regularly, while Kay Bailey Hutchison secured the second United States Senate seat in 1993 and George W. Bush won the governorship in 1994. In congressional elections, Republican seats in the House of Representatives climbed from 3 to 9 out of 30. These votes showed not only increasing strength for the party, but also appear to have marked a fundamental shift in voter loyalties. In the 1982 Republican primary, the number of participants increased over the 1978 total from 158,403 to 265,851. This spurt began a steady growth leading to the 1992 primary, in which nearly a million voters participated. At the same time, Democratic primary participation decreased from 1.8 million to 1.5 million. This grass-roots support of the Republican party showed up particularly in the growing number of Republicans elected to the state legislature. By 1992, 59 of 150 House members and 13 of 31 senators were Republicans. At the beginning of the 1990s, some analysts concluded that Texas had not only developed a vigorous two-party system but that the state also had become primarily Republican. After a hundred years as a minority party, the Republicans had become the majority.

Carl H. Moneyhon

Republic of the Rio Grande. An effort of Federalist leaders in Tamaulipas, Nuevo León, and Coahuila to break away from the Centralist government of Mexico in 1840 and to form a new confederation. Since 1835, with the ascension of Santa Anna to the presidency of Mexico, Federalist leaders throughout the nation had attempted to force a return to the federalistic Constitution of 1824. This movement was particularly strong in the northern states of Mexico, where, when the renewal of federalism failed, contiguity with the newly independent Texas contributed to secessionist sentiment. Leaders of the Federalists met at Laredo on 17 January 1840. The convention declared independence from Mexico and claimed for its territory the areas of Tamaulipas and Coahuila north to the Nueces and Medina rivers, respectively, and Nuevo León, Zacatecas, Durango, Chihuahua, and New Mexico. Among the government figures of the Republic of the Rio Grande, Antonio Canales Rosillo was elected commander in chief of the army, and José Carbajal secretary to the council. The government was moved to Guerrero, Tamaulipas, where it was to have remained temporarily. Canales was disastrously defeated by the Centralist army under Gen. Mariano Arista (24–25 March 1840) at Morales, Coahuila. Col. Antonio Zapata, Federalist cavalry commander, was captured and executed. Canales with his few remaining troops retreated to San Antonio, while the provisional government fled to Victoria, Texas. Canales then toured Texas in an effort to raise interest and aid for the continuance of his campaign. He arrived at Austin in the latter part of April 1840 and conferred with President Lamar, who, though privately interested in Canales's cause, officially gave no sanctions to him on the basis that Texas was striving to secure recognition of its independence from Mexico. Canales then went to Houston, where he was well received, and on to San Patricio, where his army was reorganizing. The growing army consisted of 300 Mexicans, 140 Americans, and 80 Indians. The principal leader of the Americans was Col. Samuel W. Jordan. Jordan and ninety men were ordered to the Rio Grande as the vanguard of the army late in June. They proceeded into the interior of Tamaulipas and captured Ciudad Victoria without a battle. From there treacherous subordinate officers led them toward San Luis Potosí, but, suspecting the treachery, Jordan changed direction and marched toward Saltillo. There, on 25 October, he was attacked by Gen. Rafael Vásquez, the Centralist commander at Saltillo, but in spite of the desertion of part of his command, managed to defend himself and return to Texas. Early in November commissioners of Canales and Arista met, and Canales capitulated at Camargo on 6 November. He was taken into the Centralist army as an officer, and Federalism was dead for the time being. *David M. Vigness*

Resacas. Former channels of the Rio Grande in southern Cameron County. *Resaca* is probably from Spanish *resacar* ("to retake"). The primary geological function of a resaca seems to be diversion and dissipation of floodwater from the river. Resacas are naturally cut off from the river, having no inlet or outlet. Before land development and water control in Cameron County, floodwater from the Rio Grande drained into resacas from surrounding terrain. Over the years portions of the resacas silted up and became bottomland, forming the remaining stretches of channel into a series of unconnected horseshoe bends. The channels themselves were either dry or contained stagnant ponds and marshes. Development of resacas as reservoirs and channels for irrigation water started in 1906, when Col. Samuel Robertson began construction of a canal to connect the Resaca de los Fresnos with a pumping station on the Rio Grande at Los Indios. Many resacas are now filled with water by pumping. Some rural resacas remain dry except in rainy weather. The ownership and administration of resacas varies according to jurisdiction. Some are owned by irrigation districts, some by municipal water corporations or utility districts, and some by owners of adjacent land who provide easement to public corporations. In urban areas resacas have been landscaped as community or residential showplaces, while those in rural areas are often left as marshlands. They serve as habitats for waterfowl, beaver, nutria, various species of amphibians and reptiles, including alligators, and various species of fish. Resaca de la Palma was the scene of a Mexican War battle on 9 May 1846; the battlesite is now covered by urban development. *Charles M. Robinson III*

Resnick, Judith Arlene. Astronaut; b. Akron, Ohio, 5 April 1949; d. 28 January 1986; m. Michael Oldak (1970; divorced); ed. Carnegie–Mellon University (bachelor's degree in electrical engineering, 1970), University of Maryland (Ph.D., 1977). She was employed by the Radio Corporation of America as a design engineer in New Jersey and Virginia in the early 1970s. Before joining NASA, she also served as a biomedical engineer at the National Institutes of Health in Bethesda, Maryland, and as a senior systems engineer for Xerox Corporation in California. She applied to NASA in 1977 and entered the astronaut-training program with 35 others in Houston in January 1978. This group included the first six women picked to participate in NASA flight preparation. After her training Resnik worked on orbiter development for the space administration and served as a technical commentator for network television coverage of the 1982 flight of the space shuttle *Columbia*. In August 1984, a year after Sally Ride became the first American woman to fly in space, Resnik made her first space flight, as a mission specialist on the seven-day maiden flight of the orbiter *Discovery*. Throughout her tenure at NASA, she was an expert in the use of the robot arm on shuttle flights, which was operated from within the aircraft to perform tasks outside of them. Her second space flight was in 1986 on the *Challenger*, where she was again assigned to be a mission specialist. She and the other six crew members of this flight were killed when the *Challenger* exploded soon after takeoff. *Debbie Mauldin Cottrell*

Rice, William Marsh. Businessman and philanthropist; b. Springfield, Massachusetts, 14 March 1816; d. New York City, 23 September 1900 (buried on the Rice University campus, Houston); m. Margaret C. Bremond (1850; d. 1863); m. Mrs. Julia Elizabeth Baldwin Brown (1867; d. 1896). Rice left school at the age of 15 to be a general-store clerk, and at 21 he purchased an enterprise of his own. After the panic of 1837 he moved to Houston, where he contracted to furnish and serve liquor in the bar of the Milam Hotel in return for the cost of the liquor, three dollars a day, and board. He was issued a headright certificate to 320 acres of Houston land and soon (1840) received a first-class license for a mercantile business from the city. With Ebenezer B. Nichols, Rice was a senior partner in the mercantile firm of Rice and Nichols, a large export and import business that was known by 1856 as William Rice and Company. In 1841 Rice offered a gold cup to the planter who brought in the first 20 bales of cotton and a silver cup to the one who brought the first 5. In 1851 he and other investors established the Houston and Galveston Navigation Company, and by 1858 he was the owner of a brig called the *William M. Rice*, which carried ice from Boston to Galveston during the summers. Rice also served as a director of the Houston Insurance Company, which insured carriers and freight. He amassed much money and land. In 1859, with other investors, Rice incorporated the Houston Cotton Compress Company. He was also an incorporator and director of several railroads, including the Buffalo Bayou, Brazos and Colorado, the Houston Tap and Brazoria, the Washington County, and the Houston and Texas Central, as well as a stage line from Houston to Austin. Rice represented the Second Ward as an alderman from 1855 to 1857 and served on the petit jury and grand jury in Harris County. By 1860 he may have been the second richest man in Texas, with real estate and personal property valued at $750,000.

Aerial view of campus, 1991. Photograph by Bob Bailey Studios, Inc. Bob Bailey Photographic Archive, CAH; CN 10374. The Rice University campus has 40 architecturally consistent buildings grouped in a quadrangle on a campus of 300 acres in the heart of Houston.

At the outbreak of the Civil War he left his home to be used as a military hospital and transferred his business to Matamoros, where he operated through the federal blockade. Though he owned 15 slaves in 1860 and served on the slave patrol for a year, he identified with the Unionist cause. After the war he moved to Dunellen, New Jersey, where he was an agent for the Houston and Texas Central Railroad. Rice retained his interest in Texas, however. In 1885 he bought the Capitol Hotel, which became the Rice Hotel, and in 1891 he endowed and incorporated the William Marsh Rice Institute for the advancement of literature, science, and art (now Rice University). Rice had accumulated a fortune of about $3 million when he moved to New York City after the death of his second wife. He was murdered by Charles F. Jones, his valet, and Albert T. Patrick, a lawyer who made a series of forgeries in order to acquire the Rice estate. Years of litigation ensued. Though Patrick was sentenced to death, he received a full pardon in 1912, when the bulk of the estate went to Rice Institute. *Andrew Forest Muir*

Rice University. A private, independent, coeducational university in Houston; chartered and endowed in 1891 by William Marsh Rice and opened in 1912 as the William Marsh Rice Institute. When Rice's estate was settled in 1904, after the sensational trial following his murder, approximately $3 million was given to the institute as a separate capital fund added to the original endowment, which had grown to almost $3.3 million. At the

time the institute opened, the endowment stood at approximately $9 million, a sum that enabled all students to attend without paying tuition—a privilege that did not end until 1965. The original charter prescribed an institution "dedicated to the advancement of literature, science, and art." The board of trustees determined that it would be a first-rate university and in 1907 appointed mathematician and astronomer Edgar Odell Lovett of Princeton University as president with directions to plan the new institution. The entering class of 77 students had an international faculty of 10 (including, for example, Julian Huxley as the first professor of biology). The *Thresher*, an independent student newspaper, began in 1916. By 1924 the freshman class was limited to about 450, and the undergraduate enrollment has been carefully controlled ever since. Under Lovett's direction Rice Institute first developed major strength in the sciences and engineering, though distinguished instruction was offered from the beginning in the humanities and architecture. The curriculum broadened, and the faculty increased greatly in size after World War II under the administration (1946–60) of physicist William V. Houston. The institute was renamed Rice University in 1960. A number of new buildings were constructed in two periods of growth, the late 1940s and the late 1950s. Graduate work, present from the beginning, was enlarged. In 1964 the university successfully sought legal authority to break the founder's charter in two regards: permission to admit students without regard to race and to charge a modest tuition. Further expansion, especially in the humanities and social sciences, came in the 1960s and 1970s. In 1961 NASA located the Johnson Space Center on land made available by Rice, and in 1962 the university established the nation's first department of space science. The *Journal of Southern History* has been published at Rice since 1959; *Studies in English Literature* was founded at Rice in 1961; and the *Papers of Jefferson Davis* project has been headquartered at Rice since 1963. In July 1985 *Rice University Studies* (formerly *Rice Institute Pamphlet*, begun in 1915) became Rice University Press. The Shepherd School of Music and the Jesse H. Jones Graduate School of Administration were added in 1973 and 1976 respectively.

The campus has 40 architecturally consistent buildings grouped in quadrangles under live oak trees on a campus of 300 acres in the heart of Houston. The student body, formerly mostly from Texas, now is predominantly non-Texan. Almost paradoxically, Rice, with its 73,000-seat stadium, continued as a charter member of the Southwest Conference until this athletic union ended. No fraternities or sororities are allowed; all undergraduates are assigned to one of eight residential colleges (the system was established in 1957) around which student life revolves. Rice University maintains a variety of research facilities and laboratories, including distinguished libraries. Rice is also associated with the Houston Area Research Center, a consortium supported by Rice, the University of Texas at Austin, Texas A&M University, and the University of Houston. A number of interdisciplinary research institutes and centers are located on the Rice campus, including the Rice Quantum Institute, the Rice Engineering Design and Development Institute, and the Computer and Information Technology Institute. The Rice Center for Community Design and Research, housed off campus, is involved with urban planning. The Office of Continuing Studies offers a wide variety of noncredit enrichment and technical short courses to thousands of Houstonians annually. In 1990 Rice hosted the annual G-7 economic conference.

John B. Boles

Rupert Richardson. Courtesy Texas State Historical Association.

Richardson, Rupert Norval. Historian; b. Caddo, Texas, 28 April 1891; d. Abilene, 14 April 1988; m. Pauline Mays (1915); 1 son; ed. Simmons College (B.A., 1912), University of Chicago (B.S., 1914), and the University of Texas (M.A., 1922; Ph.D., 1928). Richardson was principal of Cisco High School, 1915–16, and Sweetwater High School, 1916–17, before joining Simmons College. During World War I he served briefly as a second lieutenant in the army. He was associated with Hardin–Simmons University from 1917 until his death. He was dean of students (1926–), vice president (1928–), acting president (1943–), president (1945–), and president emeritus (1953–). As president he oversaw the school's dramatic expansion following World War II. When he became president emeritus, he returned to the history department. After his retirement he continued to teach courses and supervise student theses as professor emeritus. Among his many scholarly publications were *The Comanche Barrier to South Plains Settlement* (1933), *The Greater Southwest* (1934, with Carl Coke Rister), *Adventuring with a Purpose* (1952), *The Frontier of Northwest Texas* (1963), *Colonel Edward M. House: The Texas Years* (1964), and *Caddo, Texas: The Biography of a Community* (1966). He also wrote *Famous Are Thy Halls: Hardin–Simmons University As I Have Known It* (1964). His history textbook *Texas: The Lone Star State* (1943) has been through many editions. Richardson helped found the West Texas

Historical Association in 1924 and was an editor of its *Year Book* from its inception until his death. He was a member of the Texas State Historical Survey Committee from 1953 to 1967 (president, 1961–63) and received the Ruth Lester Award in 1972 for his efforts in historical preservation. He was a fellow of the Texas State Historical Association (president, 1969–70). He was also president of the Southwestern Social Science Association, the Texas Philosophical Society, and the Texas Council of Church Related Colleges and Universities. He was a Mason and a district governor of the Lions Club and was active in Baptist affairs.

Mark Odintz

Richardson, Sid Williams. Oilman and philanthropist; b. Athens, Texas, 25 April 1891; d. St. Joseph Island, 30 September 1959. He earned $3,500 in 1908 by cattle trading while still a senior in high school. He briefly attended Baylor University and Simmons College, then quit to become a salesman for an oil-well supply company, an oil scout, and a lease purchaser. He became an independent oil producer in Fort Worth in 1919. He accumulated wealth and lost it several times during the 1920s, but was well established as a millionaire by 1935, when he opened up the rich Keystone oilfield in Winkler County. From his suite of offices in Fort Worth he individually leased more oil land than did several major oil companies; operated three cattle ranches; and owned the Texas State Network (a radio and television organization), a carbon black plant at Odessa, and the Texas City Refining Company. He purchased St. Joseph Island off the Texas coast in 1936 and resided there when he wasn't in Fort Worth. In 1954, with his longtime friend Clint Murchison, he backed fellow Texan Robert Ralph Young in a successful fight for control of the New York Central Railroad by buying 800,000 shares worth $20 million. The public seldom knew of Richardson's business activities, and few knew what he looked like, for he rarely talked to reporters and did not like publicity. He was a confidant of Franklin D. Roosevelt, whom he advised at times during World War II about oil affairs. In 1952 he helped persuade his Republican friend General Eisenhower to run for president. In 1956, however, he returned to the Democrats after the president vetoed a natural-gas bill. Though he never publicized his gifts, Richardson made large contributions to civic groups, churches, libraries, and especially to Boys, Incorporated, a California charitable organization. In 1947 he established the Sid W. Richardson Foundation, designed to aid churches, hospitals, and schools in Texas. Richardson, the "bachelor billionaire," was one of the wealthiest men in the nation; estimates of his worth ranged up to $800 million. Lyndon Johnson and Sam Rayburn attended his funeral, at which Billy Graham presided. The Richardson Foundation presented to the University of Texas at Austin a $2 million gift to increase the holdings of its History of Science Collection, housed in the Harry Ransom Humanities Research Center. In appreciation the university named a new building for Richardson. In it are housed the Center for American History, the Nettie Lee Benson Latin American Collection, the Texas State Historical Association, and the Lyndon B. Johnson School of Public Affairs.

Ben H. Procter

Richardson, Texas. A residential and manufacturing suburb 10 miles north of downtown Dallas in northern Dallas and southern Collin counties. The area of waving grass and numerous springs was popular with early settlers, who formed the community of Breckinridge in the 1840s and 1850s. Breckinridge flourished until 1873, when the Houston and Texas Central Railroad bypassed it. Richardson was founded on the HTCR tracks, and the residents of Breckinridge moved to Richardson. William J. Wheeler, a local ginner, and Bernard Reilly donated 101 acres of land for the townsite and right-of-way for the railroad in 1873. The community was called Richardson when it received a post office in 1874—mostly likely named for E. H. Richardson, a contractor who built the Houston and Texas from Dallas to Denton. By 1881 Richardson was a thriving community with several stores, including general stores, groceries, and drugstores, four doctors, several cotton gins, and churches. Its population was 147 in 1904 and 400 in 1925. Transportation improved with the arrival of the Interurban, an electric railroad, on its way from Sherman to Dallas. In 1909 the community's streets were graveled, and Dallas County built a gravel road in that decade from Dallas to the Collin county line. Around the same time telephones were available in the community, and electric lights were in use. In 1922 the first official Richardson fair was held to promote interest in agriculture and livestock. It began as a purely agricultural fair, but eventually special events were scheduled at

fair time and local businesses had exhibits. In 1924 a tornado in the community killed one man, injured 13, and destroyed a number of buildings. In 1925 Richardson incorporated under a commission form of city government. The community continued its improvements with a public waterworks and the formation of a volunteer fire department in 1926. The population reached 720 in 1940. After World War II the area began to expand. Nearby communities, such as Northern Hills, were annexed. In spite of improvements Richardson remained a sleepy farming community until the 1950s. In 1950 Richardson had a population of 1,288; but by 1961 the population was 16,810. Technological industries, such as Collins Radio (1951), began moving into Richardson, and later in the decade Texas Instruments opened near the city limit. The community became known as the "electronic suburb." Other improvements in the 1950s included the formation of a police department, Terrace Park, and a community center. The arrival of Central Expressway (U.S. Highway 75) in 1954 allowed Richardson to become a suburb of Dallas, and shopping centers replaced the cotton fields. In 1956 a home rule charter and a council–manager form of government were adopted. During the 1960s land along the northern border was annexed, and industrial parks were developed. A number of businesses opened, including 22 manufacturing firms, making such things as machine parts, space tracking systems, and television cameras. The population of Richardson was 43,900 in 1970. Richardson was a popular suburb for upper-income college-educated professionals. The city boomed again in the early 1980s, slowed somewhat, then grew again in 1989 with the influx of telecommunication firms. The "electronic city" became "telecom corridor." By the 1980s there were two schools of higher learning in Richardson—the University of Texas at Dallas and Richland Community College. In addition to all the entertainment in the Dallas area Richardson had its own symphony orchestra, and the Christmas Parade was an annual event. Several museums were located in the community, including Owens Spring Creek Farm, a showcase farm with vintage sausage-making equipment, and the University of Texas at Dallas Aviation Collection. In the early 1990s 1990 Richardson had 102 manufacturing firms, with an emphasis on electronics and telecommunications. The population in 1990 was 74,840.

Lisa C. Maxwell

Richmond State School. On a 242-acre site north of Richmond; opened in April 1968 by the Texas Department of Mental Health and Mental Retardation. The school was constructed to accommodate 500 students. The first 450 were admitted in April 1968. The institution primarily serves adults in a 15-county area along the Gulf Coast from Orange County to Matagorda County. Residents are housed according to the severity of their mental disability. Plans were to house 1,500 after a second construction phase, but this enrollment has never been reached because of the department's increasing emphasis on deinstitutionalization. Richmond State School had 1,023 students in 1980, 755 in 1990, and 700 in 1994. The school offers an intensive physical-therapy program. In 1992 it opened one of the most comprehensive programs of hippotherapy (therapy using horses) in the Southwest.

Rio Grande. Rises at the Continental Divide in Rio Grande National Forest, Colorado, as a clear mountain stream, flows through New Mexico, and forms the border between Texas and

Mexico before emptying into the Gulf of Mexico. Its length varies as its course changes; in the late 1980s, according to the International Boundary and Water Commission, its total length was 1,896 miles. The official border measurement ranges from 889 to 1,248 miles, depending on how the river is measured. A huge curve in the river in Brewster County, Texas, is known as the Big Bend.

The Pueblo Indians called the river Posoge ("Big River"). The expedition of Hernando de Alvarado called it Río de Nuestra Señora in 1540. It was called the River of May by three British sailors in 1568. In 1581 the Agustín Rodríguez expedition called it the Río de Nuestra Señora de la Concepción and the Río Guadalquivir. By 1598 the Spanish were calling its lower course the Río Bravo, and in modern Mexico it is still known by that name or as the Río Bravo del Norte (bravo denotes "wild, bold, turbulent, restless"). In 1582 an expedition headed by merchant Antonio de Espejo traveled the Río Conchos to its mouth on a river he called Río del Norte ("River of the North") and Río Turbio ("Turbulent River"). Juan de Oñate is thought to have been the first to call it the Rio Grande, when in 1598 he reached its banks near the site of future El Paso. The name Río Grande del Norte later became standard. It was the Rio Grande that Fernando del Bosque named the Río de San Buenaventura del Norte in 1675, and that Father Damián Massanet may have called the Río Ganapetuán in 1691. The river was also called the Río Caudaloso ("carrying much water"), and on a 1700 map it appeared as Río del Norte y de Nuevo Mexico.

The Rio Grande was never explored as a single unit by any one person or group. Cabeza de Vaca is believed to have crossed it in 1535 or 1536, and Vázquez de Coronado in 1540. Spanish Governor Juan Bautista de Anza examined it in 1779, as did Zebulon Montgomery Pike in 1806 and John Charles Frémont in 1849. However, the river was not well mapped before the extensive work of the American and Mexican boundary commissions made necessary by the Treaty of Guadalupe Hidalgo in 1848 and by the Gadsden Purchase of 1853–54. The French, on the basis of La Salle's accidental landing on the Texas coast, made half-hearted attempts to claim that Louisiana extended to the Rio Grande. The claim was still mentioned as late as 1803, the time of the Louisiana Purchase, and was not definitely renounced until the Adam–Onís Treaty of 1819. In 1836 Texas put forth a claim, which set aside the documentary testimony of more than a century, for the Rio Grande from mouth to source as the southwestern and western boundary of the state. Stephen F. Austin, writing as secretary of state of the Republic of Texas to William H. Wharton, who was in the United States attempting to secure annexation for Texas, instructed Wharton to compromise on the southwestern boundary if he thought such a move would help get Texas into the Union. During the republic, little settlement was made below the Nueces; the Rio Grande was never actually under Texan control until authority was established by Gen. Zachary Taylor at the beginning of the Mexican War. The river was finally recognized by Mexico as the Texas boundary in the treaty of Guadalupe Hidalgo.

In a sense, the Rio Grande is two streams. Because so much water is diverted for irrigation, the river dwindles to nearly nothing at Presidio, and only water from the Río Conchos, coming out of Mexico, sustains its journey to the Gulf. Its principal tributaries, some of which are themselves greatly reduced by irrigation, are the Pecos, Devils, Chama, and Puerco rivers in the United States, and the Conchos, Salado, and San Juan in Mexico. Major cities and towns alongside the Rio Grande are Santa Fe, Albuquerque, Socorro, Truth or Consequences, Mesilla, and Las Cruces in New Mexico; and El Paso, Presidio, Del Rio, Eagle Pass, Laredo, Rio Grande City, McAllen, and Brownsville in Texas. In Mexico the primary towns and cities are Ciudad Juárez, Ojinaga, Ciudad Acuña, Piedras Negras, Nuevo Laredo, Camargo, Reynosa, and Matamoros. Mexican states bordered by the Rio Grande are Chihuahua, Coahuila, Nuevo León, and Tamaulipas. Ciudad Juárez is the largest city on the Rio Grande as well as on the international boundary, and El Paso is the second largest city on the border. The two cities would constitute one of the world's major metropolitan areas if the Rio Grande did not divide them.

Principal crops vary along the river. Colorado and northern New Mexico grow potatoes and alfalfa. Southern New Mexico and West Texas specialize in cotton, peppers, onions, and pecans. The lower Rio Grande valley raises citrus fruits, vegetables, and cotton. Agriculture and cattle raising are the leading industries along the entire Rio Grande, although maquiladoras are rapidly becoming the leading employer, especially in Mexico. The Rio Grande has never been navigable except near its mouth and, on rare occasions, to Laredo. From the San Juan Mountains in Colorado to Albuquerque, New Mexico, it is primarily a torrent flanked by spectacular gorges and mountain slopes. South of Albuquerque, however, the land flattens and supports desert flora—mesquite, creosote brush, cactus, and yucca. The water is impounded behind Elephant Butte and Caballo dams near Truth or Consequences, New Mexico, and the river downstream is used for irrigation in the Mesilla Valley of New Mexico and the 90-mile-long El Paso–Juárez valley, the oldest irrigated area in the state. In this valley are Ysleta, Socorro, and San Elizario, generally considered the three oldest towns in Texas. Sixty thousand acre-feet of irrigation water is annually promised by treaty to Mexican farmers near Juárez, although during periods of low snow melt in Colorado, this figure is reduced proportionately. At Presidio the Río Conchos enters the nearly empty Rio Grande channel and races toward the canyon-lands of Big Bend National Park. A 191.2-mile strip of the American bank called Rio Grande Wild and Scenic River begins in Big Bend National Park and runs downstream to the Terrell–Val Verde county line. The area is administered by the National Park Service, though without federal facilities. South of Redford (formerly Polvo), the Bofecillos Mountains and the Chihuahua Mountains converge to form Colorado Canyon. From there the churning Rio Grande cuts through Santa Elena, Mariscal, and Boquillas canyons. Ahead still are smaller, whitewater canyons such as Horse, Big, and Reagan canyons. Below Del Rio, Eagle Pass, and Laredo the Rio Grande skirts huge cattle ranches and farms. Broad, open valleys are the rule. The river is meandering, brown, sluggish. The scenery becomes tropical and extremely fertile; citrus groves are prominent. The river terminates in a delta at the Gulf.

All along the border, and especially in the lower Rio Grande valley, bancos have been a serious problem. These wide, usually brushy curves shaped like horseshoes or oxbows have frequently overflowed and formed new channels. Defining the exact international border became a serious issue not solved until the banco treaty of 1905. In 1933 the United States and Mexico approved the Rio Grande Rectification Treaty, which called for straightening the channel east of El Paso. The length of this part of the river was reduced from 155.2 miles to 85.6 miles, and the era of King Cotton and economic prosperity began. The subsequent Rio Grande Canalization Project straightened the Rio Grande in New Mexico from Caballo Dam south to the Texas line, roughly 100 miles. Significant agricultural help arrived for Southwest Texas in 1932, when the United States and Mexico agreed on the Lower Rio Grande Valley Flood Control Project. It strengthened and raised levees and dredged the channel and floodways. The Mexican–United States Treaty of 1944 committed both countries to the construction of two Rio Grande dams: Falcon and Amistad. The reservoirs were designed for storage capacities of five million or more acre-feet. Presidents Dwight Eisenhower and Aldolfo Ruiz Cortines dedicated Falcon Dam in October 1953. It is 50 miles downstream from Laredo. Amistad ("Friendship") Dam was finished in 1969 and is 12 miles northwest of Del Rio. At El Paso the Rio Grande caused friction in the 1870s, when the river bit deep into the banks of Mexico and gradually transferred land to the United States. The famous Chamizal Dispute was not settled until 1963, when 437 acres was ceded from downtown El Paso to Mexico. The agreement economically strengthened both cities. The international border at the two cities is now lined with concrete so that the channel will not change. A similar, but not well-publicized, incident over boundary differences took place at the twin cities of Presidio and Ojinaga. It was settled by a 1970 treaty with Mexico authorizing a land swap called the Ojinaga Cut (or Tract), which totaled 8.3 miles. Texas gave up 1,606.9 acres and Mexico 252 acres. The treaty also provided for an international floodway of 15 miles to stabilize the border further.   *Leon C. Metz*

Rio Grande Campaign. A federal campaign during the Civil War to destroy the Confederate trade with Mexico. Texas, alone among the Confederate states, shared a border with a neutral country. Although Mexican president Benito Juárez favored the North, his opponents in northern Mexico, including caudillo Santiago Vidaurri of Tamaulipas, encouraged trade with Texas and the Confederacy across the Rio Grande. A brisk commerce resulted in which Texas cotton bought much-needed foreign goods, including weapons and other military supplies. The sleepy Mexican coastal village of Bagdad grew temporarily into a bustling city, and Matamoros, 65 miles from the mouth of the Rio Grande, became the center of the trade. The *Texas State Gazette* reported in mid-1863 that Matamoros was "crowded with merchants and traders from all parts of the world" and that the sidewalks were "blocked up with goods." Unable to blockade the neutral Mexican coast, the Lincoln administration ordered Maj. Gen. Nathaniel P. Banks, commander of the Department of the Gulf at New Orleans, to interdict the lucrative trade between Texas and Mexico. On 2 November 1863 a 6,000-man invasion force from the Union Thirteenth Corps under Gen. Napoleon Dana raised the United States flag at Brazos Santiago. The outmanned Confederates soon evacuated Brownsville, and by 1 January 1864 the federal troops had pushed up the Gulf Coast to Corpus Christi, Matagorda Island, Indianola, and Port Lavaca, and up the Rio Grande as far as Edinburg and Rio Grande City. Maj. Gen. John B. Magruder, who was in command of the Confederate District of Texas, dispatched Col. John S. Ford to South Texas to gather a force to resist the Union invasion. In the meantime hundreds of Texas refugees, including many promi-

nent Unionists, arrived in Brownsville. Provisional governor Andrew J. Hamilton established a provisional government, and Col. Edmund J. Davis and Lt. Col. John L. Haynes recruited Unionists, Confederate deserters, and Hispanics into the First and Second Texas Cavalry regiments. Judge J. B. McFarland organized a provisional court that met at the Brownsville Episcopal church, while other refugees such as federal district judge Thomas H. Duval and legislator John Hancock helped recruit troops for the Union army and attempted to convince federal authorities to invade the interior of the state. The refugees formed a chapter of the Union League—an auxiliary to the Republican party—that met every Saturday at Market Hall in Brownsville. With little actual soldiering to do, aside from an expedition into Matamoros to protect the United States consulate during fighting between Mexican factions, the federal soldiers spent most of their time fighting off dust storms and smallpox.

By June 1864 Ford had collected his "Cavalry of the West," a motley assortment of 1,300 troopers, including old men and boys ineligible for Confederate conscription, Hispanics, deserters, outlaws, and mercenaries. General Banks, in preparation for the Red River campaign, had recalled more than half of the Union invasion force and ordered all of the captured territory evacuated except the area around Brownsville, Brazos Santiago, and Port Isabel. Advancing on the federals from the West, Ford's command won several sharp skirmishes against Yankee units that included the two regiments of Texas Unionists. Federal troops, unable to halt the Confederate advance, retired from Brownsville on 29 June, and the refugees scrambled to safety across the Rio Grande. Many spent the last year of the war in New Orleans. By the end of September only a 950-man garrison remained at Brazos Santiago, where they stayed, eyed closely by a few Confederate troops, until a month after the Confederate surrender at Appomattox. On 12 May 1865, elements of two regiments of federal infantry made an ill-advised advance toward Palmito Ranch, where they were routed by Ford and his cavalry the next day. The Confederates suffered only a few casualties, but they killed, wounded, or captured more than two-thirds of the Yankee force. The battle of Palmito Ranch, the last land battle of the Civil War, ended the Rio Grande campaign.

James A. Marten

Rio Grande Compact. An interstate agreement to apportion equitably the water of the Rio Grande among Colorado, New Mexico, and Texas. A preliminary compact of 1929 provided for stream-gauging stations, for construction of a reservoir in Colorado, and for equitable dividing of the river water pending the signing of a permanent compact. The agreement was signed at Santa Fe in 1938, approved by the state legislatures, and approved by Congress in 1939. The table worked out provided for Colorado and New Mexico to deliver water in accord with a formula based upon the flow of the Rio Grande and its tributaries at designated gauging stations above the state lines. A Rio Grande Compact Commission, consisting of one representative from each state, was established, the state engineers of Colorado and New Mexico serving ex officio and the Texas commissioner being appointed by the Texas governor. The United States designates a representative to sit with the commission.

Jacqueline E. Timm

Riots. Until the last half of the nineteenth century the sparseness of the population in Texas prevented riots like those in eastern cities. Because local records were similarly sparse and the state was not involved in most local incidents, information on riots that have taken place in Texas is incomplete. Only a few incidents occurred that could be termed riots before the Civil War. Though some of these would be considered riots now, these disturbances were a common experience on the frontier and were viewed more lightly. The occurrence of cowboys "taking a town," for example, which often involved some destruction of property, was usually considered an innocent diversion. Some other incidents that legally constituted authorities considered riots are now regarded in another light. Such was the first of the Anahuac Disturbances (1832), in which a group of citizens armed themselves to free Travis, Jack, and Waller, who had been imprisoned at Fort Anahuac by Colonel Bradburn. The nearest equivalent of a riot in the early days of Texas was the feud. The first and largest of these, the Regulator–Moderator War, occurred along the Sabine River between 1839 and 1844. Smaller feuds were common, especially toward the western frontier. Mob violence at times broke into rioting, generally with the object of lynching slaves or abolitionists. Most lynching, however, occurred not as the result of rioting, but as the work of vigilance committees that operated secretly.

The greatest number of riots in Texas occurred between the beginning of the Civil War and the end of the nineteenth century. Though numerous factors accounted for the sudden increase, in general the unrest stemmed from the social and economic uncertainties of the times and the sense of dispossession that dominated most segments of society. Almost invariably, racial strife was involved. Between July and December 1870, 124 arrests were made by the State Police alone for rioting. A riot in Limestone County in 1871 was typical of those that occurred during this period. When a black policeman killed a white man in Groesbeck, the animosity between African Americans and whites erupted into mob violence. Fearing threats that blacks were going to burn the town, whites throughout the county armed themselves and gathered at Groesbeck. Governor Edmund Davis declared martial law and sent in state troops; he thus averted a violent breakdown of law. In 1872 a similar riot occurred at Springfield. Often state troops were required to restore order, and members of the mobs were usually left unpunished even when they were identified. In 1877 at El Paso one of the most destructive riots in the state occurred; property damage was estimated to cost $12,000 to $31,000. The incident, the Salt War of San Elizario, was caused by a dispute over rights to use salt ponds that had for years been used by people on both sides of the border free of charge and were regarded by those people as part of the public domain. After Charles H. Howard filed a claim for the land on which the salt deposits were located, Louis Cardis encouraged Mexicans and Mexican Americans to defy the claim. Howard shot Cardis and took refuge with state troops at San Elizario, where a mob of 500 besieged them for four days. When Howard gave himself up, he was killed, and the mob overran the town. In the wake of the violence, five men were found dead and much property was destroyed. The military post at El Paso was regarrisoned, but no measures were taken against the members of the mob, many of whom were Mexican nationals.

In the 1880s and 1890s racial incidents continued to be the major cause of riots, although economic conditions also became a factor. A riot of black troops occurred at Fort Concho in 1881. About 50 blacks broke open an arms rack and invaded San Angelo, where they destroyed property and wounded a man. The violence stemmed from the killing of a black trooper and subsided after Texas Rangers were sent to the area. The Rio Grande City Riot of 1888 occurred after the arrest and subsequent killing of a Mexican-American resident. In the Beeville Riot of 1894 violence broke out between Mexicans and blacks due to increased Mexican immigration and a shortage of jobs. In 1897 state troops were called out four times to protect prisoners from mobs; in one instance they failed to protect their charge from lynching. State troops were called out in 1898 to keep peace at Houston during a streetcar strike and at Galveston during a wharf strike; on two other occasions they were called upon to protect prisoners from mobs. In 1899 the Laredo Smallpox Riot was precipitated among Mexican-American residents who protested being moved from their homes under quarantine. They gathered in hundreds and fired several shots in an encounter with city officials. Rangers were sent in to subdue the mob before any serious damage was done. That same year troops of the Texas Volunteer Guard were sent to Orange to suppress a mob that sought to drive blacks out of Orange County.

The most common cause of riots in the first half of the twentieth century was public outrage toward prisoners. Mob threats of violence to prisoners necessitated the use of state troops on four occasions in 1900. In 1901 three lynchings by mobs took place despite the calling of state troops; in two instances the troops suppressed the mobs. At Brenham rioting broke out over the employment of a black brakeman by a railway; it was suppressed after two days. In 1902 mob violence brought on the use of state troops three times. In one instance the mob hanged a prisoner before the troops arrived. Troops were called out three times to quell mob violence in 1903, twice in 1904, three times in 1905, and once in 1906. The Brownsville Raid (1906) precipitated a serious race riot involving black soldiers. Troops were needed elsewhere in 1907 and 1908; in the latter year rioting at Slocum resulted in the killing of more than 10 blacks. Other mob actions in the first decade of the century resulted from strikes at Houston in 1904 and racial tension at Ragley the same year. Riots also took place in San Antonio and Fort Worth in April and May of 1913. The Houston Riot of 1917 was started by about 150 black troops from Camp Logan, a temporary training center near the city. The riot, touched off by the arrest of a black woman, was the culmination of general uneasiness and hostility following the establishment of the camp. It resulted in the deaths of 17 people, mostly whites; the anger of an aroused white population necessitated martial law for four days. The Longview Race Riot of 1919 also resulted in the proclamation of martial law. A strike at Galveston in 1920 produced lawlessness that required the help of the Texas National Guard. Mexia was declared in a state of anarchy because of a riot and was placed under martial law from January to March 1922. The Sherman Riot of 1930 stemmed from the arrest of a black who had assaulted a white woman; rangers were called to protect the prisoner, but a mob set fire to the courthouse and virtually seized control of the town. When troops of the Texas National Guard arrived, they were attacked by the mob, and before martial law restored order, a number of buildings were destroyed. Enforcement of oil-conservation laws in the 1930s also necessitated the use of the National Guard to suppress mob lawlessness.

Tex Ritter, ca. 1939. John Lomax Papers, CAH; CN 06677. As a student at the University of Texas, Ritter studied authentic cowboy songs under the guidance of John Lomax and J. Frank Dobie. Later he went as a performer to New York, where his success on the radio led to movie contracts in Hollywood.

The guard was also called in September 1937 to suppress mob violence at Marshall and again to quell the Beaumont Riot of 1943. In Beaumont a white mob, outraged at the assault of a white woman by a black, terrorized the black section of town. Two died and 100 homes were destroyed. In 1955 the National Guard was used to control a riot at Rusk State Hospital. In May 1967 a riot that occurred among black students at Texas Southern University in Houston resulted in the death of one policeman and the wounding of two students and two police officers. Though the immediate cause of the riot was the arrest of a student, the night-long incident was related to general racial tension.

Marilyn Von Kohl

Ritter, Tex. Western movie actor and singer; b. Woodward Maurice Ritter, Panola County, 12 January 1905; d. Nashville, Tennessee, 2 January 1974 (buried in Port Neches, Texas); m. Dorothy Fay Southworth (1941); 2 sons; ed. University of Texas (1922–27). At UT, Ritter was influenced by J. Frank Dobie, Oscar J. Fox, and John A. Lomax, who encouraged his study of authentic cowboy songs. He began singing western and mountain songs on Radio Station KPRC in Houston in 1929. The following year he was with a musical troupe touring the South and the

Midwest. By 1931 he was in New York and had joined the Theatre Guild. His role in *Green Grow the Lilacs* (predecessor to the musical *Oklahoma*) drew attention to the young "cowboy," and he became the featured singer with the Madison Square Garden Rodeo in 1932. Further recognition led to his starring in one of the first Western radio programs to be featured in New York, "The Lone Star Rangers." His early appeal to New Yorkers as the embodiment of a Texas cowboy, in spite of his roots in the rural Southern music tradition, undoubtedly led to his first movie contract in 1936. Ritter appeared in 85 movies, including 78 westerns, and was among the top 10 money-making stars in Hollywood for six years. Though his movies owed much to other singing cowboys (such as Gene Autry), Ritter often used traditional folk songs in his movies rather than modern "western" compositions. Movies such as *The Utah Trail* (1938), *Roll Wagons Roll* (1939), and *Arizona Frontier* (1940) earned him a reputation for ambitious plots and vigorous action not always found in low-budget westerns. Tex Ritter's successful recordings, which began with "Rye Whiskey" in 1931, included over the years "High Noon" (1952), "Boll Weevil" (1945), "Wayward Wind," "Hillbilly Heaven," and "You Are My Sunshine" (1946). "Ranch Party," a television series featuring Ritter, ran from 1959 to 1962. In 1964 Ritter was elected to the Country Music Hall of Fame. He was president of the Country Music Association from 1963 to 1965. In 1970 he ran unsuccessfully for the United States Senate from Tennessee. His younger son, John, is a television star.

Rivas–Iriarte Expedition. The second, and most important, Spanish coastal voyage to search for La Salle's Texas colony. It found the wreckage of La Salle's ships at Matagorda Bay and made a complete circuit of the Gulf of Mexico. The circumnavigation provided the basis for a detailed diary by the chief pilot, Juan Enríquez Barroto, and his coastal map, which has not yet come to light. The voyage was made in two *piraguas* (small, open vessels equipped with oars and a single sail) built at Veracruz especially for the purpose. *Nuestra Señora del Rosario*, commanded by Martín de Rivas, was the larger. *Nuestra Señora de la Esperanza* was captained by Pedro de Iriarte. The ships were designed on the recommendations of the two chief pilots, Enríquez Barroto and Antonio Romero, who had conducted the first search voyage early in 1686, from Havana to the Mississippi River. After sailing from Veracruz on Christmas morning, 1686, the tiny ships soon encountered northers that set them back repeatedly and heavy seas that soaked the men and spoiled provisions. More than a month was required to reach Tampico, where the voyage was delayed another month to reprovision while awaiting more favorable weather. It sailed again on 8 March. Progressing along the western and northern Gulf shore, the voyagers encountered Coahuilteca, Karankawa, and Atákapa Indians. At the mouth of the Rio Grande, near three native villages, the mariners sounded the bar while naked Indians watched from the beach with bows strung. As they sailed north along Padre Island, a continuous parade of natives moved in and out of the dunes. At Cedar Bayou (called Río de Flores), the explorers found in an abandoned Indian canoe fittings from a large ship, their first sign of the French interlopers. Exploring around Matagorda Bay, which they named San Bernardo, they found the wreckage of La Salle's bark *Belle* on Matagorda Peninsula and, in the entrance channel, the rudder post of his storeship *Aimable*, which had run aground while trying to enter the bay. They nevertheless concluded, because of the shallowness of the bay, that any attempt to establish a settlement here could only have met disaster. The explorers accorded scant attention to Galveston Bay because of its shoals. On reaching the Calcasieu River, they heard news—possibly of La Salle's men living among the Indians—that caused them to turn back to make the first known exploration of both Galveston Bay and Sabine Lake. At the Calcasieu also, they made the first known European contact with the Louisiana Atákapas. With the aid of two castaways from a lost Spanish galley—one an Apalachino Indian from Florida, the other a "Mexican" boy—whom they found living among these natives, the voyagers obtained significant ethnological data.

Thanks to their shallow-draft ships, members of the Rivas–Iriarte expedition may have been the first Europeans to glimpse the shoal-studded western Louisiana coast. Because of the wide, shallow shelf, larger vessels were unable to see the shore from a safe depth, and even the wilderness-built craft of Pánfilo de Narváez and Hernando de Soto had given it a wide berth. The *piraguas* were able to explore many of the bays and inlets for the first time, including Atchafalaya Bay and the Mississippi passes. After reexploring Mobile Bay, the voyagers passed up Pensacola Bay and proceeded to San Marcos de Apalache (St. Marks, Florida) to reprovision, then returned, via Havana and the southern Gulf Coast, to Veracruz (3–4 July 1687). Although a landmark of exploration, the voyage had failed to identify the elusive "Espíritu Santo Bay or Michipipi," where the French were believed to have settled. The captains and pilots could offer only an opinion, based on the signs at San Bernardo (Matagorda) Bay, that the French settlement had failed. Until additional evidence emerged, the matter could not be put to rest.

Robert S. Weddle

River Navigation. Because of practically nonexistent overland transportation in Texas before the coming of the railroads (1860–65), the people made numerous efforts to navigate Texas rivers by steamboat. River navigation played an important role in the development of Texas before the Civil War. Although in 1821 Stephen F. Austin planned to utilize the *Lively* on the Colorado, Henry Austin's *Ariel* was the first steamboat on a Texas river. Following a few months' unsuccessful operation on the Rio Grande, the *Ariel* was moved to the Brazos in August 1830, and in December 1830, after several attempts to make New Orleans, the *Ariel* was laid up to rot near Harrisburg. In 1834, encouraged by a subscription list formed by a number of planters, Robert Wilson and William P. Harris put the *Cayuga* in service on the Brazos. The *Yellow Stone* began to ply the Brazos in 1836 and reached San Felipe in February. By 1840 there were at least two small vessels, the *Mustang* and the *Lady Byron*, operating above Brazoria. In 1840 the *Constitution*, a reclaimed ocean steamer, took a load of 300 bales of cotton over the Velasco bar, which was the principal impediment to navigation on the Brazos. On the Colorado, six miles above Matagorda, a log raft six miles long impeded navigation. Two companies were chartered to clear the river, but their attempts, as well as those of others, were unsuccessful. By 1838 the *David Crockett* and other keelboats of light draft were operating above the raft, and in the spring of 1845 the *Kate Ward*, constructed especially for Colorado trade, was launched at Matagorda. This boat had a keel of 110 feet and a beam of 24 feet, and could carry 600 bales of cotton in three feet of water. After a channel was cut through the

raft, the *Kate Ward* reached Austin on 8 May 1845. One of the first attempts to navigate the Trinity River was made by the *Branch T. Archer*, which in May 1838 ascended the river 350 miles. Although navigation on the Trinity was frequently hindered by low water, by 1840 the *Ellen Frankland* and the *Vesta* were in fairly continuous service, and when the *Ellen Frankland* was wrecked in 1844, the *Scioto Belle* replaced her. The first attempts to navigate the narrow, tortuous Buffalo Bayou were made by the *Laura* (January 1837), the *Constitution* (June 1837), the *Leonidas* (August 1837), and the *Friend* (March 1838). By 1840 there was a regular service between Houston and Galveston. A raft near Victoria hindered navigation of the Guadalupe River, but by 1841 the *Swan* had begun a fairly regular run as far as the raft. Although a canal was cleared around the raft in July 1841, the Guadalupe apparently never did a significant river trade, and the *Swan* was later purchased by a New Orleans concern that operated a line of steamers on the Red River. A hundred-mile raft above Shreveport, partially cleared by Henry Shreve in 1833, for a long time hindered navigation of the Red. Ben Milam, with the steamboat *Alps*, was the first to navigate successfully the treacherous path through the raft (1831). Because of its length and location, the Red River was the most important in Texas river navigation. After Shreve cleared the remainder of the raft in 1838, the stream was readily navigable for at least 1,600 miles of its length. By the middle of the nineteenth century there were a number of steamboats on each of the most important rivers, despite water so shallow that schedules were frequently interrupted. Downriver and coastwise shipments to Galveston kept a number of steamers in regular service to New Orleans, beginning in 1837. For several decades riverport towns occupied positions of importance in Texas commerce that they rapidly lost when the rails were laid.

Seymour V. Connor

Rivers. The 11 principal rivers of Texas drain more or less narrow watersheds that are from two to five times longer than their average widths. Consequently these streams have generally developed dendritic drainage systems, a type developed by a stream flowing across or developing upon a broad, gently dipping coastal plain. The average trend of these drainage areas is north by 45 degrees west, a general direction also parallel with the trend of the southern Rocky Mountains in West Texas. Most of the streams of Texas follow the continental slope towards the Gulf of Mexico. Others, like the Pecos River, flow at a considerable angle to this slope of the surface, the course defined by geological structures. The Colorado, Brazos, and Red rivers, which have their source in the Panhandle or in New Mexico, all flow across the Permian Red Beds and, accordingly, during periods of considerable runoff bring down a crimson flood. Others like the Pecos and Rio Grande drain areas of extensive bolson deposits and carry waters having a dull gray color. Rivers having their source on the Edwards Plateau carry lightcolored sediments during flood stages. Thus the color of the water during flood stage indicates the nature of some of the country through which the stream flows. In the southeast portions of the state such rivers as the Sabine, Neches, Trinity, and Angelina flow through areas covered by the forest of the timber belt and on through the Big Thicket to the Gulf. This general area has an annual rainfall of from 45 to 50 inches, so that, with the timbered area and the thicket to retard runoff, these streams, in their lower reaches, maintain a fairly steady flow throughout the year.

The longer rivers that have their sources in Texas or eastern New Mexico have an exceedingly large variance between their maximum and minimum discharges of water. This fluctuation is largely due to three factors: (1) the general lack of forests and other plant cover that would inhibit the runoff, (2) the absence of erosion-prevention measures and the prevalence of overgrazing, which contributes to excessive runoff during periods of considerable rainfall, and (3) the considerable amount of rain that falls in short periods of time. (Overgrazing and soil erosion are not so prevalent now as formerly.) This variation is typical of the Southwest and difficult to control. It is conducive to high flood stages followed by little or no flow. The shorter rivers, such as the Nueces, Guadalupe, and San Antonio, which rise in the southwestern Edwards Plateau, maintain a much more even flow because they are replenished constantly by springs that owe their existence to the Balcones Fault system. The streamcourses of the larger rivers flowing southeast through the central part of Texas—the Colorado, Brazos, and Trinity—are situated much nearer the northeast margin of their drainage area than the southwest boundary, probably only one-third of the drainage area lying to the northeast of these streams. Thus these streams have their larger tributaries on the west of their watershed. The Concho, San Saba, Llano, and Pedernales all flow into the Colorado from the west; the Pecan Bayou is its only important eastern tributary. In like manner the Little, Lampasas, Leon, and Bosque rivers join the Brazos from the southwest, the Navasota being the only principal tributary flowing into it from a narrow watershed on the northeast. The Trinity River is also fed mainly from the west.

The headwaters of the Rio Grande, the Pecos, the Canadian, and the Red all rise in northern New Mexico or southern Colorado. The Canadian flows almost south for about 190 miles and then flows east and slightly north across the Texas Panhandle. The Rio Grande flows slightly southwest from its source for approximately 325 miles and then assumes a direction of south by 45 degrees east along the southwestern boundary of Texas. The Red River has its source in New Mexico very close to the Canadian River and flows in the general direction of south by 77 degrees east along the northern boundary of the state. Thus, the upper portions of these rivers form a muleshoe-shaped area, closed to the northwest, which surrounds and confines the other rivers of Texas and prevents additional development of their watersheds.

The valleys and floodplains of most Texas rivers are much larger and wider than the present average runoff would suggest, the Brazos bottom being an example. It is possible that during Pleistocene times, when the ice front stood near St. Louis and Kansas City and many valley glaciers were hanging on the east slopes of the southern Rocky Mountains, cold banks of air blanketed these areas, and, as the warmer southern breezes drifted north, precipitation far in excess of anything now known fell, giving the Texas rivers many times their present runoff and developing the wide floodplains so characteristic of them.

Hal P. Bybee

Roberts, Oran Milo. Governor; b. Laurens District, South Carolina, 9 July 1815; d. Austin, 19 May 1898 (buried in the State Cemetery); m. Frances W. Edwards (1837; d. 1883); 7 children; m. Mrs. Catherine E. Border (1887); ed. University of Alabama (grad. 1836). Roberts was admitted to the bar in 1837 and served a

term in the Alabama legislature before moving in 1841 to San Augustine, where he practiced law. President Sam Houston appointed him a district attorney (1844), and Gov. James P. Henderson made him a district judge. He taught at the University of San Augustine. In 1856 he was elected to the state Supreme Court. As a champion of states' rights he was chosen to head the Secession Convention and led in the passage of the Ordinance of Secession (1861). He raised an East Texas regiment and served briefly in the Civil War before returning to Austin as chief justice of the Supreme Court, a post from which he was removed (like all Confederate officials) in 1865. Roberts was a delegate to the Constitutional Convention of 1866. With David G. Burnet he was elected United States senator, but the Texas delegation, like that of other Southern states, was not seated because of the Radical Republican majority in Congress. Roberts opened a law school in Gilmer, in 1868. When the Democrats regained control of the state, he was elected to the Texas Supreme Court. As chief justice he oversaw the rewriting of much of the state civil code. In 1878 he was elected governor. His two terms were marked by a "pay as you go" policy of fiscal responsibility, sorely needed after Reconstruction, that reduced state expenditures but temporarily slowed school growth. His lowering of taxes kept him popular. During his governorship the Capitol construction was contracted, the University of Texas was built and opened (1883), railroad mileage increased in West Texas, and the frontier became more secure. Upon leaving office (1883), Roberts became professor of law at UT, where his great influence upon the Texas legal profession earned him the nickname "Old Alcalde." He wrote several important historical works as well as a highly influential legal textbook, *The Elements of Texas Pleading* (1890). He lived in Marble Falls from 1893 to 1895, then returned to Austin. There he helped form, and became first president of, the Texas State Historical Association.

Ford Dixon

Robertson, Sterling Clack. Empresario; b. Nashville, Tennessee, 2 October 1785; d. Robertson County, 4 March 1842 (reinterred in 1935 in the State Cemetery, Austin); m. Rachel Smith; 1 son; m. Frances King; 1 son. After serving as deputy quartermaster general at the battle of New Orleans, Robertson purchased supplies and equipment for the sick and wounded on their return to Nashville over the Natchez Trace. By 1816 he was living in Giles County, Tennessee, where he owned a plantation. He was one of the 70 stockholders of the Texas Association who signed a memorial to the Mexican government asking for permission to settle in Texas (2 March 1822). In 1825, with 31 other members of Dr. Felix Robertson's party, he set out from Nashville for Texas to explore and survey Robert Leftwich's grant. Robertson remained in Texas until August 1826, when he returned to Tennessee, filled with enthusiasm for the colonization of Texas. He toured Tennessee and Kentucky in an attempt to recruit settlers. In the spring of 1830 he signed a subcontract with the Texas Association to introduce 200 families, and on 9 May of that year took Alexander Thomson as his partner. The families they brought to Texas were prevented from settling in the colony because of the Law of April 6, 1830. In 1831 that area was transferred to Stephen F. Austin and Samuel May Williams, but Robertson obtained a contract in his own name in 1834 and served as empresario of his own colony in 1834 and 1835. In 1836 he became captain of a company of Texas Rangers and was

Sterling C. Robertson. Courtesy Special Collections Division, University of Texas at Arlington Libraries.

elected a delegate from the Municipality of Milam to the convention at WashingtonontheBrazos (1–17 March 1836), where he signed the Texas Declaration of Independence and the Constitution of the Republic of Texas. He was stationed at Harrisburg to guard army equipment during the battle of San Jacinto. Robertson served as senator from the Milam District in the First and Second congresses of the republic (1836–38). Afterward he retired to his home in Robertson County, where he became the earliest known breeder of Arabian horses in Texas. He was responsible for settling more than 600 families in Texas.

Malcolm D. McLean

Robinson, James W. Provisional governor; b. in what is now Hamilton County, Indiana, 1790; d. San Diego, California, October 1857; m. Mary Isdell (1820; divorced); 5 children; m. Sarah Snider; 1 son. Robinson was admitted to the bar in Indiana and was a law partner of William Henry Harrison. When he left for Arkansas in 1828 he deserted his family. He arrived in Texas in 1833 with a letter of recommendation to Stephen F. Austin, settled at Nacogdoches, and in 1835 received title to a league of land in Joseph Vehlein's colony (now in San Jacinto County). Robinson was a delegate from Nacogdoches to the Consultation in 1835 and was elected lieutenant governor of the provisional government. The executive council of the provisional government deposed Governor Henry Smith on 11 January 1836 and named Robinson as his successor. Smith, claiming that there was no quorum present when he was deposed, refused to relinquish the office, and as a result both Smith and Robinson claimed to be governor. Robinson served in the Texas army and fought at the battle of San Jacinto as a cavalry private under William H. Smith. He was afterward (1836) living in Gonzales County when Congress elected him judge of the Fourth Judicial District, a post that automatically made him a member of the Supreme Court. He resigned in January 1840 and later opened a law practice in Austin. Robinson was wounded in the Council House Fight at San Antonio (19 March 1840). He was again in San Antonio when it was captured by Adrián Woll in September 1842 and was one of those carried prisoner to Mexico. There he opened a clandestine correspondence with Antonio López de Santa Anna and reached an agreement by which he was to be released from prison and allowed to return to Texas with terms for an agreement between Texas and Mexico. Robinson reached Galveston on 27 March 1843, conferred with President Sam Houston at WashingtonontheBrazos, obtained his release, and may have been responsible for the negotiations that resulted in an armistice of several months between Texas and Mexico. In 1850 he moved to California. In San Diego he was district attorney from 1852 to 1855 and school commissioner in 1854. He acquired considerable property and helped promote a railroad from El Paso to California. When his estate was finally distributed in 1903 his children were all dead, and 71 legatees, chiefly grandchildren, shared in the property settlement.

L. W. Kemp

Roddenberry, Gene. TV writer and producer; b. El Paso, 19 August 1921; d. Santa Monica, California, 25 October 1991; m. Eileen Anita Rexroat (1942; divorced 1969); 2 daughters; m. Majel Leigh Hudec (1969); 1 son. Roddenberry grew up in Los Angeles, where his father worked in law enforcement. He attended Los Angeles City College, the University of Miami, Columbia University, and the University of Southern California, where he studied prelaw and aeronautical engineering. In the United States Air Force in World War II he flew a B-17 Flying Fortress on 89 missions, including Guadalcanal and Bougainville, and received the Distinguished Flying Cross, the Air Medal, and several other decorations. After the war, as a pilot with Pan American Airlines, he survived a crash in the Syrian desert in which 38 of 46 passengers were killed. From 1949 to 1953 he was a sergeant with the Los Angeles Police Department, where he worked as departmental spokesman and as Chief William H. Parker's speechwriter. He also began writing for television; in the 1950s and early 1960s his scripts were produced on "Dragnet," "Naked City," "The U.S. Steel Hour," and "Goodyear Theater," among other series. He received his first Emmy award as head writer for "Have Gun, Will Travel," a western series, and produced the television series "The Lieutenant" in 1960–61. He also produced the feature film *Pretty Maids All in a Row* in 1970. Roddenberry is best remembered, however, for "Star Trek," which premiered in 1966 and ran until 1969. The series became a cult favorite, spawned numerous fan clubs, products, and conventions, and later became one of the most popular syndicated shows in reruns. Six "Star Trek" feature films had been produced by the time of Roddenberry's death; he produced the first and was executive consultant on the next three. He was also executive producer of the sequel series, "Star Trek: The Next Generation," and coauthored two books, *The Making of Star Trek* (1968) and *Star Trek—The Motion Picture: A Novel* (1979). His book *The Questor Tapes* was published in 1974. Although Roddenberry once deprecatingly described "Star Trek" as "'Wagon Train' to the stars," one critic said that it "establish[ed]

Jimmie Rodgers in his famous "thumbs up" pose, ca. 1930. Courtesy Nolan Porterfield Collection, Cape Girardeau, Missouri. Rodgers, often referred to as the "father" of modern country music, recorded 111 songs, and sold 20 million records between 1927 and 1933.

a new level of quality for television science fiction." Roddenberry received awards from the Writers Guild of America, the National Academy of Television Arts and Sciences, and other television organizations, and "Star Trek" won an Emmy, an international Hugo award for outstanding science fiction writing, and an Image award from the NAACP. In 1985 a star in Roddenberry's honor was placed in the Hollywood Walk of Fame. He was a member of the Television Academy of Arts and Sciences, the Writers Guild of America, the American Civil Liberties Union, the American Humanist Association, the Association for Professional Law Enforcement, and the Explorers Club of New York City. His second wife appeared on both "Star Trek" series under the name Majel Barrett.

Martin Donell Kohout

Rodgers, Jimmie. The "father of modern country music"; b. James Charles Rodgers, Meridian, Mississippi, 8 September 1897; d. New York City, 26 May 1933 (buried in Meridian); m. Carrie Cecil Williamson (1920); 2 daughters. Rodgers grew up on the railroad and learned songs from black railroad workers, who also taught him to play the banjo and the guitar. Tuberculosis forced him to retire, after which he went through a chain of odd jobs and migrations in the South and Southwest. He served a brief stint as an entertainer with a medicine show and for a while

was a city detective in Asheville, North Carolina, where he had moved in search of a more healthful climate. He organized the Jimmie Rodgers Entertainers in Asheville, and the group performed on the local radio station, singing both popular and country music. In 1927 he signed a contract with the Victor Talking Machine Company, and his records catapulted him to almost immediate fame. Rodgers introduced a new form to commercial hillbilly music, the blue yodel, heard best in the "Blue Yodel" series. One song of this 12-song series has remained one of the most popular of his songs and has become known as "T for Texas." He recorded 111 songs altogether and sold 20 million records between 1927 and 1933. He earned as much as $100,000 annually, but medical bills took most of it. Billed during his professional career as "America's Blue Yodeler" and "The Singing Brakeman," Rodgers, although unable to read music, enthralled radio, recording, and stage audiences. His records included "The One Rose," "The TB Blues," "In the Jailhouse Now," "Any Old Time," "Carolina Sunshine Girl," and "The Yodeling Ranger" (composed shortly after Rodgers was made an honorary Texas Ranger in Austin in 1931). His guitar technique and his blue yodel were emulated by scores of young country and western singers, including Jimmie Davis, Hank Snow, Gene Autry, Ernest Tubb, Hank Williams, and Kenneth Threadgill. For his health he moved to the Hill Country of Texas and restricted himself to performances in the South and Southwest. He lived in Kerrville, then San Antonio, and died on a recording trip. By unanimous vote he was the first person named to the Country Music Hall of Fame in Nashville (1961).

Rodríguez, Chipita. Thought for many years to be the only woman ever legally hanged in Texas; d. 13 November 1863. Most of her story, including her given name, Josefa, is conjecture. Her father is said to have fled from Antonio López de Santa Anna. Chipita moved with her father to San Patricio while young, and for many years after his death furnished travelers with meals and a cot on the porch of her lean-to shack on the Aransas River. When Cotton Road traveler John Savage was murdered with an ax, presumably for the $600 in gold that he had been carrying, Chipita was accused of robbery and murder. Recovery of the gold from the Aransas River north of San Patricio, where Savage's body was found in a burlap bag, raised substantial doubt about the motive for the crime, but Josefa Rodríguez and Juan Silvera (who sources suggest may have been her illegitimate son) were indicted and tried at San Patricio anyway. After Chipita pleaded not guilty, the jury recommended mercy, but the judge ordered her executed. For some time she was held at sheriff William Means's home in Meansville, where two attempts by a lynching mob were thwarted. According to legend, Chipita was kept in leg irons and chained to a wall in the courthouse. There, local children brought her candy and cornshucks to make cigarettes. At the time, she was described as "very old" or "about 90," but was probably in her sixties. The court records, except for a week of transcripts, were burned in a courthouse fire or lost in a flood, and many discrepancies and irregularities exist in trial accounts; e.g., the foreman of the grand jury was the sheriff who arrested her. Legend says that resident Betty McCumber drove off hangman John Gilpin when he came for her wagon to transport Chipita to the hanging tree. At least one witness to the hanging claimed he later heard a moan from the coffin, which was placed in an unmarked grave. Many tales have arisen as a result of the trial and the hanging, one of which claims that Chipita was protecting her illegitimate son. Her ghost, with a noose around its neck, is said to wail from the riverbottoms, especially when a woman is scheduled to be executed. Chipita has been the subject of two operas and numerous books, newspaper articles, and magazine accounts. In 1985 the legislature absolved her of murder. Jane Elkins, a slave convicted of murder, was hanged on 27 May 1853 in Dallas. She was actually the first woman legally hanged in the state. *Marylyn Underwood*

Rodríguez–Sánchez expedition. An important sixteenth-century Spanish missionary expedition. The advance of the northern frontier of the viceroyalty of New Spain led to the founding in 1567 of Santa Bárbara, located in what is now southern Chihuahua on one of the tributaries of the Río Conchos. Because this river flows northward to the Rio Grande, Santa Bárbara became the primary base for the exploration and colonization of New Mexico in the remaining decades of the century. On 5 June 1581, three Franciscans—Agustín Rodríguez, Francisco López, and Juan de Santa María—left Santa Bárbara to explore missionary possibilities in the country to the north. They were accompanied by an armed escort of 8 soldiers under the command of Francisco Sánchez (also called Chamuscado), 19 Indian servants, 90 horses, and 600 head of stock. The party descended the Conchos and at its junction with the Rio Grande entered the territory of the Cabris nation, described as a handsome, well-built, intelligent people, who gave the Spaniards food and told them that some years before four Christians had passed through the area—no doubt Cabeza de Vaca and his companions. The Indians added that there were more, much larger settlements upstream. The expedition continued along the west bank of the Rio Grande through the area of present El Paso and in August 1581 arrived at the Piro and Tigua pueblos of New Mexico. On 21 August the party took formal possession of the land for the king of Spain. For the remainder of the year it explored extensively in all directions, covering much of the same territory viewed by Vásquez de Coronado 40 years before. In the meantime, Fray Santa María had ill-advisedly set out on his own to report to the viceroy and was killed by Indians in September 1581, though his companions did not learn of his fate until sometime later. In early 1582 Sánchez and his men discussed the desirability of returning to Santa Bárbara to report to the viceroy, but Fray Rodríguez and Fray López announced their intention of pursuing further their missionary endeavors in New Mexico. They did not heed Sánchez's warnings of the great dangers involved and, on 31 January 1582, stayed behind when the little band returned to Santa Bárbara. The aged Sánchez died before reaching the northern outpost, but the rest of the party arrived there on April 15, after an absence of almost 11 months. Glowing accounts of great wealth in New Mexico, together with the concern about the safety of the friars, led to preparations for another expedition to the new land. Thus, the discovery by the Rodríguez–Sánchez expedition of a new route to New Mexico laid the foundation for the introduction of Spanish civilization in what is now the American Southwest. *W. H. Timmons*

Roe v. Wade. A Texas case involved in the legalization of abortion by the Supreme Court (22 January 1973). The court's ruling that, under the Fourteenth Amendment, women have a right to abortion, overturned a Texas law making all abortions (except those performed to save the life of the woman) illegal, and by implication overturned antiabortion statutes in most other states. After contraception was decriminalized by the Supreme Court in *Griswold v. Connecticut*, some women who were already pregnant sought abortions. In March 1970 a suit was filed in Dallas in a three-judge federal district court on behalf of a pregnant woman known as Jane Roe and all other women "who were or might become pregnant and want to consider all options." The suit was against Dallas district attorney Henry Wade. The court declared that the "freedom to choose in the matter of abortions has been accorded the status of a 'fundamental' right in every case the court had examined, and that the burden is on the defendant to demonstrate to the satisfaction of the court that the infringement [by the Texas abortion laws] is necessary to support a compelling state interest." Although this burden was not met and the court declared the Texas law unconstitutional, the court still refused to issue an injunction against Wade. The following day Wade announced that he would continue to prosecute physicians who did abortions. Both sides appealed, and eventually the Supreme Court agreed to hear the case. The Supreme Court's 1973 decision held that there was a constitutional right of privacy, and that it extends to abortion. Seven justices joined the majority opinion written by Justice Harry Blackmun; two justices dissented. Justices William Rehnquist and Byron White, the dissenters, asserted that there was no right of personal privacy such as that recognized by the majority. The dissent further pointed out that, since the laws of a majority of the states had restricted abortion for at least a century, the asserted right to an abortion is not "so rooted in the traditions and conscience of our people as to be ranked as fundamental." Instead of ending the legal and public debate about abortion, the *Roe* decision became the focal point for increased turmoil. At the end of the century, the debate about abortion continued—evidence that the right to an abortion is far from universally accepted. "Jane Roe" herself became an outspoken opponent of abortion. The future of *Roe* may depend upon appointments to and retirements from the Supreme Court. *Sarah Weddington*

Rogers, Ginger. Movie actress and dancer; b. Virginia Katherine McMath, Independence, Missouri, 16 July 1911; d. 25 April 1995; m. (and divorced) 5 times: to Edward "Jack Pepper" Culpepper (1928–31), Lew Ayres (1934–41), Jack Briggs (1943–49), Jacques Bergerac (1953–57), and William Marshall (1961–67). In 1922 Ginger moved to Fort Worth with her mother and adoptive father, John Logan Rogers. In 1925 she won a Dallas Charleston dance contest; the prize was a brief vaudeville contract. Beginning with "Ginger Rogers and Her Redheads," she worked the vaudeville circuits until 1929, when she took her first role in a Broadway musical comedy, *Top Speed*. That led to her film debut the same year in the Paramount picture *Young Man of Manhattan*. After several more Broadway productions, she moved to Hollywood. She made 71 motion pictures over 35 years for several studios. She was praised for her dramatic and comedic performances in such movies as *Stage Door* (1937), *The Barkleys of Broadway* (1949), *Storm Warning* (1951), and *Kitty Foyle*, for which she won an Oscar in 1940. Despite her formidable acting skills, Rogers is best remembered as the dancing partner of Fred Astaire in nine films, including *Flying Down to Rio* (1933), *The Gay Divorcee* (1934), *Swing Time* (1936), and *Top Hat* (1935). An often repeated comment about Rogers's perfection as a dance partner is that "she did everything Fred Astaire did, except backwards and in high heels." She made her final motion picture appearance in 1965 as actress Jean Harlow's mother in *Harlow*. She performed in several stage musicals until the middle to late 1960s, when she retired from show business.

John H. Slate

Roloff, Lester. Minister; b. Navarro County, 28 June 1914; d. Leon County, 2 November 1982; m. Marie Brady (1936); 1 child (and 1 adopted); ed. Baylor University (grad. 1936) and Southwestern Baptist Theological Seminary (3 years). Roloff preached at various Baptist churches before accepting the pastorate of Park Avenue (later Second) Baptist Church in Corpus Christi (mid-1940s), where he organized the Baptist Ministerial Alliance. On 8 May 1944 he launched his "Family Altar" radio program over a 250-watt station. His home church experienced phenomenal growth, and in 1946 he opened Park Avenue Christian Day School as an extension of that ministry. Success at revival preaching led Roloff to resign his pastorate go into full-time evangelism. In 1951 his ministry was incorporated as Roloff Evangelistic Enterprises. His scathing attacks on alcoholism and other national sins often triggered criticism from more liberal elements, while his renditions of Christian hymns and folk songs like "When Jesus Comes" and "The Little House on Hallelujah Street" won him considerable notice as a Gospel singer. In 1945, while chairman of the Baylor Civil Rights Platform Committee, Roloff had opposed his alma mater's decision to grant President Truman an honorary degree because of the latter's salty language and failure to uphold certain Bible standards in daily life. Many denominational leaders began branding him as "controversial," and invitations to lead revivals and serve on committees lessened. Even so, his own ministry continued to expand, and in October 1954 he organized the Alameda Street Baptist Church, which gained 374 members within its first six months. Among other enterprises, this church took over the Good Samaritan Rescue Mission, a ministry to alcoholics and addicts, in Corpus Christi; later a second such mission was opened in Big Spring. Roloff started a monthly newsletter, *Faith Enterprise*, in May 1955, and later he published a small booklet entitled *Food, Fasting and Faith*, which contained biblical guidelines to wholesome nutrition. During that time he obtained his pilot's license and started his own "airborne" ministry. After the Baptist General Convention of Texas, which owned Station KWBU, canceled Roloff's radio program, the station went broke. Roloff Enterprises bought it, moved it to Corpus Christi, and revived it as Station KCTA (for "Know Christ the Answer").

By 1956 Roloff's break with the Southern Baptist Convention was complete. In 1956 he opened the City of Refuge, a rehabilitation center in Lee County for men and boys who were addicted or in trouble with the law. The center was moved in 1964 to the Mission area. Two years later, as the City of Refuge mushroomed, the men aged 25 and older were moved to new facilities on the grounds of an antebellum plantation near Culloden, Georgia, that Roloff Enterprises bought, while the boys remained in the Valley. At Culloden the ministry started its first rehabilitation home for troubled women (1960s). In the summer of 1958 Roloff launched his Lighthouse ministry—a houseboat dormitory built in a remote fishing area on the Gulf Intracoastal Waterway, accessible only by boat or plane. Here boys and young men addicted to alcohol and drugs or on probation were isolated from civilization for periods of time, so that they could get their lives straightened out in a quiet seaside environment. Before long, additional facilities were needed, and thousands of young men in jail were sent to the Lighthouse by judges and probation officers. In 1967 Roloff started a ministry to unwed mothers, which became the Rebekah Home for Girls in Corpus Christi (1968), a successful institution that opened a branch in Hattiesburg, Mississippi. In 1969 Roloff Enterprises purchased land south of downtown Corpus Christi for its new headquarters. There Roloff established his People's Baptist Church. Dormitories and a school were erected for the Rebekah Home, as were new facilities for the City of Refuge and Lighthouse ministries. The Jubilee Home was built for troubled women, and the Lighthouse, which continued to use the Intracoastal Waterway buildings for fishing and camping, limited its ministry to young men between the ages of 18 and 25. The Anchor Home was begun for troubled boys under the age of 18, while the Peaceful Valley Home, a retirement community for Christian senior citizens, was opened near the Lighthouse facility at Mission. In all, over the next decade, Roloff Enterprises built two rescue missions and eight homes for people of all age groups in need of help.

In 1971 the Texas Department of Public Welfare sent Roloff a letter demanding that the Rebekah and Anchor homes be licensed or closed. Roloff considered the order a breach of church–state separation. The controversy that followed eventually wound up in the Supreme Court, which ruled in favor of the state (1978). Meanwhile, Roloff had been in jail twice, had been attacked by newspapers such as the Corpus Christi *Caller–Times*, and had spent months in legal counseling, appearances in court, and meetings with officials. Many thought that the new Texas Child Care and Licensing Act (1975) had been aimed specifically at Roloff Enterprises. Rather than allow the young residents of his homes to be taken to state facilities, Roloff had them sent to the ministry's homes in Georgia and Mississippi (1979). He subsequently transferred ownership of the homes to the People's Church, after which the homes were opened once more. Despite these conflicts, Roloff continued to expand his ministries. In 1982 he bought 75 acres near the San Carlos Apache Reservation in Arizona, where he set up the "Regeneration Reservation," a ministry to make disciples of young Indians. Regeneration Baptist Church became the nucleus of this enterprise. Roloff, who had often remarked how he looked forward to taking that "ride" to Heaven, was killed with four young female staff workers when their plane crashed on the way to a preaching and singing service. By the end of 1985, mounting problems with the DHS prompted the Roloff ministries to "exile" the Rebekah and Anchor Homes to Belton, Missouri, where dormitory space was temporarily provided by Calvary Bible College. In 1987 the Peaceful Valley Home in Mission was sold to help meet mounting expenses. The rescue missions and other ministries have continued to operate "by faith" from funds contributed by People's Church members and other supporters nationwide, without any government aid. The "Family Altar" program continues to air over some 120 stations throughout the United States and the West Indies, including nine 50,000-watt stations. In 1978 Marie Roloff published a biography of her husband, *Lester Roloff: Living by Faith*.

H. Allen Anderson

Ronquillo Land Grant. A Mexican desert grant of 225 leagues; now part of Presidio, Brewster, and Jeff Davis counties, Texas.

The grant would never have become historically important if silver had not been discovered there in 1880. John Spencer and his three partners bought the land around his strike in the Houston and Texas Central Railway company survey, Presidio County, from the state of Texas in 1885. The partnership later sold its claim to the Presidio Mining Company, which operated the Presidio Mine at Shafter. By 1942 the Presidio Mine had produced more than 32 million ounces of silver. Meanwhile, several claimants arose to assert rights to the land on which the silver was located. Central to their claims was the Ronquillo grant, which had been issued conditionally to José Ygnacio Ronquillo in 1832. Although Ronquillo began to fulfill the requirements of his grant, his military service forced him to move. He petitioned the alcalde of Presidio del Norte, Cesario Herrera, to waive the restrictions on his grant, since he had to leave for military reasons. Herrera provided him with a certificate to that effect. Ronquillo then sold the land, but subsequent owners found the area too difficult to settle. The last person to purchase the grant was Juana Pedrasa, who moved to Chihuahua and married Ben Leaton of Fort Leaton fame. In 1887 Leaton's heir, Victor Ochoa, set out to claim the territory through investigation into the Ronquillo grant. Leaton had already investigated Juana's claim in the 1850s but dropped the investigation when his attorney found a difficulty in the claim. In 1887 Ochoa hired Trevanion T. Teel, a San Antonio attorney, to confirm the grant for the Leaton heirs. Teel went to Juárez for research in the archives and discovered a decree he thought might prove the legality of the grant. He lost his copy before he could get it translated, however, and sent Ochoa to get another copy. Instead Ochoa substituted a forged document that confirmed the waiver of Alcalde Herrera. Teel, unaware of the switch, concluded that the grant was valid. In 1889 he filed two suits in the United States Circuit Court for the Western District of Texas on behalf of the Leaton heirs, claiming that they owned the land within the Ronquillo grant and that the state had violated agreements of the Treaty of Guadalupe Hidalgo and Article XII of the United States Constitution when they reassigned the land to the railways. One suit, against the mining companies for recognition of true ownership, requested $1 million in damages and $6,000 per month rental. The other, against the Texas and Pacific Railway Company, the Houston and Texas Central Railway Company, the St. Louis and Texas Railway Company, and the Galveston, Harrisburg and San Antonio Railway Company, asked for recognition of the grant by the court.

Meanwhile, one E. N. Ronquillo began investigations to claim the grant, asserting that the land had not been legally conveyed to the purchasers, and that it therefore could not belong to Juana Leaton, but remained the property of the heirs of José Ygnacio Ronquillo, who died in 1860 at San Elizario. E. N. Ronquillo sold his claim for a reported $100,000 to James J. Fitzgerrell of Las Vegas, New Mexico; with a partner, Fitzgerrell sold his rights to Ernest Dale Owen of Chicago and the Texas Land and Cattle Company for $4.5 million. Teel successfully challenged Ronquillo's claim by showing that his ancestor was not the same José Ygnacio Ronquillo as the one to whom the original grant had been issued. But the Leaton heirs fired Teel because he had failed to validate their claim to the land. In 1890 Teel dropped the suits he had filed in the circuit court. Owen, however, continued to attempt to legitimize his claim. In 1890 he filed seven trespass-to-try-title suits in the United States Circuit

Court against the railroad, mining companies, and other claimants. He based his original argument upon the Juárez forgery, but when the railroad and mining companies alleged that it was a forgery, he examined it and agreed that it was invalid. He therefore sent researchers to Mexico to find the original document. When it was finally found in Santa Bárbara, the decree did not have the governor's rubric. Owen bought the interests of all the contenders to title and in 1892 brought his case to trial against the Presidio Mining Company. The court held that a valid grant was issued to José Ygnacio Ronquillo in 1832, but that Alcalde Herrera was not authorized to waive the restrictions on the grant. In an appeal the United States Circuit Court of Appeals ruled in 1893 that the alcalde had no authority to make such a large grant after the Mexican colonization law of 1825. The court held that the Santa Bárbara decree was a forgery and dismissed the case. After several other suits, Owen admitted defeat and concluded his eight-year, multimillion-dollar attempt to confirm the grant. *Julia Cauble Smith*

Ross, Sul. Governor; b. Lawrence Sullivan Ross, Bentonsport, Iowa Territory, 27 September 1838; d. College Station, 3 January 1898; m. Elizabeth Dorothy Tinsley (1861); 9 children; ed. Baylor University and Wesleyan University, Florence, Alabama (A.B., 1859). The Ross family moved to Texas in 1839, and Ross began his military career while on vacation from college by leading a band of Indian auxiliaries from the Brazos Indian Reservation against the Comanches (1858); he was wounded and nearly died. After graduating, he joined the Texas Rangers and fought with Middleton Tate Johnson's troops in a notoriously unsuccessful Indian campaign. Given authority by Sam Houston, however, Ross raised his own company for frontier defense and achieved fame by the rescue of Cynthia Ann Parker in 1860. He fought in the Civil War under command of his older brother, Peter F. Ross, in the Sixth Texas Cavalry; after numerous western campaigns, he was promoted to brigadier general (1864) in command of the Texas Cavalry Brigade (Ross's Brigade), which saw action in Georgia and Tennessee. In poor health, Ross farmed for eight years after the war. He subsequently served with distinction as sheriff of McLennan County (1873–) and was chosen a delegate to the Constitutional Convention of 1875. He was elected to the state Senate in 1880 and to the governor's office in 1886. During his two terms (1887–91) agriculture, industry, commerce, eleemosynary institutions, and education flourished, and the Capitol was finished. Upon leaving office Ross became president of Texas A&M, an institution that was troubled upon his arrival but gained new growth and public confidence during his tenure. Ross was elected commander of the Texas Division of United Confederate Veterans in 1893. In 1895 he turned down the offer of a position on the Railroad Commission because accepting it would have taken him away from A&M. After his death he was praised for his "great service to Texas." Sul Ross State University in Alpine is named for him. *Judith Ann Benner*

Rubí, Marqués de. Spanish official and diarist; b. probably in Barcelona, ca. 1725; achieved the high rank of field marshal and knight commander in the Order of Alcántara before being sent to Mexico (1764). In 1765 King Carlos III appointed him inspector of frontier presidios. Rubí went to Mexico City and on 12 March 1766 set out on his inspection, traveling first to Querétaro and then to Zacatecas. In April he was joined at Durango by

Nicolás de Lafora, his engineer and mapmaker, who kept a diary of the tour, as did Rubí himself. Rubí began his inspection tour in New Mexico, moved to Sonora, and then traveled eastward to Coahuila. He crossed the Rio Grande in July 1767 and proceeded to San Luis de las Amarillas Presidio (San Sabá) by way of the upper Nueces River, where he visited the largely failed missions at El Cañón. He left San Sabá on August 4 and reached San Antonio de Béxar on 24 August 1767. From San Antonio, he traveled to Los Adaes. Subsequently, he also inspected the presidios at El Orcoquisac and La Bahía before leaving Texas at Laredo in November 1767. In all, Rubí's inspection of the northern frontier from the Gulf of California to Louisiana occupied him for 23 months, during which he traveled an estimated 7,600 miles. As a result of his inspection, Rubí recommended that Spain reorganize its frontier defenses along a cordon of 15 presidios, each about 100 miles apart, that would stretch from the Gulf of California to the mouth of the Guadalupe River in Texas. Above this "real" frontier, which closely approximated the present international boundary between the United States and Mexico, Rubí advised that only San Antonio and Santa Fe be maintained, and he urged the complete abandonment of East Texas. Finally, because of their perfidy and duplicity, Rubí recommended a war of extermination against the Lipan Apaches. He was back in Mexico City by February 1768, and he filed his official report on 10 April. More than four years passed before a royal order commonly known as the New Regulations for Presidios was issued, on 10 September 1772. The New Regulations had enormous impact on Texas. They called for the abandonment of all missions and presidios in Texas except for those at San Antonio and La Bahía; the strengthening of San Antonio by designating it the new capital of Texas; the removal of soldiers and settlers in East Texas; and the implementation of a new Indian policy aimed at establishing good relations with the northern nations at the expense of the Apaches. With respect to East Texas, Rubí's recommendations were enacted in 1773 but were soon vitiated by the return of settlers to the region and the founding of Nacogdoches in 1779. After he sailed from Veracruz in July 1768, the remainder of Rubí's life is largely obscure. He was summoned to court in 1769 to defend his proposals, and he was in Barcelona in April 1772. When Carlos III died in 1788, Rubí may have accepted retirement at about the age of 63. His diary was not known to exist until a copy was discovered in 1989 in a volume of bound documents acquired by the Barker Texas History Center at the University of Texas at Austin.

Donald E. Chipman

Ruby, George Thompson. Politician; b. New York, 1841; d. New Orleans, 31 October 1882; m. Lucy ———. Ruby was a free-born black, probably a mulatto. He lived in Portland, Maine, Haiti, and Louisiana (1864) before joining the Freedmen's Bureau at Galveston. There he administered the bureau's schools, served as a correspondent for the New Orleans *Tribune*, and taught school at a Methodist church at a salary of $100 a month. He later began publication of the short-lived Galveston *Standard*. Upon leaving Galveston he became a traveling agent for the bureau, a position in which he visited Washington, Austin, Bastrop, Fort Bend, and other counties, with the purpose of establishing chapters of the Union League as well as temperance societies. Ruby served as a traveling agent until October 1867. In 1869 he was appointed deputy collector of customs at Galveston, a position in which he

was an important patronage broker. During his tenure he was on friendly terms with Governor Edmund Davis and with such prominent white Galvestonians as Victor McMahan of the McMahan Banking House, businessman C. B. Gardiner, district judge Chauncey B. Sabin and county judge Samuel Dodge. Even though he relinquished his position with the Freedmen's Bureau, he still was affiliated with the Union League and became president of that organization in 1868. It was the league more than anything else that enabled Ruby to rise within the ranks of the Republican party, for through this organization he influenced the large black constituency of the party. Consequently, Ruby was elected delegate to the national Republican convention in 1868; he was the only black in the Texas delegation. In that same year, he also was elected a delegate to the state Constitutional Convention of 1868–69. In the election of 1869, when many whites decided not to go to the polls, Ruby was elected to the state Senate from the predominantly white Twelfth District. As senator, he became one of the most influential men of the Twelfth and Thirteenth legislatures. He introduced successful bills to incorporate the Galveston and El Paso, the Galveston, Harrisburg and San Antonio, and the Galveston, Houston and Tyler railroads, the Harbor Trust Company, and a number of insurance companies, and to provide for the geological and agricultural survey of the state. Before the Civil War, whites had dominated work on the docks of Galveston, but after 1870 the situation changed, partly because of Ruby's organizing the first Labor Union of Colored Men at Galveston. Ruby chose not to seek reelection in 1873 because the Democrats had achieved a majority in the Senate. He saw the power of the Radical Republicans declining and moved back to Louisiana, where he considered the situation more hopeful. In New Orleans he became clerk of the surveyor for the Port of New Orleans and worked with the internal revenue department. In the late 1870s he strongly supported the Exoduster movement, a popular, unorganized migration of more than 20,000 blacks from Tennessee, Mississippi, Louisiana, and Texas to the Kansas frontier, a move encouraged by heightened racial violence in the South. From 1877 to 1882 Ruby edited a newspaper for blacks, the New Orleans *Observer*.

Merline Pitre

Ruby, Jack. Killer of Lee Harvey Oswald; b. Jacob Rubenstein, Chicago, 25 March 1911; d. Dallas, 3 January 1967. At age 16 he dropped out of school and became part of the street life on Chicago's West Side. There he worked at various odd jobs, which at one time included delivering sealed envelopes for Al Capone at a dollar an errand, and engaged in years of street-fighting, often in response to anti-Semitic taunts. He moved to California in 1933 and for a while sold subscriptions to the San Francisco *Examiner*. After returning to Chicago in 1937, he was hired by Leon Cooke to assist in organizing a union of junkyard workers. After losing control of the union to Chicago racketeers, Cooke was murdered by the union president in 1939. Ruby left a few months later. It is unclear whether he was connected with the Chicago syndicate. In 1941 he worked for the Spartan Novelty Company and in late 1942 for the Globe Auto Glass Company and the Universal Sales Company. During World War II he was drafted into the United States Army Air Corps (1943) and spent the war at southern bases working as an aircraft mechanic. He received a good-conduct medal and was discharged in 1946 as a private first class. He then joined his brothers in the Earl

Products Company, which manufactured punchboard gambling devices, miniature cedar chests, key chains, and small kitchen items. In 1947 the men changed their name to Ruby and the brothers bought Jack out. He moved to Dallas and went into the nightclub business with his sister. Over the next 16 years he ran a series of mostly unsuccessful nightclubs, sold items ranging from liquid vitamin formulas to log cabins, and was arrested nine times, although no serious charges were filed. On 24 November 1963, two days after the Kennedy assassination, Ruby, then proprietor of the Carousel Club, shot and killed Lee Harvey Oswald in the basement of the Dallas City Jail. Oswald was being transferred to the county jail. Millions of witnesses watched on national television. Although he was defended by Melvin Belli on the grounds that "psychomotor epilepsy" caused him to black out consciously while functioning physically, Ruby was convicted of murder with malice and sentenced to death. In October 1966, however, the Texas Court of Criminal Appeals reversed the conviction on the grounds of improper admission of testimony and the necessity of a change of venue. The arrangements for a new trial in February, in Wichita Falls, were under way, when, on 9 December 1966, Ruby was admitted to Parkland Hospital in Dallas, apparently suffering from pneumonia. Testing quickly revealed terminal lung cancer. Ruby never married. He espoused no political affiliation or party preference, denied any involvement in a conspiracy, and maintained to the end that he shot Oswald on impulse from grief and outrage.

Joan Jenkins Perez

Rump Senate. A term applied to the 15 Radical Republican members of the Twelfth Texas Legislature, which met during the strife of Reconstruction. In the spring of 1870 the introduction of the militia bill, which provided for discretionary power of the governor in declaring martial law, caused a fight in the Senate. The 15 radicals were for the bill; 13 Democrats and 3 conservatives were opposed. Thirteen of the opponents withdrew from the Senate to prevent the presence of a quorum and so to prevent passage of the bill. The radicals then had their opponents arrested and excluded all but four of them from their seats. The four were necessary for a quorum with which the Rump Senate passed such measures as the militia bill, a law establishing the State Police, and an act increasing the appointive power of the governor. The conservative members were held under arrest some three weeks while the Rump Senate passed the radical legislation.

Runaway Scrape. The name Texans applied to their flight when Antonio López de Santa Anna began his attempted subjugation of Texas in February 1836. The first communities to be affected were around San Patricio, Refugio, and San Antonio. Residents began to leave that area as early as 14 January, when the Mexicans were gathering on the Rio Grande. When Sam Houston arrived in Gonzales on 11 March and was informed of the fall of the Alamo, he decided upon retreat to the Colorado River and ordered all inhabitants to accompany him. Couriers were dispatched from Gonzales to carry the news of the fall of the Alamo, and when they received that news, people all over Texas began to leave everything and make their way to safety. Houston's retreat marked the beginning of the Runaway Scrape on a really large scale. Washington-on-the-Brazos was deserted by 17 March, and about 1 April Richmond was evacuated, as were the settlements on both sides of the Brazos River. The further retreat of Houston toward the Sabine left all of the settlements between the Colorado and the Brazos unprotected, and the settlers in that area at once began making their way toward Louisiana or Galveston Island. East Texas around Nacogdoches and San Augustine was abandoned by 13 April. The flight was marked by lack of preparation and by panic caused by fear both of the Mexican army and of Indians. The people used any means of transportation including their feet. Added to the discomforts of travel were diseases, intensified by cold, rain, and hunger. Many persons died and were buried where they fell. The flight continued until news came of the Texan victory in the battle of San Jacinto. At first no credence was put in this report because so many false rumors had been circulated, but gradually the refugees began to reverse their steps and turn back toward home, many toward homes that no longer existed.

Carolyn Callaway Covington

Runnels, Hardin Richard. Governor; b. Mississippi, 30 August 1820; d. 25 December 1873. Runnels, whose family amassed considerable wealth in the antebellum era, moved to Texas with family members in 1842 and settled in Bowie County. He served in the state legislature from 1847 to 1855 and was speaker of the House during his last term. He was elected lieutenant governor in 1855. In 1857 Democratic party leaders, looking for a candidate besides Sam Houston (who had angered them by his U.S. Senate votes and his seeming Know-Nothingism), hit upon Runnels. With the help of his candidate for lieutenant governor, Francis R. Lubbock, Runnels won; he thus became the only person ever to defeat Houston in an election. As governor, Runnels was outspoken on behalf of states' rights and slavery. He signed the bills appropriating money for the University of Texas and establishing the State Geological Survey. He was stymied, however, in a controversy over Indian depredations. Angry settlers, harassed by Comanches, attacked Indians on the Brazos Indian Reservation and clashed with the United States Army, to whom Runnels thought the duty of frontier defense belonged. When Runnels ran against Houston in 1859, Houston won. Runnels retired to Bowie County. He attended the Secession Convention and, after the Civil War was over, was one of the "irreconcilables" at the Constitutional Convention of 1866. He had built a Greek Revival mansion in the 1850s in anticipation of a marriage that never occurred.

Cecil Harper, Jr.

Rusk, Thomas Jefferson. Soldier and statesman; b. Pendleton District, South Carolina, 5 December 1803; d. Nacogdoches, 29 July 1857 (buried in Oak Grove Cemetery); m. Mary F. (Polly) Cleveland (1827); 7 children. Rusk practiced law in Georgia and made sizable mining investments. In 1834 the managers of the company in which he had invested embezzled all the funds and fled to Texas. Rusk pursued them to Nacogdoches but never recovered the money. He did, however, decide to stay in Texas. He became a citizen of Mexico (1835), applied for a headright in David Burnet's colony, and sent for his family. After hearing Nacogdoches citizens denounce the despotism of Mexico, Rusk became involved in the independence movement. He organized volunteers from Nacogdoches and hastened to Gonzales, where his men joined Stephen F. Austin's army in preventing the Mexicans from seizing their cannon. They proceeded to San Antonio, but Rusk left the army before the siege of Bexar. The provisional government named him inspector general of the army in the Nacogdoches District, a position he filled for three months. As a delegate from Nacogdoches to the Convention of 1836, Rusk not only signed the Texas Declaration of Independence but also chaired the committee to revise the constitution. The ad interim government, installed on 17 March 1836, appointed Rusk secretary of war. When informed that the Alamo had fallen and the Mexicans were moving eastward, Rusk helped President Burnet to move the government to Harrisburg. He ordered all the coastal communities to organize militias. After the Mexicans massacred Fannin's army, Burnet sent Rusk with orders for General Houston to make a stand against the enemy, and upon learning that Santa Anna intended to capture the government at Harrisburg the Texas army marched to Buffalo Bayou. As a security measure, Houston and Rusk remained silent about their plans. Rusk participated with bravery in the battle of San Jacinto (21 April 1836). From May to October he served as commander in chief of the Army of the Republic of Texas, with the rank of brigadier general. He followed the Mexican troops westward as they retired from Texas to be certain of their retreat beyond the Rio Grande. Then he conducted a military funeral for the troops massacred at Goliad. When it appeared that the Mexicans intended to attack Texas from Matamoros, Rusk called for more troops. Though he had 2,500 soldiers by July, he maintained a defensive position.

In the first regularly elected administration, President Houston appointed Rusk secretary of war, but after a few weeks he resigned to take care of pressing domestic problems. At the insistence of friends, however, he represented Nacogdoches in the Second Congress (1837–38). While in the capital, Houston, he taught a Sunday school class. Like many prominent Texans, Rusk became a Mason. He joined Milam Lodge No. 40 in Nacogdoches in 1837 and was a founding member of the Grand Lodge of Texas, organized in Houston the same year. In the election of 1838 and in succeeding ones, friends importuned Rusk to be a presidential candidate, but he refused. As chairman of the House Military Committee in 1837, he sponsored a militia bill that passed over Houston's veto, and Congress elected Rusk major general of the militia. In the summer of 1838 he commanded the Nacogdoches militia, which suppressed the Córdova Rebellion. Rusk suspected Cherokee involvement in the rebellion, but Chief Bowl emphatically denied any collusion with Córdova. In October, when Mexican agents were discovered among the Kickapoo Indians, Rusk defeated those Indians and their Indian allies. He captured marauding Caddo Indians (November 1838) and risked an international incident when he invaded United States territory to return them to the Indian agent in Shreveport. Unrest among the Cherokees grew after the failure to ratify the Cherokee Treaty of 1836, which would have given the Cherokees title to the lands they occupied in East Texas. In July 1839 the final battle with the Cherokees and their allies was fought. Papers taken from captured Mexican agents implicated the Cherokees in a Mexican–Indian conspiracy against the Republic of Texas. Because he agreed with President Lamar's determination to remove the Cherokees, Rusk commanded part of the troops in the battle of the Neches, in which the Cherokees were driven into Oklahoma.

In 1838, Congress elected Rusk chief justice of the Supreme Court. He recognized that he was working in a system that combined Spanish and English law and practices, systems that did not always coincide. In *Milam County v. Bell* he established the rule of mandamus against public officers. He served until June 1840, when he resigned to resume his law practice. Later he headed the bar of the Republic of Texas. He and J. Pinckney Henderson, later the first governor of the state of Texas, formed a law partnership in 1841, the most famous law firm in Texas of that day. For a short time the firm also included Kenneth L. Anderson, later vice president under Anson Jones. One of the most widely known cases Rusk handled was the murder of Robert Potter, former secretary of the Texas Navy, in 1842. Rusk represented the 10 defendants, secured their bail, which had previously been denied, and obtained a dismissal before the case was to be tried on 6 May 1843. Earlier in 1843 Rusk had been called once again to serve as a military commander. Concern over the lack of protection on the frontier caused Congress to elect Rusk major general of the militia of the Republic of Texas. But he resigned in June when Houston obstructed his plans for aggressive warfare against Mexico. Rusk then turned his energies to establishing Nacogdoches University. He was vice president of the institution when its charter was granted in 1845 and president in 1846.

Rusk heartily supported annexation and served as president of the Convention of 1845, which accepted the annexation terms. Rusk's legal knowledge contributed significantly to the constitution of the new state. The first state legislature elected him and Houston to the United States Senate in February 1846. Rusk received the larger number of votes and the longer term of office. The two men forgot past differences as they worked to settle the southwest boundary question in favor of the Texas claim to the Rio Grande. Rusk supported the position of President Polk on the necessity of the Mexican War and the acquisition of California. In the debate over the Compromise of 1850, Rusk refused to endorse secession, proposed by some in the caucus of Southern congressmen. He vigorously defended Texas claims to New Mexico and argued forcefully for just financial compensation for both the loss of revenue from import duties as well as the loss of territory. As chairman of the Committee on Post Offices and Post Roads, he sponsored bills that improved services and lowered postage rates. As an early advocate of a transcontinental railroad through Texas, he made speeches in the Senate and throughout Texas in support of a southern route and toured Texas in 1853 to investigate a possible route. The Gadsden Treaty received his support since it provided an easier railroad route to the Pacific. Rusk received the approval of the state legislature for his vote in favor of the Kansas–Nebraska Act. He was a popular man in his party and was encouraged to become a presidential candidate in 1856. President James Buchanan offered him the position of postmaster general in 1857, and during the special session of March 1857 the United States Senate elected him president pro tem. Mrs. Rusk had died while Rusk was at the spring session of Congress, however. Despondent over her death and ill from a tumor at the base of his neck, Rusk committed suicide. Rusk County and the town of Rusk were named in his honor.

Priscilla Myers Benham

Ruter, Martin. Pioneer Methodist minister; b. Charlton, Massachusetts, 3 April 1785; d. Washington-on-the-Brazos, 16 May 1838; m. Sybil Robertson; 2 children; m. Ruth Young (1810); 9 children. The self-educated Ruter joined the New York Conference of the Methodist Episcopal Church in 1801 and received his deacon's and elder's orders from Bishop Francis Asbury (1803, 1805). He served churches in the New York, New England, and Philadelphia conferences and was a delegate to seven general conferences. He also served as an officer in Methodist schools that he helped to found in New Hampshire, Kentucky, and Pennsylvania. In recognition of his contributions to education, Transylvania College, Lexington, Kentucky, awarded Ruter a doctor of divinity degree in 1822. In 1820 the General Conference chose him to establish a new branch of the Methodist Book Concern in Cincinnati. During his eight years as book agent, he edited or wrote more than a dozen books, the most influential of which, *History of the Christian Church* (1832), was required reading for Methodist preachers for nearly 50 years. In May 1836 Ruter volunteered for missionary service in the new Republic of Texas. Within a year the Methodist Missionary Society established the Texas Mission, and the bishops appointed Ruter superintendent, to be assisted by Rev. Robert Alexander and Rev. Littleton Fowler. Ruter moved to Indiana and then, with David Ayres as his guide, to Texas. On 23 November 1837 they crossed the Sabine River at Gaines Ferry, where they met Robert Alexander. In the following three weeks, Ruter preached in San Augustine, Nacogdoches, and Washington-on-the-Brazos and formed a new society at Egypt. By mid-December he was in Houston, where he preached in Congress Hall and met with Sam Houston and other leaders of the government. Ruter stated his plans to establish a college and received pledges for an endowment of six or seven leagues from large landholders. He drew up several articles of a charter to be presented to the next session of the Texas Congress. Apparently he favored a site either at Bastrop or near Chappell Hill. During the following months, except for a brief and dangerous trip to Bastrop, Ruter concentrated his missionary work in the area bounded by Houston, Egypt, and Washington. In his final report to the Methodist Board of Missions, dated 26 April 1838, he stated that he and his colleagues had gathered 325 members in 20 circuits scattered across the vast prairies from the Sabine to the Colorado and from the Old San Antonio Road to the Gulf Coast. His travels on horseback had exceeded 2,200 miles. His vision was realized in 1840 with the founding of Rutersville College and the formation of the Texas Conference of the Methodist Episcopal Church.   *Norman W. Spellmann*

Rutersville College. The first chartered college in Texas; located in Rutersville, seven miles northeast of La Grange. The institution, which flourished between 1840 and 1856, was the dream of Martin Ruter, superintendent of the Methodist mission in Texas in the early days of the republic. In 1837 Ruter wrote a charter for the school, which he planned to call Bastrop College. He died on 25 June 1838, in Washington-on-the-Brazos, and a month after his death Robert Alexander, Littleton Fowler, and 10 other Methodists agreed to purchase land for the college and submitted Ruter's charter to the Congress of the republic. Initially, Congress rejected the charter because of its espousal of Methodist doctrine, but in 1840 it accepted a second charter that had been amended to eliminate any reference to religious denomination. In 1839 the first Texas conference of the Methodist Church appointed Chauncey Richardson the first president of the college and renamed it Rutersville College. The coeducational school opened on 1 February 1840 with 63 students. The town of Rutersville, which developed simultaneously with the college, donated 52 acres for the men's division and 24 for the women's division. Richardson, his wife Martha G., and Charles W. Thomas made up the original faculty. The charter was amended in February 1841 to extend the life of the school from 10 to 99 years. Congress donated four leagues of land in Fayette and Gillespie counties to the college, money from the sale of which was to pay for construction and equipment. By 1841 the enrollment of the college's two divisions reached 100, and another professor, Thomas S. Bell, was added to the faculty. The main building, completed in 1842, was a two-story wooden structure with a pair of double doors on the front, a wide chimney extending up two stories, and a bell in a tower atop the sloping roof. The ground floor of the main building held a study hall and two classrooms; the second floor served as the auditorium where examinations were given and commencement exercises were held. The women's building was constructed of limestone and included a combination study hall, recitation room, chapel, and dining room. The president's two-story home also served as the women's dormitory. Enrollment reached 194 by 1844–45, but the school began to fall on hard times. Indian attacks, departure of students for the Mexican War, and the establishment of Baylor University in 1845 caused a decline in the number of students. Richardson left the presidency in 1845 and was replaced by William Halsey. In 1848 John Rabb, treasurer of the college and attorney for the Rutersville Townsite Company, deeded lots to the trustees to be held in trust for the Texas Methodist Conference. This prompted a dispute with Fayette County, which withdrew its support of the institution. The self-perpetuating board of trustees also came under attack. A church trial for misconduct of faculty members further damaged the school's reputation. After 1850 Chappell Hill Male and Female Institute (later Chappell Hill Female College), another Methodist institution, began to compete for students. In 1856 Rutersville College was merged with Texas Monumental and Military Institute. In 1883 the Rutersville campus was purchased by the Southern German Conference of the Methodist Church, which operated it as a conference school until 1894, when the school was closed. The buildings were eventually razed, and all that remains of the college today is a Texas Centennial historical marker.

Judson S. Custer

S

SMU Law Review. Originally *Texas Law and Legislation*, a biannual review devoted to Texas legal developments; founded by the faculty of the School of Law of Southern Methodist University in 1947. The name changed to Southwestern Law Journal with the second volume, and with the third, the journal became a quarterly. Volume 2 carried the first annual survey of Texas law, expanded to cover important developments in neighboring states. After Volume 9, these annual surveys of Texas law were abandoned; they were reinitiated in 1967, with a full additional fifth issue devoted to this purpose. The format of the journal was substantially expanded in 1957. In 1990 the journal was given its present name. It and the *Journal of Air Law and Commerce* are published by the SMU Law Review Association, a nonprofit corporation. Though subject to faculty supervision, the journal is controlled and edited by a board of student editors annually elected from the staff. The staff is selected on the basis of grades and an essay competition at the end of their first year. The journal is financed by law school funds and by subscribers.

Joseph W. McKnight

Sabine Pass, Battle of. On 8 September 1863; turned back one of several Union attempts to invade Texas during the Civil War. The Union Navy blockaded the Texas coast beginning in the summer of 1861, while Confederates fortified the major ports. The North needed cotton and wanted to prevent French intervention in the Mexican civil war. In September 1863 Gen. Nathaniel P. Banks sent by transport from New Orleans 4,000 soldiers under the command of Gen. William B. Franklin to gain a foothold at Sabine Pass. A railroad ran from that area to Houston and opened the way into the interior of the state. The United States Navy sent four gunboats mounting 18 guns to protect the landing. The Confederates had constructed Fort Griffin for defense of the pass. The Davis Guards, an artillery unit under Capt. Frederick Odlum, had marked distances by stakes in the channel. The Union forces lost any chance of surprising the garrison when a blockader missed its arranged meeting with the ships from New Orleans on the evening of 6 September. The navy commander, Lt. Frederick Crocker, then formed a plan for the gunboats to enter the pass and silence the fort so the troops could land. The *Clifton* shelled the fort from long range between 6:30 and 7:30 A.M. on the eighth, while the Confederates remained under cover because the ship remained out of range. Behind the fort Odlum and other Confederate officers gathered reinforcements, although their limited numbers would make resistance difficult if the federal troops landed. At 3:40 P.M. the Union gunboats began their advance through the pass, firing on the fort as they steamed forward. Under the direction of Lt. Richard W. Dowling the Confederate cannoneers emerged to man their guns as the ships came within 1,200 yards. A shot destroyed the *Sachem* and left it powerless at the Louisiana shore. The *Arizona* backed up because it could not pass the *Sachem* and withdrew from the action. The *Clifton* pressed up the channel near the Texas shore until a shot from the fort cut away its tiller rope, after which it ran aground. The crew contin-

ued to exchange fire with the Confederate gunners until a shot hit the boiler and forced the sailors to abandon ship. The *Granite City* also turned back rather than face the accurate artillery of the fort, and the federal assault ended. The Confederates captured 300 Union prisoners and two gunboats. Franklin and the army force turned back to New Orleans, although Union troops occupied the Texas coast from Brownsville to Matagorda Bay later that fall. The Davis Guards, who suffered no casualties during the battle, received the thanks of the Confederate Congress for their victory.

Alwyn Barr

Sabine River. Rises in three main forks—Cowleech, Caddo, and South—joined by a fourth, Lake Fork, 40 miles downstream from the junction of the other three branches. At the thirty-second parallel the Sabine becomes the boundary between Texas and Louisiana. The river empties into Sabine Lake, which is formed by the confluence of the Neches and the Sabine rivers and drained by Sabine Pass into the Gulf of Mexico. The Sabine River runs 555 miles. Because rain is plentiful in its watershed, it discharges more water at its mouth than any other Texas river. Two large reservoirs have been constructed on the Sabine, Lake Tawakoni and Toledo Bend Reservoir. The forested river basin has long been the site of human habitation. Archeological excavations have discovered evidence of all stages of southeastern Indian development, beginning with the 12,000-year-old Clovis culture. Indian development reached its peak after the arrival of the Caddos about A.D. 780. The early Caddoan Period, which lasted until about 1260, saw the construction of large mounds, the southwesternmost example of the Mississippian mound-building culture. When the first Europeans entered the area in the sixteenth century, they found various groups of Caddos living along the stream. The name Sabine comes from the Spanish word for cypress, evidently given by Domingo Ramón in 1716; the stream was designated Río de Sabinas on a map of 1721 giving the route of the Aguayo expedition. The Spanish considered territory west of the Sabine, and some territory to the east, to be part of the Spanish province of Texas. After the acquisition of Louisiana by Spain, Spanish officials debated about whether the Sabine should form the eastern boundary of Texas. The capital of the province of Texas, however, was Los Adaes, on the east side of the river near the present site of Robeline, Louisiana. French traders operated along the Sabine, and both nations claimed the area. Up to the end of the eighteenth century little was known about the topography of East Texas. Some Spanish maps labeled the Sabine Río de los Adaes; others pictured both the Sabine and the Neches flowing directly and independently into the Gulf of Mexico, or depicted the two rivers joining to form one river before entering the Gulf; yet other maps showed only one river. Some mapmakers referred to the Sabine as the Río Mexicano; others used this designation for the Neches. José Antonio Pichardo, who made a close study of the Louisiana–Texas boundary in the first decade of the nineteenth century, reported all of this past confusion.

After the purchase of Louisiana by the United States, the

indefiniteness of the western boundary led Gen. James Wilkinson and Lt. Col. Simón de Herrera in 1806 to enter into an agreement establishing the Neutral Ground, which extended from the Arroyo Hondo on the east to the Sabine on the west. The Adams–Onís Treaty (1819) established the western boundary of Louisiana and the eastern boundary of Texas as beginning at the Gulf and extending up the Sabine to the thirty-second parallel. Spanish delay in ratification of the treaty and Mexican independence (1821) put the boundary again in controversy. The United States for a time claimed that the names of the Neches and Sabine rivers had been reversed, but no definite settlement was made. In 1836 the Congress of the Republic of Texas set forth the northern and eastern boundaries of the republic as stipulated in the Adams–Onís Treaty, and the United States dropped the claim to the area between the Sabine and the Neches. Despite the attempts of the Spanish to colonize the area, large numbers of Europeans did not enter the Sabine basin until the 1820s, when Americans from the southern United States began to settle there. When Mexican general Manuel de Mier y Terán was sent to the region in 1828 to report on conditions, he found that the ratio of Americans to Mexicans was nearly 10 to one. In the early days of the republic the Sabine furnished transportation for lumber and cotton from Southeast Texas. Once cargoes reached Sabine Bay, they were loaded on ships for transport to New Orleans, Galveston, and other ports. The booming river trade on the Sabine and Neches contributed to the rise of Port Arthur and Orange. The first steamships began to ply the river in the late 1840s. By the 1870s railroads had begun to replace steamboats. During the late nineteenth and early twentieth centuries the middle Sabine River basin was the site of intensive logging, and numerous sawmills were built along the banks of the river and its tributaries. Downstream, irrigation projects were built during the early 1900s. After the Spindletop oilfield boom of 1901, the Sabine basin also became the site of large-scale oil exploration. The growth of the oil and gas industry led to the development of the Beaumont–Port Arthur–Orange metropolitan area as a major site for oil refining, processing, and shipping. As a consequence of these developments, the once clean waters of the Sabine became increasingly polluted. In recent years, however, efforts have been made to clean up the stream.

Christopher Long

Sadler, Harley Herman. The "first man to make a million dollars from a tent show"; b. near Pleasant Plains, Arkansas, 4 September 1892; d. Stamford, Texas, 15 October 1954 (buried in Cameron); m. Willie Louise (Billie) Massengale (1917); 1 child. Sadler left home without completing high school to join a carnival. By the age of 22 he had worked in repertoire in Fort Worth and Waco; barnstormed to the West Coast; failed in Chicago variety; appeared in tableaux, in a medicine show, and on a Mississippi River showboat; and played under canvas for 26 weeks with Rentfrow's Jolly Pathfinders in Texas City. He then joined Roy E. Fox's Popular Players as second comedian and baritone horn player and toured much of Texas. He remained with Fox for several seasons and became first comedian with the company, entitled to top billing. With his wife he joined Brunk's No. 1 show, with Harley serving as principal comedian and stage director for this Kansas-based company. When Glen Brunk was drafted during World War I, Sadler became manager of the company. Upon Brunk's return, Sadler entered into a partnership with the Brunk organization, thus becoming manager and equal owner of the newly constituted Brunk's No. 3. Sadler took the show into Texas, where he proved an immediate success as an independent manager. "I really believe that Sadler would do business on the Sahara Desert," a correspondent wrote to *Billboard* after visiting the show. In 1922, after completing his contractual obligations with the Brunks, Sadler bought out their interest and embarked upon a career as the owner, manager, and principal comedian of Harley Sadler's Own Show. Like most tent shows, Sadler's was a family affair. Billie was business manager and leading lady. Gloria, the Sadlers' daughter, performed in the vaudeville as soon as she could walk on the stage. Sadler's mother-in-law worked backstage, his brother-in-law was boss canvasman, his brother Ferd was advance man, and Ferd's wife worked in the box office. Numerous nephews and nieces spent summer vacations working in their uncle's show. The show quickly became a favorite in the 60-odd communities of West Texas and eastern New Mexico that it visited biennially. Sadler's popularity, both onstage and off, was phenomenal. No amount of prodigal expenditure seemed to affect Sadler's prosperity until the coming of the Great Depression. In 1931, instead of cutting back, he purchased a new tent that seated 2,500 spectators and enlarged his company to over 50. But he quickly found that his audience no longer had the price of admission. An attempt to manage a circus resulted in financial disaster, and a Texas Centennial pageant entitled *The Siege of the Alamo* proved equally unrewarding. Sadler's very substantial holdings quickly melted away. Rather than declare bankruptcy, he sold all his remaining properties, paid what bills he could, and promised eventual payment on those remaining. Within two years, operating a tiny tent show in the Rio Grande valley, the showman had paid off some $25,000 in debts and returned to a state of solvency.

Around 1940, with the tent-show audiences eroded by the air-conditioned movie houses and drive-in theaters, Sadler became an independent oil operator. Like most wildcatters, he enjoyed occasional periods of plenty interrupted by prolonged stretches of famine. He continued to operate his much-reduced tent show until the death of his daughter in 1941, when he sold all of his equipment. His retirement from show business was short-lived, however. He remained intermittently active on the stage until a farewell tour in partnership with Joe McKennon in 1947. Sadler entered state politics in 1941 and was elected in 1942 as a Democrat to the Texas House from the Sweetwater district. He proved to be an honest and diligent, if somewhat naive, legislator. After serving three terms in the House and rejecting suggestions that he run for the United States House or the governorship of Texas, he lost a race for the Texas Senate. In 1950 he moved to Abilene, where he was again elected to the Texas House, and two years later ran unopposed for a seat in the Senate. In spite of his failing health, Sadler found himself unable to refuse the many requests for help that came his way. While emceeing a fund-raiser for a Boy Scout troop in Avoca, he was stricken with a heart attack. He died the following morning.

Clifford Ashby

St. Denis, Louis Juchereau de. Explorer and adventurer; b. near Quebec, 17 September 1674; d. Natchitoches, Louisiana, 11 June 1744; m. Manuela Sánchez (1716?); at least 4 children. In late 1699, St. Denis sailed from La Rochelle to Louisiana on the second expedition of Pierre Le Moyne, Sieur d'Iberville, his relative by marriage. In Louisiana he commanded a fort on the Mississippi River and another at Biloxi Bay. He also carried out important explorations to the west of the bay and upstream, where he ascended the lower Red River. These journeys brought him into contact with Karankawa and Caddo Indians and taught him invaluable lessons on how to cope in the wilderness. In response to a letter received from Father Francisco Hidalgo, the Sieur de Cadillac dispatched St. Denis and a company of men from Mobile in September 1713. The Canadianborn adventurer reached the Natchitoches villages in that same year and left some of his goods for safekeeping. From Natchitoches he traveled to lands of the Hasinai Indians and thence to Spanish outposts on the Rio Grande. At San Juan Bautista commander Diego Ramón placed St. Denis under a pleasant house arrest while awaiting instructions from Mexico City on what to do with a foreigner bearing goods banned by Spanish mercantile restrictions. While waiting, the Frenchman courted and won a promise of marriage from Ramón's beautiful granddaughter. After being ordered to Mexico City, St. Denis defended himself ably and was appointed as commissary officer of the Ramón expedition, charged with founding Spanish missions in East Texas. He returned to San Juan Bautista, married Manuela, and subsequently participated in the founding of six missions and a presidio in East Texas (1716–17). In April 1717 he returned to San Juan Bautista with a sizable amount of merchandise. But whereas he had been well received on his first visit, the death of Louis XIV and the conclusion of the War of the Spanish Succession had ended the era of Franco-Spanish cooperation. When sent to Mexico City for a second time, St. Denis fled the capital to avoid being hauled to Spain as a prisoner. He made his way to Natchitoches by February 1719. In 1721 Spanish officials permitted his wife to join him, and the couple spent their remaining years at the French outpost on the Red River. From his command at Natchitoches, St. Denis was often a troublesome thorn for Spanish Texas. Controversy continues to surround his motives and actions. He insisted that his marriage to Manuela Sánchez indicated a desire to become a Spanish subject. Suspicious Spaniards, however, saw him as a covert agent of France. His accomplishments are indisputable: St. Denis contributed to the expanded geographical knowledge of both France and Spain, brought Spanish and French settlements into close proximity, and made contraband trade a way of life on the borders of Spanish Texas and French Louisiana. On 10 January 1743, he wrote to Jean Frédéric Phélypeaux, Comte de Maurepas, at Versailles indicating that he could no longer perform his duties as commandant of Natchitoches. He also asked permission to retire to New Spain with his wife and children. That request was denied.

Donald E. Chipman and Patricia R. Lemée

St. Edward's University. Founded by Father Edward Sorin, a member of the Congregation of Holy Cross. The congregation, which had established the University of Notre Dame in Indiana in the 1840s, undertook the staffing of a school in Galveston in 1870. Sorin learned that Mary Doyle of Austin, a widow, wanted a Catholic school established there and was willing to donate her 398-acre farm south of the city for that purpose. Sorin went to Austin in 1872 and acquired the tract from Mrs. Doyle and, from Col. Willis L. Robards, an adjacent tract of 123 acres. Two Holy Cross brothers arrived in 1874 to begin working the farm, but it

was 1878 before the first class was taught in the Doyle farmhouse. By the fall of 1881 two modest frame buildings—one a dormitory—had been built on the site. That year the school was given the name St. Edward's Academy in honor of Sorin's patron, St. Edward, King of England. In 1885 the school was chartered by the state of Texas as Saint Edward's College. In 1889 the campus was moved to its present site, on the Robards tract, where an "Old Main" building, designed by Galveston architect Nicholas J. Clayton, had been built. By the early 1900s St. Edward's had an enrollment of nearly 200 students, mostly boarders from Texas and Mexico. In 1903 the main building was destroyed by fire. It was replaced by the present one, also designed by Clayton. During the generation that followed, the growth of the school was limited by competition from the rising public school system, by some years of poor crops and economic recession in the United States and Mexico, and by the impact of the Mexican Revolution and World War I. Commercial studies continued to hold a central place in the academic program. Other studies included the basics for younger students and the classics, modern languages, writing, literature, and some science for the older ones. The students, most of them between 10 and 20 years of age, were classified, as they had been in the past century, as minimi ("minims"), juniors, or seniors, according to age and advancement. In 1921 a clear line was drawn for the first time between the college and the high school departments. The minim department became the subacademy or elementary school. A second major disaster occurred when the Austin tornado of 1922 destroyed school property and killed a student.

In 1925 the college was rechartered as St. Edward's University. Faculty and staff in these years consisted mostly of Holy Cross fathers and brothers. Sisters of the Presentation, exiled from France by anticlerical legislation, were in charge of the kitchen, laundry, and infirmary of the residential department (1903–38). The most notable of the few laymen on the faculty was Billy (William J.) Disch, coach and physical education instructor from 1901 to 1911. His success led to his being hired by the University of Texas, where he won fame in a long career as baseball coach. Help from Notre Dame brought St. Edwards through the Great Depression. During World War II the university was unable to get a service-related program, and its enrollment dwindled to a handful, but the high school, converted to a military academy, did quite well. After the war the Congregation of Holy Cross reorganized administratively, and St. Edward's was assigned to the South–West Province. The new administration set to work to provide for an influx of war veterans studying under the GI Bill. The availability of war surplus buildings facilitated the expansion of the physical plant. Also significant was the establishment on campus during these years of a house of studies for religious brothers, who numbered more than 100 in some years. The long administrations of two presidents, Raymond Fleck and Steven Walsh, spanning most of the period 1957^84, brought change, innovation, and growth, including 10 new buildings. In 1967 St. Edward's High School was closed. By 1969 the faculty numbered 80, and courses were being offered in 26 majors. Before 1966, women had been admitted only for basic courses credited by the Seton program in nursing. That year, they were admitted to Maryhill College for women. In 1970 the coordinate system was discontinued, and all students were enrolled at St. Edward's. In the 1970s the university continued to develop new programs and to strengthen its existing depart-

Drafting class, Sam Houston Normal Institute, ca. 1900–1910. Courtesy TSL. Early courses of study emphasized professional subjects and teaching methods.

ments. It launched an M.B.A. program in 1970. The Mary Moody Northen Theater for the Performing Arts was completed in 1972. In 1974 St. Edward's established New College, a program for older students. In the spring of 1969 legal control of the university passed officially from the Brothers of Holy Cross to St. Edward's University Foundation. The foundation then issued a charter to St. Edward's University, Incorporated, a nonprofit corporation organized expressly to operate the university. A 22-person ecumenical board of trustees was appointed to represent the corporation and to govern the school. Four trustees were religious members; the remainder were laymen. In 1984 the board of trustees chose as president Patricia A. Hayes, the first woman and the second lay person to be named to the office. In 1991 the Dallas Cowboys began preseason training at St. Edward's. *William H. Dunn, C.S.C.*

St. Mary's University, San Antonio. A Catholic university. For 40 years after the Marianists arrived in Texas in 1852, their educational efforts were directed toward serving the primary-school children in San Antonio at St. Mary's Institute and San Fernando Cathedral school. St. Mary's had both day students and boarders. As the latter group outgrew even subsequent buildings, it became necessary to move the boarders to newly built St. Louis College in West Heights in 1894. The institute had a high school known as St. Mary's Academy and a college division which three years later was authorized by the state of Texas to give degrees for higher studies. At first utilizing the physical facilities of both the downtown and the West Heights locations, the college prospered so well that new buildings were added in 1908 and 1921. By 1923

the high school and college divisions were so large that it became impossible for them to continue sharing facilities, and the college division was moved to the St. Louis College site, where it was reorganized into schools of arts and sciences and business and became known as St. Mary's University. Evening and summer coeducational classes were started. In the same year the alumni of the downtown St. Mary's College decided to help the Marianists' work by building a much-needed gymnasium. A law school was incorporated into the university in 1934, and graduate studies began in 1936. Campus building projects have continued. The library special-collections division houses originals and copies of many documents, including the Spanish Archives of Laredo. The university became completely coeducational in 1963 and added a division of engineering in 1967. V. J. Keefe Field on campus, a baseball field, is the home of the St. Mary's Rattlers and the San Antonio Dodgers, a Texas League team. St. Mary's University enrolls more than 4,000 students in the regular term. *Robert D. Wood, S.M.*

Sam Houston State University. In Huntsville at a site formerly occupied by Austin College; the first tax-supported, teacher-training institution in Texas; originally a high school named Sam Houston Normal Institute. Its founding was aided by a grant from the George Peabody Fund (1878–79). The establishing law provided that two students from each senatorial district and six from the state at large should be admitted as "state students," whose tuition, board, lodging, and laundry would be paid by the state. These students obligated themselves to teach in the public schools of their districts for as many years as they received aid.

During the early years the school emphasized teacher training. In 1909 manual training, vocational agriculture, and home economics were added. The state-student policy was discontinued in 1910. In 1911 control of the college was vested in a normal-school board of regents and the course of study was expanded to four years, the last two years being of college level. In 1915 the curriculum was expanded to four years of college work leading to the B.A. degree. In 1923 the legislature changed the name of the school to Sam Houston State Teachers College. The institution was admitted to the Southern Association of Colleges and Secondary Schools in 1925 and subsequently to other associations. It began offering graduate courses leading to the M.A. degree in 1936, the year Sam Houston Memorial Museum was constructed as a Texas Centennial project. By 1948 the number of academic buildings had increased from 1 to 25, and the campus had expanded from 5 to 47 acres. Considerable additions subsequently occurred, including an experimental farm, an instructional aviation field, and a former POW camp. By 1960, 25 percent of the school's graduates received their degrees in fields outside of education. In 1965 the college was reorganized into six schools and renamed Sam Houston State College. It became Sam Houston State University in 1969. The university comprises four colleges: Arts and Sciences, Business Administration, Criminal Justice, and Education and Applied Science. It is a member of the Texas State University System and is fully accredited.

Joe L. Clark and Nancy Beck Young

San Angelo, Texas. County seat of Tom Green County; 220 miles northwest of San Antonio, near the geographical center of the state. The history of the frontier town began in the late 1860s across the North Concho River from Fort Concho, which had been established in 1867. As an early frontier town, San Angelo was characterized by saloons, prostitution, and gambling. Officers of nearby Fort Concho would not leave the garrison after dark. Shortly after the fort was established, Bartholomew (Bart) J. DeWitt, the founder of San Angelo, bought 320 acres of land from Granville Sherwood and, over the river, established a trading post, which was later called Santa Angela. There are several stories as to how the town was named, including one in which it was named for DeWitt's sister-in-law, a nun in San Antonio. A local historian found that DeWitt named the town in memory of his wife, Carolina Angela, who died in 1866. The name had changed to San Angela by 1883, when application was made for a post office. The proposed name of San Angela was rejected because of the ungrammatical construction. The name should be Santa Angela or San Angelo. The latter was chosen. Oscar Ruffini, the architect of many of the early business buildings in San Angelo, arrived in the town shortly after the flood of 1882, which destroyed the county courthouse in Ben Ficklin, the county seat. After the voters decided on San Angelo as the new county seat, Ruffini was asked to design and supervise the construction of the new county courthouse. Ruffini remained in San Angelo, where he was the architect of about 40 buildings in the downtown area, some of which are still in use. Fort Concho, an ample supply of water, ranching, agriculture, and the coming of the railroads all contributed to the community's growth. The fort brought a steady flow of money from the soldiers' pay, which in turn brought traders, merchants, and others who catered to the needs of the soldiers. The first legitimate business, a combination general store and saloon, was opened by William

S. Veck. San Angelo was located at the juncture of the North, South, and Middle Concho rivers and was surrounded by farms on the east and ranches on the west. The town's economy, therefore, became more diversified than that of many other frontier settlements. During the cattle boom of the 1870s thousands of longhorn cattle were watered and fed along the Concho rivers on their way to market. Richard F. Tankersley introduced cattle ranching on the South Concho as early as 1864. John Arden and Joseph Tweedy introduced sheep ranching in 1877. San Angelo became a shipping center with the coming of the Santa Fe Railroad in 1888 and the Kansas City, Mexico and Orient in 1909. Wool growers, cattle ranchers, and the railroads combined to make the town one of the leading cattle markets in Texas, the largest sheep market in the United States, and one of the leading inland wool and mohair markets in the nation.

San Angelo has one of the most diverse industrial bases in Texas. There, more than 120 manufacturing companies produce a wide variety of products, including surgical sutures, denim jeans, iron and steel, and electronic and oilfield equipment. San Angelo had become a highly rated medical center by 1989. The first hospital was a post hospital constructed at Fort Concho in the 1870s. In 1910 St. John's Hospital and Health Center, the oldest nonmilitary hospital in West Texas, was founded by the Sisters of Charity of the Incarnate Word of San Antonio. In 1912 the state legislature established the State Tuberculosis Sanatorium, which became the McKnight State Sanatorium in 1950. The Shannon Medical Center, founded in 1932 by the estate of Margaret Shannon and including the Shannon West Texas Memorial Hospital and the Medical Plaza, is the largest acute-care facility in the region. Angelo Community Hospital, a locally owned nonprofit institution organized in 1929, provides a wide range of medical services. River Crest Hospital, opened in 1988, provides psychiatric and chemical-dependency care and specialized services for adolescents, adults, and families. Baptist Memorial Geriatric Hospital is the only geriatric hospital in West Texas providing long-term care. The West Texas Rehabilitation Center is a private, nonprofit institution that provides outpatient treatment for the handicapped. San Angelo also has become widely known as a retirement center. In 1989 four communities offered low-maintenance residences.

After incorporating in 1903, San Angelo was able to establish a city-controlled educational system designed to improve its schools. Mexican Americans protested the inferior education that their children received in segregated schools by completely boycotting the Mexican-American schools in 1910–11 and 1914–15. Nevertheless, San Angelo schools remained segregated for many years. San Angelo College, established in 1928, became an accredited senior college in 1965. In 1990 Angelo State University, with an enrollment of about 6,000 students, offered 42 undergraduate and 19 graduate programs. Fort Concho, now a National Historical Landmark, is one of the best-preserved frontier forts in the United States. In 1940 the United States War Department selected San Angelo as the location for Goodfellow Air Field. In 1958 the air force changed its function from air training command to United States Air Force Security Service, offering intelligence training courses to all branches of the military. Goodfellow Air Force Base also became the home of the $100 million Strategic Air Command long-range radar unit. In 1920 the population of San Angelo was 10,050. Between 1920 and 1930, with the opening of the Permian Basin oilfield in 1923, the

San Antonio River at St. Mary's Street Bridge, by Ida Weisselberg Hadra, ca. 1883. Oil on canvas. 24" × 30". Courtesy Witte Museum, San Antonio. The winding San Antonio River has given the Alamo City an alternative nickname, "City of Bridges." The river has also proved irresistible to artists. Ida Hadra completed this painting shortly after moving to San Antonio.

population doubled to 25,308, and the establishment of Goodfellow Air Field help push the population to 52,093 in 1950. The population rose to 73,240 in 1980 and 84,474 in 1990.

Escal F. Duke

San Angelo State School. Seventeen miles north of San Angelo; grew out of a tuberculosis sanatorium founded in 1912. With the declining need for tuberculosis treatment, the facility became part of the Texas Department of Mental Health and Mental Retardation in September 1969 and was known as the San Angelo Center. Originally, adults from other facilities throughout the state were transferred to the center. The population peaked at 791 in 1979. Individuals served at that time were ambulatory and were primarily diagnosed with mild to moderate retardation. Today the majority of the population is severely retarded. In 1983 the center was given its present name. SASS is virtually self-sustaining—it provides medical, dental, therapeutic, and psychological services, as well as administrative, social, and community services to its residents. The school strives to provide an environment conducive to growth in independent living skills, opportunities for therapy, and training for each individual according to his needs. Its goal is to equip each individual for discharge, if possible, for living in a supervised community setting.

Eva W. Horton

San Antonio, Texas. At the head of the San Antonio River in Bexar County. The area was explored by Spanish expeditions in 1691 and 1709, which named the San Antonio River and San Pedro Creek. The town grew out of San Antonio de Béxar Presidio, founded in 1718, and the villa of San Fernando de Béxar, chartered by Canary Islanders in 1731. Beginning in 1718, five Spanish missions were located along the river. The presidial captain's house (later the Spanish Governor's Palace) was completed on Military Plaza in 1749, and San Fernando de Béxar Church was built by 1758. In 1773 San Antonio de Béxar became the capital of Spanish Texas. In 1778 the settlement had a population of 2,060, including mission Indians. Its circumstances were described as "miserable" by visitors. The population was poor and heterogeneous, made up of Europeans, mestizos, and a few black slaves. The missions were all secularized by 1795, and San

Antonio de Valero Mission (later, the Alamo) became a military barracks. San Antonio declared for Mexican independence in 1813; it was recaptured by Royalist forces after the battles of Alazán Creek and Medina, and the population was decimated by purges. During the Texas Revolution, San Antonio was the site of several battles, including the siege of Bexar (December 1835) and the battle of the Alamo (6 March 1836), which made it one of the most fought-over cities in North America. After the evacuation of Mexican forces, Bexar County was organized by the Republic of Texas in December 1836, and San Antonio was chartered in January 1837 as its seat. A failed attempt to negotiate the release of captives held by Comanche Indians resulted in yet another battle in the streets of the town, the Council House Fight of 1840. San Antonio was seized twice in the Mexican invasions of 1842, and the population was reduced to about 800 in 1846. After Texas entered the Union, growth became rapid, as the city became a servicing and distribution center for the western movement of the United States. The census showed 3,488 residents in 1850 and 8,235 in 1860, when San Antonio had become for the time the largest town in Texas (ahead of Galveston). Germans made up a large part of this growth; German speakers outnumbered both Spanish speakers and English speakers until after 1877. In 1861 local militia forced the surrender of the federal arsenal at San Antonio even before the state seceded on 2 March. Subsequently, San Antonio served as a Confederate depot. Several units such as John S. Ford's Cavalry of the West were formed there, though the city was removed from the fighting.

After the Civil War, San Antonio prospered as a cattle, distribution, mercantile, and military center serving the border region and the Southwest. The city was the southern hub and supplier of the cattle trail drives. An important wool market developed with the importation of merino sheep to the adjacent Hill Country. With the coming of the Galveston, Harrisburg and San Antonio Railway in 1877, San Antonio entered a new era of economic growth. The population reached 20,550 in 1880. The new immigration was overwhelmingly native-born Anglos, mostly from Southern states. In 1881 a second railroad, the International–Great Northern, reached the city from the northeast, and five railroads had built into the city by 1900. Modernization was explosive in the 1880s, comparable to growth across the United States. Civic government, utilities, street paving and maintenance, water supply, telephones, hospitals, and a power plant were all established or planned. San Antonio was once again the largest city in the state in 1900, with a population of 53,321; it remained the largest city in 1910, with 96,614 inhabitants, and 1920, with 161,379. After 1910 Mexican immigration greatly increased due to the Mexican Revolution and the development of local service industries. The confluence of Hispanic, German, and Southern Anglo-American cultures in San Antonio made it into one of America's "four unique cities" (along with Boston, New Orleans, and San Francisco). Each successive group of immigrants put its stamp upon the city, its culture, and architecture; all mingled, none quite submerging the others. Each period of growth produced characteristic and often distinguished architecture. Peculiarly, San Antonio succeeded in merging its past into the new in each generation. Old Spanish walls remain beside modern glass towers, with rows of Victorian mansions a block away, a combination that lends the city a charm sought out by millions of visitors.

San Antonio did not expand beyond its original Spanish charter land until 1940. The land was large enough to allow a number of incorporated suburbs within the metropolitan area. Like most twentieth-century American cities in the automobile age, the Alamo City's expansion was mainly horizontal, with sprawling neighborhoods but little vertical building. Although the first Texas skyscraper and several tall buildings were built in San Antonio in the early twentieth century, vertical construction did not continue, and the city's center of population steadily moved northward. San Antonio had fallen behind Houston and Dallas in population by 1930, and has remained the third largest city in the state since that time. After a period of slow growth during the 1930s, the population increased by 61 percent during the wartime boom of the 1940s, to reach 408,442 in 1950. The First United States Volunteer Cavalry was organized in San Antonio during the Spanish–American War, and in both world wars San Antonio was an important military center for the army and air forces. It has retained this status. Fort Sam Houston and Kelly, Randolph, Brooks, and Lackland Air Force bases were the city's leading economic generators for many years. In the 1950s the city grew by almost 44 percent to reach 587,718 in 1960. Thereafter it continued to grow at a more sedate pace of 10 to 20 percent a decade. In 1990 San Antonio was the third largest city in Texas, with a population of 935,933; 55.6 percent were Mexican Americans, 35.9 percent were Anglo, and 7 percent were African Americans.

Although the lack of high-paying manufacturing and finance-industry jobs has kept San Antonio in the bottom tier of average metropolitan income, the city has developed a viable economy from its stable military bases, educational institutions, tourism, and medical-research complex. By the late nineteenth century San Antonio had become a favorite retirement spot for Texans who sought its mild climate, graceful ambience, and civilized amenities; it has continued as a favored military retirement site. Medical-research facilities in San Antonio include Brooke Army Medical Center, Wilford Hall Medical Center at Lackland Air Force Base, Brooks Air Force Base, the Southwest Research Institute, the University of Texas Health Science Center at San Antonio, the Southwest Foundation for Biomedical Research, and the 1,500-acre Texas Research Park in west Bexar County. San Antonio has long been an educational center. Its first English school was organized in 1828. Ursuline Academy was established in 1851, St. Louis Academy in 1852, and the German– English School in 1858. Palo Alto College, San Antonio College, and St. Philip's College make up the Alamo Community College District. San Antonio also has five accredited universities and one accredited college: Our Lady of the Lake University, St. Mary's University, Trinity University, the University of Texas at San Antonio, the University of Texas Health Science Center, and Incarnate Word College. Churches have played an enormous role culturally, spiritually, and architecturally in the history of the city. The first Catholic churches were founded at the missions. Concepción, finished in 1754, is the oldest surviving church in Texas. San Fernando Cathedral dates to 1758. St. Mark's Episcopal Church was organized in 1859, and its building was completed in 1875. San Antonio was raised to a Catholic diocese in 1874, and the Catholic Archdiocese of San Antonio came into being in 1926. The first town council in San Antonio, organized in 1837, held meetings in English and Spanish. City government was first dominated by Hispanics, then by Anglos and Germans. Until 1955 the city government followed the classic mayor–alder-

West Side Main Plaza, San Antonio, Texas, by W. G. M. Samuel, 1849. Oil on canvas mounted on panel. 22" × 36". Courtesy of Bexar County and the Witte Museum, San Antonio. As a veteran of Indian fights and the war with Mexico, Samuel was "one of the best known characters" in San Antonio and "a dead shot." He also applied his naïve artistic abilities to a series of paintings of the city's Main Plaza.

man pattern, in which appeared a number of colorful mayors, lively elections, and no little corruption. In 1955 San Antonio opted for the council–manager form. San Antonio has 9 television stations and 19 FM and 15 AM radio stations. The city newspaper is the San Antonio *Express–News* and there are 33 other weekly and monthly publications, including 11 military. The San Antonio *Light* was published for 111 years, from 1881 to 1992.

Tourism is one of the city's most important industries, for San Antonio's many attractions, including sports, draw hundreds of thousands of visitors every year. Among the most recent features is Fiesta Texas, a $100 million, 201-acre family musical and entertainment theme park. Sea World in San Antonio is the largest marine-life theme park in the world. The famed Riverwalk, Paseo del Rio, consists of over 1½ miles of cool, shady, walks with shops, cafes, restaurants, and clubs. HemisFair '68 left a number of permanent buildings, including the Tower of the Americas, which has an observation deck and restaurant on top. The San Antonio Botanical Gardens and Conservatory is a 33-acre horticultural facility featuring the flora of Texas, ranging from the wildflowers of the Hill Country to the formal rose gardens of East Texas. The indoor collection houses exotic plants from all over the world. A few of the other attractions found in San Antonio include El Mercado, the old marketplace with a touch of Mexico; the Sunken Gardens, lush Japanese gardens preserved in a natural setting; the San Antonio Zoo, at Brackenridge Park; the Menger Hotel; the Hertzberg Circus Collection and Museum, an extensive collection of circus memorabilia; the Witte Museum; several distinguished art galleries; and the University of Texas Institute of Texan Cultures, a

museum documenting the ethnic groups that built Texas. San Antonio's major annual events include Fiesta San Antonio in April, the San Antonio Annual Livestock Show and Rodeo in February, the Texas Folklife Festival in August, and the Riverwalk Christmas Lighting in December. The Alamo (1718), Mission Concepción (1731), Mission San José (1720), Mission San Juan Capistrano (1731), and Mission San Francisco de la Espada (1741) compose San Antonio Missions National Historical Park, one of a few urban national parks in the country. Architecturally interesting sights abound: San Fernando Cathedral (1758), the Spanish Governor's Palace (1749), the Quadrangle at Fort Sam Houston (1878), the Bexar County Courthouse (1891), and the King William Historic District are but a few. San Antonio, with its unique architectural heritage dating from the Spanish era, was one of the first cities apart from the Eastern seaboard to become preservation conscious. The San Antonio Conservation Society, founded in 1924, was instrumental in saving the beautiful San Antonio River, which winds through downtown, from being paved over for a drain. The society has since become a popular and powerful organization devoted to preserving the city's unique features. Recognizing the value and impact of the city's cultural sites upon the economy and stability of the community, the city maintains a Historic Preservation office as part of planning, and has passed a model comprehensive historic-preservation code that provides tax incentives to encourage preservation and rehabilitation. The King William and Monte Vista historic districts are outstanding examples of neighborhood restoration efforts. In sports, the Alamodome is the home venue for the San Antonio Spurs of the

National Basketball Association. The Texas Open golf tournament is held each year at Oak Hills Country Club, and the R. J. Reynolds PGA Seniors Tournament is an annual event at the Dominion. Other professional sports teams include the San Antonio Missions baseball team, the San Antonio Racquets, and the San Antonio Iguanas (a National Hockey League team).

T. R. Fehrenbach

San Antonio Art Institute. Formerly adjacent to the Marion Koogler McNay Art Museum; developed from a series of art classes sponsored first by Alene Rather, supervisor of art in the San Antonio public schools (1925). In 1927 free weekly classes at the Witte Museum were offered to selected students, with muralist and sculptor Xavier González as the first instructor. In 1933 the Great Depression forced the schools to cancel funding, though classes and projects continued with the help of the State Vocational Training Department. In 1939 the San Antonio Art League sponsored a Beaux Arts Ball, the proceeds of which were used to establish the Museum School of Art, where professional artists taught. When World War II forced the school to close in 1942, Ellen Quillin, then director of the Witte, persuaded Marion Koogler McNay to house the school on her estate, Sunset Hills. The school reopened as the San Antonio Art Institute in 1943. Mrs. McNay recruited distinguished artists to lead classes, and in 1946 commercial art classes at John G. Borglum's former sculpture studio were added for the benefit of veterans. Classes in ceramics, life drawing, and portrait painting were offered at the Witte Museum. After Mrs. McNay's death in 1950 all classes took place on her estate. In 1958 Margaret Flowers funded the construction of a modern ceramics studio, and gifts in the memory of Mary Aubrey Keating substantially expanded the school's library. Alden H. Waitt, a retired major general, was director and chairman of the board for 16 years. The institute's curriculum and enrollment continued to expand during the 1960s and 1970s, thus necessitating a larger facility. The McNay trustees provided land for a new building, and retired Episcopal bishop Everett H. Jones and his wife, Helen, paid for the construction of a new building, which opened for classes in 1976. A gift from the George and Elizabeth Coates Foundation in 1979 enabled the institute to enlarge and renovate its ceramics studio. In 1980 the board decided to make the Art Institute a college of art. But in 1992, faced with financial and accreditation difficulties, the institute filed for bankruptcy and closed. *Kendall Curlee*

San Antonio Conservation Society. Responsible for the preservation of many monuments of old San Antonio; founded by Mary Rowena Maverick Green and others in 1924, after a disastrous 1921 flood resulted in flood-control measures that threatened drastic physical changes in the city. The society was incorporated in 1925 and has remained active to the present in the purchase, restoration, and operation of historic sites, beginning with the threatened downtown meander of the San Antonio River, which later became known as the Paseo del Rio. The society was afterward involved in saving or restoring other sites of great importance, including the Spanish Governor's Palace (late 1920s); San José y San Miguel de Aguayo Mission; the Espada Mission acequia; the 1850 Jeremiah Dashiell House, which served once as the society's headquarters; the buildings in José Antonio Navarro State Historical Park; the 1876 Steves Homestead in the King William Historic District, the O. Henry House, the Anton

Wulff House; and the Aztec Theater. The Anton Wulff House has served as society headquarters since 1975. The society achieved national recognition for its long-standing annual Christmas presentations of two Mexican folk dramas, *Los Pastores* ("The Shepherds") and *Las Posadas* ("The Inns"). Also popular since its inception in 1947 was Night in Old San Antonio, held each spring at the time of Fiesta San Antonio in La Villita. In accord with its interest in ecology, the society was instrumental in preserving San Pedro Park in the late 1940s and preventing Travis Park from becoming a parking lot in the 1950s. An adjunct to the organization, the San Antonio Conservation Society Foundation, was chartered by the state in 1970.

San Antonio–El Paso Mail. Between 1851 and 1881 a series of contractors carried the United States mail and passengers westward from San Antonio to El Paso. During various periods the stage line also served Santa Fe, New Mexico, and San Diego, California. Henry Skillman, with a government contract to carry the mail between San Antonio and Santa Fe via El Paso, dispatched his first mail west on 3 November 1851. By December he was offering passenger service also, despite the continual threat of Indian attack. In October 1854 Skillman formed a partnership with George Giddings, a San Antonio merchant and freighter. They continued to operate the stage line for the next three years in the face of mounting losses to the Indians. In July 1857 Giddings entered a partnership with James Birch, a wealthy New Englander who had prospered in the California express business. Giddings and Birch operated under government contract to furnish mail service between San Antonio and San Diego on a semimonthly basis; this "San–San" was said to be the first American transcontinental mail and passenger service (1957). For passengers the one-way fare, including meals, was $200. Birch's death at sea in October 1857 threatened to destroy the new company, but Giddings kept the San Antonio–San Diego Mail Line in operation by going deeply into debt. In September 1858 the Butterfield Overland Mail began operations between El Paso and California as part of its transcontinental route, and the post office department reduced the compensated portions of Giddings's line. His branch service to Santa Fe was terminated in December 1858, and by May 1860 he was receiving payment for service only between San Antonio and Fort Stockton. Giddings continued to run his coaches to El Paso at a loss. After Texas left the Union in February 1861 he obtained a Confederate government contract to provide service between San Antonio and California, but the Union authorities and hostile Indians soon crippled his operations beyond El Paso. By August 1862 he had been forced to suspend all service west of Fort Clark. Skillman operated a covert courier service between San Antonio and El Paso for Confederate agents and sympathizers remaining in the area during Union occupation. Federal troops killed him in an ambush near Presidio del Norte in April 1864.

Bethel Coopwood revived the San Antonio–El Paso service in April 1866, but by the following November he reputedly yielded control of the company to the firm of Sawyer, Risher, and Hall. Frederick Sawyer provided the financial backing, and his general superintendent, Ben Ficklin, directed field operations. Ficklin rapidly became the dominant figure in the business. He was a former Confederate officer who had seen antebellum service as a government surveyor in the West and had served as a route superintendent for the Central Overland and Pike's Peak Express

Company before overseeing the establishment of the Pony Express. During his five-year tenure as director, Ficklin reinvigorated the Texas line by rerouting the stages toward the Middle Concho River before turning west to Fort Stockton and by establishing branch routes that served northwestern Texas, Arkansas, and the Indian Territory. When Ficklin died in 1871 his assistant, Francis Taylor, took over. Taylor enlarged the company's headquarters on the Middle Concho and named the settlement Benficklin in honor of his friend. He was also instrumental in the organization of Tom Green County in 1874; in 1875 Benficklin was chosen as the county seat. After Sawyer's death in 1875, Taylor maintained the service to El Paso despite Indian raids, banditry, and charges of corruption made by political opponents. Charles Bain assumed control of the company following Taylor's death in June 1879. Despite declining revenues and losses to the Indians he kept the line functioning until the Texas and Pacific Railroad reached El Paso on 1 January 1882 and put the stage company out of business. The generally unprofitable stage line aided the state's development by introducing commercial transportation to the far west and establishing a chain of fortified relay stations that encouraged travel and settlement, as well as foreshadowing the construction of a transcontinental railroad. After the Civil War the stage line was a source of valuable intelligence about Indian movements for frontier army garrisons. Sherman called it "the skirmish line of civilization."

Wayne R. Austerman

San Antonio *Express–News*. The *Express*, named for James Pearson Newcomb's Union paper, the *Alamo Express,* was first published as a weekly in 1865 by H. Pollmar and August Siemering, who also published the *Freie Presse für Texas.* The next year it became a daily, and in 1868 it began to use Associated Press dispatches. The paper had an early circulation of 300 daily and 800 weekly subscribers. In 1875 Siemering sold his interest. Competition with the San Antonio *Herald* closed the paper in 1879, but the editor, Frank Grice, took over and eventually reorganized the business as the Express Publishing Company (1886). The *Express* constructed its own building, the first steel fireproof building in San Antonio, in 1895, by which time the paper employed 195 people. Among early employees was William Cowper Brann. Grice died in 1906 and the paper, with a circulation of 13,100 and 18,800 on Sundays, passed to his family. Frank G. Huntress became company president in 1912. Circulation had reached almost 34,000 by 1918. The company began publishing the *Evening News* that year and in 1922 became the owner and operator of radio station WOAI. A new building was dedicated on the day the stock market crashed in 1929. Photographic sports coverage was provided by homing pigeon in 1938, and the war interest increased circulation. At the end of World War II, Frank Huntress, Jr., took over management of the daily morning newspaper from his father. When a strike by Canadian loggers nearly put it out of business in 1946, the paper acquired a large block of stock in several paper mills. The *Express* also acquired radio station KYFM in 1947, KTSA in 1949, and KGBS radio–television in 1954 (renamed KENS). Cooperation between the *Express* and the *News* increased in the 1950s, and the papers eventually merged their staffs. In 1958 circulation of the *Express* was about 74,000 and that of the *News* was 75,000. Between 1960 and 1962, Harte–Hanks Communications purchased the company. In 1965 a newsroom staff of 88 celebrated the 100th anniversary of the founding of the *Express.* Rupert Murdoch purchased the paper in 1973 and in 1984 combined it with the *News* to form the *Express–News.* In 1992 competition between the *Express–News* and the San Antonio *Light* ended when the Hearst Corporation announced the closing of the *Light* and the purchase of the *Express–News.*

Frances Donecker

San Antonio *Light*. Heralded by a small, occasional paper called the San Antonio *Surprise,* which predicted that "the Evening Light w[ill] be visible January 1, 1881 . . . and will grow brighter and stronger with each issue." The paper actually appeared on 20 January, published as a daily (except Sunday) at the office of the *Texas Sun* by A. W. Gifford and James Pearson Newcomb. In 1883 Newcomb transferred management of the paper to Gifford and Tom B. Johnson. The plant was moved to an office on Commerce Street, and the paper became the *Daily Light.* In 1890 the paper was described as the only Republican daily in Texas. In 1906 the publishing company was sold to E. B. Chandler, and in 1909 the Daily Light Publishing Company bought the San Antonio *Gazette,* after which until 1911 the paper was known as the *Light and Gazette.* Edward S. (Tex) O'Reilly, author, soldier of fortune, and adventurer, was at one time managing editor. In 1911 Harrison L. Beach and Charles S. Diehl, veteran correspondents of national standing, moved to San Antonio and bought the *Light and Gazette,* which was subsequently known once more as the *Light.* They installed leased wire-news service and published the first full market reports in a San Antonio paper. The *Light* became liberal-Democratic in its political views, and under the Beach and Diehl management circulation increased from 11,000 to 25,000 copies daily. In 1924, William Randolph Hearst bought the *Light,* which by 1945 had a circulation of 70,000. In the post–World War II years the San Antonio *Light* attained circulation leadership in the city under publisher B. J. Horner and managing editor N. Dwight Allison. In 1972 the paper, with a daily circulation of 122,292 and a Sunday circulation of 160,905, was one of the leading Hearst newspapers in the United States. By 1987, however, it was operating with a deficit. Under George B. Irish, the Light continued in the early 1990s, with a circulation of 186,777. On 6 October 1992, the Hearst corporation, after purchasing the San Antonio *Express–News,* announced that it would close the *Light* if it could not find a buyer for the property. At the time, the paper employed over 600 people including 134 editorial staff. Shortly after the announcement, the paper closed.

Frances Donecker

San Antonio Missions National Historical Park. Established in 1978 by the joint efforts of the Catholic Archdiocese of San Antonio, the Texas Parks and Wildlife Department, the San Antonio Conservation Society, and the United States Department of the Interior; comprises the sites of four Spanish missions: San José y San Miguel de Aguayo, Nuestra Señora de la Purísima Concepción, San Juan Capistrano, and San Francisco de la Espada. The park began operation in 1983. The missions, beginning with San José, had undergone decades of restoration while still functioning as churches. Visitors to the park number nearly a million a year.

Gilbert R. Cruz

San Antonio River. One of the most historically important streams in Texas; rises in a cluster of springs in north central San Antonio, flows through the city, and runs thence 180 miles to its mouth on the Guadalupe River. The spring flow of the San Antonio and its principal tributaries, the Medina River and Cibolo Creek, makes the volume of the river steadier than that of most Texas streams. The San Antonio has been identified as one of the rivers crossed by Cabeza de Vaca in 1535 and as the stream called Arroyo De León by Alonso De León on his fourth expedition into Texas in 1689. The stream was named for San Antonio de Padua in 1691 by Domingo Terán de los Ríos. At the site of present-day San Antonio the Spaniards found an Indian village, which they understood the Indians to say was named Yanaguana. Father Massanet renamed the village San Antonio de Padua and offered a Mass for the soldiers and Indians gathered there. In 1709 Father Antonio de San Buenaventura y Olivares was so impressed with the location that he wanted to establish a mission there. In 1718 San Antonio de Valero Mission—the Alamo—was established on the east bank of the river and San Antonio de Bexar Presidio was set up on the opposite side. The plentiful supply of water for drinking, irrigation, and water power caused the San Antonio River rapidly to become the center of Spanish activities in the province of Texas. Other missions established in the immediate vicinity were San José y San Miguel de Aguayo and San Francisco Xavier de Náxara. In 1731 the villa of San Fernando de Bexar, which developed into the modern city of San Antonio, was founded. The same year, three missions were moved from East Texas to the San Antonio River and renamed Nuestra Señora de la Purísima Concepción de Acuña, San Francisco de la Espada, and San Juan Capistrano. In 1749 Nuestra Señora de Loreto Presidio and Nuestra Señora del Espíritu Santo de Zúñiga Mission were moved from the Guadalupe to a site on the San Antonio River that later became the town of Goliad. Another mission, Nuestra Señora del Rosario, was established about four miles upstream in 1754. The river was likewise popular with the colonial empresarios of the Mexican period, and much of the land bordering the stream was granted to colonists in the De León and Power and Hewetson colonies. When the Texas Revolution began, the river became the scene of heroic and catastrophic engagements, including the battle of Concepción, the Grass Fight, the siege of Bexar, the Goliad Massacre, and the battle of the Alamo.

Although the San Antonio River has furnished drinking and irrigation water as well as power to turn the wheels of mills, foundries, and tanneries, in recent times it has been most significant for its beauty. In the city of San Antonio, where it is spanned by more than 50 bridges, this unhurried stream runs 15 miles across 6 miles of city blocks. In 1939 a $300,000 river-beautification project, financed by a city bond issue and a WPA grant, was inaugurated. The river was made a pedestrian thoroughfare flanked by walks from all principal downtown streets. It was deepened so it would be navigable for small craft. The project included landscaping, fountains, and the construction of an outdoor theater equipped with water curtains. The network of walkways and bridges, now known as the Paseo del Rio or Riverwalk, is one of San Antonio's principal attractions. It was enhanced and extended during HemisFair '68. The old Spanish town known as La Villita has also been restored and has become one of the showplaces of the San Antonio River area.

Frances Donecker

San Antonio Symphony Orchestra.

The Germans of San Antonio had an Instrumental Verein as early as 1852 but did not form a full orchestra until the state *Sängerfest* of 1874. Orchestral life grew but then declined after World War I, until Max Reiter, a young German conductor and refugee from European anti-Semitism, drummed up enough support for a trial orchestra concert in June 1939 at the Sunken Garden. Moved by the success of this concert, the Symphony Society of San Antonio formally incorporated. Reiter staged four concerts in the symphony's first season, engaging soloists such as pianist Alec Templeton and violinist Jascha Heifetz in order to attract large audiences. In addition, he commissioned the exiled Czech composer Jaromir Weinberger to write a *Prelude and Fugue on a Southern Folk Tune* for the new orchestra. Season ticket sales grew, and by 1943 Reiter had placed the orchestra on a fully professional basis. He added a tour through the Rio Grande valley and children's concerts and began to lure the city's Hispanic population with a visit from Mexican composer–conductor Carlos Chávez, who conducted his own music. Spring 1945 witnessed the first San Antonio Grand Opera Festival. Starting with performances of *La Bohème*, Reiter established a tradition of regular opera productions that achieved considerable financial and artistic success. After Reiter died in 1950, Victor Alessandro was named his successor. Alessandro, born in Waco, had received his education from the Eastman School of Music and after graduation had gone on to conduct the Oklahoma Symphony. In San Antonio he built upon Reiter's foundations a far-reaching and varied program of his own, initiating a series of pops concerts and greatly expanding the role of the associated conductor, principal hornist George Yaeger. In 1961 Alessandro established the Rio Grande Music Festival, a week-long series of operas and concerts each spring. From his earliest years in San Antonio, Alessandro challenged his audiences with contemporary works and championed American music, especially by Texas and local composers.

Since the late 1960s the orchestra has given its concerts in pairs, one performed at the Lila Cockrell (now HemisFair) Theater, the other at Trinity University. When Alessandro died in 1976, much of the orchestra's growth, stability and artistic integrity had been directly attributable to his quarter-century tenure. He was succeeded by François Huybrechts (1978–80) and Lawrence Leighton Smith (1980–85), after which a protracted search for a new musical director and a corresponding series of guest conductors led to financial difficulties that forced the cancellation of the 1987–88 season. Many of the musicians of the San Antonio Symphony played for the newly formed Orchestra San Antonio until January 1988, when the San Antonio Symphony reinstated its season and assumed Orchestra San Antonio's remaining commitments. For the 1988–89 season Zdenek Macal served as artistic director and principal conductor. Christopher Wilkins was appointed music director designate in 1990 and became permanent music director in 1992. In 1994 the Symphony was given the first ASCAP/Morton Gould Award for Creative Programming and was recognized for its community-relevant programming by the American Symphony Orchestra League. The San Antonio Symphony has recorded for Mercury Records.

Theodore Albrecht

San Augustine, Texas.

Thirty-two miles east of Nacogdoches in north central San Augustine County. Ayish Bayou flows through the town two miles west of the public square, and Carrizo Creek has been dammed just southwest of San Augustine to form City Lake, the source of municipal water. The original inhabitants of

Activity in front of the Courthouse, San Augustine, April 1939. Photograph by Russell Lee. Library of Congress; LC-USF 34-33044-D. The current courthouse was built after a fire in 1890 destroyed a large part of the town.

the area were the Ais (Aies, Ayish) tribe of the Hasinai Indians. The first European visitors were probably part of the Moscoso expedition early in the 1540s. The Indians remained undisturbed for almost 150 years, until French traders from Natchitoches, Louisiana, ventured into the vicinity and discovered their village near the site of present San Augustine. The Spaniards returned in 1691, when Domingo Terán de los Ríos traveled through the area, cutting a path later called the Old San Antonio Road. In 1717 Father Antonio Margil de Jesús established Nuestra Señora de los Dolores de los Ais Mission near the Ais village on Ayish Bayou. After being abandoned because of the threat of a French invasion in 1719, the mission was reestablished at the site of modern San Augustine by the Marqués de Aguayo in 1721. But permanent settlement did not occur until after 1779, when the French threat became less ominous. Then Anglos and scattered remnants of the Kickapoo, Cherokee, Delaware, and Shawnee Indians immigrated from the southern states, particularly Mississippi, Alabama, Georgia, and Tennessee. Among these pioneers, who called the area the Ayish Bayou District, were John Quinalty, Susanna Horton, Martha Lewes, Edmund Quirk, and Chichester Chaplin. Antonio Leal and his wife, Gertrudis de los Santos, settled at the site of San Augustine and built a small house with corrals to accommodate mustangs rounded up by

Leal and Philip Nolan for sale in Louisiana. In 1800 Leal sold the property to Pedro Buigas, who sold it the following year to Edmund Quirk. In 1827 Ayish Bayou residents elected municipal authorities, even though the Mexican government had not officially recognized the district. Nathan Davis became the first alcalde for Ayish Bayou District, George English the first sheriff. When the Fredonian Rebellion began in 1827, most people along the bayou abandoned their homes because advancing Mexican and rebel forces threatened their safety. Despite this apparent unwillingness to take sides, these settlers soon became involved in protests against the Mexican government. They participated in the battle of Nacogdoches (1832) and sent representatives to the Convention of 1832. Sam Houston was one of their delegates to the Convention of 1833. In 1832, under the leadership of alcalde William McFarland, residents decided to construct a permanent settlement in a central location. A committee of 15 men chose the banks of the Ayish Bayou, which had been the heart of local activities since Indian occupation, and purchased the land in January 1833 from Edmund Quirk. Thomas S. McFarland surveyed their purchase and platted 356 lots on 48 city blocks in a grid pattern, perhaps the first time that such a method was used in Texas. The streets were 40 feet wide, and squares were reserved for the school, churches, municipal buildings, a market, and the jail. The following year, under alcalde Charles S. Taylor, the municipality of San Augustine was established by Mexican law. The town is named, perhaps indirectly, for St. Augustine of Hippo. Because the population of the district was more than 2,500, inhabitants could officially elect two councilmen, a clerk, a chief justice, a primary judge, and an alcalde.

In the 1830s San Augustinians took an active part in the Texas Revolution. Early in 1836 Houston was elected commander of the Texas forces at San Augustine—and afterward for all of Texas. In April the town was again abandoned during the Runaway Scrape, but citizens returned to their homes after the victory at San Jacinto. Under the Republic of Texas, San Augustine, the only sizable town in the county, became the county seat. In 1837 settlers elected a chief justice, a sheriff, a county clerk, a district clerk, a surveyor, and a coroner. That same year, the town was incorporated. But the end of the war failed to bring peace. In 1838 local resident and war hero Henry W. Augustine led a force against Mexican insurgents in the Córdova Rebellion. In July 1839 Texas troops drove the Cherokee and allied Indians out of East Texas. Settlers were also affected by the Regulator–Moderator War. But even in such turmoil, the little village continued to grow. Without the restraint of Mexican law, Protestant organizations and congregations were formed. In 1836 the San Augustine Bible Society managed to collect more than $172. In 1838 Littleton Fowler established the First United Methodist Church. The first Presbyterian congregation in Texas, with 24 members including 2 slaves, was founded by Hugh Wilson in 1838 when he began preaching at nearby Goodlaw School. That same year Jerusalem Memorial Colored Methodist Episcopal Church was built on a town lot belonging to George W. Teel. I. D. Thomas had constructed the first store in town, and a saloon, hotels, and other businesses soon developed. McFarland Lodge, the third official Masonic organization in Texas, was founded in 1837 under the leadership of William McFarland and was joined soon by Red Land Lodge No. 3 and Rising Star Chapter No. 4. That year W. W. Parker also began publishing the San Augustine *Red-Lander*. Mrs. Stewart's Female Academy was only one of several private schools in the area. Local architects Augustus Phelps and Sidney A. Sweet designed and built several impressive Greek Revival homes. The short-lived University of San Augustine was incorporated on 5 June 1837, the same day as the town. The school finally opened in 1842 only to close five years later without issuing a single degree. Wesleyan College, chartered by an act of Congress early in 1844, was only slightly more effective. A Methodist school, under the direction of Rev. Marcus A. Montrose, granted only two degrees before closing in 1847. The University of Eastern Texas, incorporated in 1848, received the property and endowment of the University of San Augustine, and its board of trustees united with the trustees of Wesleyan College. This school closed, however, after only a few years. The first post office, originally called Kendricks, opened in March 1847, but the postmaster changed the name to Ayish Bayou the following September. In March 1848 the postal facility was officially named San Augustine. Two years later Reverend Henry Samson formed the Christ Episcopal Church congregation. Throughout the republic era the customhouse at San Augustine collected duties on imports from the United States. The customs office had also served as the municipal building, but in 1854 a new two-story brick courthouse became the center of town activities. Eight new mercantile

establishments and one drugstore had opened, and Red Land Lodge No. 3 had founded the Masonic Institute to educate local children.

By 1860 San Augustine was a shipping center for cotton, but the Civil War interrupted this lucrative business. In the summer of 1861 San Augustine sent three companies into battle, and these were later followed by others. In 1862 a battalion of the Third Texas Brigade was stationed in the town to protect against invasion. Throughout the 1870s businesses struggled to recuperate but never recaptured the success of the antebellum years. In 1884 there were 600 residents. Local businesses included cotton gins, a gristmill, and two small sawmills, but the large enterprises that had once accommodated travelers remained closed. In 1890 a fire destroyed a large part of the town, but rebuilding began soon after. The old courthouse was torn down and replaced with a new one. The gristmill and cotton gins were still functioning, and seven general stores had opened. Other enterprises included two saloons and three law offices. In 1901 the Gulf, Beaumont and Great Northern Railway extended its tracks to San Augustine. The Santa Fe Railway system acquired the line in 1903 in order to transport lumber and other goods to and from the area, thus providing railroad jobs and making large sawmill operations feasible for the first time. In 1914 residents numbered 1,300. In 1927 the old courthouse was demolished and replaced with a two-story stone structure. At that time citizens had access to city-owned water, light, and sewerage utilities, as well as an ice plant and natural gas services. Children attended new schools, including a high school. The growth and development was, however, interrupted by the Great Depression. Lumber companies, having exhausted the best of the East Texas timberlands, moved out, thus eliminating an important source of income. Twenty-seven businesses closed, workers lost their jobs, and farmers had no market for their produce. Aid came in the form of such federal programs as the WPA and the CCC, as well as governmental loans. Although some sawmills eventually reopened, they could not operate at previous levels of output. By the beginning of World War II the Deep East Texas Electric Cooperative, which provided electricity for four counties, was headquartered in San Augustine. The town also had 80 businesses, including a car dealership. By 1960 the population had increased to 2,584 and the number of businesses to 130. Among the recreational facilities was the Fairway Farm Country Club, an 18-hole, 300-acre golf course considered one of the 200 toughest in the nation. In the 1970s and 1980s a public library containing 15,000 volumes opened, a new jail was constructed, and a loop was built to direct traffic around the town. The spring crafts fair and the annual Tour of Medallion Homes and Historic Places have become popular tourist attractions. Homes bearing historic medallions include those of Stephen W. Blount, Matthew Cartwright, George L. Crocket, Ezekiel W. Cullen, Almanzon Huston, and Philip A. Sublett. In 1992 the population totaled 2,337. *Vista K. McCroskey*

San Augustine *Red-Lander*. First published in 1838 by W. W. Parker, who purchased the printing press of the Nacogdoches *Texas Chronicle* and produced the paper for a little over a year before ill health forced his retirement. The paper reappeared in 1841, when its press was sold to Anson W. Canfield, former editor of the San Augustine *Journal and Advertiser*. Canfield's opposition to tariffs and support of Sam Houston made the *Red-Lander* one of the dominant political voices of the Republic of Texas, where it competed with the *Telegraph and Texas Register* and the *Vindicator* of Washington-on-the-Brazos. The *Red-Lander* and little San Augustine wielded inordinate political influence, partly because of the town's location on the Old San Antonio Road, where travelers provided a captive audience. For five dollars a year East Texans could receive a *Red-Lander* every Thursday, with the first of six pages dominated by Canfield's lengthy editorials, bawdy verse, and reprinted articles from the Boston *Whig* of two months previous, concerning everything from nearby Indian battles to the Queen of Spain's choice of suitor. The inside pages offered local announcements, such as developments at the University of San Augustine, or quotations from "hero, statesman, and sage" Andrew Jackson, as well as financial news from various cities. When Charles DeMorse established the Clarksville *Standard* in 1842, Canfield believed that the new paper represented a conspiracy against Houston. The pages of the *Red-Lander* became a battleground for Canfield and DeMorse, and the argument verged on violence when DeMorse threatened to "settle the matter with cowhide." The dispute was never resolved in print, but the tension finally eased. After the annexation of Texas, Canfield sold the *Red-Lander* to James Russell and H. M. Kinsey and joined the forces of Zachary Taylor in Corpus Christi. In 1846 the new editors printed a libelous article about the sister of Henry A. Kendall, editor of the *Shield*, a recently founded rival newspaper in San Augustine. Kendall shot Russell outside the *Red-Lander* office, and the newspaper was never able to recover. San Augustine's prosperity and prominence faded in the late 1840s. The *Red-Lander* was purchased by W. N. Harmon, who combined it with the *Shield* to form the *Texas Union*. This venture failed as well, and in 1851 B. F. Price and Benjamin F. Benton's *Redland Herald* took over the *Red-Lander* presses. Their product was more typical of small-town newspapers than its ambitious predecessor. *Randolph Lewis*

San Bernard. The only legal port in late Spanish and early Mexican Texas. San Bernard was a coastal region rather than a definite location. It was designated a port by royal decree on 28 September 1805, and the decree was renewed by the Cortes in 1820. In 1808 Spanish officials surveyed the Matagorda Bay area to obtain information for the establishment of a permanent port, but nothing was done, although agitation continued for such an establishment. There was no customhouse, the captain of Nuestra Señora de Loreto Presidio being designated as port official, and ships with business in Texas used any convenient shore for landing and taking on goods. This condition continued until Stephen F. Austin petitioned that the port of Galveston be made a legal port of entry. *Thomas W. Cutrer*

San Elizario, Texas. Also known at various times as San Elceario and San Elzeario; 15 miles southeast of downtown El Paso in southern El Paso County. Juan de Oñate reached the Rio Grande at or near the site of present San Elizario on 20 April 1598, and 10 days later took formal possession of New Mexico and all adjacent territory in the name of the Spanish king. A settlement known as the Hacienda de los Tiburcios was founded at the site, then south of the Rio Grande, sometime before 1760. It had a population of 157 in 1765. In 1789 the Spanish presidio, located in the Valle de San Elizario opposite Fort Hancock, was moved to the Hacienda de los Tiburcios; the presidio kept its old name,

however, and the settlement that grew up around it became known as San Elizario. San Elizario was second only to El Paso del Norte among local settlements for most of the nineteenth century. Merchant caravans passed through the town before the opening of the Santa Fe Trail, and Zebulon M. Pike and Peter Ellis Bean, a survivor of the Nolan expedition, were held there in 1807. In 1821, after the Mexican War of Independence from Spain, San Elizario became part of the state of Chihuahua. Mexican troops still occupied the old presidio in 1835, and it served as a nucleus for a town which by 1841 had a population of 1,018. In 1830–31 the unpredictable Rio Grande changed course, placing San Elizario and its neighboring communities on La Isla, between the old and new channels of the river. Members of the Doniphan expedition occupied the presidio in February 1847, and the next year, when the Treaty of Guadalupe Hidalgo established "the deepest channel" of the Rio Grande as the boundary between Texas and Mexico, San Elizario became part of Texas. The town lay on the Lower El Paso or Military Road from Corpus Christi to California, and hundreds of Forty-niners passed through it in the late 1840s. Companies of the Third Infantry under Jefferson Van Horne were stationed there from 1849 to 1852. In 1850, when El Paso County was officially organized, San Elizario was selected the county seat. Except for brief periods in 1854 and 1866, it remained the county seat until 1873. A post office was open in San Elizario from 1851 to 1869. During the Civil War troops of the California Column occupied the old presidio, but after the war the fort was finally abandoned for good. After 1873 San Elizario began to decline in importance. Perhaps the most notorious episode in the history of the town was the 1877 Salt War of San Elizario, in which several men died in a dispute over rights to the salt deposits just west of the Guadalupe Mountains, 90 miles to the east. After the salt war many residents of San Elizario fled across the Rio Grande to escape punishment. In 1881 the town was bypassed by the railroad in favor of El Paso. The estimated population was 1,500 in 1890, when the town had two schools and a steam flour mill. In 1904 it still had an estimated population of 1,426, but 10 years later that figure had declined to 834. In 1931 the estimated population fell to 300, but it climbed to 925 by the mid-1940s and to 1,064 by the early 1960s. In 1990 it was 4,385. *Martin Donell Kohout*

San Felipe de Austin. Unofficial capital of Stephen F. Austin's original colony; on the west bank of the Brazos River at the Old San Antonio Road crossing, a site now on I–10 two miles east of Sealy in southeastern Austin County. The town was founded in 1824 and became the first community center in the Austin colony, which stretched northward from the Gulf of Mexico as far as the Old San Antonio Road and extended from the Lavaca River in the west to the San Jacinto River in the east. By October 1823, after briefly considering a location on the lower Colorado River, Austin, with the assistance of the Baron de Bastrop, decided to establish his capital on the Brazos near the settlement at which John McFarland operated a ferry. The site chosen was on a high, easily defensible bluff overlooking broad, fertile bottomlands. The location offered a number of advantages, including a central location and sources of fresh water independent of the Brazos. In late 1823 surveyor Seth Ingram began the tasks of defining the boundaries of the five-league expanse of prairie and woodland encompassed by the municipality and platting the town proper. The town's name was proposed by the governor of the Eastern Interior Provinces, Felipe de la Garza, to honor both the empresario, Austin, and the governor's own patron saint. Although planned on the basis of the prevailing Mexican town model with a regular grid of avenues and streets dominated by four large plazas, the settlement soon began to sprawl westward from the Brazos for more than a half mile along both sides of the Atascosito Road. By 1828 the community comprised a population of about 200, three general stores, two taverns, a hotel, a blacksmith shop, and 40 or 50 log cabins. The town, generally called simply San Felipe, was the unquestioned social, economic, and political center of the Austin colony. Its population was swelled by large numbers of immigrants and other transients. Austin built a residence on Bullinger's Creek, a half mile west of the Brazos, from which he directed the government of his colony for four years before handing responsibility for the management of most affairs to the ayuntamiento of San Felipe in 1828. Regular mail service in the colony was inaugurated in 1826 when Samuel May Williams was appointed postmaster in San Felipe; with seven separate postal routes converging here, the town remained the hub of the Texas postal service until the Texas Revolution. One of the earliest newspapers in Texas, the *Texas Gazette*, began publication in San Felipe on 25 September 1829 under the editorship of Godwin B. Cotten. Gail Borden's *Telegraph and Texas Register*, which became the unofficial journal of the revolution, was first published in San Felipe on 10 October 1835. The town's notable early inhabitants also included Josiah H. Bell, James B. Miller, Noah Smithwick, and Horatio Chriesman.

Several large cotton plantations were established in the bottomlands near the town during the 1820s, and from the outset San Felipe became a trading center for the staple. By 1830 John Cummins had constructed a grist and lumber mill near the town. As stock raising developed in the vicinity, small herds of cattle were driven from the town across the country to Nacogdoches. San Felipe was located only some 80 miles above the mouth of the Brazos, and keelboats were used extensively to transport goods between the town and various coastal ports. Nevertheless, most articles of commerce were carried overland to the coast by wagon until after the revolution. Unreliable water levels and turbulence during the spring rains discouraged steamboat traffic on the Brazos as far as San Felipe, and the stream's meanders rendered the water route to the coast far longer than land routes. However, after 1830 steamboats gradually began to appear on the lower Brazos, and by 1836 as many as three steam vessels plied the waters between San Felipe and the coast. Although the settlement, like the rest of Austin's colony, was Catholic by law, no priest resided in San Felipe until the arrival of Father Michael Muldoon in 1831. Inasmuch as Austin discouraged the establishment of Protestant churches, Protestant worship in the town was confined mainly to occasional open-air meetings conducted by itinerant ministers. Not until after the revolution were the town's first churches built.

By the eve of the revolution San Felipe ranked second in Texas only to San Antonio as a commercial center. Its population in 1835 approached 600, and many more settlers resided nearby within the boundaries of the municipality. The conventions of 1832 and 1833 were held in the town, and as the site of the Consultation of 3 November 1835, San Felipe served as the capital of the provisional government until the Convention of 1836 met the following March at Washington-on-the-Brazos. After the fall of the Alamo, Gen. Sam Houston's army retreated through San Felipe. On 30 March 1836 the small garrison under Moseley Baker remaining at San Felipe to defend the Brazos crossing ordered the town evacuated and then burned it to the ground to keep it from falling into the hands of the advancing Mexican army. The terrified residents hastily gathered what few belongings they could carry before fleeing eastward—an incident known as the Runaway Scrape. By May 1836, as news of the Texans' victory at the battle of San Jacinto spread, San Felipeans began to return, and a semblance of community life was soon restored near the original townsite. Yet many families never returned, and the government of the republic was unable to resume operation in the town for want of the necessary buildings.

San Felipe was incorporated in 1837 and became county seat of the newly established Austin County. Though a courthouse was constructed, the town never recovered its former stature. By the mid-1840s the only other buildings in the settlement were six or seven log houses and a tavern. In 1846 a county election made the new community of Bellville the county seat. As the original inhabitants abandoned the town, however, they were replaced during the mid-nineteenth century by an influx of Germans. After the Civil War, freedmen began to take up residence in the community. Czechs moved into the area in the late nineteenth century, as did a large influx of Mexican immigrants during the early twentieth century; the Mexican influx resulted from an increase in the employment of Mexican migrant farmworkers in Austin County. In the mid-1870s the people of San Felipe declined an offer by the Gulf, Colorado and Santa Fe Railway to route its new Galveston–Brenham spur through their town. Instead, the railroad was sold a right-of-way through the western section of the original 22,000-acre municipal tract. In the early 1880s Sealy, four miles to the west, developed rapidly as a station of the new rail line, and many residents and businesses moved from San Felipe to the new commercial center. When the Texas Western Narrow Gauge Railway constructed its Houston–Sealy spur through the vicinity in 1882, the remaining residents of San Felipe moved southward about a half mile to a new townsite along the tracks. Proceeds from the sale of lands within the original five-league township were invested, and the resulting income enabled the town to function without taxation and to build a first-rate system of public education. But in 1899 the Texas Western, a minor carrier, abandoned its Houston–Sealy line, and by 1890 the population of San Felipe had declined to 177. It stood at 206 in 1910. In 1947 the town had 305 residents, one business, two churches, a school, and a post office. In 1990 the population was 618. Most of the original townsite on the banks of Bullinger's Creek now lies within the 4,200-acre Stephen F. Austin State Historical Park, which was dedicated in 1928 and donated to the state by the town of San Felipe in 1940. The park features an obelisk and a bronze statue commemorating the achievements of Stephen F. Austin, a replica of Austin's log house, and a monument on the site of the town hall.

Charles Christopher Jackson

San Fernando de Béxar. San Fernando de Béxar (now San Antonio) was founded in 1731 between the San Antonio River and San Pedro Creek, to the east of the presidio established at the same location in 1718. It was the first chartered civil settlement in Texas and was named in honor of the heir to the Spanish throne, the future Fernando VI. From 1773 until 1824, when Texas was joined to Coahuila, San Fernando served as the provincial capital. In 1718 Governor Martín de Alarcón established a settlement he called Villa de Béxar near the headwaters of San Pedro Creek, but civilian settlement did not materialize. Royal authorities, hoping to reduce the expense of a purely military settlement, decided on a plan to transfer 400 families of Canary Islanders to Texas, some of whom would be located near San Antonio de Béxar Presidio. The immigrants had rights as first settlers to form a town government, to receive generous land grants, and to carry the noble title of hidalgo. Logistical problems, Indian hostilities, and the unfamiliarity of the Canary Islanders with frontier conditions caused Capt. Juan Antonio Pérez de Almazán to locate the new settlers adjacent to the presidio. Throughout the Spanish period San Fernando suffered from retarded development. Apache, Comanche, and other nonsedentary Indians raided cattle and horse herds, attacked farmers in the field, and often made communications with the interior of New Spain hazardous. The proximity of the new town to the military settlement and to five Franciscan missions led to considerable friction over land, water, and livestock among the Hispanic inhabitants of the area over the next few decades. Population growth was slow; approximately 500 settlers lived in the town and presidio in 1750, and triple that number at the end of the eighteenth century. The population grew somewhat more rapidly after 1803, but rebellion and filibustering during the second decade of the nineteenth century caused a drastic decline. In 1820 the population of the town and neighboring missions was approximately 2,000. Economic activity was correspondingly limited. Agriculture was largely for subsistence and confined to irrigated farms, one on the south side of San Fernando (established in 1731), another north of town (1777), and those of the missions as these were secularized. The farms were subdivided into individual, privately owned plots. Ranching was the most profitable activity and the source of greatest friction between townspeople and the neighboring missions. San Fernando's more prominent residents acquired large landholdings along the Medina and San Antonio river valleys in the direction of Goliad, including mission lands vacated between the 1750s and 1820s. San Fernando was also the center of contraband trade between Louisiana and the interior of Mexico.

From 1811 to the mid-1830s San Fernando was the scene of political and military upheavals that further obstructed growth. In January 1811 a retired militia officer, with the assistance of some civilians, managed to gain the allegiance of the local garrison and overthrew royal officials. By March the town's leading citizens had organized a counterrevolt, for which they earned for the town the status of *ciudad* (city). The Gutiérrez–Magee expedition captured the city in April 1813, however, and held it until August, when an army under Joaquín de Arredondo defeated the filibusters at the battle of Medina. Indian depredations, inspired by the chaos in the province, unrealistic demands on the local population by the military, and the loss of a substantial number of residents who had sided with the insurrectionists, contributed to a collapse of the town's economy. During the 1820s and 1830s San Fernando suffered further as it became both politically and economically marginal to the region. The Constitution of 1824, which joined Coahuila and Texas in a single state, led to the transfer of political authority to Saltillo. San Fernando served only as the seat of the *jefe político*, as the governor's lieutenant in the department of Texas was called. In 1831 and 1834, when the departments of the Brazos and Texas were established, San

Fernando's jurisdiction was further reduced. When hostilities between Texas and the Mexican national government erupted in the autumn of 1835, San Fernando became a base of operations and scene of battles. Too exposed to Indian and Mexican attack and removed from the bulk of the new republic's population, San Fernando, renamed San Antonio, was again reduced in status to the seat of Bexar County in 1837.   *Jesús F. de la Teja*

Sanguinet and Staats. A statewide architectural firm founded in 1903 by Marshall R. Sanguinet and Carl G. Staats. Sanguinet had moved to Fort Worth in 1883. Staats, a native New Yorker, had worked for James Riely Gordon. The firm, with headquarters in Fort Worth, is best known for its contributions to the design of steel-framed skyscrapers and for establishing offices across the state. Almost every tall building constructed in Fort Worth before 1930, and for a time the tallest structures in Beaumont, Houston, Midland, and San Antonio, were designed by Sanguinet and Staats. The 20-story Amicable Insurance Company Building in Waco, completed in 1911, was for a brief time the tallest building in the Southwest. Other prominent examples include the First National Bank Building, Houston (1905), the Flatiron Building, Fort Worth (1907), the Scarbrough Building, Austin (1910), the C. F. Carter Building, Houston (1919), the South Texas Building, San Antonio (1919), the Neil P. Anderson Building, Fort Worth (1920), and the Jackson Building, Jackson, Mississippi (1923). The firm designed in a variety of styles and forms that transformed the scale and style of the state's rapidly growing cities. It also designed a number of large residences, especially on Pennsylvania Avenue in Fort Worth and Courtlandt Place in Houston, where examples still stand. Sanguinet and Staats, with branch offices in Dallas, Wichita Falls, San Antonio, Waco, and Houston, was also among the first Texas architectural enterprises to have a statewide practice. In 1922 Wyatt C. Hedrick bought a partial interest, and the firm became Sanguinet, Staats, and Hedrick, while the Houston branch operated as Sanguinet, Staats, Hedrick, and Gottlieb, under the direction of R. D. Gottlieb, a limited partner. In 1926 the founders retired and sold their share of the firm to Hedrick, who continued the practice under his own name in Fort Worth and in limited partnerships in Houston and later Dallas.
      Christopher Long

San Juan Bautista. The "gateway to Spanish Texas"; original mission founded in 1699 in Nuevo León, then reestablished the next year at the site of present-day Guerrero, Coahuila. The founding Franciscans—fathers Francisco Hidalgo, Antonio de San Buenaventura y Olivares, and Marcos de Guereña of the College of Santa Cruz de Querétaro, were assisted by soldiers under Capt. Diego Ramón. The new site, five miles from the Rio Grande, was strategically located near a series of crossings into Texas. Here San Juan Bautista, which grew by 1702 into a complex of three missions, a presidio, and a civilian settlement, served as a way station and gateway for expeditions to the Texas interior from 1700 until the Mexican War. The three missions originally stood in a tight triangle on either side of the spring-fed arroyo that supplied their water. From 1700 to 1716 the San Juan Bautista settlement was the most advanced on New Spain's northeastern frontier. As such it served as a base for exploration beyond the Rio Grande: in 1700, Father Olivares's trek to the Frio River seeking mission neophytes; Ramón's Indian campaign along the Nueces River in 1707; and the Espinosa–Olivares–Aguirre expedition to the Colorado in 1709. San Juan Bautista served also as a listening post for news of the French, who in 1699 had settled at Biloxi Bay and were exploring west of the Mississippi. The French cavalier Louis Juchereau de St. Denis arrived at San Juan Bautista from Mobile in the summer of 1714 to entice the Spaniards to illicit trade; he married the commandant's granddaughter.

In every respect San Juan Bautista was the mother of the Texas missions. In 1716 it launched an entrada to reestablish the East Texas missions abandoned in 1693, in the charge of Domingo Ramón—who later commanded the first Texas presidio—and followed up with supply expeditions. Governor Martín de Alarcón launched his founding expedition to San Antonio from San Juan in 1718, after spending the winter there. At that time Father Olivares moved San Francisco Solano Mission to the San Antonio site, where it became Mission San Antonio de Valero, later known as the Alamo. San Juan provided grain, cattle, and remounts to bolster the faltering expedition of the Marqués de Aguayo in 1721–22. Nuestra Señora de Loreto Presidio, founded by Aguayo, was commanded in succession by two members of the Ramón family from San Juan Bautista, Domingo and his son Diego III. At mid-century San Juan provided livestock and provisions to the San Xavier missions and the Apache mission on the San Saba River. After the latter was destroyed by the northern tribes in March 1758, the San Juan Bautista commandant, Manuel Rodríguez, took a company of soldiers to join the punitive expedition and remained a year in temporary command of the San Sabá garrison. The renewed missionary effort for the Apaches on the upper Nueces River was a joint enterprise of the new commandant at San Sabá and the Rio Grande missions. Soldiers of Presidio de San Juan Bautista provided escorts for travelers and supply trains to Texas, joined Indian campaigns, and played a vital role in exploration. In 1731 they escorted the Canary Islanders on the last leg of their journey to San Antonio. They assisted explorations up the Rio Grande by José de Barroterán in 1729 and Blas María de la Garza Falcón in 1735. In 1747 they reconnoitered the Rio Grande from their post to its mouth in conjunction with José de Escandón and assisted Pedro de Rábago y Terán in opening a trail from Coahuila to La Junta de los Ríos. In 1732 and 1739 troops under Manuel Rodríguez joined Apache campaigns led by Texas governor Juan Antonio Bustillo y Ceballos and José de Urrutia. Rodríguez, at age 71, led an expedition up the Rio Grande to the presidio of El Paso in 1769, engaging hostile Indians along the way.

The New Regulations for Presidios of 1772 brought great change to San Juan Bautista. With establishment of the Provincias Internas and formation of a defense line extending west to the Gulf of California, San Juan Bautista troops were involved almost continuously in Apache campaigns, both in the Bolsón de Mabimí and north of the Rio Grande. In 1775 San Juan Bautista's force was one of several to take part in the coordinated campaign extending across southwestern Texas into New Mexico and Arizona. Vicente Rodríguez, who had succeeded his brother Manuel as commandant of the presidio, at age 76 led the Rio Grande troops north to the abandoned Presidio de San Sabá, then up the Pecos River into New Mexico. On 22 November 1772 missions San Juan and San Bernardo were transferred from the College of Santa Cruz de Querétaro to the province of Jalisco. In 1781 they were again reassigned, this time to the Missionary

College of Pachuca. The missions declined sharply. By 1790 Mission San Juan, which had baptized 1,434 Indians up to 1761, had only 63 natives under instruction. In 1797 citizens of the district petitioned for division of mission lands, but not until 1829, after Mexico had won independence from Spain, were the missions actually secularized and land distribution completed. Yet, for all practical purposes, the missions had ceased to function by 1810, when the Mexican War of Independence began. San Juan—the name changed to Puesto de Río Grande after its religious significance faded—was host to key figures of both sides during the insurgence, striking a delicate balance between factions. An 1827 legislative decree changed the name again, to Villa de Guerrero, honoring the Mexican patriot Vicente Guerrero.

Even to this declining village the processions of history still came. From 10 January to 16 February 1836, Guerrero served as the staging area for Antonio López de Santa Anna's army, which was marching on San Antonio de Béxar. In March 1842 Rafael Vásquez, having looted San Antonio, withdrew to Guerrero with his plunder. In June that year Adrián Woll assembled horses and men at Presidio del Río Grande and thence launched his invasion of Texas. The last invasion force came to Guerrero during the Mexican War, when, on 9 October 1846, United States general John E. Wool encamped his Army of Chihuahua near the village. After the war, traffic shifted more and more to Laredo and Eagle Pass, leaving Guerrero in the backwater, isolated even from Piedras Negras until the new Piedras Negras–Laredo highway was routed by the town in the 1970s. The town, anchored by the *plaza de armas* of the former presidio, had significant architectural remains from the mission period at that time, but these were rapidly deteriorating. Ruins of the San Bernardo Mission church stood just north of the village. Mission San Juan Bautista, however, had been reduced to a pile of earth and stone, often disturbed by treasure hunters. A historical study published in 1968 awakened interest in Guerrero, and it became the focus of architectural, archeological, and ethnographical investigations funded by the Mexican government and the National Endowment for the Humanities. The San Juan Bautista site was partially excavated, and the San Bernardo ruins were stabilized. Guerrero remained a small village. *Robert S. Weddle*

San Marcos, Texas. County seat of Hays County, 25 miles south of Austin. It was the site of several Spanish attempts at colonization before it became the center of Anglo-American settlement in the area. The first such attempt, in 1755, saw the short-lived establishment of the San Xavier missions and the presidio of San Francisco Xavier. These were moved less than a year later, and the headwaters of the San Marcos River remained unsettled for another half century. In 1808 the Spanish governor M. A. Cordero y Bustamante sponsored the civil settlement of San Marcos de Neve near the same site, but floods and Indian raids prompted its abandonment in 1812. In November 1846 Thomas G. McGehee became the first Anglo-American to settle in the vicinity of San Marcos Springs, but William W. Moon has been identified as the original resident of the site that became San Marcos proper. Moon was soon joined by other former members of John C. Hays's company of Texas Rangers and by Gen. Edward Burleson. Caton Erhard opened the first store and post office by 1847, and the First Methodist Church began soon after. The Texas legislature organized Hays County in 1848 and designated the young community as the county seat. San Marcos

Avenue near San Marcos, 1880. Photograph by J. G. Hyde, from *Our Indian Summer in the Far West,* by Samuel Nugent Townshend (London, printed by C. Wittingham, 1880). Courtesy TSL.

already had 387 residents. In 1851 General Burleson, William Lindsey, and Dr. Eli T. Merriman took possession of 640 acres of the Juan Veramendi grant and laid out the town center. Tarbox and Brown stagecoaches linked San Marcos with Austin and San Antonio in 1848, and the town began its development as the commercial center for the cart trade between area farmers and ranchers and coastal commission merchants. It also became a center for ginning and milling local agricultural products. Slowed for a while by the Civil War, the population in 1870 had grown only to 742, but in the decade following the arrival of the International–Great Northern Railroad in 1881 it reached 2,335. In that decade the town supported two banks, an opera house, and a variety of stores, saloons, and other businesses. Cattle and cotton production in the area provided the basis for the gradual but steady growth of San Marcos as a center for commerce and transportation. The chartering in 1899 and subsequent opening in 1903 of Southwest Texas State Normal School and of San Marcos Baptist Academy in 1907 established education as an important local industry. By the 1920s San Marcos counted more than 4,000 residents. On the eve of World War II the population was estimated to be 5,500 and the town had 200 businesses. During and after the war the city's economy began to diversify and growth accelerated. Wartime demand provided the initial stimulus for development of a light industrial and manufacturing sector; it was reported after the war that the financial resources of the city had increased 500 percent from prewar lev-

els. In the 1960s, with the emergence of Aquarena Springs and Wonder Cave as important attractions, the tourist industry became a reliable and growing source of income. The expansion of Southwest Texas State University into an important regional institution, as well as the establishment in 1965 of the Gary Job Corps Training Center, not only made education the single largest employer in the city but also helped push the population from 12,713 in 1962 to 18,860 in 1972. Industrial development accelerated in the 1970s; among the 400 businesses recorded by 1980 were manufacturers of furniture, sheet-metal products, plastics, woolens, lighting fixtures, telecommunication devices, baked goods, construction materials, and tortillas. Austin's emergence as a regional metropolitan center is another cause of the remarkable growth of San Marcos since the 1950s; in 1973 Hays County and San Marcos became part of the Austin Standard Metropolitan Statistical Area. By the mid-1980s at least 20 percent of Hays County's labor force worked in Travis County. San Marcos had a population of 28,743 in 1990.

Daniel P. Greene

San Marcos de Neve. One of the last Spanish attempts at colonization in Texas; four miles below the site of present San Marcos, where the Old San Antonio Road crossed the San Marcos River. It was intended as part of a chain of defensive settlements stretching from San Antonio to Nacogdoches and was personally funded by the Spanish governor of Texas, Manuel

Antonio Cordero y Bustamante. Cordero charged Felipe Roque de la Portilla with leadership of the expedition to reestablish a Spanish presence on the San Marcos, where the San Xavier missions had been temporarily relocated 50 years earlier. Colonists were recruited from south of the Rio Grande. The first group set out from Refugio (now Matamoros) in December 1807 and by February 1808 had settled near the San Marcos crossing. Estimates of the population vary from about 50 to 80 people. A central plaza had been laid out and titles issued to 13 town lots when a flood on 5 June 1808 nearly wiped out the nascent community. The colony held out for several years, but harassment by Comanches and Tonkawas forced its abandonment in 1812.

Daniel P. Greene

San Patricio, Texas. Founded in 1829 by the empresarios James McGloin and John McMullen after they received permission from the Mexican government to settle 200 Irish Catholic families in Texas. After recruiting settlers in New York, the empresarios hired the *New Packet* and the *Albion* to transport the colonists to their new home. The first settlers arrived at El Cópano and Mesquite Landing in late October 1829 and made their way to the old mission at Refugio, where they remained for some time. They eventually chose a townsite where the *camino real* from Goliad to Laredo and the Atascosito Road from Louisiana crossed the Nueces River. It is not known just exactly when the settlers moved from Refugio to the Nueces River site; however, by 18 November 1830 the move was completed. The old Fort Lipantitlán was across the river less than two miles distant. Land commissioner José Antonio Saucedo arrived in October 1831 to issue land grants to eight settlers. A townsite four leagues square, called Villa de San Patricio de Hibernia in honor of Ireland's patron saint, had been laid out by surveyor William O'Docharty. In 1834 José María Balmaceda, the new land commissioner, returned to issue another 76 land grants. Local autonomy under Mexican rule was increased in 1834 when the municipality of San Patricio was established. It appears that the residents of San Patricio were not caught up immediately in the revolutionary spirit that prevailed over most of Mexican Texas in 1835; however, representatives from San Patricio participated in all conventions except the first. With the help of men from San Patricio, Capt. Ira Westover and his men from Goliad captured Fort Lipantitlán in December 1835. In early 1836 the Matamoros expedition began to move to the front, with the intention of marching on Mexico; on 27 February, Gen. José de Urrea surprised Col. Francis W. Johnson's men in San Patricio and killed or captured most of the unit. The Texans were buried in the Old Cemetery on the Hill. After the battle of San Patricio the Mexican army became an ever-present menace. San Patricio became a ghost town as colonists fled to Victoria and other refuges, leaving their homes and livestock unprotected. Later the municipality was declared a depopulated area, and so it remained until Gen. Zachary Taylor arrived in South Texas in 1845 and stationed a troop of dragoons in the area to reestablish law and order. When San Patricio County was created in 1836, San Patricio was designated the county seat. A post office was established in 1848, and the town was incorporated in 1853. For the next two decades it grew, as more and more settlers arrived and farming and ranching became more profitable. The overland Cotton Road crossed the Nueces River at San Patricio, and the wagon crews stopped to buy supplies and drink in the local saloon. In the 1880s San Patricio had several churches, schools, cotton gins, a gristmill, and a population of 200. After Sinton became the county seat in June 1894, San Patricio began to decline. In 1901 a citizens' group persuaded the state legislature to disincorporate the town. For over 70 years San Patricio was all but forgotten, until in 1972 the city of Corpus Christi sought to annex an area on the Nueces River that would have given it jurisdiction over the old town. The citizens of San Patricio rose to the challenge and defeated the annexation attempt; they reincorporated on 12 August 1972. An awareness of the heritage of San Patricio has caused a rebirth of interest in its history. Annual "world-championship" rattlesnake races on St. Patrick's Day have been used by the San Patricio Restoration Society as a means to raise funds to preserve the city's landmarks. Enough money was raised to rebuild the courthouse of 1872 according to original specifications; it was dedicated in 1987. In 1990 the population was 369.

Keith Guthrie

Santa Anna. Also Santana; Penateka Comanche chief, the first member of his group to visit Washington; d. 1849. He seems to have had several wives and a number of children. Carne Muerto, a Comanche war leader of the 1850s, may have been his son. After the Texas Revolution, conflicts between Comanches and settlers intensified. Santa Anna gained prominence after the Council House Fight in San Antonio (1840). With Buffalo Hump and other war chiefs, he raided a number of white settlements. He probably took part in the Linnville raid of 1840 and may have been present at the battle of Plum Creek. In 1845, however, he was persuaded to attend treaty negotiations conducted by United States officials, and by May 1846 he agreed to a treaty promising peace between his people and American citizens in Texas. Both sides ignored the treaty. The following December, Santa Anna and a party of chiefs visited D.C. Santa Anna seems to have been overwhelmed by what he saw. Thereafter, convinced that continued armed resistance against the United States was suicidal, he fully supported accommodation and attempted to use his prestige to secure a lasting peace. His conversion reduced his prestige among his people, however, and perhaps in an attempt to regain his position, he led several raids into Mexico in 1848–49, in violation of the Treaty of Guadalupe Hidalgo. The actions necessitated intervention by United States Indian agent Robert S. Neighbors. Santa Anna died with more than 300 other Penatekas in a cholera epidemic. Thereafter, the Penateka band quickly disintegrated as its remaining members joined other Comanche groups. *Jodye Lynn Dickson Schilz*

Santa Anna, Antonio López de. Mexican general and dictator; b. Jalapa, Vera Cruz, 21 February 1794; d. Mexico City, 21 June 1876; m. Inés García (1825; d. 1844); m. María Dolores de Tosta. In 1810 he became a cadet in the Fijo de Vera Cruz infantry regiment under the command of Joaquín de Arredondo. He spent the next five years battling insurgents and policing the Indian tribes of the Provincias Internas. Like most other criollo officers in the Royalist army, he fought against the movement for Mexican independence. In 1813 he served in Texas against the Gutiérrez–Magee expedition and was cited for bravery at the battle of Medina. Afterward, he witnessed Arredondo's fierce counterinsurgency policy of mass executions, and historians have speculated that Santa Anna modeled his policy and conduct in the Texas Revolution on his experience under Arredondo. He

General Antonio López de Santa Anna. Hand-colored lithograph. 23" × 16". Courtesy San Jacinto Museum of History, Houston.

once again served under Arredondo against the filibustering expedition of Francisco Xavier Mina in 1817. In 1820 he was promoted to brevet captain, and he became a brevet lieutenant colonel the following year. In March 1821 he made the first of the dramatic shifts of allegiance that characterized his military and political career by joining the rebel forces under Agustín de Iturbide in the middle of a campaign against them. He campaigned for Iturbide for a time and was promoted to brigadier general. In 1822 Santa Anna broke with Iturbide over a series of personal grievances, and he called for a republic in his Plan of Casa Mata (December 1822). After serving as military governor of Yucatán, he retired to civil life and became governor of Vera Cruz. In 1829 he defeated the Spanish invasion at Tampico and emerged from the campaign as a national hero. In the course of this campaign, he demonstrated several of his characteristic military strengths and weaknesses; he was able to pull an army together quickly and with severely limited resources, but he also combined elaborate planning with slipshod and faulty execution. He rebelled against the administration three years later and was elected president of Mexico as a liberal in 1833, but in 1834 he stated that Mexico was not ready for democracy and emerged as an autocratic Centralist. When the liberals of Zacatecas defied his authority and an attempt to reduce their militia in 1835, Santa Anna moved to crush them and followed up his battlefield victory with a harsh campaign of repression. In December 1835 he arrived at San Luis Potosí to organize an army to crush the rebellion in Texas. In 1836 he marched north with his forces to play his controversial role in the Texas Revolution. After being captured by Sam Houston, he was sent to Washington, whence he returned to Mexico. He retired to his estates at Manga de Clavo for a time, then emerged to join the defense of Mexico against

the French in December 1838 during the so-called "Pastry War." He lost a leg in battle and regained his popularity. He was acting president in 1839, helped overthrow the government of Anastasio Bustamante in 1841, and was dictator from 1841 to 1845. Excesses led to his overthrow and exile to Havana.

At the beginning of the Mexican War, Santa Anna entered into negotiations with President James K. Polk. He offered the possibility of a negotiated settlement to the United States and was permitted to enter Mexico through the American blockade. Once in the country he rallied resistance to the foreign invaders. As commanding officer in the northern campaign he lost the battle of Buena Vista in February 1847, returned to Mexico City, reorganized the demoralized government, and turned east to be defeated by Winfield Scott's forces at Cerro Gordo. Secret negotiations with Scott failed, and when Mexico City was captured, Santa Anna retired to exile. In 1853 he was recalled by the Centralists, but again power turned his head. To help meet expenses he sold the Mesilla Valley to the United States as the Gadsden Purchase and was overthrown and banished by the liberals in 1855. For eleven years he schemed to return to Mexico, conniving with the French and with Maximilian. After a visit from the American secretary of state, W. H. Seward, he invested most of his property in a vessel that he sailed to New York to become the nucleus of a planned invading force from the United States. Disappointed in his efforts, he proceeded towards Mexico, was arrested on the coast, and returned to exile. From 1867 to 1874 he lived in Cuba, the Dominican Republic, and Nassau. During this time he finally abandoned politics and wrote his memoirs. In 1874 he was allowed to return to Mexico City, where he lived in obscurity until his death. He was buried at Tepeyac Cemetery, near Guadalupe Hidalgo.

Wilfred H. Callcote

Santa Claus Bank Robbery. In Cisco; an infamous, deadly, and bungled crime. In December 1927 Marshall Ratliff, Henry Helms, and Robert Hill, all ex-cons, and Louis Davis, a relative of Helms, stole a car in Wichita Falls and headed for Cisco. They arrived on the morning of 23 December and prepared to make themselves some easy money. But during this period three or four Texas banks a day were being robbed, and in response the Texas Bankers Association had offered a $5,000 reward to anyone shooting a bank robber caught in the act. As the group neared the bank, Ratliff donned a Santa Claus suit and got out of the car. Followed by children, "Santa" joined the other three in an alley and led the way into the bank. While the robbery was in progress, a mother and girl escaped and raised the alarm, alerting chief of police Bit Bedford and most of the citizenry about the robbery. Hill shot at someone outside the bank, and a fusillade of gunfire began. Many armed citizens, sniffing the reward money, were now on hand. The robbers forced all of the people in the bank out the door and towards their car. Several potential hostages were wounded as they emerged into the alley, including Alex Spears, the bank president. Although most of the customers escaped, two small girls were taken as hostages. In a shootout in the alley, as the robbers tried to get to their car, Chief Bedford and Deputy George Carmichael were mortally wounded. Ratliff and Davis were also wounded in the shootout, Davis severely. As the four began their escape with their hostages, they realized that they were almost out of gas and one of their tires had been shot out. They drove to the edge of town, pursued by the mob, and attempted to commandeer an Oldsmobile belonging to the Harris family. Fourteen-year-old Woody Harris, who was driving, left the car but took the keys. While the robbers put their things in the Oldsmobile, Hill was wounded. The blundering foursome realized that they could not start the car, left the unconscious Davis and the money in it, and went back to their first car with their two hostages. The citizens found Davis and the money and temporarily gave up the chase. The money was returned to the bank—$12,400 in cash and $150,000 in nonnegotiable securities. The bank was riddled with bullet holes. Besides the two police officers, there had been six townspeople wounded in the shootout, but no one was sure whether the robbers or the citizens were responsible. Davis died that night at a Fort Worth hospital.

The robbers abandoned the car and the two girls several miles from town and continued on foot. They then stole two more cars in succession. The two wounded men, especially Ratliff, were doing very poorly due to their wounds, lack of food, and icy weather (it was sleeting). Eventually, the three were ambushed by Sheriff Foster of Young County at South Bend as they tried to cross the Brazos River. Another car chase followed, with a shootout in a field as the three tried to make their escape. Cy Bradford, a Texas Ranger, was involved in the firefight, and it is rumored that he hit all three men. Ratliff was hit and fell to the ground. Helms and Hill were both wounded, but they managed to escape into the woods. Several days later, after dodging an intense manhunt assisted by an airplane, the two made it into Graham and were taken into custody by lawmen without a fight. Two more men had been wounded in the manhunt from accidental gunshots, bringing the total number of wounded to eight, excluding the three surviving robbers. Helms, Hill, and Ratliff, though all wounded, survived to face trial. Hill pleaded guilty to armed robbery, took the stand on his own behalf, and in March was sentenced to 99 years in prison. He escaped from prison three times but was recaptured each time. After settling down, he was paroled in the mid-1940s, changed his name, and became a productive citizen. Helms was identified as the one who had gunned down both lawmen and was given the death sentence in late February. After an unsuccessful insanity plea, he was executed in the electric chair (6 September 1929). Ratliff was first convicted of armed robbery and sentenced to 99 years in prison, then sentenced to execution for his role in the deaths of Bedford and Carmichael, although no one could testify to having seen him fire a gun in the bank. Ratliff appealed his case and, when that failed, went for an insanity plea. He had begun acting insane the day that Helms was executed, and thoroughly convinced his jailers that he was. His mother, Rilla Carter, filed for a lunacy hearing in Huntsville. However, the citizens of Eastland County were infuriated that he had not been executed yet, and even further aggravated to know that Ratliff was attempting the insanity plea. Judge Davenport issued a bench warrant for an armed robbery charge and for stealing the Harris car, and extradited Ratliff to the Eastland County jail. There Ratliff convinced his jailers, Pack Kilbourn and Tom Jones, that he really was insane, since they had to feed him, bathe him, and take him to the toilet. On 18 November 1928 Ratliff attempted to escape, mortally wounding Jones in the attempt. A crowd began to gather the next morning and by nightfall had grown to over 1,000. They began demanding the killer. Kilbourn refused but was overpowered, and the mob rushed in and found Ratliff, whom they dragged out and

hanged. Although a grand jury was formed, no one was ever tried for the lynching. *Walter F. Pilcher*

Santa Fe County. Established in 1848; included practically all of the area of New Mexico claimed by the Republic of Texas and later by the state of Texas. At the time it was established, the Texas legislature passed a joint resolution laying before the United States Congress the assertion that Santa Fe County was a part of Texas and authorizing the governor of Texas to issue a proclamation to organize the county. The territory was made the eleventh judicial district of Texas. Spruce M. Baird was appointed chief justice, but he never held a court. In October 1848 New Mexicans held a mass meeting at Santa Fe to protest incorporation with Texas, partially because Texas was a slave state and partially because of long animosity between New Mexico and the Texas government. In 1849 Governor Bell threatened to claim the area by force. In January 1850 Santa Fe County was subdivided into Worth, El Paso, Presidio, and Santa Fe counties. Robert S. Neighbors made an unsuccessful trip to organize the counties. Later in 1850, in compliance with a section of the Compromise of 1850, Texas ceded to the United States for $10 million her claims to the upper Rio Grande area. Worth and Santa Fe counties ceased to exist, and El Paso and Presidio counties were reduced. *Seymour V. Connor*

Santa Fe Trail. One of the most historically and economically significant routes of the cattle trailing industry from 1821 to 1880. It extended from the westernmost settlements of the United States in Missouri across the Plains Indian country to the capital of New Mexico. The area may have been traversed as early as 1541 by Vázquez de Coronado, and certainly it was known to French and Spanish traders in the eighteenth century and explored by American hunters and military forces, including that under Zebulon Montgomery Pike, early in the nineteenth century. In 1821 Mexico became independent from Spain and reversed Spanish policies of exclusiveness and resistance to foreign trade. The governor of New Mexico welcomed William Becknell, the "Father of the Santa Fe Trail," Thomas James, and Hugh Glenn to begin trade. All three took goods to Santa Fe in 1822, but Becknell was the first to transport merchandise by wagons, forerunners of the prairie schooners that eventually became the most widely accepted symbol of the trail. For mutual protection the merchants generally traveled in caravans with mule or oxdrawn wagons arranged in two parallel lines so that they could be drawn into a circle quickly in case of attack. In 1829 and 1843 military escorts were furnished by the United States government, but the soldiers were rarely needed, for the cautious plains Indians seldom risked battle with well-organized caravans. The most celebrated of all the Santa Fe traders was Josiah Gregg, who between 1831 and 1843 made nearly a dozen trips over the trail and in 1844 published the classic account, *Commerce of the Prairies: The Journal of a Santa Fe Trader*. There were several variants of the trail. At least as early as 1825 the most popular route lay mostly across territory claimed after 1836 by the Republic of Texas. The Fort Smith–Santa Fe Trail crossed the future Indian Territory and the Panhandle. The Texan Santa Fe expedition was sent out by Mirabeau Lamar partly to divert trade to Texas, and in 1843, after the failure of that expedition, the expedition of Jacob Snively was authorized to attack Mexican traders on the trail to retaliate for the injustices suffered by other Texans at the hands of the Mexicans. In its later years the Santa Fe Trail became a link in the gold trail to California and in the immigrant trails to the Far West.   *H. Bailey Carroll*

Santa Rita Oil Well. In Reagan County; brought in on 28 May 1923. The land promotion was initiated in 1919 by Rupert P. Ricker, who took advantage of a 1917 law that allowed the leasing of state land for oil exploration. He and four associates made preliminary applications on 431,360 acres owned by the University of Texas. Ricker intended to promote the land deal in Fort Worth and sell enough leases to pay the filing fee—$43,136 due the General Land Office in 30 days. When he found no interest in his land deal he sold his ideas, maps, and preliminary leases for $2,500 to Frank T. Pickrell, who, with Haymon Krupp as partner, did no better at promoting the acreage. Krupp borrowed the money to cover the filing fee. He and his New York friends incorporated as Texon Oil and Land Company to raise capital, but the company stock sold too slowly to fund drilling. Pickrell then persuaded the board of directors to approve a sales promotion for certificates of interest in a 16-section block of leases called Group No. 1. Texon Oil raised over $100,000 and used some of the capital to buy used drilling equipment. The first oil test on Group No. 1 acreage was called Santa Rita No. 1, named for the saint of the impossible. Pickrell had hired an experienced driller, Carl Cromwell, for $15 a day and stock in the company. Cromwell moved his family to the lonely drilling site and drilled for 646 days. Late on 27 May 1923 the bit drilled into the dolomitic sands, called "Big Lime," just above the 3,050-foot level. Early on May 28, with no further drilling, the Santa Rita roared to life. The well attracted the attention of scouts from major oil companies, and Pickrell eventually enlisted the aid of independent oilman Mike Benedum to test the extent of his field. Benedum proved that the area was indeed rich in oil and that Santa Rita No. 1 was just a small beginning for the men who promoted it, for the University of Texas, and for other oil-rich areas of the Permian Basin. In 1940, under the leadership of the Texas State Historical Association, the original Santa Rita rig was moved to the UT campus in Austin. It commemorates a time of transformation for both the University of Texas and Texas A&M, which shared in the university's land royalties. In 1990, after almost 67 years of production, the Santa Rita No. 1 was plugged.
     Julia Cauble Smith

Satank. Also Set-Tank, Set-Angia, Sitting Bear; Kiowa warrior and medicine man; b. shortly after 1800, probably in what is now Kansas. At a time when intertribal relations on the plains were in a state of turmoil, Satank took advantage of opportunities for advancement and became a member of the elite warrior society known as the Koitsenko. This group, comprising about 10 of the bravest warriors of the tribe, was in a sense a martial caste, its prestige dependent upon success in warfare. Accordingly, Satank was first and foremost a warrior. In the 1830s and 1840s he gained special fame for highly successful expeditions against the Cheyennes, the Sacs, and the Foxes. Gradually, however, as more whites moved onto the plains, his activities became directed against them. His targets included white settlements, wagontrains, and, on occasion, army outposts. In 1864, for example, Satank was said to have been responsible for a raid on a settlement in Menard, as well as the murder of a guard at Fort Larned, Kansas. Such exploits gained him a reputation as a daring and effective warrior. Nevertheless, he seems never to have become a chief of the first order. It is likely that his path to preeminence was blocked by Dohäsan, Kiowa paramount leader from about 1833 to his death in 1866. After Dohäsan died, Satank became one of several prominent leaders, but he never succeeded in consolidating his power. By the late 1860s the Kiowas were an embattled people, bickering and without any unifying force. White settlement, the U.S. Army, intertribal warfare, and disease combined to pressure them into seeking some sort of accommodation with the white men. Consequently, in 1867 the Kiowas, along with most other tribes of the southern plains, agreed to attend the Medicine Lodge Treaty council, in what is now Barker County, Kansas. The Kiowas were represented by Satanta and Satank, now about 70 years old. Together Satank, Satanta, and several other Kiowas signed the treaty by which they agreed to move to a reservation in southwestern Oklahoma. Satank seems never to have adjusted to confinement and was absent frequently. In 1870 his son, also named Satank, was killed in Texas. Reportedly, the old man was inconsolable and, after journeying to Texas to retrieve his son's bones, killed and scalped a white man. He joined Satanta, a young warrior named Big Tree, and other discontented Kiowas, Comanches, and Plains Apaches to conduct a series of raids on settlements in North and West Texas. On 18 May 1871, Satank and his compatriots perpetrated the Warren Wagontrain Raid. Ranald Mackenzie found Satank, Satanta, and Big Tree requesting rations at Fort Sill. Satanta bragged that he was the leader of the raid and implicated the other two. General Sherman arrested and imprisoned the three and determined that they would be transferred to Fort Richardson and tried for murder by civil authorities. The indignity of being transported in chains was too much for Satank, who en route managed to escape from his handcuffs and grab a rifle, only to be felled by bullets. He was thrown from the wagon and left to die. So fearful were the Kiowas of reprisals for the Warren massacre that no one claimed the body, which was scalped by Tonkawa scouts. Eventually Satank's remains were buried, without ceremony, at the post cemetery at Fort Sill, Oklahoma. His only known survivor, a son named Frank Givins, was living in Carnegie, Oklahoma, in 1929. He was said to be a medicine man.
     Brian C. Hosmer

Satanta. Kiowa chief, also known as White Bear; b. probably in Kansas or Oklahoma, ca. 1820; d. Huntsville, 11 October 1878. From the 1830s to the 1850s he participated in campaigns against the Cheyennes and Utes and is said to have raided as far south as Texas and Mexico. By 1865 he seems to have become an important subchief, an achievement underscored by his presence, along with Guipago (Lone Wolf), Tene-angopte (Kicking Bird) and Dohäsan, principal chief of all the Kiowa bands, in negotiations leading to the Treaty of the Little Arkansas River. Afterward, settlers continued to pour across Kiowa lands, and tribesmen, unhappy with the provision that reduced their domain to a small reservation, continued to raid settlements and harass immigrants. After Dohäsan died in 1866, Kiowa unity dissolved as a number of subchiefs, including Satanta, competed for leadership in a wave of raids across the southern plains. Satanta and his party ventured into the Panhandle and, after killing James Box, captured the man's wife and four children, whom they eventually released (for a price) at Fort Dodge, Kansas. Satanta was one of his tribe's representatives at the Medicine

Satanta seated with bow and arrow. Photograph by Will Soule. Probably at Fort Sill, Indian Territory, ca. 1869–74. Courtesy Seaver Center for Western History Research, Natural History Museum of Los Angeles County; photo Soule #13.

Lodge Treaty council (October 1867), where he was called the "Orator of the Plains." The title may have referred to his long-winded speeches rather than his eloquence. Satanta and Satank signed the agreement for the Kiowas, an agreement designed to ensure peace by restricting the Plains Indians to reservations. The treaty failed to resolve the sources of conflict, however, and by early 1868 the Indians resumed warfare on white settlements. Fearing a general Indian uprising, General Sherman called on General Sheridan to restore order. Sheridan's plan materialized as the brutally effective "winter campaign" of 1868–69. This operation, a series of military engagements conducted to force the Indians to return to the reservations by destroying their homes, horses, and will to resist, achieved its fullest expression with Custer's destruction of the southern Cheyenne village on the Washita River on 23 November 1868. Alarmed by Custer's alleged willingness to kill women and children, Satanta and Guipago surrendered on 17 December, only to be arrested and held for nearly three months while the colonel reportedly sought permission to hang them. In February 1869, Tene-angopte secured their freedom by promising that the Kiowas would quit raiding and return to the reservation.

Fear of army retribution kept the Kiowas on the reservation for a while. By 1871, however, resentment over inadequate provisions had outpaced the military threat, and the Kiowas grew restless. A new series of raids that claimed the lives of 14 white Texans during the spring of 1871. For Satanta, frustration over confine-

ment was heightened when the tribe split into two factions, one led by Guipago and the other by Tene-angopte. Responding to the apparent slight, Satanta returned to the warpath and, assisted by Ado-eete (Big Tree) and Satank, led a party of some 100 Kiowas in the Warren Wagontrain Raid, or Salt Creek Massacre (18 May 1871). Responding to the survivors' horrific accounts and the settlers' calls for vengeance, Sherman dispatched Col. Ranald Mackenzie with orders to bring the offending Indians to justice. Mackenzie's expedition proved unnecessary, however, because shortly after returning from the raid Satanta and his followers journeyed to Fort Sill to claim their rations. While there, Satanta was questioned about the raid by agent Lawrie Tatum and proceeded to shock the agent by boasting that he had led the raid and was assisted by Satank and Ado-eete. Tatum turned the chiefs over to Sherman, who after hearing the same confession, ordered that the three be sent to Jacksboro, Texas, to stand trial for murder. Bound hand and foot, Satanta, Satank, and Big Tree left Fort Sill on 8 June 1871. The trial of Satanta and Ado-eete (Satank was killed on the way to Jacksboro after attacking a guard) was a celebrated event, primarily because it marked the first time Indian chiefs were forced to stand trial in a civil court. The Jacksboro jury convicted the two men and sentenced them to hang. Yet pressure from humanitarians and a fear of Kiowa retribution influenced Texas governor Edmund Davis to commute the Indians' sentences to life imprisonment. Subsequently, Satanta and Big Tree were transferred to the Texas State Penitentiary at Huntsville, where they remained for the next two years. The federal government promised the Kiowas that the two chiefs would be released upon evidence of proper behavior. As a result, from the winter of 1871–72 through the summer of 1873 the tribe remained on the reservation. In August 1873 Governor Davis, under pressure from federal Indian agents, arranged for the chiefs' parole, a very unpopular decision. Satanta and Big Tree were taken to Fort Sill and confined to the guardhouse. On 6 October, Davis, federal officials, and the Indians agreed on conditions for parole. The Kiowas agreed to remain on the reservation or risk the reimprisonment of Satanta and Ado-eete, and the two chiefs were set free.

But peace hardly outlasted the council. By late October Kiowa and Comanche warriors resumed raiding, and by the next summer, settlements in western Oklahoma and the Texas Panhandle were again under siege as war parties attempted to halt the destruction of the buffalo herds. On several occasions during the Red River Indian War, Satanta was seen with the hostiles even though he had given up his position as war leader. Consequently, in the fall of 1874 he and Big Tree were arrested again and charged with violation of parole. Big Tree was imprisoned briefly at the Fort Sill guardhouse, while Satanta, judged the more dangerous of the two, was returned to the penitentiary at Huntsville. Demoralized over the prospect of spending the rest of his life in confinement, he committed suicide by jumping out of a window. He was buried in the prison cemetery until 1963, when his grandson, Kiowa artist James Auchiah, received permission to reinter him next to Satank in the cemetery at Fort Sill.

Brian C. Hosmer

Sayers, Joseph Draper. Governor; b. Grenada, Mississippi, 23 September 1841; d. 15 May 1929; m. Orline Walton (1879). Sayers moved with his father to Bastrop in 1851, attained the rank of major in the Civil War, and then practiced law in Bastrop for 10 years. He represented Bastrop in the state legislature in 1873 and was afterward chairman of the Democratic state executive committee (1875–78). After a term as lieutenant governor (1879–81), he was elected to the United States Congress, where he served on the appropriations and naval affairs committees and secured the long-delayed payment for the Texas Rangers' frontier services. With the help of Edward M. House, Sayers was elected governor in 1898 and 1900. During his tenure the state saw several first-rank disasters, including the Galveston hurricane of 1900. After leaving office, he practiced law in San Antonio, served as a regent of the University of Texas in 1916 (and supported the university in its struggle against Jim Ferguson), chaired the Industrial Accident Board (1913–15), and served on the board of legal examiners (1922–26) and that of pardon advisors (1927–29).

Scarborough, Dorothy. Writer; b. Mount Carmel, Smith County, 27 January 1878; d. New York City, 7 November 1935 (buried in Oakwood Cemetery, Waco); ed. Baylor University (B.A., 1896; M.A., 1899), University of Chicago, Oxford University, Columbia University (Ph.D., 1917). Scarborough grew up in Waco and in 1916 began to teach at Columbia University. In 1923 Baylor University awarded her an honorary doctorate. "Miss Dottie" taught English at Baylor (1905–15) and also taught briefly in the public schools of Marlin. She also conducted a popular and influential college-men's Sunday school

Dorothy Scarborough. Courtesy Texas Collection, Baylor University, Waco.

class at the First Baptist Church in Waco. At Columbia she became a lecturer in 1919, an assistant professor in 1923, and an associate professor in 1931. Her teaching emphasis was creative writing, especially the techniques of the short story and novel. She was an early member of the Texas Folklore Society and its president in 1914–15. As a folklorist, in addition to various essays and articles, she published two major collections, *On the Trail of Negro Folksongs* (1925) and *A Song Catcher in the Southern Mountains* (1937, posthumous). She was preeminently a novelist, however, whose works dealt primarily with the plight and role of women in Texas and elsewhere, although she also had an interest in ghosts, sharecroppers, cowboys, and other local characters and settings. *In the Land of Cotton* (1923), *Can't Get a Redbird* (1929), and *The Stretch-Berry Smile* (1932) examine the crushing responsibilities of cotton farming on the children of tenant farmers and sharecroppers. These novels, plus her juvenile reader, *The Story of Cotton* (1933), vividly depict all aspects of cotton farming. Scarborough's books include *From a Southern Porch* (1919), *Impatient Griselda* (1927), *The Supernatural in Modern English Fiction* (1917), *The Unfair Sex* (serialized, 1925–26), and *The Wind* (1925). This last, controversial, novel created a furor in Texas when it was published because of its negative portrayal of frontier life on the cattle ranges around Sweetwater in the 1880s. It was made into a movie in 1927 starring Lillian Gish and Lars Hansen. That movie is probably the last great silent film, even though the producers inexplicably destroyed the artistic unity of the story by tacking on a happy ending unrelated to the ending of the novel. Scarborough also edited three books, *Famous Modern Ghost Stories* (1921), *Humorous Ghost Stories* (1921), and *Selected Short Stories of Today* (1935). Her first book was a collection of her own poetry, *Fugitive Verses* (1912). She also wrote hundreds of articles and book reviews. *Sylvia Grider*

Schiwetz, Buck. Artist; b. Edward Muegge Schiwetz, Cuero, 24 August 1898; d. near Cuero, 2 February 1984; m. Ruby Lee Sanders (1926); 1 daughter. Schiwetz studied architecture at Texas A&M. In 1922 he moved to Dallas, where he studied art and advertising and worked as a commercial artist. In 1928 he and his wife moved to New York City, where Schiwetz studied at the Art Students League and sketched for such magazines as *House Beautiful, Scribner's, Pencil Points,* and *Pictorial Review.* In 1929 he moved to Houston as partner in an advertising firm. Schiwetz found inspiration for his freelance work in the Texas coast and loosened up his linear style by experimenting in pure watercolors such as *Summer Pastime* (1931). The effect of this fluid medium on his style can be seen in such works as *Souvenir of Galveston* (1931), in which the artist used rapid scribbled lines to suggest forms. In the mid-1930s he simulated the work of Cézanne, Monet, and Van Gogh, though he did not exhibit these exercises. Schiwetz generally chose picturesque buildings, oilfields, and natural areas in Texas as his subject matter. His etchings and watercolors won the Museum of Fine Arts (Houston) purchase prize in 1933 and the Southern States Art League Watercolor Prize and the New Orleans Art Society Watercolor Prize in 1936. During the 1940s he won prizes at the Five State Show at the Philbrook Museum in Tulsa (1940), the Witte Museum in San Antonio (1944), and the Fort Worth Art Association purchase prize, Texas General (1948). In 1954 he won a prize from the American Watercolor Society in New York City.

He exhibited at the Art Institute of Chicago (1931, 1943, 1945), the American Watercolor Society (1930, 1952, 1954), the Philadelphia Watercolor Society (1930), the Grand Rapids Art Gallery (1940), and the Colorado Springs Fine Arts Center (1947). By 1948 he had had one-man shows in five Texas museums. Schiwetz also exhibited in the Architectural League of New York, the California Palace of the Legion of Honor in San Francisco, the Library of Congress in Washington, and the Knoedler Gallery in New York City.

His advertising work for oil and chemical companies also helped to establish his reputation as a recorder of the Texas scene. *The Humble Way*, a Humble Oil magazine (1945–), featured Schiwetz's sketches and watercolors of the areas where the company operated. Its popularity prompted the company to publish the first *Texas Sketchbook* of favorite Schiwetz drawings in 1952. A collection of sketches called *Buck Schiwetz' Texas* was published in 1960 with an introduction by Schiwetz's friend and former high school teacher Walter Prescott Webb. Schiwetz's sketches of Texas courthouses and other old buildings prompted interest that often saved them from demolition. His contributions to Texas were honored in 1965, when he was made a member of the Knights of the Order of San Jacinto. He was also a member of the California Watercolor Society, the Texas Watercolor Society, and the Philosophical Society of Texas. In 1966 Schiwetz retired from his position as advertising consultant in order to devote himself to his art. His visit to his brother Berthold "Tex" Schiwetz, a sculptor working in Rome, afforded him the opportunity to sketch the Italian countryside and to visit Rome, Venice, and Florence. In 1968 his *Six Spanish Missions in Texas: A Portfolio of Paintings* was published. That year his studio in Hunt, which housed many of his works and his wife's weaving and ceramics, was blown up by a butane heater.

In 1969 Schiwetz sought treatment for alcoholism. The success of his treatment galvanized his career: he mounted a 45-piece one-man show of new work in Houston six months later. In 1971 he was the subject of a 50-year retrospective at the University of Texas Institute of Texan Cultures in San Antonio. In 1972 he wrote and illustrated *The Schiwetz Legacy: An Artist's Tribute to Texas, 1910–1971*, for which he was awarded the Coral H. Tullis Memorial Award from the Texas State Historical Association in 1973. In spite of heart disease and cancer, Schiwetz served as artist-in-residence during the Texas A&M centennial celebration in 1976, and produced *Buck Schiwetz' Aggieland: A Portfolio of Eight Scenes from Texas A & M University*. Two years later he wrote and illustrated another book, *Buck Schiwetz' Memories*. He was the official state artist of Texas for 1977–78. In the mid-seventies the artist moved to Windy Hill, a ranch northwest of Cuero that belonged to Sharon Steen, his business manager. There he worked until his death. Examples of his work can be found in the Dallas Museum of Art, the Modern Art Museum of Fort Worth, the Harry Ransom Humanities Research Center in Austin, and the Museum of Fine Arts, Houston.

Kendall Curlee

Schleicher, Gustav. Entrepreneur and politician; b. Darmstadt, Hesse, 19 November 1823; d. Washington, D.C., 10 January 1879 (buried at National Cemetery, San Antonio); m. Elizabeth Tinsley Howard (1856); 7 children. Schleicher studied at the University of Giessen and worked as a civil engineer on railroad construction in Germany. He and Dr. Ferdinand L. Herff were among the leaders in a group of intellectuals who immigrated to Texas and founded a commune, named Bettina after the German literary figure and social visionary Bettina von Arnim, on the banks of the Llano River in 1847. The community was intended to prove the truth of communist ideas and light the way for relief of the troubles in Europe, which had led to sporadic attempts at revolution and were later to lead to the abortive revolt of 1848. Bettina had "friendship, freedom, equality" as its motto and "no regular scheme of government." Schleicher soon became disillusioned at this experiment in communism, however, for he learned that "the bigger the men, the more they talked, the less they worked and the more they ate," and by the time the settlement failed (within a year) he had made contacts with the other German settlers of the area. He then operated a shingle mill near New Braunfels and began, as a surveyor, to help German settlers locate land and to acquire land himself. In 1850 he moved to San Antonio, where he and others initiated the Guadalupe Bridge Company to build a toll bridge across the Guadalupe between San Antonio and New Braunfels, as well as the San Antonio and Mexican Gulf Railway. Together with Gen. Joseph E. Johnston and others he began to build a railroad from Port Lavaca to San Antonio. He was also co-owner of a restaurant in San Antonio and a member of various social organizations such as the Texas State Sängerbund. He became an American citizen in 1852. In 1853–54 he served in the Texas House of Representatives. From 1854 to 1861 he was surveyor of the Bexar Land District, which included most of the area from San Antonio to El Paso, and during his tenure he acquired title to large tracts of land, primarily on the Edwards Plateau. Beginning in 1858, he and his brother-in-law, Heinrich Dresel, published the *Texas Staats–Zeitung* in San Antonio. Schleicher was a cofounder of the San Antonio Water Company in 1858 and of Alamo College in 1860. From 1859 to 1861 he served in the Senate of the Eighth Texas Legislature.

Although Schleicher allied himself with Democrats such as Andrew J. Hamilton and with Sam Houston in supporting the Union before the Civil War, after secession his contemporaries could see in him "an emphatic advocate of the right and justice of the Secession movement." He became a captain in the Confederate Army, in charge of Gen. John B. Magruder's corps of engineers. He tried and failed to recruit a company of fellow Germans for Sibley's Brigade, and on several occasions he served, rather equivocally, as a character witness for German Texans on trial for sedition. After the war he practiced law in San Antonio, and in 1866 he was one of the incorporators of the Columbus, San Antonio and Rio Grande Railroad. He served as engineer for the construction of the Gulf, Western Texas and Pacific Railway from Indianola to Cuero. He founded the latter town as a way station and moved to it in 1872. Though he did not solicit the nomination, in 1874 he was nominated by the Democratic party and elected to Congress from the Sixth District. He soon became known for his careful research and well-considered opinions on the reestablishment of the gold and silver standard and his support of protection for the Texas frontier with Mexico. He was a member of the committees on Indian Affairs and Railroads and Canals; in his second term he was also appointed to the Committee on Foreign Affairs. His activities in support of a stable currency gained him a challenger within his own party, John Ireland, and Schleicher had to wage a bitter campaign before being nominated and reelected in 1878. He had not taken office again, however, when he died. In 1887 Elisabet Ney sculpted a bust of Schleicher, which was accidentally destroyed at the Daughters of the Republic of Texas museum in Austin sometime in the 1950s. Schleicher County is named for him.

Hubert Plummer Heinen

Schreiner College. In Kerrville; founded by Charles A. Schreiner, who placed in trust for the Presbyterian Synod of Texas $250,000 and 140.25 acres of land in Kerrville (1917), where a preparatory school–junior college was to be established a year after World War I ended. The institute's trustees, appointed by the synod, formally received the trust in 1921 and immediately took steps to build three buildings. In 1923 the school opened with a student body of about 100 and with James J. Delaney as president. The institution remained all male until 1932, when female students were admitted to the junior college as day students. Schreiner Institute continued to offer high school and junior college courses along with required military instruction until 1957, when military training was omitted from the preparatory school and became optional for those enrolled in the junior college. In 1969 the military science department was closed. In 1973 the prep school was closed, the college curriculum was expanded, and the school was renamed Schreiner College. In 1982 Schreiner became a four-year institution. The college retained its ties to the Presbyterian Church but was funded through private gifts. Before his death in 1927 Charles Schreiner donated to the institute an additional $500,000. His sons Louis A. and Gustave F. Schreiner donated more than $3 million between 1950 and 1965. Gustave Schreiner's estate also provided a permanent endowment for the college.

Joe R. Baulch

Scots. Scottish immigrants moved to Texas singly or in small groups, some as early as 1825, but they had limited success in establishing colonies, and they dispersed rapidly throughout the population. Several Scots, working both for the United States government and Scottish universities, explored and mapped Texas from around 1805 to 1835. Those settlers who came to stay fought in the Texas Revolution and were quickly followed into the new republic by nativeborn Scots or Americans of Scottish ancestry. Among noted individuals were the McLennans, who settled in central Texas (as in McLennan County); George Cupples, a prominent early Texas physician; Jesse Chisholm, a ScotCherokee trailblazer and trader; the Camerons (Ewen, John, William, and William Waldo); and Edmund Duncan Montgomery, physician and philosopher. A number of Scottish stoneworkers were brought to Texas for the construction of the state Capitol in the 1880s though labor unions opposed their employment. These granite workers were responsible for much of the work on the present Capitol and other, later, construction around the state. In 1890 the Universal Order of Scottish Clans organized several lodges in Texas. The Scottish Society of Texas was a later organization. Both were active in the 1970s and held annual clan gatherings. Since 1961 an annual "Gathering of the Clans" has been held in Salado in November. Sponsored by the Central Texas Area Museum, it features highland dancing, piping and drumming events, and Scottish field events. The 1990 census listed 36,854 persons of Scottish descent in Texas.

The Scottish Society of Texas, organized in 1963, represented 50 Scottish Highland clans in Texas. The organization was a

John Sealy. Courtesy Blocker History of Medicine Collections, Moody Medical Library, University of Texas Medical Branch at Galveston.

statewide association that sponsored annual Texas Highland Games each May. For nine years the games were held in Austin, but in 1972 they were held at McLennan Community College in Waco. The games included competition in dancing, piping, and athletic events. Judges from outside Texas, members of official governing societies, decided winners in several traditional Scottish dances, in bagpipe bands, and in individual piping. The traditional sports events included the caber toss, the sheaf toss, and the hammer throw. Other games and events were available for children. A ball and a tartan parade were also featured. The festive two-day affair was open to the public. Each year the society gave a scholarship to a McLennan Community College student who could verify a Scottish heritage. The society perpetuated Scottish traditions and provided fellowship for Scottish Americans to promote awareness of their heritage. Its official news sheet was *Heather Notes*, edited by Harry Gordon. In the early 1990s there were a number of local Scottish societies across the state, but the statewide organization seems to have languished.

John L. Davis

Sealy, John. Businessman and philanthropist; b. Kingston, Pennsylvania, 18 October 1822; d. Galveston, 29 August 1884; m. Rebecca Davis (1857); 2 children. Sealy moved to Galveston in 1846 and clerked in a mercantile business until he formed a partnership with John H. Hutchings and moved to Sabine to establish a store for the partnership. In 1854 they were joined by a third partner, George Ball, and returned to Galveston to set up Ball, Hutchings, and Company, a commission and banking business that later became the Hutchings–Sealy Bank. That year Sealy and several other business leaders in Galveston purchased several wharf companies and established the Galveston Wharf Company. In 1858 Sealy was company president. During the Civil War he helped open and maintain trade channels through Mexico for the Confederacy, but the blockade of Galveston caused the firm to move to Houston. Sealy returned to Galveston after the war and helped organize the Galveston Gas Company. In 1870 he had real property valued at $250,000 and personal property of equal value. He and his associates bought the Buffalo Bayou, Brazos and Colorado Railway in 1870 and the Houston Tap and Brazoria in 1873. In 1876 he was president of the Galveston, Houston and Henderson Railroad. In 1879, after his brother George Sealy bought the Gulf, Colorado and Santa Fe Railway, Sealy became president of that line. He resigned in 1881 because of health problems but became general manager the next year and served in that role until his death. He bequeathed $50,000 to be used for "a charitable purpose." With the money his brother and wife built John Sealy Hospital, which opened in 1890 and is a part of the University of Texas Medical Branch.

Claudia Hazlewood

Second Armored Division. Formed at Fort Benning, Georgia, 15 July 1940, under the command of Maj. Gen. Charles L. Scott. Col. George S. Patton, Jr., supervised the training and in November 1940 succeeded Scott as commander. On general maneuvers in Tennessee, Louisiana, Texas, and the Carolinas, Patton reportedly predicted that the division would be "Hell on Wheels" when it met the enemy. The nickname stuck and became part of the division patch. On 8 November 1942 the division landed on the shores of North Africa and took Casablanca. Eight months later it participated in the invasion of Sicily, fighting against the elite Hermann Göring Panzer Division. In November 1943 the Second Armored moved to England and began preparations for the invasion of Europe. It landed on Omaha Beach on D-Day plus 3, first engaging the Germans at Carentan, France. The division shattered the German defenses at St. Lo, crossed the Seine north of Paris, traversed Belgium, pierced the Siegfried Line, and entered Germany. During the Battle of the Bulge the Hell on Wheels division was part of Montgomery's 21st Army Group. Breaking out, it raced nearly 100 miles and, under mortar fire, crossed the 1,153-foot-wide Rhine in an unprecedented seven hours. On 4 July 1945 the Second Armored was the first American unit to enter Berlin. During World War II the division was recognized for distinguished service and bravery with 9,369 awards, including 2 medals of honor, 23 distinguished service crosses, and 2,302 silver stars, as well as nearly 6,000 purple hearts. In 238 battle days the Second Armored suffered 7,348 casualties, including 1,160 killed in action. The division returned to Camp Hood, Texas, in 1946 to retrain and rebuild.

Still based at Fort Hood, the Second Armored Division furnished thousands of trained replacements to units serving in the Korean War. In 1951 the Hell on Wheels division went back to Germany to serve for six years in support of NATO, then returned to Fort Hood. Several units of the division fought in Vietnam. The division sent brigades to participate in exercises in

Germany from 1973 through 1979, and in 1987 it was engaged in the largest deployment to Europe since World War II as a part of the Third Corps exercise "Referrer 87," which demonstrated the ability to deploy and fight in support of NATO. Desert Storm temporarily interrupted the deactivation of the division, begun in 1990. The division sent more than 5,000 soldiers to the Persian Gulf (1990–91). The last unit of Hell on Wheels became inactive on 2 May 1991, ending 51 years of continuous active duty. On 23 May 1991 the First "Tiger" Brigade was rededicated as the Third "Grey Wolf" Brigade of the First Cavalry Division, rejuvenating a Second Armored Division unit stationed at Fort Hood. In December 1992 the Fifth Infantry Division was redesignated the Second Armored Division, which in turn was redesignated in December 1995 as the Fourth Infantry Division (Mechanized), stationed in Colorado.

Art Leatherwood

Second Texas Infantry. A Confederate regiment; organized September 1861 in Galveston by Col. John Creed Moore to protect the coast from Northern invasion. The regiment was first billeted at cotton warehouses in Galveston, then was moved to Camp Bee in Houston to complete training. It comprised 10 companies of volunteer militia. By March 1862 the regiment had been moved to Corinth, Mississippi, to become a part of the Army of the Mississippi under by Gen. Albert Sidney Johnston. In Mississippi the Second Texas fought in the battle at Shiloh (6–7 April 1862), for which it was cited for bravery by generals P. G. T. Beauregard and Dabney Maury. Moore was promoted to brigadier general, and staff officer Lt. Col. William P. Rogers was promoted to colonel and placed in command of the regiment. Rogers led the Second Texas in a daring and successful attack on Fort Robinett, Corinth, Mississippi, on 4 October 1862. When the fort was recaptured, Rogers was killed. At Vicksburg the regiment was distinguished for its defense, under the command of Col. Ashbel Smith, of a crescent-shaped fortification that came to be known as the Second Texas Lunette, located in the center of the line of defense. There for 46 days the regiment faced daily shelling from land-based artillery and nightly bombardment from the fleet of mortar barges anchored in the Mississippi River. With the surrender of Vicksburg (4 July 1863) the Second Texas was furloughed to Texas as paroled prisoners of war. After being exchanged in November 1863, the regiment was reassembled at Camp Bee and placed under Gen. John B. Magruder, commander of the District of Texas, New Mexico, and Arizona. But the regiment, decimated by its service in Mississippi, could muster no more than a battalion of effective troops. It was never restaffed, but continued to carry the regimental designation throughout the remainder of the war. The unit was stationed in Galveston and assigned to guard the port against capture. It then participated in a last skirmish at the mouth of Caney Creek in February 1864. Rather than surrender at the cessation of hostilities, the men mutinied in May 1865 and disbanded to return to their homes, after service distinguished by gallantry under fire and devotion to duty.

Joseph E. Chance

Second United States Cavalry. "Jeff Davis's Own" regiment, an elite unit organized in 1855 specifically for service on the Texas frontier—finest horses, latest equipment and firearms, officers (mostly West Point graduates) handpicked by Secretary of War Jefferson Davis. The regiment produced 16 generals in the 6½ years of its existence, including Confederate generals Albert

Sidney Johnston, Robert E. Lee, Edmund Kirby Smith, and John Bell Hood. Johnston was the first commander; others included Lee, George H. Thomas, and Earl Van Dorn. The Second Cavalry was Lee's last command in the U.S. Army. When the unit reached Fort Belknap from Jefferson Barracks, Missouri, Maj. William J. Hardee took four companies to establish Camp Cooper, and the rest of the regiment continued south to establish regimental headquarters at Fort Mason (January 1856). Before the Civil War, the Second Cavalry was involved in some 40 engagements along the western and northern frontiers of Texas and along the Rio Grande, fighting Apaches, Comanches, Kiowas, and Mexican marauders. Various companies of the regiment also conducted scores of scouting expeditions into West and Northwest Texas, some of five and six weeks' duration. Companies of the Second Cavalry were stationed at forts Belknap, Chadbourne, Clark, Inge, Mason, McIntosh, and McKavett, and camps Colorado, Cooper, and Verde. From Texas the regiment raided Comanche villages north of the Red River in Kansas Territory (October 1858, May 1859). At the battle of Devils River (20 July 1857), Lieutenant Hood and 25 men from Company G defeated 50 Comanches and Lipan Apaches. Hood himself suffered a painful wound when an arrow pinned his hand to his saddle. During the secession crisis the regiment was ordered out of Texas and left the state via Indianola (March–April 1861). Now under the command of Maj. George H. Thomas, the regiment was assigned to Carlisle Barracks, Pennsylvania. In the fall of 1861 it became the Fifth U.S. Cavalry. In Texas the regiment had driven the Indians far beyond the fringes of settlement and had defeated the Comanches deep in their heartland. It had also helped the Texas Rangers to combat Juan N. Cortina and to bring peace to the lower Rio Grande valley. *Harold B. Simpson*

Secretary of State. Office established by the Republic of Texas and sustained in succeeding constitutions. The secretary is appointed by the governor and confirmed by the Senate and serves four years. His major duties are to attest the governor's signature and affix the state seal to proclamations, commissions to office, and other official documents; keep a file of the official acts of the governor and the legislature; compile and publish the laws; keep a roster of all elective and appointive officers in the state; administer the primary and election laws as chief election officer; issue charters of incorporation; assess and collect the franchise tax on corporations; administer the laws concerning the sale of securities; and appoint notaries public. In the early 1990s the office of the secretary of state employed more than 200 people. *Dick Smith and Laurie E. Jasinski*

Seelye, Sarah. Civil War spy; b. Sarah Emma Evelyn Edmundson, New Brunswick, Canada, December 1841; d. La Porte, Texas, 5 September 1898; m. Linus Seelye; 3 children. To avoid an unwanted marriage, she ran away from home when she was 17 disguised as a boy. She continued her male masquerade as a publisher's agent in the Midwest and in 1861 enlisted in the Second Michigan Volunteer Infantry under the alias Franklin Thompson. She served in the Union Army undetected, with assignments including nurse, regimental mail orderly, and brigade postmaster, and on special assignments for the secret service; in her secret service duty she penetrated Confederate lines "disguised" as a woman. Fearing her guise would be discovered when she became ill with malaria in 1863, she deserted and

Juan N. Seguín, by Thomas Jefferson Wright, 1838. Oil on canvas. 26½" × 24¼". Courtesy TSL. Following the example of several artists who painted the portraits of American Revolutionary heroes, Wright established himself in a Houston hotel in 1837 and invited Texas Revolutionary heroes to have their portraits made for his "Gallery of National Portraits." He probably painted Seguín's portrait in Nacogdoches the following year.

resumed a normal existence in Ohio as a female. After regaining her health she again volunteered as a nurse, but this time with the Christian Sanitary Commission at Harper's Ferry, and as a female. Under a shortened version of her maiden name, S. Emma E. Edmonds, she wrote a fanciful account of her experiences in the army, *Nurse and Spy in the Union Army* (1865). The popularity and exposure she gained from the book and its revelation that she had deserted the army led the government to cancel her pension. A congressional bill in 1884 recognized her service to the Union and granted her a pension of $12 a month. The charge of desertion was removed by Congress in 1886. In the early 1890s the Seelye family moved to La Porte, Texas, and on April 22, 1897, Sarah became a member of the McClellan Post, Grand Army of the Republic, in Houston—the only woman member in the history of the GAR. Three years after burial, her remains were transferred to the GAR plot in the Washington (German) Cemetery in Houston. *Paul F. Cecil*

Seguín, Juan Nepomuceno. Soldier and politician; b. San Antonio, 27 October 1806; d. Nuevo Laredo, Tamaulipas, 27 August 1890; m. María Gertrudis Flores de Abrego (ca. 1825); 10 children. Seguín helped his mother run his father's post office while the latter served in Congress in 1823–24. He was elected alderman in 1828 and subsequently served on various electoral

View east from Courthouse, ca. 1872–1875. Stereograph by E. K. Sturdevant. Lawrence T. Jones III Collection, Austin. Seguin became the home for many German immigrants who brought their trade skills with them. German cabinetmaker Michael Jahn established a shop on Seguin Street, clearly visible in this photograph.

boards before being elected alcalde in 1833. He acted for most of 1834 as political chief of the Department of Bexar, after the previous chief became ill and retired. In 1835 he responded to the Federalist state governor's call for support against the Centralist opposition by leading a militia company to Monclova. After the battle of Gonzales in October 1835, Stephen F. Austin granted him a captain's commission. His company was involved in the fall of 1835 in scouting and supply operations for the revolutionary army, and on 5 December it participated in the assault on General Cos's army at San Antonio. Seguín entered the Alamo with the other Texan military when Santa Anna's army arrived, but was sent out as a courier. Upon reaching Gonzales he organized a company that functioned as the rear guard of Sam Houston's army, was the only Tejano unit to fight at the battle of San Jacinto, and afterward observed the Mexican army's retreat. Seguín accepted the Mexican surrender of San Antonio on 4 June 1836 and served as the city's military commander through the fall of 1837; during this time he directed burial services for the remains of the Alamo dead. He resigned his commission upon election to the Texas Senate at the end of the year.

As the only Mexican Texan in the Senate of the republic, he served in the Second, Third, and Fourth Congress. He served on the Committee of Claims and Accounts and, despite his lack of English, was chairman of the Committee on Military Affairs. Among his legislative initiatives were efforts to have the laws of the new republic printed in Spanish. In the spring of 1840 he resigned his Senate seat to assist Gen. Antonio Canales, a Federalist, in an abortive campaign against the Centralists, but upon his return to San Antonio at the end of the year he found himself elected mayor. In this office Seguín became embroiled in growing hostilities between Anglos and Mexican Texans. He faced personal problems as well. He had gained the enmity of some residents by speculating in land. He financed his expedi-

tion in support of Canales by mortgaging property and undertook a smuggling venture in order to pay off the debt. Although he came under suspicion of having betrayed the failed Texan Santa Fe expedition, he still managed to be reelected mayor at the end of 1841. His continuing conflicts with Anglo squatters on city property, combined with his business correspondence with Mexico, incriminated him in General Vásquez's invasion of San Antonio in March 1842. In fear for his safety, Seguín resigned as mayor on 18 April 1842 and shortly thereafter fled to Mexico with his family. He spent six years in Mexico and then attempted to reestablish himself in Texas. While living in Mexico he participated, according to him under duress, in General Woll's invasion of Texas in September 1842. Afterward his company served as a frontier defense unit, protecting the Rio Grande crossings and fighting Indians. During the Mexican War his company saw action against United States forces.

At the end of the war he decided to return to Texas despite the consequences. He settled on land adjacent to his father's ranch in what is now Wilson County. During the 1850s he became involved in local politics and served as a Bexar County constable and an election-precinct chairman. His business dealings took him back to Mexico on occasion, and at the end of the 1860s, after a brief tenure as Wilson county judge, Seguín retired to Nuevo Laredo, where his son Santiago had established himself. His remains were returned to Texas in 1974 and buried at Seguin, the town named in his honor, on 4 July 1976.

Jesús F. de la Teja

Seguin, Texas. County seat of Guadalupe County, on the Guadalupe River 35 miles northeast of San Antonio. Archeological finds in the vicinity include the remains of mammoths east of Seguin and numerous Indian campsites along the streams. Eventually Spanish, Mexican, and Anglo settlements were founded at the site of future Seguin, where Tonkawa Indians had lived. By 1833 there were 40 land titles in the region. One of the most notable settlements was the ranch of José Antonio Navarro, three miles north of Seguin. In 1833 Umphries (or Humphries) Branch and his family built a cabin, said to be the first Anglo residence at the site. In 1838, 33 of the Gonzales Rangers, a volunteer group, joined Joseph S. Martin in laying out a townsite near Walnut Branch; they named the site Walnut Springs. The name was changed in February 1839 to Seguin, for Juan N. Seguín. Republic of Texas citizens petitioned to have the area made a county, and the Texas Congress responded by establishing Guadalupe County in 1842. This county was apparently never organized, however, because in March 1846, after the annexation of Texas, the new state legislature demarked a new Guadalupe County from Gonzales and Bexar counties. A post office was opened in Seguin in 1846. Seguin became the county seat of Guadalupe County and was governed by the county until it was incorporated in 1853 by a charter. The first schoolhouse was built in 1850 by John E. Park, inventor of Park's concrete. The schoolhouse, formerly known as Guadalupe High School and in the 1980s still used by St. James Catholic Church, was recognized by the state in 1962 as the oldest continuously used school building in Texas. Guadalupe College, a school for blacks, opened in 1887 and continued until 1936. In 1912 Texas Lutheran College moved from Brenham to the Louis Fritz Farm near Seguin. The local economy has generally been agricultural, though in its early years the town was a trading partner of Gonzales, New Braunfels, and San Antonio. Seguin was on the trail taken by Germans from Indianola to the Hill Country. With the influx of the German population, farming methods improved and trade increased. By the time of the Civil War Seguin residents were growing cotton, corn, and peanuts and raising hogs and cattle. After the war Seguin was occupied by Union soldiers. One of its leading citizens, John Ireland, became governor of Texas. The Seguin economy improved dramatically in the late 1920s, when oil was discovered in the Darst Creek fields 15 miles east of town. State Senator Ferdinand C. Weinert of Seguin was responsible for long-lasting prison reforms and also worked to establish the Pasteur Institute of Texas, which saved many lives in the treatment of rabies. As the twentieth century progressed Seguin attracted manufacturing and service-oriented industries to diversify its agricultural and oil-based economy. In 1990 its population was 18,823. Tourists were attracted to Max Starcke Park, the Guadalupe County Coliseum, and the County Fairgrounds, where the Texas State High School Rodeo has been held since 1984.   *John Gesick*

Selena. Singer; b. Selena Quintanilla, Lake Jackson, Texas, 16 April 1971; d. Corpus Christi, 31 March 1995; m. Christopher Perez (1992). From 1957 to 1971 her father played with Los Dinos, a Tejano band. The children performed at the family restaurant, Pappagallo, and at weddings. After 1981 the band became a professional act. In 1982 the group moved to Corpus Christi and played in rural dance halls and urban nightclubs, where Tejano music flourishes. In her late teens Selena adopted fashions sported by Madonna. She won the Tejano Music Award for Female Entertainer of the Year in 1987, and eight other Tejano awards followed. By the late 1980s she was known as the "Queen of Tejano music" and a "woman of the people." Selena y Los Dinos recorded with Tejano labels GP, Cara, Manny, and

Freddie before 1989, the year they signed a contract with EMI Latin Records. At the 1995 Houston Livestock Show and Rodeo the band attracted 61,000. Their albums include *Alpha* (1986), *Dulce Amor* (1988), *Preciosa* (1988), *Selena y Los Dinos* (1990), *Ven Conmigo* (1991), *Entre a Mi Mundo* (1992), *Selena Live* (1993), *Amor Prohibido* (1994), and *Dreaming of You* (1995). *Entre a Mi Mundo* made Selena the first Tejana to sell more than 300,000 albums. In 1993 she signed with SBK Records to produce an all-English album, but it was replaced with the bilingual *Dreaming of You*. Although the mainstream ignored her until about 1993, in 1994 *Texas Monthly* named her one of 20 influential Texans and the Los Angeles *Times* interviewed her. The band won a Grammy in 1993 and was nominated for one in 1994. Also in 1993 and 1995, *Lo Nuestro Billboard* gave the band awards in four categories. Before Selena's death, the band sold more than 1.5 million records. The 1995 album became number one on the national *Billboard* Top 200 the week of its release. By the mid-1980s Selena had crossed into the national Latino and Latin-American market. A recording with Puerto Rican band the Barrio Boyzz furthered inroads into this area. Selena y Los Dinos began to acquire a following in Mexico as early as 1986. Selena was also known to Latin-American television audiences and was featured in advertisements for such companies as Coca-Cola, AT&T, and Southwestern Bell. In 1992 she began her own clothing line. In 1994 she opened Selena Etc., a boutique–salon in Corpus Christi and San Antonio. Despite her wealth, however, she lived in the working-class district of Molina in Corpus Christi and considered herself a public servant. She worked with government agencies and businesses to combat such evils as drug abuse and domestic violence. She was murdered by Yolanda Saldivar, her first fan club founder and manager of Selena Etc. After a private Jehovah's Witness funeral, more than 30,000 viewed her casket at the Bayfront Plaza Convention Center in Corpus Christi. She was mourned across the country. *People* magazine sold a commemorative issue on her. Selena's fans compared her death to that of John Lennon, Elvis Presley, and John F. Kennedy. Governor George W. Bush proclaimed a "Selena Day."
                                                        Cynthia E. Orozco

Semicentennial of Texas Independence. Celebrations on 2 March (Texas Independence Day) and 21 April (San Jacinto Day) 1886. Meetings on 2 March included orations at Brenham, a ball in Fort Worth, and a small gathering of Galveston County veterans. The major events occurred on 21 April in most Texas towns. Parades, picnics, and speeches abounded. Waco and Belton used the occasion to break ground for new college buildings. Volunteer firemen provided leadership for many communities including Austin, Galveston, and Houston. Militia drills and athletic contests were frequent attractions. Political leaders, including Governor John Ireland, participated. The Texas Veterans Association met in Dallas for the most important celebration, at which more than 200 old soldiers received an elaborate welcome. Semicentennial speakers drew several comparisons between the Texas Revolution and the American Revolution—Sam Houston, Stephen F. Austin, and others were compared to the Founding Fathers. References to "sacred duty" were frequent, though probably less so than in discussions of the American Revolution. The emphasis was on honoring the living veterans.   *Alwyn Barr*

Semicolon Court. The derisive label given to the Texas Supreme Court that sat between 1870 and 1873, as a result of the importance this court attached to a semicolon in its decision in *Ex parte Rodriguez*. Because *Rodriguez* nullified the election of Democratic gubernatorial candidate Richard Coke, who took office despite the court's decision, subsequent opinions of the court have been highly critical. Lawyers and politicians in the late nineteenth century coined the epithet Semicolon Court. Oran Roberts, who served on the court after 1873, gave the term historical permanency when he used it in his history of the Reconstruction era, the first serious and comprehensive account of the state during this period. Roberts concluded that this court was in such disrepute that the legal profession did not even like to cite its decisions. The court was convened by the authority of the Constitution of 1869, which ended the practice of a Supreme Court circuit and required annual sessions to be held at Austin. Its three members were distinguished, and they showed independence from Davis. But nothing could counteract the damage done to the reputation of the court in *Ex parte Rodriguez*. In this case the court invalidated the general election of 1873 on the grounds that the law providing for the election did not meet constitutional specifications. The Constitution of 1869 required that all elections would be held "at the county seats of the several counties until otherwise provided by law; and the polls shall be opened for four days." For the 1873 election the legislature provided that polling would be held in precincts and the polls would be open for only one day. The court ruled that the semicolon in this section made the second clause of the provision independent, thus not open to a change by the legislature. The court's ruling made the election unconstitutional. Opponents of the Republican administration considered the decision to be political rather than based on the merits of the case, since its effect would be to keep the Davis government in office. Among Democrats the Semicolon Court was thereafter viewed with hostility. The decision in *Rodriguez* was never enforced. Davis refused to use the police powers of the state to uphold it. Coke chose to ignore it and seized power from the existing government in January 1874. His takeover ended the Semicolon Court, since he immediately implemented the constitutional amendment, also passed in the disputed election, that increased the number of judges to five and allowed the governor to appoint new ones. Coke removed the sitting justices and appointed an entirely new court. Although Roberts observed that the Semicolon Court's decisions were not respected by the legal profession of the state, its actions did become a part of the legal corpus of the state. Post-Reconstruction justices, including in one instance Chief Justice Roberts himself, declined to hear cases challenging two railroad subsidies in *Kuechler v. Wright* and *Bledsoe v. International Railroad Company*. Roberts also cited precedents from this court in other decisions. Ultimately, though the court received opprobrium for *Rodriguez*, the bad reputation of the Semicolon Court derives largely from contemporary politics rather than from a nonpolitical assessment of its merits as a judicial body. *Carl H. Moneyhon*

Senators. Until 1913 senators were chosen by state legislatures. The first popularly elected Texas senator was John Morris Sheppard of Texarkana. Most of the United States senators from Texas have been members of the Democratic party. John Tower, who took office in 1961, was the first Republican Texas senator since the days of Reconstruction. In 1985 he was succeeded by Phil Gramm, also a Republican. In 1993 Republican Kay Bailey Hutchison became the first woman from Texas elected to the Senate. The people who have represented Texas in the United States Senate belong to the Rusk and Houston successions, named for the first incumbents, Thomas J. Rusk and Sam Houston, who took office on 21 February 1846.

June Rayfield Welch

Seven Cities of Cíbola. Among the myths that propelled Spaniards into the far reaches of northern New Spain was the legend of the Seven Cities. That myth was an outgrowth of the Muslim conquest of Portugal in the early eighth century. Allegedly, in 714 seven Catholic bishops and their faithful followers had fled across the Atlantic to a land known as Antilia, the name of which, incidentally, was the source of the name Antilles, which was initially applied to the West Indian islands of the Caribbean. The Antilian islands failed to produce large quantities of gold and silver, and by 1539 lands reported on by Cabeza de Vaca and his companions were believed to contain an El Dorado known as Cíbola. In that year, Viceroy Antonio de Mendoza dispatched Fray Marcos de Niza and the African Estevanico on a reconnoitering expedition. This exploration cost the life of Estevanico at Háwikuh, the southernmost of the Zuñi pueblos in western New Mexico. On his return to New Spain, Fray Marcos reported seeing golden cities, the smallest of which was larger than Mexico City. In 1540 the followup expedition of Vázquez de Coronado captured Háwikuh and learned the true nature of it as well as other nearby pueblos. In the following year, disappointment over the Seven Cities of Cíbola prompted Coronado to launch a futile search for Quivira—an expedition that crossed the Panhandle. *Donald E. Chipman*

Shafter, William Rufus. Army officer; b. near Galesburg, Michigan, 16 October 1835; d. near Bakersfield, California, 12 November 1906; m. Harriet Grimes (1862); 1 daughter. "Pecos Bill" Shafter was captured in the Civil War and spent several months in a Confederate prison, after which he served as an officer in the Seventeenth U.S. Colored Infantry in the battle of Nashville (December 1864). He was transferred in 1867 to Texas, where he served as lieutenant colonel of the all-black Twenty-fourth U.S. Infantry on the Rio Grande. In 1868 he moved to Fort Clark. After 1870 Shafter served primarily as a field commander, in spite of serious obesity. Working under Col. Ranald S. Mackenzie, he commanded scouting expeditions and campaigns against hostile Indians. He led several excursions into the Llano Estacado and Big Bend. His most renowned feat in West Texas was the Llano Estacado campaign of 1875. Combining two companies of his 24th Infantry with parts of the Twenty-fifth U.S. Infantry and Tenth U.S. Cavalry and a company of Seminole Indian scouts, Shafter drove his men more than 2,500 miles from June to December. Often exhausted and short of water, the troops made three crossings of the Llano Estacado and swept the plains clear of Indians. The campaign also proved the plains habitable and paved the way for white settlement. Between 1876 and the end of 1878 Shafter led three campaigns into Mexico against Indians. He became colonel of the First Infantry in 1879 and the following year participated in the war against Victorio. After leaving Texas, he served in Arizona, California, and South Dakota. In Cuba in 1898, during the Spanish-American War, he commanded the largest force of United States troops that had left American soil up to that time. In 1895 Shafter received the Medal of Honor for meritorious service in the Civil War. *Paul H. Carlson*

Shamrock Hotel. In Houston; built 1946–49 by independent oilman Glenn H. McCarthy. The Shamrock was one of the most extravagantly mythologized symbols of Texas in the 1950s. Its flamboyant dedication ceremony on St. Patrick's Day, 1949, occasioned the first national media sensation to originate in Houston. Edna Ferber transformed the Shamrock into the "Conquistador" in her popular novel *Giant* (1952), and as such it was featured in the film *Giant* (1956). McCarthy planned the Shamrock as the first phase of a mixeduse complex at a site three miles south of downtown and close to the newly planned Texas Medical Center. The 18story, 1,100room hotel—the largest built in the United States in the 1940s—was conceived by McCarthy as a downtownsized hotel scaled to the convention trade but set in a suburban locale and imbued with a glamorous, resortlike atmosphere. Flanking the hotel to the north was a fivestory, 1,000car garage; to the south was the hotel's profusely landscaped garden, terrace, and swimming pool. The pool, which measured 165 by 142 feet, was repeatedly described as the largest outdoor pool in the world, so large that it could accommodate exhibition waterskiing. To celebrate the opening of the hotel, McCarthy brought 175 film stars and executives from Los Angeles and journalists from across the country. The event, to which the public was invited, was so riotous that a live network radio broadcast by Dorothy Lamour had to be canceled. The notoriety of the Shamrock's opening reinforced the early 1950s fiction of Houston—and Texas—as a place that was "larger than life," outrageously vulgar, yet oddly endearing. The conservative design of the hotel building and its opulent interiors elicited particularly caustic reactions, most famously from Frank Lloyd Wright, who toured the building shortly before its dedication. The Shamrock was designed by the Fort Worth architect Wyatt C. Hedrick. The 63 shades of green inside were to complement McCarthy's Irish heritage. During the 1950s the Shamrock was a popular social center for Houstonians. George Fuermann, in his book *Houston, Land of the Big Rich* (1951), described it simply as "Houston's Riviera." From 1949 to 1953 the hotel was the setting for "Saturday at the Shamrock," produced by the American Broadcasting Corporation. At the time this was the only nationally broadcast scripted radio program not produced in New York or Los Angeles. Despite its celebrity, the Shamrock had persistent problems with rates of occupancy and, consequently, financial performance. In 1952 McCarthy defaulted on a loan, and the property was taken over by the Equitable Life Assurance Society. In 1954, after McCarthy sold his right of redemption, the property was acquired by Hilton Hotels, which operated it until 1986 as the Shamrock Hilton. Hilton also had trouble getting enough customers to make a profit. The Shamrock's tremendous size, its distance from downtown, and the proliferation nearby of popularly priced motels put the Shamrock at a competitive disadvantage. In 1985 the Shamrock property was sold by Hilton to the Texas Medical Center, which retained the garage building but in 1987 demolished the hotel, its lanai wing, and the swimming-

pool gardens, replacing them with a surface parking lot. On St. Patrick's Day 1986, the fortieth anniversary of the groundbreaking, 3,000 people, including Glenn McCarthy, demonstrated at the hotel to protest its demolition. *Stephen Fox*

Shawnee Trail. The earliest and easternmost of the principal cattle trailing routes from Texas. Before and just after the Civil War, the Shawnee Trail gathered cattle from east and west of its main stem, which passed through Austin, Waco, and Dallas. It crossed the Red River at Rock Bluff, near Preston, and led north along the eastern edge of what became Oklahoma, a route later followed closely by the Missouri–Kansas–Texas Railroad. The drovers took over a trail long used by Indians in hunting and raiding and by southbound settlers from the Midwest; the latter called it the Texas Road. North of Fort Gibson the cattle route split into terminal branches that ended in such Missouri points as St. Louis, Sedalia, Independence, Westport, and Kansas City, and in Baxter Springs and other towns in eastern Kansas. Early drovers referred to their route as the cattle trail, the Sedalia Trail, the Kansas Trail, or simply the trail. The name Shawnee Trail may have been suggested by a Shawnee village on the Texas side of the Red River just below the trail crossing or by the Shawnee Hills, which the route skirted on the eastern side before crossing the Canadian River. Texas fever helped to quash use of the trail before the Civil War. During the war it was virtually unused. Afterward, with Texas overflowing with surplus cattle, pressure for trailing became stronger than ever. In the spring of 1866 an estimated 200,000 to 260,000 longhorns were pointed north on the trail. Although some herds were forced to turn back, others managed to get through, while still others were delayed or diverted around the farm settlements made hostile by the Texas fever problem. James M. Daugherty, a Texas drover of 16, was attacked in southeastern Kansas by a band of Jayhawkers dressed as hunters, who killed one of the Texas drovers. With six states enacting laws in the first half of 1867 against trailing, Texas cattlemen realized the need for a new trail that would skirt the farm settlements and thus avoid the trouble over tick fever. In 1867 a young Illinois livestock dealer, Joseph G. McCoy, built market facilities at Abilene, Kansas, at the terminus of Chisholm Trail. The new route west of the Shawnee soon began carrying the bulk of the Texas herds, leaving the earlier trail to fall into disuse. *Wayne Gard*

Sheep Ranching. Initiated by the Spanish, especially near missions. In the mid-nineteenth century, after a decline, Anglo-Americans revived the industry, which peaked in the mid-twentieth century. Texas today leads the nation in sheep production. Although most sheep raising in early Texas was associated with missions near San Antonio, where there were 9,000 sheep in 1727, and La Bahía, civilian ranchers included sheep and goats with cattle in their pastures, and a few sheep grazed near the East Texas missions. Spanish officials estimated that perhaps 90,000 sheep grazed on haciendas in the Rio Grande valley from near the site of present McAllen to near Laredo. Most of the sheep were *chaurros*, a gaunt breed that weighed only 60 to 80 pounds and was more important for mutton than for wool. Mission Indians wove coarse material from the wool, and ranchers in the Valley found a small market for wool south of the river. Two important systems of sheep ranching emerged. In one, often called the *partido* system, sheep owners hired individual herders to tend the animals. The herders, under contract, tended the sheep in all regards until the end of the contract. In the other system, used especially on the large haciendas, a careful hierarchy of organization existed, with authority devolving from the *haciendaro* (owner) through the sheep-expert *mayordomo* (a sort of range foreman), to *caporales* (usually three to each *mayordomo*), to vaqueros, to *pastores*. A *pastor*, the lowest in the hierarchy, had charge of about 1,500 sheep, which he accompanied by day and camped with at night, moving on foot, usually assisted by a dog.

American pioneers in Texas were slow to adopt sheep raising, except as an adjunct to the field or plantation. Those who in the 1830s and 1840 turned to significant sheep production brought changes. They introduced such breeds as the Merino and Rambouillet, which required close herding and were more important for their wool than for their mutton. With the emphasis now on wool, a new market was found in New England woolen mills. In the period of the republic and afterward, sheep ranching expanded into the hills and plateaus north and west of San Antonio. Purebred sheep were introduced in the 1840s and 1850s by Germans and Scots. During that same period many sheep were brought from the Midwest and the Ohio valley. After the Civil War a boom occurred, for several reasons. George Wilkins Kendall, a pioneer sheep rancher near Boerne, advertised widely what he saw as ideal conditions for raising sheep in Texas. New England woolen mills, which had devised new manufacturing techniques, offered favorable prices for Texas wool. And westward-moving settlers found sheep raising a profitable enterprise in the temperate but generally dry climate. The boom peaked in the 1880s and extended the industry to the far limits of West Texas. The emphasis remained on wool. Many prospective sheepmen headed for the Edwards Plateau or the TransPecos. They usually directed a band of 1,500 to 2,000 sheep and located the animals on lands leased from the state. Some were contract herders who worked under terms similar to the Spanish *partido* system. Others were large operators who brought thousands of sheep from California or purchased *chaurros* in South Texas to mix with their Merinos, Rambouillets, or other wool breeds on land they purchased from the state. Charles Schreiner of Kerrville, who provided warehouses, transportation facilities, and a unique commission-sales system for wool, played perhaps the key role in the expansion of sheep raising in the 1880s and 1890s. By 1900, although it occurred in nearly all the state's counties, sheep raising had concentrated primarily on the Edwards Plateau and in Southwest Texas. There, ranchers with large spreads adopted the Spanish system of herding, but streamlined it to suit their needs and changed some of the terms; *vaquero* was replaced by *rustler*. Some ranchers, such as Charles Callaghan and Arthur Anderson, had as many as 50 herders, 18 rustlers, and 6 *caporales*. By this time they had also begun to add goats to their flocks. Because many sheepmen were also cattle raisers, bovine herds were common on the sheep ranches of Southwest Texas.

In the early twentieth century, extensive changes came to sheep ranching. Ranchers introduced new breeds, including Corriedale, Delaine, and others that were better suited to the high, dry rangelands of the Edwards Plateau. They organized more efficient woolmarketing associations that allowed individual raisers greater advantage in dealing with New England–based wool buyers. They turned more and more to the practice of rais-

ing sheep, goats, and cattle in the same pastures. And in 1915 they organized the Texas Sheep and Goat Raisers' Association, with J. B. Murrah of Del Rio as the first president. One of the most significant developments in the early twentieth century was the adoption of meshwire ("wolfproof") fencing. The woven wire, generally with a 6inch mesh and standing 42 to 52 inches in height, was stretched between cedar posts. Builders set barbed wire along the ground to prevent wolves and coyotes from scratching under the fence, and they frequently placed one to three strands of barbed wire above the woven wire. Although expensive, the meshwire fences reduced the need for herders, cut losses to predators, and in the long run helped ranchers improve the economic yield of their operations. During the first half of the twentieth century the number of sheep in Texas grew significantly, reaching in 1943 a peak of 10,800,000. During this growth, Texas raisers produced an increasing proportion of the total sheep of the United States. In 1910 Texas accounted for only 4 percent of the total number of sheep in the country, but in 1920 the figure reached 9 percent. Ten years later, the state had become the nation's leading producer and Texas sheepmen claimed 13.8 percent of sheep raised in the United States. Even greater growth occurred in the 1930s, when Texas produced more than 20 percent of the nation's sheep. Although the number of sheep in the state declined after World War II, the state has maintained that percentage to the present.

Sheep ranching in the state includes busy seasonal activities, of which lambing is the preeminent one. In the early days in the Southwest, particularly on the Edwards Plateau, range ewes were bred in the fall—the gestation period is about 150 days—to lamb between February and May, depending on latitude and elevation of the range. The herder, acting as a midwife, carefully watched over the ewes in his flock, assisting at a difficult birth, forcing indifferent mothers to nurse their offspring, caring for orphaned lambs or lambs born to "dry" ewes, and in other ways attending to the flock so as to get the lambs through their critical first weeks. One participant called the lambing season a "month long hell of worry and toil." Some of the larger ranchers hired special crews, *hijadores* ("lambers"), composed of three or four men, to handle the task. Shearing season was likewise intense. Itinerant shearing crews did much of the work, especially on the large ranches. For the herder, shearing represented the "social season" of sheep ranching, a time when he had the companionship of others. The arrival of the crews signaled an excuse to gather for visiting, feasting, drinking, and other social activities. Shearing also was cumbersome work. In the days before electric equipment, shearing was done by hand in huge barns or in large pens covered with brush or reeds. From daybreak to dark, shearers bent over their animals, boys sat by to count sheep or apply medicine to wounds of any animal accidentally cut, and men stood at a table with twine to tie up each fleece before they carefully placed it in a sack that was 8 to 10 feet long and, when filled, weighed about 360 pounds. In such fashion shearing continued until all animals were trimmed, and then the crew moved to another ranch. Other jobs included castrating, docking, and marking. In castrating sheep in the nineteenth century, a worker held the back of the animal against his own chest with all four legs gathered together and elevated. After he cut the end of the scrotum, he pulled out both testicles and with a knife or sharp tug severed the cords. Castration produced better mutton and ensured that the ewes would be bred only by prize rams. Docking, cutting off all but two inches of the tail, was done for sanitary and reproductive reasons. Marking was done for identification. Ranchers painted their marks on freshly shorn sheep and earmarked the animals by notching one or both ears with distinctive combinations of cuts and slashes known as "corps," "lance points," or "downfalls." By using a slightly different mark each year, a rancher could tell the age of his sheep.

Today, sheep ranching in Texas is often associated with cattle and goat raising, especially on the Edwards Plateau. Wool production remains more important than mutton, and ranchers continue to experiment with new, different, and sometimes exotic breeds to improve wool quality. Ranchers have become more efficient and scientific in their operations. They rely on improved transportation, novel marketing techniques, and modern equipment. Nonetheless, many of their methods, terms, and paraphernalia can be traced back to the eighteenth-century Spanish settlers who first undertook sheep ranching in Texas.

Paul H. Carlson

Sheep Wars. The well-known conflicts between cattlemen and sheepmen over grazing rights, which took place particularly between the early 1870s and 1900. Sheep and cattle required different amounts of water, different types of food, and different manners of herding. Differences in life and equipment of the cowboy on horseback and the sheepherder on a burro or afoot also made for antagonisms. The cattleman had priority of establishment in most areas of Texas and resented encroachment of the sheepman on his domain. The cattleman was the more aggressive of the antagonists. His methods of attempting to drive out his rival ranged from intimidation to violence, directed at both the sheepman and his flock. Nomadic sheepmen or drifters were attacked by both cattlemen and settled sheepmen because of their twisting or rolling of fences to allow passage of their flocks and because they drove sheep infected with scab across the ranges. In 1875 there were clashes on Charles Goodnight's range and in the Texas–New Mexico boundary area. Schleicher, Nolan, Brown, Crane, Tom Green, Coleman, and other Central and West Texas counties were scenes of the wars. A law of 1881, which provided for appointment of state sheep inspectors and the quarantine of diseased sheep, merely resulted in driving drifters under cover. Laws that forbade sheepmen to herd sheep on the open range were ineffective because no representatives of the General Land Office were located in West Texas to delimit the open range. A law of April 1883 called for a certificate of inspection to show that sheep were free of scab before they could be moved across a county line. Legislation, along with strict enforcement of tax collections, soon put a stop to nomadic sheepherders from out of state using Texas lands. With the general rush for leasing public lands after 1884, many sheepmen could not secure adjoining pastures and had to drive their herds across ranchers' lands, the sheep grazing on the pastures as they crossed. A code was evolved that required the herder to drive his flocks at least five miles a day on level terrain or at least three miles a day in rougher country. In court action, the cowman usually won. After the law of 1884, which made fence-cutting a felony and abolished the open range, both the cattleman and the sheepman confined their herds to their own land, and the sheep wars came to an end. Despite the occasional fights between sheepherders and cattlemen in Texas, the level of violence never reached that of some other Western states. Moreover, sheepherders and cattlemen in many areas lived in peaceful coexistence, and some ranchers ran sheep, cattle, and goats together.

Vernen Liles

Shelby Expedition. A Confederate exodus to Mexico after the Civil War. A substantial number of Southerners crossed the Mexican border, either to continue the struggle or to escape an uncertain future in the United States. Among them were governors Pendleton Murrah of Texas, Henry Allen and Thomas Moore of Louisiana, and Thomas Reynolds of Missouri; former governor Edward Clark of Texas; and numerous army officers, including William P. Hardeman of Texas and John B. Magruder. Those led by Gen. Joseph Orville Shelby, former commander of the "Iron Cavalry Brigade" of Missouri, came to be called the Shelby expedition. On 1 June 1865, with his army disintegrating around him, Shelby determined to take as many of his men as would go to Mexico to continue the war. With a few hundred well-disciplined and orderly men, with all their cannons, arms, and ammunition, he marched from Corsicana through Waco, Austin, and San Antonio to Eagle Pass. Prominent persons joined them on the way. While crossing the Rio Grande at Piedras Negras, they sank their Confederate guidon in the river, in what came to be known as the "Grave of the Confederacy Incident." After selling all their arms except revolvers and carbines to the rebel forces of Benito Juárez, they were permitted to march south. They arrived in Mexico City in mid-August 1865 and offered their services to Maximilian. Although grateful, the French-installed emperor received them only as immigrant settlers subject to the liberal terms of the Decree of September 5, 1865. Many of Shelby's men accepted and joined in the establishment of the Carlota colony in Córdoba and a colony at Tuxpan. Others joined the army or went to the Pacific coast and sailed to South America or California. Shelby himself occupied the hacienda of Santa Anna and began business as a freight contractor. He moved to Tuxpan in the fall of 1866, left Mexico the next year, and returned to Missouri, where he died in 1897 at the age of 67. Because of the Mexican civil war, robbers, and attacks by dispossessed Indians, the colonies lasted only about a year. Most of the Americans returned to the United States by the end of 1867.

Art Leatherwood

Sheppard, John Morris. United States senator; b. Morris County, 28 May 1875; d. 9 April 1941; m. Lucile Sanderson (1909); survived by 3 daughters; ed. University of Texas (A.B., 1895), Yale University (LL.M., 1898). In 1902 Sheppard ran for Congress and won the seat previously held by his recently deceased father. During his 10 years in the House, most of that time in the minority, he worked unsuccessfully on legislation to insure small bank deposits, to provide other forms of low-cost credit for low-income groups, and to prohibit the shipment of alcohol into dry areas. By 1912 he established himself as an orator. Since his seat in Congress was relatively safe, he spent election years stumping for his colleagues. He was also a master of the tariff issue, in which he supported the Democratic demand for lower rates. In 1913 Sheppard won the Senate seat recently held by Joseph Weldon Bailey. From that time until 1921 he worked much more successfully than he had earlier, largely because the Democratic party was in the majority and Wilson was in the White House. Sheppard supported Wilson's policies on tariff reductions, on solutions to border conflicts associated with the Mexican Revolution, on war preparedness, and on the League of Nations. He also continued to sponsor legislation promoting rural credit programs, child labor laws, and antitrust laws. He was also an advocate of woman suffrage. On 4 April 1917, the day Congress declared war on Germany, Sheppard introduced the Prohibition amendment, which passed as the Eighteenth Amendment in 1919. For the rest of his life, Sheppard gave an address on the anniversary of ratification.

In 1920 the Republican party won the presidency and many congressional races. Sheppard had some success in the nonpartisan agricultural bloc that subsequently became the "progressive" bloc. The Sheppard–Towner Act (1921) provided for maternal and pediatric clinics and for an investigation of infant and maternal mortality. Although the law lapsed in 1929, the ideas found expression again in the Social Security Act of 1935. In 1929 Sheppard became the Senate Democratic whip. In 1932 the economic crisis of the Great Depression brought the Democrats to power in both houses of Congress and put Franklin Roosevelt in the White House. Sheppard supported the president on every issue of the New Deal except the repeal of Prohibition. Some Texans even criticized him for being a rubber stamp for the administration, especially in his support of the Court-Packing Plan (1937). In 1934, the year in which Sheppard became the most senior member of Congress, he introduced the Federal Credit Union Act, which passed with some difficulty. In his last term in the Senate his major contributions were in the field of foreign affairs. As chairman of the Military Affairs Committee, he worked on increasing spending for defense, especially for the air force. He also supported bills to aid veterans and to increase the number of cadets at West Point. Then, in response to the war in Europe, he fought for the passage of the Selective Service Act and Lend–Lease. Soon after his work on this last measure, he suffered a brain hemorrhage, from which he died. Later, General MacArthur told Mrs. Sheppard that her husband had been the first casualty of World War II. *Richard Bailey*

Sheppard Air Force Base. Just north of Wichita Falls; established by the U.S. Army Air Corps in 1940–41 on 300 acres sold by J. S. Birdwell to the government for one dollar. Later an additional 500 acres was added to the site. Construction was completed on 17 October 1941. The training facility was named Sheppard Field, in honor of Texas senator Morris Sheppard, who had recently died. Sheppard cadets were trained as mechanics of medium bombers and gliders and as glider pilots. Some of the personnel also received liaison-pilot training. The last year of the war the base became the only helicopter-pilot training school in the nation and housed a military air-traffic school. In 1945 the base reached its peak strength, 46,304, the largest concentration of American air corps troops in the world. Within six months after VJ Day, orders were issued to deactivate the field temporarily, and the city of Wichita Falls received a lease to the property. Over the next two years the National Guard used 20 of the buildings, and a few others were moved into the city for use by Wichita General Hospital and Midwestern Hospital. In April 1948 the air force asked that Sheppard Field be "frozen" to prevent further disposal of base property. Months later the base was reactivated as Sheppard Air Force Base. Over the next three

decades the airfield expanded to 5,400 acres, became the home of 3,500 permanent military personnel, annually drew just over 4,000 students including Dutch and German nationals, and employed 2,000 private citizens. Three training schools were stationed at the base. The 3750th Technical School trained students in aircraft maintenance, transportation, communication, civil engineering, and field training. During the 1960s the school became the center for Titan and Atlas intercontinental missiles. Later, Thor and Jupiter ICBM training was added. By the mid-1960s these training activities had been discontinued. The 3630th Flying Training Wing conducted two undergraduate pilot-training programs, one for West Germany and the other for South Vietnamese helicopter pilots (1965–71). From 1960 to 1965 the Strategic Air Command had an operational wing stationed at the base. The 3630th subsequently conducted aerospace rescue schools and weather instruction. The Air Force School of Health Care Sciences offers training in dentistry, medicine, nursing, and health-services administration and manages a large hospital. The population of the base reached 13,861 in 1960 but declined to 3,825 by 1990. *David Minor*

Shepperd, John Ben. Attorney and civic leader; b. Gladewater, 19 October 1915; d. Gladewater, 8 March 1990; m. Mamie Strieber (1938); 4 children; ed. University of Texas (B.A., 1938; LL.B., 1941). Shepperd emerged as a public figure through the Jaycees. In that organization he was state and national president and was thrice named one of the outstanding young men in Texas. He was selected as one of the nation's 10 outstanding young men for 1949 in a group that included future president Gerald R. Ford and future senator Charles Percy. As a strong ally of Governor Shivers, Shepperd was appointed to a brief term on the State Board of Education, organized the Texas Economy Commission, and was made chairman of an election-law reform committee. In 1950 he was appointed Texas secretary of state. Quickly becoming a leader in the dominant conservative wing of the Democratic party, Shepperd easily won the attorney general's office in 1952 and was reelected in 1954. This was a period of school-integration conflicts, labor unrest, disputes over state and federal rights, and sharp differences between state and national Democratic party leaders. Shepperd moved aggressively against boss rule in Duval County, a fight he began as secretary of state when he threw out the election of a district judge. His investigations led to 300 indictments against school and county officials, including the "Duke of Duval," George Parr. Shepperd also exposed a major cigarette-tax swindle and defended Texas against other states challenging the constitutionality of the 1953 congressional act returning the Tidelands to state ownership. In 1956 he was chosen president of the National Association of Attorneys General. That year Shepperd considered his efforts to restrict the activity of the NAACP in Texas as one of his greatest accomplishments. He also investigated Communist infiltration of labor unions.

In late 1954, shortly after Shepperd's reelection, Texas was rocked by scandal in its veterans' land program, administered by the commissioner of the General Land Office, Bascom Giles. Shivers and Shepperd both served on the Veterans' Land Board under Giles's chairmanship. Neither was implicated in the abuse of the program by land speculators, but both were cited for their frequent absences from the board meetings where the abuse occurred. Investigations by Shepperd, together with legislative committees and grand juries, led to reform of the program. Giles was indicted, convicted, and imprisoned. Yet another government scandal erupted, involving state regulation of insurance companies accused of fraudulent activities. Investigations by the attorney general, grand juries, and legislative committees led to indictments and to reform of the state's insurance department. But the veterans' land and insurance scandals provided fodder for enemies of the Shivers administration. Although Shepperd was thought by many to be the logical heir to the governor's office, in April 1956 he ruled out not only a race for governor but also the almost certain prospect of a third term as attorney general. When his term ended on 1 January 1957 he moved to Odessa to become general counsel of Odessa Natural Gasoline Company, later a subsidiary of El Paso Products Company, and to form Shepperd and Rodman, a corporate legal firm. Shepperd made his mark in his later years in historical preservation, education, and economic development. As chairman of the Texas State Historical Survey Committee (now the Texas Historical Commission) from 1963 to 1967, he was the driving force in the highway historical markers program. He was organizing chairman of the Texas Commission for the Arts and Humanities and was appointed to three terms, beginning in 1979, on the Texas State Library and Archives Commission. He led the campaign in the late 1960s to establish the University of Texas of the Permian Basin. Over 30 years he chaired dozens of community and statewide volunteer groups and worked tirelessly to bring industry to the Permian Basin. In 1984 he was named Texan of the Year by the Texas Chambers of Commerce and in 1987 was selected Outstanding West Texan by the West Texas Chamber of Commerce. One of his last major projects was the John Ben Shepperd Leadership Forum, based at the University of Texas of the Permian Basin and aimed at encouraging young people to become public leaders. *George E. Christian*

Sheridan, Philip Henry. Army officer; b. 6 March 1831 (place unknown); d. Nonquitt, Massachusetts, 5 August 1888; m. Irene Rucker (1875); ed. West Point (grad. 1853). Sheridan was apparently born sometime between his parents' emigration from Ireland and their settlement in Ohio. In 1854 he went to Fort Duncan with the First United States Infantry. In late 1855 he was transferred to the Pacific Northwest, where he served until the Civil War started. In the war Sheridan was nicknamed "Little Phil" (he was only 5'5" tall) and became one of the top three northern generals, along with Ulysses S. Grant and William T. Sherman. Though he was only a lieutenant in 1861, Sheridan was promoted to major general in 1864. He commanded divisions at the battles of Perryville (October 1862), Stones River (December 1862), Chickamauga (September 1863), and Chattanooga (November 1863). In 1864 Grant made him commander of the cavalry corps of the Army of the Potomac in the eastern theater. He led a raid on Richmond, Virginia (May 1864), devastated the Shenandoah valley (August 1864–March 1865), and helped force Lee's surrender at Appomattox (April 1865). After the war Grant ordered Sheridan to Texas with 50,000 soldiers to threaten the French-sponsored regime of Emperor Maximilian in Mexico. For more than a year Sheridan tried to persuade the French to leave Mexico. Reconstruction became his primary task, however, on 19 March 1867, when he assumed command of the Fifth Military District (Texas and Louisiana), with headquarters in New Orleans. Congressional Republicans had passed laws requiring registering voters and writing new state constitutions in the states of the Confederacy. Military-district commanders had authority to remove from office former Confederates and Democrats who resisted Reconstruction measures. Sheridan selected Gen. Charles Griffin as his subordinate in Texas. Sheridan, who was an advocate for freedmen, severely limited voter registration for former Confederates and then required that only registered voters (including black men) be eligible to serve on juries. Most of Sheridan's political appointees were staunch Unionists or Republicans. Griffin urged the removal of Governor Throckmorton, a former Confederate, on the grounds that he had been "disloyal." Although initially reluctant, Sheridan removed Throckmorton as an "impediment to the reconstruction of the State" (30 July 1867). Within a month Sheridan himself was transferred to command of the Department of the Missouri, with headquarters at Fort Leavenworth, Kansas, where he organized a successful winter campaign (1868–69) led by Lt. Col. George A. Custer against the southern Cheyennes in Indian Territory. In 1869 Sheridan became commander of the Military Division of the Missouri, with headquarters at Chicago. In this role he oversaw the army in the Red River Indian War. After Sherman retired (1 November 1883), Sheridan became commanding general of the United States Army, and on 1 June 1888, Congress promoted him to full general. His own version of his eventful career appeared in his *Personal Memoirs* (2 vols., 1888). Sheridan died on active duty. *Joseph G. Dawson III*

Sheriff. An office provided for under every Texas constitution; superseded the alguacil of Spanish and Mexican rule. The Constitution of 1876 provided that a sheriff be elected biennially in each county; the term of office was lengthened to four years by a constitutional amendment in 1954. The main duties of the sheriff are to act as a conservator of the peace and the executive officer of the county and district courts, serve writs and processes of the courts, seize property after judgment, enforce traffic laws on county roads, and supervise the county jail and prisoners. In counties of fewer than 10,000 residents he may also serve as ex-officio tax assessor and collector. *Dick Smith*

Sherman, Sidney. Soldier and entrepreneur; b. Marlboro, Massachusetts, 23 July 1805; d. Galveston, 1 August 1873; m. Catherine Isabel Cox; 2 sons. Sherman was orphaned at 12 and started working early in his life. In Newport, Kentucky, he formed the first company to make cotton bagging by machinery. He was also the first maker of sheet lead west of the Alleghenies. He became a captain of a volunteer company of state militia in Kentucky and in 1835 sold his cotton bagging plant and used the money to equip a company of 52 volunteers for the Texas Revolution. The volunteers left for Texas by steamer on the last day of 1835. That they were already regarded as soldiers in the Texas army is shown by a land certificate for 1,280 acres awarded Sherman for services from 18 December 1835 to 16 December 1836. They carried with them the only flag the Texans had for the battle of San Jacinto. Sherman and his men reached Texas the day before the election for delegates to the Convention of 1836. The company demanded and received the right to vote. They proceeded to San Felipe, where they were met by Governor Henry Smith and Sherman received his command. When Sam Houston organized his first regiment at Gonzales in March 1836,

Colonel Sidney Sherman, 1835. Oil on canvas. 30" × 25". Courtesy San Jacinto Museum of History, Houston.

Edward Burleson was made colonel and Sherman lieutenant colonel. Soon Sherman was promoted to colonel and given command of the Second Regiment of Texas Volunteers. On the retreat across Texas, he was eager to fight. At the Colorado he asked permission to recross the river and engage Joaquín Ramírez y Sesma, but was refused. At San Jacinto, Sherman commanded the left wing of the Texas army, opened the attack, and has been credited with the battle cry "Remember the Alamo." After the battle he acted as president of the board of officers that distributed captured property among the soldiers.

Afterward, President Burnet refused to accept Sherman's resignation but instead commissioned him colonel in the regular army and sent him to the United States to raise more troops. Sherman made his way to Kentucky and sent troops and clothing back to Texas. His wife returned to Texas with him. Sherman was Harris County representative in the Seventh Congress of the republic, where he served as chairman of the committee on military affairs and introduced a bill to establish the position of major general of the militia and increase protection along the western and southwestern frontiers. In 1843 he was elected major general of militia, a position he held until annexation. After annexation, he moved to Harrisburg and with the financial support of investors bought the town and the local railroad company. The town was laid out anew, and he organized the Buffalo Bayou, Brazos and Colorado Railway Company, which constructed the first rail line in the state. In 1852 Sherman was on board when the steamer *Farmer* burst its boilers; he was saved by clinging to a piece of wreckage. In 1853 the Harrisburg sawmill,

owned by Sherman and DeWitt Clinton Harris, was burned. After his residence also burned, Sherman sent his family to Kentucky, and he moved into the railroad office at Harrisburg. Then that office burned. Sherman was keeping the Island City Hotel in Galveston when the Civil War came. Appointed commandant of Galveston by the Secession Convention, he performed his duties ably until he became ill and retired to his home on San Jacinto Bay. Sherman County and the city of Sherman in Grayson County are named in his honor. One of Sherman's sons, Lt. Sidney Sherman, was killed in the battle of Galveston. *Julia Beazley*

Sherman, William Tecumseh. Army officer; b. Lancaster, Ohio, 8 February 1820; d. New York City, 14 February 1891; m. Eleanor Boyle Ewing (1850); 3 children; ed. West Point (grad. 1840). Sherman served in California during the Mexican War. In 1853 he left the army. He practiced law and was superintendent of the institution that became Louisiana State University. When Louisiana seceded from the Union, he moved to St. Louis, where he ran a streetcar company until he was appointed colonel of the newly authorized Thirteenth United States Infantry. After his fabled service in the Civil War, which culminated with his notorious "march to the sea," Sherman was made lieutenant general (1866) and given command of the Division of Missouri. After President Grant was inaugurated, Sherman was elevated to general (1869) and named commanding general of the army. Comanche and Kiowa raids along the West Texas frontier took him to Texas on a personal tour of inspection in May 1871. Accompanied by Inspector Gen. Randolph B. Marcy and a small cavalry escort, Sherman traveled northwestward from San Antonio and visited Fort Mason, Fort McKavett, Fort Concho, Fort Griffin, and Fort Belknap. Nothing that he saw on this ride altered his opinion that the frontier was pacific and that claims of Indian raids were greatly exaggerated. On the ride from Fort Belknap to Fort Richardson, however, he and his party barely missed falling victim to the war party of Satanta, Satank, and Big Tree. Only a few days later, this band of Kiowas perpetrated the Warren Wagontrain Raid near the spot where it had observed but failed to attack Sherman's entourage. On learning of the raid, Sherman ordered Col. Ranald Mackenzie to pursue the Indians across the Red River and onto their previously sacrosanct reservation. Satanta's boastful confession of his responsibility for the raid led Sherman to order his detention and that of his colleagues at Fort Sill, Indian Territory, and thereafter the United States Army's attitude toward the defense of the Texas frontier became much more aggressive—a change that led to the decisive Red River Indian War. Sherman retired from active duty in 1884 and, after 1886, made his home in New York City. His autobiography, *Memoirs of General William T. Sherman*, was published in 1875. *Thomas W. Cutrer*

Sherman, Texas. County seat of Grayson County, 75 miles north of Dallas; designated county seat by the act that established the county in 1846, and named for Gen. Sidney Sherman, a hero of the Texas Revolution. A log courthouse was among the first buildings constructed in Sherman, and settlers soon began moving into the new community, which grew rapidly as a merchandising center. A post office began operating in 1847. The town originally was on a hill just west of its present location. In 1848 Sherman was moved to a site three miles east of the original

Wagons loaded with cotton on square, ca. 1870s. Stereograph. Lawrence T. Jones III Collection, Austin. Sherman, the county seat of Grayson County, saw tremendous growth and development as a produce market for farmers during the 1870s.

location. By 1852, 400 people lived in the community, which "consisted of a row of clapboard business buildings along the east side of the public square," and, among other edifices, two saloons, a district clerk's office, a doctor's office, and a church. By the end of the decade the town had incorporated and was a stop on the Butterfield Overland Mail route. During the Civil War the Sherman area contributed the Eleventh Texas Cavalry of the Confederate Army. Despite hardships imposed by wartime, the town continued to grow and develop during the early 1860s. The community's first flour mill began production in 1861 and became the foundation of industrial development. Although outlaw bands led by Jesse James and William Quantrill appeared in Sherman during and after the war and a period of lawlessness and depression accompanied Reconstruction, the town remained active and relatively prosperous through the end of the decade. Dry-goods stores, warehouses, grocery stores, law offices, a newspaper, and two churches served the community. Sherman Male and Female High School, also known as Sherman Male and Female Institute, began accepting students in 1866; it was one of three private schools in Sherman. The town grew significantly during the 1870s, to a population of 6,000. Various new industries, including a cottonseed oil mill and a steam–powered cracker factory, began operations in 1871. In 1873 the Sherman Male and Female High School became the North Texas Female College and offered primary, preparatory, and college education. In 1876 Austin College, a male college, moved to Sherman from Huntsville. The Houston and Texas Central Railway extended its tracks to the community in 1872, thereby quickening the already rapid business and industrial expansion, but Sherman residents failed to subscribe a large enough bonus to attract the Missouri, Kansas and Texas line, which established a terminal at the new town of Denison, a few miles north of the county seat. Although after 1880 the MK&T and other national rail systems later built to Sherman, for the time being Denison

became the county's rail and marketing town. As a result of two fires in 1875 a large part of Sherman was rebuilt with better materials. By the 1880s Sherman had become "a thoroughly stable community and had pretty well lost all traces of the rawness of the frontier." A public school system was established in 1883, and, along with Austin College, North Texas Female College, and Mary Nash College, provided Sherman with a wealth of educational institutions.

By the turn of the century Sherman's population reached 10,213. During the first two decades of the twentieth century two more rail lines extended their tracks into the community, which also had the state's first electric interurban railway, linking it with Denison. The city's first hospital, St. Vincent's, opened its doors in the early 1900s. the population increased from 12,412 by World War I, to 15,031 by the mid-1920s. By the latter date Sherman's 54 industrial plants, producing such goods as flour, cottonseed oil, and hardware, earned the city the nickname "Fifth Industrial City of Texas," although it actually ranked sixth in the state in value of annual production. Served by five railroads, the town held an equal place with Denison as Grayson County's rail center. The Sherman riot of 1930 gained the town notoriety as the scene of one of the South's major race riots and destroyed most of the black businesses in the city. Although its population growth slowed during the Great Depression, 15,713 people lived in Sherman by the mid–1930s, and some 410 businesses, including 64 industrial plants, operated locally. While Kidd–Key College (formerly North Texas Female College) closed its doors in 1935, a number of private schools and colleges remained open. By the late 1940s Sherman's population had risen to 17,156. Perrin Army Air Field was constructed near the city in 1941, and during the years of American involvement in World War II, some 2,500 potential pilots a year received basic instruction at the base, which was deactivated in November 1946 and reactivated in 1948 as Perrin Air Force Base. Sherman's population rose from 20,150 in the mid-1950s to 26,100 in the mid–1960s and 30,400 in the mid–1970s, when the town was the home of about 40 manufacturing plants that turned out products ranging from salad oils and shortenings to disposable hospital products and integrated circuits. In 1990 the population stood at 31,601, and about 600 businesses employed the local workforce. The manufacturing community turned out goods including clothing, rifles, coffee, meats, hospital products, and electronic components. *Brian Hart*

Shivers, Robert Allan. Governor; b. Lufkin, 5 October 1907; d. Austin, 14 January 1985; m. Marialice Shary (1937); 4 children; ed. University of Texas (B.A., 1931; LL.B. 1933). Shivers passed the bar exam two years before he received his law degree. He was elected as a Democrat to the state Senate in 1934, at age 27 the youngest member ever to sit in that body. In World War II he served with the Allied Military Government in North Africa, Italy, France, and Germany and attained the rank of major (with five battle stars and the Bronze Star). In 1946 and 1948 he was elected lieutenant governor. In this office he initiated the practice of appointing senators to specific committees and setting the daily agenda. Subsequently, the Senate passed a right-to-work law, reorganized the public school system with the Gilmer–Aikin Laws, appropriated funds for higher education, including the Texas State University for Negroes (now Texas Southern University), and provided money for improvements of state hospitals and highways. On 11 July 1949 Governor Jester died, and Shivers assumed the governorship, which he held for the next 7_ years. He helped establish the Legislation Council, which researches and drafts bills, and the Legislative Budget Board, which sets the budget for legislative consideration. Shivers also expanded state services by pushing tax increases through the legislature. His administrations thus augmented appropriations for eleemosynary institutions, retirement benefits for state employees, aid for the elderly, teacher salaries, and improvements for roads and bridges. During his terms of office the legislature also enacted laws pertaining to safety inspection and driver responsibility, legislative redistricting (1951), and the expansion of juries and grand juries to include women in January 1955. Shivers was probably best known for defending state claims in the Tidelands Controversy, and for his break with the national Democratic party over this issue. He was instrumental in delivering the state's electoral votes in 1952 to Republican nominee Dwight D. Eisenhower. Consequently, he was accused of disloyalty to the Democratic party. He also lost support for his opposition to *Brown v. Board of Education*, which legally ended segregation. Moreover, though Shivers was never implicated in any way, his administration became tainted with corruption because of state scandals involving insurance and veterans' lands. After retiring from politics in January 1957, Shivers managed his wife's vast inherited business enterprises in the Valley, served on various bank boards, was president of the United States Chamber of Commerce and chairman of the advisory board of the Export–Import Bank of the United States, and served as a member and chairman of the board of regents at UT. In 1980 he was instrumental in securing a $5 million grant for the UT College of Communications, which soon thereafter established an endowed chair of journalism in his honor.

Ben H. Procter

Sibley, Henry Hopkins. Army officer; b. Natchitoches, Louisiana, 25 May 1816; d. Fredericksburg, Virginia, 23 August 1886; m. Charlotte Kendall (1840); 2 children; ed. United States Military Academy (grad. 1938). With a second lieutenant's commission in the Second Dragoons, Sibley saw action in the Second Seminole War. In 1847 he was promoted to captain and given command of Company I of the Second Dragoons. In the Mexican War he was brevetted a major for bravery at Medellín, near Veracruz, and fought at Cerro Gordo, Contreras, Churubusco, and Molino del Rey. In Mexico he became snowblind while attempting an ascent of Mount Popocatépetl. From 1850 to 1854 he and his company were stationed on the Texas frontier—at Fort Graham, Fort Croghan, Fort Phantom Hill on the Clear Fork of the Brazos, and at Fort Belknap, where he conceived the idea of the Sibley Tent after visiting a Comanche village. This tent, derived from a Comanche style, was conical, with a center pole affixed to a tripod at the bottom. Within it a fire could be lit, and smoke would escape through a hole in the top. The tent was spacious and comfortable in cold weather. Sibley and his company were stationed in Kansas to help quell the violence over the slavery question. In 1857 they marched through the winter to join the Mormon Expedition at Fort Bridler. In Utah Sibley was courtmartialed as a result of a feud with his regimental commander, Philip St. George Cooke. He was afterward sent to New Mexico Territory, where the Second Dragoons fought in the unsuccessful Navajo campaign of 1860. Sibley was later stationed at Fernando de Taos and at Fort Union, where he resigned from the army. He went to Richmond, Virginia, and there persuaded Jefferson Davis to adopt a grandiose plan to seize not only New Mexico but also Colorado and California for the Confederacy. Commissioned a brigadier general, Sibley went to San Antonio and helped organize three regiments of Texans into Sibley's Brigade. He then launched an invasion of New Mexico, marched his army across West Texas to Fort Bliss, and defeated Col. Edward R. S. Canby's troops near Fort Craig in the bloody battle of Valverde (21 February 1862). Moving up the Rio Grande, the "Army of New Mexico" seized Albuquerque and Santa Fe. High in the Sangre de Cristo Mountains at Glorieta Pass, Sibley's Texans beat a Union force of Colorado "Pikes Peakers" on 28 March 1862, but lost their entire supply train to a raiding party. Forced to evacuate the territory, the brigade began a disastrous retreat through the mountains. Sibley reached San Antonio in the summer of 1862, having lost a third of his men in New Mexico. He was summoned to Richmond to answer charges filed against him as a result. He assumed command of his brigade again in Louisiana in 1863. His diminishing leadership and heavy drinking became especially evident during the battle of Bisland, and he was ordered court-martialed by Gen. Richard Taylor. Although acquitted, he was removed from command. After the war Sibley went to New Orleans, Richmond, and New York, where he was recruited into the Egyptian army as a general in 1869. In Egypt he was placed in charge of the construction of coastal fortifications, but because of his growing alcoholism and incompetence, he was dismissed by the khedive in 1873. He spent his last years in poverty at Fredericksburg, Virginia, where he lived with his daughter. There he wrote magazine articles, taught French, worked on several military inventions, and continued his legal efforts to obtain royalties on the Sibley Tent.

Jerry Thompson

Síndico Procurador. The city attorney of a Spanish municipality; a voting member of the ayuntamiento or town council. The regidors, or councilmen, elected the *síndico* from among the town citizens, although the office could, like other municipal offices, be sold to the highest bidder. The duties of the *síndico procurador* varied from town to town according to local tradition. In general they included serving as official notary as well as principal legal advisor of a municipality. Additionally, the *síndico* supervised the building of fires, the upkeep of city lots, and the prevention of public gambling. He also shared with the ayuntamiento the responsibility for weights and measures and the collection of municipal funds. His chief legal duty was to serve as general counsel to the city. He represented the town in business affairs, acted as principal negotiator, and represented his area before the *audiencia*. He also ensured that local officials observed municipal ordinances and performed their duties. Although land grants were the responsibility of the regidors and the alcalde, the *síndico* was to be present when grants were made. The Spanish Constitution of 1812 did little to change the office of the *síndico*, but it required for the first time that all ayuntamientos include an attorney. *Geoffrey Pivateau*

Siringo, Charles Angelo. Cowboy, author, and detective; b. Matagorda County, 7 February 1855; d. Altadena, California, 18 October 1928; m. Mamie Lloyd (1884; d. 1890); 1 daughter; m. Lillie Thomas (1893; divorced); 1 son. Siringo made several trips on the Mississippi from New Orleans to St. Louis and back. In 1870 he was back in Texas, where he secured work as a cowboy. For six years he worked at ranches on the Coastal Plain for Joseph Yeamans, W. B. Grimes, and others. In 1871–72 he was employed as a cowboy by Jonathan and "Shanghai" Pierce on their Rancho Grande, near present-day Blessing. In 1876 Siringo became a trail driver and accompanied a herd of 2,500 longhorns over the Chisholm Trail from Austin to Kansas. He made a second trip in 1877 with one of George W. Littlefield's herds. In Dodge City he signed on with David T. Beals and W. H. "Deacon" Bates to drive a herd into the Panhandle to establish the LX Ranch. During his years as an LX cowboy Siringo met the young outlaw Billy the Kid. Later he led a posse of cowboys into New Mexico in pursuit of the Kid and his gang. Soon after his marriage he left the LX to become a merchant in Caldwell, Kansas, where he began writing his first book. *A Texas Cowboy; or, Fifteen Years on the Hurricane Deck of a Spanish Pony* (1885) established Siringo's fame as the first cowboy autobiographer and went on to become a range-literature classic. In 1886 Siringo moved to Chicago, where he obtained employment with Pinkerton's National Detective Agency. For the next 22 years he worked all over the West as a detective. He was exceptionally shrewd and successful in this work. Throughout his detective career Siringo was also frequently involved with conflicts with early labor unions. He participated in such celebrated cases as the Haymarket anarchist trial, the Coeur d'Alene miners strikes, and the trial of Western Federation of Miners Secretary "Big Bill" Haywood, who had been charged with the dynamite murder of former Idaho governor Frank Steunenburg. Although he was reputed to be a fine shot, Siringo was proud of the fact that he made most of his arrests without violence. In addition to his two marriages of record, he may have contracted one and possibly two other unsuccessful marriages. After leaving the Pinkerton Agency in 1907 Siringo retired to his ranch in Santa

Fe, New Mexico, where he wrote his second book; this one detailed his experiences as a Pinkerton detective. The original title was "Pinkerton's Cowboy Detective," but a lawsuit by the agency held up publication for nearly two years and forced Siringo to delete the name "Pinkerton" from the title and throughout the book. It was finally published as simply *A Cowboy Detective* (1912) with fictitious names replacing real ones. To vent his anger against the Pinkertons, Siringo wrote and clandestinely published a third book, entitled *Two Evil Isms, Pinkertonism and Anarchism* (1915). The Pinkertons not only succeeded in suppressing the book, they sought the extradition of Siringo from Santa Fe to Chicago to face charges of criminal libel. New Mexico governor William C. McDonald, a personal friend of Siringo's, refused the extradition request, and the matter was dropped. Siringo was appointed a New Mexico Ranger in 1916 and for two years saw active service against cattle rustlers in the southeastern part of the state.

Following his return to Santa Fe Siringo published *A Lone Star Cowboy* (1919), which he said was to take the place of *A Texas Cowboy*, on which the copyright had expired. This was followed by *History of "Billy the Kid"* (1920). Failing health and financial insolvency forced Siringo to abandon his ranch and leave Santa Fe in 1922. He moved to Los Angeles, since his children lived nearby. In poor health and living on the threshold of poverty, he tried to support himself through the sale of his books. He even flirted with the idea of becoming a cowboy actor in western movies or a screenplay writer. He worked as a film advisor and played bit parts that he probably got because of his friendship with silent screen star William S. Hart. In 1927 Houghton Mifflin published *Riata and Spurs*, a mature composite of his first two autobiographies and his only book issued by a major publisher. But Siringo's old nemesis, the Pinkertons, stopped publication by threatening a lawsuit. The book was reissued later that year with a revised subtitle and substituted material on outlaws replacing Siringo's detective experiences. Due in large part to his books, Siringo's prowess as a cowboy and Pinkerton detective were widely known in his lifetime; he met United States senators, state governors, and national officials, such diverse celebrities as Pat Garrett, Bat Masterson, Clarence Darrow, Charles M. Russell, William S. Hart, and Will Rogers, and a panoply of Western badmen. *Ben E. Pingenot*

Sitio. In Spanish Texas, a parcel of land set aside for a specific purpose, particularly in land grants. For example, a land grant known as a *sitio de ganado mayor*—a tract for raising horses, mules, and cattle—comprised 4,338 acres, also called a league. *Donald E. Chipman*

Slaughter, Christopher Columbus. Rancher; b. Sabine County, 9 February 1837; d. Dallas, 25 January 1919; m. Cynthia Jowell (1861, possibly 1860; d. 1876); 5 children; m. Carrie A. Averill (1877); 4 children. C. C. Slaughter claimed to be the first male child born of a marriage contracted under the Republic of Texas. He was a cattle drover by the age of 12. At 17 he made a trading expedition hauling timber from Anderson County to Dallas County for sale and processing Collin County wheat into flour for sale in Magnolia, Anderson County, a trip that yielded him a $520 profit. With this money he bought his uncle's interest in the Slaughter herd. Having observed the better quality of the Brazos stock, he persuaded his father to move farther west. They selected a site in Palo Pinto County, well positioned to provide beef to Fort Belknap and the nearby Indian reservations, and in 1856 the younger Slaughter drove 1,500 cattle to the new ranch. In 1859, with the outbreak of open war with Indians, he volunteered his service and was in the expedition that unexpectedly "liberated" Cynthia Ann Parker. With the withdrawal of federal protection during the Civil War, Slaughter continued to fight Indians as a lieutenant in the Texas Rangers; he also served under Capt. William Peveler in Young County in the Frontier Regiment, part of the effort to maintain frontier protection during the war. With the loss of the war and continued Indian harassment, he and other ranchers started for Mexico in search of new ranchland. During the expedition Slaughter suffered an accidental gunshot wound that incapacitated him for a year, causing a nearly ruinous decline in his cattle business. After his recovery he started a cattle drive to New Orleans in late 1867, but en route contracted with a buyer for a Jefferson packery to sell his 300 steers there for $35 a head in gold—a large sum. With his new stake he began regular drives to Kansas City in 1868, selling his herds for as much as $42 a head. He sold his Texas ranching interests in 1871 and in 1873 organized C. C. Slaughter and Company, a cattle-breeding venture, which later pioneered the replacement of the poor-bred longhorn with Kentucky-bred blooded shorthorn stock. By 1882 a herd shipped to St. Louis received $7 per hundred pounds.

Slaughter moved his family to Dallas in 1873 and a few years later dissolved his partnership with his father. About 1877 he established one of the largest ranches in West Texas, the Long S, on the headwaters of the Colorado River. Wanting to become a "gentleman breeder," he purchased in 1897 the Goodnight Hereford herd and the 1893 Chicago World's Fair grand champion bull, Ancient Briton. In 1899 he acquired the famous Hereford bull Sir Bredwell for a record $5,000. Through these purchases Slaughter's purebred Hereford herd became one of the finest in the business. Around 1898 Slaughter undertook a major land purchase in Cochran and Hockley counties. He bought 246,699 acres, leased more, and established the Lazy S Ranch, which he stocked with his Hereford herd and mixed-breed cattle from the Long S and consigned to the management of his eldest son. In 1877 Slaughter helped organize the Northwest Texas Cattle Raisers' Association (later the Texas and Southwestern Cattle Raisers Association), for which he also served a term as president (1885). He was the first president of the National Beef Producers and Butchers Association (1888), an organization formed to combat market domination by the meat-packing industry. Frequently titled the "Cattle King of Texas," Slaughter became one of the country's largest individual owners of cattle and land (over a million acres and 40,000 cattle by 1906) and was the largest individual taxpayer in Texas for years. For a time "Slaughter Country" extended from a few miles north of Big Spring 200 miles to the New Mexico border west of Lubbock. By 1908–09, however, he opened his Running Water and Long S Ranches to colonization and sale. Yet by 1911, much of the land reverted to his ownership upon the failure of the land company promoting colonization there, and under the management of Jack Alley, it was restored to profitability by 1915. Slaughter maintained strict control over his operations until 1910, when he suffered a broken hip that crippled him for the remainder of his life, compounding problems caused by his failing eyesight. He consequently turned the business over to his eldest son, George. In addition to ranching, Slaughter participated in banking in Dallas. He contributed two-thirds of the cost for the construction of the First Baptist Church in Dallas and served as vice president of the Southern Baptist Convention, as president of the state Mission Board (1897–1903), and as an executive board member of the Baptist General Convention of Texas (1898–1911). His support of a plan to retire the consolidated debt of seven Texas Baptist schools and coordinate their activities into a system capped by Baylor University assured its acceptance by the general convention in 1897. Slaughter also contributed generously to the establishment of the Texas Baptist Memorial Sanitarium (later Baylor Hospital) in Dallas.   *Joan Jenkins Perez*

Slavery. Texas was the last frontier of slavery in the United States. In fewer than 50 years, from 1821 to 1865, the "Peculiar Institution," as Southerners called it, spread over the eastern two-fifths of the state. The rate of growth accelerated rapidly during the 1840s and 1850s. The rich soil of Texas held much of the future of slavery, and Texans knew it. James S. Mayfield undoubtedly spoke for many when he told the Constitutional Convention of 1845 that "the true policy and prosperity of this country depend upon the maintenance" of slavery. Slavery as an institution of significance in Texas began in Stephen F. Austin's colony. The original empresario commission given Moses Austin by Spanish authorities in 1821 did not mention slaves, but when Stephen Austin was recognized as heir to his father's contract later that year, it was agreed that settlers could receive eighty acres of land for each bondsman brought to Texas. Enough of Austin's original 300 families brought slaves with them that a census of his colony in 1825 showed 443 in a total population of 1,800. The independence of Mexico cast doubt on the future of the institution in Texas. From 1821 until 1836 both the national government in Mexico City and the state government of Coahuila and Texas threatened to restrict or destroy black servitude. Neither government adopted any consistent or effective policy to prevent slavery in Texas; nevertheless, their threats worried slaveholders and possibly retarded the immigration of planters from the Old South. In 1836 Texas had an estimated population of 38,470, only 5,000 of whom were slaves. The Texas Revolution assured slaveholders of the future of their institution. The Constitution of the Republic of Texas (1836) provided that slaves would remain the property of their owners, that the Texas Congress could not prohibit the immigration of slaveholders bringing their property, and that slaves could be imported from the United States (although not from Africa). Given those protections, slavery expanded rapidly during the period of the republic. By 1845, when Texas joined the United States, the state was home to at least 30,000 bondsmen. After statehood, in antebellum Texas, slavery grew spectacularly. The census of 1850 reported 58,161 slaves, 27.4 percent of the 212,592 people in Texas, and the census of 1860 enumerated 182,566 bondsmen, 30.2 percent of the total population. Slaves were increasing more rapidly than the population as a whole.

The great majority of slaves in Texas came with their owners from the older slave states. Sizable numbers, however, came through the domestic slave trade. New Orleans was the center of this trade in the Deep South, but there were slave dealers in Galveston and Houston, too. A few slaves, perhaps as many as 2,000 between 1835 and 1865, came through the illegal African trade. Slave prices inflated rapidly as the institution expanded in

Texas. The average price of a bondsman, regardless of age, sex, or condition, rose from approximately $400 in 1850 to nearly $800 by 1860. During the late 1850s, prime male field hands aged 18 to 30 cost on the average $1,200, and skilled slaves such as blacksmiths often were valued at more than $2,000. In comparison, good Texas cotton land could be bought for as little as six dollars an acre. Slavery spread over the eastern two-fifths of Texas by 1860 but flourished most vigorously along the rivers that provided rich soil and relatively inexpensive transportation. The greatest concentration of large slave plantations was along the lower Brazos and Colorado rivers in Brazoria, Matagorda, Fort Bend, and Wharton counties. Truly giant slaveholders such as Robert and D. G. Mills, who owned more than 300 bondsmen in 1860 (the largest holding in Texas), had plantations in this area, and the population resembled that of the Old South's famed Black Belt. Brazoria County, for example, was 72 percent slave in 1860, while north central Texas, the area from Hunt County west to Jack and Palo Pinto counties and south to McLennan County, had fewer slaves than any other settled part of the state, except for Hispanic areas such as Cameron County. However, the north central region held much excellent cotton land, and slavery would probably have developed rapidly there once rail transportation was built. The last frontier of slavery was by no means closed on the eve of the Civil War.

American slavery was preeminently an economic institution—a system of unfree labor used to produce cash crops for profit. Questions concerning its profitability are complex and always open to debate. The evidence is strong, however, that in Texas slaves were generally profitable as a business investment for individual slaveholders. Slave labor produced cotton (and sugar on the lower Brazos River) for profit and also cultivated the foodstuffs necessary for self-sufficiency. The effect of the institution on the state's general economic development is less clear. Slavery certainly promoted development of the agricultural economy; it provided the labor for a 600 percent increase in cotton production during the 1850s. On the other hand, the institution may well have contributed in several ways to retarding commercialization and industrialization. Planters, for example, being generally satisfied with their lives as slaveholders, were largely unwilling to involve themselves in commerce and industry, even if there was a chance for greater profits. Slavery may have thus hindered economic modernization in Texas. Once established as an economic institution, slavery became a key social institution as well. Only one in every four families in antebellum Texas owned slaves, but these slaveholders, especially the planters who held 20 or more bondsmen, generally constituted the state's wealthiest class. Because of their economic success, these planters represented the social ideal for many other Texans. Slavery was also vital socially because it reflected basic racial views. Most whites thought that blacks were inferior and wanted to be sure that they remained in an inferior social position. Slavery guaranteed this.

Although the law contained some recognition of their humanity, slaves in Texas generally had the legal status of personal property. They could be bought and sold, mortgaged, and hired out. They had no legally prescribed way to gain freedom. They had no property rights themselves and no legal rights of marriage and family. Slaveowners had broad powers of discipline subject only to constitutional provisions that slaves be treated "with humanity" and that punishment not extend to the

Young Texas in Repose, by E. W. Clay, 1852. Lithograph. 14¹⁄₁₆" × 9¹³⁄₁₆". Courtesy Yale Collection of Western Americana, Beinecke Rare Book and Manuscript Library. Northern abolitionists regarded Texas as among the worst of the slaveholding states. In this cartoon the state, depicted as a depraved-looking individual, takes its ease on a slave.

taking of life and limb. A bondsman had a right to trial by jury and a court-appointed attorney when charged with a crime greater than petty larceny. Blacks, however, could not testify against whites in court, a prohibition that largely negated their constitutional protection. Bondsmen who did not work satisfactorily or otherwise displeased their owners were commonly punished by whipping. Many slaves may have escaped such punishment, but every bondsman lived with the knowledge that he could be whipped at his owner's discretion.

The majority of adult slaves were field hands, but a sizable minority worked as skilled craftsmen, house servants, and livestock handlers. Field hands generally labored "from sun to sun" five days a week and half a day on Saturday. House servants and craftsmen worked long hours, too, but their labor was not so burdensome physically. Theirs was apparently a favored position, at least in this regard. A small minority (about 6 percent) of the slaves in Texas did not belong to farmers or planters but lived instead in the state's towns, working as domestic servants, day laborers, and mechanics.

The material conditions of slave life in Texas could probably best be described as adequate, in that most bondsmen had the food, shelter, and clothing necessary to live and work effectively. On the other hand, there was little comfort and no luxury. Slaves

Sugar Harvest in Louisiana and Texas, by Franz Hölzlhuber, ca. 1860. Watercolor on paper. 6" × 8¾". Courtesy Glenbow Collection, Calgary, Alberta, Canada. Hölzlhuber, a young Austrian traveler who spent four years in the U.S., took one of the well-known "floating palaces" down the Mississippi River to visit Louisiana and Texas, where he documented the sugar harvest by slaves.

ate primarily corn and pork, foods that contained enough calories to provide adequate energy but were limited in essential vitamins and minerals. Most bondsmen, however, supplemented their basic diet with sweet potatoes, garden vegetables, wild game, and fish and were thus adequately fed. Slave houses were usually small log cabins with fireplaces for cooking. Dirt floors were common, and beds attached to the walls were the only standard furnishings. Slave clothing was made of cheap, coarse materials; shoes were stiff and rarely fitted. Medical care in antebellum Texas was woefully inadequate for whites and blacks alike, but slaves had a harder daily life and were therefore more likely to be injured or develop diseases that doctors could not treat. Texas slaves had a distinct family-centered social life and culture that flourished in the slave quarters, where bondsmen were largely on their own, at least from sundown to sunup. Although slave marriages and families had no legal protections, the majority of bondsmen were reared and lived day to day in a family setting. This was in the slaveowners' self-interest, for marriage encouraged reproduction under socially acceptable conditions, and slave children were valuable. Moreover, individuals with family ties were probably more easily controlled than those who had none. The slaves themselves, however, also insisted on family ties. They often made matches with bondsmen on neighboring farms and spent as much time as possible together, even if one owner or the other could not be persuaded to arrange for

husband and wife to live in the same place. They fought bitterly against the disruption of their families by sale or migration and at times virtually forced masters to respect family ties. Many slave families, however, were disrupted. All slaves had to live with the knowledge that their families could be broken up, and yet the basic social unit survived. Family ties were a source of strength for people enduring bondage and a mark of their humanity in a nation that had officially denied it. Religion and music were also key elements of slave culture. Many owners encouraged worship, primarily on the grounds that it would teach proper subjection and good behavior. Slaves, however, tended to hear the message of individual equality before God and salvation for all. The promise of ultimate deliverance helped many to resist the psychological assault of bondage. Music and song served to set a pace for work and to express sorrow and hope.

Slaves adjusted their behavior to the conditions of servitude in a variety of ways. Some felt well-treated by their owners and generally behaved as loyal servants. Others hated their masters and their situation and rebelled by running away or using violence. Texas had many runaways, and thousands escaped to Mexico. Although no major rebellions occurred, individual acts of violence against owners were carried out. Most slaves, however, were neither loyal servants nor rebels. Instead, the majority recognized all the controls such as slave patrols that existed to keep them in bondage and saw also that runaways and rebels

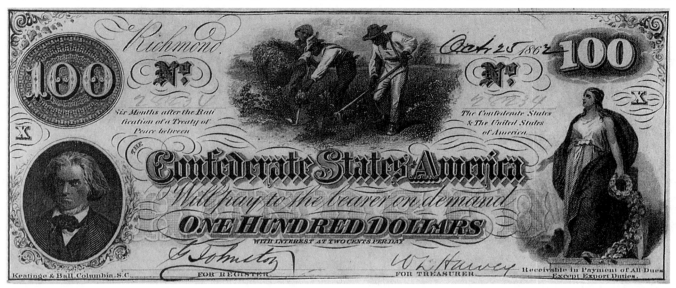

Confederate $100 bill, 1862. Courtesy Roy R. Barkley, Pflugerville, Texas. In stark contrast to the images Northerners drew of slavery, Confederate currency depicted slaves in idyllic settings.

generally paid heavy prices for overt resistance. They therefore followed a basic human instinct and sought to survive on the best terms possible. This did not mean that the majority of slaves were content with their status. They were not, and even the best-treated bondsmen dreamed of freedom. Slavery in Texas was not a matter of content, well-cared-for servants as idealized in some views of the Old South. On the other hand, the institution was not absolutely brutal or degrading. Slaves were not reduced to the level of animals, and they did not live every day in sullen rage. Instead, bondsmen had enough "room"—time of their own and control of their own lives—within the slave system to maintain physical, psychological, and spiritual strength. In part this limited autonomy was given by the masters, who generally wanted loyal and cheerful servants. Slaves increased their minimal self-determination by taking what they could get from their owners and then pressing for additional latitude. For example, although slaves worked hard, they tried to work at their own pace and offered many forms of nonviolent resistance if pushed too hard. Slaves in general were not revolutionaries who overcame all the limits placed on them, but they did not surrender totally to the system, either. One way or another they had enough room to endure. This fact is not a tribute to the benevolence of slavery, which does not exist, but a testimony to the human spirit of the slaves.

Though slaves obviously freed their owners from the drudgery of manual labor and daily chores, they were a troublesome property in many ways. Masters had to discipline their bondsmen, get the labor they wanted, and yet avoid too many problems of resistance such as running away and feigning illness. Many owners wished to appear as benevolent "fathers," and yet most knew that there would be times when they would treat members of their "families" as property pure and simple. Most lived with a certain amount of fear of their supposedly happy servants, for the slightest threat of a slave rebellion could touch off a violent reaction. Slavery was thus a constant source of tension in the lives of slaveholders.

White society as a whole in antebellum Texas was dominated by its slaveholding minority. Economically, slaveowners had a disproportionately large share of the state's wealth and produced virtually all of the cash crops. Politically, slaveholders dominated public officeholding at all levels. Socially, slaveholders, at least the large planters, embodied an ideal to most Texans.

The progress of the Civil War did not drastically affect slavery in Texas because no major slaveholding area was invaded. In general, Texas slaves continued to work and live as they had before the war. A great many did, however, get the idea that they would be free if the South lost. They listened as best they could for any war news and passed it around among themselves. Slavery formally ended in Texas on 19 June 1865 (Juneteenth), when Gen. Gordon Granger arrived at Galveston with occupying federal forces and announced emancipation. A few owners angrily told their slaves to leave immediately, but most expressed sorrow at the end of the institution and asked their bondsmen to stay and work for wages. The emancipated slaves celebrated joyously (if whites allowed it). But then they had to find out just what freedom meant. They knew that they would not be forced to labor anymore and that they could move about as they chose. But how would they make their way in the world after 1865? Blacks had maintained a degree of human dignity even in bondage (most owners had allowed them to do so), and Texas could not have grown as it had before 1865 without the slaves' contributions. Nevertheless, slavery was a curse to Texans, white and black alike. *Randolph B. Campbell*

Smith, Ashbel. Pioneer doctor and multifaceted leader; b. Hartford, Connecticut, 13 August 1805; d. near Galveston Bay, 21 January 1886 (buried in the State Cemetery); ed. Yale College (A.B. and A.M. degrees; M.D., 1828). Smith made valuable contributions to Texas in the areas of medicine, education, politics, diplomacy, agriculture and ranching, warfare, finance, transportation, and immigration. He taught in North Carolina, then studied medicine in Paris for a year. During the Paris cholera epidemic of 1832 he helped treat the sick and published a pamphlet on the disease. Upon his return to the United States

Ashbel Smith, Paris, France, 1878. Courtesy TSL.

around 1833 he established a successful medical practice in Salisbury, North Carolina. He was involved in politics in that state and became editor and half owner of the *Western Carolinian*, a nullification newspaper. In the fall of 1836 James Pinckney Henderson, a fellow North Carolinian already in Texas, persuaded Smith to move to the newly formed Republic of Texas. When he arrived in 1837 he became Sam Houston's roommate and close friend. Houston appointed him surgeon general of the Army of the Republic of Texas on 7 June 1837. In this role Smith set up an efficient system of operation and established the first hospital in Houston, a military institution. He also served as the first chairman of the Board of Medical Censors, which was established by the Second Congress of the republic in December 1837. During the devastating epidemic of yellow fever in Galveston in 1839, he treated the sick, published reports of the progress of the disease in the Galveston *News*, and, after the epidemic abated, wrote the first treatise on yellow fever in Texas. In 1848 Smith met with 10 other Galveston doctors to begin working for the formation of the Medical and Surgical Society of Galveston. When the Texas Medical Association came into being in 1853, he was chairman of the committee that drafted its constitution and bylaws. He also may have served as an early president of the board of trustees of the Texas Medical College and Hospital after it was organized in Galveston in 1873.

When Smith first came to Texas, Houston quickly recognized his diplomatic ability and in 1838 sent him to negotiate a treaty with the Comanche Indians. In 1842 Smith traveled to Europe as the *chargé d'affaires* of Texas to England and France, a position he held from 1842 to 1844. He secured ratification of a treaty of amity and commerce between England and Texas and improved the republic's relations with France, which had been disturbed by the Pig War. He was also charged with working for friendly mediation by European powers to stop Mexican threats to rein-

vade Texas, with encouraging immigration to Texas, and with learning the attitude of Russia, Prussia, and Austria toward Texas. In addition, he investigated and reported to leaders in Texas and the United States activities of the British antislavery party, which seemed potentially harmful to Texas, and the fact that two steamers were being built in England for Mexico. In 1845, as secretary of state, Smith worked with President Anson Jones to give the people of Texas a choice between remaining an independent republic and being annexed to the United States. To this end, he negotiated a treaty with Mexico, by which that country acknowledged the independence of Texas. This treaty, known as the Smith–Cuevas Treaty, angered many Texans who were avid for annexation, and Smith was burned in effigy by citizens of Galveston and San Felipe. After Texas became a state Smith served three terms (1855, 1866, and 1879) in the state legislature as a representative from Harris County. As a legislator he supported measures to aid railroad construction, validate land titles, improve common schools, found the University of Texas, and pay off the public debt. He also helped to found the Democratic party in Texas, took an active part in county and state party meetings, and represented the party several times in Democratic national conventions.

Smith rendered further military service to Texas during the Mexican War and the Civil War. He was injured at Shiloh and was cited for bravery, along with the rest of his company. He was promoted to colonel and named commander of the Second Texas Infantry, which he led in several engagements in Mississippi, including Corinth and the Tallahatchie River. During the siege of Vicksburg, he was in command of a vulnerable earthen fortification at one of the entrances to that city. After the surrender of Vicksburg, Smith was in charge of several positions in the vicinity of Matagorda Peninsula, and was credited with preventing Union invasions in that area. Toward the end of the war he was put in charge of the defenses of Galveston. After the war he and William P. Ballinger were sent by Governor Murrah as commissioners to negotiate peace terms for Texas with Union officials in New Orleans.

Smith devoted much time and energy to the cause of education, and he often urged that Texas underwrite the education of every child in the state. He was a charter member and first vice president of the Philosophical Society of Texas; one of that organization's first acts was to draw up a memorial to the Texas Congress urging the establishment of a system of public education in Texas. Smith served as superintendent of Houston Academy before the Civil War, and he was also a trustee at various times on a number of school boards in Houston and Galveston. He championed public education for African Americans and women and was one of three commissioners appointed by Governor Richard Coke to establish an "Agricultural and Mechanical College of Texas, for the benefit of the Colored Youths." This school, located five miles east of Hempstead, is now Prairie View A&M University. Smith also helped organize Stuart Female Seminary in Austin and served as a trustee on its first board. He spent his last years in an unceasing effort to establish a state university with a first-class medical branch. As president of the University of Texas Board of Regents, established in 1881, he led the effort to recruit the best professors available for the university faculty and to set up the curriculum. He also served as president of the board of visitors to the United States Military Academy at West Point in 1848.

He was a powerful orator, many of whose numerous speeches were published in newspapers and as separate monographs. He was also an able and indefatigable writer. In addition to editing the Salisbury *Western Carolinian*, he served a brief stint (December 1839–January 1840) as guest editor of the Houston *Morning Star*. His writings were published in scientific, agricultural, educational, and general magazines and newspapers in the United States and Europe. His *Reminiscences of the Texas Republic* (1876) contains much valuable material pertaining to the early history of Texas. In 1869, when the Southern Historical Society was organized, Smith was named vice president for Texas, along with Gen. Robert E. Lee for Virginia and Adm. Raphael Semmes for Alabama. Smith's experiments and innovations in agriculture and ranching were recognized internationally. He published numerous articles based on firsthand observation of the climate, soil, vegetation, and wildlife in Texas, as well as his experiences raising livestock and crops on the Gulf Coast. In 1851 he was sent as Texas delegate to the Great London Exhibition at the Crystal Palace and was named one of the judges. In May 1852 he served as superintendent of the first fair in Texas, held in Corpus Christi. He was elected the first president of the Texas State Agricultural Society when it was formed in 1853. In 1876 he was appointed by the United States Centennial Commission to act as a judge on the Jury of Awards at the Great International Exhibition in Philadelphia, and in 1878 President Rutherford Hayes appointed him one of the two honorary commissioners from Texas to the Paris International Exposition, where he was named one of the judges of agricultural products. Smith never married. He died at Evergreen, his plantation home.

Elizabeth Silverthorne

Smith, Edmund Kirby. Army officer, nicknamed Seminole Smith; b. St. Augustine, Florida, 16 May 1824; d. Sewanee, Tennessee, 28 March 1893 (buried on the campus of the University of the South); ed. West Point (grad. 1845). Smith came from a distinguished military family. He served with distinction in the Mexican War. From 1849 to 1852 he was assistant professor of mathematics at West Point. He later served under Maj. William H. Emory on the commission to survey the United States–Mexico boundary. In 1851 he was promoted to first lieutenant, and in 1855 he was assigned as a captain in the famous Second United States Cavalry, "Jeff Davis's Own," in which he saw much service on the Texas Indian frontier. He was promoted to major in 1861, and subsequently refused Col. Henry E. McCulloch's demand that he surrender Camp Colorado to Texas secessionist forces. Nevertheless, when Florida seceded, Smith resigned from the U.S. Army and accepted a commission as lieutenant colonel in the Confederate States Army. He served in the Shenandoah valley under Joseph E. Johnston. During his Confederate military career he began to refer to himself as Kirby Smith to distinguish himself from other Smiths in the Confederate Army. He became a brigadier general on 17 June 1861 and contributed materially to the Southern success at the first battle of Manassas, where he was wounded. After recovery, he was promoted to major general and assigned to duty in the West, where he commanded the District of East Tennessee and led a small army to victory at the battle of Richmond, Kentucky, on 30 August 1862. On 9 October 1862 he was promoted to lieutenant general and given command of the Trans-Mississippi Department. His competent administration of the department

and successful defense of the region against Union general Nathaniel P. Banks's Red River campaign in 1864 was marred by his inability to cooperate amicably with his principal field commander, Gen. Richard Taylor. On 19 February 1864 Smith was promoted to the rank of full general, and during this time he presided over the Marshall Conferences. He was almost the last Confederate general in the field, but in a hopelessly isolated situation he finally surrendered to Gen. Edward R. S. Canby on 2 June 1865. He subsequently served as president of the Accident Insurance Company in Louisville, Kentucky, as president of the Pacific and Atlantic Telegraph Company, as president of the Western Military Academy at Nashville, and as chancellor of the University of Nashville. In 1868 he opened a school in New Castle, Kentucky, but it burned the following year. In 1875 he became professor of mathematics at the University of the South at Sewanee, Tennessee.

Thomas W. Cutrer

Smith, Deaf. Early settler and soldier; b. Erastus Smith, Duchess County, New York, 19 April 1787; d. Richmond, Texas, 30 November 1837; m. Guadalupe Ruiz Durán (1822); 4 daughters. At the age of 11 or 12 he moved with his parents to Natchez, Mississippi Territory. A childhood disease destroyed his hearing. Smith visited Texas in 1817 and in 1821 settled near San Antonio, where he married. In 1825 he and five other men settled on the claim of James Kerr, the surveyor for the new colony of Green DeWitt, about a mile west of the site of present Gonzales. This community was the first in DeWitt's colony and one of the first American settlements west of the Colorado River. In the Texas Revolution Smith first fought with Stephen F. Austin's army at

Erastus (Deaf) Smith, by Thomas Jefferson Wright, 1836. Oil on canvas. 22" × 27½". Courtesy San Jacinto Museum of History, Houston.

the siege of Bexar and the battle of Concepción. He was responsible for the discovery of the Mexican supply train involved in the Grass Fight. He was wounded at Bexar, but remained with the army because, as Governor Henry Smith said, "his services as a spy cannot well be dispensed with." After regaining his health, Smith served as a messenger for William B. Travis, who considered him "'the Bravest of the Brave' in the cause of Texas." Smith carried Travis's letter from the Alamo on 15 February 1836. On 13 March Gen. Sam Houston dispatched Smith and Henry Karnes back to San Antonio to learn the status of the Alamo garrison. "If living," Houston reported to Thomas Jefferson Rusk, Smith would return with "the truth and all important news." Smith returned with Susanna Dickinson and her daughter. Houston first assigned Smith to the cavalry but later placed him in charge of recruits with the rank of captain. During the San Jacinto campaign he captured a Mexican courier bearing important dispatches to General Santa Anna, and on 21 April 1836 Smith and Houston requisitioned "one or more axes," with which Houston ordered Smith to destroy Vince's Bridge, reportedly to prevent the retreat of the Mexican army. Smith accomplished the mission and reported to Houston before the battle of San Jacinto. It was to Smith that Houston entrusted Santa Anna's order to Gen. Vicente Filisola to evacuate Texas. After San Jacinto, General Rusk continued to send Smith out as a scout. In 1836 the Texas Congress granted Smith the property of Ramón Músquiz in San Antonio as a reward for his military activities. Nevertheless, Smith and his family remained in Columbia. He resigned his commission in the army but raised and commanded a company of Texas Rangers that on 17 February 1837, defeated a band of Mexicans at Laredo. Soon thereafter he left ranger service and moved to Richmond, where he died at the home of Randal Jones. On hearing of his death, Houston wrote to Anna Raguet, praising Smith: "A man, more brave, and honest, never lived." Deaf Smith County is named in Smith's honor.

Thomas W. Cutrer

Smith, Henry. Provisional governor; b. Kentucky, 20 May 1788; d. Los Angeles County, California, 4 March 1851; successively married three sisters, Harriet, Elizabeth, and Sarah Gillett; 9 children. Smith moved to Texas in 1827 and settled in what is now Brazoria County. He farmed, taught school, surveyed, and took an active part in public affairs. In 1832 he took part in the battle of Velasco and was severely wounded. There is evidence that at this early date he was thinking in terms of independence for Texas. In 1833 he was elected alcalde of Brazoria and a few months later was chosen a delegate to the Convention of 1833. In 1834 the governor of Coahuila and Texas appointed Smith political chief of the newly established Department of the Brazos. As the country moved toward revolution, Smith became one of the leaders of the independence party. In the summer of 1835 he was chosen to serve on the Columbia committee of safety and correspondence and later in the same year was elected one of the delegates from his district to the Consultation. Smith urged an immediate declaration of independence and was keenly disappointed when the Consultation pledged its support to the Mexican federal Constitution of 1824. Smith had a part in preparing the organic law that served as the constitution of the provisional government. In establishing the provisional government the Consultation made an attempt to satisfy all factions. A majority of the members of the General Council were in favor of the Declaration of November 7, 1835, and were known as members of the Peace Party. Smith, one of the leaders of the War Party, was named governor and has come to be known as the first American governor of Texas.

Governor Smith did not believe in compromise and did not know the language of diplomacy. Within a short while the government was torn by strife—a condition due, at least in part, to Smith's belief that Texas was already an independent state. There were numerous other points of disagreement, including some of a personal nature, and in January 1836 the gulf between the two branches of government became so wide that cooperation was no longer possible. Governor Smith attempted to dissolve the council, and the council retaliated by impeaching the governor. In their original form, the articles of impeachment charged the governor with violation of the organic law, with failure to support the Declaration of November 7, with "official perjury," and with slandering and libeling members of the General Council. The Convention of 1836 had no time to devote to such petty squabbles, and the governor was never called upon to answer the charges made against him. Smith was not a member of the Convention of 1836 and had no place in the *ad interim* government organized by that body. His political eclipse, however, was of short duration. His friends entered his name as a candidate for the presidency in the election of 1836 and, in spite of the fact that he asked that his name be withdrawn and announced his support of Sam Houston, he received some votes. He served as secretary of the treasury during the first Houston administration. In 1840 Smith was elected to Congress. He served one term in the House of Representatives, where he was made chairman of the committee on finance and is credited with introducing several measures of importance. Afterward, he retired to his home and lived in retirement until 1849, when he succumbed to gold fever and set out for California. He died in a mining camp.

Ralph W. Steen

Smithwick, Noah. Pioneer gunsmith and memoirist; b. Martin County, North Carolina, 1 January 1808; d. Santa Ana, California, 21 October 1899; m. Mrs. Thurza N. Blakey Duty (1839); at least 4 children. The Smithwick family moved in 1814 to Robertson County, Tennessee. In 1827 Noah left his blacksmith job in Hopkinsville, Kentucky, and traveled by flatboat to New Orleans and by schooner to Matagorda Bay. He worked as an itinerant smith before settling in San Felipe. In 1830 he applied for a league of land in Stephen F. Austin's colony. When Smithwick's friend Hiram Friley sought refuge in San Felipe after killing the alcalde of Gonzales, San Felipe authorities ordered him chained with leg irons, but Smithwick gave him a file and a gun so he could escape. Friley was tracked down and shot. The authorities tried Smithwick, declared him "a bad citizen," and on 7 December 1830 banished him from Austin's colony and Texas. He was escorted to the Sabine River. Smithwick returned to Matagorda in the fall of 1835, after four years in the Redlands of East Texas and Louisiana. He arrived at Gonzales the day after the battle of Gonzales and remained to repair guns. After joining the volunteers marching towards Bexar, he took part in the battle of Concepción, but like others discouraged by the indecisive command and without winter clothing, he abandoned the siege and went to Bastrop, where he had friends. In January 1836 he joined Capt. John James Tumlinson's newly formed ranger company to defend the

Bastrop area from Indians. During the Runaway Scrape, Bastrop residents fled eastward, while Smithwick and others prepared to guard the river crossing and herd the cattle eastward. They gradually retreated southeastward searching for the army, and arrived at San Jacinto after the battle. In May, Gen. Thomas J. Rusk ordered gunsmiths to follow the Texas army from the battleground to Victoria. Smithwick did not pursue the Mexican army south of the Rio Grande, but returned to Bastrop to work as a smith and serve in the volunteer ranger corps from the fall of 1836 through 1838. He understood Spanish and occasionally served as interpreter and agent with Plains Indians seeking treaties and trading posts. After marrying, Smithwick and his wife settled in Webber's Prairie, Travis County. By 1850 they moved to Brushy Creek in Williamson County, where Smithwick ran livestock. When he flopped as a farmer, Smithwick applied for a job as armorer at Fort Croghan (present Burnet), where he worked for a while, perhaps until the fort closed in 1853. That year he paid $5,000 for the nearby saw and grist mill built by the Mormons in 1850. He and his nephew and partner, John R. Hubbard, sold their interest in 1857–58. Smithwick began a new mill on land 10 miles east of Marble Falls in the Hickory Creek settlement. As a Unionist, he received threats in 1861, sold his property, and left his nephew at the mill. Secessionists later murdered Hubbard and threw his body into a waterhole. Smithwick and a number of friends struck out for California on 14 April 1861. During the last two years of his life, he joined the Texas State Historical Association and contributed an article to the *Quarterly* (October 1898). He gradually lost his eyesight but dictated his memoirs to his daughter, Mrs. Anna Donaldson. After his death she polished the manuscript under the title *The Evolution of a State, or Recollections of Old Texas Days* (Austin: Gammel, 1900). *Margaret Swett Henson*

Social Science Quarterly. Published jointly by the Southwestern Social Science Association and the University of Texas Press; founded as the *Southwestern Political Science Quarterly* in 1920. It was the first social science journal published in the United States by a regional social science organization. The interdisciplinary character of the journal was made explicit in 1923 when the journal became the *Southwestern Political and Social Science Quarterly*. Eight years later it was renamed *Southwestern Social Science Quarterly* and in 1968, to deemphasize the regional nature of the journal, *Social Science Quarterly*. The journal publishes research, theoretical essays, position papers, and book reviews by economists, geographers, historians, political scientists, sociologists, and other social scientists. Its preference is for articles that bridge two or more of these disciplines. By the late 1980s circulation for the publication was about 2,700.

Charles M. Bonjean

Socorro, Texas. Ten miles southeast of downtown El Paso; founded in 1680, when Governor Antonio de Otermín and Father Francisco de Ayeta led Spanish and Piro Indian refugees fleeing the New Mexican Pueblo Indian Revolt to the El Paso area. In 1682 the Spanish established Nuestra Señora de la Limpia Concepción del Socorro Mission. The first permanent mission, built in 1691, was swept away by flood in 1744, and a second church was built. It was washed away in 1829, when the Rio Grande cut a new channel south of the old one, thus placing Socorro, Ysleta, and San Elizario on La Isla. The main part of the present Socorro mission was completed in 1843. By that time the town of Socorro had developed around the mission and had a population of 1,100. The town became part of Texas in 1848. For the rest of the nineteenth century Socorro remained a small farming community. Acequias supplied water for vineyards, fruit trees, and cereal grains. The construction of Elephant Butte Dam on the Rio Grande in New Mexico (1916) transformed a family-based agricultural system into one featuring large-scale cotton production on plantation-sized estates. By 1920 cotton was beginning to rival copper as the Socorro area's principal industry. The population of the community was 2,123 in the mid-1930s, but fell to 350 by 1941 and remained static for several decades thereafter. During the 1960s and 1970s developers built residential subdivisions—colonias in effect—that lacked paved streets, water, and sewer lines. Colonia residents put tremendous pressure on existing wells, as the town's population grew from 10,000 in the middle 1970s to 22,995 in 1990. Only recently has the Lower Valley Water District Authority received the necessary assistance to begin construction of new water and sewerage systems for the area. In 1985 residents blocked El Paso's plan to annex the town and voted to remain a separate corporation. Since then, Socorro has adopted ordinances and codes to halt uncontrolled growth and has instituted a historic-landmark commission to encourage historic preservation.

Martin Donell Kohout

Sokol. Means "falcon"; an organization that began in Prague, Bohemia, in 1862 and was brought to this country by Czechs; dedicated to the physical, mental, and cultural advancement of its members. The organization is modeled on the physical education of ancient Greece. The first Sokol in the United States was formed in St. Louis, Missouri, in 1865, the first in Texas in Ennis in 1908. By 1909 Sokols had been organized in Shiner, Hallettsville, and Granger. Others followed in Waco, Dallas, Fort Worth, Penelope, Guy, Seaton, Buckholts, Houston, Crosby, Rowena, Galveston, Corpus Christi, Placido, Floresville, San Antonio, and East Bernard. Many units disbanded during the Great Depression. In 1930 there were 14. In 1985 units were located in Corpus Christi, Dallas, Ennis, Fort Worth, Houston, and West. Modern gymnasiums are the trademark of Sokol, and gymnastics is part of the Sokol practice of mixing mental, moral, cultural, and physical training. The southern district of Sokol includes Texas and Oklahoma and is the fourth largest of the six districts in the United States. *Sylvia J. Laznovsky*

Solms–Braunfels, Prince Carl of. German nobleman, first commissioner general of the Adelsverein; b. Neustrelitz, 27 July 1812; d. near Kreuznach, 13 November 1875 (buried in Bad Kreuznach). Prince Carl's illustrious connections included Prince Frederick of Prussia, Queen Victoria, Czar Alexander I of Russia, King Leopold I of Belgium, and Prince Albert of Saxe–Coburg–Gotha. The trilingual prince was educated both as soldier and courtier. He secured prestigious military assignments, awards, and knightships, even though in 1839 he was sentenced by a Prussian court-martial to four months in prison for going AWOL. A secret, early, morganatic marriage (1834) dimmed his prospects after it became known, until, under duress, he consented in 1841 to the putting away of his wife and three children. That same year Carl became a captain of cavalry in the imperial army of Austria. While stationed at Biebrich, he

Prince Carl of Solms–Braunfels. Courtesy ITC.

read Charles Sealsfield's novel about Texas, William Kennedy's geography of Texas, and G. A. Scherpf's guide to immigrants to Texas. As one of the 25 members of the Adelsverein, Carl worked tirelessly to promote the growth, finances, administration, and political acceptance of the society. He lobbied his many relatives, traveled incognito through France and Belgium to the Isle of Wight, where he may have met with Prince Albert, and, along with other members, secured the covert support of England, France, and Belgium for the Texas colonial project. In 1844 Carl was appointed commissioner general for the first colony that the society proposed to establish in Texas. Provisioned with two cannons, table linens, and 12 place settings, he and his retinue traveled to the Republic of Texas, where he arrived in Galveston on 1 July 1844. A series of letters, subsequently turned into formal reports, trace the route and detail Carl's growing comprehension of North American culture, commerce, and geopolitics. In preparation to receive the German settlers and to protect them from what he considered the bad influences of the Anglo-American frontier, Carl purchased land on Matagorda Bay for the establishment of a port of debarkation named Carlshafen, or Indianola. He also traveled extensively throughout Texas and advised the Adelsverein, which already owned the right to settle Germans in the remote Fisher–Miller Land Grant, to buy even larger expanses reaching southward from the Llano River to Corpus Christi Bay and westward to the Rio Grande. Further, he communicated to Texas officials the threat of possible war with

Britain, France, Russia, and Mexico should annexation occur. After the arrival in December 1844 of the society's first settlers, some of whom he left at Indianola, or Carlshafen, the prince led the first wagontrain into the interior of Texas. Near Victoria, he left the immigrants and proceeded to San Antonio in order to conclude the purchase from Juan Martín Veramendi and Raphael C. Garza of a fertile, well-watered tract on the Guadalupe and Comal rivers. The immigrant train reached this tract on Good Friday, 21 March 1845, and founded the settlement of New Braunfels, named for the Solms ancestral castle on the Lahn River. Before Prince Carl left New Braunfels for Germany on 15 May 1845, he saw the work on the Zinkenburg, a stockade on Comal Creek, almost completed and work well underway on the Sophienburg, a fort on the Vereinsberg, a hill overlooking the old residential section of New Braunfels.

After he returned to Germany, Carl resumed his military service, from which he had been given a year's leave, and married a princess. In 1846 he published *Texas*, a clear and succinct geography and guide. During this time he also wrote a memoir, transmitted to Queen Victoria in 1846, in which he explained that Europe and the westering United States were on a collision course to dominate world trade. America would likely win this race, Carl told the queen, if the United States reached the Pacific. He suggested containment through colonization, the establishment of a powerful monarchy in Mexico, and the emancipation of the slaves as England's surest policy. Carl remained active in his support of the Adelsverein, in which his family had heavily invested. In 1847, for example, he helped to recruit the Forty, an idealistic fraternity of students that eventually settled in the Fisher–Miller Land Grant. In 1846 he left the Austrian army and became a colonel in the cavalry of the Grand Duchy of Hesse. An attempt to rejoin the Prussian army failed. In 1850 the Austrian army accepted him again, and by 1859 he had become a brigadier with command of dragoons on Lake Constance. In 1866, having also drawn Hanover into the conflict, he took part in the unsuccessful war of Austria against Prussia. As commander of an imperial corps, Carl failed, was recalled and reprimanded, but was acquitted by court-martial. He retired as a field marshal in 1868 to his residence at the estate of Rheingrafenstein on the Nahe River. He and Princess Sophie had five children. Prince Carl was characterized by one of his German contemporaries in Texas as a "Texan Don Quixote" and by an eminent German historian as the last knight of the Middle Ages.

Glen E. Lich and Günter Moltmann

Somervell, Alexander. Entrepreneur and soldier; b. Maryland, 11 June 1796; d. February 1854. Somervell moved to Louisiana in 1817 and was a planter in St. Landry Parish. In the early 1820s he moved to Missouri, where he was probably a merchant. He moved to Texas in 1833 and was granted land in Austin's second colony. He engaged in the mercantile business at San Felipe with James F. Perry. In October 1835 he joined the volunteers marching from Gonzales to Bexar and was elected major. He participated in the siege of Bexar. He enrolled in the Texas army on 12 March 1836, and on 8 April was elected lieutenant colonel of the first regiment of Texas Volunteers, succeeding Sidney Sherman. He participated in the battle of San Jacinto and remained in the army until June 1836. He served briefly as secretary of war in David G. Burnet's cabinet, then represented Colorado and Austin counties in the Senate of the First and Second congresses,

1836 to 1838. By the time he was elected brigadier general in 1839, he was living in Fort Bend County. In January 1840 he was appointed commissioner to inspect land offices west of the Brazos. The following year he was named county clerk in Austin County. In 1842 Sam Houston gave him command of a punitive expedition against Mexico in retaliation for the Mexican invasions of 1842. Houston ordered Somervell to organize the militia and volunteers and invade Mexico if the strength, equipment, and discipline of the army indicated a reasonable hope of success. Volunteers poured into San Antonio eager to pursue the enemy and invade Mexico for glory and plunder. Numbering approximately 700 men, the Somervell expedition left San Antonio on 25 November; it numbered 683 men when it reached Laredo, which was captured on 8 December. Joseph L. Bennett and 185 men returned home two days later. Somervell forced the capitulation of Guerrero. On 19 December, however, recognizing the failure of his expedition and fearing disaster, he ordered his men to disband and return home by way of Gonzales. Little energy had been shown in prosecuting the campaign, which apparently was started as a political move to appease demands for an invasion of Mexico. But the Texans were so disappointed with the order to disband that only 189 men and officers obeyed; some 308 men commanded by William S. Fisher continued to Mexico on the Mier expedition. Later that year, as a reward for his services, Somervell was appointed collector of customs for the port of Calhoun. He probably held this position until the customhouse was moved to the mainland in 1844. In partnership with two others, he helped develop the town of Saluria on northeastern Matagorda Island between 1845 and 1847. Somervell was evidently murdered. His body was found lashed to the timbers of a capsized boat in which, carrying a considerable amount of money, he had started from Lavaca to Saluria.

Robert E. Cunningham and Joseph Milton Nance

Sonnichsen, Charles Leland. Historian; b. Fonda, Iowa, 20 September 1901; d. Tucson, 29 June 1991; m. twice; ed. University of Minnesota (B.A., 1924), Harvard University (M.A., 1927; Ph.D., 1931). Sonnichsen's doctorate was in English literature. He moved to El Paso in 1931 as associate professor of English at the Texas College of Mines and Metallurgy, predecessor of the University of Texas at El Paso. He rose through teaching and administrative ranks to professor, chairman of the English Department (a post he held for 27 years), dean of the graduate school, and H. Y. Benedict Professor of English. He retired from UTEP in 1972 after a 41-year career there and moved to Tucson, Arizona, where he was editor of the *Journal of Arizona History* from 1972 to 1977 and continued to write and edit books. After arriving in El Paso, Sonnichsen turned his scholarly attention from seventeenth-century English to Southwestern history and folklore. He called his work "grassroots history" and labeled himself "genus Historianus herbidus." Sonnichsen's self-taught historical research, combined with an admired light-hearted writing touch, produced 27 books, beginning with *Billy King's Tombstone* (1942), the biography of an obscure saloonkeeper and deputy sheriff of Tombstone, Arizona, who had witnessed Geronimo's surrender. His best-known books include *Roy Bean: Law West of the Pecos* (1943), *Cowboys and Cattle Kings* (1950), *The Mescalero Apaches* (1958), *Tularosa: Last of the Frontier West* (1960), *Pass of the North: Four Centuries on the Rio Grande* (two volumes, 1968, 1980), *Colonel Greene and the Copper Skyrocket*

(1974), *From Hopalong to Hud: Thoughts on Western Fiction* (1978), and his books on Texas feuds, *I'll Die Before I'll Run* (1951), *Ten Texas Feuds* (1957), and *Outlaw: Bill Mitchell, Alias Baldy Russell* (1964). Toward the end of his life, with his eyesight failing, Sonnichsen edited a number of books, including *Geronimo and the End of the Apache Wars* (1987), *Pilgrim in the Sun: A Southwestern Omnibus* (1988), and several on Western humor, such as *The Laughing West* (1988) and *Arizona Humoresque* (1990). A few weeks before his death he completed work on a new collection of essays, "Late Harvest," which was retitled *Final Harvest* and published posthumously in 1991 by Texas Western Press. Sonnichsen was president of the Texas Folklore Society, the Western Literature Association, the Western History Association, and the Western Writers of America. He was a long-time member of the Texas Institute of Letters and the Texas State Historical Association. Among awards he received for his teaching and writing were the Bowdoin Prize from Harvard, the Friends of the Dallas Public Library Award from the Texas Institute of Letters, the Minnie Stevens Piper Professorship, the Wrangler Award of the National Cowboy Hall of Fame (twice), the Golden Spur Award and Saddleman Award of Western Writers of America, and awards of merit from the Western Historical Association and the Association for State and Local History. In 1989 he received the Barbara McCombs–Lon Tinkle Award from the Texas Institute of Letters.

Dale L. Walker

Sons of Confederate Veterans. Organized in Richmond, Virginia, 1 July 1896, under the auspices of the United Confederate Veterans. The three departments are organized into divisions. From the beginning the Texas Division has had local camps in all the major cities of the state. The organization's chief project is the preservation and maintenance of Beauvoir, last home of President Jefferson Davis, located at Biloxi, Mississippi, and owned by the Mississippi Division. Membership is open to men who are lineal or collateral descendants of those who served honorably in the Confederate Army or Navy. The general headquarters has been located in the War Memorial Building, Jackson, Mississippi, since 1955. *Mildred Webb Bugg*

Sons of Hermann. The largest fraternal insurance benefit society headquartered in Texas; founded in San Antonio in 1861. Its home offices were in San Antonio in the mid-1990s, when its 161 lodges had a membership of 80,000. Until 1920 the Texas order was part the national Sons of Hermann, organized in New York City in 1840 and named for Hermann the Defender, an early German hero known also as Arminius. In 1861 two representatives of the national grand lodge came to San Antonio to organize the first Hermann Sons lodge in Texas. The Germans of San Antonio were receptive. In 1890 the Texas grand lodge was formed; it consisted of Harmonia Lodge of San Antonio and newly formed lodges in Austin, Taylor, Temple, Waco, La Grange, Brenham, and Houston. Within a year 92 more lodges were formed. In 1896 the first sister lodge, exclusively for women, was dedicated at Sherman. In 1920 the first mixed lodge for both men and women was established in San Antonio. Currently, the order has family lodges as well as single-sex lodges. In 1920 the Hermann Sons of Texas, which by then had more members than all of the lodges in the rest of the United States combined, broke away from the national order and became autonomous. Complete transition from German to English by the Texas order was begun early in the 1930s and completed by 1937. Originally all of the members were of German extraction, but by 1965 only about half were. By 1994 membership was open to all ethnic groups. Since 1916 the order has maintained a retirement home at Comfort, and since 1954 it has operated its own summer youth camps for junior members on its campgrounds there. Local lodges offer scholarship opportunities to the youth in their communities. *Fritz Schilo*

Sons of the Republic of Texas. Organized as Deaf Smith Lodge No. 1 on 11 April 1893 at Richmond by F. M. O. Fenn; S. J. Winston was elected president. Ten days later a state society was organized in Houston with W. A. Craddock as president. The society met with the Texas Veterans Association in Waco the following year and continued to meet in conjunction with that organization for several years before becoming inactive. In 1922 the society was reactivated in Houston by Odin M. Kendall, along with several members of the original group and other descendants of early Texans. Andrew Jackson Houston was elected president. Membership was 35 the first year. The objectives of the society have been to perpetuate the memory of the founders of Texas, to encourage research, to promote the observance of Texas holidays, to preserve and mark historical sites, and to foster knowledge of the state. With the help of Jesse H. Jones, the society was influential in securing funds for the San Jacinto Monument. It helped found the San Jacinto Museum of History and promoted the observance of San Jacinto Day. Since 1951 the Sons have annually given the $1,000 Summerfield G. Roberts Award to the author of the outstanding work published on early Texas during the year. The society also awards three annual scholarships to high school seniors in an essay-writing contest. Since 1953 the organization has published *The Texian*, a periodical containing news of the society and historical articles. The Sons established David G. Burnet Park in east Harris County and assisted in establishing New Kentucky Park in the western part of the county. They also contributed to the construction of the entrance gates at the San Jacinto Battleground. In 1957 a committee met with Governor Price Daniel and discussed plans for a state archives and library building; the group was influential in helping persuade the legislature to build the structure and to give statutory standing to the Texas State Historical Survey Committee (1953). Since 1970 the society has awarded the $2,500 Presidio La Bahía Award, established by the Kathryn Stoner O'Connor Foundation, for research on Spanish Texas. In that same year the organization began financing the Spanish Texas Microfilm Center at Presidio La Bahía. An honorary branch is the Knights of the Order of San Jacinto. In 1994 the society's active membership was 3,200, with headquarters in Dallas. The society offers junior membership to persons under 18 and posthumous membership for families wishing to enroll their ancestors. *Frank E. Tritico*

Soule University. An early Methodist institution in Chappell Hill, Washington County. It replaced Rutersville College, and William Halsey, president at Rutersville, became Soule's first president. The Male Department of another early Methodist school, Chappell Hill Male and Female Institute, became the nucleus for this new male university. The Texas Conference of the Methodist Church approved plans for a central university in

Soule University, Chappell Hill. Special Collections/Tower Library, Southwestern University, Georgetown, Texas. Soule's new stone building was completed in May 1861.

1854. Prominent residents on the first board of trustees, lay and clerical, included Robert Alexander, Homer Thrall, Gabriel Felder, and Jabez Giddings. Soule University had preparatory and collegiate departments. The preparatory division opened before the university received its charter from the Sixth Texas Legislature in 1856, the year college classes began. Masons supported the new institution. Soule was under the direction of the Texas Conference of the Methodist Church, South, which provided the major financial support, although the East Texas Conference participated in administrating and financing the institution between 1856 and 1860. The university was named for Bishop Joshua Soule, a Northern Methodist bishop who visited Texas. The seven academic departments included two professorships with endowments of $25,000 each. Felder sponsored a chair of ancient and modern languages. Jared Kirby endowed another for mathematics and natural philosophy. Classes were first held in the Chappell Hill Institute building. R. J. Swearingen donated 10 acres for the university to build in a different section of town. Soule's new three-story stone building, begun in September 1858, was completed in May 1861 at a cost of $40,000. In April 1861 the trustees endowed a new chair of natural sciences.

The Civil War was disastrous for Soule University, which had the best library, endowment fund, and faculty of any Texas college before the war. Ninety-five students enrolled in the first session, and 150 were enrolled by the outbreak of the Civil War. President Halsey returned to his home in the North in 1860, and the new president, George W. Carter, from Virginia, resigned to raise a Confederate regiment. Most Soule students enlisted in the Confederate Army before the university closed in 1861. During the war, the army used the university building as a hospital; the classrooms and library were badly damaged, and school equipment was destroyed or lost. Although Soule reopened in 1867, the worst yellow fever epidemic in the area's history killed many Chappell Hill residents and Soule students. The January 1869 session had just 26 preparatory students. Enrollment failed to recover as parents from other regions of Texas refused to send their children to an area plagued by recurring epidemics and yellow fever scares. President Francis Asbury Mood could not obtain sufficient support from the board of trustees or Chapell Hill residents to pay the university's $17,000 debt because the former patrons, the plantation owners of the area, were bankrupted by emancipation. By 1871 Mood persuaded the Texas Methodist Conference to open a school in Georgetown, outside the fever belt. Mood became first president of the new institution, later called Southwestern University. Soule continued operation until 1888 with the renewed financial support of the local community, student tuition, and intermittent aid from the Texas Conference. By 1873 the school was debt-free due to its creditors' generosity. In 1878 Soule University was renamed Soule College. The Chapell Hill area itself failed to recover economically from the Civil War, and the Anglo-American Methodist residents in the region were largely replaced by non-Methodist European immigrants. Enrollment at Soule dropped from 66 in 1886 to 29 in 1887. Chappell Hill Female College used Soule's building until that institution closed. The building was eventually demolished after use as a public school. A Soule University medical department in Galveston, authorized by the trustees in 1859, enrolled 143 students in classes between 1865 and 1871, when its successor, Galveston Medical College and Hospital, was organized due to the incapacity of Soule to support the medical program any longer. The medical branch graduated 72.   *Carole E. Christian*

Southern Mercury. A leading reform newspaper that grew out of the Dallas *Mercury*, founded in 1882. In 1886 it became associated with the Farmers' Alliance and took the name *Southern Mercury*. The weekly paper, edited consecutively by J. P. Burnett, L. S. Thayer, and Samuel H. Dixon, grew with the alliance. In 1887 the publisher reported a circulation of 5,460; in 1889, 30,000. Like the alliance in Texas, the *Southern Mercury* stayed officially nonpartisan, though it looked favorably on the reform wing of the Democratic party. In 1890–91, however, conflict in the Texas alliance over whether to support Democratic governor James S. Hogg or turn to third-party politics led to the replacement of editor Dixon, an opponent of Hogg, by Milton Park. Harry Tracy, a leading third-party Texas allianceman by mid-1891, had become publisher. Park remained the editor of the *Southern Mercury* until its demise. In 1891 the paper joined the National Reform Press Association, an organization of editors advocating the formation of a third party. By October 1892 the *Southern Mercury* fully supported the People's party. The *Mercury* carried a list of state officers, the places and times of stops for any statewide speakers or lecturers, reports of local county alliance meetings, and any state policy changes. The rest of the paper consisted largely of articles, letters, and editorials explaining various platform issues. Discussion of the subtreasury, a greenback monetary system, land reform, and government ownership of the railroads and telephone and telegraph systems dominated. Occasional items focused on children or women, offered advice about farming, and discussed government events from the alliance standpoint. The peak of the *Southern Mercury*'s influence came in 1891–96, when it was the most important reform publication in the Southwest and one of the most important in the country. Its circulation, after dropping from 32,000 in 1888 to 26,000 in 1892, rose to 40,000 in 1895.

After Tracy's Dallas *Texas Advance* failed, Tracy merged the *Advance* and the *Southern Mercury* in 1894, and thereafter the *Southern Mercury* was the official state paper of the Texas Farmers' Alliance and the Texas People's party, though it continued to be published by the alliance. An attempt to publish the paper daily in early 1896 failed. When the Populists declined in Texas, the *Southern Mercury* followed. Around Milton Park and the *Mercury* in 1896 formed a group that opposed any formal cooperation with the Democrats or Republicans. The paper continued to reflect Park's politics. In 1897 the Southern Mercury Publishing Company, organized by Park, took over publication from the Texas Farmers' Alliance, and in March 1899 the *Southern Mercury* ceased to be the official paper of the alliance and the Texas People's party. Although by 1900 Park considered himself a moderate socialist and reprinted in the *Southern Mercury* material from Julius Wayland's *Appeal to Reason*, he and the *Mercury* continued to support the national Populist tickets. By 1902 Park's efforts had led him and the *Mercury* to the Allied People's party, an effort to attract socialists to the populists. In 1905 Park combined the *Southern Mercury* with the *Farmers' Union Password*, the official paper of the Texas Farmers' Union, an organization resembling the earlier Farmers' Alliance and founded in Texas in 1902. The new combination paper reported a circulation of 21,200 in 1906 and 1907. In 1908 it apparently stopped publication, perhaps the victim of the steep decline in the membership of the Texas Farmers' Union between 1906 and 1908.   *Bruce Palmer*

Southern Messenger. For many years the only English-language Catholic newspaper in Texas; originated in 1890 as a parish bulletin published by Oblate historian C. J. Smith, pastor of St. Mary's Church in San Antonio. In January 1891, under the name *St. Mary's Review*, the monthly circular grew into a semimonthly publication that six months later became a weekly newspaper. In February 1892, J. C. Neraz, bishop of San Antonio, endorsed it as official organ of his diocese and changed its name to *San Antonio Messenger*. In April the printing plant burned and the bishop decided to cancel the publication, but in October operations resumed under the direction and with the capital of L. William Menger, son of the founder of the Menger Hotel. Menger expanded the newspaper, made it regional in scope, and on 4 March 1893 changed its name to *Southern Messenger*. He edited and published it until his death in 1919. Two sons succeeded him. The *Southern Messenger* was the first statewide Catholic newspaper in Texas. It served as official publication of all the dioceses until 1935, when the Diocese of Amarillo established its own newspaper. Eventually, several dioceses and parishes started publications to serve their particular needs. But the *Messenger* continued to be published as a well-respected Catholic newspaper, approved by a long list of bishops and adopted as an official organ by the Knights of Columbus and other prominent Catholic organizations. In 1941 the Archdiocese of San Antonio founded the *Alamo Register*, which became in a few years the largest Catholic newspaper in the Southwest. In 1957 the Menger family sold the *Southern Messenger* to Robert E. Lucey, archbishop of San Antonio. The result was the merger of the two best-known names in Texas Catholic journalism into the *Alamo Messenger*, which began publication on August 4, 1957.

For the historian, the *Southern Messenger* is an important depository of news, information, and ideas, which covers seven crucial decades of recurrent debates about religious freedom and patriotism. The *Messenger* set out early to prove that no conflict existed between Catholicism and American citizenship. In 1891

Trailerville. DeGolyer Library, Southern Methodist University, Dallas, Texas, University Archives, SMU 91.12. After World War II, returning soldiers enrolling under the new GI Bill flooded the SMU campus. The area east of Bishop Boulevard, known as Trailerville, was filled with trailers housing new students.

the paper published in installments "A Catechism of the History of the United States," in which the patriotism of American Catholics, both in peace and at war, was emphasized. The newspaper also took a nativist position against the San Antonio Polish Catholic community, which had requested a Polish bishop. In other matters, the paper supported traditional Catholic causes: Irish home rule abroad, for example, and the attempt to secure public support for parochial schools at home. Although not polemic in nature, the *Review* did engage in controversies with anti-Catholic factions in San Antonio such as the Washington League, which opposed nuns as public-school teachers. The *San Antonio Messenger* had editorial confrontations with the American Protective Association, an organization rumored at the time to be responsible for the burning of the newspaper in 1892. L. William Menger was politically loyal to the United States and spiritually loyal to the Catholic Church. At the same time, as editor, he increased the *Messenger's* polemic tone in defense of Catholics against the relentless accusations of the APA. He did not hesitate to borrow arguments from national and local newspapers—including the *Iconoclast*—although the *Messenger* warned its subscribers against indiscriminately reading William C. Brann's publication. Menger favored neutrality in the Cuban conflict up to 1898, but once the United States declared war on Catholic Spain, the *Messenger* firmly supported the American cause and summoned Catholics to show their patriotism. This pattern was later repeated in both world wars. Between the wars the *Messenger* was outspoken in condemnation of the rise of Hitlerism; in this it echoed the voice of the church in Germany and elsewhere. The *Messenger* had to confront attacks from the Ku Klux Klan and other anti-Catholic organizations in the early decades of the twentieth century. During Al Smith's unsuccessful presidential campaign, the paper published in 43 installments a solid historical study on "The Catholic Question in the United States." While a long-enduring anticlerical government in Mexico drove many Mexican priests to San Antonio, Father Eugene Sugranes interviewed many of them there and published their first-hand accounts in the *Southern Messenger* (1917–41). The articles were quoted around the nation, and many prominent people sought Father Sugranes's opinion on the Mexican situation. The ultimate acceptance of Catholics by most of the Texas population in the following decades was partly made possible by the *Southern Messenger*.   *Aníbal A. González*

Southern Methodist University. In University Park, an incorporated residential district surrounded by Dallas. SMU, though related to the Methodist Church, is independent of state support and nonsectarian. The school was the project of the Texas Educational Commission, made up of representatives of the five annual conferences of the Methodist Episcopal Church, South, in Texas (1911). In 1914 the General Conference of the church made the university the connectional institution for all Methodist conferences west of the Mississippi. In 1939, with the unification of the Methodist Church, the ownership of the university was vested in the South Central Jurisdictional Conference of the Methodist Church, comprising the states of Nebraska, Kansas, Missouri, Arkansas, Louisiana, Oklahoma, New Mexico, and Texas. SMU opened in 1915 with an enrollment of 706 in two buildings on a bare hillside. The university had a staff of 195 in 1948. In the fall of 1974 the enrollment was 10,079, and the faculty numbered over 700. Buildings constructed after World War II followed the original modern Georgian style. The Owens Fine Arts Center, a complex consisting of 10 major facilities for the teaching and presentation of the arts, included art museums, theaters, and an auditorium. The university is divided into the Dedman College of Humanities and Sciences, the Meadows School of the Arts, the Edwin L. Cox School of Business, the School of Engineering and Applied Science, the School of Law, the Perkins School of Theology, and the School of Continuing Education. SMU offers 70 undergraduate degree programs and many master's and doctoral programs. The university maintains seven libraries. The Southern Methodist University Press, formerly the University Press of Dallas, was established in 1937 as the university's publishing division. A member of the Association of American Presses since 1945, the press maintains more than 100 books on its current in-print list on a broad range of topics, with emphasis on the Southwest region and Americana. The press issues two magazines: *Southwest Review* and the *Journal* of the Graduate Research Center, the latter incorporating and continuing *Field and Laboratory*, established in 1932.   *P. C. Knickerbocker*

Southwest Airlines. Headquartered in Dallas. In 1964 Rollin King acquired a small South Texas air-taxi service, Wild Goose Flying Service, and reincorporated it as Southwest Airlines. In 1967 King and Herb Kelleher planned a new venture to serve the three largest cities in Texas, offering low fares, convenient schedules, and a "no-frills" approach that was completely contrary to the standards of the established airlines. Service to Dallas, Houston, and San Antonio was already provided by Braniff Airways and Trans-Texas Airways (later Texas International Airlines), but usually as a leg of longer, interstate flights. After remarkably successful fund-raising, Air Southwest incorporated in 1967. Kelleher got state approval from the Texas Aeronautics Commission to serve Dallas, Houston, and San Antonio. The application was a state, not a federal, matter because Southwest was not proposing to fly out of state. But in February 1968 Braniff, Trans-Texas, and Continental Airlines obtained a restraining order from the Travis County District Court. Thus began a three-year legal battle that wound up in the Supreme Court, which upheld Southwest's right to fly in Texas (7 December 1970). Many consider this decision the beginning of deregulation in the airline industry. In 1971, Air Southwest became Southwest Airlines. King and Kelleher hired Marion Lamar Muse, the former president of Detroit-based Universal Airlines, to run Southwest, which had $148 in the bank and past-due bills for more than $133,000. But, using their own resources and further credit, in just 120 days the men hired and trained pilots, flight attendants, mechanics, and other personnel; completed negotiations for space at three airports; hired Bloom Advertising to design an initial campaign; and completed the purchase of three Boeing 737-200 aircraft. King, Kelleher, and Muse were able to purchase the planes at 90 percent financing, a move previously unheard of in the industry. Further skirmishes with Braniff and Texas International almost upset the scheduled opening, but on 18 June 1971 a Southwest Airlines plane flown by Capt. Emilio Salazar began service out of Love Field.

Southwest was only five months old when Muse came out with an unbelievable fare offer—$10 on the last flight of the week from Houston to Dallas. The plane was needed back in Dallas anyway for weekend servicing and the crew had been flying it back empty every week for five months. Within two weeks, the flight was carrying a full load. Muse then slashed fares on the last flight of each day in each direction to $10. By the next fall, Muse had raised regular fares from $20 to $26 and the weekend and night fare to $13. The two-tier fare system, one of the most important innovations in airline marketing history, had been born. Braniff continued to fight back by lowering its Dallas–Houston fare to just $13. In an action that became characteristic of Southwest, Muse responded with newspaper advertisements claiming, "Nobody's going to shoot Southwest Airlines out of the sky for a lousy $13," offering customers their choice of either a $13 fare or a full-fare ticket plus a fifth of premium liquor. The bottles of liquor did not cost $13, but a businessman could put the $26 fare on his expense report and take the liquor home free. Once again, a Braniff tactic backfired. With 80 percent of its customer base choosing to pay full fare, Southwest won this 1972 fare war and became the largest distributor in Texas of Chivas, Crown Royal, and Smirnoff. Braniff and Texas International were later indicted and pled nolo contendere to antitrust charges in connection with their activities involving Southwest. For further publicity, Muse clad stewardesses in hot pants and advertised the company as the "LUV" airline, a pun on its home base at Love Field. Southwest turned a profit in 1973 and has remained profitable for every year since.

Nevertheless, one of the line's longest court battles began in 1972, when the new Dallas–Fort Worth airport and the cities of Dallas and Fort Worth sued Southwest in an attempt to force the carrier to move with other airlines to the new airport. The other airlines were bound to the move by contracts. Southwest wasn't operating when the deal for the new airport was signed, however, and intended to remain at Love Field, which is considerably closer to downtown Dallas than DFW. Two years later, Southwest won the privilege to remain at Love Field as long as the field was a commercial airport. In April 1974 the Dallas City Council attempted to close Love Field to commercial traffic, but once again court rulings enabled the airport to survive. Still, the bigger airlines were not through with Southwest. In 1978, in an attempt to curb Southwest's growth, the major airlines at DFW sought support from Congress to bar flights from Love Field to anywhere outside of Texas. Finally, in 1979 a compromise known as the Wright Amendment (named after majority leader Jim Wright, D–Fort Worth) was ratified. This measure limited service from Love Field to Texas and the four bordering states. The Wright Amendment hampered Southwest's growth from Dallas Love Field, but it did not prevent the carrier from succeeding. Southwest simply grew in other directions. Meanwhile, its low fares continued to attract customers and force other airlines to discount their charges. King resigned as an officer of the company in 1976, and Kelleher eventually became chairman, president, and CEO (23 February 1982).

With the Airline Deregulation Act of 1978, which permitted competition on routes across the country that were previously virtual monopolies, Southwest again expanded. By the end of 1981 it had added service to Amarillo, New Orleans, Albuquerque, Oklahoma City, Tulsa, and 13 other cities. In 1982 it added service to San Diego, Kansas City, Las Vegas, and Phoenix—its first service to cities outside of Texas and the surrounding states. In compliance with the terms of the Wright Amendment, direct service to these cities was not available from Dallas Love Field. Since 1982 the airline has grown substantially, generally by taking advantage of opportunities in markets that are overpriced and underserved. By the late 1980s, Southwest had become the number-one airline in California, and in 1989 it officially became a "major" airline, with annual revenues exceeding $1 billion. With the inauguration of service to Baltimore in 1993, Southwest served both coasts for the first time. The acquisition of Salt Lake City–based Morris Air at the end of 1993 facilitated Southwest's expansion into new cities in the West and Northwest. In the late 1980s and early 1990s, Southwest lobbied against a proposed high-speed train between Dallas, Houston, and San Antonio, since studies showed that the train would require government subsidies of close to $100 per passenger. Since all of Southwest's fares between those cities were well below $100, the company claimed that with the same subsidy it could fly everyone in those markets for nothing. Although a contract to build the train was awarded to Texas TGV, the company was unable to raise even a fraction of the start-up funds it required, and it ultimately defaulted on its contract. Southwest has maintained a high level of public recognition through innovative advertising and public relations. Kelleher has painted Southwest planes to resemble the Texas and Arizona state flags and Shamu, the killer whale, to promote the airline's association with those states and with Sea World in San Antonio. The company also staged a famous arm-wrestling contest between Kelleher and the president of Stevens Aviation, Incorporated, of Greenville, South Carolina, to settle a dispute over rights to the advertising slogan "Just Plane Smart." Kelleher lost, but Stevens allowed Southwest to share the slogan anyway. By the early 1990s, Southwest had grown to be the nation's seventh-largest airline, with over 35 million customers a year, annual revenues exceeding $2 billion, and more than 15,000 employees in a largely unionized workforce. Although it owned under 3 percent of the nation's airline market, more than two-thirds of passengers flying in Texas did so on Southwest. In 1992 and 1993 Southwest received the industry's "Triple Crown" for best on-time performance, least lost baggage, and fewest customer complaints—thus accomplishing for two years straight something no other airline has ever done, even for a single month. Southwest is a major supporter of the Ronald McDonald Houses, which provide a home-away-from-home for families of critically ill children who are undergoing treatment at nearby medical facilities. The Southwest annual "Home for the Holidays" program, which received the President's Award for Private Sector Initiatives for 1986 and 1987, has enabled thousands of poor senior citizens to visit friends and relatives during the Christmas season at no charge. *Keli Flynn*

Southwestern Adventist College. In Keene; owned and operated by the Southwestern Union Conference of Seventh-day Adventists. It was established in 1894 as Keene Industrial Academy and chartered by the Adventist Church to train religious workers. During its initial year the academy had 56 students and 2 instructors. It operated a broom factory, a blacksmith shop, a carpentry shop, a tent factory, a bakery, and a printing office, businesses that enabled students to earn a part of their expenses and to learn a trade. The school became a 12-year academy in 1896 and added two additional years of study to its curriculum in 1916, when it was renamed Southwestern Junior College. It maintained primary, secondary, and collegiate departments and offered courses at the junior college level in

such fields as industrial arts. Between 1916 and 1963 the school gradually accumulated a 150-acre campus. In 1963 it was renamed Southwestern Union College. Since 1980 the school has been a private, four-year institution named Southwestern Adventist College. In the early 1990s it offered undergraduate degrees in a variety of fields and one graduate degree, M.A. in elementary education. The college differs from most others in the maintenance of its original emphasis upon work experience for its students. In addition to campus jobs in academic, administrative, and student service areas, the college's business conglomerate, Southwestern Diversified Industries, offers employment in its cabinet shop, bakery, car wash, motel, and graphics business. *Brian Hart*

Southwestern Baptist Theological Seminary. Grew out of the Baylor University theological department, which was established in 1901 with Benajah H. Carroll as dean. Church historian Albert H. Newman was induced to leave McMaster University in Toronto to join Carroll and Robert N. Barrett to staff the department. By 1905 the department had become Baylor Theological Seminary. Three years later the seminary separated from Baylor University and with a new name was chartered by the state. In 1910 Southwestern was moved from Waco to Fort Worth. Although the seminary was affiliated with the Baptist General Convention of Texas, which named a majority of the trustees, 10 other state Baptist bodies also cooperated in providing trustees and financial support. By 1926 the ownership of the school was transferred from the Texas Convention to the Southern Baptist Convention. It made the convention's articles of faith, "the Baptist Faith and Message," its own. These articles, revised in 1963, continue to serve as the seminary's confessional statement. From its beginning the seminary's purpose has been to prepare men and women for vocational Christian ministry. Through the years the student body has become increasingly international and interdenominational. In 1988, 43 countries and 41 denominations were represented in the multiracial student body. Classes are taught on the main campus and in off-campus centers in Dallas, Houston, Lubbock, San Antonio, and Shawnee, Oklahoma. By the close of 1988 the seminary had graduated 27,230. Southwestern has three schools—theology, religious education, and church music—each with its own faculty and degree programs. Although a few older undergraduates are admitted, the seminary is basically a graduate school. It offers a variety of master's and doctor's degrees in all three schools. It is accredited by the American Association of Theological Schools and the Southern Association of Colleges and Schools. The School of Church Music is also accredited by the National and the Texas Associations of Music Schools. Major funding for the seminary's annual budget is derived from the Cooperative Program of the Southern Baptist Convention, with additional income from an endowment. Due to the level of financing of seminary education by the convention, students do not pay tuition but only a nominal matriculation fee each semester. *W. R. Estep*

Southwestern Historical Quarterly. A publication of the Texas State Historical Association; introduced as the *Quarterly of the Texas State Historical Association* in July 1897. George P. Garrison, the first editor, served until his death on 3 July 1910. Shortly thereafter Eugene C. Barker became editor. Volume 16 appeared under the title *Southwestern Historical Quarterly*. With Volume 40 in 1937, professors Charles Hackett, Rudolph Biesele, and Walter P. Webb became editors, with Hackett as managing editor. With Volume 43 (1939–40) Webb became editor, and with Volume 46 (1942–43) H. Bailey Carroll joined him as managing editor. Webb resigned in 1946, and Volume 50 (1946–47) appeared under the editorship of Carroll, who served as editor from 1946 to 1966 and was succeeded by Joe B. Frantz at the association's seventieth annual meeting in 1966. L. Tuffly Ellis became editor in 1977, James Pohl in 1985, and Ron Tyler in 1986. A cumulative index of volumes 1 through 40 (July 1897–April 1937) was published in 1950. A cumulative index of volumes 41 through 60 (July 1937–April 1957) was published in 1960. The first 54 volumes of the *Quarterly* were reprinted in 1968. Other indexes for volumes 60 through 80 were published in 1980 and 1984. The *Quarterly* is distributed primarily to TSHA membership. In the main it has published articles dealing with Texas history. The journal has been a major source for most of the textbook accounts of Texas and Southwest history.

Southwestern University. In Georgetown; founded in April 1870 as Texas University by the five Methodist Episcopal Conferences of Texas, through a merger of four earlier "root colleges"—Rutersville College, Wesleyan College, McKenzie College, and Soule University. The institution was renamed Southwestern University under a charter of 1875. Its formation and location resulted largely from the intensive work of Francis A. Mood, who was the first "regent" (president) of the university after its opening in Georgetown in October 1873. A branch for women was established later. In its first decades Southwestern University played a central role in Methodist higher education and accreditation in Texas and initiated expansions, which included the first medical school in Texas, established in Dallas in 1903, and a School of Fine Arts. Three of the first five Rhodes Scholars from Texas were Southwestern University graduates. After the Methodist Church founded Southern Methodist University in Dallas in 1911, Southwestern redefined its role as that of a small liberal arts university. It survived with difficulty the period of social and economic uncertainties of World War I and the Great Depression. In the 1940s financial revival began, along with academic and organizational improvements and the start of a substantial building program. Graduate work was discontinued, and the university was organized into the Humanities Division, Natural Sciences Division, Social Sciences Division, and School of Fine Arts. Enrollment more than doubled during World War II with a Navy V-12 program, but dropped to fewer than 400 in 1952; it increased steadily to about 1,200 by 1993. Personnel increased from 45 faculty and 19 staff in 1952 to 136 faculty and 151 staff in 1993. Recent major building additions have included a chapel, Science Hall, Religious Activities Center, Fine Arts Center, Student Union, University Commons, and major extensions of the library.

Edwin M. Lansford, Jr.

Southwest Review. A quarterly journal of literature, the arts, and public affairs, published at Southern Methodist University; a continuation of *Texas Review*, which was first published in 1915 at the University of Texas by Stark Young and edited for more than eight years by Robert Adger Law of the university faculty. In 1924 the magazine, renamed *Southwest Review*, was transferred to

SMU by Jay Hubbell and George Bond, who served as joint editors until 1927. For the next 15 years the central figure of the editorial board was John H. McGinnis, professor of English at Southern Methodist University, who was assisted by younger colleagues and advanced students including Henry Nash Smith, Lon Tinkle, and others. During much of this time Herbert P. Gambrell of the Southern Methodist University history department served as business manager. From 1932 to 1935 Louisiana State University assumed joint responsibility with Southern Methodist University for the *Southwest Review*. This arrangement came to an end when LSU established the *Southern Review*. Whereas the *Texas Review* had generally followed a policy of cosmopolitanism, the *Southwest Review* emphasized the region. Texas writers who contributed significantly to the magazine include Sam Acheson, John A. Lomax, Mody Boatright, J. Frank Dobie, and Karle Wilson Baker. Other important southwestern contributors have been Mary Austin and Paul Horgan of New Mexico, and Stanley Vestal of Oklahoma. The *Review* published the essays of Albert Guérard between 1916 and 1959; other early contributors included Maxim Gorky, Cleanth Brooks, and Robert Penn Warren. The journal consistently gave attention to southwestern painting in articles by Jerry Bywaters, Alexandre Hogue, and others; and to regional architecture during the 1930s in articles by David Reichard Williams, O'Neil Ford, and A. B. Swank. Professor Samuel Wood Geiser of SMU wrote a series of 12 biographical essays on pioneer Texas scientists, which appeared in the magazine from 1929 to 1937 and became *Naturalists of the Frontier* (1938). The magazine was redesigned in 1985. Willard Spiegelman, the editor, and Betsey McDougall, the managing editor, announced a new focus on literary and cultural issues of more universal appeal. Recent contributors have included Quentin Bell, Amy Clampitt, Margaret Drabble, Natalia Ginzburg, James Merrill, Iris Murdoch, Howard Nemerov, and Edmund White. In the mid-1990s the *Review* was supported by grants from the Texas Commission on the Arts and the National Endowment for the Arts; it had a circulation of 1,500.

Henry Nash Smith and Willard Spiegelman

Southwest Texas State University. Established as Southwest Texas Normal School by an act of 1899. San Marcos citizens donated 11 acres on an elevation known as Chautauqua Hill, and in 1901 the legislature appropriated $25,000 for construction of a building. The school opened in 1903 with Thomas G. Harris as principal, a faculty of 17, and an enrollment of 303. In 1912 the college entered into an agreement with the San Marcos school board to use two local teachers as demonstration teachers. This arrangement was discontinued in 1914, at which time the college opened its own practice school. In 1918 the institution became a senior college, Southwest Texas State Normal College. In 1923 the name was changed to Southwest Texas State Teachers College. In 1933 arrangements were completed for the city school to become the laboratory school of the college. This unusual plan, one of the few of its kind in American colleges, continued for many years. By 1950 the campus had grown to 65 acres, the faculty to 105, and enrollment to 2,000. Enrollment was 4,461 in 1964, 6,580 in 1967, 12,894 in 1974, and 23,102 in 1991. Curriculum changes included emphasis on speech and hearing therapy courses and on the training of teachers for the orthopedically handicapped. Certification requirements met the standards of the Texas Education Agency. The legislature changed the school's name to Southwest Texas State College in 1959 and to Southwest Texas State University in 1969. During the 1960s the school gained national attention as Lyndon Johnson's alma mater. In 1975 the Sixty-fourth Legislature established the Texas State University System, to which SWTSU belongs. In 1993 the university acquired Aquarena Springs, an amusement park and archeological site. In 1995 SWTSU was organized into schools of Applied Arts and Technology, Business, Education, Fine Arts and Communication, Health Professions, Liberal Arts, Science, and the Graduate School.

Spanish Archives of Laredo. Informally called the Laredo Archives; a collection spanning from 1749 to 1872 and consisting of 3,452 handwritten official documents totaling 13,343 pages. Although the first document is dated 1749, the bulk of the collection begins in 1768, with the Spanish crown's granting of a charter for Laredo. The Spanish papers in the archives contain records of boundary surveys; land allotments; Indian raids; church, school, and social development; royal decrees and edicts; local laws and ordinances; civil and criminal litigation; census, tax, and trade statistics; and wills and estate settlements. This portion of the collection extends through the end of Mexican Texas in 1846, signaled by a document signed by Mirabeau B. Lamar, who commanded the American forces occupying Laredo. The remainder of the collection covers the period between 1846 and 1872 and consists of a few documents, written mostly in English, relating to the affairs of the city and county. For many years the collection was stored in the basement of the old county courthouse in Laredo. The archives were neglected and began to deteriorate from exposure to fire, flooding, and dampness. In 1934 an order was given to destroy the papers, but Sebron S. Wilcox, the newly appointed court reporter for the Forty-ninth District, working with the assistance of Father Florencio Andrés, a priest of the Oblates of Mary Immaculate who was serving at San Agustín Church of Laredo, rescued the archives and began restoring them. Both men worked for many years, without seeking remuneration, drying, sorting, cleaning, and identifying the documents. In 1936 the WPA undertook transcription of the Spanish documents. In 1940 the project was placed under the supervision of the Texas Historical Records Survey. It was continued by the Statewide Records Project until 1942, when the project was ended. Four copies of the transcriptions, totaling 38 volumes of typescript, were completed and filed in the National Archives in Washington, the Barker Texas History Center in Austin, the Texas State Library, and the Webb County Courthouse. Before his death (12 May 1959), Wilcox had expressed a desire that the collection be donated to a facility where it would be properly preserved and made accessible to the public. His family donated the archives to St. Mary's University, San Antonio, in 1960. In 1968 the papers were housed in a room designed for the preservation of documents. The university hired a professional archivist, Carmen Perry, who supervised preparations for a new microfilming that occurred in 1973. Legal conflict occurred after Wilcox's heirs demanded remuneration for the archives. Eventually, in December 1979, an appeals court upheld a previous decision that St. Mary's University had lawfully acquired its title to the Laredo Archives, but that the personal papers of Sebron Wilcox were to be returned to his family.

Anita C. Saxine

Spanish Missions. The Spanish mission was a frontier institution that sought to incorporate indigenous people into the Spanish colonial empire, its Catholic religion, and certain aspects of its Hispanic culture through the formal establishment or recognition of sedentary Indian communities entrusted to the tutelage of missionaries under the protection and control of the Spanish state. This joint institution of indigenous communities and the Spanish church and state was developed in response to the often very detrimental results of leaving the Hispanic control of relations with Indians on the expanding frontier to overly enterprising civilians and soldiers. This had resulted too often in the abuse and even enslavement of the Indians and a heightening of antagonism. To the degree that the mission effort succeeded, it furthered the Spanish goals of political, economic, and religious expansion in America in competition with other European-origin nations. Spanish colonial authorities enjoyed the *patronato real* (royal patronage) over ecclesiastical affairs, granted to the Spanish crown by the pope. As patrons the state authorities made the final determination as to where and when missions would be founded or closed, what administrative policies would be observed, who could be missionaries, how many missionaries could be assigned to each mission, and how many soldiers if any would be stationed at a mission. In turn, the state paid for the missionaries' overseas travel, the founding costs of a mission, and the missionaries' annual salary. The state also usually provided military protection and enforcement.

Franciscans from several of their provinces and missionary colleges in New Spain established all the missions in Texas. The ideal of the missionaries themselves, supported by royal decrees, was to establish autonomous Christian towns with communal property, labor, worship, political life, and social relations all supervised by the missionaries and insulated from the possible negative influences of other Indian groups and Spaniards themselves. Daily life was to follow a highly organized routine of prayer, work, training, meals, and relaxation, punctuated by frequent religious holidays and celebrations. In this closely supervised setting the Indians were expected to mature in Christianity and Spanish political and economic practices until they would no longer require special mission status. Then their communities could be incorporated as such into ordinary colonial society, albeit with all its racial and class distinctions. This transition from mission status to ordinary Spanish society, when it occurred in an official manner, was called "secularization." In this official transaction, the mission's communal properties were privatized, the direction of civil life became a purely secular affair, and the direction of church life was transferred from the missionary religious orders to the Catholic diocesan church. Although colonial law specified no precise time for this transition to take effect, increasing pressure for the secularization of most missions developed in the last decades of the eighteenth century.

Colonial authorities and Franciscan missionaries attempted to introduce the mission system into widely scattered areas of Texas between 1682 and 1793, with greatly varying results. In all, 26 missions were maintained for different lengths of time within the future boundaries of the state. To this number should be added San Miguel de los Adaes (the easternmost colonial Texas outpost, at a site now in Louisiana) and those missionary centers established in Mexico whose influence extended into Texas. Although most of the missions fell short of their goal, several had relative success, and all played a key role in establishing the European and mixed-race foundations of Texas. In general the missionaries sought to eradicate among missionized natives all appearances of indigenous religion and culture judged to be incompatible with or inferior to Christian beliefs and practices. However, some of the more experienced friars learned to tolerate if not encourage certain group practices originally associated with native religion, such as the *matachines* dances or even *mitotes* (native celebrations with dancing and possibly peyote), when they judged them to be relatively free of elements inadmissible in Christianity. Although the missionary strategy was to maintain as strict a vigilance as possible over the life of the missionized natives, most Indian groups in Texas were seminomadic and did not intend to adopt a year-round fixed sedentary existence, even if they voluntarily entered a mission for a time. This was especially evident when the customary seasons for food-gathering, hunting, fishing, trading, or fighting arrived. Furthermore, few Indians could have welcomed the strong regimentation of mission life, almost along monastic lines, favored by the missionaries. The effort to develop permanent indigenous mission communities was also severely hampered by the impact of periodic European-transmitted epidemics on Indian groups, which usually had slow rates of natural increase. Many mission communities were maintained only by constant new recruitment, with missionaries ranging farther and farther afield as local populations declined.

In such circumstances, the Franciscans needed a few soldiers to maintain the mission system of continued residence and strict discipline, especially among newer recruits. Soldiers were either stationed at the mission or sent out to help bring back individuals or entire groups that left. The Spanish colonization of Texas did not involve outright military conquest as a general rule, nor were people forced into entering missions. But once they entered, coercion was used when judged appropriate. Sometimes officials refused to provide such military help. In later decades Spanish civilians were at times hired as work supervisors, especially when military guards were no longer made available. On the other hand, at more solidly established mission communities such as San José y San Miguel de Aguayo (now in San Antonio), Indians themselves served as mission guards. At San José and elsewhere were Indians who preferred the benefits of permanent settlement in a mission community. A related factor in the occasional abandonment of missions by their Indian residents was the inability of the Spaniards at times to guarantee protection from raids by Apaches and subsequently Comanches in the later 1700s. Military protection from other Indians was one of the principal attractions of the missions to many Indians. This protection was essential to any foundation in such a vast territory as Texas, which was inhabited by several powerful and often belligerent tribes. And yet throughout most of the century the colonial government sought to economize by reducing its military presence in Texas. It was argued, and not without reason, that greatly increased Hispanic settlement would be a more effective and economical way of asserting control over the territory. But increased settlement was never effectively promoted except along the lower Rio Grande and in the El Paso area. Nowhere in Texas were the small and scattered settlements and missions free from attack. In the stronger mission towns Indians served very effectively as Spanish allies in the defense of their mutual home territory.

The Franciscan mission ideal of an insulated and highly controlled indigenous town was also challenged by the necessary interchange that occurred with Hispanics at adjacent military posts or civil settlements and ranches. In the frontier society and economy, limited resources—of land, labor, produce, artisans, armed defenders—were either shared or disputed among these various parties, and the indigenous people were very much a part of the total social reality. In times of common adversity or external threat, all worked together for the common good. At other times disputes over resources or rights would flare up. However, the challenges of constructing a viable community on a dangerous frontier would usually encourage gradual accommodation. The Franciscans themselves were often responsible, especially in the earlier decades, not only for the supervision of the mission community but also for the spiritual care of the local Spanish. Furthermore, the Spanish would often attend Mass at a nearby mission even if they had a separate church and perhaps even a separate pastor for themselves. In the initial founding decades the missions often held the economic advantage on the local scene, where they sometimes held extensive grants of choice land and a controlled labor supply, plus good administrators. If the mission prospered materially, its surplus helped supply the military establishments. In later decades, while the civilian population increased through birth, immigration, and the retirement of local soldier–settlers into civilian life, the Indian mission population was often decreasing. In some places the civilians found their community expansion hemmed in by the mission lands, at the same time that they were being recruited to help keep the mission economies productive. These latter circumstances increased local Hispanic pressure for secularization of the mission properties.

The Franciscans came closest to establishing their ideal system among the hundreds of Indian groups generally known as Coahuiltecans, who lived in the semiarid southern plains of what is now Texas. These hundreds of small nonallied groups of seminomads, some of which were not in fact Coahuiltecan, had a subsistence economy of hunting and gathering and were weaker militarily than both the Spanish and the encroaching predatory Indians. The missions promised them military protection and a regular, more ample food supply. In some cases the mission also provided protection from exploitation by Spanish soldiers and civilians. On the other hand, because of their seminomadic inclinations, their slow rate of natural increase, epidemics, inadequate military protection, and alternatives offered by neighboring Spaniards, mission towns were maintained only by continual recruitment to counteract steady population decline.

From 1718 through 1731 five missions that drew their members from mostly weaker groups were established near the head of the San Antonio River. The first was San Antonio de Valero, which dated from the origins of the settlement. It was followed by San José y San Miguel de Aguayo, Nuestra Señora de la Purísima Concepción, San Juan Capistrano, and San Francisco de la Espada. In varying degrees, these foundations developed as true missionary-directed indigenous towns, whose material success was evident in their churches, dwellings, granaries, workshops, irrigated fields, ranches and livestock, and regulated social and religious life. The San Antonio settlement comprised the missions, San Antonio de Béxar Presidio, and the town of San Fernando de Béxar. The area was settled enough that the missions had protection and resources to develop their own stability within a gradually coalescing community. However, the immediate proximity of the town and presidio obliged the Franciscans to engage in a losing battle to maintain strict control over the missionized Indians' relations with their neighbors. By the later 1700s the permanent Indian residents of the San Antonio missions were speaking Spanish, living as devoted Catholics, and even intermarrying with the local Hispanics. Other Indians, both local and from elsewhere, had become part of the town itself.

Two smaller Hispanic settlement complexes in the areas of present-day South and Southwest Texas also recruited among generally weaker Indian groups. The first of these began along what is now the Mexican side of the middle Rio Grande in 1700–02, when the missions of San Juan Bautista and San Bernardo were founded, together with a military post. The second, which became colloquially known as La Bahía, had a frustrating beginning near the Gulf Coast in 1722, when the mission of Nuestra Señora del Espíritu Santo de Zúñiga and an accompanying fort were founded. The La Bahía effort continued to struggle economically during its first decade (1726–36) at a new location on the lower Guadalupe River. Until adequate agriculture was finally established, the shortage of food obliged the missionaries to allow the Indians to absent themselves for their customary foraging for the greater part of the year. The La Bahía complex was finally located permanently on the lower San Antonio River in 1749. A few years later Nuestra Señora del Rosario Mission was founded across the river, primarily for Karankawas. Although the Indian towns at San Juan Bautista and La Bahía had mission structures, economies, and regimes similar to those at San Antonio, they achieved less stability and assimilation. With the exception of Rosario Mission, they had several decades of material prosperity and actually endured, although in a greatly weakened condition, past the Mexican War of Independence, which ended in 1821. But they were always confronted with episodes of temporary or permanent abandonment by some or all of the Indians for whom they were established. These two mission efforts were described in the 1790s as never having succeeded in attracting the Indians to true Christian conversion and loyalty to the Spanish state. As in other similar cases, the Indians were often described as unwilling to work and given to drunkenness and stealing. These Spanish assessments clearly indicated resistance to assimilation on the part of these groups.

Two other midcentury attempts to expand Spanish presence into Central and Southeast Texas through similar mission–fort establishments were also directed mostly to the less powerful Indian groups. But the effort at the San Xavier Missions on the San Gabriel River—San Francisco Xavier de Horcasitas, San Ildefonso, and Nuestra Señora de la Candelaria—lasted only from 1746 to 1755. This mission attempt fell victim to a multitude of obstacles: hostile Indians, the opposition of the governor, inadequate military protection and even serious misconduct on the part of the military, the seminomadic inclinations of the groups gathered there, and finally adverse weather. The few remaining missionized Indians and the friars moved temporarily to the San Marcos River for a year, and then to the Guadalupe River in 1756–58, after which this effort was finally abandoned.

Nuestra Señora de la Luz Mission, founded near the mouth of the Trinity River in 1756, was beset by unhealthful coastal conditions, official indecision, inadequate support in the early years, and, most decisively, shifting colonial frontier strategies that led to the mission's demise after only 15 years. Though never apparently resulting in a missionary-controlled village, Our Lady of Light seemed to have friendly relations with the local Orcoquiza Indians and perhaps even brought about several conversions among them. When military strategy dictated that the Spanish abandon the area, the Franciscans did so very reluctantly, while the natives pleaded for them to stay.

Most of the Indians along the lower Rio Grande were also weak, and some were already accustomed to doing seasonal migrant labor for the Spanish in nearby Nuevo León and Coahuila. But in this case colonial advisors in Mexico City successfully argued that new territory could be more effectively and economically occupied by promoting Spanish settlements with attached missions, rather than by the former strategy of founding missions and attaching forts to them. Accordingly, a major colonizing project that began there in 1749 put primary emphasis on towns, with only secondary attention to the mission efforts. Franciscans were recruited as missionaries and officially installed as such, and they were simultaneously appointed pastors to the settlements. It quickly became apparent to them that the Spanish civilians and officials as well as the Indians generally favored a loose attachment (*agregación*) of the natives to the Hispanic towns, which allowed for more flexible economic and social relations on both sides. This arrangement ran directly counter to the Franciscan ideal of the missionary-controlled, sedentary, and insulated indigenous community (*congregación*). Nevertheless, in some places, and most notably in Camargo (with jurisdiction extending into Texas), the Franciscans learned to adapt their mission approach to this situation. As a result several local Indian groups such as the Carrizos and Garzas became Christian and assimilated in varying degrees to Hispanic society.

The native groups of the southern Gulf Coast of Texas, known collectively as Karankawas, were somewhat stronger in their economy and defense than their immediate neighbors, and from the beginning they accepted only temporary or seasonal mission life. The original La Bahía Mission in 1722 in the Karankawas' own territory had foundered on this reality. And Rosario Mission, established for the Karankawas in 1754 at the final site of La Bahía, although materially sound, faced the same challenge. This and a strong nativist indigenous leader led to Rosario's temporary abandonment in 1781. When the mission was reactivated in late 1789, the Franciscan missionary effort was encountering weakened state support. Acknowledging this fact and by now quite familiar with the Karankawas' independent ways, the experienced friars accepted from the beginning a much looser social organization adapted to the Karankawas' seminomadic customs. These provided the two important things the mission could no longer guarantee: adequate food, and defense through mobility in the face of hostile raids. In 1793 Nuestra Señora del Refugio, the last mission founded in Texas, was established for the Karankawas. Refugio Mission employed the same flexible approach. In 1805 Rosario was closed, although not officially secularized, when the few remaining Karankawas associated with it were transferred to Refugio Mission as their base. This alternative missionary approach was credited with converting certain of the Karankawas to at least some Christian ways.

In other areas of what is now Texas the Franciscans were forced to accept even greater adaptations to their preferred mission system. Such was the case in the first mission villages to be established within the boundaries of future Texas, those far to the west in the El Paso district. In 1682 the Indian mission towns of Corpus Christi de la Isleta, Nuestra Señora de la Limpia Concepción de Socorro, and San Antonio de Senecú (this last site is now in Mexico) were founded by Tigua, Piro, Tompiro, and Tanoan people who had accompanied the Spanish in flight from the Pueblo Revolt in northern New Mexico. These Indians brought with them a highly developed cultural organization. Just as in their former towns to the north, the local Indian authorities, with the approval of Spanish officials, retained control over the economic and political life of their communities. In spite of the missionaries' protests, the friars were only granted spiritual jurisdiction. For a few decades there was also a mission effort among the Suma people gathered at Santa María de las Caldas in the El Paso district. Although this community was officially entrusted to secular pastors from 1730 to 1749, the Franciscans claimed that they actually had to do all the work since the pastors stayed in the distant town of El Paso itself. Living side by side with their Spanish neighbors in these new settlements, the Indian mission communities were open villages (like several other missions in what is now Texas), not the walled fortresses often portrayed as the mission model. By the nineteenth century the social interchange in these increasingly mixed Indian and Spanish towns resulted in complete Christianization and a great deal of cultural assimilation. Only the Tiguas of Ysleta retained a distinct ethnic identity, but even they were primarily Spanish-speaking and acculturated in many ways.

There were also several Indian groups at La Junta de los Ríos, the junction of the Rio Grande and the Río Conchos near the site of present Presidio in far West Texas. In the later 1600s members of these groups began engaging on their own terms in a continuing system of migrant labor and military alliance with Spaniards residing in the Conchos River district to the south in Mexico. Through these contacts many La Juntans gained a great deal of familiarity with Christianity. In 1683 some of them invited Franciscans to live among them. Among the chapels they built were those on the future Texas side of the Rio Grande in the village of San Cristóbal and that of the Tapalcolmes. Unaccompanied by military or Hispanic settlers, the missionaries had to flee several times in the next few years from regional revolts. When missions were reestablished in 1715, again without military guards or settlers, the friars found the people well-behaved but independent. Periodic attacks of Apaches and other tribes again forced the Franciscans and some natives to flee at times. The missionaries finally began to ask for a garrison and Spanish settlers, but to no avail. As a practical response some friars apparently adopted the practice of staying at La Junta only part of the year and spending the rest in the new town of Chihuahua. Through this unique missionary approach, adapted to a proud semimigrant population and lasting three-quarters of a century, many La Juntans apparently accepted an Indian-controlled process of Christianization. Several nearby tribes pressured by Apache hostilities eventually joined the La Junta settlements and also entered into this process. The La Juntans insisted that they did not want a Spanish fort or settlement established in their midst. The friars wanted a garrison, but at a respectable distance from the settlements. In late 1759, however, Presidio del Norte was built in the very heart of the settlements. The Spanish post that developed there with its own assigned chaplain quickly

replaced the separate mission effort as many Indians abandoned the district. The garrison was briefly moved elsewhere and reestablished. Any indigenous La Juntans who remained in the district soon disappeared as distinct ethnic groups, absorbed into the Hispanic society.

Still other Indian groups in Texas were large and powerful, with well-developed trade systems or wide-ranging activities that gave them alternative access through French Louisiana and later the United States to the European goods, including firearms, that they most desired. As the number of permanent Spanish military forces in the area was reduced during most of the crucial eighteenth century, the Spanish adopted the French Indian policy, which called for developing alliances with the stronger Indian groups through trade or pacts against common enemies. Mission efforts in such circumstances, most notably among the agriculturally self-sufficient Caddos in East Texas, never succeeded in establishing permanent resident Indian congregations under missionary control or in garnering many converts. An initial attempt along the Neches River in 1690–93 at the missions of San Francisco de los Tejas and Santísimo Nombre de María failed miserably. In 1716–17 another mission named San Francisco was reestablished in the same area, and five new missions were founded stretching eastward: Nuestra Señora de la Purísima Concepción de los Hainais (later Nuestra Señora de la Purísima Concepción de Acuña), San José de los Nazonis, Nuestra Señora de Guadalupe in Nacogdoches, Nuestra Señora de los Dolores de los Ais, and San Miguel de Linares de los Adaes in what is now Louisiana. But these centers never consisted of much more than a modest chapel, a missionary residence, and a few dwellings built hopefully for Indians. Relations based upon trade and military alliance offered these Indian groups all they wanted with much more freedom than the mission approach. The missionaries had to resign themselves to visiting villages and welcoming the Indians who visited the mission. Even then, the obligatory use of water in baptism carried negative connotations in Caddo understanding and further blocked conversion efforts.

In 1730–31, in reaction to the withdrawal of the local protective garrison, the supplies and official status of the three "interior" East Texas missions (those farther from the Louisiana border) were transferred to the more promising San Antonio area to help found additional missions there. After Louisiana passed from French to Spanish rule in 1763, thus eliminating the need for border defense in East Texas, the three remaining missions there were closed in 1773, along with all other Spanish foundations, in order to reduce crown expenses. When Nacogdoches was reoccupied as a Spanish civil settlement in 1779, an official mission was not reestablished there. The Franciscans assigned as pastors were primarily occupied with the settlers, although they engaged in some work with interested Indians. Although most East Texas Indians did not embrace Catholicism, a few were clearly assimilated into Spanish Catholic society, both before and after 1773. The entire East Texas missionary effort was thus carried out quite differently from the "self-contained town" model preferred by the missionaries and so often erroneously thought of as the sole Spanish missionary approach.

By the 1750s the Lipan Apaches, which consisted of several strong, mounted bands, were beginning to lose ground in Central Texas to their enemies, the Comanches and their allies, who were ranging down from the north. Under this pressure the Apaches began to be friendly to the Spanish in Central Texas;

they sought military cooperation and even encouraged Spanish outposts in their territory. The short-lived missions consequently attempted by eager Franciscans deep in contested Indian territory—Santa Cruz de San Sabá, in the vicinity of present-day Menard, and Nuestra Señora de la Candelaria del Cañón and San Lorenzo de la Santa Cruz in the upper Nueces River basin—became the target of attacks, including the disastrous annihilation of San Sabá Mission. The Apache responses to these missions demonstrated to Spanish eyes not only the Apaches' purely military motivations and lack of real interest in conversion, but also their unreliability as allies. Colonial policy therefore shifted toward systematic war against the Apaches, who in turn continued to harass Spanish settlements sporadically. Later, during the tumultuous revolutionary decade of 1811–21, Lipans and Comanches engaged in a virtual war of attrition against Spanish settlements.

By the late 1770s several factors caused the mission system to fall out of favor as an important element of Spanish frontier strategy. The weaker Indian groups who had been more ready mission recruits declined steadily in numbers due to high infant-mortality rates, European-introduced epidemics, continued hostile pressure from other Indians, demoralization, and assimilation into either other Indian groups or Spanish society. The relative success of the San Antonio missions themselves was only maintained in the later 1700s by distant recruitment among embattled groups near the Gulf Coast or in the lower Rio Grande country. Furthermore, governmental frontier policy shifted more emphatically away from maintaining missions, which were now seen not only as economic liabilities but also as against the rising spirit of liberalism. This spirit championed individual human rights and a capitalist economy advocating private rather than communal property. The growth of civilian ranching and agricultural enterprises and the governmental search for more revenue through taxes on range cattle adversely affected the mission economies along the San Antonio River. There was also increasing pressure from the growing civilian population to take over mission lands, particularly those with obviously declining Indian presence. Greater numbers of civilians were already working or even living within mission properties at the invitation of the missionaries, and they entailed increased labor costs. Conversely, in several cases there was already significant assimilation of mission dwellers into the local Spanish society. In the 1790s those missions that had clearly achieved their purpose of assimilating Indians into Spanish society and religion were either partially secularized (the San Antonio missions) or consolidated administratively (the San Antonio and El Paso missions). In the first few years of the new Republic of Mexico—between 1824 and 1830—all the missions still operating in Texas were officially secularized, with the sole exception of those in the El Paso district, which were turned over to diocesan pastors only in 1852.

In retrospect, although the Franciscans almost always sought initially to implement their ideal mission system, in practice they were forced by various Indian groups as well as by Spanish government authorities to adapt that system to local realities in most of Texas. The resultant alternative mission systems allowed much more interplay and flexibility in relations between the Indians and the Spanish. In several cases these approaches led to significant Christianization and assimilation of the Indians. In regard to the primary missionary objective of the Franciscans

Tris Speaker catching a ball. Courtesy National Baseball Library and Archive, Cooperstown, New York.

themselves, it is clear that the vast majority of the native population of Texas and even of those Indians who at one time or another resided at missions never became fundamentally Christian. On the other hand, in several places true Indian or mestizo Christian communities did develop. This was the case in the El Paso and San Antonio areas, as well as at Camargo on the lower Rio Grande. A good number of other Indians who became Christians, either through missionization or through association with Spanish communities, were assimilated individually or as families into Hispanic society. Other mission efforts such as those in East Texas, at San Juan Bautista, and at La Bahía, while apparently failing to gain a significant number of true conversions, did achieve the political goal of building a stable, economically successful Spanish presence in the contested borderlands. In these places Indians learned Spanish and came to tolerate if not welcome the Spaniards' presence.

Robert E. Wright, O.M.I.

Speaker, Tris. Baseball player; b. Tristram E. Speaker, Hubbard, 4 April 1888; d. Lake Whitney, 8 December 1958 (buried in Fairview Cemetery, Hubbard); m. Mary Frances Cuddihy (1924). In 1905 Tris attended Polytechnic College in Fort Worth. The next year, he started his baseball career as a $50-a-month player with Cleburne, of the North Texas League. In 1907 he played with Houston and the Boston Red Sox and in 1908 with Little Rock. The Red Sox recalled him in 1909, and he stayed with them through 1915. From 1916 through 1926 he played in Cleveland. In 1920, as manager at a salary of $57,000, he led Cleveland to its first pennant. In 1927 Speaker played with Washington. He finished his career with Philadelphia in 1928. After retirement he became a sales representative for an Ohio steel company and a coach in Cleveland. During his 22 years in the major leagues he recorded a lifetime batting average of .344. In 1936 he was the seventh player named to the Baseball Hall of Fame, and in 1951 he became the first athlete named to the Texas Sports Hall of Fame.   *Mary Beth Fleischer*

Spell, Lota May. Musician and author; b. Lota May Harrigan, Big Spring, 2 February 1885; d. Austin, 3 April 1972 (buried in San Antonio City Cemetery Number One); m. Jefferson Rea Spell (1910); 1 daughter; ed. privately under August Schemmel, at the Grand Ducal Conservatory, Karlsruhe (1902–05), at the University of Texas (B.A., 1914; M.A., 1919; Ph.D. in English, 1923). Because her father was a superintendent of railroads in Mexico, she received her early education from tutors. From 1905 to 1910 she performed as a pianist in Europe and Mexico. In 1910 she became an instructor in the Whitis Preparatory School in Austin. From 1910 to 1914 Mrs. Spell was head of the music department of Melrose Hall in San Antonio. From 1921 to 1927 she served as librarian of the Genaro García Library of the University of Texas. In the mid1930s she was employed by the state to identify historical sites for the Texas Centennial celebrations and to write inscriptions for the monuments placed on those sites. She was a teacher of music history and appreciation at the Texas School of Fine Arts, an associate editor of *The Musicale* (1929–33), an associate editor of the *Southwestern Musician* (1933–47), editor of *Texas Music News* (1946–48), and a contributor to numerous musical journals, including *Etude*. She devoted much of her life to developing training tools for teaching the young. From 1939 to 1971 she taught children at her studio in Austin. She prepared bulletins for the University Interscholastic League to encourage musical education in the state, including the valuable work *Music in Texas* (1936; later reprinted). Lota Spell's knowledge of German, French, Italian, Latin, and Spanish, along with her interest in music, led her into research in musical development throughout the Western Hemisphere, especially in the Southwest and Mexico, and this brought her wide recognition. Her articles appeared regularly in many important quarterlies and reviews, both musical and historical. Her research in Latin-American culture led to her book *Pioneer Printer Samuel Bangs in Mexico and Texas* (1963). She contributed articles on seventeenth-century Mexican poetess Sor Juana Inés de la Cruz and on nineteenth-century Mexican diplomat, dramatist, and theater impresario Manuel Eduardo de Gorostiza. At the time of her death she had completed manuscripts on Gorostiza and on Fray Pedro de Gante, one of the first music teachers in Mexico. A complete list of her numerous publications has yet to be compiled. Her correspondence, along with that of her husband, was given to the Latin American Collection of the University of Texas at Austin. The Spell library was purchased by the University of Texas in the early 1960s. Mrs. Spell was a member and officer of many music associations and a fellow of the Texas State Historical Association.

                                  Nettie Lee Benson

Spindletop Oilfield. On a salt dome in eastern Jefferson County; its discovery (10 January 1901) marked the birth of the modern oil and gas industry. The Gladys City Oil, Gas, and Manufacturing Company, formed in 1892, was the first company to drill on Spindletop Hill. It continued to lead in exploration of the hill until the boom occurred. Anthony F. Lucas spudded in a well on 27 October 1900 on land that adjoined the Gladys City Company lands. Only on January 10 did mud begin bubbling from the hole. Startled roughnecks fled as six tons of four-inch drilling pipe came shooting up out of the ground, followed by mud, then gas, then oil. The Lucas geyser, found at a depth of 1,139 feet, blew a stream of oil over 100 feet high until it was capped nine days later. Its flow was an estimated 100,000 barrels a day. Throngs of oilmen, speculators, and onlookers transformed Beaumont. By September 1901 there were at least six successful wells on Gladys City Company lands. Wild speculation drove land prices around Spindletop to incredible heights. One man who had been trying to sell his plot there for $150 for three years sold his land for $20,000; the buyer sold to another investor within 15 minutes for $50,000. One well, representing an initial investment of under $10,000, was sold for $1,250,000. Beaumont's population rose from 10,000 to 50,000. Legal entanglements and multimillion-dollar deals became almost commonplace. An estimated $235 million was invested in oil that year in Texas. Some made fortunes, but others lost everything.

But the overabundance of wells at Spindletop led to a rapid decline in production. After yielding 17,500,000 barrels of oil in 1902, the Spindletop wells were down to 10,000 barrels a day in February 1904. Deposits from the shallow Miocene caprock seemed to diminish. The field had not yet dried out, however. A second boom came when oil was sought on the flanks of the dome and at greater depths. On 13 November 1925 the Yount–Lee Oil Company brought in a flank well drilled to 5,400 feet. In the resulting second speculative boom the Gladys City Company participated with the Yount–Lee Oil Company and others. In 1927 Spindletop production reached its all-time annual high of 21,000,000 barrels. Within five years 60,000,000 barrels had been produced, largely from the new-found deeper Marginulin sands of the flank wells. Additional deposits were found in the Midway (Eocene) formations in 1951. Over 153,000,000 barrels of oil had been produced from the Spindletop fields by 1985.

The discovery of the Spindletop oilfield had an incalculable effect on world history. Eager to find similar deposits, investors spent billions of dollars throughout the Lone Star State in search of oil and gas. The cheap fuel they found helped to revolutionize American transportation and industry. Storage facilities, pipelines, and major refining units were built near Beaumont, Port Arthur, Sabine Pass, and Orange. By 1902 more than 500 Texas corporations were doing business in Beaumont. Many of the major oil companies were born at Spindletop or grew to major corporate size as a result of their involvement at Spindletop—the Texas Company (later Texaco), Gulf Oil Corporation, Sun Oil Company, Magnolia Petroleum Company, and Humble (later Exxon). The Spindletop oilfield again boomed in the 1950s, with the production of sulfur by Texas Gulf Sulphur Company (later TexasGulf). In 1963–66 even deeper oil production was achieved with an average well depth of 9,000 feet. The old field continued in the 1990s to yield limited oil from stripper wells and brine production. Some parts of the salt-dome cavities were being developed as storage facilities for petroleum products. In commemoration of Spindletop, a monument of Texas pink granite was placed in 1941 near the site of the Lucas gusher. The withdrawal of oil, sulfur, and brine from beneath the surface, however, caused the Spindletop dome to subside, and the monument was moved to the recreated Spindletop/Gladys City Boomtown Museum across the highway on the Lamar University campus at Beaumont. The Gladys City Company, as well as many major oil companies, continued to reap the benefit of their involvement in the discovery of the Spindletop oilfield.

Robert Wooster and Christine Moor Sanders

Sports. Texas sports have enjoyed a national reputation since Texas cowboys became famous in the pioneer days of rodeos. Today the state is best known for its high school football, although other sports long preceded these. Eighteenth and early nineteenth century travelers left vivid accounts of the sports and amusements of Spanish Texas, but nothing about the activities of the Indians. Indians competed in sports with Anglos and Hispanics, or both. Subsequently, numerous racial and ethnic groups introduced their sports to Texas, but by World War I the Anglo majority had conquered and Texas sports resembled those of the rest of the United States. Texas high school football gained widespread fame for the fanaticism of its followers, the numbers of Texas players competing at colleges across the nation, and good press. For many years, Southwest Conference football also enjoyed a national reputation for excellence. As the conference declined, however, fan interest shifted to the Dallas Cowboys and Houston Oilers of the National Football League.

The most formalized Hispanic sport was the *corrida* or bullfight, which arrived in the New World with rules and rituals intact. Although it underwent many changes in New Spain, the bullfight retained its essential character and marked most fiestas and holy days. The Spanish governor of Texas issued a proclamation in 1810 that included specifications for the location of a bullring. Although outlawed by the Texas legislature in 1891, the sport continued to flourish along the borders well into the twentieth century. Cockfighting was also popular, as was horse racing. Of greatest interest to early Anglo writers, however, were the equestrian games and contests of *charrería*, the Mexican rodeo. Developed in conjunction with *corridas* and with ranching, the activities became a major pastime in Spanish Texas.

Anglo-Texans, particularly the Texas Rangers, not only observed Hispanic sports but also participated. Rangers competed against Hispanics and sometimes Comanches in horse racing, bronc busting, roping, and the famous chicken race. Other charro contests included riding bulls and wrestling bulls to the ground by grabbing their tails. Though bullfights and public festivals helped popularize these activities, their diffusion into Anglo culture was most rapid in the cattle business. As Anglo, Hispanic, and African-American cowboys worked the cattle and drove them to market, they adopted the lingo, skills, and sports of the vaquero, thus laying the foundation for American rodeo.

Horse racing, the first really organized Anglo-Texan sport, developed almost immediately after the Texas Revolution. By importing expensive horses and forming jockey clubs, wealthy citizens of the republic soon formed a racing circuit along the Gulf Coast. Velasco, Houston, and Galveston all had rather elaborate tracks where legal betting flourished. Tracks also operated in North and East Texas. As more and more affluent Texans

Charro Mexicano, by Lino Sánchez y Tapía, ca. 1820s. Watercolor. Courtesy Gilcrease Museum, Tulsa; acc. no. 4016.336, plate XXXI.

imported and raised thoroughbred horses, however, increased state taxes on the animals made the costs prohibitive. Many tracks closed, and Texans turned their attention to the popular frontier-style match races, on which taxes had little impact. These short, two-horse road races, similar to the charro races, soon became the norm. In 1937 the legislature outlawed betting on horse racing in Texas, thus completely shutting down the remaining thoroughbred tracks, but not the breeding of fine horses. Assault, a King Ranch horse, won the Triple Crown in 1946.

Germans introduced gymnastics to Texas in the mid-nineteenth century through their turnvereins (gymnastics clubs). These organizations also provided community services such as volunteer fire companies and entertained both the public and themselves with elaborate gymnastic exhibitions. However, later generations of German Texans, though they enjoyed the social benefits of the turnvereins, lost interest in gymnastics, and many of the clubs took up bowling, which was already popular among other German-Texan organizations. They introduced nine-pin bowling, which continues in isolated Texas turnvereins today, but some of the group went on to organize the Texas Ten Pin League, which still regulates mainstream bowling in Texas. Like the turnvereins, the sokol, a gymnastic club brought by Czechs to the state, served a variety of other functions in the Czech communities. Unlike the turners, the sokols have remained true to their original mission and are engaged in gymnastics today. German Texans also formed *Schützenvereine* or shooting clubs, which sponsored the most highly organized of the many shooting contests around the state. By midcentury almost every community had some sort of gun club. Most held annual shooting tournaments and regularly scheduled matches against neighboring towns.

The exact date for the introduction of modern New York Rules baseball into Texas has eluded scholars for half a century. Games probably occurred before the Civil War, and clubs existed in Galveston, Houston, and San Antonio by 1867. Most early clubs grew out of other organizations such as hook-and-ladder companies or turnvereins. In Texas as elsewhere almost every community had at least one baseball club by the 1890s. Many Texas towns had three teams, one black, one Hispanic, one white. Each played its counterparts in neighboring communities, but never one another. Recruiting of skilled out-of-town players became commonplace when winning surpassed camaraderie and social benefits as the primary goal. Even after the introduction of professional baseball, town teams prospered until after World War I; thereafter high school and college teams gradually replaced them. Traveling professional athletes also entertained the public with contests and exhibitions of boxing, wrestling, weight lifting, and fancy rope twirling.

Little is known about women's participation in any of these activities. There are a few records of women's baseball games in the 1880s, and by the 1890s sokols and turnvereins opened their gymnastics programs to women. Organizations such as the University Interscholastic League, the National Collegiate Athletic Association, and the major leagues gradually surpassed local individuals and groups in organizing and conducting Texas sports. None of these organizations offered opportunities for women or African Americans until after World War II.

Texas high school and college sports began in the unregulated environment of the nineteenth century, and football soon proved to be king at all levels of competition. Texas high school players ultimately achieved a reputation that brought college recruiters from throughout the nation. During the twentieth century, big-time college sports came under the umbrellas of the SWC and the NCAA, while other schools formed their own conferences. The UIL attempted to control sports at the high school level, with mixed results. The biggest issues facing all these sports programs were academic integrity, racial integration, and gender equity, in that order. During the early years, high school football teams were often composed of semiprofessionals who represented their hometown or neighborhood, with few if any high school students in the lineups. The UIL attempted to change that and provide fair competition for legitimate students. They faced a long struggle against over-age students, questionable scholastic records, and all-out recruiting battles between towns. In 1919 the UIL inserted the word "white" in its membership standards. The following year black teachers founded the Texas Interscholastic League of Colored Schools. In 1923 the TILCS came under the authority of Prairie View A&M College, thereby becoming the Prairie View Interscholastic League. By 1951 the UIL offered state championships in boy's track, football, basketball, baseball, and golf and in girl's basketball. The PVIL staged state championship games in football, basketball, baseball, and track. At its peak, the UIL enrolled 6,000 schools, the PVIL 500. After a protracted struggle, the UIL dropped the color barrier in 1965, and the PVIL ceased operations four years later. Under the leadership of Roy Bedichek, Rodney Kidd, Rhea Williams, and Bailey Marshall, the UIL grew to national prominence; today it enrolls approximately 1,100 schools and sponsors nine sports each for boys and girls, in addition to contests in other educational and cultural endeavors such as music.

Though college sports organizations also faced problems with eligibility and illegal payments, they lacked any real enforcement powers until the 1950s. Before World War I several

Texas cowboys playing baseball. Photograph by Louis Melcher. Probably Fayette County, ca. 1900. Louis Melcher Collection, CAH; CN 03749.

prominent Texas colleges belonged to the Texas Intercollegiate Athletic Association, which did little to regulate their sports. Rampant abuses led L. T. Bellmont, University of Texas athletic director, to contact his counterparts throughout the Southwest and ask them to help form a conference to raise the integrity of their programs and foster competition with teams from other conferences. Bellmont envisioned wide geographic representation. Thus the original 1914 meeting to form what became the Southwest Conference attracted representatives from four states—Texas, Oklahoma, Louisiana, and Arkansas—although membership soon dwindled to two states. SWC schools won six national football titles. Coaches Dana X. Bible of Texas A&M and the University of Texas, W. M. (Matty) Bell of Southern Methodist University, O. H. (Abe) Martin of Texas Christian University, and Paul "Bear" Bryant of Texas A&M also gained national prominence and increased the conference's status. In the late 1960s, Darrell Royal of the University of Texas at Austin caused a national sensation with the introduction of the wishbone formation. An important element in SWC growth was its agreement in 1940 with the four-year-old Cotton Bowl game, whereby the conference champion became the host team. In the 1960 game Syracuse University defeated the University of Texas to capture the mythical national crown. That title was decided at the Cotton Bowl 5 times over the next 11 years.

Eleven Heisman Trophy winners have played in the Cotton Bowl, including five Texans playing for SWC teams. Two of them, Earl Campbell and Andre Ware, both African Americans, represented the vast change that began in 1964, when the first black athletes at the University of Texas competed in a track meet. The first football scholarship awarded a black player in the SWC went to Jerry LeVias of SMU in 1968, and integration in the conference continued slowly thereafter. After Congress passed Title IX of the Educational Amendments of 1972, officially outlawing discrimination on the basis of sex in schools receiving federal funding, women were quick to highlight the financial disparities in athletics, and officials faced a mandate to offer competition for women. Although the numbers of women's teams at all levels increased almost immediately, real equality remained elusive.

The glory days of the SWC and its bowl began to wane in the 1980s. Problems were exacerbated in 1987 when the NCAA shut down SMU's athletic program because of rule violations. SMU was the only school to receive the "death penalty," although the University of Houston, TCU, and Texas A&M all received NCAA sanctions of varying degrees of severity. The resulting scandals hurt recruiting and the reputation of the conference, which the University of Arkansas quit in 1990. These events, along with changes in television policies relating to both professional and amateur sports, set off a chain reaction during the 1993–94 school year. Four SWC teams (Texas, Texas A&M, Texas Tech, and Baylor) defected to the Big Eight to form the new Big Twelve Conference; the Cotton Bowl game went with them. Since the University of Houston expressed no interest in the SWC that remained, Rice, TCU, and SMU joined the Western Athletic Conference. Houston eventually joined with several other universities to form a new league, Conference USA.

By the mid-1990s Texas colleges in all organizations and divisions combined had won 21 football crowns, while men's and women's teams combined had captured 39 national track and field championships and 26 golf titles. At the opposite end, only

three basketball teams, one men's (University of Texas at El Paso, 1966) and two women's (UT Austin, 1986, and Texas Tech, 1992), have captured an NCAA Division I basketball championship. The victory by the Texas Tech women, all but one of them native Texans, was the school's first national championship. Tech star Sheryl Swoopes set a record for the most points in an NCAA tournament game by a man or woman and won five prestigious national awards, including the Babe Didrikson Award and the Associated Press Female Athlete of the Year prize. The 1966 men's champions from UTEP were the first team to start five African Americans (one Texan) in the title game. By defeating the all-white team from Kentucky, they helped end both segregation and racial quota systems in college basketball. The most successful college coaches and teams have included the University of Houston, with 16 national golf championships, all coached by Dave Williams, and UTEP, with 13 NCAA Division I men's track and field titles under Ted Banks. Abilene Christian University has won 15 NCAA Division II men's and women's track and field titles. Texas A&I won 7 NAIA Division I football championships between 1956 and 1979, six of them coached by Gil Steinke, whose teams also won 39 consecutive games. Jim Wacker coached Texas Lutheran College to two football titles in NAIA Division II, and Southwest Texas State to two in NCAA Division II. Unlike the NCAA's Division I-A, where national polls select the football champions, those teams won their titles through championship tournaments. The University of Texas at Austin has won 12 men's and women's swimming championships. Alfred "Red" Barr coached SMU to a record 17 SWC swimming titles, including 15 in a row, and produced 50 All American swimmers and divers. Under coaches Billy Disch, Bibb Falk, and Cliff Gustafson, UT Austin teams have won 62 SWC and 4 NCAA baseball championships and made a record 27 appearances in the College World Series.

Since World War II at least 81 athletes who were either born in Texas or lived in the state at the time of their competition have won Olympic gold medals. They represent 11 different sports, with track and field, the premier Olympic sport, having the largest number. The first famous Texas Olympian was Babe Zaharias of Beaumont. At the 1932 Los Angeles Olympics, she captured two gold medals and one silver and set a world record in the hurdles. Louise Ritter, a graduate of Texas Woman's University, won the gold medal in the high jump at the 1988 games and set a new Olympic record. Bobby Morrow of San Benito won more than eighty track and field titles for Abilene Christian College before capturing three golds at the 1956 Olympics. Rafer Johnson, a Hillsboro native, held several national and world records and won a gold medal in the 1960 Olympic Decathlon. He also had the honor of carrying the United States flag in the opening ceremonies in 1960, and lit the Olympic torch at the 1984 Los Angeles games. Fred Hanson of Rice University was world record holder and 1964 Olympic gold medalist in the pole vault. Randy Matson of Kilgore and Texas A&M, one of the all-time greats in shot put and discus, captured Olympic gold in the shot put in 1968. One of the youngest gold medalists was Johnny (Lam) Jones of Lampasas. By setting several records in UIL track and field meets, he qualified for the 1976 Olympics and was a member of the gold medal 4 X 100 relay team. Certainly one of the most famous American track and field athletes in recent memory is Carl Lewis. Although born in Alabama, Lewis ran track at the University of Houston and subsequently lived in Houston most of his adult life. At the 1984 Olympic Games, he matched the legendary Jesse Owens by winning four track and field gold medals. He took two golds and one silver in 1988 and two golds in 1992. During that time the Olympics dropped all pretense of amateurism, and sport made Lewis a wealthy man. David G. "Skippy" Browning, Jr., winner of eight AAU diving championships as well as the 1952 Olympic gold, was born in Boston and moved to Texas at age three. The two-time NCAA champion and three-time all American for the University of Texas died in a Navy plane crash at age 25. Romanian expatriate Bela Karoli trained elite female gymnasts at Karoli's Gym in Houston. Already the coach of world and Olympic champion Nadia Comanechi in his home country, Karoli soon put Houston on the gymnastics map and revolutionized the sport in America. His most famous pupil, Mary Lou Retton, moved to Houston to train at his gym, and captured one gold and two bronze medals at the 1984 games. She became an overnight sensation and subsequently forged a successful career as a celebrity and motivational speaker, while still living in Houston. Karoli produced many more preeminent gymnasts, including world champion Kim Zemeskal, a Houston native. He retired after the 1992 games.

Although Zina Garrison of Houston teamed with Pam Shriver to win the 1988 Olympic gold in tennis doubles, Texas has never established a reputation in tennis. The most famous and successful Texas tennis player was Wilmer L. Allison, who competed from 1922 through 1936. He won one United States singles championship and, with partner John Van Ryan, captured two Wimbledon and two United States Open doubles titles and won fourteen of sixteen Davis Cup matches. Allison coached the University of Texas team for 16 years. Texas was the site of the most famous tennis match in history, the 1973 "Battle of the Sexes" between Bobby Riggs and Billie Jean King at the Astrodome. Still considered a watershed event, the contest attracted the largest television audience ever to see a tennis match to that time. King's victory before 30,472 spectators propelled her to the forefront of the women's movement.

Texans have enjoyed notable success in individual professional sports like golf and rodeo, but despite having several teams in almost every American professional league, only two major Texas professional franchises, the Dallas Cowboys and the Houston Rockets, can claim world championships. Texans have been active in organizing and administrating professional sports since 1888, when John J. McCloskey formed the Texas League of Professional Baseball Clubs, later known simply as the Texas League. Oilman H. L. Hunt was instrumental in forming the American Football League in 1960, as well as negotiating the beginning of the Super Bowl and the merger of the AFL with the NFL. Texas women were responsible for forming the two oldest organizations of female professional athletes in America, the Women's Professional Rodeo Association in 1948 and the Ladies Professional Golf Association in 1949. Throughout the history of twentieth-century American professional team sports, new leagues have come and gone with depressing regularity, usually unable to compete financially with established organizations. Texas teams have played in most of these leagues, including the World Football League, the United States Football League, the World League of American Football, the National Women's Football League, the American Basketball Association, the Women's Basketball League, and the World Hockey Association.

San Antonio Churchill football players celebrate their state-championship victory over Temple. Photograph by Geoff Winningham. Austin, 1976. Courtesy Geoff Winningham, Houston.

The state's newest professional team, the Dallas Stars, belongs to the well-established National Hockey League.

Baseball was the first modern professional sport in the state. Texas League baseball was the major professional sport until 1962. Future stars of major league baseball such as J. H. (Dizzy) Dean, Hank Greenberg, Carl Hubbell, Brooks Robinson, and Duke Snider played their minor league ball in the Texas League. In 1962 the National League Houston Colt 45's, later the Houston Astros, made their major league baseball debut, thus ending the Texas League's dominance. Ten years later, the American League Texas Rangers opened play in Arlington. The Astros recorded a significant breakthrough in October 1993, when they named Bob Watson their new general manager. Watson is the first black in major league baseball history to hold that title. With the notable exception of pitcher Nolan Ryan of Alvin, few Texans have starred on major league baseball teams in their home state. Ryan set records for both pitching and attendance for the Astros and later the Rangers. When he retired in 1993 he was the all-time major league baseball leader in both strikeouts and bases on balls. His 27-year career is the second longest in the history of major American professional team sports. Only hockey great Gordie Howe played longer; Howe's 34-year career included a brief stint with the Houston Aeros of the now-defunct World Hockey Association. Texans in the Baseball Hall of Fame include Andrew "Rube" Foster, the "father of black baseball"; Joe Leonard Morgan, who played for the Astros from 1965 to 1972; and Frank Robinson, the first African American to manage a major league baseball team. Among major leaguers who played SWC baseball is former University of Texas All American Roger Clemens, who won the 1986 and 1987 Cy Young Award as a pitcher for the Boston Red Sox.

The first Texan to make a mark on professional football was Sam A. (Slingin' Sammy) Baugh of the Washington Redskins. He first gained notoriety as the object of a high school recruiting war in the late twenties and starred for Texas Christian University in the thirties. In 16 seasons as a quarterback he led the Redskins to two NFL championships and four divisional titles. Playing both offense and defense, he set many league records. He was elected to the Professional Football Hall of Fame in 1963. In 1962 the Dallas Texans became the last NFL team to go broke. Texas was probably not ready for professional football

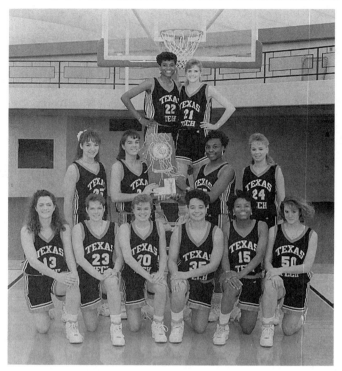

Texas Tech's 1993 NCAA Division 1 Basketball Championship Team. Photograph by Darrell Thomas. Lubbock, 1993. Courtesy Texas Tech University Athletics Department. Participation in women's sports has increased dramatically in universities across the country as a result of Title IX.

when the original Dallas Texans went broke in 1952. A more successful effort followed eight years later. The Dallas Cowboys of the established NFL and the Houston Oilers and Dallas Texans of the newly formed AFL began play in 1960. All three teams faced a struggle, but especially the Oilers and Texans, as Americans generally considered the AFL a minor league. That perception did not change until the 1970 AFL–NFL merger. The Oilers' greatest success came during the early years of the AFL. They took the league title in 1960 and 1961 but lost the 1962 championship to the Dallas Texans, who then departed for Kansas City to become the Chiefs. The Oilers lost the AFC title to Oakland in 1967 and after the merger appeared in the playoffs 10 times without winning a divisional title. In 1993, after losing 4 of their first 5 games, the Oilers won 11 in a row to capture the AFC Central Division crown, but lost in the second round of the playoffs. They also gained national attention by signing 1977 Heisman Trophy winner Earl Campbell of the University of Texas. Campbell earned the first of three NFL Most Valuable Player awards in 1978, when he was also named Rookie of the Year. In 1980 he led the league in all four rushing categories. However, the physical punishment of being virtually a one-man offense took a rapid toll, and Campbell retired in 1986. He was then number 10 on the all-time NFL rushing list; he was elected to the Pro Football Hall of Fame in 1991. The Cowboys struggled at first but made their first Super Bowl appearance in a 1971 loss to the Baltimore Colts. The Cowboys won the title in 1972, 1978, 1993, 1994, and 1996. They also won the NFC but lost the Super Bowl in 1976 and 1979. The Cowboys' first coach, Tom Landry, is

in the Pro Football Hall of Fame, where more than 25 Texans are honored. The others include former Cowboys general manager Tex Schramm, Super Bowl quarterback Roger Staubach, tackle Bob Lilly, and running back Tony Dorsett. Among the most successful Houston Oilers coaches was Andrew (Bum) Phillips, a veteran of 23 years of Texas high school and college coaching who led the Oilers from 1975 to 1980. Jack Pardee, Oilers coach in the early 1990s, was a product of high school six-man football and played his college ball at Texas A&M. He won championships coaching at both the professional and college levels before joining the Oilers.

Basketball has remained a minor sport in Texas, even though the National Basketball Association gained enormous national popularity in the late 1980s. The Rockets moved from San Diego to Houston in 1971 and twice played in the NBA championship series in the 1980s, but lost both times. They finally captured back-to-back crowns in 1994 and 1995. Neither the San Antonio Spurs, who joined the league in 1976, nor the Dallas Mavericks, begun in 1980, have won NBA championships. George Gervin of the Spurs won the NBA scoring title four times (1978, 1979, 1980, 1982). Moses Malone of Houston was the league MVP in 1979, and Hakeem Olajuwon in 1994; Spur David Robinson won the title in 1995, although the Rockets downed the Spurs for the Western Division Crown.

Nothing in the history of Texas sports equaled the 1965 opening of the Astrodome for attracting national and international attention. The first facility of its kind, the Astrodome is home to the Houston Oilers and the Houston Astros. With the nickname "Eighth Wonder of the World," the Astrodome attracted crowds of visitors and spawned a series of imitators, none of which inspired comparable hoopla. It also revolutionized many sports through the introduction of Astroturf, an artificial playing surface. The Alamodome in San Antonio, home to the Spurs, began setting records almost as soon as it opened in July 1993, when the figure-skating competition at the United States Olympic Festival drew 25,691 spectators, the largest crowd in the history of competitive figure skating.

Texans have played a greater role in the direction and leadership of rodeo than any other professional sport, and make up a significant number of hall of fame honorees. One reason is that rodeo is a native of the Southwest, with Texas the focal point, while most other major sports originated in England or New England. More Texans, at least 50, are honored by halls of fame for rodeo than for any other sport. Only cowgirl Barbara (Tad) Lucas of Fort Worth, superstar of the 1920s and 1930s, has earned a place in the National Rodeo Hall of Fame, the Prorodeo Hall of Fame, and the National Cowgirl Hall of Fame and Western Heritage Center. Bill Pickett of Austin, who invented bulldogging or steer wrestling around the turn of the century, is honored by the two halls for men. William T. Johnson of San Antonio was the most successful rodeo producer of the 1930s; he helped make rodeo a lucrative career for many athletes during the Great Depression. By World War II another Texan, western film star Gene Autry, had assumed leadership of the sport and brought it to new heights of popularity; he also greatly diminished women's competitive role. In response, several Texans, including Nancy Binford, Thena Mae Farr, and Margaret Owens Montgomery formed what is now the Women's Professional Rodeo Association. This organization made women's barrel racing a standard event on the otherwise all-male Professional

Rodeo Cowboys Association tour. Still, women's earnings fell far behind men's until the 1980s, when WPRA president Jimmie Gibbs Munroe of Valley Mills led a successful move for equal pay. Both the WPRA and PRCA had their headquarters at Fort Worth during the fifties, and today Texas is one of only three states that constitutes its own division within professional rodeo. Since official records began in 1929, Texas cowboys have won more than 90 world championships. None has been more successful than Ty Murray, a native of Arizona who later ranched and rode out of Stephenville. A six-time champion All Around Cowboy, Murray was the seventh and youngest man to reach a million dollars in rodeo winnings.

Two of the most famous golfers in American history are Texans, Ben Hogan and Babe Zaharias. After her track and field victories in the 1932 Olympics, Zaharias won myriad amateur golf titles before helping form the LPGA in 1949. From that time until her death from cancer in 1956, she dominated the women's game. The LPGA tour has never again had a star of her magnitude. The "Age of Hogan" in men's golf paralleled Zaharias's domination of women's. Between 1948 and 1953 Hogan was player of the year four times, won a total of nine victories in the four major classics, and was the leading money winner five times. Lee Treviño, a Dallas native and the first Hispanic superstar in golf, won the United States Open in 1968 and back-to-back British Opens in 1970 and 1971. In 1992 he was player of the year and topped the money list in the PGA Seniors Tour, a lucrative venture that grew out of the Austin Legends of Golf tournament. At least 10 Texas men and women have been inducted into the PGA or LPGA halls of Fame; Babe Zaharias has been honored by both.

In 1908 Galvestonian Jack Johnson became the first black man to win the world heavyweight boxing championship. His victory sparked a racial backlash that resulted in his being sentenced to federal prison. Rather than face incarceration, he escaped the country with baseball promoter Andrew (Rube) Foster and became an international hero in exile. Johnson finally surrendered his crown to Jess Willard in a 1915 bout in Havana. No other Texan held the title until George Foreman, 1968 Olympic gold medalist, captured it in 1973. Foreman, who is best remembered for waving a small American flag in the Olympic arena following his victory, won the title from Joe Frazier in 1973. He lost it to Muhammad Ali in 1974, and retired to become a minister three years later. In 1988 Foreman returned to competition. He won 25 bouts before losing to Evander Holyfield in 1991, but by then he had launched another career as a television comedian and pitchman. At the age of 46, Foreman won the International Boxing Federation's Heavyweight title in November 1994 against Michael Moorer. On 10 September 1993 the Alamodome hosted 65,000 fans who witnessed a fight between Mexican national Julio César Chávez and American Olympic gold medalist Pernell Whitaker; each held a world championship in a different division. Although the fight ended in a draw, the crowd was the largest ever to see a boxing match in Texas and the largest indoor crowd in world boxing history.

Even in so-called minor sports, Texans have periodically surged to the forefront. Adolph Toepperwein, for example, set 14 world records as a marksman and trick shooter between 1890 and 1929. His wife, Plinky, was also one of the world's best shooters. Houstonian A. J. Foyt is the most successful driver in United States Auto Club history, with 67 victories and 7 USAC champi-

onships. He was the first four-time winner of America's top race, the Indianapolis 500 (1961, 1964, 1967, 1977), and the only driver to win the Indianapolis 500 and the LeMans races in the same year. In 1984 Corpus Christi native Terry Labonte won the Winston Cup, the championship award in stock-car racing. Willie Shoemaker of Fabens was the most successful thoroughbred jockey of all time. In a career that spanned five decades, he won a record 8,833 races. He won the Kentucky Derby four times (1955, 1959, 1965, 1986) and was the first jockey to earn more than $100 million in purses. He retired in 1990.

Texas sports have changed significantly since the Spanish ranchers brought their contests across the Rio Grande in the eighteenth century. Though gradual at first, change has accelerated greatly in the past 20 years. Professional sports have eclipsed amateur and school sports, while women, Mexican Americans, and African Americans now participate in almost every facet of Texas sports. The venerable Southwest Conference has ceased to exist. Increasing amounts of money and time are invested in performers and facilities, while some Texas cities have reasonable hopes of soon hosting the Olympics. *Mary Lou LeCompte*

Stagecoach Lines. Stagecoach operations in Texas, as in other states, were closely tied to government mail contracts, which provided the finances that enabled stage companies to transport passengers and freight. Stagecoach routes provided a nineteenth-century network making travel or mail delivery possible to all communities. Postal routes were first established by the Permanent Council of the Texas provisional government in 1835. The original fifteen routes were mostly between the more populated communities of Central, South, and East Texas. Many of these early routes were served by individuals on horseback. Early stage lines were short, such as the line from Houston to Harrisburg in 1837. Houston had become the population center from which many of the early routes westward began, and by May 1839 a stage line was operating between Houston and Washington-onthe-Brazos. Later that year a line from Houston to Egypt via Richmond and another line between Houston and Austin began operation.

In 1845 the firm of Brown and Tarbox advertised a biweekly service by the Houston and Austin Mail Stage Line via Washington, Independence, La Grange, and Bastrop. This firm was probably the most prominent of the early stagers. By 1847 its Texas United States Mail Line of Stages was providing biweekly service between Houston and San Antonio, and its Western United States Mail Line of Stages supplied biweekly service between Port Lavaca and San Antonio. Also in 1847 John Sutherland began a weekly stage run from Houston to Victoria via Richmond, Egypt, and Texana. In addition, there was a desire in inland areas for connection to Gulf Coast ports, where supplies and settlers from the eastern United States and Europe were steadily arriving. Thus, by 1848 bimonthly service between San Antonio and Corpus Christi had begun. In December 1849 Harrison and Brown began weekly service between San Antonio and Lavaca via Seguin, Gonzales, Cuero, and Victoria, and in 1851 James L. Allen ran triweekly stages between San Antonio and Indianola by a similar route, with an extra stop at New Braunfels.

Stagecoach travel was fraught with danger from bandits and hostile Indians. This was especially true in frontier areas such as the country around San Antonio and Austin. Stage owners regularly reported thefts of mules and supplies, destruction of way stations, and murders of drivers, guards, and passengers by Indian raiding parties. Even so, new stage lines were being added every year as the growth in the state's population resulted in the westward expansion of the frontier and in the establishment of new towns along the stage routes.

There was also an increasing demand for stage service westward, due in no small part to the California gold rush. The San Antonio–El Paso Mail (1851–) partly filled this need, as did the Butterfield Overland Mail (1857–). At the beginning of the Civil War there were 31 stage lines operating in Texas. Except for the Butterfield and San Antonio–El Paso lines, the population centers that these lines served were primarily in the eastern half of the state. There was a route northward from San Antonio through New Braunfels, Austin, Waco, Waxahachie, Dallas, and Clarksville, operated by Risher and Sawyer. A mail route from Dallas to Fort Belknap through Weatherford made two trips a week. Other routes included a Clarksville to Waco run through Bonham, McKinney, Dallas, and Waxahachie every other day and a triweekly stage between Dallas and Palestine. These lines formed a fairly complete network of existing communities. Some lines continued to operate after the beginning of the war by signing contracts to carry mail for the Confederate states. Although the Confederate government did not have the wherewithal to sustain mail contracts in the manner of the United States Post Office Department, several Confederate States Mail stage lines operated on regular schedules out of San Antonio and other important Texas communities. A steady Confederate stage traffic plied the "Cotton Road" between Matamoros and Brownsville and the railhead at Alleyton. Southern cotton was exchanged at Matamoros for war supplies brought by ships from Europe.

In the years after the Civil War hundreds of United States mail contracts for Texas routes were let. Many were for relatively short routes between small towns, and there was stage service to nearly every Texas community. Often the same individuals bid on several contracts because long routes were bid in segments. Bidders often stipulated "four-horse coaches" or "two-horse hacks." Contracts called for biweekly, triweekly, or more frequent service and specified the day and hour for departure, arrival, and return. In January 1866 a German immigrant named August Santleben obtained a United States mail contract for service from San Antonio to Eagle Pass and into Mexico. He later wrote a book about his stagecoach experiences. In April 1866 Bethel Coopwood began service between San Antonio and El Paso, but control of the line passed to Benjamin F. Ficklin in 1867. After Ficklin's death in March 1871 the contract for this service was awarded to his partner, F. P. Sawyer of Washington, D.C., when the low bidder failed to initiate service at the required time. Sawyer operated the line through June 1875.

Although the coming of the railroads signaled the end of the stagecoach era in Texas, stage lines continued to operate from railheads into frontier areas not yet reached by rail and continued to serve bypassed rural areas. One of the last of the great Texas stagers was C. Bain and Company. Charles Bain's business operated from early 1876 into the 1880s with a route from San Antonio to Fort Concho, connecting with another Bain line from Benficklin to El Paso and Mesilla, New Mexico. Bain also operated stages between San Antonio and Laredo. However, Bain and other stage operators realized that the railroads would eventually put the stage lines out of business by winning the mail contracts. By the early 1880s the stagecoach era was essentially over, although there was some stage service in rural areas past 1900. Through the years new settlements sprang up along the stage routes and near the military posts that guarded the routes. Thus, the stagecoaches can be regarded as important in the development of Texas. Mail lines were run into sparsely settled and even uninhabited areas, where this service encouraged settlement.

Rex H. Stever

Starr, Belle. The "Bandit Queen"; b. Myra Maybelle Shirley near Carthage, Missouri, 5 February 1848; d. Choctaw Nation, 3 February 1889; m. Jim Reed (1866); 2 children. The Shirleys were Southern sympathizers and supporters of Confederate irregulars such as the raider William Clarke Quantrill. By 1864, after Carthage was burned, the family had migrated to Scyene, Texas, near Dallas. There in July 1866 a gang of Missouri outlaws who had ridden with Quantrill, including Jesse James and the Younger brothers, used the Shirley home as a hideout. Belle's relationship with Cole Younger is the subject of many stories, some of which claim that her daughter Rosie Lee, often called Pearl Younger, was his child. He denied it; the likely father was Belle's husband, the desperado Jim Reed. For a while Belle and Jim lived in Indian Territory at the home of outlaw Tom Starr, a Cherokee. After Reed was charged with murder, they went to Los Angeles (1871). Soon back in Texas, Reed became involved with the Younger, James, and Starr gangs, which killed and looted throughout Texas, Arkansas, and Indian Territory. At least one account claims that Belle disapproved of Reed's actions; most records suggest that she operated a livery barn in Dallas where she sold the horses Reed stole. Apparently no records indicate that Belle Reed was ever involved in murder, the robbery of trains, banks, or stagecoaches, or in cattle rustling. Reed robbed the Austin–San Antonio stage in April 1874, and though there is no evidence that Belle Reed participated, she was named as an accessory in the indictment. Reed was killed by a deputy sheriff at Paris, Texas, in August 1874; the story that Belle refused to identify his body in order to prevent the sheriff from claiming the reward is apocryphal. In 1878 Belle appears to have married Bruce Younger, perhaps in Coffeyville, Kansas. If that relationship existed, it soured, and she married Sam Starr in the Cherokee Nation in 1880. Belle and Sam Starr were later charged with horse stealing, a federal offense, and Belle received two six-month terms at the House of Correction in Detroit, Michigan. After this experience Belle came to be known as the Bandit Queen. In 1886 she was again charged with horse theft. This time, because of her legal skills, she was acquitted, but in the meantime her husband and an Indian policeman had shot each other to death. Belle subsequently took several lovers, including Jim July (or Jim Starr), Blue Duck, Jack Spaniard, and Jim French. An unknown assassin killed her from ambush with a shotgun. Belle Starr was not widely known until newspaper reports of her death were picked up by Richard K. Fox, the publisher of the *National Police Gazette*. When he published *Bella Starr, the Bandit Queen, or the Female Jesse James* (1889), a 25-cent novel based loosely on her life, the legends began. Belle was buried at Younger's Bend, a remote place on the Canadian River where she often lived. Her daughter later placed a headstone there, engraved with a bell, a star, and a horse, purchased with earnings she made in a brothel.

Leon C. Metz

Sketch of the Proposed Fair Grounds, by Joe Booker, 1886. Pen and ink and watercolor. 21" × 45". From the collections of the Dallas Historical Society. The first recorded State Fair of Texas was held in Dallas in 1859. It continued sporadically until it was formally chartered in 1886, when the directors voted to expand the fair with the acquisition of additional property.

State Cemetery. At a site in Austin that formerly belonged to Andrew Jackson Hamilton. When Edward Burleson died in December 1851, a joint committee of the legislature, probably inspired by the example of the Congressional Cemetery in Washington, made arrangements for Burleson's burial in what was to become a state cemetery. In 1854 the legislature appropriated money for a monument to Burleson and authorized the purchase of the land on which his grave was located. Little attention was paid to the cemetery until the Civil War, when a number of Texas officers killed in military engagements were buried there. In 1864 and again in 1866 the legislature made appropriations for enclosing the graves. In 1866 one acre of land was set aside for the burial of Union soldiers, but later their remains were moved, probably to the United States National Cemetery at San Antonio. A sexton was appointed in 1866, and in 1871 he was instructed to erect permanent markers at the graves. The cemetery was administered by the superintendent of public buildings and grounds until 1919, when it was placed under supervision of the Board of Control. It is divided into two plots. The smaller one includes some 234 marked graves of more or less prominent Texans, including Stephen F. Austin, governors, and representatives of every department of state government and every period of state history. The bodies of many prominent persons have been reinterred in the cemetery, chiefly through the effort of Louis Wiltz Kemp of the State Library and Historical Commission. The larger plot contains the marked graves of some 2,047 Confederate veterans and their widows, who died after 1889 in the Texas Confederate Home and the Confederate Woman's Home. Statuary in the cemetery includes Elisabet Ney's recumbent statue of Albert Sidney Johnston, Enrico Cerracchio's bronze bust of John A. Wharton, and Pompeo Coppini's bronze figures of S. F. Austin and Joanna Troutman. Members and former members of the Texas legislature, elective state and former state officials, and officials who have been appointed by the governor and confirmed by the Texas Senate may be buried in the cemetery. An exception to the regulations was the burial of author J. Frank Dobie in 1964 by special permission of the gover-

nor and vote of the Texas legislature. Dobie's widow was also buried there in 1974. Miriam Amanda Ferguson, buried in 1961, Daniel James Moody, buried in 1966, Allan Shivers, buried in 1985, and John B. Connally, Jr., buried in 1993, brought to 11 the number of governors interred in the State Cemetery. In the summer of 1994 Lieutenant Governor Bob Bullock, appalled at how run-down the cemetery had become, began a cleaning effort. Work was done on the sidewalks, roads, fences, and caretaker's cottage, and steps were taken to alleviate a drainage problem.

Andrew Forest Muir

State Fair of Texas. An annual event in Dallas. The Dallas State Fair and Exposition, to which the present State Fair of Texas traces its origin, was chartered as a private corporation in 1886 by a group of businessmen. After a controversy about location, C. A. Keating, speaking for the farm implement dealers, secured a charter for a separate event—the Texas State Fair and Exposition, which opened on 25 October, one day ahead of the Dallas State Fair. Exhibit facilities and a racetrack were built at each location, and both events attracted sizable crowds that fall. Attendance at the Dallas State Fair was estimated in excess of 100,000. Nevertheless, revenues for the fairs failed to meet expenses. The rival associations merged in 1887 to become the Texas State Fair and Dallas Exposition. Despite indebtedness of more than $100,000, the directors voted to expand the fairgrounds by purchasing 37 acres adjacent to the East Dallas site. Thousands came to the fair each year to view the finest racing stock, cattle sales, balloon ascents, and displays of farm machinery. Women competed for prizes in baking, preserving, and needlework. Concerts and appearances by such notables as John Philip Sousa, William Jennings Bryan, Carry Nation, and Booker T. Washington were added attractions. But the popular success of the exposition was dimmed by repeated fires, mishaps, and mounting debt. A grandstand collapsed during a firework show in 1900, and the main exhibit building burned to the ground two years later. When the Texas legislature banned gambling on horseraces in 1903, thereby eliminating the fair's main source of income, the association faced a financial crisis. To protect this valuable community asset, the Texas State Fair sold its property to the city of Dallas in 1904 under an agreement that set aside a period each fall to hold the annual exposition.

The reorganized State Fair of Texas prospered immediately, establishing new records for receipts and attendance; 300,000 people streamed through the gates in 1905. President William Howard Taft visited the fair in 1909, and Woodrow Wilson delivered a speech there in 1911. Automobile races and stunt flying exhibitions became the top attractions. Attendance passed the one million mark in 1916. World War I caused the 1918 fair to be canceled, and Fair Park was converted into a temporary army encampment. The 1920s brought significant development for the fairgrounds. A magnificent auditorium, eventually known as the Music Hall, was completed in 1925, and outstanding New York shows were presented to Texas audiences for the first time. The Texas–Oklahoma football game was established as an annual event in 1929, and in 1930 the racetrack complex was razed to permit construction of a 46,000-seat stadium that was later renamed the Cotton Bowl. In 1934, largely through the efforts of civic leader R. L. Thornton, Fair Park was selected as the central exposition site for the proposed Texas Centennial celebration. No state fair was scheduled in 1935, when construction began on a $25 million project that transformed the existing fairgrounds. The 1936 Centennial Exposition attracted more than six million people during its six-month run. A similar event on a smaller scale, the Pan American Exposition, was presented in 1937. No fairs were held during the war years of 1942–45. Under Thornton's leadership, the State Fair of Texas entered an era of unprecedented growth after World War II. Attendance topped two million in 1949.

Highlights of the 1950s included the development of an international livestock show, the installation of a monorail system, a visit from Vice President Richard Nixon, and the first appearance of Big Tex, a 52-foot cowboy figure erected in the center of the grounds. Since 1960 each exposition has been keyed to a theme. A single-day attendance record of 345,469 was set in 1966, and in 1968 the total number of fairgoers exceeded three million for the first time. Major renovation of the Cotton Bowl and Music Hall was accomplished during the 12 years that Robert B. Cullum served as state fair president. Midway accidents in 1979 and 1983 led to the adoption of a ride-safety program that is considered a model for the amusement industry. In 1986 Fair Park was designated a National Historic Landmark, and the State Fair of Texas hosted an exposition celebrating both the Texas Sesquicentennial and the fair's own 100th anniversary. The event attracted 3,959,058 visitors, the largest attendance ever recorded at an American state fair. The length of the traditional fair season has been extended from 17 to 24 days. Sponsorship by such companies as Exxon, Southwest Airlines, Dr Pepper has made it possible for the State Fair of Texas to offer its visitors a wide range of exhibits, entertainment, and services. Annual attendance in the early 1990s usually exceeded three million.   *Nancy Wiley*

State Treasurer. A state office since 1845; superseded a similar office in the Republic of Texas. The treasurer is elected and serves for four years as head of the State Treasury Department. The major duties of the office are to receive and keep state money, maintain accounts of all receipts and expenditures, collect cigarette and tobacco taxes and certain gross-receipts taxes,

serve as custodian of securities in trust, receive unclaimed property held in trust, and administer money in a local government-investment pool known as TexPool.   *Laurie E. Jasinski*

State Tree. The pecan; designated state tree by the legislature in 1919. Sentiment favoring the choice was fostered by James Stephen Hogg's request that a pecan tree be planted at his grave. The pecan is native to more than 150 Texas counties and is grown commercially in 30 more. Its commercial use in Central and West Texas greatly increased with the development of new varieties and new irrigated orchards.   *Claudia Hazlewood*

Stephen F. Austin State University. In Nacogdoches; originally one of two teachers' colleges authorized by the state legislature in 1917. The city of Nacogdoches offered the state a 200-acre site. Much of the campus is on the homestead of Thomas J. Rusk, and the president's home is on the Sam Houston tract. Because of World War I and legislative setbacks, the school did not open until 1923. Alton Birdwell was president. The 158 students were taught in the Nacogdoches public schools until May 1924. The graduate division was established in 1937. In 1945 the Forest Service of the USDA established the East Texas Branch of the Forest Experiment Station at the college, the only case in which an act of Congress named an institution to cooperate in a forestry-research program. Paul Boynton succeeded Birdwell in 1942. Enrollment in 1946–47 was 1,000. In 1949 the name of the school was changed from Stephen F. Austin State Teachers College to Stephen F. Austin State College. It was one of the fastest growing state-supported colleges in Texas during the 1960s, when government money aided in the construction of many new buildings. During the 1974–75 term the enrollment was 10,881; Ralph W. Steen was president. The school became Stephen F. Austin State University in 1969. SFASU is fully accredited. Its schools are Applied Arts and Sciences, Business, Education, Fine Arts, Forestry, Liberal Arts, Science, and Mathematics. It is governed by its own board of regents. The university confers bachelor's and master's degrees in numerous fields, as well as a doctorate in forestry. It has a cooperative Ph.D. program with Texas A&M University.   *C. K. Chamberlain*

Sterling, Ross Shaw. Governor; b. near Anahuac, February 1875; d. Fort Worth, 25 March 1949; m. Maud Abbie Gage (1898); 5 children. Sterling started with a feed store in Sour Lake (1903), bought small-town banks, acquired two oil wells that developed into the Humble Oil and Refining Company (of which he was president), and owned the Dayton–Goose Creek Railway Company in 1918. After leaving Humble he developed real estate around Houston and bought the Houston *Dispatch* and Houston Post, which he combined into the *Post–Dispatch* (later the Houston *Post*). After serving as chairman of the Texas Highway Commission in 1930, he was elected governor and served one term (1931–33). He called a special session of the legislature to deal with the depression-era agricultural emergency, but its main achievement, the Texas Cotton Acreage Control Law of 1931–32, was declared unconstitutional. He declared martial law in East Texas because oilmen were ignoring oil proration rulings of the Railroad Commission—an act the courts later said exceeded his authority. After losing his bid for a second term to Miriam Ferguson, Sterling returned to Houston and built another fortune in oil in the Sterling Oil and Refining Company

Ross S. Sterling making his first speech in his campaign for the office of governor, 1930. Ross Shaw Sterling Papers, CAH; CN 01553.

(1932–36). In addition to his presidency of this company, he was president of American Maid Flour Mills and the R. S. Sterling Investment Company, as well as chairman of the Houston National Bank and the Houston–Harris County Channel Navigation Board. His philanthropies included a large gift to Texas Christian University.

Sterne, Nicholas Adolphus. Merchant and financier of the Texas Revolution; b. Cologne, 5 April 1801; d. New Orleans, 27 March 1852 (buried originally in New Orleans, then reinterred in Nacogdoches); m. Eva Catherine Rosine Ruff (1828); 7 children. At 16 Sterne was working in a passport office when he learned that he was going to be drafted, forged a passport for himself, and immigrated to the United States. He landed in New Orleans in 1817, found mercantile employment, and studied law. Although he never practiced law in Texas, he acted as a land agent and primary judge in Nacogdoches. While still in New Orleans he became a Mason, an affiliation of great importance to him in later years. In the early 1820s he began an itinerate peddling trade in the country north of New Orleans. He used that city as a base of operations from which he ranged as far north as Nashville, Tennessee, where he met Sam Houston. The two formed a lasting relationship, which they renewed after Sterne established a mercantile house in Nacogdoches in 1826. (Houston arrived in Texas six years later.) Soon afterward, Sterne became involved with the Fredonian Rebellion. He assisted Haden Edwards and other immigrants in their resistance to the Mexican government by smuggling guns and other materials in barrels of coffee. Spies in New Orleans alerted Nacogdoches authorities to these activities, and Sterne was arrested, tried for treason, and sentenced to be shot. Because his guards were also Masons, however, he came and went as he pleased and eventually was released on the promise that he would never again take up arms against the government. Sterne adhered to the letter of this promise but not to its spirit; he assisted the Texans in the battle of Nacogdoches in 1832 and financed two companies of troops during the Texas Revolution,

but did not personally again shoulder arms against the government. Sterne officially became Catholic in order to marry Eva, though unofficially he remained a deist. Houston, one of many important guests in the Sternes' home, boarded with them when he first arrived in Texas and was baptized a Catholic in their parlor. Mrs. Sterne served as Houston's godmother, but Sterne did not serve as his godfather because the date coincided with Yom Kippur. Sterne strongly supported the movement for Texas independence. He traveled to New Orleans in 1835 as a special agent of the provisional government and personally raised and financed the New Orleans Greys. Sterne supported most of Houston's programs during the period of the republic except his benevolent Indian policy. He commanded a company of militia in the battle of the Neches (16 July 1839) and helped expel the Cherokees from East Texas. He served as postmaster at Nacogdoches (1840), as deputy clerk and associate justice of the county court, and as a justice of the peace (1841). He was deputy clerk of the board of land commissioners and commissioner of roads and revenues for Nacogdoches County. He served as a member of the board of health and was overseer of streets for the corporation of Nacogdoches. In 1847 he won election to the state House of Representatives and in 1851 was elected to the state Senate. From 1840 to 1851 he kept a diary that is now a valuable source of information on the period of the republic. Though self-educated, he served as official translator of English, French, Spanish, German, Yiddish, Portuguese, and Latin.

Archie P. McDonald

Stevenson, Coke Robert. Governor; b. Mason County, 20 March 1888; d. San Angelo, 28 June 1975; m. Fay Wright (1912; d. 1942); 1 child; m. Marguerite King Heap (1954); 1 child. Stevenson studied law on his own and passed the bar exam in 1913. He subsequently became president of the First National Bank in Junction and was involved in many business enterprises in Kimble County. He was successively county attorney (1914–18), county judge (1919–21), and state representative (1929–39); he was the first person ever to be speaker of the House for two successive terms (1933–37). He served as lieutenant governor from 1939 to 1941, when he became governor after W. Lee O'Daniel resigned to become a United States senator. Stevenson was elected in 1942 and reelected in 1944; at the end of his second term he had held the office longer than anyone else at that time. He favored soil-conservation measures, highway development, an enlarged building program for the University of Texas, and higher teachers' salaries. After he returned to ranching at Telegraph, he ran for the U.S. Senate in 1948, in a race that brought him more national attention than he had ever had. He lost the election to Lyndon B. Johnson by 87 votes, the closest margin of victory ever in a senatorial race. The election exhibited clear symptoms of fraud. After returns showed Stevenson winning, an amended return came from Precinct 13 in Jim Wells County, giving Johnson 201 votes and Stevenson 2. The voting lists from Box 13 disappeared, and the returns from neighboring Duval County were burned before the date set by law. The case went to the Supreme Court, which ruled that it did not have jurisdiction. The Senate turned down Stevenson's appeal. "Landslide Lyndon" won the election and eventually became president. Stevenson, embittered, supported Republicans for president for the rest of his life.

Eldon S. Branda

Stirpes. The Texas State Genealogical Society quarterly, named "roots" in Latin; published each March, June, September, and December. Although emphasis is placed on records of the Republic of Texas era, published material is not limited to the records of Texas. Starting in 1981 each volume was indexed by both topic and full name in the December issue. By 1987 each issue carried a full-name index. The Genealogical Society also published a 25-year topical index for volumes 1 through 25 (1961–85).   *Edna Perry Deckler*

Stockade Case. A notorious Reconstruction murder trial. On 3 October 1868, George W. Smith, the Marion County delegate to the Constitutional Convention of 1868–69, and four black men were incarcerated in the Jefferson city jail after a Republican meeting that ended in gunfire. Smith was shot at, returned fire, and, after seeking protection from the local army post, was jailed by civil authorities on the charge of assault. The next night an armed mob overpowered the guard, and, unable to dislodge Smith from his cell, shot him through the windows. The four black men were taken into the woods, where two of them were killed; the other two escaped but were later caught and brought back for trial. The military began an investigation and made four arrests on 5 December. They had planned to arrest five men that day, but William P. Saufley, grand commander of the Knights of the Rising Sun, the white supremacy group thought responsible for the slayings, had left town. By early April 1869 about 35 men had been arrested; 24 were actually brought to trial. Two of them turned state's evidence and implicated Hinche Mabry, who was serving as one of the defense attorneys. Mabry fled to Canada to avoid arrest. Most white citizens of Marion County were outraged by the military's activities. Two attorneys for the defendants, John Burke and Benjamin Epperson, went to Washington to request of John M. Schofield, the secretary of war, that the defendants be turned over to the civil courts for trial. Robert Loughery, editor of both the Jefferson *Times* and the Marshall *Texas Republican,* mounted an attack by circular to newspapers in both Texas and other states, complaining about the military's refusal to turn the case over to civilian courts or to release the prisoners on bail. Loughery's circular was sent to President Andrew Johnson, who sent it to the War Department and general in chief, asking for a full report. Gen. Joseph J. Reynolds, commander of the troops in Texas, published a circular effectively rebutting Loughery and justifying army jurisdiction in the case. In the trial (24 May–9 August 1869), described as "tortuous" by one historian, 176 witnesses were heard. The commission found three men guilty of murder and of overpowering a military guard and related violations. Four were found guilty of a lesser charge of threatening the life of Judge Colbert Caldwell; three of these were pardoned by President Grant soon after the trial. All the other prisoners were found not guilty and discharged. Those convicted of murder were sentenced to life in prison, but it is unclear whether or not they actually served time.   *Max S. Lale*

Stockdale, Fletcher Summerfield. Governor; b. Russellville, Kentucky, 1823 or 1825; d. Cuero, 4 February 1890; m. Mrs. Elizabeth Pryor Bankhead Lytle (1857; d. 1865); m. Elizabeth Schleicher (1877); 3 children. Stockdale was admitted to the bar in Kentucky. He moved to Texas in 1846 and in 1856 was one of the founders of the Powderhorn, Victoria and Gonzales Railroad

Helen Stoddard. Courtesy Special Collections, Texas Woman's University Library, Denton.

Company, which never got around to laying any track. He represented the Twenty-sixth District in the state House from 1857 to 1861 and was a delegate to both state and national Democratic conventions of the time (1859, 1860). He was a leader of the Secession Convention in Austin (1861). In 1862–63 he was a special aide to Gov. Francis R. Lubbock and in 1863 was elected lieutenant governor. In June 1865 he became governor when Gov. Pendleton Murrah fled to Mexico. The next month President Andrew Johnson appointed Andrew J. Hamilton provisional governor. Stockdale, who welcomed Hamilton to Austin, returned to Calhoun County and served as president of the Indianola Railroad. After 1873 he moved to Cuero and became a land promoter in addition to his law practice. In 1868 he was in the Texas Senate. He served in the Constitutional Convention of 1875 and was a delegate at the Democratic national conventions of 1872, 1876, and 1880, as well as a notable delegate at state democratic conventions in 1873, 1878, 1882, and 1888. His 17-year-old bride of 1877 was the daughter of Gustav Schleicher. Stockdale's portrait was hung in the capital in 1946; Stockdale, Texas, is named for him.

Stoddard, Helen. Prohibition and reform advocate; b. Helen Gerrells, Sheboygan Township, Wisconsin, 27 July 1850; d. southern California, January 1941; m. S. D. Stoddard (1873; d. 1878); 2 sons; ed. Ripon College, Wisconsin, and Genesee Wesleyan Seminary, Lima, New York (grad. 1871). The family moved to Texas in 1877 and were among the pioneer settlers of Indian Gap. In 1880 Mrs. Stoddard resigned her position in mathematics at Nebraska Conference Seminary and joined her parents in Texas, where she continued as a teacher. In the late 1880s she became interested in temperance reform through the influence of Anna Palmer, a national figure in WCTU. In 1891 she was elected to the presidency of the Texas WCTU and resigned her position at Fort Worth University. In the next 16 years she built the Texas WCTU from a membership of a few hundred to almost 1,900 dues-paying members. The TWCTU had been demoralized by the defeat of the prohibition-amendment campaign of 1887. Helen Stoddard traveled around the state lecturing, organizing new chapters, and reorganizing inactive ones. She spent the winter of 1893 lobbying successfully in Austin for the passage of a "scientific temperance-instruction law" (that is, a law requiring that children be taught the ill effects of alcohol on the human body). She was instrumental in persuading the legislature to raise the age of protection for girls from 12 to 15 in 1895 and to forbid the sale of cigarettes to minors in 1899. She lobbied successfully for a pure-food law and for statutes against cocaine, gambling, and COD liquor shipments to dry counties. Her most important lobbying work was in her stand against child labor and her effort to establish the College of Industrial Arts for girls. In 1901 Governor Sayers appointed her to the board of commissioners charged with choosing a site for the new institution. She was the only woman so chosen. She traveled more than 3,000 miles with the commission and served as secretary of the college's board of regents from 1901 to 1907. Stoddard Hall at Texas Woman's University is named in her honor. At the national level she served the WCTU as an antinarcotics lecturer and conductor of the WCTU Institute Summer Assembly in Bay View, Michigan. She spent three months in Mexico as an organizer and was twice a delegate to WCTU world conventions. Like temperance advocates generally, she supported woman suffrage, and she contributed the article on the Texas suffrage movement to Susan B. Anthony's *History of Woman Suffrage*. In 1907 she resigned the TWCTU presidency because of poor health and moved to southern California.

Judith N. McArthur

Strikes. Before the United States government began keeping records of work stoppages, no accurate means existed to determine the number of strikes in a state or the extent of participation in the strikes known to have occurred. It is clear, however that strikes occurred in Texas as early as the republic. In September or October 1838 the Texas Typographical Association, the first labor organization in Texas, struck the Houston publishers and secured a 25 percent wage increase. From then on, occasional work stoppages occurred, usually involving only a small number of workers and almost never a labor organization. Not until after the Civil War did bona fide strikes occur. Those of 1870 were typical. In January of that year, Houston telegraphers joined a short, unsuccessful nationwide strike against Western Union; in April, the Austin Typographical Union suffered a disastrous defeat; in May, Galveston brickmasons struck for a raise but returned to work without it; and in November, the engineers and brakemen on the Houston and Texas Central Railway lost their jobs as a result of a walkout over wages. The first work stoppage involving more than a handful of workers occurred in June 1872, when the management of the Houston and Texas Central Railway began requiring all employees to sign an agreement releasing the company from liability for accidents on the job. No union existed, yet almost all employees attended meetings demanding the withdrawal of the liability release, calling it a "death warrant." When the railroad refused, 80 percent of the operating employees walked out and all trains on the line stopped for several days. After supervisory personnel and new employees put most of the trains back into operation, all those remaining on strike were fired. Although the engineers were later rehired and the liability release was withdrawn, the strike was a calamitous failure for most of the workers. The number of strikes increased through the seventies, as the number of unions and labor militancy grew. The peak year until the middle eighties was 1877, when, in addition to numerous small strikes, major work stoppages occurred among dockworkers in Galveston and railway workers on the Texas and Pacific. Both the large strikes were marked by considerable violence. The dockworkers' strike saw the first use of African Americans as strikebreakers in Texas.

The first strike in Texas noted in official records occurred in 1880, when 50 employees of the draying industry stayed out 150 days but were denied an increase in wages. Between 1880 and 1886, 100 strikes occurred, involving 8,124 workers; establishments involved were closed for a total of 450 days; striking workers were out for a total of 708 days each; and the loss due to strikes was estimated at $1 million. These strikes included the Cowboy Strike of 1883, in which more than 300 cowboys in the Tascosa area struck for higher wages and better working conditions, and two strikes in Galveston, one of 280 cotton handlers lasting 64 days and the other of 150 longshoremen against the use of black laborers lasting 2 days. The first failed, the second succeeded. One of the most spectacular strikes was the Capitol Boycott in 1885—a protest against the use of convict labor. The largest number of strikes was called by the building trades unions, but the largest number of workers involved in any one industry was in transportation. The third largest group involved was the West Texas coal miners. The greatest number striking in any one year was 4,154, involved in seven strikes in 1885. Of these, 1,500 were longshoremen in the port of Galveston, and the major part of the others were in transportation. Additional thousands of Texas laborers joined the national strike of telegraphers and sectional strikes against the management of the western and southwestern railroads. In 1885 Texas ranked ninth among 40 states in number of workers involved in strikes (4,000); for the sixyear period it ranked fifteenth. Seventy-five of the 100 strikes, chiefly interstate strikes of telegraphers and railway workers, occurred in the year 1886; seventy-four of these were called by an organized labor group. Twenty-four of the twenty-five strikes between 1886 and 1894 were called by organized groups. The most significant were in the coal-mining areas, where industrial troubles were almost continuous from 1884 to 1904. In 1884, for six months, 450 coal miners carried on a losing strike against a reduction in wages. Troubles began in the mines in Erath County in 1888 and lasted for four years; Texas Rangers remained in the area for more than a year. The strike was largely unsuccessful.

After 1886 annual figures on the number of strikes are not available, but a summary for the quarter century from 1881 to 1905 shows a total of 341 strikes in Texas involving 37,000 workers. In 1903, which for the nation represents a peak year for strikes, 1,200 coal miners at Thurber remained out a total of 14,400 days and won union recognition and some changes in wages. Another strike of miners in 1910 caused a loss of 108,230 work days. Official reports from 1914 to 1926, covering World

War I, include only numbers of strikes. In Texas the number of strikes increased over the three years preceding the actual war years of 1917–18. The largest number of strikers involved was 10,000, members of the Oil Field, Gas Well, and Refinery Workers, who demanded an increase in wages and union recognition in the Oilfield Strike of 1917. After three months of unsuccessful attempts at mediation, the workers won some wage increases but lost the demand for recognition. Other strikes included 23 in the building trades, 10 in transportation, 8 in metal trades, 6 among chemical workers, 3 among miners, and 7 in the shipbuilding industry. Among the major strikes of 1919 was a general strike in the building trades in Dallas involving 10,000 workers and a strike of 1,700 coal miners that caused the loss of 52,000 workdays.

Although the years 1919–20 brought a peak of industrial unrest, no significant changes took place in the groups concerned. Strikes included 24 in the building trades, 8 in printing and publishing, 7 of railroad employees, 9 of hotel and restaurant employees, and 6 of street-railway employees. In 1921 the major industrial trouble was the participation of all Texas ports in a national strike of marine workers—the Galveston Longshoremen's Strike. In October 1921 a threatened strike of railroad workers on a national scale did not take place save for 600 workers on the International–Great Northern Railroad in Texas. Between 1922 and 1936 the number of strikes recorded annually dropped. But the mere number of strikes is little indication of the extent of industrial unrest. The 38 strikes in 1936 involved 7,058 workers; 22 strikes in 1934 involved 8,222 workers. Mandays of labor lost in 1936 totaled 93,641; mandays lost on 24 strikes in 1935 totaled 111,707. Between 1927 and 1936, 24 strikes in transportation and communication caused a loss of 253,500 work days; 38 in building and construction caused a loss of 37,200 working days; 3 strikes in agriculture and fishing caused the loss of 50,900 mandays; 9 in the textile industry caused the loss of 33,657 mandays. In 1937 shrimp workers at Palacios, under the leadership of United Cannery, Agricultural and Packing House Workers of the CIO, demanded an increase in wages and preferential union hiring. Shrimpboatmen of Sabine, Freeport, Galveston, and Point Isabel, through the Inland Boatmen's Division of the National Maritime Union, also asked for an increase in pay. In September 1938, trouble flared into open violence; one man was killed, and others were injured. Another area of persistent trouble was among garment workers in the Dallas area. Governor James Allred appointed a State Industrial Commission to investigate the Dallas Garment Workers' Strike in 1935 and the millinery workers' situation in 1937. Texas Rangers remained in the Dallas area for some time in 1937, when recurrent acts of violence kept resentment alive. The situation was the subject of a hearing by the National Labor Relations Board early in 1940.

During 1930 the number of workers involved was 538 per strike, the greatest for the period 1927–44. Six strikes involved 3,299 workers, of whom 99 percent were in two strikes in transportation and communication. One was a strike of 3,000 longshoremen against the Lykes Brothers Steamship Company that tied up 30 vessels in West Indies trade for three days. The issue on wage rates was compromised. The second largest average number of workers involved per strike was 433 in 1933. Approximately onehalf were involved in two strikes in building and construction, 475 were in textile production, 400 in tobacco

manufacture, and 300 in lumber and allied products. In 1934 the number of average workers per strike was 374, the greatest number being 1,500 in the agriculture and fishing industry. The greatest number of mandays lost in any one year of the 17-year period from 1927 to 1944 was 156,408 in 1935. In the first four years after 1939 the number of workers involved in strikes in Texas was 1 percent of those involved in the nation, but in 1945 only 11 states exceeded Texas in proportion of workers involved. The strike of the International Typographical Union against the Valley Publishing Company, which published papers in McAllen, Harlingen, and Brownsville, attracted much attention. Texas Rangers were sent into the area, and for some days the papers did not appear. The dramatic character of the picketing and some violence led to an emergency order by the city of Harlingen limiting the number of pickets. The order was tested on the question of constitutionality. In 1945 several major oil refineries were stopped by members of the Oil Workers' International demanding an increase in wages. The refineries were seized and operated by the United States Navy, the dispute was referred to a fact-finding board, and by the end of February 1946 most of the seized plants had been returned to private operation. In the same industry 450 members of a black local of the oil workers at Port Arthur struck against the Texas Company (Texaco) over racial discrimination in wages. Other strikes in 1945 included a stoppage at the Galveston Todd Dry Docks in February, at the Gulf Oil Corporation of Port Arthur in May, and at the Pennsylvania Ship Yards in Beaumont in July. In September a one-day stoppage of 10,000 workers at the Consolidated Steel Corporation shipbuilding division at Orange protested alleged discrimination against union pipefitters.

The vast changes that occurred in Texas during and after World War II are clearly exemplified by labor–management relations. The 2,500,000 mandays lost in the approximately 150 strikes during the eighteen months immediately after the war exceeded the total man-days lost in all previous strikes combined. This greatest outburst of industrial conflict in the state's history included major work stoppages in the oil, railroad, aircraft, chemical, construction, steel, and nonferrous metals industries. Causes of the strikes included the expiration of wartime nostrike pledges, the problems brought by demobilization, the drastic inflation that followed the war, and vigorous organizational drives in several industries. When this surge of labor troubles subsided, however, prewar conditions did not return. In no year of the two decades following the war did the number of strikes or mandays lost fall as low as the previous high of 64 strikes with 198,000 mandays lost established in 1937. In each year except 1963 (when only 7,000 workers struck their jobs), the number of Texans involved in labor disputes was more than twice the prewar high of 11,800 established in 1941. The average number of workers involved per strike also reached record levels after the war, with 1,025 men per strike in 1945, 977 per strike in 1946, and more than 400 per strike in 9 of the 20 years following the war. During these 20 years, 790,000 strikers lost 14,257,000 man-days in 1,680 work stoppages. Although small strikes, involving relatively few men and scant mandays lost, continued to account for the majority of these work stoppages, approximately 75 percent of the mandays lost resulted from strikes in major industries. More than 100,000 mandays were lost in strikes in the oil and gas industry in each of the years 1945, 1947, 1950, 1952, 1959, 1961, 1962, and 1963; in transportation and communication in 1946, 1947, 1950, 1953, 1963, and 1965; in the chemical industries in 1946, 1949, 1956, 1961, 1962, and 1963; in the iron and steel industry in 1946, 1952, 1956, and 1959; and in construction in 1946, 1947, 1952, 1953, 1954, 1956, 1958, 1959, 1960, 1961, and 1965. Both the industries and unions that developed most rapidly in Texas after World War II were of national or regional character; consequently, major work stoppages were less frequently purely local conflicts. The nationwide steel strikes of 1952, 1956, and 1959 affected large numbers of Texas steelworkers, and longshoremen in the state's ports took part in regional strikes in 1956, 1959, 1961, 1962, and 1965. Often nationwide strikes against particular companies, such as those against Sinclair Oil Corporation in 1945 and 1952, Southwestern Bell in 1953, and Ford Motor Company in 1964 and 1967, involved Texans.

A more mature attitude toward labor relations by the unions, management, and the public characterized the postwar decades. As a result labor disputes were more peaceful, if equally acrimonious (especially in the urban areas of high union membership and activity). Occasional fisticuffs still occurred, from those marking the oil and chemical strikes of 1945 to several fights in the farmworkers' strike of 1966–67 in the Valley. But rare was the kind of violence that marred the Lone Star Steel strike at Daingerfield in 1957, where bombings and shootings occurred and a large force of rangers and highway patrolmen was needed to restore peace.

Profound changes in the role of the strike in labor relations began in the early sixties. The federal Landrum–Griffin Act of 1959 strengthened the hand of management in union relations, especially in righttowork states, of which Texas is one. Prosperity in most of the basic industries led management to move more frequently to trade increased wages and benefits for no-strike provisions in long-term contracts. Organized labor had been successful in moving many of its industrial members into the middle class, which made them less willing (and able) to support work stoppages. Rapid technological advances rendered the strike a less useful tool for unions. In workplaces like refineries and chemical and printing plants, for example, supervisory and contract workers could maintain operations during a strike, rendering strikes much less effective. Such innovations also reduced the number of workers required in many industries. After several strikes (followed by Taft–Hartley injunctions) in the early sixties, the International Longshoremen's Association, for instance, was forced to accept containerization in Gulf ports in exchange for a guaranteed annual wage for most of its members, as the inevitable virtual disappearance of longshoreman jobs occurred. Similarly, an injunction against a national railway strike in the middle sixties culminated in reduction of the size of train crews in exchange for allowing attrition rather than massive layoffs to reduce the number of railway workers. These changes were combined with growing antiunion sentiment in business and government and a dramatic change in the makeup of the state's workforce. The result was that in the decade and a half after 1965, while the number of nonagricultural workers almost doubled the number of strikes, the number of workers involved and days idle remained essentially level. On the average, there were about a hundred strikes a year in Texas, which idled 30,000 to 40,000 workers for about a total of a million man-days (or less than .1 percent of total worktime in the state). Though changes in the categories of the Bureau of Labor Statistics reports

make precise comparison to earlier periods impossible, it is clear that a vast majority of the strikes in Texas were in the traditionally more highly unionized manufacturing, transportation, and communication and building industries.

Several of the work stoppages in this period were worthy of note. Reclassification of jobs at the American Oil Company's Texas City refinery, a result of automation, led to a year-long strike by 2,000 workers in 1962. Although a compromise ended the walkout, in time the company was able to reduce its workforce dramatically, a pattern followed by other oil and chemical installations. In 1966 a Texas branch of the California-based United Farm Workers Union began to organize the Mexican-American farmworkers in the Rio Grande valley, a move that resulted in the Starr County Strike and had broad repercussions. Though unsuccessful in gaining contracts with corporate growers, the movement highlighted serious social, health, and economic issues that have remained sources of contention. Similarly, in 1972, 2,500 workers at the Farah clothing plants in San Antonio and El Paso, more than 90 percent of whom were Mexican Americans, walked off their jobs. The Farah strike, which lasted 22 months, provoked an effective nationwide boycott of Farah products led by the AFL–CIO and other pro-union groups. Increasing activism among Hispanics in South Texas resulted in some growth in union activity there. For example, the United Auto Workers union organized the Eagle Bus Manufacturing plant in Brownsville in 1975, but was unable to secure much beyond union recognition and a grievance procedure until a strike in October 1980. The company tried to replace the 400 mostly Tejano workers with strike breakers from both sides of the Rio Grande, but was unable to secure needed skilled workers. Production before the strike was two buses per day, but at the end of two months the strike breakers had not completed a single vehicle. Under pressure from its customers, Eagle agreed to meaningful raises, a host of improved benefits, and an enhanced role for the union in shop operations. Coca Cola drivers and warehousemen in Laredo joined the Teamsters in 1977. When negotiations for a contract with increased wages and benefits stalled, they struck in March 1978. A complaint to the National Labor Relations Board led to an order for the company to bargain seriously. In January 1979, a contract granting wage increases, improved benefits, and improved job security was signed. Less traditional issues than wages and benefits motivated some work stoppages. A growing practice of contracting out repairs to nonunion workers led the 1,800 organized craft workers at Dow Chemical in Freeport to walk off the job in June 1972. After a bitter and confrontational fourmonth strike, the company agreed to contract out no more than 25 percent of its maintenance work and to grant a few selected wage increases. In what has been called the first environmental strike in America, in 1973 the 1,800 members of the Oil, Chemical and Atomic Workers at Shell Oil's Deer Park plant struck for the right of access to records to help monitor the workplace environment. After four months, the company agreed to share some information, although much less than the union had sought. The strike set a pattern, however, for other agreements on safety and environment in manufacturing industries. A regional collective bargaining arrangement between all contractors and building trade unions in the Dallas–Fort Worth area was finalized in 1971, the nation's first such arrangement. For four years this arrangement, which provided for a no-strike–arbitration process, functioned well and was viewed as a potential new pattern with national consequences. But in 1975 the contractors rejected demands for higher wages and benefits, and the largest and longest construction shutdown in the state's history followed. More than 26,000 workers in 28 unions shut down 200 contractors for 113 days. In the end, probably neither side won. By the time a compromise was reached, nonunion contractors had moved into the area; in the eighties they controlled more building jobs than at any time since the 1920s.

Little doubt exists that the relatively low number of strikes in the seventies was related to the extraordinary economic boom in Texas, fueled by soaring oil prices. Unemployment remained low, and in some oilrelated jobs wages increased an average of 17 percent a year. But even before the boom turned to bust in the 1980s, several developments began eroding the influence of organized labor and thus the use of its ultimate weapon. The reorientation of the state's economy from basic to service industries, much foreign immigration, new business practices such as "contracting out" and "downsizing," the influx of women into the workforce, increased international trade and competition, the growing migration of jobs overseas, and the increasing conservative political climate all contributed to a stagnation of union membership and, after 1982, to a precipitous decline. Additionally, a body of court decisions and NLRB rulings made it easier for management to replace striking employees, thus introducing new risks for wouldbe strikers. The effect of President Reagan's hugely popular firing of striking air-traffic controllers and decertification of their union in 1981 would be hard to overestimate. The fear of permanent replacement is cited by numerous union leaders as the greatest hindrance to union activism. As a result, collective bargaining in the eighties and nineties has more frequently been characterized by incidents such as that at the General Motors Arlington plant, where UAW members gave up benefits in 1982 and 1992 in exchange for job security for more senior employees, than by strikes. The 400 workers at the Harvey Industries plant in Athens suffered a more drastic fate. There, workers accepted a 25 percent pay cut in 1982 and a wage freeze in 1987 in order to keep their television factory working in the face of foreign competition. They struck when faced with the threat of another wage cut in early 1989, but replacements kept the plant in operation, and after several months most of the strikers gave up and went back to their jobs. Some were never rehired. In January 1991 the plant closed. In a time of massive layoffs, high unemployment, and stagnant wages, workers and unions became less willing to risk the proverbial bird in the hand.

Although the Bureau of Labor Statistics, in response to budget cuts, ceased reporting work stoppages in individual states in 1980, it is certain that strikes have declined as a factor in labor relations. Since 1982 the number of work stoppages per year in the United States has averaged between 15 and 20 percent of the number in the previous three decades. There is no reason to believe that Texas, the least unionized of the industrial states, has not followed national trends. The best estimate is that in most recent years, there have been about 20 strikes involving a few thousand workers in Texas. More and more frequently, these strikes end as did the 1992 Apple Tree supermarket strike, in which the company declared bankruptcy, a judge invalidated the union's contract, and the new Japanese owners refused to bargain. Labor is occasionally able to gain advantage at a strategic

Downtown Sugar Land, 1929. Growing sugarcane and refining sugar have been important economic assets to the community since 1843. Courtesy Imperial Sugar Company.

moment, as did the American Airlines flight attendants, who struck successfully for five days during the Thanksgiving rush in 1993. But such incidents are infrequent. Until dramatic changes occur in union effectiveness, public opinion, and the writing and administration of labor law, the strike will likely remain an ineffective tool for unions in Texas.

Ruth A. Allen, George N. Green, and James V. Reese

Sugar Land, Texas. On Oyster Creek east of the Brazos River and seven miles northeast of Richmond in northeastern Fort Bend County. The area was originally granted to Samuel M. Williams in 1828 for his service as secretary to Stephen F. Austin. Nathaniel Williams purchased the land from his brother in 1838, and there he and a third brother, Matthew, operated Oakland Plantation, which grew cotton, corn, and sugarcane. The Williams brothers established their raw-sugar mill in 1843. In 1853 Oakland Plantation was purchased by Benjamin F. Terry and William J. Kyle, who were instrumental in extending the Buffalo Bayou, Brazos and Colorado Railway through the property. A post office was established in Sugar Land in 1858. The plantation languished in the 1860s, and the post office was closed in 1886. E. H. Cunningham of San Antonio accumulated more than 12,000 acres of the property over time and invested more than $1 million in a sugar refinery, a new raw-sugar mill, a paper mill, and the 14-mile Sugar Land Railroad in the 1890s. In 1890 a second post office opened. At that time much of the labor force was leased from the nearby state prison farms. The brutal working conditions caused bitter convicts to call Sugar Land the "Hell Hole on the Brazos." From 1906 to 1908 Isaac H. Kempner of Galveston and William T. Eldridge of Eagle Lake acquired the Ellis and Cunningham plantations and the Cunningham Sugar Company, modernized the facilities, and made the community a company town for the Imperial Sugar Company, Sugarland Industries, and the Sugar Land Railroad (Missouri Pacific). In 1913 the sugar company built 8½ miles of levee, along with 20 miles of drainage ditches, to keep the Brazos from flooding Sugar Land. Between 1917 and 1928 dredging of the many shallow pools, lakes, creeks, and Oyster Creek reclaimed acreage to provide necessary drainage and more farmland. Plant disease and the high federal protective tax on cane sugar ended local cane farming by the 1920s, and thereafter raw sugar was imported for the refinery. In 1925 the population was listed at 1,000; in 1936 it was registered at 1,500, where it remained through the 1940s. In 1946 the Kempner family became sole owners of the town. By 1956 some 2,285 people called Sugar Land home. The town was incorporated in 1959, a year after Imperial Sugar and Sugarland Properties, Incorporated, also owned by the Kempner family, began selling the businesses, homes, and land for development. The town reported 3,499 residents in 1970 and 4,173 in 1980. Spurred by development from nearby Houston, the population climbed to 24,529 by 1990.   *Bettye J. Anhaiser*

Sul Ross State University. In Alpine; authorized by the legislature in 1917 as a state teachers' college and named for Lawrence Sullivan Ross. The institution was a successor to Alpine Summer Normal School (1910–). After a delay caused by World War I, in 1919 Sul Ross State Normal College began junior-college operations in 1920 with 77 students. In 1923 the institution was renamed Sul Ross State Teachers College and added courses leading to baccalaureate degrees. Graduate courses were initiated in 1933. Under the leadership of President Horace W. Morelock (1923–45) the curriculum was expanded, additional academic buildings and dormitories were constructed, the college was admitted into membership in the Southern Association of Colleges and Secondary Schools, and enrollment increased to 500. A decline during World War II was offset by the establishment of a successful United States Navy pilot-training program and a Woman's Army Corps Training School on campus. After the war, veterans increased the annual enrollments and prompted expansion of the curriculum. The college was reorganized and, in 1949, renamed Sul Ross State College. In 1969 it became Sul Ross State University. In the 1970s enrollments declined because of the opening of several new colleges in West Texas. The general education requirements were revised, and new degree programs were added. Sul Ross established a center on the campus of Southwest Texas Junior College in Uvalde. Early in its history Sul Ross State University became the cultural and educational center of the remote Big Bend region. It became a pioneer in promoting international goodwill by sponsoring 15 annual educational tours to Chihuahua, Mexico, during the 1920s and 1930s, and it continued toward the end of the century

Library Building, ca. 1948. Courtesy TSL. Since early in its history, Sul Ross State University has been the cultural and educational center of the Big Bend region.

to participate in joint endeavors with the University of Chihuahua. The Museum of the Big Bend on campus provides a depository and research facility for regional manuscript collections. The university promotes scientific research with particular emphasis on Chihuahuan Desert studies, and is involved in cooperative projects with the private, nonprofit Chihuahuan Desert Research Institute, which is headquartered on campus. Through the university's Center for Big Bend Studies, research and educational activities are conducted in the historical, cultural, and economic development of the Trans-Pecos and adjacent areas in Mexico and New Mexico. The governing body is the Board of Regents of the Texas State University System.

Earl H. Elam

Sunset Act. An important act passed in 1977 by the Sixty-fifth Legislature. It provides for a commission to review most state agencies every 12 years in order to determine if they should be continued or abolished.

Surveying. First practiced in Texas to define the boundaries of Spanish land grants. Methods varied greatly; distances were occasionally given in such units of measurement as "a cigarette's length" or "half a day's walk," and compass bearings were often inaccurate. Other surveys, slightly more accurate, made measurements in varas, cordels, and leagues. Surveyors were required by Spanish and Mexican law to point out to grantees each and every corner of the grant and to tell him "in a loud voice" that he was invested with the property pointed out. The grantee indicated his acknowledgement of the grant by throwing rocks, shouting aloud, firing guns, and making other and sundry noises. With the beginning of Anglo-American colonization, Stephen F. Austin was careful not to issue titles to colonists until a survey had been made. His instructions from the Mexican government as to surveying were printed and issued by Juan Antonio Padilla, the land commissioner; Austin's contracts with such surveyors as Horatio Chriesman, Seth Ingram, William Kincheloe, and Elias Wightman required that they use the Mexican vara as a standard unit, use the true meridian after calculating compass variation, establish corners with bearing trees at each principal corner marked with the owner's initials or with mounds of earth at least three feet high, mark every line not bounded by a river or creek so that it could be easily traced and followed, make correct notes and plots for each survey, and execute all work accurately. Austin warned surveyors to avoid leaving vacancies between tracts. The surveyor's fee was to be five dollars per Spanish mile, payable in property, or three dollars per mile, payable in cash. The early surveyors used a linked chain 20 varas long or a Gunter's chain corrected to the vara standard. They had a tendency, when land was cheap and unoccupied, to add 20 to 100 varas to each mile of line to make certain that no one was cheated; hence, a supposed section of land has often been found to contain from one to 100 acres of excess. A Jacob staff with a box compass and peep sights was used for running lines. Surveyors could not agree on the declination; some thought it should be east, others thought it should be west; others used no declination at all but simply ran a magnetic course. No compensation was made for calendar variations of magnetic north, and no correction was made for the curvature of the earth.

Despite these handicaps, the work of the first surveyors was surprisingly accurate; later surveyors in the land boom days,

Guadalupe Mountains, by John Russell Bartlett, ca. 1751. Pencil and sepia wash. 9½" × 13". Courtesy John Carter Brown Library at Brown University. Bartlett was the commissioner of the U.S. Boundary Survey, ordered to mark the boundary between the United States and Mexico in cooperation with the Mexican survey after the war with Mexico. The artists, naturalists, and surveyors who made up his command produced an unprecedented record of the southwestern border in William H. Emory's *The U.S. and Mexican Boundary Survey.* Bartlett used his own paintings in his *Personal Narrative of Explorations and Incidents in Texas, New Mexico, California, Sonora, and Chihuahua . . .* (1854).

although better equipped, were frequently less accurate. Their inaccuracies, which gave rise to land vacancy and land excess, resulted from crude equipment, incorrect methods, lack of training, and carelessness. Demands for speed often meant that surveys were not closed on the ground and that careless errors in chaining and bearings were made. In the location of railroad grants, field notes to hundreds of sections were made and filed by surveyors who were never on the land they described. One device used to speed up surveying in the prairie country was to tie a rag to a buggy wheel, drive over the lines following a magnetic compass, and count the revolutions of the buggy wheel to obtain the distance. Discrepancies and mistakes from inaccurate surveys have caused numerous and expensive lawsuits. Because of these inaccuracies, the Texas legislature has made several reforms, particularly the Statute of Limitations, to protect settlers who located on land sometimes considerably distant from that described in their patents, and House Bill No. 9 of the Forty-sixth Legislature, 1939, to protect owners of excess land from unscrupulous land grabbers.

A typical surveying party of the last quarter of the nineteenth century consisted of a chief of party, a transitman, two chainmen, one or two flagmen, a corner builder, and a cook. Iron rods

and cane poles served for flagpoles; transit stations varied between a half mile and two miles; colored oil cloth, paper, and mirrors were used for signaling. A light buggy was provided for the transitman, and the corner builder used a light wagon. A 50-vara tape was commonly employed, although old link chains, usually not longer than 20 varas, were also used. Texas surveys were not laid out by means of a regularly established system; tangible control points of well-defined base lines were never used. Description in metes and bounds has been used from the beginning, and a grid reference system has gradually been adopted. In the twentieth century surveyors in Texas used increasingly advanced technology to survey subdivisions, highways, railroads, pipelines, and wells. Surveyors are also often needed to help settle compensation cases. The Texas Surveyors Association was established in the 1940s.

Swanson's Landing. One of the first inland ports in Texas; on Caddo Lake. Peter Swanson, a civil engineer and surveyor, moved to Texas in 1833 from Tennessee and settled on the south shore of the lake, at the boundary between Texas and the United States. Swanson's Landing was thus the first port of entry through the lake. The harbor was of a comfortable depth for large riverboats. While the Caddos and Cherokees were on the warpath in Northeast Texas, Swanson had the protection of the Texas Militia under Hugh McLeod, stationed nearby at Post (Port) Caddo. In addition, the Swansons had but to step across the boundary line to find sanctuary in the U.S. Swanson constructed a dock and warehouses and opened a general store. Later he built a gristmill. Soon settlers began arriving by boat, by oxcart, on horseback, and by foot. The warehouses were soon filled with cotton, hides, and corn, all en route to New Orleans. When Texas became a state (29 December 1845), Swanson's landing was a port of entry for the resultant population surge, and Swanson prospered. He invested in land, slaves, and livestock. In April 1849 he and his wife, Amelia, made a joint will that revealed their ownership of 6,800 acres of land, slaves, and livestock. Swanson died that year, and Thomas F. Swanson took over his father's work. In 1857 Swanson's Landing was the starting point for the Southern Pacific Railroad, one of the earliest Texas railroads. The rails, cars, and other accoutrements were brought in by riverboats. The Swansons made the ties. The young people of Marshall began riding the Southern Pacific on day trips to Swanson's Landing, where they would swim, dance, picnic, and go boating. In 1861, at the beginning of the Civil War, the railroad transported to Swanson's Landing 33,000 sacks of corn and 4,274 bales of cotton. With the fall of Vicksburg, Gen. E. Kirby Smith ordered the rails to be taken up between Jonesville and Swanson's Landing and used as an extension from Jonesville to Shreveport. On 12 February 1869 the palatial sidewheeler *Mittie Stephens* burned and sank near the landing. With the removal of the track, the shifting of the riverboat to the boomtown of Jefferson, and the clearing in 1873 of the great raft from the Red River, the demise of Swanson's Landing as a port was inevitable. In the 1990s most of the land owned by Peter Swanson still belonged to his descendants. *V. H. Hackney*

Sweatt v. Painter. A celebrated and influential antisegregation case. Heman Marion Sweatt applied for admission to the University of Texas School of Law in 1946 and was denied on the basis of a "separate but equal" clause in the Constitution of 1876. Sweatt instituted mandamus proceedings to require state and university officials to enroll him. The trial judge continued the case to give the state an opportunity to establish a "separate but equal" law school, and a temporary law school was opened in Austin in February 1947. Its students had access to the state Supreme Court library, and several members of the law faculty of the UT law school taught the classes. Mandamus was then denied by the state courts of Texas pursuant to the separate but equal doctrine. But the United States Supreme Court granted certiorari and thereafter held that the equal-protection clause of the United States Constitution required Sweatt's admission to UT. He enrolled in 1950, as did several other African Americans. *Sweatt v. Painter* did not establish the invalidation of race separation per se by force of law, but moved strongly in that direction. It was clear from the opinion that a good-faith effort to supply equality of treatment without integration was insufficient. The case had a direct impact on the University of Texas in that it provided for admission of black applicants to graduate and professional programs. Undergraduate admission came later, under the influence of the *Brown v. Board of Education of Topeka* (1954) decision, which held that equality in fact was not a possibility under a policy of separation. *W. Page Keeton*

Swedes. Immigrants from Sweden began coming to Texas in 1848. They were preceded by S. M. Swenson, who immigrated in 1836. In 1848 Swenson brought 25 Swedes to Texas from Barkeryds Parish in northern Småland; they were related to one another or to Swenson and Swante Palm. They first joined Swenson in Fort Bend County, then moved with him to a large sheep and cattle ranch just east of Austin. Swenson continued to assist his countrymen in coming to Texas by advancing passage money in return for their labor. The census of 1880 recorded 364 Swedes in Texas. The depression of 1873 slowed immigration, but the movement resumed in 1878, and the 1900 census indicated 4,344 Swedes in Texas. Immigration from Sweden had practically stopped by 1910. There had also been considerable immigration into Texas from the north central states, notably Illinois. The bulk of that movement took place between 1870 and 1900, with large numbers coming in 1893 and 1894. By the 1940s there were concentrations of Swedes and their descendants around Stamford, Lyford, Melville, Brady, Fort Worth, Dallas, and Waco. Texas place names relating to Sweden or Swedes include Govalle, Lund, Manda, New Sweden, Hutto, Swedonia, East Sweden, West Sweden, Palm Valley, Swensondale, and Bergstrom Air Force Base. In 1980 there were 8,147 people of Swedish descent in the Dallas–Fort Worth Standard Metropolitan Statistical Area, 6,569 in the Houston SMSA, and 4,795 in the Austin SMSA. The 1990 census showed 155,193 persons in the state claiming Swedish descent.

Although Swedes are more numerous in Texas than in any other southern state, they have never played a dominant role in state culture or politics. They published a single newspaper, the Austin *Texas–Posten.* They sponsored two ventures in higher education, Trinity Lutheran College of Round Rock, chartered in 1906, and Texas Wesleyan College at Austin (1912). Both failed because of insufficient financial support. The Swedes in Texas today are almost completely Americanized. In 1988 a celebration entitled "New Sweden '88" commemorated the 150th anniversary of the arrival in Texas of the first Swedish immigrants. It included numerous cultural events in Central Texas, including an official visit by King Carl XVI Gustaf and Queen Silvia of Sweden. *Art Leatherwood*

Sweetwater Army Air Field. A World War II training base of the United States Army Air Forces. In 1942 the municipal airport in Sweetwater was leased to the War Department for a dollar a year and renamed Avenger Field, the winning name entered in a local newspaper contest. The field, which had been in civilian use since the late 1920s, had been improved and expanded to 920 acres by the city. Its first wartime use was for the training of a single class of British pilot cadets of the RAF by an American civilian contractor. This was followed by 10 classes of American aviation cadets and 3 classes of enlisted student pilots (1942–43). The most notable period in the history of the field began on 21 February 1943 with the arrival of the first trainees of the Women's Airforce Service Pilots, moved to Sweetwater from Houston because of heavy air traffic and bad weather. For a brief period, Avenger Field trained both men and women, but in April 1943 it became the "only all-female air base in history," except for the male instructors and support crews. Fourteen classes of WASPs, totaling 1,074 pilots, earned their wings at Avenger before the service was disbanded (20 December 1944). In 1945 facilities at the field were considerably expanded to support the combat training of P-47 Thunderbolt pilots. The end of the war brought the rapid phase-out of all training there. The field was closed in November 1945, and it reverted to peacetime use by the city of Sweetwater in 1947. During the Korean War the United States Air Force again leased the facilities (1 April 1952) as an auxiliary field for training pilots from Webb Air Force Base at Big Spring. In 1956 Avenger Field was made the site of an aircraft control and warning radar installation. In 1969 the property was once more released to the city of Sweetwater. In addition use as Sweetwater Municipal Airport, the field is now the location of the Rolling Plains campus of Texas State Technical Institute, which opened there in 1970.

James L. Colwell

Swenson, Swen Magnus. Rancher and first Swedish immigrant to Texas; b. Lättarp, Barkeryds Parish, Jönköping, Sweden, 24 February 1816; d. Brooklyn, New York, 13 June 1896 (buried at Woodlawn Cemetery, Bronx); m. Jeanette Long (1843; d. 1850); m. Susan McReady (1851); 4 children. He immigrated to America in 1836. Most accounts of his life say his ship burned in New York harbor, so he came ashore with nothing more than the clothes he was wearing. He worked as a store clerk, learned English, then worked as a railroad bookkeeper in Baltimore, Maryland, before arriving in Texas in 1838. As an agent of John Adriance of Columbia, Swenson peddled goods from a wagon labeled Columbus Supply House. Dr. George Long made him overseer of his plantation near Richmond. After the doctor's death in 1842, Swenson took charge of the plantation. In 1843 he bought a neighboring plantation, and the next year he married Mrs. Long. In 1847 he took a trip to Sweden to encourage immigration to Texas. He offered to pay the fares of immigrants in exchange for a year of their labor on his plantations. He continued this work throughout his life. After the Civil War he, his uncle Swante Palm, and a brother in Sweden began running an informal Swedish immigration service often referred to as the "Swedish pipeline." By 1850 Swenson had moved to Austin and established a mercantile business with Palm. Swenson continued to buy land; he submitted newspaper ads announcing that he would pay top dollar for headright certificates. In 1854 he invested in the Buffalo Bayou, Brazos and Colorado Railway, which gained him 100,000 acres of land in northwestern and western Texas. He eventually became one of the largest landowners in Texas, founder of the SMS Ranches. Swenson served two terms (1852 and 1856) as a Travis county commissioner, and in 1853 he became the first treasurer of the State Agricultural Society. He also expanded his mercantile business beyond the city limits, using his string of freight wagons to sell supplies to outlying forts.

During the secession crisis he agreed to help Governor Sam Houston prevent Texas secession. When the effort failed, Swenson, who by this time had sold all his slaves, stayed in Texas but remained a Unionist. Despite this, he was allowed for a time to continue his business in Austin. Acting as an agent for the Swedish government, he arranged for the export of Texas cotton abroad. Though Governor Lubbock allowed Swenson to leave the state several times, his travel caused a great outcry among politically powerful secessionists. In 1863 Swenson, in fear for his life, fled to Monterrey, Nuevo León. The next year, he went to Sweden to visit his mother. By 1865 he had gone to New Orleans and set up a large mercantile business in partnership with William Perkins; he also purchased a sugar plantation. Later that year he took his family to live in New York City, where he estab-

lished the financial house of Swenson Perkins Company. After dissolving the Perkins partnership, Swenson established the banking house of S. M. Swenson and Sons. When this business was discontinued, he became a large depositor in the National City Bank, later the First National City Bank of New York. Though he lived the last 30 years of his life in New York, he maintained his ties to Texas, operating a clearinghouse for Texas products, continuing his work as a cotton agent, and regularly visiting his extensive land holdings. In 1891 he presented his large collection of ancient coins to the University of Texas, where they were displayed at the Texas Memorial Museum.

Richard Moore

Swiss. There were plans for settlement of Swiss in Texas as early as 1819, when a group of Swiss merchants in Philadelphia proposed to settle 10,000 of their countrymen in Texas. Although their plans did not materialize, other Swiss people became interested in the opening of Texas to colonization. Louis and Henry Rueg moved to Texas in 1821 and ultimately opened a mercantile business in Nacogdoches. Simón Tadeo Ortiz de Ayala, a Creole of Guadalajara, Mexico, secured authorization from the new Mexican republic in 1822 to bring European colonists into Coahuila and Texas, with particular attention to the Swiss as well as German, Irish, and Canary Islanders; his plan was never realized. Stephen F. Austin, in a letter to Thomas F. Leaming (14 June 1830), wrote that he was considering the advantages of Swiss and German immigrants because they were opposed to slavery and did not have the Anglo-American mania for speculation. The contributions of Swiss immigrants to the history of the state have been far out of proportion to their relatively small numbers. A group of German-speaking Swiss settled the community of Schoenau, between Shelby and Industry, in Austin County. They built a hall nearby for their "Harmony Verein," where they held dances and athletic contests and organized a singing society, Helvetia Schönau Männerchor, in the 1880s. The community disappeared, but the hall was still standing and in use in 1968. The population peak of the Swiss in most Texas areas was reached in the years 1890 to 1910; during this period there were Swiss settlements in Bexar, Dallas, Austin, Fayette, Travis, and Williamson counties. Vernon, in Wilbarger County, was settled by the Swiss in 1893. The 1930 census listed 1,410 persons of Swiss extraction in Texas. They were mostly craftsmen and tradesmen, and the majority were settled in the urban centers of Galveston, Houston, and Dallas.

Swiss immigrants who have played significant roles in Texas history include Jean Louis Berlandier, botanist and zoologist for the Mexican Boundary Commission in 1828; Peter Hunter Fullinwider, first Presbyterian missionary to Texas; and John Wahrenberger, an Austin baker who in 1842 was said to have alerted the town's citizenry of the impending removal of the archives of the republic in the Archive War. Two Swiss military men were important, although little has been written about them. Johann Jacob Rahm, a Swiss member of Jack Hays's Texas Rangers, was instrumental in persuading Hays to aid Germans of Henri Castro's colony when they were stranded in San Antonio in the spring of 1844. He also aided Prince Carl of Solms–Braunfels's party when the springs and site of New Braunfels were located in 1845 and received an engraved gun from the prince in appreciation. The following year Rahm was killed in New Braunfels in a duel. C. Rohrdorf, a Swiss army colonel with the Adelsverein, was a painter and lithographer who made numerous drawings and paintings of the early German settlements of New Braunfels and Fredericksburg; he was killed in a brief gunfight between two German groups contending for the possession of Nassau Farm in 1847, and John O. Meusebach is said to have bought the art collection left by the artist. Getulius Kellersberger, brother-in-law of Johannes Romberg, moved to Texas in the late 1840s and became an internationally known surveyor and engineer. He returned to Texas to join the Confederacy during the Civil War. After the failure of the French colony of La Réunion a few Swiss made their homes in Dallas; among them were the naturalist Jacob Boll, who returned there from Europe in the 1870s, and Benjamin Lang (or

Long, as he came to be known), who was the post–Civil War mayor of Dallas and the United States commissioner for the district. Two Swiss financier–philanthropists, George Henry Hermann of Houston and Henry Rosenberg of Galveston, made outstanding bequests to their cities. Cesar Maurice Lombardi set the editorial pattern for the Dallas *Morning News* during the period of his directorship; he was also on the board of directors of the Galveston *News*. Jacob Metzger was founder of the Metzger dairies in Dallas, and Edward Walter Eberle, a distinguished naval officer from the early 1900s until the beginning of World War I, was responsible for numerous innovations in modern United States naval practices. The 1990 census listed 32,304 persons of Swiss descent in Texas.   *William T. Field*

T

Taft–Díaz Meeting. The meeting of presidents William Howard Taft and Porfirio Díaz in El Paso and Ciudad Juárez on 16 October 1909; the first meeting in history between a president of the United States and a president of Mexico. The local press called it the "Most Eventful Diplomatic Event in the History of the Two Nations." An El Paso historian has added that it was a "veritable pageant of military splendor, social brilliance, courtly formality, official protocol, and patriotic fervor." In June 1909 President Taft, desiring an expression from the Díaz government of its continued support of American investments in Mexico, wrote that he was planning a trip to the Southwest and suggested a meeting with the Mexican president at El Paso or some other convenient place on the border. The Mexican dictator readily accepted Taft's invitation, since he was convinced that his personal appearance in the El Paso–Juárez area, where there had been significant opposition to his regime, would restore his lost popularity and remind his countrymen that in spite of his years he was still in firm control. The proceedings were planned in the greatest detail by the U.S. Department of State and the Mexican Ministry of Foreign Affairs. In addition to matters of protocol, the two governments made the most elaborate arrangements for the protection and safety of the two presidents. Significantly, the area in dispute in south El Paso known as the Chamizal was declared neutral territory, the flags of neither nation to be displayed during the meeting. Taft and Díaz spent 20 minutes together at the St. Regis Hotel in El Paso. Because both presidents were bilingual there was no need for interpreters. No one else attended the meeting. Although official reports of the meeting stated that nothing of political or diplomatic significance was discussed, some have suggested that the basis was laid there for the treaty of arbitration in the Chamizal dispute that the two nations signed a year later.

Díaz then returned to Ciudad Juárez, followed by Taft an hour later. The two met at the Mexican customhouse. There, after a brief interview, they stepped outside to the front of the building under a scarlet canopy and posed for a cameraman. The resulting photograph effectively dramatized the contrast between Taft's plain appearance and Díaz's military bearing and chest full of medals. The banquet at the Ciudad Juárez customhouse dwarfed all other events of that historic occasion. The entire building had been transformed into a reproduction of one of the famous salons of Versailles. There were rich red draperies, paintings of George Washington and Miguel Hidalgo y Costilla, three traincar-loads of flowers brought from Guadalajara, a gold and silver service that had belonged to the emperor Maximilian, cut glass from Chapultepec Castle, and fine linens from the presidential palace. Soft music accompanied conversation in two languages and mutual toasts by the two presidents. With the presentation of gold goblets to the presidents as gifts from the city of El Paso, the evening came to an end. *W. H. Timmons*

Talon Children. The six children of Lucien and Isabelle (Planteau) Talon, who joined the La Salle expedition in 1684 and later fulfilled various historic roles. Their parents are believed to have married in Quebec, where two sons and two daughters were born: Marie Elizabeth (10 September 1672), Marie Madeleine (3 November 1673), Pierre (20 March 1676), and Jean Baptiste (26 May 1679). The third son, Lucien, may have been born before the family left Canada for France, where they arrived about the time La Salle began organizing his expedition to the Gulf of Mexico. When the family joined the expedition, Madame Talon was again pregnant; a fourth son, Robert, was born during the voyage. Lucien Talon, *père*, was a carpenter by trade but seems to have joined the expedition as a soldier. He is said to have been "lost in the woods" before October 1685. Marie Elizabeth contracted a fatal illness, probably in the winter of 1686. When La Salle left the settlement the last time to seek his post on the Illinois River (January 1687), he took the oldest son, Pierre, not quite 11. He intended leaving the lad, and possibly a few others, among the Hasinai (Tejas) Indians of eastern Texas to learn the language. Thus, he might form a link between these friendly natives and the 20-odd men and women left in the colony on Lavaca Bay. Whatever the plan, it was diverted by tragedy in both the group with La Salle and the one remaining in the settlement. Alonso De León, after returning to Coahuila with Jacques Grollet and Jean L'Archevêque in 1689, gathered up four of the Talon children on his 1690 entrada. He first found Pierre, who with Pierre Meunier had been living among the Hasinais, then took Marie Madeleine, Lucien, and Robert from the Karankawas on the Gulf Coast. All bore Indian tattoos on their faces and parts of their bodies; the two younger boys had forgotten their native language. Jean Baptiste Talon and another youth, Eustache Bréman, were rescued from among the Karankawas by the expedition of Domingo Terán de los Ríos in 1691.

Taken to Mexico City, the five Talon children were placed as servants in the household of the viceroy, Conde de Galve. Shortly before the ailing count ended his term and returned to Spain (in 1696), the three older boys were sent to Veracruz to be enrolled as soldiers in the Armada de Barlovento.Pierre was about 19 at the time, Jean Baptiste 16, and Lucien probably 14. They were assigned to *Santo Cristo de Maracaibo*, the flagship of Admiral Guillermo Morfi. Marie Madeleine and Robert went to Spain with the retiring viceroy and the countess. About a year later *Santo Cristo* was captured by a French vessel in the Caribbean Sea. The Talon brothers, less than cooperative in their initial interrogation by French officers, asked to be sent to Spain. They were taken instead to France, where Pierre and Jean were enrolled in naval service. Lucien, being considered too young for French military service, was employed as a servant at Oléron. The marine minister, Louis Pontchartrain, heard of the repatriates about a year later. He ordered their immediate interrogation in the hope that they would provide information useful to Pierre Le Moyne d'Iberville, who was outfitting a new voyage to the Gulf of Mexico. With French officials still confused as to the location of La Salle's colony, the Talons held the distinction of having traveled from the settlement to Mexico City. The interrogation indeed proved useful, for it revealed that they remembered much of the Indian languages: Jean Baptiste of the

Karankawas, Pierre of the Hasinais. Jean Baptiste gave the only eye-witness account of the Fort St. Louis massacre, in which he and his sisters and two small brothers had seen their mother slain. Having lived as an Indian, he gave an account of the Karankawa existence that has long been of interest to anthropologists. Pierre did the same for the Hasinais, and recounted events surrounding La Salle's death—a version somewhat different, if doubtful, from that of Henri Joutel. Although Pontchartrain failed in his effort to get the two lads on the first Iberville voyage to Louisiana, they did join the second—as soldiers in the company of Louis Juchereau de St. Denis. They remained in the colony two years, serving at "Fort Biloxi" (Fort Maurepas). But the record is silent on any part they had in explorations by St. Denis and Jean Baptiste de Bienville up the Red River. The Talon brothers, undoubtedly, were the two soldiers sent home with Iberville in April 1702 on Pontchartrain's special order, that they might "look for their woman"—their sister, who had gone from Mexico to Spain with the Condessa de Galve in 1696. Marie Madeleine, apparently, had not remained long in Spain but had failed to make contact with her brothers upon her return to France. She married Pierre Simon of Paris in 1699.

Two years later, Pierre and Jean Baptiste were in a Portuguese prison. Neither the reason for their incarceration nor its duration are known. No more is heard, directly, of Jean Baptiste. Pierre reappears a decade later on the banks of the Rio Grande with his brother Robert and his old captain, St. Denis. He at last had been called upon to retrace the road linking French territory with New Spain. It was Pierre, still wearing his Indian tattoos, who guided St. Denis through Hasinai country and interpreted for him among both Indians and, after his arrival at San Juan Bautista, Spaniards. The two brothers slipped back across the Rio Grande, while St. Denis was borne off to Mexico City, and returned to Mobile. They carried their captain's brief written message to the French governor Cadillac, which they supplemented orally. Having fulfilled this historic role, the Talons fade into obscurity.   *Robert S. Weddle*

Tampico Expedition. After his election to the presidency of Mexico in 1833, Antonio López de Santa Anna left the inauguration of the new liberal policy to the vice president, Valentín Gómez Farías, went into political retirement for a few months, and emerged as leader of the reaction. He assumed dictatorial powers, dissolving state and national legislatures. Insurrections broke out at various points. Zacatecas, Coahuila, and Texas refused to accept centralism, holding to the Constitution of 1824. In New Orleans a movement, led by George Fisher and José Antonio Mexía, began at Bank's Arcade on 13 October 1835. The members of the movement raised men and money for an expedition to attack Tampico in an effort to stir up an insurrection in the eastern states of Mexico. Mexía, who was to lead the expedition, communicated the plan to the Texas leaders, who approved it, although some, Stephen F. Austin among them, advocated an attack on Matamoros instead. Counting on the support of the liberals known to be among the members of the garrison at Tampico, Mexía and his 150 "efficient emigrants" left New Orleans on 6 November 1835 on the schooner *Mary Jane*. The vessel ran aground off the bar of Tampico on 14 November. This disaster, together with a premature uprising of the garrison the day before and the arrival of fresh troops from Tuxpan, upset Mexía's plans. On 15 November he attacked the city, held by

Gregorio Gómez; was defeated, withdrew on the American schooner *Halcyon*, and embarked for the mouth of the Brazos River, where he landed his troops on 3 December. Thirty-one prisoners were left at Tampico. Of these, three died of wounds; the others were tried by court-martial and shot on 14 December.

Tarleton State University. In Stephenville; began in 1893 when citizens raised $6,500 to build Stephenville College. Under the direction of President Marshall McIlhaney, the college operated as a private institution until 1898. The property was then transferred to the trustees of the newly established John Tarleton College, endowed by John Tarleton. It operated under trustees designated by Tarleton in his will; William H. Bruce was the first president. For a short time the school offered senior college work before reverting to junior status, with two years of high school work and two years of college work in liberal arts. Like similar schools of that period, John Tarleton College was faced with inadequate financing, and in 1916, when a movement in the legislature to establish a West Texas agricultural and mechanical college became apparent, citizens of the community and the trustees of the college offered the properties of the college to the state as a nucleus for the new school. In 1917 the legislature passed a bill establishing a branch of Texas A&M at Stephenville to be named John Tarleton Agricultural College. The school continued to offer a two-year degree, the preparatory program, and specialized study in agriculture, home economics, and military training. Citizens of Erath County raised $50,000 to purchase a 500-acre farm and additional acreage for the campus and $75,000 to become a permanent loan fund for worthy students. These assets were added to the existing property of the college and conveyed to the state. In 1926 Tarleton was accredited as a junior college, and it again focused on the liberal arts. In 1949 the name was changed to Tarleton State College. In 1953 the preparatory department closed. The college property in 1943 had an inventory value of $2 million and consisted of a 40-acre campus, 16 brick buildings, a 700-acre college farm, and a 24-acre poultry project. In 1921 an ROTC unit was established at Tarleton; in 1943, 2,500 men trained there were serving in the armed forces, and the college cooperated with the United States Army in the housing, maintenance, and instruction of 500 Army Specialized Training Program trainees. During this period affairs of the college were administered by the board of directors of Texas A&M and a local dean. Enrollment was 900 in 1950 and 3,027 in 1972. The college was accredited as a senior college in 1966. Degrees were offered in liberal arts, sciences, general business, education, and general agriculture. In 1970 a graduate program was added after gaining the approval of the Texas Higher Education Coordinating Board. In 1973 the legislature again reorganized the college and changed its name to Tarleton State University. In the early 1990s the university had a 1,200-acre ranch and a 600-acre farm complete with modern laboratories and facilities. It had a nationally recognized horse production and management program. Tarleton State University is fully accredited. It is divided into the College of Agriculture and Technology, the College of Arts and Sciences, the College of Business Administration, the College of Fine Arts, and the College of Graduate Studies.

J. Thomas Davis and Nancy Beck Young

Tarrant, Edward H. Militia general and legislator; b. South Carolina, 1799; d. near Weatherford, 2 August 1858; m. Mary

Danforth (1851). By the early 1820s Tarrant was in Tennessee, where he was elected a colonel of militia and served as sheriff of Henry County. In the 1830s he moved to Texas and settled in Red River County. In 1838 he received a league and labor of land from the Republic of Texas as part of a uniform grant made to all heads of families resident in Texas on 2 March 1836. He was elected in 1837 to the Congress of the republic but resigned shortly, having decided that he could better serve the republic by directing ranger activities against the Indians. He was chief justice (county judge) of Red River County in 1838. Tarrant practiced law, farmed, and took a leading role in militia activity against the Indians while he was chief justice. When he resigned from the post in 1839 he was one of the most prosperous men in Red River County. By popular vote on 18 November 1839 he was elected commander, with the rank of brigadier general, of an organization of Northeast Texas defenders known as the Fourth Brigade. His Indian-fighting career culminated in the battle of Village Creek in May 1841. In 1847 he ran for lieutenant governor but was defeated by John Alexander Greer. He served in the state House of Representatives,1849–53. In 1857 Tarrant moved part of his household from Italy to Fort Belknap, and when Indian depredations became frequent in that area, he again turned his attention to raising forces against them. He died en route to the fort at the home of William Fondren and was buried three times, the final time (1928) at Pioneer Rest Cemetery, Fort Worth. Tarrant County was named for him.

Tascosa, Texas. On the Canadian River in northeastern Oldham County; named for Atascosa (Spanish for "boggy") Creek, which flows into the river at the site of the original settlement. In 1876 the creek valley was first settled and was named Plaza Atascosa by *pastores* under Casimero Romero. These Hispanic sheepmen and freighters from New Mexico grazed their flocks and built adobe huts and irrigation ditches along the creeks in the area. Their settlement, 300 miles northwest of the line of settlements in 1875, and on the cattle trail through the Panhandle to Dodge City, was at the site of an easy ford over the Canadian. Romero and most of his followers remained in the vicinity until the late 1880s and 1890s, when most of them drifted with their sheep back to New Mexico. After 1875 large cattle ranches dominated the area and Tascosa became the shipping and supply point for the LIT, LX, LS, Frying Pan, and XIT ranches. Henry Kimball, the first Anglo settler in the Tascosa area, set up his blacksmith shop in 1876. A general store and saloon were also established. With the organization of Oldham County in 1880, Tascosa became the county seat. Saloons and dance halls sprang up, and a stone courthouse was built. As the Cowboy Capital of the Plains, Tascosa had more than its share of conflicts settled by fast guns. Caleb Berg (Cape) Willingham, the first sheriff of the county, shot the man who occupied the first grave in Boot Hill Cemetery. Noted outlaws, including Billy the Kid and Dave Rudabaugh, walked its streets, as did lawmen Pat Garrett, Charles A. Siringo, and others. Conflicts developed on the large ranches in 1883, when Tascosa became the scene of an unsuccessful cowboys' strike for higher wages. In 1887 the Fort Worth and Denver City Railway constructed 16 miles of track across the northeastern corner of Oldham County. Many of the businesses from Tascosa moved two miles to a new site on the railroad and across the Canadian. By 1890 the combined population of the two settlements was 350. As new towns were established

throughout the Panhandle, Tascosa declined steadily. When an election made Vega the county seat in 1915, only 15 persons remained at Tascosa. The site of old Tascosa was entirely deserted when Frenchy McCormick, widow of the town's first saloon owner, Mickey McCormick, moved to Channing in 1939. In June 1939, however, Cal Farley established his Maverick Boys' Ranch at the old townsite, offering a home and training to underprivileged boys. The newer Tascosa, on the railroad, had two stores and a population of 50 in 1947. In the 1980s the stone courthouse at old Tascosa housed a museum, and Boothill Cemetery remained as a reminder of the wild days. In 1990 the boys' ranch had a population of 485, and new Tascosa consisted of a siding and a stock pen.

Tascosa–Dodge City Trail. Linked Tascosa, Texas, and Dodge City, Kansas, the liveliest cowtowns in the West during the heyday of cattle trailing. Tascosa was almost totally supplied by freighters from Dodge hauling huge quantities of supplies for surrounding Panhandle ranches. Each of the larger stores in Tascosa freighted in 25,000 to 50,000 pounds of merchandise each month. As late as 1888 the Tascosa *Pioneer* noted that 119,000 pounds of freight had been delivered during the previous week. The general configuration of this freight trail was determined by the location of Bob and James H. Cator's ranch. Indians, Comancheros, buffalo hunters, and soldiers had moved southward across the plains, following old paths or their own instincts. There was no permanent route, however, until the Cators began making trips to Dodge City from their Palo Duro station. Their repeated use of the same tracks and crossings produced a fixed trail divided into two distinct sections: the northern half through Kansas, which was, in fact, part of the Jones and Plummer Trail; and the southern leg from Beaver, Oklahoma, to Tascosa. The trail started at Dodge City, entered Texas in Ochiltree County, and branched just south of the site of Dumas. The northern branch led to Tascosa by way of Hartley County; the southern branch hit Tascosa after turning south and then west through Potter County. Although the physical difficulties of this trail were not as formidable as those of other Panhandle trails, the great distances between way stations and the absence of settlements made it a long, lonesome haul. The trip from Dodge covered approximately 240 miles. A stagecoach took 34 hours one way, and an oxteam required from a month to six weeks for a round trip. The trail remained in use as an interstate road well past the time when other freighting trails had been abandoned. The stage line from Meade, Kansas, continued in operation until the turn of the century. Although Tascosa continued to exist until World War I, its importance as a freighting center declined as the railroads bypassed the town—the Fort Worth and Denver City in 1887, then the Chicago, Rock Island and Mexico in 1901. Area ranchers began to receive their freight from Amarillo and Channing on the railroad, and the Tascosa–Dodge City Trail was gradually abandoned.   *C. Robert Haywood*

Teagarden, Jack. Jazz musician; b. Weldon Leo Teagarden, Vernon, 20 August 1905; d. New Orleans, 14 or 15 January 1964 (buried in Los Angeles); m. Ora Binyon (1923; divorced); 2 sons; m. Adeline Barriere Gault (1942); 3 children and 1 foster child. Teagarden was married and divorced twice more in the 1930s. He and his mother played duets (trombone and piano) for silent films at a Vernon theater. At 16 Teagarden played at a concert

Jazz musician Jack Teagarden, 1920. Courtesy Duncan Schiedt, Pittsboro, Indiana.

near San Antonio with Cotton Bailey's dance and jazz band and joined Peck Kelley's Bad Boys in Houston. He made his first trip to New York in 1926 as a performer on the eastern tour of Doc Ross's Jazz Bandits. The next year he went to New York on his own and, after some vacillation, joined Ben Pollack's band, where he beat Glenn Miller for the seat of first trombone. He made his first recording in 1927 as a member of the Kentucky Grasshoppers, an offshoot of Pollack's group. Teagarden later recorded with many of America's jazz greats, including Red Nichols, Benny Goodman, and Louis Armstrong. He performed with Eddie Condon, Bix Beiderbecke, Paul Whiteman, the Dorsey brothers, Bob Crosby, Eddie Lang, Peck Kelley, and others. He was considered by many to be the greatest jazz trombonist of his era. In 1933 he signed on with Paul Whiteman's orchestra for five years. In 1939 he formed his own band, which was dissolved in 1947. He teamed up with Louis Armstrong's All-Stars for some classic recordings in the late 1940s and formed the Jack Teagarden All Stars Dixieland band in 1951. The All Stars toured Europe and Asia in 1957–59 as part of a government-sponsored goodwill tour. Teagarden developed an early appreciation of black music, especially blues and gospel. He was one of the first jazz musicians to incorporate "blue notes" into his playing. He was also among the first white jazz musicians to record with black players. He was also an excellent singer and developed a respected blues vocal style. He appeared in the movies *Birth of the Blues* (1941), *The Glass Wall* (1953), and *Jazz on a Summer's Day* (1959). He was featured on RCA Victor, Columbia, Decca, Capitol, and MGM discs. He won the 1944 *Esquire* magazine

Gold Award and was highly rated in the Metronome polls of 1937–42. Teagarden was the featured performer at the Newport Jazz Festival of 1957. He was found dead in his hotel room in New Orleans on January 15, 1964. *Charles G. Davis*

Tehuacana Creek Councils. A series of meetings of Republic of Texas officials with Indians. The first began in March 1843, when a number of tribes including the Caddos, Delawares, Wacos, Tawakonis, Lipan Apaches, and Tonkawas went to a council on Tehuacana Creek near the Torrey Brothers trading post south of the site of present Waco. Another council was held at Bird's Fort on the Trinity River in September 1843. The Wacos, Caddos, and other smaller groups met with Texans and entered into a treaty of peace that was ratified by the Texas Senate, but the absence of the Comanches caused President Houston to call another council to meet at Tehuacana Creek in April 1844. The April council convened without the Comanches. By 7 October 1844 negotiations began between Houston and contingents of the southern Comanches, Kichais, Wacos, Caddos, Anadarkos, Hainais, Delawares, Shawnees, Cherokees, Lipan Apaches, and Tawakonis. The treaty of peace and commerce signed on 9 October was ratified by the Texas Senate on 24 January 1845. A council met in September 1845, and in November a supplementary council convened at which the Wacos, Tawakonis, Kichais, and Wichitas agreed to the treaty of 9 October 1844. The last council ended on 16 November 1845. *Marie Giles*

Telegraph and Texas Register. The first Texas newspaper to achieve a degree of permanence; begun on 10 October 1835 at San Felipe de Austin by Gail Borden, Jr., Thomas H. Borden, and Joseph Baker. It became the official organ of the Republic of Texas a few months later. The advance of Santa Anna's army compelled the publishers to retire after issuing their paper on 24 March 1836. On 5 April, Baker withdrew from the firm to join the army. The press was removed to Harrisburg, and the issue for 14 April was being readied when the Mexicans captured the printers and threw the press into Buffalo Bayou. During the summer Gail Borden obtained a new press and resumed publication of the *Telegraph* at Columbia, where the Texas Congress was to meet. The first Columbia number, issued on 2 August 1836, contained a copy of the Constitution of the Republic of Texas, which had been available to very few up to that time. By the end of October the paper had 700 subscribers, besides doing the public printing. On 11 April 1837 the *Telegraph* was removed on board the *Yellow Stone* to Houston, the new capital. The first Houston issue was printed on 2 May 1837. Important changes in the management and ownership of the *Telegraph* had been made. Thomas Borden had sold his interest to Francis Moore, Jr., in March, and Gail Borden conveyed his share to Jacob Cruger in June. Under Moore's editorial control and Cruger's business management, the *Telegraph* became the unofficial link between the government and the people. The partnership continued until 1851, when Cruger sold to Moore. Moore conducted the *Telegraph* until 1854, when he sold it to Harvey H. Allen, a younger brother of Augustus C. and John K. Allen. The *Telegraph* continued as a weekly until 30 April 1855, when a tri-weekly edition was launched. Allen's conduct of the paper was not satisfactory, and a stock company purchased it in 1856. The new owners selected Edward Cushing to take charge; by a vigorous editorial policy, he succeeded in restoring the *Telegraph* to

Tehuacana Creek Indian Council, by John Mix Stanley, 1849. Oil on canvas. 17" × 24". Courtesy Susan and Pierce Butler, Nashville, Tennessee. This 1843 council, held near Torrey's Trading Post in the future McLennan County, was one of several inspired by President Sam Houston, whose Indian policy was conciliatory. Artist Stanley accompanied American commissioner Pierce M. Butler to the conference.

preeminence among Texas papers. Cushing eventually acquired all the stock and become sole owner.

From 1861 to 1865 the *Telegraph* encountered the same difficulties as other Confederate papers, particularly shortage of newsprint. Cushing resorted to printing on wallpaper and wrapping paper. When the Union forces closed the Mississippi River, he organized a pony express to gather and forward the news, which was issued as rapidly as possible either in regular or extra editions. So many extras were issued that on 6 February 1864 the *Daily Telegraph* replaced the *TriWeekly Telegraph*. Cushing spent the summer of 1865 in the North, completing arrangements for uptodate mechanical equipment for his paper and carefully studying the temper of the North. On his return he informed the South that the contest was in fact ended and counseled acquiescence. This advice was resented, and Cushing sold his paper to a syndicate but retained the job-printing department. This was the first of a series of changes in ownership and policy of the *Telegraph* that ended in its demise. The new owners of the *Telegraph* placed the paper in charge of C. C. Gillespie, who reversed the policy of Cushing. The paper rapidly lost ground, however, and the owners quickly disposed of their holding to William J. Hutchins. Hutchins made James G. Tracy, former foreman of the *Telegraph* office, business manager but retained

Gillespie as editor. Disappointed in his hopes for the paper, Hutchins sold it to William G. Webb in 1867. Webb was almost as submissive as Gillespie had been opposed to the ruling powers. This change in policy met with indifferent support, and the *Telegraph* suspended publication in the fall of 1873. In March 1874 the *Telegraph* was revived by Allen C. Gray, supported by an able editorial corps, and for a time it attained the largest circulation ever before had by any Houston paper. Nevertheless, impatient creditors and other causes again forced a suspension of publication on 11 February 1877, and the old *Telegraph* finally ceased to exist.

Television. The first television station in Texas, WBAP–TV, Fort Worth, began operating on 27 September 1947. By 1950 six stations were in operation in Texas, with three in the Dallas–Fort Worth area, two in San Antonio, and one in Houston. The rapid growth of television in its early stages prompted the Federal Communications Commission to bring all television construction to a halt in the summer of 1950 in order to allow a long-range analysis of the industry, upon which channel allocations and technical specifications could be based. At the time of the freeze only the six stations mentioned above were in existence in Texas. The ban was lifted in 1952, and other stations around the state soon began operations. In the early 1950s the San Antonio and Fort Worth stations changed from kinescope programming to broadcasting live programs by use of the coaxial cable. In 1953 four major television networks served Texas—ABC, CBS, NBC, and Dumont. In that year network broadcasting was made possible across the state through use of facilities of the Bell Telephone System, which had invested $10 million in Texas television cables and microwave relay stations. By 1973 ABC, CBS, and NBC were the major television networks, while Dumont was no longer a principal network; the Hughes Sports Network was operating in Texas, while the Westinghouse Network (not truly a network, but a program supplier) ran special dramatic programs and documentaries. Beginning in 1954 the Spanish International Network began Spanish-language television programs for the Spanishspeaking population in the El Paso–Juárez area. San Antonio joined the network the following year, Laredo–Nuevo Laredo joined in 1962, and Lubbock was added in 1970.

As an example of the early economic value of commercial television stations in Texas, the hourly rate for television time on KRLD–TV in Dallas was $750 in 1953; by 1968 the rate was $2,300 per hour. Rates varied around the state, with some of the smaller stations charging $300 per hour, but rates were increased overall by the 1970s. Over a period of 25 years the number of stations steadily increased, particularly in the larger metropolitan areas such as Houston and Dallas–Fort Worth, but some of the stations in less populated areas went out of business for lack of support. As of 6 September 1973 there were 47 major television stations and 5 satellite television stations in Texas. (A satellite station is one that is a sister–subordinate to a major station, carrying programs from the major station, but also carrying some local programs and advertising.)

The first "educational" television in the nation was KUHT, Houston, established in 1953. Others followed in Texas during the 1960s, so that by 1973 there were the following additional such stations in the state: KLRN, Austin–San Antonio; KERA, Dallas; KTXT, Lubbock; KNCT, Killeen; KEDT, Corpus Christi (the latter two connected with KLRN); and KAMU, College Station. These stations, in addition to providing locally produced programs, were connected with Educational Television (ETV), later known as National Educational Television (NET) and from 1970 as the Public Broadcasting System (PBS). In 1966 the Texas legislature provided financial aid to school districts for student ETV services, as did the National Defense Education Act. The Educational Television Facilities Act and the Elementary and Secondary Education Act provided financial aid for purchase of broadcasting equipment. The nation's first closed circuit television for university-level classroom instruction was the Texas Educational Media Program, originally called Texas Educational Microwave Project, and was operated by the University of Texas at Austin Communication Center. Plans for the project began in 1957, and the unique transmitting equipment was designed and built by Collins Radio of Dallas and bears serial number one. TEMP covered a 70mile path from Austin to San Antonio. When the system began operation it served Southwestern University in Georgetown; Texas Lutheran College in Seguin; Incarnate Word College, San Antonio College, Trinity University, St. Mary's University, and Our Lady of the Lake College in San Antonio; Southwest Texas State University in San Marcos; and the University of Texas,

Huston–Tillotson College, and St. Edward's University in Austin. By 1972 the first three schools were no longer a part of the intercollege network. The program subjects, designed to supplement college studies, varied widely. Approximately 15 courses were presented in 1971, with foreign-language instruction the most popular among member schools. A twoyear (1971–73) Moody Foundation grant underwrote the TEMP service to the five private colleges and three public universities and colleges.

Since the end of World War II the mushrooming expansion of the television industry has affected the Texas economy in the manufacturing of parts, servicing of television sets, and construction of television stations; operation of the medium has steadily increased the demand for technical and studio personnel. By the 1980s most Texans were served by local cable companies, and the proliferation of both cable services and independent stations had reduced the viewer share of the three major networks. The number of television stations in the state increased dramatically, from 69 stations in 1980 to 95 stations in 1990 and 109 in 1995. In 1995, 43 cities had one or more stations; El Paso, San Antonio, and Houston led with 8 stations each, followed by Dallas with 7, Amarillo, Austin, Corpus Christi, Lubbock, and Odessa with 5 each, and Fort Worth and Waco with 4 each. The television "dish" industry, with its satellite access to numerous stations, was cutting into the cable industry, while the older networks were losing viewing public to more specialized programming of an increasing number of sorts.

Temple, T. L. L. Lumberman and industrialist; b. Thomas Lewis Latane Temple, Essex County, Virginia, 18 March 1859; d. Texarkana, 2 October 1935; m. Georgia D. Fowlkes (1880); 5 children. Temple was orphaned at the age of 11 and went in 1876 to Arkansas, where he farmed and worked as a deputy court clerk. In Texarkana he was introduced to the lumber business, and in 1887 he became a member of Grisby, Scott, and Temple, a large sawmill operation in Wayne, Texas. In 1893 Temple organized the Southern Pine Lumber Company for the second time (after an attempt in 1891) and incorporated it in Texas with himself as president and manager. At Diboll he built a sawmill with a daily capacity of about 75,000 board feet after acquiring some 7,000 acres of timberland from J. C. Diboll. Southern Pine Lumber Company eventually became the principal one of many business interests operated by Temple and his family successors. Temple also organized the Lufkin Land and Lumber Company with E. W. and E. A. Frost and G. A. Kelley in 1900 and built a sawmill at Lufkin with a daily capacity of 100,000 board feet. Three years later he disposed of his interest in the company. Temple founded the Texas South-Eastern Railroad at Diboll and the Temple Lumber Company at Pineland; he purchased several other lumber companies and merged them into his family operations. At the time of his death he held 278,000 acres of timberland in East Texas that provided raw materials for two large pine and hardwood sawmills at Diboll and Pineland. *Bob Bowman*

Temple, Texas. Temple is in northeastern Bell County 36 miles south of Waco and 67 miles north of Austin. In 1880 Jonathan E. Moore sold 187 acres of his land to the Gulf, Colorado and Santa Fe Railway to use for a construction camp. The site was called Temple Junction by the railroad company, in honor of Bernard Moore Temple, chief engineer of the railroad; local residents called the community Mud Town or Tanglefoot. When a post office was established there in January 1881, the official name became Temple. The railroad held a sale of town lots in June 1881; there was a nucleus of railroad workers to begin with, and stores went up rapidly. In 1882 the Missouri, Kansas and Texas line was built through Temple, and the Santa Fe made the town a division point. The railroad shops added several hundred to the community population, which included doctors, lawyers, and merchants. Temple was incorporated in 1882, and by 1884 its 3,000 residents were served by three churches and a school, as well as two banks, two weekly newspapers, an opera house, a waterworks, and a wide variety of other businesses. The Santa Fe Hospital was established in Temple in 1891, King's Daughters Hospital in 1897, and Scott and White Hospital in 1904, making Temple one of the leading medical centers in the Southwest. Because of its railroad interchange and its medical facilities, it became the largest city in the county. Around 1900 it reported 7,065 residents; by 1930 this number had more than doubled, to 15,345. Local residents made several attempts to have Temple replace Belton as county seat, but these efforts failed. An interurban rail line, in operation between Temple and Belton from 1905 to 1923, helped facilitate travel to the county seat. Businesses established in Temple included the American Desk Company (1921) and a Coca-Cola bottling plant (1925). Temple Junior College opened in 1926. The Great Depression interrupted the town's steady growth, but the 1940s brought another wave of new residents. Between 1940 and 1960 the population rose from 15,344 to 30,419. In 1942 the Veterans Administration opened a new hospital in Temple, adding another dimension to the local medical facilities and making the area attractive for military retirees. By the 1970s Temple manufactures included furniture, shoes, insulation, cottonseed products, electronic products, plastics, clothing, optical supplies, woodwork, and livestock and poultry feed. In addition, Temple had a substation of the agricultural experiment station system and was the site for the state offices of the United States Soil Conservation Service. The city's population had risen to 42,483 by 1980 and to 49,851 by 1990. The Killeen–Temple metropolitan statistical area reported a population of 255,301 in 1990. *Vivian Elizabeth Smyrl*

Sculptor Allie Victoria Tennant in her studio with her full-scale model for the *Tejas Warrior*, New York, 1935. Photograph by DeWitt Ward, New York City. Courtesy Jerry Bywaters Collection on Art of the Southwest, Jake and Nancy Hamon Arts Library, Southern Methodist University, Dallas. The finished sculpture was installed over the entrance to the Hall of State in Fair Park, Dallas.

Tennant, Allie. Sculptor; b. St. Louis, Missouri, 1898 (?); d. Dallas, 19 December 1971 (buried in Oakland Cemetery). The family moved to Dallas when Allie was young. She made her first sculpture at age eight, and received her earliest artistic training from Vivian Louise Aunspaugh. She attended the Art Students League in New York City, 1927–28, 1933. She was associated peripherally with the Dallas Nine in the 1930s. She made portrait busts, full-figure commemorative works, fountain pieces, and architectural sculpture. She favored cast bronze because of its durability, but also worked with marble and sandstone. On at least one piece, *Negro Head (Negro)* (1935), now in the collection of the Dallas Museum of Art, she experimented with direct carving, a modernist rejection of the traditional processes used for bronze and marble, and a technique popular among Texas sculptors at the time. Tennant's best-known work is the nine-foot-high gilded-bronze *Tejas Warrior* (1936) over the entrance doorway of the Hall of State. The smoothly modeled contours of the Indian warrior evidence the impact of the Art Deco movement and of Paul Howard Manship's archaism on Tennant's style. In her black bronze sculpture *Negress* (ca. 1936) and in an undated sculpture of a cat, she carried simplification to a greater extreme for

expressive purposes. Her other major commissions included decorative reliefs for the Dallas Aquarium at Fair Park (1936), the James Butler Bonham memorial (1938) in Bonham; and the Antonio Navarro memorial (1938) in Corsicana. She also did the relief *Cattle, Oil, and Wheat* (1940), for the post office in Electra, funded by the WPA. She won prizes for sculptures exhibited in the Dallas Allied Arts exhibitions in 1928, 1929, and 1932, and in 1935 she won the Kiest Memorial Prize from the Dallas Art Association. She also won prizes from the Southern States Art League in 1932, 1933, and 1936. She exhibited her work at the Pennsylvania Academy of Fine Arts (1935), the Art Institute of Chicago (1935), the Kansas City Art Institute (1935), the Architectural League of New York (1938), the World's Fair in New York (1939), the Whitney Museum of American Art (1940), the National Sculpture Society (1940), and the Carnegie Institute (1941). She was elected a fellow of the National Sculpture Society in 1934, and was a member of the Dallas Art Association, the Highland Park Society of Arts, and the Southern States Art League. In 1943 Tennant and other prominent Texan sculptors founded the Texas Sculptors Group, for which she served as first president. In addition to sculpting and exhibiting her work, she lectured, contributed articles on garden sculpture to the local paper, and taught at the Dallas Art Institute. Her work is included in the collections of the Dallas Museum of Art, the Hockaday School, the University of Texas Southwestern Medical Center, and the Women's Club, all in Dallas; McMurry University, Abilene; and the Brookgreen Sculpture Gardens in Georgetown County, South Carolina. *Kendall Curlee*

Tenth United States Cavalry. A black cavalry unit authorized by Congress in the summer of 1866 with Col. Benjamin H. Grierson as regimental commander. With the exception of Henry Flipper, all of the officers were white. Most of the 12 companies of the regiment were organized at Fort Leavenworth, Kansas, and by August 1867 nine of these were stationed along the line of the Kansas–Pacific Railroad, then being constructed across the plains of Kansas and under near-constant attack by Indians. In numerous fights and skirmishes against these elusive foes the Tenth's troopers proved their courage and fighting ability. Before long, Cheyenne warriors were calling their antagonists "buffalo soldiers," a title the cavalrymen promptly and proudly accepted. The Tenth played an important role in Sheridan's winter campaign of 1868–69, which drove the hostile Southern Plains tribes into reservations in Indian Territory. At the close of these operations Sheridan assigned the Tenth the task of standing guard over the Kiowas, Kiowa–Apaches, and Comanches on their reservation. On a site that Grierson recommended and Sheridan approved, troopers of the Tenth began construction of a permanent post, first called Camp Wichita and then Fort Sill. Controlling the cooped-up raiders proved difficult for the Tenth. Under Indian policy, military forces on reservations could conduct operations against outriding raiders only when specifically called upon to do so by the resident Indian agent. Agents nominated by the Society of Friends under President Ulysses S. Grant's "peace policy" controlled Indian affairs at Fort Sill and were opposed to the use of force. Under these circumstances the Tenth could do little to stop attacks along the length of the Texas frontier. Texans and their elected representatives failed to understand the restrictions placed on the Tenth and came to regard Grierson, his officers, and his men as a collection of cowardly misfits. Grierson was falsely accused of inciting and arming Indian warriors, a charge that was denied not only by Grierson but by General Sherman, commander of the army.

The Red River Indian War (1874) changed the story. All restrictions on the army were removed, and in a campaign of five months the Tenth and a battalion of its sister regiment, the Ninth United States Cavalry, scouted more miles, destroyed more lodges and property, and captured more Indians than any other regiment in the field. In April 1875 the Tenth was transferred to the Texas frontier and headquartered at Fort Concho. For the next decade Grierson and his regiment were the principal military presence in far West Texas, and their contributions to peace, order, and settlement were significant. From forts Concho, Stockton, Davis, Quitman, and Clark, as well as from numerous camps, companies and detachments of the Tenth scouted, patrolled, and mapped thousands of square miles. Grierson's detailed reports provided invaluable information on sources of water and the nature of soils and vegetation, as well as prospects for ranching, farming, and recreational opportunities. The Tenth's presence made the opening of new roads and the construction of hundreds of miles of telegraph lines possible. In the summer of 1880 the Tenth was called upon again to prove its mettle in combat against Victorio. The Tenth outmarched and outfought the Apaches, delivered them a decisive defeat at the battle of Rattlesnake Springs, and drove them back into Mexico. After 1880 troops were no longer needed at Fort Concho, and in 1882 the headquarters of the Tenth was moved to Fort Davis. Three years later the regiment was transferred to stations in Arizona to take part in the final roundup of hostile Apache bands. In September 1886 a detachment from the Tenth Cavalry captured Mangus, the last belligerent Apache chief on the Arizona frontier. *William H. Leckie*

Tent Shows. Popular entertainment in the rural areas of the United States during the first half of the twentieth century, particularly in the Southwest, South, and Midwest. Typically, these shows featured a three-act comedy or drama interspersed with "polite" vaudeville. Great emphasis was placed upon presenting inoffensive family entertainment; the master of ceremonies frequently boasted that "nothing would be seen or heard that might offend the taste of the most fastidious." Tent shows offered a repertoire of from three to 12 plays. They reached their peak activity shortly before the Great Depression. In 1927 an article in the New York *Times* stated that the tented drama constituted "a more extensive business than Broadway and all the rest of the legitimate theatre industry put together." The Charles Harrison troupe achieved a marked success in the southern part of Texas shortly before World War I. Harrison, one of the leading playwrights of "rag op'ries" as well as an actor and manager, toured with one of the most elaborate tent theaters ever constructed. Featuring opera-house boxes and a sloping wooden floor with fixed seating, the outfit required three days to set up and a full day to dismantle. Harrison was quickly followed by Rentfrow's Jolly Pathfinders and by Roy E. Fox's Popular Players. Rentfrow, in fact, may have toured Texas as early as 1880. Fox, with headquarters in Sulphur Springs, became by 1918 the leading tent-show operator in the nation. West Texas at this time was viewing shows under canvas sent out by the Brunk brothers, an Oklahoma organization. In 1922 Harley H. Sadler's Own Show began operation. Sadler, an alumnus of the Rentfrow, Fox, and Brunk companies, was able in a few years to claim ownership of "America's Biggest and Best Traveling Stock Company." While these larger shows, often with companies of over 50, were appearing in the larger of the small towns, other troupes of varying size, some with as few as a half dozen members in the company, were playing the tiny crossroads communities. Holland and Vaye, Haverstock's Comedians, the Musical Grays, the Kennedy Sisters, the Grandi Brothers, J. Doug Morgan, Hila Morgan, Ed C. Nutt, and many other groups of players crisscrossed the vast area of Texas, bringing what was often the only commercial live entertainment ever to appear in the rural hamlets. Unlike such suspect traveling attractions as the carnival and circus, tent shows found acceptance in these farming and ranching communities. With a touring radius of no more than 200 miles, shows revisited towns on a regular basis, so that a good reputation was essential for continuing success. Although there was some opposition from owners of movie houses and from those religious sects opposed to anything associated with theater, tent shows were generally welcomed by communities. Sometimes, Wednesday evening church services would be moved to an earlier hour so that audiences could attend both the temple and the tent show on the same evening.

The tent show reached its zenith of popularity just before the depression and collapsed with the falling economy. This once widespread form of entertainment never recovered, for audiences were lured away by radio, talkies, and drive-in theaters. The introduction of air-conditioning made indoor gatherings possible in summer, and improved transportation ended the cultural isolation of rural families. The few small companies that survived turned to broad, slapstick farce centered around Toby, the red-haired, freckle-faced bumpkin who had once been one character in a much broader repertoire. The Toby Show, a burlesque of the original tent show, represented the final stages of this form of folk entertainment. World War II, with its travel restrictions and manpower shortages, extinguished most of the few remaining Toby shows. Troupes such as the Haverstock Comedians and the McKennon Players survived into the 1950s, but today, except for occasional revivals, the tent show has passed from the Texas scene.   *Clifford Ashby*

Terán de los Ríos, Domingo. First governor of the Spanish province of Texas; details of birth and death unknown. On 23 January 1691 the Conde de Gálvez appointed Terán to oversee the administration of Coahuila, Texas, and adjacent regions. Terán had been in the Spanish service in Peru for 20 years, had gone to Mexico in 1681 as a deputy of the *consulado* of Sevilla, had been captain of infantry in the castle of San Juan de Ullóa, and in 1686 was made governor of Sonora and Sinaloa, where he was successful in quelling Indian disturbances. His instructions for his Texas venture, based on suggestions by Damián Massanet, were to establish seven missions with Massanet among the Tejas Indians, to investigate rumors of foreign settlements on the coast, and to keep records of geography, natives, and products. Terán's army crossed the Rio Grande on May 28 and named the Texas rivers they crossed in their progress eastward. When they reached San Francisco de los Tejas, the governor renamed the country Nuevo Reyno de la Montaña de Santander y Santillana. On the return journey, at the site of Fort St. Louis, Terán met Gregorio de Salinas Varona, who brought him new orders for the exploration of the country. This led to a difficult march back to the missions in East Texas, where a bitter dispute with Massanet arose over Terán's seizure of mission animals to replace his depleted horse herd. Continuing on to Matagorda Bay, where he arrived on 5 March 1692, Terán was met by Juan Enríquez Barroto, who gave him instructions from the viceroy to explore the lower reaches of the Mississippi River. Terán embarked for that purpose, but bad weather caused him to abandon the project and return to Veracruz. His mission was a failure. He succeeded in founding no new missions, and the expedition added little new information about the region. After his return, he compiled a lengthy report defending his actions and detailing the dismal situation in East Texas.   *Robert Bruce Blake*

Terry, Benjamin Franklin. Confederate officer; b. Russellville, Kentucky, 18 February 1821; d. near Woodsonville, Kentucky, 17 December 1861; m. Mary Bingham (1841); six children. Terry's grandfathers were officers in the Revolutionary War, and one of them also fought in the War of 1812. His mother, separated from his father, brought him to Texas from Mississippi in 1833 or early 1834. In 1841 Terry assumed responsibility for managing the family plantation in Harris County. On 6 March 1844 the Houston

Telegraph reported that two insurgent slaves attacked Terry on his plantation with knives and axes, but "with admirable courage" he defended himself and managed to disable both men. Terry and his partner, William J. Kyle, built the first railroad in Texas, the Buffalo Bayou, Brazos and Colorado Railway (1851–56), which brought brisk trade to Harrisburg. Terry and Kyle were also awarded the contract to build the Houston Tap. Terry had purchased the Oakland sugar plantation in Fort Bend County in 1852 and became a prosperous sugar planter. In 1860 he and Kyle had real and personal property worth almost $300,000. In 1861 Terry was elected a delegate to the Secession Convention in Austin. He and two fellow delegates, Thomas S. Lubbock and John A. Wharton, conceived the idea of organizing at least one company of Texas cavalrymen for the new government. In February and March 1861 Terry was one of the senior officers aiding John S. Ford and Ebenezar B. Nichols in the campaign to disarm the federal troops at Brazos Santiago. In June 1861 Terry, Lubbock, Wharton, and perhaps as many as 50 other Texans traveled to Richmond to offer their services to the Confederate Army. Terry and Lubbock secured positions as volunteer aides to Gen. James Longstreet and were appointed colonel, a term attached as a courtesy for their volunteer service. They participated with distinction in the battle of First Manassas or Bull Run. Afterward, the Confederate War Department granted the men authority to organize a cavalry regiment. At Houston, Terry and Lubbock issued a call for volunteers that was answered by 1,170 men. The rangers were sworn into service in September, but Terry delayed their final organization until late November, when they were officially designated the Eighth Texas Cavalry, known popularly as Terry's Texas Rangers. The regiment started immediately for Virginia but en route was diverted to Nashville and then later ordered to Bowling Green, Kentucky. Terry was killed in the first battle fought by the rangers, which ended in a Confederate victory. His body was sent by train to Nashville, where the legislature adjourned and joined in a procession escorting the remains to be held in state at the Tennessee Capitol. The body also lay in state in New Orleans and then Houston, where the funeral procession was described as "the most imposing ever seen in this state." Terry County is named for B. F. Terry.   *Kenneth W. Hobbs*

Texan Santa Fe Expedition. A political–military–commercial expedition of 1841, occasioned by President Lamar's desire to get Texas in on the Santa Fe trade and establish Texas jurisdiction over the Santa Fe area, which the Republic of Texas claimed on the basis of an act of 1836. No steps had been taken to exercise control over the New Mexican settlements until 1840, when William Dryden, a resident of Santa Fe, visited Austin and, on being approached by Lamar, agreed to act as commissioner for Texas in an effort to influence the people of New Mexico to approve the change in government. John Rowland and William Workman of Santa Fe were also appointed commissioners. Dryden returned to Santa Fe with a letter from Lamar, in which the Texas president outlined the alleged benefits of joining the Republic of Texas. Without approval from the Texas Congress, Lamar on his own initiative proposed an expedition to Santa Fe to establish a trade route as well as to offer the New Mexicans the opportunity of participating in the Texas government. A call for volunteers was issued, and merchants were promised transportation and protection for their goods. William Cooke,

Richard Brenham, José Antonio Navarro, and George Van Ness were appointed civil commissioners. The military force to protect the merchants was headed by Hugh McLeod, with George Thomas Howard as second in command. George Wilkins Kendall and Thomas Falconer accompanied the expedition as guests. These, with the merchants, teamsters, and others brought the total number to 321. Twenty-one ox-drawn wagons carried supplies and merchandise for trade, which was valued at $200,000.

On 19 June 1841 the party, officially designated the Santa Fe Pioneers, set out from Kenney's Fort on Brushy Creek, 20 miles north of Austin, and traveled north. At the present site of Wichita Falls they took the Wichita River for the Red River. The Pioneers followed the valley of the Wichita for 12 days and on 17 August were deserted by their Mexican guide. They finally realized their error and sent a company out to the north to search for the Red River. On 20 August a guide returned to lead the command to the northwest. Harassed by Indians and suffering because of insufficient provisions and scarcity of water, the expedition slowly made its way to the northwest. On Quitaque Creek in the area of present northwestern Motley County, McLeod, unable to find a route by which the wagons could ascend the Caprock, divided his command, sending a party of horsemen out to seek the New Mexican settlements while he waited with the wagons and the remaining force at the foot of the Llano Estacado. The advance party, after suffering many hardships and encountering difficult traveling in crossing Quitaque and Tule canyons, finally met some Mexican traders on 12 September and sent a guide back to lead the force on into the settlements. The Texans had expected to be welcomed, but Governor Manuel Armijo of New Mexico had sent armed detachments out to await their arrival. Capt. William G. Lewis, one of the first of the advance party to reach the settlements, turned traitor and persuaded his comrades to lay down their arms on 17 September. He was again used by the New Mexicans in securing the surrender of the main force, which had crossed the Llano Estacado and was encamped at Laguna Colorada, near present Tucumcari, New Mexico, on 5 October. Thus, without the firing of a single shot, the entire expedition passed into Mexican hands. The Texas prisoners were marched to Mexico City. They were subjected to many indignities both en route and after their imprisonment in Mexico. The affair became the subject of a heated diplomatic controversy between the United States and Mexico before most of the prisoners were finally released in April 1842. Although generally considered a failure, the expedition stimulated a renewal of interest in Texas within both the United States and Mexico and formed a shaky basis for the Texas claim to western territory. *H. Bailey Carroll*

Texarkana, Texas. In extreme northeastern Texas on the Texas–Arkansas border, a short distance above the Louisiana boundary; named for its location, the three parts of its name deriving from the three states. According to one tradition, the name was derived from a steamboat known as the Texarkana, which plied the Red River as early as 1860. Others claim that a man named Swindle, who ran a general store in Red Land, Louisiana, manufactured a drink called "Texarkana Bitters." Yet another story claims that when the St. Louis, Iron Mountain and Southern Railroad was building its line through the area, Col. Gus Knobel, who made the survey, coined the name and put up

Broad Street, Texarkana, Arkansas, ca. 1875–1880. Stereograph. Courtesy TSL. Texarkana was named for its location on the Texas–Arkansas border. Texarkana, Texas, was granted a charter by the legislature in 1876.

a large sign at the site. The strategic position of Texarkana is the keynote to its history and development. The Great Southwest Trail, for hundreds of years the main line of travel from Indian villages of the Mississippi River country to those of the South and West, passed by a Caddo Indian village on the site that later became Texarkana. Seventy Indian mounds, reminders of Caddo occupation and culture, are within a radius of 30 miles of Texarkana. When the builders of the Cairo and Fulton Railroad crossed Arkansas in the late 1850s and by 1874 pushed their rails beyond the Red River to the Texas border, they met the railhead that had been extended to the state line by the Texas and Pacific. The road from the south bank of Red River was completed to the state line in 1874; Texarkana had been established in 1873 at the site where the two roads would join. The Texas and Pacific Railway Company laid out the Texas side of the town. The first business, a combination drug and grocery store operated by George M. Clark, opened in December 1873. In 1876 Texarkana, Texas, was granted a charter under an act of the state legislature. State Line Avenue, the town's main street, was laid out exactly along the dividing line between the two states. By 1896 Texarkana had a waterworks, an electric light plant, five miles of streetcar lines, gas works, four newspapers, an ice factory, a cotton compress, a cottonseed oil mill, a sewer system, brick schools, two foundries, a machine shop, a hotel, and a population of 14,000. In 1907 Texarkana, Texas, was accorded city status and granted a new charter. By 1925 the Texas side of the town had a population of 11,480, many of whom worked for one of the railroads or in processing agricultural products.

During the Great Depression the number of businesses declined from 840 (1931) to 696 (1936), but the town's economic fortunes recovered by the early 1940s, buoyed in part by the construction of the Red River Army Depot and the Lone Star Army

Ammunition Plant. In 1948 Texarkana, as the junction of four important railroad systems with eight outlets, was one of the major railroad centers of the Southwest. The city was also important as a commercial and industrial center. The industries have been built around three natural resource—abundant timber, fertile agricultural lands, and plentiful mineral deposits. While commercially one city, Texarkana consists of two separate municipalities, aldermanic in form, with two mayors and two sets of councilmen and city officials. There is a cooperative arrangement for the joint operation of fire department, food and dairy inspection, sewage disposal, environmental sanitation, and supervised recreational programs. The Federal Building has the distinction of being the only building of its kind situated in two states. The entire city in 1952 had a population of 40,490, the Texas portion reporting 24,657. By 1960 the total population reached 50,006 (30,218 in Texas and 19,788 in Arkansas). The regional economy has continued to grow at a steady pace, with more emphasis towards industry. Crops raised include cotton, corn, rice, soybeans, pecans, and truck crops; livestock and poultry accounted for 75 percent of the farm income. Industries in the area include the manufacture and marketing of lumber products, sewer tile, rockwool, sand and gravel, mobile homes and accessories, hardware supplies, tires, railroad tank cars, and paper products. Also of great importance to the economy is a federal correctional unit. Texarkana is the transportation, commercial, and industrial center for the region, as well as the hub for portions of Oklahoma and Louisiana; it is also the educational, cultural, and medical center of a metropolitan area. Texarkana College, a fully accredited junior college, includes the William Buchanan Department of Nursing. The Civic Music Association, with patrons from the entire metropolitan area, brings in artists of national and international fame. Texarkana serves the area with three major hospitals and several modern clinics. Supplying water for industrial development are Wright Patman Lake and the Millwood Reservoir in Arkansas. Both are also important recreational sites. The Texarkana area holds an annual Four States Fair and Rodeo, plus other rodeos, band festivals, and a Miss Texarkana Pageant. In 1992 Texarkana had a total population of 120,132; 31,656 of these lived on the Texas side.

Texas. The topmost structure on a river steamboat, located on the hurricane deck below or aft the pilothouse; includes the officers' quarters and other rooms. The staterooms on Mississippi River steamboats were named for states, and the officers' rooms, being the largest, were named texas. The word was in use by 1857, when Frederick L. Olmsted used it in his *Journey to Texas.*

Texas (battleship). (1) The USS *Texas*, built at the Norfolk Navy Yard and commissioned 15 August 1895; the first commissioned American steel-hulled battleship; 309 feet long. During the battle of Santiago on 3 July 1898, the *Texas* helped in the defeat of the Spanish squadron commanded by Admiral Pascual Cervera. The ship brought home the bodies of those killed on the *Maine.* In 1908 it was used as a station ship in Charleston, South Carolina. Its name was changed to USS *San Marcos* in 1911 so that the name *Texas* could be assigned to a new, more modern battleship. The *San Marcos* became a gunnery target in 1920 and was eventually sunk in Chesapeake Bay. The hulk became a hazard to navigation and was finally blasted by the Navy to send it 20 feet under the surface.

(2) The keel of the second battleship USS *Texas* was laid at the Newport News Shipbuilding Company on 17 April 1911. The ship was christened on 18 May 1912. A motion picture of the event was thought to be the first such record of a United States Navy launching. The *Texas* was commissioned for service in 1914. It was 573 feet long with a beam of 95 feet, and it displaced 27,000 tons. It had two four-cylinder steam engines developing 28,100 horsepower, driving two three-blade propellers with diameters of nearly 19 feet. The ship had 14 coal-burning boilers and was designed for a speed of 21 knots in a four-hour speed trial and 19 knots in a 24-hour endurance trial. The USS *Texas* served in the Atlantic Fleet during World War I. It was used for tactical exercises until 1918, when it operated in the North Sea. It was present at the surrender of the German Imperial Fleet in 1918, and was used to test a flying-off platform for planes in March 1919. In 1925 the ship was at the Norfolk Navy Yard to be refitted with oil-fired boilers and to have its superstructure updated. In 1927, after this modernization, it was the flagship for the commander in chief of the United States Fleet. The USS *Texas* was again involved in testing in 1938, when what later became known as radar was first being developed. In 1940–41 the ship was assigned to escort duty in the North Atlantic, and in 1942 it supported the Allied landings in North Africa. On D-Day, 6 June 1944, the *Texas* was the flagship for the bombardment group supporting the Allied landings on Omaha Beach. On 25 June 1944 it received two direct hits from German shore guns. After the damage was repaired, the *Texas* supported the landings in southern France from 14 August to 16 August 1944. By February 1945 the battleship was in the Pacific, where it supported the landings at Iwo Jima. On March 26 it supported the landings at Okinawa, and on 17 May 1944 returned to the Philippines. By mid-February 1946 the ship was back at the Norfolk shipyard for retirement and mothballing. On December 6, 1946, Texas governor Coke Stevenson accepted the Texas from the United States Navy to be used as a state shrine. In 1948, after more than 34 years of naval service, the USS *Texas* became the nation's first memorial battleship and a national historic landmark. It was permanently moored at the San Jacinto Monument. In 1983 the ship became the responsibility of the Texas Parks and Wildlife Department. By 1988 it was badly rusted and in need of repair, and was subsequently towed to the Todd Shipyard in Galveston, where major restoration was carried out. On 26 July 1990 the *Texas* was returned to the San Jacinto mooring, where it is kept open for public tours.   *Art Leatherwood*

Texas, Origin of Name. The word *texas* (vrr. *tejas, tayshas, texias, thecas?, techan, teysas, techas?*) had wide usage among the Indians of East Texas even before the coming of the Spanish, whose various transcriptions and interpretations gave rise to many theories about the meaning. The usual meaning was "friends," although the Hasinais applied the word to many groups—including Caddoan—to mean "allies." The Hasinais probably did not apply the name to themselves as a local group name; they did use the term, however, as a form of greeting: "Hello, friend." How and when the name Texas first reached the Spanish is uncertain, but the notion of a "great kingdom of Texas," associated with Quivira, had spread in New Spain before the expedition of Alonso De León and Damián Massanet in 1689. Massanet reported meeting Indians who proclaimed themselves *thecas,* or "friends," as he understood it, and on meeting the chief of the Nabedaches (one of the Hasinai tribes) mistakenly referred to him as the "governor" of a "great kingdom of the Texas." Francisco de Jesús María, a missionary left by Massanet with the Nabedaches, attempted to correct erroneous reports about the name by asserting that the Indians in that region did not constitute a kingdom, that the chief called "governor" was not the head chief, and that the correct name of the group of tribes was not Texas. *Texias*, according to Jesús María, meant "friends" and was simply a name applied to the various groups allied against the Apaches. Later expeditions by the Spanish for the most part abandoned the name Texas or else used it as an alternative to Asinay (Hasinai). Official Spanish documents continued to use it but later narrowed it to mean only the Neches–Angelina group of Indians and not a geographic area. Other putative meanings have less evidence from contemporary accounts to support them: "land of flowers," "paradise," and "tiled roofs"—from the thatched roofs of the East Texas Indians—were never suggested by first-hand observers so far as is known, though later theories connect them with *tejas* or its variant spellings. Whatever the Spanish denotations of the name Texas, the state motto, "Friendship," carries the original meaning of the word as used by the Hasinais and their allied tribes, and the name of the state apparently was derived from the same source. 			*Phillip L. Fry*

Texas A&M International University. Originally Texas A&I University at Laredo; established in 1969 as a branch of Texas A&I University at Kingsville; renamed Laredo State University in 1977, made part of the Texas A&M University System in 1989, and given its present name in 1993. It was the first exclusively upper-level institution in Texas. In September 1995 it became a four-year college. At first it shared quarters with Laredo Junior College, but now has its own campus. 		*Erika Murr*

Texas A&M University. The state's oldest public institution of higher education. In 1866 the Texas legislature voted to accept the terms of the federal Morrill Land-Grant College Act of 1862, which provided for the donation of public lands for colleges devoted primarily to teaching "such branches of learning as are related to agriculture and the mechanic arts." Earlier and subsequent land grants directly affected the development of the school. The Fourth Congress of the Republic of Texas donated fifty leagues of land (221,400 acres) for the endowment of two colleges or universities in 1839. The state legislature approved enabling legislation in 1856 providing for the sale of university lands and for the establishment of the Permanent University Fund. No public universities were built before the outbreak of the Civil War. Following the war and the acceptance of the Morrill Act, the Constitutional Convention of 1866 provided for an additional endowment of a million acres of public land for one or more state universities. This was followed in 1883 by an additional grant of a million acres of state land. Thus the Agricultural and Mechanical College of Texas became both a federal and Texas land-grant college. Under the terms of the Morrill Act, donated land from the federal government was to be drawn from the public land within the states receiving the grants, but where no such land existed, as in Texas, the secretary of the interior issued scrip entitling the state to claim unappropriated public land in the territories. In 1871 Texas received title to 180,000 acres in Colorado, the sale of which provided bonds

Horticulture students, ca. 1900–1910. Courtesy TSL. By 1910, A&M offered eight degree programs, including one in agriculture.

with a face value of $174,000. The same year the state legislature approved a bill providing for the organization of the Texas Agricultural and Mechanical College and appropriated $75,000 for the construction of academic buildings and suitable accommodations. Governor Edmund J. Davis appointed a committee of three to find a suitable site of not less than 1,280 acres. The committee selected a site near Bryan, where citizens donated 2,416 acres. The Constitution of 1876 specified that A&M College was to be a branch of a proposed University of Texas.

Following delays caused by political and financial irregularities rife in the Reconstruction era, the college opened in 1876 with 106 students and a faculty of six, headed by Thomas S. Gathright. It began as an all-male military institution with required participation in the Corps of Cadets. Subsequently, Texas A&M regularly commissioned more officers than any other institution including the service academies, and its students have achieved an outstanding record of military service in all of the wars fought since the Spanish-American War. In 1965, only after great controversy, military training became optional and the Corps of Cadets a voluntary organization. Nevertheless, the Corps of Cadets and "Aggie" traditions established by the corps continue to shape the culture of the university. A few women attended classes in the 1890s and enrolled intermittently and received degrees before 1940; women were officially admitted to Texas A&M on a limited basis in 1963 and on an equal basis with men in 1971. Just as the Corps of Cadets played a major role in the history and development of the institution, so the advent of coeducation greatly influenced the rapid growth and development of Texas A&M University in the last quarter of the twentieth century.

Despite its charter, the A&M College of Texas taught no classes in agriculture during its formative years, but stressed classical studies, languages, literature, and applied mathematics. This led to protests from farmer groups, the removal of the president and faculty in November 1879, and their replacement with new faculty and a new mandated curriculum in agriculture and engineering. Enrollment, which had climbed to 500 students, declined rapidly to about eighty students by 1883. That year the University of Texas opened in Austin under the authority of a

Final Review, ca. 1980–82. Photograph by Will Van Overbeek, Austin. Copyright ©Will Van Overbeek. Texas A&M began in 1876 as an all-male military institution with required participation in the Corps of Cadets.

separate board of regents, while A&M College functioned under the authority of its board of directors. The two Texas institutions began to battle for the meager funding then available from the state and from the Permanent University Fund. Conflicts diminished during the administration of Governor Sul Ross, who in 1891 became president of A&M. Ross's prestige and management, plus larger appropriations from the state and the founding of the Texas Agricultural Experiment Station at the college in 1887, greatly enhanced the institution. The college broadened its curriculum, particularly in the sciences and engineering. By 1910 it offered eight degree programs. In 1915 the state legislature, in cooperation with the United States Department of Agriculture, established the Texas Agricultural Extension Service, organized the Texas Forest Service, and authorized a school of veterinary medicine under the auspices of the college. During World War I the university went on a "war status." By 1918, 49 percent of the total graduates were in military service—more than from any other college or university. More than 1,200 served as commissioned officers. When the war ended, Texas A&M grew rapidly and became nationally recognized for its programs in agriculture, engineering, and military science. William Bennett Bizzell, who became president in 1914, presided over the postwar expansion until he resigned in 1925. A graduate school was organized in 1924, and programs leading to the doctorate were established in 1936. The first Ph.D. degree was awarded in 1940. In 1931, following the discovery of oil on university lands eight years earlier,

A&M and UT negotiated a settlement over the division of the Permanent University Fund by which A&M would receive a third of the revenue. Income from the fund has enabled both universities to sustain development that otherwise would have been impossible. Enrollment at A&M increased even during the difficult days of the Great Depression. Student cooperative housing projects enabled students to attend college at very low cost. Thomas Otto Walton was president of the college from 1925 until 1943, when the campus was once again on a war footing. About 20,000 Texas A&M former students served in the armed forces during World War II, some 14,000 as officers and 29 in the rank of general. The postwar period brought many changes in curriculum, administration, personnel, and student composition. Texas A&M directors organized the Texas Maritime Academy at Galveston in 1962. Gen. James Earl Rudder and Marion Thomas Harrington, who served variously as president and chancellor, guided the university through an era of unprecedented change and expansion.

Effective on 23 August 1963, the state legislature approved a bill changing the name of the college to Texas A&M University. Under the new designation "A&M" did not signify "agricultural and mechanical" but was regarded as symbolic. The new name reflected the diversified and expanded character of the institution. Enrollment surged from approximately 8,000 in 1963 to more than 25,000 by 1976, when Texas A&M celebrated its centennial. In 1990 the main campus of the Texas A&M University

System, at College Station, enrolled more than 40,000 students. Also located at College Station in 1994 was Texas A&M University College of Medicine. Texas A&M is the home of the George Bush Presidential Library. The school operated a branch campus in Koriyama, Japan, until summer 1994, when the campus closed due to a decline in enrollment. Texas A&M ranks among the top 10 United States universities in research. In 1994 Texas A&M, along with Baylor University, the University of Texas at Austin, and Texas Tech University, decided to leave the Southwest Conference to join the Big Twelve athletic conference.

Henry C. Dethloff

Texas A&M University College of Medicine. On the campus of Texas A&M University at College Station; authorized by the Texas Higher Education Coordinating Board in 1973, under an act of 1971 authorizing the foundation of a medical school associated with the Veterans Administration. James A. Knight, M.D., was appointed dean of medicine, and negotiations were completed with the VA in Washington and with Scott and White Memorial Hospital in Temple for conduct of the program. The VA awarded $17 million in support of the new program (1975). Provisional accreditation from the AMA and the Association of American Medical Colleges was granted in 1976, and the charter class entered the college in 1977. Full accreditation was awarded in 1981, the year the first class of 32 physicians graduated. In 1991 the regents of the Texas A&M University System established the Texas A&M University Health Science Center with the College of Medicine as the focal program. The medical faculty numbered over 600. The college's research budget supports faculty research as well as the operation of five research institutes (Microcirculation Research, Molecular Pathogenesis and Therapeutics, Ocular Pharmacology, Occupational Medicine, and Clinical Outcomes Assessment) and two centers (for Health Systems and Technology and for the Study of Cell Surfaces). The educational program includes graduate education leading to the M.S. and Ph.D. degrees. The juxtapositioning of a major public research university (Texas A&M), an exemplary private medical practice (Scott and White), and the medical program of a federal agency (the VA) brings the school a constellation of strengths. The clinical campus consists of Scott and White, the Olin E. Teague Veterans Center, and the Darnall Army Community Hospital at Fort Hood. In addition, the college is affiliated with the VA hospitals in Marlin and Waco as well as with other institutions in the region.

S. H. Black

Texas A&M University—Commerce. Established by William L. Mayo at Cooper in 1889 and chartered in 1890 as Mayo (or Mayo's) College, a private institution where the founder "could be at liberty to put into operation his idea of a democratic school of a college type." The building burned in 1894, and Mayo moved the school to Commerce, where it was rechartered as East Texas Normal College and began classes with 35 pupils. The school operated as an independent private college with no endowment or income except tuition and rent from dormitories. Between 1889 and 1917 more than 30,000 students received their basic education at East Texas Normal, which prepared more teachers for the public schools than any other college or university in Texas in the same period. The college had six degree programs. Mayo wanted to perpetuate his school as a state teachers' college, and he started a move to place it under the

authority of the board of regents of the state normal schools. After the legislature passed an act to do this, the board of regents paid the Mayo estate $80,000 for the institution; Mayo died in March 1917, the same month that the state purchased the plant and 50 acres of land. Commerce donated $40,000 to renovate the buildings. The board of regents of the state teachers' colleges took over the plant and staff and renamed the institution East Texas State Normal College. In 1923 the name was changed again to East Texas State Teachers College. Graduate courses were offered for the first time in 1935. After the educational scope was broadened, "Teachers" was dropped from the name (1957). In 1962 the first doctoral program was initiated. University status was authorized by the legislature in 1965, and the name was changed to East Texas State University. In 1996 the university became part of the Texas A&M University System. TAMU—Commerce is a fully accredited institution. In addition to the Commerce Campus, it has operated an upper-division institution in Texarkana since 1971 and maintains a commuter facility in Garland, a graduate branch. Its Ph.D. degree is offered in cooperation with the Federation of North Texas Area Universities.

Nancy Beck Young

Texas A&M University at Corpus Christi. Chartered 1 April 1947 as Arts and Technological College, a four-year institution affiliated with the Baptist General Convention of Texas. Its first campus was Chase Field, a deactivated naval air-training field at Beeville. In 1947 the college moved to temporary quarters at Cuddihy Field in Corpus Christi, was renamed University of Corpus Christi, and then moved permanently to a former naval radar-training school. By 1964 the institution offered bachelor's degrees in 20 fields. It was subsequently sold and became a part of the Texas A&I University System (1973). In the fall of 1974 Texas A&I University at Corpus Christi had an enrollment of 1,603. Its name was changed to Corpus Christi State University in 1977, when the system that governed the school became the University System of South Texas. In 1989 the state legislature combined this system with the Texas A&M University System. The university is divided into four colleges: Arts and Humanities, Business Administration, Education, and Science and Technology. It offers 27 undergraduate and 17 graduate degree programs. In 1993 it was given its present name.

Nancy Beck Young

Texas A&M University at Galveston. The maritime and marine branch of the Texas A&M University System; offers programs in marine curricula leading to accredited bachelor of science degrees with or without a "license option." The license option prepares graduates to take United States Coast Guard examinations for licenses as third assistant engineers or third mates in the United States Flag Fleet (Merchant Marine). The Galveston Marine Laboratory and the Texas Maritime Academy provided the foundation for what was to become Texas A&M University at Galveston. The Marine Laboratory, founded in the late 1950s by two A&M science professors, Albert Collier and Sammy Ray, conducted scientific research in oceanography and marine biology. Meanwhile, Rear Admiral Sherman B. Wetmore, United States Naval Reserve, and other interested Galvestonians successfully petitioned the Texas legislature to appropriate money to establish the Texas Maritime Academy. The academy began operation as a part of the A&M System in

1962. The Department of Oceanography of Texas A&M had obtained a building at Fort Crockett from the federal government, which also provided a training ship, the 15,000-ton *Texas Clipper*. In 1968 a gift of 100 acres of land for a campus on Pelican Island made possible an oceanography and marine-technology center. Mary Moody Northen procured a $1 million grant from the Moody Foundation. In 1971 the president of Texas A&M, Jack Williams, appointed William H. Clayton dean of the new College of Marine Sciences and Maritime Resources in Galveston. Enrollment increased from 91 in 1971 to 600 in 1979. The legislature renamed the institution the Moody College of Marine Sciences and Maritime Resources in 1972. The first "non-license" students (including women) enrolled in 1973, and women registered as cadets for the first time in 1974. The A&M regents gradually approved several additions to the curricula, in marine sciences, marine biology, marine fisheries, maritime systems engineering, and maritime administration. The two original programs of the old Maritime Academy in marine transportation and marine engineering were continued and improved. In 1981 the institution became Texas A&M University at Galveston. *Joseph G. Dawson III*

Texas A&M University at Kingsville. A law passed in 1917 to authorize a normal school in South Texas was suspended because of World War I.In 1923 the Texas legislature changed all normal schools to state teachers' colleges and authorized a new one to be located west of the 101st meridian and south of the twenty-ninth parallel. The locating board chose Kingsville for the site of South Texas State Teachers College, which opened in June 1925 with Robert Cousins as president. In 1929 the school was changed from a teachers' college to a technical school and renamed Texas College of Arts and Industries. Originally four divisions of instruction were authorized: liberal arts, industrial arts and commerce, education, and military science. By 1946 teacher training in agriculture and kindergarten had been added, and laboratory facilities in gas engineering were provided. The former Naval Auxiliary Air Station east of Kingsville was adapted to house returning World War II veterans, both students and faculty, and also to provide facilities for model farming and a stock farm. In 1967 the institution became Texas A&I University and was organized into schools of engineering, teacher education, agriculture, arts and sciences, business administration, and graduate studies. In 1977 Texas A&I, Corpus Christi State University, and Laredo State University were consolidated into the University System of South Texas. In 1989 the system was dissolved and the three universities became members of the Texas A&M University System. In 1993 Texas A&I was renamed Texas A&M University at Kingsville. The institution was one of a number of South Texas state universities that received additional funding under the South Texas Initiative passed by the Texas legislature. Its John E. Conner Museum is open to the public. The Caesar KlebergWildlife Program focuses on increasing economic returns from wildlife, grazing and brush management to benefit wildlife, and developing wildlife food and cover plants. In 1994 the university published the *Journal of South Texas* for the South Texas Historical Association. *Jimmie R. Picquet*

Texas A&M University Press. Established in 1974. The founding director, Frank Wardlaw, had previously established publishing programs at the University of Texas and the University of South Carolina. A&M Press is organized as a university department; the director reports to the university president. Its publications are devoted to advancing knowledge among scholars and to enriching the cultural heritage of the Southwest. The first title to bear the A&M imprint, *Storms Brewed in Other Men's Worlds* by Elizabeth A. H. John, appeared in September 1975. The press has developed various series featuring regional history, regional art, regional literature, natural history, and economics. It also publishes works about military history, architecture, business history, chemistry, engineering, veterinary medicine, and nautical archeology. A reprint series, Southwest Landmarks, includes fiction and nonfiction of the nineteenth and twentieth centuries. In 1979 a fire destroyed the original press offices. These were replaced in 1983 by the John H. Lindsey Building, constructed expressly for publishing. Funding for the press is derived from book sales, endowments, and support from the university. The press is a member of the Association of American University Presses. In addition to its own publications, A&M Press distributes books with various other scholarly imprints, including Rice University Press, the Texas State Historical Association,and Texas Christian University Press. *Lloyd Lyman*

Texas A&M University System. Established in 1948 with Gibb Gilchrist as chancellor; included the Agricultural and Mechanical College of Texas, Arlington State College, Prairie View Agricultural and Mechanical College, John Tarleton College, Texas Agricultural Experiment Station, Texas Agricultural Extension Service, Texas Engineering Experiment Station, Texas Engineering Extension Service, Texas Transportation Institute, and Texas Forest Service. The Texas Maritime Academy joined the system in 1962. By 1968 control of the system had passed to the office of the president. Arlington State College was transferred to the University of Texas System in 1965. From 1965 until 1969 James Connally Technical Institute was part of the A&M system, but it was separated when it became part of Texas State Technical Institute. In 1993 the A&M system added Texas A&M International University, Texas A&M University at Corpus Christi, Texas A&M University at Kingsville, and West Texas A&M University.

Texas A&M University—Texarkana. Opened in 1971 as East Texas State University Center at Texarkana, a branch of what was then East Texas State University at Commerce. TAMU—Texarkana holds accreditation and membership with the Southern Association of Colleges and Schools and the Texas Education Agency, as well as numerous other professional associations. The school is on the campus of Texarkana College. It was established to provide third and fourth year college instruction for people residing in an isolated region. Increased attention is given to adults and other nontraditional students. The majority of the student body is part-time female students with a median age of 33. The university has three academic divisions—arts and sciences, business administration, and teaching professions—and confers eight undergraduate and five graduate degrees. *Nancy Beck Young*

Texas Alcalde. Formerly the *Alcalde*; the official magazine of the Ex-Students' Association of the University of Texas at Austin; founded in April 1913, when John A. Lomax served as the association's executive secretary, and named for the "Old Alcalde," Oran Milo Roberts. In 1992 the magazine was given its present name. It features articles on the university campus, faculty, administration, and students, as well as on sports and on class reunions. It also includes general-interest stories on research discoveries, self-reported news about alumni, and news of the Ex-Students' Association and its local chapters.

Pat Maguire and May Lea McCurdy

Texas Almanac. First appeared in 1857, published by the Galveston *News*. The focus of the earliest editions was on history and state government. Somewhat later, with a focus on attracting settlers, the *Almanac* was termed an "emigrant's guide" to the state. With some gaps, the *Almanac* was published annually through 1873. Thereafter, the next edition was published in 1904 by the Dallas *Morning News* under the current designation, *Texas Almanac and State Industrial Guide*. Other hiatuses have occurred during wars or depressions. By 1950 the *Texas Almanac* had become a standard semiannual reference book on resources, industries, commerce, history, government, population, and other subjects relating to the political, civic, and economic development of Texas. *Mary G. Crawford*

Texas Antiquities Committee. Established in 1969 by the state legislature for the protection, preservation, and interpretation of the publicly owned archeological and cultural resources, antiquities, and historic buildings of Texas. With the passage of the enabling Texas Antiquities Code it became "public policy to locate, protect, and preserve all sites, objects, buildings, pre-twentieth century shipwrecks, and locations of historical, archeological, educational or scientific interest . . . in, on, or under any of the land in the State, including the tidelands, submerged land, and the bed of the sea within the jurisdiction of the state." All archeological sites on state-owned lands are state archeological landmarks and the sole property of the state. Among other functions, the TAC acts as legal custodian of all Texas archeological artifacts, provides for recovery and salvage operations, issues permits for excavation of sites for research, and serves as a public forum in this area. In 1992 the nine-member TAC board included the commissioner of the General Land Office, the executive director of the Texas Water Commission, the engineer–director of the Texas Department of Transportation, and the director of the Texas Parks and Wildlife Department. Expertise on historical matters came from the chairman of the Texas Historical Commission and an appointed historian; knowledge of archeology and curatorship came from the state archeologist, the director of a major state museum, and a professional archeologist from a recognized Texas museum or institution of higher education. Although it functions under its own board, the TAC is integrated with the Texas Historical Commission. Its first action was to enlist the cooperation of state agencies with jurisdiction over public lands in observing the Antiquities Code. The first antiquities permit on public lands was issued in 1970. An increase in subsequent years reflected accelerated development in, for instance, highway and reservoir construction. Impetus for enactment of Texas Antiquities Code legislation under consideration before 1969 was provided by the Platoro incident, in which treasure was illegally salvaged from a shipwreck off Padre Island. A major task of the newly established agency was to follow up the incident with an underwater arche-

ological investigation of the Padre Island Spanish shipwrecks of 1554. Between 1974 and 1980 the committee conducted field investigations with emphasis on resource management rather than in-depth excavation of a single site. Under the guidance of the state marine archeologist, who served as a TAC staff member, the committee focused on its preservation role by determining historic shipwreck locations and protecting them from dredging, pipeline laying, and related disturbances. The TAC also made electronic surveys covering areas where many shipwrecks probably occurred to allow companies pursuing activities such as oil and gas development to proceed without fear of damage to important sites. Other construction projects were regularly reviewed for possible effect on archeological sites or historic buildings on public lands. All new projects require environmental-impact statements. Permits are also issued to cover investigation of sites of long-established significance, such as the Alamo, where land-altering projects or archeological investigations are accorded close scrutiny. By 1982 TAC permits were also issued for restoration work on important public historic buildings.

J. Barto Arnold III

Texas Archeological Research Laboratory. A research unit of the University of Texas at Austin. In 1919 the new Department of Anthropology began to amass collections and records, a project that boomed in 1936 when funds from the WPA made possible extensive excavations by university archeologists in coastal, eastern, central, and northern Texas. The onset of World War II brought an end to the WPA programs and much of the institutionally based archeology in Texas. After the war the university revived its archeological activities and the federal government established a nationwide archeological rescue program for remains threatened by reservoir construction. As the government's investment in archeological recovery and historic preservation grew and the university's archeological graduate program expanded, the collections became increasingly important for comparative study as well as new research. However, over the years the collections had become scattered and not readily accessible, mainly because there was no central repository nor clearly designated curatorial responsibility. In 1961 the formidable tasks of consolidating and systematizing the artifact collections and site archives were begun as a cooperative venture of the Department of Anthropology, the Texas Memorial Museum, and Texas Archeological Salvage (renamed Texas Archeological Survey, then TARL-Sponsored Projects). Two years later the Texas Archeological Research Laboratory was formally recognized by the university. It was funded through Organized Research and was assigned space at the Balcones Research Center in northwest Austin. Since 1963 TARL has greatly expanded its facilities and programs. It consists of three subdivisions—Collections, Records, and Sponsored Projects. TARL Collections curates specimens from over 8,000 prehistoric and historic sites. TARL Records maintains the site-numbering system used throughout the state and curates information for over 55,000 sites. TARL-Sponsored Projects provides services to governmental and private organizations in compliance with federal and state laws protecting archeological and historic properties. TARL publications include *Studies in Archeology*, Technical Series, Archival Series, *TARL Research Notes*, and *Newsletter of Friends of TARL*. TARL continues to serve as a major repository for artifacts and site records amassed by university archeologists, as well as by archeologists working in Texas for state, federal, and private firms.

Dee Ann Story

Texas Archeological Society. Owes its beginnings to an article in *Scientific American* on the discovery in 1923 near Colorado City of an extinct bison (*Bison antiquus*) and three chert projectile points found with the bones. Cyrus N. Ray of Abilene read the article and called a meeting in October 1928 to organize a society for the study of archeology. Among the nine people who came were William C. Holden and Rupert N. Richardson. The organization named itself the West Texas Archeological Society. In 1929, after interest had become statewide, it changed its name to Texas Archeological and Paleontological Society. In 1952 the "paleontological" part was dropped. The first bulletin of the society, published in 1929 and edited by Ray, contained articles from professional and avocational archeologists. Annual bulletins have been published ever since. In 1963 the society held its first field school to train amateurs in archeological techniques. Since then the school has been conducted annually in various parts of the state. The Texas Archeological Society joined in the call for a state archeologist. In 1956 the society began publication of its quarterly newsletter.

James H. Word

Texas Blind, Deaf, and Orphan School. In Austin; established as the Deaf, Dumb, and Blind Institute for Colored Youth in 1887 by the state legislature. A $50,000 appropriation was made to buy land and construct buildings; 17 pupils and 2 teachers were present for the opening of the school. The only initial structure was an 11-room residence, but in 1888 a new two-story brick building was added. In 1919 the school was placed under the newly established Board of Control. By the 1940s the campus had 13 buildings, including dormitories, classrooms, hospital, superintendent's residence, and dining room. Instruction emphasized training in trades and industries—broom making, mattress making, shoe making and repair, tailoring, cleaning and pressing, cooking, sewing, rug making, and other handicrafts. The hospital furnished surgical, medical, dental, and nursing services; specialists for eye, ear, nose, and throat ailments were employed part-time. Students raised poultry and farm products for the school's own use. When the State Colored Orphans' Home was combined with the institute in 1943, the name of the facility was changed to Texas Blind, Deaf, and Orphan School. The school was moved to the former site of the Montopolis Drive-in Theater in 1961, after the legislature appropriated $1.5 million for the construction of 11 buildings to accommodate the 1,208 students. The school was placed under the jurisdiction of the Texas Education Agency in 1965, and its name was changed to Texas Blind and Deaf School. It was combined with the Texas School for the Deaf later that year.

James W. Markham

Texas Centennial. That is, the centennial of Texas independence; officially celebrated in 1936, although local observances began in 1935. James S. Hogg originated the idea in a speech made about 1900, and concerted action toward a plan came at a convention of the Advertising Clubs of Texas at Corsicana in 1923. The Texas Centennial Board of One Hundred was established at a meeting in Austin in 1924. A temporary Texas Centennial Commission was appointed in 1931, and in 1932 a

constitutional amendment authorizing a centennial celebration and instructing the legislature to make adequate financial provision for it was proposed. The amendment passed, and a permanent Texas Centennial Commission was appointed in June 1934. Three cities—Dallas, Houston, and San Antonio—competed to host the central exposition. The commission chose Dallas because it offered the largest cash commitment ($7.8 million), the grounds of the State Fair of Texas, and unified urban leadership headed by bankers Robert Thornton, Fred Florence, and Nathan Adams. The Texas legislature and the United States Congress each appropriated $3 million for the project. The federal government issued commemorative three-cent stamps and half dollars to observe the anniversary. Many newspapers of the state issued special centennial editions.

Events were staged all over the state throughout the year, and a map designed for centennial tourists furnished a guide to historic spots. State-wide observances of the centennial began at Gonzales in November 1935. In December San Antonio held a series of pageants to commemorate the siege of Bexar. El Paso and Livingston featured a Sun Carnival and an Indian Tribal Ceremonial in January 1936. The Galveston Mardi Gras in February featured the centennial. Houston held three celebrations: Texas Independence in March, the battle of San Jacinto in April, and the founding of Houston in August. San Antonio also had special observances in March and April. Next to the central celebration at Dallas, the most widely visited observance was the Texas Frontier Centennial at Fort Worth, which featured the "Winning of the West." The Commission of Control worked with the Advisory Board of Texas Historians, the WPA, and the Texas Highway Department to coordinate programs and to provide permanence to the centennial observance by the erection of permanent buildings, monuments, statues, and grave markers. Every county in the state received a marker indicating the date of its establishment and the source of its name. Permanent buildings that received financial assistance from the Commission of Control included the Hall of State in Dallas, the Panhandle–Plains Historical Museum in Canyon, the Texas Memorial Museum in Austin, the Sam Houston Memorial Museum in Huntsville, the Corpus Christi Centennial Museum, the West Texas Museum in Lubbock, the Big Bend Historical Museum in Alpine, the Alamo Museum in San Antonio, the Gonzales Memorial Museum, and the San Jacinto Monument and Museum of History near Houston. Historic buildings and forts were restored, and more than 20 new statues went up.

The official $25 million central exposition, occupying 50 buildings and billed as the first world's fair held in the Southwest, opened at Dallas on 6 June 1936. It featured the dual theme of history and progress. The "Cavalcade of Texas," a historical pageant depicting four centuries of Texas history, became one of the exposition's most popular attractions. The Hall of Negro Life marked an exposition milestone, the first recognition of black culture at a world's fair. The competing nonofficial Fort Worth Frontier Centennial Exposition opened on 18 July. Both expositions attracted world-wide attention. Fort Worth civic leader Amon Carter explained the difference between them: "Go to Dallas for education; come to Fort Worth for entertainment." The Fort Worth exposition closed on 14 November, the Dallas exposition on 29 November. Although attendance at both fairs (Dallas, 6,345,385; Fort Worth, 986,128) fell far short of expectations, civic leaders thought the publicity was well worth the cost. The Dallas exposition reopened on 12 June 1937 as the Greater Texas and Pan American Exposition and closed on 31 October.

Texas Christian University. In Fort Worth; Founded as Add–Ran College in 1873, when Addison and Randolph Clark moved their private school, begun in Fort Worth in 1869, to Thorp Spring. Chartered as Add–Ran Male and Female College in 1874, the school came under the control of the Christian Church in 1889, and its name was changed to Add–Ran Christian University. It moved to Waco in 1895 and became Texas Christian University in 1902. Attendance at this time averaged 350–400 students. In March 1910 a fire destroyed the main building. Fort Worth offered the institution a 50-acre campus and $200,000, and in 1911 TCU moved to its present campus. The first endowment, $25,000 from Lucas Charles Brite II, also came that year, and in 1914 Brite College of the Bible (renamed Brite Divinity School in 1963) was established. In 1911 or 1912 the university added the Fort Worth School of Medicine as a unit, but it was abandoned in 1918. A school of law was added in 1915 and closed in 1920. Edward McShane Waits began his 25-year term as president in September 1916. TCU was elected to membership in both the Southern Association of Colleges and Schools and the Southwest Conference in 1922. The school's fiftieth anniversary in 1923 was marked by a gift that assured its survival: Mrs. Mary Couts Burnett left to TCU the majority of her estate, valued at $3 million, plus half interest in several thousand acres of ranchland. Particularly when oil production began on the land, the Burnett trust became the heart of the university's endowment. The Mary Couts Burnett Library was completed in 1924, the same year in which the campus was expanded to 187 acres. During 1926 and 1927 graduate courses, offered randomly throughout the preceding years, were integrated into a separate, organized graduate school. Except for three years during the Great Depression, enrollment growth was steady during the 1920s and 1930s and reached 2,000 for the first time in 1937. By then eight permanent brick buildings were on campus, and the school had been approved by the Association of American Universities. The School of Business was established in 1938.

McGruder Ellis Sadler was elected president in 1941, and growth after World War II was rapid. A structure to house the School of Fine Arts was completed in 1949. Between 1950 and 1965, 25 buildings were constructed or acquired. By 1963 the university had purchased the 106-acre Worth Hills Golf Course adjoining the campus, bringing the total size of the campus to 237 acres. Five residence halls and a cafeteria were built on the Worth Hills land in 1964, and other construction has ensued. By the time of Sadler's retirement in 1965, Ph.D. programs were offered in psychology, physics, English, mathematics, chemistry, and history. James Mattox Moudy was TCU chancellor from 1965 to 1979. The TCU Press was formally established in 1966 (although it had operated occasionally in previous years) and began regular publication of books and monographs. Between 1965 and 1967 the university began participation in the Texas Association for Graduate Education and Research. Its library collections include the William Luther Lewis collection of rare books and an American presidency collection donated by A. M. Pate. The university won Southwest Conference championships in football in 1929, 1932, 1938, 1944, 1951, 1955, and 1958; in the

1930s and 1940s, with Leo R. (Dutch) Meyer as coach, TCU teams were considered among the best in the nation. During the fourteen years Abe Martin coached before he retired in 1966, he took teams to several bowl games and had seven players named to All-American teams. The TCU basketball team won SWC championships in 1930, 1933, 1952, 1958, 1967, 1970, and 1986; the baseball team won championships in 1932 and 1955. In 1992–93 the university was organized into six schools and colleges: Add–Ran College of Arts and Sciences, M. J. Neeley School of Business, the School of Education, the School of Fine Arts, Harris College of Nursing, and Brite Divinity School.

John Ohendalski

Texas City, Texas. On the southwestern shore of Galveston Bay seven miles from Galveston and 11 miles from the Gulf of Mexico in Galveston County; a deepwater port on the mainland. In 1891, while on a duck-hunting trip to the marshlands of a community known as Shoal Point in Galveston Bay, three brothers from Duluth, Minnesota—Jacob, Henry, and Benjamin Myers—saw that the area had potential as a major port. Other Duluth shippers joined the Myers brothers in buying 10,000 acres of Galveston Bay frontage, including Shoal Point, and renamed the site Texas City. In 1893 the Texas City Improvement Company filed the first townsite plat. The same year the post office was established. The population soon was 250, mostly from Minnesota and Michigan. In 1893 the federal government gave the Texas City Improvement Company permission to dredge an eight-foot Gulf channel to Texas City. In September 1894 the first shipment using the channel was transported. Continued dredging eventually increased the depth of the channel to 40 feet and the length of the port to 1½ miles. The company constructed a four-mile rail line to the Texas City junction of the Galveston, Harrisburg and San Antonio and the Galveston, Houston and Henderson railroads. These rail connections were extended to the Santa Fe and Southern Pacific systems. The single-track trestle pier extended into Galveston Bay and thus enabled shippers to send freight by train to Houston, where it could join the national railway systems. The Texas City Improvement Company went into receivership in 1897 and was afterward reorganized into two new companies—the Texas City Railway Terminal Company, organized to operate the railroad, and the Texas City Company, which purchased the town lots and provided water, gas, and electricity to the town. Capt. A. B. Wolvin, one of the founders of Texas City, persuaded the federal government to finance the dredging of a 25-foot channel. Work began in the summer of 1900, but the disastrous Galveston hurricane of 1900 halted operations. The Texas City port remained open, however, so that no Texas trade had to be diverted. The dredging was completed in 1905, and the federal government opened a customhouse in Texas City.

The number of ships using the Texas City docks increased from 12 in 1904 to 239 in 1910. Increased port activity came in part from the building of the Texas City Refining Company, which was chartered in 1908, a few years after the discovery of oil at Spindletop. The refinery handled midcontinent crude and for a few years was the only Texas refinery to manufacture wax and refined lubricating oil. During the next 20 years the building of tank farms, pipelines, and three more refineries firmly established Texas City as a tidewater terminal for shipment of Texas crude to the Atlantic terminal. The community established the Texas City ISD in 1905. By 1911 the number of inhabitants had grown to 1,169, and that year the city incorporated under the commission form of government. In 1913 the little coastal port was overwhelmed by the arrival of the Second Division of the United States Army, which was stationed there to guard American interests during the Mexican Revolution. Along with 14,000 troops and 3,000 animals, the military units stationed at Texas City included the First Aero Squadron. In August 1915 a hurricane completely destroyed the Texas City encampment and killed nine soldiers. The camp was moved to San Antonio—a severe economic blow to Texas City. In 1921 the Texas City Railway Terminal Company took over operation of the port with Hugh B. Moore as president. Under his leadership various industries were brought into the city, including the Texas City Sugar Refinery, bus service, tank farms for five oil companies, the Knox Process Corporation (a gasoline-cracking refinery), and the Stone Oil Company. The port also had two cotton compresses, a fig-preserving plant, a grain elevator, and various warehouse businesses.

By 1925 Texas City had an estimated population of 3,500. The Great Depression and the strong competition from Imperial Sugar Industries caused the sugar refinery to fail by 1930. Many of the stores in the business district closed, and those that remained struggled to survive. But the continued development of the oil industry contributed to economic recovery. In 1931 the Republic Oil Refinery opened to produce gasoline, chiefly from crude supplied by independent operators in the new East Texas oilfield. The business revival was quickened in 1934 when Pan-America Refinery (forerunner of Amoco), a subsidiary of Standard Oil of Indiana, started operations. By 1939 the population of Texas City had increased to 5,200. The United States commitment to the war in 1941 furthered the boom in Texas City, propelling it into fourth position among Texas ports. The plants and port were open around the clock to provide materials. More support industries, heavy construction, and port enlargements were undertaken in attempts to meet the increased domestic and wartime demands. Since the Axis threatened England and Holland, the only two tin-smelting locales in the world, the Defense Plant Corporation under Jesse H. Jones decided in 1940 to build a tin smelter in the United States. On a site donated by the Texas City Terminal Railway Company, the Tin Processing Corporation began operation of the only smelter in the Western Hemisphere. The Longhorn smelter supplied all the industrial and military needs of the free world. The M. W. Kellog pipe-bending plant and Monsanto Chemical Company also came to Texas City as national defense industries. Monsanto built a pilot plant to manufacture styrene used in synthetic rubber. During the war Texas City experienced remarkable growth; by 1950 the population was estimated at 16,620. The predicted postwar prosperity was interrupted by the Texas City Disaster, a catastrophic explosion of 16 April 1947. After the disaster, Texas City businesses rebuilt and expanded, and by 1960 the population was 32,065. This increase was largely due to additional chemical, plastics, and petrochemical industries that multiplied the tonnage through the port. Efforts to establish a navigation district and a port authority failed, and the port continued to be operated by the Texas City Terminal Railway. A second major disaster struck Texas City in 1961 when hurricane Carla brought four feet of floodwater over much of the city. In the aftermath of the storm, seawall plans that had been delayed since 1949 were completed, and construction began in 1962 on a 23-foot barrier. The last section of the seawall was completed in 1985. Because subsidence was another cause of flooding, Texas City ceased groundwater pumping and began using water from the Brazos River to supply its industries. To protect the city further from rising rainwater, in 1982 the city commissioners built an inner levee eight feet high on Moses Lake and installed Archimedes screw pumps. The city developed Moses Lake and the Texas City Dike, which extends into Galveston Bay, into recreation areas. In 1954 it built the 55-acre Nessler Civic Center, which includes a park, the library, the city hall, the stadium, and the Lowry Physical Fitness Center. In 1962 the surrounding school districts joined Texas City to establish a junior college district. The College of the Mainland opened in September 1967. The community's expansion has been to the west, with 10 major refining and petrochemical industries forming the base of the seaport. In 1990 the city population was 40,822. *Priscilla Myers Benham*

Texas City Disaster. One of the worst disasters in Texas history; began at 9:12 A.M., 16 April 1947, when the SS *Grandcamp* exploded at the docks in Texas City. The French-owned vessel, carrying ammonium nitrate produced during wartime for explosives and later recycled as fertilizer, caught fire early in the morning, and while attempts were being made to extinguish the fire, the ship exploded. The entire dock area was destroyed, along with the nearby Monsanto Chemical Company, other smaller companies, grain warehouses, and numerous oil and chemical storage tanks. Smaller explosions and fires were ignited by flying debris throughout the city. Fragments of iron, parts of the ship's cargo, and dock equipment were hurled into businesses, houses, and public buildings. A 15-foot tidal wave caused by the explosion swept the dock area. The concussion, felt as far away as Port Arthur, damaged or destroyed at least 1,000 buildings. The SS *High Flyer*, in dock for repairs and also carrying ammonium nitrate, was ignited by the first explosion; it was towed 100 feet from the docks before it exploded about 16 hours later. The first explosion had killed 26 Texas City firemen and destroyed all of the city's fire-fighting equipment, including four trucks, leaving the city helpless in the wake of the second explosion. No central disaster organization had been established by the city, but most of the chemical and oil plants had disaster plans that were quickly activated. Although power and water were cut off, hundreds of volunteers began fighting the fires and doing rescue work. Red Cross personnel and other volunteers from surrounding cities responded with assistance until almost 4,000 workers were operating; temporary hospitals, morgues, and shelters were set up. The exact number of people killed will never be known, although the ship's anchor monument records 576 persons known dead, 398 of whom were identified, and 178 listed as missing. All records of the Monsanto Company were destroyed, and many of the dock workers were itinerants and thus difficult to identify. Almost everyone in the dock area was killed, and most of the bodies were never recovered; 63 were buried unidentified. The number of injured ranged in the thousands, and loss of property totaled about $67 million. More than 3,000 lawsuits involving the United States government, since the chemicals had originated in U.S. ordnance plants, were resolved by 1956, when a special act passed by Congress settled all claims for a total of $16.5 million. Other litigation was finally settled in 1962, when the

Searching in the Ruins, the Texas City Disaster, April 16, 1947. Gelatin silver postcard print. Courtesy Rosenberg Library, Galveston, Texas.

Supreme Court refused to review an appeals court ruling that the Republic of France, owner of the *Grandcamp*, could not be held liable. The disaster brought changes in chemical manufacturing and new regulations for the bagging, handling, and shipping of chemicals. Some temporary housing was built and donated to the city, and other housing, docks, warehouses, and chemical plants were rebuilt by 1950. Public commemoration of the event began in June 1947, when the bodies of the unidentified dead were buried together in a memorial cemetery and park; in 1991 a new section was added to the park.

Texas College. In Tyler; established in 1894 by ministers of the Colored Methodist Episcopal Church; renamed Phillips University in 1909 and again Texas College in 1912. The school was accredited as a junior college in 1924 and as a four-year college in 1932; it was given a class A rating by the Southern Association of Colleges and Secondary Schools in 1948. In 1949 the enrollment reached 1,000. Although predominantly a teacher-training institution, Texas College offers vocational courses and grants degrees in the liberal arts. Especially concerned with the development of East Texas youths of limited means, the college provides financial aid through student loan and work–study programs. It housed a campus of Tyler Junior College from 1946 to 1966. The institution continued its relationship with the CME Church. It is fully accredited and has recently added programs in art, business, computer science, social work, and social science. It confers B.S., B.A., and A.A. degrees in 20 majors as well as preprofessional training in law, medicine, and the ministry. African Americans constitute 95 percent of the enrollment. *Nancy Beck Young*

Texas Commission on Alcohol and Drug Abuse. Formed in 1985 from the consolidation of drug-abuse programs of the Texas Department of Community Affairs with programs administered by the Texas Commission on Alcoholism, established in 1953. The agency administers programs for the prevention and treatment of chemical dependency and compulsive gambling. It provides assistance for statewide and community-based providers. In addition, it addresses the problem of HIV transmission by substance abuse and works with the prison system to combat chemical dependency. The Texas Commission on Alcoholism was composed of six members appointed by the governor for six-year terms. One member was required to be a physician, and at least three were to have had experience with alcoholism. Without legislative appropriations, however, the office closed after 18 months. By 1955 funds for alcoholic treatment were available only for the Board for Texas State Hospitals and Special Schools. Not until 1957 did the legislature appropriate funds for the TCA itself. In 1971 Governor Preston Smith designated the commission as the state agency to comply with the federal Comprehensive Alcohol Abuse and Alcoholism Prevention, Treatment, and Rehabilitation Act of 1970, bringing about the first state plan to prevent, treat, and control alcohol abuse. The commission subsequently designated one agency in each of the 24 state planning regions as regional alcoholism authorities. Additionally, a State Alcoholism Advisory Council was established to serve the commission. With the dissolution of the Regional Alcoholism Authorities, the State Advisory Council became a forum through which the commission listens to representatives from all areas of the state. After its concerns increased in 1985, when the agency was renamed the Texas Commission on

Alcohol and Drug Abuse, the commission was enlarged to nine members. Their duties included not only the previous ones but also those of the drug-abuse programs of the Texas Department of Community Affairs, which is now a division of the Texas Department of Housing and Community Affairs.

Richard Allen Burns

Texas Commission on the Arts. Established in 1965 as the Texas Fine Arts Commission, originally eight members appointed by the governor for six-year terms (now 18 members). The commission coordinated efforts of state agencies in developing appreciation for the fine arts in Texas and gave advice on the construction and remodeling of state buildings and works of art. The duties of the Board of Mansion Supervisors, abolished in 1965, were transferred to the commission. The commission was made permanent in 1967, and its name was changed to Texas Commission on the Arts and Humanities in 1971. The commission has the duty to foster the fine arts for Texans, to make tourism to the state more appealing, and to attract outstanding artists. It also directs the sponsorship of art lectures and exhibitions and disseminates information on Texas fine arts. It publishes an annual magazine, *Texas Arts Reach,* and a monthly publication, *Texas Commission on the Arts News.* It acts in an advisory capacity to other state agencies concerned with works of art. The commission may also accept donations of money, property, art objects, or historical relics on behalf of the state. Members are selected from all fields representing the fine arts. In 1974 a plan was undertaken for the commission to work with the Harry Ransom Humanities Research Center of the University of Texas at Austin to collect and store artifacts in the Hoblitzelle Theatre Arts Library. The collection was to serve as an official archives for Texas arts, encompassing music, dance, the visual arts, literature, architecture, and folk arts. In 1979 the agency's name was changed to the Texas Commission on the Arts. The commission also contracts with five independent organizations, including the Texas Association of Museums, to promote the arts. Before accepting grant money from the commission, the partner organization must raise matching funds.

Texas Committee for the Humanities. In 1965, Congress passed the National Foundation on the Arts and Humanities Act, which established a National Endowment for the Arts and a National Endowment for the Humanities. The Texas Committee for the Humanities, a manifestation of the NEH decision that private, nonprofit citizen committees afforded the best opportunity for promoting the humanities in the individual states, followed in 1973. Thomas Brewer led in its formation. Since NEH required all state humanities committees to focus on the relationship between the humanities and public-policy issues, the group was renamed the Texas Committee for the Humanities and Public Policy. Its first grant was awarded to KUT–FM, Austin, for a series of radio programs on the Constitutional Convention of 1974. In its 1976 reauthorizing legislation, Congress encouraged committees to undertake other kinds of humanities projects than those relating to public policy. The first director employed by the TCH board was Sandra L. Myres, of the University of Texas at Arlington. The TCH moved its office from Arlington to Austin in June 1980. The TCH has funded numerous projects in traditional humanities subjects as well as in Texas history and culture. In recognition of this shift, the organization was renamed the Texas Committee for the Humanities in 1978. From 1973 to 1982 the committee's federal resources grew dramatically as Congress increased appropriations annually to the NEH.

From 1983 to 1985 federal funding remained stabilized, although the committee received increased support from foundations and corporations. In 1986, TCH revenues were cut almost in half when federal funding dropped significantly and private sector support—weakened by the collapse of the Texas economy—diminished. From 1981 to 1985, through a combination of federal and private funding, the TCH was able to implement a number of projects on its own. It established a task force in 1981 to issue a report, *Toward Thoughtful, Active Citizens: Improving the Public School Curriculum* (1982); it inaugurated an annual Texas Lecture and Symposium on the Humanities; it took steps to publish *Texas Humanist* (later renamed *Texas Journal of Ideas, History, and Culture*); and it made plans for a major Texas Sesquicentennial project for newspapers and television stations. Federal and private revenues could not sustain many of these projects. Therefore, the TCH began to place increasing emphasis on its grant program as the primary means to meet established objectives. To accomplish its mission of stimulating public interest in the humanities, it gives awards for public humanities projects. Through the Texas Humanities Resource Center, it makes available quality packaged programs (photographic exhibits, films and print resources, etc.) to communities. The Texas Humanities Alliance, established in 1986, is a support group of contributing members whose primary mission is to assist the TCH in advancing the study of the humanities in Texas. The alliance publishes the *Texas Humanities Newsletter* quarterly. In addition, the TCH releases occasional books, drawn from TCH projects, through Texas A&M University Press. In 1983 the NEH instituted a competitive awards program for state committees. The TCH received two exemplary project awards, one for the "Texas Myths" emphasis in 1984 ($45,000), and one for "The Mexican Legacy of Texas" emphasis in 1986 ($65,000). It also received a merit award for overall excellence in programming from the NEH in 1986. Future projects for the TCH include instituting cultural and scholarly exchange programs with Mexico and developing undergraduate curriculum in the colleges and universities of Texas.

James F. Veninga

Texas Confederate Home. A home in Austin for disabled and indigent Confederate veterans; founded as a project of the John B. Hood Camp of United Confederate Veterans, which obtained a charter from the state in 1884. The United Daughters of the Confederacy cooperated in raising funds. The camp purchased a site in 1886 and opened that year. The UDC's "Grand Gift Concert and Lottery" raised over $10,800. Operating funds continued to come from public contributions until 1891, when the state assumed control and the name officially became Texas Confederate Home. The John B. Hood Camp deeded the property to the state. Management was the responsibility of a board of managers made up of five Confederate veterans appointed by the governor and a superintendent, also a Confederate veteran, who was selected by the board. The 26-acre complex on West Sixth Street had several buildings, including a large administration building and living quarters, a brick hospital, and private cottages. In 1920 the legislature established the Board of Control, abolished the board of managers of the Confederate Home, and transferred the responsibility of appointing a superintendent to the new agency. In 1949 the legislature transferred control and management to the Board for Texas State Hospitals and Special Schools. However, the Board of Control continued to handle purchases for the institution. The Board for Texas State Hospitals and Special Schools administered the home until it was closed.

During its first two years 113 veterans were admitted to the home, and from 1887 to 1953 more than 2,000 were housed in the facility. Residents numbered 312 in 1929, 80 in 1936, and 38 in 1938, when the average age of the men was 93. In 1943 only 6 Confederates were still in residence. Thomas Riddle, the last veteran, died in 1954 at the age of 108. Before that time, by act of the legislature, senile mental patients from other state institutions were transferred to the Confederate Home. After 1939 disabled veterans of the Spanish American War and World War I, as well as their wives, were admitted. In 1963 the remaining patients were sent to Kerrville State Hospital and the Austin facility was transferred to the Austin State Hospital as an annex. The buildings were razed in 1970 to make room for University of Texas married students' housing.   *Cynthia J. Beeman*

Texas County Records Inventory Project. Began in the fall of 1973, when North Texas State University received a grant under the Higher Education Act of 1965 to conduct a statewide survey of county records. The project was undertaken to provide information on existing local records for the Regional Historical Resource Depository program of the Texas State Library, to locate and preserve valuable historical research material, and to provide a database for a record-management manual for county officials. The task was a formidable one, given the fact that Texas has 254 counties. The nature, quantity, and type of records in the courthouses varied widely, and the volume was immense. While larger counties had filled warehouses with records, smaller ones had filled basements, attics, barns, and sometimes sheds or abandoned gasoline stations. Papers and volumes often lay neglected, slowly being destroyed by water, vermin, or decay. The County Records Project organized a network of volunteers from colleges and universities across the state, including historians, political scientists, and archivists, who used the inventory as field experience for their students. In addition to the academic volunteers, members of historical commissions and societies also prepared inventories in a number of counties. Often volunteer groups worked with county officials to move records in danger of being destroyed. Each county was essentially a separate project and operated out of the county courthouse. Using standard inventory forms, participants recorded such information as titles and variant titles, dates of record series, office having legal custody, forms of records, and a summary and description of contents. All records were documented and inventoried. As each office and storage area was completed, the forms were sent from the local courthouse to the project office for editing. After a recheck, the entire set of forms was edited and prepared for publication by TCRIP staff. Inventories were published by the Texas State Library.

The historical precedent for the Texas County Records Inventory Project was the WPA Historical Records Survey, a program designed to inventory county courthouse records. In Texas the program began in 1936 and published 24 inventories before World War II brought the surveys to a halt. Though the similarities between the two projects were obvious, the TCRIP decided to focus primarily on the records themselves, omitting the detailed and lengthy histories of the county and of each office of county government compiled by the WPA. With the data supplied by the inventory project, the Texas State Archives prepared a record-management manual for county officials, which provided uniform guidelines for retention and disposal of documents. Records no longer germane to the business of the county but deemed historically valuable could be transferred (with appropriate permissions) to regional depositories, thereby saving costly storage space for county government. Many counties took advantage of these programs.

In its early years the TCRIP was funded primarily by grants. In 1975 the project established an executive board of leading citizens to help raise money, and the board helped the project secure line-item funding from the Texas legislature for two sessions, 1977 to 1981. A need to cut state funds was cited as the reason for omitting the project from the State Library budget in 1981, and thus TCRIP was brought to a close. Nearly 100 county inventories had been completed; hundreds of volunteers had put thousands of hours into the work. The project became a model for other states, and materials developed by the staff, including a film, slide presentation, and handbook, were requested nationally and internationally. The TCRIP received an Award of Merit from the American Association of State and Local History in 1977.   *Mary S. Pearson*

Texas Court of Claims. Established in 1856, to handle claims against the Republic of Texas and the state, particularly land claims based upon military service. A commissioner of claims, elected by joint vote of the two houses of the state legislature, was to serve until 1 January 1858. Two years were allowed for registry of land certificates of every description, certain specified classes of certificates being exempt. The commissioner of claims was given the functions of a special commission that had been set up under an act of 1840 to investigate claims for headrights and colonization grants; this special commission had expired in 1842. Also assigned to the commissioner's office were claims growing out of an 1848 law for validation of Mexican land grants; an act of 1850 granting lands to heirs of soldiers of the Texas Revolution; and an act of 1854 allowing compensation for services and supplies furnished to the republic. Two rooms in the basement of the Capitol were set aside for the Court of Claims, and the commissioner was allowed two clerks. An act of 26 January 1858 further defined the duties of the commissioner and extended his term to 1 September 1859, when his duties were supposed to be taken over by the comptroller of public accounts. In February 1858 the legislature broadened the bases for proof of claims and authorized a larger number of specified land certificates. The Court of Claims was reestablished in 1860, and the commissioner's term of office was extended to 1862. Applications were to be made to the local district court or to the county court, that court then forwarding the claim to the Court of Claims. The commissioner was authorized to reject claims that he believed fraudulent, but persons who were thus refused were given the privilege of suit in the Travis County District Court. No special Court of Claims has existed in Texas since 1862, and since that time claims against the state have been referred by the legislature to a committee on claims in the House of Representatives.

Texas Declaration of Independence. Written and issued by the Convention of 1836 at Washington-on-the-Brazos. Richard Ellis, president of the convention, appointed George C. Childress, James Gaines, Edward Conrad, Collin McKinney, and Bailey Hardeman to the declaration committee. It is generally conceded that Childress, the chairman wrote the declaration with little help. Some evidence suggests that he brought the declaration to the convention, including the fact that the committee was appointed on 1 March and the declaration was presented the next day. The Texas edict, like the United States Declaration of Independence, contains a statement on the nature of government, a list of grievances, and a final declaration of independence. It charges that the government of Mexico had ceased to protect the lives, liberty, and property of the people; that it had been changed from a restricted federal republic to a consolidated, central, military despotism; that the people of Texas had remonstrated against the misdeeds of the government only to have their agents thrown into dungeons and armies sent forth to enforce the decrees of the new government at the point of the bayonet; that the welfare of Texas had been sacrificed to that of Coahuila; that the government had failed to provide a system of public education, trial by jury, freedom of religion, and other essentials of good government; and that the Indians had been incited to massacre the settlers. According to the declaration, the Mexican government had invaded Texas to lay waste territory and had a large mercenary army advancing to carry on a war of extermination. The final grievance charged that the Mexican government had been "the contemptible sport and victim of successive military revolutions and [had] continually exhibited every characteristic of a weak, corrupt, and tyrannical government." After the signing of the original declaration by 59 delegates, five copies of the document were dispatched to the designated Texas towns of Bexar (San Antonio), Goliad, Nacogdoches, Brazoria, and San Felipe. The printer at San Felipe was also instructed to make 1,000 copies in handbill form. The original was deposited with the United States Department of State in Washington and was not returned to Texas until after June 1896. In 1929 it was transferred from the office of the secretary of state to the Board of Control to be displayed in a niche at the Capitol, where it was unveiled on 2 March 1930.

Ralph W. Steen

Texas Department on Aging. Established in 1965 as the Governor's Committee on Aging, which was designated by the governor to administer federal funds made available through the Older Americans Act. The TDA serves more than two million older citizens, the fifth largest over-60 population in the United States. In 1957 the legislature had established an interim committee to develop legislation that would address the needs of the elderly. In 1981 the Governor's Committee on Aging was made a state agency, and its name was changed to Texas Department on Aging. The governing body is composed of nine members appointed by the governor for six-year staggered terms. The department appoints an executive director, who supervises a full-time staff and a 28-member Citizens' Advisory Council. Each council member serves for three years and represents one of the department's 28 Area Agencies on Aging. The network of these agencies provides nutrition programs, information and referral systems, employment programs, transportation systems, and in-home and other services directed toward preventing unnecessary institutionalization or life-threatening situations for the elderly.

Ben E. Dickerson

Texas Department of Agriculture. Established in 1907; headquarters in Austin; district offices in Amarillo, Beaumont, Brenham, Dallas, Houston, Lubbock, Odessa, San Antonio, San Juan, Stephenville, Tyler, and Vernon. Its consumer-services division is one of the largest in the state administration. Before TDA, official agricultural business had been conducted by the Bureau of Agriculture, Insurance, Statistics, and History, which largely ignored its responsibility to collect information and statistics on crops and livestock. Agriculture commissioner Robert Teague Milner was appointed to serve until the 1908 general election. The new agency had a staff of four, including the commissioner. Departmental duties included gathering statistics, publishing agricultural information, and holding farmers' institutes to promote advanced farming methods and practices. Under Milner the agency began to develop its role as a regulatory arm and advocate for cotton farmers. A cotton bureau was established in 1907 to prevent falsifying the size of cotton crops. In his only report to Governor Thomas M. Campbell, Milner complained that the $17,038 department budget was inadequate. In 1908 he accepted the presidency of Texas A&M. His successor, Edward Reeves Kone, frequently traveled the state to talk to farmers and give demonstrations. His commitment to the department persuaded a legislature dubious about the agency's future to increase its budget to $30,178 for fiscal year 1909–10. Subsequently, the budget grew incrementally.

Although cotton dominated Texas agriculture, prices paid to farmers rarely covered costs. Landowners and tenant farmers were unable to diversify into crops that might have pulled them out of debt. A severe drought in 1917, the driest year in Texas history, added to producers' economic woes. The department recorded crop and livestock losses in two-thirds of the state. Commissioner Fred Davis negotiated an agreement with the Texas Grain Dealers Association to furnish seed grain at cost to farmers who could afford it and on a share basis to those who could not. Through his efforts the department helped to get farmers who had food and feed to sell in contact with prospective buyers. This project was a forerunner of the agency's direct-marketing program. The agency attempted to promote a new cash crop by encouraging Texans to eat jackrabbit; it held jackrabbit dinners and published jackrabbit recipes. George B. Terrell, commissioner from 1921 to 1930, increased the department's services to farmers and promoted the state's youthful citrus industry. A fight against citrus canker doubled the number of citrus trees in Texas from one million to more than two million. In 1925 the department's duties were greatly expanded when it assumed tasks previously handled by the Department of Markets and Warehouses, including inspection of weights and measures, operation of the market news service, and supervision of gins, warehouses, and farmers' co-ops. The marketing bureau encouraged sales of more than $2.5 million in Texas agricultural products by introducing sellers to prospective buyers. Terrell continued a battle begun under Davis against the pink bollworm.

During the administration of James E. McDonald (1931–50) the Low Water Dam and Jacks and Stallions divisions were founded and eliminated. The Low Water Dam Division encouraged farmers to conserve water by building sloughs and ravines. Jacks and Stallions distributed registered and high-grade mules

UNANIMOUS

DECLARATION OF INDEPENDENCE,

BY THE

DELEGATES OF THE PEOPLE OF TEXAS,

IN GENERAL CONVENTION,

AT THE TOWN OF WASHINGTON,

ON THE SECOND DAY OF MARCH, 1836.

WHEN a government has ceased to protect the lives, liberty, and property of the people, from whom its legitimate powers are derived, and for the advancement of whose happiness it was instituted; and so far from being a guarantee for their inestimable and inalienable rights, becomes an instrument in the hands of evil rulers for their oppression.

When the Federal Republican Constitution of their country, which they have sworn to support, no longer has a substantial existence, and the whole nature of their government has been forcibly changed, without their consent, from a restricted Federative Republic, composed of Sovereign States, to a consolidated Central Military despotism, in which every interest is disregarded but that of the army and the priesthood, both the eternal enemies of civil liberty, the ever ready minions of power, and the usual instruments of tyrants. When, long after the spirit of the constitution has departed, moderation is at length so far lost by those in power, that even the semblance of freedom is removed, and the forms themselves of the constitution discontinued, and so far from their petitions and remonstrances being regarded, the agents who bear them are thrown into dungeons, and mercenary armies sent forth to force a new government upon them at the point of the bayonet.

When, in consequence of such acts of malfeasance and abduction on the part of the government, anarchy prevails and civil society is dissolved into its original elements, in such a crisis, the first law of nature, the right of self preservation, the inherent and inalienable right of the people to appeal to first principles, and take their political affairs into their own hands in extreme cases, enjoins it as a right towards themselves and a sacred obligation to their posterity to abolish such government, and create another in its stead, calculated to rescue them from impending dangers, and to secure their welfare and happiness.

Nations, as well as individuals, are amenable for their acts to the public opinion of mankind. A statement of a part of our grievances is therefore submitted to an impartial world, in justification of the hazardous but unavoidable step now taken, of severing our political connection with the Mexican people, and assuming an independent attitude among the nations of the earth.

The Mexican Government, by its colonization laws, invited and induced the Anglo American population of Texas to colonize its wilderness under the pledged faith of a written constitution, that they should continue to enjoy that constitutional liberty and republican government to which they had been habituated in the land of their birth, the United States of America.

In this expectation they have been cruelly disappointed, inasmuch as the Mexican nation has acquiesced in the late changes made in the government by General Antonio Lopez Santa Ana, who having overturned the constitution of his country, now offers, as the cruel alternative, either to abandon our homes acquired by so many privations, or submit to the most intolerable of all tyranny, the combined despotism of the sword and the priesthood.

It hath sacrificed our welfare to the state of Cohuila, by which our interests have been continually depressed through a jealous and partial course of legislation, carried on at a far distant seat of government, by a hostile majority in an unknown tongue, and this too, notwithstanding we have petitioned in the humblest terms for the establishment of a separate state government, and have, in accordance with the provisions of the national constitution, presented to the general congress a republican constitution, which was, without a just cause, contemptuously rejected.

It incarcerated in a dungeon, for a long time, one of our citizens, for no other cause but a zealous endeavour to procure the acceptance of our constitution and the establishment of a state government.

It has failed and refused to secure, on a firm basis, the right of trial by jury, that palladium of civil liberty and only safe guarantee for the life, liberty, and property of the citizen.

It has failed to establish any public system of education, although possessed of almost boundless resources, (the public domain;) and although it is an axiom in political science, that unless a people are educated and enlightened, it is idle to expect the continuance of civil liberty, or the capacity for self government.

It has suffered the military commandants, stationed among us, to exercise arbitrary acts of oppression and tyranny, thus trampling upon the most sacred rights of the citizen, and rendering the military superior to the civil power.

It has dissolved, by force of arms, the state congress of Cohuila and Texas, and obliged our representatives to fly for their lives from the seat of government, thus depriving us of the fundamental political right of representation.

It has demanded the surrender of a number of our citizens, and ordered military detachments to seize and carry them into the interior for trial, in contempt of the civil authorities, and in defiance of the laws and the constitution.

It has made piratical attacks upon our commerce by commissioning foreign desperadoes, and authorizing them to seize our vessels and convey the property of our citizens to far distant parts for confiscation.

It denies us the right of worshipping the Almighty according to the dictates of our own conscience, by the support of a National Religion, calculated to promote the temporal interest of its human functionaries, rather than the glory of the true and living God.

It has demanded us to deliver up our arms, which are essential to our defence—the rightful property of freemen—and formidable only to tyrannical governments.

It has invaded our country both by sea and by land, with the intent to lay waste our territory, and drive us from our homes; and has now a large mercenary army advancing, to carry on against us a war of extermination.

It has, through its emissaries, incited the merciless savage, with the tomahawk and scalping knife, to massacre the inhabitants of our defenceless frontiers.

It has been, during the whole time of our connection with it, the contemptible sport and victim of successive military revolutions, and hath continually exhibited every characteristic of a weak, corrupt, and tyrannical government.

These, and other grievances, were patiently borne by the people of Texas, until they reached that point at which forbearance ceases to be a virtue. We then took up arms in defence of the National Constitution. We appealed to our Mexican brethren for assistance: our appeal has been made in vain; though months have elapsed, no sympathetic response has yet been heard from the interior. We are therefore forced to the melancholy conclusion, that the Mexican people have acquiesced in the destruction of their liberty, and the substitution therefor of a military government; that they are unfit to be free, and incapable of self government.

The necessity of self preservation, therefore, now decrees our eternal political separation.

We, therefore, the delegates, with plenary powers, of the people of Texas, in solemn convention assembled, appealing to a candid world for the necessities of our condition, do hereby resolve and DECLARE, that our political connection with the Mexican nation has forever ended, and that the people of Texas, do now constitute a FREE, SOVEREIGN, and INDEPENDENT REPUBLIC, and are fully invested with all the rights and attributes which properly belong to independent nations; and, conscious of the rectitude of our intentions, we fearlessly and confidently commit the issue to the decision of the supreme Arbiter of the destinies of nations.

RICHARD ELLIS, *President.*

C. B. STEWART, THOMAS BARNETT.	Austin.	JOHN FISHER, MATT. CALDWELL,	Gonzales.	J. W. BUNTON, THOS. J. GAZELEY, R. M. COLEMAN,	Mina.	SYD. O. PENNINGTON, W. CAR'L CRAWFORD,	Shelby.
JAS. COLLINSWORTH, EDWIN WALLER, ASA BRIGHAM, J. S. D. BYROM.	Brazoria.	WILLIAM MOTLEY, L. DE ZAVALA,	Goliad. Harrisburgh.	ROBERT POTTER, THOMAS J. RUSK, CH. S. TAYLOR, JOHN S. ROBERTS,	Nacogdoches.	JAMES POWER, SAM. HOUSTON, DAVID THOMAS, EDWARD CONRAD,	Refugio.
FRANCISCO RUIS, ANTONIO NAVARO, JESSE B. BADGETT.	Bexar.	STEPH. H. EVERITT, GEORGE W. SMITH,	Jasper.			JOHN TURNER,	San Patricio.
WILLIAM D. LACY, WILLIAM MENIFEE.	Colorado.	ELIJAH STAPP, CLAIBORNE WEST, WILLIAM B. SCATES,	Jackson. Jefferson.	ROBERT HAMILTON, COLLIN McKINNEE, ALB. H. LATTIMER,	Red River.	B. BRIGGS GOODRICH, G. W. BARNETT, JAMES G. SWISHER, JESSE GRIMES,	Washington.
JAMES GAINES, W. CLARK, JR.,	Sabine.	M. B. MENARD, A. B. HARDIN,	Liberty.	MARTIN PARMER, E. O. LEGRAND, STEPH. W. BLOUNT,	San Augustin.		
		BAILEY HARDIMAN,	Matagorda.			Printed by Baker and Borden, San Felipe de Austin.	

Unanimous Declaration of Independence by the Delegates of the People of Texas, in General Convention, at the Town of Washington, on the Second Day of March, 1836. Broadsides Collection, CAH; 02853. After the Convention of 1836 voted to issue the Texas Declaration of Independence, riders carried a copy of it 40 miles down the Brazos River, where Baker and Borden printed it.

and horses over the state for breeding. McDonald's administration also saw the establishment of processing plants for Texas fruits and vegetables and the expansion of the sweet potato, tomato, citrus, black-eyed pea, watermelon, truck-farming, poultry, dairy, and nursery and floral industries. McDonald was investigated by a Texas House committee in 1935 on nine charges, including misappropriation of department funds. The House found him guilty of acts ill becoming a state official, but did not impeach him. He was reelected every two years until 25-year-old John C. White, the youngest man ever to hold the office, defeated him.

In the first major overhaul of the department, White decentralized the agency, initiated the first cooperative effort with Mexico to control insect pests, encouraged state legislation for registration and analysis of agricultural chemicals, and established laboratories to test chemical residues and contaminants before and during harvest. Under White the department inaugurated the Texas Agricultural Products marketing project to promote Texas products. It also began the Family Land Heritage Program, an annual program honoring Texas farmers and ranchers who have worked their land for 100 years or more. From 1975 to 1983 the department published *TDA Quarterly*, a glossy magazine on agricultural issues designed for a popular audience. White resigned in 1977 to become deputy United States secretary of agriculture. Governor Dolph Briscoe appointed Reagan V. Brown to succeed him. In 1978, Brown was elected under the new statute providing four-year terms for statewide elected officials. He was known for his fight for pest and predator control, especially for his effort to prevent the Mediterranean fruit fly from coming from California to Texas in 1981. He also worked to halt the spread of the obnoxious imported fire ant.

Jim Hightower became the eighth commissioner of agriculture in 1983. His major initiatives included establishing a state network of farmers' markets and wholesale-marketing cooperatives, expanding the program to help producers sell directly in international markets, updating the Texas Agricultural Products promotion (renamed the Taste of Texas program), helping farmers and ranchers get financing to build processing and marketing facilities, encouraging new agricultural development of such products as wine grapes and native plants, opening an office of natural resources to work with rural residents and farmers on farmland conservation, rural water quality, and water conservation, and increasing the department's voice in shaping national policies that affect Texas agriculture. In addition, the department's Right to Know division, established to implement the 1987 agricultural-hazards communication act, worked to keep farmers and farmworkers informed on hazardous pesticides they might encounter in their work. In 1986 the department began publishing the *Texas Gazette*, a bimonthly newsletter about department affairs, and the fall of 1987 saw the first issue of *Grassroots*, an irregularly published serial focusing on the environment and consumer topics. The department also continued its publication of numerous brochures on both specialized and popular topics, ranging from directories of agricultural cooperatives to Texas wines and wineries. In the late 1980s the department had a staff of 575 and administered 49 laws that affected numerous agriculture-related matters, including pesticide registration, egg quality, accuracy of scales and gasoline pumps, citrus-fruit maturity, seed purity, and control of fire ants.

Since the enactment of the Sunset Act in 1977 the TDA has been subject to review every 12 years by the Texas Sunset Advisory Commission. When the department came up for its first review in 1989, controversy occurred over the possibility of either making the post of agricultural commissioner an appointed one or eliminating the department entirely. Though eventually the department was continued with an elected commissioner, several changes were implemented in the agency's structure, including the establishment of a nine-member board, chaired by the agriculture commissioner, which was charged with overseeing pesticide regulation. This was an authority that had previously been granted to the commissioner of agriculture alone. In 1994 the commissioner of agriculture was Republican Rick Perry, who defeated Democrat Hightower in the 1992 election. The budget for fiscal year 1995 was $21,584,790. At that time the Texas Department of Agriculture had market and regulatory powers and administered over 50 laws. To perform its duties it had 5 regional centers, 7 suboffices, and 11 divisions.

Valerie Crosswell

Texas Department of Commerce. Established in 1987; consolidated numerous state agencies, boards, and commissions and took over the Job Training Partnership and the Community Development Block Grant program from the Texas Department of Community Affairs; originally governed by a board of six members appointed by the governor for six-year terms. In 1991 three ex-officio members, from the State Job Training Coordinating Council, the International Trade Commission, and the Texas–Mexico Authority, were added. The same year, the legislature changed the board from governing to advisory and prohibited it from involvement in the department's daily operations. The goals of the agency are to attract new businesses to Texas, to encourage expansion of existing businesses, and to improve rural economic development. In September 1991 the Community Block Grant program was transferred to the Department of Housing and Community Affairs, and the music, film, television, and multimedia programs to the governor's office. In 1989 the legislature authorized and funded foreign offices in six nations, a rural economic development fund, a product commercialization fund, and an exporters' loan guaranty program. Added in 1991 were a Texas–Mexico development fund, a rural economic development program to enhance economic development with Mexico, and a Texas–Mexico database. In the early 1990s the commission had six divisions: business development, tourism, workforce development, research and planning, intergovernmental relations, and communications. *John G. Johnson*

Texas Department of Health. Traces its beginnings to the nineteenth century, when epidemics made quarantine necessary. Although before 1879 responsibility for quarantine in Texas lay with the governor, practical application of quarantine began with local authorities. In 1879 an act amending and supplementing the Quarantine Act of 1870 authorized the governor to appoint a "medical health officer for the State"—a physician "familiar with yellow fever," old enough to have mature judgment but capable of active duty, and "pledged to the importance of both quarantine and sanitation." He was to be paid $10 a day, plus travel expenses. Later that year, $12,000 was appropriated to build quarantine stations along the coast and at the principal points of entry from other states. By 1891 the original Texas

Quarantine Department had two branches, Quarantine and Internal Sanitation, both administered by the state health officer, who was also surgeon-general ex officio. Despite the existence of a large number of disturbing health-related problems, available financial resources limited departmental activities predominantly to quarantine work. The administrative staff totaled one office assistant, except for the personnel operating the quarantine stations. The state office consisted of one dark and poorly ventilated room in the Capitol. Dr. Richard M. Swearingen, the second state health officer, wrote in 1884 that "the advances made by scientific investigators into the causes of epidemics, though positive and unquestionably in the right direction, have not been sufficient to give greater protection than heretofore, or to mitigate in any way the burdens and annoyances of quarantine." In 1903 the legislature renamed the department the Department of Public Health and Vital Statistics, even though no appropriation was made for the latter function. Early state health officers regularly appealed in vain to the legislature for additional staff to accomplish a variety of functions: enforcement of vital-statistics laws, bacteriological examination of food and water, and inspection necessary to enforce sanitary regulations. More and more, the health officers advocated the promotion of good health and the advancement of preventive techniques in order to forestall the social and economic dislocations of quarantine. In 1908 Dr. William M. Brumby described some of the goals: home hygiene for a "safe bedroom," screens to keep out insects, safe water, extermination of rodents, and sanitary laws.

Organized agitation for a state board of health had been begun by the Texas State Medical Association soon after its organization in 1869. Despite numerous rebuffs from the legislature, the association continued its advocacy for the next 40 years. The eventual result was the abolition of the Department of Public Health and Vital Statistics and the establishment of the Texas State Board of Health in 1909. The first board consisted of 7 members, all of whom had to be legally qualified physicians with at least 10 years of medical practice in Texas. The president and executive officer of the board was also designated state health officer. Texas was now able to expand its programs beyond quarantine activities. Some notable achievements during the next two decades included centralization of vital records (1909), greatly expanded education for public health (1913–14), the first sanitary inspector (1915), institution of the Bureau of Venereal Disease (1916), establishment of the Bureau of Sanitary Engineering (1917), appointment of a director of rural sanitation in order to eradicate soil-borne diseases and control soil pollution (1916), and establishment of the Bureau of Child Hygiene (1922). By 1925 activities were grouped under six bureaus: Vital Statistics; City and County Health Officers; Food and Drugs; Water, Waste Control and Inspection; Child Hygiene; and Communicable Diseases. Nevertheless, in that year only two other states made a lower per capita investment in the health of their citizens.

In 1927 the administrative agency became the Texas State Department of Health, a name that it had already used occasionally. Responsibility for selecting the state health officer was shifted from the governor to the State Board of Health. Administratively, the department remained relatively stable for the next 50 years, although it grew considerably as a result of the multiplication of public-health offices, including the Bureau of Laboratories (1928), the Division of Industrial Hygiene (1936),

the Bedding Division (1939), the independent Dental Division (1945), the Hospital Survey and Construction Division (1946), the Cancer Control Division (1947), the Water Pollution Control division (1956), and the Division of Emergency Medical Services (1956). In 1970 the first of the department's public-health regions was established in Tyler. The regional program was designed to deliver a broad range of services directly to people with no other public-health agency and to assist local health departments.

In 1974 the department again underwent reorganization, in part to align itself with new budgeting procedures advocated by the legislature. It briefly assumed the name Texas Department of Health Resources before adopting its current name. Its accomplishments include development of a state health-planning program (1975), activation of a Cancer Information Service (1976), establishment of nutrition services (1977), and development and expansion of HIV-related activities (1983–89). In 1993 the Texas Department of Health was organized into six broad areas: Family Health Services, Disease Prevention, Environmental and Consumer Health, Special Health Services, Community and Rural Health, and Departmental Administration. Its central office was in Austin, and it maintained offices in eight public-health regions throughout the state. The department is governed by an 18-member board appointed by the governor, 16 members of which must be licensed professionals with five years' professional medical experience in Texas. In 1991 the department came under the oversight of the new Health and Human Services Commission. In 1992 all environmental programs were transferred to the Texas Water Commission, and in 1993 a number of long-term-care functions were transferred to the Department of Protective and Regulatory Services. At the same time the department added a number of health services to its responsibilities.

Robert Bernstein

Texas Department of Housing and Community Affairs. Established in 1991 when the legislature merged two former agencies, the Texas Housing Agency and the Texas Department of Community Affairs. The Texas Department of Community Affairs, established in 1971, grew out of the former Division of State–Local Relations of the governor's office (1969). The Texas Housing Agency was established in 1979 to foster private investment in low-income housing. Activities of the Texas Department of Housing and Community Affairs include many of the earlier programs as well as some new ones, such as the Housing Trust Fund and the Home Investment Partnership Program, programs offering funding for housing ownership and rental assistance. All poverty and community-related programs are now under one department. TDHCA's Community Affairs and Economic Development Division administers the Community Development Block Grant, which the legislature transferred from the Texas Department of Commerce, as well as relief programs originally under the Texas Department of Human Services. In 1992 the division also managed the Weatherization Assistance, the Energy Crisis and Local Government Services programs, and the Colonia Fund. The agency's board is appointed by the governor with the advice and consent of the Texas Senate. The governor appoints the chairman.

Richard Allen Burns

Texas Department of Human Services. One of 11 human-service agencies overseen beginning in 1992 by the Health and

Human Services Commission. (The others are the Texas Department of Health, the Texas Department of Mental Health and Mental Retardation, the Texas Rehabilitation Commission, the Texas Commission for the Blind, the Texas Commission for the Deaf and Hearing Impaired, the Texas Youth Commission, the Texas Juvenile Probation Commission, the Texas Commission on Alcohol and Drug Abuse, the Texas Department on Aging, and the Interagency Council on Early Childhood Intervention Services.) The precursors of the Texas Department of Human Services began during the Great Depression: the Child Welfare Division of the Board of Control, established in 1931 but not funded until 1935; the Texas Relief Commission, in operation in 1933–34; and the Old Age Assistance Commission, established in 1936. In 1939 the legislature established the Department of Public Welfare, incorporating the earlier agencies under a more centralized control. This department administered state laws regarding assistance to the needy aged, dependent children, and blind and conducted the state's child welfare program. In 1965 the department was authorized to cooperate with the federal government in administering the antipoverty program that had been established the previous year. State funding for all assistance programs was raised from $60 million to $80 million in 1969. The department continued in the 1970s to administer four public assistance programs for needy Texans: old age assistance, aid to the blind, aid to the permanently and totally disabled, and aid to families with dependent children. The federal government provided approximately 75 percent of the assistance funds. The department also administered the Texas Medical Assistance Program (Medicaid). It served as the state agency responsible for administration of two food programs—the commodity distribution program and the food stamp program. The department's division of social services provided many services to children, adults, and families. It was intended to protect children from abuse, neglect, or exploitation. It also provided adoptive services and was responsible for licensing childcare and childplacing facilities.

In 1977 the legislature changed the name of the department to Texas Department of Human Resources. The department was restructured in 1980, with the programs categorized to reflect two major client groups: families and children, and aged and disabled persons. Voters approved a flexible spending system for welfare funding in 1981, which provided that state expenditures in this area should not exceed 1 percent of the total budget. In 1985 the DHR was renamed Texas Department of Human Services. When it came under the aegis of the new Health and Human Services Commission, the commission shifted various human-service functions and provided a permanent governing structure. Child Protective Services, Adult Protective Services, and Child-care Licensing programs were transferred to the new Texas Department of Protective and Regulatory Services. Purchased health, indigent health, and preventive health programs were subsequently transferred to the Texas Department of Health. *Vivian Elizabeth Smyrl*

Texas Department of Insurance. Authorized by the legislature under the name Department of Insurance, Statistics, and History in 1876, but began operations the year before under the state comptroller of public accounts. Subsequently, the supervision of insurance companies was handled by the commissioner of agriculture, insurance, statistics, and history (1887–1907), the

commissioner of insurance and banking (1907–13), and the State Insurance Commission, of which the commissioner of insurance and banking was a member (1913–27). In 1927 the legislature established the Board of Insurance Commissioners, composed of three members appointed by the governor for six-year terms. This board was abolished in 1957 with the establishment of the State Board of Insurance, similarly composed. The board's primary functions included chartering insurance companies, examining them periodically to see if they still met the requirements of Texas laws, licensing outofstate insurance companies to do business in Texas, and licensing insurance agents. The agency approved policy forms. It also determined rates for all fire and casualty insurance. In 1991 the state legislature inaugurated the Texas Department of Insurance, which implemented major reforms in insurance rating practices in 1992. Its new mandates ranged from massive revisions of the rules governing long-term care and Medicare supplement insurance to providing bilingual notices of insurance companies' toll-free numbers. Because its reforms strengthened the agency's efforts against insolvency by the end of 1992, Texas became the fourteenth state to win accreditation of its financial regulation program by the National Association of Insurance Commissioners. By 1994 the three-member board was replaced with one commissioner. The comptroller's office assumed the tax operations, the State Office of Administrative Hearings conducted hearings, and the Texas Workers' Compensation Commission took over worker-compensation data. Like other accredited states, Texas must undergo future periodic review by the NAIC to assure it continues to conform to NAIC standards. *Dick Smith*

Texas Department of Licensing and Regulation. The Bureau of Labor Statistics was established in 1909 to collect statistical information bearing on the commercial, social, educational, and sanitary conditions of Texas employees and their families. Later, administration of laws concerning boxing and wrestling was added. In 1956 the bureau had six divisions: Labor, Employment and Local Agency, Oil and Gas, Boxing and Wrestling, Boiler Inspection, and Accounting. It had 57 employees, 16 of whom were part-time, and was headed by a commissioner appointed by the governor for a two-year term. By 1964 the Oil and Gas Division no longer existed, but a Safety Division had been added. Functions of the bureau were to enforce laws pertaining to health, safety, and morals, as well as child labor, pay times, hours worked, the prevailing wage, and other laws. In 1973 the name was changed to Texas Department of Labor and Standards. An Administrative Division took the place of the Accounting Division, the Labor and Safety divisions were combined, and Mobile Homes and Auctioneer divisions were added. In 1989 a six-member commission began to act as the governing body, and the name was changed to Texas Department of Licensing and Regulation. The remaining labor functions were transferred to the Texas Employment Commission. The licensing agency was made an umbrella regulatory agency to oversee a variety of businesses, trades, and occupations. Besides auctioneers, manufactured housing, and professional boxing, it began to regulate tow trucks, vehicle-storage facilities, industrialized housing and buildings, and boilers, including those used in nuclear plants. Air-conditioning contractors, private personnel agencies, career counseling, and talent agencies were also under the agency's regulation. Registration of property-tax consultants and employers of certain temporary common laborers and supervision of the elimination of architectural barriers to handicapped persons were added in 1991.   *John G. Johnson*

Texas Department of Mental Health and Mental Retardation. Established in 1965; replaced the Board for Texas State Hospitals and Special Schools. The department offers services to the mentally ill and mentally retarded, designed to increase their dignity and independence. Its ultimate beginning occurred in 1861, when the first Texas mental hospital was opened in Austin. The MHMR department is now the largest Texas state agency in terms of employees (40,000 +). In the early 1990s it was the umbrella organization for 62 facilities, including 8 state hospitals, a special facility for emotionally disturbed youth, 13 state schools, 5 state centers, and 35 community mental-health and mental-retardation centers. It also included a Genetic Screening and Counseling Service and the Leander Rehabilitation Center, a recreation facility for the department's clients. The department is governed by a ninemember board of directors, each appointed by the governor for a six-year term. The board sets policy for the agency and hires a commissioner, who is the administrative head of the department and who appoints deputy commissioners for mental-retardation and mental-health services. The deputies are in charge of local facilities and their community services.

The field of mental health has metamorphosed since Texas opened its first State Lunatic Asylum in Austin. In 1925 the legislature removed the words "lunatic" and "insane" from the names of state facilities. In 1957 the legislature enacted the Texas Mental Health Code, which eliminated such terms as "lunacy," "insanity" and "unsound mind" in the law books and replaced them with "mental illness." It stipulated that epilepsy, senility, alcoholism, and mental deficiency are not mental illnesses. The code also allowed for voluntary as well as court-ordered admissions. Previously, the route to a state hospital was only through a court. In the late twentieth century most admissions remained court-ordered, however, as the state moved its focus from institutional care to community-based treatment. Texas began its move away from institutions in the late 1940s after the United States Public Health Service reported a critical need for mental-health clinics. In the 1950s four adult clinics were opened in Texas—in San Antonio, Harlingen, Fort Worth, and Dallas. In 1963 President John Kennedy signed a bill providing federal matching funds for community mental-health centers. Since then, 35 community MHMR centers have sprung up throughout the state. With a growing commitment to service outside institutional walls, MHMR has promoted the development of community programs in every county of the state. In 1974 a class-action lawsuit was filed against the department challenging conditions in state hospitals. Under this lawsuit, known as *RAJ v. Jones*, the state hospitals were placed under court monitoring. In 1992 a settlement was reached setting forth specific compliance criteria for each hospital to meet.

In the field of mental retardation, Texas began greater emphasis on care and treatment options in the community in the 1980s. The state's first institution for the mentally retarded (1917) was the State Colony for the Feebleminded. The name was changed to Austin State School in 1925. By 1992 there were 13 state schools housing about 7,000 retarded individuals, down from the alltime high of 12,000 in 1974. In the 1980s, both through policy direction and through court rulings stemming from the *Lelsz v. Kavanaugh* class-action lawsuit, the department began reducing its state-school population. This lawsuit, filed in 1974, sought improved conditions at state schools and more extensive community placement of individuals with mental retardation. A settlement reached in 1991 mandated moving retarded people to community-service assistance. Because of a dearth of facilities and services along Texas borders and in lesser populated areas, state centers were established in Beaumont, Harlingen, Laredo, El Paso, and Amarillo. Two of the five offer only mental-retardation services, while the others also offer mental-health services. The department's forensic psychiatric unit is at Vernon State Hospital, where individuals who are incompetent to stand trial or who have been found not guilty by reason of insanity receive treatment. Also key to the MHMR system is a research unit at San Antonio State Hospital, where new medication regimes are tested in collaboration with the University of Texas Health Science Center at San Antonio. As the system becomes more refined and focused, the respective missions of state schools and hospitals are expected to change markedly. For example, in the early 1990s treatment facilities for substance abuse began to be phased out at state hospitals, the services being transferred to the community centers.

Dennis R. Jones and Sheila Allee

Texas Department of Public Safety. Established in 1935 to enforce public-safety laws and to provide for crime prevention and detection. A three-member Public Safety Commission, appointed by the governor for six-year terms, oversaw the department and in turn named the director and assistant director. Originally department operations were classified into six divisions: Texas Highway Patrol, Texas Rangers, Bureau of Communications, Bureau of Intelligence, Bureau of Education, and Bureau of Identification and Records. In 1937 the state licensing of drivers was added to the tasks of the department, as was the first narcotics section. The driver's-license section was expanded in 1941 with the addition of an accident-record section, which later evolved into the Statistical Division (1946). By the early 1950s still more driver-related duties were added, with the enactment of the Motor Vehicle Inspection Act and the Safety Responsibility Act. In 1957 the DPS was reorganized into four major divisions: Identification and Criminal Records, Personnel and Staff Services, Driver and Vehicle Records, and Inspection and Planning. In 1963 the department also became responsible for the State Civil Defense Office (later the Division of Emergency Management), established to aid local governments during times of natural disaster or social upheaval. Through the years the Department of Public Safety continued to reorganize and expand its operations, forming the Criminal Law and the Traffic Law Enforcement divisions in 1968 and the administrative division in 1973, and adding an internal-affairs unit in 1978 and an automated fingerprint-identification system in 1989. In the early 1990s the DPS consisted of the director's staff and three major divisions: Criminal Law Enforcement, Traffic Law Enforcement, and Administration. In 1991 the Texas Rangers had become part of the director's staff.

Laurie E. Jasinski

Texas Department of Transportation. Originally the Texas Highway Department; established in 1917 by the state legislature.

The agency bore its original name until 1975, when it assumed the functions of the Texas Mass Transportation Commission and was renamed State Department of Highways and Public Transportation. Its chief responsibilities are to manage state highway development and public transportation systems; issue permits for the use of heavy trucks; and register motor vehicles. The Texas Highway Department was originally established only to take advantage of the 1916 Federal Aid Road Act, which granted monetary assistance to all states that had centralized, state control of road building. The legislature authorized a comprehensive system of public highways and roads in cooperation with the counties and under the direct supervision of the state highway department. The department further relieved the counties of their maintenance responsibility in1925 and ultimately required them only to furnish rights-of-way for new construction in the state road system.

Throughout the 1920s and 1930s the department was a focal point of Texas politics. The 1924 gubernatorial election of Miriam Ferguson placed the state road agency in a politically precarious situation, since control of construction and maintenance contracts meant potentially lucrative patronage to Ferguson supporters. A legislative enactment passed a year before Ma Ferguson's election staggered the terms of the highway commissioners, and she appointed all three members of the reorganized highway commission. Her appointees soon took political and monetary advantage of a vulnerable road program. Rumors of fiscal wrongdoing led Attorney General Dan Moody in November 1925 to file suit against the Ferguson-controlled highway commission. Moody alleged that several road-construction companies had received "sweetheart" contracts worth millions of dollars from the commission and that in return kickbacks had been paid to the commissioners and perhaps even to the Fergusons. The courts ruled with the attorney general and invalidated numerous road contracts. The commissioners resigned in disgrace, and by December 1925 rumors of Mrs. Ferguson's impending impeachment circulated freely throughout the state. The legislature was not, however, in session, and impeachment talk eventually subsided. The road scandals, combined with other allegations of wrongdoing in the education agency and in the functioning of the State Penitentiary at Huntsville led to Mrs. Ferguson's defeat by Moody in the August 1926 Democratic gubernatorial run-off primary. In November 1932 Mrs. Ferguson was again elected governor. Given the economic hardships of the Great Depression, the Texas Highway Department feared another round of rough-and-tumble politics in which it would be a most reluctant participant. However, Mrs. Ferguson's second gubernatorial term proved less politically volatile than her first. The depression itself was a far more dangerous enemy to the state road agency. A reduction in federal aid and in state gasoline-tax revenue caused a temporary curtailment of projects and cuts in personnel, and in 1936 led Governor Allred to advocate diverting millions of dollars of highway money into an old-age assistance program. Officials of the state road agency lobbied successfully for the defeat of Allred's plan, but the result was a forced administrative reorganization. The conflict probably also caused the resignation of state highway engineer Gibb Gilchrist, the most accomplished leader, up to that time, in the department's history.

With World War II came a sharp decline in the highway-building program. Federal aid was designated only for highway projects serving national defense, and all other "nonmilitary" projects were suspended for the duration. Highway manpower and matériel went off to Europe and the Pacific, and only minimal maintenance was accomplished at home during the war. In the postwar years the department initiated an aggressive rebuilding and expansion effort to match the growing demand for better transportation facilities. Between 1945 and 1950 Texas vehicle registrations climbed from 1.7 million to 3.1 million. To satisfy this new demand, the department moved in two directions. First, it began expressway construction in major Texas cities in 1945, supervised by the Urban Project offices. Further impetus was given to this program in 1956, when the national government passed the Federal Aid Highway Act, which provided for a nationwide interstate highway system. Second, by 1949 the agency had established a farm-to-market program to provide a coherent system of rural highways.

In the 1980s the State Department of Highways and Public Transportation was one of the nation's leading state transportation agencies. Utilizing the fiscally conservative "pay-as-you-go" basis rather than bonding, Texas has been a primary constructor of new highways. The highway department had 15,000 employees and spent nearly $5.5 billion on engineering, right-of-way, and construction, $63.6 million on planning and research, and $45.8 million on public transportation systems. The continuing expenditure of billions of dollars of public money has been essential to the state's overall economic growth. In turn, that growth has placed additional burdens upon the road agency. In 1930 the ratio of registered vehicles to miles in the state highway system was 77.9 to 1; by August 1984 it was 187.6 to one. In 1991 the Texas legislature merged the State Department of Highways and Public Transportation, the Texas Department of Aviation, and the Texas Motor Vehicle Commission to form the Texas Department of Transportation. In 1994 the department had 14,763 employees and a budget of over $3 billion.

John D. Huddleston

Texas Education Agency. Under the Gilmer–Aikin Laws, the TEA replaced the State Board of Education and the office of state superintendent of public instruction in 1949. In 1972 the TEA comprised the State Board of Education (which included the State Board for Vocational Education), the office of commissioner of education, and professional, technical, and clerical staffs. The State Board of Education, authorized by a constitutional amendment in 1928 and organized in 1929, superseded ex-officio boards established in 1866 and 1876. Before Gilmer–Aikin, the board was composed of 9 members, appointed by the governor for 6-year terms. Later, under the 1949 statute, it was composed of 21 members elected for 6year terms, with one member being elected from each congressional district of the state as the districts were constituted in 1949. The State Board of Education was the policy-forming body for the public schools; it adopted operating budgets on the basis of legislative appropriations, established regulations for the accreditation of schools, executed contracts for the purchase of textbooks, and invested the Permanent School Fund. The commissioner of education, appointed by the board as CEO of the agency for a four-year term, issued teachers' certificates and supervised the professional, technical, and clerical staffs. The agency also administered the Texas School for the Deaf, the Texas School for the Blind and Visually Impaired, and the state's vocational-rehabilitation program.

Education changes in 1984 changed the scope and direction of TEA. Six years later, TEA reorganized to become more client-centered and field-based, emphasizing communication with local school districts through the newly established Field Service Unit. In 1987 the legislature established the Legislative Education Board to oversee the implementation of state-mandated education reforms and to set public education policy, which TEA and the State Board of Education implement. TEA's divisions and their respective functions are: the Field Services Department, which provides communication between local school districts and the commissioner of education; the Department of Curriculum and Assessment, which administers the divisions of curriculum development, instructional outcomes assessment, and teacher assessment; the Department of Professional Development, which focuses on achieving a comprehensive professional development system; the Office of Programs and Instructions, which supervises the division of accelerated instruction, bilingual education, special education, services for the deaf, and migrant education; the Office of Accountability, which supervises activities related to accreditation, student achievement analysis, compliance analysis, school-district governance, special investigations, and institutional development; the Office of School Support Services, which directs policy development and supervises activities related to school support, audits, technology applications, and resource planning; and the Office of Operations, which provides services for all TEA employees and departments.

Dick Smith and Richard Allen Burns

Texas Employment Commission. Established in 1936 by the Texas legislature as the Texas Unemployment Compensation Commission; renamed in 1947. In 1933 the Wagner–Peyser Act inaugurated a federal–state system of employment offices, and in 1935 the Social Security Act included a tax to stimulate passage of state unemployment-insurance laws. In July 1935 the Texas Employment Security program started with an appropriation of $36,000 matched by the federal government. This agency replaced the National Re-employment Service, which had been a temporary branch of the United States Employment Service since 1933. In October 1936 the Texas legislature passed the Texas Unemployment Compensation Act, which accepted the unemployment insurance provisions of the Social Security Act and established the Texas Unemployment Compensation Commission. The three-member board is appointed by the governor. The commission was required to establish two coordinate divisions: the Unemployment Compensation Division and the Employment Service Division. By 1955 the agency had six departments. In 1950 the Texas Employment Service placed 484,980 persons in nonagricultural jobs, including 16,815 handicapped and 8,438 World War II veterans. The agency received 807,642 agricultural placement openings, referred 866,673 individuals, and filled 744,026 farm jobs. By 1960 the commission had 92 offices in 81 cities and towns and 2,600 employees statewide. The agency was almost ended by sunset legislation in 1983. About the same time the jobless fund went bankrupt and had to be bailed out by a federal loan. Governor William

Clements suggested that unemployed Texans could look for jobs through newspaper want ads rather than the TEC. Agency officials were caught hiring relatives, and Commissioner Richard Melado was forced to fire his daughter when she was found working at an agency office in Houston. Furthermore, an independent report concluded that the agency was topheavy with administrators. In fiscal 1991, having survived the scandal-ridden 1980s, the TEC served more than 300,000 employers, received 1,403,387 new and renewed job applications, and processed 800,970 initial unemployment claims. The commission's programs included the Communities in Schools Program, an in-school dropout prevention program; a Jobs Search Seminar, teaching applicants how to present qualifications to employers; Project Rio, Reintegration for Offenders; and Statewide Agricultural Employment Assistance Program, an employment service to agricultural employers and workers. The agency also provided immigration documentation to relieve the employer of this responsibility.

John G. Johnson

Texas Engineering Experiment Station. An engineering and technology research agency established in 1914 by the board of directors of Texas A&M to aid the industrial development of Texas. Since its inception the station has directed its efforts to the utilization of natural resources and the improvement of industrial processes. In 1994 A&M classified TEES as a branch of its Engineering Program. TEES research units in the College of Engineering include aerospace, chemical, civil, electrical, mechanical, nuclear, industrial, and petroleum engineering, as well as computer science. Technology-related divisions of TEES conduct interdisciplinary studies in eight centers in the colleges of Architecture, Business Administration, Education, Geosciences, Liberal Arts, Medicine, Science, and Veterinary Medicine. TEES also maintains regional stations at other universities—Lamar, Texas A&M International, New Mexico State, Prairie View A&M, Texas A&M at Kingsville, Texas A&M at Galveston, Texas Woman's, and West Texas A&M. TEES receives federal, state, and private funds. Typically, every state dollar invested in TEES generates four dollars in additional support through private grants and contract work. TEES work is done primarily by faculty and graduate students, though full-time researchers are also employed. Current projects include the Offshore Technology Research Center and enhanced oil recovery. Previous research focused on road and bridge building, sanitation and sewerage methods, petroleum refining, agricultural products, and aeronautical designs and installations.

Tracé Etienne–Gray

Texas Engineering Extension Service. Began as the Trade and Industrial Teacher Training Service in 1919, after the passage of the federal Smith–Hughes Act (1917). The service, administered by the Agricultural Education Department at Texas A&M, trained men from industry to teach vocational subjects in public schools. In 1924 the School of Vocational Training took over the teachers' training program. The school was dissolved in 1935, and the programs were transferred to the A&M Department of Industrial Education. By 1942 extension training had become available to water and sewerage plant operators, peace officers, public building custodians, electric linemen, and automobile mechanics. To meet wartime demands the Department of

Industrial Education established programs for firemen to set up fire-control units; for citizens in essential war industries; and for courses in job instructor training for leadmen, foremen, and supervisors in war industries and military installations. In 1945 most programs established during the war were phased out except those for firemen and supervisory training. The program for training electric linemen for rural electric cooperatives was expanded. In 1948 the board of directors established the TEES as a part of the Texas A&M College System. The service maintains 13 training divisions: Inspection Equipment and Public Work, Electric Power Training and Safety, Fire Protection, Electronics, Law Enforcement and Security, Management, Occupational and Environmental Safety (San Antonio), Small Business and Historically Underutilized Business, Telecommunications, Transportation, Water and Waste Water, and the Technology and Economic Development Division. In 1992 the TEES, now part of the Texas A&M University System, moved into new headquarters on the campus in College Station. The organization also staffs an office in Galveston. Training Centers are located in Abilene, Arlington, Corpus Christi, Houston, and San Antonio. In 1993–94 the service conducted 5,700 classes for 120,000 students. Robotics, lasers, production processes, and power generation are areas of program development.

Karen Riedel

Texas Farm Bureau. Headquartered in Waco. Following the pattern of the American Farm Bureau Federation, the Dallas County Farm Bureau was organized in May 1920. By August farmers across the state had expressed enough interest that the State Council of Agriculture and Home Economics asked the AFBF for help in establishing the Texas Farm Bureau Federation. A state headquarters was opened in Dallas, and a membership drive for 100,000 members was begun. By January 1921 enough county bureaus had been established that the first annual meeting of the TFBF was held. The delegates wrote a constitution that placed the TFBF under the umbrella of the national AFBF, and elected John Orr of Dallas president and Christopher Moser of Dallas secretary. Under the banner of "Organized for Business," the TFBF sought to promote agricultural life, cooperate in marketing, and work with the U.S. Department of Agriculture, the Texas Department of Agriculture, and Texas A&M University. Membership was open to any white farmer, landlord, or tenant who paid the $10 annual dues, which was split among the county bureau, the state federation, the newsletter *Farm Bureau News*, and the AFBF. The structure of the TFBF was on three levels—community, county, and state. The county bureau was the backbone. The state federation held annual conventions, conducted the general business, lobbied for legislation, and established cooperative marketing agencies. By the end of 1921 TFBF membership had reached 70,000. One of its more significant achievements was the establishment of the Texas Farm Bureau Cotton Association (1921) to market cotton and ensure the best profit possible for participating farmers. To do this the TFBCA pooled cotton crops, owned warehouses, and sold cotton collectively. By July 1921 the TFBCA had signed enough five-year contracts with cotton farmers to reach its 500,000-bale goal. Reorganization in the 1920s included establishment of a Women's Farm Bureau Division to provide support in membership drives, as well as formation of 14 new livestock and crop associations.

The cooperative marketing efforts failed, however, and the TFBF collapsed by 1926. Not until 1933 did a new organization appear, when the TFBF was reorganized into the Texas Agricultural Association. When the TAA affiliated again with the AFBF in 1939, the new TFBF was organized. In 1953 the annual convention changed the name to Texas Farm Bureau. Membership was 7,000 in 1945, 110,689 in 1968, 313,568 in 1983, and 320,000 in 1990. While being represented by the AFBF on national economic and political issues, the TFB assumed leadership in the state, fighting for farmers and ranchers. Over the years the TFB supported legislation about animal health, farm roads, agricultural research and education, and feed, seed, and insecticide laws. The agency also helped organize insurance companies to serve its members. In the 1960s it expanded marketing services to accelerate the sale of commodities in Europe as well as cattle and chickens within the United States. The TFB also sold its own products, such as Safemark tires and batteries, to members. In addition to the annual conventions, the bureau offered members educational institutes and a radio program, "Farm Bureau Roundup," beginning in the 1950s. Another source of TFB information was the official publication, *Texas Agriculture* (1937), which was replaced in 1985 by two new publications—*Texas Neighbors* and *Texas Agriculture Weekly*. In the early 1990s the county bureau remained the basic structure of the TFB. Membership in 1994 was 290,000 in 211 county bureaus.

Janet Schmelzer

Texas Fever. A tick-borne cattle disease that plagued the Texas cattle industry in the nineteenth century. Readers of the *Veterinarian*, an English journal, were informed in June 1868 that a "very subtle and terribly fatal disease" had broken out among cattle in Illinois. Midwestern farmers soon realized that it was associated with longhorn cattle driven north by South Texas ranchers. The cattle appeared healthy, but Midwestern cattle, including Panhandle animals, allowed to mix with them or to use a pasture recently vacated by the longhorns, became ill and very often died. Farmers often called the disease Texas fever or Texas cattle fever because of its connection with Texas cattle. States along the cattle trails passed quarantine laws routing cattle away from settled areas or restricting the passage of herds to the winter months, when there was less danger from Texas fever. Kansas, with its central location and rail links with other markets, was crucial to Texas cattle trailing. In 1885 Kansas entirely outlawed the driving of Texas cattle across its borders. This, together with restrictive legislation passed by many other states, was an important factor in ending the Texas cattle-trailing industry.

Though Texas fever was clearly associated with Texas cattle, its cause remained for many years a mystery. Various theories were proposed. One held that the longhorns ate poisonous plants that did not hurt them but that made their wastes so toxic that the smallest amount accidentally ingested by a nonimmune Midwestern cow could cause illness and death. New bacteriological discoveries of Louis Pasteur and others led scientists studying Texas fever to look for a microorganism. In 1893 Theobald Smith and Fred Lucius Kilborne of the federal Bureau of Animal Industry in Washington, D.C., announced their isolation of the pathogen of Texas fever. They named the protozoan *Pyrosoma bigeminum*. It is now recognized that either of two species of the renamed genus *Babesia* may be involved in Texas fever. From this is derived the modern name babesiosis, which is applied

Dramatization of Katherine Anne Porter's short story "The Grave" from "Katherine Anne Porter: The Eye of Memory," produced by KERA-TV, Dallas/Fort Worth, Denton. Left to right: Paul Winfield as Uncle Billy; Dina Chandel as Miranda; Yankton Hatton as Paul, and Christie Allen as Maria. Courtesy Texas Film Commission.

both to Texas fever and to infections caused throughout the world by these pathogens and other members of the same genus. Smith and Kilborne also discovered that the disease was spread by cattle ticks. After sucking blood from an infected animal, a tick would drop off into the grass and lay eggs from which would hatch young ticks already harboring the protozoan. Weeks later, the tick's progeny were still capable of infecting other cattle. Several different species of tick are now known to spread babesiosis, or tick fever.

But identification of the pathogen and vector of babesiosis still did not explain the apparent good health of the Texas cattle that carried the disease. Modern research indicates that calves are born with a natural partial resistance to infection that lasts a month or two after birth and goes away gradually. In areas like nineteenth-century Texas (and other Southern states), where the disease was widespread, the calf suffers a mild attack at an early age, then develops enough immunity to keep from being over-whelmed but not enough to rid itself of the pathogen. By the time the animal reaches adulthood, it has a shaky balance with its protozoan parasites that allows it to live in reasonably good health while remaining a carrier. Babesiosis is still a serious threat to livestock in many parts of the world. In the United States it has been eliminated by a vigorous program of cattle dip-ping, which eradicated the tick vector. King Ranch manager

Robert J. Kleberg is credited with building the first dipping vat in the state. Before the disease was eradicated in this country, non-immune American cattle were protected from it by elaborate federal quarantine laws separating Southern cattle from others in railway cars and stockyards. Northern cattle imported to the South for breeding purposes could be immunized by receiving injections of small amounts of blood from infected animals. Mark Francis of Texas A&M was a pioneer in the development of this method of immunization. *Tamara Miner Haygood*

Texas Film Commission. Promotes movies, documentaries, television series, music videos, commercials, and industrial films in Texas; established in 1971 as a result of Governor Preston Smith's promotion of the film industry in the state. The commission brought about the production in Texas of 114 theater and television movies over the next decade. The governor oversaw one state and six separate municipal film bureaus in Austin, Corpus Christi, Dallas, El Paso, Houston, and San Antonio, whose combined performance led Governor Mark White to claim that "Texas stands as a genuine 'Third Coast' alternative to the traditional production centers." A consultant estimated that film, video, and television production put about $500 million into the economy of Texas in 1980. The ultimate purpose of the commission is to stimulate local growth while attracting the profits of major motion picture and video production to the state. The commission assists media companies in finding locations, monitors the costs of filming, and assures the availability of emergency and sanitation services. It also fosters a statewide talent pool, participates in minor casting, locates extras, helps with wardrobes and props, and catalogues available personnel and technology. Texas is one of more than 40 states with film commissions. In spite of its small budget, the Texas Film Commission has helped Texas to assume the rank of fourth among the states (behind California, New York, and Florida) in the production of movies and television shows, and the industry has brought corresponding cultural and financial profits. The commission became a part of the Texas Department of Commerce in 1987. *Gary R. Edgerton*

Texas Fine Arts Association. The first organization to promote art activity throughout the state; founded in 1911 in honor of Elisabet Ney by Anna Pennybacker, Julia Pease, and others who wanted to pave the way for a state art gallery and promote the arts; still active in the late 1990s. Ella Dibrell had bought the Ney studio, Formosa, in 1908, the year after Ney's death, in order to preserve the property and its art. The site provided the group a meetingplace as well as gallery space for the semiannual art shows it instituted. The first slate of officers included Joseph D. Sayers as a vice president. During the first annual meeting, it was decided that the association would form one committee to promote the establishment of an art school in connection with the University of Texas and another to encourage legislation to establish a state arts commission. In 1909 the university was given the Ney sculpture collection at Formosa provided that it remain at the studio as long as an organization would maintain it there. In 1929 the charter for the Texas Fine Arts Association Holding Company was established to receive the Elisabet Ney Museum from the Dibrells. The association developed semiannual exhibitions, one for members in the fall and one for all Texas artists in the spring. In 1942 the association began to jury the shows. In 1927 it began a touring program that brought selected works to communities throughout Texas; within two years the association was receiving more requests for the circuit exhibitions than it could fill. Until 1929 the program was under the directorship of James Chillman, Jr., the director of the Houston Museum of Fine Arts, but in 1932 the program was moved to Austin and Jodie B. Roberdeau, secretary of the association and later its acting president, took over its administration. In 1941 the association began to publish a newsletter, *Texas Fine Arts News.* That year the members deeded the Ney Museum to the city of Austin in exchange for maintenance of the grounds and building.

In 1943 Clara Driscoll, owner of Laguna Gloria, deeded that property to the association along with a gift of $5,000. In 1942 the association began an International Exhibition of Prints and Drawings, and in 1951 it sponsored the first annual All-Texas Arts and Crafts Fair at City Coliseum. In 1953 the association held a Texas Fine Arts Festival, which was aided considerably when the Metropolitan Museum of New York offered works by old masters and contemporary New York artists. In 1961 the Laguna Gloria Art Museum, Incorporated, was made a separate chapter of the association so it could assume responsibility for the museum's operation. In 1966 the Texas Fine Arts Holding Company merged with the museum. The association retained

two persons on the museum's board of directors, maintained an office on the museum grounds, and presented two exhibitions a year—New American Talent, juried from a nationwide call for entries, and Texas Annual, for Texas artists.

Alice M. Shukalo

Texas Folklore Society. Organized by Leonidas W. Payne, Jr., who served as its first president, and John Lomax, who served as the first secretary. Killis Campbell presented the resolution for the formation of the Folk-Lore Society of Texas at the December 1909 meeting of the Texas State Teachers Association in Dallas. Charter membership, held open until 1 April 1910, totaled 92. In addition to the contributions of Lomax and Payne, the organization's philosophical groundwork also benefited from the contributions of Walter Prescott Webb, Dorothy Scarborough, and Herbert Bolton. The nonprofit society is devoted exclusively to preserving and presenting a wide variety of Texas folklore. Membership in the organization, which is the second oldest continuously functioning folklore society in the United States (the oldest being the American Folklore Society), is open to anyone interested in folklore. In April 1911 the organization held its first formal meeting in Austin at the University of Texas campus, where it maintained its first headquarters. Annual meetings have been held regularly since 1911, except for interruptions in 1918–21 and 1944–45, caused by the two world wars. The society's first official folklore publication was a monograph by William H. Thomas entitled *Some Current Folk-Songs of the Negro* (1912). The society published the first volume in its serial book-publishing program with *Publications of the Folk-Lore Society of Texas Number 1* (1916), a miscellany edited by the society's first editor, Stith Thompson, and later reprinted under title *Round the Levee* (1935). In 1923 J. Frank Dobie established the office of secretary–editor and was the first to serve in that position, which he held until 1943. During his first years in office he dissociated the society from its affiliation with the American Folklore Society, which he considered too pedantic. He also edited 16 society publications, including the classic *Legends of Texas* (*Publications of the Texas Folk-Lore Society, Number III*) (1924). In 1925 the society, which had also met occasionally with the Texas State Historical Association, voted to affiliate with the Texas Academy of Sciences. In 1943 Mody Boatright, who with Harry Ransom had for some time assisted Dobie with the society's editorial duties, became the acting secretary–editor, a post he held for the next 20 years. Under Boatright the society reestablished its connection with the American Folklore Society. In 1964 Wilson M. Hudson succeeded Boatright. In the 1960s the society transcribed an extensive collection of tapes and sponsored an annual contest for college students. Until 1971 the TFS maintained an office and archives on the campus of the University of Texas at Austin, although it was not a part of that institution. Francis Edward Abernethy of Stephen F. Austin State University became the secretary–editor of the Texas Folklore Society in 1971, and the office was moved to the SFA campus in Nacogdoches.

In addition to various newsletters and pamphlets, the society annually publishes or helps promote a book on various folklore topics; by 1996 the society had produced 54 volumes of its *Publications* series. It has also produced two special series: the five books of the Range Life series, produced between 1942 and 1945 under Dobie's editorship to preserve oral accounts of frontier life, and the five books in the Paisano Books series, produced under Hudson between 1966 and 1970 to provide an outlet for popular field folklore. The latter series bore the name of the society's emblem, the paisano or roadrunner. In 1954 the society published *Texas Folk and Folklore*, an anthology of articles from previous volumes. The society's publications are thoroughly indexed in James T. Bratcher's *Analytical Index to Publications of the Texas Folklore Society* (1973), which indexes 36 volumes, and in Herbert C. Arbuckle III's comprehensive bibliography in the society publication *T for Texas: A State Full of Folklore* (1982). Other publications of the society include *Legendary Ladies of Texas* (1981), *Hecho en Tejas: Texas-Mexican Folk Arts and Crafts* (1991), and *Corners of Texas: Publications of the Texas Folklore Society* (1983). The society had about 800 members in 1996.

Frances E. Abernethy

Texas Forestry Association. A private, nonprofit, nongovernment organization headquartered in Lufkin; organized in 1914 at Temple by a group of 20 businessmen, with William Goodrich Jones, the "father" of forestry in Texas, as first president. Objectives are to advance the cause of forestry and encourage the expansion, protection, and proper management of all forest and related resources. The founders lobbied for a state forestry agency and persuaded the legislature in 1915 to authorize the State Department of Forestry (now the Texas Forest Service). The association cosponsors annual youth forestry courses, distributes millions of pine seedlings free to East Texas youths, sponsors the tree-farm program in Texas, and awards scholarships to forestry students at Texas A&M and Stephen F. Austin State universities. It established a series of woodland walking trails and the privately financed Texas Reforestation Foundation. It cosponsors the Texas Forestry Museum at Lufkin. The TFA also publishes a monthly newspaper, *Texas Forestry*, which superseded the *Texas Forestry Association Bulletin*. The association began publishing *Texas Logger* in 1992. *E. R. Wagoner*

Texas Game and Fish Commission. The idea of managing the state's wildlife resources developed over several decades in the latter half of the nineteenth and the early twentieth century. As the population increased, especially after the arrival of the first railroads, wildlife began to decline. The state's first effort to regulate hunting occurred in 1861, when the legislature established a two-year closed season on quail. Fishing regulations, in the form of restrictions on coastal seining and netting, were instituted in 1874. In 1879 the legislature established the office of fish commissioner to enforce such regulations; the office was abolished five years later because of intense controversy surrounding the introduction of German carp to Texas waterways. In 1883, 130 counties in Texas claimed exemption from all game laws. By 1895, however, it had become clear that some regulatory office was needed to control the depletion caused by overfishing. In response to this need the legislature established the office of fish and oyster commissioner. In 1907 the legislature also gave the commissioner the responsibility for hunting regulations, and the name of the office was changed to game, fish, and oyster commissioner. The first hunting licenses were sold in 1909. In 1919 the state had only 6 game wardens to enforce regulations, and many counties continued to claim exemptions; the number of wardens was increased to 45 by 1923 and to 80 by 1928. In the 1920s the commissioner's office began developing extensive fish hatcheries in order to supplement the dwindling natural supply

of fish; restocking of deer and releases of Nilgai antelope began in the late 1920s and early 1930s.

In 1929 the duties of the commissioner were transferred to a board—the Game, Fish, and Oyster Commission—composed of six members appointed by the governor. The commission appointed an executive secretary, who acted as chief executive officer. With the commission format, the agency had more stable leadership than the earlier single-commissioner style did, and as a result it became more consistent in its policy-making and enforcement. The major duties of the commission were to enforce the laws of the state pertaining to birds, game, furbearing mammals, fish, and marine life; to issue hunting, fishing, and trapping licenses; to set open seasons and bag limits on various types of game and fish; to operate fish hatcheries; to administer game preserves; to supervise the oyster beds of the state; to control the sand, shell, and gravel in public waters; and to inform the public about wildlife resources. In 1942 the commission began publishing *Texas Game and Fish* magazine, and in 1946 it began a statewide conservation-education program. In 1951 the legislature expanded the commission to nine members and removed "oyster" from the commission's name. In 1958 the commission controlled hunting and fishing regulations in 80 counties; by 1962 hunting and fishing in 129 counties were under full or partial control of the commission. The Texas Game and Fish Commission merged with the State Parks Board in 1963 to form the Texas Parks and Wildlife Department.

Vivian Elizabeth Smyrl

Texas Gazette. An important early newspaper and the father of several more. It was a typical frontier newspaper of 4 pages an issue, 3 columns a page; it usually measured 9½ inches by 12 inches and was printed in small type. The paper was generally in English but sometimes in Spanish. Although advertised as a weekly, it was very irregular. Godwin Brown Cotten began publishing it on 25 September 1829 at San Felipe. The three major contributors were Robert McAlpin Williamson, Stephen F. Austin, and Cotten. The opinions of the latter two often clashed. Cotten sold the *Gazette* to Williamson in 1831. Williamson named it the *Mexican Citizen* and ran it until December 1831, when Cotten resumed ownership of the press and moved it to Brazoria. There he published the *Texas Gazette and Brazoria Commercial Advertiser* from April to June 1832. Daniel W. Anthony soon purchased the paper and changed the name to *Constitutional Advocate and Brazoria Advertiser* and the *Constitutional Advocate and Texas Public Advertiser*. When Anthony died of cholera in 1833, John A. Wharton took over the press and published a paper named the *Advocate of the People's Rights* until 27 March 1834. The same press was used beginning in July 1834 by Franklin C. Gray and A. J. Harris to issue the Brazoria *Texas Republican*. The *Texas Gazette*, the first enduring Texas newspaper, was the earliest Texas newspaper of which more than one issue is now extant. As the first newspaper printed in Austin's colony, it depicted the life of the colonists and therefore the growth of the colony. It provided settlers with translations of Mexican laws, brought them outside news, and allayed their fears in time of crisis. Austin's contributions enable us to trace his policy with the Mexican government. Also, Cotten set a standard for the craft of printing for later Texas newspapers and published the first printed statement of dissatisfaction with arbitrary official conduct in Texas. *Charlotte A. Hickson*

Texas Higher Education Coordinating Board. Established as the Texas College and University System Coordinating Board by the legislature in 1965 to provide unified planning and development of a comprehensive system of higher education; renamed in 1987. A study made by the Texas Legislative Council in 1950 led to the establishment of a temporary Texas Commission on Higher Education in 1953 to recommend steps for achieving a coordinated system of higher education. That commission urged the founding of a central agency to strengthen the state system of higher education through coordination and leadership of senior colleges and universities. The permanent Texas Commission on Higher Education was authorized in 1955 and given limited statutory authority, primarily in the area of developing formulas for funding public colleges and universities, program approval, and authority to review requests for establishing new wholly state-funded institutions. Establishment of a coordinating board, a high priority of Governor John Connally, was recommended after a yearlong study by a select Governor's Committee on Education Beyond the High School. The board provides statewide leadership in achieving excellence in college education through effective use of resources and the elimination of unnecessary duplication in program offerings, faculties, and campus facilities. Eighteen members, appointed by the governor and approved by the Texas Senate, serve on the board for six-year overlapping terms. No member may be professionally employed in education or serving on the board of a junior college. Members serve without pay. The board administers a number of student financial-aid programs. It appoints the commissioner of higher education as CEO of its staff. *Kenneth Ashworth*

Texas Highways. The official state travel publication; published monthly in Austin. The magazine grew out of the Texas Highway Department employee publication *Maintenance and Construction Bulletin* and originally (November 1953) carried articles about highway design and other intramural subjects. The Texas legislature passed a bill in 1959 authorizing the state to promote tourism, and one ultimate result was that in 1974 *Texas Highways*, under the guidance of editor Frank Lively, became a travel publication for the general public. In 1975 the legislature made it the official state travel publication. By early 1987 total circulation had grown to 400,000; in 1995 subscribers lived in every state and more than 100 countries. *Texas Highways* publishes articles on a wide range of subjects, including tourist attractions; historic events, individuals, and structures; ethnic groups; state and national parks; cooking and recipes; the state's major agricultural enterprises; and folklore and festivals. The magazine emphasizes historical subjects, conservation, and life in the state and has built its reputation on scenic photography. *Texas Highways* is published monthly in Austin.

Frank Lively and Jack Lowry

Texas Historical Commission. Established as the Texas State Historical Survey Committee by the Texas legislature in 1953 to survey, record, preserve, restore, and mark all phases of Texas history by working with and through state, regional, and local groups and individuals. The original 18-member committee was appointed by the governor and was composed of persons who had demonstrated interest in the preservation of Texas heritage. It had the power to prescribe uniform markers, to check the historical accuracy of inscriptions prepared for markers by any individual or group, and to certify the significance of any historic property the state determined to purchase. In 1962 the committee formed the Official Texas Historical Marker Program to record Texas historic sites in all 254 counties. The staff evaluated applications and made recommendations to the State Marker Review Board and then prepared marker inscriptions. State law authorized county judges to appoint county historical survey committees. Texas had 254 such committees in 1966. One of the objectives of the program was to place 5,000 official Texas historical markers in five years—an action deemed necessary because the state had not had an official marking program since the Texas Centennial (1936). A similar program was developed in the 1970s. In 1966 the committee established two special awards to recognize significant restoration or preservation projects— the Texas Restoration Award and the Texas Award for Historical Preservation. After 1968 the committee broadened its scope by conducting the state archeological program, a museum services program, and the National Register of Historic Places programs for the state. In 1973 the organization's name was changed to Texas Historical Commission. The THC administers a number of grant programs, including the Texas Historic Preservation Grant Program, Texas Preservation Trust Fund, and museum grants. It also administers special projects such as the Old San Antonio Road project. The commission's publications department publishes a monthly newsletter, *The Medallion*, and supervises other agency publications. The THC had 78 employees in 1992, when 15,000 volunteers were working with the commission across the state to promote historic preservations. As of that year, more than 11,000 official Texas Historical Markers had been erected. *Truett Latimer and Laurie E. Jasinski*

Texas Historical Records Survey. The Texas part of a nationwide New Deal project that provided employment to historians and others in preparing inventories of historical materials. The survey focused primarily on unpublished records and government documents. Its labyrinthine history in Texas, both under federal and state supervision, lasted from 1936 to 1942. J. Frank Davis, state supervisor of the Federal Writers' Project, began the state effort. The survey renovated and rearranged more than 10 million documents and 362,452 volumes in the state; transcribed 217,323 pages of records dating from 1731; prepared new name or subject indices to 1,169,762 property records and name indices to over four million birth, death, and marriage records; prepared new name indices to supplement the original recordings of 928,900 district and county court records; and inventoried probate papers for 392,450 estates. The probate records material eventually assembled was deposited with the San Jacinto Museum of History. The project compiled and published inventories of all federal archives in Texas. Published inventories of state, county, and municipal archives were contemplated, but only the inventories of 24 Texas county archives were ever published and distributed. Inventories of county archives published before the middle of 1940 contain a map showing the historical evolution of the county's boundary, floor plans of the county courthouse, charts depicting the evolution of county government, and a historical sketch of the county, its governmental organization, and record system. Those inventories published toward the end of the survey's operation contain merely an inventory of the records. In another phase of the survey, Joseph Milton Nance was employed (1938) as first state supervisor of the

American imprints survey to direct the inventory of public libraries in Texas for American imprints published before 1876. The imprints file was used by Ernest W. Winkler, who published a checklist of Texas imprints, 1846–62, in the *Southwestern Historical Quarterly* (April 1943–October 1948). An inventory of newspaper publishers' files in Texas, begun in 1936, was completed by the imprints survey, and a checklist of Texas newspapers to 1939, showing titles, places of publication, and location of files, was published. The historical records survey was a grandiose piece of work nobly conceived but only partially carried out. Its records were stored in the University of Texas Archives. *Joseph Milton Nance*

Texas Indian Commission. Established as the Commission for Indian Affairs in 1965, when the Board for Texas State Hospitals and Special Schools was abolished. At the time, the Alabama–Coushatta Indian Reservation was the only reservation in Texas. In 1967 the Ysleta del Sur Pueblo, or Tigua Indian Community, was added to the act. The Tiguas, from El Paso County, did not gain federal recognition as an Indian tribe until 1968. Under the 1965 act the commission was composed of three members, appointed by the governor, from East Texas. With the addition of the Tiguas the regional qualification was dropped. In 1975 the Commission for Indian Affairs was renamed the Texas Indian Commission. In 1977 the legislature added the Texas Band of the Kickapoo Indians at Eagle Pass to its jurisdiction. The Kickapoos gained federal recognition in 1984. Unlike the other tribes under the commission's jurisdiction, the Kickapoos remained trustees of the federal government and received no state money. The other major change made in 1977 required at least one member of the commission to be an Indian. The commission was initially headquartered at the Alabama–Coushatta Indian Reservation and later moved to Austin. In addition to acting as a link between the tribe and other state agencies, it oversaw the "development of the human and economic resources" of the reservations and assisted the "Texas Indian tribes in improving their health, educational, agricultural, business, and industrial capacities." A major goal of the commission was to help the tribes achieve financial self-sufficiency. The commission was required to have three public meetings a year, one at the Alabama–Coushatta Indian Reservation, one at the Tigua Indian Reservation, and one in the Dallas area, where numerous Indians resided. In 1985 the Alabama–Coushattas and the Tigua Pueblo, dissatisfied with state management of their affairs, petitioned the federal government to extend federal trust protection over their reservations. The federal government approved the request, a move that set in motion the demise of the Texas Indian Commission. In 1989 the commission came up for review under the Sunset Law. Proposed legislation that would have made it an advocacy agency rather than a supervisory one was allowed to die in the legislature. *John R. Wunder*

Texas Institute of Letters. Organized in Dallas at the Texas Centennial exposition, 9 November 1936, on the recommendation of William H. Vann, a professor of English at what is now the University of Mary Hardin–Baylor. In a speech that evening, J. Frank Dobie stated that "great literature transcends its native land, but there is none that I know of that ignores its own soil." Fifty Texans composed the charter list of members, but two of them, Fannie Ratchford and Donald Joseph, declined accep-

tance. Dobie himself at first expressed doubt about the worth of the organization, but after he had become a member he devoted himself to the work. Cokesbury Bookstore in Dallas became an early supporter of the organization and in 1938 began sponsoring annual meetings there. The first book award, in 1939, went to Dobie for *Apache Gold and Yaqui Silver*. In 1946 Carr P. Collins began funding an award of $1,000 for the best Texas book of the year, defined as one on a Texas subject or by a Texas author. Later, this became the nonfiction award when the Jesse H. Jones prize for the same sum was offered by the Houston Endowment for the best book of fiction. Both awards have continued to the present, in increased amounts. Awards funded by other individuals and organizations for poetry, short stories, scholarly authorship, journalism, children's books, and book design have been given. Fifty years after its founding, the institute awarded more than $11,000 annually. Starting in 1967 the institute cosponsored, with the University of Texas at Austin, Dobie–Paisano fellowships consisting of six-month stays, with stipends, at Dobie's 265-acre retreat, Paisano Ranch. With the exception of Katherine Anne Porter, most established Texas writers since 1936 have been associated with the Texas Institute of Letters. Porter never accepted membership. Membership is offered to persons associated with Texas who have been nominated by a member, approved by the council, and elected by the active members. The institute, whose official address varies according to residence of the secretary–treasurer, meets each spring to present awards and transact business. Its sole source of income is dues and contributions. The members are novelists, poets, essayists, historians, journalists, playwrights, and other writers, but the emphasis has always been on authorship of quality. *John Edward Weens*

Texas Instruments. Dallas-based pioneer developer of silicon transistors, integrated circuits, pocket calculators, and semiconductor microprocessors. In the early 1990s TI had 12 major locations in Texas, more than 40 major locations worldwide, and 60,000 employees. Its origins can be traced to Tulsa, Oklahoma, where John Clarence Karcher and Eugene B. McDermott, two physicists who had developed a seismographic process useful in oil exploration, started the Geophysical Research Corporation as a subsidiary of Amerada Petroleum (1924). They moved to Dallas in 1930, started a new company, Geophysical Service, Incorporated, and soon opened another laboratory in New Jersey. At the beginning of World War II GSI president Erik Jonsson, who had been hired to manage the New Jersey lab, realized that oil-exploration technology could also be used for submarine detection, and GSI began manufacturing military electronics for the government. In 1945 Patrick E. Haggerty, formerly a purchaser of GSI's equipment for the United States Navy, joined the company as manager of manufacturing, convinced that the company could exploit the rapidly developing field of military electronics. The company changed its name to Texas Instruments in 1951 and was listed on the New York Stock Exchange in 1953. TI gained a niche in the electronics industry as the first company to develop production techniques for the recently invented transistor. In 1952 Haggerty hired physicist Gordon Teal from Bell Labs, where the transistor had been invented in the late 1940s, to head the development team. To demonstrate the value of its new product, TI produced the first portable transistor radio in 1954 and soon became a primary vendor to rapidly growing IBM. Most early transistors, includ-

Texas Instruments engineer Jack St. Clair Kilby with an early integrated circuit, Dallas, ca. 1959. Courtesy Texas Instruments, Dallas. Texas Instruments became the leader in the expanding electronics industry in the late 1950s and opened a 250-acre plant in Dallas. The integrated circuit revolutionized computers.

ing those in TI's portable radios, were made from germanium. But TI engineers, against conventional wisdom, surprised the industry in 1954 by announcing production of two types of silicon transistors, developed by a team headed by Willis Adcock. By 1956, TI had total sales of $45 million, up from $3 million in 1946, and led the industry in transistor sales.

TI's early experience with silicon transistors paved the way for the invention of the silicon-based integrated circuit in 1958 by TI engineer Jack Kilby, whose concept allowed entire circuits, not simply transistors, to be made from silicon. The following year Robert Noyce of Fairchild Semiconductor in California developed an economical process for production of Kilby's circuit, and after a 10-year legal battle the two companies settled on joint patent agreements. Kilby is credited with the idea of integrating components on a silicon chip, and Noyce, who became a founder of Intel Corporation in 1968, is credited with conceiving a practical way to connect the miniature components. In 1959, in its only major merger, TI merged with the Metals and Controls Corporation of Attleboro, Massachusetts. During the 1950s the company moved into other areas, including metallurgical products, missile-guidance systems, and specialized computers. Intent on branching out into consumer electronics, chief executive Haggerty launched a research and development program in 1965 to build the first portable hand-held calculator. TI introduced that product in 1971. The same year the company received

the first patent on a microprocessor, a true "computer on a chip." Unlike dedicated integrated circuits, the first microprocessors, produced that year by both Intel and TI, were flexible and small enough to serve in a wide variety of electronic applications.

During the 1970s and 1980s the company's attempt to move beyond such relatively low-priced consumer electronics as calculators and digital wristwatches yielded mixed results. Intensified foreign and domestic competition and TI's failure to break into the microcomputer market in the early 1980s forced the company to lay off personnel and write off large losses in 1985. Certain sections of the TI microchip business still continued to be profitable, and other contracts, such as the huge ($6.8 billion) navy contract for antiradar missiles awarded to TI in 1983, helped the company to overcome difficulties that would have ruined less diversified companies. In the late 1980s TI began to prosper again, focusing on its older strengths of military and commercial electronics and funding more research and development in the expanding field of artificial intelligence and computer graphics.   *Gary Price*

Texas Iron. For most of the nineteenth century the Texas Iron was the largest collected meteorite in the world; it is still the largest preserved find from Texas. There is some evidence that this meteorite, with several others recovered between the Brazos and Red rivers, is the origin of some frontier stories of silver and precious metals on the Southern Plains. It is first mentioned in 1772 by Athanase de Mézières, who wrote of the Tawakoni Indians' excitement over it. Several Texas Indian groups had some claim to it: a Taovaya asserted in 1808 that he was its discoverer, a Comanche band claimed the land where it had fallen, and the Skidi Pawnees made it one of their deities. Since the prairie Caddos, in particular, had a sky-oriented cosmology involving meteorites, it is not surprising that the Texas Iron became an important healing shrine on the Southern Plains, the object of ceremonies and gifts. The Indian name associated with it, Comanche Po-a-cat-le-pi-le-car-re, means Medicine Rock. The rock seems to have been located in the mesquite hills east of the site of present Albany. Because ownership of it became an issue in United States–Spanish sparring over contraband trade and tribal alignments, the meteorite's story has been preserved. The first whites to see it were Anthony Glass and his party of American traders, on a mustanging expedition that delivered United States flags to Texas Indians in 1808–09. The following year George Schamp, Ezra McCall, and several other traders evaded a Spanish patrol commanded by Capt. José de Goseascochea to acquire it from the Indians in exchange for guns sorely needed against Osage raiders. The belief on the Louisiana–Texas frontier was that the 1,635-pound rock was a gigantic nugget of platinum. By 1814, however, *Bruce's American Mineralogical Journal*, after testing in New York, reported the mass to be an iron-nickel alloy meteorite. In the 1820s Professor Benjamin Silliman of Yale University, who published numerous articles on the Texas Iron in his *American Journal of Science and Arts*, collected documents on its retrieval, including the journals kept by Anthony Glass and John Maley. Silliman, who had first called the meteorite the Louisiana Iron, by the late 1830s had named it the Texas Iron. The Peabody Museum of Natural History at Yale University, where the meteorite presently resides, calls it Red River.   *Dan L. Flores*

Texas League. A professional baseball league. There was great enthusiasm for the national pastime in Texas when the State Base Ball League began in 1888. Charter franchises were located in Austin, Dallas, Fort Worth, Galveston, Houston, and San Antonio (the only charter city still participating in the league in 1990), and New Orleans fielded a replacement team late in the inaugural season. During the formative years clubs sometimes failed to make payrolls, teams folded in midseason, and occasionally the league shut down before the scheduled end of play. The Texas League did not operate in 1891, 1893, 1894, 1900, and 1901, and suspended play during World War II for three seasons. But by the early years of the twentieth century the league was securely established. The Corsicana Oilers of 1902 formed one of the legendary teams of minor league baseball, winning 27 consecutive games, including a record-setting 51 to 3 defeat of Texarkana in which the catcher hit eight home runs. In an era of independent minor league clubs, local owners could maintain a championship team for years. The Fort Worth Panthers led in Texas League history by winning six consecutive pennants from 1920 through 1925. For decades the most popular baseball event in the South was the Dixie Series, a playoff between the champions of the Texas League and of the Southern Association. A procession of great players honed their talents in the Texas League, from Hall of Famers such as Tris Speaker, Al Simmons, Hank Greenberg, Dizzy Dean, Ducky Medwick, Duke Snider, Frank Robinson, and Brooks Robinson, to modern stars like Jack Clark, Fernando Valenzuela, Orel Hershiser, Steve Sax, and Darryl Strawberry. John J. McCloskey is regarded as the "Father of the Texas League." Hall of Fame executive Branch Rickey played in the Texas League in 1904 and 1905. Other key figures have included William B. Ruggles, for decades a league executive, statistician, and historian; J. Doak Roberts, league president, 1921–29; J. Alvin Gardner, president, 1930–53; and Carl Sawatski, president, 1975–91. Numerous old Texas League ballparks offer evocative nostalgia trips for baseball buffs. In 1930 Katy Park in Waco became one of the first stadiums in organized baseball to install lights for night games. Houston's Buff Stadium and Fort Worth's LaGrave Field were showcase stadiums for minor league ball, and when LaGrave Field was rebuilt in 1950 following a fire, it was the first new baseball park to include a television booth. The central grandstand at Dudley Dome (1924) in El Paso was constructed of adobe, a unique feature in a professional ballpark in the United States, while Albuquerque Sports Stadium made available drive-in baseball for more than 100 vehicles per game just above the outfield limits. By 1994 Dudley Dome was no longer in use, and Cohen Stadium, constructed in the late 1980s, was the site of Texas League games.

Minor league baseball has flourished in Texas and flourishes still. Through the first century of the circuit's operation, a total of 38 cities in 8 states hosted Texas League teams. In Texas alone, 101 cities—more than in any other state—have supported minor league franchises. In addition to the Texas League, Texas-based minor leagues have included the Texas Association, East Texas League, Rio Grande Valley League, Panhandle–Pecos Valley League, Texas Valley League, Southwest Texas League, Southwestern League, Middle Texas League, Central Texas Trolley League, South Central League, Texas–Oklahoma League, Sophomore League, Gulf Coast League, Longhorn League, Big State League, and Lone Star League. Most of the important cities of the state have held Texas League franchises. As of 1994 only three Texas cities, San Antonio, El Paso, and Midland, were part of the eight-team Texas League loop; there have been only 15 years in which the Texas League has had an exclusively Texan makeup throughout the season. Shreveport, Alexandria, Lafayette, Lake Charles, and New Orleans have represented Louisiana. Oklahoma City and Tulsa were longtime members of the Texas League, and Ardmore fielded a team on two occasions. Albuquerque, New Mexico, and Memphis, Tennessee, once held franchises. In 1994 members of the league included Jackson, Mississippi; Little Rock, Arkansas; Wichita, Kansas; Shreveport, Louisiana; and Tulsa, Oklahoma.   *Bill O'Neal*

Texas Medical Center. A medical complex in Houston, conceived by the trustees of the M.D. Anderson Foundation in the early 1940s. In 1994 the TMC was the largest medical center in the world, with more than 675 acres and 100 permanent buildings housing 41 member institutions, which included 14 hospitals, 2 medical schools, 4 colleges of nursing, and 6 university systems. The Anderson Foundation planned the first units of the center to be the University of Texas Hospital for Cancer Research and the Baylor University College of Medicine. A 134-acre site of city-owned property, adjacent to the Hermann Hospital grounds and adjoining Hermann Park, passed to the foundation from the city in 1944, after a popular vote authorized the sale in 1943. Texas Medical Center, Incorporated, was organized and received title to the land in 1945, at which time a board of directors assumed responsibility for development and coordination under the leadership of president Ernst William Bertner. Designed to attract institutions related to health education, research, and patient care, the center assembled staffs, provided facilities, and developed programs necessary to assure the highest standards of attainment in medicine. The various programs were directed jointly by independent institutions. Between 1951 and 1955 facilities were completed for University of Texas M.D. Anderson Hospital and Tumor Institute, Methodist Hospital, Arabia Temple Crippled Children's Clinic, Texas Medical Center Library, Texas Children's Hospital, St. Luke's Episcopal Hospital, and the University of Texas Dental Branch. Expansion during 1959 and 1960 included the Texas Institute for Rehabilitation and Research, Houston Speech and Hearing Institute, Houston State Psychiatric Institute for Research and Training, Texas Woman's University, Houston Center, and the Institute of Religion. Between 1962 and 1965 Ben Taub General Hospital, a city–county charity hospital staffed by Baylor University, was completed, as was an addition to Methodist Hospital, which doubled patient care facilities to 700 beds, and the Texas Heart Institute. The City of Houston Department of Public Health opened in 1965. In 1972 the University of Texas Health Science Center at Houston joined the Texas Medical Center. The center also set up the nation's first High School for Health Professions in 1971 and the Life Flight helicopter rescue program at Hermann Hospital in 1976. In the 1980s the center added the University of Houston College of Pharmacy, the Veterans Affairs Medical Center, the Life Gift Organ Donation Center, and the Lyndon B. Johnson General Hospital. In 1993 the center enrolled 76,000 students and had 54,774 employees. TMC is especially known for patient care in heart disease, cancer, and rehabilitation.

Texas Monthly. Michael R. Levy began publishing *Texas Monthly* in February 1973. The magazine, with offices in Austin, has covered a wide variety of topics including state politics and statewide amusements. Nominated for 30 National Magazine Awards by the Columbia University Graduate School of Journalism, the magazine won in 1974 for Outstanding Editorial Achievement in Special Journalism, in 1979 for Reporting, in 1980 for Public Service, again in 1985 for Reporting, in 1990 for Photography and General Excellence, and in 1992 for General Excellence. Annually, the magazine issues the Texas Twenty, a list of the 20 most influential and outstanding Texas citizens. Every two years, following the legislative session, an issue is devoted to the best and worst legislators. In the early 1990s subscribers exceeded 308,000.

Texas Observer. An Austin journal founded in 1954 by J. R. Parton, Frankie Randolph, Minnie Fisher Cunningham, and others to advocate social justice from a progressive perspective. The first editor, Ronnie Dugger, declared the *Observer* to be politically independent. Subsequent editors included Willie Morris (later editor of *Harper's*), Molly Ivins, and Jim Hightower (later Texas commissioner of agriculture). Because of its editorial freedom, literary bent, and liberalism the *Observer* became a haven for work by such writers as William L. Brammer, Larry L. King, Elroy Bode, and Larry McMurtry. Through the years the *Observer* has covered scandals and initiated attention to civil-rights issues. Lyndon Johnson called the *Observer* "Without any question the most 'liberal' publication in my state." *The New Republic* characterized the Texas paper as "The conscience of the political community in Texas." John Kenneth Galbraith described the *Observer* as "A well-researched journal which more orthodox Texas statesmen feel should not have the protection of the First Amendment." The *Observer* has carried little advertising. From 1954 to 1967 Mrs. Randolph made up deficits totaling perhaps $250,000. In 1963 Dugger became the publisher and changed the weekly to a biweekly; by 1967 the paper was self-sustaining, though it began in 1989 to hold benefits in order to remain so.   *Ronnie Dugger*

Texas Old Missions and Forts Restoration Association. Organized in 1961 and incorporated in 1962 as a charitable and educational society to promote the preservation and restoration of Spanish missions and fort sites of Texas. The association has also promoted the restoration of San Juan Bautista, Coahuila. The association convenes at one or more of the historic sites for its annual meeting, at which historical papers are read and authoritative tours of the sites are conducted. Irregular tours of various locales related to Texas history—in Texas, Mexico, and Spain—are also sponsored by the society for its members. Since 1969 the association has published a quarterly newsletter, *El Campanario.* The society also periodically publishes, or makes available for purchase, pictures and plans of mission and fort sites for its members. Beginning in 1993 the association each year gave the Raiford Stripling award for preservation and restoration of historic sites.   *Joseph W. McKnight*

Texas Ornithological Society. Organized in 1953 at Austin, as a result of the promotional efforts of Charles McNeese and his fellow enthusiasts in the Ornithology Group of the Outdoor Nature Club of Houston. The major purposes of the society include the observation, study, and conservation of the birds of Texas and the stimulation of cooperation among ornithologists

of Texas and the Southwest. The scissor-tailed flycatcher was chosen in 1956 as the society's official bird, and the emblem of the society is a flying scissor-tail superimposed on a map of Texas. Field trips held in conjunction with the meetings of the society provide the major means of stimulating fellowship and cooperation among the membership. The society was incorporated in 1964 and granted tax-exempt status in 1974. The first publication of the society was a monthly newsletter providing news of members, the results of Christmas bird counts, migration reports, and other information regarding birds. In March 1967 the newsletter was replaced by a bulletin containing articles of a more technical nature. Since 1974 the society has published both a newsletter and a bulletin. From 1955 through 1978 the McNeese Library of Ornithology was maintained as a memorial to the first president of the society. In 1971 a Texas Bird Records Committee was established to gather distribution records and to maintain a state checklist of birds. This objective is furthered by the maintenance of a photo-record file that documents the occurrence of rare or unusual birds within the state. In 1974 the society published a *Check-list of the Birds of Texas*, which was revised and republished in 1984. Conservation is a major emphasis of the society. The first conservation platform was published in 1958 and has since been periodically revised and updated. In 1988 the society purchased an interest in the upper Texas coast woodlot known as Sabine Woods, thus providing sanctuary status for this important stopover for birds migrating over the Gulf of Mexico. The society also financially supports the study of Texas birds through small research grants and as a cosponsor of the Texas Breeding Bird Atlas Project, which was begun in 1987.   *Stanley D. Casto*

"Texas, Our Texas." The state song; adopted by the legislature in 1929, after a statewide contest; written in 1924 by William J. Marsh of Fort Worth, with lyrics by Marsh and Gladys Yoakum Wright. Alaskan statehood (1959) required modifying "largest and grandest" to "boldest and grandest."   *Charles A. Spain, Jr.*

Texas Palm. *Sabal texana* or *S. mexicana;* a native of the lower Rio Grande valley known also as Texas palmetto, Rio Grande palmetto, *palma real*, and *palma de Micharas.* The stocky palm attains 48 feet and has large, blue-green, fan-shaped leaves that form a thick, rounded crown. Its small white flowers produce an edible, dull-black berry that matures in the summer. The tree has gray to reddish-brown bark and soft reddish-brown wood. The Texas palm has a continuous range extending from the lower Rio Grande valley in Texas through eastern Mexico to Guatemala and to Oaxaca and perhaps farther north on the west coast of Mexico. In 1519 Álvarez de Pineda found a forest of the palms along a river 10 miles south of the site of present Brownsville; the trees were so numerous that he referred to the river, subsequently named the Rio Grande, as the Río de las Palmas. Texas palms were reported along the Rio Grande up to 80 miles inland from the Gulf of Mexico as late as 1852, but by 1925 agricultural clearing had severely reduced the number of the trees in Texas. By 1986 only about 100 acres of Texas palms existed in Texas, most of them clustered in 32 acres of the Audubon Society's Sabal Palm Grove Sanctuary, in Cameron County. Residents of the lower Valley once found a number of uses for the Texas palm—selling the fruit, making chair seats and roof thatching, and using the trunks as wharf posts. Texas palms have also been used as ornamental plants in parks and along streets in many southwestern Texas towns.   *Carl C. Wright*

Texas Parade. Began in 1936 as a monthly magazine that highlighted the Texas highway system; later included many subjects of interest concerning Texas, and still later focused solely on business. The magazine was originally sponsored by the Texas Good Roads Association, a voluntary, nonpolitical, nonprofit association of about 25,000 members concerned with the preservation of motor-vehicle taxes for highway construction and maintenance. It probably grew out of *Texas Good Roads Magazine*, which was published in San Marcos by the association from December 1916 to February 1918. *Texas Parade* was endorsed by the Texas Highway Department and was originally published in Houston. The founders included Buck Schiwetz as art director. Publication was interrupted from May 1943 until May 1948, when the editorial offices reopened in Austin. Though it was still focused on highway matters, the *Parade* now covered travel, history, and personalities. Topics expanded to include business, industry, and sports. The magazine became independent of the association in late 1955 and moved the corporate offices to San Antonio. In the early 1970s the *Parade* began to take more of a hard-news line and became known for its business and political analysis and coverage of topical subjects, including the newly passed liquor-by-the-drink laws and the state's probable stand on the proposed Equal Rights Amendment to the United States Constitution. By the late 1970s it was subtitled "The Business Magazine of Texas." Although not an official publication of the state, it was cited numerous times by the state legislature for outstanding promotion of Texas. The last issue of *Texas Parade* as an independent publication came out in March 1978. The magazine then merged with *Texas Business* to become *Texas Business & Texas Parade.* It was renamed simply *Texas Business* for the November 1978 issue and ceased publication in August 1988.   *W. W. Bennett*

Texas Parks and Wildlife Department. Established by the state legislature in 1963; consolidated the Texas Game and Fish Commission and the State Parks Board. The department is governed by the Texas Parks and Wildlife Commission, which is appointed by the governor. In the 1960s its immediate task was to improve the state park system by refurbishing existing facilities and acquiring new land. In 1967 voters passed a $75 million bond package to assist in parkland acquisition. Park entrance fees were instituted the next year to help retire the bond. In 1971 the legislature approved a one-cent tax on cigarettes to generate funds for park development. Between 1968 and 1976, the total amount of parkland owned by the state grew from 62,000 acres to nearly 117,000. During the 1960s the department was made responsible for the administration of the Texas Water Safety Act and for the Land and Water Conservation Fund. Also during the 1960s the state joined the Federal Aid to Commercial Fisheries research and development program, and the department renovated several of its fish hatcheries. In 1965 the department changed the name of its magazine from *Texas Game and Fish* to *Texas Parks and Wildlife.* When the Texas Endangered Species Act was adopted in 1973, the Texas Parks and Wildlife Department implemented it. In 1985 the department began Project WILD, a conservation-education program for public schools. By the late 1980s the park system included 129 parks, natural areas, and historic sites. The department was responsible for the protection and management of the fish population in more than 600 public reservoirs, 16,000 miles of streams and rivers, and 370 miles of coastline. It investigated pollution and participated in proceedings involving pollution, development, or other influences on fish or wildlife. The department employed more than 500 game wardens to enforce hunting and fishing regulations and park-safety laws. In the 1990s more than 20 million people visited Texas parks each year, and the legislature appropriated more than $102,000,000 annually to finance the operation of the Texas Parks and Wildlife Department.   *Vivian Elizabeth Smyrl*

Texas Quarterly. Originated by Harry Ransom and first published in February 1958; sought a balance among the sciences, social sciences, humanities, and fine arts. Despite its name, it was not designed to pursue regional or provincial interests alone. In its volumes leading scientists, novelists, poets, critics, scholars, statesmen, businessmen, architects, photographers, and artists had their say, delivering what the reviewer for the London *Times Literary Supplement* described as "crisp, topical essays rather than the refurbished bottom-drawer stuff." Writers included Robert Graves, Samuel Beckett, Allen W. Dulles, Frank Lloyd Wright, Aaron Copland, Robert Penn Warren, Allen Tate, J. B. Priestley, Angus Wilson, W. H. Auden, Stephen Spender, Marianne Moore, Octavio Paz, Eudora Welty, Katherine Anne Porter, Ignazio Silone, Jorge Luis Borges, Dean Rusk, and Lyndon B. Johnson. The publication also produced special numbers on Mexico, Spain, Italy, Britain, and Australia, and on the art of South America. Supplements were later issued as books, among them the *Centennial Celebration of Baudelaire's "Les Fleurs du Mal."* Paintings, drawings, engravings, and photographs by many artists, some especially commissioned by the periodical, were included. The last issue appeared in 1978.   *Thomas M. Cranfill*

Texas Rangers. In 1823, only two years after Anglo-American colonization formally began in Texas, empresario Stephen F. Austin hired 10 experienced frontiersmen as "rangers" for a punitive expedition against a band of Indians. But not until 24 November 1835 did Texas lawmakers institute a specific force known as the Texas Rangers. The organization had a complement of 56 men in three companies, each officered by a captain and two lieutenants, whose immediate superior and leader had the rank of major and was subject to the commander in chief of the regular army. The major was responsible for enlisting recruits, enforcing rules, and applying discipline. Officers received the same pay as United States dragoons and privates—$1.25 a day; however, they supplied their own mounts, equipment, arms, and rations. At all times they had to be ready to ride, equipped "with a good and sufficient horse . . . [and] with one hundred rounds of powder and ball."

    Even with such official sanctions, the rangers did not fare especially well at first. During the Texas Revolution they served sparingly as scouts and couriers, then carried out a number of menial tasks. As settlers fled east to escape advancing Mexican armies after the fall of the Alamo on 6 March 1836, the rangers retrieved cattle, convoyed refugees across muddy trails and swollen streams, and destroyed produce or equipment left behind. In fact, during the battle of San Jacinto on 21 April, they were on "escort" duty, much to their chagrin. Nor did their situation improve appreciably over the next two years, since President Sam Houston favored government economy as well as friendship with the Indians. In December 1838, however, Mirabeau B. Lamar succeeded to the presidency and immediately changed the frontier policies of the republic as well as the role of the rangers. At his behest, Congress allowed him to recruit eight companies of mounted volunteers and maintain a company of 56 rangers, then a month later to provide for five similar companies in Central and South Texas. Over the next three years the rangers waged all-out war against the Indians, successfully participating in numerous pitched battles. The most notable were the Cherokee War in East Texas in July 1839, the Council House Fight at San Antonio against the Comanches in March 1840, and the battle of Plum Creek (near the site of present-day Lockhart) against 1,000 Comanche warriors in August 1840. By the end of the Lamar administration, Texans had undermined, if not broken, the strength of the most powerful tribes. Houston, upon being reelected to the presidency in December 1841, realized that ranger companies were the least expensive and the most efficient way to protect the frontier. As a result, 150 rangers under Capt. Jack Hays figured prominently in helping repel the Mexican invasions of 1842 and in successfully protecting Texans against Indian attacks over the next three years. Hays initiated ranger traditions and esprit de corps by recruiting and training a tough contingent of men skilled in frontier warfare. Out of his command arose such famous ranger captains as Ben and Henry McCulloch, Samuel H. Walker, Bigfoot Wallace, and Robert Addison (Ad) Gillespie.

With annexation and the Mexican War in 1846, the rangers achieved worldwide fame as a fighting force. After acquitting themselves admirably during the battles of Palo Alto and Resaca de la Palma in May 1846, they became Gen. Zachary Taylor's "eyes and ears." Superbly mounted, "armed to the teeth" with a large assortment of weapons, and clearly at home in the desert wastes of northeastern Mexico, they found the "most practical route" for the American army to Monterrey. Late in September the rangers rashly set the tempo and style for Taylor's successful storming of the city. Although furloughed in October after a brief armistice, they returned early in 1847 in time to provide the general enough military information to help win the battle of Buena Vista in February. In March 1847 the theater of war shifted. An American army under Gen. Winfield Scott landed at Veracruz and quickly muscled its way into the Valley of Mexico. For the next five months the rangers under Jack Hays and Samuel Walker figured prominently in American victories. In fact, so ruthless and lethal were they against Mexican guerrillas that a hostile but fearful populace called them "los diablos Tejanos."

After the Mexican War ended on 2 February 1848, the rangers declined in importance. Since the United States had rightly assumed responsibility for protecting the Texas frontier, the rangers had no official function. Nor did the state try to enlist their services. The organization thus lost its famous captains as well as the nucleus of its frontier defenders. But after the appointment of John S. Ford as senior captain in January 1858, the rangers briefly upheld their fighting traditions. Late in the spring they moved north of the Red River to "chastise" a large band of "hostiles," in the process killing the noted Comanche chief Iron Jacket. Then in March 1859 Ford and his men were assigned to the Brownsville area, where, together with the

United States Army, they gained only limited success against the "Red Robber of the Rio Grande," Juan N. Cortina. For 14 years after this campaign, however, the rangers ceased to be either significant or effective. With the coming of the Civil War in 1861, they rushed individually to the Confederate colors. Although the Eighth Texas Cavalry was known as Terry's Texas Rangers, its founder, Benjamin F. Terry, was never a member of the state organization, nor did he necessarily recruit experienced fighters. To protect its frontiers the state had to rely on young boys, old men, or rejects from Confederate conscription. Subsequently, during Reconstruction (1865–74), either the United States army or the State Police were responsible for carrying out such duties, though they had little success.

But in 1874 the state Democrats returned to power, and so did the rangers. Texas was "overrun with bad men," with Indians ravaging the western frontier, with Mexican bandits pillaging and murdering along the Rio Grande. The legislature authorized two unique military groups to meet this emergency. The first was the Special Force of Rangers under Capt. Leander H. McNelly. In 1874 he and his men helped curb lawlessness engendered by the deadly Sutton–Taylor Feud in Dewitt County. In the spring of 1875 they moved into the Nueces Strip (between Corpus Christi and the Rio Grande) to combat Cortina's "favorite bravos." After eight months of fighting, the rangers had largely restored order, if not peace, in the area. In 1875 the Special Force enhanced its fearful reputation by stacking 12 dead rustlers "like cordwood" in the Brownsville square as a lethal response to the death of one ranger; McNelly also precipitated the "Las Cuevas War," wherein he violated international law by crossing the Rio Grande, attacking Mexican nationals, and retrieving stolen American cattle. The second military unit, designated the Frontier Battalion, was equally effective. Composed of six companies (with 75 rangers in each) under Maj. John B. Jones, the battalion participated in 15 Indian battles in 1874 and, together with the United States Cavalry, destroyed the power of the fierce Comanches and Kiowas by the end of 1875. The battalion also "thinned out" more than 3,000 Texas desperados such as bank robber Sam Bass and notorious gunfighter John Wesley Hardin; therefore, because of its very efficiency, the Frontier Battalion was no longer necessary after 1882.

For the next three decades the rangers retreated before the onslaught of civilization, their prominence and prestige waning as the need for frontier law enforcement lessened. They occasionally intercepted Mexican and Indian marauders along the Rio Grande, contended with cattle thieves, especially in the Big Bend country and the Panhandle, and at times protected blacks from white lynch mobs. By 1900 such relative inactivity persuaded critics to urge the curtailment, if not complete abandonment, of the rangers. As a result, in 1901, the legislature cut the force to four companies, each headed by a captain who could recruit no more than 20 men. Only because of the leadership and valor of such captains as J. A. Brooks, William Jesse McDonald, John H. Rogers, and John R. Hughes were the rangers able to maintain their existence—and traditions—during the lean years of the 1890s and early 1900s.

Violence and brutality soon increased along the Rio Grande, however, where the rangers continued to participate in numerous bloody brush fights with Mexican nationals. In 1910 a revolution against President Porfirio Díaz unsettled the populace on both sides of the border. In 1914, early in World War I, problems in the border country focused on Mexican nationalism, German intrigue and sabotage, and American draft dodgers. Then in 1916 Pancho Villa's raid on Columbus, New Mexico, intensified already harsh feelings between the two countries. The regular rangers, along with hundreds of special rangers appointed by Texas governors, killed approximately 5,000 Hispanics between 1914 and 1919, a source of scandal, embarrassment, and charges of brutality. In January 1919, at the insistence of Representative José T. Canales of Brownsville, the legislature overhauled the force in order to restore public confidence. During the next two months sordid stories of ranger brutality and debauchery and injustice emerged. As a result, Texas lawmakers decided to maintain the four companies but reduce the number of recruits from 20 to 15 per unit. To attract "men of high moral character" they instituted more competitive salaries, but with minimal expense accounts. They also established specific procedures for citizen complaints. After these reforms the force performed well during the 1920s, especially under the leadership of captains William L. Wright, Thomas R. Hickman, and Frank Hamer. After the enactment of Prohibition the rangers constantly patrolled the Rio Grande against tequila smugglers and cattle rustlers. They protected federal inspectors from bodily harm in the so-called "tick war" in East Texas, prevented both individual injury and property damage in labor flare-ups or Ku Klux Klan demonstrations, and tamed the lawless oil boomtowns of Miranda City, Desdemona, Mexia, Wink, and Borger.

With the Great Depression (1929–), ranger fortunes began to ebb. The legislature had to slash the budget, so that during the depression the force complement never exceeded 45. As for transportation, the rangers depended on free railroad passes or their own horses along the border. In the fall of 1932 they made a grave error in judgment: they openly supported Governor Ross Sterling against Ma Ferguson in the Democratic primary. In January 1933, upon taking office, Ma fired every partisan ranger—44 in all. The legislature then slashed salaries and budgets and further reduced the force to 32 men. Texas consequently became a haven for the lawless—the likes of Raymond Hamilton, George "Machine Gun" Kelly, and Bonnie and Clyde.

In 1935, however, James Allred became governor on a platform of better law enforcement. The legislature established the Texas Department of Public Safety. A three-person Public Safety Commission was responsible for selecting a director and an assistant director, who, in turn, oversaw three basic units: the Texas Rangers, the Highway Patrol, and a scientific crime laboratory and detection center known as the Headquarters Division. The rangers therefore became an important part of a much larger law-enforcement team. Their basic five-company structure remained intact, but changes occurred in hiring and promotion procedures. All appointments were now through examinations and recommendations, not by political patronage; each applicant had to be between 30 and 45, stand at least 5'8", and be "perfectly sound" in mind and body. Upon acceptance, each received instructions in the latest techniques of fingerprinting, communications, ballistics, and records. Each had to be a "crack shot." Although the commission established no educational provisions, each ranger had to take a written examination and submit an "intelligent" weekly report of his activities. As for promotion, seniority and performance were the all-determining factors.

For several years the rangers were apprehensive about their future because of leadership changes in the DPS. But late in September 1938, with the appointment of Col. Homer Garrison, Jr., as the new director, the rangers regained their high status. Over the next 30 years—the Garrison era—the rangers became the plainclothesmen of the DPS: they were the detectives, and the Highway Patrol officers were the uniformed state police. The rangers also expanded to six companies (each with a captain and a sergeant), with an overall complement of 45 men in 1941, 51 in 1947, and 62 in 1961. They were actually a rural constabulary, with most of the officers stationed individually in small Texas towns. The governor, however, could assign them to a case anywhere in the state. The rangers were skilled in using the modern scientific laboratory of the Headquarters Division. During the Garrison era the rangers operated at peak performance, thereby enhancing their prestige. In World War II, they rounded up enemy aliens and instructed civilians and local police in the latest defense techniques to protect generating plants, dams, factories, and industries from sabotage, while carrying out their regular duties. In the 1950s they investigated more than 8,000 cases annually. And in the 1960s their caseload increased because of the civil-rights movement and the emergence of a more populous, urban state.

When Garrison died in 1968, the DPS commissioners again reorganized and redefined ranger guidelines. Under Garrison's successor, Col. Wilson E. Speir, the force expanded to 73 men in 1969, 82 in 1971, 88 in 1974, and 94 a year later. The rangers also were highly trained and better equipped. Recruits had to be between the ages of 30 and 50, have at least eight years of on-the-job police experience, and have an intermediate certificate signifying 400 to 600 hours of classroom instruction. The DPS provided the rangers with high-powered cars equipped with the latest radio equipment as well as with a large array of sophisticated weapons and defensive armor. The state also began paying better salaries, together with such benefits as longevity pay, hospitalization insurance, and a paid life-insurance policy. As a result, the rangers evolved into the elite of Texas law enforcement. During the Garrison era such captains as Manuel T. "Lone Wolf" Gonzaullas, Alfred Y. Allee, Bob Crowder, Johnny Klevenhagen, Eddie Oliver, and Clint Peoples were instrumental in maintaining ranger tradition and performance. Subsequently, captains Bill Wilson, J. L. "Skippy" Rundell, H. R. "Lefty" Block, and Maurice Cook continued to improve the force. The training was intensified, the weaponry and crime-detection equipment became even more sophisticated, and, despite increasing case loads, the applicant list for ranger service grew. In recognition of the rangers' toughness against the criminal element and their dedication to state law enforcement, the legislature enlarged the overall complement to 99 officers (including two women) in September 1993 and again increased salaries and fringe benefits. By September 1996 the force had expanded to 105.

Ben H. Procter

Texas Rangers. An American League baseball team, headquartered in Arlington.; formerly the Washington Senators. Major league baseball came to the Dallas–Fort Worth area in 1972 when Arlington mayor Tom Vandergriff persuaded franchise owner Robert Short to move the team. After a poor first year, the great Ted Williams, the Rangers' first manager, stepped down. The 1973 season was even worse, as the club suffered through a 57–105 record and went through three managers. The highlight of the

season came in June when the first sellout crowd in Arlington Stadium history saw newly drafted 18-year-old David Clyde win his debut over the Minnesota Twins. Clyde's career quickly fizzled, however. In 1974 Short sold the club to a group headed by plastics tycoon Bradford Corbett. This transfer sparked an upswing on the field, as the club finished with a record of 84–76. This 27-game turnaround over the previous year earned Billy Martin the league's manager of the year award. First baseman Mike Hargrove was named rookie of the year, and outfielder Jeff Burroughs became the third player in major league history to be named a league's most valuable player in his second full season of play. Ferguson Jenkins also won a franchise record and league-leading 25 games. But in the next season the Rangers reverted to form, and Martin was fired in mid-season. The 1976 season was more of the same. Contrary to expectations, 1977 turned into the franchise's most successful season to date. Despite going through four managers, including Eddie Stanky for one game, the Rangers won 94 games and finished second in their division. The club slipped to 87 wins the next season but again finished second in the division. This pattern continued through the strike-shortened 1981 season, with the team having respectable records but never finishing higher than second. By this time, Fort Worth oilman Eddie Chiles had bought the club, and the Rangers plummeted in talent and record throughout the first half of the decade. The hiring of manager Bobby Valentine in 1986 saw a brief upswing, followed by two sixth-place finishes. The 1989 season saw the arrival of superstar Nolan Ryan, as well as emerging superstar Ruben Sierra. The club won 83 games. A group headed by George W. Bush had purchased the team, and fans were turning out in large numbers. The first half of the 1990s again saw some Rangers success. In 1992 and 1993 Juan Gonzalez won back-to-back league home run titles. In 1994 the highlight of the franchise's 22-year stay in Texas was finally unveiled when the Ballpark in Arlington was opened. Pitcher Kenny Rogers christened the premier ballpark in July of that year with the first perfect game by a left-hander in American League history. In 1998, when the team was owned by Tom Hicks, the Rangers won the Western Division title. The fans have accordingly embraced their team and become one of the most loyal fandoms in baseball.
Eric M. Pfeifle

Texas Regulars. A group of anti-Roosevelt Democrats who split with the Democratic party. Some Democrats resented the proliferation of government bureaus and the growth of the labor movement under the New Deal, as well as wartime restrictions, particularly the fixed prices of oil and gas. They wanted the state Democratic convention to select independent presidential electors, nominal Democrats who would decline to cast their electoral votes for Roosevelt in an effort to throw the election into the House of Representatives, where the South would have the numerical advantage. These Democrats captured the state convention in Austin on 23 May 1944 and chose electors and national delegates who would vote for Roosevelt only if the two-thirds rule, which required a two-thirds percentage of delegates for the Democratic party's presidential nomination, were restored. This plan would have strengthened the position of the South at the convention, but it had no chance of adoption at the national Democratic convention. Some of the anti–New Dealers, led by business magnate Eugene B. Germany, attempted to gain control over federal patronage in Texas by offering their electoral

votes to the Democrats. The anti-Roosevelt electors, however, were replaced with New Deal Democrats at the second Texas state convention in September 1944. They then established the Texas Regulars, hoping to divert enough Democratic votes to prevent Roosevelt from defeating Republican Thomas E. Dewey. Senator W. Lee O'Daniel, Congressman Martin Dies, and a number of oil and corporate kingpins spearheaded the movement. The Regulars opposed the New Deal and the labor unions and called for the restoration of states' rights and the white primary. Fund-raising groups sprang up, including the Committee for Constitutional Government and O'Daniel's Common Citizens Radio Committee. Although they were presented as educational organizations, these groups appeared to congressional investigators to violate the Corrupt Practices Act. The Regulars, with no candidate, polled about 12 percent of the vote, while Roosevelt received about 72 percent. The Regulars disbanded officially in the spring of 1945. Their leadership formed the nucleus of the 1948 Dixiecrat movement's leadership, disturbed by President Harry Truman's civil-rights program and even more by his position that the oil lands off the Texas coast were federal rather than state property. Liberal Democrats lost out again in the first state convention, bounced back with Governor Beauford H. Jester's help in the second one, and prompted the Dixiecrats to bolt the party in support of South Carolina governor Strom Thurmond for the presidency. The Dixiecrats finished third in Texas behind the Democrats and Republicans. The Texas Regular Dixiecratic leaders became Eisenhower Democrats in the 1950s and Republicans in the 1960s and 1970s.
George N. Green

Texas School for the Blind and Visually Impaired. In Austin; established as the Asylum for the Blind by the legislature in 1856. In 1905 the legislature changed the name to Blind Institute, and in 1915 the name Texas School for the Blind was adopted. White (including Hispanic) children between the ages of 6 and 19 were admitted by direct application to the superintendent. A fee of five dollars a week was required of those able to pay; indigents were taken free of charge. By legislative provision there was no charge for board. The school opened in a leased residence in 1857 and operated in various other quarters until 1917, when legislative appropriations enabled the institution to move to its present location. Continued appropriations have expanded the physical plant and kept it in excellent condition. The school is built on the cottage plan, with the main school building in the center. The function of the institution is to educate the blind of the state to become selfsupporting citizens. A 12-grade school offers courses similar to those offered in public schools. In 1953 oversight of the school was transferred to the Texas Education Agency. The TSB is an independent school district and participates in state and county scholastic appropriations. In the late 1960s the school was integrated and consolidated with the former Texas Blind, Deaf, and Orphan School. In the mid-1990s the school was governed by a nine-member board; three members had to be blind or visually impaired, three the parents of a blind or visually impaired person, and three experienced in working with blind or visually impaired persons. The current name of the school was adopted in 1989.
James W. Markham

Texas School for the Deaf. A state school established by the legislature in 1856 as the Texas Deaf and Dumb Asylum on a rented tract in south Austin. The school opened with three students in 1857 and grew slowly. Superintendent Jacob van Nostrand asked for funds to begin construction of a carefully designed campus. The 1858 legislature appropriated $5,000 for the purchase of the rented property and for construction. During the Civil War the school had no money for salaries; teachers and students supported themselves by farming and by making clothes from the wool of the sheep that they raised. A total of 60 students attended the school during its first 13 years. A change in the law in 1876 allowed the governor, rather than the board of trustees, to appoint the school's superintendent. Two superintendents who served during this period were Henry E. McCulloch and John S. Ford. In spite of a high turnover rate among the faculty, the school made good progress in areas such as vocational instruction. Among other new programs, the school's first monthly publication, *The Texas Mute Ranger*, forerunner of the *Lone Star*, was established in 1878. In 1883 the legislature gave the power to appoint the superintendent back to the trustees in an effort to make the position less political. A substantial building program, begun in 1875, was completed in the late 1880s. In 1893 the method of instruction at the school was changed from a strictly manual form of communication to a combined manual and oral system, and an oral department was instituted to give students a chance to develop any speech ability they might have. A deaf–blind department was organized at the school in 1900 and was maintained until 1934, when it was transferred to the Texas School for the Blind.

In 1919 the legislature established the Board of Control and placed it in charge of the deaf school. By 1923 the Texas facility was reported to be the second-largest school for the deaf in the country. It had 450 students in the mid-1940s and offered courses in a variety of trades in addition to academic instruction. Acoustic work for children with residual hearing was instituted as part of the academic training. In 1949 control of the school was given to the new Board for Texas State Hospitals and Special Schools, and the name of the facility was changed to Texas School for the Deaf. The school had gone by this name informally for years. Tensions rose, however, because the school was still categorized as an eleemosynary institution rather than an educational one. Students and teachers alike resented the stigma that society attached to "charity cases." In 1951 the legislature reclassified the school and placed it under the jurisdiction of the Texas Education Agency. The school claimed the distinction of being the oldest public school in continuous operation in the state. Beginning in 1955 several of the old buildings on campus were razed, and a completely new physical plant was built. The School for the Deaf merged with the Texas Blind, Deaf, and Orphan School in 1965. The two facilities were integrated during 1966, and the Blind, Deaf, and Orphan School became the East Campus of the School for the Deaf. The East Campus housed the school's programs in early childhood and elementary education, as well as the department for multi-handicapped deaf students. In 1981 the Texas School for the Deaf became an independent school district and was also made a state agency. It served as a resource center for other deaf-education programs. Also in 1981 Victor Galloway became the school's first deaf superintendent. In contrast to the days when deaf children were taught only certain crafts and trades, society had begun to accept that the deaf could make significant contributions. Careers in such fields as computers, teaching, and law were becoming available, and

between 40 and 60 percent of the school's graduates went on to attend a college or technical school. *Vivian Elizabeth Smyrl*

Texas Southern University. A historically black, state-supported institution established by the Texas legislature in 1947 under the name Texas State University for Negroes; took over Houston College for Negroes. The intent of the legislature was to offer African Americans a segregated university equivalent to the University of Texas. Efforts for a black university in Houston had begun in the nineteenth century when Rev. John H. Yates tried unsuccessfully to have Bishop College located in Houston, then joined other black Houstonians in organizing Houston College, also known as Houston Baptist Academy (1885). This institution, at which almost all students were in primary or secondary school, closed by the early 1920s. In 1925 Wiley College, with the support of the Houston school board, began offering extension classes for teachers in the city's black high school. With the support of school superintendent E. E. Oberholtzer, the Houston School Board voted to establish a junior college system in the city (1927), of which Houston Colored Junior College was a component. HCJC had more than 700 students in 1934 and became a four-year college the next year. It originally held classes during the evening in Jack Yates High School in the Third Ward.

In 1946 Houston College for Negroes moved to a permanent campus southeast of downtown Houston—land donated by Hugh Roy Cullen. A year later the college and its facilities were acquired by the State of Texas. The impetus of *Sweatt v. Painter* led the state to establish Texas State University for Negroes (1947). Because the goal of blacks in Houston was to end segregation, many considered the establishment of this segregated institution a mixed blessing. TSCN opened with 2,303 students. Initially it offered programs in the College of Arts and Sciences, the School of Vocational and Industrial Education, the Graduate School, and the School of Law. In 1949 the School of Pharmacy was added; in 1965 the university expanded to include a School of Business, and six years later a School of Education. That same year the School of Vocational and Industrial Education was renamed the School of Technology. In 1951 a delegation of students went to Austin to petition the legislature to remove the phrase "for Negroes" from the name of their university. After debate with opponents, the institution was renamed Texas Southern University. Under President Ralphael O'Hara Lanier (1948–55) the institution was harshly criticized, since its rationale had been undercut by the *Sweatt* decision: separate was intrinsically unequal. Lanier was accused of undermining the Law School, of fiscal mismanagement, of violating academic freedom, and of being a Communist. Nevertheless, the university grew. Under succeeding presidents the students took the lead in organizing sit-in demonstrations to force desegregation of public facilities in Houston, and a violent confrontation with police occurred (1967). The desegregation of white state universities in Texas raised ongoing questions about the continued existence of a university for blacks. Furthermore, designation of the neighboring University of Houston as a state university (1963) had brought fears that TSU might be absorbed by UH.

In 1973 the legislature designated TSU "a special purpose institution of higher education for urban programming," thus giving the institution a new *raison d'être*. In 1974 the university received authority to offer a doctorate in education. In 1984 it added a doctoral program in pharmacy and a degree in accounting. In the 1990s TSU enrolled more than 10,000 students and was organized into seven schools and colleges: the College of Arts and Sciences, the College of Pharmacy and Health Sciences, the Thurgood Marshall School of Law, the College of Education, the School of Technology, the Jesse Jones School of Business, and the Graduate School. It confers baccalaureate degrees in 78 areas, as well as numerous graduate degrees. The TSU library houses the Heartman Collection on African American history and culture, the Barbara Jordan papers, and the Mickey Leland archives. TSU also conducts research under numerous auspices, including the Minority Cancer Education Center, the Mickey Leland Center on World Hunger and Peace, and the Minority Biomedical Research Support Program. *Cary D. Wintz*

Texas Southmost College. In Brownsville; opened as Brownsville Junior College in 1926. In 1947 the institution acquired a site at the newly deactivated Fort Brown. The first classes were held on the new campus in 1948. In 1949 the Southmost Union Junior College District was established and the school was renamed Texas Southmost College. Complete separation of TSC from the public schools took place in 1950. In addition to several buildings obtained from the War Assets Administration, the college district built the Pink Bollworm Research Center and other facilities. The Civic Center, owned by the city, was on the campus and was used jointly by the city and the college. The administration and natural sciences were housed in a former hospital complex, later referred to as Gorgas Science Center, a historical landmark. In 1973 Texas Southmost College established a four-year extension program in Brownsville with Pan American University. The school, Pan American University—Brownsville, opened in 1973; it became a separate entity in 1977. In September 1991 Texas Southmost College entered into a partnership with the school, now known as the University of Texas at Brownsville.

Texas and Southwestern Cattle Raisers Association. The oldest and largest such organization in the United States; begun at Graham, Texas, 15 February 1877, under the name Stock-Raisers' Association of North-West Texas. Cattlemen in Oklahoma, New Mexico, and Indian Territory were invited to join. The call for the initial meeting had been made by leading cattlemen, among whom were James C. Loving and C. C. Slaughter. The immediate objective was to systematize the "spring work" and to curb cattle rustling. Col. C. L. (Kit) Carter was made chairman of the organizational meeting, which was held at the courthouse in Graham. Among the ranchers present was Samuel Burk Burnett. Carter was elected president and Loving was elected secretary. Such strong measures against cattle thieves were proposed at the original meeting that some present did not take membership for fear of retaliation by the lawless element. The association was incorporated in 1882. That year the system of assessment "per head" of cattle was adopted; it is still in force. In 1883 the inspection system was inaugurated. Inspectors were eventually located along the trails, at shipping points, and at terminal markets. This practice resulted in recovery of many cattle that by accident or design got into the wrong herds. The protection offered by this system drew small and large operators into the association fold, including Robert Justus Kleberg of the King Ranch and the Kokernots of West Texas. The association offered rewards to those who fingered thieves of

members' livestock (payable after conviction). In addition, from 1893 to the mid-twentieth century the association employed a staff attorney to assist with prosecution and other matters. The association listed 730,000 cattle in 1883 and 1,385,303 in 1895. By 1893 membership had so spread that the name was changed to Cattle Raisers Association of Texas. The present name was adopted in 1921, when the organization merged with the only other regional cattlemen's group remaining in Texas, the Panhandle and Southwestern Stockman's Association, which had been founded in 1880.

In 1945 membership stood at 6,000 and represented 3,500,000 cattle. Rains in 1957 brought an end to one of the Southwest's most severe and widespread droughts and resulted in a resurgence of membership, which reached a new high of 13,000. In the late 1950s the association's officers went to Florida to observe the results of screwworm eradication in the Southeast and to bring about screwworm eradication in the Southwest. The program, financed in the beginning largely from voluntary contributions by the stock industry, was perhaps of more benefit to livestock producers than any other program in the twentieth century. Working through and with the Southwest Animal Health Research Foundation and government agencies, the association played a major role in the program, which brought about an end to the pest through release of millions of radiation-sterilized screwworm flies. In 1961 the association recognized the growing importance of cattle feeding in the Southwest by establishing the cattle feeders' division, and that same year the association established award programs for Four-H members and Future Farmers of America. In little more than a decade the Southwest had become one of the nation's leading cattle-feeding areas. In 1955 there were 227,000 cattle fed in Texas, and in 1969 there were 2½ million head fed, mostly in modern feedlots utilizing tons of Texas-grown grain sorghums. Control of cattle theft continued as one of the primary objectives of the association. In 1943 the secretary of agriculture had made the association the brand-inspection agency for Texas cattle, a responsibility that significantly expanded its operations. In 1966 mechanization of the TSCRA brand records was initiated. Machines were installed to transcribe and record brand-inspection information received daily from inspectors at markets throughout Texas. Inspection records relating to missing or stolen cattle could also be retrieved speedily from the brand files. This mechanization was a great aid in the detection and apprehension of cattle thieves.

In 1979 the association founded the Texas and Southwestern Cattle Raisers Foundation, a nonprofit organization dedicated to education, research, and charitable activities to promote the cattle industry. In 1991 the field-inspector force, 33 strong, was one of the most important services offered by the association. As specially commissioned Texas Rangers, the inspectors combined legal authority with detective skills and cattle-industry knowledge. Inspectors helped recover nearly $2.5 million worth of livestock and property in 1994. The association also monitored governmental affairs on both state and national levels, representing members' interests in such areas as taxation, farm legislation, immigration, and pesticide regulation. In addition, the association offered members affordable insurance. The *Cattleman*, a monthly magazine begun in 1914, coupled with *News Update*, provided the latest in industry news, trends, and association activities. In 1991 the TSCRA had 17,000 members, predominantly in Texas, representing 2.5 million cattle. The membership

Texas Spring Palace, Fort Worth, 1890. Lithographed poster. Courtesy Mrs. C. W. Hutchison, Fort Worth. Photograph courtesy Amon Carter Museum Archives, Fort Worth; acc. no. 73.71/4. Citizens of Fort Worth organized the Texas Spring Palace, a trade fair begun in May 1890 that allowed Texas counties and cities to exhibit products from "field, forest, orchard and garden."

of the TSCRA extends over several states and includes owners of herds ranging from less than a hundred up to many thousands. Past presidents have included such prominent Texans as John Barclay Armstrong, Richard Mifflin Kleberg, Robert Justus Kleberg, Herbert Lee Kokernot, and Dolph Briscoe, Jr. Don C. King served as secretary and general manager from 1966 until 1995. Offices of the association and of the foundation are in Fort Worth, along with the Cattleman's Museum and the Waggoner Library, a research library for the cattle industry.

Larry Marshall, T. C. Richardson, and Dick Wilson

Texas Spring Palace. A fair in Fort Worth; opened on 29 May 1889. Robert A. Cameron, immigration agent for the Fort Worth and Denver Railway, devised a plan to advertise Texas by displaying all the natural products of the state under one roof in a building intended to rival the Sioux City Corn Palace and Toronto Ice Palace. The idea caught on, and the Spring Palace was built in 31 days. Its exterior walls were painted a dark bronze

green; its roof sported both turnip-shaped cupolas and a massive center dome surpassed in size only by that of the Capitol in Washington; and wheat, cotton, and other products of Texas covered the entire structure. Inside the oriental-style exhibit hall, settlers and investors could find neatly classified samples of most grains, grasses, fruits, vegetables, and minerals produced within the state. Visitors interested in aesthetic pursuits could also tour floral, historic, scientific, and art exhibits or view mosaics depicting Texas scenes—all made from natural products by the women of the state. More than 50 Texas counties contributed to these exhibits. Concerts by the Elgin Watch Factory Band and the Mexican National Band, vocal performances, political and religious orators, dances, and sporting events competed with the exhibits for the visitors' attention. A second season, scheduled for May 1890, proved especially popular but ended catastrophically. In spite of efforts to make the palace fireproof, a flash fire swept through the building on the night of May 30, leveling the structure in a matter of minutes. Although several thousand people were attending a dance in the palace that night, only one life, that of Englishman Al Hayne, was lost. Hayne died as a result of his efforts to save women and children from the burning building. A 15-year-old girl named Ada Large also heroically aided those trapped by the flames and was later given a medal by the city. Although the Spring Palace had hardly had time to establish itself as a power in the state's immigration crusade, contemporaries claimed measurable benefits for both Texas and Fort Worth as a result of the project. Newspapers in St. Louis, Boston, and New York published columns on it, for instance, thus focusing national attention on Texas and Fort Worth. As a result of this publicity, 28 percent of the visitors to the fair came from outside the state. Nevertheless, the Spring Palace was not rebuilt. A new committee was set up in 1900 to draw up plans, and the Fort Worth board of trade voted $10,000 to help. Plans eventually called for a Spring Palace auditorium, speedway, amphitheater, and theater garden. The principal motivation was to compete with the annual State Fair of Texas in Dallas. Eventually, the annual Fort Worth Fat Stock Show grew out of this sentiment, and its success, plus the inability of civic leaders to raise enough money to get the Spring Palace started again, killed the whole idea. The city's central post office and adjacent railroad yards now occupy the Spring Palace site. A monument to Al Hayne stands on Main Street.

Patricia L. Duncan

Texas State Archives. In Austin and regional centers; part of the Texas State Library. The collection comprises documents and records from all periods of Texas history. In 1836, so the Texas documents would not fall into Mexican hands, they were moved from place to place by the ad interim government as Sam Houston's retreating army moved eastward; some records were lost. The archives were subsequently moved frequently, to a succession of Texas capitals—in 1836 to Columbia, in 1837 to Houston, in 1839 to Austin. The Mexican invasions of 1842 caused the attempted move that caused the so-called Archive War. The treasurer's office burned in 1845, but with only slight loss. In 1855 the adjutant general's office burned with the irreparable loss of the muster rolls of the soldiers of the Texas Revolution. The state Capitol burned in 1881, but fortunately, few document were lost. The departments and their records were subsequently crowded into whatever space could be found until the present Capitol was completed in 1888. Concern for the archives motivated the founding of the General Land Office, which consolidated records from other land offices. An attempt at concentration of archives in the state department began in the 1850s, when the Bexar and Nacogdoches archives were transferred whole or in part to Austin and housed as the Spanish Archives. The law establishing the Department of Insurance, Statistics, and History (1876) made the Texas State Library the legal depository of the archives of the state and the office of record for all reports and papers issued by the several departments. Between September 1877 and July 1879, many documents were transferred, chiefly from the state department. After the building of the Capitol, the transfer of archives started anew and continued. Most republic-era records held by the secretary of state went to the State Library in 1904–05. More archival records were transferred in the 1930s and 1940s, when crowded conditions in the Capitol forced the departments to make room for current records.

In 1933, to alleviate the "congested condition" of state departments and to provide for management of records, the legislature instituted the Bureau of Records, under the supervision of the Board of Control. The bureau was located in the basement of the DeWitt C. Greer Building, where it provided fireproof storage and access to noncurrent records for the agencies. The space freed in the Capitol basement was allotted to the Archives and History Division of the State Library. By 1937 crowded conditions, constant damp, and the installation of a new sprinkler system made the basement a hazardous place for the archives. Although the most valuable of the records were moved that year to the main floor of the library, many remained in place, usually filling their subterranean storage areas from floor to ceiling. Expansion of the State Library's holdings in the next 10 years forced off-site storage of government publications and archives in a number of locations: the Texas Confederate Home, Camp Mabry, and a cowbarn and annex in North Austin. By 1947, when the legislature transferred records management from the Bureau of Records to the State Library, many of the records had deteriorated almost completely. The Capitol basement was finally cleared when the archives were moved to the basement of the Greer Building in 1950. Records from the cowbarn and annex were moved to warehouses in South Austin in 1952. The improved conditions did not last long, however. In 1956 a Quonset hut at Camp Hubbard in northwest Austin became the new home for the archives. This move brought on a "Second Archive War." Citizen concern and the support of Governor Price Daniel resulted in the construction of the Lorenzo de Zavala State Archives and Library Building, completed in 1961.

The 1947 law that authorized the State Library to establish and maintain a records-administration division to manage all public records of the state has helped to ensure a systematic approach to preserving the archives of Texas. By 1963 agency heads were required to establish records-management programs within their agencies. Currently, overall responsibility for state agency records rests with the State Library, assisted and advised by the Records Management Interagency Coordinating Council. The State and Local Records Program of the State Library helps schedule records, provides microfilm services, and records storage for the state. The move toward the local-records program began in 1971. Before that, county archives had been housed in county courthouses, many of which had been destroyed by fire.

The legislature established regional depositories for local records throughout the state, operated through the State Library. The 1971 law permitted local officials to offer or lend their records to the regional depositories. In 1989 the legislature strengthened the state's commitment to local-records management by requiring local-records officers to establish management procedures and prepare schedules. As the twentieth century came to an end, a new challenge to archive preservation emerged with the rapid expansion of electronic technologies. The rate of change in computer hardware and software and in electronic storage media often outpaced the ability to transfer successfully all of the archival electronic records scattered among the less essential data. Some records remain locked in outdated computers, inaccessible for all practical purposes.

The archives of the adjutant general's office consist of a large number of muster rolls and payrolls of the soldiers of the republic and of the early ranger forces of the state; some thousand or more Confederate muster and pay rolls; rolls of the State Police, state guard, and reserve militia of the Reconstruction era; rolls of the rangers of the postwar period known under several names—frontier forces, minute men, Frontier Battalion, and Texas Rangers; rolls of the militia known as the Texas Volunteer Guard, Texas National Guard, and Texas State Guard; and rolls of the soldiers of the Spanish–American War. In addition, there are enlistment papers, records of bonds and oaths, certificates of service, quartermaster's papers, ordnance papers, correspondence, and reports. The archives of the comptroller of public accounts and state treasurer comprise financial records of the republic and state. Among the most valuable records of the comptroller's office are military service records, public debt papers, and claims papers. A few school ledgers and journals, letter books and school census records of the 1850s are a part of the archives of the treasury department, the treasurer being ex officio state superintendent of education at that time. The board of education, of later establishment, preserved records dating from the 1860s and 1870s—minutes of the board, registers of county school boards, journals, ledgers, letter books, school population, records of normal schools and colleges, and other documents.

Most Texas governmental archives have been transferred to the Texas State Archives building. Notable exceptions are the most recent charters and laws, which remain in the State Department. The Land Office archives remain in the department. The archives of the Supreme Court and the attorney general's office, along with those of the Third and Fourth Civil Appeals courts, are now in the State Library. The archives of the Railroad Commission, the Texas Department of Health, and the Board of Control have also become part of the holdings. County records of interest for family research, such as deeds, wills, and marriage and probate records have been microfilmed by the Genealogical Society of Utah and are available on loan through regional depositories. Much manuscript material formerly in private hands has found its way into the state archives, some by purchase, some by gift: the papers of Mirabeau B. Lamar, the John H. Reagan papers, and the Andrew Jackson Houston collection of Sam Houston papers, donated by A. J. Houston's daughters. Regional archives hold others. Several additional collections of papers related to Sam Houston and his family have been deposited in the Sam Houston Regional Library and Research Center in Liberty. In the University of Texas library there are many mixed personal collections, notably the Stephen

F. Austin papers, the Thomas J. Rusk papers, and the Ashbel Smith papers. Other individual collections are those of Washington D. Miller, George W. Smyth, Hugh McLeod, James Morgan, David G. Burnet, and Samuel May Williams. Some are in the State Library, others in the University of Texas library, and still others (the three last named) are in the Rosenberg Library at Galveston. The Texas State Archives also hold transcripts and photostats of documents pertaining to Texas from the British Public Records Office, the Archivo General de México, the Archivo de Govierno in Saltillo, the Archivo General de Indias in Seville, the Cuban Archives at Havana, the Archives of Matamoros, and the Franciscan records from Mexico City. Microfilms of some records have been obtained. The census bureau many years ago turned over to the State Library the manuscript census records for Texas from 1850 through 1880 except the population schedule. Microfilms of this schedule of the censuses for 1850 through 1920 have been obtained. A substantial number of the Texas archives have been edited and printed. The State Library has also produced a number of microform publications of Texas archives. A number of archival documents and historic relics from various Texas collections were used in producing the CD–Rom *Victory or Death*, an interactive study of the battle of the Alamo and other Texas Revolution battles.

Harriet Smither and Jean Carefoot

Texas State Genealogical Society. Organized in 1960 in Fort Worth by Edna Perry Deckler, president of the Fort Worth Genealogical Society. Objectives are to stimulate interest in the local history and genealogy departments of libraries (including the Texas State Library), to conserve genealogical and historical research material in Texas and make it available to the public, and to distribute genealogical records. In addition to *Stirpes*, the TSGS publishes a quarterly newsletter and hosts an annual conference.

Jean Heggemeier

Texas State Historical Association. A nonprofit organization with offices on the University of Texas at Austin campus. Ten people met on the campus on 13 February 1897 to discuss the founding of an organization to promote the discovery, collection, preservation, and publication of historical material pertaining to Texas. They included academic and lay historians, a blend of membership that has been preserved until the present. George P. Garrison, Eugene Digges, and Charles Corner drafted a constitution for the organization and invited 250 persons to attend an organizational meeting held in Austin the next month. Former governors Oran Roberts and Francis Lubbock, former congressman and railroad commissioner John H. Reagan, George T. Winston, A. J. Rose, and Garrison signed the letter of invitation. About 25 persons attended the first formal meeting at the Capitol. Roberts was elected president, and Dudley G. Wooten, Julia Lee Sinks, Guy M. Bryan, and Corner were elected vice presidents. Garrison was elected secretary and librarian, and Lester Bugbee was named treasurer and corresponding secretary. The meeting was conducted by the light of two lanterns, since the lighting system failed; lanterns lighting the path of historical discovery have served as the symbol of the association ever since. Because those attending included women (Dora Arthur, Julia Sinks, and Bride Taylor) a spirited discussion over female membership developed. John S. Ford wanted to call the women "lady members" in the constitution, rather than just

"members," and he grew especially concerned over the term Fellow, which he maintained could not apply to a woman. Garrison and the women were unable to change his mind, and Ford stormed from the meeting. The officers met at the University of Texas on 23 May 1897 to plan the first official annual meeting, which was held in Austin on 17 June. In an address entitled "The Proper Work of the Association," Roberts observed that many of the members had been important figures in the making of Texas history and that their role was "not so much . . . the writing of a connected and complete history as to furnish the facts for that object in the future." In accord with this precept, the early issues of the *Quarterly of the Texas State Historical Association*, which began publication in July 1897, contained numerous letters, diaries, journals, and memoirs. The title of the publication became *Southwestern Historical Quarterly* in the volume for 1912–13.

Garrison's original title, secretary of the association, in time became director as duties of the office multiplied. The director must be a faculty member at UT and is also director of the Center for Studies in Texas History, a university department. The university provides financial support for several staff positions; other positions are funded by the association. The association continues to hold annual meetings. During the 1970s semiannual meetings also were held in other Texas cities during the fall to give members in each section of the state a greater opportunity to participate. Since 1970 annual meetings have been held in Austin in even-numbered years and in other cities in alternate years. In addition to publishing *SHQ*, the association began publishing books in 1918. The publication program proceeded on a case-by-case basis until 1940, when a formal endowment to support this activity was established. The association's members collected books and documents to improve the Texas collection in the library of the University of Texas, supported local and regional historical societies and associations, and in 1941 began the Junior Historians of Texas program. The most significant publication of the association has been the *Handbook of Texas*, edited by Walter P. Webb and H. Bailey Carroll (1952; *Supplement*, edited by Eldon S. Branda, 1976). The association published the *New Handbook of Texas* in six volumes in 1996. The TSHA had more than 3,500 members in 1995.

Archie P. McDonald

Texas State Library. In Austin; established 24 January 1839 by a joint resolution of the Third Congress of the Republic of Texas, which appropriated $10,000 for the purchase of books to be deposited in the office of the secretary of state. The first purchase—the only one made during the republic's financially strapped existence—was an 18-volume set of the *Edinburgh Encyclopedia* for $250. Ashbel Smith, however, *chargé d'affaires* to England and France 1842–45, arranged with Joseph Hume, a member of the British Parliament, a system of exchange of documents between the two governments. Exchanges were also proposed by some of the states of the United States. After annexation further accessions were provided for by an act of the Second Legislature in 1848. Under this act $300 was appropriated to pay the expense of transportation, and the secretary of state was to act as librarian. At this time the books for the use of the Supreme Court were also in charge of the secretary of state during the recesses of the court. This arrangement proved unsatisfactory, and in 1854 an act was passed that established a separate library for the Supreme Court. In 1856 another appropriation, this time of $5,000, was made for the purchase of books for the State Library. The books, selected by Elisha Pease, embraced a "large number of choice and standard works." In a bill of 1860 was an appropriation of $1,500 for the State Library to be expended under the direction of the board of commissioners of public grounds and buildings. After the Civil War the office of state librarian was established, and Robert Josselyn, one-time secretary to Jefferson Davis, was appointed to the position at a salary of $1,000 a year, which, however, was not paid, because no appropriation was made for the purpose. Josselyn was shortly removed, with all other officials, by General Sheridan as an "impediment to Reconstruction," and the library was again placed in the state department and so remained until 1876. The catalog Josselyn completed before his removal shows 5,000 volumes in the library, which was then housed in a large room on the third floor of the Capitol.

In 1872 Governor Davis appointed Joseph Lancaster librarian. He described the library as a "wreck of grandeur." Many books were mutilated, others had been stolen. Everything needed a thorough cleaning, but there was neither duster nor broom to accomplish the work. In 1874, at the end of the Reconstruction era, an act was passed authorizing the governor to appoint "a suitable person to take charge of the public halls of the capitol, including the Senate chamber, hall of the House of Representatives, public library, the capitol grounds and State Cemetery, with all the public property belonging thereto, who shall be a practical horticulturist." The Department of Insurance, Statistics, and History was established under the Constitution of 1876, and in addition to his other duties, the commissioner of the new department was to have charge and control of the State Library and of all documents transferred under the law from the other departments. The first commissioner was Valentine O. King. Between 1877 and 1880 a large number of documents, chiefly the Nacogdoches Archives, were transferred from the state department. This was the beginning of the Texas State Archives. King later donated his valuable collection of Texana to the library. When the Capitol burned on 9 November 1881, maps and charts, the *Edinburgh Encyclopedia*, Lord Kingsborough's collection of Mexican antiquities, 120 volumes of debates in the English Parliament, several bound volumes of the *Diario Gobierno*, and thousands of other books and pamphlets were lost. For the next 10 years what was left of the library was without a habitation and almost without a name. Not until 1891 did the work of building the library began anew, largely as the result of the influence of Governor James Hogg. That year the office of historical clerk was appointed, and two years later a Spanish translator and an archivist were added to the staff. The library was housed with the Department of Insurance, Statistics, and History, although in the new Capitol the doors of a large room in the north wing of the second floor were marked "State Library." This room, however, was occupied by the Supreme Court Library.

By 1901 the volumes in the library numbered 25,000, bound and in pamphlet form; four-fifths of these were government documents. The beginning of the collection of early Texas newspapers dates from this period. In 1902 a Texas Library Association was organized, aided by the Texas Federation of Women's Clubs, and in 1909 the TLA obtained legislation for the organization of the Texas State Library and Historical Commission. The act divorced the library from the Department of Insurance, Statistics, and History, new quarters were secured in the room occupied by the Supreme Court Library, and a librarian and assistant librarian were appointed. The commission was to consist of five members, including the superintendent of public instruction and the head of the department of history of the University of Texas as ex-officio members; the other three were to be appointed by the governor. In 1919 this law was amended and the governor was given power to appoint all five commissioners to serve for six-year terms. Under the original act the Library and Historical Commission was authorized to maintain a legislative reference and information section. A county library law was passed in 1917, and thereafter traveling libraries, each consisting of about 50 books, were sent out to rural schools and communities without libraries. In 1919 the work for the blind was inaugurated, and later an annual appropriation was made for the service. In 1920–21 county libraries were provided for. A *Handbook of Texas Libraries* has been issued at intervals by the Texas Library Association.

Texas had able state librarians and employees. The chief problem the library faced for more than half a century was inadequate housing. By the 1950s the situation had become alarming, and the archives division was forced to move to a quonset hut in northwest Austin. In January 1957 Governor Daniel went before the legislature and recommended that a state archives and library building be built to house the divisions of the State Library. The new building was dedicated in 1962. Of the 100,000 square feet of floor space, the library occupied 66,000 square feet; the General Land Office occupied the rest (until 1974). The first-floor foyer houses displays of historic maps, manuscripts, and artifacts. Texas State Library services include preservation of historical documents, aid to researchers, and publication and display of valuable Texana. The library administers federal and state programs to encourage library development. The federal Library Services Act (1956) and its successor, the Library Services and Construction Act (1965), provided categorical grants to public libraries. The Texas Library Systems Act (1969), the first legislation to provide state funds for public libraries, gave the Texas State Library and Historical Commission the authority to organize systems and enabled the legislature to appropriate funds for them. In 1969 the Legislative Reference Library was separated from the State Library. The Regional Historical Resources Depository Act (1971) gave the Texas State Library responsibility for administering the establishment of regional depositories. In 1972 the new Records Management Division was moved to a building in north Austin and the Texas State Library and the Texas Historical Commission began a campaign to recover items belonging to the state archives. In 1973 the library building was named for Lorenzo de Zavala. In 1973 the governing commission's name was changed to Texas State Library and Archives Commission. In 1977 an additional facility, the Sam Houston Regional Library and Research Center, was built in Liberty.

By 1982 only 1,000 cubic feet was left to store historic records in the main building, the Records Division had filled 160,000 cubic feet of its 180,000, and yearly material required from 15,000 to 25,000 cubic feet. As a regional depository of federal documents, the library received from 50,000 to 60,000 such documents annually. By 1985 a moratorium had been placed on accepting new materials from state agencies, and the library had turned down gifts of historical manuscripts from private donors

Texas Tech Administration Building soon after completion in 1925. Texas State Historical Association. The Administration Building was one of six buildings on the campus of Texas Technological College when it opened on 30 September 1925.

for lack of space. That year the legislature authorized the expansion of the Records Center Building from 48,000 to 82,000 square feet. In 1989 the Local Government Records Act placed with the State Library responsibility for reviewing and sanctioning record-management programs in each of the more than 8,800 local jurisdictions in the state. In 1991 state and local record-management functions were combined into a single State Library program. A 1947 law requires that records kept by governors are to be placed in the state archives. In 1991 the state archivist asked the attorney general to encourage former governors Clements and Briscoe to turn over their papers. Clements had already given more than 500,000 documents to Texas A&M University and had plans to give A&M the rest of the papers from his first term. The attorney general had already ruled that former governor Connally's papers had to be turned over to the state. Of recent former governors only Mark White had agreed to turn over his papers to the State Library.

Harriet Smither and Dorman H. Winfrey

Texas Tech University. At Lubbock; founded in 1923, when Governor Neff signed a bill to establish a college in West Texas to "give instruction in technological, manufacturing, and agricultural pursuits" and "to elevate the ideals, enrich the lives, and increase the capacity of the people for democratic selfgovernment." The college was governed by a ninemember board of directors appointed by the governor. The movement for a college in West Texas had begun before 1900, however. It resulted in the approval of a bill early in 1917 establishing West Texas A&M College as a branch of Texas A&M, but the bill was repealed at the next legislative session after it was discovered that Governor Jim Ferguson had falsely reported Abilene as the locating committee's choice for the site. Angry West Texans, led by the West Texas Chamber of Commerce, continued the fight. Lubbock was chosen as the location for the college, out of 37 towns that applied. Land just west of the city was purchased by the Lubbock steering committee and sold to the state. Texas Technological College opened in 1925 with 914 students and six buildings. Initially it had four schools: Agriculture, Engineering, Home Economics, and Liberal Arts. From the beginning the liberal arts school formed the largest unit in the college. Graduate education began in 1927 in the School of Liberal Arts. A Division of Graduate Studies opened in 1935 and became the Graduate School in 1954. A Division of Commerce was formed in 1942; by 1956 it had become the School of Business Administration. The School of Law and the School of Education opened in 1967. In 1968 the agriculture school became the School of Agricultural Sciences. The college grew slowly and survived a move in the legislature in 1933 to reduce sharply its size and scope. By 1939–40 enrollment stood at 4,246, and although it dropped during World War II, the college trained 4,747 men in its training detachments for the armed services. In 1969, when the college was renamed Texas Tech University, students numbered 19,490. In the reorganization, six schools became colleges (Law remained a school). The Texas Tech School of Medicine opened in 1972 on the campus as a separate entity.

Intercollegiate sports began at Tech in 1925. In 1956 the university was admitted to the Southwest Conference. In 1935 the college became a regional deposit library for government documents. By 1969 the library held some 1,200,000 volumes in support of large and growing undergraduate and graduate programs. The first Tech Ph.D. was granted in 1952. Military training began as early as 1925, and in 1936 formal A&M ROTC training began. Air Force ROTC was added in 1946. By 1990 enrollment stood at just over 25,000, and the faculty numbered 1,159. The budget in 1969 totaled $39 million; by 1990 it had risen to $219 million. The physical plant grew rapidly during the 1960s and 1970s. The university also maintained an agricultural research and educational farm of some 15,000 acres at Pantex, near Amarillo. A Lubbock County farm laboratory was added in 1974 and enhanced in 1985 by the addition of the Burnett Center for Beef Cattle Research and Instruction. The university's center at Junction opened in 1971 on a 411-acre tract; it offers regular and short courses, workshops, and retreats throughout the year. The International Center for Arid and Semiarid Land Studies was established in 1966 to promote one of the university's special missions. In the 1990s Texas Tech was a well-established state university with a broad range of undergraduate programs and over 100 programs each at the master's and doctoral levels. Its research and teaching programs in agriculture, engineering, and other disciplines have had a major impact on the economy and life of West Texas.   *Lawrence L. Graves*

Texas Tech University Health Sciences Center. Administration in Lubbock; authorized by the Texas legislature in May 1969 under the name Texas Technological College School of Medicine. When Texas Tech became a university that same year, the medical school became Texas Tech University School of Medicine. In 1979, in recognition of its expanding scope, it was renamed Texas Tech University Health Sciences Center. Lubbock had begun seeking a medical division for Texas Tech in the early 1960s. Legislators proposed the move in 1965. Several Texas cities that wanted medical schools of their own, including Amarillo, Houston, and El Paso, opposed the legislation. After the bill passed both the House and Senate but was vetoed by Governor John Connally, a heated debate followed. West Texans claimed that any new medical school should be in their area because the rest of Texas was served by the University of Texas schools and Baylor. They also argued that medical resources in West Texas were not equal to those of the rest of the state. The three largest West Texas cities—Lubbock, Amarillo, and El Paso—waged a verbal war. El Paso based its claim on having the largest source of patients for teaching purposes, Amarillo argued that it was building a new medical park that included a city hospital, and Lubbock declared that the medical school should be located on the campus of a major university. The Texas Higher Education Coordinating Board authorized the founding of two new medical schools, one in Houston under the authority of the University of Texas, and one in Lubbock under the administrative control of Texas Technological College. The Lubbock school was to utilize the medical facilities in other West Texas cities. Lubbock legislators were able to get a bill through the legislature in 1969, and Governor Preston Smith, who had supported Tech's getting a medical school since 1949, signed the bill into law. Because ad valorem taxes cannot be used for constructing educational facilities, however, the medical school could not be a part of Texas Tech University; it had to be a separate state institution. Both institutions, however, had the same persons sitting on their boards of regents, and the same individual was president of both schools. The difference between the legal status and the common conception of the medical school's dependency caused problems that still plague both TTU and TTUSM.

Proposed innovations in curriculum and instruction at the new school included shortening the period of time required to get the M.D. degree, using electronic teaching aids, introducing the students to clinical settings early in their training, using existing medical facilities instead of one large teaching hospital,

encouraging students to go into family practice, and extending programs to outlying areas. Virtually all innovations were incorporated into the school's original program but were modified in 1975 to follow more established principles. The school continues to encourage family practice, to urge its residents to remain in West Texas, and to strive to develop better rural health care. The School of Medicine opened for classes with 36 freshmen and 25 junior transfer students in August 1972 and graduated its first class in May 1974. In the 1980s Texas Tech University Health Sciences Center opened schools of nursing and allied health. TTUHSC operates four regional academic health centers, located in El Paso, Amarillo, Odessa, and Lubbock. In 1993 the School of Medicine offered M.D., M.S., and Ph.D. degrees. M.D. students typically study two years in Lubbock, then do clinical studies at the regional academic health centers in Lubbock, El Paso, or Amarillo. The Odessa campus focuses more on electives and graduate training. Slowed in part by probationary status (imposed in 1975 and removed in 1977), the School of Medicine did not increase its student enrollment as rapidly as was planned. Nonetheless, from 61 students in 1972, enrollment grew to 100 per class, plus graduates in the basic sciences and in postgraduate medical training. By 1993 the Texas Tech University School of Nursing offered B.S., M.S. and Ph.D. degrees. It had branches in Lubbock and in the Permian Basin (with campuses in Odessa and Midland), and its students participated in activities at the Regional Academic Health Centers at Lubbock and Odessa. In 1993 the School of Allied Health taught courses leading to the completion of B.S. degrees in clinical laboratory science, occupational therapy, or physical therapy and certification in emergency medical services. Linked by computer to all four campuses, the TTUHSC library, the most comprehensive medical information source in West Texas, serves private practices and hospitals in addition to the academic population. In fiscal year 1992 TTUHSC had $6,540,000 in sponsored research. In 1993 the Texas Tech University Health Sciences Center received 31 percent of its funds from state appropriations and the rest from other sources, including faculty earnings, grants, and private contributions. The Texas Tech Medical Foundation, a nonprofit corporation chartered in 1970, administers donations and grants on behalf of the TTUHSC, helping provide support for projects including research, student financial aid, and training facilities.   *Robert L. McCartor*

Texas Wesleyan College. In Austin; established by Swedish Methodists as a result of a meeting in 1907 of ministers in Waco. Rev. O. E. Olander found 21 available acres where the University of Texas law school now stands. The cost of the site was $6,300. A board of trustees was appointed (1909), a building was planned (1910), and the cornerstone was laid (1911). Texas Wesleyan College opened in 1912 with 14 students. Under Olander's leadership the school prospered through the 1920s. The Olanders, in addition to running the school, operated the Sunnybrook Dairy in Austin, which provided work for Swedish boys seeking higher education. In 1928 a large tabernacle was built on the site of the college; it was used by students as well as other religious groups in Austin. Rev. Oscar Linstrum became president of the school in 1930. Tuition for two semesters was $18 to $22, and room and board cost $15. Courses offered included English, math, social studies, science, Swedish, Christian ethics, and Bible geography. Latin, German, and Swedish literature courses were offered, and the school had a music department. Tobacco and profane language were forbidden, all students had to retire at 10 P.M., and daily attendance at chapel service was required. Students were expected to attend the Central Swedish Methodist Church in Austin.

The 1930s saw a movement away from things ethnic and a movement to be more "American." Swedish churches in Austin began to offer services in English instead of Swedish. Interest in ethnic colleges such as Texas Wesleyan declined, and the University of Texas was eager to expand. In 1931 the college's trustees accepted an offer from UT to purchase the school grounds for $135,000. The trustees also voted to continue operation of the school, and for several years the University of Texas granted the college free use of the grounds. In May 1935 the school was renamed Texas Wesleyan Academy and the number of board members was reduced from 25 to 9. In 1936 the academy agreed to lend $100,000 to Texas Wesleyan College at Fort Worth. In June of that year academic courses were discontinued, though a small music school operated for some years, and a scholarship and loan program for descendants of Swedes continued. In February 1939 Texas Wesleyan College at Fort Worth filed suit against Texas Wesleyan Academy, stating that the money from the sale of the school was church money and not private money. In June 1941 a court ruled against the academy and ordered that the loan to the Fort Worth school be canceled and that $135,000 of academy assets be turned over to Texas Wesleyan College. The academy appealed the decision but later reached a compromise. Among other provisions, the school was allowed to keep property located on East Avenue in Austin. In 1957 the academy board discontinued student loans; the music school closed in 1956. In 1961 the board of trustees officially changed the name of Texas Wesleyan Academy to Texas Wesleyan Foundation. The scholarship fund was continued until the last awards were given for the 1976–77 school year. In 1989 a Texas historical marker was placed at the site of Texas Wesleyan College. *James M. Christianson*

Texas Wesleyan University. In Fort Worth. In 1890 the Northwest Texas Conference of the Methodist Episcopal Church, South, authorized the establishment of Polytechnic College, which received a gift of 300 acres of land from Fort Worth businessmen A. S. Hall, W. D. Hall, and George Tandy. The college retained 50 acres for the campus; the remaining 250 acres became the community of Polytechnic Heights. Classes began in 1891 with 105 students. Polytechnic College established a School of Commerce in 1894. In 1899, however, the school almost closed when an outbreak of measles, meningitis, and smallpox decreased enrollment severely. In 1902 Hiram A. Boaz became president. Under his leadership the college rebounded from its initial indebtedness, enrollment surpassed 1,000, and a number of new buildings offered more classroom space and living quarters for students. Because there was no endowment for the college, Boaz proposed to found a new university to replace Vanderbilt University as the flagship school for the Methodist Church west of the Mississippi. To that end, he sought to merge Southwestern University in Georgetown with Polytechnic and house the new school at the Fort Worth site. The Educational Commission of the Methodist Church approved the idea but instead opted to develop Southern Methodist University in Dallas into such an institution. Thus the merger did not take

effect, and Boaz was appointed president of SMU. As a result of these changes in 1913–14, the institution once again suffered financial difficulties and was forced to reorganize. Polytechnic College became Texas Woman's College. During the Great Depression, again under financial duress, the college became coeducational again and was renamed Texas Wesleyan College (1935). When Texas Wesleyan Academy (formerly Texas Wesleyan College) in Austin sold its property to the University of Texas, Texas Wesleyan in Fort Worth was granted a $100,000 loan which, after litigation, changed the fortunes of the college (1941). During the presidency of Dean L. Sone, the college built eight new buildings, enrollment topped 1,000, and the college freed itself of debt in 1942. During the next two decades Texas Wesleyan College continued to prosper, offering bachelor of arts degrees in four areas and a master's program in education. After 1970, however, student enrollment slowly decreased. In the 1980s the college averaged 1,500 students in the academic year. Jon H. Fleming became president of the college in 1979 and reorganized it into four schools. He planned to move the institution to a larger campus in West Fort Worth, but financing of this venture failed to materialize, partly because of the slump in the oil industry. Enrollment dropped to 1,300, then climbed slowly. In October 1988 *US News and World Report* listed TWC as one of the top five small liberal arts schools in the country because of its resources. In 1989 the school was renamed Texas Wesleyan University. It is fully accredited. It offers bachelor's degrees in several fields and master's degrees in education and health sciences. *David Minor*

Texas Western Press. The publishing division of the University of Texas at El Paso; founded by book designer Carl Hertzog in 1952. Before this date, all printing for the school was done by the University of Texas in Austin. When financial problems arose, Hertzog made contributions out of his own pocket to keep the press in operation. Not until 1962 did the press begin to receive regular funding. *Southwestern Studies*, a quarterly series of monographs begun in 1963 by Samuel D. Myers, Jr., has been a successful project of the press. Titles have included Haldeen Braddy's Robert N. Mullin's *The Boyhood of Billy the Kid* (1967), J. J. Borden's *The Ponce de León Land Grant* (1969), John H. Haddox's *Los Chicanos* (1970), and Robert H. Thonhoff's *San Antonio Stage Lines, 1847–1881* (1971). *The Chamizal Settlement* (1963) by Gladys Gregory was reprinted in the Congressional Record and was influential in the settlement of the Chamizal Dispute. UTEP faculty publications of Texas Western include C. L. Sonnichsen's *El Paso Salt War of 1877* (1961) and Haldeen Braddy's *Hamlet's Wounded Name* (1964), *Pancho Villa at Columbus* (1965), and *Pershing's Mission in Mexico* (1966). The press evenly divides publication between faculty and nonfaculty writers. *Hugh W. Treadwell*

Texas Woman's University. Founded as a result of lobbying for a state-supported women's college led by the Grange and the WCTU, with the support of the Texas Federation of Women's Clubs and the Texas Woman's Press Association; authorized by the legislature in 1901. A commission appointed by Governor Sayers selected Denton as the site of the new school in 1902. The institution began classes in 1903 as Girls' Industrial College, with an enrollment of 186 students. Helen Stoddard, Mary Eleanor Brackenridge, and Eliza S. R. Johnson, members of the original

Gardening, College of Industrial Arts, Denton, Texas, ca. 1905. Courtesy TSL. Girls' Industrial College began classes in 1903 with an enrollment of 186 students and a faculty of 14. In 1905 the name was changed to College of Industrial Arts.

board of regents, were the first women to sit on the governing board of a Texas university. After 1927 legislative mandate required that four of the college's nine regents be women. The name of the institution was changed to College of Industrial Arts in 1905, to Texas State College for Women in 1934, and to Texas Woman's University in 1957. In the initial years of its existence TWU was essentially a junior college for rural and small-town girls seeking vocational training. Since many came from areas with limited high school facilities, the first two years of the curriculum were preparatory; high school graduates went directly to the junior class. Although inadequate funding for dormitory construction kept enrollment below 2,000 until the end of World War I, the curriculum evolved and expanded. President Francis Bralley initiated the four-year, college-level curriculum in 1914, and the first B.S. degrees were awarded the following year. The state Department of Education recognized the institution as a college of the first class in 1916, and by 1923 the liberal arts curriculum had been expanded sufficiently to qualify the college for membership in the Southern Association of Colleges and Secondary Schools. The institution was accredited by the American Association of University Women in 1925. A home extension program was set up in 1911, and that same year the college held its first summer normal school. Texas Woman's University was the first educational institution in the state to offer instruction in home economics; graduates of its teacher-training program formed an overwhelming majority of the state's secondary teachers of home economics. A degree program

in home demonstration, established in 1922, was the only one in the Southwest, and by the mid-1930s graduates of the university constituted one-third of the home demonstration personnel in Texas. The university granted its first master's degrees in 1930.

Although the Great Depression temporarily caused a sharp drop in enrollment, President Louis H. Hubbard took advantage of federal funds available through the WPA and the PWA to launch an extensive building program. A campus landmark, the Little-Chapel-in-the-Woods, was also a project of the depression. NYA recruits constructed the building. The *Pioneer Woman* statue, another landmark, was executed by Leo Friedlander and given by the state in 1938 to commemorate the Texas Centennial. In 1941 TWU became a member of the Southern University Conference. John A. Guinn, president from 1950 to 1976, oversaw a second major period of physical expansion. During this time the university also began to build a national reputation as a center for research in textiles, food, and nutrition under the direction of Pauline Beery Mack, dean of the College of Household Arts and Sciences and director of the Research Institute. Ph.D. degrees were awarded for the first time in 1953. In 1960 TWU became a member of the Oak Ridge Institute of Nuclear Studies, and in the 1960s it received a series of research grants from NASA to study the physiological effects of space flight on astronauts. Male students were admitted for the first time in 1972.

In addition to a 270-acre campus in Denton, centers in Dallas and Houston provide instruction in the health sciences and related areas. The Dallas center has two campuses—the Inwood–Parkland Campus near Parkland and St. Paul hospitals and the Presbyterian Hospital Campus on Walnut Hill Road. The Houston center is in the heart of the Texas Medical Center. The Denton campus also operates the Southwest Institute of Design, a program cooperatively conducted by the university and the fashion industry. In addition to its other holdings, the TWU library houses the Woman's Collection. In 1979 the legislature authorized the establishment of a Collection of the History of Texas Women at TWU. The collection includes the gowns of the first ladies of Texas and Texas Women: A Celebration of History, an exhibit and archives developed by the Foundation for Women's Resources in 1981. In 1976 Mary Blagg Huey, an alumna of TWU, became the seventh president and the first woman president of the university. *Joyce Thompson*

Texas Writers' Project. A WPA project. Its best-known publication was *Texas: A Guide to the Lone Star State* (1940), cosponsored and copyrighted by the state highway department for tourism development. Members of the Texas Writers' Project also wrote and published, in limited editions, a number of local guides, some of which have become collector's items. The costs of publication were usually underwritten by sponsors. Folklore formed an integral part of each work—each district collected information on legends, epigrams, and customs in its area. All districts participated in the Federal Writers' Project to locate and interview former slaves. More than 300 such interviews were collected in Texas and deposited in the Library of Congress. In addition to these works, the writers also researched histories of Texas towns and cities, transcribed old newspaper articles, wrote essays on business, industry, and architecture, and drafted outlines for walking tours of historical sites. The writers also worked on a regional series and suggested for publication such titles as "America Eats" (on regional cuisine, with recipes), "Hands That Built the Nation" (a history of handicrafts), and "The Western Range: The Story of the Grasslands" (in cooperation with the Texas Historical Records Survey). When the project closed, the University of Texas received the working papers for projected publications and an indexed inventory of all manuscripts from 1937 and 1938. The Texas State Library also received some of the unpublished materials. J. Frank Davis directed the writers' project in Texas. The University of Texas Bureau of Research in the Social Sciences sponsored the project after the federal government withdrew full funding in 1939. *John G. Johnson*

Texas Youth Commission. Established by the Texas legislature in 1957 under the title of the Texas Youth Council. Its purpose is to provide services to delinquent youths, ages 10 to 21. The agency's roots extend back to 1859, when the legislature acknowledged the need for separate correctional facilities for child offenders. In 1887 funds were approved to build the Gatesville State School for Boys, and in 1913 the Gainesville State School for Girls was approved. The age of adult criminal responsibility, which had been 8 years old in 1836 and 9 in 1856, was raised to age 17 in 1918, and the legislature replaced all criminal procedures in juvenile cases with special civil procedures in 1943. The Gilmer–Aikin Laws established the Texas Youth Development Council in 1949. It consisted of 14 members, with the commissioner of the Department of Public Welfare serving as the council's executive secretary. The Texas legislature established the

Texas Youth Council in 1957 with three appointive members serving six-year terms. Over the next two decades the organization held responsibility for the state's juvenile correctional institutions, including Gatesville State School for Boys, Mountain View School for Boys, Gainesville State School for Girls, Crockett State School, Brownwood Statewide Reception Center for Delinquent Girls, and Brownwood State Home and School for Girls. The council also had supervision over the care of dependent and neglected children at Waco State Home, Corsicana State Home, and West Texas State School. By the end of 1970 the Texas Youth Council supervised over 2,940 juveniles in schools and another 836 in homes. By the late 1960s and early 1970s the agency opened halfway houses, initiated community assistance and foster care programs, and provided for psychiatric care and instruction for independent living.

In 1971 some teenagers sued the state in a landmark federal court case known as *Morales v. Turman*. The plaintiffs alleged physical and mental abuse, segregation, and neglect. The council implemented a number of changes based on the constitutional rights of juveniles deprived of liberty. Federal judge William W. Justice ordered the closing of the facilities at Gatesville and Mountain View. He also called for the elimination of corporal punishment and segregation. The agency increased staff and supervision of services, established clear policies and procedures, and adopted a Student Bill of Rights. The council board was expanded from three to six members. The parties finally reached a settlement in 1984, and the agency was placed under federal supervision by a three-member committee for a period of four years. In the early 1980s the council supervised over 1,000 juveniles. In 1983 the legislature changed the name of the council to the Texas Youth Commission, to be governed by a six-member board appointed by the governor with Senate concurrence. In addition to administering correctional youth facilities and programs, the commission tries to meet emotional and social needs of youths through vocational and educational programs, substance-abuse programs, and maternity training for pregnant girls. A system of parole services attempts to foster a successful transition back into the community. In 1991 the Texas legislature established the Health and Human Services Commission, and the Texas Youth Commission was put under the jurisdiction of that broader agency. During the 1992 fiscal year the Texas Youth Commission supervised an average daily population of 1,163 juveniles at the state schools at Brownwood, Crockett, Gainesville, and Giddings and at West Texas State School at Pyote. The commission also oversaw an average of 88 youths at the Corsicana Residential Treatment Center. By 1994 the agency employed over 2,000 workers and had appropriations of over $108 million. *Laurie E. Jasinski*

Texian. A term applied to a citizen of the Anglo-American section of Coahuila and Texas or of the Republic of Texas. In 1835 a newspaper called the Nacogdoches *Texian and Emigrant's Guide* was published. President Lamar used the term to foster nationalism. Early colonists and leaders in the Texas Revolution, many of whom were influential during the Civil War and who were respected as elder statesmen well into the 1880s, used the word. After annexation, however, *Texan* generally replaced *Texian*, although the *Texas Almanac* used the latter term as late as 1868. *Herbert Fletcher*

Theater. Before the arrival of English-language theater in Texas, four types of performance prevailed. For centuries, Indians performed religious rituals that included elements of dance, costume, and impersonation. In Spanish Texas, colonists staged secular dramas to celebrate special occasions. Spanish missionaries presented religious dramas and cultivated a fourth type of performance, a mixture of native dance and Christian theater. Performances occurred near El Paso in 1598, at Los Adaes in 1721, and in San Antonio during the 1770s. This theatrical activity prefigured such Spanish-language folk dramas as *Los Pastores*, performed in Texas communities annually since the nineteenth century.

American newspapers reported English-language theater in Columbia as early as 1836. Professional theater arrived in Houston in 1838. Two managers, John Carlos and Henri Corri, founded competing theaters before Houstonians built their first church. Professional actors, who traveled by ship from New Orleans, played leading roles, while amateurs filled smaller parts. Sam Houston, Mirabeau B. Lamar, John S. Ford, and William B. Ochiltree were among the leaders of the Republic of Texas who participated in theater. Theaters presented serious plays and musical concerts as well as a variety of disreputable entertainments. Frontier audiences consisted mostly of men and sometimes turned rowdy. Houstonians publicly debated the morality of theater not long after its introduction there. By 1845 strolling players, or independent performers, had reached Matagorda, San Augustine, Galveston, Jefferson, and other towns on accessible trade routes. During the Mexican War, actors, including future star Joseph Jefferson, performed for United States troops in Corpus Christi and the Rio Grande valley. From 1845 to 1860, professional theater in Texas was chiefly a phenomenon of the Gulf Coast. With its bustling port, Galveston became an attractive addition to the New Orleans–based touring circuit. Small inland towns got by with amateur dramatic societies and the occasional strolling entertainer. A few original plays were written by Texans during this period, including several about the Texas Revolution, such as *The Storming of the Alamo*. After 1850, sophisticated German-language theater and opera also flourished, presented mostly by social clubs in such German towns as Fredericksburg and New Braunfels. The Casino Club in San Antonio built a series of handsome theaters for German-language performance.

The Civil War and Reconstruction brought Texas theater to a temporary halt. In the 1870s, however, railroads opened inland markets for traveling troupes. Managers of stock companies, including actor William Crisp, established short-lived resident theaters in Galveston, Houston, and San Antonio. Texans built dozens of theaters, then called opera houses, across the state, some with full scene-changing equipment, traps, and auxiliary rooms. Several of these theaters survive, the oldest being the Bastrop Casino Hall, built in 1848. Utility halls with flat floors—usually located above commercial establishments—sufficed in smaller towns. Balconies and boxes allowed blacks and women to attend in segregated sections. By the late 1880s, Texas had joined the transcontinental theater circuit. Celebrities such as Edwin Forrest, Edwin Booth, Sarah Bernhardt, Helena Modjeska, and Lillie Langtry performed in Texas. They traveled in special railroad cars and played to intense local interest. "Combination companies," complete with star players, supporting casts, sets, and costumes, toured by train, stopping every 30 to 60 miles to perform for the night. The standard mix of melodramas, Shakespearean plays, minstrel shows, and musical extravaganzas was complemented by vaudeville, or variety shows for respectable audiences, in the 1890s. Large opera houses, such as the Galveston Grand, built in 1894, employed the latest theater technology and provided opulent settings for tours from New York, Chicago, and other cultural centers.

In the 1890s, Galveston businessman Henry Greenwall became a powerful manager of a touring circuit based in Texas. The national touring system was dominated by a syndicate of

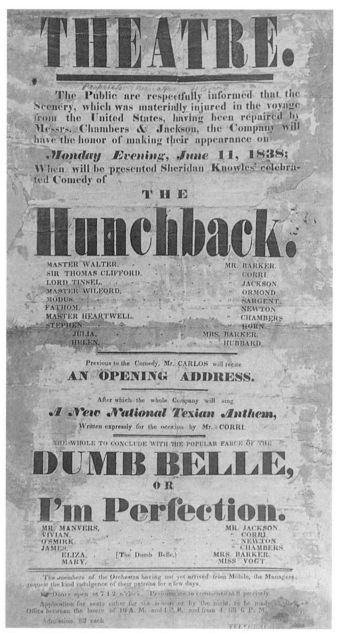

Theater bill for *The Hunchback* and *Dumb Belle, or I'm Perfection*, Houston, 1838. Broadside. Courtesy Masonic Grand Lodge Library and Museum of Texas, Waco. Theater began in Texas when a playhouse opened in Houston on 11 June 1838. The playbill for that night informed potential theatergoers that a new "National Texian Anthem" would be performed.

Adah Isaacs Menken, ca. 1860–68. Theatre Arts Collection, HRHRC. Adah Isaacs Menken grew up in Nacogdoches and became a successful actress in New York, London, and Paris. A friend of celebrities like Charles Dickens, she was said to be the most photographed woman in London.

agents and theater owners, which Greenwall opposed for a time. After 1905, theaters showed films as novelties. Recognizing a growing market, businessman Karl Hoblitzelle, who moved his headquarters from St. Louis to Dallas in 1920, built large theaters that alternately presented movies, vaudeville, and legitimate plays. Stale programs, labor problems, and the growing popularity of movies caused the decline of commercial theatrical tours. One exception was the Spanish-language troupes that fled to South Texas during the Mexican Revolution and toured until the 1930s.

While tours declined, better-educated and urbanized Texans turned to amateur theater as part of an idealistic movement of cultural improvement. Critic and scholar Stark Young organized a drama society, the Curtain Club, at the University of Texas in 1907. It remained active through the 1950s. Other drama clubs soon followed at Texas universities. The San Antonio Little Theatre grew out of a reading group founded in 1912. By the 1920s, dozens of Texas cities and towns supported amateur "little theaters." The Dallas Little Theatre won several national competitions and produced new plays by respected writers such as Paul Green. Secondary schools instituted drama programs after the first University Interscholastic League play contest in 1927. The University of Texas established the first curricular drama department in 1938; its first prestigious faculty member, Shakespeare scholar B. Iden Payne, joined in 1946.

During the Great Depression, commercial tours were confined to the largest cities, while musical entertainment reached smaller towns through tent shows. The Federal Theatre Project, part of the WPA, had little success employing theater artists in Texas, but it offered an important opportunity to pioneer director Margo Jones in Houston. After leaving the project she spearheaded the American regional theater movement, which com-

bined civic-theater idealism and subscription practices with professional artists. She also popularized intimate, arena-style staging through her book *Theater-in-the-Round*. After receiving encouragement from longtime Dallas *Morning News* critic John Rosenfield, Jones founded Theatre 47 (its name changed each season) in a small facility at the State Fair of Texas. Almost simultaneously, Jones, Nina Vance, and her collaborators founded the Alley Theatre in Houston. It turned professional in 1954. Texas theater was devastated by Jones's accidental death in 1955; she had directed on Broadway and subsequently nurtured the careers of playwrights Tennessee Williams, William Inge, and the team of Jerome Lawrence and Robert E. Lee, while proving that professional theater could thrive outside New York City.

During the 1940s and 1950s, innovative educator Paul Baker, working at Baylor University, transformed theories of creativity and theater training. He later led the Dallas Theater Center, which opened its facility, designed by Frank Lloyd Wright, in 1959. During the 1960s the Alley and the Dallas Theater Center became the state's dominant resident theaters (Margo Jones's theater had collapsed soon after her death). These theaters presented works by Texas playwrights Preston Jones, Horton Foote, and L. Ramsey Yelvington, along with American and European classic plays. Aided by large grants from the Ford Foundation, the Alley built a sizable modern theater in downtown Houston, which opened in 1968. In accordance with Baker's educational ideas, the Dallas Theater Center was never fully professionalized during his tenure, which ended in 1982. At the same time, several organizations specialized in large-scale musical productions: Casa Mañana in Fort Worth, Theatre Under the Stars in Houston, and Dallas Summer Musicals, which presented shows in the Music Hall at Fair Park. Texas produced musical talent of national import: actress Betty Buckley from Fort Worth, the

University of Texas–trained composing team of Tom Jones and Harvey Schmidt (originators of the longest-running show in American history, *The Fantasticks*), and performer–director Tommy Tune from Houston. Tune helped devise *The Best Little Whorehouse in Texas*, along with other Broadway and touring successes. The financial success of the Texas version of *Whorehouse* led Houston's PACE Concerts to enter the field of theatrical touring. By the 1990s, PACE Theatrical had become the largest producer of Broadway-scale musical tours in the country.

During the 1970s, another form of commercial theater swept the state. Dinner theaters proliferated in the suburbs of larger Texas cities, offering mostly light entertainment and food. These popular establishments declined in the 1980s, although variety entertainment continues to be served along with food at several large theaters. Outdoor performances also multiplied. The most successful was *Texas*, still presented each summer at Palo Duro Canyon State Scenic Park. Also in the 1970s, civic leaders recognized the value of historic theaters and renovated major facilities in Dallas (the Majestic Theatre), San Antonio (Majestic), Austin (Paramount), Abilene (Paramount), Texarkana (Perot) and Galveston (Grand). Smaller theaters were refurbished in Columbus, Granbury, Uvalde, and other towns. After a few failed attempts in the 1960s, a vibrant underground theater also evolved in urban areas in the late 1970s. The success of sketch-comedy troupes, such as Esther's Follies in Austin, inspired satirists Joe Sears, Jaston Williams, and Ed Howard to inaugurate the widely seen *Greater Tuna* plays. African-American and Hispanic companies began in Houston, Dallas, Fort Worth, and Austin. Experimental plays and performance art could be seen at Vortex Repertory and other venues in Austin, DiverseWorks in Houston, JumpStart in San Antonio, Caravan of Dreams in Fort Worth, and several theaters in the Deep Ellum district of Dallas.

In the 1990s the state's leading theater, the Alley, became more adventurous under artistic director Gregory Boyd. For the first time, visionary artist Robert Wilson of Waco returned to work in his home state, to direct at the Alley, the University of Texas, and Houston Grand Opera, the largest performing-arts group in the state. Wilson's "operas of images" made him one of the world's foremost avant-garde directors. Houston Grand Opera received international recognition for its breakthrough revivals of Scott Joplin's *Treemonisha* and the Gershwins' *Porgy and Bess*, and later as a leader in presenting new operas. The Alley and Theatre Under the Stars generated new Broadway-scale musicals such as *Beauty and the Beast* and *Jekyll and Hyde*. The University of Houston, along with the Alley, made an artistic home for Edward Albee. Dallas Theater Center returned to the spotlight in the 1980s under distinguished Texas director Adrian Hall, who opened a second theater and produced such new works as an adaptation of Robert Penn Warren's *All the King's Men*. In the 1990s, DTC expanded further into new work, including projects by Texas playwright Octavio Solis. Smaller towns in Texas continued to see mostly amateur theater, although some semiprofessional projects succeeded, such as Midland Community Theatre and the Shakespeare festivals in Winedale, Kilgore, and Odessa. Among Texas expatriates who made a mark on American play writing during this period were Terrence McNally of Corpus Christi, winner of multiple Tony awards, and Robert Schenkkan of Austin, Pulitzer Prize–winner for *The Kentucky Cycle*.

The early 1990s witnessed the rise of the medium-sized pro-

fessional theater company. Zachary Scott Theatre became the leader in Austin, Theatre Three in Dallas, Stages in Houston, and Stage West in Fort Worth. These more adaptable theaters discovered niches that larger resident theaters could not fill. Houston produced a professional touring troupe, the A. D. Players, which specializes in wholesome family entertainment. Dallas Children's Theatre became the state's most notable producer of plays for youth. One of the most unusual theater buildings constructed in the country during this time was the Addison Center Theater, an entirely flexible room for environmental performances. Perhaps the most significant institution in Texas theater continues to be the University Interscholastic League one-act play contest. Almost every high school participates in this spring rite, which exposes thousands of secondary-school students to theater and prepares potential trainees for the state's several large university drama programs. The ubiquity of theater in Texas, home to more than 300 producing theater companies, can be traced to the widespread influence of this contest.

Michael Barnes

Third Texas Cavalry. A Confederate regiment mustered into service by Col. Elkanah B. Greer in Dallas, 13 June 1861. With Lt. Col. Walter P. Lane as second in command, George W. Chilton as major, and Capt. Mathew D. Ector as adjutant, Greer led the 10 companies north across Indian Territory to join Brig. Gen. Benjamin McCulloch's forces near Springfield in July 1861. The unit was the first regiment of Texas volunteers to serve outside the state. Greer's troops participated in the Confederate victories at Wilson's Creek, Missouri (10 August 1861) and Chustenahlah, Indian Territory (26 December 1861). They were present but not engaged at Pea Ridge, Arkansas (7–8 March 1862), where McCulloch died. The unit, which had been consolidated with Sterling Price's command before Pea Ridge and absorbed into the army of Maj. Gen. Earl Van Dorn, was transferred to Corinth, Mississippi, in the spring of 1862. In the fever-ridden campgrounds around Corinth, 43 troopers from the Third Texas died from the effects of epidemic disease. An additional 200 officers and men were discharged as disabled, over age, or under age in the course of the general reorganization of the Confederate Army on 20 May 1862. Nevertheless, the regiment played a significant role in Gen. Pierre G. T. Beauregard's successful evacuation of Corinth on the night of 29–30 May 1862. The regiment, reorganized as part of Maj. Gen. Sterling Price's Army of the West, came briefly under the command of Col. Robert H. Cumby, who was succeeded by Col. Hinche Mabry, 26 June 1862. Mabry served as regimental commander until 29 March 1864, when he was replaced by Lt. Col. Jiles S. Boggess, who remained the unit's commander until the end of the war. The Third Texas sustained its most severe one-day loss on 19 September 1862, when 22 men were killed, 74 wounded, and 48 captured in the battle of Iuka, Mississippi. On 3–4 October the regiment participated in Van Dorn's costly and unsuccessful attack on the Union fortifications at Corinth. Two months later the Third Texas formed part of Van Dorn's cavalry column, which staged the spectacularly successful Holly Springs raid, thereby delaying Union major general Ulysses S. Grant's projected attack on Vicksburg by half a year. In February 1863 the troopers marched north into Tennessee to engage Union forces south of Nashville. There they participated in the Confederate victory at Thompson's Station (5 March). Later in the spring the regiment was ordered back to Mississippi, where it took part in the ultimately fruitless effort to defend Vicksburg and Jackson, Mississippi, against the Union advance. After the fall of Vicksburg in July 1863 the East Texans bivouacked in Mississippi for 10 months, during which time they were chiefly engaged in fending off Union raids into the interior of the state. On 16 December 1863, Col. Lawrence Sullivan Ross took over permanent command of a brigade formed from the Third, Sixth, Ninth, and Twenty-seventh Texas Cavalry regiments, and the men in these units thereafter fought together as Ross's Brigade until the end of the war. When the Third Texas capitulated to Union major general Edward R. S. Canby at Citronelle, Alabama, in May 1865, there were but 207 members of the unit left.

Douglas Hale

Thirty-sixth United States Infantry Division. The "Texas Division"; saw action in Europe during both world wars. At the outset of its federal service the division was composed mostly of Texas National Guard troops, hence its nickname. According to some sources, the arrowhead (point down) on the division's shoulder patch was thought to stand for Oklahoma, while the superimposed capital block-letter "T" was thought to stand for Texas. The "T-Patchers" mobilized at Camp Bowie, Tarrant County, in 1917. Some national guardsmen from Oklahoma supplemented the division. After a period of training in Texas, initially under Maj. Gen. Edwin St. John Greble, the division was ordered overseas under the command of Maj. Gen. William R. Smith and arrived in France in stages between 31 May and 12 August 1918. The division completed additional training in September and engaged in the Allied Meuse–Argonne offensive during most of the month of October, fighting in the Aisne valley. The Thirty-sixth advanced 13 miles against German resistance and suffered 2,601 casualties before being relieved on October 28–29, 1918. The division returned to America between April and June 1919 and was demobilized in June from federal service.

The division again entered federal service on 25 November 1940. Training began at the new Camp Bowie in Brown County under the command of Maj. Gen. Claude V. Birkhead. Additional soldiers came from several other states, but most top officers were Texans. Maj. Gen. Fred L. Walker, a regular army officer from Ohio, was posted to command the division in September 1941 and led the T-Patchers in maneuvers in Louisiana. One unit of the division, which became known as the "Lost Battalion," was shipped off to the Pacific soon after Pearl Harbor and was captured at the fall of Java. The men of the battalion spent the war in Japanese prison camps, and many died building the Burma Railroad. After more months of training, the division was sent to Africa in April 1943. The Thirty-sixth participated in hard fighting in September 1943 with other units of the United States Fifth Army under Gen. Mark W. Clark at a vulnerable beachhead at Salerno, Italy. The division was withdrawn after casualties considerably reduced its effectiveness. Subsequent personnel changes reduced the percentage of Texans to less than half. The Thirty-sixth made significant contributions to the Allied campaign in Italy and fought in two of the most controversial American actions of the war, at San Pietro and the Rapido River. In December 1943 two battalions of the division attacked the German-held town of San Pietro. Director John Huston photographed some of this combat for his grim

1945 documentary film, *The Battle of San Pietro*. Historian Martin Blumenson concluded that the Thirty-sixth was "close to exhaustion" by the end of 1943; nevertheless, units of the Texas Division were selected to undertake one of the most difficult of all military operations: crossing a strongly defended river at night. General Clark needed pressure on the German defensive line below Rome to prevent the Germans from counterattacking the projected Allied beachhead at Anzio. Further advantage would be obtained if the attack could achieve an Allied breakthrough into the Liri valley and open the push on Rome itself. General Walker had serious doubts about the Rapido operation, given the current of the river, its muddy banks and approaches, and the lack of adequate boats or bridging equipment. One source called the attempts to cross the Rapido (20–22 January 1944) a "two-day nightmare." The attack met stout German defenses, and the T-Patchers suffered heavy casualties, including 143 killed, 663 wounded, and 875 missing, but managed to participate in the continuing Italian campaign, including the capture of Rome. A fictional account by Harry Brown of one of the division's actions, entitled *A Walk in the Sun* (1944), was made into a major Hollywood movie of the same title released in January 1946 by Twentieth Century Fox. Subsequently, the T-Patchers were designated one of three infantry divisions to go ashore in Operation Anvil–Dragoon, the invasion of southern France, scheduled for August 1944. General Walker was relieved in late June and replaced by Maj. Gen. John E. Dahlquist. In contrast to the bitter battles in Italy, the "French Riviera Campaign" seemed fast-moving and met with considerable success. In the spring of 1945 the division entered Germany, where it served for six months as an occupation garrison; it returned to America in December 1945 to be demobilized. According to official reports the Texas Division ranked seventh in casualties among all United States divisions; totals of killed, wounded, and captured exceeded 19,000.

When the War Department made national guard units available to the governors of the states in 1946, the Thirty-sixth Division was reactivated. The division grew until the Texas National Guard was reorganized in 1959, when the Thirty-sixth and Forty-ninth were exchanged to achieve better geographic alignment. The Thirty-sixth was called to active duty for 12 months during the Cuban Missile Crisis (1961–62). In 1965 a separate Thirty-sixth Infantry Brigade was formed, primarily of Thirty-sixth Infantry Division units, to serve as a high-priority unit of the selected reserve force with capability of mobilizing in seven days. With reorganization of the reserve forces, however, the Thirty-sixth Infantry Division was eliminated by January 1968. A portion became part of the Seventy-first Infantry Brigade (Airborne), the only reserve-forces air brigade in the United States Army. Both the Thirty-sixth Infantry Brigade (Separate) and Seventy-first Brigade (Airborne) succeeded the Thirty-sixth Infantry Division. Lineage and honors of the division are continued by the Thirty-sixth Brigade of the Fiftieth Armored Division of New Jersey in Houston. In 1946 veterans of the unit founded the Thirty-sixth Division Association, which still meets annually.

Joseph G. Dawson III

Thompson, Ben. Gunfighter cum lawman; b. England, 11 November 1842; d. San Antonio, 11 March 1884. Thompson's parents brought him to Austin, where he took up gambling as a career. Before he was 18 he shot and killed a youth and killed a man in a knife fight in New Orleans. Though he enlisted with the Confederacy, he did not leave Texas until near the end of the Civil War. He killed a Confederate soldier and wounded several others, shot a teamster in Austin for allegedly stealing an army mule, and left the state to join Emperor Maximilian's forces in Mexico as the Civil War ended. He then returned to Texas and killed his brother-in-law, Jim Moore, who he believed was abusing his sister. Thompson was convicted and spent two years in the penitentiary at Huntsville. After his release, he went to Abilene, Kansas, and opened the Bull's Head Saloon with a partner, Philip Coe (1871). Thompson was recovering in Kansas City from a riding injury when Coe got into a shootout with Abilene marshal "Wild Bill" Hickok and was killed. Thompson then moved to Ellsworth, Kansas, with his brother Billy, who killed Ellsworth sheriff Chauncey Whitney. The brothers were forced to leave Kansas. In 1875 Thompson moved to Fort Elliott, where he befriended Bat Masterson. When Masterson shot an army sergeant in a fight over a woman, Thompson stepped in to prevent Bat from being killed by other soldiers. Afterward, the two were hired by the Atchison, Topeka and Santa Fe Railway to help settle a right-of-way dispute with the Denver and Rio Grande Railroad. Strangely, the conflict was settled in the courts rather than in the streets or saloons. After the railroad war Thompson returned to Austin and opened his own business, the Iron Front Saloon, at Sixth and Congress. One of his main competitors was Mark Wilson's Capital Theatre. On Christmas Eve in 1876, Thompson was at the Capital with several friends when a fight erupted. When Thompson tried to intervene on behalf of one of the troublemakers, Wilson emerged with a shotgun. In the ensuing fracas, Wilson fired at Thompson and was killed by three fast return shots. Thompson was ruled to have fired in self-defense. Afterward, his urbane manners and prowess with a revolver impressed the citizens of Austin enough that they elected him city marshal (1881). During his 10 months in office there were no murders, assaults, or burglaries in the city. But in 1882, while still serving as marshal, Thompson got into another fight in a saloon in San Antonio, where he killed the owner of the Vaudeville Theatre, Jack (Pegleg) Harris. He was indicted for the murder and resigned as marshal. After a sensational trial and acquittal, he returned to Austin to a hero's welcome. Shortly afterward, he brashly returned to the Vaudeville Theatre with his notorious friend John King Fisher, and the two were shot and killed by Harris's partner, Joe Foster. Residents of Austin engaged those of San Antonio in a free-wheeling, nasty debate after a coroner's jury in San Antonio ruled the killing self-defense.   *Patrick Cox*

Thrall, Homer Spellman. Methodist minister, historian, and publisher; b. Underhill, Vermont, 19 December 1819; d. San Antonio, 12 October 1894; m. Amanda J. Kerr (1847; d. 1851); m. Mrs. Amelia Trueborn West (1852); ed. Ohio University, Athens, Ohio. Thrall read letters of Martin Ruter in the *New York Christian Advocate* and determined to be a minister in the Republic of Texas. On 20 November 1842 he landed at Galveston. He was appointed first to Brazoria. He held the first camp meeting on the Guadalupe River with Texas Rangers on hand to guard against Indian raids. When the Methodist schism over slavery and principles of polity occurred in 1844, Thrall, like most Methodist ministers in Texas, joined the proposed Methodist Episcopal Church, South. The church divided Texas into two conferences, the Eastern Texas and the Texas. Thrall

remained in the latter and received his ordination as an elder from Bishop Edmund S. Janes at San Augustine in January 1845. Although he was appointed that year to Bastrop, his presiding elder changed his assignment and sent him to the Rutersville circuit. Thrall also served as principal of the male department of Rutersville College that year. In 1846 he was sent to form the Austin circuit. Until a church could be built the following year he preached in the Capitol to a congregation that included Mirabeau B. Lamar, Governor James P. Henderson, Gen. Edward Burleson, and Chief Justice John Hemphill. Between sessions of the legislature Thrall taught school in the Capitol. He purchased a lot at the corner of Congress and Cedar (Fourth Street) and supervised the construction of the first Methodist church in Austin. While riding the Washington circuit (1848–49), he served on a committee with Chauncey Richardson and Robert Alexander that established the *Texas Wesleyan Banner* (later the *United Methodist Reporter*).

Thrall was an agent for the American Bible Society in 1852–53. From 1854 to 1891 he served terms as presiding elder and circuit preacher in several districts in both the Texas Conference and the West Texas Conference. Among the districts in which he preached were Rutersville, Galveston, Austin, Victoria, Houston, Corpus Christi, San Antonio, Seguin, and Del Rio. In addition, he was a delegate to the General Conference in 1854, 1878, and 1886. He was secretary of the Texas Conference from 1852 to 1857 and of the West Texas Conference from 1882 to 1890. Thrall taught again at Rutersville College, 1853–55. In 1855 he was secretary of the commission that located Soule University at Chappell Hill. He wrote five widely read books, partly inspired by conversations with acquaintances he made when he first arrived in Texas—Emily Austin Perry, members of Stephen F. Austin's original colony, veterans of the Texas Revolution, and such political leaders as Lamar and Anson Jones: *History of Methodism in Texas* (1872), *A History of Texas* (1876), *A Pictorial History of Texas* (1879), *The People's Illustrated Almanac, Texas Handbook, and Immigrants' Guide* (1880), and *A Brief History of Methodism in Texas* (1889). After he retired in November 1891 he lived in San Antonio and wrote historical articles for the San Antonio *Daily Express*. Southwestern University honored him with a doctor of divinity degree in 1884. Thrall willed his library of 2,300 volumes to Southwestern University.   *Norman W. Spellmann*

Threadgill, Kenneth. Country singer; b. John Kenneth Threadgill, Peniel, Texas, 12 September 1909; d. Austin, 20 March 1987; m. Mildred Greer. In Austin in 1923, Threadgill met his future mentor and idol, Jimmie Rodgers. Backstage at the Tivoli Theater, Rodgers heard Threadgill imitating his yodeling and was impressed. Threadgill incorporated yodeling into his act later to make a unique style that fans loved. In 1933 he moved to Austin and began working at a service station, which he soon bought and made into Threadgill's Tavern. The tavern still sold gasoline and food. It had the first beer license in Austin after the repeal of Prohibition. At that time Threadgill did not allow dancing because dance halls that served beer had to pay an extra tax. He and his wife ran the place until World War II, when they closed for a few years. After the war the small (45-seat) tavern was packed on weekends when Kenneth Threadgill and his Hootenanny Hoots played. Wednesday nights became the hot time to congregate for beer, country music, yodeling, and the "Alabama Jubilee," the song that would usually get Kenneth to dance his patented shuffle. Such disparate characters as goat ropers, cedar choppers, frat-rats, hippies, and average Joes attended the hootenanny. Two musicians from the Hootenanny Hoots once invited some roadside hippies with musical instruments to come to Threadgill's. Thus Janis Joplin came on the scene. One night, in jest, Threadgill gave her two free beers for *not* singing. In 1970 Threadgill's huge birthday picnic was recorded in the *Congressional Record* when Congressman J. J. Pickle commended the "Father of Austin Country Music" as a legend. In his first movie soundtrack and album in the early 1980s, *Honeysuckle Rose,* Threadgill and Willie Nelson appeared together. Threadgill sang "Coming Back to Texas" and "Singing the Yodeling Blues." He received $3,000 for acting and $4,000 for the songs; he afterward sold almost two million copies of the soundtrack. In September 1981 he released Kenneth Threadgill and the Velvet Cowpasture's first album, *Long-Haired Daddy.* The title describes Threadgill himself, who had long white hair, horn-rimmed glasses, huge sideburns, and a rotund belly. His optimistic lyrics were about social stability. Some of his best-known songs were "Silver-Haired Daddy of Mine," "There's A Star-Spangled Banner Waving Somewhere," "T for Texas, T for Tennessee," and "It Is No Secret What God Can Do." Mrs. Threadgill died in 1976, and Threadgill sold the tavern in the early eighties. The establishment now thrives as Threadgill's Restaurant.   *Alan Lee Haworth*

Throckmorton, James Webb. Governor and congressman; b. Sparta, Tennessee, 1 February 1825; d. McKinney, 21 April 1894; m. Annie Rattan (1848); 10 children. Throckmorton moved to Texas with his family in 1840 and, after his father's death, went back to Kentucky to study medicine with an uncle. He returned to Texas when the Mexican War broke out and served less than three months before contracting a kidney disease that plagued him the rest of his life. Subsequently, as a surgeon's assistant and soldier, he served at Monterrey, Saltillo, and Buena Vista before his discharge in 1847. He became a prominent citizen of McKinney, especially as a supporter of education. He soon quit practicing medicine to practice law. He was elected as a Whig to the Texas House (1851), then as a Democrat to the Texas Senate (1857). He sided with Sam Houston against secession and was one of only seven delegates to the Secession Convention to vote against withdrawing from the Union. Nevertheless, he raised a Confederate company from Collin County and served extensively in the Civil War before his kidney ailment forced him to resign. In 1864 he was made brigadier general of the First Texas Frontier District. In 1865, E. Kirby Smith appointed him commissioner to the Indians, who nicknamed him "Old Leathercoat." Throckmorton presided over the Constitutional Convention of 1866 and was elected governor in June of that year. He opposed the Fourteenth Amendment on the grounds that slavery was already illegal. This stand caused conflict with Reconstruction officials and, in the general postwar chaos, helped guarantee his administration's failure. Disputes with Gen. Charles Griffin, centered on Throckmorton's refusal to support Radical Republican measures (including increased armed support for freedmen), led the general to appeal to Gen. Philip H. Sheridan, and Throckmorton was removed from office. He returned to McKinney, practiced law, and, though forbidden to hold office, joined former governors Andrew J. Hamilton and E. M. Pease in taking a public stand against the Radical

Republicans. After the General Amnesty Act (1872) he was able to run for office. He was elected to Congress (1874, 1876), where he concentrated on education and railroad legislation. He failed in an attempt to gain the Democratic nomination for governor in 1878, then was reelected to Congress three times (1882, 1884, 1886). His health prevented him from running in 1888 and thwarted a half-hearted attempt to seek the governorship again in 1892. During his later life Throckmorton worked extensively as an attorney for railroads.   *David Minor*

Thurber, Texas. Though it is a ghost town today, Thurber once had a population of perhaps as many as 8,000 to 10,000. At that time (1918–20) it was the principal site for mining bituminous coal in Texas. It was 75 miles west of Fort Worth in the northwest corner of Erath County. The coal deposits were discovered in the mid-1880s by William Whipple Johnson, an engineer for the Texas and Pacific Railway. He began mining operations there in December 1886 with Harvey Johnson. Isolation forced the operators to recruit miners from other states and from overseas; large numbers of workers came from Italy, Poland, the United States, Britain, and Ireland, with smaller numbers from Mexico, Germany, France, Belgium, Austria, Sweden, and Russia. Black miners from Indiana worked in the mines during the labor troubles of the 1880s. The force of predominantly foreign workers, many of whom spoke little or no English, enabled the company to maintain a repressive environment for many years. Following inability to meet a payroll and a resulting strike by miners, the Johnsons sold out in the fall of 1888 to founders of the Texas and Pacific Coal Company, including Robert Dickey Hunter, who became president of the new company, and H. K. Thurber of New York, for whom the town was named. Colonel Hunter chose to deal with the dissident miners, who were affiliated with the Knights of Labor, with an iron hand. The new company fenced a portion of its property and within the enclosure constructed a complete town and mining complex, including schools, churches, saloons, stores, houses, an opera house, a 200-room hotel, an ice and electric plant, and the only library in the county. Eventually the strike ended, and the miners and their families moved into the new town. In addition to the mines, the company operated commissary stores. As in the typical company town, low pay, drawn once a month, forced employees to utilize a check system between pay periods, whereby the customer drew scrip, reportedly discounted at 20 percent, for use at the company's commissary stores. In 1897 a second industry came to the town, a large brick plant. Hunter was also a partner in this operation, which, although it was separate from the mining company's holdings, used clay found on company property. A stockade, armed guards, and a barbed wire fence, which restricted labor organizers, peddlers, and other unauthorized personnel, regulated access to the town.

Despite Hunter's retirement in 1899, Thurber remained a company-dominated community. William Knox Gordon, the new manager of the Thurber properties, at first continued the established policy of suppression and antiunionism. This brought a concentrated effort by the United Mine Workers to unionize the Thurber miners. Following the induction in September 1903 of more than 1,600 members into the Thurber local of the UMW and the organization of locals of carpenters, brickmakers, clerks, meat cutters, and bartenders, the company opened negotiations with the workers and, on 27 September

1903, reached an agreement resulting in harmonious labor–management relations. Thurber gained recognition as the only 100 percent closed-shop city in the nation. Despite occasional strikes, basic labor–management harmony prevailed, and Thurber remained a union stronghold until the mining stopped in the 1920s, after railroad locomotives began to burn oil rather than coal. Gordon's discovery of the nearby Ranger oilfield in 1917 stimulated this conversion, and the change of the company name to Texas Pacific Coal and Oil Company in April 1918 signified shifting company interest toward oil production, which yielded large profits from 1917 to 1920. Declining use of coal and a resulting wage cut led to labor unrest lasting through much of the 1920s and to a strike in 1926 and 1927. Many miners accepted UMW assistance and moved to mining areas in other states. Numerous Italians returned to Italy rather than work in nonunion mines, and in 1926 the union chartered two railroad cars to return to their homeland 162 Mexicans, who likewise refused to scab. By the end of 1927 no union miners remained in the state. The company maintained operation of the brick plant until 1930, a general office until 1933, and commissary stores until 1935. By the late 1930s Thurber had become a virtual ghost town. *James C. Maroney*

Tidelands Controversy. A legal battle between the United States and Texas involving the title to millions of acres of submerged land in the Gulf of Mexico. Texas, first acquired this land by establishing and maintaining itself as an independent nation, then reserved this as well as all other unsold land when it entered the Union in 1845. Ownership of the property by the state of Texas was recognized by officials of the United States for more than 100 years. The discovery of oil under the tidelands, however, led applicants for cheaper federal leases and federal officials to assert national ownership as they had done against California and other coastal states. All states became concerned over their long-recognized titles to lands beneath their navigable waters. It became a national issue, resulting in three Supreme Court decisions against the states, three acts of Congress in favor of the states, two presidential vetoes against the states, and a major issue in a presidential campaign, before the states finally won the victory. It was the most serious conflict of the century between the states and the federal government. The federal claims were branded as an attempted "expropriation" and "steal" by outraged officials of Texas and many of the other states. In 1949 a statewide public opinion poll reported that the people of Texas considered it to be the most important public issue facing the state. Public indignation ran higher in Texas than elsewhere because this land had been dedicated to and was a source of revenue for the public schools. Furthermore, Texas held title not only under the general rule of law theretofore applicable to all states, but under the specific provisions of the annexation agreement between the Republic of Texas and the United States.

Before Texas entered the Union, the U.S. Supreme Court had written two decisions holding that lands beneath all navigable waters within the boundaries of the original states "were not granted by the Constitution to the United States, but were reserved to the States respectively" and that "the new States have the same rights, sovereignty and jurisdiction over this subject as the original States." In addition to this established rule of law, the Republic of Texas received specific assurances that the United States would respect the republic's boundaries. The

boundary beginning "in the Gulf of Mexico, three leagues from land, opposite the mouth of the Rio Grande" was written into the Treaty of Guadalupe Hidalgo in 1848. On many other occasions between 1845 and 1948 the United States recognized this boundary and Texas ownership of the submerged lands within such boundary. Thus, with no adverse claims against the title to this property, the Texas legislature authorized the School Land Board to execute mineral leases on it for the benefit of the public school fund. These leases, sold to the highest bidders, had yielded many millions of dollars before any federal claims were asserted. Other coastal states, relying upon their general title under the Constitution and the long line of Supreme Court opinions, were receiving revenues from oil, kelp, shell, sand, marl, fish, ports, docks, piers, and expensive building sites on filled land along the coasts of Florida and New York. The earliest adverse claims against any of the states were asserted by applicants for federal oil leases under the federal law, which granted leases at 25 cents per acre on any undeveloped land owned by the United States. This was not one one-hundredth of the price per acre averaged by the states for the leases they had sold under state laws. By 1950 there were 1,031 federal lease applicants who had blanketed the coasts of Texas, California, and Louisiana with applications for leases on lands already covered by state leases.

The first lawsuit asserting federal ownership of tidelands was filed by the United States against California in 1946. Because this lawsuit was based on claims broad enough to be applied against other states, the attorneys general of all other states filed an amicus curiae brief in opposition to the federal claim, and Texas attorney general Price Daniel presented oral argument on their behalf before the Supreme Court. In 1946, while the suit was pending, Congress passed a bill recognizing and confirming state ownership of the property, but this bill was vetoed by President Truman. In 1947, by a split decision, the Supreme Court decided against California. The language and theory of Justice Hugo Black's opinion were so shocking to state officials and leading lawyers of the nation that the American Bar Association, the Council of State Governments, the Governors Conference, most of the state legislatures, the National Association of Attorneys General, and the American Title Association immediately urged that Congress overthrow the result and theories announced in the decision. It became one of the most widely criticized opinions in the history of the court. Black reasoned that although the states had claimed and possessed their submerged lands in good faith under the language of numerous Supreme Court decisions, oil and other property involved might be necessary to the national defense. He asserted that the case should not be controlled by "bare legal title" or "mere property ownership." The new theory that federal "paramount rights" may be exercised to take oil and other property without compensation excited fears that all submerged state land and eventually private property might be in jeopardy. However, until after the presidential election of 1948, Texas still had hope that its special title would be recognized by federal officials. During the presidential campaign, President Truman said in Austin on 20 September 1948, "Texas is in a class by itself; it entered the Union by Treaty"—an argument endorsed even by Harold Ickes, a champion of the fight against state ownership. Nevertheless, shortly after the 1948 election, Truman directed the attorney general to file suit, and the Supreme Court decided against Texas. After a second hearing, the court reaffirmed its decision. In 1952 Congress again passed a bill restoring to the states the title to all submerged lands within their respective boundaries, but for the second time Truman vetoed the bill.

In the presidential campaign of 1952, Dwight Eisenhower made special recognition of the rights of Texas under the annexation agreement as well as the long-recognized rights of the other states under earlier Supreme Court decisions. He declared in favor of state-ownership legislation and said he would sign the bill if it were enacted again by Congress. The Democratic nominee, Adlai Stevenson, said he would veto such a bill if it were enacted again by Congress. In Texas this became the foremost issue in the 1952 campaign. The state Democratic Convention placed Stevenson's name on the ticket but then passed a resolution urging all members of the Texas Democratic party to vote for Eisenhower, and Eisenhower carried the state. In 1953 Congress made the restoration of submerged lands one of the first orders of business. Price Daniel, then United States senator, was coauthor of the legislation in the Senate, where it survived what was then the longest filibuster in Senate history (27 days) and finally won a substantial majority in both houses. Eisenhower signed the measure on 22 May 1953. A final battle was pitched against Texas in 1957, when the Republican attorney general, Herbert Brownell, filed suit against the state, alleging that its legal boundary and therefore its tideland ownership extended only three miles instead of three leagues (10.35 miles) into the Gulf. President Eisenhower publicly disagreed with the position taken by the Department of Justice. Nevertheless, Texas was forced to defend its boundary again in the Supreme Court. Texas prevailed in this lawsuit (1 June 1960) and now holds thoroughly litigated and firmly established title to its three-league Gulfward boundary and the 2,440,650 acres within that boundary. By 1987 the Texas public school fund had received nearly $2 billion from leases, rentals, and royalties on the tidelands.

Price Daniel

Tinkle, Lon. Writer; b. Julien Lon Tinkle, Dallas, 20 March 1906; d. Dallas, 11 January 1980; m. Maria Ofelia Garza (1939); three sons; ed. Southern Methodist University (A.B., 1927; A.M., 1932), Sorbonne, University of Paris (*diplome de phonetique*, 1933), and Columbia University. Tinkle taught at SMU beginning in 1932 and eventually became E. A. Lilly Professor of Literature. He became a book editor and critic for the Dallas *Morning News* in 1942. He is best known for his books, some of which focus on younger readers: *Thirteen Days to Glory: The Siege of the Alamo* (1958), reprinted as *The Alamo* (1960); (editor with Allen Maxwell) *The Cowboy Reader* (1959); *The Story of Oklahoma* (1962); (editor with Wynn Rickey) *Treson Nobel: An Anthology of French Nobel Prize-Winners* (1963); *The Valiant Few: Crisis at the Alamo* (1964); *Miracle in Mexico: The Story of Juan Diego* (1965); *The Key to Dallas* (1965); (author of preface) William Harvey Vann, *The Texas Institute of Letters, 1936–1966* (1967); *J. Frank Dobie: The Makings of an Ample Mind* (1968); *Mr. De: A Biography of Everette Lee DeGolyer* (1970); (author of introduction) Norman Kotker, editor, *Texas: A Picture Tour* (1973); and *An American Original: The Life of J. Frank Dobie* (1978). He also wrote *Les Deux Idoles*, with C. F. Zeek. Tinkle was a member of the Philosophical Society of Texas, the Texas Institute of Letters (of which he was president, 1949–52), and the Dallas Chamber of Commerce Fine Arts Committee. His many honors included a prize from the Texas Institute of Letters and a book award from the Sons of the Republic of Texas, both for *Thirteen Days to Glory* in 1959; Palmes Academiques of France; an LL.D. from St. Mary's University in 1963; and another prize from the Texas Institute of Letters for *An American Original: The Life of J. Frank Dobie* in 1979.

Stephen Earl Comer

Tips, Kern. Sportscaster; b. Houston, 23 August 1904; d. Houston, 23 August 1967; m. Nancy Tucker; 2 children; ed. Texas A&M and Rice Institute. While a student, Tips was a sports reporter for the Houston *Chronicle* (1924–26); he was subsequently *Chronicle* sports editor (1926–34). He began his radio career as a sportscaster in 1926 and became a newscaster in 1930. He was general manager of Houston radio station KPRC from 1935 through 1946. In 1947 he began a successful advertising partnership, from which he retired in 1966. He was simultaneously the "Voice of the Southwest Conference," since he spent 32 years broadcasting Southwest Conference football games. His voice was beamed around the world through the facilities of the Armed Forces Radio Service network. Tips served as a member of the board of directors of the National Association of Broadcasters (1939–40), as a member of the NBC Affiliates Council in 1941, as an advisor to the Office of War Information during World War II, and as director of Civilian Defense of Houston and Harris County (1943–45). In 1959 he was selected as the man who had contributed most to radio and television in Texas in the first annual award of the Association of Broadcasting Executives in Texas. He was recipient of the only award ever made by the Southwest Football Officials Association for distinguished service to the sport. He was voted Texas Sportscaster of the Year in a national poll for five consecutive years. Tips was the author of *Football–Texas Style* (1964).

Sylvia Gunn

Toboso Island. A name (Isla de Toboso, origin unknown) given by eighteenth-century Spaniards to Matagorda Island. Until near the end of the century, Toboso Island lay firmly in the grasp of hostile Karankawa Indians and apostates from Rosario and Espíritu Santo missions. In May 1776 Capt. Luis Cazorla of Presidio La Bahía (Nuestra Señora de Loreto Presidio) crossed the lagoon near the mouth of the Guadalupe River with 21 men to reach the island on horseback. Investigating the wreck of an English trading vessel, he found the ship on its side on the Gulf side of the island, the crew massacred by the Karankawas. In an attempt to define the island, Cazorla expressed the belief that it ran from "the port of Mata gorda" to the mouth of the Nueces River. Although this concept was slow to change, the definition was eventually narrowed to embrace only Matagorda Island. Cazorla extracted from Karankawa chiefs a pledge to stop preying on shipwrecked sailors, but the coastal natives soon returned to their old habits. Not until 1791, with one final effort to missionize the coastal denizens, was their island refuge breached again. On 5 December 1791, Fray José Francisco Garza, accompanied by a few soldiers from La Bahía, found the crossing used by the natives to reach Toboso Island, where the Indians kept horses stolen from Spanish ranches and other Indians. The feat was a high point in the "peace offensive" by Garza and Fray Manuel Julio de Silva of the College of Guadalupe de Zacatecas and pointed toward the eventual founding of Nuestra Señora del Refugio Mission. The island, "fourteen leagues long and not less than two wide," Garza recorded, had several shallow freshwater lakes, most of which dried up in summer. Even then, the Indians told him, fresh water could be obtained from holes dug in the sand. The shore was littered with fragments of wrecked vessels. Largely as a result of Garza's efforts, Mission Refugio was founded near the head of San Antonio Bay (to be moved later to the present Refugio townsite). In August 1793 Juan Cortés, the La Bahía commandant, inspected the new mission's environs with special attention to the Indians' retreat on Toboso Island. Finding the crossing that the Indians had shown Father Garza, he and his four soldiers rode their horses across the lagoon. By the time they reached the island, the animals' hooves were lacerated and bleeding from the oyster shell. The water was shallow enough that the island could be reached on foot, but thick-soled shoes were needed to protect the feet. Exploring the island from San Antonio Bay to the "Port of Matagorda," Cortés defined Toboso Island's limits. To render it ineffective as the natives' retreat, he ordered the cutting or burning of some thickets on the island near the crossing, where an ambush might be laid. Because of the lack of a permanent water source and the numerous mosquitoes and horseflies, Cortés deemed the island "more appropriately called purgatory." *Robert S. Weddle*

Toby and Brother Company. Purchasing agent for the Republic of Texas, as of 24 May 1836; composed of Thomas and Samuel Toby, businessmen of New Orleans. To obtain money for meeting outstanding obligations, purchasing supplies, and making advances to the government, the firm had been commissioned in March 1836 to sell 300,000 acres. It was appointed general agent of Texas on 10 June 1836 and commissioned to sell 500,000 acres of Texas land at a minimum of 50 cents an acre. Toby set up subagents in Louisiana, Baltimore, and New York to sell land scrip. Although the scrip was reduced to 15 cents an acre in December 1836, there was little market for the land or scrip in the winter of 1837. On 15 March 1837 the Texas treasury drew on Toby for 100,000 acres of scrip to be used by Felix Huston to purchase army supplies; Toby returned 106,640 acres in scrip. On 14 December the Congress prohibited the further sale of scrip and authorized the recall of the agency, all scrip to be returned within four months. At the close of its contract with Toby and Brother Company the state owed the firm $76,620.26. During the period of its agency, the firm disposed of 940,761 acres for cash or credit in addition to furnishing transportation and supplies for the Texas army and serving in an advisory and diplomatic capacity. Although its efforts to exchange scrip for cash were not successful, it was faithful to its obligations. The converted schooner *Swift* was renamed *Thomas Toby* in honor of the firm and became a privateer. Claims of Toby and Brother against Texas were approved by 1838, but lack of funds kept them from being fully paid at the time of Thomas Toby's death in July 1849. Thomas Toby's children attempted several times to settle their claim against the state and succeeded in 1881, when $45,000 was appropriated to pay them.

Toepperwein, Ad and Plinky. Sharpshooters. Adolph Toepperwein b. Boerne, 16 October 1869; d. San Antonio, 4 March 1962. Elizabeth Servaty b. New Haven, Connecticut, 1882; d. San Antonio, 27 January 1945. Ad was a vaudeville shooting performer when the two met. Both were working for the Winchester arms company. Plinky (from the verb *to plink*, which she coined) discovered that she was a "natural" with a rifle, and within two years of their marriage (1903) the Toepperweins were

Adolph Toepperwein in a studio photograph. Courtesy ITC. The son of a gunsmith, Toepperwein became a famous marksman who toured with a circus and then represented the Winchester Repeating Arms Company for 50 years as an exhibition publicity agent.

traveling as a team, billed as "The Famous Topperweins" (their name Americanized). Plinky became an outstanding woman marksman, representing American Powder Mills. They traveled throughout the world. Ad's first official record was made at the St. Louis World's Fair in 1904, where the two first performed together. In 1906, during a threeday exhibition, he made 19,999 hits out of 20,000 handthrown wood blocks. It was at the San Antonio fairgrounds in December 1907 that he made his famous world record, using a 1903 model Winchester .22 automatic. At about 25 feet he didn't miss a single handthrown wood chip out of 8,000 and missed only 4 out of the remaining 5,000 during 68½ hours of target shooting. He attracted crowds to exhibits wherever Winchester guns were sold. After his retirement in 1951 he conducted a shooting camp in Leon Springs and was elected to the Texas Sports Hall of Fame. The Toepperweins' displays of expertise included shooting while standing on their heads and while lying on their backs. They could also break two targets simultaneously, one in front and one behind, with the aid of a mirror. Some of Plinky's aerial targets included marbles, metal discs, apples, oranges, and eggs. Not only did she perform spectacular, crowd-pleasing stunts, she also was the first woman in the United States to qualify as a national marksman with the military rifle and the first woman to break 100 straight targets at trapshooting, a feat she repeated more than 200 times, often with a twelve-gauge Winchester model 97 pump shotgun. She was inducted into the Trapshooting Hall of Fame, Vandalia, Ohio, in 1969. She also held the world endurance trapshooting record of 1,952 of 2,000 targets in 5 hours and 20 minutes. Annie Oakley, also a member of the Trapshooting Hall of Fame, called her "the greatest shot I've ever seen." The Toepperweins had one son, who died in 1940. Ad and Plinky are buried at Mission Burial Park, San Antonio. A Toepperwein museum was opened in May 1973 on the Lone Star Brewery grounds in San Antonio to house some of the memorabilia of the team's long years of marksmanship.

Tornadoes. Most tornadoes in the United States occur along a belt skirting the eastern edge of the Great Plains from Iowa to Texas. They are most frequent in Texas during April, May, and June. Between 1916 and 1963, 1,505 tornadoes caused 865 deaths and considerable economic loss in the state. During 1957, 145 were observed touching the ground; in 1967, 232 were recorded; and in 1972, 144 tornadoes were observed in Texas. Tornadoes often appear suddenly and inflict great damage in one brief blow; towns have been flattened in minutes. One tornado hit White Deer, Higgins, and Glazier in April 1947, cut a trail 1½ miles wide, and traveled a total of 221 miles across parts of Texas, Oklahoma, and Kansas. The tornado cloud has a twisting tail, or funnel, which operates like a suction tube. The funnel moves erratically across the ground, smashing some buildings, skipping others, and changing directions. In the tornado aftermath there are inexplicable mysteries that are recounted until they become folklore. Among the oddities and freakish sights related in Texas tornado tales appear live plucked chickens, straws driven into posts, corn cobs imbedded in tree trunks, houses intact but shifted from foundations, whole large roofs displaced a few inches, and heavy equipment carried great distances. According to one account, a tornado in the Cedar Creek community in May 1868 "blew cattle into the air, lodging them in trees, sucked all water from the Brazos River for a short distance and dumped a fifty-pound fish on dry land." The destructive potential of tornadoes has increased as Texans have become more urbanized. Two tornadoes simultaneously swept through different parts of Austin on 4 May 1922, inflicting damage of $350,000 and killing 13 persons. A thoroughly photographed tornado moved slowly through Oak Cliff and West Dallas on 2 April 1957. It damaged 574 buildings, mainly homes, injured 200 persons, killed 10, and caused economic loss of $4 million.

For about 12 hours on 6 May 1930 massive turbulence occurred from West Texas to deep East Texas and as far south as Kenedy. That morning windstorms struck Austin, Spur, and Abilene; from noon until 9:30 P.M. at least 16 other places suffered severely. There were at least three separate tornadoes. At mid-afternoon tornadic winds ravaged Bynum, Irene, Mertens, Frost, and Ennis, killing 41 persons, injuring many more, and doing $2 million damage to crops and buildings. Frost was left in ruins, the jail being practically the only building that withstood the assault. Later in the evening another tornado struck Kenedy, Runge, and Nordheim, resulting in 36 lives lost, 34 injuries, and $127,000 in damages. Finally, a nighttime tornado at Bronson in

Sabine County caused additional damage and two deaths. Spur, San Antonio, and Gonzales also reported deaths because of the storm. A total of 82 persons lost their lives in the turbulence of that day, and damage totaled almost $2.5 million. A large part of Goliad was destroyed in four minutes on 18 May 1902 by a tornado that struck without warning. In a strip about two blocks wide and a mile long in the western part of town, 100 houses were ripped into rubble, as were a Methodist church, a newly constructed Baptist church and parsonage, and a black Methodist church filled with worshipers. Several hundred persons were injured, and 114 people died, almost all of whom were buried in one long trench, for there was no time to dig separate graves or conduct individual funerals. For decades to come, this was noted as the state's worst tornado catastrophe. Among the long-remembered oddities wrought by the strong wind was the fact that no pieces of steel from stoves or other household implements were ever recovered. Nor was any trace found of a long steel bridge.

Not until 11 May 1953 did a single tornado kill so many Texans again. This time, however, there was a warning. The weather bureau announced that tornadoes were a possibility somewhere along a line extending from San Angelo to Waco. Early that afternoon a tornado swept through three miles of small houses in the Lake View portion of San Angelo, and later another funnel twisted through five miles of Waco. At San Angelo 11 persons were killed and 159 were injured; the damage amounted to over $3.25 million. At Waco—immune to tornadoes, according to an Indian legend—losses were much greater. In a two-square-mile section of downtown Waco, buildings were lifted by the funnel and dropped in masses of broken bricks, splintered wood, and crushed plaster. Tons of glass flew through the air. Within seconds the business district was turned to a pile of debris. Some 196 business buildings were demolished, 376 others were damaged to the extent that they were unsafe, 2,000 automobiles were damaged, 150 homes were destroyed, 250 other homes were seriously damaged, and an additional 450 homes were less seriously damaged. Total damages cost $51 million. A total of 1,097 persons were injured and 114 perished, the same number as in Goliad half a century earlier.

In the spring of 1970 a series of tornadoes spread havoc across the South Plains. On 17 and 18 April a group of twisters hit across the country from Whitharral to Clarendon, injuring 150 people and killing 23 along two 175-mile-long paths. Plainview, reputed to have more tornadoes than any other place in the United States, suffered heavy damage, and 16 people were killed when a funnel touched down at the resort village of Sherwood Shores on Greenbelt Lake. On the night of 11 May, 17 years after the Waco disaster, a tornado swept through the business and residential districts of Lubbock. The wind turned vehicles into missiles and toppled brick buildings. When it was over, a swath eight miles long and a mile wide had been cut through the city. In a 15-square-mile area, designated as the storm area, 8,800 structures were damaged and 250 businesses and 1,040 houses were destroyed. Façades were blown off buildings of 15 and 20 stories. In addition, at Texas Tech University—not included in the storm area assessment—widespread "minor" damage amounted to a half million dollars. Altogether, 26 people were killed, 2,000 were injured, and property damage of over $200 million was sustained. On 10 April 1979, three tornadoes spawned by a massive storm system in North Texas killed 54, injured 1,807, and caused $42 million in damages. The first tornado crashed through Vernon in the afternoon; in 10 minutes it destroyed or damaged several hundred homes, killing 11 and injuring 60. The second, with a continuous ground track of almost 60 miles, hit the town of Harrold, causing one death and extensive damage. That evening a massive tornado whipped across eight miles of residential area in southern Wichita Falls, in a 1½-mile-wide swath. In less than 30 minutes 42 people died, and 3,000 homes were demolished and 600 others heavily damaged. Half of those killed were in cars the twister lifted, spun, and crushed. The storm continued into Clay County, where it caused 40 more injuries and another $40 million in damage. A lone twister roared through the isolated West Texas community of Saragosa on 23 May 1987, devastating the town and killing 29 residents. Another 121 were injured. Eighty percent of the town was laid waste, and all of its public buildings were destroyed. Most of the deaths and injuries occurred in the community hall, when the walls fell in on a kindergarten graduation ceremony attended by more than 100 persons. On 27 May 1997 an appallingly powerful tornado hit the community of Jarrell in Central Texas, killing 27 people and, it is said, pulling asphalt off of roads and not only shattering houses but twisting off pipes that protruded from concrete foundations. *Roy Sylvan Dunn*

Torrey Trading Houses. The firm of Torrey and Brothers traded widely with the Indians from 1838, when John F. Torrey arrived in Houston, until 1848, when the Torreys sold their major trading house to George Barnard. The Torreys' trading activities were a vital part of Sam Houston's peace policy and acted as a civilizing agent for the Indians. The Torreys conducted a significant fur trade, assisted in the establishment of New Braunfels, and established what was perhaps the first regional bank in the United States. John Torrey and his brothers David K. and Thomas S. Torrey built the first frame house in Houston and used it as a trading post and as a supply center for their other posts. David purchased goods in Boston and New York. The Torreys operated a trading house on the Bosque River in 1842 and established houses at Austin, San Antonio (1844), New Braunfels (1845), and Fredericksburg. Barnard opened a branch store on the Navasota River in 1843, and, at Houston's request, the firm opened a branch at the falls of the Brazos (1843–). With its official status under a law of the Republic of Texas passed in 1843, the Brazos post had a near monopoly of the Texas Indian trade. It traded goods to the Indians and, for a price, recovered stolen horses, runaway slaves, and captured Mexicans from the Indians. Indians frequently met at a council ground some four miles west of the trading post. On 16 November 1845, Thomas I. Smith and George W. Terrell made a treaty with the Kichai, Tawakoni, Waco, and Wichita groups at the post. In 1844 the Torrey brothers furnished Prince Carl of Solms–Braunfels with weapons for the Adelsverein. The brothers contracted with John O. Meusebach to provision and transport Germans from the coast inland. In the Torreys' unusual banking and credit system, the Tehuacana post served as a clearinghouse for the notes of rangers and Indians in the immediate area and for the entire border from the western edge of what is now Hood County almost to New Braunfels. The company sometimes paid advances to Indians for deerskins, who could pay the debt at the post on the Navasota River, at the falls of the Brazos, or at New Braunfels. Debts were sometimes paid by supplying six shaved

skins for each dollar borrowed. From 1844 to 1853 the trading house handled at least 75,000 deerskins. William N. P. Marlin and Leonard Williams, freighters, traveled an estimated 15,000 miles collecting and delivering pelts to Houston at $1.50 a hundred pounds in 1846 and $2 a hundred pounds in 1848. Grant and Barton, commission furriers in New York, sold skins at auction for Torrey and Brothers and later for George Barnard. In 1849 Barnard moved the Brazos post to Comanche Peak in Hood County. By 1849 the Torrey Brothers had sold their remaining interests to Barnard and moved out of Texas toward California. *Henry C. Armbruster*

Tourism. While tourism as a major source of revenue for Texas is a relatively recent phenomenon, the state's role as a visitor destination may be traced far back into history. The origin of tourism in Texas might be traced to the coastal map produced in 1519 by Alonso Álvarez de Pineda, for maps remain a keystone of modern tourist promotion. Similarly, visitor promotion in Texas could be traced to Cabeza de Vaca, whose reports in 1536 of the Seven Cities of Cíbola induced Francisco Vázquez de Coronado and 1,000 troops to make a tour of West Texas in a fruitless search for gold. Promotional literature in pre-republic Texas was beamed at potentially permanent residents, although at least one guidebook for casual visitors, Mary Austin Holley's *Tourist Guide to Texas*, was published in 1835. A number of guides to Texas were published during the republic and early statehood. In Melinda Rankin's *Texas in 1850*, the author wrote as shamelessly as any contemporary publicist that "a traveller, passing through Texas during the months of April and May, would not fail of pronouncing it to be the most charming spot on earth." Before and after the Civil War, the development of railroads in Texas gave impetus to travel for pleasure and adventure. Stagecoach, steamship, and riverboat lines sought recreational traffic by posting special excursion rates and promoting the charms and comforts of Texas with various publications. Between 1873 and 1878 commercial buffalo hunts promoted cooperatively by railroads and private entrepreneurs drew many hunters, who helped spread the state's fame as an outdoorsman's paradise, a status it has retained. The salubrious climate of Texas has long drawn visitors, and various health spas have flourished since the 1850s. The Hot Wells health resort of San Antonio, a pioneer tourist attraction throughout the last half of the nineteenth century, attracted visitors by the thousands through such imaginative devices as ostrich races. In the early 1900s the Rio Grande valley and the Texas coast, principally around Galveston, became popular as winter resorts. By 1922 the fame of Texas as a winter retreat was so well established that President Warren G. Harding vacationed at length in the Rio Grande valley. Early writers of Western novels, such as Rex Beach and Zane Grey, helped to publicize Texas as "cowboy country." The guides to Texas written in the cowland idiom by Charles A. Siringo and sold in paperback on west-bound trains are said to have outsold the Bible between 1885 and 1900.

Except for the increased construction of highways after 1917, which was a decided advantage for travelers, Texas did not formally enter into the field of tourism until the Texas Centennial year, 1936. Then, at the request of the legislature, the Texas State Highway Department established information bureaus at principal entry points to counsel visitors drawn to Texas by the celebration at Dallas. The information bureaus were so popular among visitors that the legislature asked that they be operated permanently as a service to tourists. In 1995 state tourist bureaus were located in Amarillo, Anthony, Austin, Denison, Gainesville, Langtry, Laredo, Orange, Texarkana, Valley, Waskom, and Wichita Falls. Since 1936 the highway department has published annually a new edition of an illustrated Texas travel map for tourists. Its distribution exceeded a million copies in 1967. The highway department has also published a wide range of informational, statistical, and safety materials since 1936 to assist travelers on Texas highways. Until 1958 publication of literature designed primarily to attract visitors to Texas was proscribed by the "carpetbagger clause" in the Constitution of 1876. Inserted by Texans with recent memories of Reconstruction and its herd of "carpetbaggers" and "scalawags," the constitutional provision made it unlawful to expend any state funds for the attraction of immigrants. By various court interpretations, tourists were ruled to be immigrants. In 1950 tourism surprisingly emerged as the state's fifth largest industry. In 1958, enlightened by findings that tourism in Texas was declining despite a growing $30 billion annual vacation expenditure among Americans, Texans voted a constitutional amendment to allocate tax money to attract visitors. In 1960, under the revised constitution, the Texas Highway Department published the first brochure specifically designed to lure tourists to the state. Subsequently, many promotional pieces have appeared.

In 1963 the legislature authorized the state's first tourist-advertising budget and established the Texas Tourist Development Agency as a part of the executive branch. The agency was charged to promote a responsible and accurate national and international image of Texas through creative advertising and public relations. Within the purview of the agency, Texas became the first state to base its national advertising schedules upon motivational research findings. Interviews were conducted nationwide by Belden Associates, an opinion-polling firm of Dallas, and supplemented by the national Gallup Poll to guide the agency in developing its advertising programs. Texas tourist advertising in national publications emphasized scenic and cultural variety, pleasant climate, abundant water, good accommodations, and sophisticated activities to offset the research firms' findings that large numbers of Americans considered Texas a desert land peopled largely by cowboys and oilmen and devoid of such nationally favored vacation charms as inland water, beaches, forests, mountains, historic sites, and cosmopolitan cities. In its first three years the tourist agency, in cooperation with various tourist-oriented businesses over the state, also hosted four tours of Texas for nationally known travel writers and editors, resulting in worldwide publicity on the emerging "Vacationland Texas." A $12,000 exhibit dramatizing the message of "Texas for a World of Difference," the theme of early Texas tourist advertising, was sponsored by both the tourist development agency and private businesses. It began touring the nation's principal travel and vacation shows in 1967.

Although developing and promoting tourism in Texas was the primary responsibility of the tourist agency, other state agencies were involved on an ancillary basis. The highway department remained most active in tourism through its travel and information division, operation of tourist bureaus, production of travel-promotion literature, maintenance of extensive photograph files, and tourist counseling. Many programs of the Texas Historical Commission and the Texas Parks and Wildlife

Diners enjoy mariachis on a barge at La Mansion del Rio Hotel on the Riverwalk in San Antonio, ca. 1980s. Courtesy Texas Department of Transportation/Jack Lewis. Tourism provides a major source of revenue for the state of Texas.

Department were keyed to a growing awareness of the economic importance of tourism. The Texas Commission on the Arts and the Texas Film Commission have also brought visitors. By the late 1960s the total tourism effort had helped excite increased interest of investment capital in building additional facilities to accommodate and entertain those vacationing in Texas. Some of the biggest attractions have been Six Flags Over Texas, between Dallas and Fort Worth, and HemisFair '68 in San Antonio. Other outstanding attractions included the Astrodome in Houston; the Ballpark in Arlington; Texas Stadium in Irving; Astroworld in Houston; Aquarena Springs in San Marcos; the outdoor drama *Texas*, at Palo Duro Canyon; Schlitterbahn in New Braunfels; and Seawolf Park at Galveston. The Lyndon B. Johnson Space Center in Clear Lake City has a tourist complex, Space Center Houston, built to educate and entertain visitors. A large number of cities, towns, and geographic regions, such as San Antonio, El Paso, Dallas–Fort Worth, Corpus Christi, Padre Island National Seashore, the Rio Grande valley, Guadalupe Mountains National Park, and Big Bend National Park were also considered tourist attractions. Lyndon B. Johnson's election as president caused a notable increase of tourists to the Hill Country and to sites associated with Johnson—Lyndon B. Johnson State Historical Park; Lyndon Baines Johnson Birthplace, Boyhood Home, and Ranch; and the Lyndon Baines Johnson Library. San Antonio also enhanced its marketability to tourists with its Paseo del Rio, Busch Gardens–Sea World theme park, and Fiesta Texas. Tourist information and tourist guides are available through the Texas Department of Transportation, Travel and Information Division, and the Texas Department of Commerce—Tourism Office. *Keith Elliott*

Tower, John Goodwin. United States senator; b. Houston, 29 September 1925; d. near New Brunswick, Georgia, 5 April 1991; m. Lou Bullington (1952; divorced 1976); 3 daughters; m. Lilla Burt Cummings (1977; divorced 1987); ed. Southwestern University (B.A., 1948), Southern Methodist University (M.A., 1953), London School of Economics and Political Science. Tower served in the navy in World War II and was in the navy reserve until 1989. From 1951 to 1960 he taught political science at Midwestern University in Wichita Falls. While there, he became active in the Republican party. In 1954 he ran for state representative but lost, and in 1956 he led Texas as a delegate to the Republican national convention. In 1960 he was nominated to run against Lyndon B. Johnson for senator. Johnson easily won the election but was also elected vice president. William Blakely was appointed to fill the seat that Johnson resigned, and a special election was slated for the spring. Tower led in this election and beat Blakely in the runoff on May 27. As the first Republican senator elected in Texas since 1870, he was seen by many as heralding the arrival of two-party politics in Texas. He was reelected to the Senate in 1966, 1972, and 1978. He began on two major committees: Labor and Public Welfare, and Banking and Currency. He served on the former until 1964. He remained on the Banking and Currency Committee, which in 1971 became the Committee on Banking, Housing, and Urban Affairs, throughout his Senate career. In 1965 Tower was assigned to the Senate Armed Services Committee, in which he served continuously until his retirement; he was chairman from 1981 to 1984. He also served on the Joint Committee on Defense Production from 1963 until 1977 and on the Senate Republican Policy Committee in 1962 and from 1969 until 1984. He was elected chairman of the Senate Republican Policy Committee from 1973 to 1984. In his 24-year Senate career, Tower influenced a variety of domestic and foreign policy issues. As chairman of the Senate Armed Services Committee, he worked to strengthen and modernize the nation's defenses. He was widely respected for his skills at guiding legislation through Congress. He worked to stimulate economic growth, improve opportunities for small business, improve transportation systems, and encourage strong financial institutions and systems. He was also concerned with promoting prosperity in agriculture, the energy industry, the fishing and maritime industries, and other areas of commerce particularly important to Texans.

Tower supported Barry Goldwater for president in 1964, headed Richard M. Nixon's Key Issues Committee in 1968, supported Gerald Ford for president in 1976, and worked for the Reagan–Bush tickets in 1980 and 1984, and the Bush–Quayle ticket in 1988. He was a member of the National Republican Senatorial Committee in 1962–63, 1969–70, and 1973–74 and was its chairman in 1969–70. He was a Texas delegate to the Republican National Convention in 1956, 1960, 1964, 1968, 1972, and 1980. He also chaired the National Security and Foreign Policy Platform Subcommittee in 1972, and was chairman of the National Republican Platform Committee in 1980. Tower maintained close ties with Southwestern University and served on its board of trustees from 1968 through 1991. In 1964 he received an honorary doctorate degree from the university and was named distinguished alumnus in 1968. The Tower–Hester Chair of Political Science, named for Tower and his former professor George C. Hester, was inaugurated at Southwestern University in 1975.

Tower retired from the Senate on January 3, 1985. Two weeks later President Ronald Reagan appointed him chief United States negotiator at the Strategic Arms Reduction Talks in Geneva. Tower served for 15 months in this role and gained the Soviets' respect for his negotiating skills, knowledge of the issues, and mastery of technical details. In April 1986 he resigned to pursue personal business. He was distinguished lecturer in political science at Southern Methodist University from 1986 until 1988 and chaired Tower, Eggers, and Greene Consulting, Incorporated, of Dallas and Washington from 1987 to 1991. Reagan again called Tower into government service in November 1986, when he appointed him to chair the President's Special Review Board to study the actions of the National Security Council and its staff during the Iran–Contra affair. The board, which became known as the Tower Commission, issued its report on 26 February 1987. In 1989 Tower was President George Bush's choice to become secretary of defense, but the Senate did not confirm his nomination because of his conservative political views and alleged excessive drinking and womanizing. The charges, counter-charges, and accusations of the hearings are chronicled in Tower's 1991 book, *Consequences: A Personal and Political Memoir*. In 1990 President Bush named Tower chairman of the President's Foreign Intelligence Advisory Board. Senator Tower died, along with his daughter Marian, in a commuter plane crash.

Susan Eason

Tranchese, Carmelo Antonio. Priest; b. Pomigliano d'Arco, Italy, 29 August 1880; d. Grand Coteau, Louisiana, 13 July 1956; ed. in Naples and Malta and at St. Bueno's College, North Wales. "El Padrecito," a Jesuit from 1896, was ordained a priest on 25 September 1910 in North Wales. He began his missionary life with a year in Albuquerque, then was then sent to St. Ignatius Church in El Paso. In 1915 he went to St. Andrew's in Poughkeepsie, New York, to complete his tertianship, after which he returned to El Paso, first to the Church of the Guardian Angel and then again to St. Ignatius (1928). Between 1928 and 1932 he moved back and forth between El Paso, San Jose, and Albuquerque. In 1932, Tranchese began his duties as the pastor of Our Lady of Guadalupe Church on the West Side of San Antonio, which was home for many of the city's 82,000 Mexican Americans. Working conditions and wages were poor, housing was dilapidated and disease-infested. Tranchese helped establish the Guadalupe Community Center, which, in cooperation with the Bexar County Tuberculosis Association, sponsored a health clinic that offered workshops in disease prevention and provided free vaccinations and other medical care. In 1935 he was appointed to the board of the tuberculosis association. He also encouraged efforts to improve working conditions and wages. Though he was skeptical of organized labor because he believed it Communist inspired, he supported local strikes and was particularly active in soliciting provisions and establishing breadlines for pecan workers who struck in 1935 and 1938. In October 1938, when the city's pecan companies mechanized in response to the Fair Labor Standards Act (Wage–Hour Act), throwing approximately 8,000 shellers out of work, Tranchese helped organize the Catholic Relief Association, which solicited and distributed food, clothing, and shelter. He also established a relief depot in the church, which daily supplied several thousand people with rations. He established himself as the city's major advocate for public housing, drumming up support through speeches, articles, and letters, including appeals to President Franklin Roosevelt. In 1937 he was appointed one of five charter members of the San Antonio Housing Authority and shared responsibility for persuading the United States Housing Authority and President Roosevelt to approve a project for the city. Despite threats to his life and slander of his character, he eventually contributed to the removal of some of the worst slums on the West Side and their replacement by the Alazán–Apache Courts. He also played a role in securing USHA loans and annual subsidies for courts built in other areas of the city, including Victoria Courts for Anglo families and Lincoln and Wheatley courts for blacks. The projects were completed in 1942. Tranchese served as vice chairman of the SAHA (1944–), received tributes from political dignitaries, and was featured in radio and print media. A movie agent considered making a movie about him. Tranchese initiated the first Spanish archdiocesan Sunday newsletter in Texas, *La Voz de la Parroquia*, which circulated throughout the Southwest. He also translated a folk shepherds' play, *Los Pastores*, from Spanish to English and later edited and published the play (1949). In 1953 he suffered a breakdown and was sent to St. Charles College, in Louisiana, to recuperate.   *Donald L. Zelman*

Trans-Pecos. The region west of the Pecos River, bounded by the Rio Grande on the south and west, and on the north by the thirty-second parallel, which forms the boundary with New Mexico. Most of the region's physical and cultural landscape has little in common with the rest of the state. Although it constitutes about 11 percent of the area of Texas, the Trans-Pecos has received less attention than the more populous east. It is about the same size as South Carolina. It also possesses the most varied, distinctive, and spectacular scenery in Texas. Most of the region is typified by the Texas portion of the Basin and Range physiographic province. Toward the northeast, along the western margins of the Pecos River valley, the region grades into the Great Plains. Farther south the Edwards Plateau forms the eastern boundary. A western extension of the plateau, known as the Stockton Plateau, ends at the eastern boundary of the Basin and Range. The Edwards Plateau is sharply defined farther east by the Balcones Escarpment, but northward this plateau merges almost imperceptibly into the High Plains region known as the Llano Estacado.

More than half of the entire United States–Mexico border is in the Basin and Range physiographic province, which reaches its eastern terminus in the Big Bend. Most of the area was once covered by vast seas that laid down great thicknesses of sedimentary rock. During a period of mountain building known as the Laramide Orogeny, the original horizontal structure of the sedimentary rocks was deformed into a series of folds. More recently, primarily during the Tertiary, volcanism and faulting resulted in upthrust ranges and downdropped basins. In the zone known as the Rio Grande Rift, which has been especially active during the last 25 million years, the boundary faults resulted in great vertical displacement. The Franklin Mountains of El Paso, for example, originally rose more than 25,000 feet from the floor of the original basin. In this area most of the uplifted ranges were formed along parallel faults and tilted to form what is known as rotated horst mountains. Most of the mountain ranges have a north–northwest trend. Today the basin fill is 2,000 to 8,000 feet thick. With the exception of the Rio Grande and two of its major tributaries, the Río Conchos (in Mexico) and the Pecos, the area is typified by internal drainage. Most water evaporates, and what is left seeps into the basin fill. These internaldraining basins provide significant recharge to aquifers. After the great ice age, the glacial melt filled freshwater lakes that formed remnant shorelines, terraces, large arroyos, and other features. Today the evaporation pans are associated with desert flats, playas, alkaline deposits, and sandy surfaces. The Salt Basin, just west of the Guadalupe Mountains in the Dell City area, provides numerous and obvious examples of these landforms.

Basin and Range topography offers higher elevations and greater local relief than can be found anywhere else in Texas. Although most of the state is relatively flat and less than 2,500 feet above sea level, the TransPecos basins are elevated about 4,000 feet and crossed by numerous widely spaced mountain ranges that rise an additional 2,000 to 3,000 feet. Some of the ranges, such as the Sierra Diablo and Delaware Mountains, have gentle slopes even at high elevations. Others, such as the Davis Mountains, are marked by steep slopes. The highest peak in Texas, Guadalupe Peak (elevation 8,751 feet), is located in the TransPecos, as indeed are all Texas peaks higher than 5,000 feet. In fact, no peaks east of the TransPecos in the United States or Canada rise above 6,700 feet. The lowest elevations in the TransPecos occur in the narrow Rio Grande valley, where elevations fall below 2,000 feet in the Big Bend country, and on the plains that slope eastward to the Pecos River valley, where some elevations are below 3,000 feet. The mean altitude of the region (based on planimeter calculations) is 4,100 feet. Most of the TransPecos is associated with the northern part of the Chihuahuan Desert, Mexico's largest arid zone. Only the highest elevations and the extreme eastern margin of the region receive sufficient precipitation in relation to temperature to be considered semiarid rather than true desert. In general, the average annual precipitation decreases with increasing distance from the Gulf of Mexico, the principal source of moisture for the region; the average annual precipitation is about 15 inches at Marathon (altitude 4,043 ft.) and less than 9 inches in El Paso (same altitude). In addition to the east–west variability, precipitation also increases with increasing elevation. Since the early 1970s, the region has received more precipitation—approximately two inches more at most localities. About three-fourths of the annual precipitation falls during the six warmest months of the year. The maximum precipitation occurs during July, August, and September, when the northwestward circulation of moist unstable air around the western edge of the Bermuda subtropical anticyclone produces numerous convectional thunderstorms. Also, tropical storms in the eastern Pacific Ocean are frequently of sufficient size and intensity to supply the atmosphere of the interior desert with relatively large quantities of water vapor. Analysis of satellite imagery and surface observations for summer rainfall has revealed that about 55 percent of the annual precipitation falling in El Paso is the result of tropical revolving storms, some of which reach hurricane intensity. Approximately 45 percent of the precipitated moisture was derived from the eastern, tropical Pacific and 55 percent from the Gulf of Mexico. Tropical revolving storms derived from either the Gulf of California or the Gulf of Mexico occasionally bring widespread heavy rain to the region and inflate the average annual precipitation figures. In September 1974, for instance, a series of such storms over a period of 10 days helped to raise the annual precipitation at Toyah to 21.9 inches, versus an average of 9.92 inches. The period of maximum precipitation during the warmest months is followed by a mild, dry winter during which the flow of air is generally from the west, where topographic barriers inhibit the movement of any significant amounts of moisture into the TransPecos.

The combination of clear skies, high altitudes, and southerly location enables the TransPecos to receive the highest mean annual solar radiation of any location within the United States (data from faulty sensors previously placed the maximum at China Lake, California, in the Mojave Desert). At lower elevations in the Rio Grande valley below Candelaria some of the highest temperatures in the United States are frequently recorded. In general, the TransPecos exhibits some of the highest average maximum temperatures found in Texas during the winter (second only to the Gulf Coast) and some of the lowest average temperatures in summer (second only to the Panhandle). Large diurnal ranges are common in all seasons, and frosts occur frequently in winter, even at low elevations. Aridity imposes a major constraint on vegetation in the Trans-Pecos. Soils, topography, temperatures, and precipitation variations impose secondary controls that produce significant variations in vegetation from place to place within the region. Desert grassland, the most widespread vegetation type, occupies the lowlands between about 3,600 feet and 4,600 feet. Desert shrubs, particularly creosote bush, occupy the lowest elevations, and there are indications that this type of vegetation has been expanding upslope throughout the region as a result of grassland disturbance over the last 100 years. At higher elevations the desert grassland grades into open woodland. Dense woodland is generally restricted to the higher elevations of the Davis and Guadalupe ranges. Scattered throughout the region are smaller areas of riparian, holophytic, and other vegetation types adapted to specific site conditions. Upland soils are generally shallow and unproductive. Even the deeper alluvial soils of the basins are frequently too saline to be very productive. The Rio Grande is the world's twentieth largest river in volume, the fifth largest in North America, and the only significant surface stream in the Trans-Pecos. Runoff from the mountains of Colorado and northern New Mexico is controlled by major storage dams in southern New Mexico, from which water is released for heavy irrigation in the valleys above and below El Paso and Ciudad Juárez. The average annual flow of 370,000 acre-feet at El Paso is reduced by agricultural diversions and infiltration to 109,000 acre-feet at Fort Quitman. There are long stretches with virtually no water flow between the Quitman Mountains and Presidio. The Rio Grande is replenished at Presidio by inflow from the Río Conchos, which drains the eastern slopes of the Sierra Madre Occidental in Mexico. The Conchos, the most important tributary of the Rio Grande, supplies at least 17 percent of the latter's total flow. Through Big Bend the average annual flow is about 833,000 acre-feet. By way of comparison, the flow past Rio Grande City in southern Texas averages about three million acre-feet. Except for cities immediately along the Rio Grande, Trans-Pecos settlements must depend upon subsurface water. Because of the heavy water demands of El Paso, the Rio Grande provides less than 25 percent of that city's water. Two major areas of groundwater are the basins of the Hueco Bolson, just east of El Paso, and the Salt Basin, which stretches for a considerable distance west of the Guadalupe, Delaware, and Davis mountains. The groundwater resources of the region are limited by low recharge rates and high mineral contents.

Although the El Paso area was partially explored by Europeans beginning late in the 1500s, the Trans-Pecos saw no real settlement until Texas became a part of the United States. Before the Civil War a small settlement was established on the Texas side of the river at El Paso, and some mining was taking place in Presidio County. The combination of aridity, isolation, and roving bands of Apache and Comanche Indians discouraged rural settlements in the region. The rural counties of the Trans-Pecos (away from El Paso) are still the least populated areas in Texas, and they are not growing. Population in them amounts to one inhabitant per square mile, whereas the Texas average is more than 50 per square mile. About three-fourths of the rural Trans-Pecos population lives in eight or nine small towns. Only the growth of El Paso County differs from the pattern of sparse population and minuscule growth. In general, the cultural landscape of the Trans-Pecos, like the physical one, has more in common with the Southwest than with the rest of Texas. Extensive cattle grazing is the dominant commercial land use in rural areas of the Trans-Pecos. Only small scattered areas have sufficient water for irrigation. Aridity and long-standing landtenure practices have combined to produce unusually large ranches and low animal densities in this region of predominantly private land ownership. The average working ranch is larger than 20,000 acres, compared to the state average of less than 1,200 acres. Although cattle grazing is the dominant land use in the Trans-Pecos, the region supports only about 2 percent of the cattle in Texas. They are more often worked by the stereotypical cowboy here than elsewhere. There is virtually no rainfed agriculture in the region, and even irrigated agriculture is confined to a small fraction of the land area of the lowest basins. Floodplain irrigated agriculture is found along the Pecos River valley, along the Rio Grande above and below El Paso, and in a much smaller strip near Presidio, where water from the Río Conchos replenishes the depleted Rio Grande. Irrigated agriculture based upon groundwater pumping is essentially limited to the Salt Basin around Dell City and its southward extension through Van Horn. High-quality cotton, pecans, alfalfa, and vegetables such as tomatoes, onions, and chilies are the major crops of the region. As cotton production has declined in the face of mounting costs and increased competition from other areas, pecans and vegetables have increased in importance. Water may become even less abundant in the future because of the increasing depths from which it must be pumped and the increasing cost of energy to run the pumps. Agriculture in the region is also threatened by the ongoing conversion of farmland to urban uses in the Rio Grande valley above and below El Paso. Because of the presumed lack of significant untapped groundwater reserves of acceptable quality, no new major agricultural developments are anticipated.

Although the Trans-Pecos is not especially noted for its mineral production, economically valuable deposits of various minerals are scattered throughout the region. The oilfields of West Texas extend across the Pecos River, and sulfur, talc, fluorspar, and silver are among the minerals that either are being worked at the present time or have been produced in significant quantities in the recent past. Tourism is important in such sites as Big Bend and Guadalupe Mountains national parks and the nearby Carlsbad Caverns in New Mexico. The Trans-Pecos has several other historical and recreational areas, including Hueco Tanks State Historical Park, Fort Davis National Historic Site, and Big Bend Ranch State Natural Area. The Trans-Pecos is on major transportation routes. The region sits astride the lowest, most southernmost, and generally icefree east–west corridor across the United States, a fact that brings large volumes of traffic.

Historically, El Paso del Norte was on a strategic north–south trail connecting Mexico City with Santa Fe. Today, more than 40 million people a year cross the border at this locality. The east–west route was established with the coming of railroads in 1879; additional rail routes followed and were later supplemented by a number of major energy pipelines connecting the Midland–Odessa region with the West Coast. Most recently Interstate highways 10 and 20 were built through the region. On the negative side, the ease of transportation to the region, coupled with its isolation, small population, and lack of political clout, has made the Trans-Pecos and adjoining southern New Mexico the target for dumping of everything from radioactive waste to New York fecal sludge.   *Robert H. Schmidt*

Travis, William Barret. Texas commander at the battle of the Alamo; b. Saluda County, South Carolina, 1 or 9 August 1809; d. San Antonio, 6 March 1836; m. Rosanna Cato (1828); 2 children. Travis's boyhood centered around the work of the family farm, church attendance, home schooling, and playing with area children. James Butler Bonham was one of these, but it is difficult to establish a strong relationship between Bonham and Travis in these early years. The family moved to Alabama in 1817. There they helped found the communities of Sparta and Evergreen. Travis studied law as an apprentice of James Dellet, the leading attorney in Claiborne, and became an attorney and partner. He founded the Claiborne *Herald*, joined the Masonic order, and accepted a position as adjutant of the Twenty-sixth Regiment, Eighth Brigade, Fourth Division, of the Alabama Militia. A year later he abandoned his wife, son, and unborn daughter and left for Texas. The story has been told that Travis suspected his wife of infidelity, doubted his parenthood of her unborn child, and killed a man because of it. The rumor is probably true, given its persistence, but hard evidence of it is lacking. Travis arrived in Texas early in 1831, after the Law of April 6, 1830, made his immigration illegal. He arrived at San Felipe de Austin, and on 21 May obtained land from Stephen F. Austin. He falsely listed his marital status as single. He established a legal practice in Anahuac. The purpose of the move there was to establish himself in an area where there were few attorneys while he learned the official language, Spanish. He traveled the country doing legal work and became associated with a group of militants who opposed the 1830 law. Eventually this group became known as the War Party.

Travis had many occasions to oppose the commander of the Mexican garrison at Anahuac, Col. John Davis Bradburn, a Kentuckian in the service of Mexico. Bradburn enforced the anti-immigration law, refused to allow state officials to alienate land to American settlers arriving after the passage of the law, and allegedly used materials and slaves belonging to the settlers to build his camp. The principal prerevolutionary events at Anahuac occurred in 1832 when William M. Logan of Louisiana engaged Travis to secure the return of runaway slaves being harbored by Bradburn. Logan returned to Louisiana for proof of ownership and threatened Bradburn that he also would return with help. Travis alarmed Bradburn with a note passed to a sentry that Logan had returned with a large force. Bradburn turned out his entire garrison to search for Logan, who, of course, was nowhere near the area. Suspecting Travis as the perpetrator of the prank, Bradburn sent soldiers to his law office to arrest Travis and his partner, Patrick C. Jack. They were held in a guardhouse and later in two brick kilns. Word of their arrest spread, and men

Colonel William B. Travis, by Wiley Martin, 1835. Pencil sketch. Courtesy TSL.

assembled to demand their release. The group drafted the Turtle Bayou Resolutions, which pledged their loyalty to the states'-rights Constitution of 1824, but not to the current Centralist regime, and demanded the release of the prisoners. John Austin traveled to Velasco to obtain a cannon to force Bradburn to comply. Col. José de las Piedras, commander at Nacogdoches, hurried to Anahuac. Although in sympathy with Bradburn, he realized that the Mexican forces were outnumbered. He ordered Travis and Jack released to civil authorities, who soon released them altogether. This incident began the Anahuac Disturbances of 1832, which resulted in the battles of Velasco and Nacogdoches later that summer and produced the conventions of 1832 and 1833 with their petitions for repeal of the anti-immigration law and separate Texas statehood.

In the aftermath, Travis moved his legal practice to San Felipe. In 1834 he was elected secretary to the ayuntamiento there and was accepted, despite his youth, into the councils of government. He also met Rebecca Cummings, who lived at Mill Creek, and began a courtship that resulted in a decision to marry once Travis was divorced. Rosanna Travis began divorce proceedings against her husband in 1834, charging him with desertion. They were divorced in the fall of 1835, and she remarried early the next year. She had permitted Charles Edward Travis to move to Texas, where he lived with the family of David Ayers, so that he could be near his father. Travis may not have known when the divorce became final, for he became embroiled in the rapidly moving events of the Texas Revolution in July 1835 and was constantly occupied until his death. In any event, he made no attempt to marry Rebecca Cummings.

After S. F. Austin carried the petition of the Convention of 1833 to the government in Mexico City and was incarcerated, fears for his safety cooled politics in Texas until the summer of 1835. By then Antonio López de Santa Anna had asserted full Centralist authority and reestablished a customhouse and military garrison at Anahuac under the command of Capt. Antonio Tenorio. A war group led by James B. Miller met and authorized Travis to return to Anahuac to expel Tenorio. In late June Travis led some 25 men by way of Harrisburg and Galveston Bay on an amphibious assault on Tenorio's position and captured the Mexican soldiers easily. The action alarmed the Peace Party, and for several months Travis was regarded by many Texans as a troublemaker. Gen. Martín Perfecto de Cos, Mexican military commander in the north, moved his command to San Antonio. He branded Travis and the other partisans at Anahuac outlaws and demanded that the Texans surrender them for military trial.

Travis joined the hundreds of Texans who hastened to the battle of Gonzales, but arrived too late to take part. He remained with the militia and accompanied it to the siege of Bexar. He served as a scout in a cavalry unit commanded by Randal Jones and later commanded a unit himself. He did not remain at San Antonio through the final assault in early December, but returned to San Felipe. He advised the Consultation on the organization of cavalry for the army but turned down a commission as a major of artillery. He later accepted a commission as a lieutenant colonel of cavalry and became the chief recruiting officer for the army. Governor Henry Smith ordered Travis to recruit 100 men and reinforce Col. James C. Neill at San Antonio in January 1836. Travis was able to recruit only 29 men, and because he was embarrassed he requested to be relieved. When Smith insisted, Travis reported to Neill and within a few days found himself in command of about 50 men when Neill took leave. When James Bowie arrived with 100 volunteers, he and Travis quarreled over command. They were able to effect an uneasy truce of joint command until Bowie's illness forced him to bed. Travis directed the preparation of San Antonio de Valero Mission for the anticipated arrival of Santa Anna and the main command of the Mexican army. With engineer Green B. Jameson he strengthened the walls, constructed palisades to fill gaps, mounted cannons, and stored provisions inside the fortress. He also wrote letters to officials requesting reinforcements, but only 35 men came from Gonzales to his relief, thus raising the number of the Alamo's defenders to approximately 183. Travis's letter addressed "To the People of Texas and All Americans in the World," written on 24 February, two days after Santa Anna's advance arrived in San Antonio, brought more than enough help to Texas from the United States, but it did not arrive in time to prevent the annihilation of the Texans on 6 March 1836. Travis died early in the battle from a single bullet in the head. His body and those of the other defenders were burned. The nature of Travis's death elevated him from a mere commander of an obscure garrison to a genuine hero of Texas and American history. *Archie P. McDonald*

Travis State School. Established by the legislature as the Austin State School Farm Colony, a branch of the Austin State School, in 1933. The 241-acre site was on the Colorado River about eight miles east of downtown Austin. It was intended to provide a home for mentally retarded boys who could not further benefit from training at the Austin State School and who were able to do such work as farming, dairying, gardening, and related tasks. By the mid-1940s the institution had six ward buildings, a cannery, and an administration building for its 477 boys. The colony became separate from the Austin State School in 1949. It acquired an additional 195 acres in the late 1950s and built several dormitories to accommodate its increased enrollment. Farming operations at the facility ceased in the early 1960s, and the institution changed its name to Travis State School in 1962. Ten new ward buildings and service buildings were completed in 1963. In July 1968 the school had 1,800 students, all of whom had been transferred from other institutions. A special-education program was conducted for those able to benefit from classroom instruction. In 1970 the school received a grant from the Hospital Improvement Project, which made possible the use of a unit system of treatment. A new Vocational Evaluation and Training Center, with a capacity of more than 300 residents, was opened and staffed through a grant from the Texas Rehabilitation Commission. That same year a swimming pool, an administration building, and five full-time physicians were added. School enrollment at the end of 1970 was 1,754. Female students were first admitted in 1973. The student population declined steadily in the 1970s and 1980s, as the Texas Department of Mental Health and Mental Retardation implemented plans to integrate some students into community-based programs. The school used a system known as "behavioral characteristic progression" to evaluate the training needs of students and to coordinate that training so as to help each student achieve his maximum potential. Travis State School functioned as an independent school district from 1981 to 1988; after 1988 it depended on the Manor ISD to provide academic instruction through its "mainstreaming" program. Travis closed in the mid-1990s as a result of an 18-year-old federal suit against the Texas Department of MHMR. *Vivian Elizabeth Smyrl*

Treasury Robbery. The robbery of the state treasury, one of the boldest crimes in Texas history, in 1865. As news of the Confederate surrender reached Texas, civil government and law enforcement quickly began disappearing. Governor Pendleton Murrah and many Confederate officials fled to Mexico, most other Confederate state government officials had been removed from office, and Union occupation forces had not yet arrived. Capt. George R. Freeman, a Confederate veteran from Hamilton, organized 30 volunteers to protect the city until Union occupation forces could arrive. Freeman related that on the night of 11 June 1865 he was informed by Gen. Nathan G. Shelley of Austin that a robbery of the state treasury was imminent. A prearranged signal by church bell was given to the volunteers to convene at the Christian Church, located at the southern end of Congress Avenue. To the alarm no more than 20 volunteers responded; many of these had been in church. The treasury building was located northeast of the Capitol. By the time the troops arrived the robbers were in the building and breaking into the safes. As Freeman's men approached, a brief gunfight erupted in which one of the robbers, Elex Campbell, was mortally wounded by Al Musgrove and Fred Sterzing. Freeman was wounded in the arm. Of the estimated 50 desperadoes participating in the break-in, all but one escaped. The thieves fled towards Mount Bonnell, west of Austin, carrying with them about $17,000 in specie, more than half of the gold and silver in the state treasury at the time. The gang was headed by a man known only as Captain Rapp. According to an audit delivered to Governor Andrew J. Hamilton in October 1865, a total of $27,525 in specie and $800 in Louisiana bank bills was located in the treasury at the time of the robbery. United States bonds and coupons and other securities belonging to the state school fund, amounting to several million dollars, were also in the vaults at the time. The robbers failed to escape with any of the securities. Freeman reported that $25,000 in United States coupons clipped from the bonds was found on the floor of the treasury after one of the robbers apparently dropped the package in his attempt to escape. The loot was never recovered, although some of it was found strewn between the treasury building and Mount Bonnell. Captain Freeman and his company of volunteers were later recognized by the state for their service in defending the public treasury, but the resolution providing a reward for their services never passed the legislature.

Patrick Cox

Treaty of Guadalupe Hidalgo. A treaty between the United States and Mexico, signed 2 February 1848; ended the Mexican War, recognized Texas annexation, and ceded to the United States Upper California (the modern state of California) and nearly all of the present American Southwest between California and Texas. The treaty traced the boundary between the United States and Mexico from the Gulf of Mexico up the main channel of the Rio Grande to the southern boundary of the Mexican province of New Mexico. The line followed the southern boundary of New Mexico to its western boundary and north to the first branch of the Gila River, then down the Gila to its intersection with the Colorado River, and finally along the old Spanish–Mexican division line between Upper and Lower California. The exact boundary was to be surveyed and marked by a joint Mexican–United States Boundary Commission.

The negotiation of the treaty presented many knotty problems, mostly caused by the Mexicans' sense of honor and their refusal to admit defeat. After Gen. Winfield Scott had captured Veracruz and pushed into the interior of Mexico, President Polk and Secretary of State James Buchanan sent Nicholas P. Trist, from the Department of State, to join him in the hope that with plenipotentiary powers and full instructions the two could take advantage of any crack in Mexican resolve to push through negotiations. Scott and Trist managed to establish communications with the Mexican government by way of British legation officials in Mexico City, who were anxious to see peace return before Mexico was entirely crushed. For a time the Mexican president, Antonio López de Santa Anna, seemed willing to consider a negotiated peace, and Scott decided to "encourage" him by occupying the Valley of Mexico and threatening Mexico City, goals he accomplished after several bloody but victorious battles. In August–September 1847 Trist met with Mexican commissioners to discuss terms, but the talks broke down and Scott was forced to occupy Mexico City. Thereupon Santa Anna resigned and the rest of the Mexican government fled to a provisional capital about a hundred miles to the north. At this point an indefinite deadlock might have resulted, for the weak Mexican administration succeeding Santa Anna dared not act, and the Mexican congress, which split into a number of peace and war factions, did everything possible to avoid responsibility. By the end of November, after weeks of jockeying, Trist, aided by British diplomats, managed to persuade the Mexicans to send a peace commission to Mexico City and at least exchange proposals. At that point a dispatch arrived from the impatient Polk instructing Trist to give up the effort and return home. Pressed by Scott and the other American generals and by the British, Trist decided to disobey his orders and stay. The negotiations, which lasted about a month, were delayed at every point by haggling over details and slow correspondence between the Mexican commissioners and their government, a hundred miles away, which resisted every concession. At first the Mexicans would recognize Texas territory only to the Nueces River. They also resisted the cession of New Mexico, and a particularly bitter argument arose over the cession of San Diego, which they denied had ever been a part of Upper California. The American purchase price of $15 million represented half of the original Mexican demand. When Polk received the completed treaty he was affronted by Trist's disobedience and stopped his salary. On further consideration, he decided to submit the treaty to the Senate because it met his minimum instructions concerning the boundary and because any continuation of the war risked serious disunion in the country during an election year. The nation received the treaty with relief, and the Senate approved it after a few minor changes. The execution of the treaty was generally satisfactory to both sides, except for its requirement that the United States prevent Indian raids into Mexico, an almost impossible task on a long, unsettled frontier. As Americans came to desire more Mexican territory south of the Gila River for a railroad route, a new treaty, the Gadsden Purchase, was negotiated in 1853 to make the desired changes.

David M. Pletcher

Trees. Texas has between 255 and 281 species of native trees in 91 genera and 47 plant families. Tree experts rarely agree about the figures because of controversy over the identification of some trees. Does eastern sugar maple (*Acer saccharum*) actually occur in Texas? Many Texans say yes, but eastern taxonomists say that the Texas tree is the Florida sugar maple (*A. barbatum*). Dahoon (*Ilex cassine*) and myrtle (*I. myrtifolia*) holly were recorded in Texas almost 100 years ago and have not been seen since. The definition of a tree—a plant with a trunk three inches in diameter at 4_ feet in height, with one stem only, the stem attaining 13 feet in height—is controversial and omits some plants that we normally think of as trees. The anacacho orchid tree (*Bauhinia congesta*), for instance, is not considered a tree by some experts, and yet in many landscapes it fits the definition of a tree.

Almost 50 percent of the nation's arboreal species occur in Texas, a large number primarily due to diverse climate and soils. East Texas forests are a continuation of southern pine forests and are essentially oak–hickory deciduous forests planted to pines. The coastal prairies and plains have trees that can survive periodic flooding and poor drainage. The Rio Grande plains have elements of the Mexican flora, as does the southern TransPecos. In the mountains and highlands of the TransPecos are elements of the Rocky Mountain flora. The High Plains is a short-grass prairie and is essentially treeless. The plains from the foot of the Caprock to the Western Cross Timbers are now more or less covered by shrubby mesquite (*Prosopis glandulosa*), with other scattered trees along intermittent watercourses. The Cross Timbers, both east and west, and the post oak savannah are part of the true prairie association with tall grasses in the openings and understory. The dominant trees of these regions are post oak (*Quercus stellata*) and blackjack oak (*Q. marilandica*). In the past, trees occupied only the creek banks and river valleys of the Grand Prairies and Lampasas Cut Plain, areas that were grasslands but are now mostly in cultivation to the east with ranching on the west. These prairie areas have remnants of the Midwest flora, such as bur oak (*Q. macrocarpa*). The Edwards Plateau, which was once a grassland, is now rich in tree species, the dominant tree being the escarpment live oak (*Q. fusiformis*).

More species of oak–39–than of any other tree grow in Texas. Five oaks are dwarf and classed as shrubs. Twentyfour are white oaks (i.e., they produce acorns yearly), and 15 are black (acorns need two years to mature in most cases). There are 15 oaks less than 30 feet tall, 10 oaks less than 50 feet tall, and 14 oaks over 50 feet in height. Nineteen of the oaks are "live" oaks; their leaves remain green through most of the winter. Nineteen of the oaks are adapted to the acid soils and high rainfall of East Texas, 16 are adapted to the alkaline soils of western Texas, and 4 thrive on the igneous soils and high altitudes of the mountains. Any area in Texas has an oak that can be grown for ornamental purposes. Other genera with several species include: *Crataegus* (hawthorns, 16–33), *Fraxinus* (ash, 9), *Juniperus* (juniper, 9), *Pinus* (pines, 8, with 5 species from West Texas and 3 from East Texas), *Carya* (hickories, 8), *Acacia* (acacia, 7), *Populus* (cottonwoods and poplars, 7), *Acer* (maples, 5), *Prunus* (plums, 5), *Yucca* (yucca, 5), and *Sabal* (palms, palmetto, 2). Families of plants with several tree species include Fagaceae (beech family), Rosaceae (rose family), Leguminosae (legume family), and Salicaceae (willow family). For sheer numbers of a species, no tree can even come close to the ubiquitous mesquite. This tree has now occupied well over 60 million acres of the Texas landscape and shows no sign of declining. After the mesquite, three oaks would contest for second place: from Central Texas to the Sabine, post oak; in deep East Texas, the southern red oak (*Q. falcata*), and in the Edwards Plateau escarpment, live oak.

Benny Simpson

Trinity River. Rises in three principal branches: the East Fork, the Elm Fork, and the West Fork. A fourth headstream, shorter and smaller, is known as the Clear Fork. The Trinity River proper begins a mile west of downtown Dallas and flows southeast, forming all or part of the county lines between Kaufman and Ellis, Ellis and Henderson, Henderson and Navarro, Freestone and Anderson, Anderson and Leon, Leon and Houston, and Houston and Madison counties. It then cuts across northern Walker County to form a portion of the line between Walker and Trinity counties and continues as the line between Trinity and San Jacinto and San Jacinto and Polk counties. At the northern line of Liberty County the river turns almost directly south and enters Trinity Bay just west of Anahuac. The Trinity flows 423 miles from the confluence of the Elm and West forks to the coast. It is thus the longest river having its entire course in Texas. The river rises on the North Central Plains, but most of its course is in the Coastal Plains area. The total drainage basin area is 17,969 square miles and includes all or part of 37 counties. The largest cities in the Trinity basin are Dallas and Fort Worth.

Others are Arlington, Garland, Irving, Richardson, Plano, Grand Prairie, and Mesquite. In addition to several dams on the river's tributaries, the Trinity is dammed just above Camilla in San Jacinto County to form Livingston Reservoir. Slow-moving floods are common in the middle and lower basin area. The extreme lower reaches are subject to hurricane-induced surge tides. The annual flow of the stream averages five million acrefeet but is highly irregular because the rainfall is often concentrated—hence the floods. The most disastrous Trinity flood on record was that of 1908. Reservoirs on the upper branches control flooding to a certain extent and provide municipal water supplies.

The Trinity has been identified as the stream that the Caddo Indians called Arkikosa in Central Texas and Daycoa nearer the coast, as well as the one that La Salle called River of the Canoes (1687). The name Santísima Trinidad is supposed to have first been applied by Alonso De León in 1690. The next year, Domingo Terán de los Ríos called the same stream Encarnación de Verbo. Domingo Ramón in 1716 probably applied the name Trinity to the present Brazos, for, when he later reached the Trinity, he was told by the Indians that other Spaniards called the stream the Trinity. The Marqués de Aguayo and other later explorers used the name Trinity consistently. In the colonial period the land along the lower stream was settled as far up as Anderson County. The Anahuac Disturbances were among the most historically significant events of the era. Settlement up the Trinity valley continued to advance rapidly in the period of the republic. Beginning about 1836 numerous packet boats such as the *Scioto Belle* (1844–) steamed up the Trinity River, bringing groceries and dry goods and carrying down cotton, sugar, cowhides, and deer skins. Some of the packets penetrated as far as Magnolia, 10 miles west of Palestine, and in 1854 one reached Porter's Bluff, 50 miles below Dallas. Such efforts continued, though navigation fell off during the Civil War. In 1868 *Job Boat No. 1* reached Dallas with a cargo, after a voyage of a year and four days from Galveston. In the years before 1874 nearly 50 boats continuously navigated the river as far north as Trinidad in Kaufman County and Porter's Bluff in northern Navarro County. In the peak season of 1868–69 boats carried 15,425 bales of cotton down the Trinity. With the construction of railroads to Dallas in the early 1870s the river traffic began to die. But the idea of making a port of Dallas has persisted. Over the past century the Trinity has become increasingly polluted, particularly from runoff in the Dallas–Fort Worth area. Since the early 1960s, when the river was described as "septic," efforts have been made to clean up the Trinity. The task is huge and ongoing.

Wayne Gard

Trinity University. In San Antonio; heralded by Ewing College (1848), Chapel Hill College (1849), and Larissa College (1855). After these Presbyterian antecedents failed during the Civil War, Cumberland Presbyterians opened Trinity University in Tehuacana (1869). In 1902 the institution was moved to Waxahachie, where it became a member of the Southern Association of Colleges and Schools and began to accept graduates of the defunct Fairemont Female Seminary at Weatherford as alumnae. In 1942 the Synod of Texas accepted an invitation of the San Antonio Chamber of Commerce to move Trinity University to the Alamo City, where by agreement it absorbed the University of San Antonio, a Methodist school. All credits

Ruth Taylor Theater. Courtesy Trinity University Archives. Trinity is well known for its campus design and buildings by Texas architect O'Neil Ford.

and degrees given by the University of San Antonio and its predecessors, San Antonio Female College and Westmoreland College, were acknowledged by Trinity University. In 1945 Trinity obtained its present site on the north side of the city. In 1952 the university officially moved to its new skyline campus, designed by architect O'Neil Ford. Trinity served a full century as "the college of the Synod of Texas," first of the Cumberland Presbyterian Church and, after 1906, of the Presbyterian Church in the United States of America. In 1969 the university and the synod dissolved their covenant. Although an independent university, Trinity maintains its pursuit of its original purpose, and the church renders reciprocal allegiance. According to its Statement of Institutional Purpose, Trinity intends to remain "a relatively small university in the liberal arts tradition, with a balance among the humanities, fine arts, social sciences, and natural sciences, and with the inclusion of limited and carefully selected professional programs which meet the needs of its constituency." Trinity is fully accredited and is a member of the Association of American Colleges, the Association of Texas Colleges, the Presbyterian College Union, the American Council on Education, the Independent Colleges of America, and the National Commission on Accrediting.   *Donald E. Everett*

True West. A nonfiction Western story magazine published by Western Publications of Austin; founded by Joe Austell Small in 1953 as a quarterly published by Sportsman Publishing Company. The first issue reprinted stories from a sister publication, *Western Sportsman*. The magazine became bimonthly in 1954. Topics included badmen, range wars, the gold rush, Indian fights, ghost towns, and buried treasure. The magazine ran 48 and 72 pages and sold for 25 cents. Its international circulation reached 185,000. Small was the editor and publisher. By the second issue, the magazine was published by the True West Publishing Company—apparently merely a name change and not a change of ownership. Pat Wagner assumed editorship in the early 1960s and remained until the company left Texas. The publisher chose stories by sifting "fact from rumor, lies and fiction." From 1955 until his death in 1963 Walter Prescott Webb served as historical consultant. Western Publications also carried on the publication of *Frontier Times*. Old issues of *True West*

were reissued in 1964 under another Western Publications title, *Old West*, so as not to devalue collector's copies of the original *True West*. Early contributors included J. Frank Dobie, Frederick B. Gipson, and Curtis K. Bishop. In 1979 Western Publications was sold to Chester Krause of Iola, Wisconsin; editorial offices remained in Austin until 1982, after which *True West* continued to be published as a monthly by Western Publications of Stillwater, Oklahoma.   *W. W. Bennett*

Tubb, Ernest. Country and western singer; b. Crisp, Texas, 9 February 1914; d. Nashville, 6 September 1984 (buried in Hermitage Memorial Gardens, Nashville); m. Lois Elaine Cook (1934; divorced 1948); m. Olene Adams Carter ("My Tennessee Baby," 1949); 5 children. As a teenager, Tubb was befriended by Carrie Rodgers, widow of Jimmie Rodgers. She helped him obtain a recording contract with RCA Victor in 1936. In 1940 Tubb signed with Decca Records and began commercially promoting his records through association with a flour company. As the "Gold Chain Troubador," he earned only $75 a week in salary and sold few records. He was almost ready to take a job in the defense industry when he recorded "Walking the Floor Over You," a million-record seller that paved the way to Hollywood. Tubb made several movies, joined the Grand Ole Opry in 1943, and remained a regular performer there for over 40 years. With his band, the Texas Troubadors, he kept a performance schedule that adversely affected his health and married life. By 1949 his hits numbered seven: "Blue Christmas," "Don't Rob Another Man's Castle," "Have You Ever Been Lonely," "I'm Bitin' My Fingernails and Thinking of You," "Slipping Around," "Tennessee Border No. 2," and "Warm Red Wine." Tubb recorded more than 250 songs and sold 30 million records. He was elected to the Country Music Hall of Fame in 1965. He owned a record store in Nashville and was known for his generosity to unknown artists who later became famous, including Hank Williams, Hank Snow, and Loretta Lynn. He played himself in the 1980 movie *Coal Miner's Daughter*.   *Phillip L. Fry*

Turtle Bayou Resolutions. On 12 June 1832, Anglo-American settlers opposed to the rule of Mexican commander John Davis Bradburn fled from Anahuac north to the crossing on Turtle Bayou near James Taylor White's ranchhouse. White was a loyal supporter of Bradburn. The Texas rebels had just learned that the antiadministration Federalist army had won a significant victory under the leadership of Antonio López de Santa Anna. Taking advantage of this favorable news, they aligned themselves with the Federalist cause by composing the Turtle Bayou Resolutions, which explained their attack against the Centralist troops at Anahuac in the first of the Anahuac Disturbances. They were, they claimed, not Anglos attacking a Mexican garrison, but Federalist sympathizers opposing a Centralist commandant as part of the civil war that had been in progress for two years between the Centralist administration of Anastasio Bustamante and those wanting to return to the Constitution of 1824. The four resolutions condemned violations of the constitution by the Bustamante government and urged all Texans to support the patriots fighting under Santa Anna, who was at the time struggling to defeat military despotism. A copy of the document was included in the seven-point statement of causes for taking up arms that was presented to Federalist colonel José Antonio Mexía in Brazoria on 18 July 1832. Mexía had arrived two days earlier with 400 troops and five vessels to quell a supposed movement to sever Texas from Mexico. The explanations offered by the Texas leaders satisfied Mexía, and he returned to the Rio Grande. No signatures are affixed to the extant copy of the resolutions, but seven of the Texas leaders (Wyly Martin, John Austin, Luke Lesassier, William H. Jack, Hugh B. Johnston, Francis W. Johnson, and Robert M. Williamson) signed the combined document presented to Mexía. The document was published in an extra edition of the Brazoria *Constitutional Advocate* on 23 July 1832 and appeared in Mary Austin Holley's *Texas* (1833).   *Margaret Swett Henson*

Twenty-fifth United States Infantry. A black regiment formed in 1869 in New Orleans by the consolidation of the old Thirty-ninth and Fortieth regiments under command of Col. Joseph A. Mower. The regiment was transferred to West Texas in 1870 and helped garrison forts Clark, Davis, Duncan, McKavett, Quitman, and Stockton, along with smaller subposts at Presidio, the Guadalupe Mountains, Eagle Spring, and Seven Springs, for the next decade. The Twenty-fifth initially included large numbers of former slaves and Civil War veterans. Later, recruiting efforts emphasized the North and the border states. The line officers were white. During its tour of duty in the Lone Star State, the regiment's enlisted personnel faced considerable racial discrimination. Like all units stationed on the frontier, most of its soldiers engaged in numerous routine garrison activities, road building, and mail escort. Individual companies also engaged in patrols and occasional skirmishing against Indians, and in 1878 one company participated in Colonel Mackenzie's foray into Mexico. In 1880 the regiment was transferred to Dakota Territory. It was moved to Montana in 1888. Four of its companies participated in the Wounded Knee campaign two years later. Much of the Twenty-fifth Regiment was employed as part of the army's bicycle corps during the mid-1890s. In the Spanish–American War the regiment served with distinction in the Santiago campaign. It subsequently fought in the Philippine Insurrection until 1902, when the unit was returned to the United States. In 1906 sections of the regiment's First Battalion were involved in the controversial Brownsville Raid. The regiment returned to the Philippines, 1907–09, to fight against the Moros. During World War I the Twenty-fifth remained in Hawaii, but it saw duty in the South Pacific during World War II. Its battalions were subsequently distributed among various standing divisions.   *Robert Wooster*

Twenty-fourth United States Infantry. A black regiment. On 28 July 1866, Congress reorganized the regular army into 5 artillery, 10 cavalry, and 45 infantry regiments. Six regiments were reserved for black enlisted personnel. Three years later, Congress consolidated the regular force, reducing the infantry regiments to 25. As part of this reduction, the Thirty-eighth and Forty-first regiments, two units including many former slaves, were combined to form the Twenty-fourth Infantry Regiment. On 1 November 1869, Col. Ranald S. Mackenzie, previously head of the Forty-first, assumed command of the new regiment at Fort McKavett, Texas, which had been headquarters for Mackenzie's old regiment. The following year Mackenzie was transferred to the Fourth United States Cavalry and replaced in his old command by Col. Abner Doubleday, a fellow Civil War combat veteran associated with baseball. Lt. Col. William R.

Shafter was second in command. The Twenty-fourth helped garrison several posts in West Texas and along the Rio Grande until 1880, when the regiment was transferred to Indian Territory. There it remained until the late 1890s, when it was shifted to Fort Douglas, Utah. During its years in Texas, the Twenty-fourth Infantry, like most frontier regiments, engaged largely in garrison duty, routine patrols, and minor skirmishing. Several companies, however, took part in Mackenzie's expedition toward the headwaters of the Freshwater Fork of the Brazos River in 1872 and Shafter's 1875 and 1876 forays onto the Llano Estacado. Strong contingents from the regiment also participated in Shafter's subsequent expeditions into Mexico, which were designed to interdict Indian raids into the United States. Detachments also saw action in the campaigns against Victorio. Composed entirely of black enlisted men and white officers during this period, the Twenty-fourth's soldiers encountered a good deal of racial prejudice despite their strong record in the campaigns against the Indians. During the Spanish–American War the regiment once again distinguished itself in the bloody engagements at El Caney and San Juan Hill. The following year it was sent to the Philippines, where it participated in antiinsurgency operations until 1902. In 1916 it served in the punitive expedition against Mexico. A brief stint in Texas the following year saw part of the regiment involved in the Houston Riot of 1917. In April 1942 the Twenty-fourth was sent to the South Pacific, the first black unit transferred overseas. It was used largely as a service unit in the New Hebrides until some elements saw combat on Bougainville in March 1944. Between December 1944 and August 1945 the regiment helped eliminate the remnants of Japanese defenders on Saipan and Tinian. Still segregated, the regiment was assigned to occupation duty in Japan following the war. It was afterward thrown hurriedly into action in Korea, where it came under criticism for its performance in combat and was deactivated in 1951.   *Robert Wooster*

Tyler, Texas. County seat of Smith County; 99 miles southeast of Dallas. The city was authorized in 1846 when the Texas legislature voted to establish the county and a corresponding county seat. The townsite, located near the geographic center of the county, was selected by a panel of commissioners appointed by the legislature and named for President John Tyler in recognition of his support for admitting Texas to the United States. In 1847 commissioners purchased a 100-acre site from Edgar Pollett and a townsite was laid out in 28 blocks around a central square. A log courthouse on the north side of the square served as the meeting hall and church. Another log courthouse was built in 1847 on the center of the Tyler square; it was replaced in 1852, when a new, larger, brick courthouse was constructed on the same site. Tyler was incorporated in 1850 and instituted an aldermanic form of government. A local Masonic lodge was organized in 1848 and an Odd Fellows lodge in 1851, the year the first newspaper was published. The rich soil of the surrounding area attracted numerous planters, and, buoyed by the prosperity of the surrounding farms and plantations, Tyler quickly emerged as a leading shipping and commercial center for the region. Numerous new buildings were constructed in the decade prior to the Civil War. In 1860 more than 35 percent of the total population of 1,021 was slaves. Not surprisingly, Tyler residents voted overwhelmingly for secession, and local men volunteered for army service in large numbers. During the Civil War Tyler was

Smith County Courthouse, 1876. Courtesy Texas State Historical Association. The original log courthouse (1846) was replaced in 1847 and again in 1852. This photograph shows E. L. Clay and W. W. Kidd's additions to the two-story brick structure (1876).

the site of the largest Confederate ordnance plant in Texas, and in 1863 a large Confederate prison camp, known as Camp Ford, was built four miles to the northeast. With so much of its wealth invested in slaves, Tyler and Smith County suffered from an economic depression in the early postbellum period. Economic woes were further compounded when the Texas and Pacific and the International railroads both bypassed Tyler in the early 1870s. In April 1874, however, the Houston and Great Northern began service on its branch line to Tyler. In an effort to ensure the town's prosperity, leading citizens worked to have a spur built from Tyler to Ferguson (Big Sandy). The narrow-gauge line, known as the Tyler Tap Railroad, was completed in 1877. In 1879 the Tyler Tap was acquired by the Texas and St. Louis Railway Company, which located its machine shops and hospital in the town. The Kansas and Gulf Short Line Railroad, founded the following year, also established machine shops there. Enlarged by the influx of laborers to the railroad shops, the city's population nearly tripled from 1880 to 1890. The postwar period also witnessed other important developments. The town's first bank, the Bonner and Williams Bank, was founded in 1870. Numerous new businesses were built during the 1870s, and despite fires that destroyed several city blocks, the downtown area continued to grow. A public school system was established in 1882, and by 1885 the town had Episcopal, Catholic, Baptist, Methodist, Church of Christ, and Presbyterian churches, two private colleges, public and private schools, a plow factory, three planing mills, wagon and carriage factories, an ice factory, several gristmill–cotton gins, hotels, an opera house, a waterworks, two banks, and two weekly newspapers.

Tyler achieved city status in 1907, and by 1910 it had 10,400 residents. After an election in April 1915 the city adopted the manager–commission form of government. A new three-story courthouse was built in 1909; it served the county until the present courthouse was constructed in 1954. Despite the importance

of the railroads, agriculture long remained the mainstay of the economy. During the early twentieth century cotton accounted for four-fifths of the county's agricultural income. After the mid-1890s, however, truck farming and fruit orchards became increasingly important. When a peach blight wiped out much of the fruit industry, many farmers turned to growing roses, which proved ideally suited to the climate and soil of the Tyler area. By the 1920s the rose industry had developed into a major business, and by the 1940s more than half the U.S. supply of rose bushes was grown within 10 miles of Tyler. The flourishing rose business gave rise to the Texas Rose Festival, which has become one of the city's major attractions.

Tyler remained a small agricultural and railroad city until 1930, when the East Texas oilfield discovery set off a boom. Numerous oil companies and field developers established offices in Tyler, and the city emerged as an important regional center for the oil and gas industry. The population mushroomed to more than 25,000 by 1933 and to 28,279 by 1940. During World War II the economy received a further boost with the establishment of Camp Fannin 10 miles to the northeast; this camp had a troop capacity of nearly 19,000 at the height of the war. In the 1950s industry replaced agriculture as the city's economic base. Foremost in the change was the petroleum industry, but by 1966, even though the petroleum industry still represented the largest actual monetary expenditure, the metal and fabricating industries involved more workers. The city also had extensive railroad and machine shops; manufacturers of woodwork, furniture, clothing, and fertilizer; cottonseed oil mills; and food-processing plants. By the middle 1960s Tyler had 125 manufacturing plants employing 8,000 workers. The more important industries included aluminum foundries, petroleum and chemical plants, concrete block plants, a tire factory, machinery manufacturers, and air-conditioning and refrigeration plants. Other significant industries were concerned with timber production and the manufacturing of clothing. Roses, other horticultural production, and cattle and hay production accounted for the most important sources of agricultural receipts. Tyler also emerged as the leading medical and educational center for the area. Medical facilities included the East Texas Chest Hospital (now the University of Texas Health Center at Tyler), the Mother Francis Hospital, Tyler Medical Center, and Doctors' Hospital. Higher education was provided by Texas College, which was established in 1894 by ministers of the Colored Methodist Episcopal Church, and by Tyler Junior College, originally established in 1926 as part of the Tyler public school system. The University of Texas at Tyler, established in 1971 as Tyler State College, had an enrollment of 3,725 in 1990. Tyler's population grew steadily from 51,230 in 1960 to 57,770 by 1970. Beginning in the 1980s, however, the population expanded rapidly, its growth rate at times even outpacing that of Dallas and Houston. In 1992 Tyler had 82,316 residents; approximately 75 percent of the residents of the greater Tyler metropolitan area were white, 21 percent black, and 6 percent Hispanic. The East Texas Fair, held annually in September, the October Texas Rose Festival, and the annual spring Azalea and Flower Trails festival attract visitors. Pounds Field provides airport service for the city and the surrounding region. Tyler residents also benefit from a symphony, several theaters and museums, a planetarium, municipal parks and rose gardens, and a zoo. A daily newspaper, nine radio stations, and one television station serve the area.   *Christopher Long*

U

Ugalde, Juan de. Spanish governor and army officer; b. Cádiz, 9 December 1729; d. Cádiz, 1816. He joined the Spanish army in 1738 and first saw action as a captain in 1743 against the Austrians in northern Italy. From 1749 to 1757 he fought against the Moors in North Africa and, during the Seven Years' War (1756–63), against the Portuguese. He was promoted to lieutenant colonel and dispatched in 1764 to South America, where he served as corregidor of Cochabamba, Bolivia, until 1772. He returned to Spain in 1774 and was promoted to colonel. On 26 March 1776, King Charles III appointed him governor of the province of San Francisco de Coahuila in northern New Spain. Before leaving Spain, Ugalde was also made a knight of the Order of Santiago. He took office as governor in 1777. His primary charge was to protect Coahuila from Indian attacks, specifically from the Lipan and Mescalero Apaches. Between 1779 and 1783 he conducted four campaigns against the Mescaleros in northern Coahuila and the Big Bend and Pecos River regions of Texas. For leaving the Coahuilan settlements inadequately protected while on campaign, however, he was relieved of duty in 1783. He remained in Mexico City until 1786, when he was promoted to commander of arms of the Provincias Internas. Again he took to the field in January of 1787 and combed his territory for Apaches, from the Bolsón de Mapimí in the south to the headwaters of the Colorado in the north, and from the Pecos River in the east to the Guadalupe Mountains in the west. He signed peace treaties whereby several Apache groups agreed to settle near his headquarters at Santa Rosa. Ugalde was promoted in December 1787 to commanding general of the Eastern Internal Provinces. In August 1789 he launched a lengthy campaign against the Apaches in West Texas within an area bounded now by San Antonio, San Saba, and El Paso. On 9 January 1790 he and his troops, with more than 100 Indian allies, surprised and defeated 300 Apaches at the Arroyo de la Soledad, the present Sabinal River canyon. In commemoration of this victory, the battlefield was named the Cañón de Ugalde; from it the city and county of Uvalde derived their misspelled name. After a change of viceroys, Ugalde was suspended in 1790. His service in the New World, like that of many Spaniards, was characterized by rivalries, political maneuvering, and abrupt reversals of fortune. He conducted his aggressive military actions against the Indians in disregard of the official conciliatory policy of the colonial administration, and it is debatable whether his campaigning pacified or merely antagonized the Apaches. After being ordered back to Spain, he continued in the service. He was promoted to field marshal (1797), made lieutenant general (1810), and awarded the Gran Cruz de San Hermenegildo in 1815. *Gary B. Starnes*

Union League. Also Loyal Union League, Union Loyal League, and Loyal League; a secret organization formed in the North in 1863 to bolster Northern morale and support the policies of President Abraham Lincoln. Texas Unionists in exile formed a chapter at New Orleans before the end of the Civil War. Returning exiles brought the league to Texas with them in the summer of 1865 and joined with local Unionists to form local league councils. Members pledged to vote for no one who had freely supported the Confederacy and to support only Union men for public office. In the election of 1866 the Union League supported gubernatorial candidate Elisha M. Pease against the Democratic candidate, James W. Throckmorton, but without success. In 1867 the newly established Republican party of Texas used the league to organize and mobilize newly enfranchised black voters and became an effective tool in providing identity and cohesion to its members. After General Sheridan removed Throckmorton from office on 30 July 1867 and replaced him with Pease, local league councils started identifying men for appointments to political office by the military. During the Constitutional Convention of 1868–69 rival factions of white Republicans within the convention struggled for control of the league, for the league controlled black votes and control over it ensured power in the state. The split was between the followers of Andrew Jackson Hamilton and Pease on the one hand and Edmund J. Davis and Morgan Hamilton on the other. The issues that divided them included the ab initio question, disfranchisement, division of the state, and support of the new state constitution.

At the annual Union League convention at Austin in 1868, the followers of Davis and Morgan Hamilton gained control of the league when they elected a black man from Galveston, George T. Ruby, as its first state president. Ruby pushed for immediate steps to end racial violence in the state and opposed the enfranchisement of former Confederates. He remained influential throughout Reconstruction because of his power within the league, and lent important political strength to Davis. The league's most important political action took place in 1869, when its leaders influenced the administration of President Ulysses S. Grant to throw his support to Davis in the race against A. J. Hamilton for governor. James G. Tracy of Houston, who became the state grand president of the league in the summer of 1869, was chiefly responsible for turning the national Republicans away from Hamilton.

Despite Davis's victory, however, the league was never fully organized in most of the state. At the 1870 meeting in Austin, Secretary of State James P. Newcomb became the grand president. He held this position during the rest of the league's existence. His efforts to support Davis and bring more blacks into the league produced few tangible results. The league was always stronger in the eyes of its opponents than in fact. During the congressional election of 1871 factions within the Republican party fought for control of the league, hoping to gain power over party machinery. Bolting Republicans under state treasurer George W. Honey and others attempted to replace Newcomb. The dissidents elected Johnson Reed, a black justice of the peace from Galveston, as grand president. Newcomb withstood this assault on his control with the support of national leaders of the league. The result of such in-fighting, however, limited the effectiveness of an already weak organization. After the 1871 election the Davis administration abandoned the league because it could not always be relied upon. In 1872 the league was replaced by a new group known as the National Guard. The next year, Republican leaders used a similar secret club, organized along military lines. Opponents of the Davis administration, however, generally ignored these changes and referred to all Republican clubs as the Union League. The league faded under increased suppression during and after the gubernatorial election of 1873, in which Richard Coke defeated the incumbent, Davis.

Carl H. Moneyhon

United Daughters of the Confederacy. Grew out of women's aid societies that operated throughout the South during the Civil War. Groups gathered to sew, make bandages, and entertain to raise money for the Confederate cause. During the war they cared for the sick and wounded and fed soldiers. After the war the organizations operated as auxiliaries to Confederate soldiers' homes and continued to aid during the rigors of Reconstruction. By the early 1890s the local groups had affiliated into state organizations in Missouri, Tennessee, and Georgia. Correspondence between Caroline M. Goodlett of Nashville and Mrs. L. H. Raines of Savannah resulted in a call for a meeting in Nashville to form a permanent organization. The three state groups united in 1894 for the purpose of honoring and serving the men and women of the Confederacy. Texas was represented at the meeting in Nashville by Mrs. J. C. Myers of Dallas. The Texas Division of the UDC was organized by Katie Cabell Muse in Victoria in 1896 and incorporated by the state in 1905. Texas had 84 active chapters and 3,305 members as of 1994. Some of the purposes of the organization are to honor the memory of those who served, to mark and protect places made historic by Southern valor, to collect materials for a history of the Civil War, and to assist the descendants of Confederates in securing education. The Texas Division sponsored the Texas Confederate Home and the Confederate Woman's Home when those facilities were needed. It has been active in marking historic locations—on courthouse lawns, for instance, or at the graves of Confederate soldiers. The UDC holds observances annually to remember veterans of all wars. The Mrs. Norman V. Randolph Relief Fund, established in 1910, provides a monthly assistance check to Daughters who are not in nursing homes. The UDC gives thousands of dollars in scholarships to descendants of Confederate veterans. An auxiliary organization known as the Children of the Confederacy is open to boys and girls from birth to 18 years of age descended from Confederate veterans. The Texas Division also maintains the Texas Confederate Museum in Waco *Esther F. Sims*

United States Border Patrol. Established in 1924; an outgrowth of many years of efforts to control immigration. In 1875 Congress denied entry to convicts and immoral women. The immigration statute of 1882 forbade the admission of idiots, lunatics, convicts, and persons who might become a public charge. The first Chinese exclusion law was passed that same year, and in 1885 some foreigners were denied entry on the basis of a contract-labor law. Subsequently, many of these individuals sought admission by illegal means, usually by slipping around the entry points. Thus evolved the need for a border-control force. Congress instituted a Bureau of Immigration in 1885, and in 1903 transferred its tasks to the Department of Commerce and Labor. In 1904 a small group of mounted inspectors, usually called Mounted Guards or Chinese Immigration Agents, operated out of El Paso. Though they never totaled more than 75,

they patrolled as far west as California trying to restrict the flow of illegal Chinese immigration. In those days, once an illegal had slipped past the Mounted Guards and entered the country, no officers existed to seek out and expel him. In March 1915, Congress authorized a separate group of Mounted Guards, often referred to as Mounted Inspectors. Most rode on horseback, but a few operated cars and even boats. Although these inspectors had broader arrest authority, they still largely pursued Chinese. The illegals disembarked on the Mexican west coast, walked overland to central Mexico, and rode the Mexican Central Railroad to Ciudad Juárez, Chihuahua. From there they were smuggled into El Paso and thence to various parts of the nation. Before the Immigration Act of 1917, almost no restrictions were in effect against Mexicans or Canadians, who could cross at will and go anywhere they wished. After 1917, however, both Canadians and Mexicans paid a head tax of eight dollars to immigrate into the United States. They also had to pass a literacy test. After this restriction, illegal entries from these countries flourished until the arrival of troops along the border during the Mexican Revolution and World War I (1910–20). When the war ended and the soldiers went home, prohibited crossings accelerated again.

In 1924 Congress, under authority of the Immigration Act, established the United States Border Patrol as part of the Immigration Bureau, an arm of the Department of Labor. The uniformed agency, started in El Paso, employed 450 officers. Its duties called for the prevention of smuggling, as well as the arrest of illegal entrants into the United States. Mounted Guards, policemen, Texas Rangers, sheriffs, and appointees from the Civil Service Register of Railroad Mail Clerks were employed. Congress authorized the border patrol in 1925 to assume authority over coastal operations as well as land, paying attention in particular to traffic from Cuba. Illegal travelers and smugglers had been infiltrating Florida as well as the Gulf coast. The government initially provided the agents only a badge and revolver; the uniforms did not arrive until 1928. Recruits furnished their own horses and saddles, but Washington supplied oats and hay and paid the patrolmen $1,680 annually. In 1932 the patrol was placed under the authority of two directors, one in charge of the Mexican border office at El Paso, the other in charge of the Canadian border office at Detroit. Most illegal immigrants from Mexico came only to visit their families or to work briefly in border towns. During Prohibition smuggling was a worse threat that absorbed most of the attention of the border patrol. Whiskey bootleggers avoided the bridges and slipped their forbidden cargo across the Rio Grande by way of pack mules. In intercepting these smugglers, more than one border patrolman laid down his life in dark, swampy thickets beside the river. In 1933 President Franklin D. Roosevelt united the Bureau of Immigration and the Bureau of Naturalization into the Immigration and Naturalization Service. The first border patrol academy opened as a training school at Camp Chigas, El Paso, in December 1934. Thirty-four trainees attended classes in marksmanship and horsemanship. A patrolman was not considered a horseman until he had ridden up the rugged, nearby Mount Cristo Rey. Then he had to descend, still mounted. Although horses remained the transportation of choice for many years, by 1935 the border patrol had begun installing radios in vehicles and stations. The workload and accomplishments of the force remained fairly constant until 1940, when the patrol moved out of the Department of Labor to the Department of Justice and was beefed up by 712 additional patrolmen, 57 auxiliary personnel, and added equipment; the force now employed 1,531 officers. By the end of the war, employees numbered 8,000. The force provided tighter control of the border, manned alien detention camps, guarded diplomats, and assisted the coast guard in searching for Axis saboteurs. For the first time, the border was patrolled by air.

The McCarran–Walter Act of 1952 established the immigration laws in effect today. The same year, border patrol officers were first permitted to board and search a conveyance for illegal immigrants anywhere in the United States. Illegal entrants traveling within the country were for the first time subject to arrest. In 1955 the INS split into four regional offices managed by commissioners who supervised district and border patrol sectors. During the war years and into the 1960s, while many men were absent from farms, a labor shortage developed. Farmers needed help, so the border patrol recruited Mexican nationals, called *braceros*, authorizing them to visit the United States for specific periods of time as legal agricultural workers. However, the program had serious side effects. Illegal immigration soared as those not chosen as *braceros* sought to enter the country anyway. Furthermore, with the phasing out of the program, many former *braceros* simply turned around in Mexico and crossed the Rio Grande illegally back into the United States. As illegal immigration roared out of control along the Mexican border, 62 Canadian border units were transferred south for Operation Wetback, a large repatriation project. Throughout the early 1950s a special task force of 800 border patrol officers was assigned by the United States attorney general to southern California, where thousands of illegals were rounded up and shipped home and thousands more left voluntarily. The task force moved to the lower Rio Grande valley, then to Chicago and other interior cities. Again, in spite of major successes in repatriation, many deportees simply turned around and recrossed the seriously undermanned border. In 1954 the border patrol began expelling adult Mexican males by boatlift from Port Isabel, Texas, to Veracruz. The project was discontinued two years later after nearly 50,000 illegals had been returned home. Various other flights, train trips, and bus trips originated along the border and terminated in the interior. Though partially successful, they also were expensive and were phased out primarily because of costs. Furthermore, by that time illegals had begun entering on private aircraft. In cooperation with other federal services, the border patrol began tracking suspect flights. In 1958 the El Paso office of the border patrol established a Fraudulent Document Center that was afterward moved to Yuma. During the Cuban missile crisis of the early 1960s, Cuban defectors living in Florida flew aircraft out over the ocean in an effort to harass their former homeland. The American government made this harassment illegal, and assigned the border patrol to prevent unauthorized flights. The patrol added 155 officers, but discharged 122 of them when the crisis ended in 1963. The early sixties also witnessed aircraft-hijacking attempts by various psychopaths, and President Kennedy ordered border patrolmen to accompany domestic flights and prevent takeovers. The Miami sector of the border patrol coordinated the effort. By that time the old business of alien smuggling began to involve drug smuggling. The border patrol assisted other agencies in intercepting illegal drugs from Mexico.

The border patrol of the 1990s carried out its functions with a variety of devices, including helicopters, blimps, airplanes, radar, floodlights, motion detectors, cameras, informants, dogs, vehicles, and fences and walls. Its duties were divided into several categories. A *linewatch* did surveillance of the border and apprehended illegal crossers when they enter. A *farm and ranch check* involved evaluating farms and ranches, which employ a broad variety of workers, many of them transient. *Traffic checks* were checkpoints along highways, where traffic is stopped and drivers are asked to prove their citizenship. Such checks lead frequently to the arrest of wanted criminals as well as the confiscation of tons of drugs. In *city patrol*, officers cruised various communities on foot or in vehicles seeking illegal immigrants. Finally, in the function of *transportation check*, agents constantly monitored buses, trains, and airports for undocumented aliens. In the 1990s, as the American public demands tighter control of the borders, the border patrol was again expanding and upgrading. The agents, highly trained and motivated, were taught Spanish. A significant percentage were of Hispanic origin.

Leon C. Metz

United States Naval Inactive Ship Maintenance Facility. Home of the "moth-ball fleet" at Orange, where military shipbuilding began in 1940. The office in Orange supervised construction at shipyards along the entire Texas coastline. Three shipyards in Orange produced more than 300 ships of various types during World War II. At the peak of production more than 22,000 workers were there, and the population of the town skyrocketed. After the war Orange was designated one of eight locations in which reserve vessels would be stored. The area of the shipyards, on the Sabine River, provided abundant fresh water, where ships would not corrode. Naval base facilities and 12 piers were constructed. In November 1945 the United States Naval Station at Orange was established with Capt. T. R. Cowie as commanding officer, and with the mission of providing logistical support and berthing space for the inactivation ("mothballing") of the Texas Group, Atlantic Reserve Fleet. Eventually about 150 vessels were moored there. In 1950 about 30 were reactivated for service in the Korean War, and up to 850 military personnel worked at the station. In 1959 the station was deactivated. In 1966 the Texas Group was disestablished, and the Naval Inactive Ship Maintenance Facility was commissioned with 197 ships and crafts in its custody. Ships were maintained, repaired, and kept in a state of ready remobilization. Inactivation and activation of ships, as well as all major overhaul work, were done on a contract basis by local civilian industry. In the late 1960s and early 1970s more than 160 vessels were still in custody. The facility was closed in 1975, and by 1980 all of the ships were gone. US Steel acquired some of the facilities, Lamar University at Orange used others, and the piers were sold to the Orange County navigation and port district. The navy retained 18½ acres—the site of the present United States Navy and Marine Corps Reserve Training Center. *Howard C. Williams*

University of Central Texas. A four-year private college in Killeen; established in 1973 as American Technological University to educate military personnel at Fort Hood and provide programs for business and education agencies. The name was changed in 1989. The institution closed in 1999.

Erika Murr

University of Dallas. A Catholic university. The University of Dallas charter dates from 1910, when the Vincentian Fathers so renamed their Holy Trinity College (1905). The charter became dormant in 1929. In 1954 the Sisters of St. Mary of Namur obtained it to operate a new institution that would absorb Our Lady of Victory College. After the mother superior, leery of the scope of the enterprise, withdrew sponsorship, the sisters and some fund-raising laymen induced Bishop Thomas K. Gorman to have the diocese take over sponsorship. The institution was to be owned by a board of trustees. Gorman announced that the university would be a Catholic coeducational institution welcoming students of all faiths and races and offering undergraduate work, with a graduate school to be added as soon as possible. The new University of Dallas opened to 96 students in 1956 on a 1,000-acre tract of rolling hills northwest of Dallas. Cistercian Fathers, the Sisters of St. Mary of Namur, three Franciscans, and a number of laymen composed the original faculty. The Franciscans left after three years. The Dominican Fathers joined the faculty in 1958 and established the Albert the Great Priory. The School Sisters of Notre Dame came in 1962 and established the motherhouse for their southern province on the university campus. The Cistercian Fathers now have a permanent abbey and a preparatory school for boys adjacent to the main campus. In time most of the faculty was lay people, of many faiths. A gift of $75 million from the Blakley–Braniff Foundation established the Braniff Graduate School in 1966. The Constantin Foundation endowed the undergraduate college with gifts in 1967 and 1969. The Rome Program began in 1970, and a legacy from the estate of Mrs. John B. O'Hara established the Summer Science Institute in 1973. Holy Trinity Seminary was founded in 1965 and occupied its present facilities adjacent to the main campus in 1967. The Graduate School of Management began in 1966, the year the graduate program in art was instituted. In 1973 the Institute of Philosophic Studies, a doctorate-granting program of the Braniff Graduate School and an outgrowth of the Wilmoore Kendall Politics and Literature Program, was initiated. In 1989 the university realized a long-range goal with the purchase of a permanent site for its Rome Program on a 12-acre estate in I Due Santi near Marino, Italy.

Sister Lois Bannon, O.S.U.

University of Houston—Clear Lake. At Clear Lake City; a graduate and upper-division branch of the University of Houston System, opened in 1974; bordered by the Lyndon B. Johnson Space Center and Armand Bayou Nature Center. It primarily serves the needs of the upper Texas Gulf Coast and the region's petrochemical and space industries. A council composed of the presidents of nine community colleges in the area advises the president. The institution began on a 50-acre tract donated by the Friendswood Development Company, a subsidiary of Humble Oil. It awards bachelor's and master's degrees through 78 programs in basic and applied research. It offers programs to business, industry, government agencies, and the technological industries of the region, and operates a wide range of centers, institutes, and laboratories. Faculty and administrative staff were originally drawn from the University of Houston—University Park and the nearby Johnson Space Center. Joint research in space technology and health resulted in the formation of the Research Institute for Computing and Information Systems in 1986. *Diana J. Kleiner*

University of Houston–Downtown. An open-admission undergraduate university, founded in 1974 after receiving the assets of South Texas Junior College. The Continuing Education Center and Conrad N. Hilton School of Hotel and Restaurant Management were also dedicated that year. The university was approved as a separate four-year unit of the University of Houston System in 1975. It offers undergraduate programs in arts and sciences, business, preprofessional education, public service, technology, and teacher education, as well as programs for the educationally disadvantaged, adult education, and activities in public service and research. *Diana J. Kleiner*

University of Houston System. Coordinates activities of the University of Houston—University Park and its branch campuses, Clear Lake, Downtown, and Victoria; established by the state legislature in 1977. Overall administration is conducted by a chancellor, to whom each branch president answers.

Diana J. Kleiner

University of Houston—University Park. The central campus of the University of Houston System; founded in 1926 as a result of Houston school superintendent Edison E. Oberholtzer's plans for a college. The resulting Houston Junior College began at San Jacinto High School in 1927. In 1938 a gift from Julius Settegast and Ben Taub of 108 acres of land southwest of the central city, a citywide campaign for building funds, and a donation from Hugh Roy Cullen and his wife combined to establish the campus and its first building, which opened in 1939. In 1942 the university was divided into six colleges and a graduate school. During World War II it became a training site for servicemen and produced 500 civilian pilots. The Houston ISD governed the university until it became a private institution in 1945. In 1950 the university had 14,129 students and 352 full-time faculty members. The next year, the physical plant consisted of 12 permanent buildings on 260 acres. The university established KUHT, the nation's first educational television station, in 1953. During the 1950s private foundations provided endowments and other funding, but in 1963 the institution was admitted to the state system of higher education. It was governed thereafter by a nine-member board of regents appointed by the governor. In 1960 the university chartered a foundation to develop a Texas environmental research center at the site of the former Camp Wallace near La Marque. UH began several research projects for NASA in 1962, and by 1964 research contracts in progress reached the million-dollar level annually. The university initiated a bilingual education program, an Afro-American Studies program (1969), and a Mexican-American Studies program (1972). In the early 1990s UH—University Park was divided into 13 colleges, offered 272 degree programs, and enrolled more than 33,000 students. The M. D. Anderson Library held 1.6 million volumes. Other facilities included the Sarah Campbell Blaffer Gallery, the Texas Center for Superconductivity, the Hilton Hotel School of Hotel and Restaurant Management, the Management Development Center, the Institute of Urban Studies, the Institute of Labor and Industrial Relations, the Solar Energy Laboratory, the Institute on Cardiovascular Studies, the Open University, the National College of District Attorneys, the National College of Criminal Defense Lawyers, the Continuing Education Center, and Arte Público Press, the largest publisher of Hispanic literature in the United States. *Diana J. Kleiner*

University of Houston–Victoria. An upper-level and graduate branch of the University of Houston System on the campus of Victoria College; established in 1973. UH–Victoria became a separate degree-granting institution in 1983, when it was given its current name. The university awards degrees through schools of arts and sciences, business administration, and education. Enrollment rose from 350 in 1973 to 1,108 in 1991.

Diana J. Kleiner

University of the Incarnate Word. In San Antonio; chartered in July 1881 as a Catholic college for women and operated by the Sisters of Charity of the Incarnate Word. The congregation purchased property from George W. Brackenridge's estate in 1897, and in 1900 the college was located on its 230acre tract at the headwaters of the San Antonio River adjacent to Brackenridge Park. Incarnate Word College was affiliated with the Catholic University of America in Washington in 1912. The present buildings were occupied in 1922. In 1971 the college became fully coeducational (the nursing school had always admitted men). In the early 1990s the campus comprised 56 acres and many buildings. The fully accredited university offered four undergraduate degrees and four graduate degrees. *Nancy Beck Young*

University Interscholastic League. Began at a Texas State Teachers Association meeting in Abilene in 1910. The leader of the organization effort was E. D. Shurter, who was commissioned by University of Texas President Sidney Mezes to undertake the service as part of the newly created Extension Bureau of the university. Known first as the Debating League of Texas High Schools, the league expanded its functions and in 1911 became the Debating and Declamation League of Texas Schools. In 1912 the league added a track and field meet by taking over the functions of the Interscholastic Athletic Association, which had been directed for three years by Charles W. Ramsdell. The competitive program among public schools has been expanded to include contests in dramatics, journalism, music, academics, essay writing, football, basketball, track and field, tennis, golf, and many other events. The UIL is now the oldest and largest high school association of its kind in the United States. In 1917 it began publication of its official monthly organ, the *Interscholastic Leaguer* (now *The Leaguer*), and in 1965 it opened its membership to all public schools. The organization, which operates as a nonprofit service, is divided into an academic division, an athletic division, and a music division. It is operated as an extension of the University of Texas Division of Continuing Education. Among the past presidents of the organization was Roy Bedichek (1922–48). The Texas Interscholastic League Foundation, founded in 1958, furnishes talented contest participants with college scholarships. The UIL also sponsors four student activities conferences in various parts of the state and the annual Interscholastic League Press Conference for about 1,800 students and advisors involved in school publications. In the early 1990s more than two million students annually participated in UIL activities. *Christopher Long*

University of Mary Hardin–Baylor. In Belton; originated in 1845 in Independence as the Female Department of Baylor University. Until 1971, when it became coeducational, MHB was the oldest college for women west of the Mississippi. In 1851 Baylor president Rufus C. Burleson divided the male from the female students. The latter stayed in the old frame building of Independence Academy with Horace Clark as principal and in 1855 moved into a stone building built to Clark's design. The tall stone columns of the Female Department building are all of Baylor University that stands today in Independence. In 1866 the Baptist State Convention of Texas severed the Female Department from the university and founded Baylor Female College, which operated under the original charter but was governed by a separate board of trustees. In 1886 the Baptist State Convention of Texas moved both Baylors to Central Texas—the men to Waco and the women to Belton. The original MHB building in Belton enclosed a dormitory for students and teachers, a dining hall, a library, a chapel, studios, and classrooms. In 1907 an administration and classroom building was begun. The college has always emphasized the liberal arts. At the turn of the century it had two degree programs, classical and English, the latter requiring no foreign language. These evolved into the B.A. and the B.S. degrees approved by the State Department of Education, which in 1912 recognized Baylor Female College as "a college of the first rank," and in 1913 began accepting its graduates as teachers without further examination. From the 1920s through the 1960s the college's Conservatory of Music won national acclaim. Baylor Female College was one of the founding institutions for Alpha Chi (1922), at first known as the Scholarship Society of the South.

The period of 25 years coinciding with the presidency of John C. Hardy (1912–37) saw the greatest growth in enrollment, which necessitated an expensive building program and plunged the college into debt. In 1925 Baylor Female College was renamed Baylor College for Women. In 1926 it was admitted to the Southern Association of Colleges and Universities and in 1927 to the American Association of Colleges. In the Great Depression the college was saved from bankruptcy by a gift from Mary and John G. Hardin. In gratitude the institution changed its name to Mary Hardin–Baylor College in 1934. By 1978 MHB had been reorganized as a university with five schools: arts and sciences, creative arts, business, education, and nursing. It was renamed University of Mary Hardin–Baylor at this time. In 1968 the Scott and White School of Nursing became a part of the institution. Since the admission of male students, the university has been affiliated with the National Association of Intercollegiate Athletics. It is also affiliated with the Association of American Colleges for Teacher Education, the Texas Association of Music Schools, the National Conference of Church Related Schools, and the AAUW. The university has changed its administrative policy from expansionism to restricted growth in order to house its students comfortably, to provide first-rate faculty, and to keep academic standards high. *Eleanor James*

University of North Texas. In Denton; founded as Texas Normal College and Teachers' Training Institute by Joshua C. Chilton in 1890. Classes were held on the second floor of the B. J. Wilson hardware store, on the courthouse square. The school received a state charter in 1891. By then it occupied a permanent campus, purchased by a group of Dentonites called the syndicate, at the corner of Hickory and Avenue B streets. The city government financed and constructed the first building, and nearly 185 students of various ages attended during the first year. John J. Crumley succeeded Chilton as president in 1893, and he and state Senator Emory C. Smith of Denton secured the right for the

"North Texas State Normal." Postcard, ca. 1900–1910. Courtesy TSL.

college to confer state teaching certificates. Wording in the Texas law granting this power accidentally changed the school's name to North Texas Normal College. The third president, Menter B. Terrill, enrolled a large number of preparatory students and awarded 268 teaching certificates and 24 bachelor's degrees during his presidency. Nevertheless, Denton leaders wanted a state-owned college. In 1899 state senator Charles V. Terrell introduced, and governor Joseph Sayers signed, the bill for a state charter. Money to fund the institution was not appropriated until two years later. North Texas achieved senior college status and conferred bachelor's degrees by 1917. Under President William H. Bruce (1906–) teacher training was emphasized and a teachers' demonstration school was begun. By the time Bruce retired in 1923 enrollment had reached 4,736 and North Texas had become the largest teacher-training institution in the Southwest. It changed its name to North Texas State Teachers College at Denton in 1923. Master's degree students first enrolled in September 1935. Enrollment and faculty salaries fluctuated through the Great Depression and World War II. The music department, now famous, became a member of the National Association of Schools of Music in 1941.

In 1945 a reorganization committee recommended that NT offer a general liberal arts education and develop a number of professional schools. Guided by the committee report, school officials established several new divisions, including the college of arts and sciences; schools of music, business administration, education, home economics; and the graduate school. The institution was renamed North Texas State College and given its own board of regents (since 1911 it had been governed with other state teachers' colleges by a common board). The institution conferred its first doctorate in 1953. In 1961 the college became North Texas State University. It brought Texas College of Osteopathic Medicine under its board of regents in 1975. In 1986 the Governor's Select Committee on Higher Education designated North Texas State an "emerging national research university." Since then a number of notable academic programs have been developed or strengthened, including the Hotel and Restaurant Management Program, the Professional Development Institute, the Classic Learning Core, the Information Systems Research Center, the Texas Academy of Mathematics and Science, the Center for Texas Studies, and the Institute of Applied Sciences. In May 1988 the institution was given its present name.

Robert S. La Forte

University of North Texas Health Science Center at Fort Worth. In 1972 Texas College of Osteopathic Medicine became affiliated with North Texas State University; NTSU was to provide the medical students with basic science instruction. In 1975, TCOM became a separate state-supported medical school under the direction of the NTSU Board of Regents. The college rapidly outgrew its scattered temporary facilities and began development of a central campus in Fort Worth. Its first building, opened in 1978, housed the clinical science departments, classrooms, outpatient clinics, administrative offices, and a library. Other buildings were soon necessary. Despite osteopathic medicine's traditional emphasis on teaching and clinical service, TCOM administrators believed that a strong biomedical research program was essential to the education of well-trained primary-care physicians. The first TCOM outpatient clinic opened in 1973 on Rosedale Avenue in Fort Worth. The Mobile Clinic Program also began that year, using a specially equipped van to bring medical services to eight Community Action Agency sites. In conjunction with the rapid growth of the clinical science and research programs, TCOM became one of the first medical schools in the nation to commit itself to a curriculum based on the promotion of health. At the same time, TCOM recognized its obligation to continue to train students in traditional medical skills and knowledge. In 1993 the Texas legislature recognized two decades of progress when it renamed TCOM the University of North Texas Health Science Center at Fort Worth. The center comprised the medical school, which retained the name Texas College of Osteopathic Medicine, and the Graduate School of Biomedical Sciences. TCOM's clinical services had expanded to include 6 general and family-practice clinics and 18 specialty clinics, including the DNA/Identity Laboratory and the Hyperbaric Medicine and Wound Care and Gerontology Assessment and Planning clinics. Twelve affiliated Texas hospitals served as major clinical teaching sites, the 265-bed Osteopathic Medical Center of Texas being the main teaching hospital. The graduate school formalized TCOM's 15-year history of cooperation with UNT in educating basic scientists; it offers both master's and doctoral degrees in biomedical sciences. By 1994, TCOM had graduated 1,519 osteopathic physicians. True to the osteopathic tradition, almost three-fourths are in the primary career fields of family medicine, general internal medicine, and pediatrics. TCOM has consistently produced the highest proportion of family medicine physicians of all eight medical schools in Texas. About 60 percent of TCOM graduates practice in Texas; of those, 31 percent are in communities of fewer than 25,000 people and 14 percent are in towns of fewer than 5,000.

Craig Elam and Ray Stokes

University of St. Thomas. In Houston; a coeducational Catholic university founded in 1947 by the Basilian Fathers at the request of the Bishop Christopher E. Byrne. It offers a principally undergraduate liberal arts curriculum with an emphasis on Judaeo-Christian values and a course of study in which theology and philosophy are of prime importance. More than half the student body is Catholic, but the university is open to all religious faiths. The university added a School of Theology in 1968, with a program leading to the M.Div. degree for students at St. Mary's Seminary. A master of religious education degree was added in 1969, followed by a master of arts in theology in 1982. In 1972 the School of Nursing was established with the cooperation of the Sisters of Charity of the Incarnate Word. In 1978 the School of Education, with a program leading to the M.Ed. degree, was added, and in 1979 the Cameron School of Business, offering an M.B.A. degree, was established. A center for Thomistic Studies, with M.A. and Ph.D. programs in philosophy, was founded in 1979. The physical plant has grown from the original building, the T. P. Lee mansion on Montrose Boulevard, to a 15-acre campus with more than 30 buildings. The plan of the university and several of the buildings were designed by architect Philip Johnson after the plan of the University of Virginia. The university is fully accredited. By the 1980s it had an enrollment of over 2,000. Through its Center for International Studies, the university participates with the University of Houston and Texas Southern University in the Houston Inter-University Consortium in International Studies. The Center for International Studies at St. Thomas also serves as the secretariat for the Gulf Coast Council on Foreign Affairs. The university sponsors several programs of study abroad, including a summer program in Mexico, a research project in Israel, and a semester in Rome in cooperation with the University of Dallas. The Doherty Library collections include the Hugh Roy Marshall Graduate Philosophy Library, devoted to St. Thomas Aquinas. The university is governed by a 15-member board of directors, at least 3 of whom must be Basilian priests, and an advisory board of 25 trustees. *Virginia Bernhard*

University of Texas at Arlington. The second-largest university in the University of Texas System. In 1917 local residents obtained state support for buying a former private school site and forming a branch of Texas A&M there under the name Grubbs Vocational College, a junior college with a high school department. In May 1923 Grubbs was renamed North Texas Junior Agricultural College, and 10 years later the high school unit was dropped. By 1945 students referred to the two-year college as NTAC. In 1948, in the reorganization of Texas A&M, NTAC was made a major branch. In 1949 the school was renamed Arlington State College. In 1959 ASC became a four-year college that granted undergraduate degrees in the arts and sciences, engineering, and business administration. Student enrolment was 6,388. A major building program between 1950 and 1965 saw the completion of 18 projects. The growth of Arlington and Dallas–Fort Worth provided the impetus for the rapid development of the college after 1959. In April 1965 the Texas legislature transferred Arlington State College from the Texas A&M University System to the UT System. In 1967 the college was renamed University of Texas at Arlington. In 1966 the university initiated master's programs in economics, electrical engineering, engineering math, math, psychology, and physics. The foreign language department participated in a cooperative program with the Summer Institute of Linguistics in Dallas County. Also the university participated in the Association of Higher Education, a consortium in North Texas, to introduce undergraduate and graduate courses on closed-circuit television. The Energy Research Center was established in 1968 to sponsor research in electricity generation and transmission. Centers in a dozen or so other fields were started. During the 1970s UTA initiated joint programs with UT Dallas and the UT Health Center at Dallas, including doctoral programs in the mathematical sciences, humanities, and biomedical engineering. By 1976 the university's four colleges had been joined by an Institute of Urban

Studies and by schools of social work, architecture and environmental design, and nursing, each of which was responsible for its own undergraduate and graduate programs. By the late 1980s, UTA covered 348 acres in downtown Arlington. The university joined the Fort Worth Chamber Foundation in developing an Automation and Robotics Research Institute opened in 1987 in Fort Worth. The library special collections include the Jenkins Garrett Library of Mexican War materials, the Cartographic History Collection, the Robertson Colony Collection, the Texas Political History Collection, the Texas Labor Archives, and the Minority Cultures Collection. *Samuel B. Hamlett*

University of Texas at Austin. The original University of Texas. In 1839 the Congress of the Republic of Texas ordered a site set aside for a university, but not until 1881 did the institution become a reality. Austin was chosen as the main site and Galveston for the location of the medical department. The university regents chose Ashbel Smith president, selected the faculty, and determined the curriculum. UT formally opened in its first Main Building in September 1883, though classes were held in the temporary Capitol as late as January 1884. The university is supported by the Permanent University Fund, the Available University Fund, legislative appropriations, and gifts and grants. The campus originally consisted of a 40-acre tract on College Hill set aside when Austin became the state capital. Over the years, additions have included an athletic field bought in 1897, a gift from George W. Brackenridge of 500 acres on the banks of the Colorado River in 1910, the campus of the former Blind Institute in 1925, the Cavanaugh homestead on Waller Creek in 1930, and the grounds of Texas Wesleyan College and property on Whitis Avenue in 1931. The J. J. Pickle Research Campus, a 476-acre site eight miles north of the main campus, houses research organizations in engineering, science, and the social sciences. The Montopolis Research Center is located on 94 acres in southeast Austin. Also attached to the main university are the University of Texas at Austin McDonald Observatory in Jeff Davis County, the University of Texas at Austin Marine Science Institute at Port Aransas, Winedale Historical Center near Round Top, the Bee Cave Research Center west of Austin,

Students having tea between classes in a field of bluebonnets. Courtesy Austin Public Library, Austin History Center PICA C00691. The main campus of UT originally consisted of a 40-acre tract on College Hill.

Old Main. Dallas Historical Society. In the 1930s this UT building was torn down and the current tower was built on its site.

Paisano Ranch, Sam Rayburn Library in Bonham, and the Institute of Geophysics in Galveston.

The university's old Main Building, completed in 1899 and later razed, served all purposes. To Cass Gilbert of New York, who designed the first library building and Sutton Hall, is due the Spanish Renaissance style that came to be used in most of the early campus buildings. Paul P. Cret of Philadelphia worked out a general plan of development in 1933, and his advice was sought in planning all structures built between 1932 and 1945. Because of the constitutional prohibition of the use of general revenue for buildings, temporary frame structures had to be erected to house the growing student body, especially after World War I, and the university became famous for its "Shackeresque" architecture. Oil was discovered on university land in 1923—gushers of wealth presciently anticipated by Ashbel Smith, though perhaps not in the form he envisioned. The resulting savings in the Available Fund made passage of a constitutional amendment possible in 1931, so that a bond issue for construction of fireproof buildings could be passed. A second amendment in 1947 authorized a bond issue of $15 million, $10 million of which was for the university. Of that share, $2 million was allotted to the medical branch. The enormous increase in student enrollment after World War II necessitated a second era of temporary frame buildings, some for instruction, others for housing. Nineteen buildings were constructed or acquired between 1950 and 1965, including Texas Memorial Museum, which was transferred from the state in 1959. The university was granted the right of eminent domain in 1965 to purchase property adjacent to the campus on the north, east, and south. The Lyndon Baines Johnson Library, housing presidential papers, was completed in 1971 on the university campus with university funds. It was staffed and operated by the federal government. In 1992 the physical plant of the university, valued at more than $1 billion, comprised 120 permanent buildings.

For many years, major instruction divisions at UT were called departments, and subject divisions within departments were called schools. The university was opened with an academic department (with six schools) and a law department. As the institution grew, more schools and departments were added until in 1994 the university had eight colleges and seven schools, in which it offered more than 100 undergraduate degree programs and 170 graduate degree programs. In the first year, 1883–84, the university faculty comprised eight professors, four assistants, and the proctor. Enrollment for the first long session was 221. As a result of the United States Supreme Court decision in *Sweatt v. Painter*, African Americans were admitted to the university for the first time in the summer of 1950. In the mid-1990s UT enrolled about 50,000 students in the regular terms. University employees totaled more than 20,000. In the faculty were two Nobel Prize winners and two Pulitzer Prize winners as well as numerous members of prestigious scholarly organizations.

After the example of the University of Virginia, UT planned at first to have no president. Under the regents the faculty were to have control, acting through a chairman chosen annually by themselves. John W. Mallet, Leslie Waggener, and Thomas S. Miller were chairmen before 1895, when the office of president was instituted. Waggener was president ad interim for 1895–96. Succeeding presidents have included William L. Prather (1899–1905), Sidney E. Mezes (1908–14), William J. Battle (ad interim, 1914–16), Robert E. Vinson (1916–23), William Seneca Sutton (ad interim, 1923–24), Walter M. W. Splawn (1924–27), Harry Y. Benedict (1927–37), Homer P. Rainey (1939–44), Theophilus S. Painter (acting 1944–46, president 1946–52), and Harry H. Ransom (1960–61). Between 1963 and 1967 the office of president of the main university was abolished and the chancellor of the system, Harry Ransom, assumed the additional duties. In 1967 the presidency was reestablished and Norman Hackerman became president. Lorene Lane Rogers, fifteenth president of UT Austin, was the first woman to be named president of a major state university (1974). In the 1990s the University of Texas at Austin General Libraries constituted one of the largest academic libraries in the country. It included the Harry Ransom Humanities Research Center, the Perry–Castañeda Library (the main library), the undergraduate library, the Center for American History, and the Nettie Lee Benson Latin American Collection. The earliest student publication, a literary monthly called *Texas University*, appeared in 1885 and had a long career. The first weekly newspaper, the *Alcalde* (1895–97), was forerunner of the current *Daily Texan*. The printing plant and bindery of the university issues official bulletins and has printed scholarly books. Development of the University of Texas Press on a large scale was begun in 1950. That same year the university established the office of chancellor to administer the main university and its branches: the University of Texas Medical Branch at Galveston, Texas Medical Center at Houston, Southwestern Medical College at Dallas, and Texas Western College at El Paso. James P. Hart was the first chancellor. Former students of the university were first organized in 1885 into the Alumni Association, which was renamed the Ex-Students' Association in 1914. In 1967 the Texas legislature changed the official name of the main university from University of Texas to University of Texas at Austin. UT Austin is the largest of 15 component institutions in the University of Texas System. By the end of 1992, it had granted more than 345,000 degrees. Public-welfare and research agencies conducted by the university date from 1884. In 1994, 87 organized research units were operating at the university.   *William James Battle*

University of Texas at Austin McDonald Observatory.

On Mount Locke, near Fort Davis; originally financed by a bequest from William Johnson McDonald, bachelor banker of Paris (d. 6 February 1926), who thought the observatory would improve weather forecasting and help farmers plan their work. The university, having no astronomy faculty, signed a 30-year collaborative agreement with the University of Chicago in 1932, whereby Texas financed the telescope and Chicago provided the astronomers. Warner and Swasey, of Cleveland, built the observatory, including the mechanical parts of the 82-inch telescope, then the second largest in the world. The director of the University of Chicago's Yerkes Observatory, Otto Struve, provided the telescope's concept and became the first director of McDonald Observatory in 1932. The chosen site, in the Davis Mountains, is located primarily on the cattle ranch of the pioneer settler G. S. Locke and was donated by his granddaughter Violet Locke McIvor. The location is ideal, not only because of minimal dust and artificial light, both obstacles to astronomical observation, but also because of the proportion of clear night skies. The dedication of the telescope in 1939 included a symposium attended by most of the world's leading astronomers. During World War II McDonald gained several European expatriate astronomers. Dutch immigrant Gerard P. Kuiper was director from September 1947 to December 1949 and again from September 1957 to March 1959; Struve was honorary director to 1950. Bengt Strömgren of Denmark was director from January 1951 to August 1957 and William W. Morgan of Chicago from April 1959 to August 1963. At the end of the original operating agreement between the universities of Texas and Chicago, UT had organized an astronomy department, and in September 1963 Harlan J. Smith was appointed director of the observatory and chairman of the UT Astronomy Department. Under his guidance, both the department and the observatory underwent enormous expansion, compelling him to relinquish the chairmanship in 1979. He retired as director in 1989 and was succeeded by Frank N. Bash.

The primary telescopes at McDonald and their dates of installation are: 82inch Struve reflector (1939), 36-inch reflector (1956), 107-inch reflector (1969), 30-inch lunar laser ranging reflector (1981), and 16-foot radio dish for millimeter wavelengths (1967, closed in 1988). The largest telescope, the 107-inch reflector, was partly financed by NASA for studying the close approaches of Mars in 1967 and 1969. The main coudé spectrograph, currently the world's largest, was designed by Robert G. Tull of the UT faculty and dedicated in 1968. The University of Texas Radio Astronomy Observatory was a large array of antennas, built by Austin astronomers, situated near Marfa and designed to survey the northern sky for radio sources at meter wavelengths. It was shut down in 1989 after completing the survey and was dismantled soon after. Construction of the Hobby–Eberly Telescope on Mount Fowlkes, adjacent to Mount Locke, began in 1994. Its design incorporates 91 metersized hexagonal mirrors mounted on a frame to give an effective collection area 8.5 meters in diameter. At a fixed altitude setting of 55 degrees, almost all objects in the northern sky are accessible when the telescope is appropriately turned on a vertical axis, and they can be observed for one to two hours through a moving prime focus tracker. The cost is a small fraction of that of an equivalent two-axis instrument. The project is a joint enterprise of the University of Texas at Austin, Pennsylvania State University, Stanford University, Ludwig-Maximilian University in Munich, and Georg-August University in Göttingen. All instruments at McDonald are now operated electronically under computer control. The W. L. Moody, Jr. Visitors' Information Center at the foot of Mount Locke offers exhibits, tours, and evening "star parties." McDonald also produces the bimonthly magazine *StarDate* and radio and television spots.

David S. Evans

University of Texas at Austin Marine Science Institute. At Port Aransas; a research unit of the University of Texas at Austin. Vessels from the institute have access to both the Gulf of Mexico and the bay environments of the Texas coast. Scientists and students can reach a multitude of coastal habitats including hypersaline lagoons, estuaries, mud flats, seagrass meadows, oyster reefs, barrier islands, and the vast environmental domain of the offshore continental shelf. The institute conducts research in marine biology, marine chemistry, marine geology, and physical oceanography. It has a resident staff of about 100, including scientists and support personnel. In the summer it offers upper-division and graduate courses, as well as opportunities for younger students to hear lectures, participate in field trips and research cruises, and otherwise use the facilities.

In 1892 the University of Texas Board of Regents informed Governor James S. Hogg of the need to establish a marine station on the Gulf. Early attempts to set up a facility in Galveston were unsuccessful. In 1935, UT zoologist Elmer J. Lund went to Port Aransas to investigate a massive fish kill caused by a red tide. He and A. H. Wiebe constructed a small, rough-lumber shack on the old Corps of Engineers dock. In 1940 the mayor of Port Aransas, Boone Walker, offered the university the current site, a 10-acre tract of his own property, for a biological laboratory. The Institute of Marine Science was established formally in 1941 with Lund as its first director. After World War II Lund purchased 12 acres and a building built in the 1890s from the United States Army Corps of Engineers and donated it to the university. In 1945 he established the *Publications of the Institute of Marine Science*, which was later renamed *Contributions in Marine Science* and is still published yearly by the institute. In 1946–47 two permanent frame buildings and a 200-foot pier into Aransas Pass were built. By 1961 a laboratory complex, boathouse and docks, seawater ponds, and other outdoor structures had been completed. In 1963 adjacent land was acquired, and the regents approved a $3 million expansion plan for addition laboratories and a boat basin. The name of the institute was changed in 1968 to Marine Science Institute at Port Aransas. The expansion plan was completed in 1973. In 1974 laboratory and dormitory wings and an apartment house for graduate students were built. Another building complex, completed in 1983, includes an auditorium, a library, and indoor aquaria for public display. The research vessel *Longhorn* became the institute's research flagship in 1970. In 1990 the institute had 72 acres of beachfront land. In 1973 the Texas legislature authorized the Texas Marine Science Institute as a part of the University of Texas at Austin. In 1975 the institute became the Port Aransas Marine Laboratory, was joined with the newly formed Galveston Geophysical Laboratory, and was placed under an umbrella organization called the Marine Science Institute. Both laboratories were affiliated with the Department of Marine Studies on the main campus in Austin, where the central directorate was also located. In 1984 the Institute for Geophysics in Austin was established and incorporated the Galveston Geophysical Laboratory; the Port Aransas facility once again became the sole location of the university's Marine Science Institute.

The flagship of the University of Texas fleet is the 105-foot research vessel *Longhorn*. Courtesy University of Texas at Austin Marine Science Institute.

Research ranges widely at the institute. Scientists and students work on such environmental problems as the effect of toxic chemicals and the restriction of freshwater flow into the bays and estuaries. Other research includes topics important to the understanding of the Texas Coastal Zone—for example, how nutrients are cycled, how energy is passed in food chains, how marine plant and animal species survive and reproduce in the environment, and how these organisms respond to oil spills, dredging, domestic waste, hurricanes, droughts, freezes, and other phenomena. Applied research in the culture of red drum, speckled trout, and red snapper provides fish farmers with information on stocking density, disease prevention, control of spawning, and development of inexpensive food resources at each level of the life history of cultured species. *Robert S. Jones*

University of Texas at Brownsville. On the grounds of Fort Brown; established as Pan American University—Brownsville in 1973. In 1972 the Texas Southmost College board of trustees took bids from Texas A&I University and Pan American University for the establishment of a four-year program in Brownsville, and in January 1973 the offer made by Pan American was accepted. The extension program was approved by the Texas Higher Education Coordinating Board in May. Classes began in the fall of that year, when the school had an enrollment of 262 undergraduates and 130 graduates. It offered three undergraduate degrees and three graduate degrees. In the fall of 1977 the institution became a separate entity governed by Pan American University regents but funded by the state. In 1989 it became part of the UT System under the name University of Texas—Pan American—Brownsville. In September 1991 the name was changed to University of Texas at Brownsville and the school began a partnership with Texas Southmost College. *Alicia A. Garza*

University of Texas at Dallas. In Richardson; grew out of the Graduate Research Center of the Southwest, established mainly by the founders of Texas Instruments. The center, chartered in 1961, concentrated on education and research in science and technology and was initially quartered in the Fondren Science Library at Southern Methodist University and subsequently on land at the Dallas–Collin county line. In 1967 the center was renamed Southwest Center for Advanced Study. In 1968 the coordinating board for the Texas College and University System recommended an upper-level state university in Dallas, a commuter school for juniors, seniors, and graduate students, to be named University of Texas at Dallas. UTD began classes the next year and from 1969 to 1975 enrolled only graduate students. In 1975 juniors and seniors were admitted; enrollment grew from 700 graduate students in the fall of 1974 to 3,333 students, mainly undergraduates, in 1975. The typical UTD student is 30 years old, married, and has children. Most students work and take at least one evening class. In keeping with the nontraditional nature of the student body, UTD has no social fraternities and no intercollegiate sports. It comprises seven schools: Arts and Humanities, Engineering and Computer Science, General Studies, Human Development, Management, Natural Sciences and Mathematics, and Social Sciences. The university encourages interdisciplinary studies by dispensing with discipline-based departmental structures. It offers 59 degrees, including the Ph.D. in 10 fields. In addition to its general functions, the Eugene McDermott Library is a depository for United States government publications and for state government publications. Its special collections include the Translation Library, the Arnold A. Jaffe Holocaust Collection, the History of Aviation Collection, and the Art Photography Collection. The Callier Center for Communications Disorders, which specializes in speech and hearing disorders, is part of the School of Human Development, although it is not located on the main university campus. Another off-campus university library is the University of Texas at Dallas Geological Information Library, which holds the world's largest collection of petroleum well logs and geological data. The Southwestern Legal Foundation at UTD sponsors seminars and short courses for government officials and others. UTD is accredited by the Commission on Colleges of the Southern Association of Colleges and Schools. Its main campus has 11 buildings on nearly 500 acres. Four hundred acres of its land are now being used for Synergy Park, an industrial park that focuses upon businesses that can interact with the university. *Anthony Champagne*

University of Texas Dental Branch at Houston. In the Texas Medical Center; a component since 1972 of the University of Texas Health Science Center at Houston. It began as Texas Dental College in 1905 and was a proprietary school until 1943, when it officially became part of UT. The name was changed to UT School of Dentistry by legislative act in May 1943 and to UT Dental Branch in 1958. The Dental Branch is the oldest state dental school in Texas and has provided more dentists to Texas than any other school. In addition to its DDS program it provides specialty training for endodontists, orthodontists, oral and maxillofacial surgeons, pediatric dentists, periodontists, and prosthodontists. The curriculum has included auxiliary dental programs in dental hygiene and dental assisting, though the latter program was phased out in 1991. In addition to its extensive dental clinic at the Texas Medical Center, the Dental Branch operates clinics for the indigent at Goodwill Industries in Houston, Laredo, and Brownsville. It also provides services at the Texas State Penitentiary at Huntsville. A research arm, the Dental Science Institute, established in February 1964, concentrated on microbiology of oral diseases, calcification, aging, oral malignancies, and soft-tissue diseases. The Dental Science Institute was phased out in 1995. *Don L. Allen*

University of Texas Dental School at San Antonio. Established in June 1969 and enrolled its first students the next year. In 1972 it coalesced with the other recently established University of Texas schools on the South Texas Medical Center campus to become the University of Texas Health Science Center at San Antonio. The present structure housing the dental school was dedicated in 1975, and periodic renovations have maintained the clinical and research facility. The school offers advanced education and residency programs in dental anesthesiology, dental diagnostic science, endodontics, general dentistry, oral and maxillofacial surgery, pediatric dentistry, periodontics, prosthodontics, and public-health dentistry. Other postdoctoral programs conducted in partnership with the Health Science Center's Graduate School of Biomedical Sciences combine clinical education with research experience and lead to M.S. or Ph.D. degrees. Fellowship and preceptor programs, providing comprehensive clinical training, are offered in areas such as geriatric dentistry, facial pain, esthetic dentistry, biomaterials, implantology, and maxillofacial prosthodontics. Continuing education opportunities offered by the school are a vital resource to dentists. A broadbased research program on oral health includes focused centers in microbiology and immunology of oral diseases, salivary dysfunction, dental imaging, geriatrics, dental materials, and osseous metabolism related to growth and development, regeneration, and biocompatability. The school provides clinical care and education to underserved and financially disadvantaged individuals. Affiliation agreements with institutions and clinics in locales including Brownsville, Harlingen, McAllen, El Paso, Mexico, Central America, South America, and Europe link the mission of the dental school with other professional colleagues. *Kenneth L. Kalkwarf*

University of Texas at El Paso. Opened in 1914 under the University of Texas Board of Regents as Texas School of Mines and Metallurgy; suggested by William B. Phillips of the University of Texas geology department at the International Mining Convention in El Paso in 1903. In 1919 the legislature made TSMM a branch of the University of Texas, and in 1920 the regents named it the College of Mines and Metallurgy. The broadening of undergraduate and graduate programs was reflected in subsequent name changes, to Texas Western College in 1949 and to the University of Texas at El Paso in 1967. UTEP is the second oldest academic component of the University of Texas System. When it was established, El Paso was the site of the second largest custom smelter in the world and a center of mining activity. El Pasoans gave to the state the original campus, now part of Fort Bliss, and later the first part of the present campus. The institution was moved there in 1917 after a fire. The campus features the only collection of buildings in the Western Hemisphere of Bhutanese style, reminiscent of the monastery–fortresses of the Himalayas. Noted El Paso architect Henry C. Trost designed the first buildings, and additional structures have maintained the style. El Paso Junior College (1920–27) was merged with the College of Mines in 1927. The first M.A. program began in 1940 and the first doctoral program, that in geological sciences, in 1974. Since 1976 the university has had a graduate school and six colleges: Business Administration, Edu-

Old Main, ca. 1920s. University of Texas—El Paso Library. The distinctive characteristic of the campus of UT—El Paso is the Bhutanese-style buildings. El Paso architect Henry C. Trost designed the first group of buildings, including Old Main.

cation, Engineering, Liberal Arts, Nursing and Allied Health, and Science. Both baccalaureate and graduate degrees are offered in all the colleges. The enrollment first reached 1,000 in 1939, 2,000 in 1947, 5,000 in 1962, and 10,000 in 1968, and since 1977 has exceeded 15,000. Library special collections at UTEP include military history and book design, the latter centering on Carl Hertzog, founder of Texas Western Press. The university operates the El Paso Centennial Museum, the John W. Kidd Memorial Seismic Observatory, and the Inter-American and Border Studies Center. Since it is located on the Mexican border, UTEP participates in numerous cooperative research efforts and cultural exchanges with institutions in Mexico and other Latin-American countries. Hispanics, both Mexican Americans and Mexicans, contribute significantly to life at UTEP, which is a center for conferences on linguistics, education, health problems, and other concerns shared by neighboring nations.

Nancy Hamilton

University of Texas Environmental Science Park. In the Smithville–Bastrop area. The Camp Swift Division is an animal-study area, and the Buescher Division is an ecology-study area adjacent to Buescher State Park. The idea originated in the mid-1960s with Dr. R. Lee Clark of the UT M. D. Anderson Hospital. A legislative bill to activate the park was signed in April 1971, and $100,000 was allocated for planning. The bill gave administration of the park to M. D. Anderson Hospital and permitted the hospital to receive gifts and grants from outside sources. The Buescher Division, including more than 700 acres of almost pristine forest land, was to be used in studies of flora and fauna, the effect of human beings on them, and problems of health and disease. A study compared the effects of the 500,000 visitors in 1971 in Bastrop State Park to the effects of visitors on Buescher State Park, which received about one-fourth that number of visitors. The Camp Swift Division was planned for veterinary resources and animal studies, including raising animals for experimentation. The potential uses for both divisions were myriad. In October 1972 the environmental science park became a part of the University of Texas System Cancer Center. The park remained divided into two divisions, the Carcinogenesis Research Laboratories Division in Buescher State Park and the Veterinary Resources Division near Camp Swift. Construction began on new research facilities for the study of environmental carcinogens in 1976 and was completed in September 1977. The Ralph Meadows Research Building, which housed laboratories, offices, and a library, was completed by February 1992.

University of Texas Health Center at Tyler. On the site of Camp Fannin (1943–46), a World War II infantry training base and POW camp. In 1947 the legislature authorized the purchase of the site from the federal government and chartered the East Texas Tuberculosis Sanatorium, which housed 1,000 cots in existing wooden barracks. The sanatorium was renamed East Texas Tuberculosis Hospital in 1951. In 1957 most of the army barracks were demolished and replaced with a new building. The legislature renamed the institution the East Texas Chest Hospital in 1971 and designated it a primary referral facility in Texas for treatment of pulmonary and heart disease. A $17.2 million building and expansion project for a new patient-care annex was begun in 1976 and completed in 1980. In 1980 a new six-story building was constructed and the old building was renovated for use as an administration center. In 1977 the institution joined the University of Texas System, becoming the University of Texas Health Center at Tyler. The center has the only East Texas postgraduate program to provide residency training for physicians in family medicine. The center offers clinical rotations for students in nursing, respiratory therapy, physical therapy, radiology technology, medical laboratory technology, and exercise physiology. Research in cell biology, environmental sciences, biochemistry, biomathematics, molecular biology, epidemiology, physiology, and microbiology is conducted in a biomedical research facility completed in 1987.   *John Evans*

University of Texas Health Science Center at Houston. Established by the University of Texas System regents in 1972; includes six schools and a number of special programs, centers, and institutes, all located at the Texas Medical Center. The schools are the Dental Branch, which began in 1905 as the Texas Dental College and joined the system in 1943; the Graduate School of Biomedical Sciences, begun in 1963; the School of Public Health, begun in 1967; the Medical School, begun in 1970; the School of Nursing, begun in 1972; and the School of Allied Health Sciences, begun in 1973. An executive council, made up of deans and vice presidents, advises the president on policy that affects the institution's approximately 1,100 faculty members and more than 4,000 staff members. Through its six schools, the center is also affiliated with 196 area and state hospitals and facilities, the major Houston hospital affiliations being Hermann Hospital, Lyndon B. Johnson General Hospital, the University of Texas M. D. Anderson Cancer Center, St. Joseph Hospital, and the Memorial Healthcare System. The Harris County Psychiatric Center joined UT–Houston, as it is commonly called, in 1989. Center clinics treated more than a million patients in 1995. The Health Science Center has over 170 formal affiliations, including the Houston Community College System, King's College of the University of London, Rice University, Tel Aviv University, Texas Southern University, Prairie View A&M University, Tokyo Dental College, and the University of Houston. In addition to its graduate-level training, the center offers a few undergraduate

programs. Its international educational and research programs operate in countries including China, Colombia, Egypt, England, Germany, India, Japan, Mexico, Russia, and Zambia. The center grants professional degrees in biomedical research, cytotechnology, dentistry, medical technology, medicine, nursing, nutrition and dietetics, and public health. It awards certificates in dental hygiene and cytogenetics. The schools of allied health sciences, dentistry, and nursing offer graduate and undergraduate education, and those of medicine, public health, and biomedical sciences provide only graduate work. In 1995 more than 3,000 students enrolled, not including fellows, postdoctoral students, and trainees in residency programs, and more than 900 degrees and certificates were conferred. Major research funding is supplied by National Institutes of Health grants, other federal and state grants and contracts, and fellowship awards. In fiscal year 1995 the university was awarded more than $75 million in research funding, a sum that ranked it among the top 100 research universities in the country; that year total research expenditures at the center exceeded $78 million. In 1995 endowment funds supported 16 endowed chairs, 31 endowed professorships, 11 endowed lectureships, and more than 50 other endowed awards and special funds.   *Debbie Orozco*

University of Texas Health Science Center at San Antonio. Began in 1959 when the legislature authorized South Texas Medical School. After heated debate a site on the periphery of the city, rather than downtown, was chosen. Construction of the school, located on 100 acres donated by the San Antonio Medical Foundation, was begun in 1966 and completed in 1968. Faculty was recruited as early as 1965, and students enrolled by 1966, but they attended classes in Dallas or Galveston until 1969. The first class in San Antonio had 104 students, and in 1970 the 33 students of the first graduating class received M.D. degrees. A dental school was authorized by the Sixty-first Texas Legislature in 1969. The University of Texas Dental School at San Antonio began, using temporary facilities in the medical school, in September 1970. The science faculty of the medical school developed graduate programs in anatomy, biochemistry, biophysics, microbiology, and pharmacology. In 1970 graduate programs for M.A. and Ph.D. degrees in these fields were approved by the state. Four years later physiology was added to the list. In 1972 the University of Texas Graduate School of Biomedical Sciences at San Antonio was established and assumed responsibility for the administration of these programs. The UT Health Science Center at San Antonio was also established in 1972. It was to be composed of the dental school, the graduate school of biomedical sciences, the medical school, and a school of allied health sciences. In 1969 the UT School of Nursing at San Antonio was authorized by the Texas legislature; it offered a baccalaureate degree in nursing in 1970 and a master's degree in nursing in 1972. In 1976 the board of regents reorganized the system school of nursing, and the San Antonio School of Nursing was placed administratively within the health science center. In July 1990 a Ph.D. in nursing was approved by the Texas Higher Education Coordinating Board to be offered at UTHSCSA. The B.S.N. to Ph.D. program is a partnership between the Texas Tech University Health Science Center in Lubbock and the UTHSCSA School of Nursing. The center employs more than 4,000 persons. In 1992 it received $82 million in grants, contracts, and awards. The Industry–University Cooperative Research Center,

The University of Texas Medical Department Bacteriological Lab, ca. 1910. Moody Medical Library, University of Texas Medical Branch at Galveston.

funded in 1985 by the National Science Foundation and industrial sponsors, enhanced the university's role in the community as a liaison between academic research and industry. The health science center, the Southwest Foundation for Biomedical Research, the Southwest Research Institute, and the University of Texas at San Antonio formed the Southwest Research Consortium in 1975. Research using combined facilities and expertise can be conducted among the members of the consortium that would not be possible in a single institution.

J. B. Aust

University of Texas Institute of Texan Cultures. In San Antonio; established by the state legislature in 1965 to manage the state's participation in HemisFair '68; to plan exhibits related to the history of Texas; and to house these exhibits. The ITC, a permanent state agency, was designed to study the ethnic groups that settled in Texas. It displayed relics, artifacts, and personal memorabilia, but only those that had a direct connection with telling the story of the people in each ethnic group. The exhibits made use of sound, color, movement, and atmospheric design. R. Henderson Shuffler guided the research projects and formed the original staff. The institute's continued function is to bring together, on loan, fragments of Texas history collections from museums and archives, to produce filmstrips and slide shows on

Texas history, and to publish historical pamphlets and books. ITC was put under the University of Texas System in 1969. In 1973 it became, more specifically, a part of the University of Texas at San Antonio. In 1995 the ITC had 100 regular staff members and 450 volunteer workers. In addition to maintaining 50,000 square feet of exhibits featuring 27 cultures and ethnic groups, the institute hosts the Texas Children's Festival, Pioneer Sunday, the Texas Folklife Festival, and other events.

David C. Tiller

University of Texas Medical Branch at Galveston. In March 1881, when the state legislature authorized the establishment of the University of Texas, it determined that the medical school did not have to be in the same city as the main campus. Between 1865 and 1881 Galveston doctors had organized medical societies, taught medical students in two colleges, examined candidates for licensure in Galveston County, participated on a board of health, treated indigent patients at local hospitals, and edited the state's only three medical journals. Proud of this legacy, Galvestonians lobbied for their city to be the site for the new medical school. In September 1881, 70 percent of Texas voters chose Galveston over Houston. After 10 years of political and economic struggles, the Medical Department of the University of Texas opened for instruction in October 1891 with 13 faculty members and 23 students. The UT regents added a School of Pharmacy in 1893 and assumed responsibility for the John Sealy Hospital Training School for Nurses in 1896. By 1900 the institution had graduated 259 men and 6 women as physicians, 76 men and 6 women as pharmacists, and 54 women as nurses. In 1919 it was renamed the University of Texas Medical Branch. In a classic study of all American medical schools published in 1910, Abraham Flexner concluded that UTMB was the only school in Texas "fit to continue in the work of training physicians." Displaying their esteem for both Carter and UTMB, the Association of American Colleges elected the UTMB dean, William S. Carter, as its president in 1917.

Throughout its existence UTMB has remained dedicated to patient care, teaching, and research. Expansion of the campus has accompanied expansion of programs for care of the sick, instruction of students, and research. State, federal, and private dollars have enabled the addition of major clinical facilities, including Negro Hospital (1902, 1937), Children's Hospital (1912, 1937, 1978), Woman's Hospital (1915), a psychiatric hospital (1931, 1982), a new John Sealy Hospital (1954) and John Sealy Hospital Towers (1978), ambulatory care facilities (1930, 1966, 1983), Shriners Burns Institute (1966, 1992), Jennie Sealy Hospital (1968), the Texas Department of Corrections Hospital (1983), and a vastly expanded Emergency Trauma Center (1992). As the major statewide multicategorical referral medical center, UTMB has treated a steadily increasing number of inpatients and outpatients; about 18,000 came annually during the late 1930s, and more than 350,000 by the late 1980s. A variety of educational programs evolved at UTMB. Although the School of Pharmacy was moved to Austin in 1927, the training of physicians, nurses, and other health professionals remained as central missions. By the seventy-fifth anniversary year (1965–66) 3,000 of UTMB's 5,000 physician graduates still practiced in Texas. By 1991 UTMB had conferred more than 9,000 medical degrees, 4,000 nursing diplomas or degrees, 800 master's or doctor's degrees in the biomedical sciences, and 3,000 diplomas or degrees in such allied fields as physical therapy, occupational therapy, and medical technology. The UT regents administratively centralized the latter programs into a School of Allied Health Sciences in 1968. They organized the biomedical science graduate programs into a Graduate School of Biomedical Sciences in 1979 and established two unique institutes—the Marine Biomedical Institute (1969) and the Institute for the Medical Humanities (1973).

During UTMB's first 50 years several faculty members engaged in experimental and clinical research projects. These professors included Oscar Plant in physiology, William Rose and Meyer Bodansky in biochemistry, Wilfred Dawson in pharmacology, Donald Duncan in anatomy, George R. Herrmann in internal medicine, and Robert Moore and James E. Thompson in surgery. Research activities increased dramatically after World War II, sponsored largely by government and foundation grants. The Hogg Foundation for Mental Health, the Harris and Eliza Kempner Fund, and the Moody Foundation, among others, have contributed. Approximately 700 full-time faculty members and 1,900 students participated in the instructional and research programs of UTMB's four schools and two institutes during the institution's centennial year (1990–91), when, with an annual budget of $438 million, UTMB was the fourth largest public employer in the Houston–Galveston area. The institution has had 13 chief administrative officers, among whom were John

Fannin Young Paine (1891–97), Allen John Smith (1897–98, 1901–03), William Keiller (1922–26), George Emmett Bethel (1928–35), and Truman G. Blocker, Jr. (1955–56, 1964–74).

Chester R. Burns

University of Texas—Pan American. In Edinburg; the only fully accredited four-year university in the Rio Grande valley. It began as Edinburg College, a two-year community college (1927) administered by the Edinburg School District. The Association of Texas Colleges designated Edinburg Community College a junior college in 1933. In 1942 the Edinburg School District became its board of trustees, and in the years following World War II the enrollment grew to 100 graduates a year. In 1948 the college gained regional status and secured partial state funding, along with independent legal standing. In 1950 an 8½-acre tract of property, designated the "West University," was purchased by the school. In 1951 the state legislature passed a bill allowing Hidalgo County to hold a referendum for a four-year university, and as a result Edinburg became Pan Regional College. In January 1952 the name was changed to Pan American College. By the early 1960s the college employed 80 permanent faculty members. On 1 September 1965 it was fully integrated as the twenty-second institution in the Texas System of Colleges and Universities as a state senior college. By the end of the decade state and federal money had helped with an extensive building program, which included a $1.5 million fine-arts complex. In 1970 the institution gained approval to operate graduate programs and began offering master's degrees in the arts, education, and science. By the fall of 1971 Pan American had gained full university status and changed its name to Pan American University. In 1973 a campus at Brownsville was added. In 1981 Miguel Navarez, vice president for student affairs, assumed the presidency, thus becoming the first Hispanic president of a major university in Texas. In 1989 the university merged with the University of Texas System. *Rex Field*

University of Texas of the Permian Basin. In Odessa; authorized by the Texas legislature in 1969 to accept only junior, senior, and master's degree graduate students. After long delay caused by a lawsuit concerning the validity of property deeds, transitional buildings were constructed. Classes began with an initial enrollment of 1,112 in 1973, when innovations included term tenure for faculty, modular classrooms, selfpaced instruction, no student dorms, and a sports program centering around rugby rather than the hallowed football or basketball. Enrollment was expected to be made up largely of transfers from local junior colleges; however, this proved to be erroneous, as did estimates of student numbers. Many students were older residents of the area. Experience also proved many of the innovations instituted at UTPB to be unfeasible. Selfpaced classes took a progressively minor role in instruction, mobile homes were placed on campus in 1976 to provide student housing, and the open lab was replaced with traditional lab facilities. The university was restructured in 1991, when Governor Ann Richards signed a bill adding freshman and sophomore classes.

Bobbie Jean Klepper

University of Texas Press. At the University of Texas at Austin. The press has published and distributed books, journals, and electronic publications in many fields. In addition to its concentration on Texas, it has published works on regions as remote as the Middle East and in fields ranging from natural science through anthropology to literature translations. Books bearing the imprint of the University of Texas Press were printed by the university's printing division at the request of faculty authors beginning in 1922. The press as such, under director Frank H. Wardlaw (1950–74), issued its first book in 1951, John and Jeannette Varner's translation of Garcilaso de la Vega's *The Florida of the Inca*, still in print in the 1990s. Encouraged by historian Walter Webb, Wardlaw originally emphasized regional studies and Latin American studies. In the mid-1990s that emphasis continued, with literature in translation forming an important component of the Latin-American studies program. In the 1970s the press established a journals division with three journals in its program. By 1995 it was publishing or distributing 14 journals in the humanities and social sciences, including the *Journal of Politics, Social Science Quarterly, Cinema Journal,* and *American Short Fiction,* a finalist for the 1993 and 1995 National Magazine Awards for fiction. Most of the journals published by the press are related to its book acquisitions and to the academic areas in which UT is strong. In 1977 the press moved into its present premises east of the main campus in Austin. In 1985 the press established an endowed fellowship program that provides a UT graduate a year of employment and training in book publishing. In 1995 the press was chosen to participate in a program, sponsored by the Association of American University Presses and the Coalition for Networked Information, to advance university presses in the networked information environment and to encourage cooperation between the university press, library, and computer center. In 1994 the press published 85 new books and by 1995 had 900 titles in print. UT Press distributes books worldwide for museums and other academic and cultural organizations and is the instate sales representative for the university presses of Nebraska, New Mexico, Oklahoma, and Texas Tech.

Joanna Hitchcock

University of Texas at San Antonio. Established in 1969 in northwest San Antonio. Its master plan, approved in 1971, envisioned 27 undergraduate and 15 graduate degree plans in 5 multidisciplinary colleges. The initial development of the university occurred in two phases. The first (1972–) was the construction of seven facilities between 1973 and 1976. The university began admitting graduate students in June 1973 and held classes at the Koger Center, a temporary off-campus location. In 1975 the programs moved to the newly completed campus, and in 1976 the first freshman class was admitted. The Southern Association of Colleges and Schools accredited the graduate program in 1974 and the undergraduate program in 1977. The second phase—the construction of additional buildings—was completed by 1981. In 1982 the academic program was restructured into four colleges, and an engineering division was added. In 1985 the university established a master's degree in biotechnology. UTSA was a founding member of the Southwest Research Consortium, a collaborative effort of San Antonio research institutions that includes UTSA, the University of Texas Health Science Center at San Antonio, and the Southwest Research Institute. The university's economic development centers provide services to San Antonio and South Texas businesses and communities through cooperative public–private sector arrangements. In 1986 UTSA was chosen by the American Association of State Colleges and

Medical College Building, located at 1420 Hall Street. Photo postcard, ca. 1910. Courtesy TSL.

Universities as a national model for this type of cooperation. UTSA offers primary experience in archeology. The University of Texas Institute of Texan Cultures was linked administratively with UTSA in 1986. UT San Antonio, in accord with its mandate, has developed into a comprehensive public metropolitan university. In 1989 the university offered 40 undergraduate and 20 graduate degree programs. Its library collection includes extensive materials on San Antonio, Texana, Western Americana, Spanish colonial history, and architecture. *Linda J. Whitson*

University of Texas Southwestern Medical Center at Dallas. Organized as the University of Texas Health Science Center at Dallas in 1972; renamed in 1987. The center is located near two primary teaching hospitals, Parkland Memorial and Children's Medical Center. Southwestern Medical Center comprises the Southwestern Medical School, the Southwestern Allied Health Sciences School, and the Southwestern Graduate School of Biomedical Sciences. Each is under the direction of a dean, and the entire center is under the direction of a president. Enrollment at Southwestern Medical School is limited to 200 students per entering class. In addition to the M.D. program, the school offers joint programs, in association with the Graduate School of Biomedical Science, that lead to a combined M.D.–Ph.D. This medical school developed from a private and unaffiliated medical school, Southwestern Medical College of the Southwestern Medical Foundation, which came into existence in 1943 after Baylor Medical College moved to Houston. In 1949 the college became a part of the University of Texas under the name Southwestern Medical School. In addition to the established curriculum, the medical school provides instruction to around 300 postdoctoral fellows and 900 clinical residents stationed in the primary teaching hospitals and the Veterans Affairs Medical Center in Dallas. A large and increasing continuing-education program provides courses to more than 15,000 physicians annually. The Southwestern Allied Health Sciences School developed out of degree training in medical art and illustration, a program that was attached to Southwestern Medical College at the time the school became a part of the University of Texas. The first students in allied health sciences enrolled in 1973. By 1984 the school offered B.S. degrees in such areas as allied health education, nutrition and dietetics, and gerontology. The Southwestern Graduate School of Biomedical Sciences developed from programs approved in 1953 for the Ph.D. in biophysics and microbiology. Subsequently, 14 programs leading to advanced degrees have been approved by the Southern Association of Colleges and Schools. Support for the Southwestern Medical Center derives from legislative appropriations, the Permanent University Fund, and other sources. In 1985 UT Southwestern faculty members Michael Brown and Joseph Goldstein were awarded the Nobel Prize in medicine for their work in cholesterol metabolism. Theirs was the first Nobel Prize in medicine awarded in Texas. In 1988 another faculty member, Johann Deisenhofer, a professor of biochemistry, won the Nobel Prize for chemistry along with two West Germans. In the 1990s UT Southwestern had a new 160-bed hospital—Zale–Lipshy University Hospital—and also operated the James W. Aston Ambulatory Care Center. *John S. Chapman*

University of Texas System. Reorganized in 1967; embraces general academic institutions, health science centers, a cancer center, and a nursing school. UT Austin, the largest component institution, includes the UT Austin McDonald Observatory at Mount Locke and the UT Austin Marine Science Institute in Port Aransas. Other general academic institutions within the system are UT Arlington, UT Brownsville, UT Dallas, UT El Paso, UT–Pan American in Edinburg, UT of the Permian Basin in Odessa, UT Tyler, UT San Antonio, and the UT Institute of Texan Cultures at San Antonio. The health science centers, the cancer center, and the nursing school were organized in October 1972. Under the administrative control of each of these medical units were several individual institutions. In 1995 the health science centers were UT Southwestern Medical Center in Dallas, including UT Southwestern Medical School, UT Graduate School of Biomedical Science, and UT School of Allied Health Sciences; UT Medical Branch at Galveston, including UT Medical School at Galveston, UT Graduate School of Biomedical Sciences, UT School of Allied Health Sciences, UT Marine Biomedical Institute, UT Institute for the Medical Humanities, and UT Medical Branch Hospitals; the UT Health Science Center at Houston, including UT Medical School at Houston, UT Dental Branch, UT Graduate School of Biomedical Sciences, UT School of Allied Health Sciences, UT School of Public Health, UT Mental Sciences Institute, and UT Speech and Hearing Institute; and the UT Health Science Center at San Antonio, including UT Medical School at San Antonio, UT Dental School, and UT Graduate School of Biomedical Sciences at San Antonio. UT Health Center at Tyler provided medical care to East Texas residents, as well as research and training for physicians. The UT System Cancer Center comprises the UT M. D. Anderson Cancer Center at Houston and the UT Environmental Science Park in Bastrop. The UT System School of Nursing included UT Austin School of Nursing, UT School of Nursing at El Paso, UT School of Nursing at Galveston, UT School of Nursing at Houston, and UT School of Nursing at San Antonio. The UT System is governed by a nine-member board of regents selected from different parts of the state, nominated by the governor, and appointed by the state Senate for six-year terms. It has been administered by both presidents and chancellors, among whom was Harry Huntt Ransom.

University of Texas at Tyler. Opened as Tyler State college in 1973, with upper-division classes in the abandoned O. M. Roberts Junior High School. In 1975, TSC became Texas Eastern University and moved to its permanent campus. In 1979, Governor William P. Clements, Jr., signed legislation making the university a part of the University of Texas System. UT Tyler is the only public, degree-granting university in the East Texas Planning Region, an area of 14 counties. There, students may earn bachelor's or master's degrees in 52 areas of study. Community-service programs include the Small Business Institute, Office of Business and Economic Research, Technology Partnership Organization, Family Violence Research and Treatment Center, Academic Nursing Center, and Learning Development Center. *Vista K. McCroskey*

Urbanization. Urbanization is the process of becoming urban. Living together in villages, towns, and cities is a natural condition of human life that has obtained since the beginning of civilization 10,000 years ago. Cities, for better or worse, have been deeply involved in developing the main characteristics of civilization—literacy, government, high arts, commerce, technology. Urban places have been focal points for action and ideas, and gateways for trade and migration. The future of humanity is to become urban; about half of the world's population will be living in cities in 2000. Texas shares this human legacy, for in the 1990s more than 80 percent of its citizens lived within city limits. For Texas, therefore, urbanization is practically complete. Although often unrecognized, the history of city building is one of the most significant themes in Lone Star history.

The urbanization of Texas is mainly the result of European settlement and culture. The Indian contribution is slight, since there is little in modern Texas cities that can be traced to Indian origins except perhaps genetic matter in segments of the population. This physical heritage has had very little discernible influence upon the constructed environment. Nevertheless, Indians were in some sense forerunners of urbanization in Texas. The Caddos of East Texas lived in permanent villages and may have descended from the Mound Builders of the Mississippi and Ohio River basins. Evidence at Cahokia, Illinois, suggests that these Indians possessed an urban instinct. The Pueblo Indians of Arizona and New Mexico can also be seen as village people. They contributed adobe architecture and art motifs to the Southwest. Some Indian names, moreover, remain in the language and on the maps. Places like Waco and Nacogdoches take their names from local tribes and village sites. The word *Texas*, of course, was adopted by the Spanish from a Caddo Indian word for "friend." Depending upon their degree of hostility or receptivity, Indians also influenced the location of Spanish missions and presidios as well as Anglo-American forts.

Town building in a modern sense, however, resulted primarily from Spanish and Anglo-American efforts. After the entrada of Vázquez de Coronado, the Spanish settled into a slow, deliberate northward movement out of Mexico. Pueblos (towns), presidios (garrisons), and missions (churches) were a part of this as well as ranches and farms. The monarchs ruled through these urban institutions. The Laws of the Indies (1573), moreover, prescribed town planning by dictating an elevated location, central plaza, street pattern, and sites for church, shops, government buildings, hospitals, and slaughterhouses. Today this is most clearly seen in downtown San Antonio, where the Spanish

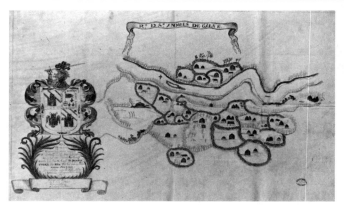

Mapa de la provincia donde habita la Nacion Casducacho (Texas) . . . Manuscript map. Courtesy TSL and Archivo General de Indias, Seville. The Caddo Indians of East Texas lived in permanent villages. This map shows a village near the site of what is now Texarkana, comprising family compounds separated by hedgerows, with a temple on the western edge and the chief's house in the center.

Governor's Palace borders Military Plaza and San Fernando Cathedral fronts Main Plaza. The plazas were built to the specifications of the old laws and have persisted to the present in shape and form. The city began as a supply depot for Spanish missions in East Texas and Louisiana in 1718. The post shortly expanded. Priests established missions, farmed irrigated fields, and laid the cornerstone of the Alamo chapel in 1744. In 1731 a small group of Canary Islanders settled nearby, started farms, parceled out town lots, and established the first official municipality in Texas, San Fernando de Béxar. San Antonio de Béxar became the provincial capital in 1772 with a 10-room, adobe Governor's Palace as headquarters for Spanish rule in Texas. San Antonio was the largest Spanish settlement in provincial Texas, with an early-nineteenth-century population of 2,500. Its success came from its central location in the province, fresh water from the spring-fed San Antonio River, remoteness from the fierce Comanches, and Spanish persistence.

Several lesser settlements also exemplified Spanish town-building. In East Texas Nacogdoches had 770 inhabitants at the end of the empire. Its history is one of abortive missionary efforts, retreat from French incursions, abandonment, fire, flood, disease, and, finally, resettlement in the late eighteenth century by a mixed group of Spaniards, Cherokee Indians, and Americans. Antonio Gil Ibarvo led the reoccupation and probably used the Law of the Indies to lay out the town in 1779. There was a public square with streets leading from the four corners in the familiar gridiron pattern. Nacogdoches, however, quickly came under the influence of westward-moving Americans. After the Louisiana Purchase in 1803 it became a gateway for land-hungry pioneers venturing out of the American Southland. James Long used the town as a staging ground for rebellion in 1819, and later inhabitants reacted to the high-handed Haden Edwards with the Fredonian Rebellion in 1826. In southern Texas the Spanish settlement of La Bahía claimed a population of 618 in 1803. It started in 1722 on Matagorda Bay at the site of La Salle's failed fort. While digging the foundations for a presidio the workers found French nails and gun fragments. To escape the unhealthful conditions on the coast and for military purposes the settlement moved in 1726 to the Guadalupe River and

in 1749 to the San Antonio River. In 1829 the Mexican government changed the name of the loosely linked presidio, mission, and civil settlement to Goliad, a name made infamous in the Texas Revolution for the willful slaughter of Texan prisoners of war. In its move northward, the Spanish Empire also scattered presidios, missions, and pueblos through the Rio Grande valley. Laredo, for example, started in 1755 as a pueblo and then acquired a mission in 1762. In late 1659 Father García de San Francisco de Zúñiga, moreover, established the first of the missions at El Paso del Norte. By the end of the century this area of the northern Rio Grande was the site of six missions, four pueblos, and a presidio. The mission area at Ysleta, now a part of El Paso, is considered the oldest settlement in Texas. It dates from the Pueblo Indian uprising of 1680, when Spanish and Indian refugees retreated from New Mexico. The Spanish culture in the Valley has been sustained over time by a continuing flow of migrants back and forth across the river. Elsewhere in Texas, however, Spanish urban influence decreased following the Texas Revolution. The Hispanic population in Texas, despised after the revolution, dropped to as little as 4 percent in the late nineteenth century. Yet the flow and ebb of the Spanish Empire left a residue of distinct architecture, gridiron street patterns, plazas, Catholicism, food, and language in Southwest Texas, as well as a heritage of ranching that became the foundation for the range cattle industry. The sounds of the Iberian past still echo in the place names—San Antonio, El Paso, Amarillo, Corpus Christi, Galveston, Laredo, San Angelo, San Marcos—while the clothing, animals, and equipment of the vaquero still haunt the American West.

The arrival of Moses Austin in 1820 at the Governor's Palace in San Antonio marks the beginning of American influence in Texas urbanization. The Spanish needed population in order to hold their northern frontiers, and Austin offered willing American pioneers. Settlement began on empresario grants with small towns used as administrative points—San Patricio (John McMullen and James McGloin), San Felipe (Stephen F. Austin), Sarahville de Viesca (Sterling C. Robertson), Gonzales (Green DeWitt), and Victoria (Martín De León). The empresarios were given more freedom than the early Spaniards to determine the shape of their towns. The American and north European immigrants brought conflicting ideas about language, slavery, free enterprise, democracy, Protestantism, and freedom of speech. The culture flowed mainly from the cresting wave of the American westward movement, and it was this Anglo-American influence that set the pattern for modern Texas cities.

Texas followed behind the urbanization curve of the United States. The state provided for incorporation in 1858 and then made later modifications in the law, including provision for home rule charters in 1912. Although statistics do not explain the how or why of urbanization, they do give a hint by marking the timing of events. In 1850 only 3.6 percent of the Texas population lived in cities of more than 2,500 people, whereas the national level was 15 percent. In 1900, when Texas moved from seventh to sixth most populous state in the nation, the urban percentage was 17.1, while for the United States the urban rate was 39.6 percent. The oil discoveries in the early twentieth century uncovered a major resource, scattered small boomtowns across the state, and later supplied a sprawling petrochemical industry along the coast from Corpus Christi to Port Arthur–Orange. In 1950 the census counted 59.8 percent urban for Texas; for the

United States it was 58.6 percent. In 1940 Texas had posted 45.4 percent, but World War II industry and military training camps pushed Texas across the half-way point and close to the national average. In 1990 in Texas, by then the third largest state, the urban population reached 81.6 percent, compared to the 77.5 percent for the United States. Only slightly more than 1 percent of the people, however, actually worked on farms and ranches. The remainder simply lived outside a defined urban space.

The common elements of American town origins, still consequential today, include gridiron street layout; wood, metal, glass, and stone buildings; promotion by land speculators; favorable transportation locations; sufficient water supply; commerce; and, sometimes, the political boost of a county courthouse or capital designation. The courthouse, a point of pride, often occupied a prominent position in the courthouse square, a block in the center of town faced by shops on four sides. In more abstract terms town building involved technology, environment, politics, economics, and individual ambition. These interacting factors can be seen at work over and over again in Texas urbanization. The urban expansion of American settlement in Texas came from east to west, along the coast, and up the rivers from the seacoast in a sequential pattern of seaports, river towns, and railroad towns. Americans were directed and limited at first by the technology of steamboats and ox wagons, then by railroads that spawned towns along the right-of-way, and at last by highways and aircraft that bound the established towns, state, and nation together into a transportation network. As they improved, these transport technologies gave ever-increasing access to the land, and carried not only trade goods and produce, but also people and ideas. They were communication linkages that worked with the technologies of information—newspapers, mail systems, schools, libraries, telephones, and telegraphs—that were the arteries of a complex interconnected urban world.

The release from Mexican rule in 1836 allowed almost unrestricted individual initiative, a characteristic of American cities, to direct the urban enterprise for the republic and the early state. One of the first endeavors was to build seaports—an obvious need—and the only large natural harbor was on the lee side of Galveston Island. Here, Jean Laffite had run his pirate base until forced out by the United States Navy in 1821, and here the renegade government of Texas poised for flight by sea in case Sam Houston failed at San Jacinto. It was a likely spot for urban enterprise. Advantage was taken by Michel B. Menard and nine associates, who bought 4,605 acres on the eastern end of the island at the harbor site in 1836. They divided the land into blocks with streets running parallel to the bay, organized a real estate company to handle sales, applied for incorporation from the Republic of Texas, and helped start a city government. Land sales began in 1838, and in the first year the company sold 700 lots. This was the American pattern: purchase of a likely site, promotion, subdivision, sale of lots, establishment of local government. Galveston was a success and developed as a rowdy port city with a variety of ethnic groups—particularly American, English, German, and African—and with a commercial focus upon the harbor. Merchants erected wharves and docks to reach the deep water offshore. Large ocean-going ships from New Orleans, New York, and Europe unloaded their cargoes of supplies for farmers and took on board the products of Texas. The settlers gained all sorts of manufactured items—guns, gunpowder, clothing, and books, for example—in exchange for cotton,

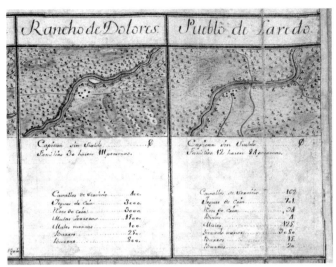

Rancho de Dolores and *Pueblo de Laredo*. Details from *Mapa general . . . de la nueba colonia de Santander*, by Don Agustin Lopez, 1758. Manuscript map. By permission of the British Library; add MS 17657: detail, Dolores/Laredo. The Spanish began modern town building in Texas. This map shows the town of Dolores, home to 111, and Laredo, home to 84, established three years earlier.

hides, pecans, and sugar. Galveston served as a transfer and storage point with an infrastructure of warehouses, banks, hotels, stores, and trading companies. Local newspapers served commerce, and the state's oldest ongoing newspaper, the Galveston *News*, began in 1842. The port also became a major entry point for immigrants and slaves. Since Galveston Island was separated from the mainland by two miles of water, trade goods were transferred to small river steamers such as the famous *Yellow Stone* that played a role in the eastward retreat of the Texan army during the revolution. These steamboats carried goods and people to and from inland trading towns on the rivers, where once more a transfer of trade items occurred, this time unloaded onto ox wagons and carts. This slow transportation system then moved the trade goods to and from the farms over crude roads cut into the wilderness.

Other seaports developed along this same general line of "breaks in transportation." On Matagorda Bay, Port Lavaca, founded in 1840, became a shipping point for cattle and even adopted the Spanish word for "cow" as its name. It competed with nearby Indianola, established as an landing point by Prince Carl of Solms–Braunfels, who marched his Germans inland to establish New Braunfels in 1845. Charles Morgan, a Gulf Coast shipper, chose Indianola over Port Lavaca for the Morgan Lines, and in the 1850s the port served as a military depot for the United States Army. It replaced Port Lavaca as county seat, gained a population of 6,000 by 1875, and ended in catastrophe. Railroads diverted trade to Galveston, and devastating hurricanes in 1875 and 1886 persuaded the survivors to abandon the site and make Port Lavaca county seat again. Velasco, which had served as a port of entry for Austin colonists, was also wiped out by a hurricane, as was Matagorda at the mouth of the Colorado River; the latter had a population of 1,400 in 1832. Farther along the coast to the west, military action established Corpus Christi as another port city. Henry Lawrence Kinney had built a trading post on the

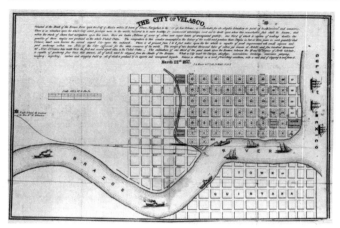

The City of Velasco, 1837. Courtesy Map Collection, Yale University Library. This map advertising Velasco clearly shows the layout on a grid similar to that of many American cities. The advertising material on the map describes Velasco's importance as seaport. A hurricane devastated Velasco in 1875, forcing its relocation and bringing about its decline.

shallow Corpus Christi Bay in 1840, but the Mexican War brought attention to the area when Gen. Zachary Taylor used the site as a base camp for his campaign into Mexico. Later, a deepening of the channel into the bay and rail service in 1873 provided Corpus Christi the opportunity to become a cattle, wool, and cotton port. Like other Gulf Coast ports, Corpus Christi suffered from hurricanes, the worst being Celia in 1970. The city, by this time, had provided itself protection with a sea wall, which, along with warning services, prevented a death toll like that inflicted during the Galveston hurricane of 1900. The Galveston storm counts as the worst natural disaster in terms of death in the history of the United States. When the Gulf waters rolled over the island, some 6,000 people died. Subsequently, Galveston protected itself by building a sea wall, raising the grade of the land, and constructing all-weather bridges to the mainland. The concentration of population in cities along the coast made people vulnerable to such storms; the hazard continues to the present. Arthur E. Stilwell, a Kansas railroad promoter, however, had a premonition about the Galveston disaster, refused to build there, and in 1895–99 constructed Port Arthur on the western shore of Sabine Lake with a canal to deep water at Sabine Pass. Port Arthur escaped the wrath of the West Indian hurricanes by its inland position, and its radial street layout gave it a unique appearance among the ubiquitous gridiron patterns.

The most important seaport in modern Texas, Houston, also profited from an inland position. The Bayou City started as a riverport town with a political connection. Its origins are typical of city promotion in early Texas. Augustus C. and John K. Allen, brothers, started the town with the inherited money of Augustus's wife, Charlotte M. Baldwin Allen. They bought land on the upper reaches of Buffalo Bayou, a navigable stream that pointed toward the fertile Brazos valley and emptied into Galveston Bay. They promoted their gridiron townsite with advertisements and a successful courtship of the Texas government. Houston, named after the hero of San Jacinto, became the temporary capital of the republic. In the first four months of 1837 the town boomed from a population of 12 to 1,500. After the

Congress moved in 1839 to Austin, the new capital, Houston slipped into the role of a commercial river town serving as a transshipment point for Galveston. Local ambition and work, however, altered the destiny of the city. Businessmen, following the example of Manchester, England, after a long struggle succeeded in obtaining federal government support in constructing a ship channel through Galveston Bay and Buffalo Bayou to a docksite near the city. The Houston Ship Channel, opened in 1914, made Houston an inland seaport that eventually became the third largest in the United States. In the process the city bypassed Galveston and left it stagnant in growth as a medium-sized city on the Gulf.

Dredging technology also benefited Port Arthur, Texas City, Galveston, Corpus Christi, Freeport, Port Aransas, Beaumont, and Brownsville. On the north bank of the Rio Grande, Brownsville, notable as a river town, resulted from military action during the Mexican War. It started as a fort named for Maj. Jacob Brown. The town that grew up around the fort, 22 miles up the Rio Grande from the Gulf, became the county seat of Cameron County in 1848, proved useful as a shipping point for contraband cotton during the Civil War, and later acquired a ship channel that served both Mexico and the United States. Another river town, Jefferson, was not so fortunate. It began in 1837 and was the county seat of Cass County from 1843 to 1852. It was located on Big Cypress Creek, where steamboats traveling from St. Louis and New Orleans on the Mississippi River, the Red River, and Caddo Lake could reach its docks. Jefferson prospered from commerce, and even developed some local manufacturing of beer, boots and shoes, and canned meat. Its success, however, depended upon the deep water at its docks, the result of a longstanding log jam on the Red River. In 1874 the United States Army Corps of Engineers destroyed the Red River Raft and the water level dropped, leaving Jefferson high and dry. The town never recovered; it remains today a charming but small East Texas town that even railroads were unable to resuscitate.

Railroads were the nineteenth-century answer for quick land transportation across the vast space of the United States. The technology—engines, track, cars—was already available from Europe and the eastern United States. Only capital and ambition were necessary to import it into Texas as the answer to the mud that sank cotton wagons to their axles on the crude roads of the Coastal Plain. At other river towns such as Houston and Brownsville the railways enhanced the port activities. Brownsville became the terminus of the Missouri Pacific and the Southern Pacific, while Matamoros, across the river in Tamaulipas, became the terminal of the Mexican National Railroad. This made Brownsville the United States gateway into Mexico. Houston had earlier begun to acquire railroads as a means to expand its trade zone in South Texas. After a faltering start, railroad construction began in 1852, when Sidney Sherman and a group of Boston investors imported equipment and started the Buffalo Bayou, Brazos and Colorado Railway along a route from Harrisburg to the Brazos valley. After it reached the Brazos River in 1856 Houstonians voted to build a seven-mile "tap" to intersect the line and divert traffic to nearby Houston. Meanwhile, Paul Bremond, with help from small investors, started the Houston and Texas Central in 1853. It grew slowly, but reached 50 miles to Hempstead in 1858. Galveston and French capitalists, with the aid of state land donations and city bonds, at the same time constructed the Galveston, Houston and

Grand Central depot on Washington Street, Houston, 1894. Courtesy Harris County Heritage Society, Houston. Houston, an already flourishing port, became the rail center of South Texas by the Civil War.

Henderson Railroad to tap the trade of Houston. This line used a trestle to reach Galveston Island in 1860, but Houston politicians blocked linkage in the Bayou City by refusing a central railroad station. The result was that at the time of the Civil War Houston had become the rail center of South Texas with lines reaching to the northwest, west, southwest, southeast, and east. This focused commerce upon Houston.

Towns touched by the magic rails gained population, quicker access to information, and commerce, while those that were bypassed suffered economic loss and prestige. New rail towns such as Sealy and Rosenberg, and eventually Temple, Childress, Amarillo, and Dalhart sprouted along the routes as the lines pushed out of the south to the north. When the Houston, and Texas Central reached Denison near the Texas–Oklahoma border in 1873 and joined the Missouri, Kansas and Texas Railway, a new era opened. Now, shipments could roll all the way from St. Louis to Houston, or even to the docks at Galveston. This meant an opening of business opportunities, an ease of migration, more information, and greater social mixing for the people of Texas cities. The northward thrust of rail lines from Houston and Galveston met a westward rail movement in North Texas. The new push began in 1873 at Marshall with grants of 20 sections of state land per mile for the Texas and Pacific Railway Company. Marshall, just west of Shreveport, Louisiana, started as a frontier community in 1839 and became a county seat in 1842. It was a headquarters for Confederate activity and a cultural center that gave it the nickname "Athens of East Texas."

The Texas and Pacific, in turn, gave it railroad shops and a moderate industrial base. Marshall was connected to Shreveport by rail in 1864, the only out-of-state connection at this time, and then joined via Jefferson with Texarkana in 1873. Texarkana, straddling the ragged northeast corner of Texas, was the site of an ancient Indian trail and Caddo village. There the Texas and Pacific joined the Cairo and Fulton Railroad, which had built across Arkansas to the border. Texarkana, a new railroad town, blossomed at the junction in 1873. The main thrust of the Texas and Pacific, however, was westward from Texarkana to Sherman and Longview to Dallas.

John Neely Bryan had promoted Dallas at a ford of the Trinity River since 1841. It became the county seat of Dallas County as various pioneers drifted in, including French refugees from a nearby defunct utopian community. By 1872 Dallas had a population of 1,200. The town provided land, bonds, and cash to attract railroads, with the result that the Houston and Texas Central arrived in 1872 and the Texas and Pacific in 1873. The population jumped to 7,000 in that depression year, and the city responded with an iron bridge across the river, a new courthouse, a city hall, and an underground water system. The depression that gripped the nation for the next three years was fortunate for Dallas. It allowed the city to consolidate its gains and forestall further railroad building until 1876. Farmers and ranchers, no longer dependent upon trade routes southward, began to buy and sell to eastern merchants. This shift wrenched the commercial orientation away from the Gulf. This period when Dallas was the western terminus of the railroads in Texas, moreover, explains the irrationality of its location. Twenty-six miles away waited Fort Worth on the geographic boundary between East and West Texas—the same boundary that separated the Old South from the West. Logically, there should be only one large city in the area. Instead, there are two, Dallas oriented to the East, Fort Worth to the West.

Fort Worth started in 1849 as a military post to guard East Texas from the Plains Indians. The fort was placed on a bluff at the confluence of the Clear Fork and the West Fork of the Trinity River, but saw only one skirmish with Indians and was abandoned in 1853 as the frontier marched westward. The barracks were taken over and used by the merchants who had established a small village around the fort. A stage line to Yuma, Arizona, began operating in 1850 and Fort Worth became a county seat in 1860, although it was not incorporated until 1873. It had been designated as the next terminus of the Texas and Pacific, but the arrival of the train was three years late. Land, money, and the free labor of the townspeople finally brought the railroad to town in 1876. Now Fort Worth could become a shipping point, for cattle and local businessmen built the Fort Worth Stockyards, which made Fort Worth the first major Texas cowtown. As editor Buckley B. Paddock of the Fort Worth *Democrat* explained, "God makes the country, but man makes the town." Within 90 days the population increased threefold, to about 3,000 people, and Fort Worth acquired the same sort of wild reputation as other frontier cattle towns. There were 13 saloons to entertain the cowboys. Still, success for the town came only after the development of a meat-packing industry in the 1890s. The Texas and Pacific, meanwhile, chugged westward into the expanse of the Great Plains. Abilene and Pecos appeared in 1881 as stops along the way, but the target was El Paso. The gold rush to California and the War with Mexico brought attention to this old Spanish settlement at the farthest western reach of the Lone Star State. Four communities on the northern side of the Rio Grande came together in the 1850s, incorporated in 1873, and felt the arrival of four railroads in 1881. El Paso became a gateway both to Mexico and to California. The rails brought industry and business to this isolated, desert land.

The urban importance of the railroad network that crisscrossed Texas was not just the starting of new towns and enhancement of others, but also the access it gave to people. The greatest decade of railroad building was the 1880s, when the number of Texas towns of 4,000 or larger increased from 11 to 20. All were served by railroads. In the 1890s the number grew to 36, and at the completion of the railroad network—13,110 miles in operation in 1910—Texas had 49 towns of more than 4,000 population. By 1920 there were 70 such towns and 30 larger than 10,000. The largest in 1920, all with more than 50,000 population, were Dallas, El Paso, Fort Worth, Houston, and San Antonio. The railroads fixed Texas cities in a spatial pattern that remained little altered by the advent of later transportation systems, though new technologies brought airplanes and airports, interurban railways, and automobiles and roads. Love Field in Dallas, for example, began as a World War I pilot-training field surfaced with weeds, mud, and jackrabbits. After the war, barnstormers occupied the field, and National Air Transport (now United Airlines) began to transport airmail from it in 1926. The city took over the airport two years later and built a terminal for passengers. This pattern was typical of the larger cities as air

transportation began to deploy across the state. Passenger service among Dallas, Fort Worth, San Antonio, Houston, and Galveston started in 1928. Electric interurban passenger trains flourished in the first four decades of the century between urban places and then declined with the popularity of automobiles and the onset of the Great Depression.

Automobiles appeared as curiosities on Texas city streets early in the twentieth century, but shortly began to influence the growth of suburbs and shopping areas. Horses became obsolete, and councils had to pass ordinances to regulate parking, speed, and traffic flow. There were more than a half million trucks and cars registered in Texas by 1922. Road building between towns, which had previously been left to the counties, was quietly taken over by the Texas Highway Department in 1917. Yet, in 1930 the state had only 7,300 miles of paved road. The depression brought opportunity, however, and in 1940 Texas roads totaled 19,000 miles. In 1950, spurred by the emergency of World War II, the total miles reached 34,000. In 1995, 183,150 miles of Highway Department roads served 14,046,517 registered vehicles. Within towns city councils experimented with various sorts of paving—wooden blocks, bricks, gravel, shell, stone blocks, planks, macadam—before settling for concrete and asphalt in the early twentieth century. Four-lane expressways began to slice through the large urban centers in the late 1940s and early 1950s, starting with Central Expressway in Dallas and the Gulf Freeway in Houston. They merged with the national interstate system, which began in 1956. The result of automotive technology is that Texas cities have become largely dependent upon private transportation, suburbs have grown, and the cities have spread over the landscape. Gasoline shortages in the 1970s made city people almost neurotic, and fear of enclosure promoted annexation fights between neighboring towns in the late 1940s and 1950s. Sprawl increased the cost of urban services such as police and fire protection, but also allowed the freedom of movement and living space that Texans seem to prefer. Automobiles and roads also provided access to recreation facilities throughout the state and contributed to tourism, a major industry that attracted visitors' annual expenditures of $17 billion by the mid-1980s. In some places such as South Padre Island, access has made possible the building of large recreation communities, a recent dimension of Texas urbanization.

The major transportation vehicles—ships, railroads, automobiles—along with factors of geography and resources, have thus placed and shaped Texas cities. In Texas history several other factors, in addition, have been influential in urbanization and deserve special mention: the oil boom, the influence of national warfare, and politics. Although petroleum had been discovered earlier it was the oil development of the first half of the twentieth century that particularly affected the cities. The gusher at Spindletop oilfield in 1901 started the rush and brought refineries and oil companies to Houston, Beaumont, and Port Arthur. Beaumont was founded in 1835, developed a lumber industry, acquired a ship channel, and became an oil boomtown in the early twentieth century. In booms, speculators swapped oil stocks in the streets, hardware stores became oil-tool suppliers, businessmen paid high prices for hallway cots in crowded hotels, oilfield workers lived in tents, people crowded into local entertainment halls, and urban facilities were overwhelmed. This boomtown phenomenon occurred over and over as small towns and villages saw the rush of oil argonauts to new fields of

University Park (looking east on Lovers Lane towards Preston). Dallas, 1946. Photograph by Frank Rogers. Courtesy Jack B. Kirven. The arrival of the automobile in Texas accelerated the growth of suburbs like University Park.

wealth. Corsicana, Batson, Humble, Wichita Falls, Electra, Mexia, Burkburnett, Ranger, Breckenridge, Luling, Conroe, Odessa, Kilgore, Longview, and Borger each hosted an oil rush. Forty-five thousand people arrived at Borger during eight months in 1926–27, for example, and two years later Texas Rangers under martial law had to clean up the town. The "Boogertown" jail was so overloaded that the rangers hand-cuffed their prisoners to a chain down the middle of the main street and called for lawmen from around the Southwest to come and claim their fugitives on the trotline.

Growth brought on by World War II resembled that of the oil booms, though earlier wars had had some impact. Austin, Marshall, Jefferson, Houston, and San Antonio had been impor-tant during the Civil War as sites of war manufacturing and mil-itary organization. San Antonio was the home of the Eighth Military District before the war, and afterwards, in 1879, became the location of Fort Sam Houston. This fort expanded during the Spanish–American War and was the largest in the United States by 1900. World War I brought large army encampments to Waco, Houston, San Antonio, and Fort Worth, and major avia-tion bases to Wichita Falls, Fort Worth, and San Antonio. The military tradition and bases remained in San Antonio after the war. With World War II, military personnel in the city amounted to about one-third of the population. World War II resulted in 5 military bases, 40 air fields, a naval air station at Corpus Christi, and 21 camps for prisoners of war in the state. Defense contracts amounted to around $600 million each year during the war years, paid for the production of ships, airplanes, uniforms, steel, gasoline, and synthetic rubber. On the Houston Ship Channel, Todd Shipyards expanded from 6,000 to 20,000 employees in four months in order to construct Liberty Ships in assembly-line fashion. North American Aviation in Dallas and Convair in Fort Worth employed 60,000 people to construct B-

24 bombers. As a result of all of this the state population jumped 20 percent and the large cities—Houston, Dallas, Fort Worth, San Antonio—doubled in population. Texas cities were now nationally important. In 1948 Houston was the fastest-growing city in the country, and in 1954 its metropolitan population exceeded a million.

In the 1940s Austin, with nearby Bergstrom Air Force Base, also doubled in population, but its existence and growth is unique in the Texas urbanization story. Austin was nourished by politics and higher education rather than by physical resources and transportation. In a minor way many Texas towns and cities benefited by hosting a political unit. The courthouse, for instance, was an anchor in the center of town that helped when towns were young. It gave them a continuing reason for exis-tence, and attracted business and residents. The largest prize, however, was the role of capital of the republic, and in 1839 the Texas Congress awarded it to Austin. The city retained the role after annexation in 1845–46. The construction of the Capitol and the various state offices ensured the success of this city on the Colorado River. Representatives, foreign diplomats, people with governmental business, and civil-service workers traveled to meet or live in Austin. The Houston and Texas Central Railroad, in response, reached the city in 1871; the International–Great Northern arrived in 1876. The capital grew respectably and is now the fourth largest metropolitan area in the state, with a sig-nificance that transcends the administration of state government. By designating Austin the site of the University of Texas in 1881, voters made the city the leader for higher education in the state.

In the larger places such as Austin, Dallas, Fort Worth, Lubbock, Houston, Waco, and San Antonio other colleges and universities gave diversity to the economy and leaven to the cul-ture. Towns evolved, moreover, where colleges became the dom-inant feature—San Marcos, Georgetown, College Station,

Prairie View, Denton, Kingsville, Plainview, Abilene, Canyon, Commerce, Edinburg, and Alpine. By and large higher education in Texas was a function of the urban centers, and even in instances where a school started in the countryside, such as Texas A&M, a town grew around it to serve the faculty and students. Colleges and universities through education and example helped to build an appreciation for visual arts, music, literature, dance, and theater in Texas, but the cultural nature of urbanization is much broader. It includes cultural venues—theaters, museums, galleries, music halls, churches, schools, and stadiums; organizations that sponsor sports teams, orchestras, bands, opera, religion, and dance; information resources such as libraries, newspapers, magazines, and radio and television stations; and recreation facilities such as parks, zoos, walkways, swimming pools, restaurants, and saloons. Recreation, education, business, and inspiration often overlap or merge, and it is the concentration of people in cities, for the most part, that supports such efforts.

In the art of architecture, the major structures of cities take on significance. The new red granite Capitol in Austin (1888) was inspired by the Capitol in Washington, D.C. Its form reflected an image of public power and virtue. In the same manner for a later generation the dramatic reverse-tiered Dallas City Hall, designed by I. M. Pei, symbolized modernity and efficiency in city government. The nineteenth-century iron-front business buildings of the Strand in Galveston revealed why the city was nicknamed "the New York of Texas." San Antonio's Tower of the Americas, built for HemisFair '68, stood as a reminder of cultural convergence, and the Astrodome in Houston was a dramatic example of human ingenuity that became widely imitated. The contemporary skylines of Dallas and Houston, because of the extensive construction in the past two decades along with a willingness to destroy old buildings, provide a showcase of modern architectural design.

Art galleries such as the Witte Museum in San Antonio, the Amon Carter Museum in Fort Worth, the Dallas Museum of Art, and the Museum of Fine Arts in Houston date from the first part of the twentieth century, although art in Texas reaches back to Indian rock art, the religious decorations of Franciscans, and nineteenth-century travelers such as George Catlin. The growth of museums, however—particularly historical museums—was largely a post–World War II phenomenon, a time when Texas was rapidly urbanizing. In similar manner music extends back to Indians, Spanish immigrants, and early American settlers. Music was taught in the early Texas cities and various bands performed, but the first symphony orchestra started in San Antonio in 1904, followed by Dallas in 1911 and Houston in 1913. Community orchestras have since developed in Amarillo, Austin, Wichita Falls, El Paso, Beaumont, Lubbock, Midland–Odessa, Corpus Christi, Fort Worth, and other cities.

Theater productions and other traveling entertainments were common in early Texas cities. Promoters built a playhouse in Houston in 1838, the same year San Augustine organized a "Thespian Corps." Theatrical interest has shown a remarkable persistence. Railroads provided access for the touring companies that flourished before and after the turn into the twentieth century, and Dallas built an opera house in 1872 in time for the arrival of the trains. Motion pictures began their urban appearance in the early twentieth century, and Little Theater groups sprang up to replace the disappearing touring companies. Local theater efforts later led to such organizations as the Margo Jones theatrical group of Dallas and the Alley Theatre of Houston. In 1922 commercial radio spread across the state from the urban centers to present dramas, news, music, religious services, and sports events. Television stations added to this activity in 1947 with the start of WBAP–TV in Fort Worth, and by 1950 the state had six stations, all broadcasting from the major cities.

Public libraries, along with the Texas State Library, flourished in the early twentieth century along with the public secondary schools that benefited from state reorganization in the 1880s. Rural libraries also existed, of course, but as urbanization progressed libraries and schools became largely urban based. The cities took up the special burden of education to raise the level of urban culture and to provide access to its benefits. Without sufficient education the opportunities of urban life mean little—a newspaper, for instance, is of small use to illiterate people. United States District Judge Woodrow Seals sensed this role when he ruled in 1977 that the Houston Public School District had to give free education to all children regardless of their citizenship status. The result is that Texas urbanization has led to enormous school districts in the major cities, with attendant problems of integration, staffing, management, expense, and facilities. Big-city problems have become big-school problems.

Other problems are part of urban development. Racial and ethnic differences have caused explosions of hatred and misunderstanding in Texas, such as the Houston riot of 1917, which left 19 people dead and led to the largest courts-martial in United States history, and the brutal lynching of Jesse Washington in Waco in 1916. The legacy of segregation, at first instituted under slavery and then continued by law and custom, has resulted in *de facto* housing separation. Hispanic barrios and black residential areas are still common in Texas cities and have attracted recent study. As the Mexican-American population of Houston began to rebuild in the early twentieth century, for example, a barrio developed near the cotton compresses at the railroad tracks and became a city within a city. It has endured, along with traditional black living areas of the Fifth Ward, where poverty and crime are egregious. The stress between and within racial and ethnic groups manifests itself repeatedly in city government, school decisions, housing, and local police relations. Crime and vice have been always a part of Texas city history, and some places gained notoriety, such as Hell's Half Acre in Fort Worth and Postoffice Street in Galveston. During Prohibition and into the 1950s the Maceo brothers in Galveston ran illegal nightclubs and casinos until finally Texas Rangers closed down the "Free State of Galveston." Lee Harvey Oswald cut down President John F. Kennedy in 1963 on the streets of Dallas, and sharpshooter Charles Whitman in 1966 killed 17 people from the tower on the Main Building at the University of Texas at Austin. Crime statistics have generally shown the rates to be worse in the larger urban places, with Dallas, Fort Worth, San Antonio, or Houston sharing the lead. There has always been a crime problem in Texas cities, of course, but a fairly recent dimension of this underside of urbanization is the severe and intractable illegal drug trade that infests the urban core.

As they expanded, large cities also developed problems of pollution. Houston was the first, as might be expected of the state's largest city; there, people began complaining of the bad air in the 1940s. In 1958 commercial airline pilots could track the path to Houston by simply following a mile-wide streak of industrial haze extending northward to Austin and Dallas. In response Harris County officials established a pollution-control division in the county health department. Because of industrial dumping and city sewage, in addition, the Houston Ship Channel in the 1960s ranked as one of the worst polluted waterways in the world. The water was 80 percent sewage; when thunderstorms flushed the channel with rain, there were massive fish kills in Galveston Bay. Harris County also attacked that problem as well and gained some success with sewage treatment by the 1980s. In addition, the large cities have had to contend with garbage disposal in ever-expanding landfills. As a beleaguered mayor of Houston, Louie Welch, said in the 1970s, "You know, when it comes to garbage, people want us to pick it up, but they don't want us to put it down again, especially if it is near their house." The problem continues.

Many of these difficulties are common in the other urbanized areas of the nation, and the solutions, personnel, and technology for modern Texas cities are often borrowed from someplace else. Seaports, river towns, railroad towns, college communities, boomtowns—there were places like these elsewhere. This fact raises a question: is there anything unusual about Texas urbanization? The answer is, "Yes," a few developments and circumstances are unusual, if only by degree. The racial and ethnic mix of Mexican Americans, African Americans, and Anglo-Americans, for example, is noticeable and varied. For Texas, where more of the Mexican-American minority lives in the southwest and more of the African-American minority in the east, this mix has provided both a basis for disharmony in politics and economics and the opportunity to enrich the culture with language, customs, and foods. Although it is a partly subjective exercise to assign a "character" or "personality" to a city or place, it is commonly done in popular literature to explain uniqueness. Texas has mixed the social customs of the West and the South, the cotton kingdom and the cattle kingdom. The slavery–cotton plantation system reached into East Texas, and the state shares the heritage of the Civil War. Some prejudice against Northerners lingers, along with some reverence for colonnaded architecture, Confederate flags, and a leisurely pace of life. In polite conversation city people still ask about family ancestry, a Southern trait, as well as occupation. Children are still sometimes taught to say "Yes sir" and "No sir," "Yes ma'am" and "No ma'am" in speaking to adults, and "you all" is a permanent plural form of "you." Juneteenth, long an informal Black holiday to celebrate emancipation, is now a state holiday. At the same time cowboy hats, boots, and jeans are regularly seen on the streets of the cities, particularly in the west. Single-story ranch-style homes are as popular as two-story Georgians everywhere. Livestock shows and rodeos are presented along with formal equestrian events and major sports matches. Chili and barbecue "cook-offs" abound. The customs from a rural Southern and Western past linger and mix on Texas sidewalks.

In the area of politics, Galveston developed the idea of the commission form of city government. Against the backdrop of the 1900 hurricane Galveston business leaders devised a form of city government whereby a designated official took charge of a specific urban function. The electorate put the scheme into effect a year after the storm, and the idea became a favorite of reformers during the Progressive Era in the United States. Commission governments spread nationwide, but because of intrinsic inefficiencies they declined in number after 1920 in

Tank farm, refineries, and petrochemical plants along banks of the Houston Ship Channel. Photograph by Ray Miller. Houston, ca. 1980. Courtesy Ray Miller, Houston. Because of industrial dumping and city sewage, the Houston Ship Channel once ranked as one of the worst-polluted streams in the world.

favor of the traditional mayor–council and council–manager form. In 1913 Amarillo became the first Texas council–manager city; it was followed by more than 50 others by 1950.

Perhaps the greatest distinctive Texas feature of Texas cities is determined by physical resources. Oil discoveries brought wealth to the state and attracted industry. This, combined with petroleum technologies and warfare, hastened the move to the cities. The quick fortune extracted by oil rigs resulted in gleaming office towers, new-rich suburbs, petrochemical plants, secondary industries and services, tax revenue, and literary stereotypes of the wealthy Texan such as Jett Rink of Edna Ferber's *Giant* (1952), or J. R. Ewing of the television show "Dallas." During the oil depression of the 1980s, however, petroleum dependence cut in the opposite direction and caused wide economic suffering, unemployment, and urban slowdown. Another major physical resource has been abundant land. There are few geographic barriers in Texas, and as a consequence cities have spread out across the landscape as far as commuters will drive. People could afford it. Single-family houses on large lots have been possible for the middle class; shopping malls have arisen in the suburbs; office clusters in suburbs have led to polynucleation; mass transportation, which depends upon density of population, has largely failed; air pollution has been dissipated. Though other American cities have built in a similar manner, particularly in the West, the pattern is more notable in Texas. The density of population in metropolitan areas of the country in 1990 was 332 people per square mile; in Texas it was 301. There was some political control of this expansion, however. Planning and zoning of the cityscape began with Dallas in 1910 and has spread to most of the larger cities, with the exception of Houston, which stubbornly has chosen to remain the nation's largest unzoned city. State urban-renewal and planning-assistance legislation, passed in 1957, moreover, has enabled Texas cities to control and alter their growth. Space, oil, commission politics, the racial and ethnic mixture, and the mingling of Western and Southern cultures have given Texas urbanization a distinctive history, while Spanish and Anglo-American principles have guided it. Most Texans now live in urban places and are a part of city culture. Texas urbanization is largely complete; only refinement and expansion remain for the future.

David G. McComb

Uvalde, Texas. Uvalde is 40 miles west of San Antonio in south central Uvalde County. It was founded by Reading W. Black, who settled there in 1853. Black and Nathan L. Stratton operated a ranch on the road between San Antonio and Fort Duncan. By 1854 Black had opened a store, two rock quarries, and a limekiln; he also prepared a garden and an orchard, repaired nearby roads, and built a permanent home. Black hired Wilhelm C. A. Thielepape as surveyor in May 1855 to lay out a town he called Encina. Seminole, Tonkawa, and Lipan–Apache Indian raids and temporary withdrawal of troops from nearby Fort Inge discouraged settlement during the first year. The return of troops to Fort Inge and the community's proximity to the road connecting San Antonio with the western United States eventually encouraged growth. In 1856 when the county was organized, the town was renamed Uvalde for Spanish governor Juan de Ugalde and was chosen county seat. In 1857 a Uvalde post office opened. The settlement centered around a mill built by Black and James Taylor in 1858. Border warfare and lawlessness prevailed until the late 1880s. In 1881 Uvalde became a shipping point on the Galveston, Harrisburg and San Antonio Railway. It was incorporated in 1888. By 1890 Uvalde had a population of 2,000 and 60 businesses. The Crystal City and Uvalde Railroad was built to Crystal City in 1911, and the Uvalde and Northern ran to Camp Wood from 1921 to 1942. Garner Army Air Field, named for John Nance Garner of Uvalde, opened in 1941. Uvalde's population increased to 5,286 in 1940, 10,293 in 1960, and 14,729 in 1990. Southwest Texas Junior College was established in 1946, and Texas A&M University operates a research and extension center in Uvalde. The fairgrounds encompass a rodeo arena, a racetrack for quarter horses, and stables and facilities for stock shows. Garner State Park is located 26 miles north of town. In 1990 Uvalde depended on agriculture for its economic base, and it was the honey capital of the world. It is also home to a United States fish hatchery, and a large asphalt mine is located out of the city limits. The Uvalde Arts Council operates a community theater and local museum in the restored opera house.

Freida R. Rogers

V

Vance, Nina Eloise Whittington. Founder of the Alley Theatre; b. Yoakum, 22 October 1914; d. Houston, 18 February 1980 (buried in Gonzales); m. Milton Vance (and soon divorced); ed. Texas Christian University (B.A., 1935), Columbia University, and the University of Southern California. She taught high school speech and by 1941 was acting in the Houston Community Players, an amateur group headed by Margo Jones. After directing over a dozen productions for her own Players Guild (1945–47), she began directing plays at Vivien Altfeld's dance studio. More than 100 people came to the first meeting, which chose the name Alley Theatre. Under Nina Vance's leadership the Alley became one of the best-known nonprofit resident theaters in the United States. Vance was responsible for the Alley Theatre's success. She fought for its early advancement to professionalism and in 1954 made the irreversible decision to "go equity"—to turn her theater into a unionized group of professionals rather than to remain in amateur status. Starting with *Season with Ginger* in 1950, she championed both classics and new plays and produced many world premieres, including *The Effect of Gamma Rays on Man-in-the-Moon Marigolds* in 1965. She directed more than 100 plays during her tenure at the Alley. She was one of the founding members of the Theatre Communications Group, a networking organization for professional regional theaters, in 1961. The same year, President John F. Kennedy invited her to serve on the advisory committee of the proposed National Culture Center. In that and other posts she traveled and consulted in Europe and brought world theater to the Alley. She was awarded an honorary doctorate by the University of St. Thomas (1969). At a memorial tribute her theater was renamed the Nina Vance Alley Theatre. *N. J. Stanley*

Vaquero. The mounted herdsman of the Spanish colonial period and his Mexican counterpart of the nineteenth century; a historical figure that, like the Anglo cowboy, has acquired romantic traits and near-mythic stature. White stock raisers were heavily influenced by Spanish ranching institutions. Particularly between 1821 and the era of cattle trailing, many Spanish stock-handling techniques passed into the Anglo way of doing things. Spanish vaqueros in colonial times were generally viewed as a rough and rowdy lot. Many operated outside the law and preyed upon unbranded cattle that roamed the vast estates of northern Mexico. Often they were mestizo or semicivilized Indians on the lower rungs of the social ladder, but they were invariably noted for their horsemanship and stock-tending skills. As ranching made its way north to Texas through the tier of provinces along the Rio Grande, these herdsmen were the vanguard of Hispanic colonization. In many cases they attached themselves to a *patrón* (in this case, an influential rancher who owned a grant of land from the king), married, and built shacks on his property. Their children were born and raised in his service, an arrangement that sometimes spanned generations. Early Anglo ranch owners in South Texas, such as the founders of the King Ranch, fell heir to this tradition, which continued well into the twentieth century. By the 1870s the vaquero's saddle, chaps, bandana, sombrero, lasso, spurs, and even elements of his expertise were so widespread that they lost their Hispanic identity and became simply "Texan." *Jack Jackson*

Vara. A Spanish unit of distance (about 33⅓ inches) used in Spanish and Mexican surveys and land grants; 5,645.4 square *varas* = an acre, 1,906.1 *varas* = a mile, and 1,000,000 square *varas* = one *labor* (177.1 acres). The word *vara*, from late Latin, originally meant a long, thin, clean branch of any tree or plant. It later came to be used for any straight stick and then for a lance. Next it came to mean a badge of office carried by mayors and judges. The *vara* eventually became a uniform and official measure.

Vaughan, Stevie Ray. Blues musician; b. Oak Cliff, 3 October 1954; d. 27 August 1990 en route to Chicago (buried at Laurel Land Memorial Park in South Dallas); m. Lenny Bailey (1980; divorced 1986). By the time Vaughan was in high school, he was playing guitar in clubs in Deep Ellum. He dropped out before graduation and moved to Austin (1971), where he slept on pool tables and couches in the back of clubs and collected bottles to earn money for new guitar strings. He played in various local bands such as Cobra and Nightcrawlers. In the late 1970s he formed Triple Threat, a group that became Double Trouble. In the early 1980s the group attracted the notice of well-established performers like Mick Jagger, who in 1982 invited Double Trouble to play at a private party in New York City. That same year the group received an invitation to play at the Montreux Jazz Festival in Switzerland—the first band in the history of the festival to play without having a major record contract. After that, Jackson Brown invited Vaughan to his Los Angeles studio for a demo session at which Stevie recorded his 1983 debut album, *Texas Flood*. David Bowie had Vaughan play lead guitar on his album *Let's Dance* and join him on his 1983 tour. Vaughan's fame immediately soared. Double Trouble followed *Texas Flood* with *Couldn't Stand the Weather* (1984), *Live Alive* (1985), and *Soul to Soul* (1986). All of the albums went gold and captured various Grammy nominations in either the Blues or Rock categories. In 1984, at the National Blues Foundation Awards, Vaughan became the first white man to win Entertainer of the Year and Blues Instrumentalist of the Year. Stevie also, however, lived the stereotypical life of a rock and roll star, full of alcohol and drug abuse. After a collapse on his 1986 European tour, he stayed sober. His fifth album, *In Step* (1989), won him a second Grammy. In 1990 Vaughan collaborated with Jimmie Vaughan, his brother, on *Family Style*, which was released after his death. Epic records released two more posthumous albums of his work, *The Sky is Crying* (1991) and *In the Beginning* (1992). Vaughan died in a helicopter crash in Wisconsin. A memorial statue of him is located on Town Lake in Austin. *Robin Dutton*

Vázquez de Coronado, Francisco. Spanish explorer; b. Salamanca, 1510; d. Mexico City, 22 September 1554; m. Beatriz de Estrada (1530s); 5 children. In 1535 Vásquez de Coronado, usually called Coronado in the United States, accompanied

Viceroy Antonio de Mendoza to Mexico, where he married. Coronado was appointed in 1538 to the city council of Mexico City and to the governorship of Nueva Galicia. In 1540, Mendoza appointed Coronado to lead an expedition to the legendary Seven Cities of Cíbola, spoken of by Cabeza de Vaca. On 22 April 1540, Coronado left Culiacán for the north. There was no gold at Cíbola (the Zuñi villages in western New Mexico and Arizona). Coronado was guided from there by an Indian called El Turco, who told stories of great rewards to be found in Quivira, a region on the Great Plains far to the east. Chasing this chimera occupied him until the early part of 1542. He traversed much of Texas—the Llano Estacado, Palo Duro and Tule canyons, and the lower Pecos country. When he returned to Mexico he was subjected to an official examination of his conduct as leader of the expedition and as governor of Nueva Galicia. He was cleared of charges in connection with the expedition, but on some of the other charges was fined and lost his commission. In Mexico City he served as councilman until his death.   *David Donoghue*

Velasco, Battle of. A prelude to the Texas Revolution; probably the first case of bloodshed in the relations between Texas and Mexico. On 26 June 1832 Henry Smith and John Austin, in charge of Texans who had gone to Brazoria to secure a cannon for use against the Mexican forces at Anahuac, squared off against Domingo de Ugartechea, commander of the Mexican fort at Velasco, who tried to prevent the passage of the vessel carrying the cannon. The Texans numbered between 100 and 150; the number of Mexicans was variously estimated at 91 to 200. Ugartechea and his garrison were forced to surrender when their ammunition was exhausted. Texan casualties were perhaps 7 killed and 14 wounded; 3 of the 14 later died of their wounds. The Mexicans had 5 killed and 16 wounded. Final terms allowed Ugartechea to surrender with the honors of war and return to Mexico aboard a ship furnished by the colonists. The formal surrender took place in camp at the mouth of the Brazos on 29 June 1832, in the form of a document signed by Texas representatives William H. Wharton and William J. Russell and Mexican representatives Juan Moret and José Rincón, with final approval by Ugartechea and John Austin.

Velasco, Texas. Originally on the east side of the Brazos River 16 miles south of Angleton and four miles from the Gulf of Mexico in southeastern Brazoria County; founded in 1831. Ten years earlier the schooner *Lively* had landed at the site with 38 men, the first of Stephen F. Austin's colonists. Nothing but a single house stood at the site until Mexico set up a customs port there and dispatched troops in 1831 to help the customs collector. Subsequently, more than 25,000 settlers entered through the port. The community developed upstream from the coast by 1835; a customhouse, salt works, and trading posts were located at Velasco during the immigration period. The town was named for a Mexican general, as was Quintana, on the opposite side of the river. According to one writer, Old Velasco became the "Boston harbor of the Texas Revolution," as the site of the battle of Velasco in 1832. A cholera epidemic reduced the population to 100 in 1834, and a mail route from San Felipe to Velasco was established in 1835. After the battle of San Jacinto, President David G. Burnet made the town the temporary capital of the Republic of Texas. Government records were housed at Fort Velasco until the first capital of Texas was established at

Columbia. Antonio López de Santa Anna signed the treaties of Velasco on 14 May 1836. Between the Texas Revolution and the Civil War, Velasco and Quintana served as summer resorts for wealthy plantation families of the region. Galveston businessmen Samuel May Williams and Thomas F. McKinney established warehouses and organized shipping of all kinds at the port. A seminary for young ladies, Velasco Female Academy, and a school for young men, taught by Oxford graduates, were established by 1838. Comfortable hotels were built to accommodate visitors and patrons of the racetrack located a short distance upriver. A local post office operated from 1846 until 1891. Antebellum Velasco had business houses, homes, a hotel, boardinghouses, wharves, and a customhouse; riverboats embarked from the wharves for Galveston and New Orleans. With completion of the first intracoastal canal to Galveston Bay in 1856, however, the town began to decline as shipping was diverted to Galveston. During the Civil War the port of Velasco was fortified by Confederate troops, and Union ships were forced to go to New Orleans for drinking water, food, and fuel. The port played an active role in the exchange of cotton for European guns, ammunition, milled goods, and medicines for army and home use. Federal vessels attempted to stop vital trade and fired upon shore defenses, patrols, and small craft seeking to outrun them. With the ruin of the plantation system after the war, Velasco and Quintana declined as resorts. In 1875 a hurricane destroyed even the old town records. By 1884, when its residents numbered 50 and local farmers shipped livestock, Velasco had been reduced to semiweekly steamer service to Brazoria and reported only a general store and a boat-builder's shop.

The new town of Velasco was surveyed and laid out in 1891, when a new Velasco post office was established. The port was officially opened by the United States secretary of the treasury on 7 July 1891. A year later over $1 million worth of lots had been sold. Promoters working throughout the Midwest advertised the Velasco Hotel and an area along the river designed as Riverside Park. By 1892 Velasco had 136 business establishments and 167 residences, an electric-light plant, and a planing mill. Jetties were built by the Brazos River Channel and Dock Company by 1897, and the newly dug deepwater port ran to a depth of 17_ feet. New settlers traveled to Houston by train, to Columbia on the Columbia Tap branch of the International and Great Northern Railroad, and by riverboat down the Brazos to Velasco. The Velasco Terminal Railway, completed around 1890, allowed passengers to proceed directly from the Columbia Tap connection at Anchor to the new town. By 1896 the community had a new lighthouse, several churches, schools, hotels, a national bank, a cottonseed oil mill, cotton gins, special and general stores, and two weekly newspapers. In that year Velasco shipped cottonseed oil, cotton, lumber, and livestock. Surfside, or Old Velasco, and Crescent Beach could be reached by electric railroad. The population was 3,000 when the Galveston hurricane of 1900 wrecked the town. Afterward, Velasco rebuilt slowly, enduring fluctuations of poverty and prosperity. By 1914, with a population of 1,000, the community had a fish and oyster plant and shipped cattle, cotton, cane sugar, and syrup. The population dropped to a low of 400 in the mid-1930s, when the town supported 12 businesses. But diversion of the Brazos River and the formation of a tidal estuary deep enough to accommodate large vessels in the old river channel subsequently revived both Velasco and nearby Freeport. Construction of chemical-industry facilities during

Veramendi Palace, San Antonio. Courtesy ITC. While Juan Martín de Veramendi was governor of Texas and Coahuila, his home in San Antonio became known as the Veramendi Palace. In December 1835 Ben Milam was killed at its entrance by a sniper.

World War II increased the population from 900 in 1940, when the city was incorporated, to 5,200 by 1950. Velasco was incorporated with Freeport in 1957. The community subsequently became part of the Brazosport industrial and port area and Brazosport ISD. *Merle Weir*

Veramendi, Juan Martín de. Mexican governor of Coahuila and Texas; b. San Fernando de Béxar, 17 December 1778; d. Monclova, 1833; m. Josefa Navarro; 7 children. With Juan José Erasmo Seguín, Veramendi accompanied Stephen F. Austin from Natchitoches, Louisiana, to Bexar (1821). He served in Bexar as collector of foreign revenue (1822–23) and was elected alternate deputy to the Mexican National Constitutional Congress (1823). The same year, he obtained a five-league grant from the ayuntamiento, but when he discovered that the land lay within Green DeWitt's colony, he petitioned for a grant somewhere else (ca. 1827) and received 11 leagues. Veramendi was the first alcalde of Bexar (1824–25). He was elected vice governor of Coahuila and Texas in 1830 and moved to Saltillo the next year. In April 1831 his daughter married James Bowie, with whom he formed a partnership to establish cotton mills in Saltillo. Veramendi became governor upon the death of José María Letona in 1832. His administration was favorable to AngloAmerican colonization and therefore unpopular with some Mexicans. He died in a cholera epidemic at his summer home.

Veterans' Land Board. Authorized by constitutional amendment in 1946, appointed in 1949; composed of the governor, attorney general, and commissioner of the General Land Office, who were to administrate the Veterans' Land Program. The board was empowered to issue $25 million in bonds, the proceeds of which were to be used for buying land to resell to Texas veterans of World War II. Later, veterans of the Korean War and the Vietnam War were included. Another constitutional amendment in 1956 changed the composition of the board to the commissioner of the General Land Office and two gubernatorial appointees. The board purchases land directly from the seller and resells it to veterans on a 30-year contract. The amount of land and money involved have varied through the years. Since inception of the program more than 130,000 loans have been made to purchase more than 4.5 million acres. An ancillary program, the Texas Veterans' Housing Assistance Program, began in 1983. It provides low-interest home loans in conjunction with mortgage loans from private lending institutions. In 1986 the Texas Veterans' Home Improvement Program was instituted. It makes loans for home improvements. These programs are self-supporting. *Dick Smith and John G. Johnson*

Vial, Pedro. Pathfinder; b. Lyons, France (mid-eighteenth century); d. Santa Fe (1814). Vial claimed he had become familiar with lands along the Missouri River before the American Revolution. He appeared in Natchitoches and New Orleans in 1779 and arrived in San Antonio in 1784 after living for a time among the Taovaya Indians. He was selected by Governor Domingo Cabello y Robles to gather information about the eastern Comanches, who were associates of the Taovayas. With Francisco Xavier Chaves, Vial spent summer 1785 within Comanchería. The following year, Cabello charged Vial with finding the most direct route between San Antonio and Santa Fe. He set out on 4 October with only one companion, Cristóbal de los Santos. His responsibilities included keeping a diary in which he was to record distances traveled, Indians encountered, and the size of native encampments. Vial soon fell ill and possibly became disoriented. In any event, he traveled northward by way of Tawakoni villages near the site of present Waco and then continued on to the Red River, where he lived for a time with the Taovayas. Thence he followed the Red and Canadian rivers westward and reached Santa Fe on 26 May 1787. This circuitous route extended a thousand miles. The next year Vial set out for Natchitoches by way of the Panhandle and the Red River. From Natchitoches he trekked to San Antonio, followed by a second journey to Santa Fe—covering in all an estimated 2,377 miles in 14 months. In successive summers (1792–93), he traveled over what later became the Santa Fe Trail, making a round trip—estimated at 2,279 miles—between Santa Fe and St. Louis, traversing a variety of Indian homelands—Apache, Comanche, Kansas, Osage, Arapaho, Pawnee, Sioux. His major explorations linked Santa Fe to San Antonio, Natchitoches, and St. Louis. Vial also served the governor of New Mexico as interpreter and agent in Indian country. In 1798 he left the Spanish to live among the Comanches, but in 1799 he resided at Portages des Sioux, north of St. Louis. By 1803 he was back in Santa Fe. His will indicated that he had never married and did not leave children. *Donald E. Chipman*

Victoria, Texas. County seat of Victoria County; largest city in the central coastal region, and the commercial focus of the surrounding counties. The town was established in 1824 by Martín De León and named Guadalupe Victoria for the first president of the republic of Mexico. It is on the Guadalupe River at a site known earlier as Cypress Grove. Guadalupe Victoria was platted by José M. J. Carbajal and developed an early importance as a stop on the La Bahía Road, as a stock-raising center, and as a shipping point for the port of Linnville. By 1834 about 300 people were living in the municipality, which was governed by a Council of Ten Friends from 1824 to 1828 and by four alcaldes from 1828 to 1836; the four were Martín and Silvestre De León, Plácido Benavides (elected twice), and John J. Linn. Though primarily a Mexican settlement, Guadalupe Victoria contributed volunteers, supplies, and arms to the Texas cause against Antonio López de Santa Anna. Its superior defensive position on the banks of the Guadalupe induced Sam Houston to order Fannin to retreat there from Goliad in 1836. After Fannin was defeated at the battle of Coleto, however, Guadalupe Victoria was occupied by the Mexican army under José de Urrea until the Texas victory at San Jacinto. Soon thereafter, the Mexican residents were ostracized; they fled, and their town, resettled by Anglos, became known as Victoria. Victoria was incorporated under the Republic of Texas in 1839. The first mayor was John J. Linn, who, together with five aldermen, set down various ordinances and concentrated on leasing ferry operations across the Guadalupe River and making the river navigable for trade. In August 1840 several citizens were killed in the great Comanche raid that destroyed Linnville. In 1846, the year the Victoria post office was established, the town suffered a terrible cholera epidemic. Victims died so rapidly that proper burials were impossible, though valiant efforts were made by German immigrant Dillman Mantz and his son and by a legendary black man called Black Peter. In spite of the epidemic, Victoria continued to grow as a trade center, especially as Indianola became an important port of entry for both goods and the thousands of immigrants who settled in the area. By 1850 Victoria had three public houses, a variety of stores, a weekly newspaper, and a courthouse. By 1860 the population was 1,986, including 521 slaves, and the town had become a major junction between Lavaca Bay ports, San Antonio, Austin, and northern Mexico. A variety of settlers—Americans, Germans, Bohemians, Italians, Jews from several countries, and Mexicans—arrived in the town by the 1880s. The San Antonio and Mexican Gulf Railroad reached Victoria in 1861, was destroyed during the Civil War in 1863, and was rebuilt by the federal occupying force in 1866. The New York, Texas and Mexican Railway reached the city during the 1880s. In 1888 L. D. Heaton, Jim Brown, and others established a mule-drawn streetcar system that operated until 1894. The four cars were named for popular ladies of the city.

County Judge J. L. Dupree sponsored the community's first highway in 1889. In 1917 a $100,000 bond issue inaugurated the era of "hard-top" streets, and Uvalde Rock Asphalt Company received a contract to improve 53 downtown blocks. A safe and vault company at Victoria was the only institution of its kind south of Cincinnati, and the Texas Continental Meat Company, established in 1883, was a harbinger of new techniques. Combining prairie grass, cattle, railroads, and business acumen, Continental pioneered in the slaughtering and packing of swine, sheep, and poultry, as well as beef. The company utilized the first refrigerator cars and manufactured from animal fats the first oleomargarine and gelatin. The second Kraft–Phoenix Cheese Corporation plant to be built in Texas, established in the city in 1934, took advantage of local dairy farming. Ranching was the area's first major enterprise and the one that ensured Victoria's early success. One of the first meat-packing plants was established there in 1869. During the 1880s changes occurred that reflected a general transition in the state from pioneer ranching and traildriving to market production. Many ranchers shifted their interests to financial institutions and commerce, which in turn supported a transformation of the cattle industry. By 1900 three banks served the area. The Victoria Advocate, the state's second oldest existing newspaper, first appeared in 1846 and by 1897 was publishing a daily edition. John Stilwell Munn, editor in the 1880s, coined the city's first and still cherished nickname—City of Roses—to express civic pride in the town's gardens. The change from riverwater to wells began with a Victoria landmark, the standpipe, constructed in 1884 and located on De Leon Plaza. This 105-foot tower leaned enough to encourage wagers on its destiny. The Casino Hall was the center of cultural events after 1854, and in 1893 the city welcomed the opening of G. H. Hauschild's Opera House. This landmark drew large audiences for nearly four decades. Before 1936, when the Texas Centennial prompted a long list of historical markers, Victoria displayed Pompeo Coppini's statue Last Stand (1912). The White Way—bronze plates on twelve lampposts around De Leon Plaza and four more on Market Square, dedicated to Victoria's pioneers—had also taken shape. In later years flowers were added below the light fixtures in imitation of a practice in Victoria, British Columbia. An old bandstand, built on Constitution Street about 1899, was moved to the center of the square in 1923 in place of the standpipe. The plaza, changed little since these alterations were made, still gives downtown Victoria a flavor of the past.

During the post–World War II era Victoria became one of the fastest-growing cities in Texas. Its historic industries have contributed to an increased prosperity. The city hosted Foster Army Air Field until 1957; afterward the facility became Victoria Regional Airport. The population grew from 16,126 in 1950 to 33,047 in 1960 and to 55,076 in 1980. In 1986 the city had a symphony orchestra, a fine arts association, a nationally recognized Bach Festival, numerous historic homes, museums, and libraries, a branch of the University of Houston that complemented Victoria College, and the Texas Zoo, the only zoo in the world that featured native Texas wildlife exclusively. Victoria also served as the medical center for a seven-county area. In 1981 Victoria became a standard metropolitan statistical area. Accessible by three U.S. highways, rail, and commercial air, Victoria MSA is also located on a barge canal connected to the Gulf Intracoastal Waterway. Business income is derived from oil, manufacturing, agribusinesses, petrochemicals, tourism, and recreation, especially hunting, fishing, and boating. In 1982 the area had 62 plants manufacturing such products as oilfield and foundry equipment, aluminum, petrochemicals, and steel. Victoria serves as the commercial focus for the counties surrounding the Victoria MSA. In 1990 the city had a population of 55,076. *Robert W. Shook*

Victorio. An Apache war chief; b. New Mexico, ca. 1825; d. Tres Castillas, Chihuahua, 15 October 1880. Victorio was a member of the Eastern Chiricahua Apaches, often referred to as the Warm Springs or Mimbreño Apaches. The legend that he was part Mexican is considered apocryphal. In the 1850s he rode with Geronimo on raids into northern Mexico, and in 1862 he was said to have joined Mangas Coloradas. After Mangas died in 1863, Victorio slowly emerged as a tribal leader, forming a band of Eastern Chiricahuas and Mescaleros into a band of about 300. In 1869 he and his band settled near Fort Craig, New Mexico, to await the completion of a new reservation near Ojo Caliente. Apparently Victorio did little raiding until after 20 April 1877, when the government ordered him and his followers to the San Carlos Reservation in Arizona. Conditions at San Carlos were abominable, and when Poinsenay, another Apache leader who had been raiding in Mexico, related his successes to Victorio,

Victorio and his aide, Loco, led several hundred Apaches off the reservation toward Mexico. He began three years of raiding in Mexico, Texas, and New Mexico. In Texas he raided mostly between Fort Davis and El Paso. He was pursued in Texas by black United States Army troopers of the Ninth and Tenth Cavalry. The Tenth was transferred temporarily from Fort Concho to Fort Davis to campaign against Victorio, who cannily eluded the army's best efforts. During most of the summer of 1880 he camped at various sites in the Quitman, Carrizo, and Guadalupe mountains. Col. Benjamin Grierson caught the Apaches at Rattlesnake Springs, but after a three-hour battle the Indians fled westward into the Carrizo Mountains and on to Mexico. Texas Rangers involved in the Victorio campaign included James B. Gillett, George W. Baylor, and 12 others, who with almost 100 civilians entered Mexico in September 1880 looking for Victorio. Gillett said that the rangers were eventually sent out of Mexico by Col. Joaquín Terrazas, noted Indian fighter and leader of the Chihuahua state militia, who also was trailing Victorio. In October 1880 Terrazas and the militia surrounded and massacred Victorio and his warriors. Only women and children survived the confrontation, and they were prisoners in Chihuahua City for the next several years.

Joseph A. Stout, Jr.

Vidaurri, Santiago. Caudillo; b. Lampazos, Nuevo León, 25 July 1809; d. June 1867; m. Juana María Vidaurri; at least 2 children. Vidaurri visited Texas in 1841 to spy on the Texan Santa Fe Expedition. Throughout the 1840s and early 1850s he worked for conservatives in the Mexican government. After the Mexican War, he became dissatisfied with conservative politics. Denouncing the regime of Antonio López de Santa Anna under a plan labeled "Restaurador de la Libertad," Vidaurri captured Monterrey on 23 May 1855 and was installed as governor and military commander of Nuevo León. His army moved rapidly into Coahuila and Tamaulipas, consolidating control throughout northeastern Mexico. He procured military supplies from merchants north of the Rio Grande. When charged with an attempt to establish the "Republic of Sierra Madre," Vidaurri insisted that his was a federalist movement in the best of liberal traditions. He cooperated with United States and Texas authorities in punishing Indians who raided the frontier, but clashed with Texan raiders of the Callahan expedition for violating Mexican territory. Vidaurri annexed Coahuila in 1856 and decreed the formation of the combined state of Nuevo León y Coahuila. For the next two years he controlled this vast territory virtually as an independent nation. Many liberals in the government of Benito Juárez distrusted the chieftain, but were forced to seek the assistance of his Army of the North in the vicious War of the Reform. In September 1858, however, the northern caudillo suffered a major defeat at the hands of the conservatives near San Luis Potosí and retreated to Monterrey to rebuild his forces. He continued to give lip service to the national liberal government, but kept his army out of battle. Furthermore, he retained all revenues collected at the Rio Grande customhouses. National liberals, including Juárez, denounced him; and some of the most able officers of Nuevo León defected to the national cause.

When Texas seceded from the United States (1861), a Yankee naval blockade closed off all Gulf ports. Confederate agents established alternative trade routes through northern Mexico,

thus allowing European goods to flow from Tampico and Matamoros into Texas, and a vast quantity of cotton to move in the other direction. Vidaurri controlled much of the region in which this lucrative trade developed. By 1862 his hold on the fiefdom seemed stronger than ever, as he extended cooperation and warm friendship to José Agustín Quintero, the able Confederate agent who resided in Monterrey. At the same time, the Texas Rangers under Rip Ford helped to protect trade north of the river. When United States forces seized Brownsville in 1863, the commerce shifted upriver to Laredo and Eagle Pass. Meanwhile, the army of Napoleon III invaded Mexico and installed Maximilian on the throne. In 1863 Juárez once again fled from the capital, reaching Nuevo León the next February. Vidaurri at first refused to allow him to enter Monterrey. Fearing rebellion by his own people, however, the governor abandoned his fiefdom and took refuge in Texas. When Juárez moved to El Paso in August 1864, a French army occupied Monterrey and Vidaurri returned. He offered his services to Emperor Maximilian and moved to central Mexico, where he became an effective member of the imperial government. When the empire collapsed in June 1867, the army of Porfirio Díaz occupied Mexico City. A squadron arrested Vidaurri and executed him without a trial as a traitor to the Mexican nation.

Edward H. Moseley

Vidor, King Wallis. Movie director; b. Galveston, 8 February 1894; d. Los Angeles, 1 November 1982; m. Florence Arto (1915; divorced 1924); m. Eleanor Boardman (divorced 1932); m. Elizabeth Hill (1932). His father was an East Texas lumberman for whom the town of Vidor was named. As a boy, King worked as a movie projectionist at a local Galveston theater. He made an amateur movie based on the Galveston hurricane of 1900 and opened his first movie company, Hotex, in Houston in 1915. He went to Hollywood at the age of 21. His career there extended from the earliest days of silent filmmaking, when he shot two-reelers on a shoestring budget, to the "Golden Age" of Hollywood, marked by the spectacular cinematic productions of David O. Selznick, with whom Vidor made *Duel in the Sun* (1946). He considered himself a Southerner and made films that championed the poor and exposed racism and the horrors of war, yet also captured the adventures and action of a lively West. His Texas roots remained apparent. Among his films are *Billy the Kid* (1930), *Our Daily Bread* (1934), *The Texas Rangers* (1936), *Northwest Passage* (1940), and *The Fountainhead* (1951). Though Vidor is noted for his collaboration with Selznick, he made most of his films with M–G–M, which produced his first highly acclaimed film, *The Big Parade* (1925), hailed as a powerful anti-war movie. Vidor made the first all-black musical, *Hallelujah!*, in 1929. *Our Daily Bread* won a League of Nations award "for its contribution to humanity" in 1934. Vidor wrote two books, *A Tree is a Tree* (1953) and *King Vidor on Filmmaking* (1972). He had a self-proclaimed sense of mission about his filmmaking, which was influenced by a Christian Scientist background. In 1920 he published a "creed" in *Variety*, a commitment to "the picture that will help humanity to free itself from the shackles of fear and suffering that have so long bound it with iron chains." Though he was nominated five times for an Academy Award for best director, he never won. In 1978, however, the Motion Picture Academy awarded him an honorary Oscar. After he retired, Vidor taught filmmaking at USC and UCLA.

Kay Sloan

Vielé, Teresa Griffin. Memoirist; b. New York City, 27 January 1831; d. Paris, October 1906 (buried 23 October 1906 in Père Lachaise Cemetery, Montmartre); m. Egbert Ludovicus Vielé (1850; divorced 1872); 8 children. The precocious Teresa, called "cette terrible Teresa" by her family, attended an exclusive girls' finishing school, made her debut in New York City, and was honored in a poem by Longfellow. She was described by a biographer as a young woman of "beauty, intelligence, fortune, but also an indomitable character." With her husband, a West Point graduate, she moved to Ringgold Barracks (Fort Ringgold), where the couple remained until 1852, when Vielé resigned his commission and opened a successful engineering-consulting firm in New York City. Within a few years after the Civil War, Teresa's temper drove Egbert to seek "spiritual solace and sympathy" in the arms of another woman, Juliette Dana, whom he later married. After the divorce, Teresa took her youngest son, Egbert, to Paris, where she presided over a literary salon and sponsored the education and career of her son, renamed Francis Vielé–Griffin, who became a leading poet and writer of the French symbolist school. Teresa made at least two brief visits to the United States: one about 1873 to kidnap her youngest daughter, Emily, from the Vielé home near Poughkeepsie; and a second about 1893 to lecture on Islam. In 1858 she published *Following the Drum": A Glimpse of Frontier Life*, a memoir of the Vielés' Texas years. Her account of life at Ringgold Barracks comments on everything from travel and landscape, flora and fauna, and food "flavored with red ants [that] tasted something like caraway seed," to Mexican neighbors, Comanche raiders, and the Merchants War. Like Jane Cazneau, she was fascinated by the life and politics of the period. She interspersed her narrative with long historical passages and her opinions on American policy in regard to the army, the Indians, and the Mexicans. She hinted strongly that the forces assigned to the frontier were inadequate and suggested that the Americans should take a more direct role in Mexican affairs. Although her comments about Indian life and customs clearly reflect common misconceptions and prejudices, she expressed an interest in the Indians and tried to understand their viewpoint, concluding that even the "bloody, brutal, licentious" Comanches had been "driven from their rightful possessions, and [one] can see, in their ignorance, many excuses for their tiger-like ferocity." Although less inclined to be sympathetic toward the Mexicans, she was curious about them, visited in their homes, and expressed concern for the Mexican "Red Man" or peón. Although her only known published work is "Following the Drum," her literary ambitions were fulfilled in her children and grandchildren. Of the five of her children who reached adulthood, four were published authors: Francis; Kathlyne, a genealogist and historian; Herman, a novelist, playwright, and artist; and Emily, a poet and novelist. Emily's daughter, Elise Strother–Tuckerman, was also a published author.

Sandra L. Myres

Vietnamese. Before 1975 the few Vietnamese living in Texas were primarily military personnel sent for training, students, and "war brides." With the collapse of the Saigon regime in April 1975 the first major influx of refugees arrived, some coming directly from Vietnam and others through resettlement camps. Despite the fact that these new residents were mostly well-educated members of the old elite who had been forced to flee from the new communist regime, some Texans did not welcome them. Public sentiment as expressed in letters to congressional representatives ran more than 10 to one against accepting the refugees. The next large immigration took place in the late 1970s as a result of the arrival of the refugees who escaped the communist regime by boat, the so-called "boat people." These were more varied in their background and included a high percentage of individuals with a Chinese heritage. Since that time many Vietnamese have moved to Texas from other cities in the United States. Their major reasons for moving to Texas were economic opportunities, the nearness of resettlement camps, the climate and geographic similarity of places like Rockport to Vietnam, and, eventually, the attraction of Vietnamese communities, including support groups, media, and stores catering to their needs. Vietnamese generally moved to urban centers such as Houston, Dallas, and Austin and to seacoast areas. By 1981 Texas had the second largest number of Vietnamese of any state (40,000), and Houston had more than any American city outside of California.

The earliest refugees had held high government or professional positions in Vietnam, but they had difficulties finding similar occupations in Texas. Many moved to other work, including blue-collar jobs and management of small stores and restaurants. The boat people were even less prepared to enter the Texas job market and usually took up blue-collar occupations. Although the majority of the boat people had been farmers, few farmed in Texas. Fishing grew in importance. Unemployment was high among Vietnamese for the first decade after their arrival, but it subsequently declined to less than 5 percent. Most Vietnamese did not gain citizenship until the 1980s. Their memories of Vietnam and the role they played there, however, make them generally strongly anti-communist. Also, because their heritage has made them suspicious of government and the law, it is difficult for the police and census takers to gain their confidence, a fact which makes it hard to estimate their number. The Vietnamese reflect their homeland's varied religious background—of Catholic, Buddhist, Confucian, and other persuasions. Some have joined Protestant churches in Texas due to efforts by local congregations to aid them. Some have congregations of their own, such as Queen of the Vietnamese Martyrs Catholic Church in Port Arthur and Holy Vietnamese Martyrs Catholic Church in Austin. The Vietnamese strongly support education, and their children graduating from institutions of higher learning at rates higher than those of most non-Asian ethnic groups. At the same time, Vietnamese population centers such as Austin, Houston, and Dallas cultivate their ethnic heritage in radio, television, theater, martial arts, publications, ethnic shopping centers, ethnic holidays and ceremonies, and other means.

The large influx of Vietnamese into Texas cities and towns led to some tension. Originally there were problems with other minorities in housing projects. The 1975 wave of Vietnamese immigrants purchased homes as soon as they were able, but did not concentrate heavily in particular sections of cities, and the housing conflicts of earlier years had relaxed by the late 1980s. Difficulties also developed in fishing industries on the coast. Small Vietnamese shops raised competition in retail business, and cultural differences at work sometimes caused conflict. A common response to these problems was the founding of organizations such as the Vietnamese Doctors Association, the Vietnamese Students Association, and the Texas Association for

Vietnamese American Education, all chapters of national organizations. In Austin an influential association, the Vietnamese Heritage Association, was formed in the late 1980s. By 1989, 14 years after the fall of Saigon and the pro-American government, more than a million Vietnamese had resettled in the United States. After a few years of struggle with the language barrier, many Vietnamese were successful professionals—doctors, lawyers, pharmacists, teachers, engineers, computer programmers. Among them, nevertheless, the "refugees' dream" remained strong—the desire to go home and reshape their old country into a free, democratic nation.

Fred R. von der Mehden

Village Creek, battle of. A running gunfight (24 May 1841) along the banks of a tributary of the Trinity River in eastern Tarrant County. Village Creek now forms the city limits of Arlington and Fort Worth, and much of the battlefield has been inundated by Lake Arlington. Indian villages along the creek served as a stronghold against the encroachments of white settlers from the east and Comanches from the west. After two expeditions in 1838 failed to locate the towns, the Indians intensified their raids on frontier settlements. In 1841 Gen. Edward H. Tarrant organized a company of 69 volunteers from the Red River counties, which rode into the Cross Timbers on May 14 and the next day captured a lone Indian, who revealed the exact locations of the Village Creek settlements. The following day the company galloped into the southernmost village with little opposition. Captains John B. Denton, Henry B. Stout, and James G. Bourland then led scouting detachments down the creek toward the Trinity River, encountering increasingly larger villages and stronger resistance. Denton was killed, Stout was wounded, and the Texans were routed. Although Tarrant, upon learning that the villages were home to over 1,000 warriors, decided to withdraw, the engagement on Village Creek had compromised the Indians' formerly secure position. In July 1841 Tarrant returned with 400 men but found the villages deserted. In September 1843 a treaty between the Village Creek tribes and the republic led to the construction of Bird's Fort, opened the region to settlement, and removed the Indians to a reservation on the upper Brazos River.

Donald S. Frazier

Visual Arts. With the exception of Indian rock art, the early visual arts of Texas are the work of travelers who brought with them the traditions of other cultures. The first picture having to do with Texas might well have been Frenchman Jean l'Archevêque's crude 1689 painting of one of La Salle's ships, an effort to persuade the Spanish governor to rescue him and his shipmate from the Indian village where they had lived ever since the La Salle expedition had disintegrated two years earlier. Father Louis Hennepin further elaborated upon La Salle's expedition to Texas with two imaginary engravings in his *A Discovery of a Vast Country in America* (London, 1698): La Salle's ship landing on the coast of Texas and the assassination of La Salle.

Spanish colonial period. There is little visual material relating to Spanish Texas, because few of the soldiers and settlers who entered Texas before 1821 could be classified as artists. There are some exceptions, the most important being the *Destruction of Mission San Sabá in the Province of Texas* and the *Martyrdom of the Fathers Alonso Giraldo de Terreros, Joseph Santiesteban*, a memorial painting attributed to Mexico City artist José de Páez.

Other Spanish Texas art consists only of several drawings of soldiers by Ramundo de Murrillo and maps and vignettes, especially the series on presidios that Joseph de Urrutia y de las Casas did while on the 1767 expedition of the Marqués de Rubí. The most outstanding examples of Spanish art and architecture in Texas are easily the Spanish missions of San Antonio. A short-lived settlement of Napoleonic exiles on the Trinity River, near the site of present-day Liberty, inspired a second group of images. Champ d'Asile lasted less than six months, but the French liberals idealized this foray into the wilderness and composed songs, poems, pictures, and books and organized tribute dinners on behalf of the refugees. Ludwig Rullmann, Louis Garneray, and the famous Horace Vernet produced imaginary depictions of the settlement, while others published sheet music, books, and caricatures, with the proceeds to go to the Texas refugees. None of these Romantic images, with the possible exception of the maps, bore any relation to the defunct colony, but they did spread the name of Texas across France and much of Europe.

Mexican period. Gen. Manuel de Mier y Terán's Comisión de Límites of 1828 produced the first important eye-witness documentation of Texas. With Mier traveled Swiss naturalist Jean Louis Berlandier and cartographer José Sánchez y Tapía, who collected specimens, kept journals, and made dozens of maps and drawings—of plants, animals, people, and communities. They compiled much material on South and East Texas, and after they returned to Mexico, Lino Sánchez y Tapía painted a series of watercolors of the people of Texas, including representatives of 16 different Indian tribes, from Berlandier's notes and sketches. Today the Berlandier material is scattered from the University of Texas at Austin to the Gilcrease Museum, the Smithsonian Institution, Yale and Harvard universities, and museums in Great Britain and Europe. It is possible that George Catlin visited northern Texas while on his 1834 trip into Indian Territory. He produced a number of pictures labeled "Texas," including *Caddo Indians Gathering Wild Grapes, Texas, Catlin and Party Stalking Buffalo in Texas, Comanche Giving Arrows to the Medicine Rock*, and *Comanche Village, Women Dressing Robes and Drying Meat*, among others. Even though Catlin scholar William H. Truettner maintains that Catlin did not cross into Texas during that trip, the pictures are still the best contemporary visual record that exist of the Caddos, Comanches, and other Texas tribes. Perhaps it was Catlin's later land speculation in Texas that led him to label the scenes as being of the state.

The number of pictures increased with Anglo-American colonization in Mexican Texas. An unknown draftsman produced four small drawings to be included as engravings in a small volume called *A Visit to Texas* (New York, 1834). Mary Austin Holley made several small, crude sketches of Houston and the Perry plantation in her diary, and Stephen F. Austin had his portrait painted on several occasions. Two portraits of him by William Howard, painted while Austin was in Mexico City in 1833, are at the University of Texas at Austin. At least one artist, William Tylee Ranney, was present at the battle of San Jacinto, but apparently chose not to depict any scenes of the event. His months in Texas probably inspired his later paintings of vaqueros roping mustangs on the prairies, but, with the exception of maps, the only pictures of the events of the Texas Revolution are imaginary: engravings in books such as John M. Niles, *South America and Mexico* (1836) and *Davy Crockett's Almanac*, sheet music such as the *Texian Grand March*, and caricatures like Edward W. Clay's *Genl. Houston, Santa Ana, & Cos.*

Republic of Texas. Most of the paintings done during the republic are either portraits or small sketches or watercolors intended for publication, primarily in immigrant guides, or for private use. At least 19 artists entered the republic, most of them from the United States. Among the limners were James Strange, perhaps a Scottish immigrant, who painted portraits of Antonio López de Santa Anna and his aide, Juan N. Almonte, soon after the battle of San Jacinto; Kentuckian Thomas Jefferson Wright, who began work on his "Gallery of National Portraits" in a Houston hotel room in 1836; and Ambrose Andrews, who arrived from New England in the fall of 1837 and spent the next four years in Houston as a naturalist and portrait painter. Among those searching for material for publication was the artist–naturalist John James Audubon, who visited Houston and Galveston with his son, John Woodhouse Audubon, in 1837 in search of additional specimens for *The Birds of America* and the prospective *Viviparous Quadrupeds of North America*. William Bissett, Charles Hooten, Edward Hall, and several unknown artists produced sketches that were published as prints in travel narratives or guides. Charles M'Laughlin illustrated Thomas Jefferson Green's *Journal of the Texian Expedition Against Mier* (New York, 1845), while an unnamed artist provided illustrations for George Wilkins Kendall's best-selling *Narrative of the Texan Santa Fe Expedition* (New York, 1844). William Bollaert, who might have been a British spy intent on keeping Texas from joining the Union, apparently did not intend his small, precise drawings for publication, and they did not become known until the twentieth century, when they wound up in the collections of the Newberry Library and historian W. Eugene Hollon edited and published Bollaert's extensive journal.

The Tehuacana Creek Councils (1843–) drew the attention of American artist John Mix Stanley, who accompanied United States commissioner Pierce Butler to the event. Two paintings by Stanley remain from this council—*Ko-rak-koo-kiss, a Towoccono Warrior* and *Indian Council, Tehuacana Creek, Texas* (both in the National Museum of American Art, Smithsonian Institution)—but others might have been destroyed in the fire that destroyed the Smithsonian in 1865, and with it, Stanley's Indian Gallery. Draftsmen and cartographers such as Friedrich Jacob Rothaas of Houston, William H. Sandusky of Austin, and Theodore Gentilz of Castroville made other drawings. Gentilz, by far the most talented of the three, moved in 1846 to San Antonio, where he documented the community's Spanish architecture and folk culture in genre scenes. He later tried his hand at historical subjects such as *Shooting of the Seventeen Decimated Texians or Drawing of the Black Beans* (private collection) and *Battle of the Alamo*, which was destroyed in a nineteenth-century fire. There was apparently at least one early effort to produce a memorial to the heroes of the battle of the Alamo. In 1843 a reporter for the New Orleans *Daily Picayune* described a monument that had been carved by a sculptor named Joseph Cox. The obelisk reportedly had military emblems carved on it, with the names of Travis, Crockett, Bowie, and Bonham etched on its four sides. The monument apparently was exhibited in New Orleans and, despite the fact that it was supposed to have been purchased by the state of Texas, was sold for the costs of the exhibition and never made it to Texas. By 1851 legends of the memorial had so grown that the *Texas State Gazette* reported that the rock had been chiseled from the walls of the Alamo by an English or German artist who had fought in the battles of Texas and who then "spent several months in this pious labor." The last word on the sculpture was that it had been spotted in the rubbish of a marble yard in New Orleans.

Early statehood. Although a number of easel paintings date from antebellum Texas (1846–61), most of the art produced then was still intended either for personal use or for publication in a book or magazine. At least 30 identifiable artists arrived in Texas during these years; most were from the United States, but a large number were from Germany. The Mexican War brought a number of American soldier–artists into the new state, including Edward Everett, Samuel Emery Chamberlain, Daniel Powers Whiting, and George C. Furber. Whiting, Everett, and Furber published some of their pictures during or shortly after the war, but Chamberlain's vibrant watercolors, accompanied by a candid and perhaps fictional journal–narrative, remained within his family until after World War II, when they were placed on the market. Historian William Goetzmann has published two volumes on Chamberlain, one each on the two main collections of his work at the San Jacinto Museum in Houston and the West Point Museum at the United States Military Academy.

Several talented artists arrived with the successive waves of Germans who immigrated in the 1840s and '50s. Carl Gustav von Iwonski accompanied his family from Hilbersdorf in Silesia (now a part of western Poland) in 1845–46, Swiss artist and naturalist Conrad Caspar Rohrdorf arrived with the Bonn Company of Naturalists in 1847, and Richard Petri and Hermann Lungkwitz arrived from Dresden in 1851. Rohrdorf reportedly drew at least 45 sketches of Texas before being shot to death near Round Top just a few months after his arrival. His panoramic view of New Braunfels was lithographed in Germany in 1851 to accompany a booklet encouraging emigration to Texas. Petri might have been the most talented of the four, but he died in 1857, shortly after arriving in Texas, leaving his major work, *Fort Martin Scott*, unfinished. Iwonski remained until 1875 painting landscapes, portraits, genre paintings, and still lifes. He did two lithographs—*Neu-Braunfels. Deutsche Colonie in West Texas* (1856) and *Germania Gesangverein, Neu Braunfels, Texas* (1857)—and several drawings for Harper's Weekly. He and W. C. A. Thielepape also experimented with a method of photographically reproducing drawings that they called "homeography." Lungkwitz, the finest landscape painter of nineteenth-century Texas, painted landscapes and cityscapes around San Antonio, Austin, and the Hill Country until his death in 1891. He also produced three handsome lithographs—of San Antonio, Fredericksburg, and Ernst Kapp's Water Cure, near Comfort.

Some artists entered the state at the behest of the federal government, and most of their work was included in a series of government publications. After the war with Mexico, the government undertook a number of surveys throughout the West, many of them documenting the unsettled regions of Texas. The first to cross Texas, even before statehood had been approved, was James W. Abert's expedition down the Canadian River in 1845. Abert was an artist of some ability, having been trained at West Point, and his published report (*A Report of an Expedition led by Lieutenant Abert, on the Upper Arkansas and Through the Country of the Comanche Indians, in the year 1845, 1846*) contains nine lithographs, including a picture of Pillar Rock (now called Chimney Peak) on the Canadian. Marcy, after attempting unsuccessfully to find the headwaters of the Red River in 1852, pub-

Bird's Eye View of the City of Houston, Texas, by Augustus Koch, 1873. Hand-colored lithograph. 24¾" × 32". Oversize Pictures file, CAH; CN 08701.

lished the first pictures of Palo Duro Canyon in his *Exploration of the Red River of Louisiana, in the Year 1852* (1853), while artist Heinrich B. Möllhausen crossed the Panhandle from east to west with Lt. Amiel W. Whipple's portion of the Pacific Railroad Survey in 1853, documenting the landscape and Kiowa culture in *Reports of Explorations and Surveys, to Ascertain the Most Practicable and Economical Route for a Railroad from the Mississippi River to the Pacific Ocean* (12 vols., 1855–61). Several talented artists participated in the joint survey of the new boundary between the United States and Mexico, including Augustus de Vaudricourt, Arthur C. V. Schott, and John B. Wyess, whose work was published in William H. Emory's *United States and Mexican Boundary Survey* (2 vols., 1857–59), and Commissioner John Russell Bartlett, who published prints after his own facile watercolors in his *Personal Narrative* (2 vols., New York, 1854). Bartlett was also responsible for the visit of Henry C. Pratt, whose View of *Smith's West Texas Ranch* documents the future site of El Paso. Pratt also did portraits of a number of people while in the area, including John Russell Bartlett (Amon Carter Museum, Fort Worth), James Wiley Magoffin (Magoffin Home State Historical Park, El Paso), and Benjamin Franklin Coons

(private collection). Carl Schuchard of San Antonio covered much of the same territory for the Texas Western Railroad, a private venture that failed but nevertheless published Andrew B. Gray's route survey, *Southern Pacific Railroad: Survey of a Route for the Southern Pacific R.R., on the 32nd Parallel* (1856), including Schuchard's pictures along the road from San Antonio to El Paso and beyond. The federal military presence on the frontier also resulted in pictures—from works of the well-known Seth Eastman, who served briefly at Fort Martin Scott, near Fredericksburg, and Capt. Arthur T. Lee, who helped establish Fort Davis in far West Texas in 1855, to those of the elusive Leon Trousset, who made sketches of Fort Davis and Fort Stockton, perhaps on commission for the government.

Other artists came either with increased immigration or because of it. Sarah Ann Hardinge arrived in Texas in 1852 in search of land that her brother had left her; she sketched, for her own and her family's enjoyment, various scenes of the country and each place where her family resided—Jacob de Cordova's plantation, Seguin, and several other plantations in the Seguin and Wilson County area. Louis Hoppe, on the other hand, might have been an itinerant laborer who worked on the two farms that he pictured in small but precise watercolors in the south central Texas communities of La Grange and Frelsburg. British artist Thomas Flintoff is an example of one who came hoping to find customers among the newly prosperous planters and businessmen who would pay him to paint their portraits. He spent most of 1852 in Texas, producing likenesses of individuals such as Pryor and Mary Bryan, Thomas Jefferson Chambers and his wife, Annie, and, posthumously, Stephen F. Austin and Edward Burleson. On his own he painted a series of watercolors of Houston, Matagorda, Indianola, and Corpus Christi, pictures that reveal the historic look of these early communities, which, like Hardinge's and Hoppe's pictures, were not known until their owners revealed them in relatively recent years. Some artists produced historically valuable images even though they only passed through the state. Austrian Franz Hölzlhuber, on a trip from his temporary home in Minnesota, visited Texas and Louisiana as part of a tour of the South and produced unique depictions of slaves harvesting sugarcane in East Texas or Louisiana and two scenes of what might well be a portion of the Big Thicket. Helmuth H. D. Holtz sketched Indianola and Matagorda, probably from his vantage point on the bark *Texana* in the harbors, and had his paintings lithographed in Germany. An unknown artist submitted drawings of Galveston, San Antonio, and New Braunfels for inclusion in Herman J. Meyer's *Universum*, a compendium of world views published in 24 volumes in Hildurghausen between 1835 and 1860. C. O. Bahr published his bird's-eye view of Galveston in Dresden, probably about 1860. Approximately half of the artists who came to Texas during these years were trained, and the others were self-taught.

Civil War. Texas was appropriately called the "dark corner" of the Confederacy, for few Civil War battles took place within its borders and only a few artists were present to document them and the other events of the years 1861–65. Unnamed artists published a series of illustrations of Texas forts in *Harper's Weekly* in 1861. Another unnamed artist, probably Iwonski, sent a series of drawings to *Harper's* as the war began. The most famous one shows the surrender of the Union Army in Texas to Confederate colonel Ben McCulloch in San Antonio. Iwonski's genre portrait of Samuel Maverick, Jr., as a member of Terry's Texas Rangers captures the enthusiasm that many Texans felt for the war, while C. H. Claus's naïve painting of the battle of the Nueces (Fredericksburg Historical Society) in 1862, coupled with a subsequent illustration in *Harper's*, depicts one of the saddest moments of the war, when a group of Confederate soldiers massacred most of a group of German Unionists who were trying to go to Mexico rather than remain in Confederate Texas. Another unfortunate episode of the war is shown in James S. McClain's lithograph *Camp Ford Texas* (ca. 1865), the prison that the Confederacy maintained at Tyler.

Gilded Age. At least four trends are noticeable between 1865 and 1900: the large number of artists who produced lithographed bird's-eye views of cities, an interest in history painting, the emergence of Texas-born artists, and the evolution of the most popular of all Texas characters, the cowboy. The bird's-eye craze affected not just Texas, but swept the country during the latter half of the nineteenth century. Almost 5,000 such views were produced of North American cities during these years by more than 50 identified artists working in 12 cities across the nation. Perhaps as many as 7 of these artists drew more than 50 lithographs of Texas cities. Although there are a number of views

of Texas cities that predate the Civil War, such as Rohrdorf's *New Braunfels*, Lungkwitz's *San Antonio*, and Bähr's *Galveston*, Camille N. Drie, probably from St. Louis, began the genre in Texas with his 1871 view of Galveston. Typically, the artist showed his sketches to the local newspaper editor, who announced to the community that the artist would produce a view of their city if there were enough subscriptions. The artist would draw the view and send it back to a lithographic plant in St. Louis or Milwaukee and move on to the next city. Six months or so later, the finished views would be delivered to the customers. Perhaps as many as 200 or 300 lithographs would be printed and usually colored by hand; in some cases, such as the 1891 view of Fort Worth, merchants purchased additional copies to use as advertisements and as many as 1,000 were printed. Augustus Koch, a German immigrant who lived in Wisconsin and the most prolific of the Texas bird's-eye-view artists, produced 19 Texas views between 1873 and 1898. Herman Brosius, probably from Wisconsin, did 4 Texas views in 1872–73, Midwesterner D. D. Morse did 3 in 1876, Henry W. Wellge of Milwaukee did 9 between 1881 and 1895, and Thaddeus M. Fowler of Pennsylvania did 13 in 1890–91. Denison is the most frequently portrayed city in the state, with 4 lithographs (by Brosius, 1872, Morse, 1876, Wellge, 1885, and Fowler, 1891). There are three prints each of Austin, Fort Worth, Galveston, and San Antonio.

The fiftieth anniversary of the Texas Revolution in 1886 stimulated most of the history painting, as artists competed to commemorate the heroes of the revolution and sell their paintings to the state for the new Capitol. The two most important history painters were Henry A. McArdle and William H. Huddle; works of both hang in the Capitol today. Theodore Gentilz, Robert J. Onderdonk, and L. M. D. Guillaume painted important works, and Louis Eyth supplied well-known illustrations for several of historian James T. DeShields's books. Huddle's most important painting is *The Surrender of Santa Anna*. McArdle's two most significant works, *Dawn at the Alamo* and *The Battle of San Jacinto* (1895), hang in the Texas Senate chamber. Onderdonk's *The Fall of the Alamo or Crockett's Last Stand* hangs in the hall of the Governor's Mansion. Huddle also painted the portraits of many Texas presidents and governors that hang in the Capitol. The Semicentennial of Texas Independence also called attention to some emerging native-born artists, most notably 19-year-old Stephen Seymour Thomas of San Augustine, who won an award of merit at the 1887 State Fair of Texas. It was the beginning of a notable career. Thomas, who was known mostly for his portraits, studied in Paris, where he later made his home. He painted dozens of portraits of distinguished sitters and developed an international reputation that culminated with an exhibition at the Los Angeles Museum in 1935. Other Texas-born artists who had begun to receive some measure of fame by the last decades of the century were Ida Weisselberg Hadra of San Antonio, who had studied with Hermann Lungkwitz, and Boyer Gonzales, Sr., of Galveston, who befriended the famous American artist Winslow Homer.

Sculptors also benefited from the desire to honor the founders of the republic. No one knows why the gifted German sculptor Elisabet Ney moved to the state in 1872, but she settled on Liendo Plantation near Hempstead with her husband, scientist and philosopher Edmund D. Montgomery, and proceeded to manage the plantation and raise her son. As the new Capitol began to take shape, she contacted Governor Oran Roberts, a family friend, and presented him with a proposal for sculpture throughout the new building. Roberts recommended the proposal, but in the end all sculpture except the Goddess of Liberty for the top of the dome was stripped from the plan, and that contract went to a Chicago monument company. Almost a decade later, Ney won a commission from the World's Fair Exhibit Association, a group of women who had organized to see that the state would be properly represented at the coming World's Fair in Chicago in 1893. Ney moved to Austin and built a studio in a suburban addition to the city, Hyde Park, where it remains today as a museum. She agreed to execute statues of Stephen F. Austin and Sam Houston for the Texas exhibit but finished only the statue of Houston in time for the fair. In 1901 she received commissions for marble sculptures of both Austin and Houston for the state Capitol and for the National Statuary Hall in the national Capitol. Later that year she also received the commission for the recumbent statue of Gen. Albert Sidney Johnston that is now in the State Cemetery. Ney expected to receive other commissions as various organizations prepared to honor the state's forebears, but was disappointed when in 1899 the Texas Confederate Veterans commission for a massive memorial went to a young Italian sculptor from New York. The bronzes that Pompeo Coppini produced for the memorial made his reputation in Texas; thereafter, he received numerous commissions from the state and other parties. Among his best known works are the Littlefield Fountain Memorial at the University of Texas at Austin, the bronzes of the Texas heroes in the Hall of State in Dallas, and the Alamo Cenotaph in San Antonio.

One of the most popular characters in history also emerged from this period, first on the pages of *Harper's Weekly* and *Leslie's Illustrated*, then on the easels of Frederic Remington and Charles M. Russell, among others. Some of the earliest pictures of the Texas vaquero, or the cowboy, surely are the roping seen in *A Visit to Texas* (1834) and William Ranney's paintings done in 1846 and based on his Texas experience of a decade before. But the cowboy did not become a popular figure until the 1860s and 1870s, when hundreds if not thousands of cowboys were herding cattle up the Western, Chisholm, and Shawnee trails. Such artists as A. R. Waud, William M. Cary, Paul Frenzeny, and Jules Tavernier published sketches in *Harper's Weekly*, and cowboy authors such as Charles Siringo (*A Texas Cow Boy*, 1885) wrote about the experience. Remington and Russell, working in New York and Montana respectively, went on to make the cowboy a national icon. In Texas, meanwhile, Frank Reaugh, who had arrived in Terrell with his family in 1876 and moved to Dallas in 1890, was popularizing longhorn cattle in much the same way that Onderdonk did the bluebonnet. Both Gutzon Borglum and Alexander Phimister Proctor, well-known American sculptors, continued the cowboy theme for several Texas works. The Trail Drivers Association commissioned Borglum to do *Texas Cowboys (Trail Drivers Monument)* (1925) as a memorial to the trail drivers, and Proctor's famous *Mustangs* (1939–40) is a prominent bronze on the UT Austin campus. Proctor also did *Robert E. Lee and the Confederate Soldier* (1935–36) for Lee Park in Dallas.

Early twentieth century. A number of communities set out to produce a more favorable atmosphere for the arts as the twentieth century dawned. Robert Onderdonk had founded the first

An exhibition held under the auspices of the San Antonio Art League, San Antonio, ca. 1894. Albumen print. Courtesy Witte Museum, San Antonio, Texas. Groups like the San Antonio Art League formed in many Texas cities in the late nineteenth century, offering artists exhibition opportunities and citizens a chance to see art.

art association in San Antonio, the Van Dyke Art Club, in 1886. When he moved to Dallas, he founded the Dallas Art Students League in 1893. Other cities followed suit. The Houston Public School Art League was founded in 1900, and in Austin the Texas Fine Arts Association was organized in 1911. The public libraries in such cities as Fort Worth sponsored art exhibitions from the turn of the century. No longer would Texas-born artists such as Seymour Thomas of San Augustine, Julian Onderdonk of San Antonio, Murray P. Bewley of Fort Worth, and Royston Nave of La Grange have to grow up in an unsupportive environment. While art organizations struggled to organize throughout the state, one of the nation's most talented painters was creating a new and modern vision of the West Texas landscape. Georgia O'Keeffe, a young Wisconsin woman who had studied at the Art Institute of Chicago and in New York and who taught at West Texas State Normal School in Canyon, incorporated the stark plains of the Panhandle into her developing aesthetic and produced startlingly new images that took New York by storm. "I lived on the plains of North Texas for four years," she later recalled. "It is the only place I have ever felt that I really belonged—that I really felt at home . . . . That was my country—terrible winds and a wonderful emptiness." After successful exhibitions, she soon moved to New York City, where she married Alfred Stieglitz, who recognized her unique talent. After Stieglitz's death, O'Keeffe settled in New Mexico, where she continued to depict the elemental beauty of the land in distinctive ways until her death in 1986.

Great Depression and World War II. Disenchanted by World War I, artists such as Thomas Hart Benton of Missouri traveled across the country in search of authentic subjects. In Texas Benton depicted the changing economy that the discovery of oil initiated. In *Cattle Loading, West Texas* (Addison Gallery of American Art, Phillips Academy, Andover, Massachusetts, 1930) he portrayed the death of the Old West and its ways, which had "gone beyond recall." On the other hand, *Boom Town* (Memorial Art Gallery of the University of Rochester, 1928), a caricature of Borger in 1926, captures the raucous energy of the

John Biggers at work on a painting. Copyright ©1962 Houston *Chronicle* Publishing Company. Reprinted with permission. All rights reserved. John Biggers, one of the most prominent African-American artists in Texas, helped found the art department at Texas Southern University.

"traditional . . . western boom town." Further battered by the stock market crash and the onset of the Great Depression, artists led in the national self-examination that resulted. Would our democratic and economic traditions survive their sternest test? Benton, John Stewart Curry of Kansas, and Grant Wood of Iowa led the national search for indigenous subjects with which to explain America to itself. Jerry Bywaters, born in Paris, Texas, and educated at Southern Methodist University and in New York, Europe, and Mexico, led a number of talented young Texas artists in this search. The Dallas Art Institute became their gathering place after Olin Travis became director, and they soon composed a vibrant regional arts community. Bywaters, Otis Dozier of Lawson, William Lester of Graham, and Alexandre Hogue of Denton painted and wrote about Texas and the Southwest in the new *Southwest Review*. Their search for Texas subjects led them back to their roots: to farm life and the landscape, people and animals, droughts and the Dust Bowl. After the establishment of the federal Public Works of Art Project in 1933, these artists turned to murals of the "American scene"—art that John S. Ankeney, director of the Dallas Museum of Fine Arts and of Region 12 of the PWAP explained, would be "taken from our actual existence and environment," that "would be salient and socially significant," and that would be accessible to all Americans. What the New Deal administrators had in mind was the eminently successful Mexican mural program of the 1920s, in which young artists covered the public buildings of Mexico City with colorful paintings. Bywaters, who had seen the Mexican muralists at work, thought that the Dallas painters had an unprecedented opportunity to interpret Texas life as only natives could.

The PWAP and the subsequent Federal Art Project, a part of the WPA, put unemployed Texas artists to work. Bywaters and Hogue turned to the history of Dallas County for a mural in Old City Hall, including Tonkawa Indians, John Neely Bryan, early settlers, the French colony La Réunion, the coming of railroads, and the building of a modern city. Dozier painted *Applied Biology and Pure Science* for the library at Texas A&M, and other Dallas artists received commissions for murals all over the state. Bywaters explained how this new Texas art fitted into the national scene in an article in *Southwest Review* (April 1936). He, Hogue, and seven associates prepared an elaborate proposal for the new Hall of State, which was to be constructed in Fair Park in Dallas as a part of the Texas Centennial celebration in 1936. They were greatly disappointed when the main contract for the hall itself went to an experienced but conservative mural artist from New York, Edward Savage. Tom Lea, an El Paso artist, received the commission for the West Texas Room, Olin Travis for the East Texas Room, Arthur Starr Niendorff for the North Texas Room, and James Owne Mahoney for the South Texas Room. The Dallas Nine, as Bywaters and his group were soon called, felt justified when the jury for the Texas gallery of the Centennial art exhibition selected much of their work to exhibit. The icing on the aesthetic cake was the construction of a new Dallas Museum of Fine Arts in Fair Park. In all, artists painted dozens of murals in public buildings in Texas as a part of various government programs.

When it appeared certain that the United States would enter World War II, *Life* magazine commissioned Tom Lea, who had done a number of post office murals, to do a series of portraits of American soldiers. Pleased with his work, *Life* employed him full-time as a war correspondent and sent him on a 100,000-mile trek during the next four years to document American involvement in England, North Africa, Italy, Egypt and the Middle East, India, and China. He was present for the marine landing on the Pacific island of Peleliu in September 1944 and ultimately produced more pictures than any of the other eight war artists that *Life* employed. After the war, he teamed up with El Paso designer Carl Hertzog to publish *Peleliu Landing* (El Paso, 1945).

After World War II. By 1948 Fort Worth was the only city in Texas that could be said to have developed a "school" of artists—that is, as Dallas critic John Rosenfield, Jr., explained the term, "a homogeneous group representing a definitely advanced aesthetic and a high average of quality in practicing it." Such a school might have developed in Dallas had not so many of the Bywaters circle left to pursue their careers elsewhere: Spruce and Lester went to Austin to help establish the art department at the University of Texas, Hogue moved to Oklahoma, Bywaters became director of the Dallas Museum of Fine Arts. But in Fort Worth, artists such as Bill Bomar, Bror Utter, Cynthia Brants, George Grammer, Flora and E. Dickson Reeder, Blanche McVeigh, and Evaline C. Sellors led the way to a new and modern aesthetic, one in which "the individual replaces the regional," as New York *Times* critic Aline Louchheim explained. The new Fort Worth Art Museum (now the Modern Art Museum of Fort Worth) resulted from the fervor. The University of Texas art department has attracted excellent artists over the years, but has not developed an "Austin school." According to Loren N. Mozley, former chairman of the department, the faculty produced art "like that which you might find anywhere in the world." Mozley himself was a painter of note, and Charles Umlauf was the best-known sculptor. The Umlauf Sculpture Garden near Zilker Park in Austin is his and his wife's gift to the city of Austin. John Thomas Biggers established the art department at the Texas State University for Negroes (later Texas Southern University) in 1949. A year later, Carroll Harris Simms, a sculptor, joined him. Both are Southerners, Biggers from North Carolina and Simms from Arkansas. Biggers taught his students to look to their African heritage, as well as their local communities, for inspiration. He painted murals based on black history and community life for various Houston organizations and traveled to Africa in 1957 to study his heritage. He published *Ananse: The Web of Life in Africa* (1962) as a result. Biggers began painting in a new style after his retirement in 1983. That same year he completed a mural in honor of Christia V. Adair, a commission from the Harris county commissioners, and in 1987 he completed a series of paintings based on shotgun houses, the premier form of African-influenced architecture, in the Third Ward in Houston. The Museum of Fine Arts, Houston, gave Biggers a retrospective exhibition in 1995.

Folk Painters. Perhaps half of the artists who came to Texas during the nineteenth century would be classified as folk artists—that is, persons without formal training whose art is often distinguished by traditional ethnic expression, unaffected by the trends of academic art. William G. M. Samuel of San Antonio, Louis Hoppe, and Annie B. McMahon, who painted *The Peter B. Faison Family* (La Grange Garden Club) about 1890 would fit into that category. So would Charles A. A. Dellschau of Houston, although he might have considered himself more an aeronautical draftsman than an artist. Dellschau, a German, spent his first few years in America as draftsman for a group of scientists who formed the Sonora, California, Aero Club. After his retirement in Houston at the turn of the century, he began working on his airship designs again. The Sonora Aero Club members had experimented with aircraft and sought information about unidentified flying objects; Dellschau's designs probably were based on their speculations. His work remained unknown for more than half a century and still has not been fully appreciated for its complexity and design.

Most folk artists paint the people and things around them or from memory, and many of them do not begin painting until

Zebras and Hyenas, by Melissa Miller, 1985. Oil on linen. 72" × 84". Photograph by George Holmes. Jack S. Blanton Museum of Art, University of Texas at Austin. Purchased through the generosity of Mari and James A. Michener, 1985.

Jermayne MacAgy during the installation of The Trojan Horse: The Art of the Machine at the Contemporary Arts Museum, Houston. Photograph by Eve Arnold, 1958. Courtesy Eve Arnold, London. Photograph courtesy Menil Collection, Houston. Museum director Jermayne MacAgy served as an inspiration to many artists and collectors in Houston and organized successful exhibitions of modern art.

late in life. Frank M. Edwards (1855–1956), who did not begin painting until he was 80 years old, filled the walls of the stone home that he built himself with murals of his cowboying days. No one noticed the work of Harold O. Kelly of Blanket until he contacted a professor at Howard Payne College to assist him in shipping some of his small canvases. The professor introduced him to Jerry Bywaters, who arranged for an exhibition of Kelly's pictures in 1950. Kelly became the resident artist at the Texas State Fair. Clara McDonald Williamson is perhaps the best known of the untutored artists who depicted life as it used to be in her native Iredell, Texas. After her husband died in 1943, she began to take art classes at SMU and the Dallas Museum of Fine Arts and painted "memory" pictures until her death in 1976. Velox Ward of Mount Vernon began painting at age 60, when he decided to give his children a picture for Christmas. He tried to evoke "the good old days" of his rural boyhood shortly after the turn of the century. When Fannie Lou Spelce of Austin began taking art classes at Laguna Gloria Art Museum in 1966, her instructor realized her natural talent and suggested that she stop taking classes and paint as she wanted to. Her popular paintings include representations of quilting bees, the country store, fairs, strawberry-picking time, and other scenes from her childhood in Dyer, Arkansas. Eddie Arning's inspiration came from a different source. A resident of the Austin State Hospital, Arning made his first drawings in 1964 with crayons supplied by one of the attendants. As his vision developed he switched to oil pastels and began to improvise on illustrations that he saw in magazines. Consuelo González Amezcua of Del Rio gained her inspiration from the fine silver and gold filigree jewelry so popular in Mexico; the result was complex and vivid drawings that she made with colored ballpoint pens, which she called "filigree art." The fact that Texas has long since become an urban state is illustrated in the paintings of Frank Freed of Houston. A Harvard graduate, veteran of World War II, and an insurance salesman,

Cadillac Ranch, by the Ant Farm, 1977. Photograph by Wyatt McSpadden. Old Route 66, 1981. Courtesy Wyatt McSpadden, Austin. This sculpture, which features 10 vintage Cadillacs half-buried in a maize field, was erected for the amazement and amusement of drivers traveling the seemingly endless distances of the Panhandle.

Freed began painting seriously at age 42 in 1948, producing naïvely drawn but complex and sophisticated canvases representing the frustration and perplexity of the times, such as *Climate of Opinion*, now in the collection of the Museum of Fine Arts, Houston.

The "threat" of modern art. Despite the enthusiastic acceptance of modern art by some Texas artists, the transition did not come without complaint. Battered by a series of incidents after World War II—the Berlin blockade, the Communist coup in Czechoslovakia, the fall of China to Communist forces, the Soviet explosion of the atomic bomb, and the subsequent exposure of successful spying on the part of Julius and Ethel Rosenberg, among others—many Texans became suspicious of the directions art was taking. In Houston an assistant school superintendent took it upon himself to remove all the art books that contained pictures of nudes from the high school libraries. In Dallas, Bywaters, as director of the museum, had kept up with such incidents throughout the country—in San Francisco, Los Angeles, New York, Washington, and Hollywood—all involving an attack upon the arts or the arts organizations. To Bywaters modern art seemed to be an easy target, so when the normally sedate Public Affairs Luncheon Club of Dallas issued a statement on 15 March 1955 declaring that the Dallas Museum of Fine Arts was "overemphasizing all phases of futuristic, modernistic, and non-objective painting and statuary," he urged that the trustees appoint a committee to deal with the complaint. Hoping that the matter would go away, the trustees declined to act. But the opposition would not go away, because it was well financed by such determined individuals as oilman H. L. Hunt. The following year the director of the public library removed a rug and a painting by Pablo Picasso from an exhibition rather than "stir up a lot of controversy." Bywaters also discovered that what one writer called the "Emily Post–Impressionist School of Bluebonnet Painters" was behind the denunciations, as local art clubs, such as the Frank Reaugh Club, the Klepper Club, the Federation of Dallas Artists, the Bassett Club, and the Oak Cliff Fine Arts Society joined the Dallas County Patriotic Council to demand that certain kinds of modern art not be exhibited in the museum. Reveau Bassett, one of the most outspoken of the museum's critics and a successful landscape painter who had frequently exhibited in the museum, vilified equally the Communists and expressionist, cubist, and futurist artists. Like many other citizens, Bassett combined whatever he did not like with the Communist threat, finally denouncing the museum for exhibiting the work of "commie artists" while not giving "good American artists . . . a chance." Bywaters and the board successfully resisted the demand to stop exhibiting modern art, but one of the casualties of the turmoil was the Museum for Contemporary Arts, which was founded in 1957 but closed its doors and merged with the Dallas Museum of Fine Arts in 1962.

Two of the most outstanding artists to come from Texas left to pursue their careers on opposite coasts. Morris Graves was born in Oregon and went to sea before landing in Beaumont, Texas, where he finished high school. His classmates there remembered him as a quiet young man who made drawings for the high school annual in 1932. He returned to the West Coast because of the hardships of the depression and finally got a job with the Federal Art Project in Los Angeles. His "Message" series of paintings, exhibited at the Museum of Modern Art in 1939, established him as one of the most important artists working in America. A member of the so-called Pacific Northwest Painters, Graves traveled and studied in China and Japan, and the impact of Oriental philosophy as well as style is evident in his mysterious paintings. *Fish Reflected upon Outer and Mental Space* (Amon Carter Museum, ca. 1943) is characteristic of his work, which he described as notations about the outside world "with which to verify the inner eye." One of the artists who had the most impact on his peers during the 1960s was Robert Rauschenberg from Port Arthur. Even in the 1990s Rauschenberg said that he did his best work in a hot, damp climate like Port Arthur's and noted that it was his suspension from the University of Texas—because, having kept frogs as pets, he refused to dissect a live frog in anatomy class—that sent him from the state when he was drafted into World War II. After the war and study at the Kansas City Art Institute, Rauschenberg went to Paris, then returned to study at Black Mountain College in North Carolina. Shortly after he arrived in New York in 1949, he established his reputation with works of art that he called "combines," made out of found objects—junk—thereby inspiring much of the pop-art movement. By the 1960s, the glut of popular culture images—television, film, photographs, printed matter—and boredom with traditional techniques had inspired him to begin making silkscreens of various images that appeared to be collages. *Rodeo Palace* (1975–76) is a nostalgic tribute to his Texas roots, conceived for an exhibition in honor of the annual Fort Worth rodeo at the Southwestern Exposition and Fat Stock Show. But his acknowledged masterpiece is *Retrospective I* (1964), a complex gathering of images including President Kennedy at a press conference that reminds one of the flicker of the nearly inescapable television screen. The premier representation of pop art in Texas is probably *Cadillac Ranch* (1981), which the Ant Farm produced on commission from Amarillo businessman Stanley Marsh III.

In Austin, meanwhile, Dave Hickey had assembled a group of young Texas artists and established a gallery that he hoped would permit them the freedom of expression to create their visions and not paint or sculpt Texas subjects per se. For four years during the 1960s, A Clean Well-Lighted Place, which took its name from a San Francisco bookstore (thence from a short story by Ernest Hemingway), was an exciting place to be. Barry Buxkamper, Terry Allen, Jim Franklin, Fred and Glenn White-head, Luis Jiménez, George Green, Bob Wade, Mel Casas, Jack Boynton, and others became a part of this experiment, which in retrospect Hickey acknowledged was ahead of its time. They attracted national attention, and some of their images live on, such as the ubiquitous armadillo that Glen Whitehead and Jim Franklin conjured.

Isolation, that characteristic of Texas that made it so difficult for artists to communicate and to inspire each other during the earlier years, finally led an outstanding American sculptor, Donald C. Judd, to leave New York in 1976 and settle in the West Texas community of Marfa. With the support of the Zia Foundation of New York, he took over the grounds of Fort D. A. Russell, thus ensuring that he had plenty of solitude and room for his large minimalist sculptures. Judd's paintings were included in a number of exhibitions, and he wrote art reviews for several journals. In 1960–62 he began the transition from painter to sculptor, finding satisfaction in the clearly defined forms, smooth surfaces, and visual clarity that he was able to achieve in his large pieces, which he usually made from light-reflecting industrial metals such as brass, copper, stainless steel, anodized aluminum, and plexiglass. Judd remained in Marfa until his death in 1994.

Ron Tyler

W

WCTU. The Woman's Christian Temperance Union was formed to promote total abstinence from alcoholic beverages and put liquor dealers out of business, in order to reduce crime, poverty, and immorality. The Texas branch was organized by Frances Willard, 1881–83. A state organization was formed at Paris on 9 May 1882, but was inactive until Jenny Beauchamp took over as president in 1883. Membership was 1,500 by 1887. WCTU members were largely middle-class evangelical Protestants. Local unions were federated into district organizations, which in turn were subunits of the state union. Children of both sexes were organized into Loyal Temperance Legions and adolescent girls into the Young or "Y" WCTU. A state journal, *The Texas White Ribbon*, was named after the badge of membership and evolved out of a newsletter launched by Mrs. Beauchamp in 1885; the Loyal Temperance Legion issued *The Texas Blue Violet*. The WCTU did not own property and never had a permanent headquarters building. State presidents included Helen Stoddard. In addition to "temperance," the WCTU structured a public and political role for women. Focusing on the drinking man's neglect and abuse of his family and speaking as "organized motherhood," the WCTU promoted an agenda of social-welfare reforms and asked for woman suffrage (1888) in the name of "home protection." After the Texas union's endorsement of woman suffrage alienated the rank and file, membership dropped to fewer than 600 and did not rebound until the 1890s. As late as 1893 Texas was the only Southern union doing even minimal suffrage work. When the state's first suffrage association, the Texas Equal Rights Association, was formed that year, WCTU women filled almost all of the offices.

The WCTU operated departments devoted to medical temperance, Sunday schools, Christian citizenship, motion pictures, literature, social purity, prisons and jails, and other areas. It pressured the legislature into establishing a boys' reformatory at Rusk so that juveniles would cease to be incarcerated with adult prisoners; campaigned to raise the age of consent as part of the fight against prostitution; and secured a law requiring alcohol education in the public schools. Helen Stoddard helped draft the legislation that established Texas Woman's University. By 1910, however, new women's organizations such as the YWCA and the Texas Congress of Mothers were offering more opportunities for social-welfare voluntarism and drawing women who a generation earlier might have joined the WCTU. Thenceforth, the WCTU worked mainly for Prohibition. Organizational growth was incremental, and union strength was concentrated in North Texas, where prohibition sentiment was strongest; attempts to establish Hispanic unions in the southern counties met with little success. Throughout the 1920s the WCTU was part of the coalition of women's organizations that made up the Joint Legislative Council, but as sentiment mounted in favor of repealing Prohibition the women concentrated heavily on opposing alcohol. By the 1930s the WCTU, like prohibition, had lost its progressive image: temperance women devoted themselves to polling political candidates for their views on alcohol; campaigning for "drys"; and protesting cigarette advertising, gambling, bathing-beauty contests, and suggestive motion pictures. Membership in 1930 was reported as 3,349 active and 335 honorary members—virtually the same as a decade earlier. Although in later years the WCTU claimed a membership of 10,000, the number of active duespaying women was probably never more than half that number. By the 1960s the organization was moribund, and its main activity was placing books and literature in educational institutions. The last president, Ruth Horner Godbey, carried on the office until the mid1970s and died in 1978 at the age of 86. *Judith N. McArthur*

WPA. Originally (1935) the Works Progress Administration, later (1939) the Work Projects Administration; a New Deal federal agency established as a relief measure during the Great Depression and phased out in 1943. To combat unemployment in Texas, Governor Miriam Ferguson issued an executive order establishing the Texas Relief Commission in March 1933. The commission, using FERA funds, enabled Texans to participate in various early New Deal programs such as construction and white-collar projects of the Civil Works Administration and the camp programs of the CCC. The FERA was discontinued in December 1935. In July of that year, Texas had established an administration in San Antonio, directed by H. P. Drought, to coordinate WPA activities. The WPA functioned in Texas until after unemployment had begun to fall off sharply in 1942. The phase-out was completed in 1943, and Drought wrote his final report in March of that year. Under the WPA 600,000 persons in Texas were helped to provide subsistence for themselves and their families. Regulations required that anyone employed by the WPA had to be the economic head of his family and had to be certified as destitute on the rolls of the Texas Relief Commission. People of both sexes and all races were employed. WPA wages in Texas ranged from $45 to $75 a month. Peak employment under the Texas WPA program was 120,000 persons, in February 1936. The peak caseload of the relief commission came in February 1939, when 218,291 of the unemployed were on relief rolls. State WPA administrator Drought blamed the increase in caseload on crop failure. In September 1939 the state relief organization was renamed the State Department of Public Welfare. The caseload remained high from 1939 to 1942, always staying between 120,000 and 150,000, while the number of workers employed by the WPA was never more than half of the caseload figure.

WPA activities were dependent on the needs and skills of the persons on relief. As its art project the state conducted an excellent survey of folk art objects for the *Index of American Design*. The original plates for this index are on deposit at the National Gallery of Art in Washington. The WPA Archeological Survey studied the Indians of Texas. In the paleontologic–mineralogic survey, WPA workers, under the supervision of scientists, worked many sites in Texas for fossils, mineral resources, and combinations of both. As war requirements increased, work became involved with mineral investigation, especially for the location of road materials and mineral resources designated as strategic. The Federal Music Project in Texas organized groups

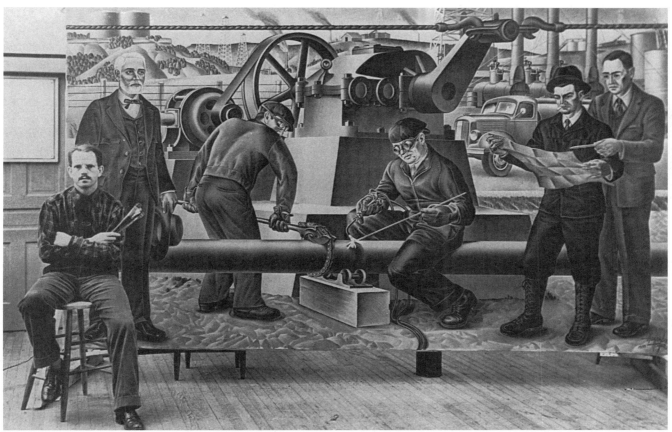

Alexandre Hogue and his mural depicting the oil industry, painted for the Graham post office, 1939. Jerry Bywaters Collection on Art of the Southwest, Jake and Nancy Hamon Arts Library, Southern Methodist University, Dallas (photography by Harry Bennett). Hogue, a member of the Dallas Nine, painted murals for the Federal Art Project from 1939 to 1941.

of musicians into ensembles including dance bands, a Mexican folk group, and two Latin-style orchestras. The program also included teaching in CCC camps, in underprivileged parts of three metropolitan areas, and in public schools having no musical curriculum. A broad adult-education program was instituted to provide instruction in such basic areas as literacy and citizenship, in vocational training and home economics, and in foreign languages and other academic subjects. Programs designed primarily to answer the needs of unemployed women were a child-protection program, for training in the care of preschool children; a clothing program, for the operation of shops that trained workers to make and repair garments and shoes for free distribution to the needy; a feeding program, which included storage and distribution of relief food, as well as the provision of school lunches, matron service, gardening, and food preservation; a housekeeping aid program, which trained women to fill positions as domestic workers and provided emergency aid in home services; and a health service program, which provided training and personnel for work in health agencies and institutions. The American Imprints Inventory employed library workers and supervisors, first as a part of the Texas Historical Records Survey program and later in cooperation with the library service program. This inventory included books, pamphlets, broadsides, broadsheets, maps, newspapers, and periodicals in public, semi-public, and private collections in the state for the period from the beginning of printing into the nineteenth century; it calen-

dared or transcribed three major manuscript collections. Copies of these materials were deposited at the University of Texas and other institutions. This program also included compilation of a list of all libraries in Texas. Other archival and literary programs were the research and records programs, which provided clerical labor to public agencies for the installation or improvement of records systems; the library training program, which covered every phase of library science; and the library service program, which gave support in labor, funds, or technical knowledge to all types of libraries in Texas. Perhaps the best known was the Texas Writers' Project, which conducted large-scale research into the state's cultural history and its geographical points of interest. This work resulted in many publications, including several state and local guides to Texas. All manuscript materials from the writers' project were deposited in the University of Texas at Austin archives.

The greatest single area of WPA public spending in Texas was construction. As in most of the other WPA projects in Texas, one-fourth of the construction costs had to be provided by sponsors. This was a regulation imposed by the Texas WPA administrators, there being no federal requirement for matching money. Construction projects included parks, swimming pools, highways, bridges, stadiums, and other public buildings. Recreational facilities were increased, but recreational leadership and organizational help were also boosted under the WPA. An attempt was made to provide leisure-time activities for persons of all ages, races, and economic groups during all seasons of the year. The WPA in Texas built and organized pre-school play centers, playgrounds, community recreation centers, toy loan centers, athletic leagues, boys' clubs, girls' clubs, and, after World War II started, centers for all branches of armed forces personnel. All recreational programs were begun with the idea of establishing permanent facilities. *Mallory B. Randle*

Waco, Texas. In central McLennan County halfway between Dallas and Austin; on the Brazos River. The city is built on the site of an ancient agricultural village of Waco Indians. About 1830 a group of Cherokee Indians moved into the area and drove the Wacos from the village. Fort Fisher, a Texas Ranger outpost and the first white settlement in the area, was established in 1837, but was abandoned after only a few months. In 1844 George Barnard began operating Torrey's Trading Post No. 2 on a small tributary of Tehuacana Creek, eight miles south of the old Waco village. A year later Neil McLennan moved onto land nearby on the South Bosque River. A log smithy was erected at the present site of East Waco in 1846 by Jesse Sutton, a blacksmith. In 1848 Gen. Thomas J. Chambers sold a two-league grant of land, including the old Waco village site, to John S. Sydnor of Galveston. Sydnor struck a deal with land agent Jacob De Cordova to divide the property and dispose of it at a dollar an acre. George B. Erath, who had first visited the area as one of the rangers stationed at the old 1837 outpost, was one of De Cordova's surveyors, and he urged that the new townsite be placed at the former Indian village. In 1848 the tract was sold to Nathaniel A. Ware and Jonas Butler of Galveston; they became De Cordova's partners in the venture. On 1 March 1849, Erath laid out the first block of the new town and lots were purchased. The property owners had earlier chosen Lamartine as the name of the new town, but Erath was successful in persuading them to call it Waco Village. When McLennan County was organized in 1850, Waco Village was selected as the county seat after De Cordova and his partners donated free lots in the town for public purposes. The first courthouse was built later that year. De Cordova induced a number of important citizens to move to the new townsite, including Capt. Shapley P. Ross, a ranger and Indian fighter, who established and operated a ferry across the Brazos. Ross also owned the town's first hotel and served as its first postmaster. By 1852 the town had Methodist and Baptist churches, and in 1854, when the town was growing rapidly, George Lambdin began publishing the Waco *Era*, the town's first newspaper. In 1856 Waco Village was incorporated as the town of Waco, and a new county courthouse was built that year. The town continued to grow as cotton culture spread along the Brazos, and by 1859 there were 749 people living there. Situated in the midst of a flourishing plantation economy, many of the town's most prominent citizens sympathized with the Southern secessionist cause during the Civil War. Seventeen companies of Confederate soldiers were raised from Waco and the surrounding countryside, and six Confederate generals were from the town. The Confederacy produced cotton cloth at Barron's Mill, part of the Waco Manufacturing Company. Postwar emancipation of the many slaves in the area led to conflicts and animosities in Waco during Reconstruction. Lt. A. F. Manning, the Freedmen's Bureau agent assigned to the town, complained in 1867 that a local grand jury refused to indict a white man accused of killing a freedman. Later that year Manning's black ward was

castrated by two local physicians and a white accomplice; when one of the doctors was arrested, the local populace became so agitated that soldiers were detached to guard the jail. Local citizens complained when the federal government confiscated the Waco Manufacturing Company, which the government claimed had been a Confederate enterprise during the war. The town's peace was also marred by a race riot during the late 1860s.

Waco's economy recovered rapidly in the years just after the Civil War. After 1868 the town was on a spur of the Chisholm Trail used by cattlemen to drive steers to market, and cattlemen and their employees often stopped in the town to buy supplies and for recreation. By 1871 between 600,000 and 700,000 cattle had been driven through the town. The economy especially began to boom after 1870, when the Waco Bridge Company opened a suspension bridge spanning the Brazos. Upon completion of the bridge, Waco was quickly reincorporated as a city. In 1871, when the Waco and Northwestern Railroad was built into the city, Waco became an important debarkation point for thousands of prospective settlers headed west and the primary shipping point for a broad area. The town had many saloons and gambling houses during the 1870s, attracting cowhands, drifters, and others who helped earn the town the nickname of "Six Shooter Junction." A red light district called the "Reservation" also grew during this period, and prostitution was legally recognized, licensed, and regulated by the city until the early twentieth century. When two other railroads, the St. Louis and Southwestern and the Missouri–Kansas–Texas lines, built into Waco in the early 1880s, the city became the hub of a transportation network linking the area's cotton farmers and nascent industries with factories and consumers across Texas and the nation. By 1884 there were about 12,000 people living in Waco, and an estimated 50,000 bales of cotton, 900,000 pounds of wool, and 500,000 pounds of hides were being shipped through the city annually. Industries in the city that year included a cotton factory producing yarns and socks, a woolens factory, two cottonseed oil mills, and two planing mills. By the 1890s Waco had become one of the most important cotton markets in the south, and many cotton agents had moved into offices around the town square. By 1898 Waco's Kirksey Woolen Mills was among the largest in the south, and the city had ice plants, grain elevators, flour mills, foundries, boiler plants, and bottling works. During the late nineteenth century artesian wells were drilled, two natatoriums were built, and the city was widely advertised as a health resort. Waco's population grew from 3,008 in 1870 to 7,295 by 1880; by 1900 there were 20,686 people living in the city, making it the sixth largest population center in Texas. Waco also attracted a number of educational institutions and in some circles was known as the "Athens of Texas" (not to disregard the town of Athens, Texas). Waco Classical School, established in 1860, became Waco University in 1861 and in 1887 merged with Baylor University, which moved to Waco at that time. In 1872 the African Methodist Episcopal Church opened Paul Quinn College. Sacred Heart Academy, a Catholic school, was founded by the Sisters of St. Mary of Namur in 1873. Other private or sectarian schools, including Waco Academy, Waco Select School, and Leland Seminary, were also operating in the city at that time. Waco Female College was first established in 1856; it closed its doors in 1893, but by 1895 Add–Ran College occupied the buildings. Add–Ran became Texas Christian University in 1902. The city's first gas plant began operation in

McLennan County Courthouse, 1901–1902. Texas Collection, Baylor University. This pink granite and white limestone courthouse was designed by architect J. Riely Gordon.

the 1880s, and by 1890 streetcars pulled by mules ran regular routes through the town. In 1891 some of the mule-drawn cars were replaced by electric cars operated by the Waco Railway and Electric Light company; by 1901 the Citizen Railway company was operating 20 electric trolleys on city streets. In the early 1890s the town began to build a system of city parks, often with land donated by private citizens.

A street-paving program began in 1905. In 1909 the city's elaborate Cotton Palace was built, and its Fall Exposition soon became one of the most popular fairs in the south; in 1913 an estimated 500,000 people visited it. An electric interurban railway that opened in 1913 connected the city with Dallas. By 1914 Waco had grown to about 35,000 residents and was becoming an important center of the state's insurance industry. The Amicable Insurance Building, a 22-story structure completed in 1911, was designed to be the tallest building in Texas at the time. During World War I Waco was selected as the site for Camp MacArthur, an infantry training base covering more than 10,000 acres of what is now the northwestern part of the city. The 35,000 troops assigned to the camp between 1917 and 1919 virtually doubled Waco's population for the duration of the war, and the city's economy boomed as its hotels were filled with soldiers' families. Encouraged by the United States Army's attempts to eliminate

temptations for the soldiers, the city's ministers and others waged an anti-prostitution campaign in 1917, and the "Reservation" was shut down. Between 1900 and 1930 the racial composition of the city changed as rural blacks moved to Waco in search of better jobs and educational opportunities. By the 1920s a black middle class had begun to appear in the city. Perhaps partially in response to this development, Waco became a center of Ku Klux Klan activity and influence during the 1920s. Lynchings had occurred in Waco in 1905, 1915, and 1916, and on at least one occasion the black victim was publicly burned in the town square; in the 1920s mobs of white citizens hanged or burned other blacks as well. In 1923 more than 2,000 Klansmen paraded through the city, and the organization boycotted businesses of people unsympathetic with its agenda. Many Waco business and political leaders at least implicitly supported the Klan during this period, and one member claimed that the Klan "controlled every office in the city of Waco" during the 1920s.

By 1930 Waco had grown to a population of 53,848, but the onset of the Great Depression undercut the city's momentum. As prices for cotton and other agricultural products fell and farmers reduced their spending, businesses in Waco were forced to lay off employees. Ultimately, many businesses closed their doors and unemployment rose. The Cotton Palace fair, long a symbol and source of the city's prosperity, was shut down. A National Youth Administration training program was set up at Baylor University. The WPA also established an office in the city and paid for the construction of University High School and other local projects. During the depression Waco also became a distribution center for the government's surplus commodities program. The 1930s saw the demise of the city's electric trolleys, which were replaced by buses in an attempt to keep up with a "progressive" trend being established in other cities around the country. Waco's population grew slightly during the 1930s, and by 1940 there were 55,982 people living there. World War II revived demand for cotton and cotton products, and the economy was invigorated by the construction of war plants and military bases in or around the city. Mattress and canvas industries grew in the city, and by 1942 Waco was the armed forces' leading manufacturer of cots, tents, mattresses, and barracks bags. The war also brought the Waco Army Flying School, established eight miles north of the city, and the Blackland Army Air Field, set up at nearby China Spring. Meanwhile, the Bluebonnet Ordnance Plant was built in MacGregor. A housing shortage developed as workers and military families moved into Waco by the thousands. In November 1943 the War Manpower Commission estimated that only four apartments were vacant in Waco and that high housing prices were causing hardships for the area's poorer residents. Near the end of the war the city was chosen to be the site of a new General Tire and Rubber plant, the first major tire factory in the Southwest.

Though the area's military installations were closed after the war, in 1948 Waco Army Air Field was reactivated as Connally Air Force Base and Waco continued to grow during the 1940s and early 1950s. By 1952 about 84,300 people were living there, and the city was the sixth largest industrial center in Texas, with more than 250 factories producing cotton goods, tires, glass, furniture, sporting goods, caskets, dry-cleaning equipment, and other products. On 11 May 1953, however, downtown Waco was ravaged by a tornado that killed 114 people and seriously injured another 145; 196 business buildings were completely destroyed, and 396 were damaged so badly that they had to be torn down. After the tornado many shoppers began to frequent suburban shopping centers, contributing to the decline of the city's downtown business district. "White flight" also contributed to urban decay, especially after the city's schools were integrated in the late 1960s. Connally Air Force Base was closed in 1966, dealing a blow to the city. By 1970 the population had declined to 95,326. The Waco Urban Renewal Project was begun in 1958 to deal with the problem of inner-city blight, and in 1967 the city was chosen for the federal government's "Model Cities" program. By 1978 the Urban Renewal Project had helped to channel more than $125 million into renovating the city's urban core. Slums were cleared and a number of new buildings were constructed, including new apartment complexes, a shopping center near Baylor University, and a convention center. The Texas Ranger Hall of Fame and Museum was dedicated in 1976. Though Waco's economy suffered a downturn in the late 1980s and early 1990s, the city worked to bring tourist dollars into the area by building a zoo at Cameron Park and attracting the Texas Sports Hall of Fame. The city's population reached 101,216 in 1980 and 103,216 in 1990. The Waco area received worldwide attention in 1993 during a confrontation between federal officers and the Davidians led by David Koresh. *Roger N. Conger*

Walker, John George. Army officer, railroad agent, and diplomat; b. Cole County, Missouri, 22 July 1822; d. Washington, D.C., 20 July 1893 (buried in Winchester, Virginia); reportedly m. Mellissa Smith (1856); m. Sophie M. Baylor (1858); at least 5 children; ed. Jesuit College (now St. Louis University). Walker was commissioned a lieutenant and served in Col. Persifor F. Smith's Mounted Rifle regiment in the Mexican War. He was severely wounded at Molino del Rey and was brevetted captain in 1847, for "gallant and meritorious conduct" at San Juan de los Llanos. After the war he saw duty in Arizona, California, Oregon, and New Mexico and became a captain in 1851. He served on the Texas frontier against the Indians from 1854 to 1856. Several of his reports describing his exploring expeditions through Navajo territory in 1859 have been published in *The Navajo Reconnaissance* (1963). Walker resigned from the United States Army on 31 July 1861 and accepted a commission as major of cavalry in the Confederate Army. The next year he was promoted to brigadier general. His Civil War service included commanding a column under Stonewall Jackson in the Confederate capture of Harpers Ferry (12–15 September 1862) and leading a division at the battle of Antietam or Sharpsburg (17 September 1862). On 8 November 1862 he was promoted to major general and transferred to the Trans-Mississippi theater. On 1 January 1863 at Little Rock he took command of a new division that had been raised and trained by Brig. Gen. Henry E. McCulloch; the unit subsequently became known as Walker's Texas Division or Walker's Greyhounds. Walker led the division with distinction during the Red River campaign (March–May 1864), but after being again seriously wounded at the battle of Pleasant Hill (9 April) he relinquished command of the unit. On 10 June he relieved Lt. Gen. Richard Taylor as commander of the District of West Louisiana. In August he was assigned to replace John B. Magruder as commander of the District of Texas, New Mexico, and Arizona. He was replaced by Magruder on 31 March 1865, on orders of Edmund Kirby Smith, commander of the Trans-Mississippi Department, who feared a massive federal invasion of the Texas coast and reportedly wanted a "fighting commander to meet it." At that time Walker was offered his choice of commanding the District of Arkansas or a division of infantry. In April he assumed command of John Austin Wharton's cavalry corps, which was camped near Hempstead, and on 12 May he was assigned command of John Horace Forney's division.

After the war he went with other senior Confederates to Mexico; lived in England, where he represented the Virginia-based Venezuela Company; and was a partner of Francis B. Hoffman of New York in the firm of Walker and Hoffman, which aimed to supply railroad iron and machinery to the Southern states while marketing Southern staples in England. On a business trip from Liverpool to Galveston in January 1867, Walker announced his intention to settle in Texas within the next few years. In 1869 he was one of two Texas agents for the Mound City Mutual Life Insurance Company of St. Louis. In November, as an agent of the Houston and Texas Central Railway, he contracted in California for 300 Chinese workers. These laborers, who became the first large group of Chinese in the South, reached Calvert, Texas, in January 1870 and began to help extend the railroad westward. In November 1871 Walker, who was reported as having resided in Jefferson, Texas, for the past year, visited Dallas on a fund-raising trip for the Texas Professorship of Applied Mathematics at Washington and Lee

University. His family appears to have resided in New Orleans from at least this time until probably the fall of 1876, when they moved to the vicinity of Winchester, Virginia, the early home of his mother-in-law.

In August 1872 Walker was engaged in establishing the Dallas *News*. The next month, he joined John Cardwell as an editor and proprietor of the Austin *Democratic Statesman*. In 1873 he accepted a position as "general emigration agent" for the Texas and Pacific Railway, a job that required him to spend much of his in New York and Philadelphia, where he boosted immigration to Texas. He also lobbied for the railroad in the Texas legislature, in Congress, and elsewhere. Walker worked for the Texas and Pacific at least through December 1876, while apparently maintaining a residence, or at least a base, in Dallas. In 1875 he was elected board member and vice president for the Dallas Herald Printing Company. In 1875 Governor Richard Coke appointed Walker a Texas delegate to the national railroad convention in St. Louis. In 1876 the Dallas *Weekly Herald* reported that Walker had bought a summer place near Winchester, Virginia, so as to be nearer the Texas and Pacific home office, but that the action would "in no way affect his domicile and citizenship in Texas." He seems to have made the Winchester home his chief residence in 1878. During Grover Cleveland's first term as president, Walker served as United States consul in Bogotá, Colombia, and as a special envoy to invite Latin-American republics to the Pan American Conference that convened in 1889. His first year of Confederate service has frequently been confused with that of another officer of the same name, who was his cousin. (This John George Walker was with Terry's Texas Rangers.) Walker's wife was the niece of John R. Baylor and the grandniece of R. E. B. Baylor. *Thomas W. Cutrer*

Walker, Samuel Hamilton. Texas Ranger and soldier; b. Prince George County, Maryland, 24 February 1817; d. Mexico, 9 October 1847. In May 1836 Walker enlisted in the Washington City Volunteers for the Creek Indian campaign in Alabama. He was stationed in Florida and apparently saw no combat. After his enlistment ended in 1837, he remained in Florida as a scout until 1841. He may also have been a railroad superintendent. He traveled to Galveston in January 1842, where he served in Capt. Jesse Billingsley's company during the Adrián Woll invasion. He then enlisted in the Somervell expedition and took part in the actions around Laredo and Guerrero. He also joined William S. Fisher's Mier expedition. Walker escaped at Salado, was recaptured, and survived the Black Bean Episode. In 1844 he joined Jack Hays's company of Texas Rangers and participated in the battle of Walker's Creek near the Pedernales River. During the engagement some 15 rangers using new Colt revolvers successfully defeated about 80 Comanches. When Gen. Zachary Taylor requested volunteers to act as scouts and spies for his regular army, Walker enlisted as a private and was mustered into federal service in September 1845. In April 1846 he formed his own company for duty under Taylor. On 28 April Walker was ambushed with his company en route to join Taylor at Port Isabel. He reached Taylor's camp the next day, and his reports caused Taylor to move his encampment. Walker performed exemplary duty as a scout and courier on numerous other occasions. His company was the only Texas unit at the battles of Palo Alto and Resaca de la Palma. He was presented a horse by the grateful citizens of New Orleans in the spring of 1846 for his numerous

exploits with Taylor's army. Walker served as captain of the inactive Company C of the United States Mounted Rifles until the outbreak of the Mexican War. When the First Regiment, Texas Mounted Riflemen, was organized in June 1846, Walker was elected lieutenant colonel. He fought in the battle of Monterrey in September, and mustered out of federal service on 2 October 1846, activated his commission as captain of the mounted rifles, and proceeded to Washington, D.C., to begin recruiting for his company. During his recruitment excursion Walker visited Samuel Colt. Colt credited Walker with proposed improvements, including a stationary trigger and guard, to the existing revolver. The new six-shooter was named the Walker Colt.

After arriving with his new company at Veracruz, Walker was detailed on 27 May 1847 to the First Pennsylvania Volunteers, stationed at Castle San Carlos de Perote to counter Mexican guerrilla activities between Perote and Jalapa. On 5 October he left Perote with Gen. Joseph P. Lane to escort a supply train to Mexico City. According to J. J. Oswandel, author of *Notes on the Mexican War*, Walker grew increasingly embittered against the enemy: "Should Captain Walker come across guerrillas, God help them, for he seldom brings in prisoners. The captain and most all of his men are very prejudiced and embittered against every guerrilla in the country." En route Lane was informed of a sizable enemy force at Huamantla and ordered an attack. With Walker's mounted rifles in the lead, the assault force reached Huamantla on 9 October. During the spirited contest that followed Walker was either shot in the back or killed by a man on foot carrying a lance. Following his death his unit took revenge on the community of Huamantla. Walker was buried at Hacienda Tamaris. In 1848 his remains were moved to San Antonio. On 21 April 1856, as part of a battle of San Jacinto celebration, he was reburied in the Odd Fellows' Cemetery in San Antonio. *Charles D. Spurlin*

Walker, T-Bone. Blues musician; b. Aaron Thibeaux Walker, Linden, Texas, 28 May 1910; d. Los Angeles, 16 March 1975 (buried in Inglewood Cemetery); m. Vida Lee; 3 children. His mother took him to Dallas, where his musical relatives and family friendship with Blind Lemon Jefferson and Huddie Ledbetter familiarized him with the blues from childhood. He taught himself guitar and married in his teens. Around 1925 he joined Dr. Breeding's Big B Tonic medicine show, then toured the South with blues artist Ida Cox. In 1929 in Dallas he cut his first record, *Wichita Falls Blues*, as Oak Cliff T-Bone. Around 1930, after winning first prize in an amateur show promoted by Cab Calloway, Walker toured the South with Calloway's band and worked with the Raisin' Cain show and several other bands in Texas, including those of Count Biloski and Milt Larkins. He also appeared with Ma Rainey, a great figure in blues history, in her 1934 Fort Worth performances. In 1935 Walker moved to Los Angeles, where he quickly made a name for himself singing and playing banjo and then guitar for black audiences in two popular nightclubs, Little Harlem and Club Alabam. Fans were attracted to his acrobatic performances, which combined playing and tap dancing. In 1935 he became the first blues guitarist to play the electric guitar. The Trocadero Club in Hollywood, where Walker had become sufficiently well known to appear as a star, welcomed integrated audiences after his 1936 performances. From 1940 to 1945 he toured with Les Hite's Cotton Club orchestra as a featured vocalist; he recorded *T-Bone Blues* with Hite in New York

T-Bone Walker. Courtesy Houston Metropolitan Research Center, Houston Public Library.

City in 1940. He was subsequently billed as "Daddy of the Blues." He also toured United States Army bases in the early 1940s and, recruited by boxing champion Joe Louis in 1942, went to Chicago, where he headlined a revue at the city's Rhumboogie Club so successfully that he returned year after year. In the mid-1940s he became a band leader, signed a recording contract with the Black and White label, and turned out some of the best titles of his long recording career, including "Stormy Monday." Many of his songs reached the Top Ten on the Hit Parade. In the 1950s he recorded under the Imperial label and worked for Atlantic Records. In 1955 he underwent an operation for chronic ulcers.

In the early 1960s Walker joined Count Basie's orchestra, appeared in Europe with a package called Rhythm and Blues, U.S.A., and played at the American Folk Blues Festival and Jazz at the Philharmonic. This began a new phase of his career, during which he appeared before largely white audiences. He was a regular attraction abroad, where his recordings made him a great favorite, and he was a participant on television shows and at jazz festivals in Monterey, California; Nice, France; and Montreaux, Switzerland. In Europe he recorded a Polydor album entitled *Good Feelin'*, which won the 1970 Grammy for ethnic–traditional recording. Among his other albums are *Singing the Blues, Funky Town,* and *The Truth.* Walker used a fluid technique that combined the country blues tradition with more polished contemporary swing, his style influenced by Francis (Scrapper) Blackwell, Leroy Carr, and Lonnie Johnson. Among those he

influenced were B. B. King, Pee Wee Crayton, Eric Clapton, Albert Collins, and Johnny Winter. Many titles from Walker's more than four decades of recording have been reissued. His funeral was attended by more than a thousand mourners.

Helen Oakley Dance

Walker County Rebellion. An incident during Radical Republican rule in Reconstruction Texas. In 1870 anarchy prevailed across much of the state despite years of military occupation. The Radical Republican–dominated Twelfth Legislature approved sweeping anticrime measures proposed by Governor Edmund Davis. Crucial components, such as the State Police and state militia, brought criticism to Davis and his supporters. These instruments of order also brought the administration into conflict with localities even as Davis tried to protect key political constituencies and solicit the support of those who viewed him with suspicion. The murder of Walker County freedman Sam Jenkins in December 1870 precipitated a major challenge to Davis. Jenkins, who had testified against several whites in an assault case, turned up dead on a road outside of Huntsville. An investigation by State Police captain Leander McNelly led to the arrest of four whites: Nathaniel Outlaw, Joseph Wright, Fred Parks, and John McParrish. With tensions high, state district judge J. R. Burnett acquitted Parks and found the others guilty on 11 January 1871. Before the men could be escorted to jail, however, gunfire broke out in the courtroom, and both Wright and McParrish escaped with the aid of Huntsville citizens. Outlaw was captured. Despite cautions from Burnett that draconian measures might only inflame tensions, Davis considered imposing martial law. By 6 February Burnett himself begged for troops as tensions rose in the area. The state Senate, reacting to Davis's handling of the previous Hill County Rebellion, hesitated. On 15 February Davis ordered Adjutant General James Davidson to Huntsville with orders to declare martial law—an order he carried out on 20 February. Davidson established a court martial two days later, tried 10 citizens, and got 7 convictions, for crimes ranging from aiding the escapees to ignoring the call for a posse. Nathaniel Outlaw received five years' imprisonment. Sheriff Cyrus Hess, accused of negligence in allowing the jailbreak, received a fine of $250. But all the defendants except Hess received pardons by the end of March 1871, after which Outlaw sued the governor and adjutant general, winning a $20,000 judgment that was overturned in 1872. Taxes assessed Walker County to defray martial law costs amounted to $7,621.09, or seventy-five cents per person. The actions of the Davis administration in Walker County drew fire from various quarters. Davis's desire to bring order to Texas served to fuel accusations of tyranny against him and the Republicans. *Ricky Floyd Dobbs*

Walker's Creek, Battle of. An important battle between Texas Rangers and Indians in 1844. Capt. John Coffee Hays left San Antonio around 1 June with 14 rangers to scout the hills to the north and west for a Comanche war party led by Yellow Wolf, which had recently been raiding into Bexar County. The party rode as far as the Pedernales River without encountering hostiles and turned back, following the Pinta Trail to its crossing of the Guadalupe River in the area of present Kendall County. The rangers camped there on 9 June and became involved in a fight with a band of Comanches, whose numbers were variously estimated at 40 to more than 200. The Indians held a brushy hill.

The fight for the hilltop, wrote Ben McCulloch, was hand-to-hand. The rangers repulsed two counterattacks on their flanks, after which the Indians fled the field and were pursued for three miles under heavy fire from the rangers' revolvers. At the end of the hour-long battle, Indian casualties were estimated at from 20 to more than 50 killed and wounded, with Yellow Wolf among the slain. Ranger losses amounted to one killed and four seriously wounded. Among the latter were Samuel Walker and Robert A. Gillespie, both thrust through the body with lances. Walker was not expected to live, but he and Gillespie both survived to become highly effective ranger captains in the Mexican War. The Houston *Morning Star* characterized the Walker's Creek fight, known also by various other names, as "unparalleled in this country for the gallantry displayed on both sides." This fight is considered to be the first in which revolvers were used in combat; a Comanche who had taken part in the battle later complained that the rangers "had a shot for every finger on the hand." According to Josiah Wilbarger, it is the Walker's Creek fight that is depicted on the cylinder of the 1847 Walker Dragoon model Colt revolver.   *Thomas W. Cutrer*

Wallace, Bigfoot. Soldier and Texas Ranger; b. William Alexander Anderson Wallace, Lexington, Virginia, 3 April 1817;

Bigfoot Wallace in San Antonio. Courtesy Western History Collections, University of Oklahoma Library. Wallace liked to ride occasionally into San Antonio, where he undoubtedly regaled folks with tales of his career and early days in Texas.

d. 7 January 1899 (buried in the State Cemetery). He was descended from Highlanders William Wallace and Robert Bruce. In 1836, when he learned that a brother and a cousin had been shot down in the Goliad Massacre, he set out for Texas to "take pay out of the Mexicans." A good many years later he told John C. Duval that he believed the account had been squared. Wallace stood six feet two inches "in his moccasins" and weighed 240 pounds, mostly muscle. He farmed near La Grange, then moved to Austin (1840). He saw the last buffalo of the region run down Congress Avenue, decided that people were getting too thick, and moved to San Antonio. He was with the Texans who fought Gen. Adrián Woll's invading Mexican army near San Antonio in 1842 and then volunteered for the Somervell and Mier expeditions. Some of his most graphic memories were of his experiences in Perote Prison. As soon as he was released, he joined the Texas Rangers under Jack Hays. He was with the rangers in the Mexican War. In the 1850s Wallace commanded, as captain, a ranger company of his own, fighting border bandits as well as Indians. He was so expert at trailing that he was frequently called upon to track down runaway slaves trying to get to Mexico. He drove a mail hack from San Antonio to El Paso and on one occasion, after losing his mules to Indians, walked to El Paso and ate 27 eggs at the first Mexican house he came to—before going on to town for a full meal. During the Civil War he helped guard the frontier against the Comanche Indians. At one time Wallace had a little ranch on the Medina River on land granted him by the state of Texas. He spent his later years in Frio County near a small village named Bigfoot, where he liked to recount the stories of a career that had made him a folk hero.
                     J. Frank Dobie

Wallace, Ernest. Historian; b. Daingerfield, 11 June 1906; d. Lubbock, 17 November 1985 (buried in Resthaven Memorial Park); m. Ellen Kegans (1926); 1 daughter; ed. East Texas State Teachers' College (B.S., 1924), Texas Technological College (master's degree, 1935), University of Texas (Ph.D., 1942). Wallace taught at Texas Tech (1936–), where he became a professor in 1946. His dissertation was published as *Charles De Morse: Pioneer Editor and Statesman* (1943). He was awarded the University of Texas Board of Regents Fellowship in 1938 and a Ford Foundation Fellowship in 1952. For several years he was a consultant to the Department of Justice in the land suits of the Kiowa, Comanche, and Kiowa–Apache Indians against the federal government. He was a leader in the Panhandle–Plains Historical Society, the West Texas Historical Association, and the Texas State Historical Association. Over the years he published numerous works on the history of Texas. With E. Adamson Hoebel he coauthored his best-known work, *The Comanches: Lords of the South Plains* (1952). He also coedited *Documents of Texas History* with David Vigness (1963) and was coauthor with Rupert N. Richardson and Adrian N. Anderson of the third and fourth editions of *Texas: The Lone Star State* (1970, 1981). His other books include *Texas in Turmoil* (1965), *Ranald S. Mackenzie on the Texas Frontier* (1964), and *The Howling of the Coyotes* (1979). Wallace was consultant for *The Great Chiefs* and *The Texans* in Time–Life Books' "Old West" series (1975–79). He was Horn Professor of History at Texas Tech from 1967 until his retirement in 1976. He received many honors, including the Action Award from the West Texas Museum Association for "outstanding contributions to the enrichment and culture of the great South Plains." Phi Alpha Theta established the Ernest Wallace Scholarship in History at Texas Tech. Wallace's papers are housed in the Southwest Collection at Texas Tech University.

H. Allen Anderson

Walter Prescott Webb Historical Society. The Texas State Historical Association's educational program for college students. It was proposed by Joe Frantz when he became director of the TSHA in 1966. The first two chapters, however, were not formed until 1973. The society is open to any undergraduate interested in Texas history. In 1974 the C. M. Caldwell Memorial Endowment Fund was set up to reward outstanding student writing and chapter achievements. The Caldwell Awards are distributed during the society's annual meeting, which is held in the spring in conjunction with the TSHA's annual meeting. Since 1982 society members have had the opportunity to publish their research in *Touchstone*, the society's annual publication. Thirty chapters of the Webb Society had been chartered by 1995.

David De Boe

War Party. The faction within the Anglo-American population of Texas that helped to sway public opinion in favor of armed conflict with the rest of Mexico in the crucial time between 1832 and 1835. The term *War Party* and its counterpart, *Peace Party*, did not denote formally constituted organizations, but were descriptive labels for the opposition. The War Party perpetrated the Anahuac Disturbances, although the term was not used until 1835, when Santa Anna's centralization of power increasingly defined the lines between the two factions. The earliest document that has been found to contain the name *War Party* is a letter of 25 July 1835 from James H. C. Miller to J. W. Smith, which suggests the arrest of the prominent leaders, reporting, "All here is in a train for peace, the war and speculating parties are entirely put down." Individuals who implicated themselves as leaders of the War Party by word or deed in agitation for action against the Mexican government in the period from 1832 to 1835 include Branch T. Archer, Moseley Baker, James Bowie, and William B. Travis

Jodella K. Dyreson

Warren Wagontrain Raid. An Indian depredation of 18 May 1871 that helped decide the fate of the Plains Indians. William T. Sherman reconnoitered the Texas frontier on his way to Fort Richardson and concluded that Texans' reports of growing Indian menace were unjustified (17 May). Meanwhile, more than 100 Indians from the Fort Sill Reservation crossed the Red River into Texas under the leadership of Satank, Satanta, Addoetta (Big Tree), and Maman-ti (Skywalker). They watched Sherman pass unmolested not a half mile from their hidden position, while Maman-ti's magic predicted an attack on the second group of whites to pass would be successful. That second group was a wagontrain belonging to a freighting contractor named Henry Warren, traveling on the Butterfield Overland Mail route. The attackers killed the wagonmaster and six teamsters and allowed five to escape. The Indians, who suffered one dead and five wounded, immediately returned to the reservation. Sherman ordered Col. Ranald Mackenzie, post commander at Fort Richardson, to pursue the Indians with three companies of his Fourth United States Cavalry. Sherman then traveled on to Fort Sill where on 27 May he personally arrested Satank, Satanta, and Big Tree. He ordered that the three prisoners be

returned to Fort Richardson and tried for murder in the civil courts in nearby Jacksboro. On the way, Satank tried to escape and was killed. On 5 and 6 July Satanta and Big Tree were tried separately, found guilty, and sentenced to hang. This was the first time Indians had been tried in civil courts. Supporters of the Quaker peace policy persuaded Governor Edmund J. Davis to commute the Indians' sentences to life imprisonment. In October 1873 they were paroled. After the Warren Wagontrain Raid, Sherman abandoned his defensive Indian policy and the Quaker peace policy as well. He began offensive operations against all Indians found off the reservation, a policy that culminated in the Red River Indian War of 1874–75 and the cessation of Indian raids in North Texas. *Allen Lee Hamilton*

Washington-on-the-Brazos, Texas. Washington-on-the-Brazos, in the upper northeastern corner of what is now Washington County, was a major political and commercial center in early Texas. The town was originally named Washington and began to be called Washington-on-the-Brazos or Old Washington only after the Civil War. Washington was a mile southwest of the junction of the Brazos and Navasota rivers, where the La Bahía Road crossed the Brazos River, 70 miles northwest of Houston and nearly 200 miles up the Brazos from the coast. In 1821 Andrew Robinson's family and other members of the Old Three Hundred settled near the future townsite. By 1822 Robinson was operating a ferry at the La Bahía crossing; in 1824 he obtained a grant of a half league from the Mexican government. A settlement named La Bahía developed at the much-traveled ferry crossing. In 1831 Robinson gave one-quarter league to his daughter Patsy and son-in-law John W. Hall. Recognizing the site's commercial potential, Hall surveyed and laid out a town in December 1833, when Methodist leader John W. Kinney built its first residence. After Captain Hall bought the remainder of Robinson's grant, he established the Washington Town Company in 1835 with Dr. Asa Hoxey, Thomas Gay, and the Miller and Somervell Company to promote sales of town lots. Hoxey, a former resident of Washington, Wilkes County, Georgia, named the new town after his hometown. Attracted by its location on the river and on or near major roads, merchants and tradesmen from neighboring communities settled in the new town. Washington's commercial growth resulted from provisioning emigrants to the interior and from the surrounding area's increasing agricultural development and population. The town was elevated on bluffs above the river and had a plentiful water supply from nearby springs; its location was therefore more healthful and less flood-prone than that of settlements at the river's edge. In December 1835 Washington became Gen. Sam Houston's headquarters and the concentration point for Texas army volunteers and supplies. By 1836 the residents numbered approximately 100.

To stimulate further growth, Washington businessmen offered an assembly hall without charge to attract the Convention of 1836 to their town. These town promoters rented the only structure large enough for deliberations, an unfinished building, from entrepreneur Noah T. Byars. Although the town had an inn, most delegates could not find lodging. At Washington between 1 and 17 March 1836 delegates signed the Texas Declaration of Independence, wrote the Constitution of the Republic of Texas, and established the ad interim government. To escape Santa Anna's army, the Texas government and the inhabitants of Washington evacuated the town. After the Texas victory at San Jacinto, the rapid influx of new settlers into the interior and the expanding agricultural cultivation in Washington's hinterland augmented the town's significance as a supply and transit point. The selection of Washington as county seat made the town a legal center. Abundant timber in the vicinity encouraged the development of sawmills, which began operating by 1837. A brickyard begun the same year also facilitated town construction. The Republic of Texas established a post office at Washington in 1836. The town was incorporated by the Texas Congress on 5 June 1837 and reincorporated under a mayor–alderman form of city government on 29 December 1837. Hall's construction of a race track, the proliferation of gambling and drinking establishments, and a spate of furloughed Texas army veterans resulted in a disorderly environment not conducive to growth. In 1837 Rev. Z. N. Morrell established the first Missionary Baptist church in Texas at Washington. Baptist, Methodist, and Cumberland Presbyterian clergymen cooperated in 1838 against mounting lawlessness. A revival led by R. E. B. Baylor and Rev. William Tryon in 1840 ended the general disorderly conduct and resulted in the formation of Washington's second Baptist church in 1841. Methodist missionary Robert Alexander's organization of a Methodist church in the town in 1837 and Martin Ruter's planning the Washington Circuit to promote the spread of Methodism helped make Washington a center of religious activities by 1838.

Commerce and population declined as a result of a depression in 1839, and Mount Vernon became county seat in 1841. In 1842, however, Washington became the capital of Texas. During Houston's second administration and the administration of his successor, Anson Jones, the Texas Congress, high courts, and foreign embassies moved in, and the town's economy and social life were correspondingly stimulated. The town was the site of peacemaking between President Houston and the Indians in the summer of 1844. Jones's inauguration and inaugural ball, as well as the session of the Texas Congress that approved annexation to the United States, occurred at Washington in 1845. When Austin became capital again in the late summer of 1845 the *Texas National Register* also moved to Austin, and Washington lost its political significance. The arrival of the steamer *Mustang* in 1842 persuaded Washington residents to develop the town, which was located near the upper limit of Brazos River navigation, as a riverport. Washington became a distribution center for commercial exchanges between the interior and the Gulf Coast. The Brazos floods of 1843–44 lowered cotton production and made navigation difficult, and Washington suffered from epidemics in 1844–45. In April 1848 town residents organized the Brazos Steamship Association to eliminate navigational obstacles. This organization bought two steamboats, the *Washington* and the *Brazos*, to initiate regular service between Washington and Velasco. From 1849 through about 1858, commerce and population in Washington increased rapidly as the town became a frequent steamboat stop and significant transit point for export of the region's profitable cotton crop. Although residents had access to merchants in Houston and Galveston, service industries catering to travelers, wholesale and retail merchandising, leather, wood, and metal fabricating, construction, and the professions flourished at this important stagecoach stop and riverport. Residents organized the Brazos River Improvements Association, which held meetings in 1854 and 1856 to obtain government assistance. In 1856 the population reached 750. At the height of its development Washington had two newspapers, four churches, two hotels, a Masonic lodge, two Odd Fellows chapters, a market house, and a commercial section with brick buildings of two and three stories. Washington was also a center of Know-Nothing political activity. The Washington *American*, an organ of the American (Know-Nothing) party, was published there in 1855 and 1856, and the town was the site of local meetings and a state Know-Nothing convention in 1855.

In 1858 Washington refused to pay the Houston and Texas Central Railroad an $11,000 bonus to link the town to the projected rail line. The new road built to Hempstead in 1858. Construction of the Houston and Texas Central to Navasota in 1859 and of the Washington County Railroad to Brenham in 1860 accelerated the rise of these towns and the decline of Washington, which had insisted on depending on river transportation. With the increasing use of railroads, however, steamboats ceased to operate on the Brazos, and the once-prosperous riverport was doomed. Most residents moved in the 1860s to Brenham or Navasota. Washington became a small supply point for the immediate vicinity. By 1884 residents numbered an estimated 175. By 1889 most of the townsite had become cultivated fields; the Presbyterian church was the only remaining church building from the era of the town's prosperity still standing in 1891. The last remaining historic structures burned in 1912. In 1899 Brenham schoolchildren under the leadership of superintendent E. W. Tarrant erected a monument to mark the site of Independence Hall, where the Texas Declaration of Independence was signed. In 1915 the state legislature appropriated funds for a park encompassing part of the townsite. Washington-on-the-Brazos has been the site of annual celebrations of Texas independence on 2 March. The Texas Centennial celebration in 1936 and the Texas Sesquicentennial celebration in 1986 have been the outstanding twentieth-century events at Washington-on-the-Brazos. The Star of the Republic Museum, built in 1970, preserves many artifacts, as well as extensive historic documentation, of the nineteenth-century town. Blessed Virgin Mary Mission, founded for slaves in 1849, is still attended by their descendants. The Texas Archeological Research Laboratory, in cooperation with the Texas Parks and Wildlife Department and University of Texas at Austin Texana Programs, conducted excavations at Washington-on-the-Brazos between 1964 and 1969.

Carole E. Christian

Water. *Artesian Wells.* Artesian wells tap the confined groundwater trapped below impermeable strata beneath the surface of the earth. Natural pressure forces the water to rise, sometimes above the surface of the earth. Although extensive drilling for artesian wells did not begin until the 1880s, in 1857 and 1858 John Pope experimented with artesian wells on the plains of West Texas, and in 1858 a bill introduced by Forbes Britton became a law authorizing the drilling of public artesian wells on the road between San Antonio and Laredo. These early experiments were typical of the many mistakes made, through lack of knowledge, in an effort to secure water in the arid part of the state. The artesian-well area is largely confined to the Coastal Plain east of the Balcones Escarpment, although there have been other isolated artesian areas, most notable of which were located at El Paso, Fort Stockton, and Balmorhea. By 1897 there were 458 flowing and 506 nonflowing wells in the Black and Grand Prairie regions, somewhat fewer on the Coastal Plain, and none on the High Plains.

Around the turn of the century there were six artesian districts in Texas: Coastal Prairie system, Hallettsville system, Carrizo system, Black and Grand prairies system, Trans-Pecos Basin system, and Stevens County and Jack County systems. At that time the city of Galveston received its water from approximately 33 artesian wells, and Houston had about 100. In 1905 the area comprising most of South Texas from 20 miles south of Corpus Christi to the Rio Grande valley was referred to as the Artesian Belt. Farmers were just beginning to realize the agricultural potential of South Texas and relied on irrigation from artesian wells to provide water to crops. In a 1905 edition of *Farm and Ranch* magazine an article stated that 200 wells were in operation, ranging in depths from 600 to 800 feet and averaging flows from 200 to 600 gallons per minute. Wells were also touted in promotional brochures, such as the ad for the town of Sarita, which estimated that an artesian well would irrigate 100 to 200 acres. Costs for digging those wells ranged from $1,000 to $1,500. Water from artesian wells was included in the general irrigation act of 1913, and in May 1931 the legislature passed a law to prevent the waste of artesian water, which had become an important source of water supply for numerous cities and irrigation projects. Throughout the later part of the twentieth century more cities looked to other options for municipal water such as the use of surface reservoirs. Though wells remained the property of the individual owner, increased government regulation became the focus of debate. According to Texas law a person can drill an artesian well for domestic or stock purposes, but the well should be properly cased. Records of depth, thickness, and the types of strata penetrated should be kept. Reports of new artesian wells are made to the Texas Water Commission. Those using wells for other than domestic needs must submit an annual report regarding the well level, quantities used, and methods of use.

Seymour V. Connor

Irrigation. Irrigation in what is now the United States it possibly had its beginnings in West Texas or New Mexico. There is evidence of a prehistoric desert agriculture in a few West Texas localities. The Spaniards found New Mexico and Arizona Indians growing crops in an arid climate by collecting and diverting run-off water to the planted fields. Brush dams caught the flow of a dry arroyo when flushed by a thundershower and watered the thirsty plants, even though no rain fell on the field itself. Records left by Vázquez de Coronado and other Spanish explorers indicate that the Indians had developed and established irrigation systems near the sites of present-day El Paso and Pecos, supplied respectively by the Rio Grande and the Pecos River. The first Europeans to practice irrigation in Texas were the Franciscans, who between 1716 and 1744 directed the construction of acequias to supply water for domestic use and irrigation at seven missions in the San Antonio area. Parts of one rock-lined *acequia madre* ("mother ditch") are still in use. The first field crop known to have been grown under irrigation in what is now called Texas was corn, which was cultivated successfully by both Indians and missionaries. In the Gulf Coast area and in the lower Rio Grande valley, salinity and high water tables have been favorable to citrus fruits, vegetables, and cotton. Grain, cotton, alfalfa, and pasture grasses are the principal crops under irrigation in the western sections of the state and on the High Plains.

Large-scale irrigation began in Texas with the construction of canals in the vicinity of Del Rio in 1868. In the 1870s development began on the Pecos River, in the lower Rio Grande valley, and in the Fort Stockton area. Modern projects began along the Coastal Plain and in the El Paso valley during the 1890s and on the High Plains in 1920. In 1913 the Texas legislature passed the first major irrigation act, which called for the establishment of the Board of Water Engineers to regulate water appropriations. A series of dry seasons (1916–18) aroused renewed interest in irrigation from storage reservoirs, and a constitutional amendment was adopted providing for the formation of water-conservation districts by landowners. Whereas the previous irrigation projects had been largely private ventures, most of the new ones were formed under the district act, and most of the former private projects were taken over by public agencies and operated as a nonprofit service to the land. The use of irrigation continued to increase throughout the first half of the twentieth century. In 1948, of the nearly 30,000,000 agricultural acres in the state, 2,884,700 acres was under irrigation. Irrigated land accounted for about 10 percent of the state's harvested acreage. Irrigation was practiced on 29,779 farms; sprinkler or overhead systems were used on more than 850. In some areas irrigation was absolutely necessary for successful agriculture. In others, rainfall was normally sufficient to sustain plant growth, but production was greatly increased by supplemental irrigation.

The major irrigation systems of the state depend upon two water sources: surface streams and underground water. The main regions that use streams are the lower Rio Grande valley, the Colorado River basin, and the Pecos River basin. Most of the water in these areas is considered good for irrigation, although the sodium content is slightly higher in the waters of the more western streams. The High Plains, the El Paso valley (also partly supplied by the Rio Grande), the Winter Garden Region, and the Gulf Coast area mainly use underground water. According to the state Board of Water Engineers, the number of wells in these areas increased from 600 in 1936 to 4,300 in 1949, and the number of acres increased from 80,000 in 1936 to 550,000 in 1949. The irrigation acreage supplied by groundwater pumped from wells was said to have expanded more rapidly in Texas than in any other area in the United States. Methods of irrigation established in various sections of the state depended upon the crops to be grown and the available water supply. In the rice belt the common method used was border flooding or pans. In the Valley the basin-flooding method was used for citrus fruit and the furrow or row method was used for vegetables and field crops. The row method was followed also for cotton and grain crops in other sections of the state.

Irrigated land in Texas increased to 3,131,534 acres by 1950. The growth was largely a result of the rapid development of irrigation on the High Plains, which was supplied exclusively with high-quality groundwater from the underlying Ogallala sands. Irrigation of the region continued to grow spectacularly—more rapidly than any development elsewhere—to 5,894,686 acres by 1974, when the High Plains was one of the largest irrigated areas in the United States and represented 65 percent of all Texas irrigation. The amount of irrigated cropland harvested increased from 10 percent in 1948 to about 25 percent during the mid-1960s, to 72 percent in 1973. In 1974 there were 8.5 million acres in Texas under irrigation. Of that total, 22 percent (more than 1,800,000 acres) was irrigated by sprinkler systems and the rest was watered by surface systems that channeled water in borders, rows, and field levees. The field levees were used mainly for rice. Many irrigation systems employed efficient pipelines or lined ditches to prevent water loss. Drip irrigation generated some interest, especially for tree crops, and was used on 4,500 acres; thereafter the method became standard for many kinds of orchard. Eighty percent of the total irrigated acreage came from water pumped from wells. Important groundwater-supplied irrigated areas included the Winter Garden Region and adjacent lands below the Balcones Escarpment, the Trans-Pecos farms of Reeves, Pecos, and Ward counties, the Marfa, Van Horn, and Dell City vicinities, and part of the Gulf Coast, as well as several north central Texas localities (where, especially during the 1960s, there was an increased use of sprinkler systems for peanut growing). Major areas supplied with surface water were the lower Rio Grande valley, portions of the Gulf Coast rice-growing area, the El Paso valley area, and alluvial lands along the lower Brazos River and other Texas rivers and tributaries. An increasing acreage in small tracts was being irrigated from small upstream impoundments.

Water availability will determine how much of the arable land in Texas is irrigated in the future. Throughout the second half of the twentieth century aquifers were being depleted faster than they could be recharged. A comprehensive Texas water plan was developed in the 1960s, and an amended one published in the 1980s offered an analysis and prediction of Texas water needs to the year 2030. In 1991 the total irrigated acres in the state had decreased to six million. The southern High Plains still accounted for the largest portion—68 percent. Of the total irrigated acres in Texas, 34 percent was watered by sprinkler irrigation. Seventy percent of all irrigation was from wells. The use of drip irrigation had increased somewhat, to 55,000 acres. Irrigated cropland produced 30 percent of the state's total harvested acreage, which accounted for 50 to 60 percent of the value of all crops produced. The decline in irrigated acreage was attributed to decreasing groundwater supplies and higher fuel prices.

Morris E. Bloodworth and Paul T. Gillett

Playas. Playas are shallow, disc-shaped basins etched in the southern Great Plains. Lakes form when surface runoff fills the basins. In Spanish, *playa* means "beach," and the word was perhaps chosen because the lakes represent essentially all of the naturally occurring surface water in a vast semiarid region—the "only beach in town." About 19,000 playas dot the prairie landscape on the southern High Plains of Texas; another 6,000 basins are located in adjacent states. Some Texas counties, such as Floyd, contain more than 1,700 playas, but the average is nearer 600 basins per county. Playas are ephemeral lakes that can reach a size of more than 200 acres, although the average is about 17 acres. Most of them are dry for much of the year and fill naturally only from the runoff of rainstorms. Playas are unlike most lakes in that water is not carried to or from them by streams or rivers. Instead, each drains a relatively small, closed watershed surrounding its basin. Nonetheless, because they are so numerous, playas collect between two million and four million acre-feet of water each year, on an aggregate of about 250,000 surface acres. Playa basins are lined with lenses of nearly impermeable clay, often the Randall type, which prevents the surface water from percolating downward into the underlying Ogallala Aquifer. Thus, without large watersheds, stream flow, or frequent precipitation, the shallow water soon evaporates, leaving

the basins dry until the next rainstorm renews the cycle. Most playa basins originated from the deflating action of strong prairie winds sweeping across the landscape. Older notions attribute formation of the basins to the wallowing of buffalo, but few if any playas were actually so formed.

Some of the earliest inhabitants of North America and later the Plains Indians may have camped near playas, but these associations are largely lost to history. Water-filled playas naturally attracted wildlife and hunters. Spearheads attributed to the Folsom (or a Folsom-like) culture have been recovered from a bed of elephant bones discovered in an ancient playa in Roberts County. Some of the larger, more permanent playas presumably served as campsites for nomadic Indians. The first mention of the playas appears in the records of the sixteenth-century trek of Vásquez de Coronado and his conquistadors as they searched fruitlessly for the legendary Seven Cities of Gold; the men were often forced to drink from what they called buffalo wallows. In 1844 an expedition of the Republic of Texas subsisted on ducks, cranes, and antelope shot near a playa as the group advanced toward Santa Fe. Although playas were unreliable sources of water, during wet years they sometimes became obstacles to travel.

Because the heavy clay soils hold some moisture even in dry years, playas often were important sources of hay at the turn of the century; tons of wild hay were sold to cattlemen, who generally considered playa-grown hay superior. Playas still contribute to agriculture on the semiarid southern High Plains of Texas, where irrigation is expensive and the Ogallala Aquifer is being depleted. About 70 percent of the playas larger than 10 acres have been excavated into deep pits for storing irrigation water and natural runoff; once in the pits, the water remains available for a second irrigation cycle. The pits are excavated with steep sides that produce a favorable ratio of surface area to volume and minimize evaporation. Though this practice vastly reduces the natural littoral zones—the shallow areas of high biological productivity that represent the foundation for aquatic food webs—playas that might usually be dry collect irrigation runoff that supports a rich community of plant life and provides surface water for wildlife. In years of normal rainfall the playas are second in importance only to the Gulf Coast of Texas as wintering grounds for waterfowl in the Central Flyway; more than a million mallards, wigeons, pintails, and green-winged teals winter on the playas. Vegetation growing in playa basins also provides cover for large numbers of ring-necked pheasants. Playas supply unique wildlife habitats in an intensively cultivated region.

Eric G. Bolen

Surface Water. Surface water constitutes the ordinary flow and underflow of rivers, streams, and lakes, as well as runoff from precipitation. There are over 6,687 square miles of inland water in Texas, ranking the state seventh among the contiguous 48 states. These inland waters are represented by 15 major river basins and 8 coastal basins. The state also has over 665 miles of coastline. More than 11,000 named streams and tributaries with a combined length of over 80,000 miles provide drainage for rainfall runoff. The total annual discharge of water from these streams has varied from around 21 million acre-feet to 55 million acre-feet, depending on whether the state is in a wet or dry period. In 1990 surface water comprised 43 percent of the water used in Texas. That total was broken down for the following uses: municipal, 26 percent or 1.79 million acre-feet; agricultural,

48 percent or 3.25 million acre-feet; industrial, 19 percent or 1.3 million acre-feet; mining, 1 percent or .06 million acre-feet; and steam-electric power generation, 5.5 percent or .37 million acre-feet. Unlike underground water, which is subject to the rule of capture, surface water and its use is regulated by the state of Texas. The Texas Natural Resource Conservation Commission (formerly the Texas Water Commission) was in 1995 the agency in Texas responsible for authorizing, enforcing, and protecting the use of surface water. A second state agency, the Texas Water Development Board, was responsible for making studies, planning, and providing financial support to public entities and leadership towards the responsible development and conservation of the state's water resources for current and future generations of Texans, their economy, and their environment. A third agency, the Texas Parks and Wildlife Department, deals with issues that affect the environment.

Surface water differs from other natural resources in that the supply is constantly being replenished, although the yield differs from year to year and the distribution varies. Surface runoff is primarily dependent upon rainfall. It is, however, influenced considerably by evaporation, transpiration, surface topography, and the capacity for infiltration of surface soils and rocks. Based on weather records over an 80-year period extending into the 1980s, precipitation amounts to 413 million acre-feet of water a year in the state; however, 90 percent of this is lost to evaporation and plant transpiration, leaving only 40 million acre-feet to recharge aquifers and flow to rivers and streams. Soil types, vegetation, surface slopes, and rainfall intensities all alter the relation between rainfall and runoff. Generally speaking, however, the relative average quantity of water in Texas streams follows the rainfall pattern across the state. Precipitation across Texas is mainly dependent on the moisture content of the onshore flow of air from the Gulf of Mexico. Its proximity to the Gulf puts all except the extreme western section of the state in the path of frequent tropical or semitropical storms. The general path of these storms is up or across the major streams. Rainfalls of more than 20 inches in 24 hours have occurred throughout the state and resulted in significant floods. Generally, moisture increases from the western to the eastern portions of the state. Less than one inch of the average annual rainfall of extreme West Texas appears as flow in the streams. The yield increases progressively to 15 inches of average annual runoff along the Texas–Louisiana border, where the average annual rainfall is 50 to 55 inches.

The first gauging station of the United States Geological Survey in Texas was established on the Rio Grande at El Paso in 1889, and a few miscellaneous measurements of Central Texas streams were made in 1894, 1895, and 1896. In 1897 Thomas Ulvan Taylor began a systematic study of a few of the principal streams of Texas for the USGS. Beginning in 1915 the USGS, in cooperation with the Board of Water Engineers, the United States Army engineers, and various other agencies, established and maintained streamflow measurement stations at numerous sites where future developments were anticipated. In 1945 there were 183 gauging stations maintained on the major rivers of Texas and their principal tributaries. In addition, stream-measurement stations on 10 important canals were in operation, and gauges at 8 reservoirs and lakes were maintained for determination of storage contents. Many miscellaneous measurements of springs and of streams at low and flood flows, as well as other special investigations of the surface-water resources, have been made by the Geological Survey. The resulting data afford material for evaluating the availability of surface-water flows of the large Texas streams. Between 1941 and 1980 the average annual runoff of Texas streams was 52 million acre-feet. Fifty percent of the total Texas runoff originates from the eastern quarter of the state, principally from six streams—the Sulphur, Sabine, Neches, San Jacinto, and Trinity rivers and Cypress Creek in Northeast Texas. The total drainage area of these East Texas streams is 46,000 miles. East Texas streams are not subject to as rapid variations in flow as are those of other sections of Texas. Usually they carry a considerable amount of flood runoff during the winter and spring months. The Brazos, Colorado, Guadalupe, Nueces, and Rio Grande basins are subject to long periods of low flow and short periods of flood flow; therefore, their runoff characteristics are quite different from those of streams in East Texas. From 70 to 90 percent of the total runoff from these basins occurs as flood flow extending only over a few weeks, except for streams such as the Devils and Guadalupe rivers, which derive a large portion of their flow from uniformly flowing springs. Historically, the Guadalupe River below New Braunfels has been the most dependable stream in the state from the standpoint of a well-sustained low flow. Comal Springs and San Marcos Springs are the principal sources for its abundant supply of water, though in the latter part of the twentieth century, increased population, pumping, and water use have threatened the stability of the springs. Surface streams in some areas also lose much water to underground formations. The stream network of the upper Nueces River basin is a principal example; it loses substantial flow as the water flows across certain sections of the Balcones Fault zone. The variations of flow of the Concho River near San Angelo in 1936 are typical of the wide range in runoff that may be expected from average West Texas streams when floods of great magnitude occur. The total runoff during that year was 869,000 acre-feet; of this amount, 96 percent occurred during a 16-day period, and 30 percent occurred in one day. The average annual runoff for this station was 146,000 acre-feet. During droughts such as that of the early 1950s the state's annual runoff shrinks drastically, and the annual yield of individual streams has an even wider variation.

Managing, tracking, and protecting the quality of existing water supplies has become increasingly important as population and industrial needs increase. Historically, because of the limited water supply that was available from the unregulated flow of all Texas streams, it was necessary that floodwater be stored and conserved for multiple uses. Over the last half of the twentieth century the number of Texas reservoirs has increased dramatically, with improved flood control and increased conservation as consequences. The state had only 8 major reservoirs in 1913. By 1930 the number had grown to 32 with a total capacity of 1,284,520 acre-feet. In 1960 there were 105 reservoirs with a total capacity of 22,746,200 acre-feet. By 1993 Texas had 212 major reservoirs in existence or under construction, with a conservation storage capacity totaling 40,825,072 acre-feet. This amounted to a total surface area of 1,695,647 acres. There are over 5,700 reservoirs in Texas of at least 10 surface acres in size. Of these reservoirs, 207 have a storage capacity of over 5,000 acre-feet and comprise 97 percent of the available surface water supplies in the state. The usable water, or conservation storage capacity of these reservoirs allocated to Texas, is 35 million acre-feet. Their total flood storage capacity is 17.4 million acre-feet, and their dependable water supply (firm yield) for the year 2000 will be 8.1 million acre-feet annually. About 86 percent or 7 million acre-feet of the total firm yield is currently being used for municipal, agricultural, mining, power-generation, and industrial purposes. Virtually all of the remaining water in the reservoirs has been committed, by the appropriation of water rights, to meet the growing municipal and industrial needs of the major metropolitan areas. From 1930 to 1993 the state's population increased from 6 million to 18 million. The development of additional supplies will become increasingly difficult since the number of new reservoir sites is limited. Many of these sites are being developed, and environmentalists are worried about the changes reservoirs cause to ecosystems. Future water-use plans are generally focused on conservation, reuse, regionalization, and the best use of existing supplies.

Texas Water Commission. The Texas Water Commission was formerly the state's primary regulatory agency for water resources. Throughout its history, the TWC was responsible for protecting surface and groundwater quality and ensuring that utility and water district customers received adequate services. The TWC also implemented state laws relating to water and enforced all laws, rules, orders, permits, licenses, and standards under its jurisdiction. Its responsibilities included certification of wastewater treatment plants, administration of surface water rights, dam safety management, water well driller regulation, and water district supervision. Other duties included ratesetting for some privately owned public water and wastewater systems and the administration of flood-control projects and the national flood insurance program. In 1992 the commission was given jurisdiction over municipal solid-waste management. Its responsibility had already included industrial and hazardous waste management and waste minimization initiatives. The TWC also coordinated state responses to oil and hazardous materials spills and regulated petroleum storage tanks. Another major program of the TWC was "Clean Texas 2000," a cooperative effort between private industry and the TWC. Participants worked voluntarily toward a goal of reducing by 60 percent the release of toxic substances, the generation of hazardous pollutants, and the disposal of solid waste in landfills during the period from 1987 to 2000. Three fulltime commissioners headed the TWC by gubernatorial appointment and served staggered sixyear terms, with one commissioner serving as chairman. The commission usually met once a week in Austin. Duties included establishing agency policy, adopting rules, consideration of permit applications, and ordering enforcement actions against violators. The commission appointed an executive director for program administration, and a general counsel, a chief clerk, an ombudsman, an independent public interest counsel, and an independent head of the Office of Hearings Examiners.

Water development in Texas began in 1905 when the first state drainage districts were established. Water-rights procedures were developed in 1913 when the Burges–Glasscock Act established the Board of Water Engineers. Between 1913 and the formal beginning of the TWC, numerous regional councils, authorities, and districts regulated various aspects of water quality and water resources. However, a statewide plan for the development, conservation, and beneficial use of Texas water was not adopted until the Water Planning Act of 1957 was signed into law. In 1962 the Texas Water Commission replaced the Board of Water Engineers. Lawmakers gave the new agency additional authority to measure, eliminate, and prevent water pollution. The TWC also began licensing well drillers, inspecting water-district construction projects, and overseeing operations of the state reclamation engineer. The agency was called the Texas Water Rights Commission from 1965 to 1977, when it was again named Texas Water Commission. In 1985 the Texas Water Commission absorbed part of the Texas Department of Water Resources and became the primary state agency for implementing state water laws. Another expansion occurred in 1992 when the TWC took over functions of the Water Hygiene Division and Solid Waste Bureau of the Texas Department of Health. The TWC also absorbed the Texas Water Well Drillers Board and the Board of Irrigators that same year. In its final year of operation (fiscal year 1993), the TWC had a budget of nearly $128 million and employed 1,800 workers. In 1991 the Texas legislature ordered the consolidation of the TWC and the Texas Air Control Board into the Texas Natural Resource Conservation Commission, effective September 1, 1993. The TNRCC became responsible for the regulation of air quality, water quality, and waste management in Texas. *Terry L. Hadley*

Texas Water Development Board. A six-member board appointed by the governor to serve as a policy-making body; established in 1957 through a state constitutional amendment. Membership consisted of overlapping six-year terms, and each board member had to be from a different section of the state. The agency's original function was to provide loan assistance to political subdivisions for the development of surface water supply projects that could not be financed through commercial channels. During the 1960s the board's responsibilities grew to include the authority to obtain and develop water conservation storage facilities, prepare a state water plan, and assume operations of the Texas Water Commission not related to the question of water rights. In the 1990s the Texas Water Development Board has a number of broad responsibilities. One primary function is still the granting of loans to local governments in order to implement flood and pollution control, wastewater treatment, and municipal solid waste management. In addition, the board provides grants and loans to economically distressed areas of the state to implement water and sewage projects, including low-interest loans to colonia residents for plumbing improvements. The agency is responsible for collecting data and conducting studies regarding agricultural water conservation, freshwater needs of Texas estuaries and bays, and surface and ground water resources. It also maintains the Texas Natural Resources Information System, a central database of information concerning the state's resources. The executive administrator's office implements the agency's policies. An administrative division provides support through services such as accounting, budget monitoring, and inventory recordkeeping. The board funds its assistance programs with state-backed bonds and federal grants to provide for a State Revolving Fund for borrowers, overseen by the office of the Development Fund manager. Loan recipients also receive engineering and technical advice from the board's engineers and archeologists. As the agency responsible for developing a state water plan, the Texas Water Development Board employs a number of research sections to assess and predict water availability, environmental impact, and water uses for both agricultural and municipal areas. The board continually collects surface and underground water information through hydrologic monitoring. It provides technical evaluation of water-resource problems and promotes programs on conservation education. By the early 1990s the agency had sold over $1 billion in bonds for the financing of water-related projects since its inception.   *Laurie E. Jasinski*

Texas Water Quality Board. The first separate state agency that was interested solely in state water-pollution control was the Texas Water Pollution Advisory Council, established in 1953. It consisted of five ex-officio members and was purely advisory. The Texas Pollution Control Act of 1961 established the Texas Water Pollution Control Board, which was empowered to issue permits and generally control pollution. The Texas Water Quality Act of 1967 established the Texas Water Quality Board, which assumed the functions, powers, duties, and responsibilities of the Water Pollution Control Board. The Texas Water Quality Board consisted of seven members: the executive director of the Texas Water Development Board, the state commissioner of health, the executive director of the Texas Parks and Wildlife Department, the chairman of the Railroad Commission, and three members appointed from the public. The Texas Water Quality Board was the chief agency to oversee water quality. It established guidelines for wastewater discharge and was involved in the administration and inspection of proposed sewage-treatment facilities and the proper appropriation of funds for such projects. The board held public hearings for permit applications, conducted research, and coordinated efforts with other state agencies to provide for effective control of water quality. The agency was organized into three divisions: administrative, central operations, and field operations, which maintained 11 district offices in the state. Two other divisions, executive and hearings and enforcement, were later added. In 1976 the agency employed 400 people. The 1977 Water Reorganization Act consolidated the Texas Water Quality Board, the Texas Water Development Board, and the Texas Water Rights Commission into the Texas Department of Water Resources. While the other two agencies continued to operate as named organizations, the Texas Water Quality Board was abolished and its duties split between the two agencies.

Texas Water Well Drillers Board. Established in 1961 as a result of a statute that required well drillers to register with the Board of Water Engineers. The board originally served as an advisory group. After the state's water agencies reorganized in 1965 the Texas Water Well Drillers Board was established by an act that gave the agency primary responsibility for the licensing and regulation of well drillers and the prevention of underground water pollution. The board was responsible for aiding the Texas Water Commission in enforcement of drilling rules. Regulations required the recording of accurate logs on drilled or altered wells. The Texas Water Commission was to receive copies of all logs. Drillers had to inform landowners of potentially hazardous or polluted wells. The board also implemented the water commission's standards for plugging wells and had the authority to plug abandoned or deteriorated ones. The board was made up of nine members appointed by the governor for overlapping six-year terms. Six of the members had to be registered water well drillers with 10 years' experience and had to represent different geographical regions—the Gulf Coast, Trans-Pecos, Central Texas, Northeast Texas, and Panhandle–South Plains. In 1991 the board had an operating budget of $188,644. The agency was abolished in 1992, and the Texas Water Commission assumed its duties.   *Laurie E. Jasinski*

Underground Water. Underground water includes all water that occurs below the earth's surface, occupying interstices or voids of pervious rocks and soil; like surface water, it is derived principally from precipitation that falls upon the earth's surface and percolates downward under gravity. Underground water in the zone of saturation may occur in either water table (unconfined) aquifers or artesian (confined) aquifers. Confined water is generally under pressure greater that atmospheric pressure, and wells penetrating a confined aquifer will permit water to rise above the confining strata. If sufficient pressure exists flowing wells may result. In the case of water table aquifers, water is derived from local precipitation; but in the case of artesian wells, water may enter the permeable strata 10 or even hundreds of miles from the point where it is intercepted by wells; hence, water taken from a well is no more a part of the land than is the water of a surface stream that crosses it. The city of Houston, for example, derives water from the Beaumont clay, from the Goliad–Willis–Lissie formations, and in smaller quantities from the Logarto clay, which outcrops approximately 100 miles to the west.

Most geologic formations in Texas contain water, but only a relatively few yield abundant supplies. Those formations yielding abundant supplies that have been classified as major aquifers include the Gulf Coast Aquifer; the Carrizo–Wilcox Aquifer, just north of the Gulf Coast Aquifer; the Trinity Group Aquifer, mainly in North and Central Texas; the Edwards–Trinity Aquifer, identified with the Edwards Plateau; the Edwards Aquifer, corresponding to the Balcones Escarpment zone; the Ogallala Aquifer, roughly coextensive with the High Plains; and the Alluvium Aquifer, in widespread areas in Texas but occurring principally in West Texas. In all, Texas has 7 major and 16 minor aquifers. They underlie approximately 76 percent of the state. The massive Ogallala Aquifer accounts for 90 percent of the total water in all the Texas aquifers. In the mid-to-late 1980s 11 million acre-feet a year was being withdrawn from aquifers in Texas. Replenishment fell far short, however, amounting to only 5.3 million acre-feet a year.

Underground water is a principal water resource in Texas, and its importance as a source of supply for municipal, industrial, and irrigation uses, as well as domestic and livestock purposes, is immeasurable. In 1990 more than half of the water used in the state was underground water; about 71 percent was for agricultural use and 21 percent for municipal use, with the remainder going to industrial needs. Many large cities and most of the smaller cities and communities in Texas supply their water needs from municipally owned wells or from a combination of surface and underground water sources. More than half of all municipal water in Texas comes from underground water. The largest single use of underground water in Texas is for irrigation. In 1990, six million acres in Texas was irrigated, and about 70 percent of all irrigation water came from underground sources. More underground water is used for irrigation in Texas than for all other uses combined. In addition to municipal and irrigation uses, many industries have developed underground water supplies for cooling and industrial processes. Underground water is particularly desirable for industry because of its uniform temperature and uniform quality at a given source. Although all underground water contains minerals derived principally from soil and rocks through which it moves, its quality and temperature generally remain constant at a given locality unless it is contaminated by human activities. Several factors have contributed to the development and widespread use of underground water as a supply source in Texas. Nearly all of the geologic formations in the state yield some water, generally in sufficient quantities for domestic and livestock purposes. Where it is available in sufficient quantities, underground water is generally cheapest to develop, since it does not need the extensive pipelines and treatment facilities required for surface supplies. Unlike surface water, which flows in definite and limited channels, underground water can often be developed at the point of use, requiring little or no transportation. Large areas of Texas deficient in rainfall and having few perennial streams still have vast quantities of underground water in storage.

Unlike surface water, which is the property of the state of Texas, underground water is the exclusive property of the owner of the land surface and subject to the rule of capture. It is subject to barter, sale, or lease and not to the complicated and often conflicting riparian and appropriative doctrines governing surface-water rights. Except for a few statutes pertaining to conservation, protection, and waste, the state of Texas does not regulate the production or use of underground water. Some local control is exercised by underground water conservation districts, which are empowered to promulgate rules and regulations for conserving, preserving, protecting, and recharging underground water reservoirs within their boundaries, including well spacing and well permitting. In the latter part of the twentieth century many areas in the state were grappling with the problems of overpumping. Land subsidence, especially in the Houston–Galveston area, has been a major concern that resulted in the establishment of a subsidence district in 1975. Also, too much pumping may result in saltwater intrusion. Increasingly, many municipalities and agribusinesses looked to more efficient conservation methods and the use of surface water.

Bernard B. Baker

Underground Water Conservation Districts. The establishment of underground water conservation districts was authorized by the state legislature in 1949. At that time the Board of Water Engineers was responsible for designating the districts to correspond with the boundaries of underground reservoirs. A district could be established through special legislation or a signed petition from landholders. In 1985 an amendment also allowed the Texas Water Commission and Texas Water Development Board to recommend the formation of a district. Agency recommendations were also subject, however, to approval by residents of a potential district in an election. Residents could veto a designation, though they risked the withholding of state funds.

A district is headed by a board of five directors elected by district voters. The directors can employ an engineer to survey underground reservoirs. Underground water conservation district boundaries must be in accordance with the boundaries of an underground reservoir, or a subdivision of a reasonably definable section of the reservoir can constitute a district. Districts are authorized to regulate the use of groundwater and can implement rules providing for the conservation, protection, and control of those resources. They can develop conservation plans and conduct research projects. The district may acquire land to build dams and may call for the installation of pumps for the recharge of an underground reservoir. It also determines and approves permits for large-volume water consumers. In a dis-

trict most new wells must be cataloged, and drillers' logs can be required. Districts have substantial limitations and often come in direct conflict with the traditional view of groundwater as private property and its use as a landowner's right. The use of the districts has also been undermined through the practice of establishing dormant districts—ones where no ad valorem taxes are levied—essentially districts in name only.

In 1992, 34 underground water conservation districts were registered with the Texas Water Commission. The High Plains Underground Water Conservation District and North Plains Groundwater Conservation District No. 2 have successfully implemented conservation and educational programs to equalize use of the Ogallala Aquifer. The Edwards Underground Water District, however, has been caught up in a battle of municipal and agricultural interests against conservation of the Edwards Aquifer. The Harris–Galveston Coastal Subsidence District, established in 1975—after the determination that the water table in the Houston area had fallen nine feet—requires stringent regulation. It restricts the amount of water that can be used and levies pumping fees. The program has successfully reduced subsidence in the Houston area, but with the inevitable side effect of increased flooding.

Laurie E. Jasinski

Water Agencies and Programs. Several units of local government in Texas have been authorized to engage in water programs. Counties, cities, and other kinds of water districts were authorized by statute to undertake certain projects. The extent to which the units actually exercised their authority, however, has varied considerably. Early in the state's development, counties were relied upon to undertake certain water functions. They were authorized to clear and improve streams for navigation and to make drainage and flood-control improvements on petition of property owners. These programs were limited, however, because constitutional provisions permitted only a special-assessment tax to finance such improvements. The county remained the only unit of local government authorized to perform these services until 1904, when the constitution was amended to permit the establishment of special districts. After that time these new units assumed most of the duties of making the improvements. Counties, however, continued to participate in water programs as administrative areas of the state government. They were responsible for enforcing state laws, including fish and game laws and water laws pertaining to water districts. Under water law statutes, the county commissioners' court was empowered to establish numerous kinds of water districts. The county board appointed the governing boards of drainage, navigation, and levee districts, and the boards of water-control and preservation districts in their county. Counties also had a certain amount of supervisory authority over general-law water districts. The county auditor had general supervision over the books and records of all the county officers, including those of the water districts.

After the constitutional amendment of 1904 that authorized the first public development of water resources, the water district became the most important unit of local government to undertake water programs. Water districts in Texas direct all the major water programs, including flood control, drainage, navigation, irrigation; domestic, commercial, and industrial water supply; and sewage disposal, power supply, groundwater control, mosquito control, soil conservation, and recreation. These tasks of supplying or controlling water often involve the construction of levees, dams, lakes, and power facilities, or the channeling, clearing, and maintenance of streams and rivers. In 1949 the Texas legislature authorized the establishment of underground water districts with local voter approval. By 1966 there were more than 793 water districts in the state, counting all districts founded under both general and special laws. The types of general-law water districts were water control and improvement, water improvement, freshwater supply, underground water conservation, irrigation, levee improvement, drainage, and navigation districts, as well as conservation and reclamation, water control and preservation, water power control, water supply, and municipal water districts. There was little control over water districts by either state agencies or the public, and this caused a great deal of criticism. The rapid multiplication of disparate, often overlapping water districts made it impossible for even the most conscientious citizen to understand their problems and activities. As a result, in 1961 the legislature enacted a provision which provided that no districts except water control and improvement districts and underground water conservation districts could thereafter be established. The legislature also empowered the Texas Water Commission to supervise and coordinate activities of water districts. The prohibition on establishing other types of districts, however, was declared unconstitutional in 1963.

Cities had a vital concern in maintaining adequate municipal water supply. Texas cities could establish municipal water systems and issue the bonds required to construct them if such construction and bonding were approved in popular elections. Cities were also authorized to construct sewer systems and sewage disposal plants, most of which had to be financed by means of voterapproved bond issues. Flood-protection measures were also undertaken by cities, since many cities were located on or near streams. Home rule cities, which had the power to improve any river or stream within the city and to levy a special assessment on property owners, especially benefited. Texas cities located on navigable streams could acquire land for the purpose of establishing and maintaining wharves, docks, railway terminals, and other aids to navigation. They could also deed this property to the federal government for the improvement of navigation. Any city situated within the territorial limits of a navigation district and having a deepwater port could purchase, construct, own, and maintain dikes, spillways, seawalls, and breakwaters to protect the city. Furthermore, the city could elevate and reclaim submerged or low lands along the waterfront, dredge channels, and build and operate dry docks, piers, wharves, and boat basins. To finance these improvements for their harbors, coastal cities could issue bonds. Texas cities could also generate, purchase, and distribute hydroelectric power, own and operate municipal electric plants, and contract with other generating agencies for electrical energy. By the 1990s there were thousands of local agencies and corporations involved in supplying water for municipal, industrial, and agricultural use. Local water suppliers mainly included municipal utility districts, cities, water-supply corporations, and private water suppliers. There were more than 1,000 municipal utility districts that, through voter approved bond elections, could develop water resources by building reservoirs, drilling wells, constructing treatment plants, or undertaking other projects.

John T. Thompson

Water Law. The complexity of the Texas law of water rights stems from its combination of Spanish law with English common law, as well as from its legal fragmentation of the hydrologic cycle. Water-rights law determines who is entitled to use the available water supply, in what quantities, and for what purposes, and often specifies when and where the water may be used. Unlike scientists, who usually regard all water as part of the endless hydrologic cycle—a natural whole—courts divide water into unrelated legal classes with different rules of law governing the ownership and use of each class. Several classes of underground and surface water are recognized, and recent attempts at weather modification bring yet another class, atmospheric moisture, into consideration. Texas law pertaining to surface-water resources is voluminous, while groundwater law is relatively sparse; as might be expected, law pertaining to atmospheric moisture is even less developed.

With respect to surface-water rights, Texas is one of several dual-doctrine states that recognize both riparian and prior-appropriation doctrines, which are dissimilar in almost every respect. The riparian doctrine, which accords water rights to those who own riparian land, was introduced into Texas over 200 years ago during the Spanish settlement of San Antonio. Hispanic legal principles and practices were continued essentially unchanged by the Mexican government after 1821 and later by the Republic of Texas until 1840. Extensive tracts of land with appurtenant water rights were granted by these governments in Texas, and today title to about 26 million acres, one-seventh of the state, can be traced to these sources. For many years Texas courts, water agencies, and water users assumed that Hispanic and pre-1840 republic land grants carried extensive riparian rights, including the right to take water from streams for irrigation, a principle with which the Texas Supreme Court agreed in the landmark case *Motl v. Boyd* (1926). However, in the 1950s, construction of International Falcon Reservoir on the Rio Grande prompted a reexamination of Hispanic water law, and it was determined in *State v. Valmont Plantations* (1961) that rights to water for irrigation and other major uses did not accrue from these grants unless expressly mentioned. Only a few specific grants of irrigation rights were made.

More comprehensive riparian rights were attached to all lands granted by the republic and state between 1840 and the Appropriation Acts of 1889–95, an era when vast tracts of Texas land passed from the government into private hands. In 1840 the Texas Congress adopted the common law of England (with some exceptions) and with it acquired the English riparian doctrine, somewhat different from the Spanish. Subsequent judicial modifications of the original doctrine gave riparian landowners the right to make reasonable use of water for irrigation or for other purposes. As early as 1872 the Texas Supreme Court pointed out the unsuitability of riparian doctrine for the arid and semiarid portions of the state and suggested legislation to impose the prior-appropriation system. The appropriation doctrine was adopted by the state near the turn of the century. Since 1895 land acquired from the state has no longer carried riparian water rights as a matter of course. Instead individuals must appropriate water rights from the state through established statutory procedures. The superior position of preexisting riparian rights has, however, been uniformly recognized by all appropriation statutes. Between 1895 and 1913 a landowner could appropriate water from a stream merely by filing a sworn statement and map with his county clerk describing the diversion. It is not surprising that under this loosely administered system, water-rights claims often overlapped, described unrealistically large irrigated acreages, or claimed more water than the stream could possibly supply. These rights are called "certified filings" because after 1913 the state recognized and recorded certified copies of the early diversions, which amounted to almost 1,000. A 1913 statute introduced a more modern and strictly administered appropriation procedure. Since that time persons have had to make application to the Texas Water Commission (now the Texas Natural Resource Conservation Commission) for permits to appropriate water from Texas streams. As of August 1975 the agency had recognized more than 10,600 water-rights claims involving almost 54 million acre-feet of water, slightly more than the state's average annual surface-water runoff of 49 million acre-feet.

State water agencies and water users have always had great difficulty in coordinating the diverse Hispanic and English riparian rights and later appropriation rights, all of which were in effect on the same streams. Because permit holders are required to file annual reports, reasonably accurate long-term records of appropriative water use are extant. However, as late as 1968 there were unrecorded water-rights claimants (riparians and some unrecorded certified filings) in all major river basins; the extent of their claims and the amount of water they were diverting each year were unknown. This perhaps large but unquantified water use made coordinated administration and management of the state's surface-water resources difficult, if not impossible. A decision on all surface-water rights was urgently needed. Adjudication on the lower Rio Grande in a massive lawsuit, *State v. Hidalgo County Water Control and Improvement District No. 18* (1969), involving 42 special water districts, over 2,500 individuals, and more than 90 lawyers, showed the futility of a purely judicial determination of water rights for the entire state. The Water Rights Adjudication Act (1967), designed to remedy the situation, set up a complex administrative and judicial adjudication procedure. All unrecorded water-rights claims were required to be filed with the TWC by 1969. Over 11,600 unrecorded claims, primarily from riparian landowners, were filed, asserting rights to more than seven million acre-feet of water. Claims were limited to the maximum amount of water diverted during any year between 1963 and 1967. After administrative determination of rights by the TWC, these findings were to be filed in district court for judicial determination of rights, and eventually certificates of adjudicated water rights were to be issued to successful claimants. Adjudication under the act began on sparsely populated southwestern stream segments in 1969 and proceeded to the northeast into the more populous river basins. Following adjudication, nebulous riparian rights and other unrecorded water rights were for the first time limited to a specific maximum quantity of water. The number of permit holders was also limited, and permits became subject to cancellation for nonuse. The potential for more efficient surface-water management, administration, and planning was greatly increased.

Diffused surface water—surface drainage over the face of a tract of land before it is concentrated into a channel or streamcourse—is another legal class of water. It retains this classification until it reaches a streamcourse, sinks into the ground, or evaporates. In Texas landowners have the right to intercept, impound, and use diffused surface water on their land. Their rights are superior to those of adjacent lower landowners and to

holders of rights on streams into which the water might eventually flow. Texas law provides that diffused surface water can be impounded in tanks by the landowner on his own property without a permit, so long as the reservoir does not exceed 200 acre-feet in storage capacity and the water is used only for domestic and livestock purposes. A permit is required if the reservoir exceeds the storage limits, if the dam is on a stream, or if the water is to be used for other purposes. Most farm tanks are shallow, have large surface areas, and lose large quantities to evaporation and percolation underground. Thousands of small, private tanks exist in some Texas watersheds, and they can have a very adverse effect on stream flow and downstream water use. During the drought of the 1950s it was calculated that more than 50 percent of surface runoff in some watersheds was intercepted by such private reservoirs. Under present Texas water law, downstream water users have no recourse to protect their existing water rights.

Water that percolates beneath the land surface becomes part of yet another legal classification, groundwater or underground water. Groundwater, a particularly important resource, provides for more than 60 percent of the state's water needs. Because of the diverse physical and hydrologic environments of Texas, excessive pumping may lead to such regional problems as land-surface subsidence and saltwater intrusion on the Gulf Coast, dwindling spring flow and stream flow in Central Texas, and groundwater depletion on the High Plains and in far West Texas. Texas law subdivides groundwater into two classes: percolating groundwater and water flowing in well-defined underground streams. Texas courts presume that all groundwater is percolating unless proved otherwise. The law about the ownership of percolating groundwater in Texas is well settled. The strict common-law or "English" rule was established by the Texas Supreme Court in *Houston & T. C. Ry. v. East* (1904). Under this rule the owner of the overlying land can pump and use the water with few restrictions, whatever the impact on adjacent landowners or more distant water users. Since the *East* case the rule has been elaborated somewhat by Texas courts but has not been modified significantly. A law passed in 1949 provides for the voluntary establishment of local conservation districts for underground water. Also, groundwater districts may be formed by special legislation and given powers significantly different from those of general-law districts. Such local districts exercise about the only control over landowner rights to groundwater. General-law districts have rather broad statutory powers, including regulatory authority over well spacing, water proration, and groundwater conservation. However, they have not implemented all these powers, and the only significant conservation rules they enforce pertain to well spacing and the control of off-farm groundwater waste.

In the era since World War II there has been increasing interest in weather modification, especially to increase rainfall and suppress hail. No Texas cases or statutes deal with possible sovereign rights to atmospheric moisture. However, Texas courts have gone further than those of any other state in finding private rights to this segment of the water resource. In *Southwest Weather Research, Inc. v. Duncan* (1958), cloud seeders were temporarily enjoined from engaging in hail suppression over plaintiffs' lands when it was claimed that precipitation was being reduced. Suggesting that landowners in Texas have a natural right to any precipitation that falls on their land, the court stated, "We believe that the landowner is entitled . . . to such rainfall as may come from clouds over his own property that nature in her caprice may provide." Subsequently, in 1967, a Weather Modification Act placed weather modification under control of the Texas Water Development Board. In 1977 the Texas Water Commission took over the issuance of licenses and permits required for weather modification operations; unlicensed activities are prohibited. Amendments allow public hearings in affected areas, and public elections may be held where a permit is requested for hail suppression. For all its increasingly complex provisions, the act does not mention the question of public and private rights to atmospheric moisture in Texas. Uncertainties as to both the direct and side effects of weather modification continue to impede it.

Conjunctive management of water resources in various phases of the interconnected hydrologic cycle is often recommended and is viewed as a desirable objective in both the original (1969) and revised (1984) Texas water plans. Omitting consideration of atmospheric moisture and diffused surface water, it is evident that coordinated use and management of surface water and groundwater in a state like Texas, where different doctrines apply to each, would be almost impossible to achieve. Water in streams, the property of the state, can be managed in the general public interest, whereas groundwater is not subject to such control. The absolute ownership rule applied to groundwater provides no basis for correlating rights in an interconnected supply. Even this brief overview of Texas water law should make it evident that the fragmented institutional structure governing water rights constitutes a formidable obstacle to achieving comprehensive and efficient water-resource management. In some areas, such as the ongoing adjudication of surface-water rights, great progress has been made. In others, the relative lack of control over groundwater and diffused surface-water use continues to cause problems. As the population of Texas grows and the demands on the state's limited water supplies increase, so do the difficulties of managing this essential resource. *Otis W. Templer*

Water Power. Water has never been an important source of industrial power in Texas because of the irregular and frequently insufficient flow of Texas rivers. As early as 1822, however, James Bryan contemplated building a gristmill on the Colorado River, and a few years later Jared E. Groce was granted land over and above his headright for constructing a gristmill and sawmill on the Brazos. About 1825 George Huff and others obtained land from the Mexican government to locate a saw and grist mill on the San Bernard, but the contract was voided in May 1825. A few mills using water power were probably built, although most of the early gristmills, sawmills, and cotton gins were powered either by steam or by oxen. Various types of water wheels could have been used to transmit power directly through shafts and belts to the mill machinery. In 1841 William Kennedy reported that he believed the streams of Texas afforded great facilities for water mills, but by 1882 there were few mills in the state over 25 years old and little utilization of water power except in localities where there were swift-moving streams with natural falls, such as a woolen manufacturing plant on the Comal River. Many of the mills had to maintain auxiliary steam plants. A natural dam and series of three falls at Marble Falls resulted in the establishment of a number of flour mills, cotton gins, gristmills, and a cottonseed oil mill. By 1890 a new type of turbine wheel had begun to replace older styles of water wheels, and some electric power was being generated by hydroelectric plants. Numerous

small power plants, such as one on the San Marcos River near Prairie Lea, were operated by private owners. The Prairie Lea mill had a dam constructed of a timber framework filled in with rocks; its turbine wheel could produce 45 horsepower under a seven-foot head. The power operated a gin, a corn mill, and a Wiley dynamo. By 1923 water power in Texas was developing a total of 12,000 horsepower, utilized for ginning cotton, grinding corn, sawing lumber, and generating some electricity. Since the early 1930s the use of water power for direct-connecting machinery has declined, but numbers of hydroelectric plants have been built both as private corporations and as federal projects. In 1946, of the 194 electric power plants in Texas 26 were hydroelectric; they generated about 15 percent of the state's electric power. In January 1967 there were 23 hydroelectric plants with a total generating capacity of 389,860 kilowatts. In the 1970s major power plant sites included International Falcon Reservoir, six sites on the Highland Lakes of the Colorado River, Amistad Reservoir on the Rio Grande, two sites along the Brazos River, six plants on the Guadalupe River, Denison Dam on the Red River, and Toledo Bend Reservoir on the Sabine River. In the later part of the twentieth century the use of hydroelectric power continued to decline relative to other means of power generation. In 1992, of the 390 generating units in Texas and 30 units outside Texas supplying power to the state, only 1 percent were hydroelectric. In 1994 there were 23 hydroelectric power plants in Texas, or, more specifically, 23 dams with power facilities. The facilities housed 44 generating units with a total generating capacity of 541.7 megawatts.

Waters–Pierce Case. Perhaps the best-known suit brought by the state of Texas against a corporation for violation of its antitrust law. In 1897 when Attorney General Martin M. Crane brought suit in state district court in Austin against Waters–Pierce Oil Company, charging that Waters–Pierce was a party to the Standard Oil of New Jersey trust agreement. The state court's ruling for the state, carrying a penalty of revocation of the company's charter and cancellation of its permit to do business in Texas, was upheld by the state's appeal courts. Early in 1900 the United States Supreme Court upheld the ruling. Waters–Pierce was a Missouri corporation operated by its founder and president, Henry Clay Pierce, who immediately began to consider methods to circumvent the decision so that he could continue to operate his company in Texas; the technicalities of the court decision gave him the opportunity he needed. By the trust agreement Waters–Pierce was Standard Oil's marketing agent in Texas, and the court decided against the company because Waters–Pierce was a party to a trust agreement and not because it was a trust operating in Texas. In 1900 Pierce enlisted the support of Joseph W. Bailey, soon to be a United States senator, who spoke to state officials, including the governor, the attorney general, and the secretary of state, most of whom were Bailey's political allies. Pierce then reorganized the company under the same name by purchasing from Standard Oil the shares that had been placed in the trust. Since the reorganized company was an independent corporation in compliance with the laws of the state, Waters–Pierce was given a new permit to do business without ever having been expelled. Public reaction to the Waters–Pierce reentry was not favorable, and Bailey's pending election to the Senate by the legislature was delayed while an investigating committee explored his connection to the case. The committee's recommendation in 1901 that Bailey be exonerated on the grounds that he had not acted improperly was approved with virtually no opposition. Bailey did not receive a fee for his efforts on behalf of Waters–Pierce; however, he failed to mention to the investigating committee that he received a personal loan of $13,300 from Pierce, a fact that eventually forced him out of office.

No direct activity regarding Waters–Pierce and Bailey flared up again until 1906, when the state of Missouri brought suit against Waters–Pierce, claiming that it was part of the Standard Oil trust. When Pierce admitted the charge while testifying in Missouri, public reaction in Texas was immediate. Bailey ran unopposed in the July 1906 Democratic primary for reelection to the Senate. The legislature voted to return him to the United States Senate on 20 January 1907, but also determined to investigate his relationship with Waters–Pierce in light of the Missouri disclosures. The investigation not only revealed Pierce's loan to Bailey but also that Bailey had received some very large fees working as an attorney for several companies and wealthy individuals. Although the legislature adopted a report in February 1907 that again exonerated him of all charges of wrongdoing, his political integrity was impaired, and he did not run again for the Senate in 1912. While Bailey's difficulties continued, Attorney General Robert V. Davidson's antitrust suit, initiated in 1906 against Waters–Pierce, was successful. The company was found guilty of violating the antitrust laws through its relationship to Standard Oil, its permit to do business in Texas was cancelled, and penalties of $1,623,000 were assessed. The decision was ultimately sustained by the United States Supreme Court, and in April 1909 Waters–Pierce paid more than $1,718,000 in fines and interest to the state of Texas. In 1909 the company's property in the state was sold for $1.4 million. The Waters–Pierce Case and the companion Bailey controversy symbolized for many Texas progressives the need for stronger regulation of corporations in the state and prepared the way for the reforms that occurred in Texas from 1906 to 1920.

Bob C. Holcomb

Waul, Thomas Neville. Confederate Army officer; b. Sumter District, South Carolina, 5 January 1813; d. Hunt County, 28 July 1903 (buried in Fort Worth); m. America Simmons (1837); ed. South Carolina College (3 years). By 1850 the Wauls had moved to Gonzales County, where he practiced law and raised cotton. Waul was appointed by the Secession Convention to the Provisional Congress of the Confederate States (1861). He ran for a seat in the Confederate Senate in November 1861 but was defeated. He then returned to Brenham and recruited Waul's Legion, for which he was commissioned colonel on May 17. He and his command were captured at the surrender of Vicksburg on 4 July 1863, but he was soon exchanged. He was promoted to brigadier general on 18 September 1863 and given command of the first brigade, formerly that of Brig. Gen. James M. Hawes, of Maj. Gen. John G. Walker's Texas Division, which he led during the Red River campaign of 1864. Afterward, Waul and his brigade were transferred to Arkansas, where, at the battle of Jenkins' Ferry on 30 April 1864, they helped to repulse federal major general Frederick Steele's attempted invasion of Texas and Waul was wounded in action. After the war Waul was elected to the state Constitutional Convention of 1866. Thereafter he practiced law in Galveston before retiring to his farm near Greenville in 1893.

Thomas W. Cutrer

Waxahachie, Texas. County seat of Ellis County, 30 miles south of Dallas. The name comes from an Indian word meaning "cow" or "buffalo" and is also the name of a local creek. Waxahachie was established as the seat of the new county in August 1850 on land donated by Emory W. Rogers, a pioneer settler. Rogers, J. D. Templeton, W. H. Getzendaner, B. F. Hawkins, and J. H. Spalding were among the first settlers in the community, which began with just over 100 residents and grew rapidly. In 1850 the first county courthouse was built and a general store and the post office opened. The community's first school of any consequence, Waxahachie Academy, was established in 1860 and operated for 37 years. The community's first bank began operation in 1868, and the first newspaper, the Waxahachie *Argus*, began publication in 1870. Waxahachie was incorporated in 1871 and adopted a mayor–alderman form of government. Four years later the state legislature granted a corporate charter to the investors in the Waxahachie Tap Railroad to construct and operate a rail line to Garrett, 12 miles east. The line was in operation in September 1879. By 1880 the population stood at 1,354. The following year the Waxahachie Tap was absorbed by the Houston and Texas Central Railway, which extended the line to Fort Worth. Six years later the Missouri, Kansas and Texas Railroad built through Waxahachie. By 1899 the city had over 100 businesses, including an electric light factory. The mule-drawn Waxahachie Street Railroad provided public transportation. The population reached 4,215 in 1900. In 1900–01 a cotton textile mill began operation; the finished plant used 4,000 bales of cotton a year to produce single-filling duck and toweling cloth. The plant doubled its capacity in 1907, but, like many of the plants constructed during the South's "cotton mill campaign" of the late nineteenth and early twentieth centuries, it eventually became unprofitable and closed down. Trinity University moved to Waxahachie from Tehuacana in 1902 and operated there until 1942. The Trinity and Brazos Valley Railway completed construction through Waxahachie in 1907. Five years later the completion of an electric interurban line from Dallas through Waxahachie to Waco further increased the town's transportation facilities. By 1920 Waxahachie had a population of 7,958 and 200 businesses. Local manufacturing plants in 1926 included cotton textile mills, a garment factory, a broom factory, and an ice and ice cream factory. When Trinity University left the town in 1942, its grounds were occupied the following year by the Southwestern Bible Institute, which later moved to Waxahachie from Enid, Oklahoma. This institution later changed its name to Southwestern Assemblies of God College and became coeducational. A branch of Navarro College is also located in Waxahachie. Although the population declined from its high of 15,720 in 1968 to 13,452 in 1977, the town became increasingly industrialized. A cottonseed oil mill, feed and poultry processing plants, and clothing, furniture, and fiberglass manufacturers all operated in the community. In 1990 Waxahachie had 18,168 residents. A yearly tour known as the Gingerbread Trail includes Victorian-style houses with gingerbread carpentry, the most popular architectural style, as well as combinations with Queen Ann's, Classic Renaissance, or Roman Doric revival. The red sandstone and granite Victorian courthouse, designed by James Riely Gordon and completed in 1897, graces the town's square. The Nicholas P. Sims Library (1905) and the octagonal Chautauqua Auditorium (1902) are examples of the 300 Waxahachie structures listed on the National Register of Historic Places. In the 1980s four movies were filmed in

Waxahachie. The town is home to the Ellis County Historical Museum and Gallery and also hosts the annual Scarborough Renaissance Faire and an annual Christmas parade and tour of homes. *Margaret L. Felty*

Wayland Baptist University. In Plainview; chartered in 1908 under the name Wayland Literary and Technical Institute. The name was changed to Wayland Baptist College in 1910 and to Wayland Baptist University in 1981. Dr. and Mrs. J. H. Wayland donated an initial gift of $10,000 and 25 acres of land on the condition that the Staked Plains Baptist Association (which proposed the college) and citizens of Plainview would raise an additional $40,000. Classes started in 1910 with 225 students from primary school to college level. After the public school system was well established, the elementary grades were discontinued, but college preparatory courses were offered until 1941. Wayland was admitted to membership in the American Association of Junior Colleges in 1926 and approved as a senior college by the Texas Department of Education in 1948. WU became one of the institutions supported by the Baptist General Convention of Texas in 1914. The BGCT elects the board of trustees. Except during periods of crisis, growth was gradual but steady in enrollment, physical plant, and academic standing. In 1951 Wayland was the first college in Texas to be integrated voluntarily. In addition to the main campus, Wayland conducts classes in Lubbock, Amarillo, Wichita Falls, San Antonio, Alaska, and Hawaii. Students may pursue bachelor's degrees; master's degrees are offered in education and business administration. The Museum of the Llano Estacado, on the campus, houses exhibits illustrating the development and the cultural heritage of the Panhandle–South Plains region. Wayland's athletic program has received wide-spread recognition and acclaim. *Florie Conway*

Weather. The location of Texas with relation to the North American continent, the warm Gulf of Mexico, and the not-far-distant Pacific Ocean guarantees a constant exchange of settled and unstable weather. The state's varied physiography, from the forests of the east and the Coastal Plain in the south to the elevated plateaus and basins in the north and west, also brings a wide variety of weather on almost any day of the year. Because of its expansive and topographically diverse nature, Texas offers continental, marine, and mountain-type climates. West of the Caprock escarpment, on the High Plains, a continental climate marked by cold winters and low humidity predominates. In the Trans-Pecos a form of mountain climate is found. The eastern two-thirds of Texas, on the other hand, has a humid, subtropical climate that is occasionally interrupted by intrusions of cold air from the north. Though variations in climate across Texas are considerable, they are nonetheless gradual.

Precipitation is not evenly distributed over the state, and variations at any one locale from year to year are apt to be pronounced. The mean annual precipitation varies from a statewide maximum of 59.20 inches at Orange, in the lower Sabine River valley of East Texas, to a minimum of 7.82 inches at El Paso, at the western tip of the state. The mean annual rainfall distribution correlates roughly with longitude and varies little from north to south across Texas. The Trans-Pecos is the driest region in the state, with an average annual regionwide precipitation of 11.65 inches, while the Upper Coast (45.93 inches) and East Texas (44.02 inches) are the wettest. At most locations rainfall for any single month will vary appreciably from the norm. Likewise, the number of days with precipitation usually is significantly abnormal. Moreover, the number of "rain days" follows the general trend of rainfall totals in that seasonal frequencies of rain days are lowest when rainfall totals are lowest. The mean number of days in January with at least .1 inch of precipitation varies from seven in East Texas to one or fewer in the Trans-Pecos; in July rain days normally are as numerous in the mountainous Trans-Pecos as in East Texas and along the upper coast. Particularly in the western half of Texas, one or two rainstorms often account for nearly all of a month's rainfall. The wet season does not occur at the same time of year in all parts of Texas. Intense and prolific thunderstorms, often moving in "squall lines," roam much of Texas in the late spring; Central, North, and East Texas receive their maximum rainfall in May. The warmest time of year is also the wettest for the High Plains and Trans-Pecos; nearly three-fourths of the total annual precipitation in these regions occurs from May to October. Tropical weather disturbances ensure that the late summer and early autumn are the two wettest periods for the part of Texas within 100 miles of the Gulf.

On the other hand, winter is the driest time of the year in nearly all of Texas. The exception is East Texas, where rainfall typically is the least substantial in July and August. December or January is normally the driest month on the High and Low Rolling Plains, as well as on the Edwards Plateau. The dry season peaks somewhat later farther east in north central and south central Texas, while on the Coastal Plain March is the driest month. Early spring is normally very dry in the Trans-Pecos; in fact, in this semiarid region, rainless spells often last several weeks at a time, and two or even three months can elapse without significant rain. Since much of the annual rainfall occurs quickly, excessive runoff often leads to flooding. The broad, flat valleys in the eastern half of Texas, where mean annual rainfall exceeds 25 to 30 inches, sustain comparatively slow runoff. When rain is heavy, these valleys store vast amounts of water before slowly releasing it into the streams. The resulting flat-crested, slow-moving flood in the lower basins causes protracted periods of inundation. By contrast, in the western half of Texas, where ground and tree cover is sparse and stream slopes are typically quite steep, high-intensity rains produce rapid runoff that frequently leads to flash flooding. The area along the Balcones Escarpment (from Austin south to San Antonio, then west to Del Rio) is one of the nation's three most flash-flood-prone regions.

Snowfall occurs at least once every winter in the northern half of Texas, although accumulations rarely are substantial except in the High Plains. Snow is not uncommon in the mountainous areas of the Trans-Pecos, though heavy snows (five inches or more) come only once every two or three winters. More often than not, snow falling in the southern half of the state melts rapidly; it stays on the ground only once or twice in every decade. Snowfall rarely is observed before early November and hardly ever occurs after mid-April. Where it is not uncommon, snow is almost always heaviest in either January or February. Mean seasonal snowfall is 15 to 18 inches in the Panhandle and 4 to 8 inches elsewhere in the High and Low Rolling Plains.

Temperatures vary considerably among the state's 10 climatic regions. Few areas escape freezing weather in a given winter. On the other hand, the heat of summer is intense everywhere.

Whereas precipitation varies longitudinally across Texas, mean annual temperature varies latitudinally. On a year-around basis, readings are the coolest in the extreme north and warmest in the far south. In mid-winter the mean daily minimum temperature varies between the upper teens in the northern periphery of the Panhandle and the low fifties in the lower Rio Grande valley; afternoon highs range from the upper forties in the extreme north to near seventy in the far south. Conversely, summer lows in the Panhandle average in the low sixties and, in the lower Valley, in the middle to upper seventies; daytime highs reach into the low nineties in both regions. All-time temperature extremes in Texas include: -23° F at Tulia (1899) and Seminole (1933) and 120° at Seymour (1936). Extended periods (more than one or two days) of subfreezing highs are rare, even in the far north. However, parts of the Panhandle generally have subfreezing temperatures for many successive winter nights. The mean number of days with freezing temperatures in the northern High Plains is 120. In this region the first autumn freeze ordinarily occurs at the end of October, and the last freeze in spring takes place in mid-April. The "freeze-free" season lengthens with distance north-to-south down the state. The mean number of days with freezes is 40 to 55 in north central Texas and 20 to 25 in south central Texas. In some years the temperature never reaches the freeze level in the Valley. Even when it does, it almost always remains below 32° F for only four to six hours or less, usually around sunrise.

Air-conditioning is desirable—indeed, now, a necessity—in all parts of Texas, as temperatures everywhere climb into the nineties numerous times in July and August. Only on Galveston Island and in the highest elevations of the Trans-Pecos do summer daytime temperatures normally fail to rise above the eighties. Nighttime readings in summer are comfortable in West Texas, where less humid air allows the temperature to drop abruptly into the sixties after sunset. In the eastern half of Texas, however, much more humid air prevents nighttime readings from dropping lower than the middle or low seventies. Heat is usually most intense in the basins of the upper Rio Grande (within and upstream from Big Bend National Park) and in the upper Red River valley, where daytime highs in summer often soar well above 100° F. Triple-digit highs are also very common in South Texas from mid-May until late September.

All of the Texas coastline is subject to the threat of hurricanes and lesser tropical storms during the summer and autumn. Vulnerability reaches a maximum during August and September, the height of the hurricane season in the Gulf of Mexico and Caribbean Sea. Hurricanes strike the Texas coast an average of one every three years. Inland, hurricanes cause damage due to high winds, including tornadoes, and flooding from excessive rainfall. Persons along the coast must also contend with storm tides. Although tornadoes can occur anytime, most of them materialize during April, May, and June. In a normal year, about 130 are sighted in Texas, 30 percent of which occur in May. On average, about 200 people are hurt and a dozen are killed annually by the twisters. Tornadoes are most likely to occur along and south of the Red River between Lubbock and Dallas; they are least likely in the Trans-Pecos. Thunderstorms occur in every month of the year, though least in winter. With an average of 60 thunderstorm days a year, East Texas is most susceptible to the severe localized phenomena fostered by the storm (hail, high winds, flash flooding). The mean annual number of thunder-

storm days diminishes from east to west across Texas; the Trans-Pecos has only about 40 such days each year. The lower Valley has fewer still (30). The peak hail frequency statewide is in May. Most hailstorms are short-lived, however, since the macroscale weather systems (such as squall lines) that generate hail move rapidly. Hailstones are usually largest in the High Plains, where hail the size of tennis balls—even baseballs—is not uncommon in the summer. Sunshine is most abundant in the extreme west, where El Paso receives an average of 80 percent of the total possible sunshine annually. Cloud cover is most prevalent along the coast, especially in the Upper Coast, where the mean annual sunshine amounts to only about 60 percent of possible.

The voluminous records kept by Spanish Texas officials mentioned the weather directly; however, through the years various other sources—diaries, travel accounts, correspondence, newspapers, and medical records of military posts—reveal that the weather in Texas was of concern to early explorers, missionaries, dignitaries, Anglo-American colonists, other immigrants, and temporary residents. By 1855 Texas had 21 weather stations reporting data that were published. The stations decreased in number during the Civil War, and by 9 February 1870, when federal weather service officially began, Texas had 14 weather stations at scattered settlements and military posts. Congress passed an act in 1890 transferring all meteorological services formerly carried on by the army signal corps to a newly constituted weather bureau under the secretary of agriculture, effective July 1, 1891. Texas had 78 stations in 1890 and 112 in 1900; the number of stations continued to increase until by the early 1970s there were about a thousand weather observers around the state, mostly citizen volunteers reporting to the federal government, in addition to 41 major stations and offices operated by the federal weather bureau (which in 1971 became a part of the National Oceanic and Atmospheric Administration). In addition, the United States Air Force air-weather service maintained stations at military installations in Texas. By 1995 the number of stations had been reduced to ten. Offices were maintained at El Paso, Brownsville, San Angelo, Midland, Amarillo, Lubbock, Corpus Christi, New Braunfels, Houston, and Dallas. *George W. Bomar*

Weatherford College. In Weatherford; the oldest junior college in the state; founded by the Phoenix Masonic Lodge, which in 1869 received a charter to establish a Masonic Institute. Classes were not held until two or three years later. In 1884 the school's name was changed to Cleveland College in honor of Grover Cleveland. Five years later the Central Texas Conference of the Methodist Episcopal Church, South, moved Granbury College, which had originally opened in 1873 as a private elementary and high school and had been under the conference's authority since 1880, to Weatherford and combined the two institutions as Weatherford College. President David S. Switzer guided the institution through the first decade under its new name. The average yearly enrollment was about 300, and the school offered classes from grade school through the fourth year of college. Switzer left Weatherford in 1902 to establish his own college, and from 1903 to 1921 the school operated intermittently; it even served briefly as an academy. In 1921 the institution was reorganized as a junior college. Weatherford Junior College was accredited by the Texas Association of Colleges and acquired a sound financial foundation through grants from the estates of J. R. Couts and Edward D. Farmer of Weatherford. In 1944

Walter Prescott Webb at a barbecue. Photograph by Russell Lee. Wimberley, ca. 1957. Russell Lee Photograph Collection, CAH; CN 03948.

Southwestern University took over operation of Weatherford as a branch institution, with the understanding that if Southwestern should discontinue the relationship, the college's facilities would then be offered to the city of Weatherford or to Parker County for the purpose of operating a public junior college. In 1949 Southwestern transferred the college to the county, and the school officially became Weatherford College of the Parker County Junior College District. In 1966 the college district purchased 90 acres and built a new campus. In 1975 the school added the Education Center facility at Mineral Wells, on property acquired from Fort Wolters. By the mid-1980s Weatherford College had extension centers in Bridgeport, Decatur, Granbury, and Jacksboro.   *David Minor*

Webb, Walter Prescott. Historian; b. Panola County, 3 April 1888; d. near Austin, 8 March 1963 (buried in the State Cemetery); m. Jane Elizabeth Oliphant (1916; d. 1960); 1 daughter; m. Terrell Maverick (1961); ed. University of Texas (B.A., 1915; M.A., 1920; Ph.D., 1932). After earning a teaching certificate in Ranger he taught at various small Texas schools and, with the assistance of his benefactor, William Hinds, eventually entered the University of Texas. He was teaching at Main High School in San Antonio in 1918, when he was invited to join the history faculty of the University of Texas. After an unsuccessful year of "educational outbreeding" at the University of Chicago, he returned to Texas determined to write history as he saw it. The result was the publication in 1931 of *The Great Plains*, acclaimed as "a new interpretation of the American West," acknowledged by the Social Science Research Council in 1939 as the outstanding contribution to American history since World War I, and winner of Columbia University's Loubat prize. In 1939, after a year as Harkness Lecturer at the University of London, Webb

became director of the Texas State Historical Association. During his tenure (to 1946), he expanded the *Southwestern Historical Quarterly* and launched a project to compile the *Handbook of Texas* (1952). With the assistance of H. Bailey Carroll, he established the Junior Historians of Texas (1940). He returned to England in 1942 as Harmsworth Professor of American History at Oxford. At the University of Texas he became famous for his books and seminars, especially those on the Great Plains and the Great Frontier, in which he developed two major historical concepts. He proposed in the Great Plains thesis that the westward settlement of the United States had been momentarily stalled at the ninety-eighth meridian, an institutional fault line separating the wooded environment to the east from the arid environment of the west. The pioneers were forced to pause in their westward trek while technological innovation in the form of the six-shooter, barbed wire, and the windmills allowed them to proceed. The Great Frontier thesis became the crux of a book of the same title, published in 1952, that Webb declared to be his most intellectual and thought-provoking. *The Great Frontier* proposed a "boom hypothesis": the new lands discovered by Columbus and other explorers in the late fifteenth century precipitated the rise of great wealth and new institutions such as democracy and capitalism. By 1900, however, the new lands disappeared, the frontier closed, and institutions were under stress, resulting in the ecological and economic problems that plagued the twentieth century. Although not universally well received at the time, the Great Frontier thesis became the sole topic of the Second International Congress of Historians of the United States and Mexico at its 1958 meeting, and the concept was again an object of discussion at an international symposium in 1972.

Webb wrote or edited more than 20 books. In 1935 he published *The Texas Rangers: A Century of Frontier Defense*, the definitive study of this frontier law enforcement agency, but regarded by Webb as being filled with "deadening facts." *Divided We Stand: The Crisis of a Frontierless Democracy* (1937) analyzed the practices of modern corporations, which Webb contended promoted economic sectionalism to the disadvantage of the South. *More Water for Texas: The Problem and the Plan* (1954) reflected his interest in the conservation of natural resources. A collection, *An Honest Preface and Other Essays*, appeared in 1959, and at the time of his death he was working on a television series on American civilization under a grant from the Ford Foundation. Webb was a charter member and later a fellow of the Texas Institute of Letters. He was also a member of the Philosophical Society of Texas and president of the Mississippi Valley Historical Association (1954–55) and the American Historical Association (1958). He received honorary degrees from the University of Chicago, Southern Methodist University, and Oxford University. He held two Guggenheim fellowships, acted as special advisor to Senator Lyndon Johnson on water needs of the South and West, and received an award from the American Council of Learned Societies for distinguished service to scholarship. The United States Bureau of Reclamation also gave him an award for distinguished service to conservation. He was killed in an automobile accident, and Governor Connally decreed that he should be buried in the State Cemetery. A statue of Webb and his old friends J. Frank Dobie and Roy Bedichek stands in Zilker Park, Austin. Webb's second wife was the widow of F. Maury Maverick of San Antonio.   *Necah Stewart Furman*

Wells, James Babbage, Jr. South Texas political boss; b. St. Joseph Island, 12 July 1850; d. Brownsville, 21 December 1923; m. Pauline Kleiber (1880); 4 children; ed. University of Virginia law school (grad 1875). In 1878 Wells formed a law partnership with Stephen Powers and settled at Brownsville. As one of the cofounders of the Democratic Blue Club of Cameron County, Powers excelled at political organization. Wells married his mentor's niece, who later became head of the Texas Association Opposed to Woman Suffrage. By his marriage Wells joined the inner circle of Democratic elite families. He also became Catholic. After Powers's death (1882), Wells consolidated his control over the Cameron County Blue Club and eventually extended his influence over the Democratic organizations of Hidalgo, Starr, and Duval counties. In each of these counties he oversaw the rise of bosses who ran their own local machines but who acknowledged Wells's leadership on regional, state, and national questions. The Brownsville attorney was the central figure in South Texas politics from the mid-1880s through the first decade of the twentieth century and continued to exercise power as the Cameron County Democratic chairman until 1920. Throughout his long career, however, he held public office (city attorney and state district judge) for only two brief periods. Although corruption and violence often tarnished the image of Democratic rule in South Texas, the key to Wells's political success was the satisfaction of constituent needs. For the influential ranchers of the valley, Wells defended sometimes suspect land claims, arranged low property-tax valuations, and lobbied for the deployment of Texas Rangers and federal troops to provide protection against cattle rustling and border raids. He relied on the ranchers to mobilize their Hispanic workers and tenants for elections, but his ties with the Mexican-American majority were not just secondhand. He welcomed the participation of prominent Mexican ranchers and businessmen in his political organization and local government, and he provided modest, informal welfare support for some of his loyal but impoverished constituents—in the tradition of the Mexican patrón and big city boss. In this he epitomized the contemporary style of Caucasian relations with Hispanic Texans. Ranchers and border-town businessmen also benefited from Wells's efforts to promote the extension of railroad construction to the lower Rio Grande valley. The resulting boom in irrigation and vegetable and fruit farming not only transformed the regional economy and attracted thousands of new settlers but ultimately proved to be Wells's political and economic undoing. Exhibiting both a progressive commitment to honest, efficient government and an aversion to Hispanic participation in politics, the new settlers eventually turned against Democratic boss rule, and Wells's machine collapsed in 1920. He also lost thousands of dollars in ill-conceived land speculation and development schemes and fell heavily into debt.

At the state level, he participated in a coalition of conservative Democrats, headed by Edward Mandell House, that dominated Texas politics between the fall of the Populist revolt in the mid-1890s and the renewal of reform under the leadership of Governor Tom Campbell in 1907. From 1900 through 1904 Wells served as the chairman of the state Democratic party, and in 1901 he even conducted an unannounced campaign for the governorship until he realized that the House faction favored another candidate. Although the conservative wing of the party revived after the end of Campbell's administration in 1911, Wells never reclaimed his past level of statewide influence. The Cameron County boss indirectly influenced national politics as well by shepherding the early congressional career of John Nance Garner, whose original district included the Valley. Despite his political astuteness and record of accomplishment, Wells could not survive the changing demographic structure in the region, the rising tide of racial animosity between Caucasians and Hispanics following the Mexican border raids of 1915 and 1916, and his loss of favor at the state level. Jim Wells County is named in his honor.

Evan Anders

Wends. A Slavic people concentrated in East Germany near Bautzen and Cottbus in the upper Spree River valley, an area long known as Lusatia; also known as Sorbs or Lusatian Serbs. They speak Sorbian, which is divided into two dialects, Upper Sorbian and Lower Sorbian. The language was originally written with Gothic letters, although since 1937 the Latin alphabet has been used. Wends have never had an independent nation, and their homeland has always been surrounded by Germans. During the Middle Ages the Wends survived the raids and massacres of German Eastland horsemen; especially during the Nazi years they were pressured to assimilate the German culture, and gradually they have adopted the German language and many customs, although they still retain a separate identity. In 1840, before overseas migration began, there were about 164,000 Wends in Lusatia. In the 1980s there were only 60,000. Outside Germany, most of the Wends settled in two areas, Australia and Texas. The desire for better economic opportunity was probably the main reason for Wendish immigration to these two places. Although scholars dispute the role of social and religious factors in the process, Texas Wends commonly express the belief that their forefathers came here solely for religious freedom. Around 1848 small groups of Wends began immigrating to Australia, where many Germans had already settled. These pioneers sent letters home, many of which were published in local newspapers, and which influenced Wends still in Europe. A small group of Wends moved to Austin County around 1849–50 and were quickly absorbed by the Germans of the vicinity. In 1853 a group of 35 Wends left Bremen for Texas. They were shipwrecked off the coast of Cuba, but eventually made their way to Galveston, and from there to the communities of New Ulm and Industry.

In the fall of 1854 a newly established congregation of nearly 600 conservative Lutheran Wends, led by John Kilian, left Germany to join their countrymen in Texas. The group constituted the only mass exodus of Wends. Traveling first by railway and steamship to Liverpool, England, the Wends embarked on an English ship, the *Ben Nevis*, for the journey to Texas. While in Liverpool, however, a number of Wends contracted cholera, and 73 of them died on board the ship. After a three-week stop in Queenstown, Ireland, to remove the sick and fumigate the ship, the *Ben Nevis* sailed for Galveston, where it arrived on 15 December 1854. Galveston was caught in a yellow fever epidemic. In December and January the Wends walked the 85 miles to New Ulm and Industry. Two lay leaders of the congregation, Johann Dube and Carl Lehmann, went ahead 30 miles and purchased a league of land in what is now Lee County. At first services were held in one room of Kilian's two-room house, but the group set aside 95 acres for a church and school, later called St. Paul's. This was the first Missouri Synod Lutheran church founded in Texas and is thus the mother church not only of the Wends, but of all conservative Lutherans in Texas. After their first tiny log church was built, individuals purchased farm acreage and town lots, built crude dugout houses for shelter, and established what became the community of Serbin. In 1860 Serbin had a post office. After 1871, however, a new railroad connection made nearby Giddings the business and commercial center of the region, and Serbin declined in both population and influence.

Over the years, due to religious dissension and economic pressures, the Wends spread throughout south central Texas. Today the leading Wendish centers are in Lee, Fayette, Williamson, Coryell, and Bell counties, especially in the towns of Serbin, Warda, Giddings, Fedor, Manheim, Loebau, Lincoln, Winchester, La Grange, Thorndale, Walburg, Copperas Cove, The Grove, Vernon, Swiss Alp, New Ulm, Industry, Noack, and Aleman. Substantial numbers of people of Wendish descent also live in Houston, Austin, and Port Arthur.

While most Wends consider themselves Germans, they have maintained an ethnic identity. Early restrictions against inter-marriage have relaxed over the years. Nevertheless, many individuals still claim there have been no intermarriages in their families since the arrival of the *Ben Nevis*. Early Wends practiced many distinctive customs, of which perhaps the most noticeable to outsiders was Wendish brides' adoption of the German Lutheran custom of wearing black wedding dresses to represent the grief and hardship of marriage. This custom died out by the 1890s. Religious conservatism militated against wearing bright colors, dancing, secular singing, or any other kind of frivolity. The Wends valued education, and today St. Paul's still has an accredited parochial school. Church congregations regularly paid for the higher education of promising young men who wanted to become pastors or teachers. Concordia University at Austin has traditionally received considerable Wendish support.

The proximity of German neighbors eventually resulted in cultural assimilation and adaptation. At the time of their migration, most of the Wends spoke Wendish and German, and those who spoke only Wendish learned German after they moved to Texas. Most of the Wends in Serbin and all of the Wends who settled elsewhere had adopted German as their primary language by World War I. The shift from Wendish to German is documented in the Giddings *Deutsches Volksblatt*, the principal German-language paper in the area. The newspaper, although largely written in German, also carried articles and letters in Wendish. By the 1930s the language had begun to die out in Texas, and few people remained who were still fluent in it. In the 1980s only a few people could still speak the language. In rural Wendish areas German continued to be used for church services until after World War II, but today it has also largely died out. The Texas Wendish Heritage Society, founded in 1971, seeks to preserve and, whenever possible, revive remnants of the Wendish culture. One project involves an attempt to translate and publish all early Wendish documents. The society, which had about 350 members in 1994, maintains a Wendish museum at Serbin and annually participates in the Folklife Festival of the University of Texas Institute of Texan Cultures at San Antonio. The art of Easter egg painting has been maintained as a Wendish tradition. Wendish Fest, an annual festival held at Serbin in September, celebrates the Wendish heritage of the area.   *Sylvia Grider*

Weslaco, Texas. Fifteen miles west of Harlingen in south central Hidalgo County. The site was part of the Llano Grande grant to

Juan José Ynojosa de Ballí (1790). In 1904 the Hidalgo and San Miguel extension of the St. Louis, Brownsville and Mexico Railway reached the site, promoted by Uriah Lott, Lon C. Hill, Jr., and others interested in developing the area through farming. The American Rio Grande Land and Irrigation Company of neighboring Mercedes, which had interest in the railroad, purchased a major portion of the Llano Grande grant and platted the West Tract in 1913. In an effort to control raids from Mexico, the United States government stationed troops along the Rio Grande in 1916 and established a camp at the Llano Grande railroad depot, located between Mercedes and the site of Weslaco. The guardsmen erected a watchtower at Progreso. In 1917 the irrigation company sold 30,000 acres to the W. E. Stewart Land Company, from which the name Weslaco is derived. The Stewart Company sold the townsite to Ed C. Couch, Dan R. Couch, R. C. Couch, and R. L. Reeves. The site was surveyed and platted in 1919 by H. E. Bennet, a civil engineer hired by Ed Couch and Reeves. A post office, the chamber of commerce, the Guaranty State Bank, a newspaper, and the Community House were all established in 1920. Electricity came in December 1920 from the Donna Light and Ice Company. In 1921 the Weslaco ISD was established, the first high school opened, and the Texas Rangers opened a Weslaco station. The Valley Experiment Station was established in 1923 under the auspices of Texas A&M. It was later renamed Texas A&M University Agricultural Research Center. A municipal ordinance of 1921 provided that the land north of the railroad tracks be designated for industry and Hispanic residences and businesses. The area to the south of the tracks was reserved for Anglo residences and businesses. Weslaco therefore developed as two towns. "El pueblo americano" the Anglo side, consisted of well-built frame houses; it had paved streets and enclosed sewers. The Mexican side featured corrugated tin shacks, unpaved roads, and outhouses. Streets north of the tracks had Spanish names, business was conducted in Spanish, and schools were established for Mexican children. In the 1928 county election the Weslaco ballot box was rejected by Judge A. W. Cameron, an incumbent official whose victory was in question. Cameron, who evidently believed that he would have won the Hispanic vote of Weslaco, testified that Mexican-American voters had been intimidated by a crowd yelling "Don't let those Mexicans in to vote. Throw them out." The protesters were allegedly led by the Citizens Republican Committee.

Construction of a railroad depot in 1927 attracted canning plants, dehydrating plants, and a box factory to Weslaco. A ground-level water reservoir was constructed in 1928. The first Weslaco "Birthday Party" was held in December 1929 and included a parade and style show. By 1930 the town's population had reached 5,300. In 1936 civic plans required all buildings in the business section to be remodeled with Spanish colonial architecture; neon lights were used to outline the new façades. In 1936 the Gibson Trailer Campground opened; at the time it was the only municipal campground for tourists in the lower Rio Grande valley. In 1939 the United States Farm Security Administration established a camp north of town on what is now Highway 83. The $250,000 camp, the first of its kind in Texas built expressly for the purpose of housing migrant farmworkers, became known as Weslaco North. The United States Fruit and Vegetable Products Laboratory conducted an experimental tract near the city. The Weslaco Citrus Growers Association was organized in 1940. The Texas A&I Citrus Center opened in 1948; experiments there yielded popular varieties of grapefruit. In 1950 the population of Weslaco was 6,883. An international bridge at the Progreso crossing south of Weslaco opened on 11 November 1954. Weslaco schools were officially integrated in 1961. Hurricane Beulah caused $100,000 in damage to the city when it struck the Valley in 1967. The town continued to be a centrally located citrus and vegetable marketing and processing center through the 1990s. Its industries centered on agricultural businesses, with some cattle feeding and clothing manufacturing. In 1970 the population was 15,313. The migrant "camp" was renamed Northside Apartments in the early 1990s, when it comprised 289 units. Weslaco's population was 21,877 in 1992, by which time the city was part of a complex metropolitan area along U.S. Highway 83. Weslaco is surrounded by many colonias, including Sun Country Estates, Expressway Heights, Sunrise, and Sunrise Hill. *Alicia A. Garza*

West, Emily D. Called the "Yellow Rose of Texas" by twentieth-century mythmakers; also erroneously called Emily Morgan by those who presumed her a slave of James Morgan; b. free in New Haven, Connecticut. In 1835 she signed a contract to work a year for James Morgan in Texas, where she arrived on the same vessel as Emily de Zavala and her children. On 16 April 1836 in New Washington she was seized by Mexican troops. General Santa Anna arrived the next day, and after three days of resting and looting warehouses, he ordered the buildings set afire and departed to challenge Sam Houston's army, which was encamped about 10 miles away on Buffalo Bayou. Emily, doubtless already a rape victim, was forced to accompany the Mexican army. With regard to the Yellow Rose legend, she may have been in Santa Anna's tent when the Texans charged the Mexican camp on 21 April, but it was not by choice. She could not have known Houston's plans, nor could she have intentionally delayed Santa Anna. Moreover, in their official reports after returning to Mexico, none of the dictator's disaffected officers mentioned the presence of a woman or even that *el presidente* was in a state of undress. After the battle Emily found refuge with Isaac N. Moreland, an artillery officer, who later made his home in Houston and served as county judge. Strangers assumed Emily was James Morgan's slave because she was black. A story was told around campfires and in barrooms that Emily had helped defeat the Mexican army by a dalliance with Santa Anna, but there is almost no evidence for this. William Bollaert's diary (1956) records a chance rumor heard in 1842 as an editorial footnote with Bollaert's name attached, a fact that led readers to believe the note was a footnote in the original manuscript. The editor's 1956 footnote launched a prurient interest on the part of two amateur historians—Francis X. Tolbert and Henderson Shuffler—who concocted the modern fiction. By then, a popular Mitch Miller song was celebrating the "Yellow Rose." Shuffler added other fictions, including that Emily's story was "widely known and often retold . . . in the 1840s." He suggested that a stone might be placed at the San Jacinto battleground "In Honor of Emily Who Gave Her All for Texas Piece by Piece." In 1976 English professor Martha Anne Turner published *The Yellow Rose of Texas: Her Saga and Her Song*, in which she credits Shuffler and adds even more undocumented details. Thus the story was full-blown for the journalistic frenzy of the Texas Sesquicentennial in 1986. The real Emily West remained in Texas until early 1837, when she asked for and received a passport allowing her to return home. Moreland wrote a note to the secretary of state saying that he had met Emily in April 1836, that she was a 36-yearold free woman who had lost her "free" papers at the battleground. She stated that she came from New York in September 1835 with Colonel Morgan and was anxious to return home. Although there is no date on the application housed in the Texas State Archives, Mrs. Lorenzo de Zavala, by then a widow, was planning to return to New York on board Morgan's schooner in March, and it seems possible that Morgan arranged passage aboard for Emily. *Margaret Swett Henson*

Western Publications, Incorporated. An Austin firm responsible for several widely read magazines dealing primarily with facets of Western Americana. The company grew out of the Sportsman Publishing Company of Austin, which initially began publication in Texas with *Western Sportsman* magazine in 1947, revived from the 1937 Colorado publication of the same name. Owner Joe Austell Small bought *Western Sportsman* during World War II, began the publishing firm, and founded many of its magazines, including *True West* (1953–), *Wanderlust* (1960), *Old West* (1964–), *Relics* (1967–), *Gold!* (1969–), which was about tales of treasure in the old West, *Badman* (1971–), and *Horse Tales* (1972–). In 1955 he purchased *Frontier Times*, which had been published by J. Marvin Hunter since 1923. Most of the stories printed in Western Publications magazines were presented as true accounts. In 1953 the company name was temporarily changed to True West Publishing Company. Small wrote lengthy editorials for many of the magazines, but Pat Wagner was listed as editor for most of the magazines. Western Publications was sold in September 1979 to Chet Krause and Krause Publications, an Iola, Wisconsin, firm, but retained editorial offices in Austin until 1982. It was sold to Bob Evans Publications in February 1984 and moved to Perkins, Oklahoma. Small was publisher emeritus and retained an address in Austin. By the late 1980s Western Publications was headquartered in Stillwater, Oklahoma, and continued to publish magazines dealing with Western Americana. *W. W. Bennett*

Western Trail. Also known as the Dodge City Trail and the Fort Griffin Trail; blazed in 1874 by cattle-drover John T. Lytle, who herded 3,500 longhorn cattle along the leading edge of the frontier from South Texas to the Red Cloud Indian Agency at Fort Robinson, Nebraska. Following the defeat of the Plains Indians in the Red River Indian War, Lytle's route supplanted the farmer-clogged Chisholm Trail to the east. By 1879 the Western Trail was the principal thoroughfare for Texas cattle bound for northern markets. Feeder routes such as the Matamoros Trail (from Brownsville) and the Old Trail (from Castroville) converged in Kerrville to form the Western Trail. The trail proceeded northward, crossing the James River near the site of present Noxville, the Llano at Beef Trail Crossing, the San Saba at Pegleg Crossing, and Brady Creek west of Brady. It left the Hill Country through Cow Gap, where minor feeder trails from Mason, San Saba, and Lampasas counties converged. It crossed the Colorado River at Waldrip and passed through Coleman, where a trail from Trickham and one of two feeders from Tom Green County merged with the trunk route. Beyond Coleman, the Western Trail fanned out to take advantage of grassy prairies; branches passed through the sites of present Baird, Clyde, and Putnam and reunited at Albany, where the Potter and Bacon

Trail (or Potter–Blocker Trail) diverged toward the Llano Estacado and Colorado pastures. The Western Trail crossed the Clear Fork of the Brazos near Fort Griffin, where the second feeder trail from Tom Green County, which ran through Buffalo Gap, joined the trunk route. Thence the Western Trail proceeded through Throckmorton, crossed the Brazos at Seymour and the Pease at the site of Vernon, and veered northeastward to leave Texas at what later became known as Doan's Crossing, on the Prairie Dog Town Fork of the Red River. Several alternative routes crossed Indian Territory to Dodge City, Kansas, on the Santa Fe Railroad, the first and most important terminus of the trail; to Ogallala, Nebraska, on the Union Pacific, the principal alternative for rail shipment; and to northern ranges. Some herds were delivered to Indian reservations on the northern plains. Several factors such as barbed wire, the introduction of meatier cattle breeds, and the settlement of the frontier contributed to the demise of the Western Trail, but a principal cause was the Texas fever controversy. The last reported drive on the Western Trail was made in 1893 by John Rufus Blocker to Deadwood, South Dakota. By then, three to five million cattle had been driven to northern pastures and markets along the route.

Jimmy M. Skaggs

West Texas A&M University. In Canyon; originally West Texas State Normal College, one of seven state-supported teachers' colleges of Texas; established 1910. Robert B. Cousins, president from 1910 to 1918, was followed in office by Joseph A. Hill, who served until 1948. In 1914 the administration building burned. In 1919 the school granted its first four-year degrees. It was admitted to the American Association of Teachers Colleges in 1922, to the Association of Texas Colleges in 1923, and to the Southern Association of Colleges and Secondary Schools in 1925. In 1923 it was renamed West Texas State Teachers College. In 1932 it was the first institution of higher learning in West Texas to offer graduate training. In 1932–33 the Panhandle–Plains Historical Society built its museum, Pioneer Hall, on the campus. In 1942 Mr. and Mrs. Allen Early gave to the college a building in Amarillo, and the Amarillo Center of the college began to offer adult education classes there. Annual enrollment averaged 1,000. The institution was renamed West Texas State College in 1949. The school received authorization from the Texas legislature in 1963 to reorganize and change its name to West Texas State University. Administrative reorganization included the college of arts and sciences with three divisions (humanities, social sciences, and science); the school of business; the school of teacher education; and the graduate school. At this time a marked expansion began on the physical plant, curriculum and program development, enrollment, and faculty, along with an increased emphasis on research, which brought about the construction of the Kilgore Research Center's first unit and cooperative research agreements with several agencies, including the National Science Foundation. In the 1990s the Kilgore Center housed the Alternative Energy Institute, which studied alternative energy sources. Of the major buildings on campus, 20 were constructed or greatly modified between 1950 and 1965. In 1990 the university joined the Texas A&M University System and in 1992 was given its present name. It offered 50 undergraduate programs and 44 graduate programs.

Nancy Beck Young

West Texas Chamber of Commerce. Founded in Fort Worth in December 1918, when representatives of some 25 counties and of 4 city chambers of commerce attended a meeting called by Dr. C. C. Gumm; the purpose was to promote West Texas. The first regional convention was held in Mineral Wells in 1919 under the presidency of C. T. Herring of Amarillo. The chamber worked for the establishment of Texas Tech, for redistricting of Texas to give West Texas more nearly proportional representation in the state legislature, and for protection of West Texas water rights. In 1922 the organization was expanded to bring in the eastern counties of New Mexico; in 1928 the San Antonio district withdrew to go into the South Texas Chamber of Commerce. In 1929 the organization was divided into 10 regions, with a regional director in each division, all subordinated to the main headquarters. Stamford was headquarters from 1918 to 1937, when the offices were moved to Abilene. The official publication of the chamber, *West Texas Today*, was published as a quarterly from 1918 to 1922, when it became a monthly. In the late 1980s the West Texas Chamber of Commerce and the other regional chambers of commerce were merged into the Texas Chamber of Commerce in Austin.

West Texas Historical Association. Organized at the Taylor County Courthouse in Abilene (1924); proposed by Royston Campbell Crane, Sr., a Sweetwater lawyer and the son of a president of Baylor University. The call for the organizational meeting was signed by Crane and six residents of Abilene, including Rupert N. Richardson and William C. Holden. The purpose of the organization is to promote the investigation, study, and preservation of the history of West Texas. In 1929 the association applied for and received a state charter of incorporation for 50 years. The association held its first annual program meeting in Cisco in 1925, and soon thereafter published the first volume of the West Texas Historical Association *Year Book*, which still appears annually and has grown to be an invaluable source of information about West Texas. Although the WTHA has never attempted to define the geographic bounds of West Texas, it has maintained its headquarters on the campus of Hardin–Simmons University. Many of its annual meetings have been in Abilene; others have ranged as far as Alpine, Lubbock, and Weatherford.

Ernest Wallace

West Texas State School. In Pyote; formerly West Texas Children's Home of Pyote. In 1958 the 697th Air Control and Warning Squadron began operations at the site of the old Pyote Air Base on University of Texas land. When that radar base closed in 1963, the Texas Youth Council began work on a children's home to be founded on the location, using existing buildings. In 1965 the Texas legislature appropriated $200,000 for renovation and purchase of equipment to found the institution. West Texas Children's Home of Pyote opened for dependent and neglected children in 1966. In the early 1980s the home changed from an orphanage to a state school for male status offenders. The name was changed to West Texas State School in 1990. The facility consists now of brick buildings with dormitory space and recreational facilities for 192 students. High school classrooms are maintained throughout the year on the campus to allow students the opportunity to earn GEDs.

Julia Cauble Smith

Whig Party. Achieved moderate success in Texas in the mid-nineteenth century. Personality dominated politics in the Republic of Texas. Sam Houston was dominant, and political groups were usually his foes or supporters. While the image and legend of Houston and other famous leaders like Andrew Jackson continued to bind political partisans, annexation brought more complex political parties to the state, as new immigrants from the United States brought their political loyalties with them. By the time of the presidential election of 1848 the rising number of immigrants had established the Whig party in Texas. The Whigs began their political career in the state with several handicaps. Sam Houston, previously a supporter of Democrat Andrew Jackson, reestablished his ties to the Democratic party. Even worse was the Whigs' long-running opposition to annexation. Whigs also had often opposed the Mexican War, which had widespread support in Texas, and the Whig candidate for president, Gen. Zachary Taylor, had earned the enmity of many Texans during the war. Despite these handicaps the Whigs held a state convention, selected a slate of presidential electors, and organized "Rough and Ready" clubs in several Texas towns. Whig newspapers were established, and party spokesmen toured the state. Taylor and Millard Fillmore, the party candidates, wound up with 31 percent of the statewide vote. They were strongest in Northeast Texas and along the coast. By 1851 Whig candidates were running for state and local offices. William B. Ochiltree was also a candidate for Congress from the eastern district that year. Though Ochiltree and the Whigs running for state office lost, in some counties, such as Harrison County, the Whigs had modest success. In the 1852 presidential election the Whigs again suffered from having a candidate generally unpopular in Texas. Texas Whigs had supported Millard Fillmore in the national convention and were disappointed when Winfield Scott received the nomination. General Scott was closely linked to the antislavery wing of the party and was roundly criticized in the Democratic newspapers of the state. Again the Texas party carried on an organized campaign led by their presidential electors and editorial spokesmen. Voter interest was low in 1852, and the Whigs garnered only 26 percent of a meager turnout. They failed to carry a single county. Bitter national debates over the slavery issue caused a rift between proslavery and antislavery Whigs and soon brought about the demise of the party in Texas. Unable to organize on a national level, the Texas Whigs drifted into other political groups. In 1853 Ochiltree drew some votes for governor, but by 1855 the Whig party was dead in Texas.

Whigs generally came from urban counties with strong interests in commerce and improved transportation. The largest slaveholders in other Southern states were likely to be Whigs, but this was less true in Texas. Conservative Unionists, however, were strongly inclined to belong to the party. The party stressed a reverential regard for the nation and a pragmatic concern for improving business conditions. It also opposed the Democrats. Many immigrants to Texas in the period of 1848 to 1854 had long opposed the Democratic party. They habitually voted for the Whigs and, despite the unpopularity of their candidates in 1848 and 1852, could not bring themselves to vote for a Democrat. The inability of the Whigs to find a strong leader around whom to rally and their inability to win elections cost them dearly. Ultimately, the Whigs' Unionist ideology, which was perhaps their greatest strength, was compromised by the debate over slavery. For Texas Whigs, slavery was a legal right to be maintained in the Union, and anyone who agitated against it not only disregarded the law but threatened the Union. Texas Whigs considered slavery a subject that should be buried because it raised tempers and held the portent of a civil war. When the Northern wing of the party refused to bury the slavery issue, the nature of the Texas Whigs' unionism and their belief in the legality and necessity of slavery compelled them to abandon their party. Over the course of the 1850s and early 1860s prominent Whigs like Ochiltree, James W. Throckmorton, and Benjamin H. Epperson searched for another party that could defeat the Democrats and achieve their purposes. They had some degree of success in the state elections of 1859, but they lost badly in their struggle to keep Texas from seceding in 1861. *Walter L. Buenger*

Whip-handle Dispatch. Letters sent from Matamoros to Texas in 1836, hidden in a hollow whip handle. The letters were written by Henry Teal and Henry W. Karnes, Texas commissioners to Mexico, by William Parsons Miller, who had been captured at Copano, and by William Howell, a Pennsylvania wool buyer resident in Matamoros. Reuben M. Potter copied Karnes's letter to make it more legible. The dispatch bore information warning the Texans that a large number of Mexican troops might possibly invade Texas in the summer of 1836. The unidentified Mexican courier bearing the whip, to be delivered to Thomas Jefferson Rusk, was intercepted by a Texas patrol near the Nueces River, and the dispatch was forwarded to the Texas War Department. Secretary of War Alexander Somervell used the Teal and Miller letters as the basis of a circular calling for an enlistment of the militia.

Whipple, Amiel Weeks. Army officer and surveyor; b. Greenwich, Massachusetts, 21 October 1817; d. Washington, D.C., 7 May 1863; m. Eleanor Mary Sherburne (1843); 4 children; ed. West Point (grad. 1841). After receiving his commission, Whipple served with the Topographical Engineers. With the United States Boundary Commission he helped survey the new boundary with Mexico west from El Paso and along the Gila River to the Pacific. He accompanied commissioner John R. Bartlett across Texas from Indianola through San Antonio to El Paso in the fall of 1850. He was chosen by the War Department to direct the survey of a possible transcontinental railroad route along the thirty-fifth parallel from Fort Smith, Arkansas, to Los Angeles—the Whipple expedition. With eleven civilian scientists, Whipple and his command left Fort Smith on 14 July 1853, worked their way up the Canadian River, and camped in what is now Shackelford County. In the Panhandle, Whipple followed trails marked by Josiah Gregg in 1840, James W. Abert in 1845, and Randolph B. Marcy and James H. Simpson in 1849. The expedition was briefly guided by Comancheros and Pueblo Indians from New Mexico who happened to be in the area. Whipple had frequent peaceful contacts with Plains Indians. On 11 September he passed by the ruins of Adobe Walls. Near the site of present-day Sanford, the expedition left the Canadian and ventured over Marcy's route across the Llano Estacado to Anton Chico, New Mexico, before pushing on to Arizona and California. At Los Angeles the expedition disbanded. In his report Whipple confirmed the feasibility of the thirty-fifth parallel route for a railroad. The expedition sparked interest through-out Europe and led to lengthy correspondence between Whipple and Wilhelm von Humboldt. Except for the Civil War and Reconstruction politics, the Canadian valley might have been included in the first transcontinental railroad. Whipple was the last of the antebellum pathmarkers to venture across the Panhandle, though he incorrectly identified some of the creeks Simpson had labeled, thus misleading many later historians who used his itinerary. He served the Union with distinction during the Civil War and was mortally wounded at Chancellorsville. Just before Whipple's death President Lincoln signed his promotion to major general of volunteers. Whipple was posthumously awarded more brevets for his wartime services, and both of his sons received presidential appointments to the military academy of their choice. Fort Whipple, now part of the Fort Myer reservation near Alexandria, Virginia, is named in his honor.

H. Allen Anderson

White Horse. Kiowa chief; Kiowa name Tsen-tainte; d. 1892. White Horse early evinced talent as a horseman and warrior. In 1867 he joined a large party of Comanches and Kiowas on a revenge raid against the Navajos, who were then living on the reservation near Fort Sumner, New Mexico. In the raid he took a captive boy whom he later adopted. Although White Horse participated in the council at Medicine Lodge Creek in Kansas, he soon cast his lot with the war faction and gained considerable notoriety during the early 1870s for his raids on Texas settlements. Whites considered him the "most dangerous man" among the Kiowas. Even after raids in the vicinity of Fort Sill were curtailed, White Horse defiantly continued his attacks south of the Red River. On 30 September 1870, for instance, he ambushed a stagecoach en route to Fort Concho and killed Martin Wurmser, a trooper who was serving as an escort. He also participated in the Warren Wagontrain Raid. While the imprisonment of chiefs Satanta and Big Tree momentarily curbed his raiding, he and Big Bow engineered another attack on a wagon train in what is now Crockett County (20 April 1872), which resulted in the death of 17 Mexican teamsters. On the way back from that foray, White Horse was wounded in the arm during a skirmish with Capt. N. Cooney's Ninth Cavalry. On 19 May, White Horse's younger brother, Kim-pai-te, was killed in a fight with L. H. Luckett's surveying crew near Round Timbers, 25 miles south of Fort Belknap. In revenge, on 9 June, with Big Bow, White Horse attacked the homestead of Abel Lee on the Clear Fork of the Brazos. Lee and his 14-year-old daughter Frances were fatally shot, his wife scalped and murdered, and the remaining three children carried into captivity. Soldiers trailed them, but the Kiowas escaped back to the reservation and held a scalp dance that went on for several nights. The Lee children remained captives for a few months before they were ransomed. After the 1872 councils and the release of Satanta and Big Tree from prison on parole, White Horse was peaceful for a time but remained with the war faction. He accompanied the intertribal war party to the second battle of Adobe Walls in June 1874 and was encamped in Palo Duro Canyon when Col. Ranald S. Mackenzie's troops attacked on 27 September. White Horse and his followers surrendered at Fort Sill on 19 April 1875. Because of the atrocities he had committed, he was among those singled out by Kicking Bird for incarceration at St. Augustine, Florida. In 1878 he was returned

with the others to the reservation near Fort Sill, where he spent his remaining years peacefully with his family.

H. Allen Anderson

White Man. Also *Whiteman*; a weekly newspaper devoted to the removal of Indians from North Texas; first published at Jacksboro in 1860. The paper reflected the sentiments of its original editors, who included H. A. Hamner, John R. Baylor, and Isaac Worrall. Hamner was known as a critic of Governor Sam Houston's frontier defense policy, as an advocate of Indian extermination, and later as a supporter of secession. Baylor was one of the most vocal critics of the state's Indian policy and, like Hamner, specifically blamed Houston for the failure to protect North Texas from Indians. The Butterfield Overland Mail came through Jacksboro and distributed the *White Man*, which may have reached more than 1,000 readers. One historian concluded that the paper was "the worst Indian condemnatory sheet in all history." Nevertheless, the looming secession issue soon took center stage. The editors used their paper to condemn Houston's support of the Union. On 29 July 1860 the offices of the *White Man* burned, and the editors blamed the fire on abolitionists. Publication resumed in Weatherford in September under the partnership of B. L. Richey, John Deavors, and Alfred Obenchain. In late 1861 the paper ceased publication. Baylor and Hamner joined the Confederate Army. *David Minor*

White Man's Union Associations. Also White Men's Primary Associations; political organizations formed in the wake of Reconstruction to maintain white control in county elections. Several counties formed associations to limit black or Hispanic suffrage. Among the earliest of these groups was the one in Wharton County, which was formed in November 1889 and grew until all qualified white voters automatically became members. The constitution of the organization claimed that its purpose was to ensure better county government, but in actual practice it was much like a political party. By nominating all county officials for the spring Democratic primary elections, the association exercised a stranglehold on the local political scene and kept the county's black and Hispanic voters from having any voice in elections or other local political matters. Minority voters could vote in the fall general elections, but that meant nothing in a one-party state where the primary was the real election. White Men's Associations were founded in Marion County (1898) and Jackson County (1902). Many other counties formed similar organizations or instituted the so-called White Primary.

Christopher Long

White Primary. The restriction of primary elections to whites; a measure designed to disfranchise African Americans and assure the dominance of the Democratic party. When the Texas legislature passed a white primary law in 1923, Texas was thrust into the center of a struggle about the constitutionality of the measure nationwide. In the years immediately following Reconstruction no statewide primaries existed, and virtually all politically involved Texas blacks were Republicans. A 1921 decision in a case (*Newberry v. United States*) not related to white primaries signaled the United States Supreme Court's willingness to treat primaries as private party functions. Texas legislators apparently concluded that the courts would not provide constitutional protection to blacks who wished to vote in primaries. In 1924 Lawrence Nixon, a black physician and member of the El Paso NAACP, challenged the new law. With help from the NAACP, Nixon's suit reached the Supreme Court as *Nixon v. Herndon.* On 7 March 1927 the court unanimously declared the white primary statute unconstitutional for violating the "equal protection" clause of the Fourteenth Amendment. The decision, however, left open the possibility that the party could do privately what the state could not do officially. The legislature replaced the 1923 law with a new statute giving the executive committee of each state party power to decide who could vote in its primary, and the Democratic executive committee adopted a resolution allowing only whites to vote in the Democratic primary. Nixon again sued and again won a temporary victory. In *Nixon v. Condon* (1932), the Supreme Court decided 5–4 that the Democratic executive committee would not have had the authority to speak for the party in banning blacks without the 1927 law that granted it that authority. Because of this indirect state role, the white primary had violated the Fourteenth Amendment. Just weeks after the second *Nixon* decision, the Texas Democratic state convention adopted its own white primary resolution to replace the executive committee's resolution. In 1934 Texas attorney general James Allred endorsed the convention's action. Many white leaders welcomed Allred's overt support for the white primary, but others attacked him. Black opponents of the white primary also faced disunity. Houston barber Richard R. Grovey and attorneys J. Alston Atkins and Carter W. Wesley initiated their own challenge to the white primary despite the tactical objections of the NAACP. The Houstonians generated some support for their cause but lost their case, *Grovey v. Townsend* (1935). Some of the Houston blacks who had split with the NAACP over *Grovey* later cooperated with the NAACP to bring the case of Lonnie E. Smith, a Houston dentist, to the Supreme Court. By this time the membership of the court had changed, and the nation's fight against Nazism in Europe was indirectly strengthening support for civil rights at home. In *Smith v. Allwright* (1944), eight justices overturned the *Grovey* decision. The majority concluded that various state laws made the Texas primary an integral part of the general electoral process. Therefore, blacks could not constitutionally be prohibited from voting in the Democratic primary even by party officials. The *Smith* decision did not end all attempts to limit black political participation but did virtually end the white primary in Texas. *Sanford N. Greenberg*

Whitfield's Legion. Also First Texas Legion and Twenty-seventh Texas Cavalry; one of the two legions that Texas provided to the Confederate States Army (the other was Waul's Legion). Though a legion was properly a regiment of mixed arms, generally composed of infantry, cavalry, and artillery battalions, Whitfield's was purely a cavalry unit. Its nucleus was a company recruited in Lavaca County in 1861 by Capt. John Wilkins Whitfield and assigned to Brig. Gen. Ben McCulloch's Army of the West at Fort Smith, Arkansas. There it was combined with three other independent cavalry companies from Texas—Capt. E. R. Hawkins's from Hunt County, Capt. John H. Broocks's from San Augustine County, and Capt. B. H. Norsworth's from Jasper County—and with one company from Arkansas, to form Whitfield's Battalion, sometimes called the Fourth Texas Cavalry Battalion. Whitfield

was promoted to major and made commander. After its participation in the battle of Pea Ridge or Elkhorn Tavern, Arkansas, on 7–8 March 1862, the battalion was dismounted and transferred east of the Mississippi River. There it was assigned to the Army of West Tennessee and fought as infantry in the battles of Iuka (19 September 1862) and Corinth (3–4 October 1862). Later that year the battalion was augmented by the recruiting of eight new companies from Texas. The Arkansas company was transferred to an Arkansas regiment, and the battalion was redesignated Whitfield's Legion or the Twenty-seventh Texas Cavalry. The regiment was then remounted and assigned to Brig. Gen. Lawrence Sullivan Ross's brigade, the famed Ross's Texas Brigade of the Army of Tennessee. There it fought in all of the principal battles in Tennessee, Alabama, and Georgia during 1863 and 1864. When Whitfield was promoted to brigadier general in May 1863 and assigned to command of a brigade, Hawkins was promoted to colonel and elevated to command of the regiment. *Thomas W. Cutrer*

Whiting, William Henry Chase. Army officer; b. Biloxi, Mississippi, 22 March 22 1824; d. Fort Columbus, Governors Island, New York, 10 March 1865 (buried at Oakdale Cemetery, Wilmington, North Carolina); m. Kate Walker (1857); ed. Georgetown College (grad. 1840) and West Point (grad. 1845). Whiting proved himself an academic genius at Georgetown and West Point. He took a commission in the Corps of Engineers and was sent to Pensacola until 1848, when he was assigned duty in Texas to scout a wagon road between San Antonio and El Paso. That partially successful expedition, the Whiting and Smith expedition, located the future southern route between the two cities. Whiting then surveyed the frontier forts of Texas and reported on them in 1850. During the 1850s he was involved in engineering projects in California, Texas, North Carolina, South Carolina, Georgia, and Florida. One of his projects in Texas appears to have been the clearing of the Colorado River raft. At the outbreak of the Civil War he joined the Confederate Army, in which he distinguished himself as an engineer. By July 1861 he was a brigadier general commanding two brigades, one of which was Hood's Texas Brigade. During the battles around Richmond, Whiting was a major general and was suffering from chronic fatigue. He asked for and received a medical furlough. In 1864 he was at Cape Fear, near Petersburg and Drewry Bluff. He was wounded in the leg at Fort Fisher and taken prisoner. He died in captivity. *Art Leatherwood*

Whitman, Charles Joseph. Mass murderer; b. Lake Worth, Florida, 24 June 1941; d. Austin, 1 August 1966; m. Kathleen Leissner (1962). The infamous tower sniper at the University of Texas was an Eagle Scout at the age of 12, a graduate from Catholic schools, and an ex-marine. He was attending UT in 1965–66. In 1966 his mother left his father and moved to Austin to be near her eldest son. On March 29 Whitman sought medical and psychiatric advice at the university health center, but he failed to return as directed for further assistance. During the predawn hours of 1 August he killed his mother and wife. About 11:30 A.M. he went to the university tower, taking with him a footlocker, six guns, knives, food, and water. After clubbing the receptionist (who later died) on the twenty-eighth floor, he killed two persons and wounded two others who were coming

View of Wichita Falls, Texas, 1890. Drawn by T. M. Fowler.

up the stairs from the twenty-seventh floor. On the observation deck of the tower, at an elevation of 231 feet, Whitman then opened fire on persons crossing the campus and on nearby streets, killing 10 more people and wounding 31 more (one of whom died a week later). Police arrived and returned his fire, while other policemen worked their way into the tower. At 1:24 P.M. police and a deputized private citizen reached the observation deck, where police officers Ramiro Martinez and Houston McCoy shot and killed Whitman. Altogether, 17 persons were killed, including Whitman, and 31 were wounded. Whitman was found to have a brain tumor, but medical authorities disagreed over its effect on his actions.   *Alwyn Barr*

Wichita Falls, Texas. In southeastern Wichita County. According to tradition, the site was acquired in a poker game by John A. Scott of Mississippi in 1837. In fact, Scott acquired the tract by purchasing Texas land certificates, which he packed away and promptly forgot. Years later the certificates were rediscovered by Scott's heirs, who commissioned M. W. Seeley to map out a townsite on the tract on the Wichita River. As platted by Seeley in July 1876, the townsite included the location of a small waterfall on the Wichita River that was later washed away, several named streets, and a town square. In a fanciful drawing that accompanied the plat, Seeley also included an imaginary lake, a steamboat on the river, and warehouses laden with cotton and other goods. The town never became a steamboat shipping center, although railroads were very important to its later devel-

opment. The first permanent settlers were the Barwise family of Dallas. They first came to the townsite on an exploring trip in 1878 and returned to stay the following year. A post office was established in 1879; the first public school opened in the fall of 1880, and the first church, First Methodist, was formally organized in 1881. By that time, according to various reports, there were between 8 and 13 families living at the townsite. During 1881 and 1882 the residents of Wichita Falls induced the Fort Worth and Denver Railway Company, then building tracks west out of Fort Worth, to run the line through the town by offering substantial property concessions along the right-of-way. The first train arrived in 1882, and the first manufacturing concern, a shingle and sorghum mill, was established along with the first lumberyard. Joseph Alexander Kemp, later to become one of the most prominent of the town's promoters, arrived in 1883 and soon established a general store. Wichita Falls became the county seat of Wichita County in November 1883. It was officially incorporated on 29 July 1889. Soon the economy was stimulated by the arrival of more railroads. At the turn of the century the Wichita Valley Railroad, the Wichita Falls Railway, the Wichita Falls and Southern Railway, the Wichita Falls and Oklahoma Railway, and the Wichita Falls and Northwestern made the town a transportation and supply center for Northwest Texas and southern Oklahoma. Frank Kell, Kemp's brother-in-law, arrived in 1896 after buying the Wichita Valley Mills Company. Kemp and Kell were the two leading promoters of the city for several decades.

By 1890 the population was 1,987, and as the town continued to grow, its leaders recognized the need for a reliable water supply. The Lake Wichita project was begun in 1900 and completed the following year. Lake Kemp and Lake Diversion were added during the 1920s, followed by Lake Kickapoo in 1947. Today the primary water supply comes from Lake Arrowhead, constructed in 1966. By 1907 the population of Wichita Falls was 5,055, and by 1909 the town had 30 miles of sidewalk, 5 miles of sewers, and more than 100 businesses. The streetcar system featured an extension to Lake Wichita that made the lake a recreation center. Soon a hotel, a domed pavilion, a racetrack, a boardwalk, and vacation cottages sprang up. The lake remained the center of recreation for the city until well after World War I, even though the hotel was destroyed by fire in 1918. Oil was discovered just west of the city in Clay County around 1903, but it was the opening of the Electra field in 1911 that triggered a shift in the economic base. By 1913 the North Texas fields were producing 46 percent of all the oil in Texas, and refineries began to appear in Wichita Falls in 1915. The discovery of the Burkburnett fields in 1918 triggered an actual boom. By 1920 there were 9 refineries and 47 factories within the city. More than a dozen major building projects were inaugurated in the downtown area during the early 1920s. In addition, the city added a municipal auditorium in 1927 and an airline passenger service in 1928. That same year the city's first commercial broadcasting station, KGKO, was established. The population of Wichita Falls in 1930, on the eve of the Great Depression, was 43,607. The community had 32 parks, 47 churches, 5 railroads, 20 schools, and 118 industrial establishments. The depression slowed growth but did not stop it, due in part to a major oil discovery at nearby Kamay in 1938. In 1940 the population was 55,200. In 1941 the economy was further bolstered by the opening of Sheppard Field, an Army Air Corps training facility. By May 1945, when the base reached its peak strength, there were 46,000 army personnel stationed there. The base was deactivated on 31 August 1946, but reopened as Sheppard Air Force Base in August 1948. By 1960 the population was 101,724, and while oil production in the area still ranked eighth in the state, it was soon eclipsed by other enterprises. By 1962 refinery activity had practically ceased.

Recognizing that change was coming, the city's leaders formed Industrial Development, Incorporated, which sought to diversify the economy by attracting other types of industries. Gates Rubber Company built a Wichita Falls plant in 1964. Sprague Electric and Johnson and Johnson followed in 1966. Tex–Color Labs arrived in 1967, followed by Town and Country Mobile Homes and Dowell Division of Dow Chemical Company in 1968. In 1970 Industrial Development merged with the Chamber of Commerce to form the Board of Commerce and Industry. This organization was successful in attracting 15 new industries during the 1970s, including Pittsburgh Plate Glass, Certain Teed, Washex, Howmet Turbine, AC Spark Plug, and Cieba Geigy. These successes produced great optimism that the new trend would continue, but it declined by the early 1980s. Moreover, several companies moved their facilities away. These included AC Plug, Johnson and Johnson, and Sprague. Meanwhile, because of the construction of a large shopping mall in the southwestern part of the city, the downtown collapsed as a viable shopping area. Wichita Falls was devastated on 10 April 1979 by one of the strongest tornadoes ever recorded. Sweeping through the southern part of the city, the storm destroyed 20 percent of all the dwellings in town and damaged or destroyed numerous business establishments. Miraculously, only 45 people were killed, although more than 3,200 were injured. The city made a rapid recovery, and within three years most of the damage had been repaired. Also, the boom in oil prices during the early 1980s caused a brief flurry of activity in business. However, when oil prices slumped again in the mid-1980s, the economy became stagnant. In 1993 Wichita Falls had a population of 97,710.

Kenneth E. Hendrickson, Jr.

Wilbarger, John Wesley. Methodist minister and author; b. Kentucky or Virginia, 1806; d. 1892. Wilbarger moved to Texas from Kentucky in 1837 at the urging of his brother, Josiah Pugh Wilbarger, who had lived near Bastrop since the late 1820s. He served as a minister for the area and assisted his brother in surveying the region. In 1833, while on a trip to Austin, Josiah was scalped by Indians and left for dead, but somehow survived. This and other tales of Indian attacks that John Wilbarger heard during his lifetime prompted him to write a compendium of such stories, which he published as *Indian Depredations in Texas* in 1889. According to Wilbarger, he began collecting material for the book around 1870 and worked on it for two decades. The 672-page book, described by one author as "the most complete compilation of accounts of Indian warfare in nineteenth-century Texas," includes more than 250 narratives of attacks and counterattacks. In his preface Wilbarger noted that many of the articles had been "written by others, who were either cognizant of the facts themselves or had obtained them from reliable sources." Wilbarger, however, claimed that he had attempted to verify all of the stories. Although Wilbarger's book depicts the Indians as unredeemable savages, it is considered a classic work of Texana and has been reprinted several times. Also noteworthy is the fact that *Indian Depredations* was illustrated with 34 woodcuts signed by T. J. Owen but subsequently attributed to O. Henry.

Christopher Long

Wilderness Areas. The five protected wilderness areas in Texas are Big Slough, in Houston County; Indian Mounds, in Sabine County; Little Lake Creek, in Sam Houston National Forest; Turkey Hill, in Angelina County; and Upland Island, in Angelina and Jasper counties. In 1936 the United States Forest Service acquired 634,000 acres from private owners, mainly timber companies. Funds were provided as part of the New Deal to rescue owners from financial difficulties and to renew payments to counties and school districts because many owners had been unable to pay their taxes on these lands. The law required the Forest Service to pay 25 percent of all receipts from timber sales to the counties and school districts. When the Forest Service acquired these lands, they included many timber stands older than 100 years. A few were open fields. Much of the cutting had been clearcutting, which removed all marketable trees; but before 1936 the loggers had abandoned their clearcuts, permitting the native vegetation to return. Early loggers therefore did less lasting harm than modern clearcutters, who follow up with bulldozing all remaining vegetation and plant a single species on each stand—loblolly or shortleaf pine. The citizens who nominated wildernesses generally proposed areas with the oldest trees. In the five areas that ultimately were designated as wildernesses, several stands appear never to have been cut. The national champion longleaf pine in Upland Island is estimated to be over 400 years old. It grows near swamp chestnut oaks up to 17 feet in circumference, not far from the state champion shagbark hickory.

Beginning with the Carter administration in 1977, the new assistant secretary of agriculture inaugurated a national evaluation of potential wildernesses. Logging and burning were deferred on 14 inventoried areas in Texas. In 1979 the secretary of agriculture announced his final wilderness recommendations to Congress. In Texas he recommended only 10,712 acres in only three wildernesses. Everything else was to be opened to clearcutting. Citizen groups immediately began to look for a congressman from Texas who would file a bill covering 10 areas totaling 65,000 acres. The Forest Service opposed anything over 10,712 acres. In 1983 the proponents finally found a sponsor—John Bryant, newly elected to Congress from Dallas County—and two cosponsors, Steve Bartlett and Martin Frost of Dallas County. Even with the help of John Seiberling, chairman of the House subcommittee on parks and public lands, the bill got nowhere until citizen support expanded in the district of Congressman Charles Wilson, where three of the wildernesses lie. He agreed to a compromise of five wilderness areas totaling 34,700 acres. That compromise was made possible by the willingness of lumber industry giant Temple–Eastex to trade some of its land inside Upland Island and Indian Mounds for Forest Service land outside. The compromise passed the House unanimously. In the Senate, Lloyd Bentsen and John Tower cosponsored the measure, which was signed by President Reagan on 30 October 1984.

Shortly after the bill passed, an opportunity arose to straighten out some irregularities in the wilderness-area boundaries resulting from timber and oil-drilling contracts granted before 1984. In 1985 the price of timber fell and the drillers hit dry holes. Also, some private owners decided they were willing to part with their lands that jutted into the wildernesses and caused irregular boundaries. In response to legislative lobbying by citizen groups, including the Texas Committee on Natural Resources, President Reagan signed a bill adding 1,200 acres to be protected wilderness areas in 1986. The Forest Service leases portions of the wildernesses for grazing of cattle from March through November, but the number of animals is relatively small. Since the Forest Service never acquired the oil and gas under most of the wilderness land, it permits seismographic exploration by private mineral owners. The East Texas Wilderness Act split two wildernesses in order to maintain a pipeline and roads leading to dwellings. The other roads have been closed off by piles of sand and are becoming vegetated, except along footpaths. By careful routing a person can walk through any of these wildernesses all day and, with rare exceptions, see only nature and a few other nature lovers.

Edward C. Fritz

Wildlife Areas. In 1994 Texas had 29 state wildlife-management areas encompassing 1.5 million acres and 18 national wildlife refuges. The areas were acquired for research and demonstration and to provide protection for unusual wildlife species and habitats. In many of the state-owned areas, supervised public hunting and fishing were permitted if surplus game existed. State wildlife areas are Candy Cain Abshier Wildlife Management Area, in Chambers County; Alazan Bayou WMA, in Nacogdoches County; Atkinson Island, near the Houston Ship Channel in Harris County, accessible only by boat; Black Gap and Elephant Mountain, in Brewster County; Walter Buck, in Kimble County; Chaparral, in Dimmit and La Salle counties; Dam B, in Jasper and Tyler counties; James E. Daughtrey, in Live Oak and McMullen counties; Engeling, in Anderson County; Granger, in Williamson County; Guadalupe Delta and Welder Flats Coastal Preserve, in Calhoun County; Gene Howe, in Hemphill County; Keechi Creek in Leon County; Kerr, in Kerr County; Las Palomas, which comprises 16 units in Cameron, Starr, Hidalgo, Willacy, and Presidio counties; Lower Neches, in Orange County; Mad Island, in Matagorda County; Matador; Pat Mayse, in Lamar County; J. D. Murphree, in Jefferson County; Old Tunnel, in Kendall County; Peach Point, in Brazoria County; Playa Lakes, in Moore, Hartley, and Castro counties; Redhead Pond, in Nueces County; Richland Creek, in Freestone County; Sierra Diablo, in Culberson and Hudspeth counties; and Somerville, in Burleson and Lee counties.

The federal wildlife refuges in Texas are Anahuac, Aransas, Attwater Prairie Chicken, Big Boggy, Brazoria, Buffalo Lake, Hagerman, Laguna Atascosa, Lower Rio Grande Valley, Matagorda Island, McFaddin, Muleshoe, San Bernard, Santa Ana, and Texas Point. Balcones Canyonlands NWR was established in 1992 in the Texas Hill Country as a preserve for the endangered golden-cheeked warbler and black-capped vireo. The two other refuge areas in Texas, Little Sandy and Moody NWRs, serve as conservation easement refuges.

Private refuges operated by the Audubon Society include South Bird Island on the Laguna Madre; Second-Chain Islands, in Calhoun County; Green Island, on the Laguna Madre at the mouth of the Arroyo Colorado; Lydia Ann Island, north of Port Aransas; and Swan Island, located at Copano Bay near Rockport. The Rob and Bessie Welder Wildlife Foundation and Refuge, another private refuge, is located northeast of Sinton.

Wiley College. In Marshall; the oldest black college west of the Mississippi; established in 1873 by the Freedman's Aid Society of the Methodist Episcopal Church and chartered in 1882. F. C. Moore was the first president. The college had a white missionary faculty and was administered by whites for its first 20 years. After a reorganization in 1892, Wiley had its first black president, Bishop Isaiah B. Scott, and black teachers gradually replaced the white faculty members. The school offered regular college courses and some vocational training. It included preparatory grades until 1922 but thereafter functioned solely as an institution of higher education. In 1907 Wiley received the first Carnegie college library west of the Mississippi. Seven of the 14 buildings on the campus in 1936 were of brick, and the total value of the plant was estimated at $350,000. Enrollment in 1945 was 420. The 46-acre campus was improved and modernized during the 1960s with an extensive building program. In 1962 Wiley and Bishop College students held sit-ins at the local Woolworth store—demonstrations that helped integrate public facilities in Marshall. In 1969 a series of nonviolent student demonstrations over faculty hiring practices, primitive dormitory facilities, and cutbacks in the intercollegiate athletic program brought approximately 100 Texas Rangers and other lawmen to the school for a massive but unsuccessful search for concealed weapons in the dorms; the school was closed down for several weeks in February and March of that year. Further demonstrations resulted in the school administration's agreement in August to improve living conditions on campus. Wiley had an enrollment of 573 in 1974 and was accredited by the Southern Association of Colleges and Secondary Schools, the Texas Education Agency, the university senate of the Methodist Church, and the American Medical Association. Wiley offers B.S. and B.A. degrees and preprofessional training in medicine, nursing, dentistry, and law. *Sallie M. Lentz and Gilbert Allen*

William P. Hobby Airport. Began in 1927 as a landing field in a 600-acre pasture. The city of Houston purchased the field in 1937, expanded it to 1,240 acres, and replaced its wooden terminal building. Houston Municipal Airport, as it was then called, was served only by Braniff Airways and Eastern Airlines. By the end of World War II the airport had paved runways, city-built hangars, and a lighting system, and four additional airlines had begun service. International flights began in 1950, when Pan American Airlines began service to Mexico City. In 1954 the city renamed the airport Houston International Airport. In 1957, KLM Royal Dutch Airlines began direct flights between Houston and Amsterdam. The 1950s saw expansion of the old terminal, construction of a new one, lengthened and strengthened runways capable of handling the new turbojet aircraft, several new hangars, and a high-intensity lighting system. In the 1960s growth continued with another addition to the terminal. In 1966 more than two million passengers passed through Houston International. The airport was renamed William P. Hobby Airport in 1967 in honor of a Texas governor and Houston civic leader. As early as the 1950s the Civil Aeronautics Administration recommended that Houston begin to plan for another airport—a recommendation that led to the opening of Houston Intercontinental Airport in 1969, when Hobby was designated a general aviation airport serving mainly private and corporate aircraft. Nevertheless, by 1971 domestic commercial carriers had returned to Hobby. In 1980 the Houston Aviation Department reported that 10 domestic passenger carriers served more than three million passengers there. Three cargo carriers were also operating out of Hobby, and 700 aircraft, including 175 jets, were based there. The city of Houston master plan to accommodate the future aviation needs of the city includes Houston Intercontinental, Hobby, and Ellington Field. *Art Leatherwood*

Williams, Samuel May. Entrepreneur; b. Providence, Rhode Island, 4 October 1795; d. Galveston, 13 September 1858; m. Sarah Patterson Scott; 9 children. Williams was apprenticed around the age of 15 to his uncle, a Baltimore commission merchant. He journeyed as supercargo to Buenos Aires, where he remained for a time mastering Spanish and Latin-American business practice. He settled in New Orleans in 1819 before departing for Texas in 1822 under the name E. Eccleston. He resumed his true identity in 1823 when Stephen F. Austin employed him as translator and clerk. For the next 13 years Williams was Austin's lieutenant. He was named postmaster of San Felipe in 1826 and appointed revenue collector and dispenser of stamped paper by the state of Coahuila and Texas the following year. He became secretary to the ayuntamiento of San Felipe in 1828. For these services he received 11 leagues (49,000 acres) of land, which he selected on strategic waterways including Oyster Creek and Buffalo Bayou. In 1835 Williams attended the legislature at Monclova and contracted for two of the 400-league grants offered by the state gov-

ernment as a means to raise funds to oppose President Antonio López de Santa Anna. He and six others were proscribed as revolutionaries, but he escaped arrest by going to the United States.

He entered a partnership with Thomas F. McKinney in 1833, McKinney, Williams and Company, and used his family's mercantile contacts in the United States to secure credit for the firm. Their commission house, located at Quintana, dominated the Brazos cotton trade until 1838, when they moved to Galveston. The firm used its credit in the United States to purchase arms and raise funds for the Texas Revolution. Neither the republic nor the state was able to repay the $99,000 debt in full, and the partners realized only a small portion of their investment in addition to the passage of favorable relief legislation. As investors in the Galveston City Company, McKinney and Williams aided in developing the city by helping to construct the Tremont Hotel as well as the commission house and wharf. McKinney withdrew from the partnership in 1842, when Henry Howell Williams assumed his brother's interest in the firm, which became H. H. Williams and Company. In 1841 the commission house received special permission from the Texas Congress to found a bank to issue and circulate paper money as an aid to commerce. In 1848 Williams activated his 1835 charter, obtained from Coahuila and Texas and approved by the republic in 1836, to open the Commercial and Agricultural Bank of Galveston, which also printed its own money. Jacksonian antibanking sentiment inspired his enemies to attack the bank through the state courts on the grounds that it violated constitutional prohibitions against banks. The Texas Supreme Court sustained the bank in 1852, but subsequent suits brought its demise in 1859.

Williams, a political supporter of Sam Houston, represented the Brazos district in the Coahuila and Texas legislature in 1835 and Galveston County in the lower house of the Texas Congress in 1839. He was an unsuccessful candidate for the United States Congress in 1846. In 1838 he received a commission to negotiate a $5 million loan in the United States and to purchase seven ships for the Texas Navy. President Houston sent him to Matamoros in 1843 to seek an armistice with Mexico, an unsuccessful ploy. Late in life, Williams lived quietly with his wife on a country estate west of the city. The Samuel May Williams House is operated now by the Galveston Historical Foundation as a museum. *Margaret Swett Henson*

Williamson, Clara McDonald. Painter; born Iredell, Texas, 20 November 1875; d. Dallas, 17 February 1976; m. John Williamson, a widower; 1 child + 2 from John's first marriage. Mrs. Williamson did not turn to painting until after her husband's death (1943). She sketched constantly, audited a drawing class at Southern Methodist University, and took evening painting classes at the Dallas Museum School. In a still-life class led by Otis Dozier, she painted her first "memory painting," *Chicken for Dinner* (1945). Her largest group of work consists of such memory paintings: e.g., *The Night Before Christmas* (1954), *Texas Barn Dance* (1951), and the extraordinary *Standing in the Need of Prayer* (1947). She also documented everyday activities such as washing clothes in *Monday* (1955) and carding, spinning, and weaving in *The Family Room* (1955). In *The Girls Went Fishing* (1945–46) a group of skinny-dipping boys are surprised by the arrival of several young women. Though such childhood memories are popular subjects for naive painters, McDonald also chose subjects unique to her time and place. She represented the

Standing in the Need of Prayer, by Clara McDonald Williamson, 1947. Oil on panel. 28" × 40". Photograph by Ulric Meisel. Courtesy Dan C. Williams and Valley House Gallery, Dallas. Naïve painter Clara Williamson began to paint after the death of her husband. To fill her days, she turned to making "memory pictures" like this one depicting a torchlight revival meeting she remembered.

cattle drive passing near Iredell in two paintings, *Git 'Long Little Dogies* (1945) and *Old Chisholm Trail* (1952). The technological developments that transformed Texas are featured in several important paintings: *The Building of the Railroad* (1949–50), for instance, and *Transportation, The Old and the New, Circa 1919, Meridian, Texas* (1963). The latter represents the first plane to land in Bosque County.

Williamson had an innate sense of design. She favored subtle color harmonies, as in *Arbor Meeting* (1957), where gray, rose, blue, and sage green suggest an early evening atmosphere. She sold her first work, an early watercolor, to Jerry Bywaters. Donald Vogel, an artist and dealer, entered her paintings in numerous competitive exhibitions throughout the state. She won the Dealey Purchase Award at the Dallas Allied Arts Exhibit in 1946, and in 1948 she was the subject of a solo exhibition at the Dallas Museum of Fine Arts. Her work was exhibited in New York, Florida, Illinois, Colorado, California, Maryland, Pennsylvania, Oklahoma, and Washington. She was represented in the 1950 exhibition American Painting Today at the Metropolitan Museum of Art in New York, and her work was included in three traveling exhibitions organized by the Smithsonian Institution, one of which toured Europe. She was honored by solo exhibitions in Dallas, San Antonio, Fort Worth, Longview, and New York. In 1966 her work was included in the

International Exhibition of Primitive Art in Bratislava, and the Amon Carter Museum organized a retrospective of her work that traveled to the Oklahoma Art Center (Oklahoma City), the Marion Koogler McNay Art Museum, and the Dallas Museum of Fine Arts. In 1969 a documentary film of Williamson's career was aired on national television. "Aunt Clara" did not court the recognition that she received. She turned down a solo exhibition in a New York gallery early in her painting career; when discussing her career in general she noted that she had refused to "sign on the dotted line" for fear that "they'd tell me what to paint, how to paint it, and when to paint." She finished her last painting, a memory picture of her home near the SMU campus, in a nursing home. Her work is included in the collections of the Dallas Museum of Art, the Amon Carter Museum in Fort Worth, the Wichita Art Museum in Kansas, the Terry Art Institute in Miami, Florida, and the Museum of Modern Art in New York.   *Kendall Curlee*

Wills, Bob. Country musician; b. James Robert Wills, Limestone County, 6 March 1905; d. 13 May 1975 (buried in Memorial Park, Tulsa); m. Betty Anderson (1942); 4 children + 2 from previous marriages. Wills was married and divorced several times before his lasting marriage to Betty Anderson. In Hall County, where the family moved in 1913, he learned to play the violin. He played

Bob Wills and the Light Crust Dough Boys, (left to right) Milton Brown, Durwood Brown, Truett Kimzey, Bob Wills, Herman Arnspiger. From Charles R. Townsend, *San Antonio Rose: The Life and Music of Bob Wills* (Urbana: University of Illinois Press, 1976). Courtesy the author.

for ranch dances in West Texas for the next 14 years. During that time he first combined frontier fiddle music with the blues and jazz he had learned from black playmates and coworkers in the cottonfields of East and West Texas. He played fiddle music with the heat of blues and the swing of jazz; his new music could as properly have been called western jazz as western swing. In 1929 Wills moved to Fort Worth. There he performed on several radio stations, organized a band that became the Light Crust Doughboys, and worked for W. Lee O'Daniel. In 1934 he moved to Oklahoma, where he made radio and musical history with his broadcasts over Station KVOOnio Rose" (1940) made him a national figure in popular music. He went to Hollywood that year and made the first of his 19 movies. He joined the army in December 1942. After World War II he had his greatest success, grossing nearly a half million dollars during some years. In 1957 he was elected to the American Society of Composers, Authors, and Publishers. In 1968 he was elected to the Country Music Hall of Fame, although he never thought of his music as "country." In 1969 the governor and legislature of Texas honored Wills for his contribution to American music, one of the few original music forms Texas and the Southwest have produced. The day after the ceremonies in Austin, Wills had the first in a series of crippling strokes. By 1973 his health had improved to the extent that he could lead some of his former Texas Playboys in a recording session for United Artists. The album, *For the Last Time: Bob Wills and His Texas Playboys,* sold more copies than any other in Wills's career and was awarded a Grammy Award by the National Academy of Recording Arts and Sciences, the highest achievement of any Wills recording or any other recording in the history of western swing.   *Charles R. Townsend*

Wilson, Dooley. Screen actor; b. Arthur Wilson, Tyler, 3 April 1894; d. 1953. Wilson began performing in vaudeville at age 12. During the 1920s he led his own band, in which he performed as a singing drummer, on a nightclub tour of Paris and London. He returned to the United States in 1930 and gave up his drums for an acting career. He performed with Orson Welles and John Hausman in Federal Theater productions and then landed a Broadway role in the musical *Cabin in the Sky.* He made his film debut in 1939. He is most famous as the pianist Sam in *Casablanca.* Director Hal Wallis allowed Wilson to sing the role, but the piano playing was dubbed. Wilson was under contract to Paramount and on loan to M–G–M. His film credits include *Keep Punching* (1939); *My Favorite Blonde, Night in New Orleans, Take a Letter Darling,* and *Cairo* (1942); *Casablanca, Two Tickets to London, Stormy Weather,* and *Hither and Hither* (1943); *Seven Days Ashore* (1944); *Triple Threat* and *Racing Luck* (1948); *Free for All* and *Come to the Stables* (1949); and *Passage West* (1951). In 1945 Wilson had a prominent role in the New York musical *Bloomer Girl.* He also acted in "Beulah," one of the first television series starring black actors, in 1951. He was on the board of directors of the Negro Actors Guild of America. He died shortly after his retirement.   *Peggy Hardman*

Windmills. Before the introduction of windmills to Texas, inhabitable land was confined to areas where a constant water supply was available. There was no way for vast areas to be settled without a life-giving supply of water. The coming of the windmill made it possible to pump water from beneath the ground, and soon whole new areas of the state were opened up to settlers. The first windmills in Texas were of the European style, built by Dutch and German immigrants for grinding meal and powering light industry. What Texans needed most, however, was a windmill that pumped water. Because of its bulk and need for constant attention, the European windmill was impractical for this purpose. The solution to this problem came in 1854, when Daniel Halladay (Hallady or Halliday) built the first American windmill in Ellington, Connecticut. He added to his mill a vane, or "tail," as it was called by Texas cowhands, that functioned to direct the wheel into the wind. The wheel was a circle of wooden slats radiating from a horizontal shaft and set at angles to the wind, designed so that centrifugal force would slow it in high winds; thus the machine was self-regulating and operated unattended. Its simple direct-stroke energy converter consisted of only a shaft and a small flywheel to which the sucker rod was pinned. This compact mechanism was mounted on a four-legged wooden tower that could be constructed over a well in one day. Railroads immediately recognized windmills as an inexpensive means of providing water for steam engines and for attracting settlers to semiarid regions through which they planned to lay track. In 1860 the Houston Tap and Brazoria Railway purchased the right to manufacture and use James Mitchell's "Wind Wheel" on its right-of-way from Houston to Wharton. By 1873 the windmill had become an important supplier of water for railways, small towns where there were no public water systems, and small farms.

Many of the very early mills were crude, inefficient, homemade contraptions. One of the popular makeshift mills was a wagon wheel with slats nailed around it to catch the wind, mounted on half an axle. The axle was fastened securely to a post erected beside the well. A sucker rod was pinned to the edge of the hub. It was stationary and worked only when the wind blew in the right direction. The windmills used later on the big ranches were the more dependable factory-made windmills. Windmills moved to the ranches when barbed wire came to

Texas in the late 1870s. At first the waterholes, springs, creeks, and rivers were fenced, so that the back lands had no access to water. In the midst of the ensuing fence cutting and fighting, some ranchers began drilling wells and experimenting with windmills. Most of these experiments were unsuccessful, however, due to lack of knowledge concerning the proper size of the windmill in relation to the depth and diameter of the well. One of the earliest successful experiments was made eight miles north of Eldorado, in Schleicher County, by Christopher C. Doty, a nomadic sheepman. Doty moved his flock into that area and found abundant water in shallow wells. By 1882, however, a drought had dried his wells; he ordered a drilling rig from Fort Scott, Arkansas, bored a 52-foot well, and erected a Star windmill, which successfully supplied water for his 4,000 head of stock.

The practice of watering stock with windmills spread rapidly over the Edwards and Stockton plateaus, into the Trans-Pecos country, and down into the Rio Grande plains. It then moved northward into the Panhandle, where Eastern land speculators began buying, fencing, and running stock on the land until it became ripe for colonization. Among the first of these speculators to indirectly bring windmills to North Texas was the Magnolia Cattle and Land Company, organized by Willa V. Johnson. In 1884 the company bought two-thirds of the state-owned land in Borden County, land that had natural water resources and had long been unofficially claimed for grazing by C. C. Slaughter. When Johnson fenced the land, Slaughter was forced into the use of windmills to supply water for his cattle. By 1886 the Matador Land and Cattle Company and the Francklyn Land and Cattle Company had begun using windmills to water stock. The largest of the Eastern land speculators, the Capitol Syndicate, began using windmills on its XIT Ranch in 1887. One XIT windmill, believed to be the world's tallest, was made of wood and stood 132 feet. By 1900 the XIT had 335 windmills in operation. On the coastal prairies of Texas the Coleman–Fulton Pasture Company put up 22 windmills in San Patricio County in 1885–86, but it was not until the King Ranch began extensive use of the windmill in 1890 that the practice began to spread rapidly over that area. By 1900 windmills were a common sight in Texas. Inhabitable land was no longer limited to regions with a natural water supply. The windmill made the most remote areas habitable.

The use of windmills brought about two of the most colorful characters of the West, the driller and the windmiller, and altered the lifestyle of another, the range rider. The driller was usually a loner and seldom seen by anyone except the range rider and windmiller. He followed the fence crews and guessed at where he might find water, then bored wells with his horse-powered drilling rig. When he was successful the windmiller followed and set up a mill. Owners of the larger ranches usually employed several windmillers to make continuous rounds, checking and repairing windmills. The windmillers lived in covered wagons and only saw headquarters once or twice a month. The early mills had to be greased twice a week, and this was the range rider's job. He kept a can (or beer bottle) containing grease tied to his saddle. When he rode up to a mill that was squeaking, he would climb it, hold the wheel with a pole until he could mount the platform, and then let the wheel turn while he poured grease over it. The range rider was always in danger of attacks from swarms of wasps, which hung their clustered cells beneath the windmill's platform; there was the added danger of falling from the tower when such attacks occurred.

The windmill industry's shift in 1888 to the backgeared, all-steel mill caused heated debates in Texas livestock and farming circles. Most ranchers and farmers welcomed the new steel windmill because its galvanized wheel and tower held up better in harsh weather; also, its gear system was better able to take advantage of the wind, thus enabling the windmill to run more hours per day. The backgeared mill could also pump deeper and larger-diameter wells. Those who favored the old wooden mill argued that the steel mill was more likely to break because of its high speed, that it was not as easily repaired as the wooden mill, and that when parts had to be ordered the steel mill might be inoperative for days. Though sales of wooden mills continued, they declined steadily, so that by 1912 few were being sold. The last major development in the windmill came in 1915. A housing that needed to be filled with oil only once a year was built around the mill's gears. This relieved the range rider of his biweekly greasing chores and somewhat diminished the windmiller's job. Because of the dependability of this improved windmill, worries over water shortages were eased for the rancher, farmer, and rural dweller. This mill was the prime supplier of water in rural Texas until 1930, when electric and gasoline pumps began to be widely used.

Though Texas became the largest user of windmills in the United States, there were never more than three active manufacturers of windmills in Texas at one time. Only two Texas manufacturers, the Axtell Company in Fort Worth and the San Antonio Machine and Supply Company, produced windmills on a large scale. The last water-pumping windmill patented in the United States, however, was invented by a native Texan, W. W. Welborn, in 1951, in the small southwestern town of Carrizo Springs. It was a specialized mill designed for pumping water from depths of 700 to 2,000 feet. By the time this giant mill had been developed, the windmill market had declined so far that it could support no new mills. At their peak in 1928, windmill manufacturers in the United States produced 99,050 units a year, 26,000 of which were exported; 50 percent of the remainder were sold in Texas. The last census of windmill manufacturers was taken in 1963; that year only 7,562 units were sold, and 3,000 of those were sold in Texas.

Windmills remained an important supplier of water for Texas cattlemen. In the late 1960s the King Ranch kept 262 mills running continuously and 100 complete spares in stock. Stocking spare mills is a common practice among ranchers who depend on the windmill to supply water for cattle in remote pastures. Because the windmill has been confined for the most part to remote areas, it has become a symbol of a lonely and primitive life, fitting for the pioneer Texans it first served.

During the 1970s researchers turned to windmills as an energy source. Due to the oil embargo and subsequent fuel crisis, the United States government increased funding for windmill research. In the 1980s the two types of modern windmills included horizontal axis and vertical axis. These new versions harness wind power and convert it into electricity. The Windmill Museum, which centers on Dutch culture, is located in Nederland, Texas. A Texas historical marker at Littlefield marks the site of a replica of the world's tallest windmill, built on the XIT Ranch. The original blew over in 1926.

Daniel B. Welborn

Women. *Woman Suffrage.* In the settlement and development of Texas, men and women were partners in hardship and work but not in politics and government. As an independent republic and as a state in the Union, Texas granted women no voting rights. The question of their voting was raised during the Constitutional Convention of 1868–69, when Tirus H. Mundine of Burleson County proposed that the franchise be conferred upon qualified persons without distinction of sex. The committee on state affairs approved this proposal, but the convention rejected it by a vote of 52 to 13. A few years later, during the Constitutional Convention of 1875, two resolutions for the enfranchisement of women were introduced. Both were referred to the committee on suffrage, but neither was reported. Through the initiative of Rebecca Henry Hayes of Galveston, the Texas Equal Rights Association was organized at a meeting in Dallas in May 1893. The association soon had auxiliaries in Denison, Dallas, Fort Worth, Taylor, Granger, San Antonio, Belton, and Beaumont. Interest in women's rights was thereby aroused. Suffrage news began appearing in Texas newspapers. A bill to enfranchise women was introduced in the Texas House of Representatives in 1895 and was referred to the committee on constitutional amendments, but was never reported. In spite of its auspicious beginning, the TERA was destined to be short-lived. Dissension arose between Hayes and the executive committee, and at the state convention in Dallas in June 1895 she was not reelected to the presidency. The association then entered a period of decline, and during 1896 it ceased to function.

Interest was revived when Annette Finnigan and her sisters, Elizabeth and Katharine, organized the Equal Suffrage League of Houston in February 1903. Through the efforts of the Houston suffragists a similar organization was established in Galveston. Delegates from the two leagues met in Houston in December 1903 and organized the Texas Woman Suffrage Association with Annette Finnigan as president. Unfortunately for the suffrage cause, the Finnigan sisters moved from the state in 1905, and without their leadership and support the association became inactive. During Finnigan's presidency the Texas Woman Suffrage Association attempted to organize leagues in several Texas cities but was unable to secure adequate local support. Throughout the state, however, there were individuals who favored votes for women. The issue was brought before the Texas legislature in 1907 when Jess A. Baker of Granbury introduced in the House of Representatives a resolution to enfranchise them. At a hearing on 21 February, Elisabet Ney, the sculptor, Helen Stoddard, president of the state WCTU, and several other women spoke in its behalf. Their efforts were of no avail, however, for the committee on constitutional amendments recommended that the resolution not be adopted.

In the spring of 1908 a woman suffrage club was formed in Austin. For several years it was the only votes-for-women organization in the state. In February 1912 an Equal Franchise Society was formed in San Antonio. Its president was Mary Eleanor Brackenridge, a prominent clubwoman and civic leader. The society held frequent meetings, sponsored public lectures, and distributed large quantities of literature. Its activities stimulated interest throughout Texas, and the time now seemed opportune for the establishment of a state-level organization. In April 1913 more than 100 persons from seven Texas cities met in San Antonio and reactivated the Texas Woman Suffrage Association. For the office of president they chose Mary Eleanor

Baylor University woman "beating the drum" for woman suffrage, Waco, 1915. Courtesy Texas Collection, Baylor University, Waco, Texas. Despite earlier efforts by such groups as the Texas Woman Suffrage Association, women in Texas won the vote only after the Texas legislature ratified the national woman suffrage amendment in June 1919.

Brackenridge. She held this office until April 1914, when she was succeeded by Annette Finnigan, who had returned to Texas. The following year Finnigan was succeeded by Minnie Fisher Cunningham of Galveston. At their convention in 1916 the suffragists changed the name of their organization to Texas Equal Suffrage Association and reelected Cunningham president. Subsequent conventions also reelected her, and she held this office until the Suffrage Association was replaced by the League of Women Voters of Texas in October 1919.

The suffragists realized that gaining the vote would not be easy. Women had long been unable to vote, and many people, including many women, thought that the status quo should not be disturbed. Custom and tradition held that government was the prerogative of men and hence outside of women's sphere, that women had no need for the ballot because men would protect them. Participation in politics would, it was thought, make women coarse and crude and would cause them to neglect their homes and their children. In the minds of many Texans woman suffrage was more than a political issue. It was a dangerous threat to the social order. In contrast, the suffragists pointed out that women were citizens and taxpayers and, as such, should be entitled to a voice in the affairs of government. Enfranchisement would not cause them to neglect their homes, nor would it make them coarse and crude. On the contrary, it would enable them to function more effectively in their traditional roles. As mothers, teachers, businesswomen, and workingwomen, they would use the ballot in behalf of better schools, playgrounds, parks, public health, sanitation, working conditions, and an improved life in general.

A formidable task of changing public opinion lay ahead. To gain support at the grassroots level, the suffragists organized leagues throughout the state. By June 1918 there were 98 such organizations. To publicize their cause they sponsored lectures and forums, conducted debates and essay contests, maintained booths at fairs and in department stores, marched in parades, made house-to-house canvasses, and sent letters and petitions to legislators and congressmen. They distributed thousands of pamphlets and kept newspapers supplied with suffrage news. With the entry of the United States into World War I, suffragist leagues supported projects and activities in behalf of the war effort. Their patriotic endeavors were important in softening the opposition to enfranchisement. The Texas Equal Suffrage Association was an affiliate of the National American Woman Suffrage Association, and for several years it was the only state-level organization working for women's enfranchisement. In January 1916, however, the Congressional Union for Woman Suffrage (later known as the National Woman's party) established a branch in Texas. It began with a membership of 100 and with Clara Snell Wolfe of Austin as state chairman. Unlike the NAWSA, the National Woman's party engaged in militant activities such as picketing the White House and burning President Wilson in effigy. The party's Texas branch announced its approval of this policy but sponsored no militant agitation in the state. Public opinion in Texas was opposed to such militancy, and the National Woman's party was unable to gain widespread support in the state. In 1915 the opponents of women's enfranchisement organized the Texas Association Opposed to Woman Suffrage. They distributed large amounts of literature but did little organizing throughout the state. The leader of the antisuffragists was Pauline Kleiber Wells, wife of James B. Wells of Brownsville.

In 1911 Jess Baker of Granbury once again raised the suffrage question in the Texas House. His resolution to enfranchise women was referred to the committee on constitutional amendments, which recommended that it not pass. Two years later T. H. McGregor of Austin introduced a similar resolution in the Senate. This resolution received a favorable committee report but was rejected by a vote of 19 to 8 when the Senate voted on its passage to engrossment. By the time of the 1915 legislative session, women's enfranchisement had become an active issue. The suffragists had done much educational work through newspaper publicity and the distribution of literature. Prospects for winning concessions from the legislature seemed good. The Texas Woman Suffrage Association established a lobby in Austin. Women throughout the state sent letters and petitions to the lawmakers. In the House the committee on constitutional amendments recommended that the suffrage resolution be adopted. When the House voted on the measure, 90 of its members voted in favor and 32 against. Since the 90 favorable votes were less than the two-thirds majority required for a constitu-

tional amendment, the resolution failed. During the two years that followed, the suffragists continued to organize and propagandize. When the legislature convened in January 1917, resolutions to enfranchise women were introduced. Once again the House voted on the question. This time 76 representatives voted in favor and 56 against. Once again the resolution failed of adoption. The governor of Texas during the 1915 and 1917 legislative sessions was James E. Ferguson, an inexorable opponent of woman suffrage. When dissatisfaction with Ferguson's conduct in office led to a movement to impeach him, the suffragists supported the anti-Ferguson movement. During the summer of 1917 he was impeached and removed from office. His successor, William P. Hobby, was friendly toward the cause.

Primary suffrage did not require an amendment of the state constitution but could be granted by a simple legislative act. At a called session in March 1918, Charles B. Metcalfe of San Angelo introduced a bill to permit women to vote in primaries. It passed the House 84 to 34 and the Senate 18 to 4. It was then signed by Governor Hobby, and Texas women thereby became eligible to participate in primary elections. In seventeen days 386,000 women registered to vote in the Democratic primary to be held on 26 July. They took an active part in the campaign and strongly supported Hobby for governor and Annie Blanton for state superintendent of public instruction. Hobby, Blanton, and other candidates favored by the women were victorious. Since Texas was predominantly Democratic, primary suffrage was almost equivalent to full enfranchisement. Women were now a force in state politics. In August 1918 Democratic conventions in 233 counties went on record in favor of woman suffrage, and in September the state Democratic convention endorsed it.

When the legislature convened in January 1919 Governor Hobby sent a message recommending that the Texas Constitution be amended to extend full suffrage to women. He also recommended that persons of foreign birth be allowed to vote only after they had acquired full citizenship through naturalization. If adopted, this citizenship requirement would take the vote from "first paper" aliens, who were at that time fully enfranchised. Without a dissenting vote, both houses passed a resolution embodying the governor's recommendations. Before becoming part of the Texas Constitution, however, the resolution had to be approved by the voters at the polls. The enfranchisement of women and the disenfranchisement of aliens were both parts of the same resolution. The two proposals could not be voted upon separately but had to be accepted or rejected as a unit. Under existing law women could not vote in the referendum on the proposed amendment since they had only primary suffrage. Aliens could vote on it, however, because they were already fully enfranchised. Under the direction of Jane McCallum of Austin the suffragists conducted a vigorous campaign. When the referendum was held on 24 May, however, the proposed amendment was defeated by a majority of 25,000 votes. The antisuffragists hailed this defeat as a mandate against votes for women. The suffragists emphatically denied this claim. They maintained that the issue had been clouded by the inclusion of the citizenship requirement and published an analysis of the returns showing that counties with large alien populations cast large majorities against the proposed amendment. The following month, June 1919, the federal woman suffrage amendment was submitted to the states. The Texas legislature convened in special session on 23 June. The following day the House

Children attending kindergarten, Canadian, Texas, ca. 1906. Photograph by Ellsworth Fuller, Oklahoma City. Courtesy Texas Memorial Museum, Austin; acc. no. 886-5. Women established the state's first public kindergartens.

adopted a resolution ratifying the federal amendment by a vote of 96 to 21. In spite of some opposition, the Senate approved it on 28 June. Texas was then hailed as the ninth state in the Union to ratify the Nineteenth Amendment. The Nineteenth Amendment encountered its strongest opposition in the South. It was opposed as a threat to states' rights and to state control of elections, partly because of the fear that the black woman's vote might increase the political influence of African Americans. These states'-rights and racial objections were raised in Texas, but they were of less concern there than in other parts of the South. Of the 11 states in the former Confederacy, only 3 ratified the Nineteenth Amendment during the 1919–20 campaign. Texas, the first of the three, yielded to the demands of the suffragists only after the movement seemed assured of success nationally.

A. Elizabeth Taylor

Women and Education. The history of Texas women with regard to education includes the struggle for equal access, the capitalization on professional opportunities in the field of education, and the continuing use of education as an avenue to further development. The earliest signs of education facilities in Texas date to the area's Spanish period, when missions established for Indians included schools that focused on training in agriculture and industry. These mission schools included training for females, such as Angelina, the Caddo for whom Angelina County was later named, who was educated by priests at San Juan Bautista around 1700. Nonmission schools were also pre-

sent in the region by the mid-eighteenth century, but by the time the area was part of Mexico in the 1820s, all signs of formal education—for either sex—had disappeared. The subsequent constitution of the state of Coahuila and Texas required the establishment of primary schools, and in the early 1830s the state made land grants to support local schools. These schools included separate primary instruction for girls, who followed a similar curriculum to that for boys, with an added emphasis on sewing, embroidery, and other domestic skills. During this same time, numerous private schools opened in Texas to provide education for the increasing number of American settlers in the state. Such facilities often afforded girls an opportunity to attend school, usually in a separate female department. Frances Trask Thompson's school in Coles Settlement (later Independence), established in 1834, is recognized as the first boarding school for girls in Texas. It was also the precursor of Independence Academy, Baylor Female College, and Mary Hardin–Baylor University. Lydia Ann McHenry opened a school for girls in Washington County in 1835.

The number of educational facilities grew during the eras of the Republic of Texas and antebellum Texas. As civic leaders, religious groups, and educational associations promoted the establishment of educational institutions, private academies for girls continued to be organized. Such schools usually had women teachers. The female department of the Methodist Rutersville College (1840), near La Grange in Fayette County, was a well-known institution of the time. Miss A. E. Madden ran the Female Academy established in San Augustine in 1840. She had taught in the United States before settling in Texas, and in her new school she combined girls' training in literature and grammar with drawing, painting, and needlework. Matagorda Academy, established in 1840, admitted both boys and girls and utilized the services of its founder, Rev. C. S. Ives, and his wife to teach their respective sexes. Though Mirabeau Lamar led the Republic of Texas to commit itself to a public school system in 1839, the actual move to put such a system in place was a slow one. Private schools remained the only choice for many Texas children, and smaller numbers of wealthy Texans sent their children to school in the United States. Either of these alternatives usually ensured the segregation and differentiation of male and female training. Many young Texas women in the midnineteenth century were taught at home schools run by their mothers. Isolation from other areas and limited resources mandated that many pioneer Texas women teach their children—both boys and girls—at home. This practice reflected an important educational contribution by women in Texas and helped produce reasonably low illiteracy rates among white Texans over the age of 20 by 1850: 12 percent for men and 20 percent for women. However, teacher Melinda Rankin noted in her *Texas in 1850* that education in the state still showed many weaknesses, and that, specifically, it lacked a "Female Seminary of high order," which could "elevate the standard of female education, which . . . has not been made in Texas as prominent an object as its importance demands."

The foundations of modern Texas public schools were laid in 1854, with the establishment of a $2 million school fund by Governor Pease. Although numerous changes in the state's approach to education came with the constitutions of 1866, 1869, and 1876, the concept of tax-funded public schools had been accepted, if not always enthusiastically, since 1854. For much of this time, schools separated by sex and race were the norm in Texas. Separation often carried other stipulations. In 1871, for example, the Texas Board of Education specified that public schools for girls devote two days a week to needlework. The Constitution of 1876 marked the first indication of a major step away from consistent separation of males and females in public schools by allowing communities to establish schools according to conditions. The first move toward coeducation in higher education in Texas came in 1865, when Baylor University approved the teaching of male and female students together. Subsequent to this, the University of Texas was coeducational from its founding in 1883, in contrast to the state's first major land-grant institution, Texas A&M (1876).

As educational opportunity for women increased in the state, so, too, did their presence in the teaching profession. After the Civil War, a gradual feminization of the educational field took place, as the depletion of male teachers resulting from the war and the general broadening of educational opportunities brought a greater need for teachers. By 1900 Texas women outnumbered men for the first time in teaching positions. Texas women subsequently pushed to attain more professional recognition as teachers, often turning to organizational efforts to help them. In 1916 Annie Webb Blanton, a graduate of the University of Texas with teaching experience in rural and city schools as well as the state normal school in Denton, led a group of women to protest their lack of influence in the Texas State Teachers

Association; she was subsequently elected president of this group. In 1929 in Austin she organized the Delta Kappa Gamma Society, a women's professional organization for teachers that grew into an international body with membership exceeding 160,000.

The changing face of higher education in Texas in the twentieth century had a direct influence on women. With the foundation of numerous teachertraining institutions in the state between 1900 and 1920, as well as the establishment of the Girls' Industrial College (now Texas Woman's University) in 1902, the opportunity to pursue formal education beyond high school, as well as to attain postsecondary teaching jobs, greatly increased for women. These opportunities were defined, or limited, in several ways. Six of the seven new normal schools admitted only white students, as did the Girls Industrial College. Women in the southern and western parts of the state found access to these institutions more difficult. Furthermore, the opportunity to continue one's education, even at a reasonably affordable state school, almost always necessitated at least middleclass income. Still, the early institutions gave Texas women increased access to education. Texas women used their education, interests, and organizational skills in a variety of classroom endeavors. Often they worked in oneroom rural schoolhouses, where they taught a span of ages and subjects and were expected to abide by strict codes of conduct, which could require modest dress, prohibit marriage, and mandate regular church attendance. Urban classrooms presented different opportunities and challenges. Leonor Villegas de Magnon, a teacher in Laredo, taught in the midst of border conflict resulting from the Mexican Revolution. She eventually turned her school into a hospital and helped the wounded from both sides of the fighting.

Creativity to meet pressing social needs marked the efforts of numerous Texas women educators in the twentieth century. Jovita Idar ran a free kindergarten in San Antonio. Jeffie O. A. Conner became the state's first black home demonstration agent and an administrator for the McLennan County schools. In Fort Worth, Edna Gladney opened the Texas Children's Home and Aid Society to educate unwed mothers and help find homes for their children. Jovita González de Mireles initiated the state's first bilingual elementary school program in Texas and wrote Spanish-language textbooks with her husband for Corpus Christi schools beginning in 1940. Increased access to higher education slowly allowed women to reach positions of leadership in these institutions. Lucy Ann Kidd–Key taught in and served as president of North Texas Female College in Sherman for 28 years before her death in 1916. The college, which closed in 1935, was wellknown for its cultural emphases and its many faculty members recruited from Europe. Mary Elizabeth Branch became the first black woman college president in Texas when she became the head of Tillotson College in Austin (now Huston–Tillotson College) in 1930. Lorene Rogers became the first woman named as president of a major state university when she took over leadership of the University of Texas at Austin in 1974; she served as its president until 1979. Mary Huey became the first female president of Texas Woman's University in 1976 and served until 1986.

Access to education also had a momentous impact on women's contributions to society, as Texas women used their intellectual attainments to advance other goals. Frequently, female leaders in club work, politics, and community service

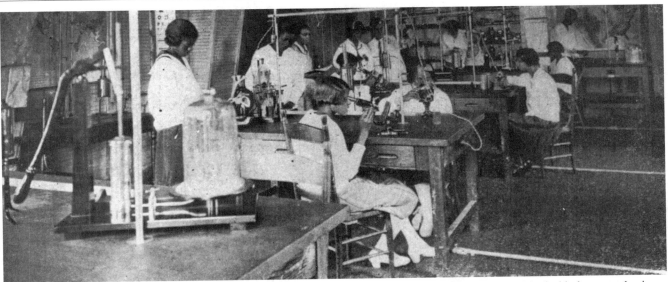

Class in physics at Mary Allen Seminary, Crockett, Texas, ca. 1927. Courtesy CAH; CN 06166. Educational opportunities for black women developed toward the end of the nineteenth century. Mary Allen Seminary opened in 1886.

held college degrees. The increasingly active women's clubs in the state generally grew out of literary societies. The Texas Federation of Women's Clubs, which began in 1897, quickly targeted education as one of its major interests by making the establishment and development of libraries in the state a priority. Julia B. Ideson, a graduate of the first library science class at the University of Texas in 1903, became the head of the Carnegie Library in Houston and later had the city's downtown library named for her. Dorothy Scarborough introduced the first college course in journalism to Baylor University. The roster of well-known Texas women with postsecondary degrees includes early-twentieth-century figures such as Anna Pennybacker (Sam Houston Normal Institute) and Minnie Fisher Cunningham (University of Texas Medical School), as well as more recent leaders such as Sarah Hughes (Goucher College) and Ann Richards (Baylor University).

Women's education also found a connection to politics in local school districts, where the view of the classroom as a woman's domain, as well as the expected interest mothers were to take in the education of their children, led women to positions of leadership. The Texas Congress of Mothers (later known as the Texas Congress of Parents and Teachers) was formed in 1909 and became a vital organization for Texas women. By the 1920s, Texas women also held increasing numbers of school board seats and school district superintendencies. Dallas and San Antonio both elected women to their school boards before 1915. Annie Blanton's election in 1918 as state superintendent of public instruction represented the first time a Texas woman was elected to statewide office and symbolized, not coincidentally, the important role of education as an avenue for women's increasing political involvement. The first woman elected to the Texas Senate, Margie E. Neal, who served four terms beginning in 1926, consistently supported education-related legislation and introduced the bill that instituted a new State Board of Education.

In the late twentieth century, Texas women continued to maintain a close relationship with educational endeavors. All of the state's public and private institutions of higher education admitted women, and Texas women were earning undergraduate degrees numbers equal to men. Texas Woman's University remained the state's premiere female school. Although it admitted males in some of its programs, it was still recognized as the largest university for women in the United States. Numerous private primary and secondary schools, such as the Hockaday School in Dallas, continued to limit their enrollment to girls. Of the state's 500,000 public school teachers, 78 percent were women in 1994. A burgeoning area of change for females in Texas schools occurred in the field of sports, where federal legislation mandating equal financial support to male and female programs helped increase the quantity and quality of women's and girls' sports. Thus, in a state long marked by educational squabbles and inequities, Texas women have fought for their access to substantial formal training, have forged important roles for themselves as educators in the state, and have used their educational opportunities to enhance their place in a variety of endeavors and as a conduit for improving society.

Debbie Mauldin Cottrell

Women and health. Women are the major consumers of health services, the majority of health caregivers, and the traditional caretakers of family health. Women's health care and particularly the conditions under which women give birth have ramifications far beyond the health and well-being of the individual mother and child; they frequently serve as a gauge for society's conscience and faith in the future. Texas women have always had a nurturing role in matters of health: as women, wives, or mothers, they were responsible for maintaining a healthy environment, preventing illness, maintaining wellness, and treating the sick and injured. Among the nomadic populations and in agricultural villages, women cared for children, prepared food and clothing, and maintained the home. In the late seventeenth century the wives of Spanish soldiers were the first European women to settle in Texas in the presidios that supported the Spanish missions. Women in Spanish Texas continued to fulfill the chief roles of homemaker and mother amid the rigors of frontier life. Midwifery was important during this

Tyrrell Public Library bookmobile, 1929. Courtesy Tyrrell Historical Library, Beaumont, Texas. This bookmobile, brought about by the efforts of women, was the first in Texas and one of the first in the nation

period, when women gave birth at home aided by friends and relatives. In 1809 Governor Manuel María de Salcedo ordered that all midwives register with the city council, pass an examination, and receive a license. This was an attempt to decrease infant mortality caused by the ignorance of women posing as midwives. Isolation from other women frequently removed the women of the Texas frontier from their sources of support, advice, and care when faced with illness. The major treatment in outbreaks of smallpox and cholera was Indian or Mexican folk medicine with prayer. Jane Long was probably the first Anglo-American woman to give birth in Texas. She, her daughter, and a slave named Kian spent the winter of 1820–21 on Bolivar Peninsula while James Long was on a military mission against Spanish forces. Kian successfully nursed Mrs. Long through both childbirth and illness during that winter. In 1850 men outnumbered women by 15,704. The housekeeping that was expected of Texas wives and mothers included care of the sick. During the turbulent decade of the Texas Revolution and Republic of Texas, women ran the farms, ranches, and plantations during their husbands' absence and organized the evacuation of their families as the Mexican armies approached. Susanna Dickinson accompanied her husband to the Alamo, where she and Andrea Castañón Villanueva served as nurses. Women in antebellum Texas, faced with the inconvenience and expense of getting a physician, turned to domestic medicine or alternatives to mainstream medicine. Women within families, particularly plantation owners' wives, assumed primary responsibility for family and slave health, nursing, dosing, and deciding when to call for professional help. Many black women, both slaves and free, also provided nursing care and midwifery services, and concocted drugs.

Texas women had access to a wide variety of domestic-medicine manuals. Popular journals and local newspapers were filled with domestic advice, remedies, and advertisements for cures. The *Southern Lady's Companion* ran articles on health and healing of special interest to women. Stores were filled with patent medicines claiming to cure ailments from cancer to coughs. From Lydia E. Pinkham's Vegetable Compound to Leidy's Female Pills, patent-medicine advertising was often directed to

women, both as consumers and caretakers of family health. Bolstered by the therapeutic confusion and reform spirit of the nineteenth century, and mirroring the notion of frailty and invalidism among middle and upper class women, patent medicines claimed cures for a multitude of female disorders. Patent medicines also provided women an alternative to orthodox treatments they considered harmful. Some nineteenth-century physicians were active in the effort to educate consumers against dangerous or fraudulent remedies. The *Texas Health Journal*, founded in Dallas in 1888 and the official organ of the Texas State Sanitary Association, characterized itself as "a monthly magazine devoted to preventative and state medicine and the exposure of medical fraud, secret remedies and quacks." The strict regulation of patent medicines that developed was accompanied by increased reliance on doctors and therefore a loss of females' ability to manage their own and their families' health. As the nineteenth century evolved, it became fashionable for male physicians in the Northeast to attend middle and upper class women during childbirth. Women in Texas also invited male physicians into their birthing rooms to take advantage of the shortened labors and painless childbirth they promised. Physicians were also called by friends or midwives when complications developed. Once there, the physician validated his presence through his practices. Such "meddlesome midwifery" was not without opponents, and Texas physicians themselves debated the pros and cons of anesthetics, forceps, and other obstetrical interventions. The rural character of the state and scarcity of regular physicians, however, made the midwife a necessity. Some Texas physicians probably enlisted the aid of midwives to assist them in covering their rural practices, and some midwives received instruction and advice from local physicians. Midwives were protected in the first medical practice act of Texas passed in 1873. But later, at the 1881 meeting of the Texas State Medical Association, the assembly opposed the part of the act permitting "ignorant and irresponsible females, without any evidence of qualification, to practice midwifery." Galveston had a training program for midwives in 1890. "Midwife" was listed as an occupation in the Galveston City Directory from 1870 through 1919. The female midwife remained the major birth attendant for Texas women at least through the turn of the twentieth century, when 75 percent of births in Texas were attended by midwives.

Nurse-training schools in Texas developed in the nineteenth century, when trained nurses established a public role for women that was fashioned from the domestic sphere and brought cleanliness, order, and respectability to the hospital. Catholic congregations of women supplied the first trained nurses in Texas; they staffed numerous hospitals, where nursing was eventually formally taught. The first nursing school in Texas was John Sealy Hospital Training School, which formally opened in March 1890 with two students and was followed by six more nursing schools in the next 14 years. Domestic virtues such as duty and self-sacrifice were a recurring theme in training schools as student nurses faced demanding physical labor, long hours, little leisure time, and exposure to serious illnesses. Nursing education became the bridge by which women extended their traditional domestic role of caring for the sick into the public world of work.

Before 1891 physicians trained in Texas received their education in proprietary medical schools and their training through

Women demonstrating for passage of prohibition statutes, Lufkin, ca. 1915. Courtesy Ora McMullen Room, Kurth Memorial Library, Lufkin, Texas. Even before they received the right to vote, women were involved in political causes, especially those relating to family and community welfare.

an apprenticeship system. Formally trained female physicians were quite new when they were first discussed in Texas publications in the midnineteenth century. Those who attempted to follow Elizabeth Blackwell, who had received her medical degree from Geneva College in 1849, were often frustrated. They frequently met opposition similar to that expressed by Fanny Fern in the *Standard* (26 March 1853): "FOR MYSELF, I prefer prescriptions written by a masculine hand; shan't submit my pulse to anything that wears a bonnet." Others, such as Mrs. Sarah J. Hale, thought that women were "better qualified by nature to take charge of the sick and suffering . . . that mothers should know the best means of preserving the health of their children," and "that female physicians are the proper attendant for their own sex in the hour of sorrow." Thus the debate over women in medicine evolved: either women had no place in medicine because they were female, belonged in medicine precisely because they were female and had important qualities to impart, or belonged in medicine in spite of the fact they were female. Early Texas female physicians trained outside Texas include Sofie D. Herzog, who practiced in Brazoria from the late 1880s until her death in 1925; Margaret Holland, the first woman to practice medicine in Harris County, whose career lasted from the 1870s to 1921; Juliet Marchant, who practiced in La Porte from 1893 to 1929; and Minnie Archer, who practiced in Houston from 1894 to 1912. Other Texas doctors trained outside the state included Ellen Lawson Dabbs, Grace Danforth, and Frances (Fanny) Leak. In 1897 Marie DeLalondre Dietzel became the first female graduate of the oldest medical school in Texas, the University of Texas Medical Branch at Galveston, which opened in 1891. Female physicians continued to graduate from that institution, an average of one every other year, until 1920.

Dr. Marie Charlotte Schaefer graduated in 1900 and after postgraduate work at the University of Chicago and Johns Hopkins, became the first female member of the faculty in 1901. She headed a department from 1912 until her death in 1927. The university also offered women a degree in pharmacology. Political activist Minnie Cunningham was one of the first women to earn that degree (1901).

In late nineteenth-century Texas, women began to influence health concerns and social reform through political action and women's organizations. The suffrage movement of the late nineteenth century strongly advocated equal access to medical education for women. The movement was also intertwined with the popular health movement, which emphasized hygiene and dress reform. Texas women's clubs were a force in the debate over prohibition, antitobacco legislation, child labor legislation, purefoodanddrug legislation, improvement of public health, sanitation, licensing standards for nurses, improved health-care facilities, and other health topics. In 1912 the *Texas Medical Journal* instituted a "women's department" conducted by the wife of the editor, Mrs. F. E. Daniel, and other physicians' wives, female physicians, and consumers. Mrs. Daniel's purpose was to devote a "few pages" of each issue to "articles of especial value to my sex." The department continued through 1914 and provided information on social issues, public-health problems, and women's health. Although far from radical, the articles encouraged women to ask interesting questions of their physicians, such as "why so many joyous healthy girls become invalids after marriage?" and "why so many children are born blind?" The women medical students of Texas were as forward-looking in the arena of women's rights as the suffragettes or the women who broke into medical education several decades earlier. The 15 female students at UTMB in 1912 lobbied to have the position for the secretary–treasurer of the student association to be a permanent female office. Their efforts were defeated by a vote of 103 to 26. However, Violet H. Keiller, Class of 1914, was elected secretary–treasurer by acclamation. She was the daughter of a member of the original faculty and later joined the staff of the medical school. In 1914 the graduating class consisted of 4 females and 40 males, and the top 2 graduates were women. In 1916 the women medical students at UTMB invited all the women physicians of Texas to a meeting. The *Texas State Journal of Medicine* listed the names of 49 women eligible to attend. The April 1916 issue of the *Journal* was devoted to Texas women of medicine. Contributors included Mary C. Harper (San Antonio), Ethel Heard and Violet Keiller (Galveston), Minnie Lee Maffett (Dallas), and Martha Wood (Houston). In 1920 Ethel Lyon Heard, a member of the faculty at UTMB, was appointed as the physician for women at the University of Texas. Almost 30 years after the first female graduated from UTMB, women were still encountering obstacles to their role in medicine. In 1926 the hospital board of John Sealy Hospital in Galveston, after vigorous debate, decided that misses Edith Bonnett and Frances Van Zandt would be allowed to serve internships, though with certain restrictions. Some of the hospital staff considered work in the male genitourinary division particularly objectionable to women, and expected that the men in this division and the marine ward would not allow women interns to treat them. The women agreed to have other work substituted during those two six-week terms. Since the hospital would need to hire two senior students to fill in for them, the women stated they would not expect the hospital to pay them room and board during those two months.

The late nineteenth and early twentieth century brought a massive attack waged by physicians on the character, cleanliness, integrity, training, abilities, and safety of the midwife. Texas physicians echoed this attack in their journals, although some admitted that midwives were still necessary. The early twentieth century was a period of struggle for professional cohesion, high standards, and the exclusion of alternative practitioners among medical professionals in general. Obstetricians were attempting to expand their influence and raise their status. To eliminate the economic competition of the midwife and general practitioner and to establish their superior expertise, obstetricians defined pregnancy and childbirth as pathologic and themselves as the only safe, successful, and qualified attendants. The substitution of scientifically trained specialists and the hospital for the lay midwife and the home removed childbirth from the female domestic sphere and placed it in the hands of "experts" in the malecontrolled professional sphere. In Galveston, with an abundance of physicians and hospitals, the percentage of midwife-attended deliveries decreased from 35 percent in 1910 to 2 percent in 1923. The campaign to eliminate the midwife was less successful in rural Texas, however. In 1924, the Bureau of Child Hygiene of the State Department of Health estimated that 4,000 midwives were practicing in Texas, and, at least in certain eastern and southern counties, midwives were attending over 50 percent of the births. The bureau concluded that many of these midwives "have no training, not even in the simplest rudiments of surgical cleanliness" and recommended licensing and training to remedy the problem. The twentieth-century public-health movement was effective in analyzing, publicizing, and helping to remedy many of the deficiencies of health care in America. In the effort

to improve maternal and infant morbidity and mortality the focus was placed on the expertise of the obstetrician. Midwives were generally recognized only as a stopgap measure by health reformers, and efforts to improve their practice were meager. Training for midwives was provided by public-health nurses in Texas through money allocated by the 1921 Sheppard–Towner law, the first federal legislation to provide federal dollars to states to improve the health of mothers and children. Opposition to Sheppard–Towner was vigorous. Physicians opposed it as socialized medicine or as government intrusion into the business of states and the domestic life of American families. Consequently, its provisions were allowed to lapse in June 1929, and none of the 14 bills introduced to reinstate it was approved. If the passage of Sheppard–Towner was the culmination of the Progressive Era women's-health movement, its defeat reveals the movement's declining effectiveness. The conservative political climate, continued opposition of organized medicine, recognition that women did not vote as a bloc, and inability to maintain a sustained women's-health movement were factors contributing to the bill's demise.

The first half of the twentieth century found the majority of women in Texas still the keepers of the home, whether that home was on a cotton farm or in an oilfield. About a third of Texas women had entered the workforce by 1930, including a growing number of married women, but most were confined to occupations seen as "women's work" (clerical jobs, retail sales, teaching, nursing). The world wars brought women into traditionally male-occupied jobs. Female nurses from Texas contributed to the war effort in both wars. During World War II an estimated 51 percent of Texas nurses were serving in the armed forces or private war industries. An extreme shortage of nurses resulted. Other female-dominated jobs in allied health sciences developed as further evidence of the specialization and professionalization of women's nurturing qualities. Physical therapists and occupational therapists have been active in Texas since the 1920s. But the legacy of midwives in Texas did not end in the mid-twentieth century. In Texas in 1970, midwives attended slightly more than 3 percent of live births. In 1983 the Sixty-eighth Legislature enacted the Lay Midwifery Act, which mandated the annual identification of persons practicing lay midwifery, delineated the scope of practice, and provided for voluntary educational preparation for those attending births. With the addition of certified nurse midwives in Texas, almost 5 percent of Texas births in 1989 were attended by midwives. This small but important resurgence in midwifery is illustrative of the different perspective of the feminist health movement of the 1960s and 1970s when compared with the earlier woman's health movement. No longer was motherhood seen as woman's primary destiny or the role that guaranteed her a public voice. Instead, motherhood is seen as one role among many available to women. Women have been encouraged to alter the terms under which care is provided and to demand demedicalization of such functions as uncomplicated childbirth.

Women's health issues remain complex and challenging. By the 1980s the majority of mothers worked outside the home, yet they still had major responsibilities for family health, whether caring for ill children or elders or decreasing fat and cholesterol in the family diet. Women were expressing skepticism about the male-dominated biomedical model and asking why women, particularly pregnant women, are so underrepresented in clinical-research trials and why research into women's health is underfunded. Women consumers of health care were attempting to understand and shape that care in a way that recognized the larger context of their lives. Whether as female AIDS activists, in foundations such as the Houston-based Susan G. Komen Breast Cancer Foundation, or Right-to-Life or Pro-Choice groups, women were becoming more active in influencing the direction of their health care. *Cheryl Ellis Vaiani*

Women and the Law. Women's progress toward equal rights in Texas has developed within a complex history of social customs, cultural traditions, and law. The Lone Star State was at first a rural society based on farming and ranching, and its legal system reflected the outlook of a traditional, family-centered, agricultural population. As the state became more urbanized after 1900, the economy drew growing numbers of women into the marketplace. By taking jobs, entering the professions, and operating their own companies, women brought unprecedented legal questions to business, industry, politics, and government that required lawmakers to consider the needs of women as individuals and not merely as members of families. Before Texas women gained equal rights, marriage was the most significant influence on their legal status. From the time of the early republic, a single woman enjoyed basic civil liberties. Although she could not vote or serve on juries, she had the right to make contracts, to sue and be sued, to choose her domicile, to own and control property, and, if widowed, to have custody of her children. A matron, by contrast, bore many of the legal disabilities of a minor. The laws regulating property and contractual rights most clearly defined the married woman's legal status in Texas. By continuing the Spanish practice of giving limited, specific rights to married women, Texans avoided the English common-law practice of vesting the wife's legal identity in her husband. Indeed, Anglo-American law confined married women more than the Hispanic system. A Texas statute enacted in 1840 guaranteed rights that women have had ever since: to own separate property (the personal effects, real estate, and stocks and bonds possessed at the time of marriage) and to share equally with their husbands the wealth amassed during marriage. Also in keeping with the Hispanic law was a statute enacted in 1856, which allowed anyone "of sound mind" to make a last will and testament. Even though she could not witness the will of another person, a matron had the right to leave her separate property, as well as her share of the community property to whomever she chose.

While securing the wife's rights to ownership, Texas statutes and court rulings gave to the husband the management of both her separate and their community property, with the justification that such control helped him fulfill his legal duty to support her and the family. The law allowed him to bring suit to protect or enforce his wife's separate interests, as well as those of the community property. In addition, her earnings were, like his, community property; as such, they also were under his control. Until 1967 and the enactment of the marital-property section of the Family Code, Texas law put a wife's salary, bonuses, and wages under her husband's control to the extent that technically only he could "contract her services to another." In other words, an employer who wished to comply strictly could not hire a woman without consulting her husband. Despite her disabilities, however, the wife was not without legal rights. Without her permission her husband could not sell any of her property, and though she needed his agreement to sell her real estate or stocks

Supporters of the Equal Rights Amendment at the Capitol. Photograph by Mike Fluitt. Austin, 1975. Courtesy of the Austin History Center, Austin Public Library; PICA 09932.

and bonds, she could "by oral consent" give away any of her personal goods. She also had a limited right to defend her separate property by appealing to the county court if her husband mismanaged it or used its proceeds for anything other than the family's support. Such a review of the husband's management could persuade the court to give control of her property to the wife. As a general rule, then, the husband served as the family's financial and economic agent. But whenever necessary the wife could assume familial responsibilities as guardian, trustee, administratrix, executrix, or receiving agent. Indeed, by vesting limited property rights in married women through separate and community property, Texas law protected families from husbands who were careless, wasteful, or victims of economic depression.

Control of their own property came slowly to married women, creeping through five acts of legislation passed over more than 50 years. In 1913 Houston attorney Hortense Ward, one of the first three women admitted to the Texas bar, led the campaign to win a law intended to enlarge married women's rights regarding their separate property. Because of numerous hasty revisions to placate critics of the original bill, the statute collided with existing property laws, and court rulings consequently sheared away some of its intended benefits. Although the new law retained the husband as sole manager of the community property, the wife acquired control of the rents and other income from her real property holdings, as well as the income from her stocks and bonds. Her husband still had to agree to the sale of her separate property, but she gained exclusive control of bank accounts in her own name. Before 1913 a husband could write checks on his wife's account and even withdraw money that she had deposited before marriage. Though the wages of employed women remained under their husbands' control as community property, women of the middle and upper classes—those most likely to own real estate and stocks and bonds—benefited from the provisions of the 1913 law. Three later statutes, passed in 1921, 1957, and 1963, dealt with married women's legal status without effectively improving it. Change in the marital property law in 1921 added nothing to a married woman's rights, though it did exempt her separate property from creditors in contracts that she made jointly with her husband. Creditors could, in such cases, claim reimbursement only from the couple's community property. Thirty-six years later, in 1957, another law allowed married women aged 21 and over the choice of whether to accept complete control of their separate property, as well as to contract freely without their husbands' signatures. For a matron who chose not to take these rights and responsibilities, the provisions of earlier statutes remained: her husband had to "join in any encumbrance of her lands" and in the sale of her stocks and bonds. Because married couples on numerous occasions had used the wife's couvert status to avoid paying debts, the 1957 law expressly stated that marriage would not excuse a wife from her obligations or from suits and court actions in connection with her contracts. Although the measure enacted in 1963 stated that married women had the contractual rights of men and single women, it made little difference. Numerous other statutes contained provisions which, in effect if not by intent, curtailed women's rights.

Historically, Texas lawmakers were more concerned with protecting the interests of families than of individuals. Of all the state's laws intended to protect the family, those relating to the homestead probably carried the most real benefits for wives without marketable skills, whether they lived in urban or rural areas. Enacted as a statute in 1839 and first written into the state's constitution in 1845, the Texas homestead-exemption law gave wife and husband virtually identical rights regarding the homestead, except that only he could choose it and decide when to leave it. Her interests, like his, were protected by the guarantee that the surviving spouse had a life estate in the family homestead, and certain provisions of the law gave her the right, under defined circumstances, to block her husband's decisions regarding the homestead. Even if the actual holdings defined as the homestead were the husband's separate property and as such would pass beyond the immediate family upon his death, his widow and single daughters (but not single sons) had the right to live on the homestead for as long as they wished. Passage in 1967 of the Marital Property Act (later part of the Texas Family Code) perpetuated these homestead provisions by giving either surviving spouse the right of lifetime use and occupancy of the homestead. Long before 1967, however, much more than the homestead laws needed to be changed. Legal measures originally intended to strengthen the family and protect women became hindrances to business as the Texas economy expanded and the state grew more urbanized. For example, the requirement of the wife's separate agreement, apart from her husband and in the presence of a notary, to the sale of the homestead might well preserve her ownership rights from her spouse's misjudgment or coercion. But along with its patronizing implications that married women lacked the business knowledge—or the good sense—to make practical decisions, this "protection" complicated property agreements. Mishandled or ignored, the provision could enable married couples to evade the terms of agreements, avoid payment of debts, and, on occasion, even renege on legal obligations.

Genuine control of property required the right to make contracts, and in this respect Texas law remained discriminatory for many years. In 1840 the Texas Congress adopted the common-law practice of barring a married woman from making contracts, and afterward the legislature enacted statutes to define specific conditions within which she could do so. In general terms, the law allowed a married man to make any contract except those expressly forbidden, while a married woman could make only those expressly allowed. If her husband failed in his legal duty to provide for her and their children, for example, the wife could draw on his separate property and pledge his credit to buy "necessaries." She had considerable latitude for such purchases, for the courts defined "necessaries" not merely as food, clothing, shelter, and medical care, but also "such things as are suitable to their condition and station in life." From frontier times the laws regulating a married woman's property and contractual rights directly affected her earning power, especially if she wished to operate a business. Both the English and the Spanish sources of Texas law were products of preindustrial societies whose trade and commerce depended at least as much on agriculture as manufacturing. Citizens of Texas, though the state was initially agrarian, increasingly made their living in nonagricultural pursuits. Even in the frontier villages, married women earned money with dressmaking and millinery, not only in their homes, but also in shops and stores. Larger numbers operated boardinghouses and schools. In small towns where people knew and associated frequently with each other, daytoday agreements about sewing orders or a child's lessons depended more on personal trust and shared values than on law or the courts. But as urban areas grew, the variety of businesses run by matrons increased rapidly, and their clients and customers expanded beyond friends and neighbors to include larger numbers of strangers. In 1900 the United States census listed 531 women in Texas who were merchants and dealers, about onethird of whom were married. A decade later the figures had more than doubled, and this count did not include the married women who operated small businesses in their homes.

At last lawmakers realized that married women who owned and ran businesses needed wider contractual rights, from which their customers and creditors also would benefit. In 1911 the legislature passed a statute giving matrons a way to remove "the disability of coverture for mercantile and trading purposes." By applying, with her husband, in writing to the district court in the county where she intended to operate her business, a married woman could regain the status of single woman specifically for the purpose of engaging in trade. The law made no provision for appealing the judge's decision, but if he agreed, she had the rights to contract freely and to sue and be sued "as in any other cases." With all her contracts now binding, her separate property became liable for her debts and obligations. Without this license to trade as a single woman, a matron could not be held to her contracts, and she could, in fact, void her agreements at will. Despite the law's obvious benefits, the courts interpreted the 1911 statute in ways that left married female merchants with several problems. Allowed to invest only her separate money in her business, a wife had to be able to prove that whatever funds she put into the firm were indeed hers and neither her husband's nor community property. In addition, at all times she must avoid mingling her goods with those purchased with her husband's credit or with community property. The joint holdings of her marriage could not go into her venture, though as manager of the community property, her husband could draw upon them at will. More problematical to her prospects for expanding her business was the fact that Texas laws defined her profits as community property, automatically subject to her husband's control and management. For this reason, a wife could not legally invest her profits in her company, and as community property her profits were liable for her husband's debts. Nonetheless, whatever the statutes stated and the courts ruled, city directories listed hundreds of married women operating businesses in their own names. Only with the enactment of the Marital Property Act in 1967 did such women gain equal contractual powers and the right to control those portions of the community property that they earned. Married women at last were equipped with the legal rights enabling them to build multi-million-dollar firms in Texas.

The Family Code carried benefits for women in addition to those affecting property. After 1967 both spouses had the right to select their respective domiciles, and in the event of separation or divorce, mothers retained equal rights with fathers regarding custody of the children. As parents, each had the legal duty to support their children. For the first time the wife, if employed, acquired the responsibility of providing for a husband unable to support himself; a housewife was not, however, required by law to take a job. The law also recognized the wife's right to retain her birth name after marriage. The Spanish law required a married woman to take her husband's name, but from the earliest days of the Republic of Texas the practice was never mandatory. The changing of a bride's name was always more a matter of custom than of law.

As a group, Texas lawmakers were never friendly to ideas about equality for women, but sometimes legislators inadvertently wrote measures that allowed both married and single women rights normally reserved for men. The Constitution of 1876 required males or "qualified electors" for fewer than a half dozen public offices, an omission which meant that, technically at least, women could hold such elected positions as governor, lieutenant governor, secretary of state, United States senator and representative (though not state senator or representative), and county or state judge. Although Texas women could not vote at any level of government until passage of the primary suffrage law of 1918, years before that date women had served on school boards in Wills Point, Denison, and Dallas. In 1917 the male voters of Marble Falls elected a woman mayor. After the Nineteenth Amendment to the United States Constitution took effect in 1920, women were eligible to serve in any office for which they were otherwise qualified. Similarly, women sometimes acquired rights through the application of federal laws. For example, in a series of important decisions the United States Supreme Court applied the due-process clause of the Fourteenth Amendment to business interests and ruled that a corporation could exercise the rights of an individual before the law. Although a married woman in Texas could not make contracts, one effect of the court's rulings was to allow a married woman member of an incorporated organization to enter into contracts for the corporation, as well as to bring suits and manage property. In 1886 the Texas legislature issued a charter to the Dallas German Ladies Aid Society, almost all of whose members were married women. The charter enumerated the basic civil liberties of a corporate body and stated the society's right to exercise them. In other situations, too, federal law expanded individual rights and activated protections that state law failed to provide or state officials neglected to enforce. Organized labor law in Texas, for example, was rarely effective until overridden by federal regulations and statutes. More than the property laws and specified rights to contract, the state's criminal code recognized a matron's separate

identity, and, in contrast to the common-law idea of husband-wife "oneness," assumed her general responsibility before the law as if she were "sole, or a man." The Texas criminal code of 1856 recognized a few situations in which marriage could cause mitigating circumstances for a woman—if, for example, she was involved in a crime "by the command or persuasion of her husband." Such modest protections, however, could not balance a married woman's lack of civil liberties, for particularly by handing down penalties after convictions, jurors had opportunities to punish women for violating accepted customs or to reward women for observing social expectations.

In all aspects of the law, social attitudes leaked through the most objective of statutes—in the drafting of bills by legislators, the rulings and interpretations of judges, and the applications by juries during trials. Probably no area of the law so much reflected customs, mores, and outright prejudices as that pertaining to divorce. When Texas was part of Mexico, the canon law regulated divorce. In 1838 the Congress of the Republic of Texas passed a law allowing the district courts to grant legal separations and divorces when "satisfied of the justice of the application," or when they found it "reasonable and proper that the application should be granted." In 1841 the Congress tightened the law by defining the causes justifying divorce: "adultery, abandonment, cruel treatment, and outrages from one toward the other such as render their living together insupportable." From that time until 1967, virtually the only objective criteria for ending a marriage were, first, the provision that either spouse was entitled to a divorce after being abandoned by the other for three years; and second, the fact that wife and husband had lived apart without cohabitation for seven years. All other grounds were evaluated by juries, and in this way community values affected each divorce petition. Juries decided which actions constituted "excesses," "cruel treatment," and "outrages" and whether such behavior made continuation of the marriage "insupportable." Although commentators considered the divorce laws more favorable to wives than to husbands, these laws demonstrated a clear acceptance of a double standard of personal and sexual behavior. A husband, for example, could win a divorce because of his wife's "amorous or lascivious conduct with other men, even short of adultery," or if she was "taken in adultery" even once. A wife could succeed with this charge only if her husband "*lived* in adultery with another woman" (italics added). On the other hand, his discovery after marriage of her "premarital unchastity, even though concealed," would not win his freedom. A husband's violence against his wife was not adequate reason for a divorce unless it was a "serious" danger and might happen again. Moreover, the jury was likely to deliberate on whether she had behaved "indiscreetly" or had somehow "provoked" her husband. His transmission of a venereal disease was grounds for divorce, as were "false and wicked imputations of a depraved and foul husband aspersing the good name of his wife." A wife's refusal of sexual intercourse might not be a cause for divorce, depending on the jury's opinions about "her condition of health, probable ill effects of childbirth, [or] the husband's age, health, virility, and the like." Consideration for the circumstances of each case undoubtedly produced decisions resulting from contemporary notions about race and class, for juries had the discretion to examine "the habits and character of the parties; their previous training and their standing in society." Clearly, some women were judged worthy of protection from violent husbands, and others were judged otherwise. Many women undoubtedly suffered the brunt of jurors' prejudices regarding their "station" in life or their "place" in society.

Legal disabilities worked equally against all married women in Texas, but minority women (and men) also faced racial and ethnic bias and discrimination. By requiring each voter in primary elections to pay a poll tax, for example, the Terrell Election Laws of 1903 and 1907 barred many African and Mexican Americans, as well as poor whites, from the elective process. Another law passed in 1923, three years after the Nineteenth Amendment enfranchised women, denied to all black citizens the right to vote in Democratic primaries. In a oneparty state, the primaries were as important as the regular elections.

For all Texas women major gains in civil liberties came as slowly as property and contractual rights. In March 1918, 22 years after the state's first suffragists organized, the legislature passed the law allowing women to vote in primary elections and party nominating conventions. In June 1919, Texas became the ninth state to ratify the Nineteenth Amendment to the United States Constitution, which took effect on 26 August 1920 and fully enfranchised American women. More than 30 years later, in 1954, Texas women first served on juries. Despite the 1963 law granting equal contractual rights with men, a total of 44 legal disabilities continued to plague married women. However reassuring this statute appeared, without the amendment or rescission of dozens of other laws, its actual effects were severely limited. For example, it left intact the 1911 law that gave matrons equal contractual rights for trade, but failed to mention married women in the professions. A married woman attorney could not sign a client's bond, and married women physicians also wondered if they actually had the right to perform various procedures required by their medical practices. Restrictions remained throughout the state's judicial rulings and statutes. After years of hard work, Dallas attorney Hermine Tobolowsky succeeded in 1971 in persuading the legislature to enact the Texas Equal Rights Amendment, which the voters ratified in 1972. The amendment established the principle of equality within the state's constitution, but any constitution is, by nature, a passive instrument of government. Its provisions become active only when its principles are applied to the writing of new statutes or used to challenge existing laws in the courts. Thus, of more real and immediate significance than the Equal Rights Amendment was passage in 1967 of the Marital Property Act, which two years later became a section of the Texas Family Code. The Marital Property Act was a comprehensive set of statutes, which, though aimed specifically at families, amended the laws regarding virtually every aspect of life in Texas, including insurance, banking, real estate, deeds, contracts, divorce, choice of domicile, child custody, and property rights. Led by Dallas attorney Louise Raggio, this revision of the state's laws amounted to a virtual revolution for women in Texas. Its major—and still largely unappreciated—effect was to give married women equal legal rights. (Single women have always enjoyed equal property and contractual rights and in 1920 and 1954, along with married women, also acquired equal political rights.) Enacted in three sections between 1967 and 1974, the Texas Family Code was the first family code in the United States.

Just as women bore disabilities under the law, so did they face strong prejudice within the profession of law. Unlike medicine and teaching, which have always borne certain indelible relationships to ageold female roles, law remained more securely ensconced within the "male realm." For many years widely accepted assumptions about their "place" in society discouraged women from studying law, the most direct way to affect the passage of legislation as well as its interpretation and application in the courts. In 1900 the federal census listed no female attorneys in Texas and in 1910, only three. During the subsequent decades the numbers of women lawyers grew slowly, to only 75 among the state's 6,651 by 1930. More than 40 years passed before the first two minority women attorneys began practicing in Texas. Charlye O. Farris, the state's first black woman lawyer, graduated from Howard University Law School in 1953; two years later Edna Cisneros became the first Hispanic woman to be licensed in Texas as an attorney. As late as 1986, women were still a mere 14 percent of the state's practicing lawyers. But the situation changed rapidly during the following decade. By 1990, 789 women received just over 40 percent of the J.D. degrees awarded by Texas law schools, and three years later nearly 13,000 female attorneys comprised 23 percent of the State Bar of Texas. By 1994, 88.1 percent of those women lawyers were Caucasian, 5.4 percent black, 4.7 percent Hispanic, 1 percent Asian, and 0.3 percent American Indian. The remaining 0.5 percent were "other."

Despite their apparent progress during the years of the suffrage campaign and their success in winning passage of legislation during the decade afterwards, women's advance into lawmaking positions evaporated. In 1925 Governor Neff appointed three woman attorneys to hear a single case, from which the sitting justices had disqualified themselves. Though making national news, the All-Woman Supreme Court remained a curiosity rather than the beginning of a new development. Women's progress onto the judicial bench remained glacial, even after Sarah Hughes was appointed the state's first female judge in 1931. Forty years later, two women held state district judgeships, two were domestic-relations judges, and one was a county judge. As late as 1981 only 11 of 330 district judges were women, and by 1990 their numbers had grown to 41 of 361, a percentage increase from 3 to 11. Despite this modest progress on the state bench, women continued to lag behind as district attorneys, advancing from 4 of 329 statewide in 1980 to only 7 in 361 by 1990. The appointment of women to the federal courts in Texas was equally slow. After nearly thirty years as a state district judge, Sarah Hughes became a federal district judge in 1961, but remained more a token than an example. In both 1980 and 1990 Texas had only three woman United States district judges, and seven others served in the state's appellate courts.

Women were also slow to claim the right to help make Texas laws. In 1931 four women sat in the state House of Representatives and only one in the Senate. During the next 40 years those figures changed very little: in 1973 five women were state representatives, one a senator. In 1981–82, 11 women were members of the Texas House, still only one of the Senate. In 1989–90 the figures were little changed at 14 and 3, respectively. Modest though noticeable improvement came suddenly, however, and by 1993 the Seventythird Legislature included 25 women among 150 representatives and 4 women among 31 senators. Perhaps such slow advances must also be sure progress, which in the future can assure women of stronger and more secure roles in Texas life and public affairs.

Elizabeth York Enstam

Women and Literature. Texas has a rich literary tradition, identified most frequently with the Anglo men writers of the early to middle twentieth century who dealt eloquently and dramatically with the birth of the republic, the efflorescence of the range cattle industry, and the discovery of oil. From the 1920s through the 1940s, Texas letters were dominated by the now-mythic figure of J. Frank Dobie, who was widely known as "Mr. Texas" and who exercised considerable control over what was published about Texas. Typical of many men of his generation, Dobie took little notice of the literary output of contemporary women writers or their predecessors. His indifference toward women writers was symptomatic of the prevailing temperament of Texas culture. According to James McComb, the "Texas Mystique" is "paternalistic, chauvinistic, wealthy, aggressive, friendly, exploitative, prejudiced, independent, optimistic, enterprising, boisterous." Furthermore, according to McComb, this characterization is "widely believed, casually followed, occasionally helpful, and painfully misleading." As McComb implies, the Texas Mystique is exclusively male.

Women, however, in spite of being ignored by the Mystique, played a crucial role in the development of Texas culture, both during the nineteenth century and afterward. Their role as homemakers and guardians of morals and culture on the frontier is undeniable, and female pioneers' lives apparently were not as romantic or dramatic as those of their male counterparts. Understandably, frontier women also succumbed to loneliness and despair more frequently than men did, and their mortality rate was probably higher. In part because they were excluded from the Mystique, the literature that Texas women have produced differs dramatically from that of Texas men. Texas women rarely have written about high times and shoot-em-ups on cattle drives or heroism during battles against Mexicans or Indians. Instead they have focused on the more human problems of personal relationships and maintaining quotidian stability during times of crisis. Women writers have also examined the universal qualities that sometimes get blotted out by the Mystique: humor, loyalty, betrayal, decency, paradox, faith, steadfastness. Women writers have neither felt an obligation to uphold the Mystique nor often consciously attacked it. Instead, they have ignored the mythic image of Texas culture and Texas people and have in the process produced another body of literature that is distinctive but not as widely known as that of the more traditional men writers.

Women have contributed to the full range of Texas literary production, from poetry to short stories to novels to journalism to personal-experience essays to scholarly articles, monographs, and books. Although nonfiction dominates much nineteenth-century writing, the best-known and most extensive literary genre has been fiction. Especially among contemporary women writers, Mexican-American women have been publishing high-quality fiction that is barely known outside of the mainstream. They write about topics even further removed from the Mystique than their Anglo counterparts. Theirs is a literature born out of the distinctive Hispanic culture of Texas, of which Spanish–English code-switching is a feature. Their subject matter is survival, triumph, and serenity in a hostile or indifferent majority world. Women writers from other ethnic groups in Texas have had limited literary production. A number of African-American women playwrights are active in the Houston area, and other contemporary black women are beginning to publish fiction that is receiving statewide and national attention.

For well over a century, a limited but solid body of scholarship has documented the growth and development of Texas women's literature. The first known descriptions of Texas women writers are to be found among the compendia of miscellaneous data that were a fixture of Victorian literary and intellectual life. Ida Raymond's *Southland Writers: Biographical and Critical Sketches of Living Female Writers of the South, With Extracts from their Writings* (1870) is the earliest known literary history written by and acknowledging Texas women writers, who were classified at the time as Southern; the South v. West debate did not emerge for several more decades. Raymond's book is essentially a biographical dictionary containing brief entries on otherwise little-known authors. In 1885 the first literary history specifically about Texas was compiled and edited by a woman, Ella Hutchins Steuart. This ambitious work—*Gems from a Texas Quarry; or Literary Offerings by and Selections from Leading Writers and Prominent Characters of Texas, Being a Texas Contribution to the World's Industrial Exposition at New Orleans, 1884–85*—anthologizes both men and women writers, including a number of women whose names are obscure or otherwise unknown today but who were apparently well-known and popular writers in their day, especially as journalists. A fascinating and ephemeral source of literary history concerning Texas women writers, and perhaps the first piece devoted exclusively to that topic, appeared on successive Sundays in the Galveston *Daily News* in 1893. Entitled "Women Writers of Texas," this two-part article by Bride N. Taylor, vice president of the Texas Women's Press Association, consisted of brief biographical sketches of 77 women authors, starting with Mary Austin Holley and concluding with a sketch of the modest Taylor herself, added by the editors. In 1896 Elizabeth Brooks published her biographical dictionary, *Prominent Women of Texas*, which includes a chapter on prominent authors. *Writers and Writings of Texas*, edited by Davis Foute Eagleton, an English professor at Austin College in Sherman, appeared in 1913. Interspersed among the men, Eagleton provided biographical sketches of nine women authors, with representative excerpts from their works. A supplement lists the names of 131 Texas women writers, with a notation of genre, such as poetry, or the titles of their significant publications. The next significant work after Taylor and Brooks devoted exclusively to women was Annie Pickrell's *Pioneer Women in Texas* (1929). The biography–anthology format of this book underscores the tenacity of this genre of writing in Texas.

Spurred in part by the Texas Centennial (1936), Texans began to seek recognition and legitimacy in national literary circles. Subsequent literary histories focused on Texas as a distinct region and on the literary genres being produced in the state rather than on the biographies of the authors. One of the earliest of these genreoriented anthologies is *A Century with Texas Poets and Poetry*, published in 1934 by Vaida Stewart Montgomery. The dominant trend in Texas literary history during this decade was to identify Texas literature as part of the larger field of southwestern literature. Dobie's idiosyncratic *Guide to the Life and Literature of the Southwest*, first published in 1929 and originally the syllabus and reading list for his course of the same name at the University of Texas, fueled this identification of Texas with the greater Southwest. This shift in focus away from the biographical and toward the regional also brought Texas women scholars and literary critics to the forefront, along with a few men scholars. Topical bibliographic guides included Mabel Major, Rebecca Smith, and T. M. Pearce, *Southwest Heritage: A Literary History with Bibliography* (1938, 1948, 1972); Florence Barns, *Texas Writers of Today* (1935); and Sister Agatha (Mary Louise) Sheehan, *Texas Prose Writings* (1936). Leonidas W. Payne's *A Survey of Texas Literature* (1928) presents some critical and bibliographic material as well as biographical information on Texas authors, including a number of women. For many years these topical and bibliographic works set the standard for Texas literary histories. They are still reasonably reliable guides, although dated. Some more recent works are *Southwestern American Literature: A Bibliography* (1980), *A Bibliographical Guide to the Study of Western American Literature* (1982), *The Texas Literary Tradition* (1983), and *Range Wars* (1988).

Since the mid-nineteenth century, the literary output of Texas women writers has been steady and varied. Although decades later many pioneer women wrote and published their memoirs of early Texas, Mary Holley published contemporaneously with the events she described. Holley, first cousin and confidante of Stephen F. Austin, was a sophisticated, well-educated, and articulate woman who moved to Texas to start a new life after the death of her clergyman husband. Her visit coincided with the birth of the Republic of Texas, and her book, *Texas*, which included one of the earliest accounts of the Texas Revolution, was primarily propaganda designed to attract settlers. Holley, though the first, was not the only woman to write best-selling nonfiction about early Texas. In 1852, Jane Cazneau (writing under the pseudonym Cora Montgomery) published *Eagle Pass*, a vivid description of the two years that she lived on the Texas side of the Rio Grande. Nearly forty years later, Fannie Chambers Gooch published a similar description of Mexican life and society as she experienced it while living in Mexico for several years, *Face to Face with the Mexicans* (1887). Another book based on the author's personal experience was Teresa G. Vielé's *Following the Drum* (1858), an account of army barracks life on the Rio Grande in 1851.

Other women turned to fiction in order to write about the dramatic events unfolding around them. In 1855 Augusta Evans Wilson published the first Texas novel by a woman, the highly sentimental and romantic *Inez: A Tale of the Alamo*, a typical nineteenthcentury potboiler that chronicled the travails of a romance between an Anglo heroine and her Tejano lover. Foreshadowing what became the hallmark of Texas women writers, Wilson eschewed concentrating on the battle of the Alamo itself, but instead emphasized the doomed love of her protagonists. In 1888, Amelia Barr's novel *Remember the Alamo* presented a more realistic treatment of Tejano–Anglo relationships during the turbulent period of the revolution. Twentyfive years later, Barr provided a detailed record of Austin social life and the city's upheaval during the Civil War in her autobiography, *All the Days of My Life* (1913). By the end of the nineteenth century, Mollie Davis, who grew up on the San Marcos River in the 1850s, wrote two novels from firsthand knowledge of Texas life: *Under the Man-Fig* (1895) and *The Wire-Cutters* (1899). *The Wire-Cutters* realistically depicts the lives of pioneer women and wouldbe cattlemen during the infamous episodes of fence cutting in West Texas in the 1880s. The book appeared three years before Owen Wister's famous *The Virginian* (1902) and four years before Andy Adams's celebrated *Log of a Cowboy* (1903), and is therefore the first "Western" novel.

Women writers did not gain further notice as significant contributors to Texas literature until the 1920s, when they began to publish fiction full of social commentary. For example, Mattie Ruth Cross's *The Golden Cocoon* (1924), which went through five editions in the first year after publication, reflects the author's knowledge of the sterile lives of North Texas tenant farmers. A year later, Dorothy Scarborough caused an uproar in West Texas with her anonymously published novel *The Wind* (1925), which depicted the harsh reality of the ranch country around Sweetwater, where she had lived as a child. Another contemporary of Cross and Scarborough, Karle Wilson Baker, was known for her poetry more than her fiction. Winifred B. M. Sanford's short stories, many of which were published in the *American Mercury*, came fresh from her observations as a curious newcomer to Wichita Falls during the 1920s oil boom. During this same decade, the most distinguished Texas writer, Katherine Anne Porter, began her career. She rejected traditional roles of women as too confining and began to explore women's interior lives in short fiction. In 1939, the newly formed Texas Institute of Letters honored Dobie's *Apache Gold and Yaqui Silver* as the best Texas book of the year instead of Porter's *Pale Horse, Pale Rider*. In spite of this snub, which she never forgave, Porter went on to national acclaim, while Dobie remained a regionalist. By the 1940s other Texas women were gaining national attention. Loula Grace Erdman, a Missouri transplant to Texas, won the Dodd–Mead *Redbook* award in 1947 for *The Years of the Locust*, a depiction of the separate viewpoints of five women attending the funeral of the family patriarch. Her other novels and stories, such as *The Edge of Time* (1950) and *The Wind Blows Free* (1952), dealt sensitively and realistically with Panhandle pioneer settlers, especially women and children.

By the 1960s, Texas women's writing had developed and matured into a more mainstream tradition, its primary Texas connection being setting rather than adherence to stereotyped Texas characters and plots. In fiction as well as other genres— poetry, children's literature, journalism, and scholarly articles and monographs—contemporary Texas women have distinguished themselves as writers dealing with universally accessible themes rather than narrow regional focus.

Sylvia Grider and Lou Rodenberger

Women and Politics. Women have historically been outsiders in politics, legally barred from voting until the twentieth century and subsequently handicapped in running for office by lack of campaign funds and exclusion from the inner sanctums of political parties. As outsiders, women have often become involved in politics to promote causes, especially those relating to family and community welfare, rather than to build careers. Although the female politician did not emerge until the late twentieth century, a long political tradition of advocacy and activism predated women's admission to formal electoral politics. In the nineteenth and early twentieth centuries middle-class women used their voluntary associations to voice opinions on public policy and seek legislative remedies for social problems. In the process they pioneered pressuregroup politics: promoting an issue before the public, mounting petition and letter-writing campaigns to state legislators, urging voters not to reelect uncooperative incumbents. In the 1880s the WCTU united women who favored prohibition as a solution to the poverty and domestic violence that often resulted when husbands drank heavily. Temperance women quickly broadened their agenda and invaded the legislature to lobby as Christian mothers for laws authorizing a boys' reformatory to keep juveniles from being incarcerated with adult criminals (1887), requiring alcohol education in the public schools (1893), forbidding the sale of cigarettes to minors (1899), and raising the age of consent for minor girls (from 10 to 12 in 1891, to 15 in 1895, and to 18 in 1918). At the same time, women participated more formally in Gilded Age politics by supporting thirdparty challenges to Democratic domination. WCTU members Jenny Beauchamp and Mary Clardy served on the platform committee of the Texas Prohibition party at the 1886 and 1890 conventions, respectively, and Beauchamp was a delegate to the national convention in 1887. Women were even more visible in the Farmers' Alliance. Female membership was as high as 43 percent in some local chapters, and Texas was the only state alliance that elected women to high office. Mary Clardy served as assistant state lecturer and Fannie Moss as secretary–treasurer in 1892; Frances Leak was elected to succeed Moss in 1894. Ellen Dabbs and Bettie Gay were among the Texas representatives to the National Farmers' Alliance convention in 1892, which gave birth to the People's party.

The Progressive era saw a decline in third-party activity but a multiplication of women's voluntary associations: the Texas Federation of Women's Clubs formed in 1897, the Texas Federation of Colored Women's Clubs in 1905, the state YWCA in 1906, and the Texas Congress of Mothers in 1909. Working independently or in collaboration, and justifying their activism as "social motherhood," the women's organizations pursued legislation to safeguard public health, provide care for dependent and delinquent children, improve the public school system, and protect working women. Women's voluntarist politics helped secure a pure-food law (1907), laws enabling public schools to institute kindergarten programs (1907, 1917), a constitutional amendment to raise the limitation on local school taxes (1908), compulsory school attendance for children between 8 and 14 (1915), a juvenile court system (1907) modeled on experiments in Chicago and Denver, state juvenile training schools for boys (1909) and girls (1913), and a mothers' pension law for widows with dependent children (1917). The 1911 child labor law was initiated by a TFWC committee with backing from the state labor commissioner and the Child Welfare Conference of Texas, a confederation of a dozen voluntary and professional associations chaired by Adella Kelsey Turner. Pressure exerted by the Congress of Mothers finally resulted in Lala Fay Watts's appointment in 1918 as first child welfare inspector of the Bureau of Labor Statistics.

Middle-class and working-class women joined forces to lobby for protective labor laws for women. Textile worker Eva Goldsmith, representing the Houston local chapter of the United Garment Workers of America, kept before the 1913 legislature a bill establishing a maximum 54-hour work week and 10hour day for women. She was consequently appointed vice chairman of the legislative committee of Texas State Federation of Labor, its only woman officer. In 1915, with lobbying assistance from the Austin chapters of the WCTU and YWCA, Goldsmith successfully promoted an amendment that restricted the workday to nine hours. A minimum-wage law for women and minors passed in 1919 (and was repealed in 1921) after women's organizations formed the Texas Women's Legislative Association to lobby for a 13-point agenda that included strengthening laws regarding child labor, working women, mothers' pensions, public education,

and prohibition. The association also secured a Woman's Division in the Bureau of Labor Statistics and the appointment of Lala Watts, head of the WCTU's Department of Women and Minors in Industry, to head it. Female lobbyists in Austin were backed by local women's clubs, mothers' clubs, and temperance unions that inundated their legislative representatives with letters and telegrams. At the same time these organized women entered local politics as "municipal housekeepers" who pressured city governments for civic and social reforms: pure water and milk supplies, sanitation services, parks and playgrounds, police matrons to oversee women prisoners in city jails, the abolition of vice districts. In Galveston the Women's Health Protective Association was more active than the city health department in demanding enforcement of sanitation ordinances and taking violators to court. A sanitation committee from the Houston Housewives' League accompanied the city health inspector to the dairies, scored them according to the league's own standards—considerably tougher than the municipal health code—and posted the scores at City Auditorium. The Dallas Federation of Women's Clubs spent five years persuading the city to build a water-filtration plant.

Women also won their first elective offices during the Progressive era. Female school reformers argued that women, as experts on child development, should be elected to school boards. Dallas became the first major Texas city to have women school trustees when clubwomen Adella Turner and Ella Tucker won seats in 1908. In San Antonio the following year Anna Hertzberg and Jeanette Noyes–Evans, president and treasurer respectively of the Woman's Club of San Antonio, campaigned successfully for two of the open school-board seats. The election was invalidated when the city's pending new school charter, with a provision excluding women trustees, was approved by the state legislature. Another new charter in 1913 removed the bar, and the clubwomen secured a provision requiring that three of the trustees be women; Hertzberg, Mrs. Atlee Ayres, and Mrs. Milton Bleim won the seats.

Women were active in state referendum campaigns on prohibition and highly visible in the local-option elections that decided whether towns and counties should be "wet" or "dry." State WCTU leaders were brought in to give orations, and thousands of women not formally enrolled in the WCTU formed temporary alliances with local chapters. They staged temperance parades and held demonstrations outside the polls, where their children helped sing and wave banners. In East Texas white and black women sometimes demonstrated together. Even though WCTU membership remained small and largely confined to evangelical churchwomen, support for prohibition was overwhelming among white women by around 1915, and the sentiment became more vocal after the country entered World War I. Sixteen organizations joined forces in the Texas Women's AntiVice Committee in the summer of 1917 to demand that liquor and prostitution be banned within 10 miles of the state's military cantonments. By 1917 there was also broad support within women's organizations for the ballot—a demand first voiced by the WCTU in 1888—and an equally strong aversion to the demagogic governor, James E. Ferguson, an intransigent opponent of both woman suffrage and prohibition. Under the leadership of Minnie Cunningham, the Texas Equal Suffrage Association unobtrusively assisted the legislative investigation that resulted in Ferguson's impeachment. When he threatened to

La Conferencia de Mujeres por La Raza, Houston, May 28–30, 1971. Program cover. Courtesy Houston Metropolitan Research Center, Houston Public Library. Hispanic women entered Texas politics when they ran on the ticket of La Raza Unida, a political party organized in 1970.

make a comeback in the 1918 election, Cunningham seized the opportunity provided by the split in Democratic ranks over "Fergusonism" to make a quiet political bargain with the progressive–prohibitionist leaders in the legislature that gave women the right to vote in primary elections. Enfranchised in March 1918, the new woman voters redeemed Cunningham's promise to vote as a bloc in July for the progressive candidate, William P. Hobby, who won by a landslide. Annie Blanton, elected state superintendent of public instruction, became the first woman to win statewide office.

Black women had been excluded from the suffrage campaign, and the white primary law kept them from sharing in white women's new electoral power. The two groups made tentative advances toward improving race relations through the state's branch of the Committee on Woman's Work of the Commission on Interracial Cooperation. The black women protested discrimination and violence, while Jessie Ames, who headed the Woman's Committee in Texas until her appointment as the first woman executive director of a state CIC (1924), urged whites to practice toleration and oppose lynching. The Texas Association of Colored Women's Clubs undertook its first lobbying project, a

home for delinquent black girls, with the assistance of Ames, who toured the state promoting the project while Ada Belle DeMent of the TACWC worked as liaison to the white clubs of the TFWC.

Women's voluntarist politics persisted even after the Nineteenth Amendment brought full enfranchisement. During the 1920s organized women continued to pursue the goals of social motherhood through the Joint Legislative Council, dubbed the "Petticoat Lobby" by legislators tired of being asked to pass "women's bills." The JLC achieved progressively less as the decade wore on, and finally disbanded in 1927. For the first decade after enfranchisement, women continued to influence gubernatorial elections in favor of progressive candidates. Former suffragist Nona Mahoney and state Democratic national committeewoman Eliza Johnson organized women for Pat Neff in 1920, helping to defeat Joseph W. Bailey, an old antisuffrage enemy. In 1924, however, Jim Ferguson avenged himself by running his wife, Miriam A. Ferguson, for governor as his proxy. The resurgence of Fergusonism, a political issue for another two decades, and of the Ku Klux Klan, which recruited many women members in Fort Worth, Dallas, and Houston, helped fragment the women's coalition. Thousands of Democratic women refused to support either Ma Ferguson or her runoff opponent, KKK activist Felix Robertson; when Ferguson won the nomination they protested by campaigning for the Republican "good government" candidate, George C. Butte, in the general election. Although Mrs. Ferguson appointed Emma Meharg the first woman secretary of state, most of the former suffragists remained allied against her. In 1926 Jane McCallum chaired a "Texas Woman Citizen's Committee" that helped reformer Dan Moody defeat Ma Ferguson for reelection. Mrs. McCallum served as secretary of state for Moody's two administrations and that of his successor, Ross Sterling.

By 1932, when Mrs. Ferguson defeated Sterling and regained the governor's office, there was no longer a visible "woman's bloc." All in all, the immediate postsuffrage decades brought little political power to women. Annie Blanton and Minnie Cunningham lost races for Congress. The Democrats resisted the attempts of the League of Women Voters and the Democratic Women's Association to secure equal representation for women on the party's state and county executive committees. Although the Republicans attracted women members in the 1920s by allotting them more positions, the GOP was only a nominal presence in a oneparty state until the 1970s. The state legislature remained overwhelmingly male, the state congressional delegation entirely so. In 1922 Edith Wilmans became the first woman elected to the legislature; Margie Neal, elected to the first of four terms in 1926, was the first woman senator. In the ensuing half century no more than four women representatives and one senator ever sat in any given session. Instead of rising, their numbers declined. There were no women at all in the Thirtyninth (1925–27) and Forty-fifth (1937–39) legislatures, and there were fewer in the 1960s than in the 1940s. During these decades women worked through the legislature to expand their legal rights. Representatives Helen Moore and Sarah Hughes first introduced a constitutional amendment to permit women to serve on juries in 1935. A new coalition of voluntary associations, including the American Association of University Women, did the lobbying and promotional work. The bill was reintroduced in every session but one until it was passed in 1953 and ratified in 1954. In

1957 the Business and Professional Women began a campaign for the Texas Equal Rights Amendment. Coordinated by Hermine Tobolowsky, it combined club pressure in the style of the presuffrage era with a decade of working to elect supportive legislators and defeat opponents; the amendment finally passed in 1971.

Black women, who suffered the double discrimination of race and sex, fought legalized racism through the NAACP. Juanita Craft of Dallas was active as an organizer, while Christia Adair helped found the Houston NAACP, of which she was executive secretary from 1943 to 1959. The association's efforts helped Hattie Mae White become the first black woman elected to the Houston school board in 1958. In 1966, when Mrs. Adair became one of the first two African Americans elected to the Harris County Democratic Executive Committee, the state convention refused to seat them. That same year redistricting made it possible for Barbara Jordan, who had lost races for the state House in 1962 and 1964, to win a seat in the state Senate; she was the first black elected since Reconstruction.

The combined effect of the civil-rights movement and the resurgence of feminism in the 1960s began to translate into higher political visibility for women by the early 1970s. The Texas Women's Political Caucus organized in 1971 to encourage women to seek public office and formulate a feminist political agenda; at the time, Barbara Jordan and State Representative Frances Farenthold were the only women in the legislature. The following year brought unprecedented achievements. Sissy Farenthold made the first serious bid for statewide office since Miriam Ferguson's final campaign in 1940; she ran strongly in the Democratic gubernatorial primary and lost narrowly in a runoff. Anne Armstrong, of the Republican National Committee, was chosen as the first woman to give a keynote address at a national party convention. Barbara Jordan became the first Texas woman elected to Congress in her own right (Lera M. Thomas had served her deceased husband's unexpired term in 1966–67) and the first black congresswoman elected from the South. Five women, the largest number ever, were elected to the state House of Representatives, including Sarah Weddington, the plaintiff's lawyer in *Roe v. Wade.*

The visibility of Hispanic women at the state level was limited before the rise of the Raza Unida party (1970). Although active in organizations such as LULAC, they had no influence in mainstream state politics. In 1972 Alma Canales ran for lieutenant governor, thus becoming the first Hispanic woman to seek high state office. Though she lost, Hispanic women in Crystal City, the birthplace of La Raza Unida, won county offices. Mujeres por la Raza groups, organized by Martha P. Cotera, encouraged more Hispanic women to seek office; two ran unsuccessfully for the legislature in 1974, and in 1976 Irma Rangel became the first to win a seat in the house. Women continued to make gains as the decade unfolded. Barbara Jordan gave the keynote address at the Democratic National Convention in 1976. By 1977, when the National Women's Conference met in Houston to formulate a political agenda, 11 women were serving in the legislature and María Elena Martínez had been elected to head the Raza Unida party.

More important in the long run, women had begun to compete successfully for local elective offices. In 1975 Lila Cockrell, who had been the first woman elected to the San Antonio City Council, became the city's first woman mayor. Carole Keeton McClellan, the first woman president of the Austin school board,

won the Austin mayoral race in 1977. Over the next 15 years Houston, Dallas, Fort Worth, El Paso, and Corpus Christi elected woman mayors.

By the 1980s women candidates had overcome the image of being long shots for office and established themselves as serious contenders. Travis county commissioner Ann Richards became the first woman in 50 years to win statewide office when she was elected to the first of two terms as state treasurer in 1982. In 1986 three women were elected to the state Senate, which had never before had more than one female member. Ann Richards gave the keynote address at the Democratic national convention in 1988 and in 1990 won an acrimonious race for governor. Women also captured both parties' nominations for state treasurer. Kay Hutchison's victory marked the first time a Republican woman had won statewide office; it was also a triumph for the Texas Federation of Republican Women. Women were elected to 12.7 percent of the legislative seats in 1990 (19 in the House, 4 in the Senate), and nineterm representative Wilhelmina Delco, an African American, became speaker pro tem.

The 1992 conventions drew national attention to the state's women politicians. Kay Hutchison was temporary president of the Republican national convention. Ann Richards chaired the Democratic national convention, which featured speeches by Barbara Jordan and former state representative Lena Guerrero, whom Richards appointed to an interim vacancy on the Railroad Commission. Guerrero's promising political career crashed a few weeks later when it was revealed that she had been falsely representing herself as a graduate of the University of Texas. She resigned from the Railroad Commission but remained in the race and was decisively defeated. In 1993, in a special election following the resignation of Lloyd Bentsen, Jr., Hutchison was elected to the United States Senate. She went on to win in the regular election of 1994.

While the majority of women officeholders continued to be clustered at the local level, sophisticated national fund-raising networks formed in the 1980s for female candidates enabled more women than ever to make serious bids for higher office. In 1992, billed nationally as the "Year of the Woman" in politics, 34 women ran for the state House, 6 for the state Senate, 3 for other state office, and 4 for Congress. They succeeded in record numbers. Twenty-four women won seats in the House and four in the Senate. Judge Rose Spector became the first woman elected to the state Supreme Court. State Senator Eddie Bernice Johnson was elected to Congress to represent the new Thirtieth District, a minority district that she helped draw while head of the state Senate's Subcommittee on Congressional Redistricting.

Judith N. McArthur

Women's Airforce Service Pilots. A World War II measure to overcome a shortage of pilots. Two efforts were organized to recruit women pilots and to free male pilots for combat duty. The United States Army Air Forces directed aviator Nancy Harkness Love to recruit women to ferry planes for the Air Transport Command. In September 1942 her group was commissioned as the Women's Auxiliary Ferrying Squadron and was stationed at New Castle Army Air Base in Wilmington, Delaware. Shortly thereafter aviator Jacqueline Cochran was appointed director of the Women's Flying Training Detachment, independent of Love's WAFS, by Gen. Henry H. Arnold, chief of the AAF. Cochran had just returned from Great Britain where, at the request of the British government, she had led 25 women pilots in ferrying aircraft for the British Air Transport Auxiliary. This was the first organized group of American women pilots to serve in the war. In 1940 and 1941 Love and Cochran had separately proposed to the United States military that American women pilots be sought, but their plans were not approved because there were more male pilots than airplanes. General Arnold had also expressed his doubts at that time about the ability of women to pilot large aircraft. The first class of Cochran's 319th WFTD, called the "guinea pigs," began training at the Municipal Airport in Houston in November 1942, one month after the WAFS was formed. The airport did not have housing for the trainees, and the establishment officer, Leoti Deaton, had difficulty finding accommodations. The women were housed in motels and private homes and were picked up each morning and driven to the airport in trailer trucks. For the first few weeks facilities at the field were primitive. Since there was not a place to change clothes, the trainees flew, attended ground school, drilled, and marched to and from the mess hall in the same pair of GI coveralls, called "zoot suits." When better quarters became available, the women were moved to Avenger Field at Sweetwater (1943). They were required to pay their own way there and the return fare if they washed out; they also had to pay for their room and board.

In August 1943 the WFTDs and the WAFS were merged into one command called the Women's Airforce Service Pilots, with Cochran as the director. The WASPs were treated as much as possible like male cadets. They marched wherever they went and lived in barracks. They received 285 hours of ground instruction and approximately 210 hours of flying time, about equally divided between PT-17s, BT-13s and AT-6s. The training period lasted seven months. Graduates of Avenger Field went on to flying assignments throughout the United States. They ferried 12,650 planes of 77 different types, including B-17s. Fifty percent of the fighters manufactured for the war were ferried by WASPs. After proving themselves as ferry pilots, the women towed targets, flew tracking, smoke-laying, searchlight, strafing, and simulated bombing missions, gave instrument instruction, and tested damaged airplanes, a dangerous task. The WASP program began on a civilian basis because it was an experiment. While the women fliers functioned in the military, they lived under civilian law. They did not receive government insurance, and hospitalization for sickness or illness was difficult to work out. In 1944 a bill proposing militarization of the WASPs was defeated in Congress, largely as a result of lobbying by male civilian pilots. By late 1944 the war in Europe was almost over, and there was a surplus of pilots. On 20 December the AAF determined there was no longer a need for the WASPs, and the program was discontinued. Twenty-five thousand women had applied to be WASPs, 1,830 were accepted, 1,074 graduated, and 38 gave their lives serving their country. They flew 60 million miles for the AAF and received high praises from their commanders. In 1977 the United States government gave the WASPs honorable discharges and veterans' benefits. *Sherwood Inkley*

Wood, George Tyler. Governor; b. Cuthbert, Georgia, 12 March 1795; d. Point Blank, Texas, 3 September 1858; m. Martha Evans Gindrat (1837). Martha Gindrat was a widow with three children; she and Wood had another child. Wood was in the Georgia legislature, 1837–38. He moved to Texas in 1839 and started a planta-

tion at Point Blank, then in Liberty County. He represented the county in the Texas Congress in 1841 and at the Convention of 1845. He was a state senator (1846), a position he resigned to command a company in the Mexican War. In 1847 he was elected governor, in which office he concentrated on the debt question, frontier defense, and the New Mexico boundary dispute. He lost to Peter H. Bell in the 1849 election, ran again in 1853, and was defeated, perhaps because he was viewed as a partisan of Sam Houston, whose reputation was at its nadir. Wood retired to his plantation. Wood County and Woodville are named for him.

J. E. Wheat

Wool, John Ellis. Army officer; b. Newburgh, New York, 29 February 1784; d. 10 November 1869 (buried in Troy, New York); m. Sarah Moulton (1809). In 1812 Wool entered the regular army as a captain in the Thirteenth Infantry; he won national acclaim for heroism at the battles of Queenston and Plattsburg and was promoted to brevet lieutenant colonel. He served as an army inspector general for 25 years, receiving special assignments in Europe, the Cherokee country, and along the Canadian border, before assuming command of the Eastern Department in 1841 as a brigadier general. In May and June 1846 Wool mustered 10 volunteer regiments in the Ohio valley for Zachary Taylor's army on the Rio Grande, then proceeded to Texas to organize a division to invade Chihuahua. In early July he landed volunteers and supplies at Camp Irwin on Matagorda Bay and laid out Camp Crockett at San Antonio for some 3,400 men. In August he sent a Texas cavalry unit under Col. William C. Young to Eagle Pass to recall and arrest Col. William S. Harney, commander of the Second Dragoons at San Antonio, who had launched an unauthorized and unsuccessful invasion of Mexico. In October, Wool released Harney from arrest, placed him in charge of the advance, and marched for the Rio Grande at Eagle Pass. He crossed into Coahuila on a pontoon bridge laid down by Capt. Robert E. Lee, but found it impossible to penetrate the cordilleras into Chihuahua and swung east to join Taylor's forces at Saltillo. Wool chose the battlefield at Buena Vista, and as field commander on 22–23 February 1847 he enabled Taylor to repulse a larger Mexican army under Antonio López de Santa Anna. At Taylor's departure for the United States, Wool commanded the occupation forces, which included Texas cavalry, in Tamaulipas, Nuevo León, Coahuila, and Zacatecas, from November 1847 until the American withdrawal from Mexico in June 1848. Wool subsequently commanded the Eastern Department (1849–53, 1857–61) and the Department of the Pacific (1854–57), and during the Civil War he commanded successively the Department of Virginia (Fortress Monroe), the Middle Department (Baltimore) and the Department of New York and New England (New York City). He retired on 1 August 1863, a regular major general, at the age of 79. *Harwood P. Hinton*

World War II Internment Camps. Although many Americans are aware of the World War II imprisonment of West Coast Japanese Americans in relocation centers, few know of the smaller internment camps operated by the Immigration and Naturalization Service. Under the authority of the Department of Justice, the INS directed about 20 such facilities. Texas had three of them, located at Seagoville, Kenedy, and Crystal City. Prisoners included Japanese Americans arrested by the FBI, members of Axis nationalities residing in Latin-American coun-

General Wool Crossing the Military Plaza, San Antonio, by Samuel Chamberlain, ca. 1867. Watercolor. 7" × 12⅛". Courtesy San Jacinto Museum of History, Houston. Chamberlain, en route to Mexico as a member of Wool's force, noted the varied audience that witnessed this 1846 scene: "wild looking Texans, Mexicans in their everlasting blankets, Negro Slaves, with a sprinkling of Lipan Indians, in full dress of paint and feathers, White women, Squaws and Senoretas."

tries, and Axis sailors arrested in American ports after the attack on Pearl Harbor. About 3,000 Japanese, Germans, and Italians from Latin America were deported to the United States, and most of them were placed in the Texas internment camps. Twelve Latin-American countries gave the United States Department of State custody of the Axis nationals. Eighty percent of the prisoners were from Peru, and about 70 percent were Japanese. The official reasons for the deportations were to secure the Western Hemisphere from internal sabotage and to provide people to exchange for American citizens captured by Japan. However, the Axis nationals were often deported arbitrarily as a result of racial prejudice and because they provided economic competition for the other Latin Americans, not because they were a security threat. Eventually, very few Japanese ever saw Latin America again, although some Germans and Italians were returned there. The majority of Texas internment-camp prisoners were Axis nationals from Latin America.

The Seagoville internment camp, built by the Bureau of Prisons as a minimum-security women's reformatory in 1941, held prisoners from Central and South America, married couples without children from the United States, and about 50 Japanese language teachers from California. The facilities at Seagoville made it the most unusual camp operated by the INS. Twelve colonial-style, red-brick buildings with cream limestone trim were surrounded by spacious lawns. Paved sidewalks and roads connected the buildings, and visitors remarked that the camp resembled a college campus. Nevertheless, a high, woven-wire fence surrounded the camp, which had a single guarded entrance. A white line painted down the middle of the paved

road that encircled the camp marked a boundary that internees could not pass. The six dormitories had single or double rooms and were furnished with chests of drawers, desks, chairs, and beds. Communal laundry, bathing, and toilet facilities were located on all floors. Each dormitory had a kitchen with refrigerators, gas stove, and dishwasher, as well as a dining room with four-person maple tables, linen table coverings, cloth napkins, and china. Internees prepared their own food under supervision. Other facilities at the Seagoville camp included a hospital and a large recreation building. A female doctor directed the hospital and supervised a staff of 6 physicians, 10 registered nurses, a dentist, and a laboratory technician. The recreation building provided a variety of activities, such as ballet and stage productions performed by internees in the auditorium. In addition, the recreation building had orchestral instruments, 12 classrooms for English and music instruction, a multilanguage library, and sewing and weaving rooms. Outside activities included gardening, farming, tennis, baseball, badminton, and walking. Although conditions at the Seagoville camp were unusually comfortable for a prison environment, the internees did have some complaints. Many resented being held at a penal institution, which was still administered by a warden, Amy N. Stannard. The prisoners also disliked the censorship of their letters and the limit on their outgoing correspondence. In late summer of 1942, the INS planned to reunite Japanese men from other internment camps with their families already at Seagoville. Anticipating this transfer, Seagoville received 50 one-room ply-wood huts from the INS detention camp at Santa Fe, New Mexico, and a large building was constructed as a kitchen and mess hall. Laundry rooms and separate male and female communal toilet and bath facilities were built. The largest population interned at Seagoville was 647. In June 1945 the Seagoville alien enemy internment camp was closed and detainees were repatriated, paroled, or moved to other INS internment camps.

In contrast to Seagoville, the Kenedy Alien Detention Camp housed only men. Before World War II, the site was a CCC camp; Kenedy business owners, in an effort to increase local prosperity, lobbied the INS to use the camp as an internment station. The camp received its first large group of prisoners on 23 April 1942, and during the course of its existence housed more than 3,500 aliens. The United States Army took over the operation on 1 October 1944, and from then until the end of the war it housed wounded and disabled German prisoners of war.

Crystal City was the location of the largest Texas internment camp administered by the INS and Department of Justice. To reduce hardships during internment and to reunite families, the INS originally intended to detain only Japanese at Crystal City, especially the many Latin-American Japanese families brought to the United States for internment pending repatriation. Germans and Italians, however, were also held in Crystal City. In the fall of 1942 the INS assumed ownership of the Farm Security Administration's migratory farmworkers' camp on the outskirts of Crystal City. Existing facilities were 41 three-room cottages, 118 one-room structures, and some service buildings. Eventually, the INS spent more than a million dollars to construct more than 500 buildings on the camp's 290 acres. Warehouses, auditoriums, administration offices, schools, clothing and food stores, a hospital, and many housing units were built. Like the camps at Kenedy and Seagoville, the Crystal City internment camp provided jobs and revenue for the town. The first German internees arrived in December 1942. The first Japanese arrived from Seagoville on 10 March 1943. In addition, prisoners were taken to Crystal City from other INS internment camps in Hawaii and Alaska (not states at the time), the United States, Puerto Rico, the West Indies, and South and Central American countries. The population of the Crystal City camp peaked at 3,326 in May 1945. Languages spoken at Crystal City included Japanese, German, Italian, Spanish, and English; ages of internees ranged from newborn to elderly. The variety of prisoners added to the complexities of camp organization and administration. Camp officials tried to arrange housing so that similar races and nationalities would be together, but even so, strong differences emerged between those who wanted repatriation and those who wanted to stay in the United States or return to the country they were expelled from. The camp was divided into separate sections for Germans and Japanese. Though no physical boundaries separated the two groups, they did not interact often. They had separate auditoriums, community centers, schools, and stores. Housing units consisted of triplexes and duplexes that shared toilet and bath facilities, three-room cottages with indoor toilet and bath, and plywood huts with central latrines and baths. Except for the huts, all housing had cold running water, kitchen sinks, and oil stoves. Administrators assigned housing and set food allowances based on the age and size of families. Token money was issued accordingly, and families purchased food at a large grocery store. Two separate, large canteens were called the German General Store and the Japanese Union Store; these stores took tokens like the central grocery. The majority of store positions were held by internees, including cashiers, store clerks,

butchers, and warehouse workers. The Japanese were provided with special foods, such as soy sauce, tofu, seaweed, dried shrimp, and large quantities of rice. Internees could participate in a paid-work program. Workers were paid 10 cents an hour and employed in all aspects of camp organization. They planted vegetables, tended orange orchards and beehives, raised pigs and chickens, washed laundry, repaired clothes and shoes, manufactured mattresses, furniture, and clothes, and made sausage and bakery items. Others worked in the stores, administration offices, hospital, or schools. Employment kept the internees busy and lessened the frustrations of internment. In many ways, the Crystal City camp resembled a bustling small town.

The Crystal City internment camp had four schools to educate the numerous children detained there. The children of Germans and Japanese who desired repatriation were sent to language schools taught by internees. The Federal Grammar and High School provided an American-style education for a mostly Japanese student body. Gaining accreditation from the Texas State Department of Education was a challenge because of teacher and school-supply shortages, as well as the difficulty of organizing classes when all students were transfers. Team sports were very popular: 32 softball teams were divided into 2 leagues with a schedule of games and tournament play-offs. A chapel with more than 30 internee priests and ministers provided worship services. Also, camp officials granted many requests for picnics by the Nueces River, which was not far outside the internment camp boundary. At Crystal City, the INS administrators tried to make camp life as normal as possible, but security constantly reminded detainees of their lack of freedom. A 10-foot fence, guard towers, and floodlights surrounded the camp. Mounted guards patrolled the perimeter of the compound, a small police force was inside the camp at all times, and vehicles were searched at the gate. Officials kept dossiers on each internee and conducted head counts every day in the housing units. All letters were censored. Prisoners met visiting friends or relatives under surveillance, although college students and American soldiers on vacation were allowed to stay with their parents. Security was a priority; Crystal City did not have any escape attempts.

With so many internees, camp officials realized a need for medical services. In December 1942 the medical division was composed of 2 nurses and a 25-cent first aid kit. By July 1943 a 70-bed hospital and clinic operated 24 hours a day. Internee doctors performed more than a thousand major and minor operations, and a Japanese pharmacist dispensed more than 30,000 prescriptions. Hundreds of babies were born at the detention station.

By July 1945 hundreds of Germans and Japanese had been repatriated from Crystal City. More than 100 had been released or paroled, 73 had been transferred to other camps, and 17 had died. In December 1945 more than 600 Peruvian Japanese left for Japan because the Peruvian government would not allow them to return to Peru. That same month, a similar number of Japanese were allowed to go home to Hawaii. Some prisoners resisted repatriation to Japan and were not allowed to return to Central and South America. In late 1947 the United States determined to let them stay. On 1 November 1947, more than two years after the end of World War II, the Crystal City internment camp closed—the last facility detaining aliens to do so.

Emily Brosveen

Wyalucing Plantation. In Marshall; the two-story brick planta-tion home of Beverly Lafayette Holcombe, built 1848–50. The house was designed to resemble a rectangular Grecian temple, with columns on all four sides. A second cottage-style residence called Westover was built on the western end of Holcombe's 100-acre tract, and the two homes were linked by a street lined with slave cabins. According to family tradition, the name Wyalucing is of Indian derivation and means "home of the friendless"; other sources translate it as "home of the warrior." Wyalucing, the scene of numerous social events in the antebellum period, served as headquarters for the Trans-Mississippi Agency of the Confederate Post Office Department. In 1865 Confederate general Joseph O. Shelby addressed the troops of his Iron Brigade from the veranda of Wyalucing just before their departure on the Shelby expedition. In 1880 the home was purchased by former slaves of Harrison County for Bishop College. Wyalucing was used as the Bishop College music hall in the 1940s. When the college moved to Dallas in 1961 the Harrison County Historical Society tried to preserve Wyalucing, but the plantation building was demolished in the early 1960s, and the land is currently the site of a low-rent housing development.

XYZ

XIT Ranch. Established to finance construction of the Capitol. In 1879 the legislature appropriated three million acres for the purpose. The existing Capitol burned in 1881, thus making construction of the new building urgent. The Capitol Syndicate was formed to manage the land; chief among its investors were John Farwell, Charles Farwell, and Amos Babcock. The syndicate established the XIT Ranch to utilize the unsettled Panhandle land until it could be sold. Babcock conducted a survey of the property and recommended that it be immediately stocked with cattle and fenced. To secure finances, John Farwell went to England and in 1884 formed the Capitol Freehold Land and Investment Company of London. By attracting wealthy British investors like the Earl of Aberdeen and Henry Seton–Karr, a member of Parliament, Farwell returned with the equivalent of roughly $5 million in American currency. From the beginning, the syndicate had intended to run cattle only until the land could be utilized for agriculture; long-range goals were to promote settlement, eventually subdivide the acreage, and gradually sell it off piecemeal. On the strength of Babcock's suggestions, it was decided to fence the entire range and erect windmills. B. H. (Barbecue) Campbell of Wichita, Kansas, was chosen by Farwell to be the XIT's first general manager. Under his direction, surveyor William S. Mabry surveyed a fence line for a horse pasture at Buffalo Springs, the ranch's first designated headquarters, and late in the spring of 1885 the first pasture fence was completed. Campbell, in the meantime, set about contracting for longhorn cattle in Central and South Texas. On 1 July 1885, the first herd of 2,500 head arrived at Buffalo Springs. They had been driven from the Fort Concho area by Abner P. Blocker, who reportedly devised the XIT brand with his boot in the dust when Campbell sought a design that could not be changed easily. Although legend persists that the brand signified "10 in Texas," since the land covered all or part of 10 counties, that theory is doubtful; some speculate that it really meant "biggest in Texas." Within the next year 781 miles of fence was built, and by November 1886 some 110,721 cattle valued at $1,322,587 had been purchased. After 1887 large-scale buying ceased, and the herd averaged 150,000 head. The first ranchhouse was built in 1886. For convenience the ranch was cut into several divisions, which eventually totaled eight in all. Each division had a section headquarters, a foreman, its quota of employees and horses, and its specific characteristics. When the Fort Worth and Denver City Railway built through the Panhandle in 1887, the new town of Channing emerged as a major shipping point. As a result it became the center of ranch activities, and the main XIT headquarters was established there. The eighth division, which came about with the building of the Pecos and North Texas line in 1898, was centered at Bovina. Another railroad shipping point was Perico, near the Farwell Park line camp in the Buffalo Springs division.

In 1887 reports of inconsistencies in the XIT's management, including inferior cattle and the presence of wanted outlaws on the range, led to an investigation conducted at the syndicate's request by state senator Avery L. Matlock from Montague. Matlock briefly took over the management and was followed by Albert G. Boyce (1888). Like his predecessor, Boyce insisted on strict adherence to the ranch laws as set up by the syndicate, including prohibitions against gambling, drinking alcoholic beverages, abusing stock, and killing beef without permission. Under his rule the XIT reached its peak with 150 cowboys who rode 1,000 horses and branded 35,000 calves in one year. In addition to its vast Panhandle acreage, the XIT maintained maturing grounds for its cattle in the northern Plains, first in South Dakota and later, in 1889, on a range north of Miles City, Montana. For 11 consecutive years, 12,500 cattle were driven annually to these northern pastures and fattened for the Chicago markets. Beginning in 1889, a program of breeding and herd improvement was launched with the introduction of Hereford, shorthorn, and Aberdeen–Angus cattle to the XIT. By the turn of the century 325 windmills and 100 dams had been erected on the XIT ranges, all at a cost of around $500,000. Fences divided the ranch into 94 pastures, and 1,500 miles of fencing had been completed. Since the XIT dominated politics in several counties, many of its employees were elected to public offices. The operation of such a huge spread meant coping with unceasing problems. Fence cutting and cattle rustling increased as smaller ranchers moved into the Panhandle and the adjacent New Mexico Territory. Consequently the XIT men, along with certain "hired guns," often formed vigilante posses that struck back at rustlers. Straight-shooting lawmen like Ira Aten were frequently hired as section foremen. Moreover, wolves and other predators, deprived of their natural prey, took a terrible annual toll among cattle, particularly during the calving season; many cowboys earned extra money by "wolfing" to obtain the high bounties established for wolf pelts. Frustrating delays in drilling wells, especially during XIT's earlier years, sometimes resulted in cattle dying from lack of sufficient water. Because of such difficulties, in addition to droughts, blizzards, prairie fires, and declining markets, the XIT operated largely without profit throughout most of its existence.

By the late 1890s the clamorings of British creditors were rising, and the Capitol Syndicate began the gradual process of selling out. George W. Littlefield, the first large purchaser, bought 235,858 acres. William E. Halsell started his Mashed O Ranch out of the old Spring Lake division by buying 184,155 acres. John M. Shelton developed the Ojo Bravo division as the Bravo and JJ ranches. As homesteaders began pouring in, a land rush occurred during the early 1900s. To promote its real estate, the syndicate established the office of land commissioner in 1905, selected F. W. Wilsey for the position, and stationed James D. Hamlin at the rail town of Farwell to represent the owners. Experimental "poor farms," as the cowboys called them, were set up, one about seven miles south of Channing and another at the short-lived townsite of Parmerton near Bovina. By the time Henry S. Boice succeeded A. G. Boyce as general manager in 1905, much of the XIT land was already being divided into small tracts and sold to farmers. In 1909 nearly all of the British bonds that had helped start the enterprise were redeemed in full, much to the satisfaction of the English investors. While the Capitol had

Ralph Yarborough campaigning for governor on the courthouse stairs. Photograph by Russell Lee. McKinney, Texas, 1954. Russell Lee Photograph Collection, CAH; CN

cost more than $3 million instead of the original projection of $1.5 million, the cost of the land being sold was increased, and the corporation fulfilled its contract. The last of the XIT cattle were sold on 1 November 1912, and land sales subsequently increased through the Capitol Reservation Lands, the new trust formed by the Farwell Estate in 1915. In 1929 the ranch still owned 450,000 acres; by 1943 that acreage had been reduced to around 350,000. The last parcel of XIT land was sold in 1963 by Hamlin Y. Overstreet, who had succeeded his late uncle as a company representative in Farwell.

The romance of the XIT Ranch, enhanced by the spread's sheer size, lives on in western lore. In the late 1920s, the Farwell Estate commissioned J. Evetts Haley to write *The XIT Ranch of Texas* (1929). It and Lewis T. Nordyke's *Cattle Empire* (1949), which is more like a novel, remain the standard accounts. Memoirs of former XIT employees, including James D. Hamlin, Cordelia Sloan Duke, and Charles E. MacConnell, have been published. The XIT Ranch records are housed in the Panhandle–Plains Historical Museum in Canyon, and the old general office building still stands in Channing. In Dalhart memories of the ranch are kept alive in the XIT Museum and the "Empty Saddles" monument, as well as the annual XIT Reunion, complete with parade and rodeo. Other West Texas towns, including Muleshoe, Farwell, and Bovina, also advertise their connection with the XIT. The old Escarbada division headquarters, home of Ira Aten while he was foreman, is now part of the Ranching Heritage Center in Lubbock. *H. Allen Anderson*

Yarborough, Ralph Webster. Senator and liberal Democratic party leader; b. Chandler, Texas, 8 June 1903; d. Austin, 27 January 1996 (buried in the State Cemetery); m. Opal Warren (1928); 1 son; ed. University of Texas law school (grad. 1927). Yarborough was appointed to the United States Military Academy at West Point in 1919 but dropped out the following year. He taught school for a time while attending classes at Sam Houston State Teachers College and paid his way through UT by working at various jobs. After several years with an El Paso law firm that included William Henry Burges and William Ward Turney among its partners, Yarborough was hired as an assistant attorney general in 1931 and was given special responsibility for the interests of the Permanent School Fund. Over the next four years he gained recognition by winning several cases against the Magnolia Petroleum Company and other major oil companies and successfully establishing the right of public schools and universities to oil-fund revenues. His work ultimately secured billions of dollars for public education. In 1936 Governor Allred appointed Yarborough to a state district judgeship in Austin; Yarborough was elected to that office later the same year. He made his first bid for statewide elective office in 1938, when he came in third in the race for attorney general. He was in the Texas National Guard in the 1930s and in the United States Army during World War II; he served in Europe and the Pacific in the Ninety-seventh Division and ended the war as a lieutenant colonel with a Bronze Star and a Combat Medal. After the surrender he spent eight months with the military government of occupation in Japan. In 1946 he returned to Austin and resumed law practice. In the 1952 Democratic primary Yarborough challenged incumbent governor Allan Shivers and lost. The campaign was the first of many in one-party Texas in which Yarborough was aligned with the progressive or liberal wing of the Democratic party against conservatives. A second primary loss to Shivers in 1954 was characterized by harsh campaign attacks on both sides, as Yarborough accused Shivers of wrongdoing in the Veteran's Land Board Scandal and Shivers countered by claiming that Yarborough supported integration and was backed by Communist labor unions. He lost another bid for the governorship to Price Daniel in 1956 in a close run-off campaign. When Daniel vacated his senatorial seat in 1957, Yarborough joined the field for the office with 21 other candidates and squeaked through the primary with 38 percent of the vote to join Lyndon Johnson in the Senate. Yarborough received the support of organized labor, the newly organized Democrats of Texas, and the recently founded *Texas Observer*.

In the Senate, Yarborough established himself as very different from the majority of his southern colleagues. After refusing to support a resolution opposing desegregation, he became one of only five southern senators to vote for the Civil Rights Act of 1957. He defeated wealthy conservative Democrat William A. "Dollar Bill" Blakley in the primary and Republican Ray Wittenburg in the election to win a full term in 1958. In 1960 Yarborough sponsored the Senate resolution leading to the Kennedy–Nixon television debate, a crucial event in the election and a model for subsequent presidential campaigns. In 1963 Yarborough was present at the Kennedy assassination; many believe his feud with conservative governor John Connally led to his sitting in the second car in the motorcade rather than with the president. Yarborough defeated George H. W. Bush, future president of the United States, in the senatorial race of 1964. In his years in the senate Yarborough supported many of the key bills of Johnson's Great Society and pressed for legislative action in the fields of civil rights, education, public health, and environmental protection. He voted for the Civil Rights Act of 1964 and was one of only three southerners to support the Voting Rights Act of 1965. Yarborough served for years on the Senate Labor and Public Welfare Committee, of which he became chairman in 1969. He sponsored or cosponsored the Elementary and Secondary Education Act (1965), the Higher Education Act (1965), the Bilingual Education Act (1967), and the updated GI Bill of 1966. He was also an advocate for such public-health measures as the Occupational Health and Safety Act, the Community Mental Health Center Act, and the National Cancer Act of 1970. He cowrote the Endangered Species Act of 1969 and sponsored the legislation establishing Padre Island National Seashore (1962),

Guadalupe Mountains National Park (1966), and Big Thicket National Preserve (1971). His interest in the preservation of Texas historical sites led him to sponsor bills to make Fort Davis and the Alibates Flint Quarries national monuments.

In 1970 Lloyd Bentsen, Jr., upset Yarborough in the primary and went on to gain the Senate seat. Yarborough's last attempt at political office, a run at John Tower's Senate seat in 1972, did not make it past the primary, where he was defeated by Barefoot Sanders. Yarborough returned to the practice of law in Austin. As an avid bibliophile and collector of Western Americana and Texana, he amassed a substantial library. He numbered J. Frank Dobie among his friends and supporters. "Smilin' Ralph" Yarborough is one of the great figures in the Texas progressive tradition, a gregarious politician who campaigned in the old energetic, back-slapping style and who believed that social welfare could be significantly improved through government action.   *Mark Odintz*

Yellow Stone. A vessel that played a major role in the Texas Revolution; well known as the first steamboat to navigate the upper Missouri River before it came to Texas. Contracted by Pierre Chateau, Jr., by permission of John Jacob Astor, the sidewheeler was built in Louisville, Kentucky, in 1831 for the fur trade. It had a tonnage of 144 and was designed for navigating the Missouri's shallow water and snags—river features also typical of the Brazos River, where the boat entered the cotton trade in 1836. The vessel made the first successful voyage from St. Louis all the way up the Missouri to the American Fur Company's Fort Union, near the mouth of the Yellowstone River, in 1832. George Catlin, who was a passenger, recorded and sketched this trip. Another journey, to Fort Pierre in 1833, was described by Prince Maximilian von Wied, a German naturalist, and painted by Karl Bodmer, a Swiss artist, who were passengers. During the winters the American Fur Company used the *Yellow Stone* on the lower Mississippi.

In late 1835 the ship, owned by Thomas Toby and registered in New Orleans, was placed in drydock there for extensive repairs and for outfitting for the Texas trade. In November 1835 the boat arrived in Brazoria from New Orleans; it then ran cotton between San Felipe and Washington-on-the-Brazos. Manned by a crew from the United States and flying the United States flag, it cleared port on 31 December 1835, with its cargo largely ammunition and its passengers mostly volunteers for the Texas army, including 47 men of the Mobile Grays. The ship arrived at Quintana at the mouth of the Brazos in early January 1836. On the Brazos it operated under the control of the merchant firm of McKinney, Williams and Company. The *Yellow Stone* was loading cotton at Groce's Landing above San Felipe when Sam Houston's army arrived on 31 March 1836 and made camp on the west side of the Brazos. Houston impressed the ship to ferry his army across the flooding river. He made an agreement with Capt. John E. Ross and his crew, pledging land in exchange for their services and promising indemnity to the boat's owners for wages and damages. The captain later presented a bill for $4,900 to the Texas government. The *Yellow Stone* was recognized as an unarmed neutral ship of the United States, and the crew was not required to bear arms. On 12 April General Santa Anna, with 750 picked men and a six-pounder, began crossing the Brazos downriver at Thompson's Ferry, and on the same day the *Yellow Stone* made the first of seven trips transporting the Texas army across to Groce's. After Houston released it, the vessel, its engine, crew, and passengers, protected by Groce's cotton bales, started down the swollen Brazos at full steam and passed the burned ruins of San Felipe on 15 April. Gen. Joaquín Ramírez y Sesma met the steamer with heavy fire, but damaged her only slightly. At Galveston Island on 26 April, President David Burnet commandeered the *Yellow Stone* to house the cabinet. On 4 May she was ordered to Buffalo Bayou, where the cabinet was to begin treaty negotiations with the defeated Santa Anna. On the return journey, on 9 May, additional passengers included Santa Anna and his staff, the wounded Houston and his staff, General Cos, and 80 wounded prisoners. The vessel then continued on to Velasco, where the treaty was being made.

Ross left the *Yellow Stone* in July 1836 and was succeeded by James H. West, who had come to Texas from Pennsylvania with the New Orleans Greys. Other later captains were William Sargeant, a San Jacinto veteran, and Thomas Wigg Grayson. Before it disappeared, the *Yellow Stone* transported the body of Stephen F. Austin and mourners from Columbia Landing downriver to Peach Point Plantation in December 1836 and moved the Texas government and the press and staff of the Telegraph and Texas Register from the Brazos to Houston in the spring of 1837. Many have tried to determine the fate of the *Yellow Stone*. One source claims without other verification that she was stranded on the Brazos in 1837 with no lives lost. The last known voucher for the vessel is dated 31 May 1837, for the passage of Dr. A. Ewing from Houston to Galveston. A ship's bell, said to be that of the *Yellow Stone*, is in the Alamo museum. Despite repeated petitions from Houston to the republic and state government after 1837, the full terms of his pledge in behalf of the crew were never met. Houston wrote in a petition that the "use of the boat enabled me to cross the Brazos and save Texas."

Lois Wood Burkhalter

Henderson Yoakum, by George R. Allen, 1849. Oil on canvas. 27" × 22". Courtesy Mary Robinson Woodward, Fort Worth.

Yoakum, Henderson King. Historian; b. Claiborne County, Tennessee, 6 September 1810; d. Houston, 30 November 1856; m. Evaline Cannon (1833); 9 children; ed. West Point (grad. 1832). In 1833 Yoakum resigned his lieutenant's commission to practice law in Murfreesboro, Tennessee. He became captain of a company of mounted militia in 1836 and served near the Sabine River under Edmund P. Gaines. In 1837 he was mayor of Murfreesboro. In 1838 he reentered the army as a colonel in the Tennessee infantry and served in the Cherokee War. He was a member of the Tennessee Senate from 1839 to 1845 and as senator urged the annexation of Texas. In 1845 he moved to Huntsville, where he was admitted to the Texas bar. In 1846 he was instrumental in making Huntsville the county seat of Walker County. At the outbreak of the Mexican War he volunteered as a private under John Coffee Hays and served at Monterrey as a lieutenant under James Gillaspie. In 1846 he returned to his law practice at Huntsville, where Sam Houston was his close friend and client. Although a member of the Methodist Church, Yoakum wrote the charter for Austin College (1849) and served as a trustee for that school from 1849 to 1856. He helped establish Andrew Female College in Huntsville and in 1849 was appointed director of the state penitentiary there. In 1853 he became "master mason" and then "high priest" of the Huntsville Lodge. In July of that year he moved to his country home, Shepherd's Valley,

seven miles from Huntsville, where in 1855 he completed his two-volume *History of Texas from Its First Settlement in 1685 to Its Annexation to the United States in 1846*, for which Houston was said to have given him much of the information. Yoakum County is named for him.

Thomas P. Yoakum

Zaharias, Babe. Athlete; b. Mildred Ella Didrikson, Port Arthur, 26 June 1911; d. Galveston, 27 September 1956 (buried in Beaumont); m. George Zaharias (1938). In 1915, Mildred's Norwegian family moved to Beaumont. She acquired her nickname during sandlot baseball games with the neighborhood boys, who thought she batted like Babe Ruth. She was recruited during her senior year in 1930 to do office work at Employers Casualty Company of Dallas and to spark the company's semi-professional women's basketball team, the Golden Cyclones. Between 1930 and 1932 she led the team to two finals and a national championship and was voted All-American each season. Her exceptional athletic versatility prompted Employers Casualty to expand its women's sports program beyond basketball. Babe represented the company as a one-woman team in 8 of 10 track and field events at the 1932 Amateur Athletic Union Championships. She placed in 7 events, taking first place in 5—shot put, javelin and baseball throws, 80-meter hurdles, and long jump; she tied for first in the high jump and finished fourth in

Babe Didrikson Zaharias, Willow Springs Golf Course, San Antonio, 1935. San Antonio *Light* Collection, ITC.

the discus throw. In 3 hours she singlehandedly amassed 30 points, 8 more than the entire second-place team, and broke 4 world records. Her performances in the javelin throw, hurdles, and high jump qualified her to enter the 1932 Olympics, where she again broke world records in all 3 events. She won gold medals for the javelin and hurdles and, despite clearing the same height as the top finisher in the high jump, was awarded the silver medal because she went over the bar head first, a foul at that time. Babe received a heroine's welcome on her return to Texas. She had started another basketball season with the Golden Cyclones when the Amateur Athletic Union disqualified her from amateur competition because her name appeared in an automobile advertisement. Her family was badly in need of money, and she turned professional to earn what she could from her status as a sports celebrity. Never hesitant to capitalize on her own abilities or to turn a profit from showmanship, she spent 1932–34 promoting and barnstorming. She did a brief stint in vaudeville playing the harmonica and running on a treadmill and pitched in some major league spring-training games; she also toured with a billiards exhibition, a men's and women's basketball team called Babe Didrikson's All-Americans, and an oth-

erwise all-male, bearded baseball road team called the House of David.

Since golf was one of the few sports that accommodated women athletes, she made up her mind to become a championship player, and between engagements she spent the spring and summer of 1933 in California taking lessons from Stan Kertes. Her first tournament was the Fort Worth Women's Invitational in November 1932; at her second, the Texas Women's Amateur Championship the following April, she captured the title. Complaints from more socially polished members of the Texas Women's Golf Association led the United States Association to rule her ineligible to compete as an amateur, thus disqualifying her from virtually all tournament play. Babe resumed the lucrative routine of exhibition tours and endorsements, impressing audiences with smashing drives that regularly exceeded 240 feet. She met Zaharias, a well-known professional wrestler and sports promoter, when she qualified at the 1938 Los Angeles Open, a men's Professional Golfers' Association tournament. After they married, Zaharias managed his wife's career. Babe Zaharias regained her amateur standing in 1943 and went on to win 17 consecutive tournaments, including the British Women's Amateur Championship (she was the first American to win it), before turning professional in 1947. The following year she helped found the Ladies Professional Golf Association in order to provide the handful of professional women golfers with a tournament circuit. She was herself the LPGA's leading money winner from 1949 to 1951. In 1950 the Associated Press voted her Woman Athlete of the Half-Century.

In April 1953 Babe underwent a colostomy to remove cancerous tissue. Despite medical predictions that she would never be able to play championship golf again, she was in tournament competition 14 weeks after surgery, and the Golf Writers of America voted her the Ben Hogan Trophy as comeback player of the year. In 1954 she won five tournaments, including the United States Women's Open. Portrayed as a courageous survivor in the press, she played for cancer benefits and maintained her usual buoyant public persona, but in June 1955 she was forced to reenter John Sealy Hospital at the University of Texas Medical Branch at Galveston for further diagnosis. She spent much of the remaining 15 months of her life in the hospital. In September 1955 she and her husband established the Babe Didrikson Zaharias Fund, which financed a tumor clinic at UTMB. Her exuberant confidence, self-congratulatory manner, and cultivation of her celebrity status irritated some fellow athletes, but she was the most popular female golfer of her own time and since. She enjoyed playing to the gallery in her golf matches, and her wisecracks and exhibitions of virtuosity delighted spectators. She was voted Athlete of the Year by the Associated Press six times. Between 1940 and 1950 she won every women's golf title, including the world championship (four times) and the United States Women's Open (three times). She established a national audience for women's golf and was the first woman ever to serve as a resident professional at a golf club. In 1955, a year before her death, she established the Babe Zaharias Trophy to honor outstanding female athletes.   *Susan E. Cayleff*

Zale Jewelry Corporation. Founded 17 March 1924 as a single store in Wichita Falls by Morris B. Zale, a Russian Jewish immigrant. The goal of selling the greatest amount of jewelry to the largest number of people at the lowest possible price introduced the concept of mass marketing to retail jewelry, a business that had previously catered exclusively to the wealthy. In order to attract a working-class clientele, Zale's offered interest-free credit with minimal down payments and low, no-interest, weekly installments—an innovation, like the extensive advertising that Zale's used. The company opened stores in Tulsa and Oklahoma City in the late 1920s, but the Great Depression postponed further expansion. After the struggle of the 1930s, Zale's began to recover and by 1939 operated 12 stores in 3 states. A shortage of available merchandise during World War II limited growth again, but at the end of the war Zale's launched a massive expansion program. In 1946 the company moved its headquarters from Wichita Falls to Dallas. It began acquiring well-known jewelry stores and operating them under their original names—Corrigan's of Houston (1944) provided the foundation for the company's highly successful Guild Division. By 1956 Zale's was operating a total of 63 stores in 10 states with gross annual sales exceeding $35 million. In 1957 Morris Zale relinquished the company presidency to his brother-in-law, Ben Lipshy. That same year Zale's went public with its stock. In 1958 Zale's began buying diamonds directly from the South African firm DeBeers. Since Zale's personnel purchased, cut, polished, mounted, and marketed diamonds, the company eliminated middlemen at each of those steps, thus reducing margins, increasing profits, and helping to maintain uniform quality.

In the mid-1960s Zale's acquired Skillern Drugstores, Karotkin Furniture Stores, Levine Department Stores, Butler Shoe Company, Cullum and Boren Sporting Goods, O. G. Wilson Catalogue Stores, Optex, Incorporated, and Sugerman, Incorporated. By 1984, however, Zale's had divested itself of all those holdings except Wilson's and returned exclusively to retail jewelry. In 1984 Zale's employed 13,500 persons in its 9 divisions and operated some 1,550 retail jewelry units. In addition to its Zale's stores, the company also operated Mission Jewelers and the leased jewelry departments in some of the country's leading department stores. The Guild Division included some of the nation's most prestigious jewelry stores, such as Bailey, Banks, and Biddle of Philadelphia. Besides its operations in the United States, Zale's also had holdings in France, Germany, India, the United Kingdom, Guam, Puerto Rico, Switzerland, Japan, and Israel. With gross sales annually surpassing $1 billion, Zale's ranked as the world's leading retail jeweler. Nevertheless, the company was involuntarily thrust into Chapter 11 bankruptcy in January 1992. At the time equal shares of the company comprising 47.5 percent were owned by Peoples Jewellers Ltd. of Toronto and Swarovski International Holding of Zurich. In 1991 the firm's four separate retail chains—Zale's, Bailey, Banks, and Biddle, Gordon's, and Corrigan's—produced $1.2 billion in annual sales. Nonetheless, Zale's faced a $1.2 billion dollar debt from the 1986 takeover by Peoples Jewellers and declining sales blamed on a nationwide recession. The company's reorganization plan included closing many of the firm's duplicate stores in shopping malls.   *Tommy W. Stringer*

Zavala, Adina de. Preservationist; b. Harris County, 28 November 1861; d. San Antonio, 1 March 1955 (buried in St. Mary's Cemetery); ed. Sam Houston Normal Institute (grad. 1881). The family lived at Galveston before moving to a ranch near San Antonio about 1873. Adina de Zavala taught school at Terrell (1884–86) and San Antonio. About 1889 she and other San

Adina de Zavala in front of the Spanish Governor's Palace, San Antonio, ca. 1930s. Adina de Zavala Papers, CAH; CN 06536.

Antonio women formed a patriotic society that became affiliated with the Daughters of the Republic of Texas in 1893. One of her greatest contributions to Texas was the preservation of a portion of San Antonio de Valero Mission, better known as the Alamo, which her group prevented from being razed in the early twentieth century. In the climactic event of that effort, in conflict with another DRT faction led by Clara Driscoll, she barricaded herself inside the north barrack of the Alamo for three days in February 1908 to protest its destruction. In 1912 she organized the Texas Historical and Landmarks Association, which placed 38 markers at historic sites. She urged the preservation of the Spanish Governors' Palace in San Antonio. In the 1930s she helped establish the location near Crockett of sites of the first two missions established in Texas by the Spanish. In 1923 Governor Neff appointed her to the Texas Historical Board, and she was one of the original members of the Committee of One Hundred appointed to plan for the Texas Centennial celebration. Miss Zavala was a charter member and honorary life fellow (1945–) of the Texas State Historical Association. She was a dedicated Catholic and a member of the United Daughters of the Confederacy, the Texas Folklore Society, and the Philosophical Society of Texas. She wrote a book, *History and Legends of the Alamo and Other Missions in and Around San Antonio* (1917); pamphlets, including *The Story of the Siege and Fall of the Alamo:*

Lorenzo de Zavala. Miniature on ivory. Courtesy San Jacinto Museum of History, Houston.

A *Résumé* (1911); and contributions to the *Handbook of Texas* (1952).   *L. Robert Ables*

Zavala, Lorenzo de. First vice president of the Republic of Texas; b. near Mérida, Yucatán, 3 October 1788; d. Texas, 15 November 1836; m. Teresa Correa y Correa (1807; d. 1831); 3 children; m. Emily West (1831); 3 children; ed. Tridentine Seminary of San Ildefonso, Mérida (grad. 1807). Zavala founded and edited several newspapers that advocated democracy. He served as secretary of the city council of Mérida (1812–14) and was imprisoned for his advocacy in the fortress of San Juan de Ullóa in the harbor of Veracruz (1814–17). In prison he studied enough medical texts to qualify him to practice medicine, and taught himself to read English. After serving as secretary of the provincial assembly of Yucatán in 1820, Zavala went to Madrid in 1821 as a deputy to the Spanish Cortes. Upon his return to Mexico, he joined the leaders of the new nation in establishing a republican government. He represented Yucatán as a deputy in the First and Second Mexican Constituent congresses of 1822 and 1824 and in the Mexican Senate from 1824 to 1826. In the following two years, marked by the struggle between the Federalists and Centralists, Zavala served intermittently as governor of the state of Mexico. When Vicente Ramón Guerrero became president, Zavala was appointed secretary of the treasury; he served from April to October 1829. When the Centralist party, led by Vice President Anastacio Bustamante, ousted Guerrero late in the year, Zavala, a strong Federalist, was forced to abandon politics and, after a period of house arrest, to go into exile in June 1830. Upon his

arrival in New York he sought to interest eastern capitalists in empresario grants he had received in 1829, which authorized him to settle 500 families in a huge tract of land in what is now southeastern Texas. In New York City, in October 1830, he transferred his interest in the grants to the Galveston Bay and Texas Land Company. After spending several months during 1831 in France and England, he resided in New York City until his return to Mexico in the summer of 1832. From December 1832 until October 1833 he again served as governor of the state of Mexico, before returning to the Congress as a deputy for Yucatán. Named by President Antonio López de Santa Anna in October 1833 to serve as the first minister plenipotentiary of the Mexican legation in Paris, he reported to that post in the spring of 1834.

When he learned that Santa Anna had assumed dictatorial powers in April of that year, Zavala denounced his former ally and resigned from his diplomatic assignment. Disregarding Santa Anna's orders to return to Mexico City, he traveled to New York and then to Texas, where he arrived in July 1835. From the day of his arrival, he was drawn into the political caldron of Texas politics. Although he first advocated the cause of Mexican Federalism, within a few weeks he became a supporter of the independence movement; he served in the Permanent Council and later as the representative of Harrisburg in the Consultation and the Convention of 1836. His legislative, executive, ministerial, and diplomatic experience, together with his education and linguistic ability, uniquely qualified him for the role he played in the drafting of the constitution of the Republic of Texas. His fellow delegates elected him ad interim vice president of the new republic. In the 25 years after 1807 when Zavala became politically active, he had demonstrated his skills as a writer in uncounted articles and editorials in newspapers in Mérida and Mexico City, and in a large number of pamphlets and memorials. He is best known as an author for his two-volume history of Mexico, which first appeared under the title *Ensayo histórico de las revoluciones de México desde 1808 hasta 1830* (Paris and New York, 1831 and 1832), and for his *Viage á los Estados-Unidos del Norte de América* (Paris, 1834), in which he described economic, political, and social phenomena he observed during his visit to the United States in 1830–31.

In the weeks after adjournment of the Convention of 1836, Zavala rejoined his family at their home at Zavala Point on Buffalo Bayou, from where they fled to Galveston Island as Santa Anna's army pursued Zavala and other Texas government figures. In accord with the Treaties of Velasco, Zavala was appointed (May 1836) one of the peace commissioners to accompany Santa Anna to Mexico City, where the general was to attempt to persuade the Mexican authorities to recognize the independence of Texas. The frustration of this plan by certain Texas military units brought an end to the peace commission. Shortly thereafter, Zavala returned to his home in poor health and relinquished his part in the affairs of state. He resigned the vice presidency on 17 October 1836. Less than a month later, soaked and half-frozen by a norther after his rowboat overturned in Buffalo Bayou, he developed pneumonia, to which he succumbed the next month. He was buried at his home in a small cemetery plot marked by the state of Texas in 1931. The plot has since sunk into Buffalo Bayou. Zavala was the grandfather of Adina de Zavala. Zavala County and several other places are named for him.   *Raymond Estep*

INDEX OF CONTRIBUTERS

Compiled by Linda Webster

The page ranges of each contributor's articles are given. The contributor's name is found at the end of the article, the last page in the page range.

INDEX

Compiled by Kay Banning and Linda Webster

Note: Boldfaced page numbers indicate a full article on this topic. Italicized page numbers indicate illustrations.
For state agencies and associations see headings under Texas.

General Tire Company, 47, 563
General Wool Crossing the Military Plaza, San Antonio (Chamberlain), 993
Gentilz, Henriette, 363
Gentilz, Théodore, 216, *363, 363,* 930, 932
Gent, Peter, 534
Gentry, Abram, 238
Gentry, Diana Rogers, 436
Geological Surveys of Texas, **364**
Geological Survey, U.S., 544, 564–65, 950
Geology, **364–68,** *365, 366, 367*
Geophysical Research Corporation, 273
Geophysical Service, Incorporated, 273
George and Elizabeth Coates Foundation, 748
George B. Dealey Library, 266
George Bush Presidential Library, 835
George Peabody Fund, 743
Georgetown Equal Suffrage League, 125
Georgetown, Lake, 368
Georgetown, Texas, **368,** 919
Georgia, 10
Gerald, G. B., 452
German, Addie, 370, 371, 708
German, Catherine, 370, 371
German, Julia, 370, 371, 708
German, Sophia, 370, 371
German settlers, *50,* **368–70**
  Adelsverein and, 102, 369
  agriculture and, 109
  American party and, 124
  antebellum Texas and, 37, 39
  architecture and, 132
  Austin and, 144
  Brenham and, 187
  Catholic Church and, 710, 714
  Comanche Indians and, 614
  Democratic party and, 60
  Dreissiger and, 289
  Fisher–Miller land grant and, 324
  Fort Martin Scott and, 340
  Forty-eighters and, 349
  Georgetown and, 368
  Indianola and, 453
  internment camps and, 90, 993, 994
  La Grange and, 505
  Latin Settlements and, 514
  limekilns and, 525, 526
  Meusebach–Comanche Treaty and, 574
  Mexican Texas and, 820
  music and, 60, 604, 605
  New Braunfels and, 616
  Pinta Trail and, 670
  post-Civil War period and, 56
  presidential election of 1860 and, 239
  prohibition and, 62, 67, 71, 686, 715
  religion and, 712
  Republican party and, 718
  San Antonio and, 746, 750
  San Felipe de Austin and, 754
  Seguin and, 769
  sheep ranching and, 772
  slavery and, 713
  Solms–Braunfels and, 787–88
  Sons of Hermann and, 789
  sports and, 802–3
  theater and, 876
  Torrey Trading Houses and, 886
  Unionism and, 49
  visual arts and, 930
  Wends and, 961, 962
  World War I and, 71, 73
German Sisters, **370–71**
Germany, 71, 72, 90. *See also* German settlers
Germany, Eugene B., 864
Geronimo, 205, 330, 344, 926
Gerrells, Helen, 812
Gershwin, George, 606, 878
Gervin, George, 806
Getzendaner, W. H., 957
Gibbons, Euell, 371
Gibbons, Reginald, 532
Gibbs, Barnett, 523, 524, 662
Gibbs Brothers and Company, 450
G.I. Bill (1966), 998
G.I. Bill of Rights (1944), 123
Gibran, Kahlil, 402
Gibson, Jewel H., 532
Gibson Trailer Campground, 962
Giddings, George, 748
Giddings, George H., 338
Giddings, Jabez, 790
Gifford, A. W., 749
Gilb, Dagoberto, 535
Gilbert, Cass, 905
Gilbert, Thomas L., 709
Gilbride, Kevin, 443
Gilchrist, Donald, 679
Gilchrist, Gibb, 836, 850
Gildersleeve, Fred, 667
Giles, Albert, 13
Giles, James Bascom, 97, 362, 774
Gillaspie, James, 682, 999
Gilleland, Daniel, 231
Gilleland, William, 453
Gillespie, C. C., 826
Gillespie, Robert Addison, 512, 862, 945
Gillett, James Buchanan, 529, 927
Gillette, Henry F., 160
Gilley's Country and Western Club, 657
Gilliam, Sam, 275, 276
Gillis, Don, 605
Gilmer, Claud, 116, 371
Gilmer–Aikin Laws, 96, 116, 300, 303, 371, 383, 778, 850, 875
Gilpin, John, 732
Gindrat, Martha Evans, 992
Ginzburg, Natalia, 795
Giordano, John, 605
Gioux, Olivier, 529
Gipson, Frederick B., 532, 895
Giraud, François P., 134
Girlstown, U.S.A., 201, **371**
Gish, Lillian, 763
Gittings, Paul L., 667
Givens, Newton C., 341–42
Givins, Frank, 761
Gladewater *Mirror,* 619
Gladney, Edna, *372, 372,* 978
Gladney Milling Company, 372
Gladys City Boom Town Museum, 162
Gladys City Oil, Gas, and Manufacturing Company, 629, 801, 802
Gladys Porter Zoo, 191
Glanville, Jerry, 443
Glass, Anthony, 858
Glass, William, 708
Glasscock, George Washington, 368
Glass–Steagall Banking Act, 84
Glenn, Hugh, 760
Glenn, John W., 364
Glenn Spring Raid, **372–73**
Glidden, Joseph, 155
Glidden, Joseph F., 122
Globe of the Great Southwest, Odessa, 629
Glomar Explorer, 447
Goat ranching, 108, 111, 114, 171, 305, *373,* **373–74,** 696, 698, 771, 772, 773. *See also* Ranching
Gockley, David, 606
Godbey, Ruth Horner, 938
Goddess of Liberty, 207, *208*
Godwin, William, 664
Goetzmann, William, 930
Goff, Lloyd, 267
Goheen, Michael, 234
Gold, 594
Gold, Bernard, 475
Goldbarth, Albert, 537
Goldbeck, Eugene, 668
Goldberg, Billy, 475
Goldberg, Irving, 475
Golden, Johnny, 282
Goldsmith, Eva, 989
Goldstein, Joseph, 913
Goldstein, Joseph L., 415
Goldwater, Barry, 97, 267, 888
Goldwyn, Samuel, 323
Golf, 805, 807, 1000
Goliad, Texas, *15,* 18, 21, 22, 27, 117, 118, 120, 374, *374,* **374–75,** 500, 885, 914
Goliad Campaign of 1835, 28, 374, 511
Goliad College, 374
Goliad Declaration of Independence, 208, 285, 374, **375,** 467
Goliad Massacre, 22, 120, 317, 374, 586, 618
Goliad State Historical Park, 500
Gómez, Francisco (El Chiclanero), 519
Gómez, Gregorio, 823
Gómez, José Manuel, 553
Gómez Canedo, Lino, 7
Gómez Farías, Valentín, 17, 21, 823
Gonzales, Boyer, Sr., 932
Gonzales, Pedro, 526
Gonzales, Simón Elías, 220
Gonzales, Texas, 18, 22, 29, 118, 119, 132, 242, *375,* **375–76,** 397, 914
Gonzales, Battle of, 17, 20, 21, **375**
Gonzales College, 376
Gonzales *Inquirer,* 619
Gonzales Memorial Museum, 602, 838
Gonzales Museum, 376
Gonzales Rangers, 769
Gonzales Ranging Company of Mounted Volunteers, 375
Gonzalez, Henry B., 95, 97, 489, 578, *579*
Gonzalez, Juan, 864
Gonzalez, Ray, 537
González, Xavier, 748
González Amezcua, Consuelo, 935
González de Mireles, Jovita, 579, 978
Gonzaullas, Manuel T. "Lone Wolf," 863
Gooch, Fannie Chambers, 988
Gooch, Tom C., 269
Good, John J., 416
Goodbread, Joseph G., 35
Goodfellow, John J., Jr., 376
Goodfellow Air Force Base, **376,** 744
Good Government League, 79, 419
Goodlett, Caroline M., 899
Goodman, Benny, 825
Good Neighbor Commission, **376–77,** 418, 640
Goodnight, Charles, 155, 193, 214, 223, *377,* **377–78,** 419, 651, 697, 773
Goodnight, Corinne, 378
Goodnight College, 378
Goodnight Ranch, 378
Goodnight–Loving Trail, 214, 377, **378**
Good Samaritan Hospital, 160
Good Samaritan Rescue Mission, 734
Good Shepherd Home for Delinquent Girls, 356
Goodwin, Sherman, 410
Goose Creek oilfield, 75, 630
Goose Island State Park, 246
Goraz, Juan Leal, 206
Gordon, Harry, 765
Gordon, James Riely, 134, *379,* **379,** 755, *941,* 957
Gordon, William Knox, 881
Goree, Thomas Jewett, 682
Goree Farm, 683
Gorgas, William Crawford, 330
Goribar, José María, 228
Gorky, Maxim, 795
Gorman, Thomas K., 645, 901
Gorostiza, Manuel Eduardo de, 801
Goseascochea, José de, 858
Gosport System, 188
Gottlieb, R. D., 755
Gouhenant, Adolph, 263
Gould, Charles N., 631, 652
Gould, Jay, 58, 202, 410, 426, 500, 512, 691–92
Gould, Lewis, 74, 77
Gould's Pumps, 546